UNITED STATES ARMY IN WORLD WAR II

Special Studies

CHRONOLOGY
1941–1945

Compiled by

Mary H. Williams

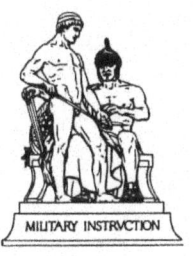

CENTER OF MILITARY HISTORY

UNITED STATES ARMY

WASHINGTON, D.C., 1989

Library of Congress Catalog Card Number 59-60002

First Printed 1960—CMH Pub 11-1

For sale by the Superintendent of Documents, U.S. Government Printing Office
Washington, D.C. 20402

UNITED STATES ARMY IN WORLD WAR II
Kent Roberts Greenfield, General Editor

Advisory Committee
(As of 17 January 1958)

Elmer Ellis University of Missouri	Maj. Gen. Oliver P. Newman U.S. Continental Army Command
Samuel Flagg Bemis Yale University	Brig. Gen. Edgar C. Doleman Army War College
Gordon A. Craig Princeton University	Brig. Gen. Frederick R. Zierath Command and General Staff College
Oron J. Hale University of Virginia	Brig. Gen. Kenneth F. Zitzman Industrial College of the Armed Forces
W. Stull Holt University of Washington	Col. Vincent J. Esposito United States Military Academy

T. Harry Williams
Louisiana State University

Office of the Chief of Military History
Maj. Gen. Richard W. Stephens, Chief

Chief Historian	Kent Roberts Greenfield
Chief, Histories Division	Col. Seneca W. Foote
Chief, Editorial and Publication Division	Lt. Col. E. E. Steck
Editor in Chief	Joseph R. Friedman
Chief, Cartographic Branch	Elliot Dunay
Chief, Photographic Branch	Margaret E. Tackley

. . . to Those Who Served

Foreword

The relationship of events in time is the essence of history. *Chronology: 1941–1945* establishes the sequence of events from the time the first bombs on Pearl Harbor on 7 December 1941 until the instrument of surrender was signed aboard the USS *Missouri* in Tokyo Bay on 2 September 1945. The other volumes in the series United States Army in World War II recount in detail the various aspects of a complex global war—individual campaigns, grand strategy, logistics, support, and so forth. In this volume the reader can see the events of the war day by day in their sequence and contemporaneity, measure the scope of the global struggle, and begin to grasp the relation of the innumerable parts to the whole.

Washington, D.C.
23 June 1958

R. W. STEPHENS
Maj. Gen., U.S.A.
Chief of Military History

Preface

The chronology is primarily one of tactical events of World War II from the time the United States was drawn into the conflict on 7 December 1941 until the surrender of Japan in 1945, with emphasis on ground action by United States armed forces. Air and naval co-operation, combat actions of foreign units—both Allied and enemy—and general events of world-wide interest are detailed within the scope of space limitations.

Geographically, events for the period from Pearl Harbor to the invasion of Normandy on 6 June 1944 are arranged in sequence from the Western Hemisphere westward around the world. From D Day to the end of the war the order is reversed, the action in western Europe taking precedence. The dates used are those of the area under discussion. Thus, the attack on Pearl Harbor is dated 7 December while the events occurring simultaneously in the Far East appear under 8 December. An exception has been made for the Gilberts and Marshalls campaign because the scene of engagement lies so near the International Date Line and also because most of the records consulted are dated west longitude.

To itemize the materials used in the preparation of this work of reference would be tedious, if not impossible. Suffice it to say that the compiler consulted extensively After Action Reports, histories of units engaged, dispatches of the Allied commanders, and other primary sources, but for correctness and completeness relied heavily on the findings of the historians who have written and are writing other volumes for the UNITED STATES ARMY IN WORLD WAR II, on the *History of United States Naval Operations in World War II* by Samuel Eliot Morison, and on *The Army Air Forces in World War II* edited by Wesley Frank Craven and James Lea Cate.

The volume is the product of a co-operative effort of the Chronology Section—first of the Historical Division and then of the Office of the Chief of Military History. To one staff member, Miss Goldie Ann Kannmacher, the compiler is especially grateful for unstinting service throughout most of the life of the project. The assistance of Miss Betty Lee Belt in the project's initial stages is gratefully acknowledged. For directing the work of the staff during a six-month absence of the compiler, acknowledgments are due Maj. John M. Baker. Members of the staff who served it ably are Mrs. Margaret Leenhouts, Miss Mary G. Schuster, Miss Ruth Upson, Miss Grace Waibel, Miss Elizabeth Stribling, and the late Mrs. Priscilla White. Miss Lauretta Plockelman and Miss Jaqueline Van Hovel contributed valuable clerical assistance.

The compiler is also grateful to Dr. Kent Roberts Greenfield for his advice and moral support. To Miss Mary Ann Bacon, who edited the volume, to Nicholas J. Anthony for the Index, and to Mr. Israel Wice, Chief, General Reference Office, and his competent assistants, who acquired the materials used, I acknowledge my great indebtedness.

Washington, D.C.
21 February 1958

MARY H. WILLIAMS

Contents

	Page
1941	3
1942	11
1943	81
1944	159
1945	365
LIST OF ABBREVIATIONS	553
LIST OF CODE NAMES	557
INDEX	563

CHRONOLOGY

1941–1945

1941

7 December

INTERNATIONAL SITUATION—Japan strikes without warning and almost simultaneously at various U.S. and British possessions in the Pacific; declares war against U.S. and Great Britain.

HAWAII—Launched from carriers of a naval task force (TF) standing 200 miles N of Oahu, Japanese planes attack Oahu between 0750 and 1000 bombing the Pacific Fleet, which, except for the carriers, is concentrated in Pearl Harbor, and AAF planes parked in close formation on Hickam and Wheeler airfields. 3 BB's are sunk, another is capsized, and 4 more are damaged; 3 CL's, 3 DD's, and other vessels are seriously damaged. 92 Navy and 96 Army planes are lost. American casualties are 2,280 killed and 1,109 wounded. Japanese lose 29 planes and 5 midget submarines.

MIDWAY—At 2135, 2 Japanese DD's bombard Midway, garrisoned by a small U.S. Marine detachment (6th Defense Bn), to neutralize it.

LIBYA—Maj Gen N. M. Ritchie's British (Br) Eighth Army, a component of Gen Sir Claude J. E. Auchinleck's Br Middle East Forces (MEF), continues offensive, begun in November, to clear Libya of German and Italian forces, which are nominally under Italian command, but actually under German Field Marshal Erwin Rommel. Objective is twofold: first, destruction of enemy concentrated in E Cyrenaica, which is in progress; second, conquest of Tripolitania. Armd elements of Br 30 Corps battle enemy tanks around Bir el Gubi. After nightfall, Br 13 Corps goes on the offensive, 10th Div driving along El Adem Ridge, key feature S of Tobruk.

USSR—German offensive (Operation BARBAROSSA, begun on 22 July 1941 by Field Marshal Walther von Brauchitsch, CinC of the German Army) to crush Soviet forces has ground to a halt on broken line from Lake Ladoga on N to Sea of Azov on S. At the extremities of front, Soviet garrisons of Leningrad and Sevastopol are besieged; on central front Germans are at outskirts of Moscow. Red Army is conducting general counteroffensive (begun on 6 December) to drive enemy westward. 3 fresh Soviet armies are exerting pressure against enemy spearheads in vicinity of Moscow. Although assured the support of satellite nations (Finland, Rumania, Hungary), Germans are at a disadvantage because of overextended supply lines and battle exhaustion.

WESTERN EUROPE—Although Adolf Hitler has by this time abandoned plans for invasion of England (Operation SEA LION) as result of defeat of Luftwaffe in Battle of Britain (8 August-31 October 1940), German planes continue active over England. RAF in turn has been making frequent attacks on European continent.

8 December

INTERNATIONAL SITUATION—U.S. and Great Britain declare war on Japan. On W side of international date line (7 December, Hawaiian time), Japanese bombard Wake and Guam, each garrisoned by small detachments of U.S. marines; British-mandated Nauru and Ocean Islands; the Philippines; British Malaya and Singapore; Thailand; Hong Kong.

P.I.—Japanese naval planes from Formosa attack Clark and Iba Fields and catch many aircraft on the ground. FEAF is reduced to almost half strength, and installations are severely damaged. Tuguegarao and Baguio are each hit by Japanese Army planes before the main strike against Clark Field. TF 5, Asiatic Fleet, under Rear Adm William A. Glassford, heads S toward safer waters. Japanese begin advance landings to acquire air bases from which to support main assault: invade Batan I., between Formosa and Luzon, without opposition.

THAILAND—Some Japanese from Indochina cross into Thailand and drive on Bangkok against negligible resistance. Others land unopposed at Singora and Patani on E coast and start SW across Kra Isthmus to assist in conquest of Malaya.

MALAYA—Japanese invade Malaya early in the morning, landing on E coast near Kota Bharu after naval bombardment of beaches, and are vigorously engaged by Lt Gen A. E. Percival's Malaya Command. Ind 3 Corps (under Lt Gen Sir Lewis Heath), which is responsible for all Malaya N of Johore and Malacca, employs Ind 9th Div against enemy in Kota Bharu area and sends Ind 11th Div, already poised to move into Thailand, across border to delay enemy on roads to Singora and Patani. Ind 9th Div, whose primary mission is to protect the 3 airfields in Kelantan (Kota Bharu, Gong Kedah, and Machang), fights losing battle for Kota Bharu, from which it starts withdrawing during night 8-9. One Ind 11th Div column, driving toward Singora, engages tank-supported enemy force 10 miles N of frontier; another, advancing toward Patani, is opposed only by Thai police forces. In conjunction with ground attacks, Japanese planes strike repeatedly at airfields in N Malaya and greatly reduce strength of RAF Far East Command. RAF, after attacking enemy shipping and troops in Kota Bharu area, withdraws from the Kelantan airfields to Kuantan, far to S. Singapore, ultimate objective of Japanese 25th Army in Malaya, is also attacked by air.

CHINA—Japanese seize International Settlement at Shanghai, and many ships are sunk or captured in its harbor; move troops toward Kowloon, on mainland across from Hong Kong.

LIBYA—Axis forces begin orderly withdrawal toward Gazala, followed closely by 13 and 30 Corps of Br Eighth Army and harassed by RAF. Skillful rear-guard action delays pursuit.

USSR—German *Army Group North* withdraws from Tichwin, on Leningrad-Vologda RR, under Soviet pressure. *Army Group Center* is slowly giving ground in Moscow area.

9 December

CENTRAL PACIFIC—Japanese continue preinvasion bombing of Wake and Guam; invade Gilbert Is.

P.I.—Continuing neutralization of airpower on Luzon, enemy bombers strike Nichols Field, near Manila.

THAILAND—Japanese occupy Bangkok without opposition.

MALAYA—Japanese force Ind 9th Div of Ind 3 Corps from Kota Bharu airfield and continue air attacks on other fields, including Kuantan. RAF abandons Kuantan airfield for Singapore I. and Alor Star airfield, on NW coast, for Butterworth. RAF bomber attack on Singora airfield (Thailand) proves very costly since fighter protection is lacking. Dutch planes arrive at Singapore to augment strength of RAF.

CHINA—Declares war on Japan, Germany, and Italy.

10 December

CENTRAL PACIFIC—Japanese invade Guam and overwhelm small U.S. garrison; continue preinvasion bombing of Wake.

P.I.—Two Japanese TF's, each consisting of some 2,000 men, arrive off N Luzon from Formosa. Landings begin simultaneously at Aparri and near Vigan, but rough sea forces alteration in plans. The Aparri force gets 2 cos ashore at Aparri and the rest at Gonzaga, over 20 miles to E; upon closing on Aparri, pushes 6 miles S and seizes Camalaniugan airstrip. The Vigan force lands small group at Pandan, near Vigan, and the rest at point 4 miles S; quickly secures Vigan and sends elements N along Route 3 toward Laoag. No opposition is offered by 11th Div (PA), which is responsible for defense of N coast. U.S. planes attack shipping of the invasion force. Capt Colin Kelly becomes the first U.S. hero of World War II in this action by hitting what was supposed to be a Japanese BB; subsequent investigation has revealed that there were no BB's present. Fighter aircraft from Batan I. provide cover for enemy. Japanese planes bomb and strafe Nichols and Nielson Fields, near Manila, and Del Carmen Field, near Clark, achieving particularly damaging results at Nichols. Cavite naval base also suffers heavily from enemy air attack. FEAF, by this time half strength, decides to confine its future activities to rcn flights.

MALAYA—Japanese gain control of waters E of Malaya and air over N Malaya. The small British Eastern Fleet is severely crippled by loss of *Repulse* and *Prince of Wales* off Kuantan to enemy planes. Adm Sir Tom Phillips, CinC Eastern Fleet, is killed in this action and is replaced by Vice Adm Sir Geoffrey Layton. As enemy continues destructive attacks on airfields in NW Malaya, RAF abandons airfield at Sungei Patani and withdraws all serviceable aircraft from Butterworth. From Butterworth, RAF bomber sq, reduced to 2 aircraft, withdraws to Taiping and RAAF fighter sq (6 repairable aircraft) to Ipoh. Japanese begin series of heavy air attacks against Penang I. Ind 9th Div withstands attacks while organizing delaying positions S of Kota Bharu. Ind 11th Div columns operating along Thailand frontier attempt to delay enemy. Far East Council is formed at Singapore.

LIBYA—Siege of Tobruk is lifted after 8 months as Pol garrison breaks out of town early in morning and joins other Br Eighth Army forces in Acroma area. Forward supply base is soon organized at Tobruk.

11 December

INTERNATIONAL SITUATION—Germany and Italy declare war on U.S., which then replies with declarations against them.

WAKE—Wake garrison (about 450 marines of 1st Defense Bn) repels invasion attempt. Japanese naval force arrives off Wake early in morning and at dawn opens fire. Shore batteries force the vessels to withdraw with landing force still embarked. 4 aircraft of VMF-211, all that remain serviceable of the original fighter sq on Wake, pursue and attack enemy force as it retires toward the Marshalls. 2 planes that survive this action intercept shore-based

Japanese aircraft that try to attack Wake later in the morning. Wake is subsequently subjected to almost daily air strikes as enemy continues softening the defense in preparation for landing.

P.I.—Japanese Aparri force on Luzon continues rapidly S along Route 5 toward Tuguegarao. Laoag and its airfield fall to Vigan force. Japanese begin mining San Bernardino and Surigao Straits. Commercial vessels withdraw from Manila Bay.

MALAYA—Ind 9th Div, Ind 3 Corps, abandons the 2 remaining airfields in Kelantan (Gong Kedah and Machang) in order to protect communications. Japanese exert strong pressure against one Ind 11th Div column on Kroh-Patani road and force the other, on road to Singora, back toward partially prepared positions at Jitra. RAF, now greatly depleted in strength, adopts policy of conducting bomber operations only at night until adequate fighter support is available and of using fighters primarily for defense of Singapore Naval Base and for protection of convoys bringing reinforcements. Ind 3 Corps troops are thus denied much close air support.

BURMA—Japanese begin offensive against lower Burma with air attack on Tavoy airdrome.

12 December

PACIFIC—U.S. troops aboard Allied convoy proceeding from Hawaii toward Far East under escort of CA Pensacola are organized as TF South Pacific and placed under command of Brig Gen Julian F. Barnes.

P.I.—Japanese make another preliminary landing, at Legaspi, S Luzon. TF of 2,500 men from Palau goes ashore unopposed and secures Legaspi and the airfield. Maj Gen George M. Parker, Jr., whose South Luzon Force consists of 41st and 51st Divs (PA), sends elements of 51st forward to delay enemy, but contact is not made for several days. Tuguegarao airfield falls to Aparri force early in morning. Japanese planes attack Luzon in force. Iba and Clark Fields are targets, with main force against Iba. Batangas is an alternate target.

MALAYA—Gen Percival decides to withdraw Ind 3 Corps from Kelantan since airfields there are already in possession of Japanese; movement of surplus supplies to rear is begun. Troops fight delaying actions while awaiting rolling stock in which to withdraw. Japanese penetrate Jitra position and force Ind 11th Div TF back to Kedah R. Ind 11th Div force, called Krohcol force, on Kroh-Patani road, also falls back under pressure and at midnight 12–13 passes to direct command of corps. Ind 12th Brig Gp is released from reserve for action on W coast.

BURMA—Japanese begin small-scale operations, using infiltration tactics. From Thailand, small force crosses into lower Tenasserim unopposed. Gen Sir Archibald P. Wavell, CinC India, is given responsibility for Burma, previously within Air Chief Marshal Sir Robert Brooke-Popham's Far Eastern Command, and is promised reinforcements to strengthen the small garrison, fighting strength of which does not exceed 30 bns during the campaign. Lt Gen D. K. MacLeod's Burma Army, charged with protecting Burma Road and Tenasserim airfields, is a heterogeneous group of Burmese, Ind, and Br forces, some poorly trained, formed into Burma 1st Div (Burma 1st and 2d Brigs and Ind 13th Brig) and Ind 16th Brig. The 16 obsolete RAF fighters on hand are augmented by sq of American Volunteer Group (AVG) fighters, which is flown in to Mingaladon from AVG base in China. Air strength is eventually increased but not enough to alter ground operations materially.

MIDDLE EAST—Gen Auchinleck receives the first of a number of notices that forces intended for Middle East must be diverted to Far East to help stem Japanese advance. First call is for Br 18th and Ind 17th Divs, 4 light bomber sqs, and AA and AT guns.

LIBYA—Eighth Army's 30 Corps moves to Libyan-Egyptian frontier to destroy isolated enemy garrisons and open communication lines. 13 Corps begins probing enemy's new line, which extends from Gazala southward.

13 December

P.I.—Enemy aircraft again attack Luzon, virtually completing destruction of U.S. Army and Navy planes in the Philippines. Del Carmen, Clark, and Nichols Fields are hit, as well as Baguio, Tarlac, Cabanatuan, and Batangas.

MALAYA—Krohcol force concentrates in positions 2–3 miles W of Kroh. Ind 11th Div begins withdrawing from Kedah R toward Gurun, a more favorable defense position in S Kedah some 30 miles S of Jitra. Fighter support is increased as sq from Singapore joins the few fighters based at Ipoh. Reports of Japanese convoy moving SSW from Saigon result in period of sharply increased Br air rcn from Malaya.

BORNEO—Small Miri detachment (Ind co and engineers), having destroyed oil fields and installations in E Sarawak and W Brunei to deny them to enemy, sails for Kuching, capital of Sarawak, where rest of the Ind bn, with local and administrative attachments, is disposed to defend airdrome. Dutch planes based on Singkawang assist RAF units on Malaya in searching for Japanese shipping heading southward from Indochina.

CHINA—British withdraw from Kowloon under pressure as Japanese continue drive on Hong Kong.

BURMA—Victoria Pt, at S tip of Tenasserim, is evacuated by British.

LIBYA—13 Corps, Br Eighth Army, opens attack on Rommel's Gazala line and meets firm resistance. Both sides suffer heavy losses.

14 December

P.I.—Japanese Vigan and Aparri detachments are placed under the same command and ordered, after the Aparri force joins the Vigan at Vigan, to march S to Lingayen Gulf. Adm Thomas C. Hart withdraws the few remaining patrol bombers of Patrol Wing 10 and 3 tenders from the Philippines, leaving very little of the Asiatic Fleet to support operations. Maj Gen Lewis H. Brereton has already withdrawn the heavy bombers of FEAF from Luzon to Del Monte airfield, Mindanao.

MALAYA—On W coast, Ind 11th Div completes withdrawal to Gurun; Japanese, in close pursuit, penetrate the new positions, night 14-15. Krohcol force is dissolved and its components, which are put under command of Ind 12th Brig, move to Baling area, about 9 miles W of Kroh. Ind 3 Corps sends small detachments to guard Grik road, which is now uncovered. On E coast, Kelantan force continues fighting withdrawal. Since airdromes on Singapore are becoming congested, preparations are being made to base air units in NEI.

15 December

P.I.—Gen Brereton receives permission to withdraw the few remaining B-17's to Darwin (Australia). Air defense of the Philippines is left to a few fighters.

MALAYA—Ind 3 Corps remains under strong pressure on W coast. During night 15-16, Ind 11th Div begins withdrawal from Gurun positions to Muda R. Garrison of Penang I. fortress, opposite Butterworth, prepares to withdraw as RAF abandons Butterworth airdrome.

USSR—On central front N of Moscow, Red Army takes Klin, on rail line to Leningrad.

16 December

HAWAII—All elements of U.S. TF 14, bearing supplies, reinforcements, and aircraft for relief of Wake, rendezvous SW of Oahu and sail for Wake.

MALAYA—Ind 11th Div completes withdrawal behind Muda R in Wellesley Province and defeats enemy efforts to secure foothold on S bank. Ind 3 Corps decides to withdraw Ind 11th Div behind Krian R. however, since it is greatly weakened by sustained fighting without benefit of tank and adequate air support. Fighting develops on Grik road N of Grik, night 16-17, as small detachment guarding the road encounters main body of Japanese Patani force thrusting toward Kuala Kangsar in effort to isolate Ind 11th Div on W coast. On E coast, Kelantan troops begin withdrawal by rail as movement of supplies and equipment is completed. Penang I. fortress is evacuated as planned during night 16-17.

BORNEO—Japanese invade British Borneo, landing on N coast at Miri (Sarawak) and at Seria (Brunei).

CHINA—U.S. War Department gives Brig Gen John Magruder, head of American Military Mission to China (AMMISCA), permission to divert Chinese lend-lease to the British, provided Chinese agree.

LIBYA—Axis forces begin withdrawal from Gazala line toward next delaying position, Agedabia. Ind 4th Div of 13 Corps, Br Eighth Army, which has been particularly hard pressed by enemy, pauses briefly to reorganize before joining other elements of corps in pursuit.

USSR—Continuing firm pressure against enemy in Moscow area, Soviet forces seize Kalinin, NW of Klin.

17 December

U.S.—In command shake up, Adm Husband E. Kimmel is replaced by Adm Chester W. Nimitz as CinC, Pacific Fleet; Lt Gen Walter C. Short, CG Hawaiian Department, is replaced by Lt Gen Delos C. Emmons; Maj Gen Frederick L. Martin, CG Air Force, Hawaiian Department, is replaced by Brig Gen Clarence L. Tinker.

MIDWAY—Marine Scout Bombing Sq 231 completes record flight from Hawaii to Midway, bolstering U.S. positions there.

P.I.—Japanese Legaspi force, advancing NW on Luzon along Route 1 toward Naga, makes its first contact with Filipino forces near Ragay. B-17's begin withdrawal from Mindanao to Australia.

MALAYA—Hard fighting continues on Grik road. Weak defense detachment is reinf but falls back under pressure of superior enemy forces. Ind 12th Brig Gp is ordered to Kuala Kangsar. Gen Percival gives Ind 3 Corps permission to withdraw to Perak R line if necessary. Perak Flotilla is formed to prevent enemy from landing on W coast between Krian and Bernam Rivers.

AUSTRALIA—Plan is drawn up for using Australia as an Allied supply base under command of Maj Gen George H. Brett.

BORNEO—Dutch planes begin 3-day series of strikes against Japanese shipping off British North Borneo.

USSR—German *Army Group South* opens offensive against Sevastopol defenses, in the Crimea, and is stubbornly opposed.

18 December

P.I.—Japanese Legaspi detachment reaches Naga (Luzon).

MALAYA—Ind 11th Div completes withdrawal behind Krian R and is held in reserve in Taiping area. Forces defending Grik road are further reinf. After visiting forward areas, Gen Percival draws up plans for withdrawal behind Perak R; decides to amalgamate certain units, among them Ind 6th and 15th Brigs (to be designated Ind 6/15 Brig) and to incorporate Ind 12th Brig Gp in Ind 11th Div.

CHINA—Japanese invade Hong Kong I., crossing straits from mainland.

19 December

P.I.—On Luzon, Japanese Legaspi detachment reaches Sipoco and is reported to be pushing toward Daet. On Mindanao, 2 enemy TF's from Palau, totaling about 5,000 men, arrive off Davao during night 19-20. Enemy planes discover and attack Del Monte airfield.

MALAYA—Enemy is active against right flank of Krian R line; on Grik road, frustrates efforts of Ind 3 Corps to recover lost ground. RAF fighters based at Ipoh are forced to withdraw to Kuala Lumpur. Ind 9th Div continues withdrawal southward in E Malaya and abandons Kuala Krai railhead.

BURMA—Japanese overrun Bokpyin, village some 100 miles N of Victoria Pt. Controversy, known as the *Tulsa* Incident, arises as a U.S. officer asks Government of Burma to impound lend-lease material at Rangoon (a valuable part of which is loaded on the SS *Tulsa* in the harbor), pending a decision on its use. At the suggestion of the senior Chinese representative in Burma, a committee is subsequently formed to determine the division of stocks.

LIBYA—13 Corps, Br Eighth Army, continues to follow withdrawing enemy, Ind 4th Div advancing along coast to Derna and 7th Armd Div across desert.

GERMANY—Hitler takes personal command of German Army, dismissing Field Marshal von Brauchitsch.

20 December

U.S.—Adm Ernest J. King is appointed CinC, U.S. Fleet.

WAKE—Patrol bomber bringing news of relief force en route to Wake arrives in Wake Lagoon.

P.I.—In another preliminary landing, Japanese invade Mindanao early in morning. Landing force goes ashore at and near Davao; after overcoming light opposition of about 2,000 Filipino troops, seizes Davao and its airfield. On Luzon, Japanese detachment starts S from Vigan toward Lingayen Gulf.

MALAYA—Indecisive fighting continues on Krian R front and along Grik road.

CHINA—Col Claire L. Chennault's AVG, based at Kunming to protect SW China and patrol Burma Road, enters combat, successfully intercepting enemy planes over Kunming. AVG is under control of Chinese Air Force.

21 December

WAKE—Japanese carrier planes begin preinvasion bombardment of defenses, supplementing attacks by shore-based aircraft. The relief force (TF 14) is within 627 miles of the island.

P.I.—3 convoys from Formosa and the Pescadores, bearing main body of Japanese *14th Army* assault force, arrive in Lingayen Gulf, Luzon, night 21-22. Filipino 11th Div makes contact with Japanese Vigan force at Bacnotan.

MALAYA—Ind 11th Div takes command of all troops W of Perak R, including those on Grik road, who are still heavily engaged, and begins withdrawal behind Perak R.

22 December

WAKE—Japanese carrier-based and land-based planes continue strong softening attacks. Of the 2 serviceable planes remaining on the island, 1 is lost in combat and the other is rendered useless when it crash-lands. Personnel of VMF-211 offer their services as infantry. TF 14, the Wake relief force, is delayed for refueling.

P.I.—Japanese begin main landings along coast of Lingayen Gulf on Luzon before dawn. One assault force goes ashore near Bauang, another at Aringay, and a third near Agoo. Forces move forward at once without serious opposition from 11th and 21st Divs (PA). 71st Inf of first Div (PA) and 26th Cav (PS) move out to help halt enemy. The Bauang assault force seizes that town, effects junction with Vigan force at San Fernando, La Union, and pushes inland toward Baguio, while the other forces overrun Rosario and face S toward Manila. U.S. submarines and a few aircraft attack enemy armada in Lingayen Gulf. 9 B-17's from Batchelor Field near Darwin attack enemy shipping off Davao, Mindanao, and then land on Del Monte Field; during night 22-23, 4 of the planes continue to Lingayen Gulf and attack transports. This is the first action in the Philippines by Australian-based planes.

MALAYA—As Ind 11th Div continues withdrawal across Perak R, RAF begins regular rcn of W coast to prevent enemy landings. Ind 9th Div completes planned withdrawal in E Malaya to positions from which to defend Kuantan airdrome and protect Ind 11th Div from attack from E.

CHINA—At meeting of Allied leaders in Chungking, Generalissimo Chiang Kai-shek offers Ch 5th and 6th Armies for defense of Burma. Gen Wavell accepts Ch 6th Army's 93d Div, elements of which are approaching border of Burma from China; regt of 49th Div is to be held in reserve on N Burma frontier.

AUSTRALIA—*Pensacola* convoy reaches Brisbane, where Gen Barnes' TF South Pacific becomes U.S. Forces in Australia (USFIA). This is the first U.S. troop detachment to arrive in Australia.

23 December

WAKE—Japanese naval force arrives off Wake about 0200 and puts ashore about 1,500 personnel of *Special Naval Landing Force*. Garrison holds out for about ii hours before being overwhelmed. TF 14, the relief force, after reaching point a little more than 400 miles from Wake, is recalled shortly before surrender of the island and retires toward Midway, the last American base remaining between Hawaii and the Philippines.

P.I.—On Luzon, General Douglas MacArthur decides to evacuate Manila and withdraw to Bataan to make a delaying stand. During night 23-24, enemy invasion force of 7,000 men arrives in Lamon Bay from the Ryukyus. Enemy invasion force sails from Mindanao for Jolo I., Sulu Archipelago.

MALAYA—Ind 3 Corps completes withdrawal of all W coast forces behind Perak R, night 23-24. Japanese planes, which so far have concentrated on airfields, begin intensive action against forward areas.

BORNEO—Japanese convoy is detected heading toward Kuching, Sarawak.

CHINA—Japanese begin drive on Changsha, Hunan Province.

BURMA—Japanese open series of strong air attacks on Rangoon, beginning battle for air supremacy that is to last until late February 1942. Exodus of civilian laborers hampers port operations in Rangoon.

LIBYA—Because of supply difficulties, which increase as pursuit progresses westward, elements of 13 Corps, Br Eighth Army, are forced to remain in place. However, Ind 4th Div seizes Barce, on coast, and forward elements Of 7th Armd Div force enemy to retire from Antelat to Agedabia.

24 December

ST PIERRE AND MIQUELON Is.—These islands, off Newfoundland, are seized by Free French.

INTERNATIONAL CONFERENCE—Anglo-American conference, called ARCADIA, opens in Washington to consider war strategy. Prime Minister Winston S. Churchill, President Franklin D. Roosevelt, and British and U.S. Chiefs of Staff attend.

U.S.—American engineers and military members of Iranian, USSR, and North African missions sail for the Middle East from New York on Army transport *Siboney*.

MIDWAY—Garrison is reinf with 2 batteries of 4th Defense Bn, which arrive from Hawaii.

P.I.—On Luzon, Adm Hart releases 4th Marines, stationed at Olongapo, to defend beaches of Corregidor. Japanese Lamon Bay invasion force, which constitutes southern prong of pincers applied against Manila, goes ashore early in morning at 3 points—Mauban, near Atimonan, and Slain. Main assault force, in center, secures Atimonan, forcing defenders back toward Pagbilao. Mauban force takes that town and pushes 5 miles W. From Slain enemy advances in 2 columns, one SW toward Tayabas Bay and the other SE along Route 1 toward the Legaspi detachment. Japanese on N Luzon consolidate beachhead and debouch on central plain to thrust sharply toward Agno R line. San Fabian and Binalonan fall, 26th Cav (PS) retiring from Binalonan across the Agno to Tayug. Planned withdrawal toward Bataan is begun in evening. USAFFE hq, except for rear echelon, and President and High Commissioner of the Philippines sail to Corregidor from Manila. Fort Stotsenburg is evacuated. Maj Gen Jonathan M. Wainwright's North Luzon Force, disposed generally along line Tayug-Urdaneta-San Carlos-Aquilar, from E to W, begins withdrawing toward Agno R line. South Luzon Force, command of which passes from Gen Parker to Brig Gen Albert M. Jones, is to withdraw northward into Bataan. Gen Parker moves to Bataan to head Bataan Defense Force, organized to prepare defensive positions.

SULU ARCHIPELAGO—Japanese invade Jolo I. in evening against light resistance from the constabulary.

BORNEO—Japanese convoy, despite attacks by Br and Dutch planes and Dutch submarines, succeeds in landing troops in Kuching area, Sarawak, early in morning. Garrison, having already destroyed Kuching airdrome, requests permission to withdraw to Dutch Borneo and is told to delay enemy as long as possible before retiring. Dutch aircraft withdraw from Singkawang, Borneo, to Palembang, Sumatra.

MALAYA—Ind 11th Div, controlling all Ind 3 Corps troops N of Slim and Bernam Rivers, is organizing defense in depth astride main road with MLR in Kampar area and rear positions near Slim R. Commander AIF Malaya, Ma) Gen Gordon Bennett (CG Aus 8th Div), assigns responsibility for N Johore to Aus 27th Brig Gp, Aus 8th Div.

AUSTRALIA—Brig Gen Henry B. Claggett takes temporary command of USFIA, pending arrival of Gen Brett from Chungking.

LIBYA—Detachment Of 7th Armd Div, 13 Corps, Br Eighth Army, enters Benghazi and finds that enemy has withdrawn.

25 December

INTERNATIONAL CONFERENCE—General George C. Marshall, U.S. Chief of Staff, proposes at the ARCADIA Conference in Washington that Far Eastern forces be placed under a unified command.

MIDWAY—Garrison is strengthened as Marine Fighter Sq 221 flies in from USS *Saratoga*.

P.I.—USAFFE hq opens on Corregidor. Rear Adm F. W. Rockwell is put in charge of all naval activities in the Philippines. North Luzon Force reaches Agno R and prepares to hold there until night 26-27. 71st Div (PA) withdraws from E flank of line to reorganize. Japanese troops from Urdaneta succeed in crossing the Agno near Tayug, night 25-26. South Luzon Force begins northward withdrawal toward Bataan. Japanese, in close pursuit, seize Sampoloc and Pagbilao.

SULU ARCHIPELAGO—Japanese complete conquest of Jolo I, increasing threat to NEI.

BORNEO—After brisk fighting in vicinity of Kuching airdrome, Sarawak, small Ind garrison breaks contact with enemy and starts on foot toward Dutch Borneo.

CHINA—Br garrison of Hong Kong surrenders to Japanese. Many Allied ships are captured or sunk off the island. At a Joint Military Council meeting to consider lend-lease transfers, Chinese representative announces that the Generalissimo has decided, because of the seizure of the *Tulsa's* cargo, that he will not co-operate with the British and will recall Ch troops.

26 December

MIDWAY—Garrison is increased by 4th Defense Bn units and ground echelon of VMF-211, who had made a futile attempt to relieve the Wake garrison.

P.I.—Naval defense forces under Adm Rockwell move to Corregidor. Manila is declared an open city. North Luzon Force, except for 194th Tank Bn, falls back from the Agno to line Santa Ignacia-Guimba-San Jose. South Luzon Force continues to withdraw in 2 columns and organizes first line of defense of Sariaya.

MALAYA—Ipoh is evacuated by Ind 11th Div troops, but Ind 12th Brig Gp fights rear-guard action at Chemor, to N.

CHINA—*Tulsa* Incident ends with conciliatory meeting between Chiang Kai-shek and Gen Magruder during which it is agreed to send an AMMISCA officer to Rangoon.

MIDDLE EAST—Gen Auchinleck is notified that 4 fighter sqs are to be transferred from Middle East to Far East; accedes to request for tanks.

NORWAY—Br Commandos (Cdos) raid German bases on islands off Norway.

27 December

FAR EAST—Lt Gen Sir Henry Pownall relieves Air Chief Marshal Brooke-Popham as Br CinC Far East.

P.I.—Luzon front is quiet as Japanese consolidate along the Agno. North Luzon Force withdraws toward next delaying line, Tarlac-Cabanatuan, where it is to make maximum delaying effort. On S Luzon, Japanese continue to pursue U.S. columns along Routes 23 and 1; on latter, Japanese break through main positions of 53d Inf and seize Candelaria.

MALAYA—Ind 11th Div rear guards (12th and 28th Brigs) begin withdrawal to defense positions near Kampar. In E Malaya, Japanese threat to Kuantan is increasing. Enemy forces near Trengganu-Pahang border are placed under arty fire.

BURMA—Lt Gen T. J. Hutton replaces Gen MacLeod as commander of Burma Army.

LIBYA—7th Armd Div of 13 Corps, Br Eighth Army, attacks Rommel's Agedabia position, which is well-suited by nature for defense, but makes no headway.

NORWAY—Br Commandos again raid enemy bases on islands off Norway.

28 December

U.S.—First contingent of construction battalions ("Seabees") is authorized in Navy.

P.I.—Japanese begin drive from the Agno toward Cabanatuan. In S Luzon, Japanese force 52d Inf (PA) back to Tiaong. Gen Jones receives orders to withdraw speedily to Bataan. 53d Inf (PA) moves to Bataan for rest and reorganization. Enemy seizes Luisiana, on Route 1, and 1st Inf (PA) withdraws westward.

LIBYA—13 Corps, Br Eighth Army, continues assault on Agedabia with 22d Armd Brig of 7th Armd Div, whose tank strength by this time has been greatly reduced because of mechanical failure. After futile effort to get behind enemy position, 22d Armd Brig falls back to El Haseiat. Both sides suffer heavy tank losses.

29 December

P.I.—On N Luzon, 91st Div (PA) holds Cabanatuan against strong enemy thrust, but Japanese succeed in crossing Pampanga R near there. Another enemy force, heading for Tarlac in 21st Div (PA) sector, reaches position just N of Tarlac. All elements of South Luzon Force withdraw quickly toward Bataan. Japanese planes attack Corregidor for the first time. Medium and dive bombers drop some 60 tons of bombs. Although wooden structures suffer heavily, little damage is done to military installations. AA fire from forts guarding Manila Bay destroys a number of bombers. 4th Marines takes responsibility for beach defense.

MALAYA—On Ind 11th Div front, Ind 12th Brig holds firmly against strong enemy attack but, since its position is becoming untenable, falls back through Kampar to Bidor, where it is held in reserve.

BORNEO—Ind detachment from Kuching, Sarawak, arrives at Sanggau, Dutch Borneo, and is placed under Dutch command.

CHINA—Establishment of China Theater under supreme command of Chiang Kai-shek, who is to be assisted by an Allied staff, is announced. Theater is to include portions of Thailand and Indochina in friendly hands.

BURMA—From Bokpyin, Japanese withdraw under pressure into Thailand.

30 December

U.S.—Forces of Naval Coastal Frontiers are placed under U.S. Fleet.

P.I.—North Luzon Force is unable to hold enemy on line Cabanatuan-Tarlac and begins withdrawal southward toward final defense positions before Bataan. From Cabanatuan, gist Div (PA) withdraws along Route 5 through Gapan toward Baliuag, NE of Calumpit. Tank bns are ordered to Plaridel-Baliuag area to defend vital Calumpit bridge over Pampanga R, across which South Luzon Force must withdraw to reach San Fernando and the road leading into Bataan, and 71st Div (PA) is dispatched to Baliuag. In center, 11th Div (PA) succeeds in delaying enemy column heading for Tarlac from Cabanatuan, 21st Div (PA) falls back from Tarlac along Route 3 toward line Bamban-Arayat. South Luzon Force, ordered to delay enemy, halts at Santiago, where ambush is arranged, but because of reverses of North Luzon Force is directed in evening to continue withdrawal and cross Calumpit bridge not later than 0600 on 1 January. 51st Inf (–) and battery of 51st FA are dispatched to assist in defense of Calumpit bridge. 2d Philippine Constabulary (PC) covers withdrawal while main body moves toward Bataan. President Manuel Quezon is inaugurated on Corregidor.

MALAYA—Japanese maintain pressure against Kampar position in W Malaya; on E coast threaten Kuantan from N in greater strength. Kuantan defense force is in process of concentrating W of Kuantan R, which is crossed by a single ferry.

LIBYA—After another costly and unsuccessful tank battle for Agedabia, during which 22d Armd Brig is rendered ineffective as a fighting force, 13 Corps of Br Eighth Army suspends assault pending arrival of reinforcements. German tanks have proved superior both mechanically and in gun power.

USSR—While German *Army Group South* continues offensive against Sevastopol, Soviet Caucasian troops make amphibious assault against E Crimea and seize Kerch and Feodosia. On central front, Germans continue to withdraw from Moscow area under Red Army pressure.

31 December

INTERNATIONAL CONFERENCE—ARCADIA conferees order joint Australian-British-Dutch-American (ABDA) Command to be established under Gen Wavell of the British Army.

P.I.—Evacuation of Manila is completed as rear echelon of USAFFE hq leaves. North Luzon Force closes in final defense positions, Bamban-Arayat, before San Fernando and Plaridel, E of Calumpit bridge. On E flank, 91st Div (PA) goes into reserve S of Baliuag, leaving 71st Div (PA) to delay enemy briefly at Baliuag; both divs then retire toward Calumpit bridge. Firm contact is made between North and South Luzon Forces in San Fernando area after latter crosses Calumpit bridge. Gen Jones is placed in command of all forces E of Pampanga R.

MALAYA—Ind 11th Div now holds relatively well-organized defense position in W Malaya, with Ind 6/15 Brig disposed on MLR at Kampar and Ind 28th Brig Gp to E. Japanese increase pressure against 28th Brig Gp. On E coast, Kuantan defense force completes concentration W of Kuantan R and destroys ferry.

CHINA—Joint Military Council is formed in Chungking.

AUSTRALIA—Gen Brett arrives from Chungking to take command of USFIA.

LIBYA—On Libyan-Egyptian frontier, S African 2d Div, assisted by 1st Army Tank Brig of 30 Corps, Br Eighth Army, attacks and penetrates Bardia fortress, on main road from Tobruk to Egypt.

USSR—Germans on southern front break off attacks on Sevastopol in order to counter Soviet thrusts from Kerch and Feodosia. On central front, Red Army troops seize Kaluga, SW of Moscow.

1942

1 January

U.S.—Declaration of the United Nations is signed by 26 nations in Washington, D. C.

Luzon—South Luzon Force, upon completing withdrawal across the Pampanga at Calumpit by 0500 and destroying bridges there at 0615, is disbanded. Its components continue withdrawal toward Bataan, and Gen Jones rejoins 51st Div (PA). Japanese move through Plaridel to Calumpit but are unable to cross the Pampanga. Covering force (elements of 71st and 91st PA Divs) withdraws from river line toward San Fernando. Meanwhile, 21st and 11th Divs (PA) continue fighting withdrawals, 91st along route Bamban-Angeles-Porac and 11th on route Malagang-San Fernando-Guagua (N of Sexmoan), arriving on line Porac-Guagua during night 1-2.

Malaya—Japanese attack Kampar position in W Malaya in force but are unable to break through. Ind 11th Div is in grave danger as enemy amphibious force lands in Utan Melentang area, at mouth of Bernam R, behind Kampar line. Ind 12th Brig Gp moves from Bidor to meet this threat. Japanese aircraft deliver first severe blow against Tengah airdrome on Singapore I.

China—Chinese request lend-lease aid for construction of road across N Burma to link with Burma Road. The projected road would extend from Ledo, India, to Fort Hertz, Myitkyina, and Lungling.

Burma—Air Vice Marshal D. F. Stevenson takes command of Allied air forces in Burma, replacing Gp Capt E. R. Manning, RAF.

Libya—30 Corps, Br Eighth Army, renews assault on Bardia after nightfall.

USSR—Red Army continues broad offensive throughout January with spectacular success in some sectors, but is unable to relieve besieged ports of Leningrad and Sevastopol.

2 January

U.S.—Lt Gen Hugh A. Drum, tentatively selected for field command in China, arrives in Washington, D. C., where he confers with various military leaders and finds opinions as to role of U.S. in China widely divergent.

Luzon—Defenders complete successful withdrawal through San Fernando, final elements clearing the town at 0200 and organize delaying positions along 10-mile front from Porac to Guagua. Holding this line are 21st Div (PA) on W, its left flank covered by 26th Cav (PS) at San Jose, S of Porac, and 11th Div (PA) on E. Japanese attack W flank in vicinity of Porac in afternoon and force 21st Div to fall back. Meanwhile, Japanese E of the Pampanga succeed in crossing the river and move to San Fernando, where they join with Japanese from Angeles. Japanese occupation force moves into Manila. Japanese planes begin daily attacks on Corregidor.

Malaya—Japanese force reaches Telok Anson via Perak R and goes ashore, greatly increasing threat to Ind 3 Corps. 1st Independent Co and Ind 3d Cav Sq defending this area are forced back through Ind 12th Brig Gp, which in turn comes under severe pressure. Although enemy attacks on Kampar position are still being contained, it is decided to withdraw to Slim R after nightfall because of precarious situation along coast. Japanese landing attempt at Kuala Selangor is frustrated by arty fire late in day.

Libya—Bardia garrison, under pressure of S African 2d Div and 1st Army Tank Brig (30 Corps, Br Eighth Army), surrenders early in day.

3 January

Allied Strategy—Gen Wavell, as supreme commander of ABDA forces, is directed to hold Malay Barrier (line Malay Peninsula-Sumatra-Java-Australia) and operate as far beyond the Barrier as possible in order to check Japanese advance; hold Burma and Australia; restore communications with the Philippines through NEI; maintain communications within theater.

Luzon—Japanese continue determined attacks on W flank of Porac-Guagua line, where 21st Div (PA) succeeds in halting enemy below Pio; exert strong pressure on E flank in vicinity of Guagua.

Malaya—Ind 11th Div completes withdrawal to Slim R line. Because of threat to communications in W Malaya, Kuantan force on E coast, which had previously been ordered to hold airdrome until to January, begins fighting withdrawal at once. Newly formed and poorly trained Ind 45th Brig, reinf, and an Ind Pioneer bn (a labor unit) arrive at Singapore and concentrate in S Malaya.

BORNEO—Japanese invade Labuan I., in Brunei Bay, without opposition. From there, detachment moves to mainland at Mempakul, thence to Weston on foot, and from Weston to Beaufort by rail.

4 January

LUZON—Continuing strong attacks against E flank of Porac-Guagua line, Japanese overrun Guagua and continue along Route 7 to Lubao, cutting planned line of retreat of 11th Div (PA). 21st Div zone (W part of line) is relatively quiet. Withdrawal from line Porac-Guagua begins under cover of darkness, 4-5, with 21st Div covering for 11th. Some cut-off elements of 11th Div make circuitous withdrawal through San Jose, while others move down Route 7 and form OPL between Lubao and Santa Cruz.

MALAYA—Ind 11th Div is under constant air attacks as it prepares defensive positions along Slim R in W Malaya. Japanese force moves S along W coast to Selangor R, then E along the river, threatening communications line at Rawang. To meet this threat, Ind 6/15 Brig Gp starts toward Batang Berjuntai.

NEW BRITAIN—Japanese begin air offensive against Rabaul, strategic base in Bismarck Archipelago, garrisoned by 1,400 men (principally 2/22d Bn of 8th Div, AIF; RAAF detachment; 100 men of NGVR; and a few RAN officers). Located at Rabaul are a fighter strip at Lakunai and a bomber strip at Vunakanu.

CHINA—Chinese halt enemy drive in Changsha area of Hunan Province.

5 January

LUZON—U.S. and Filipino troops complete withdrawal to new line extending along base of Bataan Peninsula from Dinalupihan on W to Hermosa on E. During night 5-6, withdrawal continues through Layac Junction, the funnel through which all roads into Bataan pass, final elements clearing it by 0200 after which the bridge is blown. Delaying position, called Layac line, is formed S of Layac Junction and manned by 71st and 72d Regts of 71st Div (PA), U.S. 31st Inf of Philippine Div, and 26th Cav (PS). 31st Inf, the only completely U.S. regt in the Philippines, has not yet been in action. Ration of Bataan defense force and of garrisons of fortified islands in Manila Bay is cut in half. Bataan echelon of hq is established on Bataan under Brig Gen Richard J. Marshall. Japanese continue daily air attacks on Corregidor and occasional attacks on other targets in Manila Bay area.

MALAYA—CinC Eastern Fleet moves hq from Singapore to Batavia, Java. Gen Percival, at conference in Segamat, plans for withdrawal into Johore. On Slim R front, Ind 11th Div repels enemy attack down railway.

AUSTRALIA—Gen Brett assumes duties as CG, U.S. Army Forces in Australia (USAFIA, previously USFIA).

BURMA—Hq of Ind 17th Div is established at Moulmein. Of 3 brigs that this div is to contain, only one—Ind 16th—is in Burma.

MIDDLE EAST—Gen Auchinleck is given responsibility for Iraq and Iran. Lt Gen E. P. Quinan's forces in Iraq become Br Tenth Army, corresponding to Br Ninth Army under Gen Sir Henry Maitland Wilson in Syria.

USSR—Red Army lands reinforcements on Crimean coast near Eupatoria and Sudak in effort to break siege of Sevastopol naval base, but can make little headway against firm German resistance. On central front S of Kaluga, Soviet forces hold Belev, W of Oka R. Action on northern front along Volkhov R is indecisive.

6 January

LUZON—After destructive arty exchanges in morning, Japanese having the advantage of air spotting, enemy attacks the overextended delaying line S of Layac Junction in force and makes limited penetration; enters Dinalupihan without opposition. Withdrawal of line begins during night 6-7. Japanese aerial bombardment of Corregidor ends except for nuisance raids. Enemy air attacks during first week of 1942 have resulted in little damage to fortifications.

MALAYA—On Ind 11th Div front, Ind 6/15 Brig Gp reaches Batang Berjuntai area and takes up defensive positions S of Selangor R. Kuantan force completes withdrawal from E Malaya through Jerantut during night 6-7; continues W in Raub area.

CHINA—Having accepted nomination of Chiang Kai-shek as Supreme Commander of an Allied China Theater, Chinese ask that a senior U.S. officer be sent to China to act as chief of the Generalissimo's Allied staff.

LIBYA—Br 1st Armd Div, which has recently arrived from U. K. and relieved 7th Armd Div of 13 Corps, Br Eighth Army, reaches Antelat. Port at Derna opens to traffic.

7 January

LUZON—Siege of Bataan begins as U.S. and Filipino forces complete withdrawal from Layac line. North Luzon Force becomes I Philippine Corps, containing about 22,500 men of 1st 31st, 71st, and 91st Divs (all PA), 26th Cav (PS), miscellaneous troops, and supporting weapons. Bataan Defense

Force is renamed II Philippine Corps and consists of about 25,000 men of 11th, 21st 41st, and 51st Divs (all PA), 57th Inf (PS) of Philippine Div, and supporting weapons. Defense of Bataan as far S as Mariveles Mts is divided about equally between the 2 corps, I Corps being responsible for W half and II Corps for E half. Service Command Area is located at S tip below Mariveles Mts and is the responsibility of Brig Gen A. C. McBride; in this area are 2d Div (PC)—organized on this date—provisional infantry units formed from air corps personnel, and provisional bn of Navy and Marine personnel. Defenses on Bataan are organized in depth: MLR extends from Mauban on W to Mabatang on E, a distance of 20 miles; OPL is disposed before the MLR; and rear line of defense, manned by USAFFE reserve (Philippine Div, less 57th Inf; tank group; SPM group), is being formed.

MALAYA—Japanese, in strong tank-infantry assault beginning before dawn, break through Slim R positions of Ind 11th Div and drive rapidly toward Kuala Lumpur, reaching positions a miles S of Slim village. Ind 3 Corps withdraws the Slim R line southward to Tanjong Malim, between village of Slim and road junction at Kuala Kubu. This action temporarily leaves Ind 11th Div ineffective as a fighting force. Gen Wavell arrives at Singapore.

BORNEO—Japanese in Sarawak reach frontier of Dutch West Borneo.

LIBYA—13 Corps, Br Eighth Army, patrols to Agedabia and finds that enemy has withdrawn. Convoy arrives safely at Benghazi. Because of rough seas, this port is not put into full operation.

8 January

U.S.—War Department orders that only Air Corps, AA, and service troops be sent to Australia, where emphasis will be placed on rapid build up of air forces.

Luzon—Front is quiet as Japanese regroup for drive on Bataan and U.S. and Philippine forces organize defense positions.

MALAYA—Gen Wavell visits Malayan front, where preparations are being made for withdrawal of Ind 3 Corps into Johore.

BORNEO—Japanese occupy Jesselton, British North Borneo.

9 January

Luzon—Japanese open assault on Bataan at 1500 From Dinalupihan-Hermosa area, 3 RCT's with arty support move forward, a against II Corps on E and I toward I Corps sector on W. None of the columns reaches the OPL. II Corps, defending Abucay line (from Mabatang on Manila Bay to Mt Natib) with 57th Inf (PS) on E, 41st Div (PA) in center, and 51st Div (PA) on W, opens fire on enemy combat team driving down East Road and makes patrol contact with it. To W, another Japanese column advances unmolested down trail from Dinalupihan to vicinity of Album. In I Corps area, enemy column from Dinalupihan is slowed only by demolitions while moving W along Route 7 toward Olongapo. Disposed along I Corps' Mauban line (Mt Silanganan on E to Mauban on Subic Bay) are Co K of 1st Inf (PA); 31st FA bn of 31st Div (PA) organized as infantry; and 3d Inf of 1st Div (PA). Additional troops are maintaining OPL to front.

MALAYA—Gen Percival issues instructions for withdrawal of Ind 3 Corps into Johore, where final stand before Singapore Naval Base is to be made. Corps begins withdrawal at once, executing demolition program as it goes. Ind 11th Div and line of communications troops are to delay enemy along two lines: one covering Seremban and Port Dickson, and the other covering Tampin and Malacca; Ind 9th Div is to clear Kuala Pilah and Tampin, respectively.

BORNEO—RAF planes from Malaya terminate action over Borneo with rcn flight over Kuching.

CHINA—As consideration of the U.S. role in China continues in Washington, Gen Marshall decides to recommend against sending Gen Drum to China because of the small effort that is currently to be made there.

10 January

LUZON—Gen MacArthur inspects Bataan defenses. Japanese make their first surrender demand, dropping it from the air. In II Corps area, Japanese force driving S along East Road splits, most of it moving W; both forces reach OPL along Calaguiman R below Samal and exert strong pressure against it. Enemy column pushing S in central Bataan is slowed by jungle terrain. In I Corps area, Japanese W assault force reaches Olongapo without opposition.

MALAYA—Ind 3 Corps abandons Port Swettenham and Kuala Lumpur while falling back to cover Port Dickson and Seremban area. Japanese planes, which since late December have been making night attacks on airdromes on Singapore, begin daylight raids on the airdromes.

NEI—Gen Wavell, Supreme Commander of ABDA area, flies to Java, where he confers with members of ABDA staff; establishes hq at Lembang, 10 miles N of Bandoeng.

BURMA—Commander of Ind 17th Div arrives in Burma to take charge of Tenasserim operations.

11 January

U.S.—Plan to dispatch U.S. V Corps, reinf, and air and supply forces to N Ireland (MAGNET) is approved.

LUZON—In II Corps area, Japanese advancing down E coast of Bataan drive back OPL of 57th Inf (PS), cross Calaguiman R, and after nightfall begin assault on MLR, forcing 57th Inf to fall back a little. Fighting continues throughout night 11-12. Reserves are committed and 57th Inf counterattacks, regaining most of lost ground by dawn of 12th. To W, another enemy column shifts W in sector of 41st Div (PA) and is contained by that div. Advance elements of still another column, pushing slowly S in central Bataan toward 51st Div (PA), reach, Orani R by morning.

MALAYA—Lull develops in ground action as Ind 3 Corps continues withdrawal into Johore, but enemy planes remain active and begin series of strikes against Muar.

NEI—Japanese invade NEI at 2 points. Central assault force, with air support from Jolo I., lands at rich oil center of Tarakan, off E coast of Dutch Borneo, while E assault force from Davao, Mindanao, invades Celebes at Menado and Kema. Naval paratroop force is dropped on airfield just S of Menado. Allied planes are unable to halt enemy, and the small Dutch garrisons are quickly overwhelmed. Japanese soon put Tarakan and Menado into use as air bases from which to support operations to S.

LIBYA-EGYPT—S African 2d Div of 30 Corps, Br Eighth Army, attacks Sollum, just across Egyptian border, and captures it early on 12th. 13 Corps pursues Rommel's forces toward El Agheila, a strong natural position.

USSR—Soviet forces continue to push westward on central front and cut N-S Rzhev-Brvansk RR line.

12 January

LUZON—Japanese exert strong pressure against II Corps, particularly on W, while taking up positions for concerted assault. 51st Div (PA) is hard hit and gives ground, some of which is regained after reserves are committed. In center, Japanese push back OPL of 41st Div (PA). On E coast, Japanese regain positions on S bank of Calaguiman R; to meet threat there, 21st Inf (PA) is released from reserve to assist 57th Inf (PS). In I Corps area, Japanese detachment moves by boat and seizes undefended Grande I.

13 January

LUZON—On E flank of II Corps, 21st Inf (PA) counterattacks at 0600 after arty preparation and reduces part of salient on left flank of 57th Inf (PS). Japanese are thus prevented from launching planned offensive in that area, but make progress to W against 51st Div (PA), forcing it back to MLR along Balantay R. Enemy column driving S in central Bataan, with task of turning corps' left flank, is not yet in position for attack.

MALAYA—Gen Wavell again visits front and confers with commanding officers. Withdrawal of Ind 3 Corps into Johore reaches final stage; all vehicles are being moved through Segamat. Convoy with badly needed reinforcements reaches Singapore and unloads first echelon of Br 18th Div (53d Brig Gp), AA units, and 50 Hurricane fighters with crews.

BURMA—Joint Military Council recommends construction of Ledo and Imphal roads.

USSR—Red Army has driven deep salient between German 2d Pz and 4th Armies on central front SW of Kaluga; deepens it with capture of Kirov.

14 January

INTERNATIONAL CONFERENCES—Anglo-American ARCADIA Conference ends in Washington. Among major decisions reached are: agreement to establish Combined Chiefs of Staff to direct British-American war effort; the main effort must be made first against Germany; occupation of French N Africa (GYMNAST) is of strategic importance in Atlantic area.

U.S.—As discussions are begun in Washington to consider who shall go to China instead of Gen Drum, Gen Marshall proposes Maj Gen Joseph W. Stilwell, who is being considered for command of GYMNAST.

LUZON—In II Corps area, strong Japanese pressure against W flank of 41st Div (PA) forces outposts to retire across Balantay R. 51st Div (PA) withdraws to S bank of river to tie in with 41st. Japanese enveloping column continues slowly down center of Bataan but is still N of MLR. In I Corps area, Japanese start S on W coast toward Moron in 2 columns, one by sea and the other along trail from Olongapo. Waterborne elements land about midway between Olongapo and Moron and continue S on foot. Gen Wainwright sends containing force to Moron.

MALAYA—Ind 3 Corps completes withdrawal into Johore and assumes responsibility for S part of Johore; assault elements (Aus 22d Brig of Aus 8th Div) are designated East Force and disposed astride Malacca-Segamat road. AIF Malaya (less Aus 22d Brig), responsible for NW Johore, is reinf by Ind 9th Div and Ind 45th Brig and is designated West Force. Aus 27th Brig and Ind 8th Brig Gps are astride main road and RR N of Segamat. Enemy is to be kept N of line Muar-Segamat-Mersing, if possible. Japanese overtake West and East Forces. Many cyclists are killed in ambush prepared near Gemas by elements of West Force. East Force patrols encounter enemy from Kuantan in Endau area. On this date and 15th, Dutch detachment of about 80 native troops with European officers flies from NEI to Singapore and concentrates in Labis area, N Johore, for guerrilla action against enemy communications.

USSR—Moscow announces capture by Red Army of Medyn, on central front NW of Kaluga.

15 January

ALASKA—Alaskan Air Force is activated at Elmendorf Field under command of Lt Col Everett S. Davis.

LUZON—In II Corps area, Japanese, attacking vigorously at junction of 41st and 51st Divs (PA), gain foothold on S bank of the Balantay. 51st Div commits reserves and service troops to no avail. Further reinforcements, Philippine Div (less 57th Inf) from USAFFE reserve and 31st Div (−) (PA) from I Corps, are sent forward. Japanese enveloping column in central Bataan arrives in position to turn corps' W flank and pauses to reorganize. Regrouping is conducted to E as enemy threat there diminishes. In I Corps area, the 2 Japanese columns driving on Moron converge and push closer to objective.

MALAYA—Forward elements of Aus 27th Brig Gp inflict more casualties on enemy in Gemas area before pulling back to main position. On W coast, Japanese reach N bank of Muar R and land small party between Muar and Batu Pahat, threatening communications of West Force in Yong Peng area. Boundary between West Force and Ind 3 Corps is altered to give this region, which Ind 45th Brig is defending, to 3 Corps.

ABDA COMMAND—Headed by Gen Wavell, ABDA opens officially at Batavia, Java, at noon GMT. Gen Wavell is replaced as CinC India by Gen Sir Alan Hartley.

MIDDLE EAST—U.S. War Department, learning of transfer of Iraq and Iran to Middle East Command from India Command, cables the information to chiefs of U.S. Military North African Mission and U.S. Military Iranian Mission.

16 January

INTERNATIONAL CONFERENCES—Representatives of 21 American Republics meet in Rio de Janeiro, Brazil, to provide for hemispheric solidarity against attack.

LUZON—In II Corps area, 51st Div (PA) counterattacks to restore positions on corps W flank; after making limited progress on right, is subjected to severe pressure and falls back in confusion, W flank elements making futile attempt to gain contact with I Corps on rugged terrain of Mt. Natib. Entire line on Bataan is jeopardized by enemy breakthrough in this sector. Japanese encircling force, although in position to turn W flank of corps, prepares instead to advance down Abo-Abo R valley. To E, 41st Div (PA) refuses its left flank in effort to tie in with 51st Div and, with assistance of elements of 23d and 32d Regts and quickly formed prov bn, succeeds in halting enemy. U.S. 31st Inf moves to vicinity of Abucay Hacienda, on left flank of 41st Div, and prepares to counterattack; reserve force, 45th Inf (PS), also moves toward attack positions. I Corps engages enemy for first time. Japanese cross Batalan R and attack Moron but are forced back to river line by 1st Inf and elements of 26th Cav. Cavalrymen are withdrawn after engagement because of heavy losses.

MALAYA—Japanese cross Muar R and force Ind 45th Brig from Muar, on S bank; continue landings on W coast in Muar-Batu Pahat area, increasing threat to communications. 53d Brig of Br 18th Div is released to Ind 3 Corps, which places it under Ind 11th Div command; 2 bns are dispatched to positions W of Yong Peng and the third is held in reserve at Ayer Hitam. RAF, concentrated on Singapore I, prepares to withdraw to Sumatra. Singapore airdromes are still targets of daily enemy air attacks.

BURMA—46th Brig, Ind 17th Div, arrives. Japanese attack and eventually outflank Imperial forces at Myitta, threatening Tavoy.

17 January

U.S.—War Department appoints Gen Breton commander of tactical forces in ABDA area.

LUZON—II Corps counterattacks to restore W portion of line, formerly held by 51st Div (PA), and makes limited progress. U.S. 31st Inf, moving N from Abucay Hacienda area, reaches Balantay R on left but is unable to make much headway on right. Reserves move forward to plug gap between the assault bns. Japanese encircling column begins unopposed march down Abo-Abo R toward Orion. In I Corps area, Moron defenders fall back under enemy pressure to ridge S and SE of Moron.

MALAYA—Additional reinforcements are moved into Muar-Yong Peng area as enemy continues attacks and build up. West Force withdraws bn from Segamat, and East Force releases one from Jemaluang for operations in this area.

BORNEO—Japanese force lands at Sandakan, British North Borneo.

LIBYA-EGYPT—30 Corps, Br Eighth Army, receives surrender of Halfaya garrison and takes many prisoners. 1st Free French (FF) Brig Gp was to have participated in attack on Halfaya, had the garrison not surrendered. With destruction of enemy in E Cyrenaica and reopening of communication line from there into Egypt, first phase of Libyan campaign is successfully concluded. In W Cyrenaica, 13 Corps reconnoiters enemy's El Agheila position.

18 January

LUZON—II Corps renews efforts to restore W flank positions. U.S. 31st Inf is still unable to gain Balantay R line on right and is under strong pressure along the river on left. Bn of 45th Inf (PS) reaches the Balantay to W of 31st Inf and is attached to 31st Inf. 2 other bns of 45th Inf advance toward the Balantay between 31st Inf and 41st Div (PA), but are halted short of objective. In I Corps area, Japanese increase pressure and force outposts to withdraw. Small enemy force is moving eastward unopposed to outflank E portion of line.

MALAYA—Ind 45th Brig, reinf, repels further enemy attacks in Muar-Yong Peng area and destroys a number of tanks, but landing of strong Japanese force a few miles N of Batu Pahat increases danger in this sector. In evening, Commander West Force orders withdrawal. Entire Muar front is placed temporarily under Ind 3 Corps command. During night 18-19, Ind 9th Div falls back behind Muar R, as does AUS 27th Brig Gp behind Segamat R. RAF bomber group withdraws from Singapore I. to Sumatra.

USSR—On southern front, Red Army makes deep penetration near Izyum, on Donets R in the Ukraine; gains ground E of Kursk.

19 January

LUZON—II Corps continues efforts to regain positions along Balantay R on W flank, 45th Inf (–) (PS) reaching river in region between 31st Inf (U.S.) and 41st Div (PA). 31st Inf, however, is under increasingly strong pressure. Enemy column driving down Abo-Abo R valley reaches positions near Guitol and is engaged by 31st Div and elements of 21st Div (PA). I Corps restores OPL in counterattack but is forced to abandon it after nightfall. Elements of 92d Inf (PA) are sent to block enemy infiltrators from Mt Silanganan, on corps E flank.

MALAYA—Bitter fighting continues in Muar-Yong Peng area. 53d Brig of Br 18th Div, under command of Ind 11th Div, takes responsibility for strategic positions W of Yong Peng—a defile and bridge—but loses them. Muar force (Ind 45th Brig and 2 Aus bns), now isolated, is ordered to withdraw.

BORNEO—British North Borneo is surrendered to Japanese at Sandakan.

BURMA—Japanese seize Tavoy and its airfield. Because of this, it is decided to withdraw Mergui garrison by sea to Rangoon at once, although Mergui has not yet been attacked. Balance of Ch 93d Div (6th Army) is ordered to move into Burma.

MIDDLE EAST—Gen Auchinleck issues operations instructions to Commander, British Troops in Egypt (BTE), and Commander, Eighth Army, restating that objective in Libya is Tripoli and outlining plan for defensive stand in the event the Libyan offensive cannot be continued.

USSR—Heavy fighting continues on southern front; Germans in the Crimea recapture Feodosia.

20 January

LUZON—Japanese contain repeated attacks by Philippine Div (U.S- 31st and PS 45th Regts) on W flank of II Corps while preparing for major assault to begin on 22d. After further fighting before Guitol, Japanese retire northward. In I Corps area, Japanese maintain pressure and continue infiltration into right flank from Mt. Silanganan.

MALAYA—Br 53d Brig counterattacks W of Yong Peng but is unable to recover lost ground. Muar force begins difficult withdrawal toward Yong Peng. Withdrawal of Segamat forces continues; during night 20-21, Aus 27th Brig Gp moves from Segamat R line to Yong Peng; Ind 9th Div pulls back to defensive position to E.

BISMARCK ARCHIPELAGO—More than 100 Japanese carrier-based planes attack Rabaul, New Britain, causing serious damage. Kavieng, New Ireland, is also attacked by air but in much less strength.

BURMA—Japanese cross into Burma in force and begin assault on N Tenasserim, attacking 16th Brig, Ind 17th Div, on Myawadi-Kawkareik road, near Thai border E of Moulmein, in conjunction with air attacks.

USSR—Mozhaisk, about 60 miles W of Moscow, falls to Soviet forces.

21 January

Luzon—In II Corps area, Japanese continue preparations for offensive, massing assault forces on extreme W flank of corps; contain further attempts of Philippine Div to restore W flank positions. In I Corps area, small enemy force, having circled about E flank of corps, reaches West Road in area 4 miles E of Mauban and blocks it, cutting off 1st Div troops along MLR from forces to S. Forces that can be spared from other sectors attack the Japanese block from N and S but are unable to reduce it.

MALAYA—Withdrawal of defense forces from

Muar and Segamat fronts continues. Commander of West Force is placed in charge of all troops on Yong Peng-Muar road. Muar force is supplied by air. East Force patrols ambush enemy force driving on Mersing.

CELEBES SEA—Enemy convoy is observed moving S in Celebes Sea.

BISMARCK ARCHIPELAGO—Japanese planes continue preinvasion bombardment of Rabaul (New Britain) and Kavieng (New Ireland). At Rabaul, the only coastal battery is destroyed.

NEW GUINEA—Japanese begin air offensive against New Guinea with 50-plane attack on Lae-Salamaua area.

CHINA—Chinese Government accepts proposal that Gen Stilwell act as chief of the Generalissimo's Allied staff and agrees to give him executive authority over Allied units. Ch 49th Div (6th Army) is authorized to move into Burma.

LIBYA—Axis forces, with strong air support, go on the offensive in W Cyrenaica, pushing rapidly eastward in 3 columns astride main road. Br Eighth Army's 13 Corps commander orders withdrawal to line Agedabia-El Haseiat at once and a further retreat if necessary; orders Ind 4th Div to check coastal advance toward Benghazi.

22 January

LUZON—Gen MacArthur orders withdrawal of entire Mauban-Abucay line southward to final defense position on Bataan, behind Pilar-Bagac road; withdrawal is to start after nightfall on 23d and be completed by daylight of 26th. In II Corps area, Japanese open offensive that forces Philippine Div back to positions E and S of Abucay Hacienda, approximately those held at beginning of counteroffensive on 16 January. In I Corps area, elements of 91st Div (PA), supported by Scouts of 26th Cav and tanks, attempt unsuccessfully to reduce roadblock on West Road and to reach 1st Div troops still fighting along MLR to N. Japanese begin series of amphibious operations, night 22-23, when bn embarks in barges at Moron and sails toward Caibobo Pt, below Bagac. U.S. PT boat encounters and sinks 2 vessels.

MALAYA—Six-day battle on Muar front ends in victory for Japanese. Ind 45th Brig, despite close air and naval support during the operation, is destroyed as a fighting body. Muar force destroys its vehicles and weapons and pushes toward Yong Peng by infiltration, leaving wounded behind. Batu Pahat defense force (detachment of Ind 11th Div) skirmishes with enemy on Batu Pahat-Ayer Hitam road. Ind 8th Brig Gp, 9th Div, having withdrawn from Segamat sector to positions astride main road between Labis and Yong Peng, is attacked by enemy.

East Force repels enemy attempt to cross river at Mersing. Partly trained Ind 44th Brig, reinf, and 7,000 Ind reinforcements arrive at Singapore.

MAKASSAR STRAIT—U.S. submarine attacks enemy convoy.

BURMA—Ind 16th Brig breaks off action in Kawkareik area and falls back toward Moulmein.

LIBYA—Continuing swiftly eastward, Axis forces occupy Agedabia.

23 January

U.S.—Gen Stilwell, in Washington, accepts China assignment and takes over part of staff previously selected by Gen Drum.

LUZON—Philippine Div, on II Corps W flank, withstands increasingly heavy pressure. After nightfall, II Corps begins withdrawal to final defense line. In I Corps area, Japanese maintain heavy pressure against Mauban MLR and frustrate further attempts to reduce roadblock on West Road. In Service Command Area, enemy amphibious force heading for Caibobo Pt, having lost its way during night, arrives at 2 points on SW coast, both well S of objective. About a third land at Longoskawayan Pt; the rest land at Quinauan Pt. Gen McBride, responsible for defense of S tip of Bataan except for naval reservation near Mariveles, sends Philippine Constabulary elements to Quinauan Pt, but they make little headway. Comdr Francis J. Bridget, commanding naval reservation, dispatches sailors and marines to Longoskawayan Pt; these, reinf by personnel of U.S. 301st Chemical Co and a howitzer from the Constabulary, clear Pucot Hill, but enemy returns after nightfall.

MALAYA—Rear guards from Segamat and Muar fronts complete withdrawal through Yong Peng at midnight, 23-24; West Force then comes under command of Ind 3 Corps, which is to defend central Johore and thereby protect Singapore naval base until reinforcements arrive. Japanese are to be kept N of line Batu Pahat-Ayer Hitam-Kluang-Jemaluang, if possible. Fighting continues in Batu Pahat area, and road from there to Ayer Hitam is closed. Japanese intensify air attacks.

BISMARCK ARCHIPELAGO—Japanese *Fourth Fleet* lands troops at Rabaul (New Britain) and Kavieng (New Ireland). Small Aus garrison of the important Rabaul base is soon overwhelmed. Kavieng is undefended. Japanese are now within easy striking distance of New Guinea.

SOLOMON IS.—Elements of Japanese *Fourth Fleet* invade Kieta (Bougainville) without opposition.

NEI—Japanese invasion forces move S in 2 convoys, one through Makassar Strait to Balikpapan (Borneo) and the other through Molucca Passage to Kendari (Celebes). Unopposed landings are made at both places, but convoy off Balikpapan is attacked by Dutch planes. On Sumatra, RAF reinforcements from Middle East begin arriving at Palembang, where one of the 2 airdromes is attacked for first time by enemy planes.

BURMA—Japanese planes begin period of intensified attacks on Rangoon area in effort to destroy Allied aircraft in Burma.

LIBYA—Axis troops take Antelat and Saunnu despite opposition of 13 Corps, Br Eighth Army.

USSR—Thrusting strongly SW from Valdai Hills, NW of Moscow, Red Army seizes Cholm, German center of resistance near boundary of *Center* and *Northern Army Groups*. To SE, Rzhev, another enemy center of resistance, is being encircled.

24 January

LUZON—II Corps begins disengaging and withdrawing combat troops. Japanese maintain intense pressure on Philippine Div and attack covering force, but bulk of troops withdraw successfully. Situation in I Corps area deteriorates rapidly. 1st Div, exhausted by prolonged fighting along MLR and critically in need of supplies and 'ammunition, remains under pressure. Additional strength is applied against Japanese roadblock on West Road without avail. In Service Command Area Japanese cannot be ousted from Quinauan and Longoskawayan Pts. Sailors and marines succeed, however, in regaining Pucot Hill and driving enemy back to Longoskawayan and Lapiay Pts.

MALAYA—Outline plan for withdrawal to Singapore is issued. Hard fighting continues at Batu Pahat. Japanese are approaching Kluang, in Ind 9th Div sector. Additional units (Aus MG bn and about 2,000 Aus reinforcements, many of whom are poorly trained) arrive at Singapore.

MAKASSAR STRAIT—Battle of Makassar Strait, first big naval battle of the war, occurs early in morning when 4 U.S. DD's strike at enemy shipping off Balikpapan, Borneo, with good effect.

NEI—The first of a small group of U.S. P-40's reaches Java from Australia.

NEW GUINEA—Allied forces evacuate Lae and Salamaua, which are threatened by Japanese.

AUSTRALIA—Combined Chiefs of Staff order Darwin area incorporated into ABDA Command.

BURMA—Rear elements of Mergui garrison arrive at Rangoon. Moulmein is now threatened.

LIBYA—Br Eighth Army's 13 Corps prepares to counterattack or, if enemy cannot be contained, to fall back on line Derna-Mechili as Axis offensive halts briefly.

USSR—Soviet forces on Donets front in the Ukraine break through enemy positions in Izyum area and capture Barvenkova, about 40 miles E of Lozovaya; in Valdai Hills sector to N, deepen salient between Cholm and Rzhev to vicinity of Velikie Luki, where Germans are firmly established.

25 January

MIDWAY—Shelled by Japanese submarine.

LUZON—Responsibility for defense of beach area of S Bataan passes from Gen McBride of Service Command Area to commanders of I and II Corps. II Corps continues withdrawal under air attack and with Japanese in full pursuit. I Corps abandons Mauban MLR. Withdrawal of 1st Div southward begins during morning and continues through night 25-26. Diverting enemy attention, other elements of I Corps press in on roadblock on West Road from the W. In South Sector, operations against Japanese at Quinauan and Longoskawayan Pts remain indecisive.

THAILAND—Declares war on U.S.

MALAYA—Since Batu Pahat must be abandoned at once, Gen Percival orders entire line in central Johore withdrawn. Ind 3 Corps is responsible for withdrawal operation, which begins after nightfall. Meanwhile, Batu Pahat defense force fights losing battle for that town throughout day. Ind 11th Div commander sends Br 53d Brig Gp to relief of Batu Pahat defense force, but most of the column is unable to get through. To E, enemy attacks in Ayer Hitam-Kluang area are beaten off.

BURMA—Gen Wavell, visiting Rangoon, orders Moulmein held. 16th Brig, Ind 17th Div, is disposed W of Salween R, opposite Moulmein. Ind 46th Brig is ordered to Bilin area. Lull ensues as Japanese bring up reinforcements to vicinity of Paan and Moulmein, on Salween R.

LIBYA—Speeding eastward again, Rommell's forces seize Msus. Weakened 1st Armd Div of 13 Corps, Br Eighth Army, is ordered to fall back on Mechili, leaving detachment to protect withdrawal of Ind 4th Div from Benghazi and Barce. Gen Auchinleck visits Eighth Army hq, where he remains until 1 February. Gen Ritchie revokes order for general withdrawal of 13 Corps and orders Ind 4th Div, over which he takes direct control, and 1st Armd Div to counterattack in Msus area.

26 January

LUZON—Philippine II and I Corps complete withdrawal to final defense line on Bataan in morning, closely followed by Japanese. The new line, which is to be continuous for the first time, extends from Orion on E to Bagac on W and is generally behind Pilar-Bagac road. Gaps develop in each corps sector when USAFFE withdraws Philippine

Div as its reserve. Units are hastily shifted to replace 31st (U.S.) and 57th (PS) Regts in II Corps line and 45th Inf (PS) in I Corps line. II Corps, responsible for E Bataan from coast to Pantingan R, organizes its line into 4 sectors, from E to W: Sector A, 31st Inf of 31st Div (PA); Sector B, Prov Air Corps Regt; Sector C, elements of 31st Div (PA) and remnants of 51st Div (PA); Sector D, 41st and 21st Divs (PA) and 33d Inf, less 1st Bn, of 31st Div (PA). In addition, beach defense forces are organized as Sector E. 1st Bn of 33d Inf, 31st Div (PA), and regt of PA combat engineers constitute corps reserve. Japanese patrol along E slopes of Mt Samat almost to MLR but do not discover gap in line, which exists for several hours. I Corps line, extending from Pantingan R to W coast, is divided into Right and Left Sectors: Right Sector is manned by 2d PC Regt (less one bn) on E and 11th Div (PA) on W; disposed in Left Sector are elements of 1st Div (PA) on E and 91st (PA) on W. Beach defense forces make up South Sector. 26th Cav (PS) is held in corps reserve. Japanese open offensive, driving S along West Road toward Binuangan R. 91st Div (PA) contains these attacks. In South Sector, Japanese maintain beachheads at Quinauan and Longoskawayan Pts and move reinforcements toward former. USAFFE sends 88th FA (PS) to W coast from II Corps sector, one of its gun batteries to Quinauan Pt and another to Longoskawayan Pt.

MALAYA—Japanese amphibious force lands in E Malaya at Endau and moves rapidly inland. Some damage is done to the convoy by RAF planes as it approaches Endau and by naval vessels after it has anchored, but British lose HMS *Thanet* in the action. Ind 11th Div makes another unsuccessful attempt to relieve Batu Pahat force, which withdraws by infiltration, leaving wounded behind.

NORTHERN IRELAND—First convoy of U.S. troops arrives.

27 January

LUZON—In II Corps area, Japanese begin assault against MLR in afternoon. After feint down East Road, main attack is made against Sectors C and D. Sector C is thinly manned and in the process of being reinf by 41st Inf from Sector D. Japanese force the outposts back and get small advance group across Pilar R. In I Corps area, enemy renews efforts to break through MLR on W coast and is again brought to a halt by 91st Div (PA). In South Sector, Gen Wainwright sends 3d Bn of 45th Inf to Quinauan Pt and 2d Bn of 57th Inf to Longoskawayan Pt to dislodge or destroy enemy along SW coast. Meanwhile, after preparatory fire from all available guns is conducted against Longoskawayan Pt, infantry attacks but is unable to clear it. Scouts of 2d Bn, 57th Inf, relieve naval bn there during night 27–28. Japanese are contained but cannot be cleared from Quinauan Pt. Water-borne reinforcements for this position land short of objective, between Anyasan and Silaiim Rivers, before dawn and put beach defenders, 1st Bn of 1st Philippine Constabulary, to flight. 17th Pursuit Sq, from reserve, and 2d Bn of 2d Philippine Constabulary, from MLR to N, move against Japanese but are halted about 1,000 yards from shore. Japanese are ordered, upon reinforcing Quinauan beachhead, to drive to Mariveles.

MALAYA—Gen Percival, receiving permission from Gen Wavell to retire to Singapore at his discretion, decides to withdraw at once through Johore Bahru and across causeway to Singapore. Withdrawal is to be accomplished under cover of darkness and completed during night 30–31. East Force meets no opposition as it pulls back. While elements of Ind 11th Div's Batu Pahat force fall back to Benut, the rest move to Ponggor R mouth, from which they are withdrawn by sea during the following nights. West Force fights local actions while retiring along main road and RR.

NEI—Singkawang II airfield, Borneo, under enemy attack, is ordered evacuated.

AUSTRALIA—Gen Barnes assumes command of base facilities in Australia.

LIBYA—As 13 Corps, Br Eighth Army, prepares to counterattack in Msus area, enemy renews offensive, making main effort toward Benghazi while moving strong diversionary column toward Mechili.

USSR—On Donets front, Soviet forces seize important rail center of Lozovaya, W of Izyum.

28 January

INTERNATIONAL CONFERENCES—Rio Conference of American republics ends.

U.S.—Eighth Air Force is activated at Savannah, Georgia, under Brig Gen Asa N. Duncan.

LUZON—In II Corps area, 41st Inf completes movement into Sector C line, taking up positions between 31st and 51st Div elements. Japanese renew attack against corps in evening: some cross Tiawir R in front of Sector D, where they are halted; others attempt to move forward in Sector C without success. From W coast, in I Corps area, Japanese move eastward along corps' MLR to 1st Div sector, where defense preparations are not yet completed; during night 28–29, Japanese breach MLR there and pour southward through gap. As the enemy force becomes divided in dense jungle, two pockets, called Little Pocket and Big Pocket, are formed, Little Pocket about 400 yards below MLR and Big Pocket nearly a mile behind MLR. In South Sector, Scouts of 2d Bn, 57th Inf, attack Longoskawayan Pt and advance two thirds of its length before arty support is obstructed by Pucot Hill. 3d Bn of 45th

Inf (PS) attacks enemy beachhead at Quinauan Pt, but jungle terrain and enemy make progress slow and costly. At night 3d Bn is reinf by Co B of 57th Inf. In Anyasan-Silaiim sector, 17th Pursuit Sq and Philippine Constabulary elements push almost to coast of Anyasan Bay, but Constabulary, fearing counterattack, withdraws in confusion after dark.

MALAYA—East Force continues unopposed withdrawal toward Singapore. Japanese reach Benut and continue southward behind Ind 11th Div. Gap develops between the two brigs of Ind 9th Div withdrawing along RR; 22d Brig becomes isolated from main body.

LIBYA—Ind 4th Div is authorized to withdraw from Benghazi since armored elements of 13 Corps, Br Eighth Army, are too busily engaged to assist it. Ind 7th Brig, the last to withdraw, finds its line of retreat blocked but breaks out to S and eventually makes its way back to Eighth Army.

29 January

U.S.—Combined Chiefs of Staff establish ANZAC Area, covering ocean expanses between Australia, New Zealand, and New Caledonia. This area is to be under U.S. naval command.

FIJI Is.—U.S. troops arrive in islands.

Luzon—II Corps withstands further efforts of Japanese to breach MLR. In r Corps area, troops of 1st and 11th Divs operate against Little and Big Pockets, respectively, in effort to determine their strength and disposition, and evoke sharp opposition. Scouts of 1st Bn, 45th Inf,, prepare to assist 11th Div in attack on Big Pocket. In South Sector, after half-hour arty preparation augmented by fire of mine sweeper offshore, ad Bn of 57th Inf (PS) attacks and clears Longoskawayan Pt; enemy remnants are being mopped up. 3d Bn of 45th Inf (PS) continues to make slow and costly progress at Quinauan Pt. In Anyasan-Silaiim sector, Scouts of 2d Bn, 45th Inf, prepare for attack and are reinf by 1st Bn of Philippine Constabulary and 1st Bn of 12th Inf (PA), both of these having been relieved at Quinauan Pt. Co A of 57th Inf is to guard West Road.

MALAYA—Withdrawal toward Singapore continues. Additional elements of Br 18th Div arrive at Singapore; also, a sq of obsolete light tanks arrives from India, the only tanks to reach Malaya.

NEI—Japanese occupy Pontianak, on W coast of Dutch Borneo.

IRAN—Great Britain and Soviet Union sign treaty of alliance with Iran, wherein Iran agrees to remain neutral; Britain and USSR promise to withdraw their troops from Iranian territory 6 months after hostilities with Axis cease. (Persian Corridor is to become principal route for movement of supplies to USSR.)

LIBYA—Axis main forces remain in Msus area, but elements pursue Ind 4th Div of Br Eighth Army as it falls back slowly toward Derna line.

USSR—On central front, Red Army continues to deepen salient SW of Kaluga and reports capture of Sukhinichi.

30 January

P.I—Gen MacArthur takes control of all naval forces in the Philippines.

Luzon—In Sector C of II Corps, efforts to dislodge enemy from Pilar R bridgehead fail. Indecisive fighting continues along MLR. I Corps makes slow progress against enemy pockets behind MLR. While 1st Div attempts to reduce Little Pocket, elements of 11th and 45th Regts attack Big Pocket from N and S, respectively. In South Sector, 3d Bn of 45th Inf, reinf, continues to attack Quinauan Pt beachhead. 2d Bn of same regt, reinf, supported by 88th FA battery, pushes slowly toward Silaiim R mouth.

MALAYA—British withdrawal to Singapore reaches its final stage. East Force is the first unit to cross causeway and is followed by Ind 11th Div and West Force. West Force delays withdrawal as long as possible in futile effort to recover 22d Brig of Ind 9th Div. Remnants of this brig are eventually ferried across Strait of Singapore. It is decided to withdraw Malaya Air Force to NEI except for a single squadron.

NEI—Japanese invade Ambon (Amboina), second largest naval base in NEI, and are opposed by garrison of Dutch and Australians. Allied air and naval forces have already been withdrawn because of enemy air attacks.

BURMA—Japanese open strong attack on Moulmein and seize the airdrome.

31 January

U.S.—Gen Stilwell, in memo to Gen Marshall, estimates his needs for China assignment and requests that his staff and any forces that may join it be called a task force. War Department subsequently approves designation of Stilwell's forces as U.S. Task Force in China.

Luzon—After air and arty preparation, Japanese begin attack on II Corps in evening but are halted by corps fire. Enemy regt concealed in bridgehead across Pilar R begins withdrawing under cover of darkness. I Corps continues battle against enemy pockets in sectors of 1st and 11th Divs. The pockets are now cut off from supply. In South Sector, operations against enemy beachhead at Quinauan Pt continue with little change in positions. Japanese reinforcements are ordered to the area. 192d Tank Bn (less one co) is sent to W coast to help reduce Quinauan Pt beachhead.

MALAYA—Malaya defense force completes withdrawal to Singapore Island at 0815 and blows causeway. For defense purposes, Singapore is divided into 3 sectors. Ind 3 Corps, under command of Gen Heath, consisting of Ind 11th and Br 8th Divs and corps troops, is responsible for N area. S Area, which includes Singapore town, is the responsibility of Maj Gen F. Keith Simmons, commander of Singapore Fortress troops, who has under his command in addition to fixed defenses, 1st and 2d Malayan Brigs and Strait Settlements Volunteer Force. W Area, under command of Gen Bennett, Commander AIF, is manned by Australians and Ind 44th Brig, with attachments. Activity from this time until Japanese invasion is confined to arty exchanges, air attacks, and patrolling. Chief targets for enemy planes are docks and Kalang airdrome.

BURMA—Moulmein garrison withdraws across the Salween to Martaban. 48th Brig of Ind 19th Div arrives in Rangoon and is held in reserve. Another brief lull ensues in ground action as Japanese prepare for further attacks, infiltrating across the Salween and bombing and shelling Martaban.

ETHIOPIA—Great Britain recognizes independence of Ethiopia.

IRAN—Maj Gen John N. Greely, head of U.S. Military Mission to USSR, which is to advise and assist Russians on lend-lease matters, arrives at Basra, Iraq; from there proceeds to Tehran, Iran, where he establishes his hq.

1 February

GILBERT AND MARSHALL Is.—Units of U.S. Pacific Fleet make surprise air and naval attacks on Japanese air and naval bases at Roi, Kwajalein, Wotje, Taroa, and Jaluit Islands in the Marshall group and Makin in the Gilbert group, severely damaging enemy shipping and aircraft facilities.

LUZON—II Corps prepares to attack in Sector C to clear enemy bridgehead from which Japanese continue to withdraw. I Corps continues efforts to reduce pockets S of MLR with negligible success. In South Sector, Scouts renew battle against Quinauan Pt beachhead but progress is still limited. Scout casualties by this time are estimated at 50 percent. Japanese reinforcements for Quinauan Pt are spotted, night 1-2, and attacked by remaining 4 P-40's of FEAF, motor torpedo boats, and arty and infantry weapons from shore. Enemy is forced to land instead in Anyasan-Silaiim area.

ERITREA—Placed under command of GHQ MEF.

LIBYA—Gen Ritchie orders general withdrawal of 13 Corps, Br Eighth Army, to line Gazala-Bir Hacheim in order to avoid envelopment. Ind 4th Div; which reverts to 13 Corps command, completes withdrawal to Derna line during night 1-2.

USSR—Red Army continues powerful offensive throughout February but with diminishing success as German resistance stiffens with arrival of reinforcements. Further efforts to break through to Leningrad and Sevastopol are futile, but some success is achieved in other sectors. Soviet forces in the Crimea are reinforced.

NORWAY—Puppet government is established under Vidkun Quisling.

2 February

U.S.—Gen Stilwell is designated Chief of Staff to Supreme Commander, China Theater, and is directed by War Department to "increase the effectiveness of United States assistance to the Chinese Government for the prosecution of the war and to assist in improving the combat efficiency of the Chinese Army."

LUZON—II Corps attacks to clear bridgehead, at first employing 31st Engr Bn (PA) and then reinforcing with elements of 41st Inf after opposition proves stubborn. Enemy completes withdrawal from bridgehead during night 2-3. In I Corps area, armd platoon of 192d Tank Bn and platoon of 1st Bn, 45th Inf, attempt unsuccessfully to reduce Big Pocket. In South Sector, Co C of 192d Tank Bn assists Scouts in another attack on Quinauan Pt beachhead, but results are no more satisfactory. Other Scout bns 2d Bn of 45th Inf; 3d and 1st Bns of 57th Inf) attack abreast to clear Anyasan-Silaiim sector, making slow progress except on left, where no opposition is met.

ERITREA—Personnel of U.S. North African Mission embarked on *Siboney* reach Massawa.

LIBYA—Gen Auchinleck orders Br Eighth Army to hold Tobruk as a supply base for future offensive.

3 February

LUZON—II Corps, finding enemy bridgehead clear, advances OPL in that sector. I Corps continues to make little headway against enemy pockets in sectors of 1st and 11th Divs. In South Sector, Scouts and tanks are still unable to make much progress against Quinauan Pt beachhead. Progress is also limited in Anyasan-Silaiim sector although tanks of 192d Tank Bn and arty assist Scouts there.

NEI—Japanese begin preinvasion air attacks on Java. From Kendari, Celebes, enemy aircraft strike hard at Soerabaja, Madionen, and Malang.

NEW GUINEA—Japanese begin bombing Port Moresby, garrisoned by small Aus force.

BURMA—Generalissimo Chiang Kai-shek agrees

to let Ch 5th Army take over Toungoo front. Balance of Ch 6th Army is ordered to move into Burma. Ind 48th Brig is ordered to zone of Ind 17th Div, under which it is to fight.

4 February

P.I.—USAFFE takes direct control of Panay and Mindoro garrisons, which were previously part of Visayan-Mindoro Force, established early in January under command of Brig Gen William F. Sharp.

LUZON—II Corps front is relatively quiet. In I Corps area, Japanese in Big Pocket repel still another tank-infantry attack. In South Sector, Scouts and tanks continue attack against Quinauan Pt and this time succeed in compressing enemy into small area at tip. In Anyasan-Silaiim sector, tank-infantry attacks against enemy still make slow progress.

MADOERA STRAIT—U.S.-Dutch naval force of 4 cruisers and. 7 DD's, under command of Rear Adm Karel W. Doorman of Royal Netherlands Navy, sets out to attack enemy shipping off Balikpapan but is detected and attacked by enemy planes in Madoera Strait and abandons mission. USS *Houston* and USS *Marblehead* are damaged in the action.

NEI—Small Aus garrison of Ambon I. (largely 2/21 Bn) surrenders to Japanese.

LIBYA—13 Corps, Br Eighth Army, completes withdrawal to line Gazala-Bir Hacheim and is fortifying it. Axis forces hold line Tmimi-Mechili. Lull ensues until summer during which both sides conduct harassing operations and prepare to renew offensive. British gradually relieve battle-weary forces with fresh troops as they become available.

5 February

U.S.—Caribbean Air Force is redesignated Sixth Air Force; Pacific Air Command becomes Seventh Air Force; Alaskan Air Force is redesignated Eleventh Air Force.

LUZON—I Corps plans to attack with all available forces against enemy pockets. In South Sector, Japanese are driven to edge of cliff overlooking beaches at Quinauan Pt. Little progress is made against enemy in Anyasan-Silaiim sector.

SINGAPORE—Convoy bringing final elements of Br 18th Div and some Ind reinforcements arrives. Slowest ship of the convoy, *Empress of Asia*, is sunk by enemy planes before reaching destination. Japanese air attacks on docks at Singapore prevent other ships of the convoy from unloading some of their cargo.

BURMA—Gen Wavell again visits Burma and inspects situation W of the Salween opposite Moulmein.

6 February

U.S.—Naval Coastal Frontiers are redesignated Sea Frontiers.

LUZON—In I Corps area, Japanese receive reinforcements and attack late in day to relieve pockets. While some elements increase pressure against 1st and 11th Philippine Divs, others drive toward Big Pocket until stopped by 11th Div 800 yards from objective. Small salient in corps MLR is thus formed and called Upper Pocket. In Manila Bay area, Japanese arty, emplaced along S shore of Manila Bay in vicinity of Ternate, begins daily bombardment of fortified islands. Forts Drum and Frank receive main weight of shells.

NEI—Japanese now hold Samarinda, on E coast of Dutch Borneo.

7 February

PACIFIC—ANZAC Force is placed under command of Vice Adm Herbert F. Leary, USN.

LUZON—I Corps opens all-out attack, under command of CG, Left Sector, against enemy pockets and partially encircles both. 1st Div is employed against Little Pocket. 92d Inf of 91st Div (PA) makes main attack against Big Pocket from W and is supported by elements of 11th, Philippine, and 51st Divs. In South Sector, after Scouts on left flank come up against enemy positions in Anyasan-Silaiim area and are brought to a halt, Filipino air corps troops and Constabulary bn are committed to form continuous line from Silaiim Bay to Quinauan Pt. Methodical destruction of enemy remnants at Quinauan Pt continues. Japanese relief force attempting to evacuate troops from SW coast is attacked by P-40's and shore guns and forced back to Olongapo.

8 February

MIDWAY—Bombarded by Japanese submarine.

LUZON—Lt Gen Masaharu Homma orders general withdrawal northward to more favorable positions where troops can be rested and reorganized while awaiting reinforcements for final assault on Bataan. I Corps continues battle to destroy Little and Big Pockets and completely encircles latter. Japanese escape from Little Pocket through small gap on E during night 8-9. In South Sector, resistance on Quinauan Pt ends after small naval craft from Mariveles neutralize beaches, then land party of 21st Pursuit Sq, which works inland and meets Scouts pushing toward beaches. Co of 57th Inf and platoon of 37-mm. guns are released at Quinauan for action against enemy in Anyasan-Silaiim sector. Japanese make final attempt to withdraw forces from SW coast by water and succeed in rescuing 34.

SINGAPORE—Japanese intensify bombardment and about 2045 begin landing in force on NW coast;

despite opposition at beaches, gain firm bridgehead and start toward Tengah airfield, driving wedge in Aus line in W Area.

NEW BRITAIN—Japanese seize Gasmata.

9 February

LUZON—In I Corps area, Japanese remnants from Little Pocket are destroyed while seeking to escape. 1st Div is now free to join in battle against Big Pocket, which is being compressed and from which Japanese are trying to escape. In South Sector, 2d Bn of 57th (PS) replaces 3d Bn in center of line in Anyasan-Silaiim region and makes limited progress against enemy.

SINGAPORE—Although reinforcements are sent to W Area from other sectors, Japanese reach Tengah airfield. In evening, additional enemy land in area just W of causeway. Gen Percival orders garrison to defend S part of the island, where Singapore town, Kalang airdrome, the reservoirs, and supply depots are located. Far East War Council meets for the last time.

U.K.—Pacific War Council, composed of representatives from Great Britain, Australia, Netherlands East Indies, and New Zealand, is formed in London.

10 February

CHRISTMAS I.—U.S. detachment arrives.

MIDWAY—Shelled by enemy submarine.

LUZON—I Corps is rapidly reducing Big Pocket. South Sector forces are compressing Japanese in Anyasan-Silaiim area.

SINGAPORE—Gen Wavell visits Singapore and orders the island held and all remaining RAF personnel withdrawn to NEI. Japanese deepen penetration to supply depot area. AIF Malaya, which is further reinf in W Area, falls back to line Kranji-Jurong, partially prepared switch line position; is later forced from this line.

NEI—Japanese ,continue conquest of Borneo and Celebes; on Celebes, land force at Makassar.

BURMA—46th Brig, Ind 17th Div, which has recently relieved Ind 16th Brig along the Salween in Martaban area, begins fighting withdrawal from Martaban toward Thaton, since Japanese have by-passed Martaban.

11 February

LUZON—I Corps makes substantial progress against Big Pocket, but enemy succeeds in withdrawing through gap on N side. In South Sector, Japanese fall back to Silaiim Pt, between Silaiim and Anyasan Rivers, under pressure.

SINGAPORE—Japanese gain further ground; drop appeals for the garrison to surrender.

BURMA—Additional enemy forces cross Salween in Paan area and engulf bn of Ind 46th Brig.

12 February

U.S.—Tenth Air Force is activated at Patterson Field, Ohio, and assigned to Gen Stilwell.

LUZON—I Corps regains important trail junction unopposed. In South Sector, Japanese try desperately to escape from Silaiim Pt; break through Philippine line, but are overtaken as they push N toward Silaiim R and are forced steadily toward the sea:

SINGAPORE—Japanese attack strongly at several points and make further gains. During night 12-13, beach defense forces on E and SE coasts are withdrawn to strengthen defense perimeter around town of Singapore. Supply situation is deteriorating rapidly.

MEDITERRANEAN—3 supply ships leave Alexandria (Egypt) for Malta, but all are lost to enemy before reaching destination.

ENGLISH CHANNEL—German warships *Scharnhorst*, *Gneisenau*, and *Prinz Eugen* proceed from Brest up English Channel under attack by RAF and air arm of Royal Navy.

13 February

WESTERN HEMISPHERE—U.S. and Canada approve construction of U.S. Military Highway through Canada to Alaska.

CANTON I.—U.S. detachment arrives.

LUZON—I Corps, after searching entire area of Big Pocket without finding any live Japanese, turns its full attention to the salient, Upper Pocket, in MLR. Elements released from the Big Pocket assault force join in the battle. In South Sector, troops complete destruction of enemy in Silaiim area.

SINGAPORE—Japanese further compress British on Singapore. Main thrusts are against W part of S Area; Br forward units pull back, night 13-14, to cover Alexandra area, where main ordnance depot and ammunition magazine are located. All remaining Br shipping—small ships and other light craft—sail from Singapore, night 13-14. Some personnel are withdrawn in these vessels among them Rear Adm, Malaya, and Air Officer Commanding, Far East.

NEI—Japanese overrun Bandjermasin, key point in SE Borneo.

14 February

LUZON—I Corps further reduces salient in MLR, which is now about half its original size.

ABDA COMMAND—Vice Adm Conrad E. L. Helfrich of Royal Netherlands Navy succeeds Adm Hart as commander of ABDA Combined Naval Striking Force.

SINGAPORE—Japanese continue to make main effort against W part of S Area and gain ground near Alexandra. Water supply of garrison is in danger of failing within a short time. Supplies of food and ammunition are also dwindling rapidly. Br flotilla withdrawing from Singapore is attacked by enemy naval and air forces in approaches to Bangka Strait and suffers heavily. Boat carrying Rear Adm, Malaya, and Air Officer Commanding, Far East, is driven ashore on small deserted island where the men later perish.

NEI—Japanese invade Sumatra, dropping paratroopers in Palembang area after air attack on Palembang I airdrome. Small force defending airdrome (150 Dutch infantry and about 60 RAF ground defense gunners) is forced to withdraw toward W coast, Japanese having blocked road to town of Palembang. Allied naval TF moves N to engage enemy shipping in Bangka Strait but comes under heavy air attack and retires to base. Palembang-based aircraft are attacking enemy shipping in Bangka Strait and cannot be notified in time to intercept invasion force.

IRAQ—Siboney reaches Basra where American civilian construction force debarks and proceeds by lorry to Umm Qasr, hq of Iranian District engineer, to begin construction projects. Cargo does not arrive at Umm Qasr until end of month.

15 February

LUZON—In II Corps area, Japanese attack in limited strength to ease pressure against troops withdrawing northward from I Corps sector. I Corps continues to make steady progress against salient in MLR.

SINGAPORE—Malayan campaign ends with surrender of Singapore, W anchor of Malay Barrier, to Japanese. Gen Percival meets with Japanese commander, Gen Tomoyuki Yamashita, and surrenders his forces (more than 64,000 troops—Indian, British, and Australian) unconditionally, effective at nightfall.

NEI—Japanese invasion fleet enters river mouth near Palembang, Sumatra, and unloads troops despite repeated and costly attacks by aircraft from Palembang II airdrome. Dutch and RAF personnel withdraw from Palembang, where demolition of refineries is only partially completed. Br personnel holding landing grounds in central and N Sumatra are ordered to W coast for withdrawal.

AUSTRALIA—Allied convoy with reinforcements for Koepang, Timor (Aus 2/4 Pioneer Bn and U.S. 148th FA Regt, less one bn), sails from Darwin. The units are to secure Penfoie airdrome, the only staging point on Timor for flights to Java.

BURMA—Ind 17th Div begins withdrawal behind Bilin R line, 46th Brig abandoning Thaton. Japanese follow closely and try to outflank div.

16 February

CARIBBEAN SEA—German submarines attack Aruba I., off coast of Venezuela.

LUZON—I Corps reduces salient in MLR to area 75 by 100 yards. In South Sector, enemy remnants from Silaiim Pt, attempting to escape northward, are detected about 7 miles from the point and destroyed in 2-day fight. In Manila Bay area, Japanese destroy section of pipeline on Cavite shore through which Fort Frank on Carabao I. received fresh water. Distillation plant is put into operation at Fort Frank.

NEI—Withdrawal of Br personnel and operational aircraft from Sumatra to Java is completed. Equipment is left behind at Oesthaven. Allied convoy bound for Timor is recalled to Darwin because of heavy attacks by Japanese planes.

17 February

BORA BORA—U.S. Army units arrive.

LUZON—I Corps completely restores MLR without opposition as enemy continues to withdraw.

BURMA—Japanese maintain pressure against Ind 17th Div along Bilin R and continue outflanking attempts.

MIDDLE EAST—Gen Auchinleck is ordered to release a more divs for action in Far East—Br 70th and Aus 9th. Aus 9th Div is subsequently allowed to remain in Middle East.

18 February

U.S.—War Department orders overseas contract activities throughout the world militarized. All civilian contract activities are to be terminated by 18 August 1942.

NEI—Japanese invade Bali, off E coast of Java, landing on SE coast, night 18-19. This completes isolation of Java. Br volunteer party from Batavia (Java) sails to Oesthaven (Sumatra), where equipment is salvaged and demolitions are performed without interference from enemy.

BURMA—Situation of Ind 17th Div deteriorates as Japanese gain foothold on W bank of Bilin R near Bilin and continue pressure on flanks. TF's are formed by Burma Army to protect Pegu from SE and sea approaches to Syriam.

19 February

BADOENG STRAIT—Combined Allied naval force under Adm Doorman, Royal Netherlands Navy, attacks enemy vessel off Bali, night 19-20. Although considerable damage is believed to have been done to enemy, Dutch DD *Piet Hein* is sunk and other Allied vessels are damaged.

AUSTRALIA—Darwin undergoes destructive attack by Japanese planes from carriers in Banda Sea and ground base at Kendari. Most of the shipping in the harbor, including USS *Peary* (DD), is destroyed. Virtually all the aircraft crowded on the airfield are demolished. This is the greatest single Japanese air effort since attack on Pearl Harbor.

BURMA—Ind 17th Div continues to defend Bilin R line throughout day but is ordered to fall back after dark. Mandalay receives its first enemy air attack.

20 February

U.S.—Grants billion-dollar loan to USSR.

LUZON—In Manila Bay area, Japanese arty bombardment of fortified islands reaches peak intensity.

NEI—Japanese invade Timor, where Aus 2/40th Bn defends Penfoie airdrome.

SOUTH PACIFIC—Newly formed U.S. naval TF, consisting of USS *Lexington* with screen of cruisers and DD's, heads toward Rabaul, New Britain, to disperse Japanese concentrations but when attacked by enemy planes withdraws without executing mission. Japanese suffer heavy plane losses and postpone operations scheduled against New Guinea.

BURMA—Ind 17th Div begins withdrawal behind Sittang R, 48th Brig leading.

U.K.—Maj Gen Ira C. Eaker, who is to command VIII Bomber Command, arrives by air to prepare for reception of U.S. air force (Eighth); reports to Maj Gen James E. Chaney, CG USAFBI.

21 February

LUZON—Lull settles over entire front as both sides dig in and prepare for further action. Japanese have completed withdrawal from I Corps area; diversionary forces employed against II Corps are ordered back to Balanga area.

BURMA—Removed from jurisdiction of ABDA Command and placed under command of CinC, India. 7th Armd Brig arrives at Rangoon from Middle East; is soon committed on Pegu front. Ind 17th Div continues toward Sittang bridge near Mokpalin with Japanese in close pursuit.

22 February

U.S.—President Roosevelt orders Gen MacArthur to leave the Philippines.

BURMA—Japanese open strong attacks against 2 brigs of Ind 17th Div E of Sittang R in Mokpalin area before withdrawal through Sittang bridge bottleneck can be accomplished.

U.K.—Hq of U.S. Army Bomber Command, USAFBI, is established under Gen Eaker.

23 February

INTERNATIONAL AGREEMENTS—U.S. and Great Britain sign mutual-aid agreement on settlement of lend-lease obligations.

U.S.—Enemy submarine shells Bankline Oil Refinery near Santa Barbara, California. This is the first attack of the war on U.S. mainland.

BISMARCK ARCHIPELAGO—U.S. Fifth Air Force makes first attack against Rabaul, New Britain. 6 B-17's from Townsville, Australia, strike with unobserved results.

NEI—Japanese report conquest of Ambon completed. Gen Brett flies from Java, which is in imminent danger, to Australia.

BURMA—Violent fighting for Sittang R bridgehead continues. Ind 17th Div destroys Sittang bridge at 0530 to prevent enemy from using it, although 16th and 46th Brigs are still E of the river. Remnants of these brigs eventually cross in small craft or by swimming, but battle of Sittang bridgehead is disastrous for Ind 17th Div; 46th Brig must be broken up to provide replacements.

MIDDLE EAST—Auchinleck revises plans for defense of Northern Front, instructing Br Ninth and Tenth Armies to impose maximum delay on enemy in the event of Axis offensive.

24 February

WAKE—U.S. naval TF (*Enterprise*, 2 cruisers, 7 DD's), under command of Vice Adm William F. Halsey, Jr., considerably damages Japanese positions by aerial and naval bombardment.

NEI—Evacuation of Java continues. Gen Brereton and his staff leave for India.

INDIA—Gen Stilwell arrives at Karachi.

USSR—During 10-day battle on northern front, Red Army encircles *II Corps* of German *Sixteenth Army* SE of Staraya Russa. German forces to S are containing Soviet efforts to break through to Smolensk on central front and to Dnieper bend in the Ukraine.

25 February

ABDA COMMAND—Is dissolved and defense of Java is left to the Dutch, who are to be assisted by Br, Aus, and U.S. detachments.

BURMA—Japanese are infiltrating into Pegu Yomas through gap of some 30-40 miles that exists between Burma 1st Div at Nyaunglebin and Ind 17th Div at Pegu, threatening Rangoon-Mandalay road.

INDIA—Gen Stilwell, who receives rank of Lt Gen, AUS, confers with GHQ, India, at New Delhi.

26 February

P.I.—Japanese amphibious force, consisting of a bn of infantry and a FA battery, sails from Olongapo, Luzon, for Mindoro.

AUSTRALIA—U.S. TF bound for New Caledonia reaches Australia.

INDIAN OCEAN—USS *Langley* (ACV), with 32 fighters on board, is sunk en route to Java by Japanese planes.

BURMA—Hard fighting is developing in Waw area, NE of Pegu, as enemy continues infiltration westward from Sittang R.

LIBYA—13 Corps is responsible for defenses organized in depth over 36-mile area from Gazala to Bir Hacheim. 30 Corps prepares defensive positions on frontier and has detachment at Giarabub.

27 February

U.S.—President Roosevelt, by executive order, authorizes creation of joint Mexican-U.S. Defense Commission. Brig Gen Raymond A. Wheeler, now in Iran, is named commander of SOS CBI; Gen Wheeler is also to continue as chief of Iranian Mission.

P.I.—Japanese force lands on NE Mindoro, where a town and airfield are overrun. No effort is made to secure rest of island. Enemy blockade about the Philippines is thus tightened.

JAVA SEA—Organized Allied naval resistance collapses during Battle of Java Sea. Combined naval TF under Adm Doorman attacks Japanese convoy approaching Java and is decisively defeated. Br DD's *Electra* and *Jupiter* and Dutch DD *Kortenaer* are sunk, as are Dutch cruisers *De Ruyter* and *Java*. Japanese sustain some damage but not enough to interfere with their plan for completing conquest of NEI.

INDIA—Gen Wavell arrives in New Delhi from Java.

FRANCE—British successfully raid radio location station at Bruneval during night 27-28, dropping parachute force of 120.

28 February

U.S.—War Department directive gives Gen Wheeler mission of expediting flow of supplies and equipment to Gen Stilwell.

NEI—After severe air attacks on air and naval installations, Japanese *16th Army* invades Java during night 28 February-1 March, going ashore on N coast and making main effort near Batavia. Allied planes attack enemy shipping before and during landing. Adm Doorman's naval force, split into small groups, heads toward Soenda Strait in effort to escape from Java Sea; some of the vessels are not heard from again. *Sea Witch*, with 27 crated P-40's on board, reaches Tjilatjap safely, but P-40's are destroyed to prevent them from falling into enemy hands.

BURMA—Br Imperial forces fall back on Pegu from Payagyi and Waw in anticipation of general withdrawal.

1 March

MIDWAY—MAG 22 is formed from squadrons on the island.

LUZON—Japanese *14th Army*, during period 6 January to date, has suffered severe setback on Luzon and sustained almost 7,000 casualties (2,700 killed and over 4,000 wounded).

NEI—Japanese, now in undisputed control of air and sea, make rapid progress on the ground on Java. Allied planes based on Java are virtually wiped out, many of them on the ground. After a final effort to stall enemy by air, surviving air personnel begin assembling in Jogjakarta, the last remaining airfield in Java, for withdrawal to Australia. Since Java ports are untenable, Allied naval command is dissolved and ships are directed to withdraw to Australia. U.S. DD's *Edsall* and *Pillsbury* and PG *Asheville*, as well as a few Br corvettes, are unable to make good their escape. Of Adm Doorman's original Java Sea striking force (5 cruisers and 10 DD's), only 4 U.S. DD's succeed in reaching Australia. Cruisers *Houston* (U.S.) and *Perth* (Aus) and DD's *Pope* (U.S.), *Encounter* (Br), and *Evertsen* (Dutch) are lost while trying to escape.

BURMA—Burma 1st Div covers concentration of Ch 5th Army in Toungoo area. 200th Div of the army, which is already disposed in this area, regains Nyaunglebin and Pyuntaza, on Rangoon-Mandalay road. Gen Wavell arrives in Burma and orders Rangoon held as long as possible, at least until reinforcements en route (63d Brig Gp) arrive. Ind 17th Div returns toward Waw, which is to be defended.

USSR—Soviet advance comes to a halt during March. Battle line remains about the same throughout month, despite continued fighting on all fronts.

Germans are unable to relieve isolated *II Corps*, *Sixteenth Army*, SE of Staraya Russa, but succeed in withdrawing salient SW of Kaluga; contain Soviet attacks on southern front, which are extended to region E of Kharkov.

2 March

NEI—Japanese gain further ground in Java, where Dutch are continuing to resist; claim capture of Batavia, from which NEI Government has been forced to move to Bandoeng. Many ships are scuttled off Java to prevent them from falling into enemy hands.

NEW GUINEA—Japanese begin heavy air strikes on New Guinea in preparation for invasion of Huon Gulf area.

BURMA—Japanese continue to infiltrate westward between Burma 1st and Ind 17th Divs and are swinging SW on Rangoon, bypassing Pegu.

3 March

NEI—Dutch continue losing battle for Java against superior enemy forces.

AUSTRALIA—Japanese planes strike hard at Broome, where refugees from Java are concentrated, destroying many planes on ground and in water.

BURMA—Fighting continues in Waw-Pyinbon area, NE of Pegu. 63d Brig Gp arrives at Rangoon.

4 March

HAWAII—2 Japanese planes drop total of 4 bombs near Punch Bowl crater, Oahu. No damage.

MARCUS I.—U.S. planes from carrier *Enterprise* make surprise attack on island just before dawn, achieving satisfactory results.

P.I.—Gen MacArthur is reorganizing his forces in the Philippines in preparation for his departure. Composite Visayan-Mindanao Force is divided into 2 commands. Gen Sharp retains command of forces on Mindanao; the Visayan forces are placed under Brig Gen Bradford G. Chynoweth. MacArthur's plans envisage the formation of 2 more commands. Maj Gen George F. Moore's harbor defense forces on Corregidor and other islands in Manila Bay will constitute one, the forces on Luzon the other.

NEI—Dutch continue fighting on Java and report that destruction of principal installations has been completed.

CHINA—Gen Stilwell establishes Hq, American Army Forces, China, Burma, and India, at Chungking, using his U.S. Task Force in China and AMMISCA personnel as a nucleus. Gen Magruder's directive is altered to place AMMISCA personnel at disposal of Gen Stilwell.

5 March

NEI—Dutch continue a losing battle for Java. Batavia is reported evacuated.

NEW BRITAIN—Japanese convoy bound for Huon Gulf, New Guinea, sails from Rabaul, New Britain, during night 5-6.

INDIA—Gen Breton takes command of U.S. Tenth Air Force, which is at this time extremely small, with hq at New Delhi.

BURMA—Lt Gen Sir Harold R. L. G. Alexander arrives at Rangoon to take command of Burma Army. Gen Hutton remains as Chief of General Staff. Gen Alexander at once begins offensive to close gap between Burma 1st and Ind 17th Divs. Japanese attack Pegu from W and succeed in entering the town.

USSR—Moscow announces recapture by Red Army of Yukhnov, NW of Kaluga, on central front.

6 March

AUSTRALIA—U.S. TF sails for New Caledonia.

CHINA—Gen Stilwell confers for the first time with Chiang Kai-shek in Chungking.

BURMA—Newly arrived 63d Brig, under command of Ind 17th Div, makes futile effort to clear block on Rangoon-Pegu road and relieve Pegu garrison, which is isolated. Gen Alexander orders Rangoon evacuated since situation in lower Burma is deteriorating rapidly; denial program is to be put into effect at midnight 6-7.

7 March

NEI—Japanese conquest of Java is virtually completed. Radio and cable communications with Bandoeng cease. Final reports indicate that enemy is still advancing on all fronts, that the defenders are completely exhausted, and that all Allied fighter planes have been destroyed.

NEW GUINEA—Japanese convoy arrives in Huon Gulf during night 7-8 and under cover of naval bombardment lands assault forces at Salamaua and Lae without opposition.

NEW CALEDONIA—Maj Gen Alexander M. Patch, commander-designate of New Caledonia Task Force, arrives.

BURMA—Burma Army evacuates Rangoon, moving along Prome road except for demolition forces, which are removed by sea. Loss of Rangoon seriously handicaps supply and reinforcement of Burma Army, which must now depend on air for this. Withdrawal from Rangoon is halted at Taukkyan by enemy roadblock. Bypassed force in Pegu is ordered to withdraw.

8 March

ALASKA—Brig Gen William O. Butler assumes command of U.S. Eleventh Air Force under Alaska Defense Command (Maj Gen Simon B. Buckner, Jr.). Alaska Defense Command is in turn under Western Defense Command (Lt Gen John L. De-Witt), which was designated a theater of operations early in the war.

BURMA—63d Brig and elements of 16th, with tank and arty support, clear Japanese block on Rangoon-Prome road at Taukkyan. During period 8-13 March, heavy bombers of U.S. Tenth Air Force transport troops and supplies from India to Magwe, Burma.

MIDDLE EAST—Gen Ritchie is ordered by Gen Auchinleck to provide diversion in Libya for passage of convoy to Malta. Supply situation on Malta is very serious.

9 March

U.S.—Major reorganization of U.S. Army is effective this date. GHQ is abolished and 3 autonomous commands—Army Ground Forces under Lt Gen Lesley J. McNair, Army Air Forces under Lt Gen Henry H. Arnold, and Services of Supply (later designated as Army Service Forces) under Maj Gen Brehon B. Somervell—are given responsibility for Zone of Interior functions under Gen Marshall as Chief of Staff. Field forces remain under control of War Department General Staff.

Adm King is appointed Chief of Naval Operations in addition to his post of CinC, U.S. Fleet. Adm King succeeds Adm Harold R. Stark, who will command U.S. naval forces operating in European waters.

P.I.—Gen MacArthur announces that Gen Yamashita has replaced Gen Homma as CinC of enemy forces in the Philippines.

NEI—Japanese complete conquest of Java and thereby gain control of entire NEI. With Malaya Barrier thus penetrated, Australia is in greater danger.

NEW GUINEA—Land-based planes attack Japanese convoy in Huon Gulf with unobserved results. Japanese aircraft continue neutralization of points in New Guinea.

BURMA—Burma Army forces at Taukkyan continue northward withdrawal without serious difficulty.

10 March

MIDWAY—Enemy patrol plane is shot down SW of island.

P.I.—Gen Wainwright visits Gen MacArthur on Corregidor and learns that he (Wainwright) will head Luzon Force and that his I Corps will be turned over to Gen Jones, 51st Div CG. Gen MacArthur, after his withdrawal from the Philippines, plans to remain in control of Philippine operations from Australia through Col Lewis C. Beebe, who will be deputy chief of staff of USAFFE.

NEW GUINEA—Japanese make another landing on New Guinea, at Finschhafen. U.S. planes, 104 strong, from carriers *Lexington* and *Yorktown* make co-ordinated attacks on enemy shipping and installations at Lae and Salamaua, considerably damaging shipping and airfields. A few B-17's from Townsville, Australia, follow up carrier strikes with attacks on same area. Japanese fly fighters from Rabaul, New Britain, to Huon Gulf area and continue neutralization of Port Moresby by air.

IRAN—Declared eligible for U.S. lend-lease.

11 March

P.I.—Gen MacArthur and his family and staff embark from Corregidor in 4 PT boats for Mindanao.

BURMA—Burma Army regroups in preparation for defense of upper Burma. In Irrawaddy Valley, Ind 17th Div is disposed in Tharrawaddy area. In Sittang Valley, Burma 1st Div, after successful diversionary attacks against Shwegyin and Madauk, E of Nyaunglebin, withdraws, except for 13th Brig, to positions N of Kanyutkwin. Gen Stilwell is placed in command of Ch 5th and 6th Armies. Ch 6th Army is holding Shan States. Ch 5th Army, except for 200th Div disposed in Toungoo area, is to concentrate at Mandalay.

MALTA—Military garrison is placed under command of CinC MEF. Naval and RAF garrisons are under command of CinC Mediterranean and Air Officer Commanding in Chief, respectively. Lt Gen Sir William Dobbie, Governor of Malta, remains commander in chief.

12 March

NEW CALEDONIA—U.S. TF (17,500 men) under Gen Patch reaches Noumea to assist in defense of that area.

ANDAMAN IS.—Garrison of Andaman Is. (co of British and bn of Gurkhas) is withdrawn, since loss of Rangoon makes it unfeasible to maintain this seaplane base.

BURMA—Burma Army establishes hq at Maymyo.

13 March

NEW GUINEA—Japanese, having gained firm positions in Lae-Salamaua area, replace infantry with naval forces.

SOLOMON IS.—Japanese force from *4th Fleet* sails from Rabaul, New Britain, for Buka, which is eventually seized together with other positions in N Solomons.

INDIA—First detachment of U.S. troops (Air Forces personnel) to reach CBI arrive at Karachi, having been diverted from Java.

14 March

U.S.—Joint Chiefs of Staff decide to continue on the defensive in the Pacific with forces already there and to build up forces in United Kingdom for an offensive against Germany.

P.I.—Gen MacArthur and his party reach Mindanao.

IRAN—U.S. Iranian Mission begins releasing civilian contractors in accordance with War Department directive of 18 February calling for militarization of contract activities throughout world.

15 March

LUZON—In Manila Bay area the Japanese, having emplaced additional arty along S shore of Manila Bay SW of Ternate, renew intensive bombardment of fortified islands. Shelling is conducted daily and in great force through 21 March, despite U.S. counterbattery fire. Forts Frank and Drum are particularly hard hit.

BURMA—Gen Stilwell is notified that Gen Wavell, as Supreme Commander, India, is responsible for operations in Burma.

17 March

AUSTRALIA—From Mindanao, Gen MacArthur flies to Darwin, where he will be in supreme command of forces in SW Pacific. Formal delineation of this area has not yet been agreed upon. Col Beebe, deputy chief of staff of USAFFE, is promoted to brig gen.

CBI—Air Vice Marshal Stevenson, commanding Allied air forces, moves hq from Burma to Calcutta, India.

18 March

NEW HEBRIDES—U.S. Army troops (2 cos of 182d Inf and an engr co of Americal Div) arrive at Efate to build airfield.

19 March

BURMA—Lt Gen William J. Slim arrives in Burma to take command of Imperial troops, now formed into Burma I Corps. In Sittang Valley, Japanese begin drive on Toungoo and are opposed by Ch 200th Div.

USSR—German *Army Group North* is making determined efforts to break through to *II Corps, Sixteenth Army*, in Cholm-Staraya Russa area. Red Army maintains pressure on enemy on central and southern fronts.

20 March

P.I.—Gen Wainwright learns that he has been promoted to rank of lt gen and that Washington has placed him in command of all U.S. forces in the Philippines.

LIBYA—Complying with request of 8 March for offensive action to divert enemy's attention from Malta-bound convoy, Br Eighth Army raids landing grounds in Derna and Benghazi areas after nightfall.

21 March

P.I.—Gen Wainwright, as commander of U.S. Forces in the Philippines (USFIP), which supersedes USAFFE, establishes hq on Corregidor and appoints Gen Beebe his chief of staff. Maj Gen Edward P. King, Jr., is to be commander of Luzon Force.

AUSTRALIA—Lt Gen George H. Brett, U.S. Army, becomes commander of combined air forces, retaining command of USAFIA.

CBI—Assam-Burma-China Ferry Command is activated. It consists of 25 Pan-American transports, which are soon diverted from mission of taking supplies to China in order to supply forces withdrawing from Burma.

BURMA—Burma 1st Div, upon being relieved on Toungoo front by 200th Div, Ch 5th Army, begins movement to Irrawaddy front, leaving large area S of Toungoo undefended. Gen Stilwell, now in Burma, issues orders for Ch participation in defense of line Toungoo-Prome. Ch 5th Army is charged with defense of Toungoo. Its 200th Div is reinf by attachment of Temporary 55th Div (T-55th) of Ch 6th Army, which is to move to Pyawbwe. In army reserve, Ch 22d Div is directed to Taungdwingyi, where it is to be prepared to assist British in Prome area while Ch 96th Div is to move to Mandalay. Crippling enemy air attack on Magwe airdrome reduces the already meager air force defending Burma.

LIBYA—Br Eighth Army continues raids on forward landing grounds of Axis forces as diversion for convoy to Malta. Raids are partially successful, drawing off part of enemy's aircraft, but convoy is unable to reach Malta intact and later suffers additional damage under air attack while unloading.

22 March

U.S.—President Roosevelt sends message to Gen MacArthur in Australia expressing his desire that Gen Wainwright control all forces in the Philippines; Gen MacArthur concurs.

BURMA—Japanese planes make another destructive attack on Magwe airdrome, forcing AVG and RAF aircraft to withdraw to Loiwing (on Ch frontier) and Akyab, respectively. Troops defending Burma are thus denied close air support. Gen Stilwell, upon arriving at front, begins planning for counterattack in support of Ch 200th Div at Toungoo. Chinese continue to withstand pressure against Toungoo from the S.

23 March

ANDAMAN Is.—Japanese invade islands without opposition.

24 March

U.S.—Pacific Theater is established as an area of U.S. responsibility by Combined Chiefs of Staff.

LUZON—Japanese begin intense air and arty bombardment of Bataan. Luzon-based Japanese Army and Navy planes begin thorough bombardment of Corregidor, continuing through end of March. During this period night air attacks are conducted for the first time.

BURMA—In surprise attack on Kyungon airfield, N of Toungoo, Japanese rout defenders (troops of Ch 200th Div and rear elements of Burma 1st Div) and cut rail line and road, thus partially surrounding Toungoo. Chinese fall back on Toungoo, while Burmese succeed in withdrawing to Irrawaddy front.

25 March

SOCIETY Is.—162d Inf, U.S. 41st Div, arrives at Bora Bora.

BURMA—Ch 200th Div is virtually besieged in Toungoo. Elements of T-55th Div arrive N of the town but do not attack. Burma I Corps is ordered to concentrate in Prome-Allanmyo area.

26 March

CELEBES—Japanese carrier force leaves Kendari for Indian Ocean.

BURMA—Continuing pressure against Chinese in Toungoo, Japanese seize the town as far as RR line. Ch 22d Div, which has previously been ordered to Pyinmana-Yedashe area, N of Toungoo, to counterattack in support of Ch 200th Div, arrives in position but fails to take the offensive.

27 March

U.S.—War Plans Division issues "Plan for Operations in Northwest Europe," calling for small-scale operation in autumn 1942 (SLEDGEHAMMER) as an emergency measure if Soviet forces show signs of collapsing or main Anglo-American invasion (ROUNDUP) in spring 1943 If SLEDGEHAMMER Is not required. Build-up plan for the invasion is coded BOLERO.

BURMA—Ch 200th Div continues to resist enemy onslaughts against Toungoo. On Irrawaddy front, Japanese are massing forces S of Prome. RAF planes withdraw from Akyab to India as result of heavy enemy bombing of Akyab.

FRANCE—British conduct combined operations against harbor installations at St. Nazaire, night 27-28. HMS *Campbeltown* (DD) rams main lock gate and lands troops who carry out demolitions.

28 March

LUZON—Japanese, moving into position for all-out offensive against Bataan, feint against I Corps and push in OPL of Sector D on II Corps front. Increasingly heavy air and arty bombardment of Bataan is lowering efficiency of defense force as well as destroying badly needed materiel. Efforts to run the blockade and supply the garrison with necessary items have virtually failed, and supply situation is growing steadily worse.

BURMA—Gen Alexander, at request of Gen Stilwell, agrees to attack on Irrawaddy front. Rcn elements of Burma I Corps clash with enemy at Paungde, SE of Prome.

29 March

BURMA—Going on the offensive to relieve pressure on Chinese at Toungoo and restore communications, TF of Burma I Corps attacks and clears Paungde, but its situation becomes precarious as Japanese establish themselves a few miles N at Padigon and on E bank of the Irrawaddy at Shwedaung.

30 March

U.S.—Directives are drafted for Gen MacArthur as Supreme Commander, SWPA, and for Adm Nimitz as CINCPOA, for submission to Allied governments concerned. SWPA is to include Australia, Philippines, New Guinea, Bismarck Archipelago, Solomons, and most of NEI. As Supreme Commander of SWPA, Gen MacArthur is to maintain positions in Philippines and bases in Australia; guard approaches to SWPA; halt enemy's advance on Australia; protect communications within theater; support POA forces; and be prepared to take the offensive. POA comprises N, Central, and S Pacific, all under over-all command of Adm Nimitz, and the first two under his direct

[31 MARCH–5 APRIL 1942]

command. As CINCPOA, Adm Nimitz is to maintain communications between U.S. and SWPA; support operations in SWPA; and be prepared to take offensive action. In addition to SWPA and POA, Pacific Theater is to include Southeast Pacific Area—ocean stretches W of Central and South America.

Pacific War Council is established in Washington.

Inter-American Defense Board holds its first meeting in Washington.

BURMA—Ch 200th Div withdraws from Toungoo under pressure. On Irrawaddy front, Burma I Corps TF falls back to Prome from Paungde area, leaving vehicles behind at Shwedaung. During night 30–31, Japanese attack Ind 63d Brig at Prome and soon breach defenses, exposing right flank of Ind 17th Div.

ASCENSION I.—First detachment of U.S. forces arrives to build airstrip on this small island, which lies about midway between South America and Africa.

31 March

BURMA—Ch 200th Div makes contact with Ch 22d Div N of Toungoo and withdraws N of Pyinmana as reserve. With loss of Toungoo, road to Mawchi is left undefended and Japanese, during next few days, overrun small Ch garrison at Mawchi; continue E, forcing elements of Ch T-55th Div back to Bawlake

1 April

U.S.—Pacific War Council holds its first meeting at Washington, D.C.

NEW GUINEA—Japanese from NEI land at a number of points on Dutch New Guinea coast, from Sorong on NW tip to Hollandia, during period 1–20 April; landings are virtually unopposed.

BURMA—CinC India, visiting front, agrees to immediate withdrawal of Burma I Corps to Allanmyo area, N of Prome. Japanese continue to press in on Prome.

Iraq—Dock construction project at Umm Qasr is begun after cargo of *City of Dalhart* is unloaded.

USSR—Stalemate exists along entire line. Germans of Army Group North are largely concerned during the month with extricating II Corps of Sixteenth Army from pocket SE of Staraya Russa.

2 April

INDIA—U.S. Tenth Air Force flies its first combat mission, attacking shipping off Andaman Is.; subsequently concentrates on enemy positions in Burma.

BURMA—Burma I Corps withdraws from Prome.

3 April

LUZON—Japanese open all-out offensive against Bataan line, which is by now understrength, undernourished, poorly clothed and equipped, and battle weary. After air and arty bombardment, lasting from 1000 until 1500, Japanese move forward, making main effort against Sector D, the W flank of II Corps, where 41st and 21st Divs (PA) are thinly spread and dazed as result of preliminary bombardment. 41st, on W, gives way and is rendered virtually ineffective as a fighting force, although regt on extreme W succeeds in withdrawing in an orderly fashion. Bn on W flank of 21st Div is forced to pull back. Effort to re-establish line of 41st Div after dark is partially successful. The only corps reserve unit, 33d Inf (PA), less 1st Bn, is released to Sector D as is Prov Tank Gp (–) of Luzon Force reserve. In I Corps sector to W, Japanese succeed in reaching MLR on E flank but are unable to pierce it.

BURMA—Burma I Corps continues northward withdrawal from Allanmyo area although not under enemy pressure. In Sittang Valley, Gen Stilwell begins deploying Chinese for stand at Pyinmana. Ch 22d Div is to fall back gradually on Pyinmana, where Ch 96th Div is to take over.

MIDDLE EAST—India is removed from U.S. Iranian Mission's sphere of responsibility, but Karachi remains base for the 2 U.S. Middle East missions. Gen Wheeler is relieved as chief of Iranian Mission.

4 April

LUZON—In II Corps area, Japanese attack is again preceded by demoralizing arty bombardment in conjunction with air attacks. MLR of Sector D collapses as 41st Div withdraws again and 21st Div is forced from MLR to reserve line in front of Mt Samat. After nightfall, Japanese regroup for assault on Mt Samat. Sector C has to refuse its left flank because of enemy breakthrough. Luzon Force sends 2 regts of Philippine Div—31st (U.S.) and 45th (PS)—to support II Corps.

INDIAN OCEAN—Japanese naval force in Indian Ocean sinks Br cruisers *Dorsetshire* and *Cornwall* near Colombo, Ceylon.

MIDDLE EAST—Col Don G. Shingler is notified that he is to head U.S. Iranian Mission, replacing Gen Wheeler. Iranian projects now have top priority, and construction project at Umm Qasr, Iraq, is suspended.

5 April

LUZON—After air and arty preparation, Japanese resume offensive in the II Corps area, concentrating on 21st Div, which yields Mt Samat and is left virtually ineffective as a fighting force. Corps prepares to counterattack on 6th with all available forces. Japanese invasion force of 4,852 troops sails from Lingayen Gulf toward Cebu, in the Visayan Islands.

CEYLON—Japanese carrier-based planes attack Colombo.

6 April

LUZON—II Corps counterattacks N toward reserve line in Sector D but meets enemy attack head on and falls back. On corps E flank, U.S. 31st Inf and 21st Div (PA), directed to drive N in region E of Mt Samat, are unable to reach line of departure. In center, Philippine 33d Inf, followed by 42d and 43d, endeavors to drive N between Catmon and W slopes of Mt Samat, but 33d is surrounded and presumed lost and units to rear are routed. Hq of Sector D and W flank troops are thus separated from rest of II Corps. On W, Philippine 41st Inf, followed by 45th, makes limited progress, but 45th is unable to overtake 41st and 41st becomes isolated. U.S. 31st Inf and bn of 57th Inf (PS) are assigned to Sector C, where line is withdrawn to San Vicente R. Japanese receive effective air and arty support throughout day.

ADMIRALTY IS.—Small Japanese naval force from Truk lands at Lorengau.

AUSTRALIA—Main body (Hq, 163d Regt, 167th FA Bn, and other units) of U.S. 41st Div reaches Melbourne.

BURMA—Japanese land reinforcements at Rangoon. Chiang Kai-shek, visiting Maymyo, urges that Taungdwingyi be held and agrees to provide Ch div to assist Burma I Corps. Ch 200th and 96th Divs are in position to defend Pyinmana.

MIDDLE EAST—U.S. War Department decides that no fixed installations are to be established in Iranian Mission territory.

7 April

LUZON—Japanese, attacking again in II Corps area with air and arty support, force entire corps MLR back to Mamala R line; this line, too, becomes untenable, and Americans and Filipinos withdraw under cover of darkness, 7–8, to Alangan R. 26th Cav (PS), released to II Corps from I Corps reserve, establishes holding position while line is formed along the Mamala. Meanwhile, attempts by Philippine Div units to form continuous line prove futile. Philippine Constabulary regts defending beaches are ordered into battle line. I Corps is directed to withdraw southward to Binuangan R line.

8 April

LUZON—II Corps disintegrates completely under sustained enemy attacks from ground and air. Japanese soon discover gaps in Alangan R line—held by 31st Inf (U.S.), 57th Inf (PS), 26th Cav (PS), 803d Engr Bn (U.S.), 14th Engr Bn (PS), and Constabulary troops—and stream southward at will. In final effort to stem enemy advance, Prov Coast Arty Brig (AA), serving as infantrymen, forms weak line just N of Cabcaben, but other units ordered to extend this line are unable to do so. Gen King decides to surrender Luzon Force; orders equipment destroyed during night 8–9. Of the 78,000 men of Luzon Force, about 2,000 succeed in escaping to Corregidor.

U.K.—Gen Marshall and Mr Harry Hopkins arrive in London for series of conferences with the British on BOLERO.

9 April

LABRADOR—U.S. detachment arrives.

P.I.—On Luzon, at 0330, emissaries of Gen King start to Japanese lines under white flag to arrange for surrender. Gen King surrenders Luzon Force unconditionally at 1230, and grim march of prisoners from Balanga to San Fernando follows. Fall of Bataan permits Japanese aircraft previously employed against it to devote their full attention to Corregidor. For the first time since end of March, enemy planes attack in force. Japanese arty emplaced at Cabcaben, S Bataan, opens fire on Corregidor. In the Visayan Is., Cebu I. garrison is alerted as enemy flotilla heading toward the island is spotted.

BURMA—Burma I Corps is now disposed to defend oil fields, on general line Minhla-Taung-dwingyi, a 40-mile front. Chinese are not in position to support corps because of a series of contradictory orders.

CEYLON—Trincomalee undergoes heavy air attack by Japanese planes from carriers. HMS *Hermes* (aircraft carrier) is sunk offshore.

USSR—Strong Soviet efforts to advance from Kerch area in the Crimea make little headway against stubborn enemy forces. Germans remain on the defensive on central front, containing most of Red Army thrusts; on northern front, make slow progress against firm opposition toward encircled forces in vicinity of Cholm and Staraya Russa.

10 April

VISAYAN Is.—Japanese invade Cebu I., garrisoned by about 6,500 troops under command of Col Irwin C. Scudder. Bulk of enemy assault force goes ashore on E coast at Cebu City, the rest on W coast in vicinity of Toledo. Cebu MP Regt at Cebu City and 3d Bn of 82d Inf (PA) at Toledo fight lively delaying actions before withdrawing inland from both towns under pressure. Gen Chynoweth, CG Visayan Force, whose hq is on Cebu, sends 3d Bn of 83d Inf to defend Cantabaco, where cross-island highway branches.

BURMA—Patrols of Burma I Corps find that Japanese are moving forward toward the Minhla-Taungdwingyi.

GERMANY—RAF Bomber Command drops first 2-ton bomb during attack on Essen, night 10-11.

11 April

Visayan Is.—On Cebu, 3d Bn of 83d Inf fails to stop enemy at Cantabaco, and Japanese drive rapidly eastward from Toledo with little difficulty.

Burma—Japanese open attacks against center of line Minhla-Taungdwingyi.

USSR—Germans vigorously oppose Soviet efforts to land additional forces on Crimean coast near Eupatolia. Stalemate continues on central front. On northern front, Germans continue to make slow progress toward encircled forces.

12 April

U.S.—Gen Arnold, Chief AAF, sends Gen Marshall, attending BOLERO conference in London, air plan for BOLERO, calling for establishment of Eighth Air Force in England.

P.I.—Since Japanese now control cross-island highway on Cebu, Gen Chynoweth retreats to mountains of N Cebu, where he organizes remnants of the garrison for guerrilla warfare. Japanese, employing guns on Bataan and Cavite, intensify arty bombardment of Corregidor. Enemy aircraft continue to pound the island.

Burma—Ch 38th Div of 66th Army, previously earmarked for defense of Mandalay, begins movement to Irrawaddy front to assist Burma I Corps in holding line Minhla-Taungdwingyi. During night 12-13, Japanese occupy Migyaungye, exposing W flank of Burma Army.

13 April

SOUTH PACIFIC—Vice Adm Robert L. Ghormley is designated Commander, South Pacific Area (COMSOPAC) and S Pac Forces.

BURMA—Gap develops in Burma I Corps line, and Japanese are moving N through it toward oil fields. Burma 1st Div, under pressure S of Magwe, is reinf by 7th Armd Brig (less 7th Hussars). Gen Stilwell's orders designed to avert threat to Lashio—93d Div (less regt) is directed to move to Taunggyi; 49th Div plus regt of 93d is to continue to guard Thailand border; T-55th Div is to remain in Mawchi-Loikaw area—are delivered to Ch 6th Army. Ch 66th Army, less 38th Div, is to concentrate below Mandalay.

14 April

U.K.—British Government and Chiefs of Staff accept BOLERO Plan, proposed by Gen Marshall, for build-up to attack Germany.

AUSTRALIA—Government approves directive of 30 March to Gen MacArthur as Supreme Commander, SWPA. This is the last of the nations concerned to do so.

BURMA—Yenangyaung oil fields are ordered destroyed, night 14-15; this is accomplished during next 48 hours. Japanese are moving around Ch T-55th Div in Mawchi-Loikaw area.

FRANCE—Pierre Laval is restored to power by Marshal Henri-Philippe Pétain.

15 April

BURMA—Japanese continue to press northward and are bypassing Burma 1st Div.

U.K.—Gen Eaker establishes hq of U.S. Bomber Command at High Wycombe. U.S. Eighth Air Force, which was originally to have supported GYMNAST, is now committed to U.K. instead.

16 April

VISAYAN Is.—Gen Wainwright places Gen Sharp in command of Visayan garrisons and orders him to reorganize Visayan-Mindanao Force for stand on Mindanao. Cebu I. is thus conceded to be lost. Japanese force of 4,160 invades Panay at dawn, most going ashore at Iloilo and the rest at Capiz. Landings are unopposed by Col Albert F. Christie's Panay Force of about 7,000 which retires to mountains to wage guerrilla warfare.

MALTA—Awarded the George Cross in recognition of its heroism under attack.

17 April

U.S.—Adm William D. Leahy, U.S. Ambassador to France, is recalled to Washington for consultation.

BURMA—On Irrawaddy front, Japanese block road N and S of Pin Chaung near Yenangyaung. Ch 38th Div leaves Kyaukpadaung at night to relieve isolated Burma 1st Div. To S, Ind 17th Div sends out strong columns from Natmauk and Taungdwingyi to ease pressure on Burma 1st Div, but Japanese are not diverted. On Sittang front, Ch 22d Div, ordered to delay for 2 weeks in preparation for trapping enemy at Pyinmana, is in Lewe area, but because of reverses suffered by Burma I

Corps, Gen Stilwell is forced to abandon plans for stand at Pyinmana. Japanese continue pressure against Ch T-55th Div in Bawlake-Mawchi area.

18 April

PACIFIC—Gen MacArthur assumes supreme command of SWPA, USAFFE becoming inactive. Gen Sir Thomas Blarney, CinC Australian Military Forces, is to command Allied Land Forces; Gen Brett is to head Allied Air Forces; Adm Leary, previously in command of ANZAC Force, is to command Allied Naval Forces. USAFIA, under Gen Barnes, has about the same supply and administrative functions. USAFIP, under Gen Wainwright, remains in the new command structure until its dissolution on 6 May.

VISAYAN IS.—Japanese make another unopposed landing on Panay, at San Jose.

JAPAN—Tokyo undergoes its first air attack of the war. 16 B-25's of 17th Bombardment Gp, U.S. Eighth Air Force, led by Lt Col James H. Doolittle, take off from USS *Hornet*, standing with naval TF under Adm Halsey some 800 miles from Tokyo, in morning and at 1215 begin strikes on Japanese homeland, hitting Tokyo, Kobe, Yokohama, and Nagoya with good effect. Search and fighter support are provided by planes of USS *Enterprise*. After the attack, all bombers head for China where they were to have come under control of Gen Stilwell, but because of poor weather conditions and the late hour, all crash-land or are abandoned by crews. One lands near Vladivostok and its crew is interned; 2 land in enemy territory and their crews are imprisoned, some of the flyers being executed on 15 October 1942. Adm Halsey's naval TF (the 2 carriers plus 4 cruisers, 8 DD's, and 2 oilers) withdraw safely. This is the first occasion on which medium land bombers are moved by carriers and launched off enemy shores.

BURMA—In Yenangyaung area, Burma 1st Div drives to outskirts of Twingon; Ch 38th Div clears portion of Pin Chaung. On Sittang front, Ch 22d Div is relieved by Ch 96th and withdraws N of Pyinmana. Ch 200th Div is ordered to Meiktila but does not move. Ch T-55th Div collapses under enemy attacks S of Loikaw, and communications between it and Ch 6th Army cease. Road to Lashio is thus uncovered. Elements of 93d Div, which were to have assisted T-55th, do not reach the T-55th in time to be of help.

19 April

SWPA—Gen MacArthur appoints staff of GHQ SWPA. Among members are Maj Gen Richard K. Sutherland, Chief of Staff; Gen Richard Marshall, Deputy Chief of Staff; Col Charles P. Stivers, G-1; Col Charles A. Willoghby, G-2; Brig Gen Stephen J. Chamberlain, G-3; and Col Lester G-4.

VISAYAN IS.—Japanese claim all of Cebu I.

BURMA—113th Regt, Ch 38th Div, drives into Yenangyaung and finds Japanese firmly established there; clears 3 of 5 enemy strongpoints. Burma 1st Div continues efforts to advance in Twingon area until ordered to withdraw northward, then escapes with heavy losses in men and equipment. Threat to Burma Road is increased as Japanese columns converge a few miles S of Loikaw.

20 April

VISAYAN IS.—Japanese conquest of Visayan Is. is virtually completed. Cebu and Panay are in enemy hands, although guerrillas continue to hold out in mountain areas. Small garrisons in hills of Negros, Samar, Leyte, and Bohol are too weak to interfere with enemy plans.

BURMA—Ch 38th Div troops withdraw northward from Yenangyaung toward Gwegyo and cover retreat of Burma 1st Div toward Mt Popa area. In Sittang Valley, Ch 5th Army troops fall back northward from Pyinmana. Japanese continue active in vicinity of Loikaw. Taunggyi-Meiktila road is left undefended as Chinese withdraw toward Hopong, closely followed by Japanese. 2 bns of Ch 93d Div reach Loikaw area but return at once to Kengtung. Ch 49th Div is ordered to move W.

21 April

BURMA—Japanese overtake Ch 6th Army at Hopong. Ch 49th Div is moving quickly W as ordered, and elements are committed in Mong Pawn-Loilem region.

22 April

BURMA—Gen Stilwell orders Ch 200th Div to move from Meiktila to Taunggyi to counter enemy moves in Loikaw-Loilem area. Ch 28th Div, 66th Army, concentrated in Mandalay area, is directed to move to Loilem via Hsipaw but does not do so. Ch 96th Div continues delaying action in Sittang Valley, while Ind 17th Div, 7th Armd Brig, and Ch 22d Div take up positions around Meiktila and Thazi.

23 April

BURMA—Ch 200th Div, reinf, of 5th Army engages enemy W of Taunggyi. Japanese seize Loilem. Ch 6th Army retires into China.

U.K.—Germans begin series of retaliation air attacks on cathedral cities, the first occurring night 23–24 against Exeter.

25 April

BURMA—Gen Alexander orders withdrawal to N bank of Irrawaddy from line Meiktila-Kyaukpadaung to start after nightfall. Ch 22d Div withdraws from Pyawbwe and is being encircled in Meiktila area by Japanese. Ch 5th Army force (200th Div and 1st and 2d Regts of T-55th) clears enemy from Taunggyi but is unable to halt drive toward Lashio. Gen Stilwell confers with Br and Ch commanders concerning defense of Lashio.

26 April

FANNING I.—U.S. detachment arrives.

MINDANAO—Japanese detachment from Cebu sails for Mindanao. Enemy forces already on Mindanao are exerting pressure against Digos defense force—101st FA (PA), less bn, and 2d Bn of 102d (PA).

BURMA—Gen Alexander decides to concentrate on defense of India rather than that of Burma.

27 April

U.S.—U.S. Army Air Services is formed under Maj Gen Rush B. Lincoln to take responsibility for air service from USAFIA.

CHINA—Gen Stilwell presents "Proposal to Organize and Train a Chinese Force in India" to Chiang Kai-shek and gains his approval in principle.

28 April

Mindanao—Japanese are particularly aggressive against Digos defense force.

BURMA—Ch 28th Div, 66th Army, is ordered to Lashio from Mandalay, since Lashio is in great danger.

29 April

S PACIFIC—Adm King establishes South Pacific Amphibious Force (primarily 1st Mar Div).

P.I.—On Mindanao, Japanese begin offensive to clear the island. Force of 4,852 men from Cebu lands on W coast at Cotabato and Parang and takes both towns despite opposition of ad Bn of 104th Inf, 101st Div (PA), at Cotabato and of 2d Inf of 1st Div (PA) at Parang; 3d Bn of 102d Inf is unable to prevent elements of the Parang force from establishing contact with the Cotabato force. Enemy detachment already on Mindanao, having been relieved at Davao, turns NW toward Sayre Highway, which extends from Kabacan on S to Bugo on N. The E and the W assault forces both have air support. Preinvasion air and arty bombardment of Corregidor becomes intense.

NEW GUINEA—Japanese order landing at Port Moresby.

BURMA—Japanese overrun Lashio, terminus of Burma Road, the only land route to China, just as leading elements of Ch 29th Div, 66th Army, arrive there. Blockade of China is thus completed. Ch 200th Div reaches Loilem; subsequently withdraws from this area to China. Gen Alexander decides to make a stand on line Kalewa-Katha-Bhamo-Hsenwi and orders withdrawal to this line to begin on 2 May.

MIDDLE EAST—Gen Auchinleck issues operation instructions to commanders of Br Ninth and Tenth Armies for action in the event of enemy attack through Anatolia.

30 April

Mindanao—From Cotabato, Japanese move E toward Sayre Highway via Route I and Mindanao R and reach Piket, about 8 miles from objective. Philippine forces from Cotabato move N and guard trails leading N from Route I. The Parang detachment of Japanese, having left holding force there and moved NW during night 29-30 by boat, lands S of Malabang and at dawn attacks 61st Inf (PA), disposed along Mataling R, forcing it to withdraw 4 miles northward. Action in E Mindanao is limited and indecisive.

Burma—Japanese complete conquest of central Burma. Br Imperial forces withdraw across the Irrawaddy over Ava bridge, which is destroyed at midnight. Ch 22d Div, after covering withdrawal, pulls back from Mandalay. Japanese follow withdrawal closely and begin action against Monywa, crossing river on night 30 April-1 May. Allied commanders agree that Ch 5th Army plus 38th Div will move from Katha to Imphal, India, if line Kalewa-Katha-Bhamo-Hsenwi cannot be held.

1 May

P.I.—On Mindanao, Japanese force driving N along Route I gains control of that highway as far N as Lake Lanao and virtually eliminates 61st Inf (PA). Other forces continue E unopposed toward Sayre Highway at Kabacan. Fighting in E Mindanao continues indecisive. Japanese planes and arty begin final phase of preinvasion bombardment of Corregidor.

BURMA—Japanese overrun Monywa.

INDIA—Air Service Command of Tenth Air Force is activated under Brig Gen Elmer E. Adler, with hq at New Delhi.

2 May

U.S.—Secretary of War Henry L. Stimson, in letter to Gen Greely, terminates U.S. Mission to USSR since Soviet Government has refused it diplomatic clearance as a whole.

MIDWAY—Adm Nimitz visits Midway to inspect defenses.

MINDANAO—73d Inf (PA), reinf with stragglers of defeated 61st, attempts to stall enemy advancing N along Route I. Unable to hold at SW corner of Lake Lanao, 73d withdraws N, establishes line from lake Lanao across Route I, and delays enemy briefly. Japanese detachment from Cotabato continues E toward Kabacan. Brig Gen Joseph P. Vachon, CG of Cotabato-Davao defense sector, places all available forces at Kabacan. Digos defense force, ordered to withdraw to Kabacan, starts movement during night 2-3. Cagayan defense sector is alerted as enemy convoy heading toward Macajalar Bay is sighted.

SOLOMON IS.—After enemy invasion force is detected approaching Tulagi I., off S coast of Florida I., in S Solomons, small RAAF garrison destroys installations and withdraws to New Hebrides.

BURMA—Elements of Burma I Corps (63d, 13th, and 1st Brigs) attack into Monywa while transport moves about the town toward Ye-U. Action is then broken off and Burma 1st and 2d Brigs withdraw independently while rest of Burma Army falls back toward Shwegyin.

N ATLANTIC—HMS *Edinburgh* (cruiser) is sunk during enemy attacks on homeward-bound convoy from USSR.

3 May

P.I.—Japanese amphibious force from Panay goes ashore on Mindanao about 0100 at Cagayan and Tagoloan R mouth, in Macajalar Bay, and presses S along Sayre Highway. Troops of Cagayan defense sector (PA 102d Div, formed from 61st and 81st FA and 103d Inf) oppose landing but are unable to halt enemy. In a desperate effort to hold Sayre Highway, reserves—2.95-inch gun detachment and 62d and 93d Regts (PA)—are committed, but these, too, fall back under pressure. During night 3-4, Gen Sharp orders general withdrawal. Meanwhile, other Japanese forces gain control of road to N shore, routing 73d Inf, which withdraws into hills N of Lake Lanao. Still other enemy forces arrive at Kabacan after Digos force has made good its escape, but are halted there. Preinvasion air and arty bombardment of Corregidor continues without let up. U.S. submarine succeeds in withdrawing 25 persons from the island.

SOLOMON IS.—Small Japanese force invades Tulagi, which is soon converted into a seaplane base. Learning of this, Rear Adm Frank J. Fletcher, commanding naval force cruising the Coral Sea, heads for Tulagi in carrier *Yorktown*.

4 May

P.I.—Filipinos complete withdrawal to new defense line on Mindanao and begin organizing it. 102d Div, reorganized to include the 2.95-inch gun detachment, 62d Inf, 81st FA, and 2 PS cos of 43d Inf, is stationed in Dalirig sector and 61st FA and 93d Inf in Puntian sector. 103d Inf, isolated from rest of force, is to defend Cagayan R Valley. Japanese planes are active, but front is otherwise quiet. Japanese air and arty bombardment of Corregidor reaches peak of intensity.

SOLOMON IS.—Carrier planes from the *Yorktown* attack Tulagi harbor early in modeling, opening series of Coral Sea actions. A number of enemy vessels are sunk or damaged before the *Yorktown* withdraws toward rest of Coral Sea naval force.

NEW BRITAIN—Japanese transports leave Rabaul for Port Moresby, New Guinea.

BURMA—Br Imperial forces evacuate Akyab, on Bay of Bengal. AVG abandons Loiwing for Kunming, China. Japanese occupy Bhamo and defeat Ch 29th Div at Wanting. Chiang Kai-shek orders Ch 5th Army to Myitkyina.

MADAGASCAR—Br naval and military forces under Rear Adm Syffret and Maj Gen Sturges land on N Madagascar at Courier Bay against little opposition from Vichy French.

5 May

U.S.—Lt Gen Carl Spaatz is appointed commander of Eighth Air Force, replacing Gen Duncan.

CORAL SEA—*Yorktown* rejoins *Lexington* and the combined naval force (the 2 carriers plus 7 CA's, 1 CL, 13 DD's, a oilers, and a seaplane tender) moves NW searching for enemy.

P.I.—After final day of intense bombardment, Japanese invade Corregidor, landing at North Pt during night 5-6. On Mindanao, Filipinos continue to organize defense line.

JAPAN—Imperial General Headquarters directs *Combined Fleet* to assist Army invasion of Midway and the Aleutians.

BURMA—Gen Stilwell, withdrawing toward Myitkyina, learns at Indaw that railway is blocked and enemy are in Bhamo, so decides to take his party W instead to India.

6 May

CORAL SEA—Continuing search for enemy vessels, Adm Fletcher's TF moves toward Louisiade Archipelago, leaving DD *Sims* and tanker *Neosho* behind at fueling point.

P.I.—Gen Wainwright surrenders all forces in the Philippines to Japanese unconditionally. Surrender negotiations are begun at 1030 and continued until midnight, when surrender document is signed. On Corregidor, Japanese seize Malinta Tunnel and land additional troops. Garrison of 11,000 surrenders. On Mindanao, Japanese resume attack, moving into Tankulan and pushing on toward Dalirig, which comes under arty fire.

BURMA—Ch 200th Div plus elements of T-55th, still at Taunggyi, are ordered to Myitkyina and eventually make their way to China.

LIBERIA—Initial detachment of U.S. forces arrives in Liberia.

MADAGASCAR—British hold northern ports of Diego Suarez and Antsirene.

7 May

CORAL SEA—Japanese carrier planes discover and sink DD Sims and tanker *Neosho*. Aircraft from *Lexington* and *Yorktown* encounter Japanese carrier *Shoho* off Misima I. and sink it as well as an escorting CL.

P.I.—From Manila, Gen Wainwright broadcasts terms of surrender to forces still holding out in the Philippines. On Mindanao, Japanese break off ground action but continue to employ air and arty.

MALTA—Spitfire reinforcements are being flown in from carriers *Wasp* and *Eagle*.

8 May

SWPA—Gen MacArthur recommends that an offensive be undertaken against Japanese but desires naval, air, and ground forces strengthened first.

BATTLE OF CORAL SEA—Main action occurs as Adm Fletcher's naval force encounters enemy force of 2 carriers, 4 CA's, and several DD's, main support force of a Port Moresby invasion group. In the first major naval engagement conducted entirely by carrier aircraft, Japanese carrier *Shokaku* is badly damaged. Both the *Yorktown* and the *Lexington* are damaged; *Lexington* is abandoned and sunk after the action. Both sides lose heavily in aircraft, but U.S. loss of 66 planes is considerably less than that of enemy. As a result of Battle of Coral Sea, Japanese are turned back from Port Moresby, key point in New Guinea and of vital importance to security of Australia. Coral Sea battle also marks the end of Allied defensive and paves way for a defensive-offensive period.

P.I.—Gen Wainwright dispatches messages to key officers in the Philippines, urging them to surrender their forces. On Mindanao, Japanese renew attack in evening and continue it throughout night 8-9. Defeated 62d Inf is pursued toward Dalirig.

BURMA—Japanese occupy Myitkyina.

USSR—Germans begin series of limited offensives to straighten lines in preparation for main summer offensive toward oil fields of the Caucasus. *11th Army of Army Group South* leads off in the Crimea, pushing toward Kerch.

9 May

MINDANAO—Japanese take Dalirig and rout defenders. Although forces defending Puntian sector are still intact, their position is untenable and Mindanao campaign is virtually over.

NEW GUINEA—Japanese Imperial General Headquarters orders invasion of Port Moresby suspended temporarily.

TONGA IS.—U.S. troop detachment arrives at Tongatabu.

GALAPAGOS IS.—U.S. troops arrive on the Galápagos Is., off W coast of South America.

10 May

P.I.—Gen Sharp directs Visayan-Mindanao Force to surrender. These, as well as small forces holding out on Luzon and Palawan, are reluctant to yield but do so gradually during period 10 May-9 June.

BURMA—Japanese attack Br covering force at Shwegyin.

11 May

CHINA—In retaliation for the Doolittle raid, Japanese launch strong drive in Chekiang Province.

MEDITERRANEAN—3 of 4 Br DD's attempting to halt enemy convoy are lost to Axis aircraft.

12 May

BURMA—Japanese force heading for Kengtung crosses the Salween.

USSR—While Germans continue Crimean offensive toward Kerch, Red Army opens 2-pronged attack toward Kharkov, thrusting SW across upper Donets on N and northward from Izyum salient on S. Attack at first goes well.

U.K.—First large detachment of U.S. Eighth Air Force arrives.

13 May

FIJI IS.—Americans relieve NZ forces of responsibility for Fiji Is. and prepare to reinforce positions there.

AUSTRALIA—Rear echelon of U.S. 41st Div arrives.

14 May

U.S.—Legislation establishing Women's Army Auxiliary Corps (WAAC) is enacted.

AUSTRALIA—U.S. 32d Div arrives.

BURMA—Br Imperial forces withdrawing from Burma reach Tamu, Assam.

15 May

NEW GUINEA—Aus 14th Brig Gp and 700 attached Aus AA troops start to Port Moresby to bolster positions there.

INDIA—Gen Alexander moves hq from Burma to Imphal area of India. Gen Stilwell arrives in India.

LIBYA—Br Eighth Army has completed most of its preparations for offensive, but Rommel's forces are showing signs of forestalling it.

USSR—Germans announce capture of town and harbor of Kerch, in the Crimea. Red Army continues offensive toward Kharkov.

16 May

INDIA—First detachment of SOS troops—393d QM Bn (Port) and 159th Station Hospital—arrives at Karachi.

17 May

USSR—Battle of Kharkov opens as Germans counterattack from Izyum area and in region E of Kharkov, bringing Soviet offensive to a halt.

18 May

POA—U.S. Seventh Air Force is alerted for possible enemy attack on Midway or Hawaii.

BURMA—Chiang Kai-shek orders Ch 5th Army, which now consists largely of Ch 22d and 96th Divs, to take up positions between Myitkyina and Fort Hertz. Ch 22d Div survivors reach Ledo area in July and August. Ch 96th eventually makes its way to China via Fort Hertz.

19 May

MIDDLE EAST—Gen Auchinleck issues instructions to Commander, Br Tenth Army, on action to be taken should the enemy attack through Iran from the Caucasus.

U.K.—U.S. Eighth Air Force detachment hq under Gen Eaker takes control of all U.S. Army air organizations in British Isles.

20 May

POA—Reinforcements are being hastily moved to Midway and the Aleutians, since Japanese plan to invade the islands is by now known. In the Aleutians, work on secret air base on Umnak I. is being rushed to a conclusion. Rear Adm John S. McCain takes command as COMAIRSOPAC.

BURMA—With conquest of Burma completed, Japanese (56th, 18th, 33d, and 55th Divs of 15th Army) take up defensive positions.

INDIA—Burma I Corps is placed under command of 4 Corps as rear guard reaches India.

21 May

POA—Rear Adm Robert A. Theobald, as commander of TF 8, becomes responsible for all forces, U.S. Army and naval and Canadian, in Alaska area.

GERMANY—Adolf Hitler decides to postpone projected conquest of Malta, Operation HERCULES, until Egypt is conquered.

22 May

NEW GUINEA—21st Troop Carrier Sq begins movement of some 300 troops and supplies to Wau to reinforce weak Aus group, called Kanga Force, defending Bulolo Valley. Kanga Force consists largely of troops of New Guinea Volunteer Reserve (NGVR).

23 May

ALEUTIANS—U.S. fighter aircraft land safely on runway at new air base on Umnak I.

USSR—Continuing counteroffensive in Kharkov area, Germans isolate Red Army forces in Izyum salient W of the Donets.

25 May

INDIA—Ch 38th Div (− 113th Regt, which acts as rear guard) reaches India.

26 May

HAWAII—Naval TF under Rear Adm Raymond A. Spruance, built around carriers *Enterprise* and *Hornet*, arrives at Pearl Harbor from S Pacific.

MIDWAY—USS *Kittyhawk* brings in additional air and ground reinforcements.

NEW GUINEA—Aus Kanga Force is strengthened by arrival of Aus 5th Independent Co by air.

LIBYA—Rommel prepares to resume offensive, moving armored forces around S flank of Br Eighth Army to positions SE of Bir Hacheim under cover of darkness. Br Eighth Army is now disposed with 13 Corps (50th Div; S African 1st and 2d Divs; 1st Army Tank Brig; 9th Brig of Ind 5th Div) on N and 30 Corps (1st and 7th Armd Divs; 201st Gds Brig; Ind 3d Motor Brig Gp; 29th Brig of Ind 5th Div; FF 1st Brig Gp) on S.

U.K.—Anglo-American air conference opens in London to consider allocation policy. Among those attending are Gen Arnold, Rear Adm John H. Towers, and British Chief of Air Staff Sir Charles Portal. 20-year Anglo-Soviet mutual aid agreement is signed in London.

27 May

HAWAII—Adm Fletcher's naval force, based on carrier *Yorktown*, arrives at Pearl Harbor from S Pacific.

MIDWAY—Japanese Vice Adm Chuichi Nagumo's *Carrier Striking Force* leaves Japan for Midway. Enemy transports depart from Saipan and covering cruisers and DD's from Guam for same objective.

NEW CALEDONIA—Americal Div, its name a contraction of words "America" and "New Caledonia," is activated under Gen Patch.

INDIA—USAFCBI SOS Base Section I is activated at Karachi; Base Section 2 (Calcutta) is authorized.

LIBYA—Axis forces open offensive against Gazala-Bir Hacheim line of Br Eighth Army at dawn, making main effort on S and staging demonstration on N. In 30 Corps sector, FF 1st Brig Gp holds detached strongpoint at Bir Hacheim against attack. German armored columns disposed SE of this village sweep northward toward El Adem and Acroma and are opposed by Ind 3d Motor Brig, a few miles E of Bir Hacheim, and 7th and 1st Armd Divs to N.

28 May

POA—Main body of Japanese naval force under command of Adm Isoroko Yamamoto leaves Japan for Midway. From Pearl Harbor, Adm Spruance's naval force also heads for Midway. U.S. troop detachment (500 from the Efate garrison) arrives at Espiritu Santo, New Hebrides, where bomber strip is to be built to support invasion of the Solomons.

CHINA—Chinese withdraw from Kinhwa, Chekiang Province, under pressure.

BURMA—Japanese seize Kengtung.

LIBYA—Br Eighth Army defeats enemy efforts to break out to coast in rear of Gazala positions in order to gain supply line to forces NE of Bir Hacheim.

USSR—Battle of Kharkov ends as Germans complete reduction of Red Army salient W of the Donets in Kharkov area.

29 May

LIBYA—Upon breaching mine fields in center of Br Eighth Army's position, enemy starts passing vehicles through gaps despite Br fire. Rommel's main armored forces, temporarily on the defensive until a supply route can be opened to them, fall back southward under attack by armor of 30 Corps.

30 May

POA—Adm Fletcher's *Yorktown* force sails for Midway from Pearl Harbor. Japanese TF (2 transports, 2 carriers, 2 CA's, 3 DD's) leaves Japan for Aleutians, where it is to create a diversion for the invasion of Midway and land small forces on W Aleutians. Initial detachment of U.S. troops arrives at New Zealand.

INDIA—Ch 113th Regt, rear guard covering withdrawal of 38th Div and 5th Army from Burma, crosses the Chindwin.

LIBYA—Axis forces, in effort to consolidate bridgehead at gaps in mine fields, move W under attack by Br Eighth Army and RAF. Gen Ritchie decides to counterattack on night of 31st, but accedes to request of corps commander to postpone attack 24 hours. 1st Armd Brig, which has recently arrived in Libya, is used to bring other units up to strength.

Germany—RAF opens air offensive against Germany with attack of unprecedented scale against Cologne, night 30–31. Over 1,000 planes participate; more than 2,000 tons of bombs are dropped.

31 May

LIBYA—Axis forces begin assault on Sidi Muftah, detached strongpoint of 13 Corps, Br Eighth Army, and are engaged by 150th Brig of 50th Div, to whom armored assistance is rushed. Later, 13 Corps begins preliminary phase of general counterattack but makes little headway.

1 June

AUSTRALIA—Japanese midget submarines enter Sydney harbor and sink an Aus boat.

LIBYA—Continuing attack on Sidi Muftah, enemy wipes out 150th Brig of 50th Div and much of 1st Army Tank Brig assisting it. Lull ensues as

Br Eighth Army prepares for general counterattack and enemy strengthens his salient.

2 June

POA—Naval TF's of Adms Fletcher and Spruance rendezvous 350 miles NE of Midway. The combined force (3 carriers, 7 CA's, 1 CL, 13 DD's, and 25 submarines), under command of Adm Fletcher, moves to point about 200 miles N of Midway. Reconnoitering from the Aleutians, PBY discovers 2 enemy carriers about 400 miles S of Kiska.

USSR—German *11th Army of Army Group South* begins 5-day arty preparation for assault on Sevastopol in the Crimea.

3 June

ALEUTIAN Is.—Japanese carrier-based aircraft bomb and strafe Fort Mears and Dutch Harbor, Unalaska I., in several waves.

MIDWAY—Battle of Midway opens when planes based there locate and attack elements of Japanese invasion force as it approaches.

MIDDLE EAST—22d Inf Brig Gp of Br East Africa Command sails for Madagascar to relieve Br forces.

4 June

ALEUTIAN Is.—Japanese planes from carriers again attack Dutch Harbor, Unalaska I., damaging fuel installations and a station ship. Attempts of PBY's, B-17's, and B-26's to locate and attack the carriers are largely ineffective because of poor visibility, and Japanese retire southward with light losses confined to aircraft. Subsequent efforts to find the enemy TF are futile.

MIDWAY—Japanese are decisively defeated in main Battle of Midway. Enemy carrier planes (about 80 bombers and 50 fighters) strike in force, damaging installations but leaving runways intact. Midway-based planes oppose the attack and take heavy toll of enemy planes, then, together with aircraft from the 3 U.S. carriers in the vicinity, attack enemy shipping. Japanese carriers *Kaga*, *Akagi*, and *Soryu* are hit. *Kaga* sinks at once; USS *Nautilus* sinks the damaged *Soryu*; Japanese scuttle the *Akagi*. Japanese carrier *Hiryu* scores damaging hits on USS *Yorktown*, which is abandoned and taken under tow. The *Hiryu* is in turn badly damaged by planes from *Enterprise* and *Hornet* and is scuttled at dawn of 5th. Plane losses are heavy on both sides.

LIBYA—Br Eighth Army opens counterattack with infantry after nightfall in effort to reduce enemy salient in center of line.

5 June

U.S.—Declares war on Bulgaria, Hungary, and Rumania.

MIDWAY—Despite poor visibility, U.S. planes pursue enemy force retreating from Midway and score damaging hits.

LIBYA—Br Eighth Army counterattack ends in failure. 13 Corps' 69th Brig (50th Div), supported by 32d Army Tank Brig, attacks enemy salient from N while 30 Corps, employing 9th and Loth Brigs (Ind 5th Div) and 22d Armd Brig 1st Armd Div), makes main effort from E toward Sidi Muftah but is halted short of objective. British lose 2 brigs of infantry and 4 regts of arty.

6 June

MIDWAY—USS *Yorktown*, still under tow, is hit by torpedoes from Japanese submarine as is USS *Hammann* (DD), which is alongside; both vessels sink. Despite these U.S. losses, Battle of Midway is a severe setback to the Japanese and costs them the initiative.

LIBYA—Heavy, indecisive fighting occurs as enemy begins concentrating armor in Knightsbridge area, threatening Tobruk, and at the same time intensifies action against the Bir Hacheim strongpoint.

7 June

POA—Brig Gen Howard C. Davison replaces Maj Gen Clarence L. Tinker, who was lost in Battle of Midway, as commander of Seventh Air Force.

ALEUTIAN Is.—Japanese invade western Aleutians, landing some 1,800 men on Attu and Kiska.

CHINA—Continuing drive in Chekiang Province, Japanese seize Chuhsien airfield and attack city itself.

USSR—After 5 days of heavy air and arty preparation, German *Army Group South* renews ground assault to clear the Crimea in preparation for main offensive on the rich Caucasus, moving against Sevastopol fortress. Local actions to improve positions in other sectors continue.

8 June

SWPA—As a result of the successful Midway action, Gen MacArthur proposes to Gen Marshall that a limited offensive to regain positions in Bismarck Archipelago be undertaken.

NEW GUINEA—Small party of Americans and Australians flies from Port Moresby to reconnoiter Milne Bay area for air base site. Such a base would strengthen defenses of Port Moresby.

LIBYA—Indecisive fighting continues in vicinity of Knightsbridge and Bir Hacheim. Free French, stubbornly defending Bir Hacheim, are forced to yield some ground; their supply situation is critical.

U.K.—European Theater of Operations, U.S. Army (ETOUSA) is established under command of Gen Chaney, superseding U.S. Army Forces in British Isles (USAFBI).

9 June

INTERNATIONAL AGREEMENTS—U.S. and Great Britain agree to pool food and production resources.

P.I.—Japanese conquest of the Philippines is completed, although small, isolated detachments continue to hold out. Combined U.S. and Filipino force of 140,000 is now eliminated as a fighting force. USFIP ceases to exist.

LIBYA—Free French continue to hold out at Bir Hacheim against furious ground and air attacks. Efforts to relieve them are unsuccessful.

10 June

CHINA—Chinese withdraw from Chuhsien, Chekiang Province, after 4 days of hard fighting.

LIBYA—Gen Ritchie orders evacuation of the isolated Bir Hacheim position and FF 1st Brig, assisted by 7th Armd Div, withdraws during night 10-11.

USSR—German *Army Group South* continues assault on Sevastopol in the Crimea, making slow progress against Red Army strongpoints; opens limited offensive NE of Kharkov to improve positions.

11 June

INTERNATIONAL AGREEMENTS—U.S. and Great Britain make simultaneous announcements of mutual-aid agreement with Soviet Union. The agreement permits USSR to repay lend-lease debts in kind rather than in cash.

ALEUTIAN Is.—Upon discovering enemy on Kiska, Allied aircraft begin series of long-range, small-scale attacks on the island, striking as often as the difficult weather conditions permit, in an effort to weaken enemy by attrition. Attu is beyond range of aircraft.

CHINA—Advance Section 3, under SOS, is activated in China.

LIBYA—Exploiting capture of Bir Hacheim, Axis forces surge northward toward El Adem, which protects S approach to Tobruk.

12 June

SWPA—GHQ authorizes construction of air bases at head of Milne Bay, New Guinea.

RUMANIA—U.S. air combat from Africa begins with attack on Ploesti oil fields at dawn. Heavy bomber TF (coded HALPRO), under Col Harry A. Halverson and temporarily based in Egypt, makes the attack. On return trip, several of the B-24's are forced to land in Turkey and crews are interned.

LIBYA—Indecisive tank battles occur in vicinity of El Adem and Knightsbridge.

13 June

U.S.—Gen Marshall orders establishment of a U.S. Middle East organization, U.S. Army Forces in the Middle East (USAFIME), in order to unify Middle East missions. Iraq and Iran are to come within its geographical sphere.

German submarine lands 4 enemy agents on beach at Amagansett, Long Island.

LIBYA—Axis armor decisively defeats armor of Br Eighth Army, forcing British from escarpment between El Adem and Knightsbridge. Br tank strength is dangerously depleted, and 13 Corps supply line is consequently in danger. Knightsbridge garrison (201st Gds Brig) is ordered to withdraw to Acroma.

14 June

NEW ZEALAND—First echelon of U.S. 1st Mar Div (5th Marines) arrives.

LIBYA—Gen Ritchie orders withdrawal of forward divs (S African 1st and Br 50th) of 13 Corps, since tank losses in El Adem area have left them precariously situated. S African 1st Div withdraws safely to Egyptian frontier, using coastal route. 50th Div retires SE through enemy territory. Enemy turns his attention to Acroma but can make little headway against firm opposition, although favored by superior tank strength.

15 June

LIBYA—29th Brig of Ind 5th Div (30 Corps) withstands 3 tank-supported attacks on El Adem with assistance of aircraft. Maj Gen Klopper, CG of S African 2d Div, is named commander of Tobruk fortress and instructed to defend it at all costs.

16 June

LIBYA—Gen Auchinleck authorizes Gen Ritchie to organize the garrison of Tobruk as he wishes. 4 inf brigs with supporting arty and tanks are disposed within Tobruk. Rest of Br Eighth Army is to act as mobile columns outside the fortress. Gen Klopper is authorized to withdraw the garrison if necessary. Acroma garrison holds out against enemy tank attacks. Other enemy tank columns drive on

Sidi Rezegh and feint toward El Adem. El Adem garrison withdraws after nightfall.

17 June

U.S.—German submarine lands 4 enemy agents on Ponte Vedra Beach, Florida.

MIDDLE EAST—Maj Gen Russell L. Maxwell accepts appointment as head of USAFIME.

Libya—Enemy gains control of coastal road to Bardia, completing isolation of Tobruk.

18 June

U.S.—Prime Minister Churchill arrives for series of Anglo-American conferences with President Roosevelt in Washington.

LIBYA—Axis forces drive to Gambut. This is a blow to the Tobruk garrison, since air support from forward landing grounds in Gambut area is now denied the garrison.

USSR—Germans report reduction, after 12 days of hard fighting, of northern part of Sevastopol fortifications except for one coastal fort.

U.K.—Gen Spaatz, in London, takes command of U.S. Eighth Air Force.

19 June

POA—Adm Ghormley takes command of South Pacific Area and South Pacific Force.

MIDDLE EAST—USAFIME is activated by order of Gen Maxwell, with hq in Cairo, Egypt, replacing U.S. North African Military Mission.

20 June

U.S.—President Roosevelt and Prime Minister Churchill, in a closed session in Washington, decide upon a northwest African campaign.

POA—Maj Gen Willis H. Hale becomes commander of U.S. Seventh Air Force, although Navy has operational control of the force.

LIBYA—Axis forces, with strong arty and close air support, open assault on Tobruk and penetrate deeply into the fortress, destroying tanks and arty of Br garrison. Gen Klopper receives permission to break out but is unable to do so since his transport is cut off in harbor area. 30 Corps sends 7th Armd Div to relief of Tobruk garrison, but it fails to arrive in time to assist.

USSR—Germans reach N shore of Sevastopol harbor and continue assault on last coastal fort in N fortifications.

21 June

INTERNATIONAL AGREEMENTS—Arnold-Portal-Towers agreement, stemming from London conference of 26 May and subsequent discussions in Washington, is signed. This agreement, which concerns U.S. air commitments and provides strong air force for BOLERO, is approved by U.S. Joint Chiefs of Staff on 25 June and by Combined Chiefs of Staff on a July.

LIBYA—Tobruk falls to enemy. Gen Ritchie decides to withdraw to Matruh, Egypt, and orders 13 Corps to delay enemy while 30 Corps begins organization of the Matruh position.

22 June

U.S.—Japanese submarine shells Fort Stevens military reservation in Oregon at mouth of Columbia R, doing no damage. The shelling is the first foreign attack on a continental military installation since the War of 1812 and the only one of World War II.

War Department orders all units and individuals under Gen Stilwell's command assigned under a permanent change of station to American Army Forces in "India, China, and Burma" rather than to Army Group, Washington, D.C. This is the first step in the evolution of a U.S. theater of operations on the Asiatic mainland.

SWPA—Maj Gen Robert L. Eichelberger is named commander of U.S. I Corps, replacing Maj Gen Charles F. Thompson. I Corps eventually comes under operational command of Gen Blarney, Commander Allied Land Forces. Gen MacArthur authorizes small airfield at Merauke, on S coast of Dutch New Guinea, to protect Port Moresby from the W. Initial force to garrison Milne Bay, New Guinea (2 cos and an MG platoon on loan from Aus 14th Brig at Port Moresby, sails from Port Moresby.

INDIA—First CO of USAFCBI SOS Base Section 2 assumes his duties at Calcutta.

EGYPT-LIBYA—Br Eighth Army begins withdrawal to Matruh without interference as enemy reorganizes. Small enemy force moves into Bardia. Gen Auchinleck visits Eighth Army hq,

USSR—German *Army Group South* begins limited attack in Izyum area to improve positions E of the Donets; continues battle for Sevastopol. Fall of the last of the northern coastal forts at Sevastopol is announced.

23 June

CBI—Gen Brereton is ordered to Middle East with all available bombers because of crisis there. Flight of 24 B-17's intended for China is diverted at Khartoum, Egypt, for the same reason.

MIDDLE EAST—U.S. Military Mission is redesignated Iran-Iraq Service Command under Hq, USAFIME, effective 24 June. Col Shingler, with hq at Basra, heads the new command.

LIBYA—Enemy continues preparations for drive into Egypt; forward elements are engaged by 7th Armd Div of 13 Corps, Br Eighth Army, near Sollum.

24 June

EGYPT-LIBYA—Rommel begins drive into Egypt, pushing rapidly NE and E against ineffective rear guard resistance to vicinity of Sidi Barrani. 10 Corps hq, which has recently arrived in Egypt from Syria, takes command at Matruh, releasing 30 Corps, which moves E to El 'Alamein to organize defenses. 10 and 13 Corps constitute mobile elements of Br Eighth Army.

USSR—German *Army Group South* attains its objective in Izyum area, Oskol R line; continues to make progress in battle for Sevastopol.

U.K.—Maj Gen Dwight D. Eisenhower assumes command of ETOUSA.

25 June

POA—Adm King presents his views on projected offensive to Gen Marshall.

NEW GUINEA—Gen Basil M. Morris forms new unit, called Maroubra Force, to hold Kokoda Trail over Owen Stanley Range between Port Moresby and Buna. Maroubra Force consists of Aus 39th Bn, less one co, of Aus 30th Brig and a Papuan bn of 300. Allied garrison arrives at Milne Bay.

EGYPT-LIBYA—Axis forces continue rapidly toward Matruh despite air attacks. Gen Auchinleck takes personal command of Br Eighth Army, relieving Gen Ritchie; after reviewing situation, decides to continue withdrawal from Matruh to El 'Alamein.

26 June

NEW GUINEA—Elements of Maroubra Force (Co B of Aus 39th Bn) are ordered to Kokoda.

CBI—Gen Brereton leaves for Middle East and is succeeded as commander of U.S. Tenth Air Force by Brig Gen Earl L. Naiden.

Egypt—Enemy armor breaches mine field of Br Eighth Army S of Matruh.

27 June

U.S.—By this date the 8 enemy agents that landed on Long Island and in Florida have been arrested. They have caused no damage. All are subsequently court martialed and six are executed.

SWPA—Gen MacArthur completes plan, TULSA I, for offensive to secure New Britain-New Ireland-Admiralty Is. area.

Egypt—10 and 13 Corps of Br Eighth Army are forced to withdraw eastward toward El 'Alamein when enemy infiltrates between them and partially envelops former in Matruh area.

28 June

MIDDLE EAST—U.S. Army Middle East Air Force is established in Middle East under command of Lt Gen Lewis H. Brereton. It at first consists of Halverson Detachment (HALPRO) and 9 B-17's.

EGYPT—Enemy overruns 29th Brig of Ind 5th Div as it attempts to cover withdrawal of 10 Corps in Fuka area. 10 Corps retires southward to El 'Alamein.

USSR—Germans launch main summer offensive. On N flank of *Army Group South* enemy pushes eastward toward the Don from Kursk. Battle for Sevastopol continues, with Soviet forces losing ground steadily.

29 June

U.S.—Adm King proposes to Joint Chiefs of Staff that Adm Ghormley command offensive to seize lower Solomons and that Gen MacArthur control moves against New Guinea and New Britain. This is a compromise on the question of whether the planned offensive in the Pacific shall be controlled by the Navy or by the Army.

NEW GUINEA—Co E of U.S. 46th Engrs arrives at Milne Bay to begin work on base.

China—Chiang Kai-shek, meeting with Gen Stilwell, makes 3 demands "essential for the maintenance of the China Theater of War": 3 U.S. divs, 500-plane air force in China, monthly transportation by air of 5,000 tons of supplies into China.

EGYPT—Axis forces speed eastward to within 15 miles of El 'Alamein despite action of 13 Corps, Br Eighth Army.

30 June

U.S.—Hq Co of U.S. Army Forces in the South Pacific Area (USAFISPA) is organized at Fort Ord, California.

NEW GUINEA—Aus Kanga Force, guarding Bulolo Valley, conducts its first offensive action, a raid on Salamaua. This is followed a few days later by a raid on Lae.

EGYPT—Upon completing withdrawal to prepared positions at El 'Alamein, Br 30 Corps takes responsibility for N flank and 13 Corps for S flank. 10 Corps staff is withdrawn to command Delta Force, which is to defend Alexandria and the Nile Delta.

USSR—Germans broaden offensive toward the Don in *Army Group South* sector. While *2d Army* and *4th Pz Army* continue toward the river at Voronezh, *6th Army* begins drive to E in region SE of Belgorod. In the Crimea, battle for Sevastopol is in its final stage. On N front, German *Army Group North* eliminates last of Soviet pocket W of Volkhov.

1 July

PACIFIC—TULSA II, a modified version of TULSA I, is drawn up as planning for offensive continues. 2d Marines, reinf, 2d Mar Div, sails from California in 5 ships escorted by carrier *Wasp*.

MADAGASCAR—Lt Gen Sir William Platt, CinC East African Command, takes responsibility for occupied portion of Madagascar.

EGYPT—Enemy forces make their deepest penetration into Egypt with capture of fortified position of Deir el Shein, S of the El 'Alamein fortress. Ind 18th Brig Gp, which has recently arrived from Iraq, is overrun in this action.

USSR—German *Army Group South* completes reduction of Sevastopol fortress in the Crimea and, to the N, continues toward the Don.

2 July

U.S.—Joint Chiefs of Staff issue directive prescribing occupation of New Britain-New Ireland-New Guinea area. Offensive is to be conducted in 3 phases, during which the following are to be secured and occupied: (1) lower Solomons (Santa Cruz Is., Tulagi, and adjacent positions) (Task One); (2) rest of Solomons and NE coast of New Guinea (Task Two); (3) Rabaul, New Britain, and adjacent positions in New Guinea-New Ireland area (Task Three). Target date is set as 1 August but subsequently postponed to 7 August. Navy is to command first phase and Army the second and third. Boundary between SWPA and S Pacific is to be altered to place lower Solomons within S Pacific zone.

AUSTALIA—AUs 7th Brig is directed to move to Milne Bay, New Guinea.

CBI—Chiang Kai-shek names Gen Stilwell CinC of Chinese Army in India, but Stilwell's power over the troops is restricted.

MAYOTTE I.—Br and E African troops land on island, at N end of Mozambique Channel, and secure it for seaplane base.

EGYPT—Br Eighth Army wrests initiative from Rommel as 13 Corps, on S flank, counterattacks northward in rear of enemy. With close air support, 13 Corps maintains pressure on enemy throughout month, gaining some ground and easing pressure against N and central sectors. Enemy makes repeated efforts to break through but is unable to do so; gradually extends positions S and E of 13 Corps to Qattara Depression.

3 July

U.S.—Gen Marshall authorizes creation of a mobile air force for SWPA and another for POA. Preparations for offensive in the Pacific continue at a rapid pace.

4 July

CBI—AVG is inducted into Tenth Air Force as its contract with China terminates.

EGYPT—30 Corps, Br Eighth Army, is strengthened by arrival of Aus 9th Div, which is concentrating in vicinity of El 'Alamein fortress. 13 Corps continues to attack on S flank, making slow progress.

WESTERN EUROPE—U.S. air operations against Europe are initiated. 6 U.S. aircraft manned by U.S. crews participate in RAF attack on airdromes in Holland.

5 July

USSR—Organized Soviet resistance in the Crimea ends. To N, German *4th Pz Army* has reached the Don at Voronezh, where Red Army is resisting strongly. *Army Group Center* is improving positions N of Smolensk in local actions.

6 July

CBI—Gen Stilwell issues letter of instructions setting up command structure of a theater in CBI, with "Headquarters, American Army Forces, China, Burma, and India" at Chungking and branch office at New Delhi. A few days later another branch office is established at Kunming. China Air Task Force (CATF) is activated.

USSR—Voronezh falls to German *Army Group South* after it has been evacuated by Red Army forces.

7 July

POA—Carrier *Saratoga*, followed by carrier *Enterprise*, each with supporting ships, sails from Pearl Harbor for S Pacific. Elements of the *Enterprise* support force leave main force at sea and proceed to New Caledonia to embark 1st Raider Bn.

AUSTALIA—Adm Ghormley arrives in Australia and confers with Gen MacArthur on coming offensive.

NEW GUINEA—Co B, Aus 39th Bn, leaves Port Moresby for Kokoda, traveling on foot along tortuous trail over Owen Stanley Range.

USSR—German *6th Army* effects junction with *4th Pz Army* NE of Valuiki.

8 July

PACIFIC—Gen MacArthur and Adm Ghormley recommend that offensive be postponed until SW and S Pacific forces can be strengthened. Adm Nimitz issues his final plan of attack, ordering S Pacific Force to seize Santa Cruz Is. and Tulagi-Guadalcanal area in the Solomons.

CBI—Gen Chennault takes command of CATF.

USSR—Russians announce evacuation of St Oskol, SE of Kursk.

9 July

SWPA—Aus 7th Brig commander and advance elements of the brig leave Townsville, Australia, for Milne Bay, New Guinea.

USSR—German *Army Group South* is divided into 2 groups. *Army Group A*, on S consists of *1st Pz*, *17th*, and *11th Armies*. *Army Group B* comprises *2d*, *Hungarian 2d*, *4th Pz*, and *6th Armies*. *Group A* is to seize Rostov, where major Soviet forces are believed concentrated, then continue S through the Caucasus. *Group B* is to drive along the Don to Stalingrad, thence along the Volga to Astrakhan.

10 July

U.S.—In response to recommendation of Gen MacArthur and Adm Ghormley on 8 July, Joint Chiefs of Staff rule that offensive must be conducted as planned.

NEW GUINEA—Small Allied party flies from Port Moresby to Buna area to reconnoiter for airfield site.

EGYPT—In limited offensive, 30 Corps of Br Eighth Army seizes Tel el Eisa mounds, W of El 'Alamein. Enemy makes a number of unsuccessful attempts to reduce this salient.

USSR—While *Army Group B*'s *4th Pz* and *6th Armies* drive along the Don toward Stalingrad, *1st Pz* and *17th Armies* of *Army Group A* drive on Rostov. Russians admit loss of Rossosh.

11 July

USSR—Continuing drive on Rostov, *Army Group A* overruns Lisichensk, on the Donets.

12 July

AUSTALIA—U.S. 41st Div, which has been training near Melbourne, starts to Rockhampton.

NEW GUINEA—Co B, Aus 39th Bn, advancing overland from Port Moresby, reaches Kokoda.

13 July

PACIFIC—Operation Plan TULSA-II A is drawn up. U.S. 32d Div begins movement from Adelaide to camp near Brisbane, Australia. Maj Gen George C. Kenney, CG of Fourth Air Force, is directed to take command of Allied Air Forces, replacing Gen Brett.

14 July

PACIFIC—Maj Gen Millard F. Harmon is named commander of U.S. Army Forces in South Pacific Area (COMGENSOPAC). In preparation for invasion of the Solomons, ships from SWPA (TF 44) leave Brisbane, Australia, for New Zealand, where all except I CA, which becomes part of Air Support Force, are assigned to Solomons Amphibious Force. TF 42 (submarines) is to interdict enemy shipping in Rabaul area. Adm Ghormley alerts 7th Marines, 1st Mar Div, on Samoa to be prepared to sail for the Solomons on 4 days' notice.

EGYPT—Br Eighth Army makes limited attack along and to S of Ruweisat Ridge and gains some ground.

USSR—German *Army Groups B* and *A* continue rapidly toward Stalingrad and Rostov, respectively. *4th Pz Army* is assigned to *Army Group A* for operations S of Rostov.

15 July

SWPA—Plan is drawn up for Operation PROVIDENCE, occupation by Allied forces of Buna area on N coast of New Guinea.

CBI—India-China Ferry Command is activated.

EGYPT—In tank-supported counterattack, enemy recovers part of ground lost in Ruweisat Ridge area.

USSR—Russians admit loss of Boguchar and Millerovo. German *Army Group A* continues rapidly toward Rostov, *1st* and *4th Pz Armies* reaching Kamensk, on the Donets.

16 July

U.S.—Breaks off consular relations with Finland, effective 1 August 1942. Gen Harmon, with small forward echelon of USAFISPA, starts air journey from Washington to S Pacific.

PACIFIC—Adm Ghormley issues Operation Plan No. 1-42, covering Task One of projected offensive. TF's 61 and 63 are formed. TF 61, under Vice Adm Frank J. Fletcher, is the Solomons Expeditionary Force, which includes Air Support Force under Rear Adm Leigh Noyes and Amphibious Force commanded by Rear Adm Richmond K. Turner. TF 63, under Adm McCain, consists of all Allied landbased aircraft in S Pacific.

EGYPT—30 Corps of Br Eighth Army enlarges salient W of El 'Alamein with capture of ridge 3 miles W of railway station. 13 Corps exerts pressure against S flank of enemy.

17 July

SWPA—Movement order for Operation PROVIDENCE, occupation of Buna area, New Guinea, is issued. Serial One is to leave Port Moresby on 31 July. D Day is to be 10–12 August.

U.K.—Gen Marshall, Adm King, and Harry Hopkins arrive in England to urge that SLEDGEHAMMER be undertaken in 1942.

18 July

USSR—Continuing southward on broad front, Germans take Voroshilovgrad, coal and coke center of Donets basin, and to SE reach the Don at Tsimlyansk.

19 July

SWPA—From Rabaul, Japanese invasion force of about 1,800 men sails for Buna, New Guinea. Lugger arrives at Buna with supplies and MG's of Co B, Aus 39th Bn.

CBI—Gen Stilwell submits to Chiang Kai-shek a plan, dated 18th, calling for Allied co-operation in regaining Burma as a necessary preliminary to getting aid to China.

20 July

PACIFIC—USAFIA, largely a supply organization, is discontinued, and U.S. Army Services of Supply, Southwest Pacific Area (USASOS SWPA) is established under command of Gen Richard Marshall. GHQ SWPA moves forward in Australia from Melbourne to Brisbane to be nearer scene of offensive. Maj Gen Alexander A. Vandegrift, CG 1st Mar Div, issues tactical orders for invasion of Solomons.

CBI—Dr. Lauchlin Currie arrives in China to discuss U.S.-Chinese relations with Stilwell and the Chinese.

21 July

PACIFIC—Solomons Expeditionary Force (TF 61) is ordered to rendezvous SE of Fiji Is. on 26 July. Allied planes sight and attack enemy convoy approaching New Guinea, despite poor visibility, which prevents Japanese naval planes at Lae, however, from supporting enemy. After naval gunfire bombardment of Buna, Japanese begin landing near Gona, night 21–22, forestalling Allied Operation PROVIDENCE, which was to have secured the same general area. Japanese naval forces at Salamaua provide diversion by raiding Mubo and Komiatum, and enemy submarines become increasingly active.

EGYPT—Br Eighth Army opens attack against center of enemy's line late in day, employing infantry to clear mine fields for passage of armor.

22 July

PACIFIC—98th Sq of 11th Heavy Bombardment Gp lands in New Caledonia. Solomons Amphibious Force, with 1st Mar Div embarked, sails from Wellington, New Zealand. 3d Defense Bn, final reinforcing unit, begins voyage from Pearl Harbor to join 1st Mar Div.

NEW GUINEA—Allied planes continue to attack enemy shipping off N coast, setting fire to a transport. Upon landing, Japanese Navy units move to Buna and Army forces to Giruwa. Advance force pushes inland at once from Giruwa to reconnoiter trail to Port Moresby and reaches Soputa area. Gen MacArthur orders Gen Morris, commander of New Guinea Force, to reinforce Kokoda as quickly as possible.

EGYPT—Br Eighth Army continues attack, gaining some ground but failing to break through enemy line. 23d Armd Brig, which has recently arrived from England, passes through gaps made by infantry in mine fields but is unable to gain ground and loses many tanks. NZ 6th Brig and bn of Ind 161st Brig are virtually destroyed by enemy counterattacks.

USSR—German *Army Group* A opens all-out assault against Rostov.

U.K.—British refuse U.S. proposal to launch Operation SLEDGEHAMMER.

23 July

NEW CALEDONIA—42d Sq of 11th Heavy Bombardment Gp arrives.

NEW GUINEA—Continuing along Kokoda Trail, Japanese clash with Aus Maroubra Force near Awala, forcing Australians back toward Wairopi.

24 July

FIJI IS.—431st Sq of 11th Heavy Bombardment Gp arrives.

NEW GUINEA—Lt Col William T. Owen, CO Aus 39th Bn, flies to Kokoda, which is in imminent danger. Outnumbered Maroubra Force, fighting delaying action as it falls back toward Kokoda, crosses Kumusi R and destroys Wairopi bridge across it.

USSR—Rostov falls to German *Army Group* A.

25 July

U.S.—Combined Chiefs of Staff agree upon command setup for TORCH, as GYMNAST is renamed.

POA—Adm McCain issues orders for Solomons offensive to TF 63. 26th Sq of 11th Heavy Bombardment Gp arrives at Efate, New Hebrides.

[26–31 JULY 1942]

NEW GUINEA—Japanese cross Kumusi R over improvised bridge and outflank Maroubra Force, which falls back to Oivi, 6 miles from Kokoda.

USSR—Germans claim capture of Novocherkassk, NE of Rostov.

26 July

POA—Gen Harmon takes tactical command of all U.S. Army forces in S Pacific and establishes provisional CP at Suva, Fiji Is. Solomons Expeditionary Force (TF 61), except for party bringing 3d Defense Bn across the Pacific, assembles SE of Fiji Is.

NEW GUINEA—New Guinea Force flies 30 men from Co D, Aus 39th Bn, to Kokoda; 15 of these are sent forward to Oivi. After Japanese surround Oivi position, small defense force at Kokoda (platoon of Co B and 15 men of Co D) abandons it for prepared positions at Deniki.

EGYPT—30 Corps, Br Eighth Army, launches attack on N flank after nightfall.

27 July

POA—S Pacific commanders of island bases are informed by COMSOPAC that Gen Harmon will be responsible for training Army ground and air personnel. TF 61 sails to Koro, Fiji Is., to rehearse for invasion of Solomons.

NEW GUINEA—Aus Oivi force, having broken through enemy during night 26–27, joins elements of Maroubra Force at Deniki. New Guinea Force, upon learning of evacuation of Kokoda, recalls 2 air transports bound for Kokoda with reinforcements and supplies.

EGYPT—30 Corps, Br Eighth Army, continues attack but is unable to make progress. 13 Corps, in support of 30, feints and patrols.

USSR—German *Army Group B* continues to clear Don bend near Stalingrad. 6th Army begins battle to reduce Soviet bridgehead across the Don at Kalach, W of Stalingrad.

28 July

PACIFIC—Gen Harmon arrives at New Caledonia. Gen Kenney, commander-designate of Allied Air Forces, arrives in Australia. Expeditionary Force (TF 61) begins rehearsal at Koro, Fiji Is., for invasion of Solomons. Adm Fletcher issues Operation Order No. 1-42 to TF 61.

JAPAN—Tokyo orders all-out offensive for E New Guinea, including amphibious assaults on Milne Bay and attack on Port Moresby by land and sea.

NEW GUINEA—Maroubra Force recaptures Kokoda in counterattack, but this position is in great danger as Japanese reinforcements move forward from beachhead.

CHINA—Japanese campaign in Chekiang Province, conducted in retaliation for Doolittle raid on Japan, ends.

29 July

POA—Gen Harmon shifts USAFISPA CP from Suva, Fiji Is., to Noumea, New Caledonia.

NEW GUINEA—Japanese recapture Kokoda, again forcing defenders back to Deniki. Lull ensues as Japanese consolidate and strengthen positions. Allied planes frustrate efforts of 2 enemy transports to unload troops and supplies on N coast. One returns to Rabaul without unloading. The other is disabled and subsequently sinks; troops embarked reach Giruwa by small craft.

CBI—Gen Stilwell broadens plans for offensive with "Pacific Front" proposal calling for recapture of Burma by Allied forces from Yunnan and Manipur.

30 July

U.S.—Women's Reserve is established by law in Navy and called WAVES from expression "Women Accepted for Volunteer Emergency Service."

POA—Adm Turner issues Operation Plan No. A3-42 to Solomons Amphibious Force.

NEW GUINEA—Co C of Aus 39th Bn completes march to Demki.

NEI—Japanese invade Aru, Kei, and Tanimbar Is.

EGYPT—Gen Auchinleck decides to remain on the defensive until reinforcements arrive.

USSR—German *Army Group A* establishes bridgehead across Manych R SW of Proletarskaya; *Army Group B* continues reduction of Kalach bridgehead across the Don W of Stalingrad. On central front, Soviet forces begin attacks in Rzhev area.

31 July

POA—Adm Turner's Amphibious Force, covered by Adm Noyes' Air Support Force and Adm McCain's TF 63, begins voyage to the Solomons from Fiji Is. B-17's of TF 63, from New Hebrides bases, start 7 days of attacks on Guadalcanal and Tulagi in preparation for invasion.

NEW GUINEA—Additional elements (Co A of Aus 39th Bn) of Maroubra Force reach Deniki.

1 August

CHINA—Chiang Kai-shek formally approves Gen Stilwell's proposal of 18 July for offensive and modifies the 3 demands of 29 June.

EGYPT—Activity on both sides is confined to patrolling, arty exchanges, and preparations for renewing offensive.

USSR—German *Army Group A*, to which *1st Pz Army* reverts, is fanning out S of Rostov and has cut Novorossisk-Stalingrad RR with capture of rail junction of Salsk; forward elements reach Kuban R. Heavy fighting continues in Don bend opposite Stalingrad as German *Army Group B* continues efforts to isolate Soviet forces. Red Army continues local attacks in Rzhev sector.

3 August

USSR—German *Army Group A* continues rapidly southward into Kuban area, where it is attempting to establish bridgehead, and overruns Voroshilovsk. Soviet forces continue to resist *Army Group B* in Don bend opposite Stalingrad and to attack Germans in Rzhev sector.

4 August

SWPA—Gen Kenney assumes command of Allied Air Forces, succeeding Gen Brett.

5 August

USSR—German *Army Group A* establishes bridgehead across the Kuban in Armavir-Nevinnomyssk area, threatening Maikop oil fields; claims capture of Kropotkin. Red Army units continue to fight losing battle inside Don bend near Stalingrad.

6 August

POA—Allied invasion force continues toward Solomons undetected.

NEW GUINEA—New Guinea Force takes command of all Aus and U.S. forces in Australian New Guinea (Papua and NE New Guinea).

CBI—Dr. Currie leaves China for Washington to present Gen Stilwell's "Pacific Front" plan and Chiang Kai-shek's modified demands to President Roosevelt and Combined Chiefs of Staff.

USSR—On Novorossisk-Stalingrad RR, Germans claim capture of Tikhoretsk and Russians admit loss of Kotelnikov: German *Army Group A* overruns Armavir, on Kuban R. Soviet resistance to *Army Group B* in Don bend near Stalingrad is growing weaker.

7 August

ALEUTIAN Is.—Kiska undergoes its first bombardment by surface forces. TF of cruisers and destroyers under Rear Adm W. W. Smith, part of Adm Theobald's North Pacific Force (TF 8), bombards shore installations with unobserved results. This action had been planned for 2d July but was postponed because of weather conditions.

SOLOMON Is.—After preparatory bombardment of landing areas, U.S. 1st Mar Div (−7th Marines), reinf, invades S Solomons with close air and naval support. Unloading operations are delayed by enemy air attacks during which USS *Mugford* (DD) is damaged.

At 0910, 5th Marines (−2d Bn) lands unopposed on N coast (Beach Red) of Guadalcanal about 6,000 yards E of Lunga Pt and establishes beachhead between Tenaru and Tenavatu Rivers. 1st Marines and supporting weapons follow 5th Marines ashore. 1st Bn of 5th Marines drives W along coast toward Lunga R; 1st Marines pushes SW toward Mt Austen. Advance halts for night after each of the assault forces has gained about a mile, 1st Bn of 5th Marines reaching mouth of Ilu R.

At 0740, 1st Bn of 2d Marines begins landing on S coast of Florida I., Co B near Haleta and rest at Halavo. The bn meets no opposition and is later withdrawn. At 0800, 1st Raider Bn, followed by 2d Bn of 5th Marines, lands on S coast (Beach Blue) of Tulagi without opposition. Marines clear NW end of island without difficulty, but Raiders meet bitter opposition from enemy in caves and dugouts on SE end in afternoon and are forced to halt some 1,000 yards from SE tip. Co G of 5th Marines helps hold this perimeter against enemy attacks.

At noon, 1st Para Bn invades twin islets of Gavutu and Tanambogo, which are joined by causeway, E of Tulagi; clears most the a islets despite enemy fire. From Florida I., Co B of 2d Marines makes unsuccessful attempt to land on N coast.

NEW GUINEA—Activity is confined to patrol clashes. By this time all 5 rifle cos of Aus 39th Bn are at the front and Maroubra Force contains 480 men. Because of Solomons offensive, Japanese recall convoy heading for Buna from Rabaul.

EGYPT—Prime Minister Churchill visits Br Eighth Army front.

8 August

ALLIED COMMAND—President Roosevelt and Prime Minister Churchill agree on Gen Eisenhower, CG ETO, as commander of TORCH.

SOLOMON Is.—Japanese planes continue to attack Allied shipping, destroying USS *George F. Elliott* (AP) and damaging USS *Jarvis* (DD). *Jarvis* heads for Noumea but is never heard from again.

Abandoning thrust toward Mt Austen on Guadalcanal, 1st Mar Div advances W in 2 columns. 1st Bn of 5th Marines crosses Lunga R and secures coastal village of Kukum. To S, 1st Bn of 1st Marines takes airfield and reaches E bank of Lunga R. Both Kukum and the airfield are found to have been hastily evacuated.

On Tulagi, 1st Raider Bn and 5th Marines finish clearing the island by 1500.

On Gavutu-Tanambogo, 1st Para Bn, assisted by 3d Bn of 2d Marines from div reserve, completes capture of Gavutu-Tanambogo.

BATTLE OF SAVO I.—During night 8–9, Japanese naval force of cruisers and DD's attacks Allied warships off Savo I. and inflicts heavy damage before retiring to Rabaul. As a result of the action, HMAS *Canberra* and USS *Astoria*, *Quincy*, and *Vincennes* are lost and other vessels are damaged.

EGYPT—Gen Alexander flies to Cairo, where he learns that he is to relieve Gen Auchinleck as CinC MEF. Lt Gen W. H. E. Gott, CG of Br 13 Corps, who was to have been given command of Br Eighth Army, is killed in airplane accident.

USSR—Surovikino, W of Stalingrad, falls to German *Army Group B*.

9 August

SOLOMON Is.—Amphibious and Air Support Forces of TF 61 retire, former with more than half the 60 days' supplies and elements of landing force still embarked. Of the original landing force of over 19,000, almost 17,000 are now ashore. Guadalcanal beachhead is being consolidated and work is begun on uncompleted airstrip, where air warning system is established. During 8 and 9, 2d Marines completes northern attack with occupation of Mbangai, Makambo, and Kokomtambu islets.

NEW GUINEA—Maj Gen Sydney F. Rowell, CG Aus I Corps, is designated to command New Guinea Force.

USSR—Krasnodar and Maikop fall to German *Army Group A*.

10 August

NEW IRELAND—U.S. submarine sinks Japanese cruiser *Kako* off the island.

New Guinea—Maroubra Force counterattacks toward Kokoda with 3 cos One seizes Kokoda airfield, but the others are unable to advance.

EGYPT—Gen Alexander receives directive calling for destruction of Rommel's army in Egypt and Libya.

USSR—Soviet resistance in foothills of Caucasus range is increasing, but forward elements of German *Army Group A* reach Pyatigorsk.

11 August

U.S.—Adm Leahy makes the first of many suggestions that Burma Road be reopened.

NEW GUINEA—U.S. Advanced Base in New Guinea, a logistical agency, is established by USASOS with hq at Port Moresby, which is to become a large supply and communications center. Maroubra Force abandons Kokoda airfield, night 11–12, since it is untenable.

MEDITERRANEAN—Enemy U-boats heavily attack Malta-bound convoy and sink HMS *Eagle* (aircraft carrier).

MIDDLE EAST—Iran-Iraq Service Command is redesignated Persian Gulf Service Command (PGSC); remains directly under Hq USAFIME.

USSR—Threat to Stalingrad increases as German *Army Group A* eliminates Soviet bridgehead in Don bend near Kalach.

12 August

NEW HEBRIDES—Elements of original Guadalcanal invasion force (1,390 of 2d Marines) debark at Espiritu Santo.

GUADALCANAL—TF 63, under Adm McCain, is given responsibility for getting aviation supplies, ammunition, and ground crews from Espiritu Santo to Guadalcanal. First U.S. plane, a PBY, lands on airfield, called Henderson Field after Midway hero Maj Lofton Henderson. Patrol led by 1st Mar Div Intelligence Officer embarks at Kukum to make contact with enemy in Matanikau area; upon landing, night 12–13, is wiped out, except for 3 persons, by enemy.

EGYPT—Lt Gen Sir Bernard L. Montgomery, who is to head Br Eighth Army, arrives from U.K.

USSR—Prime Minister Churchill arrives in Moscow where, during a 4-day visit, he discusses the subject of a second front in Europe with Marshal Joseph Stalin. On central front, local Soviet attacks against Rzhev reach their climax without achieving a decisive victory. Elements of German *Army Group A*, driving toward the Kuban in region E of Sea of Azov, reach Slavyansk.

13 August

NEW GUINEA—Japanese convoy, with 3,000 construction troops embarked, reaches Basabua, a short distance from Gona. Japanese attack Maroubra Force at Deniki in strength, forcing it back beyond Isurava, 5 miles from Deniki. After this victory, which firmly secures Buna-Kokoda track, enemy pauses to consolidate.

JAPAN—Imperial General Headquarters orders *17th Army* at Rabaul to take responsibility for ground operations on Guadalcanal.
MIDDLE EAST—Col Shingler becomes CO of Persian Gulf Service Command.
EGYPT—Gen Montgomery takes command of Br Eighth Army.
USSR—Germans claim capture of Elista, in Kalmyk district S of Stalingrad.

14 August

U.S.—Directive is sent to Gen Eisenhower as CinC TORCH.

15 August

GUADALCANAL—Marine rations are cut. First destroyer-transports arrive with supplies and aviation ground crews.
MIDDLE EAST—Gen Alexander takes command of MEF from Gen Auchinleck.
EGYPT—Gen Montgomery is rapidly reorganizing and strengthening Br Eighth Army, for which 10 Corps is to serve as reserve. Considering 'Alam el Halfa ridge, far in rear of El 'Alamein Line, of vital importance, 44th Div and 10th Armd Div (—9th Brig) are ordered to this area from Delta region, where they have been training. 132d Brig of 44th Div is attached to NZ 2d Div.
USSR—Germans report capture of Georgievsk.

16 August

EGYPT—Enemy installations on Egyptian front are bombed for first time by U.S. medium bombers in support of Br Eighth Army.

17 August

GILBERT Is.—Lt Col Evans F. Carlson's 2d Mar Raider Bn, consisting of 221 marines, moves by 2 submarines to Makin and begins 2-day raid on Butaritari I., during which scattered enemy forces are engaged and radio station is destroyed. Enemy planes attack the Raiders on both days. 30 marines are lost in the action.
GUADALCANAL—Adm Ghormley shifts responsibility for establishing line of communications to Guadalcanal from TF 63 to Adm Turner's TF 62. Henderson Field becomes operational. Japanese land reinforcements near Taivu Pt and in Kokumbona area, night 17-18.
USSR—German *Army Group A* establishes bridgeheads across Kuban R.
FRANCE—U.S. Eighth Air Force conducts first attack against Europe. Sq of B-24's, escorted by RAF Spitfires, bombs rail center at Rouen.

18 August

NEW GUINEA—Large Japanese detachment, embarked on 3 escorted transports, reaches Basabua undetected and goes ashore. Gen Rowell assumes command of New Guinea Force, replacing Gen Morris.
CBI—Maj Gen Clayton L. Bissell is given command of U.S. Tenth Air Force.

19 August

GUADALCANAL—5th Marines, in limited offensive, clears coastal villages of Matanikau and Kokumbona, then returns to Lunga Pt. Cos L and B attack Matanikau from E and S. Co I, moving forward by sea, clears Kakumbona. While patrolling to locate enemy radio station, Co A of 1st Marines encounters and virtually wipes out party of 34 Japanese—recently landed Army forces—near Taivu Pt.
NEW BRITAIN—Japanese reinforcements, about 1,500 in 4 transports screened by DD's, leave Rabaul for Guadalcanal.
NEW GUINEA—Leading elements of Aus 7th Div (21st Brig) arrive at Port Moresby, from which they start at once toward Isurava to bolster Maroubra Force.
EGYPT—Gen Alexander directs Gen Montgomery to hold current positions at El 'Alamein while preparing for offensive.
FRANCE—Canadian (Cdn) and Br troops, 5,000 strong, raid Dieppe for 9 hours, damaging military installations at great cost in casualties. 50 U.S. Rangers accompanied the expedition; of these, 6 were wounded and 7 were reported missing. Many German planes are destroyed by supporting Allied fighters.

20 August

U.S.—Twelfth Air Force is activated at Bolling Field, Washington, D.C.
NEW HEBRIDES—Advanced supply depots are established at Noumea and Espiritu Santo.
GUADALCANAL—First planes (advance echelon of MAG 23, 1st Mar Air Wing) arrive for duty at Henderson Field. The group consists of VMF 223 (19 F4F-4's) and VMSB 232 (12 SBD-3's). Supply and evacuation between Guadalcanal and Espiritu Santo is begun by MAG 25. 1st Mar Div units along Ilu R exchange fire with enemy moving up from E, beginning in evening.
NEW GUINEA—Japanese order amphibious assault on Milne Bay by about 1,500 men from Kavieng, New Ireland, and from Buna.
USSR—German *Army Group B* makes slow progress toward Stalingrad against stubborn resis-

tance and gains foothold across the Don in Kletskaya area. In the Caucasus, Soviet rear guards continue strong delaying action.

21 August

GUADALCANAL—In predawn attack toward airfield, about 200 Japanese attempt to gain W bank of Ilu R; the few who succeed are killed or driven back by 2d Bn of 1st Marines. Japanese remaining E of the Ilu are surrounded and destroyed in concerted attacks by 2d and 1st Bns, 1st Marines. 1st Bn crosses river upstream and attacks enemy from rear while 2d, with light tank platoon spearheading, attacks at river mouth. Japanese sustain almost 800 casualties; 15 of the enemy are captured; 35 marines are killed and 75 wounded. Lunga garrison, already strengthened by raiders and parachutists, is further increased by 2d Bn of 5th Marines from Tulagi. Rations and aviation supplies in limited quantities are landed.

SWPA—Operation Plan TULSA II-B is drawn up as planning for offensive continues.

NEW GUINEA—Japanese convoy reaches Basabua and lands reinforcements, completing quota for overland drive on Port Moresby. Aus 18th Brig reaches Milne Bay, where it joins Aus 7th Brig, CMF, which reached there in July.

USSR—Elements of German *Army Group A*, clearing E coast of Black Sea, overrun Krymskaya.

22 August

BRAZIL—Angered by the recent sinking of 5 of her ships by enemy, Brazil declares war on Germany and Italy. United Nations shipping is thus able to make full use of the comparatively short S Atlantic route via Ascension I.

ALEUTIAN Is.—After consideration of the relative merits of Tanaga and Adak as an advanced air base from which to attack Kiska, Adak has been chosen. Directive for its occupation on 30 August is issued.

SOLOMON Is.—On Guadalcanal, first U.S. Army planes, 5 P-400's of 67th Fighter Sq, arrive for duty at Henderson Field, flying there from New Hebrides. Ships bringing supplies are thus afforded greater protection, but shipments remain small. CO and staff of 2d Marines arrive on Tulagi from New Hebrides.

NEW GUINEA—Maj Gen Cyril A. Clowes takes command of Milne Force, which by this time comprises 9,458 men (7,429 Australians, 1,365 Americans, 664 RAAF). The U.S. component consists largely of engineers and AA personnel. Japanese Maj Gen Tomitaro Horii leaves for the front to take personal charge of operations. His forces now total over 11,000 men.

23 August

USSR—German *Army Group B* presses in steadily on Stalingrad, spearhead reaching the Volga; *Army Group A* gains additional ground along E coast of Black Sea and captures Elbrus.

24 August

BATTLE OF EASTERN SOLOMONS—American naval TF's, centering about CV's *Enterprise* and *Saratoga*, intercept Japanese fleet units (3 carriers, 8 BB's, 4 CA's, 2 CL's .and 21 DD's, plus the 4 transports with reinforcements for Guadalcanal) well E of Guadalcanal. Major air battle ensues (U.S. carrier planes being assisted by a few land-based planes), and Japanese sustain heavy losses before retiring northward. Japanese carrier *Ryuju*, 1 CL, and 1 DD are sunk, and other vessels are damaged. Japanese lose 90 planes; Americans, 20 planes.

GUADALCANAL—Henderson Field is subjected to almost daily air attacks and Lunga perimeter is bombarded from sea at frequent intervals. Marine fighters intercepting enemy aircraft over Henderson Field shoot down 21 for loss of 3. 11 dive bombers from the *Enterprise* land on the field and remain for 3 months.

NEW GUINEA—Gen Horii orders general offensive. Japanese amphibious forces leave for Milne Bay, those from New Ireland in a transports and the force from Buna in 7 large landing barges. Barges are detected by coastwatcher in afternoon.

25 August

BATTLE OF EASTERN SOLOMONS—U.S. carrier forces are unable to locate enemy fleet units, but U.S. Marine and Army land-based bombers attack Japanese transport force continuing toward Guadalcanal and cause it to delay landings and retire northward. Enemy transport and DD are sunk and cruiser is damaged.

NEW GUINEA—Enemy amphibious force bound for Milne Bay from Buna is stranded on Goodenough I., D'Entrecasteaux Is., when P-40's from Milne Bay destroy all 7 of their beached barges. Aircraft from Australia and Milne Bay attack enemy convoy proceeding from New Ireland toward Milne Bay but are hampered by weather conditions and fail to stop it. After shelling beaches, Japanese begin landing, night 25-26, at 3 points E of Rabi, their intended landing site, and push W at once. Elements of Aus 61st Militia Bn stationed at K. B. Mission, E of Rabi and in path of Japanese advance, engage enemy who retires at dawn of 26th to landing point. Other elements of 61st Bn are moving from Ahioma to head of Milne Bay at Gili Gili by sea and lose to the enemy 1 of 2 ketches loaded with troops.

MIDDLE EAST—Col Shingler is directed by Gen Maxwell to take responsibility for construction, maintenance, supply, and administration of installations in new PGSC area, which comprises Iraq, Iran, and parts of Saudi Arabia bordering on Persian Gulf.

26 August

GUADALCANAL—5th Marines, 1st Mar Div, prepares for limited attack to eliminate resistance on W flank of Lunga perimeter.

New Guinea—Planes from Milne Bay and Port Moresby attack Japanese in Milne Bay, destroying most of their supplies on shore and damaging large transport. After nightfall, enemy convoy bringing rest of 1,170-man force from New Ireland arrives safely in Milne Bay. Japanese make another night attack, 26-27, to W, forcing Aus militia back to Gama R line; at dawn of 27th Japanese retire once more to landing point. Meanwhile, Japanese forces in Isurava area renew overland drive on Port Moresby at dawn and force Australians (depleted 39th Bn, 30th Brig Hq, 2 cos of 53d Bn) back steadily by overwhelming pressure. Japanese supply lines, which are becoming overextended, are frequently attacked by air.

INDIA—Training center for Ch troops is activated at Ramgarh, Bihar Prov, with Col Frederick McCabe as commandant.

27 August

GUADALCANAL—1st Bn of 5th Marines lands about 1,000 yards W of Kokumbona and starts E along shore while Co I of 3d Bn pushes W from Kukum by overland trail to intercept enemy withdrawal inland. 1st Bn is halted by enemy fire about 1,500 yards E of Kokumbona. 9 more P-400's of 67th Fighter Sq arrive at Henderson Field.

NEW GUINEA—Fresh AIF troops (2/10th Bn of 18th Brig) advance unopposed to K. B. Mission during day. After nightfall, Japanese, with tanks, renew attack and split defending force, which withdraws. Japanese overland drive on Port Moresby continues, with Australians falling back gradually. Reinforcements (21st Brig) are moving to forward area to assist Australians.

USSR—German *Army Group B* continues battle for Stalingrad; *Army Group A* presses closer to oil prize of Grozny, seizing Prokhladny and reaching Terek R.

28 August

GUADALCANAL—1st Bn of 5th Marines, in flanking movement without enemy contact, returns with Co I of 3d Bn to Kukum area.

NEW GUINEA—Milne Force withstands determined frontal assaults against No. 3 airstrip. Aus 7th Brig, reinf by Americans of 709th Airborne AA Battery and of 43d Engrs, staunchly defends the strip. Other Australians continue fighting withdrawal across Owen Stanley Range.

USSR—German *Army Group A* begins assault on Novorossisk, on Black Sea.

29 August

NEW GUINEA—Orders for Aus 18th Brig to clear N shore of Milne Bay are revoked when another enemy convoy is detected approaching that area. 775 Japanese reinforcements are unloaded from the convoy. Fighting continues along overland trail to Port Moresby, but because of situation at Milne Bay and in the Solomons, *South Seas Detachment* is ordered to halt upon reaching S foothills of Owen Stanley Range. Aus 21st Brig relieves 39th Bn and elements of 53d Bn.

30 August

ALEUTIAN IS.—U.S. occupation force lands on Adak without opposition.

Guadalcanal—Japanese bombers attack shipping off coast and sink *Colhoun* (APD). Rear echelon of MAG 23 (12 dive bombers and 18 fighters) arrives at Henderson Field.

NEW GUINEA—After quiet day, Japanese attack at night in effort to secure No. 3 airstrip but are repulsed and retreat at dawn of 31st, leaving many dead. Enemy continues to gain ground in overland drive on Port Moresby.

EGYPT—During night 30-31, Axis forces open offensive against El 'Alamein Line, making main effort against 13 Corps, Br Eighth Army, on S while conducting a unsuccessful diversionary thrusts against 30 Corps.

31 August

SOLOMONS IS.—USS *Helm* (DD) tows 3 harbor patrol boats to Tulagi. USS *Saratoga* (CV) is damaged by enemy torpedo while patrolling W of Santa Cruz Is. and is forced to retire to Tongatabu for emergency repairs; on 12 September leaves there for Pearl Harbor where she remains until November.

NEW GUINEA—Australians take the offensive in Milne Bay area against demoralized enemy. 18th Brig drives E to K. B. Mission. While tide has turned against enemy in Milne Bay area, other forces continue across Owen Stanley Range toward Port Moresby. Gen Horii is ordered to go on the defensive upon crossing the range.

INDIA—Gen Stilwell agrees to SOS proposal that main base in India be established at Calcutta rather than Karachi.

EGYPT—Axis forces, against strong opposition, breach mine field on S flank of 13 Corps, Br Eighth Army, and German armor then drives through and attacks W toward W end of 'Alam el Halfa ridge until halted short of it with heavy losses. Air and arty are employed against enemy with good effect. Heavy attacks by U.S. and Br planes throughout August have seriously affected Rommel's supply position.

USSR—Although Soviet resistance along Terek R has stiffened considerably, German Army Group A secures foothold across it in Mozdok area.

1 September

JAPAN—Foreign Minister Shigenori Togo resigns and Premier Hideki Tojo is asked to assume duties of Foreign Ministry.

SOLOMON IS.—USS *Betelgeuse* lands 200 men of 6th Naval Construction Bn in Lunga area. Throughout September, Americans on Guadalcanal lack adequate fighter strength, although carrier planes that can be spared are employed at Henderson Field. Trickle of supplies to the garrison increases only slightly.

NEW GUINEA—Australians continue to make progress in Milne Bay area and to fall back slowly along trail over Owen Stanley Range. As diversion for Milne Bay forces, Japanese from Salamaua attack Aus Kanga Force guarding Bulolo Valley and seize Mubo.

MAURITIUS, RODRIGUEZ, AND SEYCHELLES ISLANDS—Transferred from command of Br Army Hq, India, to East Africa Command. These, with Madagascar, are formed into "Islands Area" under Maj Gen G. R. Smallwood.

EGYPT—Br Eighth Army repels further enemy attempts to reach W end of 'Alam el Halfa ridge and prepares for counterattack to close gap in mine field on S flank. 30 Corps is thinned out to reinf 13 Corps; 10 Corps is ordered forward.

USSR—Army Group B continues to batter defense ring about Stalingrad. Anapa, important Black Sea port, falls to Army Group A.

2 September

SAMOA—7th Marines and part of 5th Defense Bn embark for New Hebrides.

NEW GUINEA—Australians continue to clear N coast of Milne Bay but are unable to stem Japanese drive toward Port Moresby. About 1,000 Japanese reinforcements from Rabaul land at Basabua, night 2–3.

EGYPT—Massing armor S of 'Alam el Halfa ridge, enemy halts to await frontal counterattack, but Br armor remains in prepared positions.

USSR—Army Group A continues to press toward Novorossisk and Grozny. Threat to Novorossisk increases as German and Rumanian forces from the Crimea cross Kerch Strait and join other Axis forces in the area.

3 September

SWPA—Gen Kenney, Commander Allied Air Forces, makes Fifth Air Force, the U.S. component, a separate command in order to achieve greater efficiency. Fifth Air Force is given responsibility for operations in NE area; RAAF is to defend the Australian continent, particularly the Darwin area.

EGYPT—Aircraft continue to harass enemy, who begins to fall back, concentrating on supply transport, which Axis can ill afford to lose. During night 3–4, attack of 13 Corps to close gap in mine field is begun by NZ 2d Div, reinf, and evokes furious opposition.

USSR—Germans continue to push toward Stalingrad, Grozny, and Novorossisk against stubborn resistance; are reported at W suburbs of Stalingrad.

4 September

SOLOMON IS.—1st Raider Bn patrols Savo I., finding it free of enemy, and returns to Guadalcanal. U.S. destroyer-transports *Little* and *Gregory* are sunk by enemy warships in Sealark Channel, night 4–5.

NEW GUINEA—Continuing E along Milne Bay, Australians reach Goroni. After nightfall, Japanese place wounded on board ship for withdrawal.

EGYPT—13 Corps, Br Eighth Army, is still strongly opposed as it attempts to close gap in mine field.

5 September

U.S.-U.K.—Final decision is made that TORCH is to include landings at Algiers and Oran in Algeria and at Casablanca, Morocco.

SWPA—U.S. 32d and 41st Divs are assigned to Gen Eichelberger, CG U.S. I Corps.

NEW GUINEA—Japanese continue evacuation of Milne Bay under cover of darkness. About 1,300 of original force of some 1,900 are withdrawn by sea. Australians, following withdrawal closely, capture supply dump at Waga Waga.

EGYPT—Enemy opposition to 13 Corps, Br Eighth Army, as it continues battle to close gap in mine field is unabated.

6 September

NEW GUINEA—Aus 18th Brig continues to clear enemy from Milne Bay against light, scattered resistance. In Owen Stanley Range 2/14th and 2/16th Bns of 21st Brig, Aus 7th Div, fall back to Efogi Spur, beyond The Gap, where 2/27th Bn of same brig is already established.

EGYPT—13 Corps, Br Eighth Army, continues offensive, making slow progress southward against firm opposition.

USSR—Germans announce capture of Novorossisk, leading port on E coast of Black Sea. Fierce fighting continues around Stalingrad.

7 September

NEW GUINEA—Organized resistance in Milne Bay sector ceases; stragglers are eventually mopped up by Australians. Decisive defeat of Japanese removes threat to Port Moresby from Milne Bay area, but enemy drive along trail over Owen Stanley Range toward Port Moresby is still unchecked.

EGYPT—Gen Montgomery halts battle of 'Alam el Halfa before original positions have been restored, leaving enemy in possession of 4-5 mile stretch of desert on S flank. Lull ensues in ground action during which Br Eighth Army prepares intensively for offensive. Deceptive measures are taken on a comprehensive scale to conceal plans from enemy.

USSR—Soviet forces continue stubborn resistance to *Army Group B* in Stalingrad area and to *Army Group A* in vicinity of Novorossisk.

8 September

GUADALCANAL—Prov bn composed of depleted 1st Raider and 1st Para Bns moves E from Lunga Pt by sea to destroy enemy force at Tasimboko, near Taivu Pt. Debarking E of Tasimboko, the bn moves W, clashing with outposts of strong enemy force that has landed recently near Taivu Pt. Japanese holding force is driven from Tasimboko. Raiders sustain 8 casualties and kill 27 Japanese. Henderson-based aircraft support raiders. Japanese in Taivu Pt area constitute main body of new assault force, smaller group of which is in vicinity of Kokumbona.

NEW GUINEA—Gen Horii, with 5 reinf bns in assault, attacks 21st Brig of Aus 7th Div on Efogi Spur, forcing 2/27th Bn off trail and encircling 2/14th and 2/16th Bns.

9 September

U.S.—Japanese plane, launched from submarine off coast, drops incendiary bomb on mountain slope near Brookings, Oregon, causing small forest fire. This is sole bombing by plane of continental U.S. during the war.

NEW GUINEA—25th Brig of Aus 7th Div is rushed toward Owen Stanley Range front. 16th Brig of Aus 6th Div is ordered to Port Moresby.

MADAGASCAR—Br forces of East Africa Command renew offensive in order to insure safety of certain military objectives and gain air and sea control of Mozambique Channel. 29th Independent Inf Brig makes surprise landing, night 9-10, on W coast in vicinity of Majunga and seizes Majunga virtually unopposed. After being passed through by E African 22d Brig Gp, which starts toward Tananarive, 29th begins re-embarking for another landing. As diversion for Majunga landing, small landings are made on Nosy Be I., off NW coast, and at Morondava, on W coast; forces on N part of island move southward along W and E coasts.

GERMANY—RAF BC, during heavy attack on Duesseldorf, night 10-11, drops first 2-ton incendiary bomb.

11 September

ALEUTIAN IS.—Completion of runway on Adak permits stepped up air offensive against Kiska, some 250 miles distant.

GUADALCANAL—From 29 August to date, about 6,000 Japanese have arrived, landing mostly at night from DD's and destroyer-transports.

NEW GUINEA—Gen MacArthur submits to Gen Blarney a plan for accelerating operations. While Australians, upon receiving reinforcements, are to attack to drive enemy back along Port Moresby-Kokoda trail, an RCT of U.S. 32d Div is to execute wide flanking movement to E to get behind Japanese at Wairopi and thus hasten their expulsion from New Guinea. Aus 2/14th and 2/16th Bns break through enemy forces and fall back to Nauro; then yield Nauro under pressure and take up positions on ridge N of Ioribaiwa, where 2/1st Pioneer Bn and 3d Bn of 14th Brig are established.

12 September

NEW HEBRIDES—7th Marines and elements of 5th Defense Bn arrive at Espiritu Santo. Adm Turner, after conferring with Gen Vandegrift on Guadalcanal, recommends to Adm Ghormley that 7th Marines be used to strengthen Lunga defenses.

GUADALCANAL—Prov raider-parachute bn conducts reconnaissance in force along ridge, later

[13-17 SEPTEMBER 1942]

called Bloody or Edson's, S of OPL and about 800 yards E of Lunga R, to close the route of approach to Henderson Field; despite enemy fire, reaches southernmost knoll. Fire fight continues throughout night 12-13, and enemy succeeds in infiltrating.

U.K.—Gen Eisenhower officially announces assumption of command as CinC Allied Expeditionary Force for TORCH, and Allied Force Headquarters (AFHQ) is activated in London.

13 September

GUADALCANAL—Adm Ghormley orders 7th Marines to reinforce garrison. Air defense is strengthened by arrival of 12 dive bombers and 6 TBF's. Japanese launch air, naval, and ground attacks against Lunga perimeter in attempt to recapture airfield. Prov raider-parachute bn is unable to advance on Bloody Ridge and digs in on central knoll, about 250 yards N of previous bivouac area. After nightfall, main enemy assault force of at least 2 bns drives northward to northernmost knoll where Prov raider-parachute bn, with close arty support, holds firm against further determined attacks. Other Japanese, about 2 cos, attack 3d Bn of 1st Marines on E flank along Ilu R, night 13-14, but are unable to break through.

CHINA—Gen Stilwell presents to Chiang Kai-shek a proposed plan of operations for China Air Task Force, calling for defense of ferry route from India to China as primary mission.

MADAGASCAR—Gen Platt, CG E African Command, establishes hq ashore at Majunga. E African 22d Brig continues toward Tananarive, hampered chiefly by roadblocks.

LIBYA—During night 13-14, small raiding parties of Br MEF move against Tobruk and Benghazi in effort to destroy enemy supplies and installations at the ports. The Tobruk raid is made by land and sea, overland party moving from Egypt. From Kufra, motorized column moves overland more than 500 miles to Benghazi. The raids prove costly and accomplish little.

N ATLANTIC—Large Allied convoy to USSR suffers heavy losses during enemy air attacks.

14 September

ALEUTIAN IS.—Kiska undergoes its first major air raid, by 12 heavy bombers with 28 fighters from Adak.

NEW HEBRIDES—TF 65, organized to transport 7th Marines to Guadalcanal, leaves Espiritu Santo.

GUADALCANAL—Japanese break off attacks on Bloody Ridge at dawn and withdraw under air attack, leaving about 600 dead; Marine casualties are 143. 2d Bn of 5th Marines starts relief of Prov raider-parachute bn. On E flank along the Ilu, 3d Bn of 1st Marines moves 6 light tanks against enemy, but 3 are disabled; Japanese continue sporadic fire in this sector. In afternoon, Japanese attack 3d Bn of 5th Marines on ridge commanding coastal road to W sector of perimeter but are driven off. 3d Bn of 2d Marines arrives on Guadalcanal from Tulagi.

NEW GUINEA—Advance elements (2/31st and 2/33d Bns) of 25th Brig, Aus 7th Div, reach Ioribaiwa, where they take over defense of ridge from Aus 21st Brig. Japanese, with 2 full regts in line, force a further withdrawal, to Imita Ridge, the last before Port Moresby, lying 32 miles from that objective. This is the last withdrawal of Aus forces on this front.

LIBYA—To assist withdrawal of Benghazi raiding party, diversionary raids are made on Gialo and Barce.

15 September

S PACIFIC—Japanese submarines attack U.S. warships on patrol S and E of the Solomons, sinking CV *Wasp* and damaging BB *North Carolina*; latter is forced to return to Pearl Harbor for repairs.

GUADALCANAL—5th Marines, 1st Mar Div, extends positions S of Henderson Field to include Bloody Ridge. Enemy SE of Lunga perimeter continues to fire intermittently on 3d Bn of 1st Marines.

NEW GUINEA—First elements (Co E and attachments) of 126th Inf, U.S. 32d Div, fly to Port Moresby from Brisbane, Australia. This is the first U.S. infantry force to arrive in New Guinea.

16 September

ALEUTIAN IS.—Enemy, during period 27 August-16 September, transfers Attu garrison to Kiska.

NEW GUINEA—Japanese overland drive on Port Moresby grinds to a halt at Ioribaiwa. Australians are firmly entrenched on Imita Ridge, to S, where they are preparing for counteroffensive.

CHINA—Gen Chennault presents to Gen Bissell a plan for employment of CATF that calls for defense of India-China ferry route as primary mission; suggests that CATF operate directly under Stilwell and that it be detached from U.S. Tenth Air Force.

MADAGASCAR—French Governor General requests peace terms.

USSR—*Army Group B* penetrates NW suburbs of Stalingrad.

17 September

NEW GUINEA—In preparation for wide flanking movement to E, Allied rcn parties move E along S coast from Port Moresby. Party of 126th Inf, U.S. 32d Div, under Capt William F. Boice, leaves by lugger for Kapa Kapa to reconnoiter inland from there to Jaure. Another party, headed by SWPA Engineer officer Brig Gen Hugh J. Casey's deputy, Col Leif J. Sverdrup, who is already charged with locating and developing landing fields, moves towards Abau in order to reconnoiter trail inland from there. Japanese at Ioribaiwa are in a precarious position. Although within sight of Port Moresby, troops are in no condition to attack without reinforcements and supplies, neither of which can be spared.

MADAGASCAR—French plenipotentiaries receive and reject terms for cessation of hostilities.

18 September

GUADALCANAL—Improved Allied supply situation permits restoration of full rations to garrison. TF 65 arrives off Kukum and unloads rest of 1st Mar Div—4,180 of 7th Marines, reinf—plus vehicles, equipment, ammunition, and supplies. This is the first ammunition to arrive in response to request of 22 August, 3 other vessels unload aviation gasoline. TF 65 retires to Espiritu Santo with 1st Para Bn, American wounded, and 8 Japanese prisoners. Marines are patrolling aggressively from defense perimeter.

NEW GUINEA—Japanese Imperial General Headquarters orders current positions held as long as possible and Buna-Gona beachhead held as primary defensive position. Gen Horii prepares to thin lines gradually.

AUSTRALIA—Main body of 126th Inf (less arty), U.S. 32d Div, embarks at Brisbane for New Guinea.

MADAGASCAR—29th Independent Inf Brig of Br E African Command lands without opposition on E coast at Tamatave and moves inland toward Tananarive virtually unopposed. E African 22d Brig continues toward Tananarive from W coast.

19 September

GUADALCANAL—Gen Vandegrift establishes continuous defense lines, divides Lunga area into 10 sectors.

20 September

NEW GUINEA—127th Inf of U.S. 32d Div is ordered to Port Moresby.

INDIA—Base Section 2, SOS, at Calcutta, receives its first troops from Karachi.

USSR—Stubborn street fighting is in progress in Stalingrad. Town of Terek falls to German *Army Group A*.

U.K.—Outline plan for TORCH is issued; D Day is set for 8 November.

22 September

U.S.—Combined Chiefs of Staff approve plan drawn up in Washington by SOS, "The Plan for Operation of Certain Iranian Communication Facilities between Persian Gulf Ports and Tehran by U.S. Army Forces." The plan gives U.S. direct responsibility for moving supplies through Persian Corridor to USSR.

23 September

GUADALCANAL—1st Mar Div begins limited operation to W of Lunga perimeter to eliminate enemy within striking distance of Henderson Field: 1st Bn, 7th Marines, is directed to advance along N slopes of Mt Austen, cross the Matanikau, and push W to Kokumbona; 1st Raider Bn is to establish patrol base at Kokumbona at point where inland trails intersect coastal road.

NEW GUINEA—Gen Blarney arrives in Port Moresby to take direct command of New Guinea forces. Lt Gen Edmund F. Herring becomes Commander, Advance New Guinea Force, succeeding Gen Rowell. 128th Inf of U.S. 32d Div reaches Port Moresby by air and is assigned to garrison force under operational control of Aus 6th Div.

MADAGASCAR—E African 22d Brig enters Tananarive, which has been declared an open city.

USSR—German *Army Group B* continues to make slow progress in Stalingrad against bitter opposition. *Army Group A* assembles an assault force for drive on Black Sea port of Tuapse.

24 September

GUADALCANAL—1st Bn of 7th Marines engages in fire fight with enemy on NW slope of Mt Austen.

25 September

GUADALCANAL—2d Bn of 5th Marines joins 1st Bn, 7th Marines, on NW slope of Mt. Austen to continue attack against enemy in Matanikau-Kokumbona area. 2 COS of 1st Bn, 7th Marines, return to Lunga perimeter. Patrol of 1st Bn, 1st Marines, reconnoiters Koli Pt without incident.

NEW GUINEA—25th Brig, Aus 7th Div, opens counteroffensive to drive enemy back along Port Moresby-Kokoda trail, attacking strongly for Ioribaiwa.

MADAGASCAR—E Africa 22d Brig establishes contact with 29th Independent Brig, giving British control of central part of island.

26 September

GUADALCANAL—2d Bn, 5th Marines, and elements of 1st Bn, 7th Marines, reach the upper Matanikau and push N along E bank, encountering enemy fire from vicinity of Matanikau village. Arty and aircraft are employed against the enemy position. 1st Raider Bn passes through 5th Regt sector to join in attack.

MADAGASCAR—Gen Platt moves hq from Majunga to Tananarive.

27 September

GUADALCANAL—1st Raider Bn attempts to attack enemy strongpoint in Matanikau village area from rear but is unable to cross river. 2d Bn of 5th Marines attacks frontally at river mouth but cannot force crossing. 1st Bn of 7th Marines lands near Pt Cruz and takes ridge inland from beach but is prevented by fire from advancing farther; with naval and air support, returns to shore and re-embarks for Kukum. 2d Bn, 5th Marines, covers withdrawal of 1st Raider Bn and returns during night to Lunga perimeter.

NEW GUINEA—Japanese abandon Ioribaiwa Ridge under Aus pressure and are in full retreat.

28 September

NEW GUINEA—Main body of 126th Inf, U.S. 32d Div, reaches Port Moresby and is assigned to New Guinea Force to assist in advance on Wairopi.

29 September

SOLOMON IS.—Troop strength of Guadalcanal garrison is now 19,261; 3,260 troops are on Tulagi. 6th Naval Construction Bn is constructing airstrip.

MADAGASCAR—Continuing S from Tananarive, Br forces occupy Fianarantsoa. 2 cos of Pretoria Regt and a few armd cars from Diego Suarez land on SW coast at Tulear in order to secure the port, airfield, and seaplane base site for patrolling Mozambique Channel.

U.K.—U.S. fliers of 3 RAF Eagle Sqs are transferred to USAAF.

30 September

ALEUTIAN IS.—Enemy makes the first of a number of nuisance raids on Adak.

1 October

NEW GUINEA—GHQ issues plan for encirclement and reduction of Buna-Gona beachhead. Upon securing Kumusi R line from Wairopi southeastward, Goodenough I, and N coast from Milne Bay to Cape Nelson, concerted assault is to be made on Buna-Gona area. Advance will be along 3 routes: Kokoda Trail, where Australians are now pursuing enemy; from S coast to Jaure along either Rigo or Abau track, both of which are being reconnoitered; NW along coast from Milne Bay.

MIDDLE EAST—Letter of Instructions is issued to Brig Gen Donald H. Connolly, commander-designate of PGSC. CG USAFIME is to exercise administrative supervision over PGSC.

USSR—Bitter fighting continues within and near Stalingrad throughout October, German *Army Group B* making limited progress against determined resistance. Red Army efforts to relieve the besieged city, which is under severe air and arty bombardment, prove futile. Drives of German *Army Group A* are virtually halted by Soviet resistance. Red Army contains attacks toward Grozny oil fields. In NW sector of this front, fierce battles occur in Novorossisk-Tuapse area along Black Sea coast. German offensive is steadily losing momentum because of fuel shortage, heavy losses in manpower, difficult terrain, and firm opposition.

2 October

ELLICE IS.—5th Defense Bn force from Espiritu Santo, New Hebrides, occupies Funafuti.

MADAGASCAR—Br forces take Antsirabe.

3 October

INDIA—India Air Task Force is activated in upper Assam under Brig Gen Caleb V. Haynes to protect the India end of the Hump ferry route.

USSR—On Caucasian front, *Army Group A* captures Elkhotovo, within 7 miles of Darg Kokh. Fierce fighting continues in Stalingrad area.

4 October

NEW GUINEA—Capt Boice's rcn party (elements of 126th Inf, U.S. 32d Div) reaches Jaure, completing rcn of Kapa Kapa-Jaure trail, which is found to be difficult but practicable.

ENGLISH CHANNEL—Small Br party raids Sark I.

6 October

U.S.—Second Protocol for U.S. aid to USSR, covering period to 1 July 1943, is signed in Washington. 3,300,000 tons are to be sent by N Soviet ports and 1,100,000 by Persian Gulf route.

POA—Gen Harmon recommends to Adm Ghormley that projected invasion of Ndeni, Santa Cruz Is., scheduled to follow capture of Tulagi and Guadalcanal airfield, be postponed and that Guadalcanal be reinf; that naval operations in the Solomons be increased; and that adequate airdrome construction personnel and equipment be sent to Guadalcanal. Adm Ghormley decides to proceed with plan to occupy Ndeni as landing field site and agrees to reinf Guadalcanal with an Army regt and to improve airdrome facilities. 164th Inf of Americal Div is chosen to reinf Guadalcanal and 147th Inf (less 2 bns) to occupy Ndeni.

NEW GUINEA—Fifth Air Force completes movement of reinf Aus 18th Brig to Wanigela. Channel from Milne Bay to Cape Nelson has now been charted in order to permit shipment of supplies by water.

EGYPT—Gen Montgomery issues instructions for El 'Alamein offensive in Western Desert.

USSR—Oil city of Malgobek, near Grozny, falls to *Army Group A*.

7 October

GUADALCANAL—1st Mar Div, with air and arty support, opens offensive to extend perimeter westward beyond arty range of Henderson Field, moving 3 columns forward toward the Matanikau, line of departure, from Kukum area. While 5th Marines (less bn) moves along coast to conduct holding action at Matanikau R mouth, 7th Marines (less bn), followed by Whaling Group (3d Bn of 2d Marines and div scout-sniper detachment under Col William J. Whaling), advances SW with mission of crossing river and enveloping Pt Cruz. 5th Marines column soon meets opposition and drives enemy back almost to Matanikau R mouth. The other 2 columns reach Hill 65, overlooking Matanikau R, with little difficulty and halt for the night. After nightfall, attack preparations are simulated at river mouth and 5th Marines is reinf by co of 1st Raider Bn.

NEW GUINEA—U.S. 32d Div force (platoon of Co E, 126th Inf; AT and Cannon Cos; native carriers) under Capt Alfred Medendorp begins difficult march from Kalikodobu, 40 miles SE of Port Moresby, toward Jaure. The force is dependent upon airdrops for most of its supplies.

8 October

GUADALCANAL—Marine attack across Matanikau R is postponed because of heavy rains, but 5th Marines and raiders reduce enemy bridgehead on E bank in costly fighting. When Japanese plans for counteroffensive are discovered, 1st Mar Div CG changes plan of attack. Instead of driving toward Kokumbona and the Poha, marines are to raid Pt Cruz area in force and return to Lunga perimeter.

NEW GUINEA—Japanese withdrawal across Owen Stanley Range toward Kokoda slows as preparations are made for stand at Templeton's Crossing, N of Myola.

CBI—Gen Chennault delivers Wendell L. Willkie a letter for President Roosevelt asking for increased authority and air power in order to destroy Japanese Air Force in China, then attack Japanese Empire.

9 October

GUADALCANAL—Rear echelon of 2d Marines, 2d Mar Div, arrives. 164th Inf of Americal Div sails to Guadalcanal from Nouméa, New Caledonia. Whaling Group and 7th Marines force cross the Matanikau and, with arty assistance of 11th Marines, drive N to coastal area; retire eastward across Matanikau R mouth, covered by 5th Marines, concluding 3-day action during which Japanese lose nearly 700 men as against 65 marines killed and 125 wounded.

FRANCE—In heaviest daylight raid to date, about 100 U.S. heavy bombers with strong RAF and U.S. fighter support attack industrial targets at Lille. Many enemy planes are encountered and more than 100 are damaged or destroyed.

10 October

GUADALCANAL—In anticipation of enemy counteroffensive, marines strengthen defense positions and patrol aggressively. 3 bns of 1st and 7th Marines plus elements of Special Weapons Co take responsibility for E bank of the Matanikau, where permanent positions are established at river mouth. By this time, 12 P-39's of 67th Fighter Sq are at Henderson Field. B-17's are occasionally staging through the field.

NEW GUINEA—Main body of 2d Bn, 126th Inf, U.S. 32d Div, with supporting units, leaves Kalikodobu on foot for Jaure.

11 October

BATTLE OF CAPE ESPERANCE—After Japanese naval force moving toward Guadalcanal is spotted by U.S. planes in afternoon, TF of 4 cruisers and 5 DD's under Rear Adm Norman Scott, standing off Rennell I. to protect convoy bringing elements of Americal Div to Guadalcanal, moves toward Cape Esperance to engage enemy and at 2346 opens fire. During 34-minute battle, the TF sinks *Furutaka* (CA) and *Fubuki* (DD) and damages *Aoba* and *Kinugasa* (CA's). Enemy retires northward, leaving DD's *Natsugumo* and *Murakumo* to rescue survivors. U.S. losses are light: *Duncan*, *Boise*, *Salt Lake City*, and *Farenholt* are damaged; of these, only the DD *Duncan* sinks, on 12th.

MADAGASCAR—Gen Platt, CG E African Command, relinquishes command on island to Maj Gen Smallwood, General Officer Commanding Islands Area.

12 October

BATTLE OF CAPE ESPERANCE—Henderson-based planes conclude action against retiring enemy naval force, sinking DD's *Murakumo* and *Natsugumo*.

SOLOMON IS.—4 boats of MTB Sq 3, the first naval craft to be permanently based at Tulagi except for harbor patrol boats, are towed in.

CBI—Gen Stilwell requests that a second 30 Chinese divs be equipped.

13 October

GUADALCANAL—Japanese aircraft, long-range arty from Kokumbona area, and naval TF that includes 2 BB's alternate in bombarding Henderson Field during day and throughout night 13-14, severely damaging field and sharply reducing U.S. air strength. First ground force units of U.S. Army, 164th Inf of Americal Div, arrive on *McCawley* and on *Zeilin*, which also bring 210 men of 1st Mar Air Wing and 85 Marine casuals plus weapons and supplies. Unloading despite air attacks, the vessels embark 1st Raider Bn and sail for New Caledonia. Troop strength of 1st Mar Div is thus brought up to 23,088, excluding forces on Tulagi. 1st Mar Div CG divides Lunga perimeter into 5 regimental sectors, massing greatest strength on W.

CHINA—Gen Stilwell presents to Chiang Kai-shek President Roosevelt's reply of 12 October to the Generalissimo's 3 demands.

14 October

GUADALCANAL—Further enemy bombardment of Henderson Field puts it out of action temporarily, forcing aircraft to use Fighter Strip No. 1, a rough runway SE of Henderson. Strength of operational aircraft is reduced during 13th and 14th from 90 to 42. Supply of aviation gasoline is critically low, but SBD's and P-39's take to the air in effort to halt enemy convoy of transports escorted by DD's proceeding toward Guadalcanal. The planes fail to stop the convoy but sink a transport and set another vessel on fire.

NEW GUINEA—Fifth Air Force begins flying coastal force (128th Inf of U.S. 32d Div and 2/6th Aus Independent Co, under command of Brig Gen Hanford MacNider) to Wanigela. Australians advancing along Kokoda Trail are meeting stubborn opposition in vicinity of Templeton's Crossing.

15 October

GUADALCANAL—Japanese 17th Army issues tactical orders for assault on Lunga Pt, setting date tentatively for 18th. 5 escorted enemy transports unload final elements of assault force (3,000-4,000 men) and most of cargo at Tassafaronga. Aircraft from Guadalcanal and New Hebrides join in attacks on enemy, sinking 2 vessels and damaging others. Vitally needed gasoline arrives from Espiritu Santo on Army and Marine transport planes and on seaplane tender *MacFarland*.

16 October

GUADALCANAL—Japanese begin march along narrow trail from Kokumbona assembly area toward attack positions E of Lunga R. Japanese arty shelling of Lunga perimeter increases in volume and accuracy. U.S. patrol craft attack enemy coastal positions from Kokumbona to Cape Esperance. Operational aircraft number 66 after arrival of 20 F4F's and 12 SBD's. Seaplane tender *MacFarland* is seriously damaged by enemy aircraft in Sealark Channel but is salvaged by crew.

17 October

NEW GUINEA—Bitter fighting is in progress on Kokoda Trail at Eora Creek, where Japanese commit reinforcements. Abel's Field at Fasari, on upper Musa R near Mt Sapia, becomes operational. Field is named for Cecil Abel, a missionary who constructed it with assistance of native labor and equipment dropped by Fifth Air Force. First luggers reach Wanigela and continue toward Pongani with men and supplies.

U.K.—Convoys for TORCH begin assembling at Firth of Clyde.

18 October

POA—Adm Halsey succeeds Adm Ghormley as Commander, South Pacific Area.

NEW GUINEA—Air movement of most of 128th Inf, U.S. 32d Div, to Wanigela is completed. Elements are left at Port Moresby temporarily when Wanigela field becomes unserviceable because of rains. Hard fighting continues on Kokoda Trail in vicinity of Eora Creek.

19 October

U.S.—War Department agrees to equip 30 more Chinese divs.

POA—U.S. 25th Div is alerted for movement to Guadalcanal.

NEW GUINEA—Col Sverdrup's rcn party completes march along Kapa Kapa trail, which is so poor that it is rejected as a possible route of advance, to upper Musa R, where Abel's Field is already in use; searches for additional airfield sites.

MADAGASCAR—Troops of Br E African Command continue to clear S part of island and in 2 pronged attack overcome opposition at Andriamanalina.

20 October

POA—Gen Vandegrift, reporting to Adm Halsey aboard his flagship in Nouméa harbor, requests and is promised more support for Guadalcanal. Adm Halsey orders 147th Inf, which had been earmarked for invasion of Ndeni, Santa Cruz Is., to Guadalcanal. The Ndeni operation is never undertaken.

GUADALCANAL—Japanese attack is postponed to 22d, since main enveloping force has not yet reached line of departure, but patrol of supporting coastal force is taken under fire at mouth of Matanikau R and retires after 1 of its 2 tanks is hit.

NEW GUINEA—16th Brig of Aus 6th Div enters fight for Kokoda Trail, relieving 25th Brig of Aus 7th Div; continues action to clear Eora Creek area. U.S. 32d Div party under Capt Medendorp, having left elements at Laruni, where dropping ground is staked out, arrives at Jaure, where Capt Boice's party is searching for airfield sites.

CBI—Ch troops begin moving by air into India to meet Ramgarh requirements. Ch 22d and 38th Divs are being brought up to strength.

IRAQ—Gen Connolly reaches Basra, where he assumes command of PGSC, replacing Col Shingler, who remains as acting chief of staff until relieved by Col Stanley L. Scott on 20 November. Strength of PGSC at this time is about 400 officers and men of SOS and AAF and just under 1,000 American civilians.

EGYPT—Allied air action is intensified in effort to attain high degree of air superiority before Gen Montgomery's El 'Alamein offensive opens. Air superiority is achieved by assault date, 24 October.

21 October

U.S.—Adm King informs Adm Nimitz that Joint Chiefs of Staff have agreed to strengthen air forces in S Pacific by 1 January 1943.

GUADALCANAL—Japanese coastal force, with support of arty and 9 tanks, attempts to cross to E bank of the Matanikau but pulls back after losing a tank to U.S. fire.

NEW GUINEA—From Jaure, 50-man patrol of Cannon CO, U.S. Sad Div, sets out for Kumusi R Valley, where it subsequently establishes defense line and is joined by Medendorp's main group, the entire force being called Wairopi Patrol. Australians maintain pressure on enemy along Kokoda Trail, slowly gaining ground in flanking attacks.

22 October

GUADALCANAL—Japanese postpone attack on Lunga perimeter until 23d, since main assault force is still short of line of departure, but continue arty fire against Marine positions along Matanikau.

NEW GUINEA—To secure NE coast of Papua, 2/12th Bn of Aus 18th Brig embarks in 2 DD's at Milne Bay and during night 22-23 lands at a points on Goodenough I., from which submarines have withdrawn 60 of the 353 Japanese stranded there on 25 August.

INDIA—Combined planning staff conference opens to consider offensive in Burma.

ALGERIA—In preparation for TORCH, Maj Gen Mark W. Clark, deputy commander to Gen Eisenhower, and small U.S. party arrive in Algeria by submarine under cover of darkness to meet secretly with pro-Allied French party headed by Brig Gen Charles E. Mast. During the meeting Gen Mast assures Gen Clark and U.S. Consul General Robert Murphy that French will co-operate under leadership of Gen Henri Giraud.

EGYPT—U.S. advanced base hq becomes Desert Air Task Force Hq under command of Gen Brereton. Br Eighth Army moves secretly into assault positions during night 22-23.

U.K.—TORCH cargo convoy leaves for Africa.

23 October

U.S.—Forces from U.S. begin movement to N Africa in preparation for TORCH. First detachment of Western Naval Task Force, under Rear Adm Henry K. Hewitt, sails from Hampton Roads, Virginia.

GUADALCANAL—After quiet day, Japanese arty opens up at 1800 with heaviest fire to date, after which assault force (tank co and inf regt) makes determined but futile efforts to cross Matanikau R mouth and overrun 3d Bn of 1st Marines. Japanese sustain heavy losses: 600 are estimated killed and at least 8 tanks are knocked out. 1st Marines casualties are 25 killed and 14 wounded. Main enemy enveloping force, which was to have attacked simultaneously with coastal force, is not yet in position and postpones for another day its attack on S perimeter.

EGYPT—Br Eighth Army opens El 'Alamein offensive at 2140. More than 1,000 guns pound enemy batteries until 2200, then switch to enemy forward positions as Br troops move forward, 30 Corps on N making main effort and 13 Corps conducting diversionary actions on S. Heavy fighting continues throughout night.

24 October

U.S.—Final detachment of Western Naval Task Force sails from Hampton Roads for N Africa. Covering group of warships sails from Casco Bay, Maine.

GUADALCANAL—Japanese column is observed E of the Matanikau on foothills of Mt Austen in afternoon and bombarded by arty and aircraft with unobserved results. Shortly after midnight 24-25, regt of main Japanese assault force attacks S flank of Lunga perimeter, where 1st Bn of 7th Marines is thinly spread along 2,800-yard front, 2d Bn having been withdrawn to plug gap between Lunga perimeter and forward positions along the Matanikau. Marines, assisted by fire of adjacent troops—2d Bn of 164th Inf—and reinf during night by 3d Bn of 164th Inf, hold against repeated attacks, and enemy retires morning of 25th.

NEW HEBRIDES—2 U.S. naval carrier forces, based on *Enterprise* and *Hornet*, rendezvous NE of New Hebrides and come under command of Rear Adm Thomas C. Kinkaid.

NEW GUINEA—Organized resistance on Goodenough I. ceases; 250 Japanese are withdrawn to Rabaul by DD after nightfall. After exhausting overland journey, head of 2d Bn, 126th Inf, U.S. 32d Div, reaches Jaure. From there the force is to move to Buna area via Natunga and Bofu, AT and Cannon Cos protecting its rear and harassing enemy in Wairopi area.

EGYPT—30 Corps, with 4 divs in assault, secures 2 corridors through enemy mine fields on N flank of Br Eighth Army, Aus 9th and Br 51st Divs gaining one on N and NZ 2d and S African 1st Divs one on S. 10 Corps armor then begins passing through: 1st Armd Div, debouching through N corridor, breaks through mine field during night 24-25, but 10th Armd Div, using S corridor, is unable to reach W edge of mine field. On Eighth Army S flank, 13 Corps' 7th Armd and 44th Divs succeed in breaking through mine fields N of Himeimat, night 24-25, and establish small bridgehead; to S, FF 1st Brig pushes W but is driven back.

ITALY—RAF Lancasters, after flight of some 1,400 miles from Britain, attack Milan in force. This is the first daylight attack on Italy by Br planes from home bases.

25 October

BERMUDA—Air group for TORCH (carriers) sails for N Africa.

GUADALCANAL—Japanese arty and aircraft are very active during day but ground attacks are withheld until night 25-26, when 2 enemy regts attack 1st Bn of 7th Marines and 3d Bn of 164th Inf on S flank of Lunga perimeter and other enemy forces attack 2d Bn of 7th Marines E of Hill 67 and Matanikau R. Both attacks are repulsed and lull in ground action follows.

EGYPT—As El 'Alamein battle continues, Gen Montgomery decides to make main effort on N flank of 30 Corps and withhold attacks of 13 Corps in order to preserve strength of 7th Armd Div. On N flank of 30 Corps, Aus 9th Div drives N toward coastal road to Rahman; 1st Armd Div, attempting to push W in Kidney Ridge area, is unable to advance. Series of determined enemy counterattacks with strong tank support is repulsed. In 13 Corps sector, 50th Div attempts to improve positions in Munassib area with little success.

26 October

NEW HEBRIDES—172d Regt of U.S. 43d Div arrives at Espiritu Santo, but vessel bringing it, *President Coolidge*, is sunk off coast by U.S. mines.

BATTLE OF SANTA CRUZ IS.—Adm Kinkaid's naval force, upon learning of presence of Japanese naval units near Santa Cruz Is., moves forward and engages in naval air battle. 3 Japanese carriers and 2 DD's are damaged and 100 planes are destroyed. Cost is high, however, since carrier *Hornet* and DD *Porter* are sunk; 4 vessels, one of them the carrier *Enterprise*, are damaged; 20 planes are lost to enemy and 54 from other causes. This is the last time during the Guadalcanal Campaign that Japanese use carrier aircraft in close support.

GUADALCANAL—Operational aircraft on Henderson Field now total 29.

EGYPT—El 'Alamein battle continues but with decreasing momentum. 30 Corps, Br Eighth Army, improves positions in vicinity of Miteiriya Ridge and during night 26-27 succeeds in taking Kidney Ridge. Gen Montgomery decides to regroup for next phase, the breakout attack, and withdraws NZ 2d Div into reserve. Allied planes continue effective support of ground operations and disperse enemy force concentrating for attack. Enemy air action, which has been rather light thus far, increases.

USSR—Hard fighting continues in Stalingrad. In the Caucasus, Nalchik falls to *Army Group A*.

U.K.—TORCH troop convoy leaves for Africa.

27 October

CBI—Generals Wavell and Stilwell agree that Stilwell shall conduct offensive in Hukawng Valley of N Burma and occupy area Myitkyina-Bhamo; make contact with Ch forces from Yunnan. Americans are to be responsible for construction of Ledo

Road to Myitkyina; the road is eventually to link with Burma Road.

EGYPT—Enemy counterattacks strongly against Kidney Ridge, committing reinforcements that have moved up from the S, and is repulsed with heavy losses. Br Eighth Army continues regrouping for breakout assault. 7th Armd Div, reinf by brig of 44th Div, brig of 50th Div, and Greek Brig, is transferred from 13 to 30 Corps. 1st Armd Div of 10 Corps is withdrawn into reserve.

28 October

NEW GUINEA—2d Bn of 126th Inf, U.S. 32d Div, and portable hospital begin difficult march from Jaure toward Natunga and Bofu, preceded by Cos E and F, which are to secure dropping grounds.

EGYPT—After probing Br positions in Kidney Ridge area, enemy begins forming for attack but is forced by Allied aircraft to abandon it. During night 28-29, Aus 9th Div of 30 Corps, Br Eighth Army, begins northward attack toward the sea in effort to eliminate enemy's coastal salient and secure coastal road and RR. Narrow wedge is driven almost to the road despite stubborn opposition from Thompson's Post, key point in enemy's coastal positions.

29 October

WESTERN HEMISPHERE—Alaska Military Highway opens to traffic.

ALEUTIAN IS.—Japanese reoccupy Attu.

GUADALCANAL—Japanese, having suffered heavy casualties in recent battles, begin general withdrawal about this time toward Koli Pt and Kokumbona. 1st Mar Div prepares for offensive to drive enemy westward beyond Poha R. 2d Marines (− 3d Bn) is ordered to Guadalcanal from Tulagi to assist in the offensive; 3d Bn, which has been operating as mobile reserve in Lunga area, is to return to Tulagi for garrison duty. Attack is to begin on 1 November after outposts have been established W of the Matanikau and bridges have been constructed across the river.

NEW GUINEA—Japanese commit fresh forces from beachhead to hold heights at Oivi in order to cover withdrawal across Kumusi R.

EGYPT—Australians withstand determined enemy attacks against their wedge in N sector of 30 Corps and Br Eighth Army front. Gen Montgomery, learning of the presence of strong German reinforcements on N coast, alters breakout plan. Instead of pushing W along coast, he decides to shift axis of advance S in order to drive against Italians.

30 October

EGYPT—Br Eighth Army renews assault on N flank of 30 Corps during night 30-31. Aus 9th Div drives N to the sea, then pushes E, trapping large enemy force. Allied planes provide excellent tactical support, attacking accurately in small area to neutralize Thompson's Post. Most of the pocketed enemy force subsequently succeeds in escaping when tanks from W break through to assist.

31 October

GUADALCANAL—1st Mar Div completes preparations for offensive. 5th Marines and 2d Marines (−) move into attack positions along the Matanikau. During night 31 October-1 November, Co E of 5th Marines crosses the Matanikau and outposts W bank, and 1st Engr Bn constructs 3 footbridges.

1 November

GUADALCANAL—1st Mar Div, with arty, naval gunfire, and air support, launches attack toward Poha R. 5th Marines, followed by 2d Marines (less 3d Bn) in reserve, crosses footbridges over Matanikau R and drives W about 1,000 yards in 2 columns to positions short of Pt Cruz, 1st Bn, the right flank column, meeting considerable delaying opposition along coast. Whaling Group (3d Bn of 7th Marines and scout-sniper detachment) crosses the river upstream and advances W on inland route to protect left flank of 5th Marines. To forestall expected enemy landings in Koli Pt area, E of Lunga perimeter, 2d Bn of 7th Marines starts E toward Metapona R.

USSR—Close combat between Soviet garrison of Stalingrad (62d and 64th Armies) and German 6th and 4th Pz Armies of Army Group B continues, but the garrison has proved itself capable of weathering maximum effort of enemy. In the Caucasus, Red Army has frustrated every enemy effort to reach Grozny and is containing attacks toward Tuapse, but German Army Group A captures Alagir, blocking Ossetian Highway, which extends from Alagir to Kutais.

2 November

GUADALCANAL—5th Marines envelops enemy on coast at Pt Cruz. 3d Bn joins 1st Bn in coastal battle E of Pt Cruz while 2d Bn, on left, drives N to coast W of Pt Cruz and turns E, trapping enemy. 2d Marines (− 3d Bn) moves forward on left of 5th Marines to continue westward attack. Stores, ammunition, and 1 Army and 1 Marine Corps 155-mm gun battery arrive at Lunga Pt. The 2 batteries are the heaviest U.S. arty to reach the island and the first capable of countering enemy fire effectively. E of Lunga perimeter, 2d Bn of 7th Marines crosses Metapona R mouth and establishes itself near Tetere village. During night 2-3, Japanese *17th Army* lands supplies and about 1,500 men E of Koli Pt to supply and reinf Japanese already there; orders an airfield constructed.

NEW GUINEA—Aus 25th Brig, which has re-entered battle for Kokoda Trail, seizes Kokoda and its airfield, greatly facilitating supply and reinforcement of Australians in this area. Piecemeal movement by night of 128th Inf, U.S. 32d Div, less elements still at Port Moresby, by lugger from Wanigela to Pongani and Mendaropu is completed by this time and supplies are being accumulated. Gen MacArthur sets 15 November as tentative date for attack to reduce Buna-Gona beachhead and agrees to proposal by Gen Blarney that troops be transferred by air to Pongani.

EGYPT—Br Eighth Army's 30 Corps opens breakout assault, called SUPERCHARGE, at 0100. NZ 2d Div, in the lead, advances W under cover of arty barrage and secures new corridor through enemy mine fields. 9th Armd Brig passes through corridor in mine field and establishes bridgehead across track extending S from Rahman. At daybreak, the armd brig meets furious opposition from enemy AT screen and sustains over 75% casualties, but maintains the bridgehead. 10 Corps armor begins debouching through the bridgehead, and 1st Armd Div becomes strongly engaged near Tel el Aqqaqir.

3 November

GUADALCANAL—5th Marines completes reduction of Japanese pocket at Pt Cruz. 2d Marines takes the lead, 1st Bn and Whaling Group attacking W of Pt Cruz. E of Lunga perimeter, 2d Bn of 7th Marines encounters enemy moving W along coast from Tetere and is forced to retire to W bank of Nalimbiu R and await reinforcements. When information of enemy landing reaches div hq in afternoon, naval and air support is provided immediately; 1st Bn of 7th Marines is dispatched by landing craft to Koli Pt.

CBI—Generalissimo Chiang Kai-shek agrees conditionally to plans formulated during recent conference in India, promising 15 divs from Yunnan, provided Allies furnish strong sea and air forces. Gen Stilwell is to command Chinese Army in India (CAI) during Burma operations. Chiang's promise of the Yunnan divs leads to accelerated planning for reorganization of Yunnan force, called Y-Force.

EGYPT—1st Armd Div of 10 Corps, Br Eighth Army, is unable to penetrate enemy's AT screen. Since enemy is obviously withdrawing, Gen Montgomery orders attack to outflank the screen. During night 3-4, 51st Div and brig of Ind 4th Div drive quickly to Rahman track S of Tel el Aqqaqir, breaking through the screen in S sector and forcing enemy to turn it. Allied aircraft fly over 400 sorties against enemy retreating along coastal road.

4 November

GUADALCANAL—Lunga perimeter command is reorganized and garrison is reinf. 2 sectors are established, the commander of each being responsible to div hq. Brig Gen William H. Rupertus, Asst CG of 1st Mar Div, is assigned sector E of Lunga R and Brig Gen Edmund B. Sebree, Asst CG of Americal Div, the W sector. 8th Marines, reinf, of 2d Mar Div debarks from naval TF in Lunga-Kukum area and is attached to 1st Mar Div. 1st Mar Div halts westward offensive short of Kokumbona because of enemy threat E of perimeter. 2d Marines (− 3d Bn), reinf by 1st Bn of 164th Inf, after driving 2,000 yards W of Pt Cruz, breaks off attack and digs in at Pt Cruz; 5th Marines and Whaling Group return to positions E of the Matanikau. E of perimeter, Gen Rupertus and Hq and 1st Bn, 7th Marines, arrive in Koli Pt area to assist 2d Bn, 7th Marines. 164 Inf (− 1st Bn) and Co B of 8th Marines march to W bank of Nalimbiu in region S of 7th Marines and elements start N along the river. Meanwhile, the naval TF transporting 8th Marines lands forces at Aola Bay to establish airfield. Aola Force (1st Bn of 147th Inf; elements of 2d Raider Bn; 5th Defense Bn detachment; Battery K of 246th FA Bn, Americal Div; and 500 naval construction troops) establishes beachhead a little E of Aola R without opposition. Work is begun at once on airfield, but site is later found unsuitable. 2d Raider Bn is ordered to Koli Pt.

NEW GUINEA—Aus 16th Brig begins attack on Oivi and finds enemy prepared for firm stand. Col. Sverdrup by this time has cleared sites for 3 more airfields in general vicinity of Dyke Ackland Bay, the most important of these at Pongam. Fifth Air Force completes movement of rear elements of 128th Inf, U.S. 32d Div, to Wanigela.

MADAGASCAR—Governor General again seeks peace terms and accepts those rejected on 17 September.

MIDDLE EAST—Lt Gen Frank M. Andrews relieves Gen Maxwell as CG USAFIME. Gen Maxwell becomes CG SOS USAFIME.

EGYPT—Enemy, now in full retreat, is pursued W by Br Eighth Army and harassed by aircraft. 10 Corps armor clashes with Axis rear guards S of Ghazal.

5 November

GUADALCANAL— 164th Inf (— 1st Bn) crosses flooded Nalimbiu about 3,500 yards S of Koli Pt and drives N along E bank in effort to outflank enemy facing 7th Marines.

NEW GUINEA—Aus 16th Brig continues attack on Oivi against determined resistance. Aus 25th Brig moves against Gorari from Kokoda.

INDIA—Rcn of Ledo area, terminus of Ledo Road to Myitkyina, Burma, and base from which operations in N Burma, RAVENOUS, are to start, is begun.

MADAGASCAR—Hostilities cease at 1400.

EGYPT—Br Eighth Army regroups and continues pursuit of enemy. 10 Corps, now consisting of 1st and 7th Armd and NZ 2d Divs, pushes rapidly W, overcoming rear guard resistance near Fuka. 30 Corps takes up positions between El 'Alamein and Matruh. 13 Corps is given task of mopping up battle zone.

NW AFRICA—As convoys from U.S. and U.K., with assault forces for TORCH, continue toward NW Africa, Gen Eisenhower flies to Gibraltar and establishes AFHQ CP. U.S.-Br staff consists of: Adm Sir Andrew B. Cunningham, naval CinC; Brig Gen James H. Doolittle, U.S. air forces; Air Marshal Sir William L. Welsh, Br air forces (Eastern Air Command); Lt Gen K. A. N. Anderson, Br ground forces.

6 November

GUADALCANAL—7th Marines establishes bridgehead on E bank of Nalimbiu. 164th Inf (—) continues toward Koli Pt, 3d Bn reaching it after nightfall. Aola Force transports complete unloading operations and withdraw.

NEW GUINEA—Gen MacArthur arrives at Port Moresby, where advance echelon of GHQ opens, to direct operations.

EGYPT—10 Corps, Br Eighth Army, continues close pursuit of enemy, advance elements approaching Matruh bottleneck as heavy rains begin.

USSR—Fighting continues in Stalingrad area but on a diminishing scale. In the Caucasus, Red Army is strongly countering enemy efforts to reach Ordzhonikidze.

7 November

GUADALCANAL— 164th Inf enveloping force completes northward movement along E bank of the Nalimbiu to Koli Pt and joins 7th Marines. Combined force then moves E along coast without opposition to within a mile of Metapona R.

CBI—Gen Stilwell, with approval of Foreign Minister T. V. Soong, sends for Gen Wheeler to survey Ch supply situation in preparation for projected campaign in spring of 1943.

EGYPT—Br pursuit of enemy is delayed in Matruh area as heavy rainfall immobilizes supporting vehicles. Enemy seizes opportunity to withdraw some forces. By this time, 4 German and 8 Italian divs are ineffective as fighting units. British have taken 30,000 prisoners, among them 9 generals.

NW AFRICA—Gen Giraud arrives at Gibraltar for conference with Gen Eisenhower, having traveled from France by submarine and plane. TORCH invasion armada from U.S. and U.K. closes in along N African coast. U.S. transport *Thomas Stone* is torpedoed off SE Spain and disabled; troops aboard are transferred to landing boats but do not reach Algiers until after its surrender.

8 November

GUADALCANAL—7th Marines (—) and 2d Bn of 164th Inf, latter being attached to 7th Marines as reserve, move E along coast to surround enemy now disposed astride Gavaga Creek, W of Tetere. 1st and 2d Bns of 7th Marines take up positions on W and E banks, respectively, of the creek. "Tokyo Express" has been landing reinforcements along coast from Kokumbona to Cape Esperance during the period 28 October to date.

NEW GUINEA—Final elements of TF Warren (1st Bn of 128th Inf, U.S. 32d Div) are flown from Port Moresby to Wanigela; from there are moved forward by boat.

EGYPT—Br Eighth Army, although still delayed by rainfall, clears opposition in Mersa Matruh area.

NW AFRICA—Allied troops invade French NW Africa, landing on Algerian and Moroccan coasts. Warships and carrier planes provide close support.

ALGERIA—Eastern Naval Task Force lands Eastern Assault Force (RCT 39, U.S. 9th Div; RCT 168, U.S. 34th Div; 11th and 36th Brigs, Br 78th Div; Br 1st and 6th Cdo Bns), under command of Maj Gen Charles W. Ryder, USA, E and W of Algiers, beginning at 0100; 11th Brig and RCT 168 go ashore W of Algiers near Castiglione and Sidi Ferruch, and RCT 39 lands E of Algiers near Cap Matifou. As troops move forward toward Algiers against little or no resistance, 2 Br DD's, with 3d Bn of RCT 135, U.S. 34th Div, embarked, make frontal attack on Algiers Harbor in effort to take it intact; one DD is forced to withdraw; the other enters harbor and lands troops about 0530, but is forced to retire under heavy fire, leaving troops ashore. Eastern Assault Force takes Blida and Maison Blanche airfields; pushes to edge of Algiers, which capitulates at 1900.

Center Naval Task Force lands Center Assault Force (U.S. II Corps assault force, consisting of 1st Div, 1st Ranger Bn, and CCB of 1st Armd Div), under Maj Gen Lloyd R. Fredendall, USA, E and

W of Oran, beginning at 0130, a half hour behind schedule. Rangers and RCT's 16 and 18 of 1st Div land E of Oran in Arzew area; take Arzew, where harbor is secured by U.S.-Br naval landing party without opposition; thrust SW toward Oran to St Cloud, which enemy retains, and Fleurus; elements drive SE along coast to La Macta. Passing through beachhead, TF Red of CCB seizes Tafaraoui airport, 15 miles S of Oran, enabling 31st Fighter Gp planes to support operations from there. W of Oran, RCT 26 of 1st Div lands at Les Andalouses; takes Bou Sfer and Aïn et Turk but is halted short of Oran. TF Green of GCB, 1st Armd Div, debarks at Mersa Bou Zedjar, 16 miles W of Les Andalouses, and heads for La Senia airport, clearing Lourmel and reaching Sebkra d'Oran. 2d Bn of 509th Para Inf (trained as 2d Bn, 503d Para Inf) is dropped to assist in capture of La Senia and Tafaraoui airports, but drops are scattered and paratroopers arrive too late to help. Meanwhile, HMS *Walney* and *Hartland*, carrying detachments of 3d Bn, 6th Armd Inf Regt, 1st Armd Div, and Br naval landing party, are sunk by enemy fire while attempting to take Oran Harbor intact.

MOROCCO—Western Naval Task Force, scheduled to land troops at 0400, is delayed at least an hour in landing Casablanca assault forces; engages French fleet at Casablanca. Northern Attack Group TF (60th Inf of 9th Div and 1st Bn of 66th Armd Regt, 2d Armd Div) under Maj Gen Lucian K. Truscott, Jr., USA, lands on beaches N and S of Sebou R at Mehdia; attempts to reach Port-Lyautey and airfield 2 miles N but meets considerable opposition and cannot reach objective. TF of Center Attack Group (3d Div and 1st Bn of 67th Armd Regt, 2d Armd Div) under Maj Gen Jonathan W. Anderson, USA, lands NE of Fedala, sustaining serious loss of landing craft (242, 64 percent), and takes D-Day objectives. Surprised Fedala garrison surrenders and advance is continued toward Casablanca. Southern Attack Group's landing force (47th Inf of 9th Div; 2d and 3d Bns of 67th Armd Regt, 2d Armd Div; and special units) under Maj Gen Ernest N. Harmon, USA, secures 5,000-yard beachhead in Safi area and takes Safi. 2 U.S. DD's, with Cos K and L of 47th Inf, 9th Div, and naval contingent aboard, enter Safi Harbor ahead of landings; after silencing batteries with gunfire, land assault force, which takes harbor facilities without opposition.

GERMANY—Hitler reaffirms his intention of taking Stalingrad, despite very heavy losses in men and equipment, lack of reserves, and overextended supply lines.

FRANCE—Vichy France breaks off diplomatic relations with U.S.

9 November

GUADALCANAL—7th Marines, committing 2d Bn of 164th Inf to its S, completes encirclement of enemy along Gavaga Creek except for small gap on S at creek line; repels spirited attempts of enemy to break out. In preparation for renewing attack on Kokumbona, 164th Inf units (Hq, AT Co, and 3d Bn) and Co B of 8th Marines are withdrawn from Koli Pt area to Lunga perimeter.

NEW GUINEA—Advance elements of 2d Bn, 126th Inf, U.S. 32d Div, arrive at Natunga. Airlift of 126th Inf, less 2d Bn, from Port Moresby to forward area begins. Leading elements of 1st Bn, under Lt Col Edmund J. Carrier, are flown to Abel's field, since Pongani Field is temporarily unserviceable, and start toward Pongani on foot. Rest of 1st Bn (Cos D and C, less 2 platoons), under Maj Richard D. Boerem, is flown to Pongani and starts march toward Natunga.

EGYPT—Br Eighth Army resumes pursuit of enemy as weather improves. NZ 2d Div reduces opposition at Sidi Barrani and continues W.

TUNISIA—Germans invade Tunisia without opposition from French, initial elements landing on El Aouïna airport, Tunis.

ALGERIA—Gen Giraud arrives on front. Gen K. A. N. Anderson takes command of Br First Army at Algiers and prepares to move light forces as rapidly as possible to Tunis and Bizerte in order to forestall enemy seizure of these important objectives. Enemy sinks U.S. transport *Leedstown* off Algiers. Flanking attack on Oran continues to meet resistance as it reaches outskirts of city, but La Senia airport is captured and Fr resistance at St Cloud is bypassed and contained.

MOROCCO—Western Task Force establishes hq at Fedala, where Adm Hewitt, USN, transfers to Maj Gen George S. Patton, Jr., USA, command of troops ashore. French continue to resist strongly at approaches to Port-Lyautey and airport. 3d Div delays advance on Casablanca to await unloading of heavy equipment and arty. RCT 47, 9th Div, organizes Safi beachhead.

10 November

GUADALCANAL—7th Marines (−) and 2d Bn of 164th Inf continue reduction of pocket astride Gavaga Creek; make unsuccessful attempt to close gap in line. Westward offensive toward Kokumbona is renewed under command of CO, 2d Marines. 1st Bn of 164th Inf and 2d Marines (− 3d Bn) attack W from Pt Cruz with 8th Marines protecting left rear.

NEW GUINEA—Aus 16th Brig forces Japanese from Oivi toward Kumusi R mouth.

EGYPT—Br Eighth Army clears Halfaya Pass.

ALGERIA—Adm François Darlan broadcasts from Algiers order for Fr forces in N Africa to cease resistance. Troops of 1st Div and of CCB, 1st Armd Div, converge on Oran; RCT 16 has leading elements within the city by 0830; CCB columns enter Oran from S before French CG surrenders at 1230.

MOROCCO—French resistance in Port-Lyautey area ends. By noon, Twelfth Air Force fighters are landing on airfield from USS *Chenango*. U.S. forces from Fedala close in on Casablanca and prepare for concerted assault at dawn on 11th. CCB, 2d Armd Div, breaks off drive toward Marrakech from Safi area and marches toward Mazagan in order to conserve strength for attack on Casablanca.

11 November

GUADALCANAL—Westward offensive toward Kobumbona is halted because of strong indications of an all-out enemy attempt to recover Lunga area. After reaching positions a little beyond those gained on 4 November, assault force begins withdrawal across the Matanikau. E of Lunga perimeter, 2d Bn of 164th Inf closes gap on S flank of U.S. line about enemy along Gavaga Creek and drives N to beach while 7th Marines closes in from E and W. Naval force bringing reinforcements and supplies from New Hebrides arrives and begins unloading; when the 3 transports of the force are damaged by enemy aircraft, the group retires to join naval forces approaching from New Caledonia.

NEW GUINEA—Hq of 126th Inf, 32d Div, is flown to Pongani.

EGYPT-LIBYA—10 Corps, Br Eighth Army, drives last of enemy from Egypt and enters Libya, taking Bardia without opposition. 1st and 7th Armd Divs continue pursuit of enemy in Libya. NZ 2d Div pauses at frontier to reorganize.

NW AFRICA—In response to Adm Darlan's order of 10th, all resistance of Fr forces in NW Africa ceases by 0700.

MOROCCO—Western Task Force cancels attack on Casablanca because of armistice; 3d Div enters city at 0730. CCB of 2d Armd Div receives surrender of Mazagan and establishes bridgehead at Azemmour without opposition. Enemy torpedoes and sinks U.S. transport off coast.

ALGERIA—Br First Army lands elements of 36th Brig, 78th Div, at Bougie, 110 miles E of Algiers, without opposition. Hart Force—mobile TF based on 11th Brig of 78th Div—moves out of Algiers toward Bône, traveling overland.

FRANCE—Axis troops march into unoccupied France.

12 November

GUADALCANAL—Enemy pocket along Gavaga Creek is completely eliminated. The action has cost Japanese 450 killed, and the few who have eluded the trap are being harassed, while retiring toward Mt Austen, by Col Carlson's 2d Raider Bn marching W from Aola Bay. Kokumbona assault force completes withdrawal across the Matanikau. Transports and cargo ships from New Hebrides and New Caledonia arrive off Lunga Pt and begin unloading; withdraw at 1815 under DD escort after all troops, totaling about 6,000 and including RCT 182 of Americal Div, and part of the supplies are ashore, because of news that heavy Japanese naval force, including 2 BB's, is moving S toward the island. Warships remain to engage enemy.

NAVAL BATTLE OF GUADALCANAL—During night 12-13, Japanese warships are located by radar between Savo and Cape Esperance and naval battle ensues during which 2 enemy DD's are sunk and 4 damaged. Japanese retire northward without having accomplished mission of neutralizing Henderson Field before arrival of transport force. U.S. losses are heavy: AA cruisers *Atlanta* and *Juneau* and DD's *Barton*, *Cushing*, *Laffey*, and *Monssen* are sunk; 5 other vessels are seriously damaged.

NEW GUINEA—Gorari falls to Aus 25th Brig. Japanese succeed in withdrawing main forces across flooded Kumusi R, night 12-13. 2d Bn of 126th Inf, U.S. 32d Div, moves toward Gora and Bofu, Co E, in the lead, reaching Bofu. 3d Bn of 126th, upon reaching Pongani by air, starts toward Natunga.

CBI—Gen Stilwell, in memorandum to Foreign Minister Soong, suggests that a commander be chosen at once for Y-Force; that units to participate in offensive be designated and reorganized; that available 75-mm guns be sent to Yunnan; and that incompetent commanders be removed.

MIDDLE EAST—U.S. Ninth Air Force is established by order of Gen Andrews, CG USAFIME. Gen Brereton activates Hq Sq, Ninth Air Force, and IX Air Service Command. Hq and Hq Sq of 19th Bombardment Wing arrive by sea.

MOROCCO—U.S. transports *Hugh L Scott* and *Edward Rutledge* are lost off Morocco to enemy torpedoes.

ALGERIA—Br First Army takes Bône, 150 miles E of Bougie, without opposition, but enemy planes make damaging attacks later in day. 6th Cdos land by sea and secure port. U.S. transport planes drop 2 cos of 3d Para Bn at Duzerville airdrome, 6 miles SE of Bône. Paratroop Task Force (60th Troop Carrier Gp and 2d Bn of U.S. 509th Para Inf) is placed under operational control of Br First Army at Algiers.

13 November

SOLOMON IS.—Crippled Japanese BB *Hiei* is attacked by air near Savo throughout day and is subsequently scuttled.

GUADALCANAL—8 P-38's of 339th Sq, 347th Fighter Gp, arrive on fighter strip just E of Henderson Field after flight from Milne Bay.

NEW GUINEA—Australians destroy enemy rear guard at Kumusi R crossing.

LIBYA—Tobruk falls to 10 Corps, Br Eighth Army.

ALGERIA—Gen Eisenhower flies to Algiers to conclude agreement with Adm Darlan. Allied convoy arrives at Bône and unloads 17/21 Lancers Regimental Gp (later called Blade Force), 1st Para Brig (–), transport of 78th Div (–), and Advance Hq of Br First Army. Main body of 36th Brig, 78th Div, advances to Djidjelli, 40 miles E of Bougie.

14 November

GUADALCANAL—Japanese continue attempts to neutralize Henderson Field with naval gunfire in preparation for landing of reinforcements. Enemy cruiser-DD force opens fire early in the morning, but bombardment is cut short by PT boats. The enemy group, as well as large convoy loaded with some 10,000 troops, is later attacked by aircraft with excellent results. Planes of carrier TF under Adm Kinkaid, based on USS *Enterprise*, the last carrier in S Pacific, join land-based planes in attacking enemy vessels. 1 enemy CA is sunk and 3 other warships are damaged. Of 11 transports in the transport convoy, 7 are sunk, but the others continue to Tassafaronga after nightfall to unload about 4,000 troops and a few tons of supplies. In another effort to neutralize Henderson Field, Japanese move powerful warship force forward. Elements of Adm Kinkaid's naval force intercept enemy warships, night 14-15, and in long-range gun battle sink a DD and badly damage BB *Kirishima*, which is scuttled by her crew. U.S. losses in this engagement are 3 DD's sunk and 2 other warships damaged.

NEW GUINEA—New Guinea Force issues attack plan for reduction of Buna-Gona beachhead. Advance elements of 126th Inf, U.S. 32d Div, are consolidating positions at Natunga. TF Warren (128th Inf of 32d Div and Aus 2/6th Independent Co) is consolidating and patrolling in Oro Bay-Embogu-Embi area. On Kokoda Trail, Aus 25th Brig starts crossing improvised bridge at Wairopi, and Fifth Air Force drops bridging equipment.

15 November

GUADALCANAL—The 4 surviving transports of Japanese convoy are sighted at Tassafaronga and attacked by arty, naval gunfire, and aircraft from Henderson Field and the New Hebrides. All 4 are destroyed and supplies on beach are fired. This decisive defeat almost isolates Japanese on Guadalcanal.

LIBYA—10 Corps, Br Eighth Army, seizes Martuba airfields.

ALGERIA-TUNISIA—Br First Army reaches Tunisia at Tabarka, 80 miles W of Tunis. Tabarka is occupied by 36th Brig, 78th Div. 2d Bn of U.S. 509th Para Regt lands in Algeria at Youk-les-Bains, near Tébessa and 100 miles S of Bône.

16 November

NEW GUINEA—U.S. 32d and Aus 7th Divs move forward to eliminate Buna-Gona beachhead, 32d toward Buna and 7th toward Gona and Sanananda. Japanese, expected to be few and dispirited, are prepared for a determined stand and have organized a series of strong positions favored by terrain for defense. Col Yosuke Yokoyama commands all forces W of Girua R (Gen Horii having been lost at sea while withdrawing from Kokoda Trail battle) and Capt Yoshitatsu Yasuda those E of river. In Aus 7th Div sector on W, 25th Brig moves toward Gona and 16th toward Sanananda. To E, U.S. 32d Div's 126th Inf heads for Buna along axis Inonda-Horanda-Dobodura, and Warren Force (based on 128th Inf) moves along coast toward Cape Endaiadere. Although by evening Aus arty is employed to support coastal advance, Warren Force suffers severe blow when small craft bringing urgently needed supplies are destroyed by enemy planes; among personnel embarked on these is Maj Gen Edwin F. Harding, CG U.S. 32d Div, who swims to shore.

NEW BRITAIN—Japanese establish *8th Army Area* at Rabaul under command of Lt Gen Hitoshi Imamura. This command comprises 2 armies: *17th*, charged with operations in the Solomons, and *18th*, to operate in New Guinea.

TUNISIA—Br First Army continues movement into Tunisia. 1st Para Bn lands at Souk el Arba, 30 miles S of Tabarka. Several thousand Germans form bridgehead in Bizerte-Tunis area. Fr 19th Corps reports contact with German patrol on Bédja-Djebel Abiod highway. Fr forces at Oued Zarga and Mateur drive off enemy patrols.

MEDITERRANEAN—Allied aircraft from Martuba protect Malta-bound convoy, which departs from Port Said.

17 November

NEW GUINEA—Aus and U.S. forces continue toward Japanese beachhead in Buna-Gona area. U.S. 32d Div's TF Warren suffers another setback as

Japanese planes put 2 more supply luggers out of action, leaving only 1 serviceable and necessitating supply of vital items by air until more luggers become available. Wairopi Patrol reports to Aus 7th Div at Wairopi. Japanese reinforcements arrive at Basabua by DD in evening.

TUNISIA—CG Br First Army orders 78th Div to concentrate for advance on Tunis. 36th Brig of 78th Div makes contact with Germans W of Djebel Abiod, 70 miles W of Tunis. To S, 2d Bn of U.S. 509th Para Regt occupies Gafsa airfield.

18 November

GUADALCANAL—Gen Sebree, CG of W Sector, begins moving forces toward line of departure W of the Matanikau (from Pt Cruz southward along ridge containing Hills 80, 81 and 66) in preparation for full-scale westward offensive. 2d Bn of 182d Inf, covered by 8th Marines, which remains E of the Matanikau, crosses the river about 700 yards from its mouth and takes Hill 66, southernmost point of the line of departure.

NEW GUINEA—Aus 16th Brig drives to Popondetta, where airfield construction is begun, and continues toward Soputa without making contact with the enemy. U.S. 32d Div's 126th Inf is ordered to establish contact with Australians. Because of supply problems, TF Warren remains in place.

TUNISIA—36th Brig of 78th Div, Br First Army, repels German attack at Djebel Abiod, but Hart Force (11th Brig), spearheading drive, becomes isolated in region E of Djebel Abiod. Germans attack Fr forces of 19th Corps at Medjez el Bab, 35 miles SW of Tunis and 30 miles S of Mateur.

19 November

GUADALCANAL—1st Bn, 182d Inf, crosses Matanikau and moves W along shore with Co B, 8th Marines, covering left flank; digs in just E of Pt Cruz. Gap of over 1,000 yards separates 1st and 2d Bns of 182d Inf W of the Matanikau. During night 19-20, Japanese move forward from Kokumbona and open fire on 1st Bn.

NEW GUINEA—Forward elements of Aus 25th Brig encounter enemy one mile S of Gona; Aus 16th Brig makes contact with Japanese just outside Soputa. After establishing contact with Australians near Popondetta, 126th Inf of U.S. 32d Div heads for Buna but, since Japanese appear to be concentrated W of Girua R, is directed to assist Maj Gen George A. Vasey's Aus 7th Div instead. Gen Harding thus loses half his assault force; left flank of TF Warren is left exposed. 1st and 3d Bns of 128th Inf, Warren Force, attack in parallel columns, 1st Bn from Boero and 3d Bn from Simemi. Both meet accurate enemy fire from concealed positions and suffer heavy casualties; maximum gain of 200 yards is made on right along coast.

TUNISIA—Gen Louis Jacques Barré, Fr 19th Corps, rejects German ultimatum to evacuate Medjez el Bab, where German tank-infantry assaults supported by arty and air are repulsed by French aided by U.S. arty and Br troops.

USSR—Red Army opens winter offensive. After 7 1/2-hour arty preparation, 6 corps of Don Front attack from Serafimovich bridgehead across the Don NW of Stalingrad and make deep penetration in Kletskaya area. This is the beginning of a pincers movement to isolate Axis forces attacking Stalingrad. Offensive is well timed and indirectly aided by Allied offensive in NW Africa.

20 November

GUADALCANAL—Japanese attack left flank of 1st Bn, 182d Inf, early in day and force it back, but 1st Bn recovers lost ground with assistance of air and arty and drives forward until stopped by enemy fire just W of Pt Cruz. Enemy retains Pt Cruz itself. 164th Inf moves forward during night 20-21 to bridge gap between assault bns of 182d Inf.

NEW GUINEA—Advance elements of Aus 25th Brig enter Gona but are driven out after nightfall. 126th Inf of U.S. 32d Div, upon reaching Popondetta, is sent on to Soputa to assist Aus 16th Brig. Aus 16th Brig clears enemy rear guard from Soputa and continues along Sanananda track to its junction with main trail to Cape Killerton but is halted at enemy's forward defense line. TF Warren continues to meet heavy fire, which pins down 3d Bn of 128th Inf on left; 1st Bn is halted after 100-yard advance in coastal area. Col Carrier's detachment (elements of 1st Bn, 126th Inf) and Aus 2/6th Independent Co arrive at front and prepare to join in attack along coast.

LIBYA—Benghazi falls to 10 Corps, Br Eighth Army.

TUNISIA—Fr 19th Corps units, together with British and attached U.S. forces, withdraw from Medjez el Bab to Oued Zarga, 10 miles W, where forward elements of Blade Force, Br First Army, are located. Main body of Blade Force is concentrated in Souk el Arba area. Br 1st Para Bn is holding Bédja.

USSR—Continuing offensive, 3 Soviet corps of Stalingrad Front penetrate German positions S of Stalingrad.

21 November

GUADALCANAL—1st Bn, 182d Inf, clears enemy from Pt Cruz but is unable to advance any farther. To S, 164th Inf attacks from Hills 80-81 ridge line but is halted after negligible gains by Japanese, whose defenses are skilfully organized in depth and mutually supporting.

NEW GUINEA—126th Inf, U.S. 32d Div, upon reaching Soputa, is attached to Aus 76th Brig, which continues costly and fruitless efforts to advance toward Sanananda. 2d Bn of 128th Inf, U.S. 32d Div, begins drive on Buna Mission, moving from Ango along Dobodura-Buna track; upon reaching trail junction, called the Triangle, where trails to Buna Mission and Buna Village converge, is halted by well-organized bunker positions that are made more formidable by swampy terrain on both sides of the Triangle. Since no further progress can be made with forces present, 2d Bn of 126th Inf is ordered to cross Girua R and assist. Attack of Warren Force is delayed by series of mishaps, but gets under way by 1630 after air and arty preparation, which is of little benefit. Casualties are again heavy and gains negligible. 3d Bn, 128th Inf, attempting to take bridge between airstrips, is pinned down by enemy fire. Aus 2/6th Independent Co tries to secure E end of New Strip by infiltration and knocks out a few MG positions in the area. Along coast, 1st Bn of 128th Inf and Col Carrier's detachment of 1st Bn, 126th, attack abreast, gaining a few yards and destroying some MG nests. Situation improves somewhat as additional guns are brought forward and airstrip at Dobodura becomes operational.

LIBYA—B-24's of IX Bomber Command, staging out of Gambut, make successful attack on Tripoli harbor.

TUNISIA—Elements of Hart Force succeed in rejoining 36th Brig of 78th Div, Br First Army. Enemy withdraws to E bank of river at Medjez, but 78th Div is too weak to follow up and is ordered to await reinforcements. 2d Bn of U.S. 509th Para Inf withdraws from Gafsa to Fériana, 40 miles N.

22 November

GUADALCANAL—182d and 764th Regts again meet strong resistance while attempting to push W and are unable to advance. 8th Marines prepares to attack through 764th Inf.

NEW GUINEA—While Aus 25th Brig continues toward Gona, U.S. 126th Inf (−) attacks through Aus 76th Brig toward Sanananda. Maj Boerem's detachment (elements of 1st Bn) moves along road as 3d Bn advances on flanks along secondary trails. After nightfall, fresh Japanese forces attack Co L, flanking on right, to insure safety of food supply dump in line of advance and are driven off. From Soputa, 2d Bn of 126th Inf moves forward to assist 2d Bn of 128th, crossing to E bank of Girua R on rafts during evening. On Warren Force front, 3d Bn of 128th Inf secretly pulls back to positions just behind 1st Bn, though Co I holds former position astride trail just W of New Strip.

TUNISIA—36th Brig of 78th Div, Br First Army, repels attack at Djebel Abiod. 11th Brig of 78th Div completes concentration at Bédja. Fr and U.S. troops reoccupy Gafsa.

USSR—Red Army forces of Don and Stalingrad Fronts make junction at Kalach, encircling 6th Army of German Army Group B at Stalingrad.

23 November

U.S.—Bill authorizing Women's Reserve, U.S. Coast Guard (SPARS) is signed by President Roosevelt.

GUADALCANAL—After 30-minute arty preparation, 8th Marines passes through 764th Inf to continue attack westward but is unable to advance. Since the offensive has proved too costly to be continued for the time being, attack is halted along Hills 66-80-81-Pt Cruz line to await reinforcements. By this time, 84 U.S. (Army, Navy, and Marine Corps) and New Zealand planes are operating from Guadalcanal.

NEW GUINEA—Main body of Aus 25th Brig arrives at front and begins assault on Gona against determined resistance. 3d Bn of 126th Inf, U.S. 32d Div, continues toward Sanananda; Co L, on right is pinned down by fire at edge of food dump. Airfield at Popondetta becomes operational, and 4 guns are flown in and emplaced just S of Soputa. 2d Bns of 126th and 128th Regts are combined to form Urbana Force under command of CO, 128th Inf. 2d Bn of 128th Inf is slowed by extremely difficult terrain as it advances against the Triangle along main track and swamps on either side of it. Warren Force commander, Gen MacNider, is wounded while inspecting front and replaced by Col J. Tracy Hale, Jr. After ineffective preparatory fire against enemy bunkers, 1st Bn of 128th Inf and Col Carrier's detachment of 1st Bn, 126th Inf, attack along coast toward Cape Endaiadere, gaining some 300 yards against intense fire. Aus 2/16th Independent Co makes limited progress toward E end of New Strip.

LIBYA—Upon being outflanked by 7th Armd Div of 10 Corps, Br Eighth Army, enemy withdraws from Agedabia for El Agheila, where he hopes to make a successful stand.

ALGERIA—AFHQ is moved from Gibraltar to Algiers.

TUNISIA—Verbal agreement is reached that all troops N of Le Kef-Zaghouan line are to be under command of Br First Army and those S of it under Fr command.

SENEGAL—Dakar falls to Allied forces without a shot.

24 November

NEW GUINEA—Japanese continue to repel efforts of Aus 25th Brig to take Gona. 3d Bn of 126th Inf, U.S. 32d Div, pushes on toward Sanananda: 2 Aus cos join Co L in battle for food dump on right; on left, Cos I and K reach clearing W of Killerton trail, some 1,200 yards N of original starting point, but are driven back into swamp by enemy infiltrators. Urbana Force launches co-ordinated assault on the Triangle at 1428 after ineffective air and brief mortar preparation. While Co F of 126th Inf makes frontal assault in which Co H of 128th joins, Co E of 126th takes over left flank positions along Entrance Creek and Cos E and G of 128th attack on right flank. The attack, although carefully planned, is a failure. Warren Force front along coast is quiet.

CBI—Gen Stilwell is informed by U.S. War Department that little more aid, aside from existing commitments, can be provided for N Burma offensive.

LIBYA—Front is quiet generally as Gen Montgomery plans an assault on El Agheila bottleneck. Br Eighth Army forces must be regrouped and supplies and reinforcements amassed.

TUNISIA—Br First Army is ordered to advance on Tunis, with Tebourba and Mateur as first objectives. Main body of CCB, U.S. 1st Armd Div, begins move from Tafaraoui, Algeria, to Tunisia; forward elements (1st Bn of 1st Armd Regt) arrive at Bédja and are attached to Blade Force.

USSR—Soviet forces of Stalingrad Front are exploiting their breakthroughs; on central front, are attacking in vicinity of Veliki Luki and Rzhev.

25 November

NEW GUINEA—Firm Japanese opposition on entire front has resulted in virtual stalemate. Arty fire is exchanged and patrols are active in some sectors.

TUNISIA—Br First Army attacks toward Tunis. On N, 36th Brig of 78th Div advances from Djebel Abiod toward Mateur. In center, Blade Force penetrates enemy positions between Mateur and Tebourba; attached elements of CCB, U.S. 1st Armd Div, raid Djedeïda airfield, 5 miles E of Tebourba, destroying 30 planes. 11th Brig of 78th Div recaptures Medjez el Bab.

26 November

NEW GUINEA—Stalemate continues on Gona front. Further frontal and flanking attacks of 126th Inf, U.S. 32d Div, toward Sanananda make limited progress: 1st Bn (–) is pinned down on Soputa-Sanananda track after 100-yard advance; on left, 3d Bn (–) drives E to within 700 yards of Killerton trail; on right, Co L and Australians finally overrun the bitterly contested food dump. Urbana Force halts frontal and right flank attacks on the Triangle and prepares to make strong effort on left, since enemy is disposed in less strength W of Entrance Creek and terrain is more favorable. Warren Force, under personal observation of Gen Harding, makes determined effort to advance after strong air and arty preparation. Japanese retire into bunkers during bombardment and emerge afterward to meet attack. 3d Bn of 128th Inf (–) and 1st Bn of 126th (–) advance abreast, latter on left followed by 1st Bn of 128th. Little is accomplished by the attack. Co I of 128th Inf and Aus 2/6th Independent Co, charged respectively with securing W and E ends of New Strip, are unable to advance. Japanese retain air superiority over Buna front and sink lugger bound for Hariko with ammunition. 127th Inf, U.S. 32d Div, reaches Port Moresby from Australia.

TUNISIA—Br First Army continues to advance. Blade Force engages in its first armored battle on plain S of Mateur

27 November

NEW GUINEA—Three-day lull begins as preparations are made for renewing attack. Col John W. Mott, Gen Harding's chief of staff, arrives on Urbana front and takes command.

TUNISIA—Tebourba, 20 miles W of Tunis, falls to 11th Brig of 78th Div, Br First Army. German counterattack on the town, supported by tanks and dive bombers, is thrown back. CCB, U.S. 1st Armd Div, is detached from U.S. II Corps, which operated as Center Task Force at Oran, and attached to Br First Army.

FRANCE—Fr fleet is scuttled in harbor of Toulon by order of Adm Jean de Laborde to prevent it from falling into German hands.

28 November

SOLOMON IS.—Enemy submarine torpedoes *Alchiba*, off Guadalcanal, leaving only 4 undamaged cargo ships in S Pacific Force.

NEW GUINEA—Capt Medendorp's detachment (Cannon and AT Cos of 126th Inf, U.S. 32d Div) arrives on Sanananda front from Wairopi and takes up positions just behind Cos I and K, W of Killerton trail.

CHINA—Gen Wheeler reports to Gen Stilwell on Chinese SOS.

FRENCH SOMALILAND—Nearly one third of Vichy-controlled garrison of Djibouti crosses into British Somaliland and declares its adherence to the Allies.

TUNISIA—Br First Army's 11th Brig of 78th Div and elements of CCB (2d Bn of 13th Armd Regt), U.S. 1st Armd Div, reach outskirts of Djedeïda, 15 miles W of Tunis. This is the point nearest Tunis to be reached until final phase of campaign. To S, Germans evacuate Pont-du-Fahs, 35 miles SE of Tunis. At Gafsa, elements of U.S. 1st Div (3d Bn of RCT 26) are attached to 2d Bn, U.S. 509th Para Regt.

29 November

GUADALCANAL—3d Bn of 147th Inf, elements of 246th FA Bn, part of 9th (Mar) Defense Bn, and additional Seabees are landed in Koli Pt area, where an airfield, Carney, is to be constructed; Aola Bay area has been rejected as unsuitable for an airfield site.

NEW GUINEA—Allied bombers intercept enemy force of 4 DD's, proceeding without air cover, in Vitiaz Strait and turn it back, thus preventing reinforcement of Gona with fresh troops from Rabaul. Col Kiyomi Yazawa and part of enemy force that had withdrawn along W bank of the Kumusi to positions N of Gona reach Giruwa from there by barge. Lt Gen Robert L. Eichelberger, engaged in training U.S. 41st Div at Rockhampton, Australia, is ordered to New Guinea.

TUNISIA—Br First Army is stalled at Djedeïda by firm opposition, although 11th Brig of 78th Div continues fighting there. Elements of Br 1st Para Brig are dropped by U.S. transports at Depienne, 10 miles NE of Pont-du-Fahs, to take Oudna airdrome and threaten Tunis from S, but vigorous opposition prevents paratroopers from attaining their objective.

USSR—Red Army offensive, which continues to gain ground in Stalingrad sector, is expanded to the Caucasus, where attacks are begun against Terek bridgehead.

30 November

BATTLE OF TASSAFARONGA (LUNGA PT)—U.S. naval TF takes up position at entrance to Savo Sound to prevent enemy landings in Tassafaronga area; makes contact and, opens fire on enemy naval force during night 30 November–1 December, sinking DD and damaging another vessel. Enemy retires without effecting landings. USS *Northampton* (CA) is badly damaged and abandoned, and 3 other cruisers are damaged during the action.

NEW GUINEA—Gen Eichelberger, CG I Corps, flies from Australia to Port Moresby. Aus 21st Brig, having rested and reorganized after action in Owen Stanley Range, takes over attack on Gona front, relieving Aus 25th Brig. In Sanananda sector, left flank elements of 126th Inf, U.S. 32d Div, establish block behind enemy on Soputa-Sanananda trail, but frontal attacks along the trail in center and flanking attacks on right make little headway. Urbana and Warren Forces each make concerted attacks but gain little ground. Urbana Force fails in 3 attempts to take Buna Village; elements protecting flank and rear seize crossing over Siwori Creek and outpost region between there and Buna Creek, but are unable to clear Coconut Grove or advance beyond the Triangle. Warren Force, attacking toward Cape Endaiadere on right and NE edge of New Strip on left, encounters enemy's MLR in Duropa Plantation and is unable to breach it. Bren carriers that were to have spearheaded assault in this sector fail to arrive.

TUNISIA—As 11th Brig, Br 78th Div, continues losing battle at Djedeïda, Br First Army prepares for attack on Tunis by Blade Force and CCB of U.S. 1st Armd Div on 2 December. CCB is concentrated in Medjez el Bab area and Blade Force in vicinity of Chouïgui. By this time, Axis forces have about 15,500 fighting troops in Tunisia.

1 December

GUADALCANAL—8th Marines, 2d Mar Div, is withdrawn from forward positions W of Matanikau R, leaving Americal Div units to hold W sector.

NEW GUINEA—Gen Eichelberger flies to Dobodura and takes command of all troops in Buna area. Aus 21st Brig, after turning back from Giruwa 3 barge loads of Japanese attempting to reinforce Gona, attacks and captures Gona, forcing Japanese back to Gona Mission for final stand. Elsewhere, Japanese show no signs of weakening. Enemy exerts heavy pressure against roadblock (called "Huggins" after Capt Meredith M. Huggins) on Soputa-Sanananda trail and withstands frontal and flanking attacks toward it. Urbana Force makes another futile attempt to reach Buna Village after arty and mortar preparation with all available weapons. Warren Force continues attacks toward Cape Endaiadere on right and New Strip on left with little success; 1st Bn of 126th gets elements to NE edge of New Strip.

CBI—Airlift to China is removed from authority of Gen Stilwell and made part of Air Transport Command (India-China Wing, ATC).

BURMA—Japanese, having rested and refitted, start back into battle line Tengchung-Myitkyina-Kamaing-Kalewa-Akyab.

TUNISIA—Enemy forestalls offensive, intended for 2d, counterattacking strongly toward Tebourba with tanks and infantry supported by aircraft. Blade Force falls back with heavy tank losses. CCB, U.S. 1st Armd Div, is attached to Br 78th Div to help hold Tebourba area and moves forward to vicinity of Tebourba. Concentration of 78th Div, the first full div of 5 Corps, Br First Army, on Tunisian front, is now complete.

U.K.—Lt Gen Ira C. Eaker replaces Gen Spaatz as head of U.S. Eighth Air Force. Gen Spaatz flies to Algeria.

2 December

NEW GUINEA—Japanese try to reinforce bridgehead. 4 DD's, with about 800 men embarked, reach Basabua early in morning, but are forced by Allied aircraft to move on and land troops near Kumusi R mouth, about 12 miles N of Gona. Japanese maintain pressure on roadblock on Soputa-Sanananda trail, which supply party reaches, and whittle down its perimeter. Efforts to reach the block frontally and from right flank are again unsuccessful. Urbana Force attacks again toward Buna Village, in greater strength and after increased preparatory fire, but is halted short of objective. Since simultaneous attacks against Cape Endaiadere and New Strip have proved unfeasible, Warren Force concentrates on New Strip, leaving holding force (Co B, 128th Inf) on coastal track, where it fails to deceive enemy with feint toward Cape Endaiadere. Warren Force attacks after air and ground bombardment, which does little damage to enemy, but results are negligible. Gen Eichelberger visits Urbana front while his staff officers inspect Warren front. Afterwards, Gen Eichelberger relieves Gen Harding of command of U.S. 32d Div and designates Brig Gen Albert W. Waldron as his successor.

TUNISIA—Br First Army withstands another attack on Tebourba. Br tank losses are now about 40 U.S. forces (2d Bn of U.S. 509th Para Regt with 3d Bn of RCT 26, U.S. 1st Div) in conjunction with Fr troops attack Faïd Pass, 65 miles NE of Gafsa.

3 December

NEW GEORGIA—Japanese are discovered to be constructing airfield at Munda Pt, which becomes target for almost daily air attacks.

GUADALCANAL—Movement of Aola Force, less 2d Raider Bn, to Koli Pt, where airfield is to be constructed, is completed. Aola Force is joined by 18th Naval Construction Bn and rest of 9th Defense Bn.

NEW GUINEA—Situation of 126th Inf roadblock on Soputa-Sanananda trail remains precarious as Japanese continue to attack it repeatedly from all sides and to prevent forward movement of Allied units attempting to reach it. On Urbana and Warren fronts, troops are being rested and regrouped in preparation for all-out attack on 5 December. Lt Col Melvin McCreary replaces Col Mott as commander of Urbana Force. Col. Clarence A. Martin succeeds Col Hale as commander of Warren Force. Gen Eichelberger requests that 126th Inf hq be moved E of Girua R and is promised Aus troops and tanks. Japanese are successfully supplied by air.

TUNISIA—Germans continue to attack Tebourba and occupy it during night 3–4. 11th Brig, Br 78th Div, whose positions are penetrated, withdraws with heavy losses to region N of Medjez el Bab. CCB, U.S. 1st Armd Div, engages enemy on El Guessa heights, SW of Tebourba. To S, Fr and U.S. forces capture Faïd Pass.

4 December

GUADALCANAL—Carlson's raiders (2d Mar Raider Bn) reach Lunga perimeter, having marched W from Aola Bay. During the month-long journey, more than 400 enemy dead have been counted for loss of 17 raiders.

NEW GUINEA—Japanese maintain pressure against block on Soputa-Sanananda trail, Col McCreary is replaced by Col John E. Grose as commander of Urbana Force. Hq of 126th Inf moves from Sanananda to Urbana front; U.S. troops of this regt that are W of the Girua R remain under operation control of Aus 16th Brig and pass to command of Maj Bernd G. Baetcke. Advance elements of 127th Inf, U.S. 32d Div, reach Dobodura. Lines on Urbana and Warren fronts are rearranged to permit units operating under bns other than their own to return to parent bns.

ITALY—20 B-24's of IX BC, in first attack by U.S. bombers on Italy, damage docks and shipping at Naples.

5 December

U.S.—Selective Service System is placed under War Manpower Commission by Presidential executive order.

S PACIFIC—AAF units in S Pacific are to be designated Thirteenth Air Force, although this air force has not yet been formally activated.

NEW GUINEA—In Gona area, Aus 21st Brig maintains pressure on enemy; Aus 25th Brig withdraws for Port Moresby. Bn of 21st Brig, supported by elements of Aus 39th Bn, 30th Brig, moves E to keep enemy from Basabua anchorage while rest of the 39th Bn advances W because of enemy landings at Kumusi R mouth. Roadblock on Soputa-Sanananda trail remains under severe pressure, and food and ammunition of garrison are dwindling rapidly. Japanese turn back supply party attempting to reach the block and again repel frontal and flanking attacks toward it. After air and arty preparation, Urbana and Warren Forces launch all-out attacks. Some Urbana Force elements drive to within 50 yards of Buna Village; others break through to the sea; still others invest W bank of Entrance Creek except for Coconut Grove. Buna Village is completely isolated. Warren Force attack, although preceded by Bren carriers, is a total failure except on left, where slight progress is made toward bridge between strips. Warren Force suffers heavily from enemy as well as intense heat. Brig Gen Clovis E. Byers, I Corps chief of staff, replaces Gen Waldron, who is wounded, as commander of 32d Div.

TUNISIA—Combined Chiefs of Staff approve Gen Eisenhower's plan to attack on 9 December. Br First Army is handicapped by lack of advanced airfields, overextended supply lines, and lack of reserves. While preparations are being made for the attack, Allied aircraft are conducting strikes against ports to limit enemy's build-up.

6 December

NEW GUINEA—Japanese frustrate effort to supply beleaguered roadblock on Soputa-Sanananda trail with rations and ammunition. The garrison is near the end of its resources. Urbana Force prepares for another attack on Buna Village and places first "time on target" fire of the campaign on Buna Mission. Since frontal attacks by Warren Force have been futile and costly, it is decided to soften enemy positions by attrition and infiltration while awaiting arrival of tanks.

TUNISIA—German attack penetrates positions of CCB, U.S. 1st Armd Div, on El Guessa heights.

7 December

NEW GUINEA—Aus 30th Brig relieves Aus 16th Brig on Sanananda front where troops are greatly weakened by malaria as well as protracted fighting. Cos C, D, and L of U.S. 126th Inf are relieved in front line by Aus 49th and 55/53d Bns. Americans, except for those garrisoning the roadblock and holding positions W of it, are ordered to rear of Aus forces. Fresh Aus troops attack at once toward the block but cannot reach it; further effort to supply the block is also futile. Col Clarence M. Tomlinson takes command of Urbana Force, relieving Col Grose. After heavy air and arty preparation, Urbana Force again attacks Buna Village and clears trench at S edge. Elements on coast repel enemy attacks from the village and mission. Warren Force patrols intensively. Gen Eichelberger, who is in the process of moving his hq from Henahambuti to Simemi Village and of combining hqs of I Corps and 32d Div into Hq Buna Force, selects Brig George F. Wootten, CG Aus 18th Brig, who is at Milne Bay, to command future operations of Warren Force.

8 December

U.S.—JCS present to President Roosevelt proposal for recapture of all Burma, Operation ANAKIM. President agrees that Gen Stilwell must be provided means for his part of the operation-N Burma, Operation RAVENOUS.

GUADALCANAL—RCT 132 (–) of Americal Div arrives.

NEW GUINEA—Allied planes intercept convoy of 6 DD's, with fighter cover, attempting to reinforce beachhead and force it back to Rabaul. Japanese sustain heavy casualties while trying unsuccessfully to withdraw from Gona to Giruwa. Allied supply party reaches roadblock on Soputa-Sanananda trail against bitter opposition. Urbana Force, continuing battle for Buna Village, concentrates on bunker position on S edge. Newly arrived flame thrower proves so ineffective that the weapon is not used again during the campaign. Japanese fail in attempt to reinforce garrison of village with troops from mission. On Warren front, preparations are made to move guns closer to enemy bunkers as 2 more 25-pounders arrive by sea. Brig Wootten is ordered to Port Moresby. Navy agrees to provide corvettes for movement of fresh troops to Warren front.

TUNISIA—Gen Eisenhower gives Gen K. A. N. Anderson permission to withdraw Br First Army to more favorable positions from which to prepare for attack.

9 December

GUADALCANAL—Gen Patch, CG Americal Div, relieves Gen Vandegrift, CG 1st Mar Div, of responsibility for Guadalcanal. 1st Mar Div is gradually withdrawn during the month for rehabilitation.

NEW GUINEA—After preparatory bombardment from air and ground, Aus 21st Brig launches final assault on Gona area and by 1630 overcomes resistance in hand-to-hand combat. Hundreds of Japanese dead are found. Leading bn (3d) of 127th Inf, U.S. 32d Div, completes air movement to Urbana front and prepares for final assault on Buna Village.

10 December

NEW GUINEA—Japanese remaining on coast NW of Gona, now greatly depleted in strength by air attacks as well as pressure of Aus 39th Bn, are ordered to establish defensive perimeter around Napapo and await reinforcements. On Sanananda front, Allied supply party reaches roadblock and finds garrison in desperate need of relief. On Urbana front, 3d Bn of 127th Inf, U.S. 32d Div, begins relief of 2d Bn of 126th Inf, which by now is also greatly understrength. Warren Force continues to bombard and probe enemy line in effort to soften it. Aus 2/6th Independent Co is detached and returns to Aus 7th Div. Japanese are again supplied by air. Brig Wootten reports to Gen Blarney for instructions.

TUNISIA—German tank-infantry columns attack Medjez el Bab from NE and E and are repulsed. Medjez garrison of 4 Fr bns has been reinf by 1st Gds Brig (–). During night 10-11, 11th Brig of Br 78th Div and CCB of U.S. 1st Armd Div begin withdrawal to Bédja area to refit, CCB sustaining heavy loss of equipment as it withdraws.

11 December

NEW GUINEA—On Urbana front, 3d Bn of 127th Inf completes relief of 2d Bn, 126th, in line. Brig Wootten inspects Warren front, where positions are virtually static. The first of a number of freighters to bring supplies and personnel to Oro Bay arrives night 11-12 and unloads 4 light tanks of Aus 2/6th Armd Regt and supplies.

MIDDLE EAST—U.S. military personnel begin arriving in Iraq and Iran.

LIBYA—Gen Montgomery issues orders for attack on El Agheila on 14th. Air action is stepped up in preparation for the offensive.

TUNISIA—Another German attack on Medjez el Bab from N and E is repulsed. Br 6th Armd Div begins arriving in forward area. CCB, U.S. 1st Armd Div, is relieved in Bédja area by 11th Brig, Br 78th Div, and is placed in 5 Corps reserve.

USSR—Red Army retains the initiative, making progress in Stalingrad sector and in the Caucasus; sharp thrusts are continued against enemy on central and northern fronts without materially changing situation. German *6th Army*, isolated between Don and Volga Rivers on Stalingrad front, is under strong pressure. German *Army Group A* withdraws MLR in vicinity of Terek R in the Caucasus.

12 December

GUADALCANAL—2d Mar Div begins relief of Americal Div W of the Matanikau. Enemy party raids Fighter Strip 2 under cover of darkness. 2d Mar Div Signal Co and 18th Naval Construction Bn arrive.

NEW GUINEA—From Oro Bay, tanks are moved forward by sea to Hariko and hidden. Corvettes with Aus forces embarked (18th Brig Hq, 2/9th Bn, and CO of 2/10th Bn) arrive off Soena Plantation after nightfall; withdraw to Porlock Harbor after a few troops are unloaded because of news that Japanese naval force is moving on Buna.

TUNISIA—Blade Force, Br First Army, is dissolved, component elements reverting to parent units. Br 6th Armd Div is in contact with enemy E and SE of Medjez el Bab.

USSR—Germans open counterattack toward Stalingrad from Kotelnikov in effort to relieve isolated *6th Army*.

13 December

GUADALCANAL—3d Bn of 182d Inf and Co C of 2d Mar Engr Bn arrive.

NEW GUINEA—Japanese convoy of 5 DD's, bringing some 800 men (among them Maj Gen Kensaku Oda, Gen Horii's successor as commander of *South Seas Detachment*), is detected off Madang while proceeding toward beachhead and unsuccessfully attacked by Allied planes. Further futile efforts are made to supply roadblock on Soputa-Sanananda trail, which is now out of contact with rest of front. Buna Village is subjected to heavy fire in preparation for attack on 14th; after nightfall, Japanese garrison, now reduced to about 100, evacuates the village and swims for Giruwa. Corvettes return to Oro Bay under cover of darkness and finish unloading Aus troops.

LIBYA—Germans begin withdrawing from El Agheila positions early in morning, leaving rear guards and numerous mines to delay Br pursuit. 51st Div, Br Eighth Army, penetrates E sector of defenses. Western Desert Air Force harasses withdrawing enemy.

TUNISIA—5 Corps, Br First Army, is ordered to be prepared to renew drive on Tunis. Lull ensues as preparations are made for attack.

14 December

GUADALCANAL—Additional elements of Americal Div arrive.

NEW GUINEA—Japanese convoy reaches Mambare R mouth early in morning and unloads without being detected. Allied planes subsequently deliver damaging attacks on troops, supplies, and landing craft. On Sanananda front, supply party succeeds in breaking through to roadblock. W of the block, Co K and Cannon Co are relieved by Australians and move to rear. On Urbana front, Cos I and K of 127th Inf move cautiously to Buna Village after arty and mortar preparation and find it void of Japanese. Recently landed Aus forces move to Hariko from Oro Bay. Aircraft establish record for Papuan campaign by bringing 178 tons of matériel to Dobodura and Popondetta airfields.

LIBYA—Br Eighth Army continues to pursue enemy, Br 7th Armd Div taking the lead in westward push while NZ 2d Div advances rapidly SW into desert in effort to get behind enemy.

15 December

NEW GUINEA—Aus 2/7th Cav Regt begins arriving at Soputa. On Urbana front, 2d Bn of 128th Inf, employing small force of 80-odd men immediately available, attacks and encircles Coconut Grove, last enemy position on W bank of Entrance Creek. After nightfall, Dutch freighter unloads additional tanks and cargo at Oro Bay. The tanks are moved forward to Hariko and, with others already there, are organized into X Sq of Aus 2/6th Armd Regt.

LIBYA—While 7th Armd Div, Br Eighth Army, engages enemy rear guards from E, NZ 2d Div drives rapidly to coast in Merduma area to block enemy's escape on W.

TUNISIA—Br First Army is slowly building up strength. 6th Armd Div completes concentration in Tunisia and is followed early in February 1943 by 46th Div. Tanks and selected personnel of 1st Bn, 1st Armd Regt, are sent back to Oran to rejoin 1st Armd Regt, U.S. 1st Armd Div. U.S. Ninth Air Force opens offensive against Tunisian ports with raid on Sfax.

16 December

GUADALCANAL—Gen Patch orders 132d Inf, Americal Div, to occupy Mt Austen, which dominates the island, as a preliminary to major offensive to be undertaken in January. The Mt Austen sector is to be controlled by Col John M. Arthur, USMC, commander of W sector.

NEW GUINEA—Gen Eichelberger takes command of U.S. 32d Div after Gen Byers is wounded while observing operations on Urbana front. Hq of Advance New Guinea Force moves from Popondetta to Dobodura. On Urbana front, 2d Bn of 128th Inf renews attack on Coconut Grove and clears it by noon; establishes bridgehead across Entrance Creek, where engineers repair bridge, from which to attack the Triangle. Platoon of Co F, 126th Inf, called Schwartz patrol, is ordered to Tarakena, W of Siwori, to protect left flank.

BURMA—In Arakan coastal sector, Eastern Army of India Command, under Lt Gen N. M. S. Irwin, opens limited-objective offensive for Akyab I., at end of Mayu Peninsula, which at this time is lightly held by enemy. Lacking resources for an amphibious assault, as planned originally, advance is made overland by Ind 14th Div, which consists at this time of 4 Ind brigs and is later strengthened by 4 more Ind brigs and one Br brig. Ind 123d Brig, leading off, finds Maungdaw free of enemy and occupies it.

LIBYA—Enemy, by breaking into small detachments, is able to withdraw from El Agheila positions after hard fighting, but loses about 20 tanks and some 500 captured.

USSR—Red Army opens strong offensive on middle Don against Italian 8th Army, which is forced to give ground. As a result, Germans are forced to abandon efforts to relieve 6th Army on Stalingrad front. In the Caucasus, Germans withdraw Terek bridgehead.

17 December

GUADALCANAL—Mt Austen operations open with rcn in force of NE slopes by elements of 3d Bn, 132d Inf; no enemy are encountered. Advance elements of 25th Div (RCT 35) arrive.

NEW GUINEA—On Urbana front, Cos G and E of 128th Inf make fruitless and costly attack on the Triangle, which they dub "Bloody Triangle." In this action, Co G loses 10 of its 27 effectives. Orders are issued for capture of Musita I., between Buna Village and Mission, on 18th and the Triangle on 19th to pave way for assault on main objective, Buna Mission. Brig Wootten takes command of Warren Force and prepares for attack on 18th. Tanks of X Sq start toward line of departure at 1800, the noise of their motors covered by mortar fire.

BURMA—Continuing drive toward Akyab, Ind 14th Div seizes Buthidaung without opposition.

TUNISIA—Lull continues on Br First Army front. 2d Bn of U.S. 509th Para Regt and 3d Bn of RCT 26, U.S. 1st Div, raid Maknassy, 30 miles NE of Tébessa.

18 December

U.S.—JCS authorize occupation of Amchitka, less than 100 miles from Kiska, provided it is suitable for an advanced air base from which Kiska can be attacked.

ALEUTIAN IS.—Rcn party surveys Amchitka and reports that the operation is feasible.

GUADALCANAL—3d Bn, 132d Inf, advances up NW slopes of Mt Austen to Hill 35, where enemy fire is encountered.

NEW GUINEA—Aus 39th Bn, which has been joined by elements of 2/14th Bn, has reduced enemy strength at Napapo to about half and is being relieved for action on Sanananda front by Aus 2/16th and 2/27th Bns. Australians, supported by fire of Americans, begin concerted attack on Sanananda front. 2/7th Cav Regt, having moved elements into roadblock against firm opposition, attacks N along Soputa-Sanananda trail, bypassing resistance just ahead of the block. Aus 30th Brig attacks at track junction, employing 2 bns in frontal assault and another in region E of track, but makes little headway. Urbana Force attempts to clear Musita I. Elements of Co L, 127th Inf, reach the island by means of cable, but withdraw upon meeting heavy resistance. On Warren front, concerted assault against Cape Endaiadere and New Strip is spearheaded by tanks, which prove invaluable in reducing concrete and steel fortifications. After preliminary air and ground bombardment, Aus 2/9th Bn begins attack on Cape Endaiadere and soon breaks through main enemy positions and reaches objective; then drives W along coast until halted near Strip Pt by new line of bunkers. 3d Bn of U.S. 128th Inf mops up and establishes defensive perimeter in Duropa Plantation. Americans and Australians attack New Strip from S and E. While 1st Bn, 126th Inf, pushes toward bridge between the strips, elements of Aus 2/9th Bn, reinforced during day by 1st Bn of 128th Inf, reduce strongpoint at E end of New Strip and pursue enemy W along N edge of strip toward bridge. Australians sustain heavy casualties and lose 3 tanks in the action, which is otherwise highly successful. Advance elements of Aus 2/10th Bn arrive at front by sea during night 18-19.

LIBYA—Continuing pursuit of enemy, NZ 2d Div of Br Eighth Army clashes sharply with rear guards at Nofilia. After the action, pursuit is largely abandoned for administrative reasons.

19 December

GUADALCANAL—After air and arty preparation, 3d Bn of 132d Inf attempts unsuccessfully to advance from Hill 35; 3d Bn CO is killed by enemy fire. Reserve bn (1st, 132d Inf), less one co, advances to positions E of 3d Bn.

NEW GUINEA—Continuing assault on Sanananda front, Australians reduce several enemy positions just beyond track junction in frontal drive; flanking elements reach positions near roadblock. Enemy attack on the block is repulsed. Aus cavalrymen destroy enemy force 300 yards N of the block and establish new perimeter, which they call Kano Urbana Force, after air and mortar preparation, attacks the Triangle, Cos E and G of 126th Inf driving S on it while Co F blocks from below. Attack is soon halted by cross fire, which causes heavy casualties. Bn commander is lost in this action. Troops on Warren front regroup. Rest of Aus 2/10th Bn arrives at front after dark. U.S. troops to operate Oro Bay port and engineers charged with construction of road from Oro Bay to Dobodura airfields land at Oro Bay, night 19-20. Additional cargo is also brought ashore.

USSR—Soviet forces continue to gain ground in broad offensive. Assault forces from middle Don reach Kantemirovka, on Voronezh-Rostov RR N of Millerovo.

20 December

GUADALCANAL—Enemy riflemen harass flanks and rear of 132d Inf on NW slopes of Mt Austen.

1st Bn attempts unsuccessfully to locate enemy's E flank. U.S. engineers complete construction of jeep road to Hill 35.

NEW GUINEA—Australians on Sanananda front continue to reduce enemy positions beyond track junction; consolidate new Kano perimeter. On Urbana front, 2d Bn of 126th Inf, except for Co F at tip of Triangle, is withdrawn as reserve, and 127th Inf takes over attack. After preparatory bombardment, Co E attacks the Triangle under cover of smoke but is unable to advance; another attack is also unsuccessful. During this action, its first, Co E sustains 39 casualties. The decision is made to bypass the Triangle in the future. Gen Eichelberger replaces Col Tomlinson with Col Grose as commander of Urbana Force. On left flank of Urbana Force, Schwartz patrol, having clashed with enemy W of Siwori Village on 18th and 19th, is reinf with 20 men from 2d Bn, 126th Inf. Warren Force, attacking after heavy arty preparation, clears most of region E of Simemi Creek. Enemy retains only small finger of land at creek mouth. Efforts to cross 125-foot bridge W of New Strip are futile as are attempts by engineers to repair it.

21 December

U.S.—JCS direct Amchitka to be occupied as near 5 January as possible.

GUADALCANAL—Ordered to cut Maruyama Trail, Co C of 132d Inf pushes 1,000 yards S without making contact with enemy or finding trail.

NEW GUINEA—From Napapo, Gen Oda and his staff arrive at Giruwa. On Sanananda front, Australians continue to batter enemy positions in front of track junction. 49th Bn succeeds in entering the roadblock and protects supply line to it. Cavalrymen push N from Kano position toward Sanananda. Urbana Force, feinting toward the Triangle, draws enemy from bunkers and kills many with arty fire. In preparation for drive through Government Gardens to sea, Co K of 12th Inf crosses Entrance Creek in rubber boats under fire, night 21-22, to establish bridgehead above the Triangle. On left flank, Schwartz patrol meets firm resistance at Tarakena, about a mile W of Siwori, and retires eastward; 30 more men of 2d Bn, 126th Inf, reinf the patrol. Warren Force finishes clearing region E of Simemi Creek and begins to cross after patrol discovers suitable site some 1,300 yards below its mouth. The crossing is undetected by enemy.

LIBYA—Light forces of Br Eighth Army, pursuing enemy westward, overtake rear guard at Sirte and are halted.

22 December

NEW GUINEA—Gen Oda takes responsibility for Japanese beachhead from Col Yokoyama and personally directs operations on Sanananda front. Aus reinforcements (21st Brig hq and 39th Bn of 30th Brig) reach Soputa from Gona; relieve U.S. 126th Inf forces of roadblock on Soputa-Sanananda trail. Aus 21st Brig takes command of 49th Bn, 2/7th Cav, and U.S. forces from the roadblock. 30th Brig, which is responsible for clearing pockets at track junction, retains command of 36th and 55/534 Bns and rest of U.S. forces on this front. Firm opposition of seasoned Japanese troops limits efforts to advance N along the track and to clear track junction. On Urbana front, Co I of 127th Inf follows Co K across Entrance Creek, strengthening bridgehead. Other elements of 127th Inf begin to clear Musita I. after engineers repair bridge to it. On Warren front, Aus 2/10th Bn (— Co C) continues to cross Simemi Creek near Old Strip, while 2/9th plus Co C of 2/10th mops up E of the creek.

TUNISIA—5 Corps, Br First Army, renews drive on Tunis, night 22–23. 2d Coldstream Gds of 1st Gds Brig attacks Djebel el Ahmera (later known as Longstop Hill), 6 miles NE of Medjez el Bab, and partially occupies it.

USSR—In the Caucasus, Soviet forces begin strong attacks SE of Nalchik as enemy starts withdrawal of spearhead in the area. Red Army offensive continues to gain ground on Stalingrad front and in middle Don sector. Sharp Soviet thrusts toward Velikie Luki, on central front, are gaining ground.

23 December

NEW GUINEA—Virtual stalemate exists on Sanananda front, where Japanese are stubbornly defending their well-organized positions. On Urbana front, 127th Inf completes capture of Musita I. and begins firing on Buna Mission at close range; prepares to drive E across Government Gardens to sea. Warren Force continues movement across creek, where engineers repair bridge under fire, and takes up positions for concerted assault on Old Strip. Aus 2/9th Bn and 3d Bn of U.S. 128th Inf hold their positions along coast and finish mopping up region E of the creek. During night 23–24, 2 enemy vessels sink barge loaded with ammunition and strafe beach at Hariko; vessel bringing more tanks and supplies to Warren Force unloads at Oro Bay.

TUNISIA—3-day period of torrential rain begins. Elements of RCT 18, U.S. 1st Div, relieve 2d Coldstream Gds on Djebel el Ahmera and are forced to withdraw under German counterattack.

24 December

GUADALCANAL—3d Bn of 132d Inf, followed by 1st Bn in reserve, moves W without incident to Hill 31, W of summit of Mt Austen; upon attacking S toward Hill 27, is stopped short by fire from enemy strongpoint, called Gifu, between Hills 31 and 27. The Gifu position, with fixed defenses and interconnecting pillboxes, is held by about 500 Japanese.

NEW GUINEA—After arty preparation, Urbana Force, employing 127th Inf, begins drive toward the sea through Government Gardens, where enemy defenses are organized in depth and concealed by high kunai grass. Progress is very slow. Platoon of Co L discovers weak spot and drives through to line of coconut trees near coast; is surrounded there and suffers heavy casualties before escaping by circuitous route. As a diversion, elements move to Mission side of creek from Musita I. and from shallows between Buna Village and Buna Mission, but withdraw because of intense opposition. Warren Force opens attack on Old Strip after arty preparation. Aus 2/10th Bn, disposed along N edge of strip, is supported by 3 tanks while making main effort. 1st Bns of U.S. 126th and 128th Regts attack in parallel columns along S edge of strip; later 1st Bn of 128th Inf follows 1st Bn of 126th. Attack gains some 450 yards, but Japanese fire prevents movement onto the strip and knocks out the tanks.

ALGERIA—Darlan is assassinated in Algiers.

TUNISIA—Decision is made at conference between Gen Eisenhower and Gen K. A. N. Anderson to abandon attack on Tunis until after rainy season. Br First Army regains positions on Djebel el Ahmera.

25 December

GUADALCANAL—Further efforts of 3d Bn, 132d Inf, to advance toward Hill 27 are frustrated by strong opposition from Gifu strongpoint.

NEW GUINEA—Japanese beachhead is supplied by submarine. Urbana Force, with 7 cos in assault, continues efforts to secure corridor to sea through Government Gardens. After arty and mortars thoroughly cover Buna Mission, troops on Musita I. feint toward the Mission. Main attack, by Cos A and F, then opens without preparatory fire, and advance elements succeed in reaching line of coconut trees near coast where they establish defense perimeter and repel counterattacks. Other elements of 127th Inf press forward toward Cos A and F; still others continue reduction of enemy positions in Government Gardens, assisted by diversionary thrusts against the Triangle. Warren Force continues to make slow progress astride Old Strip, runway of which remains under intense fire. Co C of Aus 2/10th Bn is disposed on extreme left in an attempt to turn enemy's right flank.

LIBYA—Sirte falls to Br Eighth Army upon being outflanked by light armd force.

TUNISIA—Germans recapture Djebel el Ahmera, concluding seesaw battle for this hill dominating exits of Medjez el Bab. 1st Gds Brig withdraws to Medjez el Bab area, night 25-26. RCT 18 of U.S. 1st Div, upon relief by 1st Gds Brig, moves to Teboursouk.

26 December

GUADALCANAL—After arty and air preparation, 3d Bn of 132d Inf renews attack to S, making limited progress against strong opposition from Gifu strongpoint. 3d and 1st Bns, latter on E, dig in for night on line between Hill 31 and Gifu. Advance elements of 2d Mar Air Wing, which is to relieve 1st Mar Air Wing, arrive at Henderson field.

NEW GUINEA—On Urbana front, 127th Inf renews attack to open corridor to sea. Co C is prevented by stubborn opposition from reaching Cos A and F near the coast, but patrol gets through. Warren Force, assisted by 25-pound gun emplaced at SE end of Old Strip, succeeds at last in forming continuous line across the strip. Advance elements on flanks push to NW end and begin reduction of enemy positions there. Japanese planes from Rabaul, the first to be based there, attack Dobodura but are driven off by Fifth Air Force. Under cover of darkness, 26-27, additional Allied tanks and troops are landed at Oro Bay.

FRENCH SOMALILAND—Fighting French farce from British Somaliland moves into French Somaliland to seize 2 rail bridges and thus insure safety of rail line from port of Djibouti to Addis Ababa, Ethiopia. Action is accomplished without bloodshed.

27 December

GUADALCANAL—While 3d Bn, 132d Inf, conducts holding attack that gains little ground, 1st Bn, to E, moves S to locate enemy flanks, elements running into Gifu strongpoint instead of outflanking it.

NEW GUINEA—Japanese under Maj Gen Tsuyuo Yamagata at Napapo are ordered to move to Giruwa by sea. On Urbana front; Co B of 127th Inf breaks through to Cos A and F near coast, and Co C engages in clearing bunkers N of the gardens. Japanese defense of Old Strip slackens as withdrawal is begun. Warren Force finishes clearing runway except for stubborn bunker position to rear of dispersal bay. 52 Japanese planes raid Buna without causing serious damage; 14 are shot down. Additional Allied tanks and cargo are unloaded at Oro Bay, night 27-28. RCT 163, U.S. 41st Div, arrives at Port Moresby from Australia.

BURMA—Ind 14th Div continues unopposed drive on Akyab astride Mayu R and range. E of river, Ind 123d Brig reaches vicinity of Rathedaung. In coastal sector, Ind 47th Brig arrives at Indin and gets patrol to Foul Pt, at tip of Mayu Peninsula. Advance then halts for various administrative reasons, one being the difficulty of bringing reinforcements and supplies forward.

LIBYA—Br Eighth Army patrols cross Wadi Tamet.

TUNISIA—Br First Army repels enemy attack in Medjez el Bab area.

28 December

GUADALCANAL—Patrols of 132d Inf probe Gifu line but are unable to find gaps. Since effective strength of the assault bns now totals only 1,541, 132d Inf CO is promised fresh 2d Bn.

NEW GUINEA—Japanese garrison of Buna is ordered to withdraw to Giruwa, assisted by detachment at Giruwa, which is to attack through U.S. left flank. Urbana Force's 127th Inf gains broad corridor from Entrance Creek to line of coconut trees. Co K makes futile attempt to establish bridgehead on Mission side of Entrance Creek: some elements attempting to land from boats are turned back by fire; others begin crossing bridge between Musita I. and the Mission, but bridge becomes unusable before many are across. Volunteers from Co E enter the Triangle in evening and find strong defenses there deserted. Warren Force overcomes all organized resistance at Old Strip and swings N toward coast. Aus 2/12th Bn arrives at Oro Bay from Goodenough I, night 28-29.

CBI—Chiang Kai-shek radios President Roosevelt that although Chinese army in Yunnan will be ready for offensive by spring of 1943 as planned, the offensive cannot be undertaken unless there are additional naval forces for Bay of Bengal.

FRENCH SOMALILAND—Joins Fighting French.

LIBYA—Br Eighth Army patrols reach positions overlooking Wadi el Chebir without enemy opposition.

29 December

NEW GEORGIA—Enemy completes airfield at Munda despite frequent Allied air attacks.

GUADALCANAL—At conference at Gen Patch's CP, the decision is made to continue attack on Mt Austen. Patrol of 1st Bn, 132d Inf, finds safe route to Hill 27, S of Gifu.

NEW GUINEA—Gen Yamagata, charged with rescue of Buna garrison, arrives at Giruwa. On Urbana front, Co B of 127th Inf drives from line of coconut trees to sea SE of Buna Mission, completing corridor from Entrance Creek to coast and cutting off Japanese at Buna Mission from those at Giropa Pt. Patrol wades shallows between spits extending from Buna Village and Buna Mission without opposition. Warren Force attacks northward toward coast in area between Simemi Creek and Giropa Pt, 4 tanks spearheading. Little headway is made because of poor tank-infantry co-ordination and determined opposition; positions are consolidated at edge of coconut trees. Aus 2/12th Bn arrives at front.

LIBYA—Advance elements of Br Eighth Army (armd cars of 4th Light Armd Brig) come to a halt just W of enemy's Buerat position. Buerat and Bu Ngem are found to be free of enemy. Lull follows as British prepare to attack.

USSR—Kotelnikov, SW of Stalingrad, falls to Red Army.

30 December

GUADALCANAL—In preparation for renewing attack on Hill 27, 2d Bn of 132d Inf begins movement to forward positions. 1st and 3d Bns continue to patrol.

NEW GUINEA—Urbana Force maintains pressure against Buna Mission from SE and prepares to envelop it by attacking eastward from Buna Village and Musita I. Warren Force regroups. Advance elements of 163d Inf (1st Bn and hq), U.S. 91st Div, are flown to Dobodura and Popondetta from Port Moresby.

TUNISIA—RCT 18, U.S. 1st Div, moves to Medjez el Bab.

31 December

GUADALCANAL—2d Bn of 132d Inf reaches Hill m, E of the Gifu strongpoint, line of departure for enveloping movement.

NEW GUINEA—Urbana Force begins envelopment of Buna Mission. Co E, 127th Inf, and Co F, 128th, cross shallows E of Buna Village before dawn and, although Japanese offer strong opposition upon being alerted, advance about 200 yards along spit extending from Buna Mission. Other elements of Urbana Force maintain pressure on enemy from SE and finish clearing Government Gardens, but enemy retains positions in swamp N of gardens. Patrol contact is made between Urbana and Warren Forces. Warren Force finishes regrouping. Fresh Aus 2/12th Bn is disposed on left, 3d Bn of U.S. 128th Inf in center, and Aus 2/10th on right. With arrival of additional cargo at Oro Bay by sea, supplies moved in this manner since the first vessel arrived on 11 December total some 4,000 tons.

N ATLANTIC—Enemy naval force engaging USSR-bound convoy sustains damage to 1 cruiser and at least 3 DD's.

1943

1 January

GUADALCANAL—From Hill 11, 2d Bn of 132d Inf marches slowly S and W over precipitous terrain to SE slope of Hill 27, arriving too late in day to open assault as planned. RCT 27, 25th Div, arrives on island.

NEW GUINEA—Urbana Force attacks toward Buna Mission from SE and from the spit after heavy preparatory fire, but makes little progress. In evening Japanese are seen swimming from the Mission. Co B, 127th Inf, moves E toward Giropa Pt to assist Warren Force, which encircles enemy between Giropa Pt and Old Strip. On left, Aus 2/12th Bn, supported by 6 tanks, drives to coast at Giropa Pt and turns SE, clearing coastal strip to Simemi Creek; 1st Bn, U.S. 128th Inf, mops up bypassed pockets. On right, 3d Bn of 128th Inf and Aus 2/10th Bn make slow progress in 2-pronged attack to clear enemy entrenched in dispersal bays off NW end of Strip.

NW AFRICA—Gen Eisenhower places Gen Fredendall in command of U.S. II Corps, which is planning for Operation SATIN, capture of Sfax, Tunisia, to prevent junction of Axis armies. TF SATIN is to consist of 1st Armd Div and RCT 26 of 1st Inf Div. AFHQ takes responsibility for communications lines from Bone to Constantine, relieving Br First Army.

USSR—Encircled German *Sixth Army* on Stalingrad front, now compressed into area some 25 by 40 miles, remains under attack from all sides. Efforts to supply it by air meet with little success and are costly in aircraft. Soviet troops of Kalinin Front capture Velikie Luki, important rail center, which has been under attack for some time. Elista, S of Stalingrad in Kalmyk steppes, falls to other Red Army forces.

2 January

GUADALCANAL—Gen Harmon activates XIV Corps, consisting of Americal and 25th Divs, former reinf by 147th Inf. 2d Mar Div and other Marine ground forces are attached to corps. Gen Patch is placed in command of corps, and Gen Sebree succeeds him as commander of Americal Div. After heavy arty preparation, 132d Inf of Americal Div continues offensive against the Gifu strongpoint. 2d Bn, taking enemy by surprise, advances quickly to crest of Hill 27, S of the Gifu strongpoint, and digs in; holds firm under a number of counterattacks. 3d and 1st Bns establish lines along N and E sides of the Gifu, respectively, but gaps remain between the 3 assault bns.

NEW GUINEA—Urbana Force overruns Buna Mission in concerted assault. Organized resistance ends at 1632. Top Japanese commanders, Capt. Yasuda and Col Hiroshi Yamamoto, commit suicide. With Mission clear, Co C of 127th Inf joins Co B in attack along coast toward Giropa Pt, and by 1930 makes junction with Warren Force. Warren Force, in final attack, finishes clearing region from Giropa Pt eastward. Japanese move forward from Giruwa to rescue survivors of Buna garrison. Japanese have lost at least 1,400 men at Buna: 500 W of Giropa Pt and 900 E of it. Casualties of U.S. 32d Div and Aus 18th Brig total 2,817 (620 killed, 2,065 wounded, 132 missing). In preparation for stepping up action on Sanananda front, where stalemate has existed for some time, Gen Herring orders 25-pound arty from Buna to that area. 1st Bn and Hq, U.S. 163d Inf, take responsibility for Huggins and Kano blocks on trail to Sanananda, gradually relieving Australians, 2–4 January. Huggins is renamed Musket.

USSR—German *Army Group A* begins withdrawing *1st Pz Army* northward toward Rostov to prevent it from becoming encircled.

3 January

GUADALCANAL—1st Bn, 132d Inf, exerts pressure against E part of the Gifu and establishes contact with 2d Bn to left.

NEW GUINEA—Urbana and Warren Forces mop up.

TUNISIA—Enemy tank-infantry force, with arty and air support, overruns Fr 19th Corps troops at Fondouk. Br First Army's 5 Corps, employing 36th Brig of 78th Div, begins limited attacks to improve positions on Djebel Azag and Djebel Ajred, W of Mateur. Br 6th Armd Div conducts rcn in force on Goubellat plain.

USSR—Exploiting German withdrawal in the Caucasus, Red Army occupies Mozdok and Malgobek.

4 January

N PACIFIC—Adm Nimitz replaces Adm Theobald with Adm Kinkaid as commander, TF 8.

Rear Adm Charles H. McMorris relieves Adm W. W. Smith as commander of strike group.

GUADALCANAL—Japanese are ordered to withdraw from Guadalcanal to New Georgia Is. Final echelon of 25th Div (RCT 161) arrives. 2d Mar Div hq and 6th Marines, reinf, also land, bringing 2d Mar Div nearly up to full strength. 132d Inf completes semicircle about E part of the Gifu between Hills 31 and 27 with patrol contact between 1st and 3d Bns; halts and prepares defenses while awaiting relief. In 22 days of fighting on Mt Austen, 132d Inf has killed 400–500 Japanese and suffered 383 casualties.

NEW GEORGIA—U.S. cruiser-DD force bombards Munda airfield night 4–5.

NEW GUINEA—Japanese overrun outpost near Tarakena, forcing patrol there to swim for Siwori Village. With Tarakena spit in their possession, Japanese are able to rescue some of the survivors of Buna garrison. Gen Herring confers with commanding officers on plan for reduction of enemy W of Girua R.

LIBYA—Severe 2-day storm begins, sharply decreasing capacity of Benghazi port and forcing Br Eighth Army to make greater use of the more distant port of Tobruk. Because of this, Gen Montgomery alters plan of attack, scheduled for 15th, on Buerat position, from which Italians are already withdrawing. 10 Corps, which was to have advanced, is to remain in place while all its vehicles are used to move supplies forward from Tobruk. Size of the assault force, drawn from 30 Corps, is reduced by one div.

5 January

GUADALCANAL—Staff section chiefs of XIV Corps assume their duties. Gen Patch, in letter of instructions to 25th Div CG, Maj Gen J. Lawton Coffins, directs 25th Div to relieve 132d Inf, Americal Div, on Mt Austen and attack W some 3,000 yards. 2d Mar Div, holding coastal sector from Pt Cruz to Hill 66, is to maintain contact with N flank of 25th Div.

NEW GUINEA—Advance elements of Aus 18th Brig (2/9th Bn and brig hq) and 4 tanks of Aus 2/6th Armd Regt reach Soputa. Additional tanks and arty are kept E of the river for some time because of poor road conditions. As preliminary to allout offensive against Sanananda, 127th Inf starts NW along coast toward Tarakena.

NW AFRICA—U.S. Fifth Army is activated under Lt Gen Mark W. Clark, with hq at Oujda, Morocco. (The army was previously constituted, effective 1 December 1942, by War Department memorandum to CG ETO, dated 8 December 1942, which assigned to it I Armd and II Corps. GO 67 of Hq ETO, dated 12 December 1942, constituted the army in accordance with above War Department authority.) Gen Eisenhower activates Allied Air Force, containing both EAC and Twelfth Air Force, under command of Gen Spaatz, who retains command of Eighth Air Force as well.

TUNISIA—5 Corps, Br First Army, breaks off action on Djebel Azag and Djebel Ajred after hard fighting in heavy rain, withdrawing assault force (36th Brig, 78th Div) to original positions.

USSR—Soviet forces take Nalchik, in the Caucasus; column advancing along the Don overruns Tsimlyansk.

6 January

SWPA—Japanese convoy bound for Lae (New Guinea) from New Britain is detected and subsequently attacked by Allied planes as it proceeds toward its destination.

BURMA—Ind 14th Div, renewing offensive on Arakan front, finds Japanese firmly entrenched at Donbaik and Rathedaung. Although fighting continues at these points for many weeks, positions remain about the same.

7 January

GUADALCANAL—In preparation for offensive on 10th, 35th Inf of 25th Div leaves Lunga perimeter for Mt Austen. 147th Inf TF, under Capt Charles E. Beach, embarks at Kukum in 2 LCT's for Beaufort Bay to block trail leading N toward Kokumbona. About 50,000 Allied air, ground, and naval forces are now in Guadalcanal area.

NEW GUINEA—127th Inf continues toward Tarakena. Cos G and F, with fire support of Co E, reach positions about 500 yards from objective. Aus 18th Brig completes movement to Soputa. 2d Bn, U.S. 163d Inf, arrives on Sanananda front. Japanese convoy with reinforcements reaches Lae despite efforts of aircraft to turn it back.

IRAQ—Americans take exclusive jurisdiction over port of Khorramshahr, where first U.S. troops arrived in December 1942.

8 January

GUADALCANAL—Gen Collins issues FO I to 25th Div concerning coming offensive. 35th Inf moves secretly up Mt Austen toward line of departure.

NEW GUINEA—COS A, C, and F of 127th Inf overrun Tarakena. 163d Inf begins offensive to clear road to Sananada: 1st Bn attacks 2 enemy perimeters located between Musket and Kano, making limited progress. Allied planes continue to attack enemy convoy as it unloads some 4,000 reinforcements at Lae.

CHINA—In message to President Roosevelt, Chiang Kai-shek turns down proposal for offensive in spring of 1943.

MADAGASCAR—Gen Platt, CG Br East African Command, turns over responsibility for island, except for Diego Suarez area, to Gen P. Legentilhomme, High Commissioner for French possessions in Indian Ocean.

TUNISIA—CCB, U.S. 1st Armd Div, is detached from 5 Corps, Br First Army, and reverts to 1st Armd Div.

USSR—Gen Rokossovski, commanding Soviet forces of Don Front, sends ultimatum to Field Marshal Paulus calling for surrender of German 6th Army at Stalingrad. Soviet forces seize Zimovniki, on Stalingrad-Novorossisk rail line.

9 January

GUADALCANAL—XIV Corps Completes preparations for attack on 10th. 25th Div, which is to lead off, moves forward to line of departure. 27th Inf, on div right (N), takes up positions for assault on hill mass called Galloping Horse, between NW and SW forks of the Matanikau. 35th Inf, on left, prepares to make main effort against Hills 43 and 44, called Sea Horse, lying between the Gifu and Galloping Horse, while exerting pressure against the Gifu. 3d Bn, followed by 1st, completes wide circling movement about S flank of the Gifu to line of departure for attack on the Sea Horse. 2d Bn and Cav Rcn Tr take up positions about eastern part of the Gifu, relieving 132d Inf of Americal Div. Americal Div (−) holds perimeter defense. Capt Beach's 147th Inf TF lands at Beaufort Bay and establishes beach defenses.

NEW GUINEA—Enemy fire prevents 127th Inf from establishing bridgehead across Konombi Creek in Tarakena area. Relief of elements of 126th Inf, now greatly depleted in strength, is completed on Sanananda front. While 1st Bn, 163d Inf, continues efforts to reduce the 2 enemy pockets between Musket and Kano, 2d Bn establishes position, called Rankin after Capt Pinkney R. Rankin, astride Killerton trail W of Musket, isolating enemy in track junction. Japanese convoy departs from Lae early in morning shadowed by Allied planes. As result of recent attacks on the convoy, 2 transports have been sunk and about 80 planes destroyed.

10 January

GUADALCANAL—25th Div, reinf, begins largest and final offensive to clear Guadalcanal, immediate objectives being Galloping Horse, Sea Horse, and the Gifu strongpoint. After ½-hour arty preparation—first divisional TOT concentration of the campaign—followed by aerial bombardment, 27th Inf drives S through 2d Mar Div against Galloping Horse and clears more than half of the objective. 1st Bn on W, attacks from Hill 66 to objective, N part of Hill 57, and establishes patrol contact with 3d Bn to E. From Hill 55, 3d Bn advances 1,600 yards toward Hill 53, but is halted by stubborn opposition on Hill 52, intermediate position. 35th Inf's 3d Bn begins envelopment of S flank of Sea Horse, omitting preparatory fire, and takes preliminary objective, a small hill a short distance S of the Sea Horse, against scattered opposition. Combat patrols of 2d Bn move against the Gifu after preparatory fire but are unable to make any headway.

NEW GUINEA—COs A and C, 127th Inf, establish bridgehead across Konombi Creek in Tarakena area. Action is then suspended temporarily. 1st Bn, 163d Inf, finds 1 of the 2 enemy positions between Musket and Kano evacuated. Kano is renamed Fisk after 1st Lt Harold R. Fisk, 3d Bn, 163d Inf, reaches front.

LIBYA—Gen Montgomery briefs assault forces of Br Eighth Army on projected drive through Buerat line to Tripoli, which must be accomplished within 10 days, beginning on 15th, to avoid supply difficulties.

USSR—Since ultimatum of 8th has not brought about surrender of German 6th Army at Stalingrad, Soviet forces with strong arty and mortar support are attacking to destroy it. Field Marshal Paulus is holding out in order to cover withdrawal of endangered German spearheads from the Caucasus to Rostov.

11 January

GUADALCANAL—3d Bn Of 27th Inf, 25th Div, continues attack on Galloping Horse but is again unable to take Hill 53. Stiff opposition coupled with insufficient drinking water make action on this front very difficult. 3d Bn, 35th Inf, completes circle about the Gifu with capture of Sea Horse, where it is forced to rely on air supply until boat line can be completed. 3d Bn of 182d Inf, Americal Div, attached to 35th Inf, closes gap between Galloping Horse and Sea Horse. 2d Bn, 35th Inf, continues to meet heavy fire from the Gifu as it probes the position with combat patrols. Capt Beach's 147th Inf force, less elements holding beachhead, starts march to Vurai, SW of Kokumbona, to block this escape route from Kokumbona.

NEW GUINEA—Small Aus Kanga Force begins 3-day raid on Mubo, during which considerable damage is inflicted on enemy.

TUNISIA—6th Armd Div of 5 Corps, Br First Army, improves positions in local attack N of Bou Arada.

USSR—As Germans continue withdrawal from the Caucasus, Soviet forces occupy Pyatigorsk, Georgievsk, and Mineralnye Vody.

12 January

ALEUTIAN IS.—Small U.S. Army force under command of Brig Gen Lloyd E. Jones lands on Amchitka without opposition.

GUADALCANAL—27th Inf, 25th Div, continues attack on Galloping Horse, replacing 3d Bn with 2d, and makes limited progress toward Hill 53. CO C, 35th Inf, starts W toward corps objective along ridge SW of Sea Horse but is soon halted by enemy fire. Efforts of 2d Bn to break through the Gifu are frustrated by strong resistance.

NEW GUINEA—After arty preparation, 2 bns of Aus 18th Brig, with tank support, attack enemy positions at trail junction; 163d Inf supports assault with feints from Musket and Rankin. Japanese AT fire soon disables tanks, but Australians continue battle, progressing slowly at great cost. Japanese begin withdrawing from the junction, night 12-13

USSR—Soviet forces of Leningrad and Volkhov Fronts launch limited offensive, supported by air and arty, to raise siege of Leningrad.

13 January

POA—Gen Harmon activates U.S. Thirteenth Air Force under Brig Gen Nathan F. Twining, with hq at Espiritu Santo, New Hebrides.

GUADALCANAL—XIV Corps offensive broadens as 2d Mar Div begins coastal attack from line Pt Cruz-Hill 66, to right of 25th Div. 8th Marines, on right, attempts to advance W From Hills 80 and 81 but is halted by enemy fire. 2d Marines advances 800 yards W from Hill 66. 27th Inf, 25th Div, completes capture of Galloping Horse with reduction of Hill 53 by 2d Bn. Americans now hold 4,500-yard front extending S from Pt Cruz over Hill 66 to Hills 57 and 55. CO C, 35th Inf, is again halted by enemy fire from SW as it endeavors to push W. 2d Bn makes negligible progress against pillboxes of the Gifu strongpoint.

NEW GUINEA—Gen Eichelberger assumes duties of Commander, Advance New Guinea Force, and takes control of all Aus and U.S. troops. Gen Herring commands New Guinea Force.

14 January

INTERNATIONAL CONFERENCES—10-day Anglo-American conference opens at Anfa, near Casablanca, Morocco, to plan Allied strategy for 1943.

GUADALCANAL—In costal sector, 8th Marines of 2d Mar Div is still unable to advance because of fire from ravine W of Hills 80 and 81. 6th Marines replaces 2d Marines on div left flank. CO C of 35th Inf, 25th Div, continues vain efforts to advance W, but patrols discover route around enemy's right flank. Depleted 2d Bn, reinf by AT Co, continues fruitless efforts to reduce the Gifu strongpoint. Capt Beach's 74th Inf force reaches Vurai; moves forward to Tapananja, about 6 miles S of Sealark Channel, when patrols find Vurai area free of enemy; establishes outposts on upper Poha. Japanese land about 600 replacements near Cape Esperance to cover withdrawal of forces from Guadalcanal.

NEW GUINEA—Gen Vasey, Aus 7th Div CG, launches offensive to intercept enemy withdrawal from trail junction. While 163d Inf pushes S to block escape routes, Aus 18th Brig quickly clears enemy remnants from the junction and joins forces with 163d Inf on Sanananda and Killerton trails. Final mop up is left to Aus 2/7th Cav and 39th and 49th Bns.

LIBYA—30 Corps, Br Eighth Army, moves forward in preparation for assault on Buerat line and drive on Tripoli.

15 January

GUADALCANAL—2d Mar Div continues to make slow progress in coastal sector, despite use of tanks and a flame thrower. Co B of 35th Inf, reinf by platoon of Co, D, takes over westward attack from Co C. After ½ hour arty concentration followed by MG and mortar fire, Co B outflanks enemy position barring advance and finds it to be a bivouac area held by a single platoon. Enemy positions in the Gifu remain practically intact despite further efforts of 2d Bn, 35th Inf, to reduce them. Surrender request is broadcast to Japanese in the Gifu.

NEW GUINEA—Preparations are made for allout offensive to clear Sanananda area. Lt Col Merle H. Howe, 3d Div G-3, takes command of Urbana Force, which is to renew drive W along coast. Aus 18th Brig moves N along Killerton trail, passing through Rankin, in preparation for drive to coast. 2d Bn of 163d Inf—the Rankin force—then follows Australians northward and takes over trail junction E of a coconut plantation about 1 ½ miles N of Rankin perimeter. On Soputa-Sanananda road, 1st Bn of 163d Inf envelops enemy pocket remaining between Musket and Fisk, elements infiltrating to attack from inside the perimeter.

LIBYA—Br Eighth Army opens drive on Tripoli, moving forward in 3 columns—those on right and in center under personal command of Gen Montgomery; outflanking force on left under 30 Corps command. 7th Armd Div and NZ 2d Div, the enveloping force, drive enemy back to Wadi Zem Zem. Coastal advance by 51st Div begins at 2230 and meets little opposition. 22d Armd Brig moves forward in center prepared to assist wherever needed.

16 January

GUADALCANAL—CG XIV Corps orders a second co-ordinated westward offensive in order to extend positions through Kokumbona to Poha R; forms Composite Army-Marine Div (CAM) (consisting of 6th Marines, 182d and 147th Inf Regts, and 2d Marine and Americal Div arty units) to drive W on 3,000-yard front in coastal sector while 25th Div attacks SW on corps S flank to envelop enemy's S flank. In 35th Inf sector, Co B, reinf, advances W to corps objective, some 1,500 yards W of the Sea Horse, without opposition, gaining positions on precipice overlooking SW fork of the Matanikau. 2d Bn commander decides to make double envelopment attack against the Gifu on 17th and sends elements from Hill 27 to Hill 42 to attack from NW as other forces drive N from Hill 27.

NEW GUINEA—After preparatory bombardment, assault against enemy in Sanananda area opens. On left, Aus 18th Brig drives quickly along Killerton trail to coast and clears broad coastal strip from Cape Killerton to outskirts of Sanananda Village. On Soputa-Sanananda road, 1st Bn of 163d Inf, having been relieved of task of clearing enemy pocket by 3d Bn, attacks N, bypassing strongpoint immediately ahead to gain position some 400 yards W of road. 3d Bn finishes clearing pocket between Musket and Fisk. From trail junction E of the coconut plantation, 2d Bn of 163d Inf hacks its way SE to Soputa-Sanananda road about 1,000 yards behind enemy's main line and makes contact with 1st Bn and Aus 18th Brig. Attacking toward Sanananda from E, 1st Bn of 127th Inf makes negligible progress along coastal road.

IRAQ—Declares war on Germany, Italy, and Japan.

LIBYA—Br Eighth Army, having passed through enemy's main positions at Buerat, pushes energetically toward Tripoli, coastal force reaching Churgia and enveloping force crossing Wadi Zem Zem.

USSR—Soviet forces of Voronezh front, having opened offensive S of Voronezh several days earlier, are W of the Don at Rossosh, on Voronezh-Rostov RR, where Italian forces are routed. On Stalingrad front, progress is being made in reduction of trapped German 6th Army.

GERMANY—RAF bombers attack Berlin, night 16-17, using target-indicator bombs for first time. This is the first raid on Berlin since 7 November 1941.

17 January

GUADALCANAL—8th Marines, 2d Mar Div, upon clearing ravine W of Hills 80 and St and moving forward to positions abreast 6th Marines, withdraws from line to perimeter defense. Coastal attack, which has gained almost a mile beyond Pt Cruz since 13th, is to be continued by 182d Inf on left and 6th Marines on right. 182d Inf (less 3d Bn) moves into CAM Div line. After ineffective broadcast calling for Gifu garrison to surrender, 2d Bn of 35th Inf, 25th Div, pulls back while 2 ½-hour arty concentration is placed on the strongpoint, then returns to previous positions. Since darkness is approaching rapidly, ground attack is withheld. 27th Inf, 25th Div, which is to conduct holding action during corps' coming offensive while 161st Inf makes main effort, begins forward movement. Co C, with light MG section attached, takes up positions on ridge SW of Hill 66, called Snake.

NEW GUINEA—Advance elements of Aus 17th Brig are flown to Wan. Brig M. J. Moten, CG Aus 17th Brig, takes command of Kanga Force. Aus 18th Brig continues to clear coastal region between Wye Pt and Giruwa. Sanananda Village and Pt are overrun, but enemy retains positions W and S of Sanananda and in outskirts of Giruwa. On Soputa-Sanananda road, 163d Inf probes enemy defenses N of Fisk. 127th Inf, replacing 1st Bn with 2d, continues W along coastal road toward Giruwa, handicapped by extremely difficult and skillfully defended terrain. 3d Bn pushes S along Konombi Creek and encounters enemy outpost.

LIBYA—Br Eighth Army pursues enemy W toward Tripoli, hampered by desert terrain as well as mines and demolitions. Coastal forces reach positions 10 miles from Misurata. S column reaches Beni Ulid.

ALGERIA—U.S. II Corps' TF SATIN moves forward in preparation for drive on Sfax, but the operation is canceled.

USSR—Red Army extends its hold on Voronezh-Rostov RR with capture of Millerovo.

18 January

GUADALCANAL—Americans gain continuous line from Hill 53 northward to coast at point some 1,500 yards W of Pt Cruz. CAM Div continues W on N flank of XIV Corps with 6th Marines on right and 182d Inf on left. In 25th Div sector, 2d Bn of 35th Inf throws tight cordon about the Gifu and begins attack on it from NW.

NEW GUINEA—Japanese, although facing certain defeat, continue to offer last-ditch resistance on Sanananda front. Australians are stubbornly opposed near Sanananda and Giruwa. 163d Inf works on formidable bunker positions astride Soputa-

Sanananda road N of Fisk. 127th Inf, with Cos G and F in the lead, continues W along coast against weakening resistance and gains 300 yards.

BURMA—Ind 47th Brig opens attack on Japanese positions at Donbaik but can make little headway. Ind 123d Brig remains near Rathedaung but is threatened from the E as Japanese in Kaladan Valley skirmish in Kyauktaw area with elements protecting flank.

LIBYA—Br Eighth Army continues to pursue enemy toward Tripoli but loses contact because of terrain and obstacles. Gen Montgomery orders pursuit accelerated and continued day and night.

TUNISIA—Col Gen Jurgen von Arnim, NEW Axis commander in Tunisia, opens offensive to restore Tunis bridgehead line by recovering ground lost to French on 12-13 January and then seizing control of passes W of Kairouan.

On Br First Army front, 6th Armd Div of 5 Corps contains tank-infantry thrust down Bou Arada Valley at junction of Br and Fr sectors. Main enemy attack, in which the NEW Mark VI "Tiger" tank participates, forces Fr 19th Corps back on N flank and reaches road leading SW to Rebaa Oulad Yahia. U.S. 1st Armd Div (–) is placed under U.S. II Corps command.

USSR—Soviet forces of Leningrad and Volkhov Fronts have reopened land communications with Leningrad, isolated since fall of 1941, and hold corridor 10 miles wide to it in region S of Lake Ladoga. In the Caucasus, Red Army troops along the Manych take Divnoe while Soviet units along the Kuban overrun Cherkessk.

19 January

GUADALCANAL—182d Inf, On CAM Div left, has gained slightly more than 1,000 yards since entering line on 17th, but gap exists between it and 6th Marines. 147th Inf, upon relief at Koh Pt by Americal Rcn Sq, moves to Pt Cruz area. Japanese in the Gifu strongpoint are beginning to weaken under blows of 2d Bn of 35th Inf, 25th Div.

NEW GUINEA—Gen Yamagata withdraws from Sanananda front by launch after issuing orders for general withdrawal westward through Allied lines on 20th. Gen Oda and Col Kiyomi Yazawa are killed while trying to escape after nightfall. Australians reduce enemy position immediately S of Sanananda but are still held up along coast W of Sanananda and in outskirts of Giruwa. Japanese along Soputa-Sanananda road, now compressed into 3 pockets, withstand intensified efforts of 163d Inf to dislodge them. 127th Inf advances steadily westward along coast toward Giruwa.

BURMA—Ind 47th Brig continues attack on Donbaik but is unable to reduce enemy positions.

LIBYA—Continuing toward Tripoli, Br Eighth Army regains contact with enemy. Coastal force reaches Homs while column on left presses toward Tarhuna. 22d Armd Brig, in reserve at Zliten, prepares to drive through 51st Div—the coastal force.

TUNISIA—As German offensive continues to press Fr 19th Corps back toward Rebaa Oulad Yahia, Br First Army refuses its S flank to conform with Fr withdrawal. Br and U.S. reinforcements are sent forward, to come under Fr command upon arrival: 36th Brig Gp of Br 8th Div is given mission of interdicting road to Rebaa; CCB, U.S. 1st Armd Div, moves N from Sbeïtla to Maktar, night 19-20.

USSR—Soviet troops seize rail junction of Valuiki, NE of Kharkov, and Kamensk, N of Rostov on rail line to Voronezh.

20 January

CHILE—Severs relations with Germany, Italy, and Japan.

GUADALCANAL—3d Bn of 147th Inf (less Co I and plus Co C) begins moving into CAM Div line between 6th Marines and 182d Inf. Div attack halts to await completion of this move. Gen Collins issues orders to 25th Div for offensive on 22d. 161st Inf, upon assembling in S part of Galloping Horse, moves 2d Bn forward to Hill X, SW of Galloping Horse. 1st Bn of 27th Inf patrols toward Hill 87, meeting enemy fire upon approaching it. 2d Bn, 35th Inf, continues reduction of the Gifu.

NEW GUINEA—Aus 18th Brig continues to clear coastal region W of Sanananda, N part of Soputa-Sanananda road, and outskirts of Giruwa. 163d Inf battles the 3 pockets astride Soputa-Sanananda road. 127th Inf drives W along coast to within sight of Giruwa.

LIBYA—Br Eighth Army presses more slowly westward toward Homs-Tarhuna area as enemy resistance stiffens.

TUNISIA—Enemy continues down Rebaa Valley to Rebaa Oulad Yahia; upon gaining entrance to Ousseltia Valley, which parallels Rebaa Valley, shifts main weight of attack there and reaches Ousseltia. Many Fr 19th Corps troops are isolated in mountains to E. Gen Alphonse Juin places CCB, U.S. 1st Armd Div, under command of Gen Louis-Marie Koeltz, CG Fr 19th Corps, who orders it to Ousseltia Valley. Gen Eisenhower, having decided against Operation SATIN by U.S. II Corps, issues directive prescribing that S flank remain on the defensive and that as much as possible of II Corps be held in mobile reserve.

USSR—Troops of Gen Yeremenko's South Front (previously called Stalingrad Front) capture Proletarskaya, an Stalingrad-Novorossisk RR; some elements then force the Manych while others proceed toward mouth of the Donets.

21 January

GUADALCANAL—XIV Corps completes preparations for offensive on 22d. 2d Bn of 161st Inf, 25th Div, advances to Hill Y, SW of Hill X, where opposition is negligible. 3d Bn, 27th Inf, moves forward to Snake to follow 1st Bn—main assault force—turning over position on Hill 57 to 2d Bn. Action against the Gifu is continued by 2d Bn, 35th Inf.

NEW GUINEA—Aus and U.S. troops effect junctions along coast E of Sanananda and on Soputa-Sanananda road. 127th Inf column drives through Giruwa virtually unopposed to join Australians just W of the village. In afternoon AUS 2/9th and 2/10th Bns launch 3-pronged attack on enemy positions along coast W of Sanananda and clear all except small pocket. Aus 2/12th Bn, clearing southward along Soputa-Sanananda road from Sanananda Village, makes contact with 2d Bn of 163d Inf. 163d reduces 2 of the 3 pockets on Soputa-Sanananda road and in the course of the day kills more than 500 Japanese.

LIBYA—Br Eighth Army continues to press W toward Tripoli, 51st Div overcoming resistance in Corradini area. Learning that enemy has strengthened Tarhuna at expense of Horns front, Gen Montgomery decides to make main effort along coast.

TUNISIA—Gen Eisenhower gives Gen K. A. N. Anderson, CG Br First Army, responsibility for coordinating operations of Br, Fr, and U.S. forces. Maj Gen Laurence S. Kuter, USAAF, is assigned to Gen K. A. N. Anderson's hq as executive air commander with mission of co-ordinating air action. CCB, U.S. 1st Armd Div, with strong arty and air support, begins attack in late afternoon to drive enemy back in Ousseltia Valley and makes considerable progress until halted by darkness.

USSR—Voroshilovsk, E of Armavir, falls to Red Army.

U.K.—CCS directive regarding bomber operations from U.K. relieves VIII Bomber Command to a large extent of necessity of supporting N African operations.

22 January

GUADALCANAL—XIV Corps Opens final offensive toward the Poha R at 0630. Assault troops are supported by arty, air, and naval gunfire. CAM Div pushes W toward heights SE of Kokumbona (Hills 99 and 98) with elements of 3 regts in assault. 6th Marines, advancing along coast, is stopped by enemy fire from ravine W of Hill 94. 147th Inf in center and 182d on left are hampered more by terrain than by enemy. 147th Inf seizes Hill 95. 182d Inf makes contact with 27th Inf of 25th Div N of Hill 88. On corps S flank, 25th Div attacks toward Hill 87. 1st Bn, 27th Inf, with role of conducting holding action while 2d Bn, 161st Inf, envelops enemy's S flank, moves forward from Snake and quickly takes Hill 87, day's objective, from which enemy has withdrawn; continuing attack, also seizes Hills 88 and 89 by 1035. To exploit this advantage, div boundary is altered and 27th Inf is ordered to continue as rapidly as possible toward Kokumbona. By 1700, 27th Inf holds heights just E and S of Kokumbona (Hills 90 and 98). 2d Bn, 161st Inf, the enveloping force, advances slowly through jungle from Hill Y to Hill 87. 2d Bn, 35th Inf, assisted by a tank, forces 200-yard gap in N part of the Gifu strongpoint; repels final enemy counterattack, night 22-23.

NEW GUINEA—Papua Campaign ends in decisive defeat of Japanese. This is the first victory of the war against Japanese on land. Organized resistance on Sanananda front collapses as Aus 18th Brig eliminates last small pocket on coast W of Sanananda and 163d Inf finishes clearing Soputa-Sanananda road. Cost to each side has been heavy. Of the estimated force of 16,000 committed by enemy in Papua, about 7,000 are buried by Allied forces; prisoners, for the large part Korean and Chinese, total some 350. Aus troops sustain approximately 5,700 casualties and U.S. forces 2,788. Battle-weary 126th Inf is withdrawn from zone of combat.

LIBYA—Passing through 51st Div of Br Eighth Army, 22d Armd Brig continues coastal drive on Tripoli, reaching positions beyond Castelverde, while S column advances to within 17 miles of Tripoli.

TUNISIA—Allied attack to clear Ousseltia Valley is halted by strong opposition.

USSR—Soviet forces of Voronezh Front open assault on Voronezh. Troops of South Front overrun Salsk, on Stalingrad-Novorossisk rail line at its junction with line to Rostov. German 6th Army remains under attack at Stalingrad; Berlin admits Soviet penetration of positions from W.

23 January

INTERNATIONAL CONFERENCES—Casablanca Conference to determine strategy for 1943 ends, conferees having agreed: to continue assault against Germany, upon completion of Tunisian campaign, with conquest of Sicily (HUSKY) in July or possibly June of 1943; to give high priority to a combined bomber offensive against the European continent from the U.K.; to advance toward the Philippines through Central and SW Pacific; to build up U.S.

air forces in CBI and mount ANAKIM In fall of 1943, diverting U.S. landing craft and naval forces from the Pacific to assist; and to terminate hostilities only upon "unconditional surrender" of enemy.

GUADALCANAL—XIV Corps makes substantial progress, overrunning Kokumbona and pocketing enemy remaining E of the Poha in ravine E of Hill 99, between CAM and 25th Divs. Continuing W in coastal sector, CAM Div reaches Hill 91 on S and to N takes Hill 92. In 25th Div zone, 27th Inf's 3d Bn drives N to coast, taking Hills 98 and 99; 1st Bn seizes Kokumbona in 2-pronged attack; 2d Bn, on S flank, pushes NW to Hill 100. 2d Bn, 35th Inf, meets only slight resistance as it finishes clearing the Gifu, ending all Japanese resistance on Mt Austen.

LIBYA—Br Eighth Army columns drive into Tripoli from E and S and secure the port.

TUNISIA—Fr 19th Corps, helped by Br and U.S. units, stabilizes positions on general line Bou Arada-Djebel Bargou-Djebel Bou Dabouss. Enemy breaks off attack and consolidates newly won positions. Elements of U.S. 1st Div join CCB, U.S. 1st Armd Div, and are temporarily attached to CCB in preparation for attack on 24th to recover Kairouan Pass. Isolated Fr forces in hills E of Ousseltia Valley withdraw to positions S of Ousseltia covered by CCB, U.S. 1st Armd Div. U.S. II Corps constitutes CCC, U.S. 1st Armd Div, and gives it task of raiding Sened Station.

USSR—Red Army troops penetrate into Voronezh and begin clearing the town. Armavir, on Baku-Rostov RR, falls to other Soviet forces.

24 January

ALEUTIAN IS.—Enemy begins series of minor air raids on Amchitka.

GUADALCANAL—Continuing W in coastal sector, CAM Div reaches Hills 98 and 99 and gains contact with 25th Div. 25th Div, upon being resupplied, begins drive toward the Poha. 2d Bn, 27th Inf, attacks W from Kokumbona at 1300 and reaches Hill 102 on right and 103 on left.

TUNISIA—Implementing order of 21st for Gen K. A. N. Anderson to co-ordinate efforts of the 3 Allied nations, U.S. II Corps is attached to Br First Army. Gen Juin agrees to place Fr 19th Corps under Br First Army upon approval by Gen Giraud. Gen K. A. N. Anderson subsequently directs U.S. II Corps to take command of all ground troops S of line Morsott-Thala-Sbiba (all exclusive) -Djebel Trozza-Fondouk-Sidi Amor el Kenani (all inclusive), and N of line from the salt marshes (chotts) to Gabés. Full-scale Allied assault northward in Ousseltia Valley is canceled. Germans order attack on Faïd Pass as soon as possible. CCC of U.S. 1st Armd Div, U.S. II Corps, moving forward from Gafsa, conducts successful raid on Sened Station and retires to Gafsa as planned.

25 January

GUADALCANAL—XIV Corps, in FO 2, directs CAM Div to pass through 25th Div at Poha R and pursue enemy, now in full retreat. 25th Div, continuing advance with 2d and 3d Bns of 27th Inf, upon relief of 3d by 6th Marines on Hills 98 and 99, reaches the Poha on right and secures Hills 105 and 106 on left. 161st Inf protects corps S flank.

NEW GUINEA—Maj Gen Horace H. Fuller, CG first Div, takes operational control of all Allied troops in Oro Bay-Gona area. Aus 7th Div and U.S. 32d Div troops are relieved gradually during January and flown to Port Moresby; from there they are moved to Australia by sea.

LIBYA—Br Eighth Army, employing 7th Armd Div in pursuit of enemy to Tunisia, reaches Zavia.

TUNISIA—Gen K. A. N. Anderson, CG Br First Army, becomes responsible for all Allied forces in Tunisia as Gen Giraud agrees to place Fr 19th Corps under his command. Benito Mussolini designates Gen Giovanni Messe to succeed Field Marshal Rommel, commander of *German-Italian Panzer Army*, who is to be withdrawn because of protracted service and ill health, but the shift does not take place for some time. In Fr 19th Corps sector, CCB of U.S. 1st Armd Div and elements of U.S. 1st Inf Div, under command of Col Stark, CO RCT 26, begin clearing rear-guard resistance from Ousseltia Valley.

USSR—Red Army completes capture of Voronezh.

26 January

GUADALCANAL—25th Div, after 2d and 3d Bns of 27th Inf establish contact and are passed through at Poha R line by CAM Div, is withdrawn to guard airfields since there are indications of an enemy attempt to recover Lunga perimeter. 161st Inf, its mission unchanged, passes to control of XIV Corps. CAM Div, with 6th Marines and 182d Inf abreast, former on right, pushes forward from the Poha about 1,000 yards against light resistance.

TUNISIA—Fr 19th Corps attacks to regain Kairouan Pass in Ousseltia Valley.

USSR—Russians report substantial gains against German pocket at Stalingrad, where defenses have been penetrated.

27 January

GUADALCANAL—CAM Div, in 2,000-yard advance, reaches Nueha R.

BURMA—Royal Ind Navy launch sinks large Japanese launch loaded with Japanese troops in Mayu R.

LIBYA—Br Eighth Army's 7th Armd Div continues to pursue enemy toward Tunisia and meets stiffening resistance near Zuara.

GERMANY—U.S. Eighth Air Force makes first air attack on Germany, bombing docks at Wilhelmshaven.

28 January

GUADALCANAL—CAM Div continues W from Nueha R, eliminating sniper nests.

NEW GUINEA—Japanese make their last attempt at an overland drive on Port Moresby, striking at Wau where Australians of Kanga Force offer lively delaying opposition until rest of Aus 17th Brig can be flown in during next few days.

CHINA—T. V. Soong, Gen Chen Cheng, and Gen Stilwell reach agreement upon program to train and equip 30-division Chinese force in Yunnan.

TUNISIA—Fr 19th Corps continues to clear Ousseltia Valley, gaining control of W exit and half the length of Kairouan Pass. CCB, U.S. 1st Armd Div, is detached from corps; during night 28-29, moves to Bou Chebka. RCT 26 (less one bn) of U.S. 1st Div, ordered to Sbeïtla, breaks off action with enemy in afternoon. U.S. units remaining with French in Ousseltia Valley are 2d Bn, 26th Inf; 1st and 3d Bns of 16th Inf; 7th FA Bn; battery of 33d FA Bn; TD co; and bn of engrs. U.S. 1st Div (−RCT's 16, 18, 26) begins move from Guelma (Algeria) into Fr 19th Corps sector.

USSR—Soviet forces seize Kasternoe, rail junction between Voronezh and Kursk.

29 January

GUADALCANAL—CG XIV Corps detaches 147th Inf from CAM Div. 147th, reinf by pack howitzers of 2d Bn, 10th Marines, and Battery A of 9th FA Bn, under command of Brig Gen Alphonse De Carre, is ordered to pass through 6th Marines and continue drive along coast to Cape Esperance. 182d Inf reverts to control of Americal Div.

TUNISIA—U.S. 1st Div (−) is placed under command of Fr 19th Corps to help defend Ousseltia Valley. CCB, U.S. 1st Armd Div, reverts to U.S. II Corps.

USSR—Kropotkin, on Baku-Rostov rail line, falls to Soviet forces.

30 January

GUADALCANAL—147th Inf takes up pursuit of enemy westward. 1st Bn, on beach, reaches Bonegi R mouth but pulls back under fire from W bank; 3d Bn, on left, is halted by enemy 1,000 yards E of the Bonegi.

NEW GUINEA—Aus Kanga Force, which is being reinf by air, decisively defeats Japanese at Wau and forces them to begin retreating.

TUNISIA—In Br First Army area, Germans attack Faïd Pass and overrun it, forcing French back to Sidi Bou Zid. U.S. II Corps sends CCA, 1st Armd Div, from Sbeïtla area to help defend Faïd, but the combat command arrives too late. CCC starts NE from Gafsa toward Sidi Bou Zid-Maknassy road. CCD, with 1st Bn of RCT 168, U.S. 34th Div, attached, moves toward Maknassy. RCT 168 is concentrating in Tébessa area.

USSR—Rail junction of Tikhoretsk, S of Rostov, falls to Red Army, cutting main line of retreat of German *Army Group A* from Novorossisk area. Other Soviet forces regain oil center of Maikop. German *Army Group Don* is no longer an effective fighting body, having become separated from *Army Group A* during northward withdrawal.

GERMANY—RAF Mosquitoes make daylight attack on Berlin during celebration of tenth anniversary of Hitler's assumption of power.

31 January

GUADALCANAL—147th Inf, with arty and naval gunfire support, attempts to cross the Bonegi. Stiff resistance at river mouth prevents 1st Bn from crossing, but 3d Bn crosses about 2,500 yards inland from Tassafaronga Pt. Small party from 147th Inf sails from Beaufort Bay to Lavoro to outpost Titi area in preparation for landing by 2d Bn of 132d Inf, reinf, Americal Div; 6 of the party go ashore and suggest by radio that landing be made at Nugu Pt. 2d Bn of 132d Inf sails from Kukum for Nugu Pt at 1800. 2d and 8th Marines, 2d Mar Div, sail from Guadalcanal for New Zealand.

NEW GUINEA—Australians place arty fire on enemy in Wau area with good effect.

LIBYA—7th Armd Div of Br Eighth Army finishes clearing Zuara, near Tunisian border.

TUNISIA—Fr 19th Corps troops, Br First Army, are being withdrawn for rest and rehabilitation. U.S. 1st Div takes control of Ousseltia Valley area. In Rebaa Valley, 36th Brig of Br 78th Div repels tank-infantry attacks near Sidi Said, N of Rebaa Oulad Yahia, destroying 5 tanks of which 2 are Tigers. In U.S. II Corps area, CCA of 1st Armd Div begins action to regain Faïd Pass, but attack fails; CCC, continuing toward Eastern Dorsal, is ordered to join CCD in effort against Maknassy; CCD moves from Gafsa with task of seizing Sened Station and then reducing enemy positions near

Maknassy, but is subjected to demoralizing air attack and cannot be formed for assault.

MIDDLE EAST—Gen Brereton becomes commander of USAFIME, succeeding Gen Andrews, who is to command U.S. forces in ETO.

1 February

GUADALCANAL—Command of western pursuit passes from Gen De Carre to Gen Sebree. 1st Bn of 147th Inf, assisted by arty and naval gunfire, again attempts unsuccessfully to cross Bonegi R mouth but forces enemy rear guards from E bank. 2d Bn of 132d Inf, Americal Div, makes unopposed landing at Verahue, to rear of enemy in Cape Esperance area. During night 1-2, Japanese begin evacuation of forces by sea from Cape Esperance.

NEW GUINEA—Co G of 163d Inf, U.S. 41st Div, starts NW along coast toward Kumusi R mouth.

CBI—Generals Arnold and Somervell and Field Marshal Sir John Dill open conferences in New Delhi with Field Marshal Wavell and Gen Stilwell to prepare detailed plans for ANAKIM for submission to Chiang Kai-shek. During the conferences agreement is reached upon a series of operations, ultimate objective of which is to recapture Burma in order to attack Japan from China. Main effort would begin in November 1943,

BURMA—Ind 55th Brig, which has relieved Ind 47th Brig, attacks enemy's Donbaik positions but is no more successful than 47th had been: Of 6 supporting tanks, 2 are knocked out by AT fire and 2 others are abandoned.

TUNISIA—In Br First Army's U.S. II Corps area, CCA of 1st Armd Div continues attack toward Faïd Pass after very heavy arty preparation but makes little progress. Fr units and CCA then organize defense positions and remain in place to await reinforcements. Br First Army cancels projected attack on Maknassy because of enemy threat W of Kairouan. II Corps, protecting right flank of Allied forces, is to employ CCC and CCD of 1st Armd Div as mobile reserve near Sbeïtla, although CCD is to secure more favorable defense position 3-4 miles E of Sened Station first. Brig Gen Ray E. Porter is to command CCD temporarily, relieving Col Robert V. Maraist. CCD, reinf by 1st Bn of 168th Inf, 34th Div, attacks and captures Sened Station. CCC, almost through Maizila Pass, N of Maknassy, withdraws to Sbeïtla and thence to Hadjeb el Aïoun.

USSR—Red Army captures Svatovo, SE of Kharkov, cutting rail line from Kharkov to Donets basin.

2 February

GUADALCANAL—1st Bn, 147th Inf, succeeds in crossing Bonegi R at its mouth and makes contact with 3d Bn S of Tassafaronga Pt. 2d Bn of 132d Inf, Americal Div, begins advance northward along coast from Verahue, main body reaching Titi.

TUNISIA—In Br First Army's U.S. II Corps area, 1st Armd Div hq opens at Sbeïtla; CCD drives to ridge E of Sened, where it digs in and repels counterattack.

USSR—Final resistance of German 6th Army at Stalingrad ends, concluding epic struggle that has turned the tide against the Axis. Action in other sectors is unabated as Red Army endeavors to drive enemy as tar W as possible before spring thaw sets in. Immediate objectives are key positions of Rostov, Kharkov, and Kursk.

3 February

GUADALCANAL—147th Inf establishes line extending S from Tassafaronga Pt and patrols to Umasani R. 2d Bn, 132d Inf, patrols northward toward Cape Esperance as far as Kamimbo Bay.

NEW GUINEA—After heavy arty preparation, Kanga Force counterattacks from Wau to drive enemy back to Mubo and makes steady progress.

BURMA—On Arakan front, Ind 123d Brig unsuccessfully attacks Rathedaung.

TUNISIA—In Br First Army's U.S. II Corps area, CCD of 1st Armd Div continues attack toward Maknassy until directed to withdraw; disengages and withdraws through Gafsa toward Bou Chebka, where it passes into corps reserve. CCB arrives at Maktar and is held in Br First Army reserve. 1st Armd Div (−) defends region from Fondouk Gap to Maizila Pass, CCC covering N sector from point N of Djebel Trozza to vicinity of Sidi Bou Zid and CCA covering area to S as far as Djebel Meloussi. First Rcn Bn is held in 1st Armd Div reserve at Sbeïtla.

USSR—Continuing toward Rostov, Soviet forces take rail junction of Kushchevkaya. Other Red Army troops seize Kupyansk rail junction, SE of Kharkov. Still others cut rail line between Kursk and Orel.

4 February

GUADALCANAL—147th Inf advances about 1,000 yards westward toward the Umasani against minor opposition. Concentration of 2d Bn, 132d Inf, with its arty, transport, and supplies at Titi is completed. Japanese withdraw additional forces by sea from Cape Esperance under cover of darkness.

NEW GUINEA—Japanese, harassed by aircraft, begin retreating in disorder from Wau area. Pro-

[5-9 FEBRUARY 1942]

longed period of intensive patrolling ensues as Kanga Force attempts to intercept and destroy enemy groups, remnants of which eventually reach Mubo.

TUNISIA—Br Eighth Army has completed the conquest of Tripolitania and crossed into Tunisia, where Rommel is hastily preparing for stand at Mareth Line. Enemy rear guards are imposing maximum delay as British approach Mareth.

ALGERIA—Hq, North African Theater of Operations (NATOUSA) is established as a separate command under Gen Eisenhower at Algiers. ETO boundary is altered to give Spain, Italy, and several Mediterranean islands to NATOUSA. Gen Andrews becomes head of ETOUSA.

USSR—Red Army spearheads continue to close in rapidly on Rostov, Kharkov, and Kursk. Soviet commandos land on Black Sea coast near Novorossisk and are being engaged by German *Army Group A*, which is almost isolated in Novorossisk-Krasnodar region.

5 February

GUADALCANAL—147th Inf activity is limited to patrolling. No organized enemy forces are found E of the Umasani. 2d Bn, 132d Inf, patrols northward from Titi.

TUNISIA—In Br First Army area, 2d Bn of RCT 16, Fr 19th Corps, joins U.S. 1st Div, to which it reverts from attachment to 36th Brig of Br 78th Div.

USSR—St Oskol, on rail line SE of Kursk, falls to Soviet troops, as does Izyum, on rail line SE of Kharkov.

6 February

GUADALCANAL—161st Inf, 25th Div, passes through 147th Inf to continue pursuit of enemy (3d Bn moving along beach and 2d Bn to S) and reaches Umasani R; patrols cross the river. 147th Inf, which moves to rear, is brought to full strength with arrival of 2d Bn from Fiji Is.

NEW GUINEA—Japanese planes make belated and unsuccessful attack on Wau airdrome. In air battles during day, 24 enemy planes are destroyed and many more damaged. No Allied planes are lost.

TUNISIA—In Br First Army area, U.S. 34th Div (− RCT 168) is attached to Fr 19th Corps.

USSR—On southern front, one Soviet spearhead is about 5 miles S of Rostov; another takes Yeisk, on Sea of Azov, completing isolation of German *Army Group A* in triangle Yeisk-Krasnodar-Novorossisk. Deepening salient in the Ukraine below Kharkov, Soviet forces take Lisichansk, on the Donets.

[91]

7 February

GUADALCANAL—161st Inf, 25th Div, crosses Umasani R and advances NW to Bunina Pt; patrols reach Tambalego R. Moving forward from Titi, 2d Bn of 132d Inf, Americal Div, arrives at Marovovo. Night 7-8, Japanese destroyers make final run down the Slot to Cape Esperance to evacuate troops.

CHINA—Generalissimo Chiang Kai-shek, in letter to President Roosevelt, presents enlarged version of the 3 demands and agrees to take part in Burma offensive.

TUNISIA—In Br First Army area, 1st Ranger Bn arrives at Gafsa by air and is attached to U.S. II Corps. RCT 168 (− 1st Bn), 34th Div, is attached to 1st Armd Div.

USSR—Continuing toward Rostov, Soviet troops take Azov, on Sea of Azov. In the Ukraine, Kramatorsk, SE of Kharkov, falls to Red Army. Russians cut main highway between Kursk and Orel.

8 February

GUADALCANAL—161st Inf, 25th Div, overcomes light delaying opposition at the Tambalego and proceeds to Doma Cove. Pushing northward from Marovovo, 2d Bn of 132d Inf, Americal Div, reaches Kamimbo Bay.

AUSTRALIA—162d Inf, U.S. 41st Div, sails for New Guinea.

BURMA—Ind 77th Brig (called Chindits) under Brig Orde Charles Wingate begins guerrilla warfare program behind enemy lines: entering Burma through 4 Corps front, Chindits advance in 7 columns toward Mandalay-Myitkyina railway line.

TUNISIA—In Br First Army's U.S. II Corps area, enemy orders attack against Gafsa area with primary purpose of destroying allied forces. 1st Div's RCT 26 (− 2d and 3d Bns) is released by CCA, 1st Armd Div, to corps and moves from Sidi Bou Zid to Fériana.

USSR—Soviet columns converge on Kursk and overrun this important enemy base.

9 February

GUADALCANAL—Organized resistance on Guadalcanal ceases at 1625 with junction of 1st Bn of 161st Inf, 25th Div, and 2d Bn of 132d Inf, Americal Div, at village of Tenaro. About 13,000 Japanese (12,000 from *17th Army* and the rest naval personnel) have made good their escape to Buin and Rabaul.

TUNISIA—Kesselring, Rommel, and von Arnim modify attack plan because Americans are withdrawing from Gafsa; von Arnim is to attack Sidi

Bou Zid; Gafsa area is to be attacked later by 2 forces under Rommel's command.

USSR—Soviet troops capture Belgorod, rail junction on Kursk-Kharkov line.

10 February

NEW GUINEA—Co G of 163d Inf, U.S. 41st Div, reaches Kumusi R mouth and establishes defense perimeter.

TUNISIA—In Br First Army area, U.S. II Corps assigns 1st Armd Div responsibility for containing Axis forces at Faïd.

In Br Eighth Army area, heavy rainfall delays operations against Ben Gardane, main outpost of enemy's Mareth positions.

USSR—N of Rostov, Soviet forces cut Novocherkassk-Rostov rail line. Red Army columns converging on Kharkov take Chuguev and Volchansk.

11 February

TUNISIA—In Br First Army area, RCT 135 of U.S. 34th Div, Fr 19th Corps, begins relief of French in Pichon-Maison des Eaux region. In Djebel Rihana area, 2d Bn of RCT 26 is relieved by 2d Bn of RCT 16 and becomes U.S. 1st Div reserve. Gen Fredendall, CG U.S. II Corps, issues directive on defense of Faïd position.

USSR—S of Kharkov, Germans are forced from RR junction of Lozovaya.

12 February

SWPA—GHQ issues draft "Plans for the Seizure and Occupation of the New Britain-New Guinea-New Ireland Area," coded ELKTON.

TUNISIA—Br First Army, which has been strengthened by arrival of 46th Div during first week of February, receives orders for reorganization. Shifts are scheduled to begin on 15th.

USSR—Soviet forces take Krasnodar rail center on the Kuban and are pressing W toward Novorossisk. German escape corridor from Rostov is narrowed as Red Army troops cut main RR extending NW from Rostov at Krasnoarmeisk. Shakhty, on Rostov-Voronezh line, also falls to Russians.

13 February

TUNISIA—CinC Allied Force visits U.S. II Corps area to review disposition of forces, since an enemy attack is imminent. Axis commanders meet to review attack plans.

USSR—Germans are containing Soviet attacks toward Novorossisk, last enemy stronghold remaining in NW Caucasus. Red Army gains complete control of Rostov-Voronezh rail line with capture of Novocherkassk and Likhaya.

14 February

TUNISIA—In Br First Army's U.S. II Corps area, enemy begins strong westward push at dawn with tanks and infantry supported by arty and dive bombers. CCA, 1st Armd Div, is forced to fall back toward Sbeïtla from positions E of Sidi Bou Zid. Elements of CCA and attached 168th Inf are isolated on Djebel Lessouda, NE of Sidi Bou Zid, and on Djebel Ksaira and Garet Hadid in region SE of Sidi Bou Zid. To assist CCA, which suffers heavy tank losses, CCC, reinf by 2d Bn of 1st Armd Regt of CCB, is released by corps for counterattack on Sidi Bou Zid on 15th. Because of loss of Sidi Bou Zid on N flank of corps, Fr and U.S. forces (U.S. being 3d Bn of RCT 26, 1st Div, and 1st Ranger Bn) withdraw from Gafsa to Fériana, night 14–15

USSR—Red Army occupies Rostov, key communication center through which Germans have been extricating their forces from the Caucasus. Voroshilovgrad, already bypassed by Soviet thrust toward Stalino, also falls. Germans reorganize forces. *Army Group South* (formerly *Don*) takes control of remnants of Army Groups Don and B. 2d Army transfers to *Army Group Center. Army Group A* retains Kuban bridgehead in Novorossisk area.

15 February

NW AFRICA—Gen Alexander, selected at Casablanca Conference to head all Allied forces in Tunisia, arrives at Algiers for conference at AFHQ.

TUNISIA—In Br First Army area, Gen K. A. N. Anderson, CG, orders forces holding high ground W of Faïd withdrawn and Kasserine Pass organized for defense. In U.S. II Corps area, Hq, SOS NATOUSA, is established under Brig Gen Thomas B. Larkin. 1st Armd Div's CCC counterattacks in Sidi Bou Zid area in effort to relieve encircled forces on hills, but is unable to accomplish its mission and falls back with heavy tank losses. Most of the U.S. force on Djebel Lessouda succeeds in escaping during night 15–16. While action at Sidi Bou Zid is in progress, Gen K. A. N. Anderson directs Gen Fredendall to withdraw all forces, after isolated troops have been extricated, to positions defending Sbeïtla, Kasserine, and Fériana. Axis forces, moving cautiously against Gafsa, discover that it has been evacuated. Fr 19th Corps is quietly and gradually moving right flank forces back to Shiba.

In Br Eighth Army area, improving weather conditions permit resumption of operations toward Mareth Line.

16 February

ALEUTIAN IS.—Japanese make their last nuisance raid on Amchitka as first Allied plane lands on new fighter strip there.

GUADALCANAL—In preparation for invasion of Russell Is.—Operation CLEANSLATE—first echelon of 43d Div assault force (RCT's 103 and 169) under 43d Div CG, Maj Gen John H. Hester, arrives at Guadalcanal.

SWPA—U.S. Sixth Army is established in SWPA under command of Lt Gen Walter Krueger. Army consists of I Corps (Gen Eichelberger), 2d Engr Special Brig, and 503d Para Inf Regt; 1st Mar Div is attached.

TUNISIA—Br First Army releases CCB, U.S. 1st Armd Div, to U.S. II Corps. RCT 18, U.S. 1st Div, is released by Br 5 Corps for movement to Shiba, where positions are being strengthened. In U.S. II Corps area, enemy, anticipating evacuation of Sbeïtla, which 1st Armd Div is too weak to hold as result of heavy losses at Sidi Bou Zid, begins drive on the town late in day; despite opposition of screening force, of 1st Armd Div between Sidi Bou Zid and Sbeïtla, arrives at outskirts of latter and is briskly engaged by CCA and CCB, CCB having arrived from Maktar, as withdrawal of Americans toward Western Dorsal begins. Because of unexpectedly sharp resistance, enemy breaks off attack for night. Isolated Americans on Djebel Ksaira and Garet Hadid, under attack throughout day, make unsuccessful attempt to withdraw, night 16-17, and are virtually wiped out. From Gafsa, Germans advance 25 miles NW toward Fériana and SW through Metlaoui to Tozeur.

In Br Eighth Army area, 7th Armd Div drives into Ben Gardane, Mareth Line outpost.

USSR—Soviet troops occupy Kharkov as Axis forces withdraw toward Poltava.

17 February

SOLOMON IS.—Small party of U.S. officers sails from Guadalcanal to Russell Is. to reconnoiter in preparation for invasion; goes ashore on Banika I. after dark.

CHINA—It is announced that Gen Chen will be CG Chinese Expeditionary Force.

BURMA—Ind 55th Brig again attempts to reduce enemy position at Donbaik, on Arakan front, but is unsuccessful.

MEDITERRANEAN—Mediterranean Air Command is constituted and activated by AFHQ under Air Chief Marshal Sir Arthur W. Tedder, with unified control over all Allied air forces based in Middle East, NW Africa, and Malta. Air Vice Marshal Sir Arthur Coningham assumes command of Allied Air Support Command (AASC). Pursuant to decision reached by CCS on 20 January, AFHQ issues directives to Gen Alexander, naming him Deputy CinC of Allied Forces in French North Africa and Commander of the Group of Armies (18 Army Group, combining numbers of Br First and Eighth Armies) operating in Tunisia, effective 20 February.

TUNISIA—In Br First Army area, Fr 19th Corps withdraws W to conform with withdrawal of U.S. II Corps. RCT 18, U.S. 1st Div, is attached to Br 6th Armd Div at Sbiba. U.S. II Corps falls back to Western Dorsal and stations troops to defend passes at Sbiba (Fr 19th Corps sector), Kasserine, Dernaïa, and El Ma el Abiod. Defensive positions are being organized. CCB covers withdrawal of 1st Armd Div from Sbeïtla. Germans enter Fériana and overcome rear-guard opposition; take Thélepte air base. 3d Bn of RCT 39, 9th Div, which has moved forward from Souk Ahras (Algeria) comes under corps command.

Br Eighth Army, with 51st Div and 7th Armd Div in assault, captures Médenine and its airfields.

USSR—Red Army takes Slavyansk, rail junction N of Kramatorsk.

18 February

ALEUTIAN IS.—Adm McMorris' strike force bombards Attu, but weather conditions prevent observation of results. This is the first time naval gunfire is employed against Attu.

SOLOMON IS.—Rear echelon of Russell Is. assault force from 43d Div lands on Guadalcanal. Russell Is. rcn party returns to Guadalcanal, night 18-19, after learning that Japanese have withdrawn from the islands.

INDIA—Gen Wheeler, charged with Ledo Road construction in late December, is given responsibility for defending the road.

BURMA—Ind 77th Brig (Chindits) crosses the Chindwin unopposed; subsequently reaches and cuts Mandalay-Myitkyina railway line without interference.

MEDITERRANEAN—Mediterranean Air Command (U.S. Ninth and Twelfth Air Forces; RAF EAC, ME, Malta, Gibraltar) begins functioning. Under Mediterranean Air Command, Northwest African Air Forces (NAAF), consisting of EAC and Twelfth Air Force, is activated under command of Gen Spaatz.

TUNISIA—In Br First Army area, U.S. II Corps continues organization of defenses at passes through

Western Dorsal as enemy action subsides to rcn. Enemy stages demonstration at E exit of Kasserine Pass in evening, alerting provisional U.S. defense force (19th Combat Engr Regt and elements of 26th Inf, 1st Div). Reinforcements are moved to the pass, among them 1st Bn of 39th Inf, 9th Div. During night 18-19, CO of 26th Inf takes responsibility for defense of the pass, relieving CO 19th Engrs. As a precautionary measure, 26th Armd Brig, Br 6th Armd Div, is sent to Thala, coming under corps control.

Br Eighth Army, continuing toward Mareth Line, takes Foum Tatahouine.

USSR—*II Corps* of German *16th Army* begins withdrawal on northern front.

19 February

SWPA—Naval elements of SWPA force are redesignated U.S. Seventh Fleet.

TUNISIA—Gen Alexander, upon visiting, the front, finds situation so serious he takes command of 18 Army Group At once, a day ahead of schedule. 18 Army Group comprises Br First and Eighth Armies, Fr 19th Corps, and U. S. II Corps. Br First Army retains command of the Fr and U.S. corps. Upon taking command, Gen Alexander orders Br, U.S., and Fr forces organized under separate commands and their respective commanders at once; the front held by static troops while armored and mobile forces are withdrawn as reserve striking force; plans made to regain the initiative.

In Br First Army area, Fr 19th Corps contains German tank-infantry attack on Sbiba Pass, where strong defense force (U.S. 34th Div (−), RCT 18 of U.S. 1st Div, elements of Br 6th Armd Div, and Fr units) is stationed. In U.S. II Corps area, enemy opens attack on Kasserine Pass with tanks and infantry, supported by arty, and succeeds in gaining positions within it but cannot drive defenders out. Some reinforcements are sent forward to bolster Allied positions. CCB, 1st Armd Div, is alerted for possible commitment.

USSR—Red Army reports progress S and SW of Kharkov and announces that Kharkov-Kursk RR and highway are cleared of enemy.

20 February

SOLOMON Is.—U.S. naval force under Adm Turner leaves Guadalcanal for Russell Is. with initial assault echelon of 43d Div.

TUNISIA—Axis forces are being reorganized. Gen Messe assumes command of Italian *First Army*; Rommel's *German-Italian Panzer Army* ceases to exist. Rommel remains in Tunisia, however, a few weeks longer.

18 Army Group: In Br First Army area, Fr 19th Corps repels another enemy attack against Sbiba, after which enemy in the area shifts from the offensive to aggressive defensive. U.S. 1st Div (−) moves to Bou Chebka and reverts to U.S. II Corps. In U.S. II Corps area, enemy breaks through Kasserine Pass and thrusts N toward Thala and W toward Tébessa. Br force of all arms, based on 26th Armd Brig of 6th Armd Div, under Brig C. G. G. Nicholson, is given responsibility, under II Corps control, for co-ordinating operations to check enemy and restore positions. Nicholson's force is to operate NE of Hatab R before Thala. CCB, 1st Armd Div, under command of Nicholson, and other troops operating S of the Hatab are to defend passes in Djebel el Hamra before Tébessa. Preparations are made for counterattack on 21st.

USSR—In region S and SW of Kharkov, Soviet forces take Pavlograd and Krasnograd.

21 February

SOLOMON Is.—U.S. 43d Div invasion force lands on 3 beaches in Russell Is., 2 of them on Banika I. and the other on Pavuvu I, without opposition. Initial landing force consists of 43d Div hq, BLT's 1 and 2 and of RCT 103, 43d Cav Rcn Tr, 3d Mar Raider Bn, 11th Mar Defense Bn detachment, and 43d Signal Co. LCT's bring rest of 43d Div, less RCT 172, from Guadalcanal to Russell Is. by end of February, at which time 9,000 men are ashore.

BURMA—During night 21-22, coastal craft of Royal Ind Navy land party at Nyebon, SE of Akyab; party successfully raids enemy positions and withdraws.

N AFRICA—Gen Spaatz takes control of Western Desert Air Force (WDAF).

TUNISIA—18 Army Group: Gen Alexander orders Gen Montgomery to apply pressure against enemy's S flank as diversion for Br First Army. In Br Eighth Army area, Gen Montgomery, who is now planning for assault on Mareth Line, is not yet ready for large-scale operations but decides to risk sending small forces forward along coast and to move Fr force under Gen Leclerc (called L Force), which has recently joined Br Eighth Army and driven from Nalut to Ksar Rhilane, northward from Ksar Rhilane.

In Br First Army area, Fr 19th Corps halts probing thrust toward Sbiba with assistance of newly arrived Churchill tanks. In U.S. II Corps area, strong enemy forces continue attack from Kasserine Pass toward Thala and are barely contained short of this objective after hard fighting. Nicholson's force defending Thala is augmented by 2 Hampshires and by 2 FA bns of U.S. 9th Div, latter arriving from W Algeria after 4-day forced march. Limited enemy thrust toward Tébessa is contained by CCB of 1st Armd Div, reinf by elements of RCT 16, 1st Div.

USSR—Enemy opens counteroffensive toward Kharkov from Stalino.

22 February

TUNISIA—18 Army Group: In Br First Army's U.S. II Corps area, enemy continues offensive until afternoon, when Rommel abandons effort to drive through to Le Kef and orders withdrawal. Attack is broken off and enemy starts back toward Kasserine Pass, leaving many mines behind. 1st Armd Div assumes command of Nicholson's force at Thala and of its own CCB.

USSR—On central front, Soviet forces open offensive in Orel-Bryansk area and renew efforts to take Rzhev.

23 February

TUNISIA—Rommel assumes command of German *Army Group, Africa*, as Axis forces continue reorganization.

18 Army Group: Gen Alexander informs Gen Montgomery that situation at Kasserine has improved and orders him not to take undue risks.

In Br First Army's U.S. II Corps area, final enemy forces withdraw into Kasserine Pass during morning, followed unaggressively by Allied forces. Enemy and Allied planes are active during day.

USSR—Sumy, in the Ukraine NW of Kharkov, falls to Red Army.

24 February

TUNISIA—18 Army Group: In Br First Army's U.S. II Corps area, CCB of 1st Armd Div and 26th Armd Brig of Br 6th Armd Div continue to follow withdrawing enemy. 1st Armd Div prepares to attack to recover Kasserine Pass; attached 16th Inf, 1st Div, is to lead off on 25th. RCT 26 (−2d and 3d Bns), reverting to 1st Div control, moves to El Ma el Abiod to defend pass.

In Br Eighth Army area, Gen Montgomery orders 7th Armd and 51st Inf Divs to maintain pressure on enemy along coast and on Gabès road, respectively.

25 February

SWPA-S PACIFIC—Rough draft of long-range plan for advance to the Philippines (RENO) is drawn up.

RUSSELL Is.—Torpedo boat base at Wernham Cove becomes operational.

TUNISIA—18 Army Group: In Br First Army area, U.S. II Corps, hampered only by mines and booby traps, recovers Kasserine Pass. 9th Div is concentrating in Tébessa area under corps command.

U.K.—RAF begins round-the-clock air offensive against enemy.

26 February

SWPA—All units of the U.S. Army in SWPA and all elements of the Philippine Army called into the service of the USA are assigned to USAFFE, which has been inactive since April 1942.

BURMA—Pipeline that is to parallel Ledo Road gets high priority from CCS. Royal Ind Navy launches sink enemy launch loaded with troops and damage another N of Ramree I.

TUNISIA—18 Army Group: In Br First Army's 5 Corps area, German *5th Panzer Army*, under von Arnim, opens offensive on broad front, threatening Bédja and Medjez el Bab. On N, attacks W of Jefna are contained. Br outpost at Sidi Nsir, on road from Mateur to Bédja, is overwhelmed after vigorous battle that gains time for 46th Div to concentrate for defense of pass to Bédja. Attack on Medjez itself is repulsed, but in region to S enemy makes deep penetration that is contained N of El Aroussa. 38th Brig contains attack N of Bou Arada, but is in an exposed position because of enemy's success to N. Gen K. A. N. Anderson, to strengthen defenses of Goubellat-Bou Arada region, forms provisional div, called Y, from 38th Brig and 1st Para Brig. In U.S. II Corps area, RCT 16 reverts to 1st Div, which assumes responsibility for Kasserine Pass and for maintaining contact with 34th Div, which comes under II Corps command. 1st Armd Div is assembling as reserve S of Tébessa.

In Br Eighth Army area, Gen Montgomery sets 20 March as D Day for attack on Mareth Line (PUGILIST); expects to have sufficient troops and supplies in forward area by 4 March. Because of enemy movements, Gen Alexander warns Gen Montgomery that enemy will attack as soon as possible.

27 February

NEW GUINEA—162d Inf, U.S. 41st Div, reaches Milne Bay.

TUNISIA—18 Army Group: In Br First Army's 5 Corps area, hard fighting continues around Bédja, but enemy is unable to advance. In U.S. II Corps area, 9th Div relieves 1st Div at El Ma el Abiod and Dernaa Pass, NW of Fériana, and 1st Div assembles E of Tébessa.

28 February

SWPA—GHQ revises ELKTON plan for drive on Rabaul.

NEW GUINEA—1st Bn of 168d Inf, U.S. 41st Div, having arrived at front and relieved elements of 163d in Sanananda-Killerton-Gona area and at Kumusi R mouth, starts N from Killerton by water, leapfrogging cos.

BURMA—Construction of road from Ledo, India, crosses Burmese border. In order to subdue Kachin guerrillas in N Burma, Japanese are moving one small force toward Sumprabum, Br outpost near Fort Hertz, and another toward Tanai R in Hukawng Valley.

TUNISIA—18 Army Group: In Br First Army area, S Corps continues to contain enemy attempts to advance on Bédja. In U.S. II Corps area, enemy has now retired to Eastern Dorsal, abandoning Sbeïtla and Fériana. II Corps patrols actively.

USSR—Determined German counterattacks in upper Donets are making progress and have overrun Kramatorsk and Lozovaya. Hard fighting continues in Orel-Bryansk sector. Spring thaw is hampering operations around Kuban bridgehead and on Mius R.

1 March

BISMARCK SEA—B-24 detects Japanese convoy, well protected with fighters, en route from Rabaul (New Britain) to Huon Gulf (New Guinea).

BURMA—Sumprabum is evacuated by Br civil authorities. Japanese subsequently move into the village and continue to skirmish with Kachin levies in the area, but make no further progress toward Fort Hertz.

N AFRICA—Gen Spaatz takes command of Twelfth Air Force, an organization that has been merely a name since air reorganization of February. Twelfth Air Force is to be continued as administrative hq for U.S. Army elements of NAAF.

USSR—Moscow announces that an offensive of NW Front, begun a few days earlier by Marshal Timoshenko, has regained Demyansk, Lichkova, and Zaluchie.

2 March

BISMARCK SEA—Allied planes make damaging attacks on enemy convoy bound for Huon Gulf. Some Japanese are rescued from sinking transport and put ashore at Lae, night 2-3, by DD's.

TUNISIA—18 Army Group: In Br First Army's 5 Corps area, enemy renews attack on N along Mateur-Tabarka road near Jefna and forces 139th Brig, 46th Div, back to Sedjenane. U.S. II Corps is directed to begin limited offensive on S flank of Br First Army not later than 115 March in order to divert enemy forces from Br Eighth Army area, gain forward airfields from which Eighth Army's offensive against Mareth Line can be supported, and establish alternative supply line for Eighth Army.

In Br Eighth Army area, NZ 2d Div concentrates S of Médenine, having been rushed forward from Tripoli.

USSR—German *Army Group Center* evacuates Rzhev.

3 March

ALEUTIAN IS.—Adm Kinkaid recommends limited offensive with available forces be conducted against Attu, bypassing Kiska, the objective for which planning has been in progress for some time.

BISMARCK SEA—During heavy co-ordinated attacks, Allied planes severely cripple Japanese convoy, which has arrived off Huon Gulf. After nightfall, PT boats of Seventh Fleet destroy one of the vessels previously damaged by aircraft.

TUNISIA—German *Africa Corps* issues plan for attack from Mareth Line.

18 Army Group: In Br First Army's 5 Corps area, fighting around Bédja subsides, but enemy seizes Sedjenane, about 12 miles W of Jefna. U.S. II Corps continues to patrol actively without making contact with enemy. Sidi Bou Zid and Hadjeb el Aïoun are free of enemy.

In Br Eighth Army's 30 Corps area, enemy makes local probing attack against 81st Div positions near Mareth and is driven off with heavy casualties.

USSR—On Kharkov-Bryansk rail line, Soviet forces capture Lgov and Dmitriev Lgovsky. *1st Pz Army* of *Army Group South* reaches the Donets and overruns Slavyansk and Lisichansk.

4 March

BISMARCK SEA—Battle of Bismarck Sea ends in decisive victory for Allied land-based planes. During the running battle (1-4 March), Japanese lose the entire convoy of 8 transports and 4 DD's, many of the aircraft protecting it, and many personnel embarked in it. This is the last enemy attempt to use large vessels to reinforce positions on Huon Gulf, New Guinea.

TUNISIA—18 Army Group: In Br First Army's 5 Corps area, 139th Brig of 46th Div remains under heavy pressure along Mateur-Tabarka road and during night 4-5 falls back to Tamera, about 8 miles W of Sedjenane.

Br Eighth Army, having completed concentration of troops and weapons in forward area, is now prepared to meet enemy attack—which appears to be imminent because of troop movements in mountains W of Médenine—and is greatly superior to enemy in tanks and AT weapons.

USSR—Russians take Sievsk, S of Bryansk.

5 March

SOLOMON IS.—U.S. naval TF successfully bombards Vila and Munda, night 5-6.

TUNISIA—18 Army Group: In Br First Army's 9 Corps area, 1st Para Brig, upon relief by RCT 26 of U.S. 1st Div, moves N to strengthen 46th Div units in Tamera area, where enemy threat is still serious. U.S. II Corps continues to patrol aggressively. Rcn force of 34th Div enters Pichon, from which Germans have withdrawn, but later withdraws because of enemy forces on hills to N and S.

USSR—Red Army troops are attacking toward Staraya Russa.

6 March

RUSSELL IS.—Islands undergo enemy air attack. This is the first indication that Japanese have learned of American occupation of the islands.

TUNISIA—18 Army Group: In Br First Army's 5 Corps area, enemy maintains pressure against N flank of corps in Tamera area. In U.S. II Corps area, Gen Patton takes command of corps, relieving Gen Fredendall. As head of I Armd Corps in Morocco, Gen Patton had been preparing to command U.S. troops of projected invasion of Sicily. Maj Gen Omar N. Bradley, who is to succeed Gen Patton after operations in S Tunisia are completed, becomes deputy corps commander.

In Br Eighth Army's 30 Corps area, Rommel makes his last attack in Tunisia and is decisively defeated. Four strong thrusts toward Médenine are repulsed by British, who commit only one sq of tanks. Enemy retires after nightfall, having lost about 50 tanks.

USSR—Gzhatsk, on rail line between Moscow and Smolensk, falls to Red Army.

7 March

TUNISIA—18 Army Group: SE Algerian Command, disposed generally SW of Gafsa between U.S. II Corps and Br Eighth Army, occupies Redeyef and patrols toward Tozeur. This command, which includes Fr Camel Corps, was formed late in January under Gen Robert Boissau, previously Fr Army commander at Oran.

8 March

CHINA—Japanese cross Yangtze between Ichang and Yoyang.

TUNISIA—18 Army Group: Takes command of U.S. II Corps, but leaves Fr 19th Corps attached to Br First Army. II Corps continues planning for offensive in mid-March. Forward elements of SE Algerian Command occupy Tozeur.

In Br First Army area, 5 Corps continues to withstand pressure against N flank in Tamera area.

USSR—Red Army troops capture Sychevka, N of Vyazma, forcing enemy back toward Smolensk.

9 March

NEW GUINEA—Japanese planes attack Wau in force. This is the first of a series of heavy air attacks on strategic points in New Guinea, among them Dobodura, Oro Bay, Porlock Harbor, Port Moresby, and Milne Bay.

BURMA—Columns of Ind 77th Brig (Chindits) begin crossing the Irrawaddy R in order to harass enemy farther E.

N AFRICA—Axis reorganization of forces continues. Field Marshal Kesselring's authority aver ground, air, and sea units in the Mediterranean theater is extended. Gen von Arnim takes command of *Army Group Africa*, succeeding Field Marshal Rommel, who leaves Africa. Gen Gustav von Vaerst succeeds von Arnim as commander of *Fifth Panzer Army*.

18 Army Group: In U.S. II Corps area, 1st Div is joined in Bou Chebka area by RCT 18, which reverts to it from attachment to 34th Div.

10 March

TUNISIA—18 Army Group: In Br First Army's 5 Corps area, enemy continues to attack 46th Div positions in vicinity of Tamera. French relieve RCT 26, U.S. 1st Div, in Bou Arada area. SE Algerian Command takes Metlaoui.

In Br Eighth Army area, Fr force under Gen Leclerc (L Force), screening W flank of Eighth Army at Ksar Rhilane, repels sharp enemy attack.

USSR—NW of Vyazma, Soviet forces seize Byelyi.

11 March

CHINA—U.S. Fourteenth Air Force is activated under Maj Gen Claire L. Chennault.

TUNISIA—18 Army Group: In Br First Army area, 5 Corps remains under enemy pressure in Tamera sector.

USSR—Continuing counteroffensive toward Kharkov, enemy reaches the town, which Red Army is staunchly defending.

12 March

U.S.—Pacific Military Conference opens in Washington to plan for operations against the Japanese during 1943. During the conference, which continues through 15th, Gen Sutherland, Gen MacArthur's chief of staff, presents ELKTON plan for reduction of Rabaul, as revised on 28 February, calling for mutually supporting drives, one by SWPA forces from New Guinea to New Britain and another by S Pacific forces through the Solomons. Of great concern to the planners is the shortage of shipping in which to transport the necessary reinforcements to the Far East.

BURMA—Because of recent enemy activity in Sumprabum sector and Hukawng Valley, Gen Stilwell orders Ch troops to Ledo area. On Arakan front, Japanese are employing envelopment tactics against Br Imperial forces and are splitting them into small groups.

TUNISIA—18 Army Group: Succeeds in establishing a reserve force, Br 6th Armd and 78th Divs, under recently arrived hq of Br 9 Corps. 6th Armd Div is in the process of being refitted with Sherman tanks. In U.S. II Corps area, RCT 60 of 9th Div is attached to 1st Armd Div in preparation for coming offensive.

USSR—Germans report violent street fighting in Kharkov. Red Army takes important enemy base of Vyazma.

13 March

NEW GUINEA—Kanga Force continues to press enemy back inch by inch toward Mubo and is now N of Guadagasel.

TUNISIA—18 Army Group: Sets 17 March as D Day for U.S. II Corps' offensive, initial objective of which is Gafsa. 1st Armd Div, reinf by RCT 60 of 9th Div, begins movement from Tébessa area, where it has been refitting since 26 February, toward assembly area NE of Gafsa. Elements are formed into TF, under Col Clarence C. Benson, for detached service and move to region SW of Sbeïtla during night 13-14. In preparation for offensive, air operations are begun against enemy landing fields, although weather conditions are unfavorable.

14 March

N AFRICA—Gen Giraud restores representative government in French N Africa and suppresses organizations of Vichy origin.

18 Army Group: Gen Alexander issues policy directive regarding forthcoming offensive in Tunisia.

USSR—Germans claim capture of Kharkov.

15 March

PACIFIC—Central Pacific Force is redesignated Fifth Fleet.

NEW GUINEA—1st Bn of 162d Inf, U.S. 41st Div, occupies positions at Mambare R mouth without opposition.

TUNISIA—18 Army Group: Gen Eisenhower visits U.S. II Corps hq as preparations for offensive continue. While corps line from Shiba to Kasserine is held by 34th Div and from Kasserine to El Ma el Abiod by 9th Div, assault forces (1st Inf and 1st Armd Divs) prepare to attack on 17th. 1st Div, reinf by 1st Ranger Bn and arty and TD units, assembles in Bou Chebka area.

16 March

TUNISIA—18 Army Group: U.S. II Corps completes preparations for attack. 1st Div, which is to lead off, moves forward, night 16-17, to line of departure. 1st Armd Div is greatly hampered by muddy terrain as it moves into position to protect left flank of 1st Div.

In Br First Army's 5 Corps area, Y Div (38th Brig and 1st Para Brig) is dissolved upon relief by 3d Brig of 1st Div. This is the first unit of 1st Div to arrive in Tunisia.

Br Eighth Army, as a preliminary to main assault on Mareth Line, conducts limited attacks, night 16-17, to mislead enemy and drive in his outposts. The actions are largely successful.

17 March

BURMA—On Arakan front, Ind 55th Brig, which has previously relieved 123d in region E of Mayu R, is attacked and outflanked by enemy at Rathedaung. Assisted by Ind 71st Brig of 26th Div, 55th Brig later succeeds in withdrawing toward Buthidaung. E flank of forces W of the Mayu is thus exposed.

TUNISIA—18 Army Group: U.S. II Corps opens offensive as planned after arty and air preparation, 1st Div attacking for the first time as a div. Employing RCT's 16 and 18, reinf by bn of RCT 26, 1st Div moves into Gafsa, which enemy has evacuated, and organizes it for defense. Hamlet SE of Gafsa, is also occupied. 1st Armd Div, defending left flank, is handicapped by heavy rains but CCA moves into Zannoueh, between Gafsa and Sened, without opposition.

In Br First Army's 5 Corps area, 46th Div withdraws under pressure from Tamera.

Br Eighth Army continues local operations in preparation for assault on Mareth Line.

18 March

INDIA—308th Bombardment Gp (B-24) arrives in India to reinforce U.S. Fourteenth Air Force.

BURMA—6th Brig of Br 2d Div, assisted by 71st Brig of Ind 26th Div, makes final and vain effort to clear Donbaik. Japanese continue infiltration and envelopment tactics, leaving Imperial forces no choice but to withdraw northward. Ind 77th Brig. (Chindits) completes its crossing of the Irrawaddy, but because of increasing hardships eventually abandons plan to cut Mandalay-Lashio rail line and returns in small groups to India.

TUNISIA—18 Army Group: U.S. II Corps's 1st Div, continuing attack with attached 1st Ranger Bn, takes El Guettar without opposition. Very heavy rains immobilize 1st Armd Div, but plans are made for attack on Sened Station on 19th.

In Br First Army area, Gen Anderson orders 5 Corps, which is reinf by 1st Para Brig of Corps Franc d'Afrique and one Tabor of Fr Goumiers, to cease withdrawal and to prepare to recover at least part of lost ground as a necessary preliminary to launching major assault toward Tunis and Bizerte. Enemy is attacking in Djebel Abiod area.

19 March

TUNISIA—18 Army Group: Lull occurs on U.S. II Corps front as road conditions force postponement of attack on Sened Station. SE Algerian Command, protecting S flank of II Corps, is moving forward and has elements S of Gafsa.

Br Eighth Army completes preparations for attack on Mareth Line on 20th. NZ Corps (NZ 2d Div, Br 8th Armd Brig, LeClerc's force, and a regt each of armd cars and medium arty), formed temporarily for outflanking drive around enemy's W flank, starts wide circling movement to S from concealed positions in Foum Tatahouine area, night 19-20.

USSR—Enemy takes Belgorod, N of Kharkov.

20 March

TUNISIA—18 Army Group: In U.S. II Corps area, 1st Armd Div opens corps offensive with drive on Maknassy. While attached RCT 60, motorized, and CCC thrust toward Sened Station, intermediate objective, from NW, CCA takes more direct route, moving along road from Zannouch. Enemy is found to have evacuated Sened Station; RCT 60 occupies it; night 20-21. With Sened Station in U.S. hands, 1st Div begins eastward attack from El Guettar, night 20-21, employing attached 1st Ranger Bn and 26th and 18th Regts.

Br Eighth Army opens assault on Mareth position, constructed originally by French and improved later by Germans, in effort to break through it and Gabès gap to open country. NZ Corps openly continues enveloping movement toward El Hamma switch line in order to divert enemy's attention from E end of Mareth Line; despite very difficult terrain and enemy opposition, reaches positions a few miles short of defile between Djebels Tebaga and Melab. 30 Corps, after very heavy arty barrage, attacks in coastal sector at E end of Mareth Line at 2230, employing 50th Div, which secures foothold on fortified N bank of Wadi Zigzaou, a formidable obstacle because of its width and depth, against intense enfilade fire. 10 Corps, containing 1st and 7th Armd Divs, in army reserve, is disposed in central sector, prepared to exploit success of either of the assault forces.

21 March

TUNISIA—18 Army Group: In U.S. II Corps area, CCC and CCA of 1st Armd Div bypass Sened village, which surrenders to RCT 60, and continue E to Maknassy, placing it under arty fire in preparation for attack on 22d. 1st Div pushes eastward from El Guettar. 1st Ranger Bn, circling N of El Guettar-Maharès road (called Gumtree), gets behind enemy at Djebel el Ank defile while 26th Inf drives directly along road. In this successful action, over 700 prisoners are taken. To right, 18th Inf takes Hill 336, S of Gumtree road, and presses on toward Djebel el Mcheltat.

In Br Eighth Army area, NZ Corps makes slow progress toward El Hamma switch line. 30 Corps strengthens bridgehead on bank of Wadi Zigzaou somewhat but can get only a few tanks across. Covered by heavy arty fire, 50th Div broadens and deepens bridgehead, night 21-22.

In Br First Army area, 5 Corps is severely menaced on N as enemy forces defenders of important lateral road between Mateur and Djebel Abiod back to Djebel Abiod.

USSR—Germans claim to have closed last remaining gap in line of communications with Orel sector. Russians take Durovo, 57 miles NE of Smolensk. Operations on entire front are bogging down because of spring thaw.

22 March

TUNISIA—18 Army Group: In U.S. II Corps area, 1st Armd Div finds Maknassy free of enemy and occupies it; renewing attack, night 22-23, with CCC on N and RCT 60 on S, seizes Djebels Dribica and Bou Douaou but is unable to clear enemy from Djebel Naemia, which dominates pass E of Maknassy. 1st Div consolidates and improves positions E of El Guettar, 26th Inf probing beyond Bou Hamran, on Gumtree road, and 18th occupying Djebel el Mcheltat and moving elements S across

El Guettar-Gabès road to Djebel el Kreroua and E tip of Djebel Berda. German armored div heads NW up Gabès-Gafsa road, night 22-23, for counterthrust toward Gafsa. SE Algerian Command continues forward in conjunction with and to S of U.S. II Corps and is in contact with enemy at Djebel Bou Jerra, SW of Djebel Berda.

In Br Eighth Army area, offensive is severely handicapped by heavy rainfall. Determined enemy counterattack forces 50th Div, 30 Corps, to give ground. Since enemy reserves are now committed in coastal sector and fighting here is proving very costly, Gen Montgomery decides to switch main weight of his attack to W flank and conduct holding action on E. 10 Corps releases 7th Armd Div to 30 Corps.

Br First Army is strengthened as 1st Div completes concentration in Tunisia.

23 March

TUNISIA—18 Army Group: In U.S. II Corps area, 1st Armd Div continues futile efforts to take Djebel Naemia, where enemy is building up strength. 1st Div, by dint of hard fighting, contains 2 strong enemy thrusts toward El Guettar. Both sides sustain heavy losses. SE Algerian Command is meeting strong opposition as it continues forward to S of U.S. II Corps.

In Br Eighth Army area, 30 Corps withdraws Wadi Zigzaou bridgehead under cover of arty fire during night 23-24. Ind 4th Div begins operations to clear Médenine-Hallouf-Bir Soltane road, night 23-24. 10 Corps hq and 1st Armd Div move out after dark to join NZ Corps, which is still help up near bottleneck between Djebel Tebaga and Djebel Melab, in preparation for assault against enemy's W flank.

24 March

U.S.–JCS approve plan to occupy Attu in the Aleutians.

TUNISIA—18 Army Group: In U.S. II Corps area, 1st Armd Div attacks Djebel Naemia in greater strength but cannot dislodge enemy. Gen Patton orders the position taken during next morning's attack. Maj Gen Orlando Ward, CG 1st Armd Div, personally commands attack, which begins midnight 24-25 without arty preparation. Enemy, unable to break through positions of 1st Div on hills SE of El Guettar, maintains pressure in the area and achieves limited gains.

In Br Eighth Army area, 30 Corps is containing enemy in coastal sector by feints coupled with air attacks while preparations are made for attack against W flank of Mareth Line.

In Br First Army's 5 Corps area, enemy is at last contained on N flank, where 46th Div holds line Cap Negro-Djebel Abiod.

25 March

TUNISIA—18 Army Group: In U.S. II Corps area, 1st Armd Div's attack against Djebel Naemia at first makes some progress, but gains cannot be held. Maintaining pressure against 1st Div on hills SE of El Guettar, enemy forces 18th Inf elements to give ground on NE part of Djebel Berda; since no reinforcements for this position are available, 18th Inf defense force is ordered to withdraw from Djebel Berda. U.S. II Corps receives new directive from Gen Alexander, calling for broadened offensive; is reinf for this purpose by 34th and 9th Divs. 34th Div is to conduct limited offensive for Fondouk Gap from Sbeïtla. 9th Div (− RCT 60) and 1st Div are to open gap SE of El Guettar for passage of 1st Armd Div. 1st Armd Div is to break off offensive in Maknassy area and leave small holding force there in order to drive on Gabès.

26 March

BATTLE OF KOMANDORSKI Is.—Small naval task group under Adm McMorris encounters superior enemy surface force attempting to run Allied blockade and reinforce Japanese positions in the Aleutians. Joining battle off Komandorski Is. in the Bering Sea, enemy is forced to retire without completing his mission; his Aleutians garrisons are henceforth obliged to rely on meager supplies brought in by submarine.

TUNISIA—18 Army Group: Br Eighth Army, having adopted new plan called SUPERCHARGE, and abandoned original plan, PUGILIST, renews assault on Mareth Line in afternoon following destructive aerial bombardment that lasts for $2^{1}/_{2}$ hours. NZ Corps, leading assault against W flank of Mareth Line, jumps off at 1600 and penetrates enemy positions in defile between Djebels Tebaga and Melab. 10 Corps' 1st Armd Div, exploiting this success, breaks through the defile and pushes toward El Hamma as operations are continued through night by moonlight. Ind 4th Div, 30 Corps, clearing Médenine-Bir Soltane road, is beyond Hallouf Pass.

27 March

TUNISIA—18 Army Group: In U.S. II Corps area, 34th Div, in its first action as a div, begins drive on Fondouk Gap, moving astride road from Hadjeb el Aïoun with 2 regts abreast, 135th on left and 168th on right. Frontal and enfilading fire from heights ahead halt attack short of objective; 135th

Inf attempts to advance at night but falls back under intense fire. 133d Inf (less bn at Algiers) remains at Sbeïtla to defend it. In SE Algerian Command area, camel troops occupy Sabria and Rhidma, about 25 and 18 miles, respectively, SW of Kebili.

In Br Eighth Army area, Mareth Line collapses under blows of 10 and NZ Corps on W, but enemy retains El Hamma and escape corridor through which main body withdraws, night 27-28. Axis efforts to strengthen W flank are belated and ineffective. 1st Armd Div continues toward El Hamma and repels 2 counterattacks. New Zealanders complete difficult task of mopping up during night 27-18. Ind 4th Div, 30 Corps, completes operations to open Médenine-Bir Soltane road.

28 March

U.S.—JCS approve new directive for Gen MacArthur and Adm Halsey, altering previous directives of 2 July 1942. Operations are to be confined to the earlier Task Two, and bases are to be secured in the Trobriands. Timing is left largely to the discretion of the commanders. Gen MacArthur is to command SWPA forces and have general direction of Adm Halsey's forces in the Solomons; have strategic control of Pacific Fleet task forces engaged in the operations.

NEW GUINEA—MacKechnie Force, named after Col Archibald R. MacKechnie, CO of 162d Inf, U.S. 41st Div, is formed, largely from 1st Bn of 162d Inf, to secure Waria R mouth and Morobe harbor.

TUNISIA—18 Army Group: U.S. II Corps opens major attack toward Gabès from positions near El Guettar, employing 1st Div on left and 9th (less RCT 60) on right, in effort to force gap in enemy positions through which 1st Armd Div can attack. 1st Div, with RCT 18 on left, 26 in center, and 16 on right, renews efforts to advance astride Gumtree road and makes limited progress on left. 9th Div, in action as a div for the first time, attacks with 47th Inf from positions on Djebel Berda, previously abandoned by 18th Inf, toward Hill 369 on Djebel el Kreroua, an eastern spur of Djebel Berda. Attack is a costly failure because of well-organized enemy positions on hills and ridges and confusion arising from inaccurate maps. 1st and 3d Bns, mistaking Draa Saada el Hamra ridge for Hill 369, clear it except for Hill 290 at its tip. 2d Bn and reserve bn (1st Bn, 39th Inf) become lost for more than a day while trying to reach Hill 369. 2d Bn, 39th Inf, is sent after nightfall toward Hill 369 but meets such heavy fire from Hill 290 that main body falls back to starting point and stragglers return 36 hours later. 1st Armd Div, which has elements at Gafsa to meet threat of enemy breakthrough, is ordered to concentrate additional elements there during night 28-29.

On N flank of II Corps, 34th Div continues limited attack toward Fondouk Gap but is unable to make much headway. Camel troops of SE Algerian Command occupy Douz, S of Chott Djerid.

In Br Eighth Army area, 10 Corps continues attack toward El Hamma, from which enemy withdraws, night 28-29. NZ Corps pursues enemy northward toward Gabès. 30 Corps moves forward along main Mareth-Gabès road, hampered by mines and demolitions.

In Br First Army area, 5 Corps begins counteroffensive to recover northern road and relieve pressure on Medjez el Bab, a dangerously exposed salient. 46th Div, employing 138th Brig, 36th Brig of 78th Div, and 1st Para Brig, assisted on left flank by Corps d'Afrique and a Tabor of Moroccan Goumiers, drives steadily eastward despite heavy rainfall, which is to continue for a week. Enemy forces in this sector have thinned out.

29 March

TUNISIA—18 Army Group: U.S. II Corps' operations in El Guettar and Fondouk areas continue to make negligible progress against firm resistance. Plan of attack toward Gabès is changed by 18 Army Group late in day: 1st Armd Div is to attack on 30th in effort to break through enemy positions barring road to Gabès.

Br Eighth Army pursues enemy northward through Gabès. NZ Corps takes Gabès and Oudref. 30 Corps' 51st Div overtakes NZ Corps at Gabès. 10 Corps' 1st Armd Div advances northward from El Hamma.

30 March

TUNISIA—18 Army Group: U.S. II Corps continues efforts to break through enemy positions astride El Guettar-Gabès road. 1st Div secures most of S part of Djebel el Mcheltat. After preparatory arty concentrations, 9th Div takes part of Djebel Lettouchi, eastern spur of Djebel Berda, but cannot hold it or advance elsewhere. 1st Armd Div's TF Benson attacks through infantry at noon but is soon stopped by enemy fire and mines. Lane is cleared through mine field at pass between Djebel el Mcheltat and Hill 369, night 30-31. 34th Div, to N, continues futile efforts to reach Fondouk Gap. SE Algerian Command's camel troops occupy Kebili.

Br Eighth Army's forward elements make contact with enemy's new line along Wadi Akarit. 10 Corps is ordered to determine whether the Akarit defenses can be carried by assault with current forces. NZ Corps, having served its purpose, is abolished.

In Br First Army area, 5 Corps' 46 Div recaptures Sedjenane.

31 March

NEW GUINEA—MacKechnie Force of U.S. 41st Div moves by water to Waria R mouth and Dona airstrip.

TUNISIA—18 Army Group: In U.S. II Corps area, 1st Div's RCT's 16 and 26 attempt unsuccessfully to clear SE tip of Djebel el Mcheltat. 9th Div makes little progress against bypassed Hill 772 (on Djebel Berda) and Hill 369 (on Djebel el Kreroua). TF Benson, 1st Armd Div, attacks about noon, passing through lane cleared in mine field, and secures most of region from road to foothills at N, but loses 9 tanks. 4 more tanks are salvaged. CCA begins diversionary attack against Djebel Djebs, hill mass N of Maknassy, and evokes sharp enemy reaction. As a diversion for 34th Div's attack on Fondouk Gap, CO C of 751st Tank Bn, Co A of 813th Tank Bn, and motorized co of 109th Combat Engrs attack on NW slopes of Djebel Touila, about 5 miles S of infantry. During nights of 31 March-1 April and 1-2 April, 34th Div assault force pulls back out of range of enemy fire and establishes defensive positions, concluding the Fondouk Gap battle.

In Br Eighth Army area, Montgomery decides to await reinforcements and regroup upon learning from to Corps CG that an immediate assault across Wadi Akarit would be costly. 30 Corps, which is reinf by NZ 2d Div, is to be responsible for securing bridgehead.

In Br First Army area, 5 Corps' 46th Div gains all its objectives on N flank of corps, recovering El Aouana; enemy withdraws from Cap Serrat. Preparations are begun for next phase of attack: clearing Bédja-Medjez road and relieving pressure on Medjez. Fr 19th Corps makes contact with U.S. 34th Div at El Ala, W of Fondouk.

1 April

ALEUTIAN Is.—CINCPAC and WDC CG issue joint directive for invasion of Attu on 7 May. Adm Kinkaid as commander of North Pacific Force (TF 16, formerly TF 8) will head the operation. Under him, Adm Rockwell, Commander Amphibious Force North Pacific, is to conduct landing operations. Maj Gen Albert E. Brown's 7th Div, although trained for mechanized warfare in the desert, is to make the assault.

SOLOMON Is.—Japanese aircraft, whose attention during the preceding month has been devoted largely to Allied bases in New Guinea, attack Russell Is.

CHINA—Infantry and Arty Training Centers for Chinese Y-Force officers open.

IRAN—U.S. AAF takes responsibility for assembling aircraft for USSR at Abadan Air Base. Douglas Aircraft Company, under contract to AAF, had previously been responsible for Abadan.

TUNISIA—18 Army Group: In U.S. II Corps area, plan of attack is changed after another fruitless attempt by TF Benson of 1st Armd Div to break through enemy positions barring Gabès road. Second phase (to secure pass between Djebel Chemsi and Djebel Ben Khëir for passage of armor) is to begin at once, although enemy still retains Hill 772 on Djebel Berda and Hill 369 and pass N of it on Djebel el Kreroua. TF Benson goes on the defensive. 1st Div continues efforts to clear SE tip of Djebel el Mcheltat. 9th Div is concentrating on Hill 772, which must be cleared before operations can be continued against Hill 369. In Maknassy area, CCA of 1st Armd Div continues diversionary attack on Djebel Djebs. SE Algerian Command's camel troops are maintaining liaison with Br Eighth Army in Kebili area.

2 April

TUNISIA—18 Army Group: In U.S. II Corps area, virtual stalemate exists as enemy checks dogged efforts of infantry of 1st and 9th Divs to clear Gumtree and Gabès roads. 1st Div clears rest of Djebel el Mcheltat, but 9th is unable to take Hill 772 on Djebel Berda. Gap exists between the two divs. Diversionary action of CCA, 1st Armd Div, in Maknassy area is suspended.

3 April

NEW GUINEA—Elements of MacKechnie Force land on shore of Morobe harbor to establish defensive position.

TUNISIA—18 Army Group: Gen Alexander alerts Gen Patton to be prepared to move U.S. II Corps to N flank of Br First Army upon collapse of enemy's Wadi Akarit position; 9th Div is to move first. Hard fighting continues in U.S. II Corps area for positions dominating Gumtree and Gabès roads. 1st Div takes village of Sakket, but 9th is still checked by enemy on Hill 772.

In Br First Army's 5 Corps area, Fr naval party (detachment of goumiers and elements of Corps Franc d'Afrique) occupies Cap Serrat. Fr 19th Corps repels limited enemy thrusts W from Pichon.

4 April

TUNISIA—18 Army Group: 9 Corps, 18 Army Group reserve, prepares for offensive to recover Fondouk Gap. U.S. 34th Div, which is to participate, is transferred to 9 Corps. In U.S. II Corps area, 1st and 9th Divs continue futile efforts to clear Gumtree and Gabès roads.

Br Eighth Army, preparing for assault on Wadi Akarit line, has nearly 500 tanks concentrated in the region.

5 April

BURMA—Japanese gain control of Mayu Peninsula as far N as Indin and overrun hq of 6th Brig. By this time, Ind 26th Div has taken over the front from Ind 14th Div.

TUNISIA—18 Army Group: In U.S. II Corps area, stalemate continues as enemy halts all efforts of 1st and 9th Divs to advance. II Corps takes precautionary measures to meet enemy attack, which hostile concentrations are interpreted to indicate. When no attack materializes, it is correctly anticipated that enemy is preparing instead to withdraw. Gen Ernest Harmon assumes command of 1st Armd Div, replacing Gen Ward.

In Br First Army's 5 Corps area, 4th Div assumes command of sector NE of Bédja.

6 April

TUNISIA—18 Army Group: In U.S. II Corps area, while 1st and 9th Divs press forward toward general line intended originally for first phase, TF Benson of 1st Armd Div follows up closely and reaches road junction NE of Djebel Berda. As a diversion in the Maknassy area, CCB attacks Djebel Maïzila, and CCC demonstrates at Djebel Naemia. After nightfall enemy disengages and for the most part withdraws eastward under cover of arty fire. II Corps is ordered to apply maximum pressure on 7th.

Br Eighth Army begins assault on Wadi Akarit line, from which enemy begins withdrawing, night 6-7. 30 Corps jumps off before dawn with 51st Div on right, 50th in center, and Ind 4th on left. Progress is made, particularly on flanks, but tenacious resistance and counterattacks prevent a complete breakthrough. 10 Corps, which is to drive through 30 Corps' bridgehead, moves forward at noon. NZ 2d Div, which reverts to corps, leads drive.

7 April

SOLOMON IS.—Intensifying their aerial offensive against Allied shipping and aircraft, Japanese attack Guadalcanal area in force, employing 71 bombers and 117 fighters. 3 Allied vessels are sunk: NZ corvette *Moa*, U.S. oiler *Kanawha*, and U.S. DD *Aaron Ward*. Japanese plane losses in this action far outnumber Allied losses of 7 fighters.

TUNISIA—18 Army Group: All available aircraft of XII Air Support Command and WDAF attack enemy, who is retreating in all sectors. 9 Corps completes preparations for assault on Fondouk, designed to block northward retreat of enemy from Akarit line. Commanding officers reach agreement on final details and decide to open attack at 0300 on 8th. U.S. II Corps makes contact with Br Eighth Army and SE Algerian Command on Gafsa-Gabès road. TF Benson, ordered to push forward relentlessly and without regard to cost, advances steadily SE toward Gabès and in afternoon makes contact with 10 Corps of Br Eighth Army, then pulls back to help mop up. 9th Div begins movement to Bou Chebka area, night 7-8, turning over its sector to 1st Div, which is to conduct mopping up.

Br Eighth Army, with 30 Corps on right and 10 Corps on left, pursues rapidly retreating enemy northward to general line Cekhira-Sedkret en Noual.

In Br First Army area, 5 Corps opens offensive to clear Bédja-Medjez el Bab road and thereby remove enemy threat to Medjez. 78th Div, with close air and arty support, begins attack N of Oued Zarga.

8 April

TUNISIA—18 Army Group: 9 Corps opens attack on Fondouk before dawn, U.S. 34th Div and elements of 46th Div leading off in effort to clear gap through which 6th Armd Div is to debouch for drive on Kairouan. On the N, 128th Brig of 46th Div advances through hills E of Pichon to Djebel Rhorab. S of gap, 34th Div, with 135th Inf on N and 133d on S, is prevented by intense ground and air bombardment from reaching its first objective, lower slopes of Djebel el Haouareb, although tanks are committed in support of infantry. Attack is supported by arty fire, beginning at dawn, but scheduled air attacks are canceled because of weather conditions.

In Br First Army area, Fr 19th Corps, ordered to seize Djebel Ousselat and Eastern Dorsal in order to assist attack of Br 9 Corps, advances to positions N and NE of Pichon. 5 Corps is methodically clearing mountainous region N of Bédja-Medjez el Bab road.

9 April

TUNISIA—18 Army Group: In 9 Corps area, while infantry of 46th and U.S. 34th Divs continue efforts to clear heights dominating Fondouk Pass, 6th Armd Div is committed at 1500 to speed the operation and succeeds in forcing the pass, but at heavy cost in tanks. Meanwhile, 128th Brig of 46th Div clears Djebel Rhorab, U.S. 34th Div is unable to clear Djebel el Haouareb during day but gains its crest in night attack by 1st Bn, 133d Inf. 1st Armd Div, U.S. II Corps, moves northward to positions

N of Sidi Bou Zid, leaving RCT 60 to hold Maknassy sector.

Br Eighth Army continues pursuit of enemy northward along Gabès Gulf, 30 Corps, in coastal sector, reaching positions a few miles short of Sfax.

In Br First Army's 5 Corps area, 78th Div takes Chaouach, mountain village 4 miles NW of Medjez el Bab.

10 April

TUNISIA—18 Army Group: Gen Alexander's draft plan of 8 April for final offensive in Tunisia, Operation VULCAN, is officially approved. Br. First Army is to make main attack on Tunis. Br Eighth Army is to exert pressure to S and cut off Cap Bon from Tunis. U.S. II Corps, from positions on N flank of Br First Army, is to drive on Bizerte in conjunction with Br First Army's assault on Tunis. Fr 19th Corps is to operate on extreme S flank of Br First Army under First Army command. SE Algerian Command, pinched out after junction of U.S. II Corps with Br Eighth Army, is dissolved; its components are to operate under Fr 19th Corps. 9 Corps is to be under command of Br First Army.

9 Corps' 6th Armd Div drives quickly toward Kairouan, overcoming resistance S of that town. U.S. II Corps' CCA, 1st Armd Div, advancing N through Rebaou Pass, makes contact with 34th Div E of Fondouk.

Br Eighth Army's 30 Corps takes Sfax and continues N to La Hencha.

In Br First Army area, Fr 19th Corps now controls Djeloula Pass, between Ousseltia and Kairouan. 5 Corps continues to clear heights dominating Bédja–Medjez el Bab road.

11 April

NEW GUINEA—Two Allied merchant ships are lost to enemy aircraft that attack Oro Bay in strength.

TUNISIA—18 Army Group: 9 Corps' 6th Armd Div occupies Kairouan unopposed and makes contacts with Br Eighth Army. In U.S. II Corps area, 9th Div moves N to Br 5 Corps zone. 1st Div, which is to follow 9th to N flank of Br First Army, moves to Morsott. 1st Armd Div remains in Sbeïtla–Faïd region.

In Br Eighth Army area, Gen Montgomery holds 30 Corps hq and 7th Armd and 51st Inf Divs in reserve in Sfax area; sends Ind 4th Div and 50th Div N to join 10 Corps. Some elements of 10 Corps make contact with 6th Armd Div of 9 Corps near Kairouan while others continue northward toward Sousse. 1st Armd Div remains in place in Fauconnerie area.

12 April

NEW GUINEA—Japanese make heavy air attack on Port Moresby but do little damage.

TUNISIA—18 Army Group: It is agreed that U.S. II Corps will remain under command of 18 Army Group rather than Br First Army, but First Army is to issue the necessary orders for U.S. II Corps in order to co-ordinate its operations with First Army's drive on Tunis.

In Br Eighth Army area, Gen Montgomery, in response to request from Gen Alexander for reinforcements for Br First Army, selects 1st Armd Div and King's Dragoon Gds for the mission. 10 Corps captures Sousse and continues N.

In Br First Army's 5 Corps area, U.S. 9th Div begins relief of 46th Div. 78th Div continues clearing region NW of Medjez el Bab.

13 April

TUNISIA—18 Army Group: In Br Eighth Army area, advance elements of 10 Corps, continuing N along coast, reach AT ditch guarding enemy's next delaying position at Enfidaville. Subsequent efforts, on a limited scale, to force enemy from his Enfidaville position before it can be strengthened are futile.

14 April

NEW GUINEA—Japanese conclude series of heavy air strikes on New Guinea with strong attack on Milne Bay that causes little damage.

TUNISIA—18 Army Group: 9 Corps moves to assembly area SW of Teboursouk.

In Br First Army's 9 Corps area, U.S. 9th Div assumes command of 46th Div sector. 4th Div, in its first action, has been exerting pressure against enemy N of Hunt's Gap in conjunction with 78th Div's attack and has reached hills just SW of Sidi Nsir. 78th Div takes commanding ridges, Djebel el Ang and Djebel Tanngouche, some 8 miles N of Medjez. Fr 19th Corps has driven enemy from Eastern Dorsal as far as 10 miles N of Pichon.

15 April

ALEUTIAN IS.—Initial elements of 7th Div begin embarkation for Attu operation. Reserve force (RCT 32, less one bn) sails for Adak. Prov bn, consisting of 7th Scout Co and 7th Rcn Tr, less one platoon, leaves for Dutch Harbor where it is to transfer to a DD and 2 submarines for last lap of journey.

RUSSELL IS.—First of 2 airfields is completed on Banika I.

TUNISIA—18 Army Group: Gen Bradley assumes command of U.S. II Corps, replacing Lt Gen

George S. Patton, Jr., who returns to his previous task of preparing for invasion of Sicily.

In Br First Army area, 5 Corps' 78th Div loses Djebels el Ang and Tanngouche to enemy counterattack but recaptures former and part of latter.

16 April

CHINA—Japanese *11th Army* is concentrating forces for offensive to gain control of river shipping on Upper Yangtze in W Hupeh Province.

TUNISIA—WDAF, including U.S. Ninth Air Force, begins operating from airfields near Kairouan and Sousse.

18 Army Group: Issues instructions for coming offensive to capture Tunis and Bizerte. U.S. II Corps' hq moves from Gafsa to region 2 miles NW of Bédja. 1st Armd Div starts to Br 9 Corps zone, arty being first unit to go.

Br Eighth Army abandons attempts to force enemy, by quick jabs, from his Enfidaville position and prepares to make large-scale effort on night 19-20.

In Br First Army's 5 Corps area, 78th Div offensive has gained depth of 10 miles on 10-mile front and has freed Medjez el Bab from enemy threat. U.S. 1st Div begins relief of 4th Div NE of Bédja.

18 April

SOLOMON Is.—Adm Yamamoto is killed when P-38's from Guadalcanal shoot down plane flying him from Rabaul to the Solomons for an inspection visit.

MEDITERRANEAN—In Operation FLAX, Allied planes, which have been conducting offensive to disrupt flow of German air transport from Italy and Sicily to Tunisia since 5 April, have a particularly good day, destroying 50-70 of some 100 enemy transport planes and 16 of the escort for loss of 6 P-40's and a Spitfire. Operation FLAX, while contributing materially to the success of Operation VULCAN—final ground offensive to clear Tunisia—had been planned originally for February, before VULCAN plans had been formulated. In preparation for VULCAN, other Allied planes intensify efforts against enemy airfields, beginning night 18-19.

TUNISIA—18 Army Group: Br Eighth Army releases 1st Armd Div to Br First Army in preparation for VULCAN.

19 April

TUNISIA—18 Army Group: Plan for main assault on Tunis and Bizerte, to begin on 22d, is outlined. U.S. II Corps assumes command of new zone on N flank of Allied line at 1800, with front extending from coast E of Cap Serrat to Hill 667, 5 miles W of Heïdous. Corps Franc d'Afrique is attached to 9th Div and given zone on extreme N.

In Br First Army area, 5 Corps' N boundary is shifted S as U.S. II Corps takes over coastal region. Fr 19th Corps, holding line Karachoum-Djebel Edjehaf-W of Djebel Mansour, is maintaining patrol contact with Br Eighth Army on right.

Br Eighth Army opens assault on enemy's Enfidaville position after intensive preparatory bombardment. To Corps jumps off at 2130, with 50th Div on right, NZ 2d Div in center, and Ind 4th Div reinf by L Force on left. 7th Armd Div guards W flank. Enemy is initially forced to give ground.

20 April

TUNISIA—18 Army Group: In Br First Army area, as 5 and 9 Corps are preparing for assault on Tunis, German tank-infantry force counterattacks sharply, night 20-21, in region between Medjez el Bab and Goubellat.

In Br Eighth Army area, 10 Corps, continuing attack on Enfidaville line, takes Enfidaville and pushes northward on right but is checked on left at Djebel Garci by stubborn opposition.

21 April

ALEUTIAN Is.—Adm Kinkaid issues Operation Order I-43, providing over-all plan for capture of Attu.

TUNISIA—18 Army Group: Completes preparations for main VULCAN assault. U.S. 34th Div, having trained vigorously in vicinity of Fondouk and Maktar, begins night marches, 21-22, to new zone of U.S. II Corps.

In Br First Army area, enemy counterattack in Medjez el Bab-Goubellat area ends in costly failure. This action delays by a few hours jump-off of 46th Div, 9 Corps, on 22d.

Br Eighth Army concludes offensive operations in Tunisia. 10 Corps is so bitterly opposed at Takrouna that Gen Montgomery decides late in day to confine offensive to coastal region. Army subsequently regroups while holding current positions; offensive is never renewed.

22 April

TUNISIA—18 Army Group: Br First Army begins final phase of Tunisia Campaign. 5 Corps, making main effort astride the Medjerda, attacks enemy positions N and S of Medjez el Bab. 78th Div attacks to seize rest of Djebel Tanngouche on left; on right begins northeastward drive along Djebel el Ahmera (Longstop) ridge. To S, 1st and 4th Divs attack astride Medjez el Bab-Tunis highway, 1st Div clearing hamlet of Grich el Oued and 4th Div, Goubellat. 9 Corps attacks on Goubellat plain, between Medjez el Bab and Bou Arada, in effort to destroy enemy's armored reserve and support 5 Corps to N. 46th Div advances steadily in region N of Sebkret el Kourzia but is hampered SW of these salt marshes by enemy defenses and mines. 6th Armd Div is committed in late afternoon and upon attacking through infantry is strongly opposed by enemy armor.

23 April

NEW GUINEA—Aus Kanga Force in Mubo area is dissolved and Aus 3d Div takes over. Stalemate exists in this sector, where Australians hold broken line Mubo-Komiatum-Bobdubi.

TUNISIA—18 Army Group: U.S. II Corps begins drive on Bizerte early in morning, making main effort on right. On N flank, 9th Div, reinf by Corps Franc d'Afrique, which is disposed along coast on extreme N and directed on Kef en Nsour, attacks toward Jefna position on highway between Djebel Abiod and Mateur, key points of which are Djebel Azag (Green Hill) and Djebel Ajred (Bald Hill). While RCT 47 conducts holding action along highway, RCT's 39 and 60 make outflanking attacks in hills to N, RCT 39 attacking toward Djebel Aïnchouna and RCT 60, farther N, pushing eastward from Djebels Mergueb and Msid. Satisfactory progress is made on div flanks, but RCT 39 is slowed in center by stubborn opposition on Djebel Aïnchouna. On S flank of II Corps, 1st Div, reinf by 6th Armd Inf of 1st Armd Div, which is disposed on extreme S, attacks toward Djebel Sidi Meftah. On N, RCT 26 attempts to take Hill 575 (Kef el Goraa) but is halted short of it. In center, RCT 16 fights indecisively for Hill 400. On S, RCT 18 begins clearing N side of the Tine, and attached 6th Armd Inf is similarly employed S of the river; enemy is driven from Hill ago but retains Hill 407, to NW.

In Br First Army area, 5 Corps' 78th Div clears enemy remnants from Djebel Tanngouche and continues along Djebel el Ahmera ridge, clearing all but NE slopes. In 9 Corps area, tank battles continue on Goubellat plain, where enemy is bringing mobile reserves forward.

U.K.—CCS issue directive for establishment of an Anglo-American staff to plan for invasion of western Europe. Lt Gen Sir Frederick E. Morgan, as Chief of Staff to the Supreme Allied Commander (designate), is to head the new headquarters. The initial letters of his title, COSSAC, come to stand for his office.

24 April

U.S.—Main body of Attu invasion force sails from San Francisco for Cold Harbor, Alaska.

TUNISIA—18 Army Group: In U.S. II Corps area, 9th Div continues to press toward Jefna position. On N, RCT 60 takes Djebel Dardyss. RCT 39, in center, suffers heavy casualties as it battles determined enemy on Djebel Aïnchouna. 1st Div places softening fire on Hill 575 (Kef el Goraa) throughout day and to right, in sector of RCT 16, secures hill positions and thus removes threat of envelopment. RCT 18 seizes Hill 407 while 6th Armd Inf fights vigorously for Hill 388. Germans begin withdrawal from 1st Div front during night 24-25. At the same time RCT 168, 34th Div, takes over N flank positions of 1st Div.

In Br First Army's 5 Corps area, 78th Div continues to clear Djebel el Ahmera while 1st and 4th Divs press eastward astride Medjez el Bab-Tunis highway. In 9 Corps area, indecisive tank and infantry battles continue on Goubellat plain. Little progress is made, although 1st Armd Div is committed and follows 6th Armd Div E.

25 April

TUNISIA—18 Army Group: In U.S. II Corps area, RCT 39 of 9th Div finishes clearing Djebel Aïnchouna. Enemy begins withdrawal from 9th Div zone night 25-26. RCT 168, 34th Div, moves forward in conjunction with 1st Div units to right, taking over mopping-up operations. 1st Div follows up enemy withdrawal on S flank of corps. RCT 26 occupies Hill 575 early in day and presses on to Djebel Touta. Advance elements of RCT 18 reach W end of Djebel Sidi Meftah. 6th Armd Inf takes previously contested hills on S side of Tine R and patrols eastward.

In Br First Army's 5 Corps area, Heïdous falls to 78th Div. 9 Corps continues tank battles in vicinity of Sebkret el Kourzia without appreciable success within its own zone, but forcing enemy to withdraw exposed salient to right. Fr 19th Corps makes substantial progress as enemy withdraws salient S of Bou Arada-Pont-du Fahs road.

26 April

ALEUTIAN Is.—U.S. surface force bombards enemy installations at Chichagof Harbor and Holtz Bay, Attu. This is the second naval bombardment of Attu.

SWPA—GHQ issues ELKTON III, superseding two previous ELKTON plans, calling for mutually supporting advances in S Pacific and SWPA toward Rabaul, the whole operation being under the code name CARTWHEEL.

TUNISIA—18 Army Group: On U.S. II Corps' 9th Div front, RCT 60 swings NE toward Kef en Nsour, previous objective of Corps Franc d'Afrique, rather than SE toward Jefna position as planned, since French are unable to advance in region N of Djebel Dardyss. RCT 39, now solely responsible for outflanking the Jefna position, takes Hill Sri, SE of Djebel Aïnchouna. Continuing holding action along highway, RCT 47 finds enemy disposed in force on Hill 598, SW of Djebel Aired. 34th Div takes over zone in Djebel Grembil-Hill 575 region, between 9th and 1st Divs, and prepares for drive on Hill 609 (Djebel Tahent). Enemy positions on hills in this area are being softened by arty fire. On S flank, 1st Div gains its initial objectives, permitting 1st Armd Div to take over Tine valley zone at 2200 in preparation for armored drive through enemy's second line of defense to Mateur.

In Br First Army's 5 Corps area, 78th Div finishes clearing Djebel el Ahmera. 1st Div reaches Djebel Bou Aoukaz, 4 miles from Djebel el Ahmera. On main road to Tunis, 4th Div reaches positions 7 miles E of Medjez el Bab. 9 Corps is now opposed on Goubellat plain by 3 enemy armd divs that contain further efforts to advance. 6th Armd Div is withdrawn into reserve. Fr 19th Corps continues to pursue enemy northward toward Pont-du-Fahs, reaching Djebel Fkirine.

27 April

TUNISIA—18 Army Group: U.S. II Corps continues offensive with 4 divs in assault, its major objective now being the Jefna position, Hill 609 (Djebel Tahent), and Mateur. Column of 39th Inf, 9th Div, reaches Hill 382, NW of Djebel Azag, where it is stalled for 4 days by firmly entrenched enemy. 34th Div begins drive on Hill 609: RCT 168, on N, reaches slopes of Djebel el Hara; RCT 135, to right, drives to Hill 490, just W of 609, but is forced to withdraw. 1st Div patrols reach Djebel el Ang. 1st Armd Div begins attack on S flank of corps, CCA (6th Armd Inf, reinf) making main effort. Attack fails to gain immediate objectives—Hills 299 and 315, NE of Djebel el Ang—and elements are forced back from Hill 312, from which attack on Hill 315 was made.

In Br First Army area, 5 Corps' advance is checked by series of determined enemy counterattacks. 4th Div is forced to withdraw its left flank at Ksar Tyr.

28 April

TUNISIA—18 Army Group: In U.S. II Corps area, 9th Div continues E astride the Sedjenane, reaching Kraim Lerhmed on N and Kef Saban on S. RCT 39 clears hills generally N of Hill 382, but enemy retains 382. In center of II Corps area, main effort is made to clear approaches to Hill 609, which is hampering forward movement of 34th and 1st Divs. While 34th Div's RCT 168 clears Djebel el Hara, RCT 135 occupies Hill 490 and withstands counterattacks against it. In conjunction with 34th Div, RCT 16 of 1st Div secures foothold on Hill 531, S of 609. RCT 26 reaches Djebel el Anz against strong resistance. RCT 18, to S, clears part of Djebel Sidi Meftah. On corps S flank, CCA of 1st Armd Div takes Hill 315 and part of Hill 299, where enemy is resisting strongly.

In Br First Army area, 5 Corps is largely successful in containing enemy counterattacks along its front.

29 April

TUNISIA—18 Army Group: Gen Alexander decides to reinforce Br First Army for final push to clear rest of Tunisia.

In U.S. II Corps area, RCT 60 of 9th Div reaches Djebel Hazemat, N of Sedjenane R; pushes closer to Kef en Nsour, S of river. RCT 39 continues outflanking action toward Jefna on N while RCT 47 patrols actively toward Djebels Azag and Aired, reaching W slope of Azag. 34th Div makes limited progress against Hill 609, getting elements on S slopes. RCT 16 of 1st Div begins attack on Hill 523, strongpoint E of Hill 609, but makes little headway. Rest of 1st Div front is relatively quiet as positions on Djebel el Anz and Djebel Sidi Meftah are consolidated. CCA, 1st Armd Div, continues to clear Hill 299 against determined opposition.

30 April

ALEUTIAN IS.—Attu assault convoy arrives at Cold Harbor, where final attack plan is adopted.

TUNISIA—18 Army Group: Gen Alexander calls on Br Eighth Army to supply reinforcements for Br First Army in preparation for final assault. Gen Montgomery agrees to release 7th Armd Div, Ind 4th Div, and 201st Gds Brig, all veteran units.

U.S. II Corps makes substantial gains: On N, RCT 60 of 9th Div takes Djebel Guermach, a short distance from Kef en Nsour; RCT 39 seizes the strongly contested Hill 382 and other heights N of the Jefna position. 34th Div drives to summit of Hill 609 in tank-supported assault but is subjected to intense fire there. RCT 16, 1st Div, takes a hills E of Hill 609 but loses both to persistent counterattacks; 1st Armd Div provides tank assistance in the area. On S flank, 1st Armd Div retains Hill 299 under enemy fire, but the hill is not yet entirely free of enemy.

1 May

TUNISIA—18 Army Group: Begins regrouping for final offensive.

In U.S. II Corps area, enemy finds positions facing corps untenable and begins withdrawal, night 1–2. 9th Div suspends offensive on N flank of corps. In center, Germans make vain efforts to regain Hill 609. On S, enemy remnants are cleared from Hill 299, and 1st Armd Div is ready for drive on Mateur.

In Br First Army area, Fr 19th Corps reorganizes for final push with 3 divs: from left to right, Algerian, Moroccan, and Oran.

2 May

TUNISIA—18 Army Group: In U.S. II Corps area, 9th Div's RCT 60 occupies Kef en Nsour as enemy withdraws speedily toward Bizerte.

3 May

U.S.—Gen Marshall transmits to Gen Stilwell President Roosevelt's decision to make major U.S. air effort in China and to continue preparation for a modified ANAKIM (recapture of Burma).

MEDITERRANEAN—Gen Eisenhower decides that Br and U.S. forces to be employed in Operation HUSKY shall land abreast on SE coast of Sicily. A period of indecision by HUSKY planners (Force 141) as to landing sites thus ends.

TUNISIA—18 Army Group: Gen Alexander outlines to Gen K. A. N. Anderson his plan for final attack. 9 Corps, with 2 infantry and 2 armd divs in assault, is to make main effort, thrusting directly toward Tunis along road from Medjez el Bab. Lightning attack is planned in order to split and destroy enemy rather than compress his bridgehead, since schedule for invasion of Sicily requires quick conclusion of N African operations.

In U.S. II Corps area, 81st Armd Rcn Bn, followed by other elements of 1st Armd Div, advances to Mateur as enemy is withdrawing from it and quickly secures the town. 34th Div moves eastward toward Chouïgui, making no contact with enemy.

ETO—Gen Andrews, CG ETOUSA, is killed in plane crash in Iceland. Lt Gen Jacob L. Devers is subsequently chosen to replace him.

4 May

ALEUTIAN IS.—Attu invasion convoy leaves Cold Harbor for target, a day behind schedule because of poor weather conditions. D Day is consequently postponed to 8 May. As the convoy later approaches Attu, strong winds force a further postponement of D Day to 11 May.

BURMA—Continuing infiltration tactics, Japanese are now established on Buthidaung-Maungdaw road and resisting efforts of Br Imperial forces to oust them.

TUNISIA—18 Army Group: U.S. II Corps pushes forward in preparation for full-scale drive on Bizerte on 6th. On N flank, 9th Div and Corps Franc d'Afrique get into position for advance on Bizerte over hills N of Garaet Achkel. Corps d'Afrique improves positions W of Djebel Cheniti, commanding ridge just N of Garaet Achkel. To right, 1st Armd Div, whose next objective is Ferryville, patrols actively from Mateur. Enemy is subjecting Mateur to heavy air attacks. 91st Rcn Sq begins limited offensive for Djebel Achkel, a precipitous hill just S of Garaet Achkel commanding Mateur-Ferryville area, and meets strong opposition. On S flank of II Corps, 34th Div patrols uneventfully to Eddekhila in preparation for attack on Chouïgui Pass.

5 May

TUNISIA—18 Army Group: In U.S. II Corps area, RCT 47 of 9th Div paves way for direct assault on Djebel Cheniti by clearing hilly region NW of it. 81st Rcn Sq, 1st Armd Div, gains control of Djebel Achkel, but enemy remains on its E slopes until 11th. 1st Div moves forward to W bank of the Tine facing Djebel Douimiss. 34th Div reconnoiters toward Eddekhila in force against strong opposition. In Br First Army's 5 Corps area, 1st Div, with effective air and arty support, attacks Djebel Bou Aoukaz, on E bank of Medjerda R between Medjez el Bab and Tebourba, in order to cover left flank of 9 Corps as it drives on Tunis on 6th. The position is secured during bitter and costly fighting.

6 May

SWPA—GHQ issues Warning Instructions for Operation CARTWHEEL, drive on Rabaul.

TUNISIA—18 Army Group opens final assault, VULCAN, before dawn. Offensive is supported by massed arty fire, which at dawn is supplemented with the most intensive air bombardment yet employed in N Africa.

In U.S. II Corps area, while 47th Inf of 9th Div continues to clear hills N of Djebel Cheniti, 60th Inf passes through Corps Franc d'Afrique for frontal assault on Djebel Cheniti and clears most of it. CCA (6th Armd Inf, reinf) of 1st Armd begins attack on hills E of Mateur-Ferryville road; takes first ridge (Djebel el Messeftine), but loses it in counterattack. CCB (13th Armd Inf, reinf), to right, protects flank of CCA and starts E along Mateur-Djedeïda road. 1st Div, employing 18th and 26th Regts and with Co H of 1st Armd Regt in support, attacks across the Tine to clear Djebel Douimiss hills but is forced to withdraw to W bank, during night 6–7, where it conducts holding action. 3d Div (−RCT 7), upon arrival from Morocco,

[7-11 MAY 1943]   [109]

assembles behind 1st Div for possible commitment. 34th Div's 168th and 133d Regts drive beyond Eddekhila.

In Br First Army area, 9 Corps opens attack toward Tunis with Br 4th and Ind 4th Divs abreast, latter on left, on narrow front. After enemy line is breached, 6th and 7th Armd Divs pass through infantry and push on to Massicault, about half way to Tunis. Enemy attempts unsuccessfully to establish new line from Djedeïda to St. Cyprien.

7 May

BURMA—Ind 26th Div withdraws NW from Buthidaung under pressure.

TUNISIA—18 Army Group: Overruns both Tunis and Bizerte, splitting enemy forces.

In U.S. II Corps area, 9th Div finishes clearing Djebel Cheniti and adjacent hills to N; reconnoiters toward Bizerte as enemy resistance on N front collapses. Rcn elements of 894th TD Bn, followed closely by elements of 751st Tank Bn, enter Bizerte, where they find few enemy but many mines and booby traps. Ferryville falls to 1st Armd Div; elements driving E to cut Tunis-Bizerte road reach Oued ben Hassine and take bridge intact. 34th Div drives toward Chouïgui defile but is stopped a little short of it by enemy on Hill 242; enemy abandons the pass before dawn of 8th.

In Br First Army's 9 Corps area, 7th and 6th Armd Divs continue NE from Massicault, overrunning St. Cyprien and Le Bardo; Derbyshire Yeomanry and 11th Hussars enter Tunis in afternoon. Fr 19th Corps occupies Pont-du-Fahs.

8 May

TUNISIA—18 Army Group: In U.S. II Corps area, Corps Franc d'Afrique makes official entry into Bizerte. RCT 47 of 9th Div also enters, but withdraws while French mop up. 1st Armd Div pushes E in region S of Lac de Bizerte, clearing Djebel Sidi Mansour. Left flank elements, upon reaching Tunis-Bizerte road, drive N to Menzel Djemil. Column on right flank moves toward Protville to establish contact with British moving NE from Tunis and reaches Hill III, about midway between Mateur and Protville.

In Br First Army's 9 Corps area, while 7th Armd Div pushes northward toward U.S. II Corps zone from Tunis, 6th Armd Div, followed by 4th Div, drives SE toward Hammamet in effort to prevent enemy from making final stand on Cap Bon Peninsula and is halted abruptly at narrow Hamman Lif defile by enemy rear guards bent on keeping this line of retreat open. 1st Armd Div, released to 9 Corps from army reserve, is pushing NE from Goubellat area. 5 Corps' 1st Div and Ind 4th Div press eastward in conjunction with Fr 19th Corps. Fr 19th Corps is meeting firm resistance in hilly Zaghouan area.

9 May

CBI—Gen Wheeler, CG SOS, is directed to take charge of U.S. portion of Assam airfield project.

TUNISIA—18 Army Group: U.S. II Corps receives unconditional surrender of enemy within its zone. Thousands of prisoners, including 6 generals, are taken. 1st Armd Div drives to coast on left and makes contact with Br 7th Armd Div on right.

Br First Army continues to meet resistance in region S of U.S. II Corps zone. 9 Corps' 6th Armd Div is still held up at Hamman Lif defile. Fr 19th Corps battles enemy in Zaghouan area.

MEDITERRANEAN—Preparations are begun for conquest of Pantelleria (Operation CORKSCREW), largely by air and sea bombardment, before invasion of Sicily (Operation Husky) in order to remove this threat to HUSKY and gain an airfield from which to support HUSKY. NAAF is directed to make its full strength available for the operation. Fleet Adm A. B. Cunningham is to provide surface striking force and naval protection for movement of assault troops—Br 1st Inf Div—and maintain close naval blockade about the island. D Day is tentatively set as 11 June.

10 May

ALEUTIAN IS.—Japanese, alerted to expect assault on Attu during past week, decide that it will not be forthcoming and slacken their defenses.

TUNISIA—18 Army Group: In Br First Army's 9 Corps area, 6th Armd Div forces Hamman Lif defile in morning and thrusts rapidly to Hammamet, cutting off Cap Bon Peninsula. Advance is continued toward Bou Ficha.

11 May

ALEUTIAN IS.—U.S. 7th Div lands at widely separated points on Attu. Dense fog limits naval gunfire and air support, but helps infantry achieve complete tactical surprise. 17th Inf (less BLT 1), with 2d Bn of 32d Inf attached as reserve, makes main landing of Southern Landing Force on coast of Massacre Bay (Beaches Blue and Yellow) in afternoon; 2d and 3d Bns of 17th Inf push rapidly northward up Massacre Valley toward Jarmin (Massacre-Holtz Bay) Pass until pinned down about 1900 by intense enfilading fire from heights surrounding the valley. Platoon of 7th Rcn Tr makes subsidiary landing at Alexai Pt and joins main body at Massacre Bay without opposition. BLT 1, 17th Inf—the main assault group of Northern Landing Force—goes ashore at end of W arm of Holtz Bay (Beach Red) in afternoon; pushes southward toward Jarmin Pass to within 800 yards of its first objective, hill mass called Hill X, virtually unopposed. Prov Bn (7th Scout Co and 7th Rcn Tr, less one platoon) makes subsidiary landing on N coast W of Holtz Bay (Beach Scarlet) before dawn and moves inland unopposed toward Jarmin Pass. Gen Brown, 7th Div CG, arrives on Massacre beach and orders assault on Jarmin Pass for 12th. Mud of Attu immobilizes trucks and tractors.

CBI—Monsoon brings work on Ledo Road to a halt about 47 miles from Ledo.

TUNISIA—18 Army Group: In Br First Army's 9 Corps area, uneventful sweep around Cap Bon Peninsula by 4th Div reveals that no important enemy forces are there. 6th Armd Div reaches Bou Ficha. In Fr 19th Corps area, Axis resistance is weakening in Zaghouan sector.

12 May

INTERNATIONAL CONFERENCES—TRIDENT Conference—President Roosevelt, Prime Minister Churchill, and Combined Chiefs of Staff—opens in Washington to reconsider strategy in the light of recent events in Tunisia, the Aleutians, and the USSR.

ALEUTIAN IS.—On Attu, 7th Div, with naval gunfire and air support, continues 2-pronged thrusts toward Jarmin Pass. Frontal attacks from Massacre Bay beachhead fail to gain ground. Patrols are probing to develop enemy positions. 2d Bn, 32d Inf, goes ashore at Massacre Bay. Northern Force, finding enemy in prepared positions on Hill X, makes double envelopment attack and gains foothold on crest.

SOLOMON IS.—Allied surface vessels bombard Vila and Munda, night 12-13.

CBI—First Arakan campaign ends where it started as Ind 26th Div evacuates Maungdaw for defensive positions to N. Cost in casualties has been heavy. Factors contributing to the failure of this campaign have been the cancellation of Chinese drive into Burma from Yunnan plus unexpectedly limited action of 4 Corps from Assam.

TUNISIA—18 Army Group: Collapse of enemy resistance in the S is all but complete by nightfall. Enemy is surrendering en masse, among them Gen von Arnim, General Officer CinC, *Army Group Africa*.

In Br First Army's 9 Corps area, organized resistance collapses as 6th Armd Div drives S from Bou Ficha. Br Eighth Army's 56 Div co-operates by shelling from S. Isolated pockets of enemy remain NW of Enfidaville. Resistance in Fr 19th Corps zone ceases.

13 May

U.S.—CCS, at TRIDENT Conference, approve final outline plan for invasion of Sicily (Husky). Br and U.S. forces are to land abreast between Syracuse on SE coast and Palma on S coast on 10 July.

ALEUTIAN IS.—On Attu, further efforts of Massacre Bay force to break into Jarmin Pass are repelled by enemy. Positions remain about the same as those gained on D Day, although 2d Bn of 32d Inf is committed. Vicious and costly fighting occurs to N as enemy attempts to drive 7th Div troops from Hill X, but crest is firmly in American hands by nightfall. 3d Bn, 32d Inf, lands on Beach Red to reinforce the Holtz Bay force. Naval gunfire and air support of troops continues insofar as weather conditions permit.

NEW GUINEA—Japanese begin new series of heavy air attacks.

TUNISIA—18 Army Group: With surrender of Gen Messe, Rommel's successor, who is notified of his promotion to marshal on this date, Tunisia Campaign ends.

14 May

ALEUTIAN IS.—On Attu, Massacre Bay force, employing 2d Bn of 32d Inf on left and 3d Bn of 17th on right, continues fruitless and costly efforts to break into Jarmin Pass. Holtz Bay force prepares for strong southward attack but postpones it since 3d Bn of 32d Inf is unable to reach attack positions in time. Adverse weather conditions limit air support of troops, but surface vessels continue to bombard enemy positions.

PANTELLERIA—Mediterranean Air Command orders sea and air blockade of the island.

15 May

U.S.—CCS decide to give first priority to construction of Assam airfields; set goal of 7,000 tons a month to China, to be reached by 1 July.

ALEUTIAN IS.—3d Bn, 17th Inf, is withdrawn from Massacre Bay line on Attu, leaving 2d Bn, 32d, to continue attack. No progress is made, despite close arty support before and after jump-off. Dense fog postpones attack of Holtz Bay force until 1100. As fog is lifting it is discovered that enemy has withdrawn to ridge in center of valley, abandoning prepared positions and quantities of food and ammunition. Pursuit of enemy across open valley is slowed by enemy fire from commanding heights and is further handicapped by an Allied air strike that hits 7th Div forces by mistake. Prov bn that landed on Beach Scarlet on D Day joins main northern force.

[16-22 MAY 1943] [111]

CHINA—Because of Japanese action in central China, Chiang Kai-shek orders Gen Chen to return to defend Ichang area.

16 May

ALEUTIAN IS.—In an effort to speed operations on Attu, Maj Gen Eugene M. Landrum assumes command of assault force, relieving Gen Brown. Holtz Bay force secures foothold on N end of Holtz Valley ridge, thereby gaining control of entire ridge. Japanese, greatly outnumbered by Americans and in danger of being taken from the rear, withdraw during night 16-17 toward Chichagof Harbor for final stand. Most of Adm Rockwell's naval force retires northward to safer waters. Gen Landrum directs Capt H. B. Knowles, USN, to assume control of the remaining vessels; takes over air-ground control.

GERMANY—RAF Lancasters, in highly successful night operation, 16-17, attack and breach Moehne and Eder dams, flooding large portions of the Ruhr and disrupting electric and transportation systems.

17 May

ALEUTIAN IS.—On Attu, Holtz Bay force's 3d Bn, 32d Inf, moves forward well before dawn and by daylight finds that enemy has withdrawn. Patrols report E arm of Holtz Bay free of enemy. Massacre Bay force also finds positions previously defended by enemy abandoned and occupies Jarmin Pass. Patrol moves forward in effort to establish contact with Northern Force.

18 May

ALEUTIAN IS.—Patrol from Massacre Bay front makes contact with Holtz Bay force before dawn. Holtz Bay is put into use by Americans as landing phase ends. This improves the supply situation of Northern Force somewhat. Co K of 32d Inf sweeps entire Holtz Bay Valley, making no contact with enemy. Preparations are made for next phase of battle-attack on Chichagof Harbor. Northern Force patrol attempts unsuccessfully to locate an easier route to Chichagof than the Holtz-Chichagof Pass, which is commanded by steep Fish Hook Ridge. 1st Bn of 4th Inf arrives.

PANTELLERIA—Allied planes begin strong air offensive against Pantelleria that is to continue through 5 June. Porto di Pantelleria and Marghana airdrome are chief targets. In conjunction with air attacks, naval blockade is being maintained about the island, virtually isolating it.

19 May

ALEUTIAN IS.—On Attu, 2d Bn of 17th Inf, assisted by Co C of 32d Inf, begins attack before dawn to capture pass (later called Clevesy Pass after Lt Samuel H. Clevesy of Co H) into Sarana Valley. After heavy fighting in which 2d Bn of 32d Inf is committed, the pass is cleared by nightfall, but enemy remains on crests of 2 peaks overlooking it. On N front, Co L of 32d Inf begins operations to clear the high Holtz-Chichagof Pass at base of Fish Hook Ridge, moving from Holtz Bay up steep slope of the valley against enemy fire.

20 May

U.S.—CCS accept TRIDENT recommendations for CBI.

ALEUTIAN IS.—On S front, Co G of 17th Inf clears one of the 2 peaks dominating Clevesy Pass in morning, but efforts of 2d Bn and CO C of 32d Inf to take the other fail. Co E of 32d Inf then moves forward for night enveloping attack, scaling the steep slopes cautiously in effort to take enemy by surprise. Meanwhile, 1st Bn of 4th Inf moves through Clevesy Pass to attack heights across upper part of Sarana Valley and makes substantial progress. 3d Bn, 17th Inf, patrols along Sarana Valley and fires upon enemy located by 1st Bn, 4th Inf. Northern Force continues to clear preliminary hill line of Fish Hook Ridge.

BURMA—Gen Sir George Giffard replaces Gen Irwin as Commander of Eastern Army. Completion of 3-months' mission of Brig Wingate's Chindits is announced. About a third of the original force has been lost. Withdrawal of Chindits into India is completed early in June. The Wingate expedition, supplied wholly by air, becomes a pattern for future operations behind enemy lines.

21 May

ALEUTIAN IS.—On southern front on Attu, Co E of 32d Inf reduces last enemy strongpoint on peak dominating Clevesy Pass. 1st Bn, 4th Inf, pushes forward to ridge overlooking Sarana-Chichagof Pass and facing Fish Hook Ridge; patrols to mouth of the pass. After prolonged bombardment by all available weapons, Co L of Sad Inf, Northern Force, takes hill that has been barring its progress toward Fish Hook Ridge. Remaining 2 cos of 1st Bn, 32d Inf, land on Attu.

CHINA—Final phase of Japanese expedition in central China opens.

22 May

ALEUTIAN IS.—Southern Force, in morning attack by 3d Bn of 17th Inf, takes rest of high ground surrounding entrance to Chichagof Valley. Exploiting this success, 2d Bn of 32d Inf attacks in afternoon and drives wedge into entrance of Chichagof Valley, the easiest approach to Chichagof. Patrol contact is made with Northern Force, which remains in place, consolidating positions.

INDIA—Gen Wheeler receives directive calling for expedited program of airfield construction in Assam.

USSR—Moscow announces dissolution of Comintern.

23 May

ALEUTIAN IS.—Southern Force, employing 2d Bn of 17th Inf, begins attack on Fish Hook Ridge but is soon pinned down by enemy fire. Strong patrols of Northern Force attempt unsuccessfully to force Holtz-Sarana Pass. Direct communication between Northern and Southern Forces is possible for first time as wire is laid between the two. Coordinated attack for the Fish Hook is then planned.

TUNISIA—18 Army Group staff is disbanded, having served its purpose.

24 May

U.S.—JCS authorize planning and training for invasion of Kiska.

ALEUTIAN IS.—On Attu, efforts of 3d Bn, 32d Inf, and 2d Bn, 17th, to gain Fish Hook Ridge meet intense fire and make little headway.

25 May

INTERNATIONAL CONFERENCES—TRIDENT Conference in Washington ends. The conferees have selected 1 May 1944 as target date for cross-Channel invasion of northwestern Europe (OVERLORD). Large-scale air offensive from United Kingdom will precede OVERLORD. In the Mediterranean, operations following capture of Sicily (HUSKY) are to be designed to knock Italy out of the war. Ploesti oil fields are to be bombed from Mediterranean bases. Material to China is to be increased and communications with it opened. General approval is given U.S. "Strategic Plan for the Defeat of Japan," calling for drive on Japan through Central Pacific.

ALEUTIAN IS.—On Attu, Southern Force's 2d Bn, 17th Inf, gains toehold on crest of Fish Hook Ridge, breaking through elaborate tunnel system below summit. Northern Force, attacking with 3d Bn of 32d Inf and supported by Cos A and C of 17th, clears trench system on its side of the Fish Hook but is unable to reach crest.

TUNISIA—Combined hq is established at Sousse by representatives of forces participating in Operation CORKSCREW (conquest of Pantelleria).

26 May

ALEUTIAN IS.—Northern and Southern Forces are slowly expanding positions on Fish Hook Ridge, former moving elements to crest via route previously cleared by 2d Bn, 17th Inf. 1st Bn, 4th Inf, joins in fight for the ridge.

27 May

U.S.—Joint Staff Planners direct Joint War Plans Committee to determine troop needs and suggest target dates for invasion of the Marshalls, POA.

ALEUTIAN IS.—7th Div. finishes clearing Fish Hook Ridge. Fighter strip is being constructed at Alexai Pt.

28 May

ALEUTIAN IS.—7th Div maintains pressure on enemy, who by end of day is compressed into small part of Chichagof Harbor. Messages requesting Japanese to surrender are dropped from the air.

29 May

ALEUTIAN IS.—Japanese make strong counterattack from Chichagof Harbor before dawn, pushing rapidly toward Clevesy Pass in effort to break out into Massacre Valley. Main force of attack is spent by dawn when enemy, dispersed into small groups, is forced to go into hiding.

30 May

ALEUTIAN IS.—After a last weak counterattack, organized enemy resistance collapses on Attu. 7th Div reaches shore of Chichagof Harbor without incident. U.S. Army force under Brig Gen John E. Copeland occupies Shemya I. without opposition.

31 May

ALEUTIAN IS. 7th Div is rounding up stragglers of the defeated Japanese garrison of Attu, originally numbering about 2,500.

1 June

ALEUTIAN IS.—Plan is formulated for occupation of Kiska. U.S. Eleventh Air Force is to continue to take advantage of every break in the weather to hit Kiska while assault troops are being assembled and trained intensively at Fort Ord, California, and in the Aleutians. Surface vessels are to assist in the softening up program and cover landings.

PANTELLERIA—All-out air offensive against the island continues and is being supplemented with naval gunfire from small groups of Br vessels.

3 June

SOLOMON IS.—Adm Halsey issues basic operations plan for assault on New Georgia Is., in central Solomons, in order to secure Munda airfield, from which to support subsequent offensive against N Solomons. Adm Turner is to head amphibious forces. New Georgia Occupation Force (43d Div reinf and 1st and 4th Marine Raider bns) is to be under command of Gen Hester, CG 43d Div.

CHINA—Japanese attain their objective of capturing shipping on Upper Yangtze in W Hupeh and begin withdrawing.

ALGERIA—French announce formation in Algiers of French Committee of National Liberation, a provisional government for the French Empire.

5 June

MEDITERRANEAN—Gen Eisenhower orders head of Force 141 (planning staff that is later to become Headquarters, 15th Army Group, under Gen Alexander) to draw up plans for invasion of Italy. Gen Alexander is given command of Br 10 and 5 Corps.

6 June

PANTELLERIA—Air action against the island is intensified as second phase of air offensive opens. Main weight of attacks is against coastal batteries and gun emplacements.

7 June

SOLOMON IS.—Japanese begin another series of air attacks on Guadalcanal in effort to cut communications lines. Allied fighters intercept and destroy 23 planes for loss of 9.

8 June

ALEUTIAN IS.—Fighter strip at Alexai Pt, Attu, is completed. Japanese order Kiska abandoned. U.S. DD blockade is established about the island and aircraft continue to pound it whenever possible.

PANTELLERIA—Air offensive against the island becomes increasingly intense as invasion date approaches. Br naval forces of 8 DD's, 5 CL's, and 3 torpedo boats bombard shore batteries and harbor area. Surrender requests, dropped by aircraft, are ignored.

10 June

U.S.—In preliminary report, Joint War Plans Committee recommends Marshalls be invaded near end of October and Gen MacArthur and Adm Halsey conduct holding actions until operations in the Marshalls are concluded. This arouses unfavorable reaction in some quarters and the suggestion is soon rejected.

ETO—CCS issue directive that officially inaugurates Combined Bomber Offensive (later designated Operation POINTBLANK) against Germany.

11 June

PANTELLERIA—After preparatory naval and air bombardment, Br 1st Div lands on Pantelleria virtually unopposed. Island surrenders unconditionally at 1735. This is the first occasion on which airpower has overwhelmed an objective of this type. NAAF, during period 8 May to date, has flown 5,285 sorties against the island and dropped 6,200 tons of bombs. Fall of Pantelleria permits Allied aircraft in Mediterranean to concentrate efforts in direct preparation for invasion of Sicily (HUSKY).

LAMPEDUSA—Allied planes begin air assault on island that continues through night 11-12. Br naval TF from Pantelleria accompanying an LCI with co of Coldstream Gds embarked joins aircraft in bombarding island, night 11-12.

GERMANY—Attack by Eighth Air Force on Wilhelmshaven demonstrates the difficulty of daylight strikes on targets beyond range of fighter escort. Although B-17 losses are light, intercepting enemy planes prevent accurate bombing of the submarine-building yards.

12 June

SOLOMON IS.—Allied planes intercept large force of attacking enemy planes in Guadalcanal area and destroy 31 for loss of 6.

LAMPEDUSA—Surrenders unconditionally after further bombardment. Coldstream Gds go ashore and take charge.

13 June

CHINA—Japanese expedition in central China ends.

LINOSA—Landing party from Br DD accepts surrender of island.

GERMANY—60 B-17's of Eighth Air Force attack Kiel submarine yards and harbor against heaviest German Air Force opposition yet encountered. 22 B-17's are lost in air battle. Main Eighth Air Force attack of the day, by 102 B-17's on Bremen, is lightly opposed.

14 June

NEW GUINEA—On or near this date, U.S. 41st Div forms Coane Force, consisting of 2d and 3d Bn, 162d Inf, plus elements of 205th and 218th FA Bns, under Div Arty Commander, Brig Gen Ralph W. Coane.

CHINA—Forward echelon hq of U.S. Fourteenth Air Force is established at Kweilin.

LAMPIONE—Br naval party occupies island without opposition. Allies now control all islands in Sicily Strait.

15 June

MEDITERRANEAN—Gen Giraud is directed by Gen Eisenhower to name ground forces commander and staff to prepare plan for invasion of Corsica (FIREBRAND). Gen Giraud subsequently suggests Gen Juin as commander.

16 June

SOLOMON Is.—FO No. I, Hq, New Georgia Occupation Force, directs seizure of preliminary objectives in central Solomons in preparation for capture of Munda airfield on New Georgia I. D Day is to be 30 June. Some 120 Japanese planes attack Guadalcanal, damaging 3 ships, 2 of which must be beached. Intercepting Allied planes, 104 strong, exact heavy price, claiming almost 100 enemy aircraft destroyed. 6 Allied planes are lost.

17 June

CHINA—Gen Stilwell presents TRIDENT proposals to Chiang Kai-shek.

18 June

SOLOMON Is.—43d Div issues orders for movement to New Georgia Is. COMAIRSOPAC assigns duties for New Georgia operation to his air units.

CHINA—Gen Chennault reports to the President on operations of Fourteenth Air Force. Gen Stilwell, now commanding YOKE-Force staff (all U.S. organizations working with Y-Force), outlines to Col Dorn, his chief of staff, his mission in the program.

SICILY—Allied planes begin powerful attacks on Messina. Other targets on and in vicinity of Sicily are being pounded in preparation for HUSKY.

U.K.—Prime Minister Churchill announces that Gen Auchinleck is to replace Gen Wavell as CinC India and that Wavell will be Viceroy of India.

20 June

NEW GUINEA—Gen Krueger opens ALAMO (U.S. Sixth Army) hq at Milne Bay. 17th Brig, Aus 3d Div, is holding positions in Mubo-Lababia Ridge area against sharp enemy counterattacks that continue for next few days.

CBI—Gen Auchinleck succeeds Gen Wavell as CinC India.

LAMPEDUSA—Airfield becomes serviceable.

GERMANY—RAF Lancasters, on first RAF shuttle-bombing raid between U.K. and Africa, attack Friedrichshafen, concentrating on industrial targets, and land safely in N Africa. On return trip to Britain, the planes bomb naval base at Spezia, Italy, night 23-24.

21 June

ALEUTIAN Is.—Airfield on Shemya I. becomes operational.

SOLOMON Is.—To forestall enemy occupation of Segi Pt on S tip of New Georgia I., 4th Mar Raider Bn (−) sails there from Guadalcanal and lands unopposed.

22 June

SOLOMON Is.—Cos A and D of 103d Inf, 43d Div, and airfield survey force join Mar Raiders on Segi Pt, New Georgia I.

TROBRIAND Is.—Woodlark TF (112th Cav RCT, reinf) lands advance party on Woodlark I. without opposition, night 22-23.

GERMANY—Eighth Air Force bombers attack synthetic rubber plant at Huels in force with particularly good results. Plant is temporarily put out of operation. This is the first large-scale daylight attack to be made on the Ruhr.

23 June

TROBRIAND Is.—Kiriwina TF (RCT 158, a separate regt, reinf) lands advance elements on Kiriwina I, night 23-24, without opposition.

NEW GUINEA—Enemy pressure on 17th Brig of Aus 3d Div, in Mubo-Lababia Ridge area, eases as Japanese withdraw a little.

25 June

SICILY—Preinvasion bombardment by Allied planes continues. NAAF delivers heaviest single attack of the month on Messina, dropping more than 300 tons of bombs.

26 June

NEW GUINEA—MacKechnie Force, now assembled at Morobe where supplies have been amassed, starts movement by water to staging area at Mageri Pt, 15 miles N W of Morobe, in preparation for amphibious assault on Nassau Bay.

PANTELLERIA—33d Fighter Gp (P-40) is established on island.

U.K.—COSSAC planners select Air Marshal Sir Trafford Leigh-Mallory, air officer commanding in chief, RAF Fighter Command, to prepare air plans for OVERLORD.

27 June

SOLOMON IS.—From Segi, New Georgia I., marines of 4th Raider Bn move by sea to vicinity of Lambeti Plantation in preparation for overland march to Viru Harbor.

28 June

NEW GEORGIA I.—Marines of 4th Raider Bn begin overland journey to Viru Harbor.

29 June

SOLOMON IS.—While U.S. assault forces are sailing to central Solomons, surface force bombards Munda, Vila, and the Shortlands, night 29–30.

MEDITERRANEAN—Gen Eisenhower recommends to CCS that projected landing on heel of Italy near Taranto (Operation MUSKET) be deferred by Fifth Army. 3 other actions are under consideration: (1) invasion of toe (BUTTRESS) and instep (GOBLET); (2) landing on toe from which overland drives would be made to heel, Naples, and Rome with seaborne reinforcements moved in at Naples; (3) invasion of Sardinia (BRIMSTONE).

30 June

PACIFIC—Operation CARTWHEEL, converging drives on Rabaul by forces of S Pacific and SWPA, opens with amphibious operations against central Solomons, Trobriands, and New Guinea.

SOLOMON IS.—Ships and landing craft from S Pacific Amphib Force (organized as TF 31 under command of Adm Turner) land New Georgia Occupation Force (commanded by Gen Hester, 43d Div CG) on central Solomons. New Georgia Occupation Force is divided into Western Force (TG 31.1), which is to make main landing on Rendova I. and later take Munda airfield on New Georgia I., and Eastern Force (TG 31.2), which is to make subsidiary landings. Preceding main landing, Onaiavisi Occupation Unit (COs A and B, 169th Inf) secures Onaiavisi Entrance in uncontested landings on Sasavele and Baraulu Is.; establishes outposts on Roviana I. 172d Inf, 43d Div, of Western Force lands on Rendova I. without opposition and pushes inland 1,000 yards to search for scattered Japanese forces. Failing to receive signal to land from marines of 4th Raider Bn ashore, Viru Occupation Force (reinf Co B, 103d Inf) of Eastern Force lands instead at Segi Pt. The Mar Raiders, moving overland, reach Viru Harbor in evening. To secure Wickham Anchorage on Vangunu I., Eastern Force lands reinf 2d Bn, 103d Inf, and elements of 4th Mar Raider Bn on Vangunu at Oleana. Although landing is unopposed, Japanese resist movement of assault force toward Wickham Anchorage. Japanese aircraft are active against shipping, damaging flag ship *McCawley*, which friendly PT's later sink by mistake.

TROBRIAND IS.—Main bodies of Woodlark and Kiriwina TF's make unopposed landings on their respective islands, where airfields are to be constructed. These are the first operations to be directed by U.S. Sixth Army, operating as ALAMO Force.

NEW GUINEA—MacKechnie Force (Col MacKechnie, commander of 162d Inf, 41st Div), consisting now of 1st Bn, 162d Inf, and supporting U.S. and Aus forces, begins unopposed landing at Nassau Bay shortly after midnight 29–30, aided by lights of Aus forces ashore. Final wave, Co B, does not land until later. MacKechnie Force pushes N toward Bitoi R and S toward Tabali R, soon meeting enemy opposition. Papuan Inf Bn (PIB) scouts blocking enemy movement in Cape Dinga area, S of Nassau Bay, force enemy back toward American positions. Aus 3d Div's 15th Brig opens attack on Bobdubi Ridge, and 17th Brig maintains pressure against enemy positions in Mubo salient. All operations are commanded by New Guinea Force (Gen Herring, commander, pending arrival of Gen Blarney).

MEDITERRANEAN—As preinvasion bombardment continues, NAAF planes, in period 18–30 June, fly 883 bomber sorties and IX BC, 107 sorties, against Sicily and Italy, concentrating on supply points, ports, and marshaling yards.

1 July

Solomon Is.—43d Div troops on Rendova consolidate beachhead and continue search for enemy. On New Georgia I., marines of 4th Raider Bn seize Viru Harbor in double envelopment maneuver.

NEW GUINEA—Allied troops are consolidating positions along S arm of Bitoi R in Nassau Bay area.

CHINA—Gen Chennault designates shipping and port installations as primary targets for Fourteenth Air Force.

2 July

SOLOMON IS.— 43d Div is ordered to proceed with next task in central Solomons—capture of Munda airfield—and begins movement of assault force from Rendova to New Georgia. Enemy bombers make destructive raid on Rendova; subsequent air attacks are much less effective. Japanese warships shell Rendova, night 2–3.

TROBRIAND IS.—Work is begun on airfield at Woodlark I.

NEW GUINEA—MacKechnie Force holds firm beachhead at Nassau Bay. Contact is made with Aus 3d Div.

MEDITERRANEAN—Sicilian and Italian ports continue to receive full attention of NAAF, which, during period 12 June–2 July, drops 2,276 tons of bombs. Malta-based and Gozo-based fighters contribute cover and escort. Final phase of pre-HUSKY air offensive, beginning at this time, is directed toward knocking out enemy planes and wrecking airfields.

U.K.—Air Marshal Leigh-Mallory establishes air staff at Norfolk House.

3 July

Solomon Is.—Southern Landing Group (Brig Gen Leonard F. Wing) of Gen Hester's Munda-Bairoko Occupation Force lands 1st Bn of 172d Inf, 43d Div, on Zanana beach, about 5 air miles E of Munda, New Georgia I., without opposition. Small defense perimeter of 1st Bn is gradually strengthened during next few days. Wickham Anchorage on Vangunu I, which is to become staging point for landing craft, falls into American hands.

4 July

Solomon Is.—Co B, 103d Inf, arrives at Viru Harbor and relieves marines of 4th Raider Bn. From Zanana, 1st Bn of 172d Inf and Co A of 169th virtually unopposed move W to Barike R, line of departure for assault on Munda. As transports carrying Northern Landing Group (Lt Col Harry B. Liversedge, USMC) of Gen Hester's Munda-Bairoko Occupation Force proceed toward Rice Anchorage, night 4–5, accompanying warships bombard Vila and Bairoko Harbor and intercept Japanese DD's bringing reinforcements to Kolombangara from the Shortlands. In the ensuing action, USS Strong is lost to enemy torpedo, but Japanese effort to land troops is blocked.

CRETE—Br commandos successfully raid enemy airfields during night and withdraw safely.

MEDITERRANEAN—Gen Wladislaw Sikorski, CinC of Polish forces, is killed in plane crash near Gibraltar.

5 July

U.S.—President Roosevelt proposes to Chiang Kai-shek that Maj Gen George E. Stratemeyer coordinate air forces matters in India-Burma sector.

Solomon Is.—Gen Harmon recommends to Adm Halsey that XIV Corps staff prepare to take over on New Georgia and free Gen Hester for operations against Kolombangara. Almost all the New Georgia Occupation Force is now ashore in central Solomons, main body at Rendova. Northern Landing Group—consisting of 1st Raider Bn of 1st Mar Raider Regt, reinf by 3d Bns of 148th and 145th Regts, 37th Div—lands without opposition at Rice Anchorage, beginning at 0130. Leaving elements of 3d Bn, 145th Inf, to defend landing site, Col Liversedge's force starts S toward Dragon's Peninsula, between Enogai Inlet and Bairoko Harbor, forward elements reaching Giza Giza R. Patrol of Southern Landing Group finds Japanese force blocking Munda Trail between Zanana and Barike R.

BATTLE OF KULA GULF—U.S. naval surface force engages enemy vessels bringing second echelon of reinforcements to Kolombangara, night 5–6. Japanese lose 2 DD's and sink USS *Helena*. Force of 850 Japanese succeeds in landing at Vila.

USSR—Germans launch offensive on limited front to reduce Soviet salient at Kursk, *9th Army* pushing S from Orel and *4th Pz Army* and *Army Kempf* working northward from Belgorod. Limited progress is made at heavy cost in tanks. By this time, Axis and Soviet forces have both taken advantage of spring thaw to reorganize and refit troops. Red Army is greatly superior in strength.

6 July

ALEUTIAN Is.—U.S. naval vessels, for the first time in 11 months, bombard Kiska, supplementing intermittent efforts of aircraft to neutralize the island. Cruiser-DD TF (Rear Adm Robert C. Giffen) conducts the action and retires safely.

Solomon Is.—Heavy bombers begin series of strikes against enemy airfields on Bougainville, the next objective. Attacks are gradually increased in strength and frequency and are supplemented by medium bomber strikes on enemy shipping in the area. By this time, 43d Div's 172d and 169th Regts are on New Georgia I. 172d closes along the Barike R and 3d Bn, 169th, starts toward the river from Zanana. Japanese repulse attacks against their roadblock on Munda Trail. Col Liversedge's force reaches and crosses Tamakau R.

NEW GUINEA—3d Bn of 162d Inf, part of U.S. first Div's Coane Force, goes ashore at Nassau beachhead and begins period of active patrolling. 2d Bn, 162d Inf, takes over positions vacated by 3d Bn at Morobe.

CHINA—Fourteenth Air Force begins antishipping operations off West R estuary.

7 July

U.S.—Gen Giraud arrives in Washington to confer with President Roosevelt and military leaders.

Solomon Is.—First echelon of 145th Inf (− 3d Bn), 37th Div, sails from Guadalcanal for Rendova. On New Georgia I, 43d Div continues futile efforts to eliminate roadblock on Munda Trail between Zanana and the Barike. Continuing S, main body of Col Liversedge's force reaches Enogai Inlet and encounters enemy resistance at Triri; 3d Bn of 148th Inf reaches Munda-Bairoko Trail.

NEW GUINEA—Allied planes, in direct support of ground operations, attack Mubo area in force, dropping over 100 tons of bombs. MacKechnie Force, having pushed inland from beach to Napier, begins assault on Bitoi Ridge. Aus 2/6th Bn captures Observation Hill, an important terrain feature a mile W of Mubo.

USSR—Slow enemy advance in Orel sector N of Kursk is brought to a halt as Red Army opens counterattacks. Limited progress is being made by S prong of Axis offensive in Belgorod area.

8 July

NEW GEORGIA I.—43d Div completes reduction of enemy strongpoint astride Munda Trail; 169th Inf closes along the Barike, from which Munda will be attacked on 9th. Col Liversedge's 3d Bn, 148th Inf, establishes roadblock on Munda-Bairoko Trail and remains there. 1st Raider Bn, turning over positions at Triri to troops of 145th Inf, tries in vain to reach Enogai.

9 July

SOLOMON IS.—On New Georgia I, 43d Div, with close air, arty, and naval gunfire support, attacks W across Barike R toward Munda with 172d Inf on left and 169th on right. 172d gains about 1,100 yards but 169th makes little headway beyond the Barike and still has elements E of the river. 1st Raider Bn of Col Liversedge's force again attacks toward Enogai from Triri, using another route, but is halted by enemy fire near Enogai Pt. Both sides are moving reinforcements to central Solomons. Second echelon of 145th Inf (−3d Bn), 37th Div, sails for Rendova. Japanese land 1,200 reinforcements from the Shortlands on Kolombangara.

SICILY—Tremendous preinvasion air offensive against island results in Allied air superiority, over enemy. As convoys of Western (U.S., under Vice Adm Henry K. Hewitt) and Eastern (Br, under Adm Sir Bertram H. Ramsay) Naval Task Forces, with ground assault forces of Gen Alexander's 15th Army Group embarked, approach Sicily in preparation for early morning invasion on 10th, Br and U.S. airborne contingents take off from Tunisia and are dropped on the island during night 9-10. High winds prevailing in assault area handicap both sea and airborne forces, but latter surprise enemy and take assigned objectives, facilitating forward movement of seaborne forces when they arrive. 1st Air Landing Brig Gp of 1st A/B Div, 13 Corps, Br Eighth Army, is dropped near Syracuse to hasten capture of that port. Most of the 130-odd gliders land wide of drop zone and nearly 50 fall into the sea, but group of 8 officers and 65 men reaches and holds objective-Ponte Grande bridge. U.S. parachute task force under Col J. M. Gavin, consisting of 82d A/B Div's RCT 505 and 3d Bn of 504th Para Regt, is dropped from 226 C-47's to take high ground near Ponte Olivo airfield, NE of Gela, and assist seaborne forces of U.S. II Corps, Seventh Army, in capture of the airfield. Although drops are very widely scattered over S Sicily, objective is taken. This is the first major airborne operation to be undertaken by Allied forces in World War II and consequently becomes subject of intensive study.

USSR—Red Army opens counterattacks in Obojan region, S of Kursk. Although vigorous fighting continues N and S of Kursk for some time, Axis forces are unable to advance.

10 July

KURILE IS.—Paramushiro is bombed for first time, by B-25's from Attu.

NEW GEORGIA IS.—Maj Gen Oscar W. Griswold, CG XIV Corps, is ordered to New Georgia. Momentum of 43d Div's westward drive on Munda slows, particularly on right, where 169th Inf is brought to a halt at junction of Munda Trail with trail leading to coast at Laiana. Jungle terrain makes close air support increasingly difficult as attack progresses and is also slowing road construction. Liversedge's force clears most of Enogai area but by now is dependent upon airdrops for food and water.

NEW GUINEA—U.S. forces from Nassau Bay effect junction with Aus 3d Div troops at Buigap Creek, cutting Japanese communications between Mubo and Salamaua.

SICILY—15th Army Group: Main invasion forces of U.S. Seventh and Br Eighth Armies, with close support of Royal and U.S. Navies and Allied aircraft, land on SE coast of Sicily on broad front from point W of Licata on W to point S of Syracuse on E between 0245 and 0600; establish bridgeheads without serious difficulty.

U.S. Seventh Army, which Gen Patton activates at sea at 0001, puts 3 assault forces ashore between Licata and Capo Scaramia. Gen Truscott commands westernmost TF (3d Div, CCA of 2d Armd Div, and 3d Ranger Bn), which lands in Licata area and takes Licata and its small port. Gen Bradley, U.S. II Corps commander, commands the other two U.S. assault force. 1st Div (− RCT 18) and 1st and 4th Ranger Bns land at Gela. To E, 45th Div goes ashore near Scoglitti. Both Gela and Scoglitti, as well as Vittoria, are taken as troops push inland and along coast against light resistance. U.S. 82d A/B Div parachutists, upon making contact with 1st Div, come under II Corps command; elements take

Marina di Ragusa. Floating reserve (RCT 18 of 1st Div, and 2d Armd Div less CCA) is landed during day in region E of Gela.

Br Eighth Army (Gen Montgomery) lands to E of U.S. II Corps between Pozzallo and Syracuse. 30 Corps, with 231st Brig on right, 51st Div in center, and Cdn 1st Div on left, lands on Pachino peninsula and clears town of Pachino and airfield. 13 Corps, on E flank, employs 5th Div on right and 50th on left. While 50th takes Avola, 5th makes contact with airborne forces of Br 1st A/B Div at Ponte Grande and crosses bridge to capture Syracuse, night 10-11.

11 July

Solomon Is.—Adm Halsey selects Gen Vandegrift, commander of I Mar Amphib Corps, to head ground forces that are to invade Bougainville, which lies between S Pacific forces and Rabaul. Gen Griswold arrives at Rendova by air. On New Georgia I, supply problem is growing so acute as 43d Div's attack progresses toward Munda that 172d Inf starts quietly S to anchor left flank on coast at Laiana and shorten supply line. Enemy soon discovers the move. Command of 169th Inf, which is still held up by opposition from heights dominating Munda-Lambeti trail junction, passes to Col Temple G. Holland, former commander of 145th Inf. Liversedge's force is mopping up in Enogai area. Airfield at Segi Pt is ready for limited use by fighters.

SICILY—15th Army Group: U.S. Seventh Army reaches beachhead line Yellow (Palma di Montechiaro-Campobello-Mazzarino-Caltagirone-Grammichele) on W flank, where Gen Truscott's force expands Licata bridgehead to include Palma di Montechiaro, Naro, Campobello, and Riesi. II Corps withstands determined, tank-supported counterattacks, main force of which hits 1st Div in Gela area. 45th Div helps repel enemy and takes town of Comiso and airport and Ragusa. Airdrop of another contingent of 82d A/B Div (RCT 504) in Gela area proves costly; drops are scattered and come under both enemy and friendly fire. In Br Eighth Army area, 30 Corps expands bridgehead to Avola-Pozzallo road, seizing Pozzallo. 13 Corps makes main effort northward along coast toward Augusta.

USSR—In region S of Kursk, Axis *4th Pz Army* and *Army Kempf* join forces in drive toward Prochorovka and make limited progress.

12 July

NEW GEORGIA—172d Inf of 43d Div, now without food and water, pushes to within 500 yards of Laiana and learns from scouts that Japanese are firmly entrenched in vicinity of Ilangana. 169th Inf, up against outer defenses of Munda position, attempts to advance behind rolling arty barrage but makes little headway.

BATTLE OF KOLOMBANGARA (Second Battle of Kula Gulf)—Allied surface force under Rear Adm Walden L. Ainsworth engages enemy force bringing reinforcements to central Solomons, night 12-13; sinks Japanese cruiser but loses DD *Gwin* and suffers damage to other vessels. Despite this action, Japanese land 1,200 men on Kolombangara.

NEW GUINEA—Allied troops advancing on Mubo reduce several enemy strongpoints.

CBI—Generalissimo Chiang Kai-shek consents to TRIDENT recommendations concerning limited offensive, now called SAUCY, to reopen land route from Burma to China.

SICILY—15th Army Group: Bridgeheads are firmly established by end of day. Br and U.S. forces make contact at Ragusa.

Advance U.S. Seventh Army CP moves ashore from USS *Monrovia*. Gen Truscott's force takes Canicatti, important road junction. II Corps, despite further determined efforts of enemy to push it back to the sea, expands bridgehead. 1st Div takes Ponte Olivo airport and pushes inland toward Niscemi. Units of 45th Div in Ragusa make contact with Cdn 1st Div of Br Eighth Army.

In Br Eighth Army area, 30 Corps, overrunning Modica and Palazzolo, reaches general line Sortini-Palazzolo-Ragusa-Scicli. 13 Corps, though assisted by air and naval gunfire, is stalled by stubborn opposition at Priolo Gargallo, about half way between Syracuse and Augusta.

USSR—Red Army opens strong offensive, supported by concentrated arty fire, to reduce Axis salient at Orel, concentrating on N and E flanks. The operation is well timed, coming after enemy reserves have been committed to the unsuccessful offensive toward Kursk, which has sharply reduced tank strength. During fierce battle S of Kursk, in Prochorovka area, Axis loses over 400 tanks in vain effort to advance.

13 July

NEW GEORGIA—Adm Halsey directs Gen Harmon to take command of New Georgia operation, which is falling behind schedule. 169th Inf of 43d Div, with air and arty support, drives salient into enemy positions E of Munda with capture by 3d Bn of hill commanding Munda Trail. Inability of 1st and 2d Bns to advance, however, leaves 3d Bn in exposed position. 172d Inf reaches coast at Laiana.

NEW GUINEA—Mubo area is cleared of enemy. Aus 3d Div, assisted by fire of Americans, finishes clearing Lababia Ridge.

SICILY—First Allied fighters fly to Sicily to operate from Pachino field. Enemy planes are no longer able to offer effective resistance over the island and are reducing their efforts.

15th Army Group: Gen Alexander establishes new boundary between Br and U.S. forces, giving Eighth Army road Vizzini-Caltagirone-Piazza Armerina-Enna-S. Stefano.

U.S. Seventh Army orders Canicatti held while rcn is pushed W to Agrigento on W, where Gen Truscott's assault force has attained its immediate objective. In II Corps area, RCT 18 is released to 1st Div, from which 1st and 4th Ranger Bns are detached. 2d Armd Div (− CCA) and 1st and 4th Ranger Bns are placed in army reserve. II Corps continues efforts to close along line Yellow. 45th Div pushes N, taking Licodia and Monterosso.

In Br Eighth Army's 30 Corps area, 51st Div is slowed by enemy near Vizzini. 13 Corps begins offensive, night 13-14, in effort to break out into Catania plain. Parachutists of 1st Para Brig are dropped to seize Primasole bridge over Simeto R, the most suitable exit to Catania plain, and do so. The operation, however, is costly, since planes come under enemy and friendly fire. Seaborne commandos are landed and take another bridge in the area. 5th Div, followed by 50th, makes ground assault from vicinity of Lentini and is firmly opposed.

14 July

Solomon Is.—On New Georgia, 43d Div's left flank is reinf as 3d Bn of road Inf, with engineers and tanks attached, lands at Laiana. The bn is not committed to action at once, however. 3d Bn, 169th Inf, holds its exposed hill position under enemy fire. On Guadalcanal, 25th Div's RCT 161 is alerted for movement to New Georgia.

TROBRIAND Is.—Airfield on Woodlark I. is ready for use by C-47's.

SICILY—Messina, a primary target for Allied bombers, is particularly hard hit. 212 heavy and medium bombers drop about 800 tons of bombs.

15th Army Group: In U.S. Seventh Army area, 82d A/B Div, in army reserve, is being assembled and reinf in Gela area for operations on W flank of U.S. sector. 4th Tabor of goums of Fr N African Army lands at Licata and is attached to 3d Div. In II Corps area, 1st Div makes substantial progress, taking Mazzarino and Niscemi. CCB, 2d Armd Div, mops up in Niscemi area. Rangers, assisted by naval gunfire, seize Butera. On II Corps right flank, 45th Div takes Biscari airfield and to right reaches line Yellow near Vizzini.

In Br Eighth Army's 30 Corps area, 51st Div, assisted by U.S. 45th Div, overcomes strong opposition at Vizzini. In 13 Corps area, main assault force is stoutly opposed near Lentini but succeeds in pushing through that town toward Primasole bridge. Parachute force defending the bridge withstands strong enemy pressure throughout day and at night falls back to ridge overlooking the bridge.

ITALY—Air offensive against Italy to interdict movement of supplies and reinforcements to Sicily is intensified by NAAF, Naples being a primary target.

15 July

Solomon Is.—Gen Griswold, CG XIV Corps, takes command of New Georgia Occupation Force at midnight 15-16, relieving Gen Hester, who retains command of 43d Div. Adm Turner is relieved of posts of Commander, S Pacific Amphib Force (III Amphib Force and TF 32), and Commander, New Georgia Attack Force (TF 32), and leaves for Hawaii. 1st Bn of 145th Inf, 37th Div, lands at Zanana and is attached to 43d Div to relieve elements of 69th Inf. Co of 103d Inf is committed on left flank to plug gap in line of 172d Inf. In air battle over central Solomons, Japanese lose 45 of about 75 aircraft as against 3 U.S. planes lost. As a result, Japanese virtually stop daylight attacks.

SICILY—15th Army Group: In U.S. Seventh Army area, Gen Patton forms Provisional Corps, comprising 3d Div, reinf by 3d Ranger Bn and supporting troops, and 82d A/B Div, reinf by newly arrived RCT 39 of 9th Div and supporting troops, all under command of Maj Gen Geoffrey Keyes, to operate en W flank of U.S. Seventh Army as it swings NW. 2d Armd Div, to which CCA reverts, assembles in Campobello area under army control. 3d Div continues to patrol actively. II Corps reaches line Yellow all along its front, 45th Div on right flank co-operating with 30 Corps in vicinity of Caltagirone.

In Br Eighth Army's 30 Corps area, Cdn 1st Div, taking the lead from 51st Div, captures Grammichele and Caltagirone. In 13 Corps area, main assault force makes contact with paratroopers commanding Primasole bridge; both forces continue efforts to establish bridgehead over the Simeto.

16 July

NEW GEORGIA—As 172d Inf of 43d Div, assisted by Marine tanks, slowly expands Laiana beachhead, 1st Bn of 169th Inf attacks through 3d Bn, taking hill—later called Kelley Hill for 1st Lt John R. Kelley—where it is exposed to strong enemy pressure.

TROBRIAND Is.—First Allied plane lands on Woodlark airstrip.

SICILY—Enemy air attacks during daylight virtually cease, but night attacks are increasing.

15th Army Group: Axis troops are withdrawing to Messing peninsula, at base of which lofty M. Etna commands entire island. Gen Alexander issues directive calling for Br Eighth Army to drive enemy NE along 3 routes into Messing peninsula while U.S. Seventh Army, protecting rear of Br Eighth Army, seizes road net at Enna and cuts E-W road at Petralia.

In U.S. Seventh Army's Prov Corps area, 3d Div begins assault on Agrigento while 3d Ranger Bn takes its port, Porto Empedocle. In II Corps area, 1st Div seizes Barrafranca. 45th Div begins movement to left flank of corps.

In Br Eighth Army's 30 Corps area, Cdn 1st Div pushes northward from Caltagirone, taking Piazza Armerina, night 16-17. To ease pressure on 13 Corps to right, 91st Div is ordered to drive on Paterno, NW of Catania. 13 Corps establishes small bridgehead across the Simeto before dawn.

ITALY—Prime Minister Churchill and President Roosevelt make joint appeal to Italian people to "decide whether Italians shall die for Mussolini and Hitler—or live for Italy and for civilization."

USSR—Axis forces go on the defensive, having lost heavily in futile attempts to reduce Kursk salient and being under strong pressure in Orel area. Red Army is mounting secondary attacks on southern front against enemy's Kuban bridgehead. Main Soviet offensive against Orel salient is gaining ground.

17 July

NEW GEORGIA—43d Div withstands the only organized offensive attempted by Japanese during Munda operation, beginning night 17-18. The counterattacks at various points are generally unsuccessful.

NEW GUINEA—From Nassau Bay, Coane Force (2d and 3d Bns of 162d Inf, U.S. 41st Div, and supporting units) moves out to join Aus 3d Div in drive toward Salamaua. The attack on Salamaua, under Aus command, is a secondary effort designed to divert enemy from next main effort, which is to secure Markham Valley and Huon Peninsula and thus gain control of Vitiaz and Dampier Straits.

MEDITERRANEAN—CCS accept Gen Eisenhower's recommendations of 29 June. At a meeting between Gen Eisenhower and his commanders at Carthage to consider post-HUSKY operations, it is decided that the dual mission of knocking Italy out of the war and drawing off maximum German forces from other areas can best be accomplished by invasion of Italian mainland.

SICILY—15th Army Group: In U.S. Seventh Army's Prov Corps area, 3d Div, assisted by naval gunfire, completes reduction of Agrigento. 82d A/B Div is being moved forward to W flank by motor. Going into action on W flank of II Corps, 45th takes Pietraperzia and secures crossings of Salso R, S of Caltanissetta, while 1st Div seizes crossings 6 miles E of Caltanissetta.

In Br Eighth Army's 30 Corps area, 51st Div drives to within to miles of Paterno, crossing Simeto R. 13 Corps expands bridgehead over the Simeto in coastal sector and during night 17-18 begins northward drive on Catania with 2 brigs of 50th Div.

USSR—While continuing reduction of Orel salient, Red Army begins local attacks in region S of Izyum and SW of Voroshilovgrad. Moscow announces that positions in Orel sector held before German offensive of 5 July have been recovered.

18 July

NEW GEORGIA—XIV Corps, while preparing for final push on Munda, repels Japanese counterattacks at several points. 1st and 2d Bns of 148th Inf, 37th Div, which have landed at Zanana, try unsuccessfully to reach and relieve 169th Inf, 43d Div.

TROBRIAND Is.—Airfield on Kiriwina I. becomes operational.

NEW GUINEA—Coane Force secures S headland of Tambu Bay for supply base.

SICILY—15th Army Group: U.S. Seventh Army is directed to cut N coastal road after capture of Petralia; upon gaining line across island from Campofelice on N to Agrigento on S, is to mop up W part of island. Army advances rapidly all along line as enemy continues withdrawal to NE part of island. Prov Corps pushes NW toward Palermo, 3d Div, in the lead, reaching line Raffadali-S. Cataldo. 82d A/B Div, reinf by RCT 39 of 9th Div, begins operations on W flank of corps; attacking through 3d Div near Agrigento, seizes crossings of Fiume delle Canno, about 8 miles W of Porto Empedocle. II Corps drives NW to attack Palermo from E. 45th Div takes Caltanissetta and pushes on through S Catering. 1st Div reaches M. Capadarso area, NE of Caltanissetta.

In Br Eighth Army's 30 Corps area, 51st Div continues toward Paterno while Cdn 1st Div thrusts toward Leonforte and Adrano. In 13 Corps area, 5th Div drives toward Misterbianco, W of Catania, while 50th, on coast, continues efforts to reach Catania.

19 July

ALEUTIAN Is.—Adm Kinkaid approves plans for invasion of Kiska.

ITALY—Rome undergoes damaging air attack. More than 500 bombers of USAAF attack military objectives—Lorenzo and Littoria marshaling yards and Ciampino airfields—with about 1,000 tons of bombs.

SICILY—15th Army Group: U.S. Seventh Army makes rapid progress against light resistance. In Prov Corps area, 82d A/B Div, driving NW along coastal highway, reaches positions beyond Ribera. Casteltermini and Mussomeli fall to 3d Div. 2d Armd Div is following in order to exploit possible breakthrough. In II Corps area, 45th Div patrols actively in S. Caterina area. 1st Div, advancing on Enna, clears enemy pocket S of objective.

In Br Eighth Army's 30 Corps area, Cdn 1st Div continues toward Leonforte, bypassing Enna and reaching positions N of Valguarnera. 51st Div crosses Dittaino R at Sferro, SW of Paterno. 231st Brig, bridging gap between Cdn 1st Div and 51st Div, thrusts to within 3 miles of Agira, where it halts to await clearance of Leonforte. 13 Corps continues to meet firm resistance near Catania. 5th Div crosses the Simeto to W of 50th Div, but its supporting weapons remain S of the river.

20 July

U.S.—JCS direct Adm Nimitz to seize bases in the Gilbert Is. and on Nauru.

NEW GEORGIA—Elements of 145th Inf, 37th Div, relieve hard-pressed 169th Inf of 43d Div E of Munda. 148th breaks through enemy positions that have been checking it and prepares to relieve 145th. Trail from Laiana to Munda Trail is completed, easing supply situation. Liversedge Force, after futile attempt to take Bairoko, falls back to Enogai.

NEW GUINEA—U.S. forces begin lengthy struggle for heights (Roosevelt Ridge, Scout Ridge, and Mt Tambu) commanding Tambu Bay and Dot Inlet.

CBI—Gen Bissell is recalled to U.S. to become Assistant Chief of Air Staff, A-2, and is replaced as head of Tenth Air Force by Brig Gen Howard C. Davidson.

SICILY—15th Army Group: Gen Alexander orders U.S. Seventh Army, upon reaching coastal road (Highway 113) N of Petralia, to reconnoiter eastward along it and Highway 120 (Petralia-Nicosia-Cesarò), which parallels it to S; to drive on Palermo, which is to be a major supply base; and to secure left flank on general line S. Giuseppe-Corleone-Sciacca.

In U.S. Seventh Army's Prov Corps area, 82d A/B Div, continuing W along S coast, takes Sciacca and Menfi. 3d Div clears S. Stefano and heights N of Mussomeli. 2d Armd Div, assembled in Ribera area, is attached to Prov Corps. TF X is formed to capture Castelvetrano and airfield W of it; protect left and rear of corps' drive on Palermo. Lt Col William O. Darby heads the TF, which is composed of 1st and 4th Ranger Bns, RCT 39 of 9th Div, and supporting units. In II Corps area, 45th Div clashes with Italian delaying forces in Vallelunga area. 1st Div, in conjunction with Br units to right, takes Enna, important supply center, and drives on to Villapriola.

In Br Eighth Army area, Gen Montgomery orders reserve, 78th Div, to Sicily from Africa. In 30 Corps area, Cdn 1st Div pushes to within a few miles of Leonforte. 51st Div, from Sferro area, attacks Gerbini airfield. 13 Corps is virtually stopped by firm resistance on Catania plain.

MEDITERRANEAN—Planning for invasion of Sardinia (BRIMSTONE) is dropped because of successes in Sicilian campaign. Attention of planners becomes focused next on Naples because of its harbor and its proximity to Rome.

USSR—Mitsensk falls to Red Army, whose assault against Orel salient continues.

21 July

Solomon Is.—Small U.S. rcn party lands on Vella Lavella at Barakoma, night 21-22, in preparation for full-scale invasion. U.S. control of Vella Lavella would isolate Japanese at Vila, Kolombangara. On New Georgia, 148th Inf of 37th Div relieves 145th Inf E of Munda.

SICILY—15th Army Group: In U.S. Seventh Army's Prov Corps area, TF X seizes Castelvetrano and airport, and 2d Armd Div assembles NE of Castelvetrano prepared to exploit breakthrough, which appears imminent. 82d A/B Div takes S. Margherita and 3d Div seizes Corleone. In II Corps area, 45th Div continues NW, taking Valledolmo. 1st Div clears delaying opposition in Alimena.

In Br Eighth Army area, Gen Montgomery decides to make main effort on left, where assault forces will push around N side of M. Etna to take enemy from rear, major assault to begin on 1 August. 13 Corps and 51st Div of 30 Corps are to go on the defensive. In 30 Corps area, Leonforte falls to Cdn 1st Div, night 21-22. 51st Div falls back under enemy pressure to positions S of Gerbini airfield.

22 July

ALEUTIAN IS.—In effort to soften Japanese defenses on Kiska, U.S. warships and aircraft attack the island in force.

NEW GEORGIA—Gen Griswold orders general attack on Munda by 37th and 43d Divs on 25th. 37th Div commander takes charge of his forces on the island. RCT 161, 25th Div, arrives and is attached to 37th Div.

SICILY—15th Army Group: U.S. Seventh Army takes Palermo, on N coast, virtually completing second phase of operations. Limited mopping up must be carried out in W part of island before final phase—drive to E—can start. Prov Corps takes Palermo without a fight: While TF X thrusts W along coast protecting left and rear, 2d Armd Div is committed to action and drives rapidly NE to outskirts of Palermo. At the same time, 3d Div continues NW to positions SE of the city. Since there is no show of resistance, planned attack on Palermo is withheld and 2d Armd Div enters without opposition. City surrenders at 2000. In II Corps area, left flank elements of 45th Div make contact with 3d Div in outskirts of Palermo while others push on toward N coast. 1st Div continues N toward coast on right flank of corps, taking Bompietro.

USSR—Bolkhov, NW of Mitsensk, falls to Red Army. Soviet troops begin local offensive on northern front S of Lake Ladoga.

23 July

TROBRIAND IS.—6th Fighter Sq arrives on Woodlark to begin operations from airfield there.

SICILY—15th Army Group: Gen Alexander orders U.S. Seventh Army to exert maximum pressure eastward along Highways 113 and 120 as soon as possible, leaving elements behind to complete mop-up of W part of island. As a result of this order, preparations are made to reinforce II Corps with 3d and 9th Divs and arty units.

U.S. Seventh Army mops up in W Sicily, taking many prisoners. Engineers begin to repair badly damaged port of Palermo. In Prov Corps area, while 3d Div polices Palermo, 82d A/B Div, to which control of TF X components passes, clears Marsala-Trapani area of W coast. In II Corps area, 157th Inf of 45th Div cuts Highway 113, N coastal road, 6 miles E of Termini Imerese; while elements push W from there to Termini Imerese, rest of regt drives E along highway to positions beyond Campofelice. 179th Inf, 45th Div, takes Collesano and advances toward Castelbuono. 1st Div overcomes resistance at Petralia, cutting Highway 120, and patrols eastward.

In Br Eighth Army area, 30 Corps is meeting strong resistance as it attempts to drive E from Leonforte.

24 July

NEW GEORGIA—XIV Corps prepares for assault on Munda on 25th. 161st Inf, attached to 37th Div, runs into tenacious opposition as it tries in vain to reach line of departure.

SICILY—15th Army Group: In U.S. Seventh Army area, Prov Corps continues to mop up W part of island, taking record number of prisoners. II Corps pursues enemy eastward, 45th Div in coastal sector and 1st Div on S flank. 45th Div takes Cefalu and Castelbuono. 1st Div overruns Gangi and attacks toward Nicosia.

USSR—Red Army has recovered positions in Belgorod area, which was held by the Russians at start of German offensive on 5 July.

NORWAY—U.S. Eighth Air Force makes its first attack on Norway. 167 B-17's drop 414 tons of bombs on industrial targets at Heroya while 41 release 79 tons on naval installations at Trondheim. Only 1 plane fails to return. This is the longest flight yet undertaken by U.S. planes based in England.

25 July

Solomon Is.—Gen Twining replaces Rear Adm Marc A. Mitscher as COMAIRSOLS. Air strength of this command has increased from 235 to 539 planes since 2 April. Since invasion of Rendova on 30 June, Fighter Command alone has destroyed 316 planes for loss of 71. Enemy discontinues daylight air attacks on Rendova.

NEW GEORGIA—XIV Corps opens final offensive for Munda airfield. Although supported by naval gunfire and powerful air bombardment, assault troops can make only slow progress against strongly entrenched enemy. 43d Div, with 103d Inf on left and 172d on right, attacks on left (S) and gets elements to coast near Terere but withdraws the salient since it is exposed. 37th Div, with 145th, 161st, and 148th Regts in line from left to right, cannot begin general advance until opposition on ridge (called Bartley Ridge in honor of 2d Lt Martin E. Bartley) in front of 161st Inf is cleared and then starts to envelop enemy there. 148th advances without serious opposition but is out of contact with 161st.

ITALY—King Victor Emmanuel proclaims fall of Mussolini, whose offices are taken over by Marshal Pietro Badoglio; takes command of Italian Army.

SICILY—15th Army Group: In U.S. Seventh Army's II Corps area, 45th Div makes limited progress along N coastal road (Highway 113). 1st Div, on Highway 120, repels counterattack E of Gangi.

In Br Eighth Army's 30 Corps area, hard fighting is in progress in Agira sector.

26 July

U.S.—CCS request Gen Eisenhower to plan at once for AVALANCHE, invasion of Italy at Salerno, in order to gain Naples and nearby airfields.

ALEUTIAN IS.—Eleventh Air Force makes heaviest attack to date on Kiska, dropping 104 tons of bombs.

Solomon Is.—Adm Halsey proposes to Gen MacArthur that plans for invasion of S Bougainville mainland be dropped and that the Shortlands and Ballale, in Bougainville Strait, be secured as planned in order to provide airfields and anchorages to support future operations. Gen MacArthur later approves.

NEW GEORGIA—43d and 37th Divs are assisted by tanks and flame throwers as they continue attack on Munda after preparatory fire. 103d Inf, 43d Div, takes Ilangana and reaches coast at Kia, but 161st Inf, in 37th Div zone, makes little headway against Bartley Ridge.

SICILY—15th Army Group: In U.S. Seventh Army area, Prov Corps releases RCT 39, 9th Div, 3d Chemical Weapons Bn, and 4th Tabor of goums to II Corps to strengthen it for eastward drive. II Corps makes limited progress astride Highways 113 and 120. On Highway 113, 45th Div reaches road junction N of S. Mauro.

27 July

NEW GEORGIA—37th Div temporarily suspends attack on Bartley Ridge in center and begins assault on feature to left called Horseshoe Hill, reducing several pillboxes. 148th Inf gains tenuous contact with 161st, but gap remains between the 2 regts.

CBI—Chinese-American Composite Wing (CACW) is activated in Fourteenth Air Force at Karachi, India. The wing consists of Ch aircraft and pilots trained under lend-lease.

MEDITERRANEAN—AFHQ directs CG, Fifth Army, to prepare plans for capture of Naples and nearby airfields from which future operations in Italy could be supported. D Day, which is to depend upon phase of the moon and availability of landing craft, is tentatively set as 7 September. Br planners are already working on plans for Operation BUTTRESS, invasion of toe of Italy by 10 Corps.

SICILY—15th Army Group: In the coastal sector of the U.S. Seventh Army's II Corps area, 45th Div's RCT 180 reaches Tusa, a few miles W of S. Stefano, and elements cross Tusa R but are driven back; RCT 179 reaches S. Mauro. 1st Div clears several strongpoints while pushing toward Nicosia along Highway 120; its left flank is protected by 4th Tabor of goums and its right by 91st Rcn Sq, which also maintains contact with British.

28 July

ALEUTIAN IS.—Japanese garrison of Kiska is withdrawn by sea without detection by Allied forces, who are continuing preparations to invade the island.

Solomon Is.—U.S. rcn party returns from Vella Lavella and recommends that an advance detachment be moved to Barakoma in preparation for main landings.

NEW GEORGIA—Gen Griswold calls for replacements. 43d Div is creeping forward in small-scale actions. 145th Inf, 37th Div, continues to clear Horseshoe Hill. 3d Bn, 161st, occupies some abandoned enemy positions on Bartley Ridge.

SICILY—15th Army Group: Gen Alexander moves his hq to Sicily.

In U.S. Seventh Army area, coastal cargo vessels begin arriving at Palermo. In II Corps area, 45th Div, recrossing Tusa R, pushes a little closer to S. Stefano in coastal sector. 1st Div takes Nicosia.

In Br Eighth Army's 30 Corps area, Agira falls to left flank elements of corps.

29 July

NEW GEORGIA—XIV Corps continues to advance slowly toward Munda airfield, methodically destroying enemy pillboxes with assistance of tanks and flame throwers. Maj Gen John R. Hodge takes command of 43d Div, relieving Gen Hester, and commits 1st and 3d Bns, 169th Inf, between 172d and 103d Regts. In 37th Div zone, 145th Inf reaches crest of Horseshoe Hill but pulls back a little to more tenable positions; 161st Inf forces on Bartley Ridge continue to advance cautiously; 148th pulls back to establish contact with 161st and protect supply route, but does not quite succeed in closing the gap and is precariously situated.

SICILY—15th Army Group: In U.S. Seventh Army area, trains begin using RR line between Palermo and Cefalu. Prov Corps nearly completes its mop-up task in W Sicily. 3 small islands off Trapani (Favignana, Marettimo, and Levango) surrender to 82d A/B Div. In II Corps area, 45th Div meets increasing rear-guard resistance as it approaches S. Stefano, on N coast road, and moves elements SE in effort to outflank enemy; other elements advance to Mistretta, which enemy retains. From Nicosia, 1st Div probes to outskirts of Mistretta and eastward along Highway 120 toward Cerami without incident; goumiers clear pocket about 3 miles W of Capizzi. RCT 39 is attached to 1st Div.

In Br Eighth Army's 30 Corps area, recently arrived 78th Div, now in position to attack and reinf by Cdn 3d Brig, opens assault along axis Catenanuova-Adrano, night 29-30. In 13 Corps area, 5th Div is reinf by 2 bns of infantry and regt of tanks.

30 July

NEW GEORGIA—Alteration of boundaries gives 43d Div a wider front and places S half of Bartley Ridge within zone of 145th Inf, 37th Div. 145th Inf repels counterattack on Horseshoe Hill and shells enemy positions. 161st is reinf by 2d Bn of 145th and continues to clear Bartley Ridge. Elements of 148th gain physical contact with 161st, but main body of 148th is isolated.

SICILY—15th Army Group: In U.S. Seventh Army area, enemy continues withdrawal eastward across army front. In II Corps area, 45th Div is strongly opposed by enemy rear guards in S. Stefano area during day, but enemy withdraws from the town and from Reitano, to S, night 30-31. On Highway 120, 1st Div advances toward Troina, its patrols reaching Cerami.

In Br Eighth Army's 30 Corps area, 78th Div takes Catenanuova in morning; renews attack, night 30-31, securing heights to N and NE from which to attack Centuripe. 231st Brig, leading eastward drive on Regalbuto, is meeting severe resistance near this objective.

USSR—Enemy attempts to recover ground lost on Mius front but is unable to retain the initiative.

31 July

NEW GEORGIA—2d Bns of 161st and 145th Regts finish clearing Bartley Ridge. Enemy continues to resist on Horseshoe Hill. 148th Inf tries to return to main body.

SICILY—15th Army Group: In U.S. Seventh Army area, Gen Patton issues directive for major attack eastward toward Messina, beginning 1 August. II Corps, which is to contain 1st, 3d, and 9th Divs, and supporting units, will make main effort along Highways 113 and 120 from line S. Stefano-Mistretta-Nicosia. Prov Corps is to organize W part of Sicily and protect rear of II Corps; be prepared to furnish reinforcements to II Corps. Aircraft and naval TF 88 are to support offensive. In Corps area, 45th Div is being relieved in S. Stefano sector by 3d Div. On S flank, 1st Div advances to within 5 miles of Troina, capturing Cerami; 4th Tabor of goums, on div left flank, takes Capizzi.

In Br Eighth Army's 30 Corps area, 231st Brig is still fiercely opposed just W of Regalbuto. 78th Div attacks strong enemy position at Centuripe.

1 August

NEW GEORGIA—43d Div's road and 169th Regts—172d Inf now being pinched out—reach outer taxiways of Munda airfield without serious difficulty since main body of enemy has withdrawn. In 37th Div zone, Japanese are found to have abandoned Horseshoe Hill; 148th Inf succeeds in breaking through to main body. Hq of 25th Div and 27th Inf arrive on Sasavele; 35th Inf is alerted for movement to Munda.

SICILY—15th Army Group: In U.S. Seventh Army's II Corps area, 3d Div completes relief of 45th Div—which is transferred to Prov Corps—on N coast in S. Stefano area; continues eastward drive along coastal highway, gaining several miles. On Highway 120, 1st Div continues to press toward Troina, forward elements reaching outskirts, and begins move to outflank enemy, who is resisting strongly. 9th Div (less RCT 39 in action with 1st Div) arrives at Palermo.

In Br Eighth Army's 30 Corps area, Cdn 1st Div joins 231st Brig in assault on Regalbuto and succeeds in penetrating into the town. Enemy continues vigorous defense of Centuripe.

RUMANIA—Ploesti oil refineries are targets for first low-level, mass assault by AAF heavy bombers based in Libya. 177 B-24's, some drawn from NAAF and others on loan from Eighth Air Force, all under control of Gen Brereton, CG Ninth Air Force, conduct the attack for which pilots and crews have been intensively trained in N Africa. Oil objectives, although heavily defended, are severely damaged. Cost of this operation (TIDALWAVE) is high: 54 planes are lost, 41 of them in action. 7 of the B-24's land in Turkey.1

2 August

ALEUTIAN IS.—In preparation for invasion of Kiska, surface vessels of 2 naval TF's and aircraft of Eleventh Air Force bombard the island.

Solomon Is.—RCT 27 of 25th Div and div hq arrive on New Georgia I, where RCT 27 is given mission of defending N flank of XIV Corps and maintaining contact with 2d Bn of 148th Inf, 37th Div. XIV Corps is steadily clearing Munda airfield area.

SICILY—15th Army Group: In U.S. Seventh Army area, mines and demolitions are slowing advance of II Corps' 3d Div along coastal road. 1st Div continues efforts to envelop and reduce Troina, which enemy is defending tenaciously.

In Br Eighth Army area, left flank elements of 30 Corps gain firm control of Regalbuto and continue E while 78th Div fights indecisively in streets of Centuripe throughout day.

ITALY—Allied warning to Italian people of imminent invasion of Italy is broadcast from Algiers.

3 August

NEW GEORGIA—XIV Corps continues battle for Munda airfield and is progressing steadily. Bibolo Hill mass, just N of airfield, is cleared of enemy. 3d Bn of 148th Inf, Liversedge Force, is moving forward from Bairoko area to block northward withdrawal of enemy from Munda. S Pacific Scouts (Fijian and Solomons natives) are attached to 25th Div.

[4–7 AUGUST 1943]   [125]

SICILY—15th Army Group: In U.S. Seventh Army's II Corps area, 3d Div, supported by naval gunfire, continues E along N coast road toward Furiano R. 1st Div makes limited progress in Troina area, where enemy is still offering firm resistance.

In Br Eighth Army's 30 Corps area, enemy's Catania position, which is being thinned out, becomes untenable as 78th Div takes Centuripe, forcing enemy back across Salso R. In 13 Corps' coastal sector, 5th Div opens attack on 2-brig front, night 3–4.

USSR—Soviet offensive broadens as troops of Voronezh and Steppes Fronts open powerful drive on Kharkov, in N Ukraine. 3 Soviet fronts (West, Bryansk, and Center) are closing in on Orel.

4 August

ALEUTIAN IS.—Eleventh Air Force offensive against Kiska reaches its peak as 152 tons of bombs are dropped during 134 sorties.

NEW GEORGIA—XIV Corps continues to clear Munda area. 43d Div sector is clear except for Kokengolo Hill, N of the runway on airfield. Most of 37th Div's assault force reaches the sea.

SICILY—15th Army Group: In U.S. Seventh Army's II Corps area, 15th Inf of 3d Div, although assisted by naval gunfire, is unable to force crossing of Furiano R. RCT 7 moves by water to positions on coast behind RCT 15. After strong arty and air preparation, 1st Div makes all-out effort to take Troina but cannot break through enemy positions. In support of assault on Troina, 60th Inf of 9th Div, reinf by arty and engineer units, moves against positions N and NW of Cesaro. 9th Div (−) completes assembly at Nicosia and is attached to II Corps.

In Br Eighth Army's 30 Corps area, Cdn 1st and Br 78th Divs pursue enemy northward across Salso R. 13 Corps' 50th Div is alerted for drive on Catania. 5th Div continues toward Misterbianco.

5 August

NEW GEORGIA—Munda airfield, main objective of central Solomons campaign, falls to XIV Corps after 12 days of fighting in well-fortified jungle. 25th Div has task of driving on Bairoko and Zieta in order to clear final resistance and make contact with Liversedge Force.

NEW GUINEA—Lt Col Malcolm A. Moore takes command of newly formed Second Air Task Force based at advanced airfield recently constructed at Tsili Tsili, in Watut R Valley W of Lae, in order to facilitate operations against Lae.

SICILY—15th Army Group: In U.S. Seventh Army area, on N flank of II Corps, 3d Div opens attack on S. Fratello Ridge. 1st Div, with direct air support, continues battle for Troina, gaining positions overlooking the town. Enemy withdraws from Troina, night 5–6.

In Br Eighth Army area, 30 Corps continues toward Adrano; 13 Corps overruns Paterno, Misterbianco, and Catania.

USSR—Red Army captures Orel and Belgorod, both valuable prizes, 2d Pz Army is virtually destroyed during the Orel battle, remnants being absorbed by 9th Army. Fall of Belgorod, key enemy position on N face of Kharkov salient, greatly weakens enemy's Kharkov position.

6 August

BATTLE OF VELLA GULF—Japanese naval force taking reinforcements to central Solomons is intercepted in Vella Gulf, between Vella Lavella and Kolombangara, by U.S. naval TF under Cmdr Frederick Moosbrugger. In the ensuing night action, 3 enemy DD's are sunk but another vessel escapes. About 300 Japanese succeed in reaching Vella Lavella but over 1,500 are lost. This ends enemy plans for counterattack on New Georgia.

NEW GUINEA—Japanese order air reinforcements to Wewak.

SICILY—15th Army Group: In U.S. Seventh Army's II Corps area, 3d Div continues to attack enemy positions along Furiano R on N coast but is unable to advance. RCT 16 of 1st Div enters Troina, from which enemy has withdrawn, and pushes E until halted by opposition about a mile from the town. RCT 60, 9th Div, takes heights 7 miles N of Troina. 9th Div is reinf by 91st Rcn Sq and 4th Tabor of goums.

In Br Eighth Army's 30 Corps area, Adrano falls to 78th Div as enemy pulls out, night 6–7. 1st Div takes Biancavilla.

7 August

NEW GEORGIA—Munda airfield is ready for emergency use.

INDIA—Gen Stratemeyer arrives in India.

CHINA—Col Dorn reports that Gen Chen will not return to Yunnan from Enshih to command Y-Force until more troops and supplies are provided. At this time only 2 Ch armies have begun to reorganize.

SICILY—15th Army Group: In U.S. Seventh Army's II Corps area, 3d Div improves positions on N coast in S. Fratello region against continued strong resistance. Night 7–8, small amphibious force (2d Bn of 30th Inf, reinf) makes landing on coast 2 miles E of S. Agata, greatly facilitating progress in that area. 9th Div replaces 1st Div and begins drive on Randazzo, enemy strongpoint that on this date is target for peak air effort. 9th Div pushes E in 2 columns, one from M. Pelato, 8 miles N of Troina, and the other along Highway 120.

8 August

NEW GEORGIA—RCT 161, 25th Div, starts northward behind 1st Bn of 27th Inf to clear region W of Bairoko Harbor in conjunction with Liversedge Force, which is to clear area E of the harbor.

SICILY—15th Army Group: In U.S. Seventh Army's II Corps area, enemy is forced to fall back on N coast road and 3d Div takes S. Agata. 9th Div's 47th Inf reaches Cesaro, on road to Randazzo; 60th Inf captures M. Camolato, 6 miles NW of Cesaro.

In Br Eighth Army's 30 Corps area, Bronte falls to 78th Div.

9 August

NEW GEORGIA—25th Div column (1st Bn of 27th Inf) makes contact with Liversedge Force. 35th Inf is ordered to prepare to land on Vella Lavella.

MEDITERRANEAN—Gen Alexander directs Gen Montgomery to seize bridgehead on Calabrian coast of Italy with current resources.

SICILY—15th Army Group: In U.S. Seventh Army area, II Corps advances steadily eastward against rear-guard opposition. In coastal sector, forward elements of 3d Div reach Torrenuovo; enemy falls back to Zappulla R. 9th Div's 47th Inf advances along Cesaro-Randazzo highway, and 60th advances in difficult terrain to N. Enemy pulls back to Simeto R line, between Cesaro and Randazzo.

Since enemy is delaying advance on Messing via Randazzo in Br Eighth Army's 30 Corps sector, Gen Montgomery decides to make a greater effort along E coast with 13 Corps and commits 5th Div there to drive N in region E of M. Etna in conjunction with 50th Div.

10 August

NEW GEORGIA—1st Bn of 27th Inf, 25th Div, is attached to Liversedge Force to assist in clearing region between Bairoko Harbor and Enogai Inlet. 3d Bn of 148th Inf, 37th Div, is detached from Liversedge Force and attached to 27th Inf of 25th Div with mission of intercepting northward withdrawal of enemy from Munda.

SICILY—15th Army Group: In U.S. Seventh Army area, II Corps continues to pursue enemy eastward. In coastal sector, enemy retires to heights W of Naso and is followed by 3d Div. During night 10-11, 3d Div makes another highly successful landing on coast, outflanking enemy in Capo d'Orlando region. The amphibious force (2d Bn of 30th Inf, reinf by arty and tanks), with close air and naval gunfire support, lands 2 miles E of Capo d'Orlando and establishes positions astride main highway and RR. 9th Div elements driving along Highway 120 toward Randazzo reach road junction N of Bronte.

11 August

POA—Lt Gen Robert C. Richardson, Jr., organizes small TF (804th Aviation Engr Bn, prov AAA bn, prov air service support sq, fighter sq, and service units) to develop Baker I. as a base from which to support coming offensive in Central Pacific.

SOLOMON IS.—Adm Halsey issues orders for further operations in central Solomons. Northern Force (TF 30 under Rear Adm Theodore S. Wilkinson is to land troops (RCT 35, 25th Div, and supporting units) under Brig Gen Robert B. McClure on Vella Lavella to seize air and naval bases. Strong Japanese forces at Vila on Kolombangara will thus be bypassed. New Georgia Occupation Force is to extend its positions to Arundel and shell enemy on Kolombangara. 43d Div amphibious patrol finds evidence that Japanese are holding Baanga I.

NEW GUINEA—Fifth Air Force completes movement of Second Task Force to Tsili Tsili field.

SICILY—Allied aircraft supporting the 15th Army Group are concentrating on enemy movements and evacuation points with good effect as enemy withdraws at a rapid rate from Sicily to Italian mainland.

15th Army Group: In U.S. Seventh Army's II Corps area, as a result of the successful amphibious operation on coast, night 10-11, 3d Div overruns Naso with little difficulty and enemy retires eastward beyond Patti. 9th Div presses closer to Randazzo, passing 39th Inf through 4th on Highway 120; 60th Inf continues toward Floresta on 9th Div N flank.

In Br Eighth Army area, Gen Montgomery, anxious to prepare for imminent invasion of Italy, orders 91st Div to relieve 5th Div and 30 Corps hq to take over duties of 13 Corps hq on 13 August.

USSR—Closing in on Kharkov, some Red Army units reach Akhtyrka and others cut Kharkov-Poltava RR.

12 August

ALEUTIAN IS.—In a final preinvasion naval bombardment of Kiska, 5 cruisers and 5 DD's expend 60 tons of shells.

Solomon Is.—Advance landing party from Rendova goes ashore at Barakoma on Vella Lavella, night 12-13, to pave way for main landing on 15th and finds only stragglers. Co L of 169th Inf, 43d Div, begins landing on Baanga to establish beachhead but runs into heavy opposition and is forced to withdraw, leaving 34 men ashore.

SICILY—15th Army Group: In U.S. Seventh Army's II Corps area, 3d Div continues pursuit of enemy in coastal sector. 9th Div's 60th Inf reaches Floresta, N of Randazzo; 39th continues E along Highway 120, gaining favorable position for assault on Randazzo, but enemy withdraws, night 12-13.

In Br Eighth Army area, 30 Corps' 78th Div, which has been held up for several days S of Maletto, seizes that town.

USSR—Chuguev, SE of Kharkov, falls to Red Army as investment of Kharkov continues.

13 August

ALEUTIAN IS.—Kiska invasion force leaves Adak for target.

Solomon Is.—Elements of 169th Inf, 43d Div, land on Vela Cela, small island between New Georgia and Baanga, and reconnoiter without incident. Aircraft search for the American party on Baanga. First Allied plane lands on Munda airfield, New Georgia.

NEI—B-24's of 380th Heavy Bombardment Group, which has recently arrived in Australia as part of air reinforcements promised SWPA at Pacific Military Conference in March, attack oil center at Balikpapan, (Borneo) in force. The round trip covers 1,200 miles.

SICILY—15th Army Group: In U.S. Seventh Army's II Corps coastal sector, RCT 30 of 3d Div continues E toward Patti despite formidable roadblock at Capo Calava that requires movement about it by water. RCT 15 and 3d Ranger Bn are clearing pockets SW of Patti. In 9th Div sector, RCT 39 enters Randazzo without opposition and is passed through by RCT 47, which continues E, as does RCT 60 to N.

ITALY—Twelfth Air Force makes second large-scale attack on marshaling yards at Rome, employing 106 B-17's, 102 B-26's, and 66 B-25's with fighter escort. Some 500 tons of bombs are dropped, causing heavy damage. Fighter opposition is strong but only 2 B-26's are lost.

USSR—Soviet forces continue to improve positions in Kharkov area against determined opposition. Other Red Army troops driving on Smolensk take Spas Demensk.

14 August

INTERNATIONAL CONFERENCES—QUADRANT Conference, attended by President Roosevelt, Prime Minister Churchill, and CCS, opens in Quebec, Canada.

POA—U.S. Army Forces in Central Pacific Area (USAFICPA) is activated under Gen Richardson, who is to have charge of administration and training of ground and air forces in Central Pacific.

Solomon Is.—Brig Gen Francis P. Mulcahy, USMC, COMAIR New Georgia, opens command post at Munda airfield, New Georgia. Two sqs of Marine aircraft (F4U) arrive to begin operations. 3d Bn of 169th Inf, 43d Div, establishes beachhead on SE Baanga with 3 cos. Co L tries to rescue the force stranded there earlier but is encircled by enemy and suffers heavy casualties.

NEW GUINEA—With close air and arty support, 2d Bn of 162d Inf, U.S. 41st Div, pushes to crest of Roosevelt Ridge, but enemy retains series of ridges on Dot Inlet.

SICILY—15th Army Group: In U.S. Seventh Army's II Corps area, 3d Div speeds eastward along coast to vicinity of Barcellona. Some 9th Div elements make contact with 3d Div in Montalbano area; those on Highway 120 are passed through by RCT 18 of 1st Div, which continues pursuit E of Randazzo.

Br Eighth Army is out of contact with enemy.

ITALY—Italian Government proclaims Rome an open city.

MEDITERRANEAN—Naval plan "Western Naval Task Force Operation Plan No. 7-43" for Operation AVALANCHE, invasion of Italy at Salerno, is issued. Elements of the naval force are to make diversionary feint against beaches NW of Naples.

15 August

ALEUTIAN IS.—Allied invasion force arrives off Kiska and begins landing without opposition. Weather conditions prevent air support of the operation (COTTAGE), but Eleventh Air Force, during final phase of preinvasion bombardment from 10 August to date, has dropped 355 tons of bombs. Under command of Vice Adm Thomas C. Kinkaid, Adm Rockwell commands the amphibious force of nearly 100 ships, and Maj Gen Charles H. Corlett, USA, is in charge of landing force of over 34,000 troops. Troops employed are: 17th Inf of 7th Div, which participated in the Attu operation; 53d Inf; 87th Inf, trained in mountain fighting; 184th Inf; 1st Special Service Force; Cdn 13th Brig Gp; hq troops. 159th Inf of 7th Div, originally earmarked for the Kiska operation, is garrisoning Attu so that 17th Inf, with battle experience in the Aleutians, can be employed.

Solomon Is.—Wilkinson's Northern Landing Force puts Gen McClure's Landing Force—RCT 35 of 25th Div and supporting units—ashore on SE coast of Vella Lavella in Barakoma area, where beachhead is established without ground opposition. Japanese aircraft are very active against shipping but do little damage. Zieta, New Georgia, falls to 27th Inf, 25th Div. On Baanga, the small American beachhead is strengthened by 2d Bn of 169th Inf, 43d Div, which attacks through Co I after the latter tries in vain to reach Co L. Elements of Co L succeed in joining main body, but the co is so depleted in strength that it is sent back to Munda.

NEW GUINEA—Japanese make first air attack on new air base at Tsili Tsili.

BURMA—Work on Ledo Road is progressing very slowly. From end of March to date, only 3 miles have been constructed.

MEDITERRANEAN—U.S. Fifth Army issues Outline Plan for Operation AVALANCHE. Gen G. Castellano of Italian Commando Supremo begins negotiations for armistice at British Embassy in Madrid.

SICILY—Withdrawing enemy forces are being subjected to round-the-clock air attacks.

15th Army Group: In U.S. Seventh Army area, 157th Inf of 45th Div, under Seventh Army control, lands on N coast NW of Barcellona, night 15–16, behind forward elements of II Corps' 3d Div in order to block enemy withdrawal. In II Corps area, 3d Div continues rapidly along N coast to Spadafora. 9th Div remains in Randazzo area. 1st Div halts advance.

Br Eighth Army completes drive around M. Etna as 78th Div clears Randazzo-Linguaglossa road and 51st Div overruns Linguaglossa. 50th Div seizes Taormina, on road to Messina. Commandos with tanks land, night 15–16, on E coast at Ali in effort to cut off retreating enemy, but are too late to accomplish the mission; start inland toward Messina.

USSR—Soviet forces driving W astride Orel-Bryansk RR overrun Karachev. Hard fighting continues in Kharkov sector.

SICILY—Enemy continues withdrawal of rear guards to Italy as rapidly as possible and offers no organized opposition.

15th Army Group: In U.S. Seventh Army's II Corps area, RCT 7 of 3d Div, speeding toward Messina, reaches Divieto in coastal sector. Strong 3d Div patrols enter Messina, which is under fire from Italian coast, before midnight.

17 August

ALEUTIAN IS.—Main enemy camp on Kiska is found to be deserted. Search of the island continues.

Solomon Is.—Second echelon of Northern Landing Force arrives at Vella Lavella and unloads despite enemy air attacks. 43d Div troops on Baanga are assisted by dive bombers as well as arty but make little headway.

NEW GUINEA—Fifth Air Force begins series of heavy air attacks on Wewak and satellite fields at But, Dagua, and Boram in order to neutralize them in preparation for offensive against Lae.

SICILY—15th Army Group: Sicily Campaign ends with official entry of RCT 7, 3d Div, into Messina at 1000. Americans are joined there a little later by Br force from All. Fall of Sicily permits stepped-up air operations against the next objective, Italy.

GERMANY—315 Eighth Air Force bombers make destructive daylight attacks on aircraft plants at Schweinfurt and Regensburg, dropping 724 tons of bombs. In air battles over targets, 60 U.S. bombers are shot down, but enemy plane losses are far heavier. RAF begins massive attacks (Operation CROSSBOW) on German V-weapons experimental bases with night strike (17–18) against Peenemuende, on Baltic Sea coast, by about 570 aircraft dropping almost 2,000 tons of bombs.

16 August

SOLOMON IS.—43d Div commander personally directs operations on Baanga and commits 172d Regt (−) as well as 169th (−). Arty supports attack but progress is still slow. Enemy guns on Baanga begin shelling Munda.

MEDITERRANEAN—At conference of commanders at Carthage, final decisions are made for invasion of Italy. 13 Corps of Br Eighth Army, employing Cdn 1st and Br 5th Divs, which have been withdrawn from Sicilian battle, is to cross Strait of Messina to Calabrian coast between 1 and 4 September. This operation (BAYTOWN) is to be followed on 9 September, or not more than 48 hours later, by main assault of U.S. Fifth Army in Salerno area (AVALANCHE).

18 August

INTERNATIONAL CONFERENCES—CCS, at QUADRANT Conference in Quebec, direct Gen Eisenhower to send representatives to Lisbon to negotiate with Italians for armistice.

ELLICE IS.—Implementing directive of 20 July to establish bases from which assault on the Marshalls can be supported, advance party lands on Nanomea to reconnoiter and choose airfield site.

Solomon Is.—Japanese naval force bound for Horaniu, at Kokolope Bay on NE Vella Lavella, for purpose of establishing barge base there, is intercepted early in morning by U.S. naval force, which sinks 2 submarine chasers, 2 torpedo boats, and 1 barge. 43d Div commits another bn of 172d Inf to assault on Baanga.

MEDITERRANEAN—Air plan for support of Operation AVALANCHE is issued.

USSR—Red Army troops further improve positions about Kharkov with capture of Zmiev; S of the city.

19 August

Solomon Is.—Japanese troop-laden barges that escaped U.S. naval force on 18th succeed in unloading at Horaniu, Vella Lavella. On Baanga I., Japanese naval guns that have been shelling Munda are captured.

NEW GUINEA—Japanese abandon positions on Mt Tambu and Komiatum Ridge, last major obstacles before Salamaua, and fall back to final defensive positions.

20 August

SOLOMON IS.— 43d Div troops complete offensive on Baanga, sealing off S peninsula. Action on the island has cost the div 52 killed and 110 wounded. A search of rest of island and of islands leading N to Diamond Narrows is uneventful. Japanese withdraw from S Baanga.

NEW GUINEA—Gen Blarney takes command of New Guinea Force, releasing Gen Herring, who proceeds to Dobodura to command Aus I Corps.

21 August

Solomon Is.—Enemy planes intermittently attack vessels taking third echelon of Northern Landing Force to Vella Lavella, but cause little damage.

22 August

ALEUTIAN IS.—Uneventful search for enemy on Kiska is completed. Light casualties have been suffered by Allied forces during the operation as a result of mistaken identity.

ELLICE IS.—Advance party of 2d Mar Airdrome Bn lands at Nukufetau, where air base is to be established.

NEW GUINEA—Air offensive against Wewak has neutralized enemy airpower on New Guinea sufficiently for Allied warships (4 DD's under Capt Jesse H. Carter) to risk voyage along coast from Milne Bay to Finschhafen. After bombarding Finschhafen, night 22-23, the DD's return safely.

23 August

Solomon Is.—On New Georgia, 27th Inf of 25th Div reaches Piru Plantation after difficult march through swampland.

USSR—Enemy abandons Kharkov, having exhausted reserves in a losing battle for the city. Hard fighting is developing S of Izyum and on Mius front as powerful Soviet forces attempt to breach enemy defenses. On Mius front, Red Army troops cut Taganrog-Stalino RR.

24 August

INTERNATIONAL CONFERENCES—QUADRANT Conference at Quebec ends. OVERLORD, invasion of northwestern Europe, target date 1 May 1944, and POINTBLANK, Combined Bomber Offensive to destroy economic and military power of Germany as a prelude to OVERLORD, shall constitute the primary effort against Germany. Plans for invasion of Italy are approved, but the forces to be employed are confined to those already allotted at TRIDENT. Advances against Japan are to be made along both the Central Pacific and the SWPA route. Action in the Central Pacific is to begin with invasion of Gilberts and Marshalls. In SWPA, Rabaul will be neutralized but not captured; New Guinea will be neutralized as far W as Wewak; Manus and Kavieng are to be secured as bases from which further advances can be supported. A new Allied command, Southeast Asia Command (SEAC), is authorized to simplify command structure in Asia; Adm Lord Louis Mountbatten is to be Supreme Commander and Gen Stilwell will be his deputy. China theater is not included in SEAC; as China is an area of U.S. strategic responsibility, Gen Stilwell is responsible to Generalissimo Chiang Kai-shek. North Burma offensive is scheduled to begin in February 1944.

POA—Fifth Amphibious Force is established under command of Adm Turner.

NEW GUINEA—Aus 5th Div relieves Aus 3d Div of final operations against Salamaua; primary objective is to divert enemy attention from Lae. While Aus 5th Div is clearing heights S of Francisco R on lea, Americans of 162d Inf, 41st Div, continue operations against ridges in Dot Inlet.

25 August

Solomon Is.—Action on New Georgia I. comes to a close as Americans seize Bairoko Harbor without opposition. Japanese remnants have withdrawn to Kolombangara and Arundel. 172d Inf, 43d Div, is to secure that part of Arundel I. commanding Diamond Narrows.

MEDITERRANEAN—15th Army Group: U.S. Fifth Army issues Field Order No. 1, putting outline plan for invasion of Italy into effect. Under 15th Army Group, U.S. Fifth Army is to conduct Operation AVALANCHE In Naples area and Br Eighth Army, Operation BAYTOWN on toe of Italy.

26 August

INTERNATIONAL AGREEMENTS—U.S. and several other Allied nations extend recognition to French Committee of National Liberation.

MEDITERRANEAN—15th Army Group: AVALANCHE Operation Plan of 15 August is modified somewhat to meet changes in situation. Br and U.S. arty is in position on Sicily to support BAYTOWN.

27 August

ELLICE IS.—Rest of 2d Mar Airdrome Bn and elements of naval construction bn arrive at Nukufetau.

SOLOMON IS.—172d Inf (− 3d Bn), 43d Div, lands on SE Arundel at S tip of Nauro Peninsula without opposition. While Co A holds beachhead, rest of the force drives N to base of the peninsula.

ITALY—15th Army Group: Br rcn party lands at Bova Marina, on toe, and finds the area undefended.

USSR—Sevsk, S of Bryansk, falls to Red Army.

FRANCE—U.S. Eighth Air Force flies its first CROSSBOW mission, 187 B-17's bombing Watten.

28 August

ELLICE IS.—Forward echelon of 7th Mar Defense Bn and detachments from 2 naval construction bns land on Nanomea.1

29 August

Solomon Is.—Patrols of 172d Inf, 43d Div, start up E and W coasts of Arundel without opposition. RCT 35 of 25th Div is ordered to secure radar site on NE Vella Lavella in Kokolope Bay region, where patrols have observed considerable enemy activity.1

30 August

Solomon Is.—Elements of 1st Bn, 35th Inf, 25th Div, start N up E coast of Vella Lavella toward Kokolope Bay.

USSR—Red Army surges forward in several sectors. Forces driving on Smolensk take Yelnya. Others, in region W of Kursk, overrun Gluchov. Breaking through to Sea of Azov on Mius front, Soviet troops take Taganrog.

31 August

Solomon Is.—1st Bn of 145th Inf, 37th Div, arrives on Vella Lavella from New Georgia and relieves 1st Bn of 35th Inf, 25th Div, of perimeter defense mission so that it can move N to Kokolope Bay. U.S. patrol on Arundel encounters light opposition on E coast.

1 September

POA—Allied TF arrives on Baker I. to develop it as a base from which future operations in the Central Pacific can be supported. Airstrip is constructed within a week. This brings number of Central Pacific bases within bombing range of the Gilberts up to 5: Funafuti, Nukufetau, and Nanomea in Ellice Is.; Canton; Baker. U.S. carrier-based planes make surprise attack on Marcus I., heavily damaging installations.

Solomon Is.—In preparation for offensive against N Solomons, Air Command North Solomons is formed at Espiritu Santo under Brig Gen Field Harris, USMC. On Vella Lavella, forward elements of 1st Bn, 35th Inf, 25th Div, driving on Kokolope Bay, reach Orete Cove area, about 14 miles NE of Barakoma.

NEW GUINEA—Allied air operations are intensified in preparation for offensive against Lae. Fifth Air Force is concentrating on airfields, supply points, and shipping in New Guinea-New Britain area.

ITALY—Units of Royal Navy join aircraft and arty in bombardment of Calabrian coast in preparation for BAYTOWN.

2 September

Solomon Is.—On Arundel, final elements of 172d Inf, 43d Div—the 3d Bn—land at Nauro Peninsula.

ITALY—As NAAF completes preinvasion attacks in preparation for BAYTOWN, having intensified them against Calabrian Peninsula during past week, virtually all airfields in S Italy except Foggia and its satellites have been neutralized. U.S. bombers, during period 18 August to date, have flown almost 3,000 sorties against communication targets. Small B-17 attack on Brenner Pass temporarily interdicts the pass, the shortest route between Germany and Italy. Allied planes open intensive preinvasion attacks in support of AVALANCHE, pounding airfields within range of Salerno day and night.

USSR—Red Army is moving steadily westward toward the Dnieper on broad front from Smolensk area on N to Sea of Azov on S. Some elements cut Bryansk-Konotop RR; others take Sumy, between Konotop and Kharkov; still others are pressing toward Stalino.

3 September

Solomon Is.—172d Inf patrol, moving up W coast of Arundel, reaches Bustling Point without enemy interference. With beachhead defenses of Barakoma area on Vella Lavella now firmly established, Adm Wilkinson, CG TF 31, relinquishes command of operations.

NEW GUINEA—Allied planners meeting at Port Moresby decide to seize line Dumpu-Saidor to protect movement to Cape Gloucester. As air preparation for landing at Lae continues, the assault force assembles off Buna.

SICILY—At 1715, after units of Br Eighth Army have landed on mainland of Italy, Gen Castellano, on behalf of the Italian Government of Marshal Badoglio, signs short-term armistice at Cassibile, near Syracuse, Sicily, to became effective on 8 September, when news of it is to be made public. Because of the Italian armistice, U.S. 82d A/B Div, scheduled to drop in Capua area of Volturno Valley to block southward movement of enemy reinforcements, is to be dropped instead in vicinity of Rome where, with assistance of Italians, it will prevent German occupation of Rome.

ITALY—15th Army Group: Under Gen Alexander, invades European continent. In Br Eighth Army area, 13 Corps, under cover of air, naval, and arty bombardment, is ferried across Strait of Messina and lands on Calabrian coast between Reggio and Villa S. Giovanni at 0430; against token resistance from Italians, quickly seizes Reggio, its airdrome, and S. Giovanni and pushes northward in 2 columns, 5th Div along coastal road to Schilla and Cdn 1st Div on parallel inland route to S. Stefano. During night 3–4, commandos land at Bagnara to outflank enemy positions and speed advance.

4 September

POA—V Amphibious Corps (VAC), under command of Maj Gen Holland M. Smith, USMC, is created to train and control troops for amphibious landings in Central Pacific.

Solomon Is.—On Arundel, 2d Bn of 172d Inf, 43d Div, moves by sea to Stima Peninsula; leaving Co G to contain enemy pocket at its base, advances NW. After amphibious move from Nauro to Bustling Point, 1st Bn begins advance to secure control of entrance to Wana Wana Lagoon.

NEW GUINEA—While diversionary action by Aus 5th Div and 162d Inf of U.S. 41st Div toward Salamaua is drawing to a close, offensive operations are begun against Lae, the main objective. After brief naval gunfire preparation, 26th and 20th Brigs, Aus 9th Div, and U.S. scouts of 2d Engr Special Brig land at points 14 and 18 miles E of Lae without opposition. The Americans are placed under command of Aus 9th Div upon landing. Fifth Air Force co-operates by bombing Hopoi and driving off enemy planes that damage several LST's and LCI's of TF 76. From positions 14 miles from Lae, 26th Brig and Aus 2/17th Bn start W toward Lae.

Aus 2/13th Bn drives E from Bulu Plantation, 18 miles E of Lae, to Hopoi to secure E flank.

ITALY—15th Army Group: Gen Alexander orders 1st A/B Div to be prepared to land elements at Taranto (SLAPSTICK) on 9th in order to secure the port, airfields, and installations and establish contact with Italians in Brindisi area; cancels projected invasion of Crotone area (GOBLET) by Br 5 Corps from N Africa, thereby releasing 5 Corps hq, which is to take command of forces in heel of Italy and be prepared to advance upon order.

In Br Eighth Army area, 13 Corps moves steadily northward up Calabrian Peninsula, hampered only by skillful demolitions.

USSR—Red Army blocks last rail exit from Kharkov with capture of rail junction of Merefa, S of the city.

5 September

SOLOMON IS.—172d Inf, 43d Div, unsuccessfully attacks Japanese positions some 600 yards SE of base of Bomboe Peninsula on Arundel and strengthens block at base of Stima Peninsula after enemy counterattacks there.

NEW GUINEA—U.S. 503d Para Regt and detachment of Aus 2/4th Field Regt, transported across Owen Stanley Range from Port Moresby by Fifth Air Force, drop unopposed at Nadzab, on Markham R NW of Lae, after aircraft bomb and strafe landing zone. Paratroopers are soon joined by Aus force (2/2d Pioneer Bn and 2/6th Field Co) that has moved to Nadzab area from Tsili Tsili. Co of Papuan Inf Bn (FIB), which has also moved forward, covers W approaches to Nadzab. Nadzab airfield is quickly prepared to receive Aus 7th Div and eventually becomes a major Allied air base.

MIDDLE EAST—Gen Brereton relinquishes command of USAFIME.

ITALY—AVALANCHE assault forces begin movement from N Africa to Gulf of Salerno.

15th Army Group: In Br Eighth Army area, 13 Corps has cleared Calabrian Peninsula as far N as Bagnara on W and Bova Marina on E. 5th Div is meeting rear-guard resistance N of Bagnara.

6 September

Solomon Is.—On Arundel, 1st Bn of 172d Inf, 43d Div, secures Grant I. and W half of Bomboe Peninsula; 3d Bn holds the block at base of Stima Peninsula; 2d Bn works slowly toward base of Bomboe Peninsula.

NEW GUINEA—26th Brig of Aus 9th Div, followed by 24th Brig, which landed night 5–6, continues W toward Lae, meeting opposition for the first time at Bunga R. Advance elements of U.S. 871st A/B Engr Bn are, flown in to Nabzab.

CHINA—Gen Stilwell proposes that Ch divs under Chiang Kai-shek, both Nationalist and Communist, be employed in China to forestall Japanese reaction to U.S. Fourteenth Air Force attacks.

ITALY—Strait of Messina is now open to Allied shipping.

15th Army Group: In Br Eighth Army area, 13 Corps continues to make steady progress northward. 5th Div takes Gioia and is ordered to drive on Nicastro with 231st Brig attached.

USSR—Soviet forces take Konotop by storm.

GERMANY—U.S. Eighth Air Force dispatches 407 heavy bombers, a record number, 338 of them against factories in Stuttgart area. Weather conditions prevent attack on target, but 262 bombers attack targets of opportunity. Price of operating over Germany is again high—45 aircraft are lost.

7 September

U.S.—JCS discuss possibility of mounting invasion of Paramushiro from the Aleutians.

POA—In Central Pacific, 5,000-foot airstrip is completed at Nanomea, Ellice Is.; sq of aircraft is operating from there by end of month.

NEW GUINEA—C-47's begin flying Aus 7th Div in to Nadzab.

ITALY—15th Army Group: In Br Eighth Army area, in effort to get behind retreating enemy on W coast, 231st Brig of 13 Corps, supported by commandos, lands, night 7-8, near Pizzo, but because of speed of enemy retreat is engaged by rear guards. Main body of 13 Corps continues N toward line Nicastro-Catanzaro.

USSR—Germans announce evacuation of Stalino.

8 September

BAKER IS.—Airstrip suitable for fighters is put into use.

Solomon Is.—Since 172d Inf of 43d Div is making little headway on Arundel, 1st Bn of 169th is attached to it. Japanese move a bn of infantry from Kolombangara to Arundel in preparation for counterattack against New Georgia.

NEW GUINEA—Australians of 9th Div moving W on Lae reach flooded Busu R and find Japanese holding W bank. Japanese at Salamaua are ordered to fall back to Lae. Aus 5th Div, continuing toward Salamaua, is now at Francisco R, near the airfield.

ITALY—As AVALANCHE convoys are approaching Salerno and aircraft are completing a week of intensive, preinvasion attacks, Gen Eisenhower broadcasts news of Italian armistice at 1830 and Marshal Badoglio makes similar broadcast at 1945. This is the cue for Italian fleet and aircraft to head for prearranged points to surrender to Allied forces.

AVALANCHE convoys, divided into 2 forces (Southern Assault Force under Rear Adm Hall, USN, from Oran and Northern Assault Force under Commodore G. N. Oliver, RN, from Tripoli and Bizerte), pass from command of CinC Mediterranean to that of Adm Hewitt, USN, Naval Commander Western Task Force, upon reaching prescribed area. Learning that Germans are in Rome area in considerable strength and that Italians cannot assist operations as planned, Gen Eisenhower cancels scheduled drop of elements of U.S. 82d A/B Div there, too late to give them another mission during initial phase of Salerno operation.

USSR—Red Army recovers entire industrial region of the Donbas with occupation of Stalino.

9 September

Solomon Is.—Adm Halsey proposes that Treasury Is. and Choiseul Bay be secured as bases from which S Bougainville-Shortlands area can be neutralized, a suggestion that is not accepted by Gen MacArthur. 37th Div returns to Guadalcanal from New Georgia and subsequently trains there for Bougainville operation. On Arundel, 172d Inf of 43d Div suspends attack while arty is employed against enemy.

NEW GUINEA—Aus 9th Div begins to cross Busu R and holds bridgehead against counterattacks. 162d Inf of U.S. 41st Div, assisted by Australians, takes Scout Ridge in Dot Inlet.

ITALY—15th Army Group: Br 1st A/B Div, moving by sea from Bizerte, mounts Operation SLAPSTICK, landing on heel of Italy without opposition and taking port of Taranto.

U.S. Fifth Army, under Gen Mark Clark, invades Italy, landing at H Hour (0330) S of Salerno with U.S. VI Corps (Southern Assault Force) S of Sele R and Br 10 Corps (Northern Assault Force) N of the river. Landings and operations ashore are closely supported by aircraft and naval gunfire. By end of day, VI and 10 Corps each hold a bridgehead on shallow Salerno plain but gap exists between them. 82d A/B Div is released by U.S. Fifth Army to AFHQ. Ventotene I. surrenders. VI Corps (Maj Gen Ernest J. Dawley) goes ashore in Paestum area. 36th Div's RCT's 141 and 142, making initial assault, secure beachhead and withstand at least 4 strong tank counterattacks as enemy makes futile attempts to push the RCT's back into the sea. RCT 141, on right, is particularly hard pressed but retains shallow beachhead. Reserve—RCT 143—is committed in center upon landing. By end of day, initial objectives, except on right flank, are secured. Beachhead extends from heights just W of La Cosa Creek to Hill 386 (spur of lofty M. Soprano), Capaccio, and M. Soltane. Br 10 Corps (Lt Gen Sir

[10-11 SEPTEMBER 1943]

Richard I. McCreery), making main effort of Fifth Army, is opposed in greater force than VI Corps. 56th Div, on 10 Corps right flank, reaches its first major objective, Montecorvino airfield, but is unable to take it; patrols push to Battipaglia, which enemy also retains. 46th Div drives northward along coast toward Salerno. On left flank of corps, Br-U.S. force (Br 2d and 41st Commandos; U.S. 1st, 3d, and 4th Ranger Bns) under command of Col Darby, USA, lands on Sorrento Peninsula W of Salerno. Commandos take Vietri Sul Mare and push E toward Salerno. Rangers make unopposed landing at Maiori, on extreme left; while 4th Ranger Bn secures beachhead, others push N to M. Chiunzi, which overlooks Nocera-Pagani Valley passes leading to Naples.

USSR—Soviet forces W of Konotop take Bakhmach on rail line to Kiev. Others to N reach Desna R line S of Bryansk.1

10 September

SOLOMON IS.— 2d and 3d Bns of 27th Inf, 25th Div, are attached to 43d Div and ordered to Arundel to help 172d Inf. 27th Inf commander is to be responsible for future operations there.

NEW GUINEA—Aus 7th Div relieves U.S. 503d Para Inf at Nadzab and begins drive E toward Lae with 25th Brig Gp. Japanese at Lae are thus threatened from both E and W.

MIDDLE EAST—Maj Gen Ralph Royce takes command of USAFIME, replacing Gen Brereton.

ITALY—15th Army Group: Gen Alexander directs Gen Montgomery to maintain pressure against Germans on Eighth Army front in order to prevent their concentration against Fifth Army.

On U.S. Fifth Army's VI Corps right flank, RCT 141 of 36th Div, after reorganizing, turns S to block routes leading to beachhead; RCT 143, also protecting right flank, patrols E and SE uneventfully; RCT 142 moves against Hill 424 and Altavilla, on its slopes, taking Albanella and reaching positions on ridgeline to Roccadaspide. RCT 179, 45th Div, lands and starts northward toward Ponte Sele. Br 10 Corps continues to receive main weight of enemy opposition and fights indecisively for Battipaglia and Montecorvino airfield on right flank. In center, 46th Div takes Salerno. On left, 3d Ranger Bn withstands probing jabs against M. Chiunzi and 4th Bn patrols W along coast of Sorrento Peninsula.

In Br Eighth Army area, 13 Corps is at neck of Calabrian Peninsula on line Catanzaro-Nicastro. Enemy is accelerating withdrawal in order to reinforce Salerno area.

USSR—Soviet forces driving along edge of Sea of Azov take Mariupol. Other units establish bridgehead across Desna R in vicinity of Novgorod Severski.

11 September

ALEUTIAN IS.—Gen Butler, CG Eleventh Air Force, is transferred to ETO. Gen Butler is succeeded as head of Eleventh Air Force by Maj Gen Davenport Johnson. Eleventh Air Force sustains heavy losses during raid on Kuriles.

Solomon Is.—27th Inf (−) of 25th Div lands on W end of Bomboe Peninsula on Arundel, and 2d Bn starts E at once toward 172d Inf at base of the peninsula. Arty and, for the first time in the S Pacific, 4.2-inch mortars support the attack.

NEW GUINEA—Aus 5th Div crosses Francisco R near Salamaua airfield as Japanese begin withdrawal from Salamaua to Lae.

ITALY—15th Army Group: Brindisi falls to Br 1st A/B Div, which continues clearing heel without opposition.

U.S. Fifth Army expands beachhead on Salerno plain. Since gap still exists between U.S. VI and Br 10 Corps, boundary is moved N from Sele R line, and 45th Div assumes command of new left flank positions of VI Corps. In VI Corps area, RCT 142 of 36th Div takes Altavilla and Hill 424. On N flank of corps, Germans counterattack RCT 179 of 45th Div on bluffs overlooking Ponte Sele and force Americans back; RCT 157 is ordered to ease pressure on RCT 179 by attacking on W side of Sele R and, with 191st Tank Bn spearheading, pushes forward until halted at tobacco factory strongpoint on commanding ground across the Sele from Persano. During night 11-12, enemy withdraws from Persano but begins infiltration around Hill 424. Br 10 Corps takes Montecorvino airfield, but enemy is keeping it under heavy fire. 10 Corps is still unable to clear Battipaglia on right flank. Left flank is strengthened by elements of VI Corps (1st Bn of 143d Inf; AA battery; arty battery; co each of paratroopers, tanks, TD's, and chemical mortars; 2 engr cos), that help Rangers holding positions overlooking Nocera-Pagani Valley.

In Br Eighth Army's 13 Corps area, light forces move rapidly northward in effort to pin down enemy, taking port of Crotone on right and reaching general line Castrovillari-Belvedere on left.

MALTA—Italian fleet formally surrenders to Adm Cunningham. Germans sink BB *Roma* while it is en route to surrender.

CORSICA—Fr submarine sails from Algiers for Corsica with small Fr force embarked to help patriots clear island of Germans. Additional Fr forces are later moved to Corsica from time to time as shipping becomes available. Enemy garrison of Sardinia is being evacuated via Corsica.

U.K.—Since U.S. Ninth Air Force is soon to be transferred to United Kingdom, Gen Devers names Gen Eaker, CG U.S. Eighth Air Force, as commanding general of all U.S. Army Air Forces in United Kingdom.

12 September

NEW GUINEA—As Aus 9th and 7th Divs push toward Lae from E and W, Aus 5th Div occupies Salamaua, Salamaua airfield, and the isthmus. Japanese begin withdrawing from Lae.

ITALY—15th Army Group: Gen Alexander orders Br Eighth Army to advance as quickly as possible, despite administrative risks.

In U.S. Fifth Army area, critical period begins as enemy renews strong efforts to reduce beachhead. Airstrip is completed in Paestum area. Capri, in Gulf of Naples, is occupied by Allied forces. In VI Corps area, Germans counterattack, recovering Hill 424 and Altavilla from 142d Inf, 36th Div. Situation of 45th Div on N flank of VI Corps improves: 179th Inf occupies Persano; 157th, after seesaw battle, seizes tobacco factory barring its advance in region W of the Sele. 36th Combat Engrs takes up positions on left flank of 157th Inf. Corps begins regrouping after nightfall to strengthen exposed left flank. 179th Inf moves from Sele-Calore corridor, which 2d Bn of 143d Inf comes N to defend, to left flank of 157th Inf. Strong German counterattack forces Br 10 Corps to yield toehold on Battipaglia. 167th Brig, 56th Div, suffers heavy casualties in this action and is relieved by 201st Gds Brig. U.S. Ranger force on left flank of 10 Corps withstands enemy attacks.

13 September

Solomon Is.—On Arundel, 3d Bn of 27th Inf begins struggle for Sagekarasa I., NE of Bomboe Peninsula, while elements of 169th Inf outpost islets W of Sagekarasa. On Bomboe Peninsula, 2d Bn of 27th makes radio contact with 172d Inf.

ITALY—15th Army Group: Gen Alexander directs Gen Montgomery, CG Eighth Army, to take command of Taranto bridgehead forces (Br 1st A/B Div, which 78th Div is soon to reinforce) as soon as possible. Gen Montgomery agrees to do so at once.

U.S. Fifth Army's Salerno bridgehead is still seriously threatened as enemy counterattacks strongly astride Sele R. VI Corps barely succeeds in containing major enemy thrusts. 36th Div units begin attack to regain Altavilla but meet strong counterattacks that isolate some elements there and force rest back to La Cosa Creek. On N flank of VI Corps, Germans overwhelm 2d Bn of 143d Inf in Sele-Calore corridor and force 157th Inf of 45th Div to give ground in region W of the Sele. Since offensive operations cannot be continued with current forces, troops dig in and prepare to hold on best defensive line possible until situation improves. Two bns of 141st Inf move N from quiet southern sector. 504th Para Inf (−), 82d A/B Div, is dropped S of Sele R to strengthen bridgehead. Br to Corps contains strong tank-infantry attacks from Battipaglia. 167th Inf is committed on right flank of 45th Div and makes contact with VI Corps.

AEGEAN—Br units occupy Kos I, where RAF aircraft are soon established.1

14 September

Solomon Is.—On Vella Lavella, 1st Bn of 35th Inf, 25th Div, opens attack in Kokolope Bay area after preparatory fire and finds Horaniu vacated by enemy. 1st and 3d Bns, latter having moved forward, then organize defensive positions in this region. While 3d Bn of 27th Inf holds off enemy counterattacking on Sagekarasa, 1st Bn of 172d Inf, on Arundel, bypasses enemy positions on Bomboe Peninsula in order to come in behind 2d Bn, 27th Inf. Reinforcements are sent to Sagekarasa. Japanese begin moving rest of a regt from Kolombangara to Arundel. 8th Brig Gp, NZ 3d Div, arrives on Guadalcanal from New Caledonia, having rehearsed en route (in New Hebrides) for invasion of Treasury Is. in the Solomons.

NEW GUINEA—Crossing the Busu by newly completed bridge, 26th Brig of Aus 9th Div joins 24th Brig on W bank. 25th Brig, Aus 7th Div, continues E toward Lae, seizing Heath's Plantation.

ITALY—15th Army Group: U.S. Fifth Army, committing reserves and service troops, contains further enemy onslaughts with assistance of naval gunfire and aircraft. RCT 180, 45th Div, lands and is held in Fifth Army reserve. In VI Corps area, RCT 505 of 82d A/B Div is dropped S of Sele R and advances at once to strengthen beachhead. In behalf of Br 10 Corps, 2d Bn of U.S. 509th Para Inf is dropped behind enemy lines in Avellino area, night 14-15, to disrupt enemy communications; drop is widely scattered and paratroopers retire to hills, where they wage guerrilla warfare for the next week. Br 7th Armd Div arrives and begins unloading.

In Br Eighth . Army area, elements of Taranto bridgehead force (Br 1st A/B Div) enter Bari. 13 Corps continues northward in light strength. 5th Div is concentrating in Belvedere area.

AEGEAN—Br force occupies Leros.

15 September

U.S.—T. V. Soong presents President Roosevelt a plan for reorganization of China theater in such a way as to eliminate Gen Stilwell; subsequently seeks in other ways to have Stilwell recalled.

POA—2d Mar Div is formally attached to V Amphibious Corps as preparations for offensive in Central Pacific continue.

Solomon Is.—Maj Gen Charles D. Barrett is named CG I Marine Amphibious Corps (I MAC), but his sudden death soon afterwards forces Gen Vandegrift to resume command of I MAC before operations against N Solomons are begun.

NEW GUINEA—Australians continue toward Lae from W and E, 7th Div clearing Edward's Plantation and 9th Div taking Malahang airdrome. Gen MacArthur orders New Guinea Force to seize Kaiapit and Dumpu with assistance of U.S. planes.

ITALY—15th Army Group: Gen Alexander orders U.S. Fifth Army to continue attack across Volturno R.

U.S. Fifth Army front is relatively quiet as German activity subsides. Minor enemy thrusts are repelled. III VI Corps area, 325th Gli Inf of 82d A/B Div arrives by sea.

In Br Eighth Army's 13 Corps area, forward elements of 5th Div, attempting to make contact with VI Corps, reach Sapri. Enemy is threatened with entrapment between Eighth and Fifth Armies.

USSR—Continuing toward Kiev, Soviet forces overrun Nezhin. To N, Red Army opens strong offensive against Smolensk.

16 September

Solomon Is.—Reinforcements are sent to Arundel in preparation for stronger U.S. effort on 17th. Rest of 27th Inf (1st Bn and AT Co), platoon of 43d Cav Rcn Tr, and Marine tanks move to Bomboe Peninsula. 2d Bn, 169th Inf, reinforces 172d Inf's block at base of Stima Peninsula.

NEW GUINEA—Aus columns coverage on Lae, from which Japanese have withdrawn. 25th Brig, 7th Div, enters first and is joined there by 24th Brig, 9th Div.

ITALY—15th Army Group: U.S. Fifth and Br Eighth Armies make patrol contact near Vallo. Fifth Army makes contact with Taranto bridgehead force to form Allied line across S Italy.

U.S. Fifth Army's FO No. 2 directs RCT 180, reinf, under army command, to drive on Benevento. In VI Corps area, 504th Para Inf, 82d A/B Div, begins attack to recover Altavilla, night 16-17. Patrols of 505th Para Inf find Roccadaspide free of enemy.

In Br Eighth Army's 13 Corps area, 5th Div patrol makes contact with patrol of VI Corps and rcn elements of Cdn 1st Div make contact with Br 1st A/B Div units from Taranto bridgehead.

AEGEAN—Br force occupies Samos.

USSR—Red Army makes substantial gains, taking Novgorod Severski, SW of Bryansk; Romni, in region E of Kiev; Lozovaya, S of Kharkov; and Novorossisk, on Kuban Peninsula.

GERMANY—Berlin announces evacuation of Bryansk by German troops.

17 September

Solomon Is.—At planning conference at Port Moresby, Gen MacArthur urges that a base on mainland of Bougainville be established. On Arundel, 27th Inf (−), assisted by tanks, begins co-ordinated drive SE toward 172d Inf's block at base of Stima Peninsula. 3d Bn, 27th, suspends attack on Sagekarasa while fire is placed on enemy positions.

NEW GUINEA—GHQ SWPA decides to employ Aus 9th Div force in landing on 22d at Finschhafen, which will serve as an advanced air and light naval base. U.S. 503d Para Inf, having completed its mission in Nadzab area is withdrawn. Aus 2/6th Independent Co is flown to burned off site a few miles from Kaiapit, NW of Lae, for drive on Kaiapit, which will be used as an advanced air base from which to neutralize Wewak.

ITALY—15th Army Group: In U.S. Fifth Army's VI Corps area, 504th Inf of 82d A/B Div continues attack toward Altavilla but is pinned down by enemy fire before reaching objective. Enemy is retiring northward, however, and completes withdrawal from 45th Div front after nightfall.

In Br Eighth Army area, 13 Corps begins general advance northward with main forces toward line Potenza-Auletta.

USSR—Red Army troops occupy Bryansk.

18 September

U.S.—Joint War Plans Committee recommends retrenchment of North Pacific Force. Eleventh Air Force has already been cut to 1 heavy and 1 medium sq, a fighter gp of 4 sqs, and 1 troop carrier sq.

Solomon Is.—On Vella Lavella, Maj Gen H. E. Barrowclough, CG NZ 3d Div, takes command, replacing Gen McClure. NZ 14th Brig Gp lands to round up retreating enemy, but Japanese eventually succeed in withdrawing from the island. On Arundel, Co G, reinf, of 103d Inf arrives to reinforce 172d Inf's block at base of Stima Peninsula. Additional reinforcements are sent from mainland to 3d Bn, 27th Inf, on Sagekarasa.

ITALY—15th Army Group: In U.S. Fifth Army's VI Corps area, paratroopers of 504th Inf, 82d A/B Div, accompanied by tanks of 191st Tank Bn, enter Altavilla without opposition. 45th Div, discovering that enemy has withdrawn, patrols northward to regain contact, reaching heights between Battipaglia and Eboli and entering Persano without opposition. 3d Div, which is to relieve battle-weary 36th Div, begins landing. In Br to Corps area, 131st Brig of 7th Armd Div occupies Battipaglia without resistance.

Br Eighth Army's 5 Corps hq lands at Taranto to take command of forces holding Taranto bridgehead.

SARDINIA—Surrenders without a shot to small Allied party embarked on 2 Br MTB's, enemy having completed withdrawal from this and neighboring islands.

USSR—Rail junction of Pavlograd, S of Lozovaya, falls to Red Army.

19 September

POA—VAC estimates that the capture of Nauru with forces available will be difficult.

GILBERT Is.—Carrier and AAF planes make coordinated attacks on Tarawa, during which complete photographic coverage is obtained. The carrier force, TF 15 under Rear Adm Charles A. Pownall, includes carriers *Belleau Wood, Princeton,* and *Lexington.* 11th Bombardment Gp (Seventh Air Force) supplies the B-24's, which operate from Canton and Funafuti.

NEW GUINEA—Aus 2/6th Independent Co takes Kaiapit in lively fighting and repels repeated counterattacks.

ITALY—15th Army Group: U.S. Fifth Army gains firm control of Salerno plain. In VI Corps area, 45th Div occupies high ground overlooking Eboli; 36th Div units take Serre and Ponte Sele.

In Br Eighth Army area, 13 Corps reaches line Auletta-Potenza, 5th Div occupying former and Cdn 1st Div latter. From there, light forces are to clear to line Altamura-Potenza, then continue to Spinazzola and Melfi.

USSR—Soviet troops on Smolensk front overrun Yartsevo and Dukhovshchina. Enemy is forced to retire toward the Dnieper all along lower front as Priluki, Piryatin, Lubni, Khorol, and Krasnograd fall to troops fighting E and SE of Kiev.

20 September

Solomon Is.—27th Inf forces on Sagekarasa find that Japanese have withdrawn from the island. On the mainland of Arundel, rest of 27th Inf suspends attack while patrols try in vain to locate 172d Inf position.

ITALY—15th Army Group: U.S. Fifth Army's VI Corps is placed under command of Maj Gen John P. Lucas. 36th Div, upon turning its sector over to 3d Div, is withdrawn into reserve. 82d A/B Div is ordered to concentrate in Crotone area and be prepared to assist advance of VI Corps on army order. 3d and 45th Divs start northward into mountains, 3d driving through Battipaglia toward Acerno and 45th on right along Highway 91.

USSR—Velizh, NW of Smolensk, falls to Soviet troops.

21 September

Solomon Is.—On Arundel, 27th Inf, upon renewing assault, finds that Japanese have withdrawn from mainland of Arundel as well as islands nearby. Enemy is estimated to have lost 600 dead on Arundel. By this time Japanese have decided to abandon the central Solomons entirely and want only to escape northward.

NEW GUINEA—Amphibious assault force (20th Brig Gp, Aus 9th Div) sails from Lae for Finschhafen. Aus 22d Brig starts overland drive from Lae toward Langemak Bay. 21st and 25th Brigs, Aus 7th Div, are flown to Kaiapit from Nadzab to pursue enemy up Markham Valley to Dumpu.

ITALY—15th Army Group: Gen Alexander outlines plans for future operations in 4 phases: (1) consolidation of current positions on line Salerno-Bari; (2) capture of Naples and Foggia; (3) seizure of Rome and neighboring airfields as well as communications center of Terni; (4) eventual capture of Leghorn, Florence, and Arezzo.

In U.S. Fifth Army's VI Corps area, 3d and 45th Divs continue N over mountains toward E-W Highway 7, meeting delaying opposition just S of Acerno and W of Oliveto, respectively. 34th Div, whose 133d Inf is to reinforce VI Corps for drive on Avellino, begins landing at Paestum.

USSR—Soviet forces take Chernigov, between Gomel and Kiev.

22 September

POA—Adm Halsey issues warning order for invasion of N Solomons and directs Adm Wilkinson, who is to head landing forces, to make detailed plans. It is later decided to invade Treasury Is. and Empress Augusta Bay area of Bougainville.

SWPA—GHQ issues orders for DEXTERITY—landing on Cape Gloucester, New Britain. ALAMO Force is to make airborne and amphibious assault on Cape Gloucester; neutralize Gasmata, and then take it in shore-to-shore operation. D Day, at first set for 20 November, is finally postponed to 26 December.

NEW GUINEA—After preparatory naval bombardment, 20th Brig Gp of Aus 9th Div lands at Song R mouth, 6 miles N of Finschhafen, early in morning; establishes beachhead with little difficulty and pushes S toward Finschhafen. Fifth Air Force provides air support and intercepts enemy aircraft making ineffective attacks on the convoy.

ITALY—15th Army Group: U.S. Fifth Army directs Br 10 Corps to seize Naples and VI Corps to secure line Avellino-Teora. VI Corps is to be prepared to continue to Benevento. In VI Corps area, 3d and 45th Divs overcome opposition barring their advance: 3d occupies Acerno and 45th Oliveto.

In Br Eighth Army area, Ind 8th Div arrives from Africa. In 5 Corps area, special force (elements of 8th Div and of 4th Armd Brig), under 78th Div command, lands at Bari, night 22-23, to drive to Foggia.

USSR—Germans announce evacuation of Poltava, which is untenable. This is the last strongpoint E of the middle Dnieper. In Kuban area, Soviet forces take Anapa.

23 September

NEW GUINEA—Continuing S toward Finschhafen, Aus 20th Brig takes airfield and reaches Bumi R, where Japanese are firmly established.

ITALY—15th Army Group: U.S. Fifth Army begins general advance. Br 10 Corps, making main effort, attacks toward Nocera-Pagani Pass on left with 46th Div; 56th drives northward on Salerno–S. Severino road. Firm enemy opposition makes progress slow. In VI Corps area, 3d and 45th Divs continue northward, hampered more by extensive demolitions than by enemy. Engineers are playing important role in keeping routes of advance open.

Br Eighth Army drives enemy from Altamura.

USSR—Red Army troops push through Poltava toward Kremenchug.

24 September

POA—Vice Adm Raymond A. Spruance recommends to Adm Nimitz that an amphibious operation against Makin be substituted for projected invasion of Nauru. This plan is subsequently accepted.

Solomon Is.—First Allied plane lands at Vella Lavella airfield.

NEW GUINEA—20th Brig, Aus 9th Div, forces Bumi R, N of Finschhafen. Enemy planes again attack shipping.

NEW BRITAIN—ALAMO Scouts begin rcn of Cape Gloucester area in preparation for invasion.

ITALY—15th Army Group: In Br Eighth Army's 5 Corps area, 78th Div patrols reach Ofanto R.

USSR—Heavy fighting is in progress in vicinity of Smolensk and Roslavl.

GERMANY—Berlin announces evacuation of Smolensk and Roslavl.

25 September

NEW GUINEA—162d Inf of U.S. 41st Div, having successfully completed its mission, begins return trip to Australia. 20th Brig, Aus 9th Div, continues battle for Finschhafen.

ITALY—15th Army Group: Gen Montgomery begins regrouping Br Eighth Army to strengthen E flank. 5 Corps, which is to include 5th, 1st A/B, and Ind 8th Divs, is initially to remain in Taranto area while 13 Corps, with 78th Div on right and Cdn 1st Div on left, continues advance. 5 Corps is later to move forward behind 13 Corps and secure its left flank.

USSR—Soviet forces take Smolensk and Roslavl on central front; to S, hold E bank of the Dnieper from Kremenchug to Dniepropetrovsk. German *4th Army* falls back to positions W of Smolensk and holds.

26 September

NEW GUINEA—Japanese try in vain to destroy Aus beachhead in Finschhafen area.

CORFU—Surrenders to German force that has recently landed there.

ITALY—15th Army Group: Is directed by Gen Eisenhower to secure air bases in Rome area.

U.S. Fifth Army's Br 10 Corps continues efforts to break out into Neapolitan plain; enemy positions are beginning to weaken under its blows. To reinforce W flank, U.S. 82d A/B Div is transferred to Maiori by sea and, under 10 Corps control, takes command of Rangers. VI Corps is handicapped by autumn rains as well as demolitions, but 45th Div takes Teora and junction of Highways 7 and 91.

In Br Eighth Army area, 13 Corps patrols reach Canosa.

27 September

Solomon Is.—I MAC issues letter of instructions to 3d Mar Div for N Solomons offensive.

ITALY—Marshal Badoglio receives terms of complete instrument of surrender.

15th Army Group: In U.S. Fifth Army's VI Corps area, 3d Div reaches Highway 7 and is threatening Avellino.

In Br Eighth Army area, enemy abandons Foggia and its airfields, major objective of Eighth Army.

USSR—Soviet troops reduce enemy's bridgehead to narrow strip on Taman Peninsula when they capture Temryuk and occupy N bank of Kuban R.

GERMANY—U.S. Eighth Air Force attacks Emden port area through overcast, using H2S-equipped aircraft as Pathfinders for the first time. Of 305 bombers dispatched, 244 attack target or targets of opportunity. P-47's, with belly tanks, escort bombers all the way to target in Germany for first time.

28 September

Solomon Is.—Japanese begin withdrawing from Kolombangara after nightfall.

ITALY—15th Army Group: U.S. Fifth Army is now ready for assault on Naples by Br 10 Corps and on Avellino by VI Corps. Br 10 Corps forces enemy back through passes leading to Naples. 23d Armd Brig advances to Castellammare. Rangers seize Sala. 131st Brig, 7th Armd Div, overruns Nocera.

29 September

CHINA—Gen Stilwell issues "Program for China," in which he recommends that 60 Nationalist divs be re-formed.

ITALY—Marshal Badoglio and Gen Eisenhower sign complete instrument of Italian surrender on board HMS *Nelson*, off Malta.

15th Army Group: Gen Alexander issues instructions for future operations, to be conducted in 2 phases: (1) capture of Naples and airfields to N and Foggia airfields, while advancing to general line Sessa Aurunca-Venafro-Isernia-Castropignano-Biferno R-Termoli; (2) advance to general line Civitavecchia-Terni-Visso-S. Benedetto del Tronto.

U.S. Fifth Army directs VI Corps, upon capture of Avellino, to shift to left along general line Avellino-Montemarano-Teora. Br 10 Corps units seize bridge at Scafati. This is the only bridge now standing across the Sarno. Rcn units are pursuing retreating enemy. In VI Corps area, 3d Div units converge on Avellino and open attack on it, night 29-30.

USSR—Soviet troops occupy Kremenchug and E bank of the Dnieper in that area; continue to close in on Kiev to NW.

30 September

ITALY—15th Army Group: In U.S. Fifth Army area, Br 10 Corps has surrounded M. Vesuvius. In VI Corps area, Avellino falls to 3d Div during morning.

1 October

Solomon Is.—Adm Halsey informs Gen MacArthur of his decision to invade Bougainville at Empress Augusta Bay on 1 November and is promised maximum air assistance from SWPA.

NEW GUINEA—Aus 9th Div commits another bn to assault on Finschhafen, making 3 in all.

ITALY—15th Army Group: In U.S. Fifth Army's Br 10 Corps area, King's Dragoon Gds enter Naples during morning without opposition. This excellent port, although damaged by bombing, can be quickly restored to use.

In Br Eighth Army area, 13 Corps occupies Foggia airfields and drives northward toward line Termoli Vinchiaturo in order to safeguard the fields, 78th Div along main coastal road and Cdn 1st Div along inland route leading into mountains. Gargano Peninsula is clear of enemy.

USSR—During first week of the month, 3 Soviet army groups apply strong pressure against enemy's line along Dnieper bend and succeed in establishing small bridgeheads in vicinity of Kiev, Kremenchug, and Dniepropetrovsk.

AUSTRIA—In third attack from the Mediterranean in behalf of Combined Bomber Offensive, heavy bombers of XII BC and 3 on loan from Eighth Air Force drop 187 tons of bombs on Wiener Neustadt. Others are prevented from attacking Augsburg (Bavaria) by overcast but hit alternate targets in Germany and Italy. The Eighth Air Force B-24's return to England after this attack.

2 October

POA—27th Div, previously authorized to plan for invasion of Nauru, is notified that its mission will be to capture Makin Atoll in the Gilberts.

Solomon Is.—Japanese complete withdrawal from Kolombangara, night 2-3. Efforts of U.S. naval forces to interfere are largely ineffective and some 9,400 Japanese escape safely.

NEW GUINEA—Troops of Aus 9th Div seize village and harbor of Finschhafen and make contact with Aus 22d Brig, which has moved forward from Lae. Japanese retain Sattelberg and Wareo, both of which command Finschhafen area and must be cleared.

ITALY—15th Army Group: In U.S. Fifth Army's Br to Corps area, U.S. 82d A/B Div move, into Naples to police it while advance is being continued to the Volturno, a natural barrier covering Naples. In VI Corps area, while 3d Div drives northward toward the Volturno on left flank of corps, 34th and 45th Divs, 45th on right, are moving along separate routes toward Benevento, important road junction. To hasten advance along Adriatic coast in Br Eighth Army area, 2d Special Service Brig (commandos) of 13 Corps lands, night 2-3, near Termoli and secures the town and port; soon joins 78th Div, which, moving N along coast, secures bridgehead across the Biferno.

3 October

AEGEAN—Axis forces invade Kos I.

ITALY—15th Army Group: In U.S. Fifth Army's VI Corps area, 133d Inf of 34th Div takes Benevento and establishes bridgehead across Calore R. 34th

Div is then withdrawn to reserve, leaving 45th Div to expand bridgehead.

In Br Eighth Army area, Germans rush reinforcements forward in attempt to hurl back bridgehead across the Biferno at Termoli, and hard fighting ensues. Brig of 8th Div is landed in the bridgehead, night 3-4. Cdn 1st Div, hampered by terrain, is within 15 miles of Vinchiaturo.

4 October

AEGEAN—Germans overrun Kos I. Loss of this island, site of only Allied air base in the Aegean, endangers Samos and Leros.

CORSICA—Allied forces gain complete control of Corsica as enemy withdraws from Bastia area. Participating in expulsion of Germans were patriots, Bn du Choc, goums of 4th Moroccan Mtn Div, and small U.S. OSS party.

5 October

U.S.—JCS approve gradual strengthening of W Aleutians.

POA—CINCPAC-CINCPOA issues plan for offensive in Central Pacific. Adm Spruance is to seize Makin, Tarawa, and Apamama in the Gilberts, cover amphibious landings on each with air and naval surface forces, and deny enemy use of land bases in the Marshalls and at Nauru during the operation. D Day for landings is set for 19 November (WLT) and later postponed to 20 November (WLT).

WAKE—U.S. TF 14 begins 2-day operation against Wake in which carrier-based and land-based planes participate.

ITALY—15th Army Group: In U.S. Fifth Army area, Br 10 Corps gets forward elements to the Volturno.

In Br Eighth Army's 13 Corps area, indecisive fighting for Biferno bridgehead at Termoli continues, with Germans penetrating into Termoli itself.

6 October

Solomon Is.—Action in central Solomons comes to a close. Elements of 27th Inf, 25th Div, make unopposed landing on Kolombangara during morning. U.S. casualties during the central Solomons campaign total 1,094 killed and 3,83 wounded. Counted enemy dead, except on Vella Lavella, total 2,483. The campaign yields Allied forces 4 airfields (Munda, Barakoma, Ondonga, and Segi) within range of Bougainville, the next objective.

BATTLE OF VELLA LAVELLA—Although outnumbered 3 to 1, U.S. DD's engage enemy naval force during night 6-7 as it is withdrawing 600 Japanese from Vella Lavella. Japanese succeed in rescuing their forces but lose a DD. U.S. losses are 1 DD sunk and 2 others damaged.

NEW GUINEA—Elements of Aus 7th Div takes Dumpu with unexpected ease. This is to become a staging field for fighters.

NEW BRITAIN—ALAMO Scouts begin reconnoitering Gasmata area in preparation for invasion.

ITALY—15th Army Group: U.S. Fifth Army reaches S bank of Volturno 1, successfully concluding another phase of the Italian campaign. In Br 10 Corps area, 56th Div takes Capua.

In Br Eighth Army's 13 Corps area, 78th Div gains firm control of Biferno bridgehead at Termoli.

7 October

ITALY—15th Army Group: U.S. Fifth Army begins preparations for assault across the Volturno. Crossing date is set tentatively at night 9-10 and later postponed to night 12-13. VI and Br 10 Corps improve positions along S bank of the river.

In Br Eighth Army's 13 Corps area, another brig of 8th Div, the last to arrive in Italy, lands in Biferno bridgehead as enemy retires across Trigno R.

USSR—Soviet forces on central front overrun Nevel, rail center N of Vitebsk. Enemy resistance is stiffening all along the line and progress of Red Army is becoming less spectacular.

8 October

NEW GUINEA—Aus II Corps, under Lt Gen Sir Leslie Morshead, relieves Aus I Corps.

ITALY—15th Army Group: In U.S. Fifth Army's VI Corps area, 30th Inf of 3d Div forces enemy remnants to withdraw across the Volturno. 34th Div is to take over zone of 30th Inf and join 3d Div in assault across the river.

GERMANY—U.S. Eighth Air Force, for the first time, uses radio countermeasure called CARPET in powerful attack on Bremen and Vegesack by 357 bombers. Despite this, the attack is costly.

9 October

U.S.—Gen Arnold recommends to JCS that Twelfth Air Force be divided into two air forces to increase power of Combined Bomber Offensive. It has already been decided that Italy-based planes will assist in offensive to knock out Germany.

ELLICE IS.—Nukufetau airstrip is ready for use.

ITALY—15th Army Group: In U.S. Fifth Army's VI Corps area, 45th Div finishes clearing right flank of army. 179th Inf replaces 157th, which is withdrawn to reserve.

In Br Eighth Army area, 5th Div is transferred from 5 to 13 Corps.

USSR—Red Army eliminates final resistance on Taman Peninsula.

11 October

ITALY—15th Army Group: In Br Eighth Army area, gap is developing between 78th Div on Adriatic coast and Cdn 1st Div, and Gen Montgomery regroups units: 5 Corps, with 78th Div and Ind 8th Div under command, is given responsibility for right flank; 13 Corps is to advance on 2-div front, employing Cdn 1st and Br 5th Divs; NZ 2d Div, which is to concentrate in Taranto area by mid-November, is to be held in army reserve.

USSR—Soviet forces closing in on Gomel take suburb of Novo Belitsa.

12 October

POA—Adm Halsey issues basic plan for invasion of N Solomons.

NEW BRITAIN—U.S. Fifth Air Force begins strong air offensive against Rabaul in effort to isolate and neutralize Bismarck Archipelago. 349 aircraft participate in the surprise attack and considerably damage Japanese shipping and aircraft at cost of only 4 planes lost.

ITALY—15th Army Group: U.S. Fifth Army begins assault crossing of the Volturno on 40-mile front during night 12-13. Operations in VI Corps sector start at midnight with feint on left flank by 1st Bn of 15th Inf, 3d Div.

13 October

MAKIN—Photographic coverage of the atoll is obtained.

ITALY—Formally declares war on Germany, thereby becoming a cobelligerent of the Allies.

15th Army Group: U.S. Fifth Army establishes bridgeheads on N bank of the Volturno against sharp resistance. Engineers play an important part since enemy has destroyed bridges while making planned withdrawal. Fall rains and mountainous terrain make forward movement difficult. Weather conditions curtail NAAF support of the operation. Br 10 Corps, on W flank of army, makes main effort with 46th Div at Cancello while 7th Armd Div, in center, and 56th Div, on right, make diversionary attacks at Grazzanise and Capua, respectively. 46th Div establishes bridgehead in coastal sector, and 7th Armd Div gains toehold on N bank, but 56th Div is unable to cross at Capua. VI Corps, to right of to Corps, crosses river on 2-div front. On left, 3d Div crosses E of Capua with 34th Div to its right.

3d Div seizes M. Majulo, M. Caruso, and Piana di Caiazzo. 34th Div gains bridgehead from Piana di Caiazzo to junction of Calore and Volturno Rivers. On right flank of VI Corps, 45th Div is clearing M. Acero area with 179th and 180th Regts.

In Br Eighth Army's 13 Corps area, 5th Div, advancing along Route 87, reaches Casacalenda.

14 October

Solomon Is.—8th Brig Gp, NZ 3d Div, begins rehearsal for the Treasuries at Florida, concluding on 17th.

ITALY—15th Army Group: Unloading of supplies is transferred from Salerno to Naples.

In U.S. Fifth Army area, Gen Clark, CG, alters boundary between corps and changes plan of attack. Since 56th Div, on right flank of Br to Corps, is unable to cross the Volturno at Capua, boundary is moved E to permit it to use bridge within the Triflisco Gap, formerly 3d Div zone. 3d Div of VI Corps is to take over mission of 34th and latter is to move to right to make contact with 45th Div. 45th Div, upon reaching Piedimonte d'Alife, is to be relieved. VI Corps is to advance astride the Volturno to Venafro-Isernia area, clearing upper Volturno Valley. 3d and 34th Divs are to make converging attacks toward Dragoni, but 34th is forced to await improvement of its supply situation. Army bridgeheads across the Volturno are being expanded.

In Br Eighth Army's 13 Corps area, Cdn 1st Div takes Campobasso.

USSR—On the Dnieper bend, Soviet forces successfully conclude struggle for Zaporodzhe, industrial center of the Ukraine; others are fighting in streets of Melitopol.

GERMANY—Of 291 B-17's of U.S. Eighth Air Force attempting to bomb ball-bearing plants at Schweinfurt, 228 reach target and drop 483 tons of bombs accurately. Although severe damage is done, cost is heavy—60 B-17's lost and others damaged. As a result of these losses, daylight bombing attacks against strategic targets deep in Germany are not resumed for some time.

15 October

POA—I MAC issues final orders for invasion of N Solomons. The attack force (TF 31 under Adm Wilkinson), with ground forces of Gen Vandegrift's I MAC, will seize Treasury Is. bases on 27 October in preparation for main invasion of Bougainville on 1 November. In support will be carrier-based and land-based aircraft, surface forces, and submarines.

ITALY—15th Army Group: In U.S. Fifth Army's Br 10 Corps area, 56th Div crosses the

[16-22 OCTOBER 1943]   [141]

Volturno, using bridges in former VI Corps sector. VI Corps' 3d Div takes Cisterna, but elements are being strongly opposed near Villa and Liberi. Elements of 34th Div (2d Bn, 135th Inf) take Ruviano. Enemy withdraws from this area, night 15-16. On right flank of VI Corps, 45th Div finishes clearing to Titerno Creek and makes contact with 34th Div across the Volturno to left.

Br Eighth Army's 13 Corps pauses as Cdn 1st Div takes Vinchiaturo.

U.K.—Gen Brereton activates U.S. Army Air Forces in the U.K. (USAAFUK), which includes Eighth and Ninth Air Forces.

16 October

U.S.—JCS, accepting Gen Arnold's plan to divide Twelfth Air Force into two forces, propose to Gen Eisenhower that Fifteenth Air Force be formed from XII BC with primary mission of increasing weight of Combined Bomber Offensive.

POA—3d Mar Div, having framed at Guadalcanal for operations against Bougainville, conducts rehearsals in New Hebrides, concluding them on 20th.

NEW GUINEA—Aus 9th Div, forewarned by a captured document of imminent attack, repels the first of a series of sharp counterattacks from Sattelberg.

CHINA—Adm Mountbatten arrives in Chungking.

U.K.—Gen Brereton assumes command of reconstituted Ninth Air Force.

17 October

NEW GUINEA—Japanese continue vigorous attacks from Sattelberg after attempting to land 4 barge loads of troops, of which only one reaches shore.

ITALY—15th Army Group: In U.S. Fifth Army's VI Corps area, 3d Div finds that enemy has withdrawn from Liberi and Villa. Elements of 34th occupy Alvignano after patrols report it clear.

USSR—Red Army breaks through enemy line below Kremenchug and pushes toward Krivoi Rog. Red Army forces of Center Front, attempting to complete investment of Gomel, seize Loyev after crossing the Dnieper S of Gomel.

18 October

Solomon Is.—Air Command, Solomons, begins intensive attacks on Bougainville airfields in preparation for invasion.

ITALY—15th Army Group: In U.S. Fifth Army's VI Corps area, 3d and 34th Divs continue toward Dragoni, 3d clearing Roccaromana, and prepare to make concerted effort to take Dragoni and bridges beyond. To block enemy escape route from Dragoni, 133d Inf of 34th Div begins second crossing of the Volturno and takes railway-highway bridge there.

19 October

INTERNATIONAL CONFERENCES—Conference between Soviet, Br, and U.S. foreign ministers opens in Moscow.

U.S.—Third (London) Protocol, extending through 30 June 1944, is signed. It promises 2,700,000 tons to USSR via the Pacific route and 2,400,000 by either the N Soviet ports or the Persian Gulf.

NEW GUINEA—Aus 9th Div, assisted by arty, contains further enemy attacks in Finschhafen area.

ITALY—NAAF begins offensive against bridges, thus, during next 5 days, forcing enemy to make greater use of motor transport and coastal shipping. 15th Army Group: In U.S. Fifth Army's VI Corps area, 168th Inf of 34th Div opens attack on Dragoni before dawn and finds that enemy has withdrawn. 133d Inf finishes crossing the Volturno NE of Dragoni. 135th crosses to SE and heads toward Alife.

20 October

GILBERT IS.—Photographic coverage of Tarawa is obtained.

NEW GUINEA—Aus 26th Brig arrives by sea to reinforce Aus 9th Div at Finschhafen, where enemy attacks continue.

JAPAN—Japanese order strong force of carrier planes to Rabaul to augment land-based air strength and delay Allied progress while main perimeter defenses of Japan are being strengthened. This plan is called Operation RO.

ITALY—15th Army Group: In U.S. Fifth Army's VI Corps area, Alife falls to 34th Div and Piedimonte d'Alife to 45th Div. This concludes current mission of 45th Div, which is withdrawn into corps reserve. While 3d Div continues northward toward Mignano in region W of the Volturno, 34th Div is to drive on Capriati al Volturno in region E of the river. 133d Inf opens drive on S. Angelo d'Alife.

21 October

SWPA—ALAMO Force hq moves from Milne Bay (New Guinea) to Goodenough I.

22 October

U.S.—CCS agree to establishment of Fifteenth Air Force in the Mediterranean.

POA—I MAC directs 2d Para Bn of 1st Mar Para Regt, FMF, to land at Voza (Choiseul I), night of 27 October, to conduct diversionary raid and, if feasible, establish permanent base there.

MEDITERRANEAN—Gen Eisenhower is notified that the Fifteenth Air Force will be established under his command, effective 1 November.

ITALY—15th Army Group: In U.S. Fifth Army's VI Corps area, 133d Inf of 34th Div takes road junction S of S. Angelo d'Alife, from which enemy rear guards have withdrawn, and prepares to attack the town.

In preparation for general advance on Rome (line Pescara-Avezzano-Rome), 78th Div of Br Eighth Army's 5 Corps crosses bn over the Trigno, night 22-23.

23 October

POA—27th Div issues field order for invasion of the Gilberts.

CBI—Gen Stilwell, Acting Deputy Supreme Allied Commander, SEAC, has by now decided that he can do little more toward improving the Chinese Army, his basic mission.

ITALY—15th Army Group: In U.S. Fifth Army's VI Corps area, 133d Inf of 34th Div opens assault on S. Angelo d'Alife but is unable to take it.

USSR—Hard fighting for Melitopol ends in victory for Soviet forces.

U.K.—Prime Minister Churchill issues directive outlining mission of Adm Mountbatten as Supreme Allied Commander, Southeast Asia.

24 October

ITALY—15th Army Group: In U.S. Fifth Army's VI Corps area, 133d Inf of 34th Div takes S. Angelo and commanding ground beyond without opposition.

25 October

POA—Adm Spruance issues operation plan, which is subsequently modified somewhat, outlining organization and tasks of Operation GALVANIC, invasion of the Gilberts.

NEW GUINEA—Japanese begin withdrawing toward Sattelberg in coastal sector N of Finschhafen, suspending attacks on Aus 9th Div.

ITALY—15th Army Group: Allied commanders decide that the initiative must be retained in Italy in order to pin down enemy forces there and prevent them from massing for counteroffensive before spring 1944.

U.S. Fifth Army, with positions N of the Volturno firmly established, is ready for drive against German delaying positions in mountains from M. Massico on W coast to Matese mountains on right boundary. In VI Corps area, 135th Inf of 34th Div moves forward to take up pursuit toward Ailano, passing through 133d Inf.

USSR—On the Dnieper bend, Red Army forces overrun Dniepropetrovsk and Dnieprodzerzhinsk.

26 October

POA—Treasury Is. assault force (Rear Adm George H. Fort's Southern Force of Adm Wilkinson's TF 31) sails for target.

27 October

POA—In preparation for invasion of Bougainville, 8th Brig Gp of NZ 3d Div, under Brig R. A. Row, lands on 2 islands of Treasury group, Stirling and Mono. The small Japanese force on Mono is quickly put to flight and must be rounded up. Stirling is undefended. New Georgia-based planes support the operation. Japanese planes attack shipping with little success. 2d Mar Para Bn (Lt Col Victor H. Krulak) begins diversionary raid on Choiseul I, Solomons, landing night 27-28, and subsequently patrols actively to feign strength that is not present.

ITALY—15th Army Group: In U.S. Fifth Army's VI Corps area, 168th Inf of 34th Div is ordered to attack on 28th since elements of 135th Inf are being held up by enemy rear guards on hill S of Ailano.

In Br Eighth Army's 5 Corps area, 78th Div makes futile attempt to expand bridgehead across Trigno R. Failure is largely due to heavy rainfall.

USSR—Soviet forces break through enemy defenses beyond Melitopol, but by this time Germans have succeeded in stabilizing positions before Nikopol and at Krivoi Rog.

28 October

ITALY—15th Army Group: In U.S. Fifth Army's Br 10 Corps area, 46th Inf and 7th Armd Divs begin attack on M. Massico and M. S. Croce. In VI Corps area, 168th Inf of 34th Div finds that enemy has abandoned the hill S of Ailano.

In Br Eighth Army area, heavy rainfall forces Gen Montgomery to postpone planned attack by 13 Corps along axis Vinchiaturo-Isernia. 5 Corps continues unsuccessful efforts to expand Trigno bridgehead in coastal sector.

29 October

ITALY—15th Army Group: In U.S. Fifth Army's VI Corps area, 34th Div continues to pursue enemy northward, 135th Inf taking Pratella and

Prata. Elements of 504th Para Inf, 82d A/B Div, protecting right flank of VI Corps, reach Gallo. 3d Div continues N on left flank of corps in region W of the Volturno.

In Br Eighth Army area, 13 Corps begins attack toward Isernia, 5th Div leading off in downpour of rain, night 29–30.

30 October

INTERNATIONAL CONFERENCES—Moscow Conference of Foreign Ministers ends after considering certain politico-military issues. Although a tripartite conference (Br-U.S.-Soviet), Ch representatives have participated in some phases. Conferees agree to demand "unconditional surrender" of Germany and establish a world organization for peace. Discussions lead to establishment later in London of European Advisory Commission to study and make recommendations on problems relating to termination of the war in Europe.

31 October

POA—Adm Turner's Northern Attack Force (TF 52) begins rehearsals for GALVANIC—invasion of the Gilberts—off Hawaii. TF 31 units rendezvous W of Guadalcanal, then sail for Bougainville. Enemy airfields on S Bougainville are now unserviceable.

ITALY—15th Army Group: U.S. Fifth Army takes control of Italian 1st Motorized Gp. In Br 10 Corps area, while 7th Armd and 46th Inf Divs continue attacks on M. Massico and M. S. Croce, 56th Div, on to Corps right flank, takes Teano. In VI Corps area, some elements of 34th Div reach Fontegreca while others occupy Ciorlano, on slopes of La Croce Hill.

In Br Eighth Army's 13 Corps area, Cantalupo falls to 5th Div.

1 November

U.S.—Alaska is made a separate theater of operations. Alaska Defense Command, separated from Western Defense Command, is renamed Alaskan Department and comes under direct control of the War Department.

U.S. Military Mission to USSR is organized under Maj Gen John R. Deane to establish American airfields in USSR for shuttle bombing of enemy territory.

Solomon Is.—After preparatory naval gunfire and aerial bombardment, Northern Force of Adm Wilkinson's TF 31 starts landing 3d Mar Div, reinf, of Gen Vandegrift's I MAC on Bougainville about 0730 9th and 3d Marines, 9th on left, land abreast on N shore of Empress Augusta Bay in Cape Torokina area and establish shallow beachhead despite opposition from small but determined defense force. Elements of 2d Mar Raider Regt (Prov) land on Puruata I, off Cape Torokina, and begin to clear it. Maj Gen A. H. Turnage, 3d Mar Div CG, takes command ashore. Japanese air attacks delay unloading of cargo and surf damages many landing craft, but the operation is otherwise very successful. In support of the landings, naval vessels of TF 39 (Rear Adm A. Stanton Merrill) and carrier aircraft of TF 38 (Rear Adm Frederick C. Sherman) neutralize enemy airfields in S Bougainville-Shortlands area.

BATTLE OF EMPRESS AUGUSTA BAY—During night 1–2, TF 39 engages enemy force of cruisers and DD's proceeding toward Bougainville and forces enemy to retire after losing a cruiser and a DD.

MEDITERRANEAN—U.S. Fifteenth Air Force is activated pursuant to CCS directive of as October.

ITALY—15th Army Group: In U.S. Fifth Army area, Br 10 Corps continues to clear M. Massico-M. S. Croce hill mass on W flank of Fifth Army. 56th Div takes Roccamonfina. In VI Corps area, 168th Inf of 34th Div reaches Capriati al Volturno.

USSR—In the Crimea, Red Army troops seal off Perekop Isthmus with capture of Armyansk; make landings on E end of Kerch Peninsula.

2 November

BOUGAINVILLE—3d Mar Div is slowly expanding beachhead and organizing defenses. 3d Marines, which has had hard fighting on right flank, is exchanging places with 9th Marines. Puruata I. is cleared by noon. Carrier planes of TF 38 make 2 strikes against Bonis, continuing neutralization of airfields; before departing to refuel.

NEW BRITAIN—75 B-25's, with P-38 escort, attack Rabaul with good effect but meet the strongest opposition to be encountered by Fifth Air Force during the entire war.

BURMA—Japanese along Tarung R are withstanding efforts of 112th Rgt, Ch 38th Div, to advance; wipe out co of 1st Bn.

ITALY—15th Army Group: In U.S. Fifth Army's Br 10 Corps area, patrols of 7th Armd and 46th Inf Divs reach the Garigliano. VI Corps prepares to cross 2 divs, 45th and 34th, over the Volturno. Advance elements of 45th Div—Co F of 180th Inf—cross below Sesto Campano, night 2–3.

In Br Eighth Army area, 5 Corps begins main assault across the Trigno, night 2–3. Firm resistance is being overcome with help of arty and naval gunfire.

AUSTRIA—U.S. Fifteenth Air Force joins in Combined Bomber Offensive against Germany with damaging attack on aircraft works at Wiener Neustadt by 112 heavy bombers. Enemy puts up strong fighter and AA opposition.

3 November

POA—Northern Attack Force (TF 52) completes rehearsal for GALVANIC at Hawaii.

Solomon Is.—3d Mar Div continues to improve beachhead positions on Bougainville. At 1800, 3d Marines takes responsibility for left flank and 9th Marines for right flank. 3d Raider Bn patrol moves to Torokina I. and makes search for enemy, but finds none.

ITALY—15th Army Group: In U.S. Fifth Army's VI Corps area, 4th Ranger Bn crosses the Volturno in 45th Div zone at 1800 to block Highway 6 NW of Mignano, but is stopped short of objective. 45th Div continues crossing the Volturno. Rest of 2d Bn, 180th Inf, upon crossing SE of Presenzano at 2000, drives NW toward Rocca Pipirozzi. After strong arty preparation, 34th Div begins to cross the Volturno, night 3-4.

In Br Eighth Army area, 5 Corps is strongly opposed as it attacks S. Salvo ridge.

GERMANY—In largest daylight raid to date by U.S. Eighth Air Force, over 500 planes, led by Pathfinders, attack Wilhelmshaven port area through cloud.

4 November

U.S.—War Department Operations Division recommends that current commitments to China be fulfilled; that limited bomber offensive from China be mounted; and that only 30 Ch divs be trained and equipped, plus equipment for 3 additional divs in order to start training of ZEBRA Force.

SOLOMON IS.—2d Mar Para Bn withdraws. from Choiseul in LCI's. Bougainville beachhead is seriously threatened as Japanese naval force, including heavy cruisers, arrives at Rabaul from Truk. TF 38, with land-based air cover, is ordered to strike at Rabaul.

BURMA—112th Regt, Ch 38th Div, digs in in current positions in N Burma, since all efforts to advance have been futile and costly. 2d Bn is still short of Sharaw Ga. By this time, 1st Bn, directed against Yupbang Ga, is isolated by enemy roadblock and must be supplied by air; 3d Bn is pinned down at Ngajatzup, 30 miles SW of Ningbyen.

ITALY—15th Army Group: U.S. Fifth Army's Br ro Corps, with M. Massico and M. S. Croce hill masses under its control, prepares for assault on M. Camino by 56th Div. In VI Corps area, 2d Bn of 180th Inf, 45th Div, clears Rocca Pipirozzi and digs in an ridge to NW; makes contact with 4th Ranger Bn at Cannavinelle. 3d Bn of 179th Inf, upon crossing the Volturno S of Venafro, attacks and captures Venafro. 1st Bn follows 3d across the river. 34th Div's 133d Inf seizes S. Maria Oliveto; 168th takes Roccaravindola.

In Br Eighth Army area, 13 Corps troops enter Isernia without opposition. 5 Corps takes S. Salvo ridge, enemy having made general withdrawal in the area.

USSR—Germans are forced to yield additional ground along the Dnieper as Soviet troops press forward to its mouth opposite Kherson. Red Army units open major offensive in Kiev area, pushing S from Dnieper bridgehead and threatening the city with encirclement.

5 November

BOUGAINVILLE—In zone of 9th Marines, 3d Ranger Bn repels Japanese attack against block on local trail, called Mission Trail. Later the Rangers and 3d Bn of 9th Marines drive up Mission Trail toward its junction with Numa Numa Trail. The Numa Numa and East-West Trails are the two main trails on Cape Torokina.

NEW BRITAIN—Almost 100 carrier aircraft of TF 38 attack new enemy naval forces concentrated at Rabaul, taking enemy by surprise; despite intense AA fire, severely damage 5 cruisers and 2 DD's at cost of 10 planes lost. Later, Fifth Air Force planes bomb wharf area as enemy aircraft are searching in vain for TF 38. Enemy naval forces are severely crippled and threat to Bougainville beachhead from this source ends.

CBI—Gen Stilwell submits report to Chiang Kai-shek on SEAC planning and progress of preparations for attack from Yunnan by Y-Force.

ITALY—15th Army Group: U.S. Fifth Army begins 10-day period of gruelling action against lofty hills and mountains that form enemy's Winter Line. Designed as a delaying position, this line is disposed in front of main defense belt known as the Gustav Line. Fifth Army's efforts to breach the line during next 10 days are fruitless. In addition to a tenacious enemy, Fifth Army is adversely affected by terrain, rainy weather, and lack of reserves. In Br 10 Corps area, 56th Div, in conjunction with left flank elements of U.S. VI Corps, begins battle for M. Camino-M. la Difensa-M. Maggiore hill mass, concentrating on M. Camino. In VI Corps area, 3d Div begins outflanking attacks against positions commanding Mignano Gap: as 7th Inf columns press toward German M. la Difensa positions, which hold out for next 10 days, elements of 15th are sent northward over M. Cesima toward Cannavinelle

Hill; 30th Inf, upon passing through 45th Div's zone, night 5–6, presses W toward M. Rotondo.

In Br Eighth Army area, 5 Corps pursues enemy northward, 78th Div, on coast, pushing through Vasto. Ind 8th Div takes Tufillo.

6 November

U.S.—CCS accede to request of Gen Eisenhower for retention of landing craft. 12 U.S. and 56 Br LST's due to depart from Mediterranean are to remain until 15 December. A further extension, until 15 January 1944, is subsequently granted.

ELLICE IS.—Advance Hq, Seventh Air Force, opens at Funafuti.

SOLOMON IS.—1st Bn, 21st Marines, arrives on Bougainville to reinforce 3d Mar Div's beachhead.

INDIA—Government of India accepts offer of U.S. troops to help operate Bengal and Assam RR.

ITALY—15th Army Group: In U.S. Fifth Army's Br 10 Corps area, 56th Div continues attack toward M. Camino, elements taking Calabritto. In VI Corps' 3d Div sector, 7th Inf is still fighting for M. la Difensa; efforts of 15th Inf to take Hill 253, SE nose of M. Lungo, are unsuccessful, as are those of 30th Inf to take M. Rotondo. To E, 45th and 34th Divs batter at hills and mountains with little success.

USSR—Germans withdraw from Kiev to avoid envelopment.

7 November

POA—Southern Attack Force (TF 53) begins rehearsal for GALVANIC at Efate, New Hebrides. A Fifth Fleet carrier force, under command of Rear Adm Alfred I. Montgomery, reaches S Pacific.

BOUGAINVILLE—Beachhead undergoes its first major counterattack. Japanese DD's from Rabaul land 475 troops between Laruma and Koromokina Rivers early in morning. The troops attack at once in vicinity of Koromokina lagoon and are held off by 3d Marines, although small outpost is cut off and must be rescued by sea.

CBI—SEAC adopts TARZAN, India-based portion of general offensive in Burma, now called CHAMPION. TARZAN calls for limited offensive on Arakan coast for Akyab; drive from Imphal to Chindwin. R.; establishment of a div on RR to Myitkyina; amphibious operation against the Andamans.

11 Army Group: In Br Fourteenth Army's 4 Corps area, Japanese are becoming aggressive in Chin Hills and occupy Falam.

ITALY—15th Army Group: U.S. Fifth Army continues to battle enemy in mountains of Winter Line but makes little headway. In VI Corps sector, 34th Div organizes TF A under Brig Gen Benjamin F. Caffey, consisting of 135th Inf and supporting units, for drive on Montaquila.

USSR—Exploiting German withdrawal from Kiev, Soviet forces push on to Fastov, rail junction to SW, where they are halted by strong opposition.

8 November

BOUGAINVILLE—Gen Vandegrift (CG I MAC, pending arrival of Maj Gen Roy S. Geiger) reaches Bougainville and takes command of operations there and on the Treasuries. Advance elements of 37th Div, RCT 148, also arrive to take over left flank of beachhead and are attached to 3d Mar Div. Battle of Koromokina Lagoon ends as 1st Bn of 21st Marines, after extremely effective preparatory fire, attacks and eliminates subdued remnants of the counterlanding force.

CBI—Gen Stilwell directs Col Thomas S. Arms, of Y-Force Infantry Training Center, to activate ZEBRA Force Infantry Training Center at Kweilin.

ITALY—15th Army Group: Gen Alexander orders Fifth Army to plan for amphibious operation on W coast.

In U.S. Fifth Army's Br 10 Corps area, 56th Div withstands strong counterattacks at Calabritto and seizes hill to NE. In VI Corps area, 7th Inf of 3d Div is still unable to scale M. la Difensa, but 3d Bn of 15th Inf takes Hill 253 and 3d Bn of 30th reaches top of M. Rotondo—45th Div continues to fight for mountains north of Venafro and Pozzilli. 3d Bn, 179th Inf, opens assault on hills between Pozzilli and Filignano. 34th Div's TF A takes Montaquila.

In Br Eighth Army's 5 Corps area, 78th Div gains heights overlooking the Sangro from its mouth to Paglieta.

9 November

BOUGAINVILLE—Gen Geiger arrives on Bougainville by air: Allied dive bombers raid Koromokina Lagoon-Laruma R area.

10 November

POA—Main body of Northern Attack Force for GALVANIC leaves Pearl Harbor.

SOLOMON IS.—Gen Geiger takes command of Allied forces on Bougainville and Treasury Is.

NEW BRITAIN—Gen MacArthur cancels projected offensive against Gasmata. Fifth Air Force strongly attacks Rabaul.

ITALY—15th Army Group: In U.S. Fifth Army's VI Corps area, elements of 45th Div take hills between Pozzilli and Filignano without opposition. 1st Ranger Bn relieves other elements of 45th Div on M. Corno.

11 November

BOUGAINVILLE—Additional elements of 21st Marines arrive. Marines now hold junction of Mission and Numa Numa Trails, having killed an estimated 550 Japanese during drive up Mission Trail. In order to secure airfield site, Gen Geiger orders 3d Mar Div to drive E and 37th Div, W.

NEW BRITAIN—Powerful air offensive against Rabaul continues. Carrier planes of TF 38 and others of Adm Montgomery's force, as well as land-based RAAF and Fifth Air Force planes, attack with good effect. Japanese planes locate Adm Montgomery's group and attack it vigorously but ineffectively.

CBI—Generalissimo Chiang Kai-shek replies to Gen Stilwell's memo of 5 November at conference of Chinese National Military Council at Chungking. While agreeing to Br and Ch attack on Burma, he wants to hold Chinese back until British are attacking Kalewa. Replacements and supplies for Y-Force are to be provided.

11 Army Group: In Br Fourteenth Army's 4 Corps area, Japanese seize Haka.

ITALY—15th Army Group: In U.S. Fifth Army's VI Corps area, 45th Div commits 157th Inf between 180th and 179th for drive on Acquafondata. 2d Bn, 509th Para Inf, to which 1st Ranger Bn is attached, clears saddle of M. S. Croce.

USSR—Russians improve positions W of Kiev, seizing foothold across Teterev R, but are under pressure in Fastov area, SW of Kiev, where Germans are taking the initiative. Soviet Center Front forces attack northward toward Rechitsa, W of Gomel.

12 November

POA—Southern Attack Force for GALVANIC completes rehearsal off New Hebrides.

TREASURY IS.—8th Brig Gp, NZ 3d Div, completes elimination of small enemy garrison on Mono. For 205 Japanese dead counted, 40 New Zealanders and 12 Americans have lost their lives.

NEW BRITAIN—Japanese withdraw their carrier aircraft from Rabaul. Rabaul no longer presents a serious threat to Allied forces.

LEROS—Axis force invades Leros by air and sea.

ITALY—15th Army Group: In U.S. Fifth Army's Br 10 Corps area, 56th Div, exhausted by prolonged fighting, is to be withdrawn from M. Camino. In VI Corps area, 157th Inf of 45th Div makes limited progress toward Acquafondata but is threatened by enemy on Hills 769 and 640. 133d Inf, 34th Div, is pinched out by 135th Inf on right and 179th Inf on left; 135th Inf makes contact with 504th Para Inf, which has pushed past Fornelli to Colli and is maintaining contact with Br Eighth Army.

USSR—Continuing to advance W of Kiev, Soviet forces take Zhitomir, important rail center.

13 November

POA—Southern Attack Force for GALVANIC departs from New Hebrides. Preinvasion air operations against Gilberts are begun. B-24's from Funafuti bomb Tarawa without interception but meet unusually heavy AA fire.

BOUGAINVILLE—Gen Geiger becomes responsible to Adm Halsey as Adm Wilkinson relinquishes command. 21st Marines begins attack for junction of Numa Numa Trail with East-West Trail to ensure safety of airfield site. 129th Inf of 37th Div arrives.

NEW BRITAIN—U.S. Fifth Air Force begins preinvasion bombardment of targets in W New Britain.

CBI—Col Francis G. Brink is given responsibility for training of GALAHAD forces, a task previously held by Lt Col Charles N. Hunter. In late December the GALAHAD Force is activated as 5307th Regt (Prov).

ITALY—15th Army Group: In U.S. Fifth Army's VI Corps area, 157th Inf of 45th Div scales Hill 640 but is forced off. Hills 640 and 769 must be cleared before advance on Acquafondata can be continued.

USSR—Red Army intensifies pressure against enemy in Dnieper bend.[1]

14 November

BOUGAINVILLE—After delay to await air strike, replenishment of water supply, and repair of communications; 21st Marines, supported by 5 tanks, renews battle for trail junction and takes it. Perimeter defense is established. 148th Inf reverts to 37th Div from attachment to 3d Mar Div.

CBI—Movement orders are issued to aviation engineers and dump truck companies required to build airfields in India in preparation for arrival of B-29's.

ITALY—15th Army Group: In U.S. Fifth Army's Br 10 Corps area, 56th Div withdraws as planned from slopes of M. Camino, night 14-15.

USSR—Germans launch counteroffensive aimed at recapture of Zhitomir.

15 November

BOUGAINVILLE—Beachhead perimeter is expanded to inland defense line Dog.

CBI—Gen Wheeler is made principal administrative officer of SEAC. Similar post for Gen Auchinleck's India Command is given to Gen Sir Alan Brooke. Maj Gen William E. R. Covell succeeds Gen Wheeler as commander of SOS CBI.

BURMA—On N Burma front, Ch 38th Div is moving reinforcements forward for 112th Regt. 114th Regt arrives at front and is followed in early December by 113th. In 11 Army Group's Fourteenth Army sector, Japanese take Fort White in 4 Corps area, having forced British to abandon it.

ITALY—15th Army Group: U.S. Fifth Army halts advance in order to reorganize in preparation for another assault on the Winter Line. 7th Armd Div is withdrawn from left flank of Br 10 Corps to 15th Army Group reserve in preparation for movement to England. 46th Div takes over 7th Armd Div sector. 82d A/B Div, largely engaged in policing Naples, is also to be withdrawn to England before next offensive. 1st Armd Div begins arriving at Naples about this time.

USSR—Continuing offensive toward Rechitsa, Soviet forces cut rail line between Gomel and Pinsk.

16 November

BOUGAINVILLE—Continuous road through beachhead is completed, vastly improving supply situation.

CBI—Adm Mountbatten activates his new command, SEAC, and takes over operational control from CinC India. Movement orders are issued to U.S. forces who are to help operate the Bengal and Assam RR. Gen Stratemeyer's Hq, AAF, India-Burma Sector, virtually rejects Gen Chennault's proposals for 1944 for logistical reasons. Hump tonnage requested cannot be supplied. Since the TWILIGHT plan for B-29's to be brought to CBI is approved, priority of Fourteenth Air Force must be lowered.

LEROS I.—Enemy completes occupation of island.

ITALY—15th Army Group: In U.S. Fifth Army's VI Corps area, 36th Div moves forward to relieve 3d Div in Mignano Gap.

In Br Eighth Army area, 5 Corps is ordered to attack toward general line Ortona-Lanciano on 20 November. Adverse weather conditions subsequently force Gen Montgomery to postpone the date.

8th Div has secured small bridgehead on N bank of the Sangro and is gradually expanding it.

17 November

GILBERTS-MARSHALLS—During period 13-17 November, heavy bombers of Seventh Air Force have flown 141 sorties against Gilberts and Marshalls and have dropped some 173 tons of bombs.

BOUGAINVILLE—Final elements of 21st Marines arrive, but APD McKean is lost to enemy plane en route.

NEW GUINEA—Australians of 9th Div open assault against Sattelberg, which is suited by nature for defense. 26th, 24th, 20th, and 4th Brigs, assisted by tanks, aircraft, and arty, participate in the battle.

USSR—Some Red Army units in Kiev sector overrun Korosten, endangering enemy's supply system, but others are threatened with encirclement in Zhitomir as German counteroffensive for Zhitomir gains ground. To N, Soviet forces overrun Rechitsa and close in on Gomel.

18 November

ITALY—15th Army Group: In U.S. Fifth Army area, II Corps (Gen Keyes) is given zone of operations in center and takes command of 3d and 36th Divs. VI Corps contains 34th and 45th Divs.

USSR—Soviet troops force the Dnieper near Cherkassy, SE of Kiev, and take Ovruch, NW of Kiev, but continue to fall back under enemy pressure in Zhitomir area. To N, enemy forces in Gomel are imperiled by rapid expansion of Rechitsa salient.

19 November

CENTRAL PACIFIC—Land-based and carrier-based aircraft join in final bombardment of Gilberts, Marshalls, and Nauru in preparation for invasion of Gilberts.

BOUGAINVILLE—145th Inf of 37th Div arrives.

NEW BRITAIN—Fifth Air Force intensifies action against the island.

ITALY—15th Army Group: In Br Eighth Army's 5 Corps area, enemy completes withdrawal across the Sangro in Ind 8th Div sector.

USSR—Red Army forces abandon Zhitomir to avoid being trapped there.

20 November

GILBERT IS.—U.S. forces invade Makin and Tarawa Atolls (Operation GALVANIC), opening series of amphibious operations in Central Pacific aimed ultimately at invasion of Japan. Air and naval gunfire bombardment precede and closely support assault teams. Aerial supremacy over enemy has already been achieved. At both atolls, landing forces are beset with supply difficulties and communication failures.

MAKIN ATOLL—TF 52's landing force (27th Div's 165th Inf reinf by 3d Bn of 105th, tanks of 193d Tank Bn, and other supporting units), under Maj Gen Ralph C. Smith, invades Makin. As a preliminary to main invasion of Butaritari I., largest of the Makin group, special landing detachment sails for Kotabu at 0645 and secures the island without opposition. Invasion of Butaritari is begun on schedule at 0830, when BLT's 1 and 3 of 165th Inf start landing on Red Beaches 1 and 2 on W coast. At 1041, about 10 minutes behind schedule, BLT 2 begins landing on Yellow Beaches, located on N (lagoon) shore between On Chong's Wharf and King's Wharf. Both assault forces secure beachheads and with tank support push rapidly forward against light resistance, converging along West Tank Barrier, where enemy opposition is overcome, although small pocket remains to NW. Arty is emplaced on Ukiangong Pt.

TARAWA ATOLL—TF 53's landing force (2d Marines of 2d Mar Div, reinf by 2d Bn of 8th Marines and supporting units), under Maj Gen Julian C. Smith, USMC, invades Betio I., at SW tip of the atoll, where airfield and main enemy forces are located. Landings are made with great difficulty and very heavy casualties. Transports arrive S of assigned area and at 0507 come under fire of previously alerted enemy on Betio. While transports are moving northward out of range of enemy guns, warships attempt, with some success, to neutralize enemy positions. Aircraft deliver brief strikes before forces land. Although H Hour is postponed from 0830 to 0900, first troops do not reach shore until 0910. Marines land under direct fire, many wading from partly exposed reef that fringes coast; upon reaching shore, landing teams become intermingled and disorganized. Landings are made on 3 adjacent beaches (Red 1, 2, and 3, from W to E) on NW coast. 3d Bn of 2d Marines, the Red 1 assault force, gains beachhead on NW tip of island but is isolated there. In center, 2d Bn of 2d Marines is pinned down by enemy fire on Red 2. 2d Bn of 8th Marines, favored by more protracted naval gunfire preparation, meets less opposition on Red 3 and gains beachhead extending inland to airfield. To strengthen precarious hold on the island, 1st Bn of 2d Marines, from regt reserve, and 3d Bn of 8th Marines, from div reserve, are committed. Fortunately, counterattacks, expected after nightfall, fail to materialize, and meager gains are held. Shortly before invasion of Betio, a scout-sniper platoon clears enemy positions from main pier, partly burning it in the process.

Solomon Is.—Maj Gen Ralph J. Mitchell, USMC, relieves Gen Twining as head of Solomons Air Command. Gen Twining later takes command of Fifteenth Air Force. On Bougainville, 3d Mar Div is extending its positions in vicinity of Piva R forks against lively opposition. 37th Div is unopposed.

BURMA—II Army Group: In Br Fourteenth Army's 15 Corps area, Ind 7th Div starts across Mayu Range along two crude trails in preparation for offensive.

21 November

MAKIN ATOLL—BLT 2, 165th Inf, attacks on Butaritari I, after air and arty preparation, and overruns fortified area between West and East Tank Barriers as it pushes eastward to Stone Pier. BLT 1 mops up in W part of island and eliminates pocket near West Tank Barrier. Rcn detail lands on Kuma I. early in day, reconnoiters, and withdraws.

TARAWA ATOLL—Marines on Betio continue to meet grim opposition but strengthen their hold on the island with assistance of aircraft, arty, and naval gunfire. Further reinforcements are landed, bringing total bns ashore to 7. RCT 6 is released from V Amphibious Corps reserve to 2d Mar Div and its 1st Bn lands on Green beach, on W end of island. Rest of 8th Marines lands on Beach Red 2. 3d Bn of RCT a secures entire W end of Betio (Green Beach), while 1st and 2d Bns of RCT 2, from Red 2 and 3, push across airfield to S coast, splitting enemy forces. 2d Bn of RCT 8, on Red 3, makes little progress during day. Meanwhile, arty and naval gunfire are directed against E end of Betio to prevent enemy from escaping to next island (Bairiki), and 2d Bn of 6th Marines lands on Bairiki after preliminary bombardment that kills the few enemy there. While fighting is in progress on Betio, Co D of 2d Tank Bn starts reconnoitering other islands of Tarawa Atoll.

APAMAMA ATOLL—VAC Rcn CO. (–) lands from submarine *Nautilus* and begins reconnoitering the atoll under naval gunfire cover.

22 November

INTERNATIONAL CONFERENCES—SEXTANT Conference, attended by President Roosevelt, Prime Minister Churchill, and Generalissimo Chiang Kai-shek, opens at Cairo, Egypt, to consider war issues.

MAKIN ATOLL—After preparatory bombardment, BLT 3 of 165th Inf takes over attack from BLT 2 and drives E on Butaritari well beyond East Tank Barrier, which enemy has abandoned. Though E tip of island remains to be explored, Adm Turner declares the island captured. Gen Ralph Smith assumes command ashore. Night 22-23, Japanese are virtually wiped out when they make an unsuccessful counterattack. Steps are taken to cut off enemy's escape from Butaritari: elements of Co A, BLT 1, make waterborne move to narrow neck of island to intercept enemy; special detail moves to Kuma I. to halt enemy withdrawal there.

TARAWA ATOLL—Japanese on Betio undergo heavy air, naval, and arty bombardment as battle for the island continues. Enemy is brought under cross fire as arty is emplaced on Bairiki. Passing through 3d Bn of 2d Marines, 1st Bn of 6th Marines drives E along S coast on narrow front, making contact with 2d Marines force and continuing advance to E end of airfield. 2d Bn of 8th Marines, with elements of 3d Bn attached, presses E along N coast to E end of airfield. 1st Bn of 8th Marines, attached to 2d Marines, attacks strongpoint between Red Beaches 2 and 1 and succeeds in containing it. Thus by end of day enemy is compressed into E part of Betio beyond airfield and retains pocket between Red Beaches 1 and 2. 3d Bn, 6th Marines, lands on Green Beach and moves forward along S coast behind 1st Bn, 6th Marines. Gen Julian Smith establishes CP ashore. During night 22-23, Japanese counterattacks are repelled by 1st Bn, 6th Marines.

SWPA—As planning for invasion of New Britain continues, Gen MacArthur decides to make subsidiary effort at Arawe.

NEW GUINEA—Aus 9th Div continues to struggle for Sattelberg, 26th Brig reaching S slopes.

ITALY—15th Army Group: In Br Eighth Army area, 5 Corps now has 5 bns on N bank of the Sangro.

23 November

MAKIN ATOLL—Organized resistance on Butaritari I. ends at 1030 when advance elements of 3d Bn, 165th Inf, reach tip of island. Re-embarkation of assault forces begins.

TARAWA ATOLL—3d Bn of 6th Marines, attacking through 1st Bn, reaches the end of Betio shortly after 1300, and Gen Julian Smith reports the end of organized resistance on Betio at 1330. 8th Marines, less 1st Bn, moves to Bairiki. 2d Bn, 6th Marines, moves from Bairiki to Betio and is given task of securing rest of islands in Tarawa Atoll. 3d Bn, 10th Marines, moves to village of Eita, where 3d Platoon of Co D, 2d Tank Bn, is attached to it.

BOUGAINVILLE—3d Mar Div, still strongly opposed in Piva forks area, begins regrouping. 1st Mar Para Bn arrives.

BURMA—In N Burma, Japanese overrun CP of 112th Regt, Ch 38th Div.

ITALY—15th Army Group: In U.S. Fifth Army's II Corps area, 1st Special Service Force (SSF), a highly trained group of Canadians and Americans under Col Robert T. Frederick, is attached to 36th Div.

24 November

MAKIN ATOLL—RCT 165, less 3d Bn, leaves for Hawaii. 3d Bn and miscellaneous units are left behind to conduct minor mopping up operations and to support construction forces. Command is turned over to Col Clesen H. Tenney, Garrison Force commander. 27th Div casualties for Makin total 218, of whom 58 are killed and 8 die of wounds. Enemy casualties, aside from those subsequently inflicted during the mop-up, are estimated at 550, including 105 prisoners. Japanese submarine sinks escort carrier USS Liscome Bay off Makin; 644 persons aboard are lost.

TARAWA ATOLL—2 Marine RCT's (8th and 2d) leave for Hawaii. Embarking from Betio, 2d Bn of 6th Marines, guided by scouts of 2d Tank Bn, begins uneventful search for enemy on islands up the long east side of Tarawa Atoll.

BOUGAINVILLE—3d Mar Div makes substantial progress, gaining commanding ground in Piva forks area. Marine SBD makes successful forced landing on Torokina fighter strip, although strip has not yet been completed.

INDIA—Airfield construction personnel for Ind air bases begin arriving.

ITALY—15th Army Group: U.S. Fifth Army outlines final plan of attack to begin about 2 December. First phase calls for capture of M. Camino-M. la Difensa-M. Maggiore area, to be preceded on 1 December by capture of Calabritto. In second phase, M. Sammucro is to be cleared in conjunction with drive W along Colli-Atina road. Third phase is to be attack into Liri Valley.

In Br Eighth Army area, 13 Corps captures Castel Alfedena. 5 Corps' bridgehead N of the Sangro is now firmly established.

GERMANY—Berlin reports progress toward Korosten, USSR.

25 November

TARAWA ATOLL—After scouting about half way up E side of atoll, Co D of 2d Tank Bn is recalled to village of Eita to prepare to reconnoiter other atolls. 2d Bn, 6th Marines, continues uneventful trek up Tarawa Atoll.

APAMAMA ATOLL—Apamama Occupation Force, based on 3d Bn of 6th Marines, is en route to atoll.

BATTLE OF CAPE ST GEORGE—5 Japanese DD's bound for Buka with reinforcements are turned back to vicinity of Cape St George (New Ireland) and engaged, night 25-26, by Allied DD's, which destroy 3 Japanese DD's without suffering any damage. This concludes series of night naval engagements of the Solomon campaigns.

NEW GUINEA—Sattelberg falls to troops of Aus 9th Div.

FORMOSA—U.S. Fourteenth Air Force, in its first attack on Formosa, destroys 42 enemy planes while attacking Shinchiku airdrome.

BURMA—AAF and RAF begin series of coordinated strikes against installations in Rangoon area, despite unfavorable weather conditions.

ITALY—15th Army Group: U.S. Fifth Army's plan for amphibious operations at Anzio (Operation SHINGLE) is approved. A single infantry div, reinf, is to establish beachhead and attempt to join main body within a week. Fr increment of Fifth

Army general staff arrives from N Africa by air to prepare for arrival of French Expeditionary Corps (FEC) under Gen Juin.

USSR—Attacking in Propoisk area, N of Gomel, Soviet forces achieve breakthrough on broad front and cut highway between Gomel and Mogilev, greatly increasing peril to Germans in Gomel.

ETO—Air Chief Marshal Leigh-Mallory, heading Allied Expeditionary Air Force (AEAF), activates his headquarters. Second Tactical Air Force, RAF, and later Gen Brereton's U.S. Ninth Air Force come under AEAF.

26 November

INTERNATIONAL CONFERENCES—First part of SEXTANT ends at Cairo after inconclusive discussions concerning OVERLORD and possible expansion of operations in the Mediterranean. After considering CHAMPION—plan for offensive in Burma—the conferees have agreed that an amphibious operation will be undertaken and have received Chiang Kai-shek's promise to commit Yunnan force. Upper Burma is to be cleared in spring of 1944 to open land route to China. Also approved is TWILIGHT—plan to base B-29's in CBI. Br and U.S. conferees leave for Tehran, Iran, for further discussions.

TARAWA ATOLL—2d Bn of 6th Marines reaches Buariki, last relatively large island of atoll, and prepares to attack enemy forces believed to be there.

APAMAMA ATOLL—VAC scouts are recalled as Apamama landing force arrives and begins organizing defenses of the atoll.

BOUGAINVILLE—I MAC continues to expand perimeter of beachhead. 3d Div is now at S shore of Lake Kathleen.

CBI—Brig Gen Haydon I. Boatner, Chief of Staff and Deputy Commander, CAI, reports to Maj Gen Thomas G. Hearn, Chief of Staff, U.S. Forces CBI, that situation of Ch 38th Div is "critical."

USSR—Germans abandon Gomel, key position of central front.

GERMANY—U.S. VIII BC surpasses its 3 November record for aircraft dispatched, sending out 633 bombers, Bremen their primary target. Results are largely obscured by overcast.

27 November

TARAWA ATOLL—2d Bn, 6th Marines, clears enemy from Buariki. Small islet of Naa, at N tip, remains to be explored.

CBI—At meeting of SEAC delegation to Cairo Conference, Gen Stilwell reveals that the Generalissimo is unwilling to fulfill commitments agreed to at Cairo and wants Stilwell to hold out for airborne assault on Mandalay (TOREADOR) and 10,000 tons a month over the Hump.

ITALY—15th Army Group: In Br Eighth Army area, 5 Corps prepares to attack in Adriatic coastal sector, weather conditions at last permitting close air support. Tanks of 4th Armd Brig and transport are brought across the Sangro.

28 November

INTERNATIONAL CONFERENCES—President Roosevelt, Prime Minister Churchill, and Marshal Stalin begin conference, coded EUREKA, at Tehran, Iran.

TARAWA ATOLL—Atoll is completely secured. No Japanese are found on Naa. Marine casualties on Tarawa total 3,301. Japanese losses are estimated to be 4,690 killed, 17 captured, and 129 Koreans taken prisoner.

ITALY—15th Army Group: In Br Eighth Army area, 5 Corps begins battle of the Sangro at 2130, Ind 8th Div, in the lead, takes Mozzagrogna, night 28–29. New Zealanders follow across the Sangro.

USSR—Germans report encirclement and destruction of Soviet forces in Korosten area.

29 November

BOUGAINVILLE—Work is begun on an airstrip, called Piva Uncle, near Piva R.

NEW GUINEA—Pursuing enemy northward along Huon Peninsula coast, Australians seize Bonga, former enemy supply base, and Gusika; press toward Wareo.

ITALY—15th Army Group: In U.S. Fifth Army area, VI Corps begins limited operations on right flank of army to divert enemy from the coming main assault against M. Camino. 45th Div begins clearing region N of Filignano–S. Elia road in effort to open the road: 1st Bn of 178th Inf leads off against La Bandita (Hill 855) but cannot take it; 157th Inf, making diversionary thrusts, secures Hill 460. 34th Div, to right of 45th, begins operations to clear heights overlooking Colli-Atina road: 1st Bn of 168th Inf moves against M. Pantano, taking the first of 4 knobs; 133d Inf moves against hills between Castelnuovo and Cerasuolo.

In Br Eighth Army area, 5 Corps breaches Winter Line in its sector. Driving through Mozzagrogna, 4th Armd Brig, with excellent air support, begins to clear Sangro ridge.

30 November

INTERNATIONAL CONFERENCES—EUREKA Conference at Tehran ends. Acceding to Soviet desires to make OVERLORD the main effort, OVERLORD and ANVIL (southern France) have been given priority over all other operations. Premier Stalin has agreed to commit Soviet forces against Japan after Germany is defeated. From Tehran, Br and U.S. delegates go back to Cairo, where the SEXTANT talks will be renewed.

GILBERT IS.—2d Tank Bn scouts reconnoiter Abaiang and Marakei Atolls, N of Tarawa, finding but 5 Japanese, on former.

SWPA—Gen Krueger forms TF DIRECTOR, under Brig Gen Julian W. Cunningham, for the invasion of Arawe, New Britain, on 15 December, called 2 Day to distinguish it from main D Day invasion at Cape Gloucester later. The TF is based upon 112th Cav.

CBI—Chiang Kai-shek again agrees to CHAMPION while inspecting Chinese troops at Ramgarh.

ITALY—15th Army Group: In preparation for Operation RAINCOAT—U.S. Fifth Army's first phase of assault against Winter Line aimed at capture of Camino hill mass—diversions are begun to deceive enemy. 3d Ranger Bn feints toward S. Pietro and 23d Armd Brig feints on lower Garigliano. In VI Corps' 45th Div sector, 1st Bn of 179th Inf continues fruitless attempts to clear La Bandits. On M. Pantano, 1st Bn of 168th Inf, 34th Div, retains positions against strong counterattacks and tries unsuccessfully to gain second knob; patrols of 1st Bn, 133d Inf, move into Castelnuovo while 3d Bn advances to M. la Rocca and elements of 200th Bn move onto Croce Hill.

In Br Eighth Army area, 5 Corps finishes clearing ridge above the Sangro. 4th Armd Brig and 78th Div push toward coast, taking Fossacesia. Ind 8th Div, moving NW along ridge, reaches heights overlooking Castelfrentano. To W, New Zealanders, having crossed the Sangro with difficulty, join their bridgehead with that of corps.

USSR—Moscow announces withdrawal of Soviet forces from Korosten.

1 December

GILBERT IS.—2d Tank Bn scouts find Maiana Atoll free of enemy, concluding their mission.

ITALY—15th Army Group: In U.S. Fifth Army area, air operations are sharply increased in preparation for main assault against Winter Line. Br 10 Corps begins diversionary attack toward Calabritto at dusk, employing 139th Brig, 46th Div. Numerous obstacles and strong opposition slow advance. In VI Corps area, 45th Div continues to meet firm resistance that prevents 1st Bn, 179th Inf, from scaling La Bandits and 2d Bn from clearing crest and reverse slope of Hill 769 to S. In 34th Div sector, 1st Bn of 168th Inf remains on first knob of M. Pantano but is isolated from main body; no further progress is made by 133d Inf.

2 December

ITALY—About 30 aircraft of German Air Force attack Bari, night 2–3, with spectacular results. Bombs blow up 2 ammunition ships in the crowded harbor, and as a result 17 other ships are lost. Damage to the port reduces its capacity for 3 weeks.

15th Army Group: In U.S. Fifth Army area, Allied aircraft and arty pound enemy positions in preparation for Operation RAINCOAT. Arty concentrations are the heaviest thus far in the Italian campaign. Br 10 Corps continues attack toward Calabritto but does not take it. Despite this failure, 56th Div begins attack on M. Camino from S after nightfall. II Corps opens attack on Camino hill mass from NE, night 2–3. 1st SSF moves against M. la Difensa, 2d Regt spearheading, and clears it before dawn. In VI Corps' 45th Div sector, enemy continues stout defense of La Bandita and positions on Hill 769. 34th Div commits additional elements against M. Pantano and with great difficulty takes the second knob; Co L of 133d Inf gains Hill 1180, on S slopes of M. Marrone, in night attack, 2–3, but the regt is unable to gain further ground in the area after this.

In Br Eighth Army's 5 Corps area, Castelfrentano falls to NZ troops.

USSR—Continuing offensive in Dnieper bend, Soviet forces break through along Ingulets R and push to within 6 miles of Znamenka.

3 December

INTERNATIONAL CONFERENCES—Br and U.S. delegates, returning from Tehran, reopen SEXTANT discussions at Cairo.

SWPA—Dates for invasion of New Britain at Arawe and Cape Gloucester are finally set for 15 and 26 December, respectively.

ITALY—15th Army Group: In U.S. Fifth Army's Br 10 Corps area, 56th Div makes substantial progress, taking M. Camino (819) and Monastery Hill (963) but is forced back from latter. In II Corps area, 1st SSF units, continuing attack from M. la Difensa before dawn, reach M. la Remetanea. 142d Inf, 36th Div, begins drive on M. Maggiore and takes it. In VI Corps area, 45th Div is unable to make further progress against La Bandits or Hill 769. Elements of 3d Bn, 168th Inf, 34th Div, upon relief by elements of 135th Inf, move to first knob of M. Pantano and relieve 1st Bn, 168th Inf; 3d Bn then attacks toward third knob but is driven back.

In Br Eighth Army's 5 Corps area, Ind 8th Div and 78th Div reach Moro R, overrunning Lanciano and S. Vito. 78th Div is later relieved there by Cdn 1st Div, which has been transferred to 5 Corps from 13 Corps.

USSR—NW of Gomel, Soviet troops improve positions and take highway center of Dovsk.

ETO—CROSSBOW—operations against German secret weapon sites—is given top priority for Allied tactical air forces.

4 December

TARAWA ATOLL—Capt Jackson R. Tote, USN, Commander, Advanced Base, Tarawa, takes command, relieving Gen Julian Smith. During December and January, air bases are constructed in the Gilberts.

BOUGAINVILLE—1st Mar Para Regt arrives and is soon committed to help advance the outpost line.

CHINA—Chang-te, in Tung-ting Lake area, falls to Japanese, climaxing local offensive by *11th Army* designed to disrupt Ch troop concentrations and divert Chinese from Yunnan. Having accomplished their mission and taken the rice center of Chang-te, Japanese soon begin withdrawal.

ITALY—15th Army Group: In U.S. Fifth Army's Br 10 Corps area, 56th Div is unable to regain Monastery Hill but seizes Hills 683 and 615. In II Corps area, German counterattack forces 1st SSF from M. la Remetanea to M. la Difensa. 1st Regt moves up to assist 2d in clearing M, la Remetanea–M. la Difensa ridge. 142d Inf, 36th Div, maintains positions on M. Maggiore. In VI Corps area, 135th Inf of 34th Div relieves all elements of 168th Inf on M. Pantano. 168th has suffered heavy casualties.

ETO—Intensive aerial rcn is begun to locate German secret weapon sites.

5 December

U.S.—President Roosevelt accedes to Br wishes that BUCCANEER be canceled. CCS ask Adm Mountbatten to suggest action to be taken in the event he loses most of his landing craft.

INDIA—Japanese make strategic air attack on Calcutta, damaging dock area.

ITALY—15th Army Group: In U.S. Fifth Army's Br 10 Corps area, enemy withdraws from Monastery Hill (963) since the position is threatened by 56th Div units, which move up toward Colle, W of the hill. II Corps retains current positions on M. la Difensa and M. Maggiore, but they are being supplied only with great difficulty. VI Corps remains in place, consolidating and patrolling.

In Br Eighth Army area, 5 Corps pushes toward Ortona, whose harbor can be used for supply, Ind 8th Div crossing Moro R.

ETO—U.S. Ninth Air Force begins CROSSBOW operations. Its P-51's start escorting strategic bombers of U.S. Eighth Air Force.

6 December

U.S.—On the basis of Adm Mountbatten's estimate to CCS that no major amphibious operations can be undertaken if BUCCANEER is canceled, President Roosevelt informs Chiang Kai-shek that there can be no amphibious operation simultaneously with TARZAN; inquires whether Chiang will go ahead under the circumstances or wait until November 1944, when a major amphibious assault might be undertaken.

ITALY—15th Army Group: In U.S. Fifth Army area, Br 10 Corps seizes crest of M. Camino and for the next 3 days mops up W slopes as far as the Garigliano. In VI Corps area, elements of 179th Inf, 45th Div, reach top of Hill 769, but enemy retains positions on reverse slope.

In Br Eighth Army's 5 Corps area, Cdn 1st Div crosses Moro R.

USSR—Russians cut Smela-Znamenka RR line SW of Kremenchug.

7 December

INTERNATIONAL CONFERENCES—U.S. and Br delegates conclude SEXTANT Conference at Cairo. To gain landing craft for ANVIL, plans for amphibious operations against Bay of Bengal are canceled. Plans for north Burma campaign are unsettled. CCS set up tentative timetable for offensive against Japan as follows: seizure of Marshalls and New Britain, January 1944; Manus, Admiralties, April 1944; Hollandia, New Guinea, June 1944; and Marianas, October 1944. CCS issue directive establishing unified command in the Mediterranean, effective 10 December. Gen Eisenhower, whom President Roosevelt has already decided to make commander of OVERLORD, is to be responsible for all operations in the Mediterranean except strategic bombing.

CBI—Since Adm Mountbatten is ordered to release a large portion of his amphibious resources for use elsewhere, planning is begun for limited operation (PIGSTICK) on S Mayu Peninsula as a substitute for BUCCANEER, subject to approval of Chiang Kai-shek.

ITALY—15th Army Group: U.S. Fifth Army begins second phase of assault on Winter Line. II Corps begins envelopment movements against enemy positions in S. Pietro area astride Highway 6. In preparation for assault on M. Lungo, Italian 1st Motorized Gp relieves 1st Bn of 141st Inf, 36th Div, on SE nose (Hill 253); 2d and 3d Bns, 143d Inf, prepare for drive on S. Pietro, moving forward to line of departure on Cannavinelle Hill; 1st Bn of 143d Inf jumps off toward M. Sammucro (Hill 1205) at 1700 and gains crest before dawn of 8th. On N flank, 3d Ranger Bn attacks at dusk toward Hill 950, a mile N of M. Sammucro.

In Br Eighth Army area, 5 Corps makes unsuccessful attack on Orsogna.

8 December

NEW GUINEA—Wareo falls to Aus 9th Div, clearing way for drive on Sio.

INDIA—In preparation for offensive, 18 Japanese bombers and about 50 fighters attack Tinsukia airfield in Assam.

ITALY—15th Army Group: In U.S. Fifth Army area, II Corps continues battle for positions about S. Pietro. Italian 1st Motorized Gp begins attack on M. Lungo but makes little headway against determined resistance. 143d Inf (−) of 36th Div attacks toward S. Pietro and is soon pinned down by enemy fire; 1st Bn of 143d withstands strong counterattack on M. Sammucro. On left flank of II Corps, 1st SSF finishes clearing M. la Remetanea (907). In VI Corps area, 2d Moroccan Inf Div, first of the FEC units to arrive in Italy, begins relief of 34th Div.

USSR—Red Army, continuing offensive SW of Kremenchug, cuts Znamenka-Krivoi Rog and Znamenka-Nikolayev RR's.

ETO—Gen Arnold informs Gen Spaatz that he (Spaatz) will command U.S. Strategic Air Forces in Europe.

9 December

BOUGAINVILLE—Torokina airstrip becomes operational. 3d Mar Div begins struggle for hills around beachhead that is to last until late in the month.

CBI—Replying to President Roosevelt's message, Chiang Kai-shek asks for financial assistance and increased air strength.

ITALY—15th Army Group: In U.S. Fifth Army's Br 10 Corps area, Rocca d'Evandro falls, concluding action against Camino hill mass. In II Corps area, 2d and 3d Bns of 143d Inf continue to be held up in S. Pietro area and pull back after dark to line of departure while arty concentration is placed on enemy. Germans counterattack on M. Sammucro is repulsed. In VI Corps' 45th Div zone, Hill 769 is completely cleared, but Germans retain Lagone and La Bandita.

USSR—Rail junction of Znamenka falls to Soviet forces.

10 December

BOUGAINVILLE—Marine fighter sq flies in to operate from Torokina airstrip, which is within 220 miles of Rabaul.

MIDDLE EAST—PGSC is redesignated Persian Gulf Command (PGC); detached from USAFIME and made responsible to the War Department; and directed "to further the objective of the United States in the prosecution of the war." Gen Connolly, CG PGC, is to co-ordinate U.S. activities in the area with those of other Allied nations.

MEDITERRANEAN—CCS directive calling for unified command—Mediterranean Theater of Operations (Allied)—in the Mediterranean becomes effective, although Mediterranean Allied Air Forces has not yet been activated.

ITALY—15th Army Group: In U.S. Fifth Army area, Allied air attacks are stepped up in preparation for next phase of offensive, which is to begin on 15th. Br 10 Corps takes responsibility for M. la Difensa from 142d Inf of 36th Div, VI Corps. In II Corps area, 3d Ranger Bn, with arty support, renews attack on Hill 950 on N flank of II Corps and takes it. Activity in S. Pietro area and on M. Sammucro is on a limited scale. Current U.S. positions are being consolidated. In VI Corps area, 2d Moroccan Div takes command of zone previously held by 34th Div.

Br Eighth Army has regrouped to increase weight of attack in coastal sector, where opposition is heavy. 13 Corps, with 5th Div and NZ Div under its command, is to move N on left of 5 Corps, leaving 78th Div in previous positions under Eighth Army command. 5 Corps continues northward along coast with Cdn 1st and Ind 8th Divs. Cdn 1st Div now has bridgehead across Moro R and is pressing toward Ortona, assisted by air and naval bombardment of coastal targets.

USSR—Troops of Second Ukrainian Front resume attack, one force investing Cherkassy and another pushing toward Kirovo.

11 December

SWPA—GHQ draws up outline plan for seizure of Saidor (New Guinea).

CBI—Adm Mountbatten issues directive ordering integration of U.S. Tenth Air Force and RAF Bengal Command into Eastern Air Command (EAC). All Allied air forces in SE Asia are under command of Air Chief Marshal Sir Richard Peirse as Allied Air CinC.

ITALY—15th Army Group: U.S. Fifth Army maintains current positions against counterattacks while preparing for full-scale offensive.

12 December

ITALY—15th Army Group: In U.S. Fifth Army area, Br 10 Corps extends farther eastward to relieve final elements of VI Corps on M. Maggiore, and boundary is adjusted accordingly. In II Corps area, 142d Inf of 36th Div begins preliminary operations in preparation for assault on M. Lungo on 15th:

occupies S. Giacomo Hill, between Lungo and Maggiore, and after nightfall takes Hills 141 and 72.

13 December

SWPA—TF DIRECTOR sails from Goodenough I. for Buna, en route to Arawe, New Britain.

GERMANY—710 bombers of U.S. Eighth Air Force with P-51 escort are sent against Kiel, establishing another record for bombers dispatched. Good results are reported although bombing is by radar.

14 December

SWPA—Final plans for operation against Cape Gloucester, New Britain, are made. It is decided not to use airborne troops as planned.

ITALY—15th Army Group: U.S. Fifth Army completes preparations for offensive by II and VI Corps on 15th and begins forward movement, night 14-15.

USSR—Russians begin first phase of winter offensive. From Nevel salient, which has gradually been improved, Soviet forces push toward Vitebsk and reach outskirts. Soviet troops of Second Ukrainian Front overrun Cherkassy. Enemy recovers Radomyshl, S of Malin.

15 December

Solomon Is.—Gen Griswold, XIV Corps CG, relieves Gen Geiger, I MAC CG, of responsibility for Bougainville beachhead, where final defensive perimeter is virtually secure, although 21st Marines, 3d Mar Div, is still clearing heights near the beachhead.

NEW BRITAIN—Operation DEXTERITY opens when, as a preliminary to main invasion of New Britain, TF 76 (Rear Adm Daniel E. Barbey) lands TF DIRECTOR (112th Cav, reinf) under command of Brig Gen Julian W. Cunningham, USA, on W coast of Arawe Peninsula about 0700, after naval gunfire and aerial bombardment. Scattered opposition on the peninsula is overcome without difficulty. Before the main landing, cavalrymen try in vain to make surprise landings at Umtingalu, on mainland E of the peninsula, and on Pilelo islet. Despite alerted enemy, Tr B succeeds in landing on Pilelo and quickly clears it. Japanese planes are active against troops and shipping, attacking at frequent intervals during this and the next few days. Plans to use Arawe as a base for light naval forces never materialize, nor is the site used as an air base. Plan for Cape Gloucester landing is amended to increase size of initial assault force and limit objective of secondary landing.

NEW GUINEA—Road from Lae to Nadzab is completed.

CBI—Gen Stratemeyer takes command of EAC. Troop Carrier Command is activated. First infantry class completes 6-weeks' course at Kweilin Infantry Training Center for ZEBRA Force.

BURMA—In N, 1st Bn of 114th Inf, Ch 38th Div, tries unsuccessfully to relieve isolated 1st Bn, 112th Regt. After the attack, Japanese return to previous positions, which they proceed to strengthen.

ITALY—15th Army Group: U.S. Fifth Army renews offensive against Winter Line before dawn. On II Corps' S flank, 142d Inf of 36th Div opens attack on M. Lungo from S at dusk and advances rapidly. Second battle for S. Pietro opens about noon, with 143d Inf (−) attacking from slopes of M. Sammucro and 2d Bn of 141st advancing from M. Rotondo area. Progress is slow and costly. 1st Bn of 143d Inf, with 2d Bn of 504th Para Inf to its right, begins attack on W slopes of M. Sammucro shortly after midnight, 14-15. Paratroopers suffer heavy casualties during fruitless attempt to take Hill 687; 1st Bn is pinned down short of Hill 730. In VI Corps area, 45th Div, on S flank of corps, begins attack toward heights dominating La Rava Creek on left and toward Lagone on right: 157th Inf gains positions on Hills 640 and 470, N of La Rava Creek, and makes futile attempt to clear Fialla Hill and Hill 770, S of the creek; 179th Inf is stopped short of Lagone; platoon of 45th Rcn Tr fails in attempt to clear hill just N of Lagone, but elements of 1st Bn, 179th Inf, occupy La Bandita, farther N, without opposition after nightfall. On N flank of VI Corps, 8th Rifle Regt of 2d Moroccan Div seizes M. Castelnuovo and S. Michele Pass.

ETO—AEAF takes operational control of U.S. Ninth Air Force.

16 December

ITALY—15th Army Group: In U.S. Fifth Army's II Corps area, 142d Inf of 36th Div finishes clearing M. Lungo by 1000. Italian 1st Motorized Gp secures ridge between Hills 253 and 343 in afternoon. Further attacks on S. Pietro fail to gain ground but the position becomes untenable for enemy after fall of M. Lungo. To cover withdrawal, Germans launch strong counterattack that continues into the night 16-17. 1st Bn, 143d Inf, repels counterattack on W slopes of M. Sammucro. In VI Corps area, patrols of 179th Inf, 45th Div, find that enemy has withdrawn from Lagone. Fr troops clear hill just N of Lagone and second knob of M. Pantano.

17 December

BOUGAINVILLE—Torokina strip is put into use as staging base for Rabaul-bound fighters.

SWPA—Gen MacArthur orders Gen Krueger to prepare plans for next phase of DEXTERITY—seizure of Saidor, New Guinea, as advanced air and naval base. To perform this task, Gen Krueger forms TF MICHAELMAS under Brig Gen Clarence A. Martin, 32d Div ADC, consisting of RCT 126, reinf, 32d Div. The TF is largely that originally scheduled to invade Gasmata, New Ireland.

CBI—Generalissimo Chiang Kai-shek, in another message to President Roosevelt, again calls for financial aid and increased air strength.

ITALY—15th Army Group: In U.S. Fifth Army's II Corps area, 36th Div pursues enemy beyond S. Pietro; 1st Bn of 141st Inf relieves 1st Bn of 143d on M. Sammucro; 2d Bn of 504th Para Inf is being relieved in same area by 1st Bn. In VI Corps area, Germans are making limited withdrawal in center of corps front. After nightfall, 180th Inf of 45th Div, passing through 179th, takes M. la Posta without opposition. Germans begin withdrawal from M. Pantano positions, leaving a small number of rear-guard forces to delay pursuit.

18 December

NEW BRITAIN—Preinvasion air operations against Cape Gloucester area are intensified.

CBI—Chiang Kai-shek gives Gen Stilwell full command of Ch troops in India and in the Hukawng Valley of Burma.

CHINA—Enemy planes attack Kunming in preparation for offensive against India.

ITALY—15th Army Group: In U.S. Fifth Army's II Corps area, patrols find enemy still clinging to W slopes of M. Sammucro. VI Corps advances in center along S. Elia road as enemy withdraws. Fr troops occupy rest of M. Pantano hill mass; on road to Atina, clear Cerasuolo area.

19 December

CBI—Chiang Kai-shek rejects Adm Mountbatten's proposal for a major attack.

SICILY—AFHQ asks Seventh Army hq at Palermo to estimate requirements for planning staff to plan for an operation on scale of HUSKY.

ITALY—15th Army Group: In U.S. Fifth Army's II Corps area, 36th Div's 143d and 141st Regts attempt to clear S and W slopes of M. Sammucro from which enemy is barring access to Highway 6 and Mignano Gap, but make little headway. 15th Inf of 3d Div relieves 142d Inf on M. Lungo.

20 December

PACIFIC—At a planning conference at Port Moresby, attended by representatives of S Pacific and SWPA, it is decided that S Pacific will plan to invade Green Is. as next step in isolation of Rabaul, since no immediate action can be taken against Kavieng, New Ireland, the next objective of ELKTON III.

TREASURY IS.—Army planes fly from New Caledonia to Stirling I. to begin operations from there.

RUSSELL IS.—Army bombers move from New Caledonia to Russell Is.

NEW BRITAIN—Japanese force moving against Arawe beachhead reaches Pulie R, east of Arawe.

CBI—In reply to Chiang Kai-shek's message of 17th, President Roosevelt suggests that China carry out her part in offensive to regain Burma; promises U.S. help in reopening land route to China, which would afford greater protection to Hump air route; says the requested loan is under consideration. Chiang Kai-shek replies that Y-Force will move only if Andaman Is., Rangoon, or Moulmein are seized by Allies; that Ch troops will move into Burma without an amphibious operation if Mandalay or Lashio can be recovered.

MEDITERRANEAN—Mediterranean Allied Air Forces is activated in accordance with CCS directive of 5 December, as of 10 December. Under it are placed all air units in the Mediterranean: USAAF/NATO, all RAF elements including RAF Malta and RAF ME, and Fr and Italian units operating within the area. Air Chief Marshal Tedder is made Air CinC, with Gen Spaatz as his operational deputy. Spaatz also takes over duties of CG USAAF/NATO.

ITALY—15th Army Group: Plans for an amphibious operation by U.S. Fifth Army on W coast are canceled because of slow progress against the Winter Line and lack of sufficient landing craft.

In U.S. Fifth Army area, II Corps continues efforts to clear W slopes of M. Sammucro and reaches next objective, S. Vittore. 36th Div, in night attack 20-21, fails in attempt to clear Hill 730 and Morello Hill.

In Br Eighth Army's 5 Corps area, Cdn 1st Div pushes into outskirts of Ortona, where violent fighting ensues.

21 December

BOUGAINVILLE—Relief of 3d Mar Div in beachhead line begins.

SWPA—TF BACKHANDER (Maj Gen William H. Rupertus, USMC) conducts final rehearsal for invasion of Cape Gloucester, New Britain, at Cape Sudest, New Guinea.

CBI—Gen Stilwell arrives at Ledo to take personal charge of N Burma campaign.

USSR—Soviet salient beyond Zhlobin is under strong enemy attack.

22 December

CHINA—Continuing preparations for offensive against India, Japanese planes attack Kunming.

MTO-ETO—Gen Spaatz is ordered to take command of U.S. Strategic Air Forces in Europe at once. Gen Eaker is to command Allied air forces in the Mediterranean upon relief by Air Chief Marshal Tedder, who is to become Deputy CinC for OVERLORD. Gen Eaker is subsequently given permission to remain in ETO until he can advise Generals Spaatz and Doolittle in England and does not reach MTO until mid-January. NATOUSA directive results in reorganization of AAF elements in MTO.

ITALY—15th Army Group: In Br Eighth Army's S Corps area, Villa Grandi falls to Ind 8th Div. Cdn 1st Div continues battle for Ortona.

23 December

Solomon Is.—Army bombers begin operations from Munda airfield, New Georgia.

BURMA—In Hukawng Valley, 3d Bn of 114th Regt, Ch 38th Div, having crossed the Tanai at Kantau earlier in the month, skirmishes with enemy 9 miles from Kantau.

ITALY—15th Army Group: In Br Eighth Army's 13 Corps area, 5th Div takes Arielli. 5 Corps continues to fight for Ortona.

24 December

BOUGAINVILLE—With elimination of enemy on heights about beachhead perimeter, airfields are secure.

SWPA—ALAMO Force hq moves from Goodenough to Cape Cretin, New Guinea.

NEW BRITAIN—Preinvasion bomber effort reaches its peak in number of sorties flown, 280.

BURMA—In Hukawng Valley, 1st Bn of 114th Regt, Ch 38th Div, after arty preparation, attacks to relieve beleaguered 1st Bn of 112th in Yupbang Ga area and succeeds in joining it, although Japanese retain positions W of the river blocking crossing at Yupbang Ga.

MTO-ETO—President Roosevelt and Prime Minister Churchill announce appointment of Gen Eisenhower to post of Supreme Commander, Allied Expeditionary Force, to head OVERLORD. Gen Wilson will command Allied forces in the Mediterranean under title of Supreme Allied Commander, Mediterranean Theater (SACMED). Churchill also announces appointment of Gen Montgomery as commander of 21 Army Group, succeeding Gen Sir Bernard Paget. Gen Sir Oliver Leese is to succeed Gen Montgomery.

ITALY—15th Army Group: In Br Eighth Army's 13 Corps area, NZ 2d Div, moving to outflank Orsogna, reaches heights commanding that town on NE.

MIDDLE EAST—Gen Connolly is relieved as CG PGC by Brig Gen Donald P. Booth.

USSR—In Vitebsk sector, Russians overrun Gorodok in 2-pronged attack, bringing about collapse of whole series of defense points that depend upon it. At dawn, Soviet forces open new offensive; driving along axis of Kiev-Zhitomir highway, they breach enemy lines and soon recover ground lost to German counteroffensive and more.

ETO—U.S. Eighth Air Force makes major effort against CROSSBOW targets—German secret weapon sites—exceeding previous records in number of aircraft dispatched. Of more than 1,300 aircraft sent out, 722 are heavy bombers.

25 December

BOUGAINVILLE—First echelon of Americal Div (RCT 164) arrives to relieve 3d Mar Div.

TREASURY IS.—U.S. Navy Seabees complete fighter strip on Stirling.

NEW IRELAND—After surface bombardment of Buka to entice enemy aircraft from Kavieng, carrier TF under Adm Frederick Sherman strikes at Kavieng harbor with 86 planes but finds few shipping targets there.

NEW BRITAIN—TF BACKHANDER sails for Cape Gloucester from New Guinea. Japanese attack Arawe beachhead, forcing outposts and observation posts back.

INDIA—About 50 Japanese aircraft raid Chittagong.

TUNISIA—15th Army Group: Military leaders meeting at Tunis revive plan for amphibious landing below Rome; draft plan for 2 divs plus airborne troops and some armor to land as near 20 January as possible in conjunction with drive from S.

ITALY—15th Army Group: In U.S. Fifth Army's II Corps area, 1st Regt of 1st SSF, jumping off night 24–25, captures Hill 730 early in morning. 504th Para Inf clears several hills to N.

USSR—Soviet forces cut Vitebsk-Polotsk highway.

26 December

NEW BRITAIN—After preparatory naval gunfire and aerial bombardment, during which enemy observation from Target Hill, commanding landing beach, is masked by smoke, TF BACKHANDER, commanded by Gen Rupertus, 1st Mar Div CG, and consisting of 1st Mar Div (–), reinf, begins main invasion of New Britain at Cape Gloucester at 0746. Forested, swampy terrain is more formidable than the surprised enemy, who offers only light opposition. 7th Marines establishes beachhead, clearing

Target Hill, and is passed through by 1st Marines. Gen Rupertus establishes CP ashore. Successful secondary landings are made by reinf 2d Bn, 1st Marines, at Tauali, SW of the airdrome, and by elements of 2d Engr Special Brig on Long I. Night counterattacks are repulsed. Japanese aircraft attack the landing force, sinking 1 DD and damaging other vessels. Japanese force reaches positions NW of Arawe MLR.

ITALY—15th Army Group: In U.S. Fifth Army's II Corps area, some elements of 36th Div clear Morello Hill; others take responsibility for Hill 730. Sammucro hills are now completely cleared of enemy. In VI Corps area, 8th Rifle Regt of 2d Moroccan Div attacks Mainarde ridge, N of Atina road, unsuccessfully.

27 December

NEW BRITAIN—1st Mar Div expands Cape Gloucester beachhead despite torrential monsoon rainfall and difficult terrain. 1st Marines drives 3 miles W toward airfield without enemy interference. Co G of 158th Inf arrives at Arawe, where Japanese are becoming aggressive, in response to Gen Cunningham's request for reinforcements.

BURMA—Brig Gen Lewis A. Pick opens military road to Shingbwiyang, in Hukawng Valley. Commander of 3d Bn, 112th Inf, Ch 38th Div, is killed and the bn is later withdrawn to main body. 65th Regt of Ch 22d Div, reinf, is given mission, previously held by 3d Bn of 112th, of clearing Taro Plain plus task of pushing back into Hukawng Valley to threaten enemy's flank.

ITALY—15th Army Group: In U.S. Fifth Army's VI Corps area, Fr troops gain positions on slopes of Mainarde ridge.

USSR—In Vitebsk sector, Soviet forces cut Polotsk-Vitebsk RR.

28 December

BOUGAINVILLE—Americal Div takes command of E sector of beachhead, relieving 3d Mar Div.

NEW BRITAIN—Gen Krueger releases reserve—5th Marines, reinf—to Gen Rupertus. 1st Marines reduces prepared enemy trail block about 1,000 yards E of the airfield. Japanese attack on Arawe beachhead is repulsed.

BURMA—Ch 38th Div, attacking with 1st and 2d Bns of 114th Regt and 1st Bn of 112th, clears several enemy strongpoints along Tarung R.

ITALY—15th Army Group: In U.S. Fifth Army's VI Corps area, French continue attack on Mainarde ridge and overrun Hill 1190.

In Br Eighth Army's 5 Corps area, Germans are finally cleared from Ortona.

USSR—Soviet forces take Korostyshev, important position E of Zhitomir.

29 December

NEW BRITAIN—1st Marines secures main objective, the airfield, at Cape Gloucester with singular ease. 5th Marines arrives to reinforce beachhead and make wide sweep inland toward airfield to block enemy withdrawal. Enemy makes another unsuccessful counterattack on Arawe beachhead.

NEW GUINEA—TF MICHAELMAS issues formal orders for invasion of Saidor. D Day is tentatively set for 2 January.

BURMA—Continuing attack to clear Tarung R line, Ch 38th Div eliminates another Japanese strongpoint and forces enemy to break into small groups.

NORTH AFRICA—AFHQ informs U.S. Seventh Army planners of general objectives of ANVIL, projected invasion of S France.

ITALY—15th Army Group: In U.S. Fifth Army's Br 10 Corps area, 9th Commando makes seaborne raid just N of Garigliano R mouth to secure information for future operations. In II Corps area, combat patrols of 36th Div enter S. Vittore but are forced out. In VI Corps sector S of Atina road, Fr forces seize 3 hills on E end of M. Monna Casale and dig in.

USSR—Soviet forces overwhelm enemy at Korosten and, to S, gain control of long stretch of RR to point below Chernyakhov. Red Army troops drive W along RR toward Sarny.

30 December

BOUGAINVILLE—First Piva airstrip is completed. Fiji patrol, having advanced along Numa Numa trail, establishes outposts near coast at Ibu village, where it can observe enemy movements. Airstrip for use of Piper Cubs is cleared there.

NEW BRITAIN—Cape Gloucester airdrome is declared secure; has been taken by Marines at very light cost.

NEW GUINEA—Gen Martin learns officially that D Day for invasion of Saidor will be 2 January.

ITALY—15th Army Group: In U.S. Fifth Army's II Corps area, 34th Div relieves battle-worn 36th Div. RCT 142 is attached to 34th Div to garrison positions on M. Sammucro. In VI Corps area, 180th Inf of 45th Div attempts to clear hills astride S. Elia road in region E of Acquafondata and succeeds in getting elements on one, M. Rotondo.

USSR—Kazatin is overwhelmed by Soviet forces.

31 December

NEW GUINEA—TF MICHAELMAS sails from Goodenough I. for Saidor.

BURMA—In Hukawng Valley, elements of 113th Regt, Ch 38th Div, relieve 2d Bn of 112th in region 4 miles N of Yupbang Ga.

ITALY—15th Army Group: In U.S. Fifth Army's II Corps area, 6th Armd Inf of 1st Armd Div relieves 15th Inf of 3d Div on M. Lungo. In VI Corps area, 180th Inf of 45th Div attempts in vain to clear more hills E of Acquafondata.

USSR—Soviet forces recover Zhitomir as German garrison evacuates it. Vitebsk is almost encircled, but subsequent efforts of Red Army to take it fail.

1944

1 January

NEW BRITAIN—Brig Gen Lemuel C. Shepherd, ADC 1st Mar Div, issues first order to ADC Group, calling for attack SW toward Borgen Bay on 2d. ADC Group, as strengthened for the attack, consists of 7th Marines, reinf by bn of 5th Marines, and supporting units.

NEW IRELAND—U.S. carrier-based planes under command of Adm Frederick C. Sherman attack enemy shipping in Kavieng harbor.

NEW GUINEA—As Saidor assault force joins DD escort in Oro Bay, Allied planes pound coastline in Saidor area with over 200 tons of bombs.

CBI—Gen Stilwell creates an operations staff for ZEBRA Force.

MTO—Gen Patton turns over command of U.S. Seventh Army to Gen Clark. Gen Clark, who also retains command of U.S. Fifth Army, is to plan for Operation ANVIL. In accordance with NATOUSA directive of 22 December, AAF units are reorganized, effective this date: USAAF/NATO becomes Army Air Forces, Mediterranean Theater of Operations (AAF/MTO); XII Air Force Service Command becomes Army Air Forces Service Command, MTO (AAFSC/MTO); II Air Service Area Command becomes XV Air Force Service Command; III Air Service Area Command becomes XII Air Force Service Command; XII Air Force Engineer Command (Prov) becomes AAFEC/MTO. The new organization is approved in behalf of Gen Eisenhower by Maj Gen Walter Bedell Smith.

2 January

BOUGAINVILLE—182d Inf, Americal Div, relieves 21st Marines in line.

NEW BRITAIN—In Cape Gloucester area, Co E of 5th Marines establishes physical contact with Mar patrol from Green Beach at Dorf Pt. ADC Group attacks toward Borgen Bay with 3 bns abreast, moving around 2d Bn, 7th Marines; is halted by enemy strongpoint, which it partly envelops.

NEW GUINEA—U.S. Sixth Army's TF MICHAELMAS (RCT 126, 32d Div, reinf) makes surprise landing at Saidor under cover of smoke screen, and captures harbor and airfield. Weather conditions prevent aircraft from joining DD's in preliminary bombardment, but effective air strikes are made in co-ordination with the landing. Aus troops driving along Huon coast from Finschhafen occupy Sialum.

CBI—Maj Gen Daniel I. Sultan arrives at New Delhi to act as Gen Stilwell's deputy, freeing Stilwell of administrative burdens.

ITALY—15th Army Group: Gen Alexander orders U.S. Fifth Army to mount amphibious operation below Rome (SHINGLE) between 20 and 31 January; shortly before the assault landing at Anzio, Fifth Army is to thrust sharply toward Cassino and Frosinone; Eighth Army is to keep enemy pinned down in its sector by exerting pressure and employing deceptive measures. Air preparation for Anzio landing begins.

3 January

POA—U.S. Joint Expeditionary Force (TF 51 under Adm Turner) issues Operation Plan A6-43 for assault on the Marshalls, specifying shipping to be involved and giving pre-D=Day bombardment plan.

NEW BRITAIN—1913th Aviation Engr Bn begins work on Cape Gloucester airdrome. Japanese attack Target Hill in early morning and are beaten back. Attack of ADC Group halts at small stream, dubbed Suicide Creek, NW of Target Hill. Efforts to bridge the creek so that tanks can cross are unsuccessful.

CBI—To hasten clearing of Tanai R line, Gen Stilwell promises commander of Ch 38th Div the use of 3d Bn, 112th Regt, from reserve, provided he takes Taihpa Gain 2 days.

ITALY—15th Army Group: In U.S. Fifth Army area, II Corps prepares for final phase of assault on Winter Line, to begin on 5th. During night 3-4, 1st SSF, as preliminary for attack on M. Majo, begins clearing ridge SE of this feature. French Expeditionary Corps (FEC), under Gen Juin, takes command of zone on N flank of Fifth Army as U.S. VI Corps withdraws from line to participate in amphibious assault on Anzio. 3d Algerian Div begins relief of 45th Div.

USSR—Soviet forces take Olevsk, NW of Kiev; press beyond there to achieve first crossing of prewar frontier of Poland. Novograd Volyinsk falls, giving Russians control of another rail line from Korosten.

4 January

NEW BRITAIN—After arty preparation, ADC Group continues attack. Tanks cross improvised ramp over Suicide Creek and support marines by destroying enemy positions at point-blank range.

Assault force, now expanded to 4 bns, pushes southward without opposition to next phase line—N of Hill 150 and Aogiri Ridge.

NEW IRELAND—Carrier-based aircraft of Adm Frederick Sherman again attack Kavieng but find no ships there.

NEW GUINEA—Extensive patrolling of Saidor area is uneventful. Australians reach Cape King William, 16 miles SE of Sio.

ITALY—15th Army Group: In U.S. Fifth Army's Br 10 Corps area, in preparation for attack on Cedro Hill, 138th Brig of 46th Div establishes bridgehead across Peccia R, night 4–5, against strong opposition. In II Corps area, 1st SSF gains positions on ridge SE of M. Majo, overrunning Hill 775 and M. Arcalone. Other elements of II Corps move forward to line of departure for main offensive, overcoming some opposition en route.

USSR—Belaya Tserkov, another enemy strongpoint SW of Kiev, falls to Red Army. Advance continues toward Uman.

WESTERN EUROPE—U.S. planes begin flying supplies, under code name CARPETBAGGER, from United Kingdom to underground patriot forces in Western Europe. Full-scale supply missions will come to an end in September 1944

5 January

NEW BRITAIN—ADC Group remains in place in Cape Gloucester area, patrolling and regrouping.

NEW GUINEA—Gap between U.S. and Aus troops is narrowed to about 60 miles as Australians reach Kelanoa. U.S. patrols meet opposition at Cape Iris, W of Saidor.

BURMA—Ch 38th Div makes vain attempt to clear last strongpoint remaining between it and Tarung R.

ITALY—15th Army Group: U.S. Fifth Army begins final assault on Winter Line. Br 10 Corps withdraws Peccia R bridgehead, since tanks are un-able to cross river. M. Porchia, which dominates Cedro Hill, is still held by enemy. In II Corps area, TF A (6th Armd Inf, reinf) of 1st Armd Div pushes toward M. Porchia, reaching N-S road in front of it. 3d Bn, 135th Inf, jumping off night 4–5, clears part of village strongpoints of S. Vittore. 1st Bn, 135th, attacks toward La Chiaia, NW of S. Vittore, beginning night 4–5, but is stopped by fire from S. Giusta. In conjunction with assault of 135th Inf, 168th Inf begins move to outflank La Chiaia and takes Hill 425. 1st SSF confines its activity to probing M. Majo with patrols.

USSR—Red Army forces overrun Berdichev, rail junction SW of Kiev.

U.K.—U.S. Strategic Air Forces in Europe (USSAFE) is established in United Kingdom, under command of Gen Spaatz to co-ordinate operations of Eighth and Fifteenth Air Forces. Official abbreviation of this headquarters is changed on 4 February 1944 to USSTAF.

6 January

POA—COMCENPAC issues Operation Plan No. Cen 1-44 for invasion of Marshall Is. 7th Div FO 1 calls for occupation of Kwajalein in several phases. Maj Gen Hubert R. Harmon takes command of U. S. Thirteenth Air Force.

BOUGAINVILLE—Logistical situation improves as Prov Service Command, activated on 15 December at New Caledonia, begins operations on Bougainville.

NEW BRITAIN—ADC Group, renewing southward attack, clears Hill 150, S of Target Hill. Gen Cunningham reports to Gen Krueger the presence of enemy positions near Arawe beachhead.

NEW GUINEA—808th Aviation Engr Bn arrives at Saidor.

CBI—Since remaining landing craft are recalled to the Mediterranean, Adm Mountbatten cancels PIGSTICK. Gen Sultan warns Gen Stilwell that SEAC planners want to bypass Burma until Germany is defeated, then mount a major offensive beginning with invasion of Sumatra. Gen Stilwell in his capacity of Chief of Staff, China Theater, later decides to seed a mission (Gen Boatner, Brig Gen Benjamin G. Ferris, Col Francis Hill, and Col Brink) to Washington to present his views.

BURMA—Brig Gen Frank D. Merrill is assigned command of the GALAHAD force, whose designation is made "unit." Chinese make another unsuccessful attempt to reduce enemy strongpoint on Tarung R.

ITALY—15th Army Group: In U.S. Fifth Army's II Corps area, TF A of 1st Armd Div reaches crest on N end of M. Porchia and holds firm against counterattack. 135th Inf completes clearing S. Vittore by 1700 and drives closer to La Chiaia. 168th Inf continues outflanking movement to N, making slow progress. 1st SSF is reinf by 2 bns of 133d Inf, 34th Div, to temporarily continue operations as TF B. TF B attacks toward M. Majo from M. Arcalone, night 6–7. RCT 142 is detached from II Corps and returns to 36th Div as reserve.

ETO—Gen Order No. I of USSAFE names Maj Gen Frederick L. Anderson and Brig Gen Hugh J. Knerr as deputy commanders for operations and administration, respectively.

7 January

JAPAN—Japanese Imperial General Headquarters authorizes *Southern Army* to secure positions in

Imphal area of India when the opportunity presents itself.

CBI—Adm Mountbatten drops plans for CUDGEL, small operation in Arakan coastal sector of Burma.

ITALY—15th Army Group: In U.S. Fifth Army's II Corps area, M. Porchia falls to TF A of 1st Armd Div, making nearby Cedro Hill, in Br to Corps zone, untenable for enemy. 135th Inf occupies M. La Chiaia and continues W, clearing Hill 224 and Cicerelli Hill, between M. La Chiaia and Highway 6. 168th gains control of ridge NE of La Chiaia, contributing to success of 135th Inf. Right flank column of TF B, 1st SSF, takes M. Majo early in day and holds it against series of counterattacks while column on left attempts to reduce Hill 1109, overlooking Cervaro, without success.

USSR—Moscow announces breakthrough on 60-mile front in Kirovograd sector. Kirovograd is practically surrounded.

8 January

U.S.—War Department Operations Division planners decide that present positions in CBI should be maintained and that airpower should be built up so that CBI can support main offensive against Japan to be made in the Pacific.

SOLOMON Is.—U.S. warships under command of Adm Ainsworth bombard Shortlands, starting large fires.

MTO—Gen Eisenhower turns over command of Allied Forces in MTO to Gen Wilson. Gen Devers takes command of NATOUSA.

ITALY—15th Army Group: In U.S. Fifth Army's Br 10 Corps area, 139th Brig of 46th Div takes M. Cedro without opposition. In II Corps area, TF B outflanks and captures Hill 1109. Enemy has now been forced back to M. Trocchio and hills above Cervaro to defend approaches to Liri Valley, which leads to Rome.

USSR—Kirovograd, highway and rail center of Dnieper bend, falls to Red Army. Germans are reporting offensive in Zhlobin area.

9 January

BOUGAINVILLE—Americal Div continues relief of 3d Mar Div on Bougainville: 132d Inf enters line. Second Piva airfield, called Piva Yoke, is completed.

NEW BRITAIN—ADC Group secures foothold on Aogiri Ridge, W of Hill 150, which enemy has been told to hold at all costs since it covers a good supply route that they have constructed.

CBI—In Hukawng Valley, 112th and 113th Regts of Ch 38th Div are converging on Taihpa Ga, and 114th is active in jungle S of the Tanai. 3d Bn, 114th, begins lively action with enemy infiltrators who have surrounded its supporting battery.

11 Army Group: In Br Fourteenth Army area, 15 Corps overruns Maungdaw on Arakan front.

ITALY—15th Army Group: In U.S. Fifth Army area, II Corps orders attack on 10th, 34th Div making main effort, to secure Cervaro and M. Trocchio, final Winter Line objectives. Last elements of U.S. 45th Div are relieved by 3d Algerian Div, FEC.

10 January

NEW BRITAIN—ADC Group repels enemy charges against Aogiri Ridge, beginning at 0115, then continues attack southward toward Hill 660. Arawe beachhead is being reinforced.

NEW GUINEA—Since enemy attack on Saidor is expected, Gen Martin asks Gen Krueger for reinforcements and is granted BCT's 1 and 3 of RCT 128.

ITALY—15th Army Group: In U.S. Fifth Army's II Corps area, 34th Div's 168th Inf columns push toward Cervaro across hills N of S. Vittore-Cervaro road; 2d Bn of 135th, to left, advances NW from La Chiaia to threaten Cervaro from S; TF B, on right, heads toward Capraro Hill. Enemy strongly resists all these thrusts.

USSR—Large enemy pocket N of Kirovograd is eliminated.

11 January

NEW BRITAIN—ADC Group reaches next phase line S of Aogiri Ridge and Hill 150.

NEW GUINEA—C-47's start using Saidor airfield.

ITALY—15th Army Group: U.S. Fifth Army's II Corps closes in on Cervaro.

USSR—On central front, Russians announce resumption of offensive in vicinity of highway junction of Mozyr. Berlin has previously announced this.

GERMANY—Strategic air offensive against German aircraft industry and the German Air Force (POINTBLANK), in preparation for OVERLORD, begins. 663 heavy bombers are dispatched against plants at Oschersleben, Halberstadt, and in Brunswick area. Although extensive damage is done, aggressive enemy fighters exact a high price. Total loss is 60 bombers.

12 January

U.S.—War Department planners in Washington, considering the matter of a new directive for SEAC, reject CULVERIN—assault on Sumatra—and favor opening of a land route to China.

Advance part of U.S. Third Army leaves Fort Sam Houston, Texas, to embark for ETO.

SOLOMON Is.—Americal Div completes movement to Bougainville.

NEW BRITAIN—Arawe beachhead is now strengthened by Co B, 1st Tank Bn, 1st Mar Div, and Co F, 158th Inf.

AFHQ—U.S. Seventh Army planning group under Brig Gen Garrison H. Davidson moves from Sicily to Algiers to work on plans for ANVIL, invasion of S France. Planning headquarters for ANVIL is designated Force 163.

ITALY—15th Army Group: Gen Alexander, CG, directs U.S. Fifth Army to impose maximum losses on enemy S of Rome and to clear Rome; advance to general line Civitavecchia-Viterbo-Terni and later to Pisa-Pistoia-Florence. Long-range objective of Br Eighth Army is Faenza=Ravenna region. Importance of speed is stressed.

U.S. Fifth Army orders VI Corps (Gen Lucas) to land in Anzio=Nettuno area at H Hour (0200) on D Day (22 January) and drive on Colli Laziali. In II Corps area, 2d Bn of 168th Inf, 34th Div, overruns Cervaro; other units of the div continue to clear hills near the town. On right flank of II Corps, TF B reaches Capraro Hill. FEC, with 3d Algerian Div on left and 2d Moroccan Div on right, opens drive toward S. Elia and makes steady progress.

USSR—Russians envelop Sarny, in prewar Poland, and take it from rear. Germans are counterattacking around Vinnitsa, SW of Kiev.

13 January

PACIFIC—CINCPAC-CINCPOA Campaign Plan GRANITE outlines tentative operations to be conducted and timetable: carrier raid on Truk about 24 March in support of invasion of the Admiralties and Kavieng; capture of Eniwetok and Ujelang Atolls in the Marshalls (CATCHPOLE), 1 May; capture of Mortlock and Truk in the Carolines, 1 August; invasion of the Marianas (FORAGER), 1 November. If Truk can be bypassed, it is proposed that the Palaus be invaded on 1 August. 27th Div is alerted to prepare to seize Eniwetok.

NEW BRITAIN—ADC Group continues attack toward Hill 660 with 3d Bn, 7th Marines, but is pinned down short of objective. Arty and aerial bombardment precede the attack. 864th Engr Aviation Bn arrives to help repair Cape Gloucester airdrome.

BURMA—In Hukawng Valley, Ch 38th Div gains firm control of Tarung R line as 114th Regt reduces the last strongpoint in Yupbang Ga area. 112th, to N, has cleared region between the Tarung and Sanip Rivers. 1st Bn, 113th Regt, upon crossing the Tarung at Yupbang Ga, patrols N to Tabawng Ga.

ITALY—15th Army Group: In U.S. Fifth Army's II Corps area, 168th Inf of 34th Div finishes clearing heights overlooking Le Pastinelle and the Rapido Plain. TF B (1st SSF and 133d Inf) is dissolved, having completed its mission; RCT 133 remains in position. 2d Bn of 135th Inf reduces troublesome strongpoint (Pt 189) S of Cervaro. II Corps is now in position for assault on last hill barring access to the Rapido, M. Trocchio.

BOUGAINVILLE—Arty units of Americal Div begin relieving those of 3d Mar Div.

14 January

U.S.—President Roosevelt, in message to Chiang Kai-shek of this date, delivered on 15th, asks that Yunnan forces be committed in Burma in conjunction with operations from India; hints that if they are not, lend-lease to China may be curtailed.

NEW BRITAIN—3d Bn, 7th Marines, drives to top of Hill 660, final objective of ADC Group.

USSR—Breaking through enemy positions on broad front, Soviet forces take Mozyr and Kalinkovichi; during next few days deepen the salient.

15 January

U.S.—War Department abolishes Central Defense Command and transfers its functions to Eastern Defense Command.

NEW BRITAIN—Relief of ADC Group is begun.

NEW GUINEA—Elements of Aus 9th Div reach Sio, on N coast of Huon Peninsula.

BURMA—In Hukawng Valley, 1st Bn of 113th Regt, Ch 38th Div, followed by 3d, reaches Kaduja Ga; 2d Bn is in reserve at Yupbang Ga. 3d Bn of 114th Inf is reinf by 2d Bn of same regt.

ITALY—15th Army Group: U.S. Fifth Army successfully concludes operations against Winter Line with capture by II Corps of M. Trocchio; is now confronted by Gustav Line, which follows the Garigliano, Gari, and Rapido Rivers to Cassino and continues to Br Eighth Army boundary along hills above Cassino. U.S. Fifth Army's Br 10 Corps prepares for assault across lower Garigliano. 5th Div moves quietly forward, night 15-16. II Corps overruns M. Trocchio without a fight, Germans having withdrawn main forces across the Rapido. 135th Inf, 34th Div, takes this last height before the Rapido while 168th Inf on right and 141st Inf, 36th Div (which has relieved 6th Armd Inf on M. Porchia), on left keep pace. In FEC area, Germans abandon S. Elia, corps' objective.

USSR—Troops of Leningrad Front, having quietly concentrated W of Leningrad, open powerful offensive for that city on northern front. Other Red Army forces begin assault on Novgorod from S. ETO-COSSAC is redesignated Supreme Headquarters, Allied Expeditionary Force (SHAEF).

16 January

BOUGAINVILLE—3d Mar Div completes withdrawal from island.

NEW BRITAIN—Japanese make their last counterattack in W New Britain, a futile and costly effort to recover Hill 660. Relief of ADC Group continues. 2d Bn of 158th Inf, with tank support, attacks to reduce enemy positions near Arawe perimeter after air and arty preparation, gaining 1,500 yards.

CBI—Generalissimo Chiang Kai-shek, replying to President Roosevelt's message, threatens to discontinue supplying food and housing for U.S. forces in China after 1 March 1944 unless he is granted the previously requested billion-dollar loan or unless the U.S. will finance the Cheng-tu project at the exchange rate of 20 to 1. This arouses sharp criticism in Washington. Adm Mountbatten, in letter to Gen Marshall, offers to provide Br troops to lead Chinese Army in India, but Gen Stilwell prefers and eventually secures operational control of GALAHAD.

In Hukawng Valley of Burma, 3d Bn of 114th Regt, Ch 38th Div, crosses the Sanip but is halted by enemy pocket near junction of Tanai and Tarung Rivers. 112th Regt secures Gum Ga; subsequently pushes on to Warang, where it halts.

ITALY—15th Army Group: U.S. Fifth Army's II Corps is ordered to make main effort toward Anzio.

ETO—Gen Eisenhower takes over post of Supreme Commander, Allied Expeditionary Force.

17 January

NEW BRITAIN—Enemy positions in Arawe area are mopped up.

BURMA—In Hukawng Valley, 113th Regt of Ch 38th Div bypasses enemy position on Brangbram Stream, leaving company to contain the position, and heads for Taihpa Ga, advancing very cautiously.

ITALY—15th Army Group: In U.S. Fifth Army area, VI Corps concludes brief but strenuous amphibious training program for SHINGLE with rehearsal, called WEBFOOT, from 17th to 19th on beaches S of Salerno. Br 10 Corps opens Operation PANTHER, assault across the Garigliano, at 2100. 5th and 56th Divs, latter on right, cross in several columns and at first make good progress.

ETO—Reorganization of ETOUSA SOS into a single headquarters is announced.

18 January

ETO—Gen Eisenhower gives USSAFE administrative responsibility for all U.S. Army air forces in the United Kingdom.

19 January

NEW BRITAIN—Extensive program of patrolling is begun in W New Britain in effort to regain contact with Japanese and secure W part of the island to line Borgen Bay-Itni R.

NEW GUINEA—Saidor beachhead is by now reinf with most of RCT 128.

ITALY—15th Army Group: Hq is redesignated Hq, Allied Central Mediterranean Force (ACMF). In U.S. Fifth Army's Br 10 Corps area, 5th and 56th Divs enlarge bridgehead across the Garigliano. 5th Div gains Minturno and 56th is approaching Castelforte.

USSR—Soviet forces of Leningrad Front seize Novgorod.

20 January

ITALY—ACMF: In U.S. Fifth Army area, Br 10 Corps continues to expand bridgehead across the Garigliano, 5th Div gaining heights overlooking Capo d'Acqua Creek on coast. 201st Gds Brig is withdrawn from reserve to attack M. Scauri and concentrates S of Minturno. II Corps' 36th Div, with close air and arty support, begins assault across the Rapido in S. Angelo area with 141st and 143d Regts in evening and meets intense opposition. 34th Div makes diversionary thrust toward Cassino.

USSR—Soviet troops advancing SW from Pulkovo and SE from Oranienbaum join, encircling enemy and sealing off corridor to Gulf of Finland.

ETO—Gen Spaatz takes responsibility for all U.S. Army air forces in United Kingdom in accordance with order of Gen Eisenhower of 18th.

21 January

BURMA—Gen Stilwell decides to drive an armored spearhead, followed by infantry, down Kamaing Road to Walawbum. 113th Regt of Ch 38th Div reaches Ningru Ga, less than a mile from Taihpa Ga.

ITALY—ACMF: In U.S. Fifth Army area, VI Corps begins uneventful voyage from Naples area toward Anzio. To deceive enemy, naval forces bombard Civitavecchia and feint landings there. In Br 10 Corps area, Germans, having brought up reinforcements, begin series of strong counterattacks against Garigliano bridgehead, which extends from the river to Hill 413 and thence to Salvatito Hill. II Corps' 36th Div, which has gained a weak hold on far bank of the Rapido during night 20-21, attempts to expand and strengthen bridgehead against continued severe opposition. 1st Bn, 141st Inf, holds bridgehead across the river but is out of contact with main body, which retires to assembly areas. 1st Bn, 143d, which crossed, night 20-21, withdraws under heavy fire to E bank. Renewing attack at 1600, 3d Bn of 143d Inf succeeds in crossing S of S. Angelo and 2d Bn starts across during night 21-22.

USSR—Soviet troops capture rail junction of Mga, SE of Leningrad.

ETO—OVERLORD Is. discussed during first meeting of Gen Eisenhower with his commanders at Norfolk House, London.

22 January

POA—Main body of GALVANIC assault force, the largest U.S. force to be assembled in the Pacific thus far, sails for the Marshalls. Enemy interception of land-based planes over Kwajalein ceases.

ADMIRALTY Is.—Preinvasion air attacks begin with B-25 strike on shipping off the coast. Photo planes obtain photographs of Lorengau and Momote.

ITALY—ACMF: After brief, intense rocket bombardment of beaches, U.S. Fifth Army's VI Corps begins 3 simultaneous landings in Anzio area at 0200, completely surprising enemy, who offers but feeble resistance. Assault forces reach preliminary objectives by noon and continue toward initial beachhead line, some 7 miles inland. On right, 3d Div lands on X-Ray beaches E of Nettuno and seizes all crossings on Mussolini Canal; hard fighting develops along the canal during night as enemy reinforcements arrive, and Germans regain most of the bridges. In center, 6615th Ranger Force (Prov)—3 Ranger bns plus 83d Chemical Bn and 509th Para Inf Bn—lands near Anzio port; seizes it intact and Nettuno as well. On left, 2d Brig Gp of Br 1st Div and 2d Special Service Brig (9th and 43d Cdos) land 6 miles NW of Anzio on Peter Beach to block main road from Anzio to Albano. Allied planes provide close support for landings. Enemy aircraft make ineffective attacks. Br 10 Corps continues to meet strong enemy counterattacks against Garigliano bridgehead and loses M. Natale. Particularly hard, indecisive fighting occurs N of Tufo. In II Corps area, 36th Div continues losing battle for Rapido bridgehead, abandoning it under heavy pressure. The div suffers heavy casualties in this futile attempt to force the Rapido.

USSR—Germans announce frustration of Soviet attacks in Vitebsk sector. Red Army troops have almost encircled Vitebsk.

23 January

POA—Attack Force Reserve for GALVANIC and Majuro Attack Group sail for target.

NEW GUINEA—Australians of 18th Brig, 7th Div, helped materially by recent heavy attacks of Third Air Task Force, gain control of Shaggy Ridge, 6 miles N of Dumpu in Ramu Valley. This victory plus that at Saidor gives Allied forces control of Huon Peninsula. Japanese withdrawing to Madang are subjected to air attacks.

ALGERIA—AFHQ orders ANVIL planners to assume that 3 U.S. divs will be employed in invasion of S France.

ITALY—ACME: In U.S. Fifth Army area, VI Corps expands beachhead with little difficulty except on right flank, where 3d Div continues battle for Mussolini Canal bridges. Enemy planes make strong effort against the beachhead. Br 10 Corps withstands further enemy efforts to reduce the Garigliano bridgehead and falls back slightly in Minturno area. II Corps prepares for another assault across the Rapido, this time by 34th Div. FEC recovers M. S. Croce and is ordered to turn SW toward Terelle and Piedimonte as preparations are made to envelop Cassino from N.

USSR—Moscow announces that rains have halted Soviet offensive in Vitebsk area.

U.K.—Gen Eisenhower proposes to CCS that OVERLORD be mounted in greater strength and in a wider zone than originally planned; that airborne forces be used in the Cotentin instead of at Caen. He also recommends that target date of 1 May be postponed a month, largely because of shortage of assault craft; for the same reason he recommends that the ANVIL assault force be limited to one div.

24 January

ALGERIA—ANVIL planners learn that assault force for invasion of S France will contain but one U.S. div.

ITALY—ACMF: In U.S. Fifth Army area, VI Corps reaches initial beachhead line, where main body pauses to consolidate and await reinforcements. On left flank, 2d Brig of Br 1st Div advances to Moletta R line. On right flank, 504th Para Inf secures rest of bridges along main Mussolini Canal after relieving 3d Rcn Tr there. Ranger Force relieves 7th Inf (− 3d Bn) in quiet left sector of 3d Div front. 15th and 30th Regts, 3d Div, are disposed along W branch of canal facing Cisterna. In preparation for drive on intermediate objectives of Campoleone and Cisterna, Br 1st Div probes toward former and 3d Div toward latter. 2d Special Service Brig (9th, 10th, and 43d Cdos) is withdrawn from Anzio to Br 10 Corps zone. Enemy aircraft again attack bridgehead strongly. In Br 10 Corps area, after a last counterattack against Garigliano bridgehead, enemy goes on the defensive, having gained M. Rotondo (Hill 342), N slopes of Hill 413, and

Castelforte at great cost. In II Corps area, after 30-minute arty preparation, 133d Inf of 34th Div attacks, night 24-25, to secure bridgehead across the Rapido N of Cassino; elements reach river line but are unable to cross. FEC completes preparations for attack on N flank of southern front.

GERMANY—Berlin announces fresh Soviet offensive in Kirovograd area of the Dnieper bend.

25 January

U.S.—U.S. Third Army is relieved at Fort Houston, Texas, by U.S. Fourth Army at midnight 25-26.

BURMA—65th Regt, Ch 22d Div, whose mission is to clear Taro Plain (a responsibility previously held by 3d Bn of 112th Regt, Ch 38th Div) and then push eastward into Hukawng Valley, has encircled and eliminated enemy force during 23-24 January; 323 enemy dead are counted in gorge where the Tanai enters the Taro Plain.

ITALY—ACMF: In U.S. Fifth Army's VI Corps area, 3d Div attacks with 1st Bn of 30th Inf up Campomorto-Cisterna road and with 2d Bn of 15th up Conca-Cisterna road until stopped by enemy strongpoints. As a diversion, 504th Para Inf attacks across Mussolini Canal toward Littoria and retires after dark. On left flank of VI Corps, Br 1st Div makes limited attack for Aprilia, called the Factory, N of Carroceto, and clears it. In II Corps area, 133d Inf of 34th Div continues efforts to establish bridgehead across the Rapido N of Cassino and gets all 3 bns to W bank. Bypassing M. Cifalco, 4th Tunisian Inf, FEC, secures Le Propaia and advances to foot of Belvedere Hill. Enemy recovers part of Le Propaia in counterattack.

In Br Eighth Army area, 13 Corps assumes command of Cdn 5th Armd Div.

USSR—Red Army troops SW of Leningrad capture Krasnogvardeisk rail junction.

26 January

ARGENTINA—Severs relations with Germany and Japan.

MARSHALL Is.—B-25 strike on Maloelap, for the first time with fighter escort, destroys most of enemy air strength there.

CHINA—U.S. Ambassador to China, Clarence E. Gauss, delivers President Roosevelt's reply to Chiang Kai-shek. Roosevelt's reply proposes that a Chinese representative discuss exchange rate with Treasury officials in Washington and states that U.S. expenditures in China, beginning 1 March 1944, will be limited to U.S. $25,000,000 a month. In letter to President Roosevelt, Gen Chennault proposes that B-29's, under Fourteenth Air Force command, be used against industrial targets in Japan after air supremacy has been established in China and enemy's ocean shipping has been pounded; then, Japanese Army installations in China, Formosa, and Hainan should be attacked. Chennault warns Gen Arnold that B-29 operations from Cheng-tu area would be costly and suggests that all air forces in China be under control of commander of air forces in China.

BURMA—65th Regt, Ch 22d Div, reaches Ahawk Stream. The Ahawk Trail along this stream is the shortest route from Taro to the Hukawng Valley.

ITALY—ACMF: Continuing limited attacks toward Cisterna in U.S. Fifth Army's VI Corps area, 3d Div reduces strongpoint near Ponte Rotto. Br 1st Div repels strong enemy counterattack against the Factory. Br 10 Corps completes regrouping to renew offensive. 46th Div is committed E of Castelforte, shortening line of 56th Div. In II Corps area, advance elements of 133d Inf, 34th Div, reach edge of Hill 213 against strong opposition but at nightfall fall back to W bank of the Rapido. At 0330, 1st Bn of 135th Inf crosses one co over the Rapido just N of Cassino and presses to edge of town; after daybreak joins elements of 133d Inf in unsuccessful attack against Pt 225, between Cassino and the barracks. RCT 142, 36th Div, is attached to 34th Div to assist French in operations to N. In FEC area, 4th Tunisian Inf, 3d Algerian Div, seizes Belvedere Hill and Abate Hill; 3d Algerian Inf drives enemy from Le Propaia.

27 January

YUGOSLAVIA—Allied commando party successfully raids Hvar, night 27-28.

ITALY—ACMF: In U.S. Fifth Army's VI Corps area, 3d Div, after another futile attempt to reach Cisterna, breaks off attack to regroup for a stronger push. Br 1st Div makes slow progress N of the Factory on left flank of corps. Br 10 Corps renews attack to expand Garigliano bridgehead. 46th Div presses toward M. Jugo and 5th Div toward M. Natale. Enemy resists vigorously. In II Corps area, after hour-long arty preparation, 168th Inf and 756th Tank Bn attack through bridgehead of 133d Inf, 34th Div. A few tanks cross with great difficulty and clear lanes for infantry. 1st and 3d Bns, former on left, then cross under heavy fire and drive to vicinity of Hills 56 and 213. After nightfall 3d Bn withdraws to river and moves N along it to cross 500 yards upstream. In FEC area, 3d Algerian Div loses Abate Hill and Hill 700 to SE during strong counterattack but retains Belvedere Hill.

USSR—Red Army units gain ground in Leningrad area. Enemy is cleared from RR between Tosno and Lyuban, and Tosno is overrun.

28 January

BURMA—65th Regt, Ch 22d Div, crosses Ahawk Stream.

ITALY—ACMF: In U.S. Fifth Army's VI Corps area, assault elements of Br 1st Div reach positions 1½ miles N of the Factory, then halt to regroup for assault on Campoleone. Br 10 Corps continues struggle to expand Garigliano bridgehead. In II Corps area, 1st Bn of 168th Inf, 34th Div, after getting a few men to Hill 213, falls back to river. By dawn, 3d Bn has small bridgehead across the Rapido near Cairo. In FEC area, 3d Algerian Div repels determined counterattacks between Belvedere Hill and Le Propaia.

USSR—Red Army forces moving down Leningrad-Moscow RR capture Lyuban and drive on toward Chudovo.

ETO—Lt Gen Omar N. Bradley succeeds Lt Gen George Grunert as commander of First U.S. Army.

29 January

U.S.—In order to improve Calcutta-Assam LOC, now in Br civilian hands, Gen Marshall suggests to President Roosevelt that the LOC be placed under Anglo-American military control and that the President write Prime Minister Churchill on this matter. President Roosevelt agrees and urges Churchill to intervene personally.

NEW GUINEA—863d Aviation Engr Bn arrives at Saidor.

MARSHALL Is.—As invasion forces approach the Marshalls, carrier planes and naval vessels join in final neutralization program, supplementing action of land-based planes that has been in progress for some time. Carrier aircraft of Adm Mitscher's TF 58 thoroughly cover airfields and other targets on Kwajalein Atoll; completely neutralize Taroa airfield on Maloelap Atoll; make repeated attacks on Wotje airfield. These strikes are followed by naval bombardment by TF 58 warships. In addition, the neutralization group (TG 50.15) bombards Wotje and Maloelap. Land-based planes concentrate on Roi-Namur and Kwajalein Islands in Kwajalein Atoll and attack targets on Wotje, Maloelap, Jaluit, and Mille Atolls.

CBI—5303d Hq, commanding service units supporting the Chinese, becomes an "area command."

In Burma, Gen Stilwell's plan to block road leading from Kamaing to enemy positions along the Tanai goes astray as 1st Bn, 114th Regt, Ch 38th Div, upon arriving at front, is ordered by div CG to clear Japanese from river bank instead. 3d Bn of 114th Regt is withdrawn for rest.

YUGOSLAVIA—Allied base for coastal craft is established at Vis, already the chief base for supplying Tito's forces.

ITALY—ACMF: In U.S. Fifth Army area, VI Corps regroups in preparation for strong assault on Campoleone and Cisterna, immediate objectives before Colli Laziali. AA cruiser HMS *Spartan* and a Liberty ship are sunk during heavy enemy air attack. In Br 10 Corps area, 138th Brig, on right flank of 46th Div, reaches M. Jugo. 56th Div makes unsuccessful attack on Hill 413. In II Corps area, 168th Inf of 34th Div is strongly reinf by tanks, arty, and engineers as it renews attempts to take Hills 56 and 213 and saddle between them. Tanks, using alternate route, cross the Rapido in force, permitting all 3 bns of 168th Inf to advance rapidly to objectives, which are overrun before dawn of 30th. In FEC area, 2d Bn of 142d Inf arrives at Belvedere Hill.

USSR—With fall of Chudovo on Leningrad front, Leningrad-Moscow rail line is cleared of enemy. Germans announce their withdrawal from Smela, in the Dnieper bend. Red Army launches co-ordinated assault by troops of First and Second Ukrainian Fronts against faces of salient held by German *8th Army* in the Ukraine.

GERMANY—In the largest U.S. air strike to date, over 800 heavy bombers of Eighth Air Force attack industrial center of Frankfurt am Main, using radar.

30 January

MARSHALL Is.—Carrier planes of TF 58 continue neutralization of the Marshalls, attacking Eniwetok Atoll, where 19 planes are destroyed on the ground, in addition to targets on Kwajalein, Wotje, and Maloelap Atolls. Immediate objectives on Kwajalein Atoll—Roi-Namur and Kwajalein Islands—are pounded during 400 sorties and subjected to naval bombardment of surface vessels for 4 hours. Assault forces arrive at target after nightfall; accompanying DD's and cruisers turn aside en route to objective in order to bombard Maloelap and Wotje. Rear Adm Harry W. Hill's Majuro Attack Group (TG 51.2), consisting of reinforced 2d Bn of 106th Inf, 27th Div, and VAC Rcn Co, begins invasion of Majuro Atoll, which is to become an advance naval base, night 30-31. Scouts of VAC Rcn Tr makes unopposed landings on Calalin and Dadap Islands in the atoll.

NEW BRITAIN—Cape Gloucester airfield is ready for use.

CBI—GO 13, Hq USAF CBI, directs that XX BC be under command of Gen Stilwell, on whose behalf Gen Stratemeyer will exercise control. In Burma, 65th Regt, Ch 22d Div, gains control of Taro Plain; overruns Taro.

ITALY—ACMF: U.S. Fifteenth Air Force, with dual purpose of destroying German airpower and assisting Allied troops, attacks targets in Po Valley so successfully that German Air Force in the future sharply curtails opposition to strategic bombing during daylight.

In U.S. Fifth Army area, VI Corps launches major offensive toward Colli Laziali, forestalling planned enemy counterattack to reduce Anzio beachhead. On left, Br 1st Div and 1st Armd Div make main effort up Albano road. After sharp action, beginning night 29-30, of 24th Gds Brig to secure line of departure for 3d Brig, 3d Brig jumps off in afternoon and takes heights just S of Campoleone overpass. 1st Armd Div moves left of Albano road to attack Colli Laziali from W. On right flank of VI Corps, 1st and 3d Ranger Bns spearhead attack of 3d Div toward Cisterna, moving forward quietly, night 29-30; spotted by Germans at dawn, Rangers are ambushed and virtually destroyed within 800 yards of Cisterna. Meanwhile, efforts of 4th Ranger Bn and 3d Div to relieve the ambushed Rangers are costly and futile. 504th Para Inf makes diversionary attack along Mussolini Canal but stops short of Highway 7. In Br 10 Corps area, 17th Brig of 5th Div takes M. Natale. In 11 Corps area, 168th Inf of 34th Div repels strong enemy counterattacks W of the Rapido. In FEC area, 2d Bn of 142d Inf, U.S. 36th Div, begins attack toward Manna Farm.

U.K.—Prime Minister Churchill promises President Roosevelt that he will investigate the matter of the Calcutta-Assam LOC.

31 January

KWAJALEIN ATOLL—Under over-all command of Fifth Fleet (TF 50) commander, Adm Spruance, U.S. Joint Expeditionary Force (TF 51, commanded by Adm Turner) invades Marshalls at Kwajalein Atoll, opening Operation FLINTLOCK. Air, naval, and ground operations are well co-ordinated. Little opposition is met and U.S. casualties are extremely light. Underwater demolition team is employed for first time in the Pacific to explore beaches at W end of Kwajalein I. Southern Attack Force (TF 52, also under Adm Turner) invades S Kwajalein Atoll. Preliminary operations begin early in morning. Provisional units attached to RCT 17, 7th Div, secure channel for entry of shipping into lagoon with occupation of Cecil (Ninni) and Carter (Gea), small islets NW of Kwajalein I. Reconnaissance elements and part of Co B, 111th Inf, take Cecil without opposition by 1235 after having landed earlier by mistake on Chauncey (Gehh), where some infantrymen are left to contain enemy. Troops of another provisional force from 7th Div manage to land on Carter at 0620 and overcome opposition by 0930.

After preparatory air and naval bombardment, RCT 17 begins invasion of Carlos (Ennylabegan) and Carlson (Enubuj) at 0910, 40 minutes behind schedule. BLT 1 occupies Carlos and BLT 2, Carlson, with little trouble. Arty is put ashore on Carlson and registered on next objectives, Kwajalein I., (Porcelain) and Burton (Ebeye). Northern Attack Force (TF 53 under Rear Adm Richard L. Conolly) invades N Kwajalein. 4th Mar Div opens operations with preliminary landings by 25th Marines, reinf, on islands adjacent to main objective, twin islands of Roi-Namur (Burlesque-Camouflage), in order to secure safe passage for naval vessels into lagoon and for arty sites. 1st Bn, 25th Marines, quickly quells token resistance on Ivan (Mellu) and Jacob (Ennuebing), SW of Roi, during morning, making Jacob Pass available for shipping. In afternoon, 3d Bn, 25th Marines, takes Albert (Ennumennet), and 2d Bn seizes Allen (Ennubirr), SE of Namur, with ease. 3d Bn then proceeds to Ennugarrett (Abraham) and occupies it. Arty is brought ashore and registered on Roi-Namur.

MAJURO ATOLL—Atoll is secured without a fight as VAC scouts complete uneventful reconnaissance.

ITALY—ACMF: In U.S. Fifth Army's VI Corps area, superior enemy forces bar 3d Div from Cisterna. Br 1st Div and 1st Armd Div are stubbornly opposed from Campoleone area. Attack up Albano road halts upon VI Corps order at night. In Br 10 Corps area, 138th Brig of 46th Div reaches M. Purgatorio. In II Corps area, 168th Inf of 34th Div seizes Cairo village and repels further counterattacks. 133d begins clearing barracks area N of Cassino. In FEC area, 2d Bn of 142d Inf, U.S. 36th Div, overruns Manna Farm. French recapture Abate Hill.

1 February

U.S.—CCS agree to postpone the cross-Channel assault about a month, the exact date to depend upon weather conditions during early days of June.

KWAJALEIN ATOLL—Troops of VAC open attack for main objectives. The generally light opposition met is a tribute to the effectiveness of preliminary bombardment by naval vessels, aircraft, and arty, which was closely integrated and overwhelming. In Southern Landing Force area, 7th Div invades Kwajalein I., at S bend of the atoll, advance elements touching down at 0930. BLT's 184-3 and 32-1 land abreast, former on N, on Beaches Red 1 and 2 at W end of island and quickly secure beaches. In zone of 184th Inf enemy clings to ruins of his main beach defenses along lagoon shore. Both teams move steadily eastward to N-S Wilma Road, which connects coastal roads Will on N and Wallace on S.

BLT 32-2 attacks through BLT 32-1 in afternoon. By end of day 7th Div holds about a third of island, including W edge of airfield. Gen Corlett, 7th Div CG, lands on Carlson and takes command ashore. U.S. forces are withdrawn from Chauncey, infantry elements to Cecil and 7th Rcn Tr aboard the *Overton*. A few naval troops are left to guard barges. In Northern Landing Force area, 4th Mar Div lands 2 BLT's of RCT 23 on S shore of Roi and similar force from RCT 24 on S shore of Namur. Assault hour, set for 1000, is delayed because of boating difficulties, and landings actually occur between 1145 and noon. On Roi, which airfield largely covers, stunned and disorganized Japanese offer no effective resistance as RCT 23 speeds to N coast and clears island except for small pocket in center of airfield. RCT 24 is less fortunate on Namur, where thick vegetation and many buildings provide concealment for enemy. BLT's 2 and 3 push N abreast, 2d on right, meeting considerable opposition as Japanese rally from preliminary bombardment. BLT 2 suffers more than 50% of its casualties from powerful explosions of a blockhouse containing ammunition. Reinf by reserves from BLT 1 and tanks from RCT 23, RCT 24 reaches line extending from initial objective (O-1) on eastern shore to positions 175 yards N of O-1 on W flank. Landing Force Commander establishes CP on Namur. Enemy infiltration attempts, night 2-3, culminate in counterattack by about 100 at dawn, but attack is repelled in close combat.

BURMA—5303d hq, previously designated "area command," is redesignated Northern Combat Area Command (NCAC). The term "combat" is included to permit Gen Stilwell to retain command, since SEAC controls forces in line of communications areas. Gen Boatner heads NCAC. All Allied units, upon entering N Burma, are to be attached or assigned to NCAC, except for GALAHAD Force, which on arrival is attached to CAI and later assigned to NCAC. British hq in N Burma, Fort Hertz area, under Brig John F. Bowerman, is attached to NCAC. Engineers begin construction of permanent road in Hukawng Valley and combat road to support Ch divs. The combat road is to consist of improved Kamaing Road plus Kachin and Naga trails and is to run through Shingbwiyang, Yupbang Ga, Taihpa Ga, Maingkwan, and Tinghawk Sakan. During period 30 January-1 February, 3d Bn of 113th Regt, Ch 38th Div, moves through Taihpa Ga to attack enemy strongpoint in that area.

ITALY—ACMF: In U.S. Fifth Army's VI Corps area, 3d Div, after another futile attempt to reach Cisterna in morning, breaks off attack and digs in to meet expected enemy counterattack. Entire VI Corps is now on the defensive. Enemy build-up presages imminent counteroffensive to drive corps back into the sea. Gen Clark confers with Gen Alexander. By this time 45th Div and 1st Armd Div (– CCB) are ashore. Br 10 Corps continues efforts to expand Garigliano bridgehead against stubborn opposition. In II Corps area, 135th Inf of 34th Div attacks toward Castellone and Majola Hill with fire support of 168th from Hills 56 and 213 and reaches top of both objectives. Enemy counterattacks vigorously in region from Manna Farm to Hill 706.

USSR—Red Army troops approaching Estonian border capture Kingisepp, last Russian station on RR to Narva.

ETO—Initial Joint Plan, NEPTUNE (formulated by air, ground, and naval planners) for invasion of Normandy is issued. The code name NEPTUNE is more restricted in its connotation than the term OVERLORD; NEPTUNE applies only to movement across the Channel, seizure of a beachhead in Normandy, and the Normandy area.

2 February

KWAJALEIN ATOLL—In Southern Landing Force campaign, 7th Div meets increased resistance, which planes, arty, and naval gunfire help to neutralize as the division continues clearing Kwajalein. 2d Bn, 184th Inf, passing through 3d, advances along lagoon side of island on left while 2d Bn of 32d Inf continues attack on ocean side. Overwhelming enemy strongpoints, both assault forces soon reach Carl Road, which crosses island at E end of airfield. As advance continues toward next cross-island road, Nora, some 300 yards ahead, 3d Bn, 32d Inf, attacking through 2d Bn, crosses tank ditch and clears strongpoint, called Corn. Although forward elements of division get well beyond Nora Road, line is organized for night short of it, 3d Bn of 32d Inf taking up positions in Corn Strong Point and 2d Bn of 184th on line 75-100 yards NE of Carl Road. Elements of 7th Rcn Tr land on Chauncey, where enemy is becoming aggressive, and clear it during sharp fire fight. Japanese dead total 125. In preparation for invasion of Burton, island is searched from DD and seaplane and pounded by arty and naval gunfire. In Northern Landing Force campaign, 4th Mar Div completes mop up of Roi and capture of Namur; begins search of remaining islands of N half of Kwajalein Atoll. On Namur RCT 24, with tank support, attacks with BLT 3 on left and BLT 1 on right. Organized resistance ceases by 1215, ending battle for S Kwajalein except for mopping up. Maj Gen Harry Schmidt, 4th Mar Div CG, announces end of organized resistance on Namur at 1418. RCT 25 is given task of securing other islands of N half of Kwajalein Atoll and begins uneventful search for enemy.

SWPA—U.S. Sixth Army hq moves from Australia to Cape Cretin, New Guinea.

CBI—Replying to President Roosevelt's message of 26 January, Generalissimo Chiang Kai-shek reports that he has discussed the exchange rate, Chinese offering 30 to 1, with the Minister of Finance and reiterates offer to move Yunnan troops to Burma when large-scale amphibious operation can be undertaken.

ITALY—ACMF: Gen Clark, CG U.S. Fifth Army, orders Gen Lucas, CG VI Corps, to consolidate beachhead and prepare for defense. In Br 10 Corps area, 2d Special Service Brig fails in effort to take M. Faito. In II Corps area, 135th Inf of 34th Div presses southward toward Highway 6, 2d Bn crossing Hill 445 and pushing on toward Hill 593 while 1st Bn clears Hill 324 to E. 3d Bn of 168th Inf is committed because of counterattacks on 2d Bn. 1st Bn of 142d Inf, 36th Div, takes responsibility for M. Castellone. 133d Inf finishes clearing barracks area N of Cassino and attacks S with tank support to N end of Cassino but withdraws about 1,000 yards after nightfall.

USSR—In the Ukraine, Soviet forces attack German 6th Army on 60-mile front W of the Dnieper. First Estonian village falls to other Soviet forces. Stalin agrees to provide 6 bases for U.S. Planes in USSR.

3 February

KWAJALEIN ATOLL—Adm Hill arrives by plane from Majuro to take part in formal planning for invasion of Eniwetok with forces previously allocated as reserves for Kwajalein. Planning continues until the expeditionary force sails on 15th. In Southern Landing Force campaign, 7th Div attacks to clear rest of Kwajalein I., with Nathan Road (E-W road opposite Nob Pier) as immediate objective; assault forces encounter dense construction and must destroy blockhouses and concrete positions in detail. 1st Bn of 184th Inf advances on lagoon side, 3d Bn of 32d Inf attacks on ocean side. Beyond Nora Road; frontal attacks prove too costly, particularly in 184th Inf's zone where Co B is virtually halted along lagoon at W edge of built-up Admiralty area, that plan of attack is changed. 1st Bn, 184th, swings left to lagoon shore while 2d attacks through its right flank toward Nathan Road, forcing exposed salient into enemy positions. 3d Bn, 32d Inf, assisted by 1st Bn, continues toward Nathan Road, advance elements getting to within 100 yards of it. Numerous enemy pockets have been bypassed. Enemy counterattacks are repulsed during night. After effective naval gunfire, arty, and carrier aircraft bombardment that eliminates enemy opposition, 1st Bn of 17th Inf, 7th Div, invades Burton, 2 cos going ashore abreast (Co A on right; Co C on left) on S part of lagoon beach at 0935. After crossing S end of island, 1st Bn drives N supported by amphibian tractors and later by light and medium tanks. Opposition develops about an hour after the landing, particularly on left where Co B passes through Co C shortly before 1700. By 1900, forward elements halt for night on line that crosses island just S of Bailey Pier, a concrete structure extending into lagoon about midway up the island. 3d Bn, upon landing, takes responsibility for rear area. Illumination throughout night and fire of supporting arms help prevent enemy counterattacks. Amphibious tank detachments sent to Buster and Byron, islets (no known native names) between Kwajalein and Burton, take them without opposition.

ITALY—ACMF: Gen Alexander forms NZ 2d Div and Ind 4th Div into NZ Corps under Lt Gen Sir Bernard C. Freyberg and places the corps under U.S. Fifth Army command. VI Corps issues verbal orders to beachhead forces to prepare defensive positions at once. In II Corps area, while 1st Bn of 135th Inf, 34th Div, completes clearing Hill 324, 2d Bn, 135th, and 3d Bn, 168th, drive to within 1½ miles of Highway 6. 133d Inf attacks with tanks toward Cassino but is driven back; renewing attack in afternoon, gets forward elements to northern edge of town, where they dig in. Enemy continues to counterattack between Manna Farm and Hill 706, but the hill is cleared by 3d Bn, 135th Inf.

USSR—Soviet forces converge S of Korosun and surround 2 corps of German 8th Army. Germans make desperate attempts to relieve the besieged forces, curtailing offensive operations to do so.

4 February

KWAJALEIN ATOLL—RCT 184, in southern part of atoll, continues difficult mop-up of enemy along lagoon shore, completing this as far as Green Beach 4 by 1435. 1st Bn, 32d Inf, attacks through 2d Bn of 184th and 3d Bn of 32d toward end of island, arriving at Nate Road in a highly disorganized state. Here 2d Bn, 32d, passes through 1st Bn to complete capture of island. Advance elements reach Nero Pt, at tip of island, by 1515, but organized resistance continues until 1920. Gen Corlett announces capture of Kwajalein I., to Adm Turner at 1610. A considerable number of Japanese and Koreans surrender during the day. 1st Bn, 17th Inf, continues northward attack on Burton, this time meeting main opposition on right, in zone of Co A. At 1130, 3d Bn attacks through 1st Bn. Co K reaches NE corner of island at 1210 and Burton is completely secured by 1337. Troops of 2d Bn, 17th Inf, secure Burnet (no known native name) and Blakenship (Loi), N of Burton, capturing about 40 natives on Burnet

and subduing more than 20 Japanese and Koreans on Blakenship.
CBI—In NCAC area, Gen Stilwell alters plan of attack: Ch 22d Div is to envelop enemy in Yawngbang area. 1st Bn of 113th Regt, Ch 38th Div, reaches Kaduja Ga. After stubborn defense of Taihpa Ga area during past few days, Japanese withdraw secretly about this time.
11 Army Group: In Br Fourteenth Army area, Japanese open offensive on 15 Corps' Arakan front, 2 TF's pushing northward around E flank of Ind 7th Div while a holding force makes frontal attacks on Ind 7th Div N and NW of Buthidaung. Enveloping enemy forces overrun Taung Bazaar and head S and W.
ITALY—ACMF: In U.S. Fifth Army area, VI Corps receives plan of defense. 45th Div is to hold Moletta R line with one RCT on left flank. Newly arrived 1st SSF is to hold right flank. 1st and 3d Divs are to hold central sector. In VI Corps reserve, 1st Armd Div (– CCB) and 45th Div (– an RCT) are to be prepared to counterattack. 36th and 39th Engr Combat Regts are to help defend coastline and be prepared to assemble as corps reserve. Enemy counteroffensive against Anzio beachhead begins, night 3–4, with limited effort against Campoleone salient held by Br 1st Div. After hard fighting throughout day, British fall back to new line about a mile N of Carroceto and the Factory with heavy losses. In II Corps area, 34th Div is stubbornly opposed as it continues efforts to break through enemy positions. 3d Bn, 135th Inf, reaches S. Angelo Hill but enemy counterattack forces it back to Hill 706. 2d Bn get to within 500 yards of Hill 593. 1st Bn gains weak hold on Pt 445. 133d Inf and supporting tanks consolidate positions on N edge of Cassino; 1st Bn penetrates NE corner but is driven back; takes Hill 175.
USSR—Moscow announces that entire coast of Gulf of Finland is cleared as far as Narva R estuary, as is rail line from Novgorod to Leningrad.

out opposition. Western Force advances N from Carlos and takes 4 islands, 3 of them without opposition.
CBI—Adm Mountbatten's representatives, Axiom Mission, leave New Delhi for London and Washington, where they will present his views. 16th Brig of Gen Wingate's Special Force begins southward trek from Ledo. Wingate's long-range penetration columns are to divert enemy from Myitkyina area in behalf of Gen Stilwell, facilitate advance of CEF across the Salween from Yunnan, and impose losses on enemy in N Burma. Special Force consists of Ind 77th and 111th Brigs and 3 independent brigs 04th, 16th, 23d) formed from Br 10th Div. U.S. 5318th Air Unit, under Col Philip G. Cochran, is responsible for supplying, transporting, and evacuating Wingate's columns.
ITALY—ACMF: In U.S. Fifth Army area, VI Corps receives probing jabs, particularly in front of Cisterna. Enemy continues build-up of forces for main counteroffensive. Airstrip at Nettuno is abandoned as a permanent base because of enemy shelling. Port operations are hampered by continuing enemy air attacks. II Corps continues battle for Cassino, but cannot break through. Small force from 1st Bn of 135th Inf, 34th Div, reaches walls of Abbey and withdraws; this is the farthest advance to be made by 34th Div during battle for Cassino. Night 5–6, 1st and 3d Bns, 168th Inf, assemble on Pt 445; 1st Bn, 135th, concentrates on left flank to block enemy infiltration from Castle Hill. 1st Bn, 133d, drives S from Hill 175 to Castle Hill but is forced back to Hill 175 by strong night counterattack. 3d Bn repels counterattack at N edge of Cassino and takes another block of houses. 36th Div is ordered to move around 34th Div and be prepared to capture Piedimonte from NE.
USSR—Moscow reports Lutsk and Rovno, previously reported evacuated by enemy, occupied by troops of First Ukrainian Front.

5 February

KWAJALEIN ATOLL—While mopping up is conducted on Kwajalein I., other islands in S Kwajalein Atoll are being reconnoitered. 3d Bn, 17th Inf, finds 3 Japanese on Beverly (S Gugegwe); 1st Bn clears about 200 Japanese from Berlin (N Gugegwe). Co C with tanks then proceeds to Benson, next island to N, and secures it. 7th Rcn Tr invades Bennett (Bigej); is assisted there by 3d Bn of 184th Inf with 2 tanks; 94 Japanese are killed before island is secured. 2d Bn (–) of 17th Inf, organized into Eastern and Western Forces, continues to mop up. Eastern Force works south from N end of southeastern leg of atoll toward Bennett, taking 5 islands with-

6 February

KWAJALEIN ATOLL—In Southern Landing Force area, Western Force of 2d Bn, 17th Inf, occupies Cohen (Ennugenliggelap), next island N of Clifton (Eller), without opposition, bringing to an end offensive against S Kwajalein Atoll. Southern Landing Force losses total 142 killed, 845 wounded, and 2 missing. Japanese losses are estimated at 4,938 killed and 206 captured. Northern Landing Force continues uneventful reconnaissance of islands of N Kwajalein Atoll.
ADMIRALTY Is.—Momote and Lorengau airfields are unserviceable as result of Fifth Air Force attacks.

CBI—Responsibility for Calcutta–Assam LOC is given to Calcutta representative of GHQ, India. Port is to be controlled by an outstanding man who will be assisted by 2 deputies, one of them an American. Port director will be a civilian responsible to War Transport Department of Indian Government.

11 Army Group: In 15 Corps area, Japanese overrun headquarters of Ind 7th Div and separate it from Ind 5th Div. The headquarters is re-established later in day at Sinzweya.

ITALY—ACMF: U.S. 88th Div arrives at Naples but is not committed to action until it has received combat training.

U.S. Fifth Army takes control of supply at beachhead and control of 540th Engr Combat Regt to defend X-Ray and Nettuno beaches. About midnight 6–7, enemy begins diversionary attack on Moletta R in company strength and is engaged by 2d Bn, 157th Inf, of VI Corps. II Corps is in position for assault on last ridge (Hill 593, Monastery Hill, Castle Hill, and Cassino) barring access to Highway 6. NZ Corps takes over sector S of Highway 6, releasing elements of II Corps for action against Cassino.

USSR—Moscow announces major breakthrough by troops of Third Ukrainian Front in region NE of Krivoi Rog and Nikopol where Apostolovi, rail junction between the 2 places, is overrun. Enemy forces are trapped as the Dnieper is reached near Nikopol. On N front, E bank of the Narva N and S of Narva is free of enemy.

7 February

KWAJALEIN ATOLL—Northern Landing Force concludes uneventful search of islands of N Kwajalein, completing offensive against Kwajalein Atoll. During the action, 4th Mar Div has suffered 737 casualties, of whom 190 were killed or died of wounds. Japanese losses are 3,472 killed and 91 captured.

CBI—President Roosevelt replies to Chiang Kai-shek assuring him that the U.S. will study the exchange rate and U.S. military expenditures in China. Chinese advance $15,000,000,000 in Chinese national currency to CBI to cover U.S. expenditures for March, April, and May 1944 without specifying rate of exchange for repayment. Of this, $500,000,000 is allocated for Cheng to airfields for B-29's.

ITALY—ACMF: In U.S. Fifth Army's VI Corps area, after strong air and arty action, enemy begins main counteroffensive against Anzio beachhead at 2100 and takes Buonriposo Ridge from Br 1st Div by daybreak. Br 10 Corps makes limited attack, night 7–8, toward M. Faito in effort to reach mountains behind Castelforte and open Liri Valley, but attack is a failure. In II Corps area, 36th Div takes over Castellone=Manna Farm area and corps prepares for second drive to cut Highway 6.

USSR—Troops of Third Ukrainian Front drive to outskirts of Nikopol.

8 February

CBI—Gen Stilwell's mission to Washington reports that a major Japanese offensive is about to begin, according to estimate of situation by GHQ, India.

MEDITERRANEAN—Gen Wilson informs JCS that he must have more definite information regarding the size of ANVIL assault in order to plan campaign in Italy.

ITALY—ACMF: In U.S. Fifth Army area, VI Corps' Br 1st Div commits reserves to counter enemy offensive, and hard fighting continues throughout day in Factory area. In Br 10 Corps area, bridgehead across the Garigliano reaches its maximum depth, with 46th Div holding about 6 square miles NE of Castelforte. When 56th Div is withdrawn to reinforce Anzio beachhead, plan for drive up Ausonia Valley is abandoned and 10 Corps goes on the defensive. II Corps begins another strong effort to break through to Highway 6 in Cassino area. While 133d Inf, 34th Div, continues to struggle in Cassino, 168th opens attack on Monastery Hill, its right flank protected by 135th. 168th Inf jumps off at 0400 with 2 bns in assault but is pinned down short of Monastery Hill and suffers heavy casualties. 135th Inf repels counterattacks on right flank. 100th Bn joins rest of 133d inf in fight for Cassino and makes slow progress within and near Cassino. In NZ Corps area, Br 78th Div is placed under control of corps.

USSR—Nikopol, important manganese center in the Ukraine, falls to forces of Third Ukrainian Front assisted by troops of Fourth Ukrainian Front. German bridgehead at Nikopol is reduced.

9 February

U.S.—President Roosevelt asks Chiang Kai-shek if an American observer mission might be permitted to go to N China.

ITALY—ACMF: In U.S. Fifth Army's VI Corps area, enemy overruns strategically situated Factory and holds its against counterattacks supported by naval and air bombardment; continues attacks, night 9–10, forcing British back even farther. Relief of hard-pressed and badly depleted Br 1st Div is begun during night 9–10 by 180th Inf. II Corps is still unable to break through to Highway 6 in Cassino area.

10 February

SWPA—CG, Sixth Army, terminates Operation DEXTERITY (W New Britain and Saidor, New Guinea). 5th Aus Div and TF MICHAELMAS make patrol contact about 4 miles SE of Saidor, completing Huon Peninsula campaign. On New Britain, patrols of 1st Mar Div and RCT 112 make contact.

BURMA—11 Army Group: In Br Fourteenth Army area, 15 Corps' Ind 7th Div is isolated at Sinzweya as Japanese cut Ngakyedauk Pass and contact other forces to S. Ind 26th Div, released from Fourteenth Army reserve to assist in restoring communications, recaptures Taung Bazaar. Ind 7th Div and 16th LRP must be supplied by air from this time.

ITALY—ACMF: In U.S. Fifth Army's VI Corps area, enemy captures Carroceto RR station despite efforts of Br 1st Div with close support of air and arty to stem advance. Relief of Br 1st Div continues, night 10-11, when 179th Inf replaces 168th Brig S of the Factory. II Corps prepares for another effort to break through at Cassino.

ETO—CCS announce that D Day for OVERLORD will be postponed about 3 weeks. All LST's in the Mediterranean not vitally needed are to be returned to U.K.

11 February

ITALY—ACME In U.S. Fifth Army's VI Corps area, 179th Inf of 45th Div, assisted by 191st Tank Bn, attacks to recover the Factory. 1st Bn reaches objective but is driven back. II Corps tries again to reach Highway 6. 36th Div, with 141st and 142d Regts in assault, suffers heavy casualties while attacking in vain toward Albaneta Farm. 168th Inf, 34th Div, attacks through violent rain and snow storm toward Monastery Hill but is also unsuccessful. Gen Alexander directs Ind 4th Div, NZ Corps, to attack as soon as possible to cleat heights W of Cassino.

USSR—Shepetovka, rail center W of Kiev near prewar Polish border, falls to troops of First Ukrainian Front.

12 February

PACIFIC—TF 58, less one attack group, sails for Truk from Majuro. Allied assault force begins voyage toward Green Is.. Co B of 1st Marines, 1st Mar Div, moving by sea from Cape Gloucester, New Britain, lands on Rooke I., and begins uneventful search for enemy.

BURMA—11 Army Group: In Br Fourteenth Army's 15 Corps area, Ind 7th Div is ordered to hold its positions and contain enemy forces that Ind 26th Div and Ind 5th Div are moving against from N and S, respectively.

ITALY—ACMF: In U.S. Fifth Army's VI Corps area, 45th Div, after another unsuccessful attempt to recover the Factory, goes on the defensive. In II Corps area, 36th Div breaks off offensive on N flank of corps; in bitter fighting repels very heavy enemy counterattack preceded by extremely heavy arty barrages. NZ Corps relieves II Corps of responsibility for Cassino sector.

USSR—Soviet forces pushing toward Luga overrun important rail junction of Batetskaya and get to suburbs of Luga.

ETO—CCS issue directive to Gen Eisenhower on his duties as Supreme Allied Commander, Allied Expeditionary Force, which will invade the European continent to destroy German armed forces. Target date is set as May 1944

13 February

SWPA—Gen MacArthur directs forces of South and Southwest Pacific Areas to take Manus I., Admiralty Is.., and Kavieng, New Ireland, about 1 April in order to gain control of Bismarck Archipelago and isolate Rabaul.

ITALY—ACMF: In U.S. Fifth Army's II Corps area, Ind 4th Div, NZ Corps, begins relieving 168th Inf, which is depleted in strength. 133d Inf retains positions in Cassino. NZ Corps prepares to take over battle for Cassino. FEC is reinf by combat team of Italian 1st Motorized Gp.

USSR—Soviet forces clear E shore of Lake Peipus.

ETO—CCS order a combined bomber offensive against Germany aimed at destruction of "military, industrial, and economic systems"; disruption of communication lines and reduction of airpower.

14 February

CBI—Adm Mountbatten warns Br Chiefs of Staff of impending Japanese attack on 4 Corps after Arakan offensive is successfully concluded.

ETO—Gen Eisenhower, upon receiving CCS directive of 12 February, establishes headquarters, Supreme Headquarters Allied Expeditionary Force (SHAEF). COSSAC staff comes under control of SHAEF.

15 February

MARSHALL Is.—Eniwetok Expeditionary Group (TG 51.11 under Adm Hill) leaves Kwajalein for Eniwetok.

GREEN Is.—Amphibious force under command of Adm Wilkinson invades Green Is.. The landing force (NZ 3d Div, less 8th Brig Gp; supporting and construction units, including U.S. 976th AAA Gun Bn), headed by Gen Barrowclough of NZ 3d Div, goes ashore on Nissan I., without opposition and starts search for Japanese. Construction is begun at once for advanced-naval base. Enemy planes attempting to interfere with the operation are driven off by aircraft and AA fire.

CBI—GO 16, Hq USAF CBI, rescinding GO 13 of 30 January, removes Gen Stratemeyer from command of XX Bomber Command but gives him mission of controlling logistics and responsibility for administration of the XX BC in India; maintaining efficiency of transportation facilities between India and China; making recommendations, with approval of CG XX BC, to theater commander for missions in Southeast Asia-China area.

ITALY—ACMF: In U.S. Fifth Army area, VI Corps is reorganizing and strengthening beachhead to meet threat of enemy counteroffensive. 36th Engrs now hold part of Moletta R line, replacing most of 157th Inf. Night 15–16, 56th Div, which is in process of moving to VI Corps zone from Br 10 Corps sector, takes over left flank from positions of 36th Engrs almost to Albano road. To E, 45th Div holds front line. Br 1st Div is withdrawn for rest and refitting. In II Corps area, relief of 168th Inf is completed by Ind 4th Div. NZ Corps begins offensive to clear heights W of Cassino and establish bridgehead across the Rapido S of Cassino, night 15–16, with preliminary attack by elements of Ind 4th Div for Hill 593. The attack fails. Earlier in day, alternating air and arty bombardment destroy Benedictine Abbey of Monte Cassino, which enemy has been using extensively as a base for offensive operations.

GERMANY—RAF BC makes powerful night attack on Berlin.

16 February

MARSHALL Is.—In preparation for invasion of Eniwetok, TG 58.4 attacks and photographs the atoll. Most buildings are destroyed, 1 of 2 coastal guns on NE corner is wrecked, and Engebi airfield is left temporarily unserviceable. 14 enemy planes are estimated destroyed on the ground.

NEW BRITAIN—Campaign for W New Britain ends successfully as Army and Marine patrols make contact at Itni R.

GREEN Is.—New Zealanders discover enemy force of about 70 on S part of Nissan I.

BURMA—In NCAC area, 66th Regt of Ch 22d Div, which in conjunction with 65th was to have enveloped enemy in Yawngbang area, takes wrong trail and clears village that is mistakenly believed to be Yawngbang.

ITALY—ACMF: In U.S. Fifth Army's VI Corps area, Germans sharply increase air effort in conjunction with all-out offensive against Anzio beachhead, flying some 170-odd sorties, the peak of their performance. Instead of attacking in support of NZ Corps at Cassino as planned, Allied aircraft are diverted to support of Anzio beachhead forces. Enemy attack starts at 0630, after half-hour of arty preparation, with thrusts at various points held by 56th, 45th, and 3d Divs, main effort being against 45th on left flank. 3d Div repels all attacks before Cisterna, but enemy makes limited gains in other sectors at great cost in tanks and personnel. Germans renew attack down Albano road before midnight.

17 February

CAROLINE Is.—TF 58, less the group supporting Eniwetok operation, begins powerful 2-day strikes against Truk in effort to test enemy's strength.

ENIWETOK ATOLL—Adm Hill's Eniwetok Expeditionary Group (TG 51.11) invades Eniwetok Atoll (Operation CATCHPOLE) after preliminary naval gunfire, air bombardment, and minesweeping operations. Troops of VAC Rcn Co make unopposed landings from lagoon side on Canna (Rujoru) and Camellia (Aitsu) Islands, SE of Engebi, at 1318. Quick search reveals no Japanese and arty is brought ashore and registered on Engebi, main objective in N part of atoll. In order to insure safety of arty units, VAC scouts then take several small islands in vicinity of Canna and Camellia without enemy interference. 4th Mar Div scouts, of Co D, 4th Tank Bn, head for Zinnia (Bogon), W of Engebi, to block withdrawal from Engebi; in the darkness land by mistake on a islands below there but work back to Bogon without opposition. First day's objectives are thus secured without any American casualties. In preparation for invasion of Engebi, naval gunfire supplemented by shore-based arty fire is placed on island and underwater demolition teams reconnoiter beaches.

GREEN Is.—As New Zealanders continue elimination of enemy garrison, PT boat base is opened.

ITALY—ACME: In U.S. Fifth Army's VI Corps area, enemy commits his full strength to counteroffensive. Pressing down Albano road, Germans drive deep wedge into center of 45th Div front, between 157th and 179th Regts. Allied aerial, arty, and naval bombardment is helpful in preventing enemy breakthrough. Air effort is the heaviest yet undertaken in support of troops; about 1,100 tons of bombs are dropped. Br 1st Div (− 3d Brig) is given task of holding sector of final beachhead line in Albano road area in order to relieve pressure on 45th Div. 45th is reinf by 2d Bn of 6th Armd Inf. Br 56th Div recovers ground lost to enemy in its sector. Gen Truscott, relieved of command of 3d Div by Brig Gen John W. O'Daniel, becomes deputy commander of VI Corps. In NZ Corps area, elements of Ind 4th Div make night assault in Cassino area and reach crest of Hill 593 but are driven off. Reinforcements move up and occupy heights between Pts 450 and 445. Br 78th Div, having been delayed by deep snow, arrives in NZ Corps zone from Br Eighth Army front. Planned air support is again shifted to Anzio.

USSR—Troops of Second Ukrainian Front complete reduction of enemy pockets W of Cherkassy. Germans suffer some 100,000 casualties in this battle.

18 February

ENIWETOK ATOLL—22d Marines, supported by elements of an Army cannon company, invades Engebi after preparatory bombardment. Enemy offers organized resistance only at S tip of island, which by 1450 is declared secure. Part of the assault force re-embarks for Parry. Scouting parties begin search for enemy on smaller islands between Engebi and S part of the atoll.

CAROLINE Is.—TF 58 completes attacks on Truk during which most airfields are left unserviceable and many aircraft are destroyed on the ground and in the air. Although most of the Japanese Fleet has withdrawn, merchant shipping suffers heavily, some 200,000 tons being destroyed in harbor. Support ships intercept and sink one CL and one DD trying to escape. As a result of this action, it is decided to bypass enemy on Truk.

BISMARCK ARCHIPELAGO—Allied DD's bombard Rabaul, New Britain, and Kavieng, New Ireland.

NEW GUINEA—Maj Gen William H. Gill, 32d Div CG, arrives at Saidor and takes command. Elements of 126th Inf are pushing W in effort to destroy enemy forces bypassing Saidor.

BURMA—Gen Stilwell personally checks on location of missing 66th Regt, Ch 22d Div, and finds it and 3d Bn of 65th near CP of 66th. When main trail from Yawngbang to Lakyen is found, Japanese have withdrawn and the opportunity of trapping them is lost.

ITALY—ACMF: In U.S. Fifth Army's VI Corps area, enemy makes main effort against 45th Div. Although salient is broadened and deepened, no breakthrough can be made. Weather conditions prevent the tremendous air support of the previous day, but arty fire is still employed on large scale. 179th Inf falls back to final beachhead line, where it contains enemy. This is the deepest penetration to be achieved by enemy in Anzio beachhead. In NZ Corps area, Ind 4th Div continues limited attacks for Hill 593, taking part of it and holding against several counterattacks. Other elements of Ind 4th Div attack at 0200 toward Monastery Hill but gain little ground. Jumping off night 17-18, NZ 2d Div's 5th Brig takes Cassino station but loses it by midafternoon, 18th. Action in Cassino area subsides during late February and early March as both sides regroup.

USSR—Soviet forces overrun Staraya Russa.

19 February

ENIWETOK ATOLL—RCT 106, 27th Div, lands on lagoon shore of Eniwetok I., after naval and air bombardment. Two bns go ashore abreast, 1st Bn on right and 3d on left. Pushing through outposts, assault forces reach ocean side of island. 1st Bn then pivots to right to secure arty sites in S part of island. Strong enemy counterattack delays southward attack. 3d Bn, 22d Marines, the reserve force, is committed to strengthen 1st Bn in afternoon. 3d Bn, which was to have conducted holding action, is ordered to N end of island instead and at 1230 starts northward cautiously. Unexpectedly slow progress on Eniwetok forces postponement of attack on Parry I., scheduled for this date.

ITALY—ACMF: In U.S. Fifth Army's VI Corps area, predawn enemy attacks make slight penetration, but further efforts during morning to advance down Albano road are frustrated. TF under Maj Gen Ernest N. Harmon (6th Armd Inf less 2d Bn, 30th Inf, and supporting units) counterattacks strongly after heavy arty and air preparation and gains some 2,000 yards. 169th Brig, Br 56th Div, which has just landed, cannot get ready in time to attack in conjunction with Harmon's TF. British eliminate enemy pocket formed by enemy attack during morning. By this time enemy has committed his reserves in fruitless and costly effort to break through and tide of the battle has turned in favor of VI Corps.

20 February

ENIWETOK ATOLL—While 3d Bn of 106th Inf works slowly northward on Eniwetok I, 3d Bn of 22d Marines, assisted by 1st Bn, 106th Inf, overcomes resistance in S part of island. 1st Bn (−), 106th Inf, conducts mopping up operations on S Eniwetok I. Preparations for assault on Parry, last of the 3 big islands of the atoll, continue. Arty on Eniwetok I., is registered on Parry and supplements other bombardment. 2d Separate Pack Howitzer Bn is emplaced on Japtan I., and joins in bombardment of Parry.

JALUIT ATOLL—Carrier planes of TF 58 pound targets on atoll.

GREEN Is.—Japanese garrison is completely destroyed by this time at cost of 10 Nev, Zealanders and 3 Americans killed.

ROOKE I.—Co B, 1st Marines, withdraws after uneventful stay of 8 days.

ITALY—ACMF: In U.S. Fifth Army's area, VI Corps decisively defeats enemy in center of salient.

This ends Axis efforts to achieve a breakthrough. Enemy is maintaining pressure against flanks of salient while preparing to renew offensive.

GERMANY—USSTAF begins a week of strong air attacks against aircraft factories (ARGUMENT), dispatching powerful force of over 1,000 bombers of Eighth Air Force against a number of plants, most of them in Brunswick=Leipzig area. Several factories are reported severely damaged.

21 February

ENIWETOK ATOLL—Capture of Eniwetok I., is completed, but mopping up continues. 3d Bn, 106th Inf, reaches N tip at 1630. 3d Bn, 22d Marines, is withdrawn in preparation for invasion of Parry, which is still under large-scale preliminary bombardment. Plan for capture of Parry is completed and approved.

NEW BRITAIN—5th Marines is working eastward along N coast from Natamo toward Iboki Plantation. 3d Bn, in overland and amphibious operation, seizes Karai-ai, Japanese supply point near Cape Raoult.

ITALY—ACMF: In U.S. Fifth Army's NZ Corps area, Gen Freyberg issues plan for another assault on Cassino. In VI Corps area, relief of battle-worn 45th Div is begun: elements of Br 56th Div advance under fire, during night 21-22, to replace 2d Bn, 157th Inf, which has been isolated W of Albano road. Enemy is maintaining pressure against shoulders of salient, especially against 180th Inf.

USSR—Soviet forces break into outskirts of Krivoi Rog.

22 February

MARIANAS—Enemy planes make costly and futile efforts to turn back carrier TF 58 (Adm Mitscher) as it is proceeding toward the Marianas.

ENIWETOK ATOLL—1st Bn, 106th Inf, takes responsibility for N part of Eniwetok I., as well as S part 3d Bn is withdrawn as floating reserve for Parry I., operation. 22d Marines starts landing on Parry at 0900 as a 3-day preliminary bombardment draws to a close. During the preparatory phase, Parry receives 9444 tons of naval shells, 245 tons of arty shells, and 99 tons of bombs. 22d Marines lands on lagoon shore and meets lively resistance at once. After pushing across to ocean shore, 1st Bn on left turns N and clears N part of island by 1330; 2d Bn, which is joined by 3d Bn, drives S and by 1930 overwhelms enemy in S part of island, whereupon Parry is declared secure.

SWPA—Japanese appear to be withdrawing aircraft from *Southeast Area*. U.S. Seventh Fleet DD's operating near Rabaul and others bombarding Kavieng meet no air opposition.

BURMA—In NCAC area, Merrill receives oral orders for operation to trap Japanese.

ITALY—ACMF: In U.S. Fifth Army's VI Corps area, 3d and Br 1st Divs relieve elements of 45th Div on left flank of corps.

USSR—Soviet forces take Krivoi Rog, important industrial center in the Ukraine, by storm.

GERMANY—USSTAF employs Fifteenth Air Force as well as Eighth against German aircraft plants. From Italian bases, Fifteenth strikes at Regensburg while Eighth attacks plants at Bernburg, Aschersleben, and Halberstadt.

23 February

MARIANAS—Carrier planes of TF 58 attack enemy positions as planned, damaging shipping and destroying a number of aircraft on the ground and aloft.

ADMIRALTY Is.—Low-level aerial rcn evokes no Japanese reaction.

NEW BRITAIN—80th Fighter Sq moves to Cape Gloucester.

CBI—In NCAC area of Burma, 65th and 66th Regts, Ch 22d Div, jointly occupy Yawngbang, but too late to block retreat of enemy.

11 Army Group: In 15 Corps area of Br Fourteenth Army, Japanese, after determined but fruitless efforts to overrun Ind 7th Div at Sinzweya, begin to withdraw.

ITALY—ACMF: In U.S. Fifth Army area, VI Corps is placed under command of Gen Truscott. Enemy, continuing limited actions, wipes out those elements of Br 56th Div that have replaced 45th Div in region W of Albano road.

USSR—On northern front SW of Lake Ilmen, Soviet forces break into outskirts of Dno.

24 February

SWPA—Gen MacArthur orders Admiralties reconnoitered in force by ground forces not later than 29 February, since aerial rcn of 23d was unopposed.

NEW GUINEA—U.S. patrols from Saidor reach Biliau at Cape Iris.

CBI—In NCAC area of Burma, U.S. 5307th Prov Unit (Marauders), starts from Ningbyen on expedition to harass Japanese in Hukawng Valley, with ultimate goal of capturing Myitkyina airfield in conjunction with Chinese forces.

11 Army Group: Elements of Ind 7th Div, 15 Corps, Br Fourteenth Army, pushing over Ngakyedauk Pass, make contact with elements of Ind 5th Div.

USSR—Troops of Second Baltic Front, assisted by troops of Leningrad Front, overrun Dno. In a new offensive begun a few days ago by First White Russian Front forces, enemy bridgehead on left bank of the Dnieper S of Vitebsk is reduced and Rogachev, N of Zhlobin, is overrun.

GERMANY-AUSTRIA—Continuing offensive against aircraft industry, U.S. Eighth Air Force planes strike hard at Schweinfurt, which RAF BC further damages in night attack, and Gotha. Fifteenth Air Force attacks plants at Steyr for second successive day. Both forces are strongly opposed and engage in intense air battles.

25 February

NEW BRITAIN—2d Bn, 5th Marines, lands at Iboki Plantation without opposition.

CBI—U.S. 5307th Prov Unit, NCAC, makes contact with enemy patrols.

11 Army Group: In Br Fourteenth Army's 15 Corps area, 81st W African Div takes Kyauktaw in Kaladan valley.

ITALY—ACMF: In U.S. Fifth Army's VI Corps area, 18th Brig of Br 1st Div arrives to bolster that badly depleted div. Br 56th Div is also greatly under-strength.

USSR—First echelon of U.S. personnel for FRANTIC Mission enters USSR via PGC.

GERMANY—U.S. Eighth and Fifteenth Air Forces, concluding series of all-out attacks on German aircraft industry, closely co-ordinate their efforts against plants at Regensburg. Eighth Air Force also strikes at Augsburg (target for night attack by RAF BC), Stuttgart, and Fuerth. German Air Force opposition is directed particularly against Fifteenth Air Force, which loses nearly one fifth of its attacking force.

U.K.—Prime Minister Churchill assures President Roosevelt that the upper Burma campaign will not be curtailed for the sake of CULVERIN or any other amphibious operation. The subject of a new SEAC directive is under consideration by Allied planners.

26 February

SWPA—Alternate plans for Operation BREWER (invasion of the Admiralties) are approved. TF BREWER, based on 1st Cav Div under Maj Gen Innis P. Swift, the div CG, is constituted as the occupation force. Elements are to reconnoiter Momote airdrome area in force on 29 February, and if possible remain there. If beachhead is established, rest of the TF will reinforce it. Preinvasion softening by Fifth Air Force is curtailed by unfavorable weather conditions.

U.S.—CCS agree to suspend decision on ANVIL until situation is reviewed on 20 March and give Italian campaign "overriding priority over all existing and future operations in the Mediterranean."

USSR—Moscow reports Dno-Novosokolniki rail line clear of enemy. Soviet forces E of Pskov take Porkhov.

27 February

ADMIRALTY IS.—As reconnaissance force of TF BREWER begins loading on ships of Rear Adm William M. Fechteler's attack group at Oro Bay, PBY lands small ALAMO scouting party on SE coast of Los Negros, where Japanese bivouac area is discovered. Preinvasion air attacks are delivered against Momote and Lorengau and on New Guinea at Wewak and Hansa Bay.

USSR—Moscow announces repulse of German counterattacks against positions on W bank of Styr R in prewar Poland.

28 February

SWPA—BREWER Rcn Force (Brig Gen William C. Chase, 1st Cav Brig CG) sails for Los Negros, Admiralty Is. The scouting party there is withdrawn. Allied planes continue preinvasion attacks against the Admiralties and New Guinea targets.

ALGERIA—At AFHQ, Gen Clark is relieved of responsibility for ANVIL. Davidson continues to head ANVIL planning group (Force 163) pending assignment of new army commander.

ITALY—ACME: Allied commanders meeting at Caserta plan for drive on Rome.

In U.S. Fifth Army's VI Corps area, Germans open another offensive to reduce Anzio beachhead, making preliminary thrust against Br 1st and 56th Divs in region W of Albano road in morning; screen preparations for assault on 3d Div on right flank of corps with smoke in afternoon; begin arty preparation for next phase of assault after nightfall. In II Corps area, 36th Div is relieved on M. Castellone by elements of 88th Div and FEC. By this time only one U.S. bn is in line on southern front.

29 February

SWPA—GHQ issues outline plan for assault on Hollandia, New Guinea.

ADMIRALTY IS.—After preparatory naval and air bombardment, latter being sharply curtailed by heavy overcast, BREWER Rcn Force (2d Sq of 5th Cav, 1st Cav Div, reinf) begins landing on E coast of Los Negros I., at 0817. Momote airfield is occupied against negligible resistance by 0950. Since strength of the BREWER force is inadequate to defend the airfield, beachhead perimeter is withdrawn for night to base of Jamandilai Peninsula. Gen MacArthur and Adm Kinkaid inspect beachhead;

MacArthur orders it held at all costs. Expected counterattack develops after nightfall but is un-coordinated and fails to achieve much although enemy is superior in strength. Intermittent air and naval bombardment of Lorengau airfield on Manus and Seeadler Harbor is begun.

BURMA—11 Army Group: In Br Fourteenth Army area, 15 Corps, after prolonged fighting, completes reopening Ngakyedauk Pass.

ITALY—ACMF: In U.S. Fifth Army's VI Corps area, Germans, after exchange of arty fire, begin main offensive against right flank of VI Corps in effort to force 3d Div back to Mussolini Canal but make little headway. 2d Bn, 30th Inf, counterattacks at 1930 and recovers some of the lost ground.

1 March

ADMIRALTY Is.—On Los Negros, BREWER Rcn Force clears out infiltrators and organizes defenses while awaiting reinforcements. Japanese counterattack in evening but are unable to breach perimeter; continue infiltration attempts throughout night. Gen Krueger orders Gen Swift to seize the entire Admiralties group and begin development of air and naval bases.

BURMA—88th Regt of Ch 30th Div, NCAC, leaves Ledo for Shingbwiyang.

ITALY—ACMF: In U.S. Fifth Army's VI Corps area, enemy continues offensive against Anzio beachhead on a reduced scale. Main effort, in Ponte Rotto area, is contained by 3d Div.

2 March

LOS NEGROS—BREWER Support Force (Col Hugh T. Hoffman), consisting of 1st Sq, 5th Cav, reinf, lands; after preparatory air bombardment, joins with 2d Sq in attack that gains Momote airdrome with ease.

BURMA—In NCAC area, U.S. 5307th Prov Unit assembles across the Tanai. Advance elements of 16th LRP, Br Special Force, pushing southward from Ledo, cross the Chindwin on rafts and dinghies dropped from air near Singkaling Hkamti.

11 Army Group: In Br Fourteenth Army area, 81st W African Div, 15 Corps, captures Apaukwa but later retires to positions NW of Kyauktaw under strong enemy counterattack.

MEDITERRANEAN—Lt Gen Alexander M. Patch is designated by AFHQ as commander of U.S. Seventh Army, which is to conduct ANVIL.

ITALY—ACMF: In U.S. Fifth Army's VI Corps area, 509th Para Inf Bn withdraws to reserve upon relief by 30th Inf, 3d Div. Br troops repel limited enemy attacks on W flank of corps. 9th and 40th Royal Mar Commandos arrive and are assigned to Br 56th Div. MAAF support of Anzio beachhead forces is the heaviest to date. 351 heavy bomber sorties are flown in addition to many by medium, light, and fighter bombers.

3 March

SWPA—Preliminary planning for invasion of Hollandia, New Guinea, is continued at meeting in Brisbane by S and SW Pacific Area representatives. Since Hollandia is not within range of land-based aircraft, carrier support must be obtained. Japanese have air bases within 125 miles of Hollandia in Wakde I: Sarmi area of Dutch New Guinea.

LOS NEGROS—U.S. cavalrymen prepare to meet night counterattack, having learned of enemy's intentions of making strong effort to destroy the beachhead. Enemy attacks as expected, making no attempt to conceal his movements, but all efforts to break through are frustrated and casualties suffered are so severe that no further action on this scale is attempted.

BURMA—In NCAC area, U.S. 5307th Prov Unit moves forward to block road on either side of Walawbum, 3d Bn clearing Lagang Ga, where drop field is established. Japanese begin moving back to Walawbum, believing Americans to be there. 1st Prov Tank Gp (Chinese-American), supported by bn of Ch 65th Regt, 22d Div, reaches Ngam Ga, 5,000 yards NW of Maingkwan; repels enemy attacks during night. 64th Regt is near Ngam Ga in region E of Kamaing road. 66th, on W, is in contact with 65th as it emerges from Taro Plain.

ITALY—ACMF: In U.S. Fifth Army's VI Corps area, 3d Div withstands limited attack in Ponte Rotto sector; later in day counterattacks, regaining some ground. Enemy's final major assault against Anzio bridgehead thus ends.

4 March

GREEN Is.—Fighter field is completed and a bomber field will be late in the month.

LOS NEGROS—2d Sq, 7th Cav, and 82d FA Bn arrive to reinf beachhead. 2d Sq, 7th Cav, replaces 2d Sq, 5th Cav, in line.

CBI—At request of Gen Marshall, Gen Stilwell meets Adm Mountbatten in effort to improve relations with him and iron out major differences of opinion. The meeting is amiable and current problems are settled.

In NCAC area of Burma, 2d Bn, U.S. 5307th Prov Unit, blocks Kamaing road N of Walawbum while 3d Bn, less elements at Lagang Ga, opens fire on Walawbum from heights E of the town. Japanese make unsuccessful attempt to cross river and outflank Americans; open strong attacks against 2d Bn. 3d Bn holding force at Lagang Ga withstands organized enemy attack. 1st Prov Tank Gp, finding that Japanese have withdrawn, advances about 3 miles SE from Ngam Ga to Tsamat Ga, near Maingkwan.

ITALY—ACMF: Enemy forces facing VI Corps of U.S. Fifth Army are ordered to hold present positions and organize them for defense. Lull ensues.

GERMANY—Eighth Air Force delivers the first U.S. bomber attack on Berlin.

5 March

SWPA—Gen MacArthur, hoping to isolate Japanese forces in New Guinea and prevent buildup of enemy air strength in W New Guinea, proposes to JCS that Hansa Bay operation be canceled in favor of invasion of Hollandia during April; recommends that operations against Kavieng, New Ireland, be undertaken as planned on 1 April.

NEW GUINEA—126th Inf (− 2d Bn), 32d Div, and supporting units land without opposition at Yalau Plantation, about 30 miles W of Saidor. Aus forces have broken out of Ramu Valley. Enemy is retreating toward Madang.

LOS NEGROS—Gen Swift arrives and takes command of TF BREWER. 2d Sq of 7th Cav begins attack N across skidway upon relief in line by 2d Sq of 5th Cav.

CBI—In NCAC area, 66th Regt of Ch 22d Div outflanks and captures Maingkwan. 2d Bn, U.S. 5307th Prov Unit, maintains roadblock N of Walawbum under enemy attack until ordered to replenish supplies at Wesu Ga and then joins 3d Bn below Walawbum. 3d Bn continues blocking mission, but I & R Platoon is forced back across river. GALAHAD makes contract with 1st Prov Tank Gp moving southward about midnight and arranges to guide it to GALAHAD lines. Adm Mountbatten asks Gen Giffard, CG 11 Army Group, for details of reinforcement program for central front, where enemy is expected to begin offensive operations.

In Br Fourteenth Army area, Gen Wingate's Special Force of long-range penetration brigs (largely from Br 70th Div but called Ind 3d Div and popularly known as Chindits) begin dropping from air on Japanese lines of communications in central Burma. U.S. engineer personnel drop first, followed by 77th and 111th Brigs. No. 1 Air Commando, USAAF, under Col Cochran, Chindits' own air force, flies Chindits in and drops them on airstrip called BROADWAY, about 50 miles NE of Indaw. Another projected dropping site, PICCADILLY, some 20 miles S of BROADWAY, cannot be used since enemy has blocked it. 15 Corps begins offensive toward Maungdaw-Buthidaung road and Naaf R mouth.

USSR—Red Army opens drive in the Ukraine to destroy enemy in Dnieper bend.

6 March

BOUGAINVILLE—XIV Corps patrols discover large numbers of Japanese near Hill 700, highest ground of Empress Augusta Bay beachhead, indicating an imminent counterattack. By this time perimeter is well organized, but enemy retains control of some hills commanding it.

NEW BRITAIN—In shore-to-shore operation, Combat Team A (reinf 5th Marines, 1st Mar Div) lands about midway up W coast of Willaumez Peninsula, in vicinity of Volupai, for drive on Talasea, though scheduled air preparation is withheld because of unfavorable weather conditions. Swampy terrain and elaborate enemy defenses make progress difficult, but beachhead is expanded to depth of about 2,000 yards.

LOS NEGROS—12th Cav arrives to reinforce beachhead and joins in action at once against retreating enemy. Bridgehead is expanded to include Salami and Porlaka.

BURMA—Generalissimo Chiang Kai-shek orders Gen Stilwell to halt Chinese offensive temporarily because of Japanese offensive on Arakan front. 3d Bn, U.S. 5307th Prov Unit, repels determined attack across river and kills some 400 Japanese. Arrival of 1st Prov Tank Gp and junction between forward elements of Ch 38th Div and GALAHAD forces at Kasan Ga ends Japanese hopes of victory. Commanders of 1st Prov Tank Gp and GALAHAD arrange for co-ordinated assault on Walawbum on 7th. Japanese abandon Walawbum area.

7 March

LOS NEGROS—Elements of 5th Cav take Papitalai. 12th Cav is securing E shore of Seeadler Harbor; 2d Sq crosses to Papitalai Mission and secures beachhead. B-25 makes successful forced landing on Momote airfield.

BURMA—In NCAC area, Merrill decides to withdraw GALAHAD force S to block Kamaing Road since Ch troops are now in Walawbum area. 113th Regt, Ch 38th Div, its rear and right flank protected by 112th, closes in Walawbum area and reestablishes roadblock vacated by GALAHAD. CO of 1st Prov Tank Gp, after unsuccessfully attempting to persuade 113th Regt to join in frontal attack on Walawbum, finds 64th Regt, Ch 22d Div, agreeable to suggestion that they move S together and block Kamaing Road near Walawbum. Two blocks are established—one and two miles W of the Nambyu Stream. Tank forces intercept enemy forces on the march and disperse them.

8 March

BOUGAINVILLE—Japanese arty opens up against beachhead perimeter and Piva strips, destroying 1 B-24 and 3 fighters and damaging 19 aircraft on the ground. Allied bombers, except for small local support force, withdraw to New Georgia. Corps arty counters enemy fire and is augmented by naval gunfire and air attacks. Japanese troops, about 2 cos strong, begin attack on Hill 700, in 37th Div zone, night 8-9.

SWPA—41st Div begins move from Australia to Cape Cretin, New Guinea, where it is to stage for Hollandia.

LOS NEGROS—2d Sq, 7th Cav, secures Lombrum Plantation. This virtually completes capture of Los Negros. Supply vessels enter Seeadler Harbor without drawing enemy fire.

NEW BRITAIN—5th Marines continues toward Talasea almost unopposed, and scouts find this objective free of enemy.

CBI—In NCAC area, Gen Stilwell orders coordinated assault on encircled enemy in Walawbum area, but communication difficulties prevent the various units from complying. On W, Ch 22d Div is fighting near Kumnyen Ford. 113th Regt, Ch 38th Div, is at Wesu Ga. 1st Prov Tank Gp, after constructing ford across Nambyu Stream, enters Walawbum, but lacking infantry support pulls back to Nambyu Stream for night. Communications between Gen Stilwell and GALAHAD are restored late in evening and Merrill is ordered to halt.

11 Army Group: In Br Fourteenth Army area, Japanese launch strong drive on Imphal, in 4 Corps sector, a week before it is anticipated by SEAC, thrusting northward toward Tiddim and Tamu.

9 March

BOUGAINVILLE—Continuing attacks on Hill 700, Japanese drive small salient into line of 145th Inf, 37th Div, on saddle. Efforts to regain the saddle fail. Enemy arty fire shifts to Torokina strip.

LOS NEGROS—2d Cav Brig, reinf, lands at Salami Plantation. First echelon of Allied fighter garrison arrives at Momote airfield.

NEW BRITAIN—Marines secure Talasea airdrome without opposition. Rcn of Garua I., off Talasea, is negative.

BURMA—In NCAC area, elements of Ch 22d and 38th Divs and of 1st Prov Tank Gp enter Walawbum after Japanese have made good their escape. Fall of Walawbum gives Chinese virtual control of Hukawng Valley.

USSR—Soviet forces break into Tarnopol, where prolonged street fighting ensues.

10 March

U.S.—JCS agree on timetable for operations in the Pacific: invasion of Hollandia on 15 April, Marianas on 15 June, Palaus on 15 September, Mindanao on 15 November 1944; Formosa on 15 February 1945

BOUGAINVILLE—Japanese bn begins assault on Hill 260, in Americal Div sector, seizing South Knob from 182d Inf and holding it against counterattack. In co-ordinated counterattack, 145th Inf, 37th Div, narrows enemy salient on saddle of Hill 700 but cannot eliminate it.

ADMIRALTY Is.—On Los Negros additional service elements and aircraft arrive. Allied planes begin series of preinvasion attacks on Manus I.

BURMA—11 Army Group: In Br Fourteenth Army area, the first Japanese reaction to landing of Chindits in central Burma is an air attack on one airfield–Chowringhee.

ITALY—Hq, Allied Central Mediterranean Force is renamed Hq, Allied Armies in Italy (AAI).

USSR—Soviet forces on the offensive SW of Smela capture Uman, German air base.

WESTERN EUROPE—U.S. Ninth Air Force, which has thus far assisted Strategic Air Force, is authorized to concentrate now on preinvasion operations.

11 March

BOUGAINVILLE—As indecisive fighting for Hills 100 and 260 continues, a third Japanese force (2 bns) begins main attack toward Piva airfields, achieving 2 minor penetrations in line of 129th Inf in center of 37th Div sector. In 145th Inf sector, envelopment attack by elements of 148th Inf gains some ground on saddle of Hill 700. 182d Inf, Americal Div, is unable to regain South Knob of Hill 260.

ADMIRALTY Is.—Preliminary operations are begun in preparation for invasion of Manus I. Patrols find Bear Pt, on Manus proper, free of enemy but unsuitable for arty; seize Butjo Luo, N of Manus, where arty is to be emplaced; upon landing on Hauwei I., also N of Manus, are ambushed by enemy and withdraw with difficulty.

BURMA—11 Army Group: In Br Fourteenth Army area, airdrop of Chindits (77th and 111th Brigs) in central Burma is completed. Buthidaung falls to Ind 7th Div, 15 Corps.

ITALY—AAI: In U.S. Fifth Army area, VI Corps issues preliminary plans for resuming offensive in Albano road sector. Relief of Br 56th Div by Br 5th Div of Br 10 Corps is completed.

USSR—Red Army troops pushing down Dnieper R overrun Berislav.

12 March

U.S.—JCS issue directive to Gen MacArthur and Adm Nimitz calling for dual advance to Luzon–Formosa area by February 1945. Emirau, St. Matthias Is., is to be invaded instead of Kavieng, New Ireland; Hollandia, New Guinea, instead of Hansa Bay. Rabaul and Kavieng are to be isolated with minimum forces.

BOUGAINVILLE—Japanese are unable to exploit penetration toward Piva airfields and yield some ground to 129th Inf counterattack. Continuing attack on saddle of Hill 700, 148th Inf restores line of 145th Inf. Counterattack by 182d Inf on Hill 260 gains ground on South Knob but this cannot be held.

ADMIRALTY Is.—After preparatory bombardment, 2d Sq of 7th Cav lands on Hauwei and establishes small beachhead against strong resistance.

BURMA—In NCAC area, U.S. 5307th Prov Unit opens second drive to encircle Japanese *18th Div*. After putting 2 roadblocks behind enemy, Americans are to be relieved by Ch 38th Div. 1st Bn, 5307th, is to cut Kamaing Road S of pass through Jambu Bum ridge line, at junction of Hukawng and Mogaung Valleys; 2d and 3d Bns are to make wide circling movement to E and cut road several miles S of first block.

11 Army Group: In Br Fourteenth Army area, Ind 5th Div of 15 Corps clears enemy from Razabil area.

13 March

U.S.—Main body of U.S. Third Army hq sails from N.Y. for England.

BOUGAINVILLE—129th Inf of 37th Div, in coordinated tank-infantry counterattack, regains all ground lost to enemy in its sector. Japanese withdraw from Hill 100 area. 1st Bn of 132d Inf, Americal Div, tries in vain to recover South Knob of Hill 260.

ADMIRALTY Is.—2d Sq of 7th Cav, with tank assistance, completes clearing Hauwei I. Arty is brought ashore to assist operations against Manus.

BURMA—In NCAC area, 1st Bn of U.S. 5307th Unit reaches Makuy Bum.

Adm Mountbatten orders diversion of 30 aircraft from Hump to fly in Ind 5th Div to central front in 11 Army Group's Br Fourteenth Army area, where enemy is gaining ground. Japanese aircraft attack Chindits' BROADWAY airstrip.

USSR—Troops of Third Ukrainian Front plunge across lower Dnieper; take Kherson.

14 March

POA—Adm Nimitz proposes to make carrier strikes against Wakde-Sarmi and Hollandia before D Day in support of Hollandia operation; promises air support for landings and, for limited period thereafter, for operations ashore. Adm Wilkinson is directed to seize Emirau, St Matthias Is..

BOUGAINVILLE—129th Inf, 37th Div, improves positions during lull. Americans decide to suspend attacks on Hill 260 and to harass enemy there instead.

CBI—11 Army Group: In Br Fourteenth Army area, Ind 17th Div of 4 Corps, having been authorized to withdraw when threatened with isolation, begins withdrawal but finds route to Imphal cut by Japanese.

15 March

BOUGAINVILLE—Japanese renew attack toward Piva airfields, making slight penetration in 129th Inf line, but tank-infantry counterattack restores situation. To strengthen main attack on 129th Inf, Japanese decide to withdraw all but a screening force from Hill 260. Attack is temporarily suspended.

ADMIRALTY Is.—After preliminary arty, naval, and aerial bombardment, 8th Cav of 2d Brig, 1st Cav Div, lands on N coast of Manus I., in vicinity of Lugos Mission. 1st Sq overruns Lugos Mission and starts E along coastal road (No. 3) toward Lorengau airdrome. 2d Sq advances due S to Road No. I, an inland route to Lorengau airdrome. 7th Cav follows 8th ashore and is committed to defense of beachhead. On Los Negros, elements of 5th Cav are driving W in S part of island toward Hill 260.

CBI—In NCAC area, Ch 22d Div, with 64th and 66th Regts in assault, and 1st Prov Tank Gp are now about 3 miles N of Jambu Bum ridge line.

11 Army Group: In Br Fourteenth Army area, Japanese *15th* and *31st Divs* cross the Chindwin in strength at several widely separated points N of Tamu.

ITALY—AAI: Allied planes, in greatest air effort yet made in MTO, level Cassino with 1,200 tons of bombs. At noon, heavy arty barrage opens, and under its cover NZ Corps begins third battle of Cassino. NZ 2d Div begins clearing Cassino, where preparatory bombardment has reduced opposition in N and E part of town, but enemy is clinging stubbornly to rubble in S and W part. Ind 4th Div attacks toward Monastery Hill, making slow progress. 85th Div is arriving to reinforce U.S. Fifth Army.

USSR—Red Army forces break through enemy defenses on right bank of Bug R on wide front.

16 March

ADMIRALTY Is.—On Manus, 8th Cav, with tank support, continues twin drives on Lorengau airdrome. On Road No. 3, 1st Sq pushes about half way across the airstrip against tenacious resistance and is then relieved by 1st Sq of 7th Cav. 2d Sq drives NE along Road No. 1 toward the airfield. Softening fire is placed on enemy positions, night 16-17. On Los Negros, elements of 1st Sq, 12th Cav, make unopposed landing at Chaporowan Pt. 5th Cav forces continue to extend perimeter westward.

NEW BRITAIN—Marines clash with enemy for last time upon entering Kilu, on E coast of Willaumez Peninsula N of Numundo Plantation.

NEW GUINEA—Fifth Air Force, continuing interdiction of waterborne movements to and from Wewak, damages merchant vessel of supply convoy approaching Wewak. Wewak is left virtually undefended as Japanese withdraw fighters to Hollandia to cover the supply convoy.

CBI—Adm Mountbatten confirms verbal order of 13th for diverting Hump aircraft. Gen Stilwell asks Gen Marshall to urge Chinese to cross the Salween in order to relieve pressure on NCAC and Br Fourteenth Army fronts. In Mawlu area of central Burma, 77th Brig, Special Force, successfully engages enemy; blocks communication lines leading to N Burma; establishes airstrip.

ITALY—AAI: In U.S. Fifth Army area, NZ Corps continues stiff battle for Cassino and Monastery Hill, making limited progress.

17 March

BOUGAINVILLE—Renewing attack on 129th Inf, 37th Div, Japanese make small penetration, which is soon eliminated in tank-infantry counterattack. Positions remain static for the next few days while Japanese are assembling their forces from Hills 700 and 260 in preparation for a stronger effort against 129th Inf.

ADMIRALTY Is.—On Manus, 2d Cav Brig, in co-ordinated attack by elements of 7th and 8th Cav, overruns Lorengau airdrome, principal objective on Manus. Extensive preliminary and supporting arty fire assists materially in breaking enemy resistance at the airdrome. Lorengau airdrome is found to be inadequate as a base and another site is later found at Mokerang Plantation. On Los Negros, 1st Sq of 5th Cav seizes Hill 260, where 40-50 Japanese dead are counted.

CBI—Adm Mountbatten asks President Roosevelt and Prime Minister Churchill to ask Chiang Kai-shek for another Chinese div for Burma. In N Burma, elements of Ch 22d Div and some tanks of 1st Prov Tank Gp reach crest of Jambu Bum.

ITALY—AAI: In U.S. Fifth Army area, New Zealand troops of NZ Corps seize RR station in Cassino, where enemy continues to resist tenaciously.

USSR-POLAND—Forces of First Ukrainian Front make progress SW of Rowno, overrunning Dubno, a road and rail junction.

FINLAND—Formally rejects Soviet peace terms.

18 March

SWPA—GHQ and CINCPAC-CINCPOA issue operation plans for invasion of Hollandia. Amphibious force (Commodore Lawrence F. Reifsnider), with Emirau landing force embarked, sails from Guadalcanal for target.

ADMIRALTY Is.—On Manus, 2d Sq of 8th Cav, attacking across Lorengau R, takes Lorengau village with unexpected ease. Enemy must still be cleared from Road 2, which runs S to Rossum via Old Rossum. On Los Negros, 2d Sq of 12th Cav meets sharp resistance while reconnoitering NW of Hill 260 from Papitalai Mission perimeter. Some RAAF fighters are by now based on Momote and others arrive later in month.

NEW GUINEA—Japanese supply convoy reaches Wewak, missing naval bombardment of this objective by Seventh Fleet DD's, night 18-19.

CBI—Adm Mountbatten receives permission from Washington to keep the aircraft diverted from the Hump for one month. Gen Stilwell orders U.S. 5307th Unit to block approaches to the Tanai Valley from the S.

ITALY—AAI: In U.S. Fifth Army area, NZ Corps fights bitterly for limited gains within and near Cassino.

USSR—Red Army units pushing toward Bessarabia reach border with capture of Yampol, on E bank of the Dniester. Forces of First Ukrainian Front, after hard fighting, take Zhmerinka.

GERMANY—In heaviest attack of the war to date, RAF bombers drop over 3,000 tons of bombs on Frankfurt, night 18-19.

19 March

MANUS I.—8th Cav is given task of clearing E end of Manus; 7th is to eliminate main enemy positions on the island along Rossum road.

NEW GUINEA—Fifth Air Force planes destroy the Japanese Wewak convoy as it is moving toward Hollandia.

BURMA—In NCAC area, Fort Hertz detachment seizes Sumprabum. 2d and 3d Bns, U.S. 5307th Unit, less ORANGE Combat Team of 3d Bn, are ordered to block Kamaing Road near Inkangahtawng while ORANGE CT patrols from Janpan area.

11 Army Group: In Br Fourteenth Army area, Ind 5th Div begins movement by rail and air from Arakan sector to central front to assist in repelling enemy there.

ITALY—MATAF issues directive for Operation STRANGLE, to interdict movement of enemy supplies in Italy, calling for destruction of marshaling yards and attacks on rail lines and ports. Communication lines have been targets for bombers since early in the year.

AAI: In U.S. Fifth Army area, NZ Corps is almost halted by determined opposition in Cassino area; during night 19-20, regroups.

USSR—Troops of Second Ukrainian Front reach the Dniester on broad front and cross to W bank. To NW, enemy stronghold of Mogilev-Podolski falls to Soviet forces storming it from NE and SE. In region S of Dubno, Germans yield Kremenets to advancing Red Army.

20 March

ST MATTHIAS IS.—Landing force consisting of 4th Marines under command of Brig Gen Alfred H. Noble, USMC, lands without preparatory bombardment on Emirau I., which is undefended. Seizure of Emirau for use as a light naval and air base concludes series of CARTWHEEL offensives against Rabaul.

NEW IRELAND—In general support of landing on Emirau, U.S. warships bombard Kavieng.

ITALY—AAI: In U.S. Fifth Army area, NZ Corps continues Cassino battle until 23d without making appreciable headway.

BURMA—In NCAC area, leading tanks of 1st Prov Tank Gp reach Hkawnglaw Stream, some 4 miles S of Jambu Bum, but fall back when infantry fails to follow. 112th Regt, reinf, Ch 38th Div, is ordered to envelop Japanese below Kamaing.

USSR—Highway and rail junction of Vinnitsa falls to troops of First Ukrainian Front.

HUNGARY—Germans occupy Hungary.

21 March

LOS NEGROS—5th and 12th Cav begin concerted effort to clear rest of island. While 1st Sq, 5th Cav, and 2d Sq, 12th Cav, attempt to effect junction by drives from Hill 160 and Papitalai Mission, respectively, 12th Cav forces at Lombrum and Chaporowan push inland to cut off westward retreat of enemy.

NEW GUINEA—Patrols of U.S. 32d Div and Aus 7th Div establish contact about 8 miles from Yalau Plantation.

BURMA—After brief halt at Janpan in NCAC area, 2d Bn and elements of 3d, U.S. 5307th Unit, resume southward advance on Inkangahtawng. Elements of 64th Regt, Ch 22d Div, cut Kamaing Road, night 21-22.

MEDITERRANEAN—Gen Wilson, having reviewed the situation as directed on 26 February, recommends that ANVIL be canceled in favor of strong campaign in Italy.

ITALY—AAI: U.S. 34th Div begins to disembark at Anzio.

22 March

CBI—In NCAC area, 1st Bn of 5307th Unit finds Japanese blocking trails, so is forced to cut another.

11 Army Group: In Br Fourteenth Army area, additional elements of Wingate's Special Force are being flown to central Burma. Japanese offensive into India in 4 Corps sector has reached serious proportions.

U.K.—British Chiefs of Staff recommend that plans for ANVIL be dropped. This would insure a greater effort in Italy. Americans disagree, holding out firmly for ANVIL despite problems of acquiring sufficient shipping for it.

USSR—Pervomaisk falls to Soviet forces.

23 March

BOUGAINVILLE—Japanese begin general assault against 129th Inf, 37th Div, after dark. Counterpreparation by U.S. arty makes attack largely ineffective, but enemy achieves small penetration.

SWPA—Alamo Force FO 12 gives Gen Eichelberger's I Corps responsibility for ground operations at Hollandia. The corps is designated TF RECKLESS and is to include 24th and 41st Divs, latter less one RCT. TF PERSECUTION is organized under Brig Gen Jens A. Doe, ADC first Div, to establish air base at Aitape.

ST MATTHIAS IS.—U.S. DD's bombard Eloaue, small island off SW coast of Mussau, where patrol from Emirau has discovered that Japanese are operating small seaplane base.

BURMA—In NCAC area, U.S. forces of 5307th Unit arrive in position to block Kamaing Road in Inkangahtawng, although 1st Bn is still far behind. Patrols find enemy entrenched at Inkangahtawng. Flanking forces of 64th Inf, Ch 22d Div, join 66th Inf.

ITALY—AAI: In U.S. Fifth Army area, NZ Corps breaks off attack on Cassino. Germans have been forced into narrow zone in W edge, of the town but still hold positions commanding Cassino, including the Monastery.

USSR—Troops of First Ukrainian Front achieve breakthrough E of Tarnopol and almost complete circle around Tarnopol.

24 March

BOUGAINVILLE—Japanese try in vain to gain further ground and are decisively defeated during counterattack. This is the last enemy offensive in the Solomons, although skirmishes continue sporadically during April and May. Beachhead perimeter is subsequently expanded slightly.

Los Negros—1st Sq, 5th Cav, and 2d Sq, 12th, begin co-ordinated westward attack abreast from Hill 260 after brief arty preparation; assisted by concentrated fire on enemy positions, succeed in gaining objective heights. This is the last big action on Los Negros, although considerable time is required to mop up isolated parties.

CBI—In NCAC area, U.S. 5307th Unit attempts to envelop Inkangahtawng but finds it too strongly held. Japanese strongly oppose efforts to block Kamaing Road in this region. Learning that enemy force is moving to outflank them, 2d Bn troops withdraw to Manpin area. 3d Bn then pulls back to Ngahgahtawng to bivouac.

11 Army Group: In Br Fourteenth Army area, Maj Gen O. C. Wingate, commander of Special Force (Ind 3d Div), is killed in plane crash while flying from Imphal to Lalaghat. Brig W. D. A. Lentaigne succeeds him as commander of Chindits. To avert enemy threat on central front, preparations are being made to bring in 33 Corps and commit it in Dimapur=Kohima area, to N of 4 Corps. Br 2d Div starts to this region.

MTO-ETO—It is decided not to mount ANVIL and OVERLORD simultaneously as planned. ANVIL target date is tentatively set at 10 July and is later postponed to 15 August.

25 March

U.S.—JCS approve the liquidation of South Pacific (SOPAC) forces and transfer of units to SWPA and POA. XIV Corps hq and corps troops and 25th, 37th, 40th, 43d, 93d, and Americal Divs are transferred to SWPA. I Marine Amphibious Corps and corps troops and 1st and 3d Mar Divs are given to POA. SWPA receives Thirteenth Air Force as well as Navy and Marine air units and reinforcements for its Seventh Fleet.

MANUS Is.—Organized fighting ends as 2d Cav Brig completes clearing No. 2 Road to Rossum. Air strikes, arty, bazookas, flame throwers, and tanks are employed during the battle. Small enemy groups remain to be located and eliminated.

NEW GUINEA—Japanese withdraw their air headquarters from Wewak to Hollandia.

USSR—Proskurov falls to troops of First Ukrainian Front.

26 March

NEW BRITAIN—Allied PT base is established at Talasea.

BURMA—In NCAC area, Japanese moving N from Kamaing are harassed by aircraft. 2d and elements of 3d Bn, U.S. 5307th Unit, start from Manpin toward Nhpum Ga to block enemy force moving N. I and R Platoon delays Japanese at points between Manpin and Nhpum Ga. 65th Regt, Ch 22d Div, having moved forward from reserve positions and been reinf by elements of 66th and 64th Regts, continues drive on Shaduzup.

ITALY—AAI: Extensive regrouping is in progress and inter-army boundary is redefined. U.S. Fifth Army retains control of Br 10 Corps. Br Eighth Army takes over sectors of FEC and NZ Corps. NZ Corps is disbanded and its components pass to command of 13 Corps, which then consists of 2d NZ, Ind 4th, 3d Algerian, Br 78th, and Br 4th Divs. Pol 2 Corps takes responsibility for sector of 2d Moroccan Div. 5 Corps assumes charge of area from Palena to Adriatic coast.

USSR—Forces of Second Ukrainian Front reach Prut R on 53-mile front. Enemy troops in Kamenets-Podolsk and Tarnopol are enveloped.

ETO—Gen Eisenhower approves plan to isolate invasion area by air attacks on transportation system, particularly rail centers and facilities.

27 March

BOUGAINVILLE—Japanese begin withdrawal from Empress Augusta Bay area.

SWPA—FO 1 of TF RECKLESS specifies Humboldt Bay landing areas for Hollandia operation.

CBI—In NCAC area, main body of 2d and 3d Bns, U.S. 5307th Unit, arrive at Auche. 1st Bn and Ch 113th Regt take up positions along Nam Kawng Chaung, night 27-28.

11 Army Group: In Br Fourteenth Army area, 4 Corps is strengthened at Imphal by arrival of 2 brigs of Ind 5th Div from Arakan.

USSR—Soviet forces overrun Kamenets-Podolsk.

28 March

BOUGAINVILLE—Elements of 93d Div—RCT 25 and 1st Bn of 24th Inf—arrive at Empress Augusta Bay for combat duty. Hill 260 is found to be abandoned by enemy.

ADMIRALTY Is.—1st Sq, 5th Cav, occupies Loniu Village, Los Negros. Widespread patrolling on both Los Negros and Manus evokes little opposition.

BURMA—In NCAC area, 2d and 3d Bns of U.S. 5307th Unit reach Nhpum Ga area and establish defensive positions, 2d Bn at Nhpum Ga and 3d at Hsamshingyang. Crossing river before dawn, 1st Bn surprises enemy in camp and blocks Kamaing Road below Shaduzup; repels enemy efforts to reduce the block. Ch 113th Regt relieves Americans at the block. Japanese in this region are now caught between Ch 22d Div, disposed 4-5 miles to N, and Ch 38th Div. Japanese counterattack Ch 22d Div near Shaduzup 5 times.

ITALY—AAI: U.S. IV Corps hq, under Maj Gen Willis D. Crittenberger, arrives in Italy.

In U.S. Fifth Army's VI Corps area, 34th Div arrives at Anzio beachhead and relieves 3d Div before Cisterna.

USSR—Forces of Third Ukrainian Front overrun Nikolaev.

29 March

CBI—Gen Stilwell, conferring with Chiang Kai-shek on 28th and 29th, asks for reinforcements and is promised Ch 50th Div. A few days later Chiang Kai-shek offers Ch 14th Div.

In NCAC area of Burma, 2d Bn of 65th Regt, Ch 22d Div, enters Shaduzup. Japanese are exerting pressure against 2d Bn, U.S. 5307th Unit, at Nhpum Ga.

11 Army Group: In 4 Corps area of Br Fourteenth Army, Japanese cut Imphal-Kohima road near Kohima. Ind 50th Para Brig, which has been delaying enemy at Ukhrul, begins to retire toward Imphal. Kohima garrison is now reinforced by 161st Brig, Ind 5th Div.

ITALY—AAI: In U.S. Fifth Army area, Br 10 Corps is relieved in Garigliano sector by FEC and II Corps, latter on left.

MEDITERRANEAN—AFHQ submits outline plan for ANVIL.

30 March

CAROLINE Is.—TF 58 begins 3-day attack on targets in W Carolines in order to support coming invasion of Hollandia and to destroy enemy air and surface units.

BOUGAINVILLE—93d Div troops on island are attached to Americal Div and enter lines to gain experience.

ADMIRALTY Is.—As mopping up on Los Negros and Manus continues, operations are begun against outlying islands. After preparatory bombardment of Pityilu, 3 miles N of Lugos Mission, 1st Sq, reinf, of 7th Cav lands without opposition and virtually destroys the small Japanese garrison while searching most of the island.

NEW GUINEA—Fifth Air Force bombers, with long-range fighter escort, make first daylight attack on Hollandia.

BURMA—In NCAC area, 2d Bn of U.S. 5307th Unit withstands further enemy attacks at Nhpum Ga. 1st Bn starts to Janpan. 113th Regt, Ch 38th Div, makes contact with Ch 22d Div.

USSR—Cernauti (Bessarabia) falls to Soviet forces of First Ukrainian Front.

GERMANY—RAF BC suffers such heavy losses during night attack on Nuremberg, 30-31, that heavy night penetration is suspended temporarily. Of about 800 bombers dispatched, almost 100 are lost.

31 March

ADMIRALTY Is.—1st Sq, 7th Cav, completes mop-up of Pityilu.

NEW GUINEA—Fifth Air Force again strikes at Hollandia, achieving excellent results.

CBI—In NCAC area of Burma, 2d Bn of U.S. 5307th Unit becomes isolated as Japanese cut trail to Hsamshingyang. Merrill is flown out because of ill health.

11 Army Group: In 4 Corps area of Br Fourteenth Army, Japanese are blocking Ukhrul-Imphal road and besieging Imphal garrison, which must be supplied by air. In 15 Corps area, Br 36th Div takes tunnels on Maungdaw-Buthidaung road, but Japanese still hold part of the road.

ITALY—AAI: U.S. Fifth Army releases Br 10 Corps but retains Br 1st and 5th Divs at Anzio.

USSR—Red Army forces pushing toward Odessa take part of Ochakov, SW of Nikolaev.

1 April

CAROLINE Is.—TF 58 concludes 3-day action against W Carolines, having made air attacks on the Palaus, Yap, Ulithi, Ngulu, and Woleai. During the attacks, Japanese lose about 150 aircraft either on the ground or in the air. Enemy shipping also suffers heavily: 2 DD's, 4 escort vessels, and 104,000 tons of merchant or naval auxiliary shipping are sunk; many other vessels are damaged. Airfields and shore installations are hit. Main channel into Palau fleet anchorage is blocked by mines. The threat of Japanese naval interference from the Palaus to the approaching Hollandia operation is thus removed. TF 58 loses 20 planes.

SWPA—Naval plans for Hollandia operation are issued.

ADMIRALTY Is.—12th Cav begins operations against small islands off Mokerang. After preliminary bombardment of Koruniat I., 1st Sq moves from Mokerang Pt to the island in canoes. Finding no Japanese there, the force proceeds to Ndrilo I., which is also free of enemy.

BURMA—In NCAC area, Gen Stilwell asks that 50th and 14th Ch Divs be flown in over the Hump. ORANGE CT of U.S. 5307th Unit attacks to reopen Hsamshingyang-Nhpum Ga road but is unable to break through to 2d Bn.

ITALY—AAI: In U.S. Fifth Army area, 509th Para Inf Bn leaves Anzio beachhead. 504th Para Inf has already left there to rejoin 82d A/B Div.

2 April

NEW GUINEA—When weather conditions prevent attack on Hollandia, Fifth Air Force bombers strike instead at Hansa Bay.

BURMA—In NCAC area, Nhpum Ga remains under siege despite further efforts of 3d Bn, U.S. 5307th Unit, to break through to 2d Bn. 2 field pieces are dropped at Hsamshingyang airstrip and soon registered on enemy.

USSR—Red troops cross Prut R east of Cernauti and occupy Gertza.

3 April

U.S.—JCS directive to CBI theater stresses importance of capture of Myitkyina.

ADMIRALTY Is.—2d Sq, 12th Cav, lands without opposition on Rambutyo I., after preparatory bombardment and begins search for the few Japanese concealed there.

NEW GUINEA—Fifth Air Force, in its heaviest attack to date, again pounds Hollandia. During period 30 March to date, over 300 Japanese planes have been destroyed or damaged, most of them on the ground. Enemy air opposition from Hollandia is insignificant after this time.

CBI—Gen Stilwell, meeting at Jorhat with Adm Mountbatten and Gen Slim, learns that he may continue his N Burma campaign despite grave situation in Kohima area. It is agreed that 2 brigs of Ind 3d Div (Chindits) will assist his drive on Mogaung and Myitkyina by harassing enemy lines of communication.

11 Army Group: In Br Fourteenth Army area, skeleton staff of 33 Corps (Lt Gen Sir Montagu Stopford) arrives at Jorhat. Corps is to assist in stemming enemy offensive.

In NCAC area of Burma, efforts of 2d and 3d Bns, U.S. 5307th Unit, to open Hsamshingyang-Nhpum Ga road are again futile, although supported by air and arty. 1st Bn is directed to move as quickly as possible to Hsamshingyang.

4 April

CBI—In NCAC area, 3d Bn of U.S. 5307th Unit, making all-out effort to reach Nhpum Ga, gets to within 1,000 yards of objective. Aircraft and arty closely support attack. Feints are made to divert enemy from main battle. 2d Bn withstands very strong enemy attack against its Nhpum Ga perimeter. Ch reinforcements—forward elements of 1st Bn, 112th Regt, 38th Div—arrive at Hsamshingyang and are disposed to guard trail junction. Ch 114th Regt is given mission originally assigned to 112th of blocking road below Kamaing. Ch 22d Div's 64th Regt is to envelop left flank of enemy while 65th and 66th Regts conduct holding action in Shaduzup area.

11 Army Group: In Br Fourteenth Army area, air movement of 14th Brig, Ind 3d Div, to central Burma (ABERDEEN, in Manhton area) is completed. In 4 Corps area, Japanese begin assault on Kohima in force. 161st Inf of Ind 5th Div, which has been withdrawn from Kohima to Dimapur because of threat to latter, is ordered back to Kohima, now garrisoned by a heterogeneous force.

5 April

CBI—In NCAC area of Burma, further efforts by 3d Bn, U.S. 5307th Unit, to break through to Nhpum Ga are vain; beleaguered 2d Bn checks Japanese efforts to reduce perimeter.

11 Army Group: In Br Fourteenth Army area, 33 Corps is concentrating around Dimapur. Advance elements of Br 2d Div arrive there.

RUMANIA—U.S. Fifteenth Air Force drops 588 tons of bombs on Ploesti rail targets. Although not admitted as such, this is actually the beginning of an oil offensive in which U.S. Eighth Air Force joins, starting on 12 May.

6 April

NEW GUINEA—As a result of Fifth Air Force attacks on Hollandia, Japanese by now have only 25 serviceable planes there.

CBI—In NCAC area, ORANGE CT of 3d Bn, U.S. 5307th Unit, continues attack toward Nhpum Ga, gaining 200 yards.

11 Army Group: In Br Fourteenth Army area, Ind 7th Div begins air movement from Arakan front to Dimapur. Two Ind 7th Div brigs are to join 33 Corps at Dimapur and the third brig will join 4 Corps at Imphal. Leading elements of 161st Brig, Ind 5th Div, enter Kohima, but rest of regt is unable to break through enemy forces investing the town.

7 April

CBI—In NCAC area of Burma, 1st Bn of U.S. 5307th Unit completes difficult forced march to Hsamshingyang and prepares to join in attack toward Nhpum Ga. Elements of 3d Bn continue efforts to reach Nhpum Ga but make little progress.

11 Army Group: In 33 Corps sector of Br Fourteenth Army area, Japanese make deeper inroads at Kohima and seize main water supply. In 4 Corps area, Ind 17th Div completes northward drive along

Tiddim Road to Imphal and subsequently concentrates N of that town. Ind 23d Div troops have assisted 17th during later stages of drive to Imphal.

8 April

NEW GUINEA—Final rehearsals for Hollandia operation are begun at Taupota Bay by 24th Div and near Lae by 41st Div.

ADMIRALTY Is.—Forward echelon of XIII Bomber Command hq moves to Los Negros.

BURMA—In NCAC area, frontal and flanking attacks by 3d Bn and 250 men of 1st Bn, U.S. 5307th Unit, toward Nhpum Ga make little headway.

USSR—Soviet forces open new offensive in the Crimea.

9 April

ST. MATTHIAS Is.—On Emirau, Island Commander, Maj Gen James Moore, USMC, assumes command.

ADMIRALTY Is.—1st Sq, 12th Cav, makes unopposed landing on Pak I., and begins search for enemy stragglers. This completes action in the Admiralties of 1st Brig Combat Team. 2d Brig continues search for enemy remnants on Manus. On Los Negros, radio station and message center are established at Salami Plantation.

CBI—In NCAC area of Burma, U.S. 5307th Unit finds that Japanese have withdrawn from Nhpum Ga. No effort is made to follow, since forward movement beyond Nhpum Ga is not desirable at this time. During action at Inkangahtawng and siege of Nhpum Ga, 5307th has suffered 59 men killed and 314 wounded. Total of 379 must be evacuated because of wounds or illness.

11 Army Group: In Br Fourteenth Army area, envelopment of 4 Corps at Imphal is completed as Japanese cut E-W trail from Bishenpur to Silchar. 4 Corps must now be supplied entirely by air, a difficult task that is to become even harder with arrival of monsoon season.

10 April

NEW GUINEA—Hollandia assault forces (TF RECKLESS) complete rehearsals and being loading for movement to target.

CBI—11 Army Group: In 33 Corps sector of Br Fourteenth Army area, Br 2d Div begins operations to clear road to Kohima.

ITALY—AAI: In Fifth Army area, Germans abandon plans for attack on Anzio. 85th Div begins moving into Allied line W of Minturno.

USSR—Odessa, important Black Sea port, falls to troops of Third Ukrainian Front.

11 April

ST. MATTHIAS Is.—147th Inf assumes garrison duties on Emirau.

ADMIRALTY Is.—Gen Kenney establishes Thirteenth Air Task Force (Maj Gen St. Clair Streett) under operational control of ADVON Fifth Air Force pending arrival of Thirteenth Air Force hq in the Admiralties.

USSR—Soviet forces in the Crimea break through enemy defenses on Kerch Peninsula to seize Kerch.

12 April

ADMIRALTY Is.—Pak I., is now free of Japanese. Mop-up of Manus continues.

CBI—In NCAC area of Burma, 114th Regt of Ch 38th Div relieves 113th in line. To E, 112th is holding salient about Nhpum Ga.

11 Army Groups: In Br Fourteenth Army area air movement of another long-range penetration column, W African 3d Brig, Ind 3d Div, to central Burma is completed. 33 Corps, responsible for Kohima area, is being reinf as rapidly as possible. 23d Brig, Ind 3d Div, is relieved of task of guarding Jorhat RR and ordered S to assist Br 2d Div and cut communication lines W of the Chindwin. In 4 Corps area, elements of Ind 20th Div relieve detachment of Ind 23d Div on Tiddim Road S of Imphal.

13 April

NEW GUINEA—Elements of Aus 15th Brig, under command of Aus 11th Div, enter Bogadjim without opposition.

WESTERN EUROPE—Tactical air forces (U.S. Ninth and Br 2d) begin offensive against Normandy coastal batteries.

14 April

CBI—Chinese agree to undertake offensive across the Salween with Y=Force. Adm Mountbatten recommends to British Chiefs of Staff that N Burma campaign be confined to capture of Myitkyina.

ETO—Gen Eisenhower receives operational control of British and U.S. strategic air forces; CCS have previously had this responsibility.

15 April

U.S.—Northwest Sea Frontier (Oregon and Washington) and Alaska Sector are abolished, former coming under Western Sea Frontier (Vice Adm David W. Bagley) and latter becoming Alaskan Sea Frontier (Adm Fletcher). 17th Naval District (Territory of Alaska and its waters) is established.

[16-22 APRIL 1944]

CBI—Hq, Supreme Allied Commander South East Asia, is transferred from New Delhi, India, to Kandy, Ceylon. Gen Chennault warns Generalissimo Chiang Kai-shek to expect an enemy air offensive in China. The Generalissimo urges Gen Stilwell to advance cautiously in Mogaung Valley. Airlift of Ch 50th Div to Maingkwan is almost completed. Ch 14th Div is to follow soon.

MEDITERRANEAN—Gen Wilson (SACMED) learns that Gen Jean de Lattre de Tassigny will command French forces in ANVIL.

ITALY—AAI: Br Eighth Army is regrouping for spring offensive. Br 10 Corps relieves Pol 2 Corps in N sector.

POLAND—Tarnopol falls to Soviet forces of First Ukrainian Front.

ETO—AEAF issues over-all air plan for Operation NEPTUNE. Major plans are about completed by this time, although planning continues until late in May.

16 April

SWPA—TF RECKLESS begins voyage to Hollandia via Admiralty Is.

USSR—Soviet Independent Maritime Army captures Yalta, in the Crimea.

17 April

ADMIRALTY Is.—2d Sq, 7th Cav, having completed mop up of its assigned portion of Manus I., begins movement to Hauwei I.

CBI—Gen Stilwell orders Gen Chennault to defend B-29 bases at Cheng-tu as a primary mission.

Japanese open their last major offensive against China, crossing a div over Yellow R in Honan Province at night to assembly areas along the river.

In NCAC area of Burma, Chinese make progress down Mogaung Valley where Japanese have abandoned Warazup.

11 Army Group: In Br Fourteenth Army area, 4 Corps is going over to the offensive in Imphal area.

ETO—Directive by Gen Eisenhower to strategic air forces gives German Air Force top priority on target list. Attacks on oil plants will have twofold purpose of getting German Air Force into the air and diminishing oil supply.

18 April

CAROLINE Is.—B-24's of 5th Bombardment Gp, Thirteenth Air Force, begin series of attacks on Woleai from Momote airfield, Los Negros, in preparation for landings on Hollandia.

NEW GUINEA—TF PERSECUTION begins voyage to Aitape from Finschhafen and joins TF RECKLESS vessels moving toward the Admiralties.

[187]

USSR—Red Army continues to gain ground in the Crimea, where Balaklava is overrun.

19 April

CHINA—Two Japanese divs start S along Peiping-Hankow RR in Honan Province.

MEDITERRANEAN—Gen Wilson receives directive from CCS to launch an offensive in Italy in support of OVERLORD.

20 April

SWPA—Hollandia assault forces rendezvous near the Admiralties and begin last leg of journey to target.

ADMIRALTY Is.—Thirteenth Air Force bombardment sq equipped for night attacks completes fly-in to Momote airfield.

CBI—Adm Mountbatten returns 10 of 20 aircraft borrowed from the Hump route; the rest are returned after repairs are made.

In NCAC area, Ch 38th Div, pressing S in Mogaung Valley toward Kamaing, overruns Hill 1725, S of Tingring, which enemy has defended tenaciously in order to cover withdrawal of main forces to line Wala-Malakawng.

11 Army Group: In 33 Corps sector of Br Fourteenth Army area, Br 2d Div, advancing along Dimapur-Kohima road, reaches besieged Kohima garrison, but enemy retains Kohima and is still blocking road from there to Imphal.

ITALY—AAI: Fr 1st Motorized Div begins landing at Naples and is followed by other Fr forces in early May.

21 April

ADMIRALTY Is.—Seabees and aviation engineers complete airstrip at Mokerang Plantation, Manus I.

NEW GUINEA—As assault convoys approach Hollandia, carrier planes of TF 58 join land-based planes in smashing attacks on airfields in this region. Air attacks are supplemented by naval gunfire.

BURMA—In NCAC area, TF called END RUN is organized for drive on Myitkyina, combining Ch troops with Americans of depleted GALAHAD Force. Three combat teams are formed: K (89th Regt, Ch 30th Div, and 3d Bn of GALAHAD); H (150th Regt, Ch 50th Div; 1st Bn of GALAHAD; 3d Co; Animal Transport Regt; battery of Ch 22d Div arty); M (2d Bn of GALAHAD plus 300 Kachins). Surgical units are to accompany the force.

ETO—U.S. Eighth Air Force offensive against German oil targets, scheduled to begin on this date, is canceled because of weather conditions.

22 April

NEW GUINEA—TF's RECKLESS and PERSECUTION, assisted by aircraft of TF 58 and gunfire of

U.S. and Aus naval vessels, make unopposed landings on N coast. TF RECKLESS begins pincers operation against Hollandia region of Dutch New Guinea with landings at Tanahmerah and Humboldt Bays. 24th Div (−) quickly secures beachhead at Tanahmerah Bay, where 19th Inf (−) and 21st Inf (−) land on N at Beach Red 2 and 1st Bn, 21st Inf, goes ashore on Red 1, in Dépapré Bay. Red 2, from which principal effort was to have been made, is found to be extremely narrow, backed by swamp, and lacking a road to connect it with Red 1. Supplies must be transshipped to Red 1. 21st Inf units begin movement, Co I advancing overland, from Red 2 to Red 1, leaving 19th Inf to hold Red 2. From Red 1, 1st Bn of 21st Inf starts along trail to Lake Sentani and airfields; after reaching Jangkena, about 8 miles inland, pulls back to Kantome for night. Enemy efforts to cut the trail, night 22-23, are futile. Meanwhile, 41st Div (−) lands at Humboldt Bay. 162d Inf goes ashore on N sandspit between Humboldt and Jautefa Bays on Beaches White 1 and 2, former on N. From White 1, 2d and 3d Bns push inland to Hollandia-Pim track and northward to ridge overlooking Hollandia. Reinf rifle platoon of Co A, 162d Inf, lands on White 2 and moves S to Cape Pie, securing northern spit for landing of Cos K and L of 186th Inf. Because of mangrove swamp there, 186th Inf force proceeds by water between the sandspits to Beach White 4, on coast of Jautefa Bay N of Pim; takes Leimok Hill, Pim, and Suikerbrood Hill. Co I, 186th Inf, lands on S sandspit (Beach White 3); secures Cape Tjeweri at N tip and moves SE toward Hollekang. TF PERSECUTION, based on RCT 163, 41st Div, begins subsidiary operation to gain base at Aitape, E of Hollandia. Landing at Wapil, the force easily secures beachhead, which includes Tadji airfields; outposts E flank at mouth of Nigia R and extends W flank to Pro Mission, beyond Waitanan Creek. Base development is begun at once.

NEW BRITAIN—1st Mar Div patrol clashes with enemy for last time.

23 April

ADMIRALTY IS.—2d Sq, 12th Cav, turns over responsibility for Rambutyo I. to native police.

NEW GUINEA—In Hollandia area, 21st Inf advances beyond Sabron to small stream, where first organized resistance develops; pulls back to Sabron. Since logistics problem is becoming acute, forward movement of the regt is halted. Div reserve (2d Bn, 19th Inf) and AT and Cannon Cos of 19th and 21st Regts move to Dépapré to assist in getting supplies inland. Beaches are so congested that D+2 convoy is diverted to Humboldt Bay, where main effort must now be made. In Humboldt Bay sector, 2d and 3d Bns of 162d Inf, 41st Div, take Hollandia without opposition and heights about the town. 186th Inf advances along axis Pim-Lake Sentani; flanking elements on right clash with enemy. In Aitape area, 1st and 2d Bns of 163d Inf push W to Raihu R, 2d Bn using coastal route. 1st Bn overruns uncompleted Tadji West Strip. RCT 127 (less 1st Bn and Cos F and G), 32d Div, lands and relieves 3d Bn, 163d Inf, on E flank of beachhead. 3d Bn then moves to Tadji Plantation. Cos F and G, RCT 127, land on Tumleo and Seleo Islands and easily secure both.

CBI—Adm Mountbatten's AXIOM Mission returns to New Delhi without having gained acceptance of CULVERIN.

In NCAC area of Burma, 1st Bn of 112th Regt, Ch 38th Div, moves from Tategahtawng to relieve END RUN Force, now within a mile of Manpin. Final attack order calls for Ch 22d Div to make main effort while 112th Regt blocks from S. Subsequent efforts of Chinese to change this plan are rejected by Gen Stilwell.

24 April

U.S.—War Department Operations Division's Strategy Section states, "collapse of Japan can be assured only by invasion of Japan proper."

NEW GUINEA—U. S. 31st Div arrives at Oro Bay. Aus forces enter Madang, from which enemy has withdrawn. Markham-Ramu trough and Huon Peninsula are now secure. In Hollandia area, Tanahmerah Bay elements of TF RECKLESS continue to be beset with supply problems and confine activities to patrolling and moving supplies forward. 1st Bn, 19th Inf, moves forward from Red 2 to assist in carrying supplies inland. Scheduled airdrop of supplies is canceled because of weather conditions. In Humboldt Bay sector, 186th Inf advances to shore of Lake Sentani and seizes jetty. TF RECKLESS reserve—34th Inf, 24th Div—is transferred from Tanahmerah Bay to Humboldt Bay. In Aitape area, 163d Inf secures Aitape and Rohn Pt. After Aus engineers complete work on Tadji fighter strip, 25 P-40's of RAAF land there.

BURMA—In NCAC area, 1st and 3d Marauder Bns start to Naubum in preparation for drive on Myitkyina. 2d Bn is patrolling N of Hsamshingyang.

25 April

NEW BRITAIN—1st Mar Div turns over responsibility for island to 40th Inf Div.

NEW GUINEA—In Hollandia area, 21st Inf renews attack from Sabron although supply situation is still difficult and weather conditions again prevent airdrop. Additional forces are assigned to supply carrying. 186th Inf continues W from Humboldt Bay sector to Nefaar, some elements moving overland and others across Lake Sentani. In Aitape area, active patrolling is conducted along coast and inland. Co G, 127th Inf, occupies Ali I. Balance of an RAAF wing arrives at Tadji airfield.

26 April

NEW GUINEA—Elements of Aus 5th Div occupy Alexishafen. In Hollandia area 21st Inf, against negligible opposition, overruns Hollandia airdrome; makes patrol contact with Humboldt Bay force between Weversdorp and the airdrome. Supply situation improves as clearing weather permits airdrops. 186th Inf easily secures Cyclops and Sentani airdromes. Junction of patrols of 21st and 186th Regts closes pincers on enemy in Hollandia area. In Aitape area, 1st Bn of 127th Inf arrives.

ETO—5 naval assault forces for Normandy invasion complete assembly. One, Force U, conducts rehearsal exercise (TIGER), during which it suffers heavy damage from German E-boat attacks. Rehearsals are conducted by the other TF's in early May.

27 April

NEW GUINEA—Gen MacArthur sets target date for next offensive, Wakde-Sarmi, as 15 May. Plans are being made for invasion of Biak in early June. In Hollandia area, Cyclops airdrome is ready for limited use. Elements of 186th Inf reconnoiter two islands in Lake Sentani as well as N shore of the lake. 162d Inf seizes Cape Soeadja, at NW limits of Humboldt Bay.

CBI—Final arrangements are made for drive on Myitkyina by Marauders and for offensive across the Salween by Y=Force. Gen Merrill, who has recovered from his illness, will lead the Marauders. Chiang Kai-shek arranges details for assault across the Salween with Gen Wei Li-huang by telephone. Gen Wei has replaced Gen Chen Cheng as Ch commander of Yunnan forces.

11 Army Group: In Br Fourteenth Army area, 4 Corps is desperately resisting enemy efforts to break through to Imphal before the monsoon rains begin. Japanese hold 6 miles of trail from Imphal to Silchar. Ind 17th Div has moved S from concentration area N of Imphal and, together with elements of Ind 20th Div, is attempting to halt enemy's advance.

ITALY—AAI: In Br Eighth Army area, Pol 2 Corps takes command of M. Cassino sector from 13 Corps.

FRANCE—U.S. Eighth Air Force joins in air offensive against transportation, striking at Blainville and Châlons-sur-Marne.

28 April

U.S.—Secretary of Navy Frank Knox dies.

NEW GUINEA—First organized resistance in Aitape sector is met by outpost of 3d Bn, 163d Inf, at Kamti village. Some 200 Japanese are estimated to be in this region. TF, known as Nyaparake Force, consisting of Co C of 127th Inf reinf by elements of Co D, embarks for Nyaparake village, about 17 miles E of Nigia R, to intercept westward movement of enemy from Wewak. Landing near Dandriwad R mouth, about 8 miles E of Nyaparake, the force begins patrolling without detecting many Japanese.

CBI—As Japanese offensive in Honan gathers momentum, U.S. Fourteenth Air Force begins attacks on Yellow R bridges. Chinese-American Composite Wing is disposed to guard B-29 fields at Cheng-tu; besides this task and that of knocking out bridges across Yellow R, the force is to neutralize RR yards at Cheng-hsien and Kaifeng.

In NCAC area of Burma, END RUN Force opens drive on Myitkyina. K Force leads off, moving by indirect route that crosses Kumon Range toward Ritpong. Ch 38th Div, by frontal and flanking moves, is, slowly forcing enemy back toward Wala.

29 April

NEW GUINEA—ALAMO Force orders RCT 163, upon relief in Aitape area, to begin staging for Wakde-Sarmi operation.

BURMA—In NCAC area, Brig Gen Frank Dorn establishes Field Hq, Y-FOS, which is to accompany Gen Wei Li-huang's hq.

11 Army Group: In Br Fourteenth Army area, 16th LRP Brig of Ind 3d Div is being flown out of Burma for rest.

MEDITERRANEAN—Ground, naval, and air outline plans for ANVIL are presented to Supreme Allied Commander, Mediterranean Theater.

30 April

CAROLINE Is.—TF 58, while returning from Hollandia operation, begins 2-day air attack on Truk. Atoll.

NEW GUINEA—163d Inf withdraws outpost at Kamti village.

CBI—In NCAC area, H Force of TF END RUN starts forward behind K Force toward Myitkyina. Ch 22d Div, apparently having received permission from Chiang Kai-shek, begins aggressive action.

11 Army Group: In 4 Corps sector of Br Fourteenth Army, Ind 5th and 23d Divs are driving N toward Ukhrul, 5th on W. Ind 30th Div, less elements on Tiddim Road, contains enemy in front of Palel.

1 May

CAROLINE IS.—TF 58 completes 2-day action against Truk, during which some 120 Japanese aircraft are destroyed, about half of them on the ground.

NEW GUINEA—Upon returning to Kamti village, Co I of 163d Inf finds that Japanese have withdrawn. Little contact is made with enemy on W flank after this. Nyaparake Force moves back to Nyaparake by water and sets up outposts at Charov and Jalup.

BURMA—Air supply situation improves as Air Marshal Sir John Baldwin becomes responsible for co-ordination of activities of Troop Carrier Command with those of 3d TAF.

In NCAC area, SOS takes responsibility for Y-FOS.

ITALY—AAI: Final details of plans for drive on Rome are ironed out at meeting at Caserta.

2 May

U.S.—JCS directive orders Gen Stilwell to stockpile supplies in China in order to support Pacific operations. Hump tonnage at this time is inadequate for current U.S. operations in China.

ADMIRALTY IS.—8th Cav withdraws to Hauwei I., having accounted for 285 enemy dead and sustained losses of 4 killed and 7 wounded.

3 May

BURMA—In NCAC area, as 65th Regt and elements of 66th Regt, Ch 22 Div, continue push down Kamaing road toward Inkangahtawng, 64th Regt, Ch 22 Div, cuts Kamaing road about 500 yards S of Hwelon Stream.

4 May

NEW GUINEA—32d Div's RCT 726 and other div troops arrive at Blue Beach; div CG assumes command of TF PERSECUTION. From 22 April to date, Japanese casualties in Aitape area are estimated at 525 killed and 25 captured as against Allied losses of 19 killed and 40 wounded. Adm Barbey proposes that D Day for Wakde-Sarmi operation be postponed until 21 May in order to take advantage of higher tides and to have more time to complete preparations.

BURMA—In NCAC area, Ch 22d Div overruns Inkangahtawng, on road to Kamaing, in co-ordinated effort by air, armor, and arty. Chinese then halt in this region for some time.

5 May

ADMIRALTY IS.—8th Cav begins final mop up of Manus, which is largely clear of enemy.

BURMA—In NCAC area, K Force of TF END RUN reaches trail junction N of Ritpong; patrol starts cutting trail through jungle so that enemy can be taken by surprise from rear.

ITALY—AAI: Gen Alexander issues Operation Order No. 1, AAI, for drive through Gustav Line to Rome and pursuit of enemy thereafter to line Rimini-Pisa.

6 May

NEW GUINEA—At conference of military leaders to consider Adm Barbey's proposal that the Wakde-Sarmi operation be postponed, it is agreed that 21 May for D Day is preferable to 15 May and that the operation cannot be undertaken earlier than 16 May. Gen MacArthur, informed of this by Gen Krueger, proposes a major change: Wakde I., from which aircraft can cover future move to Biak, should be taken as planned but the Sarmi part of the operation should be cancelled, since terrain there does not appear to be of a suitable type to support heavy bomber operations. 32d Div staff becomes Hq, PERSECUTION TF. Aitape defenses are reorganized; E and W sectors, separated by Waitanan Creek, are to be held respectively by RCT 127 and RCT 726.

BURMA—In NCAC area, KHAKI CT, followed closely by ORANGE CT, cuts its way around Ritpong and emerges on trail S of village. 88th Regt, Ch 30th Div, makes unsuccessful attack on Ritpong from N. Elements of 114th Regt, Ch 38th Div, cross Nawngmi Stream.

ITALY—AAI: Gen Alexander sets 11 May as D Day for offensive.

7 May

NEW GUINEA—Nyaparake Force patrol, after clashing with strong enemy patrol across the Dandriwad R, withdraws to W bank.

NEW BRITAIN—Elements of 40th Div occupy Cape Hoskins airdrome without opposition.

BURMA—In NCAC area, TF END RUN blocks exits from Ritpong from S and during night 7-8 frustrates efforts of Japanese to withdraw.

8 May

NEW GUINEA—126th Inf completes relief of 163d in W sector of Aitape perimeter. Nyaparake Force is strengthened by arrival of rifle platoon and light MG section from Co A.

BURMA—In NCAC area, TF END RUN provides fire support for another attack by 88th Regt, Ch 30th Div, on Ritpong, but enemy retains the village. 114th Regt, Ch 38th Div, begins general advance on Kamaing, while 112th prepares to attack Warong.

ETO—Gen Eisenhower sets D Day for Normandy invasion as 5 June. This is subsequently postponed to 6 June.

9 May

NEW GUINEA—Planners meeting at ALAMO Force hq decide to undertake the Wakde-Biak operation as proposed by Gen MacArthur with forces originally assigned to the Wakde-Sarmi operation. D Day for Wakde is set for 17 May and Z Day for Biak for 27 May. Japanese withdraw their MLR to line Sorong-Halmahera. Nyaparake Force patrols, using coastal trail and an inland one paralleling it, advance almost 5,000 yards E of the Dandriwad against some resistance and retire to Babiang at dusk.

BURMA—In NCAC area, Ch 198th Div, Y=Force, is ordered to move forward to crossing site over Salween. Salween crossings are to be made night 10 or 11 May. Japanese are driven from Ritpong, and Chinese troops remain there to mop up while Marauders move S to Lazu and block trail. 114th Regt, Ch 38th Div, overruns East Wala and Hlagyi and is approaching 112th Regt's outposts just N of Manpin.

USSR—Sevastopol falls to Soviet forces.

FRANCE-BELGIUM—U.S. Eighth Air Force begins large-scale attacks on airfields, striking at Laon, Florennes, Thionville, St Dizier, Juvincourt, Orleans, Bourges, and Avord. The offensive against airfields, in which RAF BC, AEAF, and U.S. Eighth Air Force are to participate, is started less than a month before Normandy invasion so the enemy will not have time to recover by D Day.

10 May

U.S.—James V. Forrestal is appointed Secretary of the Navy.

NEW GUINEA—GHQ SWPA issues instructions for Wakde-Biak operation. After air strike by RAAF, Nyaparake Force pushes E from Babiang and takes Marubian without opposition.

CBI—In NCAC area, H and K Forces are now concentrated at Lazu.

On Salween front Y=Force begins crossing the Salween without incident, night 10-11.

ITALY—AAI: On eve of offensive, Allied dispositions are as follows: U.S. Fifth Army, with II Corps on left and FEC on right, holds sector from Tyrrhenian Sea to confluence of Liri and Gari Rivers; 36th Div is in Fifth Army reserve. Br Eighth Army has 13 Corps on left and Cdn 1 Corps behind it; Pol 2 Corps and then 10 Corps to right, and 5 Corps in Adriatic coastal sector; S African 6th Armd Div is in Eighth Army reserve.

11 May

CBI—In NCAC area, Chinese Y=Force continues crossing the Salween under cover of darkness. Three regts of 36th Div and 346th Regt, 116th Div, cross at Mengta Ferry. K Marauder Force starts toward Ngao Ga.

11 Army Group: In Br Fourteenth Army area, 4 Corps regroups. Ind 23d Div is given responsibility for Palel-Tamu road. Ind 20th Div drives N in 2 columns toward Ukhrul.

ITALY—AAI: AAI opens drive on Rome at 2300 with tremendous arty bombardment of Gustav Line by weapons of U.S. Fifth and Br Eighth Armies. While 5 Corps, under direct control of AAI, contains Adriatic coastal sector, U.S. Fifth Army's II U.S. Corps and FEC and Br Eighth Army's 13 and Pol 2 Corps attack, night 11-12. Tactical surprise is achieved, but enemy rallies quickly.

U.S. Fifth Army jumps off first, moving forward under cover of arty bombardment. U.S. II Corps, in Gulf of Gaeta coastal sector, attacks with 85th Div on left and 88th on right. 85th Div's 339th Inf makes limited progress above Scauri: elements secure positions on slopes of M. dei Pensieri and part of S. Martino Hill, but others make no progress against S. Domenico Ridge, SW of Tremensuoli. 338th Inf, co-ordinating its attack for S Ridge—so-called because of its shape—which extends SW from Tamo to Solacciano, with that of 88th Div's 351st Inf toward S. Maria Infante, is unable to take Solacciano or advance up draw between S Ridge and S. Maria Ridge. Pushing N along S. Maria Ridge from Minturno area, 351st Inf gets forward elements to Hills 146 and 150. 350th Inf, 88th Div, in co-operation with FEC to right, attacks hills SW of Castelforte and clears 3-413,316, and Ceracoli. On left flank of FEC Corps, 4th Moroccan Mtn Div attacks toward Castelforte in conjunction with left flank elements of II Corps. To right, 2d Moroccan Div overruns M. Faito and Cerasola Hill.

In Br Eighth Army area, 13 Corps attacks across the Rapido in force in region between the Liri and Cassino, employing 4th Div on N and Ind 8th Div on S. Enemy vigorously opposes crossings but bridgehead is established. Pol 2 Corps begins attack in Cassino area to right of 13 Corps at 0100, 12th. 10 Corps, on extreme right of Eighth Army, secures right flank of assault forces and demonstrates to mislead enemy.

FRANCE—Ninth Air Force begins program of attacks on selected airfields within range of Caen, hitting those at Beaumont-le-Roger and Cormeilles-en-Vexin.

12 May

NEW GUINEA—Charov outpost is withdrawn in order to strengthen base at Nyaparake.

CBI—In NCAC area of Burma, K Force clashes with enemy near Tingkrukawng and is soon pinned down by superior numbers. Ch 38th Div is now able to maintain communications between its 114th and 112th Regts; 113th is approaching West Wala and Maran.

On Salween front, 198th Regt begins clearing Mamien Pass. 36th Div, Ch 53d Army, which is to clear Tatangtzu Pass, surrounds enemy outposts at E end of it; night counterattack forces 36th Div back to the Salween.

ITALY—AAI: Aircraft join in battle for Rome at dawn.

In U.S. Fifth Army's II Corps area, enemy is resisting strongly and making determined counterattacks. Elements of 339th Inf, 85th Div, withstand attacks on S. Martino Hill and are passed through by 1st Bn, 337th, which completes capture of this feature. Co F, 339th, is isolated on M. dei Pensieri during enemy counterattack. 338th Inf makes another vain effort to drive up draw between S Ridge and S. Maria Ridge but takes Solacciano. Stiff opposition slows progress of 351st Inf, 88th Div, toward S. Maria Infante; Co F is isolated and wiped out. 350th Inf takes Ventosa village with ease and halts to await forward movement of French. In FEC area, 4th Moroccan Mtn Div, reinf by regt of 3d Algerian Div, tanks, and TD's, clears Castelforte on left and assists 2d Moroccan Div on right. 2d Moroccan Div is unable to advance. 1st Motorized Div is committed on right flank; 4th Motorized Brig assisted by armor pushes N toward S. Andrea but makes little headway. Mtn Corps, consisting of 1st, 3d, and 4th Groups of Tabors, 1st Moroccan Inf of 4th Mtn Div, and 2d Bn of Algerian Arty Regt, follows 4th Moroccan Mtn Div into Castelforte.

In Br Eighth Army's 13 Corps area, Ind 8th Div gains firm bridgehead on W bank of the Rapido and puts 2 bridges across the river, but Br 4th Div is unable to expand its small bridgehead. Pol 2 Corps, in Cassino area, seizes Phantom Ridge, NW of the Monastery, but is forced back to line of departure, where it remains for several days.

GERMANY—In powerful experimental blow at oil fields in central Germany to test enemy reaction, more than 800 heavy bombers of Eighth Air Force, escorted by U.S. and RAF fighters, attack oil plants at Zwickau, Merseburg=Leuna, Bruex, Leutzkendorf, Boehlen, and other points with 1,718 tons of bombs. Damage at Bruex, Boehlen, and Zeitz is so severe that the plants are temporarily put out of operation. Excellent results are also achieved at Merseburg=Leuna. German Air Force reacts violently and 46 bombers of Eighth Air Force and 10 Allied fighters are lost. Almost 200 enemy aircraft are claimed destroyed.

13 May

NEW GUINEA—Gen Gill decides to abandon Marubian area.

CBI—In NCAC area of Burma, when frontal and flanking attacks on Tingkrukawng by K Force fail, the village is bypassed.

On Salween front, Japanese almost wipe out a Ch bn in Mamien Pass but situation is restored after reinforcements arrive. Japanese resistance in this region ends. Regt of 53d Army crosses the Salween and attacks Japanese flank, regaining positions in Tatangtzu Pass.

ITALY—AAI: In U.S. Fifth Army area, Germans, after offering stiff resistance throughout day, begin withdrawal to next delaying position night 13-14. In II Corps area, efforts of Co F of 339th Inf, 85th Div, to break through enemy encirclement fail. 2d Bn, 338th, clears Cave d'Argilla and Hill 60, in region N of S. Martino Hill, while 1st Bn pushes from Solacciano toward Hill 126, on S Ridge. 351st Inf, 88th Div, continues toward S. Maria Infante. Renewing attack on right flank of II Corps, 350th Inf's 1st Bn seizes M. Rotondo. FEC smashes through Gustav Line in spectacular push. 2d Moroccan Div overruns M. Girofano, M. Feuci, and M. Maio in center of corps zone. Exploiting this success, 1st Mtzd Div speeds forward on right flank to S. Apollinare while 4th Moroccan Mtn Div, on left flank, clears opposition about M. Ceschito, N of road to Coreno, in skillful enveloping attack. Over 1,000 prisoners are taken. Mtn Corps, upon moving forward from Castelforte to positions N of M. Rotondo, halts until opposition can be cleared from Ceschito. Mtn Corps is organized into 3 groups. One pushes northward toward Ausonia and the other 2 drive W toward Spigno, night 13-14.

In Br Eighth Army area, 13 Corps expands Rapido bridgehead. Bridge is completed in sector of 4th Div.

14 May

NEW GUINEA—Co C, 127th Inf, withdrawing from Marubian, finds its route cut by enemy. Japanese also harass Co A at Ulau Mission. Since these positions are becoming untenable, it is decided to withdraw.

ITALY—AAI: In U.S. Fifth Army area, II Corps makes progress all along line against rearguard opposition. 338th Inf, 85th Div, clears Hill 131 of S Ridge, previously an enemy strongpoint, and outposts Formia-Ausonia road. 2d Bn, 337th

Inf, then continues toward next 85th Div objective, Castellonorato, reaching Hill 108, N of Spigno–S. Maria Infante road junction, and patrolling beyond there. 351st Inf, 88th Div, seizes Hill 126, at E end of S Ridge, and S. Maria Infante village, initial objectives. Div, with elements of 3 regts in assault, begins drive on Spigno. 350th Inf advances W across Ausente Creek to N slopes of M. dei Bracchi; 349th occupies M. dei Bracchi and, in conjunction with 351st, clears M. la Civita. In Mtn Corps area, two groups advance W to positions just E of Ausonia road, where they are stopped by enemy. Third group reaches base of Fammera escarpment, leaving containing force at Ausonia. On left flank of FEC area, 4th Mtn Div and 3d Algerian Div mop up region W of M. Majo. In center, 2d Moroccan Div, thrusting toward S. Giorgio, reaches Castellone and Cantalupo Hills; elements are pushing toward Castelnuovo. On right flank, 1st Motorized Div, advancing along the Liri, reaches S. Giorgio.

In Br Eighth Army area, 13 Corps continues to expand and strengthen Rapido bridgehead. Preparations are made for next phase of attack, to isolate Cassino in conjunction with Pol 2 Corps, on 15th, but delay of 78th Div in crossing the Rapido forces postponement of assault.

15 May

NEW GUINEA—U.S. outposts at Ulau and Marubian are withdrawn by sea to Nyaparake.

BURMA—In NCAC area, H Force reaches upper Namkwi R, about 15 miles from Myitkyina.

ITALY—In U.S. Fifth Army's II Corps area, 337th Inf of 85th Div overruns Castellonorato. To left, 3d Bn of 338th reaches junction of Highway 7 and Ausonia road. 88th Div, thrusting to Spigno, finds town undefended and in ruins; is ordered to push on to Itri at once. On left flank in FEC sector, one gp of Mtn Corps pushes steadily W along difficult mountain trails toward M. Revole. Another gp continues northward, scaling Fammera escarpment; 6th Moroccan Inf is relieved of containing role at Ausonia and joins main body. Enemy is driven from Ausonia by noon but retains La Bastia Hill to N in effort to keep control of Esperia road. 3d Algerian Div relieves holding force at Ausonia; armored elements push on to Castelnuovo, which 2d Moroccan Div has cleared earlier in day, thereby gaining control of Ausonia Defile. German fire prevents forward movement of 1st Motorized Div from S. Giorgio on right flank of FEC.

In Br Eighth Army area, 13 Corps continues working through the Gustav Line, with 78th Div moving forward between 4th Div and Ind 8th Div, in preparation for concerted assault with Poles on Cassino. Cdn 1 Corps begins passing through 13 Corps and relieving Ind 8th Div.

16 May

NEW GUINEA—TF TORNADO—Wakde assault force—begins voyage to target from Hollandia area.

CBI—In NCAC area, H Force crosses the Namkwi after confining inhabitants of Namkwi village in order to assure secrecy.

On Salween front, 593d Regt, Ch 190th Div, reaches Shweli valley near Laokai, having moved W over mountains. Rest of 190th Div is clearing strongpoints in Mamien Pass. On S flank, where enemy has thinned out in order to strengthen upper Shweli valley, elements of Ch 76th and 88 Divs are progressing rapidly toward Pingka and have taken 13 villages NE of that objective.

11 Army Group: In Br Fourteenth Army area, Kachin guerrillas gain temporary possession of Washang, about 30 miles E of Myitkyina.

ITALY—AAI: In U.S. Fifth Army area, II Corps rapidly pursues enemy. In 85th Div sector, 339th Inf, after clearing Scauri and M. Scauri, is pinched out by 338th, which drives along Ausonia road to Highway 7 and to Acquatraversa Creek. 337th Inf, pushing W from Castellonorato, meets opposition from M. Campese and halts in valley below it. 349th Inf, 88th Div, advances in conjunction with 337th Inf. Continuing toward Itri, 351st reaches M. Ruazzo and M. Mesola. In FEC area, one column of Mtn Corps completes difficult trek, almost unopposed, to M. Revole; another reaches positions S of Esperia. Elements of 3d Algerian Div secure junction of S. Giorgio-Esperia roads and hold it against counterattack. On right flank, 1st Motorized Div silences fire on S. Giorgio and drives W, pinching out 2d Moroccan DIV.

In Br Eighth Army area, Cdn 1 Corps takes over sector to left of 13 Corps and relieves Ind 8th Div. In 13 Corps area, 78th Div, assuming burden of assault, pushes NW through last defenses of Gustav Line in effort to isolate Cassino in conjunction with Poles. Pol 2 Corps, which has been reorganizing after its initial defeat, is ordered to renew offensive on 17th.

17 May

NEI—Carrier-based planes of British Eastern Fleet attack Soerabaja naval base, Java. B-24's of SWPA follow up, night 17–18, with attack on docks.

NEW GUINEA—TF TORNADO begins preliminary phase of Wakde I. operation. 163d Inf lands without opposition near Arare, on Dutch New Guinea mainland opposite Wakde I., after preparatory naval bombardment; extends flanks W to Tor R and E to Tementoe Creek. Arty is landed and registered on Wakde. Co E and Prov Groupment of shore-based arty land on Insoemanai I., and find it free of Japanese.

CBI—In surprise attack in NCAC area, H Marauder Force seizes Myitkyina airstrip. While the strip is being taken by 150th Regt of Ch 50th Div, 1st Marauder Bn seizes Pamati, site of Irrawaddy ferry. In response to request for reinforcements in order to begin assault on Myitkyina itself, elements of Ch 89th Regt are flown in from Ledo. M and K Forces are moving toward Myitkyina to assist H Force. Ind 3d Div (—) is transferred from control of Br Fourteenth Army to Gen Stilwell's command. 23d Brig remains attached to Br forces. 16th Brig has been flown out for rehabilitation. Squadron of American Dakotas is ordered diverted from Troop Carrier Command to Fourteenth Air Force to supply Yunnan Force. Bombers of Strategic Air Force are used to replace the Dakotas temporarily.

On Yunnan front, Ch force securing Huei-jen Bridge area gets forward elements to Hongmoshu village, well behind Japanese and only 24 air miles from Teng-chung, but Japanese later recover the village.

ITALY—AAI: In U.S. Fifth Army's II Corps area, 85th Div continues pursuit of enemy through Formia corridor, 338th Inf entering Formia where enemy is still resisting; 337th Inf, after strong arty concentration on M. Campese, drives to Maranola. 351st Inf, 88th Div, with 3d Bn in the lead, attempts to take M. Grande, W of Itri-Pico road, but is halted by heavy fire and tanks. 350th Inf (—), moving forward in 2 convoys to Trivio, advances on foot through Maranola to positions S of 351st Inf. In FEC area, one column of Mtn Corps is clearing region W and NW of M. Revole as far as Itri-Pico road; a second reaches positions S of M. del Lago. 3d Algerian Div enters Esperia, which is undefended, but meets strong opposition while continuing pursuit toward S. Oliva; elements begin ascent of M. Oro, key position overlooking Hitler Line. 1st Motorized Div, continuing NW along S bank of the Liri, is halted by fire from M. Oro and extensive mine fields.

Br Eighth Army begins general offensive. Cdn 1 Corps drives W on left flank of army toward Hitler Line. 13 Corps and Pol 2 Corps, in concerted attacks to isolate Cassino, make substantial progress, but Germans are keeping an escape route open and withdrawing Cassino garrison through it. 13 Corps cuts Highway 6; Pol 2 Corps recovers Phantom Ridge and captures Colle S. Angelo.

18 May

ADMIRALTY Is.—Campaign is officially terminated by CG Sixth Army. Air and naval bases have been developed. Japanese casualties during operation total 3,280 killed and 75 captured as against U.S. casualties of 326 killed, 1,189 wounded, and 4 missing.

NEW GUINEA—After preparatory bombardment, 163d Inf lands 3 cos of 1st Bn and Co F of 2d on S coast of Insoemoar I., main island of Wakde group and site of Wakde airfield; despite opposition from mutually supporting pillboxes and bunkers, clears most of airfield and island. Enemy retains NE end of the island and counterattacks unsuccessfully, night 18-19. On mainland, 3d Bn, 163d Inf, begins westward advance across Tor R, establishing small bridgehead.

BURMA—In NCAC area, Marauders begin assault on town of Myitkyina while elements of 89th Regt, Ch 30th Div, defend Myitkyina airfield. 1st Bn overruns Zigyun, S of Myitkyina. 150th Regt, Ch 50th Div, attacks from N, seizing RR station.

ITALY—AAI: In U.S. Fifth Army area, 36th Div begins movement to Anzio beachhead. In II Corps area, 338th Inf of 85th Div mops up Formia and pushes N to M. di Mola and W to M. Conca against rear-guard resistance, while 337th, swinging SW, reaches Highway 7 between Formia and Itri and thereby protects flank of 338th. 339th Inf moves forward along Highway 7, night 18-19. In 88th Div sector, 351st Inf remains in place under intense fire that abates with arrival of supporting arty; 349th reverts to control of 88th Div. FEC meets strong resistance as it attacks toward Pico. While one Mtn Corps column continues to clear left flank, another reaches heights commanding S. Oliva. 3d Algerian Div reduces opposition on M. Oro feature in conjunction with 1st Motorized Div to right and drives enemy from Monticello and S. Oliva. 1st Motorized Div continues along S bank of the Liri to Forma Quesa Creek.

Br Eighth Army completes reduction of Gustav Line in Liri Valley with capture of Cassino. Cdn 1 Corps continues toward Hitler Line at Pontecorvo. In 13 Corps area, Cassino, now in ruins, falls to 4th Div. Detachment of 78th Div thrusts to outskirts of Aquino, key position in Hitler Line. In Pol 2 Corps area, 3d Carpathian Div takes Cassino Monastery.

19 May

NEW GUINEA—Organized resistance on Insoemoar I., rapidly disintegrates, and Japanese remnants are compressed into small pocket at NE tip. Engineers begin to repair airdrome. Prov Groupment on Isoemanai is disbanded; its components return to mainland or to Wakde. Cos E and I land on Liki and Niroemoar and find them undefended. Fifth Air Force establishes radar detachments on the islands. In Aitape sector, 32d Rcn Tr replaces Cos C and D, 127th Inf, at Nyaparake. Brig Gen Clarence A. Martin, 32d Div ADC, takes command of East Sector, replacing Col Howe.

CBI–In NCAC area, at Myitkyina, 1st Bn of Marauders turns over Pamati ferry to Chinese and takes up position on Namkwi R, S of the town. K Force, approaching from N, takes Charpate without difficulty. M Force reaches Namkwi. Japanese garrison of Myitkyina is thus partially encircled. Ch 22d Div commits 65th Regt to line. Ch 38th Div, upon receiving permission from Chiang Kai-shek to push toward Kamaing, decides to send 112th Regt around E flank of enemy to block Kamaing Road S of Seton and move 114th down Kumon Range toward Mogaung.

Br Fourteenth Army commander recommends that Gen Stilwell be given command of all operations to open land route to China.

ITALY–AAI: U.S. Fifth Army orders 509th Para Inf Bn dropped in Galla di M. Orso area N of M. Romano to speed advance of II Corps. In II Corps area, 338th Inf of 85th Div finds Gaeta abandoned by enemy. Elements of 339th move toward Itri to assist 88th Div while others clear hills S of Highway 7. 351st Inf, 88th Div, captures M. Grande with ease; patrol clears stragglers from Itri, where 349th Inf soon arrives. 350th Inf takes up positions E of Itri. Germans order withdrawal of troops S of the Liri and E of Pico to line Pico–Pontecorvo. In FEC area, Mtn Corps column takes Campodimele and cuts Highway 82 near M. Vele.

In Br Eighth Army area, Cdn 1 Corps and Br 13 Corps attempt unsuccessfully to breach Hitler Line before its defenses can be organized, former in Pontecorvo area and latter at Aquino.

20 May

MARCUS I.–Carrier planes of Fifth Fleet TF begin 2-day assault on island.

NEW GUINEA–After mopping up NE tip of Insoemoar I., TF TORNADO assault force returns to mainland, turning over control of island to AAF. Japanese casualties on Insoemoar total 759 killed and 4 captured. At least 50 more have been killed on the mainland. Total U.S. casualties during the Wakde operation is 43 killed and 139 wounded; of these, Army losses were 40 killed and 107 wounded. On the mainland, Japanese efforts to recover Tor R crossing site fail. ALAMO Force warns PERSECUTION TF to expect major Japanese effort against Toem–Arare beachhead.

CBI–In NCAC area, Gen Stilwell reminds Adm Mountbatten that his (Stilwell's) forces will be released upon reaching Kamaing according to Cairo agreement. 112th Regt, Ch 38th Div, takes Warong.

On Salween front, Ch engineers complete landing strip begun on 12th.

ITALY–AAI: In U.S. Fifth Army's II Corps area, elements of 349th Inf, 88th Div, clear Fondi and drive on to M. Passignano. FEC closes in on Pico.

In Br Eighth Army area, Pol 2 Corps begins battle for Piedimonte and reaches outskirts, where indecisive fighting continues for next few days.

21 May

MARCUS I.–Fifth Fleet carrier planes conclude damaging attacks on the island.

NEW GUINEA–Wakde airstrip becomes operational. RCT 158, ALAMO Force reserve, arrives at Toem.

BURMA–In NCAC area, 3d Marauder Bn, moving S from Charpate, is halted near Radhapur and repels enemy attacks down Mogaung road.

ITALY–AAI: In II Corps sector of U.S. Fifth Army area, 85th Div, whose next objective is Terracina, lands 1st Bn, 338th Inf, at Sperlonga without opposition. 337th Inf drives overland toward Terracina, reaching positions near the town and overrunning M. S. Biagio. 88th Div takes M. Calvo and Cima del Monte. 351st Inf relieves 349th Inf forces on M. Passignano. FEC undergoes determined enemy attacks at various points. On left, one Mtn Corps gp attacks across Itri–Pico road toward Lenola. 1st Motorized Div reaches positions between M. Leucio and M. Morrone. 3d Algerian Div gains foothold in Pico but withdraws after nightfall to avoid encirclement.

FRANCE-GERMANY–AEAF fighters begin operations, called CHATTANOOGA CHOO-CHOO, against enemy train movements.

22 May

NEW GUINEA–Gen Krueger enlarges mission of TF TORNADO, whose task of securing Wakde airdrome and adjacent strip of mainland is completed. Drive is to continue W toward Sarmi, 16 miles W of the Tor. Since enemy stragglers are interfering with work on Wakde airdrome, Co L of 163d Inf moves to Insoemoar I., to mop up. In Aitape sector, Nyaparake Force, now consisting of 32d Rcn Tr and Co A, 127th Inf, continues active patrolling against increasing enemy resistance, which forces it back along beach to Parakovio.

BURMA–In NCAC area, 3d Marauder Bn withdraws to Charpate.

ITALY–AAI is preparing for major effort: Br Eighth Army against Hitler Line, and U.S. Fifth

Army to effect junction between VI and II Corps. U.S. Fifth Army revokes order to 509th Para Inf Bn and directs it to be prepared to drop in mountains above Pontine Marshes to facilitate drive of II Corps on Terracina. This does not become necessary. 36th Div closes in Anzio beachhead. In II Corps area, 337th Inf of 85th Div recovers part of M. S. Croce under enemy fire from Terracina. 338th, attacking to block Highway 7 behind Terracina, is diverted by lively action at RR tunnel. 350th Inf, 88th Div, pushes from M. Calvo toward Roccasecca; 349th secures M. Monsicardi; 351st thrusts to M. Chiavino. In FEC area, Hitler Line collapses. One Mtn Corps gp seizes Lenola and links left flank with U.S. II Corps. 7th Inf, 3d Algerian Div, and another gp of Mtn Corps converge on Pico and clear it.

In Br Eighth Army area, as a preliminary to main offensive, Cdn 1st Div of Cdn 1 Corps tries unsuccessfully to outflank enemy from left in limited attack.

23 May

NEW GUINEA—RCT 158 relieves elements of 163d Inf at Tor R mouth and begins westward drive toward Sarmi. 3d Bn is pinned down on coastal track some 400 yards E of Maffin No. I. 1st Bn crosses the Tor to assist, but darkness prevents it from joining in battle. In Aitape sector, Nyaparake Force continues to fall back, elements reaching Tadji. TF HURRICANE holds limited rehearsal for Biak.

CBI—In NCAC area, Marauders at Charpate, Burma, withstand strong enemy attack.

On Salween front, Japanese drive Chinese from hill positions on S flank.

ITALY—AAI: Opens general offensive. In U.S. Fifth Army's VI Corps area, Operation BUFFALO—attack to break out of Anzio beachhead—begins at 0630 after arty and air preparation. While 45th Div on extreme left conducts holding action, main body of VI Corps attacks enemy's Cisterna defense line. On left, 1st Armd Div, employing CCA on left and CCB on right, gets forward elements beyond the RR. In center, 3d Div, with elements of 3 regts in assault, meets strongest opposition but gets about half way to Cisterna. 1st SSF, followed by elements of 133d Inf, 34th Div, attacks on right along Mussolini Canal to RR but falls back to Highway 7 under counterattack. Almost 1,500 prisoners are taken during day. On left flank in II Corps area, 85th Div's 337th Inf pushes slowly down M. S. Croce to outskirts of Terracina; 338th presses steadily toward M. Lenano; 339th seizes Sonnino. In 88th Div sector, 350th Inf reaches Roccasecca. FEC attacks to prevent enemy withdrawal from Liri Valley; makes slow progress since enemy is intent on holding until withdrawal of Hitler Line can be completed. Mtn Corps relieves 88th Div of II Corps on M. Chiavino and seizes M. Pizzuto. 2d Moroccan Div attacks from S. Oliva area toward Pastena and 3d Algerian Div from Pico toward Ceprano against determined resistance. 1st Motorized Div guards right flank along the Liri.

Br Eighth Army opens general assault against Hitler Line. Cdn 1 Corps, employing Cdn 1st Div, pushes toward Aquino-Pontecorvo road, penetrating enemy's defense line. Cdn 5th Armd Div is ordered to attack through the gap.

24 May

WAKE—Carrier aircraft of Fifth Fleet attack Wake.

NEW GUINEA—158th Inf (TF TORNADO, assisted by tanks and flame throwers, drives slowly W along coast to Tirfoam R. In Aitape sector, Nyaparake Force continues withdrawal to defensive positions at mouth of creek about 3,000 yards W of Yakamul.

CBI—In NCAC area, Japanese drive 3d Marauder Bn from Charpate, thus recovering N approach to Myitkyina.

On Salween front, Ch 226th and 228th Regts make unsuccessful frontal attacks against ridge that forms SE end of Pingka valley.

ITALY—AAI: U.S. Fifth Army takes direct control of 36th Engr Combat Regt, with attachments, from VI Corps; orders it to push S via Littoria to link up with II Corps. VI Corps continues attack toward Cisterna after 30-minute arty preparation. 1st Armd Div drives well beyond Highway 7, CCA thrusting toward Velletri against stiffening resistance and CCB toward Cori against weakening opposition. In center, 3d Div's 30th and 7th Regts close in on Cisterna. 133d Inf, 34th Div, takes over right flank attack toward M. Arrestino from 1st SSF and advances to RR beyond Highway 7. In II Corps area, elements of 337th Inf, 85th Div, take Terracina—from which enemy has withdrawn—virtually completing current mission of corps. Engineers and rcn elements are opening road to Anzio beachhead. In FEC area, some troops of Mtn Corps are driven from crest of M. Pizzuto but recover it with aid of U.S. 88th Div; others fight seesaw battle for Vallecorsa. Germans continue effective defense of Pastena against 2d Moroccan Div thrusts. 3d Algerian Div makes little progress on right flank of FEC.

In Br Eighth Army area, Cdn 1 Corps takes Pontecorvo early in day and reduces enemy positions as far N as Aquino, which Germans retain. Attacking through breach made by infantry, Cdn 5th Armd Div reaches Melfa R and establishes bridgehead across it, night 24-25, against heavy fire.

25 May

NEW GUINEA—Command of TF TORNADO (Wakde-Sarmi) passes from Gen Doe, 41st Div ADC, to Brig Gen Edwin D. Patrick. Hq, RCT 158, replaces Hq, RCT 163, as TORNADO hq. Gen Doe is to head assault force for Biak operation. TF HURRICANE leaves Humboldt Bay for Biak in evening. Continuing W toward Sarmi, with 1st Bn in the lead, 158th Inf takes Maffin No. 1 against scattered opposition. 1st and 2d Bns cross Tirfoam and press W toward next objective, Lone Tree Hill, against strong resistance.

CBI—In NCAC area of Burma, Ind 3d Div columns begin withdrawal, some elements up Bhamo-Myitkyina road and others toward Mogaung, abandoning roadblock (BLACKPOOL) on railway near Namkwin. This is a matter of some concern to Gen Stilwell, who wants blocking of enemy on S continued. Outflanking enemy, elements of Ch 38th Div block Kamaing road at Seton, evoking strong enemy reaction.

On Salween front, Ch 88th Div is ordered to join 87th and New 28th Divs (71st Army) in drive on Lung-ling, leaving Ch 2d Army responsible for operations in Pingka=Hsiangta=Mangshih area. 2d Army orders 76th Div to bypass Pingka, leaving 226th Regt to besiege the valley. 226th maintains thin line before Pingka until Japanese yield the valley in late September. Japanese are finally forced from defensive positions at E end of Tatangtzu Pass and fall back 8 miles to another line of defense.

ITALY—AAI: U.S; Fifth Army achieves a solid front with junction of VI and II Corps during morning. Brett Force (1st Bn of 36th Engrs, TD's, and rcn elements of Br 1st Div) makes contact with 91st Cav Rcn Sq of II Corps below Borgo Grappa. Opening of Highway 7 permits supplies to move northward for assault on Rome. VI Corps overruns Cisterna, Cori, and M. Arrestino as enemy opposition collapses. Supporting aircraft take extremely heavy toll of German vehicles fleeing toward Velletri and Valmontone. Over 2,600 prisoners are taken by noon. 1st Armd Div makes little progress toward Velletri but cuts Giulianello-Velletri road just W of Giulianello. 34th Div (− 133d Inf) takes up positions behind 1st Armd Div. In center, 3d Div seizes Cisterna and Cori 3d Regt, 1st SSF, attacks through 133d Inf on right flank of VI Corps and secures M. Arrestino. II Corps is informed of impending relief by IV Corps; maintains current positions while waiting for FEC to come up abreast it to right. 339th Inf, 85th Div, crosses Amaseno R into hills W of Priverno. FEC overcomes organized resistance within its sector, at S. Giovanni Incarico on right and Vallecorsa on left. 3d Algerian Div takes former and Mtn Corps, latter. 1st Motorized Div is withdrawn as FEC reserve.

Br Eighth Army also makes rapid progress as enemy begins general withdrawal. Cdn 1 Corps expands bridgehead across the Melfa and passes infantry through armor to exploit toward the Liri. 13 Corps begins forward movement, taking Aquino without opposition and reaching the Melfa, where bridgehead is established. Pol 2 Corps secures rest of Piedimonte as Germans withdraw.

FRANCE—U.S. Eighth Air Force joins in air offensive against coastal batteries, attacking Fecamp and St Valery.

26 May

NEW GUINEA—1st Bn, 158th Inf, continues slowly W toward Lone Tree Hill. Preliminary bombardment by naval vessels and arty is poorly timed and permits Japanese to reoccupy positions previously vacated. Enemy is found to be strongly disposed on approaches to Maffin Strip.

CBI—In NCAC area, Japanese further weaken positions of Marauders in Myitkyina area with recovery of Namkwi from 2d Bn.

On Salween front, 27th Troop Carrier Sq arrives at Yun-nan-i and within 2 days is dropping badly needed supplies to Y=Force.

ITALY—AAI: In U.S. Fifth Army area, VI Corps boundary is altered to give the Factory to British. Upon completing extensive regrouping and preparatory bombardment, VI Corps renews attack at 1100. On left flank, 45th and 34th Divs, pushing toward line Campoleone Station-Lanuvio, make average gains of about 1 1/2 miles despite considerable opposition. 1st Armd Div tries in vain to reach Velletri over terrain unsuitable for armor; after nightfall withdraws to reserve, turning over its sector to 36th Div. 143d Inf, 36th Div, and rcn elements bridge broad gap between 34th and 3d Divs and apply limited pressure toward Velletri. 3d Div, assisted by TF Howze of 1st Armd Div, on left, and 1st SSF, on right, drives northward on right flank of corps to positions S and W of Artena; TF Howze cuts Velletri-Valmontone road in push toward Highway 6. In II Corps area, 339th Inf of 85th Div consolidates positions W of Priverno. 88th Div's 350th and 349th Regts advance from Roccasecca area across Amaseno Valley, beginning at 2300. In FEC area, 2d Moroccan Div overruns Pastena and advances into hills E of Castro dei Volsci, pinching out 3d Algerian Div. Falvaterra falls to 3d Algerian Div.

Br Eighth Army issues orders for regrouping while pursuing retreating enemy. Cdn 1 Corps reaches the Liri, where bridges are down. Patrols find Ceprano clear of enemy. In 13 Corps area, 6th Armd Div, driving on Arce, is checked by delaying opposition at Providero Defile. Ind 8th Div takes Roccasecca; later it attempts to outflank Arce in support of 6th Armd Div. Pol 2 Corps is being pinched out by 13 Corps on left and to Corps on right and loses contact with enemy. 10 Corps begins pursuit, with NZ 2d Div taking axis S. Biagio-Atina-Sora and Italian Liberation Corps directed along Highway 83 toward M. Cavallo.

27 May

NEW GUINEA—TF HURRICANE, consisting largely of 41st Div (− RCT 163), lands on Biak I. in Bosnek area after naval and air preparation. Against token resistance 186th Inf secures initial beachhead and trail over ridges to inland plateau N of Bosnek. 162d Inf starts W toward airfields, overcoming opposition in Parai Defile to reach Parai. Gen Fuller, commander of 41st Div and of TF HURRICANE, takes command ashore. Japanese air attack causes little damage. In Wakde-Sarmi area, 158th Inf continues drive on Lone Tree Hill and gains positions on it. Japanese begin series of attacks against beachhead—some 200 are committed against Toem, night 27-28.

CBI—In NCAC's Myitkyina area, 2d Marauder Bn, reinf by 209th Engr Combat Bn, completely spends its strength in battle just S of Charpate while endeavoring to reach Radhapur.

On Salween front, Ch force securing Huei-jen Bridge area has elements within 5 miles of Hongmoshu. Monsoon rains are restricting activities of both sides.

In China, Japanese begin second phase (*TOGO*) of *ICHI GO* operation, moving 2 divs S in region E of Hsiang R.

ITALY—AAI: In U.S. Fifth Army's VI Corps area, 45th and 34th Divs gain ground on left flank of corps against spotty resistance. 1st Armd Div is alerted for breakthrough attempt. 142d Inf, 36th Div, is to exploit breakthrough if it is achieved by armor. 36th Div commits 141st Inf NE of Velletri to plug gap existing between 143d Inf and 3d Div. On right flank of VI Corps, 3d Div's 15th Inf clears Artena. TF Howze again fails to reach Highway 6 north of Artena but holds positions dominating it. 1st SSF emplaces arty on crest of hill above Artena on extreme right. 3d Div organizes Artena area for defense and repels tank-infantry counterattacks. II Corps turns over its sector and troops, except for organic units and 85th Div, to IV Corps, night 27-28. 85th Div troops move into Sezze and hills S of Roccagorga. 350th Inf, 88th Div, seizes Roccagorga. 351st relieves 85th Div on left of 350th. FEC clears Amaseno, M. Siserno, and Castro dei Volsci.

In Br Eighth Army area, Cdn 1 Corps crosses elements over the Liri in assault boats under fire and occupies Ceprano. In 13 Corps area, elements of 78th Div start toward Ceprano to pursue enemy toward Frosinone from there. 6th Armd Div, assisted by Ind 8th Div, continues efforts to take Arce. In 10 Corps area, Italian Corps of Liberation seizes M. Cavallo from enemy rear guards. NZ 2d Div gets elements to Atina.

28 May

NEW GUINEA—While 186th Inf expands beachhead on Biak, 162d continues W toward airfields. Strong opposition develops at road junction W of Mokmer village, but leading elements (3d Bn) of 162d Inf get to within 200 yards of Mokmer airfield. Japanese counterattack strongly, forcing 3d Bn back and splitting it. 2d and 1st Bns try to clear terrace behind 3d but make little headway under fire from East Caves on dominating cliff N of Mokmer village. Small craft take ammunition and medical supplies to 3d Bn, and platoon of tanks is sent W along coastal road. Deciding that the position is untenable, Gen Fuller recalls 3d Bn to positions held night of 27th and requests reinforcements. In Wakde-Sarmi area, 158th Inf continues costly efforts to advance after preparatory arty bombardment. When forward positions become untenable, attack is halted, and assault forces are ordered back to Snaky R line. Gen Patrick requests RCT 163, scheduled for Biak, kept in Wakde area pending arrival of elements of 6th Div.

BURMA—On Salween front, Gen Wei, having decided to commit Ch 71st Army, less 88th Div already over the Salween, across the river below Hwei-tung Bridge to seize Lung-ling while a containing force attacks Japanese on Sung Shan, prepares for ferrying operations at Shihtien, 8 miles S of Hwei-tung Bridge. The Salween is rising sharply because of monsoon rains.

ITALY—AAI: In U.S. Fifth Army area, VI Corps meets increased resistance on left flank. 180th and 157th Regts, 45th Div, advance to RR W of Albano road, but 157th is forced back in counterattack. 179th Inf moves forward to fill gap along RR between 45th and 34th Divs. 34th Div, with 133d Inf on left and 168th on right, battles enemy strongpoints below Lanuvio. 3d Div patrols actively on right flank of VI Corps. 1st SSF repels enemy thrust down Valmontone road. FEC continues clearing Lepini Mountains. On right, 2d Moroccan Div is approaching Ceccano.

In Br Eighth Army's 13 Corps area, Germans withdraw from Arce, night 28-29. In 10 Corps area, NZ 2d Div reaches the Melfa and establishes bridgehead.

29 May

NEW GUINEA—On Biak, first tank battle of SWPA is fought as Japanese attempt to dislodge

2d Bn, 162d Inf, from positions W of Parai. Enemy cuts road E of Parai but counterattack restores situation. Since opposition cannot be neutralized, 162d Inf withdraws by land and sea, 2d and 3d Bns to Bosnek and Mandom and rest of RCT 162 to small defense perimeter near Ibdi. Japanese move back into Parai Defile, but achieve this success at cost of more than 500 dead. Gen Krueger orders 2 bns of 163d Inf to Biak, although Toem=Arare beachhead on the mainland is still threatened. In Wakde-Sarmi area, Gen Patrick directs 158th Inf to send I bn back across Tor R; 1st Bn is replaced by 3d and returns to relieve 3d Bn, 163d Inf, at Arare.

CBI—Gen Chennault warns of serious Japanese threat to objectives in E China and asks that Fourteenth Air Force supplies be increased so that enemy can be stopped.

On Salween front, supply situation of Chinese improves as footbridge is repaired. This is later found to be inadequate and air supply is required for Chinese in Mamien Pass.

ITALY—AAI: In U.S. Fifth Army's VI Corps area, 1st Armd Div attacks up Albano road with CCB on left and CCA on right, passing through 45th Div; clears Campoleone Station by noon but is slowed beyond there by firm opposition and suffers heavy tank losses. 45th Div's 180th Inf follows CCB northward while 179th pushes N in region E of Albano road; 157th is withdrawn into reserve. 36th Div continues holding action below Velletri. Enemy continues effective defense of Lanuvio area and inflicts heavy casualties On 34th Div. II Corps takes over sector E of Frascati between VI Corps and Br Eighth Army; assumes command of 3d Div. 337th Inf, 85th Div, closes in Rocca Mass ima-Giulianello area. In IV Corps area, relief of 88th Div is begun by FEC. 349th Inf is relieved and departs for Anzio beachhead. In FEC area, 2d Moroccan Div is taking over Siserno hill mass from 4th Mtn Div and repels enemy attack to keep Palombara Pass open until withdrawal is completed.

In Br Eighth Army area, Cdn 1 Corps begins drive on Frosinone from Ceprano and takes Pofi. 13 Corps finds Arce undefended; establishes bridgehead across upper Liri. 10 Corps takes over inactive zone of Pol 2 Corps, which is to relieve 10 Corps in Adriatic coastal sector and continue drive under AAI control.

30 May

NEW GUINEA—On Biak, 186th Inf meets few enemy as it patrols from Parai Defile eastward. 162d Inf patrols evoke opposition from Japanese in Ibdi pocket, on ridge NW of Ibdi. In Wakde-Sarmi area, 158th Inf organizes new defense line along Tirfoam R. 1st and 3d Bns, 163d Inf, leave for Biak. Japanese attack Arare perimeter after nightfall.

BURMA—Gen Boatner replaces Col John E. Mc-Cammon as head of Myitkyina TF.

ITALY—AAI: In U.S. Fifth Army's VI Corps area, enemy continues stubborn defense of Albano, Velletri, and Lanuvio. CCB, 1st Armd Div, reaches Campoleone Creek and is reinf by 157th Inf. 135th Inf, 34th Div, reduces small enemy position SW of Lanuvio 36th Div continues holding action below Velletri and at night attacks toward M. Artemisio. 1st Br Div is attached to corps at midnight. II Corps continues movement to new zone. During night 30-31, 85th Div relieves elements of 3d Div. 349th Inf, 88th Div, arrives SW of Cori and is attached to 85th Div. In FEC area, elements of 3d Moroccan Div move into Palombara Pass.

In Br Eighth Army area, Cdn 1 Corps continues toward Frosinone and makes contact with French at Ceccano.

U.K.—Loading of assault forces for OVERLORD begins.

31 May

NEW GUINEA—On Biak, TF HURRICANE continues patrolling and regroups in preparation for renewing attack. 1st and 3d Bns of 163d Inf arrive. In Wakde-Sarmi area, Gen Patrick reduces defense perimeter of TF TORNADO. Main position is between the Tor and Tementoe, but bridgehead is retained across the Tor. In Hollandia=Aitape area, Co G of 127th Inf relieves Nyaparake Force. 1st Bn, 126th Inf, begins offensive from East Sector to drive enemy back across the Drindarai, advancing against light resistance through Yakamul to Parakovio. Japanese are becoming aggressive in 127th Inf sector along the Driniumor and begin crossing the river.

CBI—On Salween Front, Ch 53d Army's supplies are replenished during period 28-31 by 27th Tr Carrier Sq.

ITALY—AAI: U.S. Fifth Army orders offensive for Colli Laziali by VI and II Corps. In VI Corps area enemy continues stout defense of Albano. 1st Armd Div is withdrawn to reserve. 34th Div is still stalled by stubborn resistance below Lanuvio. Germans thin out between Lanuvio and Velletri after nightfall. 36th Div makes substantial progress on right flank: 142d Inf takes Maschio d'Ariano and positions commanding Velletri-Nemi road; 143d moves forward to M. Artemisio; 141st pushes slowly toward Velletri. II Corps attacks toward line of departure for main offensive, I June. 85th Div, which takes over left half of II Corps line leaving right half to 3d Div, attacks with 337th Inf on left and 338th on right, securing positions on M. Artemisio, clearing Lariano, and reaching positions across Velletri-Artena road. 88th Div is attached to II Corps. IV Corps sector is taken over by 4th Mtn Div, FEC. FEC extends positions northward in Lepini Mountains to Supino and Carpineto.

In Br Eighth Army area, Cdn 1 Corps finds Frosinone undefended. 10 Corps seizes Sora.

1 June

NEW GUINEA—On Biak, TF HURRICANE begins offensive to expand perimeter. While 163d Inf holds beachhead, 186th Inf, with supporting tanks and arty, moves N to surveyed airstrip on inland plateau and repels strong enemy attacks from N and S. 2d Bn, 162d Inf, begins laborious trek northward in effort to make contact with 186th Inf on inland plateau while rest of regt probes westward from Ibdi. Japanese seize water hole in coastal sector and block main coastal road. Naval and engineer units explore 3 islands of Paidado group—Mios Woendi, Aoeki, and Owl. In Hollandia=Aitape area, ALAMO Force gives Gen Patrick permission to keep rest of 163d Inf until arrival of 6th Div detachment. In sector of TF PERSECUTION, Japanese force 1st Bn, 126th Inf, to return to Yakamul, where it will maintain base from which Harech R line can be explored from coast inland.

CBI—In NCAC area of Burma, Ch 22d Div force cuts Kamaing Road in Mogaung Valley just SE of Nanyaseik, above Kamaing. With Ch 38th Div holding Seton block below Kamaing, Kamaing garrison is in grave danger, but monsoon rainfall is slowing operations. U.S. reinforcements are being rushed to Myitkyina. 2 engr bns, GALAHAD replacements, and GALAHAD evacuees have arrived by air between 26 May and 1 June. Supplies are dangerously low, Americans having only food enough for 1 day and Chinese for 2 days. Chinese attack makes little progress. U.S. 236th Engr Bn pushes toward Namkwi with dual purpose of clearing that region and of gaining combat experience; attack fails, although elements succeed in reaching objective.

On Salween front, elements of Ch 2d Reserve and 36th Divs (54th Army) reach Shweli Valley from Tatangtzu Pass and join 593d Regt, Ch 198th Div, from Mamien Pass. Japanese are drawing off forces from upper Shweli Valley to strengthen Lung-ling area to S. Two regts of 9th Div, Ch 2d Army, cross the Salween; 76th Div of same army patrols toward Burma Road.

ITALY—AAI: U.S. Fifth Army opens offensive to destroy German *Fourteenth Army*. In VI Corps area, Br and U.S. troops continue futile efforts to break through to Albano and block escape of enemy to E. Br 1st Div, on extreme left, is unable to advance. 45th Div makes limited progress. 34th Div gains a little ground below Lanuvio. 141st Inf, 36th Div, takes Velletri after hard battle. 142d Inf consolidates positions on M. Artemisio; 143d, relieved of Maschio d'Ariano by 337th Inf of 85th Div, advances SW along the ridge. II Corps opens final offensive for Rome, aiming first at Highway 6 and Cave road. On left flank, 85th Div, with 337th Inf on left and 338th on right, attacks toward M. Ceraso against strong resistance. 349th Inf, 88th Div, is committed to right, where gap is developing, and drives to heights N of RR. On right flank of II Corps, 3d Div attacks northward in Valmontone area. 30th Inf and TF Howze, reinf by elements of 7th, make slow progress on left. On right, 15th Inf pushes to Highway 6, and 1st SSF takes high ground SE of Valmontone. 91st Cav Rcn Sq screens right flank ahead of 3d Div. IV Corps is officially withdrawn from line at 1400.

In Br Eighth Army area, Cdn 1 Corps, moving up Route 6 toward Rome, reaches Ferentino.

2 June

U.S.—CCS issue new directive to SEAC, a compromise between Br and U.S. positions. Br view that air link to China should be developed in order to support operations in the Pacific is accepted. Ground operations are to be pressed only insofar as they are of assistance to build-up of Hump tonnage. Capture of Myitkyina area of N Burma and construction of pipelines to China are to be integral parts of the main operation.

NEW GUINEA—On Biak, 186th Inf attacks W along inland plateau toward airfields; against sporadic but persistent opposition, reaches positions almost abreast those of 162d Inf in Ibdi area. 2d Bn, 162d Inf, joins 186th Inf and is attached to it. In coastal sector, 162d Inf recovers water hole, reduces roadblock, and blocks trail leading inland. Co A, 163d Inf, occupies Owi and Mios Woendi Islands. In Hollandia=Aitape area, TF PERSECUTION's 1st Bn, 126th Inf, is formed into 2 forces: Herrick Force is to hold Yakamul; Bailey Force is to patrol southward from Yakamul along the Harech.

CBI—In NCAC area of Burma, formal siege of Myitkyina begins, with Chinese tunnelling toward enemy.

On Salween front, Ch 36th Div takes Kaitou village and surrounds Chiaotou in Shweli Valley.

In China, Japanese offensive in Honan draws to a close, enemy having secured his objectives there at light cost.

ITALY—AAI: Temporarily alters interarmy boundary to permit U.S. Fifth Army greater freedom of movement.

In U.S. Fifth Army's VI Corps area, the enemy, after stubborn defense through day, withdraws main forces, night 2-3. 45th Div makes little progress toward Albano. 168th Inf, 34th Div, takes Villa Crocetta and crosses Genaro Hill to reach RR; patrols enter Lanuvio, night 2-3. 142d and 143d Regts of 36th Div advance abreast on right flank of VI Corps, seizing hills just E of M. Cavo and hills E of Tano Hill. 141st Inf reaches Highway 7 before dawn and drives W along it until relieved by 157th Inf of 45th Div, which has moved from left flank of VI Corps to Velletri area to reinforce 36th Div. 157th continues W along the highway to positions 2^1/$_2$ miles W of Velletri. RCT 361, 91st Div, closes at Velletri and is attached to 36th Div, but is not committed to action before fall of Rome. II Corps gains initial objective and enemy begins to withdraw. 85th Div, having regrouped, attacks with 339th Inf on left, 337th in center, and 338th on right. 339th, which is to finish clearing Maschio d'Ariano, takes M. Fiore. 337th seizes M. Ceraso and pushes almost to Highway 6. 1st Bn, 338th, reaches Highway 6 at S. Cesareo. 88th Div's 351st Inf overruns S. Cesareo and cuts Highway 6; 349th captures Gardella Hill. On left flank of 3d Div, TF Howze and 7th Inf drive to Labico; 7th Inf continues toward Palestrina area. 30th Inf pushes through Valmontone, which enemy has abandoned, to positions near Cave. 15th Inf takes over from 1st SSF task of guarding right flank. 1st SSF, under II Corps control, drives down Highway 6 and gains contact with FEC east of Colle Ferro at 1530. In FEC area, Lepini Mts have been cleared of stragglers by 3d Algerian and 2d Moroccan Divs.

In Br Eighth Army area, 13 Corps seizes Alatri.

U.S. Fifteenth Air Force begins shuttle bombing (coded FRANTIC) between Italy and Soviet bases. 130 bombers and 70 fighters, after attacking rail targets at Debrecen (Hungary), continue E and land at the 3 new American bases in USSR—Poltava, Morgorod, and Piryatin.

3 June

NEW GUINEA—On Biak, TF HURRICANE's 186th Inf continues W on broad front to positions N of Parai. Japanese do not oppose advance, but terrain makes progress slow. Supply line is tenuous and water must be brought inland from coast. 162d Inf (−) attempts unsuccessfully to push W through Parai Defile. It is decided that the Ibdi Pocket must be cleared before westward attacks can continue. Engineer, AA, radar, and arty units move to Owi I. In Hollandia=Aitape area, Japanese in TF PERSECUTION zone are still active around Yakamul and bypass Herrick Force to reach positions W of Yakamul.

BURMA—In NCAC area, Ch 42d and 150th Regts and 1st Bn of 89th continue attack on Myitkyina; suffering 320 casualties. Operations are to be temporarily suspended in order to avoid further casualties and to train U.S. troops.

ITALY—AAI: In U.S. Fifth Army's VI Corps area, 45th and 34th Divs push toward Albano from S and SE. 45th drives N to RR and is followed by 1st Armd Div, reinf by 135th Inf of 34th Div, which is to continue attack through 45th Div. In 34th Div sector, 168th Inf takes Lanuvio early in day; 100th Bn (Nisei) overcomes rear-guard opposition on M. du Torri by 0100 on 4th; 133d Inf overruns Genzano before dawn of 4th. 157th Inf is attached to 34th Div upon entering its sector; bypassing M. du Torri, seizes road junction on Albano road north of RR, night 3-4. 36th Div's 141st Inf takes Nemi and road junction E of Lake Albano; 142d clears crest of M. Cavo; 143d eliminates strongpoint on Tano Hill. II Corps, having regrouped extensively in order to swing W on Rome, gets into position for final assault. 85th Div pushes toward Frascati, elements reaching hills NE of town. 88th Div column drives through Colonna to final phase line S of Tor Sapienza by 0400 on 4th. 349th Inf, guarding Highway 6 near Zagarolo, is attached to 3d Div. TF Howze, which is reinf and attached to 1st SSF, drives up Highway 6 against rear-guard resistance and secures Osteria Finocchio road center. 1st SSF, upon relief on right flank by FEC, moves forward to right of TF Howze. 3d Div guards right flank while awaiting relief by FEC. 15th Inf, the first unit to be relieved, takes up positions NE of Osteria Finocchio. 7th Inf moves W in region N of Highway 6. FEC moves forward to rear of II Corps. 3d Algerian Div advances along Highway 6, relieving right flank elements of II Corps. 2d Moroccan Div takes up positions facing Paliano and Genazzano to defend right rear of FEC.

In Br Eighth Army area, Cdn 1 Corps takes Anagni.

U.K.—Loading of cross-Channel assault forces is completed.

4 June

SWPA—GHQ begins preparations for seizure of Noemfoor I., between Biak and Manokwari. The island, containing 3 airdromes, can be used as a staging area and also as base from which to cover sea lanes W of Biak.

NEW GUINEA—On Biak, 186th Inf of TF HURRICANE halts westward drive because of possible enemy attack and spends rest of day in uneventful patrolling. In Ibdi area, 162d Inf makes limited progress in clearing trail leading inland and ridge lines extending from it. In Hollandia=Aitape area, Japanese, after preparatory bombardment, counterattack Herrick Force of TF PERSECUTION in Yakamul area, forcing elements on far side of stream to retire. Bailey Force is ordered to relieve

Herrick Force and starts N toward Yakamul, bypassing enemy block on trail.

CBI—On Salween front, Chinese silence enemy fire on heights commanding Huei-jen Bridge. 88th and 87th Divs, Ch 71st Army, are converging on Lung-ling, 88th from Pingka and 87th along Burma Road. Elements of Ch New 28th Div take Lameng; others are containing Sung Shan garrison.

ITALY—AAI: U.S. Fifth Army columns, some motorized, converge on Rome against rear-guard opposition and are enthusiastically welcomed by the populace. Elements of 88th Rcn Tr of II Corps are the first to enter but cannot deepen penetration. Gen Clark designates garrison of the Eternal City: 3d Div, less one regt that will remain in the city as Fifth Army reserve; Br 1st Bn, the Duke of Wellington's Regt; 1 composite bn of FEC. 3d Div is to command the garrison forces. In VI Corps area, 1st Armd Div takes Albano and drives up Highway 7 into Rome while 36th Div, to E, advances into E suburbs. 45th and 34th Div task forces secure crossing sites below Rome. In II Corps area, 1st SSF and 88th Div columns, making main effort, 1st SSF along Highway 6 and 88th Div along Via Prenestina, are delayed W of Centocelle for about 9 hours but push on through to city. 1st SSF fans out within Rome to take Tiber bridges N of Ponte Margherita. 88th Div TF's, based on 1st Bns of 351st and 350th Regts, drive through the city and seize Ponte Milvio and Ponte del Duca d'Aosta. On left flank of II Corps, one 85th Div force drives through Frascati and along Via Tuscolana to Rome, taking Ponte Cavour there; another cuts Highway 7. FEC completes relief of 3d Div on right flank of II Corps. Forward elements of 3d Algerian Div reach Aniene R at Lunghezza. 1st Motorized Div is committed to right.

Br Eighth Army regroups in order to place 2 fresh armd divs, Br 6th and S African 6th, in van of pursuit that 13 Corps is to lead. 13 Corps takes command of S African 6th Armd Div from Cdn 1 Corps. Cdn 1 Corps is withdrawn into reserve.

U.K.—At SHAEF, Gen Eisenhower postpones D Day 24 hours, to 6 June, because of unfavorable weather forecasts.

5 June

SWPA—Gen MacArthur tells Gen Krueger that ALAMO Force will direct the Noemfoor operation.

NEW GUINEA—On Biak, Gen Krueger urges TF HURRICANE to intensify efforts to take airfields quickly. 186th Inf resumes westward attack without opposition and reaches main ridge, NE of Mokmer airfield, which 3d Bn scales. In Ibdi area, 162d Inf succeeds in clearing trail inland and making contact with 186th Inf but, despite support of naval vessels offshore, can make little headway in Parai Defile. In Hollandia=Aitape area, initial elements of 6th Div arrive at Toem and begin relief of 158th Inf, TF TORNADO. TF PERSECUTION'S Herrick Force is withdrawn from Yakamul to beachhead by water. Bailey Force completes arduous trek via perimeter of Co G, 127th Inf, 2 miles W of Yakamul, and is sent W along coast to the Driniumor, to which Co G and its supporting arty also retire. During action in Yakamul area, 1st Bn, 126th Inf, has suffered 18 killed, 75 wounded, and 8 missing and has killed 200-250 Japanese. 1st Bn of 127th Inf, which has been trying for several days to drive enemy from ridge N of Afua, makes stronger effort and finds that Japanese have abandoned the ridge.

CBI—Generalissimo Chiang Kai-shek, conferring with Gen. Stilwell, asks that B-29 tonnage be diverted to meet Japanese threat in E China. Gen Stilwell agrees to request permission if situation grows worse.

On Salween front, 20,000 troops of Ch 71st Army have crossed to W bank of the Salween. Drive on Lung-ling continues.

11 Army Group: In 33 Corps sector of Br Fourteenth Army area, battle of Kohima is successfully concluded as Br 2d Div clears Aradura Spur, S of Kohima, but Kohima-Imphal road must still be opened by 33 Corps working S and 4 Corps pushing N.

THAILAND—B-29's of U.S. XX Bomber Command, on their first mission, attack Bangkok in force.

ITALY—AAI: Gen Alexander orders vigorous pursuit of enemy to line Rimini-Pisa. Fifth Army, on W, is to seize Viterbo airfield and port of Civitavecchia, then advance on Leghorn. Br Eighth Army is to advance astride the Tiber to clear Terni and Rieti.

U.S. Fifth Army gets most of assault forces across the Tiber and pursues enemy as rapidly as possible, VI Corps using Highway 1 and II Corps, Highway 2. Fifth Army takes control of 3d Div for garrison duty within Rome. In VI Corps area, Br 5th and 1st Divs in coastal sector get advance elements to lower Tiber, where bridges must be built. 1st Armd Div's CCB spearheads advance of 36th Div and CCA, that of 34th Div. II Corps employs 85th Div on left and 88th on right as it speeds northward. 91st and 117th Cav Rcn Sqs provide flank protection. FEC crosses the Aniene and drives to the Tiber, then suspends forward movement until S African 6th Armd Div of Br Eighth Army can cross its front.

In Br Eighth Army's 13 Corps area, S African 6th Armd Div concentrates E of Rome in preparation for pursuing enemy northward along Route 3

(Via Flaminia) W of the Tiber. Br 6th Armd Div, advancing along Route 4 (Via Salaria) E of the river, makes contact with enemy outposts N of Rome. 10 Corps, which is initially to advance on Rieti, takes command of Ind 8th Div.

6 June

FRANCE—21 Army Group (Gen Montgomery, CG): Allied forces invade France, landing on coast of Normandy. Although OVERLORD is under supreme command of Gen Eisenhower, Gen Montgomery heads all land forces, Air Chief Marshal Leigh-Mallory the air forces, and Adm Ramsay the naval forces. Powerful air and naval bombardment precedes and follows landings. Strategic aircraft join with tactical in pounding assault zone. Surprise as to time and place of invasion is achieved and casualties are extremely light on all beaches except OMAHA. Naval opposition is absent and air reaction is feeble. Seaborne assault—H Hour being 0630 for Americans and a little later for British—is preceded 4-5 hours by the largest airborne operation yet attempted. 3 divs are dropped to facilitate inland movement of seaborne assault forces. Drops are scattered, but paratroopers largely accomplish their mission of securing beach exits, advancing in small groups across hedgerow country.

In Gen Bradley's U.S. First Army area, VII Corps (Gen Collins), on extreme right, lands W of Vire Estuary on UTAH Beach. Its primary mission is to seize port of Cherbourg as quickly as possible. 101st and 82d A/B Divs are dropped behind UTAH Beach in region between Ste Mère-Eglise and Carentan. 101st secures beach exits in St Martin-de-Varreville–Pouppeville region and makes contact with seaborne 4th Div; blocks roads at Foucarville, which enemy surrenders night 6-7; takes lock at La Barquette, N of Carentan, but is unable to secure crossings of the Douve on either side of Carentan as planned. Enemy is resisting strongly in Carentan–St Côme-du-Mont area. 82d A/B Div, upon dropping astride the Merderet, takes Ste Mère-Eglise but fails to gain its other objectives—crossings of the Merderet and Douve, and making contact with 101st A/B Div in Beuzeville-au-Plain area—small groups are isolated W of the Merderet. At H-2, 4th Cav Gp detachment makes unopposed landings on Iles St Marcouf. 4th Div, reinf by 359th Inf of 90th Div, lands at H Hour, 8th Inf leading, and against relatively light opposition secures beachhead; 8th Inf gets some elements to Les Forges crossroads and others to Turqueville area, but enemy retains salient between these and 82d A/B Div units at Ste Mère-Eglise. Tank-infantry TF (from 325th Gli Inf of 82d A/B Div and 746th Tank Bn) arrives in Les Forges area but is unable to break through to 82d A/B Div. 12th Inf, 4th Div, reaches Beuzeville-au-Plain area to left of foist A/B Div, and 22d advances along coast to general line Hamel-de-Cruttes–St-Germain-de-Varreville. V Corps (Maj Gen Leonard T. Gerow) lands to E of VII Corps on OMAHA Beach at H Hour but suffers heavy losses in men and equipment because of adverse surf conditions and raking fire delivered from sharply rising bluffs that command the narrow beach. 1st Div, reinf by 116th Inf of 29th Div, initially puts 116th and 16th Regts ashore; rest of 1st Div and 115th Inf of 29th land later in day. 2d and 5th Ranger Bns are attached to 116th Inf to clear Pointe du Hoe. 3 cos of 2d Ranger Bn, supported by fire from naval vessels offshore, scale steep cliff of Pointe du Hoe and take coastal battery, which enemy has abandoned; during next 2 days withstand series of sharp counterattacks against their isolated position. Other Rangers and 116th Inf (–) land between Vierville-sur-Mer and Les Moulins and overrun former. Elements of 116th Inf land E of Les Moulins and make futile effort to reach St Laurent-sur-Mer. On left flank of V Corps, 16th Inf and follow-up regts (115th, 18th, 26th) make maximum penetration of about $1^1/_2$ miles between St Laurent-sur-Mer and Colleville; 3d Bn of 16th Inf, on extreme left, takes Le Grand Hameau.

Br Second Army (Lt Gen Myles C. Dempsey) lands to E of U.S. First Army on 3 beaches (GOLD, JUNO, and SWORD) between Le Hamel and Ouistreham and presses inland toward Bayeux and Caen. In 30 Corps area, 50th Div, reinf by 8th Armd Brig, elements of 79th Armd Div, and 47th Royal Mar Cdo, lands on GOLD Beach in Le Hamel–La Rivière sector; against strong opposition at Le Hamel, drives inland toward Bayeux, reaching general line Vaux-sur-Aure–St Sulpice-Vaux-sur-Seulles–Brécy-Creuilly; makes contact with Cdn 3d Div to left. Preparations are made for attack on Bayeux at daylight. I Corps puts troops ashore on JUNO and SWORD and drives on Caen from NW and N. Well before the seaborne assault, 6th A/B Div (–) is dropped E of the Orne in Caen area; secures bridges over Orne R and Caen Canal at Bénouville and destroys coastal battery at Merville. Cdn 3d Div, reinf, lands on JUNO in Courseulles area and thrusts rapidly inland 3-6 miles; armored patrols reach Bayeux–Caen highway at Bretteville-l'Orgueilleuse. Br 3d Div, reinf, lands to left on SWORD and drives inland to Biéville, within about 2 miles of Caen, but gap exists between it and Cdn 3d Div. Germans make their only major counterattack of the day through the gap but are forced back almost to starting line.

FRANTIC—104 B-17's and 42 P-51's of U.S. Fifteenth Air Force attack airfield at Galati (Rumania), staging from bases in USSR.

ITALY—AAI: In U.S. Fifth Army area, VI Corps races northward, CCB of 1st Armd Div reaching positions about 25 miles from Rome where it is passed through at 2200 by 168th Inf, 34th Div.

In Br Eighth Army area, 13 Corps progresses rapidly W of the Tiber; S African 6th Armd Div reaches Civita Castellana. Stronger opposition E of the river makes going slower, but Br 6th Armd Div reaches Monterotondo. In 10 Corps area, Ind 8th Div pursues enemy to Subiaco.

CBI—Because of Japanese offensive in China, Gen Stilwell increases Hump allocation to Fourteenth Air Force to 8,325 tons. 1,500 more tons from B-29 allocation bring total tonnage for Fourteenth Air Force to the 10,000 Gen Chennault requested.

NEW GUINEA—On Biak, upon orders from Gen Fuller to clear Mokmer airfield at once and drive on to coast S of there, 186th Inf of TF HURRICANE prepares to drive on the airfield instead of clearing heights commanding it as planned. Attack is postponed until 7th in order to amass sufficient supplies. After receiving supply of water, 3d Bn, followed by 1st, moves down W slope of ridge in preparation for attack on airfield. 162d Inf continues to meet lively opposition in coastal sector.

POA—TF 58 sails from the Marshalls for the Marianas.

U.S.—JWPC issues study, "Operations Against Japan, Subsequent to Formosa," in which the following schedule for 1945 is suggested for planning purposes: Phase 1—take Bonins and Ryukyus and attack China coast (1 April-30 June); Phase 2—consolidate and exploit (30 June-30 September); Phase 3—invade Japanese home islands, Kyushu on 1 October and Honshu on 31 December.

7 June

FRANCE—21 Army Group: U.S. First Army continues attack toward D Day objectives. Gen Eisenhower, visiting the front, orders VII and V Corps to make speedy junction through Isigny and Carentan. VII Corps gives 101st A/B Div task of clearing Carentan. V Corps makes 29th Div responsible for seizing Isigny. In VII Corps area, 4th Div, with 22d Inf on right and 12th on left, drives northward toward line Quinéville-Montebourg until halted by strong opposition from permanent fortifications at Crisbecq and Azeville; 8th Inf columns converge on Ste Mère-Eglise, where they assist elements of 82d A/B Div in throwing back major enemy counterattack from N. Tanks of 10th and 746th Tank Bns also give valuable assistance. Other elements of 82d A/B Div clear E bank of the Merderet but are violently opposed at La Fire bridge across it and are unable to relieve isolated elements W of the river. 82d A/B Div is strengthened by arrival of 325th Gli Inf Regt in gliders and by sea. Seaborne elements (1st Bn) move forward with 8th Inf of 4th Div; the other bns are committed at La Fière and N of Ste Mère-Eglise. To S, 101st A/B Div units on N bank of the Douve temporarily suspend efforts to establish bridgeheads but receive surrender of enemy detachments from Le Port and La Barquette; 506th Para Inf (− 3d Bn) moves S from Culoville to reconnoiter in force toward the Douve but is stopped near St Côme-du-Mont. V Corps continues toward initial objectives with 29th Div on right and 1st on left. 116th Inf of 29th Div and Rangers are clearing bluffs on V Corps right flank; relief force pushing toward Rangers on Pointe du Hoe reaches St Pierre-du-Mont area. 175th Inf of 29th Div, upon landing, is given task of taking Isigny; moving between 116th and 115th Regts, advances quickly along Longueville-Isigny road, taking La Cambe before dawn of 8th; 115th Inf clears St Laurent region and pushes SW toward Louvières and Montigny. Elements of 26th Inf, 1st Div, on right flank of div, make futile attempt to reach Formigny; 18th Inf, in center, thrusts to En-granville, Mandeville, and Mosles; 16th, on left, takes Huppain. Enemy retains narrow corridor between U.S. and Br bridgeheads along Drome R to its junction with Aure R. 2d Div begins landing in evening.

In Br Second Army's 30 Corps area, 50th Div overruns Bayeux and gets 2 regts S of Bayeux-Caen highway. 47th Royal Mar Cdo begins battle for Port-en-Bessin in afternoon. In 1 Corps area, Cdn 3d Div brig pushes S of Bayeux-Caen highway.

ITALY—AAI: Gen Alexander issues new orders for pursuit of enemy. U.S. Fifth Army is to advance to general area Pisa=Lucca=Pistoia, while Eighth Army is to push toward line Florence-Bibbiena-Arezzo as rapidly as possible. 5 Corps is to remain on the defensive in Adriatic coastal sector. 2 Pol Corps will be committed only if enemy cannot be cleared from Ancona.

In U.S. Fifth Army's VI Corps area, 168th Inf of 34th Div, advancing through night 6-7, seizes Civitavecchia and its port, 40 miles NW of Rome. This port, although damaged, soon becomes valuable in supplying assault forces.

In Br Eighth Army area, 13 Corps shifts axis of advance from N to NW. S African 6th Armd Div, followed by 78th Div, turns toward Orvieto, important road center, on Viterbo-Bagnoregio road. E of the Tiber, Br 6th Armd Div swings toward Terni instead of Rieti.

CBI—In NCAC area, Chinese commanders call Gen Boatner's attention to the dangerously reduced strength of Chinese forces in Myitkyina area. Limited operations are continued there while preparations are being made for offensive on 10th.

On Salween front, Ch 88th Div of 71st Army reaches East Gate of Lung-ling. Ch 87th Div, moving along Burma Road, is approaching the city.

NEW GUINEA—On Biak, 186th Inf, assisted by arty and aircraft, drives quickly across Mokmer airfield to beach without opposition, but Japanese then subject entire area to intense fire. Supply of 186th Inf by sea is begun under fire. 162d Inf begins movement by sea of bulk of its troops in coastal sector to Mokmer airdrome via Parai in order to exert pressure against Parai Defile from Was well as E and open it to coastal traffic. Limited effort is being made against Ibdi Pocket area. Enemy's East Caves position, E of Mokmer airfield, is being neutralized by fire. In Hollandia=Aitape area, 2d Bn joins 1st Bn of 158th Inf, TF TORNADO, in Tor R bridgehead. Both patrol uneventfully toward Maffin No. 1. In TF PERSECUTION'S sector, Japanese become active about 1,300 yards W of Afua on Afua-Palauru supply line. Gap exists in outer defense line along the Driniumor, where regrouping is conducted. 1st Bn, 128th Inf, replaces 1st Bn, 126th, in N part of line.

U.S.—Gen Marshall rejects request, made by Gen Stilwell at instigation of Chiang Kai-shek and Gen Chennault, that B-29 stocks be used by Fourteenth Air Force in the event of an emergency in China.

8 June

FRANCE—21 Army Group: Contact is established between U.S. First and Br Second Armies near Port-en-Bessin.

In U.S. First Army area, VII Corps begins all-out drive on Cherbourg with 4 refits—505th Para Inf (82d A/B Div) and 8th Inf (4th Div) on W and 4th Div's 12th and 22d Regts on E. Enemy again halts assault of 22d Inf at edge of Azeville-Crisbecq fortifications; 12th Inf fights bitterly for Edmondeville. On W, attack reaches general line from Montebourg highway through Magneville to the Merderet. 82d A/B Div remains under strong enemy pressure along the Merderet. On VII Corps S flank, 101st A/B Div opens battle for Carentan in effort to effect speedy junction with V Corps: 506th Inf (−), strongly reinf, forces enemy from St. Côme-du-Mont; div then regroups along the Douve with orders to cross in vicinity of Brévands. V Corps secures D Day objectives. 116th Inf of 29th Div and Rangers succeed in relieving hard-pressed units of 2d Ranger Bn on Pointe du Hoe and push on to Grandcamp; 175th Inf continues rapid drive on Isigny and takes it with ease, night 8-9; 115th drives S to the Aure through Longueville. In 1st Div sector, Formigny falls to elements of 18th Inf from Engranville; 26th Inf, making main effort to trap enemy between U.S. and Br bridgeheads, overruns Tour-en-Bessin and, night 8-9, Ste Anne; 16th attempts to block enemy escape from Port-en-Bessin, but enemy retains escape corridor and withdraws bulk of his forces through it, night 8-9.

In Br Second Army's 30 Corps area, Port-en-Bessin falls to 47th Royal Mar Cdo early in day. 50th Div compresses enemy's escape corridor in conjunction with U.S. V Corps, taking Sully and château at Fosse Soucy, but pulls back under enemy pressure.

ITALY—AAI: Br 5 Corps, holding Adriatic coastal sector, finds that enemy is withdrawing and moves forward.

In U.S. Fifth Army's VI Corps area, 133d Inf, leading 34th Div's pursuit up Highway 1, encounters delaying opposition S of Tarquinia. II Corps, to speed advance, commits 2 TF's ahead of 85th and 88th Divs—TF Howze on left and TF Ellis (91st Cav Rcn Sq, reinf) on right. Forward elements get to within 6 miles of Viterbo before corps is halted in order to give S African 6th Armd Div right of way. Shift of interarmy boundary to left greatly narrows zone of 88th Div.

In Br Eighth Army's 13 Corps area, S African 6th Armd Div makes rapid progress toward Orvieto on left flank. E of the Tiber, Br 6th Armd Div encounters enemy positions extending W from Monte Maggiore and is held up at Passo Corese; puts infantry in the lead, night 8-9.

CBI—On Salween front, Ch 88th Div of 71st Army penetrates outer defenses of Lung-ling. Ch 87th Div reaches North Gate of the city and blocks Japanese supply route at Manio Bridge, on Teng-chung-Lung-ling road.

NEW GUINEA—Seventh Fleet PT boats begin operating from Mios Woendi. On Biak, 186th Inf of TF HURRICANE improves and consolidates positions in Mokmer airdrome area. 2d Bn of 162d Inf meets heavy fire as it advances E to rejoin parent unit and halts on ridge N of East Caves. 162d Inf completes movement of bulk of its 1st and 3d Bns to Parai. Japanese continue to resist stubbornly in Parai Defile despite pressure from W and E by elements of 163d, 186th, and 162d Regts. Elements of 162d Inf pushing W from Parai toward Mokmer airfield are strongly opposed but reach positions near Mokmer village. In Hollandia=Aitape area, 1st and 2d Bns of 158th Inf, TF TORNADO, with tank support, attack W after brief arty preparation. Considerable resistance develops, but attack progresses to within 1,500 yards of the Tirfoam.

9 June

FRANCE—21 Army Group: In U.S. First Army's VII Corps area, 4th Div makes significant progress at some points as it continues drive on Cherbourg:

on right flank, 22d Inf forces German garrison of Azeville fortifications to surrender and organizes TF BARBER to drive on Quinéville through Azeville gap; 12th Inf thrusts quickly northward from Edmondeville, reducing strongpoint at Joganville; during hard and costly fighting, 8th Inf overruns enemy positions at Magneville and drives to Ecausseville, from which enemy withdraws after nightfall. 505th Para Inf, 82d A/B Div, reinf by bn of 327th Gli Inf, makes limited progress W of Magneville; 82d A/B Div makes main effort at La Fière, where 2 bns of 325th Gli Inf, followed by 1st Bn of 508th Para Inf, cross the Merderet and secure bridgehead of sufficient depth to include all units that had been isolated W of the Merderet. 101st A/B Div prepares for 2-pronged attack on Carentan via causeway and Brévands, but its jump-off is delayed awaiting bridge repairs. V Corps attacks S toward Fôret de Cerisy on 3-div front, committing 2d Div in narrow zone between 29th and 1st. From Isigny, main body of 175th Inf, 29th Div, thrusts S to its objectives, reaching La Fotelaie, while Co K, reinf by Rcn Tr and tanks, forces crossing of the Vire R at Auville-sur-le Vey; 115th Inf crosses the Aure S of Canchy and fans out to Bricqueville, La Folie, and Le Carrefour. In center of V Corps, 2d Div's 38th Inf pushes into Trévières and begins clearing it while 9th, to E, thrusts to Rubercy. 1st Div, attacking with 18th Inf on right and 26th on left, reaches its left flank objectives, Agy and Dodigny. 2d Armd Div begins landing.

Br Second Army is pushing forward toward Tilly-sur-Seulles in 30 Corps zone and Caen in 1 Corps zone against strong opposition.

ITALY—AAI: In U.S. Fifth Army's VI Corps area, 133d Inf of 34th Div overruns Tarquinia. 361st Inf of 91st Div enters line, taking over coastal sector under command of 36th Div. Viterbo falls without a fight to CCA, 1st Armd Div, early in day. II Corps is being relieved by FEC.

Br Eighth Army establishes new boundary between 13 and 10 Corps along Tiber R. Elements of 13 Corps E of the river (Br 6th Armd and 4th Inf Divs) pass to command of 10 Corps. In 13 Corps area, S African 6th Armd Div makes contact with U.S. Fifth Army at Viterbo and pushes on toward Orvieto. In 10 Corps area, Br 6th Armd Div continues toward Terni. Ind 8th Div reaches Arsoli.

USSR-FINLAND—As prelude to main summer offensive, Soviet troops of Leningrad Front launch attacks to eliminate Finnish threat on Karelian Isthmus, between Lake Ladoga and Gulf of Finland, striking at Finnish Mannerheim Line after 3-hour preparatory bombardment.

CBI—Adm Mountbatten directs Gen Giffard, CG 11 Army Group, to clear Dimapur-Kohima-Imphal road not later than mid-July; to clear Dimapur-Kohima-Imphal Plain=Yuwa=Tamanthi region; to prepare to attack across the Chindwin in Yuwa=Tamanthi area after the monsoon.

On Salween front, Ch 71st Army begins attack on 2 of 3 hills in Lung-ling. 9th Div of Ch 2d Army blocks Burma Road 4 miles S of Mang-shih; because of disagreement between army and group army commanders, 9th Div later withdraws the block and confines its activities to patrolling.

NEW GUINEA—Engr aviation bns begin building strip on Owi. On Biak, main body of 162d Inf, TF HURRICANE continues W along coast toward Mokmer airfield against heavy fire from East Caves; makes contact with 2d Bn, which reverts to regt. Efforts are being made to discover limits of the East Caves position. In Hollandia=Aitape area, 1st and 2d Bns of 158th Inf, TF TORNADO, continue to Tirfoam R, overrunning enemy defenses en route. Forward movement from there is halted since 158th Inf is to be prepared to attack Noemfoor I. at short notice. A second RCT of 6th Div is to relieve 158th Inf. In sector of TF PERSECUTION, Japanese are found to have withdrawn from Afua-Palauru trail. Sq of RAAF Beaufighters of Wing 71 arrives at Tadji, where only 110th Rcn Sq of U.S. Fifth Air Force has been stationed from 25 May to date.

10 June

FRANCE—21 Army Group: In U.S. First Army area, VII and V Corps establish contact at Auville-sur-le-Vey, but enemy remains in Carentan. In VII Corps area, TF BARBER, on 4th Div right, makes little headway through Azeville gap toward enemy's MLR on Quinéville ridge, since enemy is disposed in strength on the TF flanks; efforts to reduce Ozeville and Château de Fontenay are futile; 12th Inf reaches positions just below Montebourg-Quinéville highway in region E of Montebourg and is well ahead of rest of 4th Div; 8th Inf gains its objectives along Le Ham-Montebourg highway. 505th Para Inf, 82d A/B Div, takes one of its objectives, Montebourg Station, but is halted a little short of the other, Le Ham. 60th Div (less 359th Inf, attached to 4th Div) attacks W toward the Douve through 82d A/B Div's Merderet bridgehead but makes little headway; 357th Inf crosses at La Fière and pushes toward Les Landes; 358th crosses at Chef-du-Pont and moves on Pont l'Abbé, getting a little beyond Picauville. 101st A/B Div begins envelopment of Carentan: 327th Gli Inf moves in from NE upon crossing the Douve near Brévands and cuts E exits from the town; bitter battle develops on W, where 3d Bn, 502d Para Inf, inches across causeway NW of Carentan under enemy fire, which supporting arty is unable to silence; elements of 401st Gli Inf make contact with V Corps units at Auville-sur-le-

Vey. 9th Div arrives and begins to debark. V Corps gains its objectives with little difficulty since German lines above Caumont have given way and gap 10 miles wide is virtually undefended. 29th Div's 115th Inf reaches Elle R line. 38th and 9th Regts of 2d Div speed through Fret de Cerisy to objectives. 18th Inf, 1st Div, reaches St Lô=Bayeux highway.

In Br Second Army area, 30 Corps commits 7th Armd Div to action in Tilly-sur-Seulles region, where enemy is resisting strongly. I Corps continues to press toward Caen.

ITALY—AAI: Br 5 Corps pursues enemy up Adriatic coast, Ind 4th Div taking Pescara and Chieti.

In U.S. Fifth Army's VI Corps area, 1st Armd Div, relieved by 36th Div on left and FEC on right, is withdrawn from line. 36th Div is responsible for entire VI Corps zone. In II Corps area, final elements of corps are withdrawn from line. In FEC area, Lt Gen Edgar de Larminat, as head of Pursuit Corps, directs advance of 3d Algerian Div on W and 1st Motorized Div on E in narrow sector, largely W of Highway 2, on Fifth Army right flank.

In Br Eighth Army's 13 Corps area, enemy rear guards are slowing S African 6th Armd Div below Bagnoregio. 4th Div reverts to corps from Br 10 Corps upon relief E of the Tiber by Ind 8th Div. 10 Corps is meeting considerable resistance below Terni. NZ 2d Div reaches Avezzano.

CBI—In NCAC area, Allied troops launch coordinated attack on Myitkyina but make little progress. In Mogaung Valley, Ch forces are pushing closer to Kamaing, which is besieged.

On Salween front, Ch 87th and 88th Divs are supplied with ammunition by air as they continue to attack hills in Lung-ling.

In China, Japanese have 5 divs along the Liu-yang R and are threatening Changsha.

NEW GUINEA—On Biak, Gen Krueger again urges Gen Fuller to secure airfields as quickly as possible. Bulk of 162d Inf, TF HURRICANE, advances cautiously W toward Mokmer airdrome. Enemy continues to resist in Parai Defile. AT Co of 162d Inf and Co A, 186th, are recalled from ridges extending W from trail inland, which they have been trying in vain to clear since 7th. In Hollandia= Aitape area, hq of TF PERSECUTION orders positions along the Driniumor improved quickly; in the event of attack, enemy is to be delayed first along line X-ray R-Koronal Creek and second at the Nigia. Main line of resistance about the airfields is to be held. Japanese patrol activity is decreasing in Driniumor area but increasing along S branches of Niumen Creek, about 3,000 yards E of the Driniumor.

U.S.—U.S. Eighth Army is activated at Memphis, Tennessee.

11 June

FRANCE—21 Army Group: In U.S. First Army's VII Corps area, 4th Div's TF Barber continues futile efforts to break through Azeville gap to Quinéville ridge in coastal sector; 12th Inf gains its objective— W end of Montebourg-Quinéville ridge—but pulls back behind Montebourg-St Floxel road since its flanks are exposed; 8th Inf digs in along Le Ham-Montebourg road when enemy fire prevents forward movement to the RR. 82d A/B Div's 505th Para Inf, making main effort with 2d Bn of 325th Gli Inf, thrusts into Le Ham under heavy fire and finds Le Ham deserted. 90th Div continues to make slow progress W of the Merderet, but partly surrounds Pont l'Abbé. 101st A/B Div presses in slowly on Carentan against unabated opposition: On right, 3d Bn of 502d Para Inf, after crossing the Madeleine R and clearing enemy strongpoints, is joined by 1st Bn; determined counterattacks are repelled and 2d Bn, 502d Para Inf, takes over line, night 11-12. While main body of 327th Gli Inf conducts holding action along canal on left, elements move in to outskirts of Carentan along Bassin Flot. Destructive fire is placed on Carentan during night 11-12, and Germans quietly abandon the town. In V Corps area, elements of 2d Armd Div (3d Bn, 41st Armd Inf Regt) are committed to strengthen bridgehead at Auville-sur-le-Vey, since VII Corps' 101st A/B is fully occupied with battle for Carentan. V Corps front is quiet except at tip of Fôret de Cerisy, where elements of 2d Div reduce strongpoint at Haute Littée crossroads.

In Br Second Army's 30 Corps area, 7th Armd Div breaks into Tilly-sur-Seulle but is forced out by enemy.

USSR-FINLAND—Continuing offensive against Mannerheim Line, Soviet forces drive wedge 15 miles deep on 30-mile front in Finnish positions.

FRANTIC—U.S. Fifteenth Air Force planes attack Focsani airfield while returning to Italy from their first shuttle bombing mission between there and USSR.

ITALY—AAI: In U.S. Fifth Army area, IV Corps (Gen Crittenberger) takes command of VI Corps sector and of 36th Div. VI Corps, which is to participate in Operation ANVIL under U.S. Seventh Army, has driven nearly 65 miles N of Rome with little difficulty, but there are indications that rear-guard opposition will soon increase. In FEC area, Montefiascone falls to 1st Motorized Div. 3d Algerian Inf Div secures Valentano.

In Br Eighth Army's 13 Corps area, S African 6th Armd Div is unable to break through enemy delaying line below Bagnoregio. In 10 Corps area, Br 6th Armd Div crosses Galantina R, from which enemy has departed, and takes Cantalupo.

CHINA—Japanese attack in strength across Liuyang R and meet little opposition from Chinese of IX War Area.

NEW GUINEA—U.S. 6th Div commander, Maj Gen Franklin C. Sibert, his hq, 20th Inf, and miscellaneous units of 6th Div arrive at Toem. On Biak, TF HURRICANE opens assault with 2 regts abreast to clear region N and W of Mokmer airfield. 186th Inf, on left along coast, easily reaches first phase line, about 1,350 yards beyond W end of runway. 162d Inf gets left flank to first phase line but is halted a little short of line of departure, extending inland from coast at Monoebaboe, on right. Japanese laborers bring news of Japanese West Caves strongpoint, some 1,000 yards NW of 3d Bn, 162d Inf. Elements of TF HURRICANE probing toward East Caves are recalled to Mokmer airdrome. Japanese in Parai Defile finally yield to pressure from E and W.

MARIANAS—As invasion convoy, after rendezvousing off the Marshalls, sails for Saipan, carrier planes of TF 58 begin preinvasion softening of the Marianas, a day ahead of schedule, with fighter sweep in afternoon that gains control of the air. Enemy losses through destruction or serious damage are estimated to be from 147 to 215 planes. Of 225 U.S. aircraft launched, only 12 are lost.

12 June

FRANCE—21 Army Group: In U.S. First Army's VII Corps area, 39th Inf of 9th Div, attached to 4th Div, is given part of 22d Inf's sector along coast and takes Crisbecq, from which enemy has withdrawn, as well as Dangueville and Fontenay-sur-Mer, forcing enemy back to his MLR on Quinéville ridge. With strong fire support, including naval, 22d Inf makes concerted assault on Ozeville and captures it; 12th Inf moves forward again to Les Fieffes Dancel, at W end of Quinéville ridge; 8th Inf makes limited attack on Montebourg, but finds it strongly held and pulls back. W of the Merderet, 90th Div commits 359th Inf, which is returned to it by 4th Div, between 357th and 358th but is still unable to make much headway; night attack, 12-13, on Pont l'Abbé by 358th overruns the town, which has been leveled by arty and aerial bombardment. 508th Para Inf of 82d A/B Div, reinf and organized as a TF, crosses the Douve at Beuzeville-la-Bastille, night 12-13, in effort to make contact with 101st A/B Div at Baupte. 101st A/B Div envelops and captures Carentan: Brig Gen Anthony McAuliffe coordinates final assault, which is made by 506th Para Inf, replacing 502d, on right and 327th Gli and to its E 501st Para Regts on left; after 501st and 506th Regts close circle about Carentan, elements of latter and 327th Gli Inf drive rapidly into the town and eliminate stragglers; to secure approaches to Carentan, 506th and 501st Regts thrust toward Baupte and Priers, respectively, but are soon stopped; 327th Gli Inf pushes SE to Montmartin-en-Graignes region and makes contact with elements of V Corps. In V Corps area, 29th Div TF (2 cos of 115th Inf) crosses the Vire to reconnoiter in Montmartin-en-Graignes area and take bridges over Vire-Taute Canal but is halted by strong opposition in Montmartin-en-Graignes region. To meet expected enemy counterattack in weak sector between VII and V Corps, elements of 2d Armd Div are ordered to Montmartin-en-Graignes area. V Corps begins attack toward St. Lô and is vigorously opposed on right. 115th Inf, 29th Div, makes futile attempt to cross Elie R SE of Ste Marguerite-d'Elle; 3d Bn crosses but is driven back with severe casualties. 116th Inf attacks through 115th in evening and succeeds in crossing. 23d Inf, 2d Div, attempts to reach Hill 192, which commands approaches to St. Lô from N and E, but is stopped at Elie R; 9th Inf, on div left, against lighter resistance, advances in conjunction with 1st Div and takes Litteau ridge. On left flank of V Corps, 1st Div, with 18th Inf on right and 26th on left, thrusts to edge of Caumont.

In Br Second Army's 30 Corps area, 50th Div maintains pressure on enemy near Tilly-sur-Seulles. 7th Armd Div begins flanking attack on right flank of corps and pushes through Livry to positions E of Caumont.

ITALY—AAI: In U.S. Fifth Army area, Civitavecchia port is opened to LST traffic. IV Corps continues pursuit of enemy northward, advancing a little less rapidly than VI Corps had, against gradually increasing resistance. 36th Div, reinf by 361st Inf of 91st Div and tanks and TD units, is in assault, its advance screened by 117th Cav Rcn Sq. TF Ramey, under Brig Gen Rufus S. Ramey, consisting of 91st Cav Rcn Sq, reinf by 141st Inf of 36th Div and supporting units, is formed to screen right flank of IV Corps and maintain contact with French. Enemy is offering delaying opposition in vicinity of Orbetello.

CBI—On Salween front, Ch 115th Inf recovers Hongmoshu, in Huei-jen Bridge area.

NEW GUINEA—On Biak, 2d Bn of 163d Inf, 41st Div, arrives; 186th Inf remains on first phase line patrolling actively while awaiting forward movement of 162d Inf to right. Regimental boundary is extended 300 yards on N; 162d Inf is still furiously opposed on right, where 3d Bn works slowly forward, advance elements gaining but 300 yards; gap of almost 900 yards exists between 3d and 2d Bns at end of day. Engineers begin repairs on Mokmer airdrome. In Wakde-Sarmi area, Gen Sibert takes command of TF TORNADO. Hq, 6th Div, becomes

[13-14 JUNE 1944]

headquarters of TF TORNADO, replacing Hq, RCT 158.

MARIANAS—Aircraft of TF 58 continue attacks to complete destruction of enemy planes and wreck airfields; attack enemy convoy attempting to escape, sinking 10-14 ships; sink a cargo vessel just off Saipan and severely damage another; sink enemy vessel in Tanapag harbor.

13 June

FRANCE—21 Army Group: U.S. First Army halts southward attack of V Corps at end of day, ordering it to hold positions while VII Corps makes main effort to cut Cotentin Peninsula and take Cherbourg. XIX Corps (Gen Corlett), which is not yet operational, is given mission of securing and deepening corridor between VII and V Corps in Carentan-Isigny region. In VII Corps' 4th Div sector, 39th Inf (attached) makes limited progress against coastal strongpoints S of Quinéville; 22d Inf gets into position for drive down ridge to Quinéville; 12th maintains positions at W end of Quinéville ridge; 8th contains enemy at Montebourg. 90th Div, whose commander is replaced, continues extremely slow advance, reaching general line Gourbesville-Pont l'Abbé. The 508th Para Inf force of 82d A/B Div reaches Baupte by 0800 as Germans withdraw hastily. Enemy makes strong effort from SW to recover Carentan and gets almost to city limits before 101st A/B Div, assisted by elements of 2d Armd Div, halts attack. 101st A/B Div then attacks with 502d Regt, which passes through 506th, on N and 501st on S and reaches line along road from Baupte to Carentan-Périers highway; 327th Gli Inf, expecting counterattack that does not materialize, pulls back to defense positions along N side of RR between Carentan and the Vire. VII Corps is now securely joined with V Corps. V Corps halts attack toward St Lô at end of day. Isolated elements of 175th Inf, 29th Div, withdraw from Montmartin-en-Graignes area; 116th Inf takes St Clair-sur-Elle and Couvains. 38th Inf, 2d Div, with strong arty support, pushes about 2 miles beyond Elle R toward St Lô. Caumont falls to 1st Div in morning. In Br Second Army's 30 Corps area, 7th Armd Div reaches Villers-Bocage, important communications center, but withdraws northward to tie in with U.S. V Corps, after enemy counterattack gets almost to road from there to Caumont. 50th Div is still held up near Tilly-sur-Seulles.

ITALY—AAI: In Br Eighth Army's 13 Corps area, S African 6th Armd Div breaks through enemy positions at Bagnoregio and pushes on toward Orvieto. In 10 Corps area, Br 6th Armd Div advances through Narni to Terni, arriving just as enemy demolishes bridge.

[209]

BURMA—In NCAC sector, hard fighting is in progress in Myitkyina area, where Japanese penetrate positions of Co K, NEW GALAHAD, but are finally halted.

CHINA—CBI theater ships trainload of arms and ammunition from Kweilin to Hengyang for Chinese IX War Area in response to information by U.S. observer group there that Chinese need them.

NEW GUINEA—Acceding to request by Gen Fuller for a fresh regt, Gen Krueger alerts 34th Inf, 24th Div, for movement to Biak on 18 June. On Biak, Mokmer airfield is repaired sufficiently for fighter planes to use it. 186th Inf, 41st Div, continues to patrol from first phase line; 162d endeavors in vain to close gap between 3d and 2d Bns; 1st Bn moves forward to protect right and rear of 162d Inf. Enemy fire from East Caves position has been neutralized enough for trucks to use coastal road.

MARIANAS—G-2 estimates that 15,000-17,600 enemy troops are on Saipan and 10,150-10,750 on Tinian. TF 58 continues aerial bombardment of the Marianas and begins naval bombardment as well in effort to destroy enemy's defenses. 7 fast BB's and 11 DD's pound W coast of Saipan and Tinian at long range with doubtful results. During further air attacks on enemy shipping, a transport is sunk and other vessels are set on fire. Mine sweepers operate off W coast of Saipan under protection of TF 58. Enemy offers no opposition to air attacks on Saipan.

U.S.—JCS ask Adm Nimitz and Gen MacArthur to comment on the following proposals: (1) advance target dates so that invasion of Formosa, tentatively planned for 15 February 1945, can be advanced; (2) bypass certain objectives, among them S Philippines, also to hasten invasion of Formosa; (3) bypass certain targets, including S Philippines and Formosa, in order to advance directly to Japan. Both men subsequently reply in the negative.

14 June

FRANCE—21 Army Group: In U.S. First Army's VII Corps area, enemy's MLR on N crumbles under attacks of 4th Div: 39th Inf (attached) overcomes strong opposition in Quinéville and finishes clearing coastal region to S with capture of Fort St Marcouf; 22d Inf clears heights W of Quinéville. 90th Div is relieved of task of driving W to the Douve by 9th Inf and 82d A/B Divs and starts pivoting northward to protect left flank of 9th Div: 357th Inf begins fighting in Gourbesville; 359th starts swing to N; 358th, after pushing about 1,000 yards W of Pont l'Abbé, is relieved by 82d A/B Div. 60th Inf, 9th Div, attacks toward Ste Colombe on narrow front as 90th Div turns N, reaching

Valognes-Pont l'Abbé highway. 82d A/B Div thrusts W astride Pont l'Abbé-St Sauveur-le-Vicomte road with 507th Para and 325th Gli Regts abreast and gains about a mile. 79th Div arrives at UTAH Beach. XIX Corps becomes operational and has under its command 29th Div, transferred from V Corps, and 30th Div, which is concentrating between the Vire and Taute.

In Br Second Army's 30 Corps area, additional enemy pressure from S forces 7th Armd Div to withdraw farther northward to Parfouru-l'Eclin area. U.S. V Corps arty assists in repelling enemy attacks.

ITALY—AAI: Gen Alexander learns that VI Corps hq will be withdrawn for ANVIL at once, 3d Div on 17 June and 36th on 27 June; 2 Fr divs are to be withdrawn to Naples area, one on 24th and the other in early July. AAI is still committed to task of clearing Italy S of line Pisa-Rimini. Advanced Hq opens at Frascati.

In U.S. Fifth Army area, Liberty ships are now able to use Civitavecchia port. IV Corps continues to push N and NW, elements taking Magliano. FEC boundary is moved W and TF under Gen Guillaume (1st Gp of Tabors and 1st Moroccan Inf) assumes responsibility for left flank.

In Br Eighth Army's 13 Corps area, Orvieto falls to S African 6th Armd Div without a struggle. 78th Div, to E, overtakes enemy rear guard and inflicts heavy losses in vehicles and guns.

CBI—In NCAC area, battle for Myitkyina continues, with Allied forces making slight progress against stiff resistance. Gaps in Allied positions around Myitkyina are being used by enemy to isolate small units. Gen Boatner orders Morris Force (Ind 3d Div TF), on E bank of the Irrawaddy opposite Myitkyina, to attack at once and is informed by its leader, Brig G. R. Morris, that Japanese command routes of approach, terrain is flooded, and men are exhausted. In Mogaung Valley, Chinese are tightening ring about Kamaing.

On Salween front, Japanese are reinforcing positions within and near Lung-ling and begin vigorous counterattacks. Of 21 bns of Ch XI Group Army in Lung-ling area, only 9 are participating in action for this city. Chinese are forced from Manio Bridge, which Japanese at once put into use.

Continuing offensive in China, Japanese take Liu-yang, increasing threat to Changsha.

NEW GUINEA—Gen Krueger orders Gen Eichelberger, CG of U.S. I Corps and of TF RECKLESS, to Biak to replace Gen Fuller as CG TF HURRICANE. 1st Bns of 162d and 186th Regts circle northward around 3d Bn of 162d Inf to positions above low ridge that is barring forward movement and then push W abreast, 1st Bn of 162d on left coming up against perimeter of Japanese West Caves strong-point. Japanese efforts to oust 1st Bns, night 14-15, fail. In Wakde-Sarmi area, rest of 6th Div arrives at Toem; 20th Inf relieves 158th Inf at the Tirfoam. 158th takes up positions on W bank of Tementoe Creek and patrols S and E.

MARIANAS—As Adm Hill's Western Landing Group, with 2d and 4th Mar Divs embarked, approaches Saipan, 2 bombardment groups under Rear Adm Jesse B. Oldendorf open fire. These, consisting of 7 old BB's, 11 cruisers, 26 DD's, a few APD's, and mine sweepers, get within closer range and achieve better results than did ships of TF 58. Underwater demolition and mine sweeping operations are conducted along coast.

15 June

FRANCE—21 Army Group: In U.S. First Army area, VIII Corps (Maj Gen Troy H. Middleton) becomes operational and has mission of establishing defensive positions from Carentan W across the Cotentin Peninsula and protecting SW flank of VII Corps, 101st A/B Div is transferred to it from VII Corps in current positions. In VII Corps area, Gen Collins decides that main effort of corps will be to cut off Cotentin Peninsula as soon as possible. 357th Inf of 90th Div completes capture of Gourbesville, but div makes little progress elsewhere; bn of 358th Inf is committed on right flank. In 9th Div sector, 47th Inf is committed on right and moves quickly to high ground W of Orglandes; 60th Inf is forced back to line of departure by strong counterattack, the last E of the Douve, but recovers about half the lost ground. Against decreasing resistance, 82d A/B Div's 505th Para Inf, after relieving 507th, drives to positions S of Reigneville; 325th Gli Inf advances to within 1,000 yards of St Sauveur-le-Vicomte. XIX Corps begins limited attacks to improve defensive positions. 30th Div, which has not yet landed all of its components, attacks with 120th Inf and takes Montmartin-en-Graignes. 29th Div's 175th Inf—upon relief, night 15-16, N of Elle R by 119th Inf, 30th Div—moves to line of departure S of river.

ITALY—AAI: Br 5 Corps continues N along Adriatic coast, 3d Carpathian Div replacing Ind 4th Div in line.

In U.S. Fifth Army area, VI Corps hq is assigned to U.S. Seventh Army for Operation ANVIL. IV Corps reaches Ombrone R line and sends patrols into Grosseto; begins crossing the river after nightfall.

In Br Eighth Army area, 13 Corps overcomes rear-guard opposition at Ficulle and Allerona. In 10 Corps area, pursuit of enemy toward Perugia is continued beyond Todi after bridge is completed at Terni.

CBI—In NCAC area, indecisive fighting for Myitkyina continues. On Salween front, Ch forces containing Sung Shan—triangular hill mass that dominates 36 miles of Burma Road where it crosses the Salween—make limited attack that overruns peak at SE corner; Ch efforts to take another, at SW corner, are unsuccessful.

JAPAN—China-based B-29's of XX BC make their first attack on Japanese homeland, dropping 221 tons of bombs on Imperial Iron and Steel Works' Yawata plant, Kyushu I.

SWPA—Planners issue RENO V, the last of the RENO series of plans, calling for establishment of air bases, between July and October, on Vogelkop Peninsula and on Morotai, latter being timed simultaneously with POA's invasion of the Palaus; invasion of the Philippines at Mindanao on 25 October in order to gain bases from which to support operations in mid-November against Philippine targets farther N; invasion of Luzon in early 1945

NEW GUINEA—On Biak, Gen Eichelberger arrives and takes command of TF HURRICANE. Forward movement is limited by enemy tank attacks from West Caves stronghold. 1st Bn, 162d Inf, presses slowly S toward ridge where 3d Bn is fighting. Efforts of 162d Inf to close gap between 3d and 2d Bns are frustrated, but the gap is narrowed to about 500 yards. Air support of the Marianas from Biak is impossible. Enemy is still interdicting use of Mokmer airdrome.

SAIPAN—U.S. VAC marines invade island, beginning at 0840, landing on W coast after saturation naval and aerial bombardment. While reserve elements conduct diversionary demonstration in Tanapag Harbor area, 2d and 4th Mar Divs make main landings near Charan Kanoa. 2d Mar Div, employing 26th Marines on N and 8th Marines on S, lands N of Afetna Pt. 4th Mar Div, with RCT 23 on left and RCT 25 on right, goes ashore S of Afetna Pt. Gap between the assault divs at Afetna Pt. is broader than expected since elements of 2d Mar Div land N of assigned beaches. Against strong opposition, including scattered tank attacks, marines press inland, overrunning town of Charan Kanoa. By end of day beachhead is about 10,000 yards long and over 1,000 yards deep in most places, but flanks are insecure and enemy retains Afetna Pt. Good progress is made in unloading reserves and supporting weapons. CP's of 2d and 4th Mar Divs are established ashore. Japanese suffer heavy casualties in determined but abortive attempts to destroy the beachhead, night 15-16. Illumination of naval star shells assists marines in the night action. 27th Inf Div, VAC reserve, is en route to Saipan; RCT 106 is detached for duty with Guam assault force.

BONIN-VOLCANO Is.—U.S. carrier-based planes attack Chichi Jima and Haha Jima in the Bonin group and Two Jima in the Volcano Is., concentrating on airfields, barracks, and fuel stores.

16 June

FRANCE—21 Army Group: In U.S. First Army area, VII Corps finishes clearing region E of the Douve and establishes bridgehead. Corps objectives are advanced as attack progresses very rapidly against retreating enemy. 90th Div employs 358th Inf in region to right of 9th Div. 9th Div attacks with 4 regts: 39th, which 4th Div has released; 359th of 90th Div, temporarily attached; 47th; and 60th. Driving rapidly through Ste Colombe, 60th Inf establishes bridgehead across the Douve before Néhou with 2d Bn; rest of 9th Div clears region E of the Douve. 82d A/B Div makes substantial gains: 325th Gli and 505th Para Regts reach St Sauveur-le-Vicomte before noon and are joined there by 508th Para Inf, which 507th has relieved at Baupte; 505th and 508th then establish bridgehead 2,000-3,000 yards deep. In XIX Corps area, 120th Inf of 30th Div takes heights commanding Vire-Taute Canal and remains there defending canal line while 29th Div, in conjunction with V Corps' 2d Div, pushes toward St Lô. 175th Inf drives against Hills 90 and 97, NW of St Lô, while 116th, reinf by bn of 115th, attacks toward NE end of Martinville ridge (Hills 147 and 150). Strong opposition halts attack well short of objectives. In V Corps area, 2d Div, with 3 regts in assault, attacks for Hill 192; 3d Bn of 38th Inf gets to within 700 yards of its crest; div attack is then halted for some time.

ITALY—AAI: In Br Eighth Army area, 13 Corps elements meet delaying opposition at Citta della Pieve. In 10 Corps area, Ind 8th Div, driving toward Perugia, overruns Bevagna and Foligno.

CBI—In NCAC area, Ch forces (149th Regt of 50th Div attached to 22d Div) in Mogaung Valley overrun Kamaing. 114th Regt of Ch 38th Div, by-passing Kamaing, effects junction with Chindits of Ind 3d Div at Gurkhaywa.

On Salween front, continuing counteroffensive in Lung-ling area, Japanese have driven Ch 87th Div back 3 miles from the city. To N, Ch 2d Reserve and 36th Divs overrun Chiaotou.

In China, Japanese open attacks on Changsha, from which Ch garrison from 4th Army is leaving for Paoching.

NEW GUINEA—Allied commanders meet to consider invasion of Noemfoor. 30 June is tentatively chosen as D Day. On Biak, TF HURRICANE continues attack with 2d Bn of 186th Inf making main effort. The bn closes gap on low ridge and develops W limits of enemy's West Caves position before withdrawing for night.

MARIANAS—Adm Spruance postpones indefinitely landing on Guam, tentatively scheduled for 18 June, since major naval battle appears to be imminent from enemy fleet movements; issues orders to meet this threat. Naval surface forces begin preinvasion bombardment of Guam. On N flank of Saipan beachhead, 2d Mar Div consolidates and strengthens present positions, committing 2d Marines on left; 8th Marines, on 2d Div right, quickly clears Afetna Pt and Charan Kanoa pier and establishes contact with 4th Mar Div. 4th Mar Div, rearranging its lines before renewing assault, commits reserves, 24th Marines. Jumping off at 1230, 4th Div advances to positions generally along 0–1 ridge line against strong resistance particularly on right where terrain is also an obstacle. Advance party of XXIV Corps Arty lands and establishes CP. 27th Div's 165th Inf lands, night 16–17.

17 June

FRANCE—21 Army Group: In U.S. First Army's VII Corps area, 9th Div, against disorganized resistance, breaks through to W coast, sealing off Cotentin Peninsula as attack continues through night 17–18. Coastal road is cut at Barneville-sur-Mer and Grande Huanville. 90th Div reaches assigned defensive line Golleville–Urville and halts. 82d A/B Div, which is to pass to VIII Corps control, is ordered to establish bridgehead S of the Douve at Pont l'Abbé. In XIX Corps area, efforts of 29th Div to advance are largely contained by enemy strongly established in gap between 175th and 116th Regts near Villiers-Fossard. 115th Inf is committed in center but is unable to reduce the enemy salient. 175th Inf, employing a single bn, is stopped on Hill 108.

ITALY—AAI: 2 Pol Corps, under AAI control, takes command of Adriatic coastal sector from Br 5 Corps, which by this time has advanced to line Teramo–Giulanova. Poles are to continue pursuit toward Ancona.

In U.S. Fifth Army area, IV Corps commits RCT 517 (Para) on right of Highway 1 to give it battle experience before it joins U.S. Seventh Army for Operation ANVIL. 36th Div continues steadily northward.

In Br Eighth Army's 10 Corps area, torrential rains begin, slowing movement. When bridge across the Tiber 3 miles N of Todi is completed, advance on Perugia continues astride the river. Ind 8th Div encounters strong opposition SE of Perugia at Bastia, where Chiasco R is forced.

ELBA—Fr TF based on 9th Colonial Inf Div, under control of AFHQ, lands on Elba and begins clearing the island. This operation, coded BRASSARD and originally planned for an earlier date, is undertaken to disrupt enemy's seaborne traffic and assist offensive on mainland.

CBI—On Salween front, Ch 88th and 87th Divs are ordered to fall back in Lung-ling area, and XI Group Army later withdraws to line Mengmao–Hwangtsoapa.

11 Army Group: In Br Fourteenth Army area, Br casualties during battle of Imphal Plain, 4 March to date, total 2,669 killed and nearly 10,000 wounded and missing. Japanese are estimated to have lost 30,000.

NEW GUINEA—On Biak, TF HURRICANE, attacking with 1st Bns of 186th and 162d Regts, clears heights commanding West Caves strongpoint. P–38's, unable to reach Wakde I., after attack on Sorong, land successfully at Owi, although the field is not yet completed. Since reinforcement of Aitape sector is being considered to meet imminent threat, Gen MacArthur offers Gen Krueger use of a regt of 31st Div.

SAIPAN—RCT 105, 27th Div, lands but is not committed to action; 2d Bn is attached to 4th Mar Div and 1st to 165th Inf. NTLF commander, Gen Holland Smith, and XXIV Corps Arty commander, Brig Gen Arthur M. Harper, set up CP's ashore. After intense preparatory bombardment, marines begin attack that gains immediate objectives except in center, where heavy enemy fire is directed from 600-yard gap existing between 2d and 4th Mar Divs in difficult terrain around Lake Susupe. On N flank of beachhead, 2d Mar Div's 2d and 6th Marines press NE and 8th Marines, reinf by elements of 29th Marines, advances due E. Enemy holds out stubbornly in coconut grove in 8th Marines sector. In 4th Mar Div zone, enemy soon pins down left flank of 23d Marines, causing gap to develop between the assault bns that is filled after dark by 3d Bn of 24th Marines. 24th Marines, in 4th Div center, and 25th Marines, on right, reach 0–2 line, 24th against strong resistance; 25th Marines, from N part of ridge W of Aslito airfield, penetrates building area N of airfield proper. 165th Inf of 27th Div, attached to 4th Mar Div, is closely supported by arty and naval gunfire as it fights for Aslito airfield and heights commanding it. Because of threat of naval battle, planes of TF 58 are diverted from support duties to conduct searches and neutralize Guam and Rota.

18 June

FRANCE—21 Army Group: Gen Montgomery, CG, issues his first written directive since invasion of France, calling for speed-up of operations to take Caen and Cherbourg.

In U.S. First Army's VII Corps area, plans are completed for drive on Cherbourg, next big objective of First Army. 9th Div improves blocking positions and frustrates enemy efforts to escape southward from Cotentin Peninsula, inflicting heavy losses. In XIX Corps area, enemy continues stubborn opposition to advance on St Lô. 3d Bn of 175th Inf, 29th Div, which 119th Inf of 30th Div has relieved at Meauffe, drives to Le Carillon and from there is sent to aid of 1st Bn of 175th Inf on Hill 108.

USSR–FINLAND—Soviet forces break through Finnish Mannerheim Line on Karelian Isthmus.

ITALY—AAI: On right flank of U.S. Fifth Army's FEC, 1st Motorized Div occupies Radicofani, which dominates Rome-Florence road.

Br Eighth Army CG decides to confine advance of 10 Corps beyond Perugia to road through Umbertide and Citta di Castello instead of along Route 71 as originally planned. 13 Corps, making main effort, is to use Route 71 and secondary road through Sinalunga. Br columns converging on Perugia are meeting delaying opposition near the town. Germans quietly abandon positions at Citta della Pieve, in 13 Corps zone, night 18-19.

CBI–In NCAC area, activity of Myitkyina TF subsides to patrolling and skirmishing.

On Salween front, in Shweli Valley, Ch 36th Div of 54th Army begins assault on Watien, and 116th and 130th Divs reach positions near Chiangtso, 4 miles SE of Watien.

In China, Japanese overrun Changsha, which Chinese have abandoned.

NEW GUINEA—On Biak, TF HURRICANE is regrouping and getting into position for final assault to clear entire region from which enemy can fire on Mokmer airfield. 34th Inf, 24th Div, arrives from Hollandia and takes over positions of 186th Inf W of Mokmer airdrome. Gen Fuller leaves Biak to take new position in SEAC. Gen Doe replaces Gen Fuller as CG of 41st Div. Gen Krueger informs Gen MacArthur that he prefers to use Cav RCT 112 to reinforce Aitape rather than break up 31st Div. Gen Krueger orders Gen Sibert to begin offensive in Wakde-Sarmi area. Sibert plans to attack W from the Tirfoam on 20th with 20th Inf, which 1st Inf is to relieve for this purpose.

SAIPAN—LCI gunboats and Marine arty defeat efforts of Japanese to move reinforcements from Tanapag Harbor to the front early in day. 2d Mar Div remains in place except on right, where coconut grove in 8th Marines' sector is cleared. 4th Mar Div drives to E coast of Saipan at Magicienne Bay, cutting island in two. 25th and 24th Marines, on right and in center, respectively, drive to O-3 line, which lies partly along E coast, but 23d Marines, on div left, fights hard to get 400 yards E of Lake Susupe, short of objective. 27th Div's 165th Inf takes ridge W and SW of Aslito airfield and the airfield itself during morning against light resistance, enemy having fallen back to Nafutan Pt. The field is renamed Conroy Field for Col Gardiner J. Conroy, commander of 165th Inf, who was killed at Makin; later, it is renamed Isley Field for Comdr Robert H. Isely, naval aviator lost over Saipan, and misspelled "Isley" consistently. Main attack, later in day, is made by RCT 165 on left and RCT 105 on right; RCT 165 gets almost to Magicienne Bay without opposition, but RCT 105 is slowed by terrain. Transports with 106th Inf are detached from Southern Attack Force and ordered to Saipan.

19 June

FRANCE—21 Army Group: Gen Montgomery schedules offensive for Br Second Army for 22-23 June. Violent storm, lasting through 22d, seriously handicaps build-up of troops and supplies.

In U.S. First Army area, VII Corps begins final drive on Cherbourg with 3 divs abreast. On left, 9th Div, attacking with 60th and 39th Regts, advances quickly northward to Helleville, St Christophe-du-Foc, and Couville; 4th Cav Sq of 4th Cav Gp, which is attached to div to screen right flank, reaches St Martin-le-Gréard; bn of 359th Inf, 90th Div, is also committed on div right flank, to hold Rocheville area. In center, 79th Div's 313th and 315th Regts attack from line Golleville-Urville, which 60th Div has previously secured; 313th reaches its objective, Bois de la Brique, but 315th, directed to bypass Valognes and cut Cherbourg highway NW of there, is halted SW of Valognes and left in position to contain town from W; 314th moves forward during night to take over div left, and 313th shifts to right flank of div. 4th Div, on VII Corps right, encounters firm opposition from forces deployed for defense of Cherbourg. 8th and 12th Regts attack on either side of Montebourg, which 3d Bn of 22d Inf finds clear of enemy, well before dawn, 8th reaching positions just SE of Valognes and 12th abreast it to right. 24th Cav Sq, 4th Cav Gp, screens right flank of 4th Div. In VIII Corps area, 82d A/B and 90th Divs are transferred to VIII Corps from VII Corps. Starting night 18-19, 82d A/B establishes bridgehead S of the Douve at Pont l'Abbé.

ELBA—French complete occupation of island.

CBI—On Salween front, Ku-tung falls to elements of Ch 2d Reserve Div pushing S toward Teng-chung. Ch 53d Army is preparing to attack Chiangtso.

NEW GUINEA—On Biak, TF HURRICANE opens co-ordinated assault for airfields after preparatory arty fire. 186th Inf, making main effort in region N and W of West Caves, reaches ridges W of Hill 320, cutting road leading S to West Caves and enveloping rear of West Caves position. Enemy opposition is scattered. New orders call for 162d

Inf to reduce West Caves while 186th continues to clear region to NW and 34th seizes Borokoe and Sorido airdromes.

SAIPAN—New phase opens as marines pivot N, 4th Mar Div moving around 2d Mar Div, to clear N part of island. 27th Div is to clear Nafutan Pt and S coast, a task presumed to be merely a mop-up mission. 165th Inf reaches S coast of Magicienne Bay without opposition. In 105th Inf sector, 3d Bn is virtually unopposed as it moves forward over rugged terrain; 1st Bn, after frontal assault on the first of a series of ridges of enemy's Nafutan position fails, moves to outflank enemy. Late in day, 1st Bn of 165th Inf is sent back to airfield to plug gap that has developed in line of 105th.

BATTLE OF THE PHILIPPINE SEA—Over the Marianas, carrier planes of TF 58 engage huge force of planes from enemy carriers and inflict crippling losses. Japanese lose over 400 aircraft; there is only superficial damage to a few vessels of TF 58 and only 17 U.S. planes are destroyed. Efforts are made to locate Japanese fleet.

20 June

FRANCE—21 Army Group: Gen Montgomery decides that Br offensive cannot begin before 25 June since arrival of VIII Corps units has been delayed.

In U.S. First Army area, VII Corps continues rapidly toward Cherbourg, 9th and 79th Divs coming up against semicircular belt of fortifications 4–6 miles from the city. 9th Div's 60th Inf moves quickly N through Vasteville to positions just short of its objective—Hill 170—E of Haut Biville; 47th follows to Vasteville, then turns E and advances short distance toward Bois du Mont du Roc. 79th Div reaches positions between St Martin-le-Gréard and Bois de Roudou. 4th Div is virtually unopposed as it moves to line from Le Thiel to Bois de Roudou, just short of enemy's MLR within its sector. In XIX Corps area, 29th Div elements, assisted by tanks and engineers, make limited and futile effort to reduce Villiers-Fossard salient.

USSR-FINLAND—Viipuri falls to Soviet forces of Leningrad Front, insuring safety of Leningrad and opening Gulf of Finland to Soviet fleet.

ITALY—AAI: Period of rapid advance northward comes to a close about this time since enemy has been able to re-form his units and strengthen his positions. Delaying line is disposed across Italy below Gothic Line, where enemy is prepared to make a stand. Pol 2 Corps, across Aso R, seizes Fermo and Pedaso.

U.S. Fifth Army is about half way between the Tiber and the Arno. IV Corps, which has met increased rear-guard opposition during past 10 days, holds line extending E from junction of Highways 1 and 73. FEC gets forward elements to Orcia R, a tributary of the Ombrone, where it is halted. 1st Motorized Div, which is to participate in ANVIL, is replaced in line by 2d Moroccan Div at midnight, 20–21.

In Br Eighth Army's 10 Corps area, 6th Armd Div enters Perugia without opposition. 13 Corps, in center and on right flank, encounters forward positions of enemy delaying line extending from Lake Trasimeno W to Chiusi.

CBI—Gen Stilwell and his force of NCAC are transferred from operational control of Fourteenth Army commander to direct control of Supreme Allied Commander. GALAHAD situation is now critical because of battle exhaustion and disease, and it is apparent that Myitkyina cannot be taken quickly. Personnel from rear area are forced to return to the battle when at all fit for duty.

On Salween front, Ch 36th Div seizes Watien, in Shweli Valley.

Vice President Henry A. Wallace arrives in Chungking, China, for talks with Chiang Kai-shek and Gen Chennault.

SWPA—During planning conference at Gen Krueger's hq, it is decided that D Day for Noemfoor should be postponed to 2 July.

NEW GUINEA—On Biak, 1st Bn of 162d Inf begins attack on West Caves strongpoint but makes little headway. 163d Inf establishes outpost on Hill 320. 34th Inf occupies Borokoe and Sorido airdromes and the village of Sorido against negligible resistance; establishes blocking positions to prevent enemy from reinforcing main battle area. On Aitape front, Japanese strengthen positions in Yakamul area and halt patrolling in this region by 128th Inf. In Wakde-Sarmi area, 6th Div begins westward attack from the Tirfoam toward Lone Tree Hill. 20th Inf drives along coast to Snaky R without difficulty but is stopped by heavy fire from defile between Lone Tree Hill and E nose of Mt. Saksin.

SAIPAN—Marines complete pivoting movement for northward drive, 4th Div coming up to right of 2d, and are on O–4 line, a little below enemy's MLR, which crosses island from just below Garapan to NW corner of Magicienne Bay. As 4th Div swings around 2d, 25th Marines encounters and reduces well-organized enemy positions on Hill 500, just W of Tsutsuuran village. 27th Div begins converging drives on Nafutan from N and W. 165th Inf, reinf by 1st Bn of 105th, attacks S toward Nafutan Pt at noon after preparatory fire and gains about 1,000 yards. 3d Bn, 105th, continues E along S coast for about 600 yards; it is then but 100 yards from 165th Inf force. 106th Inf lands on Saipan and is placed in corps reserve. 2d Bn, 105th Inf, reverts to 27th Div.

BATTLE OF THE PHILIPPINE SEA—In final phase of this major sea action, planes from TF 58 attack strong Japanese naval force well W of Saipan and sink 2 carriers, 2 DD's, and 1 tanker; severely damage 3 carriers, 1 BB, 3 cruisers, 1 DD, and 3 tankers. 16 U.S. planes are destroyed by enemy; 73 others are lost because they cannot locate carriers in darkness or because they run out of fuel. Subsequent efforts to overtake the enemy fleet are unsuccessful.

21 June

FRANCE—21 Army Group: In U.S. First Army's VII Corps area, while 9th and 79th Divs patrol and reorganize for final assault on Cherbourg, 4th Div closes along the city's main defenses to right—Hill 178—NW edge of Bois du Coudray-Hill 158. 22d Inf gets bn on Hill 158, cutting lateral road between Cherbourg and St Pierre-Eglise. At night, Gen Collins issues ultimatum to the German garrison commander, Maj Gen Karl-Wilhelm von Schlieben to surrender by 0900 22d.

USSR-FINLAND—Soviet forces of Karelian Front begin offensive on both sides of Lake Onega.

FRANTIC—U.S. Eighth Air Force begins shuttle raids between Br and Soviet bases. 114 B-17's and 70 P-51's, after bombing oil targets at Ruhland, S of Berlin, land at Soviet bases. Enemy discovers the base at Poltava and makes highly destructive attack on it by light of flares, night 21-22, causing heavy damage to aircraft and stores of ammunition and gasoline.

ITALY—AAI: In Pol 2 Corps area, advance elements reach Chienti R line, behind which enemy is prepared to make a stand, and establish small bridgehead.

In U.S. Fifth Army area, IV Corps commits 1st Armd Div, reinf by 361st Inf of 91st Div, to right of 36th Div in sector previously held by TF Ramey, since IV Corps zone is widening and resistance is increasing. 36th Div continues slowly along Highway 1. FEC is held up by determined opposition along Orcia R line.

In Br Eighth Army area, 13 Corps battles outlying positions of enemy's Trasimeno line. 78th Div takes Sanfatucchio after hard fighting but is unable to progress against hamlet of Vaiano. S African 6th Armd Div reaches heights leading to Chiusi but cannot break into the town. 13 Corps commander decides to commit reserves—4th Div and Cdn 1st Armd Brig—and continue advance on 3-div front; orders 4th Div to relieve 78th Div of positions below Vaiano on night 22-23 and be prepared to relieve rest of 78th, which is scheduled to leave the theater at end of June.

SWPA—TF CYCLONE Is. formally organized to take Noemfoor. Gen Patrick sets up temporary CP at Finschhafen.

NEW GUINEA—Owi airfield is put into use by fighters of Fifth Air Force. On Biak, 1st Bn of 162d Inf continues attack on West Caves without avail, although tanks and flame throwers are used. Japanese efforts to withdraw from the position through 186th Inf lines to NW are frustrated. 186th Inf probes enemy position, called the Teardrop, just NW of Hill 320. 3d Bn, 163d Inf, which was to have driven into the Teardrop from NW and N in conjunction with 186th Inf's pressure from S and SW, is too far N to reach it. In Wakde-Sarmi area, after probing to locate strongpoints, 3d Bn of 20th Inf renews attack toward Lone Tree Hill but meets such heavy fire from well-organized positions that it pulls back to E bank of Snaky R. Arty and mortar fire are placed on Lone Tree Hill, night 21-22.

SAIPAN—Marine action is confined to patrolling. Gen Holland Smith, preparing to make main attack on N and being informed that only 300-500 Japanese remain on Nafutan Pt, orders most of 27th Div to assemble in corps reserve and places its arty under control of XXIV Corps Arty; directs single infantry bn and platoon of tanks to continue clearing S Saipan and protect the airfield. Gen Ralph Smith requests use of RCT 105 and Gen Holland Smith agrees, but orders to this effect do not reach 27th Div until 22d. Meanwhile, 27th Div continues assault on Nafutan Pt, replacing 2d Bn of 165th Inf with 2d Bn of 105th on left of line. Day's action gains little ground. 3d Bn, 105th, reduces cave strongpoint while continuing E along S coast and at end of day is only a short distance from troops moving down from N. At 2000, before receiving word that 105th Inf may be retained, Gen Ralph Smith orders RCT 105 to conduct holding action facing Nafutan Pt and to relieve RCT 165 units by 0630 22d; upon reorganization of lines, not later than 1100 22d, to continue offensive. Gen Holland Smith orders 27th Div to reconnoiter northward toward Marines.

22 June

FRANCE—21 Army Group: In U.S. First Army area, VII Corps, receiving no reply to ultimatum begins final assault on Cherbourg fortress. Intense air preparation, beginning at 1240, does more to demoralize enemy than to damage his positions. VII Corps attack opens at 1400. On left flank, 9th Div presses NE toward Cherbourg with 60th Inf on left and 47th on right; 60th quickly takes Acqueville but is halted at edge of Flottemanville fortifications; 47th gets forward elements to slopes of Hill 171, just W of Bois du Mont du Roc. In center, 79th Div attacks with 3 regts: while 315th is clearing Hardinvast region and 314th the draws E of Tollevast, 313th makes main effort on div right astride Valognes-Cherbourg highway and thrusts to positions just S of La Mare a Canards, an enemy strongpoint. On right flank of VII Corps, 4th Div also attacks with 3 regts: on left, 8th Inf makes limited progress toward La Glacerie; 12th, in center, makes main effort toward Tourlaville but is held to small gains; to right, 22d Inf, with mission of clearing Digosville, becomes surrounded by enemy and is unable to advance.

USSR—German Air Force makes night attack on base at Mirgorod, but U.S. planes escape before the raid. Dumps and supplies are considerably damaged.

ITALY—AAI: Pol 2 Corps is forced to abandon its small bridgehead across the Chienti in Adriatic coastal sector. Activity along the river subsides to patrolling as corps moves troops and supplies forward in preparation for stronger assault.

U.S. Fifth Army continues to advance slowly, particularly in sector of FEC, where it is decided to outflank enemy holding Orcia R line. On right flank in IV Corps area, 1st Armd Div commits TF Howze between CCA on right and CCB on left.

CBI—In NCAC area, Chindits of 77th Brig, Ind 3d Div, begin assault on Mogaung and are joined by 114th Regt, Ch 38th Div. On Salween front, Japanese fall back hastily from Chiangtso toward Teng-chung, harassed by Allied planes. Ch XX Group Army has firm control of Shweli Valley, and is ready for drive on Teng-chung.

11 Army Group: In Br Fourteenth Army area, 4 and 33 Corps troops meet, reopening Dimapur-Kohima-Imphal road. Enemy offensive has failed, and Japanese are obliged to withdraw as best they can under difficult monsoon weather conditions.

NEW GUINEA—PT's land Allied rcn party on Noemfoor, night 22-23. First big cargo ships arrive at Biak. Fifth Air Force P-40's begin operations from Mokmer airdrome. 1st Bn, 162d Inf, continues to work on West Caves, using TNT charges and flame throwers, and at 1555 reports them clear. However, small groups of Japanese emerge from caves during night 22-23 and have to be eliminated by 1st Bn and 186th Inf to N. 186th Inf continues to probe the Teardrop; attempts unsuccessfully to seize 3 enemy guns that are firing from new positions NW of perimeter. In Wakde-Sarmi area, RCT 158 is relieved in preparation for Noemfoor I. operation. RCT 158 has had 70 killed, 257 wounded, and 4 missing during Wakde-Sarmi action; has killed an estimated 920 Japanese and captured 11. After air attack by P-47's from Wakde and intense arty preparation, 3d Bn of 20th Inf drives to crest of Lone Tree Hill and establishes defense perimeter. 2d Bn also reaches the crest but gap exists between the two bns. Japanese counterattack 3d Bn in evening, isolating both it and 2d Bn. Co L, 1st Inf, starts forward with supplies for 3d Bn. On Aitape front, 3d Bn of 127th Inf replaces 1st Bn at Afua.

SAIPAN—2d and 4th Mar Divs begin northward attack toward 0-5 line, extending from W coast below Garapan across Mt. Tapotchau to Laulau village on Kagman Peninsula on E. On W, left flank of 2d Mar Div, 2d Marines remains in place since it is already on 0-5; in center, 6th Marines gets elements to top of Mt. Tipo Pale, about 1,200 yards SW of top of Mt. Tapotchau, achieving greatest div gain for day; on right, 8th Marines makes slow progress toward Mt. Tapotchau, which commands entire island, over extremely difficult terrain. 4th Mar Div attacks with 25th Marines on left and 24th on right; commits 23d in center during day. 25th and 23d Regts drive almost to objective, while 24th advances rapidly along E coast. 27th Div (less 105th Inf) is ordered to attack between 2d and 4th Mar Divs, relieving left flank elements of latter to permit 4th Mar Div to shift E to cover Kagman Peninsula. 27th Div regroups units about the Nafutan position. 3d Bn of 105th Inf shifts N, relieving 1st Bn on right flank, while 2d Bn replaces 3d Bn of 165th on left. No advance is made against the strongpoint and a little ground is lost on left, where relief is accomplished with difficulty. Late in day, 2d Bn of 105th Inf is ordered to continue mop up of Nafutan Pt, a task still believed to be an easy one.

23 June

FRANCE—21 Army Group: Unloading is resumed as storm abates.

In U.S. First Army area, VII Corps penetrates outer defenses of Cherbourg. On left, 9th Div's 60th Inf overruns Flottemanville area, and 47th completes capture of Hill 171; 39th overcomes bypassed resistance near Beaudienville. 79th Div makes limited progress in vicinity of La Mare à Canards but is unable to reduce this strongpoint. In 4th Div zone, 12th Inf, assisted by tanks, advances steadily toward Tourlaville, but units flanking it make little progress.

In Br Second Army's I Corps area, 51st Div, in limited offensive, takes Ste Honorine, NE of Caen and E of the Orne. 1 Corps subsequently exerts limited pressure against enemy N of Caen without making decisive gains.

USSR—Red Army opens summer offensive on central front, where main attack, on 350-mile front, is made by First Baltic and 3 White Russian Fronts against enemy's Minsk salient in White Russia. Particularly strong pressure is applied near Vitebsk and Bobruisk. Soviet aircraft and arty lend powerful support to troops. Both German and Soviet forces have by this time completed extensive reor-

[24 JUNE 1944]

ganization, but enemy is spread thin and lacks adequate reserves.

ITALY—AAI: Gen Alexander, meeting with his commanders, proposes that AAI advance through Ljubljana gap into S Germany.

In Br Eighth Army area, elements of 13 Corps break into Chiusi after hard battle, but German counterattack isolates the troops. 4th Div takes command of sector in center of 13 Corps, between Vaiano and Lake Chiusi, relieving elements of 78th Div. In 10 Corps area, King's Dragoon Gds gain foothold on M. S. Croce.

CHINA—At meeting between Mr. Wallace and Generalissimo Chiang Kai-shek, a proposal is presented that a U.S. observer group be sent to Chinese communists to secure information and assist pilots shot down over N China. When approval is gained, the project (coded DIXIE Mission) is undertaken by 16 officers and enlisted men and 2 civilians.

NEW GUINEA—TF CYCLONE Issues FO 1 for Noemfoor operation. On Biak, 1st Bn of 162d Inf continues to probe West Caves area. 3d Bn, 163d, makes patrol contact with 186th Inf at the Teardrop. Photographs of the Teardrop indicate that Japanese are concentrated on W of the position and preparations are made for attack. 186th Inf is still unable to seize weapons firing on it from NW. In Wakde-Sarmi area, 2d Bn of 20th Inf repels dawn attack against its perimeter on Lone Tree Hill in costly fighting; after unsuccessful attempt to push N to make contact with 3d Bn, moves back down hill and up again, along route used by 3d Bn, to positions just NW of 3d Bn's perimeter. Some supplies are obtained from volunteer groups and from Co L, 1st Inf, which arrives after hard fight. Japanese make determined attempt to destroy forces on Lone Tree Hill in evening; attack in small groups through night 23-24. Gen Sibert decides to try to outflank enemy on the hill.

SAIPAN—VAC attacks northward on 3-div front as 27th Div enters center of line. 2d Mar Div's left and center regts remain in place until more progress can be made to right; 8th Marines, on div right, gains cliff commanding most practical route to crest of Mt. Tapotchau. 27th Div is slow in accomplishing relief of left flank elements of 4th Mar Div and consequently slow in opening attack up valley, called "Death Valley," which is flanked on left by hill mass of Mt. Tapotchau and on right by ridge, called "Purple Heart Ridge." Upon attacking, with 106th Inf on left and 165th on right, div meets intense opposition from cave-studded heights; progress is slow and costly, particularly on left. On right flank, 4th Mar Div attacks with 23d Marines on left and 24th on right: 23d Marines is slowed by inability of 165th Inf to advance but gets to top of Hill 600; 24th continues to make rapid progress along Magicienne Bay

[217]

and reaches 0-5 line just E of Laulau. Enemy tank-supported counterattacks down Death Valley and against Hill 600 are repelled, night 23-24. On S Saipan, 2d Bn of 105th Inf, after reorganizing throughout morning, continues attack on Nafutan position, getting platoon to top of Mt. Nafutan; rest of bn, after small initial gains, pulls back to starting line.

24 June

FRANCE—21 Army Group: In U.S. First Army area, VII Corps closes in on Cherbourg. While 9th Div's 60th Inf clears N flank, 47th and 39th Regts move in on the city, 47th toward Equeurdreville fort and Redoute des Fourches and 39th toward Octeville. In 79th Div zone, 314th Inf overruns La Mare à Canards and pushes toward Fort du Roule, while 313th, to right, keeps abreast and takes Hameau Gringer; 315th, on div left, is still clearing Hardinvast region, far to rear. 12th Inf continues to make main effort of 4th Div. Reinf by bn of 22d, the regt overcomes strong resistance in Digosville area and enters Tourlaville unopposed at night. 8th Inf reduces strong positions E of La Glacerie, on div left. 22d Inf, on div right, contains enemy in Maupertus area. 3d Armd Div, XIX Corps, arrives on Continent.

ITALY—AAI: 1st Motorized Div is the first of the French units to leave Italy for Operation ANVIL.

In Fifth Army area, IV Corps continues northward against strong rear-guard opposition, 117th Cav Rcn Sq on coast overrunning Follonica. In FEC area, Guillaume Group, reinf with light armor, crosses Ombrone R in order to continue advance in contact with 1st Armd Div of IV Corps.

In Br Eighth Army area, 13 Corps opens concerted drive northward with 3 divs. 78th Div, on 13 Corps right flank, establishes bridgehead across Pescia R with infantry, but armor is unable to follow. In center, 4th Div battles in vain for Vaiano throughout day; Germans abandon the hamlet, night 24-25. S African 6th Armd Div continues to meet stubborn opposition on left flank of 13 Corps at Chiusi. In 10 Corps area, enemy has shortened his line, which now runs through Magione, in order to shift armor W to oppose 13 Corps. Br progress up the Tiber Valley is very slow because of mountainous terrain.

NEW GUINEA—On Biak, TF HURRICANE cuts exits from the Teardrop. 2d Bn, 186th Inf, moves N and E to reach NW corner; Co K of 163d Inf blocks N exits and Co C, 163d, guards E side. In Wakde-Sarmi area, TF TORNADO begins outflanking attacks on Lone Tree Hill. Cos K and L, 1st Inf, move by sea to coast just W of the hill and establish small beachhead; try in vain to push inland to clear W side of the hill. 2d and 3d Bns, 20th Inf, assisted by Co L of 1st, make slow progress against numerous enemy defenses on top of the hill and open supply route. Co M, 1st Inf, moves along coast to assist.

SAIPAN—On W flank of V Amph Corps, 2d Marines of 2d Mar Div reaches 0-6 line at S outskirts of Garapan, where the regt must remain for some days awaiting units to right. 6th Marines is battling enemy strongpoint N of Mt. Tipo Pale. On div right, 8th Marines, reinf by bn of 29th Marines, reaches ridge within MG range of top of Mt. Tapotchau. 27th Div's zone is broadened eastward as 165th Inf is given responsibility for clearing valley E of Purple Heart Ridge; 106th Inf alone is thus responsible for clearing Death Valley. Further efforts of 27th Div to move forward are futile. 4th Mar Div veers E to clear Kagman Peninsula, 23d Marines pivoting about 24th Marines. Gap develops between marines and 27th Div because of turning movement. Against moderate resistance, div overruns Laulau and Chacha villages. Failure of 27th Div to advance, despite urging of Gen Holland Smith, results in replacement of its commander, Gen Ralph Smith. Maj Gen Sanderford Jarman, Island Commander, assumes command temporarily, pending arrival of a permanent commander. Gen Jarman's chief of staff takes control of 27th Div elements on S Saipan, where no progress is made during day, and the force on Mt. Nafutan is recalled.

25 June

FRANCE—21 Army Group: In U.S. First Army's VII Corps area, naval gunfire supplements aerial and ground bombardment as battle for Cherbourg nears its end. 9th Div's 47th Inf drives into W suburbs of Cherbourg, overrunning fort at Equeurdreville, Hameau de Tot, and Redoute des Fourches; elements reach coast but are withdrawn. 39th Inf attacks Octeville, where enemy continues to hold out. 79th Div's 314th Inf gains upper defenses of Fort du Roule against stubborn resistance; 313th gets advance elements into outskirts of Cherbourg. In 4th Div zone, 12th Inf gains its objective with drive to coast E of Cherbourg; when orders are changed to permit div to participate in capture of Cherbourg, 12th Inf enters the city and clears assigned portion in E part; 22d Inf is ordered to take Maupertus airfield.

Br Second Army opens offensive in 30 Corps zone for commanding ground in Rauray area. 49th Div, reinf by 8th Armd Brig, attacks S in region E of Tilly-sur-Seulles and makes limited progress against strong resistance. Some elements reach Fontenay; others thrust to Tessel-Bretteville area.

USSR—Soviet forces envelop Vitebsk, trapping 5 enemy divs, and cut Smolensk-Minsk highway.

ITALY—AAI: In U.S. Fifth Army's IV Corps area, port of Piombino falls without opposition to 39th Engineers. This is last day of action in Italy for 36th Div. FEC begins crossing the Orcia in strength as enemy opposition diminishes.

In Br Eighth Army's 13 Corps area, 78th Div expands its Pescia bridgehead slowly. 4th Div forces enemy rear guards from Vaiano. Enemy retains Chiusi throughout day but withdraws after nightfall, blocking exits.

CBI—On Salween front, Chinese reluctantly admit to U.S. liaison personnel with 71st Army that Japanese have routed 261st Regt, 87th Div, and that the 87th Div commander has attempted suicide. Although 8th Army is moving forward from Indochina border to reinforce troops in Lung-ling area, the battle has already been lost to small enemy force of 1,500. Ch effectives in this region have totaled 10,000. Failure at Lung-ling brings orders from Chiang Kai-shek to take Teng-chung and Sung Shan at all costs in preparation for renewing attack on Lung-ling.

NEW GUINEA—On Biak, 1st Bn of 162d Inf makes limited penetration into underground positions of West Caves. Co L, 186th Inf, seizes the enemy guns that have been firing from positions NW of perimeter. Elements of 2d and 1st Bns, 186th Inf, overrun the Teardrop, which has been largely evacuated by enemy, killing 38 Japanese. In Wakde-Sarmi area, under combined attacks of 2d and 3d Bns, 20th Inf, and 3d Bn of 1st, Japanese begin withdrawing from Lone Tree Hill, having received and inflicted heavy casualties there. 3d Bns of 63d and 1st Regts are to mop up on N while 1st Bns of 20th and 1st Regts conduct holding and mopping up operations to S.

SAIPAN—6th Marines, 2d Mar Div, is still held up by strongpoint N of Mt. Tipo Pale. To right, 8th Marines and attached elements of 29th Marines gain crest of Mt. Tapotchau, whose 1,554-foot height commands the island. Some elements of 27th Div's 106th Inf begin wide outflanking movement eastward while others continue northward pressure on enemy in Death Valley, but progress is slow. 165th Inf makes futile efforts to scale Purple Heart Ridge. On right flank of corps, 4th Mar Div easily secures all of Kagman Peninsula, sharply reducing corps front; elements are now on 0-6 line. Turning point in Nafutan battle on S Saipan comes as 2d Bn, 105th Inf, succeeds in crushing Japanese MLR on Ridge 300, which controls Nafutan Pt. Enemy's position on Saipan is by now hopeless, but fanatic resistance continues.

26 June

FRANCE—21 Army Group: In U.S. First Army's VII Corps area, 47th Inf of 9th Div attempts to clear NW section of Cherbourg but cannot gain the arsenal; 39th drives through Octeville and Cherbourg to coast, taking Gen Schlieben, fortress commander, and Rear Adm Walther Hennecke, enemy's naval commander, prisoner at St Sauveur-le-Vicomte. Schlieben refuses to surrender the entire fortress, however. 79th Div completes capture of Fort du Roule and its assigned portion of Cherbourg. 22d Inf, 4th Div, begins attack on Maupertus airfield.

Br Second Army continues limited offensive within 30 Corps zone while beginning main attack with 8 Corps. In 30 Corps zone 8th Armd Brig, spearheading attack of 49th Div, drives to outskirts of Rauray. 8 Corps attacks to E of 30 Corps with 15th and 43d Inf and 11th Armd Divs. 15th Div gets elements to Colleville and patrols to Grainville-sur-Odon. 11th Armd Div thrusts to Mouen.

FRANTIC—Eighth Air Force planes leave USSR for Italy, bombing oil plant at Drohobycz, Poland, on the way. Upon reaching Italy, the planes remain long enough to fly one mission with Fifteenth Air Force before returning to England.

USSR—Vitebsk and Zhlobin fall to Red Army as offensive continues on central front. Vitebsk is one of 3 key positions generally E of Minsk, the others being Orsha and Mogilev, which Hitler has ordered to be held at all cost.

ITALY—AAI: In U.S. Fifth Army's IV Corps area, 34th Div takes control of coastal sector, releasing 36th Div for Operation ANVIL. Para RCT 517 Is. also withdrawn from line. 34th Div has under its command RCT 442 (Nisei) (− 1st Bn), 100th Bn, 804th TD Bn, and other units. FEC completes crossing the Orcia and pushes on toward Siena. The battle along the Orcia has been costly to the French.

In Br Eighth Army's 13 Corps area, S African 6th Armd Div enters Chiusi. 4th Div moves forward to positions almost abreast 78th Div, on 13 Corps right flank, then halts to await 4th Div. 10 Corps is reinf by Ind 10th Div, which arrives to replace 6th Armd Div. Latter is to shift to 13 Corps front a little later. Ind 8th Div takes M. Pilonica.

CBI—In NCAC area, Brig Gen Theodore F. Wessels, USA, takes command of Myitkyina TF, replacing Gen Boatner who has malaria. Mogaung falls to 114th Regt, Ch 38th Div, and 77th Brig, Ind 3d Div. 77th Brig is withdrawn from action by its commander soon afterward on grounds of exhaustion despite orders from Gen Stilwell, who has operational control of the unit, for it to prevent Japanese from reinforcing Myitkyina. Fall of Mogaung permits Chinese to link up with Myitkyina TF, which thus far has been isolated from other friendly forces in Burma. On Salween front, offensive against Teng-chung is begun with air attacks by B-25's from Yun-nan-i.

In China, Japanese seize Heng-yang airfield.

NEW GUINEA—On Biak, mopping up W of Mokmer begins. 1st Bn of 34th Inf (less Co C, which is ambushed en route) seizes abandoned positions on ridge extending N from NW corner of the Teardrop. In Wakde-Sarmi area, 3d Bn of 63d Inf replaces battle-worn 2d and 3d Bns, 20th Inf, on Lone Tree Hill.

SAIPAN—In early morning, 2 LCI(G)'s attack enemy barges moving from Tanapag Harbor, sinking 1 and damaging 1. This concludes enemy attempts to counterland. In 2d Mar Div zone, 6th Marines bypasses and later reduces the stubborn pocket that has been barring advance N of Mt. Tipo Pale; 8th Marines consolidates positions on Mt. Tapotchau. 27th Div continues attack in center of corps with 106th Inf and 2d Bn of 165th. On div left, 1st Bn of 106th is held up by strongpoint, called "Hell's Pocket," at SW end of Death Valley. On right, 3d Bn of 106th and 2d Bn of 165th batter at Purple Heart Ridge from W and E slopes, respectively; enemy there is beginning to weaken. CO of 106th Inf is replaced. 4th Mar Div, to which 165th Inf (− 2d Bn) and 1st Bn of 105th are attached at night, mops up on right flank of corps. On S Saipan, 2d Bn of 105th Inf closes in on enemy in Nafutan Pt area. After nightfall, Japanese make futile breakout attempt.

27 June

FRANCE—21 Army Group: In U.S. First Army's VII Corps area, organized resistance at Cherbourg ceases during morning when Brig Gen Robert Sattler, deputy commander of the Cherbourg fortress, surrenders the arsenal to 47th Inf, 9th Div, after Allies broadcast an ultimatum. 4th Div takes over garrisoning of Cherbourg; its 22d Inf overruns Maupertus airfield and quickly clears Cap Lévy. 9th Div prepares to attack to clear Cap de la Hague. Advance engineer units arrive at Cherbourg to restore facilities. In VIII Corps area, newly arrived 83d Div takes over defensive positions on corps left flank held by 101st A/B Div.

In Br Second Army's 30 Corps area, 49th Div gains Rauray and holds it against strong counterattacks. 8 Corps secures small bridgehead across the Odon near Baron, bypassing resistance in Grainville-sur-Odon region.

USSR—Red Army overruns Orsha, NE of Minsk, and envelops Bobruisk.

ITALY—AAI: In U.S. Fifth Army area, IV Corps continues toward Highway 68. In FEC area, enemy, after resisting strongly during day, begins retiring after nightfall.

In Br Eighth Army's 13 Corps area, 4th Div drives enemy rear guards from Gioiella. In 10 Corps area, Germans begin general withdrawal in region between Lake Trasimeno and the Tiber and are being pursued by corps. Elements of 6th Armd Div find M. Pacciano and M. Bagnolo free of enemy.

CBI—On Salween front, regt of Ch Hon 1st Div, 8th Army, relieves New 28th Div, but in the process Japanese are able to recover ground lost during June. Enemy is reinforcing Sung Shan by infiltration through Ch lines.

NEW GUINEA—On Biak, Co C rejoins 1st Bn, 34th Inf. Preparations are made by 34th Inf to clear Japanese from cliffs NW of 1st Bn area. Gen Eichelberger decides that situation on Biak is now stable enough for him to leave. 1st Bn of 162d Inf, accompanied by members of 41st Counter Intelligence Detachment, patrols into innermost depths of West Caves. A hasty count reveals that at least 125 Japanese have been killed there. This is the last enemy position that can threaten Mokmer airdrome. On Aitape front, Maj Gen Charles P. Hall, CG XI Corps, takes command of TF PERSECUTION at midnight, 27-28. Reorganization and regrouping of forces is quickly undertaken. Cav RCT 112 arrives to reinforce TF PERSECUTION, which is threatened with enemy attack. In Wakde-Sarmi area, 3d Bn of 63d Inf encounters fire from few remaining MG positions as it mops up on Lone Tree Hill.

SAIPAN—6th Marines, 2d Mar Div, continues to clear div center against heavy resistance; 8th Marines, elements of which are relieved by 2d Bn, 25th Marines, starts clearing N slope of Mt. Tapotchau. 27th Div's 106th Inf again attacks Hell's Pocket on div left with 1st Bn and for first time makes some progress in reducing it. On div right, other elements of 106th arid 2d Bn, 165th, clear further ground on Purple Heart Ridge; 3d Bn of 106th, followed by 2d Bn, then drives W across Death Valley under enemy fire. On right flank of corps, 4th Mar Div gets additional elements to line O-6; attached elements of 165th Inf make substantial progress on div left, but gap develops and bn of 24th Marines is brought forward to fill it. Japanese decide to make their final stand on N Saipan on line across island from Tanapag through Hill 221 to Tarahoha, delaying in current positions as long as possible while the new line is being organized. On S Saipan, 2d Bn of 105th Inf concludes operations against Nafutan Pt, which is declared secure at 1840. 550 Japanese dead are counted. Total number estimated to have held the position exceeds 1,000, rather than the 300-500 originally thought to have been there.

28 June

FRANCE—21 Army Group: In U.S. First Army's VII Corps area, 79th Div, upon relief in Cherbourg, moves S to U.S. VIII Corps zone. 9th Div continues preparations for attack to clear Cap de la Hague.

In Br Second Army area, 30 Corps secures Brettevillette but later loses it to enemy counterattack. 8 Corps expands its Odon bridgehead near Baron and secures another, near Gavrus; fights to clear enemy from flanks.

USSR—Soviet threat to Minsk increases as Second White Russian forces take Mogilev.

ITALY—AAI: In U.S. Fifth Army area, salvage parties reach Piombino, and the port is made ready for use by Liberty ships in less than a month. In IV Corps area, 117th Cav Rcn Sq is withdrawn from line to participate in Operation ANVIL. IV Corps is pushing steadily northward, with 34th Div on left and 1st Armd Div on right, toward Highway 68, which Cecina R parallels.

In Br Eighth Army's 13 Corps area, S African 6th Armd Div reaches Chianciano without making contact with enemy. In center, 4th Div breaks through enemy positions on Casamaggiore-Frattevecchia ridge. Elements of 78th Div move forward on 13 Corps right flank to conform. In 10 Corps area, Ind 10th Div is relieving Ind 8th Div.

CBI—Vice President Wallace recommends to President Roosevelt that Gen Stilwell be replaced or that he be given a presidential representative with considerable powers as his deputy; suggests that steps be taken to meet Japanese threat in E China.

In NCAC area, 1st Bn of 42d Regt, Ch 14th Div, attacks toward Sitapur in order to cut off Japanese N of Myitkyina.

On Salween front, Japanese planes make their first appearance, dropping supplies to Sung Shan garrison.

In E China, Japanese begin assault on Heng-yang itself and for the first time in E China are being firmly opposed by Chinese.

NEW GUINEA—Amphibian vehicles conduct rehearsal for Noemfoor operation. On Biak, Gen Eichelberger turns over command of TF HURRICANE to Gen Doe and leaves the island. It is learned that 34th Inf must serve as ALAMO Force reserve for pending operation, necessitating regrouping of forces on Biak. 34th Inf continues mopping up. Japanese begin a second withdrawal (first being on 22d), with orders to prepare for guerrilla warfare; about this time begin withdrawing from East Caves. Large-scale infantry action against Ibdi Pocket ends, but the position is kept under fire from ground and air.

SAIPAN—2d Mar Div continues clearing difficult terrain N of Tipo Pale and on crest of Mt. Tapotchau. Maj Gen George W. Griner takes command of

27th Div, which completes reduction of organized resistance at Hell's Pocket on left but makes little headway and suffers heavy casualties in Death Valley proper and on Purple Heart Ridge. 4th Mar Div maintains and improves positions on right flank of corps, additional elements reaching 0-6 line; provides fire support for 27th Div.

29 June

FRANCE—21 Army Group: In U.S. First Army's VII Corps area, 9th Div—employing 47th Inf on right, 60th in center, and 4th Cav Gp (−) on left—attacks to clear Cap de la Hague; comes to a halt before enemy line through Gruchy, Gréville, and crossroads SE of Beaumont-Hague. Forts in Cherbourg harbor surrender. In VIII Corps area, 101st A/B Div is detached from corps and starts from St Sauveur-le-Vicomte to Cherbourg. In XIX Corps area, first elements of 3d Armd Div enter combat: CCA begins limited action to reduce Villiers-Fossard salient in 29th Div's line NE of St Lô in preparation for renewing drive on St Lô.

In Br Second Army area, 8 Corps, as it continues action to expand Odon bridgehead and corridor leading to it, undergoes determined counterattacks by enemy armor against W flank, which temporarily gain some ground but leave the attackers exhausted. In view of the strong concentration of enemy armor in front of 8 Corps, it is decided to break off offensive and consolidate present positions.

USSR—Germans yield Bobruisk to First White Russian troops.

ITALY—AAI: In U.S. Fifth Army's IV Corps area, 442d Inf, which has recently cleared villages of Belvedere and Sassetta, is withdrawn from center of 34th Div line and replaced by 135th Inf; 133d Inf, driving along Highway 1, is stubbornly opposed but gets to within a mile of Cecina.

Br Eighth Army takes command of Pol 2 Corps in Adriatic coastal sector. Germans begin general withdrawal in front of Eighth Army. 13 Corps commander orders 6th Armd Div to relieve 78th Div, night 3-4 July; 9th Armd Brig to move to 10 Corps sector between 30 June and 4 July. S African 6th Armd Div takes Acquaviva and Montepulciano. 4th Div advances to ridge through Petrignano and Valiano, which enemy rear guards are defending. 78th Div takes Castiglione del Lago, former enemy strongpoint N of the Pescia, without opposition.

BURMA—In NCAC area, Col Charles N. Hunter takes command of all U.S. troops at Myitkyina. 1st Bn of 42d Regt, Ch 14th Div, after making considerable progress through enemy territory, is halted by fire. Co F, NEW GALAHAD, attempts to support the bn but loses its way and is destroyed as a fighting body.

NEW GUINEA—On Biak, 34th Inf continues mopping up in region N of 186th Inf against little opposition. Mortars and tanks fire on East Caves, from which engineers have recently received fire. On Aitape front, Gen Hall reorganizes TF PERSECUTION into 3 commands—Western Defense Area (Brig Gen Alexander N. Stark, Jr.), Eastern Defense Area (Gen Gill), and Eastern Defense Command (Gen Clarence Martin). Gen Martin's command, holding outer defense line along Driniumor R, includes 3d Bn of 127th Inf, 128th Inf (less 3d Bn), and Cav RCT 112.

SAIPAN—6th and 8th Marines, 2d Mar Div, continue to clear rugged terrain on left flank of corps. 27th Div's 106th Inf, after regrouping, drives northward in Death Valley with 1st and 2d Bns of 106th Inf and 3d Bn of 105th abreast, gaining about 1,000 yards. To right, 2d Bn of 165th tries in vain to take northernmost hill of Purple Heart Ridge. 4th Mar Div, with elements of 165th Inf still attached, consolidates and improves positions on right flank of corps, meeting strong opposition on left.

30 June

FRANCE—21 Army Group: Gen Montgomery, CG, orders U.S. First Army to make breakout attack while Br Second Army continues efforts to take Caen and contains enemy between there and Villers-Bocage.

In U.S. First Army's VII Corps area, enemy's defense line on Cap de la Hague Peninsula collapses under 9th Div's attacks. 39th Inf begins exploring tip of the peninsula after nightfall. 101st A/B Div relieves 4th Div at Cherbourg and latter starts S for coming offensive. In XIX Corps area, CCA of 3d Armd Div gains its limited objectives NE of St Lô and is relieved there by 115th Inf, 29th Div.

ITALY—AAI: In U.S. Fifth Army's IV Corps area, 34th Div continues battle for Cecina: bn of 135th Inf establishes bridgehead across the Cecina R and, with assistance of tanks, defends it successfully; 133d Inf makes main effort against town of Cecina, which is still stoutly defended; to protect right flank, 168th Inf is moved forward to Cecina R by truck, and 3d Bn begins crossing without opposition.

In Br Eighth Army's 13 Corps area, 4th Div overruns Petrignano in lively fighting.

NEW GUINEA—Main body of Noemfoor attack forces leaves Toem at 1800. On Biak, 34th Inf finishes mopping up its sector, ending main phase of action on Biak, and withdraws to beach. 162d and 186th Regts move into assigned positions on main and reserve lines. In Wakde-Sarmi area, TF TORNADO completes mop up of Lone Tree Hill and surrounding region.

SAIPAN—At commander's conference on Saipan, it is decided to land on Guam on 21 July and to reinforce Southern Troops and Landing Force (III Amphib Corps) for this purpose with 77th Div. Postponement of Guam invasion allows time for 77th Div to arrive from Hawaii and permits stronger and more prolonged preliminary bombardment.

2d Mar Div continues to advance its center and right flank over difficult terrain above Tipo Pale and Mt. Tapotchau. 27th Div finishes clearing Death Valley and Purple Heart Ridge; makes contact with Marines on either flank. This successfully concludes battle for central Saipan. 4th Mar Div continues to consolidate on Kagman Peninsula and patrols deeply beyond 0-6 line.

1 July

FRANCE—21 Army Group: U.S. First Army's Field Order No. I, as amended, prescribes general offensive to be opened on 3 July by VIII Corps on W flank of army and extended progressively eastward by other corps upon order. In VII Corps area, organized resistance on Cherbourg Peninsula ceases as 9th Div pushes to tip of Cap de la Hague. V Corps improves positions slightly in limited attack by elements of 38th Inf, 2d Div.

Br Second Army repels determined counterattacks against its salient between Tilly-sur-Seulles and Caen. 30 and 8 Corps, supported by massed arty concentrations, throw enemy back and inflict heavy tank losses.

USSR—Third White Russian troops take Borisov by storm.

ITALY—AAI: In U.S. Fifth Army's IV Corps area, 34th Div's 133d Inf gets forward elements to Cecina R and clears Cecina town; 135th maintains its small bridgehead E of Cecina despite enemy efforts to destroy it; 168th crosses 3d Bn over the Cecina on div right flank before dawn. 1st Armd Div makes limited progress on right flank of corps: CCA, on E, is near Casole d'Elsa, where enemy is disposed for strong defense. FEC pushes forward toward Siena.

In Br Eighth Army area, 10 Corps, which is virtually out of contact with enemy, replaces 6th Armd Div in line with Ind 10th Div. 9th Armd Brig is arriving.

NEW GUINEA—As TF 77 (Adm Fechteler), consisting of most of combat elements of VII Amphib Force, U.S. Seventh Fleet, plus Aus units, steams toward Noemfoor with TF CYCLONE, Allied aircraft pound the island with over 200 tons of bombs, continuing a program of aerial bombardment of enemy bases there and on Vogelkop Peninsula. On Biak, TF HURRICANE begins aggressive patrolling to prevent enemy remnants from organizing for guerrilla warfare. In Wakde-Sarmi area, to insure safety of Maffin Bay staging sector, TF TORNADO begins clearing inland between the Woske and Tor Rivers. 1st Inf pushes along coast to the Woske.

SAIPAN—VAC drives toward next phase line, 0-7, which extends across northern neck of Saipan. On W flank of corps, 2d Mar Div gains about 800 yards in center and on right. In center, 27th Div gains about 600 yards on left and 400 on right against moderate opposition. 4th Mar Div maintains positions on right flank of corps and patrols uneventfully.

U.S.—Gen Marshall asks Gen Stilwell for his reaction to a possible split of CBI into two theaters, with Gen Sultan commanding in Burma and Gen Stilwell leading Chinese forces in China proper.

2 July

FRANCE—21 Army Group: Regroups in preparation for renewing offensive.

U.S. First Army commits VII Corps, with 4th, 9th, and 83d Divs under its command, between VIII and XIX Corps. VIII Corps commands 8th, 79th, 82d A/B, and Both Divs. XIX Corps retains 29th and 30th Divs. V Corps has command of 1st and 2d Inf and 2d Armd Divs. 3d Armd and 101st A/B Divs are held in First Army reserve.

USSR—Third and First White Russian forces are enveloping Minsk; latter cuts Minsk-Baranovichi RR.

ITALY—AAI: Chief of Staff, AAI, issues "Appreciation" concerning course of action after the necessary forces for ANVIL have withdrawn from Italy; concludes that offensive in Italy can be continued on a limited scale but recommends that AAI be reinf if possible in order to secure Ljubljana Gap and invade S Germany.

In U.S. Fifth Army's IV Corps area, 133d Inf of 34th Div closes along the Cecina and takes Cecina Marine at its mouth, concluding bloody action on left flank of corps. 135th consolidates and strengthens bridgehead across the Cecina then moves W, pinching out 133d. CCA, 1st Armd Div, suffers heavy losses in tanks and personnel during futile attempts to enter Casole d'Elsa. FEC takes Simignano, SW of Siena, and pushes on toward Siena.

In Br Eighth Army's 13 Corps area, patrols reach junction of Highways 71 and 75 without opposition. S African 6th Armd Div advances through Sinalunga, from which enemy has withdrawn. 4th Div takes Fojano without opposition. 10 Corps is unopposed throughout day but regains contact with enemy after nightfall.

CBI—In NCAC's Myitkyina area, Gen Wessels withdraws the Chinese forces directed toward Sitapur in order to strengthen N flank, toward which enemy is reported to be moving in strength. Fighting during the past week has resulted in little change in positions, although Ch 150th Regt and 236th Engrs have gained a few hundred yards.

On Salween front, Chinese troops begin assault on Teng-chung in violent monsoon rainfall. 348th Inf of Ch 116th Div, 53d Army, reduces 7 pillboxes $4^1/_2$ miles NW of the city. Previous medium-level and skip-bombing attacks on the city have done little harm to enemy in dugouts.

In E China, Japanese halt attack on Heng-yang to await arrival of arty at front.

NEW GUINEA—At Noemfoor, after extremely heavy and effective naval gunfire and air bombardment of assault zone, which started 80 minutes before H Hour, TF CYCLONE (RCT 158, reinf) lands at 0800 on N part of island in Kamiri airfield region without opposition. Gen Patrick assumes command ashore, relieving Adm Fechteler, who directed the amphibious phase; after inspecting Kamiri airdrome, requests that reserves—503d Para Inf—be dropped there. Light resistance develops as assault bns of 158th Inf move cautiously inland, mopping up as they go, but beachhead—800 yards deep and 3,000 yards wide—is secured. Arty is landed and put into use, and work is begun on Kamiri airdrome. TF CYCLONE inflicts over 100 casualties on enemy while suffering only 3 men killed, one of them accidentally. At Aitape, RCT 124 of 31st Div is assigned to TF PERSECUTION as reserve.

SAIPAN—On extreme left of corps, 2d Marines, 2d Mar Div, easily seizes Garapan, which has been leveled by bombardment. Gains of 800–1,200 yards are made in div center and on right. In 27th Div zone, 106th Inf advances some 400 yards on left flank and 3d Bn of 165th about 1,700 yards on right flank, but 3d Bn of 105th is held up by enemy strongpoint in center. 1st Bn, 105th, released from reserve, bypasses the strongpoint and makes contact with right flank units. Assault elements of 4th Mar Div advance right flank 1,500 yards against negligible resistance. After nightfall, Japanese fall back to their final defense line on N Saipan.

3 July

FRANCE—Field Marshal Guenther von Kluge relieves Field Marshal Gerd von Rundstedt as German Commander in Chief West.

21 Army Group: U.S. First Army opens general offensive, to become known as the Battle of the Hedgerows, on W flank. VIII Corps, in driving rain that prevents air support and hampers movement, attacks southward down W coast of Cotentin Peninsula toward La Haye-du-Puits with 79th, 82d A/B, and 90th Divs, from W to E, abreast. Progress is limited by firm opposition in hedgerow country, but 82d A/B Div gains Hill 131, NE of La Haye-du-Puits.

USSR—Minsk falls to Third and First White Russian Fronts.

ITALY—AAI: In U.S. Fifth Army's IV Corps area, 34th Div begins drive on Leghorn, employing 135th Inf on left, 442d in center, and 168th on right, and meets strong resistance. 3d Bn, 135th Inf, pushes into S edge of Rosignano, beginning bitter battle for this enemy stronghold SE of Leghorn. In zone of CCA, 1st Armd Div, Cos K and L of attached 361st Inf take over attack on Casole d'Elsa but are unable to enter the town. In FEC area, Siena falls to 3d Algerian Div during morning.

In Br Eighth Army's 13 Corps area, 78th Div finds Cortona undefended and is passed through by 6th Armd Div.

CBI—Gen Stilwell, replying to Gen Marshall's inquiry of 1st, expresses no eagerness for a field assignment in China and comments on situation in China.

11 Army Group: In 33 Corps sector of Br Fourteenth Army area, Ukhrul falls to troops of Ind 7th Div and 23d LRP Brig, but enemy remains near this important communications center.

NEW GUINEA—On Noemfoor, moving E along N coast, 2d and 3d Bns of 158th Inf extend beachhead perimeter some 1,800 yards toward Kornasoren airfield. 1st Bn of 158th Inf patrols S of Kamiri R, eliminating some stragglers. 1st Bn, 503d Para Inf, moving from Hollandia in C-47's, drops on Kamiri airfield and takes responsibility for central sector of the airfield defenses. Casualties during the airdrop are extremely high, almost 10%, although enemy offers no opposition. On Biak, elements of Co E, 542d Engr Boat & Shore Regt, and Co E of 163d Inf push into East Caves with unexpected ease. Patrolling throughout the caves is continued during next few days. Japanese 18th Army issues plan for attack in force across Driniumor R on the mainland, beginning night 10–11. RCT 124, 31st Div, begins landing at Aitape, final elements going ashore on 6 July.

SAIPAN—VAC pushes quickly toward O-7 line. On left flank, 2d Mar Div is being pinched out as 27th Div, making main effort, veers NW toward Tanapag Harbor. Attacking with 106th Inf on left, 1st Bn of 105th in center, and 3d Bn of 165th on right, 27th Div gains positions commanding Tanapag, although enemy strongpoint is delaying elements of 106th Inf near boundary of 2d Mar Div. 4th Mar Div encounters heavy fire from Hill 721 and nose jutting S from it, which holds up 3d Bn of 23d Marines on div right. Heavy fire is placed on this position, night 3-4.

VOLCANO-BONIN Is.—TF 58 makes destructive attacks on ground installations and shipping at Iwo Jima in Volcano Is.. and Haha Jima and Chichi Jima in Bonin Is.., employing naval gunfire as well as carrier aircraft.

4 July

FRANCE—21 Army Group: In U.S. First Army area, VIII Corps continues to make slow progress southward on W flank of army. 82d A/B Div takes Hill 95, overlooking La Haye-du-Puits from NE, where it remains until pinched out by 79th and 90th Divs on its flanks. VII Corps opens attack to E of VIII Corps on narrow front between swamps of Prairies Marcagéuses and Taute R. 83d Div, in action for first time, leads off toward Priers but meets firm resistance that makes progress negligible.

In Br Second Army's I Corps area, in preparation for all-out assault on Caen, Cdn 3d Div seizes Carpiquet but is held up short of its airfield for some time by enemy defenders. In 8 Corps area, 43d Div is attacking NE astride the Odon to ease pressure on 1 Corps.

USSR—Troops of First Baltic Front overrun Polotsk.

ITALY—U.S. Seventh Army moves to Naples in preparation for invasion of S France.

AAI: In U.S. Fifth Army's IV Corps area, 135th Inf, on 34th Div's W flank, clears about a third of Rosignano; 442d Inf slightly improves positions in center; to right, 168th attempts in vain to reach Castellina, key enemy position, but overruns Hill 675 (M. Vitalba); 363d Inf is committed to right of 168th and gains ground on heights E of Hill 675. CCA, 1st Armd Div, gets elements of 361st Inf into Casole d'Elsa before dawn after most of the enemy garrison has withdrawn. After this action 361st Inf is detached from 1st Armd Div and reverts to 91st Div. Subsequent action of 1st Armd Div on right flank of IV Corps is limited until time of its relief. In FEC area, 3d Algerian Div completes withdrawal from corps zone to Naples and is replaced by 4th Mtn Div.

In Br Eighth Army area, 13 Corps, with S African 6th Armd Div on left, Br 4th Div in center, and Br 6th Armd Div on right, moves forward to M. Lignano hill mass below Arezzo against sporadic resistance. 6th Armd Div, using Highway 71, most direct route to Arezzo, quickly reaches Castiglion Fiorentino but is slowed soon afterward by demolitions.

NEW GUINEA—On Noemfoor, 3d Bn of 158th Inf, continuing along N coast unopposed, takes Kornasoren airfield. 1st Bn (−) crosses Kamiri R and seizes Kamiri village without enemy interference; continues SE against scattered fire to large Japanese garden area, some 1,700 yards distant, where defensive perimeter is established for night on Hill 201. 3d Bn, 503d Para Inf, drops on Kamiri airfield, suffering casualties exceeding 8%, and relieves elements of 3d Bn, 158th Inf. Because of high casualty rate during airdrops, it is decided to fly rest of 503d Para Inf to Kamiri airfield when the field can receive C-47's safely. In Wakde-Sarmi area, Hill 225 falls to elements of 63d Inf.

POA–CINCPOA, in radio message to COMINCH, rejects suggestion of 13 June that target dates for operations in the Pacific be advanced; states that air forces should be established on Mindanao before Formosa is invaded; expresses doubt that Gen MacArthur can reach Mindanao by 25 October as hoped.

SAIPAN—VAC completes drive to northern neck of Saipan and prepares for final phase of battle in which 2 divs will advance NE on Marpi Pt and its airfield. 2d Mar Div's 2d Marines completes mop up of Garapan and forces enemy remnants into tip of Mutcho Pt, but 6th Marines is checked on ridge about 1,000 yards from coast. 27th Div, after fire fight with large group of retreating enemy, completes drive to Tanapag Plain. 106th Inf reaches seaplane base at Flores Pt and is joined by 8th Marines; eliminates the cave strongpoint to rear; in center, 1st Bn of 105th Inf reaches beach; on right, 1st Bn of 165th Inf quickly gains last ridge overlooking Flores Pt seaplane base. 4th Mar Div drives forward to Hill 767 area, taking Hill 721 and the nose from it with ease. In preparation for 2-div assault on 5th, 2 bns of 165th Inf, 27th Div, relieve 2 left flank bns of 4th Mar Div in late afternoon; during the relief, gap develops in line through which almost a hundred Japanese infiltrate, but the hole is later filled and Japanese are driven back or killed.

U.S.–JCS, in memorandum to President Roosevelt, recommend that Gen Stilwell be promoted from rank of lt gen to general; that Chiang Kai-shek be urged to place Gen Stilwell in command of all Chinese forces; that G en Sultan be given command of Chinese Corps in Burma; and that Gen Wheeler replace Stilwell as Deputy to Adm Mountbatten.

5 July

FRANCE—21 Army Group: In U.S. First Army area, 35th Div begins landing on the Continent. VIII Corps overruns RR stations of La Haye-du-Puits. VII Corps continues to make slow progress toward Priers.

ITALY—AAI: Gen Wilson, as result of decision to undertake ANVIL, issues new directive calling for AAI to advance to Po R line and from there to line Venice-Padua-Verona-Brescia; promises that U.S.

92d Div and a Brazilian div may be expected as reinforcements, former about 15 September and latter by end of October.

In U.S. Fifth Army's IV Corps area, 135th Inf of 34th Div gains about half of Rosignano as stubborn fighting continues; 442d secures positions on ridge some 2 miles E and 1 mile N of Rosignano; 168th and 363d Regts maintain and consolidate positions to right.

In Br Eighth Army area, 13 Corps meets stiffening resistance all along line. Efforts to break through to cut Highway 69 W of Arezzo fail. 4th Div takes Tuori. In 10 Corps area, Ind 10th Div reaches Umbertide. Germans are again withdrawing in front of corps. In Pol 2 Corps area, Badia falls to 3d Carpathian Div.

CBI—On Salween front, Ch 8th Army (82d, 103d, and Hon 1st Divs), which has assembled E and S of Sung Shan, begins assault on that enemy stronghold after night-long arty preparation. 2 Ch regts attack at dawn and make limited gains, which they lose to Japanese counterattack.

NEW GUINEA—On Noemfoor, 1st Bn (−) of 158th Inf, on Hill 201, repels the only major counterattack offered by Japanese during the Noemfoor operation early in morning and virtually annihilates the enemy force of 350–400. 2d Bn, 158th, prepares to land at Namber airdrome, on SW coast, while other elements of TF CYCLONE continue search for enemy. In Wakde-Sarmi area, elements of 63d Inf take crest of Mt. Saksin.

SAIPAN—VAC begins final phase of assault on island with 27th Div on left and 4th Mar Div on right. 27th Div's 105th Inf pushes slowly forward along coast and in coconut grove to E, but is stopped on right by deep canyon, called Harakiri Gulch, ideally suited for defense. 165th Inf tries in vain to enter the canyon on left but has little action on right. 4th Mar Div advances with 24th Regt on left and 25th on right, after 23d clears to line of departure in morning; is almost unopposed as it drives about 1,200 yards from line of departure to its objective for day, since enemy has been unable to establish line in this region.

6 July

FRANCE—21 Army Group: U.S. Third Army establishes hq in France at Nehou. Corps assigned to it are: VIII (now with U.S. First Army), XII, XV, and XX.

In U.S. First Army area, VIII Corps continues to close in on La Haye-du-Puits, which is nearly enveloped, but enemy is putting up a staunch defense. VII Corps commits 4th Div to W of 83d as attack toward Priers continues against unabated opposition.

USSR—Elements of First White Russian Front occupy Kovel, from which Germans have withdrawn.

ITALY—AAI: In U.S. Fifth Army's IV Corps area, 135th Inf of 34th Div continues clearing Rosignano; 168th breaks into Castellina and takes it; cuts road from there to Chianni; 363d overruns Hill 634 (M. Vase) NE of Castellina.

In Br Eighth Army area, 13 Corps is still meeting strong opposition below Arezzo, but 4th Div takes Poggio all'Olmo. 10 Corps advances rapidly until halted by new enemy delaying line. In Pol 2 Corps area, 3d Carpathian Div seizes Osima.

NEW GUINEA—On Noemfoor, after naval and air preparation, 2d Bn of 158th Inf makes amphibious assault on Namber airfield and takes it without opposition by 1240. Arty liaison plane lands there soon afterward. Aus P-40 sq arrives at Kamiri airdrome for operations. Vigorous patrolling of Noemfoor discloses few enemy. On Biak, loudspeakers are moved into East Caves in effort to induce Japanese to surrender. The few remaining alive are found to have abandoned their positions there. RCT 124 of 31st Div completes movement to Aitape from Oro Bay.

MARIANAS—In preparation for invasion of Guam, Gen Holland Smith attaches 77th Div to III Amphib Corps.

SAIPAN—After futile attempt by 27th Div to draw abreast 4th Mar Div, new orders are issued at 0900. 27th Div zone is limited in W coastal area to point just beyond Makunsha village; extends inland to include valley running S of it, dubbed Paradise Valley, and Harakiri Gulch. Marines are given responsibility for rest of island to NE. Some progress is made toward Makunsha on left, but efforts to overrun Harakiri Gulch and push to coast via Paradise Valley are largely futile. 4th Mar Div attacks with 23d, 24th, and 25th Regts abreast, from left to right, in expanded zone, making rapid progress against sporadic resistance except on left, where 23d Marines is strongly opposed while attempting to push into Paradise Valley from W and is out of contact with 24th Marines. 24th Marines gains 1,400–1,800 yards. 25th Marines moves quickly up E coast, assisted by naval gunfire, to Mt. Petosukara; accepts surrender of 700–800 civilians.

U.S.—President Roosevelt, accepting recommendations of JCS of 4th, radios Chiang Kai-shek as suggested.

7 July

FRANCE—21 Army Group: In preparation for all-out assault on Caen by Br Second Army, heavy bombers of RAF BC attack in force, night 7-8, dropping 2,662 tons of bombs on military targets.

In U.S. First Army's VIII Corps area, 79th and 90th Divs continue efforts to break through enemy positions in La Haye-du-Puits–Mont Castre Forest area and repel several counterattacks. VII Corps inches forward down Carentan–Périers road against steadily increasing resistance. XIX Corps, to E of VII Corps, opens attack with 30th Div that establishes bridgehead in St Jean-de-Day area and takes that town: after preparatory bombardment, 117th Inf forces the Vire on div left at 0430 and 120th attacks across Vire-Taute Canal to W at 1345. After nightfall, CCB, 3d Armd Div, crosses into bridgehead at Airel with mission of expanding it toward St Gilles; 113th Cav Gp moves forward on 30th Div's right flank.

ITALY—AAF: In U.S. Fifth Army's IV Corps area, 135th Inf of 34th Div completes clearing Rosignano, but enemy is holding out just beyond the town; after heavy concentrations of fire on M. Vase, enemy counterattacks and recovers it from 3d Bn, 363d Inf. FEC gets forward elements beyond Highway 68. 4th Mtn Div takes Colle di Val d'Elsa, SW of Poggibonsi. Offensive operations of FEC later subside as preparations are made for its movement to Naples area upon relief by Br 13 Corps.

In Br Eighth Army's 13 Corps area, S African 6th Armd Div retains foothold on slopes of M. Lignano against strong counterthrusts. In 10 Corps area, Ind 4th Div, which has been trained recently in mountain warfare, is concentrating S of Umbertide to re-inforce corps as it continues advance on Sansepolcro.

CBI—Br 36 Div, which has moved forward to replace 77th LRP Brig, Ind 3d Div, is transferred to command of Gen Stilwell.

In NCAC area, Myitkyina TF begins training on program for forces in reserve and those in contact with enemy.

On Salween front, Ch 8th Army continues operations to clear Sung Shan with night attack, 7–8, by 246th Regt of 82d Div. Although peak is seized, Japanese counterattack and drive Chinese off, causing 200 casualties.

JAPAN—Small force of B-29's attacks Kyushu I., night 7–8, most of planes concentrating on Sasebo naval targets. This is the third B-29 mission and the second against Japanese homeland.

NEW GUINEA—On Biak, co of 163d Inf attempts to move into Ibdi Pocket but finds enemy repairing old fortifications and building new ones. Bombardment of the position is resumed.

POA—Adm Nimitz orders his commanders to prepare for invasion of S Palaus (Angaur, Peleliu, Ngesebus) on 15 September and of Yap and Ulithi, NE of the Palaus, on 5 October.

SAIPAN—Japanese remnants, estimated to number about 3,000, make a last desperate counterattack, which overwhelms most of 105th Inf, on 27th Div left flank, as well as guns of 3d Bn, 10th Marines, before it is stemmed at 105th Inf CP. 106th Inf is committed to relieve 105th and recovers most of the lost ground, but stops a little short of 105th, isolated remnants of which are withdrawn by water. Meanwhile, 165th Inf clears Harakiri Gulch without serious opposition. 4th Mar Div continues to make rapid progress on right.

U.S.—Gen Marshall informs Gen Stilwell of action taken by President Roosevelt and urges Stilwell to maintain friendly relations with Chiang Kai-shek.

8 July

FRANCE—21 Army Group: In U.S. First Army area, VIII Corps overruns La Haye-du-Puits during attack from W by 79th Div. Newly arrived 8th Div enters line between 79th and 90th Divs. VII Corps continues efforts to advance down Carentan–Priers road against strong opposition. In XIX Corps area, 113th Cav GP, 30th Div, and 3d Armd Div expand bridgehead despite difficulty in co-ordinating movement of infantry and armor within limited sector. On W, 113th Cav Gp overruns villages of Goucherie and Le Mesnil-Veneron; late in day the group is attached to CCA, 3d Armd Div, which has crossed into bridgehead and is pushing toward Le Desert. 30th Div, with 120th Inf on right, 117th in center, and 119th on left, advances toward Le Désert and Cavigny. CCB, 3d Armd Div, gets almost to La Bernardrie; is attached to 30th Div late in day. 35th Div, which has completed landing on the Continent, is attached to XIX Corps.

In Br Second Army area, I Corps opens assault Caen at 0420, employing Cdn 3d Div on right, 59th Div in center, and 3d Div on left. Br troops penetrate into the city at NE corner. U.S. heavy bombers provide close support for the attack.

USSR—Units of First White Russian Front overrun Baranovichi.

ITALY—AAI: In U.S. Fifth Army's IV Corps area, 34th Div continues drive on Leghorn and makes some headway. 88th Div takes command of zone previously held by 1st Armd Div and attacks with 350th Inf on left and 349th on right: bypassing Volterra, div gains heights N and E of the town; 350th presses toward Laiatico, commanding strongpoint, and 349th overruns Roncalla. In FEC area, 4th Gp of Tabors attacks toward S. Gimignano, W of Poggibonsi, and takes Hill 380, 2 miles N of Highway 68.

In Br Eighth Army area, 13 Corps undergoes further enemy counterattacks. In 10 Corps area, Ind 4th Div takes command of sector W of the Tiber.

CBI—Generalissimo Chiang Kai-shek agrees in principle to President Roosevelt's request that Gen Stilwell be permitted to command Ch forces, but asks that an influential personal representative of the President's be sent to China.

On Salween front, 5 Ch divs have encircled Tengchung.

NEW GUINEA—During conference at Gen Krueger's CP, plans are made for operations in Sansapor-Mar region of the Vogelkop but on a tentative basis since terrain information is lacking. In Aitape area, Gen Krueger orders Gen Hall to reconnoiter in force across the Driniumor. The 3 commands of TF PERSECUTION are renamed to avoid confusion, Western Defense Area becoming Western Sector, Eastern Defense Area becoming Eastern Sector, and Eastern Defense Command becoming PERSECUTION Covering Force.

SAIPAN—2d Mar Div (−), with 165th Inf attached, attacks through 27th Div to clear remaining enemy from Saipan. 6th Marines reaches beach by 1830 against little opposition; 8th Marines, to E, mops up in hills and ravines. 165th Inf attacks on right from positions above Harakiri Gulch, driving through Paradise Valley. 4th Mar Div attacks toward N tip of Saipan. 23d Marines drives through Karaberra Pass to the sea by 1205. To right, 2d and 24th Marines reach assigned positions in afternoon. 25th Marines is unopposed as it continues up E coast about 600 yards.

GUAM—Warships of Southern Attack Force begin naval bombardment of Guam coastal defenses.

9 July

FRANCE—U.S. 5th Div arrives on Continent. 21 Army Group: In U.S. First Army area, VIII Corps attempts to push beyond La Haye-du-Puits but makes little headway against dual handicaps of stubborn enemy and hedgerow terrain. In VII Corps area, 4th and 83d Divs gain several hundred yards toward Périers in violent fighting, 83d overrunning St Eny. 9th Div arrives from Cherbourg and is given sector E of the Taute, previously right flank of 30th Div's zone. Boundary between VII and XIX Corps is adjusted accordingly. In XIX Corps area, while 113th Cav Gp and CCA of 3d Armd Div hold on right flank of corps, 30th Div and attached CCB continue offensive toward Hauts-Vents, immediate objective. Strong enemy counterattack in region W of main road to St Lô is checked, largely by arty fire. CCB, attacking between assault regts of 30th Div, thrusts rapidly toward Hauts-Vents along main highway until stopped short of objective by div order. Late in day CCA, 3d Armd Div, is attached to 9th Div, VII Corps.

In Br Second Army's I Corps area, Caen falls as 3d Div, driving S into the city, meets Cdn 3d Div, which enters from W. Elements of Cdn 3d Div at last take Carpiquet airfield, which enemy has defended stubbornly, and Bretteville-sur-Odon.

USSR—Lida falls to Third White Russian Front.

ITALY—AAI: In U.S. Fifth Army's IV Corps area, 34th Div's 135th and attached 442d Regts make slow progress above Rosignano; with recapture of Hill 634 (M. Vase) by 363d Inf on div right, 363d and 168th are able to continue northward; 168th thrusts into Casale and clears it before dawn of 10th. On right flank of IV Corps, 88th Div's progress is also limited by strong opposition. TF Ramey is given mission of protecting right flank of corps along Highway 68 and maintaining contact with FEC. The TF, consisting entirely of armd units, begins slow advance on road net E of Villamagna. In FEC. area, enemy forces 4th Gp of Tabors from Hill 380 after seesaw battle. 1st and 6th Moroccan Inf relieve goumiers and start toward Hill 380, regaining it before dawn of 10th. Germans apply pressure against other units, forcing back Fr salient on Highway 2.

In Br Eighth Army area, plans are made for attack by 13 Corps on Arezzo on 15th, by which time N7, 2d Div of Cdn 1 Corps will have moved forward to strengthen the assault. 13 Corps will meantime maintain pressure on limited scale against enemy below Arezzo. In Pol 2 Corps area, Italians take Filottrano after about a week of hard fighting.

NEW GUINEA—On Biak, AAF joins in bombardment of Ibdi Pocket. In Wakde-Sarmi area, 1st Bns of 1st and 63d Regts complete battle for crest of Hill 265, SW of Hill 225. This is the last enemy strongpoint in Maffin Bay region.

SAIPAN—2d Mar Div mops up additional enemy on W flank of corps; attached 165th Inf reaches coast except for company that remains behind to mop up Paradise Valley. 4th Mar Div attacks with 2d Marines of 2d Mar Div and 24th and 25th Marines and quickly reaches Marpi Pt, final objective. Saipan is declared secure by Adm Turner at 1615. Final mop up of stragglers is assigned to 2d and 4th Mar Divs, with 165th Inf still attached to latter. During the Saipan operation, Northern Troops and Landing Force suffers 14,111 casualties, about 20% of its total strength of 71,034. Of the 14,000 casualties, 3,674 are Army and 10,437 are Marine Corps. Japanese garrison of about 30,000 is virtually destroyed. Saipan is within bombing range of Japan and is to become base for B-29's.

10 July

FRANCE—21 Army Group: Gen Montgomery issues orders for offensive, calling for strong southward drive (COBRA) by U.S. First Army, which will be assisted by Br Second Army attack E and S of Caen.

In U.S. First Army area, VIII Corps advances some 3,000 yards beyond La Haye-du-Puits, 90th Div overrunning Mont Castre Forest. VII Corps continues attack with 3 divs—4th, 83d, and 9th, from W to E—and reaches general vicinity of St Eny, Tribehou, and Le Désert. In XIX Corps area, CCB of 3d Armd Div renews efforts to reach Hauts-Vents but is stopped a little short. 120th Inf, 30th Div, pulls up almost abreast CCB, forward elements reaching village of Le Rocher; 119th Inf, on 30th Div left flank, reaches positions just short of Belle-Lande.

In Br Second Army area, 1 Corps mops up within Caen. 8 Corps begins drive toward Thury Harcourt, attacking between the Odon and the Orne. 43d Div takes Eterville and Hill 112, between Eterville and Evrecy, but is unable to secure Maltot.

USSR—Field Marshal Walter Model, who has replaced Field Marshal Ernst Busch as commander of German *Army Group Center*, proposes that *Army Group North* be withdrawn behind the Dvina in order to employ elements on central front, but Hitler refuses. By this time, German *9th* and *4th Armies* have been virtually destroyed on central front. Troops of Third White Russian Front encircle Vilno.

ITALY—AAI: In U.S. Fifth Army's IV Corps area, 135th and 442d Regts, on 34th Div left flank, make slow progress toward Leghorn; on right, 133d Inf attacks through Casale and 363d moves forward abreast it. Progress on right flank of IV Corps is negligible.

CBI—On Salween front, 307th Regt of 103d Div, Ch 8th Army, is continuing costly efforts to clear enemy from Sung Shan.

11 Army Group: In Br Fourteenth Army's 33 Corps area, Japanese have been cleared from immediate vicinity of Ukhrul.

NEW GUINEA—On Biak, Cos K and L of 163d Inf push into Ibdi Pocket. In Aitape area, TF PERSECUTION begins rcn in force E of the Driniumor. 1st Bn, 128th Inf, crosses at mouth of river and drives along coast almost to Yakamul, dispersing 2 enemy groups en route. 2d Sq, 112th Cav, crosses to S and moves cautiously through jungle about a mile, making no contact with enemy. Rest of TF PERSECUTION forces in Driniumor area regroup. During night 10–11, enemy attacks W across the Driniumor in force, breaking through line of PERSECUTION Covering Force on 1,300-yard front and threatening Paup villages along coast. Co E, 128th Inf, is overwhelmed and suffers heavy casualties. Co G is also heavily hit but checks enemy onslaughts. Rcn forces E of the river are ordered to withdraw to river line.

11 July

FRANCE—21 Army Group: U.S. First Army attacks with 4 corps abreast as V Corps joins in offensive on extreme E. VIII Corps makes further progress below La Haye-du-Puits. VII Corps bears brunt of strong German counterattack on its left flank and on right flank of XIX Corps. Enemy tanks penetrate 9th Div lines in Le Désert area, but positions are restored by combined efforts of infantry, tanks, TD's, arty, and aircraft. Germans lose a number of tanks in this action. To W, 83d and 4th Divs continue forward slowly. XIX Corps opens attack on St Lô with 30th Div W of the Vire and 35th and 29th Divs E of the river. 30th Div, with less difficulty than 9th, checks enemy counterattack NW of Pont Hébert; attached CCB, 3d Armd Div, secures Hauts-Vents crossroads; 119th Inf meets increasingly strong opposition in Pont Hébert area. 35th Div attacks with 137th Inf along the Vire and 320th on left from La Méauffe–Villiers-Fossard region, but makes little headway; strongpoint at St Gilles stops 137th Inf well above Pont Hébert. 29th Div attacks on left flank of XIX Corps in conjunction with V Corps: 115th Inf progresses slowly toward La Luzerne against stubborn resistance; 116th, penetrating enemy positions, drives S through St André-de-l'Epine and then W along Martinville ridge toward St Lô. V Corps renews attack on Hill 192, NE of St Lô. 2d Div, employing 38th and 23d Regts, makes the final assault and with tremendous arty support overcomes opposition on this important feature that has withstood vigorous attacks during June; crushes enemy defense in St Georges-d'Elle area; cuts Bayeux–St Lô highway at La Calvaire.

In Br Second Army's 30 Corps area, 50th Div improves positions near Hottot against lively resistance. In 8 Corps area, 43d Div holds Hill 112 against counterattack. In I Corps area, 51st Div tries in vain to advance on Colombelles, E of the Orne.

ITALY—AAI: Orders MALLORY MAJOR, air offensive against Po R bridges, to go forward.

In U.S. Fifth Army's IV Corps area, 442d Inf, in 34th Div sector, gets almost to Pastina; 133d Inf bypasses Pastina to E but is stopped short of Hill 529; limited progress is made in other sectors of div front. 351st Inf, 88th Div, is released from reserve to continue attack on Laiatico but is pinned down short of objective.

In Br Eighth Army's 13 Corps area, NZ 2d Div begins concentrating within corps zone to assist in drive on Arezzo.

CHINA—Japanese, having completed preparations for stronger assault on Heng-yang, renew attack, and are stoutly opposed by Chinese garrison, which is assisted by aircraft.

NEW GUINEA—On Noemfoor, TF CYCLONE starts regrouping for systematic mopping up operations. 158th Inf is given N sector and 503d Para Inf the S. 2d Bn of 503d arrives, having moved by air from Hollandia to Biak and thence by sea to Namber airdrome. In Aitape area, PERSECUTION Covering Force begins general withdrawal from Driniumor R line to next delaying positions, along line of X-ray R and Koronal Creek, after futile attempt by 1st Bn, 128th Inf, to reopen Anamo-Afua trail. Gen Krueger orders positions along the Driniumor restored. On Biak, 3d Bn of 163d Inf begins steadily compressing Japanese in Ibdi Pocket.

12 July

FRANCE—21 Army Group: U.S. First Army relinquishes command of 101st A/B Div, which is to return to England for rest and training. VIII Corps makes substantial progress southward toward the Ay and Sèves Rivers as enemy opposition diminishes. 8th Div, in center, overruns Hill 92. VII Corps makes limited gains toward Raids, on Carentan-Périers road, and toward Les Champs-de-Losque crossroads against strong resistance. XIX Corps continues attack on St Lô, moving in slowly. 30th Div is still held up in Pont Hébert area. 35th makes negligible progress N of St Lô. 29th advances its right flank (115th Inf) to villages of La Luzerne and Belle-Fontaine, NE of St Lô, but 116th is practically halted on ridge leading W to St Lô. In V Corps area, 2d Div, against light resistance, finishes clearing all assigned objectives in Hill 192 area and gains firm control of highway to St Lô from Bérigny to La Calvaire.

Br Second Army is largely engaged in regrouping.

USSR—Soviet offensive is broadening. Moscow announces opening of attacks in region between Nevel and Ostrov by Second Baltic Front, which overruns Idritsa, on rail line to Riga.

ITALY—Air offensive against Po R bridges, MALLORY MAJOR, is begun by TAF medium bombers under ideal weather conditions.

AAI: In U.S. Fifth Army's IV Corps area, U.S. armored units driving on Leghorn along Highway 1 in coastal sector get beyond Castiglioncello. 34th Div makes limited progress to right: 442d Inf pushes into outskirts of Pastina, but 133d battles in vain for Hill 529, from which enemy begins withdrawing after nightfall. 363d Inf reverts to 91st Div as that div prepares to enter action. 88th Div's 351st Inf, with strong arty and mortar support, overruns Laiatico. In FEC area, 4th Mtn Div drives forward almost to S. Gimignano.

CBI—In NCAC area, Myitkyina TF, with air support, makes major effort against Myitkyina, but the attack fails. As result of poor air-ground liaison some bombs hit friendly forces.

On Salween front, Japanese continue to repel Chinese efforts to clear Sung Shan, although 2 Ch regts are committed to this task. 2-week lull ensues and Ch 8th Army breaks off attacks.

NEW GUINEA—In Aitape area, Gen Gill, CG of 32d Div and of Eastern Sector, takes control of PERSECUTION Covering Force, relieving Gen Martin, who becomes commander of Eastern Sector. Gen Gill sets up hq at Tiber and prepares for attack to recover positions along the Driniumor, dividing covering force into 2 groups: North Force, consisting of 124th Inf (less 2d Bn) reinf by 1st Bn of 128th Inf; South Force, consisting of 112th Cav and 3d Bn of 127th Inf. 2d Bn of 128th Inf, holding Tiber while reorganizing, is held in reserve. Co B, 128th Inf, moves from Tiber to Anamo in preparation for general attack. After dark, Japanese attack 2d Bn, 128th Inf, but are forced to withdraw. On Biak, about 200 Japanese escape from Ibdi Pocket.

13 July

FRANCE—4th Armd Div arrives on Continent.

21 Army Group: U.S. First Army commander approves Outline Plan for COBRA—breakout attack in St. Lô area. Minor amendments altering boundaries are subsequently made. VIII Corps continues steadily southward all along line. VII Corps makes progress on left flank, where 9th Div gets almost to crossroads at Les Champs-de-Losque. Offensive on rest of VII Corps front is virtually suspended. XIX Corps continues costly battle for St Lô. On E, 29th Div passes 175th Inf through 116th in vain attempt to drive W along highway ridge toward the city. In V Corps area, 5th Div replaces 1st Div in line. 1st Div withdraws to Colombières area in preparation for movement to VII Corps zone.

In Br Second Army area, Cdn 2 Corps becomes operational with Cdn 2d and 3d Divs under its command. 12 Corps takes command of 8 Corps sector and of 43d, 15th, and 53d Inf Divs; 11th Armd Div; 4th Armd Brig; and 31st Tank Brig.

USSR—After several days of street fighting, Vilna falls to troops of Third White Russian Front.

ITALY—AAI: In U.S. Fifth Army's IV Corps area, 34th Div gains about 3 miles toward Leghorn and to E overruns Pastina and Hill 529. 91st Div is committed in center of corps front and attacks toward the Arno with 363d Inf on left and 362d on right; presses close to Chianni and heights to E despite strong opposition. 88th Div, on IV Corps right flank, makes substantial progress against decreasing resistance. In FEC area, 4th Mtn Div overruns S Gimignano and commanding ground nearby as enemy begins withdrawal in that region. Against diminishing resistance, 2d Moroccan Div drives almost to Poggibonsi on W and to outskirts of Castellina in Chianti on E.

In Br Eighth Army's 13 Corps area, NZ 2d Div pursues enemy northward toward Arezzo, taking crest of M. Castiglione Maggiore without opposition. Corps is directed to press NW to Alpe di Poti with Ind 4th Div while Ind 10th Div protects right flank.

NEW GUINEA—On Noemfoor, 1st Bn of 503d Para Inf encounters main enemy forces remaining on Noemfoor at Hill 670, some 3 miles NE of Namber airdrome. In Aitape area, PERSECUTION Covering Force attacks to restore positions along the Driniumor. North and South Forces succeed in reaching the river, but broad gap exists between them. 1st Bn of 128th Inf, while clearing coastal sector from Anamo to the Driniumor, on N flank of North Force, decisively defeats enemy's *Coastal Attack Force* and destroys most of its arty. In region W of the Driniumor, Japanese make a number of small attacks on 2d Bn of 128th Inf, in Tiber area, and are driven off.

SAIPAN—3d Bn of 6th Marines, 2d Mar Div, occupies Maniagassa I., in Tanapag Harbor without serious opposition. This concludes Marine activities on Saipan.

U.S.—President Roosevelt, preparing to depart for Hawaii to discuss Pacific strategy with Gen MacArthur and Adm Nimitz, replies to Chiang Kai-shek's letter of 8th, agreeing to choose a political representative and urging that the way be quickly cleared for Gen Stilwell to take command of Ch forces.

14 July

FRANCE—21 Army Group: In U.S. First Army area, VIII Corps closes along Ay and Sèves Rivers, where forward movement is stopped by army order. In VII Corps area, 9th Div continues to clear Les Champs-de-Losque–Le Désert area against tenacious resistance. In XIX Corps area, 119th Inf of 30th Div captures Pont Hébert, concluding bitter struggle for this objective. Just across the Vire, 35th Div breaks through to Pont Hébert-St Lô highway. 29th Div maintains positions NE and E of St Lô. In V Corps area, commander of 5th Div assumes responsibility for former zone of 1st Div on left flank of corps.

USSR—Broadening offensive southward, troops of First Ukrainian Front attack above and below Brody, in region E of Lwow. Pinsk falls to First White Russian forces.

ITALY—AAI: Directs Br Eighth Army to take Ancona and Florence and U.S. Fifth Army, Leghorn; later, attack is to carry through the Gothic Line between Dicomano and Pistoia to the Po R line, where bridgeheads are to be established.

In U.S. Fifth Army's IV Corps area, 135th Inf of 34th Div meets little opposition as it continues toward Leghorn; 442d takes S. Pieve di Luce; 133d is approaching Usigliano. Elements of 91st Div's 363d Inf take Chianni without opposition early in day; patrols of 362d find that enemy has abandoned Terricciola. 88th Div gains about 4 miles on right flank of IV Corps, overrunning key positions at Belvedere and Villamagna. In FEC area, as enemy resistance collapses, French take Poggibonsi and continue toward Certaldo.

In Br Eighth Army's 13 Corps area, NZ troops gain summit of M. Carmucino, but German opposition then stiffens all along line.

CBI—In NCAC area, request by Maj Gen Lentaigne for withdrawal of Morris Force (of Ind 3d Div) from positions across the Irrawaddy from Myitkyina is denied. By this time the force has only 3 platoons left.

11 Army Group: In Br Fourteenth Army area, 33 Corps completes envelopment and elimination of Japanese force on Ukhrul–Imphal road, completely clearing Ukhrul area. 4 Corps, pressing down Tiddim road, has been stubbornly opposed thus far, but Japanese are beginning to weaken under attacks of Ind 5th and 17th Divs and aircraft.

POA–CINCPAC-CINCPOA issue Joint Staff Study for STALEMATE (invasion of the Palaus).

NEW GUINEA—Gen MacArthur orders TF CYCLONE to have Kornasoren airdrome ready to receive 50 P-38's by 25 July in preparation for invasion of Vogelkop Peninsula. Rcn party moves by PT boat from Noemfoor to Cape Opmarai, N coast of the Vogelkop, where it stays for 3 days gathering information upon which final plans for the operation are made. In Wakde-Sarmi area, 31st Div (less RCT 124) begins unloading at Maffin Bay to relieve 6th Div. In Aitape area, South Force narrows gap between it and North Force along the Driniumor by moving 3d Bn of 127th Inf northward, but the 2 forces are still out of contact with each other. 3d Bn of 124th Inf, North Force, kills about 135 Japanese in the gap, night 14–15.

15 July

FRANCE—21 Army Group: U.S. First Army halts offensive W of Taute R while regrouping extensively in preparation for COBRA. 4th Armd Div is temporarily held in reserve. VIII Corps, now holding initial objectives along Ay R except for town of Lessay, maintains current positions while regrouping to include 8th, 79th, 90th, 4th, and 83d Divs. VII Corps continues offensive with 9th Div while regrouping on rest of front to include 30th and 1st Inf Divs and 2d and 3d Armd Divs. Zone is extended E to Vire R when 30th Div is transferred to corps in place at 2400. 9th Div secures crossroads at Les Champs-de-Losque. In XIX Corps area, 30th Div, before its transfer to VII Corps, attacks with 117th Inf to outskirts of Le Mesnil-Durand, forcing salient into enemy positions. 35th and 29th Divs, with close air and arty support, continue battle for St Lô. 134th Inf, on left flank of 35th Div, gains N slopes of Hill 122, where it is within 2,000 yards of St Lô, but rest of div is held up well to rear in Le Carillon-Pont Hébert area. 29th Div makes main effort on left flank of XIX Corps with 116th Inf along Martinville Ridge: 2d Bn of 116th Inf succeeds in breaking through to Bayeux-St Lô highway near La Madeleine but is isolated there; 175th Inf holds its positions on left flank of div; 115th, on right flank, makes slow progress SW from La Luzerne. V Corps, upon regrouping, contains 2d and 5th Divs on inactive left flank of army.

In Br Second Army area, 12 Corps begins attack toward line Bougy-Evrecy-Maizet, between the Odon and the Orne, night 15-16, 15th Div moving forward with illumination from searchlights.

USSR—Troops of Second Baltic Front overrun Opochka.

ITALY—Allied air attacks on Po bridges between Piacenza and the Adriatic (MALLORY MAJOR) are successfully concluded, but tactical bombers subsequently continue interdiction program on an expanded scale, hitting bridges W of Piacenza and throughout Po Valley.

AAI: In U.S. Fifth Army's IV Corps area, 135th Inf of 34th Div continues rapidly toward Leghorn until hit in evening by counterattack on left flank near heights overlooking the town; enemy is driven off with aid of arty. 442d Inf advances to left rear of 168th as latter begins attack in right half of 442d's zone. 168th and 133d Regts push toward Pisa with 100th Bn filling gap between them; bypassing Lorenzana, 133d gets nearly 2 miles beyond the town. In center of IV Corps, 91st Div's 363d Inf takes Bagni di Casciana without opposition, then withdraws in preparation for assisting attack of 34th Div on Leghorn; 361st Inf replaces 362d on div right and takes Morrona, NW of Terricciola. 88th Div continues northward on right flank of corps. In FEC area, 8th Moroccan Inf takes Castellina in Chianti while 4th Moroccan mops up E of Poggibonsi. By nightfall FEC is up against enemy delaying line in Certaldo=Tavernelle area.

In Br Eighth Army area, 13 Corps opens attack on Arezzo at 0100 after strong arty preparation, employing 6th Armd Div on left and NZ 2d on right. Air support begins at dawn. 6th Armd Div drives salient into center of enemy line, and NZ 2d Div takes M. Lignano. After nightfall, Germans begin general withdrawal.

BURMA—Thus far in the siege of Myitkyina, Japanese garrison has suffered 790 dead and 1,180 wounded, and its commander is contemplating withdrawal. No co-ordinated attacks have been attempted by Myitkyina TF since 12th, but daily attacks on a limited scale have gradually constricted Japanese positions.

NEW GUINEA—In Aitape area, PERSECUTION Covering Force is still endangered along the Driniumor by gap, now 1,500 yards wide, between North and South Forces. 124th Inf, North Force, is ordered to extend southward to left flank of South Force. Japanese are becoming active in vicinity of Afua. On Biak, Americans move back into Ibdi Pocket, where Japanese are continuing to resist. Arty bombardment of the enemy position is resumed.

16 July

FRANCE—21 Army Group: In U.S. First Army area, VII Corps continues S toward Périers-St Lô road with 9th Div on right and 30th on left. 9th Div is slowed by enemy below Les Champs-de-Losque. 30th Div deepens its salient between Terrette and Vire Rivers beyond Le Mesnil-Durand. CCB reverts to 3d Armd Div from attachment to 30th Div. In XIX Corps area, 35th Div makes little headway on right flank of corps. 29th tries in vain to relieve isolated 2d Bn, 116th Inf, astride Bayeux-St Lô road and repels tank-infantry counterattacks.

In Br Second Army area, 30 Corps attacks with 59th Div toward Noyers and partially envelops this objective. 50th Div, to W, improves positions near Hottot. In 12 Corps area, while 53d Div overruns Cahier, 15th takes Gavrus, Bougy, and Esquay, in region above Evrecy.

USSR—Converging columns of Third and Second White Russian Fronts overrun Grodno, rail and road junction on route to East Prussia.

ITALY—AAI: In U.S. Fifth Army's IV Corps area, 135th Inf of 34th Div, jumping off at 0100, seizes Hill 232 and M. Maggiore (Hills 449 and 413), SE of Leghorn. 168th Inf takes Lorenzana and pushes on to vicinity of Fauglia. 2d Bn of 133d Inf seizes Usigliano and drives to within 3 miles of the Arno Valley. 91st Div continues attack in IV Corps center with 361st Inf on left and 362d on right: 361st gets within sight of Arno Valley floor against diminished resistance and holds its gains against armored counterattacks; 362d gets almost to Capannoli. 88th Div continues steadily northward on right flank of corps, accelerating advance as opposition weakens suddenly during day. Plan for relief of FEC by British is completed. FEC goes on the defensive until relief can be accomplished.

In Br Eighth Army's 13 Corps area, Br 6th Armd Div captures Arezzo, where enemy's delaying action has gained time for him to improve the Gothic Line; elements thrust to the Arno, take bridge intact, and establish bridgehead. Next objective of corps is Florence. In 10 Corps area, fall of Arezzo menaces German positions on the Alpe di Poti. Corps is now able to concentrate on drive toward Bibbiena. On right flank, enemy forces at Scheggia, on Route 3, are threatened.

NEW GUINEA—In Aitape area, 3d Bn of 124th Inf, North Force, guided by Tr E of 112th Cav, advances S to close gap in Driniumor line. Elements succeed in breaking through to South Force lines, killing about 40 Japanese. Japanese are seen crossing the Driniumor about 2,500 yards S of Afua. 1st and 2d Bns, 127th Inf, which have been released from MLR, begin mopping up W of the Driniumor. On Noemfoor, 503d Para Inf finds that enemy has withdrawn from Hill 670 and contact is again lost for a time. Kamiri airdrome is ready to accommodate an entire fighter group.

17 July

FRANCE—Rommel's participation in the war ends. Severely wounded when his car is strafed by aircraft, he is unable to continue his duties as commander of *Army Group B* and von Kluge takes over this post in addition to his other duties.

21 Army Group: U.S. First Army places 4th Armd Div under command of VIII Corps. In VII Corps area, 9th Div breaks through enemy's MLR on right flank of corps and drives quickly toward St Lô highway, while 30th Div deepens salient on left flank to La Houcharderie. In XIX Corps area, 35th Div penetrates enemy positions on right flank of corps; 137th Inf, along the Vire, reaches objective near Rampan. Enemy withdraws salient at Le Carillon, 29th Div makes further vain attempts to relieve isolated 2d Bn, 116th Inf, and push on into St Lô from W; 3d Bn, 116th Inf, reaches 2d Bn but cannot move forward from there and it too becomes isolated; 115th Inf gets elements to Martinville Ridge.

In Br Second Army area, 30 Corps makes limited progress near Noyers. In 12 Corps area, 15th Div tries unsuccessfully to break into Evrecy. 53d clears most of right flank of corps N of the Odon and begins relief of 15th Div. 8 Corps completes preparations for attack in new zone E of the Orne.

ITALY—AAI: In U.S. Fifth Army's IV Corps area, 135th Inf of 34th Div makes little progress toward Leghorn; armored units on coast cover its flank; 442d Inf takes Luciana; 168th and 133d Regts reach S edge of Arno R Valley, 168th after stiff battle for Fauglia. 361st Inf, 91st Div, drives through Ponsacco toward Pontedera; 362d advances through Capannoli and across Era R toward the Arno. Enemy resistance to 88th Div stiffens, but

3d Bn, 349th Inf, seizes Palaia. On extreme right of IV Corps, TF Ramey, consisting so far of armored units, is reinf by bn of 351st Inf and takes Montaione.

Br Eighth Army commander concludes that the Gothic Line must be assaulted by two corps up axes Florence-Firenzuola and Florence-Bologna. 13 Corps pursues enemy toward Florence. In 10 Corps area, Ind 4th Div reaches the Alpe di Poti and begins clearing that hill mass. Pol 2 Corps, with close air support, begins assault on Ancona.

NEW GUINEA—In Aitape area, PERSECUTION Covering Force closes gap in line along the Driniumor, but enemy forces another in it, night 17-18. Japanese are getting into position for attack on Afua.

18 July

FRANCE—21 Army Group: U.S. 6th Armd Div begins landing at UTAH Beach.

U.S. First Army, with capture of St Lô by XIX Corps, successfully concludes Battle of the Hedgerows, during which it has gained suitable positions from which to launch breakout attack (COBRA). In VII Corps area, 9th and 30th Divs continue steadily toward Périers-St Lô road, which patrols reach. XIX Corps completes costly struggle for St Lô. On right flank of corps, 35th Div advances rapidly southward all along line, left flank elements reaching N edge of St Lô. After 115th Inf, 29th Div, closes in on the city from NE, TF C (special force of 29th Div) attacks into the city from E and clears it by 1900. St Lô remains under enemy fire that adds to wreckage already wrought by Allied air and arty bombardment. 113th Cav Gp is attached to 29th Div to reconnoiter southward and determine extent of enemy's withdrawal.

Br Second Army begins offensive in Caen area that, despite its limited-objective nature, receives the strongest air support (7,700 tons of bombs) ever provided for ground forces in Normandy. Purpose of the offensive is to draw off German armor from U.S. First Army's breakout attack (COBRA), scheduled for 24 July. Cdn 2 Corps crosses the Orne to open exits from Caen. Cdn 2d Div is heavily engaged near Louvigny. Cdn 3d Div takes Colombelles and Giberville. 8 Corps, making main effort, attacks through bridgehead of I Corps with 3 armd divs, 11th, 7th, and Gds, from W to E. Although resistance stiffens considerably in afternoon, attack reaches general line Hubert-Folie-Tilly-la-Campagne-La Hogue-Frenouville-Cagny. 1 Corps, in supporting role, clears 3 villages W of Troarn.

USSR—Troops of First Ukrainian Front overrun Brody. To N, First White Russian forces begin westward drive from Kowel. Troops of Third Baltic Front go on the offensive S of Lake Peipus, threatening Ostrov and Pskov. Soviet forces on East Prussian border are brought to a halt at Augustow by German counterattack.

ITALY—AAI: In U.S. Fifth Army's IV Corps area, 34th Div begins final assault on Leghorn with 135th Inf and attached RCT 363 of 91st Div, latter organized as TF Williamson under Brig Gen Raymond Williamson. Attack reaches outskirts of the city, but enemy is able to extricate most of its garrison. Along coast, 804th TD Bn reaches Montenero. Elements of 361st Inf, 91st Div, reach the Arno at Pontedera by 0800; 362d arrives at last ridge commanding the river, where it is ordered to halt. 88th Div comes to a halt on last heights overlooking the Arno above Palaia. FEC renews pursuit of enemy upon finding that he is withdrawing all along front.

In Br Eighth Army's 13 Corps area, S African 6th Armd Div on left flank of corps overruns Radda in Chianti. In Arno Valley, 4th Div and Br 6th Armd Div are almost halted by the first of a series of enemy delaying lines above Arezzo, but 4th Div takes Montevarchi, on Highway 69. Ind 8th Div passes to command of corps. 10 Corps begins regrouping and shifting westward for drive on Bibbiena while conducting limited attacks. Ind 4th Div is slowly extending its hold on Alpe di Poti. Enemy is stubbornly defending heights on either side of Citta di Castello but is forced back from M. Arnato. Pol 2 Corps breaks through to Ancona on Adriatic coast.

JAPAN—Cabinet of Premier Tojo falls. A new one is subsequently formed under Kuniaki Koiso.

NEW GUINEA—Gen Sibert, 6th Div commander, relinquishes command of TF TORNADO to Maj Gen John C. Persons, 31st Div commander, in order to take charge of TF TYPHOON, comprising reinf 6th Div (less RCT 20, attached to 31st Div), for Sansapor-Mar operation in the Vogelkop, scheduled for 30 July. In Aitape area, PERSECUTION Covering Force closes gap in Driniumor R line and holds W bank of the river from the coast to Afua. Japanese withdraw both E and W under attack by 124th Inf. 127th Inf finishes clearing region between Koronal Creek and the Driniumor and is moving forward to establish patrol base on East Branch, Koronal Creek. In evening Japanese attack 1st Sq of 112th Cav, South Force, from right and rear in Afua area and force it to fall back 250 yards.

19 July

FRANCE—21 Army Group: In U.S. First Army area, XIX Corps mops up within St Lô. 113th Cav Gp finds that enemy withdrawal southward has been a' limited one. 35th Div is ordered to take over entire corps sector, relieving 29th Div. It is to be reinf by 29th Div Arty and 113th Cav Gp.

In Br Second Army's Cdn 2 Corps area, 2d Div takes Louvigny, on N bank of the Orne, and Fleury and Ifs, on S bank. 3d Div clears Faubourg de Vaucelles and Cormelles. In 8 Corps area, Cagny falls to Gds Armd Div. 1 Corps continues to fight for Troarn.

USSR—Moscow announces encirclement of some 4 or 5 German divs W of Brody.

ITALY—AAI: In U.S. Fifth Army's IV Corps area, Leghorn falls to 34th Div without serious opposition, but retreating Germans have carried out a thorough demolition program within the city and on harbor facilities. 3d Bn of 135th Inf enters first, at 0200, and is followed by 363d Inf. 100th Bn is given responsibility for policing Leghorn and 363d Inf for left flank of 34th Div while 135th Inf assembles to SW. Patrols of 363d Inf moving N of Leghorn toward the Arno meet little opposition. To E, zone of 168th Inf is expanded to include that previously held by 133d Inf. 91st and 88th Divs patrol actively in center and on right flank of corps. In FEC area, 4th Mtn Div seizes Certaldo; 2d Moroccan Div takes S. Donato, NW of Castellina.

In Br Eighth Army's 13 Corps area, S African 6th Armd Div begins clearing main ridge of the Chianti hills on left flank of corps, but stubborn enemy opposition limits progress elsewhere. Elements of Br 6th Armd Div secure new crossing site over the Arno at Laterina.

SWPA—GHQ issues Outline Plan for Occupation of Southwest Morotai.

NEW GUINEA—In Aitape area, South Force of PERSECUTION Covering Force attacks S on right flank and recovers ground lost on 18th in Afua area, but in afternoon Japanese attempt to encircle Tr A, 112th Cav, necessitating another attack. Tr A drives enemy back 600 yards SW of its original positions astride Afua-Palauru trail.

20 July

FRANCE—21 Army Group: U.S. First Army continues to prepare for COBRA, shifting 4th Div from command of VIII to that of VII Corps. In XIX Corps area, 134th Inf of 35th Div relieves TF C, 29th Div, in St Lô.

In Br Second Army's Cdn 2 Corps area, 2d Div takes St André-sur-Orne against strong opposition. In 8 Corps area, Bourguebus falls to 7th Armd Div and Frenouville to Gds Armd Div. This ends action to expand Orne bridgehead and threaten Falaise.

GERMANY—In East Prussia, near Rastenburg, attempted assassination of Adolf Hitler fails.

USSR—Soviet forces driving W from Kowel reach Bug R on 40-mile front.

ITALY—AAI: In U.S. Fifth Army's IV Corps area, 442d Inf, in 34th Div sector, establishes outpost line along Highway 67 SE of Pisa. 91st Div zone is expanded westward to include part of that previously held by 34th Div and eastward into 88th Div sector. On right flank of IV Corps, TF Ramey, moving forward with 88th Div, gains heights along Orlo R, 6 miles E of Palaia, where it halts during relief of FEC by British. In FEC area, 4th Mtn Div gains line S. Stefano-Castelfiorentino-Certaldo on left flank of corps.

In Br Eighth Army area, 13 Corps commander changes plan of attack. Since corps is soon to extend W to relieve FEC and since region between the Chianti hills and Route 2 is lightly defended by enemy, main effort is to be made on left flank, where NZ 2d and Ind 8th Divs are to attack up Route 2. S African 6th Armd Div takes M. S. Michele and M. Querciabella, permitting 4th Div and Br 6th Armd Div in Arno Valley to move forward again.

NEW GUINEA—On Biak, TF HURRICANE completes reduction of enemy positions in East Caves. Bombardment of the Ibdi Pocket continues. In Aitape area, 43d Div begins arriving. 1st and 2d Bns of 127th Inf, now at patrol base site on East Branch, Koronal Creek, where they are supplied chiefly by air, are ordered to prepare to move SE toward Afua.

MARIANAS—Volume of aerial attacks on Guam by carrier-based planes reaches peak. The island continues to be pounded by naval gunfire as well. Tinian is also under preinvasion air and naval bombardment, but on a smaller scale.

21 July

USSR-POLAND—Ostrov falls to troops of Third Baltic Front. Upon crossing the Bug W of Kowel, some elements of First White Russian Front drive toward Brest Litovsk while others advance toward Lublin.

ITALY—AAI: U.S. Fifth Army issues orders for next phase, drive to the Gothic Line. While Br Eighth Army is clearing heights N and NW of Florence, Fifth Army is to cross the Arno in vicinity of Montelupo, tentatively between 5 and 10 August, and take M. Albano, Pistoia, and Lucca. II Corps is to take over entire Fifth Army front while preparations are being made for attack. 34th Div, upon reaching the Arno, is to be detached from IV Corps and pass to army control. In IV Corps area, 91st Div begins clearing enemy from S bank of the Arno without meeting serious opposition. TF Ramey releases 1st Armd Div elements under its command. Relief of FEC in current positions is begun by British, night 21-22.

In Br Eighth Army's 13 Corps area, elements of NZ 2d and Ind 8th Divs move forward to relieve FEC. S African 6th Armd Div battles enemy on heights near Greve. 10 Corps finishes regrouping. After nightfall enemy begins withdrawing salient at Citta di Castello.

BURMA—In NCAC area, withdrawal of exhausted Morris Force of Ind 3d Div from Myitkyrna area is authorized.

NEW GUINEA—In Aitape area, Gen Hall strengthens line along the Driniumor. 2d Bn of 169th Inf, 43d Div, moves forward to Anamo. 2d Bn of 124th, released from reserve, advances to Palauru village. Tr A, 112th Cav, is replaced by Tr C. Renewing attacks in Afua area, Japanese isolate Tr C from rest of South Force in battle that continues through night 21-22. Platoon of Co I, 127th Inf, succeeds in reaching the isolated unit.

TINIAN—Preinvasion bombardment is intensified.

GUAM—After preparatory bombardment by naval vessels and carrier aircraft, U.S. marines of III Amphib Corps (Southern Landing Force land on W coast of Guam about 0830. 3d Mar Div, with 3 regts abreast, goes ashore at Asan; 1st Prov Mar Brig, with 22d Marines on left and 4th on right, lands to S at Agat. Against moderate opposition, marines push inland and by nightfall hold 2 beachheads near the ends of final beachhead line, each of them extending about a mile inland on a 2-mile front. RCT 305, 77th Inf Div, lands on S beaches to help hold the beachhead.

22 July

FRANCE—21 Army Group: In U.S. First Army's VIII Corps area, 90th Div elements move to area of St Germain-sur-Sèves but are later forced to withdraw.

In Br Second Army's 12 Corps area, 43d Div, in limited attack, takes Maltot.

FRANTIC—Renewing shuttle bombing after lapse of about a month, 76 P-38's and 58 P-51's of U.S. Fifteenth Air Force attack airfields in Rumania, claiming destruction of 56 enemy planes, and land at Soviet bases. At the same time, heavy bombers of same air force attack Ploesti oil targets in force.

USSR-FINLAND—Russians on Finnish front are now at 1940 Soviet-Finnish border.

POLAND—Soviet forces driving on Lublin overwhelm Chelm.

ITALY—AAI: In U.S. Fifth Army's IV Corps area, 34th Div begins clearing region below the Arno on left flank of corps at 2200. 91st Div finishes cleaning out its zone below the Arno.

In Br Eighth Army area, 13 Corps extends westward to take over sector previously held by FEC, including Highway 2. Ind 8th Div now holds positions, on extreme left with NZ 2d Div to its right. In 10 Corps area, Ind 10th Div takes Citta di Castello and continues N.

CBI—Gen Stilwell, in radio message to Gen Hearn, his chief of staff, establishes CBI policy on support of Chinese forces in E China. Stilwell says that Gen Chennault should admit his failure to stop Japanese by air alone to Chiang Kai-shek, who could then decide what revision should be made in allocation of Hump tonnage.

NEW GUINEA—In Aitape area, 2d Bn of 169th Inf, 43d Div, moves to right of 124th Inf, North Force, along the Driniumor. Japanese make unsuccessful attacks against North Force in effort to regain crossing of the Driniumor. Enemy continues active in Afua area. Efforts to relieve isolated Tr C, 112th Cav, are futile, and South Force is obliged to refuse its right flank, leaving Afua to enemy and Tr C isolated. On Biak, after air and arty preparation, 2 cos of 163d Inf attack Ibdi Pocket and clear it without serious opposition.

TINIAN—Softening up of island continues.

GUAM—Marines repel counterattacks on both beachheads and then expand them toward final beachhead line. 3d Mar Div thrusts salient 1,000 yards inland toward Mt. Chachao and seizes Piti Navy Yard; in shore-to-shore operation, elements begin clearing Cabras I. 1st Prov Mar Brig, reinf by RCT 305, gains Mt. Alifan and final beachhead line on S flank of corps. Gen Geiger orders 1st Prov Mar Brig to clear Orote Peninsula upon relief by 77th Div. Advance party of 306th Inf, which is to accomplish the relief, arrives to prepare for landing of rest of the regt.

23 July

FRANCE—21 Army Group: Cdn First Army (Gen Henry D. G. Crerar) takes control of Br 1 Corps on extreme E flank.

USSR—Pskov, last prewar Soviet city held by Germans, falls to forces of Third Baltic Front.

ITALY—AAI: In U.S. Fifth Army's IV Corps area, 34th Div finishes clearing to the Arno with little difficulty; 363d Inf takes Marina di Pisa by 0330 and reaches S Pisa below the Arno by 1330. All bridges over the Arno have been destroyed. Enemy is placing heavy fire on S Pisa and on port of Leghorn. 88th Div begins clearing right flank of IV Corps below the Arno and is briskly engaged at some points.

In Br Eighth Army's 13 Corps area, Tavernelle falls to NZ troops. S African 6th Armd Div makes progress on heights near Greve, taking crests of M. Domini and M. Fili. 4th Div reaches S. Giovanni.

CBI—Generalissimo Chiang Kai-shek, in message to President Roosevelt, reaffirms his willingness to place Gen Stilwell in command of Ch forces but specifies 3 conditions that must be met: (1) Chinese communists, before coming under authority of Gen Stilwell, must agree to obey orders of Chinese Government; (2) Stilwell's role must be clearly defined; (3) Chinese must have full authority for lend-lease distribution.

Adm Mountbatten outlines 2 plans of attack: CAPITAL, an attack across the Chindwin; and DRACULA, an attack on Rangoon area by seaborne and airborne forces.

On Salween front, Ch 8th Army, renewing attack on Sung Shan with 3 regts supported by direct fire of howitzers, makes substantial progress.

SWPA—Gen MacArthur radios his proposed schedule of operations to Washington: invasion of Morotai on 15 September, Talauds on 15 October, and Mindanao on 15 November.

NEW GUINEA—In Aitape area, Trs A and B of 112th Cav, upon relief by 1st Bn of 127th Inf N of Afua, attack W toward isolated Tr C while 2d Bn, 127th Inf, moves in from SE. Cavalrymen recapture Afua with little difficulty; 2d Bn reaches perimeter of Tr C. North Force frustrates further enemy efforts to secure crossing of the Driniumor, night 23-24. On Biak, final mop up of Ibdi Pocket is begun. On Noemfoor, patrols of 503d Para Inf regain contact with enemy about 4 miles NW of Inasi village, on E coast.

TINIAN—Surface vessels, arty, and aircraft successfully execute final preinvasion bombardment.

GUAM—3d Mar Div fights stubbornly to expand N beachhead; completes occupation of Cabras I., where guns are emplaced to support future operations. 306th Inf, 77th Div, lands at Agat and begins relief of 1st Prov Mar Brig in S beachhead.

24 July

FRANCE—U.S. 28th Div arrives on Continent. 21 Army Group: Air preparation for Operation COBRA is begun, but weather conditions are so unfavorable that the attack is postponed. Minor alteration of interarmy boundary becomes effective as Br 30 Corps extends W to take command of part of U.S. 5th Div zone on left flank of U.S. V Corps. 15th Scottish Div makes the relief.

POLAND—Troops of First White Russian Front overrun Lublin. Right flank elements of First Ukrainian Front cross San R NW of Lwow.

ITALY—AAI: U.S. Fifth Army begins regrouping along the Arno. Army sets new boundary between IV and II Corps, IV on W, but II Corps troops within current IV Corps zone are to remain under operational control of IV Corps until new boundary becomes effective, on or about 25 July; directs relief of infantry divs of IV Corps.

BURMA—In NCAC area, Ch 50th Div is joined by 149th Regt, which relieves portions of 42d and 150th Regts in line in Myitkyina area.

CHINA—Ch garrison of besieged Heng-yang has been without air support since 17th because of weather conditions but continues to resist strongly and has forced enemy to halt briefly to reorganize.

NEW GUINEA—TF TYPHOON embarks at Maffin Bay for Sansapor-Mar operation. In Aitape area, North Force of PERSECUTION Covering Force repels the last enemy attempts, in limited strength, to secure crossing of the Driniumor, night 24–25. The region then becomes relatively quiet. Japanese, at least 2,000 strong, are disposed on South Force's right flank and rear in Afua area and prevent 2d Bn, 127th Inf, and Tr C, 112th Cav, from breaking out.

TINIAN—Following strong preparatory bombardment, U.S. 4th Mar Div lands on NW coast, beginning at 0830, against light opposition. While landing is in progress, 2d Mar Div conducts diversionary demonstration to S and then returns to landing site and puts 1st Bn, 8th Marines, ashore to operate under control of 4th Mar Div. 4th Mar Div pushes inland and secures beachhead, which includes part of the old Ushi Pt airfield on the N.

GUAM—Gen Geiger orders attack to link the beachheads and secure Orote Peninsula on 26th. 77th Div completes relief of 1st Prov Mar Brig in S beachhead and holds it with 305th and 306th Regts abreast, 305th on N. 3d Mar Div continues to meet bitter opposition while endeavoring to take heights commanding N beachhead.

25 July

SHAEF—Gen Eisenhower directs that U.S. forces in Normandy be regrouped under a new U.S. army group, 12th. Gen Bradley will head the new command and set the time of its activation.

FRANCE—21 Army Group: U.S. First Army launches breakout assault (COBRA) in VII Corps zone as weather conditions improve. Saturation bombing by Eighth and Ninth Air Forces precedes the ground assault and stuns enemy. More than 4,000 tons of bombs are concentrated in a small area, some falling short and inflicting casualties on U.S. forces. Gen McNair, who has recently replaced Gen Bradley as commander of U.S. 1st Army Group, an organization confined to paper to deceive enemy, is killed by a bomb while watching the attack. Gen DeWitt later replaces Gen McNair. VII Corps attacks across Périers-St Lô road on narrow front at 1100 to force passage through enemy positions in Marigny-St Gilles region. 9th Div on right, 4th in center, and 30th on left advance steadily and force enemy back about 2 miles to line La Butte-La Chapelle-en-Juger-Hébécrevon. VIII Corps is reinf by attachment of 6th Armd Div, now assembled at Le Mesnil.

In Br Second Army area, Cdn 2 Corps attacks at 0330 with 2d Div on right and 3d on left, pushing a short distance along Falaise road against stubborn opposition and then breaking off attack. This action helps to divert enemy from COBRA.

FRANTIC—U.S. Fifteenth Air Force fighter bombers from Soviet bases attack Mielec airdrome (Poland), near Lwow, with good effect.

EASTERN EUROPE—Troops of Second Baltic Front cut Dvinsk-Riga road. Lwow is enveloped by forces of First Ukrainian Front. Four Soviet columns are converging on Brest Litovsk.

ITALY—AAI: In U.S. Fifth Army area, II Corps takes over sector of 88th Div on right flank of army, previously right flank of IV Corps. 88th Div finishes clearing its zone below the Arno and releases TF Ramey.

In Br Eighth Army area, 13 Corps continues drive on Florence, reaching next delaying line, extending through S. Casciano, in zones of NZ 2d Inf and S African 6th Armd Divs.

BURMA—In NCAC area, Myitkyina TF is further strengthened by arrival of 1st Bn, 90th Regt, Ch 30th Div. By now it is evident that Japanese are preparing to abandon Myitkyina.

NEI—Warships of Br Eastern Fleet bombard Sabang naval base, off N tip of Sumatra, causing extensive damage. Carrier-based aircraft attack airdromes near Sabang.

NEW GUINEA—TF TYPHOON conducts practice landing near Toem in preparation for invasion of the Vogelkop. In Aitape area, relief of Tr C of 112th Cav is finally accomplished after 4 days of strenuous efforts as Cos B and E, 127th Inf, make contact and open escape route. To exploit this success, 1st and 2d Bns, 127th Inf, attack S to Afua-Palauru trail, but enemy remains in considerable strength in this region. On Noemfoor, 503d Para Inf loses contact with Japanese, who withdraw from Inasi area. Kornasoren airfield is ready to accommodate one fighter group.

TINIAN—After repelling determined Japanese counterattack with heavy losses to enemy, 4th Mar Div continues attack and, against light opposition, considerably expands beachhead, which now includes about half of the new airfield. Additional elements of 2d Mar Div land; rest of 8th Marines is placed under operational control of 4th Mar Div.

GUAM—While 77th Div defends S beachhead, 3d Mar Div continues attacks against heights commanding N beachhead and efforts to close the 4-mile gap between it and 77th Div, but progress is still limited.

26 July

FRANCE—21 Army Group: In U.S. First Army area, VIII Corps joins in Operation COBRA, attacking at 0530 on W flank of army with 8th, 90th, and 83d Divs, from W to E. 8th Div cuts Lessay-Périers road about midway between the 2 towns. 90th establishes bridgehead across Sèves R. 83d makes minor gains. At night 79th Div begins crossing Ay R behind 8th Div. VII Corps commits additional units to exploit breakthrough. Passing through 9th Div, 1st Div seizes Marigny. CCB, 3d Armd Div, then drives through to positions W and SW of Marigny. 4th Div speeds S to La Conviniere. 2d Armd Div attacks through 30th Div on left flank of corps and takes St Gilles and Canisy. Meanwhile, 9th and 30th Divs broaden and deepen positions on flanks of the penetration. In XIX Corps area, 28th Div is attached to corps. V Corps attacks E of St Lô at 0600 after arty preparation by both Br and U.S. guns. 5th Div on right and 2d on left push forward to Vidouville-Rouxeville road.

FRANTIC—U.S. Fifteenth Air Force fighter bombers, while returning to Italy from USSR, make successful sweep over Ploesti=Bucharest area of Rumania.

EASTERN EUROPE—Soviet forces of Leningrad Front take Narva, Estonia. Elements of First White Russian Front reach the Vistula E of Radom.

ITALY—AAI: In U.S. Fifth Army area, IV Corps relieves infantry units as ordered. TF 45—consisting of 91st AAA Gp, 107th AAA Gp, and 2d Armd Gp—is organized under hq of 45th AAA Brig and replaces 34th Div on W flank. 34th Div releases 363d Inf to parent unit, 91st Div, and assembles near Rosignano.

CBI—On Salween front, Japanese defending Sung Shan request and receive air support that damages Ch batteries and brings attack to a halt temporarily. After preparatory aerial bombardment, Chinese attack Teng-chung in force with mortar and arty support and seize Lai-feng, fortified peak dominating approaches to the town. At the same time, other Ch forces attack SE wall of the town but cannot get over it.

NEW GUINEA—In Aitape area, since enemy appears to be preparing for further attacks in Afua sector, U.S. forces in this region are rearranged for defense. No large-scale attacks are forthcoming, each side being in the dark as to strength and disposition of the other's forces.

TINIAN—2d Mar Div completes landing, resumes command of 8th Marines, and is committed to action. 4th and 2d Mar Divs, with close air, naval gunfire, and arty support, make co-ordinated attack that progresses rapidly against light resistance, securing N quarter of the island. Front line extends roughly across island from points S of Faibus San Hilo Pt on W coast to Asiga on E coast and embraces Ushi Pt airfield and Mt. Lasso.

GUAM—Attack to clear Orote Peninsula opens after heavy preparatory bombardment during which 7 bns of arty are employed. 1st Prov Mar Brig, with 4th Marines on left and 22d on right, begins to clear narrow neck of the peninsula and gains 1,500 yards despite difficult jungle terrain. 3d Mar Div repels strong enemy counterattack against N beachhead and, in close combat, eliminates enemy infiltrators who have succeeded in penetrating lines.

HAWAII—President Roosevelt, Gen MacArthur, Adm Nimitz, and Adm Leahy meet at Pearl Harbor to consider strategy for the Pacific. The feasibility of bypassing the Philippines in favor of Formosa is discussed. This question remains the subject of heated debate for some time to come.

27 July

FRANCE—21 Army Group: In U.S. First Army area, VIII Corps is hampered more by delaying obstacles than by enemy opposition as it moves forward on W flank of army. 79th Div overruns Lessay, and 8th pushes southward between there and Périers. 90th Div occupies Priers and crosses the Taute just E of there. 83d Div gets patrols across the Taute on left flank of corps. First elements of 6th Armd Div (Tr A of 86th Cav Rcn Sq, mechanized) are committed through 8th Div and clear heights near Le Bingard. 13th Inf, 8th Div, is attached to 4th Armd Div. In VII Corps area, 1st Inf and 2d and 3d Armd Divs make main effort southward while other elements of corps facilitate their movement and expand positions on flanks of salient. 1st Div and CCB, 3d Armd Div, drive SW toward Coutances, reaching Camprond. 2d Armd Div thrusts spearheads to Notre Dame de Cenilly and Fervaches. XIX Corps commits 28th Div to line in preparation for attack. V Corps extends W during day to include 35th Div, which is now attacking in St LB area, and takes high ground just W and S of St Lô. 5th and 2d Divs make limited progress against strong opposition, overrunning Notre Dame d'Elle.

EASTERN EUROPE—Troops of Second Baltic Front seize Dvinsk, on Dvina R. Bialystok falls to forces of Second White Russian Front after hard battle of about a week. Columns of First Ukrainian Front take Lwow and Stanislawow.

ITALY—AAI: In Br Eighth Army's 13 Corps area, enemy falls back toward Florence as NZ 2d Div takes S Casciano.

CBI—In NCAC area of Burma, 3d Bn of NEW GALAHAD succeeds in taking northern airstrip at Myitkyina and turns it over to 209th and 236th Engr Bns to defend. Japanese garrison of Myitkyina is becoming less aggressive. On Salween front, after mopping up on Mt. Lai-feng, Chinese count some 400 Japanese dead for their loss of 1,200.

NEW GUINEA—In Aitape area, 2d Bn of 127th Inf, South Force, drives S beyond Afua-Palauru trail, but returns to starting line when enemy threatens its communications. 1st Bn, 127th Inf, and part of 1st Sq, 112th Cav, clear enemy from heights near South Force's supply base. In Wakde-Sarmi area, 6th Div, less RCT 20, begins to leave for the Vogelkop operation.

TINIAN—After preparatory bombardment, marines continue attack and advance rapidly, clearing northern third of island by 1600. Ushi Pt airfield is under repair.

GUAM—1st Prov Mar Brig continues to clear Orote Peninsula: 22d Marines advances steadily against light resistance on right, but 4th Marines is soon pinned down by fire from prepared enemy positions. In N beachhead, 3d Mar Div extends its right flank 1,500 yards and its left 200 yards across Chonito cliff but is still unable to make much progress in center toward Mt. Chachao. To accelerate link up of the 2 beachheads, 77th Div is ordered to extend its positions northward beyond Mt. Tenjo, decreasing ground to be covered by 3d Mar Div.

28 July

FRANCE—21 Army Group: U.S. First Army orders exploitation of breakthrough and rapid pursuit of disorganized enemy. VII Corps, instead of continuing SW to coast, is to drive S to left of VIII Corps. VIII Corps commits 6th and 4th Armd Divs through infantry to spearhead pursuit, 6th on W. CCA, 6th Armd Div, speeds S through 79th Div to positions SW of Coutances. CCB, 4th Armd Div, races down Périers-Coutances road and takes Coutances by 1700. With fall of Coutances, COBRA has largely accomplished its purpose. Infantrymen of VIII Corps move forward behind armor. 106th Cav Gp protects W flank of corps, advancing along coast to mouth of Sienne R W of Coutances. Many of the enemy are trapped as junction is made with VII Corps on E flank. In VII Corps area, 3d Armd and 1st Inf Divs make contact with VIII Corps near Coutances. CCB of 2d Armd Div reaches St Denis-le-Gast. XIX Corps, attacking to exploit breakthrough, extends W to include 30th Div and CCA, 2d Armd Div, in current positions. CCA thrusts S through Villebaudon to vicinity of Moyen. 30th Div drives S along W side of Vire R toward Tessy-sur-Vire. In V Corps area, 35th Div continues S along E bank of the Vire to Ste Suzanne-sur-Vire. 2d Div, whose 9th Inf has been relieved by 10th Inf of 5th Div, takes St Jean-de-Baisants. 5th Div straightens line in limited advance.

EASTERN EUROPE—Troops of First White Russian Front overrun Brest Litovsk. Jaroslaw and Przemysl, on W bank of the San, fall to forces of First Ukrainian Front.

NEW GUINEA—On Biak, organized resistance ends as mopping up of Ibdi Pocket draws to a close, but general mopping up continues for some time. The Ibdi Pocket had been held by some 800 Japanese; of these, 300 are estimated to have been killed during period 22-28 July and 154 are dead by actual count. In Aitape area, South Force of PERSECUTION Covering Force shortens lines to improve defensive positions and insure safety of its supply base, pulling back again from Afua.

TINIAN—Marines continue to advance rapidly against light resistance from retreating enemy and clear Gurguan Pt airfield.

GUAM—On Orote Peninsula, Marine and Army tank reinforcements are supplied to 4th Marines of 1st Prov Mar Brig and spearhead attack during afternoon that brings 4th Marines abreast 22d Marines at E end of the airstrip. Final beachhead line is gained as 3d Mar and 77th Inf Divs join the N and S beachheads. 3d Mar Div, reinf by 3d Bn of 307th Inf, clears Mt. Chachao and Mt. Alutom, opening road from Adelup Pt to Mt. Tenjo. Co A of 305th Inf, 77th Div, moves to top of Mt. Tenjo with little difficulty and is relieved there by 2d Bn, 307th Inf.

29 July

FRANCE—21 Army Group: In U.S. First Army area, VIII Corps continues pursuit with 6th and 4th Armd Divs abreast spearheading and motorized combat teams of infantry following. CCA, 6th Armd Div, secures crossing of Sienne R near Pont de la Roche on W flank of corps. CCA, 4th Armd Div, drives to Cerences. VII Corps' attack swerves from SW to S and reaches general line Cerences-Hambye-Percy. Enemy tank columns withdrawing along highway from Roney to St Denis-le-Gast suffer extremely heavy losses under air, arty, and tank attacks. In XIX Corps area, 29th Div is committed on right flank of corps, relieving elements of CCA, 2d Armd Div, and drives to positions E of Percy, where it is in contact with VII Corps. 30th Div meets strong opposition as it continues S along W bank of the Vire toward Tessy-sur-Vire. V Corps pushes quickly toward Torigny-sur-Vire.

ITALY—AAI: In Br Eighth Army's 13 Corps area, Ind 8th Div, on W flank of corps, reaches the Arno near Empoli. 4th Div takes M. Scalari after hard battle.

BURMA—Gen Giffard, CG 11 Army Group, orders Gen Slim, CG Br Fourteenth Army, to draw up detailed plans for CAPITAL.

NEW GUINEA—In Aitape area, Gen Hall decides to counterattack with 124th Inf, reinf by 2d Bn of 169th. 1st Bn, 169th, relieves 2d Bn, 124th, of task of patrolling Palauru=Chinapelli region. 1st Sq, 112th Cav, and 2d Bn, 127th Inf, attack to improve positions of South Force in Afua area but make little progress. Co G, 127th Inf, holding exposed outpost, is forced E under enemy attack to heights about 300 yards W of Afua.

TINIAN—2d and 4th Mar Divs continue to clear Tinian, 2d gaining ground rapidly on W but 4th slowed by considerable resistance on heights to E.

GUAM—1st Prov Mar Brig clears tenacious enemy defenders from Orote airstrip and completes capture of the peninsula by 1700. 3d Mar and 77th Inf Divs are patrolling actively from beachhead perimeter in preparation for next phase of attack.

30 July

FRANCE—21 Army Group: In U.S. First Army's VIII Corps area, 6th and 4th Armd Divs speed toward Granville and Avranches. CCB, 6th Armd Div, attacks through bridgehead of CCA and drives some 3 miles beyond Bréhal along road to Granville. CCB, 4th Armd Div, pushes into Avranches, where bridges over Sée R are captured. In VII Corps area, 1st Inf and 3d Armd Divs continue S on right flank of corps, while units to E mop up. CCA forces crossing of the Sienne at Gavray, and bridge construction is begun; CCB drives quickly toward Villedieu-lès-Poëles. XIX Corps repels strong counterattack on right flank near Percy but makes little forward movement because of strong opposition. V Corps runs into stout resistance as it continues southward. 5th Div succeeds in crossing Torigny-sur-Vire–Caumont road on left flank, but progress elsewhere is negligible.

Br Second Army, having regrouped, renews offensive with powerful air support. RAF BC and AEAF bombers drop 2,227 tons of bombs. 8 Corps, on W flank of army, attacks astride Caumont-Le Bény-Bocage road with 11th Armd Div on W and 75th Div on E, pushing beyond La Fouquerie and Les Loges. 30 Corps attacks with 43d Div on W and 50th on E to left of 8 Corps. Progress is slow, particularly on E.

ITALY—AAI: In Br Eighth Army area, NZ 2d Div begins attack on Pian dei Cerri ridge in region W of Route 2.

BURMA—In NCAC area, commander of Japanese forces at Myitkyina issues withdrawal order and commits suicide.

NEW GUINEA—On Vogelkop Peninsula, TF TYPHOON lands on N coast near Mar, omitting preparatory bombardment in order to attain surprise. 1st Inf of 6th Div, with 2d Bn on left, 1st in center, and 3d on right, lands without opposition, first wave going ashore at 0701, one minute late. Left flank advances 800 yards inland to low hills and right flank 2,500 yards W along coast to mouth of Wewe R. Amphibious force (6th Cav Rcn Tr with a mortar section and riflemen of 1st Bn, 63d Inf) lands on Middleburg I., at 0730 and then moves to Amsterdam I. Neither of these small islands is defended. TF TYPHOON has no battle casualties. Gen Sibert takes command ashore at 1020. Air assistance is not required. In Aitape area, 2d Bn of 124th Inf joins its regt on the Driniumor in preparation for counterattack in sector of North Force. South Force patrols actively. Co G, 127th Inf, is surrounded by enemy on high ground W of Afua.

TINIAN—Marines push steadily southward against increasingly stiff resistance, capturing town of Tinian and compressing Japanese into about 5 square miles at S tip of island. Island Commander takes command of Garrison Forces.

GUAM—Gen Geiger issues orders for pursuit of enemy northward on 31st.

31 July

FRANCE—21 Army Group: In U.S. First Army's VIII Corps area, 6th Armd Div's CCR, attacking in coastal sector, overruns Granville and entire div moves SE to Avranches area. At 2100 6th Armd is ordered to relieve 4th Armd Div at Avranches and secure bridges in that area. 4th Armd Div probes southward from Avranches and secures crossing of the Selune near Pontaubault. In VII Corps area, 1st Inf Div and CCA of 3d Armd Div drive rapidly to Brécey on right flank of corps and secure crossing of See R. 4th Div and CCB, 3d Armd Div, drive forward beyond Villedieu-lès-Poëles. XIX Corps continues attacks toward Tessy against heavy resistance. 30th Div overruns Troisgots, N of Tessy. V Corps drives S toward the Vire, 35th Div taking Torigny-sur-Vire.

In Br Second Army area, 8th Corps gets forward elements across the Soulevre R near Le Bény-Bocage. Gds Armd Div reaches Le Tourneur. 30 Corps takes Cahagnes and is approaching Jurques.

Cdn First Army takes command of Cdn 2 Corps.

EASTERN EUROPE—In Latvia, troops of First Baltic Front seize Jelgava, near Gulf of Riga, threatening to isolate German *Army Group North*. Third White Russian forces press forward toward East Prussia, elements entering Kaunas (Kovno), former capital of Lithuania, where street fighting is in progress. Troops of Second White Russian Front also continue toward East Prussia. Closing in on Warsaw (Poland), First White Russian Front takes Siedlce.

ITALY—AAI: In U.S. Fifth Army's IV Corps area, TF Ramey, consisting of elements of 1st Armd Div with tanks and TD's, relieves 91st Div on right flank of corps. 91st Div is transferred to II Corps to relieve 88th Div in place. II Corps now has command of 3 of the army's 4 infantry divs—88th, 91st, and 85th.

BURMA—11 Army Group: In Br Fourteenth Army area, 4 Corps hq is withdrawn to India and its components on Tiddim road are transferred to command of Hq, 33 Corps, which now has full responsibility for forcing enemy back across the Chindwin. Japanese are in full retreat down Tiddim road. 15 Corps, on Arakan front, has engaged in patrolling throughout June and July despite heavy monsoon rainfall.

NEW GUINEA—In Vogelkop area, 3d Bn of 1st Inf, 6th Div, moves by sea to Cape Sansapor and makes unopposed landing at 0844. Sansapor Plantation and Village are quickly secured and defensive positions established. Cape Sansapor is found to be unsuitable for PT base but is to become site of radar Warning installation. In Aitape area, 124th Inf, reinf by 2d Bn of 169th and dubbed TED Force, begins counterattack in North Force sector at 0800 under direction of Col Edward M. Starr. The 4 bns cross the Driniumor and advance in separate columns toward Niumen Creek, which 3 of the 4 reach, the other being halted 800 yards short by enemy rear guards. 128th Inf protects sector previously held by North Force. In sector of South Force, Co G of 127th Inf breaks out of encirclement near Afua and returns to main body. From 13 July to date, South Force has suffered almost 1,000 casualties; 260 of them within 112th Cav; over 700 Japanese are estimated to have been killed by South Force.

TINIAN—Marines continue S over rugged terrain against moderate resistance. Unusually heavy bombardment by naval vessels, aircraft, and arty precedes attack.

GUAM—3d Mar and 77th Inf Divs begin pursuit of enemy northward, 3d Mar on left, and reach first phase line, extending generally from Agana on W to Yona on E, without trouble except for skirmish at Yona, where 77th Div meets some enemy troops.

HAWAII—81st Div begins preliminary rehearsals for Palaus operation.

1 August

FRANCE—12th Army Group: U.S. 12th Army Group (Gen Bradley) becomes operational and takes command of U.S. divs engaged in France, these being divided between U.S. First and Third Armies. Gen Montgomery, however, is to retain command of all ground forces through month of August. XIX TAC of U.S. Ninth Air Force becomes operational with mission of supporting Third Army. IX TAC continues to assist First Army.

U.S. Third Army (Gen Patton) becomes operational with 4 corps under its command (VIII, XII, XX, XV) as well as Forces Françaises de l'Interieur (FFI). Operating on right of First Army and on extreme right of Allied forces, Third Army is to secure Brittany Peninsula and its valuable ports. VIII Corps, consisting of 4th and 6th Armd Divs and 8th and 79th Inf Divs, passes from First to Third Army command; with 4th and 6th Armd Divs spearheading, pours through the narrow Avranches corridor and fans out to S, SW, and W. Crossing La Selune R at Pontaubault, 6th Armd Div swings W into Brittany in 2 columns and reaches Pontorson-Antrain area. 4th Armd Div drives southward to cut off the peninsula and reaches positions near Rennes. XV Corps (Maj Gen Wade H. Haislip), consisting of 83d and 80th Inf and 5th Armd Divs, is concentrating between Sée and Selune Rivers to block enemy movement toward Avranches.

U.S. First Army, command of which passes from Gen Bradley to Lt Gen Courtney H. Hodges, directs all but V Corps to drive SE. V Corps is to take heights N of Vire and remain there until pinched out. VII Corps expands Brécey bridgehead on right flank with 1st Div reinf by CAA of 3d Armd Div. 4th Div, reinf with CCB of 3d Armd Div, pushes forward toward St Pois. 9th Div moves southward on left flank of corps. XIX Corps overruns Percy and Tessy, Percy falling to 28th Div and Tessy to CCA, 2d Armd Div. V Corps continues southward toward Vire on 2-div front after 5th Div is pinched out on right flank by British. 5th Div assembles in rear in Army reserve.

21 Army Group: In Br Second Army's 8 Corps area, 11th Armd Div overruns Le Bény-Bocage. To left, Gds Armd Div is driving on Estry. 30 Corps works forward toward Mont Pincon on right and Villers-Bocage on left. 7th Armd Div is committed to drive on Aunay-sur-Odon.

In Cdn First Army area, 2 Corps evokes strong opposition as it attacks below Caen in Tilly-la-Campagne-La Hogue area. In Br 1 Corps are, 49th Div takes control of Sannerville-Troarn sector.

MEDITERRANEAN—AFHQ changes code word for invasion of S France from ANVIL to DRAGOON. Plans for the operation are largely completed by this time. Hq of 6th Army Group (Gen Devers) is formed at Bastia, Corsica, and will eventually take control of the U.S. and Fr forces in S France.

EASTERN EUROPE—Pol underground forces revolt as Soviet offensive nears Warsaw; fighting continues throughout the next two months. First Baltic Front pushes to Gulf of Riga at point 25 miles W of Riga. Kaunas (Kovno), Lithuania, falls to Third

White Russian Front, which is headed toward Konigsberg.

CBI—Gen Stilwell, who is promoted to rank of full general, arrives in Kandy, Ceylon, and Adm Mountbatten leaves there for London to discuss future strategy in SEAC.

In China, siege of Heng-yang continues despite efforts of Chinese to break through enemy lines. U.S. Fourteenth Air Force, during period 26 May to date, has flown 4,454 sorties in support of Chinese in E China.

NEW GUINEA—PT sq begins operations from Amsterdam. LCT's are shuttling aviation engineers and equipment to Middleburg, a more suitable airfield site than the mainland of the Vogelkop. On Biak, engineers complete 4,000-foot runway at Borokoe airdrome. Mokmer airfield has been extended to 7,000 feet. In Aitape area, TED Force gets last of its 4 columns to Niumen Creek and consolidates perimeters along the creek. Japanese attack right flank of South Force in strength just as South Force is preparing a rcn in force. About 2 enemy cos make suicidal onslaughts against Tr C, 112th Cav, N of Afua, but are repulsed with heavy casualties. Tr G and elements of Co K, 127th Inf, then reconnoiter well beyond South Force's perimeter against scattered opposition.

POA—U.S. Army Forces, Pacific Ocean Areas, under command of Gen Richardson, supersedes U.S. Army Forces in Central Pacific Area and contains all Army forces of South Pacific area as well. AAF POA is activated under Lt Gen Millard F. Harmon. Adm Halsey issues outline plan for invasion of W Carolines.

TINIAN—Organized resistance comes to an end, and marines begin to mop up.

GUAM—111 Amphib Corps continues to pursue enemy northward, reaching 0-2 phase line beyond Agana-Pago Bay road.

2 August

FRANCE—Gen Eisenhower urges Gen Montgomery to press the attack.

21 Army Group: In Br Second Army area, 8 Corps is meeting stronger opposition above Vire. 11th Armd Div pushes to N outskirts of the town and patrols cross Vire-Vassy road. Gds Armd Div is brought to a halt short of Estry. Corps is reinf by 3d Div. In 30 Corps area, on right flank of corps, 43d Div continues southward toward Mont Pincon, while 7th Armd Div continues toward Aunay. On corps left flank, 50th Div takes Amaye-sur-Seulles, W of Villers-Bocage.

12th Army Group: To exploit success of. VIII Corps, orders Third Army to secure line St Hilaire-du-Harcourt-Fougères-Rennes and then clear Brittany Peninsula, bypassing St Malo if it cannot be taken easily.

In U.S. Third Army's VIII Corps area, continuing W along Brittany Peninsula, 6th Armd Div bypasses Dinan to S when strong opposition develops there. 83d Div is attached to corps to follow 6th Armd Div, replacing 79th Div. 79th Div is transferred to XV Corps for drive on Fougères. TF A (TD's, cavalry, and engrs), under Brig Gen Herbert L. Earnest, is formed to clear bypassed resistance along N coast of Brittany Peninsula. 4th Armd Div gains additional ground near Rennes. 13th Inf of 8th Div, motorized, moves forward to Rennes area.

In U.S. First Army's VII Corps area, 1st Div and attached elements of 3d Armd Div speed southward toward Mortain. 4th Div continues toward St Pois. 9th Div cuts road NE of Villedieu. Corps releases 2d Armd Div to XIX Corps. XIX corps advances steadily SE from Percy-Tessy area against moderate opposition from retreating enemy. In V Corps area, continuing S toward Vire with 35th Div on W and 2d on E, corps crosses the Vire and Soulevre Rivers.

ITALY—AAI: In Br Eighth Army's 13 Corps area, enemy begins limited withdrawal behind the Arno as NZ 2d Div maintains pressure on ridge below Florence.

GERMANY—Hitler orders counterattack between Mortain and Avranches to isolate U.S. forces in Brittany.

CBI—On Salween front, aircraft supporting Ch assault on Teng-chung succeed in breaching the thick wall at 5 places.

NEW GUINEA—On Biak, 2d Bn of 163d Inf lands at Korim Bay. In Aitape area, South Force of PERSECUTION Covering Force remains on the defensive, repelling determined enemy attacks that probably cost Japanese some 300 killed. TED Force prepares to attack S in region E of the Driniumor.

GUAM—Garrison Force takes responsibility for Orote Peninsula and Cabras I., to release additional units for movement northward. Gen Geiger orders the attack pressed toward Yigo area, where Japanese are reportedly concentrating. On right flank of corps, 77th Div, with 305th Inf on right and 307th on left, attempts to reach 0-3 line, beyond Mt. Barrigada, but finds Japanese controlling the road junction at Barrigada village, below the mountain, from well-concealed positions in jungle and halts over 2 miles short of objective. On left flank of corps, 3d Mar Div moves steadily northward, taking Tiyan airfield.

3 August

FRANCE—21 Army Group: In Br Second Army area, 8 Corps makes little progress in vicinity of Vire and Estry. 30 Corps is firmly opposed as it continues toward Mont Pincon, Aunay, and Villers-Bocage. 12 Corps, with 50th Div on right and 53d on left, gains positions along Villers-Bocage–Caen highway. 53d Div overruns Noyers and Missy.

12th Army Group: Directs Third Army to complete capture of Brittany Peninsula with minimum forces, clear region W of Mayenne R and N of Loire R, and secure crossings of the Mayenne; First Army is to extend its operations to Mayenne–Domfront area.

In U.S. Third Army's VIII Corps area, forward elements of 6th Armd Div get to within a few miles of Loudeac when attack is halted upon order to return and reduce Dinan. TF A moves forward to clear bypassed resistance in St Maio area. 13th Inf reverts to 8th Div from attachment to 4th Armd Div and begins assault on Rennes, while 4th Armd Div continues S, passing W of Rennes. In XV Corps area, 79th Div reach Fougères.

In U.S. First Army area, VII Corps overruns Mortain. 4th Div continues to close in on St Pois. 9th Div reaches positions just NW of Fort de St Sever. XIX Corps, continuing steadily SE, reaches St Sever-Calvados on right and is about half way to Vire on left. V Corps meets stiffening resistance as it approaches Vire.

USSR—Troops of First Ukrainian Front cross the upper Vistula at Baranow and within the next few days expand the bridgehead.

CBI—In NCAC area, Myitkyina falls to Myitkyina TF at 1545. Raiding force of Ch 50th Div leads final assault, which begins before dawn. Of 187 Japanese prisoners taken, most are patients. During the battle for Myitkyina, Allied forces have sustained the following losses: 972 Chinese and 272 Americans killed; 3,184 Chinese and 955 Americans wounded; 188 Chinese and 980 Americans sick. Capture of Myitkyina is a major victory and permits support of the Pacific offensive from bases in China.

On Salween front, elements of Ch 107th and 348th Regts, from 36th and 116th Divs, respectively, reach top of wall around Teng-chung just E of S corner by 1500. One platoon clings there throughout night 3–4 Ch 8th Army renews operations against Sung Shan, 308th Regt of 103d Div, armed with flame throwers, takes one of its peaks, Kung Lung-po, and, since Japanese are short of ammunition, is not counterattacked.

NEW GUINEA—In Aitape area, TED Force attacks S along Niumen Creek toward Torricelli Mts to cut E–W trails and destroy enemy. 3d Bn of 124th Inf and 2d Bn of 169th advance abreast, spearheading attack, but are soon halted. 1st Bn, 124th Inf, then bypasses enemy to W. Japanese activity against South Force in Afua area subsides after small attack early in morning fails. 1st Bn, 169th Inf, moves into perimeter of South Force from Palauru.

GUAM—Renewing attack toward Mt. Barrigada after regrouping, 77th Div finds that enemy has withdrawn northward and takes Barrigada village and its much-needed reservoir with ease. Progress beyond the village is slowed by difficult jungle terrain and small-scale opposition. 3d Mar Div continues to make steady progress on left flank of corps, taking Finegayan and driving beyond Tumon Bay area. Warships begin shelling Mt. Santa Rosa (870 ft), which dominates N part of Guam, day and night.

4 August

FRANCE—21 Army Group: Gen Montgomery orders Br Second Army to continue pivoting eastward about 12 Corps and Cdn First Army to attack toward Falaise as soon as possible.

In Br Second Army area, 8 Corps is still held up by stiff resistance in Vire and Estry areas. In 30 Corps area, 43d Div seizes Hermilly, NW of Aunay. Villers-Bocage falls to 50th Div. 12 Corps, swinging eastward toward Orne R SW of Caen, is beyond line Le Locheur–Evrecy–Esquay–Notre-Dame–Feugerolles-sur-Orne.

12th Army Group: In U.S. Third Army's VIII Corps area, planned attack on Dinan is canceled and 6th Armd Div continues toward Brest instead. Advancing through night 4–5, 6th Armd Div reaches vicinity of Carhaix, which supporting FFI forces report strongly held. TF A and elements of 83d Div reach enemy stronghold of St Maio, where prolonged struggle ensues. Rennes falls to 13th Inf, 8th Div. 4th Armd Div is driving toward Vannes.

U.S. First Army releases 5th Div to XX Corps, Third Army. In VII Corps area, 1st Div, to which 39th Inf of 9th Div and CCB of 3d Armd Div are attached, improves positions in Mortain area on right flank of corps; patrols probe southward toward Mayenne. 4th Div, which releases CCB of 3d Armd Div to 1st Div, battles vigorously but indecisively for St Pois and heights about the town. 9th Div pushes into Forêt de St Sever against strong opposition. XIX Corps is almost halted by stiffening resistance and mine fields. V Corps reaches its objectives above Vire, 2d Div continuing advance through night 4–5, and halts to permit XIX Corps to cross its front to take Vire. 30th Div is transferred to corps from XIX Corps.

FRANTIC—In response to the first direct Soviet request for air support, group of U.S. Fifteenth Air Force fighter bombers attacks airfields in Rumania and then lands at Soviet bases.

ITALY—AAI: Alters plan of attack on Gothic Line. New plan, OLIVE, calls for main effort by right flank of Br Eighth Army, which will be quietly strengthened, rather than attack against center of enemy's line as previously planned. U.S.

Fifth Army, which is to be strengthened by attaching Br 13 Corps, is to make a subsidiary attack up road from Florence to Bologna after enemy has thinned out in center.

Br Eighth Army successfully concludes campaign for central Italy as 13 Corps reaches the Arno at Florence and drives into S part of the city. Enemy has destroyed all bridges except the Ponte Vecchio. Period of extensive regrouping is begun by Eighth Army in preparation for coming assault on the Gothic Line in N Apennines.

CBI—On Salween front, Chinese break into Teng-chung, where prolonged battle for the city ensues. In 33 Corps sector of 11 Army Group's Br Fourteenth Army area, Tamu falls to Br 2d Div.

NEW GUINEA—In Aitape area, Japanese, suffering from casualties, logistic problems, and disease, withdraw southward from front of South Force in Afua area after a last desperate attack that costs them over 200 dead. South Force patrols move forward in pursuit against scattered fire and make contact with TED Force. Both the main assault force and the enveloping column of TED Force continue S in region between the Driniumor and Niumen Creek to E-W trail. Co-ordinated attack by TED Force and South Force scheduled for this date must be postponed until TED Force reaches the Driniumor.

GUAM—77th Div succeeds in reaching 0-3 line, overrunning Mt. Barrigada, and makes contact with 3d Mar Div to left, closing dangerous gap. Progress during day is slowed more by terrain than by skirmishes with enemy. 3d Mar Div is obliged to hold up its advance on left flank of corps in order to tie in with 77th Div. Gen Geiger prepares to commit 306th Inf, which is comparatively fresh, in pursuit toward Mt. Santa Rosa. 1st Prov Mar Brig (−) is relieved of defense duties on S flank and held in reserve.

5 August

FRANCE—21 Army Group: In Br Second Army area, 8 Corps is clearing enemy pockets. In 30 Corps area, Aunay falls to 7th Armd Div, which pushes on toward Thury-Harcourt. 12 Corps closes along the Orne on 7-mile front between Grimbosq and Caen.

12th Army Group: In U.S. Third Army area, VIII Corps is attacking W, SW, S, and E simultaneously. 6th Armd Div continues W toward Brest, bypassing Carhaix and reaching Huelgoat area. 83d Div attacks outer defenses of St Maio; TF A continues W along N coast of Brittany. Brittany Peninsula is cut off as CCA, 4th Armd Div, reaches Vannes. In XV Corps area, 90th Div TF seizes Mayenne. 79th Div is approaching Laval.

U.S. First Army adjusts boundary between U.S. and Br forces and gives new mission to V Corps. In VII Corps area, 1st Div, reinf, continues to consolidate positions in Mortain area and probe southward with patrols. 4th Div overruns St Pois and advances slightly beyond there. 9th Div pushes on through Forêt de St Sever. 30th Div is transferred to VII Corps from V Corps. In XIX Corps area, 29th Div progresses toward Vire despite strong opposition. V Corps is to drive through Vire to take region between Tinchebray and St Jean-du-Bois, employing 2d and 29th Divs. 29th is to remain under XIX Corps until it captures Vire. 35th Div reverts to Third Army.

ITALY—AAI: In Br Eighth Army area, 10 Corps takes crest of M. il Castello.

NEW GUINEA—In Aitape area, main body of TED Force is held up short of main E-W trail E of Afua by stubborn enemy rear guards, who are keeping Driniumor crossing, point open, but the flanking column reaches the trail about 1,500 yards E of the river.

GUAM—306th Inf enters center of 77th Div line and moves NW to pinch out 307th Inf, but is slowed by enemy rear guards. Dense jungle on div right delays 305th Inf. 3d Mar Div continues steadily northward on left flank of corps.

6 August

FRANCE—21 Army Group: Gen Montgomery orders drive to the Seine.

Br Second Army undergoes enemy counterattacks between Vire and Mont Pincon. In 8 Corps area, enemy armor penetrates positions of 11th Armd Div in Vire area, but lost ground is later recovered. Gds Armd Div is strongly engaged at Le Busq, on Vire-Aunay road. 15th Div has moved forward to Estry area but is unable to dislodge enemy from that town. 3d Div is attacking southward toward Vire. In 30 Corps area, 43d Div gains feature on Mont Pincon massif. 7th Armd Div continues attack toward Thury-Harcourt. In 12 Corps area, 59th Div attacks across the Orne in Grimbosq area late in day and establishes shallow bridgehead.

12th Army Group: Group orders establishment of bridgehead over Sarthe R in Le Mans-Alençon area.

In U.S. Third Army's VIII Corps area, CCB, on right flank of 6th Armd Div, overcomes opposition S of Morlaix and at Lesneven; CCA makes slow progress along secondary routes to S. 83d Div continues to hammer at St Maio stronghold. TF A gets beyond St Brieux as it continues W along N coast on Brittany. RCT 121, 8th Div, is attached to 83d Div for attack on Dinard, W of St Maio. 4th Armd Div is advancing on Lorient. XV Corps, with major elements now across the Mayenne, is driving rapidly on Le Mans. 79th Div takes Laval. XX Corps (Maj Gen Walton H. Walker), consisting at present of

5th Div, is reinf by 35th Div in order to protect S flank of army.

In U.S. First Army's VII Corps area, 1st Div, relieved by 30th Div in Mortain area, continues swiftly SE with 3d Armd Div to Ambrières-le-Grand and Mayenne, relieving elements of 90th Div (XV Corps) at Mayenne. 4th Div is pinched out W of St Pois. 9th Div pushes southward toward Sourdeval against strong resistance. In XIX Corps area, 29th Div breaks into Vire and clears the city. With fall of Vire to XIX Corps, V Corps is out of contact with enemy.

FRANTIC—Returning from USSR to Italian bases, fighters of U.S. Fifteenth Air Force raid rail targets in Bucharest=Ploesti area of Rumania. 76 B-17's and supporting fighters of U.S. Eighth Air Force attack aircraft factory at Gdynia (Poland) and then land at Soviet bases.

ITALY—AAI: Issues orders for preliminary operations before assault on the Gothic Line.

CBI—In NCAC area, Br 36th Div, which is moving S down RR corridor, seizes Sahmaw.

In 11 Army Group's Br Fourteenth Army area, Gen Slim directs 33 Corps to pursue enemy to the Chindwin; occupy Sittaung and, if possible, Kalewa; cross the Chindwin in Kalewa area.

NEW GUINEA—In Aitape area, Japanese rear guards that are protecting withdrawal from Afua attack TED Force before dawn and bitter fighting ensues until TED Force column laboriously outflanks enemy and forces him to withdraw in afternoon. When new enemy trail is found to have been cut about 800 yards to S of main trail, TED Force prepares to cut it and move in on Afua from SE. South Force, which has been reinf by 3d Bn of 128th Inf, starts S astride Driniumor R, meeting disorganized resistance.

P.I.—U.S. aircraft begins night harassing attacks on Davao area of Mindanao.

GUAM—III Amphib Corps drives to 0-4 line, gaining control of more than two thirds of Guam. Small but determined force of Japanese with tanks attacks 305th Inf, on 77th Div's right flank, during early morning and inflicts heavy casualties before retiring abruptly. 305th then moves forward about 1,000 yards to 0-4 line with little difficulty. 306th Inf reaches div left boundary, pinching out 307th Inf.

7 August

FRANCE—21 Army Group: In Br Second Army's 30 Corps area, 43d Div completes capture of Mont Pincon, inflicting and suffering heavy casualties during enemy counterattacks. 12 Corps maintains bridgehead across the Orne and attacks S along the river toward Thury-Harcourt.

In Cdn First Army area, 2 Corps, with Cdn 2d Div on right and Br 51st Div on left, attacks S toward Falaise at 2330 after half hour of preparatory bombardment by heavy bombers.

12th Army Group: In U.S. Third Army's VIII Corps area, 6th Armd Div closes in on Brest. Rear elements arrive outside the city too late in day to begin concerted assault, thus giving enemy time to strengthen defenses and bring up reinforcements. TF A is approaching Morlaix. 83d Div continues battle for St Malo. 4th Armd Div invests Lorient. XV Corps is rapidly approaching Le Mans.

In U.S. First Army area, Germans open strong counterattack with massed armor toward Avranches early in morning in effort to break through to the sea and split U.S. forces. Attack penetrates line at junction of XIX and VII Corps, overrunning Mortain and rolling on to Juvigny and Le Mesnil-Tôve before it can be stemmed with assistance of aircraft. In VII Corps area, 30th Div bears brunt of enemy counterblows and elements are isolated in Mortain area. To help stabilize center of corps line, 4th Div and 2d Armd Div are committed at once, latter being transferred from XIX Corps, and prep-arations are made to return 35th Div to First Army. RCT 12, 4th Div, and CCB, 3d Armd Div, are attached to 30th Div, 4th Div is reinf by RCT 39, 9th Div. Progress is made on flanks of enemy penetration, 9th Div advancing slightly near Mortain and 1st Div crossing the Mayenne and reaching St Fraimbault-de-Prières on S. XIX Corps pushes southward to relieve enemy pressure in Mortain area. In V Corps area, 9th Inf of 2d Div releases elements of 29th Div (XIX Corps) in Vire for movement to S.

USSR—By this time, Germans have about stopped Soviet summer offensive. Soviet armies have driven over 400 miles from the Dnieper to the Vistula and consequently supply and communications lines are becoming overextended.

FRANTIC—Some of the Eighth Air Force planes that bombed Gdynia on 6th attack oil refineries at Trzebinia (Poland).

ITALY—AAI: U.S. Fifth Army tentatively postpones D Day of offensive to 19 August; makes minor changes in plan of attack; promises to make available from army reserve 34th Div to II Corps and RCT 442 (−) and RCT 370, 92 Div, to IV Corps. II Corps is still to make main effort while IV Corps, whose 1st Armd Div is to be replaced by RCT 442, demonstrates in Pontedera=Cascina area.

NEW GUINEA—On Biak, 2d Bn of 162d Inf starts N along Sorido-Korim Bay track to make contact with 163d Inf, which is moving S. In Aitape area, TED Force cuts the new Japanese trail below main trail and drives westward toward the Driniumor. South Force continues to patrol actively while awaiting arrival of TED Force at the Driniumor. Japanese appear to be in full flight.

GUAM—III Amphib Corps, with air and naval gunfire support, attacks in greatest strength yet employed on Guam to clear N third of the island. 77th Div makes main effort toward Yigo and Mt. Santa Rosa on right flank of corps. After destructive preparatory bombardment, 77th Div attacks at noon with 306th Inf on left, 307th in center, and 305th on right. 307th, assisted by 306th, overcomes opposition along Finegayan-Yigo road and seizes Yigo. 305th advances slowly through jungle in coastal sector toward Mt. Santa Rosa. Enemy tanks are again active after nightfall, but U.S. lines hold firm. 3d Mar Div in center of corps front and 1st Prov Mar Brig on left flank drive northward.

8 August

FRANCE—Gen Montgomery orders U.S. forces to drive almost due N on Alençon as quickly as possible in order to make a short envelopment of enemy in Falaise-Mortain area while the broad envelopment toward the Seine is in progress.

21 Army Group: In Br Second Army area, 30 Corps makes limited progress toward Condé-sur-Noireau. 12 Corps continues to hold bridgehead E of the Orne, but efforts to thrust S along E bank toward Thury-Harcourt in conjunction with drive down W bank fail because of determined enemy counterattacks.

In Cdn First Army's 2 Corps area, Cdn 2d Div seizes Fontenay-le-Marmion and Requancourt. 51st Div overruns Garcelles-Secqueville. At 1355, following air preparation, Cdn 4th Armd and Pol 1st Armd Divs pass through infantry, former on right, to exploit southward toward Falaise, but soon meet strong opposition from enemy's MLR. Air support of the Cdn offensive during night 7-8 and on this date is the second heaviest of Normandy, exceeded only by support of British on 18 July. U.S. Eighth Air Force and RAF BC drop more than 5,200 tons of bombs.

12th Army Group: In U.S. Third Army's VIII Corps area, ultimatum calling for surrender of Brest is ignored. 6th Armd Div prepares for all-out assault on the city on 9th until enemy threat to rear forces a change in plans. Enemy div is found to be moving toward Brest via Plouvien. 1st Bn of 28th Inf, 8th Div, is attached to 6th Armd Div but does not join it until later. Bitter fighting continues in outskirts of St Malo. RCT 121, attached to 83d Div, meets strong opposition as it advances on Dinard. XV Corps envelops and overruns Le Mans and crosses Sarthe R in that area. 79th Div enters Le Mans. 2d Fr Armd Div is attached to corps to help it secure line Sées-Carrouges, both inclusive. 80th Div of XX Corps is to take over Le Mans bridgehead. In XX Corps area, 5th Div invests Angers and Nantes.

In U.S. First Army's VII Corps area, enemy continues efforts to deepen penetration of U.S. lines without avail. 30th Div elements are still isolated near Mortain. 35th Div, released to VII Corps by XX Corps, and elements of 2d Armd Div are attacking eastward near Mortain. XIX Corps makes small gains in Gathemo-Vire region.

FRANTIC—U.S. Eighth Air Force planes, returning from Eastern Command bases in USSR to England via Italy, attack airfields in Rumania.

CHINA—Japanese complete capture of Hengyang. This has far-reaching effects on Chinese politics.

NEW GUINEA—In Aitape area, most of TED Force reaches the Driniumor near Afua.

GUAM—Effective enemy resistance comes to an end. 77th Div clears Mt. Santa Rosa and virtually all of its sector.

9 August

FRANCE—21 Army Group: In Cdn First Army area, 2 Corps continues S astride Caen-Falaise road. Cdn 4th Armd Div overruns Bretteville-le-Rabet while Pol 1st Armd Div seizes Cauvicourt and St Sylvain in costly fighting. Infantry units are clearing flanks.

12th Army Group: In U.S. Third Army's VIII Corps area, 6th Armd Div, leaving small force to contain Brest, moves N to meet threat to its rear and virtually destroys enemy div in Plouvien area; makes contact with TF A near Brest. 83d Div continues assault on St Malo, where resistance is now confined largely to the Citadel. 4th Armd Div is still containing Lorient and sends elements toward Nantes. XV Corps mops up Le Mans and swings N toward Alençon, 5th Armd Div on right and Fr 2d Armd Div on left, followed by infantry. 80th Div, temporarily attached to corps, is mopping up near Le Mans. In XX Corps area, 5th Div closes in on Angers.

U.S. First Army orders a turn NE toward Argentan to meet British working southward toward Falaise to trap enemy in Vire-Mortain-Domfront-Ger region. In VII Corps area, enemy counteroffensive toward Avranches loses its momentum but heavy fighting continues. 39th Inf, 9th Div, is detached from 4th Div. In XIX Corps area, 28th Div is unable to advance in Gathemo region, but 29th moves slowly forward below Vire. V Corps orders 2d Div, whose mission is still primarily defensive, to move one reinf regt SE. 102d Cav Gp is attached to 2d Div, which relieves additional elements of 29th Div (XIX Corps) on hills near Vire.

ITALY—AAI: In Br Eighth Army area, 13 Corps completes clearing region below the Arno in Florence area.

CBI—On Salween front, Japanese raid Ch 8th Army's arty positions and supply dumps in Sung Shan sector with some success. In China, Marshal Li Chi-shen, President of the Military Advisory Council of Chungking, sends message to U.S. Consulate in Kweilin that E China war lords are about to form a provisional government in order to effect national unity and defeat Japanese; that Chiang Kai-shek will be asked to resign. U.S. attitude to this is one of watchful waiting.

NEW GUINEA—In Aitape area, Gen Gill reports to Gen Hall that resistance along the Driniumor has ceased.

GUAM—77th Div and 3d Mar Div are clearing final resistance on Guam. Bypassed enemy groups show a determination to be killed rather than surrender.

10 August

FRANCE—21 Army Group: In Cdn First Army's Br 1 Corps area, 49th Div, in conjunction with Cdn 2 Corps, advances to Vimont against strong opposition.

12th Army Group: In U.S. Third Army area, VIII Corps continues to attack Dinard and the Citadel at St Malo and to contain Brest and Lorient. 1st Bn, 28th Inf, is attached to CCA, 6th Armd Div, in preparation for attack on Hills 95 and 105 at Brest. Elements of 4th Armd Div drive rapidly E, forcing enemy back into Nantes. In XV Corps area, armored columns continue steadily northward toward Alençon and Sées. In XX Corps area, 5th Div overruns Angers. 7th Armd Div is attached to corps.

In U.S. First Army area, VII Corps, which has regained the initiative, is slowly driving enemy back toward Mortain. 9th Div improves positions NW of Sourdeval. Stubborn enemy defense of Mortain limits progress of 30th and 35th Divs toward that town. 22d Inf, 4th Div, is committed to right of 35th Div in Le Teilleul area. 2d Armd Div repels counterattack NE of Barenton. In XIX Corps area, CCA of 2d Armd Div and 28th Inf Div make co-ordinated attack on right flank of corps, overrunning Gathemo; armor then drives eastward along road toward Tinchebray. 29th Div, attacking toward St. Sauveur-de-Chaulieu on narrow front, is hard pressed by enemy and makes little headway. In V Corps area, 2d Div begins limited attacks to SE while continuing to defend Vire. 9th Inf advances to Maisoncelles=la Jourdan area where it is ordered to halt.

MEDITERRANEAN—At AFHQ Gen Wilson receives directive from Br Chiefs of Staff to proceed with DRAGOON as planned. Phase I of air operations in preparation for invasion of S France ends. During this phase (28 April to date) MAAF has dropped more than 12,500 tons of bombs. During Phase II enemy coastal batteries, radar stations, and troops are to be hit, and target area is to be isolated by destruction of highway bridges across the Rhône. To deceive enemy, similar targets are to be bombed between Via Reggio in Italy and Beziers, near French-Spanish border.

USSR—Units of Second White Russian Front force Narew R near Bialystok.

CHINA—Brig Gen Patrick J. Hurley's name is proposed to Chiang Kai-shek as President Roosevelt's representative; Donald M. Nelson is suggested at the same time as Presidential representative to study China's economy.

NEW GUINEA—On Noemfoor, 503d Para Inf regains contact with enemy near Hill 380, $2^{1}/_{2}$ miles SSW of Inasi. During the next few days 3d Bn, assisted by arty and aircraft, works in toward the hill while 1st Bn blocks escape of Japanese. In Aitape area, PERSECUTION Covering Force begins movement back to Blue Beach.

GUAM—All organized resistance on island ends as marines finish clearing their zone to N tip. In subsequent mopping up of scattered groups, several hundred Japanese are killed. Of an estimated 18,500 Japanese on Guam, those dead by actual count total a little over 10,000.

11 August

FRANCE—Gen Montgomery commends Allied forces and urges that the attack be pressed.

21 Army Group: In Second Army's 8 Corps area, 3d Div drives S across Vire-Condé road about 2 miles E of Vire and presses toward Tinchebray. 30 Corps continues slowly SE from Mont Pincon toward Cond. 50th Div, having moved forward on left flank, is beyond St Pierre-la-Vieille. In 12 Corps area, forward elements of 53d and 59th Divs, continuing S astride the Orne, reach outskirts of Thury-Harcourt. Elements E of the river patrol NE to establish contact with Cdn 2 Corps.

In Cdn First Army's 2 Corps area, while armored elements of corps are clearing opposition astride road to Falaise, 2d Div crosses Laize R at Bretteville and advances SW to link up with 12 Corps to right, and 51st Div clears left flank S of Caen-Mézidon RR. Br 1 Corps zone is expanded as corps takes command of 51st Div in place from Cdn 2 Corps.

12th Army Group: Gap between U.S. Third Army units moving N and Cdn and Br forces moving S is now about 20 miles wide. In U.S. Third Army's VIII Corps area, enemy garrisons of Dinard and St Maio's Citadel continue to hold out against 83d Div attacks. CCA, 4th Armd Div, reaches Nantes area and relieves elements of 5th Div, XX Corps, containing that city. In XV Corps area, 2d

Armd and Fr 5th Armd Divs continue steadily northward followed by infantry, meeting increasingly strong rear-guard opposition. Corps is directed by Gen Patton to push beyond Falaise although U.S. boundary is S of there. XX Corps is directed by army to attack NE to line Carrouges-Sées after assembling on line Mayenne-Le Mans; one RCT of 80th Div is to maintain bridgehead at Le Mans; 7th Armd Div is to move to rear of line of departure from its assembly area.

In U.S. First Army's VII Corps area, 9th Div makes further gains NW of Sourdeval. 30th Div, in the course of hard fighting, forces enemy back to Mortain. Below Mortain, 35th Div advances slowly, and 2d Armd Div withstands further counterattacks NW of Barenton. In XIX Corps area, 29th Div and CCA of 2d Armd Div attack heights around St Sauveur-de-Chaulieu, while 28th Div continues SE from Gathemo. V Corps improves defensive positions at and near Vire.

USSR—Troops of Third Baltic Front break through enemy defenses below Lake Peipus on 42-mile front and press northward.

ITALY—Assault force begins movement from Naples area toward target in southern France.

AAI: In Br Eighth Army area, Pol 2 Corps has cleared Adriatic coastal sector as far as Cesano R.

CBI—On Salween front, Chinese begin tunneling and mining under enemy positions remaining in Sung Shan hill mass, since other methods of attack have not resulted in taking the position.

NEW GUINEA—In Aitape area, 103d Inf of 43d Div begins relief of PERSECUTION Covering Force units remaining along the Driniumor.

U.S.—CCS confirm orders for DRAGOON to proceed as planned.

12 August

FRANCE—21 Army Group: In Br Second Army area, 8 Corps is heavily engaged 3 miles SE of Vire. In 30 Corps area, forward elements of 50th Div are within about 3 miles of Cond. 12 Corps is clearing opposition in vicinity of Thury-Harcourt.

In Cdn First Army area, 2 Corps is still held up astride road to Falaise but succeeds in linking up with Br 12 Corps to right at Barbery.

12th Army Group: In U.S. Third Army's VIII Corps area, 83d Div continues to inch forward against St Malo Citadel and Dinard. CCA, 6th Armd Div, attacks toward limited objectives at Brest but makes little headway. Late in day, div mission is changed: CCA is to contain Brest while rest of div relieves 4th Armd Div at Lorient and Vannes. VIII Corps is to relieve 5th Div units (XX Corps) at Angers. Patrols of CCA, 4th Armd Div, enter Nantes. XV Corps drives beyond Alençon and Sées toward Argentan. 2d Fr Armd Div thrusts to Carrouges. 5th Armd Div takes Sées. Infantrymen continue to follow armor closely. XX Corps is ordered to make contact with XV Corps in Alençon area and then await new orders. 5th Div moves to St Calais area, leaving containing force behind at Angers.

U.S. First Army has completely defeated enemy efforts to break through to Avranches. VII Corps recovers ground lost to enemy and relieves isolated elements of 30th Div. 3d Armd Div assembles for new mission; CCA is detached from 1st Div and CCB from 30th Div. XIX Corps releases 29th Div (less 116th Inf, which relieves 2d Div at Vire) to V Corps in current position. 28th Div, against moderate opposition, drives rapidly southward to Sourdeval on right and positions near St Sauveur-de-Chaulieu on left. CCA, 2d Armd Div, improves positions in St Sauveur-de-Chaulieu area. V Corps, employing 29th Div on right and 2d Div on left, attacks SE, 29th reaching positions overlooking St Sauveur-de-Chaulieu-Tinchebray road and 2d overrunning Truttemer-le-Grand.

ITALY—AAI: In Br Eighth Army area, 13 Corps zone is extended eastward to include sector held by 6th Armd Div. 13 Corps thus has 4 divs: NZ 2d, Br 1st, Ind 8th, and Br 6th Armd. 10 Corps now has but one div, Ind 10th.

CHINA—Generalissimo Chiang Kai-shek agrees to accept Gen Hurley and Mr. Nelson as Presidential representatives.

NEW GUINEA—On Biak, Sorido airdrome, now consisting of a 4,000-foot strip, is being used by transport planes, but the field is later abandoned.

13 August

FRANCE—12th Army Group: In U.S. Third Army's VIII Corps area, 83d Div continues to make slow progress against strongpoints at St Malo and Dinard. CCA, 6th Armd Div, batters at outer defenses of Brest without avail. Rest of 6th Armd Div moves forward to relieve 4th Armd Div at Vannes and Lorient. 4th Armd Div, finding Nantes free of enemy, moves toward St Calais. 8th Div (–) advances to Dinan from Rennes. XV Corps reaches Argentan area and is halted there by order of Gen Bradley. During next few days Germans succeed in withdrawing thousands from Falaise-Argentan trap before it can be closed. XX Corps, with Chartres as its next objective, moves forward in preparation for attack. 80th Div is pinched out by XV Corps near Alençon. XII Corps (Maj Gen Gilbert R. Cook), which is given command of 4th Armd Div (VIII Corps) and 35th Div (VII Corps), receives its first offensive mission—to drive E on Orléans and protect S flank of army. Assault forces are assembling SE of Le Mans.

In U.S. First Army's VII Corps area, 3d Armd and 1st Inf Divs swing NE around Domfront, driving rapidly toward Vire-Argentan road to constrict pocketed enemy forces. 3d Armd Div, on corps right, moves through Javron toward Ranes, making contact with Fr 2d Armd Div (XV Corps). 1st Div cuts Domfront-Alençon road in Couterne-La Chapelle Moche area. 4th and 9th Divs await new mission. 30th Div passes to control of XIX Corps. XIX Corps probes eastward, 2d Armd Div units threatening Domfront and Ger and 28th Div moving toward St Sauveur-de-Chaulieu through Sourdeval. In V Corps area, 29th Div pushes southward in direction of Ger on right flank of corps, forward elements reaching La Françaisere, E of Sourdeval. 2d Div heads for Tinchebray, overrunning Truttemer-le-Petit.

ITALY—AAI: In U.S. Fifth Army's IV Corps area, 1st Armd Div, which has been completely reorganized in the field, takes responsibility for right flank of corps, replacing TF Ramey.

In Br Eighth Army's 13 Corps area, elements of Ind 8th Div cross into N Florence via Ponte Vecchio to help Italians extend their hold on the city.

CBI—SWPA—Rcn of Manila docks, P.I., by Gen Chennault's Fourteenth Air Force evokes unfavorable reaction from both Gen Stilwell and Gen MacArthur. MacArthur warns Chennault not to bomb Manila.

NEW GUINEA—In Aitape area, relief of 127th Inf along the Driniumor is completed.

14 August

FRANCE—21 Army Group: In Br Second Army area, 8 Corps continues southward toward Tinchebray while V Corps of U.S. First Army pushes toward same objective from W. 30 Corps is closing in on Vassy and Condé. In 12 Corps area, 59th Div takes Thury-Harcourt. Advance is continued toward Falaise.

In Cdn First Army area, 2 Corps, making main effort on Falaise from N, begins attack to outflank opposition on Caen-Falaise highway. Cdn 2d Div secures bridgehead across Laize R and pushes to within 4 miles of Falaise. In support of troops, RAF BC drops 3,723 tons of bombs.

12th Army Group: In U.S. Third Army's VIII Corps area, 6th Armd Div's CCB and CCR move to Vannes and Lorient, respectively, to relieve 4th Armd Div's units. CCB finds Vannes deserted and moves on to Lorient, relieving CCR. Lorient containing force now consists of CCB, 15th Tank Bn, and 86th Cav Rcn Sq (mechanized). 83d Div continues struggle for St Malo Citadel and Dinard. 8th Div (−) joins in assault on Dinard. XV Corps mops up in Alençon-Sées-Argentan area and prepares to drive E on Dreux. XX Corps begins drive toward Chartres with 7th Armd and 5th Inf Divs, armor spearheading. XII Corps continues E toward Orléans with elements of 4th Armd Div.

In U.S. First Army's VII Corps area, 3d Armd Div drives steadily northward through Carrouges to Ranes against strong opposition as enemy struggles to keep escape routes open. 9th Div is following up. 1st Div gets forward elements well beyond La Ferté-Macé. 4th Div, disposed along the Varenne, is out of contact with enemy. In XIX Corps area, CCA of 2d Armd Div pushes E, overrunning Domfront, Lonlay-l'Abbaye, and Get. 28th Div, except for 109th Regt, which moves S toward Forêt de Mortain, goes into reserve. 30th Div moves forward behind armor. In V Corps area, 29th Div, advancing E from positions below Sourdeval-Tinchebray highway, reaches St Jean-du-Bois. 2d Div continues toward Tinchebray but is soon stopped by lively opposition.

MEDITERRANEAN—After rendezvousing off Corsica, DRAGOON convoys head for target area of southern France.

POLAND—British begin dropping supplies to Pol forces within Warsaw.

NEW GUINEA—In Vogelkop area, crippled B-24 makes successful landing on Middleburg I. airstrip.

15 August

N FRANCE—Gen Montgomery moves boundary between Br and U.S. forces northward.

21 Army Group: In Br Second Army area, 8 Corps makes contact with U.S. V Corps forces near Tinchebray. 30 Corps overruns Vassy and continues to clear region near Condé. 12 Corps progresses toward Falaise from NW.

In Cdn First Army's 2 Corps area, Cdn 4th Armd Div advances toward Falaise in region E of Caen-Falaise road. Pol 1st Armd Div establishes bridgehead across Dives R NE of Falaise.

12th Army Group: Plan to drop airborne forces W of the Seine to block enemy escape routes (TRANSFIGURE) is by now unnecessary.

In U.S. Third Army's VIII Corps area, 83d Div takes Dinard, but enemy continues effective defense of St Malo Citadel. 6th Armd Div contains Brest and Lorient. In XV Corps area, 5th Armd and 79th Inf Divs are pushing rapidly toward Dreux. Corps elements containing enemy pocket in Argentan-Falaise area (Fr 2d Armd Div, 90th Inf Div, and 80th Inf Div, less 319th Inf), are formed into Prov Corps under command of Maj Gen Hugh J. Gaffey, U.S. Third Army chief of staff. Enemy continues vigorous efforts to escape trap. In XX Corps area, 7th Armd Div reaches edge of Chartres, where heavy fighting ensues. In XII Corps area, 4th Armd Div, followed by 35th Div, pushes rapidly toward

Orléans. Elements of 35th Div are driving toward Châteaudun, NW of Orléans.

In U.S. First Army area, VII Corps progresses well against light resistance. 3d Armd Div, upon capture of Ranes, moves some elements NE toward Ecouché and others NW toward Fromental. 1st Div continues northward toward Vire-Argentan highway to left of armor. 9th Div continues to follow spearheads. In V Corps area, 29th Div secures heights S of Tinchebray; 2d Div overruns Tinchebray. This concludes current mission of corps.

S FRANCE—U.S. Seventh Army, under control of AFHQ, begins preliminary operations to isolate main DRAGOON invasion beaches on Fr Mediterranean coast about midnight 14–15. To secure left flank of assault area, SITKA Force (U.S. Special Service Force) invades small islands of Levant and Port Cros, clearing former and part of latter; ROMEO Force (Fr Commandos) lands on mainland at and E of Cap Nègre and soon clears coastal defenses and blocks coastal highway. Rosie Force (Fr Naval Assault Group) lands SW of Cannes in Theoule-sur-Mer area to secure right flank of assault area, but is unable to accomplish its mission and suffers heavy casualties. RUGBY Force (1st ABTF) drops in rear of assault beaches, beginning at 0430, and accomplishes its task of blocking off invasion coast from the interior along "Blue Line" in Le Muy-Le Luc area before H Hour. RUGBY Force is unable to clear Le Muy but overruns a number of villages. These ground operations, plus final pounding of assault zone by aircraft and naval gunfire, leave enemy incapable of offering much resistance. VI Corps (Gen Truscott) lands, 3 divs abreast, between Nice and Toulon at H Hour (0800) and moves inland against light, scattered resistance. 3d Div (ALPHA Force) lands on left flank between Bay of Cavalaire and Bay of Pampelonne; moves quickly W and N, left flank forces overrunning Cavalaire and making contact with Fr Commandos, who are placed under 3d Div, at Cap Nègre; right flank troops reach St Tropez as 1st ABTF elements and FFI are completing its capture and join in attack that clears the town and St Tropez Peninsula. Other towns taken by 3d Div are La Mole, Cogolin, Grimaud, and La Croix. In center of corps, 45th Div (DELTA Force) lands near Ste Maxime and quickly secures beaches, although town of Ste Maxime holds out until afternoon; speeds inland toward Le Muy and Fréjus. Contact is made with 1st ABTF and with friendly forces on each flank. 179th Inf is held in reserve. On right flank of VI Corps, 36th Div (CAMEL Force) lands E of St Raphaël, 141st Inf leading at H Hour and 143d following soon afterwards. 141st Inf overruns Drammont and coastal fortifications near Agay and pushes rapidly northward. 143d drives W toward St Raphaël. RCT 142, scheduled to land at 1400 W of Fréjus and take that town, is forced to land 10 miles E of the town instead when obstacles at planned site cannot be breached; starts ashore at 1532, moving to heights NE of Fréjus.

ITALY—AAI: Br Eighth Army begins large-scale shift of units to E flank in preparation for assault on Gothic Line.

SWPA—ALAMO Force issues FO for invasion of Morotai. XI Corps TF, called TRADEWIND Assault Force, under command of Gen Hall and consisting of 31st Div with RCT 126 of 32d Div as reserve, is to conduct the operation.

NEW GUINEA—On Noemfoor, Japanese succeed in withdrawing main force of some 200 toward Pakriki, on S central coast, from Hill 380, night 15–16. On Biak, 162d and 163d Regts split enemy remnants on island as they make contact on Sorido-Korim Bay track. In Aitape area, Tadji Defense Perimeter and Covering Force, consisting of 43d Div and Cav RCT 112, under command of Maj Gen Leonard F. Wing, who also commands 43d Div, takes over mission of PERSECUTION Covering Force and latter is dissolved. In Wakde-Sarmi area, 31st Div, less RCT 124, arrives. In Vogelkop area, ALAMO Force warns TF TYPHOON that enemy force of 250 has been moving along N coast from Manokwari to Sorong.

POA—III Amphib Corps, having completed its operations in the Marianas sooner than expected, is definitely committed to task of invading the Palaus next.

16 August

N FRANCE—21 Army Group: In Br Second Army's 8 Corps area, 3d Div finds Flers clear of enemy. In 30 Corps area, Condé-sur-Noireau falls to 11th Armd Div without opposition. 12 Corps, continuing SE toward Falaise, gets almost to Falaise-Condé railway line.

In Cdn First Army area, 2 Corps has virtually surrounded Falaise. Br I Corps begins general advance eastward toward the Seine in coastal sector. 6th A/B Div, on coast, finds enemy firmly established along the Dives in Cabourg area. 49th Div crosses the Dives at Mézidon. 51st Div seizes St Pierre-sur-Dives and continues toward Lisieux. 7th Armd Div is operating on corps right flank.

12th Army Group: In U.S. Third Army's VIII Corps area, 83d Div continues to batter at St Malo Citadel; releases 121st Inf to 8th Div. Elements of 8th Div are now in Brest area. XV Corps reaches Eure R and establishes bridgehead. Dreux falls to 5th Armd Div. XX Corps assembles near Chartres and establishes bridgehead across Aunay R. In XII Corps area, Orléans falls in co-ordinated assault by CCA, 4th Armd Div, and 137th Inf, 35th Div. RCT 320, 35th Div, reaches outskirts of Châteaudun.

In U.S. First Army area, VII Corps continues northward with little difficulty except in Fromental area, where 3d Armd Div is strongly opposed. XIX Corps reaches its objectives and is pinched out by British; releases CCA, 2d Armd Div, to parent unit. V Corps remains in place. 116th Inf of 29th Div defends corps front.

S FRANCE—In U.S. Seventh Army area, Army CP is established ashore W of St Tropez. Enemy garrison of Port Cros I., is resisting stoutly from fort on W end of island. 1st ABTF consolidates in rear of beachhead and overcomes opposition at Le Muy. VI Corps orders exploitation inland. 7th Inf, 3d Div, is slowed by roadblocks as it continues W along coast beyond Cap Nègre; attached Fr Commandos are clearing Cap Bénat, W of Cap Nègre. 15th Inf assembles near Collobrières. 30th Inf overruns La Guarde Freinet, Les Mayon, Gonfaron, and Collobrières to establish itself along Blue Line. 45th Div completes clearing its zone, closing along Blue Line. 36th Div is in contact with 45th Div to left and French survivors of Rosie Force on right. 142d Inf overruns Fréjus and Puget while 143d clears St Raphaël. 141st continues N along coast, seizing Theoule and taking up defensive positions near La Napoule. Fr Army B (Gen de Lattre de Tassigny), under command of U.S. Seventh Army, begins landing 2d Corps over VI Corps beaches in preparation for drive on Toulon and Marseille from Blue Line.

ITALY—AAI: Operation Order No. 3 presents plan, secretly drawn up on 4th, for breaking through Gothic Line: Br Eighth Army initially is to make main effort in Adriatic coastal sector. U.S. Fifth Army, previously unaware of this alteration in plans, is forced to change its strategy. Gen Clark issues instructions to mask build-up of II Corps from enemy. New interarmy boundary becomes effective, and 85th Div of II Corps relieves NZ 2d Div in Montelupo area. Fifth Army, upon reaching Bologna area, is to continue to Modena and exploit beyond there.

NEW GUINEA—In Aitape area, 128th Inf returns to Blue Beach from former sector of North Force along the Driniumor., 43d Div, with 169th Inf on W flank, 172d S of Tadji strips and along the Nigia, and 103d along the Driniumor, patrols without meeting organized resistance except at mouth of the Dandriwad.

17 August

N FRANCE—Hitler replaces von Kluge as commander of *OB WEST* with Field Marshal Model.

21 Army Group: Br Second Army presses southward against enemy pocket from vicinity of Flers, Condé, and Falaise.

In Cdn First Army's 2 Corps area, capture of Falaise by Cdn 2d Div narrows enemy's escape corridor. Crossing Dives R near Morteaux, Cdn 4th Armd Div drives SE toward Trun in conjunction with Pol 1st Armd Div to left.

12th Army Group: Directs First Army to clear Chambois-Trun area and, in conjunction with British, to complete encirclement and reduction of enemy pocket; orders Third Army to drive on Mantes-Gassicourt while completing capture of Brittany Peninsula; orders regrouping for above missions; adjusts boundaries.

In U.S. Third Army's VIII Corps area, opposition at St Malo ends with surrender of the Citadel to 83d Div. To speed reduction of Brittany, 2d Div and 2d and 5th Ranger Bns are allocated to corps; 29th Div is to be attached within the next 2 days. In XV Corps area, 5th Armd and 79th Inf Divs maintain their bridgeheads across the Aunay and move elements toward Mantes-Gassicourt. In XX Corps area, 7th Armd Div completes mop-up of Chartres; 5th Div blocks exits. XII Corps mops up in Orléans and Châteaudun. Enemy withdraws across the Loire on S flank.

In U.S. First Army area, VII Corps establishes positions along Vire-Argentan highway between Ecouché and Flers. 3d Armd Div overcomes strong resistance at Fromental. 9th Div is on highway in Fromental-Briouze area. 1st Div is on its objective to left and in contact with British. Regrouping must take place before further offensive action can be undertaken. V Corps takes over new zone and units previously under control of Prov Corps, Third Army, with orders to close Argentan-Falaise gap. XIX Corps is given responsibility for sector and troops previously held by V Corps. As reconstituted, V Corps consists of Fr 2d Armd Div, 80th Div (less 319th Inf), and 90th Div. 90th Div seizes Le Bourg-St-Léonard, below Chambois, against bitter opposition.

S FRANCE—In U.S. Seventh Army area, small German garrison of Port Cros I., surrenders to U.S. Special Service Force. In U.S. VI Corps area, 3d Div, with 7th Inf and attached Fr Commandos, continues to clear left flank toward Toulon, reaching Blue Line in La Londe-Les Maures area. 1st and 2d Bns of 30th Inf assemble E of Brignoles, night 17-18. On right flank, 36th Div, moving elements through Trans-en-Provence to Draguignan, also reaches Blue Line, completing assault phase; makes contact with 1st ABTF near Le Muy.

EASTERN EUROPE—Germans are strongly counterattacking about Siauliai in Lithuania. Troops of Third White Russian Front reach border of East Prussia along Sesupe R.

ITALY—AAI: U.S. Fifth Army orders attack on 8-mile front between Florence and Pontassieve on 72

[18-19 AUGUST 1944]

hours' notice after 0001, 25 August. During first phase, II Corps, raking main effort, is to take M. Morello, M. Senario, and M. Calvana; Br 13 Corps is to take M. Giovi. Attack is to penetrate Gothic Line during second phase.

In Br Eighth Army area, Pol 2 Corps postpones attack across the Cesano, planned for this time, until mine fields can be cleared.

CHINA—Gen Chennault asks Gen Hearn to send U.S. supplies to Chinese to assist them in recapturing Heng-yang, regardless of Nationalist Government's view on this matter.

NEW GUINEA—On Noemfoor, 503d Para Inf regains contact with enemy and overcomes last organized resistance. On Biak, 1st Bn of 186th Inf less Co B but reinf by Co E, lands from LCM's at Wardo Bay against token resistance. After this, enemy remnants on Biak break up into small groups without hope of making a further stand. In Vogelkop area, Gen Barnes of XIII Air Task Force reports strip on Middleburg I., ready for fighters, a day ahead of schedule.

18 August

N FRANCE—21 Army Group: In Br Second Army area, 8 Corps, now pinched out, is held in army reserve. Its transport is used by units driving toward the Seine. 30 Corps is rapidly reducing enemy pocket from N. 11th Armd Div reaches Putanges and Ecouché. 12 Corps, also compressing the enemy pocket, continues SE toward Argentan.

In Cdn First Army's 2 Corps area, Cdn 4th Armd Div seizes Trun and continues SE in conjunction with Pol 1st Armd Div to left. Stiff fighting develops in Chambois area as enemy makes furious attempts to keep escape corridor open, counterattacking vigorously from within and without the pocket.

12th Army Group: In U.S. Third Army's VIII Corps area, 2d Div, moving from First Army zone to Brest to relieve 6th Armd Div, is attached to corps. 8th Div is concentrated N of Brest, and TF A is in Morlaix area. In XV Corps area, 5th Armd and 79th Inf Divs drive quickly toward the Seine at Mantes-Gassicourt. In XX Corps area, 7th Armd Div takes over bridgehead at Dreux; 5th Div moves to Chartres. In XII Corps area, 35th Div finishes mopping up in Orléans and begins movement to Janville area. 4th Armd Div continues to clear region near Orléans.

U.S. First Army, while reducing Argentan-Falaise Pocket, regroups in preparation for future action. VII Corps mops up, maintains contact with British at Briouze, and prepares to renew offensive. V Corps, with 90th Div on right and 80th on left, attacks northward to close Falaise-Argentan gap. 90th pushes into Forêt de Gouffern while 80th advances through Bordeaux toward Argentan. Fr 2d Armd Div assists with fire and provides flank protection; CCL is attached to 90th Div.

S FRANCE—In U.S. Seventh .Army area, VI Corps overruns enemy's primary defenses in coastal sector. While 7th Inf of 3d Div continues W along Highway 98 (St Tropez-Toulon), 30th and 15th Regts drive W along Highway 7, S of Argens R. 30th Inf begins assault on Brignoles, where fighting continues throughout night 18-19. CC1, Fr 1st Armd Div, which has moved forward between 3d and 45th Divs, overcomes enemy opposition in Cabasse-Carces region. 45th Div's 179th Inf begins assault on Barjols, where enemy is putting up strong delaying opposition. Prov Armd Group, headed by Deputy Commander, VI Corps, Brig Gen Frederick B. Butler, and called TF Butler, starts NW from Le Muy area to spearhead advance inland toward Grenoble, reaching Riez. 36th Div, which is to follow TF Butler northward, moves elements against Callian, E of Fayence, where group of paratroopers is surrounded by enemy. 143d Inf, upon relief by 141st, moves to assembly area at Draguignan. In Fr Army B area, 2d Corps begins drive toward Marseille with 3d Algerian Div.

EASTERN EUROPE—Sandomierz, on W bank of the Vistula, falls to troops of First Ukrainian Front. Germans continue to counterattack strongly in Siauliai area of Lithuania in effort to reopen communications with Baltic forces.

ITALY—AAI: U.S. Fifth Army takes command of 13 Corps, Br Eighth Army, in place. In II Corps zone, 85th Div relieves 91st Div in line below Fucecchio and 91st begins training near Certaldo.

In Br Eighth Army area, Pol 2 Corps starts preliminary attack toward Gothic Line in Adriatic sector, crossing Cesano R with Italian Corps of Liberation (previously Utili Div) on left, 5th Kresowa Div in center, and 3d Carpathian Div on right.

19 August

N FRANCE—German Field Marshal von Kluge commits suicide. As a result of general uprising of Fr resistance forces in Paris, Germans ask for and are granted truce to last until 23d so that they may withdraw troops. Falaise-Argentan trap is closed as Cdn 2 Corps elements make junction with U.S. V Corps troops at Chambois. German *Seventh Army* and elements of *Fifth Panzer Army* are encircled.

21 Army Group: In Br Second Army's 30 Corps zone, 11th Armd Div reaches Argentan-Bailleu area. In 12 Corps area, 53d Div is approaching Bailleu-Trun region.

In Cdn First Army's 2 Corps area, Cdn 4th Armd Div takes St Lambert-sur-Dives, on Trun-Chambois road, and holds it against lively counterattacks.

Patrol of Pol 1st Armd Div makes contact with U.S. V Corps at Chambois. In Br I Corps area, forward elements are crossing La Vie R, although considerable resistance continues to rear.

12th Army Group: In U.S. Third Army's XV Corps area, 79th Div TF enters Mantes-Gassicourt, which is clear of enemy. 5th Armd Div starts N along W bank of the Seine toward Louviers to cut off enemy retreat across the river. In XX Corps area, 5th Div completes mop up of Chartres. In XII Corps area, Maj Gen Manton S. Eddy takes command of corps, relieving Gen Cook.

In U.S. First Army's V Corps area, 80th Div is closing in on Argentan; 90th reaches Chambois and at 1930 contacts Pol patrol, closing Falaise-Argentan gap. XIX Corps attacks N toward Evreux from Brezolle, W of Dreux, with 2d Armd Div on left and 30th Div on right, to cut off enemy from the Seine between Paris and Elbeuf. 28th Div is concentrating in Mortagne area.

S France—U.S. Seventh Army directs VI Corps to seize Aix-en-Provence while French Army B continues drives on ports of Toulon and Marseille and takes responsibility for region S of Highway 7. In VI Corps area, 3d Div completes capture of Brignoles and speeds W along Highway 7 toward Aix-en-Provence. 179th Inf, 45th Div, overcomes opposition at Barjols and thus opens route to lower Durance Valley; continues advance to Rians. Main body of TF Butler crosses the Durance at Oraison and moves N along W bank to Sisteron. Detachments moving N from Riez and along E bank of the Durance to intercept enemy forces moving southward from Grenoble converge on Digne, where enemy surrenders. 141st Inf, 36th Div, clears Callian after indecisive fighting throughout day. In Fr Army B's 2d Corps area, 1st Armd Div is protecting N flank of corps. 3 Algerian Div, after driving through Méounes, on northern road to Marseille, splits into 3 groups, called Linares, Bonjour, and Chapuis, Linares turning S into hills N of Toulon. 9th Colonial Div starts W from Collobrières area to outflank enemy in Hyères-Toulon region from the N. On S flank, 1st Div moves along coastal road toward Hyères until stopped by heavy fire near the town, then sends elements N to outflank enemy.

Italy—AAI: In Br Eighth Army's Pol 2 Corps area, 3d Carpathian Div is slowed in coastal sector by opposition at S Constanzo.

20 August

N France—Gen Montgomery directs 21 Army Group to eliminate Falaise-Argentan Pocket before driving to the Seine; elements of 12th Army Group to drive N across Br front to lower Seine in order to cut off enemy retreat.

21 Army Group: In Cdn First Army area, Br 1 Corps crosses additional elements over La Vie R. Br 7th Armd Div captures Livarot. Cdn 2 Corps frustrates final desperate enemy attempt to escape from Falaise-Argentan Pocket.

Br Second Army heads for the Seine, passing through U.S. forces in Argentan area.

12th Army Group: In U.S. Third Army's XV Corps area, 79th Div establishes bridgehead across the Seine near Mantes-Gassicourt. 5th Armd Div continues N toward Louviers. XX Corps attacks E toward the Seine, with 7th Armd Div on N and 5th Div on S, in effort to gain bridgeheads at Melun and Montereau. XII Corps attacks for bridgehead over Yonne R at Sens, 4th Armd Div spearheading.

In U.S. First Army's V Corps area, 80th Div overcomes moderate resistance at Argentan. XIX Corps continues N, elements forcing the Aure between Verneuil and Nonancourt.

S France—In U.S. Seventh Army's VI Corps area, 3d Div reaches suburbs of Aix-en-Provence. 7th Inf, upon relief by French in coastal sector, joins 3d Div. 45th Div's 157th Inf crosses the Durance in St. Paul area, using partially destroyed bridge, and takes Mirabeau and Pertuis; 180th Inf, advancing along S bank of the river, takes Peyrolles and Meyrargues. TF Butler blocks routes running S from Grenoble. 36th Div, relieved of defensive positions on E flank of corps by 1st ABTF, moves NW behind TF Butler. 1st ABTF is placed under direct command of Seventh Army and made responsible for region generally along line from Fayence to La Napoule. In Fr Army B's 2d Corps area, while Chapuis Group of 3d Algerian Div and elements of 1st Armd Div continue W toward Marseille on N flank, Chapuis Group reaching Le Camp, Linares Group continues to work southward through hills overlooking Toulon, and Bonjour Group turns SE toward Toulon. 9th Colonial and 1st Inf Divs isolate Hyères. Frontal assault against E outskirts by 1st Div fails.

Eastern Front—Red Army opens offensive against Rumania. Troops of Second and Third Ukrainian Fronts push forward with strong air and arty support toward Iasi and Kishinev. Germans continue efforts to reopen communications with Baltic forces.

Italy—AAI: U.S. Fifth Army regroups extensively in preparation for attack. IV Corps, with TF 45 and 1st Armd Div under command, takes over most of the army front, spreading thin along 55-mile line. 85th Div, in positions formerly held by NZ 2d Div, is placed temporarily under corps pending arrival of S African 6th Armd Div. In II Corps area, RCT 442 (less 100th (Nisei) Bn), attached to 88th

Div, occupies 5-mile sector W of Florence, replacing Br units.

CBI—On Salween front. after mines under enemy positions on Sung Shan are exploded, Ch troops with flame throwers clear this feature, which has held out for so long, but scattered pockets of enemy remain about Sung Shan.

SWPA—CTF 77 issues Operations Plan 8-44 for Morotai operation.

NEW GUINEA—Gen Krueger declares the Biak operation at an end. Base development is well advanced. Although airfields were not ready in time to support Marianas operation as hoped, they are to contribute materially to subsequent offensive in SWPA and POA. TF HURRICANE, during period 27 May to date, has suffered about 400 killed, 2,000 wounded, 150 injured in action, and 5 missing, aside from those removed from action because of sickness. Japanese, during the same period, have lost about 4,700 killed and 220 captured. 41st Div continues to mop up Biak for some months to come.

21 August

N FRANCE—21 Army Group: In Cdn First Army area, 2 Corps, leaving Pol 1st Armd and Cdn 3d Divs to complete reduction of Falaise-Argentan Pocket, drives E toward the Seine at Rouen.

In Br Second Army's 30 Corps area, 11th Armd Div, spearheading for corps, bypasses Gacé and drives on toward Laigle.

12th Army Group: In U.S. First Army's V Corps area, 80th Div is relieved of responsibility for its sector near Argentan by Br 30 Corps. 102d Cav Gp, which has closed in Sées area, begins rcn NE of Sées and E of Exmes. VII Corps commits 9th Div in defensive role in Mortagne area. In XIX Corps area, 2d Armd Div bypasses Verneuil and advances toward Breteuil. 28th Div moves up to clear Verneuil. 30th Div overruns Nonancourt.

In U.S. Third Army's XV Corps area, while 79th Div improves and expands bridgehead across the Seine in Mantes-Gassicourt area, 5th Armd Div continues N toward Louviers. In XX Corps area, 7th Armd Div drives to Arpajon-Rambouillet area. 5th Div overruns Etampes. In XII Corps area, 4th Armd Div captures Sens. 35th Div pushes through Pithiviers.

S FRANCE—In U.S. Seventh Army area, 1st ABTF begins clearing coastal sector around La Napoule in preparation for drive on Cannes. In VI Corps area, 30th Inf of 3d Div, assisted by FFI forces, takes Aix-en-Provence, from which most Germans have withdrawn. Gen Truscott orders 3d Div to halt on line Le Puy-Rognac until strength of enemy armor can be determined. 45th Div columns are moving on Avignon, Apt, and Volonne.

TF Butler, turning over roadblocks below Grenoble to 36th Div, drives W through Die and Crest to the Rhône Valley, destroying enemy vehicle convoy N of Livron. 36th Div shuttles to Grenoble corridor to relieve TF Butler and continues across the Durance toward Grenoble; is ordered to provide reinforcements for TF Butler in Rhône Valley. In Fr Army B area, 2d Corps continues drive on Toulon and Marseille. 1st Div takes Hyères, on E approach to Toulon. Groupe de Commandos takes Mt. Coudon and Linares Group of 3d Algerian Div neutralizes Mt. Caumes, both hilltop fortresses N of Toulon. Bonjour Group, 3d Algerian Div, gets rcn elements to Bandol, on coast W of Toulon, completing investment of Toulon. Chapuis Group, 3d Algerian Div, and elements of 1st Armd Div continue W on N flank of 2d Corps toward Marseille, reaching Aubagne.

EASTERN EUROPE—Continuing counteroffensive, Germans regain Tukums, 35 miles E of Riga.

ITALY—AAI: Orders U.S. Fifth Army, which has been pretending to build up forces in vicinity of Pisa and Fucecchio, to extend its feigned concentrations, particularly in Florence area, to cover preparations for main Br Eighth Army push.

In U.S. Fifth Army's II Corps area, 88th Div sends 350th Inf to Leghorn to assist IV Corps. Br 13 Corps prepares for limited operations across the Arno, since enemy appears to be withdrawing.

In Br Eighth Army area, Pol 2 Corps continues northward in Adriatic sector, forcing enemy to withdraw behind the Metauro R, night 21-22.

NEW GUINEA—In Wakde-Sarmi area, RCT 20 reverts to 6th Div from attachment to 31st Div.

22 August

N FRANCE—21 Army Group: In Cdn First Army's Br I Corps area, Deauville falls to Belgian Brig, under command of Br 6th A/B Div. 6th A/B Div is engaging enemy in Pont Evêque area. Br 49th Div crosses the Touques near Pont Evêque. Br 7th Armd Div thrusts beyond the Touques, passing through S outskirts of Lisieux. 2 Corps, less elements mopping up Falaise-Argentan pocket, reaches Touques R.

In Br Second Army's 30 Corps area, 11th Armd Div, speeding eastward, reaches Laigle.

12th Army Group: In U.S. First Army's V Corps area, Br 30 Corps units relieve 80th Div, from which CCL is detached and reverts to Fr 2d Armd Div. 80th and 90th Divs assemble for maintenance and rehabilitation while awaiting new orders. V Corps, now entirely out of contact with enemy, is given mission of freeing Paris. Fr 2d Armd Div is alerted for the task. 4th Div is transferred to V Corps from VII Corps. Advance into Paris is to begin at conclusion of German-FFI armistice on 23d. In XIX Corps area, 2d Armd Div continues steadily northward, overrunning Breteuil; 28th Div clears Verneuil. 30th Div reaches vicinity of Evreux.

In U.S. Third Army's XV Corps area, 79th Div holds Mantes-Gassicourt bridgehead against enemy counterattack. 5th Armd Div continues N toward Louviers despite strong opposition between Eure and Seine Rivers. XX Corps speeds toward Melun and Montereau, 7th Armd Div approaching Melun and 5th Div threatening Fontainebleau. In XII Corps area, 4th Armd Div, continuing E from Sens, overcomes opposition at Villeneuve. 35th Div reaches W outskirts of Montargis. In VIII Corps area, main body of 29th Div is moving W by motor to Brest.

S FRANCE—In U.S. Seventh Army area, 1st ABTF is reinf by 1st SSF, which is committed in center to replace Br 2d Para Brig. RCT 517 is given task of patrolling roads W and S of Larche Pass and maintaining contact with friendly forces to W. In VI Corps area, 3d Div improves positions on left flank of corps. Elements of 157th Inf, 45th Div, and FFI forces clear Apt; 180th Inf reduces light rearguard opposition in Rognes area; 179th moves toward Grenoble to join 36th Div. 36th Div units take Grenoble without opposition and reconnoiter beyond there without incident; RCT 141 starts W to Rhône Valley to back up TF Butler in Montélimar area and emplaces 2 FA bns near Marsanne to fire across the Rhône; RCT 142 arrives at Gap. In Fr Army B area, USS *Omaha* accepts surrender of garrison of Porquerolles I., off Giens Peninsula. In 2d Corps area, while 1st Div continues W toward Toulon along coast against strong resistance, Linares Group of 3d Algerian Div seizes Mt. Faron, last of the big hilltop fortresses N of Toulon, and 9th Colonial Div forces enemy from La Vallette, NE of Toulon. With reduction of Mt. Faron, a way is opened into Toulon through Dardennes ravine. On N flank, Chapuis Group of 3d Algerian Div and elements of 1st Armd Div invest Marseille.

EASTERN EUROPE—Offensive against Rumania by troops of Second and Third Ukrainian Fronts is overwhelming enemy. Iasi falls to forces of Second Ukrainian Front.

ITALY—AAI: In Br Eighth Army area, Pol 2 Corps occupies S bank of the Metauro from S. Ippolito to the coast. Italian Corps of Liberation, moving up on left flank, reaches Cagli, SW of S. Ippolito.

CBI—Adm Mountbatten returns to Ceylon from London, having presented his views on strategy there.

On Salween front, Japanese remnants around Sung Shan, during 21 and 22, make futile counterattacks against Chinese.

SWPA—TF TRADEWIND (Morotai force) issues FO No. 1.

23 August

N FRANCE—21 Army Group: In Cdn First Army area, Br 1 Corps continues to make slow progress in coastal sector. 2 Corps is heavily engaged in vicinity of Orbec.

In Br Second Army's 12 Corps area, mechanized patrols reach Bernay. In 30 Corps area, 50th Div reaches Verneuil-Breteuil area, where it halts while U.S. XIX Corps moves across its front toward Elbeuf.

12 Army Group: Attaches XV Corps and its 5th Armd and 79th Inf Divs to First Army, effective 0600 24th; alters boundary between First and Third Armies to run along line Chartres-Melun (both towns to First Army).

In U.S. First Army's V Corps area, Fr 2d Armd Div, reinf by Tr B of 102d Cav Sq, starts toward Paris along 2 routes to assist FFI forces in taking the city but is halted in Versailles-Bois de Meudon area by strongpoints and roadblocks. 4th Div, preceded by 102d Cav Gp (less Tr B) follows Fr armor along southern route and reaches Arpajon, S of Paris. In XIX Corps area, one 2d Armd Div column, bypassing Conches, which 28th Div clears, reaches Le Neubourg, while another drives toward Elbeuf. 30th Div finds Evreux free of enemy and makes contact with 5th Armd Div (XV Corps) on right.

In U.S. Third Army's XV corps area, 79th Div maintains Seine bridgehead at Mantes-Gassicourt while 5th Armd Div continues clearing region W of the Seine. In XX Corps area, 5th Div takes Fontainebleau and continues toward Montereau. 7th Armd Div closes in on Melun. In XII Corps area, 35th Div overruns Montargis.

S FRANCE—In U.S. Seventh Army area, engineers are preparing way for entry of 1st ABTF into Cannes, which patrols report clear of enemy. 1st SSF prepares to attack Grasse, important road junction on Route Napoleon (Highway 85). VI Corps concentrates on intercepting German withdrawal up Rhône Valley to Lyon, 141st Inf, 36th Div, closes in the valley and occupies MLR from Drôme R to Montélimar area; TF Butler is disposed to support 141st Inf and provide flank protection; 2d Bn of 141st, assisted by French Maquis and arty fire of TF Butler from Condillac Pass, attacks southward toward Montélimar on Highway 7 but fails in the first of many efforts to take the town. To free additional elements of 36th Div for action in Rhône Valley, 180th Inf of 45th Div relieves 142d Inf of defensive positions in N part of E (right) flank of corps. 179th Inf is attached to 36th Div in Grenoble area. 3d Div works NW toward the Rhône and finds

Martigues clear. In Fr Army B's 2 Corps area, 9th Colonial and 1st Inf Divs break into E part of Toulon and press forward to center of city. After battery on Cap de l'Esterel, at E tip of Giens Peninsula, surrenders, Fr troops land on the peninsula and clear it without opposition. Chapuis Group of 3d Algerian Div, assisted by Goums and CCI of 1st Armd Div, breaks into suburbs of Marseille from E and N. Efforts to induce the garrison to surrender fail.

RUMANIA—King Michael surrenders Rumania unconditionally to Soviet forces.

ITALY—AAI: In U.S. Fifth Army's IV Corps area, advance elements of 92d Div—RCT 370—take over part of zone held by 1st Armd Div.

CBI—War Department notifies Gen Stilwell that operations to open land route to China must be limited to construction of 2-way, all-weather road to Myitkyina and opening trail from there to China. This decision is made in order to increase manpower for Pacific offensives but limits tonnage to China over Ledo Road. Gen Hearn presents message from President Roosevelt to Chiang Kai-Shek, urging that Gen Stilwell be put in command of Chinese forces soon and commenting on conditions proposed by Chinese. Gen Hearn also informs Gen Chennault that his proposal to send U.S. supplies to E China for recapture of Heng-yang is refused.

On Salween front, Japanese commander at Lungling calls for reinforcements.

NEW GUINEA—On Noemfoor, 503d Para Inf begins concentration in Kamiri airdrome area, leaving 3 cos behind to patrol S part of Noemfoor.

24 August

N FRANCE—21 Army Group: In Cdn First Army area, Br I Corps extends right flank to St Georges-du-Vièvre, on Risle R. In 2 Corps area, Cdn 2d Div seizes Bernay and establishes bridgehead across Risle R at Nassandres. Contact is made with U.S. XIX Corps in Elbeuf area.

In Br Second Army's 12 Corps area, 15th Div is concentrating near Le Neubourg in preparation for attack across the Seine at Louviers.

12th Army Group: In U.S. First Army area, XIX Corps moves closer to Elbeuf and is interdicting Seine crossing sites with arty fire. In XV Corps area, 5th Armd Div reaches Houdebouville. In V Corps area, Fr 2d Armd Div gets a little closer to city limits of Paris against strong opposition. 102d Cav Gp units, screening for 4th Div, reach the Seine S of Paris. Ordered by Gen Bradley to push into Paris at once, 4th Div, less one RCT, attacks toward the city from S in conjunction with Fr attacks from SW. One RCT of 4th Div retains mission of securing crossings of the Seine S of Paris.

In U.S. Third Army area, XX Corps gains bridgeheads across the Seine at Melun and Montereau, 7th Armd Div establishing former and 5th Div, latter. In XII Corps area, CCA of 4th Armd Div drives E toward Troyes while CCB, to right, reaches St Florentin area and 35th Div moves up to Courtenay; CCR is moving forward to join rest of 4th Armd Div.

S FRANCE—In U.S. Seventh Army area, 1st ABTF's 509th Para Bn, followed by 1st Bn of 551st Para Inf, advances into Cannes without opposition and pushes on to Antibes. 1st SSF takes Grasse with ease; seizes Valbonne and makes contact with friendly forces from Cannes area. RCT 517, which has relieved elements of 36th Div in Fayence-Callian area, advances on left flank of 1st ABTF, taking St Vallier on Route Napoléon. In VI Corps area, 36th Div establishes MLR along Roubion R and faces S to prevent enemy movement northward: 141st Inf, on right, defends sector W from Bonlieu; 142d protects left sector of line from Bonlieu to Pré-Alps. Elements of 111th Engr Bn are disposed in front of Bonlieu. Forward elements of 3d Div reach the Rhône at Arles. In Fr Army B's 2d Corps area, organized resistance in E part of Toulon comes to an end, but Germans retain W part and dock area. Chapuis Group, 3d Algerian Div, pushes well into Marseille. CC2, 1st Armd Div, relieves U.S. 3d Div at Aix, Gardanne, and Rognac.

EASTERN EUROPE—Kishinev falls to Soviet frontal and flanking attacks.

ITALY—AAI: In U.S. Fifth Army's Br 13 Corps area, 1st Div and Ind 8th Div begin fording the Arno E of Florence to secure positions on N bank before main Fifth Army attack starts—there is no opposition.

Br Eighth Army completes preparations for attack on Gothic Line on 3-corps front. Screened by Pol 2 Corps on army right flank, Cdn 1 Corps, employing Cdn 1st Div in line, takes over narrow front just W of Pol 2 Corps. 5 Corps, with 46th Div and Ind 4th Div in line, moves to W of Cdn 1 Corps on front of about 20 miles. 10 Corps, consisting of Ind 10th Div and mixed brig group, continues to hold left flank of army. Italian Corps of Liberation, upon relief by 5 Corps, is held in army reserve.

CBI—On Salween front, Japanese reinforcements start from Mangshih to Lung-ling front.

NEW GUINEA—In Vogelkop area, Gen Sibert leaves Sansapor-Mar sector to take command of X Corps, hq of which has recently arrived from U.S. Brig Gen Charles E. Hurdis takes over Gen Sibert's posts as commander of TF TYPHOON and 6th Div.

25 August

N FRANCE—21 Army Group: In Br Second Army's 12 Corps area, 15th Div gets into position to cross the Seine at Louviers. In 30 Corps area, 43d Div establishes bridgehead across the Seine at Vernon under cover of arty fire.

12th Army Group: In U.S. First Army area, XIX Corps overruns Elbeuf, its objective; makes contact with Br forces to N. In V Corps area, Fr 2d Armd Div, bypassing resistance in Versailles area, gets forward elements into Paris from SW at 0700. 4th Div enters from S soon afterward, following Tr A, 38th Cav, which enters at 0730. FFI forces and jubilant French civilians assist in methodical clearing of scattered strongpoints within the city. German commander in Paris, Lt Gen Dietrich von Choltitz, surrenders formally to Brig Gen Jacques-Philippe Leclerc of Fr 2d Armd Div at 1515. 22d Inf, 4th Div, establishes bridgehead across the Seine S of Paris. V Corps releases 80th and 90th Divs to Third Army, which assigns them respectively to XII and XX Corps. In VII Corps area, CCB of 3d Armd Div crosses the Seine below Paris at Tilly. 1st and 9th Divs are assembling S of Paris.

In U.S. Third Army area, VIII Corps launches strong attack on Brest at 1300 after preparatory bombardment for an hour. 2d, 8th, and 29th Divs, on E, N, and W, respectively, batter at strong outer defenses of the city, making little headway. 29th Div employs TF Sugar (special 175th Inf force that consists of 2 cos of 2d Ranger Bn and elements of 86th Cav Rcn Sq as well as 175th Inf units and is commanded by Lt Col Arthur T. Sheppe of 175th Inf) on extreme right to clear Le Conquet Peninsula, where formidable *Batterie Graf Spee* is located. TF B continues clearing peninsulas S of Brest. XX Corps defends Seine bridgeheads at Melun and Montereau. 5th Div crosses Yonne R at Missy. In XII Corps area, CCA of 4th Armd Div overcomes strong opposition in Troyes.

S FRANCE—In U.S. Seventh Army's VI Corps area, 3d Div drives through Cavaillon, Orgon, and Avignon without opposition. Germans attack 36th Div's line along the Roubion at its weakest point, Bonlieu, routing the engineers and separating 141st and 142d Regts. Elements of 143d are moved forward to help plug gap. Efforts of 1st Bn, 141st Inf, and TF Butler to block Highway 7 in La Coucourde area fail. 3d Bn of 157th Inf, 45th Div, is attached to 36th Div and moves to La Coucourde area. Since 141st Inf is under constant pressure and unable to gain control of hills N and NE of Montélimar, reinforcements are moved to Crest, on the Drôme, among them 143d Inf (−). Arty and aircraft are helping troops interdict enemy withdrawal up the Rhône. In Fr Army B area, 2d Corps continues to battle enemy at Toulon and Marseille.

EASTERN EUROPE—Tartu, junction of Riga-Tallinn line, falls to forces of Third Baltic Front. Rumania declares war on Germany.

ITALY—AAI: In U.S. Fifth Army's Br 13 Corps area, driving up Route 69, which parallels the Arno, 6th Armd Div reaches Route 70 E of Pontassieve. Br 1st Div and Ind 8th Div deepen bridgehead across the Arno to left.

Br Eighth Army begins main assault on Gothic Line from Metauro R line, employing Br 5, Cdn 1, and Pol 2 Corps, from left to right, night 25-26. Enemy, taken by surprise, offers only ineffective opposition.

NEW GUINEA—Gen Krueger declares the Aitape operation at an end. During this action, Allied forces have lost about 440 killed,. 2,550 wounded, and 10 missing as against Japanese losses, by U.S. count, of 8,821 killed and 98 captured. Japanese *18th Army* has paid with $2^{1}/_{3}$ divs for vain attacks to regain Aitape area and is no longer a major threat on New Guinea. On the Vogelkop, Japanese make their first air attack on region held by TF TYPHOON.

26 August

N FRANCE—Gen Montgomery directs Cdn First Army to clear Pas-de-Calais; Br Second Army to push into Belgium; U.S. First Army to support Br drive, moving forward on axis Paris-Brussels.

21 Army Group: In Cdn First Army area, 2 Corps prepares to cross the Seine S of Rouen. Patrols of 4th Armd Div cross in evening.

In Br Second Army area, 30 Corps expands and strengthens bridgehead at Vernon.

12th Army Group: In U.S. First Army area, XIX Corps is relieved by Br forces and releases 30th Div to XV Corps. XV Corps maintains Mantes-Gassicourt bridgehead and mops up. In V Corps area, while Fr 2d Armd Div mops up scattered opposition within Paris, 4th Div returns to positions SE of the city and protects Seine bridgehead and airfields in the area. In VII Corps area, additional elements of 3d Armd Div cross the Seine and push northward rapidly.

U.S. Third Army, with gasoline running low, receives a shipment by air. VIII Corps continues to make slow progress toward Brest against firm opposition. In XX Corps area, 7th Armd Div thrusts quickly NE toward Château-Thierry and the Marne. Nogent-sur-Seine falls to 5th Div. In XII Corps area, 4th Armd Div mops up Troyes; 35th Div patrols on right flank.

S FRANCE—In U.S. Seventh Army's VI Corps area, air and arty continue to help interdict northward withdrawal of enemy. 3d Div continues steadily northward toward Montélimar overcoming rear-guard opposition at Orange. 36th Div is unable to restore line along the Roubion at Bonlieu, and Germans withdraw additional units through the gap. TF Butler is ordered to restore block on Highway 7 at La Coucourde. Corps takes direct control of 757th Inf (− 3d Bn), 45th Div. 2d Bn of 157th, moving W to reinforce 36th Div, seizes Allex, N of the Drôme and E of Livron, blocking lower reaches of the Drôme. 1st Bn assists in defending Crest. In Fr Army B's 2d Corps area, organized resistance within Toulon comes to an end, but Germans retain San Mandrier Peninsula S of the city. At Marseille, further progress is made and fortified heights of Notre Dame de la Garde, within the city, capitulate. Forward elements of corps reach the Rhône in Avignon-Arles area and begin crossing.

EASTERN EUROPE—Troops of Third Ukrainian Front, advancing along the Prut R toward Galati, reach the Danube. Troops of Second Ukrainian Front are moving through Focsani-Galati gap. Bulgaria begins surrender negotiation with Allies.

ITALY—AAI: In U.S. Fifth Army area, Br 13 Corps consolidates positions N of the Arno. In IV Corps area, S African 6th Armd Div is committed to line and begins relief of 85th Div, latter reverting to II Corps.

Br Eighth Army secures bridgeheads across the Metauro in zones of Br 5, Cdn 1, and Pol 2 Corps with little difficulty.

27 August

N FRANCE—21 Army Group: In Cdn First Army area, Br 1 Corps elements reach the Seine in coastal sector. In 2 Corps area, Cdn 4th Armd and 3d Inf Divs begin crossing the Seine between Elbeuf and Pont de l'Arche and clear Tourlaville.

In Br Second Army's 12 Corps area, 15th Div begins crossing the Seine E of Louviers and establishes bridgehead in Muids-Porte-Joie area with ease. A second crossing site, about a mile upstream, is found to be strongly defended and is abandoned. 30 Corps continues to expand and strengthen bridgehead at Vernon.

12th Army Group: Allocates priority in supply to First Army. Supplies are becoming increasingly short.

In U.S. First Army area, XV Corps attacks with 30th Div on right and 79th on left to enlarge Mantes-Gassicourt bridgehead. In V Corps area, against scattered resistance, Fr 2d Armd Div and 4th Div, former on right, drive NE to outskirts of Paris, French overcoming strong opposition at Le Bourget airfield. Generals Eisenhower and Bradley visit Paris and confer with Gen Charles de Gaulle.

In VII Corps area, 3d Armd Div speeds NE toward Soissons with 4th Cav Gp spearheading and 1st and 9th Divs following, crossing the Marne in Mieux area and taking that town.

In U.S. Third Army area, VIII Corps completes encirclement of Brest. TF Sugar, 29th Div, cuts main Le Conquet-Recouvrance highway. 83d Div moves forward to protect S flank along Loire R W of Orléans. In XX Corps area, 7th Armd Div drives NE toward Reims on broad front, followed by 5th and 80th Divs. Armored forces reach the Marne at Château-Thierry, secure crossings, and overrun that town. In XII Corps area, CCA of 4th Armd Div heads from Troyes NE toward Châlons-sur-Marne, followed by 80th Div. 35th Div protects S flank of army from Orléans to Troyes.

S FRANCE—In U.S. Seventh Army's VI Corps area, 3d Div, coming up from the S, secures positions from which to attack Montélimar. 36th Div restores line along the Roubion. TF Butler reaches Highway 7 at La Coucourde but is unable to block it. So effective is arty fire, however, that a block is formed by wrecked enemy vehicles. Aircraft and arty are taking an increasingly heavy toll of enemy columns in Montélimar-Livron sector. 45th Div (−) is probing toward Lyon from Grenoble; 179th Inf takes Bourgoin, midway between Grenoble and Lyon. 180th Inf, holding defensive positions in N part of right flank of corps in Briançon area, is relieved by Prov .Flank Protection Force, called TF Bibo, in order to move to Grenoble area. TF Bibo, commanded by Lt Col Harold S. Bibo and under Seventh Army control, consists of Tr A of 117th Cav Rcn Sq; elements of 2d, 3d, and 83d Chemical Bns; 2 platoons of 180th Inf AT Co; and battery of 171st FA Bn. In Fr Army B area, 2d Corps continues to clear environs of Toulon and city of Marseille. At 1745 bombardment of San Mandrier Peninsula, S of Toulon, is halted and Germans agree to surrender the peninsula, effective on 28th. At Marseille, Fort St Nicolas surrenders, but scattered opposition remains. In evening, German command requests interview to discuss surrender terms.

EASTERN EUROPE—Focsani falls to troops of Second Ukrainian Front; Galati, third largest city in Rumania and chief port on the Danube, to those of Third Ukrainian Front.

ITALY—AAI: Br Eighth Army makes steady progress northward toward main Gothic Line positions.

BURMA—In NCAC area, Br 36th Div, continuing down Mogaung-Mandalay RR corridor, takes Pinbaw.

NEW GUINEA—1st Bn, 158th Inf, relieves elements of 503d Para Inf remaining in S part of Noemfoor.

28 August

N FRANCE—21 Army Group: In Cdn First Army area, 2 Corps expands bridgehead toward Rouen.

In Br Second Army area, 12 Corps expands its bridgehead across the Seine. In 30 Corps area, entire 43d Div is across the Seine; bridgehead extends about 4 miles in width and 3 miles in depth.

12th Army Group: In U.S. First Army area, XV Corps continues to improve positions in Mantes-Gassicourt bridgehead. 2d Armd Div is attached to corps to pass through 79th Div and spearhead breakout. In V Corps area, Gen Gerow, in letter to Gen Pierre Joseph Koenig, Military Governor of Paris, turns over the city to the French. Fr 2d Armd Div and 4th Div continue attacks NE of Paris. 5th Armd and 28th Inf Divs are attached to corps. In VII Corps area, 3d Armd Div pursues disorganized enemy to Soissons.

In U.S. Third Army area, VIII Corps continues to batter Brest. 29th Div takes direct command of TF Sugar from 175th Inf; 116th Inf is pushing E along Le Conquet–Recouvrance highway. CCB, 6 Armd Div, leaves Lorient for Third Army zone. XX Corps is speedily closing in on Reims. In XII Corps area, CCA columns, followed by 80th Div, continue rapidly toward the Marne at Châlons-sur-Marne and Vitry-le-François.

S FRANCE—U.S. Seventh Army directs that another trap be set for retreating enemy before he reaches the Belfort Gap. While 2d Corps of Fr Army B drives N along W bank of the Rhône, VI Corps is to move N via Lyon, Beaune, and Dijon to make contact with OVERLORD forces and block off enemy from the Rhine. FFI and TF Bibo troops are driven from Briançon by enemy. In VI Corps area, 3d Div clears rear-guard opposition from Montélimar, enabling 36th Div to seize hill masses to N and NE. Corps' attention shifts to Drôme R line, where final phase of Montélimar battle is being fought. 142d Regt, 36th Div, surrounds Livron, blocking Highway 7 N of the Drôme, but most of German *Nineteenth Army* has escaped northward through the Montélimar trap. TF Butler and 143d Inf isolate Loriol, S of Livron. Withdrawing enemy traffic remains a lucrative target for aircraft and arty. 45th Div's 180th Inf moves to Grenoble; 179th continues northward toward Lyon. In Fr Army B's 2d Corps area, all resistance in Toulon area comes to an end with surrender of San Mandrier Peninsula to 9th Colonial Div. Germans also surrender Marseille. 80th German garrison commanders are captured. During the battle for these important ports, in which FFI forces have given valuable assistance, 2 German divs have been eliminated. 9th Colonial Div is given temporary mission of guarding Toulon–Marseille area. Other elements of 2d Corps continue to cross the Rhône in Avignon–Arles area.

EASTERN EUROPE—Troops of Second Ukrainian Front drive into Transylvania through Oituz Pass in the Carpathian Mts.

ITALY—AAI: In U.S. Fifth Army's Br 13 Corps area, 17th Brig of 8th Ind Div, attacking night 28-29, takes Tigliano, N of Pontassieve. 6th Armd Div, securing right flank of corps, gets column beyond Rufina, on Highway 67.

Br Eighth Army continues to gain ground toward Gothic Line, Pol 2 Corps, on right, reaching Arzilla R.

29 August

N FRANCE—Gen Eisenhower directs that main effort be made in N.

21 Army Group: In Br Second Army's 12 Corps area, 15th Div has completed crossing of the Seine and holds loop of river W of Les Andelys. In 30 Corps area, 11th Armd Div, reinf by 8th Armd Brig, takes the lead, heading toward the Somme at Amiens and reaching Mainneville area.

12th Army Group: Issues instructions for operations beyond the Seine. Gasoline shortage is acute and Third Army is given priority on supply by air.

In U.S. First Army area, XIX Corps takes over zone of XV Corps at noon and assumes command of 2d Armd and 30th and 79th Inf Divs. 2d Armd Div drives through 79th Div to Magny en Vexin. 30th Div, to right, reaches line Wy-dit-Joli-Village–Saillancourt. XV Corps reverts to Third Army control and is held in reserve. V Corps, leaving Fr 2d Armd Div behind in Paris, drives NE with 4th Div to Mitry Mory–Le Plessis area. 28th Div parades NE through Paris to its assigned attack position W of 4th Div. In VII Corps area, 3d Armd Div, spearheading drive on Laon, crosses Aisne R east of Soissons.

U.S. Third Army orders advance continued to the Meuse. In VIII Corps area, 2d Rangers of TF Sugar, 29th Div, take Pointe de Corsen as assault on Brest continues against unabated resistance. XX Corps speeds NE to Reims, which 5th Div captures. In XII Corps area, CCA of 4th Armd Div overruns Châlons-sur-Marne and Vitry-le-François.

S FRANCE—In U.S. Seventh Army area, 1st ABTF, on Mediterranean coast, begins crossing Var R. Plans are made at commanders' conference at Seventh Army hq for junction of OVERLORD and DRAGOON forces. In VI Corps' Rhône Valley sector, organized resistance at Loriol and Livron, on Highway 7, comes to an end. 36th and 3d Divs are mopping up enemy rear guards. 3d Div is to assemble at Voiron, NW of Grenoble, upon relief by French; 36th is to continue N toward Lyon. To right, 45th Div continues to probe northward with 179th and 180th Regts. In Fr Army B area, 2d Moroccan Div, in process of debarking, is ordered to extreme right flank of Seventh Army; 3d Algerian Div is to advance to its left; 9th Colonial Div is to be committed gradually.

EASTERN EUROPE—Troops of Third Ukrainian Front take Constanta, Black Sea port.

ITALY—AAI: In U.S. Fifth Army's Br 13 Corps area, 6th Armd Div column reaches Consuma, on Highway 70.

In Br Eighth Army area, as Pol 2 Corps attempts to clear Pesaro, on Adriatic coast, Cdn 1 and Br 5 Corps thrust to Foglia R, behind which enemy is moving reinforcements in effort to stem Br advance. Ind 10th Div of 10 Corps finds Bibbiena, on Route 71, abandoned by enemy.

CHINA—Japanese *11th Army*, consisting of 7 divs, starts S down RR from Heng-yang, threatening U.S. Fourteenth Air Force bases at Kweilin and Liuchow.

30 August

N FRANCE—21 Army Group: In Cdn First Army's Br I Corps area, 51st and 49th Divs, latter with Royal Netherlands Brig, begin crossing the Seine. In 2 Corps area, 2d Div crosses into Seine bridgehead, having cleared W bank of the river. 3d Div takes Rouen without opposition.

In Br Second Army area, 12 Corps drives eastward from bridgehead with 4th Armd Brig spearheading and 53d Div following. 25-mile advance brings forward elements to Gournay. In 30 Corps area, 11th Armd Div, which is relieved on right flank by Gds Armd Div, is ordered to speed on to the Somme at Amiens and advances through night 30-31.

12th Army Group: In U.S. First Army area, XIX Corps, with 2d Armd Div on left, 79th Div in center, and 30th Div on right, drives rapidly NE against light resistance. 2d Armd Div makes greatest gains, reaching positions less than 10 miles from Beauvais. V Corps continues pursuit of enemy northeastward, passing 28th Div through Fr 2d Armd Div to advance abreast 4th Div, 5th Armd Div moves forward to spearhead drive on Compiègne. VII Corps seizes Laon.

In U.S. Third Army's VIII Corps area, TF B finishes clearing Daoulas Peninsula S of Brest. 29th Div gets elements to crest of Hill 103, commanding feature in Brest defenses, but enemy retains E slopes. In XX Corps area 7th Armd Div speeds toward Verdun against scattered resistance. XII Corps drives eastward toward the Meuse, advance elements of 4th Armd Div reaching St Dizier area. To left, 80th Div is moving SE toward Bar-le-Duc. On right flank, 35th Div pushes SE from Troyes. XV Corps hq and troops are concentrating in Nangis area.

S FRANCE—In U.S. Seventh Army area, on Mediterranean coast, elements of 1st ABTF drive through Nice to Beaulieu without opposition. In VI Corps area, battle of Montélimar comes to a close as 1st Bn of 143d Inf, 36th Div, reaches junction of Drôme and Rhône Rivers. TF Butler is disbanded. Next big objective of VI Corps is Lyon, toward which 36th Div is rapidly moving along E bank of the Rhône while Fr 2d Corps pushes toward it along W bank. FFI within Lyon are alerted to assist Fr and U.S. columns when they arrive at the city. Advance elements of 45th Div cross Rhône and Ain Rivers NE of Lyon and establish roadblocks at Meximieux, Lagnieu, and Ambérieu. 157th Inf reverts to 45th Div and moves northward to join it. In Fr Army B area, 2d Corps continues its crossing of the Rhône in preparation for drive up W bank. Elements take Nimes and Montpellier. 3d Algerian Div is moving to Grenoble area to relieve 45th Div of VI Corps.

EASTERN EUROPE—Ploesti, center of Rumanian oil industry, falls to troops of Second Ukrainian Front.

ITALY—AAI: Br Eighth Army begins attack on main defenses of Gothic Line against stiffening resistance. While Pol 2 Corps continues attack on Pesaro in coastal sector, Cdn 1 and Br 5 Corps thrust across the Foglia.

SWPA—81st Div begins final rehearsals for Palau operation in Guadalcanal area.

31 August

N FRANCE—21 Army Group: In Cdn First Army area, Br 1 Corps continues to crosses the Seine on left flank of army. 2 Corps attacks eastward from Seine bridgehead with 4th Armd Div on right, 3d Div in center, and 2d Div on left. 4th Armd Div drives quickly to Forges and Buchy. 3d Div speeds along St Saens-Londinières road; 2d Div drives toward Dieppe via Tôtes.

In Br Second Army's 12 Corps area, 7th Armd Div takes the lead and, together with 4th Armd Brig, speeds toward the Somme, reaching Poix-Aumale line. In 30 Corps area, 11th Armd Div reaches Amiens and seizes bridge across the Somme intact. Gds Armd and 50th Inf Divs also reach the river, former crossing E of Amiens.

12th Army Group: In U.S. First Army's XIX Corps area, 2d Armd Div continues NE on left flank of corps to positions W of Montdidier, well ahead of 79th and 30th Divs, which reach area between Beauvais and Creil. V Corps passes 5th Armd Div through 28th and 4th Divs and continues NE with all three. On left, 28th Div, in conjunction with CCB of 5th Armd Div, closes along Oise R in Chantilly-Compiègne area and crosses elements at Pont Ste Maxence. Among towns overrun are Chantilly, Creil, Pont Ste Maxence, Verberie, and Compiègne. CCB establishes bridgehead in vicinity of Pont Ste Maxence. On V Corps right flank, CCA drives to the Aisne W of Soissons, passing through 4th Div, which follows to Villers-Cotterêts area. In VII Corps area, while 1st Div consolidates in Laon and Soissons area, 3d Armd and 9th Infs Divs continue pursuit NE to general line Montcornet-Rethel.

In U.S. Third Army area, VIII Corps temporarily suspends operations against Brest and regroups. In XX Corps area, CCA of 7th Armd Div, followed closely by 5th Div, establishes bridgehead across the Meuse at Verdun. 90th Div remains in Reims area. XX Corps advances then comes to a halt to await gasoline. In XII Corps area, CCA of 4th Armd Div reaches the Meuse at Commercy and Pont-sur-Meuse and establishes bridgehead. 80th Div, following on left, reaches Bar-le-Duc area.

S France—Hq, 6th Army Group, arrives.

In U.S. Seventh Army area, patrols of TF Bibo find Briançon free of enemy. VI Corps speeds up the Rhône Valley toward Lyon. 45th Div is concentrating in Meximieux area to protect right flank of corps, prepared to move on Bourg-en-Bresse. 3d Div, upon relief in Rhône Valley, assembles at Voiron, pre-pared to assist either 36th or 45th Div.

Eastern Europe—Troops of Second Ukrainian Front overrun Bucharest, capital of Rumania.

Italy—AAI: Gen Clark orders U.S. Fifth Army to follow withdrawing enemy. IV Corps patrols cross the Arno, night 31 August–1 September, in preparation for crossing in force and confirm the fact that enemy is withdrawing. Br 13 Corps also confirms rumors of enemy withdrawal. One 1st Div column pushes through Fiesole to Highway 6521 (Florence-Borgo S. Lorenzo); another takes M. Muscoli and M. il Pratone with ease.

Br Eighth Army penetrates Gothic Line with elements of Br 5 and Cdn 1 Corps; Pol 2 Corps continues hard battle for Pesaro.

New Guinea—Gen Krueger declares Noemfoor operation at an end. TF Cyclone has suffered 63 killed, 343 wounded, and 3 missing; has killed about 1,730 Japanese and captured 186. In Vogelkop area, CG Sixth Army, declares Sansapor operation terminated. From 30 July to date, TF Typhoon has killed about 385 Japanese and Formosans and captured 215 as against a loss of 14 killed, 35 wounded, and 9 injured.

1 September

U.K.—Br Chiefs of Staff propose airborne and amphibious assault (coded Dracula) on Rangoon.

N France—21 Army Group (Northern Group of Armies): In Cdn First Army's Br I Corps area, 49th Div, upon crossing the Seine, turns W toward Le Havre while 51st drives toward St Valery-en-Caux. In 2 Corps area, 2d Div takes Dieppe, and port is opened within a week. 3d Div thrusts to Le Trèport. 4th Armd and Pol 1st Armd Divs are driving quickly toward the Somme, former in the lead.

In Br Second Army's 12 Corps area, 7th Armd Div crosses the Somme near Airaines. 53d Div, echeloned to left rear, protects left flank of corps. 30 Corps drives rapidly NE with 11th Armd and Gds Armd Divs spearheading 11th Armd reaches St Pol-Arras road and Gds Armd bypasses Arras. 50th Div is following up.

12th Army Group (Central Group of Armies): Passes to direct command of SHAEF from command of Gen Montgomery.

In U.S. First Army's XIX Corps area, 2d Armd Div, followed closely by infantry, reaches positions NW of Cambrai. V Corps speeds toward St Quentin. 4th Div, motorized and reinf by CCA of 5th Armd Div, takes the lead, thrusting to vicinity of Chauny. Other elements of corps improve positions at and near Compiègne, where bridge construction is in progress. VII Corps swerves from NE to N. CCB of 3d Armd Div drives quickly through Vervins to La Capelle; to right, CCA, in conjunction with 9th Div, reaches Etreaupont-Aubenton area. 1st Div, on corps left flank, reaches Voyenne.

U.S. Third Army is practically immobilized by acute shortage of gasoline. Enforced lull permits enemy to build up behind the West Wall. In XX Corps area, CCR of 7th Armd Div advances to Etain along Verdun–Metz highway. 3d Cav Gp, using captured gasoline, patrols eastward toward the Moselle. In XII Corps area, CCA of 4th Armd Div expands Commercy bridgehead over the Meuse, and 80th Div crosses into it. CCB crosses the Meuse S of Commercy. 35th Div protects S flank of army. VIII Corps continues preparations for renewing all-out assault on Brest when ammunition is more plentiful; makes slight gains in limited attack in conjunction with aerial bombardment. Aircraft, warships, and arty pound Ile de Cézembre, off St Malo, in preparation for amphibious assault by 83d Div force.

S France—(Southern Group of Armies): In U.S. Seventh Army area, VI Corps is rapidly closing in on Lyon. 36th Div gets forward elements to heights commanding the city. 3d Div is moving forward behind 45th Div. 45th Div, leaving 179th Inf to defend Meximieux, moves up E bank of the Ain without opposition. In determined attacks supported by tanks and SP guns, Germans isolate 179th Inf within Meximieux at great cost; FFI forces are sent to help 179th. In Fr Army B area, 2d Corps continues toward Lyon in region W of the Rhône, overrunning Serrières and Firminy.

ITALY—AAI: In U.S. Fifth Army area, IV Corps begins pursuit of enemy across the Arno. 1st Armd Div, spearheading, crosses CCA and CCB, which push toward M. Pisano and Altopascio, respectively. On coastal flank, TF 45 finishes clearing its zone S of the Arno and crosses 100th (Nisei) Bn over the river to E of Pisa. S African 6th Armd Div, with task of taking M. Albano, begins to cross the Arno W of Empoli during afternoon. In II Corps area, 88th Div, holding narrow zone along the Arno assigned to II Corps with RCT 442 (–), also crosses the Arno in pursuit of enemy. Br 13 Corps turns Florence over to Italians.

In Br Eighth Army area, Br 5 Corps and Cdn 1 Corps penetrate main defenses of the Gothic Line on M. Gridolfo and Tomba di Pesaro, commanding Foglia I valley. Pol 2 Corps, employing elements of 3d Carpathian Div, crosses the Foglia for drive eastward toward the coast, but is held up by enemy on E slopes of Pozzo Alto.

BALKANS—Allied successes on other fronts, particularly those of Red Army, force German *Army Group F* to begin withdrawing from Greece and islands of Ionian and Aegean Seas. Main withdrawal route, rail line through Skoplje and Belgrade in Yugoslavia, is so effectively hit by U.S. Fifteenth Air Force during first half of September that air withdrawal is begun from fields in Athens area. All 3 fields are left unserviceable by Fifteenth Air Force attacks during latter half of month.

NEW GUINEA—RCT 123 of 33d Div, untried in combat, arrives at Maffin Bay from E New Guinea to protect 31st Div as it stages for invasion of Morotai I.

2 September

N FRANCE-BELGIUM—21 Army Group: In Cdn First Army's Br 1 Corps area, 49th Div continues along Le Havre Peninsula toward the port, reaching enemy outposts. 51st Div takes St Valery-en-Caux. In 2 Corps area, Cdn 4th Armd Div reaches the Somme E of Abbeville and Pol 1st Armd Div is rapidly approaching the river W of Abbeville.

In Br Second Army's 12 Corps area, 7th Armd Div drives NE from the Somme to positions beyond St Pol. 30 Corps continues northward so rapidly that planned drop of airborne forces in Tournai area is not necessary. Gds Armd Div reaches Tournai. 11th Armd Div drives to Lille area.

12th Army Group: Gen Eisenhower, at a commanders' conference, outlines plans for Third Army and V Corps of First Army to drive to West Wall (Siegfried Line) after supply situation improves.

In U.S. First Army area, XIX Corps gets advance elements into Belgium and drives toward Tournai. V Corps releases Fr 2d Armd Div, in Paris area, to First Army reserve. Corps continues steadily NE, overrunning Noyon and St Quentin, until ordered to halt on general line Landrecies-Le Cateau-Cambrai. VII Corps pursues enemy into Belgium, crossing border near Maubeuge and Hirson. 3d Armd Div drives to vicinity of Mons. 9th Div, to right, swings NE to positions near Charleroi. 1st Div moves forward to left rear of armor.

U.S. Third Army is immobilized for lack of fuel. VIII Corps continues to batter outer defenses of Brest. 2d Div takes Hill 105, dominating E approach to the city. 8th Div is battling for Hill 80 and 29th Div for Hill 103. Elements of 83d Div invade Ile de Cézembre, which surrenders. In XX Corps area, while 3d Cav Gp reconnoiters to the Moselle, 7th Armd Div feints to N from Verdun to confuse enemy, halting short of Sedan when fuel runs out. In XII Corps area, 80th Div (–) relieves CCA of 4th Armd Div in Commercy bridgehead; 319th Inf crosses the Meuse to N at St Mihiel. 2d Cav Gp patrols to the Moselle. CCB, 6th Armd Div, relieves 35th Div of task of protecting S flank between Orléans and Auxerre.

S FRANCE—In U.S. Seventh Army area, 1st ABTF regains contact with enemy and clears strongpoint at La Turbia. Prov Flank Protection Force (TF Bibo) is relieved by 2d Mor Div in Briançon area. French are to protect right flank of U.S. Seventh Army and maintain contact with 1st ABTF to S. In VI Corps area, 36th Div halts just E and SE of Lyon to permit Fr 2d Corps to take the city, which patrol reports largely clear. 179th Inf, 45th Div, restores positions at Meximieux. In Fr Army B area, Lt Gen Aim de Goislard de Monsabert takes command of 2d Corps, consisting of 1st Armd and 1st Inf Divs.

ITALY—AAI: In U.S. Fifth Army's IV Corps area, TF 45, whose 100th (Nisei) Bn patrols to the Serchio I, crosses additional elements over the Arno and clears N part of Pisa. CCA, 1st Armd Div, clears most of M. Pisano. Elements of S African 6th Armd Div gain slopes of M. Albano. In II Corps area, patrols of RCT 442, 88th Div, make contact with elements of Br 1st Div, 13 Corps, at Sesto. Later, 88th Div relieves 442d Inf for shipment to France with 349th Inf and is reinf by attachment of 91st Cav Rcn Sq, reinf. Br 13 Corps meets firm opposition N of Florence on hills Morello, Senario, Calvana, and Giovi.

In Br Eighth Army area, enemy withdrawal in front of 46th Div of 5 Corps, Cdn 1 Corps, and Pol 2 Corps permits these units to advance rapidly. Cdn 1 Corps, with Cdn 1st Div directed along Route 16 and Cdn 5th Armd Div on an inland route, speeds toward Rimini, forward elements reaching Conca I and establishing bridgehead. Pol 2 Corps finds Pesaro undefended and extends positions in coastal sector to Castel di Mezzo. Corps is now pinched out by rapid advance of Canadians.

MEDITERRANEAN—Gen Wilson, Supreme Allied Commander, Mediterranean, names Lt Gen R. M. Scobie Commander of Land Forces, Greece. His hq, the reconstituted Br 3 Corps hq in Middle East, is designated Force 140 and contains 2d Para Brig from Italy, 23d Armd Brig from Egypt, and certain Greek forces, such as local police. Eventually Force 140 is augmented by Greek Sacred Regt and Greek Mtn Brig, latter coming from Italy. Naval and air forces are allotted to Force 140, former commanded by Rear Adm J. M. Mansfield and latter by Air Commodore G. Harcourt-Smith. Gen Scobie is to secure Athens area and maintain law and order in preparation for return of Greek Government. Brig Gen Percy L. Sadler, USA, will act as deputy commander of combined hq of AMLG (Allied Military Liaison Headquarters, Greece) to handle relief and rehabilitation matters.

NEW GUINEA—In Wakde-Sarmi area, Gen Krueger declares operation terminated. Brig Gen Donald J. Myers relieves Gen Persons as commander of TF TORNADO. On Noemfoor, a second 7,000-foot runway is completed at Kornasoren airdrome. In Vogelkop area, first plane, a C-47, lands at Mar airdome.

3 September

N FRANCE-BELGIUM—21 Army Group: Gen Montgomery orders Br Second Army to drive speedily to the Rhine and secure crossing; Cdn First Army to continue to clear coastal region.

In Cdn First Army area, Br 1 Corps closely invests Le Havre, moving 51st Div from St Valery to positions on right of 49th Div. Preparations are begun for all-out assault on the elaborate fortifications of the city and port. In 2 Corps area, 4th Armd Div establishes bridgehead across the Somme in Pont Remy area, E of Abbeville, and halts there temporarily. Pol 1st Armd Div, coming up on left, crosses the river W of Abbeville.

In Br Second Army's 12 Corps area, 7th Armd Div, directed on Ghent, continues NE to Lillers, on Bethune-Aire road. 30 Corps, pressing quickly NE, crosses French-Belgian border. On left, 11th Armd Div, advancing on Antwerp, reaches positions E of Alost despite opposition in Lille-Tournai area. Gds Armd Div drives into Brussels and blocks exits from the city.

12th Army Group: In U.S. First Army area, XIX Corps remains generally S of Tournai, containing pocket SW of Mons on W. V Corps is ordered to new zone on right flank of First Army, where it is to face E and advance as quickly as possible to the Meuse. In VII Corps area, Mons (Belgium) falls to 3d Armd Div. 1st Div exerts pressure against large body of disorganized enemy pocketed in Mons-Bavai-Forêt de Mormal area.

In U.S. Third Army's XX Corps area, 7th Armd Div columns feinting toward Sedan are recalled, returning on 4th after getting enough gasoline to do so. Airfield near Reims is sufficiently repaired by this time to receive cargo planes.

S FRANCE—U.S. Seventh Army, with capture of Lyon by Fr forces, completes original mission. Permission is granted for VI Corps to continue pursuit to Belfort Gap via Lons-Le Saunier-Besançon route. 2d Corps of Fr Army B is to advance up NW bank of the Saône on axis Dijon-Epinal. In VI Corps area, 36th Div continues northward toward Macon. 117th Cav Rcn Sq, spearheading advance to right, reaches Bourg-en-Bresse and Montrevel but is strongly attacked by Germans fleeing from Meximieux and suffers and inflicts heavy losses. 3d Div is moving forward in center of corps. In Fr Army B area, 2d Corps, driving NW on left flank of army to make contact with OVERLORD forces, seizes Villefranche, N of Lyon.

ITALY—AAI: In Br Eighth Army's 5 Corps area, 46th Div secures small bridgehead across Conca R in Morciano region. Cdn 1 Corps continues to pursue enemy northward, 5th Armd Div clearing Misano.

NEW GUINEA—Plans for invasion of Morotai I. are now ready. In Vogelkop area, Mar airdrome for bombers is completed on schedule.

4 September

WESTERN EUROPE—Gen Eisenhower directs 21 Army Group and U.S. First Army toward the Ruhr and U.S. Third Army toward the Saar. Hitler reinstates Rundstedt as Commander in Chief West (OB West).

21 Army Group: In Cdn First Army's 2 Corps area, while 4th Armd Div maintains positions astride the Somme in Pont Remy sector, Pol 1st Armd Div continues NE toward St Omer. 3d Div, moving up from vicinity of Rouen, joins in advance along Pas de Calais coast.

In Br Second Army's 12 Corps area, 7th Armd Div, swinging E to bypass enemy in Bethune-Lille region, continues toward Ghent, leaving 53d Div and 4th Armd Brig to mop up. In 30 Corps area, 11th Armd Div drives into Antwerp and clears city except for N suburbs and dock area.

12th Army Group: In U.S. First Army area, XIX Corps continues elimination of Mons pocket in conjunction with 1st Div of VII Corps; releases 79th Div to Third Army. In VII Corps area, 3d Armd and 9th Inf Divs continue E to the Meuse in Namur–Dinant area. V Corps begins assembly in new zone on right flank of army, moving through rear area of VII Corps. 4th Div continues mopping up in old zone.

In U.S. Third Army area, XII Corps opens attack to outflank Nancy. On N flank, 317th Inf of 80th Div begins rcn in force of Moselle N of Nancy, reaching the river at Pont a Mousson and locating crossing sites; 318th (less battalion attached to CCA of 4th Armd Div) moves toward Marbache; 319th, on 80th Div S flank, fords the Moselle at Toul and establishes bridgehead on E bank.

S FRANCE—In U.S. Seventh Army area, Fr Army B forces protecting right flank of army reconnoiter to outskirts of Briançon. In VI Corps area, 45th Div takes Bourg-en-Bresse, having overcome resistance below the town. Corps then loses contact with enemy as it continues northward toward Besançon, strongly fortified city on Doubs I.

EASTERN EUROPE—Hostilities between Finland and the USSR cease under truce agreement.

ITALY—AAI: U.S. Fifth Army issues final orders for attack on Gothic Line. II Corps, after clearing hills Morello, Senario, Calvana, and Giovi, is to breach Gothic Line at 11 Giogo Pass, rather than at Futa Pass as planned previously, and continue to Firenzuola. Br 13 Corps is to attack along 2 routes: Dicomano–Forlì and Borgo S. Lorenzo–Faenza. In IV Corps area, CCA of 1st Armd Div thrusts to edge of Lucca. CCB overcomes delaying opposition at Altopascio road center. II Corps, which is to make main effort through zone now held by Br 13 Corps, takes over S part of its new sector and under cover of darkness begins movement into attack positions.

In Br Eighth Army area, 10 Corps, advancing along Arezzo–Cesena road (Highway 71), is in contact with outer defenses of Gothic Line. In 5 Corps area, 46th Div expands Conca bridgehead against strong resistance in S. Clemente area. 1st Armd Div moves forward to exploit possible breakthrough by 46th Div and begins bitter struggle for S end of S. Savino–Coriano ridge. Cdn 1 Corps drives forward along coast, meeting heavy fire from Coriano ridge on left. Pol 2 Corps begins moving into army reserve.

CBI—Gen Hurley and Donald Nelson arrive in India after brief stopover in Moscow.

11 Army Group: Gen Slim, commander Br Fourteenth Army, tells 15 Corps commander that his corps will contain enemy on Arakan front while 4 and 33 Corps conduct strong offensive across the Chindwin, beginning in December. In 33 Corps area, E African 11th Div, which has taken over pursuit of enemy from Ind 23d Div at Tamu, takes Sittaung without opposition; elements are moving S down Kabaw Valley toward Kalemyo.

SWPA—Elements of TF TRADEWIND at Aitape, New Guinea, conduct rehearsals for Morotai operation (INTERLUDE). Aitape and Maffin Bay are the two principal staging areas for TF TRADEWIND.

U.S. Eighth Army hq arrives at Hollandia, New Guinea.

POA—First elements of Allied convoy, with III Amphib Corps (Marine) assault force embarked; starts from the Solomons for the Palau Is.., Caroline Is..

5 September

WESTERN EUROPE—21 Army Group: In Cdn First Army's 2 Corps area, 3d Div, moving along coast, bypasses Boulogne and reaches Calais area. Enemy is prepared to defend both ports. On right flank of corps, Pol 1st Armd Div continues toward St Omer.

In Br Second Army's 12 Corps area, 7th Armd Div captures Ghent, but enemy continues to hold out in N outskirts for some days. 30 Corps consolidates and reorganizes in preparation for continuing assault.

12th Army Group: U.S. Ninth Army becomes operational, taking command of troops and zone of VIII Corps, Third Army, on Brittany Peninsula. 29th Div occupies La Trinité, which enemy has vacated.

In U.S. First Army's XIX Corps area, rcn elements of 2d Armd Div and 113th Cav Gp push deep into Belgium to general line Brussels–Gembloux. In VII Corps area, while 1st Div continues mopping up Mons pocket, taking numerous prisoners, 9th Div secures crossings of the Meuse N and S of Dinant. 3d Armd Div prepares to press on to Liége. V Corps continues assembly on right flank of army and attacks E. 5th Armd Div secures crossings over the Meuse near Sedan, CCA at Bazeilles and CCR at Mohon. 28th Div is moving up behind armor. 102d Cav Gp screens assembly of 4th Div NW of Mézières.

In U.S. Third Army area, Gen Patton orders XII Corps to cross the Moselle, secure Nancy, and be prepared to continue to Mannheim and the Rhine. In XII Corps area, on N flank of 80th Div, 317th Inf makes futile attempts to force the Moselle at Pagny-sur-Moselle and in the Blenod–Pont à Mousson area after daybreak; trying again night of 5–6 at Vandieres, Pont à Mousson, and Blenod, succeeds in getting 3d Bn (−) across at Pont à Mousson. 318th Inf attacks toward Hill 326, which commands Marbache. 319th expands Toul bridgehead to include Fort de Gondreville but is unable to reduce Fort de Villey-le-Sec. XV Corps, consisting at this time of corps hq and troops and awaiting additional forces, receives mission of protecting S flank of army in sector to right of XII Corps.

S FRANCE—In U.S. Seventh Army area, VI Corps reaches positions near Besançon. 36th Div is SW of the city, 3d Div due S, and 45th Div to NE.

USSR—Declares war on Bulgaria.

ITALY—AAI: In U.S. Fifth Army's IV Corps area, CCA of 1st Armd Div takes Lucca. S African 6th Armd Div gets forward elements to Monsummano and clears part of M. Albano. II Corps continues to move assault units forward, night 5–6. At the same time, Germans pull back from positions N of Florence.

In Br Eighth Army area, 5 Corps and Cdn 1 Corps are held up by firm opposition on S. Savino-Coriano ridge. To left rear, in 5 Corps zone, 56th Div is staunchly opposed in Croce-Gemmano region and Ind 4th Div in Pian di Castello area.

6 September

WESTERN EUROPE—21 Army Group: In Cdn First Army's 2 Corps area, 2d Div, which has moved up behind assault forces, passes through 3d Div in Calais area. 4th Armd Div is advancing toward Ghent-Bruges canal. Pol 1st Armd Div crosses canal at St Omer.

12th Army Group: In U.S. First Army's XIX Corps area, 113th Cav Gp and 2d Armd Div reconnoiter eastward to general line Tirlemont-Namur. In VII Corps area, 3d Armd Div advances E from Namur astride the Meuse and occupies Huy. 9th Div expands and strengthens its Meuse bridgeheads against determined resistance. 1st Div, leaving 16th Inf behind to complete mop up of Mons pocket, starts eastward. In V Corps area, 4th Inf and 5th Armd Divs move forward from the Meuse, 4th on left reaching Bièvre and 5th Armd overrunning Sedan.

In U.S. Third Army's XX Corps area, 7th Armd Div opens corps attack to force the Moselle. Four combat rcn columns start toward the river at 0300 to search for crossing site, screen for main assault, and strengthen 3d Cav Gp; these soon encounter strong enemy outposts. Main body of 7th Armd Div attacks at 1400, with CCA and CCB leading and CCR following CCB: on N, CCA is brought to a halt at Ste Marie-aux-Chênes; CCB is held up near Rezonville and Gorze but gets elements to canal between Noveant and Arnaville. 90th Div completes its crossing of the Meuse and assembles near Etain. In XII Corps area, 317th Inf of 80th Div abandons efforts to cross the Moselle on N flank of div after enemy overruns 3d Bn's bridgehead; 318th Inf seizes Hill 326, overlooking Marbache, and attacks at W edge of Fort de l'Avant Garde; 319th is still unable to take Fort de Villey-le-Sec. 2d Cav Gp inflicts heavy losses on retreating enemy column while making its way toward Madon I line.

S FRANCE—In U.S. Seventh Army area, Fr 2d Corps takes Châlon-sur-Saône. VI Corps, preparing to cross the Doubs at Dole, Besançon, and Baume-les-Dames, is meeting delaying opposition. Elements of 3d Div overrun Fort Fontain, night 6–7, opening way to outer defenses of Besançon. Fr 1st Corps becomes operational under command of Gen Emile Béthouart with mission of continuing toward Besançon-Belfort area on right flank of army. Corps consists of 3d Algerian Div, 9th Colonial Div, and 2d Moroccan Div. The last is to move up gradually. Corps seizes Pierrefontaine, Maîche, and St Hippolyte.

EASTERN EUROPE—Soviet forces reach Rumanian-Yugoslav frontier at Turnu-Severin, on the Danube at the Iron Gate. Other Red Army troops take Ostroleka (Poland).

ITALY—AAI: In U.S. Fifth Army area, IV Corps for the next few days confines its activities to regrouping, patrolling, and making limited advances as enemy withdraws. 1st Armd Div withdraws 11th and 14th Armd Inf Bns to reserve for possible employment with II Corps. II Corps takes command of rest of its new sector and temporarily of 1st Div and elements of Ind 8th Div (Br 13 Corps) within its zone. 88th Div is relieved by 34th Div and S African 6th Armd DIV.

In Br Eighth Army area, while preparations are being made for all-out assault on S. Savino-Coriano feature, Cdn 1 Corps gets patrols to Marano I.

CBI—Gen Hurley and Donald Nelson arrive at Chungking.

On Salween front, Japanese commander of Sung Shan forces dies.

SWPA—Elements of TF TRADEWIND at Maffin Bay conduct rehearsals for Morotai operation on New Guinea mainland E of Wakde I. On Noemfoor, Gen MacNider takes command of TF CYCLONE and RCT 158.

CAROLINE Is.—Planes from fast carriers of U.S. Third Fleet, beginning 3-day strike against the Palaus in preparation for invasion, find targets scarce as result of earlier aerial attacks by land-based planes of SWPA. During the 3-day operations, 1,470 sorties are flown; targets are also bombarded by cruisers and DD's accompanying the carriers.

7 September

WESTERN EUROPE—21 Army Group: In Br Second Army area, 12 Corps relieves elements of 30 Corps in Antwerp and Alost, freeing them for advance to NE. 30 Corps begins drive toward Meuse-Escaut Canal. Gds Armd Div advances NE from Louvain to Diest and searches for crossing sites along Albert Canal, finding bridges down 11th Armd Div searches in vain for crossings over canals N of Antwerp.

12th Army Group: In U.S. First Army's XIX Corps area, 113th Cav Gp, leading eastward movement toward Holland, reaches Albert Canal near Hasselt. In VII Corps area, 3d Armd Div drives forward to Liége. 9th Div mops up Dinant and continues E. 1st Div, having completed mop up of Mons pocket, is assembling in rear area. In V Corps area, 5th Armd Div, now immobilized by lack of gasoline, is passed through by 28th Div, which drives some 15 miles E of Sedan. 4th Div continues E on N flank of corps toward St Hubert.

In U.S. Third Army's XX Corps area, CCA of 7th Armd Div, after overcoming opposition at Ste Marie-aux-Chênes and St Privat, continues to the Moselle at Mondelange, N of Metz, and starts S toward Hauconcourt; CCB is forced to withdraw elements on canal between Noveant and Arnaville because of heavy fire, but gets other elements to the river in Dornot area, where they are under fire from both sides of the river; CCR starts forward to join in battle, but is ordered to halt until passed through by 5th Div, 5th Div begins attack toward Metz: RCT 2 is stopped by organized resistance in Amanvillers–Verneville area; RCT 11 reaches heights W of the Moselle in Dornot area. 90th Div starts toward Thionville, with 359th Inf echeloned to left rear in order to protect exposed left flank of corps; 358th advances along Landres–Fontoy axis to heights W of Trieux; 357th is halted at outskirts of Briey. 3d Cav Gp is ordered to provide flank protection for corps. In XII Corps area, 318th Inf of 80th Div, after taking Hill 356, which commands Marbache, outposts the town during night 7–8; 319th pushes up to moat of Fort de Villey-le-Sec but is driven back. 2d Cav Gp reaches Madon R, where bridge is held intact.

S France—In U.S. Seventh Army's VI Corps area, Besançon falls to 3d Div, 45th Div crosses the Doubs in Baume-les-Dames area. 36th attempts unsuccessfully to cross SW of Besançon; elements cross in 3d Div sector at Avanne. Fr 1st Corps occupies Briançon.

Bulgaria—Declares war on Germany.

Italy—AAI: In U.S. Fifth Army area, II Corps completes preparations for attack, but enemy withdrawal during night 7–8 to Gothic Line itself from delaying positions on hills N and NE of Florence (Morello, Senario, Calvana, and Giovi) makes first phase of the assault unnecessary.

In Br Eighth Army area, Cdn 1 Corps is reinf by Br 4th Div, Greek 3d Mtn Brig, and Br 25th Tank Brig.

CBI—Gen Hurley, Donald Nelson; and Gen Stilwell talk in Chungking with Chiang Kai-shek, who reiterates his willingness to let Stilwell control all Ch troops in the field but asks for new Ch SOS staffed by Americans.

On Salween front, mop-up of Sung Shan position is completed. Battle for this Burma Road strongpoint has cost Chinese 7,675 dead, most of them from Ch 8th Army, and virtually destroyed all of the estimated 2,000 Japanese on and around the position.

SWPA—Gen Eichelberger, I Corps CG, takes command of U.S. Eighth Army.

8 September

Western Europe—21 Army Group: In Cdn First Army's 2 Corps area, 2d Div invests Dunkerque. 4th Armd Div reaches outskirts of Bruges. Pol armor reaches Thielt; elements enter Dixmude.

In Br Second Army's 30 Corps area, Gds Armd Div crosses Albert Canal at Beeringen. 50th Div establishes small bridgehead over canal SW of Gheel. Both crossings meet lively opposition.

12th Army Group: In U.S. Ninth Army area, VIII Corps begins all-out assault on Brest at 1000 after preparatory bombardment, employing 2d, 8th, and 29th Divs.

In U.S. First Army's XIX Corps area, 113th Cav Gp drives almost to Maastricht (Holland) and patrols Albert Canal. 2d Armd Div reaches positions in Hasselt–St Trond area. 30th Div is moving up to attack on right flank of corps. In VII Corps area, 3d Armd Div, which is reinf by 47th Inf of 9th Div, mops up in Liége; 9th Div continues E on S flank of corps and 1st Div displaces to Huy–Faimes area on N flank. V Corps, with 4th Div on N and 28th on S, meets stronger rear-guard opposition as it continues E to positions generally between Jemelle and Margut. Corps FO 26 calls for capture of Koblenz, beyond West Wall.

In U.S. Third Army's XX Corps area, German *106th Pz Brig*, having moved forward between 359th and 358th Regts of 80th Div from Aumetz, counterattacks 80th Div CP between Landres and Mairy early in morning, but becomes disorganized and is virtually destroyed. In this action Germans lose 30 tanks, 60 half-tracks, and almost 100 other vehicles. On S flank of div, enemy force pocketed in Briey capitulates. CCA (−), 7th Armd Div, disposed along the Moselle S of Talange, is containing enemy in N part of his Metz bridgehead with exchanges of fire. Because of diverging attacks of corps units, Gen Walker attaches 2d Inf of 5th Div to 7th Armd Div and CCB of 7th Armd Div to 5th Div, although missions remain unchanged. 2d Inf continues to batter at outer fortifications of Metz against determined opposition, taking Verneville and reaching edge of Amanvillers. 5th Div gains precarious foothold on E bank of the Moselle E of Dornot. 4 cos of 11th Inf and elements of 23d Armd Inf Bn, 7th Armd Div, the latter under command of 5th Div, cross under heavy fire and are pinned down in shallow bridgehead. Efforts of 11th Inf to push on to Fort Blaise are futile and costly. In XII Corps area, Germans begin series of counterattacks against 80th Div, recovering Marbache. In XV Corps area, Fr 2d Armd Div joins corps and takes over sector between Montargis and the Marne, 79th Div is assembling in Joinville area.

S FRANCE—In U.S. Seventh Army area, on Mediterranean coast, elements of 1st ABTF take Menton and drive to Italian border. In Fr 2d Corps area, 1st Armd Div reaches Beaune, on road to Dijon. 1st Inf Div outflanks and captures Autun. In VI Corps area, 141st Inf of 36th Div follows 143d across the Doubs at Avanne; cuts highways W and NW from Besançon. Germans are beginning to withdraw from Baume-les-Dames area to avoid encirclement.

ITALY—AAI: In U.S. Fifth Army's IV Corps area, patrol of 435th AAA Bn, TF 45, crosses the Serchio and enters Vecchiano without opposition. Bridging is begun there at once. 1st Armd and S African 6th Armd Divs continue to patrol actively in effort to divert enemy attention, advancing positions slightly. Flooded Arno prevents S African 6th Armd Div from crossing reinforcements. Br 13 Corps follows up as enemy withdraws, 1st Div occupying M. Morello and M. Senario and Ind 8th Div, M. Calvana and M. Giovi. 6th Armd Div protects right flank.

In Br Eighth Army area, Gen Alexander visits army front, where he decides that operations toward Rimini cannot be continued until S. Savino-Coriano ridge is cleared; orders attack against center of Gothic Line by U.S. Fifth Army. In 5 Corps area, 56th Div intensifies efforts to take Gemmano ridge in preparation for main assault on S. Savino-Coriano ridge but makes slow progress.

CBI—Gen Hurley assumes his new duties as Presidential representative to Chiang Kai-shek.

Gen Stilwell, although not anxious to command the Chinese Army, agrees to War Department proposal that CBI Theater be split and that he be relieved of responsibility for lend-lease matters in order to concentrate on support of Pacific operations from China. Chiang Kai-shek proposes to Gen Stilwell that Ch troops from Myitkyina be employed in battle for Lung-ling.

On Salween front, Japanese, having assembled strong reinforcements, begin attack on Ch positions N of Lung-ling.

In China, Japanese forces pushing S from Hengyang overrun Ling-ling, from which U.S. Fourteenth Air Force has withdrawn. Fourteenth Air Force bases at Kweilin and Liuchow are threatened from the S too, since elements of Japanese 23d Army (2 divs and an independent mixed brig) are driving N from Canton.

U.S.—JCS issue directive to CINCSWPA and CINCPOA for invasion of the Philippines.

9 September

WESTERN EUROPE—21 Army Group: In Cdn First Army's 2 Corps area, Allied patrols moving along coast enter Ostend and Nieuport. 4th Armd Div troops cross Ghent-Bruges Canal SE of Bruges against strong opposition.

In Br Second Army's 30 Corps area, Gds Armd Div, reinf by Royal Netherlands group, extends bridgehead at Beeringen against sharp opposition. 50th Div is slowly expanding Gheel bridgehead. 11th Armd Div moves forward on right flank of corps.

12th Army Group: In U.S. First Army's XIX Corps area, 113th Cav Gp enters Holland panhandle near Maastricht. Rest of corps is getting into position for offensive, 30th Div assembling near Tongres. In VII Corps area, 1st Div crosses the Meuse at Liége and pushes E on N flank of corps. 3d Armd Div (−) heads for Verviers; CCB and attached elements of 9th Div thrust to Limbourg.

In U.S. Third Army's XX Corps area, forward elements of 80th Div drive NE to vicinity of Fontoy and Neufchef, the latter being within 8 miles of Thionville. 2d Inf of 5th Div, assisted by TF from CCA, 7th Armd Div, continues to attack W of Metz without making appreciable headway. 5th Div maintains its small Dornot bridgehead against repeated counterattacks but is unable to expand or reinforce it. In XII Corps area, corps commander orders attack on S flank to begin on 11th. Germans continue to counterattack 80th Div positions.

S FRANCE—In U.S. Seventh Army area, Fr 2d Corps continues toward Dijon, elements reaching positions about halfway between Beaune and Dijon. In VI Corps area, 45th Div overcomes opposition at Baume and drives on toward Villersexel road junction. 3d and 36th Divs cross Ognon I. In Fr 1st Corps area, Séez falls to FFI forces. This is an important communications center just SW of Little St Bernard Pass.

USSR—Accepts Bulgaria's request for an armistice and breaks off hostilities.

ITALY—AAI: In U.S. Fifth Army area, Gen Clark orders II and Br 13 Corps to attack on 10th to breach Gothic Line. Boundary between the two corps is altered to give Highway 6521 to 13 Corps. Troops move northward, following up enemy withdrawal. In II Corps area, 34th Div, with 91st Cav Rcn Sq under command, takes up positions W of

[10 SEPTEMBER 1944]

Highway 65 and 91st assembles E of the highway. 91st Cav Rcn Sq patrols as far N as M. Maggiore without incident. In Br 13 Corps area, 1st Div, having accomplished its mission of screening for II Corps, shifts eastward.

Br Eighth Army issues instructions for major effort by 5 Corps and Cdn 1 Corps to take S. Savino-Coriano ridge. Greek 3d Mtn Brig is committed along coast under command of Cdn 1st Div, Cdn 1 Corps.

NEW GUINEA—Work on Kamiri airfield, Noemfoor, is completed.

10 September

WESTERN EUROPE—Conferring with his commanders in Brussels, Gen Eisenhower decides to defer operations to open the port of Antwerp until after Operation MARKET-GARDEN to secure a Rhine bridgehead. Patrol contact is made between forces of OVERLORD and DRAGOON.

21 Army Group: In Cdn First Army area, Br 1 Corps, after very strong aerial bombardment during which almost 5,000 tons of bombs are dropped, and after naval softening of defenses, launches all-out assault on Le Havre at 1745 with 49th and 51st Divs, penetrating enemy defenses.

In Br Second Army's 30 Corps area, enemy disposed along Albert Canal continues to offer stiff opposition to forces holding bridgeheads across it, but Gds Armd Div reaches Meuse-Escaut Canal near Overpelt and establishes bridgehead.

12th Army Group: Gen Bradley orders First Army to break through West Wall and secure crossings over the Rhine in vicinity of Koblenz, Bonn, and Cologne; Third Army to secure crossings of the Rhine at Mannheim. Offensive is scheduled to open on 14th.

In U.S. Ninth Army area, VIII Corps closes up to Brest proper and finishes clearing Le Conquet Peninsula. 94th Div begins arriving in corps zone to relieve 6th Armd Div (− CCB) for action with Third Army. 83d Div is detached from corps and starts E toward Third Army front.

In U.S. First Army's XIX Corps area, 30th Div, advancing NE with little difficulty, finds Fort Eben Emael undefended. 113th Cav Gp crosses the Meuse at Liége and drives N. VII Corps speeds toward German frontier against rear-guard opposition, 1st Div reaching Battice and 3d Armd moving through Verviers. In V Corps area, 4th Div reaches general line Regne-Bastogne. 28th, in rapid strides, overruns Bastogne, Longvilly, Wiltz, Selange, and Arlon. CCA, 5th Armd Div, takes city of Luxembourg with ease and probes eastward toward Germany; CCR drives to within about 8 miles of German border.

In U.S. Third Army's XX Corps area, 90th Div progresses toward Thionville against delaying opposition. 359th Inf takes Aumetz, 357th seizes Hayange, and 358th overruns Algrange. 2d Inf, 5th Div, assisted by elements of CCA, 7th Armd Div, continues almost fruitless attacks against German line W of Metz. 10th Inf, 5th Div, begins crossing the Moselle between Noveant and Arnaville about 0200 under smoke screen, the first to be used by Third Army on large scale, taking enemy by surprise. Hills 386 and 370 and Bois de Gaumont are cleared. Enemy rallies and begins strong counterattacks from Arry, which XIX TAC helps to stem. From this time on, XIX TAC is to divert some of its planes from primary targets at Brest to assist Third Army as it fights for Moselle crossings. Since the hard-pressed bridgehead forces E of Dornot are by now completely exhausted and greatly reduced in strength, they are withdrawn, night 10-11. Engineers begin difficult task of bridging the Moselle under fire after nightfall. In XII Corps area, 80th Div's 319th Inf occupies Fort de Villey-le-Sec when enemy withdraws toward Nancy. 35th Div moves up to the Moselle in Flavigny area in preparation for assault across it with 134th Inf on left and 137th on right. 2d Bn, 134th, seizes bridge intact and crosses, but enemy destroys bridge before TD's can follow and sharply counterattacks the isolated infantrymen, some of whom escape to W bank by swimming or wading. XV Corps makes patrol contact with DRAGOON patrol at Sombernon. 79th Div completes concentration in Joinville area. 106th Cav Gp is moving through it to screen advance.

S FRANCE—In U.S. Seventh Army area, Fr 2d Corps reaches Dijon and makes patrol contact with OVERLORD forces. In VI Corps area, 36th and 3d Divs are moving against Vesoul. 45th Div, to right, is driving on Villersexel.

ITALY—AAI: In U.S. Fifth Army's IV Corps area, TF 45 gets additional elements across the Serchio at Vecchiano. CCA, 1st Armd Div, crosses elements over the river in order to clear both sides within its sector; 6th Armd Inf Bn takes Villa Basilica. S African 6th Armd Div crosses additional forces over the Arno, using bridges at Florence. II Corps opens drive toward Gothic Line at 0530 with 2 divs abreast. 34th makes steady progress on left, forward elements getting beyond M. Maggiore. 91st Div drives to the Sieve and fords it during night 10-11. Br 13 Corps attacks toward Gothic Line with 3 divs, making main effort on left in support of U.S. II Corps. 1st Div drives up Highway 6521 to the Sieve and secures bridgehead W of Berge, San Lorenzo. Ind 8th Div, handicapped by lack of roads in center of corps zone, holds current positions in M. Calvana-M. Giovi area with 2 brigs while another patrols across the Sieve at Vicchio. On E flank, 6th Armd Div takes Dicomano, on Highway 67.

In Br Eighth Army area, 5 Corps commits 46th Div to assist 56th in battle for Gemmano ridge, where Germans continue to resist stubbornly. In Cdn 1 Corps area, NZ 2d Div is attached to corps.

PALAU IS.—U.S. Third Fleet's Task Group 38.4 (fast carriers), having recently bombarded targets in Bonins, Volcanos, Yap, and Ulithi, arrives off the Palaus and begins 2-day strike against AA positions and beach defenses at Peleliu and Angaur in preparation for invasion.

11 September

WESTERN EUROPE—21 Army Group: In Cdn First Army area, Br 1 Corps, pushing into Le Havre, gains heights commanding harbor. In 2 Corps area, elements of 2d Div reach Zeebrugge. Coast of Pas de Calais, except for Boulogne, Calais, and Dunkerque, is now clear of enemy; the ports mentioned are being contained. Pol 1st Armd Div, which has met strong opposition at Ghent Canal, is moving to Ghent to relieve 7th Armd Div of 12 Corps.

In Br Second Army's 30 Corps area, Gds Armd Div strengthens bridgehead over Meuse-Escaut Canal and patrols across Dutch border to Valkenswaard. 50th Div maintains Gheel bridgehead against considerable opposition.

12th Army Group: In U.S. First Army area, V and VII Corps are ordered to reconnoiter in force to test border defenses of West Wall and if possible to make limited penetration. XIX Corps get northern prong of pincers to be clamped about enemy's Albert Canal line into action when rcn elements of 2d Armd Div cross British-held bridge at Beeringen and turn SE into XIX Corps zone N of Hasselt. By the time the southern prong, 113th Cav, has reached positions S of Vise, 30th Div has already started crossing, having discovered weak spot; 120th Inf occupies Lanaye (Holland) and seizes locks near there intact. In VII Corps area, 1st Div assembles forward elements at Aubel and Henri Chapelle. 3d Armd Div secures Eupen. 9th Div, in reserve, is assembled near Verviers. 4th Cav Gp screens right flank. In V Corps area, dismounted patrol of 85th Rcn Sq, 5th Armd Div, is the first Allied unit to cross into Germany, moving over frontier at 1805 and reconnoitering uneventfully to vicinity of Stalzenburg. 28th Div (less RCT 112, attached to 5th Armd Div) assembles W of Our R and during night 11-12 secures bridge intact.

In U.S. Third Army's XX Corps area, 358th Inf, 90th Div, clears heights W of Thionville in Volkrange area and emerges upon plain overlooking the town; 357th takes Florange and reaches the Moselle at several points S of Thionville. CCR, 7th Armd Div, joins 2d Inf, 5th Div, in attacks W of Metz: 2d Inf continues frontal assault after undergoing series of counterattacks that gain some ground and necessitate bitter fighting in effort to straighten lines S of Amanvillers; CCR, from Roncourt area, attempts without much success to get behind enemy holding up 2d Inf. 5th Div reinforces Arnaville bridgehead with 3d Bn, 11th Inf, and expands it toward Corny and Arry against severe counterattacks. XIX TAC assists with strikes on Arry and Corny. In XII Corps area, CCA of 4th Armd Div prepares to cross the Moselle; engineers attempt to construct bridge near Pagny-sur-Moselle, night 11-12, but lack equipment. After preparatory bombardment, during which deceptive site is hit, 2d and 3d Bns of 137th Inf, 35th Div, force the Moselle at Crevechamps, SE of Flavigny, but are pinned down by enemy fire; 1st Bn crosses near Neuviller-sur-Moselle, to S, late in day and pushes to Lorey. Meanwhile, one column of CCB, 4th Armd Div, crosses at Bainville-aux-Miroirs and another near Bayon against considerable resistance; bypassing Bayon, left column seizes hills overlooking Brémoncourt and during night 11-12 makes contact with 137th Inf; rest of CCB and 2d Bn of 320th Inf cross at Bayon after engineers put in bridge. Enemy force of 2 cos crosses to W bank of the Moselle and attacks fort held by elements of 134th Inf near Pont St Vincent, breaching walls, but arrival of reinforcements and well-placed arty fire eliminate this threat. 80th Div is ordered to start crossing the Moselle N of Nancy on 12th. To divert enemy attention from proposed crossing site, air strike is made on Pont à Mousson area. XV Corps opens offensive to close up to the Moselle between Epinal and Charmes while continuing to defend S flank of army. With 121st Cav Sq of 106th Cav Gp screening its advance, 79th Div moves forward by motor and on foot, 314th Inf leading: 314th Inf reaches vicinity of Charmes too late in day to attack the town; 313th drives quickly toward Mirecourt; 315th reaches positions near Neufchâteau. Fr 2d Armd Div screens S flank of army and moves CCL eastward, bypassing Andelot, to vicinity of Vittel.

S FRANCE—In U.S. Seventh Army's Fr 2d Corps area, 1st Armd Div is driving on Langres. Infantry maintains defensive line. In VI Corps area, 36th and 3d Divs are investing Vesoul, where enemy is expected to make a stand in order to hold this last escape route to Belfort. 45th Div continues drive on Villersexel, clearing Rougemont. 36th Div makes contact with Fr 2d Corps at Pont-sur-Saône.

FRANTIC—U.S. Eighth Air Force begins the last of its shuttle-bombing missions. 75 B-17's and 64 P-51's attack armament plant at Chemnitz, Germany, and proceed to FRANTIC bases in USSR.

ITALY—AAI: U.S. Fifth Army continues drive toward Gothic Line assisted by air attacks on passes through the mountains. In IV Corps area, on Ligurian coast, patrols of TF 45 reach outskirts of Viareggio. S African 6th Armd Div drives N with 3 regts, gaining ground steadily and taking Pistoia without opposition. In II Corps area, 168th Inf, on right flank of 34th Div, drives toward M. Frassino, Gothic Line outpost, pushing through Cavallina and Barberino. 91st Div, advancing along Highways 65 and 6524, approaches M. Calvi and M. Altuzzo, the latter dominating Il Giogo Pass on E.

SWPA—Elements of TF TRADEWIND from Aitape rendezvous with Maffin Bay group at Maffin Bay.

12 September

INTERNATIONAL CONFERENCES—Second Quebec Conference (OCTAGON) opens.

WESTERN EUROPE—21 Army Group: In Cdn First Army's Br 1 Corps area, German garrison of Le Havre surrenders. About 12,000 prisoners are taken. In 2 Corps area, Pol 1st Armd Div, after relieving 7th Armd Div of 12 Corps at Ghent, pushes forward to Lokeren and St Nicolas. 4th Armd Div finishes clearing Bruges area and reaches Leopold Canal.

In Br Second Army area, 12 Corps, as relieved by Cdn First Army, is moving into area Gheel-Diest-Malines Antwerp.

12th Army Group: In U.S. First Army's XIX Corps area, 30th Div, whose 117th Regt has joined 119th E of the canal and river S of Vise, drives N and NE, with 113th Cav Gp advancing NE to its right. 2d Armd Div rcn bn clears bridge site along N bank of Albert Canal and bridge is completed there at midnight. CCA begins crossing at once. VII Corps conducts rcn in force to West Wall. 1st Div thrusts at Aachen Municipal Forest, S of Aachen, where it repels counterattack. One 3d Armd Div column, driving NE from Eupen, stops for night on edge of Eynattener Wald, within about 1,000 yards of West Wall; another column probes E from Eupen, some elements reaching West Wall at Schmidthof and others reaching Roetgen, just short of West Wall. Gen Collins decides to bypass Aachen, isolating it in conjunction with XIX Corps, and drive toward Stolberg corridor. V Corps begins limited attacks toward West Wall. While 102d Cav Gp protects N flank and maintains contact with VII Corps, 4th Div advances toward St Vith against light resistance. Elements of 109th Inf, 28th Div, cross bridge over the Our and take Sevenig; elements of Moth cross German frontier to reach positions W of Grosskampenberg, on Kesfeld-Uttfeld route, coming up against West Wall.

In U.S. Third Army's XX Corps area, 90th Div eliminates all resistance W of the Moselle in Thionville area and clears Thionville W of the river except for approach to main bridge there. Germans destroy the bridge. 2d Inf, 5th Div, continues bitter fighting to improve positions and straighten lines S of Amanvillers. Arnaville bridgehead perimeter holds against co-ordinated German counterattack. At noon engineers finish bridging the Moselle, thus per-mitting tanks and TD's from CCB of 7th Armd Div to cross into bridgehead. In XII Corps area, 80th Div's 317th Inf attacks across the Moselle in Dieulouard area early in morning and finds E bank lightly held; 318th (−) follows just before noon. Weapons and vehicles start across later in day. With little difficulty the bridgehead is expanded to include Ste Geneviève, Loisy, Bezaumont, and La Côte Pelée. 137th Inf, 35th Div, and CCB, 4th Armd Div, strengthen and expand Lorey bridgehead S of Nancy. In XV Corps area, elements of 106th Cav Gp cross the Moselle N of Charmes without opposition. 79th Div's 314th Inf clears Charmes, and after dark 1st Bn fords the Moselle at Charmes; 313th clashes with enemy near Poussay; 315th converges on Neufchâteau, where enemy garrison is trapped. Fr 2d Armd Div's CCL takes Vittel and CCV clears Andelot. Germans move from Epinal in 2 columns in preparation for counterattack to free encircled forces in Vittel area.

S FRANCE—In U.S. Seventh Army's Fr 2d Corps area, armored forces reach outskirts of Langres. In VI Corps area, 45th Div repels counterattack near Villersexel. 36th and 3d Divs continue clearing Vesoul area.

RUMANIA—Signs armistice, drawn up in Moscow, with Allies, agreeing to co-operate in war against Germany and Hungary and to pay reparations. Boundary between USSR and Rumania is to be that established by Soviet-Rumanian agreement of 28 June 1940. USSR promises to return Transylvania to Rumania.

ITALY—AAI: In U.S. Fifth Army's IV Corps area, S African 6th Armd Div continues to gain ground on right flank of corps as enemy falls back to prepared positions of Gothic Line. In II Corps area, rapid advance comes to an end as outer defenses of Gothic Line are reached. 34th Div is delayed on left by mine field SW of M. Frassino but on right gains lower slopes of the mountain; 135th Inf relieves 168th, on div right. 91st Div ambitiously tries to take M. Calvi and hills (Monticelli and Altuzzo) commanding Il Giogo Pass, but can get no farther than enemy outposts. In support of corps, medium bombers strike at Firenzuola. In Br 13 Corps area, 1st Div comes up against outer positions of Gothic Line. 21st Brig, Ind 8th Div, crosses the Sieve and drives quickly northward toward M. Citerna. 6th

Armd Div is delayed on right flank of corps so that Ind 8th Div can have the right of way on Highway 67.

In Br Eighth Army area, 5 Corps and Cdn 1 Corps begin second battle for S. Savino-Coriano ridge at 2300, arty fire preceding and closely supporting assault.

CBI—Gen Stilwell suggests to Chiang Kai-shek that replacements be sent for Ch forces on Salween front, who thus far have received none, instead of using Chinese from Myitkyina.

SWPA—TF TRADEWIND convoy begins uneventful voyage toward Morotai.

P.I.—Carrier TF 38 begins 3-day strike against targets in central Philippines, meeting surprisingly weak opposition from Leyte.

PALAUS—Western Fire Support Group of Adm Fort's Western Attack Force (TF 32) arrives off the Palaus and begins naval bombardment in preparation for landings, covered by Task Group 38.4 and escort-carrier force, which make aerial attacks. Mine sweeping and clearance of underwater obstacles offshore also begins.

13 September

WESTERN EUROPE—Gen Eisenhower directs capture of two objectives: the Ruhr and a deepwater port, either Antwerp or Rotterdam.

21 Army Group: In Cdn First Army's 2 Corps area, Cdn 4th Armd Div crosses light force over Canal de Derivation and Leopold Canal NE of Bruges, night 13-14.

In Br Second Army's 12 Corps area, 15th Div takes over Gheel bridgehead, relieving 50th Div of 30 Corps, and presses on to Meuse-Escaut Canal, crossing it after nightfall. 53d Div is expanding holdings in dock area of Antwerp.

12th Army Group: In U.S. Ninth Army's VIII Corps area, German garrison of Brest refuses request to surrender although the garrison is being steadily compressed on all sides. W of Recouvrance, Fort Keranroux falls to 175th Inf, 29th Div. 8th Div has been pinched out, and 29th and 2d Divs hold area around Brest. As 94th Div continues gradual relief of 6th Armd Div, CCA is released from task of containing Lorient.

In U.S. First Army's XIX Corps area, CCA of 2d Armd Div drives E toward the Maas (Meuse), on N flank of corps, forcing enemy back several miles. 119th and most of 117th Regts of 30th Div drive toward De Geul R, between Aachen and Maastricht; a bn of 117th enters Wijk, suburb of Maastricht, but finds bridges leading to island of Maastricht down. VII Corps penetrates outer defenses of West Wall at 2 points: CCB, 3d Armd Div, breaches fortifications between Roetgen and Rott; CCA, assisted by bn of 26th Inf, 1st Div, pushes through AT obstacles to village of Nutheim, which commands road to Kornelimuenster, and into Stolberg corridor. To left, 16th Inf of 1st Div withstands small counterattacks in Aachen Municipal Forest and gets into position for assault on West Wall near Ober Forstbach. 1st Div is largely engaged in containing role at Aachen. 9th Div, to secure S flank, occupies Camp d'Elsenborn with elements of 60th Inf. In V Corps area, forward elements of 4th Div assemble near the Schnee Eifel at Radscheid and Bleialf. 28th Div, employing a bn each of 109th and 110th Regts, attacks West Wall: 109th attempts to reach heights W of Roscheid but is unable to get as far as Irsen Creek; 110th advances through Grosskampenberg without opposition but is halted about half way between there and German line. 5th Armd Div, reinf by RCT tie of 28th Div, continues to protect S flank and fires on Wallendorf area.

In U.S. Third Army's XX Corps area, 90th Div, planning to cross the Moselle in Thionville area, is ordered to extend southward to relieve forces still bitterly opposed W and N of Metz. Arnaville bridgehead forces are holding on despite critical shortage of arty ammunition and heavy fire from Fort Driant that destroys ferrying raft, damages treadway at the ford, and destroys ponton bridge under construction. CCB, 7th Armd Div, crosses into the bridgehead and attacks toward Mardigny but is soon stopped by fire from Arry. In XII Corps area, enemy has decided to abandon Nancy in order to mass forces with which to overwhelm Dieulouard bridgehead; begins determined counterattacks against the bridgehead at 0100 with forces already on hand, overrunning Ste Geneviève, Loisy, and Bezaumont before being stopped just short of American-held bridges. Counterattack of 80th Div, assisted by CCA, 4th Armd Div, which crosses into bridgehead during the action, restores original bridgehead perimeter, enemy having no immediate reserves to commit in exploitation; CCA pushes through Ste Geneviève and then rapidly E toward Château-Salins, reaching Fresnes-en-Saulnois. From Lorey bridgehead S of Nancy, 35th Div, committing 320th Inf (−) with 137th, and CCB, 4th Armd Div, speed toward the Meurthe, which CCB reaches by pushing through gap in retreating enemy forces. In XV Corps area, 1st Bn of 314th Inf, 79th Div, maintains its bridgehead opposite Charmes, which elements of 106th Cav Gp are screening; 313th Inf breaks into Poussay; 315th completes capture of Neufchâteau. CCL, Fr 2d Armd Div, discovers enemy columns preparing to drive on Vittel—one at Dompaire and the other near Ville-sur-Illon; engages them and with assistance of XIX TAC decisively defeats them, destroying 60 tanks. This is an outstanding example of effective air-ground coordination. CCD overruns Chaumont.

S FRANCE—In U.S. Seventh Army's Fr 2d Corps area, Langres falls to 1st Armd Div. In VI Corps area, Germans surrender Vesoul, on last enemy escape route to Belfort in U.S. zone. 45th Div overruns Villersexel. Corps takes more than 1,300 prisoners during day.

FRANTIC—On return trip to Italy from Soviet bases, Eighth Air Force planes attack steel works at Diosgyoer, Hungary. FRANTIC bases in USSR are now well behind front line and shuttle bombing is discontinued.

POLAND—Soviet planes begin dropping supplies to beleaguered Warsaw. Lomza, key position between East Prussia and Warsaw, falls to troops of Second White Russian Front.

ITALY—AAI: In U.S. Fifth Army's IV Corps area, 1st Armd Div, ordered to be prepared to move all but one combat command to II Corps zone on 48 hours' notice, can do no more than patrol aggressively within its broad Serchio Valley sector. S African 6th Armd Div, making main effort of corps in support of II Corps to right, continues full-scale attack on hills N of Prato and takes M. Acuto. II Corps begins general assault to force Il Giogo Pass and thus gain entrance to Po Valley. 85th Div's 338th Inf, attempting to attack through 363d Inf of 91st Div and make main effort against M. Altuzzo, is unable to locate 363d and comes to a halt well short of objective under stiff opposition; to right, 339th Inf attempts in vain to take M. Veruca; to left, 363d Inf concentrates on M. Monticelli but is unable to reach crest. 362d Inf begins drive toward Futa Pass. In a supporting role on left flank of corps, 34th Div batters at Torricella Hill, below M. Coroncina, and M. Frassino. In Br 13 Corps area, 1st Div begins attack on heights flanking Highway 6521 (Poggio Prefetto and M. Guivigiana), where enemy is firmly established. Ind 8th Div takes M. Veruca and thrusts almost to top of Alpe di Vitigliano. 6th Armd Div patrols actively on right flank of corps.

In Br Eighth Army area, 5 Corps and Cdn 1 Corps gain firm hold on S. Savino-Coriano ridge, 1st Armd Div of 5 Corps taking S. Savino and Cdn 5th Armd Div of Cdn 1 Corps, Coriano and N spur of the ridge.

CBI—Gen Hurley drafts U.S. proposals for appointment of Gen Stilwell to post of Field Commander of the Ground and Air Forces of the Republic of China and directive for Chiang Kai-shek to Gen Stilwell. The Generalissimo receives them on or before 16 September. Gen Stilwell, after receiving emissaries from the Chinese Communists, leaves for Kweilin to inspect E China positions.

SWPA—TF TRADEWIND convoy is joined by Covering Force and escort carriers as it continues toward Morotai by a circuitous route in order to maintain secrecy.

14 September

INTERNATIONAL CONFERENCES—CCS, meeting at Quebec in OCTAGON Conference, draw up new directive for Adm Mountbatten, making his primary mission the recapture of Burma as quickly as possible. DRACULA (assault on Rangoon) and that part of CAPITAL requiring air and land route to China be opened are approved with target date of 15 March 1945.

WESTERN EUROPE—21 Army Group: Gen Montgomery issues orders for next phase of offensive, to begin on 17th, calling for Br Second Army to secure crossings of the Rhine and Meuse Rivers in preparation for major drive on the Ruhr and for Canadians to open port of Antwerp and seize Boulogne and Calais. Offensive operations are virtually at a standstill while supplies are being brought forward and units regrouped.

12th Army Group Area: XXIX TAC (Prov) is activated under command of Brig Gen Richard E. Nugent to provide direct assistance to U.S. Ninth Army, whose movement to main battle front will begin upon fall of Brest. The new command is attached temporarily to IX TAC.

In U.S. First Army's XIX Corps area, CCA of 2d Armd Div reaches the Maas and crosses canal to Maastricht island late in day as Germans are withdrawing. Earlier, elements of 117th Inf, 30th Div, cross to Maastricht island and find the town undefended; some elements of 119th Inf cross the De Geul a mile N of Gulpen without opposition, but others crossing at Valkenburg under enemy fire are just able to maintain a foothold on E bank. 30th Div then halts temporarily, maintaining its De Geul bridgeheads while bridges are being built and adjacent forces come abreast. In VII Corps area, TF Lovelady (Lt Col William B. Lovelady) of CCB, 3d Armd Div, thrusts to Vicht R SW of Stolberg and crosses; engineers begin bridging the river. CCA gains 4 miles, reaching outskirts of Eilendorf, a suburb of Aachen, where it halts to await 16th Inf, 1st Div, which is moving up on left flank. On right flank of armor, 9th Div commits 47th Inf, which moves elements E into Roetgen Forest to envelop towns of Zweifall and Vicht while rest works N along Vicht R. 60th Inf force turns over Camp d'Elsepborn to 4th Cav Gp and drives N across German border, seizing Kalterherberg and trying in vain to take Hoefen-Alzen ridge in order to attack the West Wall in Lammersdorf corridor. To strengthen assault on the ridge, rest of 60th Inf is ordered SE from Eupen through the Hertogenwald to Monschau from which to attack the ridge in conjunction with forces from Kalterherberg. 39th Inf drives SE from Roetgen to Lammersdorf, then attacks N against strong portion of Scharnhorst Line but is pinned down. In V Corps area, 4th Div penetrates West Wall in the Schnee Eifel: 12th Inf cuts Schnee Eifel highway and drives NE along it, taking Hill 698; 22d reaches crest of Schnee Eifel ridge and gets one bn on E slopes overlooking Hontheim. 28th Div begins major attacks in effort to breach West Wall in its sector: 109th Inf makes futile efforts to reach Roscheid; 110th, to N, attacks toward Kesfeld and sends column through Heckhuscheid and SE to take Hill 553, enemy strongpoint on Heckhuscheid-Uttfeld highway, but can clear neither objective. On S flank of corps, CCR, 5th Armd Div, begins to cross the Sauer into Germany at Wallendorf, clearing that town and bluffs beyond.

In U.S. Third Army area, XX Corps regroups in order to place greater weight on S flank. 43d Cav Rcn Sq, assisted by team from 12th Army Group hq whose function it is to make a show of strength, is given responsibility for left flank of corps. 90th Div, leaving containing force at Thionville, shifts S, relieving elements of 7th Armd Div and 5th Inf Div W and N of Metz for action to S. Planned attack to expand Arnaville bridgehead is postponed because of deep mud that makes movement of armor almost impossible. XII Corps completes envelopment of Nancy and is seriously threatening Lunéville. In local counterattacks against 80th Div's Dieulouard bridgehead, Germans gain Ste Geneviève and Loisy. 80th Div then recovers lost ground and expands bridgehead: 3d Bn of 318th Inf takes Atton and continues N to crest of Mousson Hill; 317th Inf thrusts eastward to Mt. Toulon, which enemy retains, on left and reaches Falaise Hill, S of Landremont, where enemy force moving N from Nancy is dispersed, on right. CCA, 4th Armd Div, ordered to bypass Château-Salins, races to Arracourt-Moncourt area to block enemy movement from E and cut escape routes from Nancy. SE of Nancy, 35th Div gains positions astride the Meurthe with forward elements within 6 miles of Nancy. From the Meurthe, CCB of 4th Armd Div drives through Forêt de Vitrimont to Marne-Rhine Canal near Dombasle, cutting main road W of Lunéville. 2d Cav Gp, upon crossing the Meurthe SE of Lunéville, cuts approaches from this direction. With junction of patrols of CCA and CCB near the canal late at night, envelopment of Nancy is complete. In XV Corps area, Fr 2d Armd Div makes contact with patrol of Fr 1st Armd Div, Seventh Army, near Clefmont. CCB, 6th Armd Div, is released to Third Army with mission of protecting S flank W of Troyes, relieving Fr 2d Armd Div of this task. 79th Div is ordered, except for the bn on E bank, to remain W of the river until further notice. 313th Inf mops up Poussay and takes Mirecourt on Neufchâteau-Epinal road; 315th drives enemy rear guards from Châtenois, SE of Neufchâteau, to Ramecourt, where elements of 313th destroy them during night. Fr 2d Armd Div clashes with retreating enemy near Hennecourt.

S FRANCE—In U.S. Seventh Army's Fr 2d Corps area, Gen de Lattre directs corps to turn E and advance to left of 1st Corps; 1st Inf Div is to relieve U.S. 45th Div. In VI Corps area, 36th Div pushes from Vesoul toward Luxeuil while 3d drives on Lure. 45th Div is virtually halted along line l'Isle-sur-Doubs–Villersexel.

POLAND—First White Russian Front troops, assisted by Polish forces, take Praga, suburb of Warsaw, but Germans are prepared for a stand along line of the Narew and Vistula Rivers.

YUGOSLAVIA—Br detachment with 25-pounders lands on Peljesac Peninsula and shells Trpanj, enemy withdrawal point.

ITALY—AAI: In U.S. Fifth Army area, II Corps continues to hammer Gothic Line defenses of Il Giogo Pass but is unable to break through. 338th Inf, 85th Div, makes costly efforts to take M. Altuzzo, elements temporarily gaining hold on ridge to W of main Altuzzo ridge, later known as Peabody Peak (Capt Maurice E. Peabody, Jr., Co B commander). Enemy retains M. Veruca despite efforts of 339th Inf to clear it. 91st Div's 363d Inf is again halted short of enemy's MLR on Monticelli; reserve regt, 361st, is committed through left flank of 363d in effort to outflank enemy; 362d Inf takes M. Calvi. In Br 13 Corps area, 1st Div continues attacks on Prefetto Hill. Ind 8th Div gains crest of Alpe di Vitigliano.

In Br Eighth Army area, 10 Corps begins period of regrouping in order to release units to other sectors. 5 Corps and Cdn 1 Corps consolidate positions on S. Savino-Coriano ridge and push on to the Marano, which Cdn 1st Div of 1 Corps begins crossing.

CBI—In Kweilin, Gen Stilwell learns of Chiang Kai-shek's order for 3 Ch divs to be kept inside Kweilin to defend the city and prepares to ask for a more aggressive defense.

On Salween front, Chinese complete capture of Teng-chung, which was entered on 4 August. Since Teng-chung is lost and Chinese are vigorously resisting in Lung-ling, Japanese decide to halt their counteroffensive on Salween front.

15 September

WESTERN EUROPE—21 Army Group: In Cdn First Army's 2 Corps area, 4th Cdn Armd Div establishes bridgehead across Canal de Derivation near Balgerhoek.

[15 SEPTEMBER 1944]

12th Army Group: In U.S. Ninth Army's VIII Corps area, 2d and 29th Divs continue to make slow progress at Brest. 8th Div launches attack to clear Crozon Peninsula.

In U.S. First Army's XIX Corps area, CCB of 2d Armd Div crosses newly constructed bridge over the Albert S of Maastricht and finds that CCA has finished mopping up Maastricht island. CCB TF establishes small bridgehead across the De Geul NW of Meerssen under fire. In VII Corps area, 1st Div, less 16th Inf, has almost encircled Aachen; 16th Inf reaches Eilendorf and, fanning out from there, clears surrounding heights although enemy retains high ground near Verlautenheide village. With its left flank secured by 1st Div, 3d Armd Div heads E toward Eschweiler, battling second defense belt of West Wall, called Schill Line: CCA meets strong AT opposition near Geisberg Hill, an enemy strongpoint, and loses 6 tanks; with assistance of bn of 16th Inf, clears most of the West Wall fortifications in this area. TF Lovelady of CCB crosses the Vicht upon completion of bridge and with little difficulty achieves complete breakthrough of West Wall fortifications; driving through Mausbach toward Eschweiler, the force is stopped and pulls back to Mausbach with heavy losses in armor. TF Mills (Maj Herbert N. Mills), former TF King, of CCB, advances to vicinity of Stolberg but falls back behind TF Lovelady upon meeting tank-infantry force. 47th Inf, 9th Div, pushes through second band of West Wall defenses; 60th Inf attacks Hoefen-Alzen ridge from two directions, making no progress from Kalterherberg, but getting foothold on it N of Hoefen with elements that have driven through Monschau; 39th Inf battles strong Scharnhorst Line positions near Lammersdorf without making much headway. In V Corps area, 8th Inf goes into action on N flank of 4th Div but is unable to advance; 12th drives NE along Schnee Eifel highway, taking strongpoint at crossroads 655; dangerous gap exists between it and 22d Inf; 22d, ordered to take Brandscheid before continuing main drive, undergoes enemy counterattack near Hontheim and does not advance. 28th Div's 110th Inf, assisted by engineers who blow up roadblock, succeeds in taking key hill (Hill 553) near Kesfeld; 109th falls back a little under enemy attack and for the next two days tries in vain to drive through Roscheid. CCR, 5th Armd Div, drives through West Wall and to edge of Bettingen; attached bn of 112th Inf clears Biesdorf and moves on to Stockigt to protect SE flank.

In U.S. Third Army's XX Corps area, 90th Div begins attacks on German fortifications W of Metz, employing 357th Inf on left and 359th on right: 1st Bn, 357th, works forward to position from which to attack Kellermann works (called Fort Amanvillers by Americans) from N while 2d Bn, 359th, attacks toward Jeanne d'Arc forts, gaining some 200 yards. CCB, 7th Armd Div, and 10th Inf, 5th Div, CCB on right, expand Arnaville bridgehead in preparation for northward drive on Metz; Arry, Hill 396 NE of Arry, Lorry, Mardigny, and Vittonville are cleared. After this action, CCB halts until relieved by 2d Inf of 5th Div and reverts to parent div. Other elements of 7th Armd Div are concentrating in Arnaville bridgehead. In XII Corps area, TF Sebree (Gen Sebree, 35th Div ADC), consisting of troops from 134th Regt of 35th Div and 319th Regt of 80th Div, moves into Nancy from Toul without opposition. Germans, having assembled strong reinforcements, begin determined counterattack against Dieulouard bridgehead just before dawn after intense bombardment, recovering Atton and Ste Geneviève and thereby isolating Americans on Mousson Hill. Both sides suffer heavily during day's fighting. Advance elements of 317th Inf, 80th Div, are withdrawn from Mt. Toulon to strengthen bridgehead, and CCA, 4th Armd Div, is ordered to release 1st Bn, 318th Inf, for this purpose also. 35th Div and CCB, 4th Armd Div, reach positions on or across Marne-Rhine Canal SE of Nancy: enemy fire prevents 137th Inf from crossing the Meurthe at St Nicolas du Port, but 320th crosses Rhine-Marne Canal in Dombasle-Sommerviller area; CCB forces the canal at Crevic and Maixe, against strong opposition at latter. Elements of CCA, 4th Armd Div, are sent forward to attack enemy rear in Maixe area. XV Corps is mopping up W of the Moselle. 1st Bn of 314th Inf, 79th Div, maintains bridgehead E of the river opposite Charmes. Elements of CCB, Fr 2d Armd Div, cross at Châtel, night 15-16.

6th Army Group: Becomes operational at 0001 and assumes control of the AFHQ forces that are in France. At same time, operational control of 6th Army Group and its elements passes from AFHQ to SHAEF, a move previously agreed upon between Gen Eisenhower and Gen Wilson. Fr Army B acquires autonomy and is on a par with U.S. Seventh Army. Fr Army B regroups during next few days for drive eastward.

ITALY—AAI: In U.S. Fifth Army's IV Corps area, TF 45 occupies Viareggio. RCT 6, Brazilian Expeditionary Force (BEF), under command of Brig Gen Euclydes Zenobia da Costa, enters line, relieving 434th AAA Bn of 5-mile zone between coastal plain and Serchio valley. These are the first Brazilians to fight on European soil and the first echelon of Brazilian 1st Inf Div to arrive, the rest of the div coming later. S African 6th Armd Div continues battle for hills N of Prato, taking M. Moscoso. In II Corps area, 338th Inf of 85th Div gains ground on main Altuzzo ridge, as grinding battle continues, but is unable to break through to summit. 339th, to right, is still held up by strong opposition on M. Veruca. To left of 85th Div, 91st Div's 363d and 361st Regts cannot gain crest of M. Monticelli; continuing toward Futa Pass, 362d Inf makes limited progress up Highway 65 to positions near Montecarelli. 34th Div is still stalled near Torricella Hill on left but on right takes M. Frassino. In Br 13 Corps area, 1st Div completes capture of Poggio Prefetto. Ind 8th Div takes Le Scalette and M. Stelleto. 6th Armd Div gains hold on slopes of M. Peschiena.

Br Eighth Army drives quickly toward next delaying line, called Rimini Line, which extends from fortified S. Fortunato, guarding Highway 16 and Rimini, SW to Ceriano ridge. In 5 Corps area, Ind 4th Div clears left flank of corps as far as the Conca. Montescudo falls to 46th Div. 1st Armd Div crosses the Marano in Vecciano area on right flank of corps. Cdn 1 Corps advances steadily toward Rimini with Br 4th Div on left and Cdn 1st Div on right. While Br 4th Div clears S. Patrignano ridge, which dominates the Marano, Cdn 1st Div gets forward elements to S. Martino in M. l'Abate, commanded by S. Fortunato, where confused and bitter fighting ensues.

CBI—Gen Stilwell, arriving in Chungking from Kweilin, confers with Chiang Kai-shek, who proposes to withdraw the Salween forces unless Ch troops at Myitkyina attack toward Bhamo within a week. News of this is sent by Gen Stilwell to Gen Marshall, who is attending OCTAGON Conference, and results in alteration of strategy.

11 Army Group: In Br Fourteenth Army's 33 Corps area, Ind 5th Div, advancing down Tiddim road, establishes bridgehead across the Manipur near Tuitum. Crossing is facilitated by advance brig that has crossed earlier at Shuganu and has moved S.

MOROTAI—In preparation for landings on Morotai, Fifth Air Force planes from land bases and naval aircraft from fast and escort carriers of Third and Seventh Fleets complete program of neutralizing enemy bases within range of target, begun by land-based planes at beginning of September, with strikes on Halmahera, Batjan I. (S of Halmahera), and Celebes. Halmahera is also subjected to naval gunfire bombardment. Adm Barbey of VII Amphib Force heads naval forces as commander of attack force (TF 77). After 2 hours of preliminary naval shelling of Morotai, TF TRADEWIND (Gen Hall, CG XI Corps, ALAMO) begins landing on SW coast at 0830 without opposition. 155th and 167th Regts, 31st Div, land on beach at head of Gila Peninsula, while 124th Inf, 31st Div, lands on adjacent beach to S at W side of the peninsula. Forces from both beaches push inland about 2,000 yards to D Day objectives, taking Pitoe Drôme and clearing Gila Peninsula. Gen Persons, commander of 31st Div and TRADEWIND Assault Force, establishes CP ashore. Enemy opposition ashore is negligible, but extremely unfavorable conditions offshore hamper initial phase of landings.

PALAUS—After preparatory bombardment by Western Fire Support Group and aircraft from carriers, III (Mar) Amphib Corps (Gen Geiger) begins landing 1st Mar Div on SW shore of Peleliu I., about 0830, 1st Marines on left, 5th Marines in center, and 7th Marines on right. Japanese fire, at first light, increases as marines move inland and is particularly heavy on flanks. 5th Marines partially surrounds airfield and drives salient to center of it, well ahead of flanking forces. By end of day beachhead perimeter measures about 2,800 yards from N to S but is only 400-700 yards deep, except for salient in center. As a diversion for Peleliu landings, elements of Angaur Attack Group (Rear Adm William H. P. Blandy), standing offshore, feint landings at Babelthuap.

U.S.—JCS decide to invade central rather than S Philippines and advance target date for invasion of Leyte from 20 December to 20 October. Projected operations against Yap, Talaud, and Mindanao are canceled.

16 September

INTERNATIONAL CONFERENCES—Second Quebec Conference (OCTAGON) ends, British and American conferees having approved, for planning purposes, timing and direction of war to defeat Japan and considered the matter of occupying Germany upon its defeat. The Pacific war is to culminate in 1945 with invasion of Japan—Kyushu in October and Tokyo Plain (Honshu) in December.

WESTERN EUROPE—Hitler presents plan for Ardennes counteroffensive to his commanders.

21 Army Group: In Cdn First Army's 2 Corps area, Cdn 4th Armd Div works eastward toward Ghent-Terneuzen Canal from Balgerhoek bridgehead. Pol 1st Armd Div, on right flank of corps, makes limited progress northward toward Hulst.

In Br Second Army's 12 Corps area, 7th Armd Div relieves 53d Div at Antwerp. In 30 Corps area, 50th Div relieves Gds Armd Div at Escaut bridgehead. 43d Div concentrates NE of Diest.

12th Army Group: In U.S. Ninth Army area, 83d Div, screening former Third Army sector along the Loire, accepts surrender of German *Group Elster*, about 20,000 strong, which has been cut off by junction of Third and Seventh Armies. In VIII Corps area, 6th Armd Div (− CCB) is transferred to Third Army, 94th Div completing its relief and taking over its sector. Fort Montbarey falls to 29th Div, opening way to Brest proper from W: while 116th Inf advances toward Recouvrance, 175th drives into Brest via tunnel beneath stone wall, and 115th advances toward submarine pens. 2d Div continues to press in from N.

In U.S. First Army's XIX Corps area, TF Stokes (Lt Col William M. Stokes, Jr.), consisting of 99th Inf Bn, tank bn of 2d Armd Div, and supporting units, starts N across 9-mile gap that has developed between British and American forces because of diverging drives, crossing Willems Vaart Canal N of Maastricht. Meerssen bridgehead of CCB, 2d Armd Div, is under heavy fire; CCA crosses into 30th Div's bridgehead at Valkenburg, also under fire. 30th Div renews attack toward West Wall N of Aachen from De Geul bridgeheads with 119th Inf on left and 120th on right, elements of 120th reaching positions within 3 miles of German border. In VII Corps area, stubborn defense of Stolberg corridor nullifies corps' attacks. CCB, 3d Armd Div, tries in vain to clear Weissenberg Hill; CCA is unable to advance on N suburbs of Stolberg. To bridge 4-mile gap between the two combat commands, TF Hogan (Lt Col Samuel Hogan commanding small tank force and attached 1st Bn, 26th Inf) is formed and overruns Buesbach. 47th Inf, 9th Div, takes Vicht and Schevenhuette, the latter 10 miles inside Germany and the deepest penetration so far; 39th Inf continues to batter at West Wall near Lammersdorf and reduces strongpoint that has been delaying it for 3 days; 60th Inf, assisted by tanks, clears Hoefen on Hoefen-Alzen ridge. In V Corps area, 12th Inf of 4th Div makes fruitless and costly efforts to push NE for the next few days; 8th Inf enters center of line and drives down E slopes of the Schnee Eifel hampered more by terrain than enemy; 22d Inf is still unable to take Brandscheid but gains hill on outskirts, and elements of regt take important hill on Bleialf-Pruem highway about midway between Meisert and Sellerich. In 28th Div sector, 1st Bn of 110th Inf makes narrow penetration into West Wall, seizing lofty Losenseifen Hill as well as Spielmannsholz Hill, within a few thousand yards of objective, Uttfeld. 5th Armd Div (−), awaiting arrival of arty, remains in place on S flank of corps; 1st Bn of 112 Inf, moving through Stockem, secures small bridgehead across the Pruem at Wettlingen and holds it against strong counterattack; CCB crosses into Wallendorf bridgehead to expand it but can make little headway. At 2040, Gen Gerow, CG V Corps, halts offensive, since operations are too costly to pursue at this time.

In U.S. Third Army's XX Corps area, limited objective attacks of 90th Div W of Metz are costly and almost fruitless. CCR, 7th Armd Div, begins attack to break out of Arnaville bridgehead along Lorry-Sillegny road but is soon stopped; CCB crosses into the bridgehead early in morning and joins in attack at 1400, pushing toward Marieulles. 5th Div regroups within the bridgehead: 2d Inf relieves CCB on right flank and CCB moves to Vittonville; 11th Inf crosses another bn into bridgehead and defends N flank; 10th Inf, in center, patrols toward Fey. Hitler, revoking a previous order, calls for reinforcement of Metz salient in order to prevent encirclement of Metz. In XII Corps area, 80th Div, assisted by air and arty, decisively defeats another major counterattack against Dieulouard bridgehead; 1st Bn, 318th Inf, returning to bridgehead from E, surprises enemy and captures Ste Geneviève; 319th Inf moves into bridgehead, and its 1st Bn recovers Atton and reaches isolated troops on Mousson Hill. Retreating Germans are pursued as far as Lesménils. After this action, 80th Div mops up and reorganizes for drive to E. In Nancy sector, 35th Div's 134th Inf pushes NE of Nancy to heights N of Essey-lès-Nancy; 137th forces Meurthe R and Rhine-Marne Canal and drives to within 2 miles of Nancy; 320th, to which 2d Bn reverts from attachment to CCB of 4th Armd Div, takes Buissoncourt. Germans withdraw from Lunéville as CCR, 4th Armd Div, moves into NW part of the city and 42d Sq of 2d Cav Gp enters from SE. In XV Corps area, additional elements of 106th Cav Gp cross the Moselle and begin to reconnoiter eastward toward Mortagne R. Fr 2d Armd Div's CCV Moselle bridgehead at Châtel undergoes determined counterattack by strong armored force; enemy is checked after reinforcements are moved up to the French. In order to avoid a major engagement, French withdraw the bridgehead.

6th Army Group: In U.S. Seventh Army's VI Corps area, 36th Div takes Luxeuil and 3d Div takes Lure against light opposition.

ESTONIA-LATVIA—Soviet forces of Leningrad and Baltic Fronts open offensive about this time toward Baltic Sea, pressing toward Tallinn, Valga, and Riga.

BULGARIA—Soviet forces of Third Ukrainian Front, pushing W to block enemy withdrawal from Yugoslavia, enter Sofia, capital of Bulgaria.

GREECE—Br 9th Commandos lands without opposition on Kithira I., off S coast of Peloponnesus, to reconnoiter in preparation for landing of Force 140. Advance Coastal Forces Base is established on Kithira.

ITALY—AAI: In U.S. Fifth Army's IV Corps area, while TF 45 regroups, RCT 6 of BEF seizes Massarosa, N of Lake Massaciuccioli, and takes over that portion of 1st Armd Div front previously held by 2d Bn, 370th Inf. 1st Armd Div is ordered to begin rcn in force to block enemy withdrawal. Enemy continues to put up strong apposition on right flank of corps, but S African 6th Armd Div gains Alto Hill and M. Pozzo del Bagno. In II Corps area, 338th Inf of 85th Div reaches positions near crest of M. Altuzzo, night 16-17, where it is delayed by friendly shelling; 339th Inf is committed on extreme right, passing through elements of Br 13 Corps on slopes of M. Pratone. 91st Div's 363d and 361st Regts are unable to break through enemy defenses on Monticelli, W of Il Giogo Pass; 362d Inf continues costly efforts to reach Futa Pass, elements reaching AT ditch below S. Lucia. 34th Div advances N from M. Frassino on right but is still held up on left in vicinity of Torricella Hill.

Br Eighth Army issues instructions for pursuit beyond Rimini Line, 5 Corps along Highway 9 toward Bologna and Cdn 1 Corps along Highway 16 toward Ravenna and Ferrara. Forward progress is sharply checked as 5 Corps and Cdn 1 Corps reach enemy's Rimini Line. In 5 Corps area, 46th Div is unable to advance from Montescudo. 56th Div joins 1st Armd Div in battle for Mulazzano-La Tomba ridge N of the Marano. During night 16-17, Br 4th Div of Cdn 1 Corps crosses into corps zone and by artificial moonlight provided by searchlights clears Cerasolo ridge. In Cdn 1 Corps area, Cdn. 1st Div attempts in vain to drive enemy from S. Martino on M. (Abate; on right flank, attached Greek 3d Mtn Brig begins struggle to clear Rimini airfield.

CBI—At conference between Gens Hurley, Sultan, and Stilwell and T. V. Soong, role of a field commander is discussed. Gen Stilwell finds that his conception is greatly different from that Soong believes Chiang Kai-shek holds. President Roosevelt, in message to Chiang Kai-shek, protests the proposed withdrawal of Y-Force across the Salween. Gen Stilwell reports to JCS and others that Japanese successes against U.S. Fourteenth Air Force bases in China might prevent air support from China of operations against Formosa and the Philippines. This influences planners in favor of occupation of Luzon rather than Formosa.

MOROTAI—31st Div expands perimeter of beachhead around Pitoe Drome to distance of over 7,000 yards, E to W, and about 5,000 yards N to S. Gen Hall establishes CP ashore. RCT 125 of 32d Div, reserve force, lands and relieves elements of 124th Inf still on Gila Peninsula. Enemy begins series of small and largely ineffective air raids.

PALAUS—5th Marines, assisted by 1st Marines to left, takes most of Peleliu airfield against heavy fire from heights to N, while 7th Marines clears S tip of island except for 2 small promontories. Perimeter is extended to over 3,000 yards in length, N to S, and to maximum depth of about 2,000 yards. Gen Rupertus, 1st Mar Div CG, takes command ashore. Orders are issued to land on Angaur on 17 September.

17 September

WESTERN EUROPE—21 Army Group: In Cdn First Army's 2 Corps area, Cdn 3d Div, with strong air and arty support, begins 6-day battle for Boulogne, making slow progress against strong fortifications. Br I Corps, taking over in Antwerp sector from Br Second Army, immediately starts to clear the Schelde Estuary in order to open port of Antwerp. Cdn 2d Div, upon relief at Dunkerque by 4th Special Service Brig, moves to Antwerp where it relieves 12 Corps of task of clearing dock area N of the city. 49th Div is disposed on right flank of corps. 51st Div has been left behind at Le Havre so that its transport may be used by other units.

In Br Second Army's Br 1 A/B Corps area, First Allied Airborne Army drops 1 A/B Corps, consisting of Br 1st A/B Div (with Pol Para Brig) and U.S. 82d and 101st A/B Divs, in Holland to secure axis of advance toward Zuider Zee for Br Second Army. The airborne operation (MARKET), undertaken in daylight, H Hour being 1300, with strong air support and cover, achieves tactical surprise and at first evokes little opposition. This is the largest Allied airborne operation to be mounted thus far. Approximately 20,000 troops land from aircraft and gliders. Losses in transport planes and gliders are only 2.8%. Br 1st A/B Div, with task of seizing 3 bridges over the Neder Rijn (Lower Rhine) at Arnhem, drops as planned some 8 miles from the bridges, giving enemy valuable time, however, to move forward panzer troops already assembled near Arnhem. Small force of less than a bn from the A/B div succeeds in taking N end of highway bridge and is then isolated; Germans destroy the other 2 bridges. U.S. 82d A/B Div, charged with seizing bridges and commanding ground in Nijmegen-Grave region, takes Maas bridge at Grave and Maas-Waal Canal bridge at Heumen, as well as commanding ground of Nijmegen-Groesbeek ridge; thrusts into Nijmegen, narrowly missing chance to take the highway bridge there before Germans reinforcements arrive. To U.S. 101st A/B Div is assigned task of capturing bridges at Veghel and Son, N of Eindhoven. Veghel bridges are taken with little difficulty but enemy blows that at Son just as paratroops are approaching it. Footbridge is improvised at Son over which paratroops cross to drive toward Eindhoven. 30 Corps, spearheading assault northward by ground forces (GARDEN), attacks from Meuse-Escaut Canal bridgehead toward Eindhoven with Cads Armd Div in the lead during afternoon; despite narrow zone of attack, which is confined almost to the highway by terrain, reaches Valkenswaard. On flanks of corps, 8 and 12 Corps prepare for further crossings of Meuse-Escaut Canal, 12 Corps starting across near Lommel, night 17-18.

[17 SEPTEMBER 1944]

12th Army Group: In U.S. Ninth Army's VIII Corps area, continuing battle for Brest, 29th Div clears eastward to Penfeld R while 2d Div, to right, gets elements across old city wall. 8th Div, clearing Crozon Peninsula, reaches town of Crozon.

In U.S. First Arms XIX Corps area, 2d Armd Div expands bridgeheads at Meerssen and Valkenburg, forcing enemy back toward Sittard. 30th Div takes Heerlen on left and crosses German border E of Simpelveld on R. In VII Corps area, Germans, having moved up a fresh div, make determined counterattacks against corps. 76th Inf of 1st Div and CCA of 3d Armd Div, forewarned by heavy arty barrage, turn enemy back and inflict heavy losses. CCB of 3d Armd Div takes Weissenberg Hill before being counterattacked so strongly that it falls back a little; TF Hogan is sent to its aid. Patrol of 47th Inf, 9th Div, spots Germans forming for attack in Gressenich and takes them under fire when they emerge into the open with devastating results to enemy. Corps activity after this subsides to limited actions, largely on S flank in zone of 9th Div. In V Corps area, 4th Div, after further costly efforts to get to E edge of the Schnee Eifel forest and to take Brandscheid, almost succeeding in each case, calls off offensive and passes to aggressive defense. 28th Div brings sharp reaction from enemy while attempting to advance its almost static line. 5th Armd Div withdraws its Pruem bridgehead at Wettlingen; CCR holds against determined tank-infantry counterattack aimed at eliminating its Wallendorf salient.

In U.S. Third Army's XX Corps area, Gen Walker issues tentative plan for air-ground offensive in Metz area, Operation THUNDERBOLT. 90th Div continues limited attacks W of Metz against increasingly strong resistance. Since the price is exceedingly high and gains minute, it is decided to halt attacks in this sector. Germans counterattack between 10th and 11th Regts of 5th Div in Arnaville bridgehead but are driven off; Hill 245, E of Marieulles, falls to 2d Inf. CCA, 7th Armd Div, assisted by elements of CCB, takes Marieulles; upon relief there by 5th Div is withdrawn to reserve; CCR and CCB are ordered to continue attack toward Seille R. XII Corps forms TF under Gen Sebree of 35th Div, consisting of CCB, 6th Armd Div—which has not yet arrived in corps zone—and 734th Inf, to clear Bois de Faulx and Bois de la Rumont in conjunction with 80th Div. TF Sebree, without awaiting CCB, begins attack to clear enemy from plateau NE of Nancy late in day. 80th Div is laboriously clearing bridgehead area and preparing for future offensive. 4th Armd Div is to regroup for attack NE toward Rhine R and Darmstadt, this city replacing Mannheim as corps objective. CCB of 4th Armd Div, attacking toward Nomeny to assist 80th Div in breaking out of bridgehead, makes such slow progress that it is ordered to halt. On S flank of corps, enemy is infiltrating into Lunéville, which, however, remains in American hands. In XV Corps area, cavalry of Fr 2d Armd Div makes contact with Fr 2d Corps of Seventh Army while patrolling near Bains-les-Bains, SW of Epinal. With arrival of CCB, 6th Armd Div, which relieves CCD in Chaumont area, XV Corps' flank protection mission is limited to region between the Meuse and the Moselle. Fr 2d Armd Div, less CCL and cavalry, closes along W bank of the Moselle to S of 79th Div.

6th Army Group: In U.S. Seventh Army's VI Corps area, 36th and 3d Divs are pushing northward toward the Moselle at Remiremont against delaying opposition. 45th Div awaits relief by French on right flank of corps.

ITALY—AAI: In U.S. Fifth Army area, IV Corps begins general advance on W flank of army. TF 45 drives along coast against light opposition. RCT 6, BEF, tries to keep pace with TF 45. 1st Armd Div pushes northward, CCA astride the Serchio N of Lucca and CCB toward M. Liguana from positions N of Pescia. S African 6th Armd Div is still held to small gains on right flank of corps. II Corps succeeds in breaking through Gothic Line at Il Giogo Pass. 338th Inf, 85th Div, at last takes M. Altuzzo, 339th finishes clearing M. Veruca, and 337th takes M. Pratone. W of Il Giogo Pass, 91st Div drives to crest of M. Monticelli. Germans begin withdrawal from Gothic Line under cover of darkness, 17-18. 362d Inf, 91st Div, retains positions on M. Calvi and near S. Lucia and attacks with 1st Bn to outskirts of Marcoiano. 34th Div, on left flank of corps, is still stalemated in Torricella Hill area, but gains a little N of M. Frassino. In Br 13 Corps area, 1st Div finds M. Giuvigiana free of enemy. 6th Armd Div continues to battle stubborn enemy on M. Peschiena.

In Br Eighth Army's 5 Corps area, 46th Div begins attack across the Marano W of Vallecchia, enemy having withdrawn from positions near Montescudo. 56th Div gains ground W of Cerasolo but is held up all day in M. Oliva area to SW. On Cdn 1 Corps' left flank, Br 4th Div presses toward S. Fortunato feature, target for powerful Allied air attacks, but Cdn 1st Div is still unable to clear S. Martino in M. l'Abate.

BURMA—11 Army Group: In Br Fourteenth Army's 33 Corps area, Tuitum falls to Ind 5th Div.

MOROTAI—Action of TF TRADEWIND subsides to patrolling in order to locate small Japanese parties. Islands off SW and W coast are being outposted by 126th Inf.

PALAUS—Against strong resistance, 1st Marines on Peleliu begins clearing S end of central ridge system on W arm of island; elements start up West and East Roads, which skirt the ridges. 5th Marines pushes E to clear E arm of island, meeting scattered opposition. 7th Marines begins to clear the small promontories on S tip of island. At Angaur, naval and air bombardment precede III (Mar) Amphib Corps' landing, which takes place about 0830 on 2 beaches on E coast. Against light, ineffective fire from mortars and small arms, 322d Inf of 81st Div, from northern beach, pushes to positions generally along second phase line from N coast above Lake Aztec southward along E shore of the lake. 321st secures beachhead from Cape Ngariois on N to Rocky Pt on S, extending inland some 350 yards to first phase line. RCT 323 (corps reserve) feints landing off Angaur's W shore. Enemy counterattacks at night cause little damage and cost enemy heavily.

18 September

WESTERN EUROPE—21 Army Group: In Br Second Army's 1 A/B Corps area, in Holland, First Allied Airborne Army drops second echelon of troops and supplies. Heavy fighting occurs in Arnhem area, where Allied reinforcements are late in arriving and Germans are counterattacking vigorously. Efforts to relieve the small force at N end of Arnhem bridge fail. U.S. 82d A/B Div takes bridge over Maas–Waal Canal near Honinghutie, on main Grave–Nijmegen highway, but is unable to reach Nijmegen highway bridge and withdraws from the town, except for small besieged force. No attempt has been made to take Nijmegen RR bridge, although it is still lightly held. German counterattack is thrown back as landing zones between Groesbeek and the Reichswald are being cleared. U.S. 101st A/B Div, working S, clears Eindhoven and makes contact with Gds Armd Div moving N; attempts by elements of the div to take bridge over Wilhelmina Canal SE of Best fail, and Germans blow the bridge. Div is attached to Br 30 Corps. In 30 Corps area, Gds Armd Div, driving on through Eindhoven, reaches Wilhelmina Canal near Son; elements are clearing flanks. 12 Corps strengthens bridgeheads across Meuse–Escaut Canal near Gheel and Lommel. In 8 Corps area, 3d Div secures small bridgehead near Lille St Hubert, night 18–19.

12th Army Group: In U.S. Ninth Army's VIII Corps area, organized resistance in Brest comes to an end, but the German fortress commander escapes to Crozon Peninsula.

In U.S. First Army's XIX Corps area, Gen Corlett orders corps to prepare to attack West Wall. 2d Armd Div breaks through to Sittard. 30th Div, committing 117th Inf on left flank, makes steady progress; 119th Inf reaches positions commanding Wurm R. VII Corps, for rest of month, makes only limited attacks since its positions are insecure. 3d Armd Div fights hard for heights along the Vicht near Stolberg; CCA is endeavoring to clear high ground around Muensterbusch, W of Stolberg; CCB continues efforts to gain Weissenberg Hill. On N flank of 9th Div, 47th Inf is repelling light enemy jabs toward Schevenhuette; 39th Inf attempts to expand its positions in Lammersdorf corridor, spending rest of month in efforts to take Hill 554, SE of Lammersdorf, and a plateau between Lammersdorf and Rollesbroich; 60th Inf completes capture of Hoefen–Alzen ridge SE of Monschau. V Corps passes to command of Maj Gen Edward H. Brooks, former commander of 2d Armd Div. Gen Gerow is recalled to Washington temporarily. Corps is conducting local operations and virtual stalemate exists.

In U.S. Third Army's XX Corps area, 5th Inf and 7th Armd Divs drive toward Seille R. On left, 5th Div's 10th Inf reaches positions just short of Pournoy-la-Chétive, while its 2d Inf pushes almost to Coin-sur-Seille. CCR, 7th Armd Div, drives to edge of Sillegny against intense fire; CCB, directed toward Longueville-lès-Cheminot, is stopped by fire from Hill 223, but patrols occupy Bouxières-sous-Froidmont without opposition. In XII Corps area, 80th Div struggles to improve and expand its Dieulouard bridgehead, meeting stiff resistance in center and on right. TF Sebree, clearing region NE of Nancy, takes Pain de Sucre. 4th Armd Div is ordered to attack on 19th, CCB toward Saarbruecken and CCA toward Sarreguemines; CCB reaches Fresnes-en-Saulnois area, W of Château-Salins. On S flank of corps, Germans launch long-planned counteroffensive against Third Army, attacking toward Lunéville. 2d Cav Gp outposts fall back through the city, but CCR of 4th Armd Div, assisted by TF from CCA, stems the onslaughts and forces enemy southward; Germans withdraw to Parroy after nightfall, and as a result of this action, CCB of 6th Armd Div is ordered to Lunéville to relieve CCR; CCA, 4th Armd Div, is directed to remain in place until situation stabilizes. XV Corps is ordered to cross the Moselle at once and drive NE to Mortagne R. Crossings are begun in force during afternoon. 79th Div crosses unopposed: 314th Inf drives to Moriviller, 313th moves by truck to Ein-vaux, and 315th, in reserve, follows 313th across, night 18–19. CCD, Fr 2d Armd Div, crosses at Châtel and clears that town; CCV protects bridgehead; CCL provides flank protection W of the Moselle.

6th Army Group: In U.S. Seventh Army area, VI Corps suspends offensive operations more than 15 miles from the Moselle while regrouping is in progress. 1st Div, Fr 2d Corps, is relieving 45th Div.

POLAND—U.S. Eighth Air Force, having gained Soviet approval, flies supplies to Warsaw in response to numerous appeals. Only a small portion reaches Polish hands. This is the only U.S. mission of its kind, since Stalin refuses later requests for another.

ITALY—AAI: In U.S. Fifth Army's IV Corps area, TF 45 is approaching Pietrasanta in coastal sector. RCT 6, BEF, reaches Camaiore. CCB, 1st Armd Div, gains its objectives, Castelvecchio and M. Liguana; CCA is delayed in Ponte a Moriano area by strong opposition. S African 6th Armd Div continues to meet determined opposition above Pistoia on right flank of corps, and gap is developing between it and II Corps. II Corps, having decisively defeated enemy at Il Giogo Pass, widens breach in Gothic Line to 7 miles on either side of the pass and pushes on toward Santerno R valley. 91st Div finishes clearing M. Monticelli and reduces W defenses of Il Giogo Pass; in Futa Pass area, 362d Inf breaks enemy hold on M. Calvi but is stubbornly opposed in Marcoiano region. Enemy continues effective defense of Torricella Hill and positions N of M. Frassino in 34th Div sector. In Br 13 Corps area, Ind 8th Div takes Femmina Morta feature. 6th Armd Div, still engaged with enemy on M. Peschiena, releases 1st Gds Brig to Br 10 Corps.

Br Eighth Army opens assault on main positions of Rimini Line (S. Marino–La Torraccia–Ceriano–S. Fortunato), initially employing infantry and holding armor back for pursuit. Enemy counters strongly at all points. In 5 Corps area, Ind 4th Div pushes slowly from Faetano toward S. Marino. 46th Div, directed toward the Ausa at Serravalle, is clearing heights S of the Ausa. Assault force of 56th Div crosses the Ausa and begins attack on Ceriano ridge, making such slow progress that 1st Armd Div is ordered to cross the Ausa in force to right of 56th Div as soon as armor of 56th has crossed. In Cdn 1 corps area, Br 4th Div establishes bridgehead across the Ausa on left flank of corps. 1st Div begins assault on S. Fortunato feature.

CBI—Gen Stilwell presents plan to Chiang Kai-shek for making the best use of Ch troops defending E China.

MOROTAI—Site for bomber field is chosen at Gotalalamo village, on S coast E of Gila Peninsula, since Pitoe airfield is found to be suitable only for fighters.

PALAUS—On Peleliu, 7th Marines finishes clearing S promontories and joins with 1st Marines in assault to clear ridges of W arm. Japanese resist strongly from cluster of peaks in central ridge system and little progress is made. On Angaur, Maj Gen Paul J. Mueller, 81st Div CG, takes command ashore. Some elements of 322d Inf, 81st Div, drive salient W to phosphate plant near W coast at center of island, although mistakenly bombed by friendly planes. Others, probing along N coast between second and third phase lines, are partially isolated. 321st Inf makes slow progress inland along Southern RR and tries in vain to gain Green Beach on left, about 600 yards below Rocky Point.

19 September

WESTERN EUROPE—21 Army Group: In Cdn First Army's 2 Corps area, 4th Armd Div is clearing region W of Ghent-Terneuzen Canal and S of Leopold Canal on W flank of corps. Pol armor secures bridgehead across Canal de Hulst.

In Br Second Army area, poor weather conditions sharply curtail airlift and support of ground forces. In 1 A/B Corps area, situation in Arnhem sector grows worse: enemy constricts Br perimeter W of the town, the small force at N end of the bridge is still isolated, weather conditions prevent scheduled drop of Pol 1st Para Brig, and food and ammunition resupply falls into enemy hands. Gds Armd Div of 30 Corps, upon making contact with U.S. 82d A/B Div at Grave, joins with Americans in effort to take bridges at Nijmegen in order that advance to Arnhem can go on. Simultaneous attacks on the rail and highway bridges are halted by enemy a little short of objectives. 82d A/B Div repels light probing attacks against Nijmegen-Groesbeek ridgeline and gains firm control of Cleve-Nijmegen highway. In 30 Corps area, Gds Armd Div is engaging enemy at Nijmegen. U.S. 101st A/B Div maintains defensive positions at Eindhoven, Son, St Oedenrode, and Veghel, turning back determined counterattack toward Son. Enemy resistance near Best collapses, but the village itself remains in German hands. Enemy bombers, about 100 strong, attack Eindhoven after nightfall, inflicting heavy casualties on civilians and Br troops within the town but none on Americans stationed outside. This is the only time during fall of 1944 that long-range enemy bombers attack on large scale in the West. In 12 Corps area, 53d Div, attacking from Lommel bridgehead, reaches Eindhoven-Turnhout road near Cuizel; elements take Veldhoven and make contact with 50th Div at Mereveldhoven. In 8 Corps area, 11th Armd Div pushes northward to Leende and patrols to Heeze from 3d Div's bridgehead.

12th Army Group: In U.S. Ninth Army area, VIII Corps successfully concludes Brittany campaign as 8th Div finishes clearing Crozon Peninsula and captures Maj Gen Hermann Bernhard Ramcke, fortress commander of Brest.

In U.S. First Army's XIX Corps area, TF Stokes reaches interarmy boundary, where 99th Inf Bn remains as defense force; rest of TF reverts to parent unit. 2d Armd Div drives through Gangelt toward Geilenkirchen, forcing salient between two German armies, but enemy restores contact during counterattacks. Corps faces West Wall and prepares to attack it on 20th. In VII Corps area, CCA of 3d Armd Div gains lower slopes of Muensterbusch ridge with attached bn of 16th Inf, 1st Div; CCB and TF Hogan continue futile efforts to take Weissenberg Hill. 47th Inf, 9th Div, remains under light enemy attacks at Schevenhuette; 39th Inf, in Lammersdorf corridor, pushes more than a miles toward Rollesbroich, where it is contained by enemy, but continues to fight indecisively for Hill 554. In V Corps area, 1st Bn of 12th Inf, 4th Div, falls back a little under counterattack SW along Schnee Eifel highway; later regains former positions and some ground beyond. Germans also counterattack flanks of 5th Armd Div's Wallendorf bridgehead, but IX TAC planes go into action and force enemy back in disorder. Nevertheless, it is decided to reduce bridgehead perimeter. CCB of 5th Armd Div and a fresh bn of 112th Inf, 28th Div, are to relieve CCR and the original bn of 112th in the reduced perimeter.

In U.S. Third Army's XX Corps area, CCR of 7th Armd Div, after hard fighting at edge of Sillegny, enters and finds the town vacated by enemy, but is forced out again by extremely heavy fire and enemy counterattack; CCB drives into Seille loop and takes Longueville but is unable to take Cheminot, from which its positions are threatened. Massing forces at Coin-sur-Seille, enemy columns move forward to counterattack but are checked by air and arty. 3d Cav Gp, reinf, is designated TF Polk and given mission of protecting Moselle R line between Grevenmacher and Thionville. Bn of 5th Div is alerted for attack on Fort Driant, but for various reasons the attack is postponed from day to day. In XII Corps area, 80th Div is continuing costly efforts to expand Dieulouard bridgehead. Furious enemy counterattack drives TF Sebree from Pain de Sucre, but enemy is driven back beyond Agincourt. 137th Inf, 35th Div, begins drive through Forêt de Champenoux toward Amance Hill, a key feature, but is stopped at Château-Salins–Nancy highway. CCA of 4th Armd Div, which is spread thin in Arracourt area and has elements at Lunéville, checks series of tank-infantry assaults aimed at Nancy. More than 40 enemy tanks are estimated to be knocked out in this action. German spearheads are blunted at Lézey, on ridge W of Bezange-la-Petite, and at Rethicourt-la-Petite. The force from Lunéville rejoins CCA to assist in mopping up. Meanwhile, CCB begins attack NE toward Saarbruecken, attempting to find suitable route of advance. CCB, 6th Armd Div, relieves CCR, 4th Armd Div, at Lunéville. XV Corps gets advance elements across Mortagne R. 313th Inf, now on left flank of 79th Div, crosses at Xermaménil, where rear-guard opposition is overcome; 314th reaches the river at Gerberville but calls off attack on the town after dark; Germans withdraw, night 19-20. CCD, Fr 2d Armd Div, crosses near Vallois and reconnoiters to the Meurthe at Vathiménil, which it captures. Germans order their thin line to withdraw behind the Meurthe during night since Mortagne line has been pierced at various points.

6th Army Group: Commanders conference is held at Lyon to plan for future operations. Fr Army B is renamed Fr 1st Army.

In U.S. Seventh Army's VI Corps area, 45th Div, whose relief by Fr 1st Div continues, prepares for drive to the Moselle at Epinal on left flank of corps.

FINLAND—Signs armistice with Allies in Moscow. Soviet-Finnish boundary of 1940 is restored, but Finland yields Petsamo to USSR and leases Porkkala headland to USSR as a military base. Russians yield rights to Hangoe. Reparations are to be paid by Finland, and Allies are to have the use of Finnish ships and airfields.

ESTONIA—Troops of Third Baltic Front overrun Valga, on Estonian-Latvian border. Other Soviet forces are approaching Tallinn and Riga.

ITALY—AAI: In U.S. Fifth Army's IV Corps area, 435th AAA Bn of TF 45 reaches Montrone on coast and 434th AAA Bn drives to Pietrasanta, NE of Montrone. In II Corps area, 34th Div is still checked on left flank of corps, but 91st and 85th Divs pursue enemy northward toward the Santerno, hampered more by lack of roads than by Germans.

In Br Eighth Army area, 10 Corps releases Ind 10th Div to Eighth Army. As regrouping ends, corps front is held by a hodge podge of small units, with Wheeler Force disposed on left flank, 1st Gds Brig of 6th Armd Div in center, and Lind Force and Household Cavalry on right. Activity must necessarily be confined to patrolling. 5 Corps continues to battle Rimini Line, meeting particularly stubborn opposition in vicinity of Ceriano, but 46th Div succeeds in breaching line during night 19-20 at Torraccia after crossing the Ausa at Serravalle. In Cdn 1 Corps area, Br 4th Div seizes Acqualina feature. 1st Div begins outflanking maneuver against S. Fortunato, night 19-20, and by dawn has this strongpoint surrounded.

CBI—Two messages arrive at CBI Theater hq, one from President Roosevelt and Prime Minister Churchill to Chiang Kai-shek about decisions of OCTAGON Conference and the other a personal message in plain terms from Roosevelt to the Generalissimo demanding action. Latter is delivered personally by Gen Stilwell and greatly angers Chiang Kai-shek.

[20 SEPTEMBER 1944]   [281]

MOROTAI—Work is begun on bomber strip, dubbed Wama Drome, at Gotalalamo. Pitoe Drome becomes known as Pitoe Crash Strip.

PALAUS—On Peleliu, enemy on peaks of central ridge continues to hold up 1st and 7th Marines; however, elements of 1st, advancing along East Road, push through Asias village. 5th Marines secures E arm of the island with little difficulty. On Angaur, 81st Div commits 321st Inf and 3d Bn of 322d to main effort of clearing S Angaur and splitting enemy forces there. Little opposition is met as assault forces establish line across S Angaur from Garangaoi Cove eastward, but some resistance is bypassed on SE coast. 322d Inf (−) starts N up W coast from vicinity of the phosphate plant.

20 September

WESTERN EUROPE—21 Army Group: In Cdn First Army's 2 Corps area, Pol armor overruns Hulst and Axel.

In Br Second Army's 1 A/B Corps area, situation of Br 1st A/B Div at Arnhem is critical. The small force holding N end of bridge is forced to surrender 300 wounded to Germans, reducing its strength to about 140; other elements of the div still hold perimeter near Oosterbeek, W of Arnhem, and N of Heaveadorp Ferry at the Neder Rijn SW of Oosterbeek, but enemy is steadily gaining ground. Weather conditions continue to prevent airlift of Pol 1st Brig. Br and U.S. troops take both bridges at Nijmegen in daring and costly maneuver. While elements of Gds Armd Div (30 Corps) and U.S. 82d A/B Div push through Nijmegen to S approaches, 2 bns of 504th Para Inf, 82d A/B Div, cross the wide, swift Waal in Br assault boats downstream after air and arty bombardment of N shore and ineffective efforts to put down smoke screen. Paratroops seize N end of RR bridge and push toward highway bridge. Meanwhile, resistance at S end of the rail bridge collapses and Br tanks from Gds Armd Div storm across the highway bridge, where they are joined by U.S. paratroopers. With capture of these vital bridges, advance is continued toward Arnhem. German counterattacks on N and S edges of Nijmegen–Groesbeek ridge are unsuccessful except where U.S. outposts at Wyler are forced back. In 30 Corps area, U.S. 101st A/B Div undergoes another counterattack at Son but with help of Br tanks forces enemy back. Div then begins series of limited actions designed to throw enemy off balance. 12 Corps presses slowly toward Best and Oirschot. 8 Corps, driving toward Helmond, takes Someren.

12th Army Group: In U.S. First Army's XIX Corps area, assault on West Wall is postponed because of unfavorable flying conditions. Other deterring factors are the very short supply of arty ammunition and exposed left flank of corps. In VII Corps area, enemy decides to go on the defensive instead of counterattacking as planned. CCA, 3d Armd Div, is methodically clearing Muensterbusch area; TF Hogan, moving forward stealthily, takes enemy on Weissenberg Hill by surprise and gains crest of this much fought over prize; TF Mills, CCB, secures positions on the Donnerberg, heights commanding Stolberg from E, under smoke screen but is hit hard by enemy when smoke disappears. 1st Bn of 39th Inf, 9th Div, attached to 60th Inf, drives E from Zweifall to Weisser Weh Creek, near village of Huertgen. Bn of 60th, to right, attempts to drive SE from Zweifall in order to cut Lammersdorf–Huertgen highway at Germeter but makes little headway. In V Corps area, IX TAC again assists corps in maintaining positions.

In U.S. Third Army area, boundary between XII and XV Corps is adjusted to give Forêt de Vitrimont, Lunéville, and Forêt de Parroy to XV Corps. In XX Corps area, 10th and 2d Regts, 5th Div, renew efforts to take Pournoy-la-Chétive and Coin-sur-Seille despite weather conditions unfavorable for air support and diminishing supply of arty ammunition; 2d Bn of 10th, reinf, seizes Pournoy-la-Chétive but is greatly disorganized in the process; 1st Bn of 2d Inf, against fire from Sillegny, overruns Coin-sur-Seille. CCA, 7th Armd Div, replaces badly mauled CCR in front of Sillegny and, together with CCB, attacks toward the Seille; bypassing Sillegny, CCA reaches the river, where it comes under heavy fire; CCB also reaches the river but falls back under fire. In XII Corps area, 80th Div elements push into Bois de la Rumont. Germans counterattack 134th Inf troops of 35th Div and recover Agincourt; 137th Inf attempts in vain to drive through Forêt de Champenoux to Amance plateau; arty ammunition supply runs out. CCA, 4th Armd Div, begins attack NE toward Sarreguemines but, upon reaching Hampont on left and Dieuze area on right, returns to Arracourt region because of another enemy tank attack, this time by only 8 tanks, all of which are knocked out. The area will be systematically mopped up before the offensive is continued. Small tank duels occur as CCA sweeps through Ley and Moncourt. CCB continues efforts to advance in Château-Salins area, where secondary routes are impassable. In XV Corps area, 313th Inf of 79th Div drives through Lunéville and turns SE in effort to outflank enemy's Meurthe R line; 314th reaches the Meurthe SE of Lunéville, where it comes under heavy fire. Fr 2d Armd Div patrols from current positions; CCL moves E to rejoin main body as 45th Div of Seventh Army draws up to the Moselle.

6th Army Group: Completes regrouping.

In U.S. Seventh Army's VI Corps area, Gen Truscott orders corps to cross the Moselle and seize communications centers in the Vosges to open way to Alsatian Plain and the Rhine. 45th Div, upon crossing the Moselle at Epinal, is to seize Rambervillers and Baccarat and force the Saverne Gap. 36th Div is to cross the Moselle in Eloyes area and take St Die near Saales Pass. 3d Div is to cross the Moselle in Rupt area and seize Gerardmer near Schlucht Pass. 36th Div begins rcn in force of proposed Moselle crossing site near Remiremont. Site near Eloyes is reported to be suitable, and 141st Inf moves forward to it, night 20-21. To left, 45th Div moves up to the Moselle in Remiremont area. On corps right flank, 3d Div is advancing toward the river.

Fr 1st Army now holds sector to the right of U.S. Seventh Army, 2d Corps taking up positions in new sector to left of 1st Corps.

ITALY—AAI: In U.S. Fifth Army's IV Corps area, RCT 6 of BEF gains positions on M. Prano but cannot reach crest. 1st Armd Div regroups in order to release CCA to II Corps: 370th Inf, whose 1st Bn relieves 14th Armd Inf Bn, takes command of CCA zone. S African 6th Armd Div extends its left flank to road NE of Pescia; reinforces right flank in M. Moscoso area. In II Corps area, 91st and 85th Divs continue to pursue enemy toward the Santerno. 337th Inf, 85th Div, crosses it E of Firenzuola at S. Pellegrino. 362d Inf, 91st Div, gets into position for assault on Futa Pass, 3d Bn pushing across AT ditch near S. Lucia. Corps' reserve div, 88th, is ordered to attack through right flank of 85th Div down Santerno valley toward Imola on 21st. In Br 13 Corps area, enemy withdrawal from Casaglia Pass permits 1st Div to push rapidly eastward toward Ind 8th Div.

In Br Eighth Army area, battle for Rimini Line ends as Germans withdraw, night 20-21, behind Marecchia R under cover of drenching rain. In 5 Corps area, S. Marino, in small independent Republic of San Marino, falls to Ind 4th Div. 46th Div holds La Torraccia against counterattacks. 1st Armd Div joins 56th Div in fight for Ceriano ridge, where enemy continues to resist tenaciously throughout day before withdrawing. In Cdn 1 Corps area, Cdn 1st Div battles encircled enemy at S. Fortunato, frustrating German efforts to break out.

CBI—Gen Stilwell learns that his plan for defense of Kweilin has been accepted by Chiang Kai-shek and issues orders accordingly.

MOROTAI—Beachhead perimeter has been expanded to provide space for additional airfield construction, extending about 1,000 yards N of original site and some 10,000 yards E along shore to Sabatai R.

PALAUS—On Peleliu, firm enemy defense of central ridge system on W arm virtually halts forward movement of 1st and 7th Marines. 1st Marines is so depleted in strength that 7th Marines relieves all its troops but those along West Road. 5th Marines is mopping up E arm. On Angaur, Gen Mueller declares organized resistance at an end as 321st Inf drives to S end of island and begins mopping up scattered Japanese. Japanese remaining on Angaur are concentrated in NW part of island and are prepared for prolonged defense of a broad, deep, bowl-shaped depression in Lake Salome area. 322d Inf tries to reach the bowl from different directions, but makes little headway. Airdrome construction is begun in S part of island.

21 September

WESTERN EUROPE—21 Army Group: In Br Second Army's 1 A/B Corps area, slightly improving weather conditions permit elements (750 men) of Pol 1st Brig to drop near Driel, S terminus of Heaveadorp Ferry in Arnhem area, but by this time Germans have recovered N end of the ferry, confined British to small perimeter at Hartestein, near Oosterbeek, and destroyed the small force at N end of Arnhem bridge as it attempted to escape in small groups. In 30 Corps area, Gds Armd Div, pushing toward Arnhem from Nijmegen, is brought to a halt less than 3 miles from starting point. U.S. 101st A/B Div finds highway between St Oedenrode and Veghel free of enemy, clears infiltrators from glider landing zone, and reconnoiters along secondary highway to Schijndel, which it occupies, night 21-22.

12th Army Group: In U.S. First Army's XIX Corps area, West Wall offensive is again postponed because of weather conditions. In VII Corps area, CCA of 3d Armd Div completes mop up of Muensterbusch area; in CCB's sector, TF Mills, leaving defense of Donnerberg to TF Lovelady, drives into town of Donnerberg, a suburb of Stolberg, gaining precarious foothold. On S flank of corps, 60th Inf, 9th Div, tries in vain to push into village of Huertgen and makes very slow progress toward Germeter. V Corps authorizes withdrawal of Wallendorf bridgehead. This is accomplished before dawn of 22d, using ford since Germans have destroyed Wallendorf bridges. IX TAC gives unusually effective air support.

In U.S. Third Army's XX Corps area, 83d Div is attached to corps. 7th Armd Div continues to meet intense fire from Seille R line; two cos of armd inf of CCB ford the river S and E of Longueville after dark but withdraw at daylight of 22d to await coordinated attack. 5th Div remains in place because of ammunition shortage; 2d Bn, 10th Inf, suffers heavily under continuous enemy fire and repeated counterattacks against Pournoy-la-Chétive. In XII Corps area, 80th Div continues battle for Bois de la Rumont, where 2 bns are isolated and must be supplied by tanks. 134th Inf, 35th Div, recovers Agincourt in bitter fighting; 137th is still held up in Forêt de Champenoux. CCB, 6th Armd Div, is attached to 35th Div to assist in attack on the Amance position. Moving N from Lunéville between 35th Inf and 4th Armd Divs, CCB assembles in Forêt de Grémecey. CCA, 4th Armd Div, continues sweeping its zone, taking Bures and Coincourt with ease and reaching canal to S. Corps prepares for concerted assault by 80th and 35th Divs and CCB of 6th Armd in order to bring XII Corps' center and left abreast 4th Armd Div's salient on right flank. In XV Corps area, 313th Inf of 79th Div, leaving bn at Lunéville where fighting continues in streets, drives SE along the Meurthe, clearing Moncel and halting under fire at edge of Fort de Mondon; 315th (−) moves into Lunéville and takes up defensive positions. Against heavy fire, 3d Bn of 314th crosses the Meurthe near St Clement but is unable to advance across open ground leading to Forêt de Mondon and withdraws after dark.

6th Army Group: In U.S. Seventh Army area, VI Corps begins crossing the Moselle. On left flank, 157th Inf (−) of 45th Div, having shuttled to Epinal area, begins crossing XV Corps' bridge at Châtel, night 21-22, and moves to Vaxoncourt; 3d Bn, with task of clearing Thaon before crossing, gets patrols into the town and wades the river near Igney. 179th Inf of 45th Div moves up to the river in Arches area; 180th, ordered to clear Epinal, works forward to heights overlooking the town. 36th Div, in center of corps, is first to secure crossing: 1st and 3d Bns, 141st Inf, ford the river at Eloyes while 2d Bn clears Eloyes as far as the river bank; 143d follows 141st across to clear rest of Eloyes and exploit bridgehead, taking Hill 783 overlooking the town; 142d is moving on Remiremont against firm opposition and penetrates into W part of town. Enemy is delaying advance of 3d Div toward the Moselle.

In Fr 1st Army area, the 2d Corps, which has been reinf for coming offensive, is moving forward to gain contact with enemy.

ITALY—AAI: In U.S. Fifth Army's IV Corps area, TF 45 extends positions along coast to Forte dei Marmi. RCT 6, BEF, tries unsuccessfully to take M. Prano. Reorganized CCA, 1st Armd Div, starts to II Corps zone. Left flank elements of S African 6th Armd Div reach Serra. In II Corps area, 338th Inf of 85th Div seizes Firenzuola; 339th takes M. Frena and M. Coloreta; 337th is withdrawn to reserve. 91st Div, to W, gets advance elements of 361st and 363d Regts to the Santerno; 362d, against rear-guard opposition, clears S. Lucia and M. Gazzaro and enters Futa Pass, but enemy retains hill dominating it to W. On left flank of corps, 133d Inf of 34th Div at last clears Torricella Hill; 168th is withdrawn from reserve and enters line between 133d and 135th Regts. On right flank of corps, 88th Div is committed through right flank of 85th Div and, with 349th Inf on left and 350th on right, starts quickly down Santerno valley toward Imola. In Br 13 Corps area, 1st Div is half way between Crespino and Marradi. 6th Armd Div takes M. Peschiena.

Br Eighth Army pursues retreating enemy toward the Marecchia. 5 Corps finds Ceriano ridge abandoned and gets patrols to the river before dawn of 22d. Strength of 1st Armd Div and 56th Div is so badly depleted that the divs must be reorganized. 56th Div is ordered to withdraw from line on 22d. In Cdn 1 Corps area, Br 4th Div gets patrols across the Marecchia, night 21-22. Cdn 1st Div mops up the S. Fortunato position and establishes bridgehead across the Marecchia W of Rimini; attached Greek 3d Mtn Brig, having cleared airfield S of Rimini, enters the coastal city, from which enemy has withdrawn.

SWPA—Gen MacArthur radios U.S. Chiefs of Staff that he can mount a major assault on Luzon about 20 December as result of acceleration of the Leyte invasion; suggests that the Formosa operation may be unnecessary if Luzon is occupied.

MOROTAI—Radar is established on Raoe I., off W coast.

PALAUS—On Peleliu, progress of 1st Mar Div against central ridges is still negligible. On Angaur, elements of 322d Inf break into Lake Salome bowl on NW Angaur but pull back for night since their positions are untenable. Attack is preceded by heavy volume of arty fire and bombardment of the position by naval planes. 321st Inf is alerted for movement to Peleliu so that 1st Marines can be withdrawn from there. 322d Inf thus becomes responsible for S Angaur as well as the stubborn pocket on NE end.

RCT 323, III Amphib Corps reserve, leaves the Palaus for Ulithi.

22 September

WESTERN EUROPE—Gen Eisenhower, conferring with his top commanders at Versailles, gives top priority to the opening of the Schelde approaches to Antwerp, since a deep-water port is needed in order to sustain main Allied offensive of enveloping the Ruhr from the N. Offensive is to be conducted by 21 Army Group, assisted by U.S. First Army. Boundary between 21 and 12th Army Groups is adjusted, effective on 25th, to extend NE from Hasselt through Bree, Weert, Deurne, and Venray (all to 12th Army Group) to the Maas at Maashees and along the river to original boundary

N of Maastricht. This boundary change gives XIX Corps of U.S. First Army a corridor W of the Maas that contains more than 500 square miles and includes the extensive swampland of the Peel Marshes. To secure this corridor, XIX Corps is to have 2 new divs, 29th Div from Brest and 7th Armd Div from Moselle R sector near Metz. Since supply requirements of the Ruhr offensive are to be met fully first, Third Army is to limit its action to that permitted by the supply situation.

21 Army Group: In Cdn First Army's 2 Corps area, 3d Div receives surrender of Boulogne garrison. 4th Armd Div has cleared as far N as Leopold Canal and on right flank has reached Schelde Estuary. With capture of Terneuzen by Pol armor, enemy is confined to "Breskens Pocket," region N of Leopold Canal and W of Savojaards Plaat.

In Br Second Army's 1 A/B Corps area, Br 1st A/B Div is still isolated and under heavy pressure N of the Neder Rijn near Arnhem. Air resupply is impossible because of weather conditions. Elements of 30 Corps make contact with the Pol detachment at Driel and bring DUKW's loaded with ammunition and supplies for 1st A/B Div. Mud is too deep for the DUKW's, but group of Poles succeeds in crossing supplies on rafts, night 22–23. U.S. 82d A/B Div clears S bank of the Waal 3 miles E of highway bridge. In 30 Corps area, 43d Div, taking over attack toward Arnhem from Gds Armd Div, gets elements to Driel, but main body is held up far to S by determined opposition. Germans make major counterattack against Veghel, main effort coming through village of Erp. U.S. 101st A/B Div, to whom reinforcements are rushed, forces enemy back from Veghel, but Germans cut highway between there and Uden. 12 Corps is slowly improving positions W of Eindhoven. 8 Corps, continuing toward Helmond, takes Weert.

12th Army Group: U.S. First Army goes on the defensive along most of its line. XIX Corps postpones offensive against West Wall indefinitely. In VII Corps area, CCB of 3d Armd Div, under smoke screen, withdraws both TF Lovelady and TF Mills from Donnerberg area to Stolberg, where TF Hogan has cleared enemy from S part of town; CCB then goes on the defensive and makes contact with CCA at Muensterbusch; the div comes to a halt within 3 miles of its objective, Eschweiler. Germans make all-out counterattack against 47th Inf, 9th Div, at Schevenhuette but are driven back with extremely heavy losses; 60th Inf breaks off attack for Huertgen village in order to send reinforcements to Schevenhuette; these are not required there but later attack to ease pressure on the single 60th Inf bn in Huertgen Forest, where close, indecisive fighting rages for next 3 days. V Corps remains on the defensive.

In U.S. Third Army's XX Corps area, enemy evacuates Cheminot, since it has become an untenable pocket between XX and XII Corps. 7th Armd Div prepares to attack across the Seille on 23d. 2d bn of 10th Inf, 5th Div, withstands further enemy attacks against Pournoy-la-Chétive, this time from SE of the town. In XII Corps area, elements of 80th Div continue to fight in Bois de la Rumont. CCB, 6th Armd Div, circling W and S from Forêt de Grémecey to take enemy in Amance area from rear, clears strongly occupied Armaucourt. 134th Inf, 35th Div, attacks into Bois de Faulx at noon; 137th pushes through rest of Fort de Champenoux, from which enemy flees under air and arty attack, abandoning Amance plateau. 6th Armd Div (−) assembles in Fort de Grémecey to clear this region and screen between 80th Inf and 4th Armd Divs. CCA, 4th Armd Div, halts German tank-infantry attack toward Moyenvic in region W of Juvelize and inflicts heavy losses on enemy. In XV Corps area, 79th Div progresses slowly: on left, Germans make local attacks from Forêt de Parroy toward Lunéville; 315th Inf loses and recovers a portion of Lunéville; 313th, delayed by counterattack at Moncel, cannot advance into Forêt de Mondon; 4 cos of 314th Inf ford the Meurthe but, since they cannot advance without support from tanks and arty, halt to await bridging. Fr 2d Armd Div crosses the Meurthe between Flin and Vathiménil, night 22–23; patrols through S part of Forêt de Mondon to La Vezouse R at Benamenil but is driven back.

6th Army Group: In U.S. Seventh Army's VI Corps area, 157th Inf of 45th Div maintains bridgehead at Igney while 179th crosses the Moselle at Arches and clears Archettes; 180th continues to clear Epinal, from which enemy begins withdrawing. 36th Div finishes clearing Eloyes and is attacking Remiremont.

ESTONIA—Soviet forces seize Baltic prize of Tallinn.

ITALY—AAI: In U.S. Fifth Army's IV Corps area, S African 6th Armd Div is ordered forward in pursuit since enemy appears to be withdrawing from positions above Pistoia. II Corps virtually completes operations against the Gothic Line and is ready for drive N to Radicosa Pass and NE to Imola. 362d Inf, 91st Div, completes reduction of Futa Pass defenses; other elements of 91st Div establish outposts across the Santerno. On left flank of corps, enemy opposition to 34th Div is weakening: 135th Inf takes M. Citerna, NW of Santa Lucia; 168th seizes Hill 1134, E of Montepiano. 91st Cav Rcn Sq, screening left flank, finds Vernio abandoned by enemy. 85th Div pushes toward M. la Fine on right to assist 88th Div and toward M. Canda on left in support of 91st Div's attack for Radicosa Pass. On right flank of corps, 88th Div continues rapidly along

Santerno R valley, outdistancing 85th Div, and boundary is altered to give M. la Fine, except for western spur, to 88th Div. In Br 13 Corps area, Ind 8th Div completes occupation of Giogo di Villore without opposition.

In Br Eighth Army area, 5 Corps, with Ind 4th Div on left, 46th Div in center, and 1st Armd Div on right, attacks across the Marecchia, night 22-23, and begins struggle for ridges N of the river. 56th Div withdraws from line; its 168th Brig ceases to exist as a fighting unit. In Cdn 1 Corps area, Br 4th Div establishes bridgehead across the Marecchia on left flank of corps, and 5th Armd Div prepares to attack through it. NZ 2d Div takes command of coastal sector, releasing Cdn 1st Div and attached Greek 3d Mtn Brig for welcome rest.

PALAUS—On Peleliu, Japanese continue effective defense of central ridges and are bringing up reinforcements. 1st Mar Div observation planes are operating from the airfield. On Angaur, elements of 322d Inf again push into the bowl in Lake Salome area from the S but retire at night.

ULITHI—RCT 323, 81st Div, lands without opposition and begins securing the atoll.

23 September

WESTERN EUROPE—21 Army Group: In Br Second Army area, clearing weather conditions permit last serials of U.S. 101st and 82d A/B Divs and rest of Pol 1st Brig to be brought into Holland. Pol forces are landed at Grave as reserve for 82d A/B Div. Gen Dempsey orders that fly-in of Br 52d Div be held up. In 1 A/B Corps area, aircraft and arty of 30 Corps help 1st A/B Div maintain bridgehead at Hartestein, near Arnhem. During night 23-24, about 250 Pol paratroopers cross with supplies for 1st A/B Div. In 30 Corps area, 43d Div continues efforts to break through to Driel and succeeds in getting additional elements there; one brig drives into outskirts of Elst. With arrival of Pol forces at Grave, U.S. 82d A/B Div releases Coldstream Gds Gp, which has been assisting it, to Gds Armd Div. 506th Para Inf, U.S. 101st A/B Div, reopens Veghel-Uden highway and makes contact with Br armor moving SW from Uden. Enemy continues attacks toward Veghel, although seriously threatened by advance of 8 Corps toward Helmond.

12th Army Group: In U.S. Third Army's XX Corps area, 7th Armd Div drops plans for crossing the Seille upon receiving orders to join XIX Corps of First Army. 1st Bn of 10th Inf, 5th Div, relieves the weakened 2d Bn at Pournoy-la-Chétive, night 23-24. CCR, 6th Armd Div, is attached to corps as mobile reserve and moves to Jarny area on 24th. In XII Corps area, 80th Div extends eastward in center and on right as Germans withdraw, but enemy retains hill mass E of Serrières. 35th Div clears Bois de Faulx of enemy rear guards, capturing many. 4th Armd Div rests after its lively tank battles. In XV Corps area, 79th Div clears Fort de Mondon, 3d Bn of 314th Inf suffering heavy casualties during frontal assaults. Fr patrol crosses La Vezouse R and takes Domjevin but Germans restore positions along the river. After nightfall, final enemy remnants fall back across river to organize new defense line.

6th Army Group: In U.S. Seventh Army's VI Corps area, 157th Inf of 45th Div is unable to expand bridgehead toward Girmont; 179th takes Mossoux and cuts road leading NW from there; 180th clears that part of Epinal W of the Moselle and crosses at 3 points near there. 36th Div's 142d Inf finishes clearing Remiremont and begins crossing the Moselle; other elements of div are pushing northward. 7th Inf, 3d Div, reaches the Moselle across from Rupt and about midnight begins crossing over bridge, which is found to be intact.

In Fr 1st Army area, Gen de Lattre revises his plan of attack as result of Gen Truscott's decision to make main effort with U.S. Seventh Army while Fr forces provide flank protection. He calls for offensive limited in strength to one combat command of Fr 1st Armd Div and one RCT of Fr 1st Inf Div. The armor is to attack on axis Mélisey-Le Thillot; infantry is to conduct diversionary attacks.

ESTONIA—Red Army troops reach Gulf of Riga at Paernu.

ITALY—AAI: In U.S. Fifth Army's II Corps area, 34th Div, with capture of Montepiano by 133d Inf, is through Gothic Line. 91st Div rests in preparation for its next task—clearing M. Oggioli, W of Radicosa Pass. 338th Inf, 85th Div, pushes slowly northward from M. Coloreta; 337th, replacing 338th in line, takes W part of M. la Fine. 88th Div, committing 351st Inf between 349th and 350th, reaches line. M. la Fine-M. della Croce. In Br 13 Corps area, 1st Div occupies Poggio Cavalmagra and pushes on toward Palazzuolo on left and Marradi on R. Ind 8th Div occupies M. Villanova.

In Br Eighth Army area, 5 Corps is vigorously engaged with enemy N of the Marecchia on delaying line S. Arcangelo-Poggio Berni-Montebello. Cdn 1 Corps continues to pursue enemy toward Uso R. 5th Armd Div takes responsibility for left flank of corps, releasing Br 4th Div for reserve.

GREECE—Br Special Boat Sq, Mediterranean, is dropped on Araxos, on NW coast of the Peloponnesus, to seize airfield from which retreating enemy can be harassed and to occupy Patras.

CBI—Gen Hurley sends report to President Roosevelt on situation and tells him of the Generalis-simo's reaction to his (Roosevelt's) message.

On Salween front, Japanese send rescue column to extricate garrison of Pingka.

MOROTAI—Work is begun on another airfield, called Pitoe Drome, about 1,200 yards N of Wama Drome.

PALAUS—On Peleliu, RCT 321 of 81st Div arrives from Angaur and is attached to 1st Mar Div. After relieving 1st Marines on left flank just N of third phase line, N of village of Ngarekeukl, RCT 321 reconnoiters along coast to Garekoru, near fourth phase line, without difficulty. Efforts to make general advance northward, however, fail because of intense fire from center ridges. 7th Marines has task of supporting drive of infantry. On Angaur, 322d Inf again drives into Lake Salome bowl from S but pulls back again when forward positions become untenable.

24 September

WESTERN EUROPE—21 Army Group: In Cdn First Army's Br 1 Corps area, Cdn 2d Div establishes bridgehead across Antwerp-Turnhout Canal S of St Leonard. Elements of 49th Div reach Turnhout.

In Br Second Army's 1 A/B Corps area, 2 cos of 43d Div cross the Neder Rijn in assault boats during night 24-25 but are unable to reach British-held perimeter at Hartestein. Pol forces on S bank lack assault boats for crossing. Lt Gen B. G. Horrocks, CG 30 Corps, issues and within a few hours revokes order for 43d Div to prepare to cross at Renkum. In 30 Corps area, other elements of 43d Div continue to fight for Elst and Bemmel. Continuing attacks toward Veghel, Germans cut highway NE of village of Koevering, between St Oedenrode and Veghel. In 8 Corps area, Deurne falls to 11th Armd Div.

12th Army Group: In U.S. Third Army area, Gen Patton, in accordance with order from Gen Eisenhower, halts offensive operations for aggressive defense, calling for limited actions, as supplies permit, to improve defensive positions. In XX Corps area, 5th Div begins relief of 7th Armd Div in line. In XII Corps area, 80th Div prepares to attack to Seille R line on 26th. CCB, 4th Armd Div, holds its perimeter between Château-Salins and Fresnes-en-Saulnois against determined tank-infantry attacks that P-47's help repulse. Heavy enemy fire continues from Fort de Château-Salins, however. Germans lose about 300 dead and 11 tanks in this action.

6th Army Group: In U.S. Seventh Army's VI Corps area, 157th Inf of 45th Div seizes Girmont; 180th continues clearing Epinal. 36th Div is pushing NE toward St Die; 141st Inf takes St Amé, E of Remiremont. 3d Div clears Rupt of snipers and expands bridgehead to include La Roche and Maxonchamp.

ITALY—AAI: In U.S. Fifth Army area, IV Corps releases additional elements of 1st Armd Div for use on II Corps front, retaining only CCB. S African 6th Armd Div, protecting left flank of II Corps, replaces 11th Armd Brig in line with 12th Motorized Brig; 11th Armd Brig then pushes N along Highway 6620 to S. Ippolito while rest of div pursues enemy up Highways 64 and 66. In II Corps area, 34th Div, driving toward M. Bastione with 168th and 135th Regts, gains crest of M. Coroncina and holds it against counterattack; overruns Roncobilaccio. 91st Div, attacking with 362d and 361st Regts toward M. Oggioli, reaches line from Covigliano westward; during night 24-25, 363d Inf replaces 362d in line. While 337th Inf, 85th Div, consolidates positions on M. la Fine and patrols, 338th, to left, continues slowly toward M. Canda and gets into position for assault on it. 88th Div runs into strong resistance at M. Acuto and undergoes vigorous counterattacks as it continues toward Imola. In Br 13 Corps area, 1st Div takes Palazzuolo and Marradi, but enemy is holding out on M. Gamberaldi. Ind 8th Div reaches Marradi-S. Benedetto road. 6th Armd Div advances to S. Benedetto in Alpe, on Highway 67.

In Br Eighth Army area, 5 Corps secures heights N of the Marecchia from Montebello to Poggio Berni to S. Arcangelo, and 46th Div, in center, establishes bridgehead across the Uso, taking Camerano on far bank.

GREECE—RAF personnel arrive at Araxos by sea and together with Special Boat Sq move on to Patras. Commander of Land Forces, Adriatic, controls this operation.

BURMA—In NCAC area, Br 36th Div encounters enemy in strength while probing southward from Namma and suspends forward movement until mid-October.

PALAUS—On Peleliu, 321st Inf attacks after air, naval, and arty bombardment, driving through Garekoru to fourth phase line on left. Co E, on right, starts along east-west trail, soon called 321st Inf Trail, through central ridge system running from West Road S of Garekoru to East Road in effort to pocket strong enemy forces in Umurbrogol Mts, S part of the ridge system. Japanese counterattack at fourth phase line causes 321st Inf to fall back a little, but positions are largely restored. Gap develops between infantry and 7th Marines, since latter, to right rear, has to clear ground that 321st Inf should have taken. On Angaur, when appeal to enemy to surrender produces only 2 prisoners, arty fire is placed on the pocket throughout rest of day and ensuing night.

ULITHI—RCT 323, 81st Div, secures rest of Ulithi without opposition. The atoll becomes an excellent base for Pacific Fleet during operations against the Philippines.

25 September

WESTERN EUROPE—New boundary between 21 and 12th Army Groups becomes effective.

21 Army Group: In Cdn First Army's 2 Corps area, 3d Div, having moved up to Calais from Boulogne, begins all-out assault after preparatory bombardment. Pol armor is moving from E flank of 2 Corps to E flank of Br 1 Corps.

In Br Second Army's 1 A/B Corps area, it is decided to withdraw bridgehead N of the Neder Rijn in Arnhem sector under cover of darkness, 25-26. Leaving wounded behind, Br 1st A/B Div starts crossing the river, some by ferry and others swimming. U.S. 101st A/B and Br 50th Divs partially envelop enemy's roadblock near Koevering, and Germans abandon it after nightfall. 30 Corps clears Elst and Bemmel. 8 Corps takes Helmond and Gernert, NE of Eindhoven; makes patrol contact with 30 Corps in St Antonis area.

12th Army Group: Assigns sector now held by V Corps to Ninth Army. First Army is to participate in main drive of 21 Army Group on the Ruhr by taking Aachen and protecting right flank of British.

In U.S. First Army area, XIX Corps takes responsibility for corridor containing Peel Marshes from the British, who by this time have cleared it as far as Nederweert-Wessem Canal except for triangular position about Wessem. Belgian 1st Brig, although attached to Br 8 Corps, holds outposts S of the canal within new zone of corps. 7th Armd Div from Third Army and 29th Div from Brest are to be employed by corps in clearing new sector. In VII Corps area, elements of 60th Inf, 9th Div, fighting in forest on S flank of corps, are by this time so weakened that they are almost incapable of continuing the battle.

In U.S. Third Army area, Gen Patton lists priorities for limited attacks. In XX Corps area, 5th Div, extending southward, completes relief of 7th Armd Div and withdraws to new MLR, pulling back its outpost line. Corny and Pournoy-la-Chétive, secured at great cost, are abandoned in the retrograde movement. 83d Div, with task of clearing rear guards from N flank of corps W of Sauer and Moselle Rivers, reaches W bank of the Moselle at Remich. TF Polk then moves S to Thionville area. In XII Corps area, 35th Div is relieving 6th Armd Div (−) in Forêt de Grémecey sector. In powerful counterattacks against salient held by CCA, 4th Armd Div, German *Fifth Pz Army* column drives through Marsal and Moyenvic to Vic-sur-Seille where contact is made with German *First Army*. Enemy also thrusts sharply at other points of CCA's perimeter and overruns Moncourt; CCB, turning over its positions W of Château-Salins to 35th Div, moves to S of CCA, between Rethicourt and the canal.

6th Army Group: In U.S. Seventh Army's VI Corps area, 45th Div completes clearing Epinal. 36th Div is attacking toward Bruyères and Tendon. 3d Div takes over St Amé area from 36th Div.

In Fr 1st Army area, the 2d Corps opens limited offensive with 1st Armd Div, whose third combat command has now joined it, and 1st Inf Div. Progress is limited because of firm opposition.

ITALY—AAI: In U.S. Fifth Army's IV Corps area, TF 92 (Brig Gen John S. Wood, 92d Div ADC), consisting of 370th Inf of 92d Div and CCB of 1st Armd Div, takes command of zone previously held by 1st Armd Div. Elements of S African 6th Armd Div move to M. Casciaio, W of M. Coroncina, and relieve 34th Cav Rcn Tr of task of screening left flank of II Corps. In II Corps area, 34th Div progresses slowly toward M. Bastione on left flank of corps. 91st Div takes M. Beni, below M. Oggioli, on right but makes little headway on left under fire from M. Bastione. 338th Inf, 85th Div, attempts to outflank enemy on M. Canda by attacking first toward Torre Poggiolli to NE, but is unable to gain this objective; 3d Bn, 339th Inf, tries to assist attack on Torre Poggiolli but is stopped by opposition from Montarello. Boundary between 85th and 88th Divs is altered in preparation for strong effort by 88th Div on 26th to break through last heights before Imola. 337th Inf of 85th Div takes responsibility for M. la Fine, releasing 349th Inf of 88th Div. Br 13 Corps battles for heights commanding Palazzuolo, Marradi, and S. Benedetto. Several attempts by 1st Div to take M. Gamberaldi fail. Ind 8th Div begins attack on M. di Castelnuovo, where enemy resists strongly. 6th Armd Div, previously ordered to Eighth Army front, is directed to remain in place and contain enemy on right flank of corps.

In Br Eighth Army's 5 Corps area, Ind 4th Div is delayed in crossing the Uso on left flank of corps by fire from Cornacchiara on far bank, but enemy withdraws, night 25-26. 46th Div expands its Uso bridgehead toward Canonica. 1st Armd Div, after establishing bridgehead across the Uso at S. Arcangelo and Highway 9, is relieved there by 56th Div. In Cdn 1 Corps area, 5th Armd Div secures bridgehead across the Uso.

CBI—Generalissimo Chiang Kai-shek refuses to accept Gen Stilwell as commander of Ch forces.

MOROTAI—TF TRADEWIND Is. dissolved. Gen Hall, as CG XI Corps, is responsible for continuing base development.

PALAUS—On Peleliu, 7th Marines continues to support attack of 321st Inf, 81st Div, and extends left flank to release elements of 321st for main push. On left, 321st Inf patrols northward along coast almost to fifth phase line against light resistance. 5th Marines moves forward to join with 321st Inf in attack to clear N part of island. Right flank elements of 321st Inf continue clearing lateral trail through central ridge system, meeting strong opposition. On Angaur, 322nd Inf, whose efforts to push into the Lake Salome bowl from the S have all ended in failure, attempts in vain to find suitable route of advance into bowl from N coast. Engineers then begin construction of road for an attack from ENE.

26 September

WESTERN EUROPE—21 Army Group: In Br Second Army's 1 A/B Corps area, daylight halts withdrawal of 1st A/B Div; about 300 remain on N bank of the Neder Rijn; some of these later escape southward. Although MARKET-GARDEN has not accomplished major objectives of gaining bridgehead beyond the Neder Rijn, outflanking the West Wall, securing positions from which to attack the Ruhr: or bringing about the collapse of the enemy in this area, it has gained valuable ground and improved Allied positions. Both U.S. divs are still badly needed. 101st A/B Div front is stabilized as engineers remove mines and reopen St Oedenrode-Veghel road.

12th Army Group: In U.S. Ninth Army area, VIII Corps, now consisting of 2d and 8th Divs and corps troops, starts by rail and motor to concentration areas in rear of V Corps, First Army.

In U.S. First Army's VII Corps area, to ease pressure on the weak bn of 60th Inf, 9th Div, in Huertgen Forest, 60th Inf commander moves 2 bns—attached bn of 39th Inf and his reserve bn—southward from the contested ridge to cut Lammersdorf-Huertgen highway at its junction with road leading NW to Zweifall.

In U.S. Third Army's XX Corps area, Gen Walker orders limited attack on Fort Driant to begin on 27th, regardless of weather. XIX TAC begins daily attacks on Metz forts. 3d Bn of 359th Inf, 90th Div, makes limited attack to clear road between Gravelotte and St Hubert's Farm in preparation for large-scale attack. In XII Corps area, 4th Armd Div slightly reduces its MLR on right flank of corps in order to improve defensive positions, and enemy quickly moves into Juvelize and Coincourt without opposition. 80th Div makes vain effort to close up to Seille R line in limited attack against well-dug-in enemy: elements of 318th Inf attempt unsuccessfully to take Mt. St Jean while 317th Inf force makes futile effort to push into Moivron. 35th Div completes relief of 6th Armd Div in Forêt de Grémecey area, 6th Armd Div becoming corps reserve, although CCB is still linking 80th and 35th Divs in Leyr corridor. Enemy begins series of attacks to regain Forêt de Grémecey in evening, driving in 35th Div's outposts.

ITALY—AAI: In U.S. Fifth Army's IV Corps area, TF 92 begins advance along Serchio valley N of Pescia. Continuing along Highway 6620 on right flank, elements of S African 6th Armd Div reach slopes of M. Gatta. Div halts advance of 24th Gds Brig up Highway 66 NW of Pistoia but continues up Highway 64 with 12th Motorized Brig. In II Corps area, 34th Div meets strong opposition in Bruscoli-Gambellate Creek area. 91st Div, with capture of M. Freddi, is ready to attack M. Oggioli. 85th Div again attacks unsuccessfully toward Torre Poggiolli, employing 1st Bns of 338th and 339th Regts; 2d Bn of 338th tries in vain to take Sambuco; 3d Bn, 339th, seizes Montarello. 88th Div takes M. Pratolungo on left, pushes toward Castel del Rio in center, and on right takes M. del Puntale. 1st Armd Div, less CCB, is gradually being committed to protect exposed right flank of corps. In Br 13 Corps area, 1st Div continues futile frontal assault on M. Gamberaldi and at night begins moving elements toward M. Toncone in effort to outflank enemy. Ind 8th Div suspends attack on M. di Castelnuovo. On right flank of corps, 6th Armd Div's 61st Brig drives along Route 67 to Bucconi without opposition.

In Br Eighth Army's 5 Corps area, Ind 4th Div establishes bridgehead across the Uso in vicinity of Cornacchiara but meets firm resistance from heights beyond when trying to expand bridgehead. 46th Div crosses additional elements over the Uso and secures Canonica. 56th Div advances along Highway 9 from S. Arcangelo to positions about halfway to Savignano. In Cdn 1 Corps area, Cdn 5th Armd Div enlarges bridgehead across the Uso. Brig of NZ 2d Div reaches the Uso in coastal sector. Greek 3d Mtn Brig Gp is attached to NZ 2d Div and takes up positions on right flank.

During meeting at Gen Wilson's headquarters at Caserta, Italy, final arrangements are made for orderly reoccupation of Greece. Gen Scobie is to control all guerrilla forces operating within Greece. Security battalions—political police formed to eliminate ELAS bands—are outlawed.

PALAUS—On Peleliu, 321st Inf and 5th Marines each cut across W arm of Peleliu, forming 2 pockets of enemy. 2d Bn, 321st, completes clearing 321st Inf trail, cutting off enemy to S in Umurbrogol Mts. 3d Bn, 5th Marines, pushes across the peninsula to N, isolating enemy on Amiangal Mt, at N tip. Other elements of 5th Marines drive N along W coast almost to tip of island. On Angaur, 322d Inf gains foothold in N part of Lake Salome bowl and clears positions along SE rim.

27 September

WESTERN EUROPE—21 Army Group: Field Marshal Montgomery orders Gen Crerar to clear the Schelde as quickly as possible.

In Br Second Army area, enemy aircraft make large-scale but futile efforts to destroy Nijmegen bridges.

12th Army Group: In U.S. Third Army's XX Corps area, 359th Inf of 80th Div, after further efforts in greater strength to gain road from Gravelotte to St Hubert's Farm, breaks off attack; 358th Inf, having been relieved by TF Polk, moves to right of 359th, replacing 3d Cav Rcn Sq. 5th Div begins limited attacks against Fort Driant, outer bastion of Metz barring N approach to the city; after ineffective aerial bombardment at low level, 2d Bn of 11th Inf attacks at 1415 but is unable to reach main works and withdraws to original positions. In XII Corps area, massed enemy tanks again attempt to drive in 4th Armd Div's salient, making main effort on S flank where they succeed in taking Hill 318, SE of Arracourt, which commands road to Nancy; subsidiary thrusts at Bezange-la-Petite and Xanrey are largely contained. 35th Div, holding Forêt de Grémecey salient with 134th Inf on left and 137th on right, undergoes sharp counterattacks. German columns push toward Grémecey and Pettoncourt from Chambrey, reaching latter. When reinforcements from 320th Inf of 35th Div arrive, enemy falls back toward Chambrey. Other enemy forces make limited penetration into NE edge of the forest after infiltrating from Fort de Château-Salins, but most of lost ground is recovered. 6th Armd Div is alerted for possible action with 35th Div.

ITALY—AAI: In U.S. Fifth Army's IV Corps area, TF 92 makes substantial progress up Serchio valley; takes responsibility for zone of 24th Gds Brig, which is to assist in drive up Highway 6620. S African 6th Armd Div column, moving along Highway 64, reaches Collina. In II Corps area, 34th Div continues to advance slowly on left flank of corps against strong opposition. 91st Div begins assault on M. Oggioli and makes slow progress with assistance of supporting weapons and aircraft. 85th Div reaches crest of Torre Poggiolli and clears Sambuco. 88th Div takes hill dominating Highway 937 on left, Castel del Rio in center, and M. Battaglia, key feature on road to Imola, on right; 2d Bn, 350th Inf, establishes itself on M. Battaglia and soon undergoes the first of a series of determined enemy counterattacks. In Br 13 Corps area, 1st Div seizes M. Toncone, jeopardizing enemy on M. Gamberaldi. Ind 8th Div begins flanking maneuver against M. di Castelnuovo. 1st Gds Brig returns to 6th Armd Div from 10 Corps front.

In Br Eighth Army's 5 Corps area, Ind 4th Div is virtually halted by enemy on ridges on left flank of corps. 46th Div expands its bridgehead slightly and holds gains against counterattacks. 56th Div, finding further progress toward Savignano barred by enemy on Castelvecchio ridge, patrols while awaiting reinforcements. Cdn 1 Corps issues instructions for future action of troops upon relief, scheduled to begin on 29th, by Pol 2 Corps. It is subsequently decided to employ Pol 2 Corps in another sector and keep Cdn 1 Corps in coastal zone. Forward elements of corps are approaching the Fiumicino. S. Mauro di Romagna and La Torre are clear of enemy.

PALAUS—On Peleliu, elements of 321st Inf begin attack on N side of Umurbrogol Pocket, which 7th Marines is helping to contain, and meet intense enemy fire. 1st Bn drives N, clearing Kamilianlul Mt with ease and making contact with 5th Marines at junction of East and West Roads. Some elements of 5th Marines continue clearing resistance on Amiangal Mt, while others push to end of island, Akarakaro Pt. On Angaur, 322d Inf surrounds Lake Salome bowl and gains positions along inside of it. Methodical elimination of doomed enemy there ensues.

28 September

WESTERN EUROPE—21 Army Group: In Cdn First Army's 2 Corps area, 3d Div pushes into Calais and takes the Citadel.

In Br Second Army area, Germans make particularly strong counterattack against Eindhoven-Arnhem salient in futile effort to take highway bridge at Nijmegen.

12th Army Group: In U.S. First Army's XIX Corps area, Gen Corlett orders offensive to clear Peel Marshes. 7th Armd Div is to attack from N while Belgian 1st Brig, which comes under corps control, and 113th Cav Gp make secondary effort on S.

U.S. Third Army directive places Metz first on priority list. In XII Corps area, bitter, indecisive fighting occurs on S flank of 4th Armd Div, where enemy makes repeated and determined efforts to break through to Arracourt; CCB gains and then loses crest of Hill 318, as fighting continues into night 28-29, digging in on reverse slope near crest; Germans take Hill 293, to SW, and reach E edge of Bois du Benamont. 35th Div undergoes enemy counterattacks all along line, the most determined being against NE edge of Fort de Grémecey, where ground is lost but largely regained in counterattack. Attack from Jallaucourt against W flank of div perimeter is broken up by arty fire. Enemy forces again reach Pettoncourt before being checked. XV Corps begins limited attack to clear Forêt de Parroy. 79th Div, with 315th Inf on left and 313th on right, jumps off in afternoon after air preparation, pushing into edge of the forest.

ITALY—AAI: In U.S. Fifth Army's IV Corps area, TF 92 gains control of east-west Highway 12 along Lima Creek between Fornoli and S. Marcello; takes Lucchio. Units regroup as right boundary of corps is shifted E to Gambellate and Setta Creeks: sector of S African 6th Armd Div on right flank is sharply reduced to permit concentrated effort along Highway 6620 in support of II Corps; right boundary of RCT 6, BEF, is moved eastward to include Serchio R. II Corps finds that enemy has abandoned former strongpoints in Radicosa Pass. 135th Inf, 34th Div, seizes M. Bastione; 361st Inf, 91st Div, gains crest of M. Oggioli; M. Canda falls to 338th Inf, 85th Div. Germans counterattack desperately in effort to force 2d Bn of 350th Inf, 88th Div, from its exposed salient on crest of M. Battaglia, driving back forward outposts. Reinforcements (Co K) and supplies are moved forward to 2d Bn. In Br 13 Corps area, 1st Div finds that enemy on M. Gamberaldi has withdrawn.

In Br Eighth Army's 5 Corps area, Ind 4th Div suspends operations on left flank of corps while awaiting reinforcements. 46th Div gives a little ground under strong counterattack. 56th Div, beginning assault on Castelvecchio ridge, night 27-28, gets elements to top but is forced to fall back at daylight and break off the attack; elements succeed in reaching the Fiumicino N of Sacignano on right flank. 1st Armd Div hq passes to Eighth Army control. 2d Armd Brig is put under 46th Div. Cdn 1 Corps reaches positions generally along the Fiumicino. Co of Cdn 5th Armd Div crosses but is wiped out by enemy. Operations, except for patrolling, are almost at a standstill after this because of heavy rains and flooding.

BURMA—11 Army Group: In Br Fourteenth Army area, 15 Corps is ordered to go on the offensive on Arakan front in order to clear Chittagong and Cox's Bazaar as well as Naaf R estuary.

PALAUS—On Peleliu, 321st Inf units finish clearing N part of Umurbrogol Pocket to previously designated line. 1st Bn and 5th Marines continue clearing N part of W arm. 3d Bn, 5th Marines, lands on 3 small islands off coast—Ngesebus, Kongauru, and an unnamed one—and begins clearing them. On Angaur, 322d Inf continues clearing enemy pocket inside the bowl, suffering its highest casualties for a single day on the island, about 80.

29 September

WESTERN EUROPE—21 Army Group: In Cdn First Army's 2 Corps area, armistice for withdrawal of civilians interrupts battle at Calais. In Br I Corps area, Pol 1st Armd Div moves into line on right flank of corps and begins clearing northward to right of 49th Div.

In Br Second Army area, German swimmers damage bridges at Nijmegen with submarine charges, but the bridges are soon repaired. 12 Corps reaches Hertogenbosch-Oss RR, SW of Nijmegen.

12th Army Group: In U.S. First Army's XIX Corps area, while 7th Armd Div moves through Br zone to positions from which to attack southward in Peel Marshes, Belgian 1st Brig and 113th Cav Gp open attacks from S toward Roermond but make little headway against unexpectedly strong resistance. Belgian 1st Brig is held up at triangular position in Wessem area. 29th Div completes move from Brittany into corps zone, and its arty relieves that of 2d Armd Div. In VII Corps area, 39th Inf of 9th Div, after several days of indecisive fighting, takes Hill 554, within West Wall SE of Lammersdorf. The regt's penetration is now a little more than 2 miles wide.

In U.S. Third Army area, Gen Patton approves plan for XX Corps to attack Fort Driant again, beginning on 3 October. In XII Corps area, CCR of 6th Armd Div returns to parent unit from XX Corps zone; CCA moves to Champenoux, S of Pettoncourt. 4th Armd Div, effectively supported by air, decisively defeats enemy forces attempting to reach Arracourt and drives them southward, where they go on the defensive. Furious and confused fighting rages in Forêt de Grémecey, where 35th Div counterattacks early in morning to regain road to Fresnes-en-Saulnois and enemy pushes S from Fresnes; 137th Inf is unable to clear enemy from E part of the forest, but 3d Bn of 320th, counterattacking between 137th and 134th Regts, reaches N edge of woods, and 134th Inf overruns Han. XV Corps passes to control of U.S. Seventh Army.

ITALY—AAI: In U.S. Fifth Army's IV Corps area, elements of RCT 6, BEF, take Stazzema; 3d Bn relieves 3d Bn of 370th Inf, TF 92, in place. CCB, 1st Armd Div, is detached from TF 92 and, with Br 74th Light AA Regt under its command, receives mission of driving along Highway 64. S African 6th Armd Div pushes northward along Highway 6620 in effort to come abreast II Corps to right. In II Corps area, 34th Div repels counterattack on left at Montefredente and on right reaches Fornelli. 91st Div, with 362d and 363d Regts in assault, drives about 2 miles N of Radicosa Pass astride Highway 65. 85th Div remains in place, consolidating and patrolling. Troops of 350th Inf, 88th Div, are still hard pressed on M. Battaglia, where enemy counterattacks continue; entire 350th Regt is ordered to this position and turns over defense of right flank to CCA, 1st Armd Div. In Br 13 Corps area, enemy withdraws from M. di Castelnuovo. Engineers are opening Marradi–S. Benedetto road, which by now is secure. Corps issues instructions for regrouping in order to take over zone E of Firenzuola–Imola road. 1st Div replaces 66th and 2d Brigs in line with 3d Brig.

Br Eighth Army is hampered all along line by heavy rains and flooding. 5 Corps advances its right flank, night 29–30, taking Savignano and Castelvecchio ridge without opposition, as Germans make limited withdrawal. Patrols cross the Fiumicino.

CBI—Strong Ch labor force begins work on trail between Myitkyina and Kunming via Tengchung and is assisted by small group of U.S. engineers.

PALAUS—Adm Fort's Western Attack Force (TF 32) takes command in W Carolines from Adm Wilkinson's Joint Expeditionary Force (TF 31), releasing Adm Wilkinson for action against the Philippines. On Peleliu, 7th Marines takes responsibility for completing reduction of Umurbrogol Pocket, releasing 3d Bn of 321st Inf, which then starts N along route previously taken by 1st Bn, clearing bypassed resistance as it moves. Other elements of 321st Inf relieve 5th Marines on Ngesebus and Kongauru Islands. 5th Marines continues to clear Amiangal Mt. On Angaur, 322d Inf clears floor of Lake Salome bowl and forces enemy to NW rim and NW tip of island.

MOROTAI—Pitoe Crash Strip, the original airstrip on Morotai, is ready for use by fighters. This field is subsequently abandoned.

30 September

WESTERN EUROPE—21 Army Group: In Cdn First Army's 2 Corps area, 3d Div resumes attack on Calais after armistice ends at noon. Organized resistance ceases by evening and mopping up is begun. In Br 1 Corps area, Pol 1st Armd Div takes Merxplas, NW of Turnhout.

In Br Second Army area, 8 Corps is on general line Weert-Meijel-Deurne-Boxmeer and thence along the Maas in Cuijk area.

12th Army Group: In U.S. First Army's XIX Corps area, 7th Armd Div, from positions near Oploo, attacks S in corridor W of the Maas during afternoon, pushing toward Vortum and Overloon and soon running into determined resistance; attacks to clear the corridor from S continue to make little headway. 115th Inf, 29th Div, relieves 2d Armd Div in Gangelt-Teveren area.

In U.S. Third Army's XII Corps area, 4th Armd Div, after a successful sweep S of Xanrey, goes on the defensive in a quiet sector. In a desperate attempt to recover Forêt de Grémecey, Germans make strong attack against both flanks of 35th Div's perimeter, breaching lines of 134th and 137th Regts within the forest. So grave is the situation that the corps commander, about 1420, orders 35th Div to fall back behind the Seille after dark, but Gen Patton directs counterattack by 6th Armd Div to restore situation. 35th Div, committing its last reserves, manages to hang on and enemy begins planned withdrawal.

6th Army Group: In U.S. Seventh Army's XV Corps area, 79th Div continues to meet strong opposition in Forêt de Parroy. Elements of Fr 2d Armd Div assist 45th Div of VI Corps in attack on Rambervillers.

RUMANIA-YUGOSLAVIA—Troops of Third Ukrainian Front, having secured the Iron Gate–Turnu-Severin-Orsova area, where the Danube passes through the Transylvanian Alps—cross the Danube in force and push toward Belgrade.

ITALY—AAI: In U.S. Fifth Army's IV Corps area, RCT 6 of BEF advances its right flank to Fornoli, at junction of Serchio R and Lima Creek. TF 92 thrusts to La Lima, at junction of Highways 66 and 12. S African 6th Armd Div, upon reaching upper slopes of M. Catarelto, is abreast II Corps. In II Corps area, 351st Inf of 88th Div seizes M. Cappello after hard fighting. 88th Div troops on M. Battaglia are almost driven off by further enemy attacks. Corps is now ready for drive on Po Valley and Bologna, although wearied by recent fighting and hampered by heavy rains. In Br 13 Corps area, 1st Div's 3d Brig remains on M. Toncone while Marradi-Palazzuolo road is being repaired. 17th Brig, Ind 8th Div, reaches S. Adriano, on road to Faenza.

In Br Eighth Army's 5 Corps area, Ind 4th Div clears enemy from Tribola. 46th Div takes Montalbano and patrols as far as the Fiumicino. Corps begins general attack, night 30–1. Ind 4th Div takes M. Reggiano and Borghi before dawn, but 46th Div in center and 56th on right are unable to force the Fiumicino.

MOROTAI—Wama Drôme is ready for emergency use.

PALAUS—Adm Fort, Commander of Western Attack Force, declares Peleliu, Angaur, Ngesebus, and Kongauru occupied. On Peleliu, 1st Bn of 321st Inf relieves 5th Marines on Amiangal Mt, which is not yet completely clear of organized resistance although marines report over 1,170 Japanese killed or captured there, far more than the 500 recently estimated to be on the mountain. 7th Marines begins attacks to reduce Umurbrogol Pocket; progress during the next few days is very slow.

1 October

WESTERN EUROPE—21 Army Group: In Cdn First Army's 2 Corps area, mop-up of Calais is completed during morning. In Br I Corps area, Cdn 2d Div begins drive W across Antwerp-Turnhout Canal toward Beveland Peninsula through N suburbs of Antwerp. 49th Div is engaging enemy N of St Leonard. Pol armor crosses Dutch frontier on right flank of corps.

In Br Second Army area, Germans make another strong but futile attempt to reach Nijmegen bridges, pushing S from Arnhem.

12th Army Group: In U.S. Ninth Army area, XXIX TAC of U.S. Ninth Air Force, which is to support Ninth Army, is detached from IX TAC and becomes an independent body. VIII Corps, consisting of 2d and 8th Divs and supporting units, prepares to take over sector of V Corps, First Army.

U.S. First Army spends most of its time during October encircling and reducing Aachen, from which drive on Cologne is to begin. In XIX Corps area, two-pronged attack to clear Peel Marshes continues to gain little ground. Main offensive of corps, attack on West Wall between Aachen and Geilenkirchen, cannot be undertaken as planned on this date because of poor weather conditions.

In U.S. Third Army's XX Corps area, elements of 83d Div (Co C of 329th Inf) reach outskirts of Grevenmacher, on W bank of the Moselle N of Remich. In XII Corps area, 35th Div is clearing enemy from Forêt de Grémecey, thrusting to edge of woods at some points. CCR of 6th Armd Div moves S from Pettoncourt and clears Chambrey, where it is relieved by 137th Inf, and CCA moves around W edge of the forest through Jallaucourt to seize Lemoncourt-Fresnes ridge, which it turns over to 134th Inf. This about ends battle of Forêt de Grémecey. On N flank of corps, 80th Div begins limited attacks to improve positions W of Seille R; CO of 318th Inf attempts unsuccessfully to take farm strongpoint that controls Pont Mousson-Nomeny road.

6th Army Group: In U.S. Seventh Army's XV Corps area, 79th Div commits 314th Regt in Forêt de Parroy: moving forward from Croismare, 314th gradually pinches out 313th and continues attack to right of 315th. Progress within the forest is still very slow. Elements of Fr 2d Armd Div, in conjunction with attack of 45th Div (VI Corps), cut Rambervillers-Baccarat road.

ITALY—AAI: In U.S. Fifth Army's IV Corps area, troops of S African 6th Armd Div on M. Catarelto are forced to give ground under strong enemy counterattacks. TF 45 and RCT 6 of BEF are joined under operational command of Maj Gen Enrice Gaspar Dutra, Brazilian Minister of War. II Corps begins offensive toward Bologna at 0600 after arty preparation. Enemy resists stubbornly from improvised strongpoints. On left flank of the 34th Div, 168th Inf drive down Sambro Valley until stopped by strongpoint on Hill 789; 133d attempts to take M. del Gallete but is halted short of crest and cannot clear village of Cedrecchia. 91st Div attacks toward Loiano with 363d Inf on left and 362d on right but is soon held up in Monghidoro area. 339th Inf, 85th Div, heading for M. Bibele, takes La Martina and begins clearing ridge to E; on right, 337th Inf dears the ridge as far as Spedaletto. 88th Div, although still heavily engaged on right flank at M. Battaglia, attacks with 349th Inf to protect right flank of 85th Div in region E of Sillaro R, taking Belvedere. In Br 13 Corps area, work continues on Palazzuolo-Marradi road in 1st Div zone. 19th Brig, Ind 8th Div, begins assault on M. Cavallara.

In Br Eighth Army area, Gen McCreery, formerly 10 Corps commander, takes command of Eighth Army, relieving Gen Sir Oliver Leese, who will head Allied Land Forces in Asia. In 5 Corps area, Ind 4th Div, whose scheduled relief by Ind 10th Div must be delayed because of flooding conditions, advances left flank of corps toward the Fiumicino, pushing toward S. Martino and taking Montecchio without opposition. Activity on rest of corps front comes to a standstill along the Fiumicino. In Cdn 1 Corps area, stalemate continues along the Fiumicino. Plans to attack are made and canceled from time to time because of rain.

GREECE—From Kithira I., British Advance Coastal Forces base and 9th Commandos move by sea to Poros Bay to reconnoiter, leaving elements of Greek Sacred Regt on Kithira. Greek Naval Port parties land on Mytilene (Lesbos), Lemnos, and Levita.

2 October

WESTERN EUROPE—21 Army Group: Field Marshal Montgomery decides to drive SE against the Ruhr from Nijmegen rather than continue northward. Gen Eisenhower asks that the 2 U.S. divs with Br Second Army be returned as soon as possible.

12th Army Group: In U.S. First Army's XIX Corps area, after aerial preparation that is none too successful and arty bombardment that virtually eliminates enemy flak, 30th Div begins corps' assault on West Wall, attacking across the shallow Wurm R between Aachen and Geilenkirchen. 117th Inf of 30th Div, crossing at Marienberg, reduces band of pillboxes within its sector and takes Palenberg;

119th, crossing at Rimburg, is strongly opposed from Rimburg castle and Rimburg woods and cannot get beyond RR embankment. Armor attempts to assist the assault but is mired on E bank of river. Enemy counterattack, delayed until about midnight by interdictory fire, is quickly repelled. Diversionary attack by 115th Inf of 29th Div, NW of Geilenkirchen, overruns Hatterath, Birgden, and Kreuzrath and penetrates into Schierwaldenrath despite strong opposition. 7th Armd Div is assisted by Br and U.S. arty as well as aircraft as it continues effort to clear corridor W of the Maas. TF of CCB takes Vortum, but efforts to invest Overloon fail and enemy begins series of counterattacks. To S, Belgian 1st Brig breaks off action in Wessem area since it is greatly outnumbered by enemy. 113th Cav Gp makes little progress toward Roermond; establishes small bridgehead across Saeffler Creek. Corps troops receive heavy volume of arty support during day. V Corps orders attack through West Wall toward Bonn, target date 7 October.

In U.S. Third Army's XII Corps area, elements of 319th Inf, 80th Div, continuing limited attacks, take the farm strongpoint; 318th makes limited attack on Serrières that is unsuccessful and costly; elements of 317th get into position for attack on Sivry.

6th Army Group: In U.S. Seventh Army's XV Corps area, 79th Div is still strongly opposed in Forêt de Parroy, although 106th Cav Rcn Sq, screening N flank of corps, is assisting in N part of the forest. In VI Corps area, Grandvillers falls to 179th Inf, 45th Div.

POLAND—Germans suppress insurrection of patriots in Warsaw after prolonged and bloody fighting during which possibly 250,000 Poles perish.

ITALY—AAI: Boundary between U.S. Fifth Army and Br Eighth Army is moved about a mile E of Highway 67.

In U.S. Fifth Army's IV Corps area, 24th Gds Brig of S African 6th Armd Div continues futile efforts to take M. Cataretto. In II Corps area, 34th Div clears Cedrecchia but cannot take M. del Galletto or Hill 789 until after enemy pulls back, night 2-3. 91st Div seizes Monghidoro and reduces enemy defenses in this region. 85th Div's 339th Inf is laboriously clearing enemy from Idice valley; 337th works on ridge between the Idice and Sillaro Rivers, taking Hill 751 but bypassing pockets of enemy. 88th Div's 349th Inf continues to clear region E of the Sillaro. Enemy maintains pressure on M. Battaglia, where Br 6th Armd Div (13 Corps) begins relief of 350th Inf.

In Br Eighth Army's 5 Corps area, Ind 10th Div begins relief of Ind 4th Div. Elements of Ind 4th continue drive on S. Martino.

SEAC—British Chiefs of Staff and War Cabinet have decided that DRACULA (attack on Rangoon) cannot be undertaken in March 1945 as hoped without detracting from the main effort in Europe. Adm Mountbatten, having concluded planning for CAPITAL (drive on Mandalay) and DRACULA at reduced cost in response to request from the Prime Minister, issues directives calling for CAPITAL to be undertaken at once and DRACULA about November 1945. NCAC part of CAPITAL is to be conducted in two phases: clearing to line Indaw–Kunchaung–Sikaw–Namhkam by mid-December; to line Lashio–Mongmit–Thabaikkyin by mid-February 1945. General tasks, of NCAC are to defend air route to China and overland communications; secure that part of Assam and upper Burma within its zone.

CBI—On NCAC front, gasoline deliveries to Myitkyina by pipeline are begun.

PALAUS—On Peleliu, 321st Inf finishes clearing and mopping up Amiangal Mt on N part of W arm, having killed at least 175 Japanese. 7th Marines continues attacks on Umurbrogol Pocket. On Angaur, 322d Inf suspends costly assault against enemy pocket on NW part of the island. The pocket, known to cover an area of less than 500 yards from E to W and 150 yards from N to S, is subjected to close-in fire.

3 October

WESTERN EUROPE—RAF BC breaches Westkapelle Dike along W edge of Walcheren I., causing extensive flooding.

12th Army Group: In U.S. First Army's XIX Corps area, 117th Inf of 30th Div reaches Uebach and begins clearing house-to-house resistance; is overtaken there by CCB, 2d Armd Div, which has crossed the Wurm at Marienberg to expand bridgehead northward while infantry works S to establish contact with VII Corps. The small bridgehead becomes very congested and neither armor nor infantry is able to get beyond Uebach. 119th Inf, 30th Div, takes Rimburg castle and woods, the latter in flanking and frontal assaults, but can go no farther; its bridgehead is only 800 yards deep. On left flank of corps, 7th Armd Div replaces CCA with CCR as efforts to invest Overloon continue.

In U.S. Third Army's XX Corps area, 90th Div begins limited attack toward Maizières-lès-Metz to secure line of approach to Metz from the N and gain experience in attacking fortifications: 2 cos of 357th Inf reach large slag pile overlooking the town from NW with little difficulty. At noon 5th Div renews limited attacks on Fort Driant, S of Metz, with close arty support and smoke screen, although weather conditions prevent planned aerial bombardment; 2d Bn of 11th Inf, reinf by Co B, combat engineers, and tanks, attacks SW and NW edges; Co, B forces gap in S part and Co G follows it through; fighting is confused and costly, with Germans emerging from tunnels to counterattack after nightfall. In XII Corps area, 2d Bn of 317th Inf, 80th Div, finishes clearing Sivry by 0555. Corps line in center and on right flank is now firmly re-established.

6th Army Group: In U.S. Seventh Army's XV Corps area, 79th Div, assisted by tanks, makes limited progress in Forêt de Parroy, outflanking enemy roadblock.

ESTONIA—Troops of Leningrad Front land on Dagoe (Hiiumaa), off Estonian coast at entrance to Gulf of Riga, and begin clearing the island.

ITALY—AAI: In U.S. Fifth Army's IV Corps area, enemy withdraws from M. Catarelto early in day. 11th Armd Brig, S African 6th Armd Div, reaches M. Vigese, where enemy is firmly established. In II Corps area, 168th Inf of 34th Div drives through Campiano to lower slopes of Hill 747; 133d takes M. del Galletto. 91st Div pursues enemy northward to within a mile of Loiano. 85th Div's 339th Inf, against weakening resistance, thrusts almost to Quinzano and takes I Boschi; 337th continues to clear ridge between Idice and Sillaro Rivers, beating off counterattacks against Hill 751 and taking Hill 628 to N. 349th Inf, 88th Div, pushes forward to Sassoleone; Br 6th Armd Div continues relief of 350th on M. Battaglia, where fighting has been extremely costly. In Br 13 Corps area, 1st Div's 3d Brig begins stiff battle for M. Ceco.

In Br Eighth Army's 5 Corps area, Ind 10th Div takes command of Ind 4th Div's sector on left flank of corps. Latter passes to corps reserve.

PALAUS—On Peleliu, 7th Marines gains hold on ridges along E side of Umurbrogol Pocket.

U.S.—JCS direct Gen MacArthur to seize bases on Luzon from which to support future operations. Adm Nimitz is to provide cover and support for the Luzon operation; invade Iwo Jima in January 1945 and the Ryukyus, with assistant of SWPA aircraft, 2 months later.

4 October

WESTERN EUROPE—Bombers widen gap in Westkapelle Dike on Walcheren I.

21 Army Group: In Cdn First Army's Br 1 Corps area, Cdn 2d Div, continuing Win region N of Antwerp toward Zuid Beveland, has cleared Merxem-Eekeren area.

12th Army Group: In U.S. Ninth Army area, VIII Corps assumes responsibility for sector between First and Third Armies previously held by V Corps.

In U.S. First Army's XIX Corps area, enemy, having massed reinforcements, counterattacks strongly, particularly against Uebach, where he is thrown back by combined efforts of 117th Inf of 30th Div, armor, and arty; 119th Inf repels attack on its S flank. After considerable delay because of enemy attacks, CCB of 2d Armd Div attacks from Uebach—TF Hinds (Col Sidney R. Hinds) on left, taking objective heights about Hoverhof, a mile N of Uebach, and continuing beyond there to high ground E of Zweibruggen, and TF Disney (Col Paul A. Disney) on right, gaining about 800 yards toward Geilenkirchen-Aachen highway at cost of 11 tanks and heavy casualties. 119th Inf is unable to advance from Rimburg woods; at night moves TF Cox (Lt Col William C. Cox), northward to envelop enemy barring advance. 120th Inf attacks W of the Wurm at Kerkrade; Germans counter strongly but withdraw during night. Continuing limited attacks, 115th Inf of 29th Div takes Breberen, on the far side of Saeffler Creek, where it is relieved by 113th Cav Rcn Sq, but is unable to clear woods near Hatterath and loses 4 Co K in Schierwaldenrath. 7th Armd Div continues to fight hard but indecisively near Overloon. 113th Cav Gp, having suffered heavy losses, breaks off action S of Peel Marshes. V Corps changes target date for West Wall offensive to 10 October; directs 28th and 4th Divs to reconnoiter in force to E beginning on 6 October.

In U.S. Third Army's XX Corps area, 90th Div units maintain positions on slag pile NW of Maizières-lès-Metz while plans are being made to attack the town itself. 5th Div sends Co K, 2d Inf, to Fort Driant to assist hard-pressed elements of 11th Inf there. Enemy positions are slowly and laboriously being cleared. Germans from tunnels again counterattack after nightfall. In XII Corps area, German predawn counterattack isolates elements of 317th Inf, 80th Div, in Sivry. Both sides move up reinforcements. Co E attempts in vain to reach Americans within the town. Remnants of the isolated force succeed in rejoining main body.

6th Army Group: In U.S. Seventh Army's XV Corps area, 315th Inf of 79th Div reaches N-S road through Forêt de Parroy near its junction with main E-W road, but 314th, to right, is checked by enemy counterattack. In VI Corps' area, 3d Div's 7th Inf begins assault on Vagney, SW of Gerardmer. In Fr 1st Army's 2d Corps area, the Fr 1st Armd Div begins attack to envelop and take Le Thillot but is soon brought to a halt by determined opposition in Longegoutte and Gehan forest N of the town and in Servance-Château Lambert area to S.

ITALY—AAI: In U.S. Fifth Army's II Corps area, 168th Inf of 34th Div holds positions on slopes of Hill 747; 133d clears M. Venere. 91st Div is halted short of Loiano by stiff opposition. 339th Inf, 85th Div, takes Quinzano and reaches slopes of M. Bibele; 338th moves forward to relieve 339th, night 4-5; 337th gains Hill 566, far in advance of flanking forces. 88th Div gets into position to attack Hill 587, N of Sassoleone. Br 13 Corps is reinf by fresh 78th Div, whose 38th Brig starts forward to relieve 88th Div (II Corps). 3d Brig, 1st Div, continues futile efforts to take M. Ceco.

In Br Eighth Army area, 5 Corps orders attack across the Fiumicino to begin night 6-7. Meanwhile, Ind 10th Div struggles to advance left flank of corps to the river, crossing elements over the Uso early in day and beginning assault on heights (Sogliano al Rubicone-S. Martino ridge) intervening between there and the Fiumicino.

BURMA—11 Army Group: In Br Fourteenth Army's 33 Corps area, E African 11th Div overruns Yazagyo, in Kabaw Valley. Ind 5th Div is closing in on Tiddim.

MOROTAI—Gen Krueger declares Morotai operation at an end, although mopping up continues. Japanese dead on Morotai total 102; prisoners, 13. At least 200 are estimated killed on barges between Morotai and Halmahera. Allied casualties number about 30 killed, 85 wounded, and 1 missing. Wama field is put into use by aircraft. Permanent fighter garrison arrives and CVE's are able to leave.

PALAUS—On Peleliu, 7th Marines continues attacks on Umurbrogol Pocket but by end of day is so depleted in strength that it is no longer an effective fighting force.

5 October

WESTERN EUROPE—21 Army Group: In Cdn First Army area, Br 1 Corps gets forward elements on left to Alphen, SW of Tilburg.

12th Army Group: In U.S. First Army's XIX Corps area, CCB of 2d Armd Div on left flank overruns villages of Zweibruggen and Frelenberg and continues toward Geilenkirchen; on right, cuts Geilenkirchen-Aachen highway but is unable to reach Beggendorf, its objective. CCA, reinf by 3d Bn of 116th Inf, 29th Div, moves into bridgehead at Uebach to assist 30th Div. 117th Inf, 30th Div, attacks SE from Uebach toward Alsdorf but is soon halted; working S from Uebach area, TF Cox of 119th Inf reaches positions E of Merkstein-Herbach and clears ridge behind objective ridge except for a pillbox at its S tip. Strong opposition continues to keep 7th Armd Div from Overloon, though the town is almost encircled. Germans are assisted by heavy arty fire, which corps counters with 99 missions, despite dwindling supply of arty ammunition. German Air Force strikes at Palenberg in some strength but causes little damage. In VII Corps area, adverse weather conditions prevent 9th Div from launching attack toward Schmidt, an important objective commanding Roer R and Schwammenauel Dam, one of a series of Roer dams. V Corps closes in new zone in Monschau-Losheim area.

In U.S. Third Army's XX Corps area, 5th Div maintains foothold at Fort Driant against heavy fire from surrounding forts. ADC Brig Gen A. D. Warnock takes command of a TF that is being assembled to continue operations against the fort; 1st Bn (—Co A) of 10th Inf relieves Cos B and G of 11th at the fort, night 5-6. On N flank of corps, elements of 329th Inf, 83d Div, assisted by arty and fighter bombers, finally clear Grevenmacher after nightfall. XII Corps orders 3-div attack to begin on 8th. Regrouping follows, with 26th Div moving into line. Several days of aerial and ground bombardment serve to weaken enemy positions in zone of projected attack.

6th Army Group: In U.S. Seventh Army's XV Corps area, 315th Inf of 79th Div makes unsuccessful attempt to outflank enemy at main road junction in Forêt de Parroy and elements become temporarily isolated; 314th is held up near junction and at clearing in S part of the forest. With about half of the forest cleared, 79th Div goes on the defensive while preparing for new effort to break through. In VI Corps area, 7th Inf of 3d Div continues assault on Vagney; 15th Inf reduces quarry strongpoint near Cleurie after almost a week of hard fighting.

In Fr 1st Army area, 2d Corps concentrates against the heights N of the Moselle in Longegoutte and Gehan forest, Fr 3d Algerian Div making main effort. Enemy is slowly forced up slopes of the high ground in Fort de Longegoutte.

EASTERN EUROPE—From Siauliai area of Lithuania, troops of First Baltic Front push in force toward the Baltic and East Prussia in effort to cut off German *Army Group North*, leaving Second and Third Baltic Fronts to continue drive toward Riga. Far to the S, Second Ukrainian forces launch offensive from Arad area of Rumania into SE Hungary, pressing NW toward Szeged and Budapest, on route to Vienna.

ITALY—AAI: U.S. Fifth Army issues alternative instructions for continuing attack after reaching Highway 9 (Bologna-Faenza) based on assumptions that enemy may or may not have withdrawn from Valle di Commachio-Apennines pocket by that time. IV Corps orders regrouping and continuation of attack toward La Spezia. S African 6th Armd Div, reinf by CCB of 1st Armd Div presses to direct command of army in order to achieve closer co-ordination with II Corps to right. This leaves IV Corps so weakened that it is incapable of making a major effort. TF 92, now consisting of 370th Inf and 2d Armd Gp (434th and 435th AAA Bns with supporting tanks and TD's) under command of

Maj Gen Edward M. Almond, turns over sector E of Serchio valley to 107th AAA Gp (Br 39th, 47th, and 74th Light AA Regts) and assumes responsibility for coastal sector previously held by TF 45, with orders to attack for M. Cauala, on approach to Massa. RCT 6 of BEF, as training exercise, is to continue along Serchio valley toward Castelnuovo. In II Corps area, 168th Inf of 34th Div reaches Hill 661, NW of M. Venere, but enemy retains Hill 747 to rear; 133d takes Monzuno and finishes clearing M. Venere area. 91st Div, committing 361st Inf on right, attacks with 3 regts after preparatory arty fire and takes Loiano and M. Bastia. 85th Div takes M. Bibele on left and holds positions on Hill 566 on right. 88th Div is held up by strong opposition on Hill 587. In Br 13 Corps area, 1st Div, committing 2d Brig to left of 3d, prepares to renew assault on M. Ceco, night of 6th, after strong arty preparation.

In Br Eighth Army's 5 Corps area, Ind 10th Div, after bitter fighting, succeeds in taking Sogliano-S. Martino ridge and forcing enemy back across the Fiumicino.

PALAUS—On Peleliu, action against Umurbrogol Pocket is limited as 5th Marines begins relieving 7th Marines.

6 October

WESTERN EUROPE—21 Army Group: In Cdn First Army area, 2 Corps opens assault on Breskens Pocket, Cdn 3d Div forcing Leopold Canal N of Maldegem and establishing small bridgehead against stubborn resistance.

12th Army Group: In U.S. First Army's XIX Corps area, Gen Corlett issues orders late in day, as corps' West Wall bridgehead is being firmly established, halting further advance until link-up has been made with VII Corps. 2d Armd Div, instead of driving E to secure crossings of the Roer, is to maintain current positions on N flank of the bridgehead while assisting 30th Div to push SE. CCB, 2d Armd Div, is stopped by enemy on left flank less than 1,600 yards from Geilenkirchen; on right takes villages of Beggendorf and Waurichen, the latter NE of Uebach. CCA joins 117th Inf in attack to SE that receives close air support and overruns crossroads hamlet about halfway between Uebach and Alsdorf; CCA column thrusts E almost to Baesweiler. TF Cox of 119th Inf, 30th Div, undergoes counterattack that overruns 4 pillboxes before it is checked; these are later recovered. Bn of 120th Inf, relieved by 29th Div at Kerkrade, moves to Rimburg woods. Germans are again aided by massed arty fire, but after day's action offer less resistance. Costly effort to clear Peel Marshes comes to an end as 7th Armd Div breaks off attack. The div has gained less than 2 miles in this operation and is still within Br zone. In VII Corps area, 39th and 60th Regts of 9th Div attack at 1130, after preparatory bombardment, in Huertgen Forest toward Schmidt against tenacious opposition. In V Corps area, Gen Gerow resumes command of corps.

In U.S. Third Army's XX Corps area, relief of elements of 357th Inf on N flank of 60th Div by TF Polk permits preparation for attack on Maizières-lès-Metz on 7th. Heavy enemy fire fails to dislodge Americans from the slag pile to NW. TF Warnock, which is strengthened by elements of 3d Bn, 2d Inf, and 7th Combat Engr Bn, prepares to renew attack on Fort Driant on 7th.

6th Army Group: In U.S. Seventh Army's VI Corps area, 3d Div continues battle for Vagney and clears enemy from positions astride Tendon-Le Tholy road.

In Fr 1st Army's 2d Corps area, the enemy counterattacks prevent Fr forces from progressing against heights N of the Moselle and isolate forward elements.

ESTONIA—Soviet forces of Leningrad Front land on Oesel (Saarema), off coast of Estonia, and begin clearing the island.

ITALY—AAI: In U.S. Fifth Army area, S African 6th Armd Div takes M. Vigese in surprise attack under cover of heavy mist, and pushes on toward M. Stanco. In IV Corps area, TF 92 begins protracted struggle in coastal sector for M. Cauala. In II Corps area, 168th Inf of 34th Div finishes clearing left flank of corps, Germans having withdrawn from Hill 747; is subsequently withdrawn to reserve; 91st Cav Rcn Sq screens left flank; 133d Inf, faced with difficult supply problems, presses toward Monterumici hill mass. In 91st Div zone, 363d Inf, after clearing Monzuno-Loiano road, is pinched out; 362d attacks enemy delaying line based on M. Castellari; 361st makes slow progress on E flank of div. Withdrawing 339th Inf to reserve, 85th Div continues attack with 338th and 337th Regts; 338th pushes toward Castelnuovo di Bisano and La Villa in effort to bring left flank abreast 337th Inf. 88th Div continues efforts to take Hill 587 on right flank of corps; relief of 350th and elements of 351st Regts on right flank of div is completed. In Br 13 Corps area, 3d Brig of 1st Div, attacking in evening, gains precarious hold on slopes of M. Ceco.

In Br Eighth Army area, 5 Corps postpones general assault across the Fiumicino for 24 hours. 20th Brig, Ind 10th Div, makes preliminary attack toward M. Farneto, dominating feature NW of Sogliano, pushing through Strigara and gaining crest before dawn of 7th.

CBI—Gen Hurley delivers to Chiang Kai-shek President Roosevelt's reply, in which the President agrees to recall Gen Stilwell but declines to put another U.S. officer in command of Chinese troops.

Gen Stilwell will command Ch troops in Burma and in Yunnan Province but will be relieved of responsibility for lend-lease matters. Gen Sultan is to be responsible for Hump tonnage.

PALAUS—On Angaur, particularly heavy fire is placed on enemy pocket at NW tip of island, and 322d Inf feints attack, luring enemy into exposed positions.

7 October

WESTERN EUROPE—21 Army Group: In Cdn First Army's 2 Corps area, Cdn 2d Div, which is meeting stiff resistance in Woensdrecht region, is transferred to corps from Br I Corps. 2 Corps is now responsible for first phase of operation to open Antwerp port—clearing Zuid Beveland as well as the Breskens Pocket S of the Schelde. Cdn 3d Div gets reinforcements to N bank of Leopold Canal against strong resistance that prevents bridging.

12th Army Group: In U.S. First Army's XIX Corps area, 30th Div, assisted by CCA of 2d Armd, makes substantial gains and takes about 1,000 prisoners: 117th Inf thrusts to Aldsdorf; CCA reaches Baesweiler; 119th Inf, assisted by air strike on Merkstein, reaches positions across the Wurm from Kerkrade. This puts 30th Div within about 3 miles of Wuerselen, where contact with VII Corps is expected to be made. 1st Bn of 115th Inf, 29th Div, makes successful retaliatory raid on Schierwaldenrath. In VII Corps area, 9th Div continues attack in Huertgen Forest toward Schmidt. Forward elements reach edge of woods near Aermeter and Richelskaul, but main body is held up far behind. In V Corps area, 28th and 4th Divs advance to line of departure for West Wall offensive.

In U.S. Third Army's XX Corps area, 3d Bn of 329th Inf, 83d Div, takes Echternach, on W bank of the Sauer, after nearly a week of fighting. With capture of Wormeldange by 331st Inf, region W of the Moselle in Luxembourg area is cleared. Germans strongly counterattack Co F of 357th Inf, 90th Div, on slag pile NW of Maizières-lès-Metz. While enemy is thus engaged, Cos E and G bypass the slag pile and push into the town, clearing N half and gaining foothold in factory area. Germans move up reinforcements at night. TF Warnock, employing 1st Bn of 10th Inf, 5th Div, attacks to expand positions at Fort Driant, making limited progress at great cost; 2 platoons are cut off and destroyed; at night, 3d Bn of 2d Inf is committed.

6th Army Group: In U.S. Seventh Army's VI Corps area, Vagney falls to 7th Inf of 3d Div.

ITALY—AAI: In U.S. Fifth Army area, S African 6th Armd Div gets 2 cos of Frontier Force Rifles to crest of M. Stanco, where they are out of communication with main body and are forced back to Prada. In IV Corps area, TF 92 tries in vain to reinforce troops driving on M. Cauala with tanks and TD's, but the weapons are unable to cross swollen streams. In II Corps area, 133d Inf of 34th Div continues toward .Monterumici hill mass; 1st Bn blocks Highway 6620 at Gardeletta; 135th Inf relieves elements of 133d in order to maintain pressure from S while 133d makes outflanking movement to W, night 7-8. Attack by 362d Inf, 91st Div, on M. Castellari fails. 338th Inf, 85th Div, takes Castelnuovo di Bisano but is still short of La Villa; 337th is unable to advance from Hill 566. 349th Inf, 88th Div, continues to attack on Hill 587 and seizes ridge below Il Falchetto Hill; to right, 351st is able for the first time to attack in force. In Br 13 Corps area, 3d Brig of 1st Div maintains weak hold on slopes of M. Ceco. 19th Brig, Ind 8th Div, clears M. Cavallara.

In Br Eighth Army area, 5 Corps opens attack across the Fiumicino in evening with heavy volume of arty support. Assault is preceded by light and fighter bomber strikes on enemy positions. Ind 10th Div and 46th Div make the attack while 56th Div simulates attack in Savignano area. 20th Brig, Ind 10th Div, under heavy enemy pressure on M. Farneto, is unable to gain the initiative, but 25th Brig secures positions on ridge between Roncofreddo and S. Lorenzo. 128th Brig of 46th Div seizes Montilgallo and pushes W toward Longiano and S toward S. Lorenzo.

CBI—In NCAC area, Ch 22d Div, which has been training for fall offensive since capture of Myitkyina, begins movement to Kamaing.

MOROTAI—Fighters based on Morotai begin covering AAF bomber attacks against the Philippines.

POA—CINCPOA publishes Joint Staff Study that is based for preliminary planning for invasion of Iwo Jima, Volcano Is., in Nanpo Shoto.

PALAUS—On Peleliu, ground attacks are temporarily suspended after futile attempt by 3d Bn, 5th Marines, assisted by tanks, to compress Umurbrogol Pocket.

8 October

WESTERN EUROPE—Boundary between 21 and 12th Army Groups is moved back to former position, giving British responsibility for Peel Marshes corridor W of the Maas.

21 Army Group: In Br Second Army Area, 8 Corps takes command of U.S. 7th Armd Div and Belg 1st Brig, including U.S. attachments. These units, upon relief in current positions by 11th Armd Div, start relief of Br units within their zone.

12th Army Group: In U.S. First Army's XIX Corps area, 30th Div's hopes of making a speedy junction with VII Corps at Wuerselen are soon dashed by enemy opposition on E flank. 119th Inf, following Wurm R valley southward, gets 1½ miles beyond Herzogenrath; 120th Inf, whose relief at Kerkrade has been completed by 29th Div, is committed between 119th and 117th and takes 2 hamlets; 117th Inf, upon reaching railroad W of Mariadorf, is counterattacked strongly by fresh enemy forces from Mariadorf, part of whom push to Alsdorf, where they are halted. Both sides suffer heavy losses and 117th Inf pulls back to edge of Alsdorf; bn of 120th Inf moves up to reinforce 117th Inf. CCA, 2d Armd Div, seizes Oidtweiler, NE of Alsdorf. In VII Corps area, 1st Div begins attack to encircle Aachen in conjunction with XIX Corps: while 18th Inf pushes northward through Verlautenheide, 26th is getting into position to drive through heart of the city from E; 16th Inf holds defensive line near Eilendorf. Tanks and TD's arrive by nightfall to help assault regts of 9th Div break out of Huertgen Forest toward Schmidt. In V Corps area, 28th Div encounters outlying positions of enemy's West Wall defenses.

In U.S. Third Army's XX Corps area, 2d Bn of 357th Inf, 90th Div, fights from house to house within Maizières-lès-Metz for some time to come without clearing rest of the town. Confused and bitter fighting continues at Fort Driant without much change in positions. In XII Corps area, after an hour of preparatory bombardment, corps begins concerted drive toward Seille R at 0615. 6th Armd Div, making main effort, takes Moivron, where it is relieved by 80th Div; in conjunction with 80th Div envelops and takes Jeandelincourt, clears Bois de Chenicourt, though enemy retains town of Chenicourt, and seizes Arraye-et-Han. To left, 80th Div's 318th Inf takes Manoncourt; 319th seizes Lixières, Mt Toulon, and Sivry; 317th clears Mt St Jean. 35th Div closes up the Seille on its left flank, taking Ajoncourt and Fossieux. P-47's assist with attacks on heights between Moivron and Jeandelincourt.

6th Army Group: In U.S. Seventh Army's VI Corps area, 7th Inf of 3d Div moves from Vagney NE to Sapois.

In Fr 1st Army's 2d Corps area, the 3d Algerian Div gains crest of Longegoutte heights after several days of bitter fighting.

ITALY—AAI: In U.S. Fifth Army's IV Corps area, TF 92 reaches slopes of M. Cauala but is forced back by enemy fire. In II Corps area, CCA of 1st Armd Div is attached to 34th Div. 34th Div continues attack on Monterumici hill mass, 135th Inf working slowly forward from S and 133d from W. 362d Inf, 91st Div, gets elements to crest of M. Castellari, night 8-9; 361st makes substantial progress to E, clearing villages E of M. Castellari, cutting Highway 65 at La Fortuna, and pushing to edge of Livergnano escarpment, a feature strongly favored by nature for defense. 338th Inf, 85th Div, forces enemy back to M. delle Formiche; 337th is still unable to progress appreciably from Hill 566. 349th Inf, 88th Div, upon reaching crest of Hill 587, finds it undefended; elements seize Il Falchetto Hill. In Br 13 Corps area, 3d Brig of 1st Div gains summit of M. Ceco, but enemy retains heights nearby. On right flank of corps, 6th Armd Div thrusts along Highway 67 to edge of Portico but cannot force an entrance; elements probe toward Tredozio.

In Br Eighth Army's 10 Corps area, hq, 1st Armd Div, arrives and takes command of corps forces. In 5 Corps area, since 20th Brig of Ind 10th Div is still held up on M. Farneto, 10th Brig is committed to outflank enemy, some elements pressing toward Montecodruzzo on left and others taking S. Paola on right. Ind 25th Brig takes S. Lorenzo and drives toward Roncofreddo. 46th Div is working toward Longiano.

GREECE—Br forces from Araxos have reconnoitered along N coast of the Peloponnesus to Corinth, which is free of enemy; elements of 9th Commandos are in Nauplia, on Gulf of Nauplia S of Corinth.

9 October

WESTERN EUROPE—21 Army Group: In Cdn First Army area, 2 Corps continues clearing Breskens Pocket. Amphibious assault force of Cdn 3d Div lands at E end of the pocket, taking enemy by surprise and establishing bridgehead; other elements of div expand holdings N of Leopold Canal in Maldegem area. 4th Armd Div exerts pressure on enemy positions at E end of the canal. Germans continue vigorous defense of Zuid Beveland causeway, holding 2d Div to slight gains in Woensdrecht area.

In Br Second Army area, 1 A/B Corps returns to United Kingdom.

12th Army Group: Gen Bradley decides to shift Ninth Army hq to N flank of army group, where it is to take command of XIX Corps of First Army in place; leave VIII Corps in current positions and attach it to First Army. These changes are to become effective on 22 October. 12th Army Group takes direct control of 94th Div from Ninth Army.

In U.S. First Army's XIX Corps area, 119th Inf of 30th Div drives through Bardenberg to N Wuerselen; 120th is kept from Euchen and Beek, villages astride road to Bardenberg, by enemy force crossing its front en route to Bardenberg; 117th clears Schaufenberg and tries unsuccessfully to reach Mariadorf, then is authorized to go on the defensive in Alsdorf-Schaufenberg region. At night, enemy force reaches Bardenberg and routs small holding force of 119th Inf, isolating main body of that regiment in N Wuerselen; 119th Inf reserves attempt to regain Bardenberg from the N but are stopped at the village. In VII Corps area, 1st Div continues operations against Aachen. 9th Div attacks to break out of Huertgen Forest; assisted by tanks, forward bn of 60th Inf emerges in Richelskaul area and 2 platoons of 39th Inf at Wittscheidt. In V Corps area, planned attack on West Wall is postponed until 11 October.

In U.S. Third Army's XX Corps area, it is decided to break off costly action against Fort Driant. Indecisive fighting continues within Maizières-lès-Metz. In XII Corps area, CCA of 6th Armd Div, attacking through CCB attempts to take final objective of div, plateau W of Létricourt; elements clear woods SW of Létricourt but column to right comes under heavy fire from Chenicourt and cannot reach Létricourt; CCB sends reinforcements forward. To left, 80th Div advances abreast or nearly so of armor. This ends corps' offensive toward the Seille. 80th Div gradually takes over positions won by armor and improves them. Germans retain Létricourt and from time to time mount small, ineffective counterattacks. Enemy force breaks into Fossieux, where it is engaged by 35th Div. Corps front is largely quiet for rest of month and early days of November. Regrouping and rotation of front-line troops is thus possible.

6th Army Group: In U.S. Seventh Army's XV Corps area, 79th Div makes all-out effort to clear rest of Forêt de Parroy, gaining main road junction in center and thereby making enemy positions untenable. Germans withdraw from the forest after nightfall.

In Fr 1st Army's 2d Corps area, the 3d Algerian Div forces the Moselotte in Thiéfosse-Saulxures region and takes village of Trougemont.

ITALY—AAI: In U.S. Fifth Army area, boundary between U.S. II and Br 13 Corps is altered to permit 88th Div, on right flank of II Corps, to concentrate fully on northward drive and to give 13 Corps for Santerno R valley. S African 6th Armd Div regroups for another effort against M. Stanco, giving CCB responsibility for left flank along Highway 64. In IV Corps area, TF 92 pushes to top of M. Cauala without opposition but later in day is forced to withdraw. Next 2 days are devoted to preparations for another assault. RCT 6 of BEF, pushing northward along the Serchio, halts near Barga to avoid possible enemy counterattack. In II Corps area, 34th Div continues to make slow progress against Monterumici hill mass. 91st Div repels counterattack from Livergnano, mops up, and prepares for co-ordinated effort against formidable Livergnano escarpment: Co K of 361st Inf reconnoiters to edge of Livergnano, where it is cut off from main body; Cos E and G move to positions above Bigallo and are pinned down. 338th Inf, 85th Div, now well ahead of 337th, prepares to attack M. delle Formiche in conjunction with attack of 91st Div; 1st Bn outflanks La Villa. 337th Inf prepares for full-scale effort against Hill 578, peak of Monterenzio hill mass. 349th Inf, 88th Div, begins clearing ridge leading to M. delle Tombe; 351st reaches edge of Gesso. In Br 13 Corps area, 78th Div, reinf, takes responsibility for M. Battaglia and M. Cappello, on left flank of corps; 1st Gds Brig, 6th Armd Div, remains on M. Battaglia but comes under command of 78th Div. Ind 8th Div gets into position for attack on M. Casalino.

In Br Eighth Army area, 10 Corps, upon regrouping in connection with arrival of 1st Armd Div hq, pursues retreating enemy northward along Highway 71; rcn elements find M. Castello and Mercato Saraceno clear. In 5 Corps area, hard fighting develops at S. Paola as Germans make unsuccessful attempt to recover it. 138th Brig, 46th Div, relieves 25th Brig, Ind 10th Div, on ridge N of Roncofreddo.

SEAC—Prime Minister Churchill asks Adm Mountbatten to meet him in Cairo to consider premonsoon operations. T. V. Soong presents to Gen Hurley an aide memoire from Chiang Kai-shek denouncing Allied strategy in southeast Asia. Gen Stilwell is blamed for loss of E China but the criticism falls indirectly upon President Roosevelt.

POA—In Warning Order for invasion of Iwo Jima, CINCPOA designates Fifth Fleet Commander, Adm Spruance, as commander of the operation (CTF 50); Vice Adm Richmond K. Turner, Commander Amphibious Forces, Pacific, to command joint Expeditionary Force (TF 51); Lt Gen Holland M. Smith, USMC, CG, Fleet Marine Force, Pacific, as commander of Expeditionary Troops (TF 56). 20 January 1945 is set tentatively as invasion date. Expeditionary troops are to be mounted in Hawaiian area and in the Marianas.

PALAUS—On Peleliu, 5th Marines renews attack on Umurbrogol Pocket but makes little headway.

MARCUS I.—Bombarded by warships of Third Fleet task group.

10 October

WESTERN EUROPE—12th Army Group: In U.S. First Army's XIX Corps area, after further efforts to clear Bardenberg, reserve bn of 119th Inf, 30th Div, withdraws at night to permit shelling of enemy there; 120th Ind seizes Birk crossroads, which controls road to Bardenberg, thus jeopardizing enemy forces at Bardenberg; 30th Div claims 20 German tanks during fighting on 9th and 10th. In VII Corps area, so favorable do the prospects of closing the Aachen gap appear that 1st Div delivers ultimatum calling for surrender of the city within 24 hours. In Huertgen Forest, Germans overrun the

2 forward platoons of 39th Inf of 9th Div in Wittscheidt area early in day; 39th Inf later recovers lost ground and takes Germeter without opposition; 60th Inf units re-enter the woods and seize road junction almost a mile SW of Richelskaul.

In U.S. Third Army area, III Corps hq (Maj Gen John Milliken), which has recently arrived on the Continent, is assigned to Third Army. In XII Corps area, 35th Div clears enemy from Fossieux.

6th Army Group: In Fr 1st Army area, the 2d Corps expands Moselotte bridgehead to Planois, on E-W road to La Bresse. Hopes of a quick lateral thrust to secure that communications center are dashed when corps is asked to extend northward to line Fougerolles-Remiremont-Le Tholy-Gerardmer, effective on 14th, to relieve S flank units of U.S. Seventh Army. No further effort is made at this time to extend holdings along N bank of the Moselotte.

EASTERN EUROPE—Soviet troops of First Baltic Front break through to the Baltic Sea near Memel (Lithuania), which is being invested; to left thrust to Niemen R at NE border of Prussia. Forces of Third Ukrainian Front cut Nis-Belgrade RR at Velika Plana (Yugoslavia).

ITALY—AAI: In U.S. Fifth Army area, S African 6th Armd Div makes another futile attempt to take M. Stanco, getting almost to crest before being driven back. II Corps opens third phase of offensive toward Bologna. 34th Div tries in vain to outflank the Monterumici hill mass. In 91st Div zone, 361st Inf makes main effort against Livergnano escarpment' without appreciable gains. Efforts to relieve Co K in Livergnano fail; most of the co is captured by enemy. 2d Bn of 338th Inf, 85th Div, its left flank protected by 2d Bn of 363d Inf, 91st Div, attacks lofty M. delle Formiche but, although strongly supported by air and arty, is stopped short of crest; 337th, reinf by 1st Bn of 338th, makes some progress toward Hill 578 of Monterenzio hill mass. In 88th Div zone, 350th Inf attacks through 349th on left flank of div in effort to come abreast 85th Div to left, reaching Hill 339, above II Falchetto Hill, on left and positions near M. delle Tombe on right; 351st Inf makes little headway against Gesso ridge. In Br 13 Corps area, 2d Brig of 1st Div takes command of div front, relieving 3d Brig. Ind 8th Div gains positions near top of M. Casalino.

In Br Eighth Army's 5 Corps area, German opposition along the Fiumicino collapses with capture of Spaccato by Ind 10th Div. 46th Div takes Longiano and La Crocetta. 56th Div patrols across the river on right flank of corps. Cdn 1 Corps regroups for drive across the Fiumicino. Rcn elements of 1st Div cross at Savignano di Romagna without opposition; bridging is begun at the crossing site.

RYUKYU Is.—Fast carrier task force of Third Fleet successfully attacks Okinawa, depleting enemy's air and surface strength there and damaging airfields and facilities. Aerial photographs of the island are obtained.

PALAUS—On Peleliu, 5th Marines makes limited progress against Umurbrogol Pocket.

11 October

WESTERN EUROPE—12th Army Group: In U.S. First Army's XIX Corps area, reserve bn of 120th Inf, 30th Div, captures Bardenberg with little difficulty, opening route to N Wuerselen. In VII Corps area, with expiration of surrender ultimatum, Aachen is subjected to heavy aerial and arty bombardment; patrols of 1st Div probe enemy defenses. 60th Inf, 9th Div, holds road junction in Huertgen Forest against counterattack and tries unsuccessfully to take another, between first junction and forester's lodge of Jaegerhaus. Enemy resistance to rear is weakening. 39th Inf tries in vain to cross open ground between Germeter and Vossenack; elements, moving along draw from Wittscheidt, gain positions N of Vossenack.

In U.S. Third Army's XX Corps area, 83d Div reverts to VIII Corps, Ninth Army, in place and XX Corps' N boundary is moved S to Sierck-les-Bains. TF Polk is given mission of defending N flank of corps W of the Moselle.

6th Army Group: In U.S. Seventh Army area, VI Corps issues instructions for drive to the Meurthe, calling for capture of Bruyères and Brouvelieures, followed by attack on St Dié. To deceive enemy, heavy program of fire is begun against approaches to Gerardmer.

In Fr 1st Army area, the 2d Corps concentrates on clearing region S of the Moselotte.

EASTERN EUROPE—Soviet troops of Second Ukrainian Front force the Tisza (Tisa) River on broad front at Szeged, Hungary's second largest city, seriously threatening Budapest; others are battering Debrecen, in region E of Budapest; still others, assisted by Rumanians, take Cluj, capital of Transylvania.

ITALY—AAI: In U.S. Fifth Army's IV Corps area, TF 92 begins another assault on M. Cauala in evening. RCT 6, BEF, takes Barga. In II Corps area, 133d Inf of 34th Div withdraws to reserve upon relief by CCA, 1st Armd Div. Further efforts to clear Monterumici hill mass accomplish little. 91st Div strengthens its assault on Livergnano escarpment, committing 363d on right, but makes slow progress; elements of 363d reach top of escarpment. 2d Bn of 338th Inf, 85th Div, gains crest of M. delle Formiche in costly fighting while 3d Bn clears E slopes; 337th

Inf inches forward toward Hill 578 of Monterenzio hill mass. 350th Inf, 88th Div, gains foothold on M. delle Tombe; 351st continues efforts to clear Gesso ridge. In Br 13 Corps area final enemy counterattack against M. Battaglia is repelled.

In Br Eighth Army's 5 Corps area, 56th Div, upon relief on right flank of corps by 1st Div of Cdn 1 Corps, is withdrawn to reserve and reduced to a skeleton force. Boundary between 5 Corps and Cdn 1 Corps is altered to place Highway 9 within zone of Cdn 1 Corps. Ind 10th Div and 46th Div continue toward the Savio and Cesena, seizing Montecodruzzo, heights E of the Rubicone at Montiano, and Montenovo. In Cdn 1 Corps area, 1st Div strengthens and expands bridgehead across the Fiumicino, moving along Highway 9 almost to the Rigossa. NZ 2d Div establishes 2 bridgeheads across the Fiumicino N of Savignano without opposition and, during night 11-12, takes Gatteo.

CBI—Generalissimo Chiang Kai-shek asks that President Roosevelt recall Gen Stilwell immediately.

P.I.—Carrier aircraft of Third Fleet attack Luzon to neutralize enemy airpower there.

12 October

WESTERN EUROPE—21 Army Group: In Br Second Army's 8 Corps area, 3d Div attacks southward against Peel Marshes salient, clearing Overloon. U.S. 7th Armd Div provides diversionary demonstration along Deurne-Venray road.

12th Army Group: In U.S. First Army's XIX Corps area, 30th Div with objective of taking Wuerselen and closing Aachen gap, is prevented from doing this by series of enemy counterattacks aimed at widening the Aachen corridor and forcing corps back to line Bardenberg-Euchen. Germans are thrown back at Birk, SE of Bardenberg, and at N Wuerselen with aid of aircraft and arty, but new panzer units are identified, indicating major reinforcement of the region. Corps regroups to meet this threat. In VII Corps area, in preparation for main assault on Aachen, 3d Bn of 26th Inf, 1st Div, dears factory district between Aachen and Haaren. Air and arty bombardment of Aachen continues. In Huertgen Forest, German counterattack severs MSR of 39th Inf, 9th Div, on E-W trail leading into Germeter. Forward elements N of Vossenack, although not under attack, are recalled to help restore situation. In V Corps area, CCA of 5th Armd Div leaves for XIX Corps sector, where it will be held in army reserve.

In U.S. Third Army's XX Corps area, 3d Bn of 357th Inf, 90th Div, moves into Maizières-lès-Metz to bolster weary 2d Bn. Last elements of 5th Div withdraw from Forêt Driant, night 12-13. In XII Corps area, 26th Div relieves 4th Armd Div on right flank of corps.

EASTERN EUROPE—Troops of Second Ukrainian Front take Oradea (Transylvania), continue battle for Debrecen (Hungary), and cut Belgrade-Budapest RR at Subotica (Yugoslavia).

ITALY—AAI: In U.S Fifth Army's IV Corps area, TF 92 pushes to crest of M. Cauala but is again forced to retire. Efforts to take M. Cauala are suspended for next few days. In II Corps area, 135th Inf of 34th Div extends eastward as it continues, in conjunction with CCA of 1st Armd Div, to attack Monterumici hill mass. 91st Div get additional elements up Livergnano escarpment but is unable to clear it. 3d Bn of 338th Inf, 85th Div, attacks N through 2d Bn on crest of M. delle Formiche; Germans defend Hill 578 against attacks of 337th Inf. 88th Div continues to attack M. delle Tombe and clears Gesso ridge. In Br 13 Corps area, Ind 8th Div is assigned positions SW of M. Ceco to ease strain on 1st Div.

Br Eighth Army is ordered to release Ind 4th Div and Greek 3d Mtn Brig for service outside Italy. In 5 Corps area, corps presses from the Rubicone toward the Savio and Cesena. Ind 10th Div advances its left flank to M. dell'Erta, E of the Savio; elements crossing the Rubicone to N are held up in Sorrivoli. Attacking across the Rubicone on right flank of corps, 46th Div takes Casale.

CORFU-ALBANIA—Br commando force from Land Forces, Adriatic, lands on Corfu and in Sarande area of S Albania.

GREECE—Advance detachment of Br 4th Para Bn and Royal Engrs is dropped in Megara area to secure and repair airfield. Piraeus and Kalamata are found to be clear of enemy.

FORMOSA—In preparation for invasion of Leyte, TF 38, Third Fleet, begins series of powerful carrier aircraft strikes against Formosa to neutralize enemy air and naval power, evoking strong opposition.

SWPA—Gen MacArthur issues orders for invasion of Luzon, to be undertaken by U.S. Sixth Army's I Corps (6th and 43d Divs, reinf) and XIV Corps (37th and 40th Divs, reinf). 25th Inf and 11th A/B Divs, RCT 158, 6th Ranger Bn, and 13th Armd Gp constitute reserve and follow-up forces. Various service units are assigned as army and corps troops.

PALAUS—On Peleliu, Gen Geiger opens III Amphib Corps CP ashore and declares assault and occupation phase at an end. 1st Mar Div is now responsible only for the Umurbrogol Pocket. 321st Inf takes responsibility for eastern arm of the island and begins relieving Marine units. Island Garrison Force takes over region S of the Umurbrogol Pocket.

13 October

WESTERN EUROPE—Germans launch first V-bomb against Antwerp, which, next to London, proves to be the primary target for these weapons.

21 Army Group: In Br Second Army's 8 Corps area, 3d Div attacks from Overloon toward Venray, 3 miles distant, against strong opposition.

12th Army Group: In U.S. First Army's XIX Corps area, 116th Inf of 29th Div, having turned over positions W of the Wurm at Kerkrade to 1104th Combat Engr Gp, takes over attack to close Aachen gap: reinf by tanks from 2d Armd Div, 116th begins frontal assaults against Wuerselen on narrow front that invites concentrated enemy fire; little progress is made during this and the next two days. In VII Corps area, 26th Inf of 1st Div begins all-out assault on Aachen: while 2d Bn fights from house to house within the city, 3d pushes to base of Observatory Hill, one of 3 heights commanding the city from the N, the others being Salvator Hill and the Lousberg. In Huertgen Forest, 60th Inf, 9th Div, gains its objective, Road Junction 471; 39th seals off enemy penetration and begins drive to recover lost ground.

In U.S. Third Army area, XX Corps' plan for stronger assault on Maizières-lès-Metz is abandoned as result of Third Army order freezing all arty ammunition above 3-inch.

6th Army Group: In U.S. Seventh Army's XV Corps area, 79th Div, working eastward from Forêt de Parroy, takes Emberménil.

EASTERN EUROPE—Soviet troops of Second and Third Baltic Fronts overrun Riga, capital of Latvia and important naval base on Gulf of Riga. This success, coupled with recent drive to the Baltic in Memel area of Lithuania, has trapped a large German force in W Latvia. Soviet offensive on Baltic front is soon suspended.

ITALY—AAI: In U.S. Fifth Army area, 12th Motorized Brig of S African 6th Armd Div renews attack on M. Stanco early in morning after arty preparation and, assisted by diversionary thrust to E of Grizzana, captures objective; CCB, on left flank, takes Bombiana, on Highway 64. In II Corps area, 34th Div partially outflanks enemy on Monterumici hill mass from E; 168th Inf is shifting eastward to M. delle Formiche. Enemy hold on Livergnano area is beginning to weaken under blows of 91st Div and arty and aerial bombardment. 361st Inf of 91st Div gains Hill 603, above Livergnano, and village of Casalino, NW of Livergnano; 363d Inf clears E part of the plateau. 337th Inf, 85th Div, at last takes Hill 578 and reduces opposition on Monterenzio hill mass; during night 13–14, is relieved by 339th Inf. 2d Bn of 350th Inf, 88th Div, crosses Sillaro R W of Hill 339, night 13–14, and drives northward through weak spot in enemy defenses; 351st Inf thrusts toward M. Spadura from Gesso ridge until stopped by counterattack. In Br 13 Corps area, 78th Div begins attack on M. la Pieve.

In Br Eighth Army's 5 Corps area, Ind 10th Div takes Sorrivoli but is held up near M. delle Vacche. 46th Div seizes Carpineta, night 13–14. In Cdn 1 Corps area, some elements of NZ 2d Div are held up by strongpoint at S. Angelo, but others patrol to the Rigossa.

GREECE—Br commandos (9th Cdo) and Sq B of Greek Sacred Regt land at Piraeus and secure Kalamata airfield in preparation for main landing on 15th. Rest of 4th Para Bn and Royal Engr force are dropped at Megara; after securing the airfield these forces move overland to Athens and Kalamata without opposition. U.S. 51st Troop Carrier Wing participates in Br occupation of S Greece (Operation MANNA) during period 13–18 October, taking in personnel and equipment.

CBI—Gen Hurley recommends to President Roosevelt that Gen Stilwell be relieved and that another U.S. officer be named to command Chinese Army.

FORMOSA—TF 38 continues air strikes to neutralize Formosa. Cruiser *Canberra* is badly damaged by enemy torpedo.

SWPA—VII Amphibious Force, with elements of Leyte invasion force embarked, sails from Hollandia for target. GHQ issues instructions for capture of air base in San Jose area of Mindoro, from which further operations against the Philippines will be supported and small shore-to-shore operations will be conducted to deceive enemy on Luzon. For this task, Sixth Army forms Western Visayan Task Force under Brig Gen William C. Dunckel during early November. The force eventually consists primarily of RCT 19 of 24th Div and 503d Para RCT, a separate unit. 21st Inf of 24th Div, less 3d Bn, is allocated as the reserve force; 3d Bn is to conduct deceptive operations.

MOROTAI—Medium bombers begin operations from the island.

PALAUS—On Peleliu, RCT 321 is alerted to relieve marines at Umurbrogol Pocket, where some progress is being made against W side. On Angaur, 322d Inf begins final push to eliminate enemy pocket on N Angaur.

14 October

WESTERN EUROPE—21 Army Group: In Cdn 2 Corps area, land approach to Breskens Pocket from E is secured by Cdn 3d Div at Isabella, tip of Savojaards Plaat.

12th Army Group: In U.S. First Army's VII Corps area, 26th Inf of 1st Div continues to make slow progress in Aachen and on Observatory Hill. 9th Div commits elements of 47th Inf to insure safety of Road Junction 471 in Huertgen Forest.

6th Army Group: In Fr 1st Army's 2d Corps area, 3d Algerian Div finishes clearing Forêt de Gehan and takes Cornimont, but by this time is so weakened that offensive is broken off.

ITALY—AAI: In U.S. Fifth Army area, S African 6th Armd Div finds Grizzana undefended. In II Corps area, enemy clings to Monterumici defenses despite attacks by 135th Inf of 34th Div and CCA of 1st Armd Div. At noon 1st Armd Div takes command of 135th Inf and CCA. 133d Inf shifts eastward to 91st Div zone. 91st Div improves positions in Livergnano area and takes Querceta. Germans abandon Livergnano village. 339th Inf, 85th Div, pushes northward from Hill 578. 2d Bn of 350th Inf, 88th Div, takes Hill 373, N of Hill 339; 351st Inf, ordered to consolidate on Gesso ridge, breaks off attacks. In Br 13 Corps area, 78th Div continues attacks toward M. la Pieve.

In Br Eighth Army area, 2 Pol Corps takes command of 10 Corps sector and troops on left flank of army with orders to drive on Forlì. 5 Corps continues to clear heights E of the Savio, 46th Div seizing M. dei Pini, beyond Carpineta. In Cdn 1 Corps area, 1st Div takes village of Bulgaria. Elements of NZ 2d Div clear S. Angelo, night 14–15.

YUGOSLAVIA—Soviet and Yugoslavia forces are converging on Belgrade, which is encircled.

CBI—Gen Stilwell flies to E China, where Chinese are preparing to take the offensive.

FORMOSA—TF 38 achieves its purpose of neutralizing Formosa, where some 280 enemy planes have been destroyed since 12th, but another cruiser, *Houston*, is damaged by Japanese torpedo. Part of the TF withdraws from Formosa area in effort to lure enemy fleet into the open.

SWPA—III Amphibious Force, with elements of Leyte invasion force that have reached Manus from Hawaii aboard, sail for Leyte.

POA—CG, Fleet Marine Force, Pacific, designates CG, V Amphibious Corps (Gen Schmidt, USMC) as Landing Force Commander (CTG 56.1) for Iwo Jima operation and directs him to prepare plans.

PALAUS—Adm Fort turns over control of all operations in the Palaus to Adm Hoover, heading Forward Area Central Pacific (TF 57). On Peleliu, 81st Div prepares to relieve marines at Umurbrogol Pocket while defending eastern arm of the island, recalling 2d Bn of 321st Inf from offshore islands. On Angaur, attack and occupation phase is terminated by III Amphib Corps, although pocket still remains at NW tip.

15 October

WESTERN EUROPE—21 Army Group: Is strengthened by attachment of U.S. 104th Div from Ninth Army. Div is to join Br I Corps under Cdn First Army in action to open port of Antwerp.

12th Army Group: In U.S. Ninth Army area, VIII Corps is reinf by newly arrived 9th Armd Div.

In U.S. First Army's XIX Corps area, 116th Inf of 29th Div and supporting tanks from 2d Armd Div continue efforts to close Aachen gap with frontal attacks but by this time have gained only 1,000 yards. New plan of attack to speed line-up with VII Corps is formulated. In VII Corps area, 3d Bn of 26th Inf, 1st Div, gains most of Observatory Hill, N of Aachen, but Germans counterattack sharply and recover positions in N part; since 16th Inf line near Eilendorf is under strong enemy pressure, 1st Div is ordered to suspend Aachen offensive temporarily. 9th Div's drive on Schmidt ends far short of objective; both sides have suffered heavy casualties; 39th Inf recovers all ground lost recently and still holds Wittscheidt and Germeter. V Corps releases CCB, 5th Armd Div, which moves to VII Corps area as First Army reserve.

6th Army Group: In U.S. Seventh Army's XV Corps, area 313th Inf of 79th Div tries in vain to dislodge enemy from hill mass E of Forêt de Parroy. VI Corps opens drive on Bruyères from N, W and S. 179th Inf, 45th Div, begins clearing woods N of the town in effort to cut Bruyères-Brouvelieures road. 36th Div attacks on W with attached 442d Inf (Nisei), which includes 100th Bn, recently arrived from Italy, and on S with 143d Inf along road from Fays. 3d Div begins secret move N in preparation for drive on St. Dié.

FINLAND—Soviet forces of Karelian Front clear enemy from port of Petsamo.

ITALY—AAI: In U.S. Fifth Army area, S African 6th Armd Div comes up abreast II Corps to right; with occupation of heights NE of Grizzana, gains control of lateral Highway 6424. In II Corps' 1st Armd Div sector, enemy continues to defend Monterumici, although this position is being outflanked. 34th Div, less 135th Inf, prepares to attack in new zone. 91st Div consolidates positions N of Livergnano. 85th Div holds line astride Idice R beyond M. delle Formiche and Monterenzio hill mass. 88th Div extends its left flank northward beyond Hill 369 to positions abreast 85th Div while regrouping and consolidating on right flank. Br 13 Corps, ordered to take responsibility for Gesso ridge from II Corps, begins relief of U.S. 88th Div there with 78th Div.

In Br Eighth Army area, 5 Corps takes M. delle Vacche and M. Burratini without opposition but is halted short of M. Reale and M. Romano. In Cdn 1

Corps area, Gambettola falls to NZ 2d Div without a fight.

GREECE—After delay while mines are being cleared, Gen Scobie's Force 140 (Br 3 Corps and Greek troops) arrives off Piraeus in evening and goes ashore. Gen Scobie, upon landing, sets up his hq in Athens and orders retreating enemy pursued by land and harassed by air.

SEAC—Adm Mountbatten leaves Kandy (Ceylon) for Cairo to meet Prime Minister Churchill.

CBI—NCAC opens offensive to clear N Burma and open supply route to China (CAPITAL), pushing southward from Myitkyina toward line Katha-Shwegu-Bhamo almost unopposed. Br 36th Div, which has been moving S in Burma Railway corridor during the monsoon season, continues drive with 29th Brig from Namma area and is followed by Ch 50th Div. In center, Ch 22d Div moves SE from Kamaing area in region between the RR corridor and Myitkyina-Bhamo road in effort to secure bridgehead over the Irrawaddy at Shwegu. Ch 38th Div attacks on E flank to secure Bhamo-Mansi area, with 113th Regt leading. In addition to Ch New Sixth and New First Armies, NCAC now has under its command Ch 1st Separate Regt, U.S. 475th Inf (containing GALAHAD survivors) and U.S. 124th Cav (Texas National Guard), which is to be combined into 5332d Brig (Prov), later called TF MARS, with strength of about a div.

ANGAUR—First plane lands on airfield.

P.I.—Task group of TF 38 attacks Luzon airfields.

16 October

WESTERN EUROPE—21 Army Group: Field Marshal Montgomery halts offensive operations except those to speed opening of Antwerp port.

In Cdn First Army's 2 Corps area, Zuid Beveland Isthmus is virtually sealed off with capture of Woensdrecht by Cdn 2d Div. Cdn 3d Div continues to reduce Breskens Pocket S of the Schelde. The pocket is about half its original size.

In Br Second Army's 8 Corps area, 3d Div reaches outskirts of Venray. CCB, U.S. 7th Armd Div, establishes bridgehead across canal on Deurne-Venray road.

12th Army Group: In U.S. First Army area, army closes ring about Aachen as patrols of XIX and VII Corps establish contact on Ravels Hill at 1615. In XIX Corps area, 116th Inf of 29th Div continues to batter Wuerselen, 30th Div attacks southward astride Wurm R with 119th Inf; patrol makes contact with a patrol of 18th Inf, 1st Div, VII Corps. 120th and 117th Regts of 30th Div make limited attacks within their respective sectors. In VII Corps area, Germans react promptly and vigorously to closing of Aachen gap, attempting to overrun roadblock on Aachen-Wuerselen highway, night 16-17. 16th Inf, 1st Div, stabilizes positions in Eilendorf area.

6th Army Group: In U.S. Seventh Army's VI Corps area, 45th and 36 Divs, against firm opposition, close in on Bruyères, column from S pushing through Laval.

In Fr 1st Army's 2d Corps area, 3d Algerian Div and Fr 1st Armd Div begin attack to pierce enemy's winter line in the Vosges, pressing toward heights E of the Moselotte against violent opposition.

EASTERN EUROPE—Forces of Third White Russian Front launch offensive to break into East Prussia, which Germans are prepared to defend.

ITALY—AAI: In U.S. Fifth Army area, 6th S African Armd Div, in conjunction with II Corps to right, renews northward attack between the Reno and Setta Rivers. II Corps begins final phase of attack toward Bologna, making main effort in center; left flank is still held up below Monterumici hill mass. 91st Div drives N astride Highway 65: passing through 361st Inf, 362d heads for Lucca; 361st attacks along Highway 65 in center, elements pushing W of Casalino to protect left flank; 363d advances toward M. Belmonte to help 34th Div take the feature. 34th Div attacks with 2 regts abreast: on left, 133d drives through 91st Div on narrow front toward M. Belmonte, target for arty and aerial bombardment. Searchlights provide illumination for night action. At this time the use of artificial moonlight is still in the experimental stage. 168th Inf of 34th Div attacks through 338th Inf of 85th Div on broad front between Zena Creek and Idice R, heading for M. della Vigna, N of M. delle Formiche. E of the Idice, 85th Div's 338th Inf attacks toward M. Fano while 339th attacks toward ridge above Monterenzio, taking Hill 622. 88th Div drives toward M. Cuccoli-M. Grande ridge on right flank of corps: 350th Inf makes no headway toward M. Cuccoli, but 349th takes M. delle Tombe and reaches S. Clemente. New boundary between II and Br 13 Corps, effective 2330, passes between M. delle Tombe and M. Spadura, sharply reducing zone of 88th Div. In Br 13 Corps area, 78th Div completes relief of U.S. forces on Gesso ridge.

In Br Eighth Army area, 5 Corps clears M. Romano and M. Reale, night 16-17. Elements of 20th Brig, Ind 10th Div, establish small bridgehead across the Savio near its confluence with the Borello on S flank of corps. In Cdn 1 Corps area, Cdn 1st Div advances quickly toward Cesena, elements crossing Pisciatello R. Orders are issued for concerted attack on Cesena by Cdn 1 and Br 5 Corps. NZ 2d Div takes Bulgarno without opposition.

YUGOSLAVIA—Soviet and Yugoslav forces are fighting side by side in streets of Belgrade. Nis, on Sofia-Belgrade RR line, is now free of enemy.

CAROLINE Is.—On Peleliu, RCT 321 of 81st Div, takes responsibility for completing reduction of Umurbrogol Pocket and is relieving marines there. Fresh forces, 1st Bn of 323d Inf, from Ulithi are assisting 321st Inf. At Ngulu Atoll, elements of 81st Div begin clearing the atoll, which lies between Yap and the Palaus.

17 October

WESTERN EUROPE—21 Army Group: In Br Second Army's 8 Corps area, Venray falls to 3d Div. 11th Armd Div attacks E through bridgehead of CCB, U.S. 7th Armd Div; latter pushes S along E bank of canal.

6th Army Group: In U.S. Seventh Army's XV Corps area, 44th Div, untried in combat, closes in Lunéville area; 114th is attached to 79th Div. In VI Corps area, 45th and 36th Divs are slowed by strong opposition as they continue to close in on Bruyères. In Fr 1st Army's 2d Corps area, 3d Algerian Div and Fr 1st Armd Div make limited gains but at such high cost that Gen de Lattre calls a halt and corps goes on the defensive. Army commander decides to drive on Belfort in 1st Corps zone.

ITALY—AAI: In U.S. Fifth Army's IV Corps area, patrol of TF 92 reaches crest of M. Cauala, night 17–18. In II Corps area, co-ordinated attack by CCA, 1st Armd Div, and 135th Inf against Monterumici hill mass makes little progress. 91st Div takes Lucca and improves positions to E. 91st Inf and 1st Armd Divs are alerted to expect enemy spoiling attack and take precautionary measures to insure continuance of corps offensive to E. Particularly heavy enemy fire is directed against Livergnano area. 34th Div is clearing slopes of M. Belmonte and takes crest of M. della Vigna. 85th Div continues forward above Monterenzio. 350th Inf, 88th Div, presses on toward M. Cuccoli and 349th comes up abreast. In Br 13 Corps area, 21st Brig of Ind 8th Div begins assault on M. Pianoreno. 1st Div's 66th Brig attacks in M. Ceco area.

In Br Eighth Army area, Pol 2 Corps opens offensive toward Forlì in evening, although all its forces have not yet assembled. 5th Kresowa Div leads off, pushing toward Galeata from S. Piero in Bagno area, its right flank protected by Br 1st Armd Div. 5 Corps is meeting strong opposition at Acquarola and Celincordia. 4th Div begins relief of 46th Div, night 17–18.

GREECE—Military Liaison Headquarters, Greece (until 3 October designated Allied Military Liaison Headquarters, Greece) begins arriving in Athens to distribute relief supplies.

P.I.—To insure safe passage of main Leyte invasion force into Leyte Gulf, 6th Ranger Bn makes preliminary landings on small islands at approaches to the gulf after preparatory bombardment. Co D lands on Suluan I., and rest of 6th Ranger Bn, less Co B, lands on Dinagat I. Neither landing is opposed, and channel light is set up on Dinagat. Landing of Co B on Homonhon I., is postponed because of rough sea. Mine sweeping is begun off Leyte. Leyte convoys of III and VII Amphibious Forces make visual contact. Elements of TF 38 continue to neutralize Luzon.

18 October

WESTERN EUROPE—At conference in Brussels, Gen Eisenhower issues plan for offensive, with tentative dates. First priority for 21 Army Group is to open Antwerp port. Br Second Army is to be prepared to drive SE between the Meuse and Rhine about 10 November to support U.S. advance across the Rhine. U.S. First Army is to cross the Rhine in Cologne area between 1 and 5 November. U.S. Ninth Army, after covering N flank of First Army while it is pushing to the Rhine, is to help First Army envelop and clear the Ruhr. U.S. Third Army will cover right flank of First Army and refrain from offensive operations until it has sufficient logistical support.

12th Army Group: In U.S. First Army area, Maj Gen Raymond S. McLain succeeds Gen Corlett, whose health is impaired, as CG XIX Corps. In VII Corps area, Germans are making strenuous efforts to break encirclement of Aachen. 1st Div, strongly reinf, renews assault on Aachen; 26th Inf takes Observatory Hill and is methodically clearing heart of the city. TF Hogan, 3d Armd Div, is committed to help 26th Inf clear commanding ground overlooking the city. Bn of 110th Inf, 28th Div, is brought from V Corps sector to reinforce 1st Div and close gap between 26th Inf elements within Aachen and 1106th Engrs S of the city. Although this bn is given a defensive role, it is soon drawn into battle for the city.

6th Army Group: In U.S. Seventh Army's VI Corps area, 36th Div breaks into Bruyères and clears most of town.

ITALY—AAI: In U.S. Fifth Army's II Corps area, 34th Div makes limited progress on slopes of M. della Vigna but cannot break through enemy positions on M. Belmonte. 339th Inf, 85th Div, reaches fork in main ridge between Idice and Sillaro Rivers N of Monterenzio. 88th Div is slowly clearing approaches to M. Cuccoli–M. Grande ridge and bringing reserves forward. In Br 13 Corps area, 6th Armd Div, turning over responsibility for right flank of corps along Highway 67 to 26th Armd Brig Gp, takes over right flank of 78th Div sector from M. Battaglia to the Imola road and resumes command of 1st Gds Brig, already disposed on M. Battaglia; 61st Brig relieves 38th Brig of 78th Div on M. Cappello and latter moves to Gesso ridge. 36th Brig, 78th Div, finds M. la Pieve undefended. 21st Brig, Ind 8th Div, gains ground S of M. Pianoreno, from which enemy has withdrawn.

In Br Eighth Army's Pol 2 Corps area, 5th Kresowa Div takes Galeata without opposition. In 5 Corps area Acquarola and Celincordia fall to Ind 10th Div and 46th Div, respectively. Ind 10th Div is ordered to attack across the Savio. In Cdn 1 Corps area, NZ 2d Div begins crossing the Pisciatello at 2300. Cdn 1st Div takes Ponte della Pietra. Greek 3d Mtn Brig is withdrawn from line in preparation for departure from Italy.

CZECHOSLOVAKIA—Fourth Ukrainian Front pours into E Czechoslovakia on broad front from Poland, driving through Carpathian passes.

GREECE—Greek Government returns to Athens.

CBI—Gen Stilwell is ordered to return to Washington. President Roosevelt informs Chiang Kai-shek of Stilwell's recall, adding that while no other U.S. officer will be named to command Ch forces, Gen Wedemeyer is available to act as the Generalissimo's chief of staff, a proposal that is acceptable to Chiang Kai-shek.

BURMA—11 Army Group: In Br Fourteenth Army's 33 Corps area, after hard fighting on approaches to Tiddim earlier in the month, Ind 5th Div enters the town without opposition.

JAPAN—Tokyo orders major counter offensive, SHO, against forces threatening inner defense of Japan to begin upon spotting U.S. invasion force en route to Leyte, P.I. This is to affect operations not only in the Pacific but on the Asiatic mainland as well.

PALAUS—On Peleliu, 321st Inf completes relief of 1st Mar Div elements at Umurbrogol Pocket and continues attacks to reduce it. The pocket is now about 400 yards from E to W and about 850 yards from N to S, 1st Mar Div has suffered 6,526 casualties on the island, a large portion of them at the pocket. On Angaur, enemy pocket on NW tip of island is compressed into small zone about 100 yards long and 50 yards wide.

P.I.—Co B, 6th Ranger Bn, lands on Homonhon I., without opposition and sets up channel light. Underwater demolition teams begin uneventful rcn of landing areas under cover of naval gunfire bombardment. Seventh Fleet protects assault convoy as it approaches Leyte and begins preinvasion bombardment. Third Fleet continues neutralization of Luzon and guards San Bernardino and Surigao Straits.

19 October

WESTERN EUROPE—21 Army Group: In Cdn First Army's 2 Corps area, newly arrived 52d Div enters action, taking over Cdn 3d Div's bridgehead N of Leopold Canal and continuing reduction of Breskens Pocket. Junction is made between Leopold Canal and Savojaards Plaat bridgehead forces.

12th Army Group: In U.S. First Army's VII Corps area, German resistance at Aachen is diminishing rapidly; efforts to break encirclement from outside the city cease and the garrison is told to fight to the finish. 26th Inf, 1st Div, continues to clear the city and takes Salvator Hill. TF Hogan, 3d Armd Div, seizes Lousberg heights and is given task of cutting Aachen-Laurensberg highway.

6th Army Group: In U.S. Seventh Army's VI Corps area, 36th Div completes capture of Bruyères. 3d Div—less 30th Inf, which remains in Le Tholy area—closes in assembly area behind 45th Div in preparation for drive on St Dié.

ITALY—AAI: In U.S. Fifth Army area, elements of 6th S African Armd Div gain positions on slopes of M. Salvaro, though elements to right are still short of M. Alcino, SE of M. Salvaro. In II Corps area, since 34th Div has been unable to break through in center of corps front, main effort is shifted to right flank toward M. Grande and M. Cerere. After reaching favorable positions for attack and saturation bombardment of M. Grande area by aircraft and arty, 88th Div attacks in evening, taking M. Cerere with ease and reaching crest of M. Grande by dawn of 20th, 24 hours ahead of schedule. 85th Div assists 88th and gains lower slopes of M. Fano. 34th Div, still short of M. Belmonte and to rear of 85th Div, pauses to regroup. Positions of 91st Inf and 1st Armd Divs on left flank of corps are virtually unchanged. In Br 13 Corps area, 78th Div attacks toward M. Spadura and M. dell'Acqua Saluta with 38th and 36th Brigs, respectively, taking latter and gaining precarious hold on M. Spadura. 21st Brig, Ind 8th Div, clears M. Pianoreno. 77th Brig gets elements to top on M. Casalino, but they are driven off. 1st Div's 66th Brig gains firm hold on M. Ceco and pushes toward M. delle Valle.

In Br Eighth Army's Pol 2 Corps area, 5th Kresowa Div finds Civitella di Romagna undefended. In 5 Corps area, 46th Div closes in on Cesena; elements push into S part of the city in vain effort to take bridge. 4th Div takes command of 46th Div sector, but elements of 46th Div remain in S part of Cesena. Ind 10th Div moves rest of 20th Brig across the Savio to Falcino area; establishes another small bridgehead across the Savio with elements of 25th Brig from Roversano, night 19-20. Cdn 1 Corps releases Greek 3d Mtn Brig to Eighth Army control. Rapid progress is made all along front except in coastal region. While Cdn 1st Div is closing in on Cesano, NZ 2d Div reaches road extending NE from there.

BURMA—In NCAC area, 29th Brig of Br 26th Div takes Mohnyin, where enemy has abandoned large supplies of stores and ammunition.

P.I.—Leyte assault convoy moves safely to Leyte under protection of Seventh Fleet. Underwater demolition teams complete rcn of assault areas. Preinvasion bombardment continues.

20 October

WESTERN EUROPE—21 Army Group: In Cdn First Army area, Br 1 Corps, protecting right flank of I Corps, opens drive toward Bergen-op-Zoom–Tilburg highway with Cdn 4th Armd Div on left, 49th Div in center, and Pol 1st Armd Div on right.

12th Army Group: In U.S. First Army's VII Corps area, 26th Inf of 1st Div, which is being assisted by elements of 110th Inf, 28th Div, forces enemy to W and SW suburbs of Aachen.

In U.S. Third Army's XX Corps area, enemy heavily shells 90th Div elements at Maizières-lès-Metz. In XII Corps area, P-47's of XIX TAC breach dam and release waters of Etang de Lindre to forestall later flooding of Seine R by Germans.

6th Army Group: In U.S. Seventh Army area, two fresh U.S. divs (100th and 103d) arrive at Marseille. In VI Corps area 179th Inf of 45th Div attacks for Brouvelieures after preparatory fire and gains heights commanding the town; 180th Inf, which has been pushing toward the Mortagne R from Fremifontaine area, tries in vain to break through enemy defenses along the river. 3d Div begins drive on St Dié, employing 7th Inf, which heads for Vervezelle, NE of Bruyères.

ITALY—AAI: In U.S. Fifth Army area, S African 6th Armd Div maintains positions on M. Salvaro under repeated enemy counterattacks and gains slopes of M. Alcino. In II Corps area, 88th Div continues offensive on right flank of corps, 350th Inf reaching top of M. Cuccoli and taking Farneto. To forestall enemy counterattacks against M. Grande hill mass, aircraft and arty interdict all approaches. 88th Div is reinf by 337th Inf of 85th Div, which gradually relieves 350th Inf of positions on ridge W of Farneto. Rest of corps front is virtually static. In Br 13 Corps area, Germans recapture M. Spadura from 8th Div. 21st Brig, Ind 8th Div, begins drive on M. Romano.

In Br Eighth Army's 5 Corps area, Germans destroy bridge in Cesano as 4th Div reaches it, but elements of 12th Brig wade the river near bridge site. 25th Brig, Ind 10th Div, strengthens bridgehead in Castiglione area and takes S. Carlo; to S, elements of 20th Brig secretly cross the Borello. In Cdn 1 Corps area, Cdn 1st Div attacks across the Savio with 2 cos but cannot hold bridgehead.

In coastal sector, Cesenatico is occupied after enemy withdraws.

HUNGARY—Germans are forced from Debrecen.

YUGOSLAVIA—Belgrade falls under combined blows of Third Ukrainian Front and Marshal Tito's Yugoslav Army. Yugoslavs announce capture of Dalmatian port of Dubrovnik.

EGYPT—Prime Minister Churchill arrives in Cairo from Moscow and discusses strategy for southeast Asia with Adm Mountbatten.

PALAUS—Gen Mueller, 81st Div commander, takes responsibility for ground operations in the Palaus from III Amphib Corps. Elements of 81st Div seize Pulo Anna I., in Sosoral Group, between Palaus and Morotai.

P.I.—U.S. Sixth Army invades Leyte, landing on E coast in vicinity of Tacloban, the capital, and Dulag at approximately 1000. Two firm beachheads are established, but at end of day they are nearly 10 miles apart. In a preliminary operation, 21st Inf of 24th Div lands well to S in vicinity of Panaon Strait at 0930 and secures the strait without opposition. Before landings, naval guns pound assault zone, beginning at 0600, and lifting for a time at 0850 for air strike on Dulag area. Aircraft provide close support throughout day. Advance echelon of GHQ opens on Leyte at noon. X Corps lands 2 divs abreast on N in vicinity of Tacloban. On N flank, 1st Cav Div, with 7th Cav of id Brig and 12th and 5th Cav of 1st Brig, lands and clears San Jose, Tacloban airstrip, and Cataisan Peninsula; makes contact with 24th Div to left. 24th Div, with 34th Inf on N and 19th on S, meets heavy fire after initial waves have landed; against strong opposition seizes Hill 522, key terrain feature N of Palo commanding N entrance to Leyte Valley, and secures bridgehead averaging a mile in depth. XXIV Corps lands near Dulag with 96th Div on N and 7th on S. 96th, with 383d Inf on N and 382d on S, is slowed by harassing fire and difficult terrain but takes San Jose, positions astride Labiranan R, and Hill 120; pushes inland about 2,500 yards on N and 1,300 on S; makes contact with 7th Div to left. 7th Div lands with 32d Inf on N and 184th on S; gets forward elements on N across Highway 1 and on S takes Dulag and reaches edge of airstrip, where counterattacks are repelled, night 20-21. 3d Bn, 17th Inf, lands in afternoon and secures right flank by establishing bridgehead S of Daguitan R at Dao.

21 October

WESTERN EUROPE—12th Army Group: Gen Bradley orders Ninth, First, and Third Armies to prepare for drive to the Rhine, 5 November target date for Ninth and First and 10 November for Third.

In U.S. First Army's VII Corps area, German commander of Aachen garrison surrenders at 1205, concluding struggle that has cost enemy heavily in badly needed reserve strength.

6th Army Group: In U.S. Seventh Army's XV Corps area, 9th Div launches full scale assault on heights E of Forêt de Parroy, with 313th Inf on left, 315th in center, and 314th on right. Some progress is made against strong opposition. In VI Corps area, 179th Inf of 45th Div enters Brouvelieures after main body of enemy has withdrawn and begins to clear rear-guard opposition. As 7th Inf continues toward St Dié, clearing Domfaing, 3d Div commits 15th Inf to left; 15th Inf pressure S of Brouvelieures aids 45th Div. 36th Div is improving positions E of Bruyères.

ITALY—AAI: In U.S. Fifth Army area, S African 6th Armd Div commits fresh troops on M. Salvaro and completes capture of M. Alcino. II Corps positions remain virtually the same. In Br 13 Corps area, 38th Brig of 78th Div makes another unsuccessful attempt to take M. Spadura. 21st Brig, Ind 8th Div, pushes almost to summit of M. Romano.

In Br Eighth Army's Pol 2 Corps area, 5th Kresowa Div, pressing NW toward Route 67, which leads to Forlì, takes Strada S. Zeno in Rabbi R valley and summit of M. Grosso. 5 Corps expands its 3 bridgeheads across the Savio despite heavy rainfall and rapidly rising water. Ind 10th Div's 20th Brig pushes toward M. Cavallo on left flank of corps while 25th Brig attacks to expand bridgehead from S. Carlo. 4th Div completes capture of Cesena and crosses additional forces over the Savio there, although handicapped by lack of permanent bridge. In Cdn 1 Corps area, Cdn 1st Div at 2000 begins attack across the Savio with 2d Brig, supported by diversionary fire of 3d Brig, and secures bridgehead.

HUNGARY—Elements of Second Ukrainian Front pushing W from Szeged reach the Danube at Baja, S of Budapest.

LEYTE—Japanese decide to make a strong effort to defeat Americans instead of fighting delaying action as planned.

U.S. Sixth Army: Generals Krueger, Sibert, and Hodge take command ashore of Sixth Army, X Corps, and XXIV Corps, respectively. In X Corps area, 2d Brig (7th Cav) of 1st Cav Div seizes Tacloban and S half of hill to SW; 1st Brig (12th Cav on right and 5th on left) drives W, taking Utap and Caibaan. 34th Inf, on N flank of 24th Div, undergoes determined enemy counterattack, beginning at 0100, in Pawing area. Arty and Seventh Fleet aircraft assist after daylight in routing enemy, more than 600 of whom are killed. 2d Bn then attacks ridge to W but cannot take it. 19th Inf clears far slope of Hill 522 and, with strong fire support, takes Palo. In XXIV Corps area, 96th Div's 383d Inf begins working around Catmon Hill, which is actually a series of hill positions. 1st Bn secures Labiranan Head but, since Japanese remain in this area, pulls back to Labiranan R. 2d Bn gains positions 300 yards N of Tigbao and 3d Bn, positions 1,110 yards NE of the barrio. 382d Inf drives an Tigbao but is slowed by pillboxes as well as swampy terrain. 7th Div attacks toward Dulag and Burauen airfields with 32d and 184th Regts. 32d, against considerable opposition, gets forward elements (2d and 3d Bns) to regimental beachhead line. 184th Inf easily takes Dulag airstrip by 0900 and continues W to positions about 1,000 yards beyond beachhead line, but gap exists between it and 32d Regt.

PALAUS—On Angaur, opposition, except from stragglers, is overcome by this time. Airfield is ready for bombers. About 1,300 Japanese have been killed and 45 captured on Angaur to date. Total U.S. casualties through this date are 264 killed and 1,355 wounded or injured.

22 October

WESTERN EUROPE—21 Army Group: In Cdn First Army's 2 Corps area, Breskens falls to Cdn 3d Div. Breskens Pocket is now less than half its original size. In Br I Corps area Cdn 4th Armd Div reaches Esschen.

In Br Second Army area, 12 Corps begins westward offensive to clear region W of the Maas. 15th Div heads for Tilburg and 7th Armd and 53d Inf Divs, followed by 51st Inf Div, towards Hertogenbosch.

12th Army Group: Major regrouping is begun in preparation for offensive toward the Rhine. Ninth Army hq moves from positions in Luxembourg between First and Third Armies to left flank of First Army, where it takes command of zone and troops of XIX Corps. N boundary of VII Corps thus becomes N boundary of First Army. First Army takes control of zone and troops of VIII Corps, placing new S boundary of First Army along previous boundary between Ninth and Third Armies.

In U.S. Third Army's XII Corps area, 26th Div, untried in combat as a unit, makes limited attack to gain experience and to improve positions E of Arracourt, securing ground W of Moncourt with support of troops from 704th TD Bn.

6th Army Group: In U.S. Seventh Army's XV Corps area, 79th Div finishes clearing high ground E of Forêt de Parroy. In VI Corps area, 3d Div advances steadily NE along Mortagne R toward St Dié. 179th Inf, 45th Div, completes mop up of Brouvelieures; 180th forces the Mortagne E of Fremifontaine but falls back under enemy fire.

FINLAND—From Petsamo, troops of Soviet Karelian Front drive on to Norwegian frontier.

EAST PRUSSIA—Soviet forces, after penetrating outer defense lines along NE frontier of East Prussia, are brought to a halt short of Insterburg. Activity in this area soon subsides and positions remain about the same until January 1945

YUGOSLAVIA—With the fall of Sombor, SW of Subotica, Allied forces control most of E bank of the Danube as far N as Hungarian town of Baja.

MEDITERRANEAN—Lt Gen Joseph T. McNarney replaces Gen Devers as head of NATOUSA.

ITALY—AAI: In U.S. Fifth Army area, S African 6th Armd Div continues toward crest of M. Salvaro in drenching rain. II Corps receives verbal orders to continue offensive on right flank to line Ribano Hill-M. Castelazzo, then to Highway 9. Accordingly, 88th and 85th Divs jump off, night 22-23, and get about a mile beyond M. Grande by dawn, taking Hill 568, M. Castellaro, and Hill 459. Rest of corps regroups to provide reserve force. 91st Div is reinf by 135th Inf of 34th Div; 362d and 363d Regts are withdrawn from line and Div zone is narrowed. 34th Div is gradually to extend its front, under cover of darkness, to include part of that formerly held by 91st Div. Br 13 Corps is ordered to take M. Spadura and continue northward between Imola and Castel San Pietro roads. 78th Div places fire on M. Spadura. Enemy withdrawal to E permits other units of corps to advance. 21st Brig, Ind 8th Div, takes M. Romano without opposition.

In Br Eighth Army's 5 Corps area, Ind 10th Div expands its Savio bridgeheads westward, 20th Brig pushing almost to crest of M. Cavallo. 4th Div is unable to progress from its bridgehead until heavy equipment can be crossed to it. In Cdn 1 Corps area, Cdn 1st Div is handicapped by the swollen Savio and is unable to cross supporting weapons into bridgehead. Cdn 5th Armd Div relieves NZ 2d Div in line and resumes command of 5th Armd Brig, previously known as Cumberland Force; elements moving up coast take Cervia and Pisignano.

LEYTE—U.S. Sixth Army: In X Corps area, 7th Cav of 2d Brig, 1st Cav Div, mops up Tacloban and takes rest of hill to SW. 8th Cav is placed under control of 2d Brig and takes up positions W of 7th Cav, except for Tr C, which moves to Anibong Pt. 5th Cav of 1st Brig, after laborious effort to advance over difficult terrain W of Caibaan, is ordered to halt and maintain current positions. 34th Inf, 24th Div, assisted by arty fire and naval aircraft, secures Pawing area with capture of hill to W. 19th Inf repels counterattacks against Palo, killing 91 Japanese, and mops up. In XXIV Corps area, after nightlong shelling of Labiranan Head, 1st Bn of 383d Inf, 96th Div, recaptures it while other elements of regt seize San Roque on Highway 1. 382d Inf takes Tigbao and Canmangui and sets up 3 night perimeters: one at Mati, one 800 yards E of Bolongtohan, and one 500 yards SE of Tigbao. 32d Inf, 7th Div, gets about halfway to Burauen against sporadic resistance. 184th, assisted by aircraft of Seventh Fleet, advances more rapidly, gaining 2,800 yards before being ordered to halt until 32d Inf can come abreast. 17th Inf, less 3d Bn, assembles in Dulag airfield area.

23 October

WESTERN EUROPE—21 Army Group: In Cdn First Army's Br I Corps area, U.S. 104th Div, inexperienced in combat, begins moving into line along Antwerp-Breda highway between 49th Div and Pol 1st Armd Div. On left flank of corps, Cdn 4th Armd Div swings W from Esschen toward Bergen-op-Zoom to seal off Beveland Isthmus, along which Cdn 2d Div of 2 Corps is preparing to drive.

12th Army Group: Front is generally quiet as preparations for offensive in November continue.

6th Army Group: Gen Eisenhower, in personal letter to Gen Devers, orders Sixth Army Group to protect S flank of 12th Army Group in coming offensive toward the Rhine.

In U.S. Seventh Army's XV Corps area, 44th Div commits 71st Inf to action, relieving elements of 79th Div of newly won positions E of Forêt de Parroy. In VI Corps area, 3d Div is meeting stronger resistance as it approaches Les Rouges Eaux, on road to St Dié. To left, 180th Inf of 45th Div succeeds in establishing bridgehead across Mortagne R E of Fremifontaine, from which to push NE toward Raon-l'Etape. On right flank, 36th Div extends positions E of Bruyères to Biffontaine; 1st Bn of 141st, attempting to secure heights N of La Houssière, becomes isolated in Forêt Domaniale de Champ.

ITALY—AAI: In U.S. Fifth Army area, S African 6th Div, attacking in force toward M. Salvaro, drives to summit; elements to right begin assault on M. Termine. In IV Corps area, TF 92, after unsuccessful attempt to push NE from M. Cauala, goes on the defensive in coastal sector. In II Corps area, enemy counterattacks and recovers Hill 459 from 85th Div. Elsewhere on right flank of corps, counterattacks are repulsed and bypassed pockets cleared. At night, 2d Bn of 351st Inf, 88th Div, attacks toward Vedriano and Co G takes Vedriano by dawn of 24th. 133d Inf, 34th Div, seizes M. Belmonte. In Br 13 Corps area, 78th Div, renewing assault on M. Spadura with 11th and 38th Brigs, clears this feature. 1st Div takes M. Cornazzano without opposition; gains ground N of M. Ceco. 21st Brig, Ind 8th Div, seizes M. Giro and pushes on toward M. Colombo; 17th takes M. Casalino.

In Br Eighth Army's 5 Corps area, Ind 10th Div reaches crest of M. Cavallo ridge, which extends northward to Bertinoro, commanding Highway 9; enemy begins to pull back. Savio R is subsiding and reinforcements are crossed into 4th Div's bridgehead. In Cdn 1 Corps area, Cdn 1st Div maintains bridgehead across the Savio but is unable to strengthen it. 11th Brig, Cdn 5th Armd Div, reaches the Savio to R.

BATTLE OF LEYTE GULF—Major 3-day naval battle opens as submarines discover and attack elements of Japanese *Combined Fleet* steaming toward the Philippines to eliminate U.S. threat to Leyte. Surface vessels and carrier aircraft of Third and Seventh Fleets and Japanese land-based planes later join in the action.

LEYTE—U.S. Sixth Army: At ceremony in Tacloban, Gen MacArthur restores Philippine Civil Government under President Sergio Osmena. In X Corps area, 8th Cav of 2d Brig, 1st Cav Div, charged with task of securing control of San Juanico Strait between Leyte and Samar and cutting off Japanese movement, begins operations toward this end. Rcn party moves by LCI from Tacloban through San Juanico Strait to Babatngon, on N coast, and on return reconnoiters ferry termini that connect Leyte and Samar, the Leyte terminus being at Guintiguian and the Samar terminus at La Paz, without incident. Other elements of the regiment move to Diit R and secure bridge in preparation for drive on Santa Cruz, on Carigara Bay. Japanese party raids Palo at night, using Filipinos to deceive Americans, but is dispersed and leave behind 60 dead. 1st Bn, 34th Inf, begins attack on Hill C, blocking passage into Leyte Valley on N side of Highway 2 at W edge of Palo, a strongly defended feature. 2d Bn, 19th Inf, reaches what it believes to be crest of Hill B, which also blocks entrance into Leyte Valley. 2d Sq of 12th Cav, 1st Cav Div, relieves 1st Bn, 19th Inf, on Hill 522; 1st Bn of 19th Inf is ordered to attack Hill 85, S of Palo. XXIV Corps area, 96th Div is facing acute supply shortage, which limits forward movement. 383d Inf, less 1st Bn, attacking at noon, crosses Guinarona R and reaches positions W of Pikas. 382d is largely engaged in patrolling. Tanks of 767th Tank Bn act as spearhead for 7th Div as it continues drive on Burauen in effort to take San Pablo airfield. 17th Inf (–), reinf by 2d Bn of 184th, leads troops, attacking through 32d and 184th Regts, which then follow. Tanks arrive at Burauen and scatter enemy forces. Infantrymen drive through Julita and San Pablo and seize San Pablo airfield.

PALAUS—AT and Cannon Cos relieve infantry of responsibility for eliminating the few remaining enemy on Angaur.

24 October

WESTERN EUROPE—21 Army Group: In Cdn First Army's 2 Corps area, methodical reduction of Breskens Pocket continues. Cdn 2d Div begins drive along Beveland Isthmus, leaving containing forces at its neck.

12th Army Group: Front remains generally static.

6th Army Group: In U.S. Seventh Army's XV Corps area, 44th Div, committing 324th Inf, completes relief of 79th Div. In VI Corps area, 3d Div commits its full strength to drive on St Dié as 30th Inf, having moved N, joins in attack to right of 7th. 179th Inf, 45th Div, takes town of Mortagne, on enemy side of Mortagne R.

In Fr 1st Army area, Gen de Lattre issues secret instructions to 1st Corps for offensive toward Belfort, INDEPENDENCE. 1st Corps is to be strongly reinf for the operation. Extensive deceptive measures are taken to conceal place of projected attack and take enemy by surprise.

ITALY—AAI: In U.S. Fifth Army area, M. Termine falls to S African 6th Armd Div. In II Corps area, Germans regain Vedriano and capture most of Co G, 351st Inf, 88th Div, there. 88th and 85th Divs continue attack on right flank of corps during night 24-25 but make little headway. In Br 13 Corps area, 78th Div consolidates positions on M. Spadura. 61st Brig, 6th Armd Div, pushes toward M. Taverna, reaching Orsara.

In Br Eighth Army's 5 Corps area, Ind 10th Div drives quickly toward Ronco R on S flank of corps; 4th Div advances its left flank to road junction of Madonna di Cerbiano and its right, along Highway 9, to Castellaccio. Cdn 1 Corps pursues retreating enemy toward Ronco R.

CBI—Theater is split in two theaters, India-Burma Theater (IBT) and China Theater (CT), to be headed respectively by Lt Gen Daniel I. Sultan and Maj Gen Albert C. Wedemeyer. Gen Chennault is temporarily in charge of China Theater, pending assumption of command by Gen Wedemeyer.

BATTLE OF LEYTE GULF—Seventh Fleet units engage and destroy Japanese naval force moving against Leyte via Surigao Strait, night 24-25. Third Fleet elements, after crippling another Japanese naval force, moving toward San Bernardino Strait, sails northward to attack enemy decoy force that has been sighted, thus leaving San Bernardino Strait unguarded.

LEYTE—U.S. Sixth Army: In X Corps area, 1st Sq of 7th Cav, 1st Cav Div, moves by water to Babatngon and sets up defense perimeter, from which patrols move along N coast. Tr C, reinf, of 8th Cav, after delay because of Japanese air attack on shipping in Tacloban harbor, which causes minor damage, sails to La Paz, Samar; establishes beach-

[25 OCTOBER 1944]

head and blocks road to Basey; after nightfall repels enemy thrust against the block. Main body of 1st Sq, 8th Cav, begins overland journey northward along Highway 1 and reach Guintiguian. Control of Juanico Strait is thus secured. In Palo area, 1st Bn of 34th Inf takes Hill Nan without opposition; is passed through by 3d Bn, which takes the next Hill, Mike—before Hill C—also without opposition, preliminary fires having been highly effective. 2d Bn, 19th Inf, continues efforts to take Hill B, finding enemy well entrenched on a crest higher than its own. Co K, 19th Inf, moving S along Highway 1 in effort to make contact with XXIV Corps, takes San Joaquin, S of Palo. In XXIV Corps area, 96th Div's 383d Inf, still beset by supply problems, holds current positions and patrols to locate possible supply routes to rear. Patrol finds enemy established at Tabontabon. 382d takes Anibung and Hindang. In 7th Div zone 17th Inf clears Burauen and, after brief pause, starts toward Dagami. 1st Bn, 32d Inf, turns NW toward Buri airstrip from San Pablo airfield but is so strongly opposed that it falls back to San Pablo with assistance of 3d Bn.

25 October

WESTERN EUROPE—21 Army Group: In Cdn First Army's 2 Corps area, Cdn 2d Div, working slowly W along Beveland Isthmus, reaches Rilland. In Br 1 Corps area, U.S. 104th Div drives N with 3 regts abreast toward Zundert.

12th Army Group: In U.S. First Army area, boundary between VII and V Corps is temporarily altered to give V Corps responsibility for Schmidt. V Corps takes command of 9th Div, less 47th Inf which is at Schevenhuette. 28th Div begins relief of battle-worn 9th Div in preparation for drive on Schmidt.

6th Army Group: In U.S. Seventh Army's XV Corps area, 44th Div withstands repeated counterattacks against its positions E of Forêt de Parroy. Fr 2d Armd Div is ordered to attack on right flank of corps in support of VI Corps before 1 November. In VI Corps area, Gen Brooks, former commander of V Corps, takes command of corps, replacing Gen Truscott. 36th Div attempts in vain to relieve isolated bn of 141st Inf N of La Houssière.

NORWAY—Driving into Norway from Finland, Soviet forces of Karelian Front clear Kirkenes.

ITALY—AAI: In U.S. Fifth Army area, elements of S African 6th Armd Div wade Setta Creek and take Hill 501, below M. Sole. In II Corps area, further efforts to deepen M. Grande salient, night 25-26, are costly failures. 362d Inf, 91st Div, is attached to 88th Div and prepares to assist in attack. In Br 13 Corps area, 61st Brig of 6th Armd Div gets elements to M. Taverna, night 25-26, but withdraws them because of tenuous supply situation.

In Br Eighth Army area, 5 Corps reaches the Ronco from heights across from Meldola to Highway 9. 4th Div, which replaces 12th Brig with 10th, takes Forlimpopoli without a fight. Attack across the Ronco begins night 25-26, Ind 10th Div establishing small bridgeheads S and N of Meldola and 4th Div crossing 2 cos NW of Selbagnone and 2 others at Highway 9. Cdn r Corps continues to pursue enemy toward the Ronco, coastal elements reaching the Bevano.

BURMA—NCAC offensive continues against light resistance. 29th Brig of Br 36th Div, which has progressed 23 miles from Namma against negligible opposition, skirmishes with enemy in Mawpin area.

BATTLE OF LEYTE GULF—Aircraft and surface forces of Third and Seventh Fleets decisively defeat Japanese *Combined Fleet* and continue to attack it as it begins to retire. Seventh Fleet units defeat a force that has moved through San Bernardino Strait while Third Fleet turns back the decoy force to N.

LEYTE—U.S. Sixth Army: Patrol contact is established between X and XXIV Corps at 1430. In X Corps area, on N Leyte, Japanese aircraft attack Babatngon harbor. 1st Sq of 7th Cav, 1st Cav Div, during the next few days explores coast of Carigara Bay and finds few Japanese there. 8th Cav is consolidating and improving positions in Juanico Strait area. 2d Sq of 8th Cav, because of supply difficulties, is ordered to remain in position along Diit R and patrol rather than continue drive toward Santa Cruz. In Palo area, 3d Bn of 34th Inf takes Hill C. 2d Bn, 19th Inf, gains crest of Hill B after enemy defenders have followed their customary practice of retiring from it for the night. 1st Bn, 19th, takes Hill 85. Reduction of these heights clears entrance into N Leyte Valley. 3d Bn, 19th Inf, starts toward Pastrana, reaching Castilla. In XXIV Corps area, patrol of 383d Inf, 96th Div, moves N through Tanauan and makes contact with Co K of 19th Inf, 24th Div. Co. K, reinf, attacks Tabontabon but withdraws when it finds the town too strongly held to take. 382d Inf seizes Aslom and Kanmonhag. After preparatory bombardment, 2d and 3d Bns of 32d Inf, 7th Div, preceded by tanks, continue attack toward Buri airstrip. 3d Bn reaches edge of the field but 2d is halted by elaborate defenses at edge of woods to N. 17th Inf, opposed from ridge N of Burauen and E of the road to Dagami, makes limited advance while concentrating for another drive toward Dagami, clearing E spur of the ridge and probing road to barrio of Buri.

PALAUS—On Peleliu, 323d Inf, which has arrived from Ulithi begins relieving 321st Inf.

26 October

WESTERN EUROPE—21 Army Group: In Cdn First Army's 2 Corps area, brig of 52d Div makes amphibious assault on Beveland from Terneuzen landing on S coast near Baarland and establishing bridgehead. Cdn 2d Div continues to push W along Beveland Isthmus. Cdn 3d Div is steadily reducing Breskens Pocket. In Br I Corps area, U.S. 104th Div gets into position for attack on Zundert.

In Br Second Army's 12 Corps area, 53 Div overruns 's Hertogenbosch.

12th Army Group: In U.S. Ninth Army's XIX Corps area, troops of 102d Div enter combat for first time, 406th Inf attached to 30th Div, 405th to 2d Armd, and 407th to 29th Div.

In U.S. First Army's V Corps area, 28th Div takes responsibility for zone previously held by 39th and 60th Regts of 9th Div. 9th Div (−) goes back to Camp Elsenborn. 5th Armd Div, to which CCA reverts from attachment to XIX Corps, moves to rear of 4th Div.

In U.S. Third Army's XX Corps area, action at Maizières-lès-Metz centers about strongly held Hôtel de Ville. Co K of 357th Inf, 90th Div, reaches the hotel but is driven back.

6th Army Group: In U.S. Seventh Army's VI Corps area, 3d Div continues toward St Dié under exceptionally heavy arty fire, 7th Inf, in center, overrunning Les Rouges Eaux. On left flank of corps, 45th Div is clearing Forêt d'Housseras and working toward Raon-l'Etape. 36th Div, on S flank, is relieving its isolated 141st Inf force, which begins drive to W in effort to break out.

HUNGARY—Soviet forces of Fourth and Second Ukrainian Fronts link up near Mukacevo in E Hungary.

ITALY—AAI: Heavy rains and flooding slow operations all along line.

In U.S. Fifth Army area, S African 6th Div halts efforts to take M. Sole; elements on Hill 501 are virtually isolated. In II Corps area, flash flood prevents commitment of 362d Inf across the Sillaro as planned. 88th and 85th Divs are given verbal orders to break off offensive and organize defensive positions on more tenable ground. In Br 13 Corps area, 17th Brig of Ind 8th Div pushes to Lutirano and Tredozio. 61st Brig, 6th Armd Div, after repelling attack against Orsara and making another futile attempt to take M. Taverna, confines its activities to patrolling.

In Br Eighth Army's Pol 2 Corps area, 5th Kresowa Div, having cleared M. Mirabello-M. Colombo ridge, sends elements into Predappio Nuovo, on Rabbi R, but is forced back. In 5 Corps area, Ind 10th Div consolidates bridgeheads across the Ronco, but 4th Div is unable to hold on without tank support and suffers heavy losses while withdrawing. Since the river is now in flood, corps operations temporarily come to a standstill. Cdn 1 Corps makes little progress because of flooding.

BURMA—In NCAC area, Ch 22d Div, attacking in center of NCAC front, reaches old Chindit airstrip, BROADWAY, 27 miles SE of Hopin, where it remains for a few days to recover from arduous march over hills.

BATTLE OF LEYTE GULF—Battle ends as Japanese Fleet retires with the following losses: 3 BB's, 1 large and 3 light carriers, 6 heavy and 4 light cruisers, and 9 DD's. U.S. losses are 1 light carrier (*Princeton*), 2 escort carriers, 2 DD's, and 1 DE.

LEYTE—U.S. Sixth Army: In X Corps area, 24th Div, having cleared northern approaches to Leyte Valley, attacks inland. 2d Bn, 34th Inf, drives steadily along Highway 2 to Santa Fe. From Castilla, 3d Bn of 19th continues to outskirts of Pastrana, where entrance into the town is barred by a strong fortress. In XXIV Corps area, 382d Inf of 96th Div attempts to take Tabontabon, Japanese supply center, but after reaching edge of the barrio is forced back to Guinarona R. Div arty shells the barrio through night 26-27. 383d Inf's Co E conducts rcn in force against San Vicente Hill, N tip of Catmon Hill, but is forced to withdraw. Japanese withdraw main body of troops from Catmon Hill. 3d Bn, 381st Inf, starts N along Highway 1 toward Tanauan to secure N flank of beachhead along road Tanauan-Dagami. 32d Inf, 7th Div, continues battle for Buri airfield with 2d and 1st Bns, moving through fortifications to positions around edge of the field. 17th Inf, leaving 2d Bn of 184th Inf behind to contain enemy on ridge and moving its 3d Bn forward by truck from Dao, attacks with 1st, 2d, and 3d Bns toward Dagami, reaching positions about 600 yards S of Guinarona.

PALAUS—On Peleliu, RCT 323 takes control of operations against Umurbrogol Pocket. 321st Inf has lost 146 killed and 469 wounded on Peleliu. Umurbrogol Pocket now averages about 600 yards from N to S; although about 475 yards wide on N, deep salients have been driven southward into it; Japanese retain a few caves along E side; S part of the pocket is less than 350 yards wide. A period of unfavorable weather conditions begins, during which RCT 323 improves defenses.

27 October

WESTERN EUROPE—21 Army Group: In Cdn First Army's 2 Corps area, forward elements of Cdn 2d Div reach Beveland Canal, at W end of Beveland Isthmus, and cross during night 27-28. 52d Div expands Baarland bridgehead to Oudelande. In Br 1 Corps area, Bergen-op-Zoom falls to Cdn

4th Armd Div, 413th Inf of U.S. 104th Div, assisted by effective arty preparation and attached Br tanks, takes Zundert by storm.

In Br Second Army's 8 Corps area, Germans, following heavy arty barrage, open strong tank-infantry attack toward Asten in effort to divert Allied strength from main battle front, penetrating lightly held positions of U.S. 7th Armd Div along Canal de Deurne and Canal du Nord, W of Venlo. Germans take Meijel, near junction of the two canals, and penetrate line at Heitrak, on Meijel-Deurne highway, and near Nederweert. CCA of U.S. 7th Armd Div seals off penetration pear Nederweert; CCB is relieved by Br 11th Armd Div in order to counterattack on 28th.

12th Army Group: In U.S. Third Army's XX Corps area, 357th Inf of 80th Div, employing 4 small teams, again attempts in vain to take Hôtel de Ville in Maizières-lès-Metz.

6th Army Group: In U.S. Seventh Army's VI Corps area, 3d Div presses slowly in on St Dié against heavy fire. 36th Div's isolated bn is too weak to break out, but some progress toward it is made by Nisei troops. First efforts to drop supplies by air fail. Subsequent attempts achieve some success.

In Fr 1st Army area, Gen de Lattre, at conference with Gen Devers at Vittel, presents his plan for offensive toward Belfort and gains Gen Devers' approval. The Fr drive is to coincide with general Allied offensive in November and is to open on 13th.

HUNGARY—Troops of Fourth Ukrainian Front take Ungvar (Uzhorod) on NE border. This completes Soviet conquest of Carpatho-Ukraine (Ruthenia before March 1939).

ITALY—AAI: In U.S. Fifth Army's Br 13 Corps area, 26th Armd Brig Gp, following up enemy withdrawal on right flank of corps, occupies Rocca S. Casciano, on Highway 67.

In Br Eighth Army's Pol 2 Corps area, elements of 5th Kresowa Div recapture Predappio Nuovo. In 5 Corps area, Ind 10th Div crosses additional elements over the Ronco, night 27-28. In Cdn 1 Corps area, plans to relieve Cdn 1st Div and Cdn 5th Armd Div cannot be carried out at this time because of weather conditions. Advance elements of corps across the Bevano in coastal sector are withdrawn.

BURMA—In NCAC area, U.S. 124th Cav arrives in training area.

CHINA—Japanese renew offensive to take U.S. air bases in E China (ICHIGO), heading toward Kweilin and Liuchow.

LEYTE—U.S. Sixth Army: In X Corps area, 1st Bn of 34th Inf, 24th Div, advances through 2d Bn to Mudburon R without opposition. After night-long shelling of Pastrana, 3d Bn of 19th Inf enters the town and with assistance of 1st Bn mops up. In XXIV Corps area, 382d Inf of 96th Div again attacks Tabontabon. 1st and 3d Bns push through NW part of the town to positions about a mile to NW, but 2d Bn is held up in the town and establishes night perimeter in center of it. 383d Inf patrols in vicinity of San Vicente and San Vicente Hill in effort to locate enemy positions. Sixth Army releases 381st Inf from reserve to corps. 32d Inf, 7th Div, against surprisingly light resistance, clears Buri airstrip by 1130. 17th Inf, reinf by platoon of engineers to repair bridges, continues drive on Dagami, reaching positions some 2,200 yards S of the town.

28 October

WESTERN EUROPE—Gen Eisenhower issues directive for November offensive, calling for destruction of enemy W of the Rhine, establishment of bridgeheads across the river, and drive into Germany.

21 Army Group: In Cdn First Army's Br 1 Corps area, U.S. 104th Div takes Rijsbergen, about halfway between Zundert and Breda, and pushes toward Rosendaal-Breda highway.

In Br Second Army's 12 Corps area, Tilburg falls to 15th Div. In 8 Corps area, U.S. 7th Armd Div begins two-pronged attack to recover Meijel, CCB driving SE along Deurne-Meijel highway and CCR TF moving along Asten-Meijel road. Small gains are made against severe opposition.

12th Army Group: In U.S. Third Army's XX Corps area, while one co of 357th Inf, 90th Div, makes diversionary attack N of Hotel de Ville in Maizières-lès-Metz, while 3 cos enter factory area in preparation for attack.

6th Army Group: Issues letter of instruction for reduction of enemy W of the Rhine and capture of Strasbourg.

In U.S. Seventh Army's XV Corps area, enemy makes limited withdrawal, night 28-29, pulling back to line Leintrey-Blémerey.

ITALY—AAI: In U.S. Fifth Army's IV Corps area, RCT 6 of BEF outflank Gallicano, in Serchio Valley. II Corps, now greatly understrength after six weeks of hard fighting, is ordered in writing to halt offensive and establish defensive positions.

In Br Eighth Army's 5 Corps area, Ind 10th Div crosses more elements over the Ronco, night 28-29, and begins attack from bridgehead S of Meldola. Cdn 1 Corps is withdrawn into reserve as 12th Lancers, under 5 Corps command, relieves Cdn 1st Div on left flank and TF known as Porter Force, under Eighth Army command, takes over coastal sector from Cdn 5th Armd Div.

BULGARIA—Signs armistice with Allies. By its terms, Bulgaria will relinquish portions of Greece and Yugoslavia acquired in 1941, make certain reparations yet to be determined, and place armed forces at the disposal of the Soviet high command.

YUGOSLAVIA—Announces capture of Split, capital of Dalmatia and Adriatic port, to Partisan forces.

BURMA—In NCAC area, 713th Regt of Ch 38th Div encounters patrols from enemy's OPL along Taping R near Bhamo but routes them in order to reach the river at Myothit. 112th and 114th Regts are to make wide enveloping maneuver in order to turn the enemy line.

LEYTE—U.S. Sixth Army: In X Corps area, 1st Bn of 34th Inf, 24th Div, followed by 2d Bn, drives through Alangalang to Mainit R and dislodges enemy from steel bridges spanning it. 3d Bn makes contacts with 79th Inf S of Santa Fe. 1st Bn, 79th Inf, blocks road N of Binahaan R near Macalpe; 2d establishes perimeter at Tingib. 1st Cav Div regroups: 1st Sq of 12th Cav moves to Castilla to relieve 24th Div of responsibility for rear areas so that latter may drive on Jaro; 2d Cav Brig is ordered to advance on Carigara; 2d Sq of 8th Cav is to establish base at San Miguel, secure Cavite, and patrol as far N and NW as Barugo road, maintaining contact with 1st Sq, 7th Cav; 1st Sq of 7th Cav, while holding positions at Santa Cruz and Babatngon, is to concentrate in Barugo=Carigara area and patrol S and SE. Tr C of 7th Cav moves by water from Babatngon to Barugo and overland to Carigara, where prolonged fire fight ensues; withdraws to Barugo late in afternoon. In XXIV Corps area, 2d Bn of 382d Inf, 96th Div, finishes clearing Tabontabon and continues toward Kiling. 381st Inf begins attack on E slopes of Catmon Hill at noon. 2d Bn gets almost to Labir Hill, but 1st receives such accurate fire at foot of the hill that it pulls back to vicinity of line of departure. 2d Bn of 32d Inf, 7th Div, is alerted for drive on Abuyog on 29th. 3d Bn is ordered to Guinarona. 17th Inf makes slow progress toward Dagami. 2d Bn, in the lead, suffers heavy casualties.

29 October

WESTERN EUROPE—21 Army Group: In Cdn First Army area, 2 Corps is rapidly clearing S Beveland and completing reduction of Breskens Pocket. 52d Div and Cdn 2d Div establish contact on S Beveland and 52d Div takes Goes. Br 1 Corps, upon reaching Bergen-op-Zoom–Tilburg road, is directed northward to secure crossings of Mark R. Breda falls to Pol 1st Armd Div.

In Br Second Army's 8 Corps area, Germans attack in force from Meijel toward Liesel and Asten, taking Liesel from CCB, U.S. 7th Armd Div, and pushing CCR units back about halfway up road toward Asten. During night, 15th Div (which has completed its mission with 12 Corps) and a tank brig are sent to reinforce corps. 75th Div relieves CCB near Liesel and CCR SE of Asten. U.S. 7th Armd Div, upon relief, concentrates about Nederweert and Weert.

12th Army Group: In U.S. Third Army's XX Corps area, 3 cos of 357th Inf, 90th Div, omitting arty preparation, attack from factory area at Maizières-lès-Metz into section S of Hôtel de Ville; 2 others attack from N. Most of the town is cleared by dark.

6th Army Group: In U.S. Seventh Army's VI Corps area, 45th Div moves into Bru and Jeanménil, which enemy has successfully defended for the past month, without opposition. Drive on Raon-l'Etape continues to right. 3d Div improves positions near St Dié. In 36th Div zone, 442d Inf pushes closer to isolated 1st Bn of 141st Inf in Forêt Domaniale de Champ.

ITALY—AAI: In U.S. Fifth Army area, elements of GCB, S African 6th Armd Div, on left flank of div, take Palazzo, W of Highway 64.

In Br Eighth Army's 5 Corps area, enemy garrison at Meldola is threatened with encirclement as Ind 10th Div begins attacks from bridgeheads and S of the town. 4th Div prepares for another attack across the river since flood waters are subsiding.

INDIA-BURMA—On Salween front, Gen Wei Li-huang's Chinese Expeditionary Force, closely supported by U.S. Fourteenth Air Force, renews offensive, attacking toward Lung-ling with Ch 200th Div in the lead. Japanese have been thinning out.

In NCAC area, Br 36th Div, having paused briefly at Mawpin, resumes southward drive down RR corridor.

LEYTE—Since 77th Div will apparently not be needed on Leyte, Gen MacArthur transfers it from control of Gen Krueger to that of Adm Nimitz.

U.S. Sixth Army: In X Corps area, 3d Bn of 34th Inf, 24th Div, takes the lead in drive to Jaro, reaching the town at 1700 after having cleared opposition en route to Galotan. 19th Inf defends S flank of div; Co K establishes roadblock at Ypad. 2d Cav Brig, 1st Cav Div, continues assembling in Barugo area, 1st Sq joining Tr C there. In XXIV Corps area, 2d Bn of 381st Inf, 96th Div, takes Labir and Catmon Hills with ease. 1st Bn jumps off at noon and makes contact with 2d Bn. 1st Bn, 383d Inf, is relieved on Labiranan Head and passes to Sixth Army reserve. Withdrawing depleted 2d Bn to reserve, 17th Inf of 7th Div continues attack toward Dagami with 1st and 3d Bns and breaks into S part of town. From Burauen, 2d Bn of 32d Inf moves without incident along Highway 1 to Abuyog. 7th Cav Rcn Tr, preceding it, pushes on toward Baybay.

30 October

WESTERN EUROPE—21 Army Group: In Cdn First Army's 2 Corps area, Cdn 2d Div completes drive across S Beveland, reaching E end of Walcheren causeway. Cdn 3d Div is nearing end of action to reduce Breskens Pocket. In Br 1 Corps area, 415th Inf, spearheading for U.S. 104th Div, reaches the Mark and attempts to take bridge near Standdaarbuiten, but Germans blow it.

In Br Second Army area, 12 Corps makes patrol contact with 1 Corps. 7th Armd Div drives W to Oosterhout and makes contact with Pol 1st Armd Div of 1 Corps there. In 8 Corps area, enemy makes final effort to advance in Peel Marshes but is brought to a halt.

12th Army Group: In U.S. First Army area, V Corps outlines further action to be taken by 28th Div after it seizes its first objective, line Vossenack–Schmidt.

In U.S. Third Army's XX Corps area, 357th Inf of 90th Div completes capture of Maizières-lès-Metz, thus opening route to Metz from the N.

6th Army Group: In U.S. Seventh Army's VI Corps area, elements of 45th Div seize St Benoit, on Rambervillers-Raon-l'Etape road. 3d Div now holds broad salient W of St Dié and the Meurthe from vicinity of Nompatelize on N to Traintrux on S. In 36th Div zone, 442d Inf at last makes contact with and relieves 1st Bn of 141st Inf.

ITALY—AAI: In U.S. Fifth Army area, Germans begin series of counterattacks toward Palazzo that last for several days, but CCB of S African 6th Armd Div holds firm. In IV Corps area, RCT 6 of BEF seizes Lama hill mass, N of Barga. During October corps has conducted a training program for inexperienced 1st Div, BEF, and 92d Div as the units arrived.

In Br Eighth Army's Pol 2 Corps area, Germans withdraw from Caminata region. In 5 Corps area, 10th Div takes Meldola, from which enemy has withdrawn, but runs into strong opposition as it pushes on toward Rabbi R. 4th Div tries in vain to get patrols across the Ronco on N flank of corps.

P.I.—AAF SWPA issues instruction for air support of the Mindoro operation by Gen Kenney's U.S. Far East Air Force, comprising Fifth and Thirteenth Air Forces. Fifth Air Force is to be the "assault air force" but Thirteenth Air Force, RAAF, carrier-based planes of U.S. Third and Seventh Fleets, and land-based planes of Seventh Fleet are also to assist as are B-29's of U.S. Twentieth Air Force.

LEYTE—U.S. Sixth Army: In X Corps area, 3d Bn of 34th Inf, 24th Div, starts toward Carigara along road from Jaro but is halted almost at once by Japanese. 2d and 1st Bns are given supporting roles as 3d Bn renews efforts to advance up the road without getting beyond outskirts of Jaro. Co K, 19th Inf, makes contact with elements of XXIV Corps at Lopdak. Co C skirmishes with enemy at Rizal. Gen Krueger orders relief of 21st Inf, 24th Div, in the quiet Panaon Strait area by a bn of 32d Inf. In XXIV Corps area, 2d and 3d Bns of 383d Inf, 96th Div, attack San Vicente from Guinarona R and find the barrio and hill of the same name undefended. 17th Inf, 7th Div, completes capture of Dagami in morning and spends rest of day mopping up. Contact is made with X Corps units across Binahaan R north of Dagami by means of message dropped by air and with 96th Div on E by patrols, concluding current mission of 17th Inf. 7th Div, on its beachhead line, is ordered to move elements from Abuyog to Baybay and be prepared to move to W coast.

31 October

WESTERN EUROPE—21 Army Group: In Cdn First Army's 2 Corps area, Cdn 2d Div starts W across Walcheren causeway from S Beveland but is halted by enemy fire. Amphibious assault forces at Breskens and Ostend prepare to land on Walcheren. In the Breskens Pocket, only small enemy groups remain in coastal area. Cadzand and Knocks are free of enemy. In Br 1 Corps area, while main body of corps is closing along the Mark, advance elements attempt unsuccessfully to establish bridgeheads. 1st Bn of 415th Inf, U.S. 104th Div, crosses NE of Standdaarbuiten in assault boats early in day but is encircled by enemy counterattacking force and withdraws after nightfall. Elements of Pol 1st Armd Div cross the river E of Zevenbergen, but they too are forced back to S bank. Enemy fire prevents bridging.

In Br Second Army area, 12 Corps overcomes opposition at Raamsdonk; releases 53d Div, which has completed its current mission with corps, to 8 Corps for action in Peel Marshes. In 8 Corps area, Maj Gen Lindsay McD. Silvester is replaced as commander of U.S. 7th Armd Div by Maj Gen Robert W. Hasbrouck, former CCB commander. Div front is confined to Nederweert area as Belgian 1st Brig, along Nederweert-Wessem Canal, is detached. The Belgian force is augmented by a Br armored brig. 15th Div regains Liesel.

6th Army Group: In U.S. Seventh Army's XV Corps area, Fr 2d Armd Div, with CCV on left and CCD on right, drives SE from Forêt de Mondon, taking enemy by surprise and overwhelming his forward positions Montigny, Merviller, and N part of Baccarat are cleared; other elements of div provide diversion on S flank, taking Menarmont and Nossoncourt, SW of Baccarat. In VI Corps area, 15th Inf of 3d Div attacks at night, turning northward in region W of the Meurthe.

HUNGARY—Broadening operations toward Budapest, elements of Second Ukrainian Front force the Tisza and push into Kecskemet, where street fighting ensues.

ITALY—AAI: In Br Eighth Army's 5 Corps area, Ind 10th Div progresses rapidly toward the Rabbi as enemy resistance weakens. 4th Div establishes 2 bridgeheads across the Ronco between Selbagnone and Highway 9.

SEAC—Adm Mountbatten, having returned to Kandy from meetings with Prime Minister Churchill at Cairo, at or near this time proposes to CCS that Phases 1 and 2 of CAPITAL be completed; Arakan and Akyab be cleared (Operations ROMULUS and TALON, respectively) in order to release main body of 15 Corps for use elsewhere; forward base on Kra Isthmus be seized in March 1945; Rangoon be taken after the 1945 monsoon; Malaya be invaded regardless of the monsoon.

INDIA-BURMA—11 Army Group: In Br Fourteenth Army area, 4 Corps hq returns from India and opens near Imphal with Ind 19th Div under command about this time.

In NCAC area, Br 36th Div, against stiffening resistance, reaches Mawlu.

CHINA—Gen Wedemeyer assumes command of U.S. Forces, China Theater. His primary task is to conduct air operations from China, with logistical support from IBT.

LEYTE—U.S. Sixth Army: In X Corps area, while 3d Bn of 34th Inf, 24th Div, is engaged in clearing hill around Jaro, 2d Bn passes through in attack toward Tunga. 19th Inf protects S flank of 24th Div and blocks enemy escape routes. Elements move up to Jaro and make contact with 24th Div. In XXIV Corps area, 96th Div is mopping up Catmon Hill sector. Co G of 32d Inf, 7th Div, starts from Abuyog toward Baybay.

1 November

WESTERN EUROPE—21 Army Group: In Cdn First Army area, 2 Corps begins an all-out assault on Walcheren. Continuing attack on causeway from S Beveland, Cdn 2d Div gains a few hundred yards but is forced back. From Breskens, Cdn 4th Cdo of 4th Sp Service Brig, under 52d Div command, followed by 155th Brig of 52d Div, crosses estuary to S coast near Flushing and begins clearing that town. From Ostend, 41st, 47th, and 48th Cdos of 4th Special Service Brig and Dutch cdo force move to W coast, land at gap in Westkapelle dyke, and seize Westkapelle; some elements turn NE along coast while others drive SE toward Flushing, Rcn force is sent to N Beveland. Planned air support is curtailed when missions from U.K. are canceled because of weather conditions. Warships and support craft provide close naval support, but latter suffer heavily from enemy fire and mines. Br 1 Corps prepares for co-ordinated attack across the Mark.

In Br Second Army area, 12 Corps finishes clearing its sector S of the Maas except for small region between Afwaterins Canal and the river. In 8 Corps area, 53d Div goes into line on right flank of corps along Wessem Canal SE of Nederweert and Belgian 1st Brig and Br 4th Separate Armd Brig are attached to it. U.S. 7th Armd Div prepares for limited offensive to secure NW bank of Canal du Nord.

12th Army Group: In U.S. Third Army area, Gen Patton and his commanders draw up plans for Third Army offensive. After First Army's attack on D Day, XII Corps will attack on D plus 1, XX Corps on D plus 2, and III Corps will eventually be responsible for mopping up Metz pocket. Regrouping is in progress. In XX Corps area, 5th Div reoccupies Arnaville bridgehead S of Metz, relieving 95th Div. XII Corps, in preparation for offensive, makes limited attack with 319th Inf, 80th Div, to clear Seille R bend in Létricourt-Abaucourt area and quickly takes both towns.

6th Army Group: In U.S. Seventh Army's XV Corps area, Fr 2d Armd Div' after completing capture of Baccarat, driving to the Blette R at Herbéviller and Mignéville, and helping 117th Cav Rcn Tr (VI Corps) take Bertrichamps, halts to await relief. In VI Corps area, 100th Div arrives in corps zone to relieve 45th Div on N flank. 3d Div's 15th Inf seizes La Bourgonce, in valley NW of St Dié.

MEDITERRANEAN—North African Theater of Operations (NATOUSA) is redesignated Mediterranean Theater of Operations (MTOUSA).

ITALY—AAI: In Br Eighth Army's 5 Corps area, Ind 10th Div reaches the Rabbi at Collina and Grisignano, but 4th Div is halted short of Forlì airfield by sharply increased resistance.

HUNGARY—Germans are driven from Kecskemet, communications center SE of Budapest.

GREECE—With withdrawal of enemy from Florina and Salonika, only rear-guard forces remain S of Yugoslav border.

LEYTE—Japanese land reinforcements at Ormoc.

In U.S. Sixth Army's X Corps area, 1st Bn of 34th Inf, 24th Div, executes wide flanking movement through Tuba; 2d Bn followed by 3d continues along Jaro-Carigara road and finds that enemy has withdrawn hastily. By end of day, 1st Bn, in the lead, is within 1,000 yards of Sagkanan. As plans for concerted assault on Carigara are being made, Japanese begin undetected withdrawal from the town toward hills near Limon. In XXIV Corps area, 96th Div completes mop up of entire Catmon Hill area. 1st Bn of 32d Inf, 7th Div, relieves 21st Inf of 24th Div in Panaon Strait area.

2 November

WESTERN EUROPE—21 Army Group: Field Marshal Montgomery orders extensive regrouping after Schelde Estuary and SW Holland are cleared in preparation for offensive by Br Second Army to destroy enemy bridgehead W of the Maas as prerequisite for Rhineland battle.

In Cdn First Army's 2 Corps area, 157th Brig of Br 52d Div relieves Cdn 2d Div forces at Walcheren causeway, where enemy continues to resist tenaciously; to ease pressure, elements of 156th Brig cross Slooe Channel about 2 miles S of the causeway after nightfall; Flushing is cleared of enemy. Br 1 Corps attacks across the Mark late in day after heavy arty preparation. 49th and U.S. 104th Divs establish bridgeheads, 104th in Standdaarbuiten area and 49th to W. 104th, with 413th and 415th Regts in assault, clears village of Standdaarbuiten.

In Br Second Army's 8 Corps area, CCA of U.S. 7th Armd Div begins limited attacks to clear enemy from Canal du Nord. 53d Div makes patrol contact with U.S. XIX Corps near Maeseyck.

12th Army Group: In U.S. First Army's V Corps area, 28th Div, after hour-long arty preparation, begins drive on Schmidt: 2d Bn, 112th Inf, with tank support, seizes Vossenack ridge, but main effort by rest of regt to drive SE from Richelskaul toward Kommerscheidt and Schmidt is stopped at once; 109th Inf gets elements to woods line overlooking Huertgen on N flank, but 110th is unable to advance on S flank.

In U.S. Third Army area, Gen Bradley, while visiting Army hq, asks if Third Army can begin offensive alone, since First Army cannot attack until British release 2 U.S. divs; he is told that Third Army can attack on 24-hour notice. Third Army offensive will begin when weather conditions permit softening of enemy; in the event of poor weather conditions, XII Corps will attack on 8 November. In XX Corps area, 10th Armd Div enters line in Fort Driant sector.

6th Army Group: In U.S. Seventh Army's XV Corps area, elements of VI Corps begin relieving Fr 2d Armd Div in SE part of XV Corps sector, but French retain positions along the Blette for some days to come. In VI Corps area, 100th Div begins relief of 45th Div, 399th Inf replacing 179th in line. Pushing northward NW of St Dié, 15th Inf of 3d Div takes Nompatelize without opposition, but enemy still holds La Salle, to S.

In Fr 1st Army area, Gen de Lattre is charged with conduct of Operation INDEPENDENCE.

ITALY—AAI: U.S. Fifth Army issues instructions, confirming verbal orders of 30 October, for future operations during current winter lull, calling for consolidation of the Bologna salient and limited action on its flanks. In Br 13 Corps area, on right flank, command of 26th Armd Brig's sector on Highway 67 passes to Pol 2 Corps and intercorps boundary is adjusted accordingly. Ind 8th Div's zone is broadened to include M. delle Valle area, previously held by 1st Div.

In Br Eighth Army area, 5 Corps remains in place because of tenuous communication lines. 128th Brig, 46th Div, relieves Ind 10th Div, which withdraws to reserve.

YUGOSLAVIA—Partisans seize Dalmatian port of Zara.

BURMA—11 Army Group: In Br Fourteenth Army's 33 Corps area, Ind 5th Div reduces enemy strongpoint, known as Vital Corner, below Tiddim, with assistance of air and arty bombardment.

LEYTE—U.S. Sixth Army: With clearance of entire Leyte Valley, army completes second phase of battle for Leyte. In X Corps area, 1st Cav and 24th Inf Div forces converge on undefended Carigara, near N entrance to Ormoc Valley, and make contact. In XXIV Corps area, 382d Inf of 96th Div relieves 3d and 1st Bns of 17th Inf, 7th Div, in vicinity of Dagami and engages enemy W of Dagami. Co G of 32d Inf, 7th Div, reaches Baybay, on W coast, at 2200. Main body of 32d Inf is alerted for move to Abuyog.

PALAUS—As weather conditions improve, 323d Inf of 81st Div opens attack to complete reduction of Umurbrogol Pocket on Peleliu but makes little headway.

3 November

WESTERN EUROPE—21 Army Group: In Cdn First Army's 2 Corps area, Cdn 3d Div finishes clearing Breskens Pocket. Some 12,500 prisoners have been taken during the operation. Substantial progress is made by Br 52d Div, reinf by 4th Special Service Brig, on Walcheren I. Assault forces from Westkapelle join with those from Flushing. Positions in E Walcheren are extended. In Br 1 Corps area, German delaying line along the Mark collapses as 49th Div and U.S. 104th Div expand bridgeheads, but many strongpoints remain. Pol 1st Armd Div establishes bridgehead near Zevenbergen on right flank of corps; Cdn 4th Armd Div, on left flank, improves positions in Steenbergen area.

In Br Second Army's 8 Corps area, CCA of U.S. 7th Armd Div continues to clear NW bank of Canal du Nord, overrunning villages of Horik and Ospel.

12th Army Group: In U.S. First Army's V Corps area, 112th Inf of 28th Div crosses Kall R and takes Kommerscheidt and Schmidt, but 110th and 109th Regts make little or no progress on flanks. Schmidt is on MSR of enemy in Lammersdorf Corridor.

In U.S. Third Army area, XX and XII Corps issue orders for offensive. XX Corps is to eliminate the Metz garrison, secure crossing of the Sarre in Saarburg area, and, upon order, continue offensive toward NE. XII Corps, attacking between 5 and 8 November, is to seize Faulquemont, secure Rhine bridgehead between Oppenheim and Mannheim, and, tentatively, push to Darmstadt area. In XX Corps zone, 3d Cav Gp moves forward at night to eliminate small enemy pocket W of the Moselle at Berg-sur-Moselle.

6th Army Group: In Fr 1st Army's 2d Corps area, 3d Algerian Div, in limited attack toward Gerardmer, arouses strong opposition.

ITALY—AAI: U.S. Fifth Army is assigned 366th Inf, a separate regt, but the unit does not arrive at Leghorn until 91st.

In Br Eighth Army's 5 Corps area, local attack by 4th Div brings such sharp enemy reaction that it is decided to attack in strength when weather conditions improve. Positions across the Ronco are gradually strengthened during the next few days in preparation for renewing offensive.

INDIA-BURMA—On Salween front, Ch Hon 1st Div recovers Lung-ling, scene of hard fighting for some months.

In NCAC area, Ch 22d Div reaches the Irrawaddy in vicinity of Shwegu without opposition and prepares to cross.

LEYTE—Japanese reinforcements moving up Ormoc Valley are hit with good effect by aircraft.

U.S. Sixth Army: Issues order for converging drive on Ormoc by X and XXIV Corps. In X Corps area, 34th Inf of 24th Div takes Capoocan with ease and continues toward Pinamopoan until held up by enemy strongpoint. In XXIV Corps area, 1st Bn of 382d Inf, 96th Div, attacks W of Dagami toward ridge, later called Bloody Ridge, moving through rice paddy, but is so heavily opposed that it withdraws after nightfall. One 2d Bn column advances to Patok and another moves up to reinforce 1st Bn. 1st Bn withstands strong counterattack, night 3-4.

4 November

WESTERN EUROPE—21 Army Group: In Cdn First Army area, first mine sweepers reach Antwerp. In 2 Corps area, Br 52d Div and commandos are methodically clearing Walcheren. Junction is made between forces at causeway and those who have crossed Slooe Channel. Enemy is being cleared from N coast. In Br 1 Corps area, 49th and U.S. 104th Divs continue to push N toward the Maas in center of corps. Pol 1st Armd Div, on right flank, takes Geertruidenberg. Steenbergen, on left flank, is encircled. 104th Div is directed to move to Aachen when released from current mission.

In Br Second Army's 8 Corps area, CCA of U.S. 7th Armd Div continues to clear NW bank of Canal du Nord.

12th Army Group: In U.S. First Army's V Corps area, Germans counterattack vigorously toward Schmidt and Kommerscheidt, regaining former. A few tanks that have reached Kommerscheidt help materially in turning enemy back. 109th Inf, 28th Div, withstands determined enemy attack to N; on S, 110th makes limited progress and takes Simonskall.

In U.S. Third Army's XX Corps area, 3d Cav Gp takes hill overlooking Berg but is driven off in counterattack.

6th Army Group: In U.S. Seventh Army's VI Corps area, 3d Div continues to clear For de Mortagne W of St Dié and open ground to N, where La Salle is now clear. 36th Div is clearing Forêt Domaniale de Champ and pushing toward Corcieux on S flank of corps.

ITALY—AAI: In U.S. Fifth Army area, IV Corps takes command of S African 6th Armd Div's sector and U.S. troops (CCB, 1st Armd Div) attached to that div; releases 92d Div to Fifth Army control to hold Serchio Valley and coastal sector on left flank of army. In Br 13 Corps area, 1st Gds Brig of 6th Armd Div completes relief of 1st Div in line. 1st Div then moves to relieve 88th Div and elements of 85th Div, U.S. II Corps, to W.

HUNGARY—Soviet forces of Second Ukrainian Front seize Cegled and Szolnok, on rail line to Budapest. Autumn rains and stiffening opposition in environs of Budapest are beginning to slow Red Army.

YUGOSLAVIA—Sibenik, on Dalmatian coast, falls to Partisans.

BURMA—11 Army Group: In Br Fourteenth Army's 33 Corps area, Ind 5th Div clears Kennedy Peak, another enemy strongpoint S of Tiddim.

LEYTE—U.S. Sixth Army: X Corps, directed to take up defensive role against seaborne attack in Carigara area and to patrol to locate sites for arty within range of Ormoc, regroups. After patrol of 34th Inf, 24th Div, finds that enemy has fallen back, advance continues through Colasian and Pinamopoan to edge of ridge later called Breakneck Ridge. In XXIV Corps area, 1st Bn of 382d Inf, 96th Div, continues attack W of Dagami toward Bloody Ridge and gains about 1,000 yards against light opposition. Main body of 2d Bn moves up behind 1st. Japanese counterattacking on night 4-5 are turned back by arty fire and leave 254 dead behind.

5 November

WESTERN EUROPE—21 Army Group: In Cdn First Army area, 2 Corps continues to make rapid

[6-7 NOVEMBER 1944]

progress on Walcheren I. Br 1 Corps gets forward elements to the Maas. U.S. 104th Div, less elements of 414th Inf that are to help Pol 1st Armd Div take Moerdijk, prepares to move to Aachen.

In Br Second Army's 12 Corps area, 51st Div finishes clearing enemy from S bank of the Maas. In 8 Corps area, U.S. 7th Armd Div approaches Meijel area from S, and 15th Div begins drive on Meijel from N.

12th Army Group: In U.S. First Army's V Corps area, 28th Div withstands infantry counterattacks against Kommerscheidt, but Germans infiltrate MSR and gain control of Kall bridge. Steady enemy fire on Vossenack is weakening U.S. defenders there. To help 112th Inf in drive on Schmidt on 6th, TF R (Col Ripple, CO of 707th Tank Bn) is formed, containing bn of 110th Inf, tanks, and TD's. In VII Corps area, poor weather conditions prevent opening of offensive.

In U.S. Third Army's XX Corps area, 3d Cav Gp, after heavy fire on enemy positions, clears Berg and hill to N. XII Corps is ready to open offensive, but awaits order from Gen Patton. Rain falls intermittently.

6th Army Group: U.S. Seventh Army directive calls for reduction of enemy W of the Rhine and capture of Strasbourg. XV Corps is to attack on D Day, taking Sarrebourg and forcing the Saverne Gap. VI Corps, not later than D plus 2, is to attack through Vosges passes to take Strasbourg. In VI Corps area, 45th Div, into whose line additional elements of 100th Div are gradually being introduced, pushes in slowly toward Raon-l'Etape. 3d Div continues to clear region W of the Meurthe from St Dié area northward. 36th Div is still engaged in Forêt Domaniale de Champ.

In Fr 1st Army's 2d Corps area, 3d Algerian Div, continuing limited offensive toward Gerardmer, gains Rochesson, Menaurupt, and heights near these villages.

ITALY—AAI: In U.S. Fifth Army's IV Corps area, 1st Div of BEF takes command of CCB, 1st Armd Div, in place. Corps zone, from W to E, is now manned by 107th AAA Gp, Brazilian 1st Div, and S African 6th Armd Div.

In Br Eighth Army area, improving weather conditions permit Allied aircraft to begin softening up strikes in preparation for attack by 5 Corps on Forli.

LEYTE—U.S. aircraft attack enemy forces moving up Highway 2.

U.S. Sixth Army: In X Corps area, 1st Cav Div begins prolonged program of patrolling in central mountains of Leyte. 21st Inf returns to 24th Div and relieves 34th Inf at Breakneck Ridge, W of Pinamopoan. In XXIV Corps area, 382d Inf of 96th Div continues attack on Bloody Ridge after arty prepa-

[319]

ration and, with assistance of co of tanks, is reducing enemy positions there.

6 November

WESTERN EUROPE—21 Army Group: In Cdn First Army area, 2 Corps clears Middelburg, on Walcheren I. Br 1 Corps continues to eliminate scattered strongpoints S of the Maas. Pol 1st Armd Div, assisted by elements of U.S. 104th Div, begins attack on Moerdijk, on enemy's escape route. Main body of 104th Div starts to Aachen.

In Br Second Army area, U.S. 7th Armd Div is ordered to return to 12th Army Group in preparation for offensive. 15th Div continues limited action N of Meijel.

12th Army Group: In U.S. First Army's VII Corps area, 4th Div, moving from V Corps zone to Zweifall area, is ordered to release 12th Inf, which, under command of 28th Div, V Corps, is to begin relief of elements of 28th Div at once. In V Corps area, 28th Div repels further attacks against Kommerscheidt but is forced from E end of Vossenack. Relief of 109th Inf by 12th Inf of 4th Div cannot be accomplished on night 6-7 as planned. Attack on Schmidt by TF R is postponed.

ITALY—AAI: In U.S. Fifth Army's IV Corps area, TF 45 assumes command of coastal sector from 107th AAA Gp. In Br 13 Corps area, Ind 8th Div takes M. Monsignano without opposition.

In Br Eighth Army area, Pol 2 Corps moves forward following limited enemy withdrawal. In region W of Highway 67, 3d Carpathian Div takes M. Chioda and M. Pratello. 5th Kresowa Div, E of the highway, seizes M. Testa, E of Dovadola.

INDIA-BURMA—In NCAC area, 64th Regt of Ch 22d Div crosses the Irrawaddy and overcomes light opposition in Shwegugale.

CHINA—Japanese threat to Kunming, which is besieged, is by now a matter of serious concern to China Theater hq.

LEYTE—U.S. Sixth Army: X Corps is ordered by Gen Krueger to drive as quickly as possible down Highway 2 to secure Ormoc. 21st Inf, 24th Div, probes Breakneck Ridge in preparation for attack southward. Forward elements of 3d Bn are forced back to beach near Colasian by intense enemy fire. 1st Bn attempts in vain to get into position to support assault on Breakneck Ridge. In XXIV Corps area, 382d Inf of 96th Div clears all but isolated pockets on Bloody Ridge, despite well-prepared enemy positions.

7 November

WESTERN EUROPE—21 Army Group: Cdn First Army takes direct control of final mopping up operations on Walcheren I. Br 1 Corps sector is now largely clear, although Germans continue to hold out in Moerdijk. Elements of 414th Inf, U.S. 104th Div, upon relief by British in Moerdijk area, rejoin parent div.

In Br Second Army's 8 Corps area, U.S. 7th Armd Div reverts to 12th Army Group. Final assault on Meijel is delayed to await 12 Corps' drive from SW.

12th Army Group: In U.S. First Army area, V Corps, after disastrous enemy counterattacks against 28th Div, decides to withdraw Kali R bridgehead. 28th Div loses Kommerscheidt but holds along N woods line overlooking the village. Force of engineers and tanks clears E part of Vossenack and turns defense of the village over to 2d Bn, 109th Inf. 12th Inf, 4th Div, relieves 109th Inf on N flank N of Germeter.

In U.S. Third Army area, Gen Patton orders offensive to open on 8th, although heavy downpour of rain at this time gives little promise of air assistance.

6th Army Group: In Fr 1st Army area, 2d Corps is beating off counterattacks SW of Gerardmer. Noise of this action helps cover movement of units southward in preparation for attack by 1st Corps toward Belfort.

ITALY—AAI: In Br Eighth Army area, 5 Corps opens offensive toward Forlì at 2250 after heavy arty preparation. While 4th Div attacks Forlì airfield, 46th Div, to left, drives N from Grisignano toward S. Martino in Strada.

INDIA-BURMA—In NCAC area, Shwegu falls to Ch 22d Div, which is ordered to garrison it with 64th Regt while attacking with 65th and 66th toward Man-tha.

LEYTE—U.S. Sixth Army: X Corps begins southward drive on Ormoc along Highway 2. 21st Inf, 24th Div, reinf by 3d Bn of 19th, attacks toward spur of lie ridge 400 yards to its front after massed fire on enemy positions but cannot take it; establishes night perimeters at edge of Breakneck Ridge. Co G, 19th Inf, advances toward Hill 1525, about 2,600 yards SE of Limon, in support of 21st Inf's attack, but halts far E of objective. In XXIV Corps area, 382d Inf of 96th Div, with all 3 bns in assault, continues attack on Bloody Ridge, overrunning enemy positions and killing an estimated 474 Japanese. Co E remains in Patok area.

8 November

WESTERN EUROPE—21 Army Group: Begins extensive regrouping in order to place Br Second Army along the Meuse facing eastward.

Cdn First Army completes mop up of Walcheren I., where prisoners total about 8,000, concluding offensive to secure approaches to Antwerp. Br 1 Corps extends E, taking over sector formerly held by 12 Corps of Br Second Army, and assumes command of 7th Armd Div and attachments.

12th Army Group: In U.S. Ninth Army area, XIII Corps (Maj Gen Alvan C. Gillem, Jr.) enters line on extreme left of army group, occupying narrow sector between XIX Corps and Br 30 Corps. Under XIII Corps command are 102d Div, less 406th Inf—attached to 2d Armd Div of XIX Corps—and 84th Div.

In U.S. First Army's VII Corps area, 104th Div is attached to corps and begins relief of 1st Div. V Corps begins withdrawing Kali bridgehead.

U.S. Third Army opens offensive toward the Sarre. XX Corps makes final preparations for assault on Metz fortified area. By dawn 60th Div, which is to make main effort, completes secret move to Forêt de Cattenom in preparation for attack across the Moselle through Koenigsmacker and the Maginot Line. 10th Armd Div is moving N to attack in conjunction with 60th Div. 95th Div begins diversionary action (CASANOVA) at 2100 when Co C, 377th Inf, crosses the Moselle in assault boats just S of Uckange after an engineer detachment clears E bank; against light resistance Co C moves inland some 400 yards, but accurate enemy fire prevents bridging; simultaneously with the river crossing, 2d and 3d Bns of 377th Inf begin clearing enemy pocket W of the Moselle in vicinity of Maizières-lès-Metz. 83d Div is transferred to XX Corps from VIII Corps but because of restrictions on its use will provide only fire support. XII Corps begins drive toward the Sarre at 0600 after preparatory fire. 80th Div, with 3 regts abreast on N flank, attacks across Seille R, taking Eply, Nomeny, and Aulnois-sur-Seille. 35th Div, with 137th Inf on left and 320th on right, 320th having passed through 134th, attacks in center: 137th seizes Malaucourt and Jallaucourt; 320th, in conjunction with 26th Div to right, attempts to reach Morhange plateau but is stopped at Fresnes-en-Saulnois on left and short of Bois d'Amélécourt on right. 26th Div employs 3 regts abreast on right flank of corps: 104th Inf, reinf by 2 small TF's, seizes Vic-sur-Seille and Seille bridges there; 101st overruns Moyenvic and takes its bridge, then begins costly action for Hill 310 (Côte St Jean); feinting toward Dieuze on right flank of corps, 328th Inf seizes Bezange-la-Petite and Moncourt; 2d Cav Gp, attached to 26th Div, protects S flank of corps along Marne-Rhine Canal.

6th Army Group: In U.S. Seventh Army area, XV Corps issues field order for offensive to begin on 13 November. Infantry of 44th and 79th Divs are to breach enemy positions; Fr 2d Armd Div is then to drive through the gap to exploit.

ITALY—AAI: In Br Eighth Army's Pol 2 Corps area, 3d Carpathian Div is clearing hills between Modigliana and Dovadola and takes Dovadola. 5th Kresowa Div presses toward Castrocaro, gaining M. delta Birra without opposition. 5 Corps makes slow progress in Forlì area. After nightfall, 46th Div begins attack across the Rabbi, 128th Brig crossing at S. Martino in Strada and 138th Brig, upstream from there.

GREECE—Ind 4th Div arrives in Salonika; elements move to Thrace to avert threat of civil war between EAM, now in control there, and nationalist guerrillas.

BURMA—Adm Mountbatten issues directive calling for Operation ROMULUS, to clear Arakan coastal sector.

11 Army Group: In Br Fourteenth Army's 33 Corps area, Ind 5th Div finishes clearing enemy from region S of Tiddim with unopposed occupation of Fort White, previously an enemy strongpoint.

LEYTE—Japanese land another div at Ormoc about this time and send it into mountains of central Leyte.

U.S. Sixth Army: In X Corps area, 24th Div's 21st Inf, despite a raging typhoon, continues attack on Breakneck Ridge with 2d Bn assisted by Co L but cannot force enemy back. 2d Bn of 19th Inf succeeds in clearing ridge, which has been barring its advance, but is still short of Hill 1525; elements move 1,000 yards W to occupy the next ridge. 1st Bn of 21st Inf drives to Hill 1525. In XXIV Corps area, patrols of 382d Inf, 96th Div, locate enemy force about 2,600 yards W of Patok.

9 November

WESTERN EUROPE—21 Army Group: In Cdn First Army area, Br 1 Corps finishes clearing region S of the Maas. 2 Corps takes over Nijmegen sector from 30 Corps and assumes command of U.S. 82d A/B, U.S. 101st A/B, Gds Armd, 43d Inf, and 50th Inf Divs and of 8th Separate Armd Brig.

In Br Second Army area, 12 Corps enters line along the Meuse to right of 8 Corps and takes command of 53d and 51st Divs and Belgian 1st and 8th Separate Armd Brigs in place.

12th Army Group: In U.S. Ninth Army's XIII Corps area, 7th Armd Div arrives in corps zone from Br Second Army Sector.

In U.S. Third Army area, XX Corps launches full-scale attack to encircle and reduce Metz and is assisted by powerful air attacks by Eighth and Ninth Air Forces on Metz–Thionville region. At 0330 assault bns of 359th and 358th Regts, 90th Div, start across the Moselle at Malting and Cattenom, surprising enemy and gaining bridgehead. Since the swollen river and enemy fire prevent immediate construction of bridges, supporting weapons cannot be crossed. 359th Inf takes Malting, Hunting, Petite-Hettange, Métrich, and Kerling; to S, 358th clears Basse Ham and gains hold on W part of Fort Koenigsmacker; 357th (–), crossing later in day, takes town of Koenigsmacker without opposition. 95th Div expands and strengthens its small Uckange bridgehead, bypassing Bertrange; elements of 377th Inf W of the river take woods N of Semécourt, slag pile S of Maizières-lès-Metz, Château Brieux. 5th Div begins attack across Seine R south of Metz by footbridge and assault craft: 2d Inf and 2 bns of 10th Inf establish bridgehead 6,000 yards deep and 5,000 yards wide, 2d Inf on right taking Cheminot without opposition and 10th clearing resistance at Hautonnerie Farm. In XII Corps area, 80th Div, assisted by aircraft and advance of friendly forces on its flanks, gains most of Delme Ridge. 6th Armd Div crosses the Seille in 80th Div sector in preparation for drive on Faulquemont; advance party of CCB advances to positions W of Alemont while armored infantry assists 80th Div in mopping up Nomeny area. In 35th Div sector, CCB of 4th Armd Div is committed through 137th Inf, which then follows armor, and drives forward in 2 columns, one reaching Hannocourt and the other halting short of Fonteny, where enemy holds prepared positions. 137th Inf, 35th Div, takes Delme village in conjunction with attack by 80th Div on Delme Ridge; 320th Inf, after clearing Fresnes area, concentrates on Bois d'Amélécourt and pushes into the forest, where enemy is well entrenched; 134th Inf is committed to right with mission of clearing E part of Forêt de Château-Salins. 100th Inf, 26th Div, clears enemy from Château-Salins; attached TF takes Morville-lés-Vic and continues toward Hampont; 101st Inf is attempting to outflank Hill 310 and seizes Salival. CCA, 4th Armd Div, is ordered to attack through 100th Inf on 10th.

6th Army Group: In U.S. Seventh Army's VI Corps area, 100th Div completes relief of 45th Div and takes over its mission of protecting N flank of corps and clearing Raon-l'Etape area W of the Meurthe. 45th Div moves to rest area and passes to Seventh Army control. 103d Div enters line in 3d Div sector, relieving 7th Inf.

ITALY—AAI: In U.S. Fifth Army area, II Corps front is narrowed as 1st Div of Br 13 Corps takes command of sector previously held by 88th Div and elements of 85th. In Br 13 Corps area, Ind 8th Div, pushing northward as enemy makes limited withdrawals, takes M. Budriatto.

In Br Eighth Army's 5 Corps area, 4th Div clears enemy stragglers from Forlì. 46th Div reaches Montone R at S. Varano, where it is held up by enemy from opposite bank; platoon crosses later at Terra del Sole but is isolated and lost.

BURMA—In NCAC area, Br 36th Div resumes advance with 72d and 29th Brigs, 72d on W. 72d Brig has moved forward during lull in Mawlu sector.

CHINA—Generalissimo Chiang Kai-shek, urged by Gen Wedemeyer to order Y-Force troops to exploit retreat of Japanese from Lung-ling to Mangshih, agrees to do so. After the order is issued, Ch XII Group Army (53d, 2d, and 71st Armies) starts toward Mangshih.

LEYTE—Japanese convoy lands reinforcements at Ormoc but is forced to withdraw under air attack before equipment and ammunition can be unloaded. The vessels are destroyed on their return journey by U.S. aircraft.

U.S. Sixth Army: In X Corps area, 24th Div is ordered to make co-ordinated effort to clear Breakneck Ridge and commanding ground S of Limon on 10th. 21st Inf continues bitter struggle for the ridge, gaining ground slowly in frontal attacks. To assist 91st Inf, 34th Inf is ordered to move elements into position to harass enemy rear. 2d Bn, 19th Inf, is placed under control of 21st Inf and moves toward Hill 1525 to relieve 1st Bn, 21st Inf. 1st Bn, leaving Co A to await arrival of 2d Bn, 19th Inf, begins attack to cut Ormoc road S of Limon, but is recalled to help Co A beat off counterattack against Hill 1525. 1st Bn is forced to fall back to Pinamopoan area. In XXIV Corps area, heavy rainfall prevents 382d Inf, 96th Div, from attacking enemy W of Patok.

10 November

WESTERN EUROPE—12th Army Group: U.S. First Army alters boundary between VII and V Corps to give V Corps responsibility for Huertgen in Kleinhau. In VII Corps area, 12th Inf, which reverts to 4th Div from attachment to 28th Div of V Corps, undergoes a determined counterattack on plateau SW of Huertgen that engulfs 2 cos and forces remnants back to S third of the plateau. Because of weakened state of the regt, CCR of 5th Armd Div is attached to corps. 104th Div completes relief of 1st Div. In V Corps area, elements of 28th Div make limited progress toward woods line near Huertgen.

In U.S. Third Army's XX Corps area, enemy mounts tank-infantry counterattack at 0300 that overruns Kerling and threatens Petite-Hettange before 359th Inf of 90th Div, helped by massed arty fire on Kerling, contains the onslaught; 357th begins assault on Métrich group of fortifications SE of Koenigsmacker, partially reducing it; 358th continues efforts to take Fort Koenigsmacker, elements bypassing the fort to reach Bois d'Elzange ridge. 1st Bn of 377th Inf, 95th Div, maintains Uckange bridgehead and is supplied by air; action to finish clearing enemy salient W of the Moselle has been broken off by rest of 377th Inf since Hauconcourt is now flooded; 2d Bn, 378th Inf, starts to Thionville to reconnoiter in force across the Moselle. Bridge is completed at Malling site about midnight. 2d Inf of 5th Div, its left flank covered by 10th, continues NE to left and rear of XII Corps' CCB, 6th Armd Div, taking Pagny-lès-Goin, Silly-en-Saulnois, and road junction E of latter; relieves armor at Vigny and Buchy, on intercorps MSR. In XII Corps area, 6th Armd and 80th Inf Divs advance rapidly on N flank of corps in spite of mud, mines, and congestion on highways. CCB of 6th Armd Div, in conjunction with 5th Div (XX Corps), drives through Vigny and Buchy while CCA pushes to Luppy. 80th Div gains nearly 8 miles. CCB, 4th Armd Div, attempts to swing elements from Hannocourt to Fonteny but finds enemy blocking route at Viviers. 137th Inf of 35th Div moves up behind armor, clearing Viviers in hard fight and pushing beyond Laneuveville-en-Saulnois to Fonteny area; 320th Inf drives from Bois d'Amélécourt into Forêt de Château-Salins while 134th advances on Gerbécourt. CCA, 4th Armd Div, drives through left flank of 26th Div, forward elements reaching Hampont. 101st Inf of 26th Div continues flanking attacks toward crest of Hill 310, gaining ridge NE of the hill and positions in Bois St Martin.

6th Army Group: In U.S. Seventh Army's VI Corps area, enemy resistance W of the Meurthe is weakening noticeably. Continuing northward along the river, 15th Inf of 3d Div takes Etival. 103d Div relieves 30th Inf, 3d Div, in line. 142d Inf of 36th Div, which has been inching SE through Forêt Domaniale de Champ from Les Rouges Eaux, finds Vanemont and La Houssière, at SE edge of the forest, undefended.

ITALY—AAI: In U.S. Fifth Army's Br 13 Corps area, Ind 8th Div finds M. Ponpegno clear and pushes on to M. Bassana.

In Br Eighth Army's 5 Corps area, 4th Div runs into intense opposition as it attempts to advance from Forlì.

BURMA—In NCAC area, Br 36th Div comes up against enemy's MLR in Pinwe area of RR corridor. Ch 38th Div successfully turns enemy OPL along the Taping in Bhamo area and emerges onto Bhamo plain.

CHINA—Japanese take Kweilin and Liuchow from Ch garrisons without difficulty. Next Japanese objective is Kweiyang.

PACIFIC—77th Div, en route to New Caledonia, is ordered to Leyte.

LEYTE—U.S. Sixth Army: In X Corps area, elements of 1st Cav Div begin extensive patrolling of central mountains. 24th Div opens all-out effort to clear enemy from rest of Breakneck Ridge. While

21st Inf continues frontal attacks, 1st Bn of 34th Inf and 2d Bn of 19th attack toward commanding ground S of Limon. From Capoocan, 1st Bn of 34th moves by LVT's along coast of Carigara Bay for 7 miles, lands, and advances inland to ridge near Belen. In XXIV Corps area, 382d Inf of 96th Div renews attack with 1st and 3d Bns and completes occupation of Bloody Ridge and its sector without opposition.

11 November

WESTERN EUROPE—21 Army Group: Br Second Army continues to regroup in order to help U.S. Ninth Army in offensive in Roer Valley NE of Aachen. 30 Corps takes up positions on S flank of army, including region formerly held by U.S. XIII Corps from Maeseyck to Teveren, 2 miles SW of Geilenkirchen. Corps takes operational control of U.S. 84th Div, less 335th Inf.

12th Army Group: In U.S. Ninth Army's XIX Corps area, 335th Inf of 84th Div is attached to 30th Div at Wuerselen. 102d Div turns over part of its sector to Br 30 Corps.

In U.S. First Army area, VIII Corps takes command of 83d Div from XX Corps.

In U.S. Third Army's XX Corps area, 90th Div nearly doubles size of its bridgehead: 359th Inf, after repelling local counterattacks, pushes to ridges ahead, blocks crossroads SE of Rettel, and outposts Kerling, but enemy retains Oudrenne on its S flank; 357th, leaving elements behind to complete reduction of Métrich works, drives quickly to high ground NW of Breistroff-la-Petit, well ahead of flanking regts; on S flank, where Fort Koenigsmacker surrenders, main body of 358th Inf works along Bois d'Elzange ridge, taking Hill 254. Moselle flood waters reach their crest and begin to subside. 2d Bn of 378th Inf, 95th Div, supported by combat engineers, establishes bridgehead across the Moselle at Thionville and begins assault on Fort Yutz; 377th maintains small bridgehead in Bertrange area. Continuing quickly NE on S flank of corps, 2d Inf of 5th Div reaches Aube and Dain-en-Saulnois, near Nied Française R. In XII Corps area, 6th Armd Div, assisted by 80th Div, drives to Nied Française R and establishes bridgeheads. One CCB TF of 6th Armd Div takes bridge near Sanry-sur-Nied and crosses while another reaches W bank of the river at Remilly; CCA column and 317th Inf of 80th Div seize bridge at Han-sur-Nied and establish bridgehead; another CCA force and 318th Inf reach the river at Baudrecourt 2 miles S of Han-sur-Nied, and construct treadway bridge. CCB 4th Armd Div, and elements of 137th Inf, 35th Div, are still held up at Fonteny but push into the village. 320th and 134th Regts, 35th Div, continue through Forêt de Château-Salins, from which enemy begins withdrawing main forces. CCA, 4th Armd Div, and 104th Inf, 26th Div, push forward on S flank of corps, CCA to positions between Conthil and Rodalbe and 104th Inf taking Rodalbe. 101st Inf, 26th Div, completes capture of Hill 310 and secures firm positions on Koecking ridge.

6th Army Group: In Fr 1st Army area, 1st Corps commander requests and receives permission to postpone INDEPENDENCE from 13th to 14th in order to complete preparations.

ITALY—AAI: In U.S. Fifth Army's Br 13 Corps area, limited attack by Ind 8th Div from M. S. Bartolo fails.

In Br Eighth Army's Corps area, 4th Div breaks through just beyond Forlì and advances toward the Montone.

BURMA—In NCAC area, Br 36th Div halts after futile efforts to outflank enemy in Pinwe area.

CHINA—U.S. Fourteenth Air Force planes attack Heng-yang with such success that Japanese are forced to confine future operations from this field to army co-operation flights.

LEYTE—U.S. Sixth Army: In X Corps area, 21st Inf of 24th Div continues assault on Breakneck Ridge after preparatory bombardment, 1st Bn gaining ridge that is its immediate objective but halting short of crest. 1st Bn of 34th Inf, which is out of rations, moves to Agahang, about 3,800 yards NW of Limon, and obtains food from Filipinos.

VOLCANO Is.—Warships of Third Fleet and land-based bombers bombard Iwo Jima airfields.

12 November

WESTERN EUROPE—21 Army Group: In Br Second Army area, 30 Corps takes responsibility for U.S. Ninth Army's N flank as far S as Wurm R.

12th Army Group: In U.S. First Army's VII Corps area, two cos of 12th Inf, 4th Div, break through to the isolated forces on plateau SW of Huertgen, but they too become encircled.

In U.S. Third Army's XX Corps area, the Germans, in effort to reach Malling bridge, counterattack in regimental strength with support of tanks and assault guns against 359th Inf, 90th Div, forcing outposts from Kerling and again threatening Petite-Hettange, but are driven off with heavy losses. Malling bridge is destroyed by enemy arty fire after 2 TD's have crossed. 357th Inf of 90th Div, which has been joined by its reserve bn, continues attack along Bois de Koenigsmacker ridge, pushing beyond Breistroff-la-Petit to positions overlooking Inglange; 358th gains line Elzange-Valmestroff and both of these villages. Bridge construction is begun at Cattenom. On S flank of corps 2d Inf, 5th Div, crosses into 6th Armd Div's bridgehead at Sanry-sur-Nied (XII Corps zone) and during night 12-13 repels enemy counterattack. 5th Div regroups for northward drive on Metz, 11th Inf extending its right flank to the Seille. In XII Corps area, CCB of 6th Armd Div expands Sanry bridgehead and outposts main road junction between Bazoncourt and Berlize. One CCA TF attacks toward Faulquemont from Han-sur-Nied bridgehead, overcoming strong resistance at Herny; another crosses the Nied Française at Baudrecourt. German efforts to stop 50th Div in triangle between Nied Française R and Rotte Creek subside when 6th Armd Div TF pushes S and outflanks enemy, and the creek is bridged at points. Corps alters plan of attack, giving 6th Armd Div mission of securing high ground S of Faulquemont and extending its zone southward. After 137th Inf of 35th Div seizes Faxe, restoring contact between columns of GCB, 4th Armd Div, CCB pursues enemy to Oron and takes bridge across Nied Française at Oron while 137th advances in region to E; 320th Inf clears rest of Forêt de Château-Salins and is withdrawn to reserve; 134th drives to Bellange, where it halts upon order. 26th Div, having regrouped to turn 101st Inf E along S slopes of Koecking ridge and place 328th in center on Koecking ridge, continues attack on S flank of corps. Germans, committing armored reserve, succeed in halting CCA, 4th Armd Div, and 104th Inf, 26th Div: CCA column drives through Rodalbe toward Bermering but is forced back to Bois de Conthil to await tank replacements; all-out German counterattack regains Rodalbe and virtually destroys 3d Bn of 104th Inf there; right flank column of CCA takes Hill 337, SE of Lidrezing; elements recover Conthil and reopen MSR. 104th Inf, badly depleted in strength, establishes itself along Conthil-Lidrezing road, where it forms an exposed salient. 328th Inf of 26th Div, reinf by bn of 101st, begins clearing forest on Koecking ridge, reaching Berange Farm, where stubborn strongpoint is overrun; 101st attempts unsuccessfully to take St Medard and then breaks off attack.

6th Army Group: In U.S. Seventh Army's VI Corps area, 100th Div begins attack on N flank of corps to outflank Raon-l'Etape with 399th and 397th Regts, leaving 398th and rcn tr to maintain current positions along the Meurthe: assault regts cross the river at Baccarat to attack Raon from the rear and block enemy movement. 103d Div takes command of sector W of St Di between 15th Inf of 3d Div and 36th Div. 36th Div is slowly improving positions near Corcieux.

ITALY—AAI: In Br Eighth Army area, Pol 2 Corps attacks toward line Castrocaro-Converselles-Lucia, S of Faenza, in conjunction with 5 Corps. In 5 Corps area, 4th Div is held up N of Highway 9 at S. Tome, a little short of the Montone. 138th Brig, 46th Div, attacks across the Montone SW of Forlì.

YUGOSLAVIA—Kumanovo, on Skoplje-Nis rail line, is now in Allied hands.

SEAC—Allied Land Forces South East Asia (ALFSEA) is activated under Lt Gen Sir Oliver Leese. The new hq consists of former Hq, 11 Army Group, previously under Gen Giffard, and some U.S. officers; has control over Br troops, NCAC, CAI, and Ch forces within SEAC. Lt Gen Raymond A. Wheeler takes over Gen Stilwell's former post of Deputy Supreme Allied Commander, SEAC.

CHINA—East China Air Task Force, formed by Gen Chennault to help Ch troops defend E China airfields from bases W and E of enemy-held corridor, begins arriving at Suichwan and goes into action within a week.

LEYTE—U.S. Sixth Army: In X Corps area, 21st Inf of 24th Div gains crest of Breakneck Ridge shortly after noon but is unable to advance S along Highway 2 from there. 1st Bn of 34th Inf, after receiving its first airdrop of supplies, moves through Consuegra to Cabiranan. 2d Bn, 19th Inf, blocks Highway 2 south of Limon and maintains the block with difficulty until 23d.

13 November

WESTERN EUROPE—21 Army Group: In Cdn First Army's 2 Corps area, Cdn 3d Div takes over sector formerly held by U.S. 82d A/B Div; A/B div reverts to First Allied Airborne Army.

12th Army Group: In U.S. Third Army's XX Corps area, 359th Inf of 90th Div recovers Kerling and moves through dense mine fields to establish contact with 357th near Oudrenne; 358th continues down Bois d'Elzange ridge, hampered more by mines than by enemy, to positions near Inglange. Cattenom bridge is opened to traffic, and vehicles and weapons begin crossing in a steady stream. 2d Bn of 378th Inf, 95th Div, completes reduction of Fort Yutz and takes Basse Yutz; final elements of 1st Bn, 377th, cross into Uckange bridgehead, where Bertrange and Imeldange are easily cleared and enemy counterattack is repulsed. 5th Div drives N on Metz: 11th Inf, on left, takes ground around Fey, Pournoy-la-Chétive, and Coin-lès-Cuvry; 10th overruns Forts Aisne and Yser, S of Bois de l'Hôpital; elements of 2d, having crossed the Nied Française S of Sanry-sur-Nied, take Ancerville. Engineers construct bridge near Ancerville. Enemy efforts to drive 2d Inf of 5th Div back across the Nied during night fail. In XII Corps area, German counterattack against Sanry bridgehead forces outpost of CCB, 6th Armd Div, back, but main line holds; CCB is ordered to turn over Sanry bridgehead to 5th Div (XX Corps) and move SE; one CCA column continues toward Faulquemont assisted by 317th Inf of 80th Div; another clears enemy from Arraincourt.

CCB, 4th Armd Div, and 35th Div begin drive on Morhange, important communications center: CCB, followed by 137th Inf, pushes through Villers-sur-Nied to positions N of Marthille on left and to ridge commanding Achain on right; 134th Inf clears Achain on left and reaches Rougemont Ridge on right. 328th Inf, 26th Div, continues slowly through woods on Koecking ridge under heavy fire; 101st is still checked to right rear at St Médard and Haraucourt, exposing right flank of 328th.

6th Army Group: In U.S. Seventh Army area, XV Corps begins offensive NE toward Sarrebourg with 44th Div on left, 79th on right, and 106th Cav screening N flank. 44th, with 324th and 71st Regts in assault, attacks toward Avricourt from Leintrey area, coming under heavy fire. 79th Div attacks with 314th and 315th Regts from Montigny area and drives to outskirts of Ancerviller. In VI Corps area, attack of 100th Div on N flank of corps is delayed by German counterattack, which is repelled with aid of arty fire. Germans begin burning St Dié in preparation for withdrawal.

In Fr 1st Army area, Prime Minister Churchill and Gen de Gaulle visit Gen de Lattre at Besançon. In 1st Corps area, blizzard prevents even limited action.

ITALY—AAI: In U.S. Fifth Army's Br 13 Corps area, Ind 8th Div renews assault on M. S. Bartolo and takes it in hard fighting.

In Br Eighth Army's 5 Corps area, 138th Brig of 46th Div expands Montone bridgehead to M. Poggiolo area; 128th Brig takes S. Varano. Depleted 167th Brig, 56th Div, is committed on Highway 9, between 4th and 46th Divs.

GREECE—Anglo-Greek agreement of 9 March 1942 is amended in order to place Greek armed forces under British high command. All of Greece has now been liberated.

BURMA—ALFSEA: In Br Fourteenth Army's 33 Corps area, Ind 5th Div and E African 11th Div make patrol contact near Kalemyo.

LEYTE—U.S. Sixth Army: In X Corps area, 21st Inf of 24th Div gains 400-600 yards as it continues to clear Breakneck Ridge. 1st Bn of 34th Inf reaches its objective, Kilay Ridge (named for Henry Kilay, a Filipino soldier who owned it), without opposition. This commanding position lies about 700 yards W of Highway 2 where 2d Bn, 19th Inf, is maintaining roadblock.

14 November

WESTERN EUROPE—21 Army Group: In Br Second Army area, 12 Corps opens offensive to reduce enemy bridgehead W of the Maas in Roermond-Venlo area, attacking across Nord and Wessem Canals with 53d and 51st Divs while 7th Armd Div takes locks at Panheel.

12th Army Group: In U.S. First Army's V Corps area, greatly weakened 28th Div begins moving to VIII Corps sector; 109th Inf relieves 112th, the first unit to be withdrawn, and is reinf by 2d Ranger Bn.

In U.S. Third Army's XX Corps area, Oudrenne falls to 359th Inf, 90th Div; 358th cuts Inglange-Distroff road and clears Distroff. 90th Rcn Tr links bridgeheads of 80th and 95th Divs, providing 10th Armd Div a protected route of advance. Bailey bridge is completed at Thionville during morning, and CCB of 10th Armd Div starts across it in afternoon. CCA of 10th Armd Div and 3d Cav Gp cross at Malling, latter to screen in Sarre-Moselle triangle. 95th Div, which has been engaged largely in containing enemy bridgehead W of Metz, begins attacks W of the river with 379th Inf after arty preparation: while 2d Bn works around to rear of Forêt Jeanne d'Arc and holds off counterattacks, 1st Bn begins reduction of fortifications known as the Seven Dwarfs, taking the 3 northern works and attempting in vain to gain the next, Forêt Bois la Dame. The regt is isolated in these advanced positions, though, and must be supplied by air. E of the Moselle, 2d Bn of 378th Inf, 95th Div, takes Haute-Yutz and opens assault on Forêt d'Illange; 1st Bn, 377th Inf, is heavily engaged at Bertrange and Imeldange. 10th and 11th Regts, 5th Div, drive northward abreast toward Metz while 3d Bn, 2d Inf, moves to Sorbey area; 11th clears woods SW of Fort Verdun and takes Prayelle Farm; 10th cleans out S half of Bois de l'Hôpital. In XII Corps area, Gen Eddy limits 80th Div's mission to clearing high ground S of Faulquemont. CCA of 6th Armd Div attacks toward Côte de Suisse, a ridge extending from Landroff to Thicourt, taking Brulange, Suisse, and Landroff. Germans begin series of determined attempts to recover Landroff at dusk, pushing into the village. CCB, 4th Armd Div, and 137th Inf, 35th Div, close in on Morhange, seizing Destry and Baronville in bitter fighting. 134th Inf, 35th Div, moves forward to right. CCA, 4th Armd Div, sweeps through Bois de Kerpeche, extending NE from Koecking ridge, and gets elements to Guebling. 328th Inf, 26th Div, continues to clear Koecking forest, from which enemy begins withdrawing, night 14-15.

6th Army Group: In U.S. Seventh Army's XV Corps area, 44th Div continues to battle enemy near Leintrey. 79th overcomes opposition at Ste Pôle and Ancerviller.

In Fr 1st Army area, 1st Corps opens offensive toward Belfort Gap, attacking astride the Doubs at noon with 2d Moroccan Div assisted by 5th Armd Div on left and 9th Colonial Div on right. Tactical surprise is achieved and gains are made all along front.

NORWAY—Norwegian government-in-exile announces that Norwegian troops under Col Arne Dahl have landed in Norway to operate with Soviet Karelian forces against Germans on Arctic front.

ITALY—AAI: In Br Eighth Army's 5 Corps area, 4th Div reaches the Montone in region N of Highway 9. Advancing along the highway, 167th Brig of 56th Div crosses the Montone. S of Highway 9, 46th Div continues toward Samoggia R.

YUGOSLAVIA—Yugoslavs announce fall of Skoplje, which has been main staging point for enemy forces withdrawing from Greece.

SEAC—Sir Trafford Leigh-Mallory is lost in air crash while en route to take over position as Air Commander in Chief, SEAC. Air Marshal Sir Guy Garrod is later appointed to this position.

BURMA—In NCAC area, Ch 22d Div, upon taking Mantha with ease and blocking road from Bhamo, is ordered to continue drive to Si-u. Ch 38th Div's 114th and 113th Regts are converging on Bhamo: 114th, pressing W toward the town, is bitterly opposed by enemy in Momauk area, 8 miles E of Bhamo; 113th, upon crossing the Taping at Myothit, moves W along S bank of the river toward Bhamo.

LEYTE—U.S. Sixth Army: In X Corps area, Gen Krueger orders Gen Sibert to commit 32d Div, originally intended to operate on S Samar, in zone of 24th Div in order to relieve elements of that div. Cav RCT rig arrives on Leyte and is placed under corps control. Breakneck Ridge is now largely clear, but Japanese still retain several adjacent spurs. 1st Bn, 34th Inf, patrols actively on Kilay Ridge. Supplies for the bn are hand carried by Filipinos from Consuegra. In XXIV Corps area, 32d Inf of 7th Div is ordered to start N to Damulaan-Caridad area and upon order to advance upon Ormoc.

15 November

WESTERN EUROPE—12th Army Group: In U.S. First Army's VII Corps area, 12th Inf of 4th Div breaks through to the 4 encircled cos on plateau SW of Huertgen and withdraws them, but by now the regt holds only S edge of the plateau.

In U.S. Third Army's XX Corps area, 358th Inf of 80th Div is hit hard by counterattack that reaches Distroff, but forces enemy to retire; 357th attacks toward ridge between Budling and Buding until stopped by fire from Hackenberg works; 359th passes into reserve as 10th Armd Div begins to attack. CCB of 10th Armd Div drives slowly along road E of Kerling hampered by obstacles; pushing SE toward Bouzonville, CCA takes Lemestroff. 95th Div troops E of the Moselle are formed into TF Bacon (Col Robert L. Bacon) to drive S on Metz, although 2d Bn of 378th Inf and 1st Bn of 377th are not yet in contact; 2d Bn of 378th captures Illange forts, ending organized resistance in N part of div zone; 1st Bn of 377th joins TF Bacon after enemy is finally cleared from Bertrange and Imeldange. 95th Div broadens offensive W of Metz, employing 378th and 377th Regts, less elements attached to TF Bacon: 378th takes Fort de Fèves, at N end of Canrobert works, and heights SW of Bois de Woippy; 377th, making main effort, drives S of Maizières-lès-Metz to La Maxe and Woippy, seizing La Maxe and beginning assault on Woippy; after dark patrol contact is made between 377th and 378th Regts; enemy pressure against 379th Inf, on S, eases somewhat. 5th Div improves positions and regroups for final push to Metz: 11th Inf takes Augny and reaches edge of Frescaty airport; 10th finishes clearing Bois de l'Hôpital and enters Marly, where bitter fighting ensues; 2d repels enemy drives toward Sanry bridge from Sorbey area and clears Mécleuves. In XII Corps area, 6th Armd Div, assisted by elements of 319th Inf of 80th Div, drives enemy from Landroff; armored TF takes Côte de Suisse. CCB, 4th Armd Div, reaches Metz-Sarrebourg RR but is ordered to halt since its flank is exposed and since its movement is confined to roads. 35th Div advances through Morhange, which enemy has abandoned, to Metz-Sarrebourg RR. Against light resistance, 328th Inf of 26th Div pushes forward in E part of Koecking woods; 2d Cav Gp and 101st Inf are pursuing retreating enemy toward Dieuze. CCA, 4th Armd Div, is forced to yield Guebling, since enemy cannot be driven from ground commanding the village, and withdraws this salient won at great cost.

6th Army Group: In U.S. Seventh Army's XV Corps area, 44th Div continues toward Avricourt. 79th presses northward toward Vezouse R, clearing Halloville, NE of Ancerviller. In VI Corps area, 100th Div penetrates enemy positions N of Raon-l'Etape. 103d Div prepares for its first offensive mission—to clear hill mass just SW of St Dié.

In Fr 1st Army area, 2d Corps, with 3d Algerian Div on N and 1st Div on S, moves forward to keep pace with friendly forces on flanks. 3d Algerian Div reaches Le Tholy. 1st Corps makes excellent progress except on extreme right along Swiss frontier. 2d Moroccan Div, assisted by 5th Armd Div, drives beyond Arcey, on road to Héricourt. 9th Colonial Div, with capture of Colombier-Fontaine, Ecot, and Ecurcey, opens route to Hérimoncourt.

HUNGARY—Pushing toward Budapest from E, Soviet forces take Jaszbereny.

ITALY—AAI: In U.S. Fifth Army's Br 13 Corps area, 8th Ind Div troops push into Modigliana, where contact is made with Pol 2 Corps.

BURMA—In NCAC area, U.S. 475th Inf begins march from Camp Landis to help Ch 22d Div in Si-u area. Ch 38th Div has blocked main routes from Bhamo.

In Br Fourteenth Army's 33 Corps area, Br role in Phase 1 of CAPITAL is nearly completed with unopposed capture of Kalemyo. 15 Corps passes to direct command of ALFSEA.

MAPIA Is.—U.S. Eighth Army, in its first offensive, begins amphibious assault to clear islands, 160 nautical miles NE of Sansapor. Little opposition is met by the assault force, elements of 31st Div. Captain Lord Ashbourne (RN) heads naval forces during this and subsequent operations against Asia Is.

LEYTE—U.S. Sixth Army: In X Corps area, 112th Cav is attached to 1st Cav Div and given responsibility for Capoocan=Carigara=Barugo area of N coast on 16th. 128th Inf, 32d Div, is to attack S through 21st Inf, 24th Div, toward Ormoc. Forward elements of 21st Inf are about 1,500 yards N of Limon. 24th Cav Rcn Tr joins 1st Bn, 34th Inf, on Kilay Ridge to patrol westward. 1st Bn patrols push E toward Ormoc road in futile effort to make contact with 2d Bn, 19th Inf.

16 November

WESTERN EUROPE—21 Army Group: In Br Second Army's 8 Corps area, 15th Div finds Meijel clear of enemy. In 12 Corps area, patrols reach Zig Canal, SE of Meijel.

12th Army Group: U.S. Ninth and First Armies open co-ordinated offensive to clear Roer Plain between the Wurm and the Roer. Combined airground effort is called Operation QUEEN. Air phase of QUEEN marks greatest close support effort yet made by Allied air forces, Br and U.S. strategic and tactical air forces joining in the assault on relatively small zone of attack and dropping 10,000 tons of bombs.

In U.S. Ninth Army area, XIX Corps attacks for crossing of the Roer at Juelich at 1245. CCB, 2d Armd Div, pushes toward Gereonsweiler on left flank of corps from Waurichen and Beggendorf, seizing Immendorf, Floverich, and Puffendorf. Puffendorf is in outer ring of Juelich defenses. Efforts of one column to take Apweiler are costly and unsuccessful, but another column seizes hill 700 yards NE of Puffendorf on highway to Gereonsweiler. In center, 29th Div, committing a bn each from 115th and 175th Regts, attacks from Baesweiler-Oidtweiler area toward Aldenhoven en route to Juelich but is stopped close to line of departure near villages of Siersdorf and Bettendorf. 30th Div, reinf by regt of 84th, attacks S in Wuerselen area with 3 regts abreast, 117th taking Mariadorf and 120th overrunning Euchen; little progress is made in Wuerselen.

In U.S. First Army area, VII Corps opens attack of First Army at 1245, pushing toward Dueren and Cologne to secure Roer R crossings, with 104th Inf, 3d Armd, 1st Inf, and 4th Inf Divs from left to right. 104th Div makes main effort on right with 414th Inf, reinf by bn of 415th, driving toward the Donnerberg (Hill 287) and Eschweiler Woods; enemy opposi-tion from commanding ground of the Donnerberg limits progress, but elements secure weak hold on Birkengang, suburb of Stolberg NW of the Donner-berg; rest of 104th Div conducts limited actions to N without making appreciable headway. CCB, 3d Armd Div, attacks in Stolberg corridor toward 4 villages at W base of Hamich Ridge. TF Mills loses 15 tanks in vain effort to take Hastenrath and Scherpenseel. TF Lovelady seizes Kottenich and Werth. 1st Div, reinf by 47th Inf of 9th Div, makes main effort of corps from Schevenhuette, pressing through Huertgen Forest toward Langerwehe and Juengersdorf; 47th Inf gets bn into Gressenich; 16th and 26th Regts attack in Huertgen Forest astride Schevenhuette-Langerwehe highway, 26th Inf on right, but lack tank support and advance slowly; 16th reaches edge of woods overlooking Hamich. 4th Div, reinf by CCR of 5th Armd Div, attacks on broad front in Huertgen Forest at scene of earlier battles in effort to break through between Scheven-huette and Huertgen, making main effort on left in order to support 1st Div: elements of 8th Inf on N and 22d Inf in center make extremely slow progress against well-organized positions within the forest; 12th Inf can scarcely move on plateau SW of Huertgen.

In U.S. Third Army's XX Corps area, 357th Inf of 90th Div, silencing guns of the Hackenberg, takes ridge beyond; 358th seizes Inglange and Metzervisse. CCB, 10th Armd Div, reaches Kirschnaumen; CCA's TF Chamberlain (Lt Col Thomas C. Chamberlain) gets beyond Laumesfeld while TF Standish (Lt Col Miles L. Standish) takes Ste Marguerite. TF Bacon, 95th Div, starts S toward Metz along E bank of the Moselle, advancing steadily 4 1/2 miles to Trémery. In region W of the Moselle, 377th and 378th Regts take up pursuit as Germans begin withdrawing their bridgehead, abandoning Woippy; 379th Inf, strengthening its attack, takes St Hubert Farm and Moscou Farm. 5th Div attacks N toward Metz: 11th Inf contains Verdun Forts and is heavily engaged at Frescaty airfield; 10th finishes clearing Marly and pushes on toward Magny; 2d is largely engaged at Nied Française R line, but bn pushes toward Frontigny. In XII Corps area, CCA of 6th Armd Div and 318th and 319 Regts of 80th Div attack toward Faulquemont, supported by massed fire from Côte de Suisse, and seize high ground S of town; during the advance, enemy is driven from 5 towns and about 1,200 prisoners are taken.

6th Army Group: In U.S. Seventh Army's XV Corps area, 79th Div gains ground toward Vezouse R, overrunning Barbas. Fr 2d Armd Div, which is to exploit expected breakthrough of infantrymen, clears Nonhigny with rcn elements of CCR. In VI Corps area, road Div clears part of triangular hill mass SW of St Dié.

In Fr 1st Army area, 1st Corps overruns Ste Marie and pushes on toward Montbéliard on left; thrusts to Roches-lès-Blâmont on right.

ITALY—AAI: In U.S. Fifth Army area, Br 13 Corps pauses to regroup so that troops may be rotated.

In Br Eighth Army area, 5 Corps halts along line of Montone and Cosina Rivers and regroups. 56th Div forces are withdrawn from line.

BURMA—In NCAC area, Br 36th Div is still held up in RR corridor by stubborn opposition in Pinwe area. 2 cos are isolated by enemy roadblock and have to be withdrawn.

LEYTE—U.S. Sixth Army: In X Corps area, 1st and 3d Bns of 128th Inf, Sad Div, begin drive on Ormoc, passing through 21st Inf, 24th Div, on Breakneck Ridge. 1st Bn is soon halted but 3d pushes forward 350 yards without opposition. Patrols of 1st Bn, 34th Inf, are still unable to make contact with 2d Bn, 19th Inf. 24th Div has defensive role of protecting Jaro-Ormoc trail.

17 November

WESTERN EUROPE—21 Army Group: In Br Second Army area, 12 Corps gets forward elements to the Maas across from Roermond and takes Wessem.

12th Army Group: In U.S. Ninth Army's XIX Corps area, CCB of 2d Armd Div withstands determined counterattacks against Immendorf and Puffendorf but loses hill NE of latter; another attempt to take Apweiler fails; CCA commits TF A to drive through Puffendorf toward Ederen but cannot get beyond Puffendorf. 29th Div employs 1st Bn of 116th Inf, attached to 115th Inf, against Setterich—on main highway and needed to support tanks of 2d Armd Div—but is unable to take it; nor do assault forces to S succeed in clearing either Siersdorf or Bettendorf. 30th Div makes progress in heavily built up area on S flank of corps, taking village of Heengen on N and on S clearing rest of Wuerselen and overrunning Broichweiden.

In U.S. First Army's VII Corps area, 104th Div, renewing effort to advance its right wing with heavy volume of fire support, is still firmly opposed from the Donnerberg and makes slow progress, although Birkengang is largely cleared. TF Mills of CCB, 3d Armd Div, gains weak hold on S part of Hastenrath and Scherpenseel, but since its flank is exposed by failure of 104th Div to advance, is precariously situated; enemy fire from Eschweiler Woods and the Donnerberg takes heavy toll of CCB's armor, which by nightfall is at half its original strength. In 1st Div sector, 47th Inf eliminates rear-guard opposition from Gressenich; 16th Inf, with tank support, advances almost to Hamich while 26th gains few hundred yards to right. Enemy continues to contain efforts of 4th Div to advance through Huertgen Forest. In V Corps area, 110th Inf of 28th Div is relieved by elements of 8th Div and moves to VIII Corps sector.

In U.S. Third Army's XX Corps area, 10th Armd Div fans out to pursue enemy toward the Sarre, closely supported by aircraft. 357th Inf, 90th Div, cleans out Hackenberg fortifications, which are found leveled by direct fire, and takes Klang; 358th seizes Metzeresche. Germans begin withdrawing in front of div after nightfall. TF Bacon, 95th Div, gets almost to Metz, stopping for night within sight of Fort St Julien. W of the Moselle, 95th Div continues toward Metz, 377th Inf reaching suburb of Sansonnet. Against weakened resistance, 5th Div continues northward toward Metz: 11th Inf clears most of Frescaty Airfield, but is stopped on right by fire from Fort St Privat; 10th is halted at Fort Queuleu but gets patrols to city limits; 2d withdraws elements E of the Nied Française in order to strengthen drive on right flank of div and pushes northward beyond Frontigny. XII Corps regroups and shifts boundaries in preparation for final push to the Sarre. CCB rejoins 4th Armd Div. Germans begin general withdrawal, night 17-18.

6th Army Group: In U.S. Seventh Army's XV Corps area, Avricourt falls to 44th Div. 79th Div reaches Vezouse R line in Blâmont-Cirey area and begins crossing. CCB, Fr 2d Armd Div, seizes Badonviller, near junction of XV and VI Corps front, and pushes on to Brémenil. In VI Corps area, 100th Div prepares for full-scale attack on Raon from N, 398th Inf crossing the Meurthe at Baccarat. 103d Div finishes clearing heights SW of St Dié; during night 17-18, patrols into St Dié, from which enemy is withdrawing. 36th Div patrols enter Corcieux, where enemy has already applied the torch.

In Fr 1st Army's Western French Forces area, Gen de Larminat organizes Forces Françaises de l'Ouest (FFO) to safeguard coast of Bay of Biscay from I. de Ré and La Rochelle on N to Royan and Pointe de Grave on S. CP has recently moved from Paris to Cognac. 1st Corps breaks through outer defenses of Belfort along line of the Lisaine and Gland Rivers. Among towns taken are Héricourt, Montbéliard, and Hérimoncourt.

ITALY—AAI: In Br Eighth Army's Pol 2 Corps area, hard fighting develops on M. Fortino, N of Converselle, which enemy loses and then regains in counterattack.

ALBANIA—German resistance in Tirana ends.

CHINA—From Kweilin-Liuchow area, Japanese begin drive on Kweiyang, possession of which would open way to Kunming, Hump terminus, and Chungking.

MANUS I.—77th Div sails for Leyte.

LEYTE—U.S. Sixth Army: In X Corps area, 3d Bn of 128th Inf, 32d Div, gets to within 500 yards of Limon, but 1st Bn is still held up by enemy on slopes of Corkscrew Ridge. 1st Bn of 34th Inf at last makes contact with 2d Bn of 19th Inf after pushing across ridge and Ormoc road. Efforts to clear another ridge fail, and Co B becomes isolated. During the day the bn is attached to 32d Div.

U.S.—CCS approve Adm Mountbatten's proposal of late October to clear Arakan coast; reject the Kra Isthmus operation; ask for plan to develop Cocos Is., as staging base.

18 November

WESTERN EUROPE—21 Army Group: In Br Second Army area, 30 Corps begins offensive to reduce Geilenkirchen salient (Operation CLIPPER), driving NE with 43d Div on left and U.S. 84th Div, reinf by Br Drewforce (flail tanks and searchlight battery), on right. 43d Div secures Tripsrath and most of Bauchem. 334th Inf, 84th Div, takes Prummern; continuing assault after nightfall with aid of searchlights, gains position dominating Sueggerath but is unable to take high ground—called Mahogany Hill—NE of Prummern. Geilenkirchen is now surrounded on 3 sides.

12th Army Group: In U.S. Ninth Army's XIX Corps area, CCB of 2d Armd Div, after repelling minor counterattack against Immendorf, takes Apweiler in limited attack, then pauses while 29th Div is clearing Setterich. 29th Div, with close tank and arty support, makes substantial progress, 116th Inf, to which 1st Bn reverts, gaining firm foothold in Setterich and other elements penetrating outer defenses of Juelich to take Siersdorf and Bettendorf. 30th Div continues to mop up Broichweiden and seizes Warden, SE of Mariadorf, after being twice driven off.

In U.S. First Army's VII Corps area, 104th Div seizes most of the Donnerberg and breaks into Eschweiler Woods as enemy opposition slackens. TF Mills of CCB, 3d Armd Div, assisted by reserves, takes Hastenrath and Scherpenseel, but loses its leader, Lt Col Herbert N. Mills, who is replaced by Col John Welborn; CCB then goes on the defensive. 16th Inf, 1st Div, committing its full strength, takes Hill 232, key to Hamich Ridge, and clears most of town of Hamich as 26th Inf continues slowly toward its first objective, Laufenburg Castle. Enemy makes several strong efforts to regain Hamich and Hill 232. 4th Div advances in Huertgen Forest, where 8th Inf, in 1,000-yard drive, penetrates outer defenses of approach to Dueren and 22d reaches positions astride road leading E to Grosshau, but gap exists between the regts.

In U.S. Third Army's XX Corps area, 10th Armd Div continues to pursue enemy, CCB columns reaching Launstroff and Schwerdorff and CCA detachment reaching the Nied opposite Bouzonville; finding damaged bridge N of Bouzonville near Filstroff, the CCA force begins crossing. 90th Div races southward to cut off retreating enemy; 358th Inf, upon reaching Luttange, is withdrawn for much needed rest; 359th is committed and gets elements across the Nied at Condé Northen; 90th Rcn Tr seizes Avancy. 357th Inf, on div left, is slowed by AT ditches, mines, and craters. TF Bacon, 95th Div, pushes into NE part of Metz, overrunning Fort St Julien and Fort Bellacroix; 95th Div forces W of Metz reach the Moselle and find all bridges except one blown; 377th Inf clears island formed by Hafen Canal and the river; 378th patrol starts across the Moselle bridge into Metz but Germans blow the bridge, and other elements of regt begin assault on Fort Plappeville; 379th Inf drives to the Moselle at Moulins-lès-Metz, where bridge is down. 5th Div advances into Metz from S: 11th Inf, leaving elements behind to contain Fort St Privat, pushes into the city and begins clearing S part; some elements of 10th drive into Metz while others remain behind at Fort Queuleu; 2d Inf advances northward as quickly as possible in effort to make contact with 90th Div and complete encirclement of Metz, overrunning Courcelles-sur-Nied and Ars-Laquenexy. XII Corps renews drive toward the Sarre with 2 divs abreast after preparatory fire. 50th Div remains in place, blocking in Faulquemont area. 35th Div, attacking with 137th Inf on left and 320th on right, takes Bistroff and positions E of Vallerange. 26th Div attacks to right of 35th against enemy's Dieuze–Bénestroff line: 104th Inf, on left, pushes through Bois de Bénestroff; 101st recaptures Guebling with assistance of tanks and TD's and drives to edge of Bourgaltroff, but Co F becomes isolated and is not heard from again.

6th Army Group: In U.S. Seventh Army's XV Corps area, 79th Div begins assault on Fremonville; elements find Blâmont clear of enemy. In VI Corps area, 100th Div attacks Raon-l'Etape, 397th Inf pushing into town and 398th starting across Plaine

R. 36th Div is closing along the Meurthe on S flank of corps and gains positions overlooking Gerardmer. In Fr 1st Army's 1st Corps area, 5th Armd and 2d Moroccan Divs are closing in on Belfort on N flank of corps. 1st Armd Div, assisted by 9th Colonial Div, drives 7 miles through Belfort Gap between Rhine-Rhône Canal and Swiss border to Delle; from Allaine R, where enemy is holding out at Morvillars, 1st Armd Div reconnoiters E toward the Rhine, taking Faverois, Courtelevant, Suarce, and Joncherey.

ESTONIA—Soviet forces renew efforts to win control of Gulf of Riga, stepping up action against German garrison, which is clinging tenaciously to S tip of Oesel I.

ITALY—AAI: Br Eighth Army orders co-ordinated attack toward Faenza by 5 Corps and Pol 2 Corps, beginning on 20th. In Pol 2 Corps area, 3d Carpathian Div takes over from 5th Kresowa Div in M. Fortino area and prepares to attack.

LEYTE—U.S. Sixth Army: In X Corps area, 3d Bn of 128th Inf, 32d Div, halts on ridge 500 yards N of Limon to await 1st Bn, which is still battling enemy on Corkscrew Ridge. Positions of 1st Bn, 34th Inf, on Kilay Ridge are seriously threatened and under heavy fire; Co C succeeds in relieving Co B in forward positions.

19 November

WESTERN EUROPE—21 Army Group: In Br Second Army's 30 Corps area, 334th Inf of U.S. 84th Div continues to clear Prummern area and tries in vain to take Mahogany Hill; 333d attacks up Wurm R valley toward Wurm, taking Geilenkirchen and Sueggerath. 405th Inf, U.S. 102d Div, is attached to U.S. 84th Div early in day with understanding that it will be committed only if absolutely necessary. In 12 Corps area, 51st Div takes Helden and Panningen and makes contact with 15th Div of 8 Corps.

12th Army Group: In U.S. Ninth Army's XIX Corps area, CCB of 2d Armd Div repels determined counterattack against Apweiler. CCA, reinf by bn of 119th Inf, 30th Div, attacks in 2 columns from Setterich and Puffendorf toward spur of high ground between Ederen and Freialdenhoven, one column reaching positions near Freialdenhoven. 29th Div clears rest of Setterich and AT ditch E of the village and then advances to take villages of Duerboslar and Schleiden. 30th Div's 117th inf, with powerful support of heavy weapons, easily takes St Joeris and Kinzweiler.

In U.S. First Army's VII Corps area, 104th Div mops up and shifts main weight of attack to Eschweiler-Weisweiler industrial complex N of Inde R. On N flank of 1st Div, 47th Inf column drives NW along Hamich Ridge from Hill 232 to base of Hill 187; 16th Inf finishes clearing Hamich and pushes to S part of Bovenberger Wald; reserve regt, 18th, begins attack in center of div line toward Langerwehe—previously objective of 26th Inf—reaching vicinity of Wenau; 26th Inf, whose objectives are now Juengersdorf and Merode, commits reinforcements and advances to positions less than 500 yards from Laufenburg Castle. 4th Div suspends eastward attacks in order to consolidate and try to close gap between 8th and 22d Regts. Boundary between VII and V Corps is shifted N above Huertgen so that the 2 corps can co-ordinate operations to clear Huertgen-Grosshau area. CCR, 5th Armd Div, is transferred to 8th Div of V Corps. In V Corps area, 8th Div completes relief of 28th Div in Vossenack-Schmidt area. Gen Hodges orders corps to begin offensive on 21st (instead of waiting as planned until VII Corps has broken through enemy defenses W of the Roer) in order to assist VII Corps. 8th Div prepares for action on N flank of corps toward Huertgen and Kleinhau; 121st Inf is to attack first and is ordered to move at once to Huertgen Forest, where it will pass through 12th Inf, 4th Div.

In U.S. Third Army area, XX Corps closes circle around Metz as 90th, 95th, and 5th Divs join hands. 90th Div concludes its operations against Metz and halts upon order along Nied R: 357th Inf drives to the Nied W of Boulay-Moselle; 359th plugs enemy escape route at Les Etangs; Rcn Tr establishes contact with 5th Div; 358th Inf, resting in rear area, is attached to 10th Armd Div. TF Bacon, 95th Div, is clearing streets in NE part of Metz; 377th and 378th Regts drive into Metz from NW, crossing the Moselle. 5th Div continues to clear S part of Metz; 2d Inf makes contact with 90th Div N of Retonfey and 10th Inf makes contact with 95th Div near Vallières. 10th Armd Div, in order to speed drive to the Sarre, withdraws CCA's Nied bridgehead, night 19-20, and blows the bridges; CCB is meeting stiffer opposition as it approaches Merzig and the Sarre. 3d Cav Gp, which has been pushing into triangle formed by the Sarre and Moselle, is halted on N flank of corps by fire from Orscholz Switch Line. In XII Corps area, CCB of 6th Armd Div begins attack through 137th Inf of 35th Div a and, assisted by the 137th, takes Bertring and Gros-Tenquin; Virming falls to 320th Inf. 26th Div commits its full strength to attack against Dieuze-Bénestroff line, meeting stiff opposition from German forces covering general withdrawal, which is accomplished night 19-20: 100th and 101st Regts fight in vain for Marimont and Marimont Hill (Hill 334) during day but move forward as enemy withdraws after nightfall; 328th Inf, reinf by elements of 4th Armd Div, is committed against Dieuze and, upon German withdrawal, enters together with 2d Cav Gp and takes bridge intact. CCA, 4th Armd

Div, enters battle in zone of 26th Div, recapturing Rodalbe and helping 320th Inf of 35th Div to take Virming.

6th Army Group: In U.S. Seventh Army's XV Corps area, 44th Div, pushing toward Sarrebourg, takes Ibigny and St Georges. German line along the Vezouse in Blâmont-Cirey area collapses as 79th Div completes capture of Fremonville and CCR, Fr 2d Armd Div, takes Cirey. To exploit breakthrough, CCL begins drive to secure Saverne Gap, through which advance can be continued to Strasbourg. 79th Div, instead of helping 44th Div take Sarrebourg, is to exploit success of Fr armor and protect S flank of corps. VI Corps closes along the Meurthe and prepares to attack across it. CCA, 14th Armd Div, is attached to corps. 100th Div, already E of the Meurthe, continues to advance in Raon area, 398th Inf pushing S across the Plaine to gain control of road SE from the town and 397th working on quarry strongpoint at edge of town. Div Rcn Tr and 117th Rcn Sq advance to Badonviller without opposition.

In Fr 1st Army's 1st Corps area, 2d Moroccan Div, supported by 5th Armd Div, reaches Châlonvillars, suburb of Belfort. 1st Armd Div tries unsuccessfully to open route to Dannemarie so that 5th Armd Div may drive on Cernay via Fontaine; continuing rcn eastward along 3 routes on right flank, gets elements to the Rhine at Rosenau at 1830. French are thus first of the Allied forces to reach the Rhine, but on a narrow front in sector where road net is too poor to support an advance in strength. Among villages taken, Seppois is the first in Alsace to be recovered by the French.

GREECE—Land Forces Greece and Military Liaison Greece are integrated as Headquarters Land Forces and Military Liaison Greece, under Gen Scobie.

BURMA—In Br Fourteenth Army's 4 Corps area, Ind 19th Div begins crossing the Chindwin at Sittaung.

ASIA IS.—In U.S. Eighth Army area, elements of 31st Div invade Asia Is., 100 nautical miles NW of Sansapor.

LEYTE—77th Div, en route to Leyte, is ordered to release detachment of some 1,200, upon landing, for projected operation against Mindoro.

U.S. Sixth Army: In X Corps area, 1st Bn of 128th Inf, 32d Div, continues efforts to drive enemy from Corkscrew Ridge. 1st Bn of 34th Inf, still under heavy fire on Kilay Ridge, withdraws 100 yards N, abandoning knoll on S.

20 November

WESTERN EUROPE—21 Army Group: In Br Second Army area, 12 Corps continues toward the Maas with 49th Div, supported by elements of 4th Separate Armd Brig, and 51st Div. 51st finds villages on the river SW of Venlo clear of enemy. In 30 Corps area, 334th Inf of 84th Div eliminates resistance in environs of Prummern with help of Br flame-throwing tanks, but enemy retains heights to NE. Strong opposition is slowing other elements of corps.

12th Army Group: In U.S. Ninth Army's XIX Corps area, 2d Armd Div, assisted by attached Br tanks, renews all-out drive in heavy rainfall; CCB employs 3 TF's against Gereonsweiler and takes the town; one CCA TF overruns Ederen and another clears Freialdenhoven. 29th Div, after seizing village of Niedermerz, makes 2-pronged attack on Aldenhoven, in second defensive arc of Juelich defenses, and takes the town. 30th Div consolidates on right flank of corps; using attached 17th Cav Sq, maintains contact with 104th Div of VII Corps.

In U.S. First Army's VII Corps area, 104th Div is fighting in Rohe-Hehlrath-Duerwiss region. In 1st Div sector, 47th Inf is unable to take Hill 187, on Hamich Ridge; some elements of 18th Inf clear Wenau early in day and cross Wehe Creek to continue drive on Langerwehe while others drive into Heistern and push halfway through the village; 26th Inf seizes Laufenburg Castle and drives along trail leading E toward Merode. 4th Div, beset with supply problems, narrows gap within its line somewhat. During 5 days of fighting in Huertgen Forest, the div has gained only 1½ miles, and that at high cost.

In U.S. Third Army's XX Corps area, 95th and 5th Divs continue methodically to clear rear-guard opposition within Metz and contain forts about the city. Preparations are made for final drive to the Sarre. CCA, 10th Armd Div, moves up behind 3d Cav Gp; CCB, continuing toward Merzig, reaches Hill 378 but pulls back to Hill 383 because of fire from Merzig area. In XII Corps area, 80th Div conducts rcn in force on N flank of corps, seizing bridge at Faulquemont and establishing bridgehead N of Nied Allemande R. CCA, 6th Armd Div, drives toward Hellimer crossroads, followed by 137th Inf of 35th Div. 137th upon emerging from Bois de Freybouse, is disorganized by enemy counterattack. CCA, 4th Armd Div, followed by 320th Inf, secures Francaltroff. 26th Div advances quickly behind retreating enemy, elements of 101st Inf reaching Torcheville, W of Munster. Corps orders CCA, 6th Armd Div, to attack to gain Sarre R crossings in 35th Div zone and CCB of 4th Armd Div to advance through Mittersheim in 26th Div zone; CCA of 4th Armd Div is recalled from Francaltroff area to assembly area near Conthil.

6th Army Group: In U.S. Seventh Army's XV Corps area, Fr 2d Armd Div commits CCD on N flank of corps in effort to outflank Saverne Gap from N while CCL continues enveloping maneuver from S; CCD crosses the Sarre N of Sarrebourg and drives eastward in 2 columns, one toward Phalsbourg, at W entrance to the gap, and the other toward La Petite Pierre, to N; CCL encounters stiffening resistance in vicinity of Wolfsberg Pass, SW of Saverne, and CCV is committed to assist in that area. In VI Corps area, 3d Div, with 30th Inf on left and 7th on right, crosses the Meurthe in Clairefontaine-St Michel area before dawn to spearhead drive, beginning at 0645, on Strasbourg via Saales. Attack is preceded by intense arty preparation and closely supported by XII TAC. Enemy, stunned by bombardment and threatened by successes of Allied forces on both flanks of VI Corps, is incapable of resisting effectively. 3d Div gains substantial bridgehead including towns of Le Paire, Hurbache, and La Voivre. 100th Div, protecting left flank of corps, attacks eastward from Raon-l'Etape area. 409th and 410th Regts, 103d Div, cross the Meurthe in 3d Div zone, night 20-21, to drive toward St Dié. On S flank of corps, 36th Div's 143d Inf seizes ridge commanding Anould and Clefcy.

In Fr 1st Army area, 2d Moroccan Div and CC6, 5th Armd Div, now under army command, break info Belfort, where fighting continues for next few days. In 2d Corps area, 3d Algerian Div occupies Gerardmer without resistance. 1st Div takes Plancher-lès-Mines and Champagney. In 1st Corps area, elements of 1st Armd Div reach outskirts of Mulhouse. St Louis, French suburb of Swiss Basle, is now largely clear. 5th Armd Div attacks toward Fontaine and Cernay, meeting strong opposition on Rhine-Rhône Canal S of Fontaine.

ITALY—AAI: In Br Eighth Army's 5 Corps area, enemy positions are heavily hit by air. 46th Div, as preliminary to main assault, which is postponed until 21st, begins to clear Cosina loop N of Castiglione and takes Castiglione.

INDIA-BURMA—On Salween front, Chinese of XI Group Army push through Mangshih, whose airfield is soon used to land supplies.

MAPIA-ASIA Is.—U.S. Eighth Army's operations are successfully concluded. The islands are to become sites for loran and radar stations.

LEYTE—U.S. Sixth Army: In X Corps area, 1st Bn of 128th Inf, 32d Div, is still held up on Corkscrew Ridge. CO C of 34th Inf joins main body of 1st Bn on Kilay Ridge, abandoning forward positions. Co B tries unsuccessfully to recover knoll lost on 19th. Ammunition supply is critically low.

21 November

WESTERN EUROPE—21 Army Group: In Br Second Army's 12 Corps area, 49th and 51st Divs advance steadily toward Venlo. 53d Div attacks at 1930 to clear Roermond bridgehead. 30 Corps makes little headway as attack continues in downpour of rain against strong enemy opposition. Efforts of U.S. 84th Div to reach villages of Muellendorf, Wurm, and Beeck fail. Permission is requested and received to use 405th Inf, U.S. 102d Div, to protect SE flank.

12th Army Group: In U.S. Ninth Army area, XIX Corps begins final phase of drive to the Roer. Boundary between 29th and 30th Divs is adjusted to permit all 3 divs to drive on Juelich. CCB, 2d Armd Div, seizes heights around Gereonsweiler and undergoes strong counterattack on a hill 1,000 yards N of Gereonsweiler; here, within sight of the Roer, CCB halts. CCA advances to about 1,000 yards beyond both Ederen and Freialdenhoven. 116th Inf, now on N flank of 29th Div, seizes Engelsdorf, from which 3d Bn attacks for Koslar; 2d Bn of 175th enters Bourheim after German garrison, scheduled for relief, withdraws, but is forced out when the enemy relief force moves into the town after dark. 120th Inf, 30th Div, assisted by 743d Tank Bn, thrusts quickly to Fronhoven, within 4 miles of the Roer.

In U.S. First Army's VII Corps area, 104th Div clears Rohe and Hehlrath and is fighting within Duerwiss. On N flank of 1st Div, 47th Inf masses fire of 20 bns of weapons on Hill 187 in effort to break resistance on Hamich Ridge and interdicts the hill with fire through night 21-22; 18th Inf, after repelling counterattack in Heistern and clearing rest of the village, commits its reserve bn and continues toward Langerwehe astride Wehe Creek until stopped abruptly at Hills 207 and 203; 26th Inf advances slowly toward Merode. In V Corps area, after preparatory bombardment by 8th Div and corps arty plus some guns of VII Corps, 121st Inf of 8th Div attacks through 12th Inf of 4th Div (VII Corps) on plateau SW of Huertgen, where enemy has checked previous efforts to advance. Progress is limited by thick woods containing numerous obstacles.

In U.S. Third Army's XX Corps area, CCA of 10th Armd Div, attacks N through TF Polk toward Saarburg with TF Standish on left and TF Chamberlain on right but is soon halted by obstacles of Orscholz Switch Line; CCB, now on the defensive W of Merzig, falls back a little under enemy counterattack, and its sector is quiet for the next few days; 358th Inf of 90th Div, attached to 10th Armd Div, is ordered northward to zone of CCA. As fighting continues within Metz, preparations are made for full-scale drive toward the Sarre. 90th Div along W bank of the Nied, is turning NE. 5th Div is ordered to relieve 95th so latter can make main effort toward the Sarre to right of 90th Div. In XII Corps area, 80th Div expands its Nied bridgehead and makes contact with XX Corps. CCA of 6th Armd Div and 137th Inf of 35th Div, in co-ordinated drive, take Fremestroff and Hellimer. 320th Inf of 35th Div attacks toward Grening. 104th Inf of 26th Div takes Montdidier and Albestroff, the latter an important road center, but elements in Albestroff become isolated and are destroyed. From Dieuze, TF of CCB, 4th Armd Div, drives eastward to Loudrefing.

6th Army Group: U.S. Seventh Army permits either XV or VI Corps to take Strasbourg, previously the objective of VI Corps, which is making slower progress than XV. Both corps are to be prepared to cross the Rhine if the opportunity to do so with ease presents itself. In XV Corps area, one TF of CCD, Fr 2d Armd Div, drives through La Petite Pierre to Alsatian Plain at Bouxwiller, but the other is unable to clear Phalsbourg; pushing through Wolfsberg Pass, column of CCL emerges on Alsatian Plain at Birkenwald. 44th Div takes Sarrebourg, which has been outflanked. In VI Corps area, 100th Div takes Moyenmoutier without a fight and advances toward Senones. 3d Div expands Meurthe bridgehead, taking St Jean d'Ormont. Enemy positions in St Di become untenable as 103d Div gains heights commanding the town. 36th Div crosses 143d Inf over the Meurthe at St Leonard and 141st Inf near Clefcy and advances toward Fraize. CCA, 14th Armd Div, which has been attached to corps, is driving forward on N flank toward Schirmeck to cut enemy escape routes to NE.

In Fr 1st Army area, 1st Corps is almost halted by violent German counterattack that forces 5th Armd Div troops from Suarce and Lepuix and severs Delle-Basle road near Courtelevant, endangering Fr forces in vicinity of the Rhine and Mulhouse. In Alps Sector, U.S. 44th AAA Brig takes over area previously held by U.S. 1st A/B TF. It will defend right flank along Franco-Italian border.

ITALY—AAI: In Br Eighth Army's Pol 2 Corps area, 3d Carpathian Div begins attack on M. Fortino-M. Ricci ridge S of Faenza, taking M. Fortino and pushing northward. 5 Corps opens general offensive toward Faenza with close air support. Ind 10th Div, on N flank, is pinned down along the Montone W of Villafranca. 4th Div, in center, gets elements across the river in region N of Highway 9 but is forced to withdraw them. On S flank, 46th Div continues to clear Cosina R loop N of Castiglione.

BURMA—Gen Stratemeyer inactivates Third TAF so that 221st Gp may provide close support for Br Fourteenth Army, and 224th Gp for Arakan offensive.

On NCAC front, Ch 38th Div continues to close in on Bhamo. 114th Regt, bypassing enemy outpost at Subbawng, which detachment of 113th is containing, drives into Shwekyina.

CHINA—Gen Wedemeyer formally presents his recently formulated ALPHA Plan to concentrate Ch forces in Kunming area as quickly as possible and place them under command of China's best general in order to avert threat to Kunming—to Chiang Kai-shek. Gen Chen Cheng is recommended for command of ALPHA forces, but Chiang Kai-shek prefers Gen Ho Ying-chin. American assistance will consist of maximum air support and liaison officers to advise Ch Army.

LEYTE—U.S. Sixth Army: In X Corps area, 128th Inf, less 1st Bn, which is to contain Corkscrew Ridge, is ordered to capture Limon and secure crossing of Leyte R tributary to S. In preparation for attack, fire is placed on enemy positions along Highway 2 during night. Action on Kilay Ridge is confined to patrolling and fire exchanges. Supplies brought by hand from Consuegra are being supplemented by airdrops. In XXIV Corps area, 3d Bn of 32d Inf, 7th Div, moves from Baybay to position just S of 2d Bn. Arty is being emplaced at Damulaan.

22 November

WESTERN EUROPE—21 Army Group: In Br Second Army's 8 Corps area, 15th Div occupies Sevenum and Horst, NW of Venlo. In 12 Corps area, 53d Div reaches the Maas across from Roermond. 49th and 51st Divs are converging on Venlo. In 30 Corps area, U.S. 84th Div's 334th Inf takes high ground NE of Prummern (Mahogany Hill) in surprise assault; 333d, after underpass in Sueggerath is cleared permitting tanks to assist, advances to within 500 yards of Muellendorf, advance platoon reaching the village, where it is wiped Out. 405th Inf, U.S. 102d Div, attacks toward Beeck but makes little progress.

12th Army Group: In U.S. Ninth Army's XIX Corps area, Germans, instead of falling back behind the Roer as expected, have committed fresh forces to stiffen their line. CCA, 2d Armd Div, pushes into Merzenhausen but is forced back to SW edge. In center of corps front, Germans drive elements of 175th Inf, 29th Div, from Bourheim before daylight and block efforts to re-enter; 116th Inf fights unsuccessfully for Koslar. 30th Div runs into stiff opposition, but 120th Inf takes village of Erberich; elements drive into Lohn but are forced to withdraw.

In U.S. First Army's VII Corps area, 104th Div seizes Eschweiler during morning after night attack, overruns Nothberg, finishes clearing Duerwiss, and drives toward Puetzlohn. This success earns the div the task of continuing drive to the Roer instead of stopping at the Inde as planned. In 1st Div zone, 47th Inf finishes clearing Hamich Ridge without opposition; 18th Inf is still held up in valley of Wehe Creek by enemy on Hills 207 and 203; 26th

Inf is ordered to confine its action to limited attacks to assist 18th. Renewing attack in Huertgen Forest, 4th Div's 8th and 22d Regts feint eastward while slipping elements around enemy; forward elements of 8th Inf reach heights at Gut Schwarzenbroich, the first objective, while advance force of 22d reaches positions 700 yards W of Grosshau; depleted 12th Inf begins attack to secure right flank of 22d and advances very slowly. In V Corps area, 121st Inf of 8th Div continues almost futile efforts to advance SW of Huertgen.

In U.S. Third Army's XX Corps area, mopping up in Metz ends, and 5th Div begins relief of 95th. Forts holding out about the city (Verdun, St Privat, St Quentin, Plappeville, Driant, and Jeanne d'Arc) are isolated and do not present a serious threat. Corps orders broad offensive toward the Sarre, beginning on 25th, with 10th Armd Div on left, 90th Div in center, and 95th Div on right. 95th making main effort, is to secure crossings of the river between Saarlautern and Pachten. Continuing efforts to break through stubborn enemy positions of Orscholz Switch Line, TF Standish of CCA, 10th Armd Div, advances to Nennig on left and Tettingen on right but is forced back from both; TF Chamberlain makes limited penetration through dragon's teeth to right. In XII Corps area, new plan of attack will pinch out 35th and 26th Divs along Maderbach Creek. CCB, 6th Armd Div, and 137th Inf, 35th Div, seize Leyviller and St Jean-Rohrbach. Grening falls to 320th Inf of 35th Div. 104th Inf of 26th Div attempts to envelop Albestroff, from which enemy withdraws, night 22-23; 328th Inf, having moved by truck from Dieuze to reinforce the understrength 101st Inf in a sector nearly impassable because of flooding, mines, and other obstacles, seizes Munster. From Loudrefing, CCB column of 4th Armd Div drives E through Mittersheim; CCA assembles at Conthil.

6th Army Group: In U.S. Seventh Army's XV Corps area, columns of Fr 2d Armd Div driving S from Bouxwiller and N from Birkenwald converge on Saverne. VI Corps pursues retreating enemy, mobile TF's spearheading. 100th Div takes Senones and advances toward St Blaise. 3d Div speeds to positions near St Blaise and Saales. St Di falls to 409th Inf, 103d Div, without opposition; 411th Inf establishes bridgehead near Saulcy. Strong enemy opposition to 36th Div's bridgehead on S flank of corps forces 141st Inf to pull back W of the river, but 143d remains E of the river. Corps releases 45th Div and CCA, 14th Armd Div, to XV Corps.

In Fr 1st Army's 2d Corps area, 1st Div takes Giromagny, piercing enemy line along the Savoureuse. 1st Corps recovers lost ground and drives into Mulhouse.

FINLAND—Finnish forces, complying with armistice terms by following up enemy withdrawal, reach Norwegian border.

ITALY—AAI: In U.S. Fifth Army's II Corps area, 88th Div re-enters line, taking over zone of 85th Div. 91st Div is relieved in line by 34th Div and 1st Armd Div. Br 13 Corps finishes regrouping and is disposed, from left to right: 1st Div, 78th Div, 6th Armd Div' Ind 8th Div.

In Br Eighth Army area, Pol 2 Corps continues northward along ridge toward M. Ricci. 5 Corps establishes bridgeheads across the Cosina in zones of 4th and 46th Divs, night 22-23.

LEYTE—U.S. Sixth Army: In X Corps area, 2d and 3d Bns of 128th Inf, 32d Div, attack S astride Highway 2 and take Limon, virtually completing battle of Breakneck Ridge. Bypassed pockets are eliminated by mid-December. Forward elements of 128th Inf cross the tributary of the Leyte R south of Limon. 1st Bn of 34th Inf, under heavy enemy attack on Kilay Ridge, is forced to compress its defense perimeter to avoid encirclement. In XXIV Corps area, 7th Div is ordered to assemble in Baybay area as quickly as possible. 11th A/B Div, although not originally intended to operate on Leyte, is ordered to relieve 7th Div, less 17th Inf, so 7th can clear E shore of Ormoc Bay.

23 November

WESTERN EUROPE—21 Army Group: In Br Second Army area, 30 Corps goes on the defensive and releases U.S. 84th Div to U.S. Ninth Army's XIII Corps at 1800. Further efforts earlier in day to take Wurm and Beeck have failed.

12th Army Group: In U.S. Ninth Army's XIX Corps area, CCA of 2d Armd Div takes about half of Merzenhausen and halts to consolidate. Elements of 175th Inf, 29th Div, takes Bourheim in strenuous fighting; Germans soon begin counterattacks, which continue for next 3 days. Elements of 120th Inf, 30th Div, take Lohn and hold it against 2 counterattacks; elements of 119th Inf, assisted by diversionary fire from Erberich, clear Pattern; 30th Div then halts attack to await clearance of Kirchberg and Inden.

In U.S. First Army's VII Corps area, 104th Div breaks into Puetzlohn and Weisweiler, where enemy is resisting strongly. 47th Inf, on N flank of 1st Div, attacks toward Huecheln but is soon halted; 16th seizes Rosslershof Castle, SE of Wilhelmshoehe, where it comes under heavy enemy pressure; 18th takes Hill 207. Forward elements of 8th Inf, 4th Div, are driving steadily NE in Huertgen Forest while other elements battle enemy at Gut Schwarzenbroich; 22d Inf remains near Grosshau but does not risk an attack. In V Corps area, 121st Inf of 8th Div, although helped by light tanks, makes little progress SW of Huertgen. Germans counterattack but cannot break through.

In U.S. Third Army's XX Corps area, 358th Inf of 90th Div takes over attack from CCA of 10th Armd Div, attempting to push through Orscholz line to villages of Sinz and Muenzingen with 3d and 2d Bns: 3d Bn clears Campholz woods E of Tettingen; 2d is disorganized by friendly fire which is falling short. In preparation for drive to the Sarre, 90th Div extends northward, relieving elements of GCB. 5th Div completes relief of 95th, which moves to right of 90th Div. In XII Corps area, 6th Armd Div regroups for drive to the Sarre. Elements of 137th Inf, 35th Div, push into Hilsprich, which is needed for the armored attack, but are forced back to St Jean-Rohrbach. 104th Inf, 26th Div, reoccupies Albestroff but is too disorganized to continue attack: 328th Inf takes over its sector and attacks toward line Vittersbourg-Honskirch-Altwiller. CCB column of 4th Armd Div, driving E from Mittersheim, reaches W bank of the Sarre at Fenétrange. 25th Cav Rcn Sq crosses at Bettborn and makes contact with patrols of 44th Div (XV Corps).

6th Army Group: In U.S. Seventh Army's XV Corps area, Fr 2d Armd Div drives into Strasbourg and clears the city, but enemy retains small bridgehead at Kehl bridge. Germans abandon Phalsbourg, at W end of Saverne Gap. As infantry is being shifted through the gap toward Haguenau and Soufflenheim, Germans begin series of counterattacks N of Sarrebourg, forcing corps to regroup to meet threat. Most of 44th and 45th Divs as well as 106th Cav Gp are disposed at W side of Saverne Gap. In VI Corps area, 3d Div takes Saulxures and Saales; in conjunction with 100th Div to left, overruns St Blaise. 2 regts of load Div are moving to outflank Steige pass, while the third, on S flank, at-tacks in conjunction with 36th Div in region W of Ste Marie. 143d and 141st Regts, 36th Div, are closing in on Fraize, 143d taking Mandray.

In Fr 1st Army area, 2d Corps takes Château-Lambert but progress elsewhere is negligible. Corps is ordered to open route of advance for CC6, which, with 2d Moroccan Div, has been placed under corps command. In 1st Corps area, Germans for the second time cut route to the Rhine in vicinity of Seppois.

ESTONIA—With elimination of enemy pocket on S Oesel I., Soviet forces now control entrance to Gulf of Riga.

HUNGARY—Rail junction of Cop (Csap), which has changed hands several times during last few weeks, falls to Red Army.

ITALY—AAI: In Br Eighth Army area, Pol 2 Corps secures M. Ricci. 5 Corps consolidates bridgeheads across the Cosina. Enemy begins withdrawal toward next water barrier, the Lamone. Ind 10th Div is strongly opposed, however, on right flank of corps along the Montone N of Highway 9.

LEYTE—U.S. Sixth Army: In X Corps area, 128th Inf of 32d Div improves and consolidates positions S of Limon and for the next few days patrols actively. 112th Cav, which has been patrolling Mt Minoro area, is ordered SW toward Highway 2 to relieve pressure on 32d Div. Kilay Ridge sector is relatively quiet. In XXIV Corps area, 77th Div begins unloading on Leyte and is assigned to corps. Battle of Shoestring Ridge opens as Japanese attack sector of thinly spread 32d Inf, 7th Div, along Palanas R, forcing limited withdrawal.

24 November

WESTERN EUROPE—12th Army Group: In U.S. Ninth Army area, new boundary between XIX and XIII Corps becomes effective.

In U.S. First Army's VII Corps area, 104th Div takes Puetzlohn but is opposed from house to house in Weisweiler. TF Richardson (Lt Col Walter B. Richardson), consisting of elements of 3d Armd Div plus bn of 47th inf, is formed to drive on Huecheln, Wilhelmshoehe, and Frenzerburg Castle. After laboriously clearing mine field, the TF seizes Huecheln. 18th Inf, 1st Div, continues toward Langerwehe, elements reaching Schoenthal, but is still unable to take Hill 203. In V Corps area, 121st Inf of 8th Div continues efforts to reach edge of woods overlooking Huertgen; by this time has suffered 600 battle casualties. To hasten attack, CCR of 5th Armd Div is ordered to assist on 25th, moving along exposed Germeter-Huertgen highway, since 121st has been unable to clear a safer route along Weisser Weh valley.

In U.S. Third Army's XX Corps area, 358th Inf of 90th Div continues assault on Orscholz line: 3d Bn, attacking toward Tettingen and Butzdorf after halting enemy counterattack, gets elements into Butzdorf, where they are isolated; 2d Bn, reinf during day by 1st, breaks into Oberleuken, but cannot oust enemy. In XII Corps area, 1st Bn of 134th Inf, 35th Div, helped by tanks and intense preparatory shelling, takes Hilsprich. 328th Inf, 26th Div, continues attack against enemy rear-guard line Vittersbourg-Altwiller; 101st makes vain and costly attempt to take Château strongpoint in center of Bois de Bonnefontaine. GCB, 4th Armd Div, crosses the Sarre in XV Corps zone at Romelfing and Gosselming and turns NE: N column takes up blocking positions on high ground W of Postroff; S column brushes aside resistance at Kirrberg and clears Baerendorf in house-to-house fighting.

6th Army Group: Penetrates enemy line along the Vosges. Gen Eisenhower, beginning tour of inspection of 6th Army Group front, attends conference of commanders, where it is decided to clear region W of the Rhine before attempting an assault across it. U.S. Seventh Army is to drive N to help Third Army. Fr 1st Army is to reduce Colmar Pocket, enemy's bridgehead W of the Rhine. Boundary between 12th and 6th Army Groups will be altered.

In U.S. Seventh Army's XV Corps area, Fr armor in Strasbourg will be seriously threatened unless it can be bolstered by infantrymen. Germans continue pressure from the N in region N of Sarrebourg. In VI Corps area, forward elements of 3d Div reach Rothau. 103d Div continues outflanking movement against Steige, clearing Lubine, to SW. 142d Inf spearheads eastward drive of 36th Div, reaching Ban-de-Laveline and La Croix-aux-Mines.

In Fr 1st Army area, 2d and 1st Corps are ordered to converge on Burnhaupt as quickly as possible to pocket enemy forces in Alsace. 2d Corps clears Grosmagny and Petit-Magny, on road to Rougemont-le-Château. 1st Corps withstands heavy pressure in Mulhouse area; is largely concerned with keeping routes to the Rhine open.

ITALY—AAI: In U.S. Fifth Army's IV Corps area, TF 45 captures M. Belvedere but Germans later regain it.

In Br Eighth Army area, Pol 2 Corps presses toward Marzeno R on broad front against disorganized resistance. In 5 Corps area, 4th Div drives toward the Lamone in region just N of Highway 9. 46th Div crosses the Marzeno R on S flank of corps. Ind 10th Div remains E of the Montone on N flank of corps.

CHINA—Japanese in S China, attempting to gain contact with their forces garrisoning Indochina, take Nanning.

LEYTE—U.S. Sixth Army: In X Corps area, 1st Bn of 34th Inf, 24th Div, repels minor counterattack against Kilay Ridge. In XXIV Corps area, 1st Bn of 184th Inf is attached to 32d Inf of 7th Div but cannot be committed without permission of 7th Div. 32d Inf recovers some ground previously lost on Shoestring Ridge and holds perimeter—about 2,000 yards long and less than 1,500 yards deep—against vigorous counterattack, night 24-25.

JAPAN—111 B-29's attack Tokyo from bases in the Marianas, the first of many similar raids.

25 November

WESTERN EUROPE—12th Army Group: In U.S. Ninth Army's XIX Corps area, 29th Div continues to hold off enemy at Bourheim and gets elements of 116th Inf into Koslar, where they become isolated.

In U.S. First Army's VII Corps area, 104th Div extends its hold on Weisweiler. Inde R valley to W is now clear. TF Richardson takes Wilhelmshoehe; suffers heavy losses while trying to advance across open Roer Plain to Frenzerburg Castle. 16th Inf, 1st Div, attempts unsuccessfully to reach Weisweiler-Langerwehe highway; assisted by 2 tanks, platoon of 18th Inf gets almost to crest of Hill 203, where it clings. 8th Inf, 4th Div, reaches positions a little more than a mile from the edge of Huertgen Forest; in conjunction with CCR, 5th Armd Div (V Corps), 22d Inf attacks toward Grosshau but cannot take it; 4th Div suspends attacks for several days after this. In V Corps area, CCR of 5th Armd Div joins 121st Inf, 8th Div, in attack toward Huertgen but, halted by large crater and mines, withdraws.

In U.S. Third Army area, XX Corps opens drive to the Sarre. In 10th Armd Div zone on N flank, 358th Inf continues to batter at Orscholz line: 3d Bn, assisted by aircraft and tanks, seizes Tettingen and relieves the isolated troops at Butzdorf, but pulls back from Butzdorf; 1st and 2d Bns continue to fight within and near Oberleuken, 2d Bn reaching top of Hill 388; it is decided to withdraw 358th Inf, which by now is unfit to continue attack. 90th Div, with 359th Inf on left and 357th on right, drives steadily toward the Sarre reaching Oberesch, within 4 miles of the river. 95th Div, supported by arty of 5th Div and of III Corps, attacks across the Nied on right flank of corps—377th Inf on left and 378th on right—and pushes into Maginot Line, where Germans have abandoned fortifications; takes towns of Boulay, Momerstroff, Narbefontaine, and Hallering. In XII Corps area, 80th Div, with 42d Cav Sq screening its N flank, attacks with 3 regts supported by armor, overrunning main enemy positions on N flank of corps. 6th Armd Div, reinf by elements of 134th Inf, begins drive toward Maderbach Creek, greatly hampered by craters, mud, mines, and enemy fire: CCB, driving toward Puttelange, gets forward elements to the Maderbach at Remering; CCA, aided by air strike, takes Valette. 328th Inf, 26th Div, penetrates enemy line and captures Vittersbourg; Co, G, 101st Inf, clears the Château strongpoint in Bois de Bonnefontaine, and Co K makes futile attempt to clear N edge of the woods. CCB of 4th Armd Div, after checking determined counterattack against Baerendorf, is reinf and reorganized before continuing attack late in afternoon.

6th Army Group: In U.S. Seventh Army area, boundary between XV and VI Corps is moved N of Strasbourg. In XV Corps area, elements of 44th Div and 106th Cav Gp halt enemy column advancing on Schalbach after making slight withdrawals. Fr armor continues to clear Strasbourg area. 79th and 45th Divs consolidate N and NW of Strasbourg. CCA, 14th Armd Div, makes contact with 3d Div of VI Corps near Schirmeck and is again attached to VI Corps. In VI Corps area

100th Div, on N flank, reaches Grandfontaine. 36th Div outflanks and captures Ste Marie, gaining control of roads to Sélestat and Ribeauville.

In Fr 1st Army area, 2d Corps finds that enemy has withdrawn along most of its front to avoid encirclement. 1st Corps makes slow progress toward Burnhaupt. In Alps Sector, ETOUSA orders U.S. 1st ABTF to proceed to Soissons, Lyon, and Mourmelon at once.

HUNGARY—Red Army troops are clearing Csepel I., in the Danube just S of Budapest.

ITALY—AAI: In Br Eighth Army area, Pol 2 Corps gets advance elements across the Marzeno W of Marzeno village. In 5 Corps area, 4th Div reaches the Lamone in S. Barnaba-Scaldino area E of Faenza. This advance permits Ind 10th Div to cross elements over the Montone at Highway 9 and push northward toward enemy's switch line that extends generally from Casa Bettini on the Montone to region N of Scaldino on the Lamone. 46th Div maintains bridgehead across the Marzeno but is unable to break out. Porter Force, in Adriatic coastal sector, is placed under command of Cdn 1 Corps.

BURMA—In NCAC area, Japanese in Pinwe region of RR corridor who have been holding up Br 36th Div are ordered to fall back toward central Burma.

LEYTE—U.S. Sixth Army: Gen Krueger halts work on airfields. In X Corps area, Co A, the most advanced unit of 1st Bn, 34th Inf, 24th Div, on Kilay Ridge, repels heavy enemy counterattack, night 25-26. In XXIV Corps area, 32d Inf of 7th Div contains another enemy counterattack, which is made in less strength after nightfall. 511th Para Regt, 11th A/B Div, starts difficult westward trek over mountains from Burauen toward Mahonag, 10 miles distant, to ease pressure on corps units driving on Ormoc.

POA—CINCPOA issues Operation Plan 11-44 for invasion of Iwo Jima. Fifth Fleet commander is to seize Iwo and develop air bases there. Invasion date is tentatively set for 3 February 1945.

26 November

WESTERN EUROPE—12th Army Group: In U.S. Ninth Army's XIX Corps area, to counter German shelling, corps arty program is doubled in spite of ammunition shortage. 29th Div troops in Bourheim, helped by reserves and aircraft, contain the most powerful attack to be made by enemy on this objective; isolated forces of 116th Inf in Koslar are supplied by air. Gen McLain, CG XIX Corps, orders the attack toward the Roer continued all along line.

In U.S. First Army's VII Corps area, 104th Div, pushing through Weisweiler, seizes Frenz. Infantry elements of TF Richardson, supported by long-range fire of armor, reach Frenzerburg Castle but cannot gain entrance to the medieval structure. 4th Div consolidates positions in Huertgen Forest; 12th Inf at last gets into position N and W of Huertgen to protect S flank of 22d Inf. In V Corps area, 121st Inf of 8th Div, reinf by bn of 13th, continues drive on Huertgen: finding that enemy has withdrawn from woods, attacks toward the village but is halted between the woods and the village.

In U.S. Third Army's XX Corps area, CCA of 10th Armd Div relieves 358th Inf, which reverts to 90th Div and remains on the defensive; CCB extends N wing of corps eastward toward the Sarre with little difficulty. 90th and 95th Divs continue steadily northeastward in center and on right flank of corps, 95th Div penetrating Maginot Line. 95th Div zone is extended southward to include wedge-shaped region containing Bois de Kerfent. Germans surrender Verdun forts to 5th Div. In XII Corps area, 80th Div approaches St Avold against strong rear-guard opposition. CIA, 6th Armd Div, drives through Fort de Puttelange but comes under such heavy fire upon emerging that it falls back through the woods; CCB mops up along the Maderbach with infantrymen but cannot get tanks through mud. Skillful rear guards keep 328th Inf, 26th Div, from Honskirch. 4th Armd Div begins co-ordinated attack with the a TF's of CCB E of the Sarre toward enemy's next MLR along Wolfskirchen-Eywiller-Durstel road but is slowed by terrain, which contains a number of flooded streams; CCA crosses the Sarre and moves eastward across rear of GCB.

6th Army Group: In U.S. Seventh Army area, XV Corps is still under heavy pressure from the N. VI Corps halts advance of 100th Div, which is to move to XV Corps front. 3d Div emerges from the Vosges onto Alsatian Plain at many points. 103d seizes Steige and Ville, important points on Giessen R.

Fr 1st Army continues efforts to close pincers on enemy by junction of 2d and 1st Corps at Burnhaupt, but progresses slowly. Germans for the third time cut communication line to the Rhine in 1st Corps zone.

HUNGARY—Soviet troops take Hatvan and threaten Budapest.

ITALY—AAI: In Br Eighth Army's 5 Corps area, 46th Div succeeds in reaching the Lamone on S flank of corps, but enemy is holding on firmly to switch line positions between the Lamone and Montone on N flank of corps. Heavy rains bring lull in offensive.

YUGOSLAVIA—Marshal Tito agrees to let Br naval and air force personnel use certain ports and airfields temporarily.

BURMA—In NCAC area, Br 36th Div, replacing 72d Brig with 29th, patrols actively in Pinwe area.

LEYTE—U.S. Sixth Army: In X Corps area, 1st Bn of 34th Inf, 24 Div, relieves Co A with Co C on Kilay Ridge. The bn is highly vulnerable to enemy attack from different directions and is maintaining positions with use of arty. In XXIV Corps area, Japanese make another night attack, 26-27, on Shoestring Ridge, about 200 enemy troops gaining positions in bamboo thicket within American lines, but 400 Japanese dead are counted at conclusion of the action.

27 November

WESTERN EUROPE—21 Army Group: U.S. 101st A/B Div is relieved in Cdn 2 Corps sector.

12th Army Group: In U.S. Ninth Army's XIX Corps area, CCA of 2d Armd Div finishes clearing Merzenhausen and hills near there. 29th Div clears to the Roer except for 2 strongpoints in Juelich: Kirchberg falls to 115th Inf, which attacks from Pattern, taking enemy by surprise; elements of 116th Inf make contact with isolated forces in Koslar. 120th Inf, 30th Div, attacks with attached bn of 119th Inf toward Altkirch but is halted short of objective.

In U.S. First Army's VII Corps area, 104th Div mops up in Weisweiler-Frenz sector. Elements of 47th Inf, TF Richardson, at Frenzerburg Castle, repel enemy counterthrust but are still unable to gain entrance. 18th Inf of 1st Div extends its positions on Hill 203 to crest but enemy retains reverse slopes. 4th Div continues to consolidate and improve positions in Huertgen Forest; elements of V Corps relieve 12th Inf near Huertgen. In V Corps area, 8th Div, with increased fire support, continues attack toward Huertgen and gains hold on NE and W edges.

In U.S. Third Army's XX Corps area, 10th Armd Div breaks off action toward Saarburg after laboriously clearing enemy infiltrators from Tettingen and repelling counterattack against Borg. Enemy retains Oberleuken and Nennig. Gen Walker directs 3d Cav Gp to relieve CCA and screen N flank of corps; orders 10th Armd Div to face E. 90th Div, now well ahead of flanking forces, halts near the Sarre and prepares for final drive to the river. 95th Div advances rapidly, 377th Inf reaching positions within a mile of German border and 378th reaching Falck and Dalem. Co-ordinated drive by 90th and 95th Divs is ordered for 29th. Bn of 10th Inf, 5th Div, is attached to 95th Div and takes responsibility for Bois de Kerfent, at boundary of XX and XII Corps, relieving elements of 80th Div. In XII Corps area, 80th Div enters St Avold, from which enemy has withdrawn, and regains contact near Seingbouse. Div's attack has forced general enemy withdrawal across the Maderbach, so 6th Armd Div remains in place. 328th Inf, 26th Div, occupies Honskirch and 101st moves into Altwiller without a fight. CCB and CCA, 4th Armd Div, attack E of the Sarre, overrunning Wolfskirchen, Eywiller, and Gungwiller; CCA tries unsuccessfully to break into Durstel.

6th Army Group: Boundary between 12th and 6th Army Groups is moved northward through West Wall defenses, narrowing zone of 12th.

In U.S. Seventh Army area, Gen Eisenhower orders army to attack N to help Third Army gain Saar Basin. In XV Corps area, 100th Div arrives in Sarrebourg sector and relieves elements of 44th Div. German threat to corps from the N subsides, but positions are still vulnerable on this wing. Fr 2d Armd Div passes to operational control of VI Corps. In VI Corps area, elements of 3d Div relieve Fr 2d Armd Div at Strasbourg. French prepare to drive S along the Rhine. CCA, 14th Armd Div, advances SE through Obernai toward Barr and Erstein to block exits from the Vosges and help southward drive of Fr armor. 103d Div presses toward Barr-Sélestat road, elements taking Le Hohwald. From Ste Marie, 36th Div is driving E on Sélestat.

ITALY—AAI: In U.S. Fifth Army area, Br 13 Corps is ordered to go on the offensive as soon as weather conditions permit. Ind 8th Div loses contact with enemy.

In Br Eighth Army area, army issues orders for major winter offensive in early December. In Pol 2 Corps area, enemy resistance E of the Lamone in region S of Faenza is virtually at an end. In 5 Corps area, NZ 2d Div replaces 4th Div in line. Canadians of 1 Corps relieve right flank elements of Ind 10th Div N of Casa Bettini so that latter can make a concentrated effort to take bridge at Casa Bettini, badly needed for deployment of Cdn 1 Corps in Adriatic coastal sector. In 10 Corps area, Cremona Gp arrives between 27 November and 3 December.

CHINA—Gen Wedemeyer presents to Chiang Kai-shek a plan to furnish munitions to Chinese Communists. The proposal is rejected.

PALAUS—Hostilities on Peleliu end. Approximately 13,600 Japanese have been killed on Angaur, Peleliu, and small islands off Peleliu; prisoners total about 400. 81st Div and attached units have suffered over 3,275 casualties, including 542 killed. Reinf 1st Mar Div casualties total about 1,250 killed and 5,275 wounded.

LEYTE—Bn of 306th Inf, 77th Div, leaves Leyte for operation against Mindoro.

U.S. Sixth Army: In X Corps area, 1st Bn of 34th Inf, 24th Div, on Kilay Ridge, learns from patrol that help is coming; undergoes strong counterattack from E and its supply line to Consuegra is temporarily cut. In XXIV Corps area, 1st Bn (−) of 184th Inf moves from Caridad to Damulaan to help 32d Inf, 7th Div; attacks toward Albuera, clearing enemy from the bamboo thicket within 32d Inf's zone. 109 enemy dead are counted. 32d Inf and 1st Bn, 184th, establish defense perimeters and repel light infiltration attempts during night. Japanese begin operation to regain airfields. Corps has learned of enemy plan to capture airfields in Burauen area and is taking countermeasures.

28 November

WESTERN EUROPE—Port of Antwerp is opened to traffic.

12th Army Group: In U.S. Ninth Army area, XIX Corps virtually finishes clearing its zone to the Roer. CCA, 2d Armd Div, takes Barmen and reaches the river near there. In 29th Div zone, Koslar is found free of enemy but the 2 strongpoints in Juelich area must still be cleared. 30th Div commits bn of 120th Inf in battle for Altkirch, which is cleared, but Germans retain small triangle between Inde and Roer Rivers. Offensive halts temporarily.

In U.S. First Army's VII Corps area, 104th Div reaches Inden and Lammersdorf and takes bridge at Inden intact. Frenzerburg Castle has been abandoned by enemy. 1st Div secures Langerwehe and Juengersdorf. On S flank of corps, 12th Inf of 4th Div begins attack to close gap between 8th and 22d Regts in Huertgen Forest. In V Corps area, 8th Div, attacking from 3 sides, at last secures Huertgen. Maj Gen Donald A. Stroh, div CG, is replaced by Brig Gen William G. Weaver. Aircraft and arty join in attacks against Kleinhau, the next objective, which armor is to attack. Gen Hodges directs corps to continue offensive.

In U.S. Third Army's XX Corps area, 95th Div gains positions roughly abreast 90th Div to N; 377th Inf pushes into Germany; 378th is slowed by opposition from woods E of Falck but makes some progress. In XII Corps area, 317th Inf of 80th Div fights hard for Farebersviller, elements entering and clearing part of the town. About 2000, Germans with tanks attempt unsuccessfully to drive Americans from Farebersviller. 328th Inf, 26th Div, mops up W of Canal des Houillères de la Sarre; 101st is sent to Burbach to support 4th Armd Div E of the Sarre in drive on Sarre-Union scheduled for 1 December. 26th Div is to extend northward to take over most of zone held by 35th Div. 4th Armd Div, in preparation for the Sarre-Union attack, is laboriously clearing villages E of Drulingen-Sarre-Union highway, CCB taking Berg.

6th Army Group: In U.S. Seventh Army's VI Corps area, Fr 2d Armd Div starts S from Strasbourg in 2 columns, reaching Erstein area, where enemy is resisting strongly. CCA, 14th Armd Div, also meets firm resistance in vicinity of Erstein as well as at Barr. Elements of 36th Div find Liepvre, on Ste Marie-Sélestat road, and Koenigsbourg Château, SE of Liepvre, undefended.

In Fr 1st Army area, 2d and 1st Corps converge at Burnhaupt at 1430 and pocket enemy forces in Alsace. Junction is made by CC4 of 5th Armd Div, 1st Corps, and CC6, under command of 2d Moroccan Div of 2d Corps. Germans soon attempt to break out of encirclement. In Alps Sector, 100th Bn of RCT 442 relieves 1st SSF on Franco-Italian frontier.

ITALY—AAI: In U.S. Fifth Army area, Br 13 Corps takes Casola Valsenio and M. Taverns without opposition.

In Br Eighth Army's 5 Corps area, Ind 10th Div suspends operations against Casa Bettini bridge because of weather condition. Cdn 1 Corps is concentrating in forward positions in order to attack along Adriatic coast.

BURMA—In NCAC area, Ch 38th Div maintains pressure on main northern defenses of Bhamo with 114th Regt; math has mission of entering the city but has been unable to do so.

CHINA—Japanese 11th Army, acting independently and against orders, drives across Kwangsi-Kweichow border although it has been ordered to halt at border. Gen McClure assumes position of chief of staff to Gen Wedemeyer.

PALAUS—Elements of 81st Div begin to clear Kayangel Atoll, N of Kossol Passage.

P.I.—CTF 77 issues operation plan for invasion of Mindoro. Adm Kinkaid, heading Allied naval forces, gives Rear Adm Arthur D. Struble, as commander of Mindoro Attack Group (TG 78.3), U.S. Seventh Fleet, responsibility for amphibious phase.

LEYTE—U.S. Sixth Army: In X Corps area, Japanese try to recover Kilay Ridge, night 28-29, moving onto it in strength and isolating Co C, 34th Inf, on SW end. 12th Cav, mopping up in Mt Badian-Hill 2348 region, about 5 miles NE of Kananga, inches westward from this time until 9 December. In XXIV Corps area, 32d Inf of 7th Div, now greatly weakened, is to be withdrawn to reserve while 184th and 17th Regts continue battle for Shoestring Ridge; 2d Bn, 184th, relieves 2d Bn, 32d Inf, at Damulaan; 1st Bn, 184th, falls back a little at the bamboo thicket under counterattack. 11th A/B Div, with task of securing mountain exits into Leyte Valley, completes relief of 7th Div, less 17th Inf; defends Buri and Bayug airfields and patrols.

29 November

WESTERN EUROPE—12th Army Group: In U.S. Ninth Army area, XIII Corps begins drive toward the Roer before dawn, omitting arty preparation. 84th Div, on left flank of corps, makes main effort toward Lindern and high ground NE of Beeck with 335th Inf: about 100 men of 3d Bn reach Lindern at daybreak and hold there until reinforcements, including tanks, arrive much later in day; enemy efforts to regain the village are repulsed; 2d Bn begins assault on heights NE of Beeck against strong opposition. 333d Inf provides fire support for 335th; in conjunction with 113th Cav conducts demonstration against Beeck. 102d Div makes secondary effort on S flank of corps, 405th Inf advancing along Lindern-Linnich highway to right of 84th Div and elements to right gaining limited objective in preparation for next assault. 7th Armd Div is held in corps reserve.

In U.S. First Army's VII Corps area, 104th Div retains hold on Inden and Lammersdorf though enemy tries to recover them and blows bridge at latter. 2 COS of 26th Inf, 1st Div, push into Merode, where they are isolated and almost destroyed during counterattack. 4th Div renews attack all along line in Huertgen Forest and finds that enemy has strengthened his defenses during lull in fighting; 8th Inf makes negligible progress toward road center at E edge of the forest; 12th Inf closes gap between 8th and 22d; 22d, in frontal and flanking attacks supported by armor, takes Grosshau and cuts road to Gey. 5th Armd Div, less CCR, is attached to corps. In V Corps area, CCR TF of 5th Armd Div, under Lt Col William A. Hamberg, drives into Kleinhau and clears the village. During night 29-30, 1st Bn of 13th RCT relieves TF Hamberg but abandons 2 roadblocks on hill, seriously hampering VII Corps' later attack on Grosshau. Huertgen and Kleinhau are important objectives from which coming battle for Brandenberg-Bergstein ridge can be waged.

In U.S. Third Army's XX Corps area, 90th and 95th Divs launch co-ordinated attack to reach the Sarre. 90th Div, with little difficulty, gets patrol to the river. 95th is strongly opposed on Saar heights in front of Saarlautern and undergoes 10 counterattacks, but gains general line Kerprich-Hemmersdorf-St Barbara-Merten. In Metz area, Fort St Privat falls to 5th Div. In XII Corps area, enemy recovers all of Farebersviller from 317th Inf, 80th Div, although tanks and TD's have moved forward to assist infantrymen; 318th Inf is ordered to relieve 317th. TF of CCA, 4th Armd Div, takes Durstel.

6th Army Group: In U.S. Seventh Army's XV Corps area, 114th Inf of 44th Div takes Tieffenbach. 45th Div improves positions along N bank of the Moder in Rothbach-Mertzwiller region. In limited objective attack, 79th Div's 314th Inf clears Niederschaeffolsheim, near Haguenau. In VI Corps area, Erstein falls to Fr 2 Armd Div. 411th Inf, 103d Div, seizes Barr and Andlau. CCA, 14th Armd Div, pushes S through Barr along E edge of the Vosges. 36th Div mops up near Liepvre and to S finds Le Bonhomme free of enemy.

HUNGARY—Forces of Third Ukrainian Front have joined in offensive to left of Second Ukrainian troops and, in conjunction with Yugoslav partisans, have crossed the Danube near Yugoslav-Hungarian frontier S of Budapest and driven toward Lake Balaton in region N of Drava R. Mohacs and Pecs are free of enemy. Berlin reported a Soviet bridgehead W of the Danube in this region much earlier in the month.

ITALY—AAI: In U.S. Fifth Army area, Br 13 Corps takes Fontanelice without a fight. Germans recapture M. Castellaro from 1st Div.

In Br Eighth Army's 5 Corps area, brig of 56th Div S of Faenza passes to command of 46th Div. 7th Armd Brig starts from Recanati, S of Ancona, to 5 Corps zone in preparation for December offensive.

POA—CINCPOA recommends that invasion of Mindoro and Luzon be postponed until air strength on Leyte can be built up.

LEYTE—U.S. Sixth Army: In X Corps area, Japanese continue attacks on Kilay Ridge, but 1st Bn of 34th Inf, 24th Div, succeeds in relieving Co C. At urgent request for reinforcements, 2d Bn of 128th Inf, 32d Div, moves forward, Co G, the first to arrive, immediately reinforcing Co C. In XXIV Corps area, elements of 184th Inf, 7th Div, recover some ground at bamboo thicket but are unable to clear enemy from the thicket; repel 3 heavy enemy counterattacks.

30 November

WESTERN EUROPE—21 Army Group: In Br Second Army area, 8 and 12 Corps have reduced enemy's bridgehead W of the Maas to small pocket at Blerick, across from Venlo.

12th Army Group: In U.S. Ninth Army's XIII Corps area, 102d Div takes over burden of attack: while 405th Inf continues to fight along Lindern-Linnich highway, 406th drives to edge of Linnich and 407th clears enemy from Welz, within a mile of the Roer. 335th Inf, 84th Div, overcomes resistance within Beeck, but enemy retains heights to NE.

In U.S. First Army's VII Corps area, 104th Div finishes clearing Lammersdorf and secures N half of Inden. 8th Inf, 4th Div, continues costly efforts to get through Huertgen Forest; 12th, advancing more than 1,000 yards, reaches edge of woods W of Gey

[1 DECEMBER 1944]

but is too weak to attack the village; 22d reinf by bn of 5th Armd Div, attempts to secure Grosshau clearing and forest between Grosshau and Gey in order to swing NE toward Dueren; some elements reach edge of woods overlooking Gey, but rest of force suffers heavily while trying to come abreast.

In U.S. Third Army's XX Corps area, 10th Armd Div attacks toward the Sarre on N flank of corps, CCB on right reaching the river opposite Merzig, where bridges are down. 359th Inf, 90th Div, occupies Fremersdorf, on W bank of the Sarre, without opposition; 1st Bn of 357th crosses the Nied in assault boats near Niedaltdorf and pushes on to Bueren, which enemy is defending. After consolidating positions, 95th Div continues attack toward the Sarre, gaining heights commanding Saarlautern: 377th Inf mops up Ste Barbara on left and advances right wing to Felsberg; 378th takes hill S of Felsberg. TF Bell (Col Robert P. Bell), consisting of 5th Div's 10th Inf (−), 5th Rcn Tr, and supporting units, is formed to cover exposed right flank of 95th Div and attached to that div. In XII Corps area, positions are generally static except on right, where 4th Armd Div gets into position for assault on Sarre-Union with capture of heights overlooking Mackwiller.

6th Army Group: In U.S. Seventh Army's VI Corps area, Fr 2d Armd Div and CCA, 14th Armd Div, continue S on E flank of corps; CCA clears St Pierre. 103d Div, now concentrated about Epfig, S of St Pierre, follows CCA southward toward Sélestat. Elements of 36th Div get into position for attack on Châtenois, W of Sélestat.

HUNGARY—Troops of Second Ukrainian Front take Eger, NE of Budapest, and are closing in on Miskolc.

ITALY—AAI: In U.S. Fifth Army's Br 13 Corps area, Germans take Casa Nuovo from 1st Div. In Br Eighth Army's 5 Corps area, Ind 10th Div renews attack toward Casa Bettini bridge and takes Albereto, breaching switch-line positions.

BURMA—In NCAC area, Br 36th Div finds Pinwe free of enemy.

CHINA—Generalissimo Chiang Kai-shek decides to move Ch 22d and 38th Divs from Burma to China for defense of Kunming. Ch 14th Div is eventually substituted for 38th, so that current operations in Burma will suffer less. Gen Wedemeyer informs JCS and Adm Mountbatten of the Generalissimo's decision. Chiang Kai-shek also agrees to provide 270,000 replacements for ALPHA by 1 April 1945 but refuses request to supply arms to Ch forces of IX War Area.

P.I.—Projected Mindoro operation is postponed for 10 days by Gen MacArthur in order to release shipping and naval support forces for landing in Ormoc area on Leyte. Final target dates for Mindoro and Luzon are 15 December 1944 and 9 January 1945, respectively.

LEYTE—U.S. Sixth Army: In X Corps area, 112th Cav, which has been driving S to ease pressure on 32d Div in Limon area, halts at ridge E of Highway 2 about 5,000 yards SE of Limon; unable to progress farther because of strong opposition, cavalrymen dig in and drive off enemy patrols. In XXIV Corps area, battle of Shoestring Ridge ends successfully as elements of 184th Inf, 7th Div, clear the bamboo thicket and establish night perimeter on forward slope of the ridge.

1 December

WESTERN EUROPE—12th Army Group: In U.S. Ninth Army's XIII Corps area, Linnich falls to 406th Inf, 102d Div; 405th Inf gains objective heights along Lindern-Linnich highway by double envelopment. In XIX Corps area, 116th Inf of 29th Div begins attack to reduce the 2 enemy positions W of the Roer opposite Juelich—one a group of buildings called Hasenfeld Gut and the other the Juelich *sportplatz*, an athletic field; both are protected by enemy fire from commanding ground E of the Roer and accessible only through open terrain; assault forces are soon pinned down by enemy fire. In U.S. First Army's VII Corps area, 104th Div gains some ground in S part of Inden. 8th Inf, 4th Div, still trying in vain to get out of Huertgen Forest, has gained less than 1,000 yards during 3 days of hard fighting; 22d Inf, committing its reserves, finally emerges to establish thin line along woods overlooking Gey. Gen Collins orders attack halted. Since 16 November, 4th Div has made maximum gain of a little more than 3 miles at exceedingly high cost. 47th Inf reverts to 9th Div from attachment to 1st Div. In V Corps area, elements of 28th and 121st Regts of 8th Div have cleared a portion of Tiefen Creek bottom land on right flank and of Brandenberger Wald on left flank, to provide a measure of safety for armored drive along Kleinhau-Brandenberg highway, which follows ridge line.

In U.S. Third Army area, XX Corps continues to clear enemy positions W of the Sarre in preparation for assault across the river. 10th Armd Div is overcoming relatively weak opposition in Merzig sector. 90th Div is rapidly cleaning out its sector S of Merzig. Air preparation precedes 95th Div's attempt to reach arid cross the Sarre: medium bombers attack Saarlautern, Ensdorf, and Fraulautern; fighter bombers interdict movement E of the river. Resistance continues stiff, however, as 95th Div attacks, making main effort with fresh 379th Inf: 377th takes Felsberg and begins clearing Ste Barbara; 378th gains hill near Berus but is unable to reach Bisten; 379th attacks through 377th toward Saarlautern. TF Fickett (Col E. M. Fickett), consisting of 6th Cav Gp and 5th Ranger Bn, assembles near St Avold to screen S flank of corps, relieving TF Bell, components of which revert to 5th Div. 5th Div, still containing forts in Metz area, is assigned narrow front to right of 95th Div in preparation for drive to the Sarre across Warndt salient. 6th Cav TF is to protect right of 5th Div. In XII Corps area, CCB of 4th Armd Div and 101st Inf of 26th Div open co-ordinated drive on Sarre-Union against lively opposition: 3d Bn of 101st clears Sarre-Union but, since it cannot take hill N of the town, pulls back for night; 1st Bn clears Bannholtz woods; CCB secures Hill 318, N of Mackwiller. 80th and 35th Divs and 6th Armd Div are ordered to make limited attack on 4th to straighten left and center of corps line.

6th Army Group: In U.S. Seventh Army's XV Corps area, 44th Div is meeting strong resistance in vicinity of Tieffenbach. 45th Div is likewise opposed in Zinswiller-Meitesheim area. 79th Div, reinf by 94th Cav Rcn Sq of 14th Armd Div, clears Schweighausen. In VI Corps area, Fr 2d Armd Div continues southward along the Rhine. 103d and 36th Divs are converging on Sélestat. CCA, 14th Armd Div, is withdrawn to corps reserve.

EASTERN EUROPE—In E Czechoslovakia, Soviet troops cross to W bank of Ondava R in vicinity of Humenne and Trebisov. Germans are containing attacks by troops of Second Ukrainian Front in vicinity of Miskolc, NE of Budapest in Hungary, but Third Ukrainian forces SW of Budapest gain ground NE and N of Pecs.

ITALY—AAI: In U.S. Fifth Army area, Br 13 Corps alters plan of attack because of enemy withdrawals. First phase calls for capture of M. Penzola by 6th Armd Div.

Br Eighth Army continues preparation for offensive on 3d. In 5 Corps area, Ind 10th Div secures Casa Bettini bridge over the Montone and is relieved on right flank by Cdn 1 Corps troops. Cdn 1 Corps moves assault forces across the Montone via bridge at Casa Bettini.

BURMA—Gen Stratemeyer issues general order, effective 4 December, reorganizing EAC.

On NCAC front, Ch 30th Div, with 90th Regt in the lead, is moving southward from Bhamo area toward Namhkam over rough terrain.

CHINA—Gen Wedemeyer directs Gen Chennault to make main effort of Fourteenth Air Force in defense of air line to China and SOS; in addition to providing logistical support of U.S. military activities, to support certain Ch forces in China Theater. On Salween front, Ch forces take Che-fang.

NEW GUINEA—Australians take over from U.S. troops at Aitape.

LEYTE—Japanese food supply is exhausted by this time.

U.S. Sixth Army: In X Corps area, after preparatory fire, Co E of 128th Inf, 32d Div, attacks through CO C of 34th Inf, 24th Div, to clear knolls on SE end of Kilay Ridge, taking the first. 1st Bn, 34th Inf, is ordered to withdraw from the ridge but is unable to do so for several days. 112th Cav attempts in vain to clear ridge SE of Limon. In XXIV Corps area, warning order for assault on Ormoc is issued.

PALAUS—Elements of 81st Div complete occupation of Kayangel Atoll.

2 December

WESTERN EUROPE—21 Army Group: In Cdn First Army's 2 Corps area, Germans breach dyke area on the Neder Rijn near Arnhem and flood region to SW, forcing corps to withdraw Waal R bridgehead to rail line running W from Elst.

12th Army Group: In U.S. Ninth Army's XIII Corps area, 334th Inf of 84th Div takes Leiffarth and high ground NE of Beeck and Lindern. 407th Inf, 102d Div, makes co-ordinated effort against Roerdorf and Flossdorf, taking former. In XIX Corps area, 116th Inf of 29th Div continues struggle for the 2 strongpoints in Juelich area.

In U.S. First Army's VII Corps area, 104th Div finishes clearing Inden and its entire zone W of the Inde; at 2300, 415th and 414th Regts, supported by fire of 413th, start across the river at Inden, taking enemy by surprise. 1st Div is ordered to straighten line by clearing Luchem and then prepare for relief; 1st Div has gained less than 4 miles during 15 days of hard fighting. 22d Inf, 4th Div, repels counterattack from Gey with help of arty. In V Corps area, TF Hamberg of CCR, 5th Armd Div, attacks down Kleinhau-Brandenberg highway under fire from Kommerscheidt-Schmidt ridge but is stopped by mine field; interdictory fire is placed on enemy during night while mines are being cleared.

In U.S. Third Army's XX Corps area, 10th Armd Div, with capture of Dreisbach before dawn, finishes clearing its zone W of the Sarre; CCB is then held in reserve while CCA outposts W bank of river between 3d Cav Gp and 90th Div. 90th Div, night 2–3, begins extending southward in preparation for attack across the Sarre in Dillingen area. 95th Div is again supported by aircraft as it fights for crossing of the Sarre in Saarlautern area; 2d Bn, 379th Inf, drives into Saarlautern and begins house-to-house battle in W part of town; St Barbara falls to 377th Inf; 378th forces enemy from Pikard; arty observation plane spots bridge intact leading to Saarlautern and 379th Inf prepares to seize it. 3d Bn of 11th Inf, 5th Div, joins 10th Inf in attack through SW part of Forêt de la Houve. In XII Corps area,

101st Inf of 26th Div finds enemy in possession of Sarre-Union and is obliged to clear it once more; 104th Inf elements move forward to strengthen hold on the town. 4th Armd Div cuts roads extending eastward to Domfessel and to Voellerdingen from Sarre-Union; with air support defeats enemy efforts to reopen these escape routes; Gen Patton orders div withdrawn as soon as possible after its relief by XV Corps. 35th Div relieves CCB, 6th Armd Div, near Puttelange, night 2–3. 6th Armd Div extends northward to take over part of 80th Div's MLR.

6th Army Group: Group commander, Gen Devers, orders U.S. Seventh Army to regroup by 5 December for main assault northward. French are to have full responsibility for reducing Colmar Pocket.

In U.S. Seventh Army's XV Corps area, 44th Div takes Waldhambach. 45th drives into Engwiller and clears Meitesheim. In VI Corps area, Fr 2d Armd Div drive comes to a halt in Kogenheim-Freisenheim region and div reverts to Fr 1st Army. 103d and 36th Divs begin clearing house-to-house opposition in Sélestat.

Fr 1st Army is reinf by U.S. 36th Div. Gen de Lattre orders converging drives against Colmar Pocket from N and S, aimed at the Rhine at Neuf-Brisach.

EASTERN EUROPE—Red Army continues strong attack toward Budapest. Troops of Fourth Ukrainian Front expand Ondava R bridgehead in Czechoslovakia, while those of Second Ukrainian Front hammer at fortifications in Miskolc area (Hungary). Third Ukrainian forces in SW Hungary press N and NW on broad front between the Danube and Drava Rivers.

ITALY—AAI: Br Eighth Army makes limited advances in preparation for general offensive. 10 Corps, which is responsible for deceptive measures, takes command of 26th Armd Brig, 6th Armd Div. Cdn 1 Corps begins clearing enemy's switch-line positions between the Montone and the Lamone.

BURMA—In Br Fourteenth Army's 33 Corps area, E African 11th Div reaches the Chindwin at Kalewa.

CHINA—Gen Wedemeyer presents Chiang Kai-shek a proposal, suggested by Col David D. Barrett of the American Observer Group in Yenan, to form 3 communist regts in Yenan, to be equipped by U.S. SOS, for use in Nationalist territory under command of a U.S. officer. The plan is rejected. Later in December, Gen McClure drafts plan for U.S. airborne units of technicians to go into communist China and informally presents it to the two factions for approval. Japanese column driving on Kweiyang reaches Tu-shan.

LEYTE—U.S. Sixth Army: In X Corps area, Cos E and F of 128th Inf, 32d Div, extend southward on Kilay Ridge against firm resistance. 1st Bn of 34th Inf, 24th Div, is ordered by 128th Inf commander to remain on the ridge until further notice. 112th Cav continues efforts to dear ridge SE of Limon and sends Tr A toward Highway 2 to make contact with 32d Div.

3 December

WESTERN EUROPE—21 Army Group: In Br Second Army area, with 12 Corps capture of Blerick, across from Venlo, Second Army finishes clearing W Bank of the Maas.

12th Army Group: In U.S. Ninth Army area, XIII Corps reaches the Roer. Flossdorf falls to 407th Inf, 102d Div. In XIX Corps area, commander of 116th Inf, 29th Div, is replaced as futile efforts to reduce the Juelich strongpoints continue.

In U.S. First Army's VII Corps area, 104th Div extends Inde bridgehead eastward beyond Lucherberg. Enemy, having recovered from surprise of night crossing, is countering strongly. 16th Inf (−), 1st Div, assisted by tanks and TD's, seizes Luchem. 330th Regt, 83d Div, from VIII Corps sector begins relief of 4th Div, which is eventually to move to Luxembourg. In V Corps area, 8th Div continues to clear flanks of main assault in Brandenberger Wald and Tiefen Creek area, while TF Hamberg of 5th Armd Div, with effective air support, renews drive down Kleinhau-Brandenberg highway and seizes Brandenberg. The usually inactive German Air Force appears in strength in afternoon, about 60 ME-109's attacking without causing serious damage and at cost of at least 19 shot down. With enemy on commanding ground near Brandenberg, Americans are precariously situated but no reinforcement is possible since TF Boyer (Lt Col Howard E. Boyer) of CCR, 5th Armd Div, temporarily attached to 28th Inf of 8th Div, is clearing enemy strongpoint in Vossenack.

In U.S. Third Army's XX Corps area, 1st Bn of 379th Inf, 95th Div, seizes bridge leading to Saarlautern-Saarlautern-Roden road, but the bridge cannot be used immediately because of enemy efforts to destroy it with fire; 2d and 3d Bns clear most of Saarlautern; other elements of 95th Div move forward to river line. 10th Inf, 5th Div, clears Creutzwald in hard battle; 6th Cav Gp and 2d Ranger Bn repel counterattacks W of Lauterbach. In XII Corps area, counterattacking enemy force from Oermingen drives into Sarre-Union before being checked by 26th Div defenders of the town.

6th Army Group: In U.S. Seventh Army's XV Corps area, 44th Div is delayed by enemy at Ratzwiller but 45th takes Zinswiller. 100th Div begins drive on Bitche, passing 398th Inf through 44th Div. VI Corps continues to clear Sélestat.

EASTERN EUROPE—In NE Hungary, Soviet forces of Second Ukrainian Front overrun Miskolc, key point in enemy's defense line NE of Budapest and important center of war industries.

ITALY—AAI: Br Eighth Army opens offensive toward Bologna with 3 corps abreast. Pol 2 Corps, which is to secure left flank of army by clearing foothills to left of 5 Corps, jumps off at 2300. 5 Corps attacks along Highway 9 toward the Santerno. Cdn 1 Corps, in Adriatic coastal sector, continues toward Ravenna and the Santerno with Cdn 1st Div on left and Cdn 5th Armd Div on right, Cdn 1st Div enveloping and taking Russi and Cdn 5th Armd Div seizing Godo, on Russi-Ravenna road, night 3–4.

SEAC—Adm Mountbatten agrees to permit Ch 22d and 38th Divs to move from Burma to China to defend Kunming.

BURMA—In Br Fourteenth Army's 33 Corps area, E African 11th Div establishes bridgehead across the Chindwin at Kalewa, where bridging is undertaken under fire. Ind 20th Div secures bridgehead across the river to N in Mawlaik area, crossing a brig; uses Kalewa site for crossing rest of division.

CHINA—Japanese 11th Army halts its unauthorized drive into Kweichow Province toward Kweiyang as its supplies run out.

LEYTE—U.S. Sixth Army: In X Corps area, Tr G of 112th Cav tries unsuccessfully to scale steep slopes of ridge SE of Limon. Tr A makes contact with 126th Inf W of Hill 1525 without incident. In XXIV Corps area, at commanders conference, Maj Gen Archibald V. Arnold orders 7th Div to clear region S of Talisayan R, including Hills 918, 380, and 606, beginning on 5th.

4 December

WESTERN EUROPE—12th Army Group: In U.S. Ninth Army area, XIII Corps has cleared its sector W of the Roer except for Wurm and Muellendorf and suspends offensive until 18th.

In U.S. First Army's VII Corps area, 104th Div improves bridgehead across Inde R. Upon completion of bridges, supporting weapons cross. In V Corps area, 8th Div withholds armored attack on Bergstein while awaiting reinforcements, but infantrymen continue to clear flanks of the Brandenberg-Bergstein ridge. TF Boyer of 5th Armd Div eliminates the Vossenack strongpoint.

In U.S. Third Army's XX Corps area, 95th Div regroups hastily to exploit capture of Saarlautern bridge; 3d Bn, 379th Inf, crosses bridge and begins prolonged struggle for suburb of Fraulautern, which is within West Wall; 1st and 3d Bns repel tank-infantry counterattack; 378th Inf takes Lisdorf, on the Sarre just S of Saarlautern. 10th Inf, 5th Div, withstands counterattack on S flank of corps; 3d Bn, 11th, takes up positions to right of 10th and begins attack to clear region between Roselle and Sarre Rivers. XII Carps begins final drive toward the Sarre and West Wall. 80th Div, with 318th Inf in assault, attacks after intense, effective arty preparation and takes Farebersviller and hills to NE. CCA, 6th Armd Div, attacks toward Mont de Cadenbronn. 35th Div attacks across the Maderbach before dawn, taking enemy by surprise: 134th Inf seizes Puttelange; 320th, to right, is soon checked by enemy fire. 104th Inf, 26th Div, eliminates enemy remnants in Sarre-Union during methodical mop-up. 4th Armd Div, learning of German retreat, begins pursuit across Eichel Creek, CCB crossing advance force at Voellerdingen; CCA comes under accurate fire at Domfessel.

6th Army Group: In U.S. Seventh Army's VI Corps area, toad and 36th Divs finish clearing Sélestat. 36th Div takes control there, relieving 103d Div forces.

EASTERN EUROPE—Fighting continues NE and SW of Budapest. Soviet and Yugoslav troops clearing region between the Danube and Sava Rivers in Yugoslavia overrun Mitrovica.

ITALY—AAI: In U.S. Fifth Army's Br 13 Corps area, 6th Armd Div, jumping off night 4–5, clears most of M. Penzola.

In Br Eighth Army area, Pol 2 Corps takes Montecchio. In 5 Corps area, 46th Div is attacking toward Piedura ridge against strong resistance. Cdn 1 Corps takes Ravenna and reaches the Lamone, cutting Highway 16 where it crosses the river; 1st Div begins attack across the Lamone, night 4–5.

CHINA—In the course of reorganizing the government to make it more progressive and efficient, Chiang Kai-shek names T. V. Soong premier as well as foreign minister. Gen Wedemeyer asks that B-29's, which are a strain on Hump tonnage, be moved from China.

P.I.—U.S. Seventh Air Force bombers begin harassing night attacks on Luzon airfields. On Leyte, Gen Krueger, CG Sixth Army, orders attack on 5 December to destroy enemy in Ormoc area, with X Corps moving southward astride Highway 2 to support XXIV Corps. In X Corps area, 1st Bn of 34th Inf, 24th Div, begins withdrawal from Kilay Ridge toward Pinamopoan. 112th Cav continues futile efforts to clear ridge SE of Limon.

XXIV Corps prepares for assault on Ormoc with 7th Div by land and 77th Div by sea. 184th Inf of 7th Div gets patrols as far N as Balogo 776th Amph Tank Bn after dark moves to waters 1,000 yards W of Balogo.

5 December

WESTERN EUROPE—12th Army Group: In U.S. First Army's VII Corps area, 104th Div withstands determined counterattack against Lucherberg. 9th Div is arriving from V Corps zone and begins relief of 1st Div. In V Corps area, TF Boyer of CCR, 5th Armd Div, renewing drive on Bergstein, pushes 3 prongs into the village and clears it but is threatened from Castle Hill (Burg-Berg) to E.

In U.S. Third Army's XX Corps area, 1st and 3d Bns of 379th Inf, 95th Div, continue to attack toward Saarlautern-Roden and Fraulautern, respectively, without making much headway; 2d Bn crosses into bridgehead and drives through 1st Bn to edge of Saarlautern-Roden, where counterattack is repulsed; 3d Bn breaks into S part of Fraulautern; 2 bns of 378th Inf cross the Sarre at Lisdorf and drive to edge of Ensdorf. On S flank of corps, Lauterbach falls to 5th Div without a fight. In XII Corps area, 35th Div gets patrols to the Sarre; 2d Bn, 134th Inf, drives to SE outskirts of Sarreguemines. CCA, 6th Armd Div, also patrols to river line, in region N of Sarreguemines. 2d Cav Gp, advancing along Roselle R on left flank of corps, patrols across German frontier near St. Nicolas. CCA, 4th Armd Div, crosses creek at Domfessel and pushes N toward Rohrbach-lès-Bitche, an important communications center, but is halted with heavy losses short of Bining; CCB drives to Schmittviller. 26th Div closely follows 4th Armd Div.

6th Army Group: U.S. Seventh Army begins general attack northward toward Maginot Line and West Wall with reorganized XV Corps on left and VI on right. XV Corps, consisting of 44th and 100th Inf Divs and 12th Armd Div, pushes forward with infantry, 44th taking Ratzwiller and 100th overrunning Wimmenau and Wingen. VI Corps (3d, 45th 79th, and 103d Inf Divs and 14th Armd Div) drives northward with 45th and 79th Divs: elements of 45th reach Mertzwiller, which enemy is defending stubbornly.

In Fr 1st Army area, alteration of interarmy boundary gives French full responsibility for reduction of German bridgehead W of the Rhine in Colmar area; Fr 1st Army is reinf for the task by U.S. 36th Div and Fr 2d Armd Div.

EASTERN EUROPE—Third Ukrainian Front progresses rapidly in center, where forward elements reach Lake Balaton; left flank elements driving along N bank of Drava R overrun Szigetvar. Berlin reports Soviet crossing of the Danube near Vukovar.

ITALY—AAI: In Br Eighth Army area, Pol 2 Corps, after taking M. Rinaldo and securing left flank of army, halts until 5 Corps can reduce opposition on Pideura ridge. In 5 Corps area, 46th Div continues to make slow progress against Pideura ridge. In Cdn 1 Corps area, 1st Div is forced to abandon its bridgehead across the Lamone on left flank of corps. Mopping up is conducted E of the Lamone for the next few days while bridging is underway.

SEAC—U.S. Tenth Air Force begins airlift of Ch 14th Div from Burma to China. Ch 22d Div is to prepare for similar movement.

BURMA—In NCAC area, Japanese send strong TF toward Bhamo to assist withdrawal of beleaguered garrison. This force of about 3,000 starts N from Namhkam in evening. Ch 30th Div continues southward drive toward Namhkam against enemy opposition from hill positions.

LEYTE—U.S. Sixth Army begins offensive against Ormoc. In X Corps area 112th Cav is still stalemated on ridge SE of Limon. 32d Div prepares to drive down Highway 2. In XXIV Corps area, 776th Amph Tank Bn, moving N by sea beyond Balogo, lands in Tabgas area to fire on hills in front of 7th Div; continues northward by sea to reconnoiter Calingatngan region, then returns to bivouac area. 7th Div attacks with 184th Inf on left and 17th on right: 184th secures line from beach some 300 yards S of Balogo on left to heights SE of Palanas R on right; 3d Bn crosses the Palanas and scales first ridge of Hill 380. Co K, 32d Inf, plugs gap between 184th and 17th Regts. 17th Inf takes ridge W of Hill 918. 77th Div, at Tarragona beach assembly area on E coast of Leyte, begins loading supplies and equipment for landing below Ormoc.

6 December

WESTERN EUROPE—12th Army Group: In U.S. First Army's V Corps area, counterattacking enemy force pushes into Bergstein but is driven back. Gen Weaver is granted permission to use 2d Ranger Bn to reinforce the small group at Bergstein.

In U.S. Third Army's XX Corps area, 90th Div begins attack across the Sarre at 0415, crossing in assault boats between Rehlingen and Wallerfangen and establishing small bridgehead in Pachten-Dillingen area; 357th Inf, on N, advances its left flank about $1^{1}/_{2}$ miles but is soon pinned down on right; 358th pushes to edge of Pachten and Dillingen. 95th Div, with 5 bns across the Sarre, continues efforts to take Saarlautern-Roden, Fraulautern, and Ensdorf portion of West Wall against tenacious resistance. 5th Div continues to clear to the Sarre on S flank of corps and in Metz area accepts surrender of St Quentin works. In XII Corps area, 6th Armd and 35th Inf Divs clear W bank of the Sarre from Grosbliederstroff to Wittring. 35th, assisted by tanks of 6th Armd, pushes into Sarreguemines and clears W sector. 6th Armd Div, its current mission completed, extends northward to protect N flank of corps. 35th Div is ordered to attack across the Sarre in conjunction with 26th Div on 8th. 26th Div continues rapidly toward the Sarre. 4th Armd Div gains foothold in Singling and overruns Bining before being halted to await relief by 12th Armd Div of XV Corps.

6th Army Group: In U.S. Seventh Army's XV Corps area, 44th Div takes Montbronn while 100th clears Meisenthal and surrounds Mouterhouse. In VI Corps area, enemy counterattack recovers N part of Mertzwiller from 45th Div forces.

In Fr 1st Army's 2d Corps area, U.S. 36th Div is strongly opposed at Ostheim and Guemar but takes latter.

EASTERN EUROPE—Red Army broadens and intensifies offensive toward Budapest, Berlin announces, attacking in force on either side of the Hungarian capital and crossing elements from Csepel I., to W bank of the Danube S of the city. Rumanian troops are helping Soviet forces clear NE Hungary. Moscow reports substantial gains by Third Ukrainian Front forces all along front. Soviet and Yugoslav forces clearing region between the Danube and Sava in N Yugoslavia take rail and road center of Sid.

ITALY—AAI: In U.S. Fifth Army's Br 13 Corps area, 19th Brig of Ind 8th Div, completes movement to W flank of corps to operate under 1st Div.

In Br Eighth Army area, 10 Corps moves to Macerata from Perugia.

BURMA—In NCAC area, U.S. 475th Regt is ordered to relieve Ch 22d Div in Mo-hlaing area, about a mile N of Tonk-wa. About this time, Japanese TF starts across the Shweli toward Tonk-wa.

LEYTE—U.S. Sixth Army: In X Corps area, repeated efforts of 112th Cav to eliminate enemy on ridge SE of Limon fail. In XXIV Corps area, 7th Div continues northward drive on Ormoc, taking Balogo, Hill 918, and Kang Dagit; some elements are on the Palanas R and others are on a ridge of Hill 380. 77th Div loads for landing in Ormoc Bay at Deposito and sails with DD and Fifth Air Force protection for target area. About 150 Japanese attack Buri strip, surprising defense force and entering woods N of the strip.

7 December

WESTERN EUROPE—12th Army Group: In U.S. Ninth Army's XIX Corps area, commander of 116th Inf, 29th Div, reports that continued efforts to take the Juelich strong-points will be fruitless; during the past 6 days the regt has suffered heavy casualties and is unfit to continue the action; 115th Inf replaces 116th and prepares to continue the assault.

In U.S. First Army's VII Corps area, 9th Div completes relief of 1st Div and takes responsibility for Luchem-Langerwehe-Juengersdorf-Merode region. 1st Div, except for 16th Inf, which is attached to V Corps, moves to rest areas. 83d Div, less 329th inf, takes over zone of 4th Div on S flank of corps, with 8th Inf of 4th Div under its command. 4th Div (— 8th Inf) passes to VIII Corps control. V Corps virtually finishes clearing its sector to the Roer. 2d Ranger Bn pushes to crest of Castle Hill, where it is under heavy fire and repels 2 counterattacks. When a platoon advances to reinforce the rangers, enemy withdraws hastily. CCR of 5th Armd Div pulls back from Bergstein during night but by this time 28th Inf of 8th Div has advanced almost to the village from the S.

In U.S. Third Army's XX Corps area, 90th Div attempts to improve and consolidate bridgehead in Pachten-Dillingen area with little success: 357th Inf establishes thin perimeter on N flank and holds it against major counterattack but is separated from 358th Inf in Dillingen-Pachten area by fortified West Wall belt; enemy fire continues to prevent construction of vehicular bridge, but footbridge is improvised and the bridgehead resupplied during night 7-8. 95th Div continues to battle West Wall positions in its Saarlautern bridgehead: 379th Inf makes limited progress in Saarlautern-Roden; 377th takes over fight for Fraulautern; 378th is virtually at a standstill in Ensdorf area and its 2d Bn is still W of the Sarre. 10th Inf, 5th Div finishes clearing its sector and ties in with 95th Div; in Metz area, Fort Plappeville surrenders to 2d Inf. XII Corps regroups for assault on West Wall between Saarbruecken and Zweibruecken by 35th and 26th Divs. 80th Div withdraws to rear upon relief by 6th Armd Div and 2d Cav Gp. 35th Div is still engaged at Sarreguemines. 4th Armd Div is being relieved by XV Corps. 26th Div reaches positions within sight of Maginot Line forts at Wittring and Achen.

6th Army Group: In U.S. Seventh Army's XV Corps area, 44th Div is approaching Enchenberg against lively opposition. 100th Div seizes Mouterhouse. 12th Armd Div begins relief of 4th Armd Div (XII Corps). In VI Corps area, 94th Cav Rcn Sq and elements of 19th Armd Inf Bn attached to 79th Div begin attack on Gambsheim. 103d Div is committed between 45th and 79th Divs.

Fr 1st Army opens attack on Colmar Pocket in 1st Corps zone while 2d Corps is containing determined counterattacks in Ostheim, Guemar, and Mittelwihr areas. 1st Corps drives on Cernay and Thann, 2d Moroccan Div taking Bischwiller and establishing bridgehead at Pont d'Aspach.

EASTERN EUROPE—Right wing elements of Third Ukrainian Front clearing region between the Danube and Lake Balaton seize Adony, about 25 miles S of Budapest, and Enying, less than 20 miles from Szekesfehervar; center elements report S bank of Lake Balaton clear; left flank forces clearing region between Lake Balaton and the Drava take Barcs. Moscow announces that the Germans are bringing reinforcements from Italy and the Western Front to defend Budapest. Yugoslavia reports several crossings of the Danube near Vukovar in Slovenia by Soviet and Yugoslav units. Berlin claims that German withdrawal from Montenegro and W Serbia "progressed according to plan."

ITALY—AAI: In Br Eighth Army's 5 Corps area, village of Piedura falls to 46th Div, but enemy retains ridges near there.

LEYTE—Fifth Air Force and Army and Marine land-based planes join in attacks on enemy convoy of 6 transports and 7 escort vessels heading for Leyte with reinforcements. The entire convoy is believed to have been destroyed.

U.S. Sixth Army: In X Corps area, enemy continues to cling stubbornly to ridge SE of Limon, preventing 2d Sq of 112th Cav from advancing. 1st Sq reaches Leyte R, where it makes contact with Tr A and 126th Inf of 32d Div. In XXIV Corps area, 77th Div, after naval gunfire preparation, begins unopposed landing at Deposito at 0707 and moves inland at once, 307th Inf clearing Ipil and 305th reaching Bagonbon R. Although opposition ashore is light, shipping in Ormoc Bay undergoes 16 enemy air attacks by an estimated 45-50 planes, of which 36 are believed to have been shot down. Suicide planes severely damage 5 vessels, 2 of which, USS *Mahan* (DD) and transport *Ward*, must be sunk. 7th Div pushes on toward Ormoc, 184th Inf reaching Tabgas R and 17th taking Hill 380. This virtually completes battle of the ridges, although fighting continues for several days before div reaches its objective, Talisayan R. Fighting continues in Buri airstrip area. 1st Bn of 149th Inf, 38th Div, gains hold on SW edge, making contact with 1st Bn of 187 Gli Inf, 11th A/B Div.

8 December

WESTERN EUROPE—12th Army Group: In U.S. Ninth Army's XIX Corps area, 29th Div's 115th Inf reduces Hasenfeld Gut and *sportplatz* strongpoints in Juelich area with help of assault guns and smoke.

In U.S. First Army area, VII Corps is ordered to attack on 10th to clear region between Inde and Roer Rivers and approaches to Dueren, corps' objective. In V Corps area, bn of 13th Inf relieves Rangers on Castle Hill. In their 2-day stay there, Rangers have lost more than 1/4 of their original strength.

In U.S. Third Army's XX Corps area, 357th Inf is again subjected to major counterattacks in 90th Div's Dillingen bridgehead, but forces enemy back in hand-to-hand fighting; local enemy counterattacks keep 358th Inf largely on the defensive, although elements push across RR tracks to take Dillingen station; reserve regt, 359th, crosses into bridgehead, night 8-9. 95th Div is very slowly expanding its Saarlautern bridgehead, fighting from house to house and from pillbox to pillbox; 2d Bn, 378th Inf, joins parent regt in Ensdorf after crossing river in assault boats. 6th Cav Gp takes over sector on S flank of corps from elements of 5th Div. After receiving surrender of Fort Driant, 2d Inf of 5th Div turns over Metz sector, where Fort Jeanne d'Arc is still holding out, to 87th Div of III Corps. In XII Corps area, 35th Div attacks across the Sarre, 134th Inf crossing by bridge S of Sarreguemines and 320th by boats in region to E; 134th clears Sarreinsming and pushes NE under heavy fire from Sarreguemines; 320th, whose 3d Bn is unable to cross until night 8-9, establishes bridgehead and with aid of arty and fighter-bombers halts counterattack as it is forming. 26th Div attacks Maginot Line within its sector after arty and air preparation: 328th Inf begins assault on Fort Wit-tring and Grand Bois, fighting through night 8-9; 104th, to right, easily takes 4 mutually supporting forts in Achen area.

6th Army Group: In U.S. Seventh Army's XV Corps area, 12th Armd Div completes relief of 4th Armd Div (XII Corps) in place. 44th Div pushes into Encherberg and 100th into Lemberg, but enemy is defending both towns. VI Corps is conducting deception program to lead enemy to expect Rhine crossing in Strasbourg area or attack in vicinity of Bischwiller. 45th Div begins attack on Niederbronn. In 79th Div zone, 94th Cav Rcn Sq clears Gambsheim.

In Fr 1st Army area, 2d Corps is still undergoing lively counterattacks. U.S. 36th Div troops are driving on Kayserberg. 1st Corps gains foothold in Thann.

EASTERN EUROPE—Soviet forces, Berlin admits, "widen their breach" N of Budapest. Troops of Third Ukrainian Front clearing region between Lake Balaton and the Danube are roughly 10 miles from Szekesfehervar. Germans are warding off breakthrough attempts between Lake Balaton and the Drava.

ITALY—AAI: In U.S. Fifth Army's Br 13 Corps area, enemy abandons rest of M. Penzola.

In Br Eighth Army area, 5 Corps begins relief of 46th Div with Ind 10th Div.

BURMA—In NCAC area, Japanese take Tonkwa from outnumbered Chinese. In Br Fourteenth Army area, 4 Corps hq moves from Imphal to Tamu and is placed under Lt Gen Messervy, who succeeds Lt Gen Sir Geoffrey Scoones. Corps is to move secretly southward down the Gangaw Valley to S flank of army, where it will seize bridgehead over the Irrawaddy in Pakokku area and thrust toward Meiktila and Thazi.

LEYTE—U.S. Sixth Army: In X Corps area, 1st Sq of 112th Cav begins action to locate and sever Japanese supply line to ridge SE of Limon. In XXIV Corps area, 307th Inf of 77th Div (reinf by 2d Bn of 306th and supported by arty, Co A of 776th Amph Tank Bn and Co A of 88th Chemical Weapons Bn) drives N astride Highway 2 from Ipil toward Camp Downes, less than a mile from Ormoc. Platoon of Co A, 776th Tank Bn, moving by sea, reconnoiters Camp Downes area, meeting enemy fire. 305th Inf protects S flank of div, holding perimeter from Ipil area S to Baod R. Americans consolidate positions in Buri airfield area.

VOLCANO Is.—B-29's and warships join B-24's in bombardment of Iwo Jima.

9 December

WESTERN EUROPE—12th Army Group: In U.S. Ninth Army area, 75th Div is assigned to army and on 11th further assigned to XVI Corps. In XIX Corps area, 30th Div is ordered to secure region between Inde and Roer Rivers within its zone.

In U.S. First Army area, army maintains and improves defensive positions.

In U.S. Third Army's XX Corps area, 90th Div commits its full strength to Dillingen bridgehead battle: 359th Inf begins clearing mutually supporting fortifications between 357th and 358th Regts, easing pressure on right flank of 357th; 357th holds its weak perimeter on N flank of the bridgehead against repeated counterattacks that are debilitating to both sides; supply situation of 358th, fighting indecisively along RR tracks in Dillingen, improves as rafting operations are begun in afternoon and first tank crosses by treadway ferry in evening, but 359th and 357th Regts must still rely on assault boats, carrying parties, and aircraft for reinforcement and supply. 95th Div continues almost futile efforts to expand Saarlautern bridgehead; supply problem is intensified by rapidly rising Sarre R. With relief of 10th Inf on S flank of corps by 6th Cav GP, 5th Div is able to assemble in preparation for attack on West Wall. In XII Corps area, 35th Div's bridgeheads across the Sarre continue to receive heavy enemy fire, but 2 Class 40 bridges are completed by midnight; 1st Bn of 137th Inf is sent to Sarreguemines to mop up in W part of city, since 134th Inf can make little headway until this is done; 320th moves forward more rapidly because of 26th Div's action to right. 328th Inf, 26th Div, completes capture of Fort Wittring by dawn and after daylight finds that enemy has abandoned Fort Grand Bois; 104th Inf is pushing steadily toward Gros Réderching. In III Corps area, 87th Div is assigned to XII Corps to replace 26th Div, and 346th Inf starts by truck to Gros Réderching area.

6th Army Group: In XV Corps area, CCA of 12th Armd Div, driving NE on left flank of corps, takes Singling. Enchenberg falls to 44th Div and Lemberg to 100th. In VI Corps area, 45th Div clears Niederbronn. 79th Div overruns Bischwiller and pushes to edge of Haguenau.

In Fr 1st Army area, 2d Corps is still strongly opposed but clears Mittelwihr. In 1st Corps area, 2d Moroccan Div continues clearing Thann. 4th Mtn Div is meeting vigorous opposition at Lutterbach.

EASTERN EUROPE—Moscow confirms German reports of Soviet breakthrough NE of Budapest, announcing that forces of Second Ukrainian Front have reached the Danube bend at Vac. Other troops of this front, having crossed to W bank of the Danube from Csepel I., S of Budapest, gain contact with troops of Third Ukrainian Front at Lake Velencei, between the Danube and Lake Balaton. Budapest is thus about two-thirds encircled. Sofia announces that Bulgar and Yugoslav Armies, assisted by Soviet aircraft, have completed the expulsion of Germans from Serbia and Macedonia during the last few days.

ITALY—AAI: In U.S. Fifth Army's Br 13 Corps area, 78th Div extends eastward to M. dell'Acqua Saluta-M. deb Verro area as 6th Armd Div prepares to continue offensive.

In Br Eighth Army area, 5 Corps contains determined counterattacks but in so doing is too weakened to exploit this success and suspends offensive.

BURMA—In NCAC area, Japanese forces from Tonk-wa reach Mohlaing, where Ch 22d Div CP is located. U.S. 475th Inf, which is arriving in this area, joins Chinese in counterattack that restores positions. 113th Regt, Ch 38th Div, has been unable to penetrate into Bhamo; 114th adopts American suggestion of taking full advantage of supporting arty and aircraft and is working forward methodically in N defenses. S of Bhamo, elements of Ch 90th Regt, 30th Div, become isolated during Japanese counterattack.

CHINA—Failure of 2 Ch armies (5th and 53d) to concentrate for defense of Kunming endangers success of ALPHA plan and brings protest from Gen Wedemeyer to Chiang Kai-shek, who replies that he is keeping the 5th back to defend Kunming.

LEYTE—Last of Japanese reinforcements arrive at Palompon.

U.S. Sixth Army: In X Corps area, 112th Cav continues efforts to dislodge enemy from ridge SE of Limon and to cut enemy's supply line. In XXIV Corps area, convoy arrives with supplies and rest of 306th Inf, 77th Div. 307th Inf, passing 1st Bn of 306th Inf through 2d Bn of that refit, continues toward Camp Downes and takes it. 3d Bn, 306th Inf, is committed to protect E and center of beachhead. 305th Inf secures region NE of Camp Downes and protects NE flank of div. 2d Bn of 511th Para Inf, 11th A/B Div, joins 3d Bn at Mahonag, from which patrols are being sent out. 1st Bn, 149th Inf, drives N across Buri airstrip but is forced back to S edge by enemy fire. 1st Bn, 382d, probes to locate enemy and contains night counterattack against its perimeter.

10 December

INTERNATIONAL AGREEMENTS—France and USSR sign treaty of alliance in Moscow.

WESTERN EUROPE—12th Army Group: In U.S. First Army area, VII Corps begins co-ordinated attack to clear W bank of the Roer and city of Dueren, employing 104th Inf, 3d Armd, 9th Inf, and 83d Inf Divs. Elements of 414th Inf, 104th Div attack toward village of Schophoven and Pier; penetrate into Pier but are forced out. In 9th Div zone in center, elements of 3d Armd Div, assisted by 60th Inf, thrust to Obergeich and gain positions in Echtz; elements of 39th Inf driving SE from Obergeich get into position for assault on Merode and Schlicht. 83d Div pushes into villages of Gey and Strass, NE of Grosshau, with 331st and 330th Refits; 329th Inf advances on left flank.

In U.S. Third Army's XX Corps area, Germans make all-out effort to destroy Dillingen bridgehead, counter-attacking all along line. 90th Div contains the onslaughts but cannot move forward. In 95th Div's Saarlautern bridgehead, 377th Inf deepens penetration into Fraulautern but 378th and 379th Refits are prevented by counterattacks from advancing. In XII Corps area, main body of 137th Inf, 35th Div, crosses the Sarre to clear E part of Sarreguemines and begins house-to-house battle. 134th and 320th Refits push toward Blies R. Gros Réderching falls to 104th Inf, 26th Div. 87th Div begins relief of 26th Div; latter, as relieved, moves to Metz in III Corps zone.

6th Army Group: In U.S. Seventh Army area, newly arrived 63d and 42d Divs, whose refits are organized as TF Harris and TF Linden, respectively, are assigned to army. In XV Corps area, CCA of 12th Armd Div takes Rohrbach-lès-Bitche. 44th Div secures crossroads below Petit Réderching in brisk fighting. In VI Corps area, 45th Div seizes Reichshoffen and Gundershoffen. 79th takes Marienthal and Kaltenhouse but is still held up at Haguenau. Crossing the Zintzel, 102d Div troops clear N part of Mertzwiller. 117th Cav Rcn Sq relieves 94th Cav Rcn Sq at Gambsheim.

In Fr 1st Army's 1st Corps area, 2d Moroccan Div completes capture of Thann. 9th Colonial Div reduces last enemy bridgeheads W of the Rhine between Kembs and Swiss border.

EASTERN EUROPE—Second Ukrainian Front pushes in toward Pest, portion of Budapest E of the Danube. Germans are withstanding Soviet attacks SW of Budapest and near Miskolc. In N Yugoslavia, Soviet and Yugoslav forces driving toward Vinkovci penetrate into Vukovar, Yugoslavia reports.

ITALY—AAI: In Br Eighth Army area, Cdn 1 Corps begins attack across the Lamone late in day.

BURMA—In NCAC area, Br 36th Div completes its part of Phase 2, CAPITAL, ahead of schedule as patrols enter Indaw and Katha. Later in month, div crosses the Irrawaddy at Katha and drives toward Kyaukme. Japanese forces working toward Bhamo to assist withdrawal of garrison penetrate positions of Ch 30th Div S of Bhamo; vigorous counter-attack forces enemy to go on the defensive. U.S. 475th Inf, less 1st Bn in Shwegu area, is concentrated in Mohlaing-Tonk-wa area, where it will conduct holding action while Ch 22d Div flies to China.

CHINA—Gen Wedemeyer urges Chiang Kai-shek to order troops of Y-Force on Salween front to take Wanting, at NE exit of Shweli Valley where Ledo Road is to meet old Burma Road. Chinese halted offensive operations with fall of Che-fang on 1st. Japanese in S China link up with Japanese *French Indochina Garrison Army,* thus opening route for movement of 2 divs in small groups into Indochina. This, plus their push into Kweichow, which ended on 3 December, marks high tide of Japanese invasion of continent of Asia.

LEYTE—U.S. Sixth Army: In X Corps area, 32d Div continues to press southward as does 112th Cav of 1st Cav Div to E. 2d Sq, 112th Cav, is relieved by 2d Sq, 7th Cav, on ridge SE of Limon and passes to army control. 12th Cav prepares to attack to reduce strongpoint in Mt Cabungaan area. In XXIV Corps area, 77th Div, supported by arty and naval vessels, takes Ormoc. Co A of 776th Amph Tank Bn moves into the city at 0900, before infantry assault begins, and starts shelling buildings there. 307th and 306th Refits, former driving along highway and latter to E, attack northward and clear the city. 7th Div continues forward toward 77th Div. 11th A/B Div defeats dispirited counterattack in Burauen area by enemy bn that has made its way over mountains from Ormoc Bay. 1st Bn of 149th Inf, 38th Div, attacks and clears Buri airfield area. In a final major effort against Burauen airfields, beginning at 1930, Japanese force Fifth Air Force personnel to fall back, but positions are restored in counterattack.

11 December

WESTERN EUROPE—12th Army Group: In U.S. First Army's VII Corps area, enemy continues successful defense of Pier and Schophoven, but elements of 415th Inf, 104th Div, take Merken and Vilvenich. 60th Inf, 9th Div, and armor of 3d Armd Div overrun Geich. CCR of 3d Armd Div, reinf by bn of 60th Inf, makes futile and costly effort to take Hoven. 39th Inf of 9th Div seizes Merode and Schlicht. In V Corps area, 2d Div closes in corps zone and is attached to corps. In VIII Corps area, 106th Div, with 14th Cav Gp attached, takes over positions in the Schnee Eifel formerly held by 2d Div.

In U.S. Third Army's XX Corps area, 357th Inf of 90th Div withdraws a little on N flank of Dillingen bridgehead in order to shorten front and secure supply lines; 359th and 358th Regts attempt in vain to find passage through fortified belt between them; 359th loses 3 pillboxes during counterattack; 90th Rcn Tr takes responsibility for W bank of the Sarre so that the covering force previously deployed there can be used to strengthen the bridgehead. 95th Div expands Saarlautern bridgehead in costly fighting: 377th Inf pushes to center of Fraulautern; 378th clears about 5 city blocks in Ensdorf; progress of 379th in Saarlautern-Roden is negligible. In XII Corps area, 137th Inf of 35th Div finishes clearing Sarreguemines, except for a few snipers, and blocks at Frauenberg; main body of div continues toward Blies R; at night, div prepares to, attack across the Blies on 12th. 328th Inf, 26 Div, continues toward German frontier.

6th Army Group: In U.S. Seventh Army's XV Corps area, 44th Div elements take Petit Réderching; others reach Siersthal. In VI Corps area, Haguenau falls to 79th Div.

ITALY—AAI: In U.S. Fifth Army's Br 13 Corps area, 6th Armd Div is ordered to attack for Tossignano, night 12-13.

In Br Eighth Army's Cdn 1 Corps area, 1st Div and 5th Armd Div gain bridgeheads across the Lamone and push to Fosso Vecchio Canal. Tanks are unable to cross into bridgehead. Porter Force is dissolved, but elements continue to assist 5th Armd Div.

BURMA—In Br Fourteenth Army's 4 Corps area, advance elements of 268th Brig reach Indaw.

CHINA—Gen Wedemeyer drafts directives for ALPHA that Chiang Kai-shek later approves. Gen Ho is to command ALPHA forces, but Gen Chennault will command air forces in the area. U. S. SOS will assist Gen Ho in supply matters. ALPHA forces are to complete concentration in Kweiyang area, protect Kunming and Kweiyang, and train reserves.

ULITHI—Fast carrier groups of U.S. Third Fleet leave for Luzon.

LEYTE—Leyte-based planes of Fifth Air Force begin mission in support of coming invasion of Mindoro.

U.S. Sixth Army: In X Corps area, 1st Sq of 12th Cav, 1st Cav Div, reduces strongpoint N of its perimeter in Mt. Cabungaan area after intense preparatory fire. Patrols of 2d Sq, 7th Cav, probe both sides of ridge SE of Limon before general frontal and flanking attack is begun behind arty bombardment; advance stops for night at base of the hill. 128th Inf, 32d Div, begins patrolling Limon area. XXIV Corps gains firm control of Ormoc Bay as advance elements of 7th Div overtake 77th Div troops at Ipil. Japanese forces on Leyte are thus divided. 77th Div attacks from Ormoc with 307th and 306th Regts but makes little progress. 305th Inf's 2d and 3d Bns enter line between 307th and 3d Bn of 306th, leaving regt's 1st Bn just S of Camp Downes on extreme right flank. Japanese attempts to land reinforcements at Ormoc Bay, night 11-12, are frustrated. A few Japanese succeed in landing but are unable to take an active part in the battle for Ormoc corridor.

12 December

WESTERN EUROPE—12th Army Group: In U.S. First Army's VII Corps area, 104th Div takes Pier in 2-pronged assault and forces enemy to withdraw across the Roer. Elements of 60th Inf, 9th Div, drive into Mariaweiler. Hoven is cleared of enemy. CCR, 3d Armd Div, and 60th Inf finish clearing most of region W of the Roer NW and W of Dueren during day. 39th Inf, 9th Div, begins clearing Derichsweiler.

In U.S. Third Army's XX Corps area, situation in Dillingen bridgehead improves. 357th Inf, 90th Div, mops up bypassed resistance within its sector and 359th and 358th establish contact, opening corridor through fortified belt through which tanks are moved to 357th. Vehicular ferry is put into operation. Effective smoke screen permits delivery of tanks and TD's to bridgehead. Limited progress is made in Saarlautern bridgehead by 95th Div. Combat efficiency of both 90th and 95th Divs has been lowered sharply because of insufficient reinforcements and exhaustion. In XII Corps area, 35th Div begins attack across the Blies early in morning: 1st Bn, 134th Inf, crosses and begins to clear Habkirchen, gaining weak hold there; 320th Inf, assisted by tanks, clears Bliesbruck, on near side of the river, in preparation for crossing. 328th Inf, 26th Div, gets forward elements across German border and its relief is begun by 87th Div, night 12-13.

6th Army Group: In U.S. Seventh Army area, XV Corps is virtually halted by Maginot fortifications in Hottviller-Bitche area, but CCA, 12th Armd Div, reaches Bettviller, its objective. VI Corps commits 14th Armd Div between 103d and 79th Divs. 79th Div enters Soufflenheim as enemy pulls back toward West Wall; begins clearing Seltz.

In Fr 1st Army area, Gen de Lattre alters plan of action, calling for capture of Colmar and Cernay but deferring drive to the Rhine at Brisach unless circumstances are favorable. 2d Corps is to make main effort through Colmar to Rouffach, where it will link up with 1st Corps coming from Cernay. 1st Corps is so spent that it suspends offensive until 15th.

ITALY—AAI: In U.S. Fifth Army's Br 13 Corps area, Germans, counterattacking at dawn, temporarily force back outpost of 19th Ind Brig on M. Cerere. 6th Armd Div begins second phase of its offensive, night 12-13, employing 61st Brig, which gets elements into Tossignano, where they come under heavy pressure.

In Br Eighth Army's Cdn 1 Corps area, 5th Armd and 1st Inf Divs advance from Fosso Vecchio to Naviglio Canal, which runs from Faenza to the sea, and attack across it, night 12-13. 1st Div gains bridgehead N of Bagnacavallo, but 5th Armd Div is forced back to the Fosso Vecchio.

BURMA—In ALFSEA area, 15 Corps begins offensive (ROMULUS) to clear Arakan coastal sector and gain air and naval bases from which to support future operations. While Ind 25th Div pushes southward along Mayu Peninsula toward Akyab, W African 82d Div begins clearing Kalapanzin Valley in Buthidaung area and W African 81st Div attacks in Kaladan Valley in vicinity of Kyauktaw.

LEYTE—U.S. Seventh Fleet Task Groups 78.3 and 77.3 leave Leyte Gulf for Mindoro; together with TG 77.12, which has sailed from Kossol Roads, move through Surigao Strait into Mindanao Sea, night 12-13.

U.S. Sixth Army: In X Corps area, 32d Div straightens lines S of Limon and during night 12-13 shells enemy positions ahead of it on Highway 2 as far S as Lonoy. XXIV Corps chases off enemy vessel sighted near Linao at dawn. 77th Div consolidates positions just N of Ormoc while amassing supplies and arty.

13 December

WESTERN EUROPE—21 Army Group: Br Second Army starts regrouping for offensive to clear region between the Maas and the Rhine. 30 Corps, which will at first be employed, turns over its sector and troops to 12 Corps.

12th Army Group: In U.S. Ninth Army's XIX Corps, area, 30th Div, in limited attacks, clears most of region between Inde and Roer Rivers.

In U.S. First Army's VII Corps area, 104th Div reaches the Roer on 4-mile front. 39th Inf, 9th Div, finishes clearing Derichsweiler. This virtually ends current mission of corps. V Corps opens offensive for Roer and Urft dams, employing 78th Div (untried as yet in combat), 2d Div, and 99th Div. 78th Div is held up near Kesternich. 2d Div is slowed by obstacles and enemy fire in center of corps. 99th Div attacks in Monschau Forest and gains preliminary objectives.

U.S. Third Army draws up plans for air-ground assault on West Wall. III Corps accepts surrender of last of the Metz forts—Jeanne d'Arc. In XX Corps area, 90th Div prepares for all-out effort to take rest of Dillingen on 15th, regrouping and building up supplies. 95th Div makes very slight progress in Saarlautern bridgehead, although elements of 2d Inf, 5th Div, are committed with 377th Inf to guard bridge. In XII Corps area, 35th Div strengthens its hold across the Blies; 1st Bn, 134th Inf, undergoes enemy counterattacks in Habkirchen, beginning early in morning, and is forced back toward river; 3d Bn joins in battle for Habkirchen; bn of 320th Inf crosses the Blies at Bliesbruck and takes Hill 321; small force from 137th Inf crosses N of Habkirchen but is pinned down.

6th Army Group: In U.S. Seventh Army's XV Corps area, 44th Div begins struggle for Fort Simershof, near Hottviller, which is barring forward movement. In VI Corps area, 14th Armd Div attacks between road and 79th Divs, CCA taking Soultz-sous-Forêts. 79th Div completes capture of Seltz and overruns Niederroedern.

EASTERN EUROPE—Forward elements of Second Ukrainian Front thrust to within 6 miles NE and 8 miles E of Budapest.

ITALY—AAI: In U.S. Fifth Army's Br 13 Corps area, 61st Brig of 6th Armd Div gets additional elements into Tossignano. 36th Brig of 78th Div begins attack for Parocchia di M. Maggiore, night 13-14, but is unable to reach top and withdraws at dawn.

In Br Eighth Army's Cdn 1 Corps area, 1st Div maintains bridgehead across Naviglio Canal against severe counterattacks.

BURMA—In NCAC area, 114th Regt, Ch 38th Div, breaks through northern defenses of Bhamo and is pushing into central part. In Tonk-wa area, U.S. 475th Inf quickly repels enemy attack.

P.I.—As U.S. Seventh Fleet task groups move W through Mindanao Sea, covered by CVE aircraft, which make a few air strikes, enemy planes, including kamikazes, begin strikes that damage Adm Struble's flagship, *Nashville*, and USS *Haraden*, both of which turn back.

LEYTE—U.S. Sixth Army: In X Corps area, 32d Div makes limited progress southward; southernmost elements are isolated from main body and out of food. Japanese counterattack, night 13-14, penetrates CP of 126th Inf. Enemy is driven back before dawn. 2d Sq of 7th Cav, 1st Cav Div, again attempts to take ridge SE of Limon but cannot advance. In XXIV Corps area, 305th Inf, making main effort of 77th Div, is held up in Cogon area, N of Antilao R on Highway 2 just N of Ormoc, where enemy is strongly entrenched and holds blockhouse strongpoint. Special TF under Col Paul L. Freeman, consisting of Cos E and L, is unable to take the blockhouse by storm. 306th Inf assists 305th with fire. 307th, on left flank, drives W along Ormoc-Linao road and takes Linao. Enemy positions in Cogon area are shelled during night 13-14. 32d Inf, 7th Div, starts NE from Ormoc Bay in effort to make contact with 11th A/B Div moving W.

14 December

WESTERN EUROPE—12th Army Group: In U.S. Ninth Army's XIX Corps area, 30th Div troops finish clearing region between Inde and Roer Rivers.

In U.S. First Army's VII Corps area, factory between Mariaweiler and Dueren is cleared of enemy. V Corps continues offensive but makes little headway.

In U.S. Third Army's XX Corps area, 90th Div continues attack preparations. Vehicular ferry is put out of action by enemy fire. 95th Div makes little progress in expanding Saarlautern bridgehead. In XII Corps area, 35th Div continues battle for Habkirchen, crossing 2d Bn and Co K of 134th Inf over river to join in attack. Bailey bridge is put across the river to the village, night 14-15. 87th Div, which has been moving toward Rimling, takes that village, but resistance is stiffening.

6th Army Group: In U.S. Seventh Army's XV Corps area, elements of 100th Div attacking Fort Schiesseck, near Bitche, are pinned down by enemy fire. In VI Corps area, Lembach falls to 45th Div. 103d Div encounters strong rear-guard opposition at Climbach. 79th Div column drives to outskirts of Lauterbourg.

ITALY—AAI: In U.S. Fifth Army's Br 13 Corps area, 6th Armd Div loses contact with elements within Tossignano and fighting for this objective ceases after futile efforts to take it.

In Br Eighth Army area, Pol 2 Corps renews offensive, night 14-15, pushing forward to left of 5 Corps and in conjunction with it. 5 Corps, after regrouping, jumps off, night 14-15, with Ind 10th Div on left and NZ 2d Div on right, Ind 10th attacking toward Pergola ridge and NZ 2d in Colle area, W of Faenza. In Cdn 1 Corps area, 5 Armd Div forces Naviglio Canal to right of 1st Div and establishes bridgehead.

BURMA—In NCAC area, Japanese garrison of Bhamo prepares to withdraw. U.S. 475th Inf repels another enemy attack on Tonk-wa, after which activity subsides to patrolling; makes patrol contact with Br 36th Div at Katha.

CHINA—Gen Wedemeyer starts on field inspection trip.

P.I.—Planes of U.S. Third Fleet's fast carrier groups begin attacks on Japanese airfields on Luzon. Japanese continue air attacks on the Mindoro-bound task groups of U.S. Seventh Fleet.

LEYTE—U.S. Sixth Army: In X Corps area, 126th and 127th Regts of 32d Div, pressing slowly southward down Highway 2, come up against enemy's MLR on series of ridges commanding Highway 2 and for the next few days can make only minor gains. 2d Sq of 7th Cav, 1st Cav Div, succeeds in dislodging enemy from ridge SE of Limon. 12th Cav, which has been patrolling in Mt Cabungaan area, is ordered W to block Highway 2 South of 32d Div and then attack N toward that div. In XXIV Corps area, 305th Inf of 77th Div reduces opposition in Cogon area, TF Freeman taking the blockhouse and road junction N of Ormoc to sever enemy's line of communication. On div right flank, 184th Inf relieves 306th Inf in line. 32d Inf, 7th Div, is advancing steadily over precipitous terrain toward 511th Para Inf, 11th A/B Div.

15 December

WESTERN EUROPE—12th Army Group: In U.S. First Army area, V Corps continues to gain ground slowly. 78th Div secures Kesternich but enemy infiltrates in some strength and isolates elements.

In U.S. Third Army's XX Corps area, 90th Div opens assault for rest of Dillingen and Prims R bridge on Dillingen-Saarlautern road under smoke screen with 359th Inf on left and 358th on right; attack penetrates enemy MLR in Dillingen sector and gets well into the town. Lull develops after this and 90th Div suspends attack. 95th Div continues slow advance in Saarlautern bridgehead. In XII Corps area, 134th Inf of 35th Div, assisted by tanks and TD's, takes Habkirchen; to left, 137th Inf is driven out of Breiterwald with very heavy losses in enemy counterattack. 87th Div is also bitterly opposed but 347th Inf takes Obergailbach and heights overlooking the Blies.

6th Army Group: In U.S. Seventh Army's VI Corps area, CCA of 14th Armd Div, seizes Riedseitz; CCB takes Salmbach and Schlerthal. One 79th Div column clears Lauterbourg and another reaches Lauter R at village of Schiebenhardt.

[16 DECEMBER 1944]

Fr 1st Army begins offensive against Germans W of the Rhine in Colmar area. 2d Corps, making main effort, penetrates to Orbey.

EASTERN EUROPE—Red Army troops cross Ipely (Ipel) R north of Budapest and establish bridgehead on Czechoslovak soil at Sahy.

ITALY—AAI: In Br Eighth Army area, Pol 2 Corps pushes forward on left flank of army across the Sintria R toward the Senio. In 5 Corps area, Germans struggle to prevent encirclement of Faenza, exerting strong pressure on NZ forces in Colle area and bringing Ind 10th Div to a halt short of Pergola during day but withdrawing, night 15-16. Cdn 1 Corps joins and consolidates bridgeheads across Naviglio Canal N of Faenza and spends the next few days improving bridgehead.

BURMA—In NCAC area, Japanese garrison of Bhamo escapes through Ch lines early in morning and the relief force S of the town begins to disengage. Ch 38th Div moves into Bhamo. CAI and Y=Force are only 50 air miles apart. 112th Regt, Ch 38th Div, which was recently withdrawn from Bhamo battle, is driving on Namhkam. Elements of U.S. 475th Inf move from Mo-hlaing to Tonk-wa area.

In Br Fourteenth Army area, 15 Corps makes rapid strides on Arakan front. W African 82d Div takes Buthidaung and establishes bridgehead across the Kalapanzin.

MINDORO—Western Visayan Task Force invades Mindoro at 0735 after preparatory bombardment. 19th Inf, 24th Div, lands between Caminawit Pt and San Agustin; reinf 503d Para Inf, less Co C, on beach fronting San Agustin; Co C, 503d, across river mouth from San Agustin. From San Agustin, 3d Bn of 503d Para Inf drives inland about 8 miles to final beachhead line, securing airstrip, sugar plant, and village of San Jose without opposition. 19th Inf also drives inland to final beachhead line, the only contact with enemy being made at Caminawit Pt. Western Visayan Task Force suffers no casualties. Adm Struble turns over command ashore to Gen Dunckel. Airdrome construction is begun at once and new site, about 2 miles NW of White Beach, is selected. Although there is no ground opposition, enemy planes continue to attack shipping, destroying 2 LST's and causing minor damage to other vessels. Unloading proceeds rapidly, permitting LSM's and APD's of Task Group 78.3 to withdraw ahead of schedule.

LEYTE—U.S. Sixth Army: In X Corps area, 1st Sq (−) of 12th Cav Regt starts W toward Highway 2, reaching previously selected drop area, a banana plantation about 1,800 yards E of Lonoy; rest of regt joins 1st Sq there by 17 December. In XXIV Corps area, with port of Ormoc sealed off, 77th Div pauses to consolidate. 32d Inf, 7th Div, makes contact with 11th A/B Div's 511th Para Inf, Co G of which enters its lines. Co G has been isolated for 4 days. It is decided to withdraw 1st and 3d Bns of 32d Inf to clear pockets in Ormoc area and let 2d Bn continue eastward to establish contact with rest of 511th Para Inf force.

16 December

WESTERN EUROPE—21 Army Group: In Br Second Army area, 30 Corps begins concentrating in Nijmegen area for drive on Krefeld, scheduled to begin on to January.

12th Army Group: Field Marshal von Rundstedt opens all-out counteroffensive in the Ardennes early in morning, taking Americans by surprise and penetrating lines of U.S. First Army. *6th Pz Army* on N and *5th Pz Army* on S press vigorously toward the Meuse on broad front, former directed ultimately toward Albert Canal in Maastricht-Antwerp area and latter toward Brussels-Antwerp area. Enemy paratroopers dropped behind U.S. lines to seize key points succeed in disrupting communications and causing widespread confusion.

In U.S. Ninth Army's XIII Corps area, in conjunction with offensive against First Army, enemy counterattacks in vicinity of Leiffarth and penetrates 84th Div line, but positions are soon restored.

In U.S. First Army's VII Corps area, 9th and 83d Divs contain enemy thrusts toward Mariaweiler and Guerzenich. Elements of 5th Armd Div reach the Roer in Bilstein area. Corps releases 1st Div to V Corps. In V Corps area, German counteroffensive hits S flank of corps and VIII Corps line to S. 99th Div holds back enemy in Hofen area, S of Monschau, on N but gives ground to S and Germans penetrate almost to Buellingen. Continuing offensive to N, 2d Div seizes road junction on Hofen-Rocherath road in Monschau Forest. 78th Div repels counterattack against Rollesbroich but is unable to take Kesternich. 2d Ranger Bn is attached to 78th Div. VIII Corps' 106th Div (reinf by 14th Cav Gp), 28th Div, 9th Armd Div, and N flank elements of 4th Div all fall back under enemy onslaughts. Germans drive several miles W, cutting main N-S highway between Our and Clerf Rivers, encircling Echternach, and threatening St Vith. CCB, 9th Armd Div, is attached to 106th Div to help defend St Vith.

In U.S. Third Army area, XX Corps releases 10th Armd Div to VIII Corps. 95th Div continues battle to expand Saarlautern bridgehead. Its relief is begun, night 16-17, by 5th Div. 6th Cav Gp is attached to III Corps. III Corps is assigned zone between XX and XII Corps. Holding its front are 6th Cav Gp (TF Fickett) on N and 6th Armd Div, formerly of XII Corps, on S. 26th Div remains at Metz to train replacements. In XII Corps area, 35th and 87th Divs continue to clear outer positions of West Wall. News of the Ardennes counteroffensive cancels plans for corps assault on West Wall.

6th Army Group: In U.S. Seventh Army area, VI Corps gets elements of all its assault divs to German border. 45th Div troops take Bobenthal and Nothweiler. 103d Div bypasses Wissembourg, which CCA of 14th Armd Div occupies. CCB of 14th Armd Div and 79th Div are coming under heavy fire from the Bien Wald.

ITALY—Field Marshal Sir Harold R. L. G. Alexander becomes Supreme Allied Commander, Mediterranean Theater (AFHQ), replacing Field Marshal Sir Henry Maitland Wilson, who becomes head of British Joint Staff Mission in Washington, succeeding the late Field Marshal Dill. Gen Clark assumes command of Allied Armies in Italy, redesignated 15th Army Group, and is replaced as head of U.S. Fifth Army by Lt Gen Lucian K. Truscott, Jr.

In Br Eighth Army area, Pol 2 Corps continues to clear region E of the Senio on left flank of army. In 5 Corps area, Ind 43d Brig, operating with NZ 2d Div and with specific purpose of clearing Faenza, does so with ease. NZ 2d Div reaches the Senio. Ind 10th Div takes Pergola.

BURMA—In NCAC area, U.S. 124th Cav moves forward from Myitkyina area toward Bhamo to join in action.

In Br Fourteenth Army's 4 Corps area, Pinlebu and Banmauk fall to Ind 19th Div. From Banmauk, patrol reaches Indaw and makes contact with Br 36th Div, NCAC.

CHINA—Learning from Brig Gen Frank Dorn, U.S. adviser to ALPHA forces, that Ch 57th Army is refusing to move to defend Kunming, Gen McClure protests to Chiang Kai-shek, and part of the army is flown to Kunming area. Few of the Ch forces are in place as planned to stop enemy short of Kunming. Chinese Communist leader Chou En-lai terminates negotiations between Nationalist and Communist Chinese.

MINDORO—During this and the next few days, action is limited to patrolling in beachhead area and organizing defenses about airfield perimeter. Japanese continue air attacks on shipping. Seventh Fleet detachments sail for Leyte.

LUZON—U.S. Third Fleet continues air attacks on Luzon and in evening starts eastward to refuel.

LEYTE—Airfield in Tanauan area becomes operational.

U.S. Sixth Army: In XXIV Corps area, 2d Bn of 32d Inf, 7th Div, starts eastward along Talisayan R bank toward 511th Para Inf of 11th A/B Div. While 305th Inf, 77th Div, takes Cogon and clears that area, 307th pushes toward Valencia, reaching San Jose. 306th starts N behind 307th

17 December

WESTERN EUROPE—12th Army Group: Reinforcements are being sent to Ardennes sector to defend vital road centers. 2 airborne divs, 82d and 101st, of XVIII Corps (A/B), First Allied Airborne Army, are released from SHAEF reserve for action on Ardennes front.

U.S. Ninth Army releases 7th Armd Div to VIII Corps and 30th Div, whose zone an XIX Corps front is taken over by 29th Div, to V Corps.

In U.S. First Army area, VII Corps, while rounding up paratroopers and guarding against possible airborne attack, continues to press its right flank toward the Roer. 83d Div clears Roelsdorf and Lendersdorf. 9th Div, gains ground slowly just W of Dueren; releases RCT 47 to V Corps. V Corps is fully occupied holding current positions N of breakthrough and delaying German offensive, which continues to gain ground slowly toward Malmédy. 1st and 30th Divs are getting into position to counterattack; 26th Inf of 1st Div is attached to 99th Div. RCT 47, 9th Div, assembles in Eupen area. In VIII Corps area, disorganized 14th Cav Gp continues to fall back on N flank of corps. German columns isolate 2 regts (422d and 423d) of 106th Div in Schnee Eifel salient and push on through Heuem toward St. Vith. Elements of 7th and 9th Armd Divs are committed to defense of St Vith. In 28th Div zone, Germans drive almost to Wiltz. Corps releases CCR of 9th Armd Div from reserve to block Bastogne-Trois-Vierges road. 4th Div halts enemy S of Osweiler and Dickweiler, but units are isolated at a number of points. 10th Armd Div arrives in vicinity of Luxembourg city.

In U.S. Third Army's XX Corps area, 5th Div continues to relieve 95th in Saarlautern bridgehead. Engineers complete bridge in Ensdorf area.

6th Army Group: In U.S. Seventh Army area, XV Corps is still stalled by opposition from Forts Simershof and Schiesseck. VI Corps virtually halted at outer defenses of West Wall.

In Fr 1st Army area, 2d Corps overruns Keintzheim.

EASTERN EUROPE—Elements of Second Ukrainian Front push to within 5 miles of Budapest.

ITALY—15th Army Group: In U.S. Fifth Army's Br 13 Corps area, Ind 8th Div's sector is now so narrow, because of Pol 2 Corps advance, that it is held by a single brigade, the 17th.

In Br Eighth Army's Pol 2 Corps area, 5th Kresowa Div begins relieving 3d Carpathian Div along the Senio. In 5 Corps area, Ind 43d Brig tries in vain to advance from Faenza. Ind 10th Div secures small bridgeheads across the Senio N and S of Tebano, but no strong effort can be made to expand them until supply situation improves and environs of Faenza are cleared.

CHINA—Hump Tonnage Allocation and Control Office is established in Rear Echelon, China Theater Hq.

MINDORO—Patrolling and work on defenses continue.

LEYTE—U.S. Seventh Fleet Task Groups 77.3, 78.3, and 77.12 safely reach Leyte Gulf from Mindoro.

U.S. Sixth Army: In X Corps area, 32d Div progresses slowly S of Limon. 127th Inf, to S of 126th, remains in place while 126th attempts to come abreast. In XXIV Corps area, 307th Inf of 77th Div attacks at 1415, after arty and air preparation, toward Valencia and reaches edge of the airfield. 306th stops for night 500 yards S of its objective, Cabulihan. 305th gains positions along Tambuco-Dolores road and clears Tambuco.

18 December

WESTERN EUROPE—21 Army Group: In Br Second Army area, 8 Corps extends southward to line Meeuwen-Maeseyck.

12th Army Group: In U.S. Ninth Army's XIII Corps area, 84th Div attacks for its last objective, Wurm and Muellendorf, and takes both with ease.

In U.S. First Army's VII Corps area, 83d and 9th Divs finish clearing their respective zones. Corps extends southward because of Ardennes breakthrough to take over part of V Corps zone, new boundary running from Eupen area to the Roer near Dedenborn. With boundary change, 8th and 78th Divs and attachments pass to corps control in current positions. Corps releases CCA of 3d Armd Div and 9th Div, less RCT's 47 and 60, to V Corps, 104th Div takes responsibility for 9th Div zone as well as its own and is reinf by RCT 60. 78th Div, reinf by 2d Ranger Bn and 102d Cav Gp, is to hold road center N of Konzen and Paustenbach knoll. V Corps' mission, on its smaller front, is to stabilize line Monschau-Butgenbach-Malmédy-Stavelot. Corps holds firmly at Butgenbach and Elsenborn ridge but enemy continues to move W through gap S of Butgenbach. RCT 26 reverts to 1st Div, which joins in action to keep enemy from Malmédy, combing woods near Eupen and organizing perimeter defense of Waimes. 99th Div is attached to 2d Div. Germans now hold Honsfeld and Buellingen; push into Stavelot. 30th Div recovers most of Stavelot NW of the Amblève R; organizes defense positions in Malmédy-Stavelot area; blunts enemy spearheads at Stoumont and Habiemont. In VIII Corps area, 106th Div's encircled 422d and 423d Regts try in vain to break out toward Schonberg. 7th Armd Div is too heavily engaged at St Vith to assist with eastward push. Germans occupy Recht and cut St Vith-Vielsalm road at Poteau but CCA recovers Poteau. 14th Cav Gp, which falls back to Petit Thier, is transferred from 106th Div to 7th Armd Div control. 28th Div is unable to stop enemy in its zone and becomes completely disorganized. Germans get almost to Houffalize and Bastogne, smash through roadblocks of CCR, 9th Armd Div, on Bastogne-St Vith road. Troops of 4th Div and 10th Armd Div remaining S of the breakthrough are placed under Third Army command. CCB, 10th Armd, remains with VIII Corps to help defend Bastogne; CCA attacks N and E through 4th Div to Berdorf and Echternach areas. 4th Div mops up infiltrators beyond Osweiler and Dickweiler and repels thrust from Dickweiler.

In U.S. Third Army's XX Corps area, 90th Div, attacking cautiously with 2 bns, clears most of Dillingen against surprisingly light resistance. 5th Div takes charge of Saarlautern bridgehead, and attacks at once, gaining ground. 95th Div—less 378th Inf, which continues to be responsible for Ensdorf area—is withdrawn from combat. In XII Corps area, 2d Bn of 320th Inf, 35th Div, takes Nieder Gailbach in hard fighting. 87th Div breaks off attack upon order.

6th Army Group: In U.S. Seventh Army's VI Corps area, elements of 45th Div attack across the Lauter into Budenthal but are isolated there.

In Fr 1st Army area, 2d Corps overruns Ammerschwihr.

EASTERN EUROPE—Red Army forces reach Hungarian-Czechoslovak border on 70-mile front N of Miskolc and are crossing it.

CHINA—B-29's of XX BC, hitherto employed against industrial targets in Japan, make strong attack in conjunction with Fourteenth Air Force on Hankow, Japanese supply base and industrial center, with good effect. Participating in the attacks are 77 B-29's and 200 planes of Fourteenth Air Force. Thick smoke arises from incendiaries dropped. Other attacks follow later, but on a smaller scale.

LEYTE—U.S. Sixth Army: In X Corps area, 126th Inf of 32d Div works slowly forward S of Limon and closes gap between it and 127th Inf. 12th Cav, 1st Cav Div, patrols and prepares to drive on Lonoy and Kananga. In XXIV Corps area, 307th Inf of 77th Div takes Valencia and its airstrip without opposition. 306th overtakes 307th at Valencia and makes patrol contact with 305th. 305th blocks off road to Dolores. Southern part of Ormoc Valley from Ormoc to Valencia is now clear.

19 December

WESTERN EUROPE—Allied commanders conferring at Verdun decide to halt offensives toward the Rhine and concentrate on reducing enemy salient in the Ardennes.

21 Army Group: Because of Ardennes counteroffensive, Field Marshal Montgomery abandons plan to employ 30 Corps, Br Second Army, in Nijmegen area and orders it to assemble in Louvain-St Trond-Hasselt region to hold Meuse R line.

12th Army Group: U.S. Ninth Army is ordered to go on the defensive.

In U.S. First Army area, VII Corps remains generally in place. In V Corps area, 2d and 99th Divs repel further attacks and start toward new defensive positions from which they will defend Elsenborn ridge. 9th Div (− RCT 47, which is already in corps zone, and RCT 60) takes up defensive positions in 2d Div zone, relieving elements of 2d and 99th Divs. 1st Div holds line E of Malmédy. CCA, 3d Armd Div, relieves 18th Inf, 1st Div, of defense of Eupen. 30th Div holds at Stavelot and engineers blow bridge across the Amblève R there; keeps enemy from Stoumont in costly battle. CCB, 3d Armd Div, is attached to corps to assist 30th Div. XVIII Corps (A/B) takes responsibility for region generally S of the Amblève R, including Houffalize, key road center between St Vith and Bastogne, with mission of holding N flank of enemy. 82d A/B Div, which reverts to corps, upon closing at Werbomont relieves 30th Div troops in that region. 3d Armd Div, less CCA and CCB, passes to corps control and starts toward Hotton-Le Grand Pré area. In VIII Corps area, hope of relieving beleaguered 422d and 423d Regts of 106th Div in the Schnee Eifel fades. 7th and 9th Armd Divs (−) are aggressively defending region just E of St Vith. 112th Inf, 28th Div, is attached to 106th Div. 28th Div is ordered to abandon Wiltz and return to friendly lines by infiltration; withdraw from Diekirch area. 101st A/B Div arrives at Bastogne, which enemy has almost encircled. Also employed in defense of Bastogne area are CCB of 10th Armd Div and remnants of CCR, 9th Armd Div, the latter coming under control of 101st A/B Div.

U.S. Third Army forms provisional corps from former First Army units S of the Ardennes salient, 4th Div and 10th Armd Div (− CCB); the corps is to hold enemy on S flank of the penetration and plug gap existing between it and elements of 9th Armd Div and 28th Div near Ettelbruck. XX Corps begins withdrawal from hard-won positions E of the Sarre. 5th Div maintains foothold E of the river at Saarlautern, but 378th Inf of 95th Div is ordered to withdraw from Ensdorf. III Corps is ordered N for attack against S flank of enemy in the "bulge."

TF Fickett and 6th Armd Div pass to XII Corps control. In XII Corps area, 35th Div halts attack to consolidate in preparation for relief. 4th Armd Div and 80th Div are being transferred to III Corps.

6th Army Group: U.S. Seventh Army is ordered to go on the defensive. In XV Corps area, 44th Div finds that enemy has abandoned Fort Simershof and Hottviller. Fort Schiesseck, barring access to Bitche, continues to hold out.

ITALY—15th Army Group: In Br Eighth Army area, 5 Corps, renewing offensive night 19-20, clears Faenza area sufficiently for deployment of 56th Div. Cdn 1 Corps begins attack, night 19-20, to break out of Naviglio Canal bridgehead.

BURMA—In Br Fourteenth Army's 4 Corps area, Ind 19th Div takes Wunthe.

In 33 Corps area, Br 2d Div, having moved forward from Kohima, crosses the Chindwin at Kalewa and is relieving E African 11th Div.

LUZON—Planned bombardment of island by large carriers of U.S. Third Fleet is canceled because of weather conditions.

MINDORO—Western Visayan Task Force, helped by Mindoro guerrillas, begins series of patrol actions along S, W, and NW shores of Mindoro and rcn of small islands offshore.

LEYTE—Japanese *35th Army* learns that it must manage with its current resources.

U.S. Sixth Army: Alters intercorps boundary to give Libongao to XXIV Corps. In X Corps area, 127th Inf of 32d Div continues to battle enemy S of Limon. 1st Sq of 12th Cav, 1st Cav Div, protecting E flank of 32d Div, relieves 2d Bn, 126th Inf. 12th Cav attacks toward Lonoy, on Highway 2, and seizes this barrio. In XXIV Corps area, 307th Inf of 77th Div attacks N astride Highway 2 toward Libongao, gaining nearly 3 miles; 306th, to W, pushes toward Palompon road, which patrols reach; 305th defends Valencia area.

20 December

WESTERN EUROPE—21 Army Group: Takes operational control of U.S. forces N of Ardennes breakthrough, U.S. Ninth and First Armies.

In U.S. Ninth Army's XIII Corps area, 84th Div is attached to First Army and starts to Marche (Belgium). 102d Div takes responsibility for corps front. In XIX Corps area, 29th Div takes over defense of corps front. 2d Armd Div is released as army reserve.

In U.S. First Army's VII Corps area, 5th Armd Div resumes attack toward the Roer, blocking Winden-Untermaubach highway and pushing into Untermaubach and into Schneidhausen, which enemy is defending stoutly. Although 84th Div is

[20 DECEMBER 1944]

attached to corps, it is verbally attached to XVIII Corps until 22d, pending arrival of VII Corps in new zone. In V Corps area, 2d and 99th Divs complete withdrawal to new defensive positions before Elsenborn ridge and organize secondary defense line. Germans make slight penetration in line of 99th Div W of Wirtzfeld but are sealed off and destroyed. 1st Div clears assigned region S of Eupen and contains attacks in Butgenbach-Faymonville area. 9th Div takes over new zone on N flank of corps. 30th Div, in Malmédy-Stavelot sector, is attached to XVIII Corps. In XVIII Corps (A/B) area, CCB of 3d Armd Div, is attached to 30th Div and assists in attack on La Gleize and Stoumont, which enemy defends effectively. Elements of 30th Div continue to defend Stavelot and Malmédy. 3d Armd Div (− CCA and CCB), upon closing in Hotton area, attacks eastward to secure Manhay-Houffalize road. 82d A/B Div is attempting to establish contact with friendly forces in Vielsalm-St Vith area, pushing toward Vielsalm and Hebronval. VIII Corps units defending St Vith (7th Armd Div, 106th Div, CCB of 9th Armd Div, and 112th Inf of 28th Div) pass to control of XVIII Corps. Enemy pressure on St Vith is undiminished. Elements of 10th Armd Div, 101st A/B Div, and 705th TD Bn fight their way out of local encirclement on perimeter of larger encirclement of Bastogne area. 101st A/B Div extends defensive line to W and SW of Bastogne, assisted by remnants of CCR, 9th Armd Div, and CCB, 10th Armd Div, both of which are later attached to it, along with 705th TD Bn and stragglers from other units. Marvie, SE of Bastogne, is cleared in course of tank battle. Some 25 miles SE of Bastogne, 109th Inf of 28th Div establishes defensive line Ettelbruck-Oberfeulen-Merzig and also has forces near Ermsdorf backing up CCA of 9th Armd Div, to which it is attached. Enemy now holds Waldbillig, 6 miles W of Echternach. SW of Bastogne, 28th Div hq and remnants of 110th Inf block Neufchâteau-Bastogne highway. In effort to halt enemy, engineers block roads and demolish bridges as far W of Bastogne at St Hubert. During day, operational control of corps passes to Third Army.

12th Army Group: In U.S. Third Army area, III Corps moves its hq from Metz to Arlon (Belgium), and 4th Armd and 26th and 80th Inf Divs are assembling in Arlon-Luxembourg area. Elements of CCB, 4th Armd Div, push to Bastogne area and make contact with 101st A/B and 10th Armd Divs; are temporarily attached to VIII Corps. 80th Div takes up reserve battle positions on heights N and NE of Mersch. In Prov Corps area, Gen Patton strengthens corps by attaching 5th Div, CCA of 9th Armd Div, and RCT 109th of 28th Div. CCA, 9th Armd Div, is further attached to 10th Armd Div.

[357]

CCA, 10th Armd Div, withdraws to assembly area as 4th Div moves up to take over its positions near Echternach. Tanks assist 12th Inf of 4th Div in futile effort to relieve isolated infantry in Echternach. In XX Corps area, 378th Inf of 95th Div completes withdrawal from Ensdorf to positions W of the Sarre. XII Corps zone is taken over by XV Corps at midnight.

6th Army Group: In U.S. Seventh Army area, newly arrived 10th Div, its regts organized as TF Herren, is attached to army. XV Corps, with fall of Fort Schiesseck to 100th Div, concludes offensive in this region and extends westward to St Avold to release XII Corps for action in the Ardennes.

ITALY—15th Army Group: In Br Eighth Army's 5 Corps area, 56th Div begins to clear region between Naviglio Canal and Lamone R, working northward from Faenza. NZ, 2d Div is clearing northward between Naviglio Canal and the Senio. In Cdn 1 Corps area, enemy is forced back behind the Senio, night 20-21, under pressure of 1st Div and 5th Armd Div.

BURMA—In Br Fourteenth Army's 4 Corps area, Kawlin falls to Ind 19th Div.

CHINA—Continuing inspection of China Theater, Gen Wedemeyer urges that Y=Force resume offensive toward Wanting on Salween front in effort to link up with CAI forces as soon as possible, but Y=Force does not comply until late in December. At meeting of IBT and CT leaders in Kunming, Gen Wedemeyer explains his plan for controlling ALPHA.

MINDORO—Aircraft begin arriving to operate from Hill Drome. Under direction of small party from 503d Para Inf, guerrilla force of 50 moves by water from Agustin to Pasugi-Pianag area without incident.

LEYTE—U.S. Sixth Army: In X Corps area, 12th Cav of 1st Cav Div attacks from Lonoy S along Highway 2 toward Kananga, reaching positions near that barrio. Elements of 126th Inf, 32d Div, clear last resistance within regimental sector S of Limon. 127th Inf then relieves 1st Bn, 126th, which assembles to rear. 128th Inf is alerted to move to W coast. In XXIV Corps area, 307th Inf of 77th Div overcomes strong opposition at Libongao and continues N toward road junction. 306th quickly reaches Palompon road; 1st Bn then advances W along it to Togbong R and other elements of the regt drive E along road toward its junction with Highway 2. During night 20-21, 77th Div conducts its most intensive arty bombardment of enemy positions of the Leyte Campaign. 2d Bn of 32d Inf, 7th Div, continuing E to establish contact with 511th Para Inf of 11th A/B Div, is delayed by enemy entrenched on 2 ridges.

21 December

WESTERN EUROPE—21 Army Group: U.S. Ninth Army is reinf by Br 51st Div as its zone expands. XIX Corps releases 2d Armd Div to First Army; takes over VII Corps sector at 2400. Under its command, in current positions, are 104th, 83d, 5th Armd (− CCR), 8th, and 78th Divs, from N to S. XIII Corps takes over former XIX Corps front and 29th Div. XVI Corps releases 75th Div to First Army.

In U.S. First Army area, CCA of 5th Armd Div pushes about half way through Schneidhausen; CCB gains approximately half of Untermaubach. RCT 60, 9th Div, is detached from 104th Div and moves to Ouffet (Belgium). Corps is to operate next against N flank of German salient. In V Corps area, 9th Div, reinf by 102d Cav Gp, rounds up enemy in Monschau area. 99th Div breaks up enemy formations with arty fire. CCA, 3d Armd Div, reverts to parent unit and moves from Eupen to Werbomont area. 1st Div contains further attacks toward Elsenborn ridge. In XVIII Corps (A/B) area, CCB of 7th Armd Div withdraws from St Vith at night; CCA contains attack near Poteau; CCR clears Vielsalm–Poteau road. CCB, 9th Armd Div, is attached to 7th Armd Div. 82d A/B Div's 504th Para Inf clears Cheneux and Monceau, forcing enemy back across the Amblève R; 505th improves positions from the Salm at Trois Ponts to vicinity of Grand Halleux; 508th and 325th Gli Inf occupy line Vielsalm–Hebronval–Regne, making no contact with enemy; div makes contact with friendly troops in St Vith area. 30th Div is unable to take La Gleize and Stoumont; continues to defend Stavelot and Mal-médy. 3d Armd Div, to which CCA reverts, contains enemy at Hotton; continues efforts to secure Manhay-Houffalize road. 84th Div is organizing perimeter defense of Marche.

12th Army Group: In U.S. Third Army's VIII Corps area, enemy lays siege to Bastogne and extends westward; crosses Neufchâteau–Bastogne highway in force. Ammunition and food supplies of Bastogne garrison are running low. Prov Corps troops are transferred to XII Corps. CCA, 10th Armd Div, tries unsuccessfully to recover Waldbillig. CCA of 9th Armd Div and CCR of 10th Armd Div are formed into CCX, 10th Armd Div. 4th Div repels attacks toward Consdorf and Osweiler; is out of communication with troops in Echternach. RCT 10, 5th Div, is attached to 4th Div. XII Corps opens forward CP in Luxembourg. 35th Div's relief is completed.

EASTERN EUROPE—Berlin reports fierce fighting SW of Budapest between Lake Balaton and the Danube where troops of Third Ukrainian Front are again on the offensive. Germans continue to withdraw from the Balkans.

ITALY—15th Army Group: In U.S. Fifth Army's Br 13 Corps area, 6th Armd Div takes command of M. dell'Acqua Saluta-M. del Verro sector from 78th Div.

In Br Eighth Army's Pol 2 Corps area, 5th Kresowa Div, having relieved 3d Carpathian Div, begins mopping up E of the Senio. 5 Corps continues to clear northward astride Naviglio Canal. Cdn 1 Corps overruns Bagnacavallo and reaches the Senio in Cotignola-Alfonsine area, but enemy retains positions along the river on both flanks.

BURMA—In NCAC area, Ch 114th Regt of 38th Div, with orders to cut Burma Road in Ho-si area, is now near U.S. 5332d Brig.

In ALFSEA area, 15 Corps is making such rapid progress on Arakan front that Adm Mountbatten holds commanders conference at Calcutta to discuss exploitation and presents alternative plans for assault on Akyab. By this time, river craft have been launched in the Kalapanzin to assist Ind 24th Div.

MINDORO—Japanese, having received reinforcements by air for defense of Mindoro, attack resupply convoy moving toward that island, destroying 2 LST's and damaging other shipping. From Pasugi-Pianag area, patrol of guerrillas and 503d Para Inf sail N to Sabalayan; from there move on foot to Mamburao to reconnoiter toward Palauan and Abra de Ilog.

LEYTE—U.S. Sixth Army: Effects junction between X and XXIV Corps just S of Kananga at 1645, opening Highway 2 from Ormoc to Pinamopoan and gaining complete control of Ormoc Valley. In X Corps area, 12th Cav attacks and takes Kananga; makes patrol contact with 77th Div to S. In XXIV Corps area, 3d Bn of 306th Inf, 77th Div, continues E along Palompon road to its junction with Highway 2, then N along the highway toward Kananga, making contact with Tr A of 12th Cav at 1645. 307th reaches road junction N of Libongao without trouble and assists 306th Inf. On div W flank, 1st Bn of 306th Inf, after concentrated arty preparation, takes ridge commanding Togbong R bridge site and outposts it but is driven off. In preparation for next task of 77th Div—drive W and seize Palompon—arty is emplaced near San Jose within range of Palompon.

22 December

WESTERN EUROPE—21 Army Group: In U.S. Ninth Army's XIX Corps area, 5th Armd Div clears Untermaubach and Schneidhausen before being relieved in line by 8th and 83d Divs. 8th Div attack on Obermaubach fails.

In U.S. First Army's V Corps area, Germans breach lines of 1st Div at Butgenbach and of 9th Div in Monschau Forest but are unable to exploit their success. In XVIII Corps (A/B) area, withdrawal of delaying forces in St Vith area through 82d A/B Div line begins. 82d A/B Div is under strong pressure along the Salm in Trois Ponts area. 30th Div column captures Stoumont. 3d Armd Div maintains roadblocks at strategic points and attempts to clear Hotton area. VII Corps, reconstituted to consist of 75th and 84th Inf Divs and 2d Armd Div, is rapidly concentrating in Durbuy-Marche area of Belgium and organizing defensive line. 84th Div completes perimeter defense of Marche and establishes counter-reconnaissance screen to S and SW.

12th Army Group: In U.S. Third Army's VIII Corps area, Brig Gen McAuliffe, acting CG 101st A/B Div, refuses German demand for surrender of Bastogne. Garrison is holding under heavy fire and sharp attacks. 28th Div troops blocking road SW out of Bastogne at Vaux-lès-Rosières are forced back to Neufchâteau. U.S. ammunition shortage is becoming acute and weather conditions prevent aerial resupply. III Corps begins northward drive to relieve Bastogne. On W, 4th Armd Div columns reach Burnon and Martelange. 26th Div, to right, marches about 16 miles before making contact with enemy in Rambrouch-Grosbous area. After 5-mile advance, 80th Div runs into stiff resistance at Merzig and Ettelbruck but clears most of Merzig. XII Corps, in new zone along E border of Luxembourg, attacks with 4th Div SW of Echternach but is held to small gains. 10th Armd Div maintains positions NE of Luxembourg and straightens lines. 5th Div closes N of Luxembourg. 35th moves from Puttelange to Metz. 2d Cav Gp assembles near Vatimont. In XX Corps area, 90th Div completes withdrawal of Dillingen bridgehead.

BURMA—In NCAC area, 29th Brig of Br 36th Div, moving down the Irrawaddy, gets patrols to Tigyaing, from which Japanese have withdrawn. From Tigyaing the brig is to cross the river for drive on Mongmit while rest of div closes in on Mongmit from N.

LEYTE—U.S. Sixth Army: In X Corps area, 127th Inf of 32d Div reaches Lonoy. 1st Bn of 34th Inf, 24th Div, aided by mortar platoon brought forward by sea, clears Tuktuk. In XXIV Corps area, 2d and 3d Bns of 305th Inf, 77th Div, start W from Valencia toward coast at Palompon, passing through 1st Bn of 306th at Togbong R and continuing across Pagsangahan R toward Matagob. Engineers follow closely to work on bridges.

23 December

WESTERN EUROPE—21 Army Group: In U.S. Ninth Army's XIX Corps area, 83d Div, whose relief in line is begun, drives to edge of Winden in limited attack.

In U.S. First Army's V Corps area, 1st Div restores line at Butgenbach, as does 9th Div in Monschau Forest. RCT 60 reverts to 9th Div. 5th Armd Div is attached to corps. In XVIII Corps (A/B) area, 7th Armd Div, remnants of 106th Div, RCT 112 of 28th Div, and CCB of 9th Armd Div withdraw from St Vith area as planned, moving through lines of 82d A/B Div. Assault on La Gleize by 30th Div is unsuccessful. 3d Armd Div passes to control of VII Corps in place. In VII Corps area, 3d Armd Div attempts to clear Hotton-Soy road but makes little headway; loses key road junction SE of Manhay. Germans penetrate 84th Div positions between Hargimont and Rochefort. 4th Cav Gp, with mission of screening along Lesse R, organizes defensive positions between Ciney and Marche. CCA, 2d Armd Div, organizes Ciney for defense and starts toward Buissonville. 75th Div, in corps reserve, establishes outposts along the Ourthe R.

12th Army Group: In U.S. Third Army area, improving weather conditions permit extensive air support, particularly in Bastogne area, where supplies are dropped to the garrison. In VIII Corps area, enemy continues to press in slowly on Bastogne. In III Corps area, CCA of 4th Armd Div clears Martelange and continues 2 miles up Arlon-Bastogne highway while CCB, on secondary road, drives to Chaumont, from which it is ousted in counterattack; CCR begins drive toward Bigonville (Luxembourg). 26th Div's 104th Inf clears Grosbous and pushes on to Dellen and Buschrodt; 328th occupies Wahl. 80th Div seizes Heiderscheid and holds it against counterattacks; finishes clearing Merzig; takes Kehmen; continues to battle enemy at Ettelbruck. Roadblocks on div's S flank are turned over to XII Corps. In XII Corps area, attack SW of Echternach still gains little ground. 10th Armd Div continues action to shorten and improve its line. 35th Div passes to Third Army control.

EASTERN EUROPE—Soviet forces succeed in encircling about three fourths of Budapest. Moscow confirms reports that Third Ukrainian Front is on the offensive in vicinity of Szekesfehervar, SW of Budapest.

ITALY—15th Army Group: In U.S. Fifth Army area, because of indications of enemy build-up in W sector during past few days, 92d Div in Lucca area will be reinf with 2 brigs of Ind 8th Div and 2 RCT's of 85th Div plus chemical, tank, and arty bns. In Br 13 Corps area, Ind 8th Div seizes M. della Volpe and M. Tondo with ease and, less 17th Brig, is ordered to Fifth Army's W flank to avert threat of enemy attack there.

BURMA—In Br Fourteenth Army's 33 Corps area, Ind 19th Div takes Kokoggon.

MINDORO—New airfield, called Ellmore Field, on S bank of Bugsanga R, is ready for limited use.

LEYTE—U.S. Sixth Army: X Corps begins advance W toward coast from Highway 2. 1st Cav Div, on S flank, leads off, moving slowly over difficult terrain unopposed by enemy. 32d Div reconnoiters with 127th and 128th Regts in preparation for drive W. In XXIV Corps area, in preparation for assault on Palompon by land and sea, 77th Div arty and Fifth Air Force planes pound the town. Reinf 1st Bn, 305th Inf, which is to make the amphibious assault, moves to Ormoc. 305th Inf (− 1st Bn) continues overland drive toward Palompon, pushing through Matagob under heavy fire. Enemy efforts to penetrate U.S. lines, night 23–24, fail.

POA—CG V Amphib Corps Landing Force issues preferred plan for invasion of Iwo Jima, VAC LANDFOR Operation Plan 3-44, calling for landing of 4th and 5th Mar Divs abreast on SE Iwo Jima on D Day, tentatively set as 19 February. 3d Mar Div is to be held in floating reserve until released to corps.

24 December

WESTERN EUROPE—21 Army Group: In Br Second Army's 30 Corps area, 29th Armd Brig clashes with enemy spearheads between Dinant and Ciney.

In U.S. Ninth Army's XIX Corps area, 83d Div, in limited attacks, clears about two thirds of Winden and 8th improves positions near Obermaubach. 104th Div takes responsibility for N part of 83d Div zone, turning over its positions in Inden-Pier-Schophoven region to 29th Div.

In U.S. First Army's V Corps area, 1st Div repels another enemy bid for Butgenbach. 5th Armd Div closes in Eupen area and is held in reserve. In XVIII Corps (A/B) area, 30th Div overruns La Gleize and releases CCB, 3d Armd Div. 82d A/B Div is under strong pressure in Manhay area; loses Manhay, although elements of 7th Armd Div are pressed into action in that region. 17th A/B Div is being flown to France from England and subsequently operates under VIII Corps. In VII Corps area, Germans reduce 3d Armd Div's roadblock at Belle Haie, on road to Manhay; CCR columns attacking E from Hotton and W from Soy clear Holton-Soy road. Elements of 75th Div enter combat for first time: RCT's 290 and 289 are attached respectively to CCR and CCA, 3d Armd Div. In 84th Div zone, Germans drive through Verdenne. CCA, 2d Armd Div, reaches Buissonville; 4th Cav Gp, attached to 2d Armd Div to cover its assembly and maintain contact with adjacent units, makes contact with British at Sorinne.

12th Army Group: In U.S. Third Army's VIII Corps area, heavy fighting continues around Bastogne perimeter. The city is badly damaged by air attacks. 11th Armd Div, released from SHAEF reserve to corps on 23d, is held in mobile reserve W of the Meuse. Combat engineers are guarding Meuse R line and blocking approaches to bridges. In III Corps area, CCB of 4th Armd Div is meeting lively opposition S of Chaumont, as is CCA at Warnock; CCR seizes Bigonville. 318th Inf (−), 80th Div, is attached to 4th Armd Div. 6th Cav Gp (TF Fickett) arrives from XX Corps front to guard W flank of corps in Neufchâteau area; 6th Cav Rcn Sq is assigned sector between 4th Armd and 26th Inf Divs. 26th Div secures Rambrouch and Koetschette but is held up at Arsdorf and Hierheck. 80th Div contains determined counterattacks. In XII Corps area, 5th Div, to which RCT 10 has reverted, relieves left flank elements of 4th Div and attacks toward Haller and Waldbillig, making slow progress. 2d Cav Gp, designated TF Reed, relieves right flank units of 4th Div along the Moselle. CCA, 10th Armd Div, captures Gilsdorf and Mostroff on Sauer R.

6th Army Group: Warns that enemy is massing for offensive.

In Fr 1st Army's 2d Corps area, U.S. 3d Div clears Bennwihr, concluding operations in Colmar sector.

EASTERN EUROPE—Red Army narrows enemy escape gap from Budapest to less than 20 miles. Moscow reveals that Third Ukrainian Front, in 3-day-old offensive, has achieved breakthrough SW of Budapest in Lake Velencei-Danube R sector and has surged forward 25 miles, overrunning more than 160 towns and villages; with capture of Szekesfehervar and Biske, key points in outer defenses of Budapest, western escape routes from the besieged city are closed. Other troops of this front are pushing in on Budapest from the SW.

BURMA—In Br Fourteenth Army's 33 Corps area, Br 2d and. Ind 20th Divs overcome strong Opposition in Pyingaing.

LEYTE—U.S. Sixth Army: In X Corps area, 1st Cav Div continues steadily W against scattered resistance, 12th Cav wading swamps in its sector. 32d Div, with 127th and 128th Regts in assault, starts W toward coast on N flank of corps, slowed more by terrain than resistance. In XXIV Corps area, 1st Bn (reinf) of 305th Inf, 77th Div, embarks at Ormoc and at 2000 sails for Palompon, the convoy protected by PT boats. 305th Inf, less 1st Bn, is lightly opposed as it continues W along road to Palompon.

VOLCANO Is.—Two Jima undergoes air-surface bombardment.

25 December

WESTERN EUROPE—21 Army Group: In Br Second Army area, 30 Corps is disposed along W bank of the Meuse from Givet to Liége.

In U.S. Ninth Army area, Br 51st Div is withdrawn from army reserve and transferred to First Army as reserve: In XIX Corps area, 83d Div completes capture of Winden and is alerted for movement to First Army zone. 8th Div gains additional ground near Obermaubach and begins assault on that town.

In U.S. First Army area, V Corps maintains defensive positions and has only light patrol contact with enemy. In XVIII Corps (A/B) area, 82d A/B Div, to shorten line, withdraws from Vielsalm salient upon order, pulling back to general line Trois Ponts–Basse-Bodeux–Bra–Manhay. 7th Armd Div is reinf by RCT 424, 106th Div; tries vainly to recover Manhay. 30th Div clears region N of the Amblève R between Stavelot and Trois Ponts. VII Corps, directed to go on the defensive, conducts limited attack to stabilize right flank of First Army. 3d Armd Div attacks toward Grandménil and crossroads just E, which enemy has recently seized, and reaches edge of town; is establishing defensive line in Werpin-Amonines area. TF cut off in Marcouray radios that it is starting toward Soy through enemy territory. 84th Div recovers Verdenne, but an enemy pocket remains between there and Bourdon. CCB, 2d Armd Div, seizes Celles, blocking enemy's westward advance on Dinant; reconnoiters to Sorinne and Foy Notre Dame; CCA occupies Havrenne.

12th Army Group: In U.S. Third Army area, VIII Corps maintains Bastogne perimeter against pressure from all sides. In III Corps area, CCR, moving to W flank of 4th Armd Div from Bigonville, launches surprise attack and gains road from Vaux-les-Rosières to Chaumont; CCB and CCA seize Chaumont, Hollange, and Tintage. 26th Div TF begins struggle for Eschdorf, gaining weak hold there; other elements of the div clear Arsdorf. 319th Inf, 80th Div, clears its sector to the Sauer and makes contact with 26th Div; assisted by 317th, contains counterattacks and drives almost to Kehmen. Ettelbruck is found clear. In XII Corps area, 5th Div takes Waldbillig and Haller.

6th Army Group: In U.S. Seventh Army area, advance elements of XXI Corps (Maj Gen Frank W. Milburn) arrive.

EASTERN EUROPE—Troops of Third Ukrainian Front cut last of western rail exits from Budapest and narrow escape gap to 9 miles.

ITALY—15th Army Group: In U.S. Fifth Army area, S African 6th Armd Div is placed under direct command of army. IV Corps takes command of 92d Div's sector. 19th and 21st Brigs, Ind 8th Div, are in Lucca area. Enemy patrols in Serchio Valley begin probing, night 25–26.

LUZON—Allied air attacks on island are intensified as preparations for invasion continue.

LEYTE—U.S. Eighth Army relieves U.S. Sixth Army of responsibility for Leyte-Samar area. Sixth Army is thus free for the Luzon operation. Work is progressing well on Tacloban, Dulag, and Tanauan airfields.

U.S. Sixth Army: In X Corps area, 1st Cav and 32d Inf Divs continue W toward coast, 32d supplied by air. 1st Bn, 127th Inf, disperses Japanese force of 300–400. In XXIV Corps area, after preparatory fire, 1st Bn (reinf) of 305th Inf, 77th Div, lands unopposed N of Palompon and seizes barrios of Buaya and Look as well as Palompon; patrols push NE and S. 305th Inf (−) makes very slow progress along road to Palompon against dug-in enemy pockets.

26 December

WESTERN EUROPE—21 Army Group: In Br Second Army area, 30 Corps takes command of 6th A/B Div and releases 43d Div to 12 Corps.

In U.S. Ninth Army's XIX Corps area, 83d Div is transferred to VII Corps, First Army, and turns over its sector to 8th Div. 8th Div clears Obermaubach and is working on pocket to S.

In U.S. First Army area, army halts enemy's westward drive short of the Meuse. German supply lines are now overextended, and stalled armor becomes a lucrative target for aerial attacks. XVIII Corps (A/B) maintains defensive positions and defeats enemy efforts to break through to the Meuse. In VII Corps area, 3d Armd Div stabilizes its front except on left, where contact has not yet been established with 7th Armd Div; seizes Grandménil and heights S of Soy-Hotton road. 84th Div reduces enemy pocket between Verdenne and Bourdon; hurls back enemy thrust toward Ménil. 2d Armd Div repels counterattacks in Celles area and against Havrenne and Frandeux, inflicting heavy losses on enemy.

12th Army Group: In U.S. Third Army area, armored units break through to Bastogne. In III Corps area, forward tanks of CCR, 4th Armd Div, push through Assenois to Bastogne, but vehicles are unable to follow. 101st A/B Div is temporarily attached to corps. CCA, 9th Armd Div, is detached from 10th Armd Div, XII Corps, and attached to 4th Armd Div for employment on W flank. 26th Div closes along the Sauer, winning Eschdorf in lively battle, and begins crossing. 80th Div, after clearing Scheidel, is halted in Kehmen area and transferred in place to XII Corps. Intercorps boundary is adjusted accordingly. 35th Div is attached to III Corps to assist in action against S flank of

Ardennes salient. In XII Corps area, 5th Div improves positions in Echternach area and takes Berdorf. 6th Armd Div, transferred to corps from XX Corps, moves into Luxembourg and relieves 10th Armd Div. Latter passes to XX Corps control. 109th Inf reverts to 28th Div (VIII Corps) from attachment to 10th Armd Div.

6th Army Group: In U.S. Seventh Army area, army finishes regrouping. XV Corps, holding line from St Avold to Bitche, now consists of 106th Cav Gp and road, 44th, and 100th Divs. VI Corps is disposed between Bitche and the Rhine and contains TF Hudelson and 45th and 79th Divs.

EASTERN EUROPE—Third Ukrainian Front virtually closes ring around Budapest; captures fortress city of Esztergom.

ITALY—15th Army Group: In U.S. Fifth Army area, 1st Armd Div, in army reserve, moves to Lucca. In IV Corps area, Germans begin series of counterattacks against 92d Div positions astride the Serchio, forcing general withdrawal after outposts are driven back.

BURMA—In Br Fourteenth Army's 15 Corps area, Ind 25th Div reaches Foul Pt, at tip of Mayu Peninsula, well ahead of the expected time. Japanese decide to withdraw from Akyab.

CHINA—Gen Wedemeyer, meeting with Chiang Kai-shek, Ambassador Hurley, and T. V. Soong, proposes that the food, clothing, and pay of Chinese Army be improved; informs the Generalissimo that plans are being made for offensive (BETA) against Kweilin, Liuchow, and Canton.

MINDORO—Japanese naval surface force, despite air attacks, arrives off Mindoro and about 2300 begins bombarding beachhead.

LEYTE—U.S. Eighth Army: In X Corps area, 1st Cav and 32d Inf Divs continue W over rough terrain. 34th Inf, 24th Div, prepares to clear NW part of Leyte Peninsula. Cos F and G sail at 2300 through Biliran Strait to Gigantangan I., where they spend the night. In XXIV Corps area, 77th Div remains in place in Palompon sector.

27 December

WESTERN EUROPE—21 Army Group: In U.S. First Army's XVIII Corps (A/B) area, 30th Div maintains defensive positions while regrouping. 508th Para Inf, 82d A/B Div, continues drive NE of Bra. 7th Armd Div recaptures Manhay early in day. 9th Armd Div is reinf by RCT 112 of 28th Div. In VII Corps area, Germans are infiltrating toward Sadzot in zone of CCA, 3d Armd Div, where front line is held by RCT 289. 84th Div clears pocket in Verdenne area. 2d Armd Div columns envelop Humain and clear stubborn resistance there. 83d Div, upon closing in Havelange area, begins relief of 2d Armd Div.

12th Army Group: In U.S. Third Army's VIII Corps area, 17th A/B Div takes over Meuse R sector. In III Corps area, trucks and ambulances roll into Bastogne on road opened by CCR, 4th Armd Div, ending siege of the city. 4th Armd Div and reinforcements from 9th Armd and 80th Inf Divs are broadening corridor to Bastogne and attempting to open Arlon-Bastogne highway. From S bank of the Sauer, 35th Div attacks northward between 4th Armd Div and 26th Div, 137th Inf taking Surre and 320th, Boulaide and Boschleiden. 26th Div pushes northward through 101st A/B Div, clearing Mecher-Dunkrodt and Kaundorf. In XII Corps area, 80th Div checks attack in Ringel area and blocks roads N and NE of Ettelbruck. 6th Armd Div takes responsibility for sector S of the Sauer between Ettelbruck and Mostroff. Beaufort, N of Waldbillig, falls to 11th Inf, 5th Div. 4th Div patrols find Echternach undefended. In XX Corps area, 80th Div patrols aggressively and conducts raids to keep enemy pinned down. 5th Ranger Bn is attached to 95th Div.

6th Army Group: In U.S. Seventh Army area, XXI Corps (36th Inf and 12th Armd Divs) arrives. VI Corps is reinf by TF Harris (63d Div), TF Herren 60th Div), and TF Linden (42d Div).

EASTERN EUROPE—Budapest is completely encircled as elements of Second Ukrainian Front clear island in the Danube N of the city and establish contact with Third Ukrainian forces. Fighting is in progress in E and W suburbs.

ITALY—15th Army Group: In U.S. Fifth Army area, first echelon of 10th Mtn Div arrives. In IV Corps area, enemy forces further withdrawal of 92d Div, but elements of Ind 8th Div pass through 92d and make patrol contact with enemy.

BURMA—In NCAC area, U.S. 124th Cav, upon completing its march to Momauk, begins reorganization for combat.

In Br Fourteenth Army area, 15 Corps commander recommends that operations against Akyab be advanced to 3 January.

LEYTE—In U.S. Eighth Army's X Corps area, Cos F and G of 34th Inf, 24th Div, sail from Gigantangan I., to Taglawigan, on NW coast of Leyte Peninsula, and land without opposition, taking Taglawigan; proceed by sea and overland to Daha, which is also secured. Co G, reinf, moves S by sea to San Isidro area and goes ashore. 1st Bn, meanwhile, ordered to take San Isidro, moves overland from Calumbian to heights overlooking the town. In XXIV Corps area, 3d Bn of 305th Inf, 77th Div, takes heights 600 yards ahead as it continues W along Palompon road against tenacious resistance. 2d Bn is to move forward by water. 1st Bn,

[28-30 DECEMBER 1944]

305th Inf, remains in Palompon area, patrolling and awaiting rest of regt.

VOLCANO Is.—Iwo Jima undergoes air-surface bombardment. Commander Joint Expeditionary Force (CTF 51) publishes Operation Plan A25-44, directing CG Expeditionary Troops to seize Iwo Jima and begin development of the island as an air base.

28 December

WESTERN EUROPE—Gen Eisenhower and Field Marshal Montgomery meet at Hasselt (Belgium) to plan offensive.

21 Army Group: In U.S. Ninth Army's XIX Corps area, 8th Div completes reduction of pocket S of Obermaubach.

In U.S. First Army's V Corps area, final enemy ef-fort to force 1st Div from Elsenborn defenses fails. In XVIII Corps (A/B) area, corps zone is relatively quiet. CCB, 9th Armd Div, and RCT 112 move into position to back up 3d Armd Div and 75th Inf Div. In VII Corps area, 75th Div, less RCT's 289 and 290, is attached to XVIII Corps. Germans infiltrating in sector of CCA, 3d Armd Div, take Sadzot but are driven out. 83d Div is relieving 2d Armd Div and takes responsibility for sector E of line Buissonville-Rochefort; elements push into Roche-fort. 2d Armd Div regroups.

12th Army Group: In U.S. Third Army's VIII Corps area, 11th Armd Div is transferred to corps from SHAEF reserve. III Corps makes limited progress against delaying opposition between Sauer and Wiltz Rivers. 35th Div continues drive on S flank of enemy salient despite very heavy fire SW of Villers-la-Bonne-Eau. 26th Div makes slight progress toward Wiltz. Elements of 80th Div attached to 4th Armd Div revert to parent unit. 6th Armd Div is transferred to corps from XII Corps. XII Corps is ordered on the defensive in afternoon. 80th Div repels attack for Ringel.

6th Army Group: In U.S. Seventh Army area, XV Corps releases 87th Div, which has been attached to it since 20th while reliefs were in progress.

ITALY—15th Army Group: U.S. Fifth Army postpones projected offensive toward Bologna, the Serchio Valley reversals being a contributing factor. In IV Corps area, enemy begins to withdraw in Serchio Valley, and troops of Ind 8th Div gradually push northward during next few days.

LEYTE—In U.S. Eighth Army's X Corps area, 5th and 12th Cav Regts of 1st Cav Div reach W coast at Tibur, barrio N of Abijao. 1st and 2d Bns of 34th Inf, 24th Div, take San Isidro against light resistance. In XXIV Corps area, 2d Bn of 305th Inf, 77th Div, moves by LCM's from Ormoc to Palompon; 3d Bn continues overland drive, gaining about 1,000 yards.

MINDORO—Ellmore Field is now fully operational.

29 December

WESTERN EUROPE—21 Army Group: In Br Second Army area, 30 Corps begins relief of U.S. 2d Armd Div on W flank of U.S. VII Corps.

In U.S. First Army area, V Corps front is quiet, with both sides on the defensive. XVIII Corps (A/B) zone is also virtually static. 75th Div is attached to corps and takes over zone of 7th Armd Div. VII Corps mops up infiltrators and patrols. 83d Div releases 331st Inf to 3d Armd Div; attacks toward Rochefort with 329th, making slow progress.

12th Army Group: In U.S. Third Army area, VIII Corps prepares for drive on Houffalize. 11th Armd Div moves to vicinity of Neufchâteau. 87th Div is released to corps from SHAEF reserve. In III Corps area, CCA of 4th Armd Div opens Arlon-Bastogne highway. 35th Div is clearing Villers-la Bonne-Eau-Lutrebois region; advance elements make contact with 101st A/B Div forces at Marvie, SE of Bastogne. 26th Div continues toward Wiltz against increasing resistance. Units in Bastogne (101st A/B Div, reinf, and elements of 9th Armd Div) revert to VIII Corps. 6th Armd Div is transferred to III Corps from XII Corps and assembles between Arlon and Neufchâteau.

EASTERN EUROPE—Street fighting starts in Budapest as Soviet forces break into the city from W.

BURMA—NCAC and Br Fourteenth Army fronts are linked as patrols of Br 36th Div establish contact with Ind 19th Div. On Arakan front, 15 Corps now holds Rathedaung and Kudaung I.

LEYTE—In U.S. Eighth Army's X Corps area, 1st Cav Div reaches W coast and takes Villaba, N of Tibur. 32d Div gains its W coast objectives to N of 1st Cav Div, 127th Inf taking heights commanding Antipolo Pt and 128th reaching high ground overlooking Tabango and Campopo Bays. Troops of 34th Inf, 24th Div, are eliminating small enemy groups along coast. In XXIV Corps area, 3d Bn of 305th Inf, 77th Div, after advancing 650 yards along road to Palompon, is pinned down by enemy. Prov Mtn Force gets into position for drive E along Palompon road.

30 December

WESTERN EUROPE—21 Army Group: In U.S. First Army's XVIII Corps (A/B) area, 7th Armd Div releases RCT 424 to 106th Div. 75th Div holds positions previously occupied by RCT 424. VII Corps turns over region SW of line Marche-Namur to British. Germans abandon Rochefort.

12th Army Group: In U.S. Third Army area, VIII Corps opens drive on Houffalize. 11th Armd

Div progresses slowly and at heavy cost. 87th Div takes Moircy but loses it in counterattack later in day. 9th Armd Div is ordered to Sedan area as SHAEF reserve. In III Corps area, Germans again attempt to cut Arlon–Bastogne highway and isolate Bastogne, reaching Lutrebois and surrounding 2 cos of 137th Inf, 35th Div, in Villers-la-Bonne-Eau. On left flank of corps, 6th Cav Gp is relieved by elements of VIII Corps.

6th Army Group: Reiterates warning of possible enemy attack. TF Harris (−) is transferred from VI to XV Corps.

EASTERN EUROPE—While Third Ukrainian Front continues street fighting in W Budapest, Second Ukrainian Front breaks into E part of city.

BURMA—In Br Fourteenth Army area, 33 Corps takes Kaduma.

MINDORO—Second resupply convoy arrives. Under enemy air attack while en route, the convoy loses 3 merchant ships, 2 DD's, 3 LST's, and 2 LCM's at or near the island. Most of 3d Bn, 21st Inf, arrives.

LEYTE—In U.S. Eighth Army's X Corps area, 1st Cav Div makes contact with 32d Div NE of Villaba. In XXIV Corps area, 77th Div begins 2-pronged attacks to open Palompon road. While 3d Bn, 305th Inf, continues W to point some 1,000 yards SW of Tipolo, Prov Mtn Force attacks E until stopped about 4 miles E of Palompon. Japanese withdraw main forces, night 30–31. Co C, 305th Inf, moves by water to Abijao, N of Palompon, and burns the town; continuing N, gains radio contact with 1st Cav Div in Villaba area.

31 December

WESTERN EUROPE—21 Army Group: In U.S. First Army's VII Corps area, 83d Div, to which 331st Inf reverts, takes over zone of 3d Armd Div and is reinf by RCT 290, 75th Div.

12th Army Group: In U.S. Third Army area, VIII Corps takes command of 4th Armd Div. Elements of 87th Div capture Remagen and close in on Moircy. CCR, 11th Armd Div, drives to Pinsamont and Acul while CCB attacks Chenogne. In III Corps area, one 6th Armd Div column secures high ground near Wardin; another advances to outskirts of Rechrival. 35th Div is unable to relieve isolated forces in Villers-la-Bonne-Eau, and they are presumed lost. Germans still hold Lutrebois. 26th Div repels counterattack and reorganizes. Corps arty places TOT's on Wiltz.

ITALY—15th Army Group: U.S. Fifth Army has regained most of the ground lost by IV Corps in Serchio Valley and positions are about the same as they were at the end of October.

Br Eighth Army has worked northward astride Naviglio Canal between the Senio and Lamone Rivers in 5 Corps zone to Granarole, but enemy holds Granarole. Preparations are made for limited attacks to bring entire army up to the Senio.

BURMA—In NCAC area, U.S. 475th Inf, upon relief at Tonk-wa by Ch 50th Div, which is now operating in center, starts march toward Mong Wi area, where 5332d Brig is to assemble for its first operation as a brig. Ch 1st Separate Regt, which was to be a part of 5332d Brig, will be held in NCAC reserve.

In Br Fourteenth Army's 33 Corps area, Kabo falls to Br 2d Div.

MINDORO—Japanese continue air attacks on shipping, sinking PT tender and badly damaging a DD. Platoon of Co F, 19th Inf, lands at Bulalacao, on S coast almost 25 miles SE of San Jose.

LEYTE—In U.S. Eighth Army's X Corps area, 1st Cav Div repels several counterattacks against Villaba. 77th Div (XXIV Corps) begins relief of 1st Cav Div. In XXIV Corps area, 77th Div's 305th Inf finishes clearing Palompon road. 3d Bn and Prov Mtn Force make contact 2 miles NE of San Miguel. 77th Div estimates that, during period 21–31 December, it has killed 5,779 Japanese at cost of 17 killed.

POA—Commander Fifth Fleet issues Operation Plan 13-44, directing Joint Expeditionary Force to secure Iwo Jima, begin base development there, establish military government, and withdraw assault forces at conclusion of capture and occupation phase. 19 February is confirmed as D Day.

1945

1 January

U.S.—Southern Defense Command is absorbed into Eastern Defense Command.

WESTERN EUROPE—German Air Force is unusually active, employing some 800 aircraft and damaging airfields in Holland, Belgium, and France.

12th Army Group: CG 66th Div takes over 94th Div's mission of containing enemy in vicinity of Lorient and St Nazaire (France).

U.S. Third Army continues Ardennes counteroffensive with VIII and III Corps. In VIII Corps area, 87th Div takes Moircy and Jenneville. 11th Armd Div attacks with CCA toward Hubermont, stopping E of Rechrival, and with CCB clears Chenogne and woods to N. CCA, 9th Armd Div, drives toward Senonchamps. 101st A/B Div, in Bastogne area, gives fire support to 11th Armd Div on its left and 6th Armd Div (III Corps) on its right. 17th A/B Div relieves 28th Div in Neufchâteau area. III Corps contains enemy salient SE of Bastogne, 4th Armd Div holds corridor into Bastogne and supports 35th Div with fire. 35th Div partially clears Lutrebois and reaches crossroads SE of Marvie, but makes no headway in vicinity of Villers-la-Bonne-Eau (Belgium) and Harlange (Luxembourg). In region E of Bastogne, 6th Armd Div takes Neffe, Bizery, and Mageret, but then loses Mageret.

6th Army Group: Germans launch offensive, designated Operation NORDWIND, against U.S. Seventh Army. In XV Corps area, two-pronged enemy thrust forces 106th Cav Gp, 44th Div, and 100th Div to give ground. 44th Div bears brunt of enemy's right flank drive, which penetrates positions NW of Rimling. 100th Div, caught between the 2 attack forces, withdraws its right flank, exposed by withdrawal of TF Hudelson (VI Corps); enemy infiltrators are cleared from Rimling, on left flank. Elements of TF Harris (63d Div) help check enemy. RCT 141, 36th Div, moves up to plug gap between XV and VI Corps. In VI Corps area, enemy drives salient into left flank of corps S of Bitche. TF Hudelson's thin line is pushed back on left to Lemberg-Mouterhouse area. 45th Div contains enemy along line Philippsbourg-Neuhoffen-Obersteinbach and mops up infiltrators in Dambach. Reinforcements from TF Herren (10th Div) and 79th Div are rushed to 45th Div, whose boundary is moved W. CCB, 14th Armd Div, moves to guard Vosges exits. 79th Div's right flank is extended to include Rhine sector from Schaffhouse to Gambsheim area.

EASTERN EUROPE—Fighting continues within and around Budapest, where Russians are slowly eliminating besieged German garrison.

BURMA—Br Fourteenth Army moves its hq from Imphal to Kalemyo, where joint army-air hq is established to insure close co-operation.

CHINA—Gen Wedemeyer radios the War Department his plans to have U.S. officers advise Chinese ALPHA Force from gp army hq down to regimental level.

P.I.—Operations to deceive enemy about Allied intentions against Luzon begin with limited action on Mindoro to clear NE part of island. Subsequent deceptive measures conducted on S Luzon are on a much smaller scale than anticipated and have little effect on the main operation. On Mindoro, control of Western Visayan TF passes from U.S. Sixth to U.S. Eighth Army. Co I, 21st Inf, moving by water from San Jose, lands on E coast at Bongabong without incident and marches northward toward Pinamalayan. On Leyte U.S. Eighth Army mops up, a tedious business that lasts until 8 May 1945. 77th Div of XXIV Corps is ordered to relieve 1st Cav and 32d and 24th Inf Divs of X Corps.

CAROLINE Is.—Elements of 321st Inf, U.S. 81st Div, land on Fais I., SE of Ulithi, and begin search of the island.

2 January

WESTERN EUROPE—21 Army Group: In Br Second Army's 30 Corps area, 53d Div assumes responsibility for Marche-Hotton sector (Belgium), relieving U.S. 84th Div; boundary between 30 Corps and U.S. VII Corps is adjusted.

12th Army Group: In U.S. Third Army's VIII Corps area, Gerimont falls to 87th Div; Mande St Etienne to 11th Armd Div; and Senonchamps to CCB, 10th Armd Div (attached to 101st A/B Div), and CCA, 9th Armd Div. 4th Armd Div protects and enlarges corridor leading into Bastogne from the S and helps III Corps clear woods near Lutrebois. In III Corps area, 6th Armd Div's CCB enters Oubourcy and Michamps but is driven out of latter; unsuccessfully attacks Arloncourt; CCA takes Wardin; div withdraws to high ground W of

Michamps-Arloncourt-Wardin for night. 35th Div continues fight for Lutrebois. 28th Cav Sq of TF Fickett (6th Cav Gp) is committed between 134th and 137th Regts, 35th Div. 26th Div's 101st Inf advances N in area SW of Wiltz.

6th Army Group: U.S. Seventh Army CP is moved from Saverne to Lunéville. In XV Corps area, enemy pressure forces 44th Div's right flank back past Gros Réderching and causes 100th Div's right flank to fall back farther. In VI Corps area, Germans maintain pressure against reinf 45th Div, particularly on its W flank, former zone of TF Hudelson. Fighting occurs at various points along Bitche salient. TF Herren's 276th Inf takes up switch positions in Wingen-Wimmenau-Rosteig area. CCA, 14th Armd Div, organizes outposts at Vosges exits around Bouxwiller. Center and right flank units of corps begin withdrawal to prepared positions on Maginot Line. 79th Div takes over S portion of Rhine R line held by TF Linden (42d Div).

EASTERN EUROPE—Germans are mounting strong counterattacks NW of Budapest in effort to break encirclement of the Hungarian capital.

ITALY—15th Army Group: Br Eighth Army begins series of limited actions to finish clearing E bank of the Senio. In Cdn I Corps area, 5th Armd Div attacks northward toward the sea, taking Conventelle.

BURMA—In NCAC area, U.S. 475th Inf begins crossing the Shweli over makeshift bridge put in by 138th Regt, Ch 50th Div, which crossed late in December.

P.I.—Convoys of Luzon Attack Force are assembling in Leyte Gulf. First echelon, Minesweep-ing and Hydrographic Group (TG 77.6), leaves Leyte Gulf for Luzon and is soon spotted and attacked by enemy planes, including kamikazes. On Mindoro, guerrilla patrol is reinf for attack on Palauan by Co B, 503d Para Inf, which moves to Mamburao. Work begins on one of two heavy bomber fields to be constructed. Enemy planes attacking airfields, night 2–3, destroy 22 aircraft.

POA—VAC LANDFOR Operation Plan 3-44 for invasion of Iwo Jima is approved.

3 January

WESTERN EUROPE—21 Army Group: U.S. First Army starts counteroffensive to reduce enemy's Ardennes salient from N. VII Corps attacks SE toward Houffalize with 2d Armd Div followed by 84th Div on right, and 3d Armd Div followed by 83d Div on left. 2d Armd Div gains Trinal, Magoster, positions in Bois de Tave, Freineux, Le Batty, and positions near Belle Haie. 3d Armd Div takes Malempré and Floret and from latter continues SE on Lierneux road to Groumont Creek. 75th Div, after attack passes through its line, continues mopping up S of Sadzot. In XVIII Corps (A/B) area, 82d A/B Div, in conjunction with VII Corps' attack, thrusts SE, improving positions. As a diversion, 30th Div pushes small forces S of Malmédy and then withdraws them as planned.

12th Army Group: In U.S. Third Army's VIII Corps area, elements of 87th Div are temporarily surrounded in woods E of St Hubert. 17th A/B Div attacks N late in day in region some 5 miles NW of Bastogne. NE of Bastogne, 101st A/B Div and 501st Para Inf are clearing Bois Jacques. TF Higgins (elements of 101st A/B Div and CCA, 10th Armd Div) is organized to block enemy attacks toward Bastogne. CCA, 4th Armd Div, continues to defend corridor into Bastogne. 28th Div defends the Meuse from Givet to Verdun. In III Corps area, 6th Armd Div repels enemy thrusts W of Michamps and places heavy arty concentrations on Arloncourt, Michamps, and Bourcy; to S, attempts to clear high ground near Wardin and takes road junction S of the town. 35th Div gains about two thirds of Lutrebois and crossroads W of Villers-la-Bonne-Eau (Belgium) but is unable to take Harlange (Luxembourg). East of Harlange, 26th Div continues attack in region N of Mecher Dunkrodt and Kaundorf.

In U.S. Fifteenth Army area, main body moves from Le Havre to Suippes.

6th Army Group: Is assigned defense of Strasbourg.

In U.S. Seventh Army area, XV Corps withstands further pressure and on left slightly improves positions. Germans deepen penetration at boundary of 44th and 100th Divs, entering Achen, from which they are ousted in counterattack. CCL, Fr 2d Armd Div, pushes into Gros Réderching but is unable to clear it. Attempt by 44th Div to relieve French there fails. 36th Div (—RCT 141) assembles near Montbronn. In VI Corps area, enemy expands Bitche salient, entering Wingen and Philippsbourg. 45th Div withstands pressure against Reipertsweiler, NW of Wingen, and contains attacks in Sarreinsberg-Meisenthal area. Center and right flank elements of corps complete withdrawal to Maginot positions.

ITALY—15th Army Group: In Br Eighth Army's Cdn I Corps area, 5th Armd Div reaches Canale di Bonifica Destra del Reno as it continues northward. 1st Div begins attack to clear enemy pocket between it and Br 5 Corps in Cotignola area, crossing Naviglio Canal and taking Granarolo in conjunction with attack by 5 Corps from S. In 5 Corps area, elements of 56th Div and of 7th Armd Brig as well as sq of Kangaroos (armored infantry carriers) push northward from Felisio area, clearing the Senio bank as far N as S. Severo.

BURMA—In ALFSEA area, 15 Corps invades Akyab (TALON), omitting preparatory bombardment since no opposition is expected. From landing craft in Naaf R, 3d Cdo Brig lands and is followed by brig of Ind 25th Div from Foul Pt.

In Br Fourteenth Army's 33 Corps area, Br 2d Div occupies Ye-u.

CHINA—On Salween front, Ch 9th Div (2d Army) breaks into Wanting, at Sino-Burmese border, but is driven out in night counterattack.

P.I.—Bombardment and Fire Support Group (TG 77.2), proceeding toward Luzon, shoots down a kamikaze plane. On Mindoro, guerrilla force of about 70 unsuccessfully attacks Japanese at Pinamalayan. From Mindoro, Co K of 21st Inf moves to Marinduque I. to help guerrillas destroy Japanese remnants concentrated at Boac in NE part of island.

FORMOSA-RYUKYUS-PESCADORES—In preparation for invasion of Luzon, carrier planes of U.S. Third Fleet begin attacks aimed primarily against enemy aircraft and shipping at Formosa. Secondary effort is made against the Ryukyus and Pescadores. Weather conditions severely limit scope of operations.

4 January

WESTERN EUROPE—21 Army Group: In Br Second Army area, 30 Corps opens offensive W of the Ourthe R, protecting U.S. First Army right. From Marche-Hotton road, 53d Div drives S abreast U.S. VII Corps. 6th A/B Div meets determined opposition S of Rochefort.

In U.S. First Army's VII Corps area, 2d Armd Div captures Beffe, contains counterattacks near Devantave, seizes Lamorménil, and reaches edge of Odeigne. 3d Armd Div takes Baneux, Jevigne, and Lansival and gains bridgehead at Groumont Creek. In XVIII Corps (A/B) area, 82d A/B Div advances its line to include Heirlot, Odrimont, wooded heights N and NE of Abrefontaine, St Jacques, Bergeval, and Mont de Fosse; on extreme left patrols push to the Salm.

12th Army Group: In U.S. Third Army's VIII Corps area, 87th Div attack is halted by resistance near Pironpré. Attack of 17th A/B Div evokes strong reaction in Pinsamont-Rechrival-Hubermont area. Enemy attacks in 101st A/B Div sector are ineffective. In III Corps area, 6th Armd Div is repeatedly attacked in Mageret-Wardin area E of Bastogne, and withdraws to shorten line. 35th Div clears Lutrebois but is still unable to take Harlange. 26th Div gains a few hundred yards.

6th Army Group: In U.S. Seventh Army's XV Corps area, 44th Div tries vainly to clear Frauenberg and Gros Réderching. In limited attack, 36th Div takes hill between Lemberg and Goetzenbruck. In VI Corps area, 45th Div, continuing fight to reduce Bitche salient, drives to outskirts of Wingen; attacks NE across Wingen-Wimmenau road to ease pressure on Reipertsweiler; fights to open Reipertsweiler-Wildenguth road, taking Saegmuhl and making contact with elements cut off in Wildenguth; clears about half of Philippsbourg. TF Linden's line along the Rhine is extended to include zone held by TF Herren.

BURMA—In ALFSEA area, 15 Corps completes occupation of Akyab, key port and air base on Arakan front.

In NCAC area, U.S. 475th Inf finishes crossing the Shweli. U.S. 124th Cav reconnoiters for crossing site over the Shweli while awaiting airdrop.

P.I.: Japanese planes attack TG 77.6 and TG 77.2 as they continue toward Lingayen Gulf. One CVE is so badly damaged that it has to be sunk. At the request of Gen MacArthur, Adm Halsey orders TF 38 to extend its coverage of Luzon southward on 6th. Main body of Luzon Attack Force sorties from Leyte Gulf after nightfall. X Corps, U.S. Eighth Army, terminates offensive operations on Leyte. Japanese planes continue active over Mindoro and destroy an ammunition ship.

FORMOSA-RYUKYUS-PESCADORES—TF 38 continues strikes against enemy airpower and shipping but weather conditions again sharply curtail action. As a result of the 2-day attack, 110 Japanese planes are destroyed; 12 ships are sunk; and 28 other vessels are damaged. 18 planes of TF 38 are lost in combat.

CAROLINE Is.—81st Div troops on Fais complete search of the island and are withdrawn.

5 January

WESTERN EUROPE—21 Army Group: In U.S. First Army's VII Corps area, 2d Armd Div's main effort against Consy makes little headway; elements move toward Dochamps and clear part of Odeigne. 3d Armd Div is slowed by rear-guard action in Bois de Groumont but seizes Lavaux and enters Lierneux. 75th Div moves to Aisne R. In XVIII Corps (A/B) area, 82d A/B Div makes progress all along line and repels counterattacks near Bergeval.

12th Army Group: In U.S. Third Army's VIII Corps area, 87th Div meets resistance near Bonnerue and Pironpré, W of Bastogne. Rest of corps maintains defensive positions. In III Corps area, 35th Div continues to fight for negligible gains.

6th Army Group: Fr First Army is to take responsibility for defense of Strasbourg upon relief of U.S. elements in that area by French. Relief is scheduled for 2400 but is interrupted by enemy attack.

In U.S. Seventh Army area, XV Corps clears Germans from Frauenberg and Gros Réderching.

VI Corps makes slow progress against Bitche salient in 45th Div sector. Most of Wingen and rest of Philippsbourg are cleared. On corps right flank, Germans establish bridgehead across the Rhine in Gambsheim area, crossing between Killstett and Drusenheim and overrunning Offendorf, Herrlisheim, and Rohrweiler. TF Linden, hit while executing reliefs, launches two-pronged assault toward Gambsheim: TF A moves from Weyersheim to W bank of Landgraben Canal; TF B attacks from Killstett but is stopped just N of there.

ITALY—15th Army Group: U.S. Fifth Army orders extensive regrouping. RCT 135 moves from IV Corps zone to II Corps area, reverting to 34th Div. 86th Mtn Inf, 10th Mtn Div, is attached to IV Corps.

In Br Eighth Army area, 5 Corps and Cdn 1 Corps complete limited attacks to improve Winter Line positions. The two corps link up along the Senio between Cotignola and S. Severo. Cdn 1 Corps advances to the Reno except on extreme right.

BURMA—In NCAC area, elements of 90th Regt, Ch 30th Div, begin crossing the Shweli.

CHINA—22d Div, Ch New Sixth Army, completes move to China.

P.I.—Kamikaze attacks on TG's 77.2 and 77.6 continue, causing damage to a number of vessels. Almost all of the estimated 30 attackers are destroyed. CVE planes intercept and damage 2 enemy DD's. On Mindoro, Palauan falls to composite force of guerrillas and 503d Para Inf troops. Another platoon of Co F, 19th Inf, arrives at Bulalacao and joins in march NE toward Paclasan and Dutagan Pt.

VOLCANO-BONIN Is.—Iwo Jima undergoes coordinated air-surface bombardment by land-based aircraft of Seventh Air Force and cruiser-DD task group. Surface vessels also bombard Chichi and Haha. PB4Y's photograph Iwo Jima.

6 January

WESTERN EUROPE—21 Army Group: In U.S. First Army's VII Corps area, 2d Armd and 84th Inf Divs make converging attacks toward Consy, taking positions E and W of the town, respectively. 2d Armd Div continues toward Dochamps, completes occupation of Odeigne, and makes contact with 3d Armd Div on Manhay-Houffalize road. 3d Armd Div cuts Laroche-Salmchâteau road at its intersection with Manhay-Houffalize road and captures Fraiture, Lierneux, and La Falise; 83d Armd Rcn Bn clears Bois Houby. In XVIII Corps (A/B) area, 82d A/B Div consolidates. To protect its left flank, 30th Div attacks S toward Spineux and Wanne with RCT 112, 28th Div.

12th Army Group: In U.S. Third Army's VIII Corps area, enemy gets tanks into Bonnerue, lightly held by 87th Div. 87th Div makes limited attack toward Tillet. In III Corps area, 6th Armd Div holds against repeated counterattacks. 35th Div attacks into woods NE of Lutrebois and maintains positions in Villers-la-Bonne-Eau area; 6th Cav Sq of TF Fickett is committed near Villers-la-Bonne-Eau. In XII Corps area, 80th Div's 319th Inf crosses Sure R near Heiderscheidergrund and captures Goesdorf and Dahl.

U.S. Fifteenth Army becomes operational. Maj Gen Ray E. Porter is in command.

6th Army Group: In U.S. Seventh Army's XV Corps area, attack to restore MLR on right flank of 44th Div halts on line extending along S edge of Bois de Blies Brucken to area just N of Gros Réderching. In VI Corps area, 45th Div makes slow progress against left and center of Bitche salient and on E contains counterattacks on Philippsbourg. Germans continue build up W of the Rhine on E flank of corps. 79th Div clears Stattmatten (where encircled elements of TF Linden are relieved), Sessenheim, and Rohrweiler; reaches edge of Drusenheim. Further efforts of TF Linden to gain Gambsheim are fruitless.

ITALY—15th Army Group: U.S. Fifth Army continues to regroup, RCT 365 moving from II to IV Corps zone and returning to command of 92d Div.

BURMA—In NCAC area, heavy rains begin as U.S. 475th Inf goes into bivouac in Mong Wi area and U.S. 124th Cav makes its way toward Mong Wi. Ch 38th Div gains distinction of being first CAI unit to return to Chinese soil: 112th Regt reaches Loiwing, from which it patrols across the Shweli to Namhkam.

P.I.—TG's 77.2 and 77.6 reach Lingayen Gulf area and begin naval bombardment and mine sweeping. Damaging enemy air attacks persist in spite of strong effort against Luzon by planes of TF 38, CVE's covering TF 77.2, and FEAF. Japanese score against shipping during period 2-6 is 2 ships sunk and 30 damaged. However, enemy force of some 150 aircraft on Luzon at the beginning of the year has been reduced to about 35 planes, and air action drops off sharply after this. On Mindoro, Pinamalayan, which Japanese have recently abandoned, is reoccupied by fresh enemy troops from Luzon. Co I, 21st Inf, and guerrillas join in attack there, forcing enemy back toward Calapan.

7 January

WESTERN EUROPE—21 Army Group: In Br Second Army's 30 Corps area, 53d Div takes Grimbiermont.

In U.S. First Army's VII Corps area, co-ordinated attacks of 2d Armd and 84th Inf Divs toward Laroche-Salmchâteau road, intermediate objective before Houffalize, make notable progress. Dochamps and Marcouray fall. Only rear guards remain in Consy area. 3d Armd Div seizes Regne, Verleumont, Sart, and Grand Sart. In XVIII Corps (A/B) area, 82d A/B Div, in rapid advance of 2–3 miles, clears most of angle formed by Laroche-Salmchâteau road and Salm R. Some elements secure positions on ridge just N of Comté; others, during advance to Salm R line, clear Goronne, Farniers, Mont, and Rochelinval. RCT ire seizes Spineux, Wanne, and Wanneranval.

12th Army Group: In U.S. Third Army's VIII Corps area, 87th Div continues attack on Tillet and is engaged sporadically in Bonnerue area. 17th A/B Div takes Rechrival, Millomont, and Flamierge and reaches outskirts of Flamizoulle. In III Corps area, 6th Armd Div remains under strong pressure in Neffe-Wardin region E of Bastogne. 35th Div makes limited attack toward Lutrebois-Lutremange road, halting just short of it. In XX Corps area, CG 94th Div takes command of sector previously held by 90th Div.

6th Army Group: Boundary between U.S. Seventh Army and Fr 1st Army is shifted N, giving French responsibility for Strasbourg area.

In U.S. Seventh Army's VI Corps area, 45th Div, on left flank of Bitche salient, reaches heights overlooking Althorn and overcomes final resistance within Wingen. On corps E flank, 79th Div organizes TF Wahl (elements of 313th, 315th, and 222d Inf; CCA of 14th Armd Div; 827th TD Bn) to operate in N part of div front since enemy threat to Maginot Line positions S of Wissembourg is serious. Germans drive back outposts at Aschbach and Stundweiler. In Gambsheim bridgehead area, efforts of 314th Inf, 79th Div, to clear Drusenheim are unsuccessful; Fr 3d Algerian Div takes over attack toward Gambsheim from Killstett.

EASTERN EUROPE—In Hungary, Germans continue efforts to relieve the Budapest garrison, which is being methodically destroyed, and capture Esztergom, NW of the city.

ITALY—15th Army Group: In Br Eighth Army area, Pol 2 Corps withdraws from line, turning over its sector and 5th Kresowa Div to 5 Corps.

BURMA—In Br Fourteenth Army's 33 Corps area, Ind 19th and Br 2d Divs are converging on Shwebo, Ind 19th pushing into E outskirts.

P.I.—Underwater demolition teams begin search for underwater obstacles in Lingayen Gulf as preinvasion aerial and naval bombardment of Luzon continues. On Mindoro, Japanese planes for the first time are conspicuously absent from San Jose area.

8 January

WESTERN EUROPE—21 Army Group: In U.S. First Army's VII Corps area, 4th Cav Gp and 84th Div pursue enemy on right of corps to Marcourt and Cielle; other elements of 84th Div start clearing woods S of main road junction SE of Manhay, 2d Armd Div drives on Samrée, CCA moving S from Dochamps and CCB pushing SE along Salmchâteau-Samrée Road. 3d Armd Div gains intermediate objective line, taking Hebronval, Ottre, Jouvieval, and Provedroux. In XVIII Corps (A/B) area, 82d A/B Div consolidates along line Grand Sart-Salmchâteau-Trois Ponts and clears Comté.

12th Army Group: In U.S. Third Army's VIII Corps area, enemy drives 87th Div units from Bonnerue and maintains pressure in Tillet region. Some 17th A/B Div elements gain and then lose high ground N of Laval and others are forced out of Flamierge. In III Corps area, 6th Armd Div recovers lost ground in Neffe-Wardin sector. TF Fickett occupies zone between 35th and 26th Divs, along high ground before Villers-la-Bonne-Eau, Betlange, and Harlange.

6th Army Group: In U.S. Seventh Army's XV Corps area, enemy enters Rimling. 100th and 36th Divs improve positions in local attacks. In VI Corps area, 45th Div makes slight progress against W flank of salient; TF Herren becomes responsible for E flank. 79th Div withstands pressure near Aschbach and moves reinforcements to Soultz-Rittershoffen area. Enemy checks efforts to reduce Gambsheim bridgehead. 314th Inf is unable to advance in Drusenheim or SE of Rohrweiler. CCB, 12th Armd Div, attacks with 714th Tank Bn toward Herrlisheim.

ITALY—15th Army Group: In U.S. Fifth Army area, 85th Div (−) starts from IV Corps zone to II Corps area.

BURMA—In NCAC area, U.S. 475th Inf at Mong Wi is ordered to move forward for action.

CHINA—Chinese Training and Combat Command is split. Chinese Training Center is to operate a command and general staff school and service schools. Chinese Combat Command is to control operations of ALPHA Force and provide liaison sections for each of the major Ch commands under Gen Ho.

P.I.—Preinvasion aerial and naval bombardment of Lingayen Gulf area continues. Mine sweeping is completed.

POA—CG V Amphibious Corps Landing Force issues alternate plan for invasion of Iwo Jima, No. 4-44, calling for landing on western beaches. The preferred plan, 3-44, is subsequently followed on D Day.

9 January

WESTERN EUROPE—21 Army Group: In U.S. First Army's VII Corps area, 84th Div mops up near Consy, takes commanding ground at Harze, and clears woods S of main crossroads SE of Manhay. 2d Armd Div continues toward Samrée, which is subjected to heavy arty fire. 83d Div attacks through 3d Armd Div, gaining line from Bihain—which is entered but not captured—W to point NE of Petite Langlir. In XVIII Corps (A/B) area, 82d A/B Div finishes mopping up within its zone. In 30th Div sector, RCT 424 (106th Div) takes over Wanne-Wanneranval region, formerly held by RCT 112 (28th Div).

12th Army Group: In U.S. Third Army's VIII Corps area, 87th Div continues to fight near Tillet; elements are clearing Haies-de-Tillet woods. 506th Para Inf, 101st A/B Div, attacks with CCB, 4th Armd Div, and CCB, 10th Armd Div, toward Noville, gaining 1,000 yards. 501st Para Inf takes Recogne. III Corps launches attack to trap and destroy enemy in pocket SE of Bastogne. 90th Div attacks through 26th toward high ground NE of Bras, taking Berle and crossroads on Berle–Winseler road. 26th Div's gains are slight but include heights NW of Bavigne. CCA, 6th Armd Div, co-ordinating closely with 134th Inf of 35th Div, advances to high ground SE of Marvie and feints toward Wardin. 137th Inf of 35th Div attacks Villers-la-Bonne-Eau.

6th Army Group: In U.S. Seventh Army's XV Corps area, local attack by 100th Div gains Hill 370, S of Rimling, but since this region is becoming untenable, div withdraws left flank to Guising to tie in with 44th Div. VI Corps makes very slow progress against Bitche salient, but TF Herren's 276th Inf occupies Obermuhlthal. On NE flank of 79th Div, German tank-infantry attack against 242d Inf, TF Linden, overruns Hatten and reaches Rittershoffen; counterattack drives Germans back to Hatten and partly regains that town. In Gambsheim bridgehead region, CCB of 12th Armd Div seizes part of Herrlisheim, but 79th Div is still thwarted in Drusenheim and SE of Rohrweiler. Elements of 232d Inf along canal E of Weyersheim are ordered back to organize Weyersheim for defense.

ITALY—15th Army Group: U.S. Fifth Army announces decision to postpone offensive until 1 April or thereabouts in order to await arrival of fresh troops, build up ammunition supplies, have more favorable weather conditions, and regroup and rest assault forces. In IV Corps area, 86th Mtn Inf of 10th Mtn Div enters line in TF 45's sector, relieving AAA units in region NW of Pistoia. In II Corps area, 85th Div begins relief of Br 1st Div, 13 Corps, in M. Grande area.

LUZON—After preparatory aerial and naval bombardment U.S. Sixth Army, under Gen Krueger, begins landing on shores of Lingayen Gulf at approximately 0930. Gen MacArthur is in over-all command. Seventh Fleet commander, Adm Kinkaid, heads Luzon Attack Force (TF 77). Two corps land abreast, XIV on right and I on left, without opposition. XIV Corps, with 40th Div on right and 37th on left, each with 2 regts in assault, is virtually unopposed while pushing inland to an average depth of 4 miles, its flanks near Calasiao on E and Port Sual on W. I Corps, more strongly opposed, is less successful. Its beachhead by end of day is narrower and shallower than that of XIV Corps and contains several gaps between assault forces. 6th Div, employing 2 regts, gains line from Dagupan to Pantalan R and has elements at Bued R crossing, S of San Fabian. 43d Div attacks with 3 regts to positions in vicinity of San Jacinto, Binday, and Hills 470, 247, and 385.

POA—In support of the Luzon operation, carrier planes of TF 38 attack airfields and shipping in Formosa, Pescadores, and Ryukyus areas despite unfavorable weather conditions. TF 38, under cover of darkness, then enters Japanese-controlled waters of South China Sea, passing between Luzon and Formosa without arousing enemy. At Formosa, B-29's of XX Bomber Command augment attacks of the carrier aircraft. Seventh Air Force continues raids on Iwo Jima in Volcano Is., and B-29's of XXI Bomber Command make another of their sporadic attacks on Japan, aiming at Musashino aircraft plant in Tokyo.

10 January

WESTERN EUROPE—21 Army Group: In Br Second Army's 30 Corps area, 51st Div, which has taken over attack from 53d, reaches Laroche.

In U.S. Ninth Army's XIX Corps area, 78th Div, in local attack, reaches slopes of hills overlooking Kall R.

U.S. First Army prepares to broaden attack on 13th, VII Corps thrusting toward line Houffalize-Bovigny and XVIII Corps toward St Vith. In VII Corps area, most of Laroche-Salmchâteau road, intermediate objective of corps, is cleared. 84th Div patrols toward Laroche. 2d Armd Div captures Samrée and clears Laroche-Salmchâteau road within its zone. 83d Div takes Bihain, advances slightly in region N of Petite Langlir, and crosses Ronce R east of Petite Langlir. In XVIII Corps (A/B) area, elements of 82d A/B Div secure bridgehead across Salm R near Grand Halleux.

12th Army Group: In U.S. Third Army's VIII Corps area, 87th Div captures Tillet. Renewing attack toward Noville, 101st A/B Div clears portion of Bois Jacques. 4th Armd Div units, having passed through 6th Armd Div, attack NE with elements of 101st A/B Div toward Bourcy but cease attack upon order. III Corps continues attack, with greatest progress on right (E) flank. On left flank, 6th Armd Div furnishes fire support for neighboring VIII Corps units and outposts N sector of line reached by 4th Armd Div. Elements of 35th Div take Villers-la-Bonne-Eau and high ground NW. Betlange falls to 6th Cav Sq and Harlange to 28th Cav Sq. One 90th Div regt advances from Berle to heights overlooking Doncols; another fights indecisively for Trentelhof strongpoint. Elements of 26th Div reach high ground SW of Winseler.

6th Army Group: In U.S. Seventh Army's VI Corps area, elements of 45th Div enter Althorn, on left flank of Bitche salient, but are unable to clear it. Otherwise, the salient is unchanged despite continued fighting about its perimeter. On 79th Div's N flank, indecisive fighting occurs at Hatten; bn of 315th Inf is committed there and 2d Bn, 242d Inf, recalled; another bn of 315th assembles in Rittershoffen. To S, enemy maintains Gambsheim bridgehead. Elements of CCB, 12th Armd Div, are virtually surrounded at Herrlisheim, but tanks sever enemy lines in order to reinforce infantry within the town.

ITALY—15th Army Group: In U.S. Fifth Army's IV Corps area, 92d Div takes responsibility for Serchio Valley sector. Ind 8th Div, less 17th Brig, is placed in army reserve.

BURMA—In NCAC area, 114th Regt of Ch 38th Div, which is to move around S end of Shweli Valley and cut Namhkam-Namhpakka trail, crosses the Shweli. U.S. 124th Cav, after delay at the Shweli because of swollen waters, is assembled E of the river.

In Br Fourteenth Army's 33 Corps area, Shwebo falls under combined attacks of Br 2d and Ind 19th Divs. Ind 20th Div takes Budalin after prolonged struggle. In 4 Corps area, E African 28th Brig and Lushai Brig are assisted by heavy air strike in Gangaw area, where enemy is firmly entrenched.

CHINA—In effort to reopen the Canton-Hengyang stretch of the Canton-Hankow RR, Japanese move forward as quietly as possible about this time.

LUZON—In U.S. Sixth Army area, army reserve begins landing. In XIV Corps area, 185th Inf of 40th Div takes Labrador while 160th pushes along Highway 13 toward Aguilar, reaching Umanday area. Because of gap developing between the two regts, 108th Inf (less 3d Bn) is committed in Polong area. 148th Inf, 37th Div, speeds inland to San Carlos; elements continue to Army Beachhead Line. One 129th Inf column moves without opposition to Malisiqui, within 2½ miles of Army Beachhead Line, while another reaches Army Beachhead Line at Dumpay and maintains contact with 148th Inf. In I Corps area, 6th Div drives S and SE to Mapandan and vicinity of Santa Barbara. 43d Div's 103d Inf takes San Jacinto without opposition and pushes on toward Manoag and Hill 200; 169th and 172d Regts run into organized defense positions on hills confronting them; 169th takes Hill 470 and drives on Hill 351 and 318; 172d Inf clears Hill 385 and moves slowly toward Hill 351.

11 January

WESTERN EUROPE—21 Army Group: In Br Second Army's 30 Corps area, patrols of 6th A/B Div reach St Hubert and make contact with U.S. VIII Corps.

In U.S. Ninth Army's XIX Corps area, 78th Div finishes clearing hill positions overlooking Kall R.

In U.S. First Army's VII Corps area, Laroche, in 84th Div sector, is cleared of enemy; 4th Cav Gp patrol covers portion E of the Ourthe R. 83d Div secures road junction on Bihain–Lomre road and attacks Petite Langlir and Langlir. In XVIII Corps (A/B) area, 75th Div takes up positions along Salm R that were held by 82d A/B Div. 106th Div assumes control of right of 30th Div zone.

12th Army Group: In U.S. Third Army's VIII Corps area, 87th Div's 347th Inf finishes clearing Haies-de-Tillet woods and occupies Bonnerue, Pironpre, Vesqueville, and St Hubert, from which enemy has withdrawn. Germans are also withdrawing from 17th A/B Div zone in vicinity of Heropont, Flamierge, Mande St Etienne, and Flamizoulle. In III Corps area, Germans are retiring from pocket SE of Bastogne. Elements of all divs of corps are converging on Bras. 6th Armd Div takes over sector E of Bastogne formerly held by 4th Armd Div (VIII Corps); elements attack toward Bras, clearing woods near Wardin. 35th Div gains additional high ground in Lutrebois–Lutremange area. TF Fickett clears Wantrange and attacks Tarchamps, then moves into zone of TF Scott (mainly 26th Div units) as it advances on Sonlez. TF Fickett reaches Sonlez by midnight and makes contact with 80th Div. Elements of TF Scott clear forest E of Harlange then, in conjunction with TF Fickett, secure heights SW of Sonlez. 90th Div overcomes resistance around Trentelhof, cuts Bastogne–Wiltz road at Doncols, and advances on Sonlez. 26th Div improves positions on right flank of corps. In XII Corps area, 80th Div takes Bockholz-sur-Sure and high ground S of Burden. 2d Cav Gp clears Machtum, enemy's last position W of the Moselle.

6th Army Group: In U.S. Seventh Army's VI Corps area, 45th Div clears Althorn, at W of Bitche salient, but falls back under enemy pressure in Wildenguth-Saegmuhl-Reipertsweiler region;

276th Inf makes limited gains on heights between Lichtenberg and Obermuhlthal. Enemy renews attacks against 79th Div's Maginot positions S of Wissembourg, reinforcing troops in Hatten, where 2d Bn of 315th Inf is enveloped, and wresting about two thirds of Rittershoffen from 3d Bn, 315th Inf. Elements of CCA, 14th Armd Div, counterattack from Kuhlendorf but are stopped short of Rittershoffen. CCB, 12th Armd Div, withdraws from Herrlisheim and takes up defensive positions W of Zorn R.

ITALY—15th Army Group: In U.S. Fifth Army's Br 13 Corps area, 17th Brig of Ind 8th Div joins parent div in army reserve upon relief on right flank of corps by elements of 13 and 5 Corps.

BURMA—In Br Fourteenth Army's 4 Corps area, after Gangaw is captured by E African 28th Brig and Lushai Brig, corps is able to advance quickly toward the Irrawaddy in Pakokku area for drive on Meiktila.

FORMOSA—Fifth Air Force begins small night attacks on the island with B-24's.

SWPA—GHQ orders 11th A/B Div, U.S. Eighth Army, to be prepared to land on Luzon at Nasugbu and Tayabas Bays in late January. Plan to land XI Corps at Vigan is dropped.

LUZON—In U.S. Sixth Army area, RCT 158, part of army reserve, begins drive up Route 251 toward Rabon and relieves elements of 172d Inf, 43d Div. XIV Corps is largely on Army Beachhead Line by end of day. 40th Div consolidates in Dulig-Labrador-Uyong area, finds Aguilar in the hands of Filipino guerrillas, and makes contact with 37th Div E of Aguilar, 37th Div organizes defensive positions along Army Beachhead Line; patrols actively and establishes outposts; maintains contact with 1 Corps. RCT 145, all of which is now ashore, establishes defense positions along Route 261. In I Corps area, 6th Div finds Filipino guerrillas in control of Santa Barbara; moves 3½ miles S to Balingueo. 103d Inf, 43d Div, takes Manoag without opposition; gains positions on slopes of hill mass that Hill 200 crowns; establishes contact with 6th Div. 169th tries in vain to take Hill 318: gains weak hold on Hill 560. 172d, under intense fire, snakes little headway. Corps front is rapidly widening and extends nearly 30 miles from S to N. With elimination of small enemy force at Boac, Marinduque I. is now secure.

12 January

WESTERN EUROPE—21 Army Group: In U.S. First Army VII Corps area, 2d Armd Div attacks in vicinity of junction of Manhay-Houffalize and Laroche-Salmchâteau roads: CCA takes Chabrehez, continues about a mile S in Bois de Belhez, and reduces strongpoint E of Bois de St Jean; CCB captures Les Tailles and Petite Tailles. On 3d Armd Div right, 83d Armd Rcn Bn drives S through TF Hogan (CCR) at Regne, crosses Langlir R, and clears Bois de Cedrogne E of Manhay-Houffalize road and blocks road there running W from Mont le Ban. TF Hogan moves to Bihain and clears high ground SW of the town. 83d Div completes capture of Petite Langlir and Langlir and gains bridgehead S of Langlir-Ronce R. In XVIII (A/B) Corps' 106th Div sector, bridgehead is established across Amblève R south of Stavelot.

12th Army Group: In U.S. Third Army's VIII Corps area, enemy continues withdrawing. 87th Div takes Tonny, Amberloup, Lavacherie, Orreux, Fosset, Sprimont, and road junction NE of Sprimont. 17th A/B Div recaptures Flamierge. Flamizoulle is found to be heavily mined. Renuamont, Hubermont, and villages to SW are held by light, delaying forces. In III Corps area, CCA of 6th Armd Div captures Wardin and advances to within a few hundred yards of Bras; 357th mops up Sonlez and continues to high ground SE of Bras; 359th repels attacks on crossroads NE of Doncols.

6th Army Group: In U.S. Seventh Army's VI Corps area, enemy has shifted from aggressive offensive to stubborn defensive in Bitche salient. Efforts of 45th Div to regain ground lost on 11th are only partly successful. 14th Armd Div attacks to relieve 315th Inf, 79th Div, in Hatten and Rittershoffen; CCA clears part of Rittershoffen. Situation in Gambsheim bridgehead is unchanged.

EASTERN EUROPE—Soviet forces open powerful winter offensive. With strong arty support, First Ukrainian Front leads off, attacking W from Sandomierz bridgehead over the Vistula in S Poland. Battle for Budapest continues with Red Army deepening penetration into the city.

BURMA—In ALFSEA's 15 Corps area, 3d Cdo Brig lands on Arakan coast at Myebon after air and naval bombardment and establishes firm beachhead, which enemy without success soon attempts to destroy.

In NCAC area, U.S.-Ch convoy starts along Ledo Road from Ledo, India.

SOUTH CHINA SEA—TF 38, still unmolested by enemy, makes surprise air attacks on enemy shipping off French Indochina and on airfields and shore installations from Saigon N to Tourane. Shipping targets are plentiful, including several convoys, and the TF destroys some 40 ships and damages others.

LUZON—In U.S. Sixth Army's XIV Corps area, 40th Div's 185th Inf takes Port Sual, W terminus of Army Beachhead Line, without a fight and continues W toward Alaminos. 37th Div is consolidating on Army Beachhead Line; elements move into Bayambang and Urbiztondo without opposition. In

I Corps area, 6th Div (less RCT 63) is ordered to conduct holding action along line Malisiqui-Catablan-Torres until situation in 43d Div sector improves and is moving forward toward that line. RCT 158, released from army reserve to corps late in day, moves elements to Rabon and Bani and patrols to Damortis. Corps attaches RCT 158 to 43d Div; to further strengthen 43d Div, commits RCT 63 (–) of 6th Div to right of RCT 158 to close gap between 158th and 172d Regts. RCT's 158 and 63 are to secure Damortis-Rosario road. Elements of 43d Div take Hill 560 and are attacking toward Hills 318 and 200.

MINDORO—Entire 21st Inf assembles at Pinamalayan for drive on Calapan, where Japanese force is now concentrated. Guerrilla patrol reaches Wawa, on N coast near Abra de flog.

POA—Joint Expeditionary Force (TF 51), less elements in the Marianas, begins rehearsals in Hawaiian area for landing on Iwo Jima, concluding them by 18 January.

13 January

WESTERN EUROPE—21 Army Group: In Br Second Army area, 30 Corps' Ardennes mission is completed as 51st Div reaches Ourthe R line southward from Laroche.

In U.S. First Army area, VII Corps pushes steadily toward Houffalize. On right flank, 4th Cav Gp and 84th Div clear several towns and villages. CCA, 2d Armd Div, reaches positions about 1½ miles N of Wibrin; CCB advances in Bois de Cedrogne to points 5-6 miles due N of Houffalize. 3d Armd Div's CCR cuts Sommerain-Cherain road at its junction with road to Mont le Ban and contains Mont le Ban while CCB takes Lomre. After clearing passage through woods S of Langlir for 3d Armd Div, 83d Div mops up and regroups. XVIII Corps (A/B) opens offensive, employing 106th Div on right and 30th on left. 106th Div, with 424th Inf on right and 517th Para Inf on left, attacks SE from junction of Amblève and Salm Rivers toward La Neuville-Coulee-Logbiermé-Houvegnez line, reaching positions near Henumont. 30th Div drives S from Malmédy area toward Amblève R, gaining positions near Hédomont, in Houyire woods, and in Thirimont area.

12th Army Group: In U.S. Third Army's VIII Corps area, advance elements of 87th Div reach Ourthe R and make contact with British. 17th A/B Div takes Salle, N of Flamierge, without opposition. 11th Armd Div, which has relieved elements of 101st and 17th A/B Divs, attacks N with CCR and CCA along Longchamps-Bertogne axis, cutting Houffalize-St Hubert highway near Bertogne. Bertogne is enveloped. 506th Para Inf, 101st A/B Div, seizes Foy, on Bastogne-Houffalize highway; 327th Gli Inf advances through 501st Para Inf in Bois Jacques toward Bourcy. In III Corps area, 6th Armd Div drives northward, CCB partially clearing Mageret. 90th Div drives enemy from Bras and gains Hill 530. 35th Div and TF Fickett are pinched out near Bras. 26th Div moves units into positions NE and E of Doncols as boundary between it and 90th Div is moved W.

6th Army Group: In U.S. Seventh Army area, XXI Corps (Maj Gen Frank W. Milburn) becomes operational, assuming responsibility for defense of left flank of army and taking control of 106th Cav Gp and 103d Div in place. It is to continue organization of defensive positions. In VI Corps area, 45th Div makes minor gains against Bitche salient. TF Herren (−274th Inf) moves to right flank of corps. 14th Armd Div takes command of Hatten-Rittershoffen sector, assisted by 79th Div: CCA and 3d Bn of 315th Inf continue to fight in Rittershoffen; CCR secures W third of Hatten and makes contact with 2d Bn of 315th Inf; efforts of CCB to cut roads N and NE of Hatten fail.

ITALY—15th Army Group: In U.S. Fifth Army's II Corps area, 34th Div relieves 88th Div in line.

BURMA—In ALFSEA area, 15 Corps strengthens Myebon bridgehead. Ind 25th Div begins landing.

LUZON—With scattered strikes at Lingayen Gulf, major enemy air attacks on Luzon Attack Force come to an end.

In U.S. Sixth Army area, Gen Krueger takes command ashore. In XIV Corps area, elements of 185th Inf, 40th Div, move along coast of Lingayen Gulf to site chosen for seaplane base in Cabalitan Bay and find that Allied Naval Forces have already secured it without enemy interference. Wawa falls to elements of 37th Div. In I Corps area, 6th Div gains its holding line, Malisiqui-Catablan-Torres. In 43d Div zone, RCT 158 takes Damortis without a struggle. Attacking from Alacan area, 63d Inf gets about halfway to Hill 363, its first objective. Hills 580 and 318 are practically cleared by 172d and 169th Regts, respectively.

14 January

WESTERN EUROPE—21 Army Group: In U.S. First Army's VII Corps area, 84th Div gains its final objectives, taking Nadrin, Filly, Petite Mormont, and Grande Mormont; 4th Cav Gp patrol makes visual contact with U.S. Third Army patrol. 2d Armd Div seizes Wibrin, Cheveoumont, Wilogne, and Dinez. 3d Armd Div takes Mont le Ban and Baclain. 83d Div clears Honvelez and high ground near Bovigny. In XVIII (A/B) Corps' 106th Div sector, 517th Para Inf clears Henumont and continues S; 424th Inf secures Coulee and Logbiermé. Some elements of 30th Div attack toward Hédomont and Thirimont, night 13–14, and take Hédomont before dawn; other elements clear Villers and Ligneuville and gain bridgeheads across Amblève R at these points.

12th Army Group: In U.S. Third Army's VIII Corps area, 17th A/B Div's 507th Para Inf secures Bertogne, from which enemy has fled, and 194th Gli Inf takes Givroulle; both regts continue to Ourthe R. TF of CCA, 11th Armd Div, clears Falize woods and drives along Longchamps–Compogne highway until stopped by heavy fire. 101st A/B Div continues attack toward Noville–Rachamps–Bourcy area. Elements are forced out of Recogne and Foy, but both are regained in counterattacks. Enemy is cleared from Cobru. Tank TF of CCB, 11th Armd Div, followed by infantry TF, enters Noville but withdraws under intense fire. In III Corps area, CCA of 6th Armd Div clears woods E of Wardin and captures Benonchamps; CCB finishes clearing Mageret. Elements of 90th Div drive toward Niederwampach. Having cleared small pockets during night, 26th Div moves combat patrols against enemy S of Wiltz R. In XX Corps area, 94th Div opens series of small-scale attacks to improve defensive positions in Saar–Moselle triangle S of Wasserbillig, a strongly fortified switch position of West Wall; 376th Inf takes Tettingen and Butzdorf. 95th Div moves two bns to objectives in Saarlautern bridgehead area and then withdraws them as planned.

6th Army Group: In U.S. Seventh Army's XXI Corps area, RCT 142 of 36th Div moves to 103d Div zone to cover relief of that div by TF Herren. In VI Corps area, enemy continues vigorous defense of Bitche salient. 45th Div makes slight gains along its perimeter. 14th Armd Div battles enemy in Rittershoffen and Hatten.

EASTERN EUROPE—Berlin reports new Soviet offensive in Schlossberg (Pillkalen) region of NE East Prussia. Red Army offensive in Poland broadens as First and Second White Russian Fronts attack, former from bridgeheads over the Vistula S of Warsaw and latter from Narew R bridgeheads N of the capital. In S Poland, First Ukrainian Front forces Nida R and cuts Kielce–Cracow RR. Heavy fighting continues in Budapest with German garrison slowly giving ground. Germans are steadily withdrawing forces from Yugoslavia.

ITALY—15th Army Group: U.S. Fifth Army activates a new regt, 473d, using personnel of AAA units previously under TF 45 and dissolving 45th AAA Brig.

BURMA—In Br Fourteenth Army's 33 Corps area, Ind 19th Div secures bridgehead across the Irrawaddy at Thabaikkyin, evoking speedy and violent reaction from Japanese. The enemy mistakes the div for 4 Corps as hoped and, to avert threat to Mandalay, rushes reserves forward thus weakening other sectors. For the next month, Ind 19th Div withstands repeated and determined counterattacks.

LUZON—In U.S. Sixth Army's XIV Corps area, 40th Div's Rcn Tr reaches Alaminos; 160th Inf drives S along Route 13 from Aguilar to Mangatarem. Pushing S across the Agno, 129th Inf of 37th Div takes Bautista; 37th Div Rcn Tr finds Camiling undefended. In I Corps area, 6th Div continues holding action and patrols actively. In 43d Div zone, 158th Inf attacks toward Rosario but meets such heavy fire in defile near Amlang that it pulls back approximately to its starting line; 63d Inf seizes Hill 363. After taking Hill 351, which has been bypassed, and mopping up on Hill 580, 172d Inf secures Hills 585 and 565 and pushes on toward Hill 665; upon spotting enemy moving down Route 3, is ordered to attack on 15th for junction of Routes 3 and 11. 169th Inf mops up on Hill 318; prepares to attack Hill 355. 103d Inf establishes outpost about 1½ miles SE of Pozorrubio.

LEYTE—In U.S. Eighth Army's XXIV Corps area, 96th Div relieves 11th A/B Div of tactical responsibility on Leyte and sends 2 bns to Samar I. to relieve 8th Cav, 1st Cav Div, of garrison duty at Catbalogan. Night 14–15, 7th Div sends TF, composed of 3d Bn of 184th Inf, 776th Tank Bn, and elements of 718th and 536th Amtrac Bns, on amphibious mission to secure Camotes Is.

15 January

WESTERN EUROPE—21 Army Group: In Br Second Army's 12 Corps area, in preparation for Operation BLACKCOCK—To clear triangular enemy salient between the Meuse and Roer–Wurm Rivers from Roermond southward—elements of 7th Armd Div seize Bakenhoven (Holland) about a mile NW of Susteren as line of departure for main attack by 7th Armd Div on left flank of corps.

On U.S. First Army's VII Corps right, 84th Div consolidates. 2d Armd Div clears Achouffe, Mont, and Tavernaux and sends patrols to Ourthe R and into Houffalize, which has been vacated by enemy. 3d Armd Div attacks with CCR toward Vaux and Brisy, taking Vaux, and with, CCB toward Cherain and Sterpigny. Elements of CCA are committed as reinforcements. Bn of 83d Div attacks Bovigny but is unable to take it. In XVIII Corps (A/B) area, 75th Div attacks across the Salm before dawn and seizes Salmchâteau and Bech. 106th Div consolidates and clears Ennal. 30th Div takes Beaumont, Francheville, Houvegnez, and Pont; improves positions S of Ligneuville; clears N part of Thirimont. V Corps opens offensive to clear heights between

Buellingen and Amblève and to protect left flank of XVIII Corps. 1st Div, reinf by RCT 23 of 2d Div, attacks SE with 23d Inf on right, 16th in center, and 18th on left; gains Steinbach, neighboring village of Remonval, and N half of Faymonville, but is held up S of Butgenbach by heavy fire.

12th Army Group: In U.S. Third Army's VIII Corps area, CCA of 11th Armd Div takes Compogne and Rastadt and reaches Vellereux; falls back W of Vellereux under counterattack in Rau de Vaux defile. CCB bypasses Neville and clears woods to E. 506th Para Inf, 101st A/B Div, occupies Neville. In III Corps area, 6th Armd Div, employing 320th Inf of 35th Div, overcomes house-to-house resistance in Oubourcy; CCB takes Arloncourt; CCA clears heights SW of Longvilly. 358th Inf of 80th Div meets unexpectedly strong resistance as it resumes NE attack; 1st Bn makes forced march into 6th Armd Div sector to attack Niederwampach from Benonchamps area and gains town after arty barrage by 14 FA bns. 357th Inf battles strongpoints in and around RR tunnels along Wiltz R valley while 359th starts to Wardin. In XX Corps' 94th Div zone, 1st Bn of 376th holds Tettingen and Butzdorf against counterattack while 3d Bn takes Nennig, Wies, and Berg.

6th Army Group: Issues preliminary instructions for attack against Colmar Pocket by Fr First Army, which for some time has been engaged in aggressive defense of the Vosges.

In U.S. Seventh Army's VI Corps area, local actions occur around Bitche salient perimeter. 14th Armd Div continues fight for Rittershoffen and Hatten.

EASTERN EUROPE—Red Army offensive is extended southward in Poland as Fourth Ukrainian Front begins drive in Carpathian Mts from vicinity of Sanok, SW of Cracow. To the N, First Ukrainian Front takes Kielce.

ITALY—15th Army Group: In U.S. Fifth Army area, S African 6th Armd Div, which has been under army command, is placed under control of II Corps in current positions.

BURMA—At conference in Myitkyina, Gens Wedemeyer, Stratemeyer, and Sultan agree that an AAF hq should be set up in China to command U.S. Tenth and Fourteenth Air Forces.

In NCAC area, inaugural convoy from Ledo reaches Myitkyina, where it halts to await clearance of enemy ahead. Ch 30th Div takes Namhkam with ease, gaining control of lower end of Shweli Valley.

In Br Fourteenth Army's 33 Corps area, Ind 19th Div secures another bridgehead across the Irrawaddy, at Kyaukmyaung.

CHINA—Japanese begin offensive for Suichwan airfields, driving along Chaling-Lienhwa road.

SOUTH CHINA SEA—TF 38, severely handicapped by weather conditions, launches air strikes against shipping, airfields, and ground installations at Formosa and along coast of China from Hong Kong to Amoy. Because of deteriorating weather conditions, some of the planes are diverted to Mako Ko in the Pescadores and others to Prates Reef.

LUZON—In U.S. Sixth Army's XIV Corps area, elements of 40th Div begin probing in Dasol Bay Balinao Peninsula area, where action is insignificant through 18th. 2d Bn of 160th Inf takes San Clemente, forcing enemy party back toward Camiling. Elements of 129th Inf and 37th Rcn Tr, 37th Div, intercept the enemy party near Camiling and disperse it. In I Corps area, 6th Div, while continuing holding action, extends left flank to Cabanbanan, between Manoag and Urdaneta. Patrols find enemy in possession of Urdaneta and Cabaruan Hills. In 43d Div zone, 158th Inf, assisted by arty, naval gunfire, and aircraft, begins clearing the defile near Amlang, on road to Rosario; 63d Inf drives N in effort to make contact with 158th but stops for night well S of Amlang; 172d Inf clears Hill 665 and reaches Damortis-Rosario road within 1 1/2 miles of Rosario; 169th, unable to take Hill 355 from W and S, prepares to strike from E; 103d gains most of Hill 200 area.

CAMOTES—Protected by Fifth Air Force planes and PT boats, 7th Div TF lands unopposed on N and S tips of Ponson I.

MINDORO—2d Bn of 21st Inf, driving on Calapan, meets delaying opposition along Gusay Creek. 503d Para Inf, which has been assisting guerrilla forces, terminates operations on Mindoro.

16 January

WESTERN EUROPE—21 Army Group: In Br Second Army area, 12 Corps opens Operation BLACKCOCK, 7th Armd Div driving NE and seizing Dieteren (Holland).

In U.S. First Army's VII Corps area, VII Corps of First Army and VIII Corps of Third Army establish contact near Houffalize. 2d Armd Div occupies that part of Houffalize N of Ourthe R. Enemy resistance continues on left flank of corps. 3d Armd Div captures Sommerain, Cherain, and Sterpigny but is unable to take Brisy. Attempt to get tank force from Cherain to Rettigny fails. 83d Div consolidates along E edge of Bois de Ronce. In XVIII Corps (A/B) area, 75th Div makes slow progress E of the Salm. After gaining objective line, 106th Div mops up, 424th Inf along 75th Div boundary and 517th Para Inf on high ground NW of Petit Thier. 30th Div clears rest of Thirimont and pushes S toward junction of Recht-Born road with Malmédy-St Vith road, which enemy is blocking. In V Corps area, 1st Div captures Ondenval and rest of Faymonville, but progress in woods S of Butgenbach is negligible.

12th Army Group: In U.S. Third Army's VIII Corps area, CCA of 11th Armd Div takes Vellereux and pursues enemy through Mabompré; CCB, after advancing NE through Wicourt, secures high ground S of Houffalize. Attack of 502d Para Inf, 101st A/B Div, is halted near Bourcy, but 506th Para Inf captures Vaux and. Rachamps. In III Corps area, 6th Armd Div continues NE toward Moinet: 320th Inf, attached, takes Michamps; TF Lagrew, CCA, advances through Longvilly. 90th Div clears heights E of Longvilly and seizes Oberwampach and Shimpach.

Lt Gen Leonard T. Gerow assumes command of U.S. Fifteenth Army.

6th Army Group: 28th Div is attached to U.S. Seventh Army but will operate under control of Fr 1st Army.

In U.S. Seventh Army's VI Corps area, 45th Div, on E flank of Bitche salient, withstands pressure near Obermuhlthal. CCA of 14th Armd Div is halted in Rittershoffen and CCR loses ground in Hatten. In 79th Div sector, elements of 232d Inf intercept German force at Dengolsheim and drive it back to Dahlhunden. 12th Armd Div attacks to reduce Gambsheim bridgehead: infantry elements of CCB cross river SE of Rohrweiler but fall back to Rohrweiler when enemy fire prevents construction of bridge for armor; CCA, attacking from Weyersheim toward Offendorf, makes better progress but fails to reach objective.

EASTERN EUROPE—Radom (Poland) falls to First White Russian Front; First Ukrainian Front is driving on Czestochowa and Cracow.

BURMA—In NCAC area, U.S. 5332d Brig gets into position for attack on Burma Road in Namhpakka area, between Hsenwi and Wanting. 114th Regt, Ch 38th Div, continues toward Namhkam-Namhpakka trail, reaching Ta-kawn.

CHINA—China Theater is notified that B-29's will be moved to the Marianas.

SOUTH CHINA SEA—TF 38 planes attack shipping, airfields, and ground installations along Chinese coast from Swatow to Luichow Peninsula and at Hainan I. Main effort is against Hong Kong, where good concentration of shipping is found. Results against shipping and aircraft are disappointing but important ground installations are hit. Enemy air strength proves surprisingly weak.

LUZON—Airstrip in Lingayen Gulf area becomes operational.

In U.S. Sixth Army area, XIV Corps' zone is extended to cover region from Bayambang W into Zambales Mtns. Bridges are to be constructed over the Agno for use of heavy equipment. Regrouping and widespread patrolling ensue. In I Corps area, 25th Div is attached to corps from army reserve to secure line Binalonan-Urdaneta and enters line between 6th and 43d Divs, whereupon 6th prepares to move on Urdaneta and the Cabaruan Hills. 43d Div attempts to take Rosario and junction of Routes 3 and 11 but makes little headway. 103d Inf, assisted by tanks, virtually finishes clearing Hill 200 area; elements move into Pozorrubio. During night 16-17, Japanese make local counterattacks but are driven back with heavy losses.

MINDORO—19th Inf, upon establishing outpost at Bulalacao, finds that the area is infested with Japanese.

17 January

WESTERN EUROPE—21 Army Group: In Br Second Army's 12 Corps area, some elements of 7th Armd Div advance NE from Dieteren and seize Echt while others move S and take Susteren.

In U.S. First Army's VII Corps area, 3d Armd Div mops up and improves positions near Cherain and Sterpigny. 331st Inf, 83d Div, starts to clear high ground SW of Courtil. In XVIII Corps (A/B) area, 75th Div seizes Petit Thier, Vielsalm, and neighboring villages, 106th Div is pinched out by 75th and 30th Divs. 30th Div is unable to reduce roadblock at junction of Recht-Born and Malmédy-St Vith roads. In V Corps area, 1st Div, making main effort on right, fights to clear defile S of Ondenval through which 7th Armd Div will pass in attack on St Vith. 23d Inf attacks toward high ground N and NW of Iveldingen, pocketing enemy in N part of the Wolfsbusch and moving slowly through the Rohrbusch.

U.S. First Army reverts to U.S. 12th Army Group at midnight 17-18.

12th Army Group: In U.S. Third Army's VIII Corps area, Bourcy and Hardigny fall to 101st A/B Div. Having cleared enemy from area between Bastogne and Ourthe R, corps goes on the defensive. In III Corps area, 6th Armd Div meets heavy resistance near Bourcy-Longvilly road. 90th Div resists enemy efforts to regain Oberwampach and clears wooded area S of RR track. XII Corps completes preparations for attack: 87th Div takes over 4th Div zone along the Sauer from Echternach to Wasserbillig, with 4th Div now on left and 2d Cav Gp on right; 4th Div takes responsibility for portion of 5th Div zone.

6th Army Group: In U.S. Seventh Army's XXI Corps area, TF Herren (− 274th Inf) takes command of 103d Div sector. In VI Corps area, 103d Div takes over TF Herren's sector and 274th Inf in position. 1st Bn of 315th Inf, attached to 14th Armd Div, attacks toward Rittershoffen, where CCA is still engaged, but cannot reach the town; CCR withstands enemy pressure in Hatten. Germans continue to be aggressive in 232d Inf's sector of 79th Div front, occupying Roeschwoog, Dengolsheim, Stattmatten, and part of Sessenheim; counterattack clears Sessenheim. 12th Armd Div makes little headway against Gambsheim bridgehead: CCB is again held up at river SE of Rohrweiler; CCA gains precarious foothold in Herrlisheim with 17th Armd Inf Bn, but 43d Tank Bn is cut off outside the town and wiped out.

EASTERN EUROPE—First White Russian Front overruns Warsaw, capital of Poland. Second White Russian Front now holds Ciechanow, to N. Speeding rapidly W from Kielce, First Ukrainian Front forces Warta R and occupies Czestochowa.

ITALY—15th Army Group: In U.S. Fifth Army's II Corps area, 85th Div takes command of sector previously held by Br 1st Div (13 Corps), having completed relief of that div. Boundary between II and Br 13 Corps is altered accordingly. Br 1st Div is placed under AFHQ control and is later sent to Middle East.

BURMA—In NCAC area, U.S. 5332d Brig clears Japanese outpost from Namhkam village, within 3 miles of Burma Road, and begins to clear ridge, which this village surmounts. Ch 38th Div, less 114th Regt, is ordered to advance toward Wanting to secure trace of Ledo Road.

LUZON—In U.S. Sixth Army area, Gen MacArthur directs Gen Krueger to speed drive on Manila and Clark Field. XIV Corps continues preparations for offensive. In I Corps area, 6th Div begins push on Cabaruan Hills with 20th Inf and on Urdaneta with 1st Inf. 25th Div attacks in center of corps with 27th Inf on right and 161st on left: 27th reaches Binalonan-Urdaneta road; 161st pushes to Binalonan, where enemy is offering lively opposition. 103d Inf, 43d Div, takes Pozorrubio, from which most Japanese have withdrawn. 63d Inf is attached to 158th Inf to help clear heights commanding Damortis-Rosario road in Amlang-Cataguintingan region. 158th takes ridge about 1,000 yards NE of Damortis.

18 January

WESTERN EUROPE—21 Army Group: In Br Second Army's 12 Corps area, 7th Armd Div, on left flank of corps, seizes Schilberg (opening highway from there to Sittard) and Heide, NE of Susteren. In center, 52d Div goes on the offensive along German-Dutch frontier and clears several German towns.

12th Army Group: In U.S. First Army area, VII Corps improves positions near Cherain and Courtil. In XVIII Corps (A/B) area, 75th Div clears part of Burtonville. 30th takes Poteau and surrounds roadblock at junction of Recht-Born and Malmédy-St Vith roads. In V Corps area, 1st Div repels counterattack in densely wooded Rohrbusch; eliminates pocket S of Amblève R in the Wolfsbusch; makes slow progress in woods S of Butgenbach. In U.S. Third Army's VIII Corps area, 11th Armd Div assumes responsibility for line from Hardigny to Bourcy. 17th A/B Div takes over line from Hardigny to Houffalize. In III Corps area, though German attack on Oberwampach is repulsed by 90th Div, enemy shelling of the town increases. XII Corps opens offensive at 0300 when 4th and 5th Divs attack abreast N across the Sauer between Reisdorf and Ettelbruck, surprising enemy. 4th Div, attacking with RCT 8, reaches heights commanding Our R between Longsdorf and Hosdorf. To W, 5th Div attacks with RCT's 10 and 2, capturing hills along N bank of the Sauer and towns of Ingeldorf and Erpeldange; elements start clearing Bettendorf and Diekirch, securing a third of the latter. 319th Inf, 80th Div, takes Nocher but fails to gain high ground W of Masseler. Supporting attack, 87th Div demonstrates river crossing. 2d Cav Gp supports 94th Div (XX Corps) with fire and river crossing demonstration. In XX Corps area, 94th Div loses Butzdorf during determined enemy counterattack but holds at Tettingen.

6th Army Group: Directs Fr 1st Army to begin double envelopment of Colmar Pocket on 20 January.

In U.S. Seventh Army's VI Corps area, enemy infiltration in Bitche salient NE of Reipertsweiler isolates 3d Bn of 157th Inf, 45th Div; attempts to relieve the bn are ineffective. Indecisive and costly fighting continues in Rittershoffen-Hatten area. Germans are increasingly active S of Hatten and overrun TF Linden's positions in Sessenheim and Bois de Sessenheim. 12th Armd Div continues losing battle against bridgehead, which enemy has reinforced: CCA relinquishes its hold on Herrlisheim; attack to relieve CCA elements trapped in the town fails.

In Fr 1st Army's 2d Corps area, U.S. 28th Div begins relief of U.S. 3d Div, night 18-19.

EASTERN EUROPE—In Hungary, Second Ukrainian Front clears that part of Budapest E of the Danube. Soviet armies in Poland are rapidly approaching German Silesia.

ITALY—15th Army Group: U.S. Fifth Army releases Br 13 Corps, consisting now of 6th Armd and 78th Divs, to control of Br Eighth Army in place. U.S. Fifth Army thus gets a new right boundary.

BURMA—In NCAC area, U.S. 5332d Brig gains hold on Loi-kang ridge, commanding Burma Road, and gets arty into position to fire on the road. Japanese move reinforcements to Namhpakka area.

LUZON—U.S. Sixth Army orders XIV Corps to drive S beyond the Agno in force from current general line Bayambang-Urbiztondo-Bogtong. In I Corps area, 1st Inf of 6th Div takes Urdaneta while 20th continues to probe into Cabaruan Hills without making contact with main enemy forces. 161st Inf, 25th Div, clears Binalonan. From Palacpalac, 2d Bn of 769th Inf, 43d Div, attacks through Bobonan to road junction near Sison; maintains roadblock there under strong enemy pressure. 758th and 63d Regts begin attack on ridge called Blue Ridge, near Amlang; although progress is slow the assault regts gain contact with each other.

CAMOTES—From Ponson I., 7th Div TF (3d Bn of 184th Inf, reinf) moves by sea to Poro I. and establishes beachhead.

19 January

WESTERN EUROPE—21 Army Group: In Br Second Army's 12 Corps area, Germans are cleared from Stevensweerd in 7th Armd Div sector. 52d Div overruns Isenbruch, Breberen, Saeffelen, and Broichhoven; elements cross Dutch border, taking Koningsbosch, W of Bocket, and making contact with 7th Armd Div near that village.

12th Army Group: In U.S. First Army's VII Corps area, 4th Cav Gp takes over sector of 2d Armd Div, 3d Armd Div gains its final objectives, clearing Brisy, Rettigny, Renglez, and rest of zone as far S as Ourthe R. 83d Div cleans out woods in its zone and sends elements into Bovigny and Courtil. In XVIII Corps (A/B) area, 75th Div is dislodging enemy from Grand Bois and withstands pressure near Burtonville. 30th, against light resistance, captures Recht, reduces roadblock at junction of Recht-Born and Malmédy-St Vith roads, continues to clear woods S of Recht-Born road, and takes high ground in Bois d'Emmels SE of Poteau. 7th Armd Div closes in attack positions near Waimes. In V Corps area, 1st Div opens passage through which 7th Armd Div will drive on St Vith; against greatly decreased resistance, div clears Iveldingen, Eibertingen, Montenau, and Schoppen. In U.S. Third Army's XII Corps area, 4th Div gains heights overlooking the Our NE of Bettendorf; in conjunction with 5th Div clears Bettendorf, but is unable to reduce strongpoint across the Sauer from Reisdorf. 5th Div takes rest of Diekirch and occupies Bastendorf. In XX Corps area, 302d Inf of 94th Div is clearing bypassed fortifications to allow passage of CCA, 8th Armd Div. CCA, 8th Armd Div, assembles near Koenigsmacker.

6th Army Group: In U.S. Seventh Army's VI Corps area, 157th Inf of 45th Div receives intensified fire and contains counterattacks from Bitche salient; efforts to relieve encircled 3d Bn continue. Though enemy is less aggressive in Rittershoffen-Hatten area, 74th Armd Div is unable to improve positions. Germans mount strong attacks S of Hatten. To avert threat of a breakthrough to Haguenau, 74th Armd Div's 25th Tank Bn moves to Hochfelden. 79th Div attacks toward Sessenheim with attached units of 103d Div, which enter the town but are driven out. Germans surround 2d Bn, 374th Inf, in Drusenheim but elements escape. 12th Armd Div withdraws for relief and contains enemy attack at line of relief. RCT 143, 36th Div, takes up defensive positions in Rohrweiler-Weyersheim region.

EASTERN EUROPE—Moscow confirms German reports of new Soviet offensive against East Prussia, where Third White Russian Front now holds Schlossberg (Pillkalen). Continuing rapidly across Poland, First White Russian Front takes Lodz; First Ukrainian Front seizes Tarnow and Cracow; Fourth Ukrainian Front has reached Gorlice, S of Tarnow.

BURMA—In ALFSEA's 15 Corps area, Kantha, on Myebon Peninsula, falls to 25th Ind Div.

In NCAC area, 114th Regt of Ch 38th Div cuts Namhkam-Namhpakka trail. U.S. 5332d Brig craters Burma Road and continues to clear heights overlooking it.

LUZON—In U.S. Sixth Army area, XIV Corps begins advance toward Clark Field, gaining line Camiling-Paniqui-Anao 24 hours ahead of schedule. On right, 160th Inf of 40th Div drives down Route 13 to Nambalan. One column of 129th Inf, 37th Div, drives to Carmen and patrols as far as San Manuel without incident; another advances to Moncada, where Japanese are driven off; a third reaches Paniqui. 148th Inf moves into positions along Camiling-Paniqui road—Route 55. In I Corps area, 169th Inf of 43d Div moves reinforcements to 2d Bn at road junction near Sison, but Japanese regain the position. 103d Inf begins 2-bn assault on Hill 600, E of Pozorrubio road.

CAMOTES—7th Div TF on Poro is clearing the island and making few contacts with enemy.

MINDORO—21st Inf troops overcome enemy opposition along Gusay Creek.

20 January

INTERNATIONAL AGREEMENTS—Provisional National Government of Hungary signs armistice agreement in Moscow with Great Britain, United States, and USSR.

WESTERN EUROPE—21 Army Group: In Br Second Army's 12 Corps area, 7th Armd Div reaches village of St Joost. 52d seizes Bocket and Waldfeucht (Germany) and Echterbosch (Holland). 43d Div attacks on right flank of corps in Germany, taking

Langfroich and relieving elements of 52d Div in Breberen. 12th Army Group: In U.S. First Army's XVIII Corps (A/B) area, 75th Div clears to SE edge of Grand Bois. 30th mops up to S edge of Bois de Born and Bois d'Emmels, last ridge before St Vith. 7th Armd Div attacks S toward St Vith through Ondenval defile, with Deidenberg and Born as immediate objectives: CCA drives beyond Deidenberg, but CCB, held up by mines and deep snow, is unable to take Born.

In U.S. Third Army's VIII Corps area, CCR of 11th Armd Div, finding that enemy has withdrawn from area E of Hardigny-Bourcy line, moves forward 2 miles, establishing line through Boeur, Wandesbourcy, and Bois aux Chênes. 17th A/B Div advances beyond Tavigny. In III Corps area, CCA of 6th Armd Div captures Moinet and Hill 510 to E. Elements of 358th Inf, 80th Div, meet heavy fire as they approach Derenbach and are forced to withdraw; N of Oberwampach a bn of 359th Inf captures Chifontaine and Allerborn. 328th Inf, 26th Div, establishes bridgehead across Wiltz R 2 miles S of Oberwampach. In XII Corps area, 4th Div, committing RCT 12 on left of RCT 8, continues attack N of the Sauer, clearing angle formed by junction of Sauer and Our Rivers, bypassing Longsdorf to gain positions just N and occupying Tandel. 5th Div takes Kippenhof, Brandenburg, and commanding ground near latter. 318th Inf, 80th Div, secures Burden without opposition. In XX Corps area, 1st Bn of 301st Inf, 94th Div, attacks toward Orscholz but is halted short; 302d clears fortifications and repels counterattacks. 95th Div decisively defeats counterattacks in Saarlautern bridgehead.

6th Army Group: In U.S. Seventh Army area, VI Corps starts orderly withdrawal to new defensive positions along Rothbach Rau-Moder R line at nightfall. 45th Div makes unsuccessful attempt to reach encircled 3d Bn, 157th Inf, elements of which infiltrate to main body. Some troops of 2d Bn, 314th Inf, escape from Drusenheim but rest of bn is reported missing in action.

Fr 1st Army opens offensive to eliminate Colmar Pocket, attacking with 1st Corps from the S. 1st Corps employs 2 divs (4th Moroccan Mtn Div on W and 2d Moroccan Inf Div on E) reinf by armor of 1st Armd Div along axis Cernay-Ensisheim. Weather conditions are poor and progress is so slow that initial corps objective, Ensisheim, is not reached until early February. In 2d Corps area, U.S. 28th Div completes relief of U.S. 3d Div and takes command of sector from Sigolsheim SW to Le Valtin. Corps prepares to join in offensive to reduce Colmar Pocket.

EASTERN EUROPE—East Prussia is being enveloped by Third and Second White Russian Fronts: Third takes Tilsit; Second, thrusting N toward East Prussia from Poland, gets elements across SW border near Tannenberg. First White Russian and First Ukrainian Fronts continue W in Poland toward Germany, former in general direction of Berlin and latter toward Silesia. In the Carpathians, Fourth Ukrainian Front takes Nowy Sacz in Poland and Bardejov, Presov, and Kosice (Kassa) in Czechoslovakia. Hard fighting is reported in Szekesfehervar region of Hungary, SW of Budapest, as Germans attempt to break through to the Danube.

BURMA-CHINA—While official Allied convoy from Ledo is waiting at Myitkyina, small truck convoy led by Lt Hugh A. Pock of Oklahoma reaches Kunming, China, via Teng-chung cutoff—hastily repaired but still very rough—completing 16-day trip from Myitkyina. This secondary route is of little practical value. Ch 9th Div on Salween front finds Wanting clear of enemy. Forward elements of Ch 38th Div (CAI) make patrol contact with Chinese of Y-force near Muse. U.S. 5332d Brig improves positions near Burma Road.

SWPA—Gen Eichelberger recommends to Gen MacArthur that 11th A/B Div make a single landing on Luzon, at Nasugbu Bay, instead of the two (Nasugbu Bay and Tayabas or Balayan Bays) originally contemplated. This would solve problems of air and naval support.

LUZON—In U.S. Sixth Army area, Gen Krueger asks Allied Air Forces not to bomb bridges S of the Agno since they are needed to speed drive on Manila. In XIV Corps area, 160th Inf of 40th Div gets forward elements to within 4 miles of Tarlac; 8th begins to follow 160th southward. Forward elements of 37th Div reach Victoria, which is undefended, and patrol beyond there. In I Corps area, 25th Div, with 27th Inf on right and 161st on left, opens drives on Asingan and San Manuel. 169th Inf (less 2d Bn) of 43d Div attacks Mt Alava and gets elements to crest. 103d gains positions on S part of Hill 600.

CAMOTES—7th Div TF is reconnoitering Pacijan I. without incident.

MINDORO—Bulk of 2d Bn, 19th Inf, moves to Bulalacao to destroy enemy in that region in patrol actions.

21 January

WESTERN EUROPE—21 Army Group: In Br Second Army's 12 Corps area, 52d Div clears villages of Hontem and Selsent; moves into Braunsrath without opposition. 43d Div finds Schierwaldenrath clear.

12th Army Group: In U.S. First Army's VII Corps area, 84th Div takes over former 83d Div–3d Armd Div sector and prepares to attack toward Gouvy-Beho region, between Houffalize and St

Vith. Patrols find Rogery free of enemy. In XVIII Corps (A/B) area, 75th Div clears rest of Grand Bois. 7th Armd Div overcomes house-to-house opposition in Born. 508th Para RCT takes over Deidenberg-Eibertingen area. In V Corps area, 1st Div meets stiff opposition as it attempts to improve positions NE of Schoppen; establishes outposts and sends patrols through Bambusch woods in region S of Schoppen.

In U.S. Third Army's VIII Corps area, shift in corps boundaries puts Bois de Rouvroy, NE of Buret, within corps zone and transfers Bastogne to juris-diction of III Corps. New boundaries run on the N through Laroche and Ourthe to Thommen and on the S through Neufchâteau, Bastogne, and Holdingen to Thommen. Elements of CCA, 11th Armd Div, reach Buret. 17th A/B Div continues advance NE of Tavigny. III Corps advance to NE gains momentum. 6th Armd Div clears Crendal, Troine, Baraques de Troine, Lullange, Hoffelt, and Hachiville. 90th Div's 358th Inf takes Derenbach, Hill 480, and Boevange-les-Clervaux; 359th secures Hill 520, Hamiville, and Wincrange. Some 26th Div units across Wiltz R in vicinity of Winseler clear Noertrange and Bruhl; others, in conjunction with 6th Cav Gp, enter Wiltz and mop up pockets of resistance. In XII Corps area, 4th Div captures Longsdorf but is unable to take Fuhren. 5th secures Landscheid and Lipperscheid. Renewing offensive, 80th Div's 318th Inf takes Bourscheid and Welscheid and woods between these and the Sauer; 317th is unable to get units across river to N of Bourscheid but takes Kehmen. In XX Corps area, 94th Div halts attack on Orscholz because of heavy casualties to 1st Bn, 301st Inf; 302d Inf holds Tettingen and Nennig against strong counterattack.

6th Army Group: In U.S. Seventh Army's XV Corps area, CCB of 10th Armd Div closes in area NE of Fenétrange. In VI Corps area, main body of corps completes withdrawal to new MLR, along line Althorn-Rothbach-Niedermodern-Haguenau-Bischwiller. 79th Div's OPL in Camp d'Oberhoffen area is pushed back by enemy.

EASTERN EUROPE—Fanning out from Tilsit, NE East Prussia, Third White Russian Front reaches Kurisch Sound on right and takes Gumbinnen on left; Second White Russian Front presses steadily N toward East Prussia on wide front and takes East Prussian town of Tannenberg. First White Russian and First Ukrainian Fronts continue W in Poland; latter crosses into Silesia, Germany, in region W of Czestochowa and takes several Silesian towns.

BURMA—In ALFSEA's 15 Corps area, brig of Ind 26th Div, after co-ordinated air and naval bombardment, lands on N coast of Ramree I. and captures Kyaukpyu. Ind 25th Div now holds all of Myebon Peninsula.

In NCAC area, U.S. 5332d Brig establishes perimeter defenses along W side of Burma Road but does not block the road; makes contact with 114th Regt of Ch 38th Div, which is to block road to N.

FORMOSA-RYUKYUS-PESCADORES—TF 38 makes powerful air attacks on shipping and airfields at Formosa, Sakishima Gunto, Okinawa, and the Pescadores. About 10 oilers and freighters are sunk and other vessels are damaged. At the airfields some 100 grounded planes are destroyed. Japanese counter with determined attacks on the warships, severely damaging the CV *Ticonderoga*. Fighters of Fifth Air Force make their first attack on Formosa.

LUZON—In U.S. Sixth Army area, XIV Corps drives beyond day's objective, line Tarlac-Victoria, and is ordered to continue toward Clark Field, although its E flank is exposed for over 20 miles. 160th Inf, 40th Div, takes Tarlac without opposition; elements push on to San Miguel. Advance elements of 37th Div reach vicinity of La Paz. I Corps is to seize line Victoria-Guimba in strength while protecting left flank of XIV Corps. 103d Inf of 43d Div, continuing assault on Hill 600, gains military crest. 158th and 63d Regts finish clearing Blue Ridge, near Amlang. 63d Inf is then withdrawn into corps reserve. 172d Inf, clearing heights commanding Rosario, is reinf by Philippine 2d Bn, 121st Inf.

22 January

WESTERN EUROPE—21 Army Group: In Br Second Army's 12 Corps area, 7th Armd Div fights indecisively near Montfort. 52d Div takes Laffeld and Obspringen. Waldenrath falls to 43d Div.

12th Army Group: In U.S. First Army's VII Corps area, 84th Div and attached elements of 3d Armd Div seize Gouvy and Beho. 4th Cav Gp sector is pinched out. In XVIII Corps (A/B) area, 75th Div takes Commanster and woods to NE. 30th Div secures Hinderhausen, Sart-lez-St Vith, Ober Emmels, and Nieder Emmels. 7th Armd Div's CCA, assisted by task force of CCB, clears Hunningen. Rcn party from 38th Armd Inf Bn is prevented by roadblock from entering St Vith.

In U. S. Third Army's VIII Corps area, units of CCA, 11th Armd Div, enter Bois de Rouvroy and cross Luxembourg border without encountering enemy. 17th A/B Div occupies Steinbach and Limerle. In III Corps area, CCB of 6th Armd Div enters Basbellain; CCA takes Asselborn and Weiler. 359th Inf of 90th Div occupies Donnange, Deiffelt, Stockem, and Rumlange; elements of 357th move to Boxhorn and Sassel. 26th Div and 6th Cav Gp finish clearing Wiltz and secure Eschweiler, Knaphoscheid, and Kleinhoscheid. 28th Cav Sq proceeds through Weicherdange. In XII Corps area, 4th Div gains ground along W bank of Our R and takes Walsdorf but is still unable to clear Fuhren. 5th Div continues N with 10th Inf on right and 11th on left, taking Gralingen and high ground E of Nachtmanderscheid. 80th Div elements move into Wiltz area, using routes cleared by 6th Cav Gp. In XX Corps area, enemy regains about half of Nennig from 302d Inf of 94th Div.

6th Army Group: In U.S. Seventh Army's XV Corps area, 101st A/B Div closes in Drulingen-Sarraltroff region. VI Corps improves defenses and regroups. Because of enemy concentrations, OPL of 103d Div is withdrawn from Offwiller and outposts of 79th Div pull back to Moder R line.

In Fr 1st Army area, 2d Corps begins southward drive on Colmar, in region between Sélestat and Ostheim, which, in conjunction with 1st Corps' northward attack, is aimed at enveloping and destroying the Colmar Pocket. The 3 assault divs—U.S. 3d, 5th Armd, and 1st Moroccan Inf—are protected by Fr 2d Armd Div, holding Rhine Plain. U.S. 3d Div leads off, attacking at 2100 SE across Fecht R at Guemar. To W, U.S. 28th Div conducts raids, night 23-23.

EASTERN EUROPE—In East Prussia, Third White Russian Front takes Insterburg; Second White Russian Front seizes Allenstein and Deutsch-Eylau. In Poland, First White Russian Front captures Inowroclaw, threatening Bromberg, and Gniezo, on road to Posen. First Ukrainian Front, fighting astride Polish-Silesian border, seizes Silesian towns of Konstadt and Gross Strehlitz.

ITALY—15th Army Group: U.S. Fifth Army issues instructions for training program to be undertaken in preparation for spring offensive.

BURMA—In ALFSEA's 15 Corps area, 3d Cdo Brig lands at Kangaw, on Arakan front, after preparatory bombardment. Enemy soon reacts sharply, since forces along coast to S are being cut off.

In Br Fourteenth Army's 33 Corps area, Ind 20th Div takes Monywa (enemy's last port on the Chindwin), which has been defended vigorously for several days, and Myinmu, on the Irrawaddy. In 4 Corps area, Ind 7th Div, which has replaced E African 28th Brig in line, takes Tilin.

In NCAC area, CAI becomes responsible for clearing rest of Burma Road as Chiang Kai-shek orders Chinese Expeditionary Force to assemble N of Sino-Burmese border. At night, Gen Sultan announces that the Burma Road is open. U.S. 5332d Brig gets patrols to ridge across Burma Road, but is refused permission to do more than patrol and interdict traffic on the road.

CHINA—Japanese, between 19th and present time, have occupied key bridges and tunnels on Canton-Hankow RR.

FORMOSA—Philippine-based heavy bombers of Fifth Air Force begin daylight strikes on Formosa, attacking Heito air base.

SWPA—Gen MacArthur orders U.S. Eighth Army to land one RCT of 11th A/B Div on Luzon at Nasugbu for reconnaissance in force. If Tagaytay Ridge can be taken with ease, the entire div will then concentrate there and patrol to N and E. The landing will be made on 31 January

LUZON—Allied planes begin preinvasion bombardment of Corregidor. Airstrip at Mangaldan becomes operational.

In U.S. Sixth Army's XIV Corps area, forward elements of 40th Div reach Capas, N of Bamban. 37th Div extends its right flank to San Miguel to maintain contact with 40th Div and with left flank elements takes La Paz. Scattered contacts have been made recently with enemy in Moncada and La Paz areas. In I Corps area, 27th Inf of 25th Div continues toward Asingan against little opposition. 161st, driving on San Manuel, takes hill NW of objective. 2d Bn of 169th Inf, 43d Div, with tank and arty support, renews attack on Hill 355 but is unable to take it.

MINDORO—3d Bn, 21st Inf, moves by sea to N coast at Estrella.

RYUKYU IS.—Planes of TF 38 photograph and attack Ryukyu targets including Okinawa and neighboring islands. After this action, TF 38 returns to Ulithi, arriving there the 25th.

23 January

WESTERN EUROPE—21 Army Group: In Br Second Army's 12 Corps area, 7th Armd Div is still held up by strong opposition near Montfort. 52d Div has little difficulty in clearing Aphove area and begins assault on Heinsberg. 43d Div takes Straeten and Scheifendahl with ease.

12th Army Group: In U.S. First Army's VII Corps area, 84th Div seizes Ourthe and is clearing commanding ground between there and Beho. In XVIII Corps (A/B) area, St Vith falls to 7th Armd Div: CCB attacks S through CCA and overcomes moderate resistance within the town. SW of St Vith, 75th Div takes Maldingen and Braunlauf while 30th secures Weisten, Crombach, and Neundorf.

In U.S. Third Army's VIII Corps area, CCA of 11th Armd Div establishes liaison with 17th A/B Div and continues patrolling in vicinity of Bois de Rouvroy. In III Corps area, CCA of 6th Armd Div takes Biwisch and Trois Vierges. CT Miltonberger (RCT 134, 35th Div, attached), passing through CCB, occupies Basbellain and heights to SE. 359th Inf, 90th Div, clears Bischent woods; 357th attacks across Clerf R, seizing hills on either side of draw W of Hupperdange. 1st Bn of 357th captures Binsfeld. 28th Cav Sq clears Eselborn and makes contact with enemy at Clerf and Drauffelt. Night 23-24, elements of TF Fickett attempt to take Clerf and Mecher and gain latter. In XII Corps area, Fuhren falls to 4th Div. 5th Div elements reach vicinity of Nachtmanderscheid and Hoscheid but are unable to secure either of these. On 80th Div front, 317th Inf, attacking NE toward the Clerf, reaches high ground just W of Wilwerwiltz and Enscherange; 319th crosses the Wiltz at Merkols and Kautenbach and clears Merkols. 346th Inf of 87th Div occupies Wasserbillig, at confluence of Sauer and Moselle Rivers. In XX Corps area, Germans, mounting strong tank-infantry counterattacks against 94th Div, regain Berg, but 302d Inf, employing attached bn of 376th bolstered by elements of CCA, 8th Armd Div, recaptures Nennig while 3d Bn, 302d, holds Wies and helps close gap between there and Nennig. 3d Cav Gp is given new sector between 94th and 95th Divs.

6th Army Group: In U.S. Seventh Army's VI Corps area, enemy forces left flank of 103d Div back past Rothbach.

In Fr 1st Army's 2d Corps area, 1st Moroccan Div crosses Ill R between Illhaeusern and Illwald, to N of U.S. crossing site. Supporting vehicles use bridge at Illhaeusern, though that town is not completely cleared for several days. U.S. 3d Div continues S toward Canal de Colmar: 7th Inf clears Ostheim; 30th crosses Ill R and reaches outskirts of Holtzwihr, but supporting armor is unable to cross and infantry is forced back to river line at Maison Rouge. Elements of 254th Inf, attached to 3d Div, drive to Weiss R line near Sigolsheim.

EASTERN EUROPE—In NE East Prussia, Third White Russian Front captures Wehlau, between Insterburg and Koenigsberg. Second White Russian Front captures Ortelsburg and progresses toward Elbing; in N Poland, seizes Brodnica and Lipno. Polish cities of Bromberg and Kalisz fall to First White Russian Front. First Ukrainian Front reaches Oder R line near Breslau (Silesia) on 37-mile front. Germans fighting toward the Danube in Hungary force Russians from Szekesfehervar. Second Ukrainian Front has gone on the offensive N of Miskolc and in conjunction with Fourth Rumanian Army takes a number of Czechoslovakian towns and communities.

BURMA—In NCAC area, convoy from Ledo starts forward from Myitkyina toward China. Continuing S along the Irrawaddy, 29th Brig of Br 36th Div reaches Twinnge.

LUZON—In U.S. Sixth Army's XIV Corps area, 160th Inf of 40th Div runs into opposition at Bamban but secures the town, airfield, and crossing site over Bamban R. Moving to left of 160th, 108th seizes Concepcion. Rcn elements S of Concepcion drive off enemy force at Magalang. In I Corps area, 2d Bn of 169th Inf, 43d Div, continues to meet strong resistance on Hill 355. From Hill 600, 3d Bn of 103d Inf moves back to Pozorrubio; 2d Bn advances to Bobonan. 172d Inf gains ridge at W edge of Pugo Valley.

CAMOTES Is.—7th Div TF clearing Poro I. runs into opposition on Hill 854.

24 January

WESTERN EUROPE—21 Army Group: In Br Second Army's 12 Corps area, 7th Armd Div overruns Weerd, Aandenberg, and Montfort. 52d Div completes capture of Heinsberg; occupies Haaren without opposition. 43d Div clears Schleiden and Uetterath.

12th Army Group: In U.S. First Army area, VII Corps is pinched out as 84th Div clears rest of its zone. In XVIII Corps (A/B) area, 75th Div takes Aldringen, concluding its Salm R drive. 30th Div improves positions E of Neundorf. CCB, 7th Armd Div, is clearing region S and SE of St Vith. In V Corps area, 1st Div, renewing offensive, advances steadily against moderate resistance: 16th Inf clears Bambusch woods; 18th captures Moderscheid; 26th takes Buellingen-Butgenbach-St Vith road junction at N edge of the Richelsbusch and continues SW on Buellingen-St Vith road.

In U.S. Third Army area, VIII Corps, instead of being pinched out as anticipated, receives additional territory on its right flank as advance elements approach St Vith. 17th A/B Div takes over the new region while continuing advance toward Thommen and Landscheid. In III Corps area, as direction of corps attack changes from NE to E, CCA of 6th Armd Div secures area within Trois Vierges-Wilwerdange-Binsfeld triangle and takes Holler and Breidfeld. Elements of 26th and 90th Divs become responsible for sector along W bank of Clerf R formerly held by TF Fickett. 90th Div repels predawn attack NE of Binsfeld; supporting armor crosses river at Trois Vierges and reaches Binsfeld; 359th Inf attacks across river to area N of Urspelt. 26th Div crosses river SE of Weicherdange and organizes on high ground. In XII Corps area, 4th Div consolidates along W bank of Our R from Vianden to confluence of Our and Sauer Rivers. 5th Div clears village NW of Vianden; also clears Nachtmanderscheid, and Hoscheid. 80th Div completes capture of Kautenbach and takes Alscheid and Enscherange. In XX Corps area, 94th Div, though supported by assault guns of 8th Armd Div, is unable to clear Berg but gains small bridgehead through AT obstacles. Scheduled attack through Berg by CCA, 8th Armd Div, has to be postponed.

6th Army Group: In U.S. Seventh Army's VI Corps area, enemy forces outpost of 45th Div from Saegmuhl. 103d Div repels German attempts to penetrate MLR at Bischoltz and Muhlhausen but is forced to readjust its OPL. In 79th Div sector, Germans attack across the Moder between Neubourg and Schweighausen, night 24-25, penetrating 222d Inf's MLR and seizing W portion of Schweighausen.

In Fr 1st Army's 2d Corps area, Fr and U.S. troops fight to expand Ill R bridgehead. French are stopped by enemy tanks concealed in woods near Elsenheim. U.S. 3d Div continues toward Canal de Colmar; 7th Inf moves S toward Houssen; taking over from battered 30th Inf, 15th Inf attacks from Maison Rouge and reaches edge of woods near Riedwihr.

EASTERN EUROPE—Berlin reports Soviet offensive in Latvia. Third and Second White Russian Fronts make further progress in East Prussia. In German Silesia, First Ukrainian Front overruns industrial centers of Oppeln (on the Oder) and Gleiwitz; N of Breslau, elements clear Trachenberg and, across Polish border, Rawicz.

ITALY—15th Army Group: In U.S. Fifth Army's II Corps area, 88th Div reenters line after brief rest, relieving 91st Div.

BURMA-CHINA—Ch New First Army commander promises Brig Gen Robert M. Cannon, NCAC chief of staff, to open Burma Road by 27th. Salween campaign comes to an end as Gen Wei's Chinese Expeditionary Force halts to await relief by CAI. Negotiations between Chinese Nationalists and Chinese Communists, broken off since 16 December, are resumed.

LUZON—In U.S. Sixth Army's XIV Corps area, 160th Inf of 40th Div comes up against enemy's OPLR on hills generally W of Bamban; takes one hill. 145th Inf of 37th Div gains line from Concepcion SW to Bamban R. In I Corps area, 161st Inf of 25th Div begins assault on San Manuel and against firm opposition gains toehold within the barrio. 43d Div regroups for coordinated effort on 25th to clear heights dominating roads in Pozorrubio-Sison-Rosario-Camp One area. Stark Force consists of 103d and 169th Regts and 3d Bn of 63d. Yon Force is formed of 63d, less 3d Bn. RCT 158 and 172d Inf are designated MacNider Force. 2d Bn, 169th Inf, reaches crest of Hill 355. Elements of 158th Inf begin assault on ridge NW of Cataguintingan; enemy is firmly entrenched on the ridge.

MINDORO—2d Bn, 21st Inf, moves into Calapan.

VOLCANO IS.—Iwo Jima is target for coordinated air-naval bombardment. B-29's of XXI BC, on training mission, and B-24's of Seventh Air Force concentrate on airfields and shipping. Naval bombardment, by warships of TG 94.9, is curtailed sharply by deteriorating weather conditions. No interception is met over target.

25 January

WESTERN EUROPE—21 Army Group: In Br Second Army's 12 Corps area, 7th Armd Div captures Linne and Putbroek and continues NE toward river line. 52d Div takes Kirchhoven without opposition and patrols toward Wurm R. 43d Div reaches the Wurm between Heinsberg and Randerath; patrols find Horst and Randerath clear.

12th Army Group: In U.S. First Army's XVIII Corps (A/B) area, CCB of 7th Armd Div consolidates in immediate vicinity of St Vith while CCA and RCT 424 take Wallerode and Medel, respectively. In V Corps area, 1st Div's 16th Inf gains Amblève and Mirfeld with ease; 18th advances from Moderscheid to Buellingen-St Vith road.

In U.S. Third Army's III Corps area, bulk of corps is now across Clerf R, attacking E toward ridge road known as "Skyline Drive," the Luxemburg-St Vith road paralleling Our R. CCB, 6th Armd Div, gains positions astride Weiswampach-Huldange road. 359th Inf, 90th Div, takes Hupperdange and Grindhausen; 357th seizes Heinerscheid and Lausdorn. 26th Div's 101st Inf, together with elements of 6th Cav Gp, occupies Clerf; 328th Inf takes Reuler and Urspelt. In XII Corps area, RCT 11 of 5th Div continues N, taking Merscheid. 317th Inf, 80th Div, clears Wilwerwiltz and establishes bridgehead across the Clerf; captures Pintsch, E of the river. In XX Corps area's 94th Div zone, 8th Armd Div TF takes Berg; elements of 302d Inf enlarge gap through AT defenses.

6th Army Group: In U.S. Seventh Army area, XV Corps assumes command of XXI Corps sector and troops (106th Cav Gp, 275th and 276th Regts of TF Herren, and 10th Armd Div less CCB). In VI Corps area, Germans penetrate 103d Div positions, reaching Schillersdorf and Nieffern, and force back OPL from Kindwiller. 103d Div restores MLR between Muhlhausen and Schillersdorf. As result of enemy penetration on left of 79th Div line, TF Wahl is reorganized to consist of 222d Inf, 314th Inf, 232d Inf, CCB of 14th Armd Div, the Rcn Tr, and elements of 781st Tank Bn; force clears Schweighausen and part of Bois de Ohlungen. Germans attack across the Moder between Haguenau and Kaltenhouse in sector of 242d Inf but are driven back across river.

In Fr 1st Army area, U.S. XXI Corps Hq and Hq Co is attached to army. In 2d Corps area, French make slow progress in Elsenheim woods, where armor is held up by enemy tanks. U.S. 3d Div's 7th Inf, assisted by armor, enters Houssen; 15th renews attack on Riedwihr and gets elements into town late at night; 254th, relieved along Weiss R by U.S. 28th Div, attacks toward Jebsheim.

EASTERN EUROPE—Third and Second White Russian Fronts are compressing German pocket in East Prussia. First Ukrainian Front takes Ostrow, SW of Kalisz in Poland, and Oels, in German Silesia. Berlin reports that Russians are attempting to cross the Oder at Steinhau and between Gleiwitz and Brieg.

BURMA—In ALFSEA area, Gen Leese orders 15 Corps to develop air bases at Akyab and Kyaukpyu; open Taungup-Prome road and secure bridgehead at Taungup; clear rest of Arakan coast. W African 82d Div, driving S toward Kangaw, occupies Myohaung.

In NCAC area, 113th Regt of Ch 38th Div attacks to finish opening Burma Road. Ch 30th Div is to concentrate in Hosi-Namhpakka area.

CHINA—Gen Wedemeyer informs Chiang Kai-shek that he is sending Gen McClure to Kunming to head Chinese Combat Command.

JAPAN—Tokyo orders *China Expeditionary Forces* to concentrate on seacoast and in N China rather than to move into interior.

LUZON—In U.S. Sixth Army's XIV Corps area, while 160th Inf of 40th Div is working on enemy positions on hills W of Bamban, 108th moves forward to assist with local attacks on scattered pockets. 37th Div, while protecting E flank of corps, begins pushing its right flank southward: 145th Inf takes Mabalacat East Airfield and reconnoiters S to Mabalcat. In I Corps .area, toad Inf of 43d Div takes Hills 600 and 800, bypassing Hill 700. 169th clears Hill 1500, and 3d Bn of 63d Inf takes Bench Mark Hill to N. 158th continues efforts to gain ridge NW of Cataguintingan. 72d takes Hill 900, overlooking Highway 11, which leads to Baguio.

U.S.—Gen Joseph W. Stilwell is assigned as commander of Army Ground Forces, succeeding Lt Gen Ben Lear, who has been named deputy commander to Gen Eisenhower.

26 January

WESTERN EUROPE—21 Army Group: In Br Second Army area, 12 Corps successfully concludes Operation BLACKCOCK. Small enemy bridgehead remains at Vlodrop, but no immediate effort is to be made to eliminate it.

In U.S. Ninth Army area, XIII Corps' 102d Div and attached 11th Cav Gp attack, night 25-26, and clear Brachelen-Himmerich-Randerath triangle W of the Roer against negligible resistance.

12th Army Group: In U.S. First Army's XVIII Corps (A/B) area, 7th Armd Div improves positions near St Vith; attached RCT 424 clears Meyerode.

In U.S. Third Army's VIII Corps area, corps elements advance NE into region N of Weiswampach as enemy continues withdrawal behind West Wall. 17th A/B Div, now beyond Wattermal (Belgium) is replaced by 87th Div, whose 376th Inf takes Espeler. Corps zone widens several miles to S to include 90th Div positions formerly held by 6th Armd Div (III Corps) E of Lausdorn. 90th Div occupies Lieler. In III Corps area, 90th Div and 6th Armd Divs exchange zones after CCB of 6th Armd takes Weiswampach. 17th A/B Div is taking up positions within corps zone. 26th Div's 328th Inf secures Fischbach; 101st clears Marnach and high ground E of Clerf and Drauffelt. In XII Corps zone, 4th Div is being withdrawn from line. RCT 11 of 5th Div captures Hoscheiderdickt; 5th Cav Rcn Tr clears Schlindermanderscheid. 80th Div expands bridgehead across the Clerf: 317th Inf takes Lellin-gen and Siebenaler and reaches positions near Bock-holz. 76th Div takes over former 87th Div zone. In XX Corps area, elements of 94th Div and of attached 8th Armd Div clear Butzdorf and drive toward Sinz. 95th Div improves positions in Saarlautern bridgehead area.

6th Army Group: In U.S. Seventh Army's VI Corps area, 45th Div is virtually out of contact with enemy. Activity subsides on toad and 79th Div fronts. 103d clears enemy remnants from Schillersdorf and completely restores MLR. TF Wahl restores 79th Div MLR. 101st A/B Div closes in Hochfelden area.

In Fr 1st Army's 2d Corps area, 1st Moroccan Div is clearing Illhaeusern-Jebsheim road. 5th Armd Div prepares to attack toward Brisach. U.S. 3d Div makes substantial gains: 7th Inf clears Houssen and Rosenkranz; 15th takes Riedwihr; 254th gets elements into Jebsheim.

EASTERN EUROPE—Red Army drives salient between East Prussia and Danzig as Second White Russian Front captures Marienberg and reaches Gulf of Danzig NE of Elbing. Koenigsberg is being invested by Third White Russian Front. In Poland, Soviet forces are encircling Thorn and Posen. First Ukrainian Front seizes Hindenburg (Silesia).

ITALY—15th Army Group: U.S. Fifth Army outlines deceptive measures to be taken in order to keep enemy pinned down during winter lull.

BURMA—In ALFSEA's 15 Corps area, Royal Marines from East Indies Fleet invade Cheduba I., SW of Ramree I., with support of naval aircraft.

In NCAC area, Ch 38th Div troops, working along Burma Road, get to within 5 miles of Ch Y-Force.

LUZON—In U.S. Sixth Army area, Gen Krueger orders rapid drive on Manila. XIV Corps, in addition to securing Clark Field area, is to cross the Pampanga at Calumpit; reconnoiter S and SE to line Hagonoy-Malolos-Plaridel. I Corps is to continue attack on left and advance right flank S and SE; reconnoiter to Cabanatuan. In XIV Corps area, 40th Div develops enemy OPLR on hills W and SW of Bamban: 160th Inf clears Hills 636 and 600; 108th presses toward Hill 5. 37th Div's 145th and 148th Regts advance to general line Culayo-Magalang, taking Magalang and Clark Field Runway No. I, 1½ miles NW of Culayo. In I Corps area, 158th Inf of 43d Div finishes clearing ridge NW of Cataguintingan. Some elements of 172d secure Rosario; other elements are moving toward Udaio road junction.

MINDORO—Camina Drome is ready for use by heavy bombers. Enemy resistance in Bulalacao area comes to an end.

POA—Operation Plan CINCPOA 11-44 (Iwo Jima) becomes effective. Commander Fifth Fleet takes control of all forces assigned to Central Pacific Task Forces for invasion of Iwo Jima.

27 January

WESTERN EUROPE—21 Army Group: In U.S. Ninth Army's XIX Corps area, boundary change between Ninth and First Armies extends 78th Div sector southward to Gemund. Preparations are made to clear the new region.

12th Army Group: In U.S. First Army's XVIII Corps (A/B) area, CCB of 7th Armd Div is slowly clearing Bois de St Vith.

In U.S. Third Army's VIII Corps area, 87th Div occupies several towns in area S of St Vith. 90th continues to clear W bank of Our R; 358th Inf, attacking N across border of Luxembourg, secures Lascheid (Belgium). In III Corps area, 26th Div is being withdrawn from line, but elements clear Munshausen. In XII Corps area, RCT 11 of 5th Div takes Weiler and Wahlhausen while 5th Rcn Tr clears Consthum and Holzthum. A TF based on 317th Inf, 80th Div, clears high ground W of Hosingen and captures Bockholz, Neidhausen, Dorscheid, and Marburg, concluding div's drive. In XX Corps area, 94th Div elements drive to edge of Sinz but are forced back by heavy casualties.

6th Army Group: In U.S. Seventh Army area, VI Corps makes light contact with enemy. 101st A/B Div assumes control of Moder R sector from Schweighausen to 103d Div boundary. TF Linden (− 242d Inf) closes in Château Salins area and reverts to army reserve.

In Fr 1st Army's 2d Corps area, French clear Elsenheim road and forest and head for Jebsheim. U.S. 3d Div's 30th Inf takes Holtzwihr and Wickerswihr; 254th clears large portion of Jebsheim.

EASTERN EUROPE—White Russian troops overrun the Masurian Lake region of East Prussia and continue investment of Koenigsberg. In Poland, encirclement of Thorn and Posen by Red Army is completed. First Ukrainian Front makes progress in clearing industrial region of Upper Silesia. In central Czechoslovakia, Fourth Rumanian Army captures Dobsina.

BURMA—In NCAC area, blockade of China is broken as Ch 38th Div, assisted by arty and armor, links up with Y-Force troops on Burma Road, opening land route to China. Ch 30th Div, moving to Hosi-Namhpakka area to take up position to N of U.S. 5332d Brig, gets forward elements to village 3 miles W of the U.S. force. This leaves an escape gap for Japanese.

In Br Fourteenth Army's 4 Corps area, Pauk falls to Ind 7th Div.

CHINA—Gen Wedemeyer, having investigated the matter of negotiations with communist Chinese, informs Gen Marshall that his command has been told to support the Nationalist Government and that it has been forbidden to negotiate with communist Chinese without approval of Chiang Kai-shek.

LUZON—U.S. Sixth Army receives major reinforcements as 1st Cav Div, 32d Div, and 112th Cav RCT arrive at Lingayen Gulf. In XIV Corps area, continuing operations W of Bamban, 40th Div has secured Manila RR and Route 3 from Bamban S to Mantitang. 37th Div quickly takes Culayo and Dau and pushes on to Angeles, which is undefended. In I Corps area, as 27th Inf of 25th Div reaches Asingan without difficulty, 161st continues costly fighting at San Manuel. Damortis-Rosario road is opened with junction of 172d and 158th Regts at Cataguintingan, in 43d Div zone.

LEYTE—11th A/B Div (−RCT 511), U.S. Eighth Army, conducts limited rehearsal for invasion of Nasugbu, Luzon. The naval force, TG 78.2 (Adm Fechteler) then sails for target.

POA—Joint Expeditionary Force (−) for the Iwo Jima operation departs from Hawaii for the Marianas, completing movement by 5 February and resupplying in Marianas until 7 February.

28 January

WESTERN EUROPE—12th Army Group: U.S. First Army opens drive toward West Wall and Euskirchen before dawn. XVIII Corps (A/B) attacks NE with 1st Div on N and 82d A/B Div on S. 1st Div's 16th Inf takes Valender, 18th gains Heppenbach and Hepscheid, and 26th clears Richelbusch. 82d A/B Div attacks through 7th Armd Div with 325th Gli Inf on N and 504th Para Inf on S, clearing woods up to Wereth and taking Herresbach. 7th Armd Div concludes St Vith drive with reduction of stubborn hill positions in Bois de St Vith.

In U.S. Third Army's VIII Corps area, most of corps has reached Our R. 87th Div takes over St Vith sector. 4th Div enters line between 87th on N and 90th on S, occupying Burg Reuland-Maspelt sector. 90th Div's 358th Inf captures Weweler and Stoubach; 357th clears all but the river towns in its zone and reconnoiters for crossing sites near Oberhausen. In III Corps area, elements of 6th Armd Div make unsuccessful attack on Kalborn. TF Fickett maintains flank contact between 17th A/B Div and XII Corps. In XII Corps area, 80th Div assumes responsibility for former 4th Div zone. 5th Div continues to clear W bank of Our R and secures Putscheid. In XX Corps area, 94th Div improves positions slightly in limited attack.

6th Army Group: In Fr 1st Army area, U.S. XXI Corps assumes tactical control of new zone between Fr 2d and 1st Corps and has mission of assisting in reduction of Colmar Pocket by attacking toward Brisach and effecting junction with Fr 1st Corps, a task formerly given to Fr 2d Corps. U.S. 28th and 3d Divs are attached in place and XXI Corps is strengthened by attachment of Fr 5th Armd Div and U.S. 75th Div. On corps W, 28th Div maintains positions from Le Valtin to Ill R about 2 miles NE of Colmar; 3d Div is clearing region N of Canal de Colmar from its juncture with Ill R east to Wickerswihr; Fr 5th Armd Div is assembled in 3d Div zone; 75th Div CP opens at Ribeauville. 254th Inf (attached to 3d Div) is unable to take S part of Jebsheim. Fr 2d Corps has new mission of driving E to the Rhine along axis Guemar-Markolsheim.

EASTERN EUROPE—Germans yield Memel to First Baltic Front, and Soviet conquest of Lithuania is complete. Russians close ring about Koenigsberg and compress enemy pocket in central part of East Prussia with capture of Bischofsburg and Sensburg; enemy holds out in Elbing and exerts pressure NW of Allenstein. Thrusting toward Germany on broad front, Red Army troops take Pol border cities of Sepolno, Czarnkow, and Leszno and, across Silesian border, Guhrau. To the S, First Ukrainian Front completes capture of major industrial cities along border of Upper Silesia and Poland, taking Beuthen in Silesia and Katowice in Poland. In the Carpathians, Fourth Ukrainian Front drives to Poprad (Czechoslovakia).

ITALY—15th Army Group: In U.S. Fifth Army's IV Corps area, entire 10th Mtn Div is placed under TF 45 in order to provide it with experience in combat.

BURMA—In NCAC area, first convoy from Ledo resumes journey toward Kunming, crossing border of China. Ceremonies are held at Mu-se, and Generalissimo Chiang Kai-shek renames the road the Stilwell Road. U.S. 5332d Brig makes an unsuccessful limited attack in its zone.

LUZON—In U.S. Sixth Army's XIV Corps area, 129th Inf of 37th Div attacks W from Culayo area toward Clark Field and Ft Stotsenburg; although enemy's OPLR is soon encountered, takes 2 Clark Field runways and reaches SE corner of Ft Stotsenburg. Elements of 145th Inf move NW from Angeles to keep abreast 129th. 37th Rcn Tr patrol and elements of 148th Inf reach San Fernando. 160th Inf of 40th Div, working along Hill 636-Hill 620 ridge N of Bamban R, takes Hill 620 and drives 1,200 yards beyond; narrows its front as right flank comes under heavy opposition from enemy's MLR. In I Corps area, as 161st Inf finishes clearing San Manuel, 25th Div continues attack with 35th and 27th Regts, former on right, leaving 161st behind in San Manuel area.

MINDORO—19th Inf is concentrated in San Jose area, having completed offensive operations on Mindoro.

29 January

WESTERN EUROPE—12th Army Group: In U.S. First Army's XVIII Corps (A/B) area, 1st Div captures Buellingen and patrols toward Muerringen and Honsfeld; pinched-out 16th Inf is withdrawn as reserve. 82d A/B Div's 325th Gli Inf captures Wereth and is then passed through by 508th Para Inf, which takes Holzheim, Medendorf, and high ground near Eimerscheid.

U.S. Third Army launches attack to penetrate West Wall and protect First Army right flank. In VIII Corps area, 87th, 4th, and 90th Divs attack abreast from heights W of Our R. 345th Inf, 87th Div, captures Schlierbach and Setz, 347th closes in on Neidingen and Breitfeld. 8th Inf of 4th Div is held up near Lommersweiler, but 12th bypasses Hemmeres as it drives across Our R and advances into Elcherath. 90th Div, whose mission is to protect right flank of corps on E side of Our R, crosses river and German border: 357th Inf crosses near Oberhausen and takes Welchenhausen; 358th crosses near Stupbach and captures that town. III Corps is now on its objective, N-S ridge and road controlling the Clerf and Our valleys. 6th Armd Div patrols aggressively; on its left flank CT Miltonberger clears Kalborn. In XX Corps area, 26th Div takes over Saarlautern bridgehead sector from 95th Div.

6th Army Group: In Fr 1st Army's U.S. XXI Corps area, 3d Div crosses Canal de Colmar, 7th Inf reaching Bischwihr and 15th advancing to N edge of Muntzenheim; although enemy remnants hold out in Jebsheim, 254th Inf clears to canal S of there and thrusts toward Rhône-Rhine Canal E of the town.

EASTERN EUROPE—Germans continue stubborn defense of Koenigsberg and Elbing in East Prussia. First White Russian Front invades Pomerania, taking German towns of Schoenlanke and Woldenberg. In the Carpathian sector, Fourth Ukrainian Front gains Nowy Targ, on S border of Poland.

BURMA—In NCAC area, 114th Regt of Ch 38th Div, the closest unit to enemy withdrawing from Burma Road, suffers heavily from enemy attacks; a single Ch co blocking the road about 80 miles from Lashio is almost annihilated. This ends efforts to block the road. U.S. 5332d Brig is under heavy fire as it attempts to improve positions along W side of the road.

CHINA—Gen Ho, commander of ALPHA forces, presents plan in line with Gen Wedemeyer's views for 36-division offensive force to be divided among six area commands about Kunming. This plan is later adopted and with slight modification goes into effect in February. The 36-division force is swelled to 39 divisions with return of New First Army in June. Japanese occupy U.S. Fourteenth Air Force base of Suichwan.

MINDORO-MARINDUQUE—Western Visayan TF is dissolved. X Corps assumes responsibility for security of the islands. CG 24th Div arrives at San Jose on SW Mindoro to take control of all Army troops attached to corps. Fifth Air Force hq moves to Mindoro.

30 January

INTERNATIONAL CONFERENCES—Preliminary phase of ARGONAUT (Malta-Yalta) Conference begins at Malta with Anglo-American discussions. This portion of ARGONAUT is coded CRICKET.

WESTERN EUROPE—21 Army Group: In U.S. Ninth Army's XIX Corps area, 78th Div begins drive southward to clear to Roer R line along N edge of Monschau Forest. 310th and 311th Regts advance abreast, 310th taking Konzen and 311th gaining most of Kesternich and clearing Huppenbroich. CCA of 5th Armd Div, attached to 78th Div, secures Eicherscheid. 35th Div is attached to XVI Corps.

12th Army Group: In U.S. First Army area, V Corps enters attack to breach West Wall, employing 9th, 99th, and 2d Divs from N to S. 9th takes Rohren and reaches edge of Monschau Forest E of Alzen. 393d Inf of 99th Div advances to Elsenbuchel woods E of Elsenborn. 38th Inf, 2d Div, captures Wirtzfeld and Krinkelt and gets elements to Rocherath; 9th Inf units gain hill position between Wirtzfeld and Muerringen. In XVIII Corps (A/B) area, 1st Div captures last of 3 enemy-held towns W of German frontier in its zone: 18th Inf secures Honsfeld and Hunningen; 26th takes Muerringen. 82d A/B Div, employing 325th Gli Inf, 508th Para Inf, and 504th Para Inf, from N to S, continues NE to Honsfeld-Losheim RR line, clearing Eimerscheid and Lanzerath en route.

In U.S. Third Army's VIII Corps area, RCT 346 of 87th Div attacks Andler and Schonberg; 345th takes Rodgen and attacks Heuem. 4th Div makes little progress but does clear Lommersweiler and Hemmeres. Elements of 359th Inf, 90th Div, enter Steffeshausen and capture Auel; 358th secures Steinkopf; in 357th Inf sector, tanks cross ford constructed by engineers at Welchenhausen. III Corps units push forward to clear W bank of Our R, meeting light resistance except in S where 28th Cav Sq of TF Fickett and 193d Gli Regt of 17th A/B Div launch limited attacks to establish OPL.

6th Army Group: In Fr 1st Army's U.S. XXI Corps area, 28th Div takes limited objectives on E-W road N of Colmar. 3d Div is supported by Fr 5th Armd Div as attack continues. 7th Inf takes Bischwihr and Wihr-en-Plaine; 15th clears Muntzenheim, Fortschwihr, and Urschenheim; 254th overcomes final resistance in Jebsheim but is unable to reach junction of Colmar and Rhône-Rhine Canals. In 2d Corps area, main enemy body is withdrawing from corps front. 1st Moroccan Div clears woods E of Illhaeusern.

EASTERN EUROPE—Russians tighten ring around Koenigsberg and take Marienwerder in East Prussia. Red Army troops cross from Poland into Germany at a number of points NW of Bromberg and W of Posen and take Stolzenburg, 70 miles from Berlin.

BURMA—In ALFSEA's 15 Corps area, Ind 25th Div, having withstood intense opposition against its Kangaw bridgehead, goes on the offensive and takes Kangaw village. W African 82d Div continues S toward Kangaw from Myohaung.

In NCAC area, main body of Ch 38th Div is at junction of Ledo and Burma Roads directed toward Lashio. With Ch 30th Div (−) established N of Hpa-pen village between 114th Regt of Ch 38th Div and U.S. 5332d Brig, preparations are made for combined attack by Ch 30th Div and Americans to clear heights near Hpa-pen and thus block enemy escape from Burma Road, but attack is postponed until 2 February at request of Chinese.

CHINA—Gen Wedemeyer orders officers of China Theater not to negotiate with Chinese Communists.

LUZON—In U.S. Sixth Army area, Gen Krueger issues detailed orders for continuation of attack. XIV Corps is to drive S on Manila with 37th Inf and 1st Cav Divs to line Malolos-Plaridel-Cabanatuan. I Corps, reinf by 32d Div, will drive on San Jose. XI Corps is to move along Route 7, across base of Bataan Peninsula, to Dinalupihan-Hermosa area in order to make contact with XIV Corps. In XIV

Corps area, 129th Inf of 37th Div overruns Ft Stotsenburg and Sapangbato; begins attack on enemy's MLR on heights to W; right flank elements clear hills in Dolores area. Other elements of 37th Div patrol along Route 3 to within a mile of Calumpit. 160th Inf, 40th Div, battles enemy's MLR N of Bamban R, making slow and costly progress. 108th, in local advances, now holds Hill 5 and Thrall Hill, virtually completing reduction of pockets in that area. In I Corps area, 6th Div reconnoiters in force toward Talavera and Munoz. 1st Inf secures Talavera area without difficulty but 20th, in limited attack on Munoz, is pinned down about 1,000 yards short. 32d Div (−126th Inf, in army reserve) passes to corps control and is committed on left flank of 25th Div. XI Corps, which is transferred from command of Adm Struble to that of Gen Hall and from Eighth to Sixth Army, gains all of its initial objectives. RCT 34 of 24th Div, leading assault, quickly takes town of Subic and drives to Kalaklan R, where Japanese force defending Route 7 bridge is driven off; crosses the river and seizes Olongapo. With unopposed capture of Grande I. in an amphibious operation by 2d Bn of 151st Inf, 38th Div, corps gains control of Subic Bay.

Leyte-Samar—In U.S. Eighth Army area, XXIV Corps continues mopping up on Leyte while relief of X Corps by Americal Div is begun. 1st Bn of 182d Inf, Americal Div, is sent to Samar to relieve 3d Bn of 381st Inf, 96th Div, in Catbalogan area.

31 January

Western Europe—21 Army Group: In U.S. Ninth Army's XIX Corps area, 78th Div gains its objectives and makes contact with U.S. First Army at Widdau. 311th Inf takes rest of Kesternich and 310th captures Imgenbroich. CCA of 5th Armd Div, after clearing southward from Eicherscheid, is released by 78th Div.

12th Army Group: In U.S. First Army's V Corps area, 9th Div clears Widdau and drives into Monschau Forest to bend in Monschau-Schleiden road. 99th Div makes progress in Monschau Forest E of Elsenborn. 2d Div completes capture of Rocherath and continues NE. XVIII Corps (A/B) advances well into Buchholz Forest, where German border is crossed. 1st Div gets almost through forest near Neuhof. To the S, 82d A/B Div clears large portion of the forest, reaching positions a little short of line Neuhof-Losheim-Manderfeld.

In U.S. Third Army's VIII Corps area, in 87th Div sector, RCT 346 captures Andler and Schonberg; 345th takes Amelscheid, Heuem, and Alzerath; 347th occupies Laudesfeld. 4th Div clears Elcherath and Weppeler. 90th Div makes contact with enemy E of Our R: 359th Inf advances through Bei Auel and Auel, engages enemy in positions around Winterspelt and Wallmerath, then bypasses them to advance on Gros Langenfeld and cut main road from Winterspelt to Pronsfeld; 358th captures Heckhalenfeld.

6th Army Group: In U.S. Seventh Army's VI Corps area, 36th Div opens attack at 2100 on Oberhoffen-Drusenheim axis to clear region W of the Rhine to the S.

In Fr 1st Army's U.S. XXI Corps area, 3d Div is still assisted by Fr 5th Armd Div. 7th Inf overcomes resistance at Horbourg, on outskirts of Colmar, and Fr armor continues beyond the town; 15th Inf is unable to take Durrentzen; 254th Inf reaches Rhône-Rhine Canal W of Beltenzenheim. Attack of 75th Div through 3d Div, scheduled for this date, is postponed.

Eastern Europe—Continuing reduction of enemy pocket in East Prussia, Soviet forces clear Heilsberg and Friedland. Red Army drives spearhead to Jestrow in Pomerania, and in Brandenburg takes Landsberg Meseritz, Schwiebus, and Zuellichau. German garrison of Budapest continues to hold out in W part of city.

Burma—In NCAC area, plans for Sino-American attack on heights in Hpa-pen area on 2d continue, although Ch 30th Div wants it postponed until 3d. Elements of Br 36th Div moving SE toward Mongmit, reach Shweli R in Myitson area and send patrol across it.

Luzon—U.S. Sixth Army, holding in reserve 32d Div's 126th Inf, 13th Armd Gp (less 44th Tank Bn), and 112th Cav RCT, begins final phase of drive on Manila. In XIV Corps area, 129th Inf of 37th Div attacks toward hill mass—called Top of the World—about 1,300 yards from W edge of Ft Stotsenburg and gets halfway up forward slopes. 138th Inf seizes crossing sites over the Pampanga at Calumpit late in day. 1st Cav Div starts toward Manila from Guimba, employing 5th and 8th Cav Regts, each with a motorized sq spearheading. Preceding the motorized forces, Prov Rcn Sq crosses the Pampanga and takes Santa Rosa, S of Cabanatuan, without opposition. On right flank of corps, 40th Div is clearing mountains W of Clark Field and Ft Stotsenburg. In I Corps area, 20th Inf of 6th Div continues limited attack on Munoz but is unable to take it. Patrols of 25th Div find Umingan, div's next objective, strongly held by enemy. XI Corps, leaving RCT 34 to hold at Olongapo and keeping RCT 151 of 38th Div in reserve, begins drive across base of Bataan Peninsula with 152d and 149th Regts of 38th Div. 152d, taking Route 7, reaches vicinity of enemy position, called Zigzag Pass, beginning about 3 miles NE of Olongapo. 149th moves along trail to N without opposition.

[1 FEBRUARY 1945]

In U.S. Eighth Army area, 188th Gli Inf of 11th A/B Div lands on W coast of Luzon in Nasugbu area after naval gunfire bombardment; takes Nasugbu, Wawa, and Lian and drives inland toward Tagaytay Ridge without opposition. So successful is this operation that 187th Gli Inf is landed at once and Gen Eichelberger asks Fifth Air Force to drop 511th Para Inf on 2 February instead of on 3d.

CAMOTES—7th Div TF finishes clearing Poro I. and prepares to return to Leyte.

MINDORO—21st Inf (−) moves from NE Mindoro, where about 135 Japanese have been killed in Pinamalayan Calapan region, to San Jose area. Leaving platoon on Marinduque, Co D, 21st Inf, returns to Mindoro.

1 February

WESTERN EUROPE—21 Army Group: U.S. Ninth Army prepares for Operation GRENADE, large-scale offensive across the Roer. In XIII Corps area, 5th Armd Div is attached to corps. In XIX Corps area, 78th Div continues to mop up in Imgenbroich-Kesternich sector; CCA, 5th Armd Div, is detached and joins parent unit, to which it reverts.

12th Army Group: In U.S. First Army's V Corps area, 102d Cav Gp, protecting N flank and maintaining contact with Ninth Army, relieves elements of 9th Div in Rohren and Widdau. 9th, 99th, and 2d Divs (from N to S) continue offensive for dams on Roer and Urft Rivers. 9th Div drives eastward, taking road junction on Hofen-Harperscheid road about half way through Monschau Forest. 99th Div, after gaining objectives in Monschau Forest and being pinched out by 9th and 2d Divs, is withdrawn to reserve. 2d Div moves NE from Rocherath (Belgium) across German border to join 9th Div. In XVIII Corps (A/B) area, 1st Div, continuing attack through N part of Buchholz Forest with 26th Inf on left and 18th on right, drives E about 1,500 yards against scattered resistance. 82d A/B Div consolidates; 517th Para Inf is attached to it. Patrols of both assault divs probe West Wall defenses.

In U.S. Third Army area, VIII Corps continues attack to breach West Wall along the Schnee Eifel. On N, 347th Inf of 87th Div takes Manderfeld (Belgium) and Auw (Germany). 4th Div, in center, advances almost 4 miles into Germany to positions overlooking Bleialf: Urb and Muetzenich fall to 8th Inf and Ihlren, Schweiler, and Winterscheid to 12th. 90th Div gets into blocking position on S flank of corps: bn of 359th Inf captures Gros Langenfeld and 358th Inf takes Heckuscheid. III Corps maintains and improves defensive positions in Luxembourg along ridge between Our and Clerf Rivers; patrols to and across the Our. RCT 134, detached from 6th Armd Div, leaves to rejoin 35th Div. In XX Corps area, except for limited-objective attack by 94th Div, corps front is static. Elements of 1st Bn of 302d Inf, 94th Div, clear half of Campholz woods, SE of Tettingen.

6th Army Group: In U.S. Seventh Army area, XV Corps maintains and improves defensive positions. TF Harris (63d Div) is dissolved and 63d Div (−253d, 254th, and 255th Regts) is attached to corps. In VI Corps area, 36th Div continues toward the Rhine: 2d Bn of RCT 142 crosses the Moder and enters Oberhoffen, where indecisive fighting ensues. CCB, 14th Armd Div, is attached to 36th Div and makes diversionary attack E of Oberhoffen, withdrawing at dusk. 117th Cav Rcn Sq, attached to 36th Div, clears Stainwald woods, N of Gambsheim. Rest of corps front is static throughout February: activity is confined to aggressive defense of current positions, occasional raids across the Moder, and training.

Fr 1st Army continues operations against Colmar Pocket. 2d Corps, against disorganized resistance, completes task of clearing Rhine Plain from Erstein on N to Artzenheim on S; overruns Artzenheim. In U.S. XXI Corps area, 3d Div's 15th and 30th Regts, with Fr armor in support, drive S along Rhine-Rhône Canal toward Neuf-Brisach, reaching positions just N of that town. 75th Div, with 2 regts abreast, drives S toward Andolsheim from sector formerly held by 3d Div. 28th Div, on corps W flank, starts S toward Colmar at 2100. 1st Corps continues to clear region S of Thur R between Cernay and Ensisheim. Both Cernay and Ensisheim remain in enemy hands.

EASTERN EUROPE—Red Army continues reduction of enemy within East Prussia; in Poland, takes Torun communications center on the Vistula by storm and maintains pressure on encircled Posen; in Germany, invests Schneidemuehl, thrusts to Ratzebuhr, continues toward the middle Oder and Berlin; in Hungary, continues elimination of Budapest garrison.

BURMA—In NCAC area, main body of Br 36th Div starts crossing Shweli R in Myitson region under enemy fire.

LUZON—In U.S. Sixth Army's XIV Corps area, 1st Cav and 37th Inf Divs drive quickly southward toward Manila. Prov Rcn Sq of 1st Cav reaches Gapan. Elements of 5th and 8th Cav Regts cross the Pampanga N and S of Cabanatuan and clear most of that town. Motorized elements of 8th Cav reach Santa Rosa. 37th Div's 148th Inf drives down Route 3 to Labangan R; some elements then advance E toward Plaridel until stopped at Plaridel airfield while others continue down Route 3. To W, 145th Inf column takes Hagonoy without opposition. In I Corps area, 6th and 25th Divs attack E to cut Highway 5 at San Jose. 6th Div commits 1st and 3d Bns,

20th Inf, against Munoz but is still unable to enter. 27th Inf of 25th Div, assisted by 35th Inf, attacks toward Umingan and gets elements into the barrio. 32d Div, blocking southward movement of enemy from Cagayan Valley, gets elements to San Nicolas, SW entrance to Villa Verde Trail, which joins Highway 5 at Santa Fe. On N flank of corps, 43d Div and RCT 158 consolidate on hills and ridges commanding Damortis-Rosario-Pozorrubio road. In XI Corps area, 152d Inf of 38th Div, approaching Japanese MLR at Zigzag Pass, gains less than 1,000 yards. 149th, following trail (which bends sharply northward instead of paralleling Route 7), is about 4,000 yards N of Route 7.

In U.S. Eighth Army area, when 188th Inf of 11th A/B Div meets delaying opposition in defile between Mt Cariliao and Mt Batulao, short of Tagaytay Ridge, planned drop of 511th Para Inf on the ridge is postponed until 3d. Fifth Air Force planes from Mindoro support fighting.

MOROTAI—Japanese aircraft raid Morotai 82 times during period 12 September to date.

2 February

INTERNATIONAL CONFERENCES—British-American discussions of war strategy at Malta end.

WESTERN EUROPE—21 Army Group: In U.S. Ninth Army's XIX Corps area, 78th Div passes to operational control of V Corps, First Army, in place.

12th Army Group: In U.S. First Army's V Corps area, advance elements of 9th and 2d Divs emerge from Monschau Forest and head toward Dreiborn and Schleiden, respectively. 9th Div's 60th Inf, assisted by 39th, reaches high ground SW of Dreiborn; 47th Inf clears heights near Hammer. 2d Div's 9th Inf takes Schoneseiffen and Harperscheid; 23d, to rear, continues NE attack in Monschau Forest. 99th Div is transferred to XVIII Corps (A/B) but remains in place. In XVIII Corps (A/B) area, 1st and 82d A/B Divs, jumping off at 0400, overrun pillboxes, dragons' teeth, and other fortifications at West Wall. 1st Div emerges from Buchholz Forest near Ramscheid. Attacking through 505th Para Inf, 325th Gli Inf of 82d A/B Div breaches West Wall and takes Udenbreth and Neuhof; 504th Para Inf, following, gets about 2 miles SE of Neuhof. 30th and 84th Divs are detached from corps.

In U.S. Third Army's VIII Corps area, 87th Div gains assigned objectives in attacks that continue during night 2-3. On div left, 347th Inf takes Losheim during night 2-3; 346th attacks on div right at night and secures Krewinkel before dawn of 3d. 8th Inf, 4th Div, drives to high ground W of Radscheid; 12th gets elements of 2d Bn into Bleialf. 90th Div patrols and consolidates. In XII Corps' Both Div zone, TF Oboe (4th Armd Div −) clears Hosdorf, on W bank of Our R, in local attack. In XX Corps area, elements of 1st Bn of 302d Inf, 94th Div, continuing limited attacks, clear rest of Campholz woods.

6th Army Group: In U.S. Seventh Army's VI Corps area, 36th Div continues fight for Oberhoffen and attacks Rohrweiler. Helped by tanks and TD's, RCT 142 (−) clears S and SE part of Oberhoffen; CCB of 14th Armd Div pushes NE from Bischwiller to assist in Oberhoffen but is held up by enemy fire. Elements of RCT's 143 and 142 wade the Moder to make co-ordinated attack on Rohrweiler; capture the town and bridges to SE. Farther S, RCT 141 prepares to attack Offendorf and Herrlisheim; its movement along Weyersheim-Gambsheim road is slowed by floods.

In Fr 1st Army's U.S. XXI Corps area, 7th Inf of 3d Div, with tank support, drives S through Artzenheim astride highway between Rhine-Rhône Canal and Rhine R toward Biesheim, NE of Neuf-Brisach. 75th Div overruns Andolsheim and moves SE toward Neuf-Brisach. Upon reaching edge of Colmar, 28th Div pauses to let tanks of 5th Armd Div enter first; city is captured but mopping up continues.

BURMA—In NCAC area, Japanese force Br 36th Div to withdraw its small bridgehead across the Shweli. 124th Cav, U.S. 5332d Brig, takes heights in Hpa-pen area in sharp battle. 88th Regt, Ch 30th Div, gives little assistance.

FRENCH INDOCHINA—Gen Wedemeyer relays to Washington news that Japanese are ordering Fr forces to disarm and disperse. In response to Fr requests for help, U.S. Fourteenth Air Force gives some assistance, although China Theater boundary is not clearly defined and Indochina is believed to be within Chiang Kai-shek's China Theater.

LUZON—In U.S. Sixth Army's XIV Corps area, main assault forces of 1st Cav Div reach Sabang-Baliuag sector. Elements of 5th Cav move eastward to vicinity of Norzagaray. Patrols make contact with 37th Div elements near Plaridel and elements of 6th Div, I Corps, N of Cabanatuan. One column of 148th Inf, 37th Div, takes Plaridel while another reaches Bocaue and patrols toward Marilao. Some elements of 145th Inf drive through Malolos to San Juan and others to Bulacan. Forward elements of corps are on general line Marilao-Santa Maria-Norzagaray. 129th Inf of 37th Div completes its tasks in Ft Stotsenburg area and prepares to join in 37th Div's drive on Manila. 108th Inf, 40th Div, shifts S to replace 129th; 185th Inf takes over positions vacated by 108th on W flank of 40th Div. I Corps has advanced sufficiently by this time to insure safety of XIV Corps from enemy counterattacks from the E. While 20th Inf, 6th Div, continues struggle for Munoz without making much headway, other elements of div prepare for assault on San Jose, 63d Inf cutting Highway 5 NE of Munoz and 1st Inf seizing bridge crossing along Rizal–San Jose road. 25th Div pushes into Umingan where 27th Inf is left to mop up while 35th Inf continues E toward Lupao. 161st Inf begins wide enveloping movement S of Lupao. In XI Corps area, 38th Div's 152d Inf is pinned down by stiff opposition from Zigzag Pass. 149th, far to N, is out of contact with enemy and returns to Santa Rita; ordered to retrace its steps along trail, which leads toward Dinalupihan, does so without incident.

In U.S. Eighth Army area, 11th A/B Div drives to within 2 miles of W end of Tagaytay Ridge.

LEYTE—In XXIV Corps area, 77th Div concludes combat operations on the island. Americal Div is to relieve it for future operations on Okinawa. 7th Div's special TF returns to Leyte from the Camotes, leaving 2d Bn, 94th Inf (PA), to garrison Poro and Pacijan.

3 February

WESTERN EUROPE—21 Army Group: In U.S. Ninth Army area, the following divs are assigned to army: 30th, 83d, 2d Armd, 84th, and 95th. The first three are attached to XIX Corps; 84th Div is attached to XIII Corps; 95th Div is designated army reserve. In XVI Corps area, 35th Div completes assembly SE of Maastricht (Holland).

12th Army Group: In U.S. First Army's V Corps area, 1st Bn of 311th Inf, 78th Div, swims the flooded Roer at Dedenborn and captures that town. CCR, 7th Armd Div, is attached to 78th Div to participate in drive on Schwammenauel, important Roer R dam near Hasenfeld. Jumping off before dawn, 9th Div's 90th Inf overcomes house-to-house resistance in Dreiborn and seizes Herhahn; 47th clears Einruhr. 2d Div continues toward Schleiden: 9th Inf takes Berescheid and Ettelscheid: 23d captures Bronsfeld. In XVIII Corps (A/B) area 1st Div continues to battle West Wall obstacles and slightly improves positions NW of Ramscheid; patrols find Ramscheid free of enemy. RCT 395 of 99th Div is attached to 1st Div and moves into position for attack. 82d A/B Div withstands strong counterattacks and consolidates.

In U.S. Third Army area, VIII Corps is directed to attack SE to the Pruem. 87th Div consolidates and its Rcn Tr occupies Roth. 8th Inf, 4th Div, clears Halenfeld and Buchet; 2d Bn of 12th Inf completes capture of Bleialf. III Corps is assigned new N and S boundaries that increase its zone from about 7 to some 18 miles in width. Necessary reliefs are begun late in day.

6th Army Group: In U.S. Seventh Army's XV Corps area, TF Herren is dissolved and units are absorbed into 70th Div, which is attached to corps. In VI Corps area, RCT 142 of 36th Div continues to clear Oberhoffen until relieved there by CCB, 14th Armd Div. RCT 143, reinf by bn of 142d Inf, seizes Drusenheim woods but is unable to retain much of it. S of the Moder, RCT 143 takes 2 bridges and a road junction but is later forced to withdraw. RCT 141 attacks N from Stainwald across flooded terrain to S outskirts of Herrlisheim but is forced back by counterattack.

In Fr 1st Army's U.S. XXI Corps area, 3d and 75th Divs continue toward Neuf-Brisach. 7th Inf of 3d Div clears Biesheim against vigorous opposition. 75th Div makes slow progress in Forêt Domaniale. 12th Armd Div, attached to corps to speed drive S. from Colmar toward 1st Corps, attacks through 28th Div at Colmar. CCB seizes bridgeheads across Ill R in vicinity of Sundhoffen and Ste Croix en Plaine; CCR drives S astride Colmar–Rouffach road. 28th Div, upon completing mop-up of Colmar, joins Fr armor in blocking along the Vosges in region W and S of Colmar. 1st Corps finishes first phase of mission against Colmar Pocket—clearing S bank of Thur R between Cernay and Ensisheim; prepares to drive N across the Thur to make contact with U.S. XXI Corps. Wittelsheim and Pul-versheim are among towns cleared of enemy.

BURMA—Adm Mountbatten receives directive from CCS assigning the liberation of Burma as his first task and of Malaya as his next. Burma must be cleared with forces on hand unless reinforcements can be sent from Europe.

In NCAC area, 29th Brig of Br 36th Div loses contact with enemy in Twinnge area as it moves E toward Mongmit. 475th Inf, U.S. 5332d Brig, attacks to clear rest of Loi-kang ridge and makes substantial progress.

CHINA—Japanese seize Namyung.

LUZON—In U.S. Sixth Army area, Gen MacArthur orders Manila Bay reopened, a task that entails clearing Bataan, Corregidor, and S coast of the bay in Ternate area. In XIV Corps area, 1st Cav Div, when forward elements reach city limits of Manila, is given permission to enter and does so. 37th Div, whose progress is slower, is to clear narrow zone along waterfront. Slowed because they have to move on foot and cross numerous streams, forward elements of 37th Div are still short of Manila, at Meycauayan. 129th Inf arrives in Calumpit area. In I Corps area, 1st Inf of 6th Div pushes forward to positions S and SW of San Jose. 1st Bn of 35th Inf, 25th Div, is unable to take Lupao and 3d Bn prepares to join in attack. In XI Corps area, RCT 34, under corps control, takes over assault on Zigzag Pass from 152d Inf, 38th Div, but is up against Japanese MLR and makes little headway.

In U.S. Eighth Army area, 511th Para Inf of 11th A/B Div is dropped along Tagaytay Ridge. Drops are widely scattered, but paratroopers are unopposed and make contact with 188th Inf at W end of the ridge and seize road junction at E end. With the ridge secured, plans are made to employ 511th Inf in northward advance on Manila.

4 February

INTERNATIONAL CONFERENCES—U.S.-Br-Soviet conference (MAGNETO) opens at Yalta in the Crimea to consider Allied strategy and related political issues. This is second phase of ARGONAUT.

WESTERN EUROPE—21 Army Group: In U.S. Ninth Army's XVI Corps area, 35th Div starts relief of Br 52d Div. In XIII Corps area, 29th Div, occupying positions along the Roer before Juelich, is transferred in place from XIII to XIX Corps.

12th Army Group: Preparations are made for 12th Army Group to participate with 21 Army Group in large-scale offensive to the E, scheduled to open on 10 February.

U.S. First Army is instructed to attack in Dueren area in conjunction with Ninth Army on left and to assume aggressive defensive on right, halting drive on Euskirchen. In V Corps area, 311th Inf of 78th Div, attacking E from Kesternich shortly after midnight 3–4, takes Ruhrberg and high ground around it as a preliminary to main assault through West Wall fortifications for approaches to Schwammenauel Dam. 102d Cav Gp takes over defense of Dedenborn, Ruhrberg, and Einruhr. On 9th Div left, 47th Inf seizes Wollseifen and reaches Urft Lake, where end of Dam 5 is secured; 39th, on right, repels counterattack against Herhahn and pushes toward Gemund, taking Morsbach. Elements of 9th Inf, 2d Div, make limited attack to high ground between Ettelscheid and Scheuren. In XVIII Corps (A/B), 1st Div continues assault on West Wall. 395th Inf, committed on N, drives NE, past Hill 628 to wooded heights SW of Hellenthal; 26th takes Hollerath; 18th consolidates in Ramscheid area. 99th Div begins relief of 82d A/B Div. Para RCT 517, detached from 82d A/B Div and attached to 78th Div (V Corps), moves to Bergstein area.

U.S. Third Army units regroup as result of intercorps boundary changes and new missions. In VIII Corps area, while units on corps flanks consolidate and regroup, 4th Div, attacking with 8th Inf on N and 22d on S, breaches outer defenses of West Wall along the Schnee Eifel ridge NE of Brandscheid. 90th Div is relieved of positions on S flank of corps by elements of 6th Armd Div (III Corps) and 11th Armd Div: 6th Armd Div takes over zone W of Our R; CCR of 11th Armd Div begins relief of elements E of the Our at night. 90th Div prepares to help 4th in attack on. Brandscheid and to continue attack SE to Pronsfeld. III Corps completes series of reliefs made necessary by new boundaries and assumes responsibility for its enlarged zone. On N, elements of 90th Div are relieved in place by elements of 6th Armd Div. 6th Cav Gp, after being relieved of its zone on former S flank of corps by elements of 17th A/B Div, displaces S and relieves elements of 5th Div (XII Corps). Corps retains defensive mission. In XII Corps area, regrouping is begun in preparation for offensive across Our and Sauer Rivers through West Wall. 5th Div, relieved by 6th Cav Gp (III Corps), takes over new zone between 80th and 76th Divs and begins relief of 417th Inf, 80th Div, which is attached to it.

6th Army Group: In U.S. Seventh Army's VI Corps area, activity subsides on 36th Div front, where CCB of 14th Armd Div holds all but NW corner of Oberhoffen and elements of RCT's 143 and 142 clear Drusenheim woods.

In Fr 1st Army's U.S. XXI Corps area, 3d and 75th Divs improve positions near Neuf-Brisach, 3d in region between Rhine R and Rhine-Rhône Canal and 75th between Rhine-Rhône Canal and Ill R. GCB, 12th Armd Div, holds bridgeheads across the Ill until relieved by 109th Inf, 28th Div. CCA captures Hattstatt, on Colmar-Rouffach road, but CCR meets strong opposition NE of there and is unable to progress. 28th Div, assisted by Fr 10th Div, blocks along Fecht R on corps W flank. Fr 2d Armd Div is attached to corps with mission of driving S on E flank upon order. 1st Corps attacks N across flooded Thur R toward XXI Corps and makes rapid progress. 4th Moroccan Mtn Div, in the lead, overruns Guebwiller, on road to Rouffach, and reaches S edge of Rouffach after nightfall. On Thur R line, Cernay is found to be free of enemy and preparations are made for assault on Ensisheim.

ITALY—15th Army Group: In U.S. Fifth Army's IV Corps area, 92d Div begins limited attack to improve positions in Serchio Valley, employing. 366th Inf (−) W of the river and 365th Inf on E side. Attack recovers Gallicano, Castelvecchio, and Albiano from enemy with ease.

BURMA-CHINA—First convoy from Ledo, led by Gen Pick, makes triumphal entry into Kunming, China.

On NCAC front, 475th Inf of U.S. 5332d Brig finishes clearing Loi-kang ridge, from which most Japanese have withdrawn. Future action of the U.S. force is limited to patrolling and arty exchanges.

LUZON—In U.S. Sixth Army's XIV Corps area, elements of 1st Cav Div within Manila conduct local patrolling while awaiting arrival of reinforcements; attempt unsuccessfully to take Quezon Bridge across Pasig R. 2d and 3d Bns of 148th Inf, 37th Div, move into N part of Manila and make contact with cavalrymen. In I Corps area, 1st Inf of 6th Div, assisted by aircraft, seizes San Jose—Highway 5 gateway to Cagayan Valley—and blocks approaches. 63d Inf is unable to advance northward toward San Jose. 20th commits 3 bns against Munoz and receives strong fire support but is still unable to reduce this strongpoint. Attacking from N and S, 35th Inf of 25th Div reaches edge of Lupao, where enemy continues to hold out. Japanese forces on N and S Luzon are separated as elements of 161st Inf reach San Isidro. In XI Corps area, 34th Inf is unable to make progress against enemy positions at Zigzag Pass and is attached to 38th Div, which is to make strong effort on 5th.

U.S. Eighth Army begins drive on Manila from S. 511th Para Inf, motorized, of 11th A/B Div moves along Route 17 and then Route 1 to Paranaque, 4 miles from the city, where it encounters main enemy defenses S of the city.

5 February

WESTERN EUROPE—21 Army Group: In U.S. Ninth Army area, boundary between Ninth and First Armies is shifted N to general line Liége–Aachen–Cologne. In XIX Corps area, responsibility for corps zone passes to VII Corps, First Army, which takes control of 8th and 104th Divs in place. 113th Cav Gp is detached from 8th Div and attached to 29th.

12th Army Group: In U.S. First Army area, VII Corps begins move from billeting areas in Belgium to Roer R line in Germany. The relatively inactive new zone, formerly held by XIX Corps of Ninth Army, is defended by 104th Div on left and 8th Div on right. In V Corps area, 78th Div opens drive for Schwammenauel Dam at 0300. 309th Inf, on left, thrusts NE from vicinity of Rollesbroich to high ground N of Strauch-Steckenborn fortified zone, where it digs in to prevent enemy movement northward; on right, 2d Bn of 311th Inf advances toward Hechelscheid from Ruhrberg, but is slowed by rough terrain and opposition at Woffelsbach and stops a little short of objective; in center, attached CCR of 7th Armd Div attacks later in morning for Strauch and Steckenborn from the Witzerath-Kesternich road and secures both. 39th Inf, 9th Div, mops up toward Olef R and Gemund. 9th Inf, 2d Div, gets Co A into Scheuren; 38th Inf, committed at 0300, passes through 23d Inf and gains weak hold on Hellenthal. In XVIII Corps (A/B) area, 1st Div clears toward banks of Clef and Prether Rivers from Blumenthal southward until relieved at night by 99th Div. Having relieved 82d A/B Div before dawn, 99th Div is now responsible for entire corps zone; RCT 395 reverts to 99th Div and RCT 424, 106th Div, is attached. Upon relief, 1st Div (—RCT 16) and 82d A/B Div move to assembly areas at Aywaille and Salmchâteau (Belgium), respectively.

In U.S. Third Army's VIII Corps area, 22d Inf of 4th Div takes stubbornly defended crossroads in the Schnee Eifel NE of Brandscheid and from there sends column SW into Brandscheid, where strong opposition is overcome; another column moves E from the crossroads and clears high ground overlooking Sellerich. 8th Inf attacks NE along Schnee Eifel ridge and secures crossroads in Schlausen Bacher Wald. Farther NE on the Schnee Eifel ridge, some elements of 87th Div take crossroads SE of Kobscheid; others clear portion of Losheim-Pruem road near Krewinkel. 90th Div supports 4th Div attack on Brandscheid with demonstration against Habscheid and Hollnich. 11th Armd Div assumes responsibility for its portion of former 90th Div zone.

6th Army Group: In U.S. Seventh Army area, VI Corps regroups and continues toward the Rhine. 79th Div is relieved by 36th and 101st A/B Divs. 101st A/B takes over new zone that includes about half of 79th Div sector and extends front line eastward along S bank of the Moder. 103d Div occupies sector formerly held by 506th Para Inf of 101st A/B Div. On 36th Div front, 68th Armd Inf Bn of 14th Armd Div, attached to RCT 142, presses slowly toward NW edge of Oberhoffen. RCT 142 consolidates positions in Bois de Drusenheim and makes local gains despite heavy enemy fire. CCB (—), 14th Armd Div, moves to assembly area. 117th Cav Rcn Sq relieves RCT 141 of Zorn Canal outposts; patrols find Offendorf free of enemy.

In Fr 1st Army area, Colmar Pocket is cut in two as U.S. XXI and Fr 1st Corps make firm junction. Enemy remnants W of Ill R are isolated and offer but sporadic resistance. In U.S. XXI Corps area, CAA of 12th Armd Div, jumping off early in morning, drives quickly S from Hattstatt and enters Rouffach at 0512; shortly afterward, makes contact with 4th Moroccan Mtn Div of Fr 1st Corps, which had arrived at S edge of town earlier. CCR clears Herrlisheim-près-Colmar, NE of Hattstatt, and is relieved there by 28th Div. On W flank of corps, 28th Div improves positions along Ill R south of Colmar and along Fecht R west of Colmar. 75th Div makes important gains in region between Ill R and Rhine-Rhône Canal, overrunning Appenwihr, Hettenschlag, and Wolfgantzen. On corps E flank, 3d Div's 30th Inf starts S in region between Rhine-Rhône Canal and Rhine R, bypassing Neuf-Brisach, night 5–6; 1st Bn remains behind to reconnoiter Neuf-Brisach. 1st Corps effects junction with XXI Corps along line from Ill R at Oberentzen westward. 9th Colonial Div opens assault on Ensisheim and at 2230 enters the city.

EASTERN EUROPE—Red Army troops in Prussia reach middle Oder on broad front within about 30 miles of Berlin and outflank fortified cities of Kuestrin and Frankfurt. Berlin reports Soviet forces across the upper Oder below Breslau, N and S of Brieg. Fighting continues within beleaguered cities of Posen and Budapest.

ITALY—15th Army Group: In U.S. Fifth Army's IV Corps area, 92d Div's 366th Inf takes Calomini without difficulty but is held up by resistance on slopes of M. Faeto. Across the Serchio, 365th Inf drives beyond village of Lama to slopes of Lama di Sotto ridge, commanding Castelnuovo, where it encounters violent opposition. Indecisive fighting on these heights astride the Serchio continues for next few days.

LUZON—SWPA hq approves plan to reopen Manila Bay, a mission that is assigned to XI Corps. Air action against Corregidor is intensified.

In U.S. Sixth Army area, Gen MacArthur orders Japanese in N Luzon contained while main effort is directed against Manila area. In XIV Corps area, additional elements of 37th Div and 1st Cav Div move into Manila, where responsibility for clearing N part of the city is divided between the two divs. Both push S toward Pasig R line, where Japanese demolitions cause huge fires. In I Corps area, 20th Inf of 6th Div makes very little headway at Munoz; 1st Inf takes Rizal. Lupao remains under attack by 35th Inf of 25th Div. 32d Div begins drive up Villa Verde Trail with 2d Bn, 127th Inf, which has been patrolling from Santa Maria, where the trail enters the mountains, since 31 January. In XI Corps area, 38th Div continues costly fighting for Zigzag Pass; attached RCT 34 withdraws a little. Fresh 151st Inf is ordered to relieve RCT 34 and join in assault on this position. 149th Inf, upon reaching Dinalupihan and making contact with patrol of XIV Corps, is placed under corps control and directed to advance W along Route 7 toward the Zigzag in conjunction with eastward attacks.

In U.S. Eighth Army area, 511th Inf of 11th A/B Div progresses slowly northward toward Manila, crossing damaged Paranaque bridge and driving along Route 1.

6 February

WESTERN EUROPE—21 Army Group: In U.S. Ninth Army area, XVI Corps becomes operational and takes control of Br 12 Corps sector of Br Second Army. Br 7th Armd Div is attached for operations only. 35th Div completes relief of Br 52d Div and takes over its sector. During period 6–21 February, corps defends its zone, employing 35th Div on right and Br 7th Armd Div on left; 8th Armd Div is held in reserve. In XIII Corps area, CCB of 5th Armd Div is attached to toed Div in preparation for Operation GRENADE.

12th Army Group: In U.S. First Army area, advance elements of 69th Div start toward Montenau (Belgium) from vicinity of Liesse (France). In V Corps area, 78th Div's 310th Inf, reinf by bn of 309th and tanks, attacks before dawn toward Schmidt-Harscheid-Kommerscheidt region but meets stiff opposition and gains less than 1,000 yards. Hechelscheid falls to 2d Bn, 311th Inf. CCR, 7th Armd Div, assists 309th Inf in mopping up Steckenborn area and takes over defense of Hechelscheid sector. Para RCT 517 attacks at midnight 5–6 from Bergstein toward Schmidt-Nideggen road but is held up by mine field. Co A of 39th Inf, 9th Div, takes limited objective near Olef R east of Morsbach. Scheuren falls to 1st Bn of 9th Inf, 2d Div, and Hellenthal to 38th Inf. Corps assumes responsibility for zone of XVIII Corps (A/B) at 1800; 99th Div and 106th Div (–) are attached in place. XVIII Corps (A/B) begins movement to Huertgen region. 1st Div's RCT 16, with 14th Cav Gp attached, is attached to 8th Div.

In U.S. Third Army's VIII Corps area, German resistance to corps' assault on West Wall stiffens. In local attacks, 87th Div takes road junction on Losheim-Pruem road near Roth but is unable to gain crossroads in the Schnee Eifel E of Kobscheid. 8th Inf of 4th Div, in conjunction with S flank elements of 87th Div, continues to clear the Schnee Eifel ridge. Relief of 3d Bn of 22d Inf, 4th Div, in Brandscheid by 1st Bn of 358th Inf, 90th Div, is interrupted by determined enemy counterattack toward that town, but attack is repulsed after some hours of fighting; other elements of 22d Inf attack at noon and seize Hontheim, Sellerich, and Herscheid. 90th Inf and 11th Armd Divs open coordinated attack SE through West Wall defenses before dawn, surprising enemy and quickly gaining immediate objectives. 359th Inf, 90th Div, takes Habscheid by daybreak but is then delayed by opposition around the town. CCR of 11th Armd Div advances about 2 miles through West Wall fortifications to seize Hill 568, S of Habscheid; patrols enter Lutzkampen, Grosskampenberg, and Berg, but are only able to remain in Berg. III Corps begins rcn in force E of the Our, night 6–7. Assault elements of 6th Armd and 17th A/B Divs start to the Our at 1900; by midnight 6th Armd troops are at W bank of river near Kalborn and Dahnen and 2d Bn of 507th Para Inf, 17th A/B Div, is crossing N of Dasburg.

6th Army Group: In U.S. Seventh Army's XV Corps area, CG of 63d Div takes command of sectors held by 253d and 255th Regts and those units revert to 63d Div from attachment to 44th Div; 255th conducts limited attacks to improve defensive positions. Advance party of 101st Cav Gp closes in 106th Cav Gp sector. In VI Corps area, on 36th Div front, 68th Armd Inf Bn, though fighting hard in Oberhoffen, makes little headway. RCT 143 occupies Herrlisheim without opposition; relieves 117th Cav Rcn Sq in Offendorf. Both Herrlisheim and Offendorf are found to be heavily mined.

Fr 1st Army begins final phase of operations against Colmar Pocket. U.S. XXI Corps completes southward movement and turns E toward the Rhine. 3d Div finishes clearing its zone along the Rhine on N flank of corps and seizes Neuf-Brisach. Elements of 30th Inf are led by civilian into Neuf-Brisach and easily clear the fortress city of the few enemy remaining there. Elements of Fr 2d Armd Div pass through 3d Div and drive S between Rhine-Rhône Canal and Rhine R toward 1st Corps, clearing Oberaasheim. Pivoting SE about 3d Div, 75th Div reaches Rhine-Rhône Canal line S of Neuf-Brisach and sends elements forward to relieve French at Oberaasheim. 28th Div, having passed through 12th Armd Div, drives E to Rhine-Rhône Canal on S flank of corps. 12th Armd Div provides fire support for 28th Div, blocks exits from the Vosges, and eliminates isolated pockets of enemy. Fr 5th Armd Div, now in reserve near Colmar, helps clear Vosges pockets. In Fr 1st Corps area, 1st Armd Div, disposed along Ill R from Oberentzen to Reguisheim on corps E flank, pauses to await bridging and is passed through by infantry. 2d Moroccan Inf Div crosses Ill in Meyenheim-Reguisheim area and drives E to Rhine-Rhône Canal, capturing Hirtzfelden. 9th Colonial Inf Div completes capture of Ensisheim by dawn and attacks E from there on corps S flank, reaching edge of Harth woods; elements just N of Mulhouse drive N from Modenheim to Baldersheim. On W flank of corps, 4th Moroccan Mtn Div blocks Vosges exits. Organized resistance in the Vosges ceases.

EASTERN EUROPE—Moscow confirms German report of Soviet bridgeheads across the upper Oder between Breslau and Oppeln where Red Army forces have penetrated enemy defenses along W bank of the river. Troops of First Ukrainian Front, after seizing bridgeheads N and S of Brieg, link up W of the river, encircling Brieg, which is then taken by assault; among other towns secured are Ohlau, Grottkau, and Lowen. Russians continue to destroy German pockets in East Prussia and in cities of Posen and Budapest.

SEAC—Because of successes in Burma, Adm Mountbatten issues directives calling for formulation, as soon as possible, of plans to capture Rangoon and later Singapore.

P.I.—GHQ SWPA directs Eighth Army to plan for Operation VICTOR III against Palawan and for VICTOR IV against Sulu Archipelago.

LUZON—In U.S. Sixth Army's XIV Corps area, 37th Div and 1st Cav Div have cleared most of Manila N of Pasig R. 40th Div is ordered to speed action to clear right rear of corps. 160th Inf, with tank and air support, secures foothold on McSevney Pt, W nose of Storm King Mountain. In I Corps area, Japanese continue stubborn defense of Munoz, target of very heavy arty concentration, and Lupao. Enemy withdrawal routes from Munoz are cut. 32d Div suspends attack up Villa Verde Trail while consolidating current positions about 1,500 yards N of Santa Maria. In XI Corps area, 149th Inf of 38th Div starts W toward Zigzag Pass, where enemy positions are worked over thoroughly by aircraft, now based on San Marcelino airstrip, and by arty. 152d Inf continues eastward and penetrates enemy line late in day. 151st relieves 34th Inf.

In U.S. Eighth Army area, 511th Para Inf of 11th A/B Div gains about 500 yards toward Manila. 188th Inf moves forward in preparation for attack on Nichols Field.

7 February

WESTERN EUROPE—21 Army Group: In U.S. Ninth Army's XIII Corps area, 84th Div relieves 102d of responsibility for Linnich-Himmerich sector. In XIX Corps area, 30th Div takes over defense of W bank of the Roer from Kirchberg to Merken; 113th Cav Gp is transferred to 30th Div from attachment to 29th Div.

12th Army Group: In U.S. First Army's V Corps area, 78th Div renews attack with 3 regts abreast after 30-minute arty preparation: 309th Inf, on left, encounters mines and heavy fire while advancing on Kommerscheidt, which it captures; in center, 310th soon clears high ground SW of Schmidt and elements assist in main attack; 311th, on right, is bitterly opposed as it fights toward Schmidt and Harscheid, but clears W part of Schmidt and reaches SW section of Harscheid. CCR, 7th Armd Div, mops up bypassed pockets to rear of 78th Div. 82d A/B Div moves a task force (TF A), based on Para RCT 505, to Bergstein area to operate under V Corps control in the dam region. Para RCT 517, attached in place to TF A, finds region before it, SE of Bergstein, again mined by enemy and is unable to advance. 9th and 2d Divs defend and consolidate their positions. 69th Div is assigned to First Army, which attaches it to V Corps.

In U.S. Third Army's VIII Corps area, enemy strongly resists efforts of corps to deepen penetrations of West Wall. 87th Div, employing 345th and 346th Regts, takes crossroads E of Habscheid in the Schnee Eifel and clears Losheim-Pruem road northward from there. 4th Div drives SE toward Pruem: 8th Inf seizes Wascheid and reaches outskirts of Gondenbrett; 22d secures Ober Mehlen and heights overlooking Steinmehlen. 90th Div commits its full strength against the main West Wall defenses about Habscheid, methodically eliminating numerous pillboxes under heavy fire; Hollnich falls to 359th Inf. CCR, 11th Armd Div, is unable to advance beyond Hill 568, since progress of 90th Div is insufficient to protect its N flank; tanks and TD's are moved forward to support infantry elements on the hill; 41st Cav elements regain Lutzkampen and organize commanding ground at W outskirts of Grosskampenberg. CCB closes in Weiswampach area. In III Corps area, assault elements of 6th Armd and 17th A/B Divs finish crossing the Our R and German border during morning. 6th Armd crosses elements of 44th and 9th Armd Inf Bns (CCR) near Kalborn and Dahnen, respectively; two cos of 2d Bn, 507th Para Inf, 17th A/B Div, cross N of Dasburg. Enemy puts up strong resistance after recovering from surprise. 6th Armd Div constructs bridges and moves additional forces across river during day. XII Corps attacks across Our and Sauer Rivers between Vianden and Echternach, 5th Div starting 0100 and 80th at 0300. Though arty support is strong, swift current of river and heavy fire from West Wall limit numbers crossing and prevent bridging. On left, 80th Div crosses elements of 319th Inf (1st Bn and 2d Bn, less one Co) NW of Wallendorf and elements of 318th (2d Bn and Co L of 3d) N of Dillingen. Small bridgeheads are secured by both regts. 319th takes Wallendorf after nightfall. As a diversion for 80th Div, attached elements of 4th Armd Div (51st and 53d Armd Inf Bns) conduct demonstrations. To the SE, 5th Div, with elements of three regts abreast, attacks across the Sauer near Weiterbach and Echternach. With great difficulty, a few troops of 2d Bn, 10th Inf, on N, and of 2d and 3d Bns, 11th Inf, in center, succeed in crossing; attached 417th Inf (76th Div) gets 2½ cos of 1st Bn across river on S. In XX Corps area, 94th Div, attacking with 3 bns of 301st Inf, clears Sinz except for one house and high ground NW of the town; 2d Bn of 302d Inf attacks enemy pocket between Campholz woods and Tettingen, which has withstood pressure of 1st Bn, 302d, earlier in month, and takes four pillboxes. 26th Div begins series of local actions in Saarlautern-Roden bridgehead sector; elements of 3d Bn, 104th Inf, raid enemy positions in Fraulautern and withdraw. TF Polk (3d Cav Gp, reinf) patrols across the Saar near Merzig, night 7-8.

6th Army Group: In U.S. Seventh Army's VI Corps area, in 36th Div sector, 68th Armd Inf Bn fights in NW Oberhoffen until relieved by 1st Bn, 142d Inf. RCT 143 continues to consolidate positions in Bois de Drusenheim and pushes forward from Herrlisheim and Offendorf. 79th Div is detached from corps and reverts to army control.

In Fr 1st Army area, U.S. XXI Corps closes along the Rhine from Balgau northward. Continuing S between Rhine-Rhône Canal and the Rhine, Fr 2d Armd Div seizes Heiteren and Balgau and pushes toward Fessenheim. 75th Div sends elements to Heiteren to relieve French. Mopping up operations continue on rest of corps front. In Fr 1st Corps area, 1st Armd Div crosses Ill R over bridge constructed at Ensisheim and overtakes infantry along Rhine-Rhône Canal. 9th Colonial Inf Div closes along Rhine-Rhône Canal to S.

CHINA—Japanese occupy Kanchow, U.S. Fourteenth Air Force base.

LUZON—In U.S. Sixth Army's XIV Corps area, 37th Div extends E to take responsibility for most of Manila N of the Pasig, thus releasing 5th and 8th Cav Regts, which are to clear E suburbs as far S as the Pasig. Ordered to attack across the Pasig at once, 37th Div turns over part of its zone to a provisional organization, Special Security Force, and crosses 3d and 2d Bns of 148th Inf in assault boats. 185th Inf, on N flank of 40th Div, begins attack toward Snake Hill North in region W of Storm King Mountain. In I Corps area, battle for Munoz ends victoriously for 20th Inf, 6th Div. Japanese columns attempting to escape are virtually wiped out. In Lupao, enemy continues to hold out against 35th Inf, 25th Div. 2d Bn of 127th Inf, 32d Div, renews drive up Villa Verde Trail, which at this point winds about a bowl-shaped depression and is exposed to enemy fire from commanding terrain. In XI Corps area, 151st and 152d Regts of 38th Div are slowly and methodically reducing enemy strongpoints along Highway 7 on W; 149th Inf drives rapidly W to vicinity of Balsic.

In U.S. Eighth Army area, 11th A/B Div, with arty and air support, begins drive on Nichols Field. 511th Inf makes slight progress along Route 1 toward SW corner, but 188th Inf cannot reach its intended line of departure along Cut-Cut Creek.

8 February

WESTERN EUROPE—21 Army Group: Cdn First Army, employing Br 30 Corps, begins Operation VERITABLE to clear region between the Maas and Rhine Rivers. 30 Corps, with Cdn 2d and Br 15th, 53d, and 51st Divs disposed from left to right, attacks from general line Nijmegen-Mook at 1030 after effective arty preparation, meeting light resistance except on right but hampered by mines and flooded terrain. Cdn 2d Div accomplishes its mission, overrunning Wyler in lively fighting; Br 15th Div seizes Kranburg; Br 53d 51st Divs clear heights NW and SW of the Reichswald, respectively.

[8 FEBRUARY 1945]

On extreme N, Cdn 3d Div opens amphibious attack over flooded terrain at 1800 and easily clears Zyfflich and Zandpol. Scheduled air support is curtailed sharply by weather conditions.

12th Army Group: In U.S. First Army's V Corps area, 78th Div renews assault on Schmidt before dawn: 3d Bn of 310th Inf, passing through 311th Inf, overcomes determined resistance in E part of town; 1st Bn relieves pressure on 3d by clearing high ground SE of Harscheid. 311th Inf's 3d Bn easily secures Harscheid while rest of regt clears region between Schmidt and Urft Lake. 505th Para Inf, 82d A/B Div, makes contact with 78th Div near Kommerscheidt; 508th Para Inf is placed under operational control of corps and begins relief of 517th Para Inf SE of Bergstein. 2d Div relieves 9th Div and takes control of its sector and RCT 39 in place. 9th Div (−RCT 39) starts N to Strauch-Steckenborn region in order to attack toward Schwammenauel Dam; 309th Inf and 311th Inf (−3d Bn) of 78th Div are attached to 9th Div upon their relief by 505th Para Inf. RCT 424 of 106th Div, attached to 99th Div, relieves 394th Inf in place. XVIII Corps (A/B) assumes responsibility for VII Corps sector S of Kreuzau. 1st Div takes over zone of 8th Div and defends it with RCT 16 and attached 14th Cav Gp, which revert to it. From Salmchâteau area of Belgium, 82d A/B Div, less elements fighting with V Corps, moves to vicinity of Rott (Germany).

In U.S. Third Army's VIII Corps area, 345th Inf of 87th Div, in two-pronged attack, seizes Olzheim and high ground to S and E. 4th Div arouses even greater resistance as it presses toward Pruem, but 8th Inf takes large part of Gondenbrett and 22d clears Ober Mehlen; 12th Inf is committed on div S flank. 90th Div continues to batter main fortifications, largely pillboxes, of West Wall: 358th Inf, clearing region generally S of Brandscheid, is unable to take Hill 519 but makes contact with 359th Inf near Habscheid; 359th works on pillboxes toward div rear near Habscheid; possession of Hill 511, SE of Habscheid, is hotly contested throughout day, but elements of 357th Inf succeed in retaining it. CCR, 11th Armd Div, remains in position on Hill 568, since there is still no lateral contact between it and 90th Div. CCB establishes contact with 6th Armd Div (III Corps) W of the Our. In III Corps area, CCR of 6th Armd Div expands its N bridgehead and moves additional elements across river. 44th Armd Inf Bn completes crossing in morning and secures two bridge sites near Kalborn; 9th Armd Inf Bn finishes crossing at S bridgehead near Dahnen, too late in day to expand bridgehead. Farther S, 2d Bn of 507th Para Inf, 17th A/B Div, maintains small bridgehead N of Dasburg but is unable to enlarge it; patrol of platoon strength from 513th Para Inf, which had crossed the Our, night 7-8, is

[397]

forced to withdraw. In XII Corps area, 80th and 5th Divs slowly expand their bridgeheads and move additional units into them. 80th Div's 319th Inf (−) improves positions on high ground NE of Wallendorf and after nightfall moves Co D across river; most of 3d Bn, 318th Inf, crosses near Dillin-gen and helps 2d Bn expand bridgehead. 5th Div succeeds in reinforcing elements of 10th and 11th Regts across the river with a few boat loads of personnel; rest of 1st Bn and entire 2d Bn of 417th Inf cross. Mopping up operations are carried out within 5th Div bridgehead and some houses in Weiterbach are cleared of enemy. In XX Corps area, 301st Inf of 94th Div completes capture of Sinz and takes several pillboxes to SE; elements of 302d clear last two pillboxes between Campholz woods and Tettingen. Elements of 104th Inf, 26th Div, continue local actions against Fraulautern and occupy a city block.

6th Army Group: In U.S. Seventh Army's XV Corps area, elements of 276th Inf, 70th Div, are forced from OPLR by enemy fire. In VI Corps area, enemy continues to stubbornly resist RCT 142 of 36th Div in NW Oberhoffen. RCT 143 moves E through Bois de Drusenheim and establishes outpost. CCB, 14th Armd Div, reverts to parent unit from attachment to 36th Div.

In Fr 1st Army area, U.S. XXI Corps completes offensive as Fr 2d Armd Div reaches Fessenheim and finds 1st Armd Div of Fr 1st Corps already there. Units mop up. In 1st Corps area, 1st Armd Div, after driving E from Rhine-Rhône Canal to Fessenheim and clearing that village, moves S along the Rhine toward Chalampé, capturing Blodelsheim. To S, meanwhile, other elements of corps clear Harth forest and reach the Rhine near Hombourg and Petit Landau. The small enemy bridgehead W of the Rhine now contains but 4 villages—Rumersheim, Bantzenheim, Chalampé, and Ottmarsheim.

ITALY—15th Army Group: In U.S. Fifth Army's IV Corps area, 92d Div, while continuing fruitless struggle for heights on either side of the Serchio, giving ground under counterattack in region E of the river, begins limited attack in coastal sector with 3d Bn of 366th Inf (organized as TF 1) on left, 370th Inf in center, and 371st Inf on right. Advance is slowed by opposition and numerous mines, but TF 1 crosses Cinquale Canal and turns inland, 370th Inf gains about a mile, and 371st advances 800 yards.

BURMA—In NCAC area, 26th Brig of Br 36th Div establishes bridgehead across the Shweli near Myitson and holds it against enemy fire.

LUZON—In U.S. Sixth Army's XIV Corps area, while 1st Cav Div forces are clearing E suburbs of Manila, 37th Div expands and strengthens its bridgehead S of the Pasig, crossing 1st and 2d Bns of 129th Inf into it. On right flank of corps, 40th Div's 185th Inf continues attack toward Snake Hill North; 160th gains most of McSevney Pt and holds positions against series of counterattacks; 108th attacks W from Top of the World toward series of hills about 1,500–2,000 yards distant, numbered 5, 3, 4, and 6, from N to S, and takes Hill 5. I Corps, with capture of Lupao by 35th Inf of 25th Div, finishes clearing central plain. On Villa Verde Trail, 2d Bn of 127th Inf, 32 Div, pauses to consolidate and patrol. In XI Corps area, 38th Div continues 2-pronged attack against Zigzag Pass but is still stubbornly opposed. 149th Inf is running into strong opposition.

In U.S. Eighth Army area, 511th and 188th Regts of 11th A/B Div make slow progress against Nichols Field and gain contact near SW corner.

9 February

INTERNATIONAL CONFERENCES—ARGONAUT ends after conferees have agreed to plan for an invasion of Japan after defeat of Germany. Defeat of Germany, it is now believed, will come about 1 July 1945 After Japanese will to resist has been weakened by air and naval blockade and intensive aerial bombardment, Japan itself will be invaded. The pace of the Pacific war, however, will be slowed until the capitulation of Germany. USSR (as a reward for intervention in war against Japan) is to acquire holdings in Manchuria.

WESTERN EUROPE—21st Army Group: In Cdn First Army's Br 30 Corps area, rapid amphibious advance continues. Cdn 3d Div clears Mehr, Niel, Keeken, and Milligen and patrols to the Rhine. 15th Div overruns West Wall defenses at Nuetterden and reaches heights near Materborn; patrols to outskirts of Cleve. From Nijmegen, 43d Div begins drive through 15th Div toward Goch, reaching Nuetterden. Moving E through N part of the Reichswald, 53d Div clears Stuppelburg feature and high ground SW of Materborn. 51st Div drives through S part of the Reichswald toward Hekkens road center and cuts Mook-Gennep road.

12th Army Group: In U.S. First Army's V Corps area, 9th Div, passing through 78th Div and assisted by it, makes final drive on Schwammenauel Dam. To protect N flank of 9th Div, 78th Div's 310th Inf, reinf by bn of 311th, clears region N of Schmidt-Hasenfelde road and blocks Harscheid–Nideggen road. 9th Div's 90th Inf clears to the Roer within its zone and secures most of Hasenfelde; 311th Inf (–), after driving SE and clearing N bank of Urft Lake to within a few hundred yards of Schwammenauel Dam, is passed through by 309th, elements of which reach N end of the dam and capture the control house. Relieved by 508th Para Inf near Bergstein, 517th Para Inf assembles near Huertgen; 505th Para Inf moves E toward the Roer in region W of Abenden. 106th Div assumes responsibility for sector held by RCT 424 on corps S flank; RCT 424 reverts to it.

In U.S. Third Army's VIII Corps area, 3d Bn of 345th Inf, 87th Div, captures Neuendorf, but efforts of div Rcn Tr to make contact with 4th Div Rcn Tr at Willwerath are frustrated by enemy in that town. On 4th Div N flank, 8th Inf completes capture of Gondenbrett, clears Hermespand, and crosses elements over the Pruem; 22d seizes Nieder Mehlen; 12th partly clears Steinmehlen. 90th Div makes substantial progress through West Wall fortifications: on N, where enemy is falling back, 358th Inf takes Hill 519 and advances 2,000 yards; enemy's stubborn defense of region between 90th Inf and 11th Armd Divs is unabated, but contact is established between the two divs. 11th Armd Div defends current positions and patrols. In III Corps area, CCR of 6th Armd Div expands and consolidates bridgehead E of the Our. Junction is made between div's N and S bridgeheads, and contact is made with 17th A/B Div to S. Armor crosses the river over newly completed Bailey bridge. 17th A/B Div prepares for relief by 6th Armd Div. In XII Corps area bridgeheads across the Our and the Sauer are further strengthened and expanded by 80th and 5th Divs. In 80th Div zone, 3d Bn of 319th Inf is unable to cross into Wallendorf bridgehead, but rest of 318th Inf crosses near Dillingen. By end of day 5th Div has 2d Bn of 10th Inf, 1st and 2d Bns of 11th, and 3 bns of 417th across the Sauer in Weiterbach-Echternach region. In XX Corps area, enemy repels efforts of 301st Inf, 94th Div, to clear Bannholz woods, E of Sinz. 5th Ranger Bn is transferred from 26th to 94th Div control and relieves elements of 302d Inf on 94th Div right flank. In Saarlautern bridgehead, 104th Inf of 26th Div takes a number of buildings.

6th Army Group: In U.S. Seventh Army's XV Corps area, 101st Cav Gp begins relief of 106th Cav Gp. CCB, 10th Armd Div, reverts to parent unit from corps control. 254th Inf, 63d Div, is attached to 100th Div and relieves 274th Inf, 70th Div; 274th reverts to 10th Div control. VI Corps has little contact with enemy except in Oberhoffen, where 1st Bn of RCT 142, 36th Div, engages in house-to-house fighting.

Fr 1st Army completes reduction of Colmar Pocket, leaving German 19th Army virtually destroyed as an effective fighting force. Unremitting efforts of planes of U.S. XII TAC and Fr 1st Air Corps contribute greatly to the success of this operation. In U.S. XXI Corps area, 254th Inf reverts to 63d Div from attachment to 3d Div. Fr 1st Corps eliminates the small bridgehead in Chalampé area and Germans blow bridge at Chalampé, concluding operations on Alsatian plain of France.

ITALY—15th Army Group: In Br Eighth Army area, Cdn I Corps begins Operation GOLDFLAKE, movement to ETO, where it will join Cdn First Army.

BURMA—In ALFSEA area, 15 Corps completes capture of Ramree I.

CHINA—Chinese SOS is organized.

LUZON—U.S. Sixth Army releases 112th Cav RCT to 1st Cav Div. In XIV Corps area, 37th Div units fighting S of the Pasig in Manila make very small gains against tenacious resistance. 1st Cav Div forces clearing E suburbs reach the Pasig and begin crossing. In 40th Div zone, 185th Inf gets into position for assault on Snake Hill North; 160th continues to hold on McSevney Pt; 108th takes Hills 3 and 4 and pushes toward Hill 6. In I Corps area, after repelling predawn counterattack, 2d Bn of 127th Inf, 32d Div, continues attack to clear Villa Verde Trail but is soon checked by enemy fire. In XI Corps area, 38th Div continues to eliminate enemy positions in the Zigzag.

In U.S. Eighth Army area, 11th A/B is meeting intense opposition at Nichols Field.

10 February

WESTERN EUROPE—21 Army Group: In Cdn First Army area, Br 30 Corps is hampered by extremely poor road conditions and congestion as well as stiffening resistance. Cdn 3d Div pushes almost to Cleve-Rhine Canal. 43d Div is held up at Cleve and Materborn. 15th Div partly clears Cleve against strong resistance. 51st Div closes in on Hekkens and, night 10–11, crosses elements over flooded Niers R north of Gennep. Cdn 2d Div is detached from corps.

In U.S. Ninth Army area, Germans have destroyed outlets to Roer R dams in First Army zone to S, flooding proposed crossing sites of Ninth Army and forcing postponement of its attack across the Roer. Army continues preparations and special training for Operation GRENADE.

12th Army Group: In U.S. First Army's V Corps area, 310th Inf of 78th Div continues to protect N flank of 9th Div; 311th (−) reverts to 78th Div. 9th Div's 90th Inf mops up Hasenfeld before dawn and prepares for river crossing there; 309th consolidates at N end of Schwammenauel Dam and sends patrols across it, but blown bridge across the sluice way prevents crossing in force. CCR, 7th Armd Div, reverts to parent unit from attachment to 78th Div. Entire corps zone W of the Roer is cleared by nightfall. 82d A/B Div drives E with 508th and 505th Para Regts, reaching high ground overlooking the Roer E and SE of Bergstein; 517th Para Inf is detached from div.

In U.S. Third Army's VIII Corps area, 87th Div goes on the defensive and rest of corps prepares to do likewise. 8th Inf, 4th Div, consolidates bridgehead E of the Pruem and 22d Inf pushes a short distance toward Pruem; 12th Inf completes capture of Steinmehlen and gets a bn to the river line across from Nieder Pruem. 358th Inf, 90th Div, advances to positions overlooking the Pruem R; 359th clears last three pillboxes on div right flank. CCR of 11th Armd Div resumes attack, reducing a number of bunkers and pillboxes S and SE of Hill 568. In III Corps area, CCA of 6th Armd Div begins relief of 17th A/B Div. CCB relieves CCR of bridgehead E of the Our and makes contact with 11th Armd Div (VIII Corps). Corps is assigned to First Army and prepares to move to zone of XVIII Corps (A/B). Command of corps sector and of 6th Armd Div and 6th Cav Gp in place passes to VIII Corps at 2400. In XII Corps area, 80th Div's 319th (less 3d Bn) and 318th Inf, assisted by co of 317th, continue to improve and expand bridgeheads in Wallendorf-Dillingen area; elements of 318th clear Biesdorf after nightfall. 5th Div crosses rest of 10th and 11th Regts and with these expands Weiterbach-Echternach bridgehead into West Wall; 417th mops up within the bridgehead. Two footbridges are constructed near Echternach, the first of a number of bridges to be put in within corps zone. In XV Corps area, 10th Armd Div, released by Seventh Army to Third Army, starts to Metz area, where it is attached to XX Corps. In XX Corps area, 376th Inf of 94th Div begins relief of 301st in position. 2d Bn, 376th, attacks into Bannholz woods after heavy arty preparation but is driven out. 26th Div, employing 2d and 3d Bns of 104th Inf, expands Saarlautern bridgehead, capturing a number of buildings.

6th Army Group: In U.S. Seventh Army's XV Corps area, 10th Armd Div starts to Third Army front. In VI Corps area, 2 bns of RCT 142, 36th Div, continue heavy fighting in Oberhoffen. RCT 143 attacks Drusenheim but is forced to withdraw; elements are relieved by RCT 141.

EASTERN EUROPE—In East Prussia, important port of Elbing and communications center of Preussisch Eylau fall to Second and Third White Russian troops, respectively.

ITALY—15th Army Group: In Br Eighth Army area, Cdn 1st Div takes command of Cdn I Corps sector.

BURMA—In NCAC area, Myitson falls to Br 36th Div troops.

In Br Fourteenth Army's 4 Corps area, E African 28th Brig takes Seikpyu.

P.I.—Samar Task Force (consisting largely of 1st Bn of 182d Inf, Americal Div, and guerrillas) is formed under Brig Gen L. H. Slocum, Americal Div CG. GHQ SWPA establishes boundary between U.S. Sixth and Eighth Armies. Sixth Army is responsible for Luzon and Eighth for all islands to S—about two thirds of land area of the Philippines.

LUZON—33d Div arrives from Morotai. In U.S. Sixth Army's XIV Corps area, opposition in S Manila is so stubborn and losses to 37th Div are so great that it is decided to increase volume of arty bombardment. 129th and 148th Regts, 37th Div, reach line Estero de Tonque-Estero de Paco. 1st Cav Div regroups, committing 112th Cav RCT along line of communications to permit 12th Cav to move into Rosario Heights. Div expands positions S of the Pasig and makes patrol contact with 37th Div near Paco Station. In center of 40th Div zone, 160th Inf finds that Japanese have abandoned McSevney Pt and pushes on toward final objective, Object Hill, gaining positions on Snake Hill West and Scattered Trees Ridge. In I Corps area, 3d Bn of 127th Inf, 32d Div, relieves 2d Bn on Villa Verde Trail. In U.S. Eighth Army area, as 11th A/B Div continues to clear enemy positions around Nichols Field it is transferred to command of XIV Corps, Sixth Army, and directed to maintain pressure on the airfield and determine location of enemy positions near the field and at Cavite.

LEYTE—X Corps takes command of tactical operations on Leyte and Samar. 92d Div (PA) is attached to Americal Div to help mop up. XXIV Corps closes in staging areas on E coast of Leyte.

11 February

INTERNATIONAL AGREEMENTS—U.S., Great Brittain, and USSR issue Yalta Declaration outlining conclusions reached at ARGONAUT Conference.

WESTERN EUROPE—21 Army Group: In Cdn First Army area, Br 30 Corps continues to advance despite increasingly strong resistance and flooded terrain. 3d Cdn Div reaches Cleve-Rhine Canal; 15th Div completes capture of Cleve; 43 Div maintains positions SW of Cleve and takes Materborn and Hau; 53d Div continues to clear the Reichswald; 51st Div takes important road centers of Hekkens and Gennep.

12th Army Group: U.S. First Army begins period of regrouping in accordance with letter of instructions of this date outlining plans for assault across the Roer. In V Corps area, TF A is detached from corps and reverts to 82d A/B Div. 69th Div begins relief of 99th Div in line. Upon relief, 99th moves to vicinity of Waimes (Belgium). In III Corps area, advance detachment of corps starts toward First Army zone.

In U.S. Third Army area, VIII Corps goes on the defensive and shifts boundaries. Units now under corps command, from N to S, are 87th, 4th, 90th, 11th Armd, and 6th Armd Divs and 6th Cav Gp. 4th Div readjusts positions before defending Pruem R line from Olzheim to Watzerath, relieving elements of 345th Inf, 87th Div, to N and elements of 358th Inf, 90th Div, to S. 8th Inf in bridgehead E of the Pruem and elements of 12th Inf on W bank of river opposite Nieder Pruem are withdrawn. 3d Bn of 22d Inf enters Pruem and starts systematic search for enemy within the town. 90th Div begins limited objective attacks long before dawn: 3d Bn of 357th Inf advances to line N of Masthorn; 358th Inf, after futile predawn efforts by Co I to take Watzerath, attacks with three bns and captures Watzerath and Weinsfeld. At conclusion of attacks, 90th Div regroups: 357th Inf relieves 11th Armd Div elements to S during night. 6th Armd Div takes command of 17th A/B Div zone. CCB maintains bridgehead E of the Our. Upon relief, 17th A/B Div starts to Châlons-sur-Marne area (France), where it is to be under SHAEF control; bridgehead N of Dasburg is abandoned. In XII Corps area, 319th Inf (− 3d Bn) of 80th Div continues reduction of West Wall fortifications within Wallendorf bridgehead; 318th clears high ground overlooking Bollendorf and mops up in Dillingen area; 2d Bn of 317th Inf crosses river, night 11-12, in zone of 318th Inf, to which it is attached. 5th Div finishes clearing high ground along the Sauer within its zone and on the N opens attack on Bollendorf; 417th Inf is detached but, complying with orders for 76th Div to secure S portion of corps bridgehead, continues action in current zone and captures Echternacherbruck. Boundary between 5th and 76th Divs is adjusted. In XX Corps area, 10th Armd Div completes assembly in Metz area. 376th Inf, 94th Div, completes relief of 301st and latter is withdrawn to reserve. 104th Inf, 26th Div, improves positions in Saarlautern bridgehead area despite strong resistance.

6th Army Group: In U.S. Seventh Army's XV Corps area, 101st Cav Gp completes relief of 106th Cav Gp and assumes command of its sector; 106th is withdrawn as reserve. 12th Armd Div is attached to corps and takes over screening mission formerly held by CCB, 10th Armd Div. In VI Corps area, RCT 142 of 36th Div continues to fight in Oberhoffen.

In Fr 1st Army's U.S. XXI Corps area, 75th Div is detached from corps and reverts to control of army.

EASTERN EUROPE—Moscow confirms German reports of fighting NW of Breslau in German Silesia with announcement of 4-day-old offensive in that region during which troops of First Ukrainian Front have crossed the Oder NW of Breslau and broken through German defenses along W bank to seize Steinhau, Lueben, Haynau, Liegnitz, Neumarkt, and Kanth, thus, in conjunction with assault of forces SE of Breslau, threatening the Silesian capital with encirclement and menacing less imminently the city of Dresden (Germany), 80-odd miles to W. In NE Germany, Soviet forces overrun Deutsch Krone. Other Red Army troops are eliminating enemy garrisons of Schneidemuehl and Posen; claim capture of 45 city blocks in Budapest.

ITALY—15th Army Group: In U.S. Fifth Army's IV Corps area, 92d Div breaks off limited attacks, both in coastal sector, where bridgehead across the Cinquale Canal is withdrawn, and in Serchio Valley. Little change in positions has resulted.

LUZON—In U.S. Sixth Army's XIV Corps area, 11th A/B Div presses northward toward Manila against decreasing resistance, reaching Pasay, a suburb, and clearing part of Nichols Field; makes patrol contact with 8th Cav outpost. To N, 37th Div and 1st Cav Div continue to clear Manila. In I Corps area, 161st Inf of 25th Div is ordered to advance from San Isidro area toward Puncan. 1st Bn is to move to Balaho and establish observation posts commanding Highway 5. 3d Bn of 127th Inf, 32d Div, begins drive up Villa Verde Trail but is forced back to starting point. For next few days, action in that region is confined to probing by both sides. XI Corps has advanced sufficiently against the Zigzag for 151st Inf to be released.

POA—Joint Expeditionary Force begins final rehearsals for Iwo Jima operation, off W coast of Tinian in the Marianas.

12 February

WESTERN EUROPE—21 Army Group: In Cdn First Army's Br 30 Corps area, 3d Cdn Div takes Kellen and Warbeyen and relieves Br 15th Div of responsibility for Cleve. 15th Div is stubbornly opposed as it attempts to push toward Calcar. 43d Div seizes Bedburg, a necessary action before continuing drive on Goch, but is unable to make any headway along Hau-Goch road. 53d Div continues to clear the Reichswald and withstands strong pressure from E edge. 51st Div advances in S part of the Reichswald and to right takes Heien, S of Gennep.

12th Army Group: In U.S. First Army area, Advance Hq of III Corps moves to Zweifall (Germany) to take over zone of XVIII Corps (A/B). XVIII Corps (A/B) becomes responsible for sector now held by 82d A/B Div. In V Corps area, 78th Div relieves elements of 9th Div and is transferred in place to XVIII Corps (A/B); 309th Inf and 1st Bn of 311th revert to 78th Div from attachment to 9th Div. 9th Div takes over sector of 2d Div.

In U.S. Third Army's VIII Corps area, 4th Div completes capture of Pruem. Zone of 11th Armd Div is extended southward as CCB relieves 86th Cav Rcn Sq of positions on N flank of 6th Armd Div. 41st Cav Rcn Sq, detached from 11th Armd Div and attached to 6th Armd, closes at Knaphoscheid. 6th Cav Gp captures that part of Vianden (Luxembourg) W of the Our. In XII Corps area, contact is made at Bollendorf between 80th and 5th Div bridgeheads and, within 80th Div zone, between those of 319th and 318th Regts at E edge of Wallendorf. 319th Inf finishes its crossing of the Our and continues reduction of stubbornly defended pillboxes on N flank of corps bridgehead; 318th improves positions S of Cruchten. Tanks and TD's cross into 5th Div bridgehead, where 10th Inf completes capture of Bollendorf and continues N. In 76th Div zone, 3d Bn of 385th Inf relieves 1st Bn of 417th in place and is attached to 417th, which continues slowly E along N bank of the Sauer. XX Corps maintains defensive positions. In 26th Div zone, 328th Inf begins relief of 104th on MLR.

6th Army Group: In U.S. Seventh Army's XV Corps area, Fr 2d Armd Div is attached to corps. In VI Corps' 36th Div sector, RR station and factory in NW Oberhoffen, last points of resistance, are set on fire.

ITALY—15th Army Group: In Br Eighth Army's 13 Corps area, Ind 10th Div takes command of sector previously held by 78th Div.

BURMA—In Br Fourteenth Army's 33 Corps area, Ind 20th Div begins crossing the Irrawaddy in Myinmu-Allagappa sector W of Mandalay, night 12-13, against little opposition.

LUZON—In U.S. Sixth Army's XIV Corps area, Japanese remaining in Manila are isolated as 5th Cav and 12th Cav, latter replacing 8th Cav, drive W to shores of Manila Bay, overrunning Neilson Field. In co-ordinated assault by 188th Regt and part of 187th, 11th A/B Div, Nichols Field is largely cleared of enemy. 40th Div advances its flanks, 108th Inf taking Hill 6 and 185th taking Snake Hill North, but is stubbornly opposed in center, where progress is slow. In I Corps area, 33d Div comes under corps control to relieve 43d Div and RCT 158. Corps is regrouping for drive N into Caraballo Mts. 27th Inf, 25th Div, relieves 1st Inf, 6th Div, at San Jose and improves positions along Highway 5 35th Inf moves to Rizal and probes northward with patrols toward Pantangan. 6th Div occupies positions along E coast, bisecting enemy forces on the island. In XI Corps area, RCT I of 6th Div starts S from Dinalupihan for operation to clear Bataan.

VISAYAN PASSAGE—Gen Eichelberger issues basic plan for Eighth Army's part in clearing Visayan Passage.

13 February

WESTERN EUROPE—21 Army Group: In Cdn First Army's Br 30 Corps area, Cdn 3d Div patrols toward Emmerich. 15th Div, driving on Calcar, captures Hasselt. 43d Div takes strongly defended hill feature near Cleve Forest (just E of the Reichswald) and screens it. 53d Div overcomes final opposition in the Reichswald and links up with elements of 51st Div there.

U.S. Ninth Army releases 95th Div to operational control of Br 8 Corps.

12th Army Group: In U.S. First Army area, III Cops assumes responsibility for zone of XVIII Corps (A/B) and operational control of 1st and 78th Inf and 82d A/B Divs in place. 14th Cav Gp is detached from 1st Div and attached to III Corps. Elements of 78th Div occupy Blens. Period of limited activity ensues, during which corps defends W bank of the Roer within its zone, patrols actively, rotates troops, and prepares for assault across the Roer. XVIII Corps (A/B) CP closes at Zweifall (Germany) and opens at Epernay (France) as corps prepares to engage in planning and training activities for Operation VARSITY. In V Corps area, 69th Div completes relief of 99th and takes over its zone; 99th closes in assembly areas in Belgium.

In U.S. Third Army area, VIII Corps engages in routine defensive activities along the Pruem and Our Rivers until 18 February. In XII Corps area, 80th Div's 319th and 318th Regts continue to mop up and 319th takes Amleldingen; 317th, to which 2d Bn reverts, prepares to cross river. 10th Inf, 5th Div, takes Ferschweiler and positions on high ground around it; 11th drives to edge of Ernzen. 417th Inf, 76th Div, continues to clear S portion of bridgehead and on N co-ordinates with 5th Div near Ernzen. XX Corps front remains quiet, but patrols are active. 328th Inf, 26th Div, completes relief of 104th in Saarlautern bridgehead.

6th Army Group: In U.S. Seventh Army's VI Corps area, 36th Div's advance to E is halted by flooded terrain along Moder and Rhine Rivers; RCT 142 continues to hold Oberhoffen.

EASTERN EUROPE—Red Army completes capture of Budapest after a month and a half of fighting. In German Silesia, Soviet forces gain ground NW of Breslau, encircling Glogau and seizing Beuthen.

ITALY—15th Army Group: U.S. Fifth Army releases Ind 8th Div, which has been in army reserve, to Br Eighth Army. In II Corps area, 91st Div relieves 34th Div in line.

In Br Eighth Army area, Hq Pol 2 Corps takes command of 3d Carpathian Div and Friuli Group sector.

BURMA—In NCAC area, 26th Brig of Br 36th Div is holding its Shweli bridgehead against increasing resistance. In Br Fourteenth Army area, as Ind 20th Div expands its bridgehead across the Irrawaddy in 33 Corps sector, Ind 7th Div begins crossing in Nyaungu area in 4 Corps zone, assisted by diversionary thrusts of E African 28th Brig toward Yenangyaung oil-field area.

LUZON—In U.S. Sixth Army's XIV Corps area, 37th Div and 1st Cav Div are clearing stubborn strongpoints on approaches to Intramuros in Manila. 11th A/B Div completes mop-up of Nichols Field area. In 40th Div zone, 108th Inf takes Hill 7, another of the numbered series, but is driven off. I Corps continues to regroup. 33d Div relieves RCT 158 in Damortis-Rosario-Pozorrubio sector. 25th Div relieves 6th Div on line San Jose-Rizal-Bongabon-Cebu. In XI Corps area, mine sweeping and naval gunfire bombardment of Corregidor is begun in preparation for landings. 38th Div finishes clearing Zigzag defenses except for a final strongpoint between 152d and 149th Regts.

POA—Final rehearsals for Iwo Jima operation are concluded off coast of Tinian.

14 February

WESTERN EUROPE—21 Army Group: In Cdn First Army's Br 30 Corps area, 3d Cdn Div takes village on the Rhine opposite Emmerich. 15th Div is bitterly opposed as it attempts to reach Moyland from Hasselt, on road to Calcar. 43d Div withstands strong pressure in vicinity of Cleve Forest. 53d Div fights for high ground N of Asperberg, making slow progress. 51st Div overruns Kessel in night attack, 14-15, and is reinf by 32d Gds Brig of Gds Armd Div, which takes Hommersum.

12th Army Group: In U.S. Third Army area, XII Corps has firm control of bridgehead through West Wall and is consolidating it and preparing for drive to Pruem R. 80th Div improves positions in N portion of bridgehead; 317th Inf crosses river and begins clearing enemy from Bollendorf area. 5th Div's 10th Inf expands bridgehead northward toward Schankweiler; 11th takes Ernzen. On S flank of bridgehead, 417th Inf of 76th Div takes hill positions, reduces pillboxes, and helps 5th Div capture Ernzen.

6th Army Group: In Fr 1st Army area, U.S. XXI Corps releases 28th Div to control of Seventh Army.

EASTERN EUROPE—Red Army overruns Schneidemuehl (NE Prussia); in German Silesia, gains ground NW and SW of Liegnitz.

ITALY—15th Army Group: In Br Eighth Army area, Cdn I Corps replaces Br 6th Armd Div on right flank of corps with Cremona Group, an Italian formation, as Br 6th Armd Div prepares for transfer to ETO.

[15 FEBRUARY 1945]   [403]

CHINA—During meeting at Gen Wedemeyer's hq, Plan BETA, to open coastal port, is presented to Chiang Kai-shek, who approves it.

LUZON—In U.S. Sixth Army area, XIV Corps continues to battle strongpoints in Manila. In I Corps area, 33d Div relieves 43d Div and patrols actively. 25th Div, less 161st Inf, is redeploying for drive on Balete Pass. 6th Div, less 1st Inf, assembles in preparation for movement S of Pampanga R. In XI Corps area, while 38th Div is concluding action against the. Zigzag, where firm contact is made between 149th and 152d Regts, corps begins operations to clear Bataan Peninsula, the first of a series of operations to reopen Manila Bay. East Force (RCT 1 of 6th Div, reinf) begins drive S along E coast of the peninsula from Orani, reaching Pilar. South Force (RCT 151, 38th Div), after loading at Subic and Olongapo, sails from Subic Bay for Mariveles.

LEYTE—In U.S. Eighth Army area, X Corps forms provisional TF (1st Philippine Inf (less 1st and 2d Bns) and 1st Bn of 182d Inf, reinf) to clear NW coast of Samar and islands in San Bernardino Strait.

POA—Gunfire and Covering Force (TF 54, under Rear Adm B. J. Rodgers) and Support Carrier Group of Amphibious Support Force (TF 52, commanded by Rear Adm W. H. B. Blandy) leave Saipan for Iwo Jima for pre-D-day operations.

15 February

WESTERN EUROPE—21 Army Group: Cdn First Army commits another corps, Cdn 2, in Operation VERITABLE. Cdn 2 Corps becomes responsible for left sector of Br 30 Corps front from line Grave-Groesbeek-Cleve-Emmerich northward. Cdn 3d Div is attached in place; takes Huisberden, E of Cleve, and relieves Br 15th Div of positions S and W of Moyland. During period 15 through 25 February, corps conducts limited attacks with Cdn 3d and 2d Divs in general direction of Calcar, immediate objective, and regroups in preparation for concerted assault. In Br 30 Corps area, main effort is directed against obstacles before Goch, next big objective. 15th Div, except for a brig temporarily attached to Cdn 3d Div, is withdrawn to rest in preparation for drive through 43d Div on Goch. 43d Div fights hard for hill features E of Cleve Forest. 53d Div continues toward Asperberg. 51st Div pushes toward Asperden.

12th Army Group: In U.S. Third Army's XII Corps area, 80th Div continues consolidation of N part of corps bridgehead. Elements of 5th Div continue N toward Schankweiler and patrol to Pruem R; 2d Inf relieves 10th of its portion of bridgehead.

417th Inf, 76th Div, reduces additional pillboxes and clears high ground N of Minden; 2d Bn is relieved in line by 2d Bn, 385th Inf, night 15-16. In XX Corps area, 2d Bn of 302d Inf, 94th Div, takes several pillboxes and shelters E of Campholz woods but loses them in strong night counterattack. 26th Div slightly improves positions in Saarlautern bridgehead in limited attack by 328th Inf.

6th Army Group: In U.S. Seventh Army area, XV Corps opens limited offensive to straighten and shorten front line by eliminating enemy salients at Gros Réderching in 44th Div sector and at Wilferding in 63d Div zone. 44th Div, leading off, attacks with 324th Inf through Buschenbusch woods against light resistance; in center, 71st Inf thrusts NE, capturing Rimling and reaching objective; on left, 114th Inf, despite enemy fire in vicinity of Bellevue Farm, attains regimental objective on other side of Bois de Blies Brucken. 63d Div, to advance its right flank and tie in with 44th Div's left, attacks with 255th Inf to clear Bois de Blies Brucken. To left of 44th Div, 100th Div conducts strong diversionary raids.

In Fr 1st Army area, U.S. 3d Div is detached from U.S. XXI Corps and attached to Fr 2d Corps.

EASTERN EUROPE—While troops of Second White Russian Front improve positions N of Bromberg in NW Poland, forces of First Ukrainian Front seize Gruenberg, in N Silesia, and enter Brandenburg.

BURMA—In Br Fourteenth Army's 33 Corps area, Ind 20th Div is beginning to meet strong opposition as it is expanding and consolidating its Irrawaddy bridgehead. In 4 Corps area, Ind 7th Div expands Irrawaddy bridgehead to Pagan and elements still W of the river take Pakokku.

LUZON—In U.S. Sixth Army's XIV Corps area, bitter fighting continues within Manila. 40th Div, to right rear, continues to clear enemy from hills in its zone. 185th Inf gains its final objective—Hill 1500. 108th is attempting to regain Hill 7 and 160th to clear objectives in div center. I Corps assumes responsibility for portion of XIV Corps zone lying generally N of E-W line through Tarlac. RCT 158 assembles in vicinity of Tarlac, passing to army reserve. 126th Inf, 32d Div, occupies San Manuel-Asingan-San Nicolas triangle, releasing entire 127th Inf for drive up Villa Verde Trail. In XI Corps area, 38th Div completes mop-up of enemy's Zigzag position. After preparatory bombardment, South Force lands on Mariveles coast at 1000. Gen Chase takes command ashore, relieving Adm Struble, CTG 78.3. No opposition is met, but Japanese counterattack, night 15-16—the last organized enemy effort on E coast—is repulsed.

16 February

WESTERN EUROPE—21 Army Group: In Cdn First Army's Br 30 Corps area, 43d Div drives toward escarpment overlooking Goch. 53d Div reaches Asperberg and finds bridge blown. 51st Div captures Asperden. 52d Div, taking over 51st Div right, clears Afferden, night 16-17.

12th Army Group: In U.S. Third Army's XII Corps area, elements of 80th, 5th, and 76th Divs engage in local actions to improve bridgehead positions and patrol actively. Relief of 417th Inf, 76th Div, by 385th is completed, night 16-17. In XX Corps area, 94th Div begins regrouping for offensive. 328th Inf, 26th Div, continues local action to improve positions in Saarlautern bridgehead.

6th Army Group: In U.S. Seventh Army's XV Corps area, 63d Div continues limited attack in right part of its sector until objective is reached and line in Gros Réderching area is straightened. 44th Div repels counterattacks. In VI Corps area, 42d Div (formerly TF Linden) begins relief of 45th Div. XXI Corps reverts to control of Seventh Army from attachment to Fr 1st Army.

EASTERN EUROPE—Red Army completes circle about Breslau, Silesia.

ITALY—15th Army Group: U.S. Fifth Army orders limited attack by IV Corps, beginning 20 February, to improve positions W of Highway 64.

In Br Eighth Army's 13 Corps area, Ind 10th Div takes over part of 6th Armd Div's sector in preparation for relief of the armd div by Folgore Group, which has not yet been in action. 5 Corps takes command of Cdn 1st Div in place.

BURMA—In ALFSEA's 15 Corps area, brig of Ind 25th Div lands on Arakan coast near Ru-ywa, W of An, to operate in conjunction with W African 82d Div moving down from N in effort to block enemy withdrawal toward Prome. Landing is supported by aircraft and by arty that has been emplaced secretly on small island nearby. Japanese offer little opposition. In Br Fourteenth Army's 33 Corps area, Ind 20th Div consolidates Irrawaddy bridgehead, but enemy is bringing heavy pressure to bear against it and hard fighting continues for the next few days.

LUZON—In U.S. Sixth Army's XIV Corps area, 108th Inf of 40th Div regains Hill 7 and continues W, turning right flank of Japanese line. I Corps patrols aggressively to determine routes of advance on Baguio and Balete Pass. 1st Bn, 161st Inf, establishes observation posts in hills commanding Highway 5. In XI Corps area, after intensive preparatory bombardment by aircraft and naval vessels, Rock Force (503d Para RCT and reinf 3d Bn of 34th Inf, 24th Div) starts landing on Corregidor about 0830: Fifth Air Force begins dropping 503d Para RCT; 3d Bn of 34th Inf arrives by sea from Mariveles and starts ashore about 1030. Beachhead is established and contact made between paratroopers and 34th Inf troops without serious difficulty since enemy is shaken by preparatory bombardment and is taken completely by surprise.

IWO JIMA—Intensive preinvasion bombardment begins. TF's 52 and 54 arrive off the island and start naval and air bombardment and mine sweeping. Aircraft from escort carriers co-ordinate with Marianas-based bombers in pounding Iwo Jima while planes of TF 58 (fast carrier force) deliver simultaneous attacks on Japan in general support of the Iwo operation.

MARIANAS—Joint Expeditionary Force (TF 51) leaves Saipan for Iwo Jima.

17 February

WESTERN EUROPE—21 Army Group: In Cdn First Army area, Br 30 Corps closes in on Goch. 43d Div clears escarpment NE of the town; 53d maintains positions on the escarpment to right of 43d; 51st and attached elements of Gds Armd Div move in on the W and clear Hassum.

75th Div is assigned to U.S. Ninth Army and placed under operational control of Br Second Army.

12th Army Group: In U.S. First Army's V Corps area, 9th Div (− RCT 39) is transferred to III Corps at 2400 and starts to zone of 82d A/B Div near Huertgen. 2d Div takes over former 9th Div zone and is reinf by RCT 39 of that div.

In U.S. Third Army area, XII Corps in local actions expands and consolidates Our-Sauer bridgehead. 385th Inf, 76th Div, takes responsibility for S portion of bridgehead from 417th Inf. In XX Corps area, 328th Inf of 26th Div continues limited action in Saarlautern bridgehead.

6th Army Group: In U.S. Seventh Army area, XV Corps begins second phase of limited offensive to straighten and shorten line, employing 70th Div on left flank against heights SW of Saarbruecken. 276th Inf tries in vain to take Oeting but gains hills commanding the town. 274th seizes Kerbach and Behren. 275th pushes toward Lixing and Grosbliederstroff. In conjunction with 10th Div, 63d Div's 253d Inf drives northward toward woods beyond Auersmacher, which elements reach; gains weak hold on Auersmacher. 255th Inf conducts diversionary raids across Blies R. 44th Div holds its line against determined counterattacks. 100th Div defends right flank of corps and also engages in diversionary raids. In VI Corps area, 42d Div completes relief of 45th Div and takes command of its sector at 2400. 79th Div, in reserve, is transferred to XVI Corps of Ninth Army.

[18 FEBRUARY 1945]

BURMA—In ALFSEA's 15 Corps area, Ind 25th Div expands bridgehead on Arakan coast to Ru-ywa village against continued light resistance.

In NCAC area, Br 36th Div holds Shweli R bridgehead, which is supplied entirely by air, against major enemy counterattack.

CHINA—Gen Wedemeyer warns Generalissimo Chiang Kai-shek that enemy may try to take airfields at Hsian, Laohokou, and Chihchiang. Changting is the only airfield still held by U.S. Fourteenth Air Force in E China.

LUZON—In U.S. Sixth Army area, XIV Corps begins intensive fire against Intramuros in Manila in preparation for assault. 6th Div, less RCT 1, is transferred to XIV Corps from I Corps in order to participate in offensive to clear region E of Manila and thus insure safety of that city. In I Corps area, 43d Div (less RCT 169) is placed in army reserve; RCT 169 is given mission of holding W part of Central Plain N of line Tarlac-Palauig and W of the Agno. In XI Corps area, East Force, now backed up by units released from the Zigzag (149th Inf, 38th Rcn Tr, and supporting units), starts W on Bataan along Pilar-Bagac Road without opposition. From Mariveles, South Force is working northward. Rock Force is methodically clearing Corregidor. 1st Bn, 503d Para RCT, arrives there by landing craft.

MINDORO—U.S. Eighth Army activates Palawan Task Force (composed of 41st Div's 186th Inf, reinf, and under command of Brig Gen Harold Haney) to make amphibious assault—Operation VICTOR III—on Palawan on 28 February. 41st Div is also to clear Zamboanga Peninsula (Mindanao) beginning 10 March.

IWO JIMA—Fifth Fleet surface vessels and carrier-based and land-based planes continue to pound Iwo Jima as underwater demolition teams go into action.

JAPAN—Carrier planes of TF 58 again provide general support of the imminent Iwo operation with attacks on Tokyo.

18 February

WESTERN EUROPE—21 Army Group: In Cdn First Army area, Br 30 Corps begins assault on Goch: passing through 43 Div, 15th Div reaches N outskirts of the town; 51st Div enters Goch from the NW. Upon being passed through, 43d Div gradually works E from Goch area.

12th Army Group: In U.S. First Army's III Corps area, 9th Div begins relief of 82d A/B Div and takes over its zone. Upon relief, 82d A/B starts to assembly area near Walheim (Germany) and from there later moves to vicinity of Reims (France).

In U.S. Third Army area, VIII Corps renews offensive, attacking S toward XII Corps zone through West Wall defenses in region W of the Pruem. Early morning assault without arty preparation takes enemy by surprise, and the assault divs—90th Inf and 11th Armd—overrun numerous pillboxes and other obstacles. On N, 90th Div's 358th Inf takes hill commanding Pronsfeld from the NW; 359th seizes Kesfeld. Attacking on narrow front in co-ordination with 90th Div, CCR of 11th Armd Div gains Grosskampenberg and Leidenborn. 4th Div zone is extended slightly S as elements of 12th Inf relieve elements of 358th Inf, 90th Div, near Pronsfeld. 4th Div sends out combat patrols as diversion for 90th Div attack. On corps S flank, 6th Cav Gp secures small bridgehead E of the Our between Gemund and Biewels and builds footbridge. XII Corps attacks NE toward Pruem R against scattered resistance. On left, 80th Div's 318th Inf takes Cruchten and drives toward Hommerdingen; 317th captures Stockigt and advances on Nusbaum; 319th contains enemy remaining in West Wall fortifications and releases 51st Armd Inf Bn, which reverts to 4th Armd Div. 5th Div, to the right, crosses Enz R and drives to W bank of the Pruem from vicinity of Peffingen southeastward: 2d Inf, making main effort, takes Schankweiler; 11th clears W bank of the Pruem to SE. 385th Inf, 76th Div, consolidates positions to right of 5th Div. In XX Corps area, 94th Div completes preparations for attack. In Saarlautern bridgehead, 328th Inf of 26th Div consolidates, repels counterattacks, and clears a few more buildings.

6th Army Group: In U.S. Seventh Army's XV Corps area, 10th Div overruns Oeting and pushes on toward Forbach on left; in center, takes Etzling and reaches ridge S of Stiring Wendel; on right, clears Lixing and Grosbliederstroff. Enemy infiltrators recover Auersmacher from elements of 253d Inf, 63d Div. In VI Corps area, 45th Div passes to army reserve. XXI Corps completes movement to Morhange area.

ITALY—15th Army Group: In U.S. Fifth Army's IV Corps area, in preparation for main attack on M. Belvedere and M. Castello in order to improve positions W of Highway 64, 1st Bn of 86th Inf, 10th Mtn Div, begins scaling the steep Sarasiccia-Campania cliff to left at 1930, taking enemy by surprise and gaining objectives during night 18-19. Main assault force of 10th Mtn Div moves secretly to base of Belvedere-Gorgolesco feature, night 18-19.

LUZON—In U.S. Sixth Army area, XIV Corps continues preassault fire on Intramuros in Manila and is cleaning out approaches to it. In I Corps area, RCT 169 of 43d Div relieves elements of 40th Div in NW part of revised I Corps zone. Patrol of

35th Inf, 25th Div, finds Pantalbangan clear. In XI Corps area, South Force contacts East Force at Limay on Bataan. Rock Force continues clearing Corregidor.

U.S. Eighth Army conducts offshore rcn of Capul, Dalupiri, and Biri Islands, N of Luzon.

Iwo Jima—Preinvasion bombardment continues, with special attention to landing beach area.

Japan—TF 58 sails from Japan area for Iwo to assist in invasion when weather conditions prevent further attacks on Japan.

19 February

Western Europe—21 Army Group: In Cdn First Army area, Br 30 Corps continues battle of Goch, where enemy is resisting from street to street.

12th Army Group: In U.S. First Army's V Corps area, 99th Div reverts to First Army control from attachment to corps.

In U.S. Third Army's VIII Corps area, 358th Inf of 90th Div seizes Masthorn and a hill W of Pronsfeld; 359th takes Ober and Nieder Uttfeld and heads for hill N of Houf; TF Gassman (90th Rcn Tr and tanks) is organized to cover right flank of 357th Inf and moves toward Binscheid. CCR, 11th Armd Div, captures Herzfeld and mops up in Leidenborn area. Many more pillboxes are reduced. 6th Cav Gp crosses platoon of 28th Sq over the Our just N of Vianden and constructs footbridge at crossing site; 6th Sq reinforces its bridgehead between Gemund and Biewels. In XII Corps area, 80th Div, continuing NE toward the Pruem with 318th and 317th Regts, clears Hommerdingen, Freidlingerhohe, and Nusbaum. 319th begins envelopment of enemy remaining within West Wall positions; elements capture Niedergegen. 5th Div, employing 2d Bn of 2d Inf, clears Stockem; 11th Inf is withdrawn to reserve upon relief by elements of 385th Inf, 76th Div, and 10th Inf. Boundary between 5th and 76th Divs is adjusted. On S flank of corps, TF of 2d Cav Gp crosses the Moselle at Ehnen under cover of darkness and captures road center of Wincheringen. XX Corps opens attack to clear Saar-Moselle triangle. After intense arty preparation, 94th Div attacks with 3 regts abreast (376th, 301st, and 302d with 5th Ranger Bn attached, from left to right) at 0400 to clear initial objective, Borg-Munzingen highway and ridge. Attack, closely supported by air and arty, goes well, breaching West Wall switch line defenses on broad front on left and overrunning towns of Oberleuken, Keblingen, Faha, and Munzingen. At 1800, RCT 376 is attached to 10th Armd Div, which is assembling in Perl-Basch area to attack through 94th Div. 26th Div and TF Polk continue aggressive defense of current positions.

6th Army Group: In U.S. Seventh Army's XV Corps area, 276th Inf of 70th Div breaks into Forbach and begins street fighting there. 253d Inf, 63d Div, recovers Auersmacher and takes Kleinblittersdorf. In VI Corps area, 14th Armd Div relieves right flank elements of 103d Div.

Eastern Europe—Vigorous fighting is reported on Samland Peninsula (Prussia) as Germans attempt to escape westward from Koenigsberg. In NW Poland, Red Army troops are pressing northward toward Danzig and have encircled Grudziadz. Soviet forces in Silesia continue attacks against Breslau garrison and in region NW of Breslau.

Italy—15th Army Group: In U.S. Fifth Army's IV Corps area, 10th Mtn Div maintains positions on Sarasiccia-Campania ridge against counterattacks and at 2300 begins main attack on Belvedere-Gorgolesco mass with 87th and 85th Regts, omitting arty preparation in effort to surprise enemy. Substantial progress is made during night against sporadic resistance.

Burma—In ALFSEA's 15 Corps area, Japanese begin determined operations against Ind 25th Div's bridgehead at Ru-ywa.

In NCAC area, 30th Div of Ch New First Army takes Hsenwi.

Luzon—In U.S. Sixth Army's XIV Corps area, intensive bombardment of Intramuros continues. With capture of Object Hill by 160th Inf, 40th Div's current mission on right flank ends. RCT 1 rejoins 6th Div. In I Corps area, 33d Div begins limited attacks to clear Bench Mark and Question Mark Hills, NE of Sison. 1st Bn of 161st Inf, 25th Div, assisted by aircraft and arty and mortar fire, begins operations against enemy positions NW of Lumboy, clearing the first of a series of 4. In XI Corps area, East Force suspends drive across Bataan Peninsula while 149th Inf searches for enemy positions. Rock Force repels Japanese counterattack on Corregidor. Probing of Ternate area on S coast of Manila Bay is begun.

S Philippines—In U.S. Eighth Army area, X Corps begins series of amphibious operations to clear shipping route through San Bernardino Strait to port of Manila. Prov Task Force of Americal Div lands elements at Allen, on NW tip of Samar, and 1st Bn of 182d Inf on Capul I., at W entrance to San Bernardino Strait. The landing parties begin search for enemy.

Leyte—Americal Div units are eliminating enemy pocket in Villaba area.

Iwo Jima—V Amphibious Corps (VAC): After intense preparatory bombardment by warships and carrier-based and land-based planes, VAC Landing Force (TG 56.1, commanded by Gen Schmidt, USMC) goes ashore on SE coast, beginning at 0900.

Two RCT's each of 4th and 5th Mar Divs land abreast against initial light resistance. As attack progresses inland, enemy fire becomes increasingly heavy, particularly on right, and marines incur heavy casualties and loss of equipment. On right flank of corps 4th Mar Div, with RCT 25 on right and RCT 23 on left, lands on Beaches Blue 1 and Yellow 2 and 1, from right to left; right flank elements turn right to secure Beach Blue 2, while rest of div attacks frontally across heights commanding beaches to E edge of Airfield I. On corps left, 5th Mar Div, with RCT's 27 and 28, lands on Beaches Red 2 and 1 and Green 1, from right to left, and drives across island to heights overlooking W coast; left flank elements turn S toward Mt Suribachi, highest point of the island and located on S tip, while those to right start N. Tanks and arty, as soon as landed on fireraked beaches, go into action.

20 February

WESTERN EUROPE—SHAEF opens forward headquarters at Reims. 20th Armd Div arrives on Continent.

21 Army Group: In Cdn First Army's Br 30 Corps area, Bailey bridge over the Meuse at Gennep is opened to traffic. Enemy continues to resist strongly in S part of Goch. 43d Div makes contact with Cdn 3d Div, a Corps; upon relief by 15th Div, which is pushing toward Udem, returns to Cleve for rest.

12th Army Group: In U.S. First Army's VII Corps area, 99th Div (− 394th Inf) is attached to corps and moves to Aubel and Clermont areas. In V Corps area, 28th Div is attached to corps to relieve 2d Div in line.

In U.S. Third Army's VIII Corps area, main opposition to corps centers in Lichtenborn, in 90th Div sector, from which enemy fire is direct and intense as Germans attempt to protect withdrawal. 359th Inf, 90th Div, breaks through woods E of Ober and Nieder Uttfeld; 2d Bn, 357th, takes Houf and hill to N but TF Gassman and Co A are unable to clear Binscheid; 358th is held in reserve. CCR, 11th Armd Div, clears Sengerich and heights around the town against decreasing opposition. Along the Our, 6th Armd Div renews offensive: making main effort on N, CCB overruns West Wall fortifications within its zone, N of Dahnen, gaining about 2 miles, while CCA provides diversionary fire and smoke, largely in Dasburg area. 6th Cav Gp expands and strengthens Our R bridgeheads. In XII Corps area, 318th Inf of 80th Div reaches favorable position for assault on heights S of Mettendorf; 317th dears high ground N of Nusbaum, crosses Enz R, and captures Enzen; 319th continues reduction of West Wall positions within its sector. 5th Div mops up along W bank of the Pruem; elements of 2d Inf take Halsdorf. 358th Inf, 76th Div, continues to consolidate bridgehead positions and destroy pillboxes. East of the Moselle, contact is made between 2d Cav Gp and 10th Armd Div, XX Corps, at Wincheringen. In XX Corps area, 10th Armd Div, reinf by RCT 376 of 94th Div, enters offensive to clear Saar-Moselle triangle. On left, RCT 376 clears Kreuzweiler and Thorn and CCR overruns Palzem, Dilmar, Sudlingen, Wehr, Helfant, and Rommelfangen. On right, CCA takes Kirf, Meurich, Kelsen, Dittlingen, Korrig, and Fisch. Pressing E toward the Saar, 301st Inf of 94th Div clears Kollesleuken and Freudenberg while 302d takes Weiten and Orscholz.

6th Army Group: In U.S. Seventh Army's XV Corps area, 276th Inf, 10th Div, continues street fighting in Forbach; 275th takes Alsting, Zinzing, and Hesseling villages.

ITALY—15th Army Group: In U.S. Fifth Army's IV Corps area, 10th Mtn Div after gaining crest of M. Belvedere and M. Gorgolesco during early morning hours, drives toward saddle of ridge leading to M. Torraccia.

LUZON—In U.S. Sixth Army area, XIV Corps continues preparations for assault on Intramuros in Manila. 6th Div completes relief of 2d Cav Brig, 1st Cav Div, in Novaliches-Balera area. 7th Cav, 2d Cav Brig, seizes crossings of Mariquina R in Ugong-Rosario area. In I Corps area, 1st Bn of 161st Inf, 25th Div, gains control of 3 of the 4 enemy positions under attack NW of Lumboy. In XI Corps area, 1st Inf, renewing westward drive on Bataan Peninsula, reaches W coast at Bagac.

S PHILIPPINES—In U.S. Eighth Army's X Corps area, Americal Div's Prov TF sends land and amphibious patrols from Allen, on Samar, along NW coast to Lavezares. Elements make uncontested landing on Macarite I. and cross channel to establish beachhead on Biri I., at E entrance to San Bernardino Strait.

IWO JIMA—VAC enlarges beachhead against stubborn opposition. 4th Mar Div, reinforcing each of its assault RCT's with a BLT of RCT 24–div reserve—overruns Airfield 1. After repelling predawn counterattack, 5th Mar Div continues drives to N and S. With tanks spearheading, RCT 27, reinf by bn of div reserve—RCT 26—drives slowly N on left flank of corps while RCT 28, assisted by flame-throwing tanks and close naval gunfire support, works S toward Mt Suribachi—from which enemy is pouring a heavy volume of fire—systematically reducing the numerous emplacements in its path. Maximum gain, 1,000 yards, is made in center of corps. Casualties to men and equipment continue to be high; tank casualties, after 2 days of bitter fighting, are estimated as 20% to 30%

21 February

WESTERN EUROPE—21 Army Group: In Cdn First Army's Br 30 Corps area, 51st Div overcomes final resistance in Goch.

12th Army Group: In U.S. First Army's III Corps area, RCT 39 reverts to 9th Div from attachment to 2d Div.

In U.S. Third Army's VIII Corps area, 359th Inf of 80th Div seizes Strickscheid and Euscheid; 357th, assisted by aircraft, takes high ground above Lichtenborn, clears Stalbach, and assists TF Gassman in capturing Binscheid; 358th clears draw between Halenbach and Hickeshausen and takes both towns. CCR, 11th Armd Div, widens breach in West Wall, seizing Roscheid and reducing pillboxes to NE and NW. 41st Cav Rcn Sq, detached from 6th Armd Div, assembles near Lascheid. 6th Armd Div makes good progress E of the Our: 9th Armd Inf Bn, driving S and bypassing pillboxes along E bank of river, seizes Dahnen and Dasburg; 50th Armd Inf Bn moves E and clears Reipeldingen and Daleiden. In XII Corps area, 318th Inf of 80th Div clears high ground S of Mettendorf; 317th is checked by heavy fire as it attempts to reach heights W of Niehl. 319th Inf, reinf by 53d Armd Inf Bn of 4th Armd Div, envelops and destroys enemy in West Wall positions between Our and Gay Rivers with capture of Roth; also clears Korperich and Lahr. 385th Inf, 76th Div, clears additional pillboxes within its zone. 2d Cav Gp withdraws its task force at Wincheringen to positions W of the Moselle. In XX Corps area, 10th Armd Div, against disorganized resistance, drives to final objective in Saar-Moselle triangle and attacks toward Kanzem and Wiltingen bridges: CCR clears Rehlingen, Nittel, Temmels, and Fellerich; CCA takes Wawern and clears to the Saar to N and E; CCB enters battle, driving NE on Saarburg, which it largely clears; attached RCT 376, 94th Div, mops up to the Saar in Ockfen area. 94th Div (−) clears eastward to the Saar within its zone, between Orscholz and Saarburg, overrunning a number of towns and villages. 5th Ranger Bn is detached from 94th Div and attached to TF Polk, whose zone is extended northward.

6th Army Group: In U.S. Seventh Army's XV Corps area, 276th Inf of 10th Div gains about a third of Forbach as street fighting there continues. 274th and elements of 275th capture Spicheren and reach heights beyond commanding Saarbruecken and Stiring Wendel; withstand determined enemy efforts to regain the strategic heights during next few days. In VI Corps' 36th Div sector, RCT 141 is relieved by 9th Zouave Regt, Fr 3d Algerian Inf Div, in accordance with boundary change directed on 13 February.

ITALY—15th Army Group: In U.S. Fifth Army's IV Corps area, 10th Mtn Div continues toward crest of M. Torraccia against strong opposition. Brazilian 1st Div begins attack toward M. Castello with 1st and 11th Regts, gaining the feature and taking village of Abetaia.

BURMA—In Br Fourteenth Army's 4 Corps area, elements of Ind 17th Div open drive toward Meiktila from Nyaungu bridgehead.

LUZON—In U.S. Sixth Army area, XI Corps successfully concludes operations on Bataan Peninsula with junction of East Force and South Force S of Bagac. Casualties: about 50 killed or missing. Japanese dead total about 200. Small Japanese force remains in Mt Natib area but it is eventually destroyed. Corps takes command of 40th Div in current positions in Zambales Mtns. 40th Div rests while Japanese positions are being neutralized by air.

IWO JIMA—After preparatory air, naval, and arty bombardment, VAC attacks N toward Airfield 2 and S toward Mt Suribachi. Progress is slow and costly; effective tank strength at end of day is about 50%. While clearing northward to positions generally along phase line O-1, which includes S part of Airfield 2, assault forces encounter severe opposition from well-organized enemy positions around Airfield 2. RCT 21, 3d Mar Div, released as corps reserve, lands on Beaches Yellow to support attack on Airfield 2 and is attached to 4th Mar Div. RCT 28, 5th Mar Div, is viciously opposed as it continues methodical reduction of enemy positions but reaches base of Mt Suribachi. 5th Mar Div CP opens ashore. Enemy makes several local counterattacks and repeated infiltration attempts, night 21-22. Although Americans control air over Iwo, a few Japanese planes get through to attack shipping; sink *Bismarck Sea* and damage other vessels before being shot down.

22 February

WESTERN EUROPE—21 Army Group: In Cdn First Army's Cdn 2 Corps area, Moyland, on road to Calcar, falls to Cdn 2d Div.

12th Army Group: In U.S. First Army's III Corps area, 82d A/B Div clears corps sector. In V Corps area, 2d Ranger Bn is attached to 102d Cav Gp.

In U.S. Third Army's VIII Corps area, enemy resistance to corps disintegrates. On 80th Div N flank, 359th Inf clears its zone and patrols to the Pruem at Lunebach; 357th quickly overruns Lichtenborn; 358th, reinf by newly formed TF Spiess, takes Arzfeld, Holzchen, and heights extending from SW of Heckeshausen to SE of Neurath. 11th Armd Div gains its final objectives: CCR clears Eschfeld and Reiff; attacking through Eschfeld after its capture, CCB pushes to div S boundary, where contact is made with 6th Armd Div. CCB, 6th Armd Div, takes Irrhausen and Olmscheid.

[23 FEBRUARY 1945]

Elements of CCA cross the Our and relieve units of CCB within Dasburg, then drive S along E bank, taking Preischeid and Afer; W of the Our, 15th Tank Bn, after supporting the crossings, moves S and captures Ober Eisenbach, completing reduction of West Wall positions within div zone. 6th Cav Gp crosses rest of 28th Sq over the Our at Vianden, where Bailey bridge is completed, and makes contact with 80th Div (XII Corps) at Obersgegen. XII Corps consolidates positions and begins regrouping. 80th Div's 318th Inf mops up near Mettendorf and drives toward Nieder Geckler and Sinspelt; 319th clears Geichlingen. Under command of 80th Div, CCB of 4th Armd Div begins attack through 319th Inf about midnight 22-23; 53d Armd Inf Bn reverts to CCB from attachment to 319th Inf. 5th and 76th Divs regroup for assault across the Pruem. 5th Div's 2d Inf relieves elements of 317th, 80th Div, as 5th Div boundary is moved northward. In 76th Div zone, 304th Inf is relieved of positions along the Sauer between Steinheim and Girst by 2d Cav Gp; 385th continues to clear its zone W of the Pruem. 2d Cav Gp is to defend line of Sauer and Moselle Rivers from Steinheim to Grevenmacher. In XX Corps area, 10th Armd Div clears rest of Saar-Moselle triangle; attempting to secure bridgehead across the Saar near Ockfen, attached RCT 376 of 94th Div is prevented from crossing before dawn by lack of assault boats and in afternoon by heavy enemy fire, but succeeds in crossing during night 22-23. To the S, 94th Div begins crossing 302d and 301st Regts in assault boats in Staadt (opposite Serrig)-Taben region in morning and partly clears Serrig against determined resistance. Elements of TF Polk and attached 5th Ranger Bn clear region between old and new N boundaries.

6th Army Group: In U.S. Seventh Army's XV Corps area, 276th Inf of 10th Div gains control of two thirds of Forbach while other elements of div are clearing objective heights below Saarbruecken. In VI Corps area, new boundary between U.S. Seventh and Fr 1st Armies becomes effective at 2300 upon relief of RCT 143, 36th Div, by elements of 3d Algerian Div, Fr 2d Corps. CG Fr 3d Algerian Div takes responsibility for sector E of 08.2 Easting.

ITALY—15th Army Group: In U.S. Fifth Army's IV Corps area, enemy still clings to crest of M. Torraccia, but all 10th Mtn Div objectives to left are now clear. Brazilian 1st Div consolidates positions on M. Castello and extends slightly northward.

BURMA—In Br Fourteenth Army's 4 Corps area, 2 mechanized brigs of Ind 17th Div and the 255th Tank Brig are committed to drive on Meiktila from Nyaungu bridgehead.

CHINA—Gen Chennault learns that Ch forces under Gen Hsueh Yueh in E China have at last received arms from Chungking, well after fall of Suichwan.

LUZON—In U.S. Sixth Army area, XIV Corps continues preparations for final assault on Intramuros in Manila. In region E of Manila, 6th Div and 1st Cav Div attack across the Mariquina toward line Taytay-Antipolo-Montalban, cavalrymen driving through Taytay. I Corps begins drive toward Balete Pass. 35th Inf, 25th Div, attacks with 2d Bn along crude trail leading N from Rizal through Pantabangan and with 1st Bn toward Pampanga R valley. 2d Bn, 161st Inf, is ordered to clear final enemy position, called Bryant Hill, NW of Puncan. 127th Inf of 32d Div, with arty and air support, renews attack on Villa Verde Trail, taking knoll positions in the bowl. 33d Div gains Question Mark and Bench Mark Hills, concluding 4 days of limited attacks on these objectives; subsequently probes toward Baguio.

IWO JIMA—VAC continues northward attack toward phase line O-2—extending generally from Tachiiwi Pt on E coast to Motoyama village in center to W coast S of Hiraiwa Bay—after preparatory bombardment; is virtually pinned down by resistance from main enemy defenses consisting of mutually supporting pillboxes on high ground between Airfields 1 and 2. 4th Mar Div, passing RCT 21 of 3d Mar Div through RCT 23, continues attack with RCT 25 on right and RCT 21 on left, latter making frontal attack against Airfield 2. 5th Mar Div, passing RCT 26 through RCT 27 and reinforcing it with bn of RCT 27, continues slowly N on left flank of corps but is forced back to O-1 line when gap develops on right flank. RCT 28 works slowly around base of Mt Suribachi, encircling it except for 400 yards on W coast. Enemy continues local counterattacks and infiltration attempts under cover of darkness.

23 February

WESTERN EUROPE—21 Army Group: In U.S. Ninth Army area, Operation GRENADE begins at 0330, following heavy arty preparation lasting for 45 minutes. XIII and XIX Corps attack across the Roer while XVI Corps stages demonstration at jump-off time. Enemy is taken by surprise and assault troops move forward rapidly against light to moderate resistance, but engineers putting in bridges are greatly handicapped by swift current of river as well as accurate enemy ground fire and aerial attacks on crossing sites that delay movement of rear elements and supporting armor. In XVI Corps area, as a diversion for Operation GRENADE, 79th Div's 314th Inf and 35th Div's 320th Inf move forward to positions overlooking the Roer. In XIII Corps area, 84th and 102d Divs cross the Roer at Linnich and Roerdorf, respectively. On the left,

84th Div's 334th Inf makes excellent progress against unexpectedly light resistance, clearing Koerrenzig, Rurich, and Baal. On the right, 102d Div, employing 407th Inf on left and 405th on right, takes Glimbach, Gevenich, and Boslar. XIX Corps uses 29th and 30th Divs in its assault across the Roer, 29th on left making main effort. 29th Div crosses in Broich-Juelich area, with 115th and 175th Regts on left and right, respectively: 115th seizes Broich and heights NE and SE of the town, blocks Mersch-Pattern road, and patrols toward these towns; 175th Inf's crossing at Juelich is delayed because of bridging difficulties, but large portion of Juelich is cleared and a containing force is left at the Citadel; 3d Bn of 116th Inf, attached to 175th to help mop up Juelich, crosses the Roer in afternoon. RCT 330, 83d Div, moves to Schleiden area and is attached to 29th Div. 30th Div crosses in vicinity of Schophoven: 119th Inf seizes villages of Selgersdorf, Altenburg, and Daubenrath, and at 2300 opens attack for Hambach. To the S, 120th clears villages of Selhausen and Krauthausen and begins attack on Niederzier.

12th Army Group: In U.S. First Army area, VII Corps, after 45 minutes of intense preparatory fire, attacks across the Roer at 0330. Two regts of 104th Div and two of 8th Div, each of them initially employing two assault bns, cross abreast in vicinity of Dueren. On the N, 104th Div's 415th Inf takes Huchem and Stammeln while 413th clears Birkesdorf and that part of Dueren N of RR. On the S, 8th Div's 13th Inf enters Dueren S of RR; 28th, driving on Stockheim, passes through woods just W of town. Swift current of river presents greater obstacle than enemy, though bridging operations are slowed by German fire. 394th Inf and 324th Engr Bn rejoin 99th Div in vicinity of Aubel (Belgium).

In U.S. Third Army's VIII Corps area, enemy resistance is becoming increasingly disorganized. 357th Inf, 90th Div, overruns Kopscheid and pushes to Pruem R line at Waxweiler, where enemy blows bridge, and Manderscheid; 358th and TF Spiess clear Lauperath area and capture Krautscheid, Heilbach, Upperhausen, and Berkoth. 11th Armd Div, pinched out, consolidates and maintains contact with 90th Div on E and 6th Armd Div on S. CCB, 6th Armd Div, takes last of its objectives, Jucken and heights near that town and Olmscheid; makes contact with 6th Cav Gp at Karlshausen, which it bypasses and contains; and heads for Ober Geckler in effort to contact XII Corps. CCA mops up within its bridgehead E of the Our; 15th Tank Bn crosses at Ober Eisenbach and clears region southward between Our and Irsen Rivers. In XII Corps area, 80th Div mops up and clears Ober Geckler; CCB, 4th Armd Div, takes Nieder Geckler and pushes on to Sinspelt, where bridge is captured intact. Boundary between 5th and 76th Divs is moved N, and 304th Inf of 76th Div relieves elements of 10th Inf within new zone. 76th Div continues mopping up W of the Pruem. In XX Corps' 10th Armd Div zone, RCT 376 gains its objectives E of the Saar and clears Ockfen. Against heavy fire, 94th Div continues crossing troops into Serrig bridgehead, first by assault boats and later by foot bridge erected near Taben, and completes capture of Serrig; on W bank of the Saar, 94th Rcn Tr clears Krutweiler. 5th Ranger Bn and 3d Bn of 101st Inf, 26th Div, are attached to 94th Div; upon relief in Orscholz area by 3d Bn of 101st Inf, 5th Rangers cross the Saar. TF Polk, in support of operations to the N, conducts fire demonstration against enemy positions E of the Saar, particularly in Merzig area, and patrols actively. 26th Div continues aggressive defense of Saarlautern bridgehead sector and slightly improves positions in limited attack.

6th Army Group: In U.S. Seventh Army's XV Corps area, 275th and 274th Regts, 10th Div, improve positions below Saarbruecken while 276th mops up in Forbach. In VI Corps area, 36th Div begins relief of mist A/B Div on its left.

EASTERN EUROPE—Moscow announces collapse of enemy resistance in Arnswalde (Pomerania) and Posen (Poland). In Silesia, Russians continue fighting in suburbs of Breslau and push into S part of the city.

ITALY—15th Army Group: In U.S. Fifth Army's IV Corps area, 10th Mtn Div is still short of crest of M. Torraccia but Brazilian 1st Div seizes M. della Casselina and Bella Vista. In II Corps area, 1st Armd Div, with RCT 135 of 34th Div attached, takes responsibility for left flank of corps, relieving S African 6th Armd Div, which passes to army reserve.

SEAC—At a commanders' conference in Calcutta, the decision is made to push overland toward Rangoon in Burma and not to make an amphibious assault before the monsoon.

LUZON—In U.S. Sixth Army's XIV Corps area, 37th Div begins assault on Intramuros, final enemy stronghold in Manila, at conclusion of powerful program of arty bombardment. 145th Inf enters by Quezon and Parian Gates; 3d Bn, 129th, works its way through Mint building after crossing the Pasig in assault boats. Stunned by preliminary bombardment, enemy at first offers light resistance but later rallies. 2d Cav Brig, 1st Cav Div, drives E and NE from Taytay area, meeting fire from enemy's *Shimbu* line. 20th Inf, 6th Div, crosses the Mariquina and takes edge of heights S of San Mateo; gives ground a little under enemy fire after nightfall. Elements of 11th A/B Div, in amphibious, overland, and airborne operation, take Japanese internment camp at Los Banos. In I Corps area, Co B of 35th Inf, 25th Div, reaches Pantabangan. 27th

Inf prepares to attack strong enemy force located by patrols during the wide movement to E. On Villa Verde Trail, 127th Inf of 32d Div completes reduction of enemy positions within the bowl. In XI Corps area, Rock Force now holds W part of Corregidor. 40th Div renews attack to clear final enemy positions in Zambales Mtns of Luzon, employing 108th and 185th Regts.

S PHILIPPINES—In U.S. Eighth Army area, Americans turn control of Biri over to 1st Filipino Inf and return to Samar. Japanese have lost 72 killed and Americans, 3. Verde I. attack force—reinf rifle co of 1st Bn, 19th Inf—leaves Mindoro for Verde I.

IWO JIMA—Surface vessels, aircraft, and arty continue to support VAC closely as it attacks toward O-2 line, making main effort in center against Airfield 2. Limited progress is made on flanks, but enemy retains re-entrant in center. RCT 24, reinf by bn of RCT 25, relieves RCT 25 on 4th Mar Div right flank and gains a little ground, but RCT 21 is unable to advance except on extreme right. On left flank of corps, RCT 26 of 5th Mar Div is also slowed by heavy enemy fire. RCT 28, continuing assault on Mt Suribachi, gets elements to summit, where American flag is raised; completes circle about the mountain and is methodically eliminating enemy on slopes. 4th Mar Div CP opens ashore. 3d Mar Div, less RCT's 21 and 3, is released to corps from Expeditionary Troops Reserve but remains afloat. 2d Mar Div is designated area reserve.

24 February

WESTERN EUROPE—21 Army Group: In Cdn First Army's Br 30 Corps area, 53d Div, making main effort of corps, drives slowly on Weeze from Goch.

In U.S. Ninth Army's XIII Corps area, after unsuccessful enemy attempt to regain Rurich, 335th Inf of 84th Div attacks to enlarge bridgehead, passing through 334th at Baal and turning NW toward Doveren, which falls to 1st Bn assisted by newly arrived armor. 102d Div withstands enemy thrusts against its right flank early in day, then attacks, swinging due N to clear villages of Kofferen and Dingbuchhof on left and Hompesch and Hottorf on right. Treadway bridge is completed at Linnich, permitting arty to follow. CCB, 5th Armd Div, is detached from 102d Div and moves to vicinity of Baesweiler, reverting to parent unit. In XIX Corps area, 29th Div's 175th Inf completes capture of Juelich and reduces the Citadel with assistance of flame-throwing tanks. Elements attacking due E along Juelich-Steinstrass road take Stetternich and make contact with 30th Div. 3d Bn, 116th Inf, is detached from 175th Inf. At night, 116th Inf relieves elements of 175th, and RCT 330 relieves 115th Inf.

30th Div completes capture of Hambach by 0130, gains all of Niederzier by 0630, and clears Grosse Forst and Lindenberger Wald portions of Staats Forst Hambach by 2130. 117th Inf crosses the Roer and attacks NE from Niederzier area toward Steinstrass at 1630, but encounters mine fields and felled trees that halt supporting armor; infantry elements dismount from tanks and continue to within 1,000 yards of Steinstrass. Zone of 30th Div, which would have been pinched out by 29th at Steinstrass, is extended, and 30th Div is ordered to continue toward Neuss.

12th Army Group: In U.S. First Army area, VII Corps expands Roer R bridgehead toward corps bridgehead line E of Elle R and moves additional units into it. 415th Inf, 104th Div, clears Oberzier and more than half of Arnoldsweiler; at midnight 24-25, opens drive on Ellen; 413th mops up in Dueren and takes marshaling yards NE of the city. 8th Div's 13th Inf continues to clear S Dueren and suburbs; 28th takes Krauthausen and Niederau but pulls back slightly NW of Stockheim. In V Corps area, relief of 2d Div by 28th is completed by 0230 and 28th assumes responsibility for sector, 2d Div retaining that portion formerly held by 9th Div.

In U.S. Third Army's VIII Corps area, 90th Div, in limited attacks, clears its right flank with capture of Bellscheid, Ringhuscheid, and Ober and Nieder Pierscheid. Preparations are made for relief of 90th Div by 6th Armd Div and 6th Cav Gp. CCA, 11th Armd Div, is attached to 87th Div; rest of 11th Armd Div is held in corps reserve. 6th Armd Div gains its final objectives: CCB takes Leimbach, Neuerburg, and Muxerath and continues S to make contact with 80th Div (XII Corps) N of Ober Geckler; Sevenig falls to combat patrol of CCA. 6th Cav Gp seizes Karlshausen in conjunction with 6th Armd Div and easily overruns Herbstmuhle, Rodershausen, Koxhausen, Berscheid, Nasingen, and Bauler. In XII Corps area, elements of 318th Inf, 80th Div, clear high ground N of Ober Geckler, where contact is made with 6th Armd Div (VIII Corps). CCB, 4th Armd Div, reaches Outscheid and Brimingen against moderate resistance. 5th and 76th Divs begin crossing the Pruem, night 24-25. In XX Corps area, 10th Armd Div expands RCT 376's Ockfen bridgehead toward Schoden and Beurig and moves 3 armd inf bns, under CCA control, into it by assault boats since enemy fire prevents bridging. 94th Div's 301st and 302d Regts expand Serrig-Taben bridgehead under heavy fire; last bn W of river crosses into it; 5th Ranger Bn, driving NE behind enemy lines to cut Irsch-Zerf road, reaches positions overlooking the road, where it is isolated. Engineers build treadway bridge at Taben. TF Polk continues destructive fire demonstration with all available weapons. 26th Div fails to gain ground in another limited attack in Saarlautern bridgehead.

6th Army Group: In U.S. Seventh Army's XV Corps area, 63d Div, renewing limited attack northward, completes reduction of Welferding salient with capture of Buebingen and Bliesransbach and heights between.

ITALY—15th Army Group: In U.S. Fifth Army's IV Corps area, 10th Mtn Div reaches summit of M. Torraccia during morning and Brazilian 1st Div clears La Serra. 92d Div, which has been reinf by attachment of separate 473d Inf, extends its zone to include that formerly held by TF 45, taking responsibility for W half of corps from the coast to boundary of 10th Mtn Div's zone.

BURMA—In Br Fourteenth Army's 33 Corps area, Br 2d Div starts crossing the Irrawaddy at Ngazun, W of Mandalay, bringing swift enemy reaction. In 4 Corps area, Ind 17th Div, continuing toward Meiktila, takes Taungtha, Japanese supply base.

LUZON—In U.S. Sixth Army's XIV Corps area, 37th Div overcomes organized resistance in Intramuros. Fire is placed on last 3 strongpoints in Manila: the Legislative, Finance, and Agriculture buildings. Against increasing resistance, 2d Cav Brig, 1st Cav Div, drives toward Antipolo, reaching positions less than 2 miles from that objective. 6th Div attacks with 2 regts: 63d takes Montalban and San Isidro; 20th reaches heights S of Mataba. In I Corps area, while 35th Inf of 25th Div patrols, 1st Bn of 27th Inf continues to clear Highway 5. 2d Bn of 127th Inf, 32d Div, passes through 3d Bn in Villa Verde Trail sector. In XI Corps area, Rock Force clears all of Corregidor except 3,000 yards at E end of the island. 40th Div continues action against enemy positions in Zambales Mtns of Luzon, committing 160th Inf in assault on Sacobia Ridge.

S PHILIPPINES—U.S. Eighth Army Area Command, under Maj Gen Frederick A. Irving, relieves X Corps of responsibility for closing phase of mop up on Leyte, Samar, and the Camotes. Americal Div, under control of the new command, continues operations against enemy in Villaba on Leyte and attacks to clear San Bernardino Strait. Verde I. attack force lands without opposition on NE corner of Verde I. shortly after midnight, 24–25.

IWO JIMA—After preparatory bombardment, VAC attacks toward limited objective line O–A, extending across island 800 yards N of Airfield 2 in region between lines O–1 and O–2. Both flanks reach O–A line and enemy re-entrant in center is eliminated. RCT 28, 5th Mar Div, continues to mop up on Mt Suribachi. Corps CG establishes CP ashore. 3d Mar Div, less RCT's 21 and 3, lands and is assigned zone in center of corps; div CP is established ashore. Seaplane base is established.

25 February

WESTERN EUROPE—21 Army Group: In Cdn First Army's Br 30 Corps area, 53d Div, about a mile from Weeze, halts drive upon order. 15th Div, after relief by 3d Div, is withdrawn from line; its sector on left flank of corps is taken over by 3d Div and Gds Armd Div.

In U.S. Ninth Army's XVI Corps area, 35th Div begins crossing the Roer at Linnich to join in offensive. XIII Corps presses northward toward Erkelenz. 84th Div's 335th Inf, reinf, takes Houverath; 334th clears Hetzerath and Granterath. 405th Inf, 102d Div, after 3d Bn clears Ralshoven, drops back to protect div's right flank and is replaced by 406th; 407th Inf takes Loevenich; 406th clears Katzem and a number of villages. CCB, 5th Armd Div, crosses the Roer and assembles S of Hottorf. In XIX Corps' 29th Div zone, RCT 330 captures Pattern, Mersch, and Muentz; 116th secures Welldorf and from there continues to Guesten, sending elements N that seize Serrest; 175th Inf is pinched out. 30th Div's 119th Inf takes Hollen and Rodingen; 117th clears Steinstrass and opens assault on Lich.

12th Army Group: In U.S. First Army area, VII Corps completes capture of Dueren and reaches bridgehead line. On 104th Div left, 415th Inf battles during night 24–25 for Ellen and rest of Arnoldsweiler, taking both. 413th secures heights NE of Arnoldsweiler and at 2100 begins drive toward Morschenich from bridgehead line. 414th, com-mitted on div right, attacks at 0300 toward Merz-enich, which is clear by noon, and at 2100 begins drive on Golzheim. With corps bridgehead thus established, 4th Cav Gp is committed on N flank and 3d Armd Div prepares to enter line. Elements of 4th Cav Gp relieve 415th Inf in Oberzier and Ellen and make contact with Ninth Army. 13th Inf, 8th Div, mops up final resistance in S Dueren and takes barracks; passing through 13th Inf, 121st captures Binsfeld and part of Girbelsrath; 28th clears most of Stockheim and takes Rommelsheim. III Corps opens assault across the Roer with 1st Div. 2d and 3d Bns, 16th Inf, cross over bridges in VII Corps zone and drive S from Niederau to secure crossing sites Within div zone; 2d Bn takes Kreuzau and Drove; 3d is stopped by enemy at Stockheim. Using newly constructed bridge in div zone, 1st Bn of 16th Inf crosses in afternoon and drives S from Kreuzau. 26th Inf begins crossing later in afternoon, 2d Bn closing in Kreuzau and 3d Bn in Niederau.

In U. S. Third Army's VIII Corps area, CCA of 11th Armd Div moves to Manderfeld area and, during night 25–26, begins relief of 247th Inf on left flank of 87th Div. 87th Div prepares for attack to clear remaining West Wall defenses on N flank of corps. 6th Armd Div takes over new zone W of the

Pruem and relieves elements of 90th Div (359th and 357th Regts) within it. 6th Cav Gp relieves elements of 6th Armd Div in Neuerburg and routs enemy in fire fight at Scheuren. In XII Corps area, 80th Div clears Mettendorf and mops up to rear of 4th Armd Div, to which CCB reverts. 4th Armd Div regroups while continuing attack. CCB (51st Armd Inf Bn, 37th Tank Bn, and supporting units) drives E against disorganized resistance, crossing the Pruem at Hermesdorf and establishing bridgehead across the Nims at Rittersdorf. CCA (10th Armd Inf Bn, 8th Tank Bn, and supporting units) moves from Brimingen to the Pruem and starts across at Oberweis, night 25-26. Contact is made with 80th Div forces clearing Oberweis. 5th Div crosses 2 bns of RCT 2 (1st and 3d) and 3 of RCT 10 over the Pruem near Peffingen and drives NE toward Bitburg. RCT 2, on left, takes Wettlingen and high ground to NE; W of the Pruem, 2d Bn clears Olsdorf and Bettingen. On right, RCT 10 seizes Peffingen and reaches positions W of the Nims, overrunning Ingendorf. Bn of RCT 11 also crosses the Pruem and relieves elements of 2d Inf, to which it is temporarily attached. 2 bns of RCT 304, 76th Div, cross the Pruem at 5th Div crossing site early in morning and clear Holsthum; by midnight 1st Bn, 385th Inf, is across the river and 3d Bn of 304th is crossing. In XX Corps area, since enemy continues to prevent bridging in 10th Armd Div zone, CCB crosses the Saar in Taben area of 94th Div zone, driving through Irsch toward Zerf; CCA and CCR prepare to cross; RCT 376 slowly improves and expands Ockfen bridgehead. 94th Div's 301st and 302d Regts expand Serrig-Taben bridgehead against heavy fire; isolated 5th Ranger Bn withstands strong pressure with aid of arty and improves positions S of Irsch-Zerf road. Treadway bridge is put in at Serrig.

6th Army Group: In U.S. Seventh Army area, XV Corps organizes and defends current positions. In VI Corps area, 36th Div completes relief of 101st A/B Div and takes command of new sector.

ITALY—15th Army Group: In U.S. Fifth Army's IV Corps area, first phase of limited offensive W of Highway 64 ends as organized resistance on M. Torraccia and in La Serra area collapses.

In Br Eighth Army's 13 Corps area, first elements of Folgore Gp arrive in corps zone. In 5 Corps area, Cdn participation in the Italian campaign ends. Cdn 1st Div turns its sector over to Ind 8th Div. By mid-March Cdn I Corps will be in action in ETO.

BURMA—In Br Fourteenth Army's 4 Corps area, Ind 17th Div takes Mahlaing.

LUZON—In U.S. Sixth Army area, XIV Corps continues preparations for assault on last 3 strongpoints in Manila. 2d Cav Brig, 1st Cav Div, is checked for some days by stubborn enemy in Antipolo area. 6th Div is also strongly opposed. 63d Inf mops up and patrols toward Mt Pacawagan. 20th gets to within about a mile of Mt Mataba peak. 1st Inf, less 2d Bn, is committed in center and directed toward Wawa and Wawa Dam; advances through San Mateo. In I Corps area, 2d Bn of 35th Inf, 25th Div, reaches vicinity of Carranglan with ease; repels counterattack, night 25-26. 1st Bn closes in Pantabangan. 27th Inf continues to clear hill commanding Lumboy and Highway 5. 161st Inf completes capture of Bryant Hill NW of Puncan. In XI Corps area, 2d Bn of 151st Inf, 38th Div, replaces 3d Bn of 34th Inf, 24th Div, on Corregidor, where 1,000 yards are gained along E end of island. On Luzon, 185th Inf of 40th Div completes its mission with capture of Hill 1700. 160th clears most of its sector.

IWO JIMA—VAC, with 3 divs abreast, continues attack toward O-2 line, making main effort in center where, by end of day, E-W strip and two thirds of N-S strip of Airfield 2 are secured. 3d Mar Div, resuming command of RCT 21 and passing RCT 9 through it, begins attack in center for rest of Airfield 2 and gains several hundred yards under heavy fire from heights commanding both runways. On right flank of corps, 4th Mar Div employs RCT 24 on right and RCT 23, which is released from corps reserve, on left; secures portion of E-W runway of Airfield 2 within its sector. On left flank, RCT 26 of 5th Mar Div remains in place waiting for 3d Mar Div to come abreast. RCT 28 continues to mop up on Mt Suribachi. Airfield 1 is ready for emergency use.

JAPAN—Major effort of XXI BC B-29's against Tokyo with incendiary bombs demonstrates clearly the effectiveness of this weapon, which is still being used experimentally; leads to change in XXI BC tactics from daylight precision attacks on industrial targets, which have proved none too successful, to night fire attacks on Japanese urban areas. TF 58 begins 2-day strike on targets in Tokyo area.

26 February

WESTERN EUROPE—21 Army Group: In Cdn First Army area, Cdn 2 Corps begins Operation BLOCKBUSTER—to take Calcar and Udem and exploit between them to Xanten. As regrouped, corps now consists of Cdn 4th Armd Div, Br 11th Armd Div, Cdn 2d Armd Brig, Cdn 2d and 3d Inf Divs, and Br 43d Div. Cdn infantry leads off at 0430 and the 2 armd divs join in attack, which continues during night 26-27. First day's advance gains escarpment S of Calcar, Keppeln, and positions near Udem.

In U.S. Ninth Army's XVI Corps area, 137th Inf of 35th Div, attacking NE from Doveren, drives through Bruck toward Hueckelhoven; 134th, seizing bridge at Hilfarth, crosses the Roer and gains bridgehead almost a mile deep. In XIII Corps area, 84th Div cuts Erkelenz-Gerderath road and assists 102d Div with TD fire on Erkelenz. Golkrath falls to 335th Inf and Matzerath to 334th. Continuing N with 407th Inf on W and 406th on E, 102d Div clears Tenholt, Kueckhoven, Bellinghoven, and Wockerath, then launches concerted assault on Erkelenz, which falls after moderate resistance. Advancing N on right flank of corps, CCB of 5th Armd Div clears Terheeg, Hauthausen, and Mennekrath. In XIX Corps area, 29th Div attack gains momentum: Hasselsweiler and Gevelsdorf fall to 330th Inf; 116th, after completing capture of Guesten early in day, is replaced on right flank by 115th, which takes Speil, Ameln, and Titz. 30th Div's 120th Inf captures Kalrath; 117th clears Oberembt, Kirch, and Troisdorf. 113th Cav Gp and CCB of 2d Armd Div take up defensive positions on 30th Div right flank.

12th Army Group: In U.S. First Army area, on VII Corps' N flank 24th Sq of 4th Gp moves through Hambach Forest, making contact with enemy at NE edge; Tr B of 4th Sq reconnoiters toward Esch, passing through Steinstrass. 3d Armd Div, after crossing into bridgehead and being reinf by 13th Inf of 8th Div, spearheads attack NE. On div left, CCB, employing TF's Welborn and Lovelady, drives through woods to outskirts of Elsdorf, Wuellenrath, and Berrendorf; CCA, blocking on the S with TF's Kane and Doan, takes Buir and Blatzheim; reinf 83d Armd Rcn Bn, advancing between CCB and CCA, attempts to secure bridgehead across Erft Canal near Bergheim but halts at Manheim, which it takes with assistance of TF Kane. Morschenich falls to 413th Inf, 104th Div, and Golzheim to 414th before dawn; 415th Inf, passed through by 4th Cav Gp, is held in reserve. In 8th Div zone, 121st Inf completes capture of Girbelsrath and takes Eschweiler, then continues NE without making contact with enemy; 28th clears rest of Stockheim and captures Frauwullesheim and villages near Rommelsheim. Elements of 104th and 8th Divs follow in wake of 3d Armd Div, occupying captured towns. In III Corps area, 1st Div expands bridgehead to E and SE against moderate resistance: 16th Inf clears Soller; 26th takes Udingen, Leversbach, Rath, and Boich; 18th relieves 8th Div (VII Corps) of responsibility for Stockheim and takes Jakobwuellesheim. 9th Div's 39th Inf, reinf by 1st Bn of 60th, crosses the Roer in 1st Div zone and assembles near Boich.

In U.S. Third Army's VIII Corps area, CCA of 11th Armd Div completes relief of left flank elements of 87th Div and engages in defensive patrolling. At 1500, 87th Div, with elements of 345th and 346th Regts in line, attacks N toward Hall- schlag and Ormont; strong resistance and obstacles of all types are met as attack continues through the night. 6th Armd Div maintains defensive positions along the Pruem and searches for crossing sites. 6th Cav Gp takes up defensive positions along the Pruem from Waxweiler southward and relieves 358th Inf of 90th Div, which passes to SHAEF reserve. In XII Corps area, 80th Div finishes clearing region W of the Pruem on corps N flank; 319th Inf takes Phillipsweiler and Mauel. CCB, 4th Armd Div, seizes high ground N of Bitburg but is unable to clear Erdorf, on Kyll R; CCA closes in Rittersdorf area. 5th Div's RCT 2, 3d Bn of which crosses the Pruem and joins in advance, pushes NE to Nims R, taking Stahl and Birdingen; RCT 10 clears Messerich and Dockendorf on W bank of the Nims and crosses to take Ober and Nieder Stedem; RCT II crosses the Pruem and begins attacking through 10th Inf. 76th Div regroups in preparation for drive to the Moselle at Trier and attacks E and S from Holsthum bridgehead: elements of 304th Inf secure bridgehead across the Nims in vicinity of Wolsfeld; 1st Bn of 385th pushes S from Holsthum toward Irrel; 417th (−) closes in Holsthum area and prepares to attack from Wolsfeld bridgehead. 2d Cav Gp continues to defend S flank and moves elements into Wasserbillig. In XX Corps area, 10th Armd Div and 94th Div expand and join Ockfen and Serrig bridgeheads; jointly clear Beurig area, permitting heavy ponton bridge to be put in at Saarburg. CCB, 10th Armd Div, driving along Irsch-Zerf road, relieves pressure on 5th Ranger Bn (attached to 94th Div) S of the road and reaches Zerf; CCA crosses the Saar in 94th Div zone and moves to Irsch; CCR starts from Nittel toward Beurig. 94th Div prepares to attack toward high ground from Hamm to Geizenberg to protect drive of 10th Armd Div on Trier. 101st Inf, 26th Div, takes command of Saarlautern bridgehead, relieving 328th Inf.

6th Army Group: In U.S. Seventh Army area, 101st A/B Div is detached from VI Corps.

BURMA—In Br Fourteenth Army's 33 Corps area, Ind 19th Div begins strong southward push toward Mandalay. In 4 Corps area, Ind 17th Div, continuing toward Meiktila, seizes airstrip at Thabutkon.

LUZON—In U.S. Sixth Army area, XIV Corps begins assault on last 3 strongpoints in Manila. Elements of 63d Inf, 6th Div, reach crest of Mt Pacawagan but are forced back after nightfall by heavy fire. Japanese defeat efforts of 1st Inf to take Mt Mataba. 20th Inf troops advance up southernmost slopes of the mountain. In I Corps area, 2d Bn of 35th Inf, 25th Div, reaches Carranglan, but Japanese cut regimental supply line. In XI Corps area, 40th Div completes its immediate mission in Zambales

Mtns sector when 108th Inf captures Hill 12. Rock Force concludes operations on Corregidor, except for mopping up, by 1600.

S PHILIPPINES—U.S. Eighth Army is directed to plan for operations against Panay and N Negros. As VICTOR III Attack Group (TG 78.2 under Adm Fechteler) and Close Covering Group (TG 74.2 under Rear Adm R. S. Riggs) sail from Mindoro for Palawan covered by Fifth and Thirteenth Air Forces, intensive aerial bombardment of Puerto Princesa area of Palawan begins. Americal Div completes encirclement of enemy forces in NW coastal sector of Leyte. Div's Prov TF finishes clearing S part of San Bernardino Strait from NW Samar through Balicuatro I. and W to Capul and Naranjo Is.

IWO JIMA—Although still closely supported by air, naval, and arty bombardment, VAC progress toward O-2 line is measured in hundreds of yards as enemy resistance continues strong. RCT 9, 3d Mar Div, again making main effort in center of corps, is supported by massed arty fire on heights commanding Airfield 2 as it inches forward. On right flank of corps, 4th Mar Div withdraws RCT 24 to reserve and continues attack with RCT 25 on right and RCT 23 on left; latter gains up to 300 yards, reaching SW slopes of Hill 382, where enemy is firmly entrenched. RCT 26, 5th Mar Div, pushes N on left flank of corps, center elements ahead of those on flanks, which are echeloned on left rear to commanding ground overlooking W coast and on right rear to conform with advance of 3d Mar Div. Observation planes land on Airfield 1 and start spotting for arty. AAA begins neutralization of Kangoku and Kama Rocks, off W coast.

27 February

WESTERN EUROPE—21 Army Group: In Cdn First Army's Cdn a Corps area, Br 43d Div overruns Calcar and Grieth, latter on the Rhine. Cdn 2d Inf and Cdn 4th Armd Divs enter Hochwald Forest, E of Udem, and gain positions between there and Balberger Forest to S. Cdn 3d Div clears Udem and Br 11th Armd Div drives from Udem toward Kervenheim. In Br 30 Corps area, Cdn offensive eases pressure on corps. 52d Div moves E from Afferden area and takes over 51st Div sector. 3d Div cuts Udem–Weeze road.

In U.S. Ninth Army's XVI Corps area, 35th Div advances rapidly E of the Roer against moderate resistance: 137th Inf clears Altmyhl, Myhl, Gerderath, and Gerderhahn; 134th takes Millich, Schauffenberg, Ratheim, Luchtenberg, Orsbeck, Wassenberg, and 2 other towns. 15th Cav Gp is detached from 35th Div and, under corps control, relieves 8th Armd Div of positions S of Roermond between the Roer and Meuse. CCA, 8th Armd Div, crosses the Roer at Hilfarth and heads for Wegberg. In XIII Corps area, 84th Div organizes motorized task force (TF Church, based on 334th Inf) for breakthrough attack since enemy appears to be thoroughly disorganized. Spearheaded by Co B, 771st Tank Bn, the TF drives about 10 miles N from Matzerath to road junction SE of Waldniel, where opposition is met. Beeck, Wegberg, Rickelrath, and many villages are cleared. 11th Cav Gp is attached to 84th Div for screening duty. On right flank of corps, CCB of 5th Armd Div, though handicapped by extremely muddy terrain, gets elements to Guenhoven and S edge of Rheindahlen before bogging down. 102d Div's 406th Inf attacks through the halted armor, clearing Rheindahlen and continuing N; 405th Inf, to right, reaches E-W railway line between Wegberg and Rheydt. In XIX Corps area, 29th Div advances to E-W road between Erkelenz and Garzweiler against token resistance: 175th Inf takes Holzweiler, Kuckum, Keyenberg, and Borschemich; 116th clears Immerath, Pesch, and Otzenrath; 115th seizes Opherten and Jackerath. RCT 330 reverts to 83d Div from attachment to 29th. 30th Div advances N to line Garzweiler-Koenigshoven: Garzweiler falls to 120th Inf and Koenigshoven to 119th. 2d Armd Div (−CCB) assembles across the Roer for offensive to the Rhine and is reinf by 331st Inf of 83d Div.

12th Army Group: In U.S. First Army area, VII Corps advances steadily across Cologne Plain despite enemy's stubborn defense of approaches to Cologne. 4th Cav Gp takes Tollhausen and Esch. CCR, 3d Armd Div, gains two bridgeheads across the Erft, TF Hogan crossing bridge at Glesch and TF Richardson wading across at Paffendorf. 83d Armd Rcn Bn clears Grouven and Zieverich but finds Erft bridge out. CCB task forces take Elsdorf, Wuellenrath, Berrendorf, and Giesendorf. CCA's TF Kane takes Heppendorf and Sindorf while TF Doan, in conjunction with 8th Div, clears Bergerhausen and part of Kerpen. 104th and 8th Divs follow 3d Armd Div closely, mopping up and occupying captured towns. RCT 395, 99th Div, assembles near Stolberg. In III Corps area, 16th Inf of 1st Div clears Frangenheim and Vettweiss; attacking toward Neffel R at 1900, 18th Inf reaches Kelz and Irresheim. 9th Div's 39th Inf, reinf, attacks S through 1st Div bridgehead and takes Thum and Nideggen; begins drive on Berg. 90th Inf (−) crosses the Roer and assembles near Rath. 14th Cav Gp, with mission of protecting S flank of corps, crosses the Roer and closes in Drove area. In V Corps area, 69th Div begins limited attacks for ridge E of Prether R to insure safety of Hellenthal-Hollerath highway as MSR, 271st Inf taking Dickerscheid and 273d, Giescheid.

In U.S. Third Army's VIII Corps area, 87th Div makes limited gains toward Ormont and Hallschlag. CCA, 6th Armd Div, establishes small bridgehead across the Pruem: 9th Armd Inf Bn crosses near Manderscheid and seizes Heilhausen. Elements of CCB cross to N but are forced back by heavy fire. In XII Corps area, 317th Inf of 80th Div, crossing the Pruem on N flank of corps, takes Wissmannsdorf. CCB, 4th Armd Div, clears Nattenheim and Fliessem while CCA takes Matzen. RCT's II and 10, 5th Div, drive E abreast, cutting Bitburg-Trier highway: RCT II enters S outskirts of Bitburg and overruns Masholder and Moetsch; RCT 10 clears Esslingen. RCT 2 organizes positions along W bank of the Nims. 76th Div pushes SE toward Trier from the Wolsfeld bridgehead: 304th Inf takes Meckel and Gilzem; 417th thrusts toward Idesheim and Welschbillig. Between the Pruem and Nims, 1st Bn of 385th Inf clears Irrel; 2d Bn, crossing the Pruem and Nims, takes Niederweis. In XX Corps area, CCA of 10th Armd Div begins drive on Trier, moving N through CCB at Zerf to Pellingen area, where extensive mine fields are found. CCB leaving elements to block to S and E of Zerf, follows CCA and takes Baldringen. CCR completes its crossing of the Saar in 94th Div zone and moves N of Irsch-Zerf road to protect MSR. 94th Div's RCT 376, attached to 10th Armd Div, and 301st and 302d Regts expand Ockfen-Serrig bridgehead N and NE. TF Polk (3d Cav Gp) is attached to 94th Div and its sector passes to control of 104th Inf, 26th Div.

BURMA—In Br Fourteenth Army's 33 Corps area, Japanese opposition to Ind 20th Div subsides and Irrawaddy bridgehead is firmly established. In 4 Corps area, brig of Ind 17th Div is flown in to Thabutkon from Palel as rest of div reaches outskirts of Meiktila.

LUZON—In U.S. Sixth Army's XIV Corps area, 148th Inf of 37th Div clears stubborn enemy from most of Legislative building in Manila. 145th relieves 3d Bn of 129th. 63d Inf, 6th Div, holds Mt Pacawagan against heavy opposition. 1st Inf positions in Mt Mataba area are untenable and Cos I and L withdraw; Co C is unable to progress against the mountain and also falls back. In I Corps area, 27th Inf of 25th Div captures Japanese plan for defense of Balete Pass. 35th Inf reopens line of communication.

S PHILIPPINES—In U.S. Eighth Army area, an 81-mm. mortar section of 19th Inf is sent to Verde I. Advance party lands on Lubang I. to establish roadblock.

IWO JIMA—VAC continues attack toward O-2 line after intense preparatory fire. In center, RCT 9 of 3d Mar Div penetrates enemy positions to secure rest of Airfield 2 and heights beyond. RCT 23, making main effort of 4th Mar Div, reaches top of Hill 382 but withdraws to more favorable position for night; RCT 25 is delayed on left by troublesome pocket near Minami but gains ground along E coast. 5th Mar Div, replacing RCT 26 with RCT 27, advances slowly but steadily N on left flank of corps. First detachment of PBM search planes arrives at seaplane base.

28 February

WESTERN EUROPE—21 Army Group: In Cdn First Army's Cdn 2 Corps area, Br 43d Div continues SE along the Rhine on left flank of corps. Cdn 2d Inf and Cdn 4th Armd Divs deepen penetration into the Hochwald and between there and Balberger Forest. Cdn 3d Div, followed by Br 11th Armd Div, advances to Balberger Forest.

In U.S. Ninth Army area, XVI Corps' 35th Div gains 3½ miles: 137th Inf takes Rogden, Wildenrath, and Station Vlodrop; 134th seizes Ophoven, Steinkirchen, Effeld, Birgelen, and Rosenthal; 320th Inf task force (TF Byrne) prepares for motorized drive on Venlo (Holland) some 200 miles N. CCA of 8th Armd Div, pushing N past Wegberg, overruns Merbeck and Tetelrath; CCB and CCR, upon relief by 15th Cav Gp, cross the Roer at Hilfarth, CCB sending task force N that captures Arsbeck and CCR moving to Wegberg area. In XIII Corps area, 84th Div, against stiffer resistance, gains about 2 miles. One 334th Inf column begins clearing Waldniel while another drives to Birgen. 102d Div continues N, 406th Inf taking Hardt and 405th clearing Hehn and Vorst. 5th Armd Div remains in position as reserve and protects right boundary of corps. XIX Corps overruns numerous towns and villages during rapid advance. 29th Div drives quickly toward Munchen-Gladbach with 175th and 116th Regts. In 5-8-mile advance from Otzenrath-Garzweiler region, 2d Armd Div reaches positions within 5 miles of Neuss and 6 miles of the Rhine. 30th Div improves positions in limited attacks and is pinched out by 2d Armd Div.

12th Army Group: In U.S. First Army's VII Corps area, 3d Armd Div expands shallow bridgeheads at Glesch and Paffendorf and crosses armor over newly completed bridge at Paffendorf; repels tank-infantry counterattack on Paffendorf bridgehead. RCT 395 of 99th Div is attached to div to help expand Paffendorf bridgehead. CCA, relieved at Sindorf by 104th Div and at Kerpen by 8th, moves to assembly area; TF Kane relieves 83d Armd Rcn Bn in Zieverich and latter moves back to Grouven. 104th Div mops up W of the Erft and prepares to cross. While 3d Bn of 121st Inf, 8th Div, mops up stragglers in Kerpen, 1st and 2d Bns attack for Moedrath, wading Erft Canal to reach W edge. In

[28 FEBRUARY 1945]

III Corps area, 18th Inf of 1st Div clears several towns along Neffel R; 16th takes Gladbach by noon and Luxheim in night attack. Div gives TF Davisson mission of screening N flank corps and attaches it to 18th Inf. 32d Sq, 14th Cav Gp, is attached to 1st Div to protect that div's S flank. 39th Inf, 9th Div, clears Berg and heights between Berg and Thum; 60th assists in capture of Berg; 47th crosses the Roer and clears Abenden. Elements of 60th and 47th Regts clear rest of E bank of the Roer within div zone. 311th Inf, 78th Div, crosses the Roer in 9th Div zone and drives S to secure crossing sites for main div crossings. 9th Armd Div (−) crosses the Roer; CCB attacks S from assembly area at Soller in afternoon. In V Corps area, 69th Div clears rest of objective heights E of Prether R from Honningen to Rescheid.

In U.S. Third Army's VIII Corps area, enemy opposition to 87th Div is unabated, but 345th Inf gains Neuenstein. To S, corps attacks across the Pruem in force, starting before dawn. 4th Div's 8th Inf takes Klienlangenfeld while 22d captures Dausfeld. 6th Armd Div enlarges its bridgehead: crossing near Lunebach, CCB outposts Pronsfeld and captures Lunebach, Lierfeld, and Merlscheid; 9th Armd Inf Bn expands its bridgehead and is passed through by 44th Armd Inf Bn, which takes Dackscheid and Eilscheid. Elements of 6th Cav Gp cross at Wax-weiler and clear that town. Enemy opposition to crossings is at first light but becomes heavy later in day. In XII Corps area, 317th Inf of 80th Div drives N between Pruem and Nims Rivers, taking Liessem and Niederweiler; rest of div is out of contact with enemy. CCB, 4th Armd Div, attacking toward Sef-ferweich and Malbergweich, is halted by enemy in woods N of Nattenheim; CCA patrols and estab-lishes contact with 5th Div. 5th Div clears to W bank of Kyll R within its zone: Bitburg and Irsch fall to RCT 11; Roehl and Scharfbillig to RCT 10; Suelm, Dahlem, Trimport, and Idenheim to RCT 2. 76th Div continues SE between Pruem and Kyll Rivers toward Trier, clearing Hofweiler, Ittelkyll, Idesheim, Helenenberg, and Eisenach. In XX Corps area, continuing N toward Trier, CCA of 10th Armd Div, followed by CCB, breaches mine field near Pellingen and clears Paschel and Obersehr. 94th Div's RCT 376, still attached to 10th Armd Div, and 301st and 302d Regts continue to clear pillbox resistance and expand Ockfen-Serrig bridgehead to NE, protecting 10th Armd Div's drive on Trier. 26th Div maintains and improves positions in Saarlautern bridgehead.

6th Army Group: U.S. Seventh Army regroups as XXI Corps takes over zone on left flank. In accordance with orders of 25 February, 63d and 70th Inf Divs, 12th Armd Div, and 101st Cav Gp, all formerly within XV Corps zone, pass to control of XXI Corps in current positions. XV Corps holds defensive line with 44th and 100th Divs and has 106th Cav Gp in reserve.

EASTERN EUROPE—Moscow announces capture of Pomeranian communications centers of Neustettin and Prechlau and further gains in Breslau (Silesia).

ITALY—15th Army Group: In U.S. Fifth Army's IV Corps area, 10th Mtn Div and 1st Div of BEF complete regrouping for second phase of limited offensive to secure heights W of Highway 64.

BURMA—In Br Fourteenth Army's 4 Corps area, Ind 17th Div begins assault on Meiktila against strong opposition.

LUZON—In U.S. Sixth Army area, Gen Krueger orders XIV Corps to open Balayan and Batangas Bays, SW Luzon. With reduction of opposition in Legislative building, only the Agriculture and Finance buildings remain to be cleared in Manila. Co C of 63d Inf, 6th Div, reaches crest of Mt Pacawagan, which is largely clear. 1st Inf suspends attack as regrouping of div is ordered before continuation of offensive. In I Corps area, 2d Bn of 35th Inf, 25th Div, starts toward Puncan, its supply route protected by 1st Bn. In XI Corps area, 188th Inf (− 2d Bn), reinf, of 11th A/B Div gets into position for assault on Ternate region of S coast of Manila Bay. 43d Div begins relief of 40th Div in Zambales Mtns sector.

S PHILIPPINES—In U.S. Eighth Army area, TF VICTOR IV (41st Div, less RCT 186, reinf, under Maj Gen Jens A. Doe) is activated on Mindoro for assault on Zamboanga area of Mindanao I. and parts of Sulu Archipelago. At Palawan, Attack Group VICTOR III (TG 78.2) arrives off Puerto Princesa at dawn; after air and naval bombardment lands assault waves of RCT 186, reinf, 41st Div, without opposition. Town of Puerto Princesa and its airfields are quickly seized and radar installations are established. In shore-to-shore operation, 2d Bn lands at Iwahig R mouth and moves inland. CG Palawan TF takes command ashore. On Samar, 1st Bn of 182d Inf, Americal Div, and 1st Filipino Inf begin advance to clear Mauo area. Lubang I. attack force leaves Mindoro.

IWO JIMA—VAC continues attack toward O-2 line, several hundred yards distant, prepared to continue upon order toward next objective, O-3 line, which includes Airfield 3, under construction, and most of northern part of the island. 3d Mar Div, still making main effort in center of corps, passes RCT 21 through RCT 9 and presses N under rolling arty barrage, overrunning Motoyama village and reaching commanding ground overlooking Airfield 3; in 4th Mar Div zone, RCT 23 is still vigorously opposed on Hill 382; RCT 25 gains additional ground along E coast, but enemy pocket remains near Minami. On left flank of corps, RCT 27 of 5th Mar Div gains forward slopes of Hill 362, S of Nishi. RCT 28, which as corps reserve has been mopping up in Suribachi area, prepares to join in assault on northern front and releases BLT 3 to 5th Mar Div.

1 March

WESTERN EUROPE—21 Army Group: In Cdn First Army's Br 30 Corps area, 3d Div clears Kervenheim. 2 Cdn Corps makes slow progress through the Hochwald and Balberger forests and toward Sonsbeck.

In Br Second Army area, 8 Corps releases U.S. 75th Div (− RCT 289) to U.S. XVI Corps, Ninth Army.

In U.S. Ninth Army area, on XVI Corps N flank, 35th Div's TF Byrne (based on 320th Inf) speeds more than 20 miles N from Wildenrath area of Germany and captures Venlo in Holland; surprised enemy yields 20 towns and villages; RCT's 137 and 134 follow TF Byrne, mopping up bypassed pockets. 15th Cav Gp, which has been defending Roer R line in Holland from Roermond to Vlodrop, crosses the Roer at Orsbeck (Germany) and heads N toward Venlo. CCA, 8th Armd Div, moves to Waldniel; CCR closes at Wegberg; CCB remains at Arsbeck. 79th Div is transferred to XIII Corps. XIII Corps begins co-ordinated attack before dawn with 84th and 102d Divs: Speeding N from Birgen area, motorized TF Church of 84th Div overruns Boisheim and is then dissolved; 333d Inf captures Duelken and passes through Suechteln to reach Niers Canal at Oedt; 335th follows 333d Inf to Suechteln; 11th Cav Gp, attached to 84th Div, extends screen to Boisheim. Employing 405th and 406th Regts, 102d Div overruns Viersen and secures bridgehead over Niers Canal. CCB of 5th Armd Div relieves RCT 407 of 102d Div in line. CCA, attacking from Hardt area, crosses Niers Canal and enters Anrath, which it captures before dawn of 2 March. In XIX Corps area, Munchen-Gladbach falls to 29th Div; final assault by 175th and 116th Inf abreast, latter on right, meets moderate resistance. 2d Armd Div, employing CCA on left and CCB on right, speeds N over Cologne Plain for gains of up to 9 miles. CCA takes Kleinenbroich, crosses Nord Canal over bridges captured intact, and continues N to line Willich-Osterath, clearing both those towns. CCB heads for Adolf Hitler bridge at Uerdingen, moving via Grefrath and Buettgen to Nord Canal, where treadway bridge is put in; during night 1–2 continues on to Bovert. CCR follows CCA, mopping up bypassed resistance. 83d Div is committed to right of 2d Armd Div: 331st Inf (− bn), operating under attachment to CCB until noon when it reverts to parent unit, clears to the Erft SW of Neuss, overrunning Holzheim and Grevenbroich; 1st Bn of 329th Inf begins assault on Neuss and is joined there, night 1–2, by 2d Bn of 330th, which protects left flank. 30th Div mops up W of Erft Canal within zone; 113th Cav Gp is detached and passes to corps reserve. 95th Div is released from army reserve to corps; RCT 379 is attached to 2d Armd Div and starts to Kleinenbroich area while rest of div begins assembling near Juelich.

12th Army Group: In U.S. First Army area, VII Corps continues attack toward Cologne and the Rhine from the Erft. 3d Armd Div and attached RCT 395 of 99th Div expand bridgeheads over the Erft in Glesch-Paffendorf region, taking Bergheim and Kenten and woods to E; 83d Armd Rcn Bn crosses at Paffendorf after dark to clear line of departure for CC Howze (CCR). 4th Cav Gp, after elements secure high ground NE of Glesch in order to protect left flank of bridgehead, is detached from 3d Armd Div and attached to 99th Div. Attacking across Erft Canal before dawn, elements of 104th Div's 413th and 414th Regts overrun Quadrath, Ichendorf, and Horrem. 8th Div effort is against Moedrath and neighboring heights: while 121st Inf (−) maintains pressure from W edge of town, 2 bns of 28th cross the Erft to left and push S toward Moedrath. III Corps drives steadily E toward the Rhine. On 1st Div left flank, 18th Inf takes Wissersheim, Rath, Pingsheim, and Dorweiler while 16th, to right, overruns Eggersheim and crosses Neffel R. 26th Inf passes through 16th during evening. Attacking in 9th Div zone, CCB of 9th Armd Div secures Mueddersheim, Disternich, and Sievernich early in day; relieved of these towns by 39th Inf of 9th Div, CCB continues E from the Neffel toward Roth R. 9th Div, directed toward the Rhine at Bad Godesberg, attacks with 39th Inf on left and 60th on right, clearing Froitzheim, Ginnick, Thuir, Muldenau, and ridge W of Embken. To right, CCA of 9th Armd Div, after closing in Drove and moving to Berg, drives SE to Wollersheim, where it is halted by strong resistance. CCA is reinf by 3d Bn of 310th Inf, 78th Div, and CCB by 1st Bn of 310th. 311th Inf of 78th Div, driving S along E bank of the Roer to secure bridge sites, clears region between Abenden and Blens, overcomes opposition at Hausen, and reaches positions just N of Heimbach; bridge is put in at Blens and 309th Inf starts across it late in day. V Corps is principally engaged in consolidating current positions. On N flank, 102d Cav Gp prepares to cross the Roer S of Schmidt and sends patrols of attached 2d Ranger Bn across to

[1 MARCH 1945]

secure concentration area on E bank. 2d Div organizes TF S, based on 38th Inf, in preparation for crossing the Roer to S. 69th Div, continuing limited attacks for high ground E of Prether R with elements of 271st and 273d Regts, seizes Hescheld and heights near Schnorrenberg.

In U.S. Third Army area, VIII Corps, disposed astride the Pruem, continues E against strong resistance, particularly on the N. 87th Div, its left flank protected by attached CCA of 11th Armd Div, battles fortified positions on N flank of corps with elements of 3 regts, reducing strongly defended pillboxes and clearing Ormont. 4th Div makes limited progress in bridgehead E. of Pruem R and crosses 12th Inf into it. 6th Armd Div expands Pruem R bridgehead, CCB clearing Matzerath and CCA improving positions to S by patrolling extensively. Bailey bridge is completed at Lunebach. On corps S flank, 6th Cav Gp finishes its crossing of Pruem over newly completed Bailey bridge at Waxweiler: 6th Sq takes Lascheid; 28th secures Lambertsberg, Gremelsheid, and Hargarten and attacks unsuccessfully toward Pluetscheid. Gp establishes contact with 6th Armd Div on N and XII Corps on S. In XII Corps area, continuing N between Pruem and Nims Rivers, 80th Div's 317th Inf overruns Oberweiler and Schleid; 318th moves S to 76th Div zone. Between the Nims and Kyll, CCB of 4th Armd Div, with close air and arty support, takes Sefferweich and Malbergweich. 5th Div maintains positions along W bank of Kyll R. 76th Div clears generally southward toward Trier and line of Kyll and Moselle Rivers: 417th Inf secures Mohn and Newel and reaches the Kyll near Kordel; 304th takes Olk and is passed through at Olk by 385th, which continues S. In XX Corps area, 10th Armd Div, reinf by RCT 376 of 94th Div, enters Trier, important communications center, in afternoon and begins to clear it; Moselle bridge is taken intact, night 1-2. CCB overtakes CCA and joins it in fight for Trier. RCT 376 overruns some 30 pillboxes E of the Saar and clears Wiltingen. 94th Div, reinf by 3d Cav Gp (TF Polk) and 5th Ranger Bn, expands Saarburg bridgehead, protecting 10th Armd Div's right flank and blocking enemy's escape from Trier: on left, 302d Inf expands positions NE to Hentern, Schomerich, Paschel, Lampaden, and Obersehr; firm opposition to right prevents 301st from making much headway. 26th Div continues aggressive defense of Saarlautern bridgehead sector. 65th Div is attached to corps.

6th Army Group: Detachment d'Armee des Alpes (DA ALPS) is established under 6th Army Group with responsibility for Alpine sector along Franco-Italian border from junction of France, Switzerland, and Italy to the Mediterranean. French General Doyen heads the command, which consists of Fr and U.S. forces. Fr 27th Alpine Inf Div holds left flank as far S as Mt Thabor; two Fr regts, 66th and 141st Alpine Inf Regts, are disposed in central sector; U.S. 44th AAA Brig holds right flank. Detachment d'Armee de l'Atlantique (DA ATL) is new designation for forces previously known as "French Forces of the West" or "Western French Forces."

U.S. Seventh Army, with XXI, XV, and VI Corps abreast, holds defensive line generally along the Saar, Rothbach, and Moder Rivers between Emmersweiler (Germany) and Oberhoffen (France).

Fr 1st Army remains on the defensive along the Rhine, protecting right flank of U.S. Seventh Army and of 6th Army Group.

ITALY—15th Army Group: In U.S. Fifth Army area, IV Corps postpones limited offensive on right flank scheduled for this time because of weather conditions.

In Br Eighth Army's 13 Corps area, Folgore Gp begins relief of 6th Armd Div.

MIDDLE EAST—USAFIME takes over NW Africa from MTOUSA and is redesignated Africa-Middle East Theater (AMET).

LUZON—In U.S. Sixth Army's XIV Corps area, 5th Cav clears Agriculture building, leaving a single strongpoint in Manila—the Finance building. RCT 145, including 1st Bn, which is garrisoning Intramuros, passes from control of 37th Div and Sixth Army to Provost Marshal General, USA FFE. In region E of Manila, 6th Div regroups for further action against enemy's *Shimbu* line, extending N from Antipolo to Mt Oro, while 1st Cav Div to S continues to probe to develop this line. In I Corps area, 33d Div continues to probe toward Baguio from S while Philippine Guerrilla Forces, North Luzon, under Lt Col Russell W. Volckmann, are exerting pressure toward the summer capital from the N. 32d and 25th Divs continue limited actions along Villa Verde Trail and Highway 5, respectively, toward Cagayan Valley and ultimately Balete Pass. 2d Bn of 127th Inf, 32d Div, encounters strongpoint in outer perimeter defenses of Salacsac Pass on Villa Verde Trail at Cabalisian R and is delayed by pillbox opposition. Other elements of 32d Div are working forward along Arboredo and Ambayabang Valleys. On Highway 5, 25th Div columns are converging on Puncan and Digdig.

S PHILIPPINES—In U.S. Eighth Army area, aircraft begin preinvasion bombardment of Zamboanga area of Mindanao and of islands of Panay and Negros. After naval and aerial bombardment, 1st Bn of 21st Inf, reinf, lands on Lubang I., at W end of Verde I. Passage, and clears Tilic. Most of the island, the largest in the Lubang Group, is cleared with ease within the next few days. Elements of Co E, 21st Inf, move to Verde I. from Mindoro. On

Palawan, RCT 186 of 41st Div secures Puerto Princesa Harbor, assuring virtual control of the island.

IWO JIMA—VAC attacks toward Line O-3 from positions generally along Line O-2 in center and on left but far to rear on right. 3d Mar Div attacks with RCT 21 but upon encountering well-organized enemy position about 1,000 yards due E of Motoyama village, commits RCT 9 as well. RCT 21 secures W part of Airfield 3, but RCT 9 makes little headway against savage opposition. On right flank of corps, RCT 24 of 4th Mar Div relieves RCT 23 on div left and fights throughout day about base of Hill 382; RCT 25 slows its advance to tie in with RCT 24 and hammers at enemy re-entrant near Minami. Contact between 4th and 3d Mar Divs is maintained with difficulty. 5th Mar Div, confronted with W flank of enemy's cross-island defenses, replaces RCT 27 with RCT 28 and completes capture of Hill 362. 3d Bn, 26th Marines, is committed to plug gap between div and 3d Mar Div, relieving elements of RCT 21 of this task. U.S. fighter makes emergency landing on Airfield I.

RYUKYU IS.—Aircraft and surface vessels of TF 58 bombard a number of targets in the Ryukyus chain, one of them, Okino Daito, within 450 miles of Kyushu.

2 March

WESTERN EUROPE—21 Army Group: In Cdn First Army's Br 30 Corps area, 53d Div clears Weeze and heads for Geldern. Winnekendonk falls to 3d Div.

In U.S. Ninth Army's XVI Corps area, TF Byrne of 35th Div pushes rapidly from Venlo NE into Germany, via Straelen and Nieukerk, and takes Sevelen. 15th Cav Gp closes at Venlo to screen 35th Div left flank and make contact with Cdn First Army. 8th Armd Div speeds N: CCA passes through RCT 134 of 35th Div and drives through Lobberich to Wachtendonk; CCB overtakes CCA at Wachtendonk, where bridge is out, and pulls back to Wankum; from Wegberg, CCR moves through Lobberich to Grefrath. In XIII Corps area, 84th Div crosses Niers Canal near Suechteln and Oedt. With 333d Inf effectively blocking on the left, 335th advances through St Tonis and begins assault on NE part of Krefeld: RCT 334 passes through 335th Inf's bridgehead and heads N from St Tonis toward the Rhine, moving along axis Inrath-Rath. 405th and 406th Regts, 102d Div, drive to Krefeld and begin attack on SE portion of town. Despite strong rear-guard opposition, CCA of 5th Armd Div drives on Fischeln and, after brief halt S of objective to permit 102d Div to move on Krefeld, captures the town and turns it over to XIX Corps units. In XIX Corps area, 29th Div, pinched out, consolidates in Munchen-Gladbach. Continuing N toward Uerdingen, 2d Armd Div's CCA advances through Krefeld Oppum; CCB reaches S edge of Krefeld Oppum. CCR withstands strong counterattack against Schiefbahn. 83d Div's 329th Inf completes capture of Neuss before dawn and secures W approach to Rhine R bridge there, but enemy blows the bridge; elements of 330th head for bridge at Oberkassel; bn of 331st moves from the Erft to the Rhine. Determined tank-inf counterattack from Kapellen against 83d Div right flank is contained. 30th Div relieves elements of 331st Inf as its zone is extended to Holzheim.

12th Army Group: In U.S. First Army's VII Corps area, 99th Div, with mission of clearing to the Rhine on N flank of corps and protecting Ninth Army's flank, crosses 4th Cav Gp and 393d Inf over the Erft near Glesch: 4th Cav Gp overruns Bedburg, Broich, Buchholz, and Frimmersdorf; helps 393d Inf take Neurath. 3d Armd Div meets organized resistance as it expands bridgehead NE: On left, CC Howze's TF Hogan pushes through Wiedenfeld and Garsdorf to Auenheim while TF Richardson, attacking from line of departure secured early in day by 83d Armd Rcn Bn, clears Niederaussem; after RCT 395 reduces Fortuna factory area E of Bergheim, TF's Kane and Doan of CC Hickey (CCA) cross the Erft and capture Oberhausen in concerted assault. 104th Div defends bridgehead E of the Erft and regroups. 8th Div, continuing assault on Moedrath with elements of 28th and 121st Regts, overcomes sharp resistance there; 28th Inf column takes Habbelrath and heads for Grefrath. In III Corps area, 1st Div, continuing E toward the Rhine with 18th Inf on left and 26th on right, overruns Gymnich, Lechenich, Poll, and Erp. 14th Cav Gp is relieved of mission of protecting corps S flank and attached to 1st Div. CCB, 9th Armd Div, still operating in 9th Div zone, reaches Roth R at Friesheim, Muelheim, and Wichterich and establishes bridgehead at Friesheim. Other elements of CCB and bn of 39th Inf, 9th Div, converge on Niederberg and secure it night 2-3, CCB attacking through Weiler and Borr and 39th Inf from Erp area. Elsewhere in 9th Div zone, 47th Inf takes Fuessenich, Geich, Bessenich, and Roevenich while 60th clears Juntersdorf and Embken. CCA, 9th Armd Div, attacking in 78th Div zone, clears Wol-lersheim and Langendorf. 78th Div crosses last of its combat elements over the Roer and secures firm bridgehead, permitting bridging operations to continue: 311th Inf, assisted by 2d Bn of 310th, expands bridgehead, clearing Heimbach and positions near that town and Hausen; attacking through the bridgehead, 309th Inf captures Vlatten, Eppenich, and part of Buervenich. V Corps continues to consolidate positions. 102d Cav Gp crosses the Roer in force.

In U.S. Third Army's VIII Corps area, 87th Div improves positions around Ormont against determined resistance, taking some 60 pillboxes. 4th Div, with 3 regts in assault, is slowed by terrain and lively opposition E of the Pruem and makes negligible gains; efforts to take Weinsheim, Gondelsheim, and Nieder Pruem are unsuccessful. 6th Armd Div gets forward elements to Nims R: against disorganized resistance, 44th Armd Inf Bn of CCA thrusts E to the Nims NW of Heisdorf, bypassing and later clearing that town, and crosses dismounted troops to E bank after enemy blows bridge; to left, CCB clears Ober and Nieder Lauch, Winringen, and Dingdorf. 6th Cav Gp's 28th Sq takes Pluetscheid and heights to S; well-organized resistance to left slows 6th Sq, but elements reach Nims R and enter Reuland. 90th Div passes to corps control from SHAEF reserve and is directed to attack through 6th Armd Div on 4 March. XII Corps begins assault crossings of the Kyll at midnight 2-3, when 5th Div opens attack for bridgehead between Erdorf and Philippsheim. 4th Armd Div provides diversionary fire. On corps N flank, 80th Div remains in position except for 80th Rcn Tr, which captures Heilenbach. 76th Div, on corps S flank, clears most of its zone N of the Moselle and W of the Kyll and makes contact with XX Corps: 417th Inf, temporarily reinf by bn of 318th Inf of 80th Div, takes Kordel, Butzweiler, Lorich, Besslich, and Aach; 385th secures region W of Trier; 2d Cav Gp, attached to 76th Div, crosses 2d Sq over the Sauer near Steinheim to screen right flank along E bank of the Sauer and N bank of the Moselle. In XX Corps area, 10th Armd Div completes capture of Trier. Continuing N, CCB finds Kyll R bridge near Ehrang out. Konz Karthaus falls to elements of CCA. RCT 376 clears Filzen peninsula and Kommlingen. CCR blocks to E of Trier and after nightfall starts toward Sweich in effort to gain bridge there. 94th Div continues to expand Saarburg bridgehead, which by now is 6-8 miles deep, and withstands local counterattacks.

ITALY—15th Army Group: In Br Eighth Army's 5 Corps area, Cremona Gp, assisted by Italian partisans of 28th Garibaldi Brig, begins attack for Comacchio Spit between Lake Comacchio and the Adriatic.

BURMA—In Br Fourteenth Army's 33 Corps area, Ind 20th Div and Br 2d Div link their Irrawaddy bridgeheads W of Mandalay.

LUZON—In U.S. Sixth Army area, I Corps is ordered to press attack northward as XIV Corps is winding up battle for Manila. On Villa Verde Trail, 2d Bn of 127th Inf, 32d Div, reduces the strongpoint barring its progress. On Highway 5, 2d Bn of 35th Inf, 25th Div, seizes Puncan and 3d Bn begins assault on Digdig. In XI Corps area, 43d Div completes relief of 40th Div. 40th Div, less 103d Inf, which is given garrison duty on Leyte, assembles in army reserve. Rock Force finishes clearing Corregidor, to which Gen MacArthur pays return visit. For Japanese losses of about 4,500 killed and 20 captured, in addition to some 200 killed while trying to escape and about 500 sealed in caves or tunnels, American casualties number over 1,000 killed, wounded, injured, or missing. Para RCT 503 remains on Corregidor for garrison duty.

S PHILIPPINES—In U.S. Eighth Army area, 1st Bn of 132d Inf, reinf, leaves Leyte for amphibious operations against Burias and Ticao Islands. On Samar, Co C of 182d Inf, Americal Div, drives to outskirts of Mauo and is joined there by Co B, which reports Mt Bermodo deserted. On Palawan, 186th Inf of 41st Div patrols actively to locate enemy, meeting fire near Hill 1125, N of Iratag.

IWO JIMA—VAC, now in control of about two thirds of island, attacks in greater strength in order to exploit gains in center. 3d Mar Div, in center of corps, gains control of Airfield 3, which enemy continues to rake with fire; continues N into 5th Mar Div zone to Hill 362; RCT 9 is virtually pinned down on div right. 4th Mar Div, its combat efficiency greatly reduced by casualties and fatigue, continues to clear rough terrain abounding in pillboxes, caves, and underground passages on right flank of corps: RCT 24 concentrates on clearing reverse slope of Hill 382 and RCT 25 on reducing enemy reentrant near Minami. On left flank of corps, RCT 28 of 5th Mar Div makes slow progress in attack on Nishi ridge. Additional elements of RCT 26 are committed on div right as 5th Mar Div zone is broadened by northeastward attack of 3d Mar Div. Artillery support is limited by proximity of opposing forces and tank support by increasingly difficult terrain. Unloading begins on western beaches. Airfield 1 is ready for use by transport planes.

3 March

WESTERN EUROPE—21 Army Group: Contact is made between Cdn First and U.S. Ninth Armies. 1st Cdo Brig, attached to 52d Div, Br 30 Corps, and 15th Cav Gp of U.S. XVI Corps make the junction at Walbeck, SW of Geldern.

In U.S. Ninth Army's XVI Corps area, TF Byrne of 35th Div meets firm opposition and its progress is limited to small advance E of Sevelen. 8th Armd Div, pinched out by 35th Div and XIII Corps, is withdrawn as reserve. Before being recalled, CCB crosses newly constructed bridge at Wachtendonk and captures Aldekerk; CCR crosses the Niers at Muelhausen and drives NE to Schaephuysen-Toenisberg area. In XIII Corps' 84th Div sector,

RCT 334 meets and overcomes first determined resistance at Rath and continues toward Homberg; 335th Inf finishes clearing NE Krefeld early in day and pushes toward the Rhine at Moers; 333d Inf continues blocking mission on left flank. 102d Div completes capture of SE Krefeld during morning. 5th Armd Div is given mission of mopping up on corps N flank in Orsoy area and sends CCR NE for this purpose. In XIX Corps area, 29th Div passes to army reserve but remains in Munchen-Gladbach. 2d Armd Div, reinf by 379th Inf of 95th Div, continues N over Cologne Plain: From Niederbruch-Krefeld Oppum area, CCA pushes through Viertelsheide; CCR is attached to CCA and, moving through E outskirts of Krefeld, heads for Kaldenhausen, halting SW of town upon order; CCB fights bitterly for W approach to Uerdingen bridge, which is weakened by explosion but still intact. 3d Bn of 330th Inf, 83d Div, reaches bridge at Oberkassel, which enemy destroys; 331st mops up until relieved by 329th. 95th Div gets into position for attack.

12th Army Group: In U.S. First Army's VII Corps area, on 99th Div left, 24th Sq of 4th Cav Gp takes Grevenbroich and Wevelinghoven; in center, 3934 Inf drives NE from Neurath to village of Muchhausen, W of Ramrath; 394th, committed on right, advances from Wiedenfeld area to Rommerskirchen. 395th Inf reverts to 99th Div from attachment to 3d Armd Div at 0001 and 3d Bn, after moving to Neurath, attacks E and captures Sinsteden. 4th Cav Gp is detached from 99th Div at 1800 and attached to 3d Armd Div. 3d Armd Div jumps off early in day, with CC Howze on left and CC Hickey on right, each employing 2 task forces, and drives to Stommeln and Pulheim. CC Boudinot (CCB) attacks later in day between CC's Howze and Hickey, TF Lovelady assisting CC Howze in reducing lively opposition in Stommeln and TF Welborn easily clearing Sinnersdorf. Air support at Stommeln is highly effective. 83d Armd Rcn Bn starts toward Roggendorf and the Rhine. Pushing E toward Cologne with elements of 415th and 414th Regts, 104th Div takes Glessen and Dansweiler, clears high ground E of Horrem, and begins attacks against Koenigsdorf. E of Moedrath, 8th Div's 28th Inf captures Grefrath and Bottenbroich before dawn and at 1930 opens attack for Frechen. In III Corps area, 1st Div reaches the Erft and gets elements across: 18th Inf takes Dirmerzheim while 26th seizes Blessem and Liblar. 14th Cav Gp begins relief of 18th Inf along Erft Canal. CCB, 9th Armd Div, completes drive to the Erft, reaching Weilerswist and Lommersum, and is attached to 9th Div; small Weilerswist bridgehead is taken over, night 3-4, by 1st Div, whose boundary is moved S. From Niederberg, elements of 39th Inf, 9th Div, advance with armor to Lommersum and, night 3-4, establish bridgehead there; 47th Inf takes Ober Elvenich and Ober Wichterich; 60th captures Zulpich and begins attack toward Nemmenich. CCA, 9th Armd Div, takes Merzenich and continues E to Sinzenich. 9th Armd Div is given zone between 9th and 78th Divs and directed to drive on Euskirchen and secure crossings of the Erft in that region. For this purpose, CCA is reinf, night 3-4, by 2d Bn of 310th Inf, 78th Div, and RCT 60 of 9th Div. CCR closes in forward assembly area near Zulpich. On corps S flank, 78th Div's 311th Inf defends Heimbach bridgehead while 309th continues attack, clearing rest of Buervenich, assisting 9th Armd Div in reduction of Sinzenich, and taking Linzenich and Loevenich. In V Corps area, 102d Cav Gp advances to high ground S of Heimbach. TF S of 2d Div crosses the Roer at Heimbach and drives S toward Gemund; 23d Inf improves positions W of Gemund, occupying Malsbenden. 28th Div patrols aggressively about Schleiden. Employing bn of 271st Inf, 69th Div finishes clearing high ground E of Prether R.

In U.S. Third Army's VIII Corps area, 87th Div, with tank and TD support, makes slow progress generally N of Ormont and in vicinity of Reuth. Enemy continues stubborn resistance to 8th Inf of 4th Div in and about Gondelsheim; good progress is made to right, where 22d Inf clears Weinsheim and positions W of Fleringen and 12th overcomes negligible resistance in Nieder Pruem and takes Rommersheim. CCB, 11th Armd Div, crosses Pruem R and attacks toward the Kyll through 4th Div bridgehead, clearing Fleringen; numerous mines are found, but opposition is generally light. 6th Armd Div completes drive from the Pruem to the Nims. One CCB column clears Giesdorf and continues northward through woods to make contact with 4th Div on left; another drives to the Nims and crosses just N of Schoenecken. One CCA column clears Wetteldorf and Schoenecken; another, following 44th Armd Inf Bn across the Nims, clears E bank to right of 44th. 90th Div (− 358th Inf) assembles E of Pruem R, relieves CCB of 6th Armd Div after nightfall, and prepares to drive E through CCA. 6th Cav Gp crosses Nims R in Reuland-Lasel area and clears Reuland and that part of Lasel W of the river. In XII Corps area, 5th Div, with 2 regts abreast, secures small bridgehead E of the Kyll: 11th Inf, on left, clears Metterich and presses toward Erdorf and Badem while 10th takes Gondorf and Huettingen. 76th Div mops up along Kyll and Moselle Rivers and at 2400 begins crossing 304th Inf over the Kyll near Trimport; TF Onaway (17th Armd Gp Hq and Hq CO, 702d Tank Bn, 2 motorized bns of 385th Inf, and supporting units) is formed to exploit bridgehead. On corps N flank, 318th Inf rejoins 80th Div and re-

[4 MARCH 1945]

lieves elements of 4th Armd Div in place. 4th Armd Div assembles near Bitburg in preparation for attack through 5th Div bridgehead. 89th Div is attached to corps. In XX Corps area, CCR of 10th Armd Div continues toward Sweich, halting at Ruwer R line near Eitelsbach, where bridge is out. Other elements of 10th Armd Div patrol along the Moselle and make contact with adjacent friendly units. RCT 376 is detached from 10th Armd Div and reverts to 94th Div, which consolidates positions to right of 10th Armd Div and relieves 3d Cav Gp of quiet sector W of the Saar. 3d Cav Gp, with mission of holding region W of the Ruwer, moves to new zone and relieves CCR of 10th Armd Div.

6th Army Group: In U.S. Seventh Army area, XXI Corps begins limited attacks in zones of 70th and 63d Divs to improve positions. 70th Div, assisted by CCA of 12th Armd Div and Fr Lorraine Div, attacks toward objectives beyond Forbach-Saarbruecken road. 276th Inf clears Forbach and blocks road to Stiring Wendel; 274th gets elements into Stiring Wendel and to Metz highway NE of there. 253d Inf, 63d Div, attacks toward the Hahnbusch and adjacent heights, employing Co C of 253d Inf and 1st Bn of 255th. Attack is halted a little short of the woods by enemy fire. Elements of 63d Div conduct diversionary raids in support of main action.

ITALY—15th Army Group: In U.S. Fifth Army area, reinforcements for the spring offensive are arriving and by the end of month fighting strength is increased sharply, particularly in arty and infantry. IV Corps opens second phase of limited offensive, attacking toward ridges NE of M. Torraccia and M. Castello. 10th Mtn Div, with 86th Inf on left and 87th on right, pushes about 2 miles northward, taking M. Terminale and M. della Vedetta and blocking road at Pietra Colora. 1st Div of BEF co-ordinates closely with 10th Mtn Div, moving forward to right of that div.

In Br Eighth Army's 5 Corps area, 56th Div gains firm hold on E bank of the Senio near S. Severo as Cremona Gp continues attack at base of Comacchio Spit.

LUZON—In U.S. Sixth Army's XIV Corps area, 37th Div overcomes final resistance within Manila. Elements of 11th A/B Div conclude operations to clear Manila Bay with reduction of resistance in Ternate area. In I Corps area, 35th Inf of 25th Div seizes Digdig and is eliminating pockets in vicinity of Puncan as other elements of the div work toward Puncan, on Highway 5.

S PHILIPPINES—In U.S. Eighth Army area, 1st Bn of 132d Inf, reinf, lands on Burias and Ticao Islands without opposition. Ticao is free of enemy. Uneventful search of Burias is begun. Verde I. is now secure and American forces withdraw. Total enemy casualties there are 82 killed. On Palawan, 1st Bn of 186th Inf attacks toward Hill 1125 but is pinned down by intense fire.

IWO JIMA—VAC makes slow progress toward O-3 Line against increased resistance. In center, 3d Mar Div's RCT 9 is still unable to reach Hill 362, in region E of Motoyama, but RCT 21 reaches Hill 357, NE of Airfield 3, and moves elements SE in effort to outflank Hill 362 and help RCT 9 capture it. Left flank elements of 3d Mar Div on the Hill 362 N of Airfield 3 are relieved by elements of RCT 25, 4th Mar Div, as 4th Mar Div zone is expanded eastward. 5th Mar Div, with RCT 28 on left and RCT 26 on right, continues battle for Nishi ridge on left flank of corps. On corps' right flank, 4th Mar Div's RCT 24 secures rest of Hill 382; RCT 23 passes through RCT 25 on div right and isolates enemy pocket near Minami.

4 March

WESTERN EUROPE—21 Army Group: In Cdn First Army area, Cdn 2 Corps makes substantial gains as resistance suddenly slackens. Br 43d Div, clearing W bank of the Rhine, pushes SE toward Xanten, taking Appeldorn and Vynen; Cdn 2d and 3d Divs, respectively, complete clearing Hochwald and Balberger forest; Cdn 4th Armd Div assembles in Balberger forest to await further action; Br 11th Armd Div maintains positions S of Balberger forest. In Br 30 Corps area, 53d Div clears Geldern and Issum; makes contact with U.S. 35th Div at Geldern.

In U.S. Ninth Army's XVI Corps area, TF Byrne of 35th Div presses slowly NE toward the Rhine against strong resistance, reaching Camperbruch area; RCT 137 moves to Rheurdt and attacks unsuccessfully toward Lintfort; RCT 134 contains enemy in Geldern area and is passed through by elements of Cdn First Army. 35th Div is reinf by 15th Cav Gp, which is blocking enemy movement along Issum-Wesel road, and CCB of 8th Armd Div, which is to assist in drive on Lintfort. In XIII Corps area, CCR of 5th Armd Div overcomes house-to-house resistance in Repelen and to SE cuts enemy escape route, the Rheinberg-Moers road. CCA and CCB close in assembly areas near Kempen. 335th Inf, 84th Div, drives to the Rhine, overrunning Moers and Baerl; Rheinhausen RR bridge across the Rhine at Baerl is still standing but is well defended by enemy rear guards. 334th Inf presses NE toward Admiral Scheer highway bridge, which connects Duisburg and Homberg. 102d Div is held in reserve. In XIX Corps area, 95th Div, to which RCT 379 reverts from attachment to 2d Armd Div, begins attack toward the Rhine on N flank of corps. 378th Inf, on N, drives through Uerdingen to the Rhine and clears part of N Uerdingen; efforts of 379th Inf, on S, to reduce pocket near Adolf Hitler bridge are only partially successful as German rear guards put up determined resistance. 2d Armd Div concludes its Cologne Plain operations, capturing Kaldenhausen and mopping up Uerdingen, Kaldenhausen, and Viertelsheide areas.

12th Army Group: In U.S. First Army's VII Corps area, 99th Div, employing 3 regts, speeds NE along the Erft on broad front, overrunning more than 30 towns and villages and halting a little short of Erft-Rhine junction, on line Derikum-Uekerath. Finding Roggendorf strongly held, 83d Armd Rcn Bn of 3d Armd Div bypasses it to take Hackhausen and patrol to the Rhine near Worringen before dawn; then, in conjunction with TF Lovelady of CC Boudinot, temporarily under its command, captures Roggendorf and Worringen and holds them against counterattacks. 4th Cav Gp, attacking toward the Rhine in left part of 3d Armd Div sector, seizes Hackenbroich, Delhoven, and Shaberg. 104th Div pierces outer defenses of Cologne in fighting that starts at midnight 3-4 and continues into night 4-5. Brauweiler, Loevenich, Freimersdorf, and Widdersdorf fall to 415th Inf and Koenigsdorf, Buschbell, and Weiden to 414th. 413th Inf relieves 3d Armd Div forces in Busdorf, Sinthern, and Geyen. 28th Inf, 8th Div, captures Frechen and is passed through, night 4-5, by 121st Inf. In III Corps area, 14th Cav Gp completes relief of 18th Inf, 1st Div, and organizes defensive positions along Erft Canal. 1st Div's 26th Inf clears Bliesheim and Ober Liblar and secures bridgehead across the Erft while 16th Inf mops up Weilerswist. Continuing operations E of the Erft, 39th Inf of 9th Div takes Derikum and Hausweiler; bn of 47th overruns Frauenberg early in day. CCB of 9th Armd Div, under 9th Div command, drives S from Lommersum to Bodenheim; during night 4-5 secures bridgehead across the Erft, clearing Wuescheim and Gross Buellesheim. 9th Armd Div attacks E at 1400: CCR, on N, drives to Erft R line N of Euskirchen; CCA captures Euskirchen. In 78th Div zone, 309th Inf clears Uelpenich, Duerscheven, and Enzen; 311th Inf assembles in Langendorf-Buervenich-Merzenich area for attack SE. In V Corps area, 102d Cav Gp, with mission of protecting corps N flank, secures line Vlatten-Hergarten-Duttling SW to 2d Div zone near Gemund. 2d Div's TF S captures Gemund and overcomes stubborn pillbox resistance along N bank of the Urft; passing through TF S, 9th Inf drives rapidly NE about 4,500 yards; co of 23d Inf meets determined resistance upon crossing Olef R just S of Gemund and withdraws. 28th Div seizes Schleiden and begins relief of elements of 2d Div S of Gemund. 69th Div extends northward and relieves 110th Inf, 28th Div.

In U.S. Third Army's VIII Corps area, 87th Div reduces some 110 pillboxes on N flank of corps: 347th and 346th Regts clear to Kyll R line, taking Scheid, Hallschlag, Kronenburgerheutte, and Kerschenbach; on right, 345th seizes Schoenfeld and Reuth. 4th Div presses eastward all along line, overrunning Gondelsheim and Schwirzheim and mopping up resistance bypassed by 11th Armd Div at Buedesheim and Wallersheim. CCB drives rapidly E past Buedesheim and Wallersheim until halted near the Kyll in vicinity of Lissingen by fire from E bank of river. CCA reverts to 11th Armd Div from attachment to 87th Div and assembles W of the Pruem. 90th Div attacks E through 6th Armd Div toward Kyll R against light resistance: 357th Inf, on left, clears Nieder and Ober Hersdorf and continues toward Kopp; 359th takes Seiwerath and Neustrassburg, making contact with 6th Cav Gp at Neustrassburg; 358th, in reserve, assembles E of the Pruem. 6th Armd Div assembles in Arzfeld area in SHAEF reserve. 6th Cav Gp advances rapidly E of the Nims, clearing rest of Lasel, Wawern, Huscheid, Barbach, Balesfeld, and Neuheilenbach; makes contact with XII Corps on right. In XII Corps area, 80th Div's 318th Inf and Rcn Tr reconnoiter N toward corps boundary, gaining contact with VIII Corps. 5th Div expands Kyll R bridgehead to include Erdorf, Badem, Dudeldorf, and Ordorf. 76th Div's 304th Inf completes its crossing of the Kyll and captures Hosten, Auw, Preist, Orenhofen, and Speicher; RCT 417 is attached to 10th Armd Div (XX Corps); 2d Sq of 2d Cav Gp completes screening along the Moselle and assists 385th Inf in screening Kyll R line. Scheduled attack of 4th Armd Div through 5th Div bridgehead is postponed to await further expansion of the bridgehead. In XX Corps area, CCA of 10th Armd Div begins drive on Sweich bridge; crossing Ruwer R near Eitelsbach, where bridge is later put in, the column pushes 1,500 yards NE against firm opposition. CCB takes commanding ground near Ehrang; crosses a dismounted infantry co over the Kyll. RCT 417 of 76th Div (XII Corps) is attached to 10th Armd Div as it prepares for breakout assault toward Wittlich. 94th Div regroups while continuing to defend and consolidate bridgehead.

6th Army Group: In U.S. Seventh Army's XXI Corps area, 276th Inf of 10th Div pushes from Forbach into Forbach Forest; elements clear Mari-enau, W of Forbach; 274th Inf gets additional elements into Stiring Wendel, where street fighting continues. 63d Div's 253d Inf partially clears the Hahnbusch and takes Birnberg hill nearby.

EASTERN EUROPE—Red Army troops break through to Baltic coast, splitting enemy forces remaining in Pomerania and severing communication lines between Danzig and Stettin. Second White

Russian troops reach coast at Koeslin while elements of First White Russian Front thrust to coast near Kolberg. Other forces of First White Russian Front drive to the Oder SW of Stargard, overrunning Pyritz.

ITALY—15th Army Group: In U.S. Fifth Army's IV Corps area, 10th Mtn Div makes substantial progress, 87th Inf taking M. Acidola, Madonna di Brasa, and M. della Croce, while 86th clears its objective, M. Grande d'Aiano. Brazilians of 1st Div take over 10th Mtn Div positions E of Pietra Colora.

In Br Eighth Army's 5 Corps area, Cremona Gp takes Torre di Primaro, a commanding feature from which operations can be continued later against Comacchio Spit.

BURMA—In Br Fourteenth Army's 4 Corps area, Ind 17th Div has now largely completed capture of Meiktila.

LUZON—In U.S. Sixth Army area, XIV Corps orders continuation of drive to E against *Shimbu* line on 8 March; gives 11th A/B Div, reinf by RCT 158, task of clearing Balayan and Batangas Bays on S Luzon. In XI Corps area, elements of 43d and 38th Divs make contact at Tiaong; 43d then begins westward push into Zambales Mtns W of Clark Field.

S PHILIPPINES—In U.S. Eighth Army area, Co B of 186th Inf, with flame-thrower assistance, secures Hill 1125 on Palawan. On Samar, Mauo region is searched carefully for enemy.

IWO JIMA—VAC continues attack with 3 divs, each employing 2 RCT's abreast, but is unable to advance appreciably. B-29 makes emergency landing on Iwo Jima.

JAPAN—XXI BC employs 192 B-29's in precision attack on Musashino aircraft factory at Tokyo. This raid ends precision bombardment phase of XXI BC operations against Japanese aircraft industry.

5 March

WESTERN EUROPE—21 Army Group: In Cdn First Army's Cdn 2 Corps area, Br 43d Div and Cdn 2d Div are converging slowly on Xanten, enemy's last strong position W of the Rhine; Cdn 3d Div fights hard for high ground N of Sonsbeck. In Br 30 Corps area, 43d Div pushes NE from Issum toward Alpen.

In U.S. Ninth Army's XVI Corps area, TF Byrne of 35th Div clears Camperbruch and Camp; RCT 137, bolstered by CCB of 8th Armd Div, captures Lintfort and Rheinberg and, organized as TF Murray, prepares to drive on Wesel; RCT 134 is withdrawn to reserve.

In XIII Corps area, CCR of 5th Armd Div reaches the Rhine at Orsoy, capturing that town and Rheinkamp, and fires on enemy columns attempting to escape; contact is made with 8th Armd Div, XVI Corps. In 84th Div sector, enemy explosion damages Rheinhausen bridge; 334th Inf takes Homberg in lively fighting and approaches to Admiral Scheer bridge, but enemy destroys the bridge. In XIX Corps area, 95th Div overcomes negligible resistance W of the Rhine within its zone, concluding corps' part of Operation GRENADE. While 378th Inf, supported by 377th, drives NE from Uerdingen to Rheinhausen, where bridges are destroyed, 379th eliminates pocket near Adolf Hitler bridge in S Uerdingen. Div outposts the Rhine from Uerdingen N to Essenburg. 95th Div relieves CCA, 2d Armd Div, which withdraws to assembly area; CCB, leaving Rcn Co of 67th Armd Regt, reinf, to defend Rhine R line, begins movement to assembly area.

12th Army Group: In U.S. First Army's VII Corps area, 99th Div continues toward the Rhine, Co K of 393d Inf reaching it at Grimlinghausen, 395th Inf taking Delrath and several small villages, and 1st Bn of 394th capturing Nievenheim. On 3d Armd Div N flank, 4th Cav Gp and 83d Armd Rcn Bn are clearing W bank of the Rhine: former takes Horrem and Dormagen as well as I. G. Farben factory and brick plant; 83d Armd Rcn Bn works SE along the Rhine from Worringen area past Langel to positions opposite Leverkusen. To S, 3d Armd Div and 104th Div begin assault on Cologne early in day and enter the city during morning. 3d Armd Div, with CC Boudinot on left and CC Hickey on right, each employing 2 TF's, drives SE into the city, overrunning a number of suburban communities. Continuing E toward Cologne with 415th and 414th Inf, 104th Div clears Junkersdorf and penetrates 4,000 yards into the city. 8th Div attack to E is continued by 121st Inf, which, by dawn of 6th, holds Bachem, Gleul, Stotzheim, Burbach, and Alsstadten and is pressing toward Huerth; resuming attack at 2400, 28th Inf takes Berrenrath and Knapsack before dawn of 6th. Boundary between III and VII Corps is shifted S and extended to tile Rhine S of Cologne; this leaves gap between the two corps that extends eastward from the Erft between Moedrath and Liblar. In III Corps area, 14th Cav Gp, to which 32d Sq reverts from attachment to 26th Inf of 1st Div, begins clearing the pocket between the two corps. 1st Div's 26th Inf thrusts to high ground SW of Dorf Pingsdorf and to Walberberg; 16th reaches Roesberg and Merten and captures Metternich. E of the Erft, 47th Inf of 9th Div takes Gross Vernich, Schwarzmaar, Mueggenhausen, and Neukirchen; elements of 39th clear Schneppenheim and Strassfeld. RCT 60 reverts to 9th Div from attachment to CCA, 9th Armd Div. 9th Armd Div, to which CCB reverts from 9th Div, attacks across the Erft toward Stadt Meckenheim and Rheinbach: CCB, replacing CCR in line, drives toward former, taking Klein Buellesheim, Esch, and Ludendorff; CCA advances toward Rheinbach from Euskirchen, capturing Cuchenheim, Roitzheim, Weidesheim, and Odendorf. 78th Div's 311th Inf, attacking through 309th, overruns Obergartzem, Firmenich, Satzvey, Antweiler, Rheder, Billig, and Stotzheim; upon being passed through, 309th clears Elsig, Weiskirchen, and Euenheim. In V Corps area, 102d Cav Gp takes Irnich, Schwerfen, Gehn, Kommern, Schaven, and Ober Gartzem as enemy falls back toward the Rhine. After displacing to Buervenich area, 23d Inf of 2d Div attacks S and captures Berg, Floisdorf, and Eicks; TF S is dissolved and 3d Bn, 38th Inf, continues attack S of Gemund, taking heights in Nierfeld area before being relieved by 28th Div. 28th and 69th Divs prepare for offensive action. On corps S flank, 106th Div extends right and left flanks of 424th Inf to make contact with 69th Div on N and U.S. Third Army on S; patrols E to determine extent of enemy's withdrawal.

In U.S. Third Army's VII Corps area, 87th Div's current mission is concluded as 345th Inf clears heights E of Reuth. Div organizes TF Muir (Co A of 345th Inf, 87th Rcn Tr, and supporting weapons) upon being given new objectives. 4th Div drives NE, clearing Duppach and Oos; one of two hills N of Oos is secured at request of 11th Armd Div. CCB, 11th Armd Div, halts after short advance to NE to await clearance of second hill N of Oos by 4th Div. 90th Div, whose N boundary is extended to include Gerolstein, advances to the Kyll on broad front and starts across the river: 357th Inf clears Lissingen, Hinterhausen, and Birresborn and begins fording the Kyll in Birresborn area at 2300; 359th, after reaching river line to S, prepares for attack through 357th 358th starts toward Lissingen. 6th Cav Sq, 6th Cav Gp, moves from S to N flank of corps and begins relief of elements of 87th Div; 28th Sq continues clearing S flank of corps until pinched out by 90th Div and XII Corps. In XII Corps area, 80th Div zone W of the Kyll is clear, except for small pocket in Usch-St Thomas area, with capture by 318th Inf of Neidenbach and Malberg. 4th Armd Div attacks NE through 5th Div bridgehead: 25th Cav Rcn Sq, screening left flank, clears Kyllburgweiler, Seinsfeld, and Steinborn; CCB thrusts rapidly to Salm area, overrunning towns of Meisburg, Weidenbach, Wallenborn, and Salm; to right, CCA, though hampered by difficult roads, takes Gindorf and continues to Oberkail. Bridgeheads of 5th and 76th Divs are joined N of Speicher. 5th Div expands bridgehead to include Orsfeld, Pickliessem, and Philippsheim. 304th Inf, 76th Div, mops up bypassed resistance within its bridgehead; TF Onaway begins movement into bridgehead; 2d Sq of 2d Cav Gp relieves 385th Inf of screening mission W of the Kyll. In XX Corps' 10th Armd Div zone, RCT 417 (— 2d Bn) passes through CCA, to which it is temporarily attached, in Ruwer R bridgehead near Eitelsbach and expands the bridgehead 1,500 yards to NE; CCB, reinf by 2d Bn of 417th Inf, moves another co, of dismounted infantry across the Kyll near Ehrang. 94th Div, after comparatively quiet day in which Ollmuth is taken without opposition, during night 5-6 undergoes strong counterattack, largely in zone of 302d Inf, that penetrates positions. 65th Div, assembled in Ennery area, begins its first combat mission—relief of 26th Div in Saarlautern bridgehead sector—during night 5-6.

6th Army Group: In U.S. Seventh Army's XXI Corps area, 276th Inf of 10th Div continues to clear Forbach Forest and woods NW of Marienau; 274th completes capture of Stiring Wendel. 63d Div, reinforcing attack on the Hahnbusch with an additional co, finishes clearing the woods and peak to N, its objective.

EASTERN EUROPE—First White Russian troops overrun Stargard, outer bastion of Stettin.

ITALY—15th Army Group: In U.S. Fifth Army area, IV Corps completes second phase of limited offensive. While 86th Inf mops up on left flank of 10th Mtn Div, 87th reaches final phase line at Castel d'Aiano and 85th, committed on right flank, pushes forward to M. della Spe, where it holds fast against enemy counterattacks, night 5-6. 1st Div of BEF outflanks Castelnuovo and gains positions beyond overlooking Vergato.

BURMA—In ALFSEA's 15 Corps area, 25th Ind Div, on Arakan coast, takes Tamandu, where forward supply base for DRACULA is organized before div moves to Akyab. In Br Fourteenth Army's 33 Corps area, Ind 19th Div, continuing steadily S toward Mandalay, crosses Chaungmagyi in Madaya area.

LUZON—U.S. Sixth Army field order transferring 37th Div from XIV Corps to direct control of army for garrison duty in Manila and releasing RCT 158 from army reserve to XIV Corps goes into effect. In XIV Corps area, 11th A/B Div, reinf by RCT 158, begins operations to open Balayan and Batangas Bays, S Luzon. 158th Inf drives E along Route 17 on Balayan Bay until stopped by opposition near Langanan. In I Corps area, Philippine Guerrilla Forces, N Luzon, now control N coast of island W of Cagayan R mouth; control W coast, except for Vigan, S to San Fernando area. 33d Div continues northward toward Baguio and San Fernando, threatening to close pincers on Japanese between it and the guerrillas. Elements of 32d Div continue to battle Salacsac Pass defenses on Villa Verde Trail. 25th Div completes mop-up of Puncan area, open-

[6 MARCH 1945] [427]

ing Highway 5 from San Jose to Digdig and concluding first phase of drive on Cagayan Valley.

S PHILIPPINES—U.S. Eighth Army assigns 19th Inf, 24th Div, mission of clearing Romblon Is. On Palawan, 2d Bn of 186th Inf reaches Hill 1445 (near Iratag), which enemy is prepared to defend.

IWO JIMA—VAC remains in place, improving current positions and reorganizing for concerted attack on 6th. 2d Mar Div is released as area reserve. RCT 3, 3d Mar Div, held in Expeditionary Troops Reserve, afloat, is released and leaves for base camp.

6 March

WESTERN EUROPE—21 Army Group: In Cdn First Army's Cdn 2 Corps area, Br 43d and Cdn 2d Divs slightly improve positions before Xanten under heavy fire and prepare for concerted assault on the town. Cdn 3d Div concludes its mission as it drives into Sonsbeck and makes contact with 3d Div, Br 30 Corps. Cdn 4th Armd Div attacks from Sonsbeck toward Veen. In Br 30 Corps area, 53d Div continues slowly toward Alpen, on road to Wesel.

In U.S. Ninth Army area, Operation GRENADE—drive from the Roer to the Rhine—is successfully concluded. In XVI Corps area, 35th Div completes drive to the Rhine and mops up Rheinberg. 30th Div is transferred from XIX to XVI Corps. In XIII Corps area, CCR of 5th Armd Div mops up most of zone assigned to it around Orsoy. XIX Corps defends W bank of Rhine within zone.

12th Army Group: In U.S. First Army's VII Corps area, 395th Inf of 99th Div overcomes weak resistance W of the Rhine on corps N flank, taking the 4 remaining towns, among them Udesheim, and a zinc works. 3d Armd Div zone is cleared except for small pocket in NE Cologne: along the Rhine just N and NW of Cologne, CC Boudinot, assisted by TF Hogan of CC Howze, secures Feldkassel (SE of Fuehlingen), Merkenich, Niehl, and Merheim; CC Hickey, with TF's Kane and Doan in assault, drives steadily through Cologne to the Rhine, clearing N part of city except for small pocket. 104th Div, continuing assault on Cologne with 415th and 414th Inf, clears most of S part of city, and gets patrols to the Rhine; Efferden falls early in morning to 414th Inf. 8th Div again conducts day and night attacks toward the Rhine S of Cologne: by daylight of 7th, 121st Inf holds Huerth, Hermulheim, and Kendenich and 28th Inf has Kalscheuren and Meschenich. In III Corps area, corps attack is directed SE instead of due E as a result of boundary changes. 14th Cav Gp continues to make good progress clearing pocket between VII and III Corps. Closing in tin Bonn from the N, 1st Div's 26th Inf seizes Dorf Pingsdorf, Badorf, Eckdorf, Schwadorf, and Walberberg; 16th clears Trippelsdorf, Merten, Roesberg, Hemmerich, Waldorf, Dersdorf, and Ullekoven. 9th Div, employing elements of 3 regts, expands Erft bridgehead, taking Heimerzheim, Dunstekoven, Ollheim, and Buschoven. 9th Armd Div attack is directed toward junction of Rhine and Ahr Rivers: CCB overruns Miel, Morenhoven, Flerzheim, and Stadt Meckenheim; CCA drives almost to Bad Neuenahr, clearing Palmersheim, Ober Drees, Rheinbach, Wormersheim, Altendorf, Gelsdorf, Bettelhoven, Bollingen, and Lantershofen. 311th Inf of 78th Div clears Nieder Kastenholz, Flamersheim, Schweinheim, Queckenberg, Loch, Schlebach, and Merzbach; 309th concentrates in Flamersheim area. V Corps pursues enemy toward Rhine and Ahr Rivers. 102d Cav Gp seizes Antweiler, Wachendorf, Kalkar, Kirspenich, and Arloff. Mounting infantry on tanks and TD's, 2d Div, with 23d Inf on left and 9th on right, gains up to 7 miles SE toward the Ahr and clears some 25 towns to reach general line Iversheim-Noethen-Pesch. From Gemund-Schleiden region, 28th Div presses SE toward the Ahr with RCT 110 on left and RCT 112 on right: RCT 110 gets some forward elements to Zingsheim and others to Kall and Soetenich; RCT 112 takes Golbach, Rinnen, and road junction near Eichen. 69th Div, with 3 regts abreast, drives eastward to gain contact with fleeing enemy, advancing past Oberhausen, Blumenthal, Reifferscheid, Zingsheid, Wildenburg, and Ober Wolfert. On corps S flank, 424th Inf of 106th Div consolidates, patrols, and maintains contact with friendly forces on flanks.

In U.S. Third Army's VIII Corps area, 6th Cav Gp, to which 6th Sq reverts, completes assembly on N flank of corps and takes over new mission of protecting N flank and maintaining contact with First Army; 6th Sq completes relief of 347th Inf and 1st Bn of 346th, 87th Div. Continuing attack with 346th and 345th Regts and TF Muir of latter, 87th Div clears along Kyll R line and gets elements across: Stadtkyll, Niederkyll, Glaadt, Juenkerath, Schueller, Krimm, Goennersdorf, Lissendorf, Birgel, and Staffeln are overrun. 4th Div, after completing capture of high ground N of Oos and taking Roth early in morning, follows CCB of 11th Armd Div to the Kyll, with 22d Inf on left and 12th on right; during night 6-7, crosses to relieve CCD and expand bridgehead. CCB, meanwhile, drives to the Kyll at Ober and Nieder Bettingen and against strong opposition secures small bridgehead by fording river. On 90th Div left flank, 358th Inf, reinf by TF Kedrovsky (90th Rcn Tr and TD's), motors to Lissingen, crosses the Kyll dismounted, and overruns Gerolstein; 357th, after securing heights E of crossing site and towns of Michelbach, Niederbach, and Buescheich, is passed through by 359th (— 1st

Bn), which crosses at Birresborn and drives NE to clear Gee and high ground near Gerolstein; 1st Bn, 359th, crosses the Kyll to right to clear rest of Muerlenbach and occupy Densborn. Construction of bridges over the Kyll is begun. In XII Corps area, 318th Inf eliminates last enemy pocket W of the Kyll in 80th Div zone. Drive of 4th Armd Div toward the Rhine gains momentum: CCB speeds through Ober Stadtfeld, Puetzborn, Daun, Darscheid, and Schoenbach and outposts Ulmen; CCA abandons right flank attack because of poor roads and follows CCB, reaching Salm-Wallenborn-Uedersdorf area, 5th Div improves and strengthens positions E of the Kyll. 2d Inf crosses into bridgehead and drives E to Oberkail, where bridge is out; foot elements enter Schwartzenborn but are driven out during night. 11th Inf clears northward along E bank of the Kyll to Kyllburg, taking Wilsecker and Etteldorf. In 76th Div zone, TF Onaway drives through 304th Inf's bridgehead to Herforst; 42d Sq of 2d Cav Gp crosses into bridgehead in preparation for clearing right flank of div and corps. In XX Corps area, CCB of 10th Armd Div crosses additional elements into Kyll R bridgehead near Ehrang; enemy fire prevents construction of bridge at crossing site. Ruwer R bridgehead is expanded by RCT 417 (−) to include Mertzdorf, Ruwer, and Kenn. 94th Div partly restores its bridgehead positions, but enemy infiltrators remain along Zerf-Pellingen road. 26th Div, as relieved by 65th, moves to 94th Div zone and begins relief of that div: 328th Inf crosses the Saar and relieves 2d Bn of 301st Inf and 3d Bn of 376th on 94th Div right flank.

6th Army Group: In U.S. Seventh Army's XXI Corps area, 10th Div continues to clear Forbach Forest and woods NW of Marienau; patrols reach outposts of West Wall.

EASTERN EUROPE—Troops of Second White Russian Front complete reduction of Grudziadz, key point in enemy's defense system on the lower Vistula in Poland; continue along Polish corridor toward Danzig; destroy encircled enemy forces SW of Koeslin (German Pomerania). First White Russian Front forces make substantial gains in N Pomerania, where Belgard and other points are cleared.

ITALY—15th Army Group: In U.S. Fifth Army's IV Corps area, 81st Cav Rcn Sq is detached from 1st Armd Div (II Corps) and attached to IV Corps to relieve elements of 1st Div of BEF and pinch out the rest. 1st Div of BEF later moves to left of 10th Mtn Div. In II Corps area, 34th Div relieves 88th Div astride Highway 65.

LUZON—In U.S. Sixth Army area, XIV Corps is ordered by Gen Krueger to relieve 1st Cav Div with 43d Div, less one RCT. Enemy positions are being softened with aerial and arty bombardment in preparation for renewed ground attack. In 11th A/B Div sector, elements of 158th Inf reach Lemery, across Pansipit R from Taal. I Corps is ordered by Gen Krueger to speed action toward Balete Pass-Santa Fe-Imugan area. Elements of 80th Inf, 33d Div, assemble at Damortis for drive on Aringay. On Villa Verde Trail, 1st Bn of 127th Inf, 32d Div, crosses Cabalisian R and drives E toward Salacsac Pass No. 2. 25th Div drives N astride Highway 5 toward Putlan with 161st Inf on W and 27th on E. 35th Inf's 1st Bn starts wide enveloping move NE from Carranglan to secure high ground about 5,000 yards NE of Putlan. 3d Bn, upon relief at Digdig by 27th Inf, starts rcn up Old Spanish Trail toward Salazar.

S PHILIPPINES—In U.S. Eighth Army area, 21st Inf patrols find 2 other islands of Lubang Group free of enemy. On Palawan, Japanese on Hill 1445 repulse attacks of 2d Bn, 186th Inf. On Burias, 1st Bn of 132d Inf gains first contact with enemy.

IWO JIMA—After the most intensive massed arty preparation of this operation, supplemented by naval gunfire, VAC renews efforts to break through to O-3 line but is still so bitterly opposed that progress is negligible. In center of corps, RCT 21 of 3d Mar Div achieves maximum gain of corps—about 200 yards. Progress on flanks is limited to 100 yards or less. 4th Mar Div, passing RCT 23 through left flank of RCT 24, pushes SE toward coast with 2 regts abreast, while RCT 25, on right, supports assault with fire and mops up in Minami area. 5th Mar Div attacks an hour before rest of corps, with RCT's 27, 26, and 28, from right to left, and gains 50-100 yards except on left, where no progress is made. Seventh Air force fighters land on Airfield 1 to support ground operations.

7 March

WESTERN EUROPE—21 Army Group: In Cdn First Army's Cdn 2 Corps area, further efforts of Cdn 4th Armd Div to take Veen are fruitless. Preparations for all-out assault on Xanten continue. In Br 30 Corps area, 52d Div begins relief of 53d near Alpen.

U.S. Ninth Army front, except for limited offensive by XVI Corps to extend its N flank to Wesel, is quiet, with activity confined to patrolling W and E of the Rhine, making preparations for assault crossing of the Rhine, policing, and regrouping. In XVI Corps area, 35th Div attacks N, as corps boundary is extended to Wesel, but makes little headway: TF Murray is halted at outskirts of Ossenberg. Div is reinf by attachment of RCT 291, 75th Div. 79th Div is attached to corps upon release by XIII Corps. In XIII Corps area, CCR of 5th Armd Div completes mop-up in Orsoy area and turns that town over to XVI Corps. 11th Cav Gp reverts to corps control from attachment to 84th Div and is given security mission.

12th Army Group: In U.S. First Army's VII Corps area, Cologne, third largest city in Germany, falls to 3d Armd and 104th Inf Divs, which overcome organized resistance during morning and declare the city secure by 1600. 3d Bn of 413th Inf is committed on 104th Div right for final drive and advances through S outskirts of Cologne to the Rhine. While 121st Inf, 8th Div, mops up Kendenich and clears Fischenich, 28th drives to the Rhine at Rodenkirchen and Godorf, clearing part of Rodenkirchen and Al of Godorf. Resistance within corps zone is now confined to an isolated pocket in Rodenkirchen-Weiss-Surth region of 8th Div sector. In III Corps area, 9th Armd Div, in momentous drive, reaches junction of Rhine and Ahr Rivers and establishes bridgeheads across both. CCB advances in two columns, one heading toward Remagen and the other toward Sinzig. N column overcomes light resistance in Remagen and, finding Ludendorff RR bridge standing though damaged and prepared for demolition, starts across the Rhine to high ground near Orsberg. Corps plans are hastily changed in order to exploit this unexpected advantage. Instead of clearing southward from Remagen along W bank of the Rhine, CCB moves N column across the bridge as rapidly as possible and brings up S column, which has meanwhile seized Sinzig and Ahr bridge there. Crossings start in afternoon and continue throughout night 7-8, 27th Armd Inf Bn leading, followed by weapons and 52d Armd Inf Bn. 9th and 78th Divs prepare for action in Remagen bridgehead. 7th Armd Div is attached to corps and assembles in Zulpich area before taking over 9th Div zone. 9th Div releases RCT 47 to CCB, moving it to Remagen, and prepares to commit RCT 60 in bridgehead. RCT air of 78th Div prepares to cross the Rhine. On 9th Armd Div S flank, CCA drives to the Ahr at Bad Neuenahr and Heimersheim, taking the two towns and bridges there intact; late in day Tr A of 89th Cav Rcn Sq is moved to Sinzig to release CCB's S column for operations across the Rhine. On corps N flank, 14th Cav Gp finishes mopping up between VII and III Corps. 1st Div reaches edge of Bonn and prepares to attack the city: 26th Inf overruns Bruhl, Berzdorf, and Sechtem; 16th clears Bornheim, Botzdorf, Brenig, Roisdorf, and Alfter. In 9th Div zone, 39th Inf thrusts to positions just short of Bad Godesberg while 60th gets elements within 2,000 yards of Duisdorf and overruns Witterschlick, Volmershoven, and Rottgen. On S flank of corps, 78th Div drives SE to Ahr R: attacking through Pith Inf, 309th reaches the river near Dernau and at Ahrweiler and secures 3 rail and 2 vehicular bridges intact. In V Corps area, 102d Cav Gp, driving SE, reaches Ahr R in Altenahr-Kreuzberg area, 2d Div thrusts SE through Munstereiffel for maximum gains of 10 miles on left where 23d Inf reaches the Ahr in Kreuzberg-Bruck region and takes bridge at Kreuzberg intact; 9th Inf, on right, advances 5 miles SE against moderate resistance. 28th Div also reaches the Ahr and clears Blankenheim. 69th Div clears most of its zone, taking Hecken, Kreuzberg, Schmidtheim and Dahlem; patrols between Dahlem and Blankenheimerdorf. 106th Div's 424th Inf moves E on corps S flank toward Simmer R until pinched out by 69th Div and U.S. Third Army, then begins period of rehabilitation and training. 7th Armd Div is detached from corps.

In U.S. Third Army's VIII Corps area, 87th Div, with 346th, 347th, and 345th Regts in line from left to right, thrusts rapidly NE toward Ahr R: 346th clears Esch; 347th, jumping off night of 6-7, seizes Feusdorf, Allendorf, and Ripsdorf; 345th and TF Muir take Wiesbaum and Mirbach. Expanding bridgehead secured by 11th Armd Div, 4th Div's 22d Inf takes Hillesheim while 12th secures Bolsdorf, Dohm, and Bewingen. CCB, 11th Armd Div, having been relieved E of the Kyll by 4th Div, moves S toward Lissingen; CCA crosses newly completed bridge in 90th Div zone at Lissingen and attacks through 90th Div bridgehead taking Dockweiler, Dreis, Boxberg, and Kelberg. Enemy makes firm stand at Kelberg, vital road center, but is unable to halt CCA. 358th Inf, on 90th Div N flank, improves bridgehead for passage of 11th Armd Div and extends it NE toward Dreis, and Ober Ehe; 359th captures Kirchweiler, Hinterweiler, and Waldkenigen; 90th Rcn Tr clears Salm Wald. In XII Corps area, CCB of 4th Armd Div, leapfrogging tank-infantry teams with excellent effect, advances to high ground overlooking the Rhine S of Andernach along axis Ulmen-Kaisersesch-Dungenheim-Kehrig-Polch-Ochtendung CCA follows without opposition, halting near Ochten-dung. CCR crosses the Kyll at Erdorf and follows in trace of other combat commands. On 5th Div left, motorized 11th Inf speeds NE behind armor, occupying Darschied, Daun, Puetzborn, and Salm; 2d Inf takes Gransdorf, regains Schwartzenborn, and clears Eisenschmitt; 10th, in limited attack before dawn, seizes Spangdahlem, Spang, and Dahlem. In 76th Div zone to S, TF Onaway clears Binsfeld and Niederkail; 304th Inf takes Beilingen and, night 7-8, Arrenrath; 42d Cav Sq overruns Schleidweiler and Zemmer. In XX Corps area, one 10th Armd Div column drives NE toward Wittlich while others converge on Sweich: CCA, passing through Kyll R bridgehead of 76th Div (XII Corps) in Hosten area, reaches Orenhofen; CCB clears Ehrang and

Quint and is passed through by dismounted infantry of CCR, who turn E toward Sweich; RCT 417 (−) expands Ruwer R bridgehead to high ground opposite Sweich. 94th Div continues to clear infiltrators from Saarburg bridgehead; 301st Inf (− 3d Bn), its relief completed by 26th Div, closes in rear assembly area. Under cover of darkness, 65th Div continues relief of 26th Div, which in turn relieves right flank elements of 94th.

6th Army Group: In U.S. Seventh Army area, XXI Corps halts limited attacks to await extensive rcn.

ITALY—15th Army Group: In Br Eighth Army area, boundary between Pol 2 Corps and Br 5 Corps is altered in order to narrow zone of latter in preparation for spring offensive. Regrouping of troops is about completed. Pol 2 Corps extends well across Highway 9 to S. Severo, 5th Kresowa Div relieving NZ 2d Div and left flank elements of 56th Div, 5 Corps, and reverting to command of Pol 2 Corps. NZ 2d Div is withdrawn to reserve. Ind 8th Div, 5 Corps, which is reinf by Jewish Brig during most of March, conducts river crossing exercises over the Montone. Pol 2 Corps is reinf by Ind 43d Brig-previously under command of 56th Div-and 7th Armd Brig.

BURMA—In NCAC area, 112th Regt of 38th Div, Ch New First Army, occupies Lashio, successfully concluding second phase of CAPITAL.

In Br Fourteenth Army's 4 Corps area, Japanese are making determined efforts to recover Meiktila and succeed, by capturing Taungtha, in cutting off Ind 17th Div troops at Meiktila.

LUZON—Hq USAFFE closes on Leyte and opens at Manila.

In U.S. Sixth Army's XIV Corps area, 6th Div and 1st Cav Div continue preparations for coordinated drive eastward against *Shimbu* line. Arty and aerial bombardment destroys or uncovers enemy positions. In 11th A/B Div zone, 158th Inf advances through undefended Taal and gains several miles to E and S, completing first phase of attack. 187th Inf joins in the attack: 1st Bn, attacking in 2 columns N of Lake Taal, advances rapidly against slight resistance. In I Corps area, 1st Bn of 130th Inf, 33d Div, takes Aringay bridge and town without opposition and probes toward Mt Magabang. Opposition to 1st Bn of 127th Inf, 32d Div, on Villa Verde Trail is so stiff that 3d Bn starts from Santa Maria in effort to outflank enemy. 25th Div continues N astride Highway 5 with 161st and 27th Regts; 1st Bn, 35th Inf, gains heights NE of Putlan with ease.

S PHILIPPINES—U.S. Eighth Army designates Americal Div (−) to clear Cebu, Bohol, and Negros Oriental, and small islands adjacent. On Palawan, troops of 186th Inf are still unable to clear Hill 1445 although supported by arty and mortar fire as well as aircraft.

IWO JIMA—VAC begins assault in center before dawn, withholding preparatory fire and moving forward with great secrecy. RCT 21 of 3d Mar Div captures the Hill 362 E of Motoyama but RCT 9, to right, is pinned down after limited advance at daybreak. Elements on extreme left of div continue to attack in conjunction with 5th Mar Div but are unable to advance. 5th Mar Div, again attacking with 3 Regts abreast on left flank of corps, makes limited progress on right and in center; on left, where terrain is a greater handicap than enemy, overruns Hill 215 and gains up to 600 yards. On right flank of corps, 4th Mar Div's RCT's 23 and 24 advance slowly but RCT 25 is unable to move and continues to mop up rear areas. Island Commander takes responsibility for base development. Since use of naval gunfire is now greatly restricted, most of Gunfire and Covering Force (TF 54) leaves for Ulithi.

8 March

WESTERN EUROPE—21 Army Group: In Cdn First Army's Cdn 2 Corps area, Br 43d and Cdn 2d Divs, in concerted assault on Xanten, clear the town. Cdn 4th Armd Div is still held up before Veen. Br 52d, 3d, and Guards Armd Divs pass from Br 30 to Cdn 2 Corps control as Cdn 2 Corps takes over Br 30 Corps sector on the Rhine from Wesel to Emmerich at 1800. Br 11th Armd Div, now under command of 8 Corps, Br Second Army, moves to Louvain area. In Br 30 Corps area, Hq and 51st Div revert to Br Second Army.

In U.S. Ninth Army's XVI Corps area, TF Byrne of 35th Div takes Huck and Millingen, SE of Alpen; TF Murray makes slow progress within Ossenberg and clears factory area; RCT 291 takes over right sector of 35th Div zone and makes contact with 84th Div (XIII Corps). 15th Cav Gp is detached from 35th Div and reverts to corps control.

12th Army Group: In U.S. First Army's VII Corps area, 28th Inf clears remaining resistance W of the Rhine in 8th Div and VII Corps zone in morning, whereupon corps sector is extended S to include Bonn. 4th Cav Gp reverts to corps from attachment to 3d Armd Div and extends left flank to junction of Erft and Rhine Rivers, relieving 99th Div. 104th Div takes over 8th Div zone; 8th Div (− 13th Inf, still attached to 3d Armd Div) assembles as reserve. 1st Div, attacking toward the Rhine at Bonn, is attached to corps and reinf by CC Howze of 3d Armd Div. From Roisdorf-Alfter area, RCT 16, on 1st Div left, drives E to the Rhine and clears N end of Bonn; RCT 18, to right, pushes NE into Bonn, taking Duisdorf, Lengsdorf, Endenich, Odekoven, Lessenich, and Messdorf. Contact is made

[8 MARCH 1945]

between the two teams within Bonn and patrols are sent to the Rhine. 14th Cav Gp, attached to 1st Div, maintains contact between 1st and 104th Divs and relieves 26th Inf of 1st Div in place. III Corps is largely concerned with build-up and expansion of Remagen bridgehead. Traffic congestion proves a more serious handicap than enemy opposition, though Germans make strong attempts to knock out the bridge by air and with arty. CCB of 9th Armd Div, reinf by RCT 47, completes crossing into bridgehead. Reinf 1st Bn of 60th Inf, 9th Div, and RCT 311 of 78th Div also cross the Rhine. By end of day bridgehead extends in $1^{1}/_{2}$- mile arc about Erpel, with Linz, on right, partly cleared. W of the Rhine, CCA remains along Ahr R and, with elements of 310th Inf, expands bridgehead S of the river to include Laehndorf. On corps N flank, 1st Div and attached 14th Cav Gp are transferred to VII Corps and boundary is adjusted accordingly. 9th Div continues attacks until 1715, when 7th Armd Div takes over its zone: RCT 39 occupies Bad Godesberg and is attached to 7th Armd Div; RCT 60, fighting for limited objective near Duisdorf, is also attached to 7th Armd Div except for reinf 1st Bn, which is under 9th Armd Div control. 7th Armd Div is unopposed as it begins clearing its zone W of the Rhine. 9th Div hq, all combat elements now being detached, begins movement to take over Rhine bridgehead. 2d Div (V Corps) assumes responsibility for 78th Div zone, relieving 309th Inf in line; RCT 309 is then attached to 9th Armd Div. In V Corps area, 102d Cav Gp of 2d Div and 28th Div finish clearing their sectors N of the Ahr and consolidate positions along the river. 272d Inf clears rest of 69th Div zone, advancing to Waldorf, Ripsdorf, and Hungersdorf, in region S of the Ahr.

In U.S. Third Army area, VIII Corps drives rapidly toward the Rhine against scattered resistance. On N flank, 6th Cav Gp is pinched out by V Corps and 87th Div. 87th Div gains all its objectives by noon, advancing to Hungersdorf and Dollendorf, seizing bridge intact over the Ahr at Ahrhutte, and making firm contact with V Corps. Brushing aside ineffective resistance, 11th Armd Div continues toward the Rhine: CCA takes road center of Mayen, where engineers put in bridge, and continues toward Andernach; CCB, upon crossing the Kyll at Lissingen, drives NE, taking Mannebach, where enemy pocketed between First and Third Armies puts up strong opposition. Rest of 11th Armd Div crosses the Kyll and follows CCB. To rear of 11th Armd Div, 90th Div engages in widespread, unopposed patrolling. While zed and 12th Regts improve current positions, 4th Div drives rapidly NE with TF Rhine (8th Inf, reinf) to Honerath area. In XII Corps area, 4th Armd Div mops up W of the Rhine and searches for crossing sites: CCB clears Saffig-Ketting region; CCA, to right, overruns Bassenheim, Wolken, Rubenach, Kaerlich, and Muelheim. From positions overlooking Andernach Koblenz highway, div effectively attacks enemy convoys, swelling the already impressive total of enemy losses in personnel and equipment. 11th Inf of 5th Div continues to follow armor and is attached to 4th Armd Div; 2d presses NE toward Klein Kyll R and moves TF Graham (reinf 2d Bn) to Uedersdorf in preparation for attack to S; 10th Inf takes over Schwartzenborn-Gransdorf region from 2d Inf. In 76th Div zone, TF Onaway consolidates along the Salm in Burg-Bruch area and releases 1st Bn of 385th Inf to parent unit; 1st Bn of 385th Inf takes Lanscheid; 304th Inf seizes Niersbach and Greverath; 42d Cav Sq makes contact with 304th Inf at Greverath and takes Gladbach. In XX Corps area, CCA of 10th Armd Div drives E from Orenhofen sector toward Salm R through Heidweiler, Naurath, Dierscheid, and Erlenbach to vicinity of Sehlem. Completion of Ehrang bridge permits CCR to complete crossing of the Kyll and seize Sweich. RCT 417 (−) defends and improves Ruwer bridgehead. 94th Div drives enemy remnants from Saarburg bridgehead and prepares to resume offensive instead of withdrawing to rear as planned, since new boundary is established between it and 26th Div, running generally E from Saarburg.

6th Army Group: U.S. Seventh Army is being strengthened for mid-March offensive against West Wall. 6th Armd Div is released to XV Corps from SHAEF reserve.

ITALY—15th Army Group: In U.S. Fifth Army's II Corps area, 1st Armd Div makes limited attack to improve positions on left flank of corps, taking village of Carviano, NE of Vergato.

LUZON—In U.S. Sixth Army area, XIV Corps begins eastward drive against *Shimbu* line with 6th Div and 1st Cav Div, former on N. 1st Inf, 6th Div, having been relieved in precarious positions on Mts Pacawagan and Mataba by 63d Inf, attacks against unexpectedly light opposition and gains initial objectives. 1st Cav Div, with 5th, 12th, 7th, and 8th Cav Regts abreast from N to S, attacks toward hills near Antipolo, taking one, Bench Mark 11. In 11th A/B Div sector, 158th Inf mops up and patrols while 187th Inf columns converge on Talaga and advance beyond that town until stopped by strong opposition from Hill 660. In I Corps area, Co C of 130th Inf, 33d Div, seizes Mt Magabang, NE of Aringay. 1st Bn of 35th Inf, 25th Div, takes Putlan, on Highway 5, but Japanese destroy Putlan bridge to N.

S PHILIPPINES—In U.S. Eighth Army area, 41st Inf force sails for Zamboanga, Mindanao, from Leyte. To assist guerrillas in holding Dipolog airfield there, Cos F and G of 91st Inf, 24th Div, are flown in. On Palawan, Co G of 186th Inf reaches top of Hill 1445 without incident. This ends organized resistance on Palawan. Patrols are searching for enemy remnants. Palawan Force later seizes Busuanga I., off S tip of Palawan, and Balabac and Pandanan Islands as well.

IWO JIMA—VAC attacks toward coast after arty and naval gunfire preparation, 4th Mar Div leading off at 0620 and 3d and 5th Mar Divs following at 0750. A few hundred yards are wrested from enemy in some sectors. In center, 3d Mar Div's RCT 21 gets elements to O-3 line; RCT 9 starts toward coast from Hill 362, gaining about 400 yards. 4th Mar Div; profiting a little by early hour of attack, makes limited progress in zone of RCT 23 but is unable to advance its right flank; withstands counterattack in force against left flank. 5th Mar Div, attacking on left flank of corps with 3 regts, gains some ground on left. First detachment of carriers leaves Iwo for Ulithi.

9 March

WESTERN EUROPE—21 Army Group: Field Marshal Montgomery issues instructions for crossing the Rhine N of the Ruhr. Germans abandon their Wesel bridgehead across the Rhine, night 9-10, and blow the last remaining bridge.

In Cdn First Army's Cdn 2 Corps area, Br 43d and Cdn 2d Divs clear last enemy positions in immediate vicinity of Xanten. Cdn 4th Armd Div breaches mine fields before Veen and captures that town. Br 52d Div advances slowly NE toward the Rhine.

In U.S. Ninth Army's XVI Corps area, TF Byrne of 35th Div inches forward to Drupt, NE of Alpen, and, night 9-10, is passed through by RCT 134; TF Murray completes capture of Ossenberg and pushes N past Borth and Wallach.

12th Army Group: In U.S. First Army's VII Corps area, German resistance W of the Rhine ends as 1st Div's RCT's 16 and 18 complete capture of Bonn by 1600. 99th Div is transferred to III Corps and moves to Stadt-Meckenheim area. In III Corps area, 9th Div takes command of Remagen bridgehead; div's troops revert to it. Combat elements of 78th Div (RCT's 311 and 309, and 310th Inf) are detached from 9th Armd Div and attached to 9th Div. CCB, 9th Armd Div, is also attached to 9th Div. RCT 309 crosses the Rhine and is committed in bridgehead; RCT 60 of 9th Div completes its crossing and 1st Bn, reinf, is committed. Enemy, though still offering no concerted opposition to bridgehead, puts up sharp local resistance as 9th Div expands bridgehead to include half of Honnef, Rheinbreitbach, Scheuren, Bruchhausen, rest of Linz, and positions beyond these towns. Firm opposition is met in Honnef and counterattack against center of bridgehead causes local withdrawal. Ludendorff bridge continues to be objective for German air attacks and arty fire. Corps zone W of the Rhine is cleared of enemy. 7th Armd Div defends W bank of the river between Bonn and Remagen. CCA, 9th Armd Div, defends Ahr R line; releases 2d and 3d bns of 310th Inf, 78th Div, to 9th Div for operations E of the Rhine after elements of 2d Div (V Corps) effect relief of the 2 bns in bridgeheads S of the Ahr. In V Corps area, 2d Div's 23d Inf advances to the Rhine along axis Bruck-Sinzig; 9th Inf drives E to rear of 23d; 38th Inf moves along Bad Neuenahr-Konigsfeld road to edge of Konigsfeld, S of the Ahr. RCT 110, 28th Div, temporarily attached to 2d Div, relieves 9th Inf in place.

In U.S. Third Army area, VIII Corps completes drive to the Rhine. On 11th Armd Div left flank, CCB gains heights overlooking the Rhine near Brohl; CCA reaches the river at Andernach and clears most of that city. Passing through 87th and 4th Divs, both of which are then out of contact with enemy, 6th Cav Gp drives E without opposition and establishes contact with 11th Armd Div. TF Rhine completes 4th Div's mission, clearing Honerath, Adenau, Rodder, and Reifferscheid be-fore being passed through. 87th Div begins period of rest, maintenance, and training. 90th Div dis-places to Kelberg area and sends elements on to Mayen. In XII Corps area, 4th Armd Div, directed to secure Moselle bridge at Treis if possible, regroups. CCB, with 51st Armd Inf Bn and 35th Tank Bn under command and former components transferred in place to CCR, moves S to Carden, on river opposite Treis, but finds bridge wrecked. CCR and CCA continue clearing W bank of the Rhine, taking river towns between Andernach and Koblenz. 5th Div's 2d Inf, employing leapfrog tactics, makes rapid progress, clearing Bleckhausen, Manderscheid, Bettenfeld, and Pantenburg; elements are motored to Darscheid and Puetzborn in preparation for drives SE. On corps S flank, elements of 385th Inf, 76th Div, capture Grosslittgen; Musweiler falls to 304th Inf, temporarily reinf by bn of 385th; TF Onaway is disbanded; 42d Cav Sq crosses Salm R in Dreis-Bruch area and attacks toward Dreis and Bergweiler. 89th Div begins concentration to rear of 76th Div. In XX Corps area, CCA of 10th Armd Div closes along Salm R, clearing Hotzerath, Rievenich, and Sehlem, and turns N to Dorbach area, where bridge is put in and bridgehead established. Driving NE through CCR, CCB takes Foren and Bekond. CCR clears commanding ground E of Sweich. RCT 417 (−) withstands enemy efforts to compress bridgehead NE of Ruwer R. 94th Div regroups to place 376th Inf on N, 301st on S, and 302d in reserve; 376th relieves elements of 3d Cav Gp within its sector. At 2400, 3d Cav Gp is detached from 94th Div and reinf by attachment of 16th Cav Gp, which becomes operational at this time; the 2 cav gps combine to form 316th Prov Cav Brig. 65th Div relieves final elements of 26th Div before dawn and aggressively defends Saarlautern bridgehead sector.

6th Army Group: In U.S. Seventh Army area, 71st Div is attached to XV Corps.

ITALY—15th Army Group: In U.S. Fifth Army's IV Corps area, elements of 10th Mtn Div improve positions N of Castelnuovo with unopposed capture of M. Valbura and M. Belvedere.

BURMA—In Br Fourteenth Army's 33 Corps area, Ind 19th Div breaks into Mandalay, where lively fighting ensues.

LUZON—In U.S. Sixth Army's XIV Corps area, 6th Div and 1st Cav Div continue eastward attacks. 12th Cav of latter reaches slopes of Hill Bench Mark 9. Elements of 187th Inf, 11th A/B Div, begin assault on Hill 660 but are unable to take it. In I Corps area, 136th Inf of 33d Div is ordered to maintain pressure against enemy with patrols on Kennon Road; 123d is to patrol N and E of Pugo; 1st Bn of 130th is to patrol N and E of Mt Magabang. 3d Bn of 127th Inf, 32d Div, completes march to Villa Verde Trail to eliminate opposition blocking progress there. 161st Inf column, 25th Div, drives through Anabat to positions within 1,000 yards of Putlan, on Highway 5. 1st Bn, 35th Inf, remains at Putlan bridge site under heavy fire.

S PHILIPPINES—In Eighth Army area, naval bombardment of Zamboanga area, Mindanao, is begun in preparation for offensive. Final elements of Americal Div leave Samar, where 1st Filipino Inf is to complete search for enemy. On Lubang, Co E of 19th Inf relieves 1st Bn of 21st. By end of month the island is turned over to guerrilla forces. For American losses of 8 killed, Japanese suffer 250 killed by mid-March.

IWO JIMA—VAC continues efforts to clear rest of Iwo Jima- 3d Mar Div breaks through to coast in corps center, splitting enemy forces remaining on the island; continues reduction of bypassed pockets in div rear. On right flank of corps, 4th Mar Div gains ground along boundary of RCT's 23 and 24 but is unable to advance its flanks. 5th Mar Div on corps left flank, is still checked on right and in center but pushes slowly forward along W coast. Adm Turner (CTF, Joint Expeditionary Force) departs for Guam after turning over command to Adm Hill, who is redesignated Senior Officer Present Afloat Iwo Jima.

JAPAN—XXI BC begins powerful fire raids on Japanese cities, night 9-10. This marks a radical change in previous tactics of precision bombardment attacks against industrial targets. From this time until end of the war, XXI BC—and from time to time carrier planes of fast carrier force—concentrates on wearing down Japanese will to resist in preparation for invasion of Japan.

10 March

WESTERN EUROPE—21 Army Group: In Cdn First Army's Cdn 2 Corps area, battle of the Rhineland (Operations VERITABLE and BLOCKBUSTER) is successfully ended. Cdn 2d Div is almost unopposed as it pushes SE along Xanten-Rheinberg road. Cdn 4th Armd Div makes flank contact with friendly forces. Br 52d Div easily clears to the Rhine and makes contact with Cdn and U.S. forces on flanks.

In U.S. Ninth Army's XVI Corps area, RCT 134 continues 35th Div's drive toward Wesel, overrunning Buederich. TF Byrne is dissolved and 320th Inf proceeds to Sevelen as reserve. TF Murray is pinched out and releases CCB of 8th Armd Div to parent unit. 75th Div regains command of RCT's 291 and 289 from 35th Div and Br 8 Corps, respectively, and establishes CP in Germany to left of 84th Div (XIII Corps).

12th Army Group: In U.S. First Army's VII Corps area, shift in boundary between Ninth and First Armies places 4th Cav Gp sector within Ninth Army zone and the gp is relieved in place by 113th Cav Gp of XIX Corps. Corps maintains defensive positions along the Rhine with 3d Armd Div, 104th Div, and 1st Div in line; 8th Div and 4th Cav Gp remain in assembly areas. In III Corps area, 9th Div further expands Remagen bridgehead against stubborn resistance. 9th and 78th Divs complete movement into bridgehead and 99th Div starts crossing the Rhine. N flank of bridgehead is expanded beyond Honnef, though enemy retains strong hold on Honnef, and S flank is enlarged to include Dattenberg; progress in center is slower, but line is pushed forward to Hills 244 and 411. Sharp counterattacks continue, forcing 47th Inf, in center, to fall back slightly. Germans continue persistent air and arty attacks against Ludendorff bridge and make similar attacks on newly constructed treadway bridge. Elements of 7th Armd Div occupy the westernmost of two small islands in the Rhine W of Honnef. In V Corps area, elements of 23d Inf, 2d Div, move S along the Rhine and clear half on Nieder Breisig; 3d Bn of 9th Inf reaches the Rhine near Rheinbeck. Patrolling S and SE to destroy enemy pocket to its right, 102d Cav Gp reaches Dedenbach, Nieder Zissen, Waldorf, and Gonnersdorf, all S of the Ahr. 102d Gp, less 102d Sq, is alerted for movement to new zone on short notice; 102d Sq continues mopping-up mission under command of 2d Div. 106th Div is transferred to U.S. Fifteenth Army, which will undertake security mission W of the Rhine.

In U.S. Third Army area, VIII Corps units mop up within prescribed zones. 6th Cav Gp, to left rear of 11th Armd Div, patrols actively along S bank of Ahr R to locate stragglers and maintain contact with First Army. 11th Armd Div holds Rhine R line and methodically clears sector W of the Rhine, overrunning a number of towns: CCB establishes contact with V Corps, completing encirclement of large body of enemy remaining W of the Rhine between First and Third Armies; CCA, to right, mops up in Andernach; CCR mops up to SW of CCA. 90th Div finishes mopping up within its zone. 4th Div is detached from corps and attached to Seventh Army. In XII Corps area, 4th Armd Div continues to mop up W of the Rhine from Andernach to Koblenz and N of the Moselle from Koblenz to Cochem. Driving SE from Darscheid, 5th Div's TF Graham reaches the Moselle at Cochem; 1st Bn of 2d Inf drives SE from Puetzborn to take Udler, Gillenfeld, Strohn, Nieder and Ober Winkel, Immerath, and Strotzbusch; 3d Bn, 2d Inf, is relieved by 10th Inf. 76th Div's 385th and 304th Regts reach positions astride line of Klein Kyll-Lieser Rivers from Karl to Wittlich; on right flank, 42d Cav Sq, after clearing Dreis and Bergweiler, moves elements through 10th Armd Div (XX Corps) at Wittlich to Dorf and Flussbach. 80th Div is transferred to XX Corps. XX Corps prepares for concerted breakout from Saarburg bridgehead on 13 March and is reinf by 80th Div. 10th Armd Div gains final objectives in Wittlich area and begins clearing toward the Moselle: CCA easily takes Wittlich and Bombogen and high ground between; CCB establishes bridgehead across the Salm in Sehlem area, where bridge is put in, and clears Esch, Karmes, and Clausen; CCR cleans out Lorsch-Polich-Ensch bend of the Moselle; expanding Ruwer bridgehead, RCT 417 (−) clears Kirsch, Longuich, and heights near Mertesdorf. 3d Cav Gp occupies Kasel and Riol and begins relief of RCT 417 in Ruwer bridgehead; 3d Sq, relieved by elements of 43d Sq and 94th Div, assembles in Konz Karthaus area.

6th Army Group: Fr 1st Army is directed to continue defense of current zone along the Rhine on right flank of 6th Army Group; probe enemy positions E of the Rhine; effective 13 March, turn over 3d Algerian Inf Div, reinf, now on left flank of 2d Corps, to U.S. VI Corps.

ITALY—15th Army Group: In Br Eighth Army's 13 Corps area, Ind 10th Div begins relief of U.S. 85th Div on M. Grande.

BURMA—In NCAC area, Br 36th Div columns converge on Mongmit and take it.

INDOCHINA—Japanese, fearing a U.S. amphibious operation against French Indochina in which Fr troops might participate, begin expulsion of Fr garrisons from key positions.

LUZON—In U.S. Sixth Army's XIV Corps area, 1st Inf of 6th Div gains about 300 yards, taking small ridge N of Bench Mark B. Intense air and arty bombardment of *Shimbu* line on 10 and 11 March takes heavy toll of Japanese forces forming for major effort against 6th Div. Advance elements of 1st Cav Div reach crest of Bench Mark 9. 11th A/B Div is directed to clear Batangas and drive to second phase line. 3d Bn, 158th Inf, gets into position to attack toward Calumpan Peninsula. Assisted by air strike, 1st Bn of 187th Inf clears most of Hill 660. 511th Inf columns start S along Route 1 for Santa Anastasia and E along S shore of Laguna de Bay virtually unopposed. In I Corps area, 25th Div columns converge in Putlan sector of Highway 5. 27th Inf relieves 1st Bn of 35th at bridge site N of Putlan with 3d Bn and joins with 161st Inf forces S of Putlan to clear opposition from there S to Digdig. 35th Inf turns its full attention to reconnoitering up Old Spanish Trail. In XI Corps area, 43d Div turns over its sector to 38th Div and releases RCT 169 to that div. By this time, 43d Div has penetrated final enemy positions.

S PHILIPPINES—In U.S. Eighth Army area, Romblon and Simara attack forces sail from Min-doro. On Mindanao, following air and naval gunfire preparation, 41st Div (− RCT 186) lands on Zam-boanga Peninsula virtually unopposed; secures Wolfe airfield and village of San Roque and advances on Mindanao City. Gen Doe takes command ashore and Gen Eichelberger lands to inspect beachhead. Guerrillas, helped by the 2 COS of 21st Inf, 24th Div, gain firm control of Dipolog and its airfield.

IWO JIMA—On right flank of VAC, 4th Mar Div continues SE toward coast against decreasing resistance, RCT 23 on left and RCT 25 on right, each bolstered by a bn from RCT 24. RCT 23, pushing through Higashi, gets forward elements to within 400 yards of beach and patrols to coastline at Tachiiwi Pt. RCT 25 eliminates enemy re-entrant on div right but is unable to keep pace with RCT 23. 3d Mar Div's RCT 21 clears right half of its sector; RCT 9 makes little headway against troublesome pocket on extreme right of div zone. 5th Mar Div is practically halted on left flank of corps by rugged and well defended terrain, but RCT 28, on left flank, inches forward to S rim of rocky gorge about 200 yards wide and 700 yards long.

11 March

WESTERN EUROPE—21 Army Group: In U.S. Ninth Army's XVI Corps area, patrols of 134th Inf, 35th Div, take Fort Blucher, concluding div's drive

[11 MARCH 1945]

toward Wesel. 15th Cav Gp is attached to 75th Div, which is to defend corps front. 8th Armd Div, in reserve, is given rear area security mission. 75th Div relieves 5th Armd Div of responsibility for Kempen-Repelen area; 5th Armd polices rear area of corps.

12th Army Group: In U.S. First Army's III Corps area, RCT's 309 and 311 revert to 78th Div and 39th Inf (−) of 9th Div is attached as 78th Div becomes responsible for N flank of Remagen bridgehead. Attacking with 39th and 309th Regts, 78th Div makes slow progress toward Cologne-Frankfurt Autobahn against determined resistance. In center of bridgehead, 9th Div continues attack with 310th, 60th, and 47th Regts, making small gains in vicinity of Hill 448 and Hargarten. 99th Div completes move of its RCT's across the Rhine, takes over S flank of bridgehead, and attacks SE and S with 3934 Inf on left and 394th on right; 393d Inf gains a few hundred yards, but 394th drives 3,000 yards S along E bank of the Rhine, clearing Leubsdorf and Ariendorf. Released by VII Corps, 14th Cav Gp assembles in Remagen area, and 18th Sq takes over defense of Rhine bridges from 9th Div. In V Corps area, 2d Div improves positions, along the Rhine, 23d Inf completing capture of Nieder Breisig and making contact with 9th Inf, which has meanwhile cleared Rheinbeck and Ober Breisig.

In U.S. Third Army area, VIII Corps continues to mop up W of the Rhine. Because of change in boundaries, V Corps relieves elements of 11th Armd Div N of 05 horizontal grid line; 90th Div prepares to relieve elements of 11th and 4th Armd Divs along the Rhine to S, but change of orders immediately transfers it to XII Corps. XII Corps continues mopping up along the Rhine and Moselle and prepares for assault across the Moselle. Boundary between 5th Inf and 4th Armd Divs is altered at 2400 to give 5th Div responsibility for former zone of CCB along the Moselle; at the same time, RCT 11, having effected relief of CCB, reverts to parent unit. 5th Div finishes clearing its sector. 89th Div continues movement into assigned zone between 5th and 76th Divs and relieves elements of those divs within its zone. In 76th Div sector, 42d Cav Sq reaches Hasborn and Bausendorf; 304th Inf and 2d Cav Sq advance rapidly toward Moselle R line on right flank of corps, former pressing S and SE from Wittlich and latter clearing enemy from Sweich-Piesport sector. In XX Corps area, CCA of 10th Armd Div, reinf by 2d Bn of 417th Inf, begins drive toward the Moselle at Bullay, halting at Bausendorf, where Alf R bridge is out; CCB and CCR begin concentration in Trier area. RCT 417, less 2d Bn, reverts to 76th Div, XII Corps, at 2400; earlier in day, 1st Bn is forced from hill near Mertesdorf by counterattack. 316th Prov Cav Brig (3d and 16th Cav Gps) re-

[435]

groups to defend N flank of corps from the Moselle S to 94th Div zone with 3d, 43d, 16th, and 19th Sqs in line, from left to right; from assembly area at Veckring (France), 16th Cav Gp moves up and relieves 43d Sq with 16th Sq and 3d Sq with 19th Sq. Other units of corps continue preparations for coming offensive. 80th Div starts from XII Corps zone toward E bank of the Saar opposite Saarlautern.

EASTERN EUROPE—Soviet forces are investing the Baltic ports of Danzig and Gdynia. Berlin reports slight penetrations of German positions in Kuestrin area as Soviet forces expand Oder bridgeheads.

ITALY—15th Army Group: In Br Eighth Army area, 10 Corps takes command of left flank elements of Pol 2 Corps, Friuli Gp, and Ind 43d Brig, and of sector currently held by them, placing it between 13 Corps and Pol 2 Corps. In 5 Corps area, 78th Div replaces 56th Div in line, permitting 56th Div to prepare for offensive.

SEAC—Adm Mountbatten announces that a regt of U.S. 5332d is to leave for China at once, the rest of the brig on 1 April.

BURMA—In Br Fourteenth Army's 33 Corps area, Ind 19th Div continues battle for Mandalay, taking hill strongpoint commanding NE part of the city.

LUZON—U.S. Sixth Army issues basic plan for its part in clearing Bicol Peninsula and Visayan Passage. RCT 158, currently assisting 11th A/B Div, XIV Corps, in clearing S Luzon, is to make amphibious assault against Legaspi, in Bicol Peninsula, and will assemble at staging area by 17th; 511th Para Inf of 11th A/B Div, less one bn, will serve as army reserve for the operation. In XIV Corps area, 43d Div begins relieving 1st Cav Div, which is now generally on first phase line except at Antipolo. 1st Inf, 6th Div, gets into favorable position to exploit advance eastward. 2d Bn drives nearly a mile E to trail junction while 3d Bn seizes Bench Mark B. After nightfall, Japanese begin series of abortive counterattacks, all small, against 6th Div. Efforts to penetrate positions of all 3 regts fail. In 11th A/B Div sector of S Luzon, 2d Bn of 158th Inf clears Batangas and immediate vicinity while rest of regt is cleaning out region to W and NW. 1st Bn, 187th Inf, completes capture of Hill 660. 3d Bn, 511th Inf, is brought to a halt by Japanese firmly entrenched on Mt Bijang. In I Corps area, 33d Div consolidates and patrols toward Galiano, about 10 miles W of Baguio. 127th Inf, 32d Div, is still held up by strong enemy defense of Salacsac Pass positions on Villa Verde Trail. As 25th Div's 27th and 161st Regts continue forward astride Highway 5, 3d Bn of 35th Inf seizes Salazar, an Old Spanish Trail. 43d Div, less RCT 169, is transferred to XI Corps from XIV Corps.

S PHILIPPINES—In U.S. Eighth Army area, 163d Inf of first Div secures airfield and Zamboanga City on Mindanao and pushes toward Pasananca. 162d extends positions toward Caldera Pt. East entrance of Visayan Passage is now secure and Filipino guerrillas take over occupation of Burias and Ticao Islands, releasing 1st Bn of 132d Inf, which returns to Leyte. Co C, reinf, 19th Inf, makes unopposed landing on Romblon shortly after midnight 11-12.

IWO JIMA—4th Mar Div, VAC, overcomes organized resistance within its zone on right flank of corps except for stubborn pocket on div right. In center of corps, 3d Mar Div's RCT 21 mops up and protects right flank of 5th Mar Div while RCT 9 develops enemy pocket on div right. Withdrawing RCT 26 from line, 5th Mar Div continues attack on left flank of corps with RCT 27 on right and RCT 28 on left. Terrain, as well as enemy, makes progress slow despite close arty support.

12 March

WESTERN EUROPE—21 Army Group: In U.S. Ninth Army's XVI Corps area, 75th Div takes over defense of corps sector along the Rhine and with its 290th Inf relieves 35th Div. 35th Div prepares to move to rear for rest and rehabilitation.

12th Army Group: In U.S. First Army's III Corps area, in N part of Remagen bridgehead, 78th Div withstands counterattacks against Honnef, where isolated pockets of enemy remain, and with 39th Inf drives E toward Kalenborn; 1st Bn of 310th Inf reverts to div from attachment of 9th Armd Div and is attached to 311th Inf. In center, 9th Div is strongly opposed in Kalenborn and Hargarten areas, but enters Hargarten late in day. CCB, 9th Armd Div, is detached from 9th Div and passes to corps reserve. 99th Div, in S part of bridgehead, gains initial objectives in region between Hargarten and Hoenningen. V Corps, out of contact with enemy, begins period of consolidation of positions W of the Rhine and preparations for crossing.

In U.S. Third Army area, VIII Corps completes organized mop-up W of the Rhine. CCB, 11th Armd Div, withdraws S of 05 horizontal grid line, the new V-VIII Corps boundary. XII Corps continues to mop up and prepares for attack across the Moselle. 89th Div enters combat for the first time, driving through 5th and 6th Divs, with 353d Inf on left and 355th on right, toward Cochem-Alf sector of the Moselle. 76th Div continues to clear toward the Moselle to right of 89th Div, employing 385th Inf on left and 304th on right, and reaches river line in zone of 304th at Kesten and Piesport; 2d Cav Gp screens Piesport-Sweich sector with 2d Sq and withdraws 42d Sq to Gladbach as reserve. 90th Div, directed to attack with 5th Div across the Moselle, moves assault regts to Moselle R line. XX Corps completes preparations for offensive. Clearing Bausendorf with dismounted inf and taking bridge near Olkenbach, CCA of 10th Armd Div drives from Alf R to the Moselle; on commanding ground opposite Bullay it is relieved by 76th Div of XII Corps. 1st Bn of 417th Inf, after regaining hill near Mertesdorf in surprise attack before dawn, is relieved by 3d Cav Gp, which improves positions SE of Mertesdorf under heavy enemy fire.

6th Army Group: U.S. Seventh Army is regrouping extensively for assault on West Wall. 3d and 45th Divs are attached to XV Corps.

EASTERN EUROPE—First White Russian Front forces capture Kuestrin, enemy stronghold astride the Oder on E approach to Berlin, after prolonged fighting; continue reduction of German bridgehead E of Stettin. Troops of Second White Russian Front close in on Danzig and Gdynia, thrusting to Gulf of Danzig N of Gdynia.

BURMA—In Br Fourteenth Army's 33 Corps area, Ind 20th Div is rapidly clearing region SW of Mandalay and takes communications center of Myotha.

LUZON—In U.S. Sixth Army's XIV Corps area, 6th Div commits 20th Inf to attack against *Shimbu* line, repels further small-scale enemy counterattacks. 20th Inf, driving E on left flank of div, gains its objective. 1st Cav Div is withdrawn from line for well-earned rest. 43d Div holds positions to S of 6th Div, previously zone of 1st Cav Div. Patrol of 103d Inf finds Antipolo undefended and in ruins. In 11th A/B Div sector of S Luzon, 3d Bn of 158th Inf drives on Mabini, at neck of Calumpan Peninsula, until stopped N of Mainaga by Japanese. Strong Japanese positions on Mt Bijang are being neutralized by aircraft and arty. In I Corps area, 2d Bn of 128th Inf, 32d Div, on Villa Verde Trail, is attached to 127th Inf in order to increase pressure toward Salacsac Pass No. 2. 3d Bn of 35th Inf, 25th Div, holds roadblock on Old Spanish Trail a little N of Salazar, but efforts to continue along this axis are abandoned as impracticable.

S PHILIPPINES—In U.S. Eighth Army area, 162d Inf reaches Recodo on Caldera Pt, Mindanao, and finds abandoned enemy positions. Co C drives to Masilay, NW of San Roque. Elements of 3d Bn reach village 1,500 yards NE of San Roque, which Japanese are defending stoutly. Co B of 19th Inf lands on Simara without opposition at dawn after naval bombardment and diversionary air attack on another part of island. On Romblon, Co C of 19th Inf takes Romblon town with ease and begins clearing scattered opposition elsewhere on the island.

[13 MARCH 1945]   [437]

Iwo Jima—4th and 3d Mar Divs, VAC, mop up their respective sectors and reduce pockets of resistance remaining on each of their right flanks. 5th Mar Div is assisted by air, naval gunfire, arty, and tanks as it continues assault on final defenses of enemy—network of mutually supporting pillboxes and prepared positions on broken terrain of N Iwo Jima. Although little ground is gained, enemy positions are softened and many caves and pillboxes overrun. Iwo Jima airfields are renamed South, Center, and North Airfields.

13 March

Western Europe—12th Army Group: In U.S. First Army's III Corps area, 78th Div continues to meet strong resistance as it expands bridgehead to NE: 311th Inf, further strengthened by attachment of 60th Armd Inf Bn of 9th Armd Div and 78th Rcn Tr, occupies Rhine island just W of Honnef, mops up within Honnef, and presses slowly NE over difficult terrain; 309th co-ordinates its attack to NE with that of 39th, which secures high ground immediately W of Kalenborn. 9th Div completes capture of Hargarten and makes limited gains in Kalenborn-Notscheid-Hargarten region. On S flank, 99th Div consolidates and withstands local counterattacks. In V Corps area, 102d Cav Gp (−) and 38th Sq are directed to start to Saverne area on 14th; 102d Sq is detached from 2d Div but remains in position.

In U.S. Third Army's VIII Corps area, 6th Cav Gp takes over defense of the Rhine from Andernach southward, relieving elements of 11th and 4th Armd Divs. 87th Div starts concentrating in Koblenz-Lehmen sector along the Moselle and relieves CCA, 4th Armd Div. XII Corps completes preparations for assault across the Rhine. 4th Armd and 5th Inf Divs regroup. 90th Div's reserve regt 358th, assembles W of Mertloch. 89th and 76th Divs clear most of their zones along the Moselle from Cochem to Sweich. 417th Inf, 76th Div, completes assembly as reserve. XX Corps attacks SE from Saarburg bridgehead at 0300 after heavy arty preparation. Rugged terrain and West Wall defenses make progress slow. 94th Div, with 302d Inf on N and 301st on S, crosses Ruwer R by ford and bridge and takes Bonerath, Holtzerath, Schondorf, and Bergheid (village W of Heddert). 80th Div drives through 94th and 26th Divs: 318th Inf, on left, breaks through enemy lines to block the one good road through Wadern Forest at a point near center of forest; 317th captures Greimerath. 26th Div, with 104th and 328th Regts in assault, moves slowly forward; TF D (reinf and motorized 3d Bn of 104th Inf) fights abreast 80th Div, slowly clearing roadblocks on Zerf-Britten road. In conjunction with main attack, 65th Div makes diversionary attacks in Saarlautern bridgehead area on right flank of corps. On corps left flank, 3d Cav Gp undergoes determined counterattacks; 16th Sq, 16th Cav Gp, is pinched out and moves NE to relieve 43d Sq, which withdraws as reserve. 19th Sq, 16th Cav Gp, clears Morscheid-Sommerau ridge and both towns. Final elements of 10th Armd Div close in Trier area, where brief maintenance and rehabilitation program is conducted.

6th Army Group: U.S. Seventh Army continues to regroup in preparation for offensive. In XXI Corps area, patrols report evidence of enemy withdrawal and 10th Div takes up pursuit at once, driving N toward Sarre R. In VI Corps area, 3d Algerian Inf Div of Fr 2d Corps is attached to VI Corps in current positions.

Italy—15th Army Group: Boundary between U.S. Fifth and Br Eighth Armies is adjusted to run just E of Idice R valley and M. Belmonte as Ind 10th Div of Br 13 Corps takes responsibility for M. Grande hill mass from 85th Div of U.S. II Corps.

Burma—In ALFSEA's 15 Corps area, elements of Ind 26th Div conduct final amphibious operation on Arakan coast, landing on mainland in vicinity of Letpadan to cut Ru-ywa-Taungup road.

Luzon—U.S. Sixth Army postpones Legaspi operation for a week, permitting RCT 158 to remain in XIV Corps line a while longer. In XIV Corps area, 6th Div repels further piecemeal counterattacks with little difficulty. Elements of 103d Inf, 43d Div, reach W base of Bench Mark 7. TF consisting of Co B, reinf, motors N from Taytay along Laguna. de Bay coast; makes contact with div rcn troops in Morong and Maybancal. In 11th A/B Div sector, 3d Bn of 158th Inf is unable to outflank enemy strongpoint N of Mainaga and is jeopardized as enemy, in amphibious operation, blocks road behind it at Baliti R. After further aerial and arty pounding of Mt Bijang, 511th Inf of 11th A/B Div renews attack and gets up slopes but is forced off. For next few days aircraft and arty conduct softening bombardment. In I Corps area, 1st Bn of 161st Inf, 25th Div, is directed to attack through 2d Bn in Putlan area, on Highway 5, for Norton's Knob, a spur of Balete Ridge about 1,500 yards SW of Kapintalan.

S Philippines—In U.S. Eighth Army area, Japanese resistance on Mindanao N of San Roque and S of Pasananca stiffens.

Iwo Jima—4th and 3d Mar Divs, VAC, continue to mop up and reduce small enemy pockets within their sectors. 5th Mar Div encounters fewer pillboxes and makes relatively good progress on right flank. Since ridges in this area extend from center of island to W coast, attack will be from E to W. Tanks, flame throwers, and arty are again employed to flush enemy from concealed positions, but restricted area denies troops air support. Co B, Amphib Rcn Bn, lands on Kangoku and Kama Rocks, off W coast, and secures these small islands without opposition.

14 March

WESTERN EUROPE—12th Army Group: In U.S. First Army area, VII Corps regroups in preparation for action E of the Rhine. 8th Div (− 13th Inf) takes over 1st Div zone on S flank of corps. Zone of 104th Div is extended W to include region formerly occupied by 8th Div. In III Corps area, Germans shift bulk of their arty fire from Rhine bridges to troops, but continue frequent air attacks against the bridges, employing many jet planes. Of 372 enemy planes attacking the bridges during 7-14 March, 80 are shot down by AA fire. Despite hilly terrain and lively resistance, 78th Div presses slowly N toward Konigswinter and NE toward the autobahn; secures objectives near Aegidienberg, Rottbitz, and Kalenborn. Continuing E in center of bridgehead, 9th Div gets some elements into Lorscheid and others just short of Notscheid. 99th Div's 395th Inf, released from reserve, drives 1,200 yards E on S flank of bridgehead while rest of div holds current positions. 7th Armd Div places cable across the Rhine.

In U.S. Third Army's VIII Corps area, 11th Armd Div, assembled as corps reserve, defends corps N flank and maintains contact with First Army. 87th Div closes in new zone along the Moselle, where it defends Koblenz-Lehmen sector with 346th Inf and patrols across river. XII Corps begins drive from the Moselle to the Rhine at 0200. 90th Div, with 2 regts in assault, crosses in Kattenes-Moselkern region and clears heights E of river: 357th Inf, on left, takes Alken, Brodenbach, Noerdershausen, Udenhausen, Herschwiesen, and Oppenhausen, but is unable to gain Pfaffenheck; 359th secures Burgen and part of Morshausen and Macken; 358th, in reserve, crosses at Hatzenport and assembles in Brodenbach. Crossing the Moselle to right of 90th Div, 5th Div, with 11th Inf on left and 2d on right, seizes Treis, Lutz, and Eveshausen and commanding ground near these towns; 10th remains W of river. Engineers put in bridges. 89th and 76th Divs clear all but small pockets W and N of the Moselle. 2d Cav Gp (− 2d Sq) is detached from 76th Div and moves to Kollig area. In XX Corps area, 94th Div moves forward about 1,500 yards to positions within Osburger Hoch Wald and clears Heddert. 80th Div is largely engaged in mopping up, but 2d Bn of 318th Inf reaches Weiskirchen, where it is isolated by enemy infiltration; 1st Bn of 319th Inf starts toward Bergen. 104th and 328th Regts of 26th Div continue slowly SE to right of 80th Div. On corps right flank, 65th Div continues limited action and aggressive patrolling in Saarlautern bridgehead sector. 316th Prov Cav Brig is active on N flank of corps: 16th Sq, 16th Cav Gp, attacks toward Waldrach but is halted at edge of town by stubborn opposition; 3d Sq, 3d Cav Gp, takes Nieder Fell and Fell.

6th Army Group: U.S. Seventh Army completes preparations for West Wall offensive, moving assault forces to forward assembly areas. In XXI Corps area, 101st Cav Gp, on left flank of corps, joins 10th Div in pursuit of enemy northward. 80th push into Germany and patrol to S bank of Sarre R.

BURMA—In NCAC area, air movement of U.S. 5332d Brig (MARS) to China is begun.

In Br Fourteenth Army's 33 Corps area, Ind 19th Div clears city area of Mandalay but enemy retains Fort Dufferin, target for heavy air attacks and close-range arty fire for next few days.

LUZON—In U.S. Sixth Army's XIV Corps area, 6th Div continues to repel small counterattacks. All enemy efforts to mount a concerted counterattack have proved unsuccessful and costly. 20th Inf gains positions on approaches to Mt Mataba. 1st Inf runs into well-organized enemy positions. 43d Div, less 169th Inf, begins full-scale attack against enemy's *Shimbu* line, employing 172d Inf on left and 103d on right; initial objective is heights E and N of Morong R valley. Jumping off from positions N of Antipolo, 172d comes up against outer defenses of strong enemy position on Sugar Loaf Mountain. 103d moves additional elements to Bench Mark 7 area. Co B TF continues rapidly up Morong R valley against scattered resistance.

S PHILIPPINES—In Eighth Army area, 162d Inf begins converging drive on Mt Capisan, Mindanao, with 1st and 2d Bns while 3d Bn works on the village strongpoint NE of San Roque; clears San Roque and gains trail junction 500 yards NW of Masilay. 163d Inf, with air support, seizes Pasananca road junction.

IWO JIMA—VAC raises American flag on Iwo at 0930. 4th and 3d Mar Divs continue to mop up and considerably reduce pockets in their respective sectors. 4th Mar Div begins re-embarkation. 5th Mar Div, committing RCT 26 between RCT's 28 on left and 27 on right, renews assault on N Iwo Jima and gains up to 600 yards on right, although left flank remains in about the same position. Air support of the operation ends with P-51 strike in behalf of 5th Mar Div.

15 March

WESTERN EUROPE—21 Army Group: In Cdn First Army area, Cdn I Corps takes up positions in NW Europe, having transferred gradually from Italy.

12th Army Group: In U.S. First Army's VII Corps area, RCT 26 of 1st Div, the first unit of VII Corps across the Rhine, crosses in III Corps zone in preparation for attack through 78th Div. In III Corps area, 78th Div pushes a little closer to the autobahn with 311th and 39th Regts while 309th reorganizes. 311th gains up to 2,000 yards and 39th clears Schweifeld. 9th Div completes capture of Lorscheid and takes Notscheid. With elements of 3 regts in assault, 99th Div expands bridgehead some 2,500 yards to SE and E, taking several terrain features and villages. Air attacks on bridges decrease during day. In V Corps area, 102d Cav Gp (−) is detached from corps and attached to VI Corps, Seventh Army.

In U.S. Third Army's VIII Corps area, 87th Div prepares for assault across the Moselle to clear Koblenz and region to S between the Moselle and Rhine Rivers. In XII Corps area 2d Cav Gp (−2d Sq), upon crossing the Moselle at Hatzenport, relieves left flank elements of 90th Div. 90th Div commits elements of 1st Bn, 358th Inf, on left to assist 357th Inf and drives SE with 3d Bn of 358th to gain Dieler, Ney, Halsenbach, and Kratzenburg; on right, 359th Inf completes capture of Morshausen and clears Beulich, Mermuth, and Ober and Nieder Gondershausen. 5th Div expands bridgehead SE, taking Lieg, Dommershausen, and Dorweiler. 4th Armd Div is committed in bridgehead and attacks toward Nahe R at Bad Kreuznach: CCA advances through 90th Div's bridgehead, clearing Liesenfeld and Schwall; CCB, driving through 5th Div, clears Beltheim, Goedenroth, Laubach, and Simmern and takes bridge over Simmer R. Enemy columns withdrawing in disorder before armor suffer heavily from combined action of troops, tanks, arty, and aircraft. 89th and 76th Divs improve positions along the Moselle and patrol actively; former begins limited attacks to clear Moselle loop near Alf. In XX Corps area, elements of 16th Cav Gp clear Waldrach. 94th Div drives about 10,000 yards E as resistance slackens: 302d Inf takes Hill 708 and Reinsfeld; 301st clears Schillingen, Kell, and Gusenburg; 376th starts toward Schillingen. In 80th Div zone, 318th Inf (−) mops up and prepares for drive on Weis-kirchen to relieve trapped 2d Bn; 317th clears Waldholzbach and Scheiden and reaches Mitlesheim area; 319th takes Bergen and clears toward Britten and Losheim. 26th Div pushes slowly forward to positions near Saarholzbach, passing 101st Inf through 328th.

6th Army Group: U.S. Seventh Army Opens UNDERTONE—offensive to break through West Wall and, in conjunction with Third Army to N, clear the Saar-Palatinate triangle, within the confines of the rivers Rhine, Moselle, and Lauter-Sarre. Three corps attack abreast, XV in center making main effort. Elements jump off at 0100 to achieve tactical surprise. In XXI Corps area, 63d Div attacks on right flank of corps SE of Saarbruecken to develop West Wall positions and clears Fechingen, Eschringen, and Ensheim. On left flank of corps, 101st Cav Gp and 10th Div mop up S of the Sarre; 70th Div attacks toward Saarbruecken in afternoon but gains little ground before breaking off attack to patrol vigorously. In XV Corps area 45th and 3d Divs, passing through 44th Div, drive N into Germany. 180th Inf, 45th, crosses the Blies to advance along W side while 157th pushes northward along E side of the river. From Rimling area, 3d Div drives N toward West Wall and Zweibrucken. 100th Div attacks toward Bitche on E flank of corps, clearing Schorbach and 2 Maginot forts and reaching heights in Reyersviller area. VI Corps attacks across the Rothbach and Moder Rivers with 4 inf divs abreast, assisted by armor of 14th Armd Div. On left, 42d Div reaches positions commanding Baerenthal and cuts Baerenthal-Mouterhouse road. 103d Div drives to positions near Zinswiller. 36th Div takes Bitschhoffen and penetrates enemy line along the Moder. On right flank of corps, 3d Algerian Div, reinf by elements of Fr 5th Armd Div, drives toward Lauterbourg from Oberhoffen area but is soon stopped by heavy fire.

EASTERN EUROPE—German pocket in East Prussia is split as troops of Third White Russian Front break through to the coast SW of Koenigsberg.

ITALY—15th Army Group: In U.S. Fifth Army's II Corps area, elements of 1st Armd Div try in vain to establish outpost in Salvaro, on left flank of corps.

BURMA—In Br Fourteenth Army's 4 Corps area, Ind 17th Div continues to hold out in Meiktila although still isolated and dependent upon air supply. To assist in this area, 9th Brig of Ind 5th Div is being flown to Meiktila. Two mechanized brigs of Ind 5th Div are moving overland from Jorhat to aid Ind 7th Div on W flank of corps.

LUZON—In U.S. Sixth Army's I Corps area, 127th Inf of 32d Div continues hard fighting on Villa Verde Trail; 2d Bn of 128th Inf gets to within 500 yards of Imugan; where it is brought to a halt by enemy. On Highway 5, 1st Bn of 161st Inf, 25th Div, begins assault on Norton's Knob, where entrenched Japanese throw back repeated attacks for next 10 days. 35th Inf is ordered to relieve 1st Bn of 27th so 27th Inf may apply its full force against Mt Myoko. XI Corps, with new mission of attacking vigorously against center of *Shimbu* line, takes over XIV Corps zone E and NE of Manila and the divs (6th and 43d, less RCT 169) operating there.

XIV Corps has penetrated outer positions of enemy in Montalban-Antipolo area. 6th Div, reinf by 112th Cav RCT, is to hold on left in Montalban area while advancing its right flank eastward in conjunction with 43d Div to S. In 43d Div zone, Japanese on Bench Mark 7 are almost encircled by 103d Inf. Co B TF gains ground commanding Teresa from S to E. 172d Inf is checked by opposition from Sugar Loaf. In W sector of corps, 38th Div continues to clear toward Mt Pinatubo. XIV Corps, with 1st Cav Div and 11th A/B Div under command, can now give its full attention to clearing S Luzon. In 11th A/B Div zone, Co C of 158th Inf reaches and clears Mabini, on Calumpan Peninsula. Continuing S toward Mabini, 3d Bn is stopped by resistance about a mile short.

S Philippines—In U.S. Eighth Army area, Panay invasion force sails from Luzon for target, convoy protected by Fifth and Thirteenth Air Forces. On Mindanao, 1st Bn of 163d Inf, 41st Div, clears heights N and E of Pasananca Reservoir with little difficulty while 2d Bn pushes 1,000 yards N of the Santa Maria and establishes line running N to Pasananca road junction. San Roque airfield becomes operational. On Romblon, Co C of 19th Inf reaches far side of island in overland and shore-to-shore movements. About 70 Japanese are estimated to remain in SW part of Romblon.

Iwo Jima—4th and 3d Mar Divs, VAC, further reduce pockets of enemy within their sectors. 5th Mar Div gains 400 yards on right and 200 in center; RCT 28, on div left, remains in place supporting assault forces with fire. Naval support, except for illumination, ceases.

16 March

Western Europe—12th Army Group: In U.S. First Army area, VII Corps takes over N flank of Remagen bridgehead. 78th Div is attached in place and continues to expand bridgehead northeastward: 311th Inf, reinf by elements of 310th, clears most of Konigswinter while 309th takes Hovel and Aegidienberg and cuts Cologne-Frankfurt Autobahn. 39th Inf and 60th Armd Inf Bn revert respectively to 9th Inf and 9th Armd Divs from attachment to 78th Div. RCT 310, less 1st and 2d Bns, reverts to 78th Div. RCT 18, 1st Div, assembles E of the Rhine. 4th Cav Gp and 104th Div relieve 3d Armd Div along the Rhine, night 16-17. In III Corp's 9th Div zone, now N flank of corps, 39th Inf takes Kalenborn, 47th gains a little ground near Vettelschoss, and 60th takes Strodt. 99th Div gains up to 4,000 yards as it continues E and S through Honningen Wald: driving E, 395th and 393d Regts, 395th on left, reach objective heights W of Wied R, overrunning a number of villages; advancing S, 394th Inf enters Honningen, where indecisive fighting ensues. Enemy offers a little less ground resistance and ceases air attacks on bridges.

In U.S. Third Army's VIII Corps area, 87th Div begins assault across the Moselle early in day, crossing 347th and 345th Regts in Winningen-Kolberg region against light resistance. Clearing SW along E bank of the Moselle, 347th takes Dieblich, Dieblicherberg, Nieder Fell, and positions near Waldesch. 345th thrusts NE through Lay to outskirts of Koblenz. Corps releases 11th Armd Div to XII Corps and takes control of 28th Div from V Corps. In XII Corps area, 2d Cav Gp, to which 2d Sq reverts from attachment to 76th Div, is directed to protect N flank of corps. 42d Sq completes relief of N flank elements of 90th Div and 2d moves to Kollig. 90th Div's 357th Inf continues to meet lively opposition in Pfaffenheck area; after taking Ehr, 3d Bn of 358th swings NE toward 357th; TF Spiess (90th Rcn Tr, reinf), organized to clear Boppard-St Goar sector of the Rhine, crosses the Moselle at Hatzenport and drives rapidly to the Rhine, taking Weiler, Hirzenach, Rheinbay, Karbach, Holzfeld, Werlau, and Hungeroth; RCT 359 is attached to 4th Armd Div. 4th Armd Div speeds SE to Nahe R near Bad Kreuznach and secures bridgehead: on right CCB crosses at Oberhausen and Bad Muenster and continues S to Dreineiherof and Hochstatten; CCA reaches the Nahe at Gensingen and halts, since bridge is out. 5th Div sweeps SE against negligible resistance: TF Breckenridge (motorized 10th Inf (less 2d Bn) reinf) crosses into bridgehead and moves S along right flank to Reidenhausen; 2d Inf thrusts to Hundheim area; 11th reaches positions near Simmern; 2d Bn of 10th Inf clears Moselle bend E of Cochem. 89th Div, with 353d Inf on left and 354th on right, starts across the Moselle in assault boats in Bullay area at 0330 and presses toward Grenderich on left and Hill 409, E of Enkirch, on right, gaining shallow bridgehead; elements W of the Moselle take Alf and Ernst. Engineers put in Class 40 bridge at Bullay. 11th Armd Div is attached to corps and starts to Lutzerath-Buchel assembly area. XX Corps commits armor in breakout assault. 10th Armd Div, with CCB on left and CCA on right, drives through 94th and 80th Divs and is reinf by RCT's 301, 94th Div, and 318, 80th Div. In closely co-ordinated thrusts toward the Prims, CCB and 94th Div clear to line Hermeskeil-Nonnweiler while CCA and 80th Div advance to line Ober Morscholz-Noswendel-Nieder Losheim-Wahlen. Pressing S toward Merzig, 26th Div clears Saarholzbach and Mettlach; TF D (a rifle co, tanks, TD's, and engineers) crosses Seffers R to clear Rimlingen.

[17 MARCH 1945]

6th Army Group: In U.S. Seventh Army's XXI Corps area, 63d Div continues attack to develop West Wall positions on right flank of corps. In XV Corps area, while 45th and 3d Divs continue attacks against outer defenses of West Wall, tooth Div finishes clearing Bitche and environs. In VI Corps area, 42d Div penetrates enemy positions near Baerenthal. 103d clears Zinswiller and Oberbronn and reaches outskirts of Reichshoffen. After massed arty fire, 142d Inf of 36th Div crosses Zintzel R and captures Mertzwiller; 141st continues drive in Haguenau Forest; motorized column of 143d (1st Bn, reinf) speeds toward Soultz until stopped by enemy below Eberbach. German withdrawal on right flank of corps permits 3d Algerian Div to move forward rapidly.

EASTERN EUROPE—From Szekesfehervar region of Hungary, Soviet forces open drive on Vienna.

BURMA—In NCAC area, CAI troops reach Hsipaw, NE of Kyaukme. Joint Chiefs of Staff suggest that U.S. TF MARS and Ch 38th, 50th, and 30th Divs be flown to China in transports of NCAC as well as those of China Theater and ATC.

LUZON—In U.S. Sixth Army's I Corps area, 35th Inf of 25th Div, leaving 3d Bn to maintain roadblock on Old Spanish Trail in Salazar area, starts forward to relieve 1st Bn, 27th Inf. In XI Corps area, 6th Div prepares to renew eastward drive against *Shimbu* line. 172d Inf, 43d Div, is still unable to progress in Sugar Loaf Hill area; 103d seizes Bench Mark 20, 1 ½ miles N of Teresa, and drives to crest of Bench Mark 7, last enemy strongpoint W of Morong R Valley. In XIV Corps area, 3d Bn of 158th Inf reaches Mabini. This completes capture of Calumpan Peninsula.

S PHILIPPINES—In U.S. Eighth Army area, in preparation for assault landing by 40th Div on Panay, arty cub planes are flown in to guerrilla-built airstrip in N part of island. On Mindanao, Co F of 162d Inf, 41st Div, reinf, moves by water from Zamboanga to Basilan I. and lands without opposition after 30-minute naval gunfire bombardment by a DD.

IWO JIMA—Iwo Jima is declared secure at 1800, though enemy continues to hold out on northern tip. RCT 25 eliminates pocket on 4th Mar Div right flank; RCT 23 is relieved by RCT 24 and re-embarks. 3d Mar Div, whose left boundary is changed, relieves left flank elements of 5th Mar Div with RCT 21, which, after arty preparation, drives N to coast at Kitano Pt against scattered resistance; RCT 9 overcomes organized resistance on div right flank. 5th Mar Div's RCT 26 inches forward 200 yards while RCT 28 continues clearing along gorge across its front and supports RCT 26 with fire; RCT 27, upon relief by 3d Mar Div, assembles as reserve. Center Airfield is operational.

17 March

WESTERN EUROPE—12th Army Group: In U.S. First Army's VII Corps area, 1st Div begins attack E of the Rhine toward Sieg R: 18th Inf, on left, passes through 309th Inf, on 78th Div right, and takes limited objectives in Grafenhohn-Huscheid region; 26th takes crossroads E of Himberg and drives on Hill 363, S of Wullscheid. Elements of 16th Inf assemble E of the Rhine. 78th Div regroups and provides fire support for 1st Div. 3d Armd Div, held in reserve, releases 13th Inf to 8th Div and recovers CC Howze from attachment to 1st Div. In III Corps area, Maj Gen James A. Van Fleet takes command of corps, relieving Gen Milliken. Ludendorff RR bridge collapses while under repair but other bridges have been constructed. Ground opposition continues to slacken. 9th Div cuts autobahn near Windhagen, overruns Vettelschoss, and partly clears high ground along the Wied E of Strodt. 99th Div gains initial objectives. While 394th Inf overcomes strong opposition in Honningen, 393d clears Hausen and Solscheid and 395th consolidates along the Wied and searches for crossing sites. 18th Sq, 14th Cav Gp, is attached to 99th Div.

In U.S. Third Army's VIII Corps area, 345th Inf of 87th Div crosses 2d Bn over the Moselle near Guels after 3d Bn clears Moselweiss, then attacks E through Koblenz with 2d and 3d Bns while 1st remains in S outskirts; about a third of the city is cleared in house-to-house fighting. 347th Inf presses SE toward the Rhine, overrunning Waldesch, entering Rhens, and reaching positions near river bend NW of Osterpai. Bridges are completed at Winningen and Kobern. 28th Div is assembling in Nieder Mendig sector. In XII Corps area, 357th Inf of 80th Div seizes Boppard against light resistance; elements of 358th clear St Goarer Stadtwald; TF Spiess finishes clearing along the Rhine from Boppard to St Goar and receives surrender of latter. 2d Cav Gp, attached to 80th Div since that unit is to extend right boundary along the Rhine to Bingen, relieves 80th Div of Boppard-St Goar-Oberwesel sector and makes contact with VIII Corps. On 4th Armd Div right, CCB enlarges Nahe bridgehead and in evening begins assault on Bad Kreuznach. CCA fords the Nahe and thrusts toward Sprendlingen, overrunning Ippesheim, Biebelsheim, and Zotzenheim. TF Breckenridge, 5th Div, gets advance elements to Waldboeckelheim but rest of column and 2d Inf halt near Tiefenbach; 11th Inf reaches Riesweiler, Argenthal, and Ellern. 89th Div expands and consolidates Bullay bridgehead and is passed through by 11th Armd Div. 11th Armd Div begins drive toward the Rhine at Worms at noon: CCB moves through Atlay and Lauzenhausen to

Buechenbeuren area; 41st Cav Rcn Sq advances to right, taking Loetzbeuren and Wahlenau; on div left, CCA drives through Kappel toward Kirchberg. In XX Corps area CCB of 10th Armd Div crosses the Nahe near Turkismuhle; CCA closes along W bank of the Prims on right flank of div. 94th and 80th Divs make substantial gains in conjunction with armor. 94th Div reaches Birkenfeld, its objective. 80th Div establishes bridgehead across the Prims in Krettnich-Nunkirchen area. 101st Inf of 26th Div takes Brotdorf, Honzrath, and Dueppenweiler; 104th seizes Prims R bridge at Huettersdorf; 328th clears Merzig and Haustadt. 65th Div prepares for breakout attack from Saarlautern bridgehead. 261st Inf (−) crosses the Saar near Menningen and clears heights S of Merzig in preparation for drive on Dillingen. On N flank of corps, 316th Prov Cav Brig finishes clearing MSR, the Trier–Hermeskeil road. 16th Cav Gp begins relief of 3d Cav Gp, which is to assemble in reserve at Trier. 12th Armd Div is attached to corps to exploit 94th Div breakthrough and starts to forward assembly areas.

6th Army Group: Generals Eisenhower and Patton visit Seventh Army hq at Lunéville to discuss liaison between Third and Seventh Armies.

In U.S. Seventh Army's XXI Corps area, 63d Div continues efforts to break through West Wall on right flank of corps. 12th Armd Div, which was to have exploited through 63d Div, is transferred to XX Corps, Third Army. In XV Corps area, 45th and 3d Divs reach West Wall fortifications in Zweibrucken area. VI Corps advances rapidly all along line as resistance slackens sharply. On left, 42d Div gains up to 6 miles, clearing Bannstein, Stuzelbronn, Baerenthal, Philippsbourg, Dambach, Neunhoffen, and Niedersteinbach; 117th Cav Rcn Sq seizes Mouterhouse. 103d Div overruns a number of towns and villages, among them Niederbronn, Reichshoffen, and Woerth. Motorized column of 143d Inf, 36th Div, pursues enemy to Bieberbach R near Gunstett, where bridge is down; 142d Inf follows 143d northward; 141st continues clearing Haguenau Forest. 3d Algerian Div continues rapidly N on right flank of corps.

BURMA—In Br Fourteenth Army's 33 Corps area, Japanese continue to hold Fort Dufferin, in Mandalay. Br 2d Div takes Ava Fort, at bend of the Irrawaddy S of Mandalay.

LUZON—In U.S. Sixth Army's I Corps area, 27th Inf of 25th Div begins attack along ridge leading to Mt Myoko, on Balete Ridge 5,500 yards SE of Balete Pass. In XI Corps area, 6th Div attacks eastward against *Shimbu* line with 20th and 1st Regts, 20th on N, while 63d Inf holds along general line San Mateo Montalban San Isidro, gaining day's objectives. Elements of 1st Inf fall back under counterattack, however. 172d Inf, 43d Div, continues futile efforts to reduce Sugar Loaf Hill. With S entrances to Morong R Valley secure, 103d Inf patrols toward Pantay, NE of Bench Mark 20. In XIV Corps area 188th Inf (− 1st Bn) of 11th A/B Div relieves RCT 158 in Batangas.

S PHILIPPINES—In U.S. Eighth Army area, Japanese on Mindanao are firmly established at Masilay and Pasananca. 162d Inf, 41st Div, improves positions near San Roque, capturing hill. 163d advances NW of Pasananca. On Palawan, 1st Bn of RCT 186 leaves for Zamboanga, Mindanao, to joint 41st Div.

IWO JIMA—RCT 24 of 4th Mar Div relieves RCT 25, which re-embarks; continues mopping up div zone on right flank of corps. 3d Mar Div mops up within its sector. Enemy is confined to such a small portion of N Iwo Jima that arty support of 5th Mar Div is impossible. 5th Mar Div pockets enemy forces, including their commander, Lt Gen Tadamichi Kuribayashi, in area 700 yards long and 200-500 yards wide. RCT 26, after advancing its right and center to N coast, presses S and W toward rocky gorge, along which RCT 28 remains.

18 March

WESTERN EUROPE—12th Army Group: In U.S. First Army's VII Corps area, 78th Div, driving N along E bank of the Rhine with 311th Inf on left and 310th on right, secures Nieder and Ober Dollendorf and high ground dominating Konigswinter bridge site. 18th Inf, on left flank of 1st Div, takes commanding ground and 2 villages NE of Brungsberg; 26th, on right, clears Orscheid, Wullscheid, Hill 363 S of Wullscheid, and Stockhausen. 16th Inf completes its crossing of the Rhine and relieves elements of 18th Inf and of 78th Div. In III Corps area, 9th Div, pressing toward initial objective line along Pfeffer and Wied Rivers, clears Windhagen and Ober Windhagen, improves positions E of Vettelschoss, and gains high ground along the Wied in Strodt area. 99th Div mops up and patrols along the Wied to locate crossing sites. 18th Cav Sq relieves elements of 394th Inf.

In U.S. Third Army s VIII Corps area, 345th Inf of 87th Div clears most of Koblenz and places direct fire on Fort Constantine, which continues to hold out. 347th makes progress to S despite observed enemy fire from across the Rhine, clearing rest of Rhens and taking Brey and Niederspay. 6th Cav Gp, whose zone is extended S to junction of Rhine and Moselle Rivers, prepares for relief by 28th Div, which completes assembly in Nieder Mendig area. XII Corps issues orders for drive to Mainz–Worms sector of the Rhine: 90th Div is to take Mainz; 4th Armd Div, previously ordered to Mainz, is re-

[18 MARCH 1945]

directed to Worms. In 90th Div zone, 2d Cav Gp holds Boppard-Oberwesel sector of the Rhine; TF Spiess mops up from Oberwesel to Nieder Heimbach; 358th Inf clears from Nieder Heimbach to Bingerbruch. 359th Inf reverts to 90th Div at 2400. CCB of 4th Armd Div captures that part of Bad Kreuznach E of the Nahe and attacks toward Volxheim and Wollstein, clearing part of Volxheim; CCR mops up resistance bypassed by CCB; CCA takes Sprendlingen, Gau Bickelheim, St Johann, and Wolfsheim with little difficulty. Continuing S, elements of TF Breckenridge, 5th Div, reach Gemuen-den-Mengerschied-Sargenroth area. 2d and 11th Regts clear through woods to vicinity of Weitersborn, Seesbach, Pferdsfeld, Ippenscheid, Winterbach, Begroth, Argenschwang, and Dalberg. 11th Armd Div speeds S to Nahe R and crosses elements, although bridges are wrecked: on right, 41st Cav reaches the river at Fischbach; CCB crosses some elements at Kirn and others at Kirnssulzbach; advancing through Kirchberg, CCA reaches river line near Simmern unt Dhaun. Closely co-ordinated air and ground action results in heavy losses to enemy withdrawing in confusion. RCT 355, 89th Div, crosses the Moselle at Alf and follows 11th Armd Div, to which it is attached for motorized mopping up. To rear of 11th Armd Div, 89th Div expands positions E of the Moselle and makes contact with 5th Div to left. 76th Div establishes bridgehead across the Moselle SE of Wittlich, crossing 304th Inf in Wehlen-Lieser-Kesten area and clearing Muelheim, Filzen, Wintrich, Reinsport, Nieder Emmel, and Mustert. In XX Corps area, 16th Cav Gp, completing relief of 3d Cav Gp, passes to corps control to screen N flank. 94th Div pursues disorganized enemy to Baumholder. 12th Armd Div, with CCR on left and CCB on right, begins drive through 94th Div toward the Rhine in Worms area. 10th Armd Div, pressing forward in multiple columns, reaches St Wendel area. CCA begins assault on St Wendel, target for 2 hours of direct fire; elements prepare to continue pursuit of enemy falling back toward Kaiserslautern. CCB gets forward elements to Thalichtenberg area. 80th Div follows 10th Armd Div closely by motor and on foot. 104th Inf, 26th Div, takes Gresaubach, Thalexweiler, Aschbach, and Dirmingen while 101st clears Lebach, Bubach, and Kalmesweiler; 328th assembles at Haustadt as reserve. Beginning breakout assault from Saarlautern bridgehead, 65th Div's 261st Inf takes Dillingen; 259th and 260th improve positions in Saarlautern bridgehead but fail to break out.

6th Army Group: U.S. Seventh Army is planning for assault across the Rhine. In XXI Corps area, engineers assisting 63d Div breach gap in dragon's teeth of West Wall N of Ensheim and Ommersheim. In XV Corps area, 45th and 3d Divs begin assault on pillboxes and dragon's teeth of West Wall. 100th Div starts withdrawal from line in Bitche area as 71st Div relieves it. In VI Corps area, 42d Div, crossing into Germany, reaches West Wall defenses on left flank of corps. 103d Div advances rapidly northward across German border, taking Bobenthal and bridges over the Lauter there; runs into opposition below Niederschlettenbach. Crossing Bieberbach R over newly completed bridge, some elements of 36th Div seize Dieffenbach and others take Surbourg. 14th Armd Div is moving forward to exploit through 36th Div. Orders for 3d Algerian Div to revert to Fr 1st Army upon reaching the Lauter are altered to permit French to continue to Erlen R. The div pursues retreating enemy on right flank of corps to within a mile of German border.

EASTERN EUROPE—Troops of First White Russian Front complete capture of town and port of Kolberg (Pomerania), last enemy pocket on Baltic coast between Polish corridor and Stettin Bay.

ITALY—15th Army Group: In U.S. Fifth Army's II Corps area, Italian Legnano Gp is attached to corps and placed under command of 91st Div, later relieving 2 regts of that div. 85th Div passes to army reserve.

LUZON—In U.S. Sixth Army's I Corps area, 33d Div TF (1st Bn, 130th Inf, reinf) assembles near Bauang for rcn in force of Bauang-Naguilian area. Japanese, under increasing pressure from Filipino guerrillas on N and Americans on S, are ordered to withdraw from San Fernando on 20th. 25th Div at last overruns the enemy positions N of Putlan that have been delaying it for some days. Next objective on Highway 5 is Kapintalan, some 4½ air miles N of Putlan. In XI Corps area, 2d Bn of 20th Inf, 6th Div, attacks NE, night 18–19, toward Mt Baytangan. 1st Inf, in limited action, recovers ground lost in counterattack. 1st Bn of 103 Inf, 43d Div, drives to S end of Bench Mark 23. 3d Bn attacks toward Mt Tanauan and gains positions on slopes. 38th Div commander requests and receives permission to reconnoiter Caballo I. In XIV Corps area, 158th Inf turns over responsibility for Calumpan Peninsula to AT Co. Guerrilla patrol reports Mt Bijang clear of enemy.

S PHILIPPINES—In U.S. Eighth Army area, VICTOR I Attack Group (TG 78.3 under Adm Struble) lands 185th Inf, 40th Div, on S Panay after brief naval gunfire bombardment of landing beaches in Tigbauan area. Landing is unopposed and assault forces move rapidly E and NE toward Iloilo, forward elements reaching Arevale, 10 miles E of Tigbauan. 2d Bn, 160th Inf, follows 185th Inf ashore and takes responsibility for NW edge of beachhead. 40th Rcn Tr columns drive to Alimodian and Santa Barbara. CG, 40th Div, assumes command ashore. In Mindanao area, elements of Co. F, 162d Inf, 41st Div, move from Basilan I. to Malamaui I. where search for enemy is uneventful.

IWO JIMA—3d Mar Div relieves RCT 24, 4th Mar Div, with RCT 9, whereupon RCT 24 re-embarks. RCT's 9 and 21, 3d Mar Div, patrol and mop up from this date until relieved by garrison forces. 5th Mar Div is methodically reducing final pocket of resistance: RCT 28 conducts holding action along S rim of the rocky gorge across its front and provides fire support while RCT 26 works forward slowly from N to E. Elements of 5th Mar Div not engaged in combat begin re-embarking.

JAPAN—In preparation for Operation ICEBERG (invasion of the Ryukyus), carrier planes of TF 58 attack Japanese homeland to neutralize enemy airfields on Kyushu. The strikes are highly effective, resulting in heavy damage to airfields and installations and destruction of many aircraft on the ground and in the air.

19 March

WESTERN EUROPE—12th Army Group: In U.S. First Army's VII Corps area, continuing N along the Rhine, 78th Div's 311th Inf takes Romlinghoven, Obercassel, and positions dominating bridge site while, 310th overruns Busch, Bennert, and Heisterbacherrott. 1st Div meets stubborn opposition as it drives enemy 1,000–3,000 yards farther NE and E from the Rhine: Eudenbach falls to 18th Inf; 26th reaches Gratzfeld by daylight and presses E toward airfield. First Class 40 bridge over the Rhine is completed. Corps units W of the river regroup. 8th Div relieves 413th Inf, 104th Div, and begins relief of 4th Cav Gp. 7th Armd Div is attached to corps and defends W bank of the Rhine to S of 8th Div. In III Corps area, 9th Div, continuing E throughout day and night with 39th and 47th Regts, secures initial bridgehead line by dawn of 20th. 99th Div, directed to secure commanding ground along general line Solscheid–Hammerstein, extends right flank S past Rheinbrohl and Hammerstein in limited attack. In V Corps area, elements of 9th Inf, 2d Div, clear Rhine island near Namedy.

In U.S. Third Army area, VIII Corps zone W of the Rhine is cleared as 87th Div gains its objectives. 345th Inf completes capture of Koblenz and 347th clears Oberspay. 28th Div relieves 6th Cav Gp of holding positions along the Rhine. Corps gradually becomes responsible for W bank of the Rhine from Boppard to Bingen and for 76th Div, which is to defend it, as 2d Cav Gp of XII Corps is relieved there. 385th Inf, first of 76th Div units to reach new zone, begins relieving 2d Cav Gp and is attached to corps. In XII Corps area, 2d Cav Gp displaces S along the Rhine to its junction with the Nahe, relieving 358th Inf and TF Spiess of 90th Div. 90th Div attacks across the Nahe toward the Rhine at Mainz. 358th Inf, on left, after crossing the Nahe at Bretzenheim, drives to Aspisheim and Dromersheim and outposts Welgesheim. 359th crosses the Nahe at Bad Kreuznach and drives to Wolfsheim, Vendersheim, St Johann, Sprendlingen, Hackenheim, and Volxheim. TF Spiess crosses into bridgehead and assembles. 4th Armd Div makes rapid progress against weakening resistance. CCB overruns Wollstein, Gumbsheim, Siefersheim, Wonsheim, Eckelsheim and Wendelsheim. CCA takes Vendersheim, Sulzheim, Wallertheim, Rommersheim, and Schimsheim. With close air support softening resistance immediately ahead, 11th Armd Div breaks through last enemy defense positions on high ground S of the Nahe and pursues demoralized enemy E toward the Rhine; objective is changed to the Rhine just S of Worms, rather than Worms, which 4th Armd Div is to take. From Fischbach, 41st Cav Rcn Sq drives to Medard and Odenbach and makes contact with 12th Armd Div of XX Corps, on right. CCB overruns enemy defenses S of the Nahe; races to Meisenheim and takes Glan R bridge; continues forward to Alsenz R at Rockenhausen, where bridge is secured. Rear elements of CCA battle enemy pocket at Rohrbach while others ford the Nahe at Martinstein, overrun enemy's MLR at Merxheim, and continue to Meisenheim. CCR follows CCB and assists in handling horde of prisoners. To rear of armor, 5th and 89th Divs clear southward to the Nahe from Bad Kreusnach westward. Upon dissolution of TF Breckenridge of 5th Div, RCT 10 is attached to 4th Armd Div. 304th Inf, 76th Div, expands Moselle bridgehead sufficiently to permit bridging at Muelheim and makes contact with XX Corps; Graach, Bernkastel, Andel, Monzelfeld, Longkamp, and Gornhausen are easily cleared. XX Corps continues rapidly E toward the Rhine. 16th Cav Gp displaces eastward to screen N flank. 94th Div gains 22 miles in zone of 302d Inf and 12 miles in zone of 376th. 12th Armd Div's CCR bypasses resistance at Lauterecken, which 94th Div eliminates. CCB, directed toward autobahn bridge over the Rhine N of Mannheim, passes through 94th Div at Baumholder and with TF Norton on left and TF Field on right reaches positions beyond Winnweiler. CCA joins in eastward drive, following the other assault columns. 10th Armd Div drives E with 3 CC's abreast to positions near Kaiserslautern. 80th Div clears Kusel, helps 10th Armd Div clear St Wendel, which it outposts, and moves elements E from St Wendel area. Elements of 26th Div reach Ottweiler. 65th Div expands Saarlautern bridgehead: 261st Inf takes Nalbach, Piesbach, Bilsdorf, and Saarwellingen; 260th is pinched out after clearing Saarlautern

[20 MARCH 1945]

and Saarlautern-Roden; 259th takes Fraulautern and Ensdorf.

6th Army Group: In U.S. Seventh Army's XXI Corps area, 63d Div, continuing assault on West Wall, destroys many pillboxes. On left flank of corps, 70th Div renews attack for Sarre R crossings and Saarbruecken; at night, gets patrol of 276th Inf across the river without opposition. CCA, 6th Armd Div, is attached to 63d Div to exploit expected breakthrough. In XV Corps area, 45th and 3d Divs continue assault on West Wall, destroying numerous pillboxes and bunkers. 45th Div overruns Alschbach, Blieskastel, and Webenheim. Forward elements of 3d Div reach positions E of Zweibrucken. In VI Corps area, 42d Div progresses slowly against West Wall fortifications on left flank of corps. 103d Div is strongly opposed near Nieder Schlettenbach and Reisdorf. Lively fighting is in progress in Wissembourg Gap as 36th Div clears Wissembourg and continues across German border to Ober Otterbach and positions to E. Elements of CCA, 14th Armd Div, cross the Lauter NE of Schleithal. Fr Groupement Monsabert is organized from 3d Algerian Div and attached elements of 5th Fr Armd Div to continue operations beyond the Lauter. Crossing the Lauter into Germany, Groupement Monsabert seizes Scheibenhard and Lauterbourg.

BURMA—In Br Fourteenth Army's 33 Corps area, Ind 19th Div is still unable to break into Fort Dufferin, but aircraft breach the thick wall. Ind 20th Div column drives through Pyinzi to Pindale, in region S of Mandalay.

LUZON—In U.S. Sixth Army's I Corps area, 33d Div TF takes Bauang town and bridge with little difficulty. In XI Corps area, 2d Bn of 20th Inf, 6th Div, reaches positions some 1,200 yards W of Mt Baytangan during morning. 1st Inf renews attack and gains ground to right of 20th Inf. 172d Inf, in effort to envelop Sugar Loaf Hill, moves 2d Bn through 103d Inf to Mt Caymayuman to strike from rear. 3d Bn, 103d Inf, continues clearing Mt Tanauan, where enemy is offering strong opposition. Platoon of 2d Bn, 151st Inf, 38th Div, from garrison of Corregidor, lands on E end of Caballo I. without opposition; locates enemy defenses in center of the island, against which softening bombardment is conducted for the next week. In XIV Corps area, patrol of 511th Inf, 11th A/B Div, and guerrillas occupy Mt Bijang without opposition. RCT 158 begins attack for 3 hills in Cuenca area: 2d Bn reaches 2 of the hills with ease, but 3d Bn, attacking the third, Mt Macolod, is stopped short of Cuenca by intense fire.

S PHILIPPINES—In U.S. Eighth Army area, in preparation for assault landing on Cebu, Thirteenth Air Force starts intensive bombardment. On Mindanao, 1st Bn of 186th Inf arrives at Zamboanga, where American control is being extended. Elements of Co F, 162d Inf, on Malamaui I., return to Basilan. On Panay, one 185th Inf column continues toward Iloilo until halted by enemy defenses at Molo. Another seizes Carpenter bridge across Iloilo R north of Molo before Japanese can destroy it. A third column seizes Mandurriao and its airfield without opposition. Japanese, after nightfall, attempt to escape into mountains through guerrilla lines at Jaro and are largely successful.

IWO JIMA—5th Mar Div's RCT 26, assisted by fire of RCT 28, maintains pressure against final enemy pocket, moving forward slowly. 4th Mar Div completes re-embarkation.

JAPAN—For the second successive day, carrier planes of TF 58 strike at Japanese homeland, concentrating on enemy fleet units in Kure-Kobe area. Despite extremely heavy AA fire, carrier planes damage at least 16 Japanese warships and a number of other vessels. Enemy planes hit USS *Franklin* (CV) and leave it burning. During afternoon TF 58 withdraws southward, covering the disabled *Franklin* and conducting fighter sweeps over Kyushu airfields.

20 March

WESTERN EUROPE—12th Army Group: In U.S. First Army's VII Corps area, continuing N along the Rhine toward the Sieg, RCT 311, on 78th Div left, reaches Geislar; 309th Inf passes through 310th to continue right flank drive and advances rapidly. 16th Inf, committed on 1st Div left, takes objective towns of Stieldorferhohn and Oberpleis; 18th captures Berghausen and Bennerscheid and commanding heights and villages near these; against heavy opposition, 26th cuts Eudenbach-Buchholz road and gains objectives in vicinity of airfield. CC Howze, 3d Armd Div, is attached to 1st Div and relieves elements of 16th Inf. 4th Cav Gp, upon relief by 8th Div, moves S to defensive positions along the Rhine in Bonn area. III Corps continues limited attack to SE with 394th Inf, 99th Div, improving positions.

In U.S. Third Army's XII Corps area, 76th Div continues relief of 2d Cav Gp along the Rhine and withdraws its Moselle bridgehead on S flank of corps. 2d Cav Gp, under 90th Div command, crosses 42d Sq over the Nahe at Bretzenheim and drives N to S edge of Bingen. Driving quickly toward Mainz with 358th Inf on left, 359th in center, and TF Spiess on right, 90th Div reaches Wackernheim, Ober Olmer Wald, Klein Winternheim, Ebersheim, Mommenheim, and Selzen; 357th crosses the Nahe. 5th Div crosses the Nahe and clears eastward toward the Rhine and Oppenheim; RCT 11, in the lead, reaches

Gau Odernheim-Spiesheim-Woerrstadt region. 4th Armd Div gets forward elements to the Rhine at Worms and blocks roads leading to the city. On right flank of corps, 11th Armd Div continues rapid advance toward the Rhine and gets CCB within 4 kilometers of the river. 89th Div crosses the Nahe and moves forward behind 11th Armd Div, clearing bypassed resistance. In XX Corps area, 94th Div gains up to 23 miles, advance elements (2d Bn of 302d Inf) reaching Dirmstein, E of Gruenstadt. CCR, 12th Armd Div, reaches Gruenstadt area; CCB's TF Norton reaches the Rhine N of Mannheim, night 20-21, and TF Field moves to Freinsheim area to assist 92d Cav Rcn Sq as it drives E on div right flank. 80th Div's 319th Inf seizes and outposts Kaiserslautern; 317th halts at Enkenbach and Neukirchen, NE of Kaiserslautern. Bypassing Kaiserslautern to N and S, 10th Armd Div drives E to Neukirchen-Enkenbach-Hochspeyer area.. 26th Div mops up around Ottweiler. 65th Div pushes E to Kirschhof-Dilsburg area. 3d Cav Gp moves from Trier to Saarlautern to protect S flank of corps and is attached to 65th Div. Contact is made with Seventh Army to right.

6th Army Group: U.S. Seventh Army breaks through West Wall fortifications in zones of XXI and XV Corps. In XXI Corps area, 70th Div, on left flank of corps, occupies Saarbruecken without opposition and makes contact with XX Corps, Third Army. 63d Div achieves complete breakthrough of West Wall to right: 254th Inf reaches Ober Wurzbach; 255th moves forward through West Wall into Hassel and St Ingbert TF Harris, 3d Bn of 254th Inf, reinf, is created to clear Neukirchen area. CCA, 6th Armd Div, after exploiting through 63d Div to Homburg against light opposition, reverts to parent unit. In XV Corps area, 45th and 3d Divs break through West Wall defenses in their respective zones. With capture of Homburg, 45th completes its immediate mission. 3d Div pushes forward into Zweibrucken and takes bridges intact. 6th Armd Div (− CCA) passes through 3d Div to exploit to the Rhine, advancing rapidly. In VI Corps area, 42d Div is virtually halted by effective enemy defense of West Wall positions on left flank of corps. 103d Div is also slowed by strong opposition but takes Nieder Schlettenbach. Left flank elements of 36th Div reach Dorrenbach area. CCA, 14th Armd Div, attacks in Wissembourg Gap and reaches main defenses of West Wall at Steinfeld, which it begins clearing. Groupement Monsabert is slowly clearing the Bien Wald on right flank of corps. 4th Div is attached to corps.

EASTERN EUROPE—Troops of First White Russian Front overrun Alt Damm (Pomerania) and eliminate last German bridgehead across the Oder, opposite Stettin. In East Prussia, forces of Third White Russian Front capture Braunsberg. Red Army maintains pressure against Baltic ports of Gdynia and Danzig.

BURMA—In Br Fourteenth Army's 33 Corps area, Ind 19th Div, at Mandalay, breaks into Fort Dufferin and finds that enemy has withdrawn.

In NCAC area, Br 36th Div reaches Mogok and turns SE toward Kyaukme.

LUZON—In U.S. Sixth Army's I Corps area, 33d Div TF moves N toward San Fernando from the Bauang sector in attempt to link up with guerrilla forces of N Luzon. Japanese withdraw from San Fernando under cover of darkness. On Highway 5, Co C of 161st Inf, 25th Div, takes fork of ridge W of Norton's Knob while rest of 1st Bn continues fruitless attack on Norton's Knob. 3d Bn relieves Co C. In XI Corps area, 6th Div gains several hundred yards, reaching heights commanding Bosoboso R, and pauses to mop up and reconnoiter. Japanese make determined counterattack against 172d Inf of 43d Div on Mt Caymayuman, night 20-21. 3d Bn of 103d Inf suspends attack on Mt Tanauan while that area is being neutralized with fire. In XIV Corps area, 3d and 1st Bns of 158th Inf continue attack toward Cuenca and Mt Macolod. Patrol reports Cuenca undefended.

S PHILIPPINES—In U.S. Eighth Army area, X Corps is designated as VICTOR V TF to seize Malabang-Parang-Cotabato area of Mindanao and clear region E of Zamboanga Peninsula. 24th and 31st Divs are placed under control of X Corps. 41st Div and Para RCT 505 are to be held in army reserve. On Mindanao, Co F (−) of 162d Inf returns to Zamboanga from Basilan I. Cos K and L, 121st Guerrilla Regt, and platoon of Co F, 162d Inf, remain on Basilan to provide security. On Panay, elements of 185th Inf drive quickly through Molo to Iloilo, which is secured with ease. Organized resistance on Panay has collapsed. Japanese groups withdrawing toward the mountains from Jaro are intercepted by 40th Rcn Tr and 3d Bn and harassed by aircraft. Search of the island continues.

IWO JIMA—RCT 26, 5th Mar Div, pushes slowly NW toward the sea along draw that crosses front of RCT 28. RCT 28 continues to support attack with fire and begins gradual withdrawal of elements from line as attack progresses across its front. Transports with garrison force—RCT 147—arrive off island.

21 March

WESTERN EUROPE—12th Army Group: In U.S. First Army's VII Corps area, 78th Div concludes drive to the Sieg: 311th Inf reaches the river at Meindorf; 310th takes Hangeler, Niederpleis, Muelldorf-Siegburg, and Menden. 4th Sq, 4th Cav Gp,

[21 MARCH 1945]

is attached to div to defend river line and relieves elements of 311th and 310th Regts along the Sieg. CC Howze, 3d Armd Div, is also attached to 78th Div and drives N with TF Richardson to the Sieg on div right flank, partly clearing Buisdorf; 309th Inf follows armor and mops up. 1st Div progresses NE toward the Sieg. 16th Inf clears Uthweiler, Rott, Soven, Pleiserhohn, Westerhausen, and Buchholz; 18th takes Eisbach, Ruebhausen, and Kurtscheid; in limited attack, 26th secures Germscheid. RCT 413, 104th Div, upon crossing into bridgehead E of the Rhine, is attached to 1st Div and begins relief of 26th Inf. 8th Div relieves 414th and 415th Regts, 104th Div, in line. III Corps prepares for breakout assault. RCT 38 of 2d Div, V Corps, and CCB of 9th Armd Div take over part of 99th Div zone. At midnight 21-22, 9th Armd Div is transferred to V Corps. V Corps goes on the offensive. 2d Div begins crossing the Rhine via III Corps bridges and LCVP's at 0400. RCT 9, upon relief W of the river by 69th Div, closes in vicinity of Rheinbrohl E of the Rhine. 69th Div is moving forward to W bank of the Rhine.

In U.S. Third Army's VIII Corps area, 76th Div completes relief of 2d Cav Gp, XII Corps, along the Rhine from Boppard to Bingen and passes to corps control. In XII Corps area, 42d Sq of 2d Cav Gp takes Bingen and extends positions along the Rhine to Frei Weinheim; 2d Sq, disposed along the Rhine between Frei Weinheim and Mainz, is in contact with 90th Div near Mainz. 90th Div closes in on Mainz and clears most of its zone W of the Rhine. 357th Inf is committed between 359th Inf and TF Spiess. 5th Div clears its zone W of the Rhine, RCT 11 reaching the river at Oppenheim and Nierstein. RCT 10, which reverts to parent unit, mops up Worms and begins assembly. 4th Armd Div drives N along W bank of the Rhine with CCB on right and CCA on left, clearing region between Worms and Oppenheim; CCR assembles in Stein Bockenheim area to block roads on div S flank. 11th Armd Div completes its second drive to the Rhine by 0800, when CCB takes final objective, airport S of Worms. CCB, to which 41st Cav is attached, enters Worms, which is in ruins, and withdraws to assembly area near Weinsheim. RCT 355 reverts to 89th Div from attachment to 11th Armd Div. XX Corps gets additional elements to the Rhine between Worms and Mannheim and takes up positions for assaults on Ludwigshafen and Speyer. Elements of 302d Inf, 94th Div, reach the Rhine near Petersau; 376th advances to W edge of Ludwigshafen. 12th Armd Div's CCA reaches outskirts of Ludwigshafen and is passed through by elements of 94th Div, which it prepares to assist in attack on the city. CCR and CCB (− TF Field) complete drive to the Rhine and, upon relief along W bank by 94th Div, move to assembly area. TF Field and 92d Cav Rcn Sq head for Speyer (which is also objective of 10th Armd Div), reaching edge of Mutterstadt. 10th Armd Div drives S on broad front toward Speyer: CCA reaches Neustadt and Dannstadt; CCR clears Rinnthal, Annweiler, and Queichambach, W of Landau; CCB reaches Densieders, NE of Pirmasens, and positions near Rinnthal. 80th Div (−) moves to forward assembly areas E of Kaiserslautern. 26th and 65th Divs continue E until ordered to halt. Former, advancing generally toward Neustadt, is to remain W of vertical 20 grid line and S of horizontal 90 grid line. 65th Div is to assemble in Neunkirchen area and 3d Cav Gp, which is detached from it, in Ottweiler region for rehabilitation and training.

6th Army Group: U.S. Seventh Army CP moves forward from Luneville to Sarreguemines. In XXI Corps area, organized resistance collapses. 63d Div's TF Harris clears Neunkirchen area. 63d Div is then transferred to XV Corps. 70th Div is withdrawn as army reserve. In XV Corps area, 6th Armd Div moves rapidly eastward to the Rhine, which CCA reaches at Rhein-Durkheim; makes patrol contact with Third Army at Worms. 179th Inf, 45th Div, follows CCA while rest of div mops up. In VI Corps area, 42d Div, renewing attack on West Wall at 1900 after air and arty preparation, finds that enemy has abandoned his first belt of pillboxes. 102d Div TF (2d Bn, 409th Inf, and elements of 761st Tank Bn) drives into Reisdorf. 36th Div overruns a number of enemy strongpoints within its sector. CCA and CCR, 14th Armd Div, continue clearing Steinfeld against determined opposition. Groupement Monsabert is still engaged in clearing the Bien Wald.

In Fr 1st Army area, DA ALPS completes relief of U.S. Forces within limits of Alpine Front Command.

BURMA—In Br Fourteenth Army's 33 Corps area, organized resistance within Mandalay ceases. Br 2d Div opens road from Ava to Mandalay while Ind 10th Div thrusts to Wundwin.

CHINA—Japanese begin drive on Laohokon airfield, moving by night.

LUZON—In U.S. Sixth Army's I Corps area, troops of 130th Inf, 33d Div, link up with Filipino guerrillas of U.S. Army Forces in the Philippines, North Luzon, in vicinity of San Fernando without opposition. Co F of 130th Inf finds Naguilian and its airstrip undefended. Guerrillas of 121st Inf occupy San Fernando without opposition. West coast of Luzon is now clear. 3d Bn of 161st Inf, 25th Div, attacks along ridge extending to Crump Hill, about 1,000 yards W of Kapintalan, against accurate fire that stalls advance until 8 April. 27th Inf, 25th Div, beats off determined counterattack on ridge leading to Mt Myoko. In XI Corps area, after air and arty preparation, 1st Inf of 6th Div attacks and gains 600–800 yards; blocks trail running N from Antipolo to Wawa. Captured document indicates enemy is reinforcing this area. Japanese resistance to 172d Inf, 43d Div, collapses. Mt Caymayuman, Mt Yabang, and Sugar Loaf Hill are cleared with ease. Until 26 March, 172d Inf mops up and patrols. 3d Bn of 103d Inf drives to crest of Mt Tanauan. Co B, reinf by guerrillas, advances 2 miles N of Bench Mark 23 and crosses New Bosoboso R below barrio of the same name. In XIV Corps area, 158th Inf drives rapidly E without opposition from Cuenca to slopes of Mt Macolod.

S PHILIPPINES—In U.S. Eighth Army area, Co B, having completed clearing Simara, joins Co C on Romblon. By this time 118 Japanese have been killed on Simara for U.S. losses of 10 killed. From Panay, amphibious patrol of 2d Bn, 160th Inf, lands on Guimaras I. and searches it uneventfully.

22 March

WESTERN EUROPE—12th Army Group: In U.S. First Army area, VII Corps consolidates, regroups, and conducts limited attacks for line of departure from which to make co-ordinated breakout assault. CC Howze, assisted by 309th Inf, finishes clearing 78th Div zone and reverts to 3d Armd Div. On 1st Div left, 16th Inf receives excellent air support as it clears toward stream running SE from Hennef. Relief of 1st and 3d Bns, 26th Inf, is completed by RCT 413. 104th Div, less RCT 413, moves E of the Rhine and releases 414th Inf to 3d Armd Div. III Corps begins limited attacks across Wied R, night 22–23, surprising enemy who offers little opposition. 9th and 99th Divs start crossing at 2200 and 2400, respectively, 9th Div employing 60th Inf and 99th Div, 395th and 393d Regts. 18th Cav Sq reverts to 14th Cav Gp and assembles near Ariendorf. 7th Armd Div, no longer required to defend W bank of the Rhine, prepares to cross the river. V Corps, attacking SE with RCT 38 of 2d Div and CCB of 9th Armd Div abreast, clears region between the Rhine and Wied Rivers and secures bridgehead across latter. RCT 38, co-ordinating with 99th Div of III Corps, clears Datzeroth on left and on right takes Segendorf, Rodenbach, and other villages in the vicinity. CCB crosses the Wied and overcomes considerable opposition in Neuwied. Since CCB's commander, Brig Gen William Hoge, is released by div to head 4th Armd Div, CCA hq crosses the Rhine to take command of attack and troops previously attached to or supporting CCB. Class 40 treadway bridge is constructed over the Rhine at Hommingen. 28th Div, holding W bank of the Rhine to right of 2d Div, reverts to corps control as result of interarmy boundary change.

In U.S. Third Army area, XII Corps completes drive to the Rhine and begins assault crossing. 90th Div, employing 3 bns each of 358th and 359th Regts, breaks into Mainz and overcomes half-hearted resistance there; 357th Inf maintains defensive positions to right and clears Weisenau; TF Spiess is dissolved upon relief by 5th Div Rcn Tr. 2d Cav Gp conducts river-crossing demonstration NW of Mainz and relieves elements of 358th Inf at Mainz. CCA, 4th Armd Div, assembles near Springlingen. 5th Div reorganizes for assault across the Rhine at Oppenheim and at 2200 begins crossing 1st and 3d Bns, RCT 11, with little difficulty. 11th Armd Div completes mop-up of its sector and prepares for relief by 80th Div, XX Corps. 94th Div, XX Corps, relieves elements of 41st Cav along the river in accordance with local boundary change. 89th Div prepares to cross into 5th Div's Rhine bridgehead. In XX Corps area, 94th Div forms TF Cheadle (RCT 376 and CCA, 12th Armd Div) for attack on Ludwigshafen that penetrates Friesenheim, Mundenheim, and Rheingonheim. As 94th Div zone is extended N, elements of 89th Div, XII Corps, within it, are relieved by 302d Inf. 12th Armd Div attacks to secure bridge across the Rhine in vicinity of Speyer or Germersheim: CCR takes Boehl, Iggelheim, and Hafsloch; CCB moves to Mutterstadt and, with 92d Cav Rcn Sq temporarily attached, turns S and begins assault on Speyer. 10th Armd Div columns converge on Landau and take it. 26th Div begins assembly near Alzey in preparation for operations with XII Corps.

6th Army Group: In U.S. Seventh Army area XXI Corps takes command of 71st and 100th Divs in Bitche area and will cover right flank of XV Corps as it advances to the Rhine. In XV Corps area, 3d and 45th Divs are directed to search for Rhine crossing sites. 45th Div advances to the Rhine. Elements of 3d Div move forward behind armor. 6th Armd Div, less elements on W bank of the Rhine, moves to assembly areas. In VI Corps area, 42d Div finds that enemy has abandoned West Wall positions within its sector and pushes forward with ease through Dahn. 103d Div TF reaches Klingenmuenster and makes contact with Third Army while other elements clear Silz. Pushing through Dorrenbach, 36th Div closes in on Bergzabern, destroying numerous pillboxes. 14th Armd Div completes capture of Steinfeld. Groupement Monsabert makes local gains in the Bien Wald. Since German withdrawal routes are blocked, enemy columns are profitable targets for aircraft and arty.

EASTERN EUROPE—Troops of Third White Russian Front continue reduction of German pocket in East Prussia. Second White Russian forces make slow progress against fortifications about Danzig and Gdynia. Moscow announces that troops of First Ukrainian Front have broken through enemy positions W and S of Oppeln (Silesia). Berlin reports intensified Soviet breakthrough attempts between Lake Balaton and the Danube in Hungary.

ALFSEA—At a meeting of commanders in Monywa, the problem of air supply is discussed. It is agreed that CAI be moved from Burma as quickly as possible to ease supply situation of Br Fourteenth Army, but Adm Mountbatten is not willing to use transport from SEAC for this purpose.

LUZON—In U.S. Sixth Army's I Corps area, 128th Inf of 32d Div is ordered to relieve 127th Inf on Villa Verde Trail. 35th Inf, 25th Div, moving toward Balete Pass along Putlan R Valley, is halted by strong opposition. In XI Corps area, 1st Bn of 20th Inf, 6th Div, begins attack toward wooded area about 600 yards ahead. 1st Inf patrols and mops up. Co B of 103d Inf, 43d Div, driving up Bosoboso R Valley, takes Mt Balidbiran and is joined there by Co C, 3d Bn, 103d, mops up on Mt Tanauan. 169th Inf, 43d Div, is relieved in 38th Div line by 2d Bn of 152d Inf, 38th Div.

S PHILIPPINES—In U.S. Eighth Army area, Americal Div, less RCT 164, conducts amphibious rehearsal for Cebu landing in Leyte Gulf and sails for target. On Panay, Co G of 185th Inf lands on Inampulugan I. to reconnoiter and destroys mine control station.

NEI—Japanese make the last of a prolonged series of air attacks against Morotai.

POA—TF 58 joins Logistic Support Group S of Okinawa and replenishes fuel, ammunition, and provisions in preparation for operations against Okinawa. During period 18-22 March, TF 58 has contributed materially to the success of the imminent invasion of Okinawa by destroying 528 enemy planes, damaging 16 surface vessels, and hitting ground installations.

IWO JIMA—Assisted by flame-throwing tanks, RCT 26 of 5th Mar Div continues tortuous advance NW toward the sea while RCT 28 conducts holding action along S perimeter of the pocket and supports assault with fire. RCT 27 begins re-embarking.

23 March

WESTERN EUROPE—21 Army Group: Begins Operation PLUNDER (assault across the Rhine N of the Ruhr) at 2100 after strong air and arty preparation. While Cdn First Army holds Allied left flank from Emmerich W to North Sea, Second Army begins assault crossings.

In Br Second Army's 30 Corps area, after intense arty preparation, 51st Div leads assault, crossing the Rhine near Rees at 2100 and heading for Rees. In 12 Corps area, 1st Cdo Brig crosses the Rhine NW of Wesel at 2200 and begins assault on that city.

12th Army Group: In U.S. First Army's VII Corps area, while 78th Div consolidates on corps' N flank, 1st Div continues limited attacks to expand bridgehead. Jumping off at 2000, 18th Inf takes Wellesburg before midnight; 16th Inf begins attack for crossings of the Hauf, stream running SE from Hennef, late at night. 104th Div (−), having relieved elements of 9th Div (III Corps) and of 1st Div during night 22-23, takes over zone on right flank of corps at 0130; RCT 413 reverts to it from attachment to 1st Div. With 2 bns of 415th Inf on left and bn of 413th on right, 104th Div begins limited attacks to E at 2100, gaining 400-1,000 yards and overrunning airfield E of Eudenbach. 3d Armd Div (−) crosses the Rhine. Advance elements of 86th Div, newly arrived on Continent, reach corps zone. In III Corps area, 9th and 99th Divs expand bridgehead E of the Wied. 60th Inf of 9th Div clears Strauscheid, Rahm, Weissenfels, Neschen, and several small villages between the river and the autobahn. 99th Div, with 395th Inf on left and 393d on right, pushes E past Breitscheid, Rossbach, Waldbreitbach, Nieder Breitbach, and Kurtscheid; 393d reaches final objective a little beyond Kurtscheid shortly after midnight 23-24. 7th Armd Div starts assembly E of the Rhine, night 23-24. 14th Cav Gp, relieved of traffic control and bridge-guarding mission in Remagen area by 8th TD Gp, moves 32d Sq across Rhine to assembly area near Leubsdorf. V Corps expands bridgehead E of the Wied. RCT 38, 2d Div, clears Wolfenacker, Ehlscheid, Rengsdorf, Melsbach, and Altwied. CCA, 9th Armd Div, expands bridgehead slightly in limited attack. 2d Div's RCT 23 crosses the Rhine. 69th Div completes move to the Rhine in Bad Neuenahr region and takes responsibility for sector, completing relief of 2d Div.

In U.S. Third Army's VIII Corps area, 6th Cav Gp takes over Koblenz-Boppard sector along the Rhine, relieving 87th Div. 89th Div is transferred to corps from XII Corps. In XII Corps area, 5th Div gets 4 regts and supporting weapons across the Rhine and establishes firm bridgehead 8 miles wide and 5 miles deep. On left, RCT 2 takes Astheim; in center, RCT 11 clears Trebur, Wallerstaedten, and Geinsheim; on right, RCT 10 seizes Leeheim and Erfelden and presses toward Dornheim; RCT 357 of 90th Div, temporarily attached to 5th Div to cover right flank of bridgehead, crosses the Rhine and moves elements to Erfelden area to relieve RCT 10. Engineers work on bridges, completing Class 40 treadway. 90th Div (− RCT 357) and 4th Armd Div prepare to cross the Rhine. 26th Div is attached to corps and during night 23-24 takes over Mainz-Nackenheim sector from 90th Div; 2d Cav Gp is detached from 90th Div and attached in place to 26th Div. 11th Armd Div begins concentration in Alzey area and relieves 4th Armd Div of Oppenheim–Worms sector of the Rhine. In XX Corps area, after heavy arty preparation, 94th Div's TF Cheadle renews attack on Ludwigshafen, clearing suburbs and entering city proper late in day; because of determined opposition, 301st Inf is committed on N and relieves elements of TF Cheadle. Since Rhine bridge at Speyer is out, 12th Armd Div's CCR attempts to establish bridgehead at Germersheim, thrusting S through Geinsheim and Friesbach to Weingarten, where stiff resistance is overcome with aid of air support. CCB enters Speyer from N and begins to clear moderate resistance. Driving S toward Lauterbourg with CCB on right and CCA on left, 10th Armd Div makes contact with Seventh Army units moving N and is attached to Seventh Army.

6th Army Group: In U.S. Seventh Army area, XV Corps releases 6th Armd Div to Third Army; while patrolling along W bank of the Rhine and relieving elements of Third Army within its zone, trains assault forces for crossing of the Rhine. In XXI Corps area, 10th Armd Div is attached to corps. In VI Corps area, 103d and 36th Divs are mopping up W of the Rhine. 143d Inf of 36th Div advances through Bergzabern. CCB, 14th Armd Div, gets elements to Herxheim and Germersheim. CCA takes Schaidt and presses eastward. Groupement Monsabert is strongly opposed from West Wall positions and suffers heavy casualties.

EASTERN EUROPE—Troops of Second White Russian Front reach Gulf of Danzig between Danzig and Gdynia, splitting German defenders of these port cities. Troops of Third White Russian Front maintain pressure against enemy pocket in East Prussia. Offensive of First Ukrainian Front continues to gain ground in Upper Silesia.

ITALY—Gen Heinrich von Vietinghoff succeeds Field Marshal Kesselring as supreme commander of enemy forces in Italy.

BURMA—In Br Fourteenth Army's 33 Corps area, Ind 20th Div column drives from Wundwin northward to Kume. In 4 Corps area, Myingan falls to Ind 7th Div, which is by now being assisted by elements of Ind 5th Div. Fighting continues at Meiktila, where enemy is still trying to oust Ind 17th Div.

LUZON—In U.S. Sixth Army area, Fifth Air Force begins series of attacks on Legaspi area in preparation for amphibious assault there. In I Corps area, Gen Krueger, to speed operations toward Baguio, attaches RCT 129 of 37th Div to corps, which in turn attaches it to 33d Div. 128th Inf, 32d Div, begins relief of 127th on Villa Verde Trail. 2d Bn, 128th, withdraws from Imugan area to Batchelor. XI Corps is directed to press operations to destroy enemy in Antipolo-Montalban-Ipo area, to complete opening of Manila Bay by capturing islands of El Fraile, Caballo, and Carabao, and to establish contact with XIV Corps E of Laguna de Bay in order to close gap between the corps. 20th Inf, 6th Div, is ordered to be prepared to take Mt Mataba. 1st Bn reaches woods toward which it started on 22d. 1st Inf gains most of its objective line. 2d Bn of 103d Inf, 43d Div, relieves 3d Bn on Mt Tanauan and drives N toward New Bosoboso. In XIV Corps area, 1st Cav Div relieves 511th Para Inf, 11th A/B Div, for Legaspi operation. 187th Inf takes responsibility for capture of Mt Macolod.

S PHILIPPINES—In U.S. Eighth Army area, Co G of 185th Inf returns to Panay from Inampulugan I. On Leyte, RCT 108 of 40th Div completes relief of 164th Inf, Americal Div.

POA—Br carrier task force (TF 57 under command of Vice Adm Sir Bernard Rawlings) is assigned to U.S. Fifth Fleet and sorties from Ulithi; the task force is to neutralize air installations in Sakishima Is., Ryukyu Chain, in support of Okinawa operation.

24 March

WESTERN EUROPE—21 Army Group: In Br Second Army's 30 Corps area, 51st Div is unable to overcome determined resistance by enemy paratroopers at Rees. In 12 Corps area, 1st Cdo Brig clears large part of Wesel in street-to-street fighting. 15th Div, which is to make main effort of corps, crosses the Rhine N of Xanten, starting at 0200, and overruns Mehr and Haffen. XVIII Corps (A/B) of First Allied Airborne Army, under operational control of Br Second Army, drops two airborne divs—Br 6th and U.S. 17th—E of the Rhine in region N and NW of Wesel, starting at about 1000. Airdrops of troops and a day's supplies are successfully executed; resupply by air is not required. Both assault divs take initial objectives, reaching Issel R and securing crossings, and make contact with each other and with Br 12 Corps. On the N, Br 6th A/B Div overruns Hamminkeln; to the S, 17th A/B Div takes Diersfordt and high ground to E. Strong enemy counterattacks N of Wesel are contained, night 24-25. U.S. 13th A/B Div is not employed in Operation VARSITY—the airborne drop E of the Rhine—because of insufficient airlift.

U.S. Ninth Army begins assault across the Rhine. XVI Corps, after an hour of intensive arty preparation, leads off at 0200 when 30th Div, with 119th, 117th, and 120th Regts abreast from N to S, starts across in Buderich-Wallach-Rheinberg region. To the S, 79th Div, employing 315th and 313th Regts abreast, begins crossing at 0300 after similar arty preparation; 314th crosses later in day. 30th Div gains firm bridgehead 6-10 kilometers deep S of Wesel, clearing a number of towns and villages, among them Spellen, Ork, Mehrum, Lohnen, Friedrichsfeld, Stockum, Worde, and Moellen. 79th Div, on the N, clears Stapp and Dinslaken; to the S overruns Overbruch, Vier Linden, and Walsum. 75th Div crosses 1st Bn of 290th Inf in order to defend bridges. By end of day, 19 bns of inf and several of supporting weapons are E of the Rhine and bridgehead is established with minimum of casualties.

12th Army Group: In U.S. First Army area, VII Corps, continuing limited attacks in zones of 1st and 104th Divs, expands bridgehead to assigned line of departure for breakout assault. Though enemy contests every inch gained and makes frequent and determined counterattacks, 1st Div, with effective air support, expands N perimeter of bridgehead, fighting into night 24-25: 16th Inf, reinf by bn of 26th, clears Geisnach and Lichtenberg; 18th takes Heuchel and part of Uckerath. 104th Div gains all limited objectives required on S flank of bridgehead, including high ground NE of Eudenbach and road junctions near airfield. On corps N flank, 1st Bn of 310th Inf, 78th Div, eliminates strongpoint NW of Menden. In III Corps area, 9th Div continues limited action to expand bridgehead E of the Wied with 60th Inf, clearing Borscheid; at 2200 commits 39th and 47th Regts to left in region W of the Wied. 99th Div renews limited attack eastward with 395th Inf at 2200, pressing toward the autobahn. In V Corps area, RCT 38, 2d Div, expands Wied bridgehead several more kilometers and clears Gladbach and Ober Bieber. CCA of 9th Armd Div holds current positions.

In U.S. Third Army area, VIII Corps completes preparations for assault across the Rhine. 89th Div moves into corps zone. XII Corps expands and strengthens Rhine bridgehead and commits armor through it in effort to break through to the Main. Enemy reacts more strongly and makes futile attempts to destroy bridges by air. 5th Div enlarges bridgehead to include Bauschheim, Nauheim, Gross Gerau, Dornberg, and Dornheim. As 90th Div completes movement across the Rhine to positions on 5th Div right, RCT 357 reverts to it. Driving NE with 359th Inf on left and 357th on right, 90th Div relieves 10th Inf, 5th Div, at Erfelden and Dornheim and reaches line Buettelborn-Griesheim. 4th Armd Div begins drive through bridgehead toward the Main. CCA crosses Rhine in morning and is followed in afternoon by CCB and at night by CCR. 104th Inf, 26th Div, is attached to 4th Armd Div to block on right flank and starts across river, night 24-25. CCA advances to edge of Ober Ramstadt; CCB, blocking to S for CCA, clears Stockstadt, Hahn, and Hahnlein; CCR moves to Pfungstadt. 26th Div (− 104th Inf) prepares to cross the Rhine; 101st Inf takes responsibility for Rhine bridges. 6th Armd Div is attached to corps and prepares to join in drive to the Main. XX Corps completes operations W of the Rhine and has firm contact with Seventh Army on right. After nightlong fight, Ludwigshafen falls to 94th Div in morning when N and S assault forces meet in center of city. 12th Armd Div completes its mission, capturing Speyer in zone of CCB in morning and Germersheim in zone of CCR after nightfall, and is detached from corps; CCA reverts to it from attachment to 94th Div. Germans destroy bridge at Germersheim. 11th Armd Div is transferred to XX Corps from XII Corps in place and retains current defensive mission.

6th Army Group: In U.S. Seventh Army area, plans to drop airborne forces E of the Rhine are canceled. XV Corps continues preparations for assault across the Rhine. Under cover of darkness, 24-25, assault forces begin assembly near the river and small party reconnoiters E bank. In VI Corps area, 36th Div completes drive to the Rhine and captures Leimersheim. Fr forces reach Erlen R, clearing Kandel, Rheinzabern, and Neupfotz. XXI Corps takes control of 12th Armd Div.

EASTERN EUROPE—Moscow announces that troops of Third Ukrainian Front on the offensive SW of Budapest have advanced about 44 miles on broad front and captured numerous towns, among them Szekesfehervar, Mor, Zirc, Veszprem, and Enying.

ITALY—15th Army Group: Orders for spring offensive are issued, calling for preliminary action by Br Eighth Army to begin on 10 April followed by main assault of U.S. Fifth Army. The 10 April attack date is later changed to 9 April. Separate 442d Inf returns from France to rejoin U.S. Fifth Army.

LUZON—Hq, Fifth Air Force, is established at Fort Stotsenburg.

In U.S. Sixth Army's XI Corps area, 1st Bn of 20th Inf, 6th Div, tries in vain to reach knoll about 500 yards to E. 1st Inf finishes clearing its zone with capture of ridge overlooking Bosoboso R. 2d Bn of 103d Inf, 43d Div, pauses below New Bosoboso while enemy positions ahead are being softened with fire. In XIV Corps area, 1st Cav Div and 11th A/B Div begin converging drives on Lipa in areas to N and S of Lake Taal, respectively. 1st Cav Div, on N, takes Santo Tomas with ease. 1st Cav Brig relieves 7th Cav in Los Banos area, night 24-25. 188th Inf, 11th A/B Div, reinf by 3d Bn of 511th Para Inf and TD units, starts northward drive against scattered resistance. 187th Inf, 11th A/B Div, opens drive on Mt Macolod against strong opposition. 511th Para Inf, less 3d Bn, is being held in reserve for Legaspi operation. RCT 158 concentrates in Lemery for the same operation and passes to army control.

S PHILIPPINES—In U.S. Eighth Army area, 40th Div is alerted for Negros Occidental operation. Covering Group (cruiser-DD force under Rear Adm R. S. Berkey) for Cebu operation leaves Subic Bay for target. On Mindanao, 162d Inf of 41st Div, reinf by 1st Bn of 186th, attacks Mt Capisan and secures it. Entire Sinonog R area is now cleared of organized resistance. For the next few days 162d Inf consolidates and mops up.

IWO JIMA—RCT 28, 5th Mar Div, takes responsibility for completing reduction of final resistance on Iwo; enemy pocket is confined to area 50 yards square on coast. Gen Kuribayashi is reported to be alive and holding out in a cave, but his hiding place is never discovered.

RYUKYU Is.—Mine sweeping begins under cover of naval and aerial bombardment.

25 March

WESTERN EUROPE—21 Army Group: In Br Second Army's 30 Corps area, 51st Div clears Rees except for small pocket. 43d Div takes over left flank of corps front E of the Rhine. In 12 Corps area, 15th Div overruns Bislich. In U.S. XVIII Corps (A/B) area, Br 1st Cdo Brig, as it is completing reduction of Wesel, is transferred to corps from Br 12 Corps and attached to U.S. 17th A/B Div. Corps consolidates positions, straightens lines, and eliminates enemy pocketed between Br 6th A/B and U.S. 17th A/B Divs. Jumping off at 1500 with 194th Gli Inf on N and 507th Para Inf on S, 17th A/B Div crosses Issel Canal and drives to Phase Line LONDON, some 3,000 yards E of Wesel.

In U.S. Ninth Army's XVI Corps area, 30th Div, continuing assault E of the Rhine during night 24-25 and on 25th, gains about 4 miles all along its front; on the N clears Hunxe and makes contact with Br 1st Cdo Brig. 79th Div pushes about 2 miles eastward. 134th Inf, 35th Div, reinf as a TF and attached to 79th Div, crosses the Rhine E of Rheinberg, night 25-26. 15th Sq, 15th Cav Gp, crosses the Rhine to relieve 30th Div on island S of Wesel between Lippe R and Lippe Canal. Resistance is gradually stiffening.

12th Army Group: In U.S. First Army area, VII Corps opens co-ordinated assault to break out of bridgehead at 0400, as 3d Armd Div, reinf by 414th Inf of 104th Div, passes through 1st and 104th Divs to spearhead drive on Altenkirchen, initial objective. Attacking with two CC's abreast, CC Boudinot on left and CC Hickey on right, 3d Armd Div gets about half way to Altenkirchen in 6-9 mile advance. On left, TF Welborn of CC Boudinot, pushing through Uckerath and Kircheib, reaches positions near Hasselbach; TF Lovelady advances through Griesenbach to Fiersbach. On right, CC Hickey's TF Kane thrusts past Limbach, Sessenheim, and Kescheid to Ahl Creek while TF Doan drives to Flammersfeld area via Asbach and Schoneberg. 83d Armd Rcn Bn protects left flank and CC Howze follows the two assault commands, prepared to assist either. 1st and 104th Divs mop up in wake of armor. 1st Div mops up S of the Sieg within its zone, overrunning a number of villages and terrain features. 104th Div (−) follows armor closely, gaining up to 5 miles. 78th Div begins relief of 1st Div along the Sieg and, in limited attack by elements of 309th Inf, clears strongpoint S of the river near Hennef. 4th Cav Gp (−) is relieved of defensive position in Bonn area by corps security elements; 4th Sq, upon relief along the Sieg by 78th Div, reverts to gp control. III Corps joins in First Army's large-scale offensive, making rapid progress eastward. On 9th Div left, 39th and 47th Regts clear div zone between Pfeffer and Mehr Rivers, 47th pinching out 39th; E of Wied, 60th Inf thrusts past Ober Steinbach, Krunkel, and Epgert. Speeding about 3 miles E with 395th and 393d Regts, 99th Div cuts autobahn near Willroth and takes a number of towns and villages to right; 394th Inf crosses the Wied. 7th Armd Div completes assembly E of the Rhine to spearhead corps breakout attack. In V Corps area, RCT 38, after adjusting positions to protect N flank of 2d Div and being passed through by 23d Inf, is attached to 9th Armd Div; 23d Inf drives E about 6 kilometers and is itself passed through by 9th, which continues E to Grenzhausen. CCA, 9th Armd Div, continues SE along the Rhine, taking Bendorf and Vallendar. 102d Cav Rcn Sq moves up to Neuwied.

In U.S. Third Army area, VIII Corps begins attack across the Rhine. 87th Div crosses, starting at midnight 24-25, in Braubach-Boppard region and establishes bridgehead against firm opposition, particularly on left where determined counterattack develops and is contained. 347th Inf (− 2d Bn) on div left, starts clearing Braubach and reaches outskirts of Ober Lahnstein; since 2d Bn is unable to cross, 2d Bn of 346th is attached to 347th and crosses river to assist in clearing Braubach. To S, 345th Inf thrusts to edge of Lykershausen. In XII Corps area, 16th Cav Gp, transferred to XII Corps from XX Corps, relieves 2d Cav Gp of defensive mission along the Rhine from Bingen to Mainz; 2d Cav Gp is detached from 26th Div. 6th Armd Div begins drive toward the Main at Frankfurt, crossing the Rhine at Oppenheim and passing through 5th Div. CCB crosses first and advances NE to vicinity of Walldorf and Langen; CCA reaches the Main between Ruesselsheim and Raunheim, coming under heavy AA fire from Frankfurt; CCR assembles to rear of CCA in Gross Gerau area; 4th Armd Div breaks through to the Main near Hanau and Aschaffenburg and establishes bridgeheads. On left, CCA reaches the river at Klein Auheim, just S of Hanau, where bridge is seized and small bridgehead is established at Grossauheim. From Hahnlein, CCB, on right, speeds to the Main S of Aschaffenburg, taking a rail and highway bridge and establishing bridgehead in Schweinheim area; elements enter Aschaffenburg but are withdrawn to guard bridge. CCR displaces to Dieburg to block between there and Eberstadt and sends TF to Darmstadt, which is virtually undefended. 5th Div's RCT 2 clears to S bank of the Main within its zone; RCT 10, to right, seizes Hassloch and Koenigstaedten. Driving NE toward the Main between Frankfurt and Hanau with 359th Inf on left and 358th on right, 90th Div cuts autobahn and gets forward elements of both regts to Langen; to right, TF Spiess, reorganized to exclude 90th Rcn Tr, enters Darmstadt from the W as 4th Armd Div TF enters from E, and the city is easily cleared. 328th Inf, 26th Div, relieves 101st Inf of defensive mission along the Rhine, permitting 101st to move to Darmstadt; 104th, still attached to 4th Armd Div, protects right flank of that div after completing river crossing. XX Corps enjoys brief lull during which it prepares to force crossings of the Rhine. 94th Div conducts rehabilitation and training program in Baumholder area. 80th Div closes in Rockenhausen assembly area. Seventh Army units begin relief of 11th Armd Div along the Rhine: 3d Div of XV Corps relieves CCB and all elements of CCA S of grid line 33.

6th Army Group: U.S. Seventh Army, having cleared the industrially important Saar Palatinate in conjunction with Third Army to N, regroups to continue offensive across the Rhine. VI Corps releases 4th and 42d Divs to XXI Corps and takes control of 71st and 100th Divs from XXI Corps. Corps will defend W bank of the Rhine while XV Corps and, later, XXI Corps attack across the river. Fr armor eliminates enemy bridgehead at Maximiliansau.

EASTERN EUROPE—In East Prussia, Heiligenbeil falls to Third White Russian Front forces. Troops of Second White Russian Front overrun Oliva, suburb of Danzig. Red Army offensive from Hungary toward Austria broadens as troops of Second Ukrainian Front start W to right of Third Ukrainian forces and clear Esztergom, Felsoegall, and Tata.

ITALY—15th Army Group: In Br Eighth Army area, 10 Corps takes command of Jewish Brig from 5 Corps. In 13 Corps area, Lt Gen Sir John Harding, new corps commander, arrives.

CHINA—U.S. Fourteenth Air Force personnel withdraw from Laohokon airfield after destroying installations. This is the last of the Fourteenth Air Force bases to fall to enemy. Subsequent Japanese thrusts toward bases at Sian and Ankang are stopped short of their objectives by Chinese.

LUZON—In U.S. Sixth Army's I Corps area, 128th Inf of 32d Div completes relief of 127th Inf on Villa Verde Trail and prepares to continue attack toward Salacsac Pass and Santa Fe. 3d Bn of 35th Inf, 25th Div, turns over roadblock on Old Spanish Trail to guerrilla forces, concluding American operations on this crude trail. 27th Inf, working along ridge toward Mt Myoko, has by now gained 4,000 yards and is up against enemy outposts. In XI Corps area, 1st Bn of 20th Inf, 6th Div, patrols and places arty fire on enemy positions ahead. 1st Inf prepares to relieve 20th of positions along Bosoboso R. 2d Bn of 103d Inf, 43d Div, seizes barrio of New Bosoboso and ridges commanding it, limiting Japanese escape routes to a single trail running NW from the barrio. To close this route 100, 1st Bn begins attack on Hill 1200, which commands it. In XIV Corps area, one 1st Cav Div column pushes from Santo Tomas toward Tanauan; another drives into Los Banos with ease. 188th Inf, 11th A/B Div, makes contact with 187th SE of Mt Macolod. 187th pauses briefly in Mt Macolod area to patrol and probe.

S PHILIPPINES—In U.S. Eighth Army area, X Corps issues orders for future operations on Mindanao. 24th Div is to land in Malabang area on 17 April. Five days later, 31st Div is scheduled to land in Parang area. 185th Inf assembles for operation against Negros. Cebu Attack Group, commanded by Capt Albert T. Sprague, USN, joins Covering Group off Cebu.

IWO JIMA—RCT 28, 5th Mar Div, completes reduction of final pocket of resistance on Iwo in morning. RCT 26 starts re-embarking.

RYUKYU Is.—Preinvasion aerial and naval bombardment continues, though mine-sweeping operations prevent naval surface vessels from moving up to within effective range of Okinawa. Underwater demolition teams go into action.

26 March

WESTERN EUROPE—21 Army Group: In Br Second Army area, 30 Corps expands bridgehead toward the Issel. 51st Div completes capture of Rees and thrusts toward Isselburg; 43d Div, advancing to left of 51st, reaches Millingen. In 12 Corps area, 15th Div reaches the Issel at Ringenberg and is passed through by 53d Div reinf by 4th Armd Brig. 7th Div moves up to spearhead drive on Rheine. In XVIII Corps (A/B) area, Br 6th A/B and U.S. 17th A/B Divs drive E abreast against progressively weakening resistance, to next phase line, NEW YORK, extending from Ringenberg on N to Lippe R near Krudenberg on S. 1st Cdo Brig is held in reserve in Wesel area. Build up E of the Rhine progresses rapidly as bridges are opened. Br 6th Gds Armd Brig crosses, night 26-27.

In U.S. Ninth Army's XVI Corps area, 30th Div expands bridgehead another 4 miles E, though resistance is strong and wooded terrain difficult, and on the N partly clears Gahlen; 190th Inf of 75th Div is attached. In 79th Div sector to the S, 35th Div TF relieves 315th Inf and gains 3-5 kilometers; the TF then reverts to 35th Div, whose 137th Inf crosses the Rhine and prepares to attack between 30th and 79th Divs. Against sporadic resistance, 314th Inf of 79th Div pushes east 1-2 miles, but 313th remains in position; 315th begins relief of 314th late in day. 8th Armd Div begins crossing the Rhine. 15th Cav Gp reverts to corps control and assembles E of the Rhine near Dinslaken; elements on Lippe R–Lippe Canal island are relieved by 75th Div. XIII Corps becomes responsible for XIX Corps sector and takes operational control of 95th Div (− RCT 377) and 113th Cav Gp. RCT 377 is attached to 2d Armd Div. XIX Corps prepares to move to new zone on N flank of army.

12th Army Group: In U.S. First Army's VII Corps area, CC Hickey's TF's Kane and Doan, on 3d Armd Div right, break through enemy defenses and drive through Altenkirchen to Hachenburg and Wahlrod. On left, however, stubborn opposition makes progress of CC Boudinot so slow and costly, despite close air-ground cooperation, that attack is broken off in afternoon and CC Howze is committed between CC's Boudinot and Hickey. Attacking with TF's Hogan and Richardson, CC Howze mops up Altenkirchen and continues E toward Nister R, reaching positions near Eichelhardt. 1st Div, employing elements of 3 regts, clears region S of the Sieg as far E as Eitorf, taking a number of towns and villages. 78th Div continues relief of 1st Div along the Sieg, permitting latter to follow armor eastward. 104th Div (−) eliminates scattered resistance while advancing some 12 miles E behind armor. III Corps drives armored spearheads through infantry in pursuit of disorganized enemy. 7th Armd Div, jumping off at 0200 in center of corps, thrusts toward Lahn R and Limburg. CCR attacks from Vettelschoss, TF Griffin moving steadily E to Ailertchen and TF Brown, after bypassing resistance and rubble at Dierdorf, advancing so rapidly to 2 of its objectives, Obertiefenbach and Heckholzhausen, that it overtakes retreating enemy and inflicts severe losses. CCR is directed to turn NE to secure crossings of Dill R. CCA, organized into TF's Rhea, Wemple, and King, drives SE along the autobahn toward Limburg until contact is made with 9th Armd Div (V Corps) at Montabaur, then swerves NE toward Wetzlar as plans are hastily changed to leave reduction of Limburg to V Corps. 9th and 99th Divs drive E abreast behind armor. 9th Div advances to Holz R and secures crossings: after reaching the river at Puderbach, 47th Inf is passed through by 39th, which speeds E to Muendersbach and Herschbach; to right, 60th Inf secures Horhausen by daylight and continues to the Holz at Raubach, securing crossing there and stream crossings to E at Elgert, Maroth, and Marienhausen. On 99th Div left, 394th Inf, passing through 395th, reaches objective high ground E of Dierdorf; 393d drives to Gros and Klein Maischeid. In V Corps area, 2d Div continues attacks with 9th and 23d Regts, taking Alsbach, Hilgert, Baumbach, Ransbach, and defensive positions on N flank of corps. 9th Armd Div, reinf by 38th Inf of 2d Div, drives spearheads E through forward elements of 2d Div to the Lahn at Limburg and Diez. From Bendorf area, CCB advances generally along Cologne-Frankfurt Autobahn to the Lahn near Limburg, moves 4 tanks across bridge there before enemy blows it, then clears the city with dismounted infantry. Upon relief at Vallendar by CCR, CCA drives rapidly to the Lahn at Diez, where bridges are out. RCT 272, 69th Div, crosses the Rhine.

In U.S. Third Army area, VIII Corps expands and strengthens Rhine bridgehead. 347th Inf continues to meet lively resistance in Braubach–Ober Lahnstein area, N flank of 87th Div bridgehead, but completes capture of Braubach. Against moderate resistance, 345th Inf drives salient E to include Gemmerich. 346th Inf is committed between 347th and 345th; after crossing the Rhine at Boppard drives NE to Dachsenhausen. TF Sundt (elements of 607th TD Bn, 87th Rcn Tr, co of 346th Inf, tanks, and arty) follows 346th Inf to Dachsenhausen. Treadway bridge is completed at Boppard under extremely adverse circumstances. 3d Bn of 385th Inf, 76th Div, crosses the Rhine and relieves elements of 87th Div, to which it is temporarily attached, at Lykershausen. At 0200, 89th Div starts across the Rhine in Wellmich-Oberwesel region under intense fire: on left, 354th Inf (−) secures Weyer, Nochern, Liersched, Patersberg, and St Goarshausen; 353d, reinf by bn of 355th, captures Dorscheid, Kaub, Bornich, and Weisel; TF Johnson (motorized bn of 355th Inf plus supporting weapons and engrs) crosses at Boppard and moves along E bank capturing Kestert; TF Engel (89th Rcn Tr and TD co) follows TF Johnson, mopping up. 6th Cav Gp, organized as TF Fickett, prepares to cross the Rhine. In XII Corps area, 6th Armd Div reaches S bank of the Main at Frankfurt and under intense arty fire forces crossing into Frankfurt: CCA drives to Sachsenhausen and enters Frankfurt via damaged bridge at Niederrad;

moving through Langen and Springlingen, in 90th Div zone, CCB reaches the Main and captures Offenbach; on extreme right, CC 86 (86th Cav Rcn Sq) reaches the river near Offenbach; CCR bivouacks S of Niederrad and releases elements to CCA and CCB. 4th Armd Div holds shallow bridgeheads across the Main against ground and air attacks and is reinf by 328th Inf of 26th Div, which passes 2 bns through CCA's bridgehead in Hanau area and is assisted by CCA in clearing opposition in Grossauheim. Upon relief along the Main by 26th Div, 4th Armd Div is directed to drive N on Gruenberg. 5th, 90th, and 26th Divs move rapidly toward the Main in wake of armor, forward elements of each reaching the river line. 5th Div's RCT 2 takes Raunheim; RCT 10 captures Rhine-Main airport, Kelsterbach, and Schwanheim; RCT II makes progress in woods S of Frankfurt and starts crossing 3d Bn into Frankfurt bridgehead. 90th Div reaches the Main in zone of 359th Inf, which takes Buergel, Muehlheim, and Rumpenheim; forward elements of 357th reach Hausen; TF Spiess mops up along div right flank and clears Offenthal. 26th Div, with 101st Inf on left and 104th on right (104th reverting to div from attachment to 4th Armd Div), clears most of its zone on right flank of corps to the Main and makes contact with Seventh Army; 328th Inf, released to 4th Armd Div, is motorized for movement from the Rhine to the Main. 2d Cav Gp crosses the Rhine to protect corps flanks and maintain contact with adjacent friendly units: 2d Sq (−Tr C) takes responsibility for left flank along S bank of the Main from Gustavburg to Kelsterbach, relieving RCT 2 and elements of RCT 10, 5th Div, and is attached to 5th Div; 42d Sq screens right flank from Gernsheim to Altheim and relieves right flank elements of 26th Div. In XX Corps area, 80th Div starts to Mainz in preparation for assault crossings of Rhine and Main Rivers. 45th Div of XV Corps, Seventh Army, relieves final elements of CCA, 11th Armd Div, along the Rhine N of grid line 33. 3d Cav Gp assembles in vicinity of Kriegsfeld.

6th Army Group: U.S. Seventh Army CP closes at Sarreguemines and opens at Kaiserslautern. XV Corps begins assault across the Rhine with 45th and 3d Divs at 0230 after saturation bombardment of far shore in 3d Div zone. On N, 45th Div, with 179th and 180th Regts in assault, crosses near Hamm and Rhein Durkheim and drives to corps bridgehead line, the N-S autobahn along E edge of Jaegersburger Wald, clearing Biblis and Gros Hausen and making contact with Third Army on left and 3d Div on right. Opposition to crossing is at first strong, resulting in loss of many landing craft, but soon eases. 3d Div, with 30th and 7th Regts in assault, crosses near Worms and Mannheim. Opposition is light at first as result of overpowering preparatory bombardment, but enemy rallies to resist strongly later. Clearing Burstadt, Lampertheim, Bobstadt, and Sandhofen, 3d Div pushes into Lorcher Wald toward corps objective, the autobahn on far side. Reserve elements cross into bridgehead later in day. Corps releases 63d Div to XXI Corps and takes control of 12th Armd Div from XXI Corps.

EASTERN EUROPE—Troops of Third White Russian Front are completing mop-up of enemy remnants in East Prussia. Second White Russian Front continues fight for ports of Danzig and Gdynia; second line of defense has now been breached and fighting is in progress along third and last line. In Czechoslovakia, troops of Second Ukrainian Front take communications center of Banska Bystrica. Continuing W through Hungary toward Austria, Third Ukrainian Front seizes Papa and Devecser.

ALFSEA—Gen Leese directs Adm Mountbatten to draw up plans for modified DRACULA since overland drive on Rangoon is not making the desired progress.

LUZON—In U.S. Sixth Army's I Corps area, 129th Inf of 37th Div is ordered to relieve 130th Inf of 33d Div upon arrival in Bauang area and to reconnoiter along Highway 9 from Naguilian toward Baguio. 1st Bn of 161st Inf, 25th Div, begins final assault on Norton's Knob, on Highway 5, after Japanese positions there have been heavily bombarded. In XI Corps area, 1st Bn of 20th Inf, 6th Div, is being relieved in line by 1st Inf. In XIV Corps area, 1st Cav Div elements push S on Highway 19 through Tanauan to Malvar. 188th Inf, 11th A/B Div, probes toward Lipa. 187th renews attack toward Mt Macolod but makes little headway against strong opposition.

S PHILIPPINES—In U.S. Eighth Army area, Americal Div (− RCT 164) lands 3 bns (1st and 3d Bns of 182d Inf and 1st Bn of 132d) abreast on Cebu near Talisay after an hour of naval gunfire bombardment. Enemy opposition consists of scattered fire, but mine field disables 8 landing vehicles and delays inward movement. After breaching the mine field, 182d Inf drives through Talisay toward Cebu City, dispersing delaying force about half way there, and by end of day holds Mananga R crossings and line through foothills along highway from Pardo to Mananga R. 132d Inf drives about 2 ½ miles NE to line running through Basak. Guerrillas have not secured the reservoir as directed and this task is assigned to 182d Inf.

IWO JIMA—Enemy makes final attack on Iwo in early morning. 200 or more attempt to infiltrate bivouac area; at least 196 are killed. Capture and occupation phase of Iwo operation ends at 0800 when Gen Chaney assumes title of Island Commander. Commander Forward Area takes responsibility for defense and development of Iwo Jima. 5th Mar Div turns over its zone to 3d Mar Div and continues to re-embark. RCT 9 of 3d Mar Div and RCT 147 (AUS) are now jointly responsible for defense of Iwo Jima. RCT 21, 3d Mar Div, re-embarks for return to Guam. Japanese suffer and exact heavy casualties during their losing battle; for the first and last time, inflict about as many casualties on U.S. forces as they suffer. The enemy force of almost 23,000 defending the island is practically annihilated. U.S. casualties exceed 20,000, about one third of the total assault force strength of some 60,000; more than 5,500 are killed in action. The Iwo victory gives the U.S. an air base for operations against the Japanese Empire, affords protection for previously captured Pacific bases, and tightens sea and air blockade of Japan.

RYUKYU Is.—Invasion stage of Operation ICEBERG starts with preliminary landings by 77th Div, reinf, on Kerama Is. to secure seaplane base and fleet anchorages in preparation for main invasion of Okinawa. After naval and aerial bombardment, 4 BLT's of 77th Div land on as many islands of the Kerama group almost simultaneously: BLT 3, RCT 305, lands first, at 0804, on Aka I. and with little difficulty secures town of Aka and clears two thirds of the island; BLT 1, RCT 306, seizes Geruma I., where howitzers are unloaded to support future operations; BLT 2, RCT 306, takes Hokaji I. without opposition; BLT 1, RCT 305, secures about a third of Zamami I. and holds firm against counterattacks. So successful are scheduled landings that a reserve force (BLT 2, RCT 307) lands on Yakabi I. in afternoon and clears it with ease. Patrols of Fleet Marine Force Amphib Rcn Bn, attached to 77th Div, land on Keise I., within arty range of most of southern Okinawa, and find it free of enemy. Warships and planes from fast and escort carriers of Fifth Fleet support ground operations. Enemy air reaction to the invasion is light, consisting largely of uncoordinated attacks on shipping by suicide planes. Air and long-range naval, gunfire bombardment of Okinawa continues. British carrier task force (TF 57) begins neutralization of Sakishima Is.

27 March

WESTERN EUROPE—21 Army Group: In Br Second Army's 30 Corps area, 51st Div reaches the Issel at Isselburg and is relieved by Br 3d Div. 43d Div reaches Mechelen. In 12 Corps area, Raesfeld falls to 7th Armd Div. XVIII Corps (A/B) advances rapidly through Wesel Forest and gains up to 9,000 yards. Br 6th A/B Div reaches Phase Line PARIS by daybreak; upon order to exploit gains, continues E to Erle. U.S. 17th A/B Div's 194th Gli Inf takes positions near Erle–Schermbeck road. 6th Gds Armd Brig, reinf by 513th Para Inf (−) of U.S. 17th A/B Div, attacks toward Dorsten through elements of U.S. 17th A/B Div, night 27–28.

In U.S. Ninth Army's XVI Corps area, 119th Inf of 30th Div completes capture of Gahlen and continues E; 117th, turning N, clears Besten; 120th takes commanding ground near Kirchhellen. 35th Div, with 134th Inf on left and 137th on right, attacks between 30th and 79th Divs from positions near Kirchhellen and gains several hundred yards before encountering stiff resistance. 79th Div presses slowly southward toward the Ruhr, clearing Schmachtendorf, Wehofen, and Sterkrade Holten; some elements cross Emser Canal E of Orsoy and others halt at line of canal. 8th Armd Div closes in assembly areas E of the Rhine. 290th Inf, 75th Div, is detached from 30th Div and attached to 8th Armd Div.

12th Army Group: In U.S. First Army's VII Corps area, 3d Armd Div's CC Hickey makes spectacular dash to Dill R at Herborn and Burg and secures crossings; continuing E throughout night 26–27 and on 27th, CC Howze reaches Loehnfeld and positions near Heisterberg. 1st and 104th Divs continue to follow armor, former clearing resistance to Breitscheidt and latter advancing unopposed to within 3 miles of Dill R. 78th Div consolidates on wide front along the Sieg. 4th Cav Gp (−) assembles E of the Rhine to relieve 1st Div progressively of Stromberg–Roth sector. 86th Div closes in assembly areas W of the Rhine. In III Corps area, 7th Armd Div drives NE to Dill R between Herborn and Wetzlar against scattered resistance. CCR gains crossings at Sinn, Edingen, and Katzenfurt; CCA crosses at Asslar and Hermannstein. 9th and 99th Divs follow armor closely. 9th reaches Dill R line and relieves CCR of responsibility for crossings in Sinn–Katzenfurt region; is reinf by 32d Sq, 14th Cav Gp. 99th Div drives to Sainscheid–Wilsenroth–Friekhofen–Niederzeuzheim region, S of Westerburg. In V Corps area, 2d Div finishes clearing its zone and mops up stragglers. Diez surrenders to CCA, 9th Armd Div, which crosses dismounted infantry over the Lahn on improvised footbridge; some CCB elements take Lahn bridge at Aumenau intact, while others take up positions at Hadamar and on W bank of the Lahn at Weilburg; CCR displaces to Offheim area, near Limburg, crosses the Lahn, and drives SE along Cologne–Frankfurt Autobahn toward Niedernhausen in effort to make contact with U.S. Third Army. 69th Div crosses additional elements over the Rhine and attacks E of the river with RCT 272, clearing region across from Koblenz, where Luftwaffe citadel at Ehrenbreitstein is captured, and taking Lahn R towns of Bad Ems and Nassau. 106th Cav Rcn Sq clears high ground

[27 MARCH 1945]

between Gel and Latin Rivers just E of RCT 272; relieves CCA, 9th Armd Div, at Diez, night 27-28.

In U.S. Third Army area, VIII Corps continues to enlarge and strengthen Rhine bridgehead. 87th Div expands bridgehead to Lahn R line on N, where contact is made with First Army, and to general line Bergnassau-Scheuern-Holzhausen road on right, overrunning approximately 20 towns. 89th Div crosses the last of its combat elements over the Rhine and expands bridgehead toward Wiesbaden; forward units take Bogel on N, Strueth in center, and reach Lorch on S; 335th Inf (–) is committed on right flank. TF Fickett, upon being relieved along the Rhine by 78th Div, drives E through 87th and 89th Divs toward Giessen-Frankfurt Autobahn, forward elements reaching Hohenstein. 76th Div, night 27-28, crosses 385th (–) and 417th Regts over the Rhine at Boppard; 304th holds W bank of the river from Delhofen to Bingerbruck and guards bridges. In XII Corps area, 6th Armd and 4th Armd Divs are relieved by infantry of Main R bridgeheads in preparation for breakout drive to N. Enemy fire delays bridging operations. 5th Div takes over Frankfurt bridgehead and finishes crossing 3 bns (2d and 3d of 10th Inf and attached 3d Bn of 11th) into the city, which it is methodically clearing. RCT 11 continues to clean out woods S of the Main and takes Walldorf. 90th Div mops up its zone S of the Main between Offenbach and Hanau. 4th Armd Div is relieved of Hanau-Aschaffenburg sector of the Main and bridgeheads by 26th Div, to which 328th Inf reverts and 2d Cav Gp (– 2d Sq) is attached. Helped by CCA of 4th Armd Div, elements of 328th and 101st Regts, 26th Div, slowly expand Hanau bridgehead; Grosskrotzenberg is cleared, but enemy resists from house to house in Hanau. 1st Bn, 104th Inf, relieves CCB of bridgehead near Aschaffenburg. Other elements of 26th Div cover bank of the Main and block along line Dieburg-Babenhausen. 2d Cav Gp continues to screen N and S flanks of corps, moving eastward as its positions are uncovered by adjacent friendly forces. 16th Cav Gp is transferred to XX Corps. In XX Corps area, 80th Div completes preparations for assault across the Rhine and Main in Mainz area: RCT 317 closes in Mainz; RCT 319 crosses the Rhine at Oppenheim, in XII Corps zone, and assembles in Bischofsheim area for assault across the Main. 16th Cav Gp is attached to 80th Div but remains in place temporarily.

6th Army Group: DA ALPS begins clearing Petit St Bernard Pass on Franco-Italian border W of Aosta (Italy).

Fr 1st Army is directed to regroup quickly for assault across the Rhine in Germersheim area.

In U.S. Seventh Army area, XV Corps pursues enemy toward the Main. 45th Div, with 3 regts abreast, speeds NE some 16 miles; patrols to the Main. To S, 3d Div also advances rapidly toward the Main. 44th Div crosses the Rhine and secures right flank of corps, relieving 7th Inf of 3d Div in Sandhofen. 12th Armd Div crosses the Rhine.

EASTERN EUROPE—Troops of Second White Russian Front break into Danzig and Gdynia and street fighting ensues. First Ukrainian Front overruns Silesian towns of Strehlen (S of Breslau) and Rybnik (E of Ratibor); forces of Fourth Ukrainian Front overrun Zory and Wodzislaw, SE of Ratibor. In Hungary, troops of Second and Third Ukrainian Fronts continue W toward Austria.

ITALY—15th Army Group: In U.S. Fifth Army's II Corps area, 1st Armd Div troops take Salvaro without a fight.

LUZON—In U.S. Sixth Army's I Corps area, 2d Bn of 129th Inf, 37th Div, relieves 3d Bn of 130th Inf, 33d Div, in Naguilian area and seizes Burgos. 128th Inf, 32d Div, opens battle for Salacsac Pass No. 2 on Villa Verde Trail. Well-organized, interlocking enemy positions in this region have been delaying progress along Villa Verde Trail for some time since troops must investigate the numerous caves. Troops of 161st Inf, 25th Div, complete capture of Norton's Knob and hold it against night counterattack. In XI Corps area, as final elements of 1st Bn, 20th Inf, 6th Div, withdraw to reserve, rest of 20th Inf prepares for drive on Mt Mataba. 1st Inf completes relief of 20th Inf and prepares to drive N to clear region S of junction of Bosoboso and Mariquina Rivers. 2d Bn of 151st Inf, 38th Div, in shore-to-shore move from Corregidor, lands on Caballo and begins clearing the island, which Japanese are garrisoning with well-entrenched force of about 400. In XIV Corps area, 1st Cav Div, less strongly opposed than 11th A/B Div, is directed to take Lipa. 8th Cav continues S along Route 19 to within 5,000 yards of Lipa; 7th Cav drives E from Tanauan against light resistance. 188th Inf of 11th A/B Div secures Lipa Hill, S of Lipa, and gets elements to within a mile of Lipa.

S PHILIPPINES—In U.S. Eighth Army area, only light resistance is met as Japanese withdraw from Cebu City to strong hill positions commanding it. Americal Div forces seize Cebu City and continue forward. Elements of 182d Inf secure reservoir area and turn it over to guerrillas. Co G of 132d Inf lands on Cavit I., in Cebu Harbor, and searches uneventfully for enemy. From Palawan, regt Hq and 3d Bn, RCT 186, leave for Mindanao.

KERAMA Is.—On Zamami I., BLT 1 of RCT 305 patrols actively and locates one organized enemy position. BLT 3 of RCT 305 disperses force of 75 Japanese on Aka I. RCT 306 lands on Tokashiki I., BLT's 1 and 2 pushing northward abreast, slowed by difficult terrain; BLT 3, initially in reserve, lands to clear S part of island and patrols to S tip. Kuba I. and Amuro I. are taken without opposition by Co G of RCT 307 and Co B of RCT 305, respectively. Japanese suicide planes continue to attack surface vessels.

JAPAN—As preparations for invasion of Japan continue, Tinian-based B-29's of 313th Bombardment Wing inaugurate a strategic night mining program to complete the blockade of the islands. This, combined with further intensive day and night aerial bombardment by other aircraft and submarine action in waters about Japan, yields excellent results. By midsummer Japan's merchant fleet is fatally crippled.

28 March

WESTERN EUROPE—Gen Eisenhower alters direction and plan of final Allied drive. Objective is changed from Berlin, toward which Soviet forces are moving rapidly, to Leipzig. 12th rather than 21 Army Group is to make main effort.

21 Army Group: Br Second Army, on right, breaks out of bridgehead and begins drive to the Elbe. In Cdn 2 Corps area, Cdn 3d Div, attacking toward Emmerich, reverts to corps from attachment to Br 30 Corps in current positions. Br 30 Corps reaches general line Haldern-Isselburg-Anholt. In 12 Corps area, 53d Div overruns Shede and begins assault on Bocholt. 7th Armd Div thrusts past Heiden to Borken. In XVIII Corps (A/B) area, 6th A/B Div speeds from Erle to Lembeck; is transferred to Br 8 Corps control at 2400. U.S. 17th A/B Div's 507th Para Inf overruns Wulfen and starts motorized column to Haltern, night 28-29, to relieve 6th Gds Armd Brig. 6th Gds Armd Brig, reinf, reaches Dorsten early in day and drives rapidly NE to Haltern. 1st Cdo Brig passes to Br 8 Corps control.

In U.S. Ninth Army's XVI Corps area, 8th Armd Div attacks through 30th Div with CCA and CCR, pushing toward Dorsten. CCA reaches SW approaches, where lively fighting ensues. 30th Div improves N flank positions in limited attack. 35th Div's 3-regt attack in Kirchhellen region makes limited progress. 79th Div, pressing S against the Ruhr, makes little headway on left but on right overruns a number of towns and villages, among them Hamborn and Neumuhl.

12th Army Group: U.S. Fifteenth Army, with XXII and XXIII Corps under its command, is assigned twofold mission of containing bypassed pockets at Lorient and St Nazaire in coastal sector of France and occupying, organizing, and governing the Rhine sector in Germany. As U.S. advance continues E of the Rhine, Fifteenth Army will move forward to provide security for rear areas. U.S. First and Third Armies effect junction N of Idstein.

In U.S. First Army's VII Corps area CC Boudinot of 3d Armd Div, attacking through CC Hickey, drives E practically unopposed, TF Lovelady reaching Lahn R and seizing Marburg and TF Welborn halting at Runzhausen; CC Howze advances to Dill R and secures Dillenburg. Div, ordered to swing N toward Paderborn to complete encirclement of the Ruhr in conjunction with Ninth Army, passes 83d Armd Rcn Bn through CC Howze at Dillenburg to secure turning line Dillenburg-Marburg; the armd rcn bn seizes Bottenhorn and Holzhausen. 1st Div clears Breitscheidt and drives enemy E of Biersdorf and Daaden, while 104th Div (−) advances E 10 miles behind armor. 4th Cav Gp begins progressive relief of 1st Div on successive objectives along the Sieg to E of 78th Div. Myth Div begins relief of 8th Div in defensive positions along W bank of the Rhine. In III Corps area, 7th Armd Div, jumping off shortly after midnight 27-28 from Dill R line, drives NE to Lahn R and secures crossings between Marburg and Giessen and communications centers E of the Lahn. CCR's TF Griffin crosses S of Marburg to gain objectives in Schroeck-Beltershausen region and makes contact with 3d Armd Div (VII Corps) at Marburg. TF Brown crosses in Roth-Bellnhausen area and continues to Ebsdorf. CCA meets determined resistance as it approaches Giessen but succeeds in entering and clearing the city; since bridge there is damaged, treadway bridge is constructed over the Lahn. CCB, having displaced eastward, is committed between CCR and CCA and secures crossings of the Lahn N of Giessen and road centers E of the Lahn. Bypassing resistance near Rodheim, CCB advances to Wissmar, which it is obliged to capture before continuing; TF Erlenbusch clears Wissmar, crosses the Lahn, and captures Wieseck and Grossen Buseck; from Wissmar, TF Chappuis turns N, taking Ruttershausen and crossing the Latin to clear Staufenberg, Mainzlar, Daubringen, Lollar, and Alten Buseck. 7th Armd Div thus gains all of its objectives and is directed to assemble in Marburg area to continue attack to N. 9th Div speeds E to W bank of Lahn R in Niederwalgern-Odenhausen region. 99th Div's 393d Inf clears to Dill R line NW of Wetzlar, relieving armor of crossings in Asslar-Hermannstein region; 395th is pinched out S of Merenberg; 394th motors to Giessen area. 14th Cav Gp displaces to vicinity of Lahr, W of Weilburg, and its 18th Sq is attached to 99th Div. 28th Div (−) is transferred to III Corps from V Corps. In V Corps area, 9th Armd Div assembles along the Lahn. CCR makes contact with Third Army on Cologne-Frankfurt Autobahn N of Idstein and withdraws to the Lahn. 2d Div relieves CCB at Hadamar and Limburg. 69th Div finishes crossing the Rhine and takes over sector cleared by RCT 272.

[28 MARCH 1945]

In U.S. Third Army's VIII Corps area, 87th Div makes substantial progress despite congested roads at boundary of First and Third Armies: 346th Inf clears its zone and establishes CP in advance of troops at Lindenholzhausen, across Cologne-Frankfurt Autobahn; 345th reaches Kirberg; TF Sundt takes Katzenelnbogen; 347th displaces eastward on N flank of corps as attack progresses. From Nastatten area, 76th Div drives rapidly E, with 385th Inf on left and 417th on right, toward Kamberg and Idstein and, ultimately, Usingen. TF Fickett reaches Cologne-Frankfurt Autobahn N of Idstein and makes contact with 9th Armd Div (V Corps). 89th Div moves SE against spotty resistance: TF Johnson reaches Bad Schwalbach and halts; 354th Inf moves forward behind TF Johnson; 353d, clearing Hinter Wald, is strongly opposed in vicinity of Nieder and Ober Gladbach; 355th, reinf by components of TF Engel as that TF is dissolved, overcomes severe resistance at Lorch. XX Corps begins assault NE across the Rhine. 80th Div attacks simultaneously across the Rhine and Main Rivers at 0100: 317th Inf leads assault across the Rhine at Mainz and is followed by 318th; 319th crosses the Main in Bischofsheim area. Opposition is moderate and by end of day 80th Div holds firm bridgehead in Mainz area, including towns of Kostheim, Kastel, Biebrich, Ervenheim, Wiesbaden, Bierstadt, Igstadt, Auringen, Hochheim, Wicker, Massenheim, and Delkenheim. 3d Cav Gp moves 3d Sq to Mainz area to guard bridges. As Corps attacks in center of army zone, boundaries are altered and 5th Inf and 6th Armd Divs, in and near Frankfurt, are attached to corps in place; 11th Armd Div passes to XII Corps control. XII Corps begins breakout attacks across Main R. 90th Div starts across in assault boats in Doernigheim area at 0300 and by noon holds firm bridgehead for debouchment of armor, despite stiff local resistance on left. Assault regts—357th on left and 358th on right—clear 5-6-mile bridgehead. Footbridge and ferry are completed during morning and entire div and supporting weapons are across by end of day. 6th Armd Div starts crossing into 90th Div's bridgehead in early afternoon and drives rapidly N against scattered resistance. CCB, in the lead, takes Enkheim, Bergen, Vilbel, Massenheim, Dortelweil, Nieder Eschbach, and Nieder Erlenbach; CC 86 spearheads assault, driving to positions just S of Friedberg; CCA follows CC 86 to region N of Hochstadt. Meanwhile, on corps right, 4th Armd Div crosses treadway bridge at Grossauheim in single column, starting at 0300, and drives N with CCA on right, CCB on left, and CCR to rear prepared to assist either of the other columns. After reducing resistance at Ostheim, CCA speeds to Gruenberg, its objective.

[459]

CCB meets little resistance as it advances to positions NE of Gruenberg and outposts Beltershain. CCR closes in Muenzenberg. On Main R line, 5th Div continues fight for Frankfurt, crossing RCT 2, 1st Bn of RCT 10, and 2d Bn of RCT 11 into the city and clearing most of it; 1st Bn of RCT 11 takes portion of Frankfurt S of the Main. 26th Div continues blocking mission to E and S and completes reduction of Hanau by 0630; 45th Div (Seventh Army) takes over bridgehead near Aschaffenburg. 2d Cav Gp is released from screening mission and detached from 5th and 26th Divs. 11th Armd Div begins move to the Main at Hanau and is attached to corps to fight abreast 4th Armd Div; CCA crosses the Rhine and assembles in Bischofsheim area. 6th Armd and 5th Inf Divs pass to control of XX Corps in place as XIIXX Corps boundary is altered.

6th Army Group: In U.S. Seventh Army's XV Corps area, 45th Div reaches the Main near Obernau and establishes bridgehead across the river: 157th Inf crosses and pushes toward Aschaffenburg and Schweinheim, a suburb of Aschaffenburg; 179th starts across behind 157th; 180th closes along the river. 3d Div speeds toward the Main to S and is passed through on its right flank by 12th Armd Div. Forward elements of 12th Armd Div clear the Odenwald. 44th Div drives S along the Rhine and across the Neckar toward Mannheim and Heidelberg. Burgomaster of Mannheim tries unsuccessfully to arrange for surrender of the city. XXI Corps begins crossing the Rhine to operate in region S of XV Corps. 10th Armd and 63d Inf Divs complete crossing and assemble. In VI Corps area, 103d Div begins relief of 71st Div along the Rhine from Oppau to S of Speyer. 36th Div maintains defensive positions along the Rhine.

EASTERN EUROPE—Troops of Second White Russian Front capture naval base of Gdynia and clear W part of Danzig. Continuing W along S bank of the Danube in region E of Budapest, Second Ukrainian forces take Gyoer.

ITALY—15th Army Group: U.S. Fifth Army inactivates separate 366th Inf, placing its personnel in 224th and 226th Engr General Service Regts.

BURMA—Burma Defense Army, renamed Burma National Army, rises in revolt against Japanese in central and S Burma. Adm Mountbatten establishes Air and Ground Supply Committee to study air supply situation and recommend improvements.

In Br Fourteenth Army's 4 Corps area, Japanese begin withdrawing from Meiktila sector, night 28-29.

LUZON—In U.S. Sixth Army's I Corps area, 1st Bn of 129th Inf, 37th Div, joins 2d Bn and the combined force consolidates NE and E of Burgos for next few days. 3d Bn is responsible for San Fernando area. 35th Inf, 25th Div, is directed to halt drive on Balete Pass via Putlan R Valley since 27th Inf is making better progress on Mt Myoko; is to remain in present positions temporarily, then block E approach to Putlan Valley and attack N through 1st Bn of 27th Inf. In XI Corps area, 1st Bn of 1st Inf, 6th Div, drives 600 yards N from Mt Baytangan area. 2d Bn, 20th Inf, attacks toward Mt Mataba, gaining ridge position. 3d Bn also joins in attack, but progress is slow. In XIV Corps area, 1st Cav Div forces drive to outskirts of Lipa and San Agustin. To N, 12th Cav seizes Mayondon Point and reaches corps objective line within its sector. 187th Inf, 11th A/B Div, attacks from 2 directions in vain effort to gain saddle between Mt Macolod and Bukel Hill.

S PHILIPPINES—In U.S. Eighth Army area, 40th Div forces on Panay embark at Iloilo for Negros Occidental. On Cebu, 182d Inf, in 2-pronged assault by 2d and 3d Bns, seizes Lahug Airfield. 1st Bn secures bypassed Hill 30 and attempts to clear Go Chan Hill, a spur of Hill 31, as well but finds it too strongly defended. 32 pillboxes are destroyed on Guadalupe Road E of Go Chan. Co E, 132d Inf, secures Mactan I. and Opon Airfield without opposition.

KERAMA Is.—BLT 3, RCT 305, meets no further opposition on Aka I. Other elements of RCT 305 are eliminating the enemy position on Zamami. RCT 306 seizes town of Tokashiki on Tokashiki I.

29 March

WESTERN EUROPE—21 Army Group: In Br Second Army's Cdn 2 Corps area, Cdn 3d Div continues clearing Emmerich against strong resistance. Netterden falls to Cdn 2d Div. In 12 Corps area, 7th Armd Div drives on Rheine, passing through Sudlohn and Stadtlohn. From Bocholt, 53d Div drives toward Winterswijk. 8 Corps attacks to exploit breakthrough on right flank of army, employing 11th Armd Div on left and 6th A/B Div on right, and makes rapid progress toward Osnabrueck. 11th Armd Div reaches Beikelort, SE of Ahaus, and 6th A/B Div drives to Coesfeld. In XVIII Corps (A/B) area, 6th Gds Armd Brig, relieved in Haltern before dawn by motorized elements of U.S. 17th A/B Div, proceeds to Duelmen and from there starts toward Buldern. U.S. 17th A/B Div's 194th Gli Inf is shuttled to Duelmen by motor. U.S. 2d Armd Div (XIX Corps, U.S. Ninth Army) begins passing through and relieving U.S. 17th A/B Div.

In U.S. Ninth Army's XVI Corps area, CCA of 8th Armd Div clears SW part of Dorsten; elements push E toward Marl and Polsum. Some units of CCR drive N to assist CCA at Dorsten while others continue E, overrunning Feldhausen and Schoven. 30th Div maintains defensive positions. 35th Div's 134th Inf takes Gladbeck but firm enemy resistance holds other regts to negligible gains. Continuing S with 314th and 315th Regts, 79th Div gets left flank to Emser Canal S of Sterkrade and right flank to Rhine-Herne Canal. 29th Div is attached to corps.

12th Army Group: In U.S. First Army's VII Corps area, 3d Armd Div, swerving N from Marburg, pursues disorganized enemy about 50 miles N toward Paderborn: on left, CC Howze's TF Kane reaches Brilon and TF Doan reaches Thuelen; to right, CC Boudinot columns halt just short of Marsberg and Mengeringhausen. 1st and 104th Divs move forward to left and rear of armor, respectively. RCT's 13 and 28, 8th Div, assemble E of the Rhine and begin mopping up region just S of the Sieg between Roth and Wahlbach, thus releasing elements of 1st Div and 4th Cav Gp for operations elsewhere. 78th Div continues to defend S bank of the Sieg to left of 8th Div and relieves elements of 4th Cav Gp in place. 86th Div completes relief of 8th W of the Rhine. In III Corps area, 7th Armd Div begins drive N for Edersee dam and crossings of Eder R. TF Brown jumps off early in morning to clear CCR's assembly area—Kirchhain-Amoeneburg-Kleinseelheim quickly clearing all but Kirchhain, where resistance is so severe that TF Beatty is committed. Elements of TF Brown bypass Kirchhain to reach Bracht. TF Griffin advances to Buergeln area. CCB, on right, drives N to Kirchhain, taking over attack on that city and troops already engaged there at 1600 and completing its capture by 1800. CCB retains control of TF Beatty but releases attached elements of TF Brown upon fall of Kirchhain. CCA, relieved at Giessen by 99th Div, is held in reserve. 9th Div maintains defensive positions along W bank of Lahn R. After motoring to Wissmar area, 395th Inf of 99th Div mops up W of Staufenberg and establishes OPL east of that city; 394th relieves CCA, 7th Armd Div, at Giessen and outposts region to E; 393d occupies Wetzlar. 28th Div starts assembling E of the Rhine. V Corps shifts its attack from E to N, using 9th Armd Div to spearhead drive toward Eder R. From Latin R, 9th Armd Div sweeps NE to Gleen R line between Kirchhain and Kirtorf with two CC's abreast, relieving III Corps elements at Giessen. On left, CCB crosses the Lahn at Weilburg and drives to Schweinberg area while CCA, followed by CCR, advances from Aumenau to Kirtorf. 2d Div, riding tanks, TD'S, and organic vehicles, moves forward behind armor. 69th Div mops up stragglers in rear areas.

In U.S. Third Army's VIII Corps area, 347th Inf, on 87th Div N flank, relieves V Corps of responsibility for Diez-Limburg area; TF Sundt, spearheading div attack, reaches corps boundary. 345th cuts autobahn near Niederselters and clears that town. On 76th Div left, 385th Inf clears Kamberg against vigorous opposition; 417th, to right, drives through Idstein to Oberems-Kroftel-Wuestems area. TF Fickett gets advance elements, on left flank, to Giessen-Bad Nauheim highway in vicinity of Grossen Linden. 354th Inf, 89th Div, reaches Bad Schwalbach and relieves TF Johnson, which is dissolved, then continues toward corps boundary; 353d clears resistance in vicinity of Ober and Nieder Gladbach and takes Hausen; 355th and Rcn Tr clear Rhine bend W of Wiesbaden. In XX Corps area, 6th Armd Div (with CC's A, B, and 86 in assault) rolls northward astride autobahn practically unopposed, reaching objective NE of Steinbach in region E of Giessen; attack passes through Friedberg, Bad Neuheim, Grossen Linden, and many smaller towns. 80th Div mops up within Mainz bridgehead and expands it NE on right to Koenigstein; attached 16th Cav Gp crosses the Rhine to screen left flank and drives to line Eltville-Neudorf-Georgenborn, W of Wiesbaden. 65th Div closes in Schwabenheim area and, during night 29-30, begins crossing 260th and 261st Regts over the Rhine; 261st is attached to 6th Armd Div. 5th Div completes capture of Frankfurt, which it then polices. 3d Cav Gp crosses the Rhine and drives NE along right flank of 6th Armd Div to Karben area without opposition. Action of 6th Armd Div and 3d Cav Gp opens autobahn as MSR for corps. 71st Div is attached to corps. 94th Div is transferred to XXII Corps, Fifteenth Army. In XII Corps area, 4th Armd Div drives rapidly E: CCB captures Lauterbach, its objective; CCA, moving through Ulrichstein and Herbstein, takes Grossenlueder; to open MSR, CCR advances to right of CCA through Nidda to Herbstein, which it outposts; RCT 359 (−3d Bn) of 80th Div is attached to div, motorized, and employed as blocking force on right. 11th Armd Div moves to the Main at Hanau and begins drive through 26th Div's bridgehead toward Fulda: CCA is brought to a halt at Rothenbergen; CCB follows CCA across the Main but coils off road for night at Ravolzhausen. 90th Div mops up to general line Burg Grafenrode-Kaichen-Windecken. 26th Div clears bypassed re-sistance in Hanau-Lieblos region and in Langen-diebach and Rueckingen. 2d Cav Gp starts crossing 42d Sq over the Main, night 29-30, to maintain contact between 26th Div and Seventh Army.

6th Army Group: In U.S. Seventh Army's XV Corps area, 45th Div runs into firm opposition for the first time E of the Rhine as it attempts to expand Main bridgehead. Enemy is resisting 157th Inf attacks from house to house in Aschaffenburg and Schweinheim. 179th Inf attacks E in Sulzbach area. 180th crosses the Main and drives through Sulzbach. 3d Div reaches the Main at Woerth and prepares to cross. 12th Armd Div continues eastward drive with CCA on left and CCB on right. 44th Div moves into Mannheim, from which German garrison has withdrawn. XXI Corps directs 10th Armd Div to pass through elements of 3d and 44th Divs in preparation for drive S of the Neckar. Elements of 10th Armd Div move forward to search for crossing sites over the Neckar. 63d Div begins relief of 44th Div (XV Corps). 101st Cav Gp assembles E of the Rhine. In VI Corps area, 103d Div completes relief of 71st Div and assumes control of its sector. Div passes to Seventh Army control. 71st Div is detached and starts to Third Army sector. 36th Div turns over its sector to 3d Algerian Div and passes to army control. 102d Cav Gp is also detached from corps and starts from corps sector.

In Fr 1st Army area, DA ALPS clears most of Petit St Bernard Pass and breaks off attack.

EASTERN EUROPE—Troops of Third White Russian Front mop up remnants of encircled enemy groups SW of Koenigsberg in East Prussia. Fighting continues in E part of Danzig. In Hungary, troops of Third Ukrainian Front drive to Austrian frontier, capturing Szombathely, Koeszeg, and Kapuva.

BURMA—In Br Fourteenth Army area, Ind 7th Div (less 33d Brig, which is assisting Ind 5th Div of 4 Corps in Taungtha-Meiktila area) is transferred from 4 to 33 Corps control.

LUZON—In U.S. Sixth Army's XI Corps area, elements of 43d Div gain positions on Hill 1200, commanding last enemy escape route, which runs NW from New Bososobo. 1st Inf, 6th Div, pushes forward to within about 300 yards of its objective. Some 20th Inf elements consolidate on ridge near Mt Mataba while others continue attack under intense fire. In XIV Corps area, 8th Cav of 1st Cav Div seizes Lipa and its airdrome and establishes contact with 11th A/B Div near there. Highway 19 is now open for traffic from Calamba to Batangas. 7th Cav pushes to San Andres. Elements of 187th Inf, 11th A/B Div, driving W on Mt Macolod, clear part of Dita, on Route 417.

S PHILIPPINES—In U.S. Eighth Army area, reinf platoon of Co F, 185th Inf, lands at Patik in Negros Occidental Province, Negros I., and secures Bago R bridge, which is urgently needed for drive on Bacolod, in lively action with bridge guards. Main body of 185th Inf goes ashore near Pulupandan unopposed; using Bago R bridge, drives N to outskirts of Bacolod. While 132d Inf patrols actively on Cebu, 182d battles enemy on Go Chan Hill, securing it in costly battle. Japanese explosives blow up E spur of Go Chan, causing heavy American casualties, particularly to Co A, which is withdrawn from line. 76 pillboxes are destroyed. On Mindanao, organized resistance in Zamboanga sector collapses as 3d Bn, 163d Inf, gains heights near Mt Pulungbatu, but mopping up continues for some time. Philippine guerrilla forces land on Masbate after LCI bombardment and soon take town of Masbate.

RYUKYU Is.—77th Div completes capture of Kerama Is. RCT 305's BLT 1 withdraws from Zamami and BLT 2, the garrison force, takes over. BLT 3, RCT 305, withdraws from Aka after mopping up the island. RCT 306 secures rest of Tokashiki and withdraws, except for BLT 1, which remains to patrol until end of month. The anchorage and seaplane base are put into operation. With approaches to Okinawa landing beaches now cleared of mines, naval surface vessels move in to pound assault area at close range. Aircraft continue to bombard Okinawa. Underwater demolition teams reconnoiter Hagushi beaches. Elements of TF 58, after uneventful search for enemy fleet units off Japan, attack Kyushu airfields and enemy shipping on return trip to Okinawa.

30 March

U.K.—Prime Minister Churchill writes Gen Marshall, asking that U.S. air resources be made available for support of British drive on Rangoon.

WESTERN EUROPE—21 Army Group: In Br Second Army's Cdn 2 Corps area, Cdn 3d Div completes capture of Emmerich. Elten falls to Cdn 2d Div. 30 Corps breaks out of bridgehead and heads for Lingen. Gds Armd Div and 43d Div advance rapidly, former bypassing and containing Groenlo. In 12 Corps area, Winterswijk falls to 53d Div. 7th Armd Div reaches Ahaus. In 8 Corps area, 6th A/B Div and 11th Armd Div reach Ems R at Greven and Ensdetten, respectively, after driving 14 miles NE. In XVIII Corps (A/B) area, 16th Gds Armd Brig reaches Buldern early in morning. U.S. 17th A/B Div is placed under command of U.S. XIX Corps at 0600. Corps reverts to First Allied Airborne Army at same time and its zone is divided between Br 8 and U.S. XIX Corps.

In U.S. Ninth Army's XVI Corps area, 75th Div moves E of the Rhine in preparation for attack through 30 Div and 8th Armd Div. Some elements of CCA, 8th Armd Div, are pinned down E of Marl but others take Polsum. CCR reaches Buer Hassel. 35th Div pushes from Gladbeck to Buer and to the SW clears Bottrop and Eigen. 314th Inf, 79th Div, drives S of Sterkrade Buschhausen to Emser Canal, concluding div's mission; relief of right flank elements of 35th Div is begun. 15th Cav Gp is attached to XIX Corps.

12th Army Group: In U.S. Fifteenth Army area, XXII Corps becomes operational at noon with mission of defending, occupying, organizing, and governing Neuss–Bonn sector along W bank of the Rhine. Corps temporarily has control of 95th Div, Ninth Army, and 86th Div, First Army, pending relief by Fifteenth Army units.

In U.S. First Army's VII Corps area, leading elements of 3d Armd Div get to within 2 miles of Paderborn. Resistance is scattered at first but stiffens as assault columns approach city. On left, determined resistance halts CC Howze's TF Richardson at Nordborchen and TF Hogan at Wewer. On right, CC Boudinot's TF Welborn, after reaching forest NE of Etteln, has its lines severed by infiltrators, and TF Doan of CC Hickey is committed to open route of advance; TF Lovelady is halted in Wrexen area, SW of Scherfede. While driving toward front lines, div CG, Maj Gen Maurice Rose, is fatally shot by the enemy. 104th Div continues to advance rapidly behind armor, 413th Inf reaching Arolsen and Adorf and forward elements of 415th stopping near Heringhausen. 4th Cav Gp, whose relief is completed by 78th Div, moves via Hackenburg and Dillenburg to Eibelhausen and from there attacks N, forward units reaching Beddelhausen and Markhausen. 1st Div, with elements of 3 regts in line, pushes N to line Strassebersbach-Hainchen-Irmgarteichen-Gernsdorf-Rudersdorf-Rodgen, thereby gaining heights dominating Siegen. 8th Div completes movement to new zone E of the Rhine and continues attack with 13th and 28th Regts to destroy enemy S of the Sieg within zone, largely accomplishing mission. In III Corps area, 7th Armd Div speeds N to line of Ederstau See and Eder R, captures Edersee Dam intact, and secures crossings of Eder R. CCR, on left, advances to the Eder without opposition and sends patrols to N bank. CCB organizes TF Lohse for attack on Edersee Dam, but TF Wolfe (a sub-task force of TF Brown, CCR) reaches the dam first and captures it while temporarily attached to CCB. TF Chappuis, followed by attached TF Beatty, drives to river line on right and seizes six bridges between Hemfurth and Bergheim. 99th Div, relieved at Wetzlar by elements of V Corps, assembles near Krofdorf-Gleiberg. 14th Cav Gp displaces to vicinity of Frankenbach. In V Corps area, 9th Armd Div continues N to the Eder and secures crossings. CCB drives to Bad Wildungen: some elements clear the town and cross 7th Armd Div (III Corps) bridge to establish bridgehead while others cross at Wega and move along the river to take bridge at Bergheim. CCA advances to Fritzlar, where bridge is blown and enemy offers organized resistance from ground and air: some elements cross 6th Armd Div (XX Corps) bridge at Sennern and attack Fritzlar from the rear while others take airfield S of Fritzlar. 2d Div continues rapid advance to rear of armor. 69th Div takes over new zone SW of Weilburg and begins movement into it; elements move to Wetzlar and relieve III Corps units.

In U.S. Third Army's VIII Corps area, 87th Div completes its mission as TF Sundt; reversing its course, drives W and joins 345th Inf, which is moving E. Continuing toward Usingen, 76th Div is halted at Finsternathal, Dorfweil, and Schmitten by opposition from German officer candidates; 304th Inf (−) crosses the Rhine to protect right flank along Cologne-Frankfurt Autobahn. TF Fickett gets elements to Butzbach, on Giessen-Bad Nauheim highway, completing its mission. 89th Div reaches corps boundary from Neuhof to Eltville and begins mopping up bypassed pockets. In XX Corps area, 6th Armd Div exploits breakthrough N of Frankfurt, pressing relentlessly toward Kassel and reaching Eder R in Zenner-Wadern area and the Fulda near Ober Beisheim, a little short of objective; among numerous towns, overruns Romrod, Alsfeld, Treysa, Borken, and Homberg. CCR starts to Remsfeld area. 80th Div releases 318th Inf to 6th Armd Div for motorized follow-up operations; 319th Inf motors to Grossen Buseck area, near Giessen. 65th Div, less elements attached to 6th Armd Div, continues to cross the Rhine and advances NE behind 6th Armd Div, mopping up insignificant bypassed resistance. 3d Cav Gp thrusts NE to final objectives in Wallenrode-Hebles area, between Romrod and Lauterbach. 71st Div motors to Rockenhausen assembly area. In XII Corps area, 4th Armd Div, turning NE, pursues enemy toward Hersfeld: CCB overcomes some resistance at Niederaual and Asbach and begins attack on Hersfeld, but falls back to Asbach area for night; CCA reaches its objective, high ground between Hersfeld and Vacha. 90th Div (− RCT 359) is motorized for follow-up operations behind 4th Armd Div and moves to general line Rudingshain-Breungeshain-Herchehain. 11th Armd Div completes its crossing of the Main near Hanau and continues drive toward Fulda. CCA, despite close air and arty assistance, is unable to take Gelnhausen. Reinf 41st Cav Rcn Sq (−) moves forward to open route for CCA: bypassing Gelnhausen, the column drives to outskirts of Schlierbach. CCR moves to Mittel Gruendau to contain Gelnhausen. On div left, CCB advances rapidly through Huettengessas and Buedingen to Nieder Seemen. 26th Div, with 328th Inf on left and torst on right, continues to mop up to rear of 11th Armd Div, reaching Michelan-Leisenwald area; 104th Inf, which has moved up to Hanau region, is relieved there by 2d Cav Gp and displaces to Budinger Wald. 2d Cav Gp finishes crossing the Main and screens right flank of corps NE of Hanau with 2d Sq; 42d Sq is relieved of screening mission below Third Army boundary by 106th Cav Gp of XV Corps.

6th Army Group: In U.S. Seventh Army's XV Corps area, 157th Inf of 45th Div is still held up at Aschaffenburg but clears Schweinheim. Rest of div is moving steadily forward. 3d Div crosses the Main at Woerth and establishes bridgehead. 12th Armd Div continues E, CCA driving through Amorbach to Schippach and positions near Nassig and CCB getting lead elements to Hardheim area. 44th Div, passed through and relieved in Mannheim area by 63d Div of XXI Corps, is held in reserve. In XXI Corps area, 101st Cav Gp makes contact with 12th Armd Div, XV Corps, and secures bridgehead line. 4th Div completes its crossing of the Rhine and advances E through elements of 12th Armd Div. 63d Div, after relieving 44th Div, XV Corps, crosses the Neckar in Wieblingen area. CCA and CCB, 10th Armd Div, cross Neckar R and move S.

EASTERN EUROPE—Troops of Second White Russian Front complete capture of Danzig. In Silesia, Soviet units are eliminating encircled enemy forces at Glogau and Breslau. Some elements of Second Ukrainian Front open offensive along border of Czechoslovakia and Hungary, speeding W across Hron and Nitta Rivers toward Slovak capital of Bratislava. Other elements of this front continue to clear S bank of the Danube in Hungary. Some elements of Third Ukrainian Front drive into Austria from vicinity of Hungarian town of Koeszeg while others gain ground W of Lake Balaton; still others, assisted by Bulgarian troops, thrust quickly southward from Lake Balaton to the Drava R along border of Hungary and Yugoslavia.

BURMA—In NCAC area, Br 36th Div, continuing SE from Mogok, reaches Kyaukme, where junction is made with Ch 1st Sep Regt. This brings operations on NCAC front virtually to an end, since Chiang Kai-shek has obtained Adm Mountbatten's promise to halt along line Lashio-Hsipaw-Kyaukme. In Br Fourteenth Army's 33 Corps area, Kyaukse falls to Ind 20th Div after hard fighting. In 4 Corps area, with Meiktila secure, Ind 17th Div and 255th Tank Brig start S toward Pyawbwe.

LUZON—In U.S. Sixth Army's I Corps area, 1st Bn of 35th Inf, 25th Div, is ordered to block E approach to Putlan Valley. 3d Bn relieves 1st Bn of 27th Inf on Highway 5 near Kapintalan. 3d Bn, 27th Inf, attacks through 2d Bn along ridge leading to Mt Myoko. In XI Corps area, 103d Inf of 43d Div is chosen to drive S and establish contact with XIV Corps. 172d Inf is to relieve 103d in current positions. 1st Bn of 1st Inf, 6th Div, continues attack but because of heavy enemy fire its gains are small. 3d Bn, 20th Inf, continues to fight toward Mt

Mataba. As XIV Corps objective is moved E to line Lucena-Pagsanjan, 12th Cav of 1st Cav Div continues eastward, encountering enemy position near Calauan. 1st Bn of 187th Inf, 11th A/B Div, is unable to progress in Mt Macolod sector.

S Philippines—In U.S. Eighth Army area, 185th Inf clears Bacolod with ease as enemy retires eastward on Negros into mountains in Patog-Negritos area. 40th Rcn Tr, probing eastward from Pulupandan, establishes contact with enemy's secondary line of defense near Atipuluan. 160th Inf, less 2d Bn, lands on Negros. On Cebu, 182d Inf clears rest of Hill 31, destroying 9 pillboxes.

Ryukyu Is.—Activity in Kerama Is. is limited to patrolling. Rcn and demolition around Okinawa proceed satisfactorily under protective cover of planes and naval gunfire. Preinvasion air and naval bombardment continues.

31 March

Western Europe—21 Army Group: In Br Second Army area, Cdn 2 Corps takes Hoch Elten feature. In 30 Corps area, Gds Armd Div thrusts to Haaksbergen, on road to Enschede. In 12 Corps area, 7th Armd Div, driving on Rheine, reaches Neuenkirchen. 53d Div advances to Alstatte. In 8 Corps area, 6th A/B and 11th Armd Divs gain bridgeheads across the Ems.

In U.S. Ninth Army area, XIII Corps starts crossing the Rhine at Wesel, 5th Armd Div in the lead. 102d Div and 17th A/B Div, with Br 6th Gds Armd Brig attached, are attached to corps in place. In XVI Corps area, 75th Div, with 289th and 291st Regts abreast, passes through 8th Armd Div and attacks E on N flank of corps after half hour of arty preparation, gaining about 4 miles. Upon being passed through by 75th Div, CCA of 8th Armd Div is withdrawn to assembly area; CCR, attacking at 0300, drives E to positions 1,000 yards E of Langenbochum. 75th Rcn Tr closes gap between 75th Inf and 8th Armd Divs. On corps S flank, 35th Div advances 2 miles, clearing a number of towns and villages.

12th Army Group: U.S. Fifteenth Army takes command of coastal sector of France and forces disposed there—reinf 66th Div and Fr troops of FFO, French Forces of the West—with responsibility for containing Lorient and St Nazaire pockets. XXII Corps' zone is extended N to Homberg as corps takes control of 102d Div, Ninth Army. 82d A/B Div, First Allied Airborne Army, is attached to corps and prepares to move from base camps in France to the Rhine, where it will relieve 86th Div.

In U.S. First Army's VII Corps area, Brig Gen Doyle O. Hickey assumes command of 3d Armd Div; Col Doan is put in charge of former CC Hickey; Lt Col Boles becomes head of former TF Doan. Paderborn defenders firmly oppose 3d Armd Div columns as they maneuver into position for final assault on the city. CC Howze, employing flame throwers, drives enemy from Nordborchen and Wewer. In CC Boudinot sector, TF Boles (formerly Doan) of CC Doan (formerly Hickey) destroys enemy pocket holding up Welborn's advance and TF Welborn drives to Haxtergrund; TF Lovelady withstands pressure in Scherfede area until 104th Div units arrive, then moves NW to Ebbinghausen. Mopping up to rear of armor, 413th Inf of 104th Div gains 35 miles and blocks enemy escape route from Rimbeck; 415th halts in Hallenberg-Medebach area to counter threat of enemy breakout from Winterberg and Willingen; TF Laundon (Div Rcn Tr, reinf) blocks main road at Brilon. 1st Div, with mission of blocking in region SW of Paderborn, starts to new zone: 16th Inf, upon relief by 8th Div, motors to Bueren without incident and from there blocks to W and NW and makes contact with 3d Armd Div on right; 26th Inf follows 4th Cav Gp N and prepares to block to W from Ruethen; 18th Inf is relieved by 8th Div during day. 4th Cav Gp, with 24th Sq on right and 4th on left, displaces N against stubborn delaying action to block to left of 1st Div in Ruethen-Brilon region; right column halts near Hallenberg and left near Laasphe. 9th Div is attached to corps and starts to zone between 4th Cav Gp and 8th Div. 8th and 78th Divs maintain defensive positions along the Sieg on left flank of corps; 8th Div continues to clear its zone and prepares for assault on Siegen. In region E of Siegen, 121st Inf of 8th Div clears Salchendorf, Helgersdorf, Deuz, and Grissenbach; elements of 13th Inf overrun Kirchen, SW of Siegen. In III Corps area, 7th Armd Div's CCR and CCB defend newly won positions along the Eder and are passed through by elements of V Corps. 9th Div is attached to VII Corps. 99th Div starts to Gemuenden area. 18th and 32d Cav Sqs revert to 14th Cav Gp, which is assigned defensive sector W of Lahn R formerly occupied by 9th and 99th Divs. 8th TD Gp relieves 14th Cav Gp of responsibility for Dill R bridges. 28th Div (−) closes in assembly areas E of the Rhine. In V Corps area, 9th Armd Div establishes bridgehead across Diemel R in Warburg area. CCB overcomes lively resistance at Wethen, then crosses river to take Ossendorf, Rimbeck, Noerde, and Menne. CCA reaches and clears Warburg and continues N across Diemel R to Daseburg. CCR, with mission of protecting corps E flank from Fritzlar northward, completes mop up within Fritzlar, relieving elements of CCA, and continues N behind CCA. 2d Div reaches positions just N of Ederstau See.

[31 MARCH 1945]

In U.S. Third Army area, VIII Corps, except for 76th Div, mops up stragglers. 385th Inf, 76th Div, drives to Usingen and partly clears it; 417th overcomes lively resistance in Finsternthal-Dorfweil-Schmitten region and continues NE past Hausen-Arnsbach to vicinity of Usingen. TF Fickett is dissolved. XX Corps is slowed by enemy defense line along Fulda and Eder Rivers. 6th Armd Div continues toward Kassel and establishes small bridgehead across the Fulda at Malsfeld. CCA, upon crossing the Eder on div left, pushes slowly toward Kassel, which is firmly held, reaching Werkel-Nieder Vorschutz area. CCB and CC 86 search bank of the Fulda for crossing sites; CCB establishes bridgehead at Malsfeld, crossing infantry elements at destroyed bridge site; CC 86 discovers RR bridge standing, though damaged, N of Malsfeld and prepares to cross. Ultimate objective of 6th Armd Div is changed from Leipzig to Weimar, but Muhlhausen remains immediate objective. 80th and 65th Divs, less elements attached to 6th Armd Div, continue follow-up operations to rear of 6th Armd Div, 80th Div driving toward Kassel. 65th Div completes its crossing of the Rhine. 3d Cav Gp moves on Heilenstadt and Mulhausen, but is halted near Fulda R line by strong delaying action. 16th Cav Gp reverts to corps from attachment to 80th Div; Gp Hq and 16th Sq move to Alsfeld-Kassel area to protect corps N flank. In XII Corps area, 4th Armd Div, with CCB on left and CCA on right, jumps off in afternoon toward objectives near Eisenach, reaching positions near Berka: CCB overruns Hersfeld and continues rapidly to Bosserode; main body of CCA halts for night at Wolfershausen with forward elements outposting Dankmarsheim. CCR moves from Herbstein to Hersfeld. 90th Div's 357th and 358th Regts advance behind 4th Armd Div to general line Nieder Jossa-Kruspis-Grossenmoor; TF Spiess, its usefulness ended, is dissolved. On 11th Armd Div left, CCB drives from Nieder Seemen to Grossenlueder and is followed as far as Reichlos by CCR. CCA, moving along route cleared by Cav Comd, reaches Walroth-Mueldorf area while Cav Comd (41st Cav Rcn Sq) blocks to SE. 26th Div follows 11th Armd Div toward Fulda. 2d Cav Gp continues screening mission on right flank of corps; 42d Sq assembles at Spielberg. 71st Div is attached to corps and, upon crossing the Rhine at Oppenheim, assembles near Housenstamm, SE of Frankfurt.

6th Army Group: In U.S. Seventh Army's XV Corps area, 157th Inf of 45th Div continues to clear Aschaffenburg with close air and arty support. Rest of div makes substantial progress. 3d Div expands Main R bridgehead. 12th Armd Div is transferred to XXI Corps. Corps takes control of 14th Armd Div from VI Corps. In XXI Corps area, 12th Armd Div spearheads corps attack toward Wuerzburg-Schweinfurt Kitzingen region and is followed on left by 42d Div and on right by 4th Div. CCA speeds forward to Wertheim area and CCB drives toward Ochsenfurt. 10th Armd Div continues S along the Rhine, clearing Sandhausen, Leimen, St Ilgen, and Bammenthal. From Heidelberg, 63d drives E to Neckargemund. In VI Corps area, 100th Div begins relief of 63d Div, XXI Corps.

Fr 1st Army begins assault crossings of the Rhine. In Fr 2d Corps area, 3d Algerian Div crosses in vicinity of Speyer while 2d Moroccan Inf Div crosses to right in Germersheim area. Germans, taken by surprise, are unable to stem the advance but offer heavy fire at some points.

EASTERN EUROPE—In upper Silesia, troops of First Ukrainian Front overrun Ratibor, Moravian Gap outpost. Troops of Second Ukrainian Front take Nitra and force Vah R to seize Galanta, 28 miles from Bratislava. Right flank elements of Third Ukrainian Front push toward Sopron (Hungary) and Wiener Neustadt (Austria); elements in Raba R valley of Hungary seize Vasvar, Koermend, and Szentgotthard.

LUZON—In U.S. Sixth Army's I Corps area, 128th Inf of 32d Div continues battle for Salacsac Pass No. 2 on Villa Verde Trail, capturing one hill, but is forced from crest of another. 3d Bn of 27th Inf, 25th Div, attacks along ridge leading to Mt Myoko. In XI Corps area, advance elements of 103d Inf, 43d Div, start S to seize Santa Maria Valley and make contact with 1st Cav Div. 1st Inf, 6th Div, regroups and patrols. In XIV Corps area, 12th Cav of 1st Cav Div seizes Calauan, from which enemy has now withdrawn. 5th Cav relieves elements of 7th Cav in San Agustin area and drives E along route N of and paralleling that of 7th Cav. In Mt Macolod sector, elements of 187th Inf, 11th A/B Div, gain positions on Bukel Hill. 188th Inf continues forward against scattered opposition.

S PHILIPPINES—In U.S. Eighth Army area, 185th Inf, on Negros, patrols toward Talisay in preparation for attack. 160th Inf moves to Bacolod and patrols from there. On Cebu, Americal Div prepares for all-out assault on hill defenses commanding Cebu City and beats off night attacks.

RYUKYU Is.—420th FA Gp and attachments are landed on the 4 small islands of the Keise group to support impending operations on Okinawa. 77th Div, except for the small garrison on Zamami, withdraws from Kerama Is. As against the low U.S. casualties of 31 killed and 81 wounded during operations on the Keramas, 530 Japanese have died and 121 have been captured. 1,195 civilians have been taken prisoner. 77th Div captures and destroys more than 350 suicide boats in the Keramas, heretofore an enemy suicide boat base.

1 April

WESTERN EUROPE—21 Army Group: Takes direct command of Br I Corps from Cdn First Army.

Br Second Army continues from the Rhine toward Hamburg-Wittenberg sector of the Elbe and has forward elements across Dortmund-Ems Canal, immediate objective and enemy's first line of organized resistance. Cdn 2 Corps, on left flank of Br Second Army, expands and strengthens Emmerich bridgehead. 30 Corps presses toward Dortmund-Ems Canal at Rheine. 8 Corps expands bridgeheads of 6th A/B and 11th Armd Divs over Dortmund-Ems Canal toward Osnabrueck.

U.S. Ninth Army effects junction with U.S. First Army at Lippstadt, sealing off the rich industrial Ruhr and trapping the whole of *Army Group B* and two corps of *Army Group H*. In XIII Corps area, 5th Armd Div spearheads drive toward the Weser, bypassing Muenster, which 17th A/B Div prepares to assault. While CCR, 5th Armd, drives to the Ems at Greffen, CCB moves to Warendorf and reconnoiters to Telgte. 84th Div begins assembly E of the Rhine. 11th Cav Gp also crosses to screen N flank of corps from Coesfeld eastward. In XIX Corps area, CCB, 2d Armd Div, drives SE to Lippstadt and makes contact with 3d Armd Div of VII Corps, First Army, closing noose about the Ruhr. CCA takes Cologne-Berlin Autobahn pass through Teutoburger Wald but cannot gain passages near Oerlinghausen and Augustdorf. 83d Div and 15th Cav Gp, driving E across Muenster Plain, mop up bypassed resistance and protect right .flank of corps along Lippe R. 8th Armd Div is attached to corps for drive on Paderborn. 30th Div assembles in Drensteinfurt area, between Muenster and Hamm; 113th Cav Gp is attached to it at 2400 to protect left flank. XVI Corps continues clearing region S of Haltern. 75th Div, reinf by 116th Inf of 29th Div, attacks with 3 regts abreast on left flank of corps, elements passing through 8th Armd Div zone. 134th Inf presses toward Zweig Canal, overrunning Recklinghausen; 137th completes drive to Rhein-Herne Canal; 320th mops up along Rhein-Herne Canal. 79th Div, defending right flank of corps, extends a little eastward to relieve elements of 35th Div. 29th Div completes assembling E of the Rhine.

12th Army Group: In U.S. First Army's VII Corps area, TF Kane of 3d Armd Div moves quickly to Lippstadt and establishes contact with XIX Corps. Paderborn falls to 3d Armd Div in concerted assault from SW, S, and SE. 1st Div (—) moves to region SW of Paderborn to block enemy movement from the Ruhr (ROSE) pocket. 104th Div, less 414th Inf, continues to fight on two fronts and is reinf on left by 4th Cav Gp. 413th Inf improves positions W of Rimbeck while 415th, far to left rear, defeats enemy attempt to break out of the Ruhr in Winterberg-Medebach area. 9th Div is also employed to block enemy escape from the Ruhr and attacks N, NW, and W with 3 regts. 8th and 78th Divs continue active along Sieg R line. 8th Div clears its sector S of the Sieg and begins assault on Siegen and commanding ground N of the river. XVIII Corps (A/B), transferred from First Allied Airborne Army to First Army command to operate against Ruhr pocket, establishes CP at Dillenburg. III Corps mops up while awaiting further orders. 99th Div closes in Gemuenden area. In V Corps area, 9th Armd Div expands Diemel R bridgehead N of Warburg and makes contact with 104th Div (VII Corps) at Rimbeck. CCR, protecting right flank, is relieved on right by 102d Cav Gp, which has just returned from VI Corps zone. 2d Div (less 38th Inf, attached to 9th Armd Div) completes concentration in Sachsenhausen area and establishes contact with 104th Div. 69th Div is in the process of moving from Weilburg-Wetzlar region to new assembly area in general vicinity of Naumburg.

In U.S. Fifteenth Army's XXII Corps area, 97th Div takes over zone of 95th Div in vicinity of Neuss. 95th Div, upon relief, is attached to XIX Corps, Ninth Army, and starts assembling E of the Rhine. 101st A/B Div is attached to corps to relieve 97th Div and starts from base camp to corps zone.

6th Army Group: In U.S. Seventh Army area, XV Corps meets effective opposition only around Aschaffenburg. While 2d and 3d Bns of 157th Inf, 45th Div, continue frontal assault from the S, fighting from house to house within the city, 1st Bn gains heights NE of the city. Other elements of 45th Div, as well as 106th Cav Gp to left and 3d Div to right, are pushing NE against scattered resistance. 14th Armd Div is attached to corps. XXI Corps continues E and NE with 12th Armd Div spearheading, 42d Div following on left, and 4th Div on right. Against determined opposition, armored columns close in on Wuerzburg on left and Koenigshofen on right, beginning assault on latter. 101st Cav Gp, screening right flank of corps, is attached to 4th Div. VI Corps drives SE astride the Neckar against disorganized resistance and makes contact with French forces on right flank. 10th Armd Div spearheads advance, followed on left by 63d Div and on right by 100th Div. CCR, on left flank, thrusts SE along E side of the Neckar toward Jagst R, reaching positions beyond Alfeld. CCA reaches general line from W bank of the Neckar through Hueffenhardt and Hoffenheim to Dielheim, SE of Wiesloch. CCB, on right flank, drives S to Bruchsal and then turns E to Stettfeld-Ubstadt area.

[1 APRIL 1945]

In U.S. Third Army's VIII Corps area, 76th Div finishes clearing its sector, concluding offensive of corps in current zone W of Frankfurt-Bad Nauheim Autobahn. Usingen and a number of other towns are secured. In XX Corps area, 6th Armd Div drives E from the Fulda, leaving Both Div (to which RCT 318 reverts) task of clearing Kassel. CCB crosses at Malsfeld and pushes E through Spangenberg. 80th Div drives N astride the Fulda, forward elements getting to within 3 miles of the city. 65th Div, less 261st Inf, which is attached to 6th Armd Div, is concentrating to rear of 3d Cav Gp. 5th Div continues to police Frankfurt area. XII Corps, having outdistanced XX and XV Corps, continues NE with both flanks vulnerable, 4th and 11th Armd Divs spearheading and 90th and 26th Divs following. CCB, 4th Armd Div, reaches the Werra and establishes small infantry bridgehead, permitting construction of ponton bridge, night 1-2. CCA and CCR follow CCB. 90th Div, less elements attached to 4th Armd Div, remains in place to facilitate movement of armor. 11th Armd Div, ordered to drive eastward on right flank of corps to Arnstadt and Kranichfeld via Meiningen and Thuringer Wald, attacks N into 90th Div zone near Schlitz and then E, CCB reaching Kaltensundheim area and CCA advancing to Frankenheim and Reichenhausen. Rest of div is following. 26th Div continues mopping up to rear of 11th Armd Div; 101st Inf begins assault on Fulda. 71st Div, assem-bled in reserve near Hanau with defensive mission, moves to intercept bypassed SS force N of Hanau. 2d Cav Gp, screening right flank of corps, pushes NE toward Bad Orb.

In Fr 1st Army area, 2d Corps expands Rhine bridgehead, cutting Karlsruhe-Frankfurt highway in vicinity of Mingolsheim and Bruchsal on left and reaching Linkenheim on right.

EASTERN EUROPE—Troops of First Ukrainian Front complete destruction of German garrison of Glogau, on the Oder in Silesia. Second Ukrainian Front continues W astride the Danube toward Vienna; elements N of the river reach positions within 13 miles of Bratislava. Troops of Third Ukrainian Front overrun Sopron (Hungary); push farther NW toward Wiener Neustadt and Vienna (Austria); with assistance of Bulgarians, continue clearing region SW of Lake Balaton in Hungary.

ITALY—15th Army Group: In Br Eighth Army area, 5 Corps begins series of preliminary operations to improve positions on right flank and divert enemy to this sector in preparation for main offensive to left. 2d Cdo Brig opens Operation ROAST—to clear Comacchio Spit between the lake and the sea—night 1-2, moving by water to W bank of the spit after considerable delay when craft bog down in mud of the shallow lake.

BURMA—Br Fourteenth Army takes command of Br 36th Div, which has completed its mission with NCAC. While conducting limited attacks to clear rest of central Burma, British are regrouping to make main effort with 4 Corps (Ind 5th and 17th Divs and 255th Tank Brig) down Mandalay-Rangoon RR while 33 Corps (Br 2d, Ind 7th, and Ind 20th Divs plus Ind 268th Inf Brig) shifts SW to drive along Irrawaddy R Valley on Army right flank toward Prome. Ind 19th Div, under army command, is to mop up behind 4 Corps.

LUZON—In U.S. Sixth Army area, Legaspi Attack Group (TG 78.4) lands RCT 158, reinf, in Legaspi area, Bicol Peninsula, after preparatory aerial and naval bombardment. Landing is unopposed and the assault forces quickly secure Legaspi port, town, and airstrip as well as Libog. 2d Bn encounters resistance near Daraga. Gen MacNider takes command ashore. In I Corps area, on Villa Verde Trail, 128th Inf of 32d Div recovers ground lost to Japanese during counterattack on 31st, but operations during next few days are curtailed sharply by torrential rains. 3d Bn of 27th Inf, 25th Div, secures ridge leading to Mt Myoko and until 9 April works on spur W of its crest. In XI Corps area, 43d turns S flank of *Shimbu* line as 172d Inf mops up Hill 1200. Main body of 103d Inf concentrates in Maybancal area and reconnoiters for routes of advance. In XIV Corps area, elements of 7th Cav, 1st Cav Div, reach Alaminos. 5th Cav continues eastward to N of 7th. 2d Sq, 12th Cav, begins attack on strongly defended Imoc Hill, about 4,000 yards SW of Calauan. Against decreasing resistance 1st Bn of 187th Inf, 11th A/B Div, secures Bukel Hill. 2d Bn has now opened Route 416 from Cuenca to Dita.

S. PHILIPPINES—In U.S. Eighth Army area, 185th Inf of 40th Div drives to outskirts of Talisay on Negros. Elements of 160th Inf take Granada. On Cebu, 2d Bn of 182d Inf, Americal Div, begins assault on Bolo Ridge, less than a mile NW of Guadalupe, making slow progress against well organized positions consisting of numerous pillboxes and cave and tunnel defenses.

OKINAWA—Joint Expeditionary Force (TF 51, Adm Turner) lands Tenth Army on SW shore of Okinawa in vicinity of Hagushi at approximately 0830, following intensive naval and aerial bombardment by supporting forces of Fifth Fleet. Northern Attack Force (TF 53, Rear Adm Lawrence F. Reifsnider) puts marines of 6th and 1st Mar Divs, III Amphibious Corps, ashore N of Bishi R while Southern Attack Force (TF 55, Rear Adm J. L. Hall, Jr.) lands 7th and 96th Divs, XXIV Corps, S of the river. Japanese offer little opposition as assault units move inland to gain beachhead of about

15,000 yards in length and 4,000-5,000 yards in depth. As a diversion, 2d Mar Div feints landing on SE shore of Okinawa. Air opposition is light but kamikazes, destined to play a more important role as the campaign progresses, cause some damage to shipping. In U.S. Tenth Army's III Amphib Corps area, 6th Mar Div, employing 22d Regt on N and 4th on S, takes Yontan airfield with ease. 1st Mar Div lands to S and, with 7th Regt on N and 5th on S, speeds E beyond Sobe in conjunction with XXIV Corps to S. In XXIV Corps area, 7th Div moves quickly eastward with 17th Inf on left and 32d on right, seizing Kadena airfield. 96th Div, to S, moves forward to secure commanding ground S and SE of its beaches, pushing to river beyond Chatan on coast.

2 April

WESTERN EUROPE—21 Army Group: Hq Netherlands District takes over zone of Br I Corps as hq of that corps passes to Br Second Army command.

In Cdn First Army's Cdn t Corps area, 49th Div opens drive on Arnhem from Nijmegen bridgehead. Cdn 2 Corps, which reverts to Cdn First Army from attachment to Br Second Army, drives N toward Doesburg and Zutphen.

In Br Second Army area, 30 Corps closes along Twenthe Canal and armored elements continue toward Lingen. In 12 Corps area, 7th Armd Div enters Rheine, on Dortmund-Ems Canal, but enemy is stubbornly defending airfields in the area. 8 Corps continues toward Osnabrueck.

In U.S. Ninth Army's XIII Corps area, 17th A/B Div, to which RCT 507 reverts, envelops and enters Muenster, clearing all except heart of city. 5th Armd Div continues rapidly toward the Weser, CCB columns advancing to Borgholzhausen region and CCR reaching edge of Herford. In XIX Corps area, 2d Armd Div continues battle for Teutoburger Wald passes, hampered by terrain, blown bridges, and roadblocks. CCA, assisted by elements of CCR, cuts main road from the autobahn to Bielefeld and gets elements to outskirts of Oerlinghausen. CCB moves forward through Teutoburger Wald along Detmold road to Hiddesen area. RCT 377 reverts to 95th Div from attachment to 2d Armd Div. RCT 119, 30th Div, is attached to 2d Armd Div. 83d Div continues clearing right flank of corps along the Lippe and maintains and strengthens small bridgehead at Hamm. 30th Div, less RCT 119, starts toward Teutoburger Wald to relieve 2d Armd Div units. 8th Armd Div continues E against scattered resistance; CCB is vigorously engaged at Neuhaus, NW of Paderborn. In XVI Corps area, 75th Div reaches Dortmund-Ems Canal from Datteln southward. 134th Inf, 35th Div, reaches Zweig Canal in Meckinghoven area and is there relieved by elements of 75th Div; 137th and 320th Regts defend positions along Rhein-Herne Canal.

12th Army Group: In U.S. First Army's VII Corps area, 3d Armd Div consolidates in Paderborn area; elements enter Dahl without opposition. 1st Div organizes defensive positions from which to block enemy movement from the W. 413th Inf, 104th Div, takes Rimbach; 415th decisively defeats another enemy counterattack toward Medebach and later drives W to E part of Kuestelberg. 9th Div secures Zueschen and Winterberg on right, Berleberg and Berghausen in center, and Girkhausen and Neu Astenberg on left. Corps zone is narrowed as 78th and 8th Divs pass to control of XVIII Corps (A/B) in place. XVIII Corps (A/B) takes over sector bounded by Rhine, Ruhr, Lenne, and Sieg Rivers. 78th Div defends S bank of the Sieg on left flank. 8th Div continues fight for Siegen and Netphen and heights N of the Sieg. In III Corps area, CCA of 7th Armd Div is attached to VII Corps and starts to Medebach area. In V Corps area, 9th Armd Div maintains Diemel R bridgehead against strong opposition on left, where CCB drives off counterattacking tank-infantry forces. 2d Div continues to mop up and takes responsibility for Eder bridges in Affoldern area. 102d Cav Gp is given mission of screening right flank of corps and maintaining contact with Third Army.

In U.S. Third Army area, VIII Corps starts NE to new zone in preparation for attack between XX and XII Corps. In XX Corps area, 6th Armd Div completes crossing the Fulda at Malsfeld and, with CCA and CCB abreast, drives toward the Werra and its tributary, the Wehre. Some elements reach the Werra in Bad Sooden area and search for crossing site while others secure bridgehead at Reichensachen. 80th Div pushes into outskirts of Kassel against determined resistance and tank-infantry counterattacks. 65th Div attacks E across the Fulda on right flank of corps with 260th and 259th Regts abreast, latter on right, and makes rapid progress against scattered resistance. 3d Cav Gp, ordered to defend left flank of corps, is relieved along the Fulda by 6th Cav Gp, night 2-3. In XII Corps area, CCB of 4th Armd Div expands Creuzburg bridgehead to Neukirchen. After ponton bridge is completed at Sprichra, CCA gains heights commanding that town. Ground opposition is light but German Air Force is active against both bridge sites. 90th Div begins crossing the Werra near Berka and Bengendorf. 11th Armd Div thrusts quickly to the Werra N and S of Meiningen. CCB establishes small bridgehead at Wasungen. CCA gains bridgehead in Grimmenthal area; elements take bridge at Vachdorf. Far to rear of armor, 26th Div finishes clearing Fulda area. 2d Cav Gp and 71st Div engage bypassed enemy N of

Hanau. After German SS column attacks rear of 2d Cav Sq, overrunning Waldensberg, 71st Div commits its full strength in this region: 5th Inf joins 14th W of Budingen in effort to force enemy E into Budinger Wald while 66th moves to block E exits from the woods. Forward elements of 2d Cav Gp reach Bad Orb.

6th Army Group: In U.S. Seventh Army's XV Corps area, 157th Inf of 45th Div continues assault on Aschaffenburg, where resistance is undiminished. 1st Bn drives into the city from NE. 14th Armd Div attacks NE through infantry toward Neustadt and Ostheim with CCA on left and CCB followed by CCR on right. Retreating enemy offers little opposition. In XXI Corps area, CCA of 12th Armd Div patrols eastward toward Wuerzburg, meeting no organized resistance, and is reinf by 222d Inf, 42d Div, which clears Marienburg, on W bank of the Main opposite Wuerzburg. CCB awaits repair of bridge across the Main at Ochsenfurt. CCR, reinf by 2 bns of 22d Inf, 4th Div, overcomes opposition in Koenigshofen. 232d Inf, 42d Div, clears region N and W of the Main in Wertheim-Marktheidenfeld area and forces crossing at Homburg; 242d drives N along the Main to positions beyond Bronn R. 8th Inf, 4th Div, clears region just SW of Wuerzburg; 1st Bn moves to Ochsenfurt and is ferried across the Main to establish small bridgehead, night 2–3. In VI Corps area, 10th Armd Div is slowed by rearguard action in some sectors as it continues S, SE, and E toward Heilbronn. Left flank elements of CCA, however, reach Bockingen, across the river from Heilbronn. 63d and 100th Divs continue to mop up to rear of armor.

In Fr 1st Army's 2d Corps area, 3d Algerian Inf Div clears Oestringen, Ubstadt, and Bruchsal. In region W of Bruchsal, 2d Moroccan Inf Div occupies Hochstetten and Karsdorf. Valluy Groupement (Fr 9th Colonial Inf Div) begins crossing the Rhine near Leimersheim and makes contact with 2d Moroccan Inf Div of 2d Corps.

ITALY—15th Army Group: In Br Eighth Army's 5 Corps area, 2d and 9th Cdos, 2d Cdo Brig, establish bridgehead on W shore of Comacchio Spit while 43d (Royal Mar) Cdo clear tongue of land between the Reno and the sea to attack the spit from E.

SEAC—Adm Mountbatten, meeting with military leaders in Kandy to plan for capture of Rangoon, decides to mount an amphibious assault from Akyab and Kyaukpyu by one div, supported by armor and a composite bn of airborne troops, before the monsoon, not later than 5 May.

LUZON—In U.S. Sixth Army area, RCT 158 develops defense position in Legaspi area of Bicol Peninsula, which enemy has organized to insure control of Route 1—running northward from San Bernardino Strait. 1st Bn is halted by fire from Bantog. 2d withdraws through Daraga after relieving elements isolated near there. In I Corps' 33d Div sector, 3d Bn of 129th Inf joins 2d in drive up Highway 9 toward Baguio and 1st Bn goes into reserve. 3d Bn of 35th Inf, 25th Div, begins clearing ridge dubbed "Fishhook" in Kapintalan region of Highway 5. In XI Corps area, 1st Inf of 6th Div renews northward attack with 2d Bn but gains little ground. 20th Inf begins co-ordinated attack with 1st and 3d Bns after arty preparation. 63d and 20th Regts are ordered to exchange places. In XIV Corps area, 5th Cav of 1st Cav Div reaches San Pablo. 7th Cav is pushing toward Mt Malepunyo.

In U.S. Eighth Army area, 185th Inf pushes into Talisay on Negros and clears the town and airfield; continues toward Silay, halting at Guinhalaron R, where bridge is down. Elements of Co B, 160th Inf, probe toward Concepcion and meet heavy fire. On Cebu, 2d Bn of 182d Inf gains positions on lower slopes of Bolo Ridge; is relieved by 1st Bn, 132d Inf. 3d Bn, 132d, encounters enemy position S of Talamban and withdraws while naval gunfire bombards it. In Sulu Archipelago, 2d Bn, reinf, 163d Inf, 41st Div, lands unopposed on Sanga Sanga I., in Tawi Tawi group, after naval and aerial bombardment of nearby Bongao I. After securing airfield and making contact with Filipino guerrillas, who already hold most of island, elements of 2d Bn move to Bongao I. and establish beachhead.

RYUKYU Is.—Convoy, with 77th Div embarked, is attacked by suicide planes while withdrawing from Kerama Is. and suffers some damage.

U.S. Tenth Army rapidly continues inland on Okinawa against light resistance. Kadena and Yontan airfields are ready for emergency use and arty spotting planes are flown ashore. In III Amphib Corps area, 6th Mar Div clears peninsula NW of Hagushi and pushes into foothills of Yontan-Zan. Enemy is disposed for strong defense of ridges and hills of this mountainous region. 1st Mar Div commits 2 bns of 1st Marines on fight as zone of attack widens; drives to line Ishimmi-Kutoku-Chatan. In XXIV Corps area, 7th Div employs 184th Inf troops to plug gap existing on left flank. 17th Inf reaches heights commanding Nakagusuku Bay and patrols to E coast, cutting the island in two. 32d Inf reduces strongpoint S of Koza. Enemy strongpoint near Mombaru delays center elements of 96th Div, but flanks are extended past Shimabuku on left and to vicinity of Futema on right.

3 April

WESTERN EUROPE—21 Army Group: In Br Second Army's 30 Corps area, Gds Armd Div reaches Dortmund-Ems Canal in Lingen area. In 12 Corps area, 52d Div mops up Rheine, relieving 7th Armd Div of this task. 8 Corps makes steady progress toward Osnabrueck.

In U.S. Ninth Army's XIII Corps area, 17th A/B Div completes reduction of Muenster. 5th Armd Div reaches the Weser, where bridges are down. CCB columns advance to Bergkirchen, W of Minden, and positions SE of Bad Oeynhausen. Bypassing Herford, CCR columns drive NE along autobahn to the Weser near Vennebeck, receiving surrender of Bad Oeynhausen. CCA moves forward toward Herford, crossing Dortmund-Ems Canal near Hiltrup. 84th Div starts toward the Weser in wake of 5th Armd Div. 102d Div is attached to corps and, night 3-4, crosses the Rhine at Wesel. XIX Corps, while continuing E into Germany, begins attack on Ruhr pocket. 30th Div relieves 2d Armd Div of positions in Teutoburger Wald, RCT 117 taking over passes formerly held by CCR and CCA on left and RCT 120 relieving CCB units W of Hiddesen and clearing part of Forst Berlebeck, which extends SE from Teutoburger Wald. 2d Armd Div gets into position for drive E to the Weser. CCR column drives SE to Mackenbruch and cuts Oerlinghausen-Lage road. One CCA TF attacks SE in evening through Osterheide to Lage while others overrun Oerlinghausen, assisted by CCR's flanking movement, and clear region about Pivitsheide. CCB advances through Forst Berlebeck and seizes Berlebeck. 83d Div, which releases 15th Cav Gp to 95th Div and takes control of 113th Cav Gp (− 125th Sq) from 30th Div, continues to clear along Lippe R on right flank of corps; relieves elements of 8th Armd Div in Neuhaus and mops up that town; turns over positions generally W of 30th N-S grid line, including Hamm bridgehead, to 95th Div. In afternoon, 8th Armd Div opens assault against Ruhr pocket, driving SW with CCA and elements of CCR. CCA moves along Paderborn-Soest highway to Erwitte area. CCR, closing in Lippstadt area, sends TF Walker to Elsen to relieve pressure on CCB and moves TF Artman to Weckinghausen. 95th Div begins relief of 83d Div and prepares to join in assault on Ruhr pocket. XVI Corps defends current positions and prepares to attack with 75th Div across Dortmund-Ems Canal. Co E of 291st Inf, 75th Div, crosses the canal.

12th Army Group: U.S. First Army directs XVIII Corps (A/B) and III Corps to attack in conjunction with Ninth Army to destroy enemy S of the Ruhr and E of the Rhine; VII and V Corps are to regroup in order to continue attack to E. In VII Corps area, 3d Armd and 1st Inf Divs maintain and improve defensive positions. 3d Armd Div makes contact with 8th Armd Div (XIX Corps). 413th Inf, 104th Div, takes Scherfede and Hardehausen while 415th reduces opposition in Kuestelberg. At 2400 CCA, 7th Armd Div, relieves elements of 415th Inf in Kuestelberg and is attached to 9th Div. 39th Inf, 9th Div, clears region W of Zueschen-Winterberg road but falls back a little at one point; elements of 47th Inf take Oberkirchen; 60th Inf secures Westfeld and relieves elements of 39th Inf in Neu Astenberg. In XVIII Corps (A/B) area, 97th Div is moving forward to take over left sector from 78th Div. 8th Div continues slowly NW along the Sieg. 13th Inf overcomes organized resistance in Siegen and seizes commanding ground to NW; 121st is still strongly opposed in Netphen but makes progress to right. III Corps prepares to attack on 5 April to reduce that part of the Ruhr pocket between Lenne and Ruhr Rivers, co-ordinating with XVIII Corps (A/B) to left. 32d Cav Sq, 14th Cav Gp, upon relief by 8th TD Gp, relieves CCB, 7th Armd Div, along the Eder. 99th Div starts W to Schwarzenau area. V Corps maintains and improves defensive positions. 69th Div completes assembly in Naumburg area and relieves CCR, 9th Armd Div, which assembles in Warburg area.

In U.S. Third Army area, VIII Corps continues concentration in new zone for attack to limiting line Muhlhausen-Langensalza-Gotha. 89th Div, concentrating in Hersfeld area, releases RCT 355 to 4th Armd Div. 4th Armd Div is transferred in place to corps from XII Corps at 2400. In XX Corps area, 6th Armd Div crosses the Werra and thrusts toward Muhlhausen. CCB, in the lead, crosses the Wehre at Reichensachen, clearing that town and Eschwege; crosses the Werra at Gross Burschla and drives to Heyerode. CCA, unable to cross in Bad Sooden area, follows CCB. CCR guards Eschwege and river line between Wanfried and Heldra. 80th Div continues lively battle for Kassel, clearing part of the city. 65th Div advances rapidly on right flank of corps: 260th Inf reaches line Reichensachen-Langenhain, where it is held up by friendly armor with road priority; to right, 259th crosses the Werra-3d Cav Gp assembles in Fritzlar area. 76th Div is transferred to corps from VIII Corps and is assembling in vicinity of Homberg. XII Corps directive orders advance to halt along line Gotha-Suhl. CCB, 4th Armd Div, gains positions commanding Gotha while CCA advances to Hoerselgau area. 90th Div clears Berka-Vacha sector E of the Werra. 11th Armd Div drives well into Thuringer Wald, German small arms manufacturing center. CCB pushes to Oberhof. CCA reaches Suhl and clears S part in house-to-house battle. 26th Div drives toward the Werra to rear of 11th Armd Div, forward elements reaching Schwarzbach. Germans N of Hanau are driven into Budinger Wald and encircled there by co-ordinated action of first Div, 2d Cav Gp, and XX Corps' 5th Div. 2d Sq, 2d Cav Gp, is attached to 71st Div and intercepts small enemy parties pushing toward Wirtheim.

[3 APRIL 1945] [471]

In U.S. Fifteenth Army's XXII Corps area, 94th Div closes in vicinity of Krefeld and relieves 102d Div along the Rhine. 102d Div is attached to XIII Corps, Ninth Army. 20th Armd Div is attached to corps.

6th Army Group: In U.S. Seventh Army's XV Corps area, Aschaffenburg surrenders to 157th Inf, 45th Div, concluding stiff battle. Other assault forces of corps continue quickly NE. CCB, 14th Armd Div, takes Lohr. In XXI Corps area, 222d Inf of 42d Div (attached to CCA, 12th Armd Div) opens frontal assault on Wuerzburg; 2d Bn forces the Main before dawn and establishes bridgehead in W part of Wuerzburg; 1st Bn crosses later and expands bridgehead to right. 232d Inf, 42d Div, moves to Marienburg and prepares to cross the Main; 242d reaches the Main about 10 miles N of Wuerzburg and searches for crossing site. 8th Inf, 4th Div, completes its crossing at Ochsenfurt and CCB, 12th Armd Div, also crosses after bridge is repaired. CCR, after closing in Sonderhofen assembly area and releasing attached elements of 4th Div, drives rapidly E, forward elements reaching N-S railway line at edge of Herrnberchtheim. In VI Corps area, CCR of 10th Armd Div establishes shallow bridgehead across the Jagst in Griesheim area, N of Heilbronn, against strong resistance. CCA prepares for assault crossing of the Neckar in Heilbronn area; meets intense fire from enemy entrenched along the river. CCB drives rapidly E on Heilbronn against moderate resistance, reaching Kirchhausen-Schluchtern region. 63d Div runs into troublesome pockets of resistance as it continues clearing region N of the Jagst on left flank of corps. 397th Inf, 100th Div, drives E toward Heilbronn; 399th, pinched out by Fr forces to right, assembles in Sinsheim area; 398th relieves 255th Inf, 63d Div, along the Neckar. Fr 1st Army is directed to expand bridgehead to line Lichtenau-Pforzheim-Ludwigsberg and capture Karlsruhe and Pforzheim; be prepared to clear the Black Forest. 2d Corps pushes E toward the Neckar on left and S toward Karlsruhe. Valluy Groupement drives on Karlsruhe to right of 2d Corps. DA ALPS opens fight for Mt Cenis pass.

EASTERN EUROPE—Troops of Second Ukrainian Front continue W toward Vienna on broad front: those N of the Danube in Czechoslovakia take eastern suburb of Bratislava and to right rear overrun Kremnica with aid of Rumanian troops; elements S of the Danube cross Austro-Hungarian border S of Bratislava. Troops of Third Ukrainian Front in Austria overrun important industrial center of Wiener Neustadt and cut roads and rail lines between there and Vienna. Left flank elements of Third Ukrainian Front and Bulgarian troops continue clearing region SW of Lake Balaton in Hungary; forward units cross Hungarian-Yugoslav border.

ITALY—15th Army Group: In U.S. Fifth Army's IV Corps area, 92d Div, less 365th and 371st Regts, which are exchanged for RCT 442 and 473d Inf, passes to army control for diversionary attack along Ligurian coast toward Massa and La Spezia.

LUZON—In U.S. Sixth Army area, RCT 158 makes limited progress against enemy positions on ridge running southward from Daraga. In XI Corps area, 169th Inf is detached from 43d Div and, with 112th Cav, forms Baldy Force to protect N flank of corps and probe toward Ipo, N end of enemy's *Shimbu* line. During night 3-4, 103d Inf of 43d Div concentrates secretly on slopes of Mt Sembrano and begins advance to establish contact with 1st Cav Div. 1st Inf, 6th Div, suspends ground attack while enemy positions ahead are being pounded by aircraft, mortars, and arty. 63d Inf is directed to renew attack against Mt Montalban. On Caballo I., tanks are brought forward but cannot reach enemy positions. In XIV Corps area, 187th Inf of 11th A/B Div, which now has foothold on saddle between Mt Macolod and Bukel Hill, moves to Lipa area, leaving 1st Bn behind to contain and maintain limited pressure on bypassed Japanese on Mt Macolod. 188th Inf is joined by its 1st Bn and releases 3d Bn, 511th Inf, for reserve. Patrol of 188th enters Tiaong without opposition. 2d Bn, 187th Inf, takes responsibility for Lipa-Lipa Hill area.

S PHILIPPINES—In U.S. Eighth Army area, 185th Inf, fording Guinhalaron R on Negros, advances through Silay to Imbang R. 40th Rcn Tr platoon probing along Silay-Guimbalon road meets heavy fire near latter. 1st Bn, 160th Inf, places fire on Concepcion area. Gen Eichelberger grants request for RCT 164 to move to Cebu from Leyte. On Cebu, 1st Bn of 132d Inf finishes clearing Bolo Ridge. Positions delaying 3d Bn are pounded by air. A co, reinf, of 2d Bn, 108th Inf, lands on Masbate at town of Masbate to help guerrillas gain control of the island. On Romblon, organized enemy resistance ceases.

OKINAWA—U.S. Tenth Army spotting planes start operating on Okinawa. In III Amphib Corps area, 6th Mar Div extends control over Yontan-Zan hill mass in 7,000-yard drive; advances its left flank to base of Ishikawa Isthmus. 1st Mar Div advances its right flank to E coast; reconnoiters Katchin Peninsula and along E coast as far N as Hizaonna. F6F makes successful forced landing on Yontan airfield. XXIV Corps pivots right to attack due S with 7th Div on E and 96th on W. 32d Inf, 7th Div, drives quickly S along E coast to Kuba; 184th Inf starts passing through left flank elements of 96th Div. 96th Div, which commits 382d Inf between 381st and

383d, is unable to reach Unjo but to W reaches general line Atanniya-Futema-Chiyunna-Isa.

U.S.—Gen Marshall assures the British that U.S. air resources will not be withdrawn from Burma before 1 June or capture of Rangoon.

JCS designate Gen MacArthur Commander in Chief, U.S. Army Forces, Pacific, and Adm Nimitz commander of all naval forces in the Pacific.

4 April

WESTERN EUROPE—21 Army Group: In Br Second Army area, 30 Corps establishes bridgehead over Dortmund-Ems Canal in vicinity of Lingen. 12 Corps gains bridgehead across Dortmund-Ems Canal in Rheine area. In 8 Corps area, some 6th A/B Div elements enter Osnabrueck while others bypass the city and thrust to the Weser at Minden.

12th Army Group: U.S. Ninth Army reverts to 12th Army Group from control of 21 Army Group. In XIII Corps area, 17th A/B Div organizes perimeter defense of Muenster. Efforts of 5th Armd Div to secure Weser bridges intact at Minden and Rinteln are futile. Forces of 8 Corps, Br Second Army, enter Minden before surrender of its garrison can be arranged and Germans blow bridges. CCA, U.S. 5th Armd Div, mops up pockets of enemy within Herford. Assault elements of 84th Div assemble near Bad Oeynhausen, night 4-5, for attack across the Weser. 102d Div moves forward rapidly to rear of 5th Armd and 84th Inf Divs, mopping up isolated pockets. In XIX Corps area, 2d Armd Div progresses rapidly on left, where one CCA column advances from Lage to Lemgo and thence to approaches to the Weser and another clears Pivitsheide and continues to vicinity of Gross Berkel; CCB, slowed by terrain and opposition, advances from Berlebeck to Kreuzenstein. 30th Div, protecting left flank of corps, maintains defensive positions; in limited attacks overruns Hiddesen and Detmold. To right, 83d Div makes main effort with TF Biddle—strongly reinf 113th Cav Gp—and employs 329th and 331st Regts close behind it to mop up; 330th Inf defends Lippe R line from Lippstadt westward. 95th Div begins assault on Ruhr pocket: attacks S across Lippe R and Canal in Hamm-Lippborn area with 379th and 378th Regts, former on left; forward elements reach Dinker. 15th Cav Gp screens Lippe R along div right flank. 8th Armd Div continues assault on Ruhr pocket: one CCA column thrusts S to Mohne R line while another clears Erwitte and drives toward Androchte; CCR overruns Overhagen, Stirpe, Norddorf, Ebbinghausen, and Voellinghausen. In XVI Corps area, 75th Div attacks in strength across Dortmund-Ems Canal early in morning, employing 291st Inf on left, attached 116th in center, and 289th on right; overruns Waltrop, Henrichenburg, Ickern, and part of Brambauer. 35th Div regroups to give 134th Inf center of line along Rhein-Herne Canal.

In U.S. First Army's VII Corps area, 3d Armd Div prepares to renew eastward offensive. 1st Div is being pinched out by 8th Armd Div, XIX Corps. 104th Div clears its two zones against decreased resistance: 413th Inf cleans out Forst Hardehausen and seizes Holtheim and Kleinenberg; 415th Inf and 4th Cav Gp scour Briloner Stadt-Forst. In 9th Div sector, CCA of 7th Armd Div drives NW, taking Hildfeld, Gronebach, and Niedersfeld; 39th Inf seizes terrain features in Gronebach-Winterberg area; 60th takes Alt Astenberg; 47th defends S flank, repelling determined counterattacks against Oberkirchen. Upon relief by 99th Div (XVIII Corps), 1st and 3d Bns of 47th Inf move to Kuestelberg area. 9th Div forms TF Birks, consisting of CCA of 7th Armd Div and 47th Inf, at 2000 and at midnight the div plus attachments passes to control of III Corps in place. In XVIII Corps (A/B) area, 97th Div begins relief of 78th Div along S bank of the Sieg on left flank of corps; RCT 387 joins 78th Div and is attached to it. 8th Div withstands severe counterattacks against Siegen and Netphen and makes limited progress elsewhere. III Corps completes preparations for assault against Ruhr pocket. V Corps remains on the defensive, mopping up.

In U.S. Third Army's XX Corps area, 6th Armd Div, advancing in multiple columns with close air support, encircles Muhlhausen and sends strong patrols into the city. CCA moves N and CCB S about the city, closing noose at Koerner. Defeated garrison of Kassel surrenders to 80th Div. 76th Div completes, assembly in Homberg area and advances NE toward Langensalza to clear bypassed resistance. 5th Div is detached from corps and held in army reserve, retaining security mission in Frankfurt area. On N flank of corps, 3d Cav Gp's 3d Sq begins clearing Ober Meiser-Obervellmar road NW of Kassel. VIII Corps becomes operational in new zone between XX and XII Corps and attacks E. 65th Div, on right flank of XX Corps, is transferred to corps in place and continues E on left flank of VIII Corps. RCT 261 reverts to 65th Div from attachment to 6th Armd Div and guards N flank. 259th Inf gets advance elements to Creuzberg area. 260th, assembled near Datterode, prepares to motor E. In center of corps, 89th Div, less RCT 355, shuttles E to forward assembly areas; 353d Inf moves to Berka-Lauchroeden region and relieves elements of 90th Div (XII Corps). 4th Armd Div is transferred to corps from XII Corps in place, present right flank of VIII Corps, and releases RCT 359 to 90th Div, CCB receives surrender of Gotha and moves to Muehlberg area. CCA drives SE to

Ohrdruf. 6th Cav Gp, ordered to clean out stragglers in rear area, clears region W of the Fulda and crosses to follow 65th and 89th Divs eastward. 87th Div is ordered to assemble in Friedewald area but lacks transportation to move at once. In XII Corps area, 90th Div continues E against sporadic resistance, 357th Inf taking Marksuhl and Moehra and 358th seizing Merkers, where Nazi art treasures, gold, and uniforms are discovered in salt mine. 11th Armd Div, its mission substantially completed within limits of corps restraining line, engages in limited action to consolidate and improve current positions and open lateral routes between CCA and CCB. CCA captures Suhl, liberating many slave workers from arms factories. CCR begins clearing zone between CCB and CCA. 26th Div assault regts reach the Werra in Schmalkalden-Wasungen area and start across it. 71st Div and 2d Cav Gp complete reduction of pocket N of Hanau, eliminating threat to MSR. 71st Div relieves 42d Sq, 2d Cav Gp. 17th Armd Gp, to which 2d Cav Sq is attached, takes over mission of guarding MSR.

In U.S. Fifteenth Army's XXII Corps area, 101st A/B Div completes relief of 97th Div. 82d A/B Div takes over sector of 86th Div.

6th Army Group: In U.S. Seventh Army area, XV Corps continues rapid drive NE through Spessart Mountains. CCB of 14th Armd Div reaches outskirts of Gemuenden. In XXI Corps area, after engineers complete bridging in Wuerzburg area, 232d Inf of 42d Div and elements of CCA, 12th Armd Div, cross under smoke screen. 232d works N and then E into Wuerzburg while 222d, attached to CCA, pushes S and E, clearing a large portion of the city against last-ditch resistance. CCB expands Ochsenfurt bridgehead N to include Erlach. 92d Cav Rcn Sq clears heights E of Obernbreit while CCR overruns Gnoetzheim and Herrnberchtheim. 8th Inf, 4th Div, presses northward in Ochsenfurt bridgehead in conjunction with CCB. 22d and 12th Regts launch attack in Koenigshofen area and make slow progress on wooded heights. VI Corps is so strongly opposed along the Neckar and Jagst Rivers as it opens assault on Heilbronn that it is forced to change plan of attack. 10th Armd Div begins attack on Heilbronn in sector of CCA where 3d Bn of 398th Inf, 100th Div, forces the Neckar at Neckargartach before dawn and establishes shallow bridgehead against sharp opposition. 100th Div is then given task of continuing frontal assault while 10th Armd Div conducts outflanking maneuver to attack from the rear. 100th Div reinforces Neckar bridgehead in afternoon with 2d Bn, 397th Inf. CCA clears Frankenbach-Neckargartach sector along W bank of the Neckar while CCB clears region SW of Bockingen; CCR withdraws bridgehead across the Jagst N of Heilbronn. 399th Inf begins clearing right flank of 100th Div, reaching positions W of Bockingen. On left flank of corps, 63d Div continues E in region N of the Jagst, committing 255th Inf between 254th and 253d. Two bns of 253d establish bridgehead across the Jagst in Griesheim-Herbolzheim area against firm opposition.

Fr 1st Army captures Karlsruhe in assault by Valluy Groupement and elements of 2d Corps. DA ALPS breaks off operations in Mt Cenis area where it has been under strong enemy pressure.

EASTERN EUROPE—Fourth Ukrainian Front and Czechoslovak troops open offensive toward Moravian Gap, driving W along border of Poland and Czechoslovakia from positions SW of Nowy Targ (Poland). Important communications center of Bratislava (Czechoslovakia) falls to troops of Second Ukrainian Front. In Austria, forces of Third Ukrainian Front push to within 2 miles of Vienna. Elements of Third Ukrainian Front and Bulgarian troops finish clearing Germans from Hungarian soil and continue to pursue them into Yugoslavia.

ITALY—15th Army Group: In Br Eighth Army's 5 Corps area, 2d Cdo Brig on Comacchio Spit is brought to a halt by enemy on far bank of Canale di Valetta and is relieved, night 4–5, by 56th Div. Subsequent efforts of 56th Div to cross the canal are so strongly opposed that this subsidiary action is broken off. Operation FRY—occupation of 4 small islands in Lake Comacchio—is carried out, night 4–5, without opposition by troops of Special Boat Service and 28th Garibaldi Brig.

LUZON—In U.S. Sixth Army area, 1st Bn of RCT 158, moving northward to positions NW of Busay, attacks southward along ridge on left flank while 2d and 3d Bns are attacking frontally below Daraga. Progress for next week is very slow since enemy must be destroyed in detail. In I Corps' 33d Div sector, 129th Inf patrol runs into heavy fire near Salat, about 3 ½ air miles SE of Burgos. In XI Corps area, 103d Inf, less 2d Bn, 43d Div, secures Santa Maria Valley, seizing Mabitac, Sinaloan, and Famy. Supporting weapons astride N-S highway block enemy escape. 2d Bn drives E along highway through Macatunao. 63d Inf, 6th Div, begins relief of 20th Inf and takes over its sector. In XIV Corps area, 5th Cav of 1st Cav Div, probing S with patrols from San Pablo, makes contact with 11th A/B Div forces in Tiaong area, completing isolation of Japanese on Mt Malepunyo. 188th Inf, 11th A/B Div, after contact is gained with 1st Cav Div, assembles S of Tiaong.

S PHILIPPINES—In U.S. Eighth Army area, 1st Bn of 160th Inf on Negros moves into Concepcion from which enemy has withdrawn. 2d Bn, 185th Inf, clears Guimbalon, important enemy supply base.

On Cebu, 182d Inf drives from Go Chan Hill against Horseshoe Ridge, about 800 yards to N, and takes it.

OKINAWA—In U.S. Tenth Army's III Amphib Corps area, corps CG assumes command ashore and moves CP ashore. 6th Mar Div closes along base of Ishikawa Isthmus, the L plus 15 line, and starts up the isthmus. 1st Mar Div clears its zone of action as remaining elements reach E coast. XXIV Corps meets stiffening resistance while pressing southward toward hill mass extending from Urasoe-Mura to Ouki. 96th Div, with 383d Inf on right and 382d on left, advances down W coast to Uchitomari area and pushes E flank units forward more than 2 miles beyond Nodake. 7th Div, employing 184th Inf on right and 32d on left, meets organized resistance W of Kuba on ridge surmounted by ruins of an ancient castle and falls behind.

IWO JIMA—RCT 9, 3d Mar Div, turns its portion of island over to Army RCT 747 and prepares to re-embark for Guam.

5 April

WESTERN EUROPE—21 Army Group: In Cdn First Army area, Cdn I Corps finishes clearing region between Nijmegen and the Neder Rijn. Cdn 2 Corps establishes bridgehead across Twenthe Canal in region E of Ijssel R and clears Almelo.

In Br Second Army's 30 Corps area, 43d Div, on left flank, holds Hengelo. To right, 3d Div captures Lingen. 72 Corps expands and strengthens bridgehead across Dortmund-Ems Canal. 8 Corps clears rest of Osnabrueck and continues to close along the Weser.

12th Army Group: In U.S. Ninth Army's XIII Corps area, 77th A/B Div (less RCT 794 under control of XIX Corps) is transferred to XVI Corps and starts to Duisburg region. 84th Div prepares for assault crossing of the Weser near Minden. 5th Armd Div stands by to lend engineer and other assistance. 102d Div continues rapid drive eastward toward the Weser, gaining 20-35 miles a day. In XIX Corps area, 2d Armd Div reaches the Weser S of Hameln and establishes bridgehead with 4 TF's and 2 arty bns. On left, one CCA TF crosses in assault boats in vicinity of Ohr and, when bridge is completed, is followed by another. CCB drives to the Weser in Emmern-Grohnde area; crosses one column in assault boats near Grohnde and another in sector of CCA. By the end of day, CCA bridgehead extends from Rohrsen to Voremberg; CCB holds Hajen, Frenke, Brockensen, and Heyen. 83d Div continues NE toward the Weser to right of 2d Armd Div, clearing many towns. Aided by air strikes, 95th Div expands and strengthens its bridgehead S of the Lippe against diminishing resistance. 377th Inf attacks S across the Lippe toward Soest in afternoon, passing through 379th Inf, and reaches positions beyond Wiltrop. 8th Armd Div, reinf by 194th Gli Inf of 77th A/B Div, continues W toward Soest: CCA columns converge on Altenmellrich; CCB, attacking through CCR, reaches line Weslarn-Lohne. 95th Inf and 8th Armd Divs prepare for concerted assault on Soest. In XVI Corps area, 75th Div straightens left sector of its bridgehead line and finishes clearing Brambauer.

U.S. First Army joins in battle to destroy Ruhr pocket, at first employing III Corps. XVIII Corps (A/B) regroups for co-ordinated assault on Ruhr pocket: 86th Div starts assembly in corps zone; RCT 347 is attached to 97th Div. 8th Div is still firmly opposed as it continues attack N of the Sieg; maintains positions in Siegen area against further counterattacks and mops up in Netphen. III Corps begins attack on Ruhr pocket, employing 9th Div on N, 7th Armd Div in center, and 99th Div on S. On 9th Div right flank, TF Birks clears Wiemeringhausen, Brunskappel, Assinghausen, Bruchhausen, Wullmeringhausen, and Elleringhausen. 39th Inf seizes Silbach while 60th drives into woods NE of Oberkirchen and cuts Oberkirchen-Nordenau road. 32d Sq, 14th Cav Gp, moves to Willingen area and is attached to 9th Div to protect its right flank. CCB, 7th Armd Div, attacks W through 9th Div to edge of Winkhausen, which elements bypass to reach positions near Grafschaft. 99th Div, with 394th and 393d Regts in assault, 394th on right, takes Latrop, Aue, and Muesse and thrusts toward Wingeshausen. VII Corps, now relieved of responsibility for the Ruhr pocket, starts E toward the Weser. At noon 3d Armd Div moves forward in 4 parallel columns—from left to right, TF's Boles and Kane of CCA and TF's Welborn and Lovelady of CCB; against scattered resistance gains up to 22 miles, CCA reaching Ottbergen-Rheder area and CCB advancing to Siddessen and Willegassen. 104th Div regroups. V Corps, ordered to drive to line Duderstadt-Schlotheim, attacks with 2d and 69th Divs abreast. On left, 2d Div, with RCT 23 on left and RCT 9 on right, drives quickly E through 9th Armd Div elements to Hofgeismar on left and to heights overlooking the Weser N of Hann Muenden on right. Elements attached to 9th Armd Div revert to 2d Div. On right flank, 69th Div relieves 80th Div, Third Army, in Kassel area, where RCT 271 remains to guard installations, and continues E with RCT 273 on left and RCT 272 on right to Fulda R line between Hann Muenden and Kassel, crossing elements at Steele and beginning attack toward junction of Fulda, Weser, and Werra Rivers at Hann Muenden.

In U.S. Third Army's XX Corps area, CCA and CCB of 6th Armd Div clear Muhlhausen by 0905. CCB then moves to Schlotheim area. CCA drives SE

[5 APRIL 1945]

and advance elements begin assault on Langensalza from the NW as elements of 65th Div (VIII Corps) push to same objective from the SW. 80th Div begins attack E from Kassel but is halted by change of orders and relieved by 69th Div (V Corps). 76th Div continues eastward toward Werra and Wehre Rivers: RCT 385 begins attack on Grossalmerode; RCT 304, to right, reaches the Wehre at Niederhone, W of Eschwege, and takes bridge. VIII Corps boundaries are altered to give corps former XII Corps zone. 65th Div continues toward line Muhlhausen-Langensalza. 259th Inf, on right, gains control of most of Langensalza by nightfall. Elements of 353d Inf, 89th Div, move into Eisenach after enemy agrees to surrender it, but pulls back upon learning that Germans are returning. Against light resistance, 354th Inf advances E on div left to line Henningsleben-Warza, S of Langensalza, and halts to await relief by XX Corps. 4th Armd Div remains in place awaiting relief. 6th Cav Gp is relieved of mopping up mission in corps rear. XII Corps, in preparation for drive SE upon order, begins regrouping and patrolling SE to secure line of departure. 90th Div, now out of contact with enemy and disposed within zone of VIII Corps, consolidates N of the Werra. CCA, 11th Armd Div, in limited attack, presses slowly toward crest of Thuringer Wald. CCR opens lateral routes between CCB and CCA, then drives on Meiningen, taking it and nearby airport. Div halts offensive when it receives warning order to expect new orders, and CCR turns Meiningen over to 26th Div forces who arrive there in evening. 328th Inf, 26th Div, completes crossing the Werra, overruns Schmalkalden, and establishes contact with 90th Div on left; elements of 101st relieve CCR at Meiningen; 104th, upon relief by 71st Div units in Fulda area, motors E to screen right flank from Ulster R eastward. 71st Div, with mission of protecting right flank of corps, starts to Fulda area. 42d Sq, 2d Cav Gp, screens S flank from Fulda to Ulster R.

6th Army Group: In U.S. Seventh Army's XV Corps area, converging columns of armor and infantry take Gemuenden. While CCB, 14th Armd Div, drives into Gemuenden from the W, 2d Bn of 7th Inf, 3d Div, crosses the Main and pushes into the town from SE, making contact with the armor. In XXI Corps area, CCA of 12th Armd Div completes its crossing of the Main at Wuerzburg and in conjunction with elements of 42d Div overcomes resistance there; starts drive on Schweinfurt. After CCB seizes bridge at Kitzingen, 8th Inf of 4th Div establishes small bridgehead there. CCR clears Seinsheim and Ippesheim. 22d and 12th Regts, 4th Div, continue to clear region E of Koenigshofen. In VI Corps area, 100th Div continues frontal assault on Heilbronn. 10th Armd Div, in an outflanking maneuver, crosses 3d Bn, 397th Inf, into Neckargartach bridgehead and expands the bridgehead southward into N part of Heilbronn; crosses 1st Bn, 397th Inf, over the Neckar at center of Heilbronn in effort to speed operations. 399th Inf consolidates positions on div right flank W of the Neckar. 398th (−) attacks in support of and to right of 63d Div: 2d Bn crosses the Neckar in Offenau area while its organic vehicles cross farther N in 63d Div zone. 63d Div is directed to face S instead of E. On right flank, some elements of 253d Inf push E along S bank of the Jagst toward Hardehauser Wald while others fight from house to house within Moeckmuehl. 255th Inf reaches general line Merchingen-Ober Kessach-Widdern; 254th consolidates in Osterburken-Merchingen area. CCB, 10th Armd Div, after clearing Bockingen and passing into reserve, moves southward along the Neckar and makes contact with French troops near Lauffen. CCR of 10th Armd Div, followed by CCA, attacks through 63d Div to Rengershausen-Roth area.

In Fr 1st Army's 2d Corps area, 3d Algerian Inf Div, assisted by CCS of 5th Armd Div, drives to Neckar R line S of Heilbronn on left flank of corps. 2d Moroccan Inf Div, reinf by CC's 4 and 6 of 5th Armd Div, pushes toward Pforzheim, next objective of corps. Valluy Groupement begins clearing region S of Karlsruhe, where enemy has fortified valley positions, and N spurs of Black Forest.

ITALY—15th Army Group: In U.S. Fifth Army area, 92d Div begins diversionary attack in Ligurian coastal sector toward Massa with 370th Inf on left and 442d on right. 370th Inf, moving up Highway 1, gets advance elements more than 2 miles toward objective before falling back under counterattack. 442d takes M. Fragolita and M. Carchio. In IV Corps area, 1st Armd Div is attached to corps. In 11 Corps area, 34th Div moves to Idice Valley sector, previously held by 91st Div, and 91st Div takes over zone of 34th astride Highway 65.

In Br Eighth Army's 5 Corps area, 56th Div begins Operation LEVER—to clear wedge of land between the Reno and SW shore of Lake Comacchio—attacking across the Reno, night 5-6.

USSR—Notifies Japanese ambassador in Moscow it wishes to denounce 5-year neutrality pact signed with Japan on 13 April 1941.

BURMA—Br Fourteenth Army releases Ind 19th Div to 4 Corps

LUZON—In U.S. Sixth Army's XI Corps area, 63d Inf of 6th Div is ordered to attack Mt Mataba. While main body of 103d Inf, 43d Div, patrols, 3d Bn, motorized, moves S along Laguna de Bay coast to Lumban and seizes bridge over Pagsanjan R. On Caballo I., 2d Bn, 151st Inf, is trying to reduce enemy positions with ignited diesel oil. In XIV Corps area, resistance to 1st Cav Div eases. 5th Cav makes contact with 43d Div (XI Corps) in Lumban area, on E shore of Laguna de Bay. 12th Cav completes clearing Imoc Hill area near Calauan. 7th Cav, pushing toward Mt Malepunyo from N, gets forces on Mapait Hills. 187th Inf, 11th A/B Div, takes Talisay and probes in W foothills of Mt Malepunyo while 188th mops up S and SE of Mt Malepunyo.

S PHILIPPINES—U.S. Eighth Army announces completion of Visayan Passage mission, although mopping up is still in progress. Romblon I. is turned over to guerrillas. 139 Japanese and 17 Americans have been killed there. On Negros, 160th Inf is pushing toward Hill 3155, later called Dolan Hill, which commands approaches to Patog. On Cebu, Americal Div forces strengthen positions and patrol while awaiting RCT 164 to assist in enveloping assault.

RYUKYU Is.—U.S. Tenth Army begins rcn of Eastern Islands, off Okinawa, employing FMF Amphib Rcn Bn. In III Amphib Corps area, 22d Marines of 6th Mar Div, spearheading northward drive up Ishikawa Isthmus, reaches Atsutabaru-Kin line. 1st Mar Div mops up and patrols to S; reconnoiters Yabuchi Shima, off Katchin Peninsula, with negative results. XXIV Corps CP closes on board USS *Teton* and opens ashore. 96th Div encounters well-organized enemy positions near Uchitomari and Ginowan that limit its progress. 383d Inf, on W, makes unsuccessful attack on Cactus Ridge, 600 yards SE of Mashiki. 382d gains 400-900 yards. 7th Div moves S to positions almost abreast 96th Div.

JAPAN—Gen Koiso's cabinet resigns and is succeeded by another under Adm Kantaro Suzuki.

6 April

WESTERN EUROPE—21 Army Group: In Br Second Army's 30 Corps area, Gds Armd Div drives from Lingen toward Bremen. 12 Corps finishes clearing Rheine area.

12th Army Group: In U.S. Ninth Army area, XIII Corps opens assault across the Weser at 0500. 335th Inf, 84th Div, crosses in assault boats S of Minden and just S of village of Neesen under cover of darkness, taking enemy by surprise and gaining bridgehead astride Weser Gebirge. 334th Inf crosses into bridgehead, night 5-6, over bridges erected by engineers. In XIX Corps area, CCA of 2d Armd Div thrusts NE to the Leine at Schulenberg and takes bridge intact. CCB clears Harderode, Esperde, and heights S of Heyen. CCR crosses the Weser at Grohnde and drives NE toward Burgstemmen, reaching Elze. 30th Div, with RCT 117 on left and RCT 120 on right, speeds eastward behind 2d Armd Div, clearing N flank of corps to the Weser; takes responsibility for Weser bridge sites; crosses 2 bns of RCT 117 over the Weser at Ohr and bn of RCT 120 at Grohnde. 83d Div gets forward elements to the Weser in Bodenwerder-Holzminden area, to right of 2d Armd Div; 3d Bn, 329th Inf, crosses at Bodenwerder and clears Halle. In Ruhr pocket sector, 377th Inf of 95th Div begins clearing Soest; 378th secures portion of Hamm E of Hamm-Soest RR in 2-pronged assault from Hamm bridgehead and from NE. CCB column, 8th Armd Div, reaches Ost Oennen, SW of Soest. In XVI Corps area, 75th Div thrusts S toward Ruhr R just W of Dortmund in effort to sever communication lines of trapped enemy and block movement from Dortmund westward. 35th Div releases 320th Inf to 75th Div. 17th A/B Div, less 194th Gli Inf, is attached to corps and relieves 79th Div of defensive positions along Rhein-Herne Canal from the Rhine NE, on right flank of corps. 79th Div gets into position for attack S toward Ruhr R in region just W of Gelsenkirchen and relieves elements of 320th Inf, 35th Div, along Rhein-Herne Canal. 29th Div displaces eastward to Sendenhorst-Ahlen region, SE of Muenster, and is held in army reserve.

In U.S. First Army area, XVIII Corps (A/B) begins co-ordinated assault against Ruhr pocket, heading N and NW toward the Ruhr in vicinity of its junction with the Rhine. 78th Div, disposed along S bank of the Sieg from Dattenfeld to Brachbach, attacks N across the river at 0500–309th Inf on left and 310th on right—and secures bridgehead about 6,000 yards deep. 8th Div attacks at 0600, after ½-hour arty preparation: 13th Inf takes Seelbach, barracks just NW of Siegen, and Weidenau; 121st seizes Eschenbach and Lutzel; 28th reaches Erndetebrueck. On left flank of corps, 97th Div completes relief of 78th Div and takes command of its sector along S bank of the Sieg. In III Corps area, TF Birks of 9th Div continues northward, clearing several towns, and at 1930 is dissolved. Siedlinghausen falls to 39th Inf. 60th Inf takes a number of terrain features NE of Oberkirchen. CCB, 7th Armd Div, reaches Gleidorf; CCR moves forward to Oberkirchen area. 99th Div overruns Ober Fleckenberg and Wingeshausen and commanding ground near these towns. In VII Corps area, 3d Armd Div meets determined opposition, particularly on left, as it approaches the Weser. 104th Div (−) completes assembly on right flank of corps and relief of V Corps elements within its zone; moves eastward toward the Weser to right of 3d Armd Div. 4th Cav Gp is detached from 104th Div. 16th Inf, 1st Div, displaces to forward assembly area. In V Corps area, 2d Div reaches the Weser and secures bridgehead. From Hofgeismar, RCT 23 drives to W bank in Veckerhagen-Vaake area, where it is relieved by 38th Inf, and at 1930 begins unopposed crossing in assault boats at Veckerhagen. RCT 9 clears wooded heights along W bank of the Weser to right. On 69th Div left flank, RCT 273 closes in on Hann Muenden, at junction of Werra, Weser, and Fulda Rivers, elements reaching the Werra at Laubach. RCT 272 is approaching the Weser to right.

In U.S. Third Army's XX Corps area, 6th Armd Div's mission is concluded as Langensalza, under assault by elements of CCA and VIII Corps' 65th Div, capitulates. 86th Div begins move from Kassel area to Gotha. RCT 385, 76th Div, reaches the Werra, capturing Grossalmerode, Trubenhausen, and Bad Sooden; crosses the Wehre at Niederhone to reach Eschwege area. RCT 304 speeds E from the Wehre by motor to vicinity of Schonstedt. 3d Cav Gp assembles S of Kassel when boundary change places it within V Corps zone. In VIII Corps area, 65th Div completes capture of Langensalza by 0745 and is disposed along restraining line Muhlhausen–Langensalza before noon. 353d Inf, 89th Div, overcomes strong opposition at Eisenach; 354th moves around 353d to vicinity of Waltershausen; RCT 355 reverts to div and moves to Ohrdruf area to screen right flank of div. 4th Armd Div remains in Gotha-Ohrdruf area. 87th Div moves forward on right flank of corps and relieves 90th Div and elements of 328th Inf, 26th Div, of XII Corps. In XII Corps area, 357th and 358th Regts, 90th Div, upon relief N of the Werra, assemble S of the river; 359th joins 26th Div, to which it is attached with mission of relieving 11th Armd Div in Zella Mehlis–Oberhof area. 11th Armd Div is ordered to secure assembly area along line Schleusingen–Hildburghausen in preparation for drive on Bayreuth. 26th Div, continuing E, relieves 11th Armd Div and establishes outposts near Themar. 71st Div closes in Fulda area and relieves 2d Cav Gp of task of screening right flank of corps from there eastward.

6th Army Group: XV Corps continues rapid northeastward advance. CCB and CCR columns of 14th Armd Div fan out on right flank. CCA continues toward Neustadt. In XXI Corps area, 42d Div troops and CCA, 12th Armd Div, drive NE toward Schweinfurt. CCB crosses the Main at Kitzingen and in conjunction with CCR to right overruns Markbreit, Obernbreit, and Mainbernheim, completing its mission. CCR also attains its objective upon reaching Iphofen and Einersheim. 8th Inf, 4th Div, mops up in Main bend N of Ochsenfurt. 22d and 12th Regts clear Koenigshofen area and start SE abreast toward Bad Mergentheim. Corps prepares to pivot SE about 4th Div. In VI Corps area, 100th Div continues struggle for Heilbronn, where assault forces, without aid of armor, inch forward in NE and W portions of the city. 398th Inf (−) is firmly opposed near Jagstfeld while attempting to expand Offenau bridgehead S toward Heilbronn. 253d Inf, on right flank of 63d Div, withstands strong pressure along the Jagst and completes capture of Moeckmuehl. 254th and 255th Regts mop up on N flank between Bad Mergentheim and Berlichingen. While CCR, 10th Armd Div, blocks on left flank of corps, repelling counterattack in Roth area, CCA speeds SE, forward elements reaching Crailsheim area. Enemy infiltrates across MSR between Bad Mergentheim and Crailsheim, night 6-7. Corps releases CCB to 10th Armd Div.

In Fr 1st Army's 2d Corps area, elements of 5th Armd Div assisting 3d Algerian Inf Div on left flank of corps reach the Neckar at Lauffen. 3d Algerian begins to clear Stromberg Forest. 2d Moroccan Inf Div, reinf by elements of 5th Armd Div, reached Enz R at Muehlacker on left, N outskirts of Pforzheim in center, and clears Stein and Koenigsbach on right. Valluy Groupement continues clearing fortified region about Karlsruhe, taking Durlach.

EASTERN EUROPE—Some elements of Second Ukrainian Front clearing region N of the Danube reach Morava R line NE of Vienna on 37-mile front while others to S close in on Vienna from the E. Troops of Third Ukrainian Front are clearing southern suburbs of Vienna.

ITALY—15th Army Group: In U.S. Fifth Army area, 92d Div continues attack toward Massa with 442d Inf, enemy fire preventing 370th from jumping off. 442d takes M. Cerreta and begins attack on M. Belvedere.

In Br Eighth Army's 5 Corps area, 56th Div expands its bridgehead across the Reno.

LUZON—In U.S. Sixth Army's Legaspi sector, 1st Bn of 158th Inf continues southward along ridge to trail running W from Daraga, about a mile S of Busay. 2d Bn reaches Route 160, which extends from Legaspi to Daraga. AT Co, reinf, in shore-to-shore operation to clear Sorsogon Province, moves from Legaspi to Bacon, where Bicol Peninsula is but 5 miles wide, and lands unopposed; drives overland to Sorsogon. In I Corps area, on Highway 9, Co G of 129th Inf, under 33d Div control, becomes isolated from main body of 2d Bn while executing envelopment maneuver in Salat area. 126th Inf, 32d Div, moving eastward to N of 128th, reaches Salacsac Pass area and takes Hill 519. 25th Div, astride Highway 5, continues pressure toward Kapintalan. In XI Corps area, 2d Bn of 63d Inf, 6th Div, opens assault on Mt Mataba after preparatory arty fire. 20th Inf, whose relief by 63d is completed, probes toward Mt Oro and Mt Pacawagan. 103d Inf column of 43d Div, driving along shore of Laguna de Bay, makes contact with Tr B of 5th Cav, 1st Cav Div (XIV Corps), at Santa Cruz, giving Sixth Army a solid front in S Luzon. In XIV Corps area, elements of 1st Cav and 11th A/B Divs are fighting in foothills at N and W approaches of Mt Malepunyo hill mass. 7th Cav holds Mapait Hills and elements reach Onipa R. 187th Inf, with 3d Bn of 511th attached, drives NE from Talisay toward Malarya Hill and Sulac.

S PHILIPPINES—In U.S. Eighth Army's Sulu Archipelago area, 41st Div detachment, having cleared Bongao I. with ease, returns to Sanga Sanga I.

RYUKYU Is.—Japanese make belated but all-out air effort against shipping and Okinawa beaches. Of some 400 planes involved, about three fourths are destroyed. Kamikazes sink 2 DD's, a mine sweeper, 2 ammunition ships, and an LST; damage other shipping. Preinvasion air strikes against Ie Shima are intensified.

In U.S. Tenth Army's III Amphib Corps area, 6th Mar Div, passing 4th and 29th Marines through 22d Marines, continues up Ishikawa Isthmus to line across it extending eastward from Chuda. In XXIV Corps area, troops of 383d Inf, 96th Div, clear half of Cactus Ridge in the course of hard fighting. 382d moves forward in region E of Ginowan road. On 7th Div right flank, 184th Inf, with close fire support and flame throwers, overruns elaborate outpost position on pinnacle some 1,000 yards SW of Arakachi. 32d Inf advances in coastal sector with little difficulty.

PACIFIC—U.S. Army Forces in the Pacific (AFPAC) is established under Gen MacArthur, with headquarters in Manila. The new command includes forces formerly assigned to U.S. Army Forces in the Far East and of U.S. Army Forces in POA.

7 April

WESTERN EUROPE—21 Army Group: In Br Second Army's 8 Corps area, 6th A/B Div and 11th Armd Div establish bridgeheads across the Weser at Minden and Stolzenau, respectively, and drive toward the next river line, the Leine.

12th Army Group: In U.S. Ninth Army's XIII Corps area, 84th Div completes its crossing of the Weser and expands bridgehead substantially. 102d Div continues eastward, clearing scattered pockets. 11th Cav Gp is given mission of screening N flank of corps from the Weser to the Leine. In XIX Corps area, 2d Armd Div, ordered to halt upon reaching general line of Sarstedt-Hildesheim road, attains objective and suspends offensive operations. 83d Div clears its zone W of the Weser except for small portion in Polle area and makes rapid progress E of the Weser. 330th Inf rejoins div. Continuing operations against Ruhr pocket, 95th Div's 377th Inf finishes clearing Soest by 0730 and attacks toward Werl until pinched out; 379th pushes into Werl; 378th finishes clearing Hamin and several suburbs. TF Twaddle (Maj Gen Harry L. Twaddle, 95th Div CG) is formed to complete action against Ruhr pocket in conjunction with XVI Corps. The TF consists of 8th Armd and 95th Inf Divs plus their attachments and supporting forces. TF Twaddle organizes TF Faith, under Brig Gen Don C. Faith, composed of 377th Inf, 194th Gli Inf, and supporting units, and gives it mission of clearing region between Ruhr and Mohne Rivers, protecting left flank of TF Twaddle, and maintaining contact with friendly forces on left. CCB columns, 8th Armd Div, drive on Werl in afternoon, reaching West Onnen and positions near Gerlingen. CCA clears and holds sector along Mohne R SE of Soest. CCR starts from Lippstadt to Soest area. In XVI Corps area, 75th Div continues S toward Ruhr R in center and right of its zone, 290th Inf seizing Frohlinde and Kirchline and 291st clearing most of Castrop Rauxel. On left flank, extending N to Lippe R, 320th Inf replaces 116th, which rejoins 29th Div in army reserve. 79th Div attacks S across Emscher and Rhein-Herne Canals in region between Gelsenkirchen and Essen at 0300, with 313th Inf on left and 315th on right, and drives salient to railway at Katernburg. 35th Div expands positions along Rhein-Herne Canal eastward. 17th A/B Div maintains defensive positions along right flank of corps.

In U.S. First Army area, XVIII Corps (A/B) attack broadens as 97th Div goes on the offensive for the first time, committing its right flank regt, 386th, in assault on Ruhr pocket after arty preparation. Crossing the Sieg in assault boats, 386th gains up to 4,000 yards against light resistance and maintains contact with 78th Div to right. 78th Div, despite well-defended enemy strongpoints, gains up to 5,000 yards. 8th Div advances about 4,000 yards and withstands counterattacks against Seelbach on left. 86th Div, less RCT 341, completes assembly in corps zone. In III Corps area, 9th Div drives rapidly W on right flank, where 47th Inf, becoming a part of reformed TF Birks, clears Gevelinghausen, Esshoff, Nuttlar, Ostwig, Bestwig, and Heringhausen. 39th Inf seizes Altenfeld, Elpe, and Heinrichsdorf while 60th moves forward in wooded region N of Oberkirchen and clears Rehsiepen, Ober Sorpe, and Mittel Sorpe. CCB, 7th Armd Div, hurls back counterattacks against Gleidorf; assisted by air and arty, overcomes lively opposition in Schmallenberg. CCR, attacking on div right flank, envelops and captures Holthausen. CCA reverts to div. In 99th Div zone, 394th Inf gains about 5,000 yards in region W of Schmallenberg; 393d overcomes resistance in Oberhundem. 28th Div, performing security mission, is detached from corps at 2400 and passes to command of First Army. In VII Corps area, 3d Armd Div closes along the Weser and finds all bridges down. 1st Div prepares to force the river on left flank of corps. At 1400, TF Taylor is formed—consisting of

[7 APRIL 1945]

RCT 26 (− 1st Bn), 1st Div, and reinf 4th Cav Gp, under Brig. Gen. George A. Taylor—to secure region E of Ruhr pocket between XIX and III Corps and maintain contact with adjacent friendly forces. The task force operates under corps command. 104th Div, less 414th Inf, drives to the Weser on right flank of corps and gets elements across it. With TF Laundon (104th Rcn Tr, reinf) spearheading, 413th and 415th Regts reach the river in vicinity of Gieselwerder and Bursfelde respectively. 1st Bn, 415th, crosses in Bursfelde area while 3d Bn moves S and crosses in V Corps zone. In V Corps area, 2d Div continues movement across the Weser at Veckerhagen and expands bridgehead toward Dransfeld. Supporting vehicles cross upon completion of treadway bridge. Aided by arty, air, and armor, 69th Div reaches the Werra from Hann Muenden to Witzenhausen, establishes bridgeheads, and makes contact with 2d Div on left. RCT 273 captures Hann Muenden; crosses there and at Laubach to clear Altmuenden, Lippoldshausen, Wiershausen, and commanding ground NE of Hann Muenden; moves elements along S bank to Oberode. RCT 272 reaches Witzenhausen just as enemy blows bridges; starts crossing in assault boats while engineers construct ponton bridge.

In U.S. Third Army's XX Corps area, 6th Armd Div, less CCR, defends current positions in Muhlhausen area. CCR, assisted by 3d Bn, 304th Inf, moves NW to help 76th Div, eliminating enemy forces falling back from the Werra toward Muhlhausen. RCT 417, 76th Div, continues mopping up W of the Werra, reaching Bad Sooden area; from Eschwege area RCT 385 pushes N along E side of Wehre R toward Allendorf and Volkerode; RCT 304 reaches line from vicinity of Klettstedt to Graefentonna area, E of Langensalza. 80th Div concentrates in Gotha area and relieves elements of 4th Armd Div. In VIII Corps area, enemy counterattack overruns 3d Bn of 261st Inf, 65th Div, in Struth, but situation is restored with assistance of elements of XX Corps and aircraft. Elements of 65th Div relieve 87th Div forces at Gerstungen. 353d Inf, 89th Div, clears region SE of Eisenach to line Wutha-Ruhla; 354th drives S across right front of div, entering Friedrichroda; 355th screens div right from Seebergen to Woelfig. 87th Div drives quickly E on right flank of corps with 2 regts abreast: 345th reaches Tanbach area; 347th reaches Oberhof, where it establishes contact with 11th Armd Div (XII Corps) and repels counterattack, night 7-8. 6th Cav Gp moves some elements to Eschwege area to protect left flank of corps and others to Eisenach to maintain order. In XII Corps area, 11th Armd Div starts clearing assembly zone in preparation for drive on Bayreuth. 26th Div, disposed in Meiningen-Suhl region, mops up southward toward Themar and Schleusingen, both of which fall to 11th Armd Div. RCT 14, 71st Div, closes in Kaltensundheim area, where it protects right flank of corps. Elements of 2d Cav Gp screen line Bettenhausen-Meiningen until uncovered by 106th Cav Gp of Seventh Army.

6th Army Group: In U.S. Seventh Army's XV Corps area, CCA of 14th Armd Div takes Neustadt, on Saale R, with ease but right flank forces are slowed by strong resistance. In XXI Corps area, 42d Div is given task of capturing Schweinfurt, ball-bearing center, and is reinf by CCA, 12th Armd Div. Continuing NE, div gains 8-10 miles; right flank elements establish bridgehead E of the Main at Volkach. 22d and 12th Regts, 4th Div, continue SE on right flank of corps against scattered resistance: 22d Inf clears Bad Mergentheim while 12th Inf drives to Tauber R line. In VI Corps area, 100th Div slowly expands its positions in Heilbronn: 398th Inf commits 1st Bn to assist 2d in Offenau bridgehead. Since frontal attacks against Hardehauser Wald have failed, 63d Div begins enveloping maneuver: while 253d Inf continues E, 3d Bn of 255th establishes bridgehead across the Jagst at Widdern to block on E and eventually join 253d Inf at Lampoldhausen. 255th (−) and 254th Regts clear a number of towns astride the Jagst to NE. CCA, 10th Armd Div, captures Crailsheim; elements drive W in effort to attack Heilbronn from rear and effect junction with 100th Div, thereby pocketing enemy opposing 63d Div. CCB rejoins div and starts SE toward Bad Mergentheim-Crailsheim highway. RCT 324, 44th Div, is directed to move to VI Corps zone.

EASTERN EUROPE—Elements of Third Ukrainian Front break into S part of Vienna, where street fighting ensues.

ITALY—15th Army Group: In U.S. Fifth Army area, 442d Inf of 92d Div clears M. Belvedere after hard fighting. 2d Bn, 473d Inf, is committed to left, where enemy guns continue to hold up advance. Strettoia, E of Highway 1, is being bypassed.

In Br Eighth Army's 5 Corps area, 56th Div expands Reno bridgehead to Fossa di Navigazione.

LUZON—In U.S. Sixth Army area, RCT 158 continues efforts to extend control over Legaspi area. Airstrip at Legaspi becomes operational. In I Corps area, Gen Krueger, to speed operations in the N, releases rest of 37th Div, less 145th Inf, to corps. In 33d Div sector, Co G, 129th Inf, is still isolated in Salat area. On Villa Verde Trail, elements of 126th Inf, 32d Div, capture Hill 518 in Salacsac Pass area. 128th Inf, with air and arty support, launches general assault against Japanese hill positions in this region. 25th Div columns astride Highway 5 are enveloping Kapintalan. In XI Corps area, Baldy Force begins reconnaissance in force toward Ipo Dam. XIV Corps is directed to seize E coast towns of Mauban and Atimonan, on Lamon Bay, and prepare for advance SE into the Bicols. Elements continue pressure toward Mt Malepunyo. 187th Gli Inf, 11th A/B Div, seizes Malarya Hill. Elements of 188th Inf move E through Candelaria to establish contact with Filipino guerrillas moving W through Sariaya.

S PHILIPPINES—In U.S. Eighth Army area, rest of 2d Bn, 108th Inf, arrives on Masbate. On Cebu, 3d Bn of 132d Inf advances 1,000 yards NW from vicinity of Hill 27 toward Hill 26 but withdraws under counterattack. On Negros, Para RCT 503 arrives at Pulupandan.

BATTLE OF EAST CHINA SEA—Japanese fleet units heading toward Okinawa are intercepted by planes of TF 58, which sink BB *Yamato*, CL *Yahagi*, and 4 DD's and damage 2 other DD's. Kamikaze plane damages USS *Hancock*, but TF 58 shoots down 54 aircraft for loss of 10.

RYUKYU IS.—In U.S. Tenth Army area, fighter aircraft arrive on Okinawa. Amphib Rcn Bn, FMF Pac, completes reconnaissance of Eastern Islands, finding enemy on but one. In III Amphib Corps area, 6th Mar Div reaches line Nago-Taira, at base of Motobu Peninsula, and begins reconnaissance of the peninsula. In XXIV Corps area, 383d Inf of 96th Div completes capture of Cactus Ridge while 382d advances in region E of Ginowan road. 184th Inf makes main effort of 7th Div. After unsuccessful frontal assaults on hill 1,000 yards W of Minami-Uebaru, elements of 184th take this strong enemy outpost in enveloping maneuver.

8 April

WESTERN EUROPE—21 Army Group: In Cdn First Army's Cdn 2 Corps area, Cdn 4th Armd Div, driving NE toward Oldenburg, crosses Ems R in Meppen-Lathen area. Cdn 3d Div takes Zutphen and thrusts toward Deventer. Pol 1st Armd Div is released to corps and is moving to corps zone.

In Br Second Army's 30 Corps area, Gds Armd Div, overcoming sharp resistance E of Lingen, continues NE toward Bremen. In 12 Corps area, 7th Armd Div is rapidly approaching the Weser. 8 Corps reaches the Leine SE of Nienburg.

12th Army Group: In U.S. Ninth Army area, 29th Div, in army reserve, takes responsibility for security of rear area in large sector extending from the Rhine to Dortmund-Ems Canal initially and gradually extending eastward. In XIII Corps area, 84th Div gains bridgehead objectives and on the N reaches the Leine. 334th Inf takes bridge over the Leine near Guemmer. 333d takes up defensive positions about Weetzen. CCR of 5th Armd Div, ordered to secure Leine R crossing S of Hannover and block enemy escape, moves S into XIX Corps zone to cross the Weser at Hameln, then returns to XIII Corps zone. CCB garrisons Minden and CCA remains in Herford area. 102d Div continues to mop up W of the Weser. 11th Cav Gp crosses the Weser and screens N flank of corps to the Leine. In XIX Corps area, 2d Armd Div improves defensive positions in limited attacks and regroups for future action. 30th Div continues to follow armor eastward. 83d Div continues E on right flank of corps, crossing the Leine at several points in Alfeld-Greene area, and reaches assigned objective, line Gandersheim-Westfeld, S of Hildesheim. 331st Inf starts across the Weser, 3d Bn crossing at Heinsen and clearing Bevern. TF Twaddle continues operations against Ruhr pocket. TF Faith clears region between Mohne and Ruhr Rivers E of line Allengen-Hirschberg-Meschede. CCB, 8th Armd Div, drives W through Werl and captures Ost Buederich. CCR clears westward toward Werl-Wickede road. 95th Div continues W in region between Hamm and Unna-Soest rail line, clearing numerous towns. In XVI Corps area, 75th Div, with effective air and arty support, completes capture of Castrop Rauxel and drives to edge of Luetgendortmund. 79th Div expands bridgehead S of Rhein-Herne Canal beyond Schonnebeck. 17th A/B Div moves elements of 507th Para Inf across the canal to protect exposed right flank of 79th Div by clearing to Berne Canal.

In U.S. First Army's XVIII Corps (A/B) area, 386th Inf of 97th Div expands Sieg bridgehead northward; 1st Bn of 387th, to its left, attacks across the Sieg, broadening bridgehead westward. Forward elements of 78th Div seize Waldbrol, Lichtenberg, and Freudenberg. 8th Div makes substantial gains, especially on right, where resistance is light and 28th Inf reaches Wurdinghausen-Rinsecke region, well ahead of main body. 86th Div prepares to attack on right flank of corps. 13th Armd Div starts from Homberg area to join in operations against Ruhr pocket. In III Corps area, TF Birks of 9th Div continues W, overrunning Velmede, Halbeswig, and Wehrstapel, and begins to clear Meschede; 39th Inf takes Ramsbeck, Werden, Westernboedefeld, and Boedefeld; 60th secures terrain features NE and N of Fredeburg. CCB, 7th Armd Div, clears Obringhausen and provides fire support for attack of CCR on Fredeburg; in vigorous, day-long fighting, CCR clears most of Fredeburg. 99th Div's 394th Inf, co-ordinating closely with 7th Armd Div, clears Wormbach, Felbecke, Selkentrop, Werntrop, and part of Saalhausen; 393d takes Selbecke and reduces bypassed resistance W of Milchenbach. 5th Div, less 11th Inf, is attached to corps. VII Corps establishes firm infantry bridgehead across the Weser and prepares to pass armor through it. On left flank, 1st Div crosses 18th Inf in Beverungen area and 16th Inf

[8 APRIL 1945]

in Wehrden area and gains bridgehead including Fuerstenberg, Derenthal, Meinbrexen, and Lauenfoerde. To right, 104th Div expands and strengthens Weser bridgehead: 413th Inf crosses at Gieselwerder, starting at 0400; 415th completes crossing on div right. CCR, 3d Armd Div, crosses at Gieselwerder and assembles in Imbsen area. TF Taylor, no longer required for defensive mission along Ruhr pocket, is dissolved. In V Corps area, 2d Div completes its crossing of the Weser and drives rapidly E about 10 miles: on left, 23d Inf clears Gottingen and continues SE; 9th Inf thrusts through Reinhausen into Forst Reinhausen; 38th Inf gets into position to protect left flank E of the Weser. On 69th Div left flank, RCT 273 mops up in Hann Muenden area; RCT 272, to right, completes crossing the Werra, drives to Leine R in Nieder Gandern-Hohengandern sector, and establishes bridgehead; RCT 271 (−) is moving forward to relieve RCT 273. 9th Armd Div starts to assembly area E of the Weser.

In U.S. Third Army's XX Corps area, RCT 417 of 76th Div moves to defensive positions E of Eschwege. RCT 385 and CCR, 6th Armd Div, continue to clear region N and NE of Eschwege. RCT 385 reaches Allendorf and Volkerode and relieves elements of CCR at Volkerode. RCT 304 holds line E of Langensalza and extends it NW, uncovering part of zone of CCA, 6th Armd Div. 80th Div, leaving 319th Inf at Gotha to maintain order, starts E toward Erfurt with 317th Inf on left and 318th on right. In VIII Corps area, 65th Div, whose zone on left flank of corps is being uncovered by XX Corps, passes into reserve. 89th and 87th Divs continue clearing Thuringer Wald against scattered but determined opposition. 6th Cav Gp assembles in reserve in Thal-Seebach area. 4th Armd Div, upon relief by 89th Div and XX Corps' 80th Div, assembles in Gotha area. XII Corps finishes clearing to line of departure from which to attack SE in force. On left flank, 90th Div (−) moves to Thuringer Wald, where it takes over Zella Mehlis sector and, with 359th and 358th Regts in assault—359th reverting to it from attachment to 26th Div—clears eastward to vicinity of Gehlberg on left and Stutzenbach on right. Clearing Thuringer Wald to right of 90th Div, 26th Div's 328th and 101st Regts reach Nahe R line from Schmiedefeld to Rappelsdorf and establish contact with CCA of 11th Armd Div at Rappelsdorf. 11th Armd Div completes occupation of its assembly area. 71st Div clears to general line Meiningen-Marisfeld-Juchsen. 42d Sq, 2d Cav Gp, pushes SE on right flank of corps to Juchsen-Nordheim area.

6th Army Group: In U.S. Seventh Army area, XV Corps continues attack in Hohe Rhon hills with infantrymen of 3d and 45th Divs. 3d Div is reinf by CCB of 14th Armd Div. CCA and CCR, 14th Armd Div, assemble. 44th Div is transferred to VI Corps. In XXI Corps area, 42d Div meets strong opposition from outer defenses of Schweinfurt: on left, 232d Inf drives to line Alt Bessingen-Schwebenried; in center, CCA, 12th Armd Div, and 242d Inf units reach Werneck and Ettleben; on right, 222d Inf maintains Volkach bridgehead and positions W of the Main. 12th Armd Div begins reconnaissance in force to SE, employing 92d Cav Rcn Sq on left and 101st Cav Gp on right. 22d and 12th Regts, 4th Div, patrol actively SE on right flank of corps. In VI Corps area, 100th Div continues bitter street fighting in Heilbronn and crosses reinforcements into bridgehead there. To N, 398th Inf is still strongly opposed in Jagstfeld area as it attempts to expand Offenau bridgehead to Odheim. 63d Div pushes S on left flank of corps to clear region between Jagst and Kocher Rivers. 10th Armd Div alters plan of attack, heading NW from Crailsheim area toward 63d Div rather than due W toward 100th Div. Germans are offering strong opposition in vicinity of Crailsheim. RCT 324, 44th Div, is attached to 10th Armd Div.

In Fr 1st Army's 2d Corps area, 3d Algerian Inf Div finishes clearing its zone W of the Neckar as far S as the Enz at Bissingen. Groupements Schlesser and Navarre overrun Pforzheim and, in conjunction with Valluy Groupement, clear Dietenhausen, Ellmendingen, and Diedingen to W. 2d Moroccan Inf Div gains further ground N of the Enz and establishes bridgehead S of the river in vicinity of Muehlhausen.

EASTERN EUROPE—Soviet forces of Third White Russian Front begin all-out assault on Koenigsberg (East Prussia), having broken through outer defenses from NW and S. Elimination of German garrison oaf Breslau (Silesia) continues. Second Ukrainian Front pushes right flank elements northward in Czechoslovakia toward Moravian frontier and to left establishes bridgeheads across Morava and Danube Rivers E and NE of Vienna. Troops of Third Ukrainian Front gain ground in S and W Vienna; some elements bypass the city and head W toward Linz while others speed southward from Wiener Neustadt area toward Graz.

ITALY—15th Army Group: In U.S. Fifth Army area, 473d Inf replaces 370th in coastal sector and continues attack up Highway 1 while 370th moves to Serchio Valley positions previously occupied by 473d Inf.

CHINA—Strong Japanese patrols begin probing Chinese outpost positions W of Paoching in preparation for drive on Chihchiang.

LUZON—In U.S. Sixth Army area, patrols of AT Co, RCT 158, reach Bulan, on W coast of Bicol Peninsula. In I Corps area, Gen Swift orders drive on Baguio hastened. 37th Div is to make main effort along Highway 9 while 33d Div is opening other routes, among them Galiano-Baguio and Kennon roads. 123d Inf has elements beyond Galiano, on the crude Pugo-Baguio trail, and on Mt Calugong, about 5 ½ miles SW of Baguio. 129th Inf is still held up in Salat area of Naguilian-Baguio highway. 136th Inf reaches positions about midway between Rosario and Baguio on Kennon road. Along Villa Verde Trail, 32d Div troops continue battle for Salacsac Pass, the saddle between Hills 504 and 505. On Highway 5, 161st Inf, 25th Div, reaches W slope of Crump Hill, about 1,000 yards W of Kapintalan, and pauses until 35th Inf can clear Kapintalan. In XI Corps area, air and arty fire saturates Mt Mataba as 63d Inf, 6th Div, prepares to renew ground assault. 43d Div mops up and patrols extensively. In XIV Corps area, some elements of corps probe eastward toward Lamon Bay; others maintain pressure on Mt Malepunyo. 187th Inf, 11th A/B Div, occupies Sulac, in W foothills of Mt Mataasna Bundoc.

S PHILIPPINES—In U.S. Eighth Army area, 3d Bn of 132d Inf takes ridge 2,000 yards NW of Hill 27 on Cebu and holds it against night counterattack. Co E, 182d Inf, and guerrillas move against Hill 20, between the Reservoir and Race Course. On Negros, 3-regt assault is ordered to prevent enemy from improving positions in mountainous interior. Enemy positions are pounded by aircraft.

OKINAWA—In U.S. Tenth Army's III Amphib Corps area, battle for Motobu Peninsula begins as columns of 29th Marines, 6th Mar Div, move forward to fix enemy positions. In XXIV Corps area, 383d Inf of 96th Div, with air, arty, and naval gunfire support, presses toward Kakazu Ridge and makes unsuccessful attacks on its approaches. Japanese employ spigot mortar fire for the first time. 382d Inf is virtually halted since friendly forces on its flanks cannot advance. 184th Inf, 7th Div, attacks toward 2 strongpoints—Tomb Hill, 1,000 yards NW of Ouki, and Triangulation Hill, 1,000 yards NW of Tomb Hill–taking the latter. 32d Inf continues to gain ground on E in coastal sector.

9 April

WESTERN EUROPE—RAF BC sinks *Admiral Scheer* during attack on Kiel, night 9-10.

21 Army Group: In Br Second Army area, 30 Corps advances E and NE of Lingen, Gds Armd Div reaching positions beyond Fuerstenau and 43d Div crossing Hase R. 3d Div passes to 12 Corps command. In 12 Corps area, 7th Armd Div reaches the Weser in Hoya area and establishes bridgehead. 8 Corps crosses Leine R, making contact with U.S. forces to right, and starts toward Aller R at Celle.

12th Army Group: In U.S. Ninth Army's XIII Corps area, 84th Div gets into position for assault on Hannover from N, NW, and W. CCR, 5th Armd Div, crosses the Leine S of Hannover and drives rapidly toward line Uetze-Peine en route to Oker R, cutting autobahn near Vohrum. CCA, directed toward line Celle-Uetze and thence to the Aller R, moves to Hameln to cross the Weser. Congestion there, where 102d Div is also crossing, delays CCA, which is ordered to attack instead in S portion of corps zone. 407th Inf, 102d Div, motors to new assembly areas and begins clearing Obernkirchen region, E of the Weser. XIX Corps is relieved of responsibility for Ruhr pocket by XVI Corps, which takes command of TF Twaddle, and prepares to renew eastward drive. XVI Corps, now commanding all Ninth Army forces operating against the Ruhr, further compresses the pocket. 75th Div, closely supported by aircraft and arty, presses S: 290th Inf takes Dorstfeld, at W edge of Dortmund; 289th clears Luetgendortmund; 291st blocks roads on right flank of div. 35th Div, less 320th Inf, drives S across Rhein-Herne Canal to positions N and E of Gelsenkirchen. 79th Div, continuing S with 3 regts—314th passing through elements of 315th and 313th—overruns Kray, Frillendorf, and Steele to reach the Ruhr and split enemy forces; prepares to drive E toward Dortmund. 507th Para Inf, 17th A/B Div, protecting right flank of 79th Div, reaches Berne Canal, its objective. TF Twaddle continues W toward Unna and Kamen. 8th Armd Div's CCB takes Holtum, Hemmerde, Westhemmerde, and Stockum; CCR continues W along N bank of the Ruhr; CCA holds Mohne R sector. 378th and 379th Regts, 95th Div, gain ground toward Kamen. TF Faith is rapidly clearing region between the Mohne and the Ruhr and makes contact with First Army on left.

In U.S. First Army's XVIII Corps (A/B) area, 97th Div further expands and strengthens bridgehead N of the Sieg on left flank of corps, crossing rest of 387th Inf into it at dawn and 303d Inf at 1800. 303d opens assault on Siegburg and clears about two thirds of the city. 386th Inf, on right flank, mops up bypassed pockets. 78th Div, committing 311th Inf between 309th and 310th, moves northward on broad front, reaching positions near Nuembrecht and Oberwiehl on left, Denklingen-Erdingen region in center, and Bueschergrund on right. 8th Div's zone is narrowed as 86th Div takes over right flank from 28th Inf. Continuing NW with 13th and 121st Regts, 8th Div reaches Olpe-Rahrbach region, a gain of 5-10 miles. 86th Div begins attack on right flank of corps with 342d Inf, which advances northward in narrow zone to Hotolpe-Altenhundem area. 341st Inf reverts to div from attachment to 97th Div. Corps prepares for double envelopment of the Ruhr pocket S of the Ruhr: 13th Armd Div, which is attached to corps, is to constitute left prong of pincers after debouching through 97th Div's bridgehead. 8th and 86th Divs are to form the right prong. 78th Div will maintain direct pressure in center. In III Corps area, 5th Div, less 11th Inf, closes in Olsberg area and attacks W with RCT 10 through TF Birks, 9th Div; 32d Cav Sq protects left flank. TF Birks finishes clearing Meschede and is dissolved. 39th Inf continues NW against light resistance, clearing Berlar on right. Altenilpe and Ober Henneborn fall to 60th Inf. Continuing NW with CCR on right and CCB on left, 7th Armd Div overruns numerous towns and villages and reaches general line Mailar-Ober Landenbeck-Kobbenrode. 394th Inf, 99th Div, secures Bracht and ridge to SW; 395th clears Saalhausen-Langener sector N of the Lenne; 3934 finishes clearing region S of the Lenne and crosses elements. In VII Corps area, 3d Armd Div passes through infantry bridgehead across the Weser and drives quickly toward Nordhausen. On left, CCR reaches Northeim and Levershausen area. CCB reaches Leine R north of Gottingen and bridge construction is begun. CCA, in reserve, crosses the Weser and follows CCR. 1st Div completes its crossing of the Weser and with 16th and 18th Regts expands bridgehead eastward; 26th Inf, motorized, attacks through 16th toward Einbeck: 4th Cav Gp is attached to 1st Div. 104th Div follows 3d Armd Div closely and makes contact with 1st Div S of Uslar; right flank elements take Barterode and drive toward Bovenden. In V Corps area, 9th Armd Div prepares to attack E through 2d and 69th Divs and is reinf by motorized elements of 38th Inf, 2d Div, and of 273d Inf, 69th Div. 2d and 69th Divs continue E against light resistance.

In U.S Third Army's XX Corps area, 3d Cav Gp relieves RCT 385 of 76th Div and, in conjunction with elements of CCR of 6th Armd Div, attached to 76th Div, finishes clearing N flank of corps. RCT 385 motors to right flank of 76th Div SE of Langensalza and clears Doellstaedt, Grossfahner, Gierstadt, and Kleinfahner. 80th Div continues toward Erfurt. CCB defends N flank of 6th Armd Div and clears Toba; CCA zone on right is completely uncovered by advance of friendly forces. In VIII Corps area, 89th and 87th Divs continue attack abreast, reaching positions generally along corps restraining line; are ordered to make limited attacks eastward from there on 10th. 3534 Inf finishes clearing 89th Div left flank; 354th, reinf by bn of 355th, clears Georgenthal and Finsterbergen; 355th continues to protect right flank of div and overruns Grafenhain. Continuing E with 345th and 347th Regts, 87th Div reaches vicinity of Stutzhaus on left and takes high ground E of Oberhof on right; 346th Inf moves elements NE to protect N flank of div and maintain contact with 89th Div. 4th Armd Div is transferred to XX Corps. XII Corps improves positions in limited action and prepares to renew offensive on 10th.

6th Army Group: In U.S. Seventh Army's XV Corps area, 45th and 3d Divs gain corps objectives in Hohe Rhon hill mass and corps prepares to drive SE on Nuremberg. In XXI Corps area, 42d Div, despite close air support, meets increasingly strong resistance as it closes in on Schweinfurt. 12th Armd Div—less CCA, which is assisting 42d Div—reconnoiters SE. 4th Div activity is limited to patrolling on right flank of corps. In VI Corps area, 100th Div continues efforts to join N and S bridgeheads in Heilbronn. 398th Inf is still stubbornly opposed in Jagstfeld area as it attempts to expand Offenau bridgehead. On right flank of 63d Div, elements of 255th Inf driving SW in Hardehauser Wald and 253d Inf pushing E join forces and finish clearing the woods, reaching N bank of Kocher R to S. 255th Inf (—) reaches the Kocher at Weissbach and establishes bridgehead. 254th, to left, reaches line Ingelfelden-Weldingsfeld and reconnoiters toward 10th Armd Div sector. 10th Armd Div, assisted by RCT 324 of 44th Div, withstands strong enemy pressure against Crailsheim and MSR between there and Bad Mergentheim.

In Fr 1st Army area, 2d Corps expands Enz bridgehead and to the W gains ground in spurs of Black Mountains SE of Ettlingen. Valluy Groupement, now reinf by CC2 of 1st Armd Div, gains ground in region S of Ettlingen.

EASTERN EUROPE—Organized resistance in East Prussia virtually ends as Koenigsberg fortress falls to troops of Third White Russian Front and Germans fall back to Samland Peninsula. Other Soviet forces are steadily extending control over Vienna.

ITALY—15th Army Group: In U.S. Fifth Army area, 92d Div pushes forward to outskirts of Massa, its first objective. In IV Corps area, 371st Inf is attached to corps in place and boundary between IV and II Corps is altered accordingly. 371st takes over left sector of 1st Div, BEF, on M. Belvedere, permitting Brazilians to shift NE and reduce sector of 10th Mtn Div.

Br Eighth Army opens final offensive in Italy, attacking in evening with Pol 2 and Br 5 Corps, latter making main effort, after air preparation on an extensive scale, lasting for $1^1/2$ hours, and arty bombardment of enemy positions. Flame throwers are used along the Senio just ahead of infantry and assist materially in reducing opposition at the river banks. Pol 2 Corps attacks with 3d Carpathian Div, clearing to E bank of the Senio against strong resistance; using 5 Corps' bridge, establishes bridgehead N of Highway 9 in S. Severo-Felisio sector. In 5 Corps area, NZ 2d and Ind 8th Divs, former on left, establish bridgeheads across the Senio in Lugo area. 10 Corps, with Italian Friuli Group and Jewish Brig under its command, attacks across the Senio, night 9-10, to divert enemy from main action, establishing bridgehead in Cuffiana area by dawn. 13 Corps holds defensive positions on left flank of army.

CBI—Gen Wedemeyer meets with officers of Tenth Air Force and India-Burma Theater to discuss projected move of Tenth Air Force to China.

LUZON—In U.S. Sixth Army's Legaspi sector, RCT 158 overcomes resistance near Daraga and secures junction of Highways 1 and 160. Widespread patrolling of Sorsogon Province indicates that Japanese are now concealed in hills around San Francisco, about 5 miles NE of Bulan. In I Corps area, 37th and 33d Divs prepare for strong effort against Baguio, 148th Inf of 37th Div moving from Manila to Naguilian area. Cos E and F, 129th Inf, try in vain to reach isolated Co G on Naguilian-Baguio road. 3d Bn moves to base of mountain mass called Three Peaks in preparation for attack on Monglo. 130th Inf, 33d Div, relieves elements of 123d Inf at Galiano. 32d Div assault toward Salacsac Pass, on Villa Verde Trail, gains some ground. Elements of 27th Inf, 25th Div, finish clearing spur W of Mt Myoko, from which Japanese have been barring forward movement. In XI Corps area, air and arty continue to neutralize Mt Mataba. Elements of 38th Div that have been pushing along Sacobia R toward Mt Pinatubo have gained several thousand yards during last few days. In XIV Corps area, some elements of 1st Cav and 11th A/B Divs speed E toward the coast, establishing contact at Lucban, and others are maintaining pressure on Mt Malepunyo.

S PHILIPPINES—In U.S. Eighth Army area, Americal Div gets into position on Cebu to place enfilade fire on enemy positions in mountainous interior. RCT 164 arrives at Cebu City at night. On Negros, 40th Div begins concerted effort to eliminate enemy in mountains, employing 503d Para Inf on left, 185th Inf in center, and 160th Inf on right. 503d, driving SE from Napilas area toward Manzanares, is soon halted by enemy fire. 185th drives E toward Lantawan, gaining 6,000 yards and clearing hill position. 160th, moving NE toward Hill 3155 later called Dolan Hill, reaches its base. 2d Bn of 186th Inf, 41st Div, begins shore-to-shore operations to clear Calamian Is., N of Palawan, with unopposed landing on Busuanga I. In Sulu Archipelago, RCT 163 (less 2d Bn), 41st Div, makes unopposed landing on Jolo and begins clearing it. 2 weeks of aerial bombardment and preliminary naval bombardment by Seventh Fleet precede landing.

RYUKYU IS.—In U.S. Tenth Army's III Amphib Corps area, 29th Marines of 6th Mar Div continues to explore Motobu Peninsula in effort to develop enemy positions there. In XXIV Corps area, battle for Kakazu Ridge, key feature in enemy's Shuri defense system, starts as 2 bns of 383d Inf, 96th Div, storm up the ridge in surprise attack beginning before dawn. Under enemy fire and frequent counterattacks, the regt withdraws. Both sides suffer heavy casualties. 184th Inf, 7th Div, captures Tomb Hill with assistance of massed fire. 32d Inf continues to advance along E coast. 27th Div (− RCT 105) lands to reinforce corps.

10 April

WESTERN EUROPE—21 Army Group: In Cdn First Army's Cdn 2 Corps area, Cdn 3d Div takes Deventer and continues northward toward Leeuwarden. Cdn 2d Div drives on Groningen against scattered resistance. Cdn 4th Armd Div pushes beyond Soegel toward Oldenburg.

Br Second Army's 30 Corps continues NE toward Bremen. In 12 Corps area, 53d Div, from the Hoya bridgehead across the Weser, attacks NE toward Soltau. 8 Corps continues toward Celle sector of the Aller R.

12th Army Group: In U.S. Ninth Army's XIII Corps area, 84th Div attacks and takes Hannover. 5th Armd Div, spearheading drive toward final objective, the Elbe, reaches and crosses Oker R: CCR captures bridge in Ahnsen area; CCA crosses the Oker on right flank of corps and reaches Meine, N of Braunschweig. 102d Div continues to mop up rear area. In XIX Corps area, 2d Armd Div renews eastward drive: CCA advances in 3 columns to Hallendorf area, SW of Braunschweig; CCB columns, to right, speed to the Oker at Schladen, where bridge is secured, and Gross Dohren, to SW. 30th Div shuttles E on left flank of corps from Hameln area, with RCT 117 on left and RCT 120 on right, and reaches Fuhse Canal, W of Braunschweig. 83d Div, with 329th Inf on left and 330th on right, drives E on right flank of corps from Westfeld-Seesen sector, left flank elements taking several towns in region N of Harz Mountains and right flank units fighting slowly forward through Harz Mountains. In XVI Corps area, 75th Div progresses steadily S toward Witten sector of the Ruhr against slackening resistance, forward elements taking Dueren and Stockum; establishes contact with TF Twaddle E of Brambauer. 35th Div screens right flank of 75th Div on left and clears Gelsenkirchen and suburbs on right. 79th Div advances E along the Ruhr against scattered resistance (313th Inf on left and

314th on right) and clears Bochum. After regrouping and relieving elements of 79th Div, 17th A/B Div attacks S with 507th Para Inf and takes Essen without opposition. In sector of TF Twaddle, 8th Armd Div gets into position for final assault on Unna, a target for aircraft. In conjunction with CCB, 95th Div's 379th Inf drives through Luenern and Muehlhausen on left and on right takes Kamen. TF Faith finishes clearing its zone except for Neheim and Arnsberg.

In U.S. First Army's XVIII Corps (A/B) area, 13th Armd Div begins crossing the Sieg in Siegburg area. One CCA column proceeds to Breidt area and another reaches positions near Siegburg. CCB thrusts to Agger R and establishes bridgehead with 2 rifle cos. 97th Div completes capture of Siegburg and supports crossing of 13th Armd Div over the Sieg. 78th Div, against delaying opposition, pushes steadily NW to general line Nuembrecht-Eckenhage-Hillmicke. 8th Div drives rapidly NW to Valbert-Wegeringhausen area. 86th Div's 342d Inf presses NW toward Attendorn. In III Corps area, RCT 10 of 5th Div continues rapidly W to Wenne R and takes bridge intact near Berge. RCT 2 secures bridgehead across the Wenne on high ground E of Grevenstein. 9th Div continues attack with 39th Inf on right and 60th on left until pinched out. 7th Armd Div commits CCA between CCR and CCB and drives steadily NW in multiple columns. 394th Inf, 99th Div, pushes through Odingen and Ober Elspe; 393d takes Halberbracht; 395th clears Meggen and Kickenbach. In VII Corps area, 3d Armd Div continues rapid advance on Nordhausen, CCB columns, on right, reaching Klein and Gross Werther, just SW of objective, and CCR reaching Silkerode, Bockelnhagen, and Zwinge. 1st and 104th Divs continue to follow armor closely. In V Corps area, 9th Armd Div passes through 2d and 69th Divs to spearhead attack to E: on left, CCB reaches Hain area, S of Nordhausen; CCA, in center, drives to positions beyond Ebeleben; on right, CCR overruns Schlotheim and gets forward elements to Freienbessingen. 2d and 69th Divs mop up to rear of armor.

In U.S. Third Army area, XX Corps continues E with 76th Div on left and 80th on right and prepares to commit armor to spearhead drive to the Elbe. 76th Div, with RCT's 304 and 385 abreast, 304 on left, advances to assigned objective, Straussfurt-Kuehnhausen rail line, with little difficulty; RCT 417 then relieves RCT 304. Against scattered resistance, 80th Div closes in on Erfurt and partially encircles it. 6th and 4th Armd Divs prepare to attack E abreast through 76th and 80th Divs. Elements of 6th Armd Div within First Army zone are relieved by 9th Armd and 69th Inf Divs (V Corps). 3d Cav Gp assembles N of Gotha and will protect left and right flanks of corps. In VIII Corps area, 89th and 87th Divs continue E abreast. 89th Div, with 355th Inf on left and 354th on right, drives to Gera R at Rudisleben, Arnstadt, and E of Espenfeld. 87th Div's 345th Inf takes Stutzhaus and continues to vicinity of Crawinkel; 347th, to right, reaches edge of Geraberg. Div forms TF Sundt (Div Rcn Tr, Co K of 346th Inf, and supporting units) to spearhead drive to the Saale on 11th, followed by 3d Bn of 346th Inf, motorized; rest of 346th Inf prepares to attack through 345th. 65th Div closes in assembly area in vicinity of Berka. XII Corps opens offensive to SE. 11th Armd Div, with close arty and air support, drives quickly to vicinity of Coburg, its immediate objective, against sporadic delaying action. On left, CCA blocks N and NE exits from the city. CCB reaches Wiesenfeld area, just N of Coburg, and reconnoiters in force toward the city, drawing AT fire. Heavy fire is placed on Coburg throughout night. 71st Div follows 11th Armd Div, mopping up. 26th Div pushes SE over difficult terrain of Thuringer Wald to NE of 71st Div. On left flank of corps, 90th Div continues E through Thuringer Wald, 359th Inf reaching Ilmenau and 358th, Neustadt.

U.S. Fifteenth Army takes command of 28th Div (− RCT 112), which starts to Juelich area. XXIII Corps takes over sector W of the Rhine to right of XXII Corps.

6th Army Group: In U.S. Seventh Army area, XV Corps holds current positions and patrols SE while preparing to continue offensive. CCB reverts to 14th Armd Div. In XXI Corps area, 42d Div, supported by powerful medium bomber attack and continuous arty fire, drives to within 3 miles of Schweinfurt against tenacious resistance. 232d Inf circles northward, overrunning Zell and Hambach; 242d holds current positions in center; 222d continues N along W bank of the Main to Bergrhein-feld. CCA of 12th Armd Div, assisting 42d Div, drives N along E bank of the Main, overrunning Unter and Ober Spiesheim and Alitzheim. CCB clears Stadt-Schwarzach, Klein Langheim, and Castell. CCR, followed by 101st Cav Gp, drives SE to Weigenheim and Geckenheim. Renewing offensive on right flank of corps, 4th Div's 22d Inf pushes SE to line Bartenstein-Niederstetten while 12th, to left, overruns Laudenbach. RCT 324, 44th Div, is attached to 4th Div. Corps objective line is extended to Blaufelden. In VI Corps area, 100th Div gets its two bridgeheads in Heilbronn to within a city block of each other. In Offenau bridgehead to N, 398th Inf continues to battle stubborn enemy. On N flank of corps, 253d Inf of 63d Div consolidates along the Kocher; 255th expands Kocher bridgehead southward; 254th pushes S to general line Kunzelsau-Jagstberg and makes contact with 10th Armd Div at Wolfsoelden. 10th Armd Div begins to withdraw its Crailsheim salient in compliance with army order and starts concentration in 63d Div zone.

In Fr 1st Army area, 2d Corps expands bridgehead S of the Enz and to right reaches Neuenburg and Dobel plateau. Valluy Groupement breaks through enemy defenses S of Karlsruhe. DA ALPS opens assault on l'Aution, commanding terrain in Alpes Maritimes province.

ITALY—15th Army Group: In U.S. Fifth Army area, 92d Div enters Massa, from which enemy has withdrawn.

In Br Eighth Army's Pol 2 Corps area, 3d Carpathian Div presses forward from the Senio toward the Santerno to left of 5 Corps, taking Solarolo and reaching Lugo Canal. In 5 Corps area, NZ 2d and Ind 8th Divs attack toward the Santerno. 78th Div force crosses the Senio between the two at Cotignola. 56th Div begins overland and amphibious operations toward Bastia in flooded coastal area. 167th Brig advances along the Reno while 169th, reinf by 40th (Royal Marine) Cdo, moves by water toward Menate, threatening enemy from rear.

BURMA—In Br Fourteenth Army's 4 Corps area, columns of Ind 17th Div and 255th Tank Brig converge on Pyawbwe and with air assistance capture this key point on Mandalay-Rangoon railway.

LUZON—In U.S. Sixth Army area, RCT 158, after securing Legaspi area, begins rcn of islands in Albay Gulf and prepares to send elements to help AT Co in San Francisco area. In I Corps' Baguio area, Sablan-Salat region is cleared as Cos E and F of 129th Inf, 37th Div, establish contact with Co G in advanced position. 3d Bn begins assault up Three Peaks and gets to within 100 yards of top. 27th Inf, 25th Div, gives 1st Bn task of continuing offensive for Mt Myoko and withdraws 3d Bn into reserve. Salacsac Pass No. 2 falls to 128th Inf of 32d Div, concluding prolonged and costly battle for this gateway to Cagayan Valley. In XI Corps area, 63d Inf of 6th Div, having suspended ground attacks on Mt Mataba for several days while enemy positions there were being neutralized, renews assault and gets elements to the summit, but Japanese continue to defend positions on this feature for the next week. XIV Corps columns drive to coast at Lamon Bay, sealing off Japanese forces in the Bicols. Elements of 1st Cav Div take Mauban while units of 11th A/B Div seize Atimonan.

S PHILIPPINES—In U.S. Eighth Army area, Gen Suzuki is lost at sea while withdrawing from Cebu toward Mindanao. Hill 26 on Cebu falls to elements of 132d Inf. Co E, 182d, rejoins regiment after clearing Hill 20 in conjunction with guerrilla forces. On Negros, 160th Inf is pinned down by heavy fire at foot of Dolan Hill and for next few days reconnoiters extensively. In preparation for amphibious assault on Bohol, advance party of 3d Bn, 164th Inf, lands at Tagbilaran to secure guides.

RYUKYU Is.—3d Bn of 105th Inf, 27th Div, under command of Eastern Islands Attack and Fire Support Group (TG 51.19), lands on Tsugen Shima after preparatory aerial and naval gunfire bombardment and begins search for isolated enemy groups.

In U.S. Tenth Army's III Amphib Corps area on Okinawa, 29th Marines of 6th Mar Div is enveloping Japanese positions on Yae-Take hill mass, Motobu Peninsula. Some elements reach Toguchi, on coast NW of Yae-Take, and others are at Itomi, NE of Yae-Take. In XXIV Corps area, 96th Div, with unusually heavy fire support, attacks with 2 regts, 383d and 381st, toward Kakazu Ridge; gains positions on it in costly fighting but is unable to drive enemy off. 7th Div makes limited progress in region to E, 184th Inf consolidating and 32d pressing toward Ouki.

11 April

WESTERN EUROPE—21 Army Group: In Cdn First Army's Cdn 2 Corps area, Cdn 1st Div attacks W across Ijssel R toward Apeldoorn while rest of corps continues northward on broad front. Pol 1st Armd Div, now operating to right of Cdn 2d Div, employs motorized elements in pursuit of enemy.

In Br Second Army area, 30 Corps makes steady progress toward Bremen. In 12 Corps area, some 53d Div elements cross Leine R at Westen but others are held up in Rethem area. 8 Corps gets forward elements to Aller R line near Celle.

12th Army Group: In U.S. Ninth Army's XIII Corps area, 5th Armd Div continues toward the Elbe: CCR columns reach Ohrdorf, SE of Wittingen, and Rohrberg; CCA, to right, reaches Poritz, W of Bismark. 84th Div starts toward the Elbe in left sector of corps zone, leaving 335th Inf in Hannover as corps reserve. In right sector of corps, forward elements of 102d Div reach the Leine near Pattensen, S of Hannover. In XIX Corps area, advance elements of CCB, 2d Armd Div, in record drive of 57 miles, reach the Elbe S of Magdeburg. CCA gets columns to Wolfenbuettel, Schoppenstedt, and Immendorf area. At 0200, 30th Div begins assault across Fuhse Canal W of Braunschweig with RCT's 117 and 120. RCT 117 seizes airfield SW of Braunschweig and enters W part of city. RCT 120 takes rail bridge over the Oker SE of the city and blocks eastern exits; cavalry units, driving through 5th Armd Div zone, block N and NE exits. 329th Inf, 83d Div, clears Halberstadt and Groeningen; 330th and reformed TF Biddle are clearing large wooded area to right. In XVI Corps area, 75th Div, employing 289th, 290th, 291st, and 320th Regts during course of the day, reaches the Ruhr at Witten

[11 APRIL 1945]

and takes 2 bridges intact; clears Witten, Armen, Eichlinghofen, and Brechten. 35th Div (−) closes along the Ruhr W of Witten, between 75th and 79th Divs. 79th Div, reversing its course to drive W with 313th and 315th Regts, reaches the Ruhr SW of Essen and establishes small bridgehead at Kettwig. Driving SW with 507th and 513th Para Inf, 17th A/B Div clears scattered opposition from Mulheim-Duisburg sector of the Ruhr; 507th Para Inf gains small bridgehead at Mulheim and turns it over to 79th Div. In sector of TF Twaddle, 8th Armd Div, passing CCA through CCB, takes Unna; CCR continues W in region S of Unna. Pushing SW toward Dortmund, 95th Div's 378th and 379th Regts reach line Gahmen-Grevel-Asseln. In Ruhr-Mohne pocket, TF Faith overruns Neheim and pocket NE of Arnsberg, leaving only Arnsberg to be cleared. 15th Cav Gp, its front now uncovered by 75th and 95th Divs, releases 17th Sq to TF Faith to replace 194th Gli Inf.

In U.S. First Army's XVIII Corps (A/B) area, CCB of 13th Armd Div, bypassing Troisdorf, drives through Wahnerheide and Urbach, forward elements reaching initial objective near Dunnwald, W of Berg Gladbach; to right, one CCA TF advances along autobahn through Lohmar while another is clearing opposition in Breidt area; CCR crosses the Sieg. 97th Div assists armor, mopping up bypassed resistance. 78th Div continues NW against spotty delaying resistance to Drabenderhohe-Bielstein area on left, Gummersbach in center, and Dummling, near Berg Neustadt on right. 28th Inf passes through 13th Inf, on 8th Div left, and drives rapidly NW to Kierspe area while 121st thrusts to Verse River dam. On right flank of corps, 342d Inf of 86th Div overruns Attendorn. In III Corps area, 5th Div expands Wenne bridgehead: on right, 5th Cav Rcn Tr and RCT 10 clear Forst Rumbeck to general line Rumbeck-Hellefeld; RCT 2 pushes westward, taking Westerfeld, Weninghausen, Linnepe, and Grevenstein. 11th Inf is relieved of security mission in Frankfurt. 7th Armd Div gets into position to drive W across fronts of 5th and 99th Divs. On left flank of corps, 99th Div continues NW in region E of the Lenne to positions near Serkenrode, Fretter, and Weringhausen. 9th Div, now out of action, releases RCT 47 to VII Corps. In VII Corps area, CCB of 3d Armd Div captures Nordhausen and turns it over to 104th Div troops. To left, CCA and CCR attack toward Harz Mts: CCA takes Osterode and Herzberg; CCR secures Bartolfelde, Osterhagen, Tettenborn, and Neuhof, turns them over to 104th Div troops, and assembles NW of Nordhausen. Moving through Nordhausen, 83d Armd Rcn Bn takes Obersachswerfen, Gudersleben, and Woffleben. 414th Inf, less 2d Bn, reverts to 104th Div. 1st and 104th Divs move forward rap-

idly behind armor. In V Corps area, 9th Armd Div speeds eastward, followed closely by 2d and 69th Divs. CCB, 9th Armd Div, reaches N-S line through Ringleben on left. CCA, in center, reaches Sachsenburg area, W of Heldrungen. On right, CCR reaches Rothenberga-Hardisleben region.

In U.S. Third Army area, XX Corps passes armor through infantry and drives quickly to the Saale. During day's advance, Buchenwald concentration camp near Weimar and Allied prisoner camp in Bad Sulza area are overrun. Passing through 76th Div, 6th Armd Div drives E, with CCB and CCA abreast and CCR following, to the Saale SW of Naumberg; crosses the river at Koesen, Kleinheringen, and Camburg. 4th Armd Div, attacking abreast and to right of 6th Armd, with CCB and CCA abreast and CCR following, moves E through 80th Div, bypassing Erfurt and Weimar. CCB, on left, reaches Ulrichshalben-Schwarbsdorf area, a little short of the Saale. CCA reaches the Saale S of Jena but finds bridges down and halts for night in Goeschwitz area. Mopping up to rear of armor, 76th Div reaches Buttstaedt area. 80th Div closes circle about Erfurt with 317th and 318th Regts and moves 319th eastward along autobahn behind 4th Armd Div. 3d Cav Gp takes responsibility for protecting flanks of corps, 3d Sq on left flank and 43d Sq on right. In VIII Corps area, 89th Div reaches line Gutendorf-Tonndorf-Kramchfeld-Wizleben; forms TF Crater (motorized elements of 1st Bn of 3534 Inf, 89th Rcn Tr, and supporting units) for dash to the Saale on 12th. 87th Div proceeds quickly toward Stadtilm on left and Bad Blankenburg on right. 65th Div starts to new assembly area at Waltershausen. 28th Sq, 6th Cav Gp, is given mission of protecting N flank of corps and closing gap between 89th and 87th Divs. In XII Corps area, Coburg surrenders to 11th Armd Div, which prepares to drive to Hasslach R line between Marktzeuln and Kronach; CCR TF finds Neustadt undefended. RCT 5, 71st Div, is attached to 11th Armd Div to occupy Coburg and clear woods to W. 71st Div units continue to mop up behind armor, forward elements reaching Rottenbach area. 26th Div takes Eisfeld without opposition and reaches Steinheid-Schalkau road. 90th Div advances rapidly as organized resistance collapses on left flank of corps, 359th Inf thrusting beyond Langenwiesen and Gehren and 358th beyond Gross Breitenbach; reconnaissance forces push through Konigsee.

6th Army Group: In U.S. Seventh Army area, XV Corps opens drive SE of Nuremberg at 1500 with 45th Div on left and 3d Div on right, progressing rapidly. 106th Cav Gp probes ahead of assault divs. In XXI Corps area, 42d Div regts converge on Schweinfurt and clear the city while CCA, 12th Armd Div, blocks enemy escape to E from positions commanding Schweinfurt–Bamberg highway. CCB pushes to Markt Bibart. CCR columns and 101st Cav Gp are maneuvering into position to pocket enemy in Uffenheim area. 4th Div, reinf by RCT 324 of 44th Div, opens drive SE toward Rothenburg. 12th and 22d Regts, 12th on left, making main effort, reach general line Baldersheim–Roettingen–Laudenbach. In VI Corps area, 100th Div forces within Heilbronn link up and clear about three fourths of the city. 398th Inf reaches the Kocher N of Heilbronn, overrunning Jagstfeld and Hagenbach and gaining positions near Odheim. 255th Inf, 63d Div, expands Kocher bridgehead S of Weissbach against strong opposition and is passed through by elements of 10th Armd Div. 254th Inf establishes bridgehead across the Kocher in vicinity of Ingelfingen and probes toward Kunzelsau. 10th Armd Div completes concentration in 63d Div zone and crosses elements of CCA over newly completed treadway bridge in Weissbach area.

In Fr 1st Army area, 2d Corps continues clearing along the Enz, reaching Calmbach and valley S of Dobel; to left maintains bridgehead across the Enz. Valluy Groupement reaches Murg R SE of Rastatt from Gaggenau to Gernsbach and envelops Rastatt.

ITALY—15th Army Group: In U.S. Fifth Army area, 442d Inf of 92d Div takes Carrara, from which enemy has withdrawn. 473d Inf continues to meet strong opposition to left, where 758th Tank Bn (–), reinf, is committed late in day.

In Br Eighth Army area, 10 Corps finds enemy positions covering the Senio abandoned and moves forward in pursuit. Pol 2 Corps reaches the Santerno. 169th Brig, 56th Div, lands near Menate and takes that town and Longastrino while 167th continues overland attack on right flank.

BURMA—In Br Fourteenth Army's 4 Corps area, Ind 5th Div, with armored force spearheading, passes through Ind 17th Div at Pyawbwe and drives to Yamethin. The armored force drives through the town but infantry forces are delayed there by stubborn opposition.

CHINA—Six ration purchasing commissions are sent into the field, beginning at this time, to procure supplies for ALPHA.

LUZON—In U.S. Sixth Army area, one column of 158th Inf moves by truck to Malabog and thence bn foot to Camalig, which is undefended; another moves to SW slopes of Tagaytay Ridge. These advances place the regt in position for assault on Cituinan Hill mass from N and S. In I Corps area, 129th Inf of 37th Div pushes forward along Highway 9 toward Baguio and reduces opposition on Three Peaks. Elements of 33d Div drive E toward Asin from Galiano. Japanese are reacting strongly to 32d Div's penetration of Salacsac Pass, offering heavy fire and local but sharp counterattacks. 35th Inf, 25th Div, continues attacks toward Kapintalan while 161st holds on Crump Hill and reconnoiters toward Balete Ridge. In XI Corps area, 38th Div has largely accomplished its mission of destroying enemy W of Clark Field and Fort Stotsenburg, where over 5,500 enemy dead have been counted. In XIV Corps area, patrols of 1st Cav and 11th A/B Divs, from Mauban and Antimonan respectively, establish contact on coast of Lamon Bay. Other elements of these divs maintain pressure on Mt Malepunyo and Mt Mataasna Bundoc.

S PHILIPPINES—In U.S. Eighth Army area, rehearsal is conducted at Mindoro for amphibious operation to secure Malabang-Parang-Cotabato area of Mindanao. On Cebu, elements of Americal Div secure Coconut Hill and prepare for assault on Babay Ridge. 164th Inf, less 3d Bn, is moving to Mananga R assembly area near barrio of Taup. On Bohol, 3d Bn of 164th Inf, Americal Div, lands without opposition at Tagbilaran and probes N and E with motorized patrols. Co I motors to Candijay, on E coast, and sets up roadblock. On Negros, 40th Div continues co-ordinated attacks but makes slow progress.

RYUKYU Is.—Enemy begins strong, 2-day air effort against U.S. shipping in bid to regain Okinawa. TF 58, receiving weight of attacks, abandons support missions to keep off attackers. Suicide plane damages the CV Enterprise, which must withdraw to Ulithi for repairs. Other vessels suffer lighter damage. 27th Div units complete clearing Tsugen Shima, where Japanese casualties total 234 killed.

U.S. Tenth Army orders 77th Div to land on Ie Shima on 16th, an operation previously scheduled as Phase II of Operation ICEBERG, although Phase I is still in progress. In III Amphib Corps area, 6th Mar Div has frequent, sharp clashes with enemy on Motobu Peninsula as extensive patrolling continues. By now enemy positions in mountainous Yae-Take area are fairly well fixed. In XXIV Corps area, 96th Div continues futile efforts to take Kakazu Ridge under intense fire. Elements of 32d Inf, 7th Div, push into Ouki but are forced to retire since tanks cannot follow. Virtual stalemate exists all along corps front on approaches to Shuri.

12 April

WESTERN EUROPE—21 Army Group: In Cdn First Army area, Cdn I Corps opens assault on Arnhem. At 2240, 49th Div crosses the Ijssel near Westervoort to attack from the rear while other units provide diversion S of Arnhem.

In Br Second Army area, 30 Corps now has 3 divs in assault: 43d on left, Gds Armd in center,

[12 APRIL 1945]

and newly arrived 51st on right. In 12 Corps area, 53d Div clears Rethem and establishes bridgehead across the Leine there. In 8 Corps area, 15th Div passes through 6th A/B Div and enters Celle, on Aller R.

12th Army Group: U.S. Ninth Army releases 29th Div to operational control of XVI Corps, but the div retains its current security mission in army rear. In XIII Corps area, 5th Armd Div completes dash to the Elbe, CCR reaching the river at Wittenberge and Werben and CCA in Tangermuende area, but is unable to secure bridges as hoped. 84th and 102d Divs continue to clear toward the Elbe in left and right sectors of corps, respectively. 11th Cav Gp screens N flank of corps. In XIX Corps area, CCB of 2d Armd Div establishes small infantry bridgehead across the Elbe in Randau area, S of Magdeburg. CCA and CCR speed toward the Elbe at Magdeburg and block exits from Magdeburg. 30th Div completes capture of Braunschweig and drives about 35 miles E toward the Elbe. 329th Inf, 83d Div, reaches the Elbe at Barby, SE of Schoenebeck. 330th continues to clear Harz Mts and block main roads there. 331st, after assembling in Derenburg area, drives E, forward elements taking Nienburg, on Saale R. In XVI Corps area, 75th Div continues to clear region N of the Ruhr between Witten and Westhofen; 289th Inf relieves 137th Inf, 35th Div. 134th Inf maintains and improves positions along the Ruhr; 320th is relieved by 95th Div and 75th Rcn Tr. On W flank of corps, 17th A/B Div begins relief of 79th Div N of the Ruhr; 507th Para Inf patrol receives formal surrender of Duisburg- 79th Div, as relieved, assembles for occupation duties in sector N of the Ruhr; withdraws its small bridgehead at Kettwig. In zone of TF Twaddle, 8th Armd Div mops up in Unna area and at 2400 passes to army control as reserve. 378th Inf, 95th Div, breaks into E part of Dortmund, where lively fighting ensues; 379th, to left, thrusts rapidly SW toward the Ruhr; TF Faith contains Arnsberg on the N while 5th Div of III Corps, First Army, attacks the city from the S.

In U.S. First Army's XVIII Corps (A/B) area, as enemy withdrawal becomes increasingly hasty and more and more prisoners are being taken, presaging a speedy end of the Ruhr pocket, corps establishes stop line and extends boundaries of 97th, 78th, and 8th Divs to it; provides alternate plans of advance in the event 78th Div reaches Hueckeswagen-Wipperfuerth area, final objective of armor, before 13th Armd Div. CCB, 13th Armd Div, closes on initial objective in Dunnwald area and reorganizes CCA takes Altenrath and thrusts toward Rath; CCR follows CCB, mopping up. 87th Div continues clearing region to rear of armor. 78th Div column pushes into woods near Engelskirchen on left; center and right columns speed to Thier-Klueppelberg region, threatening Wipperfuerth. 8th Div drives to Kreuzberg-Oberbruegge area, SW of Luedenscheid. 86th Div drives about 4 miles NW on right flank of corps; at 2200 forms TF Pope (reinf 3d Bn of 342d Inf) to drive through 8th Div to Luedenscheid. In III Corps area, RCT 10, on 5th Div right, captures Arnsberg and Wennigloh; RCT 2 reaches the Rohr in Hachen-Recklinghausen area and establishes bridgehead; Sad Cav Sq, operating with RCT 2, clears region between Rohr R and Sorpe Staubecken Lake as far S as Seidfeld. 7th Armd Div speeds W some 15 miles, passing through 5th Div on right and cutting across front of 99th Div on left; CCA reaches Hoevel and Balve on right; CCR seizes Neuenrade. Continuing steadily NW, 99th Div reaches general line Rohrenspring-Roenkhausen. In VII Corps area, CCR of 3d Armd Div takes Obersdorf, Polsfeld, and Blankenheim; CCA secures Sangerhausen; CCB overruns Holdenstedt, Wolferstedt, and Allstedt; 83d Armd Rcn Bn, on right flank, reaches Oberroeblingen, Niederroeblingen, and Allstedt. 1st Div and attached 4th Cav Gp are mopping up along edge of Harz Mts, where bypassed enemy is almost encircled; 26th Inf pushes into W edge to Clausthal-Zellerfeld. 413th Inf, 104th Div, enters Bad Lauterberg and seizes Sachsa and Ellrich; 414th blocks Harz Mts exits NE of Nordhausen; 415th moves elements forward to Kelbra, Wallhausen, and Oberroeblingen. In V Corps area, CCB of 9th Armd Div, after gaining positions near the Saale in vicinity of Delitz and Bad Lauchstaedt, is directed to assemble; CCA crosses Unstrut R at Nebra and continues to Pettstaedt area, NW of Weissenfels, where it assembles; CCR crosses the Saale near Naumberg and drives E through Naumberg to Weissenfels-Zeitz road, then SE toward Zeitz, elements abandoning drive NW toward Weissenfels upon learning that bridge there is down. 2d and 69th Divs, following armor, gain 25-30 miles.

In U. S. Third Army's XX Corps area, 6th Armd Div continues E from the Saale to Weisse-Elster R and gains crossings. One CCB column, finding Weisse-Elster bridges down, turns N into V Corps zone to seize bridge at Pegau and continues to Audigast; another bypasses Zeitz to N and searches for crossing over Weisse-Elster R. CCA is held up on left by strongpoint W of Zeitz but on right takes bridge across Weisse-Elster at Rossendorf and establishes infantry bridgehead before bridge is lost to time bomb. CCR moves E in effort to secure bridge at Zeitz and reaches Kretzschau, just W of Zeitz. 4th Armd Div closes along the Saale where bridges are down and crosses, initial elements in rubber boats and by ferry and rest over newly constructed bridges; CCB crosses the Saale N of Jena and clears Kunitz and Laasan; CCA crosses S of Jena and drives NE to Beulbar-Ilmsdorf-Scheiditz area; CCR moves to Mellingen area and sends force N to mop up between CCB and CCA. 76th Div, motorized, follows 6th Armd Div toward Zeitz, RCT 304, in the lead, reaching vicinity of Hollsteitz. In concerted assault, 317th and 318th Regts of 80th Div clear Erfurt; 319th receives surrender of Weimar and heads for Jena. VIII Corps drives E to the Saale against decreasing resistance. On left, TF Crater spearheads attack of 89th Div, moving through Bad Berka to the Saale in Rothenstein area; 355th Inf mops up resistance bypassed by TF Crater and seizes Tannroda; 354th progresses slowly S of Kranichfeld. TF Sundt of 87th Div reaches the Saale near Rudolstadt. 346th Inf assists TF Sundt and takes Ehrenstein and Altremda. 347th overruns Bad Blankenburg. In XII Corps area, 11th Armd Div, with CCA on left and CCB on right, drives SE from Coburg to Hasslach R against light opposition; establishes bridgeheads at Kronach and Marktzeuln. CCR turns Neustadt over to 71st Div and moves S to Ebersdorf. 71st Div continues forward behind armor. 26th Div overruns Lauscha, Steinach, Sonneberg, and Oberlind. 90th Div gains about 10 miles virtually unopposed, reaching positions S of Bad Blankenburg from Beulwitz area on left to Bock and Teich area on right. Continuing to protect right flank of corps, 42d Sq of 2d Cav Gp reconnoiters to the Main in Schney area and establishes small bridgehead at Miehelau.

6th Army Group: In U.S. Seventh Army's XV Corps area, 45th and 3d Divs, driving SE across the Main, get into position to attack Bamberg. In XXI Corps area, 42d Div mops up scattered resistance in Schweinfurt; attached CCA, 12th Armd Div, establishes contact with 3d Div (XV Corps). CCB pushes SW to Markt Nordheim area. CCR and 101st Cav Gp encircle enemy in Uffenheim area. 4th Div continues SE astride the Tauber toward Rothenburg with 12th and 22d Regts abreast while 8th and 324th Regts mop up on left and right flank of div, respectively. In VI Corps area, Heilbronn falls to 100th Div after 9-day battle. CCA, 10th Armd Div, crosses TF Hankins (61st Armd Inf Bn) into Kocher bridgehead S of Weissbach and expands it to Neuenstein. CCR follows CCA across the Kocher. 63d Div continues to clear enemy positions astride Kocher R line.

In Fr 1st Army area, 2d Corps finishes clearing its zone as far as the Enz and improves positions in bridgehead across the river. Valluy Groupement clears Baden Baden and Rastatt. DA ALPS completes reduction of l'Aution, but enemy holds Roya R valley.

ITALY—15th Army Group: U.S. Fifth Army postpones offensive, scheduled for this date, 24 hours because of weather conditions. 92d Div, along Carrione Creek, is beset with supply problems until engineers reopen road between Massa and Carrara during day.

In Br Eighth Army's Pol 2 Corps area, 3d Carpathian Div establishes bridgehead across the Santerno. 5 Corps takes many prisoners as enemy line along the Santerno collapses and Germans withdraw beyond Massa Lombardo. 56th Div's 169th and 167th Brigs link up near Longastrino and push westward toward Bastia. 78th Div is committed through 8th Ind Div's bridgehead to exploit enemy withdrawal; 36th Brig turns W toward Sillaro R while 38th, strongly reinf with armor, prepares to drive N on Bastia.

BURMA—In Br Fourteenth Army's 33 Corps area, Kyaukpadaung, communications center between Chauk and Meiktila, falls to 33d Brig of Ind 7th Div.

LUZON—GHQ SWPA establishes CP in Manila.

In U.S. Sixth Army area, 1st and 3d Bns, RCT 158, begin two-pronged assault on Cituinan Hill mass, which enemy is defending stubbornly. 2d Bn (−) motors S along Route 1 to Bulan area to clear San Francisco region of Sorsogon Province. In I Corps area, 129th Inf of 37th Div, spearheading drive on Baguio along Highway 9, is stopped short of Monglo by fire from hills commanding the highway. Elements of 80th Inf, 33d Div, push into Asin but further progress in this area is delayed by tenacious enemy defense of complex tunnel system. Other elements of 33d Div are clearing Pugo-Tuba trail. Renewing northeastward attack on Mt Myoko, 27th Inf troops of 25th Div seize hill called Pimple near the crest. 2d Bn of 35th Inf relieves 3d Bn on Fishhook feature and reconnoiters. In XI Corps area, Baldy Force, having developed enemy positions in Ipo area during reconnaissance in force, returns to original position. In XIV Corps area, 1st Cav Brig, less 12th Cav Regt, relieves 11th A/B Div forces in region E of Mt Malepunyo and starts SE into the Bicols. 511th Inf, less 3d Bn, is released from army reserve to 11th A/B Div and takes responsibility for Mt Malepunyo sector, permitting 187th Inf to return to Mt Macolod, which has been bypassed.

S PHILIPPINES—In U.S. Eighth Army area, Americal Div on Cebu begins final drive on Babay Ridge. 182d Inf, attacking toward Hill 21 with 2 bns abreast, penetrates trench system just below military crest and repels several counterattacks during night. 2d Bn, 132d Inf, attacks from Guadalupe Ridge while rest of regt harasses enemy to right. 1st Bn, 164th Inf, moves secretly into position to attack from the rear and gets to within 1,200 yards of top of the ridge. On Bohol, 3d Bn (less Co I) of 164th Inf moves toward Sierra Bullones in central

Bohol, where main Japanese forces are reported to be disposed.

NEI—93d Div, U.S. Eighth Army, assumes tactical control of Morotai, relieving 31st Div.

RYUKYU Is.—Enemy air effort shifts from TF 58 to ships anchored at Okinawa and the picket line, with suiciders still playing a major role. Two Allied ships are sunk, one of them the DD *M. L. Abele*, and a number of other vessels are hit. Ground reconnaissance of Minna I., S of Ie Shima, by Amphib Rcn Bn of FMF Pac, during night 12-13, discloses no enemy troops.

In U.S. Tenth Army's XXIV Corps area, action on Okinawa is confined to patrolling and mopping up bypassed pockets, except for further abortive efforts by elements of 96th Div to take Kakazu Ridge. After intense preparatory bombardment, Japanese begin a series of counterattacks in evening, mainly against 96th Div. American lines hold, but some enemy succeed in infiltrating.

U.S.—President Franklin Delano Roosevelt dies suddenly in Warm Springs, Georgia.

13 April

WESTERN EUROPE—21 Army Group: In Cdn First Army area, Cdn I Corps continues battle for Arnhem. Cdn 1st Div, driving toward Apeldoorn, is transferred to I Corps from 2 Corps.

In Br Second Army area, 30 Corps, continuing toward Bremen, reaches Cloppenburg-Goldenstedt area. 3d Div returns to corps to assist in drive on Bremen. 12 Corps expands Rethem bridgehead toward Soltau. 8 Corps continues toward Uelzen.

12th Army Group: In U.S. Ninth Army area, 8th Armd Div, upon relief in XVI Corps zone by 95th Div, moves to Wolfenbuettel area, where it is held in army reserve. CCB (−) proceeds to Halberstadt to defend right flank of XIX Corps. In XIII Corps area, 5th Armd Div, mopping up along the Elbe, clears a number of towns, among them Tangermuende. 84th and 102d Divs continue eastward toward the Elbe. In XIX Corps area, CCB of 2d Armd Div, unable to expand Elbe bridgehead, moves S at night to new site in Elbenau-Gruenwalde area. CCA and CCR contain Magdeburg and probe into its outskirts. 30th Div forces reach the Elbe on left flank of corps. 83d Div establishes bridgehead across the Elbe at Barby with elements of 329th and 331st Regts. RCT 330 passes to corps control and continues clearing Harz Mts in conjunction with VII Corps, First Army. In XVI Corps area, 75th Div clears all of its sector N of the Ruhr from Witten to Westhofen except for town of Herdecke. 79th Div begins occupation of new sector, relieving elements of 75th and 35th Divs. 35th Div, less 134th Inf, which is temporarily attached to 79th Div, passes to operational control of XIX Corps. 17th A/B Div performs military government duties on W flank of corps and is joined by 194th Gli Inf. In TF Twaddle sector, 95th Div's 378th Inf, reinf by bn of 377th, completes capture of Dortmund, which Allied planes have left in ruins. 379th Inf completes drive S to the Ruhr; as regimental zone is extended to Westhofen, moves 3d Bn westward toward this final objective. TF Faith is dissolved at noon when 15th Cav Gp takes over its Ruhr sector. At 2400, TF Twaddle is dissolved, but 95th Div retains control of 15th Cav Gp.

In U.S. First Army area, XVIII Corps (A/B) pursues rapidly withdrawing enemy. After regrouping, CCB of 13th Armd Div, followed by CCR, thrusts northward from Dunnwald area; CCA drives to positions near Bensburg. 97th Div pushes northward behind armor, mopping up. 78th Div reaches line extending from Wipperfuerth southwestward; on right flank takes Wipperfuerth and Hueckeswagen, final objectives of 13th Armd Div, without a fight. 8th Div, replacing 121st Inf on right with 13th, races NW toward stop line SW of Hagen, 28th Inf heading for Schwelm and 13th Inf reaching Milspe-Vorde area. On right flank of corps, 86th Div's 341st Inf, motorized, dashes from Hilchenbach to stop line in Hagen area; 342d Inf seizes Luedenscheid and heads for Hohenlimburg; 343d clears Herscheid, Huinghausen, and Plettenberg. In III Corps area, RCT's 10 and 2 of 5th Div drive NW between Ruhr and Honne Rivers to line Herdringen-Holzen-Boeingsen. CCA, 7th Armd Div, assisted by left flank elements of 5th Div, moves NW toward Hemer. 99th Div, with 394th Inf on right, 395th in center, and 3934 on left, advances quickly on left flank of corps, clearing resistance bypassed by 7th Armd Div m region S and SW of Sorpe Staubecken Lake. 14th Cav Gp takes over zone of 9th Div. 9th Div (− RCT's 47 and 60) is attached to VII Corps. In VII Corps area, 3d Armd Div drives E to Saale R at Alsleben, Nelben, and Friedeburg and crosses dismounted elements; constructs bridges, night 13-14. 1st Div and attached 4th Cav Gp begin systematic clearing of Harz Mts. 100th Div continues to block along S perimeter of Harz Mts on left rear and drives E on right; organizes TF Kelleher (414th Inf (−) and Div Rcn Tr, strongly reinf) to spearhead drive to the Saale and Halle. 9th Div (−) assembles in Nordhausen area and regains control of RCT 47. RCT 39 begins relief of 414th Inf, 104th Div, near Nordhausen. In V Corps area, CCA of 9th Armd Div drives E through Naumberg to the Weisse-Elster in vicinity of Pegau and then goes on the defensive. CCB awaits bridge construction at Weissenfels. CCR, upon securing bridge NE of Zeitz, abandons attack on Zeitz and crosses to reach positions S of Leipzig.

2d Div, following armor closely, approaches Saale R in vicinity of Merseburg. RCT 271, 69th Div, reinf by reserve TF under command of CO, 777th Tank Bn, clears portion of Weissenfels W of the Saale and crosses elements in assault boats; RCT 272 gets advance elements to Hohenmoelsen.

In U.S. Third Army's XX Corps area, 6th Armd Div continues to cross Weisse-Elster R and secures additional bridges. Using a bridge at Pegau and another captured at Profen, in First Army zone, CCB crosses and drives SE to Lucka area. CCA crosses additional elements at Rossendorf, where ford and treadway bridge are put in, and rest over bridge captured at Schkauditz. From Rossendorf, column drives NE to Breitenbach. In conjunction with RCT 304 of 76th Div, CCR starts across river near Zeitz under intense fire. RCT 304, 76th Div, forces the Weisse-Elster and begins assault on Zeitz. Bypassing Jena, which 80th Div clears, 4th Armd Div races E from Mulde bridgeheads, crossing Weisse-Elster R and establishing bridgeheads over Zwick Mulde R in 70-odd-mile drive. CCB establishes bridgehead across the Zwick Mulde at Wolkenberg and CCA another, in vicinity of Ober Winkel and Crumbach. VIII Corps mops up W of the Saale, over which all vehicular bridges are destroyed, and establishes bridgehead on right. 89th Div, with 355th and 353d Regts abreast, clears Rothenstein-Beutelsdorf sector W of the Saale and dissolves TF Crater. 87th Div, with 346th and 347th Regts abreast, clears its sector to the Saale; crosses elements at Etzelbach, Schwarza, and Saalfeld by ford and foot bridges and establishes firm bridgehead. 65th Div starts toward Arnstadt to mop up stragglers. 6th Cav Gp continues to defend left flank of corps. In XII Corps area, 11 Armd Div, continuing rapidly SE along muddy, secondary roads, takes Kulmbach and cuts Kulmbach-Bayreuth road before it is ordered to halt; probes toward Bayreuth, next objective of corps. 71st Div mops up toward Kulmbach. 26th Div reaches general line Steinbach-Fortschendorf-Steinberg-Kronach. 90th Div advances to general line Lothra-Gleima-Rottersdorf; reconnaissance elements seize Selbitz R bridge SE of Lichtenberg. On right flank of corps, 42d Sq of 2d Cav Gp reaches Thurnau area, NW of Bayreuth.

In U.S. Fifteenth Army's XXII Corps area, 28th Div is attached to corps and takes responsibility for Juelich sector.

6th Army Group: In U.S. Seventh Army's XV Corps area, elements of 45th and 3d Divs break into Bamberg and begin clearing it. XXI Corps' objective line is extended to include Feuchtwangen, Ansbach, and Fuerth. 42d Div moves elements SE in preparation for assault on Fuerth, W of Nuremberg, and releases CCA, 12th Armd Div, to parent unit. CCB clears toward Aisch R SW of Neustadt;

CCR eliminates enemy pocket within its zone to right. 101st Cav Gp, reconnoitering to SE of armor, finds enemy disposed along line Adelshofen-Steinach-Burgbernheim-Windsheim; releases 101st Sq to 4th Div. 4th Div, with 12th, 22d, and 324th Regts, from left to right, in assault, advances to line Freudenbach-Lichtel Schrozberg-Blaufelden on right flank of corps. VI Corps advances rapidly all along line as resistance weakens; is directed to secure line Poppenweiler-Crailsheim, from which to reconnoiter SE, and be prepared to attack SE. 100th Div clears region about Heilbronn and pushes E and SE. CCA, 10th Armd Div, takes Oehringen and drives SW and W toward Heilbronn, establishing contact with 100th Div. 63d Div gains all its objectives on N flank of corps with ease: 253d Inf crosses the Kocher and reaches Brettach R in Neuenstadt Langenbeutingen area; 255th reaches Neuenstein area; 254th consolidates around Kunzelsau and clears southward to general line Kupferzell-Rueblingen.

In Fr 1st Army area, Valluy Groupement, reinf by CC3 of 1st Armd Div, speeds S over Baden Plain E of the Rhine, overrunning Buehl; left flank elements push through Black Forest toward Freudenstadt in conjunction with right flank elements of 2d Corps.

EASTERN EUROPE—Soviet forces of Third Ukrainian Front, supported by those of Second Ukrainian Front, complete capture of Vienna.

ITALY—15th Army Group: U.S. Fifth Army again postpones offensive because of unfavorable weather. 92d Div is unable to advance its left flank across Carrione Creek but pushes toward Parmignola Canal in center and to vicinity of M. Pizzaculo on right.

In Br Eighth Army area, boundary between Pol 2 and Br 5 Corps is altered, narrowing front of Pol 2 Corps, whose axis of advance now extends through Medicina and Budrio. Pol 2 Corps expands Santerno bridgehead. In 5 Corps area, NZ 2d Div and 36th Brig of 78th Div push rapidly W toward Bastia in conjunction with action of 56th Div to right. 56th Div's 24th Gds Brig, reinf by 9th Cdo, makes amphibious assault on Chiesa del Bando, NE of Argenta, but is held up by enemy established along Fosso Marina.

BURMA—In Br Fourteenth Army's 33 Corps area, Ind 20th Div seizes Taungdwingyi.

CHINA—Japanese open full-scale drive on Chihchiang, making main effort along road from Paoching.

LUZON—In U.S. Sixth Army area, RCT 158, less 2d Bn, continues indecisive battle for Cituinan Hill area for next week. 2d Bn, reinf by AT Co, attacks toward San Francisco, in Sorsogon Province, meeting heavy fire from hills around the town.

In I Corps area, 129th Inf of 37th Div, clearing hills commanding Highway 9, reaches position 300 yards W of Monglo. 27th Inf, 25th Div, continues northward attack on Mt Myoko, taking a feature called the Wart. XI Corps continues to probe enemy positions in mountains of central Luzon. On Caballo I., last of Japanese are eliminated. TF (Co F (–) of 151st Inf and engineers) blows up Fort Drum on El Fraile I. with ignited fuel oil. In XIV Corps area, 5th Cav of 1st Cav Div, advancing SE toward Calaug, finds prepared enemy positions that are unoccupied. As 8th Cav closes in on enemy positions in Mt Mataasna Bundoc area, 11th A/B Div prepares for final assault against Mt Malepunyo and Mt Macolod.

S PHILIPPINES—In U.S. Eighth Army area, assault forces for Mindanao operation embark at Mindanao and Leyte. On Cebu, Americal Div continues battle for Babay Ridge: 182d Inf secures Hill 21; 1st Bn, 164th Inf, makes slow progress against strong opposition; 132d Inf attempts in vain to secure Hill 25, N of Guadalupe road, and for next few days destroys pillboxes and seals caves. Japanese are ordered to abandon their Cebu City defenses on night of 16th. On Negros, 185th Inf of 40th Div repels predawn counterattack by about 50 Japanese in vicinity of San Juan, killing most of the force. RCT 503 reaches positions about 1,000 yards S of Manzanares and pauses for several days to patrol. 160th Inf draws heavy fire from Hill 3155.

RYUKYU Is.—Preinvasion bombardment of Ie Shima is intensified. Underwater demolition teams begin reconnaissance of beaches.

In U.S. Tenth Army's III Amphib Corps area, 6th Mar Div prepares to attack well-organized enemy positions on Yae-Take hill mass of Motobu Peninsula. Some elements of 22d Marines moving up W coast of Okinawa reach N tip at Hedo; others are reconnoitering along E coast and inland. XXIV Corps is fully occupied mopping up enemy infiltrators and repelling further counterattacks.

14 April

WESTERN EUROPE—21 Army Group: Cdn First Army takes command of Netherlands District. Cdn 1 Corps clears Arnhem except for isolated pockets and is approaching Apeldoorn. Cdn 2 Corps continues northward on broad front; on left takes Zwolle without opposition and advances to Meppel area.

Br Second Army continues toward Bremen, Soltau, and Uelzen. 15th Div of 8 Corps drives into outskirts of Uelzen.

12th Army Group: In U.S. Ninth Army's XIII Corps area, 11th Cav Gp races eastward to the Elbe, screening N flank of corps, which is becoming exposed as British swerve northward. 5th Armd Div, when orders for an assault across the Elbe are revoked, mops up most of it's sector along the river. Forward elements of 84th and 102d Divs reach the Elbe, overtaking armor. U.S. and political prisoners are released during day at Salzwedel. Evidence of mass Nazi atrocities is found at Gardelegen. In XIX Corps area, 2d Armd Div, unable to put bridge or ferry across the Elbe and consequently unable to supply CCB infantry E of the river with armor, withdraws bridgehead in afternoon. CCR, upon relief in Magdeburg area by CCA, crosses the Elbe at Barby and takes over left flank of 83d Div bridgehead; is attached to 83d Div. 83d Div finishes crossing 329th and 331st Regts plus their attachments and 2 FA bns. RCT 137, 35th Div, takes up positions along W bank of the Elbe from Tangermuende to Grieben on left flank of corps, relieving 125th Cav Rcn Sq; RCT 320 comes under corps control. 30th Div clears several towns within its zone W of the Elbe. CCB, 8th Armd Div, is attached to corps and screens right flank. XVI Corps concludes operations against Ruhr pocket within its zone. 75th Div receives surrender of Herdecke and is relieved by 79th Div. 17th A/B and 79th Inf Divs continue occupation mission; latter establishes contact with 8th Div of XVIII Corps, First Army. 95th Div finishes clearing its sector; makes contact with 79th Div; relieves 15th Cav Gp of screening mission along the Ruhr. 15th Cav Gp is attached to 29th Div for military government duty.

In U.S. First Army's XVIII Corps (A/B) area, 13th Armd Div begins final phase of its Ruhr assault—drive NE from Berg Gladbach-Bensburg region toward Wipperfuerth—but rapid progress of units to right necessitates change of plans, and div is directed to drive N with CCA on left and CCB on right to establish contact with Ninth Army. 97th Div continues mopping up to rear of 13th Armd Div. 78th Div reaches positions W of Burscheid on left, enters Wermelskirchen, which is declared an open city, in center, and reaches heights overlooking Lennep on right. 28th Inf, 8th Div, clears Schwelm and continues N while 13th Inf, to right, reaches the Ruhr in Wetter area and establishes contact with Ninth Army. 341st Inf, 86th Div, captures Hagen; 342d continues toward Hohenlimburg; 343d clears many towns and villages along Lenne R on right flank. In III Corps area, RCT's 10 and 2 of 5th Div finish clearing region between Ruhr and Honne Rivers; RCT 11 completes movement to div zone from Frankfurt. CCA, 7th Armd Div, reaches edge of Hemet by noon but suspends assault until 2030 in futile effort to negotiate peaceful entry, then attacks and clears the town. 99th Div continues to mop up resistance bypassed by 7th Armd Div and relieves CCR in Neuenrade-Garbeck sector. In VII Corps area, 3d Armd Div, when bridges across the Saale are completed in morning, finishes crossing and drives rapidly NE toward line of Elbe and Mulde Rivers in vicinity of Dessau. 1st Div, despite difficult terrain and numerous defended roadblocks, pushes deeper into Harz Mts. While 413th Inf, 104th Div, maintains positions about Harz Mts and establishes contact with 1st Div, TF Kelleher jumps off at noon for Halle and forward elements reach the Saale near Lettin; 415th Inf moves E behind TF Kelleher. 9th Div begins attack with 47th and 39th Regts to clear E portion of Harz Mts. In V Corps area, CCA of 9th Armd Div consolidates along Weisse-Elster R line and at 1400 attacks E to vicinity of Lobstadt. CCB crosses newly completed bridge and prepares to follow CCA eastward. CCR reaches Borna area, overrunning Breitingen and factory area at Deutzen. 9th and 23d Regts of 2d Div reach the Saale N of Merseburg and 23d establishes bridgehead, using damaged railway bridge; at 1400, 38th Inf, reinf by 3d Bn of 9th, crosses bridge at Weissenfels and drives slowly N under accurate fire massed to protect synthetic rubber and gasoline factories at Merseburg and Leuna. 69th Div's RCT 271, reinf, completes capture of Weissenfels; RCT 272 drives to Weisse R at Luetzkewitz, NE of Zeitz.

In U.S. Third Army's XX Corps area, 6th Armd Div breaks through enemy defenses along the Weisse-Elster and drives E to Zwick Mulde R, bypassing resistance in towns and villages. One CCB column reaches the Zwick Mulde at Rochlitz and establishes bridgehead while another halts near river line in Carsdorf area. CCA, also attacking in 2 columns, reaches Spora on left and Oberkossa on right. CCR completes its crossing of river at Zeitz and Rossendorf and, though 76th Div is responsible for clearing Zeitz, destroys many German AA batteries as it drives SE through that city; forward elements reach Altenburg but await reinforcements before attacking. In 76th Div zone, RCT 417 relieves RCT 304 of task of mopping up Zeitz, and RCT 304 speeds E by motor toward Altenburg; RCT 385 reaches positions E of Weisse-Elster R near Zeitz. While CCB, 4th Armd Div, expands Wolkenberg bridgehead and takes 2 bridges at Penig, CCA columns, followed by CCR, clear Limbach and Wustenbrand. 318th Inf, 80th Div, moves rapidly E behind armor; 319th clears Gera and continues E; 317th maintains order in Gera and Jena but is relieved at Weimar by 5th Ranger Bn. VIII Corps sets restraining line extending from N boundary S along Zwick Mulde R to Wilkau, thence SW along autobahn to S boundary. 355th and 353d Regts, 89th Div, speed E from the Saale to general line Moeckern-Zwackau-Arnshagen. Upon completion of bridge near Saalfeld, TF Sundt again spearheads 87th Div advance, reaching Peuschen: 346th Inf drives about 3 miles E from Ettelbach crossing site, and 347th gets elements to Schmorda. 28th Sq, 6th Cav Gp, after crossing the Saale in XX Corps zone, drives E in zone of 89th Div to Weisse-Elster R in Gera-Weida sector. In XII Corps area, TF of CCB, 11th Armd Div, drives SE on Bayreuth in 2 columns. Confusion arises as elements of 14th Armd Div, Seventh Army, are found to be heading for same objective, but the CCB TF continues to N and W edges of the city. When surrender negotiations fail, Bayreuth is softened by intense air and arty bombardment and entered on N by CCB column. Meanwhile, 71st Div is given task of clearing Bayreuth; RCT 14, reinf by elements of 5th Inf, begins assault at 1830, clearing W part and relieving 11th Armd Div elements there. 42d Sq, 2d Cav Gp, blocks S and SE exits from the city. 26th Div reaches N-S autobahn W of Hof in vicinity of Selbitz, Muenchberg, and Streitau. Assault regts of 90th Div close along line of Saale R, Saale Stau Lake, and Selbitz R, overrunning Lobenstein. Using bridge captured by 90th Rcn Tr SE of Lichtenberg, 358th Inf establishes bridgehead and clears Blankenberg.

6th Army Group: In U.S. Seventh Army area, XV Corps finishes clearing Bamberg and pushes on toward Nuremberg. In XXI Corps area, 42d Div, employing 222d Inf on left and 232d on right, pursues enemy SE astride Wuerzburg-Nuremberg road. 12th Armd Div attacks SE to right of 42d Div, with CCB followed by CCA on left, CCR on right, and 101st Cav Gp reinf by 92d Cav Rcn Sq between the combat commands. CCB closes along the Aisch and establishes small bridgehead at Dietersheim before bridge collapses. Using ford at Lenkersheim and bridge at Ipsheim, 101st Cav Gp gains bridgehead across the Aisch. CCR overruns several towns on right flank of div. 8th Inf shuttles SE on 4th Div left flank to follow CCR closely while other elements of 4th Div push closer to Rothenburg. In VI Corps area, 100th Div, advancing E and SE from Heilbronn area toward Loewenstein with 3 regts abreast, reaches general line Talheim-Unt Heinriet-Weiler and relieves elements of CCA, 10th Armd Div, in vicinity of Bitzfeld. 10th Armd Div finishes clearing its zone and begins turning it over to 100th and 63d Divs. 63d Div consolidates, relieves elements of CCA, 10th Armd Div, near Oehringen, and makes contact with 100th Div.

In Fr 1st Army area, DA ATL opens offensive to clear Gironde Estuary, concentrating initially on Royan sector on N side of the river.

ITALY—15th Army Group: U.S. Fifth Army opens final offensive in IV Corps zone. In Ligurian coastal sector, 92d Div makes very little headway during next few days although arty is in position to counter fire of enemy guns. IV Corps attacks toward Po Valley after preparatory air and arty bombardment, advancing in region between Samoggia and Reno Rivers, the latter paralleling Highway 64. On left, 1st Div of BEF assists main effort of 10th Mtn Div in center, taking Montese. 10th Mtn Div clears Pra del Blanco basin, seizing Torre Iussi and Rocca di Roffeno. On right flank of corps, 1st Armd Div pushes toward Suzzano on left and begins bitter fight for Vergato, on Highway 64, on right.

In Br Eighth Army area, 10 Corps extends W to take over zone vacated by 13 Corps on left flank of army. This thinning of forces brings to an end planning for offensive operations, but elements of corps cross the Santerno to assist Pol 2 Corps' attack in Imola area. Jewish Brig is pinched out by Polish forces and withdraws to reserve. Pol 2 Corps outflanks and takes Imola, on Highway 9. 13 Corps, with Ind 10th Div under its command, takes over new zone between Pol 2 Corps and Br 5 Corps, leaving Folgore Gp and 6 infantry bns behind to strengthen 10 Corps. NZ 2d Div drives to the Sillaro and is transferred in place to 13 Corps from 5 Corps, enabling 5 Corps to concentrate on northward drive against Argenta Gap on right flank of army. In 5 Corps area, 36th Brig of 78th Div reaches Sillaro R and 38th pushes N to the Reno at Bastia. Enemy retains firm hold on Bastia, however. Resistance NE of Argenta continues to hold up 56th Div forces there but others push forward toward Bastia.

CHINA—*China Expeditionary Forces* is ordered by Tokyo to move 4 divs to central and N China. As a result, it is decided to withdraw from Hunan-Kwangsi RR, which links Hengyang, Kweilin, Liuchow, and Yung-ning, E China air bases. Gen Ho's chief of staff presents bold plan for campaign to halt Japanese drive on Chihchiang, calling for massing of troops on flanks of enemy and double envelopment. This plan is adopted and proves effective.

LUZON—In U.S. Sixth Army area, 2d Bn of RCT 158 continues attack toward San Francisco after air strikes but makes little headway. Co I moves up Route I to Iriga. Rest of regt is held up to N but probes northward. In I Corps area, after aerial bombardment, 148th Inf of 37th Div attacks SE through 129th Inf to Monglo, on Highway 9, elements moving to edge of hill, called Hairpin Hill, about 900 yards W of Monglo.

RYUKYU Is.—In U.S. Tenth Army's III Amphib Corps area, 6th Mar Div, assisted by aircraft, ground fire, and naval vessels, opens 2-pronged assault against Yae-Take hill mass on Motobu Peninsula. While 4th Marines (− 3d Bn, reinf by 3d Bn, 29th Marines) drives eastward, 1st and 2d Bn of 29th Marines press W from Itomi. Gains are limited by strong opposition and rough terrain, but 4th Marines secures positions on first ridges. On XXIV Corps front, action subsides after final Japanese counterattack is repulsed before dawn. 383d Inf, 96th Div, is withdrawn from line. 27th Div prepares to enter corps line.

15 April

WESTERN EUROPE—21 Army Group: In Cdn First Army's Cdn I Corps area, 49th Div completes capture of Arnhem. Cdn 5th Armd Div begins drive from there to Zuider Zee. Cdn 1st Div continues toward Apeldoorn. Cdn 2 Corps progresses toward line Leeuwarden-Groningen-Oldenburg and begins to clear Groningen.

In Br Second Army's 30 Corps area, 3d, 43d, and 51st Divs continue toward Bremen. Gds Armd Div zone is now clear. In 12 Corps area, 53d Div, advancing along Walsrode-Soltau road, gets elements beyond Kirchboitzen. 8 Corps continues to fight in Uelzen.

12th Army Group: In U.S. Ninth Army's XIII Corps area, 5th Armd Div continues to mop up along the Elbe. Additional elements of 84th and 102d Divs close along the river. In XIX Corps area, RCT 134 of 35th Div takes over sector along the Elbe from Grieben to vicinity of Colbitz Forest. RCT's 117 and 120 finish clearing 30th Div zone W of the Elbe. 2d Armd Div, less CCR, maintains defensive positions in Magdeburg sector, CCB holding W bank of the Elbe from Westerheusen to Schoenebeck. 83d Div expands Elbe bridgehead E of Barby. RCT 320, 35th Div, is attached to 83d Div and, after assembling W of the Saale, opens attack to clear right flank of corps between the Saale and Elbe, taking Tornitz and Werkleitz, then crossing the Saale and seizing Gross Rosenburg. Engineers, after nightfall, begin work on treadway bridge at Breitenhagen, SE of Barby, as a precautionary measure for Barby bridgehead. 330th Inf continues to mop up in Harz Mts and establishes contact with 1st Div of VII Corps, First Army. XVI Corps zone along the Ruhr, during period 15-18 April, grows steadily smaller as result of action by III and XVIII Corps (A/B) of First Army against Ruhr pocket S of the Ruhr. 75th Div starts assembling near Brambauer.

In U.S. First Army's XVIII Corps (A/B) area, 13th Armd Div (− CCR) drives N against considerable opposition to Wupper R in Opladen area; CCB, on right flank, clears Opladen. CCR is attached to 13th Inf, 8th Div. Following armor closely, 97th Div's 303d Inf takes large I.G. Farben chemical works near Leverkusen and continues to the Wupper while 387th and 386th Regts reach Berg Neukirchen-Burscheid railway. Enemy only offers token resistance to 78th Div, which reaches positions E of Solingen on left, overruns Remscheid and Ronsdorf in center, and captures Lennep and drives to edge of Wuppertal on right. 28th Inf of 8th Div reaches the Ruhr N of Schwelm and is passed through by 13th and 121st Regts, which start W abreast, former on right; 13th, reinf by CCR of 13th Armd Div, overruns Hattingen; from Schwelm assembly area, 121st gains about 3 miles toward Wuelfrath. 86th Div finishes clearing its sector along Lenne R up to the Ruhr except for scattered pockets. In III Corps area, 5th Div completes offensive operations in the Ruhr and is passed through by 7th Armd Div. While RCT's 10 and 2 remain in place along S bank of the Ruhr, 11th Inf clears region W of Meriden between Iserlohn and the Ruhr. CCR, 7th Armd Div, drives W from Meriden in two columns and reaches Kalthof area. 99th Div continues NW to general line Iserlohn-Kesbern-Altena. In VII Corps area, CCB of 3d Armd Div establishes shallow bridgehead across Mulde R near Torten, using wreckage of a bridge; elements to right reach Thurland area. CCR clears all except NE edge of Koethen and sends elements W toward Bebitz. CCA is committed on div right facing Dessau and reaches line Quellendorf-Koernitz-Fernsdorf. Reconnoitering on extreme right of div, 83d Armd Rcn Bn finds Wolfen and Bitterfeld strongly held but secures Reuden, Thalheim, and Sandersdorf. 1st and 9th Divs continue methodical elimination of enemy in Harz Mts for next few days. In V Corps area, CCA of 9th Armd Div reaches Thierbach-Kirzscher-Stockheim region NW of Borna, bypassing Borna, which CCB takes without opposition. CCR reaches Mulde R line, clearing Grimma on left and taking bridges in Colditz-Lastau area on right. 2d Div clears Merse-burg and Leuna by 0800, then crosses 23d Inf over the Saale at Merseburg and moves 9th Inf S after dark to clear German AA positions in zone of 69th Div. Forward elements of 69th Div reach positions due S of Leipzig on S flank of corps, pushing through Zeitz.

In U.S. Third Army's XX Corps area, 6th Armd Div crosses the Mulde, CCB at Rochlitz and rest of div at Lunzenau, and continues E to limiting line, where div halts to await arrival of Red Army forces. CCA takes 3 bridges across Zachopau R near Mittweida. 76th Div mops up in Zeitz and Altenburg and pushes elements rapidly eastward in order to take over 6th Armd Div's Mulde bridgehead. CCB, 4th Armd Div, improves positions in Bergstadt area and takes Chemnitz R bridges at and N of Draisdorf. CCA patrols toward Chemnitz and receives surrender of Siegmar. 80th Div follows 4th Armd Div closely: 319th Inf clears Grimmitscha and most of Glauchau; 318th prepares to take over bridgehead overlooking Chemnitz. VIII Corps directs 89th Div to establish bridgehead over Zwick Mulde R in vicinity of Wickau and to make contact with XX Corps. Committing 354th Inf between 355th and 3534, 89th Div drives to line of Weisse-Elster and Weida Rivers between Gera and Zeulenroda and begins crossing after nightfall. 6th Cav Gp crosses Weisse-Elster R on left flank of corps and moves E and SE in zone of 89th Div. Thrusting SE toward Weisse-Elster R, 87th Div's 346th Inf reaches Kleinwelschendorf, just W of Zeulenroda; TF Sundt drives to Pausa area; 347th Inf reaches Langenbach. 65th Div is notified that it will be returned to XX Corps. In XII Corps area, 11th Armd Div, its mission completed, remains in assembly areas. RCT 14, 71st Div, assisted by elements of 2d Cav Gp, continues to mop up within Bayreuth. Rest of 71st Div completes drive to corps restraining line on SW flank of corps, extending generally from Gefrees to Bayreuth. In center of corps, 26th Div reaches restraining line from Hof to Gefrees. On NE flank, 90th Div continues toward Plauen-Hof road and clears most of Hof.

In U.S. Fifteenth Army area, XXII Corps is made responsible for Aachen area.

6th Army Group: In U.S. Seventh Army area, XV Corps gains ground toward Nuremberg. In XXI Corps area, 42d Div's 222d and 232d Regts reach Aisch R line in Neustadt area. CCB, 12th Armd Div, completes its crossing of the Aisch at Dietersheim and thrusts SE to Scheller and Kotzenaurach; rorst Cav Gp drives SE through Linden to Zenn R; CCR is halted by stubborn opposition in vicinity of Westheim. 8th Inf, 4th Div, attacks SE toward Ansbach in conjunction with CCR of 12th Armd Div. 12th and 22d Regts push a little closer to Rothenburg against stronger resistance. VI Corps attacks SE with 100th and 63d Divs abreast, 100th on right, each div employing 3 regts abreast. 100th Div clears Unt Gruppenbach on right, begins outflanking Loewenstein in center, and on left drives to Neuberg-Buchhorn region, S of Pfedelbach. From right to left, 63d Div reaches Michelbach; positions near Waldenburg and Westernach; Goggenbach; Steinkirchen; and Nesselbach.

In Fr 1st Army area, 2d Corps continues to clear Black Forest in conjunction with Valluy Groupement and is thrusting toward Nagold R. 1st Corps crosses elements over the Rhine N of Kehl without opposition. Valluy Groupement, assisted by 1st Corps elements E of the Rhine, clears Kehl; forward elements overrun Offenburg and continue S in Baden Plain to outskirts of Lahr; left flank elements continue clearing Black Forest. In DA ATL area, after intense air and arty bombardment of enemy fortifications in Royan sector, Fr forces push to edge of that city. Fr troops across the Gironde in Pointe de Grave sector drive salient into enemy positions in vicinity of Vensac.

ITALY—15th Army Group: In U.S. Fifth Army's IV Corps area, 10th Mtn Div takes M. Pigna and M. Mantino but is unable to advance its exposed left flank. 1st Armd Div seizes Suzzano and continues to fight from house to house in Vergato. II Corps joins in offensive after intensive aerial preparation, attacking toward Bologna in region E of Highway 64, night 15-16. S African 6th Armd Div and 88th Div lead off at 2230; 91st and 34th Divs attack at 0300. In support of offensive, Legnano Gp demonstrates vigorously on right flank of corps. Enemy offers strong resistance all along line, but S African 6th Armd Div takes M. Sole by 0530.

In Br Eighth Army area, Pol 2 Corps reaches Sillaro R and begins crossing. 13 Corps drives toward Budrio, employing NZ 2d Div initially and committing 10th Ind Div later. In 5 Corps area, 78th Div turns over positions along the Sillaro on left flank of corps to Commandos in order to concentrate against the Argenta Gap. Enemy continues effective defense of Bastia against attacks of 78th and 56th Divs.

LUZON—In U.S. Sixth Army area, main body of RCT 158 continues almost futile attacks on Cituinan Hill mass from N and S. I and R Platoon drives N on Route 27. 2d Bn, RCT 158, makes two-pronged assault on San Francisco and takes the town. In I Corps area, troops of 148th Inf, 37th Div, after air strike on Hairpin Hill, clear it; push forward on Highway 9 beyond Quioeng. Elements of 130th Inf, 33d Div, attack unsuccessfully toward ridge W of Asin Tunnels. Ground assault on the tunnel positions is suspended for the next few days while enemy positions are being softened by bombardment. 1st Bn of 27th Inf, 25th Div, attacks across ravine from the Wart toward hill 300 yards ahead. 2d Bn, 35th Inf, takes hill in its sector. In XI Corps area, protracted fighting by 38th Div in Mt Pinatubo area is virtually concluded as 152d Inf column, which has moved E from W coast, makes contact with elements of 149th Inf on Mt Pinatubo. In XIV Corps area, 511th Inf of 11th A/B Div opens eastward drive on Mt Malepunyo hill mass.

S PHILIPPINES—In U.S. Eighth Army area, Americal Div troops on Cebu continue battle to destroy enemy on heights commanding Cebu City. On Bohol, 3d Bn of 164th Inf, Americal Div, makes contact with Japanese force N of Ginopolan. On Negros, 40th Div remains in place while air and arty are softening enemy positions in Negritos-Patog area. 108 aircraft drop 170 tons of bombs. Gen Sibert alters plan of amphibious operations against Mindanao since guerrilla forces there are reported to have taken Malabang. 24th Div, except for bn of 21st Inf, is to land in Parang area. The excepted bn will go ashore as planned at Malabang.

RYUKYU Is.—Arty lands on Minna I. to support invasion of Ie Shima. Air and naval bombardment of Ie Shima continues.

In U.S. Tenth Army's III Amphib Corps area, fighting on Motobu Peninsula, Okinawa, is bitter and costly as 6th Mar Div continues to press in on Yae-Take hill mass under heavy and effective fire from dominating terrain. XXIV Corps front remains static. 27th Div enters corps line.

JAPAN—Carrier planes of TF 58 attack Kyushu airfields with good effect but are unable to neutralize them completely.

16 April

WESTERN EUROPE—RAF BC sinks the *Luetzow* during daylight attack on Swinemuende.

21 Army Group: In Cdn First Army area, Cdn 2 Corps seizes Leeuwarden and Groningen.

In Br Second Army area, 30 Corps closes in on Bremen, forward elements of 3d Div reaching Brinkum, just S of the city. In 12 Corps area, 7th Armd Div, driving on Soltau, gets advance elements beyond Walsrode. In 8 Corps area, 15th Div is still strongly opposed in Uelzen.

12th Army Group: In U.S. Ninth Army's XIII Corps area, 84th and 102d Divs, former on left, relieve 5th Armd Div along the Elbe. 5th Armd Div is to clear rear area of stragglers, who threaten supply routes; releases attached elements of 84th and 102d Divs. Corps zone is extended southward to include 35th Div sector along the Elbe; 35th Div (− RCT 320) is attached to corps. In XIX Corps area, 35th Div shifts a little southward to relieve elements of 30th Div. 30th Div regroups as result of boundary change. 2d Armd Div maintains defensive positions about Magdeburg and along the Elbe to right and prepares for assault on Magdeburg in conjunction with 30th Div. 83d Div maintains bridgehead E of Barby despite strong counterattack against CCR of 2d Armd Div; RCT 320 continues to clear region between the Saale and Elbe. Enemy places arty fire on Elbe bridges and makes ineffective air attacks against them from time to time. CCA, 8th Armd Div, is attached to corps. In XVI Corps area, 79th Div, whose zone is uncovered by 8th and 86th Divs of XVIII Corps, relieves 116th Inf of 29th Div, SW of Muenster.

In U.S. First Army's XVIII Corps (A/B) area, 13th Armd Div columns, preceded by 93d Cav Rcn Sq, drive N across the Wupper in vicinity of Opladen, CCA on left advancing through Langenfeld and Hilden to region E of Duesseldorf and CCB pushing through Haan and Gruiten to Mettmann area. Crossing the Wupper to rear of armor, 97th Div drives rapidly N to general line Hilden-Solingen, but enemy retains Solingen. 78th Div, against little or no resistance, finishes clearing its sector and is pinched out by 8th Div; Elberfeld and Wuppertal are among towns overrun. 8th Div continues W, 13th Inf thrusting to Velbert area and 121st gaining final objective in Wuelfrath area. 86th Div consolidates on right flank of corps. In III Corps area, resistance in E part of Ruhr pocket collapses early in day as Germans indicate desire to surrender en masse. 7th Armd Div, with CCR again in assault, starts W toward the Lenne but halts at 0630 to await surrender negotiations. 99th Div also renews attack, with 3 regts in line, but halts at 0850 pending surrender of enemy forces, last of which—the Iserlohn garrison-capitulates by 1230. Each of the two assault divs takes more than 20,000 prisoners during the day. 7th Armd Div starts to new assembly area in vicinity of Gottingen. VII Corps is directed to halt along line of Elbe and Mulde Rivers pending arrival of Soviet forces. 3d Armd Div maintains bridgehead across the Mulde and extends right flank southward along the river. CCR overcomes resistance in Bernburg, closing that Harz Mts exit to enemy; to right finishes clearing Koethen and seizes nearby Klepzig and Merzien. CCA overruns Libbesdorf and continues NE toward Dessau; elements begin sweeping Forst Haldeburg, S of Dessau. CCB holds Mulde bridgehead near Torten and continues bridging operations under fire; to right overruns a number of towns. 104th Div continues assault on Halle against tenacious resistance and gets bulk of forces across the Saale. On W flank of corps, 1st and 9th Divs gain additional ground in Harz Mts. In V Corps area, CCA of 9th Armd Div reaches the Mulde in Bennewitz-Grimma area. CCR column crosses and clears Colditz. CCB completes assembling in Wettewitz area. 2d Div consolidates and pushes 3–5 miles eastward, 38th and 23d Regts coming abreast and squeezing out 9th. 69th Div pushes NE toward Leipzig, left flank elements halting at Zwenkau, in outer defenses of the city, and right flank elements reaching positions SE of Leipzig.

In U.S. Third Army's XX Corps area, 6th Armd Div turns over Zwick Mulde bridgehead to RCT 304 of 76th Div and begins maintenance and rehabilitation program. 76th Div closes along Zwick Mulde R, RCT's 304 and 417 relieving CCA and CCR of 6th Armd Div. 4th Armd Div turns over Zwick Mulde bridgehead to 318th and 319th Regts, 80th Div. VIII Corps pushes E and SE against scattered resistance. 6th Cav Gp, developing enemy positions ahead of 89th Div, takes Weisse-Elster bridges at Berga and Knottengrund and turns them over to 89th Div; pushes E to N–S rail line running through Werdau. 89th Div reaches Pliesse R and begins assault on Werdau on left, in center drives into Werdauer Wald, and on right reaches Weisse-Elster R in vicinity of Greiz. Assault forces of 87th Div cross Weisse-Elster R on right flank of corps and forward elements reach positions beyond corps restraining line, the autobahn. On left, 346th Inf captures Zeulenroda, crosses the Weisse-Elster, and drives to vicinity of Brockau. TF Sundt drives SE across Weisse-Elster R to Mechelgruen, E of limiting line. 347th Inf overruns Plauen and reaches autobahn to E on left and drives to Oelsnitz, beyond restraining line, on right. XII Corps consolidates along restraining line and patrols actively. 71st Div completes mop up of Bayreuth. 90th Div clears rest of Hof and improves defensive positions in limited attacks.

In U.S. Fifteenth Army area, 422d and 423d Regts of 106th Div and Div Rcn Tr are attached to 66th Div for training purposes.

6th Army Group: In U.S. Seventh Army's XV Corps area, 45th and 3d Divs continue drive on Nuremberg and 45th breaks into suburbs. In XXI Corps area, 42d Div, crossing Aisch R, overruns Neustadt and drives rapidly toward Fuerth; 242d Inf enters line between 222d and 232d Regts. 12th Armd Div continues SE toward Ansbach in center of corps with 3 combat commands in assault as CCA opens attack on div left. 8th Inf, 4th Div, continues toward Ansbach while 12th and 22d Regts gain positions just N and W of Rothenburg, respectively, and 324th Inf drives SE on div right. In VI Corps area, 10th Armd Div attacks SE through infantry. CCA, on right, reaches Gleichen-Heuholz area. To left, CCB thrusts toward Schwaebisch Hall, forward elements reaching vicinity of Suelz. 100th and 63d Divs, each with elements motorized, follow armor on right and left, respectively. Elements of 100th Div push through Loewenstein.

In Fr 1st Army area, 2d Corps overruns Calw, on Nagold R. 3d Algerian Inf Div, which has relieved 2d Moroccan Inf Div on the Enz, begins clearing woods S of Pforzheim. 1st Corps starts forward for action against enemy in Black Forest. Valluy Groupement reaches Nonnenweier. In DA ATL area, French overrun Royan, on N side of Gironde Estuary, and begin clearing NW between the Gironde and Le Seudre Rivers. Other French forces in Pointe de Grave sector push N to E–W line through Talais.

EASTERN EUROPE—Red Army opens all-out offensive toward Berlin in early morning hours, attacking along Oder and Neisse Rivers. On northern front, troops of Third White Russian Front are clearing enemy from Samland Peninsula, East Prussia. On Southern front, Second Ukrainian Front gains ground SE of Bruenn (Czechoslovakia) and N of Vienna. Troops of Third Ukrainian Front continue to clear region W of Vienna and overrun Fuerstenfeld, E of Graz.

[17 APRIL 1945]　　[499]

ITALY—15th Army Group: In U.S. Fifth Army area, IV Corps makes substantial gains as enemy begins to fall back. 10th Mtn Div, still spearheading, takes Tole, M. Mosco, and Monzuno. 1st Armd Div secures M. Pero and finishes clearing Vergato. 1st Div of BEF begins relief of left flank elements of 10th Mtn Div. In II Corps area, enemy continues vigorous defense of its positions facing corps. S African 6th Armd Div takes M. Caprara and M. Abelle. 88th Div seizes Furcoli but is unable to reach crest of M. Monterumici. 91st Div, attacking toward M. Adone, M. Posigliano, Pianoro, and M. Arnigo, makes slow progress astride Highway 65. 34th Div, directed toward Sevizzano Ridge on right flank of corps, reduces fortified position on Gorgognano Ridge.

In Br Eighth Army's Pol 2 Corps area, Ind 43d Brig seizes Medicina, on road to Budrio. In 5 Corps area, enemy is at last forced to yield Bastia, and lively battle for Argenta Gap begins.

BURMA—In Br Fourteenth Army's 4 Corps area, advance elements of Ind 5th Div occupy Shwemyo against light resistance but are under enemy fire from Shwemyo Bluff.

LUZON—In U.S. Sixth Army area, 2d Bn of RCT 158, after repulsing determined counterattack on San Francisco, attacks and clears entire area. With S tip of Bicol Peninsula clear, northern exits of San Bernardino Strait are safe for Allied shipping. In I Corps area, elements of 148th Inf, 37th Div, overcome strong opposition on heights E of Highway 9 near Yagyagan. In XI Corps area, 1st Inf of 6th Div begins attack on ridge called "Woodpecker" near junction of Bosoboso and Mariquina Rivers. After 2 days of preparatory air and naval bombardment, 1st Bn of 151st Inf, reinf, lands on Carabao I., final objective in Manila Bay, and secures it without opposition. In XIV Corps area, 11th A/B Div's 511th Inf captures Mt Malepunyo and Mt Dalaga. Elements of 8th and 7th Cav, 1st Cav Div, have pocketed enemy N and NW of Mt Mataasna Bundoc.

S PHILIPPINES—In U.S. Eighth Army area, Americal Div forces on Cebu make slow progress against heights commanding Cebu City. Enemy begins planned withdrawal after nightfall. On Negros, torrential rains ground aircraft but arty continues bombardment of enemy positions. In Sulu Archipelago, RCT 163 of 41st Div mops up scattered resistance on Jolo.

RYUKYU Is.—Japanese make major air effort against Okinawa and TF 58, despite further attacks by planes of TF 58 on Kyushu airfields. Suicide planes sink the DD Pringle and damage a number of other ships, among them the carrier Intrepid. After preparatory bombardment by warships and aircraft, 77th Div, less 307th Inf, begins landing on S and SW coast of Ie Shima about 0800, 305th Inf on right and 306th on left. Assault forces move rapidly inland, hampered more by numerous mines than by enemy opposition; take the airfield and clear about two thirds of the island. 305th Inf repels enemy counterattacks after nightfall in brisk fighting. Permission is requested and granted to use 307th Inf on Ie. On Okinawa, III Amphib Corps' 6th Mar Div employs 7 bns in final, all-out assault on Yae-Take ridges. 4th Marines, attacking with its 3 bns and attached 3d Bn of 29th Marines, moves forward on southern and western ridges while 29th Marines probes from NE. 1st Bn, 22d Marines, closes gap between 4th and 29th Marines. XXIV Corps regroups and moves up supplies in preparation for full-scale attack on 19th.

17 April

INTERNATIONAL AGREEMENTS—United States and USSR sign Fourth Protocol for aid to Soviet Union, granting 2,700,000 tons via the Pacific and 3,000,000 via the Atlantic.

WESTERN EUROPE—21 Army Group: In Cdn First Army's Cdn I Corps area, Apeldoorn falls to Cdn 1st Div. Thrusting toward Zuider Zee through Barneveld, Cdn 5th Armd Div cuts Amersfoort-Apeldoorn highway.

In Br Second Army area, 30 Corps continues to meet strong opposition at outskirts of Bremen. 12 Corps, now reinf by Gds Armd Div, is approaching Soltau on right and speeding toward Harburg on left. In 8 Corps area, 15th Div continues battle for Uelzen. To left, 11th Armd Div drives toward Lueneburg. 6th A/B Div crosses the Ilmenau SE of Uelzen.

12th Army Group: In U.S. Ninth Army's XIII Corps area, 29th Div is attached to corps to assist 5th Armd Div in pushing left flank of corps northward to the Elbe, since gap exists between U. S. and British forces. CCA, 5th Armd Div, prepares to clear Forst Knesebeck, S of Wittingen, and is reinf by elements of 102d and 84th Divs. CCB blocks roads E of the forest. CCR mops up its sector S of Salzwedel. In XIX Corps area, after preparatory aerial bombardment, 30th Div and CCA of 2d Armd Div open assault on Magdeburg about 1500. 30th Div pushes into N and NW part of city and CCA into S and SW part, clearing about two thirds of objective. CCB, 2d Armd Div, maintains defensive positions along the Elbe. 83d Div improves positions in Elbe bridgehead E of Barby. 320th Inf continues to clear between Saale and Elbe Rivers. CCA, 8th Armd Div, closes in Seehausen area and is held in reserve. In XVI Corps area, 75th Div completes assembling near Brambauer.

In U.S. First Army's XVIII Corps (A/B) area, CCA of 13th Armd Div takes German CP W of Mettmann and halts for night near Ratingen; CCB soon establishes contact with 8th Div in Wuelfrath area and by 1800 reaches Duisburg, where contact is made with Ninth Army; CCR reverts to div from attachment to 8th Div. 97th Div reaches final objective, clearing Solingen on right and reaching Duesseldorf on left; stop line is moved to N to permit attack on Duesseldorf on 18th. 78th Div consolidates and mops up; Pith Inf motors from Wuppertal to Dillenburg area. 8th Div completes its offensive as 13th Inf clears rest of sector S of the Ruhr, including Werden. 86th Div continues light mopping up operations along right flank of corps and prepares to join Third Army. III Corps continues to round up prisoners and prepares to depart for Third Army zone. 5th Div begins taking over corps zone, relieving CCR of 7th Armd Div and 99th Inf Div. 7th Armd Div is transferred to V Corps. 99th Div starts toward assembly area in vicinity of Trossenfurt, NW of Bamberg. In VII Corps area, 3d Armd Div is clearing and consolidating its sector S of the Elbe and W of the Mulde; begins withdrawing bridgehead in Torten area, night 17-18. One CCR TF thrusts N from Koethen area to Aken, on the Elbe; another circles SE from Aernburg area to div right flank to clear Bobbau-Steinfurth-Jessnitz sector and enters former. CCA finishes clearing Forst Haldeburg, just S of Dessau. Negotiations for surrender of Halle having failed, 104th Div's TF Kelleher renews assault on the city, some elements continuing S and others moving into city from E. By end of day about two thirds of the city is clear. 413th Inf assists TF Kelleher in closing escape routes from Halle. 415th Inf reaches Sandersdorf on left and Roitzsch on right. 1st and 9th Divs make progress in Harz Mts, on W flank of corps, though resistance is still strong. 1st Div takes Braunlage, Zorge, and Tanne and relieves elements of 9th Div in Hasselfelde. At 2000, 4th Cav Gp is transferred from 1st Div to 9th Div control. 60th Inf, on 9th Div left, reaches Maegdesprung area; 47th in center clears Pansfeld and Degenershausen; and 39th on right reaches Aschersleben, Guesten, and Ilberstedt. In V Corps area, 9th Armd Div mops up along the Mulde and patrols northward. 2d and 9th Divs close in on Leipzig from W and S.

In U.S. Third Army area, XX Corps regroups on quiet front for final drive into Austria. 65th Div, assembling in Bamberg area, is transferred to corps from VIII Corps. In VIII Corps area, 6th Cav Gp secures corps limiting line on left and pushes S across zone of 87th Div toward limiting line on right. 89th Div completes capture of Werdau and establishes bridgehead across Zwick Mulde R in vicinity of Zwickau; on right clears Greiz and takes Reichenbach after aerial softening of the city. 87th Div closes along limiting line on corps right flank and gains additional ground beyond it. 346th Inf pushes beyond the autobahn to Lengenfeld and Treuen. TF Sundt extends positions beyond the autobahn to Bergen area. Elements of 347th Inf occupy Theuma. XII Corps maintains defensive positions, patrols, and regroups; prepares to renew attack to SE on 19th. 71st Div, upon relief along line Bayreuth-Gefrees by 11th Armd Div, moves S to relieve 14th Armd Div (XV Corps).

In U.S. Fifteenth Army area, XXII Corps releases 20th Armd Div to First Army.

6th Army Group: U.S. Seventh Army orders attack to swerve from SE to S. In XV Corps area, 45th and 3d Divs converge on Nuremberg and begin clearing it against furious opposition. CCA and CCB, 14th Armd Div, assemble near Berg; CCR maintains positions along line Creussen-Buchau until relieved by 71st Div. In XXI Corps area, 42d Div pursues enemy to edge of Fuerth. CCA, 12th Armd Div, in conjunction with 232d Inf, 42d Div, clears Gadolzburg and Zautendorf. CCB seizes Heilbronn. CCR, continuing toward Ansbach, reaches Weihenzell-Bruenst area. Motorized TF of 8th Inf, 4th Div, thrusts to outskirts of Ansbach while rest of regt works southward through woods to Ober Felden area. 12th Inf takes Rothenburg. Other elements of div clear villages in region SW of Rothenburg. VI Corps is directed to speed to Swiss border and block enemy escape from the Black Forest. 44th Div, less RCT 324, is transferred to VI Corps from XXI Corps. 10th Armd Div, in conjunction with 100th Div on right and 63d on left, makes substantial progress. CCA columns reach vicinity of Huetten, Schuppach, and Gailsbach. CCB takes Suelz, assists 254th Inf of 63d Div in clearing about half of Schwaebisch Hall, and clears most of Michelfeld and Bibersfeld. 100th Div gains ground in hills E and SE of Loewenstein and down Neckar R Valley toward Beilstein. 63d Div opens assault on Schwaebisch Hall and is clearing enemy from this region.

In Fr 1st Army area, 2d Corps overruns Freudenstadt, splitting German 19th Army; to left, takes Nagold and Horb. 1st Corps takes command of Groupement Valluy (9th Colonial Inf Div and CC3 of 1st Armd Div), which is to constitute the right prong of a pincer maneuver to encircle the Black Forest. In addition to Groupement Valluy, 1st Corps has under its command 1st Armd Div, 4th Moroccan Mtn Div, and reserve units. Groupement Valluy overruns Oberkirch after heavy fighting in this region. In DA ALPS area, Germans withdraw hastily from Roya R Valley. DA ATL clears most of Royan pocket on N side of the Gironde. Forces on S side of the river push northward until halted by AT ditch.

ITALY—15th Army Group: In U.S. Fifth Army area, 92d Div continues to pin down enemy forces in Ligurian coastal sector but gains ground very slowly. 473d Inf crosses Parmignola Canal and pushes toward Sarzana. In IV Corps area, 10th Mtn Div makes rapid progress, taking M. Ferra, S. Prospero, and M. Moscoso. 1st Div of BEF continues relief of left flank elements of 10th Mtn Div. 85th Div (which has moved to IV Corps zone, contrary to plans for it to operate under II Corps when boundary of that corps is moved W) begins relief of 1st Armd Div on right flank of corps. As relieved, 1st Armd Div shifts from right to left flank of corps to protect exposed left flank of 10th Mtn Div. II Corps continues to battle stubborn enemy on heights below Bologna. S African 6th Armd Div tries in vain to take M. S. Barbara. 88th Div gains summit of Monterumici. 91st Div makes little progress W of Highway 65 but is approaching Pianoro on the highway and crest of M. Arnigo to E. 34th Div clears heights in Sevizzano-Gorgognano area and reaches slopes of Dei Mori Hill.

Br Eighth Army issues instructions for pursuit of enemy to the Po. 10 Corps pursues enemy to Gaiana R, where contact is regained. In Pol 2 Corps area, Ind 43d Brig is detached from corps and placed under command of NZ 2d Div. Corps gets advance elements to Gaiana R W of Medicina but cannot force crossing; to left takes Castel S. Pietro on Highway 9. In 13 Corps area, NZ 2d Div reaches Gaiana R, where it is also held up by enemy on far bank. 5 Corps is converging on Argenta Gap against strong opposition. 78th Div clears Argenta village.

BURMA—Adm Mountbatten issues directive for modified DRACULA, calling for amphibious and airborne operations to capture Rangoon.

LUZON—In U.S. Sixth Army's I Corps area, 148th Inf of 37th Div comes up against enemy's final defensive line before Baguio as elements reach Irisan R, where bridge is out. Further progress along the road to Baguio is delayed for the next few days by enemy's stubborn defense of ridges near the bridge site. 130th Inf, 33d Div, is still held up in Asin Tunnels region. 32d Div continues clearing heights in Salacsac Pass region of Villa Verde Trail. Japanese are still defending Kapintalan sector of Highway 5 against attacks of 25th Div. In XI Corps area, 63d Inf of 6th Div clears N tip of Mt Mataba, eliminating final resistance in this area. After further vain efforts to clear Woodpecker Ridge, near junction of Bosoboso and Mariquina Rivers, 1st Inf suspends attack and patrols actively. In XIV Corps area, attack of 2d Cav Brig, 1st Cav Div, on W slopes of Mt Mataasna Bundoc makes slow progress. 511th Inf, 11th A/B Div, turns N toward this hill mass, the last enemy stronghold in S Luzon.

S PHILIPPINES—In U.S. Eighth Army area, after preparatory naval gunfire and aerial bombardment, VICTOR V Attack Group (TG 78.2, Adm Noble) lands assault units of 24th Div, X Corps, on Mindanao without opposition. Main body goes ashore in Parang area and 3d Bn of 21st Inf lands just N of Malabang. Despite congestion on beach, main assault force moves rapidly inland and seizes Parang and heights commanding Polloc Harbor. 3d Bn of 21st Inf, finding guerrillas in possession of Malabang as reported, patrols southward toward Parang and N toward Polloc Harbor. 24th Div CG takes command ashore. On Cebu, Americal Div finds that enemy has withdrawn from Babay Ridge and occupies Hills 22 and 25. On Bohol, Cos K and L of 164th Inf open attack on Japanese N of Ginopolan. On Negros, 40th Div renews co-ordinated attack. 503d Para Inf reaches outer defenses of enemy on lower slopes of Banana Ridge. 185th Inf is halted at tank trap after gaining 1,600 yards. 160th Inf advances about 1,000 yards. In Sulu Archipelago, Jolo I. is now clear except for Mt Daho. Aircraft, arty, and mortars pound this last enemy strongpoint for next few days.

RYUKYU Is.—On Ie Shima, 306th Inf of 77th Div holds current positions while awaiting 305th Inf, which has fallen behind. 305th drives E toward Iegusugu Mt, which dominates entire island and is dubbed "the Pinnacle," and Ie town, elements reaching edge of the town. 2d and 3d Bns, 307th Inf, land on S coast and attack NE through elements of 305th Inf, meeting tenacious resistance from strong Japanese defenses organized in depth on ridge called "Bloody Ridge" and a rise on it known as "Government House Hill." On Okinawa, III Amphib Corps' 6th Mar Div breaks enemy organized resistance on Motobu Peninsula with capture of summit of Yae-Take hill mass; inflicts heavy casualties on Japanese.

18 April

WESTERN EUROPE—21 Army Group: In Cdn First Army's Cdn I Corps area, Cdn 5th Armd Div reaches Zuider Zee, isolating enemy forces and virtually ending offensive operations of corps. Corps subsequently closes along line of Grebbe and Eem Rivers, where it remains until end of the war. Cdn 2 Corps zone is largely clear, though enemy continues to oppose Cdn 4th Armd Div SW of Oldenburg.

In Br Second Army area, 30 Corps prepares for assault on Bremen. 12 Corps captures Soltau and continues toward Harburg. In 8 Corps area, Uelzen falls to 15th Div and Lueneburg to 11th Armd Div. 5th Div, now under corps command, is concentrating E of Osnabrueck before advancing to the Baltic.

12th Army Group: In U.S. Ninth Army's XIII Corps area, CCA of 5th Armd Div, after driving through Forst Knesebeck unopposed, assembles at Steimke and releases attached elements of 102d and 84th Divs. In XIX Corps area, organized resistance in Magdeburg ceases after assault elements of 30th Inf and 2d Armd Divs clear their respective portions and make contact. 83d Div forces E of the Elbe regroup to improve defensive positions within bridgehead; repel counterattack toward bridge at Breitenhagen. Elements of RCT 320 take Dornbock, W of the Elbe. 330th Inf continues to mop up in Harz Mts. CCB, 8th Armd Div, attacking in woods S of Derenburg, clears to Langenstein-Heimburg road. Air attack forces enemy from Forst Heimburg. XVI Corps' mission of protecting Ninth Army's right flank is successfully concluded. 29th Div starts to XIII Corps zone.

In U.S. First Army area, XVIII Corps (A/B) overcomes organized resistance in the Ruhr and begins mopping up stragglers. German forces under Field Marshal Model have suffered staggering losses in men and materiel in the Ruhr. Prisoners taken during the operation total 325,000, more than twice the number of enemy estimated to have been encircled. In XVIII Corps (A/B) area, CCA of 13th Armd Div drives W through Ratingen to the Rhine while CCB remains at Duisburg. In 97th Div sector, 303d Inf drives through Duesseldorf virtually unopposed. 78th Div, with new mission of guarding First Army rear, continues movement to Dillenburg area. 8th Div searches for bypassed enemy. 86th Div passes to control of Third Army. In VII Corps area, 3d Armd Div continues clearing its zone and establishes contact with XIX Corps on left. CCB completes withdrawal of Mulde bridgehead in Torten area. CCR, reinf by 83d Armd Rcn Bn and elements of CCA, attempts to secure Jessnitz-Wolfen-Greppin sector on div right flank and reaches Reuden and Thalheim. TF Kelleher, 104th Div, continues house-to-house fighting' in S part of Halle, clearing most of the city. 1st Div continues E and NE in Harz Mts and establishes contact with Ninth Army. 60th Inf, 9th Div, overruns Maegdesprung and Friedrichsbrunn; 47th clears Meisdorf and Opperode and begins assault on Ballenstedt; 39th Inf and 4th Cav Gp, organized as TF X and largely motorized for swift advance on div right, reach Quedlinburg. In V Corps area, 2d and 69th Divs begin co-ordinated assault on Leipzig. 23d and 38th Regts of 2d Div push into W Leipzig and clear to Weisse and Pliesse Rivers. 69th Div, employing 273d Inf, attacks NW and W into Leipzig. 9th Inf, 2d Div, takes German AA positions E of Lutzen. RCT 271 is attached to 2d Div and continues to fight in Zwenkau area, overrunning Eythra and driving N toward Leipzig.

7th Armd Div closes in Gottingen in SHAEF reserve.

U.S. Third Army regroups extensively and starts side slipping southward for final drive SE to Austria and Czechoslovakia. VIII Corps clears to corps restraining line and takes control of XX Corps sector and of 4th and 6th Armd and 76th Inf Divs in place. 6th Armd and 76th Inf Divs maintain current positions along restraining line and patrol; 76th Div begins relief of 4th Armd Div. 89th Div attains all its objectives: 355th and 354th Regts expand Zwick Mulde bridgehead toward Oelsnitz, overrunning Zwickau, Wilkau, and many other towns; makes contact with 76th Div on left; 353d Inf takes a number of towns E of the autobahn on right flank of div. 6th Cav Gp assembles on right flank of corps, where 28th Sq relieves elements of 90th Div (XII Corps) and patrols toward Czechoslovakian border. XII Corps regroups as result of boundary change and prepares to attack SE toward Chain on 19th. 2d Cav Gp's 42d Sq, upon relief in Bayreuth area by 11th Armd Div, moves to Hof area; after relieving left flank elements of 90th Div now N of corps left boundary, maintains contact with VIII Corps and patrols toward Czechoslovakia. 357th Inf of 90th Div shifts S, relieving 328th Inf, 26th Div. 90th and 26th Divs push strong reconnaissance to front in preparation for general drive to SE. Patrol of 358th Inf, 90th Div, thrusts across Czechoslovakian border near Prex at 0955, being the first Allied troops to do so. In 26th Div zone, 104th Inf pushes E to Kirchenlamitz and Weissenstadt; 101st consolidates between Gefrees and Voitsumra; 357th assembles in vicinity of Berneck. XX Corps turns over its sector and 3 divs to VIII Corps and starts to Bamberg area. 80th Div releases positions overlooking Chemnitz to 76th Inf and 4th Armd Divs- 76th Div relieves 4th Armd Div in line. XII Corps passes to Third Army control from First Army and starts to extreme right flank in Bavaria. 5th Armd Div takes over entire zone formerly held by corps, relieving 14th Cav Gp and 8th TD Gp in place; is placed under Third Army control. 86th Div is attached to corps and starts to Windsheim area.

In U.S. Fifteenth Army's XXII Corps area, 94th Div takes over zone formerly held by 101st A/B Div; 101st A/B Div prepares for move to Wurzburg area in Seventh Army zone.

6th Army Group: In U.S. Seventh Army's XV Corps area, 45th and 3d Divs deepen penetration into Nuremberg against stiff resistance. In XXI Corps area, 42d Div enters Fuerth and, in conjunction with elements of XV Corps, blocks all exits from Nuremberg. 12th Armd Div, directed to attack along axis Ansbach-Feuchtwangen-Lauchheim, concentrates in Ansbach area. While CCA reconnoiters Ansbach-Feuchtwangen road, CCB and CCR overrun northern part of Ansbach in co-ordinated assault; 101st Cav Gp moves forward to screen S flank of div. 4th. Div continues southward and begins relief of 324th Inf with 22d. In VI Corps area, 10th Armd Div advances 9 miles as enemy resistance slackens. CCA, in conjunction with 398th Inf of 100th Div, captures Mainhardt, Grab, and Ob Rot and continues SE through Hansen. CCB helps 63d Div complete capture of Schwaebisch Hall and mops up in Michelfeld and Bibersfeld; after regrouping, continues S along Kocher R to positions beyond Fichtenberg on right and to vicinity of Gross Altdorf on left. 397th Inf, 100th Div, clears toward Murr R at Sulzbach; 399th runs into considerable opposition on heights NE of Beilstein in Neckar R Valley. 254th Inf, 63d Div, mops up Schwaebisch Hall and clears to general line Ruppertshofen-Croeffelbach; 255th clears Eltershofen-Celbingen area NE of Schwaebisch Hall; 253d mops up W and SW of Schwaebisch Hall to line Sanzenbach-Uttenhofen. 44th Div, less RCT 324, closes in corps zone.

In Fr 1st Army area, 2d Corps begins drive on Stuttgart. From Freudenstadt, 5th Armd Div and 2d Moroccan Inf Div advance NE along the Neckar to Rottenburg and Herrenberg. 3d Algerian Inf Div finishes clearing forest S of Pforzheim. 1st Corps makes progress in Black Forest sector, clearing Obertal, Oppenau, Gengenbach, and Lahr. DA ATL completes reduction of Royan pocket and in Pointe de Grave sector crosses AT ditch and reaches Soulac.

ITALY—15th Army Group: U.S. Fifth Army moves boundary between IV and II Corps W. In IV Corps area, 10th Mtn Div reaches Sulmonte-S. Chierlo area astride Lavino Creek and takes almost 3,000 prisoners. Forces flanking it are regrouped to enable the mountain troops to concentrate in center for rapid pursuit. 1st Div of BEF takes over from left flank elements. 1st Armd Div, whose relief on right flank of corps is completed, moves forward rapidly on left flank of corps astride the Samoggia. 85th Div releases right flank elements of 10th Mtn Div and moves forward, on right flank of corps. In II Corps area, enemy is retreating all along line. S African 6th Armd Div finds S. Barbara ridge undefended and patrols to junction of Reno R and Setta Creek without incident, 88th Div takes ridge extending W from Furcoli and speeds northward to within a mile of M. Mario. Elements on Furcoli ridge are pinched out. 91st Div takes M. Adone, M. Posigliano, Pianoro, and M. Arnigo. 34th Div seizes Dei Mori Hill.

In Br Eighth Army's 13 Corps area, NZ 2d Div establishes bridgehead across the Gaiano. 5 Corps gains Argenta Clap, through which it is to force enemy back across the Po. 6th Armd Div is released from army reserve to corps to exploit toward Ferrara and takes up positions on left flank.

BURMA—In Br Fourteenth Army's 4 Corps area, Ind 5th Div completes clearing Shwemyo Bluff and drives S on Pyinmana.

LUZON—In U.S. Sixth Army area, assault forces of RCT 158 attacking Cituinan Hill from N and S are 2,000 yards apart. 2d Bn, having turned over responsibility for mopping up Sorsogon Province to guerrillas, gets into position near Malabog to attack the hill from E. In I Corps area, 148th Inf of 37th Div fights for ridges astride Highway 9 near Irisan bridge site, clearing one and part of another. In Mt Myoko sector, some elements of 27th Inf, 25th Div, continue efforts to clear hill 300 yards N of the Wart while others attack toward hill 600 yards from the Wart. In XI Corps area, 145th Inf of 37th Div and 20th Inf of 6th Div complete exchange of sectors. 145th Inf, now responsible for Novaliches watershed area, is directed to attack toward Mt Pacawagan, about 3,000 yards N of Mt Mataba, on 21st. Mt Pacawagan commands approaches to Wawa. 1st Inf, 6th Div, takes high ground overlooking Mariquina R after costly fighting. On El Fraile I., 38th Div patrol enters Fort Drum, a burned out shell, and finds 69 enemy dead. In XIV Corps area, 187th Inf of 11th A/B Div renews attack on Mt Macolod and gains positions on SE slope.

S PHILIPPINES—In U.S. Eighth Army area, X Corps CP opens at Parang on Mindanao, and Gen Sibert assumes command ashore. 24th Div begins amphibious and overland drives on Fort Pikit en route to Kabacan road junction, a key position. 2d Bn, 21st Inf, and force from 533d Engr Boat and Shore Regt, divided into 2 groups, make amphibious drives up 2 branches of Mindanao R and take Cotabato and Tamontaca without opposition; elements continue upstream and seize undefended Lomopog, 22 miles from Cotabato. RCT 19 starts overland drive southward along Highway 1, aided after nightfall by illumination of naval star shells. On Negros, 40th Div, assisted by aircraft, continues assault on strong enemy defense positions, making slow progress. 185th Inf inches forward from the tank trap in its sector. Elements of 160th reach military crest of Hill 3155 but are forced to withdraw. On Palawan, elements of Co G, 186th Inf, 41st Div, in shore-to-shore operation, secure Balabac I., off S tip of Palawan.

RYUKYU IS.—On Ie Shima, war correspondent Ernie Pyle is killed by enemy sniper. 77th Div continues to make main effort against Bloody Ridge from S and W with 307th Inf helped by 305th, but vicious opposition makes progress very slow. 1st Bn, 305th Inf, is attached to 307th to protect right flank. 3d Bn, 305th, drives into Ie town but pulls back to more tenable positions in outskirts. 306th Inf makes substantial progress against lighter opposition in region N of Iegusugu, pushing eastward to line from NE base of Iegusugu to NE coast. Disabled B-29 lands on Okinawa. U.S. Tenth Army CP opens ashore on Okinawa. In III Amphib Corps area, marines pursue enemy northward across Itomi-Manna road; subsequently patrol extensively and reduce bypassed pockets in N Okinawa. In XXIV Corps area, Co G of 106th Inf, 27th Div, in preparation for main attack of corps on 19th, crosses Machinato Inlet secretly, starting at 1630, and secures Machinato village to enable engineers to bridge the inlet. A footbridge is completed by midnight and 106th Inf troops start across it without arousing enemy.

19 April

WESTERN EUROPE—21 Army Group: In Br Second Army area, 30 Corps, reinf by 52d Div, begins assault on Bremen. While 3d Div attacks the portion W of the Weser frontally, 52d Div, with elements of 43d Div under command, begins crossing the Weser to strike at the city from the SE. In 12 Corps area, 7th Armd Div, driving rapidly N, cuts Bremen-Hamburg Autobahn. In 8 Corps area, 11th Armd Div reaches the Elbe in Lauenburg area.

12th Army Group: In U.S. Ninth Army's XIII Corps area, 5th Armd Div is assisted by arty and aircraft in destroying enemy troops attempting to escape through its zone. 44th Sq, 11th Cav Gp, moves out to contain and determine strength of enemy seeking to move through Forst Kloetze toward Harz Mts. XIX Corps maintains and improves defensive positions along the Elbe. 113th Cav Gp closes along the Elbe on right flank of corps from Breitenhagen southward, relieving RCT 320 of 83d Div, which in turn relieves CCR of 2d Armd Div on N flank of 83d Div bridgehead. 83d Div continues to improve positions E of the Elbe and comb Harz Mts to right rear. 8th Armd Div passes to corps control and CCA and CCB revert to it; prepares to clear Blankenburg area, at E edge of Harz Mts. XVI Corps begins period of regrouping, occupation, and military government. Its zone includes all Ninth Army territory W of the Weser and is held by: XVI Corps Arty, with 15th Cav Gp attached; 95th Div; 79th Div, with 18th AAA Gp attached; and 17th A/B Div.

In U.S. First Army's XVIII Corps (A/B) area, 8th Div extends W to the Rhine, relieving 13th Armd Div. 13th Armd and 97th Inf Divs prepare to join Third Army. 78th Div is placed under direct control of First Army. In VII Corps area, CCR of 3d Armd Div endeavors to oust enemy from Bobbau-Steinfurth and Wolfen, on right flank of div, partially clearing both towns; CCA and CCB columns gain ground near Torten; other elements of CCA seize a number of towns generally N of Koethen. TF Kelleher, 100th Div, completes capture of Halle by 1055 and then clears Radewell and Dieskau. 413th Inf attacks through 415th toward Delitzsch and reaches Zschernitz. 415th improves positions near Bitterfeld and clears Petersroda, just E of Roitzsch. Against crumbling resistance, 1st Div moves forward in Harz Mts: 26th Inf begins attack on hill that commands div sector; 16th takes Elbingrode and Huettenrode; 18th clears S part of Thale. Organized resistance in 9th Div zone ends as div reaches N boundary of corps and makes contact with adjacent friendly units. Enemy pocket continues to hold out SE of Ballenstedt. TF X is dissolved. In V Corps area, 2d and 69th Divs complete capture of Leipzig.

In U.S. Third Army area, VIII Corps consolidates along restraining line and patrols eastward. Boundary on right is altered to extend along N boundary of Bavaria to Czechoslovakian border. 6th Cav Gp continues patrolling toward Czechoslovakia. 4th Armd Div assembles as reserve. XII Corps attacks SE, air and arty softening resistance to front with very good effect. 11th Armd Div, with CCA on left and CCB on right, converges on Grafenwohr and clears it; is ordered to halt there. 26th Div, with 3 regts abreast, drives almost due S to general line Trostau-Birk. 90th Div advances SE on left flank of corps: 358th Inf, on left, takes Rehau and pushes toward Selb; 357th, on right, gets forward elements to Wunsiedel. XX Corps issues order for final drive into Austria, designating 71st Div (temporarily under XV Corps) and 65th Div as initial assault forces and 80th Inf and 13th Armd Divs (13th under XVIII Corps) as reserve; 3d Cav Gp will protect flanks of corps. 71st Div continues SE toward Amberg. 80th Div closes in assembly area and conducts training and rehabilitation. III Corps continues movement to Bavaria and takes control of 20th Armd Div from First Army.

In U.S. Fifteenth Army area, XXIII Corps relieves elements of 10th Div in Koblenz and Pfalz areas.

6th Army Group: In U.S. Seventh Army area, XV Corps continues assault on Nuremberg, breaking into the inner walled city. 42d Div, transferred to corps from XXI Corps, clears Fuerth, a western suburb of Nuremberg, and pushes into Nuremberg. 14th Armd Div, with mission of protecting left flank and rear of 45th Div, relieves 106th Cav Gp of this task. XXI Corps takes command of 63d Div, previously on left flank of VI Corps, in place. CCR and CCB, 12th Armd Div, complete capture of Ansbach, relieving elements of 4th Div there, and push quickly toward Feuchtwangen. Moving E to block enemy escape from Nuremberg, CCA estab-

[19 APRIL 1945]

lishes roadblocks at Schwabach and Bertholdsdorf and patrols between them. 101st Cav Gp, protecting S flank of armor, regains command of 101st Sq from 4th Div. 8th Inf, 4th Div, reaches Roedenweiler area; 12th reaches line Bottenweiler-Wildenholz-Theuerbronn; 22d completes relief of 324th, which is detached from div and corps, and pushes S to line Michelbach-Gailroth-Schoenbronn-Rossbuerg-Schainbach; 4th Rcn Tr clears Rot am See and maintains contact with 63d Div. 63d Div, with 255th, 254th, and 253d Regts, from right to left, is clearing region E of the Kocher between Schwaebisch Hall and Crailsheim. In VI Corps area, 10th Armd Div, achieving complete breakthrough, speeds almost 20 miles southward. CCA crosses Rems R at Lorch and continues to Fils R, taking bridge at Faurndau, near Goeppingen. CCB, bypassing Schwaebisch Gmuend, crosses the Rems W of that city and pushes eastward. 398th Inf, 100th Div, crosses the Murr at Murrhardt; 397th reaches the Murr at Sulzbach and begins assault on that town; 399th overruns Beilstein and Ilsfeld. 117th Cav Rcn Sq is attached to 100th Div and given sector on extreme right between 399th Inf and the Neckar. 44th Div, with mission of mopping up in rear and protecting flanks of armor, attacks S through 63d Div with 71st and 114th Regts. 71st follows CCA and 114th, CCB. RCT 324 reverts to 44th Div; 2d Bn, motorized, follows CCB southward. 103d Div is moving into corps zone.

In Fr 1st Army area, 2d Corps continues toward Stuttgart with 3d Algerian Inf Div on left and 5th Armd Div and 2d Moroccan Inf Div on right. 1st Corps, clearing W part of Black Forest, reaches Biberach-Mahlberg area. In DA ATL area, Fr forces in Pointe de Grave sector seize Le Verdon.

EASTERN EUROPE—Moscow confirms German reports of Soviet offensive toward Berlin on central front, stating that bridgeheads have been established across Oder and Neisse Rivers during the last 3 days. Some Red Army forces are thrusting toward Berlin from Oder bridgehead W of Kuestrin. Others have forced the Neisse between Cottbus and Goerlitz and are advancing in the direction of Dresden. Rothenburg, NW of Goerlitz, falls to Second Polish Army. Ukrainian troops continue toward Bruenn and Moravska Ostrava and gain additional ground N of Vienna.

ITALY—15th Army Group: U.S. Fifth Army issues orders for pursuit to the Po. 92d Div is to advance in Ligurian coastal sector when enemy withdraws and be prepared to renew attack toward La Spezia. IV Corps is to secure Panaro R line W of Camposanto and be prepared to take Po crossings between Ostiglia and Borgoforte. II Corps will continue drive on Bologna, clear Panaro R line E of Camposanto and be prepared to cross the Po between Ostiglia and Sermide. IV Corps pursues enemy, now in full retreat, toward the Po. 10th Mtn Div gets to within sight of the Po plain, seizing Mongiorgio and getting advance elements to road junction 3 miles NE of M. S. Michele. 1st Armd Div and 85th Div move forward on corps flanks, echeloned to rear. II Corps shifts W while continuing pursuit against spotty, but skillful, rear-guard action in order to make main effort W of the Reno with S African 6th Armd Div and 88th Div. 88th, less 350th Inf on M. Mario, is pinched out E of the Reno and takes up positions W of the river to right of 85th Div (IV Corps). S African 6th Armd Div prepares to cross the Reno in Pradura area. 91st and 34th Divs continue pursuit E of the Reno. 91st, taking command of 350th Inf, which clears M. Mario—last of 88th Div objectives E of the Reno—veers NW, eliminating scattered strongpoints. 34th Div, swinging W to take over sector of 91st Div W of Highway 65, takes hills N of M. Arnigo. Legnano Gp, which has been assisting 34th Div, begins attack astride Idice R to advance right flank of corps.

In Br Eighth Army area, Pol 2 Corps breaks through positions along the Gaiana and pursues enemy. 13 Corps drives to within sight of Budria; is ordered to continue attack across the Idice. 5 Corps is improving positions in Argenta Gap area.

BURMA—In Br Fourteenth Army's 33 Corps area, Ind 20th Div columns reach the Irrawaddy and take Magwe and Myingun.

LUZON—Gen MacArthur directs U.S. Sixth Army to seize reservoirs NE of Manila, a task subsequently undertaken by XI Corps. In the Bicols, RCT 158 attacks Cituinan hill mass from 3 directions for the next week, progressing slowly but methodically with aid of aircraft and arty. In I Corps' Highway 9 sector, 148th Inf of 37th Div clears all ridges S and NW of Irisan R bridge site, but enemy retains ridge positions to NE. 130th Inf of 33d Div, endeavoring to open Galiano-Baguio road, is still engaged in Asin tunnels area. 123d Inf probes along Pugo-Tuba trail. 127th Inf, 32d Div, relieves 128th in Salacsac Pass area of Villa Verde Trail and makes contact with 126th Inf to N. 25th Div's 35th Inf is clearing draws near Kapintalan on Highway 5. 2d Bn, 27th Inf, withstands counterattack on its perimeter on Mt Myoko and continues efforts to advance. In XI Corps area, 6th and 38th Divs are ordered to exchange sectors so that 6th Div may have an opportunity to rest. 145th Inf, under command of 6th Div, patrols actively toward Mt Oro and Mt Pacawagan. In XIV Corps area, elements of 1st Cav Div and of 11th A/B Div maintain pressure on Mt Mataasna Bundoc but make little headway against stubborn opposition. On Mt Macolod, Japanese are compressed into small pocket during 2-bn assault by 187th Inf, 11th A/B Div.

S PHILIPPINES—In U.S. Eighth Army's X Corps area, main body of 2d Bn, 21st Inf, remains at Lomopog and patrols to Highway 1 on Mindanao while Co F and elements of Boat and Shore Regt continue up Mindanao R to Ulandang; small party moves farther upstream toward Fort Pikit and lands without opposition at Paidu Pulangi. 19th Inf advances steadily along Highway 1 despite difficult road conditions. Floating reserve—34th Inf—lands at Parang and elements start up Mindanao R to assist the amphibious attack forces. On Cebu, 132d Inf is directed to move elements along E coast road. On Negros, 40th Div continues attack against enemy defenses near Negritos and Lantawan. Elements of 160th Inf again push up Hill 3155 and are again forced back. On Bohol, Co I of 164th Inf is directed to move forward from Candijay to assist main attack of 3d Bn.

RYUKYU Is.—On Ie Shima, 307th and 305th Regts of 77th Div continue futile efforts to take Bloody Ridge and Ie town; 3d Bn of 307th, bypassing main enemy positions, reaches base of Iegusugu on E.

In U.S. Tenth Army area, XXIV Corps launches general assault on Okinawa against outer belt of Shuri defenses after tremendous preparatory bombardment in which naval vessels, 27 bns of arty, and aircraft participate. Aircraft make the largest single strike of the campaign. Landing force conducts diversionary feint off SE coast. Bombardment has little effect against well-organized network of cave and tunnel positions and corps gains are modest and costly. On W flank, 106th Inf of 27th Div is halted at W end of Urasoe-Mura Escarpment. After unsuccessful attacks on Kakazu Ridge, 105th Inf bypasses it to get elements on top of the escarpment, but this leaves gap between 27th Div and 96th Div. 22 tanks are lost in fight for Kakazu Ridge. In center, 381st Inf of 96th Div pushes through Kaniku and gains positions on forward slopes of Nishibaru Ridge while 382d gets toehold on N-S Tombstone Ridge between Kaniku and Nishibaru. 7th Div is held up by intense opposition from Rocky Crags on right and Skyline Ridge, E anchor of enemy line, in coastal sector. 32d Inf gains positions on Skyline Ridge but is unable to hold them.

20 April

WESTERN EUROPE—12th Army Group: In U.S. Ninth Army's XIII Corps area, 29th Div, with 115th Inf on left and 116th on right, attacks NE toward the Elbe on left flank of corps; reaches line Esterholz-Schostorf-Wittingen and relieves British units on left. 5th Armd Div gets into position to attack to right of 29th Div. 36th Sq, 11th Cav Gp, assists 44th in containing Forst Kloetze and probing into it. In XIX Corps area, 8th Armd Div, with CCA on W and CCB on E, attacks to clear E edge of Harz Mts, relieving 330th Inf of 83d Div of this task; against sporadic resistance takes Heimburg and Blankenburg. 30th Div defends and governs a sector of the Elbe that includes Magdeburg and relieves elements of 2d Armd Div within its zone. 2d Armd Div, upon relief in S part of Magdeburg and along the Elbe to Schoenebeck, moves to occupation zone generally S of Braunschweig and relieves elements of 8th Armd Div. CCR reverts to 2d Armd Div from attachment to 83d Div. 113th Cav Gp is relieved of flank security mission, since VII Corps of First Army has reached the Elbe to right, but remains along W bank of the Elbe from Breitenhagen southward. In XVI Corps area, 17th A/B Div is relieved of responsibility for Duisberg by XVIII Corps (A/B).

In U.S. First Army area, XVIII Corps (A/B) is directed to turn over Ruhr sector to Ninth and Fifteenth Armies and prepare to join Br 21 Army Group, beginning 25 April. 8th Div becomes responsible for security of entire corps zone, relieving 97th Div. In VII Corps area, CCR of 3d Armd Div clears Bobbau-Steinfurth, W part of Jessnitz, Wolfen, and Greppin; moves elements northward to Klein Kuehnau, just W of Dessau. 3d Armd Div prepares for concerted assault on Dessau. On 104th Div left flank, 415th Inf begins assault on Bitterfeld at 0130 and clears about a third of the town; 413th Inf, in center, drives E to Delitzsch; 414th, on right flank, pushes eastward beyond Rackwitz and Schladitz. Organized resistance in Harz Mts ends and 1st and 9th Divs mop up final opposition. In V Corps area, 2d and 69th Divs begin relief on 9th Armd Div in line. Elements of CCB take Klein Krostitz with ease.

In U.S. Third Army area, VIII Corps maintains current positions and patrols actively. In XII Corps area, 11th Armd Div, as it consolidates and improves positions in Grafenwoehr area, discovers huge cache of enemy materiel and munitions. Moving up close behind armor, 26th Div reaches general line Erbendorf-Pressath-Stegenthumbach. After arty preparation on Selb, 358th Inf of 90th Div clears it and speeds SE through Arzberg; 347th drives through Marktredwitz to Fuchsmuehl and Friedenfelds. 42d Sq of 2d Cav Gp takes As, E of Rehau, and is assisted there by 2d Sq, which takes up screening positions on left flank of corps. 97th Div is arriving in corps zone to protect left flank. XX Corps attacks SE through elements of XV Corps toward the Danube in Regensburg area with 71st and 65th Divs abreast. 71st Div progresses slowly over difficult terrain and encounters troublesome pockets of resistance in Haag area on left, woods S of Auerbach in center, and Neuhaus-

Velden area on right. To right, 65th Div, while in the process of closing in Altdorf assembly area, attacks with RCT's 260 and 259 abreast. RCT 260 reaches line Lauterhofen-Trautmannshofen while RCT 359 advances to Neumarkt and clears northern third of the town. 13th Armd Div starts from XVIII Corps (A/B) sector toward assembly area in vicinity of Eschenau. III Corps issues instructions for attack to SE from new zone on right flank of Third Army, with 14th Cav Gp in narrow zone on left, 99th Div in center, and 86th Div on right. Assault forces are to move to forward assembly areas behind XV Corps, Seventh Army, on 21st, relieve elements of XV Corps within assigned zone, reconnoiter SE to line Unterferrieden-Roth-Weiszenburg, and be prepared to attack SE from reconnaissance line on 22d. 86th Div closes in Windsheim area.

In U.S. Fifteenth Army area, XXIII Corps, upon relieving elements of 10th Div in Hessen area, completes occupation of 12th Army Group zone assigned to it.

6th Army Group: In U.S. Seventh Army's XV Corps area, Nuremberg falls under co-ordinated blows of 42d, 3d, and 45th Divs. In XXI Corps area, CCB and CCR of 12th Armd Div converge on Feuchtwangen, which CCB clears with ease. CCA moves to Feuchtwangen upon relief near Nuremberg by XV Corps and drives S, preceded by 101st Cav Gp, to Dinkelsbuehl, where it halts briefly to await bridging. 4th Div gains 6-8 miles against disorganized resistance; elements of 22d Inf reach outskirts of Crailsheim. On right flank of corps, 63d Div continues S, clearing pockets of resistance E and SE of Schwaebisch Hall. In VI Corps area, CCA and CCB of 10th Armd Div, thrusting SW across Fils R, converge on Kirchheim, div objective, and clear it. 44th Div follows armor closely and takes responsibility for Rems and Fils crossings; 114th Inf occupies Schwaebisch Gmuend and blocks on exposed left flank between there and Gaildorf. In W sector of corps, 100th Div drives rapidly southward toward Stuttgart, 398th Inf pushing through Althuette to Eselshalden, 397th overrunning Sulzbach and Backnang and continuing S, and 399th reaching Winnenden area.

In Fr 1st Army area, 2d Corps, in conjunction with VI Corps of U.S. Seventh Army, almost completes investment of Stuttgart. 1st Corps works southward through Black Forest and Baden Plain in multiple columns. On left, 1st Armd Div (−) pushes toward the Danube in vicinity of Sigmaringen and Tuttlingen. In center, an armored force designated Groupement Le Bel drives to the Danube at Donaueschingen. On right, CC3 of 1st Armd Div reaches Ettenheim and outskirts of Kaiserstuhl.

DA ATL completes reduction of Pointe de Grave pocket.

ITALY—15th Army Group: U.S. Fifth Army emerges from the Apennines onto Po plain. In IV Corps area, 10th Mtn Div, still in the lead, crosses Route 9 in vicinity of Ponte Samoggia, where the highway crosses Samoggia R. To left rear, 1st Armd Div reaches Crespellano. To right rear, 85th Div reaches Gesso; elements turn E to Casalecchio, Bologna suburb, to block withdrawal of disorganized enemy. In II Corps area, 88th Div, attacking on W flank of corps W of the Reno, reaches positions between Casalecchio and Gesso. S African 6th Armd Div crosses to W side of the Reno and speeds northward to vicinity of Casalecchio. E of the Reno, 91st Div pursues enemy toward Bologna in region W of Highway 65. 133d Inf, 34th Div, drives quickly toward Bologna along Highway 65 while Legnano Gp advances right flank of corps.

In Br Eighth Army area, 10 Corps reaches Idice R, following up enemy withdrawal. In Pol 2 Corps area, forward elements cross the Idice in vicinity of Highway 9, night 20-21, and speed toward Bologna. In 13 Corps area, NZ 2d Div, leading corps advance, reaches the Idice and establishes bridgehead across it. In 5 Corps area, enemy begins retreating hastily before corps.

BURMA—In Br Fourteenth Army's 33 Corps area, Br 2d Div and Ind 268th Brig complete envelopment and reduction of stubborn enemy pocket in Mt Popa region.

CHINA—Air-ground liaison teams are rushed to Chihchiang area to help avert enemy threat.

LUZON—In U.S. Sixth Army's I Corps area, elements of 148th Inf, 37th Div, seize ridge NE of Irisan bridge site in flanking attack. 2d Bn and 1st Bn (less Co A) of 130th Inf, 33d Div, assemble N of Asin tunnel ridge to attack from N. Continued fighting in other sectors results in little change in positions. In XI Corps area, 145th Inf continues to probe toward Mt Pacawagan and arty pounds it. XIV Corps maintains pressure on Mt Mataasna Bundoc and continues attack on Mt Macolod, clearing latter except for one pocket.

S PHILIPPINES—In U.S. Eighth Army's X Corps area, 19th Inf of 24th Div continues along Highway 1 on Mindanao toward Fort Pikit, dispersing enemy force some 3 miles E of Manauangan. Of about 80 Japanese encountered SE of Lomopog, 31 are killed. Elements of 34th Inf take over river and roadblock at Ulandang. On Cebu, 3d Bn of 132d Inf, Americal Div, in amphibious move up coast from Cebu City, lands near Danao without opposition and begins extensive patrolling to intercept retreating enemy groups. On Bohol, 3d Bn of 164th Inf, Americal Div, materially assisted by preparatory mortar fire, routs Japanese in Ginopolan area. On Negros, 185th Inf, 40th Div, reaches Lantawan Plateau and starts to clear it. 160th continues futile efforts to take Hill 3155.

RYUKYU IS.—On Ie Shima, main effort of 77th Div shifts from S to N, where 306th Inf succeeds in enveloping the Pinnacle (Iegusugu Mountain). 307th and 305th Regts continue attack on the S, getting upon Bloody Ridge.

In U.S. Tenth Army area on Okinawa, XXIV Corps inches forward in some sectors against furious opposition. 165th Inf, 27th Div, committed on right flank, is stalled for the next week by enemy position called "Item Pocket," N of Gusukuma. 106th and 105th Regts battle for Urasoe-Mura Escarpment against bitter opposition from West and East Pinnacles, key features near Iso Village. 2d Bn, 105th, bypasses East Pinnacle and reaches the escarpment but is surrounded there by Japanese. 1st Bn, 105th, is given task of eliminating bypassed resistance in Kakazu area and progresses well during day, but Japanese reoccupy the area in strength, night 20-21. 96th Div clears rest of Tombstone Ridge and continues attack for Nishibaru Ridge. 7th Div is unable to advance in Rocky Crags area but gains weak hold on Ouki Hill, between Hill 178 and Skyline Ridge. In III Amphib Corps area, 6th Mar Div finishes clearing Motobu Peninsula. Except for small enemy groups, corps zone on N Okinawa is now clear. Mopping up and rcn of small islands off shore continue.

21 April

U.S.—JCS approve BETA, projected operation to take Canton-Hong Kong area and thus secure coastal port. This plan is subsequently revised and known by code names RASHNESS and CARBONADO.

WESTERN EUROPE—12th Army Group: In U.S. Ninth Army's XIII Corps area, 29th Div, driving NE against light resistance, reaches general line Guelden-Dalldorf-Salkau-Gielau-Erpensen. 5th Armd Div attacks to right from line' Daehre-Salzwedel. CCA, on left, reaches Gaddau area against opposition so firm that it delays jump-off of CCR until 1500; one CCR column clears woods near Bombeck while another advances along Salzwedel-Luechow road to Saasse. 84th Div attacks to clear Wahrenberg-Pretzetze sector along the Elbe, employing two bns of 335th Inf and one of 333d; reaches line Gorleben-Gartow-Kapern. 11th Cav Gp and 175th Inf of 29th Div eliminate enemy in Forst Kloetze. In XIX Corps area, 83d Div relieves RCT 320 in Elbe bridgehead with 330th Inf. RCT 320 reverts to 35th Div. 8th Armd Div completes mop up of Harz Mts, reaching army boundary at Michaelstein and Cattenstedt. 2d Armd Div elements begin search of Forst Konigslutter.

In U.S. First Army area, XVIII Corps (A/B) is ordered to assemble in Uelzen-Lueneburg-Celle area by 30 April to protect Br Second Army E flank; be prepared to secure Elbe bridge site; and to participate in further operations on army order. Corps will command Br 6th A/B Div and U.S. 7th Armd, 8th Inf, and 82d A/B Divs. 13th Armd and 97th Inf Divs pass to Third Army control. In VII Corps area, 3d Armd Div, with maximum arty support, begins assault on Dessau, employing elements of three combat commands; clears SW part of city in house-to-house battle. While two CCA TF's push NE through Alten into Dessau, CCR column mops up Klein and Gross Kuehnau, just W of the city, and CCB TF drives N to Dessau, where it is pinched out by CCA. Other elements of 3d Armd Div continue to clear along the Mulde on right flank of div. 104th Div finishes clearing its sector to Mulde R line, taking rest of Bitterfeld and Delitzsch. 1st and 9th Divs mop up in Harz Mts; 9th Div prepares to move E to relieve 3d Armd Div elements along the Mulde. In V Corps area, 2d and 69th Divs complete relief of 9th Armd Div along the Mulde. 9th Armd Div moves to Borna-Taucha region as reserve. 1st Bn of 271st Inf, 69th Div, begins assault on Eilenburg. Mopping up is conducted throughout corps zone.

In U.S. Third Army's VIII Corps area, 28th Sq of 6th Cav Gp finishes clearing right flank of corps to Czechoslovakian border and crosses to reach Rossbach and Gottmannsgruen. In XII Corps area, 11th Armd Div continues combing Grafenwohr area and prepares for drive on Weiden and Chain. Arty pounds Weiden throughout night 21-22. 26th Div attacks with 104th Inf on left and 328th on right, 101st being pinched out, and reaches line Parkstein-Schwarzenbach-Kaltenbrunn-Gressenwohr, overtaking 11th Armd Div, which it begins relieving of guard duty at Grafenwohr. 90th Div thrusts quickly SE with 358th and 357th Regts abreast, 358th driving through Mitterteich to Falkenberg and 357th taking Windischeschenbach and positions near Wildenreuth; blocking along left flank, 90th Rcn Tr overruns Tirschenreuth while 359th Inf clears Schirnding and Waldsassen. XX Corps establishes restraining line Hahnbach-Lauterhofen-Neumarkt since III Corps has not yet closed along its right flank. 71st Div reduces stubborn enemy pockets on its flanks and cuts Sulzbach-Nuremberg highway and rail line. 65th Div clears many villages en route to limiting line and gains about half of Neumarkt. 3d Cav Gp gets into position to attack through 71st and 65th Divs. 80th Div starts to Nuremberg to relieve 3d Div, Seventh Army. In III Corps area, 14th Cav Gp assembles in Fuerth area and prepares to take over assigned sector on left flank of corps as it is uncovered by 14th Armd Div (XV Corps), which is pushing S across corps front. 394th Inf, 99th Div, relieves 42d Div (XV Corps) of responsibility for

[21 APRIL 1945]

Fuerth. 86th Div concentrates in vicinity of Ansbach. 20th Armd Div closes in Oberzenn area.

6th Army Group: In U.S. Seventh Army area, XV Corps regroups for drive on Munich and probes southward. 3d Div, under army control, is responsible for security of Nuremberg. In XXI Corps area, CCA of 12th Armd Div speeds S from Dinkelsbuehl, toward the Danube, reaching Elchingen and Bopfingen. CCB starts S from Feuchtwangen toward the Danube. 4th Div continues S, gaining 6-8 miles along entire front. 8th Inf, heading for Ellwangen, gets advance elements to Stocken. TF Rodwell (12th Inf (motorized), 4th Rcn Tr, and supporting units) is formed for attack on Aalen and drives S through 22d Inf to vicinity of Jagstzell, between Crailsheim and Ellwangen. 22d Inf clears Crailsheim with little difficulty. 63d Div makes substantial gains on right flank of corps against light resistance; 255th Inf sends motorized TF's forward to block exits from Gaildorf and Schwaebisch Gmuend. In VI Corps area, CCA of 10th Armd Div consolidates in Kirchheim until relieved by 103d Div; CCB drives SE to Westernheim and Donnstetten; CCR advances to Gosbach. 44th Div follows on heels of armor with 71st Inf on right and 324th on left; 114th Inf continues to block Schwaebisch Gmuend-Gaildorf sector. 103d Div closes in corps zone and advances S behind armor, passing through elements of 44th and 100th Divs. 410th Inf relieves 10th Armd Div forces at Kirchheim; 411th, after taking Schorndorf and Rems crossings, gets elements beyond Hegenlohe; 409th follows 411th. On W flank of corps, 100th Div seizes bridges across the Rems and drives to within 2 miles of Stuttgart; 398th Inf assembles at Winnenden upon relief by 410th Inf of 103d Div. Seventh Army sets corps W boundary along the Neckar from Stuttgart E to junction with the Fils and thence S to Rottweil; revokes provision of field order directing corps to advance S beyond line Rottweil-Sigmaringen.

In Fr 1st Army's 2d Corps area, 5th Armed Div enters Stuttgart from the S and quickly occupies the city. In 1st Corps area, 1st Armd Div speeds SE to the Danube on left flank of corps: left column reaches Sigmaringen; right column crosses the Danube in Tuttlingen area and drives to Stockach, within a few kilometers of Lake Constance. Groupement Le Bel reaches Swiss frontier at Schaffhausen. Elements of Groupement Valluy overrun Emmendingen and Frieburg. Other Fr forces cross the Rhine and seize Vieux Brisach.

EASTERN EUROPE—Red Army is developing pincers movement against Berlin. Forces of First White Russian Front, constituting right prong, continue broad frontal assault on the city from the E, penetrating into suburbs. Elements of First Ukrainian Front that form left prong wheel northward

[509]

toward the German capital while others of the front continue W toward Dresden and Leipzig.

ITALY—15th Army Group: U.S. Fifth Army drives into Bologna, its objective for many months, and races toward the Po across open ground containing excellent road network. In IV Corps area, TF Duff (Brig Gen Robinson E. Duff), consisting of tanks, TD's, engineers, and infantry, spearheads pursuit by 10th Mtn Div, reaching Panaro R at Bomporto and taking bridge intact. 1st Armd Div and 85th Div advance on flanks of 10th Mtn Div. In II Corps area, 3d Bn of 133d Inf, 34th Div, mounted on tanks, drives into Bologna during morning, shortly after the city has been entered by Pol forces, and is joined there later in day by rest of 133d Inf, Legnano Gp, and right flank elements of 91st Div. 34th Div is placed under army command to garrison Bologna. Legnano Gp goes into corps reserve. To left, 91st Div takes M. Sabbiuno, S of Bologna. S African 6th Armd Div moves forward to exploit, heading for S. Giovanni road center, NW of Bologna. 88th Div passes through S African 6th Armd Div near this objective and takes S. Giovanni, night 21-22.

In Br Eighth Army area, 10 Corps is pinched out upon fall of Bologna and reverts to army reserve. In Pol 2 Corps area, 9th Bn of 3d Brig, 3d Carpathian Div, reaches center of Bologna by 0600. Army then orders corps into reserve. In 5 Corps area, 6th Armd Div reaches Poggio Renatico. Ind 8th Div is withdrawn from reserve to drive on Ferrara so that 6th Armd Div can push W.

BURMA—In Br Fourteenth Army's 33 Corps area, Ind 7th Div surrounds Yenangyaung, where enemy delaying force is prepared to make firm stand to cover withdrawal to Allanmyo. In 4 Corps area, Ind 5th Div continues rapidly S toward Toungoo, leaving 9th Brig to assist Ind 17th Div in clearing Pyinmana.

CHINA—Air movement of Ch 22d Div to Chihchiang (Operation ROOSTER) is begun. Ch 14th Div follows some days later, transported on trucks manned by U.S. 475th Inf. Japanese are progressing westward toward Chihchiang, making main effort along road from Pao-ching. Their spearheads are being engaged in Keosha Tungkow area. On flanks, enemy forces are threatening Wukang, NW of Hsinning, and hold positions on mountain called Paima Shan.

LUZON—In U.S. Sixth Army's I Corps area, battle of Irisan R bridge site ends as 148th Inf, 37th Div, takes last of the ridges; upon completion of temporary bridge, crosses to continue drive on Baguio. 130th Inf, 33d Div, begins attack on Asin tunnel positions from N. 35th Inf, 25th Div, finally captures Kapintalan, opening Highway 5 as far N as Kapintalan Ridge. Elements of 27th Inf on Mt.

Myoko take the hill 300 yards N of the Wart. In XI Corps area, after heavy strikes and massed arty fire, 6th Div begins assault on Mt Pacawagan with attached 145th Inf. 63d Inf provides fire support from N tip of Mt Mataba. 152d Inf, 38th Div, is directed to relieve 1st Inf, 6th Div, in positions near junction of Bosoboso and Mariquina Rivers. In XIV Corps area, 187th Inf of 11th A/B Div eliminates final pocket of enemy in Mt Macolod area and turns this region over to guerrilla forces. Route 417 is now clear.

S PHILIPPINES—In U.S. Eighth Army area, X Corps seizes undefended Fort Pikit on Mindanao. Amphibious force and company of 3d Bn, 34th Inf, move by water to the fort, which patrol from gunboats occupies. Rest of 3d Bn, 34th Inf, arrives later on foot.. On Highway 1, 19th Inf captures road junction at Dilap. On Bohol, 3d Bn of 164th Inf, Americal Div, pursues enemy northward from Ginopolan, eliminating several small groups. On Negros, 40th Div continues offensive agains Negritos-Lantawan-Hill 3155 area. 160th Inf gains military crest of Hill 3155.

RYUKYU Is.—On Ie Shima 77th Div captures the Pinnacle and holds Bloody Ridge against final counterattack, crushing organized resistance on the island, which is declared secure at 1730. Mopping up begins. Japanese casualties during the bitter, 6-day battle total 4,706 killed and 149 captured.

In U.S. Tenth Army's XXIV Corps area on Okinawa, 27th Div, on W flank of corps, continues costly attacks on Item Pocket N of Gusukuma, Kakazu, and the Pinnacles on Urasoe-Mura Escarpment without making much headway but clears mines from road leading to the escarpment so armor can move forward. 96th Div attempts unsuccessfully to clear S slope of Nishibaru Ridge and village of Nishibaru. 184th Inf, 7th Div, reinf by Co B of 17th Inf, is unable to gain Rocky Crags, but 32d Inf pushes to N slope of Skyline Ridge on E flank of corps.

22 April

WESTERN EUROPE—12th Army Group: In U.S. Ninth Army's XIII Corps area, 29th Inf and 5th Armd Divs continue rapidly toward the Elbe. CCA advances N to Lueneburg-Dannenberg road W of Metzingen, then moves one column E through Metzingen to Pussade and another W to Goehrde and NE to Weitzetze; makes contact with British on left. CCR columns converge on Luechow, which surrenders, then continue N along two routes toward Dannenberg. 84th Div finishes clearing its sector along the Elbe NW of Wittenberge. In XIX Corps area, 113th Cav Gp takes responsibility for left flank of 83d Div sector W of the Elbe. 2d Armd Div mops up rest of stragglers in Forst Konigslutter. Corps is assigned zone of occupation. 30th and 83d Divs will remain along the Elbe and 2d and 8th Armd Divs will take up positions in rear. XVI Corps zone is expanded to correspond closely with boundary of Westphalia Province. 5th Div, occupying portion of Westphalia S of the Ruhr, is attached to corps and will be relieved by 75th Div.

In U.S. First Army's XVIII Corps (A/B) area, 75th Div (XVI Corps) relieves 8th Div of portion of Ruhr sector as new boundary between Ninth and First Armies becomes effective. VII Corps begins regrouping as battle for Dessau nears an end. 3d Armd Div continues fight for Dessau, clearing all except NE tip. 104th Div maintains positions along the Mulde and regroups. 8th Armd Div (XIX Corps) begins relief of 1st Div in Harz Mts sector and takes command of its sector at noon. 4th Cav Gp reverts to VII Corps control from attachment to 9th Div. In V Corps area, CCB of 9th Armd Div assembles in vicinity of Rotha, where it becomes responsible for guarding utilities and factories. 2d Div repels counterattack E of the Mulde in Grimma area and clears woods in this region. With intensive arty support, 1st Bn of 271st Inf, 69th Div, continues to dear Eilenburg. VIII Corps is transferred from Third to First Army control as Third Army attack veers from E to S. Its mission is to defend current front, protect S flank of First Army, and maintain contact with Third Army. 4th Armd Div passes to direct control of First Army.

In U.S. Third Army's XII Corps area, main bodies of CCA and CCB, 11th Armd Div, move forward from Grafenwohr to join advance elements, then drive S along parallel routes: CCA quickly clears Weiden and continues S to Nabburg; CCB, to right, reaches Schwarzenfeld and establishes bridgehead across the Naab there. CCR moves forward, elements reaching the Naab at Wernberg. 26th Div follows armor to Wernberg-Amberg area. 358th Inf, 90th Div, takes Ploessberg and Floss while 357th clears woods and villages E of Weiden. 2d Sq, 2d Cav Gp, screens As-Arzberg area; 42d Sq extends screen to Rossbach and Thonbrunn in Czechoslovakia. 97th Div is attached to corps and begins relieving 2d Cav Gp. In XX Corps area, 3d Cav Gp, reinf, organized as a combat team, spearheads corps attack toward the Danube, driving SE through 71st and 65th Divs in 4 columns, 3d Sq on left and 43d on right. 3d Sq seizes Naab R bridge at Burglengenfeld and establishes bridgehead. 43d overruns concentration camp N of Hohenfels; attempts vainly to gain Naab R bridge at Heitzenhofen before enemy can blow it. Because of bold action by cavalrymen, infantry attack meets little resistance. RCT 5, 71st Div, overruns Sulzbach-Rosenberg and Rosenberg; motorized elements of RCT 14, reinf with tanks, clear Amberg; RCT 66 continues to clear div right flank. 65th Div, con-

[22 APRIL 1945]

tinuing SE with RCT's 260 and 259, reaches general line Kastl-Engelsberg-Wiesenacker-Ob Buchfeld but on right rear is unable to oust enemy from position in S part of Neumarkt. 13th Armd Div closes in Eschenau assembly area and is attached to corps. III Corps postpones attack, since its zone is not yet sufficiently cleared by XV Corps; displaces SE, gradually taking over assigned zone from XV Corps.

6th Army Group: In U.S. Seventh Army's XXI Corps area, CCA TF's of 12th Armd Div reach the Danube at Lauingen and Dillingen; seize bridge prepared for demolition at Dillingen and establish bridgehead on S bank. CCB reaches the Danube in Hoechstadt area but is unable to find a bridge intact. CCR begins mopping up in Bopfingen-Lauchheim area and makes unsuccessful attack on Lauchheim. 101st Cav Gp mops up to rear of armor and gets forward elements to the Danube at Lauingen. In 4th Div zone, TF Rodwell thrusts to outskirts of Aalen; 8th Inf reaches Ellwangen but is unable to clear it; 22d drives to Adelmannsfelden area, W of Ellwangen. 63d Div clears most of its zone N of the Rems between Schwaebisch Gmuend and Aalen and takes Rems bridge at Unt Boebingen. In VI Corps area, forward elements of 10th Armd Div's CCB column reach the Danube at Ehingen, where bridges are out. Div is directed to cross the Danube at Ehingen and attack toward Ulm. 44th, 103d, and 100th Divs move forward, clearing opposition to rear and on flanks of armor.

In Fr 1st Army area, 2d Corps consolidates positions in Stuttgart area; begins clearing enemy from Swabian Jura S of Tuebingen. In 1st Corps area, 1st Armd Div, turning E, drives rapidly along the Danube toward Ulm. From Schaffhausen, Groupement Le Bel advances E to NW shore of Lake Constance near Stockach. In the Baden Plain, Groupement Landouzy (9th Colonial Inf Div) reaches Neuenburg and Muhlheim.

EASTERN EUROPE—Troops of First White Russian Front gain additional ground in E suburbs of Berlin. First Ukrainian Front continues N toward Berlin and W toward Dresden; Berlin reports spearheads of these in outer defense zone of the capital. In Czechoslovakia, troops of Fourth Ukrainian Front capture road center of Troppau, NW of Moravska Ostrava.

ITALY—15th Army Group: In U.S. Fifth Army's IV Corps area, TF Duff races to S. Benedetto Po. 10th Mtn Div assembles along S bank of the Po. 1st Armd Div, bypassing Modena, on Highway 9, pushes toward the Po with CCA; CCB protects left flank and, against rear-guard opposition, crosses the Panaro SE of Modena. 85th Div reaches the Panaro at Camposanto and takes bridge before enemy can destroy it. Bridging equipment intended for II Corps is released to IV Corps in preparation for attack across the Po. In II Corps area, S African 6th Armd Div spearheads pursuit, moving columns toward the Panaro at Camposanto on left and Finale on right in effort to secure crossings. The left column, upon reaching Camposanto, is diverted eastward toward Bondeno in effort to establish contact with Br Eighth Army and both it and the right column run into rear-guard opposition S of Finale. 351st Inf, 88th Div, crosses the Panaro between Camposanto and Finale and establishes bridgehead, night 22–23.

In Br Eighth Army area, 13 Corps get forward elements to the Reno. In 5 Corps area, 78th Div reaches the Po di Volano, a few miles from the Po. 6th Armd Div column reaches Bondeno. Ind 8th Div pushes to outskirts of Ferrara, which 78th Div is also approaching.

BURMA—Lt Gen Kimura orders withdrawal of bulk of Japanese forces from Rangoon to Pegu and Moulmein. In Br Fourteenth Army's 33 Corps area, Yenangyaung, largest of the Burmese oilfields, falls to Ind 7th Div. In 4 Corps area, Ind 5th Div reaches Toungoo 3 days ahead of schedule; leading elements continue S to Oktwin.

LUZON—In U.S. Sixth Army's I Corps area, 129th Inf of 37th Div attacks through 148th toward Baguio, gaining about 4,000 yards, then suspends attack while approaches are being cleared to prevent enemy reinforcement of the city. 130th Inf, 33d Div, continuing assault on Asin tunnel positions, gains heights over first tunnel; elements are pushing toward Mt Mirador, at W outskirts of Baguio. 32d Div troops continue to fight from hill to hill along Villa Verde Trail. 1st Bn of 27th Inf, 25th Div, eliminates resistance between its hill position N of the Wart and hill farther N while Co G makes wide enveloping move to base of Lone Tree Hill, at junction of Kapintalan and Balete Ridges 2,000 yards from Balete Pass. In XI Corps' 6th Div sector, 145th Inf continues attack on Mt Pacawagan but is unable to advance. XIV Corps takes control of Bicols sector and of RCT 158 engaged there. Attack to clear Cituinan Hill continues to progress slowly. Corps has by now virtually surrounded Mt Mataasna Bundoc. 11th A/B Div, given mission of clearing Mt Malepunyo area, is reinf by 8th Cav and 2d Sq of 7th. Div regroups and maintains pressure on enemy.

S PHILIPPINES—In U.S. Eighth Army's X Corps area, 31st Div, less 2d Bn of 167th Inf on Morotai, lands on Mindanao and begins relief of 24th Div elements, freeing them for push across the island to Davao Gulf. 19th Inf, 24th Div, continues along Highway 1 to point about 3 miles SE of Balabac. From Fort Pikit, 3d Bn of 34th Inf moves overland to junction of Highway 1 with Sayre Highway, which it takes, and continues to vicinity of Kabacan.

Japanese forces on Mindanao are thus divided. Amphibious forces move upstream and secure ferry crossing in Kabacan area. In Sulu Archipelago, troops of RCT 163, 41st Div, overrun Mt Daho, last organized enemy position on Jolo I., with ease. On Palawan, reinf platoon of Co G, 186th Inf, 41st Div, makes unopposed landing on Pandanan I., off S tip of Palawan. Liberation of Palawan Province is virtually completed. On Cebu, 3d Bn of 182d Inf moves W by truck from Cebu City to Toledo and then N along coastal road to Tabuclan. On Bohol, 3d Bn regains contact with Japanese, who have dug in N of barrio of Nanod, and is pinned down.

RYUKYU Is.—Japanese air activity against shipping in Okinawa area increases. In U.S. Tenth Army's XXIV Corps area, 27th Div slightly improves positions on W flank of corps but Japanese retain Item Pocket, Kakazu, and most of Urasoe-Mura Escarpment. TF Bradford (Brig Gen William B. Bradford, 27th Div ADC), consisting of elements of 27th, 7th, and 96th Divs with supporting units, is formed to destroy the Kakazu Pocket. 383d Inf, 96th Div, relieves battered 382d and, with 2d Bn of 382d attached, attempts to take saddle in Nishibaru Ridge; elements seize Nishibaru Village. 7th Div's right flank is still held up at Rocky Crags; on left flank, 32d Inf holds current positions on Skyline Ridge and patrols.

23 April

WESTERN EUROPE—Heinrich Himmler offers to surrender German forces to Western Allies during conference at the Swedish consulate in Luebeck. The offer is subsequently rejected by the Allies, who call for unconditional surrender on all fronts.

21 Army Group: In Br Second Army area, 12 Corps enters Harburg, on the Elbe opposite Hamburg.

12th Army Group: In U.S. Ninth Army's XIII Corps area, 29th Div continues toward the Elbe against light opposition. 5th Armd Div finishes clearing its sector along the Elbe; Dannenberg surrenders to CCR after brief fire fight. In XVI Corps area, 55th AAA Brig takes responsibility for N part of 95th Div zone. 75th Div begins relief of 5th Div S of the Ruhr.

U.S. First Army releases 4th Armd Div to Third Army as reserve. In VII Corps area, enemy resistance in corps zone ceases at 2100, by which time 3d Armd Div has cleared Dessau and its entire sector. 9th Div (− RCT 60) thoroughly combs Harz Mts. 4th Cav Gp begins security mission in Quedlinburg Aschersleben Klostermansfeld area that continues until end of war. In V Corps area, 1st Bn of 271st Inf, 69th Div, finishes clearing Eilenburg.

In U.S. Third Army's XII Corps area, CCB and CCA of 11th Armd Div drive quickly from Naab R to Cham, which CCB clears with ease, completing current mission of div. Roads in div zone are clogged with thousands of prisoners and slave laborers. 104th Inf, 26th Div, advances unopposed to Dautersdorf-Neuenburg area; 328th gets forward elements to Schoengras. 358th Inf, 90th Div, overruns Flossenburg—where large concentration camp and an aircraft factory are secured—and Waldthurn; 357th takes Albersrieth (W of Waldthurn), Kaimling, and Michldorf; 359th is relieved by 2d Cav Gp as far S as Tirschenreuth and displaces SE to continue blocking along left flank of div. 97th Div closes in corps zone; continuing relief of 2d Cav Gp, takes over line As-Arzberg. 11th Armd Div is directed to continue SE to effect junction with Soviet forces near German-Austrian border; 26th Div, echeloned to right rear of armor, will protect right flank of corps along the Danube and secure bridges; 97th and 90th Divs and 2d Cav Gp are to contain enemy in Czechoslovakia and seize passes along border. In XX Corps area, 3d Cav Gp continues rapidly toward the Danube, 3d Sq turning over Naab R bridgehead at Burglengenfeld to 71st Div. 71st Div speeds SE, bypassing pockets of resistance. 5th Inf, on left, clears Schwandorf while 66th, on right, presses toward Regensburg. 65th Div advances rapidly, committing 261st Inf on right flank through elements of 259th; takes Griffenwang and Kittensee on left and Hardt and See on right; to rear, final resistance is overcome at Neumarkt. In III Corps area, 14th Cav Gp moves SE on left flank of corps, elements entering XX Corps zone to relieve 65th Div forces on hill S of Neumarkt. 14th Armd Div is transferred to corps to spearhead attack S in center of corps front while 99th Div follows. 99th Div, after waiting for 14th Armd Div to cross its front, jumps off in afternoon with 394th Inf on left and 395th on right and advances to line Allersberg-Holpoltstein. 86th Div continues SE on right flank of corps.

U.S. Fifteenth Army issues instructions for expansion of Army zone of occupation to include First and Ninth Armies' portion of Rheinprovinz E of the Rhine and 6th Army Group's remaining portion of Pfalz, Saarland, and Hessen W of the Rhine. In XXIII Corps area, 54th AAA Brig takes over Koblenz subarea, relieving XXII Corps of that portion W of the Rhine and 8th Div (XVIII Corps (A/B)) of portion E of the Rhine.

6th Army Group: In U.S. Seventh Army area, XV Corps takes command of 20th Armd Div to spearhead drive on Munich, 45th Div to follow on left and 42d on right. 45th and 42d Divs are driving S toward the Danube to clear routes of advance for armor. In XXI Corps area, CCA of 12th Armd Div, reinf by elements of CCB, strengthens and expands Dillingen bridgehead. CCR overruns Lauchheim. 4th Div gains its objectives and is ordered to continue to the Danube. 8th Inf drives through Ellwangen to Westhausen. Aalen falls to TF Rodwell, which also takes Unter Kochen. 22d Inf reaches objective W of Aalen. 63d Div, clearing region N of the Rems, is ordered to continue as rapidly as possible to the Danube. As relieved of garrison duties at Nuremberg, 3d Div begins assembly in corps zone and is attached to corps for drive on Augsburg. In VI Corps area, 10th Armd Div continues closing along the Danube and begins crossing near Ehingen and Erbach shortly after midnight, 23-24. CCR is reinforced for drive on Ulm. 44th Div follows armor to the Danube, which 71st Inf crosses near Ehingen. Against lively opposition, 103d Div closes enemy's escape corridor SE from Stuttgart: 410th Inf, reinf by bn of 409th, pushes slowly toward Urach and Muensingen; 411th clears Neuffen, Metzingen, Reutlingen, Pfullingen, and Honau. Div is reinf by 117th Cav Rcn Sq and 781st Tank Bn. 100th Div mops up pockets E of Stuttgart and N of the Neckar; elements of 397th Inf, crossing the Neckar, clear Koengen and cut autobahn to W.

EASTERN EUROPE—Red Army forces break into Berlin proper and to the S reach the Elbe where junction with Allied forces of the Western Front is imminent. First White Russian troops enter Berlin from the E while those of First Ukrainian Front enter from the S. Oranienburg, N of Berlin, and Frankfurt-on-Oder are also overrun by First White Russian forces and Cottbus, SE of Berlin, by troops of First Ukrainian Front. Left flank elements of First Ukrainian Front take Pulsnitz, NE of Dresden, and thrust to the Elbe in Torgau area.

ITALY—15th Army Group: U.S. Fifth Army shifts boundary between IV and II Corps W, giving Highway 12 to II Corps. In IV Corps area, 10th Mtn Div crosses the Po in assault boats and establishes bridgehead on N bank. CCA, 1st Armd Div, reaches the river at Guastalla and Luzzaro; CCB reaches Secchia R south of Highway 9. 85th Div thrusts to the Po at Quingentole. 1st Div of BEF, which has been moving forward on left rear of corps, takes Marano and Vignola. 34th Div is attached to corps to screen left flank along Highway 9. In II Corps area, TF of S African 6th Armd Div pushes through Finale and establishes contact with Br 6th Armd Div to E. After securing bridgehead across the Panaro at Camposanto and driving quickly northward toward the Po, div is directed toward the Po at Felonica, on right flank of corps, and turns NE. Pursuit continues with 3 divs abreast. 88th Div reaches the Po near Carbonara, overtaking and capturing many enemy troops as they prepare to withdraw across the river. 91st Div drives quickly toward the Po against scanty opposition.

Br Eighth Army adjusts boundary between 13 and 5 Corps to run N from the Reno to the Po, since zone of latter has gradually widened to about 50 miles. 13 Corps establishes bridgehead across the Reno. 6th Armd Div is attached to corps to drive to the Po to right of NZ 2d Div. Ind 10th Div is withdrawn from battle. In 5 Corps area, Ind 8th Div takes Ferrara and reaches the Po to N at Pontelagoscuro. 6th Armd Div reaches the Po N of Bondeno; makes contact with U.S. forces near Finale.

LUZON—In U.S. Sixth Army's I Corps area, after aerial bombardment of Mt Mirador area, SW of Baguio, 2d Bn of 129th Inf, 37th Div, drives toward it, reaching cemetery, where it comes under heavy fire from ravine between there and the mountain. Some elements of 130th Inf, 33d Div, clear heights over second Asin tunnel while others motor to Irisan and march toward Asin. 123d Inf, moving laboriously along the Pugo-Tuba Trail, sends 1st Bn to assist 130th against Mt Mirador. 161st Inf, 25th Div, concludes lengthy battle for Crump Hill. 35th Inf closes gap between it and 161st and attacks northward from the Fishhook. In XI Corps area, 6th Div continues assault on Mt Pacawagan with RCT 145, methodically reducing mutually supporting positions. XIV Corps maintains pressure on Mt Mataasna Bundoc.

S PHILIPPINES—In U.S. Eighth Army's X Corps area, town of Kabacan on Mindanao falls to 3d Bn of 34th Inf, 24th Div. 19th Inf reaches Fort Pikit and relieves 34th Inf units there. 24th Div is to drive W along Highway 1 to Davao Gulf while 31st Div drives N along Sayre Highway. On Cebu, 2d Bn of 132d Inf moves by water to SE coast near Tooc and patrols to locate enemy. 2d and 3d Bns enter Danao and overcome organized resistance in this region. Coastal sector is subsequently combed for scattered enemy groups. On W coast, 3d Bn of 182d Inf, assisted by guerrillas, seizes positions in vicinity of Tabuclan; later probes eastward while guerrillas push N. Except for mopping up, offensive operations are completed by this time. On Bohol, 3d Bn of 164th Inf, Americal Div, again attacks Japanese N of Nanod after arty preparation and forces them to withdraw.

RYUKYU Is.—In U.S. Tenth Army's XXIV Corps area on Okinawa, 27th Div completes capture of Urasoe-Mura Escarpment within its sector and wipes out counterattacking force. Resistance to 96th Div slackens and div gains most of high ground within its zone in Nishibaru-Tanabaru area. 1st Bn (less Co B) of 17th Inf, 7th Div, occupies Rocky Crags with ease while 32d Inf patrols and seals caves on Skyline Ridge.

24 April

WESTERN EUROPE—21 Army Group: In Br Second Army area, 30 Corps gets into position for assault on Bremen. 8 Corps closes along the Elbe in Lauenburg area.

12th Army Group: In U.S. Ninth Army's XIII Corps area, 29th Div relieves 5th Armd Div along the Elbe. 84th Div remains along the river awaiting arrival of Soviet forces.

In U.S. First Army's VII Corps area, 9th Div takes responsibility for 3d Armd Div sector along the Mulde and is reinf by CCA and CCR of 3d Armd Div. In V Corps area, 2d Div withdraws elements from E bank of the Mulde, except for outposts and bridge guarding details, upon order. Wurzen surrenders to 1st Bn of 273d Inf, 69th Div. In VIII Corps area, 6th Armd and 76th Inf Divs, ordered to withdraw elements E of the Mulde to conform to new restraining line along that river, begin adjusting defensive positions.

In U.S. Third Army's XII Corps area, CCB of 11th Armd Div drives SE from Cham along Alpine highway to Regen and clears the city with help of air and arty. 26th Div continues SE unopposed to Ragen R line W of Chain; crosses 104th Inf at Roding and 328th in Walderbach-Reichenbach area. 358th Inf, on 90th Div's left flank, overcomes resistance along Vohenstrauss-Waidhaus road and thrusts SE to Eslarn area; 357th clear Vohenstrauss, seizes bridge at Burgtreswitz, and continues SE to Pullenried and Teunz; 359th moves forward to attack through 358th, turning over positions to 2d Cav Gp. 2d Cav Gp extends screen S of Tirschenreuth to Floss-Flossenburg area and turns over positions on N to 97th Div. In XX Corps area, 3d Cav Gp reaches the Danube, 3d Sq between Naab and Regen Rivers and 43d in Riegling-Poikam area, and finds bridges destroyed. In effort to take Regen R bridge at Regenstauf, motorized RCT 14 of 71st Div speeds SE from Amberg, crosses the Naab at Burglengenfeld, and reaches the bridge, which enemy succeeds in destroying; crossing at first in assault boats and later by newly constructed treadway bridge, RCT 14 captures Regenstauf. 5th Inf reaches the Regen to left of RCT 14 and, since no vehicular crossings are found, crosses Regenstauf bridge behind RCT 14, night 24-25. 66th Inf continues S between Naab and Regen Rivers against light resistance. 260th Inf, 65th Div, drives almost to the Danube, clearing Schoenhofen, Eilsbrunn, and Bergmatting; to right, 261st, thrusting through Hemau, overruns Painten; 259th is pinched out. III Corps begins co-ordinated attack SE toward the Danube. 14th Cav Gp attacks on left flank of corps in afternoon; 18th Sq, making main effort, heads for Kelheim, located on N bank of the Danube and astride Ludwigs Kanal, clearing Waldorf; 32d Sq reaches Ludwigs Kanal to right. In center of corps, 14th Armd Div jumps off at 0600 with CCB and CCR in assault, CCB on left, and reaches the Altmuhl at Beilngries and Gungolding. Bridging of the Altmuhl is begun under heavy enemy fire. 99th Div, with RCT 394 on left and 395 on right, follows armor closely. On right flank of corps, 86th Div attacks with 342d Inf on right and 341st on left; 342d reaches the Altmuhl in Eichstatt area.

In U.S. Fifteenth Army area, XXII Corps takes up positions E of the Rhine, relieving 8th Div of XVIII Corps (A/B); 94th Div occupies Duesseldorf area while corps arty takes over Cologne area E of the Rhine. In XXIII Corps area, 28th Div, though still officially attached to XXII Corps, begins relief of 36th Div, Seventh Army, in Regierungsbezirk Saarland.

6th Army Group: In U.S. Seventh Army's XV Corps area, 45th and 42d Divs continue rapidly southward toward the Danube. In XXI Corps area, CCA of 12th Armd Div, which is reinf in Dillingen bridgehead by 15th Inf of 3d Div and which releases attached elements of CCB, overruns Binswangen and begins attack on Wertingen. CCB crosses the Danube at Dillingen and pushes S to positions near Burgau. CCR, after assembling in vicinity of Lauingen, moves SW along the Danube in search of bridges. 101st Cav Gp protects left flank of armor and moves elements W astride the Danube. 4th Div speeds S toward the Danube, TF Rodwell reaching Giengen. 63d Div, leapfrogging bns, advances rapidly S to Gerstetten-Geislingen area. In VI Corps area, CCR of 10th Armd Div and 324th Inf of 44th Div drive NE along N bank of the Danube to Ulm and clear the city in co-ordinated assault. CCA and CCB, 10th Armd Div, and 71st Inf, 44th Div, drive quickly from the Danube to the Iller R and Canal, where blown bridges halt advance. 114th Inf, 44th Div, moves to intercept Germans retreating from Muensingen toward Ehingen but fails to make contact. Assault forces of 103d Div finish clearing to line Muensingen-Metzingen against diminishing resistance, overrunning Urach, Wittlingen, and Muensingen. 100th Div remains in Stuttgart area, mopping up stragglers.

In Fr 1st Army area, 2d Corps completes thrust through Swabian Jura to Sigmaringen area, dividing encircled German forces between the Neckar and the Danube. In 1st Corps area, one 1st Armd Div column drives to Ulm, which falls to U.S. VI Corps, while another closes along the Iller to right. Destruction of enemy in Black Forest continues. On right flank, Groupement Landouzy (9th Colonial Inf Div) overruns Loerrach and reaches Swiss frontier at Basel. Elements of Groupement Valluy reach

Wehr. Forces of 10th Military Region cross the Rhine and seize Kembs Dam intact.

EASTERN EUROPE—First White Russian and First Ukrainian Fronts join forces inside Berlin and deepen penetration toward heart of city. Elements are sweeping around the city to cut enemy escape routes.

ITALY—15th Army Group: In U.S. Fifth Army area, 92d Div, which has reduced Gothic Line positions on Ligurian coast except at Aulla, is ordered to drive along coast to Genoa while pushing inland along Highways 62 and 63 toward Parma and Reggio. In IV Corps area, elements of 10th Mtn Div start northward toward Villafranca airport, SW of Verona. 85th Div establishes bridgehead across the Po at Quingentole without opposition. 34th Div relieves elements of 1st Armd Div on Highway 9 and takes Reggio. N of the highway, elements of 1st Armd Div block enemy escape routes E of Taro R. In II Corps area, 88th Div crosses 2 regts over the Po. 91st Div reaches the Po near Sermide and at night crosses 362d Inf. S African 6th Armd Div reaches the Po at Felonica.

In Br Eighth Army's 13 Corps area, NZ 2d Div and 6th Armd Div establish bridgeheads across the Po, night 24-25, 2d NZ at Gaiaba and 6th Armd at Stienta. In 5 Corps area, Ind 8th Div leads attack of corps across the Po, crossing at and to W of Pontelagoscuro, night 24-25.

BURMA—Japanese Gen Kimura moves his headquarters to Moulmein. One of the 3 airfields at Toungoo becomes operational.

LUZON—In U.S. Sixth Army's I Corps area, 3d Bn of 130th Inf, 33d Div, drives E to within about 2,000 yards of Baguio while 2d Bn of 129th Inf, 37th Div, clears the cemetery on approaches to Mt Mirador. 1st Bn, 129th, moves about 300 yards along Highway 9, coming under heavy fire. Rest of 2d Bn of 27th Inf, 25th Div, joins Co G at base of Lone Tree Hill; 3d Bn passes through 1st to continue attack along Mt Myoko.

S PHILIPPINES—In U.S. Eighth Army area, 24th Div launches drive on Mindanao toward Digos, on Davao Gulf. 34th Inf, leading, reaches Saguing, 30 miles E of Digos. 31st Div is directed to drive N on Sayre Highway to its junction with Kibawe–Talomo trail, a mission assigned to 124th Inf, which will shuttle to Kabacan area to begin the drive. On Bohol, 3d Bn of 164th Inf is systematically searching the island to destroy disorganized enemy remnants.

RYUKYU Is.—On Ie Shima, systematic mopping up continues. American casualties through this date total 172 killed, 902 wounded, and 46 missing in action.

In U.S. Tenth Army area, XXIV Corps pushes through first line of enemy's Shuri defenses on Okinawa with ease, except on W flank, Japanese having withdrawn southward, night 23-24. TF Bradford closes the gap between 27th and 96th Divs without opposition, but Japanese continue to resist in Item Pocket. 96th Div easily takes all of Nishibaru Ridge, Tanabaru Escarpment, ridge to S, and Hill 143. 7th Div eliminates final opposition in Hill 178 area.

25 April

WESTERN EUROPE—21 Army Group: Br Second Army takes operational control of U.S. XVIII Corps (A/B), which retains command of U.S. 8th Div, at noon for action in final drive from the Elbe to the Baltic. 30 Corps enters Bremen and begins to clear the city.

12th Army Group: In U.S. Ninth Army area, XIII Corps ends offensive, except for patrolling across the Elbe, and begins occupation phase. Elbe R line is held by 29th, 84th, and 35th Divs, from left to right. 5th Armd Div moves to rear and CCB relieves RCT 407 (−), 102d Div, of responsibility for protecting MSR; RCT 407 reverts to 102d Div. In XVI Corps area, 75th Div takes command of 5th Div sector S of the Ruhr. 5th Div prepares to move to Third Army area. 17th A/B Div is transferred to Fifteenth Army. XVI Corps zone, divided into five parts, is occupied and governed by 79th Div with 18th AAA Gp attached; 75th Div; 95th Div; 55th AAA Brig; and XVI Corps Arty with 15th Cav Gp attached.

In U.S. First Army's VII Corps area, RCT 39 joins 9th Div along the Mulde and completes relief of 3d Armd Div, to which CCA and CCR revert. In V Corps area, 69th Div makes patrol contact with Soviet forces in vicinity of Riesa and Torgau. 1st Bn, 271st Inf, crosses the Mulde at Eilenburg to clear Kultzschau, just E of the river. 2d Div maintains positions along the Mulde and patrols E of the river. In VIII Corps area, 6th Armd and 76th Inf Divs complete withdrawal to W bank of the Mulde except for small detachments that remain E of the river to facilitate patrolling.

In U.S. Third Army's XII Corps area, CCB of 11th Armd Div drives SW from Regen to Tittling, W of Ilz R; crosses the Ilz and seizes Perlesreut and bridges across Ohe R near Prombach. After advance elements of CCA find road near Zwiesel cratered and impassable, CCA follows CCB route SE through Regen to Kirchdorf, then turns E to Schwarzach and S to Grafenau; advance elements continue E to Kreuzberg. 26th Div reaches the Danube near Zeitldorn on right and Neukirchen-Mitterfels-Steinach area on left. In 90th Div sector, 359th Inf, reinf by 90th Rcn Tr, attacks through 358th, speeding SE to positions NW of Waldmuenchen; 357th continues SE to Schwarzach R in Roetz-Schoenthal area and sends 1st Bn to Chain to block enemy movement toward the redoubt region; 358th blocks along

Czechoslovakian border in Eslarn-Schoensee area and clears several Czechoslovakian villages. 2d Cav Gp, upon relief by 303d Inf of 97th Div, shifts S, relieving elements of 90th Div. On extreme left flank of corps, 97th Div attacks NE toward Cheb (Czechoslovakia), with 386th Inf on left and 387th on right; gains heights N of the city and begins assault on the city. In XX Corps area, 71st and 65th Divs reach the Danube and relieve 3d Cav Gp along it; 43d Cav Sq moves to right flank of corps to screen from Hemau to the Danube. 71st Div, ordered to attack across the Danube, night 25-26, and assist 65th Div's assault on Regensburg with fire, pushes S with all possible speed, 5th Inf pivoting about 14th to advance on left and abreast it. 14th Inf reaches the Danube and clears Donaustauf and Walhalla. 5th closes along the river to left in Frengkofen area. On left flank of div, 66th Inf reaches the Danube at Regensburg and begins clearing portion of the city N of the river: 65th Div prepares for assault cross-ing of the Danube at 0200 on 26th, 260th Inf displacing to forward assembly areas and 261st clearing Waldorf and assisting in capture of Kelheim. In III Corps area, 14th Cav Gp seizes Kelheim, where Danube bridge is down, and searches for crossing site over Ludwigs Kanal. 99th Div reaches the Altmuhl, clearing Dietfurt and Kinding, and starts across the river. 342d Inf, 86th Div, captures Eichstatt and establishes small bridgehead over the Altmuhl there; 341st is clearing wooded region near Gungolding bridge site.

In U.S. Fifteenth Army's XXII Corps area, 417th FA Gp relieves 82d A/B Div in Cologne sector; 82d A/B will move to Uelzen region for operations under XVIII Corps (A/B). In XXIII Corps area, 54th AAA Brig takes over Koblenz district E of the Rhine and rest of Koblenz district W of the Rhine to boundary with Saarland, Pfalz, and Hessen. 28th Div is attached to corps and takes responsibility for military government of Saarland and Hessen W of the Rhine and Pfalz (except for Landkreise Speyer, Landau, Germersheim, and Bergzabern).

6th Army Group: In U.S. Seventh Army's XV Corps area, 45th and 42d Divs reach the Danube, 42d clearing Donauwoerth. In XXI Corps area, CCA of 12th Armd Div defends Dillingen bridge and finishes clearing Wertingen; 15th Inf then reverts to 3d Div. CCB, driving W in region S of the Danube in search of crossing sites, takes Rettenbach and Limbach; elements thrust to Offingen but are forced back to Rettenbach. CCR continues SW along N bank of the Danube and makes contact with 63d Div N of Guenzburg. 3d Div, less 30th Inf, completes movement into Dillingen bridgehead. 7th Inf attacks eastward from Wertingen area in evening. 30th Inf takes up blocking positions N of the Danube on left flank of div. Forward elements of 4th and 63d Divs reach the Danube and start crossing. Most of 8th and 12th Regts, 4th Div, are across at Lauingen by end of day. 1st and 2d Bns of 254th Inf, 63d Div, cross by damaged bridge near Riedheim and take Leipheim; repel tank-supported counterattack. In VI Corps area, 324th Inf of 44th Div and CCR of 10th Armd Div cross the Danube at Ulm and clear Neu Ulm. Upon completion of bridge at Dietenheim, CCB crosses the Iller and speeds S to Kellmunz area. CCA is unable to cross near Iller-rieden since heavy fire prevents completion of bridge there, but elements cross over Dietenheim bridge and move N to block S and E exits from Ulm. 71st Inf, 44th Div, crosses the Iller at Dietenheim and drives N, clearing Voehringen. 114th Inf (−) assembles in Laupheim. 117th Cav Rcn Sq is attached to 44th Div to maintain contact with French forces 103d Div completes move to left rear of 44th Div and drives SE, advance elements reaching the Danube NE of Ulm. 115th Cav Gp and 107th Cav Rcn Sq are attached to toad Div. 100th Div, in Stuttgart area, passes to direct control of army.

In Fr 1st Army area, 2d Corps drives E from Reutlingen-Sigmaringen area to destroy enemy remaining in Swabian Jura. In 1st Corps area, Germans make a desperate effort to escape to the Bavarian Alps, mustering their forces in the Black Forest and attacking between Villingen and the Swiss frontier. 1st Corps, countering promptly, is reinf by 5th Armd Div and part of 3d Algerian Inf Div of 2d Corps and effectively supported by air.

EASTERN EUROPE—Germany is split into two separate parts as patrols of First Ukrainian Front establish contact with U.S. forces of Western Front on the Elbe near Torgau. While fighting continues within Berlin, elements of First White Russian and First Ukrainian Fronts complete circle about the city with junction NW of Potsdam. In East Prussia, troops of Third White Russian Front overrun Pillau, at tip of Samland Peninsula. On southern front, forces of Second Ukrainian Front are fighting in outskirts of Bruenn (Czechoslovakia).

ITALY—15th Army Group: In U.S. Fifth Army area, 92d Div completes reduction of Gothic Line positions in Ligurian coastal sector with capture of Aulla. In IV Corps area, 85th Inf of 10th Mtn Div takes Villafranca airfield, where it is overtaken by special pursuit TF under Col William O. Darby. TF Darby moves on toward Verona. CCA, 1st Armd Div, crosses the Po to intercept retreating enemy W of Lake Garda. 34th Div takes Parma, at junction of Highways 9 and 62. In II Corps area, 88th Div reaches Verona after nightfall and clears scattered opposition there by dawn of 26th. 91st Div reaches Cerea, on Highway to, where extremely heavy casualties are inflicted on enemy forces attempting to withdraw. S African 6th Armd Div begins crossing the Po at Felonica.

In Br Eighth Army's 5 Corps area, Ind 8th Div drives from its Po bridgehead along Highway 16 to the Adige. 56th Div and Cremona Gp cross the Po, 56th near Polesella and Cremona Gp in coastal area.

BURMA—Preparations for DRACULA, amphibious assault on Rangoon, are completed. In Br Fourteenth Army's 4 Corps area, 5th Ind Div captures Pyu and is passed through by 17th Ind Div, which is to continue overland drive on Rangoon.

CHINA—Gen Wedemeyer receives radio from Gen Marshall giving tonnage figures to be delivered to China by ATC during May, June, July, and August. These, because of European redeployment needs, are less than the estimated requirements for BETA. On flank of main Japanese drive on Chihchiang, Ch 58th Div is forced to fall back, leaving small garrison at Wukang.

LUZON—In U.S. Sixth Army's I Corps area, 2d Bn of 129th Inf, 37th Div, begins assault on Mt Mirador while 1st Bn, less Co C, organizes defensive position on Quezon Hill, which overlooks Baguio. Reinf co with tanks probes into Baguio. 1st Bn of 130th Inf, 33d Div, attacks through 3d, taking southernmost peak of Mt Mirador and beginning assault on Dominican Hill, which overlooks Baguio from S, in conjunction with 1st Bn, 123d Inf. 123d Inf arrives at Tuba, 2½ miles SW of Baguio. Under cover of darkness, 25–26, 2d Bn of 161st Inf, 25th Div, attacks toward Kembu Plateau, about 2,000 yards NW of Kapintalan. In surprise attack, 2d Bn of 27th Inf takes Lone Tree Hill. In XI Corps area, 152d Inf of 38th Div relieves 1st Inf, 6th Div, near Woodpecker Ridge and begins patrolling this region. In 6th Div sector, RCT 145 continues reduction of Mt Pacawagan positions. XIV Corps continues action against Cituinan Hills and Mt Mataasna Bundoc. Japanese order withdrawal of forces to Mt Banahao, about 18 miles from Malepunyo hill mass, beginning on 27th.

S PHILIPPINES—In U.S. Eighth Army area, 34th Inf of 24th Div, continuing toward Digos on Mindanao, reaches positions 15 miles from Davao Gulf. On Cebu, 164th Inf (less 3d Bn) of Americal Div loads and sails for Negros Oriental.

RYUKYU Is.—In U.S. Tenth Army area, XXIV Corps is largely occupied with preparations for coordinated attack on Okinawa against enemy's next line of defense, improving positions, and patrolling extensively. Enemy positions are brought under air, naval, and arty bombardment. On W flank of corps, 27th Div, during next few days, makes limited efforts to improve positions and continues operations against Item Pocket. 96th Div remains in place. Elements of 17th Inf advance right flank of 7th Div to slope of Horseshoe Ridge, N part of Kochi Ridge, between villages of Onaga and Kochi.

U.S.—United Nations Conference on International Organization opens at San Francisco, California.

26 April

WESTERN EUROPE—21 Army Group: In Cdn First Army area, Cdn 2 Corps reports NE Holland clear except for small region of coast at Ems estuary.

In Br Second Army area, 30 Corps completes capture of Bremen. 12 Corps closes along the Elbe opposite Hamburg. U.S. XVIII Corps (A/B) begins rail and motor movement from the Ruhr and Cologne sectors to new zone along the Elbe.

12th Army Group: In U.S. Ninth Army's XIII Corps area, elements of 102d Div relieve 35th Div along the Elbe. 35th Div moves to Hannover area to guard installations. 175th Inf reverts to 29th Div from attachment to corps and relieves 335th Inf, 84th Div, along the Elbe.

In U.S. First Army's VII Corps area, 104th Div patrol makes contact with Soviet forces at Pretzsch. 3d Armd Div closes in Sangerhausen area, where it performs security mission and engages in rehabilitation and training. In V Corps area, U.S. and Soviet forces make firm contact at Torgau when regimental commander of 273d Inf, 69th Div, meets commanding officer of 173d Regt, Soviet 58th Guard Div. 272d Inf, 69th Div, displaces along Eilenburg–Torgau road to guard it.

In U.S. Third Army's XII Corps area, 11th Armd Div completes its mission. CCA, after overtaking advance elements at Kreuzberg, drives S to Freyung and E to Unter Grainet; patrols across Austrian border near Lackenhausen. Continuing SE from Ohe R, CCB takes Waldkirchen and pushes E to Wollaberg; patrols to positions overlooking Austrian border near Gollnerberg. Driving SE along N side of the Danube, 26th Div reaches Muehlen-Berg area, between Ruhmansfelden and Deggendorf. 357th Inf, 90th Div, fans out to block roads E and SE of Cham. To left, 90th Rcn Tr and 359th Inf continue SE along Czechoslovakian border, 359th Inf clearing Waldmuenchen in hard fighting and reaching Furth-Raenkam area and the reconnaissance forces taking Furth, Raenkam, and Degelberg. 2d Cav Gp extends screen in Czechoslovakia. 97th Div completes capture of Cheb. XX Corps begins assault across the Danube at 0200 when 65th Div, on right, starts crossing 260th and 261st Regts SW of Regensburg; strong opposition develops, particularly in zone of 261st Inf, but firm bridgehead is established including towns of Matting, Grasslfing, Oberndorf, Nieder Gebraching, and Lengfeld. 259th Inf starts across river at 1800. On left flank of corps, 71st Div, delayed by terrain and small pockets of resistance, jumps off at 0400. 14th Inf crosses in Donaustauf-Sulzbach area and 5th, to left, in vicinity of Frengkofen; bridgehead extends as far S as Regensburg-Straubing road and several small towns are overrun. Assault regts are each reinf by bn of 66th Inf, which cross by boat and ferry. 13th Armd Div moves from Eschenau assembly area to vicinity of Parsberg, in preparation for a crossing of the Danube. In III Corps area, 14th Cav Gp, on left flank of corps, patrols actively while awaiting bridge construction. 14th Armd Div crosses the Altmuhl, CCB over bridge at Beilngries and CCR, preceded by elements of 86th Div and followed by CCA, over bridge at Gungolding; with 3 combat commands in assault, proceeds rapidly S to the Danube, CCB reaching Neustadt, CCA Menning, and CCR Mailing. 99th Div's 394th and 395th Regts also drive rapidly to N bank of the Danube from Altmuhl bridgeheads. 341st Inf, 86th Div, crosses the Altmuhl at Gungolding before dawn and advances quickly toward the Danube; 342d Inf, after being relieved in Eichstatt area by 343d, speeds to the Danube at Ingolstadt, capturing that town, and begins to cross the river.

6th Army Group: In U.S. Seventh Army's XV Corps area, 45th and 42d Divs attack across the Danube, 45th with 3 regts abreast in vicinity of Merxheim and Bergoldsheim and 42d employing 242d and 232d Regts in vicinity of Schaefstall and Altisheim; establish firm bridgeheads. In XXI Corps area, CCA of 12th Armd Div is relieved of Dillingen bridgehead by 3d Div and moves to assembly area. CCB establishes contact with 63d Div at Bubesheim and Guenzburg and then assembles. 101st Cav Gp, ordered to reconnoiter SE in 12th Armd Div zone, advances to Wertach R at Hiltenfingen and takes bridge intact. 3d Div expands Dillingen bridgehead E and SE toward Werk Kanal and Augsburg, overrunning several towns and villages; 30th Inf crosses into bridgehead. 8th and 12th Regts, 4th Div, push S from the Danube to Dinkelscher-ben-Horgau area; 22d, leaving elements to guard Lauingen bridge, assembles S of the Danube. 63d Div crosses the Danube in force in Leipheim-Guenz-burg area and clears Bubesheim. In VI Corps area, bridge is completed across the Iller at Voehringen in morning and used by elements of CCA of 10th Armd Div and 71st Inf of 44th Div. CCA speeds SE through Babenhausen to Mindelheim. CCB drives S along E side of Iller Canal to its objective, Memmingen, where many Allied war prisoners are liberated. CCR follows CCA to Babenhausen, then drives E toward Landsberg, advance elements reaching Wertach R at Turkheim. 90th Cav Rcn Sq screens left flank of div. Upon completing mop up of Neu Ulm, 324th Inf of 44th Div starts to assembly area; 71st and 114th Regts continue forward behind armor. 103d Div crosses the Danube NE of Ulm: 409th Inf drives to Guenz R in Ellzee area; 410th reaches line Asch-Weiszenhorn; 411th assembles in reserve S of the Danube.

In Fr 1st Army area, 1st Corps, closing along the Swiss border from Basel to Lake Constance, completes encirclement of enemy in Black Forest. Noose about the enemy is closed as Valluy Groupement joins forces with rest of corps; CC3 reverts to 1st Armd Div. Enemy pocket W of Tutlingen is rapidly being destroyed. Groupement Le Bel enters Constance.

EASTERN EUROPE—Moscow announces fall of port and city of Stettin to troops of Second White Russian Front who have forced the lower reaches of the Oder and broken through German defenses W of the river. Street fighting continues in Berlin, with Germans gradually yielding to overwhelming pressure. Some elements of First White Russian Front push NE of Berlin while others clear region W and SW of Frankfurt. Troops of First Ukrainian Front take Torgau and Strehla, on W bank of the Elbe. Fighting for Silesian capital of Breslau continues, with Moscow reporting gains in W part of city. Troops of Second Ukrainian Front seize armaments center of Bruenn (Czechoslovakia). On northern front, forces of Third White Russian Front begin clearing Frische Nehrung (East Prussia), crossing canal to this narrow strip of land from Pillau.

ITALY—15th Army Group: In U.S. Fifth Army's IV Corps area, TF Darby of 10th Mtn Div enters Verona at 0600 and finds 88th Div (II Corps) in control; starts along E side of Lake Garda to cut off enemy escape routes. 85th Div establishes bridgehead across the Adige in Verona area and, after pushing through Adige Line, which is largely unmanned, in hills to N, passes to army control. 1st Div of BEF reaches Collecchio, SW of Parma, where enemy pocket is eliminated. 34th Div drives along Highway 9 toward Piacenza but is halted a little short, at Nure R, by delaying force. 371st Inf, detached from 92d Div, has been pinched out on left flank of corps and passes to army control. CCA, 1st Armd Div, starts W along Highway 11 toward Lake Como to block enemy escape between there and Lake Garda. In II Corps area, 91st Div reaches the Adige at Legnago and starts crossing. S African 6th Armd Div expands Po bridgehead toward the Adige. From Verona, 88th Div turns E toward Vicenza.

In Br Eighth Army's 13 Corps area, NZ 2d Div reaches the Adige W of Badia and establishes bridgehead across it, night 26-27. In 5 Corps area, 56th Div reaches the Adige above Rovigo and secures bridgehead.

BURMA—In Br Fourteenth Army's 4 Corps area, Ind 17th Div, continuing overland toward Rangoon, reaches Daik-u.

[27 APRIL 1945] [519]

Luzon—In U.S. Sixth Army's I Corps area, Mt Mirador falls to 129th Inf, 37th Div. In 33d Div sector, 1st Bn of 130th Inf and 1st Bn of 123d Inf find Dominican hill virtually deserted by enemy. 2d Bn of 161st Inf, 25th Div, secures approach to Kembu Plateau and for the next few days mops up and patrols.

S Philippines—In U.S. Eighth Army area, 34th Inf of 24th Div continues toward Digos on Mindanao, hampered by demolitions and delaying obstacles left behind by Japanese. 124th Inf, 31st Div, gets into position for drive up Sayre Highway. 2d Bn, which is to lead, arrives at Pikit by water. On Negros, RCT 164 (less 3d Bn) of Americal Div makes unopposed landing on SE coast of Negros Oriental in vicinity of Looc, N of Dumaguete. 1st Bn lands first and takes Dumaguete airfield and city without incident. 2d Bn follows 1st Bn ashore and moves inland to San Antonio, thence S to Ocoy R, where small enemy group is encountered. Contact is made during day with 40th Div Rcn Tr, which has driven down from the N, and with Filipino guerrillas. In Negros Occidental, fighting continues on slopes of Hill 3155, where enemy continues to hold out against 40th Div forces. 185th Inf finishes clearing Lantawan Plateau and releases 2d Bn to 160th Inf in order to strengthen assault on Hill 3155.

Ryukyu Is.—On Ie Shima, 77th Div, having completed mop up of island, turns over command to ISCOM Ie Shima.

U.S. Tenth Army learns that projected invasion of Miyako, in Sakishima Group, is postponed indefinitely. III Amphib Corps, tentatively earmarked to undertake the Miyako operation instead of V Amphib Corps as planned originally, is thus free for commitment in S Okinawa. On Okinawa, XXIV Corps begins assault on next Shuri defense line after extensive preparatory fire. 165th Inf, 27th Div, continues reduction of Item Pocket while 105th Inf pushes forward to Nakama and organizes defensive positions. 96th Div, with 381st Inf on right and 383d on left, attacks for Maeda Escarpment, also called Big Escarpment, the E part of Urasoe-Mura Escarpment. Maeda Escarpment has at its E tip a lofty rock formation designated Needle Rock. Elements of div reach crest of the escarpment, where they meet furious opposition from enemy on reverse slopes. Supporting armor, however, pushes into village of Maeda, on reverse slope. 17th Inf, 7th Div, tries in vain to advance around W and E sides of Kochi Ridge though it gains weak hold on E side with platoon of Co G.

27 April

Western Europe—21 Army Group: In Br Second Army area, U.S. XVIII Corps (A/B) opens CP at Uelzen and its troops are concentrating in this area. 82d A/B Div is directed to relieve Br 5th Div along the Elbe by 30 April; be prepared to seize limited bridgehead in Bleckede area.

12th Army Group: U.S. Ninth and First Armies maintain and adjust defensive positions. 1st Div, transferred from VII to VIII Corps, prepares to extend VIII Corps zone southward into Czechoslovakia by relieving 97th Div of XII Corps.

In U.S. Third Army's XII Corps area, patrol of CCA, 11th Armd Div, reaches Czechoslovakian border N of Bischofsreuth without opposition. 26th Div drives across Regen-Deggendorf road and clears Deggendorf. 90th Div organizes defensive positions, mops up, and patrols along Czechoslovakian border, finding enemy disposed N and NE of Furth. 2d Cav Gp improves positions in Czechoslovakia. 97th Div mops up in Cheb. XX Corps expands Danube bridgehead, passes armor through it, and receives surrender of Regensburg. Regensburg, though an objective of 65th Div, surrenders to 71st Div without a fight. 71st Div thrusts SE through Traubling and Moosham to Sengkofen and is passed through by elements of 13th Armd Div. 65th Div expands Danube bridgehead to Traubling on left and Teugn on right, overrunning Abbach and Peising in center and making firm junction between the two assault regts; moves 260th Inf into Regensburg. 13th Armd Div begins drive to secure Isar R crossing and ultimately effect junction with Soviet forces. CCB halts for night in Pfatter-Moosham-Geisling area. CCA, ordered to cross 65th Div bridge SW of Regensburg, and CCR, which is to follow CCB, are held up in Deuerling area by mired approaches to the bridge. In III Corps area, 14th Armd Div regroups and mops up along the Danube; CCR relieves 86th Div troops in Ingolstadt. 99th Div establishes bridgehead across the Danube: 393d Inf, passing through 394th, crosses in assault boats in vicinity of Eining, SW of Kelheim, and captures Eining and Straubing; 395th attempts to cross in Neustadt area but is so firmly opposed that it turns N and follows 393d across at Eining. 342d Inf, 86th Div, completes its crossing of the Danube at Ingolstadt early in morning, rear elements using newly completed footbridge, and is passed through by 343d Inf, which thrusts quickly S toward the Isar; 341st reaches the Danube and starts crossing.

6th Army Group: In U.S. Seventh Army's XV Corps area, 45th and 42d Divs continue southward, 42d Div passing 222d Inf through 242d. 20th Armd Div prepares to attack through infantry toward Munich. In XXI Corps area, CCA of 12th Armd Div drives SE to the Lech at Landsberg. CCB moves forward to Langerringen. CCR drives SE through Markt Wald to W bank of the Wertach in Kirchsiebnach-Ettringen area. 3d Div closes in on Augsburg, 7th Inf reaching Werk Kanal and driving S along it on the city and 15th continuing SE to W outskirts. 4th Div's 8th and 12th Regts continue to follow armor SE; 8th Inf secures bridgehead across the Lech at Schwabstadl with 2 cos. 63d Div, continuing leapfrog tactics, also follows armor closely. 36th Div, which is concentrating in corps zone, begins relieving 63d Div. VI Corps pursues enemy, which is in full retreat, toward Austria and the vaunted but mythical National Redoubt. CCR, 10th Armd Div, drives to Landsberg area, making contact with elements of 12th Armd Div (XXI Corps), then turns S. From Mindelheim, CCA drives SE to Lech R at Schongau. From Memmingen area, CCB pursues enemy toward Fuessen, one column reaching Markt Oberdorf and another taking Kempten without a struggle. 71st and 114th Regts, 44th Div, continue southward on heels of armored columns. 103d Div also follows armor closely: 411th Inf follows CCR to Landsberg area and begins clearing this city where Hitler was imprisoned in 1923; 409th heads for Schongau, intercepting and destroying enemy columns of horse-drawn vehicles; 410th gets forward elements to Kaufbeuren. Advance elements of 101st A/B Div close in Memmingen area.

Fr 1st Army virtually finishes clearing its zone.

EASTERN EUROPE—Troops of Second White Russian Front drive rapidly W on broad front along the Baltic in Pomerania, forward elements taking Prenzlau and Angermuende. Fighting continues in Berlin, where Soviet troops have cleared about three fourths of the city. Elements of First White Russian Front overrun Spandau, NW suburb of Berlin, Potsdam, and Rathenow.

ITALY—15th Army Group: U.S. Fifth Army continues to pursue disorganized enemy. 92d Div reaches Genoa, on Ligurian coast. In IV Corps area, resistance by enemy div trapped S of the Po below Cremona comes to an end; 2 more divs are being eliminated in region S of Highway 9. CCB follows CCA, 1st Armd Div, across the Po and turns W also to block enemy escape routes.

CHINA—Chinese, materially assisted by air, are maintaining defensive positions before Ankang and Sian air bases and gradually taking the offensive.

LUZON—In U.S. Sixth Army's I Corps area, battle for Baguio ends as columns of 37th and 33d Divs converge on the summer capital and overrun it. 2d Bn of 27th Inf, 25th Div, reinf by Co B of 35th Inf, starts S along Kapintalan Ridge, where Japanese are firmly entrenched, in effort to make contact with 1st Bn of 35th Inf, which is working N along it. 3d Bn, 27th Inf, continues to clear Mt Myoko. 2d Bn, 35th Inf, gains ridge 600 yards N of Fishhook. In XI Corps area, RCT 145 (attached to 6th Div), assisted by air and arty, gains crest of Mt Pacawagan. In XIV Corps area, 1st and 3d Bns, RCT 158, make contact on main ridge of Cituinan hill mass. 11th A/B Div, with close air and fire support, launches co-ordinated assault on Mt Mataasna Bundoc, final organized enemy position in S Luzon, frustrating enemy plans to withdraw. Some ground is gained against firm opposition.

S PHILIPPINES—In U.S. Eighth Army's X Corps area, Gen Eichelberger draws up plan of attack to clear rest of Mindanao. Japanese apparently intend to make a final stand in hills NW of Davao City. 162d Inf, 41st Div, will move up from Zamboanga to guard communication lines and thus free X Corps to press attack. RCT 108, 40th Div, is to land at Macajalar Bay and move S along Sayre Highway to establish contact with 31st Div forces moving N, thus splitting the island. In order to make a double envelopment of Davao area, elements of 24th Div are to drive N along Davao Gulf from Digos and units of 31st Div are to press SE from Kibawe area on Sayre Highway. Forward elements of 34th Inf, 24th Div, reach crossroads at Digos and are held up by enemy. Aircraft and arty pound the strongpoint. 2d Bn of 124th Inf, 31st Div, starts up Sayre Highway toward its junction with Kibawe-Talomo Trail; at 2200 clashes with enemy force of bn size moving forward to attack and virtually destroys it by dawn of 28th. On Negros, forward elements of 2d Bn, 164th Inf, reach ridge leading to Palimpinon. 1st Bn scouts region W of Dumaguete City.

RYUKYU Is.—Japanese begin 2-day series of strong air attacks against shipping in Okinawa area. In U.S. Tenth Army area, XXIV Corps takes control of 77th Div. Some 27th Div elements fight vigorously for limited gains in Yafusu area while others virtually eliminate Item Pocket. 96th Div, although assisted by tanks and armored flame throwers, makes slow progress in center of corps, especially on right, where Japanese continue tenacious defense of Maeda Escarpment; some elements gain saddle between 2 hills on the escarpment and others work forward through Maeda village. 17th Inf, 7th Div, is still held up at Kochi Ridge strongpoint and assault bns—1st and 2d—are unable to gain contact.

28 April

WESTERN EUROPE—21 Army Group: In Cdn First Army area, Cdn 2 Corps, with task of clearing Wilhelmshaven-Emden peninsula and the two cities, is reinf by Br 3d Div.

In Br Second Army area, 8 Corps prepares for assault crossing of the Elbe in Lauenburg area before dawn of 29th. In U.S. XVIII Corps (A/B) area, 8th Div completes assembling in Lueneburg area and releases 13th Inf to 82d A/B Div's 505th Para Inf, which is to establish bridgehead across the Elbe in Bleckede area, night 29-30.

[28 APRIL 1945]

12th Army Group: In U.S. Ninth Army's XIX Corps area, 329th Inf of 83d Div occupies Zerbst, E of the Elbe, from which 125th Sq of 113th Cav Gp will move eastward to establish contact with Soviet forces.

In U.S. First Army area, VII Corps takes command of V Corps sector and of 2d and 69th Inf and 9th Armd Divs at 1800.

In U.S. Third Army's XII Corps area, 11th Armd Div patrols actively and moves arty forward for drive toward Passau. 26th Div continues SE to general line Hengersberg-Roggersing-Stracking-Thurmansbang. 90th Div continues to probe along Czechoslovakian border and clears Fichtenbach, N of Furth; organizes TF for drive on Nyrsko. 2d Cav Gp gains ground E of Eisendorf in Czechoslovakia. In limited attack, 387th Inf of 97th Div seizes Cheb airfield and neighboring villages, concluding action in this area. 1st Div, VIII Corps, begins relief of 97th Div. In XX Corps area, CCB of 13th Armd Div drives quickly SE along the Danube to the Isar at Platting. CCR and CCA cross the Danube in sectors of 71st and 65th Divs, respectively, CCR closing in Dengling area and CCA near Thalmassing. 71st Div, with 5th Inf on left and 66th on right follows armor SE toward the Isar on left flank of corps. 80th Div, in order to follow armor in zone to right of 71st Div, is relieved in Nuremberg by 16th Armd Div; RCT's 318 and 319 assemble S of Regensburg, passing through 65th Div. 3d Sq, 3d Cav Gp, crosses the Danube in zone of 71st Div and takes up positions on right flank of that division; 43d crosses in 65th Div zone and moves forward to protect right flank of corps. 65th Div polices Regensburg. In III Corps area, 14th Cav Gp assembles S of Ludwigs Kanal and the Altmuhl in order to cross the Danube in 99th Div zone. 14th Armd Div crosses the Danube and continues rapidly SE toward the Isar; CCA, in the lead, takes Steinbach and approaches Moosburg. 99th Div expands Danube bridgehead to line Abensberg-Muehlhausen-Geibenstetten. 341st Inf, 86th Div, completes its crossing of the Danube and with 3434 advances toward the Isar; by end of day, forward elements are within 5 miles of the river. 23d Cav Rcn Sq, 16th Armd Div, is attached to 86th Div to protect its right flank.

6th Army Group: In U.S. Seventh Army's XV Corps area, 20th Armd Div opens drive on Munich, passing through 42d and 45th Divs, which then follow. CCA and CCB, CCA on right, drive rapidly southward over parallel routes. In XXI Corps area, 12th Armd Div, with attached 101st Cav Gp leading, starts across the Lech to block passes into Bavarian Alps to SE. Using rail bridge at Landsberg as soon as it is repaired for vehicular use, 101st Cav Gp crosses and drives E to Ammer See and SE along Weilheim road to Rott. At 2030, CCA starts across bridge behind cavalry. CCR crosses the Wertach at Hiltenfingen. 15th and 7th Regts of 3d Div converge on Augsburg and capture it with little difficulty; 30th Inf crosses the Lech near Gersthofen and starts toward Munich. At 2225, 3d Div is detached from corps and attached to XV Corps for drive on Munich. 8th Inf, 4th Div, maintains Lech bridgehead at Schwabstadl while 12th continues southward toward the Lech in same area and prepares to cross upon completion of bridge. 22d Inf moves SE to cross the Lech. 36th Div takes responsibility for 63d Div zone in right sector of corps. Fr 2d Armd Div, en route to corps zone, is attached to corps. In VI Corps area, all elements of 10th Armd Div reach the Lech and search for crossing sites while engineers work on bridges; right flank elements cross Austrian border near Fuessen. CCB, continuing pursuit throughout night 27–28, gets one column to Fuessen in morning; another column crosses Austrian border to reach heights S of Fuessen. CCA maintains positions in Schongau while awaiting bridge construction and reconnoiters for crossing site as far S as Lechbruck. CCR follows CCA to Schongau. 71st and 114th Regts, 44th Div, speed S behind armor, 71st Regt assisting armor at Fuessen and elements of 114th crossing Austrian border in vicinity of Steinach; elements of 324th Inf are released from reserve and help French capture Wertach, W of Fuessen. 103d Div loses contact with enemy on left flank of corps: 411th Inf completes capture of Landsberg; 409th assembles at Schongau; 410th reaches the Lech near Lechbruck.

In Fr 1st Army area, 1st Corps opens final drive toward Vorarlberg (Austria, advancing SE with 1st Armd Div followed by 2d Moroccan Inf Div on left and 4th Moroccan Mtn Div followed by 5th Armd Div on right. From Biberach, left column drives to Leutkirch. Right column thrusts from Pfullendorf to Ravensburg.

ITALY—Benito Mussolini is intercepted by partisans while fleeing Italy and executed by a firing squad in a village on Lake Como.

15th Army Group: In U.S. Fifth Army area, Alessandria, on Highway 10, falls to 92d Div. In IV Corps area, 1st Div of BEF relieves 34th Div in Piacenza area on Highway 9 and continues to mop up trapped enemy units. 34th Div moves N to Brescia area to round up enemy remnants to W. 1st Armd Div reaches Lake Como, near Swiss border. 10th Mtn Div is placed under army control as it continues clearing E shore of Lake Garda. In II Corps area, 88th Div clears enemy from Vicenza. S African 6th Armd Div starts crossing the Adige at Legnago.

In Br Eighth Army's 13 Corps area, 6th Armd Div crosses the Adige and drives to Monselice. NZ 2d Div column moves through Monselice to Padua during night 28-29 and finds partisans in possession of the town. 5 Corps attacks toward Venice with 56th Div.

BURMA—In ALFSEA's 15 Corps area, 82d W African Div occupies Taungup, which patrols had found clear of enemy in mid-April, completing reconquest of Arakan coast. In Br Fourteenth Army's 33 Corps area, Allanmyo, on road to Prome, falls to Ind 20th Div.

LUZON—In U.S. Sixth Army's I Corps area, 37th and 33d Divs prepare to clear northward from Baguio. In effort to exploit toward Balete Pass from Lone Tree Hill, 25th Div attaches 3d Bn of 35th Inf to 27th Inf. 3d Bn, 27th Inf, when relieved on Mt Myoko by 3d Bn, 35th, is to move to Lone Tree Hill sector. Co A, 35th Inf, overtakes Co F on ridge 1,300 yards NNE of Kapintalan and starts NE to establish contact with 27th Inf but is soon pinned down. 3d Bn, 27th Inf, gets to within 40 yards of crest of Myoko hill mass. XI Corps is directed to regroup for drive on Ipo Dam. In XIV Corps area, Japanese resistance in Cituinan hill mass collapses, concluding organized resistance in the Bicols. 11th A/B Div continues attack in Mt Mataasna Bundoc area with 511th Inf on S and 8th Cav and 188th Inf on N. Some progress is made, but gap of 2 miles exists between N and S forces.

S PHILIPPINES—In U.S. Eighth Army's X Corps area, 2d Bn of 34th Inf, 24th Div, seizes Digos, cutting Mindanao in two. 19th Inf attacks N through 34th toward Davao. 2d Bn of 124th Inf, 31st Div, gains over 4 miles along Sayre Highway, reaching positions beyond Atoman. On Negros, 2d Bn of 164th Inf in Negros Oriental continues to clear heights near Palimpinon while 1st Bn moves to Luzuriaga to drive W in region S of 2d Bn. Contact with enemy is light. In Negros Occidental, 2d Bn of 185th Inf returns to parent unit after assisting 10th Inf in attack on Hill 3155, on slopes of which Japanese are still clinging. Guerrillas replace 2d Bn in this sector. Ground attack on Hill 3155 is suspended for some days while patrols develop enemy positions and fire softens them.

RYUKYU Is.—In U.S. Tenth Army's XXIV Corps area, lively fighting continues in Yafusu area of Okinawa on 27th Div front. Japanese hold Maeda Escarpment against 96th Div attacks. Co K, 381st Inf, moves through 27th Div zone toward strongpoint, called Apartment House, S of the escarpment but is forced back with heavy losses. In 7th Div zone, 3d Bn of 17th Inf replaces 1st Bn W of Kochi Ridge and attempts unsuccessfully to outflank enemy positions. 32d Inf attacks toward Kuhazu but is stopped short by heavy fire. Armored flame throwers push into the village, however.

29 April

WESTERN EUROPE—21 Army Group: In Br Second Army area, 30 Corps, with task of clearing Cuxhaven peninsula, takes command of Gds Armd Div. 8 Corps opens final drive of army, from the Elbe to the Baltic, at 0200 when 15th Div, reinf by Cdn 1st Brig, crosses the Elbe in Lauenburg area and establishes bridgehead. In U.S. XVIII Corps (A/B) area, 505th Para Inf, the first of 82d A/B Div forces to reach the Elbe, and attached 13th Inf of 8th Div relieve Br 5th Div along the Elbe.

12th Army Group: In U.S. Ninth Army's XIX Corps area, 125th Sq of 113th Cav Gp moves E of the Elbe to Zerbst and reconnoiters in effort to establish contact with Soviet forces.

In U.S. First Army area, VII Corps maintains current positions, patrols, and regroups. 9th Div shifts right to relieve 415th Inf, 104th Div, along the Mulde. CCA and CCR, 9th Armd Div, start to assembly area in vicinity of Jena. V Corps starts S to new zone. In VIII Corps area, 1st Div completes relief of 97th Div on left flank of XII Corps and takes responsibility for its sector.

U.S. Third Army releases 5th Div to XII Corps. In XII Corps area, CCB of 11th Armd Div attacks SW toward Passau to clear 26th Div zone E of Ilz R and N of the Danube, reaching Hutthurm. Continuing SE along the Danube, 26th Div reaches general line Spitzendorf-Otterskirchen and makes contact with 11th Armd Div. 80th Div TF, driving from Neukirchen, finds Nyrsko undefended. 2d Cav Gp (−) moves to Zwiesel to secure pass NE of Regen and screen along Czechoslovakian border. In XX Corps area, 13th Armd Div doses along the Isar and establishes bridgehead. CCB, assisted by arty fire and smoke screen, crosses 2 cos at Platting, where engineers begin construction of bridge. CCR, in center, drives to the Isar in Landau area. On right flank of div, CCA reaches the Isar at Landshut. Preparations are made to cross the entire div over bridge at Platting. 80th Div completes its crossing of the Danube. RCT's 318 and 319 follow 13th Armd Div by motor. RCT 317 assembles in vicinity of Koefering. 71st Div advances rapidly toward the Isar against light resistance and is ordered to seize Isar crossings in vicinity of Hanau and Zeholfing. 43d Sq, 3d Cav Gp, moves forward to protect right flank of corps from the Danube to the Isar. In III Corps area, 14th Cav Gp crosses the Danube in 99th Div zone and heads for the Isar. 99th Div advances to the Isar against little or no resistance, securing line Pfettrach-Bruckberg-Moosburg. CCA, 14th Armd Div, reaches the Isar at Moosburg and pre-

[29 APRIL 1945]

pares to force crossing; sends column NE along the Isar to Altdorf, where heavy fire is met from Landshut. CCR and CCB assemble NW of Landshut in Furth-Schatzhofen area; CCR prepares to take control of CCA forces at Altdorf and from there attack Landshut. Continuing SE on right flank of corps, 86th Div crosses Amper Kanal; continues to the Isar, capturing Friesing; begins crossing the Isar in assault boats under heavy fire, night 29-30.

6th Army Group: In U.S. Seventh Army area, XV Corps, with 20th Armd Div spearheading and 3d, 42d, and 45th Inf Divs also in assault, races to outskirts of Munich, overrunning Dachau concentration camp. 106th Cav Gp protects left flank of corps. In XXI Corps area, 12th Armd Div completes its crossing of the Lech at Landsberg and drives SE until ordered to proceed S instead toward Innsbruck. 101st Cav Gp takes Weilheim and Diessen and secures bridges across Ammer R; moves elements NE along E bank of Ammer See toward Munich upon hearing that the Nazi government there is overthrown. 12th Armd Div follows cavalry SE to Weilheim; attacking S through cavalry there, CCA reaches Oberau and makes contact with 10th Armd Div of VI Corps. 22d and 12th Regts, 4th Div, cross the Lech in Schwabstadl area and drive E to W bank of Amper R; 8th Inf maintains Lech bridgehead and sends elements to Augsburg to relieve elements of 3d Div. At dusk, 36th Div, with RCT's 141 and 142 in assault, starts SE from Landsberg area to mop up in wake of armor, crossing Lech R, night 29-30. In VI Corps area, 10th Armd Div attacks across Lech R: CCA crosses at Schongau and drives SE through Saulgrub to Partenkirchen; CCB crosses at Fuessen and drives S beyond Reutte; CCR follows CCA across the Lech to block in vicinity of Saulgrub. 71st Inf, 44th Div, co-ordinates its attack closely with that of CCB, 10th Armd Div, and secures Vils approach to narrow pass to Reutte; 114th drives S toward Gran, making some progress despite winding paths over mountainous terrain; elements of 324th attempt to clear Wertach-Jungholz pass but are held up by enemy. 409th Inf of 103d Div advances with CCA of 10th Armd Div from the Lech at Schongau to Partenkirchen area; 411th, upon relief at Landsberg by 101st A/B Div, moves to Unterammergau; 410th crosses the Lech at Lechbruck and clears road from Steingaden to Buching.

In Fr 1st Army's 1st Corps area, one 1st Armd Div column advances from Leutkirch to Kempten while another thrusts along Iller R valley to edge of Immenstadt. 5th Armd Div overruns Friedrichshafen, on Lake Constance, and to left drives to vicinity of Wangen.

EASTERN EUROPE—Second White Russian Front continues W along Baltic coast, right flank elements seizing Anklan, on road to Stralsund, and others driving into Mecklenburg. Fighting continues in heart of Berlin. In Czechoslovakia, troops of Second Ukrainian Front gain ground E of Bruenn and S of Olmuetz. Berlin admits loss of Austerlitz, SE of Bruenn, and reports that Soviet forces have launched attack NW of Moravska Ostrava.

ITALY—15th Army Group: Representatives of Gen Vietinghoff, commander of German *Army Group Southwest*, sign instrument of unconditional surrender, effective 2 May, at Caserta.

In U.S. Fifth Army's IV Corps area, 1st Div of BEF completes mop up of enemy forces cut off in the Apennines, receiving surrender of 2 div commanders. Milan is found to be in hands of partisans. 1st Armd Div takes up positions near the city and reconnoiters to Ticino R. In II Corps area, 91st Div and S African 6th Armd Div reach and cross the Brenta. Former is driving E along Highway 53 toward Treviso and latter is using parallel route to S. S African 6th Armd Div makes contact with Br Eighth Army at Padua.

In Br Eighth Army's 13 Corps area, NZ 2d Div advances along Route 14 toward Trieste, reaching the Piave, where bridge is down. 5 Corps takes Venice.

BURMA—In Br Fourteenth Army's 4 Corps area, Ind 17th Div reaches outskirts of Pegu.

CHINA—By this time 15,624 men of Ch New Sixth Army are at Chihchiang. Detachment of Ch 14th Div reaches Ankiang within next few days.

LUZON—In U.S. Sixth Army's XIV Corps area, RCT 158, leaving 3d Bn to mop up stragglers in Camalig area, starts northward. 1st Bn advances along Route 1 to Pauili R while 2d Bn, reinf by AT Co, moves along Route 27. 511th Inf, 11th A/B Div, takes its objective, Hill 2610 at Mt Malepunyo hill mass, and Hill 2480, assigned objective of 188th Inf moving down from N.

S PHILIPPINES—In U.S. Eighth Army's X Corps area, forward elements of 19th Inf, 24th Div, push through Coronon and Astorga on Mindanao to positions near Darong airfield. Co K, 34th Inf, arrives in Guma area, NW of Digos, to contain bypassed pocket. On Sayre Highway, 3d Bn of 124th Inf, 31st Div, attacks through 2d Bn, reducing Japanese roadblock and gaining 7,000 yards although enemy has destroyed bridges. On Bohol, 3d Bn (less Co 1) of 164th Inf leaves for Cebu. Guerrillas, assisted by Co I, are responsible for completing mop up. Japanese casualties total 104 killed and 16 captured for American losses of 7 killed and 14 wounded. On Negros, 2d Bn, 164th Inf, meets heavy fire as it continues to clear heights near Palimpinon.

RYUKYU IS.—In U.S. Tenth Army's XXIV Corps area on Okinawa, 77th Div begins relief of 96th Div, whose combat efficiency has been sharply reduced by action on Maeda Escarpment in center of corps zone. 307th Inf moves onto top of the escarpment, replacing 381st Inf. 96th Div withstands enemy counterattacks and infiltration attempts all along its line early in day. 383d Inf drives salient toward Shuri, taking Hill 138, from which direct fire can be placed on Shuri. 7th Div is unable to advance in Kochi Ridge sector and suffers heavy casualties from enemy fire. 32d Inf tries in vain to get tanks from the coast to Onaga to ease pressure on 17th Inf at Kochi Ridge.

30 April

WESTERN EUROPE—Adolf Hitler commits suicide in his bunker at the Reichschancellery, Berlin, after having selected Adm Karl Doenitz as his successor.

21 Army Group: In Br Second Army area, 8 Corps expands and strengthens Elbe bridgehead at Lauenburg. 6th A/B Div begins crossing into it to operate on right flank of 15th Div. U.S. XVIII Corps (A/B), now consisting of corps troops and 8th Inf, 82d A/B, and 7th Armd Divs, begins drive from the Elbe to the Baltic to right of 8 Corps. 82d A/B Div, which releases 13th Inf except for 3d Bn to 8th Div and is reinf at 1800 by RCT 121 of 8th Div, leads off: 505th Para Inf crosses in Bleckede area at 0100, using Buffaloes of 4th Royal Tank Regt, Br 79th Armd Div, and engineer assault boats; against light resistance establishes small bridgehead, which includes Bandekow on left and Stiepelse on right. Attached elements of 8th Div begin crossing late in day to relieve left flank of 505th Para Inf in the bridgehead.

12th Army Group: In U.S. Ninth Army's XIX Corps area, 3d Platoon of Tr C, 125th Cav Sq, 113th Cav Gp, makes contact with Soviet 121st Div at Appolensdorf at 1330.

U.S. First Army CG meets CG, Soviet 5th Guard Army, on E bank of the Mulde at Eilenburg at 1300. Junction of U.S. and Soviet forces is formally celebrated later in day. VII Corps releases 9th Armd Div at 2400. VIII Corps becomes responsible for supply and administration of 9th Armd Div, which is held in SHAEF reserve. 415th Inf of 104th Div relieves 291st Inf of 69th Div. V Corps takes responsibility for new zone on right of VIII Corps along Czechoslovakian border and assumes command of 1st and 97th Divs from VIII and XII Corps, respectively. 1st Div holds line from Cheb to point just S of Adorf, with 6th Cav Gp to left and 97th Div to right.

In U.S. Third Army's XII Corps area, 11th Armd Div, with CCA and CCB in assault, drives SE along right lank of corps to Austrian border. CCA, on div left, advances to border town of Wegscheid, where firm opposition is overcome. From Hutthurm, CCB drives to Austrian border in Ober Kappel area; halts to await outcome of battle for Wegscheid and sends advance elements across border to Crettenbach. CCR, upon relief by 5th Div, moves from Freyung to Wollaberg to protect N and W flanks of div. 104th Inf, on left flank of 26th Div, drives SE unopposed to positions beyond Hauzenburg. 328th Inf closes along Ilz R on div right flank and establishes bridgehead with 1st and 3d Bns at Strasskirchen. 90th Div, in limited attack, gains ground in woods E of Waldmuenchen in Czechoslovakia. In XX Corps area bridge over the Isar is completed at Platting at 1930 and 13th Armd Div begins crossing shortly afterward. CCR, after unsuccessful attempts to cross in Landau area, is relieved by 71st Div and moves toward Platting bridge. 66th and 14th Regts, 71st Div, dose along the Isar and, after massed, direct fire against enemy entrenched on heights across the river, start across under cover of smoke and supporting fire at 1645. Since swift current prevents use of standard assault boats, crossings are made in storm boats equipped with motors, by flying ferry, and over 2 damaged rail bridges. Both regts cross and establish bridgehead, which includes towns of Zeholfing, Zulling, Usterling, and Landau. Work is begun on floating treadway bridge at Landau after nightfall. 318th Inf, 80th Div, crosses the Isar over RR bridge at Mamming and moves SW toward Dingolfing. In III Corps area, 14th Cav Gp reaches the Isar on left flank of corps. 99th Div attacks across the Isar: 393d Inf begins crossing in vicinity of Landshut; 395th crosses in Moosburg area to cover bridging operations of 14th Armd Div and secures line Kochbauer–Langenpreising. CCR, 14th Armd Div, dears portion of Landshut N of the Isar and assembles for crossing at Moosburg, where engineers put in ponton bridge. Dismounted elements of CCA cross at Moosburg and drive beyond Mittl Isar Kanal. CCB starts across the Isar over Moosburg bridge at night. Foot elements of 86th Div's 342d and 343d Regts complete crossing the Isar on right flank of corps; continue to Mittl Isar Kanal and start across it in vicinity of Eitting; attached aid Cav Rcn Sq crosses over XVI Corps bridge SW of Freising. Engineers construct treadway bridge at Freising.

6th Army Group: In U.S. Seventh Army area, XV Corps converges on Munich and clears the city with ease; takes bridges over the Isar there intact. In XXI Corps area, CCA of 12th Armd Div, after driving NE to Schwaiganger in effort to secure another route to Innsbruck, is ordered to assemble in

Murnau area. CCB, preceded by 101st Cav Gp, drives to Loisach R in Sindelsdorf area and halts to await bridge construction. CCV, Fr 2d Armd Div, is attached to 12th Armd Div. 22d and 12th Regts, 4th Div, drive quickly to the Isar; 12th Regt takes Loisach and Isar bridges in vicinity of Wolfratshausen. 36th Div speeds SE through Weilheim, RCT 141 reaching Loisach R line W of Bad Toelz on left and RCT 142 reaching Murnau-Klein Weil-Eschenlohe area on right. In VI Corps area, some elements of CCA, 10th Armd Div, driving E from Partenkirchen toward Innsbruck, reach vicinity of Klais; other elements move W to open lateral route to CCB. CCB attacks to open Fern Pass, pushing slowly SE to Lermoos and then SW along main road to hairpin curve near Fernstein, where it is halted by roadblock. CCR moves to Garmisch, W of Partenkirchen. Div is ordered to halt and await passage of infantry. 71st Inf, 44th Div, co-ordinates closely with CCB and secures Reutte and Lermoos road nets; 114th Inf drives SE through Haldensee pass to Weissenbach, thence SW along the Lech to Forchach; elements of 324th Inf move through Wertach-Jungholz pass, capture Jungholz, and reconnoiter from there. 409th Inf, 103 Div, assists CCA, 10th Armd Div, as it drives E toward Innsbruck; 411th moves S to Farchant; 410th reconnoiters in vicinity of Partenkirchen. Instructions are issued for continuing attack: 101st A/B Div is to police Kaufbeuren-Saulgrub-Wertach-Kempten area; 10th Armd Div is to be passed through by 103d Div, which will drive to Innsbruck, and by 44th Div, which will drive to Imst.

In Fr 1st Army's 1st Corps area, 1st Armd Div meets firm resistance near Immenstadt. 5th Armd Div gets left flank elements to Staufen and on right clears Lindau and thrusts across Austrian border to vicinity of Bregenz. DA ATL troops land on Oleron I., off Gironde Estuary, and begin to clear ineffective opposition. The operation is supported by Fr naval units, which neutralize W coast, and by U.S. and Fr tactical aircraft. Night 30 April-1 May, Fr commandos land on E coast in vicinity of Pointe d' Arceau and push toward St Pierre d'Oleron and Dolus. On the Fr mainland, other Fr units start toward La Rochelle.

EASTERN EUROPE—On southern front, Moravian Gap stronghold of Moravska Ostrava falls to troops of Fourth Ukrainian Front.

ITALY—15th Army Group: In U.S. Fifth Army area, 92d Div reaches Turin, which is undefended; 473d Inf links up with Fr troops on Franco-Italian border. 10th Mtn Div eliminates resistance at head of Lake Garda; 85th Inf crosses the lake to Gargnano and moves on without incident to Riva. IV Corps task force formally occupies Milan. Legnano Gp moves to Brescia area to assist in mopping up.

II Corps is reinf by 85th Div. 91st Div speeds to Treviso, N of Venice. This ends eastward drive of corps.

In Br Eighth Army's 13 Corps area, NZ 2d Div troops cross the Piave and continue to Porto Gruaro, on route to Trieste. Pursuit forces of 6th Armd Div establish contact with Americans at Treviso and thrust toward Belluno and Udine.

BURMA—In ALFSEA's 15 Corps area, main body of DRACULA assault force sails for Rangoon. In Br Fourteenth Army's 4 Corps area, Ind 17th Div breaks into Pegu and begins clearing the city.

CHINA—Ch 58th Div again falls back under enemy pressure, this time to prepared positions in Wa-wu-tang area.

LUZON—In U.S. Sixth Army's XI Corps area, 6th and 38th Divs complete exchange of sectors and 38th Div takes control of RCT 145, 37th Div, on Mt Pacawagan. 152d Inf, 38th Div, is directed to prepare to attack Woodpecker Ridge. XIV Corps overcomes organized resistance in Malepunyo Mt area, but pockets remain to be mopped up.

S PHILIPPINES—In U.S. Eighth Army's X Corps area, 19th Inf of 24th Div advances on Mindanao to within 4 miles of Davao, seizing Daliao airstrip and Talomo; 21st Inf moves forward to follow 19th Inf northward and clear region NW of Talomo R. 3d Bn of 124th Inf, 31st Div, though hampered by rear-guard opposition and demolitions, makes substantial progress up Sayre Highway. On Negros, 1st Bn is ordered to move to Malabo and attack, in order to ease pressure on 2d Bn, 164th Inf, on heights near Palimpinon.

RYUKYU Is.—U.S. shipping losses inflicted by enemy during period 26 March to date total: 20 ships sunk, 14 of them by suiciders; 157 damaged, 90 of them by suicide attacks. The cost to Japanese has been heavy in aircraft. Naval forces destroy more than 1,100 enemy planes in addition to the many shot down by AA guns and aircraft.

In U.S. Tenth Army's XXIV Corps area on Okinawa, 1st Mar Div begins relief of 27th Div on W flank of corps, 1st Marines relieving 165th Inf and probing southward toward Asa R line. 77th Div takes responsibility for 96th Div zone and continues costly battle for Maeda Escarpment. 17th Inf, 7th Div, is still unable to make progress against Kochi Ridge, but 1st Bn of 32d Inf gains positions on ridge SW of Kuhazu.

1 May

WESTERN EUROPE—News of Hitler's death is made public.

21 Army Group: In Br Second Army area, 8 Corps, having secured initial bridgehead some 15 miles wide and 8 miles deep, passes 11th Armd and

5th Inf Divs through it; 11th Armd, on left, makes main effort toward Luebeck. 15th Div drives NW along the Elbe to Geesthacht, about 16 miles from Hamburg. 6th A/B Div passes to control of U.S. XVIII Corps (A/B) in place. U.S. XVIII Corps (A/B) expands Elbe bridgehead up to 9 miles against light resistance. On left flank, Br 6th A/B Div completes its crossing and expands bridgehead to include Zweedorf, Nostorf, and Boizenburg. 8th Div regains control of elements previously attached to 82d A/B Div and attacks with them between Br 6th A/B and 82d A/B Divs, seizing Zahrensdorf. 82d A/B Div, committing 504th Para Inf to right of 505th, thrusts to Forst Carrenzien. CCB, 7th Armd Div, is attached to 82d A/B Div and will operate in conjunction with 325th Gli Inf.

12th Army Group: U.S. Ninth Army, its offensive operations ended, maintains positions along the Elbe with XIII Corps on left and XIX Corps on right and continues occupation mission in zone of XVI Corps to rear. Mass surrender of Germans, particularly in XIII Corps zone, continues until end of the war. Boundaries are gradually adjusted to conform with German political boundaries. XVI Corps, occupying Westphalia, Lippe, and Schaueburg Lippe, is adjusting internal boundaries to facilitate military government. 378th Inf, 95th Div, moves to Bremen Enclave Military District, where it passes to control of 21 Army Group and is attached to 30 Corps, Br Second Army.

U.S. First Army, holding a 160-mile front from junction of the Elbe and Mulde Rivers at Dessau on the N to Ronsperk (Czechoslovakia) on the S, faces a disorganized enemy incapable of preventing Red Army from closing up on a solid front. In V Corps area, 97th Div, disposed along German-Czechoslovakian border on right flank of corps and army, improves positions in limited attacks.

In U.S. Third Army's XII Corps area, 11th Armd Div drives SE from the Austrian border to Klein Muehl R and secures crossings. CCA, on left, seizes bridge E of Peilstein and gets forward elements to Oepping. Main body of CCB halts at Lembach while elements search for crossings to E and NE, taking bridge at Krondf and establishing small bridgehead. CCR, after opening lateral communications between CCA and CCB, moves to Kasberg. 41st Cav follows CCB to Wildenranna and patrols to the Danube in search of crossing sites. 26th Div, with 104th and 328th Regts in assault and 101st screening right flank of corps and div, advances SE behind armor in right half of corps sector: 104th Inf crosses Austrian border in vicinity of Messnerschlag; 328th, to right, eliminates bypassed resistance N of Passau. 5th Div completes assembling in corps zone and, with RCT's 10 and 11 abreast, RCT 10 on left, advances to left rear of armor, forward elements crossing Czechoslovakian border on left and Austrian border on right. 2d Cav Gp, screening German-Czechoslovakian border between 5th and 90th Divs, seizes Eisenstein pass into Czechoslovakia. Left flank elements of 90th Div are passed through on left flank of corps by 97th Div (V Corps). Div continues limited attacks, emerging from woods between Waldmuenchen (Germany) and Domazlice (Czechoslovakia). 4th Armd Div is attached to corps. In XX Corps area, 13th Armd Div finishes crossing the Isar at Platting and drives to the Inn. CCB reaches the Inn in Eisenfelden area and tries in vain to take Marktl bridge. CCA thrusts to the Inn opposite Braunau and searches for crossing site. CCR reaches Unt Tuerken, between Marktl and Braunau. Moving forward from Regensburg area, 65th Div follows armor across the Isar at Platting: 261st Inf drives SE along the Danube to Sandbach on left and Aldersbach on right; 259th passes through 261st to take up assigned sector to its right; among towns cleared by div are Osterhofen, Pleinting, Aldersbach, and Vilshofen. 71st Div, attacking with 3 regts abreast, expands Isar bridgehead SE of Landau to Eichendorf, Arnstorf, and Simbach. Floating treadway bridge is put in at Landau for use of heavy transport and arty. On right flank of corps, 318th Inf of 80th Div clears Dingolfing and from there and Mamming drives SE across Vils R, clearing Reisbach; 319th crosses the Isar in Nieder Viebach area and drives SE, forward elements reaching the Vils. III Corps gets all elements across the Isar and speeds SE toward the Inn in effort to take bridges before enemy can destroy them. 99th Div completes its crossing of the Isar at Landshut and with RCT's 393 and 394 abreast, 393 on left, drives to line Vilsbiburg-Velden. 14th Cav Gp crosses at Landshut, night 1-2. Upon completing crossing at Moosburg, 14th Armd Div drives SE with CCA on left and CCB on right, passing elements through 99th Div and continuing advance during night 1-2. On right flank of corps, 86th Div organizes TF Pope (bn of 342d Inf (reinf and motorized) and 23d Cav Rcn Sq of 16th Armd Div), which heads for Wasserburg, where Inn R bridge is reported intact. Div, with RCT 342 on left and RCT 343 on right, pushes SE from vicinity of Mittl Isar Kanal to Erding.

6th Army Group: In U.S. Seventh Army area, XV Corps mops up Munich sector. In XXI Corps area, CCR of 12th Armd Div drives SE from Starnberg across Isar R in 4th Div zone to Holzkirchen, thence along autobahn, forward elements reaching the Inn. CCA follows CCR to Holzkirchen. CCB, Fr 2d Armd Div, assembles in vicinity of Uffing. 12th Inf, 4th Div, drives SE to Thankirchen and Hechenberg; 22d Inf gets 2 cos across the Isar in Unter Schaeftlarn area; 8th Inf (−) shuttles forward to screen left flank of div W of the Isar. 101st Cav Rcn Sq, 101st Cav Gp, which is attached to 4th Div to screen left flank E of the Isar crosses Loisach and Isar bridges near Wolfratshausen. RCT 141, 36th Div, begins assault on Bad Toelz, elements driving into the city and capturing Field Marshal von Runstedt. VI Corps continues southward through the Alps toward Innsbruck and Imst, passing 103d and 44th Divs through 10th Armd Div. On left flank, 103d Div heads for Innsbruck; RCT 409, making main effort, crosses Austrian border S of Mittenwald and reaches Seefeld. 3d Bn of 71st Inf, 44th Div, gets into position for assault on Fern Pass through the Alps. 114th Inf continues SW along the Lech, clearing Rauth; in effort to secure lateral contact with 71st Inf, elements drive E toward Tarrenz from road junction S of Elmen. 101st A/B Div is moving to Miesbach area of Bavaria.

In Fr 1st Army's 1st Corps area, left flank elements of corps overrun Immenstadt and Sonthofen. Right flank units clear Austrian city of Bregenz. DA ATL finishes clearing Oleron Island, concluding operations in Gironde enclave. Drive on La Rochelle continues.

EASTERN EUROPE—Speeding W along Baltic coast, troops of Second White Russian Front seize Stralsund naval base and communications center. Soviet forces within Berlin deepen penetration.

ITALY—15th Army Group: In U.S. Fifth Army's IV Corps area, 1st Div of BEF gets elements to Alessandria, where 92d Div is contacted. Contact between corps and 92d Div has been made earlier at Pavia, 34th Div relieves elements of 1st Armd Div on Ticino R NW of Milan. In 11 Corps area, 85th Div begins clearing Piave Valley, previously the responsibility of 88th Div, permitting latter to concentrate on Brenta Valley. Corps is directed to clear Highway 49 in preparation for drive through Brenner Pass to Austria.

In Br Eighth Army's 13 Corps area, NZ 2d Div, continuing toward Trieste; reaches Monfalcone and makes contact with Yugoslav troops of Marshal Tito near there.

CHINA—Gen Wedemeyer selects Gen Stratemeyer to command Army Air Forces, China Theater, with both Tenth and Fourteenth Air Forces under his headquarters.

NEI—Aus 26th Brig, 9th Div, lands on Tarakan I., off NE Borneo, and begins to clear this oil prize.

LUZON—In U.S. Sixth Army's I Corps area, 33d Div's 136th Inf effects junction with 123d, opening up Kennon road to Baguio. 32d Div continues to clear heights in Salacsac Pass area. 25th Div is strengthened for final effort against Balete Pass by attachment of RCT 148, 37th Div. 161st Inf, with close fire support, launches attack against Kembu Plateau with 2 bns abreast. In XI Corps' 38th Div sector, RCT 145 consolidates on crest of Mt Pacawagan. 43d Div is directed to begin drive to Ipo on 7th. In XIV Corps area, 5th Cav of 1st Cav Div, pushing SE into the Bicols, is attached to RCT 158. 1st Bn, RCT 158, reaches Anayan, at junction of Highways 1 and 27, without opposition. 3d Bn is ordered to establish contact with 2d Bn, which is advancing W on Route 27.

S PHILIPPINES—In U.S. Eighth Army's X Corps area, 19th Inf of 24th Div closes in on Davao, Mindanao, against strong opposition, bypassing and containing Hill 550, which commands approaches to the city. Leading elements of 21st Inf reach Bayo, 3 miles N of Dalaio. On Sayre Highway, 3d Bn of 124th Inf, 31st Div, reaches Misinsman, where Japanese force is routed in fire fight. Japanese positions in Kibawe area are targets for air attacks. On Negros, 2d Bn of 164th Inf, Americal Div, gains another knob on Cuernos de Negros ridge (Negros Oriental) and holds against counterattacks. Under cover of heavy arty fire, 185th Inf, 40th Div, attacks for Virgne Ridge (Negros Occidental), target for extensive aerial bombardment for several days, and gains control of this feature with ease. On N flank, 503d Para Inf pushes forward onto Banana Ridge. 160th Inf remains on slopes of Hill 3155 (Dolan), which is still being pounded by fire and probed by patrols.

OKINAWA—In U.S. Tenth Army's XXIV Corps area, 1st Mar Div completes relief of 27th Div in line and takes responsibility for W sector of corps front. 1st Marines continue futile and costly efforts to reach Asa R line. 1st Bn of 307th Inf, 77th Div, attempts unsuccessfully to scale precipitous E edge of Maeda Escarpment with cargo nets and ladders; elements succeed in getting to the top but are driven off in night counterattack. Efforts of 3d Bn to take the Apartment House strongpoint also fail. In 7th Div zone, 184th Inf relieves 32d Inf in line by 1730. Enemy infiltrators delay the relief. Co L, 184th, penetrates to Gaja Ridge, night 1-2, but withdraws. 17th Inf, except for mopping up Onaga, remains in place while approach routes to Kochi Ridge are being cleared.

2 May

WESTERN EUROPE—21 Army Group: Br Second Army seals off Schleswig-Holstein and Denmark as elements reach the Baltic. In 12 Corps area, 53d Div passes through 8 Corps bridgehead and turns W toward Hamburg. In 8 Corps area, Luebeck falls to 11th Armd Div. U.S. XVIII Corps (A/B) gains final objective, general line Wismar-Schwerin-Ludwigslust-Doemitz. Br 6th A/B Div drives to the Baltic coast against negligible resistance, taking Gadebusch, Labow, and Wismar; 3d Para Brig makes contact with Soviet 1st Motorcycle Bn of 3d

Tank Corps at Wismar at 2100. 8th Div, attacking with 121st Inf followed by 28th, secures Hagenow and Schwerin without opposition. Passing 325th Gli Inf, reinf by CCB of 7th Armd Div, through 505th Para Inf, 82d A/B Div pushes eastward, clearing Ludwigslust, Eldena, and Doemitz. At 2130, Lt Gen von Tippelskirch surrenders German *Twenty-first Army* unconditionally to 82d A/B Div. 7th Armd Div (− CCB) starts across the Elbe.

12th Army Group: In U.S. Ninth Army area, XIII Corps gains its first contact with Red Army: 84th Div patrols meet Russians in vicinity of Balow and Abbendorft at 1630 and 1730, respectively; at 2130, 29th Div makes patrol contact with Red Army.

In U.S. First Army's V Corps area, 1st and 97th Divs improve positions along Czechoslovakian frontier in limited attacks. 2d Div is transferred to V Corps from VII Corps and begins relief of 97th Div and XII Corps' 90th Div.

In U.S. Third Army's XII Corps area, CCA of 11th Armd Div drives S from Oepping through Rohrbach to the Muehl at Neufelden and starts fording infantry elements mounted on tanks without opposition. Main body of CCB remains at Lembach; failure of road net in Krondf area prevents crossing of the Klein Muehl there. CCR moves forward to Peilstein. 26th Div continues SE along the Danube to rear of armor, reaching Klein Muehl R in Aus-tria. To left, RCT 11 of 5th Div clears to the Gross Muehl in Austria and crosses; RCT 10 gains additional ground in Czechoslovakia on div left. 359th Inf, 90th Div, pushes toward Vseruby. In XX Corps area, 261st Inf of 65th Div reaches the Inn at Passau on left and at Neuhaus, opposite Schaerding, on right; 2d Bn clears most of Passau while 1st, with close fire support, begins assault crossing of the Inn at Neuhaus. Forward elements of 259th Inf reach the Inn S of Neuhaus. 13th Armd Div closes along N bank of the Inn to right and after establishing small bridgeheads is ordered to assemble N of the river. CCA negotiates successfully for surrender of Braunau. 71st Div drives quickly SE toward the Inn, motorized elements of 66th and 5th Regts seizing Inn R dams near Egglfing and Ering, respectively, and establishing shallow infantry bridgeheads over the dams into Austria. Engineers begin work on the dams so that vehicles can cross. 80th Div, with 318th Inf on left and 319th on right, reaches the Inn in vicinity of Braunau and Winhoering, overtaking armor. III Corps continues SE toward the Inn until ordered to refrain from crossing the Inn. Forward elements of 14th Cav Gp reach the Inn in vicinity of Neuoetting and make contact with XX Corps to left. 99th Div gets almost to the Inn. CCB, 14th Armd Div, reaches the river SE of Aschau and takes bridge intact. To left, CCA reaches the river in vicinity of Muehldorf and establishes small infantry bridgehead, withdrawing it upon order. 86th Div, replacing RCT 343 with RCT 341, drives SE to Haag with 2 RCT's abreast; TF Pope reaches outskirts of Wasserburg before being halted and is then dissolved. After breaking off attack, corps units begin assembly in assigned areas N of the Inn.

6th Army Group: In U.S. Seventh Army's XV Corps area, 86th Div is attached to corps. 3d Div prepares to drive on Salzburg. In XXI Corps area, CCR of 12th Armd Div, directed to drive on Innsbruck, closes along the Inn and drives S along it to Degerndorf area while CCA and CCB remain in current positions. CCV, Fr 2d Armd Div, which is to follow CCR, advances from Uffing assembly area to the Isar at Bad Toelz. 101st Cav Gp moves to Bad Aibling area to screen N flank of armor. Against disorganized resistance, 12th Inf, 4th Div, drives to Tegern See while 22d crosses newly completed bridge near Unter Schaeftlarn and drives SE to Miesbach-Gusteig area. RCT 141, 36th Div, finishes clearing Bad Toelz area, elements crossing the Isar to clear E part of city. In VI Corps area, RCT 409 of 103d Div continues S toward the Inn, taking Aul- and Reith; other elements of div move to forward assembly areas and begin negotiations for surrender of Innsbruck. 71st Inf, 44th Div, clears Fern Pass in enveloping maneuver: while 3d Bn attacks frontally from N, 1st Bn, led by party of Austrian soldiers, move to Fernstein and drives N along highway to attack from rear, surprising Germans. Main body of 114th Inf, preceded by 44th Cav Rcn Tr, continues along Lech R Valley; elements driving toward Tarrenz reach Boden.

In Fr 1st Army area, 1st Corps reaches Obersdorf on left and Goetzis (Austria) on right.

EASTERN EUROPE—Soviet forces complete capture of Berlin.

ITALY—15th Army Group: Hostilities come to an end as surrender terms become effective.

In Br Eighth Army's 13 Corps area, NZ 2d Div receives surrender of Trieste. 10 Corps hq starts to Naples for movement to the Far East.

BURMA—In ALFSEA's 15 Corps area, Gp Capt Grandy lands his plane on Mingaladon airfield and enters Rangoon, where he confirms information painted on roof of jail that Japanese have gone. Aerial bombardment of Rangoon area, which has been intensive since 26 April, halts. Ind 26th Div troops land astride Rangoon R from small craft and move toward Rangoon unopposed. Seaborne phase of DRACULA is preceded by airdrop of 23d Bn, 50th Ind Para Brig, in vicinity of Elephant Pt, about 20 miles S of Rangoon. Paratroopers move inland without difficulty.

In Br Fourteenth Army's 33 Corps area, Ind 20th Div seizes Prome, cutting last escape route of Japanese remnants in Arakan sector. In 4 Corps area, Ind 17th Div completes capture of Pegu.

CHINA—5th Div, Ch 94th Army, makes contact with enemy at entrance to Wuyang Valley.

LUZON—In U.S. Sixth Army's I Corps area, 33d Div is ordered to relieve 37th Div elements in Baguio area on 5th so 37th, less RCT 145, can concentrate to exploit expected breakthrough in Balete Pass–Santa Fe–Imugan area. 25th Div is to take Santa Fe, at junction of Highway 5 and Villa Verde Trail, after opening Balete Pass. 32d Div will continue E along Villa Verde Trail. 161st Inf, 25th Div, gains positions on Kembu Plateau as battle for this feature continues. Region E of Highway 5 at head of draw 2,000 yards S of Balete Pass is now clear. In XI Corps area, 145th Inf completes mop up of Mt Pacawagan. After arty preparation, 152d Inf of 38th Div attacks to edge of Woodpecker Ridge. In XIV Corps area, 2d and 3d Bns of RCT 158 effect junction at Mabatobato, opening all of Route 27. 1st Bn, which has moved from Anayan to Pili, gains patrol contact with 5th Cav, 1st Cav Div, at San Agustin. Japanese forces in the Bicols are now located at Mt Isarog, NE of Anayan; 158th Inf and 5th Cav patrols probe this area actively for about the next 2 weeks.

S PHILIPPINES—In U.S. Eighth Army's X Corps area, RCT 108 is detached from 40th Div for amphibious operations at Macajalar Bay, Mindanao. 19th Inf, 24th Div, is still stubbornly opposed as it attempts to force Davao River but succeeds in establishing small bridgehead. While 1st Bn, 21st Inf, pushes on toward Mintal, 2d Bn, in conjunction with elements of 34th Inf, clears most of Libby airfield. On Sayre Highway, 1st Bn of 124th Inf, 31st Div, takes the lead, advancing rapidly. On Negros, 1st Bn of 164th Inf, Americal Div, crosses Ocoy R in Negros Oriental and drives through Badiang; Co C pushes on toward Ticala along Ticala Valley and Co B drives up ridge toward Odlumon. Forward movement halts when Japanese cut supply line. 2d Bn is patrolling extensively. For the next few days, 185th Inf of 40th Div consolidates positions on Virgne Ridge in Negros Occidental and patrols.

OKINAWA—In U.S. Tenth Army's XXIV Corps area, 1st Mar Div attacks S on W flank of corps toward Asa R with 2 regts abreast, 1st Marines on right and 5th Marines on left. Gains are negligible and exceedingly costly since enemy has excellent observation of this area and puts up accurate fire. 307th Inf, 77th Div, continues futile efforts to take Maeda Escarpment. In 7th Div zone, 1st Bn of 17th Inf tries in vain to gain knob of Kochi Ridge. 184th Inf gains and later loses Gaja Ridge. Japanese commanders decide to mount a major counteroffensive on the 4th.

3 May

WESTERN EUROPE—21 Army Group: Field Marshal Montgomery refuses offer of German delegation to surrender all German forces in the north, including those opposing the Red Army.

In Br Second Army area, 12 Corps receives surrender of Hamburg. 7th Armd Div crosses the Elbe to help 53d Div occupy the city. 8 Corps pursues enemy toward Kiel Canal. In U.S. XVIII Corps (A/B) area, 7th Armd Div concludes offensive operations of corps, driving N along left flank to the Baltic W of Kluetz unopposed. Contact is established with Soviet forces.

12th Army Group: In U.S. First Army's V Corps area, 2d Div closes in corps zone and continues relief of 97th Div (V Corps) and 90th Div (XII Corps).

In U.S. Third Army's XII Corps area, 11th Armd Div continues SE toward Linz, its final objective. CCA advances SE to Gramastetten and Rottenegg. CCB follows CCA across river at Neufelden and drives E on div left flank to Zwettl, cutting main N-S road to Linz. 328th Inf, 26th Div, continues SE on right flank of corps but is slowed by friendly armor just ahead; at 2200 is attached to 11th Armd Div. 101st Inf continues to screen right flank of 26th Div. 104th remains in place. 5th Div patrols aggressively. 359th Inf, 80th Div, receives surrender of Vseruby; 357th establishes outpost line across Czechoslovakian border on div right flank. 4th Armd Div closes in assembly area near Regen. XX Corps is directed to veer from SE to E and establish contact with Soviet forces as soon as possible. 65th Div gets most of its forces across the Inn and prepares to cross rest at Neuhaus when bridge is completed. 261st Inf completes capture of Passau and clears Schaerding, on the Inn; pushes rapidly SE toward Linz, leading elements reaching Waizenkirchen. Elements of 260th mop up in woods between Sandbach and Passau. CCB, 13th Armd Div, withdraws its small bridgehead at Neuoetting. 71st Div crosses bulk of its forces into Austria over Ering and Egglfing dams, which are opened to heavy traffic during day, and expands bridgehead, forward elements of 66th Inf reaching Ried. 80th Div overtakes 13th Armd Div at Braunau. 43d Sq, 3d Cav Gp, extends screen along corps right flank to the Inn. III Corps completes movement into assembly areas and with minimum forces mops up N of the Inn.

6th Army Group: In U.S. Seventh Army's XV Corps area, 3d Div, with 7th Inf in assault, speeds toward Salzburg. In XXI Corps area, CCR of 12th Armd Div continues S along the Inn toward Innsbruck, crossing Austrian border and reaching positions near Reisach. CCV, Fr 2d Armd Div, is directed to drive on Berchtesgaden, rather than follow CCR to Innsbruck, and advances E along autobahn to Sulzbach. 4th Div remains in place, mopping up and preparing for relief by 101st A/B Div, which is moving into its zone. RCT 141, 36th Div, reaches Tegern See on left and Lenggries area on right; elements of RCT 142 make contact with VI Corps units at Wallgau. In VI Corps area, 103d Div continues negotiations for surrender of Innsbruck. RCT 409 reaches the Inn at Telfs and Zirl, taking bridge at Telfs; pushes E along the river to Innsbruck. Elements of 410th Inf clear several small towns in region W of Mittenwald Seefeld road. At 2030, RCT 411 (−) starts motorized movement from Mittenwald toward Brenner Pass in effort to establish contact with Fifth Army troops in Italy. 71st Inf, 44th Div, drives S from Fern Pass to Nassereith and from there 1st Bn continues toward Imst while 2d moves E along highway toward Innsbruck and makes contact with elements of 103d Div at Telfs. 114th Inf TF reaches Tarrenz, NW of Imst.

In Fr 1st Army area, 1st Corps continues S along the Iller and Rhine, reaching Feldkirch on the Rhine.

EASTERN EUROPE—Continuing W through Mecklenburg and Brandenburg on broad front, troops of Second White Russian Front effect junction with British forces of Western Front along line Wismar-Wittenberge. To left, troops of First White Russian Front reach the Elbe SE of Wittenberg and link up with U.S. forces of Western Front.

BURMA—In ALFSEA's 15 Corps area, 36th Brig of Ind 26th Div enters Rangoon while 71st Brig moves into Syriam, across the river from Rangoon. 23d Para Bn defends W bank of Rangoon R from Thakutpin to Elephant Pt.

LUZON—In U.S. Sixth Army's I Corps area, 3d Bn of 161st Inf, 25th Div, prepares to attack Mt Haruna, commanding feature W of Balete Pass. In XI Corps area, 6th Div relieves final elements of 38th Div in Kembu sector. 38th Div regroups for coordinated attack with 145th Inf toward Wawa Dam. 152d Inf temporarily suspends action against Woodpecker Ridge while patrolling and consolidating. Fifth Air Force begins series of strikes on Ipo area as 43d Div is moving secretly into position for ground attack. Baldy Force is dissolved, RCT 169 reverting to 43d Div. In XIV Corps area, 8th Cav and Tr F of 7th Cav revert to parent div from attachment to 11th A/B Div. RCT 158 probes in Mt Isarog area to locate and destroy enemy remnants in the Bicols.

S PHILIPPINES—In U.S. Eighth Army's X Corps area, 3d Bn of 19th Inf, 24th Div, clears Davao, Mindanao, which is in ruins, and patrols to Santa Ana. Forward elements of 124th Inf, 31st Div, overrun Kibawe and its airstrip and secure junction of Sayre Highway with Talomo Trail; elements then advance SE along Talomo Trail. On Negros, 1st Bn of 164th Inf, Americal Div, tries in vain to reopen supply line in Negros Oriental.

OKINAWA—In U.S. Tenth Army's XXIV Corps area, 1st Mar Div continues to receive heavy, accurate enemy fire and makes little headway on W flank of corps. Elements of 307th Inf, 77th Div, reach top of Maeda Escarpment, where they come under heavy fire from reverse slope. Coordinated attack on Kochi Ridge by 1st and 3d Bns of 17th Inf, 7th Div, fails. Japanese begin their only major counteroffensive of the Ryukyus Campaign on night 3-4, sharply stepping up air attacks and arty fire and attempting landings behind American lines on W and E coasts. The amphibious operations are costly failures: 500-800 Japanese are killed, and most of their landing craft are destroyed. The enemy forces that succeed in landing are soon rounded up and wiped out.

4 May

WESTERN EUROPE—21 Army Group: Germans sign instrument of surrender of armed forces in Holland, NW Germany, and Denmark at 1820, to become effective at 0800 5 May.

12th Army Group: In U.S. Ninth Army area, XIII Corps commander meets with Soviet III Cav Corps commander. 29th Div is transferred to XVI Corps.

U.S. First Army begins to turn over its troops to other U.S. armies as First Army hq prepares to return to the U.S. for redeployment to the Pacific. VII Corps loses contact with enemy as Red Army closes up solidly along its front. V Corps is assigned 9th Armd and 16th Armd Divs and at 1930 passes to control of Third Army for final drive on Karlsbad (Karlovy Vary) and Pilsen (Plzen). 9th Armd Div, assembling in vicinity of Weiden, releases CCA to 1st Div for drive on Karlsbad. 16th Armd Div, performing security duties in Nuremberg, is directed to move to Waidhaus area upon relief by elements of 4th Div.

In U.S. Third Army's XII Corps area, enemy in Linz and Urfahr places heavy fire on 11th Armd Div columns as they threaten these objectives. From Zwettl, CCB drives SE to Alterberg area; 41st Cav continues SE, taking Gallneukirchen, where CCB is ordered to halt and attempt to make patrol contact with Soviet forces. CCR relieves CCB elements at Zwettl and takes responsibility for guarding div N flank. CCA makes slow progress in Gramastetten-Rottenegg area; abandons plan to attack Urfahr from the NW and prepares to circle N and E to attack from NE. RCT 328, 26th Div, joins CCA and is reinf by a medium tank company. Though AA fire keeps XIX TAC from Linz, fighter bombers assist CCA with strikes NW of Linz. Arty is brought forward to support assault on Linz and begins pounding the area. 104th Inf, 26th Div, drives quickly SE on right flank of corps until ordered in afternoon to halt. 5th and 90th Divs prepare to attack to clear passes into Czechoslovakia through which 4th Armd Div will attack toward Prague. 2d Div of V Corps completes relief of 90th Div on left flank of corps and new V–XX Corps boundary becomes effective. In XX Corps area, 65th Div completes its crossing of the Inn at Neuhaus and, with 260th Inf on left and 261st on right, continues E toward Linz, reaching Eferding. 71st Div, employing 66th Inf on left, 14th in center, and 5th on right, speeds SE by foot and motor to Traun R, taking Wels and Lambach and bridges at both cities and cutting main highway between the cities. 80th Div continues to cross the Inn at Braunau; 317th Inf speeds SE to Voecklabruck; TF Smith (both Rcn Tr and tanks) drives SE to Schwanenstadt. 3d Cav Gp also crosses the Inn at Braunau. While 43d Sq screens right flank of corps from the Inn to Neumarkt, arranging for surrender of Neumarkt by telephone, 3d Sq precedes 80th Div toward the Enns and helps reduce strongpoint at Voecklabruck.

6th Army Group: In U.S. Seventh Army's XV Corps area, 7th Inf of 3d Div, crossing into Austria, advances through Salzburg to Berchtesgaden without opposition. 106th Cav Gp, reconnoitering ahead of 3d Div, accepts surrender of Salzburg. Other elements of corps move forward to Austrian border unopposed. In XXI Corps area, 12th Armd Div, after continuing toward Innsbruck and Berchtesgaden, is placed in army reserve and releases attached CCV, 2d Fr Armd Div, and 101st Cav Gp (–). CCR reaches Kufstein area (Austria), where it is relieved by 36th Div. Advancing toward Berchtesgaden, CCV, 2d Fr Armd Div, reaches Bad Reichenhall. 4th Div is relieved by 101st A/B Div, which completes movement into corps zone and is attached to corps, and starts for Neumarkt area for occupation duty within Third Army zone; 8th Inf and 101st Cav Rcn Sq are attached to 101st A/B Div. RCT 506, 101st A/B Div, moves toward Berchtesgaden. RCT 141, 36th Div, clears banks of Tegern and Schlier Lakes, including towns of Tegernsee and Schliersee, and continues southward. RCT 142, after relieving CCR of 12th Armd Div along the Inn, attacks S. In VI Corps area, 103d Div accepts formal surrender of Innsbruck at 1015; 410th Inf polices and garrisons the city; meanwhile, 411th Inf completes motor journey through Innsbruck to Brenner Pass by 0150 and at 1051 effects junction with Fifth Army's 88th Div in Italy; 3d Bn, 409th Inf, reinf by tanks, drives quickly along Inn R to Worgl, where XII Corps is contacted. In 44th Div zone, 324th Inf, motorized, speeds S through Fern Pass, passing through elements of 71st Inf at Dollinger, and clears Imst; continues SW toward Landeck with final objective of blocking Resia Pass into Italy, overrunning Mils and Wenns. Officers of German *Nineteenth Army* enter 44th Div lines to discuss surrender terms.

In Fr 1st Army's 1st Corps area, 2d Moroccan Inf Div, on left flank of corps, pushes S toward the Inn in St Anton area while 5th Armd Div thrusts SE from Feldkirch toward same objective. DA ATL halts on current line SE of la Rochelle to await surrender negotiations.

ITALY—15th Army Group: I and R Platoon of 349th Inf, 88th Div, establishes contact with U.S. Seventh Army at Vipiteno, S of Brennero, on Austro-Italian frontier.

BURMA—Vice Adm Mountbatten, having decided to omit Operation ROGER (capture of Phuket I., off Kra Isthmus, as forward base for ZIPPER, assault on Malaya), asks for 11th Aircraft Carrier Sq of British Pacific Fleet as close support force for ZIPPER. Request is denied, but Mountbatten is promised an additional escort carrier and 2 general purpose carriers.

LUZON—In U.S. Sixth Army's I Corps area, elements of 161st Inf, 25th Div, seize Mt Haruna, 300 yards W of Balete Pass, and for some days to come remain there patrolling and consolidating. 2d Bn, 27th Inf, has advanced along Wolfhound Ridge about 3,000 yards from Lone Tree Hill and 3d Bn is relieving it. In XI Corps area, 145th Inf opens co-ordinated attack after arty preparation, 1st Bn on left, 3d in center, and 2d on right. Left flank elements get about halfway to Wawa but withdraw to more tenable position at San Isidro under cover of darkness. Progress otherwise is slow because of terrain as well as enemy opposition. 152d Inf, 38th Div, renews attack on Woodpecker Ridge but makes little headway.

S PHILIPPINES—In U.S. Eighth Army area, 2d Bn of 108th Inf returns to Leyte from Masbate, where 118 Japanese and 7 Americans have lost their lives. Filipino guerrillas are responsible for final mop up. In X Corps area, 24th Div forces mop up in Davao area, Mindanao, while 124th Inf of 31st Div probes northward with patrols from Kibawe. RCT 162, 41st Div, arrives at Parang from Zamboanga. On Samal I., I and R Platoon of 19th Inf, 24th Div, lands to reconnoiter. On Negros, 1st Bn of 164th Inf, Americal Div, continues efforts to reopen supply line in Negros Oriental.

OKINAWA—In U.S. Tenth Army area, III Amphib Corps (6th Mar Div and corps troops) is displacing southward. 27th Div takes over sector vacated by 6th Mar Div. In XXIV Corps area, Japanese open ground phase of their counteroffensive early in morning and it too is a costly failure. Arty pieces, brought out into the open to provide powerful support, are profitable targets for U.S. counter battery fire. Japanese troops attack line of 7th Div and 306th Inf, 77th Div, in force but are unable to achieve a breakthrough. Enemy survivors are caught in the open and subjected to destructive fire. Suicide planes are more successful than enemy ground or amphibious forces. From evening of 3 May until evening of 4th, 17 American ships are sunk at cost to enemy of 131 planes destroyed. Japanese maintain their well-organized Shuri defenses while conducting their counteroffensive and prevent much forward movement of corps. 1st Mar Div, although not directly involved in the counteroffensive, suffers extremely heavy casualties while attacking W of Machinato airfield. 307th Inf, 77th Div, against vicious opposition, improves positions on Maeda Escarpment.

5 May

WESTERN EUROPE—21 Army Group: Group halts offensive operations at 0800, when cease-fire order becomes effective. Military government is subsequently established within British zone, and on 25 August 21 Army Group is redesignated The British Army of the Rhine.

12th Army Group: In U.S. Ninth Army's XIX Corps area, 83d Div begins withdrawing Elbe bridgehead because of imminent arrival of Soviet troops. 30th Div establishes contact with Red Army forces at the Elbe.

In U.S. Third Army's V Corps area, 1st Div prepares for drive on Karlsbad and in limited attack by 18th Inf improves right flank positions near Cheb. 97th Div, with 303d Inf on left, 387th in center, and 386th on right, attacks toward Pilsen, taking Trstenice, Chodova Plana, Plana, and Bor and investing Stribro. In XII Corps area, Urfahr-Linz industrial center falls to 11th Armd Div. From Gramastetten area, CCA drives NE to Zwettl, then southward to heights overlooking Urfahr, at which point arty bombardment of Urfahr-Linz area is lifted; TF Wingard enters Urfahr at 1100 and soon afterward crosses the Danube bridge there into Linz, which surrenders promptly; at 1800, RCT 328 moves into Linz, relieving TF Wingard. Capture of Urfahr-Linz highway and rail bridges, which have been prepared for demolition, cuts off escape of Germans in Czechoslovakia to the redoubt area. From Gallneukirchen, CCB sends 41st Cav patrols E and SE well beyond line set as boundary between U.S. and Soviet forces—the rail line running generally N and S about 12 miles E of Linz. In left sector of corps zone, stage is set for drive on Prague. 2d Sq, 2d Cav Gp, speeds northward into Czechoslovakia to Klatovy, where garrison surrenders; 42d Sq gets elements to Prasily. To right, 90th and 5th Divs, respectively, clear Regen and Freyung Passes into Czechoslovakia for debouchment of armor. 90th Div, with RCT 357 in assault, opens Zwiesel-Zelezna Ruda-Dobra Voda road through Regen Pass. 5th Div, with RCT's 10 and 2 abreast, attacks N and NE across Tepla R, RCT 10 opening Freyung-Kunzvart-Hor Vltavice road and RCT 2 cutting Volary-Kunzvart road. 4th Armd Div reconnoiters routes toward Prague and prepares to attack on 6th. XX Corps establishes restraining line along the Enns. On left flank, 65th Div's 260th Inf relieves XII Corps forces in Linz; 261st reaches Enns R and overruns town of Enns. From Traun R, 71st Div drives eastward unopposed, advance elements of 5th Inf reaching the Enns at Steyr. 3d Sq, 3d Cav Gp, precedes 80th Div to Steyr and takes bridge intact; 43d Sq extends screen on right flank of corps to Atter Kammer See. 80th Div (less 318th Inf, which remains S of Braunau, and 1st Bn of 319th Inf, which moves by train from Braunau to Voecklabruck) closes along the Enns to right of 71st Div and patrols beyond the river.

6th Army Group: Hostilities cease as *Army Group G*, consisting of German *First* and *Nineteenth Armies*, accepts Allied surrender terms at Haar, in Bavaria. The surrender is officially to take effect at noon on 6 May, but both sides order immediate cessation of fighting. In VI Corps zone of Seventh Army front, 324th Inf of 44th Div occupies Landeck without opposition.

BURMA—Ind 26th Div of 15 Corps completes reconquest of Burma with occupation of Rangoon, but large-scale mopping up must still be conducted to destroy *Burma Area Army*.

CHINA—Gen Wedemeyer proposes to Gen Stratemeyer that he (Stratemeyer) command a smaller air force than that originally contemplated. Gen Stratemeyer does not favor the suggestion.

LUZON—In U.S. Sixth Army's I Corps area, 25th Div continues reduction of enemy defenses of Balete Pass. 3d Bn, 27th Inf, finishes clearing Wolfhound Ridge. In XI Corps area, 2d Bn of 145th Inf gains positions at base of Sugar Loaf Hill on regimental right; in center, 3d Bn reaches base of Mt Binicayan. 152d Inf suspends attack on Woodpecker Ridge while reorganizing. Combat elements of 43d Div complete assembling for attack toward Ipo, scheduled to begin night 6-7.

S PHILIPPINES—In U.S. Army's X Corps area, 1st Bn of 34th Inf, 24th Div, attacks heights N of Bancal, making slow progress against entrenched enemy. 3d Bn joins Co K in Guma area to strengthen efforts against bypassed pocket there. 31st Div patrol moving N along Sayre Highway finds enemy force disposed to hold woods N of Lake Pinalay, later dubbed Colgan Woods for Capt A. T. Colgan. On Negros, 1st Bn of 164th Inf reopens supply line in Negros Oriental. While main body of 2d Bn moves to Badiang area to assist 1st Bn, Co G begins attack on strongpoint that patrols have discovered SE of Odlumon.

OKINAWA—In U.S. Tenth Army's XXIV Corps area, Japanese renew unsuccessful efforts to break through early in morning, concentrating against U.S. line near junction of 77th and 7th Divs; some 450 penetrate between Route 5 and Kochi to regain Tanabaru town and Tanabaru Ridge, cutting supply road of 7th Div. While 306th Inf, 77th Div, is containing enemy onslaughts, 307th gains reverse slope of Maeda Escarpment and holds against determined counterattacks during night 5–6. In 7th Div zone, elements of 17th Inf battle enemy infiltrators in Tanabaru area.

6 May

WESTERN EUROPE—12th Army Group: U.S. Ninth Army takes control of VII and VIII Corps from First Army at 1800. In XVI Corps area, 115th Inf (reinf) of 29th Div moves to Bremen area to relieve 378th Inf, 95th Div. In XIX Corps area, 83d Div completes withdrawal of Elbe bridgehead and turns over its zone to 30th Div, to which 113th Cav Gp is attached. Corps' contact with enemy ends as Soviet forces arrive along the Elbe in 30th Div zone at 1700.

In U.S. Third Army's V Corps area, 1st Div, on left flank of corps, attacks toward Karlsbad on broad front: 26th Inf, on left, takes Schoenbach; Kynsperk falls to 16th, in center; 18th, on right, clears Sangerberg and Mnichov. CCA, 9th Armd Div, attached to 1st Div, attacks through 16th Inf along Cheb-Falknov road, head of column reaching Rudolec. 16th Armd Div attacks through 97th Div, on right flank of corps, toward Pilsen. CCB, making main effort, drives along Bor-Pilsen road and captures Pilsen, site of Skoda munitions plant. CCR drives through Pilsen to assigned high ground E of the city. 97th Div reaches assigned objectives within its zone. XII Corps opens drive on Prague, Czechoslovakia. 4th Armd Div speeds NE unopposed through Regen and Freyung Passes into Czechoslovakia: CCB, on left, reaches Vel Bor; CCA advances to Strakonice and sends TF eastward to Pisek. To left, 2d Cav Gp clears Planice and pushes toward Zinkovy. 90th and 5th Divs follow 4th Armd Div NE. 26th Div, to which 328th Inf (–) reverts from attachment to 11th Armd Div, relieves 11th Inf of 5th Div and drives NE to Vlatava R line SE of Volary; forward elements cross the river. On right flank of corps, 11th Armd Div patrols deep inside Soviet territory without making contact with Red Army. In XX Corps area, 65th Div (less 260th Inf, which is policing Linz) closes along Enns R on left flank of corps and consolidates along W bank. 66th Inf, 71st Div, reaches the Enns to right of 5th, from Steyr southward, and relieves 80th Div forces along W bank; 5th Inf elements move N from Steyr and secure Ernsthofen dam and heights on E bank. Elements of 80th Div start S at 1700 from positions N of Kirchdorf. 3d Cav Gp takes responsibility for new zone, which includes Atter Kammer See and Traun Gmundner See.

6th Army Group: Surrender of *Army Group G* to Allied forces becomes effective at noon.

BURMA—In ALFSEA's 15 Corps area, Japanese 28th Army is isolated from rest of *Burma Area Army* as 71st Brig, Ind 26th Div, pushing N along Rangoon road, establishes contact with Ind 17th Div of 4 Corps, Br Fourteenth Army, at Hlegu.

NEI—Japanese are forced from Tarakan town, Tarakan I.

LUZON—In U.S. Sixth Army's I Corps area, 25th Div continues to work forward toward Balete Pass, 161st Inf completing capture of Kembu Plateau and seizing junction of the plateau with Balete Pass Ridge. In XI Corps area, 3d Bn of 149th Inf is attached to 145th Inf to hold Mt Pacawagan while 145th devotes its attention to eastward drive; relieves 1st Bn, 145th Inf, which has been brought to a halt on regimental left flank. 2d Bn, 145th Inf, gains top of Sugar Loaf Hill. 3d Bn reaches positions just below crest of Mt Binicayan. After nightfall, 43d Div opens drive on Ipo, employing 103d Inf on right and 172d on left. U.S. air and arty break up planned enemy counterattack before it can get under way.

S PHILIPPINES—In U.S. Eighth Army's X Corps area, 3d Bn of 34th Inf, 24th Div, attacks bypassed enemy pocket in Guma area of Mindanao but gains no ground. In Sayre Highway sector, 1st Bn of 124th Inf, 31st Div, assisted by air strikes and mortar fire, begins assault on Colgan Woods, where enemy is firmly entrenched. 3d Bn, in an outflanking maneuver, gains positions N of the enemy strongpoint. 155th Inf moves up behind 124th in Kibawe area. On Negros, in preparation for general drive southward in Negros Oriental, 2d Bn, 164th Inf, seizes ridge between 1st Bn and Co G. Co G continues attacks on enemy strongpoint SE of Odlumon. In Negros Occidental area, 185th Inf of 40th Div seizes high ground E and S of Virgne Ridge and attacks along the ridge onto Patog Plain. Para RCT 503 is also pressing toward Patog Plain.

OKINAWA—In U.S. Tenth Army's XXIV Corps area, stubborn resistance on right flank of corps virtually halts 1st Mar Div. Pivoting eastward, 1st Marines attacks unsuccessfully for Hill 60, ½ mile SE of Yafusu, while warding off Japanese attacks from reverse slope of Nan Hill, 200 yards N of Hill 60. Progress of 5th Marines against strongly fortified hills and ridges S of Awacha is negligible. 7th Marines fills gap resulting from pivoting of attack. In center of corps, 307th Inf of 77th Div, moves forward from Maeda Escarpment to S slopes of Hill 187. Some elements of 17th Inf, 7th Div, fight for knob of Kochi Ridge while others continue to eliminate enemy infiltrators in Tanabaru area. 184th Inf is patrolling extensively.

7 May

WESTERN EUROPE—German High Command surrenders all land, sea, and air forces unconditionally to Allied forces. The surrender act is signed at Reims at 0141 B Central European Time, to become effective at 0001 B 9 May. Upon receipt of this news in the field, all offensive operations are immediately halted, and organization of defensive positions is begun.

EASTERN EUROPE—Troops of First White Russian Front reach the Elbe N and SE of Magdeburg. The long-besieged city of Breslau (Silesia) falls to forces of First Ukrainian Front. In Czechoslovakia, Ukrainian troops continue clearing Olmuetz area.

LUZON—In U.S. Sixth Army's XI Corps area, 1st Bn of 145th Inf attacks SE from Mt Pacawagan for ridge extending to Wawa, meeting determined opposition. Rest of regt holds current positions and patrols. After aerial and arty preparation, 152d Inf renews attack for Woodpecker Ridge but for the next week is held to small gains. 43d Div continues toward Ipo, gaining about 8,000 yards.

S PHILIPPINES—In U.S. Eighth Army's X Corps area on Mindanao, Co C of 21st Inf, 24th Div, moves N from Mintal toward Talomo R to intercept enemy; meets intense fire and withdraws. Aircraft and arty pound the enemy positions. While Japanese pocket in Guma area is being softened by aerial and arty bombardment, 3d Bn of 34th Inf patrols. In Sayre Highway sector, 1st Bn of 124th Inf, 31st Div, makes slow progress against enemy in Colgan Woods. 3d Bn advances to Maramag Airfield No. I, SW of Maramag. On Negros, Co G of 164th Inf, assisted materially by air and arty bombardment, reduces the enemy strongpoint SE of Odlumon in Negros Oriental. Preparations for general southward advance continue. In Negros Occidental area, Para RCT 503 effects junction with 185th Inf, 40th Div. Patrols find evidence of enemy withdrawal from Patog Plain.

OKINAWA—U.S. Tenth Army takes direct command of operations on S Okinawa. Gen Hodge orders seizure of line Asa-Dakeshi-Gaja by the 8th in preparation for co-ordinated army offensive southward. In III Amphib Corps area, 1st Mar Div, which reverts to corps control, continues to fight vigorously in its zone. 1st Marines, still under heavy fire from reverse slope of Nan Hill, makes another futile effort to take Hill 60. 5th Marines is held up for the next week by opposition S of Awacha. XXIV Corps, with 77th Div on right and 7th on left, presses slowly southward toward Shuri and Yonabaru. 305th Inf, 77th Div, relieves 307th Inf. Some elements of 17th Inf, 7th Div, finish clearing Tanabaru area of enemy infiltrators while others improve positions on Kochi Ridge; still others drive on Zebra Hill, just S of Kochi town, until stopped by enemy strongpoint. 184th Inf takes Gaja Ridge with ease.

8 May

U.S.—President Harry S. Truman proclaims 8 May V-E Day.

WESTERN EUROPE—12th Army Group: U.S. First Army turns over last of its units to adjacent U.S. armies.

In U.S. Third Army area, XII Corps establishes contact with Red Army. 11th Armd Div makes the junction, concluding its mission: CCA patrol (Tr A of 41st Cav) meets Soviet units at Amstetten. XX Corps also gains contact with Soviet forces, 65th Div in vicinity of Strengberg and 71st Div at St Peter. This concludes mission of corps.

EASTERN EUROPE—Resistance in Latvia ceases as German *Sixteenth* and *Eighteenth Armies* begin surrendering to forces of Leningrad Front. Dresden and Goerlitz fall to troops of First Ukrainian Front, elements of which push S across Czechoslovakian border toward Prague. Troops of Fourth Ukrainian Front overrun Olmuetz.

LUZON—In U.S. Sixth Army's XI Corps area, 145th Inf renews 3-bn attack, 1st Bn taking ridge extending to Wawa and blocking trail in Mariquina R gorge about 600 yards S of Wawa, 3d trying in vain to advance up slopes of Mt Binicayan, and 2d taking Sugar Loaf Hill. 3d Bn of 149th Inf relieves 1st Bn of 145th of all responsibility for Mt Pacawagan.

S PHILIPPINES—In U.S. Eighth Army's X Corps area on Mindanao, 1st Bn of 21st Inf, 24th Div, establishes bridgehead across Talomo R north of Mintal, evoking strong enemy reaction. Co E, 19th Inf, relieves Co F on forward tip of Hill 550. In Sayre Highway sector, 124th Inf of 31st Div continues efforts to clear Colgan Woods, replacing 1st Bn with 2d. 3d Bn patrols in Maramag Airfield No. I area. On Samal, Co K, 19th Inf, lands after arty preparation and patrols to locate enemy. On Negros, 164th Inf, with 2 bns abreast, attacks southward in Negros Oriental, slowly but steadily wresting ground from stubborn enemy defenders as fighting continues through rest of month.

OKINAWA—Rain hampers ground, air, and naval operations. In U.S. Tenth Army's III Amphib Corps area, 22d Marines, 6th Mar Div, relieves 7th Marines, 1st Mar Div, on W coast N of the Asa. 1st

Marines, 1st Mar Div, concentrates on blasting enemy from caves on reverse slope of Nan Hill in preparation for renewing assault on Hill 60. In XXIV Corps area, limited attack by 305th Inf of 77th Div brings sharp enemy reaction. 184th Inf, 7th Div, slightly improves positions in E coastal sector.

9 May

WESTERN EUROPE—All hostilities in the European Theater of Operations are officially terminated at 0001 B as surrender act becomes effective.

EASTERN EUROPE—Resistance on Eastern Front is limited to Czechoslovakian and Austrian areas, where enemy is retreating W and SW as rapidly as possible. On northern front, German remnants along coast of Gulf of Danzig start surrendering to forces of Third and Second White Russian Fronts. First, Fourth, and Second Ukrainian Fronts pursue enemy westward in Czechoslovakia; Prague falls to forces of First Ukrainian Front. Troops of Third Ukrainian Front driving W in Austria reach Amstetten and Graz and make contact with U.S. forces near Amstetten.

BURMA—In ALFSEA area, W African 82d Div, now under direct command of ALFSEA and moving S along Arakan coast from Taungup, enters Sandoway.

LUZON—In U.S. Sixth Army's I Corps area, battle for Balete Pass nears the end as 27th and 161st Regts, 25th Div, establish contact in this region. In XI Corps area, 3d Bn of 145th Inf seizes Mt Binicayan; 2d Bn improves positions near Sugar Loaf Hill; 1st Bn patrols in Wawa sector. In XIV Corps area, patrol of 158th Inf eliminates enemy party in the Bicols, the only Japanese met in this area.

S PHILIPPINES—In U.S. Eighth Army area, RCT 108 convoys leave Cebu and Leyte for Macajalar Bay operation, Mindanao. In X Corps area on Mindanao, 1st Bn of 21st Inf, 24th Div, holds its Talomo R bridgehead against strong opposition. Efforts to bridge the river fail. Continuing attack on Guma pocket after air strike, Co K of 34th Inf finds that Japanese have withdrawn. 124th Inf, 31st Div, suspends ground attacks in Colgan Woods for next few days while enemy positions are being softened by aircraft and mortar fire.

OKINAWA—In U.S. Tenth Army area, Gen Buckner orders general attack by army to begin on 11th. While holding action is conducted in center, troops on flanks will attempt double envelopment of enemy's Shuri positions. In III Amphib Corps area, 6th Mar Div prepares to attack across Asa R on W flank of corps. Engineers construct footbridge during night. 1st Marines, 1st Mar Div, finishes clearing Nan Hill, then attacks and takes Hill 60. 5th Marines is endeavoring to pocket enemy in region S of Awacha where stubborn opposition continues. In XXIV Corps area, 77th Div's frontal assaults toward Shuri make little headway. Since enemy has organized a series of strongpoints on heights N of Shuri that must be methodically reduced, div tactics are to attack in small area with one regt after all available supporting weapons have softened it, while another regt supports the attack with fire and mops up. On left flank of corps, 382d Inf of 96th Div relieves 17th Inf of 7th Div. Most of the Japanese have been cleared from their Kochi positions.

10 May

LUZON—In U.S. Sixth Army's XI Corps area, 145th Inf mops up and patrols within its sector. 152d Inf, 38th Div, continues almost futile efforts to advance in vicinity of Woodpecker Ridge. 43d Div advance slows as troops approach Ipo.

In U.S. Eighth Army's X Corps area of Mindanao, RCT 108 lands on shore of Macajalar Bay at 0830 after uneventful mine sweeping and aerial and naval gunfire bombardment and, assisted by Filipino guerrillas, establishes beachhead without opposition. 2d Bn starts SE along Sayre Highway to make contact with 31st Div forces moving N along it, gaining 5 miles. 155th Inf, which has been probing down Talomo Trail toward 24th Div sector, is relieved by 167th Inf; 167th will continue to explore the trail. Japanese guns on Samal I. shell CP area of 19th Inf, 24th Div. 1st Bn, 21st Inf, withdraws its bridgehead across the Talomo in evening. After arty preparation, 2d Bn of 19th Inf begins attack to destroy bypassed enemy force on Hill 550, which commands Davao.

OKINAWA—In U.S. Tenth Army's III Amphib Corps area, 22d Marines, 6th Mar Div, begins attack across Asa Estuary at 0300, rear elements wading after Japanese destroy the footbridge. Against increasingly strong resistance marines push forward through Asa and establish bridgehead 350 yards deep and almost a mile wide. Bailey bridge is constructed, night 10-11, for heavy weapons. 1st Mar Div, under heavy fire from Shuri, makes little progress: 1st Marines is unable to advance; 7th Marines reaches Dakeshi Ridge and attacks it unsuccessfully. In XXIV Corps area, 77th Div continues laborious reduction of enemy positions N of Shuri. 383d Inf, 96th Div, relieves 184th Inf, 7th Div, and prepares to attack toward Conical Hill, E anchor of enemy's Shuri defense line. 383d Inf reaches crest of Zebra Hill and holds it against enemy counterattack at night.

11 May

EASTERN EUROPE—Soviet forces finish clearing Czechoslovakia and Austria and begin to mop up isolated remnants. Contact is made with U.S. forces in vicinity of Chemnitz (Saxony), Pilsen (Czechoslovakia), and Linz (Austria).

CHINA—Gen Wedemeyer writes Gen Marshall that he (Wedemeyer) is reviewing plans for increasing air strength in China and opening a seacoast port because of reduced ATC tonnage offered on 25 April and because of drain on Hump tonnage during Japanese drive on Chihchiang. Gen Ho's ALPHA forces have halted Japanese drive on Chihchiang by outflanking maneuvers and are forcing enemy back. Ch 18th and 100th Armies have blunted enemy's N spearheads in Paima Shan area; 18th recovers Shanmen. On main axis of Japanese advance, Pao-ching–Chihchiang road, Japanese set fire to Kaosha village. Ch 94th Army has successfully turned enemy's S flank and is now just 8 miles S of Paoching–Chihchiang road, well E of Tungkow.

LUZON—In U.S. Sixth Army's I Corps area 1st Bn of 35th Inf, 25th Div, and 3d Bn of 27th Inf establish contact on Kapintalan Ridge, where over 200 caves have been sealed and almost a thousand Japanese dead counted. 25th Div is directed to continue N with 161st Inf advancing W of Highway 5, 35th astride it, and 27th E of it toward Villa Verde Trail, Santa Fe, and heights E of Santa Fe. In XI Corps area, 43d Div troops driving on Ipo reach slopes of Hill 815, about a mile below objective.

S PHILIPPINES—In U.S. Eighth Army's X Corps area on Mindanao, RCT 108, pushing steadily down Sayre Highway, reaches positions commanding Del Monte Airfield. Filipino guerrillas seize Cagayan. 21st Inf, 24th Div, reinf by 1st Bn of 34th, is directed to clear region NE of Talomo R in vicinity of Mintal. 2d Bn, 19th Inf, makes little headway against enemy on Hill 550 despite ground fire and air support. On Samal, Co K, 19th Inf, searches for enemy guns that continue to fire on Davao, Mindanao. On Negros, 185th Inf, reinf by 3d Bn of 503d Para Inf, opens southward drive along Terukini and Kasagi Ridges toward Hill 4055 in Negros Occidental, progressing very slowly during rest of month. Bombardment of Dolan Hill by arty and aircraft is intensified for next few days as 160th Inf prepares to renew ground assault.

NEW GUINEA—6th Aus Div seizes Wewak.

OKINAWA—U.S. Tenth Army, after 30-minute arty preparation to neutralize enemy guns and strongpoints, launches co-ordinated attack with III Amphib Corps on right and XXIV Corps on left. On III Amphib Corp's W flank, 22d Marines of 6th Mar Div expands positions S of the Asa, some elements on coast reaching positions at N outskirts of Amike, which command the capital city of Naha, and others taking hill 800 yards S of Asa. 7th Marines, 1st Mar Div, gains foothold on Dakeshi Ridge despite intense fire from Wana Ridge to S, but 1st Marines is still virtually halted by fire from Shuri Heights. 5th Marines encircles enemy forces in region S of Awacha. In XXIV Corps area, columns of 306th Inf, 77th Div, begin attacks toward Chocolate Drop Hill (Hill 130), NE of Ishimmi, and Flattop Hill to SE, which dominates Dick hill mass in 96th Div zone, but meet intense fire and make little headway. 382d Inf, 96th Div, consolidates on Zebra and tries unsuccessfully to push forward to Dick hill mass; 383d begins attack for Conical Hill, gaining positions on hills at NW approaches.

12 May

SEAC—Preparations for Operation ZIPPER—invasion of Malaya—are in progress. Part of the assault forces—Force W (amphibious), 15 Corps, 224th Gp (air), and newly formed 34 Corps, all under Lt Gen O. L. Roberts—are now assembled in India for reorganization, rest, and training. Other assault forces that can be spared are concentrated in Rangoon area, from which the ZIPPER forces from Burma will be mounted.

LUZON—In U.S. Sixth Army's XI Corps area, 43d Div columns are converging on Ipo; Japanese are driven from Hill 815.

S PHILIPPINES—In U.S. Eighth Army's X Corps area on Mindanao, some elements of RCT 108 take Del Monte Airfield while others advance to positions SW of Tankulan. 155th Inf is directed to continue 31st Div's northward drive along Sayre Highway toward RCT 108. 124th Inf renews attack on Colgan Woods strongpoint and overcomes resistance there. 21st Inf, 24th Div, supported by massed arty fire, attacks NW along Talomo R with 1st Bn on left and attached 1st Bn of 34th Inf on right. 2d Bn, 19th Inf, assisted by air strikes, makes limited progress on Hill 550. 3d Bn, 34th Inf, asks and receives permission to remain in Guma area until its relief can be physically accomplished by 162d Inf rather than return to Digos at once. On Samal, aircraft and arty bombard suspected enemy gun positions.

OKINAWA—In U.S. Tenth Army's III Amphib Corps area, while 3d Bn of 22d Marines, 6th Mar Div, remains on W coast above Naha, Co G, to E, pushes forward to Sugar Loaf Hill, key point in Shuri defenses SE of Amike, but is forced back with heavy casualties. 7th Marines, 1st Mar Div, gains most of Dakeshi Ridge. 1st Marines, veering westward in order to advance, must be supplied by air. In XXIV Corps area, 305th Inf of 77th Div continues extremely slow advance generally along Route 5 toward Shuri. 306th temporarily suspends action against Chocolate Drop and assists 305th. 382d Inf, 96th Div, continues attack toward Dick hill mass with negligible results but takes hill 600 yards S of Zebra. 2d Bn, 382d Inf, gains weak hold on N spur of Conical Hill, whereupon div is ordered to intensify frontal attacks on the hill.

13 May

EASTERN EUROPE—Red Army completes offensive operations, overcoming last German resistance in Czechoslovakia.

BURMA—In ALFSEA area, W African 82d Div reaches Gwa without opposition, concluding operations in Arakan sector.

CHINA—Gen Wedemeyer has by this time decided that he cannot receive the Tenth Air Force in China for several months and so informs Gen Stratemeyer. Gen Chennault's Fourteenth Air Force is to move to Chungking to command air forces based in China.

LUZON—In U.S. Sixth Army area, I Corps finishes clearing Balete Pass, gaining access to Cagayan Valley. In XI Corps area, 43d Div gets elements to within sight of Ipo Dam.

S PHILIPPINES—In U.S. Eighth Army's X Corps area, RCT 108, continuing down Sayre Highway on Mindanao, runs into strong opposition from Mangima Canyon and is delayed in the area for several days. 155th Inf, 31st Div, passes through 124th and drives N along Sayre Highway in effort to establish contact with RCT 108; on Talomo Trail, elements of 167th Inf reach Pulangi R. 21st Inf, 24th Div, makes slow progress northward along Talomo Trail; 3d Bn, 34th Inf, moves forward from Guma area to assist 21st Inf in clearing Talomo R Valley; 2d Bn, 19th Inf, progresses slowly against Hill 550. On Samal, Co K, 19th Inf, unsuccessfully attacks enemy position.

OKINAWA—In U.S. Tenth Army's III Amphib Corps area, 6th Mar Div, although supported by heavy volume of fire, continues to gain ground slowly and with heavy casualties. 3d Bn, 29th Marines, is committed in region E of 22d Marines. 1st Marines, 1st Mar Div, tries in vain to take Hill 55—part of S wall of Wana Draw. 7th Marines completes capture of Dakeshi Ridge but suffers heavy casualties while attacking through town of Dakeshi toward Wana Ridge, N wall of Wana Draw. In XXIV Corps area, 306th Inf, 77th Div, renews costly attacks for Chocolate Drop Hill; tries in vain to take Flattop. 382d Inf, 96th Div, attacks toward 2 hills of Dick hill mass, taking one of them; pressing frontal assault in E coastal sector, 383d Inf succeeds in penetrating eastern end of Shuri line by driving to NE crest of Conical Hill and holding there against determined counterattacks; some elements of 383d Inf fighting NW of Conical Hill reach slopes of Charlie Hill but are unable to take crest.

14 May

CHINA—Movement of MARS (U.S. 5332d Brig (Prov)) from Burma to China is completed. The move started on 14 March.

LUZON—In U.S. Sixth Army's I Corps area, 27th Inf of 25th Div attacks northward from Balete Ridge. In XI Corps area, forward elements of 43d Div reach Ipo Dam. General assault on the dam is ordered for 17th.

S PHILIPPINES—In U.S. Eighth Army's X Corps area, on Mindanao, RCT 108 temporarily suspends drive down Sayre Highway to await supplies. 155th Inf, 31st Div, continues N along the highway; on Talomo Trail, 167th Inf troops are slowed by scattered delaying opposition and difficult terrain as they push toward barrio of Sanipon. From Bancal, 3d Bn of 34th Inf, 24th Div, attacks northward astride road leading to Mintal in conjunction with 21st Inf clearing Talomo R Valley but is soon halted; flanking attack on Hill 550 by elements of 19th Inf makes little headway; rest of 3d Bn, 19th Inf, is ordered to Samal, where enemy guns are still a threat to Davao from the N.

OKINAWA—In U.S. Tenth Army's III Amphib Corps area, 22d Marines of 6th Mar Div charges Sugar Loaf and gains feeble hold. 1st Marines, 1st Mar Div, after unsuccessful attempt to take Wana Ridge and make contact with 7th Marines, is relieved by 5th Marines. In XXIV Corps area, 306th Inf of 77th Div, greatly depleted in strength, continues vain efforts to take Chocolate Drop and Flattop. 382d Inf, 96th Div, improves positions on Dick hill mass; 383d extends control over Charlie and reaches crest of King Hill to S.

15 May

INDIA—Base Section No. 1 (Karachi) is inactivated. As a result, the other sections within SOS are given new designations.

BURMA—In Br Fourteenth Army area, Ind 26th Div, now under army command as it moves N along Rangoon Prome road, links up with Ind 20th Div, 33 Corps, moving S along the road.

LUZON—In U.S. Sixth Army area, XI Corps prepares to renew attacks on Woodpecker Ridge and Ipo Dam.

S PHILIPPINES—In U.S. Eighth Army's X Corps area on Mindanao, RCT 108, with air and arty support, renews attacks in Mangima Canyon sector of Sayre Highway against strong opposition. Elements of 124th Inf, 31st Div, guarding installations in rear area repel counterattack by about 100 Japanese, killing 72. 79th Inf, 24th Div, is ordered to drive NE from Davao area to effect junction with Filipino guerrillas moving SW; elements of 21st and 34th Regts continue clearing Talomo R Valley; attack on Hill 550, where Co G, 34th Inf, relieves 2d Bn, 79th Inf, is suspended; Co F repels counterattacks after nightfall. On Samal, main body of 3d Bn, 79th Inf, joins Co K. Japanese withdraw from the island about this time. On Negros, 160th Inf renews assault on Dolan in Negros Occidental, the target for extensive aerial and arty bombardment, and clears it except for pocket on N spur.

OKINAWA—In U.S. Tenth Army's III Amphib Corps area, small Marine force on crest of Sugar Loaf (I officer and 79 men of 22d Marines, 6th Mar Div) withdraws under fire when its position becomes untenable. 7th Marines, 1st Mar Div, suspends assault on Wana Ridge while Japanese positions are being softened with ground fire, air strikes, and naval gunfire. In XXIV Corps area, 305th Inf, 77th Div, inching forward on right flank of div, has suffered heavy casualties and is at 1/4 strength. On div left, 307th Inf attacks through 306th toward Chocolate Drop and positions near crest of Flattop. Japanese counterattack unsuccessfully after nightfall. 382d Inf, 96th Div, continues to battle enemy on Dick hill mass. 383d improves positions on spurs of Conical Hill; elements advance up NW spur but are out of contact with others to E.

16 May

CHINA—Gen Eaker, AAF Hq, tells Gen Wedemeyer that Gen Chennault will be replaced regardless of other considerations.

LUZON—In U.S. Sixth Army's I Corps area, 3d Bn of 27th Inf, 25th Div, is delayed by strongpoint on E edge of Bolong Plateau. In XI Corps area, 149th Inf begins relieving 145th in Mt Pacawagan area. 152d Inf opens all-out attack for Woodpecker Ridge after preparatory bombardment, gaining weak hold on military crest and forward slopes of Twin Peaks. In XIV Corps area, Gen MacNider reports the Bicols secure.

MINDANAO—In U.S. Eighth Army's X Corps area, 3d Bn of 767th Inf, 31st Div, advancing along Talomo Trail, runs into strong delaying opposition that virtually halts it for more than a week about a mile N of Sanipon. Continuing operations to clear Talomo R Valley, 3d Bn of 34th Inf, 24th Div, gains a little ground and digs in to consolidate for next few days.

OKINAWA—In U.S. Tenth Army's III Amphib Corps area, 6th Mar Div, attacking with 2 regts toward Sugar Loaf, experiences its worst day of combat on Okinawa as enemy continues to resist viciously. In 1st Mar Div zone, M-7's and tank-infantry teams of 5th Marines try to neutralize Wana Draw. 1st Bn, 7th Marines, attacks up Wana Ridge but is forced back to N base. In XXIV Corps area, 77th Div continues to battle enemy N of Shuri with 305th Inf on right and 307th on left. Efforts of 307th to take Chocolate Drop and Flattop are again futile. 383d Inf, 96th Div, improves positions on regimental left, where supporting tanks reach outskirts of Yonabaru, but is unable to oust Japanese from Love Hill, W of Conical Hill.

17 May

LUZON—In U.S. Sixth Army's XI Corps area, 149th Inf of 38th Div continues relieving 145th and patrols without incident; 152d Inf pauses to consolidate and patrol in Woodpecker Ridge area. In final assault by 3 regts after intensive preparatory bombardment, 43d Div takes Ipo Dam intact. Japanese still hold Osboy Ridge, however.

MINDANAO—In U.S. Eighth Army's X Corps area, 1st Bn, 19th Inf, 24th Div, starts NE to contact guerrilla forces; 2d Bn of 21st Inf, driving toward Tugbok, meets strong opposition, which arty and aircraft help to neutralize.

OKINAWA—In U.S. Tenth Army area, Gen Buckner takes control of all forces ashore and is responsible for defense and development of captured positions. Adm Hill replaces Adm Turner as Commander TF 51 and will control air defenses and naval forces. In III Amphib Corps area, while badly mauled 22d Regt, 6th Mar Div, conducts holding action, 29th Marines continues attack for Sugar Loaf after heavy naval gunfire, air, and arty bombardment. Striking from the E after 1st and 3d Bns have opened approach from W end of Crescent Hill, 2d Bn drives to crest of Sugar Loaf but falls back when ammunition is exhausted. 5th Marines, 1st Mar Div, continues to fire into Wana Draw; 2d Bn attacks Hill 55, in its mouth, and gains positions on W slope. 3d Bn, 7th Marines, relieves exhausted 1st Bn and continues efforts to take Wana Ridge without success. In XXIV Corps area, Co E of 307th Inf, 77th Div, in surprise, predawn attack, advances to Ishimmi Ridge, W of town of Ishimmi; there it is dangerously exposed to enemy fire from all sides and cannot be reinforced. 3d Bn secures positions around Chocolate Drop and drives off counterattacking enemy; drives to crest of Flattop but is driven off. 305th Inf continues slow advance on right flank of div. 96th Div commits 3d Bn, 381st Inf, on E flank, where it relieves Cos E and F, 383d, in preparation for drive S down 800 yard ridge extending from Conical peak to Sugar Hill.

18 May

CHINA—In Fukien Province, Chinese recover Foochow.

BURMA—Movement of CAI (Ch 30th, 38th, and 50th Divs) from Burma to China is begun.

LUZON—In U.S. Sixth Army's XI Corps area, 149th Inf completes relief of 145th and takes responsibility for its sector. 145th is held in reserve. 152d Inf renews assault on Woodpecker Ridge but continues to progress slowly. 43d Div extends control over Osboy Ridge and opens Metropolitan Road from Bigti to Ipo.

MINDANAO—In U.S. Eighth Army's X Corps area, RCT 108, completing capture of Mangima Canyon, is able to advance rapidly southward along Sayre Highway. 1st Bn of 19th Inf, 24th Div, reaches positions near lower end of Sasa airfield. Tugbok falls to 2d Bn, 21st Inf, which halts for a few days to patrol and consolidate.

OKINAWA—In U.S. Tenth Army's III Amphib Corps area, Sugar Loaf falls to 29th Marines, 6th Mar Div; regt also consolidates positions on northern slope of Crescent Hill and seizes part of Horseshoe, commanding feature just SW of Sugar Loaf. 1st Mar Div continues seesaw battle for Wana Draw and Wana Ridge. 5th Marines further softens enemy positions with tank and M-7 fire while engineers clear lower slopes of the ridge. 3d Bn, 7th Marines, makes another fruitless effort to take Wana Ridge. In XXIV Corps area, 305th Inf of 77th Div slightly improves positions on Highway 5; 307th is still unable to take Chocolate Drop or Flattop but improves positions about former. 382d Inf, 96th Div, succeeds in holding crest of Dick Hill under fire from Flattop and starts clearing reverse slope. 3d Bn, 381st Inf, opens attack for Sugar Hill.

19 May

LUZON—In U.S. Sixth Army's I Corps area, 25th Div, ordered to clear area W of Highway 5 as far as Imugan and N and W of Santa Fe, is reinf by 126th Inf, 32d Div. In XI Corps area, 152d Inf confines its activity against Woodpecker Ridge to local probing for next few days. Enemy resistance to 43d Div in Ipo area ends and mopping up is begun.

MINDANAO—In U.S. Eighth Army's X Corps area, 19th Inf of 24th Div, passing 2d Bn through 1st, continues NE up coastal road to Panacan. 2d Bn, 34th Inf, will renew attack on Hill 550.

OKINAWA—In U.S. Tenth Army's III Amphib Corps area, 6th Mar Div consolidates positions and relieves depleted 29th Marines with 4th Marines. 5th Marines, 1st Mar Div, further neutralizes enemy positions in Wana Draw. 3d Bn, 7th Marines, continues assault on Wana Ridge until the 7th Marines is relieved by 1st Marines. In XXIV Corps area, beleaguered Co E of 307th Inf, 77th Div, withstands severe pressure on Ishimmi Ridge throughout day; at night, when relief force arrives, withdraws with very heavy casualties. Other elements of regt continue to consolidate positions around Chocolate Drop. Direct fire is placed on Flattop and Dick Hill. 382d Inf, 96th Div, is slowly expanding hold on reverse slope of Dick Hill. Elements of 383d Inf reach W end of King Hill, NW of Conical peak, but are driven off. 3d Bn, 381st Inf, continues southward attack toward Sugar Hill.

20 May

CHINA—Japanese are redeploying to defend Japan. They begin pulling back from Ho-chih, in Kwangsi Province on branch line to Kweiyang.

MINDANAO—In U.S. Eighth Army's X Corps area, 155th Inf of 31st Div drives northward along Sayre Highway to positions commanding Malaybalay; meets heavy enemy fire. 3d Bn of 19th Inf, 24th Div, returns to Davao from Samal I. 2d Bn, continuing N along coastal road, reaches Tibungko. 2d Bn, 34th Inf, begins assault on Hill 550, holding limited gains against violent night counterattacks. 3d Bn, 34th Inf, renews attack along Bancal-Mintal road in effort to contact 21st Inf; reaches positions within 400 yards of road junction E of Mintal.

OKINAWA—In U.S. Tenth Army's III Amphib Corps area, 4th Marines, 6th Mar Div, attempts to clear rest of Horseshoe and Crescent features, which command Sugar Loaf, making limited progress on Horseshoe; repels enemy counterattacks at night, inflicting more than 200 casualties. 5th Marines, 1st Mar Div, seizes Hill 55 and advances into Wana Draw; 1st Marines takes crest of Wana Ridge in 2-pronged assault. In XXIV Corps area, 307th Inf of 77th Div finishes clearing Chocolate Drop and takes Flattop. 382d Inf, 96th Div, gains additional ground on reverse slope of Dick Hill. 3d Bn, 381st, pushes forward slowly toward Sugar Hill.

21 May

INDIA—BURMA—SOS merges with theater Hq, IBT G-4 replacing SOS commander. SOS is inactivated.

LUZON—In U.S. Sixth Army's XI Corps area, 38th Div commander orders 149th Inf to patrol Wawa area carefully. Patrols report enemy established on the dam itself. 3d Bn, 152d Inf, renews attack on Woodpecker Ridge with fire support of 1st and 2d Bns; crosses the ridge to draw between there and Regimental Objective Hill.

MINDANAO—In U.S. Eighth Army's X Corps area, 155th Inf of 31st Div, ordered to clear Malaybalay-Kalasungay region, temporarily halts northward drive up Sayre Highway and takes Malaybalay, Japanese supply base, with ease. 1st Bn of 19th Inf, 24th Div, attacking N through 2d Bn, reaches Bunawan. To block enemy escape from 34th Inf E of Talomo R, 3d and 1st Bns, 21st Inf, cross the river N of Mintal and 1st Bn pushes northward. 3d Bn, 34th Inf, renews attack but cannot advance despite air support. After heavy preparatory fire, Co G, 34th Inf, secures rest of Hill 550, from which Japanese have now withdrawn.

OKINAWA—In U.S. Tenth Army's III Amphib Corps area, 6th Mar Div continues to clear toward the Asato R on W flank of corps, fighting for Horseshoe and Crescent in Japanese Sugar Loaf defense system. Elements clear part of tunneled interior of the Horseshoe but efforts of others to expand hold on Crescent fail. 1st Mar Div is attacking toward Shuri Ridge, last feature covering Shuri Castle on W; makes slow progress against reverse slope of Wana Ridge and resists enemy efforts to regain forward slopes. In XXIV corps area, 77th Div replaces 305th Inf, just N of Shuri on Route 5, with 306th. Co A, 307th Inf, reaches base of Jane Hill, SW of Flattop, where it is isolated until the 30th and exposed to intense fire. 382d Inf, 96th Div, drives to edge of Oboe Hill 1,000 yards E of Shuri, and is halted there by enemy for some days. With capture of Sugar Hill by 3d Bn of 381st Inf, E slopes of Conical Hill are clear and enemy's right flank is turned. 184th Inf, 7th Div, starts southward along E coast at 1900 to envelop Shuri. Japanese decide to withdraw southward from Shuri.

22 May

INDIA–BURMA—Gen Stratemeyer's hq learns that C-54's are on the way to India. Because of redeployment needs, this is unexpected.

LUZON—In U.S. Sixth Army's I Corps area, elements of 27th Inf, 25th Div, are 2,000 yards SE of Santa Fe. In XI Corps area, platoon of Co A, 149th Inf, attacks to eliminate enemy position on Wawa Dam but is brought to a halt by fire. 152d Inf renews all-out attack and gains final objectives in area near junction of Mariquina and Bosoboso Rivers with assistance of flame-thrower tanks.

MINDANAO—In U.S. Eighth Army's X Corps area, RCT 108, continuing steadily southward along Sayre Highway, reaches positions near Impalutao. 155th Inf, 31st Div, after taking undefended Kalasungay, continues drive up Sayre Highway, surprising enemy force and inflicting heavy casualties. 2d Bn of 19th Inf, 24th Div, attacks through 1st Bn and reaches Tambongan. 1st Bn, 21st Inf, gains ground E of the Talomo, but gap still exists between it and 3d Bn, 34th Inf.

OKINAWA—In U.S. Tenth Army area, rains, intermittent during past few days, become frequent and heavy during rest of month and early June, hampering operations. Japanese begin withdrawing their supplies and wounded from Shuri. III Amphib Corps, with supporting armor immobilized by mud, curtails its activities sharply. 4th Marines, 6th Mar Div, reaches N bank of the Asato R, on W flank, and send patrols across it at night. In XXIV Corps area, 383d Inf of 96th Div struggles for next few days to reduce Love Hill defenses in region W of Conical peak. 184th Inf, 7th Div, drives forward unmolested through ruins of Yonabaru to hills beyond.

23 May

LUZON—In U.S. Sixth Army's I Corps area, 27th Inf of 25th Div is still stalled in spite of tank assistance. In XI Corps area, 1st Bn of 152d Inf pushes N toward Mariquina R.

S PHILIPPINES—In U.S. Eighth Army's X Corps area on Mindanao, entire Sayre Highway is opened as 155th Inf gains contact with RCT 108 S of Impalutao. 2d Bn of 19th Inf, 24th Div, reaches Ising area and makes patrol contact with Filipino guerrillas. 1st Bn, 21st Inf, takes road junction 1,700 yards N of Talomo bridge. Arty pounds area between it and 34th Inf. On Negros, 160th Inf overcomes final opposition on Dolan Hill in Negros Occidental with capture of pocket on N spur. 185th Inf continues slowly southward toward Hill 4055, final enemy strongpoint in Negros Occidental.

OKINAWA—In U.S. Tenth Army's III Amphib Corps area, 6th Mar Div begins drive from the Asato to the Kokuba on W flank of corps. Since patrols S of the Asato are but moderately opposed, 2 bns of 4th Marines cross under smoke screen and start southward. In XXIV Corps area, 184th Inf of 7th Div, after securing line of departure from which 32d Inf can push W to envelop Shuri, protects left flank and rear of Sad Inf- 32d Inf, whose supporting armor is immobilized by mud, starts W along Naha-Yonabaru valley and reaches positions a mile SW of Yonabaru without great difficulty.

24 May

MINDANAO—In U.S. Eighth Army's X Corps area, 2d Bn of 19th Inf, 24th Div, effects junction with Filipino guerrillas near Tagum R. 21st and 34th Inf troops clearing Talomo R Valley continue efforts to link up.

RYUKYU Is.—In U.S. Tenth Army area, Japanese intensify air activity, night 24-25, concentrating on airfields on Okinawa and Ie Shima, as well as shipping offshore. Some airborne troops are landed on Yontan field and destroy or damage a number of aircraft before being rounded up and killed. In III Amphib Corps area on Okinawa, elements of 6th Mar Div Rcn Co cross the Asato, which engineers bridge, and enter NW Naha without opposition. In XXIV Corps area, Japanese attack troops of 382d Inf, 96th Div, on Oboe Hill in company strength and force 2 cos of 1st Bn off. 1st Bn is reduced to co strength. Japanese retire leaving 150 dead. 2d Bn, 383d Inf, replaces 2d Bn, 382d, on Oboe. 5th Marines, 1st Mar Div, patrols to Asato. 32d Inf, 7th Div, begins probing to develop enemy defenses that cross Yonabaru valley SE of Shuri. 184th Inf extends positions slightly southward. Enemy counterattacks toward Yonabaru, night 24-25, achieving limited penetration of 32d Inf line.

25 May

CHINA—Maj Gen Henry S. Aurand assumes duties as head of SOS.

MINDANAO—In U.S. Eighth Army's X Corps area, 19th Inf of 24th Div consolidates for next few days and prepares to drive W on Mandog. 21st and 34th Regts continue to clear Talomo R Valley; 34th finds hill strongpoint that has been delaying it undefended.

OKINAWA—In U.S. Tenth Army's III Amphib Corps area, 4th Marines, 6th Mar Div, gains Machishi and most of ridge line W of there. Div Rcn Co completes its crossing of the Asato and only meets stragglers as it pushes through the part of the city W of N-S canal.

U.S.—Joint Chiefs of Staff approve directive for Operation OLYMPIC, invasion of Japanese home islands, scheduled for 1 November 1945

26 May

CHINA—Continuing redeployment for defense of Japan, Japanese withdraw from Yung-ning, severing land route to Indochina. Chinese recapture Nanning.

LUZON—In U.S. Sixth Army's I Corps area, 27th Inf of 25th Div finally clears ravine N of Balete Pass and gets patrol into Santa Fe. In XI Corps area, 151st Inf of 38th Div, on left of 149th, has cleared Wawa Road and secured supply route. Reinf platoon from Co A closes in on Wawa but is forced to withdraw; in another attempt secures the barrio.

MINDANAO—In U.S. Eighth Army's X Corps area, Co I of 167th Inf, 31st Div, bypasses enemy positions on Talomo Trail to reach Pulangi R near Sanipon. 1st Bn moves forward to assist 3d Bn.

OKINAWA—III U.S. Tenth Army area, Japanese combat units begin withdrawal from Shuri and are targets for aircraft, arty, and naval gunfire. In XXIV Corps area, 184th Inf of 7th Div drives southward along E coast to next ridge line with ease, but 32d Inf incurs heavy casualties while attempting vainly to take Dick Hill in Japanese defense line E of Chan.

27 May

LUZON—In U.S. Sixth Army's I Corps area, rest of 1st Bn, 27th Inf, 25th Div, moves into Santa Fe. This concludes corps' mountain fighting and bitter struggle for Villa Verde Trail. RCT 145 passes to corps control from XI Corps and reverts to 37th Div. In XI Corps area, 149th Inf of 38th Div is ordered to take Wawa Dam, from which enemy appears to be withdrawing. 1st Bn, jumping off in afternoon, drives to within 50 yards of the dam, where it is halted by enemy fire, and falls back to position 200 yards W of the dam for night.

MINDANAO—III U.S. Eighth Army's X Corps area, Filipinos of guerrilla 118th Inf and elements of 167th Inf, 31st Div, establish bridgehead across the Pulangi near Sanipon. Progress of 167th Inf along Talomo Trail from this point is extremely slow for the next month. 91st and 34th Regts, 24th Div, establish contact, concluding action to clear Talomo R Valley.

RYUKYU Is.—Japanese open two-day air strikes on shipping. In U.S. Tenth Army's III Amphib Corps area on Okinawa, co of 2d Bn, 22d Marines, 6th Mar Div, crosses the Asato and advances through Rcn Co to deepen penetration into W part of Naha. Opposition is still negligible. In XXIV Corps area, 32d Inf of 7th Div is unable to dent enemy's strong defense line covering Shuri.

POA—Adm Halsey, Third Fleet commander, takes control of all naval forces attached to Fifth Fleet at midnight 27-28, and the figure "5" in TF designations is changed to "3." TF 58 becomes TF 38 and Vice Adm. John S. McCain succeeds Vice Adm. Marc A. Mitscher as its commander.

28 May

BURMA—Br Twelfth Army, under command of Gen Stopford, formerly commander of 33 Corps, which is disbanded, establishes hq at Rangoon and takes control of all Allied troops in Burma, with responsibility for future operations within and from Burma. Hq, Fourteenth Army, is withdrawn to India to take command of 15 and 34 Corps for Operation ZIPPER. In addition to 4 Corps (Ind 5th, 17th, and 19th Divs), Br Twelfth Army has under its command Ind 7th Div reinf by Ind 268th Brig, Ind 20th Div, and 6th Brig of 2d Br Div. The Twelfth Army also has operational control over W

African 82d Div and E African 22d Brig, as well as Burma National Army.

LUZON—In U.S. Sixth Army's I Corps area, 37th Div is directed to relieve 25th Div in Santa Fe sector and drive N astride Highway 5 toward Aritao on 31st. Elements of 128th Inf, 32d Div, take Imugan and establish contact with 126th Inf, which has been attached to 25th Div. Corps is ordered to exploit breakthrough. Philippine guerrilla forces are placed under corps and ordered to capture Cervantes. In XI Corps area, 1st Bn of 149th Inf takes Wawa Dam without opposition. This is the last major objective of corps E of Manila.

NEGROS—In U.S. Eighth Army area in Negros Oriental, 164th Inf finishes clearing enemy from ridge positions and begins extensive mopping up operations.

OKINAWA—Continuing air attacks in strength, Japanese planes hit a number of ships and sink USS *Drexler* (DD). More than a hundred enemy planes, including kamikazes, are shot down. This is the last strong enemy air effort against Okinawa. In U.S. Tenth Army area, weather conditions improve briefly, permitting more extensive action. In III Amphib Corps area, marines of 22d Regt, 6th Mar Div, in. Naha push forward to the Kokuba estuary with ease but evoke strong reaction when trying to reconnoiter Ona-Yama I., in Naha Harbor. Engineers bridge the canal in Naha after nightfall. 29th Marines relieves 4th Marines and advances almost to the Kokuba. 5th Marines, 1st Mar Div, takes Beehive Hill on lower end of Shuri Ridge. In XXIV Corps area, 32d Inf of 7th Div confines its activity to patrolling; 184th Inf is held up by opposition at Hill 69, N of Karadera village.

29 May

LUZON—In U.S. Sixth Army area, I Corps prepares for operation to clear Cagayan Valley. 37th Div is to attack through 25th Div toward Aritao while Philippine guerrilla forces seize Cervantes. Each will then be prepared to move into Cagayan Valley. 25th and 32d Divs have security missions. 129th Inf, 37th Div, motors to Santa Fe for drive on Aritao.

MINDANAO—In U.S. Eighth Army's X Corps area, 19th Inf of 24th Div opens westward drive on Mandog, last enemy defensive position at N edge of Davao Plain, employing 3d Bn and assisted by aircraft.

OKINAWA—In U.S. Tenth Army's III Amphib Corps area, 6th Mar Div drives eastward with 29th Marines on left and 22d on right. 22d Marines crosses canal into E Naha, where enemy is prepared to make a stand. 1st Bn of 5th Marines, 1st Mar Div, takes Shuri Ridge, S of Wana Draw, and crosses into 77th Div zone to occupy undefended Shuri Castle at 1015. Bypassing enemy opposition, 1st Marines moves forward and relieves 1st Bn, 5th Marines. In XXIV Corps area, 77th Div is pressing southward toward Shuri. On 7th Div left, 184th Inf continues to battle enemy at hill near Karadera.

30 May

SEAC—Adm Mountbatten meets in Delhi with commanders of Operations ZIPPER and MAILFIST (conquests of Malaya and Singapore, respectively) and decides that these operations shall at first be under command of 34 Corps and that hq of Fourteenth Army and 15 Corps shall be moved in about D plus 50.

OKINAWA—In U.S. Tenth Army's III Amphib Corps area, 2d and 3d Bns of 22d Marines, 6th Mar Div, cross canal in Naha and attack through 1st Bn; assisted by direct tank fire, take Hill 27 at SE edge of Naha. 1st Mar Div forces in Shuri are being supplied by air and carrying parties. XXIV Corps makes substantial gains as enemy rear-guard opposition weakens. 77th Div takes 3 hills E of Shuri (Dorothy, Jane, and Tom), former strongpoints in enemy's inner defenses of Shuri; find an elaborate network of cave defenses on Dorothy. Right flank elements of 77th Div cross into III Amphib Corps zone and begin attack for 100 Meter Hill. 96th Div pushes forward all along its front, clearing most of its zone N of Yonabaru-Shuri-Naha road. Among hill positions taken are Hen Hill, which enemy has successfully defended for 9 days, Love Hill, and reverse slope of Oboe. In coordinated westward attack, 32d Inf of 7th Div seizes Oak, Ella, and June Hills, SW of Yonawa; patrols of 184th Inf push into Chinen Peninsula without incident.

31 May

SEAC—Since British and U.S. interests in Asia are now widely divergent, U.S. Air Forces units, including Tenth Air Force and U.S. components of EAC, are withdrawn from SEAC and returned to operational control of AAF. EAC is inactivated. India-Burma Theater is to support China as a diversion for operations in the Pacific while SEAC prepares to recapture Malaya and Singapore.

LUZON—In U.S. Sixth Army's I Corps area, 129th Inf of 37th Div opens northward drive into Cagayan Valley from Santa Fe along Highway 5. Forward elements reach positions 6,000 yards N of Santa Fe. TF Connolly (Maj Robert V. Connolly, 123d Inf) is organized and attached to the guerrilla U.S. Army Forces in the Philippines (Northern Luzon) for drive on Aparri. The TF, about 800 men, will drive NE along Route 3; upon arrival in Aparri area will be reinf by bn of guerrillas.

NEGROS OCCIDENTAL—In U.S. Eighth Army area, organized resistance ends as enemy withdraws from last strongpoint, Hill 4055, into mountains.

MINDANAO—In X Corps area, 2d Bn of 19th Inf, 24th Div, joins 3d Bn in drive toward Mandog.

OKINAWA—In U.S. Tenth Army's III Amphib Corps area, 6th Mar Div, continuing E along heights N of the Kokuba, runs into strong rear-guard opposition in vicinity of Hill 46. Enemy positions are softened by direct tank fire and arty bombardment. 1st Marines, 1st Mar Div, is withdrawn as reserve and will mop up in Shuri sector. In XXIV Corps area, 77th Div, after taking 100 Meter Hill, pushes into ruins of Shuri, from which Japanese have withdrawn in an orderly fashion, and is pinched out by friendly forces on flanks. 96th Div finishes clearing its zone and establishes contact with 1st Mar Div. Continuing to press W, 7th Div overcomes resistance on hills near Chan, completing its current mission.

1 June

SEAC—Adm Mountbatten informs Chiefs of Staff that he has decided to postpone D Day for ZIPPER from late August to 9 September.

LUZON—In U.S. Sixth Army's I Corps area, 129th Inf of 37th Div continues rapidly northward against scattered resistance.

MINDANAO—In U.S. Eighth Army's X Corps area, 19th Inf of 24th Div continues westward during next few days, getting into position for assault on Mandog.

OKINAWA—Since enemy has made good his escape from Shuri, U.S. Tenth Army begins southward pursuit, abandoning envelopment maneuvers aimed at splitting Japanese forces on Okinawa. In III Amphib Corps area, after clearing Hill 46, 6th Mar Div seizes Shichina and northern branch of the Kokuba. To E, 5th Marines, 1st Mar Div, are patrolling across the Kokuba. At night, 6th Mar Div Rcn Co crosses Kokuba estuary to reconnoiter in preparation for amphibious operations against Oroku Peninsula. XXIV Corps, upon regrouping, pursues enemy southward. 96th Div, on right flank, relieves 32d Inf of 7th Div and begins to clear opposition near Chan. 77th Div covers rear of 96th Div and mops up in Shuri area. 7th Div, shifting E, pushes southward on E flank of corps with 17th Inf on right and 184th on left, clearing 2 hills of rearguard opposition.

2 June

LUZON—In U.S. Sixth Army's XI Corps area, 43d Div completes mop up of Ipo area.

OKINAWA—In U.S. Tenth Army's III Amphib Corps area, 7th Marines of 1st Mar Div takes up positions along the Kokuba, releasing 6th Mar Div, which is to conduct amphibious operation against Oroku Peninsula. In XXIV Corps area, 96th Div, after cleaning out Chan area, speeds southward in pursuit of enemy for next few days, as does 7th Div to E.

3 June

LUZON—In U.S. Sixth Army's I Corps area, forward elements of 129th Inf, 37th Div, reach positions 9,500 yards N of Santa Fe.

OKINAWA—In U.S. Tenth Army's III Amphib Corps area, 1st Mar Div thrusts S across the Kokuba, 7th Marines moving forward to seal off Oroku Peninsula and 5th Marines driving southward to vicinity of Gisushi. In XXIV Corps area, 96th and 7th Divs continue quickly southward. 305th Inf, 77th Div, plugs gap developing between the corps. Patrol of 184th Inf, 7th Div, reaches SE coast of Okinawa near Hyakuna, cutting off Chinen Peninsula; 32d Inf starts reconnoitering the peninsula.

4 June

LUZON—In U.S. Sixth Army's I Corps area, 129th Inf of 37th Div patrols to Aritao.

OKINAWA—In U.S. Tenth Army area, intercorps boundary is shifted W to place Yaeju-Dake Escarpment within XXIV Corps zone. In III Amphib Corps area, after preparatory bombardment, 6th Mar Div lands 4th Marines, followed by 29th Marines, on N Oroku Peninsula. Pushing inland, marines clear about half of Naha airfield. 6th Rcn Co seizes Ono-Yama I. in Naha Inlet with ease, killing the few Japanese there. 7th Marines, 1st Mar Div, advances farther SW along base of Oroku Peninsula. 1st Marines drives S through 5th Marines. XXIV Corps, advancing rapidly against scattered resistance and swerving SW because of boundary change, reaches line Iwa-Minatoga. In coastal sector, 7th Div wades across Minatoga R.

5 June

LUZON—In U.S. Sixth Army's I Corps area, 1st Bn of 129th Inf, 37th Div, seizes Aritao during morning and presses on; 145th Inf is in Aritao area.

OKINAWA—In U.S. Tenth Army area, rains end but armor is still mired down and supply lines are dangerously overextended. In III Amphib Corps area, Japanese on Oroku Peninsula put up determined opposition that limits gains, but 6th Mar Div seizes most of Naha airfield. 7th Marines, 1st Mar Div, continues SW to seal off the peninsula while 1st Marines speeds S to Iwa area. XXIV

Corps drives to within 1,000-1,500 yards of enemy's final defense line on S Okinawa, extending from Yuza on W to E coast at Gushichan and containing 3 formidable terrain features: Yuza-Dake Escarpment, Yaeju-Dake Escarpment, and Hill 95.

6 June

LUZON—In U.S. Sixth Army area, I Corps pursues completely disorganized enemy through Bambang to Magat R; destroys delaying force at bridge and fords the river. In XIV Corps area, 5th Cav reverts to 1st Cav Div.

MINDANAO—In U.S. Eighth Army's X Corps area, 19th Inf of 24th Div gains positions from which to make final assault on Mandog.

OKINAWA—In U.S. Tenth Army's III Amphib Corps area, 6th Mar Div clears rest of Naha airfield on Oroku Peninsula and advances its right flank along coast but is brought to a halt in center of the peninsula by tenacious enemy on Hill 57. To protect right flank of 1st Mar Div as it moves S, 22d Marines is released from corps reserve to establish line across base of Oroku Peninsula. 7th Marines pushes forward to vicinity of Dakiton. In XXIV Corps area, rapid pursuit ends as corps approaches enemy's new defense line. After moving through Yunagusuku, 1st Bn of 381st Inf, 96th Div, attempts to drive up Yaeju-Dake Escarpment but meets intense fire when coming within range of enemy guns and falls back. 7th Div advances its right flank very slowly but its left is held up at ridge extending NE from Hill 95.

7 June

CHINA—Gen McClure directs Chinese armies of Kwangsi Command (not a part of ALPHA Force) to prepare to open Operation CARBONADO—to clear Hong Kong-Canton area—with assault on Fort Bayard. 3 ALPHA armies (8th, 54th, and New First) are to join in the CARBONADO offensive. In Hunan Province, Chinese stop pursuing the Japanese forces, whose offensive they halted short of Chihchiang in May. The pursuit ends at Paoching, the point from which the Japanese had begun their offensive.

LUZON—In U.S. Sixth Army's I Corps area, 3d Bn of 129th Inf, 37th Div, pursues enemy toward Solano.

MINDANAO—In U.S. Eighth Army's X Corps area, 19th Inf of 24th Div begins assault on Mandog.

OKINAWA—In U.S. Tenth Army's III Amphib Corps area, Japanese on Oroku Peninsula, determined to resist until death, are delaying 6th Mar Div, but marines clear Hill 57 strongpoint with aid of tanks. 1st Mar Div continues southward. 7th Marines reaches coast N of Itoman, sealing off Oroku Peninsula. XXIV Corps, while awaiting supplies for strong attack, conducts limited probing actions. Aircraft and arty pound Japanese defense line to neutralize it.

8 June

LUZON—In U.S. Sixth Army's I Corps area, 145th Inf of 37th Div, attacking through 129th Inf, drives through Solano to junction of Highways 4 and 5; while main body pushes on to within 1,000 yards of Bagabag, patrols probe to Magat R east of Bagabag to secure crossing of Highway 5 over it.

OKINAWA—In U.S. Tenth Army's III Amphib Corps area, 6th Mar Div is slowly pocketing enemy in Tomigusuki sector of Oroku Peninsula against vicious opposition. 1st Mar Div drives southward toward enemy's final defense line. XXIV Corps continues preparations for all-out assault on Yaeju-Dake Escarpment. Port of Minatoga is opened for use, easing supply situation. 7th Div works slowly forward on E flank of corps in limited action, but enemy retains firm hold on Hill 95; 32d Inf, which has been patrolling on Chinen Peninsula, relieves 184th Inf on div's left flank.

U.S.—Gen Marshall queries Gen Wedemeyer as to why the air forces in China have not been put under command of Gen Stratemeyer, who has been raised in rank for that purpose.

9 June

LUZON—In U.S. Sixth Army area, I Corps cuts Japanese escape routes from Cagayan Valley. 1st Bn of 145th Inf, 37th Div, seizes Bagabag and blocks road NW of the barrio while 3d Bn secures crossing of Magat R east of Bagabag on Highway 5.

MINDANAO—In U.S. Eighth Army's X Corps area, 19th Inf of 24th Div penetrates enemy's last defensive position on Mindanao with capture of Mandog. Marine aircraft are unusually active over island during day.

OKINAWA—In U.S. Tenth Army's III Amphib Corps area, enemy's last chance to escape from Oroku Peninsula is lost as 4th and 22d Marines of 6th Mar Div establish contact. 1st Mar Div is approaching Kunishi Ridge, where Japanese are firmly established for final stand on Okinawa. XXIV Corps continues preparations for concerted assault on Japanese defense line. 7th Div attacks on E flank of corps with elements of 2 regts. 3d Bn, 17th Inf, advances to SE end of Yaeju-Dake Escarpment; 1st Bn, 32d Inf, tries unsuccessfully to take Hill 95 and ridge in front of it, but eliminates some enemy positions.

10 June

BURMA—In Br Twelfth Army area, Loilem falls to Detachment 101—guerrillas led by OSS personnel. Detachment 101 has been clearing Shan Hills since end of NCAC campaign.

CHINA—Chinese forces pursuing enemy toward Liuchow take I-shan.

PACIFIC—AFPAC and USAFFE are consolidated.

LUZON—In U.S. Sixth Army's I Corps area, 37th Div is relieved of all security duties S of Aritao; 1st Bn, 148th Inf, is to take over Bagabag area so 145th Inf can continue along Highway 5; 145th Inf runs into accurate fire from heights commanding Orioung Pass and almost comes to a halt; 1st Bn, 148th Inf, drives N along Highway 4 to S edge of Lantap.

NEI—Aus 9th Div lands on mainland of Borneo at Brunei Bay and on islands of Labuan and Muara. Allied aircraft and Seventh Fleet support the operation.

OKINAWA—In U.S. Tenth Army's III Amphib Corps area, bitter fighting continues on Oroku Peninsula, where 6th Mar Div compresses Japanese into area 1,000 yards by 2,000 yards. In local counter attacks after nightfall, 200 Japanese lose their lives. 7th Marines, 1st Mar Div, takes ridge just N of Tera and drives through Itoman; 1st Marines seizes hill W of town of Yuza but pays heavy price in casualties. XXIV Corps begins all-out assault on Japanese defense line, with tank support that is now adequate. While 383d Inf, 96th Div, is pressing toward town of Yuza, 381st gets 2 cos to intermediate ledge in saddle between Yaeju-Dake and Yuza-Dake peaks. 17th Inf, 7th Div, employs softening fire extensively against its portion of Yaeju-Dake; 32d Inf, assisted by naval gunfire as well as arty and flame-throwing tanks, secures key ridge in front of Hill 95 at coast line.

11 June

CHINA—Japanese regain I-shan from Chinese.

LUZON—In U.S. Sixth Army's I Corps area, 145th Inf of 37th Div battles enemy at Orioung Pass, gaining some ground; 1st Bn, 148th Inf, neutralizes strongpoint in Lantap, patrols into Santa Lucia, and drives N to Lamut R.

OKINAWA—In U.S. Tenth Army's III Amphib Corps area, 6th Mar Div, in strong effort to eliminate enemy on Oroku Peninsula, compresses Japanese into area 1,000 yards square. 7th Marines, 1st Mar Div, tries vainly to cross open ground leading to Kunishi Ridge; 1st Marines takes Hill 69, W of Ozato. In XXIV Corps area, 383d Inf of 96th Div reaches town of Yuza but withdraws under heavy fire from the S; 381st gets entire 1st Bn to ledge of saddle between Yaeju-Dake and Yuza-Dake peaks, holds there against early morning counterattack, and places neutralizing fire on caves on Yaeju-Dake peak. 17th Inf, 7th Div, continues to neutralize positions and prepares for night assault on Yaeju-Dake; enemy's entire line on Yaeju-Dake Escarpment is endangered as elements of 32d Inf take Hill 95 on E flank.

12 June

LUZON—In U.S. Sixth Army's I Corps area, 6th Div takes responsibility for Highway 5 S of Bayombong, relieving 37th Div, which is to concentrate on clearing Cagayan Valley. 1st Bn of 129th Inf, 37th Div, relieves 1st Bn, 148th, of responsibility for security of Highway 4 N of Bagabag so latter can follow 145th Inf along Highway 5. Continuing attack on Orioung Pass, 145th Inf pushes through it; clears town of Orioung and drives N to commanding ground N of Balite.

OKINAWA—In U.S. Tenth Army's III Amphib Corps area, Japanese resistance on Oroku Peninsula begins to crack as converging columns of 6th Mar Div maintain pressure and further reduce the small pocket. Some of the enemy defense force continue to resist but others are committing suicide or surrendering. In 1st Mar Div zone, 7th Marines, advancing at 0300 under cover of darkness, gains positions on W end of Kunishi Ridge. 1st Marines mops up and consolidates on Hill 69 and patrols toward Kunishi Ridge. In XXIV Corps area, 383d Inf of 96th Div drives through Yuza again but is held up short of Yuza peak; 381st, with 3 bns in assault on div left, drives to base of Yaeju-Dake Escarpment and by envelopment maneuver reaches positions on steepest part. Predawn assault by 17th Inf, 7th Div, takes enemy by surprise and gains the regt its assigned portion of the escarpment. Japanese still hold Yaeju-Dake peak but SE end of their defense line has been penetrated.

13 June

CHINA—Gen Wedemeyer writes Gen Marshall that since Japanese withdrawals have virtually eliminated Phase I of projected offensive against Canton-Hong Kong area, plans are being made to use Nanning-Liuchow Kweilin area as base for the operation. Japanese still hold Liuchow and Kweilin but are expected to abandon them soon.

LUZON—In U.S. Sixth Army's I Corps area, Gen Beightler, in order to exploit capture of Orioung Pass, organizes an armored column (37th Rcn Tr reinf by a platoon of light tanks and supported by a co of motorized infantry) and attaches it to 145th Inf, 37th Div. The armored column pushes into plain of Cagayan Valley, driving through Cordon to Santiago. Elements of 148th Inf start forward to Orioung area. Japanese counterattack and block the road in Orioung Pass for night. 20th Inf, 6th Div, relieves 129th Inf of highway security S of Bayombong.

NEI—On Borneo, Australian forces capture Brunei town.

OKINAWA—In U.S. Tenth Army's III Amphib Corps area, organized resistance on Oroku Peninsula ends. 6th Mar Div, during 12th and 13th, bags a record number of Japanese prisoners, 159 in all. By dawn, 7th Marines, 1st Mar Div, has 6 cos clinging to positions on Kunishi Ridge under heavy fire that exacts 140 casualties. Marines are being supplied by aircraft and tanks. XXIV Corps, assisted by armored flame throwers, is destroying in detail Japanese in their cave positions. Battleground is now generally level except for some coral outcroppings. Japanese are still firmly entrenched on commanding ground of Yuza-Dake and Yaeju-Dake peaks and on Hills 153 and 115, from W to E.

14 June

BURMA—Adm Mountbatten attends Burma Victory Parade in Rangoon and while in Rangoon continues to plan for ZIPPER (recapture of Malaya). The operations will be mounted on 9 September, as planned, but on a drastically reduced scale.

CHINA—Chinese recover I-shan and pursue enemy toward Liuchow.

LUZON—In U.S. Sixth Army's I Corps area, Highway 5 at Orioung Pass is cleared of enemy block. Armored column followed by 1st Bn of 145th Inf, 37th Div, drives through Ipil to Echague; from Santiago, 3d Bn, 145th Inf, starts along road running SW to Oscariz thence NE to Cabatuan and E to Cauayan where it joins Highway 5; 148th Inf, less security details at San Luis and Cordon, moves to Santiago area. XIV Corps turns responsibility for the Bicols over to Filipino guerrillas.

OKINAWA—In U.S. Tenth Army's III Amphib Corps area, 6th Mar Div is mopping up on Oroku Peninsula. 7th Marines, 1st Mar Div, holds firmly on W end of Kunishi Ridge under enemy fire. To ease pressure, 2d Bn, 1st Marines, attacks toward E end of the ridge at 0300; gains and holds this objective despite violent opposition. Tanks play an important role in the Kunishi Ridge battle, moving troops and supplies forward, evacuating the wounded, and blasting enemy from their positions. XXIV Corps continues to destroy enemy's elaborate cave defenses. 383d Inf, 96th Div, is still held up short of Yuza peak, but 381st drives to top of Yaeju-Dake peak. 7th Div is clearing Hills 153 and 115 on E flank of corps.

U.S.—Joint Chiefs of Staff direct Generals MacArthur and Arnold and Adm Nimitz to prepare plans for immediate occupation of Japan in the event that foe suddenly collapses or capitulates.

15 June

BURMA—In Br Twelfth Army area, 101st Detachment, OSS, successfully concludes its mission of clearing Shan Hills. Detachment is disbanded in July.

LUZON—In U.S. Sixth Army's I Corps area, Cervantes, on Highway 4, falls to Philippine guerrilla forces in North Luzon. 145th Inf, 37th Div, continues advance into Cagayan Valley; 1st Bn pushes N on Highway 5 to Ganano R; 3d Bn eliminates enemy strongpoint some 4,000 yards from Santiago, on road to Cabatuan. XI Corps takes over sector of XIV Corps and control of 11th A/B Div, 1st Cav Div, and RCT 158. XIV Corps prepares to conduct operations in N Luzon as directed by Eighth Army.

OKINAWA—In U.S. Tenth Army's III Amphib Corps area, 6th Mar Div, exploring elaborate underground defense system of Japanese hq on Oroku Peninsula, finds nearly 200 Japanese dead. Among them are commanding officer and several members of his staff who have committed suicide. Marines of 1st Mar Div on W and E ends of Kunishi Ridge are unable to expand their positions and suffer further casualties. 2d Bn, 5th Marines, relieves 2d Bn, 1st Marines, on E end of the ridge after nightfall. 8th Marines, 2d Mar Div, lands on Oroku Peninsula and is attached to 1st Mar Div. XXIV Corps continues to work toward Yuza peak on W and Hills 153 and 115 on E, clearing Japanese positions methodically as it goes. Elements of 382d Inf, 96th Div, replace center elements of 383d and succeed in taking N slope of Yuza peak.

NEI—Islands of Labuan and Muara, off Borneo, are now clear of enemy.

16 June

LUZON—In U.S. Sixth Army's I Corps area, 37th Div columns converge on Cauayan: 2d Bn of 148th Inf, passing through 1st Bn of 145th on Highway 5, drives on to Cauayan; 2d Bn, 145th Inf, advancing through 3d Bn, 145th Inf, moves to Cauayan via Cabatuan; from Cauayan, 2d Bn of 148th Inf continues N toward Naguilian.

OKINAWA—In U.S. Tenth Army's III Amphib Corps area, 6th Mar Div prepares to attack on S Okinawa. 7th Marines, 1st Mar Div, advances slightly on Kunishi Ridge and gains visual contact with 5th Marines to E. In XXIV Corps area, 382d Inf of 96th Div completes relief of 383d in line and continues assault on Yuza-Dake hill mass. Yuza-

Dake peak falls at last to 381st Inf. 7th Div's 17th and 32d Regts are clearing last commanding ground—Hills 153 and 115.

17 June

LUZON—In U.S. Sixth Army's I Corps area, 2d Bn of 148th Inf, 37th Div, preceded by armored column, seizes Naguilian after forcing Cagayan R near there.

OKINAWA—In U.S. Tenth Army area, III Amphib Corps gains ground on Kunishi Ridge, where enemy resistance weakens perceptibly after fresh U.S. troops are committed. 22d Marines, 6th Mar Div, replaces 2d Bn of 7th Marines, 1st Mar Div. In XXIV Corps area, final defense line of Japanese 32d Army collapses. 7th Div completes capture of Hills 153 and 115.

U.S.—Gen Arnold, in letter to Gen Wedemeyer, asks that Gen Stratemeyer replace Gen Chennault as head of air forces in China.

18 June

LUZON—In U.S. Sixth Army's I Corps area, elements of 148th Inf, 37th Div, continuing N on Highway 5 with armored column spearheading, take Ilagan airfield and cross Ilagan R. Upon completion of treadway bridge across the Cagayan at Naguilian, armor and vehicles cross.

MINDANAO—In Eighth Army's X Corps area, organized resistance on Mindanao ends as 3d Bn of 163d Inf, 24th Div, reaches Calinan, 8 miles from Tugbok.

OKINAWA—In U.S. Tenth Army area, Lt Gen Simon B. Buckner, Jr., is killed by enemy shell while visiting observation post of 8th Marines, 2d Mar Div. Gen Geiger, USMC, replaces him as commander of Tenth Army. In III Amphib Corps area, 6th Mar Div drives steadily forward on W flank of corps against sporadic resistance, but 1st Mar Div is desperately opposed near Medeera on E flank. Attack by 5th Marines against Hill 81, W of Medeera, fails. 8th Marines, 2d Mar Div, enters action, replacing elements of 7th Marines. In XXIV Corps area, 96th Div meets intense opposition near Aragachi and Medeera on right flank of corps. 7th Div, with 184th Inf on right and 32d on left, advances southward on E flank of corps against weakening resistance.

JAPAN—U.S. bombers begin attacks on secondary cities.

19 June

CHINA THEATER—Issues detailed plans for operation against Fort Bayard, which is to be taken on 1 August for use as forward supply base for main effort against Canton-Hong Kong area. India-Burma and China Theaters are both to support the operation.

LUZON—In U.S. Sixth Army's I Corps area, 3d Bn of 148th Inf, 37th Div, completes its crossing of the Cagayan, using newly constructed ponton treadway. It is passed through by 1st Bn, which drives to Moranoa and destroys small delaying force. The armored column moves E along the river and captures 5 enemy tanks.

OKINAWA—U.S. Tenth Army is reaping substantial results from psychological warfare program that has been going on for some time. 343 Japanese surrender. In III Amphib Corps area, 6th Mar Div continues southward on W flank of corps against scattered resistance. In 1st Mar Div sector, some elements of 8th and 5th Regts reach S coast; other elements of 5th Marines are still held up at Hill 81. In XXIV Corps area, 96th Div continues to battle enemy in Aragachi-Medeera area without making appreciable headway. To E, 7th Div presses on toward Udo and Mabuni.

20 June

CHINA—Gen Wedemeyer transmits to Gen Marshall his approval of Gen Arnold's recommendations of the 17th. Gen Stratemeyer is to command China Theater Air Forces. Under him, Generals Chennault and Davidson will head respectively the SAF and TAF.

LUZON—In U.S. Sixth Army's I Corps area, Philippine guerrilla units seize Tuguegarao, about midway between Aparri and Ilagan. Co B of 6th Ranger Bn, part of TF Connolly, crosses Cagayan R and enters Aparri without opposition, night 20-21. Spearheaded by armor, 1st Bn of 148th Inf, 37th Div, eliminates enemy position on Highway 5 about 4,000 yards N of Ilagan.

S PHILIPPINES—In U.S. Eighth Army area, Operations VICTOR I (Panay-Negros Occidental), VICTOR II (Cebu-Bohol-Negros Oriental), VICTOR III (Palawan), and VICTOR IV (Zamboanga) are officially closed.

NEI—Aus forces expand positions on Borneo with unopposed landing at Lutong, in Sarawak.

OKINAWA—U.S. Tenth Army takes almost a thousand prisoners, establishing a record. Japanese pocket in Medeera area in center of army front is still resisting strongly. In III Amphib Corps area, 29th Marines, on 6th Mar Div right, reaches S coast against light opposition, but 4th Marines is progressing more slowly in Kiyamu area. Japanese on Hill 81 continue to delay 5th Marines, 1st Mar Div. In XXIV Corps area, 96th Div takes Aragachi but cannot clear Hill 85, within the Medeera pocket. 32d Inf, 7th Div, reaches Hill 89, near Mabuni, where Japanese hq is located underground.

21 June

LUZON—U.S. Sixth Army directs XI Corps CG to be prepared to mount one Para inf bn for drop on Aparri area to prevent enemy's escape from there. In I Corps area, 148th Inf of 37th Div continues Cagayan Valley drive against scattered resistance. Ranger patrols from Aparri establish contact with Filipino guerrilla forces. 63d Inf, 6th Div, presses forward toward Kiangan; 20th Inf reaches Pingkian. 25th Div elements operating on Old Spanish Trail close in on Susuga Pass from N and S.

OKINAWA—In U.S. Tenth Army's III Amphib Corps area, 6th Mar Div clears most of its zone. Hill 81 falls to 1st Mar Div. In XXIV Corps area, Japanese in the Medeera pocket continue to hold out on Hill 85, in 96th Div zone. 7th Div cleans out Hill 89 pocket near Mabuni.

22 June

CHINA—Japanese set fire to Liuchow in preparation for withdrawal. Chinese are in outskirts.

LUZON—In U.S. Sixth Army's XI Corps area, advance party of 8 persons flies N to mark landing area for airborne drop near Aparri. In I Corps area, attack elements of 148th Inf, 37th Div, take Tumauini, on Highway 5, and continue N to stream 9,000 yards SE of Cabagan; 129th Inf assembles at Tumauini to take over northward drive. Filipino guerrillas are forced from Tuguegarao under heavy fire. TF Connolly secures Dugo and Camalaniugan in Aparri area. 25th Div elements open Old Spanish Trail through Susuga Pass.

OKINAWA—U.S. Tenth Army completes capture of Okinawa and conducts flag-raising ceremony. Lt Gen Mitsuru Ushijima, commander of Japanese 32d Army, and his chief of staff commit suicide. U.S. battle casualties, during this last and most costly campaign against the Japanese, total 49,151, of which 12,520 are killed or missing and 36,631 wounded. About 110,000 Japanese are killed and 7,400 captured. Ship losses to enemy action, largely air, during the campaign total 36 sunk and 368 damaged. Japanese suffer heavy losses in aircraft, 7,800. American possession of Okinawa, with its air and naval bases, brings the war much closer to the Japanese homeland, the next objective in the Pacific.

NEI—Organized enemy resistance on Tarakan I., off Borneo, ceases.

23 June

BURMA—Gen Wheeler, USA, becomes commander of India-Burma Theater, replacing Gen Sultan.

LUZON—In U.S. Sixth Army's I Corps area, Fifth Air Force transports drop TF Gypsy under Lt Col Henry A. Burgess, consisting of reinforced 1st Bn of 511th Para Inf, 11th A/B Div, at airfield a few miles S of Aparri, at 0900. Parachutists and their glider-transported equipment land safely and without opposition. TF passes to control of corps. Parachutists establish contact with guerrillas and push S toward 37th Div. 37th Div, meanwhile, passing 129th Inf through 148th, speeds northward 11 miles on Highway 5.

OKINAWA—In U.S. Tenth Army area, Gen Stilwell, USA, relieves Gen Geiger, USMC, as commander of Tenth Army. Both corps begin systematic mopping up operations, working northward.

24 June

LUZON—In U.S. Sixth Army's I Corps area, TF Gypsy continues southward; 129th Inf of 37th Div pushes northward 5½ miles and patrols vigorously on flanks.

S PHILIPPINES—In U.S. Eighth Army area, 164th Inf of Americal Div returns to Cebu from Negros Oriental. Army zone, except for Mindanao, is now clear.

25 June

LUZON—In U.S. Sixth Army's I Corps area, TF Gypsy, supplied by air, finds Gattaran undefended and advances to positions about 2,000 yards S of Duman R. 129th Inf, 37th Div, with air and arty support, takes Tuguegarao and Penablanca without incident.

26 June

INTERNATIONAL CONFERENCES—United Nations Conference on International Organization ends in San Francisco. United Nations Charter is signed by the participating nations but is not ratified until 24 October.

CHINA—Chinese forces take Liuchow airfield.

LUZON—In U.S. Sixth Army's I Corps area, 129th Inf of 37th Div and TF Gypsy effect junction near Alcala on Highway 5. 37th Div takes command of TF Connolly, TF Gypsy, and Filipino guerrillas in the area.

MINDANAO—In U.S. Eighth Army's X Corps area, 167th Inf of 31st Div, which has been creeping forward along Talomo Trail, reaches Pinamola.

RYUKYU IS.—To enlarge air warning net in Okinawa area, special task group (TG 31.24) lands on Kume I. without opposition. The task group consists of troops from FMF Rcn Bn with one reinf rifle co from 1st Mar Div and small naval force. The island is subsequently covered by patrols.

JAPAN—B-29's of XXI BC begin night attacks on Japanese oil refineries.

27 June

LUZON—In U.S. Sixth Army's I Corps area, 129th Inf of 37th Div reaches Aparri, ending Cagayan Valley drive. This virtually concludes the Luzon Campaign as well.

29 June

RYUKYU IS.—Kume I. is declared secure.

30 June

P.I.—Luzon Campaign ends officially at midnight 30 June-1 July. U.S. Sixth Army turns over to U.S. Eighth Army the task of concluding operations on Luzon and regroups extensively for its next assignment, invasion of Japan (Operation OLYMPIC). Eighth Army takes command of XIV Corps, which will conduct the final mop up on Luzon. Two large pockets of enemy remain on N Luzon: about 11,000 Japanese are estimated to be concealed in Sierra Madre Mountains; and an estimated 12,000 are established in Kiangan-Bontoc area. Operations to eliminate these pockets continue until end of the war. Under XIV Corps command are 6th, 32d, 37th, and 38th Inf Divs plus Filipino guerrilla forces on the island. 24th Div is chosen for the final amphibious operation in the Philippines—a landing on Mindanao at Sarangani Bay. On Mindanao, X Corps continues to mop up until end of war.

RYUKYU IS.—U.S. Tenth Army completes mop up of Okinawa.

1 July

CHINA—Ch forces take Liuchow town.

NEI—Balikpapan, Borneo, target for strong aerial attacks for the past month and for naval gunfire since 24 June, is invaded by Australian forces after a final, intense 2-hour bombardment. U.S. Seventh Fleet puts the assault force, 7th Aus Div, ashore and supports the operation. Japanese resistance is light at first but increases as Australians drive inland.

2 July

S PHILIPPINES—In U.S. Eighth Army area, RCT 368 of 93d Div takes responsibility for Zamboanga sector on Mindanao and for islands of Palawan, Jolo, and Sanga Sanga, relieving troops of 41st Div, Sixth Army.

RYUKYU IS.—Campaign is officially ended.

NEI—Aus 7th Div takes Balikpapan, Borneo, and its oil installations; subsequently extends holdings in this area.

4 July

CHINA—Party of U.S. officers flies from India to Chungking to organize Hq, AAF, China Theater.

MINDANAO—In U.S. Eighth Army's X Corps area, 24th Div's Sarangani TF organizes to clear Sarangani Bay area by overland and amphibious operations. Patrol of 24th Rcn Troop (part of TF) sails from Talomo to Glan on southeast shore of bay, delivers arms to guerrilla 116th Inf, 106th Div, and in cooperation with guerrillas begins to clear east shores of bay.

5 July

NEI—Aus troops, covered by Allied warships, cross Balikpapan Bay, Borneo, and land on W shore at Penadjim Pt without opposition. Other Australian forces are extending control over key parts of Borneo.

6 July

CHINA—Gen Chennault requests and is soon granted permission to retire.

8 July

MINDANAO—In U.S. Eighth Army's X Corps area, 24th Div's Sarangani TF continues limited operations. Prov infantry bn of U.S. Army AAA troops and Combat Company of guerrilla 118th Inf, 106th Div, start southeast overland from Lake Buluan toward Sarangani Bay. Expeditionary Bn of guerrilla 108th Div starts overland southwest toward bay from Davao Gulf. Patrol of 24th Rcn Troop and elements of guerrilla 116th Inf reach Dadjangas on northwest shore of bay to reconnoiter for main landing.

9 July

NEI—Aus and Dutch forces complete encirclement of Balikpapan Bay, Borneo.

10 July

JAPAN—Carrier-based and land-based planes open powerful and sustained attacks on Japan in preparation for invasion. Airfields and industrial targets in Tokyo area are hit. Japanese air reaction is light.

INDIA—Naval personnel arrive in India for air movement to China, where they are to assist in Fort Bayard operation.

12 July

P.I.—In U.S. Eighth Army's XIV Corps area on Luzon, Kiangan falls to 6th Div, but Japanese continue to hold out in the area. Thousands of gallons of napalm have been dropped on enemy pocket in Kiangan area during last few days. 32d Div is advancing along Highway 11 against the other enemy pocket on N Luzon, in Sierra Madre Mountains. On Mindanao, in X Corps area, 1st Bn of 21st Inf, 24th Div (part of Sarangani TF), lands on north shore of Sarangani Bay against no opposition. Prov bn from Lake Buluan reaches point 20 miles northwest of bay; Expeditionary Bn of guerrilla 108th Div reaches point 15 miles northeast of bay; guerrilla 116th Inf clears additional areas along bay's shore.

13 July

MINDANAO—In X Corps area, contact is made between 1st Bn, 21st Inf, and Prov bn from Lake Buluan at point 15 miles northwest of Sarangam Bay.

15 July

MINDANAO—In X Corps area, guerrilla 116th Inf and Expeditionary Bn, 108th Div, make contact 10 miles northeast of Sarangani Bay, marking contact between all elements of 24th Div's Sarangani TF.

16 July

INTERNATIONAL CONFERENCES—Terminal Conference opens at Potsdam, Germany, to draw up terms for Japanese surrender and discuss military and political issues connected with the termination of hostilities. Representatives of the Soviet Union, Britain, and the United States attend.

U.S.—An atomic bomb is tested successfully at Los Alamos, New Mexico.

17 July

JAPAN—Units of Br Pacific Fleet join with U.S. Third Fleet warships in bombarding Japan. Japanese offer no opposition. This is the first of a series of combined American-British assaults on Japan.

18 July

GUAM—U.S. Army Strategic Air Forces is established at Guam under Gen Spaatz.

NEI—Advance elements of Aus 7th Div find Sambodja oil center on Borneo undefended.

20 July

MINDANAO—In U.S. Eighth Army's X Corps area, Co F of 34th Inf, 24th Div, lands on Balut I. at entrance to Sarangani Bay and searches the island, finding few Japanese.

23 July

CHINA—Hq, U.S. Tenth Air Force, opens at Kunming.

25 July

MINDANAO—In X Corps area, last organized Japanese resistance in Sarangani Bay sector collapses. Patrols mop up a few more Japanese until 11 August.

26 July

INTERNATIONAL AGREEMENTS—Potsdam ultimatum is issued, calling for Japan to surrender unconditionally or face "utter destruction."

27 July

CHINA—Chinese break into Kweilin and by end of month clear rear-guard opposition. Other Chinese forces take Tanchuk airfield.

30 July

JAPAN—Rejects the Potsdam ultimatum. Nevertheless, Gen Marshall, in behalf of the Joint Chiefs of Staff, directs Gens MacArthur and Wedemeyer and Adm Nimitz to co-ordinate plans for the surrender.

2 August

INTERNATIONAL CONFERENCES—TERMINAL Conference ends at Potsdam.

5 August

CHINA—Ch 13th Army takes town of Tanchuk. Ch 58th Div recaptures Hsinning.

6 August

JAPAN—B-29 drops an atomic bomb on Hiroshima.

GUAM—Final details for operation against Fort Bayard are worked out on Guam between representatives of the China and the Pacific Theaters.

7 August
LUZON—Advance detachment of Hq, U.S. First Army, arrives to prepare for operations against Japan.

8 August
USSR—Declares war on Japan, effective on 9 August.

9 August
JAPAN— Atomic Bomb is dropped on Nagasaki.
MANCHURIA—Soviet Forces pour into Manchuria.

10 August
JAPAN—Japanese Government offers to surrender "without prejudice to the Emperor's position."

11 August
U.S.—Replies to Japanese surrender offer.

12 August
U.S.—War Department suspends projected operations against Fort Bayard since end of hostilities is imminent.
KOREA—Soviet troops move into Korea.

13 August
U.S.—Surrender documents, approved by President Truman, are sent to Gen MacArthur.

14 August
JAPAN—Accepts Allied unconditional surrender terms. 11th A/B Div moves by air from the Philipines to Okinawa en route to Japan.

15 August
PACIFIC—Gen MacArthur receives notice that he is Supreme Commander for the Allied Powers. All offensive action against Japan comes to an end.

19 August
LUZON—Japanese delegation arrives in Manila for conference on formal surrender arrangements.

20 August
LUZON—The Japanese delegation leaves Manila for Tokyo with instructions about the occupation of Japan and signing of final peace terms.

28 August
JAPAN—Occupation of Japan, delayed 48 hours by typhoon, begins as advance party arrives there.

30 August
JAPAN—Occupation of Japan in force is begun by U.S. forces. 11th A/B Div is flown to Atsugi Airfield, and 4th Marines, 6th Mar Div, lands at Yokosuka Naval Base.
HONG KONG—Br naval force reoccupies that British colony.

2 September
INTERNATIONAL AGREEMENTS—Hostilities with Japan officially end with signing of instrument of surrender aboard the USS *Missouri* in Tokyo Bay. U.S. Army battle casualties during World War II total 936,259, or about 9 percent of the 10,420,000 military personnel who served in the U.S. Army and Army Air Forces.

(On 31 December 1946, hostilities are declared terminated by Presidential proclamation.)

Glossary of Abbreviations

AA	antiaircraft
AAA	antiaircraft artillery
AAF	Army Air Forces
AAFEC	Army Air Forces Engineer Command
AAFSC	Army Air Forces Service Command
AAI	Allied Armies in Italy
AASC	Allied Air Support Command (Mediterranean)
ABDA	Australian-British-Dutch-American
ABTF	airborne task force
ACMF	Allied Central Mediterranean Force
ADC	assistant division commander
AEAF	Allied Expeditionary Air Force (Europe)
AFGH	Allied Force Headquarters (Mediterranean)
AFPAC	U.S. Army Forces in the Pacific
ALFSEA	Allied Land Forces South East Asia
AMET	Africa-Middle East Theater
AMLG	Allied Military Headquarters, Greece
AMMISCA	American Military Mission to China
amph	amphibian
amphib	amphibious
amtrac	amphibian tractor
AP	transport
APD	transport, high-speed
armd	armored
ASC	Air Support Command
AT	antitank
ATC	Air Transport Command
Aus	Australian
AUS	Army of the United States
AVG	American Volunteer Group (China)
BB	battleship
BC	bomber command
BCT	battalion combat team
BEF	Brazilian Expeditionary Force
BLT	boat landing team
bn	battalion
Br	British
brig	brigade
BTE	British Troops in Egypt
CA	heavy cruiser
CACW	Chinese-American Composite Wing
CAI	Chinese Army in India
CAM	Composite Army-Marine
CATF	Chinese Air Task Force
Cav	Cavalry
CBI	China-Burma-India
CC	combat command
CCA	Combat Command A
CCB	Combat Command B
CCC	Combat Command C

[554] [GLOSSARY OF ABBREVIATIONS]

CCD	Combat Command D
CCL	Combat Command L
CCR	Combat Command R
CCV	Combat Command V
CC1	Combat Command 1
CC2	Combat Command 2
cdo(s)	commando(s)
CG	commanding general
Ch	Chinese
CinC	Cornmander in Chief
CINCPAC	Commander in Chief, U.S. Pacific Fleet
CINCPOA	Commander in Chief, Pacific Ocean Areas
CL	light cruiser
CMF	Citizen Military Forces (New Guinea)
co	company
CO	commanding officer
COMAIRSOLS	Commander Air Forces, Solomons
COMCENPAC	Commander Central Pacific
COMINCH	Commander in Chief
COMSOPAC	Commander South Pacific
COSC	Combined Operational Service Command
COSSAC	Chief of Staff to the Supreme Allied Commander (designate)
CP	command post
CT	China Theater, combat team
CTF	commander, task force
CV	aircraft carrier
CVE	aircraft carrier, escort
DA ALPS	Detachment d'Armée des Alpes
DA ATL	Detachment d'Armée de l'Atlantique
DD	destroyer
div	division
E	east, eastern
EAC	Eastern Air Command (CBI)
EAM	Ethniko Apeleftherotiko Metopo (National Liberation Front, Greece)
cngr(s)	engineer(s)
ETOUSA	European Theater of Operations, USA
FA	field artillery
FEAF	Far East Air Force
FEC	French Expeditionary Force
FF	Free French
FFI	Forces Françaises de l'Intérieur
FFO	Forces Françaises de l'Ouest
FMF	Fleet Marine Force
FO	field order
Fr	French
G-2	Intelligence section of divisional or higher headquarters
G-4	Supply and evacuation section of divisional or higher headquarters
Gds	Guards
GHQ	General Headquarters
gli	glider
GMT	Greenwich mean time
GO	general orders
gp	group
HALPRO	Air operation against Rumanian oil fields, 1942
hq	headquarters
I.	Island
IBT	India-Burma Theater

[GLOSSARY OF ABBREVIATIONS]

Ind	Indian
Inf	Infantry
Is	Islands
ISCOM	Island Commander
JCS	Joint Chiefs of Staff
JWC	Joint War Plans Committee
LANDFOR	landing force
LCI	landing craft, infantry
LCI(G)	landing craft, infantry, gun'
LCM	landing craft, mechanized
LCVP	landing craft, vehicle and pi i–.A.
LOC	line of communications
LRP	long-range penetration
LST	landing ship, tank
M.	Mont, Monte, etc. (Italy and'Sicily only)
MAAF	Mediterranean Allied Air Forces
MAC	Marine Amphibious Corps
MAG	Marine Aviation Group
Mar	Marine 6
MATAF	Mediterranean Allied Tactical Air Force
ME	Middle East
MEF	Middle East Forces
MG	machine gun
MLR	main line of resistance
MP	military police
MSR	main supply route
MTB	motor torpedo boat
mtn	mountain
MTOUSA	Mediterranean Theater of Operations, USA
N	north, northern
NAAF	Northwest African Air Force
NATO	North African Theater of Operations
NCAC	Northern Combat Area Command (Burma
NEI	Netherlands East Indies
NGVR	New Guinea Volunteer Reserve
NTLF	Northern Troops and Landing Force
NZ	New Zealand
OPL	outpost line
OPLR	outpost line of resistance
PA	Philippine Army
Pac	Pacific
Para	parachute
PBM	patrol search plane
PC	Philippine Constabulary
PG	patrol vessel, gunboat
PGC	Persian Gulf Command
PGSC	Persian Gulf Service Command
P.I.	Philippine Islands
PIB	Papuan Infantry Battalion
POA	Pacific Ocean Areas
Pol	Polish
prov	provisional
PS	Philippine Scouts
pt	point
PT	patrol vessel, motor torpedo boat
Pz	Panzer
QM	quartermaster

R	river
RAAF	Royal Australian Air Force
RAF	Royal Air Force
rcn	reconnaissance
RCT	regimental combat team
regt	regiment
reinf	reinforced
RN	Royal Navy
RR	railroad
S	south, southern
S.	San, Sant, Santa, etc. (Italy and Sicily only)
SACMED	Supreme Allied Commander, Mediterranean
SAP	Strategic Air Force
SBD	"Dauntless" single-engine Navy scout-bomber
SEAC	Southeast Asia Command
sep	separate
SHAEF	Supreme Headquarters, Allied Expeditionary Fc
SOPAC	South Pacific
SOS	Services of Supply
SPM	self-propelled mount
sq	squadron
SS	*Schutzstaffel* (Elite Guard)
SSF	Special Service Force
STLF	Southern Troops and Landing Force
SWPA	Southwest Pacific Area
TAP	Tactical Air Force
TD	tank destroyer
TF	task force
TOT	time on target
tr	troop
U.K.	United Kingdom
U.S.	United States
USA	U.S. Army
USAAF	U.S. Army Air Forces
USAAFUK	U.S. Army Air Forces in the United Kingdom
USAFBI	U.S. Army Forces, British Isles
USAFFE	U.S. Army Forces, Far East
USAFIA	U.S. Army Forces in Australia
USAFICPA	U.S. Army Forces in Central Pacific Area
USAFIME	U.S. Army Forces in the Middle East
USAFISPA	U.S. Army Forces in the South Pacific Area
USASOS	US. Army Services of Supply
USFIA	U.S. Forces in Australia
USFIP	U.S. Forces in the Philippines
USMC	U.S. Marine Corps
USN	U.S. Navy
USSAFE	U.S. Strategic Air Forces in Europe
USSR	Union of Soviet Socialist Republics
USSTAF	U.S. Strategic Air Forces
VAC	V Amphibious Corps
W	west, western
WDAF	Western Desert Air Force

Glossary of Code Names

ABERDEEN	Chindit stronghold near Manhton, Burma.
ALAMO	Code for U.S. Sixth Army while operating as a special ground task force headquarters directly under GHQ SWPA.
ALPHA	Plan to defend Kunming and Chungking.
ALPHA	U.S. 3d Division force for southern France operation.
ANAKIM	Plan for recapture of Burma.
ANVIL	Early plan for invasion of southern France.
ARCADIA	U.S.-British conference held in Washington, December 1941–January 1942.
ARGONAUT	International conference held at Malta and Yalta, January–February 1945.
ARGUMENT	USSTAF air operations against German aircraft factories, February 1944.
AVALANCE	Invasion of Italy at Salernb.
AXIOM	Mission sent by SEAC to Washington and London in February 1944 to urge CULVERIN.
BACKHANDER	Task force for operations on Cape Gloucester, New Britain.
BARBAROSSA	German offensive against USSR, 1941.
BAYTOWN	British invasion of Italy on Calabrian coast.
BETA	Plan to open port on coast of China.
BLACKCOCK	British 12 Corps operation to clear enemy salient between the Meuse and Roer-Wurm Rivers from Roermond southward.
BLACKPOOL	Chindit roadblock on railroad near Namkwin, Burma.
BLOCKBUSTER	Canadian 2 Corps offensive in Calcar-Udem-Xanten area.
BOLERO	Build-up of U.S. forces and supplies in United Kingdom for cross-Channel attack.
BRASSERD	Operations against the island of Elba.
BREWER	.Operations in the Admiralties.
BRIMSTONE	Plan for capture of Sardinia. Canceled.
BROADWAY	Drop site for Chindits, about fifty miles northwest of Indaw, Burma.
BUCCANEER	Plan for amphibious operation in Andaman Islands. Canceled.
BUFFALO	Operations to break out of Anzio (Italy) beachhead.
BUTTRESS	British operation against toe of Italy.
CAMEL	U.S. 36th Division force for southern France.
CAPITAL	Attack across the Chindwin River to Mandalay.
CARBONADO	Revised BETA.
CARPETBAGGER	Air operation from United Kingdom to drop supplies to patriot forces in Western Eurooe.
CARTWHEEL	Converging drives on Rabaul by South Pacific and SWPA forces.
CASANOVA	U.S. 95th Division diversionary action during operations against Metz.
CATCHPOLE	Operations against Eniwetok and Ujelang Atolls, Marshall Islands.
CHAMPION	Late 1943 plan for general offensive in Burma.
CHATTANOOGA CHOO CHOO	AEAF operations against enemy train movements in France and Germany.
CLEANSLATE	Invasion of Russell Islands.
CLIPPER	British 30 Corps offensive to reduce Geilenkirchen salient.
COBRA	U.S. First Army operation designed to penetrate the German defenses west of St Lô and secure Coutances, France.
CORKSCREW	Conquest of Pantelleria.
COTTAGE	Invasion of Kiska, 1943.
CRICKET	Malta portion of ARGONAUT Conference.
CROSSBOW	RAF operations against German V-weapons experimental bases.

CUDGEL	Planned small-scale operation on Arakan coast, Burma. Canceled.
CULVERIN	Plan for assault on Sumatra.
CYCLONE	Task force for Nocmfoor.
DELTA	U.S. 45th Division force for southern France.
DEXTERITY	Operations against Cape Gloucester, New Britain.
DIRECTOR	Task force for invasion of Arawe, New Britain.
DIXIE	Mission of U.S. observers to Chinese communists.
DRACULA	Plan for attack on Rangoon, 1944.
DRAGOON	Final code for invasion of southern France.
ELKTON	Plan for seizure of New Britain, New Guinea, and New Ireland area.
END RUN	Task force of GALAHAD survivors used in drive on Myitkyina, Burma.
EUREKA	International conference at Tehran, November 1943.
FIREBRAND	Invasion of Corsica, 1943.
FLAX	Air operation to disrupt flow of German air transports from Italy to Sicily and Tunisia.
FLINTLOCK	Operations in the Marshall Islands.
FORAGER	Operations in the Marianas.
FRANTIC	AAF shuttle bombing of Axis-controlled Europe from bases in United Kingdom, Italy, and USSR.
FRY	Occupation of four islands in Lake Comacchio, Italy.
GALAHAD	American long range penetration groups (Burma).
GALVANIC	Operations in Gilbert Islands.
GOBLET	Invasion of Italy at Cotrone. Canceled.
GOLD	Normandy beach assaulted by troops of British 30 Corps, 6 June 1944.
GOLDFLAKE	Movement of Canadian I Corps from Italy to ETO.
GRANITE	Plan for operations in POA in 1944.
GRENADE	21 Army Group large-scale offensive from the Rocr to the Rhine.
GYMNAST	Early plan for Allied invasion of northwest Africa.
HERCULES	German plan to invade Malta. Canceled.
HURRICANE	Assault force for Biak, New Guinea.
HUSKY	Allied invasion of Sicily, July 1943.
ICEBERG	Invasion of the Ryukyu Islands.
ICHIGO	Japanese operation to take U.S. air bases in east China.
INDEPENDENCE	French offensive toward Belfort, France.
INTERLUDE	Rehearsal for Morotai operation.
JUNO	Normandy beach assaulted by troops of Canadian 3d Division, 6 June 1944.
LEVER	Operation to clear area between Reno and southwest shore of Lake Comacchio Italy.
LONDON	XVIII Corps (A/B) phase line near Wesel, Germany.
MAGNET	Movement of first U.S. forces to Northern Ireland.
MAGNETO	Yalta portion of ARGONAUT Conference.
MAILFIST	Capture of Singapore, 1945.
MALLORY MAJOR	Air offensive against Po River bridges, Italy.
MANNA	British occupation of southern Greece.
MARKET-GARDEN	Operation to secure bridgehead over Rhine River.
MARS	U.S. task force (5332d Brigade (Provisional)), CBI.
MICHAELMAS	Task force for seizure of Saidor, New Guinea.
MUSKET	Projected landing on heel of Italy near Taranto, 1943.
NEPTUNE	Actual 1944 operations within OVERLORD. Used for security reasons after September 1943 on all OVERLORD planning papers that referred to target area and date.
NEW GALAHAD	American long range penetration groups (Burma).
NEW YORK	XVIII Corps (A/B) phase line in Ringenberg-Krudenberg area, Germany.
NORDWIND	German offensive against U.S. Seventh Army, January 1945.
OCTAGON	U.S.-British conference at Quebec, September 1944.

[GLOSSARY OF ABBREVIATIONS]

OLIVE	Attack on Gothic Line, Italy.
OLYMPIC	Plan for March 1946 invasion of Kyushu, Japan.
OMAHA	Normandy beach assaulted by troops of U.S. V Corps, 6 June 1944.
OVERLORD	Allied cross-Channel invasion of northwest Europe, June 1944.
PANTHER	British 10 Corps drive across the Garigliano, Italy.
PARIS	XVIII Corps (A/B) phase line west of Erie, Germany.
PERSECUTION	Assault force for Aitape operations, New Guinea.
PICCADILLY	Drop site for Chindits, Burma.
PIGSTICK	Limited operation on south Mayu Peninsula. Canceled.
PLUNDER	21 Army Group assault across the Rhine north of the Ruhr.
POINTBLANK	Combined bomber offensive against Germany.
PROVIDENCE	Occupation of Buna area, New Guinea, 1942. Canceled.
PUGILIST	Attack on Mareth Line, Tunisia, 1943.
QUADRANT	U.S.-British conference at Quebec, August 1943.
QUEEN	12th Army Group operation on Roer Plain between Wurm and Rocr Rivers.
RAINCOAT	Assault on Camino hill mass, Italy.
RASHNESS	Revised CARBONADO plan.
RAVENOUS	4 Corps plan for recapture of northern Burma.
RECKLESS	Assault force for Hollandia operation.
RENO	SWPA plans for operations in the Bismarck Archipelago, along northern coast of New Guinea and thence to Mindanao, P.I.
RO	Japanese air operation to augment Rabaul air forces and delay Allied offensives.
ROAST	Operation to clear Comacchio Spit, Italy.
ROGER	Capture of Phuket Island, off Kra Isthmus, Burma.
ROMEO	French commando force that lands at Cap Nigre, Mediterranean.
ROMULUS	Arakan part of CAPITAL plan.
ROOSTER	Operation to fly Chinese 22d Division to Chihchiang.
ROSE	Ruhr pocket, April 1945.
ROSIE	French naval force that lands southwest of Cannes.
ROUNDUP	Plan for major U.S.-British cross-Channel operation in 1943.
RUGBY	Airborne force that drops to rear of southern France assault beaches.
SATIN	Plan for U.S. II Corps operation against Sfax, Tunisia. Canceled.
SAUCY	Limited offensive to reopen land route from Burma to China.
SEA LION	Planned German invasion of United Kingdom. Canceled.
SEXTANT	International conference at Cairo, November and December 1943.
SHINGLE	Amphibious operation at Anzio, Italy.
SHO	Japanese plan to counterattack U.S. forces in Western Pacific.
SITKA	Force that takes islands of Levant and Port Cros, Mediterranean.
SLAPSTICK	Airborne drop at Taranto, Italy.
SLEDGEHAMMER	Plan for limited cross-Channel attack in 1942.
STALEMATE	Invasion of the Palaus.
STRANGLE	Air operation to interdict movement of enemy supplies in Italy.
SUPERCHARGE	British 30 Corps breakout, Egypt, 1942.
SUPERCHARGE	Revised plan of assault on Mereth Line, March 1943.
SWORD	Normandy beach assaulted by troops of British 3d Division, 6 June 1944.
TALON	Akyab part of CAPITAL plan.
TARZAN	India-based portion of general offensive in Burma.
TED	Task force in Aitape area, New Guinea
TERMINAL	International conference, Potsdam, Germany, 16 July-2 August 1945.
THUNDERBOLT	Offensive in Metz area.
TIDALWAVE	Low-level heavy bomber attack on Ploesti, Rumania, 1943.
TIGER	One of the rehearsal exercises for OVERLORD.
TOGO	Second phase of ICHIGO operation.
TORCH	Allied invasion of northwest Africa.
TOREADOR	Airborne assault on Mandalay.

TORNADO	Assault force for Wakde-Sarmi area, New Guinea.
TRADEWIND	Force for Morotai.
TRANSFIGURE	Plan to drop troops west of Seine River to block enemy escape routes. Canceled.
TRIDENT	U.S.-British conference held at Washington, May 1943.
TULSA	GHQ SWPA's first outline plan for operations directed at the capture of Rabaul.
TWILIGHT	Plan to base B–29's in CBI.
TYPHOON	Task force for Sansapor-Mar operation, New Guinea.
UNDERTONE	U.S. Third and Seventh Army offensive to break through West Wall and clear the Saar-Palatinate triangle, within the confines of the Rhine, Moselle, and Lauter-Sarre.
UTAH	Normandy beach assaulted by troops of U.S. VII Corps, 6 June 1944.
VARSITY	Airborne drop east of the Rhine.
VERITABLE	Canadian First Army operation to dear area between Maas and Rhine Rivers.
VICTOR I	Panay and Negros Occidental operation.
VICTOR II	Cebu, Bohol, and Negros Oriental operation.
VICTOR III	U.S. Eighth Army operations against Palawan.
VICTOR IV	U.S. Eighth Army operations against Sulu Archipelago and Zamboanga area of Mindanao.
VICTOR V	U.S. Eighth Army operations against western Mindanao.
VULCAN	Final ground offensive to dear Tunisia, 1943.
WEBFOOT	Rehearsal for SHINGLE.
YOKE	All U.S. organizations working with Y-Force, CBI.
ZEBRA	U.S.-sponsored Chinese division in east China.
ZIPPER	Plan for assault on Malaya, 1945.

UNITED STATES ARMY IN WORLD WAR II

The multivolume series, UNITED STATES ARMY IN WORLD WAR II, consists of a number of subseries which are: The War Department, The Army Air Forces, The Army Ground Forces, The Army Service Forces, Defense of the Western Hemisphere, The War in the Pacific, European Theater of Operations, Mediterranean Theater of Operations, The Middle East Theater, The China-Burma-India Theater, The Technical Services, Special Studies, and Pictorial Record.

The War Department
    Chief of Staff: Prewar Plans and Preparations
    Washington Command Post: The Operations Division
    Strategic Planning for Coalition Warfare: 1941–1942
    Strategic Planning for Coalition Warfare: 1943–1944
    Global Logistics and Strategy: 1940–1943
    Global Logistics and Strategy: 1943–1945
    The Army and Economic Mobilization
    The Army and Industrial Manpower

The Army Ground Forces
    The Organization of Ground Combat Troops
    The Procurement and Training of Ground Combat Troops

The Army Service Forces
    The Organization and Role of the Army Service Forces

The Western Hemisphere
    The Framework of Hemisphere Defense
    Guarding the United States and Its Outposts

The War in the Pacific
    Strategy and Command: The First Two Years
    The Fall of the Philippines
    Guadalcanal: The First Offensive
    Victory in Papua
    CARTWHEEL: The Reduction of Rabaul
    Seizure of the Gilberts and Marshalls
    Campaign in the Marianas
    The Approach to the Philippines
    Leyte: The Return to the Philippines
    Triumph in the Philippines
    Okinawa: The Last Battle

The Mediterranean Theater of Operations
    Northwest Africa: Seizing the Initiative in the West
    Sicily and the Surrender of Italy
    Salerno to Cassino
    Cassino to the Alps

The European Theater of Operations
    The Supreme Command
    Logistical Support of the Armies, Volume I
    Logistical Support of the Armies, Volume II
    Cross-Channel Attack

    Breakout and Pursuit
    The Lorraine Campaign
    The Siegfried Line Campaign
    The Ardennes: Battle of the Bulge
    Riviera to the Rhine
    The Last Offensive

The Middle East Theater
    The Persian Corridor and Aid to Russia

The China-Burma-India Theater
    Stilwell's Mission to China
    Stilwell's Command Problems
    Time Runs Out in CBI

The Technical Services
    The Chemical Warfare Service: Organizing for War
    The Chemical Warfare Service: From Laboratory to Field
    The Chemical Warfare Service: Chemicals in Combat
    The Corps of Engineers: Troops and Equipment
    The Corps of Engineers: The War Against Japan
    The Corps of Engineers: The War Against Germany
    The Corps of Engineers: Military Construction in the United States
    The Medical Department: Hospitalization and Evacuation; Zone of Interior
    The Medical Department: Medical Service in the Mediterranean and Minor Theaters
    The Medical Department: Medical Service in the European Theater of Operations
    The Medical Department: Medical Service in the War Against Japan
    The Ordnance Department: Planning Munitions for War
    The Ordnance Department: Procurement and Supply
    The Ordnance Department: On Beachhead and Battlefront
    The Quartermaster Corps: Organization, Supply, and Services, Volume I
    The Quartermaster Corps: Organization, Supply, and Services, Volume II
    The Quartermaster Corps: Operations in the War Against Japan
    The Quartermaster Corps: Operations in the War Against Germany
    The Signal Corps: The Emergency
    The Signal Corps: The Test
    The Signal Corps: The Outcome
    The Transportation Corps: Responsibilities, Organization, and Operations
    The Transportation Corps: Movements, Training, and Supply
    The Transportation Corps: Operations Overseas

Special Studies
    Chronology: 1941–1945
    Buying Aircraft: Materiel Procurement for the Army Air Forces
    Civil Affairs: Soldiers Become Governors
    The Employment of Negro Troops
    Manhattan: The U.S. Army and the Atomic Bomb
    Military Relations Between the United States and Canada: 1939–1945
    Rearming the French
    Three Battles: Arnaville, Altuzzo, and Schmidt
    The Women's Army Corps

Pictorial Record
    The War Against Germany and Italy: Mediterranean and Adjacent Areas
    The War Against Germany: Europe and Adjacent Areas
    The War Against Japan

Index

Aach: 421
Aachen: 269-71, 273, 275, 287, 292, 294-95, 298-308, 318-19, 323, 393, 496
Aachen Municipal Forest: 269-70
Aalen: 509, 511, 513
Aandenberg: 382
Aaron Ward: 103
Abadan air base: 102
Abaiang Island: 151
Abate Hill: 165, 167
Abau: 56
Abau Track: 57
Abaucourt: 316
Abbach: 519
Abbendorft: 528
Abbeville: 261-62
ABDA. *See* Australian-British-Dutch-American Command.
Abel, Cecil: 59
Abel's Field: 59-60, 65
Abemama Island. *See* Apamama Island
Abenden: 398, 417-18
Abensberg: 521
ABERDEEN: 185
Abetaia: 408
Abijao: 363-64
Abo-Abo River: 15-16
Abra de Ilog: 358, 373
Abraham (Ennugarrett) Island: 167
Abrefontaine: 367
Abucay: 13
Abucay Hacienda: 15, 17
Abuyog: 314-17
Acerno: 136-37
Achain: 325
Achen: 346-47
Achouffe: 374
Acquafondata: 146, 157-58
Acqualina: 280
Acquarola: 305-06
Acquatraversa Creek: 193
Acquaviva: 221
Acqueville: 215
Acroma: 4, 39, 41
Acul: 364
Adak Island: 51-52, 54-55, 57, 104, 127
ADC Group (USMC): 159-63
Addis Ababa: 78
Adelmannsfelden: 511
Adelshofen: 492
Adelup Point: 238
Adenau: 432
Adige Line: 518
Adige River: 517-18, 521-22
Adler, Brig. Gen. Elmer E.: 35
Admiral Scheer: 482
Admiral Scheer Bridge: 423, 425
Admiralty area (Kwajalein): 169

Admiralty Islands campaign: 129, 152, 162, 164, 170, 175-88
Casualties summary: 190, 194
offensive plan completed: 43-45
staging area for Philippines: 303, 329
Adolf Hitler Bridge: 418, 424-25
Adony: 346
Adorf: 462, 524
Adrano: 120, 123, 125
Adriatic coast sector: 138, 140, 142, 145, 150, 153, 183, 191, 199, 204-05, 207, 210, 212, 216, 219, 221, 231-33, 247, 250-53, 259, 262, 277, 279, 283, 296, 306, 313, 318, 319, 337, 338, 339, 344, 397, 412, 421
Advance New Guinea Force: 75, 84
Aegean Islands: 134-35 138-39, 146-47, 261, 292
Aegidienberg: 438, 440
Aermeter: 297
Afetna Point: 211-12
Afferden: 404, 415
Affler: 409
Affoldern: 468
Africa, Northwest, recovery of. *See* Northwest Africa campaign.
Africa-Middle East Theater: 419
Afua: 202, 205-06, 216, 229, 231-45
Afwaterins Canal: 316
Agahang: 323
Agana: 240-41
Agat: 234-35
Agay: 249
Agedabia: 6, 8-9, 13, 17, 69
Agger River: 485
Agincourt: 280-81, 283
Agira: 121-23
Agno River: 8-9, 374, 376, 378-79, 405
Agoo: 7
Agriculture Building (Manila): 412, 417, 419
Agrigento: 119-20
Aguilar: 371-72, 374
Agy: 206
Ahaus: 460, 462
Ahawk Stream: 165-66
Ahawk Trail: 165
Ahioma: 59
Ahl Creek: 452
Ahlen: 476
Ahnsen: 484
Ahr River: 427, 429, 431-34
Ahrhutte: 431
Ahrweiler: 429
Ailano: 142
Ailertchen: 454
Ain River: 259-60
Aïn et Turk: 65
Ainsworth, Rear Adm. Walden L.: 118, 161
Air and Ground Supply Committee (Burma): 459

Air bombardment of Europe. *See* Combined Bomber Offensive against Europe.
Air Commando, 1st (AAF): 178
Air Corps: 13, 22. *See also* Army Air Forces.
Air Force Engineer Command (Prov): 159
Air Force Service Commands
 XII: 159
 XV: 159
Air Forces
 3d Tactical: 190, 333
 Fifth: 25, 53, 58-59, 63-67, 69, 74, 78, 126, 128, 130-31, 136-37, 140, 143-47, 170, 176, 181, 184-85, 194, 206, 215-16, 274, 315 346-47 349-50, 372, 375, 380-81, 387, 389-90, 404, 415, 440 450-51, 530, 548
 Sixth: 22
 Seventh: 22, 38, 40, 42, 136, 145, 147, 344 368, 370, 383, 428
 Eighth: 19, 33, 37-38, 42, 50, 72, 82, 89, 113-14, 122, 124, 128, 130, 132, 137-41, 144, 152 154, 156, 160, 176, 178, 185, 187, 189, 191-92, 197, 203, 215, 219, 236, 244, 245, 268, 271, 273
 Ninth: 66, 75, 93, 105 124, 134, 141, 150, 152, 154, 179 186, 191, 236, 240, 321
 Tenth: 23, 27-28, 31, 35, 43-44, 50, 55, 121, 153, 345, 375, 484, 527, 537, 542, 550
 Eleventh: 22, 28, 112, 122, 125, 127, 133, 135
 Twelfth: 50, 66, 82, 93, 96, 127, 139, 141
 Thirteenth: 72, 84, 160, 183, 186-87, 315, 415, 440, 445
 Fourteenth: 97-98, 114-16, 123, 132, 147, 149, 165, 189, 194 199, 204-05, 241, 248, 259, 266, 276, 314, 323, 342, 355, 375, 387, 390, 396, 405, 453, 527, 537, 550
 Fifteenth: 141-43, 148, 160, 167, 175-76, 185, 201, 203, 207, 219, 236-37, 242, 244, 261
 Twentieth: 315
 Alaskan: 15, 22
 Caribbean: 22
 Far East: 3-4, 6, 21, 315, 368
 Middle East: 43
 Strategic: 194
 Western Desert: 74, 94, 103, 105
Air Service Area Commands
 II: 159
 III: 159
Air Service Commands
 IX: 66
 X: 35
Air Support Command, IX: 103

Air Transport Command
   India-China Ferry Command: 45
   India-China Wing: 71
   operations in CBI: 71
   transport of reinforcements to China: 441
Air Unit, 5318th: 170
Airaines: 260
Airborne Antiaircraft Battery, 709th: 52
Airborne Divisions. *See also* Glider Infantry Regiments; Parachute Infantry Regiments.
   11th (187, 188, 511th): 301, 334, 337, 339, 347, 349, 352-54, 357, 372, 374, 379, 381, 385, 388, 390-96, 398-402, 410, 417, 423, 425-26, 428, 430-31, 433-37, 440, 442, 445, 450-53, 455, 457, 460-61, 464-65, 467, 471, 473, 476-78, 480, 482, 484, 486, 488, 490, 493, 497, 499, 501, 503, 505, 510-11, 520, 522-23, 530, 546, 548, 551
   13th (88th, 326th, 515th): 450
   17th (193d, 194th, 513th): 360, 362, 365-67, 369, 371-74, 377, 379-82, 384, 387, 392, 394, 396-400, 450, 452-54, 456, 458, 460, 462, 464, 466, 468, 470, 472, 474, 476, 478, 480, 482, 485, 487, 489, 491, 493, 504, 506, 515
   82d (504th, 505th, 325th): 117-23, 131-32, 134-38, 143, 146-47, 154-56, 203-13, 222-24, 276-79, 281, 284-85, 288, 321, 324, 354, 356, 357-62, 366-71, 385-93, 395, 397, 399-402, 404-05, 408, 464, 473, 508, 516, 519-20, 522, 524, 526, 528
   101st (327th, 401st, 502d, 506th): 203-10, 219, 221-22, 229, 276, 278-79, 281-82, 284-85, 287-88, 321, 338, 354, 357, 359, 361-63, 365-67, 370-71, 373-76, 381, 384-85, 393, 410, 413, 414, 466, 473, 502, 520, 523, 525, 527, 530-31
Airborne Engineer Battalion, 871st: 131
Airborne Task Force, 1st: 249-50, 252-55, 258-59, 261, 266, 333, 337
Aircraft, Army
   first launching from carriers: 34
   H2S-equipped: 137, 144
   internment in Turkey: 41, 124
Aircraft carriers. *See also by name.*
   first engagement between: 37
   first launching of land bombers from: 34
Aire: 262
Airel: 226
Aisch River: 492, 494, 496, 498
Aisne River: 258, 260, 367
Aitape operation: 182, 187-90, 195-96, 199-202, 205-07, 212-14, 216, 221, 223, 225, 227-50, 256, 263, 269, 342
Aitsu Island: 173
Aix-en-Provence: 252-53, 255
Ajoncourt: 298
Aka: 456
Aka Island: 456-57, 460, 462

Akagi: 40
Akarakaro Point: 289
Aken: 500
Akhtyrka: 126
Akyab operation: 30, 36, 71, 75, 78, 145, 316, 351, 358, 362, 367, 384, 426, 469
Alacan: 373
Alagir: 62
'Alam el Halfa: 50, 53-54
Alaminos: 372, 374, 467
ALAMO FORCE: 114-15, 136, 139, 141, 156, 176, 182, 189, 191, 195, 200-202, 220, 249, 274. *See also* Armies, Sixth.
Alangalang: 314
Alangan River: 32
Alaska Defense Command: 28, 38, 143
Alaska Sector (USN): 186
Alaskan Air Force: 15, 22
Alaskan Department: 143
Alaskan Sea Frontier (USN): 186
Alatri: 201
Albanella: 133
Albaneta Farm: 172
Albania, operations in: 301, 329
Albano: 164, 167, 173-76, 179, 198-202
Albay Gulf islands: 486
Albereto: 341
Albersrieth: 512
Albert Canal: 265, 267-69, 353
Albert (Ennumennet) Island: 167
Albert River: 273
Albestroff: 333-35
Albiano: 392
Albuera: 339
Album: 13
Alcala: 548
Alcan Highway: 23, 62
Alchiba: 70
Aldekerk: 421
Aldenhoven: 327, 331
Aldersbach: 526
Aldringen: 382
Aldsdorf: 297
Alemont: 321
Alençon: 243, 245-48
Alessandria: 521, 527
Aleutian Islands Campaign: 40-129. *See also* Attu Island; Kiska Island.
   air-naval actions: 38, 40, 57, 88, 93, 100, 106, 112-13, 116, 121-22, 124-27
   as base for assault on Paramushiro: 132
   enemy naval support: 36
   enemy seizure: 38-40
   enemy supply situation: 100
   Komandorski Islands naval battle: 100
   recovery of: 88, 93, 96, 100, 102, 104-06, 108-14, 116, 120-29, 139
   reinforcement of: 38
Alexai Point: 109, 112-13
Alexander, Gen. Sir Harold R. L. G.: 30, 35, 50, 94-95, 102, 104-05, 107-08, 159
   CG of Allied forces in Tunisia: 92

Alexander, Gen. Sir Harold R. L. G.—Continued
   as CG of Burma Army: 27
   as CG of 18 Army Group: 94
   as CG of 15th Army Group: 113, 117-19, 120-23, 131, 133-36, 138, 145, 162, 168-69, 172, 190, 202, 204, 210, 217, 266
   as CG of MEF: 49-50
   Deputy CinC of Allied Forces in French North Africa: 93
   directive on drive on Rome: 190
   directive on Egypt-Libya: 49
   directive on Gafsa offensive: 98, 100
   plan for final offensive in Tunisia: 104
   and SACMED: 354
   transfer to India: 38
Alexandra: 23
Alexandria: 43
Alexishafen: 189
Alf: 436, 439-40, 443
Alf River: 435
Alfeld: 466, 480
Alfonsine: 358, 366, 368
Alfter: 429-30
Algeria-French Morocco Campaign: 64-66. *See also* Northwest Africa Campaign; Tunisia Campaign.
Algiers
   AFHQ moved to: 69
   Allied command conference: 92
   conference with French leaders: 60
   French Committee of National Liberation formed: 113, 130
   landings at: 53, 64-67
   NATO established: 91
Algrange: 267
Ali: 128
Ali Island: 189
Alife: 141
Alimena: 121
Alimodian: 443
Alitzheim: 485
Alken: 438
Allagappa: 401
Allaine River: 330
Allanmyo: 30-31, 509, 522
Allen, Samar: 406-07
Allen (Ennubirr) Island: 167
Allendorf: 429, 479, 481
Allengen: 480
Allenstein: 381, 386
Aller River: 482, 484, 486, 489
Allerborn: 379
Allerona: 210
Allersburg: 512
Allex: 257
Allied Air Force (NW Africa): 82
Allied Air Forces (P.I.): 379
Allied Air Support Command: 93
Allied Airborne Army, First. *See* First Allied Airborne Army.
Allied Armies in Italy: 179-354. *See also* Army Groups, 15th.
Allied Central Mediterranean Force: 163-78. *See also* Allied Armies in Italy.
Allied Expeditionary Air Force: 150, 154, 187, 191, 195, 239

[INDEX]

[565]

Allied Expeditionary Force
  activated: 55
  Eisenhower as Supreme Commander: 152, 156, 163. *See also* Eisenhower, General Dwight D.; Supreme Headquarters, Allied Expeditionary Force.
Allied Force Headquarters. *See also* Eisenhower, General Dwight D.; Supreme Headquarters, Allied Expeditionary Force.
  activated: 55
  Alexander named Deputy CinC: 93
  command conference: 92
  control of Seventh Army: 249
  meetings with Soviet Army: 496, 498, 512-17, 519, 521-23, 526-30, 532-33, 536
  moves to Algiers, 69
  moves to Gibraltar: 64
  plans for invasion of Italy: 123-24, 126-30
  plans for Southern France Campaign: 155, 157, 159, 162, 164, 171, 176-77, 240, 246, 249
  reconstitution of commands: 93
  relinquishes 6th Army Group to SHAEF: 273
  staff structure: 64
Allied Land Forces, South East Asia: 324-58
Allied Naval Forces, Luzon: 373
Allstedt: 489
Almelo: 474
Almond, Maj. Gen. Edward M.: 296
Alor Star: 4
Alost: 262, 264
Alpe di Poti: 230, 232-33
Alpe di Vitigliano: 271-72
Alpen: ?95, 425, 427-28, 430, 432
ALPHA: 249, 333, 341, 348, 350, 354, 365, 369 387. *See also* Chungking; Kunming.
ALPHA Force: 248. *See also* Southern France Campaign.
Alpine Front Command (Fr.): 447
Alpine Highway: 514
Alsace-Ardennes Campaign: 274, 353-83
Alsbach: 454
Alschbach: 445
Alscheid: 382
Alsdorf: 295-98
Alsenz River: 444
Alsfeld: 463, 465
Alsleben: 491
Alsstadten: 425
Alstatte: 464
Alsting: 407
Alt Astenberg: 472
Alt Bessingen: 481
Alt Damm: 446
Altamura: 136-37
Altavilla: 133-35
Altdorf: 507, 523
Alten: 508
Alten Buseck: 458
Altena: 496
Altenahr: 429
Altenburg: 410, 494, 496
Altendorf: 427

Altenfeld: 478
Altenhundem: 482
Altenilpe: 483
Altenkirchen: 452, 454
Altenmellrich: 474
Altenrath: 489
Alterberg: 530
Altheim: 455
Althorn: 369, 371, 380
Althuette: 507
Altisheim: 518
Altkirch: 338-39
Altmuenden: 479
Altmuhl River: 514, 516, 518, 521
Altmyhl: 415
Alto Hill: 276
Altopascio: 261, 263
Altremda: 490
Altwied: 449
Altwiller: 335, 338
Alvignano: 141
Alzen: 271, 273, 275, 278, 387, 448, 450
Alzerath: 388
Amagansett: 41
Amance Hill: 280-81, 283-84
Amanvillers: 265, 268-69
Amaseno: 198
Amaseno River: 197
Amaseno Valley: 197
Amaye-sur-Seulles: 241
Ambayabang Valley: 419
Amberg: 504, 510, 514
Ambérieu: 259
Amberloup: 372
Amblève: 375, 383
Amblève River: 355-56, 358, 361, 372-74, 377
Ambon: 20, 22, 25
Ambrières-le-Grand: 244
Amchitka Island: 75-76, 88, 93
Ameln: 414
Amelscheid: 388
American Military Mission to China: 27
American republics, solidarity meeting: 15, 19
American Volunteer Group: 5, 7, 36, 44
Amersfoort: 499
Amiangal Mt.: 288-89, 291, 293
Amiens: 258-59
Amike: 536
Amlang: 374-75, 377-78, 380
Ameldingen: 402
Ammer River: 523
Ammer See: 521, 523
Ammerschwihr: 355
Amoeneburg: 460
Amorbach: 463
Amoy: 375
Amonines: 361
Amper Kanal: 523
Amper River: 523
Amphibious Corps, Marine. *See* Marine Amphibious Corps.
Amphibious Forces (USN,)
  III: 119, 303, 305
  V: 129
  VII: 222, 274, 302, 305
  North Pacific: 102
  Pacific: 299

Amphibious Reconnaissance Battalion, FMF: 438, 456, 476, 480, 491, 548
Amphibious Support Force (USN): 403
Amphibious Tank Battalions
  536th: 374
  718th: 374
  776th: 344-45, 348-49, 374
Amsterdam Island: 239, 241
Amstetten: 534-35
Amuro Island: 458
An: 404
Anabat: 433
Anagni: 201
ANAKIM: 73, 88, 90, 108. *See also* Burma, recovery of.
Anamo: 229-30, 234
Anao: 378
Anapa: 53, 137
Anatolia: 35
Anayan: 527, 529
Ancerville: 324
Ancerviller: 325, 326
Ancona: 204, 212, 230, 232-33, 340
Andaman Islands: 28, 30-31, 145, 152, 155
Andel: 444
Andelot: 268-69
Andernach: 429, 431-32, 434, 437
Anderson, Maj. Gen. Jonathan W.: 65
Anderson, Gen. Sir Kenneth A. N. (Br.): 87-88, 92, 95, 99, 108
  CG of Allied forces in Tunisia: 88
  CG of British forces, AFHQ: 64
  CG of First Army: 65
Andlau: 340
Andler: 387-88
Andolsheim: 389-90
Andrews, Lt. Gen. Frank M.
  accidental death: 108
  activates Ninth AF: 66
  CG of U.S. Forces in ETO: 90-91, 108
  CG of USAFIME: 63
Andriamanalina: 60
Androchte: 472
Anfa Conference: 84
Angaur Attack Group (USN): 274
Angaur Island: 226, 268, 276, 278-79, 281-83, 285-86, 288-91, 293, 297, 302-04, 306, 308, 310
Angeles: 11, 385-86
Angermuende: 520
Angers: 246-47
Ango: 69
Anholt: 458
Anibong-Point: 309
Anibung: 311
Aniene River: 202
Ankang: 453, 520
Ankiang: 523
Anklan: 523
Annen: 487
Anould: 332
Annweiler: 447
Anrath: 418
Ansbach: 492, 496, 498, 500, 502-04, 509
Antelat: 8, 12, 18

[INDEX]

Antiaircraft Artillery Battalions
    434th: 273, 280, 295
    435th: 266, 280, 295
    976th: 172
Antiaircraft Artillery Brigades
    44th 333, 419
    45th: 237, 374
    54th: 512, 516
    55th: 512, 515
Antiaircraft Artillery Groups
    18th: 504, 515
    91st: 237
    107th: 237, 296, 319
Antibes: 255
Antilao River: 352
Antimonan: 8, 480, 486, 488
Antipolo: 409, 412-13, 419, 431, 435-36, 438, 440, 448, 450
Antipolo Point: 363
Antrain: 240
Antsirabe: 57
Antsirene: 3 8
ANVIL: 150, 152, 157, 159, 162, 164, 171, 176, 177, 182-84, 189, 207, 210, 212, 217, 219-20, 222, 224, 240. *See also* DRAGOON; Southern France Campaign.
Antweiler: 426-27
Antwerp: 262, 264-65, 267, 269-71, 274, 276, 283, 292, 294, 297, 302-05 309, 318, 320, 339, 353
Antwerp-Turnhout Canal: 286, 292
Anyasan River: 19-23
ANZAC Area: 20
ANZAC Naval Force (Allied): 22
Anzio Campaign: 145, 149, 155-56, 159, 162-82, 184-86, 194, 196-202
Aoba: 58
Aoeki Island: 200
Aogiri Ridge: 160-61
Aola Bay: 63, 66, 71-72
Aosta: 457
Apamama Island: 139, 148-50
Aparri: 4, 542-43 547-49
Apartment House area (Okinawa): 522, 527
Apaukwa: 177
Apeldoorn: 423, 486, 491, 493, 495, 499
Apennines, operations in: 243-507, 523
Aphove: 381
Apostolovi: 171
Appenwihr: 393
Appolensdorf: 524
Aprilia: 165
Apt: 253-54
Apweiler: 327-30
Aquino: 194-97
Arad: 295
Aradura Spur: 202
Aragachi: 547
Arakachi: 478
Arakan coast: 75, 82, 90, 93, 98, 110, 145, 161, 170, 172, 178, 181, 183, 185, 240, 263, 290, 316, 321, 329, 333, 351, 353, 358, 363, 367, 372, 381, 384, 404-05, 426, 437, 522, 529, 535, 537
Arare: 193, 195, 199
Arawe: 149, 151, 154-57, 160-63

Araxos: 285-86, 298
Arayat: 10
Arboredo: 419
ARCADIA (Washington) Conference: 8-10, 14
Arce: 197-99
Arcey: 326
Arches: 283-84
Archettes: 284
Ardennes-Alsace Campaign: 274, 353-83
Arevale: 443
Arezzo: 136, 204, 224-25, 227-28, 230-33, 263
Argens River: 251
Argenta: 492, 495, 497, 499, 501, 503, 505
Argentan: 245, 247-53
Argentina: 165
Argenschwang: 443
Argenthal: 441
ARGONAUT Conference: 387, 390, 392, 398, 400
ARGUMENT: 175. *See also* Combined Bomber Offensive against Europe.
Arielli: 156
Ariendorf: 435, 448
Aringay: 7, 428, 430-31
Aritao: 542-43, 545
Arles: 255, 257-58
Arloff: 427
Arlon: 267, 357, 359, 462-64
Arloncourt: 365-66, 375
Armaucourt: 284
Armavir: 48, 88
Armies
    First: 166, 203-34, 236-71, 273, 275-76, 278-79, 281-86, 287-308, 311-12, 315-20, 322-23, 325-64, 366-77 379-95, 397 402, 404-08, 410-12, 414-16, 418, 420, 422, 424, 425, 427, 429-30 432-42, 444-46 448-49, 451-52, 454, 456-60, 462, 464, 466, 468, 470, 472, 474, 476, 478, 480, 482, 485, 487, 489, 491-93, 495, 497, 500, 502, 504, 506, 508, 510, 512, 514-15, 517, 519, 521-22, 524, 528-30, 533-34, 550
    Third: 162, 165, 180, 225, 240-70, 272-75, 277-78, 280-302, 305, 307-08, 312-32, 334-95, 397, 408, 410-12, 414, 416-17, 419-22, 424, 426-27, 429, 431-32, 434-42, 444-49, 451-60, 463, 465, 467-68, 470, 472, 474, 477, 479, 481, 483, 485, 487, 489, 492, 494, 496, 498, 500, 502, 504, 506-08, 510-12, 514-15, 517, 519, 521-22, 524, 526, 528-34
    Fourth: 165
    Fifth: 82, 115, 123, 128-29, 132-47, 149-86, 191-202, 204-08, 210, 212-37, 240, 242-44, 248, 250-53, 255-61, 263-67, 269-77, 279-80, 282-315, 317-19 321-23, 325, 327-28, 334, 336, 338-42, 344, 346-48, 350-52, 354, 258-59, 361-64, 368-75, 377, 381, 383-84, 386, 392, 394, 397, 401-02 404-10, 412-13, 417, 419, 423, 425-26, 428, 431, 433, 437, 439, 443, 451,

Armies—Continued
  Fifth—Continued
    457, 459, 471, 475, 477, 479, 481, 483, 486, 488, 490, 492, 494-95, 497, 499 501, 503, 505, 507, 509, 511, 513, 515-18, 520-21, 525, 527
  Sixth: 93, 114-15, 136, 139, 141, 159, 169, 172, 194, 260, 301-02, 307-61, 365, 370-92, 394-97, 399-410, 412-14, 416-17, 419, 421, 423, 425-26 428, 430-31 433-43 445-51 453, 455, 457, 459, 461, 463, 465, 467, 469, 471, 473, 475, 477, 479, 481, 484, 486, 488, 490, 492, 495, 497, 499, 501, 503, 505, 507, 509, 511, 513, 515, 517, 51920, 522-23, 525, 527, 529-38, 540-49. *See also* ALAMO FORCE.
  Seventh: 117-28, 155, 157, 159, 162, 177, 207, 212, 249-69, 271-75, 277-78, 280-87, 290-300, 302-22, 324-29 331, 333-47, 349-52, 354-57, 361-63, 365-69, 371-85, 388-94, 396-410, 412-14, 417, 419, 423-24, 426, 428, 430-31, 433-34 436-39 441-43, 445-48, 450-53 455, 457, 459, 461, 463, 465-66, 469, 471, 473, 475, 479, 481, 483, 485, 487, 490, 492, 494, 496, 498, 500, 502, 504, 507-09, 511-12, 514, 516, 518-19, 521, 523-24, 526, 528-29, 531
  Eighth: 207, 263, 265, 327, 331-32, 361-65, 367, 372, 374, 381, 385, 388-401 403, 405-07 411-12, 415-17 419, 421, 423, 425, 427-28, 430-31, 433-34, 436-38 440-43, 445-46 448-50 452-53, 455, 457, 460-61, 464-65, 467, 471, 473, 476, 478, 480, 482, 484, 486, 488, 490, 493, 497, 499, 501, 503, 506, 507, 510-11, 513, 515, 517, 519-20, 522-23, 525, 527, 539-44, 546-50
  Ninth: 263, 265, 267, 270-71, 273-74, 276, 278-79, 287-88, 292, 294, 298, 303, 305, 307-08, 312, 320-23 327-44, 346-48 351-56, 358-61, 363, 370-71, 384-85, 387-95, 399, 402, 409, 411-13, 415-16, 418-19, 421, 423, 425, 427-30, 432-34 436, 450, 452, 454, 458: 460, 462, 464, 466, 468, 470-72, 474, 476, 478, 480, 482, 484, 486, 489, 491, 493, 495, 497, 499, 502, 504, 506, 508, 510, 512, 514, 515, 517, 519, 521-22, 524, 526, 528, 530, 532-33
  Tenth: 467, 469, 471, 476, 478, 480, 482, 484, 486, 488 491, 493, 495, 497, 499, 501, 504, 506, 508, 510, 92-13, 515, 517, 519-20, 522, 524-25, 527, 529-31 533-49
  Fifteenth: 366, 368, 376, 433-34, 458, 462, 464, 466, 471, 473, 485, 492 496, 498, 500, 502, 504, 506-07, 512, 514-16
Armor, German, superior in Libya: 10
Armored Corps
  I: 82, 97
  II: 82

[INDEX]

Armored Divisions
  1st: 64-66, 70-75, 81, 83, 86-95, 98-104, 106-09, 147, 158, 160-62, 167-68, 170, 173, 196-201, 204, 206-07, 215-17, 220, 222-24, 226, 234, 240, 244, 248, 252, 255, 261, 263, 264, 266-67, 271, 275, 277, 279, 282-83, 286-88, 290-91, 298, 300-301 303, 305-06, 318-19, 334, 362, 410, 428, 431, 439, 457, 475, 495, 497, 499, 501, 503, 505, 507, 509, 511, 513, 515-16, 518, 520-21, 523, 527
  2d: 65-66, 117-19, 121-22, 206-09, 222, 230, 237-38, 240-41, 244-48, 250, 252-54, 258-60, 263-65, 268-71, 273, 275-78, 290-91, 293-98, 302-03 312, 320, 327, 329-34 338-39, 356, 358-63, 365-70, 372-75, 378, 391, 414-16, 418, 420, 422-25, 454, 460, 466, 468, 470, 472, 474, 476, 478, 480, 484, 486, 489, 491, 493, 495, 497, 499, 502, 504 506, 508, 510
  3d: 217, 221-22, 226-28, 230-31, 237-42, 244, 247-50, 256-58, 260-71, 273, 275-76, 278, 280-82, 284, 305-06, 327-29, 335-36 349-50, 355-64, 366-70, 372-76, 378-80, 412, 414-16, 418, 420, 422, 424-25, 427, 429-30, 433, 440-41, 445, 447-49, 452, 454, 456, 458, 460, 462, 464, 466, 468, 470, 472, 474, 476, 478, 481, 483, 485, 487, 489, 491, 494, 496, 498, 500, 502, 504, 506, 508, 510, 512, 514-15, 517
  4th: 229-30, 232, 237-49, 251-61, 263, 268-70, 272-73, 275, 277-78, 280-81, 283-91, 301, 321-26, 328, 330-31, 333-47, 356-57 359-66, 370-71, 390, 396, 405, 408-11, 413-14 416-17, 419, 421, 423-24, 426, 428-29, 431-32, 434-35, 437, 439-44, 446-51, 453, 455, 457, 459, 461, 463, 465, 467-68, 470, 472-73, 475, 477, 479, 481-82, 485, 487, 489-90, 492, 494, 496, 498, 502, 504, 510, 512, 520, 526, 529, 531-33
  5th: 240, 245, 247-55, 258-60, 263-65, 267-68, 270, 272-73. 275, 277, 280, 301, 303, 312, 322, 327, 330, 335-36, 340-41, 343-46, 353, 356-60, 387-89, 394, 411-12, 414-16, 418, 420, 422-23, 425, 427-29, 435, 464, 466, 468, 470, 472, 474, 480, 482, 484, 486, 489, 491, 493, 495, 497, 499, 502, 506, 508, 510, 512, 514-15
  6th: 232, 236-48, 251, 258, 261, 267, 270, 272, 274, 277-78, 280, 283-85, 287-92, 298-99, 321-28, 330-31, 333-38, 342, 344-46 356, 362-76, 379-84, 386, 389, 392, 394, 396-401, 407-14, 416-17, 419-22, 424, 431, 445-48, 450-55 457, 459, 461-63, 465, 467-68, 470, 472, 474-75, 477, 479, 481, 483, 485, 487, 489-90, 492, 496, 498, 502, 514-15

Armored Divisions—Continued
  7th: 246-48, 250-57, 259-62, 264-70, 272-73, 275, 277-78, 280-81, 283-87, 289-91, 293-95, 297, 301, 304-05, 313-21, 340, 354-63, 376, 378-85, 391, 393-95, 399, 429, 431-33 438, 444, 448-49, 452, 454, 456, 458, 460, 462, 464, 468 470, 472, 474, 476, 478, 480, 483, 485, 487, 489, 491, 493, 496, 498, 500, 502, 508, 524, 526, 528-29
  8th: 378, 382-84, 394, 415-16 418, 420-21, 423, 425, 428, 430, 432-33, 435, 454, 456, 458, 460, 462-64, 466, 468, 470, 472, 474, 476, 478, 480, 482, 485, 487, 489, 491, 493, 497, 499, 502, 504, 506, 508, 510
  9th: 303, 353-59 361-65, 417-18, 420, 422, 424-27 429, 431-32 436-37 440, 447-49, 451-52, 454, 456-60, 462, 464, 466, 468, 470, 474, 481, 483, 485, 487, 489, 4 91-92 494, 496, 498, 500, 508, 510, 521-22, 524, 530, 533
  10th: 317, 320, 325-32, 334-38, 341-42, 353-62, 365-66, 370, 380, 383, 398-400, 406-11, 413-14, 416-17, 419, 421, 423-24, 426, 428-32, 434-37, 440, 442-44, 446-48 450, 459, 461, 463, 465-66, 469, 471, 473, 475, 477, 479, 481, 483, 485-86, 488, 490, 492, 494, 498, 500, 503, 505, 507, 509, 511, 513-14, 516, 518, 520-21, 523, 525, 527
  11th: 360, 363-65, 373-77, 379-81, 392-94, 396-401, 405-08, 410-12, 414, 419, 422, 424, 426-27, 429, 431-32, 434-38, 440-44, 446-48, 450-51, 453, 455, 459, 461, 463, 465, 467-68, 470, 473, 475, 477, 479, 481, 485, 487, 490, 492, 494, 496, 500, 502, 504, 506, 508, 510, 512, 514-15 517, 519, 521-22, 524, 526, 528-30, 532-34
  12th: 345-49 351, 362, 369-72, 376-78, 391-93, 395, 400, 07, 423, 442-44, 446-48, 450-51, 455, 457, 459, 461, 463, 465-66, 469, 471, 473, 475, 477, 479, 481, 483, 485, 487-88, 490, 492, 494, 496, 498, 500, 502-05, 507, 509, 511-14, 516, 518-21, 523-26, 528-29, 531
  13th: 480, 483, 485, 487, 489 491, 493, 495-97 500, 502, 504, 507-08, 511, 518-19, 521-22, 524, 528-29
  14th: 331, 333-34 336, 338-42 345, 351-52, 354, 365-66, 369, 372-76, 378, 383, 389-93, 397, 406, 439, 443, 445-48 450, 465-66, 469, 471, 473, 475, 477, 479, 481, 485, 494, 500, 504, 508, 512, 514, 518-19, 521-24, 526, 528
  16th: 521, 526, 530, 533
  20th: 407, 471, 500, 504, 509, 512, 519, 521, 523

Armored Groups 2d: 237, 295
  13th: 301, 388
  17th: 422, 473
  Provisional, Seventh Army. See Task Forces, Butler.
Arms, Col. Thomas S.: 145
Army Air Forces. See also Air Corps.
  Abadan base: 102
  absorbs AVG: 35
  absorbs Eagle Squadrons: 57
  constituted: 28
  first troops reach CBI: 29
  plane losses in Hawaii: 3
  Provisional Regt on Bataan: 19
  withdrawal of units from SEAC: 542
Army Air Forces Engineer Command, MTO: 159
Army Air Forces, India-Burma Sector: 147
Army Air Forces, MTO: 159
Army Air Forces, POA: 241
Army Air Forces Service Command: 159
Army Air Services: 33
Army Ground Forces constituted under McNair: 28
Stilwell succeeds Lear as head: 384
Army Group, Washington, D.C.: 42
Army Groups
  1st: 236
  6th: 240, 260, 273, 275, 277-78, 280-81, 283-87, 291-300, 302-26, 328-29, 331, 333-52, 354-57, 360-94, 396-410, 412-14, 417, 419, 423-24, 426, 428, 430-31, 433-34, 436-39, 441-43, 445-48, 450-51, 453, 455, 457, 459, 463, 465-66, 469, 471, 473, 475, 477, 479, 481, 483, 485, 487, 490, 492, 494, 496, 498, 500, 502, 504, 507, 509, 511-12, 514, 516, 518-19, 521, 523, 524, 526, 528-33
  12th: 236, 240-74, 276, 278-79, 281-487, 489-500, 502, 504, 506-12, 514-19, 521-24, 526, 528-34
  15th: 113, 117-47, 149-63, 354-531. See also Allied Armies in Italy; Allied Central Mediterranean Force.
  Central Group of Armies: 260
  Northern Group of Armies: 260
  Southern Group of Armies: 260
Army Service Forces: 28
Armyansk: 143
Arnaville: 264-65, 267-70, 272-73, 275, 277, 316
Arnhem: 276, 278-79, 281-82, 284-85, 287-289, 292, 342, 468, 488, 491, 493, 495
Arnim, Col. Gen. Jurgen von: 86, 91, 95, 97, 110
Arno River: 214, 229, 232-36, 238, 241, 243, 246, 253, 255-57, 260-61, 266-67
Arno-Rome Campaign: 164-267
Arno Valley drive: 233-44, 246-70
Arnold, Maj. Gen. Archibald V.: 344

Arnold, General Henry H.: 153, 165. *See also* Army Air Forces.
 CG of AAF: 28
 completes Normandy air plan: 33
 at London air conference: 39, 41
 orders Stratemeyer to head China air forces: 547
 plans for occupying Japan: 546
 plans for recovery of Burma: go recommends division of Twelfth Air Force: 139, 141
Arnoldsweiler: 411-12
Arnsbach: 465
Arnsberg: 485, 487, 489
Arnshagen: 494
Arnstadt: 467, 485, 492
Arnstorf: 526
Arnswalde: 410
Arolsen: 462
Around-the-clock bombing of Germany: 95
Arpajon: 253-54
Arracourt: 272, 280-81, 289-90, 308
Arraincourt: 324
Arras: 260
Arraye-et-Han: 298
Arrenrath: 429
Arry: 267-68, 270, 273
Arsoli: 206
Ars-Laquenexy: 329
Arsbeck: 416, 08
Arsdorf: 360-61
Artena: 197-98, 200
Arthur, Col. John M. (USMC): 75
Artificial moonlight, use of Germany: 329
 Italy: 276, 304
 Normandy: 131
 Philippines: 503
Artzenheim: 389-90
Aru Island: 47
Aruba Island: 24
Arundel Island: 126, 129-36
Arzberg: 506, 510, 512
Arzew: 65
Arzfeld: 408, 424
Arzilla River: 258 As: 506, 510, 512
Asa: 534-36
Asa River and Estuary: 525, 527, 529, 534-36
Asan: 234
Asato River: 540-41
Asbach: 452, 463
Ascension Island: 31, 51
Asch: 518
Aschaffenburg: 453, 457, 459, 461, 463, 465-66, 469, 471
Aschau: 528
Aschbach: 369, 443
Aschersleben: 175, 500, 512
Ashbourne, Capt. Lord (RN): 327
Asheville: 26
Asia Islands: 327, 331-32
Asias: 281
Asiga: 237
Asin: 488, 490, 497, 501, 505, 507, 509, 511, 513
Asingan: 379, 381, 385, 403
Aslito airfield: 212-13
Aslom: 311

Aso River: 214
Asperberg: 402-04
Asperden: 403-04
Aspisheim: 444
Assam airlift of supply to China from: 55, 57, 60-61, 110, 116, 147, 150, 155, 180-81, 187, 190, 200, 202, 205, 235, 271, 293, 297, 329, 342, 344, 355, 540
 operations in: 38, 109-10, 112, 153
Assam-Bengal railway: 145, 147
Assam-Burma-China Ferry Command, AAF: 29
Assam-Calcutta Line of Communications: 166-67, 171
Asselborn: 380
Asseln: 487
Assenois: 361
Assingshausen: 474
Asslar: 456, 458
Asten: 313-14
Astheim: 449
Astorga: 523
Astoria: 49
Astrakhan: 45
Atanniya: 472
Athens: 261-62, 302, 304-05
Atina: 149-50, 155, 157, 198
Atipuluan: 464
Atlanta: 66
Atlantic, Battle of, Allied losses: 55, 79
Atlay: 441
Atoman: 522
Atomic bomb, first test and use: 550
Atsugi airfield: 551
Atsutabaru: 476
Attack Force Reserve (USN): 164
Attendorn: 485, 487
Atter Kammer See: 532-33
Atton: 272-73, 275
Attu Island
 air-naval actions: 93, 106, 109-10
 enemy garrison strength: 112
 enemy seizure of: 40-41, 55, 62
 recovery of: 96, 100, 102, 104-06, 108-13, 127
Aubagne: 253
Aube: 323
Aubel: 268, 407, 410
Aubenton: 260
Auche: 183
Auchinleck, Gen. Sir Claude J. E. (Br.): 9, 24-25, 28, 35, 38, 4142, 47
 CG of Br Eighth Army: 43
 CG of MEF: 49-50
 commands in India: 114, 146
 commands in Iraq and Iran: 12
 defines Tripoli as objective: 16
 inspects Br Eighth Army: 18, 42
 sets Tobruk as supply base: 21
Audigast: 489,
Aue: 474
Auel: 387-88
Auenheim: 420
Auerbach: 506
Auersmacher: 404-06
Augny: 326
Augsburg: 138, 176, 513, 518-21, 523
Augusta: 118

Augustdorf: 466
Augustow: 233
Auland: 528
Auletta: 135-36
Aulla: 515-16
Aulnois-sur-Seille: 320
Aumale: 259
Aumenau: 456, 460
Aumetz: 265, 267
Aunay River: 249-50
Aunay-sur-Odon: 240-43
Aurand, Maj. Gen. Henry S.: 541
Aure River: 205-06, 252
Auringen: 459,
Ausa River: 279-80
Ausente Creek: 193
Ausonia: 192-93
Ausonia Defile: 193
Ausonia Valley: 171
Austerlitz: 523
Australia
 accepts MacArthur as commander of SWPA: 33
 aircraft transferred from P.I. to: 6
 as Allied supply base: 6
 base facilities headed by Barnes: 19
 classes of troops for build-up: 13
 control by SWPA: 30-31
 defense directive: 11
 effect of loss of NEI on: 28
 enemy air attacks: 27
 MacArthur arrives: 29
 U.S. troops arrive: 8, 32
Australian Army units
 Corps
  I: 129, 139
  II: 139
 Divisions
  3d: 106, 114-15, 117-18, 120, 129
  5th: 129, 131-34, 172, 189
  6th: 54, 56, 60, 536
  7th: 50, 54-56, 60, 67-68, 74, 84, 88, 131, 132-36, 139, 164, 182, 549, 550
  8th: 8, 12, 14
  9th: 24, 61-62, 131-32, 134-38, 141-42, 147, 149, 153, 162, 527, 545-47
  11th: 186
 Brigades
  4th: 147
  7th: 44-45, 51-52
  14th: 38, 42
  15th: 115, 186
  16th: 54, 60, 63-65, 67-69, 72-73
  17th: 85, 89, 114-15
  18th: 51, 52, 54, 58, 60, 74, 82, 84-87, 164
  20th: 131, 136-37, 147
  21st: 50, 52, 54-55, 71-73, 77, 136
  22d: 14, 136, 138
  24th: 131, 134-35, 147
  25th: 54-56, 60, 63-64, 66-72, 133-36
  26th: 131, 134, 141, 147, 149, 527
  27th: 8, 14-16

[INDEX]

[569]

Australian Army units–Continued
  Brigades–Continued
    30th: 52, 72-73, 75, 77
    36th: 77
  Regiments
    2/4 Field: 131
    2/6 Armored: 74-75, 82
    2/7 Cavalry: 75, 77, 84
  Battalions
    2/1 Pioneer: 54
    2/2 Pioneer: 131
    2/4 Pioneer: 24
    2/6: 117
    2/9: 74, 76-77 82, 87
    2/10: 52, 74, 76-77, 79, 81, 87
    2/12: 60, 78-79, 81, 87
    2/13: 131
    2/14: 54, 75
    2/16: 54, 69, 75
    2/17: 131
    2/20: 22
    2/27: 54, 75
    2/31: 55
    2/33: 55
    2/40: 25
    3/14: 54
    39th: 43-48, 52, 72-73, 75, 77, 84
    49th: 73, 76-77, 84
    53d: 52
    55/53: 73, 77
    61st Militia: 51-52
    Papuan: 43, 115, 131
  Companies
    2/6 Field: 131
    2/6 Independent: 59, 64, 67-70, 74, 135-36
    5th Independent: 39
  Miscellaneous Forces
    X Tank Squadron: 75
    Bailey: 200-202
    East: 14-15, 17, 19-20
    Kanga. See Wau.
    Maroubra: 43, 46-50
    Milne: 51-52
    New Guinea: 46-50, 56-57, 67, 84, 115, 129, 135
    West: 14-17, 19-20
Australian-British-Dutch-American Command
  absorbs Darwin area: 18
  activated: 10, 15
  Burma transferred to India from: 25, 29
  directive for defense of Far East: 11
  Helfrich CO of Striking Force: 24
  inactivated: 26
  Lembang command conference: 13
Australian Imperial Force, Malaya: 8, 14, 23
Austria
  advance on, from east: 295, 441, 453, 455, 457, 461, 463, 465, 467, 471, 473, 477, 479, 481, 483, 492, 498, 505, 535-36
  advance on, from south: 527
  advance on, from west: 500, 502, 504, 512, 517, 520-21, 524-29, 531-33
  Combined Bomber Offensive against: 138, 143-44, 176

Austria–Continued
  meetings of Allied forces: 535-36
  meetings of Fifth Army and 6th Army Group: 530-31
Autun: 266
Auville-sur-le Vey: 206-07
Auw: 389, 424
Auxerre: 261
Ava: 35
AVALANCHE: 122, 127-32. See also Salerno.
Avanne: 265-66
Avancy: 329
Avellino: 134, 136-38
Avezzano: 142, 207
Avignon: 253, 256-58
Avola: 118
Avord: 191
Avranches: 239-41, 244-45, 247
Avricourt: 325-26, 328
Awacha: 533-36
Awala: 46
Axel: 281
AXIOM Mission: 170. See also South East Asia Command.
Ay River: 229-31
Ayer Hitam: 15, 17-18
Aywaille: 393
Azemmour: 66
Azeville: 204-07
Azov: 91
Azov Sea: 91, 130, 133

B-29 aircraft, China as station for: 146, 147, 149, 150, 187, 189, 202, 204-05, 344
Baal 410-11
Baanga Island: 126-29
Baarland: 312
Babatngon: 310-11, 314
Babay Ridge: 488, 490, 493, 501
Babelthuap Island: 274
Babenhausen: 457
Babeshausen: 518
Babiang: 191
Baccarat: 282, 292, 315-16, 324, 328
Bachem :425
Bachnang: 507
BACKHANDER: 155-56. See also Cape Gloucester.
Baclain: 373
Bacnotan: 7
Bacolod: 461, 464-65
Bacon: 477
Bacon, Col. Robert L.: 326-30
Bad Aibling: 528
Bad Berka: 490
Bad Blankenburg: 487, 490
Bad Ems: 456
Bad Godesberg: 418, 439, 431
Bad Kreuznach: 439-41, 443-44
Bad Lauchstaedt: 489
Bad Lauterberg: 489
Bad Mergentheim: 477, 479, 483
Bad Muenster: 440
Bad Nauheim: 461, 463, 467
Bad Neuenahr: 427, 429, 432, 449
Bad Oeynhausen: 470, 472
Bad Orb: 467, 469
Bad Reichenhall: 531
Bad Schalbach: 459, 461

Bad Sooden: 468, 470, 477, 479
Bad Sulza: 487
Bad Toelz: 525, 527-28
Bad Wildungen: 462
Badem: 422, 424
Baden Baden: 490
Baden Plain: 492, 496, 507, 511
Badia: 225, 518
Badiang: 529, 533
Badoglio, Marshal Pietro (It.)
  heads Italian Government: 122, 131-32, 137-38
  role in armistice agreement: 132, 137-38
Badonviller: 328, 331
Badorf: 427
Baerendorf: 335-36
Baerenthal: 439, 441-42
Baerl: 423
Baesweiler: 296-97, 327, 411
Baetcke, Maj. Bernd G.: 72
Bagabag: 544-45
Bagac: 17-19, 405, 407-08
Bagley, Vice Adm. David W.: 186
Bagnacavallo: 351, 358
Bagnara: 131
Bagni di Casciana: 231
Bagno: 305
Bagnoregio: 204, 207, 209
Bago River: 461
Bagonbon River: 347
Baguio: 3, 5, 7, 384, 404, 409, 419, 426, 435, 450, 455, 469, 481-82, 484, 486, 488, 490, 501, 505, 509, 511, 513, 515, 517, 520, 522, 527, 529
Bailer Pier (Kwajalein): 169
Bailleu: 251
Bains-les-Bains: 277
Bainville-auv-Miroirs: 268
Bairiki Island: 148-49
Bairoko Harbor: 116-17, 121, 124-26, 129
Baja: 308-09
Bakenhoven: 374
Baker Island: 126, 130, 132
Bakhmach: 133
Baku: 88-89
Balabac: 511
Balabac Island: 432, 503
Balaho: 401
Balaklava: 187
Balanga: 25, 32
Balantay River: 14-16
Balayan Bay: 379, 417, 425-26
Balberger Forest: 415-16, 418, 423
Bald Hill (Djebel Ajred): 106
Baldersheim: 395, 488
Baldringen: 416
Baldwin, Air Marshal Sir John: 190
Balera: 407
Balesfeld: 424
Balete Pass: 403-04, 409, 419, 428, 442, 449, 460, 511, 522, 527, 529-32, 535, 537, 541
Balete Ridge: 437, 442, 488, 511, 533
Balgau: 396
Balgerhoek: 272, 274
Bali Island: 24-25
Balicuatro Island: 415
Balikpapan: 17-18, 22, 549

Balikpapan Bay: 549
Balinao Peninsula: 375
Baling: 6
Balingueo: 372
Balite: 545
Baliti River: 437
Baliuag: 10, 390
Balkans. *See country by name.*
Ballale Island: 123
Ballenstedt: 502, 504
Balogo: 344-46
Balow: 528
Balsic: 396
Baltic Sea sector. *See also country by name.*
  air attacks on: 128
  drive on, from east: 275, 295, 300, 302, 424, 435, 443, 446, 520, 523, 527
  drive on, from west: 501, 515, 522, 524, 527, 529
Balut Island: 550
Balve: 489
Bamban: 10-11, 381-85
Bamban River: 382-83, 386, 388
Bambang: 544
Bamberg: 488, 490, 492, 494, 500, 502
Bambusch Woods: 380, 382
Bammenthal: 465
Ban-de-Laveline: 336
Banana Ridge (Negros): 501, 527
Bancal: 532, 537, 539
Bandekow: 524
Bandjermasin: 23
Bandoeng: 27
Bandoeng Strait: 25
Bandol: 253
Baneux: 367
Bangka Strait, naval-air action in: 24
Bangkok: 3-4, 202
Bani: 373
Banika Island: 9-3-94, 104
Bankline Oil Refinery: 25
Banmauk: 354
Bannholtz Woods: 342, 398-99
Bannstein: 442
Banska Bystrica: 455
Bantog: 469
Bantzenheim: 397
Baod River: 348
Bar-le-Duc: 259-60
Barakoma: 121, 123, 126-27, 130, 139
Baranovichi: 222, 226
Baranow: 242
Baraques de Troine: 380
Baraulu Island: 115
Barbach: 424
BARBAROSSA: 3
Barbas: 328
Barberino: 269
Barbery: 247
Barbey, Rear Adm. Daniel E.: 154, 190, 274
Barby: 489, 491, 493, 495, 497, 499
Barce: 8, 18, 55
Barcellona: 127-28
Barcs: 347
Bardejov: 379
Bardenberg: 298-301
Bardia: 10-11, 42, 66
Barenton: 246-47

Barga: 299-300, 315
Bari: 134, 136-37, 151
Barike River: 116-17
Barjols: 251-52
Barmen: 339
Barnes, Maj. Gen. Julian F.: 5, 19, 251
Barneveld: 499
Barneville-sur-Mer: 212
Baron: 219-20
Baronville: 325
Barr: 338-40
Barrafranca: 120
Barré, Gen. Louis Jacques (Fr.): 68
Barrett, Maj. Gen. Charles D. (USMC) 135
Barrett, Col. David D.: 343
Barrigada: 241-42
Barrowclough, Maj. Gen. H. E. (NZ): 135, 172
Bartenstein: 485
Barterode: 483
Bartley, 2d Lt. Martin E.: 122-24
Bartley Ridge: 122-24
Bartolfelde: 487
Barton: 66
Barugo: 314, 327
Barvenkova: 18
Basabua: 49-51, 53, 68, 72
Basak: 455
Basbellain: 380-81
Basch: 406
Basey: 311
Basilan Island: 441, 444-46
Basel: 332-33, 514, 518
Basse-Bodeux: 361
Basse Ham: 321
Bassenheim: 431
Bassin à Flot: 207
Bastendorf: 378
Bastia, Corsica: 139, 240
Bastia, Italy: 212, 486, 490, 492, 495, 497, 499
Bastogne: 267, 354-67, 369-71, 373, 376, 380
Bataan Defense Force: 8, 12-13
Bataan Peninsula
  consolidation of positions: 12
  enemy assault: 13, 22, 31-32
  enemy bombardment: 30-32
  final defense position: 17-19
  MacArthur inspects defenses: 13
  recovery of: 387-88, 391, 401, 403, 405-08
  siege of: 12-13
  supply situation: 121, 30-31
  surrender demand: 13
  withdrawal to: 8-11
Batalan River: 15
Batan Island: 3-4
Batang Berjuntai: 12
Batangas: 5, 434-35, 442, 461
Batangas Bay: 417, 425-26
Batavia
  ABDA Command opens in: 15
  British Eastern Fleet moves to: 12
  enemy seizure of: 26-27
Batchelor: 450
Batetskaya: 172
Batjan Island: 274

Battalions. *See* Airborne Engineer Battalion, 871st; Amphibious Reconnaissance Battalion, FMF; Amphibious Tank Battalions; Antiaircraft Artillery Battalions; Chemical Weapons Battalions; Engineer Aviation Battalions; Engineer Combat Battalions; Field Artillery Battalions; Infantry Battalions; Marine Corps Airdrome Battalion, 2d; Marine Corps Defense Battalions; Marine Corps Engineer Battalions; Marine Corps Field Artillery Battalions; Marine Corps Raider Battalions; Quartermaster Port Battalion, 393d; Ranger Battalions.
Batterie Graf Spee: 256
Battice: 267
Battipaglia: 133-36
Batu Pahat: 15-19
Bauang: 7, 443-46, 455
Bauchem: 13 29
Baudrecourt: 323-24
Bauler: 411
Baumbach: 454
Baume-les-Dames: 264-66
Baumholder: 443-44, 453
Baupte: 208-09, 211
Bauschheim: 451
Bausendorf: 435-36
Bautista: 374
Bavai: 262
Bavaria
  operations in: 502, 504, 527
  surrender of German forces in: 532-33
Bavarian Alps: 5, 16, 521
Bavigne: 370
Bawlake: 31, 33-34
Bay of Biscay: 328
Bayambang: 372, 376 378
Baybay: 314-17, 333-34
Bayeux: 203-04, 207, 228, 231
Bayo: 527
Bayombong: 545-46
Bayon: 268
Bayreuth: 477, 479, 492, 494, 496, 498, 500, 502
BAYTOWN: 128-30. *See also* Calabria.
Bayug: 339
Bazeilles: 263
Bazoncourt: 324
Beach, Capt. Charles E.: 82-84
Bear Point: 179
Beaudienville: 216
Beaufort, Borneo: 12
Beaufort, France: 362
Beaufort Bay: 82-83, 89
Beaulieu: 259
Beaumont: 374
Beaumont-Hague: 221
Beaumont-le-Roger: 191
Beaune: 258, 266
Beauvais: 259
Bebitz: 496
Bech: 374
Bedburg: 401, 420
Beddelhausen: 462
Bédja: 67-70, 74, 95-96, 102-05
Beebe, Brig. Gen. Lewis C.: 28-29

[INDEX]

Beeck: 332-34, 340, 342, 415
Beehive Hill (Okinawa): 542
Beek: 298
Beeringen: 265-66, 268
Beffe: 367
Beggendorf: 295-96, 327
Begroth: 443
Beho: 379-81
Behren: 404
Bei Auel: 388
Beightler, Maj. Gen. Robert S.: 545
Beikelort: 260
Beilingen: 429
Beilngries: 514, 518
Beilstein: 500, 503, 505
Bekond: 432
Belaya Tserkov: 160
Belen: 323
Belev: 12
Belfort Gap: 258, 262, 264, 268, 271, 305, 310, 313, 317, 320, 323, 325, 329, 330-32
Belgard: 428
Belgian Brigade, 1st: 253, 287, 289-90, 293, 297, 315-16, 321
Belgorod: 43-44, 92, 99, 116-17, 122, 125
Belgrade: 261, 291, 300-301, 303-04, 307
Bell, Col. Robert P.: 341-42
Bella Vista: 410
Bellange: 324
Belle-Fontaine: 229
Belle Haie: 360, 366
Belle-Lande: 228
Belleau Wood: 136
Bellevue Farm: 403
Bellinghoven: 414
Bellnhausen: 458
Bellscheid: 411
Belluno: 525
Beltenzenheim: 388
Beltershain: 459
Beltershausen: 458
Beltheim: 439
Belvedere: 133-34, 221, 230, 292
Belvedere Hill: 165-66
Bemmel: 286
Ben Gardane: 92-93
Benamenil: 284
Bench Mark Hills (Luzon): 384, 406, 409, 431, 433-35 437-38, 440-43, 448
Bendorf: 452, 454
Bénestroff: 329-30
Benevento: 135, 137-38
Bengal and Assam Railroad: 145, 147
Bengal Bay: 78, 152
Bengal Command (RAF): 153
Bengendorf: 468
Benghazi: 9, 13, 17-20, 29, 55, 68, 82
Beni Ulid: 85
Bennerscheid: 445
Bennert: 444
Bennett, Maj. Gen. Gordon (Br.): 8, 21
Bennett (Bigej) Island: 170
Bennewitz: 498
Bennwihr: 360
Benonchamps: 374-75
Bénouville: 203

Bensburg: 491, 493
Benson, Col. Clarence C.: 98, 101-03
Benson Island: 170
Benut: 19-20
Berange Farm: 324
Berchtesgaden: 529, 531
Berdichev: 160
Berdorf: 355, 362
Berescheid: 391
Berg: 339, 375, 382-83, 394, 415, 417-18, 426, 500, 517
Berg Gladbach: 487, 493
Berg Neukirchen: 495
Berg Neustadt: 487
Berg, sur-Moselle: 318-19
Berga: 498
Berge: 485
Bergen: 438-39, 459, 500
Bergen-op-Zoom: 307, 309, 312, 314
Bergerhausen: 415
Bergeval: 367
Berghausen: 445, 468
Bergheid: 437
Bergheim: 414, 418, 420, 462
Bergkirchen: 470
Bergmatting: 514
Bergnassau: 457
Bergoldsheim: 518
Bergrheinfeld: 485
Bergstadt: 496
Bergstein: 340, 344-46, 392, 394-95, 397-99
Bergweiler: 432, 434
Bergzabern: 448, 450
Bergzabern Landkreis: 516
Bérigny: 229
Bering Sea, Komandorski Islands naval battle: 100
Berislav: 179
Berka: 465, 468, 470, 472, 485
Berkey, Rear Adm. R. S.: 452
Berkoth: 410
Berlar: 483
Berle: 370-71
Berlebeck: 4719, 472
Berleberg: 468
Berlichingen: 477
Berlin
  air attacks on: 85, 89, 173, 178, 215
  drive on, from east: 379, 387, 389, 394, 436, 498, 505, 509, 511, 513, 516, 518, 520, 523, 527-28
  drive on, from west: 458
  first U.S. air attack on: 178
Berlin (North Gugegwe) Island: 170
Berlize: 324
Bermering: 324
Bernam River: 11
Bernay: 254-55
Bernburg: 175, 498, 500
Berne Canal: 480, 482
Berneck: 502
Bernkastel: 444.
Berrendorf: 414-15
Berrenrath: 425
Berscheid: 411
Bertholdsdorf: 505
Bertinoro: 310
Bertogne: 373-74
Bertrange: 321, 323-26
Bertrichamps: 316

Bertring: 330
Berus: 341
Berzdorf: 429
Besançon: 262-66, 325
Bessarabia sector: 181, 184
Bessenich: 420
Besslich: 421
Best: 278-79, 281
Besten: 456
Bestwig: 478
BETA: 362, 508. *See also* Canton; Hong Kong; Kweilin; Liuchow.
Betelgeuse: 53
Béthouart, Gen. Emile (Fr.): 264
Bethune: 262
Betio Atoll: 148-49
Betlange: 369, 371
Bettborn: 335
Bettelhoven: 427
Bettendorf: 327-29, 377-78
Bettenfeld: 432
Bettenhausen: 479
Bettingen: 273, 413
Bettviller: 351
Beulbar: 490
Beulich: 439
Beulwitz: 490
Beurig: 411, 414
Beutelsdorf: 492
Beuthen: 386, 402
Beuzeville-au-Plain: 203
Beuzeville-la-Bastille: 208
Bevagna: 211
Bevano River: 311, 313
Beveland Canal: 312
Beveland Isthmus: 292, 309-12, 314-16
Beverly (South Gugegwe) Island: 170
Bevern: 480
Beverungen: 429
Bewingen: 429
Bezange-la-Petite: 280, 289, 320
Bezaumont: 269-70
Beziers: 246
Bhamo: 35-36, 61, 197, 174, 304, 314, 322, 326-27, 333, 339, 342, 345, 348, 349, 351-54
Biak Island
  in air support of Marianas: 211
  first tank battle in SWPA: 198-99
  operations on: 189-91, 196-202, 204-23, 225-31, 234-35, 238, 241, 244, 247, 249, 251, 253
Bialystok: 237, 246
Biancavilla: 125
Bibbiena: 204, 232-33, 259
Biberach: 505, 521
Bibersfeld: 500, 503
Biblis: 455
Bibo, Lt. Col. Harold S.: 257-58, 260-61
Bibolo Hill: 124
Bicol Peninsula: 435, 437, 450, 452, 467, 469, 471, 477, 479-81, 484, 486, 490, 499, 505, 511, 522, 527, 529-30, 535, 538, 546
Bidor: 10
Biebelsheim: 441
Bieberbach River: 442-43
Biebrich: 459
Bielefeld: 468
Bielstein: 487

Bien Wald: 354, 446-48
Biersdorf: 458
Bierstadt: 459
Biesdorf: 273, 399
Biesheim: 390-91
Biéville: 203
Bièvre: 264
Biewels: 405-06
Biferno River: 138-39
Biffontaine: 309
Big Escarpment. *See* Maeda Escarpment.
Bigallo: 299
Bigej Island: 170
Bigonville: 359-61
Bigti: 539
Bihain: 370-72
Biliau: 175
Bilin: 14, 18
Bilin River: 24-25
Biliran Strait: 362
Billig: 426
Bilsdorf: 444
Bilstein: 353
Binahaan River: 314-15
Binalonan: 8, 376-78
Binday: 370
Bingen: 441, 444-45, 447, 452
Bingerbruch: 443
Bingerbruck: 457
Bining: 345-46
Binscheid: 46-48
Binsfeld: 381-82, 412, 429
Binswangen: 514
Binuangan River: 19, 32
Bir el Gubi: 3
Bir Hacheim: 21-22, 26, 39-41
Bir Soltane: 100-101
Birgden: 293
Birgel: 427
Birgelen: 416
Birgen: 416, 418
Biri Island: 406-07, 411
Birk: 299, 301, 504
Birkenfeld: 442
Birkengang: 327-28
Birkenwald: 333-34
Birkesdorf: 410
Birnberg Hill: 424
Birks, Col. Hammond D.: 476, 478, 480, 483
Birresborn: 426, 428
Birtlingen: 414
Biscari: 119
Bischent Woods: 381
Bischofsburg: 386
Bischofsheim: 457, 459
Bischofsreuth: 519
Bischoltz: 383
Bischwihr: 386-87
Bischwiller: 346-48, 380, 390
Bishenpur: 186
Bishi River: 467
Biske: 360
Bislich: 452
Bismarck Archipelago: 30-31, 40
Bismarck Archipelago Campaign: 140, 154-338 *See also* Admiralty Islands; New Britain; New Guinea; New Ireland.
Bismarck Sea: 408

Bismarck Sea naval-air battle: 96
Bismark: 486
Bissell, Maj. Gen. Clayton L.: 50, 55, 60, 121
Bissingen: 481
Bisten: 342
Bistroff: 329
Bitburg: 413-14, 416-17, 423
Bitches 343, 351-52, 356, 362, 365-78, 439, 441, 443, 448
Bitoi River: 115, 117
Bitschhoffen: 439
Bitterfeld: 496, 504, 506, 508
Bitzfeld: 494
Biwisch: 381
Bizerte, drive on: 65, 67, 99-110
Bizery: 365
Black Forest: 471, 475, 492, 496, 498, 500, 503, 505, 507, 514, 516, 518
Black Mountains: 483
Black Sea sector: 186, 259
BLACKCOCK: 325. *See also* Meuse River; Boer River; Roermond; Wurm River.
BLACKPOOL: 197
Blainville: 189
Blarney, Gen. Sir Thomas (Aus.): 42
  CG of Allied Land Forces, SWPA: 34
  CG of New Guinea forces: 56, 74, 115,129
  New Guinea offensive, plan for: 54, 63
Blâmont: 328-29, 331
Blandy, Rear Adm. William H. B.: 274 403
Blankenberg: 494, 504
Blankenburg: 506
Blankenheim: 429, 489
Blankenheimerdorf: 429
Blankenship (Loi) Island: 169-70
Blatzheim: 414
Blaufelden: 485, 492
Bleckede: 519-20, 524
Bleckhausen: 432
Bleialf: 270, 275, 389-91
Blémerey: 313
Blenod: 263
Blens: 402, 418
Blerick: 340, 343,472, 474
Blessem: 422
Blette River: 316-17
Blida: 64
Blies River: 349-52, 404, 439
Bliesbruck: 350-51
Bliesheim: 424
Blieskastel: 445
Bliesransbach: 412
BLOCKBUSTER: 433 *See also* Calcar; Udem; Xanten.
Blodelsheim: 397
Bloody Ridge (Guadalcanal): 54-55
Bloody Ridge (Ie Shima): 501, 503, 506, 508, 510
Bloody Ridge (Leyte): 318-20, 323
Bloody Triangle (New Guinea). *See* Triangle, The (New Guinea).
Blue Ridge (Luzon): 378, 380
Blumenthal: 393, 427
Boac: 367, 372
Boatner, Brig. Gen. Haydon L.: 150, 160, 168, 199, 204, 210, 219

Bobbau: 500
Bobbau-Steinfurth: 504, 506
Bobdubi Ridge: 106, 115
Bobenthal: 354, 443
Bobonan: 378, 382
Bobruisk: 216, 219, 221
Bobstadt: 455
Bocaue: 290
Bocholt: 458, 460
Bochum: 485
Bock and Teich: 490
Bockelnhagen: 485
Bocket: 378
Bockholz-sur-Sure: 371, 384-85
Bockingen: 469, 473, 475
Boden: 528
Bodenheim: 424
Bodenwerder: 476
Boedefeld: 480
Boehl: 448
Boehlen: 192
Boeingsen: 491
Boerem, Maj. Richard D.: 65, 69
Boero: 68
Boeur: 379
Boevange-les-Clervaux: 380
Bofu: 61-62, 66
Bogadjim: 186
Bogel: 457
Bogon Island: 173
Bogtong: 378
Boguchar: 45
Bohol Island: 34, 430, 486, 488, 490-91, 497. 501, 506-07, 510, 512, 513, 515, 523, 547
Boice, Capt. William F.: 55-57, 60
Boich: 414
Bois aux Chênes: 379
Bois d'Amélécourt: 320-22
Bois de Belhez: 372
Bois de Benamont: 289
Bois de Bénestroff: 329
Bois de Blies Brucken: 368, 403
Bois de Bonnefontaine: 335-36
Bois de Born: 379
Bois de Cedrogne: 372-73
Bois de Chenicourt: 298
Bois de Conthil: 324
Bois de Drusenheim: 393, 396-97
Bois de Faulx: 277, 284-85
Bois de Freybouse: 331
Bois de Gaumont: 267
Bois de Groumont: 367
Bois de Kerfent: 337-38
Bois de Kerpeche: 325
Bois de Koenigsmacker Ridge: 323
Bois de la Brique: 213
Bois de la Rumont: 277, 281, 283-84
Bois de l'Hôpital: 324-26
Bois d'Elzange Ridge: 322-24
Bois de Meudon: 254
Bois d'Emmels: 378-79
Bois de Ohlungen: 383
Bois de Ronce: 375
Bois de Roudou: 214
Bois de Rouvroy: 380-81
Bois de St. Jean: 372
Bois de St. Vith: 385
Bois de Sessenheim: 377
Bois de Tave: 366
Bois de Woippy: 326

[INDEX]

Bois du Coudray: 215
Bois du Mont du Roc: 214-15
Bois Houby: 368
Bois Jacques: 366, 371, 373
Bois St. Martin: 322
Boise: 58
Boisheim: 418
Boissau, Gen. Robert (Fr.): 97
Boizenburg: 526
Bokpyin: 7, 10
BOLERO: 30, 33, 42. *See also* Normandy Campaign, planning phase.
Bolkhov: 122
Bollendorf: 400-402
Bollingen: 427
Bolo Ridge: 467, 469, 471
Bologna, drive on: 232, 243, 250, 276, 291-363, 497-509
Bolong Plateau: 538
Bolongtohan: 309
Bolsdorf: 429
Bombardment and Fire Support Group (TG 77.2): 367
Bombardment Groups
  5th: 187
  11th: 46, 136
  17th: 34
  308th: 98
  313th: 458
Bombardment Squadrons
  26th: 46 42d: 46
  98th: 46
  431st: 46
Bombardment Wing,
  19th: 66
Bombeck: 508
Bomber Command, AAF: 33
Bomber Commands
  VIII: 25, 72, 87, 150
  IX: 69, 115
  XII: 138, 141
  XIII: 186
  XX: 166, 173, 202, 211, 226, 355, 370
  XXI: 370, 383,
Bombiana: 302
Bomboe Peninsula: 131, 133-35
Bombogen: 434
Bompietro: 122
Bomporto: 509
Bondeno: 511, 513
Bône: 66, 67, 81
Bonegi River: 89-90
Bonerath: 437
Bonga: 150
Bongabon :403
Bongabong: 365
Bongao Island: 469, 478
Bonin Islands air-naval actions: 211
  seizure plans: 204
Bonis: 143
Bonlieu: 255-57
Bonn: 267, 293, 427, 429-32, 445, 452, 462
Bonnerue: 367-69, 371
Bontoc: 549
Booth, Brig. Gen. Donald P.: 156
Bopfingen: 509, 511
Boppard: 440-41, 443-44, 447, 449, 452, 454, 457
Bor: 532-33

Bora Bora: 24, 30
Boram: 128
Bordeaux: 251
Borello River: 304, 307
Borg: 338, 406
Borgen Bay: 159, 163
Borghi: 291
Borgo Grappa: 197
Borgo S. Lorenzo: 260, 263, 267
Borgoforte: 505
Borgolzhausen: 468
Borisov: 222
Borken: 458, 463
Born: 375-80
Borna: 494, 496, 508
Borneo
  Allied retirement to: 9
  attacks on enemy shipping: 6
  British North Borneo surrendered: 16
  enemy air attacks on: 19
  enemy seizure of: 5-6, 8-10, 13, 15
  installations destroyed by Allies: 5
  RAF retirement from: 13
  recovery of: 527, 545-50
Bornheim: 429
Bornich: 454
Borokoe: 214, 241
Borr: 420
Borscheid: 451
Borschemich: 415
Borth: 432
Boschleiden: 362
Boslar: 410
Bosnek: 198-99
Bosoboso River and Valley: 446, 449, 451, 453, 457, 499, 501, 510, 540. *See also* New Bosoboso; New Bosoboso River
Bosserode: 465
Bottenbroich: 422
Bottenhorn: 458
Bottenweiler: 505
Bottrop: 462
Botzdorf: 429
Bou Arada Valley: 83, 86, 88, 95, 106
Bou Chebka: 89-90, 94, 97-98, 103
Bou Ficha: 109-10
Bou Hamran: 99
Bou Sfer: 65
Bougainville Island
  air-naval actions: 116, 140-41, 143-45, 153-55, 161, 179
  armor actions: 146, 180-81
  casualties: 146
  Empress Augusta Bay naval battle 143
  enemy landings and reinforcements: 17, 145
  Rabaul, enemy threat from: 144-45
  recovery of: 122-23, 132, 135-36, 138-63, 179-84
  supply situation: 147
  U.S. reinforcements: 145-47, 149, 152, 156
Bougainville Strait: 123
Bougie: 66
Bougy: 231
Boulaide: 362
Boulay: 336
Boulay-Moselle: 330
Boulogne: 263, 268, 271, 276, 284, 287

Bourcy: 366, 371, 373, 374, 376-77, 379
Bourdon: 361
Bourg-en-Bresse: 260, 262-63
Bourgaltroff: 329
Bourges: 191
Bourgoin: 257
Bourguebus: 233
Bourheim: 332-34, 336-37
Bourscheid: 380
Bouxières-sous-Froidmont: 278
Bouxwiller: 333-34, 366
Bouzonville: 326, 329
Bova Marina: 130
Bovenberger Wald: 330
Bovenden: 483
Bovert: 4 18
Bovigny: 370, 373-74, 378
Bowerman, Brig. John F. (Br.): 168
Boxberg: 429
Boxhorn: 380
Boxmeer: 291
Boyer, Lt. Col. Howard E.: 343-45
Bra: 361-62
Brachbach: 476
Brachelen: 384
Bracht: 460, 483
Bradford, Brig. Gen. William B.: 512, 515
Bradley, Lt. Gen. Omar N.: 97, 117. *See also* Armies, First; Army Groups, 12th; Corps, II.
  CG of First Army: 166
  CG of II Corps: 104
  CG of 12th Army Group: 203, 236, 240, 247, 255, 257, 267, 298, 307, 317
Brambauer: 472, 474, 484, 495, 499
Brandenberg: 340-44, 379
Brandenberger Wald: 341, 343
Brandenburg: 388, 403, 530
Brangbram Stream: 163
Brandscheid: 273, 275, 277, 392-94, 397
Bras: 370-73
BRASSARD: 212-13
Bratislava: 463, 465, 467, 471, 473
Braubach: 452, 454
Brauchitsch, Field Marshal Walther von (Ger.): 1, 7
Braunau: 526, 528-29, 531-32
Braunlage: 500
Braunlauf: 381
Braunsberg: 446
Braunschweig. *See* Brunswick.
Braunsrath: 379
Brauweiler: 424
Brazil, declares war on Germany and Italy: 51
Brazilian Expeditionary Force: 225, 273, 275, 277, 279, 282-83, 290-92, 296, 299-300, 313, 315, 319, 408-12, 417, 423, 425-26, 428, 483, 495, 499, 501, 503, 513, 518, 521, 523, 527
Breakneck Ridge (Leyte): 318-26, 328, 334
Breberen: 294, 378-79
Brécey: 239-40
Brechten: 487
Brécy: 203

[573]

Breda: 309, 313-14
Bree: 283
Bregenz: 525, 527
Bréhal: 239
Breidfeld: 382
Breidt: 485, 487
Breistroff-la-Petit: 323
Breitenbach: 492
Breitenhagen: 495, 502, 504, 506
Breiterwald: 352
Breitfeld: 386
Breitingen: 494
Breitscheid: 449, 456, 458
Bremen: 113, 139, 150, 478, 480, 484, 486, 491, 493, 495, 497, 499, 501, 504, 514-15 517, 533
Bremen Enclave Military District: 526
Bremen-Hamburg Autobahn: 503
Brémenil: 328
Brémoncourt: 268
Brenig: 429
Brenner Pass: 130, 527, 530-51
Brennero: 531
Brenta River: 523, 527
Brenta Valley: 523, 527
Brereton, Maj. Gen. Lewis H.: 6
  as CG of ABDA tactical forces: 15
  as CG of Desert Air TF: 60
  as CG of Middle East Air Force: 43
  as CG of Ninth Air Force: 141
  as CG of IX Air Service Command: 66
  as CG of Tenth Air Force: 27, 43
  as CG of USAFIME: 42-43, 90, 133
  as CG of USAAFUK: 141
  directs assault on Rumania: 124
  transfers from Java to India: 25
Brescia: 224, 521, 525
Breskens Pocket: 284, 296-98, 302, 304, 306, 308, 310, 312, 314-17
Breslau: 382-83, 394-95 400-402, 404, 406, 410, 417, 457, 463, 481, 518, 534
Brest: 242-49, 251, 254, 256-61, 265, 267, 270-71, 273-75, 277-79, 284, 287
Brest Litovsk: 234, 236, 238
Brett, Maj. Gen. George H:
  as CG of Allied Air Force, SWPA: 29, 34, 45, 48
  as CG of Australia supply base: 6
  as CG of USAFIA and USFIA: 10, 12
  transfers from Java to Australia: 25
Brettach River: 492,
Bretteville-le-Rabet: 245-46
Bretteville-l'Orgueilleuse: 203, 218
Bretteville-sur-Odon: 227
Brettevillette: 220
Breteuil: 253-54
Bretzenheim: 444-45
Breungeshain: 463
Brévands: 205-06
BREWER: 176-78. See also Admiralty Islands campaign.
Brey: 442
Brezolle: 252
Briançon: 257-58, 260-61, 263, 265
Bricqueville: 206
Bridget, Comdr. Francis J. (USN): 17
Brieg: 384, 394-95
Briey: 265

Brignoles: 250-52
Brilon: 460, 464
Briloner Stadt Forst: 472
Brimingen: 411, 413
BRIMSTONE: 115, 121. See also Sardinia.
Brindisi: 131, 133
Brink, Col. Francis G.: 146, 160
Brinkum: 497
Briouze: 250-51
Brisach: 351, 384, 386
Brisbane: 8, 177
Brisy: 374-75, 378
Britain, Battle of: 3
British Air Force. See Royal Air Force.
British Army units
  Army Groups
    11: 145-46, 148, 161, 170-72, 175-89, 191, 193, 202, 206, 212, 216, 223, 228, 230, 238, 240, 243-44, 263, 274, 277, 290, 295, 306, 316-18, 321, 324
    18: 93-110, 112
    21: 203-72, 274, 276, 278-79, 281-92, 294-98 301-21, 323-34, 338, 340 342-43, 351, 353, 355-56, 358-85, 387-96, 398-409, 411-13, 415-161 418, 420-21, 423, 425, 427-28, 430, 432-34, 436, 438, 449-50, 452, 453, 456, 458, 460, 462, 464, 466, 468, 469, 472, 474, 476, 478, 480, 482, 484, 486, 488, 491, 493, 495, 497, 499, 501, 504, 506, 512, 514-15, 517, 519-20, 522, 524-27 529-30, 532
  Northern Group of Armies: 260
  Armies
    First: 65-75, 77, 81-83, 86-110
    Second: 203-10, 213, 216, 218-22, 224-29, 231-34, 236, 239, 241-71, 274, 276, 278-79, 281-82, 284-92, 297-98, 301-02, 304-05, 308, 312-21, 323, 325, 327-34, 340, 343, 351, 353, 355, 356, 360-61, 363, 365, 367-68, 370-71, 373-84, 394, 404, 08, 430, 449, 450, 452-53, 456, 458, 460, 462, 464, 466, 468-69, 472, 474, 476, 478, 480, 482, 484, 486, 488, 491, 493, 495, 497, 499, 501, 504, 508, 512, 514-15, 517, 519-20, 522, 524-27, 529
    Eighth: 3-6, 8-22, 28-29, 38-50, 52-54, 60-70, 74-79, 82-89, 91-105, 107, 110, 117-29, 131-47, 149-53, 155-57, 159, 162, 165, 174, 183, 187, 189, 191-202, 204-07, 209-15, 217-28, 230-39, 241-43, 246-68, 270-72, 274, 276-77 279-80, 282-83, 285-326, 328-30, 332-54, 356-58, 364, 366, 368-69, 377, 399, 401-02, 404, 413, 419, 421, 423, 425, 430, 434-35 437, 451, 453, 467, 469, 473, 475, 477, 479,

British Army Units—Continued
  Armies—Continued
    Eighth—Continued
      483-84 486, 488, 490, 492, 495, 497, 499, 501, 503, 505, 507, 509, 511, 513, 515, 517-18, 522-23, 525, 527-28
    Ninth: 12, 25, 35
    Tenth: 12, 25, 35, 38
    Twelfth: 541, 545
    Fourteenth: 146-48, 161, 170, 172, 175-87, 189, 191, 193-95, 202, 212, 214, 216, 223, 228, 230, 238, 240, 243-44, 263, 274, 277, 290, 295, 306, 316-18, 321, 325, 327, 331, 333, 343, 344, 347, 350, 353-54, 356-57, 360, 362-67, 369, 371-72, 374-75, 381, 385, 399, 401-04, 408-09, 412-14, 416-17, 421, 425-26, 430, 433, 435-36, 438-39, 442, 445-47 449-50, 459, 461, 463, 467, 475, 486, 488, 490, 492, 499, 503, 505, 507, 509, 511, 517-18, 522-23, 525, 528, 533, 537, 541.
  Army of the Rhine: 532
  Burma: 5, 9, 27-28, 33, 36
  Eastern Army in Burma: 75, 111
  Corps
    1 Airborne: 276, 278-79, 281-82,284-88, 298
    1 Burma: 29-34, 36, 38
    1: 203-04, 206-07, 216, 224, 226-28, 232-33, 235, 240, 246, 249, 252-53 255, 257, 259-62, 267-69, 276, 281, 286-87, 290-92, 294-95, 297, 303, 307-08, 311-21, 466, 468
    3: 262, 304
    5: 72, 74, 77, 81-83, 86, 93, 95-109, 113, 131, 136-37, 140, 142-45, 147, 149-53, 155-57, 183, 191, 204-05, 207, 210, 212, 255-57 259-64, 266-68, 270-72, 274, 276-77, 279-80, 282-83, 285-304, 306, 308-22, 324-26, 328, 330, 332-42, 344-45, 347-48, 352-54, 356-58, 364, 366, 368-69, 372, 404, 413, 421, 423, 425, 430, 435, 453, 467, 469, 473, 475, 477, 479, 483-84, 486, 490, 492, 495, 497, 499, 501 503, 505, 507, 509, 511, 513, 515-16, 518, 522-23
    8: 219-22, 224, 228-29, 232-33, 239-43 246-49 251, 276, 278-79, 281, 284-87, 291, 297, 302, 304-05, 313-21, 330,333, 340, 355, 402, 418, 430, 433, 458, 460, 462, 464, 466, 468, 470 472, 474, 480, 482, 484, 486, 489, 491, 493, 495, 497, 499, 501, 504, 514, 520, 522, 524, 525, 527, 529

[INDEX]

British Army Units—Continued
  Corps—Continued
    9: 98, 102–110
    10: 43, 50, 53, 61–64, 66–69, 82, 99–105, 113, 132–34, 136–47, 151–53, 157, 160–67, 169, 171, 173, 183–84, 187, 191, 198–200, 203–04, 206–07, 209–14, 217, 219–222, 225–26, 232–35, 243, 247, 259, 263, 272, 279–80, 289, 298–99, 303, 338, 343, 346, 435, 453, 484, 488, 495, 501, 507, 509, 528
    12: 229, 231–32, 234, 241–49, 251, 255–60, 262–64, 268–70, 274, 276, 278–79, 281, 284, 290, 308, 312–16, 319–21, 325, 327–28, 330–33, 340, 343, 351, 361, 375–79, 381–84, 394, 449–50 452–53, 456, 458, 460, 462, 464, 468–70, 472, 474, 476, 480, 482, 484, 486, 489, 491, 495, 497, 499, 501, 504, 512, 517, 527, 529
    13: 3–10, 12–14, 16–22, 26, 39–45, 47, 52–54, 60–62, 117–21, 123, 125–26, 128, 131–44, 149, 151, 153, 156, 165, 183, 189, 191–95, 197–99, 201–02, 204–07, 209–11, 213–15, 217–28, 230–38, 240, 243, 246–48 251, 253, 255–64, 266–67, 269, 271–72, 274, 276–77, 279, 282–83, 285–92, 294–313, 317–19 321–23, 325, 327–28, 334, 338–42 344, 346–48, 350–52, 354, 358–59, 370, 372, 377, 401, 404, 413, 419, 434–35 437, 453, 484, 495, 497, 501, 503, 505, 507, 511, 513, 515, 518, 522–23, 525, 527–28
    30: 3–5, 10, 14–16, 26, 39–47, 52–53, 60–64, 82, 84, 96–97, 99–104, 118–27, 203, 205–10, 218–20, 222, 228, 231–32, 235, 239–49, 251, 253–54, 256–65, 267, 269–70, 274, 276, 278–80, 282, 284–87, 320–21, 323, 329, 331–34, 351, 353, 356, 360–61, 363, 365, 367–68, 370–71, 373, 396, 398–408, 411–12, 415, 418, 420–21, 423, 425, 427–28, 449, 452–53 456, 458, 462, 464, 466, 468, 472, 474, 476, 480, 482, 484, 486, 488, 491, 495, 497, 499, 501, 504, 514–15, 517, 522, 526
    34: 536, 541–42
  Divisions
    1st Airborne: 117–18, 131–33, 135, 137, 276, 281, 284–55, 287–88
    1st Armoured: 12, 18, 3 9–40, 61–64, 66, 99–101, 105–06, 271, 274, 279, 282–83, 285, 287, 290, 298–99, 305

British Army Units—Continued
  Divisions—Continued
    1st Burma Infantry: 5, 26–30, 33–34
    1st Infantry: 98, 100, 105–06, 108–09, 113, 164–67, 170–73, 175–76, 184, 197, 199–200, 202, 247, 255, 256, 260–61, 264, 266–67, 269, 271–72, 274, 277, 282–53, 285–92, 294–98, 300–301, 305–06, 309, 317–18, 321, 334 341, 346, 370, 377
    2d Infantry: 185–87, 202, 243, 356, 360, 364, 367, 369, 371, 412, 421, 442, 447, 463, 507, 541
    3d Infantry: 203, 224, 226–27, 241, 243, 246, 249, 275, 279, 301–02, 304–05, 415, 420, 427, 430, 456, 491, 495, 497, 504, 520
    4th Infantry: 103–07, 109–10, 183, 191–94, 206–07, 215, 217–22, 225, 233–35, 238, 265, 274 276–77, 279–80, 283, 285, 305–12, 314–16, 318, 320–26, 333–34, 336–38
    5th Infantry: 118–21, 123, 125–26, 128, 131–32, 134–37, 140, 143, 153, 156, 162–63, 165, 167, 179, 184, 202, 501, 519, 522, 526
    6th Airborne: 203, 249, 253, 361, 367, 371, 450, 452–54, 456, 458, 460, 462, 464, 466, 472, 478, 489 499, 508, 524, 526–27
    6th Armoured: 74–75, 81, 83, 86, 93–95, 98, 103–04, 106–07, 109–10, 203–08, 214, 219–24, 231, 233–34, 247, 256, 258–59, 266, 268–71, 274, 277, 279–80, 283, 286–89, 293–94, 298–99, 305, 310–13, 317–18, 334 342–44 348 350–52, 358, 377, 402, 419, 503, 509, 511, 513, 515, 522, 525
    6th Infantry: 202, 233
    7th Armoured. 7–9, 12, 39, 41–43, 61–62, 64, 66, 69, 74–75, 84, 88–89, 93, 95, 99–100, 104–05, 107, 109, 134, 136, 138, 140, 142–43, 147, 207–10, 232–33, 240–41, 243, 249, 252–53, 259–63, 268–69, 274, 308, 325, 374–78, 380–83, 394, 453, 456, 458, 460, 462, 464, 468, 470 480, 482, 497, 504, 529
    10th Armoured: 50, 61
    11th Armoured: 219, 229, 232, 239–41, 243, 249, 251, 253, 258–62, 265–66, 279, 286, 297, 305, 313 413, 415–16, 423, 430 460, 462, 464, 466, 478–79, 501, 504, 525, 527
    11th East African: 263, 295, 325, 343–44, 356

British Army Units—Continued
  Divisions—Continued
    15th Infantry: 219, 229, 231–32, 235, 239, 243, 255–58, 270, 308, 313, 315, 319, 327, 330, 333, 396–403, 405, 407, 412, 450, 452–53, 489, 493, 497, 499, 501, 522, 524, 526
    18th Infantry: 5, 14–16, 20–22
    36th Infantry: 184, 191, 226, 244, 257, 286, 304, 311, 314, 316, 322–23, 328, 337–38, 341, 349, 352, 354, 356, 363, 382, 388–91, 397, 399, 402, 405, 434, 446, 463, 467
    43d Infantry: 219, 224, 228–29, 234, 239, 241–44, 256, 258, 274, 284–86, 321, 329 361, 378–83 398–405, 407, 423, 425, 427, 430, 415–16, 432, 452–53, 456, 462, 474, 482, 488, 495, 504
    44th Infantry: 50, 61–62
    46th Infantry: 75, 92, 95–106, 133, 137, 140, 142–43, 147, 151, 161, 165–67, 171, 255, 261–63, 268, 274, 276–77, 279–80, 282, 285–91, 297–303, 305–06, 317, 320–21, 324–26, 332–34, 336–37 340 344–45, 347
    49th Infantry: 218–19, 240, 246, 249, 253, 259–62, 267, 276, 286, 290, 292, 307, 309, 317–18, 331–33, 468, 488, 495
    50th Infantry: 39–41, 61–62, 99–100, 103–05, 118–21, 125–26, 128, 203–05, 208–09, 226, 225, 231, 239, 242, 246–47, 254, 259–60, 265–66, 265, 270, 274, 278, 257, 321
    51st Infantry: 61, 63, 74, 85–87, 93, 95–96, 101, 103–04, 118–21, 126, 128, 216, 225, 244–46, 249, 259–62, 267, 276, 308, 319, 321, 325, 330–33, 358, 361, 370, 373, 396, 398–405, 408, 415, 430, 449–50, 452–53, 456, 489, 495
    52d Infantry: 306, 312, 314, 316–18, 377–83, 392, 394, 404, 415, 421, 428, 430, 432–33, 470, 504
    53d Infantry: 228, 321–32, 242, 246, 251, 259–60, 262, 270, 274, 279, 308, 312, 315–17, 321, 325, 332–33, 365, 367–68, 370, 396, 398, 400, 404, 411–12, 420, 423, 427–28, 453, 458, 460, 462, 464, 484, 486, 489, 495, 527, 529
    56th Infantry: 110, 133–34, 139–41, 143–46, 151–52, 163, 165–66, 171, 173–77, 179, 264, 266, 276–77, 279 283, 285, 287–91, 297, 300–301, 325–26, 328, 340 356–57, 366, 423, 430, 435, 473

British Army Units—Continued
  Divisions—Continued
    56th Infantry—Continued
      475, 477, 479, 486, 488, 490, 492, 495, 497, 516, 518, 522
    59th Infantry: 226, 231, 243, 246, 248
    70th Infantry: 3, 24, 170, 178
    78th Infantry: 64, 66-72, 74, 81-82, 86, 89, 91, 98, 101, 103-07, 121, 123-28, 134, 137-40, 142, 145, 147, 151, 153, 174, 183, 193-94, 198, 204, 210, 215, 217-21, 223, 295, 299, 302-09, 334, 348, 351, 358, 377, 401, 435, 486, 490, 492, 495, 497, 501, 511
    79th Armoured: 203, 524
    81st West African: 176-77, 351
    82d West African: 351, 353, 384, 387, 404, 522, 535, 537, 541
    Guards Armoured: 232-33, 23941, 243, 259-62, 264-68, 274, 276, 278-80, 282, 284, 321, 402, 404, 412, 430, 454, 456, 458, 460, 462, 464, 469, 476, 480, 482, 488, 495, 499, 522: 95, 98
  Brigades
    1st Air Landing: 117, 119
    1st Armoured: 39
    1st Army Tank: 10-11, 39
    1st Burma: 5
    1st Commando: 421, 449-50, 452, 454, 458
    1st Guards: 74, 77-78
    1st Malaya: 21
    1st Parachute: 67, 71, 95, 97-99, 101
    2d Burma: 5
    2d Commando: 467, 469, 473, 486, 492, 497
    2d Malaya: 21
    2d Parachute: 254., 262
    2d Special Service: 138, 164, 169
    3d Commando: 367, 372, 381
    3d West African: 186
    4th Armoured: 79, 150-51, 229, 259, 316, 331, 453
    4th Special Service: 276, 316-17
    7th Armoured: 25, 33-34 340, 366, 430
    8th Armoured: 203, 218-19, 258, 321
    9th Armoured: 63, 221-22
    9th Infantry: 50
    14th Infantry: 170, 185
    16th Infantry: 170, 194
    22d Armoured: 9-10, 40, 85-86
    22d East African: 54-56, 542
    22d Infantry: 40
    23d Armoured: 46, 151, 262
    23d Infantry: 170, 186, 194
    23d LRP: 223
    25th Tank: 265
    28th East African: 371-72, 381, 399, 402
British Army Units—Continued
  Brigades—Continued
    29th Armoured: 360
    31st Tank: 229
    32d Army Tank: 40
    38th Infantry: 95, 98
    53d Infantry: 14-16, 18
    69th Infantry: 40
    72d Infantry: 322, 338
    132d Infantry: 50
    50th Infantry: 39
    201st Guards: 39, 41, 163
    255th Tank: 409, 463, 467, 486
    Lushai: 371-72
  Regiments
    17/21 Lancers: 67
    74th Light AA: 290, 296
    Coldstream Guards: 113
    Duke of Wellington's: 202
    King's Dragoon Guards: 217
  Battalions
    1st Commando: 64
    1st Parachute: 67-68
    2d Commando: 133
    3d Parachute: 66
    4th Parachute: 301-02
    6th Commando: 64, 66
    9th Commando: 138, 157, 164-65, 169, 177, 275, 292, 298, 302
    40th Commando: 13 8, 164, 169, 177
    41st Commando: 133, 316
    47th Royal Marines Commando: 203-05, 316
    48th Commando: 316
  Groups
    16th LRPG: 172, 177, 189
    39th Light AA: 296
    47th Light AA: 296
  Forces
    Advance Coastal: 275, 292
    Blade: 67-68, 70-71, 74
    140: 262, 275, 304
    W: 536
    Delta: 43
    Drewforce: 329
    Hart: 66, 68-69
    Krohcol: 5-6
    Lind Task: 280
    Special (Wingate): 91, 111, 170, 177-78,181-83
British Commonwealth. See United Kingdom; commonwealths by name.
British Chiefs of Staff. See also Combined Chiefs of Staff.
  ARCADIA Conference: 6
  plans for recovery of Mandalay: 260, 293
  plans for recovery of Myitkyina: 186
  plans for Southern France: 182, 246
  proposed assault on Rangoon: 260, 293
  warned of enemy offensive in Burma 172
British Joint Staff Mission: 354
British Navy. See Royal Navy.
British Troops in Egypt: 16
British War Cabinet: 293

Brittany Peninsula: 240-43, 250, 263, 279, 290
Britten, 437 439
BROADWAY (Burma): 178, 120, 312. See also Indian Army units, Divisions, 3d and Brigades, 77th LRP (Chindits).
Brockau: 498
Brockensen: 474
Brodenbach: 432
Brodnica: 382
Brody: 230, 232-33
Brohl: 432
Broich: 410, 420
Broichhoven: 378
Broichweiden: 328-28
Bromberg: 381-82, 387, 403
Bronn River: 469
Bronsfeld: 391
Bronte: 126
Brooke, Gen. Sir Alan: 146
Brooke-Popham, Air Chief Marshal Sir Robert: 5, 9
Brookings (Oregon), bombed by Japanese plane: 54
Brooks, Maj. Gen. Edward H.: 278, 311
Broome: 27
Brotdorf: 442
Brouvelieures: 300, 303, 307-08
Brown, Maj. Gen. Albert E.: 102, 110-11
Bru: 314
Bruch: 432
Bruchhausen: 432, 474
Bruchsal: 466-67, 469
Bruck: 413, 429, 431-32
Bruckberg: 522
Bruenn: 498, 505, 516, 518, 523
Bruenst: 500
Bruex: 192
Bruges: 265-66, 269-70
Bruges-Ghent Canal: 264, 266, 268
Bruhl: 380, 429
Brulange: 325
Brunei: 5-6, 546
Brunei Bay: 545
Bruneval: 26
Brungsberg: 442
Brunskappel: 474
Brunswick: 161, 175, 484, 486, 489, 506
Bruscoli: 288
Brussels: 256, 262-63, 267, 353
Brussels, conference on drive on Germany: 305
Bruyères: 287, 300, 303-09
Bryansk: 14, 95-96 125, 128, 130, 133, 135
Bryant Hill (Luzon): 409, 413
Bu Ngem: 79
Buariki Island: 150
Buaya: 361
Bubach: 443
Bubesheim: 512
BUCCANEER: 152. See also Andaman Islands.
Bucconi: 288
Bucharest: 237, 244, 260
Buchau: 500
Buchel: 440

[INDEX]   [577]

Buchenwald: 487
Buchet: 391
Buchholz: 420, 445, 447
Buchholz Forest: 388-90
Buchhorn: 496
Buching: 523
Buchy: 259, 322
Buckner, Lt. Gen. Simon B.: 28, 535, 538, 547
Budalin: 371
Budapest: 295, 300-301, 308, 316, 318, 326, 337, 340-44, 346-49, 351 353-54, 358-66, 369, 372, 374, 377, 379, 388-89, 384-95, 401- 02, 451, 458
Budenthal: 355
Buderrich: 450
Buding: 326
Budingen: 469
Budinger Wald: 463, 469-70
Budling: 326
Budrio: 492, 497, 499, 505
Buebingen: 412
Buechenbeuren: 442
Bued River: 370
Buederich: 433
Buedesheim: 424
Buedingen: 463
Buehl: 492
Buellingen: 353, 355, 375, 382-83, 386
Buer: 462
Buer Hassel: 462
Buerat: 79, 82-85
Bueren: 341, 464
Buergel: 455
Buergeln: 460
Buervenich: 420, 422, 424, 426
Buesbach: 275
Buescheich: 427
Bueschergrund: 482
Buettelborn: 451
Buettgen: 418
BUFFALO: 196. *See also* Anzio Campaign.
Bug River: 180, 233-34
Bugsanga River: 360
Buigap Creek: 117
Buin: 91
Buir: 414
Buisdorf: 447
Buissoncourt: 275
Buissonville: 359-60, 363
Buka Island: 28-29, 149, 156
Bukel Hill: 460, 465, 467, 471
Bulacan: 390
Bulalacao: 364, 368, 376, 379, 385
Bulan: 481, 484, 490
Buldern: 460, 462
Bulgaria
 armistice with Allies: 257, 313-14
 joins Allies: 265
 operations in: 257, 264-65, 275
 U.S. declares war on: 40
 USSR accepts request for armistice: 266
 USSR declares war on: 264
Bulgaria, Italy: 303
Bulgarian forces: 463, 467, 471, 473
Bulgarno: 304
Bulge, Battle of: 353-83

Bullay: 435-36, 440-41
Bulolo Valley: 38, 43, 53
Bulu Plantation: 131
Bumi River: 137
Buna: 43, 45-46, 48-49, 56-57, 61, 63, 67-79, 81-82, 131, 154
Buna Creek: 71
Buna-Gona beachhead: 439 45-46, 48-49, 56-57, 61, 63, 67-79, 81
Buna Mission: 69, 73, 75, 77-79, 81
Buna Village: 69, 71-75, 77-79
Bunawan: 540
Bunga River: 131
Bunina Point: 91
Buonriposo Ridge: 171
Burauen: 308-11, 314, 337, 339, 349
Burbach: 339, 425
Burden: 371, 379
Bures: 283
Buret: 380
Burg: 431, 456
Burg-Berg: 345-47
Burg Grafenrode: 461
Burg Reuland: 386
Burgau: 514
Burgen: 438
Burgbernheim: 492
Burgess, Lt. Col. Henry A.: 548
Burglengenfeld: 510, 512, 514
Burgos: 457, 459-60, 473
Burgstemmen: 476
Burgtreswitz: 514
Buri: 311-13, 339, 346-49
Burias Island: 421, 423, 428, 436
Burma. *See also* China; China-Burma-India Theater; Chiang Kai-shek, Generalissimo; India; India-Burma Theater; Stilwell, Lt. Gen. Joseph W.; Wedemeyer, Gen. Albert C.
 ABDA directive on defense of: 11
 Air-Ground Supply Committee: 459
 air-naval actions: 31, 89, 94-95, 116, 149, 179-80, 183, 185, 187, 189-90, 192, 229-30 317, 333, 371-72, 404, 438, 445, 528
 air supply of withdrawal: 29
 airborne operations and reinforcements: 178-80, 182, 184-87, 200, 2359 367, 438, 441, 449, 469, 501, 528
 Alexander CG of Burma Army: 27
 Alexander moves headquarters to India: 38
 Allied reinforcements: 15-17, 21, 25, 27-28, 157, 183-85, 194, 236, 304, 313, 439
 Allied withdrawal: 29, 34-38
 armor actions: 163, 177-78, 180-82, 190
 AVG, air reinforcement by: 5
 British forces, strength: 5
 Burma Corps formed: 29
 Canton-Hong Kong, recovery in support of: 547
 casualties: 165, 186, 212, 231, 242
 CCS directive on recovery: 391
 Central Burma Campaign: 387-550
 Chiang inspects defenses: 32
 Chinese forces in defense of: 8-9
  See also Yunnan Force.

Burma—Continued
 construction of Ledo and Imphal roads recommended: 14
 defense of, secondary to that of India: 35
 enemy air offensive: 8, 16, 18
 enemy conquest completed: 38
 enemy offensives: 5-10, 171-72, 178-79, 182, 187, 198, 406, 430
 enemy secures central Burma: 35
 fall of: 3-38
 guerrilla activities: 91, 93, 96-97, 111, 183, 193
 lend-lease matériel, impounding of: 7, 9
 LRPG activities: 146, 186, 200, 209, 214, 221, 223, 226, 237. *See also* British Army units, Forces, Special (Wingate); Merrill's Marauders; Wingate, Brig. Orde C.
 Maymyo becomes hq: 28 .
 movement of forces to China: 435, 438, 441, 537, 539
 NCAC and Fourteenth Army link-up: 3, 63
 recovery of.: 60-61, 63, 70, 73, 83, 87-88, 90-91, 93-99, 103, 108-11, 118, 125, 128-29, 138, 143-52, 154-63, 165-66, 168-202, 204-14, 216, 219-21, 223, 226, 228-31, 234-42 244, 257, 260, 263, 266, 270-72, 274, 276-77, 280, 286, 290, 293, 295, 297 304, 306-07, 311-12, 313-14, 316-23, 325-28, 331, 333, 337-39, 341-54 356-60, 362-69, 371-92, 395, 397, 399, 401-06, 408-10, 412-14, 416-17, 421, 425-26, 430, 433-39 441-42 445-47, 449-50 455, 459, 461 463, 467, 469, 475, 486, 488, 490, 492, 499, 501, 503, 505, 507, 509, 511, 515, 517-18, 522-23, 525, 528-33, 535-37, 539-41, 545-46
 Slim commands Imperial forces in: 29
 Stevenson commands Allied air in: 11
 SOS reorganization: 539
 Stilwell commands Chinese in: 297
 Stilwell commands combined forces: 155
 Stilwell withdraws into India: 36
 supply situation: 27, 172, 184, 186; 190, 197, 199-200, 207, 214, 405, 439, 449, 459
 transferred from ABDA Command to CinC, India: 25, 29
 Wavell charged with defense of: 5, 22, 26, 31
Burma, 1942, Campaign: 1-38
Burma Defense Army: 459
Burma-India Campaign: 31-385
Burma National Army: 459, 542
Burma railway corridor: 304, 314, 322, 3283 337
Burma Road: 34-35, 49, 62, 200, 202, 205-06, 211, 265, 349, 358, 376-81, 383-85, 387. *See also* Ledo Road.
Burnet Island: 169
Burnhaupt: 336-37, 339
Burnon: 359

[578]   [INDEX]

Burscheid: 493, 495
Bursfelde: 479
Burstadt: 455
Burton (Ebeye) Island: 167–69
Burtonville: 377–78
Busay: 473, 477
Busch: 444
Busch, Field Marshal Ernst: 228
Buschbell: 424
Buschenbusch Woods: 403
Buschoven: 427
Buschrodt: 359
Busdorf: 424
Buster Island: 169
Bustling Point: 130–31
Busu River: 132, 134
Busuanga Island: 432, 484
But: 128
Butaritari Atoll: 50, 147–49
Butera: 119
Butgenbach: 355, 357–60, 375–77, 382
Buthidaung: 75, 98, 108–09, 170, 178–79, 184, 351, 353
Butjo Luo Island: 179
Butler, Brig. Gen. Frederick B.: 251–59
Butler, Brig. Gen. William O. 28, 133
Butterworth: 4, 6
BUTTRESS: 115. *See also* Italy, Allied operations on mainland.
Buttstaedt: 487
Butzbach: 463
Butzdorf: 335–36, 374–75, 377, 384
Butzweiler: 421
Buzz bombs. *See* V weapons.
Byelyi: 97
Byers, Brig. Gen. Clovis: 73, 75
Byron Island: 169

Cabagan: 548
Cabalisian River: 419
Cabalitan Bay: 373, 428
Caballo Island: 22, 25, 29, 443, 445, 450, 457, 471, 475, 493
Cabanatuan: 5, 9–10, 385, 387–90
Cabanbanan: 375
Cabaruan Hills: 375–78
Cabasse: 251
Cabatuan: 546
Cabcaben: 32
Cabiranan: 324
Cabourg: 249
Cabras Island: 235, 241
Cabulihan: 355
Cadzand: 315
Cactus Ridge (Okinawa): 476–78, 480
Caen, drive on: 164, 191, 203–04, 206–07, 212–14, 216, 221–22, 224–28, 232, 240, 242–43, 245–46, 248
Caen Canal: 203
Caffey, Brig. Gen. Benjamin F.: 145
Cagayan: 536
Cagayan River and Valley: 36, 390, 393, 419, 426–27, 486, 537, 542, 544–49
Cagli: 254
Cagny: 232–33
Cahagnes: 239
Cahier: 231
Caibaan: 308
Caibobo Point: 17

Cairo, Egypt
  British conference on SEAC strategy: 299, 304, 307, 316
  SEXTANT Conference: 148, 150–52
Cairo, Italy: 166–67
Calabria: 128, 130–31, 133
Calabritto: 145, 149, 151
Calaguiman River: 13–14
Calais: 263–64, 268, 271, 287, 289–92
Calalin Island: 166
Calamba: 461
Calamian Island; 484
Calapan: 368, 373, 375, 383, 389
Calasiao: 370
Calaug: 493
Calauan: 464–65, 467, 476
Calcar: 401–03, 408, 413, 415
Calcutta Allied command conferences: 358, 410
  enemy air attack: 152
  SOS base section at: 39, 42, 53, 56
Calcutta–Assam Line of Communications: 166–67, 171
Caldera Point: 436
Calingatngan: 3 45
Calinan: 547
Callian: 251–52, 255
Calmbach: 488
Calomini: 394
Calore River: 134, 138, 140
Caltagirone: 118–20
Caltanissetta: 120
Calumbian: 362
Calumpan Peninsula: 434, 436, 440–41, 443
Calumpit: 10–11, 384, 388, 391
Calw: 498
Camaiore: 279
Camalaniugan: 45, 48
Camalig: 488, 523
Cambrai: 260–61
Camburg: 487
CAMEL: 249
Camellia (Aitsu) Island: 173
Camerano: 286
Camiling: 374–75, 378
Camina Drome: 385
Caminata: 315
Caminawit: 353
Camino Hills: 151–53
Camotes Islands: 374–75, 378–79, 382, 389, 391, 412
Camp: 425
Camp d'Elsenborn: 270–71, 312
Camp d'Oberhoffen: 380
Camp Downes: 348–50
Camp Landis: 327
Camp One: 3 83
Campania: 405
Campbeltown: 30
Camperbruch: 423, 425
Campholz Woods: 335, 389–90, 396–97, 403
Campiano: 294
Campobasso: 140
Campobello: 118–19
Campodimele: 195
Campofelice: 120, 122
Campoleone: 164, 166–67, 170
Campoleone Creek: 199

Campoleone Station: 197, 199
Campomorto: 165
Campopo Bay: 363
Camposanto: 505, 511, 513
Camprond: 237
Canadian Army units
  Army, First: 235, 239–42, 244–70, 272, 274, 276, 279, 281, 284, 286–87, 289–92, 294–98, 302–04, 306–21, 324, 342, 396, 398–408, 411–13, 415–16, 418, 420–21, 423, 425, 427–28, 430, 432–33 438, 449, 466, 468, 474, 480, 484, 486, 488, 491, 493, 495, 497, 499, 501, 517, 520
  Corps
    1: 191, 193– 202, 227, 255–57, 259, 265, 267–68, 270–74, 276–77, 279–80, 282–83, 285, 287–90, 292, 300–304, 306–13, 337–39, 342–45, 349–53, 356–58 366, 368, 399, 402, 413, 438–39, 468, 474, 488, 491, 493 495, 499, 501
    2: 229, 232–33, 236, 239–40, 244–66, 268–70, 272, 274, 276, 2799 284, 287, 289–92, 296–98, 302, 304, 307–12, 314–19, 3219 324, 338, 342, 403, 407, 413, 415–16, 418, 423, 425, 428, 430, 432–33, 458, 460, 462, 464, 466, 468, 474, 484, 486, 491, 493, 495, 497, 501, 517
  Divisions
    1st Infantry: 118–21, 124–25, 128, 131, 135–41, 151–53, 155–56, 196, 255, 261, 267, 272, 274, 276–77, 279–80, 282–83, 285, 300–10, 313, 344–45, 350–52, 357, 366, 399, 404, 413, 486, 491, 495, 499
    2d Infantry: 229, 232–33, 236, 244–46 248 250, 255, 260, 264–65, 268, 276, 286, 292, 294, 297–98, 304, 309–12, 314–16, 396, 399, 403, 408, 413, 415–16, 423, 425, 427, 430, 432–33 460, 462, 484, 486
    3d Infantry: 203–04, 226–27, 229, 232–33, 236, 253, 257, 259–60, 262, 263–64, 276, 284, 287, 289, 291, 296–98, 302, 304, 306, 308, 312, 315, 317, 324, 397–403 407, 412–13, 415–16, 418, 423, 425, 427, 458, 460, 462, 471, 480, 483–84
    4th Armored: 245, 248, 250–51, 256–57, 259–62, 264–66, 269–70, 272, 274, 279, 284, 298, 307–09, 312–13, 317, 413, 415–16, 423, 427–28, 430, 432–33, 480, 484, 501
    5th Armored: 165, 196, 261–62, 271, 285, 287–88, 290, 309–10, 313, 344, 350–52, 357, 366, 495, 501

[INDEX]

Canadian Army units—Continued
  Brigades
    1st Armored: 215
    2d Armored: 413
    13th Infantry: 127
    Regiment, Animal Transport: 187
Canal de Colmar: 382-83, 386
Canal de Derivation: 270, 272
Canal de Deurne: 313
Canal de Hulst: 279
Canal des Houillères de la Sarre: 339
Canal du Nord: 313, 316-18, 3 25, 418
Canale di Bonifica Destra del Reno: 366
Canale di Valetta: 473
Canberra, HMAS: 49
Canberra, USS: 302
Cancello: 140
Candelaria: 9, 480
Candijay: 488, 506
Canicatti: 118-19
Canisy: 237
Canmangui: 309
Canna (Rujuru) Island: 173
Cannavinelle: 144
Cannavinelle Hill: 144-45, 152
Cannes: 249, 253-55
Canonica: 287-88
Cannon, Brig. Gen. Robert M.: 383
Canosa: 137
Canrobert: 326
Cantabaco: 32-33
Cantalupo: 143, 207
Cantalupo Hill: 193
Canton: 266, 362, 371, 381, 403, 508, 517, 544-45, 547, 549, 551
Canton Island: 23, 130, 136
Cap Bénat: 250
Cap Bon: 104, 109-10
Cap de la Hague: 219-22
Cap de l'Esterel: 255
Cap Lévy: 219
Cap Matifou: 64
Cap Nègre: 100, 249-50
Cap Serrat: 102, 105
Capaccio: 132
Capannoli: 231-32
Capas: 3 81
Cape Cretin: 156, 169, 179
Cape Dinga: 115
Cape Endaiadere: 67, 69, 71-72, 75-76
Cape Esperance: 59, 64, 66, 84, 89-91
  naval-air battle: 58-59
Cape Gloucester: 131, 136, 151, 154-57, 159-60, 162, 166, 172, 175
Cape Hoskins: 190
Cape Iris: 160, 175
Cape Killerton: 68, 70, 83-85, 96
Cape King William: 160
Cape Nelson: 57-58
Cape Ngariois: 278
Cape Opmarai: 230
Cape Pie: 188
Cape Raoult: 175
Cape Soeadja: 189
Cape St. George, naval battle: 149
Cape Sansapor: 240
Cape Sudest: 155-56
Cape Tjeweri: 18 8
Cape Torokina: 143-44, 149, 153-54, 179

CAPITAL: 235, 238, 271, 293, 304, 316, 327, 349. *See also* Chindwin River; Mandalay.
Capiz: 33
Capizzi: 123-24
Capo Calava: 127
Capo d'Acqua Creek: 163
Capo d'Orlando: 126
Capo Scaramia: 117
Capoocan: 318, 323, 327
Capraro Hill: 161
Capri Island: 134
Capriati al Volturno: 141, 143
Capua: 131, 139-40
Capul Island: 406, 415
Caraballo Mountains: 401
Carabao Island: 22, 24-25, 29, 450, 499
CARBONADO: 508, 544. *See also* Canton; Hong Kong.
Carbonara: 513
Carces: 251
Carden: 432
Carentan: 203-10, 226, 229
Carhaix: 242-43
Caribbean Air Force: 22
Caridad: 326, 339
Carigara: 314-18, 327
Carigara Bay: 311, 323
Carl Road: 168
Carlos (Ennylabegan) Island: 167, 170
Carlson, Lt. Col. Evans F. (USMC,): 50, 66, 72
Carlson (Enubuj) Island: 167-68
Carlson's Raiders. *See* Marine Corps Raider Battalions, 2d.
Carmen: 378
Carney airfield: 71
Caroline Islands: 162, 164, 167, 169, 172-74, 179, 190, 211, 226, 230, 240-41, 249, 259, 263-64, 268, 270, 274, 276-79, 281-83, 285-86, 288-97, 299-303, 305-12, 317, 338-39, 342, 350, 365, 367
  in support of Hollandia operation: 184, 187, 189
Carpathian Mountains: 258, 306, 313, 375, 379, 386-87
Carpenter bridge: 445
CARPET: 139.
CARPETBAGGER: 160. *See also* French Forces of the Interior; Guerrilla forces.
Carpineta: 302-03
Carpineto: 200
Carpiquet: 224, 227
Carranglan: 413-14, 428
Carrara: 488, 490
Carrier, Lt. Col. Edmund J.: 65, 68-69
Carrione Creek: 490, 492
Carroceto: 165, 170, 172
Carrouges: 245, 247-48
Carsdorf: 494
Carter, Capt. Jesse H. (USN): 129
Carter (Gea) Island: 167
Carthage conference on Italy invasion: 120, 128
CARTWHEEL: 106, 108, 115, 182. *See also* Rabaul.
Carviano: 431
Casa Bettini: 337-39 341-42
Casa Nuovo: 341

Casablanca
  Allied landings: 63, 65-66
  Conference: 84, 87
Casacalenda: 140
Casaglia Pass: 282
Casale: 227-28, 301
Casalecchio: 507
Casalino: 302, 304
Casamaggiore: 220
CASANOVA: 320. *See also* Metz.
Cascina: 244
Casco Bay: 61
Caserta: 176, 190, 288, 523
Casey, Brig. Gen. Hugh J.: 56
Casole d'Elsa: 222-24
Casole Valsenio: 339
Cassibile: 131
Cassino: 159, 162-65, 167, 169-75, 180-82, 191-94
Castel Alfedena: 149
Castel d'Aiano: 426
Castel del Rio: 288-89
Castel di Mezzo: 262
Castel San Pietro: 309, 501
Castelbuono: 122
Castelfiorentino: 234
Castelforte,: 163, 165, 171, 191-92
Castelfrentano: 151
Castell: 485
Castellaccio: 310
Castellammare (di Stabia): 138
Castellano, Gen. G. (It.): 128, 131
Castellina: 224-25, 233
Castellina in Chianti: 230-31
Castellone: 168, 171, 193
Castellone Hill: 193
Castellonorato: 193
Castelnuovo: 150-51, 193, 296, 394, 426, 433
Castelnuovo di Bisano: 296-97
Castelvecchio: 279, 289-91, 392
Castelverde: 87
Castelvetrano: 121
Castermini: 121
Castiglion Fiorentino: 224
Castiglioncello: 229
Castiglione, Algeria: 64
Castiglione, Italy: 307, 332-33
Castiglione del Lago: 221
Castilla: 311-12, 314
Castle Hill, Germany: 345-47
Castle Hill, Italy: 170-71
Castro dei Volsci: 197-98
Castrocaro: 321, 324
Castrop Rauxel: 478, 480
Castropignano: 138
Castrovillari: 133
Casualties, U.S., total in war: 551
Cataban: 373
Cataguintingan: 377, 383-85
Cataisan Peninsula: 307
Catania: 119-21, 125
Catanzaro: 132-33
Catbalogan: 374, 388
CATCHPOLE: 162, 173. *See also* Marshall Islands.
Catenanuova: 123-24
Catmon: 32
Catmon Hill: 308, 312, 314, 316

[579]

Cattenom: 321, 323-24
Cattenstedt: 508
Cauayan: 546
Caumont: 207-09, 239 S
Cauvicourt: 245
Cavaillon: 256
Cavalaire: 249
Cavalaire Bay: 249
Cavallina: 269
Cavalry Brigade, 316th Provisional: 433, 435, 438, 442
Cavalry Division, 1st (5th, 7th, 8th, 12th): 176, 180, 307-10, 312, 314, 317, 319, 322-23, 327, 349-50, 352, 355-57, 360-65, 374, 385, 387-92, 394-402, 407, 409-10, 412-13, 419, 428, 430-31, 433-36, 440, 450-51 453, 455, 457, 460-61, 464-65, 467, 469, 471, 473, 476-78, 484, 486, 488, 493, 499, 505, 511, 522, 527, 529-30, 544, 546
Cavalry Groups
  2d: 261, 264-65, 272, 275, 278, 320, 326, 330, 345-46, 359-60, 371, 376-77, 406-09, 414, 421, 424, 426, 428-29, 431-32, 434-36, 438-41, 443-45, 447-50, 452, 455, 457, 459, 461, 463, 465, 467, 470, 473, 475, 477, 479, 481, 490, 492, 494, 496, 502, 504, 506, 510, 512, 514, 516-17, 519, 521-22, 526, 532-33
  3d: 260-61, 264-65, 280, 287, 289, 296, 300, 318-19, 325, 330-32, 338, 382, 396, 410-11, 06, 419, 423, 433-38, 442-43, 446-47, 455, 459, 461, 463, 465, 467-68, 470, 472, 477, 483, 485, 487, 508, 510, 512, 514, 516, 521-22, 529, 531-33
  4th: 203, 213, 221, 257, 268, 271, 359-60, 369, 371, 373, 378, 380, 412, 414-15 418, 420, 422, 424-25, 430, 433, 440, 444-47, 452, 456, 458, 460, 462, 464, 466, 476, 479, 483, 489, 491, 500, 502, 510, 512
  6th: 342-43, 347-48, 353, 360, 364, 366, 368, 371, 380-83, 387, 392, 399-401, 405-07, 409-11, 413-14, 417, 419-22, 424, 426-27, 431-32 434, 437, 442, 444, 449 454, 456, 468, 473, 475, 479, 481, 487, 492, 494, 496, 498, 500, 502, 504, 508, 524
  11th: 384, 415, 418, 429, 466, 478, 480, 489, 493, 504, 506, 508
  14th: 350, 353-55, 394, 397, 402, 415, 417, 420, 422, 424, 425, 427, 429, 431, 435, 436, 442, 448-49, 456, 458, 462, 464, 470, 474, 491, 502, 507-08, 512, 514, 516, 518, 521, 524, 526, 528
  15th: 415-16, 418, 420-21, 423, 430, 435, 452, 454, 462, 466, 470, 472, 487, 491, 493, 504, 515
  16th: 433, 435, 437-39, 442-44, 452, 457, 461, 465

Cavalry Groups—Continued
  101st: 395, 398, 400, 417, 438-39, 461, 463, 466, 481, 485, 488, 490, 492, 494, 496, 503-05, 507, 511, 514-15, 521, 523, 525, 527-28, 531
  102d: 245, 253-55, 263, 269, 355, 358, 389, 392, 408, 418, 420, 422, 424, 426-27, 429, 431, 433, 437, 439, 452
  106th: 238, 267-70, 275, 293, 325, 335-36, 362, 365, 373, 383, 395, 398, 400, 417, 463, 466, 479, 487, 504, 523, 531
  113th: 226-27, 232-33, 263-69, 289-90, 293-94 340, 393, 395, 414, 418, 433, 454, 466, 472, 504, 506, 510, 521-22, 524, 533
  115th: 516
Cavalry Regiments
  5th: 176-78, 180-83, 307-09, 363, 388-90, 396, 401, 419, 431, 465-67, 469, 473, 476, 477, 493, 527, 529, 544
  7th: 177-81, 184, 187, 307-11, 314, 349-50 352, 407, 431, 451, 457, 461, 465, 467, 469, 476, 478, 499, 511, 530
  8th: 180-81, 190, 309-11, 314, 374, 388-89, 396, 401, 431, 457, 461, 490, 493, 499, 511, 522, 530
  12th: 178, 181-86, 188, 307-08, 310, 314, 339-50, 352-53, 355-58 360, 363, 400-401, 431, 433, 460, 464-65 467, 476
  26th (Philippine Scouts): 7, 8, 11, 12, 15, 17, 19, 32
  38th: 256
  112th: 114, 151, 154, 172, 213, 220-21, 228-29, 232-36, 238-41, 247, 326-27, 335, 341-49, 385, 388, 399-400 440, 471
  124th: 304, 313, 354, 362, 371, 390
Provisional, 1st Cavalry Division: 388-89
Cavalry Squadrons
  17th: 331
  24th: 213
Cave: 200-201
Cave d'Argilla: 192
Cavigny: 226
Cavit Island: 457
Cavite: 4, 314, 400
Cebu: 402
Cebu Attack Group (USN): 453
Cebu Covering Group (USN): 452-53
Cebu City: 455, 457, 465, 484, 493, 497, 499, 507, 512
Cebu Harbor: 457
Cebu Island: 31-34, 430, 445, 449, 452-53, 455, 457, 460-62, 464-65, 467, 469, 471, 474, 476, 480, 482, 484, 486, 488, 490, 493, 497, 499, 501, 506-07, 512-13, 517, 523, 535, 547-48
Ceccano: 198-99
Cecil (Ninni) Island: 167-68
Cecina: 221-22
Cecina Marine: 222
Cecina River: 220-22
Cedrecchia: 292-93

Cefalu: 122-23
Cegled: 318
Cekhira: 103
Celbingen: 503
Celebes Island: 14, 274
Celebes Sea: 17
Celincordia: 305-06
Celle: 482, 484, 486, 489, 508
Celles: 361
Center Assault Force (NW Africa): 64-66
Center Attack Group (NW Africa): 65
Centocelle: 202
Central America, waters controlled by Pacific Theater: 30-31
Central Burma Campaign: 387-550
Central Defense Command (United States): 162
Central Europe Campaign: 448-536
Central Pacific: 4. *See also* Central Pacific Campaign; Eastern Mandates Campaign.
  controlled by POA: 30-31
Central Pacific Campaign: 3-152
Central Pacific Task Forces (Iwo Jima): 385
Central Plain (Luzon): 405
Centuripe: 124-25
Ceprano: 196-99
Ceracoli Hill: 194
Cerami: 123-24
Cerasola Hill: 191
Cerasolo: 276-77
Cerasuolo: 150, 155
Cerea: 516
Cerences: 238
Ceriano: 274, 279-80, 282-83
Cernauti: 184-85
Cernay: 331-32, 346, 351, 379, 389, 391-92
Certaldo: 230-31, 233-34, 251
Cervantes: 542, 546
Cervaro: 161-62
Cervia: 309
Cesano: 306-07
Cesano River: 247, 251
Cesaro: 121, 125-26
Cesena: 263, 301, 304, 306, 308
Cesenatico: 307
Chabrehez: 372
Chacha: 218
Chalampé: 397-99
Chaling: 375
Châlon-sur-Saône: 264
Châlons-sur-Marne: 189, 257-58, 400
Châlonvillers: 331
Cham: 502, 508, 512, 514-15, 517
Chamberlain, Lt. Col. Thomas C.: 327, 332, 334
Chamberlin, Brig. Gen. Stephen J.: 34
Chambois: 250-52
Chambrey: 289, 292
Champagney: 33 2
Champenoux: 290
CHAMPION: 145, 150-51. *See also* Burma, recovery of.
Chan: 541, 543
Chaney, Maj. Gen. James E.
  CG of ETO: 41
  CG of Iwo garrison: 455-56
  CG of USAFBI: 25

[INDEX]

Changsha: 8, 12, 207, 210-11, 213
Chang-te: 152
Changting: 405
Channel Islands: 23, 57
Chantilly: 259-60
Chaouach: 104
Chaporowan Point: 181-82
Charan Kanoa: 211-12
Charleroi: 261
Charlie Hill (Okinawa): 537
Charmes: 268-70, 273
Charov: 190, 192
Charpate: 195-96, 198
Chartres: 247-52, 254
Chase, Maj. Gen. William C.: 176, 403
Chatan: 468-69
Château Brieux: 321
Château de Fontenay: 206
Château Lambert: 294, 335
Château-Salins: 270, 272, 278, 280, 283, 286-87, 321, 385
Château-Thierry: 256-57
Châteaudun: 249-50
Châtel: 273, 275, 278, 283
Châtenois: 272, 341
CHATTANOOGA CHOO CHOO: 195. *See also* Normandy Campaign, air attack phase.
Chauk: 490
Chaumont: 271, 277, 359-61
Chauncey (Gehh) Island: 167-68
Chaungmagyi River: 426
Chauny: 260
Cheb: 516-17, 519, 521, 524, 532-33
Cheduba Island: 384
Che-fang: 342, 349
Chef-du-Pont: 206
Chekiang Province: 37, 39-41, 47
Chelm: 23 4
Chemical companies, in defense of Bataan: 17
Chemical Weapons Battalions
  2d: 257
  3d: 123, 257
  83d: 164, 257
  88th: 348
Cheminot: 280, 284, 321
Chemnitz: 268, 496, 502, 536
Chemnitz River: 496
Chen Cheng, Gen.: 89, 93, 111, 125, 189, 333
Chenango: 66
Cheneux: 358
Cheng-hsien: 189
Cheng-to: 163, 165, I 71, 187, 189
Chenicourt: 298-99
Chennault, Maj. Gen. Claire L.: 7, 147, 251, 255, 310, 324, 342, 350, 409, 537
  asks increased authority: 58
  CG of Fourteenth Air Force: 97, 114-15, 550
  commands CATF: 45
  commands China air forces: 547
  commands China SAF: 547
  on efficacy of air offensive: 187, 199, 204-05, 235, 248
  plan for CATF operations: 55, 60
  proposes air assault on Japan: 165
  replacement forecast: 538

Chennault, Maj. Gen. Claire L.—Continued
  retirement: 549
  Wallace-Chiang conference: 214, 217
Chenogne: 364-65
Cherain: 373-77
Cherbourg, drive on: 203, 205-06, 209, 212-22, 227
Cherkassy: 147, 153-54, 174
Cherkessk: 86
Chermor: 9
Chernigov: 136
Chernyakhov: 157
Cheveoumont: 373
Chianciano: 220
Chiang Kai-shek, Generalissimo: 36, 38, 46, 116, 187, 202, 205, 218, 270, 272, 274, 279, 282, 354, 381, 384, 386, 390, 463. *See also* Burma; China; China-Burma-India Theater; China Theater; India; South East Asia Command.
  approves Chinese force in India: 33
  and CATF: 55
  denounces Allied strategy in SEAC: 299
  demands for maintaining China Theater: 43, 48
  demands for military and financial aid: 112, 114, 118, 144, 146, 153, 155, 163, 165, 169
  demands naval forces for Bay of Bengal: 78
  demands seizure of Andamans and other areas: 155
  demands Stilwell recall: 301-02, 306
  directive to Stilwell: 271, 276
  on division of CBI: 224-27, 230, 235, 266, 310
  first conference with Stilwell: 27
  gives Stilwell command of troops: 44, 155
  halts offensive in Burma: 178
  heads China Theater: 10
  inspects Burma defenses: 32
  and Kunming planning conference: 357, 362
  leadership, internal threats to: 246
  moves forces from Burma: 341, 344
  and negotiations for use of Communist Chinese: 132, 171, 214, 217, 343, 385
  offers forces for defense of Burma: 8, 21-22, 32
  and plan for Chungking and Kunming: 333, 348, 350
  and plans for Kweilin-Liuchow-Canton: 403
  and proposal for U.S. officer to command Chinese forces: 222-27, 230, 235, 255, 265-66, 271, 276, 287, 296, 302, 306
  proposes SOS for China: 265
  protests Salween withdrawal: 276
  receives OCTAGON decisions: 280, 285
  rejects proposal to supply communists: 338
  relation to Stilwell defined: 129
  requests U.S. officer as chief of staff: 12-14, 17
  Roosevelt's replies to demands: 59, 280, 285

Chiang Kai-shek, Generalissimo—Continued
  at SEXTANT Conference: 148, 150-52
  and Stilwell's request for thirty divisions: 59
  and support of Burma operations: 60-61, 63, 70, 78, 83, 90, 111, 118, 125, 128, 129, 138, 144, 146, 150-53, 155, 162-63, 169, 181, 184, 186, 189, 195, 276, 281, 322, 341, 349
  U.S. political representatives to: 220, 226-27, 230, 235, 246-47, 263-66
  Wallace-Chennault conference: 214, 217
  and Wedemeyer: 306, 405
Chiangtso: 213, 216
Chianni: 225, 229-30
Chianti Hills: 233-34
Chiaotou: 200, 211
Chiasco River: 212
Chichagof Harbor and Pass: 106, 111-12
Chichi Jima: 211, 224, 368
Chief of Naval Operations, King appointed: 28
Chief of Staff to Supreme Allied Commander (designate)
  Leigh-Mallory selected to make, air plans for OVERLORD: 114
  Morgan appointed: 106
  redesignated SHAEF: 163
Chieti: 207
Chifontaine: 379
Chihchiang: 405, 481, 492, 495, 507, 509, 517, 523, 536, 544
Chienti River: 215-16
Chiesa del Bando: 492
Chile, breaks with Axis nations: 86
Chin Hills: 145
China. *See also* Chiang Kai-shek, Generalissimo; Burma; China-Burma-India Theater; China Theater; India; India-Burma Theater; South East Asia Command; Stilwell, Lt. Gen. Joseph W.; Wedemeyer, Lt. Gen. Albert C.
  air build-up: 98, 146-47, 149-50, 161, 165-66, 171, 173
  aircraft diverted to Middle East: 42
  airlift of supply to: 45, 55, 57, 60, 71, 110, 116, 147, 150, 155, 180-81, 187, 190, 200, 204-05, 235, 271, 293, 297, 329, 342, 344, 355, 540
  Allied offensives in: 303, 314, 495, 509
  American Mission becomes CBI: 27
  base for B-29 aircraft: 146-47, 149-50, 187, 189, 202, 204-05, 304
  base for bombardment of Japan: 189, 202, 204-05, 211, 349, 351, 355
  casualty summaries: 238, 265
  CATF established: 44-45
  Chennault heads CATF: 45
  China Defensive Campaign: 44-531
  China Offensive Campaign: 532-51
  Chinese-American Composite Wing: 123, 189
  control of AVG: 7
  Currie mission to: 46, 48
  declares war on Axis powers: 4

[581]

China—Continued
  Drum proposed for field command: 11, 13–14, 17
  enemy blockade broken: 385
  enemy offensives: 4–10, 35, 37, 39–41, 47, 371, 375, 381, 384, 387, 391, 396, 447, 481, 492, 495, 507, 509
  enemy reinforcements: 255, 266
  enemy threats to air bases in: 187, 198–99 202, 204–05, 248–49, 259, 266, 276, 282, 313, 324, 329, 375, 387, 396, 405, 409, 4479 453, 495, 507, 509, 5179 520, 523
  government reorganized: 344
  high tide of Japanese invasion: 349
  Joint Military Council formed: 10
  land supply route to: 161, 168, 195, 255, 271, 291, 293, 304, 372, 375, 379, 382, 385–86, 392. *See also* Burma Road; Ledo Road.
  lend-lease to: 6, 123, 162, 235
  and Moscow Foreign Ministers Conference: 143
  movement of forces to and from Burma: 9, 21–22, 32, 163, 435, 438, 441, 537, 539
  National Military Advisory Council conference: 146, 246
  negotiations for use of Chinese Communists. *See* Chinese Communist forces.
  operations in: 97, 105, 111, 113, 152, 155–56, 187, 189, 198, 200, 202, 204, 207–08, 210–14, 216, 218–20, 223, 225–29, 235–38, 241–43, 245–47, 251, 253–559 259, 264–66, 272, 279, 286, 302–03, 306, 313–14, 318–19, 322–24, 329, 332, 336, 339, 342–44, 348–50, 369, 371, 375–76, 379, 381, 383–85, 387, 391–92, 396, 399, 403, 405, 409, 447, 453, 481, 484, 488, 492, 495, 507, 509, 517, 520, 523, 525, 527, 529, 532, 536–39, 541, 544–45, 547–51
  pipeline supply through Burma: 95, 220, 293
  plans for recovery of ports: 204, 403, 517, 536, 544
  recovery of Burma necessary to: 46–48
  request for U.S. officer as chief of staff: 11–14, 17
  Stilwell's role in. *See also* Stilwell, Lt. Gen. Joseph W.
    attempts to have recalled: 134–35, 220, 296, 301–02, 306
    blamed for losses: 299
    named chief of staff: 21
    proposal for Chinese force in India: 33
  as supply base for Pacific: 190, 200, 204–05, 242, 517, 536, 540
  supply situation: 488, 517, 520
  threats to Chiang's leadership: 246
  and *Tulsa* incident: 9
  U.S. forces in: 20–21, 27, 163, 435, 438, 441, 537

China—Continued
  U.S. officer proposed as commander of Chinese forces in: 11, 13–14, 222–27, 230, 235, 255, 265–66, 271, 276, 287, 296, 302, 306
  U.S. political representatives in: 220, 226–27, 230, 235, 246–47, 263–66
  U.S. Task Force in: 20–21, 27
  Wallace-Chiang-Chennault conference: 214, 217
  War Department, mission to: 160, 171
  war theater, demands for maintaining: 43, 48, 59. *See also* Chiang Kai-shek, Generalissimo.
  Y-Force. *See* Yunnan Force.
China-Burma-India Theater. *See also* Chiang Kai-shek, Generalissimo; China; China Theater; Chinese Army; India-Burma Theater; South East Asia Command; Stilwell, Lt. Gen. Joseph W.; Sultan, Lt. Gen. Daniel I.; Wedemeyer, Lt. Gen. Albert C.; Wheeler, Lt. Gen. Raymond A.
  activated: 20–21, 27
  air actions in: 44, 55, 147, 155, 216, 219–20, 223, 228, 238, 241
  air build-up: 98, 146–47, 149–50, 161, 165–66, 171, 173
  air organization: 30, 44–45, 55, 71, 165
  aircraft diverted to Middle East: 42
  airlift supply to China. *See* China, airlift of supply to.
  Allied planning conferences: 8, 26, 143, 146, 177, 185, 214, 217, 246
  Assam-Burma-China Ferry Command activated: 29
  assignments to, directive on: 42
  Burma
    defense made secondary to India: 35
    operations in. *See* Burma, fall of; Burma, recovery of.
    plans for recovery: 60–61, 63, 70, 73, 87–88, 90–91
    Stilwell heads Allied forces in: 155, 297
  Calcutta base section: 53, 56
  casualty summaries: 165, 186, 212, 231, 242, 238, 242
  CCS accepts TRIDENT plans: 111
  and Chennault: 45, 58
  Chiang inspects Burma defenses: 32
  China Defensive Campaign: 44–310
  Chinese forces in support of: 209, 235, 241, 251, 255, 279, 362
  Chungking command conference: 8
  command structure defined: 44
  control of Calcutta–Assam LOC: 166–67, 171
  division into two theaters: 222–27, 230, 235, 266, 310
  enemy air and naval actions: 152–53, 156
  enemy air offensive: 8, 16, 18
  enemy ground offensives. *See* Burma; China; India.
  excluded from SEAC: 129
  first U.S. troops arrive: 29

China-Burma-India Theater—Continued
  guerrilla operations: 91, 93, 96–97, 111, 183, 193
  hq established at Chungking: 27
  India
    Allied withdrawal into: 36
    Chinese forces in: 33, 163
    enemy drive on: 156
    headquarters moved to: 38
    Stilwell heads Chinese in: 155
  India Air Task Force: 57, 60, 71
  India-Burma Campaign: 31–310
  India-China Ferry Command: 45
  India-China Wing, ATC: 71
  land supply route to China: 161, 168, 195, 255, 291, 293, 304 *See also* Burma Road; Ledo Road; Stilwell Road.
  Ledo and Imphal roads to connect with Burma: 11, 14
  Long Range Penetration Groups: 146, 186, 200, 209, 214, 221, 223, 226, 237
  mission to War Department: 160, 171
  offensive against enemy shipping: 115–16, 132, 165
  operations in China. *See* China, operations in.
  pipeline supply of China through: 95, 220, 293
  planning conferences: 8, 143, 146, 177, 185, 214, 217, 246
  plans for recovery of Myitkyina: 185–86
  preparation for reception of B–29's: 146–47, 149
  Slim heads Imperial forces in: 29
  SOS: 265
    advance sections: 41
    and Assam airfield: 109, 112
    base sections: 39, 42, 53, 56
    Covell commands: 146
    directive on: 26
    first troops arrive: 38
    and Ledo Road: 93
    Wheeler commands: 26, 64, 70
  Y-FOS: 190
  Stevenson heads Allied air: 11
  Stilwell
    attempts to have recalled: 134–35, 220, 296, 301–02, 306
    conference by: 26
    as head of CBI: 25, 27, 44. *See also* Stilwell, Lt. Gen. Joseph W.
    proposed as head of Chinese in India: 33
  Stilwell-Mountbatten conferences: 177, 185
  supply situation: 27, 172, 184, 186, 190, 197, 199–200, 207, 214
  TRIDENT plans accepted by CCS: 111
  U.S. forces redesignated CBI: 20–21, 27
  U.S. troops for Bengal-Assam RR: 145
  Wallace-Chiang-Chennault conferences: 214, 217
  Y-Force in defense of. *See* Yunnan Force.

[INDEX]

China Defensive Campaign: 44-531
China Expeditionary Forces: 384, 495
China Offensive Campaign: 532-51
China Theater. *See also* Chiang Kai-shek, Generalissimo; China; China-Burma-India Theater; Chinese Army; India-Burma Theater; South East Asia Command; Stilwell, Lt. Gen. Joseph W.; Wedemeyer, Lt. Gen. Albert.
AAF, China Theater, activated: 549
activation: 10, 310
air actions in: 314, 316, 323, 342, 542, 549
air organization: 375, 484, 527, 532, 536-38, 542, 547, 549
airborne operations: 345, 349, 354, 438, 441, 449, 507, 509, 520
airlift supply from India: 329, 342, 344, 355, 540
Allied offensives. *See* China, operations in.
Allied planning conferences: 357, 362
Aurand heads SOS: 541
Chennault heads SAF: 547
China Defensive Campaign: 44-531
China Offensive Campaign: 532-51
Chinese forces in, support of: 209, 235, 241, 251, 255, 279, 362
Davidson heads TAF: 547
enemy offensives. *See* China, enemy offensives.
enemy shipping, offensive against: 374, 376
enemy threats to air bases. *See* China, enemy threats to air bases.
Hump Tonnage Allocation and Control Office: 355
Indochina inclusion undefined: 390
negotiations for use of Chinese Communist forces. *See* Chinese Communist forces.
operations in. *See* China, operations in.
pursuit of enemy: 532-33, 539, 541, 544-46, 548
SAF in: 547
separation from CBI: 235, 266, 310
SOS in: 265, 399, 541
Stratemeyer heads air forces in: 527, 544, 547, 549
supply situation: 488, 517, 520
support of Canton-Hong Kong recovery: 547
TAF in: 547
U.S. forces in: 435, 438, 441, 537.
Wedemeyer as commander: 310, 316, 352, 357. *See also* Wedemeyer, Lt. Gen. Albert C.
Y-Force in. *See* Yunnan Force.
Chinapelli: 239
Chindits. *See* Indian Army units, Divisions, 3d and Brigades, 77th LRP (Chindits).
Chindwin River: 39, 93, 145, 177, 180, 186, 206, 235, 238, 240, 244, 263, 271, 304, 316, 327, 331, 343-44, 349, 356, 381, 430

Chinen Peninsula: 542-44
Chinese-American Composite Wing: 123, 189, 301
Chinese Army. *See also* Burma; China; Chiang Kai-shek, Generalissimo; Stilwell, Lt. Gen. Joseph W.
in Burma offensive: 59, 61, 63, 70
Chinese Combat Command: 369, 384
Chinese Expeditionary Force: 60-61, 63, 70, 78, 83, 90, 93, 110, 125, 314, 381, 383
Chinese Training and Combat Command: 369
Chinese Training Center: 369
Ramgarh training center: 52, 60
Stilwell appointed CinC: 21, 44, 63
30-division program: 89, 144
60-division program: 138
training by U.S. *See* Yunnan Force; Zebra Force.
Chinese Army units
Armies
New First: 304, 383, 387, 406, 430, 544
2d: 197, 200, 206, 322, 367
4th: 211
5th: 22, 26, 28-29, 34-36, 383, 348
6th: 8, 16-17, 22, 28-29, 33-34
New Sixth: 304, 368, 523
8th: 218, 220, 225-26, 228-29, 235, 242, 246, 265, 544
13th: 550
18th: 536
53d: 192, 199, 213, 223, 322, 348
54th: 200, 213, 544
57th: 354
66th: 33-35
71st: 197-98, 202, 205-06, 218, 322
94th: 529, 536
100th: 536
Chinese Army in India: 353, 357, 368, 379, 381, 383, 441, 449, 539
Group Armies
9th: 210
11th: 212, 332
12th: 322
20th: 216
Divisions
Honorable 1st: 220, 225, 318
2d Reserve: 200, 211, 213
5th: 529
9th: 200, 206, 367, 379
14th: 184, 187, 220-21, 341, 345, 509, 523
22d: 29-31, 33-35, 38, 60, 157, 165-66, 169, 173-75 177-84, 187-90, 195, 200, 211, 297, 304, 312, 318-20, 326-27, 341, 344-46, 348-49, 368, 509
28th: 34-35, 197 202, 228
29th: 35-36
30th: 177, 187, 189-90, 194, 236 342, 345, 348-49 368, 375, 384-85 387-90, 406, 441, 539

Chinese Army Units—Continued
Divisions—Continued
36th: 192, 200, 211, 213-14, 242
38th: 33-35 38-39 60, 143-44, 146, 149-50, 154, 156-63, 165-66, 168, 170, 178-80, 182, 184-92, 195, 197, 200, 211, 216, 219, 304, 314, 322, 326, 333, 339, 341, 344, 348, 351, 353, 358, 371, 376-80, 384-85, 387, 430, 441, 539
49th: 8, 17, 33-34
50th: 184, 187, 194, 211, 236, 242, 304, 364, 366, 441, 539
55th: 29-31, 33-35, 37
58th: 517, 525, 550
76th: 193, 197, 200
82d: 225-26
87th: 197, 202, 205, 207, 211-12, 218
88th: 193, 197-98, 202, 205, 207, 212
93d: 16, 33-34
96th: 29, 31-32, 34, 38
103d: 225, 228, 242
116th: 191, 213, 223, 242
130th: 213
190th: 193
198th: 191, 200
200th: 26, 28-32, 34-35, 37, 314
Regiment, 1st Separate: 463
Tank Group, 1st Provisional (Chinese-American): 177-82
Chinese Communist forces
Chiang demands control of: 235
delegation to Stilwell: 271
negotiations for use of: 132, 171, 214, 217, 338, 343, 354, 383, 385, 387
proposals for use and supply of: 132, 171, 214, 217, 235, 338, 341, 343, 385
U.S. observer group with: 171, 214, 217, 343
Chittagong: 156, 290
Chiusi: 214-15, 217-19
Chiyunna: 472
Chocolate Drop Hill (Okinawa): 536-39
Chodova Plana: 532
Choiseul Bay: 132
Choiseul Island: 142, 144
Cholm: 18, 29, 32
Choltitz, Lt. Gen. Dietrich von: 256
Chonito cliff: 238
Chott Djerid: 101
Chotts, The: 88
Chou En-lai: 3 54
Chouïgui: 71, 108
Chouïgui Pass: 108-09
Chowringhee: 179
Christie, Col. Albert F.: 33
Christmas Island: 23
Chuda: 478
Chudovo: 166
Chuguev: 92, 127
Chungking
Allied leaders' conference: 8
hq of CBI: 27

Chungking—Continued
    loss and recovery: 329, 333, 348, 350, 357, 365, 369, 381, 409, 488, 536-37, 544, 549
    National Military Council conference: 146
    U.S. officer as commander, conference on: 265, 276
    Wallace-Chiang-Chennault conference: 214, 217
Churchill, Winston S.: 181, 325. *See also* British Chiefs of Staff; Combined Chiefs of Staff; United Kingdom.
    appoints Auchinleck to command in India: 114
    at ARCADIA Conference: 8
    asks for air support for Rangoon: 462, 472
    Burma recovery, assurances on: 176
    Calcutta-Assam LOC, on control of: 166-67, 171
    agrees on Eisenhower to command TORCH: 48
    at EUREKA Conference: 150-51
    inspects Eighth Army: 48
    Italians, appeal to: 120, 124
    appoints Montgomery to head: 21 Army Group: 156
    at Moscow conference: 49
    Mountbatten conference in Cairo: 299, 304, 307, 316
    outlines mission of SAC, SEAC: 142
    plans for Rangoon and Mandalay: 293
    at QUADRANT Conference: 127-29
    at SEXTANT Conference: 148, 150-52
    Stalin conferences: 49
    transmits decisions of OCTAGON to Chiang: 280
    at TRIDENT Conference: 110-12
    at Washington Conference, June 1942: 42
Churgia: 85
Chuhsien: 40-41
Chynoweth, Brig. Gen. Bradford G.: 27, 32-33
Ciampino: 121
Cicerelli Hill: 161
Ciechanow: 377
Cielle: 369
Cima del Monte: 195
Ciney: 359-60
Cinquale Canal: 397, 401
Ciorlano: 143
Cirey: 328, 331
Cisterna di Littoria: 141, 164-68, 170, 173, 184, 196-97
Citta della Pieve: 210, 213
Citta di Castello: 213, 233-35
Cituinan Hill: 488, 490, 492, 497, 503, 505, 511, 517, 520, 522
City of Dalhart: 31
Civita Castellana: 204
Civitavecchia: 13 8, 162-63, 202, 204, 208, 210
Civitella di Romagna: 306
Claggett, Brig. Gen. Henry B.: 9
Clairefontaine: 332
Clark Field: 3, 5, 377-78, 380, 384-86, 388, 425, 488

Clark, Lt. Gen. Mark W.: 82, 132, 149, 168-69, 202, 250, 260, 266. *See also* Armies, Fifth; Army Groups, 15th.
    arrival in Algeria: 60
    CG, 15th Army Group: 354
    CG, Fifth and Seventh Armies: 159
    plans for Southern France: 176
Clausen: 434
Clausthal: 489
CLEANSLATE: 93. *See also* Russell Islands.
Clefcy: 332-33
Clefmont: 272
Clerf: 382-84
Clerf River and Valley: 353 381-84, 386 389
Clermont: 407
Cleurie: 295
Cleve: 279, 398-401, 403, 407
Cleve Forest: 402-03
Cleve-Rhine Canal: 399-400
Clevesy, Lt. Samuel H.: 111
Clevesy Pass: 111-12
Clifton (Eller) Island: 170
Climbach: 352
CLIPPER: 329. *See also* Geilenkirchen.
Cloppenburg: 491
Close Covering Group (TG 74.2): 415
Clowes, Maj. Gen. Cyril A. (Aus.): 51
Cluj: 300
Clyde, Firth of: 59
Coane, Brig. Gen. Ralph W.: 113, 116, 120
Coast Artillery Brigade (Provisional): 32
Coastal Attack Force (New Guinea): 230
COBRA: 227, 229, 232, 235-39
Cobru: 374
Coburg: 485, 487, 490
Cochem: 434, 436-37, 440
Cochran, Col. Philip G.: 170, 178
Coconut Grove: 71, 73, 75
Coconut Hill: 488
Cocos (Keeling) Islands: 329
Coesfeld: 460, 466
Cognac: 328
Cogolin: 249
Cogon: 352, 354
Cohen (Ennugenliggelap) Island: 170
Coin-lès-Cuvry: 324
Coin-sur-Seine: 278, 280-81
Coincourt: 283, 288
Colasian: 318-19
Colbitz Forest: 495
Cold Harbor: 106, 108
Colditz: 496, 498
Colgan, Capt. A. T.: 532
Colgan Woods: 532-36
Colhoun: 52
Colle 152, 352-53
Colle di Val d'Elsa: 226
Colle Ferro: 201
Colle San Angelo: 194
Collechio: 518
Collesano: 122
Colleville: 203, 219
Colli: 146, 149-50
Colli Laziali: 162, 166-67, 199

Collina: 289, 316
Collins, Maj. Gen. J. Lawton: 82, 86, 203, 210, 215, 269, 341
Collobrières: 250, 252
Colmar Pocket: 336, 343, 345-46, 351, 353, 360, 375, 377, 379, 381, 386-93, 395, 398
Cologne: 39, 267, 292, 305, 327, 393, 415, 418, 422, 424-25, 427, 429, 435, 440, 454, 456, 458-59, 514, 516-17
Cologne-Frankfurt Autobahn. *See* Frankfurt Autobahn.
Cologne Plain: 415, 418, 422, 424
Colombelles: 228, 232
Colombier-Fontaine: 326
Colombières: 229
Colombo: 31-32
Colonna: 201
Comacchio Spit: 421, 423, 425, 467, 469, 473
Combined Bomber Offensive against Europe
    around-the-clock operations commence: 95
    Austria: 138, 143, 144, 176
    CCS directive: 113, 172
    daylight raids postponed: 140
    Eisenhower directive: 187
    fighter escort for: 113, 137-38, 152, 154, 161, 192
    Germany: 85, 89, 95, 111, 113-14, 128, 130, 132, 137-40, 143-44, 150, 152, 154, 156, 161, 166, 172-73, 175-76, 178, 181, 184, 187, 192, 201, 203, 207, 215, 219, 234, 236, 268
    H2S-equipped aircraft in: 137, 144
    Hungary: 201, 271
    losses: 128, 132, 140, 161, 176, 184, 192, 215
    Poland: 219, 236, 244
    radar, use of: 154, 166
    radio countermeasures, use of: 139
    Rumania: 112, 124, 185, 203, 207, 234, 237, 242, 244-45
    shuttle system: 114, 138-39, 143, 175, 201, 203, 207, 215, 219, 234, 236-37, 242, 244, 245, 268, 271
    USSTAF in: 175
    V-weapons sites, attacks on: 128, 130, 152, 156
Combined Chiefs of Staff. *See also* British Chiefs of Staff; Joint Chiefs of Staff.
    agreement to establish: 14
    ANZAC area established: 20
    Burma and Malaya, directives on recovery of: 271, 274, 391, 543
    Burma pipeline approved: 95
    China, directive on airlift supply of: 200, 271, 517
    Combined Bomber Offensive, directive on: 113, 172
    order Darwin merged into ABDA: 18
    relieve VIII BC of support of North Africa: 87
    Eisenhower, directive to: 172
    Fifteenth Air Force, agreement to establish: 141-43

[INDEX]

Combined Chiefs of Staff—Continued
 Italy, in support of OVERLORD, directive on: 187
 Italy, plans for invading: 110-12, 115, 120, 122
 Japan, plan for defeat of: 152, 274. *See also* Japan, strategic plans for defeat of.
 landing craft allocation: 145, 152
 Mediterranean, unified command established for: 152-53, 155
 Myitkyina recovery, plans for: 200
 Normandy Campaign, plans for: 33, 42, 164
 Normandy Campaign, staff established for: 106
 Pacific theater established: 30
 Persian Corridor, approve movement of supplies through: 56
 at QUADRANT Conference: 127-29
 SEAC strategy, Mountbatten's proposals for: 316, 329
 Southern France, plans for: 176, 247
 strategic air forces, relinquish control of: 186
 TORCH command structure agreement: 46
 TRIDENT Conference plans: 110-12
 Tunisia attack plan approved: 73
Combined Fleet (Japanese): 310-12
Comintern, dissolution of: 112
Comiso: 118
Commander, Central Pacific. *See* Spruance, Adm. Raymond A.
Commander in Chief, Pacific Fleet. *See* Nimitz, Adm. Chester W.
Commander in Chief, Pacific Ocean Areas. *See* Nimitz, Adm. Chester W.
Commander in Chief, Southwest Pacific Area. *See* MacArthur, General Douglas; Southwest Pacific Area
.Commander in Chief, U.S. Fleet. *See* King, Adm. Ernest J.; Navy, United States; United States Fleet.
Commander in Chief, West
 Kluge succeeds Rundstedt: 223
 Model succeeds Kluge: 250
 Rundstedt reinstated: 262
Commander, South Pacific. *See* Ghormley, Vice Adm. Robert L.; Halsey, Adm. William F.
Commando forces, British. *See also* British Army units, Brigades and Battalions.
 Norway islands raid: 9
 in Italy: 131-33
 in Sicily: 119, 128
Commando forces, Dutch: 316
Commando forces, French: 249-50, 53-54
Commando Supremo: 128
Commanster: 380
Commercy: 260-61
Compiègne: 259-60
Compogne: 374-75
Comté: 369
Conca: 165
Conca River: 262-63, 274
Concepcion, Luzon: 382-83

Concepcion, Negros: 469, 471, 473
Conches: 254
Condé Northen: 329
Condé-sur-Noireau: 245-50
Condillac Pass: 254
Conical Hill: 535-40
Coningham, Air Vice Marshal Sir Arthur: 93
Connolly, Brig. Gen. Donald H.: 57, 60, 153, 156
Connolly, Maj. Robert V.: 542, 547-58
Conolly, Rear Adm. Richard L.: 167
Conroy, Col. Gardiner J.: 213
Conroy Field: 213
Consuegra: 324, 326, 333, 339
Consuma: 259
Consy: 367-70
Conthil: 323, 331, 339
Convoys: 55, 79
Cook., Maj. Gen. Gilbert R.: 247, 252
Cop (Csap): 335
Copeland, Brig. Gen. John E.: 112
Coral Sea naval and air actions: 36-37
Corcieux: 318, 324, 328
Cordon: 546
Coreno: 192
Corfu Island: 137, 301
Cori: 196-97, 199
Coriano: 263-64, 266-67, 270-72
Corinth: 298
CORKSCREW: 109-14
Corkscrew Ridge: 329-33
Corleone: 121
Corlett, Maj. Gen. Charles H.: 127, 168-69, 209, 278, 289, 296, 305
Cornacchiara: 287-88
Cormelles: 233
Corn Strong Point (Kwajalein): 168
Cornimont: 303
Cornwall: 31
Corny: 268, 287
Coronon: 523
Corps: *See also* Armored Corps.
 I: 42, 53, 73, 93, 182, 210, 301, 370-391, 393-96, 398-407, 409-10, 412-14, 416-17, 419, 421, 423, 426, 428, 430-31, 433-37, 439, 441-43, 445-46, 448-50 453, 455, 457, 459, 463, 465, 467, 469, 473, 477, 479, 481, 484, 486, 488, 490, 493, 495, 497, 499, 501, 503, 505, 507, 509, 511, 513, 515, 517, 519-20, 522, 527, 529-33, 535-45, 547-49
 II: 64-65, 70, 81, 85-86, 88-109, 117-28, 147, 149, 151-73, 176, 184, 191-202, 205-07, 234-36, 240, 244, 250-53, 261, 263-67, 269, 271-72, 276-77, 279, 282-84, 286-313, 318, 321, 334 368-70, 373, 375, 377, 383, 402, 410, 428, 431, 437, 439, 443, 457, 475, 483, 497, 499, 501, 503, 505, 507, 509, 511, 513, 515-16, 518, 521, 523, 525, 527

Corps—Continued
 III: 300, 316, 336, 347-49, 351, 353, 356-57, 359-77, 379-82, 384-87, 389, 391-92, 394, 396-402 404-05, 408, 412, 414-15, 417-18, 420, 422, 424-25, 427, 429, 431-33, 435-42, 444-45, 447-49, 451-52, 454, 456, 458, 460, 462-64, 466, 468, 470, 472, 474, 476, 478-80, 483, 485, 487, 489, 491, 493, 495, 498, 500, 504, 507-08, 511-12, 514, 516, 518-19, 521-22, 524, 526, 528-29
 IV: 184, 198-200, 207-08, 210, 212, 214-37, 240, 244, 248, 252-53, 255, 257, 260-62, 264-65, 267, 269, 271, 273, 275, 277, 279-80, 282-84, 286-301, 305, 309, 313, 315, 318-19, 336, 361-64, 368-71, 386, 392, 394, 397, 401, 404-10, 412-13, 417, 419, 423 425-26, 428, 433, 471, 475, 483, 494-95, 497, 499, 501, 503, 505, 507, 509, 511, 513, 515-16, 518, 520-21, 523, 525, 527
 V: 14, 203-11, 222, 228-31, 235, 237-65, 267-70, 272-73, 275 277-78, 280-82, 284, 287-88, 292-99, 301, 303, 305, 311-12, 315, 317-20, 322, 325, 328, 330, 332 334-36, 338-40, 342-47, 350-61, 363, 374-78, 380, 382-83, 387-95, 397, 402, 404-08, 411, 415, 417-18, 420, 422 424-27, 429, 431-37, 439-40, 444, 447-49, 451-52, 454, 456, 458-60, 462 464, 466, 468, 470, 472, 474, 476-77, 479, 481, 483, 485, 487, 489, 491, 494, 496, 498, 500, 502, 504, 508, 510, 512, 514-15, 517, 521-22, 524, 526, 528-33
 VI: 132-47, 150-55, 157-59, 162-79, 196-202, 204-10, 249-69, 271-72, 275 277-79, 282-87, 291-98, 300, 303-19, 321-22, 324-29, 331-52, 354-55, 362, 364-85, 388-93, 395-402, 404, 406, 408-10, 413-14, 419, 420, 422, 424-27, 429-33 435 438-42, 444-45, 448-49, 451-52, 454, 456, 458, 460, 462, 464, 466, 468, 470, 472, 474, 476, 478, 480, 483, 485, 487, 489, 491, 494-96, 498, 500, 502, 504, 506, 508, 510, 512, 514-15, 517, 519, 521-22, 524, 528, 530, 533
 VII: 203-22, 224-33, 236-51, 253, 256-71, 273, 275-76, 279, 280-82, 284, 287-90, 293, 295-308, 311, 319-20, 322-23, 326-47, 349-51, 353-59, 361-82, 393 397 407 410-12, 414-16, 418, 420, 422, 424-27, 429-33 435 438-42, 444-45, 448-49, 451-52, 454, 456, 458, 460, 462, 464, 466, 468, 470, 472, 474, 476, 478, 480, 483, 485, 487, 489, 491, 494-96, 498, 500, 502, 504, 506, 508, 510, 512, 514-15, 517, 519, 521-22, 524, 528, 530 533
 VIII: 210, 212-14, 219-30, 233-34, 236-51, 254, 256-61, 263, 265, 267, 270, 273-74, 276, 278-79,

Corps—Continued
  VIII—Continued
    288, 292, 294, 298, 300, 303, 308, 320, 323, 325, 343, 350, 353–77, 379–82, 384–95 397–402 405–08, 410–12, 414, 416–17, 419–22, 424, 429, 431–32 434–42 444, 447, 449, 451–52, 454, 457, 459–60, 463, 465, 467–68, 470, 472, 475, 477, 481, 483, 485, 487, 490, 492, 494, 496, 498, 500, 502, 504, 506, 508, 510, 514–15, 519, 522, 524, 533
  X: 255, 307, 310–53, 355–65, 367, 387–88, 403, 406–07, 412, 446, 453, 501, 503, 506, 507, 510–11, 513, 520, 522, 523, 525, 527, 529–44 547, 549, 550
  XI: 220, 249, 274, 287, 372, 387–88, 390–91, 393–96, 398–99 401–08, 411–14, 417, 421, 425, 434, 436, 439, 441–43, 445–46, 448–51, 453, 455, 457, 460–61, 463, 465, 467, 469, 471, 473, 475–77, 479, 482, 484, 486, 488, 490, 493, 497, 499, 501, 503, 505, 507, 510–11, 513, 517, 520, 522, 525, 527, 529–42, 546, 548
  XII: 225, 240, 247–49 251–61, 263–70, 272–73, 275, 278, 280–81, 283–95, 298–301, 307–08, 316–32, 334–63, 368, 371, 376–80, 382–86, 390, 392, 396–411, 413–14, 416–17, 419, 421–22, 424, 426, 428–29, 431–32, 434–42, 444–45, 447–49, 451–52, 454, 457, 459, 461, 463, 465, 467–68, 470, 472–73, 475, 477, 479, 481, 483, 485, 490, 492, 494, 496, 498, 500, 502, 504, 506, 508, 510, 512, 514–15, 517, 519, 521–22, 524, 526, 528–34
  XIII: 320–21, 323, 334–35, 340–44, 353, 355–56, 358, 384, 389, 391–92, 394–95 409, 411–12, 414–16, 418, 420–21, 423, 425, 427–28, 430, 433, 464, 466, 468, 470–72, 474, 476, 478, 480, 482, 484, 486, 491, 493, 495–97 499, 502,489, 504, 506, 512, 514–15, 517, 526, 528, 530
  XIV: 81–85, 87–89, 116–17, 119–20, 122–25, 154, 178–79, 183, 212, 214, 301, 370–92, 394–407, 409–10, 412–14, 416–17, 419, 421, 423, 425–26, 428, 430–31 433–43, 445–46, 448, 450–51, 453, 455, 457, 460–61, 463–64, 467, 469, 471, 473, 476–77, 479–80, 482, 484, 486, 488, 490, 493, 497, 499, 501, 503, 505, 510–11, 513, 517, 520, 522–23, 525, 527, 529–30, 535, 538, 544, 546, 549–50
  XV: 225, 240–59, 263, 266–70, 272–73, 275, 277–78, 281, 283–85, 290, 292–95 299, 302–05, 308–11, 313, 316–17 319–20, 325–29, 331, 333–38, 340, 342–43, 345–52, 354, 356–57, 362–70, 380–81, 383, 389, 391, 394, 397–401, 403–10, 412–13, 417, 419, 431, 433, 436, 439, 441–43, 445–48, 450–51, 453, 457,

Corps—Continued
  XV—Continued
    459, 461, 463, 465–67, 469, 471, 473, 475, 477, 479, 481, 483, 485, 487, 490, 492, 494, 496, 498, 500, 502, 504, 506–09, 511–12, 514, 516, 519–19, 521, 523–24, 526, 528–29, 531
  XVI: 348, 358, 387, 391–92, 394, 404 409, 412–13, 415–16, 418, 420–21, 423, 425, 427–30, 432–33, 450, 452, 454, 456, 458, 460, 462, 464, 466 468, 470, 472, 474, 476, 478, 480, 482, 484, 486, 489, 491, 493, 495, 497, 499, 502, 504, 506, 510, 512, 515, 524, 526, 530, 533
  XVIII: 356–63, 366–78, 380–94, 397, 399, 401–02, 450, 452–53, 456, 458 460, 462, 466, 468, 470, 472, 474, 476, 478, 480, 482–83, 485, 487, 489, 491, 493, 495, 497, 500, 502, 504, 506–08, 510, 512, 514–17, 519–21, 524, 526–27, 529
  XIX: 209–14, 217, 221–22, 226–33, 237–48, 250, 252–56, 258–71, 273, 275–79, 281–82, 284–85, 287, 289–305, 308, 312, 317, 320, 323, 327–39, 341–43, 346, 348, 351–52, 354, 356, 358, 360–61, 363, 371, 387–89, 391, 393, 395, 409–12, 414–16, 418, 420, 422–23, 425, 427, 454, 460, 462, 466, 468, 470, 472, 474, 476, 478–80, 482, 484, 486, 489, 491, 493, 495, 497, 499, 502, 504, 506, 508, 510, 521–22, 524, 526, 532
  XX: 225, 240, 242–43, 245–48 250–54 2, 272–73, 275 277–78, 280–82, 284–90, 292–302, 307 312–31, 333–57, 359–60, 362, 369 374–75, 56–62, 26470377–86, 389–90, 396–411, 413–14, 416–17, 419 421, 423–24 426 428–29 431–32 434–44 446–48 450–53 455457 459 461–63, 465 467–68, 470 472 474–75 477 479 481, 483 485 487 489 492 494 496 498 500 502, 504 506, 508 510 512 514 516–17, 519, 521–22, 524 526 528–30, 532–34
  XXI: 361, 373–74, 376 383, 386–93, 395–400, 402–03, 405, 417, 419, 423–24, 426, 428, 430, 437–39, 441–43, 445–48, 450–51, 453, 455, 459, 461, 463, 465, 469, 471, 473, 475, 477, 479, 483, 485, 487 490, 492, 494, 496, 498, 500, 502, 504, 507, 509, 511–12, 514, 516, 51821, 523–24, 526, 528–29, 531
  XXII: 458, 461–62, 464, 466, 471, 473, 485, 492, 496, 500, 502, 512, 514, 516
  XXIII: 458, 485, 504, 507, 512, 514
  XXIV: 307–23, 326, 333–42, 344–65, 374 387–88, 391, 400, 467–69, 471, 476–78, 480, 482, 484, 486, 488, 491, 493, 497, 499 504 506, 508, 510, 512–13, 515, 517, 519–20, 522, 524–25, 527, 529–48
  Provisional (Third Army): 248, 250, 356–58

Corps—Continued
  Provisional (Seventh Army): 119–24
Corradini: 87
Corregidor Island
  enemy air attacks on: 9–12, 30, 32–33, 35–36
  enemy artillery bombardment of: 32–33, 35–36
  enemy assault on: 36–37
  evacuation of personnel by submarine: 36
  garrison capitulates: 37
  harbor defense forces organized: 27
  Luzon Force escapes to: 32
  marines dispatched to: 8
  naval forces shifted to: 9
  Philippine government moved to: 8
  recovery of: 381, 391, 394, 402, 404–06, 411–13, 415, 421, 445, 457
  U.S. bombardment of: 381, 394, 402
  USAFFE hq opens on: 9
  USFIP hq opens on: 29
Corsica: 114, 133, 139, 248
Cortona: 223
Cosina River: 328, 332–35
Cotabato: 35–36, 446, 448, 503
Cote de Suisse Ridge: 325–26, 328
Cote St. Jean: 320–23
Cotentin Peninsula: 164, 209–10, 212–13, 223
Cotignola: 358, 366, 368, 486
COTTAGE: 127. See also Kiska.
Cottbus: 505, 513
Coulee: 373–74
Counterintelligence Corps Detachment, 41st: 220
Courcelles-sur-Nied: 329
Courier Bay: 36
Courmeilles-en-Vexin: 191
Courseulles: 203
Courtelevant: 330, 333
Courtenay: 255
Courtil: 376–78
Coutances: 227–28, 237–38
Couterne: 248
Couvains: 209
Couville: 213
Covell, Maj. Gen. William E. R.: 146
Coventelle: 366
Covigliano: 286
Cox, Lt. Col. William C.: 294–96
Cox's Bazaar: 290
Cracow: 374–76, 378
Crailsheim: 477, 479, 481, 483, 486, 492, 505, 507, 509
Crawinkel: 485
Creil: 259–60
Cremona: 5 20
Crendal: 380
Crerar, Gen. Henry D. G. (Br.): 235, 289
Crescent Hill: 538–40
Crespellano: 507
Crespino: 283
Crest: 253, 256–57
Crete: 116
Crettenbach: 524
Creuilly: 203
Creussen: 500
Creutzwald: 343
Creuzburg: 468, 472

[INDEX]

Crevechamps: 268
Crevic: 273
CRICKET Conference: 387, 390
Crimea sector: 44, 186–87
Crisbecq: 204–05, 208
Crittenberger, Maj. Gen. Willis D.: 184, 207
Croce: 264
Croce Hill: 151
Croeffelbach: 503
Croismare: 292
Crombach: 381
Cross-Channel attack. See Normandy Campaign
CROSSBOW: 128, 130, 152, 156
Crossroads 655 (Germany): 273
Crotone: 131, 13 3, 13 6
Crozon: 277
Crozon Peninsula: 273, 277–79
Cruchten: 401, 405
Crumbach: 492
Crump Hill: 447, 482, 488, 513
Csepel Island: 337, 346, 348
Cuchenheim: 426
CUDGEL: 161. SEE ALSO Arakan Coast.
Cuenca: 445–46, 448, 467
Cuernos de Negros Ridge: 527
Cuffiana: 484
Cuijk: 291
Cuizel: 279
Culayo: 385–86
Culoville: 204
CULVERIN: 161, 176, 188. See also Sumatra.
Cumberland Force (Can.): 309
Cunningham, Adm. Sir Andrew (RN): 64, 109, 133
Cunningham, Brig. Gen. Julian W.: 151, 154, 157, 160
Currie, Lauchlin: 46, 48
Cushing: 66
Cut-Cut Creek: 396
Cuxhaven: 522
CYCLONE: 215. See also Noemfoor Island.
Cyclops airdrome: 189
Cyrenaica: 3, 16–17
Czarnkow: 386
Czechoslovakia
 meetings of Allied forces in: 536
 operations in, from east: 306, 342–43, 353, 355, 379, 382, 385–86, 455, 463, 465, 471, 473, 481, 498, 505, 511, 518, 523, 525, 534–37
 operations in, from west: 502, 504, 508, 510, 512, 516–17 519, 521–22, 524, 526, 528–33
Czestochowa: 376–77, 380

Daaden: 458
Dachau: 523
Dachsenhausen: 454
Dackscheid: 417
Dadap Island: 166
Dadjangas: 549–50
Daehre: 508
Daet: 7
Dagami: 311–15, 317–18
Dagoe (Hiiumaa) Island: 294
Dagua: 128
Daguitan River: 307

Dagupan: 370
Daha: 362
Dahl: 368, 468
Dahl, Col. Arne (Nor.): 326
Dahlem: 417, 429
Dahlhunden: 376
Dahn: 448
Dahnen: 394, 396–97, 407–08
Daiku: 418
Dain-en-Saulnois: 323
Dakar: 69
Dakeshi: 537
Dakeshi Ridge: 534–37
Dakiton: 544
Dalberg: 443
Daleiden: 408
Dalem: 338
Daliao airfield: 525, 527
Dalirig: 36–37
Dalldorf: 508
Dalupiri Island: 406
Dambach: 365, 442
Damortis: 373, 375, 377, 385, 390, 402, 428
Dampier Strait: 120
Damulaan: 326, 333, 339
Danao: 507, 513
Dandriwad River: 189–91, 250
Dangueville: 208
Danmarsheim: 465
Dannemarie: 331
Dannenberg: 510, 512
Dannstadt: 447
Dansweiler: 422
Danube River: 257, 264, 291, 308–09, 337, 340, 343–49, 358, 360, 362, 377, 379, 382, 449, 459, 463, 467, 471, 477, 481, 506–07, 509–19, 521–22, 526, 528, 532
Danzig: 384, 406, 424, 428, 435–36, 446, 449–50, 453, 455, 457, 459, 461, 463
Dao: 307, 312
Daoulas Peninsula: 259
Daraga: 467, 469, 471, 473, 477, 484
Darby, Col. William O.: 516, 518
Darby's Rangers: 121–22, 133–34, 164, 167, 516, 518. See also Ranger Battalions.
Dardennes Ravine: 254
Darlan, Adm. François (Fr.): 66, 67, 77
Darmstadt: 277, 318, 453
Darong: 523
Darschied: 428–29, 432, 434
Darwin: 6, 18, 24–25, 53
Dasburg: 394, 396–97, 400, 407–09
Daseburg: 464
Dasol Bay: 375
Datteln: 468
Dattenberg: 433
Dattenfeld: 476
Datterode: 472
Datzeroth: 448
Dau: 385
Daubenrath: 410
Daubringen: 458
Daun: 428–29
Dausfeld: 417
Dautersdorf: 512
Davao: 7, 35, 244, 520, 522, 525, 527, 530, 531, 535–39

Davao Gulf: 511, 513, 515, 517, 520, 549
Davao Plain: 542
Davao River 529
Davidson, Brig. Gen. Garrison H.: 162, 176
Davidson, Brig Gen. Howard C.: 40, 121, 547
Davis, Lt. Col. Everett S.: 15
Dawley, Maj. Gen. Ernest J.: 132
Daylight air raids postponed: 140. See also Combined Bomber Offensive against Europe.
Deane, Maj. Gen. John R.: 143
Death March in Philippines: 32
Death Valley (Saipan): 217–22
Deuville: 253
Debrecen: 201, 300–301, 307
DeCarre, Brig. Gen. Alphonse: 89–90
Dedenbach: 433
Dedenborn: 355, 391–92
Degelberg: 517
Degerndorf: 528
Degenershausen: 500
Deggendorf: 517, 519
DeGeul River: 270–71, 273, 275
Dei Mori Hill: 501, 503
Deidenberg: 379–80
Deiffelt: 380
Deir el Shein: 44
Del Carmen field: 4–5
Del Monte airfield: 6–7, 536
Delhi conference on Malaya-Singapore: 542
Delhofen: 457
Delhoven: 424
Delitz: 489
Delitzsch: 504, 506, 508
Delkenheim: 459
Delle: 330, 333
Dellen: 359
Delme: 321
Delme Ridge: 321
Delrath: 425
DELTA Force 249. See also Southern France Campaign.
Dempsey, Lt. Gen. Myles C. (Br.): 203, 285
Demyansk: 96
Dengling: 521
Dengolsheim: 376–77
Deniki: 47, 49
Denklingen: 482
Denmark: 527, 530
Densborn: 428
Densieders: 447
Dépapré Bay: 188
Depienne: 71
Deposito: 346–47
Derenbach: 379–80
Derenburg: 489, 502
Derenthal: 481
Derichsweiler: 350–51
Derikum: 424
Dernaïa Pass: 93, 95
Derna: 7, 12, 18, 20–21, 29
Dernau: 429
Dernborg: 451
Dersdorf: 427
Desna River: 133

Dessau: 494, 496, 498, 500, 506, 508, 510, 151, 215, 26
Destry: 325
Detachment d'Armee de l'Atlantique: 419, 494, 496, 498, 500, 503 ,505, 507, 525, 527, 531
Detachment d'Armee des Alpes: 419, 447, 457, 461, 471, 473, 486, 490, 500
Detmold: 468, 472
Deuerling: 519
Deurne: 283, 286, 291, 301, 304, 313
Deutsch-Eylau: 381
Deutsch Krone: 401
Deutzen: 494
Deuz: 464
Devantave: 367
Deventer: 480, 484
Devecser: 455
Devers, Lt. Gen. Jacob L.: 313, 343
  CG ETO: 108
  CG NATOUSA: 161, 309
  CG 6th Army Group: 240
  names Eaker commander of USAAF in UK: 134
DeWitt, Lt. Gen. John L.: 28, 236
DEXTERITY: 136. See also Cape Gloucester.
Diamond Narrows: 129
Dick Hill (Okinawa): 536-39, 541
Dickerscheid: 415
Dickweiler: 354-55
Dicomano: 230, 263, 268
Die: 253
Dieblich: 440
Dieblicherberg: 440
Dieburg: 453 457
Dieffenbach: 443
Diego Suarez: 37, 57, 83
Diekirch: 356, 377-78
Dielheim: 466
Diemel River: 464, 466, 468
Dierdorf: 454
Dierscheid: 431
Dieler: 439
Dieppe: 50, 259-60
Diesfordt: 450
Dieskau: 504
Diessen: 523
Diest: 264, 269, 274
Dietenhausen: 481
Dietenheim: 516
Dieteren: 375-76
Dietersheim: 494 496
Dietfurt: 516
Dietlingen: 481
Dieulouard: 269-70, 272-73, 275, 278, 280
Dieuze: 281, 320, 326, 329-30, 333-34
Diez: 454, 456-57, 461
Digdig: 419, 421, 423 427-28, 434
Digne: 252
Digos: 35-36, 515, 517, 519-20, 522-23, 536
Digosville: 216-17
Diit River: 310-11
Dijon: 258, 262, 266-67
Dilap: 510
Dill, Field Marshal Sir John: 90, 354
Dill River: 454, 456, 458, 464
Dillenburg: 458, 462, 466, 500, 502

Dillingen: 342, 345-52 355 359 396-400, 442-43, 511-14, 516, 518
Dilmar: 407
Dilsburg: 446
Dimapur: 183, 185, 187, 206, 216
Dinagat Island: 305
Dinalupihan: 12-13, 387, 391, 394, 401
Dinan: 241-42, 247
Dinant: 263, 265, 360-61
Dinard: 243, 245-48
Dinez: 373
Dingbuchhof: 411
Dingdorf: 421
Dingolfing: 524, 526
Dinkelsbuehl: 507, 509
Dinkelscherben: 518
Dinker: 472
Dinslaken: 451, 454
Diosgyoer: 271
Dipolog: 431, 434
DIRECTOR: 151, 154. See also Arawe.
Dirmerzheim: 422
Dirmingen: 443
Dirmstein: 446
Disney, Col. Paul A.: 294
Disternich: 418
Distroff: 325-26
Dita: 461, 467
Dittaino River: 121
Dittlingen: 407
Dives River: 248-50
Divieto: 128
Divisions. See Airborne Divisions; Armored Divisions; Cavalry Division, 1st; Composite Army-Marine Division; Infantry Divisions; Marine Corps Divisions.
Divnoe: 86
DIXIE: 217. See also Chinese Communist forces, U.S. observer group with.
Dixmude: 265
Djebel Abiod: 67-70, 99-100, 106
Djebel Achkel: 108
Djebel Aïnchouna: 106-07
Djebel Aïred: 81-82, 106-07
Djebel Azag: 81-82, 106-07
Djebel Bargou: 88
Djebel Ben Kheir: 102
Djebel Berda: 100-103
Djebel Bou Aoukaz: 107
Djebel Bou Dabouss: 88
Djebel Bou Jerra: 100
Djebel Chemsi: 102
Djebel Cheniti: 108-09
Djebel Dardyss: 106-07
Djebel Djebs: 102
Djebel Douaou: 99
Djebel Douimiss: 108
Djebel Dribica: 99
Djebel Edjehaf: 105
Djebel el Ahmera: 77-78, 105-07
Djebel el Ang: 104-05, 107
Djebel el Ank: 99
Djebel el Anz: 107
Djebel el Hamra: 94
Djebel el Haouareb: 103
Djebel el Hara: 107
Djebel el Kreroua: 100-102
Djebel el Mcheltat: 99, 101-02
Djebel el Messeftine: 108

Djebel Fkirine: 107
Djebel Garci: 105
Djebel Grembil: 107
Djebel Guermach: 107
Djebel Hazemat: 107
Djebel Ksaïra: 92-93
Djebel Lessouda: 92
Djebel Lettouchi: 101
Djebel Maïzila: 103
Djebel Mansour: 105
Djebel Melab: 99-100
Djebel Meloussi: 90
Djebel Mergueb: 106
Djebel Msid: 106
Djebel Naemia: 99-100, 103
Djebel Ousselat: 103
Djebel Rihana: 92
Djebel Rhorab: 103
Djebel Sidi Mansour: 109
Djebel Sidi Meftah: 106-07
Djebel Tahent: 107-08
Djebel Tanngouche: 104-06
Djebel Tebaga: 99-100
Djebel Touila: 102
Djebel Touta: 106
Djebel Trozza: 88, 90
Djebel Djedeïda: 70-71, 108-09
Djeloula Pass: 104
Djibouti: 70, 78
Djidjelli: 67
Dmitriev Lgovsky: 96
Dnieper River and Basin: 25, 130, 136-38, 140-42, 144, 146-47, 151, 161, 165-66, 169, 171, 176, 178-80, 244
Dnieprodzerzhinsk: 142
Dniepropetrovsk: 137-38, 142
Dniester River and Basin: 181-82
Dno: 170, 175
Doan, Col. Leander L.: 464
Dobbie, Lt. Gen. Sir William (Br.): 28
Dobel Plateau: 486, 488
Dobodura: 67, 69, 72, 74-76, 78-79, 97
Dobra Voda: 532
Dobsina: 385
Dochamps: 367-69
Dockendorf: 414
Dockweiler: 429
Dodigny: 206
Doe, Maj. Gen. Jens A.: 182, 197, 213, 220, 417, 434
Doellstaedt: 483
Doemitz: 527-28
Doenitz, Adm. Karl: 524
Doernigheim: 459
Doesburg: 468
Dog Line (Bougainville): 146
Dohm: 429
Dolan Hill (Negros): 476, 484, 486, 493, 503, 506, 508, 510, 519, 522, 527, 536, 538 ,540
Dole: 264
Dollendorf: 431
Dollinger: 531
Dolores, Leyte: 355
Dolores, Luzon: 388
Dolus: 525
Doma Cove: 91
Domazlice: 526
Dombasle: 272-73
Domfaing: 308

[INDEX]

Domfessel: 343–45
Domfront: 242, 245, 248
Dominican Hill: 517, 519
Domjevin: 285
Dommershausen: 439
Dompaire: 270
Don River and Basin: 43–51, 68, 75–76, 82, 85, 132, 471
Dona airstrip: 102
Donaueschingen: 507
Donaustauf: 516, 518
Donauwoerth: 516
Donbaik: 82, 86, 90, 93, 99
Doncols: 371–73
Donets River and Basin: 39, 45, 87, 90–91, 96
Donnange: 380
Donnerberg. See Hill 287.
Donnstetten: 509
Doolittle, Maj. Gen. James H.: 156
  CG AFHQ U.S. air forces: 64
  leads first air attack on Japan: 34
Doorman, Rear Adm. Karel W. (Dutch): 22, 25–26
Dorbach: 432
Dorf Pingsdorf: 425, 427, 434
Dorf Point: 159
Dorfweil: 463, 465
Dormagen: 425
Dorn, Brig. Gen. Frank: 114, 125, 189, 354
Dornbock: 502
Dornheim: 449 451
Dornot: 265–67
Dorothy Hill (Okinawa): 542
Dorrenbach: 446, 448
Dorscheid: 385, 454
Dorsetshire: 31
Dorsten: 456, 458, 460
Dorstfeld: 482
Dortelweil: 459
Dortmund: 476, 482, 487, 489, 491
Dortmund-Ems Canal: 466, 468–70, 472 474 480
Dorweiler: 418, 439
Dot Inlet: 121, 127, 129, 132
Doubs River: 263–66, 325
Douglas Aircraft Company: 102
Douve River: 203–06, 208–13
Douz: 101
Dovadola: 319, 321
Doveren: 411, 413
Dovsk: 151
Doyen, Gen. (Fr.): 419
Draa Saada el Hamra: 101
Drabenderhohe: 487
DRACULA: 235, 260, 271, 293, 426, 455, 501, 517, 525, 528. See also Rangoon.
Dragoni: 40–41
Dragons Peninsula: 116
DRAGOON: 240, 246–49, 258, 267. See also ANVIL; Southern France Campaign.
Draguignan: 250–51
Draisdorf: 496
Drammont: 249
Dransfeld: 479
Drauffelt: 382, 384
Drava River: 340, 343, 345, 347, 463
Dreiborn: 390–91

Dreineiherof: 440
Dreis: 429, 432, 434
Dreisbach: 342
Drensteinfurt: 466
Dresden: 401, 505, 509, 511, 513, 534
Dreux: 248–49, 251–52
Drexler: 542
Driel: 282, 284–85
Drindarai River: 199
Driniumor River: 199, 202, 205, 207, 221, 223, 227–36, 239–41, 243–48, 250
Drohobycz: 219
Drôme River: 204, 254, 256–59
Dromersheim: 444
Drove: 412, 415, 418
Drulingen: 339 381
Drum, Lt. Gen. Hugh A.: 11, 13–14, 17
Drupt: 432
Drusenheim: 368–70, 379, 388, 391–92, 399
Dubno: 181–82
Dubrovnik: 307
Dudeldorf: 424
Duderstadt: 474
Duelken: 108
Duelmen: 460
Dueppenweiler: 442
Duerboslar: 330
Dueren: 327, 329, 341, 347, 349–50, 352, 354, 392, 410–12, 484
Duerscheven: 424
Duerwiss: 331–33
Duesseldorf: 497, 500, 502, 514
  first two-ton incendiary bomb dropped: 54
Duff, Brig. Gen. Robinson E.: 509, 511
Dugo: 548
Duisburg: 423, 474, 487, 489, 500, 502, 506
Duisdorf: 429–31
Dukhovschchina: 136
Dulag: 307–09, 361
Dulig: 372
Dumaguete: 519–20
Duman River: 548
Dummling: 487
Dumpay: 371
Dumpu: 131, 135–36, 139, 164
Duncan: 58
Duncan, Brig. Gen. Asa N.: 19, 36
Dunckel, Brig. Gen. William C.: 302, 353
Dungenheim: 429
Dunkerque: 265, 268, 276
Dunnwald: 487, 489, 491
Dunstekoven: 427,
Duppach: 426
Durance River and Valley: 252–53
Durbuy: 359
Durlach: 477
Duropa Plantation: 71, 76
Durovo: 99
Durrentzen: 388
Durstel: 337–38, 340
Dutagan Point: 368
Dutch East Indies. See Netherlands East Indies.
Dutch Harbor: 40, 104
Dutra, Maj. Gen. Enrice Gaspar (Braz.): 292

Duttling: 424
Duzerville: 66
Dvina River: 228, 237
Dvinsk: 236–37
Dyke Ackland Bay: 63

Eagle: 37, 49
Eaker, Maj. Gen. Ira C.
  CG of Eighth Air Force: 72
  CG of MAAF: 156
  CG of U.S. air units in U.K.: 38, 134
  establishes Bomber Command: 25, 33
  warns of Chennault relief: 538
EAM (Greek National Liberation Front): 321
East Africa Command (Br.): 44, 53–57, 59–60, 63–64, 83
East Caves (Biak): 198, 205–06, 208–09, 220–21, 223, 225, 234
East China Sea naval battle: 480
East Indies. See Netherlands East Indies.
East Indies Campaign: 11–46
East Indies Fleet (RN): 384
East Pinnacle (Okinawa): 508, 510
East Prussia, operations in: 374, 378–89, 394–95, 399–400, 439, 446, 448, 450, 453, 455, 461, 481, 483, 498, 505, 516, 518
East Tank Barrier (Makin): 148
East Wala: 191
East-West Trail (Bougainville): 144, 146
Eastern Air Command (Allied): 153–54, 342, 542
Eastern Air Command (RAF): 82, 93, 96
Eastern Assault Force (Algiers): 64
Eastern Defense Area (and Sector) (New Guinea): 221, 227, 229
Eastern Defense Command (New Guinea): 221, 227
Eastern Defense Command (U.S.): 162, 365
Eastern Dorsal: 89, 103–04
Eastern Europe, operations in. See under country.
Eastern Fleet (RN): 4, 12
Eastern Force (TG 31 .2): 115
Eastern Front, operations on. See under country.
Eastern Island: 476, 480
Eastern Islands Attack and Fire Support Group (TG 51 .11): 486
Eastern Mandates Campaign: 152–210
Ebbinghausen: 464, 472
Ebeleben: 485
Eberbach: 441
Ebersdorf: 490
Ebersheim: 445
Eberstadt: 453
Ebeye Island: 167–69
E-boats (Ger.): 189
Eboli: 136
Ebsdorf: 458
Ecausseville: 206
Echague: 456
Echt: 376
Echterbosch: 378
Echternach: 297, 353, 355, 357–59, 362, 376, 396, 398–99

Echternacherbruck: 400
Echtz: 349
Eckdorf: 427
Eckelsheim: 444
Eckenhage: 485
Ecot: 326
Ecouché: 249-51
Ecurcey: 326
Eddekhila: 108-09
Eddy, Maj. Gen. Manton S.: 252, 325
Eder Dam: 111
Eder River: 460, 462-65, 468, 470
Ederen: 328, 330-32
Edersee Dam: 460, 462
Ederstau: 462, 464
Edinburgh: 36
Edingen: 456
Edmondeville: 205-06
Edsall: 26
Edson's Ridge (Guadalcanal): 54-55
Edward Rutledge: 66
Edward's Plantation: 135
Eekeren: 294
Eem River: 501
Efate: 145
Eferding: 531
Effeld: 416
Efferden: 427
Efogi Spur: 54
Eger: 341
Eggersheim: 108
Egglfing: 528-29
Egypt, operations in. *See also* Libya.
  Alexander arrives in: 49
  Allied withdrawal to: 41
  communications with Cyrenaica reopened: 16
  Egypt-Libya Campaign: 41-92
  enemy drive on: 43-66
  enemy supply situation: 53
  first U.S. air attack in: 50
Egypt-Libya Campaign: 41-92
Ehingen: 511, 513-14
Ehlscheid: 449
Ehnen: 406
Ehr: 440
Ehrang: 421, 424, 426, 428-29, 431
Ehrenbreitstein: 456
Ehrenstein: 490
Eibelhausen: 462
Eibertingen: 378, 3 80
Eichel Creek: 344
Eichelberger, Lt. Gen. Robert L.: 182, 210-11, 220, 379, 388, 401, 434, 471, 520
  commands Advance New Guinea Force: 84
  commands Allied forces on New Guinea: 84
  commands at Buna: 71-73, 75
  commands I Corps: 42, 53, 93
  commands 32d Division: 75
  commands U.S. Eighth Army: 265
Eichelhardt: 484
Eichen: 427
Eichendorf: 526
Eichlinghofen: 487
Eichstatt: 514, 516, 518
Eicks: 426

Eierscheid: 387-88
Eigen: 462
Eighth Army Area Command (S Philippines): 412. *See also* Infantry Divisions, Americal.
Eilenburg: 508, 510, 512, 515, 517, 524
Eilendorf, 271 273, 298, 303-04
Eilsbrunn: 514
Eilscheid: 417
Eimerscheid: 386-87
Einbeck: 483
Eindhoven: 276, 278-79, 284, 287, 288
Einersheim: 477
Eining: 519
Einruhr: 391-92
Einvaux: 278
Eisbach: 447
Eisenach: 417, 465, 475 477 479
Eisendorf: 521
Eisenfelden: 526
Eisenhower, Gen. Dwight D.: 81-82, 86-87, 137, 142, 183, 204. *See also* Allied Force Headquarters; European Theater of Operations; Supreme Headquarters, Allied Expeditionary Force; campaigns by name .
  approval of MTO air redesignations: 159
  assumes command of ETO: 43
  CCS directive to Supreme Commander: 172
  CG of MTO: 152-53, 155, 161
  commands forces in NW Africa: 48, 55
  conference with Darlan: 67
  conference with Giraud: 64
  and control of strategic air forces: 186
  decides to abandon Tunis drive: 77
  directive on Combined Bomber Offensive: 187
  directives on drive on Germany: 262, 267, 270, 273, 283, 286, 282, 305, 309, 313, 335-36, 338, 363, 442, 458
  directives on Normandy breakout: 213, 236, 241, 257-58
  directive on NW Africa: 50
  divides Twelfth Air Force in two: 141
  inspects II Corps: 92, 98
  on landing craft allocation: 145
  as Supreme Commander: 152, 156, 163
  plans for invasion of Italy: 113, 115, 120, 122, 124
  plans for Normandy Campaign: 106, 112, 129, 150, 152, 156, 164, 167, 191, 202
  plans for seizure of Corsica: I 14
  reorganizes SOS headquarters: 163
  role in Italian surrender: 128, 131-32, 137-38
  Tunisia campaign plan approved: 73
Eisenschmitt: 429
Eisenstein: 526
Eisfeld: 487
Eita: 149
Eitelsbach: 423-24, 426
Eitorf: 454
Eitting: 524
El Adem Ridge: 3, 39

El Agheila: 14, 16, 69-70, 74-76
El Ala: 102
El Alamein: 43-45, 50, 53-55, 58, 60, 66
El Aouana: 102
El Aouïna: 65
El Aroussa: 95
El Fraile Island: 450, 493, 503
El Guessa: 72-73
El Guettar: 99-101
El Hamma: 99-101
El Haseiat: 9, 17
El Ma el Abiod, 93, 95, 98
El Sollum. *See* Sollum
ELAS (Communist Hellenic People's Army): 288
Elba Island: 212-13
Elbe River, drive to: 458, 466, 484-86, 489, 491, 493-95, 497-500, 502, 504, 506, 508, 510, 512-22, 524, 526, 528-30, 532-34
Elbenau: 491
Elberfeld: 498
Elbeuf: 252, 254-57
Elbing: 382, 384, 386-87, 399
Elbingrode: 504
Elbrus: 51
Elcherath: 386, 388
Elchingen: 509
Eldena: 528
Electra: 26
Elephant Point (Burma): 528, 530
Elgert: 454
Elista: 50, 81
Elkhotovo: 57
ELKTON: 92, 96, 98, 106, 155. *See also* New Britain Island; New Guinea Campaign; New Ireland campaign.
Ella Hill (Okinawa): 542
Elle River: 207-10, 411
Ellen: 411-12
Eller Island: 170
Elleringhausen: 474
Ellern: 441
Ellice Islands: 128-32, 139
Ellmendingen: 481
Ellmore Field: 360, 363
Ellrich: 489
Ellwangen: 509, 511, 513
Ellzee: 518
Elmen: 527
Eloaue Island: 182
Eloyes: 282-84
Elpe: 478
Elsdorf: 414-15
Elsen: 470
Elsenborn: 355-58, 363 387-88
Elsenbuchel Woods: 387
Elsenheim: 383, 385
Elsig: 426
Elst: 285-87, 342
Elten: 462
Eltershofen: 503
Eltville: 461, 463
Elzange: 323
Elze: 476
Emberménil: 302
Embi: 67
Embken: 418, 420
Embogu: 67

[INDEX]   [591]

Emden: 137, 520
Emirau: 180-82, 186
Emmendingen: 509
Emmerich: 402-03, 430, 449, 458 460, 462, 466
Emmern: 474
Emmersweiler: 419
Emmons, Lt. Gen. Delos C.: 6
Empoli: 238, 261
Empress Augusta Bay: 136, 138, 143, 178, 183
Empress Augusta Bay naval battle: 143
Empress of Asia: 22
Ems River: 462, 464, 466, 480, 517
Ems-Dortmund Canal: 466, 468-70, 472 474, 480
Emser Canal: 456, 460, 462, 478
Enchenberg: 346-48
Encounter: 26
END RUN: 187-90. *See also* Myitkyina, recovery of.
Endau: 14-15, 19
Endenich: 430
Enfidaville: 104-05, 110
Engebi Island: 173-74
Engelsberg: 511
Engelsdorf: 332
Engelskirchen: 489
Engineer Aviation Battalions
  803d: 32
  804th: 126
  808th: 160
  863d: 166
  864th: 162, 187
  1913th: 159, 187
Engineer Battalion, 14th (Philippine Scouts): 32
Engineer Boat and Shore Regiments
  533d: 503, 506
  542d: 223
Engineer Combat Battalions
  32d (Philippine Scouts): 32
  109th: 102
  209th: 198, 237
  236th: 200, 223, 237
  1106: 306
Engineer Combat Group, 1104th: 302
Engineer Combat Regiments
  19th: 94
  36th: 170, 173, 196
  39th: 170, 218
  43d: 52
  46th: 43
  540th: 171
Engineer General Service Regiments
  224th: 459
  226th: 459
Engineer Special Brigade, 2d: 93, 131, 157
England. *See* United Kingdom. English Channel escape of German battleships: 23
  raid on Sark Island: 57
Engranville: 204-05
Engwiller: 343
Eniwetok Atoll: 162, 166, 169, 172-75
Eniwetok Expeditionary Group (TG 51.11): 172-73
Enkenbach: 446
Enkheim: 459
Enkirch: 440

Enna: 119-21
Ennal: 374
Ennery: 426
Enns: 532
Enns River: 531-33
Ennubirr Island: 167
Ennugarrett Island: 167
Ennugenliggelap Island: 170
Ennumennet Island: 167
Ennylabegan Island: 167, 170
Enogai Inlet: 116-18, 121, 126
Ensch: 434
Enschede 464
Enscherange: 382
Ensdetten: 462
Ensdorf: 341, 345-47, 350, 354-57, 445
Ensheim: 439, 443
Enshih: 125
Ensisheim: 379, 389, 391-93, 395-96
Enterprise: 25, 27, 34, 38, 40, 44, 51, 61, 67, 488
Entrance Creek: 70, 73, 75-78
Enubuj Island: 167-68
Enying: 346, 451
Enz River: 405, 407, 477, 481, 483, 486, 488, 490, 498
Enzen: 407, 424
Eora Creek: 59-60
Epernay: 402
Epfig: 341
Epgert: 452
Epinal: 262, 268-69, 272, 277, 280, 282 87
Eply: 320
Eppenich: 420
Equeurdreville: 217-18
Era River: 232
Erbach: 513
Erbendorf: 506
Erberich: 333-34
Erding: 526
Erdingen: 482
Erdorf: 414, 421-22, 424, 429
Erfelden: 449 451
Erft Canal: 414-16, 418, 422, 424
Erft River: 418, 420, 422, 424-25, 427, 430
Erfurt: 481, 483, 485, 487 490
Ering: 528-29
Eritrea: 21
Erkelenz: 412, 414-15
Erlach: 473
Erle: 456, 458
Erlen River: 443 451
Erlenbach: 431
Ermsdorf: 357
Erndetbrueck: 476
Ernst: 440
Ernsthofen Dam: 533
Ernzen: 402
Erp: 284, 420
Erpel: 431
Erpeldange: 377
Erpensen: 508
Erstein: 338-40, 389
Ervenheim: 459
Erwitte: 470, 472
Escaut River. *See* Schelde Estuary and River.
Esch: 414-15, 426, 429 434
Eschdorf: 361

Eschenau: 507, 511, 518
Eschenbach: 476
Eschenlohe: 525
Eschfeld: 408
Eschringen: 439
Eschwege: 470, 475, 477, 479
Eschweiler: 273, 284, 330, 333, 380, 414
Eschweiler Woods: 327-29
Eselborn: 382
Eselshalden: 507
Eslarn: 514, 516
Espeler: 384
Espenfeld: 485
Esperde: 476
Esperia: 193-94
Espiritu Santo, as staging area: 39, 49-50, 53-57 59, 61, 66, 130
Esquay: 231, 242
Esschen: 308-09
Essen: 478, 485, 487
Essenburg: 425
Essey-lès-Nancy: 275
Esshoff: 478
Esslingen: 416
Esterholz: 506
Estero de Paco: 400
Estero de Tonque: 400
Estonia, operations in: 168-69, 171, 237, 275, 280, 284-85, 294, 296, 330, 335
Estrella, Luzon: 381
Estrella, Mindoro: 381
Estry: 240-43
Esztergom: 362, 369, 453
Etain: 260, 264
Etampes: 253
Etang de Lindre: 307
Eterville: 228.
Ethiopia, recognized by U.K.: 21
Etival: 322 :
Etreaupont: 260
Ettelbach: 494
Ettelbruck: 356-57, 359, 361-62, 377
Etteldorf: 428
Etteln: 462
Ettelscheid: 391-92
Ettenheim: 507
Ettleben: 481
Ettlingen: 483
Ettringen: 519
Etzelbach: 492
Etzling: 405
Euchen: 298, 301, 327
Eudenbach: 444-45, 449, 451
Euenheim: 426
Eupatoria: 12, 33
Eupen: 268-69, 271, 355-58 360
Eure River: 249, 254
EUREKA Conference: 150-51
European Advisory Commission instituted: 143
European Theater of Operations. *See also* Eisenhower, Gen. Dwight D.; Supreme Headquarters, Allied Expeditionary Force.
  activated under Chaney: 41
  Andrews as CG: 90-91
  boundaries altered: 91
  COSSAC established: 106
  Devers succeeds Andrews: 108

European Theater of Operations—Con.
  Eisenhower assumes command: 43
    hostilities cease: 534-35
    redeployment of units to Pacific: 528, 530, 550
    SAF headed by Spaatz: 156
    supersedes USAFBI: 41
Euscheid: 408
Euskirchen: 385, 392, 422, 424, 426
Evertsen: 26
Eveshausen: 438
Evrecy: 228, 231-32, 242
Evreux: 252, 254
Executions of prisoners of war: 34
Exeter: 34
Exmes: 253
Expeditionary Troops, Iwo Jima: 299, 363, 411, 427
Eynattener Wald: 269
Eythra: 502
Eywiller: 337-38

Factory, The (Anzio): 165-66, 170-72, 197
Faenza: 162, 263, 291, 295, 330, 333, 337-38, 340, 351-57
Faetano: 279
Faha: 406
Faibus St. Hilo Point: 237
Faïd Pass: 72, 88-90, 92, 104
Faimes: 265
Fais Island: 365, 367
Falaise: 233, 236, 242, 244-53
Falaise Hill: 272
Falam: 145
Falcino: 306
Falck: 338-39
Falize Woods: 374
Falkenberg: 508
Falknov: 533
Falvaterra: 197
Fammera: 193
Famy: 473
Fanning Island: 35
Far East, unified command for: 9
Far East Command (RAF): 4, 5, 9, 24
Far East Air Force: 3-4, 6, 21, 315, 368
Far East Council: 4, 23
Farchant: 525
Farebersviller: 339-40 344
Farenholt: 58
Farneto: 307
Farniers: 369
Fasari: 59
Fastov: 145-46
Faubourg de Vaucelles: 233
Fauconnerie: 104
Fauglia: 231-32
Faulquemont: 318, 321, 324-25, 328-29, 331
Faurndau: 505
Faverois: 330
Favignana Island: 123
Faxe: 324
Fayence: 251-52, 255
Faymonville: 357, 375-76
Fays: 303
Fechingen: 439
Fecht River: 381, 392-93

Fechteler, Rear Adm. William M.: 176, 222-23, 385, 415
Fedala: 65-66
Fecamp: 197
Felbecke: 450
Feldhausen: 460
Feldkassel: 427
Feldkirch: 530-31
Felisio: 366, 484
Fell: 438
Fellerich: 408
Felonica: 513, 515, 517
Felsberg: 341
Felsoegall: 453
Femmina Morta: 279
Fenétrange: 335, 380
Feodosia: 10, 16
Ferentino: 200
Fériana: 69, 91-93, 95-96
Fermo: 214
Fern Pass: 525, 527-28, 530-31
Fernsdorf: 496
Fernstein: 525, 528
Ferrara: 276, 503, 509, 511, 513
Ferris, Brig. Gen. Benjamin G.: 160
Ferryville: 108-09
Ferschweiler: 402
Fervaches: 237
Fessenheim: 396-97
Feuchtwangen: 492, 502-04, 507, 509
Feugerolles-sur-Orne: 242
Feusdorf: 429
Fey: 275, 324
Fialla Hill: 154
Fianarantsoa: 57
Fichtenbach: 521
Fichtenberg: 503
Fickett, Lt. Col. E. M.: 342, 353, 356, 360, 366, 368-69, 371, 373, 382, 386-87, 454, 457, 459, 461, 463, 465
Ficulle: 210
Field Artillery Battalions
  82d: 177
  97th: 89
  167th: 32
  205th: 113
  218th: 113
  246th: 63, 71
Field Artillery Groups
  14th: 516
  420th: 465
Field Artillery Regiments
  88th (Philippine Scouts): 19-20
  148th: 24
Fiersbach: 452
Fiesole: 260
Fighter aircraft. *See also* Fighter Groups; Fighter Squadrons.
  in Combined Bomber Offensive: 113, 137-38, 152, 154, 161, 192
  first to operate from Sicily: 119
Fighter Groups
  31st: 65
  33d: 114
  347th: 67
Fighter Squadrons
  67th: 51-52, 58, 122
  80th: 175
  339th: 69

Fighter Strips Nos. 1 and 2 (Guadalcanal): 59, 74
Fiji Islands
  native forces: 124, 157
  Solomons, staging area for: 46-47
  U.S. troops arrive: 20, 38
Filignano: 145, 150
Filly: 373
Filottrano: 227
Fils River: 505, 507, 509
Filstroff: 329
Filzen: 443
Filzen Peninsula: 421
Finale: 511, 513
Finance Building (Manila): 412, 417, 419
Finegayan: 242, 245
Finland
  agreement with USSR on territorial boundaries: 280
  armistices with Allies: 181, 263, 280, 334
  operations in: 206-07, 213-15, 234, 263, 280, 303, 308, 311, 334
  U.S. breaks relations with: 45
Finschhafen: 28, 129, 135-38, 141-42, 159, 187, 215
Finsterbergen: 483
Finsternathal: 463, 465
Firenzuola: 232, 263, 269, 282-83, 291
Firmenich: 426
Firminy: 261
FIREBRAND: 114. *See also* Corsica.
First Allied Airborne Army: 276, 278, 324, 354, 450, 462, 464, 466
First Support Group (TG 77.2): 367-68
  first two-ton bomb dropped: 32-33
Fisch: 407
Fischbach: 384, 443-441
Fischeln: 420
Fischenich: 429
Fish Hook Ridge (Attu): 111-12
Fishhook Ridge (Luzon): 469, 490, 513, 520
Fisk: 83-86
Fisk, 1st Lt. Harold R.: 83
Flume delle Canno: 120
Fiumicino River: 289-92, 295-97, 300-301
Flamersheim: 427
Flamierge: 369, 371-73
Flamizoulle: 369, 371-72
Flammersfeld: 452
Flattop Hill (Okinawa): 536-39
Flavigny: 267-68
FLAX: 105
Fleet Marine Forces, Pacific: 299, 303
Fleets. *See also* Navy, United States; Task Forces, Navy; United States Fleet.
  Third: 264, 268, 274, 299-301, 306, 310-11, 315, 323, 350, 352, 354, 356, 367, 550
  Fifth: 98, 145, 167, 195-96, 299, 337, 364, 385, 405, 456, 467, 541
  Seventh: 44, 96, 175, 181, 183, 205, 222, 274, 306-11, 315, 339, 351-52, 354-55, 370, 484, 545, 549
  Asiatic: 3
  Central Pacific: 98
  Pacific: 6
Fleringen: 422

[INDEX]

Flers: 249-50
Flerzheim: 427
Fletcher, Rear Adm. Frank J.: 36, 37, 39-40 45, 47, 186
Fleurus: 65
Fleury: 233
Fliessem: 06
Flin: 284
FLINTLOCK: 167. See also Marshall Islands campaign.
Floisdorf: 426
Florange: 268
Florence: 136, 162, 204, 213, 230, 232, 234 236-37, 241, 243, 246, 248, 250, 253, 255, 260-61, 264-65, 267
Florennes: 190
Flores Point: 224
Floresta: 126-27
Floret: 366
Florida, German agents landed by submarine in.: 42-43
Florida Island: 48, 140
Florina: 316
Floss: 510, 514
Flossdorf: 342-43
Flossenburg: 512, 514
Flottemanville: 215-16
Floverich: 3 27
Flushing: 316-17
Flussbach: 434
Flying Tigers. See American Volunteer Group.
Focsani: 207, 257
Foggia: 130, 136-38
Foggia-Naples Campaign: 128-63
Foglia River: 259, 261
Fojano: 222
Foligno: 211
Follonica: 217
Fondi: 195
Fondouk: 81, 88, 101-05
Fondouk Gap: 90, 100-103
Fontaine: 331-32
Fontainebleau: 254
Fontanelice: 340
Fontegreca: 143
Fontenay: 218
Fontenay-le-Marmion: 245
Fontenay-sur-Mer: 208
Fonteny: 321-23
Fontoy: 265-66
Foochow: 539
FORAGER: 162. See also Mariana Islands.
Forbach: 405-10, 423-24
Forbach Forest: 424, 426, 428
Force 141 (15th Army Group): 113
Force 163 (Southern France): 162, 176
Force U (Normandy): 189
Forces Françaises de l'Interieur. French Forces of the Interior.
Forces Française de l'Ouest: 328, 464
Forchach: 525
Foreign Ministers Conference, Moscow 141, 143
Foren: 432
Forêt de Cattenom: 320
Forêt de Cerisy: 206-07
Forêt de Champenoux: 280-81, 283-84

Forêt de Château-Salins: 286, 288, 32124
Forêt de Gehan: 303
Forêt de Grémecey: 283-84, 287-92
Forêt de la House: 342
Forêt de l'Avant Garde: 264
Forêt de Longegoutte: 285
Forêt de Mondon: 283-85, 315
Forêt de Mormal: 262
Forêt de Mortagne: 318
Forêt de Mortain: 248
Forêt de Gouffern: 251
Forêt de Parroy: 281, 284, 290-95, 299 302-03, 308-09, 311
Forêt de Puttelange: 337
Forêt de St. Sever: 242-43
Forêt de Vitrimont: 272, 281
Forêt d'Housseras: 312
Forêt Domaniale de Champ: 309, 314, 318-19, 322 391
Forges: 25 9
Forli: 263, 303, 305, 308, 316, 319-24
Forlimpopoli: 311
Forma Quesa Creek: 194
Formia: 192, 194
Formigny: 204-05
Formosa air and naval attacks on: 149, 165, 276, 302-03, 367, 370, 372, 375, 380-81
  plans for seizure of: 179, 204, 209, 224, 235, 237, 283, 301
Fornelli: 146, 290
Fornoli: 290-91
Forrestal, James V.: 191
Forst Berlebeck: 470
Forst Carrenzien: 526
Forst Haldeburg: 498, 500
Forst Hardehausen: 472
Forst Heimburg: 502
Forst Kloetze: 504, 506, 508
Forst Knesebeck: 499 502
Forst Konigslutter: 508, 510
Forst Reinhausen: 481
Forst Rumbeck: 487
Fort, Rear Adm. George H.: 142, 271, 291, 303
Fort Aisne: 324
Fort Amanvillers: 273
Fort Ava: 442, 447
Fort Bayard: 544 547 549-51
Fort Bellacroix: 329
Fort Blaise: 266
Fort Blucher: 434
Fort Bois la Dame: 325
Fort Constantine: 442
Fort de Gondreville: 263
Fort de Fèves: 326
Fort de Villey-le-Sec: 263-65, 267
Fort d'Illange: 325-26
Fort Driant: 270, 280, 288-90, 293-99, 301, 317, 334, 347
Fort Drum: 450, 493 503
Fort du Roule: 217-19
Fort Dufferin: 438, 442, 445-46
Fort Eben Emael: 267
Fort Fontain: 264
Fort Frank. See Carabao Island.
Fort Grand Bois: 347-48
Fort Hertz: 38, 96, 168, 181

Fort Hughes. See Caballo Island.
Fort Jeanne d'Arc: 273, 325, 334, 347, 351
Fort Keranroux: 270
Fort Koenigsmacker: 321-23
Fort Mears: 40
Fort Mills. See Corregidor Island.
Fort Montbarey: 274
Fort Ord: 112
Fort Pikit: 503, 506-07, 510-11, 513, 519
Fort Plappeville: 329, 334 346
Fort Queuleu: 328-29
Fort St. Julien: 328-29
Fort St. Marcouf: 209
Fort St. Nicholas: 257
Fort St. Privat: 328-29, 334 340
Fort St. Quentin: 334 345
Fort Schiesseck: 352, 354 356-57
Fort Simershof: 351, 354 356
Fort Stevens: 42
Fort Stotsenburg: 8, 386, 388, 390, 451, 488
Fort Verdun: 325, 327 334 337
Fort White: 147, 321
Fort Wint: 14, 388
Fort Wittring: 347-48
Fort Yser: 324
Fort Yutz: 323-24
Forte del Marmi: 283
Fortschendorf: 482
Fortschwihr: 387
Fortuna: 420
Forward Area, Central Pacific (TF 57) 303
Fossa di Navigazione: 479
Fossacesia: 151
Fosse Soucy: 205
Fosset: 372
Fossieux: 288-300
Fosso Marina: 492
Fosso Vecchio: 351
Fosso Vecchio Canal: 350
Foucarville: 203
Fougères: 241-42
Fougerolles: 300
Foul Point: 78, 362, 367
Foum Tatahouine: 94, 99
Foy: 373-74
Foy Notre Dame: 361
Fraiture: 368
Fraize: 333 335
Francaltroff: 331
France. See also Free French forces; French Forces of the Interior; Western Europe, operations in.
  Allied air attacks on: 50, 58
  Ardennes-Alsace Campaign: 353-83
  Committee of National Liberation: 131- 130
  Normandy Campaign: 203-34
  Northern France Campaign: 236-72
  occupied France. See Vichy France.
  provisional government formed: 113, 130
  Southern France Campaign: 249-72
  treaty with USSR: 349
Francheville: 374
Francisco River: 129, 132-33
Frandeux: 361

Frangenheim: 415
Frankenbach: 462, 473
Frankenheim: 467
Frankfurt-am-Main: 166, 181, 452-55, 457 459, 461, 463, 465, 467, 472, 487, 493
Frankfurt-am-Oder: 394 513, 518
Frankfurt Autobahn: 435, 440, 454, 456-58, 463
Franklin: 445
FRANTIC: 176, 201, 203, 215, 219, 234, 236-37, 242, 244-45, 268, 271. *See also* Combined Bomber Offensive against Europe.
Frascati: 199, 201-02, 210
Frattevecchia Ridge: 220
Frauenberg: 350, 367, 424
Fraulautern: 341, 344-46, 349-50, 396-97, 445
Frauwullesheim: 414
Frechen: 422, 424
Fredeburg: 480
Fredendall, Maj. Gen. Lloyd R.: 64, 81, 92, 97
Frederick, Col. Robert T.: 149
Free French forces: 40-41. *See also* French Army units.
Freeman, Col. Paul L.: 352
Frei Weinheim: 447
Freialdemhoven: 330-32
Freidlingerhohe: 406
Freienbessingen: 485
Freimersdorf: 424
Freineux: 366
Freinsheim: 446
Freisenheim: 343
Freising: 524
Fréjus: 249-50
Frelenberg: 295
Fremersdorf: 341
Fremestroff: 333
Fremifontaine: 307-09
Fremonville: 329, 331
French Air Force unit, 1st Air Corps: 398
French Army units
  Armies
    1st: 280, 282-83, 285, 287, 294-96, 298-300, 303-05, 310, 313, 317-20, 323, 325-28, 330-37, 339, 343, 345-49, 351, 353-55, 360, 367, 369, 375-77, 379, 381-93, 395-98, 400, 402-09, 419, 434, 443, 447, 457, 461, 465, 467, 469, 471, 473, 475, 477, 481, 483, 486, 488, 490, 492, 494, 496, 498, 500, 503, 505, 507, 509, 511, 514, 516, 518, 520-21, 523, 525, 527-28, 530-31
    Army B: 250-59, 261-65, 273, 280
  Corps
    1st: 264-66, 272, 282, 287, 305, 310, 320, 323, 325-37, 339, 346-49, 351, 379, 381, 386, 389, 391-93, 395-98, 500, 503, 505, 507, 509, 511, 514, 516, 518, 521, 523, 525, 527, 529-31

French Army units—Continued
  Corps—Continued
    2d: 250-59, 261-62, 264, 266-69, 271-72, 277-78, 282-83, 294-96, 298-300, 303-05, 318-20, 326, 332, 334-37, 339, 346-48, 351, 353-55, 360, 377, 379, 381-83, 385, 89, 403, 409, 434, 465, 467, 469, 471, 473, 475, 477, 481, 483, 486, 488, 490, 492, 496, 498, 500, 503, 505, 507, 509, 511, 514, 516
    19th: 67-69, 72, 74, 81, 86, 88, 94, 97, 102-10
    Camel: 97, 101-02
    Franc d'Afrique: 99, 101-02, 105-06, 108-09
    French Expeditionary: 149-50, 153-55, 157, 159, 161-62, 164-67, 172, 176, 183-84, 191-202, 206-08, 210, 213-19, 222-24, 226-27, 229-31, 233-35
    Mountain: 192-97
    Pursuit: 207
  Divisions
    1st Armored: 251-55, 261, 266, 268, 271-72, 285, 287, 294, 304-05, 330-32, 379, 395-97, 483, 492, 500, 507, 509, 511, 514, 518, 521, 523
    1st Moroccan: 252-55, 261, 266, 272, 278, 280, 285, 287, 332, 334 381-82, 384, 387
    1st Motorized: 187, 192-97, 202, 207, 211-14, 217
    2d Armored: 245-48 250-51, 253-59, 261, 266, 268-73, 275, 277-78, 280-81, 284, 291-92, 311, 315, 317, 320, 328, 331, 333-35 338-43, 345, 366, 381, 392, 395-97, 401, 521, 525-26, 528-31
    2d Moroccan: 153-54, 157, 162, 183, 191-93, 197-201, 214, 227, 229, 231, 233, 261, 264, 325-26, 330-32, 336, 339, 346, 348-49, 379, 395, 465, 469, 475, 477, 481, 498, 503, 505, 521, 531
    3d Algerian: 159, 161-62, 165-66, 183, 192-97, 201-02, 207, 223-24, 251-55, 259, 264, 295, 298-99, 303-05, 318-19, 326, 332, 369, 408-09, 434, 437, 439, 441-43, 445-46, 461, 465, 469, 475, 477, 481, 498, 503, 505, 516
    3d Moroccan: 199
    4th Moroccan Mountain: 139, 191-92, 348, 379, 392-93, 395, 446, 453, 500, 521, 531
    4th Mountain: 192-93, 199-200, 224, 226, 229, 233-34
    5th Armored: 247, 325-26, 330-33, 339, 381, 384, 386-91, 395, 439, 445-46, 475, 477, 503, 505, 509, 516, 521, 523, 525, 531

French Army units—Continued
  Divisions—Continued
    9th Colonial: 212-13, 252, 254-55, 258 264 325-26, 330, 349, 393, 395-96, 469, 500, 511, 514
    10th Infantry: 392
    27th Alpine: 419
    Algerian: 108
    Lorraine: 423
    Moroccan: 108
    Oran: 108
  Brigade, 1st: 16, 39, 41, 61
  Groupements
    Bonjour: 252-53
    Chapuis: 252-55
    Landouzy: 511, 514
    Le Bel: 507, 509, 511, 518
    Linares: 252-54
    Monsabert: 445-48, 450, 498, 500
    Navarre: 481
    Schlesser: 481
    Valluy: 469, 471, 473, 475, 477, 481, 483, 486, 488, 490, 492, 496, 509, 514-15, 518
  L Force: 94, 97, 99, 105
French Forces of the Interior: 240, 242, 249 253-54, 256 258-60, 266
French Morocco: 64-66
French Naval Assault Group: 249
French Navy, scuttles units: 70
Frengkofen: 516, 518
Frenke: 474
Frenouville: 232-33
Frenz: 337-38
Frenzerburg Castle: 335-39
Fresnes-en-Saulnois: 270, 278, 286, 290, 292, 320-21
Fretter: 487
Freudenbach: 492
Freudenberg: 407, 480
Freudenstadt: 492, 500, 503
Freyberg, Lt. Gen. Sir Bernard C. (NZ): 169, 175
Freyung: 517, 524, 532
Freyung Pass: 532-33
Frieburg: 509
Friedberg: 459 461
Friedeburg: 491
Friedenfelds: 506
Friedewald: 473
Friedland: 388
Friedrichroda: 479
Friedrichsbrunn: 502
Friedrichsfeld: 451
Friedrichshafen: 114, 523
Friekhofen: 456
Friesbach: 450
Friesenheim: 448
Friesheim: 420
Friesing: 523
Frillendorf: 482
Frimmersdorf: 420
Frische Nehrung: 518
Fritzlar: 462-64, 470
Frohlinde: 478
Froitzheim: 418
Fromental: 249-50
Fronhoven: 332

[INDEX]

Frontigny: 327-28
Frosinone: 159, 198-200
FRY: 421, 467, 475. *See also* Lake Comacchio and its islands.
Fubuki: 58
Fucecchio: 251, 253
Fuchsmuehl: 506
Fuehlingen: 427
Fuerstenau: 482
Fuerstenberg: 481
Fuerstenfeld: 498
Fuerth: 176, 492, 498, 500, 502, 504, 508-09
Fuessen: 520-21, 523
Fuessenich: 420
Fuhren: 380-82
Fuhse Canal: 484, 486
Fuka: 43, 64
Fukien Province: 539
Fulda: 461, 463, 465 467-68, 475, 477
Fulda River: 463, 465, 467-68, 473-74, 477
Fuller, Maj. Gen. Horace H.: 88, 198, 204, 207, 209-10, 213
Funafuti Island: 57, 130, 136, 145-46
Furcoli: 499 503
Furiano River: 125
Furth: 517, 519, 521, 523
Furutaka: 58
Futa Pass: 263, 271, 274, 276, 279, 282-84
Futema: 469, 472

Gabès: 88, 95, 99-103
Gabès Gulf: 104
Gacé: 253
Gaddau: 50 8
Gadebusch: 527
Gadolzburg: 500
Gaeta: 195
Gaffey, Maj. Gen. Hugh J.: 248
Gafsa: 68-69, 71, 88-93, 97-101, 103, 105
Gaggenau: 488
Gahlen: 454 456
Gahmen: 487
Gaiaba: 5 15
Gaiana River: 501, 503, 505
Gaildorf: 507, 509
Gailroth: 505
Gailsbach: 500
Gaja Ridge: 527, 529, 534
GALAHAD: 146, 160, 163, 168, 178-79, 187, 200, 214, 304. *See also* Long Range Penetration Groups; Merrill's Marauders; Wingate, Brig. Orde Charles.
Galanta: 465
Galantina River: 207
Galapagos Islands: 37
Galati: 203, 207
Galeata: 305-06
Galiano: 435, 482, 484, 488, 505
Galla di Monte Orso: 195
Gallicano: 313, 392
Gallneukirchen: 530, 532
Gallo: 143
Galloping Horse (Guadalcanal): 83-84, 86

Galotan: 314
GALVANIC: 142-47, 164. *See also* Gilbert Islands.
Gama River: 52
Gambellate Creek: 288, 290
Gambettola: 304
Gambsheim: 346-47, 349, 365, 368-72, 376-77 389-90
Gambut: 42, 69
Ganano River: 546
Gandersheim: 480
Gangaw: 371-72
Gangaw Valley: 347
Gangelt: 280, 291
Gangi: 122
Gap: 254
Gap, The (New Guinea): 54
Gapan: 10, 389
Garaet Achkel: 108
Garangaoi Cove: 281
Garapan: 214, 216, 218, 223
Garbeck: 494
Garcelles-Secqueville: 245
Gardanne: 255
Gardelegen: 493
Gardella Hill: 201
Garekoru: 286
Garet Hadid: 92-93
Gargano Peninsula: 138
Gargnano: 525
Gari River: 162, 191
Garigliano River: 143, 151-52, 157, 162-66, 168, 171, 184
Garmisch: 525
Garrod, Air Marshal Sir Guy: 326
Garsdorf: 420
Gartow: 508
Garzweiler: 415-16
Garua Island: 179
Gasmata: 23, 136, 139, 145, 155
Gathemo: 245-47
Gattaran: 548
Gatteo: 301
Gau Bickelheim: 443
Gau Odernheim: 446
Gaulle, Gen. Charles de: 257, 325
Gauss, Clarence E.: 165
Gavaga Creek: 64-66
Gavin, Col. James M.: 117
Gavray: 239
Gavrus: 226, 231
Gavutu Island: 48-49
Gay River: 408
Gazala Line: 4-6, 21-22, 26, 39
Gdynia: 244, 435-36, 446, 449-50, 455, 457, 459
Gea Island: 167
Geckenheim: 485
Gee: 428
Geertruidenberg: 318
Geesthacht: 526
Gefrees: 496, 500, 502
Gehan Forest: 294-95
Gehh Island: 167-68
Gehlberg: 481
Gehn: 426
Gehren: 487
Geibenstetten: 521
Geich: 350, 420
Geichlingen: 409

Geiger, Maj. Gen. Roy S. (USMC): 145-46, 154, 235-36, 239, 241, 243, 274, 301, 547-48
Geilenkirchen: 280, 292-96, 323, 329-30
Geinsheim: 449-50
Geisberg Hill: 273
Geislar: 445
Geislingen: 514,519
Geisnach: 451
Geizenberg: 414
Gel: 457
Gela: 117-19
Geldern: 420-21, 423
Gelnhausen: 463
Gelsdorf: 427
Gelsenkirchen: 476, 478, 482, 484
Gemas: 14-15
Gembloux: 263
Gemert: 287
Gemmano: 264, 266, 268
Gemmerich: 454
Gemuenden: 443, 464, 466, 473, 475
Gemund: 385, 392-93, 405-06, 422, 424, 426-27
Genaro: 201
Genazzano: 201
General Headquarters, U.S. Army, abolished: 28
General Staff, War Department. *See* War Department General Staff.
Gengenbach: 503
Gennep: 398-401, 407
Genoa: 515, 520
Gensingen: 440
Genzano: 201
George F. Elliott: 48
Georgenborn: 461
Georgenthal: 483
Georgievsk: 50, 84
Ger: 245, 248
Gera: 494, 496
Gera River: 485
Geraberg: 485
Gerardmer: 282, 294, 300, 318-20, 330, 332
Gerbécourt: 322
Gerberville: 280
Gerbini: 121
Gerderath: 414-15
Gerderhahn: 415
Gereonsweiler: 327, 331-32
Gerimont: 365
Gerlingen: 478
German Army units
 Army Groups
  A: 45-54, 56-58, 61-62, 74, 81, 89, 91-92
  Africa: 95, 97, 110
  B: 45, 47-51, 53-57, 62, 92, 232, 466
  Center: 4, 18, 44, 92, 96, 228
  Don: 89
  F: 261, 532-33
  H: 466
  North: 4, 18, 29, 31, 44, 228, 239, 295
  South: 6, 10, 37, 40-45, 92, 96
  Southwest: 523

German Army units—Continued
Armies
First: 287, 532
First Panzer: 45, 48, 81, 96
Second: 43, 45, 92
Second Panzer: 14, 125
Fourth: 14, 137, 228
Fourth Panzer: 43-45, 62, 116, 118
Fifth Panzer: 95, 97, 25 I, 287, 353
Sixth: 43-45, 47, 62, 69, 74-75 81, 83, 85, 87, 90, 169
Sixth Panzer: 353
Seventh: 251
Eighth: 166, 169
Ninth: 116, 125, 228
Eleventh: 37, 40, 45
Fourteenth: 200
Sixteenth: 25, 27-28, 534
Seventeenth: 45
Eighteenth: 534
Nineteenth: 258, 398, 500, 531-32
Twenty-first: 528
Army Kempf: 116, 118
German-Italian Panzer: 88, 94
Corps
Africa: 96
II: 25, 27, 29, 31, 94
Brigade, 106th Panzer: 265
Group Elster: 274
Germany. See also Hitler, Adolf.
Allied air attacks on V-weapons sites: 128, 130, 152, 156
Allied air losses in: 128, 161, 176, 184, 192
Argentina breaks with: 165
around-the-clock bombing: 95
Brazil declares war on: 51
Bulgaria declares war on: 265
Central Europe Campaign: 448-536
Chile breaks with: 86
China declares war on: 4
Combined Bomber Offensive against: 39, 54, 85, 89, 95, 111, 113-14, 128, 130, 132, 137-40, 143-44, 150, 152, 154, 156, 161, 166, 172-73, 175-76, 178, 181, 184, 187, 192, 201, 203, 207, 215, 219, 234, 236, 268
daylight raids on, postponed: 140
declaration of war on U.S.: 4
Eisenhower directive on bombing of: 187
Hitler takes control of army: 7
Iraq declares war on: 85
Italy declares war on: 140
meetings of Allied forces: 496, 498, 512-17, 519, 521-23, 526-30, 532-34,536
operations in east: 250, 295, 300, 304, 309, 374, 378-89, 394-95, 399-401, 404, 406, 410, 417, 424-26, 428, 435-36, 439, 443, 446, 448-50, 453, 455, 457, 459, 461, 463, 465, 467, 481, 483, 498, 505, 509, 511, 513, 515-16, 518, 520, 523, 527-28, 530 534, 535
operations in west: 268-534

Germany—Continued
as primary enemy: 14, 29, 160, 398
radio countermeasures in bombing: 139
Rhineland Campaign: 271-447
Rumania declares war on: 256
surrender in northwest: 530
surrender negotiations: 512, 529-30, 532-34
two-ton bomb dropped: 32-33
unconditional surrender policy toward: 143
use of fighter escort against: 113, 137-38, 152,154, 161, 192
use of H2S-equipped aircraft against: 137, 144
use of radar in bombing: 154, 166
Germersheim: 448, 450-51, 457 465
Germersheim Landkreis: 516
Germeter: 281-82, 300-301, 303, 320, 335
Germscheid: 447
Gernsbach: 488
Gernsdorf: 462
Gernsheim: 455
Gerolstein: 426-28
Gerow, Lt. Gen. Leonard T.: 203, 258, 275 278, 296, 376
Gerstetten: 514
Gersthofen: 521
Gerstungen: 479
Gertza: 185
Geruma Island: 456
Gesso: 299-304, 307, 507
Gevelinghausen: 478
Gevelsdorf: 414
Gevenich: 410
Gey: 340-42, 349
Geyen: 424
Ghazal: 63
Gheel: 265-66, 269-70, 278
Ghent: 262-63, 268-69
Ghent–Bruges Canal: 264, 266, 268
Ghent–Terneuzen Canal: 274, 279
Ghormley, Vice Adm. Robert L.: 33, 42, 43, 44-45, 50, 54-55, 57-58, 59
Gialo: 55
Giarabub: 26
Giberville: 232
Gibraltar, site of AFHQ: 64, 69
Gielau: 508
Giengen: 514
Glens Peninsula: 254-55
Gierstadt: 483
Giescheid: 415
Giesdorf: 422
Gieselwerder: 479, 481
Giesendorf: 415
Giessen: 457-58 460-61, 463
Giessen River: 337
Giffard, Gen. Sir George: 11, 178, 206, 238, 324
Giffen, Rear Adm. Robert C.: 116
Gifu River strongpoint: 77-79, 81, 88
Gigantangan Island: 263
Gila Peninsula: 274, 276, 279
Gilbert Islands: 164
air and naval actions: 21, 136, 139-41, 146-48, 152
casualty summaries: 149-50

Gilbert Islands—Continued
enemy seizure: 4
JCS directive on recovery of: 121, 129
recovery of: 50, 136-52
Gili Gili: 52
Gill, Maj. Gen. William H.: 174, 192, 221, 229, 246
Gillem, Maj. Gen. Alvan C., Jr.: 320
Gillenfeld: 434
Gilsdorf: 360
Gilzem: 416
Gindorf: 426
Ginnick: 418
Ginopolan: 497, 501, 507, 510
Ginowan: 476,.478 480
Giogo di Villore: 285
Gioia: 132
Gioiella: 220
Giraud, Gen. Henri: 88, 114
arrival at North African front: 65
conferences with Allied leaders: 60, 64, 116
restores civil government in Africa: 98
Girbelsrath: 412, 414
Giromagny: 334
Girkhausen: 468
Girmont: 285-86
Gironde River and Estuary: 494, 496, 498, 500, 525, 527
Giropa Point: 78-79, 81
Girst: 409
Girua River: 67-69, 72, 82
Giruwa: 46-47, 71, 73-74 76, 78, 81, 85-87
Gishushi: 543
Giulanova: 212
Giulianello: 197, 199
Givet: 361, 366
Givroulle: 374
Giza Giza River: 116
Glaadt: 427
Gladbach: 417, 431, 436, 451
Gladbeck: 460, 462
Glan: 549
Glan River: 444
Gland River: 329
Glassford, Rear Adm. William A.: 3
Glauchau: 496
Gleen River: 460
Gleichen: 498
Gleidorf: 476, 478
Gleima: 492
Gleiwitz: 383-84
Glesch: 415-16, 418, 420
Glessen: 422
Gleul: 425
Glider Infantry Regiments
187th: 347 389 401, 430-31, 433-35, 450-53, 455, 460-61, 464-65, 467 471, 476, 478, 480, 482, 490, 503, 505, 510
188th: 389-90, 392, 395-96, 398, 401, 417, 442, 451, 453, 455, 457, 465, 471, 473, 476, 480, 522-23
Glimbach: 410
Glogau: 402, 463, 467
Gluchov: 130
Gneisenau: 23
Gniezo: 381

Gnoetzheim: 473
Go Chan Hill: 460-62, 474
GOBLET: 115, 131, 133, 136
Goch: 398, 401, 403-08, 410
Godo: 344
Godorf: 429
Goedenroth: 439
Goehrde: 510
Goennersdorf: 427
Goeppingen: 505
Goerlitz: 505, 534
Goes: 314
Goeschwitz: 487
Goesdorf: 368
Goetzenbruck: 367
Goetzis: 528
Goggenbach: 496
Golbach: 427
GOLD Beach: 203. *See also* Normandy Campaign, landing phase.
Goldenstedt: 491
GOLDFLAKE: 399 *See also* Canadian Army units, Corps, I.
Golkrath: 414
Golleville: 212-13
Gollnerberg: 517
Golzheim: 412, 414
Gomel: 136, 140-41, 147, 150-51
Gona: 43, 45-46, 48-49, 56-57, 61, 63, 67-79, 81, 88, 96
Gona Mission: 71
Gondelsheim: 421-22, 424
Gondenbrett: 396-98
Gondorf: 422
Gonfaron: 250
Gong Kedah: 3-5
Gonnersdorf: 433
Gonzaga: 4
Goodenough Island: 51, 57, 60-61, 141, 154, 156, 158
Gora: 66
Gorari: 64, 66
Gorgognano Ridge: 499, 501
Gorleben: 508
Gorlice: 378
Gornhausen: 444
Gorodok: 156
Goroni: 53
Goronne: 369
Gorze: 264
Gosbach: 509
Gosselming: 335
Gotalalamo: 279, 281
Gotha: 176, 470, 472, 477, 479, 481, 485
Gothic Line: 214-516
Gott, Lt. Gen. W. H. E. (Br.): 49
Gottingen: 481, 483, 498 502
Gottmannsgruen: 508
Goubellat Plain: 81, 99 105-07, 109
Goucherie: 226
Goumier troops: 99, 101, 109, 119, 123-25, 139, 192, 210, 226-27, 255
Gourbesville: 209-10
Gournay: 259
Gouvy: 379-80
Government Gardens (New Guinea) 76-79
Government House Hill (Shima) 501
Gozo Island: 116

Graach: 444
Grab: 503
Graefentonna: 479
Grafenau: 515
Grafenhain: 483
Grafenhohn: 441
Grafenwohr: 504, 508, 510
Grafschaft: 474
Grainville-sur-Odon: 219
Gralingen: 381
Grammastetten: 529-30, 532
Grammichele: 118-19
Gran: 523
Granada: 467
Granarolo: 364, 366
Grand Bois: 378-80
Grand Halleux: 358, 370
Grand Sart: 369
Grandcamp: 205
Grande Huanville: 212
Grande Island: 14, 388
Grande Mormont: 373
Grandfontaine: 337
Grandménil: 361
Grandvillers: 293
Grandy, Group Capt.: 528
GRANITE: 162. *See also* Admiralty Islands campaign; Caroline Islands; Mariana Islands; Marshall Islands campaign; Palau Islands; Truk Atoll.
Gransdorf: 429, 431
Granville: 239
Grant Island: 131
Granterath: 412
Grasses 254-55
Grasslfing: 517
Gratzfeld: 444
Grave: 276, 278-79, 285, 403
Gravelotte: 288-89
Graz: 481, 498, 535
Grazzanise: 140
Great Britain. *See* United Kingdom.
Grebbe River: 501
Greece
  agreement with Bulgaria on territory: 313-14
  Allied Military Liaison Headquarters in: 262, 305, 325, 331
  armed forces under British: 325
  government restored: 262, 288, 306
  guerrilla activities: 288, 321
  Land Forces and Military Liaison Headquarters: 331
  Naval Port Parties: 292
  operations in: 261, 275, 285-86, 288, 292, 298, 301-02, 305, 316, 321, 325-26, 331
  role of EAM and ELAS: 288, 321
Greek Army units
  3d Mountain Brigade: 265, 267, 276, 283, 255, 258, 301, 306
  Greek Brigade: 62
  Mountain Brigade: 262
  Sacred Regiment: 262, 292, 302
Greely, Maj. Gen. John N.: 21
Green Hill (Tunisia): 81-82, 106
Green Islands: 155, 172-74, 177
Greene: 480
Greffen: 446
Grefrath: 418, 420, 422

Gregory: 53
Greimerath: 437
Greiz: 498 500
Grémecey: 289
Gremelsheid: 419
GRENADE: 389-99, 409, 427 *See also* Rhine River; Roer River.
Grenderich: 440
Grening: 333-34
Grenoble: 251-54, 257-59
Grenzhausen: 452
Greppin: 502, 506
Gresaubach: 443
Gressenich: 277, 327-28
Gressenwohr: 508
Greve: 234-35
Grevel: 487
Greven: 462
Grevenbroich: 422
Grevenmacher: 280, 292, 295, 409
Grevenstein: 485, 487
Greverath: 431
Gréville: 221
Grich el Oued: 105
Grieben: 493, 495
Griesenbach: 452
Griesheim: 451, 471, 473
Grieth: 415
Griffenwang: 512
Grik: 6-7
Grimaud: 249
Grimbiermont: 368
Grimbosq: 243
Grimlinghausen: 425
Grimma: 496, 498, 510
Grimmenthal: 468
Grimmitscha: 496
Grindhausen: 383
Griner, Maj. Gen. George W.: 220
Grisignano: 316, 320
Grissenbach: 464
Griswold, Maj. Gen. Oscar W.: 117-19, 121, 123, 154
Grizzana: 302-03
Grodno: 231
Groenlo: 462
Groeningen: 486
Groesbeek: 276, 278-79, 281, 403
Grohnde: 474, 476
Gronebach: 472
Groningen: 484, 495 497
Gros Hausen: 455
Gros Langenfeld: 388-89
Gros Réderching: 348-49, 366-68, 403-04
Gros-Tenquin: 330
Grosbliederstroff: 345, 404-05
Grosbous: 359
Grose, Col. John E.: 72-73, 76
Grosmagny: 336
Gross Altdorf: 503
Gross Berkel: 4'72
Gross Breitenbach: 487
Gross Buellesheim: 424
Gross Burschla: 470
Gross Dohren: 484
Gross Gerau: 451, 453
Gross Kuehnau: 508
Gross Maischeid: 454
Gross Muehl River: 528
Gross Rosenburg: 495

Gross Strehlitz: 381
Gross Vernich: 425
Gross Werther: 485
Grossalmerode: 475, 477
Grossauheim: 453, 455, 459
Grosse Forst: 41
Grossen Buseck: 458, 463
Grossen Linden: 461
Grosseto: 210
Grossfahner: 483
Grosshau: 329-30, 334, 336, 340-41, 349
Grosskampenberg: 269-70, 394, 396, 405
Grosskrotzenberg: 457
Grosslittgen: 432
Grossenlueder: 461, 465
Grossenmoor: 465
Grottkau: 395
Groumont Creek: 366-67
Groups. *See* Antiaircraft Artillery Groups; Army Groups; Cavalry Groups; Field Artillery Groups.
Grouven: 415-16
Grozny: 52-53, 57, 62
Gruchy: 221
Grudziadz: 406, 428
Gruenberg: 403, 455 459
Gruenstadt: 446
Gruenwalde: 491
Gruiten: 497
Grunert, Lt. Gen. George: 166
Guadagasel: 98
Guadalcanal Campaign: 48-94
Guadalcanal Island
  air and naval actions: 47, 50-53 55, 58-59, 61, 66-67, 70-71, 74, 103
  casualty summary: 82
  control assumed by Army: 73
  enemy air attacks: 51, 59, 113-14
  enemy reinforcements: 51, 54, 63-64, 67
  enemy resistance ends: 91
  enemy withdrawals: 82, 84, 91
  first Army troops arrive: 58-59
  landing operations: 48
  line of communications shifted: 50
  naval battle: 66-67
  Nimitz orders seizure: 45
  staging area for Emirau: 181
  staging area for Palaus: 259
  staging area for Russells: 93-94
  supply situation: 50-51, 53, 56, 59, 66
  U.S. air reinforcement: 50-53, 55, 57-59, 61, 67, 69, 78
  U.S. reinforcements: 50, 55-63, 71 ,73-75, 91 ,134
  U.S. strength figures: 57, 59, 82
Guadalupe: 460, 467, 490, 493
Guagua: 11-12
Guam
  enemy air attack: 3-4
  fall of: 4
  Garrison Force: 241
  Japan air offensive, base for: 550
  recovery of: 211-12, 222, 225, 227, 234-46
Guastalla: 513
Gudersleben: 487

Guebling: 325-26, 329
Guebwiller: 392
Guelden: 508
Guelma: 89
Guels: 441
Guemar: 346, 381, 386
Guemmer: 480
Guenhoven: 415
Guenz River: 518
Guenzburg: 516, 518
Guerrilla forces
  air supply of: 160
  in Burma: 91, 93, 96-97, 111, 183, 187, 193
  in France. *See* French Forces of the Interior
  in Greece: 288,321
  in Philippines: 356-58, 366-68, 372-73, 375, 399-400, 419, 426, 433-34, 436, 441, 443, 445-48, 453, 455, 457, 462, 469, 471, 476 480, 482, 486, 497, 501, 503, 510, 513, 519, 522-23, 531, 535-36, 538, 540-43, 546-50
  in Yugoslavia: 307, 314, 317-18, 340
Guerzenich: 353
Guesten: 02, 414, 500
Guhrau: 386
Guillaume, Gen. Augustin (Fr.): 210, 217
Guimaras Island: 448
Guimba: 9, 380, 388
Guimbalon: 471, 473
Guinarona: 312, 314
Guinarona Hill: 315
Guinarona River: 310, 312, 315
Guinhalaron River: 469, 471
Guintiguian: 310-11
Guising: 370
Guitol: 16
Gulf of Danzig: 384, 436, 450, 535
Gulf of Finland: 163, 170, 206, 214
Gulf of Gaeta: 191
Gulf of Nauplia: 298
Gulf of Riga sector: 239-40, 285, 294, 302, 330, 335
Gulpen: 271
Gum Ga: 163
Guma: 523, 532-37
Gumbinnen: 380
Gumbsheim: 444
Gummersbach: 487
Gumtree Road (Tunisia): 99, 101-02
Gundershoffen: 349
Gunfire and Covering Force (TF 54): 403, 430
Gungolding: 514, 516, 518
Gungwiller: 338
Gunstett: 442
Gurguan Point airfield: 238
Gurkhaywa: 211
Gurun: 5-6
Gusay Creek: 375, 378
Gusenburg: 439
Guishichan: 544
Gusika: 150
Gustav Line: 144-47, 149-58, 162, 190-92, 194-201
Gustavburg: 455

Gusteig: 528
Gusukuma: 508, 510
Gut Schwarzenbroich: 334
Gutendorf: 487
Gwa: 537
Gwegyo: 34
Gwin: 118
GYMNAST: 14, 46. *See also* Northwest Africa Campaign.
Gymnich: 420
Gyoer: 459
Gzhatsk: 97

H2S-equipped aircraft: 137, 144
Haag: 506, 528
Haaksbergen: 464
Haan: 497
Haar: 532
Haaren: 301, 382
Habbelrath: 420
Habiemont: 355
Habkirchen: 350-52
Habscheid: 393-97
Hachen: 489
Hachenburg: 454
Hachiville: 380
Hackenberg: 326-28
Hackenbroich: 424
Hackenburg: 462
Hackenheim: 444
Hackhausen: 424
Hadamar: 456, 458
Hadjeb el Aïoun: 90, 96, 100
Hafen Canal: 329
Haffen: 450
Hafsloch: 448
Hagen: 491, 493
Hagenbach: 488
Hagenow: 528
Hagonoy: 385, 389
Haguenau: 335, 340, 348-50, 378, 380, 383
Haguenau Forest: 441-42
Hagushi: 462, 467, 469
Haha Jima: 211, 224, 368
Hahn: 451
Hahnbach: 508
Hahnbusch: 423-24, 426
Hahnlein: 451, 453
Hales-de-Tillet Woods: 370-72
Hain: 485
Hainan Island: 165, 376
Hainchen: 462
Hairpin Hill (Luzon): 495 497
Haislip, Maj. Gen. Wade H.: 240
Hajen: 474
Haka: 146
Halavo: 48
Halberbracht: 485
Halberstadt: 161, 175, 486, 491
Halbeswig: 480
Haldensee: 525
Haldern: 458
Hale, Col. J. Tracy, Jr.: 69, 72
Hale, Maj. Gen. Willis H.: 42
Halenbach: 408
Halenfeld: 391
Haleta: 48
Halfaya (Hellfire) Pass: 16, 66

[INDEX]

Hall, Maj. Gen. Charles P.: 220-21, 227, 234, 239, 246, 249, 274, 276, 287, 388
Hall, Rear Adm. J. L., Jr.: 132, 467
Halle: 476, 491, 494, 498, 500, 502, 504
Hallenberg: 464
Hallendorf: 484
Hailer: 360-61
Hallering: 336
Hallouf Pass: 100
Halloville: 326
Hallschlag: 414, 06, 424
Halmahera Island: 191, 274, 295
HALPRO (Halverson Detachment). *See* Middle East Air Force; Ploesti
Halsdorf: 407
Halsenbach: 439
Halsey, Adm. William F.: 60, 116, 118, 367
  commands Fifth Fleet forces: 541
  commands SOPAC: 59
  commands Wake task force: 25
  ELKTON naval forces controlled by SWPA: 101
  objection to stress on Marshalls: 113
  plan for Carolines: 241
  plans for Solomons: 113-14, 122, 123, 126, 132, 136, 138, 140, 146
Haltern: 458, 460, 466
Halverson, Col. Harry A.: 41
Hambach: 410-11, 485
Hambach Forest (Staats Forst Hambach): 411, 414
Hamberg, Lt. Col. William A.: 340, 342-43
Hamborn: 458
Hamburg: 466, 512, 517, 526-27, 529
Hamburg Autobahn: 503
Hambye: 238
Hameau de Tot: 2 18
Hameau Gringer: 217
Hamel-de-Cruttes: 203
Hameln: 474 480 482, 484
Hamich: 327, 329-30
Hamich Ridge: 327-33
Hamiville: 380
Hamm: 414, 455, 466, 468, 470, 472, 476, 478, 480
Hammamet: 109
Hamman Lif: 109
Hammann: 40
Hammer: 390
Hammerstein: 444
Hamminkeln: 450
Hampont: 281, 321-22
Hampton Roads: 60-61
Han: 290
Hanau: 453, 455, 457, 459, 461, 463, 467, 469-70, 473, 522
Hancock: 480
Haney, Brig. Gen. Harold: 405
Hangeler: 446
Hangoe: 280
Hankow: 355, 371, 381
Hankow-Peiping railway: 187
Hann Muenden: 474, 477, 479, 481
Hannocourt: 321-22
Hannover: 480, 482, 484, 486, 517
Hansa Bay: 176, 178, 180, 185
Han-sur-Nied: 323-24

Haraden: 351
Harakiri Gulch (Saipan): 225-27
Haraucourt: 325
Harburg: 499, 501, 512
Harcourt-Smith, Air Commodore G. (RAF): 262
Hardehausen: 470
Hardehauser Wald: 475, 479, 483
Harderode: 476
Hardheim: 463
Hardigny: 376-77, 379
Harding, Maj. Gen. Edwin F.: 67-68, 70, 72
Harding, Lt. Gen. Sir John: 453
Hardinvast: 215-17
Hardisleben: 487
Hardt: 416, 418, 512
Harech River: 200
Hargarten: 419, 435-37
Hargimont: 359
Hariko: 70, 74-75, 77
Harlange: 365-67, 369, 371
Harmon, Maj. Gen. Ernest N.: 65, 103, 174
Harmon, Maj. Gen. Hubert R.: 160
Harmon, Maj. Gen. Millard F.: 116, 118
  activates XIV Corps: 81, 84
  activates Thirteenth Air Force: 84
  arrival at New Caledonia: 47
  commands AAFPOA: 241
  commands SOPAC tactical forges: 47
  commands USAFISPA: 45
  plan for Solomons: 57-58
Harper, Brig. Gen. Arthur M.: 212
Harperscheid: 389-90
Harris, Brig. Gen. Field (USMC): 130
Harscheid: 394-95, 397-98
Hart, Adm. Thomas C.: 6, 8, 24
Hartestein: 282, 285-86
Harth Woods: 395, 397
Hartley, Gen. Sir Alan (Br.): 15
Hartland: 65
Harz Mountains: 484, 487, 489 491, 494-96, 498, 500, 502, 504, 506, 508, 510, 512
Harze: 370
Hasborn: 435
Hasbrouck, Maj. Gen. Robert W.: 315
Hase River: 482
Hasenfeld Gut: 341, 347, 391
Hasenfelde: 398-99
Hassel: 446
Hasselbach: 452
Hasselfelde: 500
Hasselt: 265, 268, 283, 356, 363, 402
Hasselsweiler: 414
Hasslach River: 487, 490
Hassloch: 453
Hassum: 404
Hastenrath: 327-29
Hatab River: 94
Hatten: 370-78
Hatterath: 293-94
Hattingen: 496
Hattstatt: 392-93
Hatvan: 337
Hatzenport: 438-40
Hau: 400-401
Hauconcourt: 265, 322
Hauf River: 449

Hausen: 418, 420, 441, 455, 461, 465, 503
Haustadt: 44-43
Hauseweiler: 424
Haut Biville: 214
Haute-Littée: 207
Haute-Yutz: 325
Hauthausen: 414
Hautonnerie Farm: 321
Hauts-Vents: 227-28
Hauwei Island: 179-80, 187, 190
Hauzenburg: 524
Havelange: 362
Havrenne: 361
Hawaiian Islands casualty summary: 3
  enemy air attacks: 3, 27
  Pearl Harbor attack: 3
  Seventh Air Force alerted: 38
  Short replaced by Emmons: 6
  Spruance TF arrives: 38
  staging area for TWO: 299, 373, 385
  Tinker heads air force: 6
Haxtergrund: 464
Hayange: 267
Haynau: 401
Haynes, Brig. Gen. Caleb V.: 57
Headquarters Land Forces and Military Liaison, Greece: 331
Hearn, Maj. Gen. Thomas G.: 150, 235, 251, 255
Heath, Lt. Gen. Sir Lewis M. (Br.): 21
Heaths Plantation: 134
Heaveadorp Ferry: 281-82
Hébécrevon: 236
Hebles: 463
Hebronval: 357-58 369
Hechelscheid: 393-'94
Hechenberg: 526
Hecken: 429
Heckeshausen: 408
Heckhalenfeld: 388
Heckholzhausen: 454
Heckhuscheid: 272, 389
Heddert: 437-38
Hedgerows, Battle of the: 223-32
Hedo: 493
Hédomont: 373-74
Heengen: 328
Heerlen: 277
Heeze: 279
Hegenlohe: 509
Hehlrath: 331-32
Hehn: 416
Heide: 377
Heidelberg: 459 465
Heiden: 458
Heiderscheid: 359
Heiderscheidergrund: 368
Heïdous: 105-06
Heien: 401
Heidweiler: 431
Heilbach: 410
Heilbronn: 469, 471, 473, 475, 477, 479, 481, 483, 485, 488, 490, 492, 494, 500
Heilenbach: 421
Heilenstadt: 465
Heilhausen: 416
Heiligenbeil: 453
Heilsberg: 388

Heimbach: 418, 420, 422
Heimburg: 502, 506
Heimersheim: 429
Heimerzheim: 427
Heinerscheid: 383
Heinrichsdorf: 478
Heinsberg: 381-83
Heinsen: 480
Heintzenhofen: 510
Heirlot: 367
Heisdorf: 421
Heisterbacherrott: 444
Heisterberg: 456
Heistern: 331-32
Heiteren: 396
Heito: 381
Heitrak: 313
Hekkens: 398-400
Helden: 330
Heldra: 470
Heldrungen: 487
Helena: 116
Helenenberg: 417
Helfant: 407
Helfrich, Vice Adm. Conrad E. L. (Dutch): 24
Helgersdorf: 464
Hellefeld: 487
Hellenthal: 392-94, 415
Helleville: 213
Hellfire Pass: 16, 66
Hellimer: 331, 333
Hell's Pocket (Saipan): 219-21
Helm: 52
Helmond: 281, 284-85, 287
Hemau: 514, 516
Hemer: 491, 493
Hemfurth: 462
Hemmerde: 482
Hemmeres: 386-87
Hemmerich: 427
Hemmersdorf: 340
Hen Hill (Okinawa): 542
Henahambuti: 73
Henderson, Maj. Lofton (USMC)
Henderson Field: 49-59, 61, 66-67
Hengelo: 474
Hengersberg: 521
Hengyang: 209, 219-20, 223, 228, 236, 241, 245, 251, 255, 295, 323, 371, 495
Hennecke, Rear Adm. Walther (Ger.) 219
Hennecourt: 272
Hennef: 448-49, 452
Henningsleben: 475
Henri Chapelle: 268
Henrichenburg: 472
Hentern: 419
Henumont: 37
Heppenbach: 385
Heppendorf: 415
Hepscheid: 385
Herbach: 295
Herbéviller: 316
Herbolzheim: 473
Herborn: 456
Herbstein: 461, 465
Herbstmuhle: 411
Herchehain: 463
HERCULES: 38 *See also* Malta.
Herdecke: 491, 493

Herdringen: 491
Herford: 468, 470, 472, 480
Herforst: 428
Hergarten: 424
Herhahn: 391-92
Héricourt: 326, 329
Hérimoncourt: 326, 329
Heringhausen: 462, 478
Hermannstein: 456, 458
Hermes: 32
Hermesdorf: 413
Hermeskeil: 440, 442
Hermespand: 398
Hermilly: 242
Hermosa: 13, 387
Hermulheim: 427
Herny: 324
Herrnberchtheim: 471, 473
Heropont: 371
Heroya: 122
Herrenberg: 503
Herresbach: 385
Herrick Force (New Guinea): 200-202
Herring, Lt. Gen. Edmund F. (Aus.): 56, 81-82, 84, 115, 129
Herrlisheim: 368-72, 377, 390-91, 395-96
Herrlisheim-près-Colmar: 393
Herschbach: 454
Herscheid: 394, 491
Herschwiesen: 438
Hersfeld: 463, 465, 470
Hertogenwald: 271
Herxheim: 450
Herzberg: 487
Herzfeld: 406
Herzogenrath: 298
Hescheld: 419
Hessen: 507, 512, 516
Hesseling: 407
Hester: 113, 115-16, 119
Hester, Maj. Gen. John H.: 93
Hettenschlag: 393
Hetzerath: 412
Heuchel: 451
Heuem: 354, 387-88
Heuholz: 498
Heumen: 276
Hewitt, Vice Adm. Henry K.: 60, 65, 117, 132
Heyen: 474, 476
Heyerode: 470
Hickam Field: 3
Hickeshausen: 408
Hickey, Brig. Gen. Doyle O.: 464
Hiddesen: 468, 470, 472
Hiei: 67
Hierheck: 360
Higashi: 434
High Commissioner of Philippines, moves to Corregidor: 8
Highway 1 (Italy): 202, 205, 212, 214-15, 221, 229, 475, 479, 481
Highway 1 (Leyte): 307, 309, 311-12, 314
Highway 1 (Luzon): 393-94, 396, 434, 469, 484, 490, 495, 523, 527
Highway 1 (Mindanao): 503, 506-07, 510-11, 513
Highway 2 (Italy): 202, 207, 227, 234-35, 239

Highway 2 (Leyte): 310, 312, 319-20, 324-25, 333-35, 341-343-45, 348, 351-53, 356-58, 360.
Highway 3 (Italy): 202-03, 232
Highway 3 (Luzon): 374, 376, 385, 388-89, 543
Highway 4 (Italy): 203
Highway 4 (Luzon): 544-46
Highway 5 (Luzon): 389-91, 393, 401, 404, 412-13, 421- 423, 427-28, 430-31, 433-35, 437, 439, 443, 446, 455, 463, 469, 477, 479, 482, 501, 505, 509, 529, 536, 539, 542, 544-48
Highway 5 (Okinawa): 533, 536, 539-40
Highway 6 (Italy): 144, 152, 155, 161, 169, 171-72, 194, 197-98, 200-202
Highway 7 (France): 251-52, 254, 256-58
Highway 7 (Italy): 136-37, 167, 193-97, 201-02
Highway 7 (Luzon): 387-88, 390, 394, 396
Highway 9 (Italy): 276, 287-88, 295, 301, 309-11, 316, 324-26, 333, 335-37 344, 430, 484, 495, 501, 507, 511, 513, 515-16, 518, 520
Highway 9 (Luzon): 455, 469, 477, 482, 488, 490, 493, 495, 497, 499, 503, 505, 515
Highway 10 (Italy): 516, 521
Highway 11 (Italy): 518
Highway 11 (Luzon): 374, 376, 384, 550
Highway 12 (Italy): 290-91, 513
Highway 13 (Luzon): 371, 374, 378
Highway 14 (Italy): 523
Highway 16 (Italy): 261, 274, 276, 344, 517
Highway 17 (Luzon): 393
Highway 19 (Luzon): 455, 457, 461
Highway 23 (Luzon): 9
Highway 27 (Luzon): 497, 523, 527, 529
Highway 49 (Italy): 527
Highway 53 (Italy): 523
Highway 55 (Luzon): 378
Highway 62 (Italy): 515-16
Highway 63 (Italy): 515
Highway 64 (Italy): 286, 288-90, 299, 302, 314, 404-05, 413, 417, 495, 497
Highway 65 (Italy): 267, 269, 274, 290, 298, 304, 428, 475, 499, 501, 505, 507
Highway 66 (Italy): 286, 288, 291
Highway 67 (Italy): 234, 258, 268, 270, 286, 288, 293, 298, 305, 308, 313, 317, 319
Highway 68 (Italy): 219-20, 226-27
Highway 69 (Italy): 225, 233, 256
Highway 70 (Italy): 256, 259
Highway 71 (Italy): 213, 222, 224, 259, 263, 299
Highway 73 (Italy): 214
Highway 75 (Italy): 222
Highway 82 (Italy): 195
Highway 83 (Italy): 198
Highway 85 (France): 254-55

[INDEX]

Highway 87 (Italy): 140
Highway 91 (Italy): 136-37
Highway 98 (France): 251
Highway 113 (Sicily): 121-24, 126-27
Highway 120 (Sicily): 121-24, 126-27
Highway 160 (Luzon): 477, 484
Highway 251 (Luzon): 372
Highway 261 (Luzon): 372
Highway 416 (Luzon): 467
Highway 417 (Luzon): 461, 510
Highway 937 (Italy): 289
Highway 6424 (Italy): 303
Highway 6521 (Italy): 260, 266-67, 271
Highway 6524 (Italy): 269
Highway 6620 (Italy): 286, 288-90, 297
Hiiumaa Island: 294
Hilburghausen: 477
Hilchenbach: 491
Hilden: 497
Hildesheim: 475, 480
Hildfeld: 472
Hilfarth: 414-16
Hilgert: 454
Hill Drome: 357
Hill, Col. Francis: 160
Hill, Rear Adm. Harry W.: 166, 169, 172-73, 210, 433 538
Hill B (Leyte): 310-11
Hill C (Leyte): 310-11
Hill X (Attu): 110
Hill X (Guadalcanal): 86-87
Hill Y (Guadalcanal): 87
Hill 3 (Luzon): 398-99
Hill 4 (Luzon): 398-99
Hill 5 (Luzon): 385, 388, 398
Hill 6 (Luzon): 398, 401
Hill 7 (Luzon): 402, 404
Hill 11 (Guadalcanal): 79, 81
Hill 12 (Luzon): 415
Hill 20 (Cebu): 482, 486
Hill 21 (Cebu): 490, 493
Hill 22 (Cebu): 501
Hill 25 (Cebu): 493 501
Hill 26 (Cebu): 480, 486
Hill 27 (Cebu): 480, 482
Hill 27 (Guadalcanal): 77-79, 81-82, 92
Hill 27 (Okinawa): 542
Hill 30 (Cebu): 460
Hill 31 (Cebu): 460, 464
Hill 31 (Guadalcanal): 77-78, 82
Hill 35 (Guadalcanal): 75-76
Hill 42 (Guadalcanal): 85
Hill 43 (Guadalcanal): 83
Hill 44 (Guadalcanal): 83
Hill 46 (Okinawa): 543
Hill 52 (Guadalcanal): 83
Hill 53 (Guadalcanal): 83-85
Hill 55 (Guadalcanal): 83-84
Hill 55 (Okinawa): 537-39
Hill 56 (Italy): 165-66, 168
Hill 57 (Guadalcanal): 83-84, 87
Hill 57 (Okinawa): 544
Hill 60 (Italy): 192
Hill 60 (Okinawa): 533-35
Hill 65 (Guadalcanal): 58
Hill 66 (Guadalcanal): 68-69, 82-85
Hill 67 (Guadalcanal): 61
Hill 69 (Okinawa): 542, 545

Hill 72 (Italy): 154
Hill 80 (France): 261
Hill 80 (Guadalcanal): 68-69, 84-85
Hill 81 (Guadalcanal): 68-69, 84-85
Hill 81 (Okinawa): 547-48
Hill 85 (Leyte): 310-11
Hill 87 (Guadalcanal): 86-87
Hill 88 (Guadalcanal): 87
Hill 89 (Guadalcanal): 87
Hill 89 (Okinawa): 547-48
Hill 90 (France): 211
Hill 90 (Guadalcanal): 87
Hill 91 (Guadalcanal): 88
Hill 92 (France): 229
Hill 92 (Guadalcanal): 88
Hill 94 (Guadalcanal): 87
Hill 95 (France): 224, 246
Hill 95 (Guadalcanal): 87
Hill 95 (Okinawa): 544-45
Hill 97 (France): 211
Hill 98 (Guadalcanal): 87-88
Hill 99 (Guadalcanal): 87-88
Hill 100 (Guadalcanal): 88
Hill 102 (Guadalcanal): 88
Hill 103 (France): 259, 261
Hill 103 (Guadalcanal): 88
Hill 105 (France): 246, 261
Hill 105 (Guadalcanal): 88
Hill 106 (Guadalcanal): 88
Hill 108 (France): 212-13
Hill 108 (Italy): 193
Hill 111 (Tunisia): 109
Hill 112 (France): 228
Hill 115 (Okinawa): 546-47
Hill 120 (Leyte): 307
Hill 122 (France): 231
Hill 126 (Italy): 192-93
Hill 130 (Okinawa): 536-39
Hill 131 (Italy): 192
Hill 138 (Okinawa): 524
Hill 141 (Italy): 154
Hill 143 (Okinawa): 515
Hill 146 (Italy): 191
Hill 147 (France): 211
Hill 150 (France): 211
Hill 150 (Italy): 191
Hill 150 (New Britain): 160-61
Hill 153 (Okinawa): 546-47
Hill 158 (France): 215
Hill 170 (France): 214
Hill 171 (France): 215-16
Hill 175 (Italy): 170
Hill 178 (France): 215
Hill 178 (Okinawa): 508, 515
Hill 187 (Germany): 330-32
Hill 187 (Okinawa): 534
Hill 192 (France): 208, 211, 228-29
Hill 200 (Luzon): 371-73, 375-76
Hill 201 (Noemfoor): 224-25
Hill 203 (Germany): 332-33, 335-36, 338
Hill 207 (Germany): 332-34
Hill 213 (Italy): 165-66, 168
Hill 215 (Iwo Jima): 430
Hill 221 (Saipan): 220
Hill 223 (France): 278
Hill 224 (Italy): 161
Hill 225 (New Guinea): 224, 227
Hill 232 (Germany): 329-30
Hill 242 (Tunisia): 109
Hill 244 (Germany): 433

Hill 245 (France): 277
Hill 247 (Luzon): 370
Hill 253 (Italy): 145, 153-54
Hill 254 (France): 323
Hill 260 (Bougainville): 179-81, 183
Hill 260 (Los Negros): 150-83
Hill 265 (New Guinea): 227
Hill 287 (Germany): 281-82, 284, 327-92
Hill 290 (Tunisia): 101
Hill 293 (France): 289
Hill 299 (Tunisia): 107-08
Hill 310 (France): 320-23
Hill 312 (Tunisia): 107
Hill 315 (Tunisia): 107
Hill 316 (Italy): 191
Hill 318 (France): 289, 342
Hill 318 (Luzon): 371-73
Hill 320 (Biak): 213-15
Hill 321 (France): 351
Hill 324 (Italy): 168
Hill 326 (France): 263-65
Hill 334 (France): 330
Hill 336 (Tunisia): 99
Hill 337 (France): 324
Hill 339 (Italy): 300, 303
Hill 342 (Italy): 145, 154, 157, 164, 192
Hill 343 (Italy): 154
Hill 350 (Tunisia): 106
Hill 351 (Luzon): 371, 374
Hill 355 (Luzon): 374-75, 381-83
Hill 356 (France): 265
Hill 357 (Iwo Jima): 423
Hill 362 (Iwo Jima): 418, 420-21, 423, 430, 432
Hill 363 (Germany): 441-42
Hill 363 (Luzon): 373-74
Hill 369 (Italy): 303
Hill 369 (Tunisia): 101-02
Hill 370 (France): 267, 370
Hill 373 (Italy): 303
Hill 378 (Germany): 331
Hill 380 (Italy): 226-27
Hill 380 (Leyte): 344-47
Hill 380 (Noemfoor): 246, 249
Hill 382 (Iwo Jima): 415-16, 418, 420-21, 423
Hill 382 (Tunisia): 107
Hill 383 (Germany): 331
Hill 385 (Luzon): 370-71
Hill 386 (France): 267
Hill 386 (Italy): 132
Hill 388 (Germany): 336
Hill 388 (Tunisia): 106
Hill 396 (France): 273
Hill 400 (Tunisia): 106
Hill 407 (Tunisia): 106
Hill 409 (Germany): 440
Hill 411 (Germany): 433
Hill 413 (Italy). See M. Maggiore.
Hill 424 (Italy): 133-34
Hill 425 (Italy): 160
Hill 445 (Italy): 169
Hill 448 (Germany): 435
Hill 449 (Italy). See M. Maggiore.
Hill 459 (Italy): 309
Hill 460 (Italy): 150
Hill 470 (Italy): 154
Hill 470 (Luzon): 370-71

Hill 480 (France): 380
Hill 490 (Tunisia): 107
Hill 500 (Saipan): 214
Hill 501 (Italy): 311–12
Hill 504 (Luzon): 482
Hill 505 (Luzon): 482
Hill 510 (France): 379
Hill 511 (Germany): 397
Hill 513 (Tunisia): 107
Hill 518 (Luzon): 479
Hill 519 (Germany): 397–98
Hill 519 (Luzon): 477
Hill 520 (France): 380
Hill 522 (Leyte): 307–08, 310
Hill 523 (Tunisia): 107
Hill 529 (Italy): 228–29
Hill 530 (Belgium): 373
Hill 531 (Tunisia): 107
Hill 550 (Mindanao): 527, 534–40
Hill 553 (Germany): 272–73
Hill 554 (Germany): 278, 280, 290
Hill 560 (Luzon): 372–73
Hill 565 (Luzon): 374
Hill 566 (Italy): 295–98
Hill 568 (Germany): 394, 396–97, 399
Hill 568 (Italy): 309
Hill 575 (Tunisia): 106–07
Hill 578 (Italy): 299–303
Hill 580 (Luzon): 373–74
Hill 585 (Luzon): 374
Hill 587 (Italy): 295–98
Hill 593 (Italy): 169–71, 173–74
Hill 598 (Tunisia): 107
Hill 600 (Luzon): 378–80, 382
Hill 600 (Saipan): 217
Hill 603 (Italy): 302
Hill 606 (Leyte): 344
Hill 609 (Tunisia): 107–08
Hill 615 (Italy): 152
Hill 620 (Luzon): 386
Hill 622 (Italy): 304
Hill 628 (Germany): 392
Hill 628 (Italy): 294
Hill 634 (Italy): 225, 227
Hill 636 (Luzon): 385–86
Hill 640 (Italy): 146, 154
Hill 660 (Luzon): 431, 433–35
Hill 660 (New Britain): 161–63
Hill 661 (Luzon): 296
Hill 665 (Luzon): 374–75
Hill 667 (Tunisia): 105
Hill 670 (Noemfoor): 230, 232
Hill 675 (Italy): 224
Hill 683 (Italy): 152
Hill 687 (Italy): 154
Hill 698 (Germany): 272
Hill 700 (Bougainville): 178–81
Hill 700 (Italy): 165
Hill 700 (Luzon): 384
Hill 706 (Italy): 168–70
Hill 708 (Germany): 439
Hill 721 (Saipan): 223–24
Hill 730 (Italy): 154–57
Hill 747 (Italy): 294, 296
Hill 751 (Italy): 293–94
Hill 767 (Saipan): 224
Hill 769 (Italy): 146, 151–53
Hill 770 (Italy): 154
Hill 772 (Tunisia): 102
Hill 775 (Italy): 160
Hill 783 (France): 283
Hill 789 (Italy): 292–93

Hill 800 (Luzon): 384
Hill 815 (Luzon): 536
Hill 819 (Italy): 144–46, 149–53
Hill 854 (Poro Island): 382
Hill 855 (Italy): 150
Hill 900 (Luzon): 384
Hill 907 (Italy): 151–53
Hill 915 (Leyte): 344–46
Hill 950 (Italy): 152–53
Hill 963 (Italy). *See* Monastery Hill.
Hill 1109 (Italy): 161
Hill 1125 (Palawan): 421, 423, 425
Hill 1134 (Italy): 284
Hill 1180 (Italy): 151
Hill 1190 (Italy): 157
Hill 1200 (Luzon): 453, 461, 467
Hill 1205 (Italy): 149, 152–55, 157
Hill 1445 (Palawan): 427–28, 430, 432
Hill 1500 (Luzon): 384, 403
Hill 1525 (Leyte): 320–22, 344
Hill 1700 (Luzon): 413
Hill 1725 (Burma): 187
Hill 2348 (Leyte): 339
Hill 2480 (Luzon): 523
Hill 2610 (Luzon): 523
Hill 3155 (Negros). *See* Dolan Hill (Negros).
Hill 4055 (Negros): 536, 540, 543
Hillesheim: 429
Hillmicke: 485
Hilsprich: 335
Hiltenfingen: 518, 521
Hiltrup: 470
Himberg: 441
Himeimat: 61
Himmerich: 384, 395
Himmler, Heinrich: 512
Hindang: 311
Hindenburg: 384
Hinderhausen: 380
Hinds, Col. Sidney R.: 294
Hinter Wald: 459
Hinterhausen: 426
Hinterweiler: 429
Hiraiwa Bay: 409
Hirohito, Emperor: 550
Hiroshima: 550
Hirschberg: 480
Hirson: 261
Hirtzfelden: 395
Hirzenach: 440
Hitler, Adolf: 219, 228, 275, 520, 524–25. *See also* Germany.
  appeal to Italians: 120
  Ardennes plans: 274
  assassination attempted: 233
  death reported: 525
  decision to abandon SEA LION: 3
  decision to postpone HERCULES: 38
  heads German Army: 7
  replaces Kluge with Model: 250
  Mortain-Avranches plan: 241
  reinstates Rundstedt: 262
  Stalingrad, determination to secure: 65
  tenth anniversary of power: 89
Hitler Line: 194–200
Hizaonna: 471
Hkawnglaw Stream: 182
Hlagyi: 191
Hlegu: 533

Ho, Gen. Ying-chin: 333, 350, 369, 387, 495, 536
Hoch Elten: 464
Hochfelden: 378, 384
Hochheim: 459
Ho-chih: 539
Hochspeyer: 446
Hochstadt: 459
Hochstatten: 440
Hochstetten: 469
Hochwald Forest: 415–16, 418, 423
Hodge, Lt., Gen. John R.: 123, 308, 534
Hodges, Lt. Gen. Courtney H.: 240, 330, 339
Hoechstadt: 511
Hoefen: 271, 273, 275, 278
Hoenningen: 436
Hoerselgau: 470
Hoevel: 489
Hof: 494, 496, 498, 502
Hofen: 353, 389
Hoffelt: 380
Hoffenheim: 466
Hoffman, Col. Hugh T.: 177
Hofgeismar: 474, 476
Hofweiler: 417
Hogan, Lt. Col. Samuel: 275, 277, 280–81, 284, 305–06, 372, 415, 420, 427, 454, 462
Hoge, Brig. Gen. William M.: 448
Hohe Rhon Hills: 481, 483
Hohenfels: 510
Hohengandern: 481
Hohenlimburg: 491, 493
Hohenmoelsen: 492
Hohenstein: 457
Hokaji Island: 456
Holdenstedt: 489
Holdingen: 380
Holland. *See* Netherlands.
Holland, Col. Temple G.: 118
Hollandia
  Carolines in support of: 184, 157, 189
  enemy landing: 31
  plans for recovery: 177, 179
  recovery of: 152, 176, 178–89, 193, 199, 200–202, 205–07, 213, 223, 229,263
  staging area for P.I.: 302
Hollange: 361
Hollekang: 188
Hollen: 412
Holler: 382
Hollerath: 392, 415
Hollnich: 393 396
Hollsteitz: 490
Holpoltstein: 512
Holsthum: 413–14
Holthausen: 478
Holtheim: 472
Holtum: 482
Holtz Bay Pass and Valley: 106, 109–12
Holtzerath: 437
Holtzheim: 386
Holtzthum: 385
Holtzwihr: 382, 385
Holz River: 454
Holzen: 491
Holzchen: 408
Holzfeld: 440
Holzhausen: 458

[INDEX]

Holzheim: 418, 420
Holzkirchen: 526
Holzminden: 476
Holzweiler: 415
Homberg: 422-23, 425, 463-64, 470, 472, 480
Hombourg: 397
Homburg: 446, 469
Homma, Lt. Gen. Masaharu: 22, 28
Hommerdingen: 405-06
Hommersum: 402
Hommingen: 448
Homonhon Island: 305-06
Hompesch: 411
Homs: 86-87
Honan Province: 187, 189, 200
Honau: 513
Honerath: 431-32
Hong Kong
  air attacks on: 375-76
  fall of: 3, 7, 9
  recovery of: 375-76, 508, 544-45, 547, 551
Hongmoshu: 194, 198, 208
Honinghutie: 278
Honne River: 491, 493
Honnef: 432-33, 436-37
Honningen: 417, 440-41
Honningen Wald: 440
Honsfeld: 355, 386-87
Honshu Island, plans for seizure of: 204, 274
Honskirch: 335 337-38
Hontem: 379
Hontheim: 272-73, 394
Honvelez: 373
Honzrath: 442
Hoover, Rear Adm. John H.: 303
Hopkins, Harry: 32, 46
Hopoi: 131
Hopong: 34
Hor Vltavice: 532
Horanda: 67
Horaniu: 128-29, 134
Horb: 500
Horbourg: 3 88
Horgau: 518
Horhausen: 454
Horii, Ma). Gen. Tomitaro: 51, 53-54, 56, 67, 74
Horik: 317
Hornet: 38, 40, 61
  projects first attack on Japan: 34
Horrem: 418, 422, 425
Horrocks, Lt. Gen. B G. (Br.): 286
Horseshoe Hill (New Georgia): 123-24
Horseshoe Ridge (Cebu): 474
Horseshoe Ridge (Okinawa): 517, 539-40
Horst: 333, 383
Hoscheid: 382
Hoscheiderdickt: 3 84
Hosdorf: 377, 390
Hosi: 358, 384, 395
Hosingen: 385
Hosten: 424, 429
Hôtel de Ville (Mazières-lès-Metz) 312-14
Hotolpe: 482
Hotton: 356-61, 365, 367
Hottorf: 411-12

Hottot: 228, 231
Hottviller: 351, 356
Hotzerath: 43 2
Houdebouville: 255
Houf: 406-07
Houffalize: 355-58, 363, 366, 368-70, 372-77, 379
Housenstamm: 465
Houssen: 3 83-84
Houston: 22, 26, 303
Houvegnez: 373-74
Houverath: 412
Houyire Woods: 373
Hovel: 440
Hoven: 350
Hoverhof: 294
Howe, Lt. Col. Merle H.: 84, 195
Howze, Col. Hamilton H.: 197-98, 200-201, 205, 216
Hoya: 482, 484
Hpa-pen: 3 87-8 8, 390
Hron River: 463
Hsamshingyang: 183-85, 188
Hsenwi: 35, 376, 406
Hsian: 405
Hsiang River: 198
Hsiangta: 197
Hsinning: 509, 550
Hsipaw: 34, 441, 463
Hsueh, Gen. Yueh: 409
Hubermont: 365, 367, 372
Hubert-Folie: 232
Huchem: 4 I o
Huck: 43 0
Huecheln: 334-35
Hueckelhoven: 03
Hueckeswagen: 489, 491
Hueffenhardt: 466
Huei-jen: 194, 198, 202, 208
Huelgoat: 243
Huels: 114
Huertgen: 281-82, 284, 288, 317, 322-23, 326-27, 330, 332, 334-40, 394, 398, 404
Huertgen Forest: 284, 288, 296-303, 327-31, 334, 336-41
Huerth: 425, 427
Huetten: 500
Huettengessas: 463
Huettenrode: 504
Huettersdorf: 442
Huettingen: 422
Huggins: 71, 81
Huggins, Capt. Meredith M.: 71
Hugh L. Scott: 66
Huinghausen: 491
Huisberden: 403
Hukawng River and Valley: 61, 63, 70, 96, 98, 155-58, 161-63, 165, 168, 175, 179-80
Huldange: 383
Hulst: 274, 281
Humain: 362
Humboldt Bay: 183, 188-89, 197
Humenne: 342
Hump, The. *See* China-Burma-India Theater, airlift supply to China.
Hump Tonnage Allocation and Control Office: 355
Hunan Province: 495 544
Hundheim: 440

Hungary
  armistice with Allies: 378
  Combined Bomber Offensive against: 201, 271
  operations in: 182, 295, 300-301, 307-09, 312-13, 316, 318, 326, 335 337 340-41, 343-49, 351, 353-55, 358-66, 369, 372, 374, 377, 379, 382, 388-89, 394 401-02, 441, 449 451, 453, 455, 457, 459, 461, 463, 465, 467, 471, 473
  U.S. declares war on: 40
Hungeroth: 440
Hungersdorf: 431
Hunningen: 380, 387
Hunter, Col. Charles N.: 146, 221
Hunting: 321
Hunts Gap: 104
Hunxe: 452
Huon Gulf and Peninsula sector: 27-28, 96, 120, 150, 159, 162, 164, 172, 188
Hupeh Province: 105, 111, 113
Huppain: 204
Huppenbroich: 387
Hupperdange: 381, 383
Hurbache: 332
Hurdis, Brig. Gen. Charles E.: 255
Hurley, Maj. Gen. Patrick J.
  Kunming planning conference: 357, 362
  recommends Stilwell recall: 302
  reports on China situation: 285
  representative to China: 220, 226-27, 230, 235, 246-47, 263-66
  U.S. officer to command Chinese, proposal for: 271, 276, 296, 302, 306
HURRICANE: 196. *See also* Biak Island.
Huscheid: 424, 441
HUSKY: 87, 108-10, 112-14, 116. *See also* Sicily Campaign.
Hutthurm: 522, 524
Hutton, Lt. Gen. T. J. (Br.): 9
Huy: 264-65
Hvar: 165
Hwangtsoapa: 212
Hwei-tung Bridge: 198
Hwelon Stream: 190
Hyakuna: 543
Hyères: 252-53

I. G. Farben: 425, 495
Iasi: 252, 254
Iba airfield: 3, 5
Ibdi: 199-202, 205, 220, 226-29, 231, 234-35, 238
Ibigny: 331
Iboki Plantation: 175-76
Ibu: 157
ICEBERG: 456. *See also* Ryukyu Islands campaign.
Ichang: 97, 111
Ichendorf: 418
ICHIGO: 198. *See also* China, air bases, enemy, threats to.
Ickern: 472
Idice River and Valley: 293-94, 303-05, 437, 475, 505, 507
Idenheim: 417
Idesheim: 416-17

Idritsa: 229
Idstein: 458-59, 461
Ie: 501, 503-04, 506
Ie Shima: 478, 488, 491, 493, 497, 499, 501, 503-04, 506, 508, 510, 515, 517, 519, 540
Iegusugu Mountain: 501, 504, 506, 508, 510
Ifs: 233
Iggelheim: 448
Igney: 283-84
Igstadt: 459
Ihlren: 389
Ijssel River. *See* Issel River.
Il Falchetto Hill: 297-98, 300
Il Giogo Pass: 263, 269, 271-72, 276-77, 279
Ilagan airfield: 547
Ilagan River: 547
Ilangana: 118, 123
Ilberstedt: 500
Ile de Cézembre: 260-61
Ile de Ré: 328
Iles St. Marcouf: 203
Iller River: 382-83, 386, 391-93, 395-96
Iller River and Canal: 514, 516, 518, 523 530
Illerrieden: 516
Illhaeusern: 382, 384, 387
Illumination, battlefield. *See* Artificial moonlight, use of.
Illwald: 352
Ilmenau: 485
Ilmenau River: 499
Ilmsdorf: 490
Iloilo: 33, 443 445-46, 460
Iloilo River: 445
Ilsfeld: 505
Ilu River: 48, 50-51, 55
Ilz River: 515, 522, 524
Imamura, Lt. Gen. Hitoshi: 67
Imbang River: 471
Imbsen: 481
Imeldange: 324-26
Imgenbroich: 388-89
Imita Ridge: 55
Immendorf: 327-29, 486
Immenstadt: 523, 525, 527
Immerath: 415, 434
Imoc Hill: 467, 476
Imola: 282-84, 286-87, 289, 291, 305, 309 495
Impalutao: 540
Imphal: 35, 145, 161, 179-80, 183-87, 189, 202, 206, 216, 230, 316, 347, 365
Imphal Plain: 206, 212
Imphal Road: 14
Imst: 525, 527, 530-31
Imugan: 428, 439, 450, 529, 539, 542
Inampulugan Island: 499-50
Inasi: 235, 246
Incendiary bomb, first two-ton: 54
Indaw: 178, 293, 349-50 354
Inde River: 330, 333, 336, 339, 342-44, 347-48, 351-52
Inden: 334, 339-42, 360
INDEPENDENCE: 310, 317. *See also* Belfort Gap.
India Air Task Force: 57, 60, 71

India-Burma Campaign: 31-385
India-China Ferry Command: 45
India-China Wing, ATC: 71
India Command (Br.): 15, 114, 146, 147
India. *See also* China-Burma-India Theater; India-Burma Theater.
 aircraft withdrawn from Burma: 30
 B-29's, preparation to receive: 146, 147, 149
 Chinese forces in: 33, 163
 enemy air and naval actions: 152-53, 156
 Hartley succeeds Wavell as CinC, India: 15, 26
 Stilwell heads Chinese troops in: 155
 Stilwell conference: 26
 U.S. control of Calcutta-Assam LOC: 166-67, 171
 U.S. troops for Bengal-Assam railway: 145
 War Transport Department: 171
 Wavell appointed Viceroy: 114
India-Burma Theater. *See also* Chiang Kai-shek, Generalissimo; China; China-Burma-India Theater; China Theater; Chinese Army; South East Asia Command; Stilwell, Lt. Gen. Joseph W.; Sultan, Lt. Gen. Daniel I.; Wheeler, Lt. Gen. Raymond A. activation: 310
 air actions: 314, 342, 542
 Air-Ground Supply Committee: 459
 air support of China: 542
 airborne operations: 345, 349, 354, 438, 441, 449, 507, 509, 520
 airlift supply of China: 329, 342, 344, 355, 540
 Allied planning conferences: 357, 362
 base sections inactivated: 537
 Central Burma Campaign: 387-550
 enemy offensives. *See* Burma, fall of; Burma, recovery of.
 India-Burma Campaign: 310-85
 land supply route to China from: 372, 375, 379, 382, 385-86, 392. *See also* Burma Road; Ledo Road.
 movement of forces to China: 435, 438, 441, 537, 539
 NCAC and 14th Army link-up: 363
 operations in Burma. *See* Burma, fall of; Burma, recovery of.
 separation from CBI: 222-27, 230, 235, 266, 310
 SOS reorganization: 537, 539
 Sultan as commander: 310, 548
 supply situation: 439, 449, 459
 support of recovery of Canton-Hong Kong: 547 549
 Wheeler succeeds Sultan: 548
Indian Army units
 Corps
  3: 3-8, 11, 13-18, 21
  4: 38, 91, 110, 145-46, 172, 179-80, 182-87, 189, 191, 202, 216, 230, 240, 263, 316, 331, 347, 350, 354, 356-57, 371-72, 374, 381, 385, 399, 402-03, 408-09, 412-14, 416-17, 425, 430, 439, 450, 459 461, 463 467 475 486,

Indian Army units—Continued
 Corps—Continued
  4—Continued
   488, 499, 503, 509, 511, 517-18, 523, 525, 529, 533, 541
  15: 148, 161, 170-72, 175-80, 184, 240, 263, 290, 316, 327, 351, 353 358 362-63, 367 372-73, 378 380-81, 384, 387 399 404-06, 426, 437, 522, 525, 528, 530, 532-339, 536, 541-42
  33: 183, 185-87, 202, 216, 223, 228, 230, 240, 243-449, 263, 274, 277, 295, 306, 317-18, 321, 325, 327, 343-44, 356, 360, 364, 367, 369, 371, 374-75, 381, 401-04, 412, 414, 416, 421, 426, 433, 435-36, 438, 442, 445-47, 450, 461, 463, 467, 490, 492, 505, 507, 509, 511, 522, 528, 537 541
 Divisions
  2d: 99, 183
  3d: 178-79, 183, 185-86, 189, 194, 197, 210-11, 216, 219, 226, 230, 234
  4th: 6-8, 17-18, 20-21, 63, 100-101, 105, 107, 109, 169, 172-74, 180, 183, 207-10, 226, 230 232-33, 255 264 274, 279, 282, 285, 287-94, 301, 306, 321
  5th: 39-41, 43, 171-72, 175, 180-81, 183-85, 189, 230, 274, 277, 295, 306 317-18, 321, 325, 439, 450, 461, 467, 488, 499, 503, 509, 511, 517, 541
  7th: 148, 170-72, 175, 179 185, 223, 381, 385, 402-03, 439, 450 461, 467, 490, 509, 511, 541
  8th: 137, 140, 145, 147, 150-53, 156, 191-93, 197-98, 202, 204, 206-07, 211-12, 219-20, 233-35, 238 247-48, 255-56, 258, 264, 266-67, 269-72, 274, 279 282, 285-89, 291-92, 297, 299-301, 305-09, 312, 317-18, 321-23, 325, 327, 334, 338, 346, 351, 354, 359, 361-63, 371-72, 402, 413, 430, 484, 486, 490, 509, 511, 513, 515-16
  9th: 3-5, 7, 11-14, 16-18, 20
  10th: 219-20, 222, 225, 230, 235, 247, 255, 259, 280, 292-302, 304, 306-17, 333, 335-39 341-42, 347, 352-54, 401, 404, 434, 437 495, 497, 513
  11th: 3-13, 15-21
  14th: 75, 78, 82, 103
  17th: 5, 12-13, 15-16, 18, 22-28, 31, 33-34 185-86, 189, 230, 408-09, 412-14, 416-17, 425, 430, 439, 450, 463, 467, 486, 488, 509, 517-18, 523, 525, 529, 533, 541
  19th: 21, 316, 331, 354, 356-57, 360, 363, 369, 371, 374-75, 414, 426, 433, 435, 438,

[INDEX]

Indian Army units—Continued
  Divisions—Continued
    19th—Continued
      445-46, 467, 475, 541
    20th: 186, 189, 191, 344, 360, 371, 381, 401-04, 416, 421, 436, 445, 447, 450, 463, 467, 492, 505, 522, 528, 537, 541
    23rd: 186, 189, 191, 263
    24th: 358
    25th: 351, 362, 367, 373, 378, 380, 387, 404-06, 426
    26th: 98-99, 103, 109-10, 172, 307, 380, 436, 528, 530, 532-33, 537
  Brigades
    1st: 36
    3d Motorized: 39
    6th: 7, 99, 103
    6/15: 7, 10, 12
    7th: 20
    8th: 14, 17
    9th: 40
    10th: 40
    12th: 5-7, 9-11
    13th: 5, 28, 36
    15th: 7
    16th: 5, 12, 16-18, 23, 25, 28
    18th: 44
    22d: 20
    28th: 9-10
    29th: 39, 41, 43, 54, 56, 304, 307, 311, 322, 338, 359
    43d: 430, 435, 499, 501
    44th: 17
    45th: 11, 14-17
    46th: 15, 18, 23-25
    47th: 78, 86, 90
    48th: 21-22, 25
    50th Parachute: 184, 528
    55th: 90, 93, 98
    63d: 26-28, 31, 36
    71st: 98-99
    77th LRP (Chindits): 91, 93, 97, 99, 111, 170, 178-79, 181, 216, 219, 226
    111th: 170, 178-79
    123d: 75, 78, 86, 98
    161st: 46, 184-85
    268th: 350, 467, 507, 541
  Regiment, 44th Infantry: 21
  Cavalry Squadron, 3d: 11
  Battalions
    23d Parachute: 530
    Pioneer: 11
  Company, 1st Independent: 11
Indian Navy. *See* Royal Indian Navy.
Indian Ocean, enemy naval operations in: 30-31
Indin: 78, 103
Indochina: 218, 336, 349
  air and naval attacks on coast: 372
  enemy cuts land route to: 541
  enemy seizure: 390, 434
  enemy withdrawal reported: 5
  theater control definition: 10, 390
Infantry Battalions (Separate)
  99th: 279
  100th: 151, 171, 201. *See also* Infantry Regiments, 442d.
  Provisional (AAA troops); 549

Infantry Brigade, 53, 32d Provisional: 304 358, 364, 376-81, 390-92, 435, 438, 537 *See also* Task Forces, MARS.
Infantry Divisions
  1st (16th, 18th, 26th): 64-66, 71-72, 75, 77-79, 81, 88-89, 91-109, 117-25, 127-28, 203-09, 222, 229-30, 237-44, 247-50, 256-57, 260-71, 273, 276, 280, 298-307, 320, 322, 327-36, 338-40, 342-43, 345-46, 353-60, 363, 375-80, 382-83, 385-94, 397, 402, 412, 414-15, 417-18, 420, 422, 424-25, 427, 429-33, 438-42, 444-45, 447-49, 451-52, 454, 456, 458, 460, 462, 464, 466, 468, 470, 472, 476, 478-81, 483, 485, 487, 489, 491, 494-96, 498, 500, 502, 504, 506, 508, 510, 519, 521, 522, 524-528, 530, 532-33
  2d (9th, 23d, 38th): 204, 206-09, 211, 222, 228-29, 231, 237-38, 242-51, 256, 261, 265, 270, 273, 275, 276, 288, 292, 350-51, 353 355-57, 375-76, 387-95, 397 401, 404, 407-08, 411, 419, 422 424-27, 429, 431-33, 435, 437, 444, 447-49, 451-52, 454, 456, 458 460, 463, 466, 468, 474, 476-77, 479 481, 483, 485, 487, 489, 492, 494, 496, 498, 500, 502, 504, 506, 508, 510, 514-15, 521, 528-29, 531
  3d (7th, 15th, 30th): 65-66, 108-09, 117, 119-20, 124-28, 136-41, 143-45, 147, 155, 158, 164-65, 167-68, 170, 173, 175-77, 194, 196-202, 210, 249-58, 260, 262, 264-65, 267-69, 272, 275, 277, 282-83, 285-87, 294-95, 297-98, 303, 306-10, 312-19, 321-22, 324, 332-38, 345, 360, 377, 379, 381-93, 395, 398, 403, 436, 439, 441-43, 445-46, 448, 453, 455, 457, 459 461, 463, 465-66, 475, 481, 483, 487, 490, 492,498, 500, 502, 507-09, 513-14, 516, 518-21, 523, 528-29, 531
  4th (8th, 12th, 22d): 203-09, 213-19, 221-22, 225, 227-28, 230, 233, 236-37, 239-46, 248 253-60, 263-65, 267, 269-70, 272-73, 275, 277, 280, 294, 297, 312, 319-20, 322-23, 326-32, 334-42, 346, 353-60, 362, 376-80, 382, 384, 386-401, 405, 417, 419-22, 424, 426-27, 429, 431-32, 434, 463, 465-66, 469, 471, 473, 475, 477, 479, 481, 483, 485, 488, 490, 492, 494, 496, 498, 500, 503-05, 507, 509, 511, 513-14, 516, 518, 521, 523, 525-28, 530
  5th (2d, 10th, 11th): 227, 229-31, 235, 237-40 242 244-47 250-58, 260, 265-69, 272-73, 275, 277-80, 287, 289, 293-97, 301, 316, 321-32, 334-38, 341-48, 351, 353-62, 376-86, 392 396-407 409-11, 413-14, 416-17, 419,

Infantry Divisions—Continued
  5th (2d, 10th, 11th)—Continued
    421-24, 426, 428-29, 431-32, 434-41, 443-49, 451-53, 455, 457, 459, 461, 472, 480, 483, 485, 487, 489, 491, 493, 496, 500, 510, 512, 515, 522, 524 526, 528-29, 531-33
  6th (1st, 20th, 63d): 198, 200, 202, 206, 208, 210, 214, 230, 233, 238-40, 255, 301, 370-78, 380, 383-84, 388-91, 393-94, 396, 401-10, 412-14, 416-17, 419, 430-31, 433-40, 442-43, 445-46, 448-51, 453, 457, 460-61, 463-65, 469, 471, 473, 475, 477, 482, 486, 499, 501, 503, 505, 510-11, 513, 517, 520, 525, 530, 545-46, 548-50. *See also* Infantry Regiments, 1st, 2th, and 63d.
  7th (7th, 32d, 184th): 102, 104, 109-12, 127, 160, 167-70, 307-17, 326, 333-37, 339-41, 344-47, 349-50, 352-54, 357, 374-75, 378-79, 382, 389, 391, 467-69, 471, 476, 478, 480, 482, 484, 486, 488, 506, 508, 510, 512-13, 515, 517, 519-20, 522, 524-25, 527, 529-30, 532-35, 540-48 *See also* Infantry Regiments, 17th, 32d, and 184th.
  8th (13th, 28th, 121st): 222, 226, 229-30, 237, 240-43, 245-49, 251, 256, 261, 265, 270, 273, 276, 279, 288, 292, 328, 330, 332, 334-39, 343-44, 346-47, 355, 358, 360-61, 363, 392-94, 397, 410-12, 414-16, 418, 420, 422, 424-25, 427, 429-30, 433, 438, 444-45, 447, 458, 460, 462, 464, 466, 468, 470 472, 474, 476, 478, 480, 482-83, 485 487, 489, 491, 493, 495-98, 500, 502, 504, 506, 508, 510, 512, 514-15, 520, 522, 524, 526, 528
  9th (39th 47th 60th): 64-65, 93-95, 98-109, 119-28, 207-22, 227-32, 236-37, 240-50, 253, 256-57, 260-61, 263-66, 268, 270-73, 275, 277-79, 281-82, 284, 287-90, 295-303, 311-12, 327-33, 335, 338, 341, 345-46, 349-51, 353-59, 387-93, 395, 397-99, 401, 404-05, 408, 411, 414-15, 417-18, 420, 422, 424-25, 427 429 431-33, 435-42, 444, 448-49, 451-52, 454, 456, 458, 460, 464, 466, 468, 470, 472 474, 478, 480, 483, 485, 487, 491, 494, 496, 498, 500, 502, 504, 506, 509, 510, 512, 514, 515
  10th Mountain (85th, 86th, 87th): 362, 368, 370, 386 405-10, 412, 417, 423, 425-26, 428, 433, 483, 495, 497, 499, 501, 503, 505, 507, 509, 511, 513, 515-16, 518, 521, 525
  24th (19th, 21st, 34th): 182, 186, 188, 209, 213, 302, 307-09, 311-28, 336-40, 342-44, 353, 359, 362-63, 365, 375-76, 378-79, 381, 383, 386, 388-89, 391, 393-95, 404,

[605]

[INDEX]

Infantry Divisions—Continued
  24th (9th, 21st, 34th)—Continued
    406, 411-13, 416, 419, 421, 427-28, 431-34, 440, 446, 453, 497, 501, 503, 505-07, 510-11, 513, 515, 517, 519-20, 522-23, 525, 527, 529-44, 549-50, See also Infantry Regiments, 19th, 21st, and 34th.
  25th: (27th, 35th, 161st): 59, 75, 81- 88, 91, 119, 121-30, 133-35, 139, 183, 301, 376-79, 381, 383, 385-86, 388-91, 393-94, 396, 398, 401-04, 406-07, 409-14, 416-17, 419, 421, 423, 426-28, 430-31 433-35, 437-39, 441-43, 446-47, 449, 453, 455, 457, 460, 463, 465, 467, 469, 477, 479, 482, 484, 486, 488, 490, 493, 497, 501, 503, 505, 509-11, 513, 515, 517, 519-20, 522, 525, 527, 529-33, 535-42, 548 See also Infantry Regiments, 27th, 35th, and 161st.
  26th: (101st, 104th, 328th): 295, 301, 308, 320-26, 329-31, 333-39, 342-50, 353, 357, 359-64, 366-67, 369-71, 373-74, 376, 379-80, 382-86, 396-400, 402-06, 410-11, 414, 416-17, 419, 426, 428, 430-31, 433, 437-40, 442-44, 446-53, 455, 457, 459, 461, 463, 467-68, 470, 473, 475, 477, 479, 481, 485, 487, 497, 522, 524, 526, 528-31, 533
  27th (105th, 106th, 165th): 138, 142, 147-49, 162, 166, 174, 211-27, 484, 486, 488, 495, 497, 50,4 506, 508, 510, 512, 515, 517, 519-20, 522, 525, 527, 531 See also Infantry Regiments, 105th, 106th, and 165th.
  28th (109th, 110th, 112th): 235, 237, 240 245-48 252-54,258-59, 263, 265, 267, 269-70, 272-73, 275, 277, 280, 294, 297-98, 305 307 311-12, 315, 317-20, 322, 325, 328, 330, 353-57, 359, 362-63, 366, 368-70, 376-77, 379, 381, 383, 386-87, 389-93, 395, 402, 407, 411, 422, 424-27, 429, 431-32, 440-42, 444, 448, 456, 460, 464, 478, 480, 485, 492, 514, 516
  29th (115th, 116th, 175th): 203-14, 221-22, 228-33, 238, 243-50, 254, 256, 258-59, 261, 263, 265, 270, 273-76, 284, 290-91, 293-98, 302-04, 311, 327-34, 336-39, 341-43, 346-47, 354, 356, 358, 360, 392-93, 395, 410-12, 414-16, 418, 420, 422 460 466, 476, 478, 480, 489, 493, 497, 499, 502, 506, 508, 510, 512, 514-15, 517, 528, 530, 533
  30th (117th, 119th, 120th): 210-11, 213, 222, 226-32, 236-39, 242-48, 252-54, 256-59, 265-71, 275-76, 278, 292-301, 304, 312, 323, 327-34, 338-39, 351-52, 354-62, 366, 368, 370-71, 373-82, 390-91,395, 410-12, 414-16, 418, 420, 427, 450-52, 454, 456, 458, 460, 462, 466, 468, 470, 472, 476, 480, 484,

Infantry Divisions—Continued
  30th (117th, 119th, 120th)—Continued
    489, 491, 493, 495, 497, 499, 502, 506, 510, 532-33
  31st (154th, 155th, 167th): 188, 212-13, 223, 225, 230, 233, 249, 253, 261, 274, 276, 327, 331, 446, 453, 491, 511, 513, 515, 519-20, 522-23, 525, 527, 529-41, 548. See also Infantry Regiments, 155th and 167th.
  32d (126th, 127th, 128th): 38, 45, 53-60, 88, 155, 159, 174, 178, 182, 188, 190, 195, 229, 249, 276, 326-32, 334-35, 340-43, 345, 347, 349-52, 356-57, 359-65, 385, 387-89, 394-96, 398-401, 403, 409, 411-12, 419, 421, 426, 428, 430, 433, 435-36, 439, 449-50, 453, 457, 465, 467, 477, 479, 482, 484, 486, 488, 501, 505, 511, 525, 529, 539, 542, 549-50. See also Infantry Regiments, 126th, 127th, and 128th.
  33d (123d, 130th, 136th): 261, 400-403, 406, 409, 419, 426, 430-31, 433, 435, 443, 445-47, 450, 455, 457, 469, 473, 479, 482, 484, 488, 490, 497, 501, 505, 507, 509, 511, 513, 515, 517, 519-20, 522, 527, 529 542-43, 547-48. See also Infantry Regiments, 123d, 130th, and 136th.
  34th (133d, 135th, 168th): 64, 89-92, 94-95, 97-98, 100-109, 136, 138-47, 149-53, 155, 157, 160-73, 182, 184, 196-202, 204-06, 219-35, 237, 244 264, 266-67, 269, 271, 274, 276-77, 290, 283-90, 292-94, 296-306, 309, 334, 368, 373, 402, 410, 428, 475, 499, 501, 503, 505, 507, 509, 513, 515-16, 518, 521, 527
  35th (134th, 137th, 320th): 224, 226, 228-33, 237-39, 241, 243-49, 251, 253-57, 259-61, 267-70, 272-73, 275, 277, 280-81, 283-85, 287-92, 298-300, 320-26, 329-31, 333-35, 342-52, 354-56, 358-59, 361-71, 373, 375, 381, 386-87, 389, 391-92, 394, 409, 412-16, 418, 420-21, 423, 425, 427-28, 430 432-36, 452, 454, 456, 458, 460, 462-64, 466, 468, 472, 476, 482, 484, 487, 489, 491, 493, 495, 497, 508, 515, 517
  36th (141st, 142d, 143d): 132-34, 136, 147, 151-55, 157, 160, 162-67, 169-72, 176, 191, 194, 196-202, 206-08, 210, 212, 215, 218-19, 249-62, 264-69, 272, 275, 277, 282-87, 303-15, 318-19, 322, 324, 328, 330, 332-47, 362, 365-67, 369, 374, 378, 389-93, 395-402, 408-10, 413, 439, 441-43, 445-48, 450-51, 459, 461, 514, 520-21, 523, 525, 527-28, 530-31
  37th (129th, 145th, 148th): 116-17, 119-26, 130, 132, 145-48, 179, 180-83, 301, 370, 371-75, 378-

Infantry Divisions—Continued
  37th (129th, 145th, 148th)—Continued
    81, 383-402, 410, 412, 416, 419, 423, 426, 450, 455, 457, 459-60, 477, 479, 481-82, 484, 486, 488, 490, 493, 495, 497, 499, 501, 503, 505, 507, 509-11, 513, 515, 517, 519-20, 522, 525, 527, 529-35, 538-39, 541-49. See also Infantry Regiments, 129th, 145th and 148th.
  38th (149th, 151st, 152d): 347, 349, 388, 390-91, 393-96, 398-99, 401-03, 405-06, 408, 413, 425, 434, 440, 443, 445, 449, 457, 475-76, 484, 488, 497, 499, 503, 505, 510, 517, 525, 527, 529-35, 538-42, 549. See also Infantry Regiments, 149th, 151st, and 152d.
  40th (108th, 160th, 185th): 183, 188, 190, 301, 370-75, 378-79, 381, 384-85, 388, 390, 395-96, 398-406, 408, 411-15, 417, 421, 441, 443-44, 448-50, 452-53, 460-61, 464-65, 467, 469, 471, 473, 476, 480, 484, 488, 493, 497, 501, 503, 506-08, 510, 519-20, 522, 527, 529, 533-36, 538-40. See also Infantry Regiments, 108th, 160th, and 185th.
  41st (162d, 163d, 186th): 30, 32, 38, 45, 53, 78, 79, 91-92, 96, 98, 101-02, 113, 115-16, 120, 127-28, 131-32, 137, 179, 182, 186, 188, 197-98, 208-09, 213, 253, 405, 417, 420-21, 423, 425 427-28, 430-32, 434, 436, 438, 440-42, 444-46, 452, 457, 462, 469, 478, 484, 499, 503, 512, 520, 531, 536, 547. See also Infantry Regiments, 162d, 163d, and 186th.
  42d (222d, 232d, 242d): 349, 362, 366-68, 370-71, 376-77, 383, 385, 404, 439, 441-43, 445-46, 448, 453, 465-66, 469, 471, 473, 475, 477, 479, 481, 483, 485, 487, 492, 494, 496, 498, 500, 502, 504, 507-09, 512, 514, 516, 518-19, 521, 523
  43d (103d, 169th, 172d): 61, 93, 94, 113, 115-33, 135, 183, 234-35, 247, 249-50, 301, 370-86, 390, 401, 403, 405, 417, 421, 425, 428, 434-43, 446, 448-51, 453, 461, 463, 465, 467, 471, 473, 475-77, 482, 527, 530, 532-39, 543. See also Infantry Regiments, 103d, 169th and 172d.
  44th (71st, 114th, 324th): 305, 309-11, 320, 325, 328, 331, 333, 335-36, 338, 340, 342-43, 345-51, 356, 362, 365-68, 370, 394 403-04, 417, 439, 457, 459, 461, 463, 479, 481, 483, 485, 488, 500, 503, 505, 507, 509, 511, 513-14, 516, 518, 520-21, 523, 525 527-28, 530-32

[INDEX]

Infantry Divisions—Continued
   45th (157th, 179th, 180th): 117-24, 128, 133-41, 143-47, 150-55, 157-59, 161, 168, 170-75, 196-202, 248-54, 256-61, 263-69, 271-72, 277-78, 280-87, 291-93, 303-10, 312, 315-17, 319, 321, 334-36, 340, 342-43, 345-49, 352, 354-55, 362, 365-69, 371-74, 376-79, 383, 404-05, 436, 439, 441-43, 445-48, 455, 457, 459, 461, 463, 465-66, 468, 471, 481, 483, 487, 490, 492, 498, 500, 502, 504, 507, 512, 514, 516, 518-19, 521, 523
   63d (253d, 254th 255th): 349, 362, 364-65, 389, 394, 398, 403-06, 412, 417, 423-24, 426, 439, 441-43, 445-47, 455, 459, 461, 463, 465-66, 469, 471, 473, 475, 477, 479, 481, 483, 485-86, 488, 490, 492, 494, 496, 498, 500, 503-05, 507, 509, 511, 513-14, 516, 518, 520-21
   65th (259th, 260th, 261st): 419, 426, 428, 430, 433, 437-38, 442-47, 461, 463, 465, 467-68, 470, 472-73, 475, 477, 479, 481, 485, 487, 492, 496, 500, 504, 506-08, 510, 512, 514, 516-17, 519, 521, 526, 528-30, 532-34
   66th (262d, 263d, 264th): 365, 464, 498
   68th (271st, 272d, 273d): 394-95, 400, 402, 415, 417, 419, 422, 424, 426-27, 429, 431, 447, 449, 454, 456, 458, 460, 463, 466, 470, 474-75, 477, 479 481, 485, 487, 489, 492, 494, 496, 498, 502, 504, 506, 508, 510, 512, 514-15, 517, 521, 524
   70th (274th, 275th, 276th): 357, 362, 365-67, 369-70, 373-74, 376, 383-88, 391, 397-98, 404-10, 417, 423-24, 426, 428, 437-39, 445-47, 504, 507
   71st (5th, 14th, 66th): 433, 443, 448, 453, 459, 461, 463, 465, 467-70, 473, 475, 477, 479, 481, 485, 487, 490, 492, 494, 496, 498, 500, 504, 506, 508, 510, 512, 514, 516-19, 521-22, 524, 526, 528-30, 532-34
   75th (288th, 280th, 291st): 348, 358-60, 363-64, 366-67, 371, 374-82, 386, 388-93, 395-96, 400, 404, 418, 428, 433, 435-36, 451, 454, 456, 462-64, 466, 468, 470, 472, 474, 476, 478, 480, 482, 484, 486-87, 489, 491, 493, 495, 499, 510, 512, 515
   76th (304th, 385th, 417th): 384, 392, 396-411, 413-14, 416-17, 419, 421-22, 424, 426, 428-29, 431-32, 434-40, 443-45, 447, 454, 457, 459, 461, 463, 465, 467, 470, 472, 475, 477, 479 481, 483, 485, 487, 490, 492, 494, 496, 498, 502, 514-15

Infantry Divisions—Continued
   77th (305th, 306th, 307th): 222, 225, 234-36, 238-46, 314, 322, 329, 331, 335, 338, 344-65, 391, 456-58, 460, 462, 465, 469, 488, 499, 501, 503-04, 506, 508, 510, 519-20, 524-25, 527, 529-30, 532-40, 542-43. See also Infantry Regiments, 305th, 306th, and 307th.
   78th (308th, 310th, 311th): 351-53, 355, 358, 370-71, 385, 387-95, 397-402, 417-18, 420, 422, 424, 426-27, 429, 431-33, 435-42, 444-49, 451-52, 454, 456-58, 460, 462, 464, 466, 468, 470, 472, 476, 478, 480, 482-83, 487, 489, 491, 493 ,495-97, 500, 502, 504
   79th (313th, 314th, 315th): 210, 213-20, 222-24, 226, 230, 237-38, 240-43, 245, 248, 250-54, 257-59, 262, 266-70, 272-73, 277-78, 280-81, 283-84, 290-95, 299, 302-03, 305, 309-10, 320, 325-26, 328-29, 331, 336, 340, 342, 345-54, 362, 365-66, 368-73, 376-81, 383-84, 393, 396, 404, 409, 418, 428, 450-52, 454, 456, 458, 460, 462, 466, 476, 478 480, 482, 484-85, 487, 489, 491, 493, 497, 504, 515
   80th (317th, 318th, 318th): 245, 247-48, 250-53, 256-61, 263-70, 272-73, 275, 277-78, 281, 283-86, 288, 292-94, 298-99, 316, 320-29, 331-32, 336-40 342-44, 346, 356-57, 359-63, 368, 371, 377, 379-86, 392, 396-411, 413-14, 416-17, 419, 421-22, 424, 426, 428, 434-35, 437-40, 442-44, 446-48, 453, 455, 457, 459, 461, 463, 465, 467-68, 470, 472, 474-75, 477, 479, 481, 483, 485, 487, 490, 492, 494, 496, 498, 502, 504, 508, 521-22, 524, 526, 528-33
   81st (321st, 322d, 323d): 240, 259, 278-79, 285-88, 303, 305, 307, 317, 338-39, 342, 365, 367. See also Infantry Regiments, 321st, 322d, and 323d.
   83d (329th, 330th, 331st): 219, 222, 224-25, 227-28, 230, 237, 240-50, 257, 260-61, 267, 274, 282, 287, 292, 294-95, 297, 300, 320, 323, 343, 346, 349, 353-55, 358-64, 366, 370-76, 378-79, 390, 410, 412, 415, 418, 420, 422, 466, 468, 470, 472, 474, 476, 478, 480, 484, 486-87, 489, 491, 493, 495, 497, 499, 502, 504, 506, 508, 510, 521, 533
   84th (3334, 334th 335th): 320, 323, 329-34, 340, 342, 353, 355-56, 358-62, 365-66, 368-71, 373-74, 379-82, 390-91, 395, 409-12, 414-16, 418, 420-23, 425, 429-30, 433, 466, 470, 472, 474, 476, 478, 480, 483-84, 486, 489, 491, 493, 495, 497, 499, 502, 508, 510, 514-15, 517, 528

Infantry Divisions—Continued
   85th (337th 338th 339th): 180, 186, 191-202, 205, 240, 250-52, 257, 271-74, 276-77, 280, 282-90, 292-307, 309-10, 312, 318, 321, 334, 359, 369, 370, 377, 434, 437, 443, 501, 503, 505, 507, 509, 511, 513, 515-16, 518, 525, 527
   86th (341st, 342d, 343d): 449, 456, 458, 460, 462, 464, 474, 478, 480, 482-83, 485, 487, 489, 491, 493, 496-98, 500, 502, 507, 509, 512, 514, 516, 518-19, 521 523-24, 526, 528
   87th (345th 346th, 347th): 347-50, 352, 354-55, 363-65, 367-73, 376-77, 382, 384-91, 393-95, 397-400, 01-12, 414, 416-17, 419-22, 424, 426-27, 429, 431-32, 438-42, 444, 449, 452 454, 457, 459-60, 463, 473, 477, 479, 481, 483, 485, 487, 489-90, 492, 494, 496, 498, 500
   88th (349th, 350th, 351st): 171, 176, 191-202, 205, 226-36, 240, 252-53, 261, 264, 282-307, 309-12, 318, 321, 334, 373, 383, 428, 497, 499 501, 503, 505, 509, 511, 513, 515-16, 518, 521, 527, 531
   89th: (353d, 354th 355th): 423, 432, 435-41, 443-44, 446-49, 451, 454, 457, 459, 461, 463, 470, 472-73, 475, 477, 479, 481, 483, 485, 487, 490, 492, 494, 496, 498, 500, 502
   90th (357th, 358th, 359th): 203, 206-13, 222-24, 226, 228, 230, 234, 237, 240, 243-44, 248, 250-53, 256-57, 264-70, 272-73, 275, 277, 288-89, 293-94, 296-97, 299, 301, 307, 312-15, 320-30, 332, 334-38, 340-42, 345-52, 355, 359, 362, 369-77, 379-90, 392-94, 396-400, 405-09, 411-12, 414, 421-22, 424, 426-29, 431-32, 434-45, 447-51, 453, 455, 457, 459, 461, 463, 465, 467-68, 470, 472-73, 475, 477, 481, 485, 487, 490, 492, 494, 496, 498, 502, 504, 506, 508, 510, 512, 514-19, 522, 524, 526, 528-29, 531-33
   91st (361st, 362d, 363d): 201, 206, 208, 215, 223-26, 228-36, 240, 251, 267, 268, 271-72, 274-77, 278-80, 282-90, 292-306, 309, 311-12, 334 3.83 402, 443, 475, 499, 501, 503, 505, 507, 509, 513, 515-16, 518, 523, 525
   92d (365th 370th, 371st): 225, 244, 255, 282, 287-91, 295-301, 305, 309 315 359, 361-62, 368, 371, 392 394 397, 401, 412, 471, 475, 477, 479, 481, 483, 486, 488, 490, 492, 494, 501, 505, 515-16, 520-21, 525, 527 See also Infantry Regiments, 370th and 371st.
   93d (25th, 368th, 369th): 183-84, 491, 549
   94th (301st, 302d, 376th): 267, 270, 274, 298, 365, 369, 374-75 377-86, 388-90, 396-400, 403-11, 413-14, 417, 419, 421, 423-24, 426,

Infantry Divisions—Continued
  94th, (301st, 302d, 376th)—Continued
    428, 430-35, 437-40, 442-44, 446-49, 450-51, 453, 461, 471, 502
  95th (377th 378th, 379th): 316, 320-26, 328-32, 334-57, 362, 374, 379, 382, 384, 386, 391, 402, 418, 422-25, 454, 462, 466, 468, 470, 472, 474, 476, 478, 480, 482, 484-85, 487, 489, 491, 493, 504, 512, 515, 526, 533
  96th (381st, 382d, 383d): 307-23, 374, 388, 467-69, 471-72, 476, 478, 480, 482, 484, 486, 488, 491, 495, 506, 508, 510, 512-13, 515, 517, 519-20, 522, 524-25, 535-48 *See also* Infantry Regiments, 381st, 382d *and* 383d.
  97th (303d, 386th, 387th): 466, 470, 472-74, 476, 478, 480, 482-83, 485, 487, 489, 491, 493, 495, 497, 500, 502, 504, 506, 508, 510, 512, 514, 516-17, 519, 521-22, 524, 526, 528-29, 532-33
  99th (393d, 394th 395th): 351, 353-58, 387-94, 397, 400, 402, 406-07, 415-16, 418, 420, 422, 424-25, 427, 430, 432-33, 435-42, 444-45, 447-49, 451-52, 454, 456, 458, 460, 462, 464, 466, 470, 472, 474, 478, 480, 483, 485, 487, 489, 491, 493-94, 496, 498, 500-501, 508-09, 512, 514, 516, 518-19, 521-22, 524, 526, 528
  100th (397th 398th, 399th): 307, 316-17, 319, 321, 324-26, 328-33, 335, 337-38, 343, 345-46, 352, 357, 362, 365-66, 369-70, 398, 403-04, 417, 439, 441, 443, 448, 453, 465-669, 469, 471, 473, 475, 477, 479, 481, 483, 485, 488, 490, 492, 494, 496, 498, 500, 503, 505, 507, 509, 511, 513-14, 516
  102d (405th, 406th, 407th): 312, 320, 323 330 332-33, 340-43, 356, 384, 394-95, 409-12, 414-16, 418, 420, 422-23, 464, 470-72, 474, 478, 480, 482, 484, 486, 489, 491, 493, 495, 497, 499, 502, 515, 517
  103d (409th, 410th, 411th): 307, 321-22, 324, 326, 328, 332-38, 340-46, 349, 351-52, 354, 362, 373-74, 376, 378, 381-85, 393, 406, 439, 441-43, 445-48, 450, 459, 461, 505, 509, 511, 513-14, 516, 518, 520-21, 523, 525, 527-28, 530-31
  104th (413th, 414th, 415th): 303, 309, 311-13, 315, 317-20, 322, 327-45, 349-51, 355, 358, 360, 393, 410-12, 414-16, 418, 420, 422, 424-25, 427, 429-31, 433, 438, 440, 444, 447-49, 451-52, 454, 456, 458 460, 462, 464, 466, 468, 470, 472, 474, 476, 479, 481, 483, 485, 487, 489, 491, 494, 498, 500, 502, 504, 506, 508, 510, 517, 522, 524

Infantry Divisions—Continued
  106th (422d, 423d, 424th): 350, 353-57, 359, 361, 363, 370-76, 383-84, 393-94, 397-98, 426-27, 429, 433-34, 499
  Americal (132d, 164th, 182d): 29, 39, 58-59, 63, 66, 68, 71, 74, 81-83, 85, 89-91, 156-57, 159, 161-62, 179-80, 183-84, 388, 391, 399-400, 403, 406-07, 412, 415, 417, 421, 423, 428, 430, 433, 436, 449-50, 455, 457, 460-62, 464-65, 467, 469, 471, 474, 476, 480, 482, 484, 486, 488, 490-91, 493, 497, 499, 501, 506-07, 510, 512-13 515, 517, 519-20, 522-23, 525, 527, 529-34 542 548. *See also* Infantry Regiments, 132d, 164th, *and* 182d.
  Composite Army-Marine: 85-89
  Philippine (31st, 45th, 57th): 12-13, 15-19, 22, 31-32. *See also* Infantry Regiments, 31st (Philippine Scouts), 45th (Philippine Scouts), *and* 57th (Philippine Scouts).
Infantry Regiments
  1st: 213, 217-18, 222, 239-40, 377-78, 388, 391-94, 401, 403, 405-08, 413-14, 416-17, 431, 434-35, 438, 442-43, 445, 448-51, 453, 455, 457, 460-61, 463, 465, 469, 471, 499, 501, 503, 510, 517. *See also* Infantry Divisions, 6th.
  4th: 111-12
  17th: 109-12, 127, 167, 169-70, 307, 309-15, 317, 334, 339, 345, 468-69, 510 513, 517, 519-20, 522, 524-25, 527, 529-30, 533-35, 543-45, 547. *See also* Infantry Divisions, 7th.
  19th: 188, 302, 308-16, 320-25, 327-29, 353, 364, 368, 376, 379, 386, 411, 416, 427, 433, 436, 440, 503, 506-07, 510-11, 513, 523, 525, 527, 529-31, 534-44 *See also* Infantry Divisions, 24th.
  20th: 208, 210, 213-19, 233, 238, 253, 377-78, 388-90, 393-94, 396, 410, 412-14, 436, 438, 442-43, 445, 449-51, 453, 455, 457, 460-61, 463-64, 469, 473, 477, 503, 546, 548. *See also* Infantry Divisions, 6th.
  21st: 188-89, 302, 307, 315-16, 319-25, 327-28, 364-65, 367-68, 373, 375, 378, 381, 383, 388-89, 419, 428, 431-32, 434, 497, 501, 503, 506, 525, 527, 529, 531, 534-41. *See also* Infantry Divisions, 24th.
  24th: 183
  25th: 183. *See also* Infantry Divisions, 93d.
  27th: 81, 83-88, 124, 126, 128-29, 133-36, 139, 377, 379, 381, 385-86, 390-91, 401, 410-13, 416, 428, 430, 434, 435, 439, 441-42, 447-48, 453, 460, 463, 465, 467, 484,

Infantry Divisions—Continued
  27th—Continued
    486, 490, 493, 497, 503, 505, 509-11, 515, 517, 520, 522, 531-32, 535-38, 540-41. *See also* Infantry Divisions, 25th.
  31st: 12, 15-16, 19, 31-32. *See also* Infantry Divisions, Philippine.
  32d: 104, 109-12, 167-69, 307-17, 326, 333, 335-37, 339, 345, 352-55, 357, 468-69, 471, 478, 482, 484, 486, 488, 506, 510, 512-13, 522, 524-25, 527, 540-45, 547. *See also* Infantry Divisions, 7th.
  34th: 188, 209, 213-14, 219-21, 307-16, 318-19, 322-32, 334, 336-40, 342-44, 359, 362-63, 388, 391, 393-95, 404-06, 411-13, 415, 421, 506-07, 510-11, 513, 515, 517, 519-20, 522-23, 529, 532-41, 550. *See also* Infantry Divisions, 24th.
  35th: 75, 82-88, 124, 126-27, 130, 134, 386, 390-91, 393-94, 396, 398, 401, 406, 409-10, 412-14, 416-17, 421, 423, 428, 430-31, 433-36, 439, 441, 449, 453, 460, 463, 469, 482, 488, 490, 497, 505, 509, 513, 52,0 522, 536. *See also* Infantry Divisions, 25th.
  45th (Philippine Scouts): 15, 16, 19-21, 31-32. *See also* Infantry Divisions, Philippine.
  53d: 127
  57th (Philippine Scouts): 14-15, 18-23, 32. *See also* Infantry Divisions, Philippine.
  63d: 218-20, 224-25, 227, 239, 373-75, 377-78, 380, 383-84, 391, 393, 412-14, 416-17, 431-42, 469, 471, 473, 475, 477, 482, 486, 501, 510, 548. *See also* Infantry Divisions, 6th.
  87th: 127
  103d: 93-94, 114, 116, 119, 122-24, 135, 247, 250, 371-72, 374-80, 382-84, 436-38, 440-43, 445-46, 448-51, 453, 463, 465, 467, 471, 473, 475, 477, 533. *See also* Infantry Divisions, 43d.
  105th: 148, 212-21, 223-26, 486, 506, 508, 519. *See also* Infantry Divisions, 27th.
  106th: 166, 174-75, 211, 213-14, 217-21, 223-24, 226, 504, 506, 508. *See also* Infantry Divisions, 27th.
  108th: 371, 379, 382, 384-85, 388, 390, 398-99, 401-04, 411, 415, 450, 471, 480, 520, 529, 535-37, 539-40. *See also* Infantry Divisions, 40th.
  111th: 167
  123d: 262, 433, 482, 484, 505, 513, 517, 519, 527, 542-43, 547-48. *See also* Infantry Divisions, 33d.
  124th: 223, 225, 229-35, 239-40, 242, 249 274 276 515, 519-20, 522-23, 525, 527, 529-31, 533-38
  125th: 276

[INDEX]

Infantry Regiments—Continued
  126th: 54-58, 60-62, 65-77, 83, 87, 155, 159, 174, 178, 190, 199, 200, 202, 205, 249, 277, 344, 347, 352, 355-57, 388, 403, 477, 479, 505, 539, 542. See also Infantry Divisions, 32d.
  127th: 56, 70, 72-792 81-83, 85-87, 188-90, 192, 195, 199, 202, 216, 221, 229-30, 232-36, 238-41, 248, 352 355-57, 359-61, 363 394, 396, 398-401, 403, 409, 411-12, 419, 421, 428, 430, 433, 435-36, 439, 449-50, 453, 505. See also Infantry Divisions, 32d.
  128th: 56, 59, 63-64, 67-70, 72, 75-78, 81, 161, 163, 205, 214, 221, 228-30, 240, 244, 250, 327-35, 339-40, 342-43, 350 356 360, 363, 436, 438, 449-50, 453, 457, 465, 467, 477, 479, 486, 505, 542. See also Infantry Divisions, 32d.
  129th: 146, 179-82, 371, 374-75, 378, 386, 388, 390-91, 397-98, 400, 410, 416, 450, 455, 457, 459-60, 469, 473, 477, 479, 482, 484, 486, 488, 490, 493, 495, 511, 513, 515, 517, 519, 542-46, 548-49. See also Infantry Divisions, 37th.
  130th: 428, 430-31, 433, 443, 447, 455, 457, 484, 490, 497, 501, 505, 507, 509, 511, 513 ,515 517, 519. See also Infantry Divisions, 33d.
  132d: 73, 75-79 81-83, 89-91, 161, 180, 421, 423, 428, 436, 455, 457, 460-61, 469, 471, 480, 482, 486, 490, 493, 506-07, 513. See also Infantry Divisions, Americal.
  136th: 433, 482, 527. See also Infantry Divisions, 33d.
  138th: 388
  145th: 116-17, 119, 121-24, 130, 147, 179-80, 372, 383-86, 389-90, 410, 416, 419, 503, 505, 507, 510, 511, 513, 517, 520, 525, 527, 529-35, 538-39, 541, 543-46. See also Infantry Divisions, 37th.
  147th: 58, 60, 63, 71, 81-87, 89-91, 186, 446, 456, 474
  148th: 116-17, 120-24, 126, 145-46, 179-80, 371, 378, 385-86, 388, 390, 392-93, 396, 400, 416, 484, 495, 497, 499, 501, 503, 505, 507, 509, 511, 527, 545-48. See also Infantry Divisions, 37th.
  149th: 347, 349, 388, 390-91, 394-96, 398, 402-03, 405-06, 497, 533-34, 538-42. See also Infantry Divisions, 38th.
  151st: 388, 394-96, 401, 403, 405-06, 408, 413, 445, 457, 475-76, 493, 499, 541. See also Infantry Divisions, 38th.
  152d: 388, 390-91, 395-96, 402, 449, 497, 510, 517, 525, 529-32, 534-35, 538-40. See also Infantry Divisions, 38th.
  155th: 274, 533, 535-37, 539-40. See also Infantry Divisions, 31st.
  158th: 114, 157, 162-63, 195-99, 202, 205-06, 209-10, 216, 223-25,

Infantry Regiments—Continued
  158th—Continued
    229, 257, 264, 301, 372-75, 377-78, 380, 383-85, 390, 401-03, 425-26, 428, 430-31, 434-37, 440-43, 445-46, 448, 452, 467, 469, 471, 473, 477, 479, 481, 484, 486, 488, 490, 492, 495, 497, 499, 503, 505, 511, 520, 523, 527, 529-30, 535, 546
  159th: 127
  160th: 371, 374-75, 378-80, 382-86, 388, 395, 398-400, 403, 406, 412-13, 443, 448, 464-65, 467, 469, 471, 473, 476, 484, 486, 493, 501, 503, 506, 508, 510, 519, 522, 527, 536, 538, 540. See also Infantry Divisions, 40th.
  161st: 82, 85-88, 91, 121-24, 126, 377-79, 381, 383, 385-86, 391, 393, 401, 404, 406-07, 409, 413, 428, 430, 433-35, 437-38 446-47, 455, 457, 482, 488, 513, 517, 519, 527, 529-31, 533, 535-36. See also Infantry Divisions, 25th.
  162d: 30, 91, 95-96, 98, 101, 113, 115-16, 120, 127-28, 131-32, 137, 188-89, 198-202, 204-18, 220-21, 244, 249, 436, 438, 441-42, 444-46, 452, 520, 531, 536. See also Infantry Divisions, 41st.
  163d: 32, 78-79, 81-87, 90, 92, 96, 188-90, 193-200, 205, 208, 214-15, 217, 223, 226, 228-29, 235, 241, 244, 249, 436, 438, 440, 442, 462, 469, 484, 499, 512, 547. See also Infantry Divisions, 41st.
  164th: 58-59, 61, 63-66, 68-69, 156, 450, 471, 476, 484, 486, 488, 490-91, 493, 497, 501, 506-07, 510, 513, 515, 517, 519, 520, 522-23, 525, 527, 529-34, 542, 548. See also Infantry Divisions, Americal.
  165th: 147-49, 212-21, 223-27, 508, 519, 525. See also Infantry Divisions, 27th.
  167th: 274, 511, 535, 537-38, 541, 548. See also Infantry Divisions, 31st.
  169th: 93, 115-21, 123-24, 126-28, 132, 134-35, 234-35, 239-40, 242, 250, 371-75, 377-79, 381-84, 405, 434, 449, 471, 530. See also Infantry Divisions, 43d.
  172d: 61, 94, 115-19, 122-24, 128-36, 250, 371-75, 380, 382-85, 438, 440-42, 445-46, 448, 463, 467, 533. See also Infantry Divisions, 43d
  182d: 29, 63, 66, 68-69, 74, 83, 85-89, 159, 179-80, 388, 403 406 417, 421, 455 457 460-62, 464, 467 469 474, 482 486, 490, 493 512-13. See also Infantry Divisions, Americal.
  184th: 127, 167-70, 307-10, 312, 336, 339-41, 344-45, 347, 352, 374, 378, 469, 471, 478, 480, 482, 484, 486, 510, 527, 529 534-35, 540-44, 547. See also Infantry Divisions, 7th.

Infantry Regiments—Continued
  185th: 371-73, 390, 396, 398-99, 401, 403, 411, 413, 443, 445-46, 449-50, 453, 461, 464-65, 467, 469, 471, 473, 484, 493, 501, 503, 508, 519, 522, 527, 529, 533-34, 536, 540. See also Infantry Divisions, 40th.
  186th: 188-89, 198-202, 200-05, 207-18, 221, 251, 405, 417, 420-21, 423, 425, 427-28, 430, 432, 442, 445, 452, 457, 484, 503, 512. See also Infantry Divisions, 41st.
  305th: 234-36, 238, 241, 243-45, 347, 349-50, 352, 354-56, 359-64, 456-57, 460, 46, 499, 501, 503-06, 508, 535-40, 543. See also Infantry Divisions, 7th.
  306th: 235-36, 243-45, 338, 348-50, 352, 354-59, 456-58, 460, 462, 499, 501, 504, 508, 532-33, 536-38, 540. See also Infantry Divisions, 77th.
  307th: 238, 241, 244-45, 347-50, 352, 354-58, 456, 458, 501, 503, 506, 508, 524, 527, 529-30, 532-34, 538-40. See also Infantry Divisions, 7th.
  321st: 278-279, 281-82, 286, 288-91, 293, 301-03, 305-06, 311-12, 365, 367. See also Infantry Divisions, 81st.
  322d: 278-79, 281-83, 285-86, 288-91, 293, 297, 302. See also Infantry Divisions, 81st.
  323d: 278, 283, 285, 287, 305, 311-12, 317. See also Infantry Divisions, 81st.
  366th: 318, 459
  368th: 549. See also Infantry-Divisions, 93d.
  370th: 481. See also Infantry Divisions, 92d.
  371st: 483, 518. See also Infantry Divisions, 92d.
  381st: 312-14, 388, 471-72, 486, 506 519, 522 524 538-40, 54447. See also Infantry Divisions, 96th.
  382d: 307-14, 317-23, 349, 471-72, 476, 478, 480, 482, 506, 512, 535-41, 546. See also Infantry Divisions, 96th.
  383d: 307-15, 472, 476, 478, 480, 482, 484, 486, 495, 512, 519, 524, 535-41, 545-46. See also Infantry Divisions, 96th.
  442d: 219, 221, 223-24, 227-34, 244, 252, 261, 303, 314-15, 339, 451, 471, 475, 477, 479, 488. See also Infantry Battalions (Separate), 100th.
  473d: 374, 412, 471, 479, 481, 488, 501, 525
  475th: 304, 327, 346, 348-49 351-53, 364, 366, 369, 391-92, 509. See also Merrill's Marauders; Provisional Unit, 5307th
Ingeldorf: 377

Ingelfelden: 483
Ingelfingen: 488
Ingendorf: 413
Inglange: 323-25, 327
Ingolstadt: 518-19
Ingulets River: 151
Inkangahtawng: 181-83, 186, 190
Inn River: 526, 528-29, 531
Innsbruck: 523-25, 527-31
Inonda: 67
Inowroclaw: 381
Inrath: 420
Insoemanai Island: 194
Insoemoar Island: 194-95
Insterburg: 309, 381-82
Inter-American Defense Board meeting: 30-31
INTERLUDE: 263. *See also* Morotai Island.
International Settlement (Shanghai): 4
Intramuros (Manila): 402, 405-07, 409-10, 412, 419
Intrepid: 499
Ionian islands: 137, 261, 292, 301
Ioribaiwa Ridge: 54-57
Ipel River: 353
Iphofen: 477
Ipil, Leyte: 347-48, 350
Ipil, Luzon: 546
Ipo: 450, 471, 490, 527, 530, 532-36, 539, 543
Ipo Dam: 479, 522, 537-38
Ipoh: 4-5, 7, 9
Ippenscheid: 443
Ippesheim: 441, 475
Ipsheim :494
Iran. *See also* Persian Gulf Command; Persian Gulf Service Command.
    AAF takes over Abadan base: 102
    construction projects: 24
    contract activities militarized: 29
    included in USAFIME: 41
    lend-lease agreements: 28
    MEF alerted for defense of: 38
    military aid to USSR through: 141. *See also* Union of Socialist Soviet Republics.
    military mission to: 8, 32, 74
    mission relieved of responsibility for India: 31
    part of PGSC: 52
    Shingler heads mission to: 31
    Tehran Conference: 150-51
    transfer to MEC: 12, 15
    treaty with U.K. and USSR: 20
    Wheeler heads mission to: 26
Iran-Iraq Service Command: 42, 49
Iraq
    Axis powers, declares war on: 85
    British forces become Tenth Army: 12
    dock construction: 31, 495
    Khorramshahr, U.S. takes over: 82
    and Middle East commands: 12, 15, 41, 52
    military mission to: 74
Iratag: 421, 427
Iriga: 495
Irisan River: 501, 503, 505, 507, 509, 513

Irmgarteichen: 462
Irnich: 426
Iron Gate (Gorge): 264, 291
Irrawaddy River and Valley: 28-31, 33-35, 97, 99, 194, 210, 230, 304, 318, 348-49, 359, 372, 374-75, 381-82, 401-04, 412, 06, 421, 442, 467, 505
Irrel: 414, 416
Irresheim: 415
Irrhausen: 408
Irsen Creek: 270
Irsch: 411, 413-14, 06-17
Irsen River: 410
Irving, Maj. Gen. Frederick A.: 412
Irwin, Lt. Gen. N. M. S. (Br.): 75, 111
Isa: 472
Isabella: 302
Isar River: 519, 521-28
Isely Field: 213
Isely, Comdr. Robert H. (USN): 213
Isenbruch: 378
Iserlohn: 496, 498
Isernia: 138, 140, 142-44
I-shan: 545-46
Ishikawa Isthmus: 471, 474, 476, 478
Ishimmi: 469, 536
Ishimmi Ridge: 538-39
Isigny: 204-06, 109
Ising: 540
Island Command, Ie Shima: 519
Islands Area (Br.): 53, 59
Isley Field. *See* Isely Field.
Iso: 508
Issel Canal: 452
Issel River: 450, 453, 456, 474, 486, 488
Isselburg: 453 456 458
Issum: 423, 425
Isurava: 49-50, 52
Italian Army units
    Armies
        First: 94
        Eighth: 75
        German-Italian Panzer: 88, 94
    Corps, Liberation: 198, 251, 254-55
    Division, Utili: 251
    Brigade, 28th
        Garibaldi: 421, 473
    Groups
        1st Motorized: 143, 152-54, 172, 227
        Cremona: 338, 402, 421, 423, 425, 516
        Folgore: 404, 413, 419, 495
        Friuli: 402, 435, 484
        Legnano: 443, 497, 505, 507, 509, 525
Italian Navy, surrender of: 133
Italy
    Allied air and naval actions in: 115-16, 119-21, 127-32, 134, 140-41, 143, 151, 153-54, 163-64, 166-67, 171-74, 177, 180, 192, 197
    Allied airborne operations in: 131-32, 134, 195-96
    Allied armored actions in: 132-33, 160, 165-66, 169, 173, 192-94
    Allied operations on mainland: 112, 129, 131-534

Italy—Continued
    as Allied shuttle base for bombing Germany: 139, 175, 201, 207, 219, 237, 244-45, 271
    Anzio Campaign: 164-96
    Apennines, operations in: 243-507, 523
    Brazil declares war on: 51
    CCS plans for invasion of: 120, 122, 127-29
    Chile breaks with: 86
    China declares war on: 4
    declares war on Germany: 140
    declares war on U.S.: 4
    effect of southern France operations on: 171, 176, 182, 222
    employment of artificial moonlight in: 276, 304
    fall of Mussolini: 122
    first daylight raid from Britain on: 61
    first attack by IX Bomber Command on: 72
    included in NATO: 91
    Iraq declares war on: 85
    meetings of Allied forces in: 525, 527, 530-31
    Naples-Foggia Campaign: 128-63
    North Apennines Campaign: 267, 473
    plans for invasion of: 84, 87, 109-20, 113, 115, 120-22, 124, 126-30
    Valley Campaign: 475-534
    Rome-Arno Campaign: 164-267
    Rome declared open city: 127
    Sicily Campaign: 110-28
    surrender negotiations: 120, 124, 128, 131-32, 137-38
    surrender of German forces in: 523, 528
    Vietinghoff replaces Kesselring: 450
    winter lull: 370-91
Item Pocket: 508, 510, 512, 515, 517, 519-20
Itni River: 163, 173
Itoman: 544-45
Itomi: 486, 495, 504
Itri: 193-95
Ittelkyll: 417
Ivan (Mellu) Island: 167
Iveldingen: 376, 378
Iversheim: 427
Iwa: 543
Iwahig River: 417
Iwo Jima Campaign: 211, 224, 297, 299, 303, 323, 337, 348, 363-456, 474
    air and naval actions in: 211, 224, 268, 294, 323, 348, 360, 363, 368, 370, 383, 404-08, 411-12, 415, 428, 432, 437-38, 440
    airfields seized: 407-09, 411-18, 420-21, 423, 428, 437, 441, 456
    armor support in: 407-08, 421, 437, 449
    casualty summary: 456
    departure of naval elements: 430, 432-33, 440
    first B-29 lands: 425
    garrison force assumes control: 430, 446, 455-56

[INDEX]

Iwo Jima Campaign—Continued
  supported by raids on Japan, 370, 405–06, 413
  underwater demolition teams: 405

Jackerath: 415
Jacob (Ennuebing) Island: 167
Jacob Pass: 167
Jaegerhaus: 300
Jaegersburger Wald: 455
Jagst River: 466, 471, 473, 475, 477, 479, 481
Jagstberg: 485
Jagstfeld: 477, 481, 483, 488
Jagstzell: 509
Jakobwuellesheim: 414
Jallaucourt: 290, 292, 320
Jaluit Atoll: 21, 166, 174
Jalup: 190
Jamandilai Peninsula: 176
Jambu Bum: 180–82
Jane Hill (Okinawa): 540, 542
Jangkena: 188
Janpan: 181–82, 184
Janville: 251
Japan
  air offensive against: 146–47, 149–50, 165, 187, 189, 202, 204–05, 211, 226, 336, 349, 351, 355, 370, 405–06, 413, 433, 444–45, 458, 462, 497, 499, 547–50
    atomic bomb used in: 550
    B–29 assaults begin: 211, 226
    China as base for: 189, 202, 204–05, 211, 349, 351, 355
    first attack on Japan: 34
    Marianas as base for: 227, 336, 376, 458, 550
  Allied naval attacks in home areas: 462, 549–50
  Argentina breaks with: 165
  British declare war on: 3
  Chile breaks with: 86
  China declares war on: 4
  high tide of Asia invasion: 349
  preparations for invasion of: 188, 204, 209, 274, 398, 541, 549–50
  Iraq declares war on: 85
  JCS decision on defensive: 29
  Koiso succeeds Tojo: 233
  MacArthur recommends offensive against: 37
  occupation of: 546, 550–51
  Soviet forces against: 151, 398, 550
  strategic plans for defeat of: 112, 126, 129–30, 132, 135, 139, 147, 152, 204, 224, 230, 235–237, 294, 299, 398, 541
  surrender negotiations: 550–51
  Suzuki succeeds Koiso: 476
  Tojo succeeds Togo: 53, 233
  U.S. declares war on: 3
  USSR declares war on: 475, 550
Japanese Army units
  Armies
    8th: 67
    11th: 105, 152, 259, 339, 344
    14th: 7, 26

Japanese Army units—Continued
  Armies—Continued
    15th: 38
    16th: 26
    17th: 50, 59, 63, 67, 91
    18th: 67, 223, 256
    23d: 266
    25th: 3–4
    28th: 533
    32d: 547–48
    35th: 356
    Burma Area: 532–33
    French Indochina Garrison: 349
    Southern: 160–61
  Divisions
    15th: 180
    18th: 38, 180
    31st: 180
    33d: 38
    55th: 38
    56th: 38
Japanese Navy
  Carrier Striking Forces leaves for Midway: 39
  Combined Fleet: 36
  Fourth Fleet: 17, 28
  Hawaii losses: 3
  Special Naval Landing Force: 8
Japanese-American troops. See Infantry Battalions (Separate), 100th; Infantry Regiments, 442d.
Japtan Island: 174
Jarman, Maj. Gen. Sanderford: 218
Jarmin Pass: 109–11
Jarny: 285
Jaro, Leyte: 314–16, 328
Jaro, Panay: 445–46
Jaroslaw: 238
Jarvis: 48
Jaszbereny: 326
Jaufeta Bay: 188
Jaure: 56–58, 60–62
Java
  ABDA conference at Lembang: 13
  Allied attacks on: 193,
  Allied naval losses :26–27
  fall of: 18, 21, 24–28
  Wavell leaves for India: 26
Java (Dutch): 26
Java Sea, Battle of: 26
Javron: 248
Jeandelincourt: 298
Jeanménil: 314
Jebsheim: 384–87
Jefna: 95–96, 106–07
Jelgava: 239
Jemaluang: 15, 17
Jemelle: 265
Jena: 487, 489–90, 492, 494, 522
Jenneville: 365
Jerantut: 12
Jesselton: 13
Jessnitz: 500, 501, 506
Jestrow: 388
Jet aircraft, introduction of: 438
Jevigne: 367
Jewish Brigade: 430, 453, 484, 495
Jitra: 5
Joganville: 206
Jogjakarta: 26

Johnson, Maj. Gen. Davenport: 133
Johore, fall of: 8, 12–15, 17–18
Johore Bahru: 19
Joint Chiefs of Staff. *See also* Arnold, Gen. Henry H.; British Chiefs of Staff; Combined Chiefs of Star; King, Adm. Ernest J.; Marshall, Gen. George C.
  approve liquidation of SOPAC: 183
  approve plan for invasion of Japan: 541
  approve plans for Aleutians: 76, 100, 112, 139
  ARCADIA Conference: 8
  and Canton-Hong Kong: 508
  China as supply base for Pacific: 190
  directive on Gilberts: 121, 129
  directive on Hollandia: 178, 180
  directive on SWPA offensive: 44, 101
  on division of CBI: 224–27, 230, 235, 266, 310
  division of Twelfth Air Force: 139, 141
  Germany set as primary enemy: 29
  Ghormley proposed as Solomons commander: 43
  MacArthur as commander of SWPA offensive: 43
  Normandy air plan approval: 42
  plans for Japanese surrender: 550
  plans for Myitkyina: 185–86
  plans for occupation of Japan: 546
  plans for Pacific offensive: 179–80, 209
  plans for seizure of Paramushiro: 132
  plans for Philippines: 266, 274, 283, 294
  plans for Southern France: 171
  proposal for recovery of Burma: 73
  and reinforcement of China by air: 441
  ruling on SOPAC offensive: 45
  Stilwell report on air bases: 276
  strengthen air forces in SOPAC: 60
Joint Expeditionary Force (Marshalls): 159, 167
Joint Expeditionary Force (Palaus): 291
Joint Expeditionary Force (Volcanos): 299, 363–64, 385, 401, 404, 433, 467
Joint Mexican-U.S. Defense Commission: 26
Joint Military Council (Chungking): 10
Joint Staff Planners: 112
Joint War Plans Committee: 112–13, 135, 204
Joinville: 266–67
Jolo Island: 8–9, 484, 499, 501, 512, 549
Joncherey: 330
Jones, Brig. Gen. Albert M.: 8, 10–11, 28
Jorhat: 185–86, 439
Jouvieval: 369
Juchsen: 481
Jucken: 410
Juelich: 327, 329, 331–329, 338–39, 341–43, 346–47, 392, 410–11, 418, 485, 492
Juengersdorf: 327, 330, 339, 346

[611]

Juenkerath: 427
Juin, Gen. Alphonse (Fr.): 86, 88, 114, 150, 159
Julita: 310
June Hill (Okinawa): 542
Juneau: 66
Jungholz: 523, 525
Junkersdorf: 425
JUNO Beach: 203. *See also* Normandy Campaign, landing phase.
Juntersdorf: 420
Jupiter: 26
Jurong: 23
Jurques: 239
Juvelize: 284, 288
Juvigny: 244
Juvincourt: 191

K. B. Mission: 51-52
Kavacan: 35-36, 503, 511-13, 515
Kabaw Valley: 263, 295
Kabo: 364
Kachin guerrillas: 96, 187, 193
Kachin Trail: 168
Kadena airfield: 468-69
Kaduja Ga: 162, 170
Kaduma: 364
Kaerlich: 431
Kaga: 40
Kagman Peninsula: 216, 218, 222
Kaiapit: 135-36
Kaichen: 461
Kaifeng: 189
Kaimling: 512
Kairouan: 86, 90, 103-05
Kairouan Pass: 88-89
Kaisersesch: 429
Kaiserslautern: 443-44, 446-47, 455
Kaiserstuhl: 507
Kaitou: 200
Kakazu Ridge pocket: 482, 484, 486, 488, 491, 506, 508, 510, 512
Kako: 49
Kang Dagit: 346
Kalach: 47, 49, 69
Kaladan Valley: 8, 176, 351
Kalaklan River: 388
Kalamata: 301-02
Kalang: 21, 23
Kalapanzin River and Valley: 351, 353, 358
Kalasungay: 539-40
Kalborn: 386, 394, 396-97
Kaldenhausen: 422, 424
Kalemyo: 263, 325, 327, 365
Kalenborn: 436-38, 440
Kalewa: 35, 71, 146, 244, 343-44, 356
Kalinin: 6, 81
Kalikodobu: 58
Kalinkovichi: 162
Kalisz: 382, 384
Kalkar: 427
Kall: 427
Kall River: 317, 319-20, 370-71
Kalmesweiler: 443
Kalmyk sector: 81
Kalrath: 414
Kalscheuren: 427
Kaltenbrunn: 508
Kaltenhouse: 349, 383

Kaltensundheim: 467, 479
Kalterherberg: 271-73
Kalthof: 496
Kaluga: 10, 14, 20, 26-27
Kama Rock: 415, 438
Kamaing: 71, 163, 166, 168, 177-78, 180-83, 185, 187, 190, 195, 197, 200, 207, 210-11, 297, 304
Kamberg: 459, 461
Kamen: 482, 485
Kamenets-Podolsk: 183
Kamensk: 45, 86
Kamikaze attacks
 Okinawa: 456, 458, 468-69, 478, 480, 488, 491, 499, 525, 532, 542
 Philippines: 347, 351, 366-67
Kamilianlul Mountain: 289
Kamimbo Bay: 90-91
Kamiri: 223-24, 232, 267
Kamiri River: 233-24, 255
Kampar: 8-11
Kamti: 189-90
Kananga: 339, 355, 358
Kanawha: 103
Kanchow: 396
Kandel: 451
Kandy: 187, 469
Kanga Force (Aus.): 38-39, 43, 539 83, 85, 89-91, 98, 106
Kangaw: 381, 384, 387
Kangoku Rock: 415, 438
Kaniku: 506
Kanmonhag: 311
Kano: 76, 81-83
Kantau: 156
Kantemirovka: 76
Kanth: 401
Kantha: 378
Kantome: 188
Kanzem: 408
Kanyutkwin: 28
Kaosha: 536
Kapa Kapa: 56-57, 60
Kapern: 506
Kapintalan: 437, 443, 447, 463, 469, 477, 479, 482, 488, 501, 505, 509
Kapintalan Ridge: 509, 511, 517, 520, 522, 536
Kappel: 442
Kappelen: 420
Kapuva: 461
Karaberra Pass: 227
Karachev: 128
Karachi SOS bases: 31, 39, 53, 56, 123, 492, 537
Karachoum :105
Karadera: 542
Karai-ai: 175
Karbach: 440
Karben: 461
Karelian Isthmus: 206, 213, 215
Karl: 434
Karlsbad (Karlovy Vary): 530, 532-33
Karlshausen: 410-11
Karlsruhe: 467, 471, 473, 475, 477, 486
Karmes: 434
Karsdorf: 469
Kasagi Ridge: 536
Kasan Ga: 178
Kasberg: 526
Kasel: 434

Kassel: 463, 465, 467-68, 470, 472, 474-75, 477
Kasserine Pass: 92-95, 98
Kastel: 459
Kasternoe: 89
Kastl: 511
Katchin Peninsula: 471, 476
Katernburg: 478
Katha: 35, 304, 349, 352
Katowice: 386
Kattenes: 438
Katzem: 412
Katzenelnbogen: 459
Katzenfurt: 456
Kaub: 454
Kaufbeuren: 525
Kaunas (Kovno): 239-40
Kaundorf: 362, 366
Kautenbach: 382
Kavieng: 16-17, 129, 155-56, 159-60, 162, 172, 174-75, 179, 180, 182
Kawkareik: 16-17
Kawlin: 357
Kayangel Island: 339, 342
Kayserberg: 347
Kazatin: 157
Kebili: 101-02
Keblingen: 406
Kecskemet: 316
Kedah River: 5
Keeken: 398
Keeling Islands: 329
Kef el Goraa: 106
Kef en Nsour: 106-08
Kef Sahan: 107
Kehl: 335, 496
Kehmen: 359, 361, 380
Kehrig: 429
Kei (Kai) Island: 47
Keintzheim: 354
Keise Islands: 456, 465
Kelanoa: 160
Kelantan: 3-6
Kelberg: 429, 432
Kelbra: 489
Kelheim: 514, 516, 519
Kell: 439
Kellen: 401
Kellermann works: 273
Kelley Hill: 119
Kelley, 1st Lt. John R.: 119
Kellmunz: 516
Kelly, Capt. Colin P., Jr.: 4
Kelsen: 407
Kelsterbach: 455
Kelz: 415
Kema: 14
Kembs: 349
Kembs Dam: 515
Kembu Plateau: 517, 519, 527, 529-30, 533
Kempen: 423, 435
Kempten: 520, 523, 525
Kendari: 17-18, 30
Kendenich: 427, 429
Kengtung: 34, 37, 39
Kenn: 428
Kennedy Peak: 318
Kenney, Lt. Gen. George C.: 45, 47,48, 53, 186, 315
Kennon Road (Luzon): 433, 482, 527

[INDEX]

Kenten: 08
Keosha: 509
Keppeln: 413
Kerama Retto: 456-58, 460, 462 464-65, 469
Kerbach: 404
Kerch: 10, 32, 37-38, 186
Kerch Peninsula: 143, 186
Kerch Strait: 53
Kerkrade: 294, 296-98, 302
Kerling: 321-24, 326
Kerpen: 415-16
Kerpich: 340
Kerschenbach: 424
Kervenheim: 415, 418
Kesbern: 496
Kescheid: 452
Kesfeld: 269, 272, 405
Kessel: 402
Kesselring, Field Marshal Albert: 91, 97, 450
Kesten: 436, 443
Kesternich: 351-53, 387-89, 392-93
Kestert: 454
Ketting: 431
Kettwig: 487, 489
Keyenberg: 415
Keyes, Maj. Gen. Geoffrey: 119, 147
Kharkov: 26-27, 37-41, 90-98, 125-31
Kherson: 144, 180
Khorol: 136
Khorramshahr: 82
Kia: 123
Kiangan: 548-50
Kibawe: 515, 520, 527, 530-31, 533
Kickenbach: 485
Kidney Ridge (Egypt): 61-62
Kiel: 113, 154, 482
Kiel Canal: 529
Kielce: 374-75, 377
Kierspe: 487
Kieta: 17
Kiev sector: 133, 135-36, 138, 144-47, 156, 159-60, 162, 172
Kilay, Henry: 325
Kilay Ridge: 325-27, 330-40, 342-44
Kiling: 314
Killerton Trail. See Cape Killerton.
Killstett: 368-69
Kilu: 181
Kimmel, Adm. Husband E.: 6
Kimura, Gen. (Jap.): 511, 515
Kin: 476
Kinding: 516
Kindwiller: 383
King, Maj. Gen. Edward P., Jr.: 29, 32
King, Adm. Ernest J.
 appointed CNO: 28
 CINC, U.S. Fleet: 7, 28
 and command in Pacific: 43
 urges SLEDGEHAMMER implementation: 46
 views on Pacific offensive: 43, 224
King Hill (Okinawa): 537, 539
Kingisepp: 168
King's Wharf (Butaritari): 148
Kinhwa: 39
Kinkaid, Vice Adm. Thomas C.: 61, 67, 81, 96, 102, 105, 120, 127, 176, 339 370

Kinugasa: 58
Kinzweiler: 330
Kippenhof: 379
Kirberg: 459
Kirch: 414
Kirchberg: 334, 338, 395, 442-43
Kirchboitzen: 495
Kirchdorf: 515, 533
Kircheib: 452
Kirchen: 464
Kirchenlamitz: 502
Kirchhain: 460
Kirchhausen: 471
Kirchheim: 507, 509
Kirchhellen: 456, 458
Kirchhoven: 383
Kirchline: 478
Kirchsiebnach: 519
Kirchweiler: 429
Kirf: 407
Kirishima: 67
Kiriwina Island: 114-15, 120
Kirkenes: 311
Kirn: 443
Kirnssulzbach: 443
Kirov: 14
Kirovo: 153
Kirovograd: 161, 165
Kirrberg: 335
Kirsch: 434
Kirschhof: 446
Kirschnaumen: 327
Kirspenich: 427
Kirtorf: 460
Kirzscher: 496
Kishinev: 252, 255
Kiska Island: 40-41, 48, 51, 54, 55, 75, 96, 112-13, 116, 120-29
Kitano Point: 441
Kithira Island: 275, 292
Kittensee: 512
Kittyhawk: 388
Kitzingen: 465, 475, 477
Kiyamu: 547
Klais: 525
Klang: 328
Klatovy: 532
Klein Auheim: 453
Klein Buellesheim: 426
Klein Krostitz: 506
Klein Kuehnau: 506, 508
Klein Kyll River: 431, 434
Klein Langheim: 485
Klein Maischeid: 454
Klein Muehl River: 526, 528
Klein Weil: 525
Klein Werther: 485
Klein Winternheim: 445
Kleinblittersdorf: 406
Kleinenberg: 472
Kleinenbroich: 418
Kleinfahner: 483
Kleinhau: 322, 330, 339, 340-43
Kleinheringen: 487
Kleinhoscheid: 380
Klienlangenfeld: 417
Kleinseelheim: 460
Kleinwelschendorf: 496
Klepzig: 498
Kletskaya: 50-51, 68
Klettstedt: 479

Klin: 6
Klingenmuenster: 448
Klopper, Maj. Gen. (Br.): 41-42
Klostermansfeld: 512
Kluang: 17-18
Klueppelberg: 489
Kluetz: 529
Kluge, Field Marshal Guenther von
 CG of Army Group B: 232
 becomes CinC West: 223
 succeeded by Model: 250
 suicide: 251
Knaphoscheid: 380, 401
Knapsack: 425
Knerr, Brig. Gen. Hugh J.: 160
Knightsbridge: 40-41
Knocks: 315
Knottengrund: 498
Knowles, Capt. H. B. (USN): 111
Knox, Frank: 189
Kobbenrode: 483
Kobe: 34, 445
Kobern: 441
Koblentz: 265, 267, 431-32, 434, 437-42, 444, 449, 456, 504, 512, 516
Kobscheid: 410
Kochbauer: 524
Kocher River: 481, 483, 485, 488, 490, 492, 503, 505
Koch: 517, 533-34
Kochi Ridge: 517, 519-20, 522, 524-25, 527, 529-30, 534-35
Koecking Forest: 325-26
Koecking Ridge: 323-25
Koefering: 522
Koeltz, Gen. Louis-Marie (Fr.): 86
Koengen: 513
Koenig, Gen. Pierre Joseph (Fr.): 258
Koenigsbach: 477
Koenigsberg: 241, 382, 384-87, 406, 439, 461, 481, 483
Koenigsbourg Chateau: 339
Koenigsdorf: 422, 424
Koenigshofen: 466, 469, 473, 475, 477
Koenigshoven: 415
Koenigsmacker: 320-22, 378
Koenigstaedten: 453
Koenigstein: 461
Koepang: 24
Koermend: 465
Koerner: 472
Koernitz: 496
Koerrenzig: 410
Koesen: 487
Koeslin: 425, 428
Koeszeg: 461, 463
Koethen: 496, 498, 500, 504
Koetschette: 360
Koevering: 286-87
Kofferen: 411
Kogenheim: 343
Kohima: 183-87, 202, 206, 216, 356
Koiso, Gen. Kuniaki: 233, 476
Kokengolo Hill: 125
Kokoda: 43-47, 49, 58, 63-64
Kokoda Trail: 43, 46, 54, 56-60, 63, 67
Kokoggon: 360
Kokolope Bay: 128, 130, 134
Kokomtambu Island: 49
Kokuba River and Estuary: 540, 542-43

Kokumbona: 50, 52, 54, 56, 58-59, 62-66, 68, 82-83, 85, 87-88
Kolberg: 425, 440, 443
Koli Point: 56, 62-65, 71-72, 86
Kollesleuken: 407
Kollig: 438, 440
Kolombangara: 97, 110, 115-18, 121, 125-26, 129, 132, 134, 138-39
Kolombangara (Second Kula Gulf) naval battle: 118
Komandorski Islands naval battle: 100
Kommern: 426
Komiatum: 46
Komiatum Ridge: 106, 129
Kommerscheidt: 317-20, 342, 394-95, 397
Kommlingen: 421
Kongauru Island: 290-91
Konigsee: 487
Konigsfeld: 432
Konigswinter: 438, 440, 442
Koningsbosch: 378
Konombi Creek: 83, 85
Konotop: 130, 132-33
Konstadt: 381
Konz Karthaus: 421, 434
Konzen: 355 387
Kopp: 424
Kopscheid: 393-94
Kordel: 419, 421
Korea: 551
Korim Bay: 241, 244, 249
Kornelimuenster: 270
Koromokina Lagoon: 145
Koromokina River: 145
Koronal Creek: 207, 229, 233-34
Kornasoren: 223-24, 230, 236, 262
Korosten: 147, 149-51, 157
Korostyshev: 157
Korosun: 169
Korperich: 408
Korrig: 407
Kortenaer: 26
Koruniat Island: 184
Kos Island: 134, 138-39
Kosice (Kassa): 379
Koslar: 332-33, 336-39
Kossol Roads: 351
Kostheim: 459
Kota Bharu: 3-4
Kotabu Island: 147
Kotelnikov: 48, 74, 79
Kottenich: 327
Kotzenaurach: 496
Kowel: 225, 232-34
Kowloon: 4-5
Koxhausen: 411
Koza: 469
Kra Isthmus: 3, 316, 329, 531
Kraim Lerhmed: 107
Kramatorsk: 91, 93, 96
Kranburg: 396
Kranichfeld: 467, 487, 490
Kranji: 23
Krasnoarmeisk: 92
Krasnodar: 49, 91-92
Krasnograd: 94, 136
Krasnogvardeisk: 165
Kratzenburg: 439
Kraufbeuren: 520
Krauthausen: 410-11

Krautscheid: 410
Kray: 482
Krefeld: 273, 353, 420, 422, 471
Krefeld Oppum: 420, 422
Kremenchug: 137-38, 141, 153
Kremenets: 182
Kremnica: 471
Krettnich: 442
Kretzschau: 489
Kreuzau: 397, 412
Kreuzberg: 429, 489, 515, 517
Kreuzenstein: 472
Kreuzrath: 293
Kreuzweiler: 407
Krewinkel: 390, 393
Krian River: 6-7
Kriegsfeld: 455
Krimm: 427
Krinkelt: 387
Krivoi Rog: 141-42, 153, 171, 175
Krofdorf-Gleiberg: 462
Kroftel: 461
Kroh: 5
Kronach: 487, 490, 492
Krondf: 526, 528
Kronenburgerheutte: 424
Kropotkin: 48, 89
Krudenberg: 454
Krueger, Gen. Walter: 93, 114, 151 155,157, 160-61, 177, 190, 195, 199, 202, 207, 209-10, 212-14, 227, 229, 253, 256, 260, 264, 308, 314-15, 319, 326, 337, 344, 370, 373, 377, 379, 384, 387, 417, 428, 450, 479
Krulak, Lt. Col. Victor H. (USMC) 142
Krunkel: 452
Kruspis: 465
Krutweiler: 410
Krymskaya: 51
Ksar Rhilane: 94, 97
Ksar Tyr: 107
Kuala Kangsar: 6
Kuala Krai: 7
Kuala Lumpur: 7, 13
Kuala Pilah: 13
Kuala Selangor: 11
Kuantan airfield: 3-4, 7-11
Kuantan River: 10
Kuba: 471, 474
Kuba Island: 458
Kuban Peninsula: 135, 137
Kuban River: 48-50, 86, 92, 96, 120, 137
Kuching airdrome: 8-10, 13
Kuckum: 415
Kudaung Island: 363
Kueckhoven: 414
Kuehnhausen: 485
Kuestelberg: 468, 470, 472
Kuestrin: 394, 435-36, 505
Kufra: 55
Kufstein: 531
Kuhazu: 522, 525
Kuhlendorf: 372
Kukum: 49, 52, 56-58, 63, 82, 89
Kula Gulf naval battles: 116, 118
Kulmbach: 492
Kultzschau: 515
Kuma Island: 148

Kumanovo: 324
Kume: 450
Kume Island: 548-49
Kumnyen Ford: 179
Kumon Range: 189, 195
Kumusi River: 46-47, 57, 60, 62, 65-67, 71-72, 90, 92, 96
Kunchaung: 293
Kung Lung-po: 242
Kunishi Ridge: 544-47
Kunitz: 489
Kunming
defense of: 7, 155-56, 291, 319, 329, 333, 341, 344, 348, 350, 354, 357, 365, 369, 379, 384, 386, 387, 392, 488, 536, 544
planning conferences: 356, 362
transfer of AVG to: 36
Kunzelsau: 485, 488, 492
Kunzvart: 532
Kupferzell: 492
Kupyansk: 90
Kure: 445
Kuribayashi, Lt. Gen. Tadamichi: 442, 452
Kurile Islands, raids on: 117, 133
Kurisch Sound: 380
Kursk: 16, 43, 89-92, 94, 116-18, 120, 130
Kurtscheid: 447, 449
Kusel: 444
Kushchevskaya: 90
Kuter, Maj. Gen. Laurence S.: 87
Kutoku: 469
Ku-tung: 213
Kwajalein Atoll: 21, 160, 164, 166-73
Kwangsi Command (Chinese): 544
Kwangsi Province: 339, 495, 539
Kweichow Province: 339, 344, 349
Kweilin: 114, 209, 246, 259, 266, 272, 274, 282, 313, 322, 329, 362, 403, 495, 517, 545, 550
Kweilin Training Center: 145, 154
Kweiyang: 322, 329, 343-44, 350, 539
Kyaukme: 349 441, 446, 463
Kyaukmyaung: 375
Kyaukpadaung: 33-35, 490
Kyaukpyu: 380, 384, 469
Kyaukse: 463
Kyauktaw: 86, 176-77, 351
Kyll River: 414, 417, 419, 421-22, 424, 426-29, 431
Kyllburg: 428
Kyllburgweiler: 426
Kynsperk: 533
Kyungon: 30
Kyushu Island
air raids on: 444-45, 462, 497, 499
plans for seizure of: 204, 275

La Bandita: 150-51, 153-54
La Barquette: 203-04
La Bastia Hill: 193
La Bernardrie: 226
La Bourgonce: 316
La Bresse: 300
La Butte: 236
La Calvaire: 228-29
La Cambe: 204
La Capelle: 260

[INDEX]

La Chapelle-en-Juger: 236
La Chapelle Moche: 248
La Conviniere: 237
La Cosa Creek: 132, 134
La Côte Pelée: 269
La Coucourde: 256-57
La Croce Hill: 143
La Crocetta: 300
La Croix: 249
La Croix-aux-Mines: 336
La Falise: 368
La Ferté-Macé: 248
La Fière: 204, 206
La Folie: 206
La Fortuna: 298
La Fotelaie: 206
La Fouquerie: 239
La Françaisere: 248
La Glacerie: 216-17
La Gleize: 357-60
La Guarde Freinet: 250
La Haye-du-Puits: 223-28
La Hencha: 104
La Hogue: 232, 240
La Houcharderie: 232
La Houssière: 309, 3 11, 322
La Lima: 291
La Londe: 250
La Luzerne: 228-29, 231
La Macta: 65
La Madeleine: 231
La Mare à Canards: 216-17
La Martina: 292
La Maxe: 326
La Méauffe: 228
La Môle: 249
La Napoule: 250, 252-53
La Neuville: 373
La Paz, Luzon: 380-81
La Paz, Samar: 310
La Petite Pierre: 332-33
La Rava Creek: 154
La Rivière: 203
La Roche: 286
La Rochelle: 328, 525, 527, 531
La Salle: 317-18
La Senia: 65
La Serra: 412-13
La Spezia: 295, 471, 505
La Tombs Ridge: 276
La Rorraccia: 279
La Torre: 289
La Trinité: 263
La Turbia: 261
La Vallette: 254
La Vezouse River: 284-85
La Vie River: 252
La Villa: 296-97, 299
La Voivre: 332
Laasan: 489
Laasphe: 464
Lababia Ridge: 114, 118
Labangan River: 389
Labico: 201
Labir Hill: 314
Labiranan Head: 308-09, 314
Labiranan River: 307-08
Labis: 15, 17
Laborde, Adm. Jean de (Fr.): 70
Labow: 527
Labrador, Luzon: 371-72

Labrador Peninsula: 32
Labuan Island: 12, 545-46
Lac de Bizerte: 109
Lackenhausen: 517
Lae: 17-18, 82-83, 96, 125, 128-36, 138, 154, 186
  Allied assault on: 43-46
  Allied evacuation of: 18
  enemy air attacks: 17
  enemy landing: 27-28
  U.S. attack on shipping: 28
Laffeol: 380
Laffey: 66
Lagang Ga: 177-78
Lage: 470, 472
Lagnieu: 259
Lagone: 153-54
Laguna de Bay: 434, 437, 450, 475-77
Lahn River: 454, 456-58, 460, 464
Lahr: 408, 458, 496, 503
Lahug airfield: 460
Laiana: 117-19, 121
Laiatico: 226, 228-29
Lai-feng Mountain: 237-38
Laigle: 253
Laize River: 246, 248
Lake Albano: 201
Lake Aztec: 278
Lake Balaton: 340, 345-48, 358, 449, 463, 467, 471
Lake Bizerte: 109
Lake Buluan: 549-50
Lake Chiusi: 217
Lake Comacchio and its islands: 421, 467, 473 ,475
Lake Como: 518, 521
Lake Constance: 509, 511, 518, 523
Lake Garda: 516, 518, 521, 525
Lake Ilmen: 175
Lake Kathleen: 150
Lake Ladoga: 3, 86, 122, 206
Lake Lanao: 35-36
Lake Onega: 215
Lake Peipus: 172, 232, 247
Lake Pinalay: 532
Lake Salome: 282-83, 285-86, 289-91
Lake Sentani: 188-89
Lake Susupe: 212-13
Lake Taal: 430, 451
Lake Trasimeno: 214-15, 220
Lake Velencei: 3.48, 360
Lama: 394
Lama di Sotto Ridge: 394
Lama Hills: 315
Lambach: 531
Lambertsberg: 419
Lambeti Plantation: 115, 118
Lameng: 202
Lammersdorf: 271-73, 275, 278, 280-81, 288, 290, 317, 339-40
Lamon Bay: 480, 482, 486, 488
Lamone River: 335-38, 343-45 349-50, 357, 364
Lamopog: 506
Lamorménil: 367
Lampaden: 4 ,119
Lampedusa Island: 113-14
Lampertheim: 455
Lampione Island: 114
Lampoldhausen: 479
Lamut River: 545

Lanaye: 268
Lanciano: 147, 151
Land Forces, Adriatic (Br.): 286, 301
Land Forces, Greece (Br.): 262, 331
Landau: 447-48, 522, 524 526
Landau Landkreis: 516
Landeck: 531-32
Landgraben Canal: 368
Landing craft allocations
  Mediterranean: 145, 155, 160, 172
  Normandy: 164, 172
  SEAC: 160
Landing Force, VAC (USMC): 303, 360, 366, 369, 406
Landrecies: 261
Landremont: 272
Landres: 265
Landroff: 325-26
Landrum, Maj. Gen. Eugene M.: 111
Landsberg: 518-21, 523
Landsberg Meseritz: 388
Landscheid: 380, 382, 385, 431
Landshut: 522-24, 526
Laneuveville-en-Saulnois: 322
Langanan: 426
Langel: 425
Langemak Bay: 136
Langen: 452-53, 455
Langenbach: 496
Langenbeutingen: 492
Langenbochum: 464
Langendiebach: 461
Langendorf: 420, 424
Langener: 483
Langenfeld: 497
Langenhain: 470
Langenpreising: 524
Langensalza: 470, 472, 475, 477, 479, 481, 483
Langenstein: 502
Langenwiesen: 487
Langerringen: 519
Langerwehe: 327, 330-32, 335-36 339, 346
Langfroich: 379
Langley: 26
Langlir: 371-73
Langlir River: 372
Langres: 268-69, 271
Lansival: 367
Lantap: 545
Lantawan: 484, 506-08, 510, 519
Lantershofen: 427
Lanuvio: 197-201
Lanzerath: 387
Laoag airfield: 4-5
Laohokon: 405, 447, 453
Laokai: 193
Laon: 191, 258-60
Lapiay Point: 18
Larche Pass: 254
Lariano: 199
Larkin, Brig. Gen. Thomas B.: 22
Larminat, Lt. Gen. Edgar de (Fr.): 207, 328
Laroche: 368-73, 380
Laruma River: 145
Laruni: 60
Lascheid: 408, 419
Lasel: 422, 424

Lashio: 33-35 99, 155, 293, 387, 430, 463
Lastau: 496
Laterina: 233
Lathen: 480
Latin America. *See* American republics.
Latrop: 474
Lattre de Tassigny, Gen. Jean de (Fr.) 187, 250, 272, 285, 305, 310, 313, 317, 325, 343, 351
Latvia, operations in: 229, 236, 239-40, 253, 275, 280, 302, 383, 534
Laubach: 439, 477, 479
Lauchheim: 502, 511
Lauchroeden: 472
Laudenbach: 485, 488
Laudesfeld: 388
Lauenburg: 504, 514, 520, 522, 524
Lauenfoerde: 481
Laufenburg Castle: 329-31
Lauffen: 475, 477
Lauingen: 511, 514, 516, 518
Laulau: :216-18
Laumesfeld: 327
Launstroff: 329
Lauperath: 410
Laupheim: 516
Laurensberg: 306
Lauscha: 490
Lausdorn: 383-84
Lauter River: 352, 355, 439, 443, 445
Lauterbach: 343, 345, 461, 463
Lauterbourg: 352, 439, 445 ,450
Lauterecken: 444
Lauterhofen: 507-08
L' Aution: 486, 490
Lauzenhausen: 441
Lavacherie: 372
Laval: 243, 304 369
Laval, Pierre: 33
Lavaux: 367
Lavezares: 407
Lavino Creek: 503
Lavoro: 89
Lay: 440
Layac junction: 12
Layton, Vice Adm. Sir Geoffrey (RN): 4
Lazu: 191
Le Bardo: 109
Le Batty: 366
Le Bény-Bocage: 239-40
Le Bingard: 237
Le Bonhomme: 340
Le Bourg-St. Léonard: 250
Le Bourget airfield: 257
Le Busq: 243
Le Camp: 252
Le Carrefour: 206
Le Carillon: 213, 231-32
Le Cateau: 261
Le Conquet Peninsula: 256-58, 267
Le Désert: 226, 228, 230
Le Grand Hameau: 203
Le Grand Pré: 356
Le Ham: 206-07
Le Hamel: 203
Le Havre: 260-62, 267-69, 276, 366
Le Hohwald: 338
Le Kef: 69, 95
Le Locheur: 242

Le Luc: 249
Le Mans: 243-45 247
Le Mesnil-Durand: 231, 236
Le Mesnil-Tôve: 244
Le Mesnil-Veneron: 226
Le Muy: 249-51
Le Neubourg: 254-55
Le Paire: 332
Le Pastinelle: 162
Le Plessis: 258
Le Port: 204
Le Propaia: 165-66
Le Puy: 253
Le Rocher: 228
Le Saunier: 262
Le Scalette: 274
Le Seudre River: 498
Le Teilleul: 246
Le Thiel: 214
Le Thillot: 285, 294
Le Tholy: 296, 300, 306, 326
Le Tourneur: 239
Le Tréport: 260
Le Valtin: 379.386
Le Verdon: 505
Leahy, Adm. William D.: 33, 49, 237
Lear, Lt. Gen. Ben: 384
Leary, Vice Adm. Herbert F. (Aus.): 22, 34
Lebach: 443
Lech River: 519-21, 523, 525, 527-28
Lechbruck: 521, 523
Lechenich: 420
LeClerc, Brig. Gen. Jacques-Philippe: 94, 97, 99, 105, 256
Ledo: 170, 177, 194
Ledo Road: 11, 14, 38, 61-62, 64, 93, 95-96, 99, 110, 118, 128, 155, 255, 349, 372, 375, 377, 379, 382, 386-87, 392. *See also* Stilwell Road.
Leedstown: 65
Leeheim: 449
Leende: 279
Leese, Gen. Sir Oliver (Br.)
  commands Allied land forces in Asia: 292, 324, 384
  commands Eighth Army: 156-292
  directive on Rangoon recovery: 455
Leeuwarden: 484, 495 497
Legaspi: 5, 8, 435, 437, 451-52, 467, 469, 471, 477, 479, 484, 486
Legaspi Attack Group (TG 78.4): 467
Legentilhomme, Gen. P. (Fr.): 83
Leghorn (Livorno): 136, 202, 223, 226, 228-33, 235, 253, 318
Legislative Building (Manila): 412, 416-17
Legnago: 518, 521
Lehmen: 437-38
Leidenborn: 405-06
Leiffarth: 342, 353
Leigh-Mallory, Air Chief Marshal Sir Trafford
  commands AEAF: 150
  commands Normandy air forces: 114, 116, 203
  commands SE Asia Air Command 326
Leimbach: 411
Leimen: 465
Leimersheim: 451, 469

Leimok Hill: 188
Leine River: 476, 478, 480-83, 486, 489
Leintrey: 313, 325
Leipheim :516, 518
Leipzig: 175, 458, 465, 491, 496, 498, 500, 502, 504, 509
Leisenwald: 463
Lellingen: 384
Lembach: 352, 526, 528
Lembang: 13
Lembeck: 458
Lemberg: 347-48, 365, 367
Lemery: 428, 452
Lemestroff: 326
Lemgo: 472
Lemnos Island: 292
Lemoncourt: 292
Lend-lease
  to China: 6, 9, 11, 123, 162, 235
  Iran-U.S. agreements: 28
  Tulsa Incident: 7, 9
  United Kingdom: 7, 9, 25
  USSR: 41, 56-57, 141, 499
Lendersdorf: 354
Lengenfeld: 500
Lengfeld: 517
Lenggries: 530
Lengsdorf: 430
Leningrad sector: 3, 11, 21, 84, 86, 162-66, 170, 206, 214
Lenkersheim: 494
Lenne River: 468, 470, 483, 487, 493, 496, 498
Lennep: 493, 495
Lenola: 195-96
Lentaigne, Maj. Gen. W. D. A. (Br.) 183, 230
Lentini: 119
Leonforte: 120-22
Leopold Canal: 269-70, 279, 284, 296-98, 306
Lepini Mountains: 198, 200-201
Lepuix: 333
Lermoos: 525
Leros Island: 134, 139, 146-47
Les Andalouses: 65
Les Andelys: 258
Les Champs-de-Losque: 229-31
Les Etangs: 330
Les Fieffes Dancel: 208
Les Forges: 203
Les Landes: 206
Les Loges: 239
Les Maures: 250
Les Mayon: 250
Les Moulins: 203
Les Rouges Eaux: 309, 312, 322
Les Tailles: 372
Lesbos Island: 292
Lesménils: 275
Lesneven: 243
Lessay: 230, 237
Lesse River: 359
Lessenich: 430
Leszno: 386
Letpadan: 437
Létricourt: 299, 316
Lettin: 494
Leubsdorf: 435 449
Leuna: 494 496
Leutkirch: 521, 523

[INDEX]

Leutzkendorf: 192
Levango Island: 123
Levant Island: 249
LEVER: 475. *See also* Lake Comacchio and its islands; Reno.
Leverkusen: 425, 495
Leversbach: 414
Levershausen: 483
Levita Island: 292
Lewe: 33
Lexington: 25, 28, 36-37, 136
Ley: 281
Leyr: 288
Leyte Campaign: 305-549
Leyte Island
   fall of: 34
   recovery of: 270, 274, 283, 301-03, 305, 365, 367, 374, 385, 388-89, 391, 400, 403, 406, 421, 431, 436, 450, 471, 493, 531, 535
Leyte Gulf: 305, 351, 366-67, 449
Leyte Gulf naval battle: 310-12
Leyte Peninsula: 362
Leyte River: 333-34 347
Leyte Valley: 307, 310-12, 317, 339
Leyviller: 334
Lézey: 280
Lgov: 96
Li, Marshal Chi-shen: 246
Lian: 389
Libbesdorf: 498
Libby airfield: 529
Liberi: 141
Liberia, U.S. forces in: 37
Liblar: 422, 425
Libog: 467
Libongao: 356-58
Libya. *See also* Egypt, operations in.
   Allied operations: 3-16, 18, 26, 28-29, 38, 67-70, 74-79, 82-89
   Allied thrust to Egyptian frontier: 5
   Axis drive on Egypt: 39-43
   Axis withdrawal toward Gazala Line: 4
   Cyrenaica offensive by Axis, 1942: 17-22
   directive to Alexander: 49
   diversion in favor of Malta convoy: 28-29
   first phase of Allied campaign ended: 16
   lull in operations: 22
   Tripoli as objective: 16
Licata: 117-19
Lich: 412
Lichkova: 96
Lichtel: 492
Lichtenau: 471
Lichtenberg: 372, 451, 480, 482, 494
Lichtenborn: 407-08
Licodia: 119
Lida: 227
Lidrezing: 324
Lieblos: 461
Lieg: 439
Liége: 263, 265-67, 361, 393
Liegnitz: 401-02
Lieler: 384
Lienhwa: 375
Liepvre: 339-40
Lierfeld: 417

Lierneux: 366-68
Lierscheid: 454
Liesel: 314-15
Liesenfeld: 439
Lieser: 443
Lieser River: 434
Liesse: 394
Liessem: 417
Ligneuville: 374
Liguria coast sector: 269, 471, 475, 494, 501, 505, 515-16, 520
Likhaya: 92
Liki Island: 194
Lille: 58, 261-62
Lille St. Hubert: 278
Lillers: 262
Lima Creek: 290-91
Limay: 406
Limbach: 452, 494, 516
Limbourg: 266
Limburg: 454, 456, 458, 461
Limerle: 380
Limon: 316, 320, 322-24, 327, 329-30 333-35, 341-52, 355-57
Linao: 351-53
Lincoln, Maj. Gen. Rush B.: 33
Lindau: 525
Linden: 496
Lindenberger Wald: 411
Lindenholzhausen: 459
Lindern: 340-42
Lingayen Gulf: 6-7, 367-70, 373, 376, 385
Lingen: 462, 468-69, 472, 474, 476, 480, 482
Ling-ling: 266
Linguaglossa: 128
Linkenheim: 467
Linne: 383
Linnepe: 487
Linnich: 340-41, 395, 409, 411-12
Linosa Island: 113
Lintfort: 423, 425
Linz: 431-32, 481, 529-33, 536
Linzenich: 422
Lipa: 451, 455, 457, 460-61, 471
Lipa Hill: 457, 471
Lipno: 382
Lippborn: 472
Lippe: 526
Lippe Canal: 452, 454, 472
Lippe River: 452, 454, 466, 468, 470, 472, 474, 478
Lipperscheid: 380
Lippoldshausen: 479
Lippstadt: 466, 470, 472, 478
Liri River and Valley: 149, 161, 171, 191, 193-99
Lisaine River: 329
Lisbon: 128, 131
Liscome Bay: 149
Lisdorf: 344-45
Lisichensk: 45, 91, 96
Lisieux: 249, 253
l'Isle-sur-Doubs: 272
Lissendorf: 427
Lissingen: 424, 426-27, 429, 431
Lithuania, operations in: 239-40, 250-51, 295, 300-302, 386
Litteau Ridge: 208
Little: 53

Little St. Bernard Pass: 266
Littoria: 120, 165, 196
Liuchow: 259, 266, 313, 322, 329, 362, 403, 495, 517, 545-46, 548-49
Liu-yang: 210
Liu-yang River: 207-08
Livarot: 252
Livergnano: 298-303, 305
Liversedge, Lt. Col. Harry B. (USMC) 116-18, 121, 124-26
Livron: 253, 257-58
Livry: 208
Lixières: 298
Lixing: 404-05
Ljubljana Gap: 217, 222
Lobberich: 420
Lobenstein: 494
Lobstadt: 494
Loch: 427
Lodz: 378
Laehndorf: 431
Loehnfeld: 456
Loerrach: 514
Loetzbeuren: 442
Loevenich: 412, 422, 424
Loewenstein: 494, 496, 498, 500
Logbiermé: 373-74
Logistic Support Group (Ryukyus): 449
Lohmar: 487
Lohn: 333-34
Lohne: 474
Lohnen: 451
Lohr: 471
Loi Island: 169-70
Loiano: 292, 294-96
Loi-kang Ridge: 377, 391-92
Loikaw: 33-34
Loilem: 34-35, 545
Loire River: 242, 250, 257, 274
Loisach: 525, 527
Loisach River: 525
Loisy: 269-70, 272
Loiwing: 30, 36, 368
Lokeren: 269
Lollar: 458
Lombrum Plantation: 179, 182
Lommel: 276, 278-79
Lommersum: 422, 424
Lommersweiler: 386-87
Lomopog: 503, 507
Lomre: 371, 373
Lomza: 271
Londinières: 259
London
   AFHQ activated: 55
   conference on SEAC plans: 241, 254
LONDON: 452. *See also* Wesel.
Lone Tree Hill (Luzon): 511, 515, 517, 522, 531
Lone Tree Hill (New Guinea): 197-98, 214-20, 221
Long Island (New Britain): 157
Long Island, German agents landed on: 41, 43
Long Range Penetration Groups: 146, 186, 200, 209, 214, 221, 223, 226, 237. *See also* Infantry Regiments, 475th; Merrill's Marauders; Wingate, Brig. Orde Charles; Units, independent, 5307th Provisional.
Longastrino: 488, 490

Longchamps: 373-74
Longegoutte: 294-95, 298
Longiano: 297-98, 300
Longkamp: 444
Longoskawayan Point: 17-20
Longsdorf: 377, 379-80
Longstop Hill (Tunisia): 77-78, 105-07
Longueville: 204-05
Longueville-lès-Cheminot: 278, 280, 282
Longuich: 434
Longvilly: 267, 375-76
Loniu Village: 183
Lonlay l'Abbaye: 248
Lonoy: 351, 353 355-57, 359
Lons: 262
Looc: 519
Look: 361
Lopdak: 315
Lorch: 457, 459, 505
Lorcher Wald: 455
Lorengau: 32, 164, 170, 176-77, 180-81
Lorengau River: 181
Lorenzana: 231
Lorenzo: 120
Lorey: 268-70
Lorich: 421
Lorient: 243-48, 258, 270, 365 458, 464
Loriol: 258
Lorry: 273, 275
Lorsch: 434
Lorscheid: 438-39
Los Alamos atomic test: 550
Los Banos: 410, 451, 453
Los Negros Island: 164, 186-87
Losenseifen Hill: 275
Losheim: 295, 387-88, 390, 393-95, 439
Lothra: 492
Loudeac: 242
Loudrefing: 333-34
Loudspeakers, used in New Guinea: 225
Louisiade Archipelago naval actions: 37
Lourmel: 65
Lousberg Heights: 302, 306
Louvain: 264, 356 430
Louviéres: 204
Louviers: 252-57
Louvigny: 232-33
Love Hill (Okinawa): 538, 540 542
Lovelady, Lt. Col. William B.: 271, 273, 282, 284, 327, 414, 42, 424, 452, 458, 462, 464, 474
Lowen: 395
Lower Rhine. *See* Neder Rijn.
Loyev: 141
Lozovaya: 19, 92, 96, 135
Lubang Islands: 416-17, 419, 428, 433
Lubao: 12
Lubine: 336
Lublin: 234-35
Lubni: 136
Lucas, Maj. Gen. John P.: 136, 162, 169
Lucban: 484
Lucca: 204, 234, 263-64, 304-05, 359, 361-62

Lucchio: 290
Lucena: 464
Luchem: 342-43, 346
Lucherberg: 343, 345
Luchtenberg: 415
Luciana: 232
Lucka: 492
Ludendorff: 426
Ludendorff Bridge: 429, 432-33, 441
Ludwigs Kanal: 514, 516, 521
Ludwigsberg: 471
Ludwigshafen: 447-48, 450-51
Ludwigslust: 527-28
Luebeck: 512, 526-27
Lueben: 401
Luechow: 508, 510
Luedenscheid: 489, 491
Lueneburg: 499, 501, 508, 510, 520
Luenern: 485
Luetgendortmund: 480, 482
Luetzkewitz: 494
Luetzow: 497
Luftwaffe: 3, 34, 365
Lugo: 484
Lugo Canal: 486
Lugos Mission: 180
Luichow Peninsula: 376
Luisiana: 9
Lullange: 380
Lumban: 475-76
Lumboy: 406-07, 413
Lunebach: 408, 417, 419
Lunéville: 272, 275, 277-78, 283-84, 305, 366, 442, 447
Lunga Point: 50-66, 72, 82, 88
Lunga Point naval battle: 71
Lunga River: 48-49, 59, 62-63
Lung-ling: 197-98, 200, 202, 205-07, 210-12, 218, 255, 166, 272, 314, 318, 322
Lunzenau: 496
Lupao: 391, 393-96, 398
Luppy: 322
Lure: 272, 275
Lutirano: 312
Lutong: 547
Lutrebois: 363-69, 371
Lutremange: 369, 371
Lutsk: 170
Luttange: 329
Lutterbach: 348
Lutz: 438
Lutzel: 476
Lutzen: 502
Lutzerath: 440
Lutzkampen: 394, 396
Luxembourg, operations in: 267, 297, 308, 343 354 357-59, 362 365-66, 380, 383, 385, 389. *See also* Western Europe.
Luxeuil: 272, 275
Luxheim: 417
Luzon. *See also* Luzon Force; Philippine Islands.
  capitulation: 37
  enemy air attacks: 3-5
  enemy casualties: 26
  enemy landings: 3-5, 7-8, 17
  FEAF withdrawal: 4, 6
  pursuit of U.S. forces: 9

Luzon—Continued
  recovery of: 211, 294, 283, 301, 302, 304-06, 340-41, 344, 352-550
  U.S. air attacks: 4-5, 21
Luzon Attack Force (TF 77): 366-67, 370, 373
Luzon Campaign: 353-540
Luzon Force: 28-29, 31, 32
Luzuriaga: 522
Luzzaro: 513
Lwow: 230, 235-37
Lykershausen: 452, 454
Lyon: 254, 257-62, 280, 337
Lyuban: 165-66

M. Abelle: 499
M. Acero: 140
M. Acidola: 425
M. Acuto: 271, 286
M. Adone: 499, 503
M. Albano: 234, 261, 264
M. Alcino: 306-08
M. Altuzzo: 269, 271-73, 276-77
M. Arcalone: 160
M. Arnato: 233
M. Arnigo: 499, 501, 503, 505
M. Arrestino: 196-97
M. Artemisio: 199-200
M. Bagnolo: 220
M. Bassana: 322
M. Bastia: 296
M. Bastione: 286-87, 290
M. Belmonte: 304-06, 309, 437
M. Battaglia: 289-94, 299, 301, 305
M. Belvedere: 36, 405-07, 433 477, 479, 483
M. Beni: 287
M. Bibele: 292, 295-96
M. Budriatto: 321
M. Burratini: 303
M. Calvana: 251, 261, 263, 265-67
M. Calvi: 269, 272, 277, 279
M. Calvo: 195-96
M. Camino: 144-46, 149-53
M. Camolato: 126
M. Campania: 405-06
M. Campese: 193-94
M. Canda: 284, 286-87, 290
M. Capadarso: 120
M. Cappello: 291, 299, 305-06
M. Caprara: 499
M. Carchio: 475
M. Carmucino: 230
M. Caruso: 140
M. Casalino: 299-300, 306, 309
M. Casciaio: 287
M. Cassino and its abbey: 173, 182, 187, 194
M. Castellari: 296-98
M. Castellaro: 309, 340
M. Castello: 299, 405, 408-09, 423
M. Castellone: 169, 176
M. Castelazzo: 309
M. Castelnuovo: 154
M. Castiglione Maggiore: 230
M. Catarelto: 291-94
M. Caula: 296-301, 305, 309
M. Cavallara: 292, 297
M. Cavallo: 198, 200, 308-10
M. Cavo: 201

[INDEX]

M. Ceco: 294-98, 301, 305-06, 309
M. Cedro: 160-61
M. Ceraso: 201
M. Cerere: 306, 351
M. Cerreta: 477
M. Ceschito: 192
M. Cesima: 144
M. Chiavino: 196-97
M. Chioda: 319
M. Chiunzi: 133
M. Cifalco: 165
M. Citerna: 269, 284
M. Colomobo: 309, 312
M. Coloreta: 283, 285
M. Conca: 194
M. Cornazzano: 309
M. Corno: 145
M. Coroncina: 271, 286-87
M. Cuccoli: 304-05, 307
M. dei Bracchi: 193
M. dei Pensieri: 191-92
M. dei Pini: 303
M. dei Torri: 201
M. del Galletto: 292-94
M. delta Birra: 321
M. delta Casselina: 410
M. dell'Acqua Saluta: 306, 348, 358
M. della Croce: 285, 425
M. del Lago: 194
M. della Spe: 426
M. della Torraccia: 407-10, 412-13, 423
M. della Vedetta: 423
M. della Vigna: 304-05
M. della Volpe: 359
M. dell'Erta: 301
M. delle Formiche: 298-304
M. delle Tombe: 299-301, 304
M. delle Vacche: 302-03
M. delle Valle: 306, 317
M. del Puntale: 288
M. del Verro: 348, 358
M. di Castelnuovo: 287-89, 291
M. di Mola: 194
M. Domini: 235
M. Faeto: 394
M. Faito 169, 171, 191
M. Fano: 304, 306
M. Farneto: 296-98
M. Ferra: 501
M. Feuci: 191
M. Fili: 235
M. Fiore: 201
M. Fortino: 329-30, 333
M. Fragolita: 475
M. Frassino: 269, 271, 274, 276-77, 279
M. Freddi: 288
M. Frena: 283
M. Gamberaldi: 286-90
M. Gatta: 288
M. Gazzaro: 2 83
M. Giovi: 251, 261, 263, 265-67
M. Giro: 309
M. Girofano: 192
M. Giuvigiana: 277
M. Gorgolesco: 405-07
M. Grande: 194-95, 304-07, 309-11, 370
M. Grande d'Aiano: 425, 434, 437
M. Gridolfo: 261
M. Grosso: 308
M. Guivigiana: 271

M. il Castello: 243
M. il Pratone: 260
M. Jugo: 165-66
M. l'Abate: 274, 276-77
M. la Chiaia: 160-61
M. la Civita: 193
M. la Difensa: 144-45, 149, 151-53
M. la Fine: 284-87
M. la Pieve: 302-03, 306
M. la Posta: 155
M. la Remetanea: 151-53
M. la Rocca: 151
M. Lenano: 196
M. Leucio: 195
M. Lignano: 224, 226, 231
M. Liguana: 277, 279
M. Lungo: 145, 152-55, 158
M. Maggiore: 144, 149, 151-54, 163-64, 166, 191, 205, 231, 267
M. Majo: 159-61, 192-93
M. Majulo: 140
M. Mantino: 497
M. Mario: 503, 505
M. Marrone: 151
M. Massico: 142-44
M. Mesola: 193
M. Mirabello: 312
M. Monna Casale: 157
M. Monsicardi: 196
M. Monsignano: 319
M. Monterumici: 296-305, 499, 501
M. Monticelli: 269, 271-72, 274, 276-75,279
M. Monzuno: 499
M. Morello: 251, 261, 263, 265-66
M. Morrone: 195
M. Mosco: 499
M. Moscoso: 273, 282, 501
M. Muscoli: 260
M. Natale: 164-65, 167
M. Oggioli: 285-90
M. Oliva: 277
M. Oro: 194
M. Pacciano: 220
M. Pantano: 150-52, 154-55
M. Passignano: 195
M. Pelato: 126
M. Penzola: 342, 344, 347
M. Pero: 499
M. Peschiena: 274, 277, 279, 283
M. Pianoreno: 305-06
M. Pigna: 497
M. Pilonica: 219
M. Pisano: 261
M. Pizzaculo: 492
M. Pizzuto: 196
M. Poggiolo: 325
M. Ponpegno: 322
M. Porchia: 160-62
M. Posigliano: 499, 503
M. Pozzo del Bagno: 276
M. Prano: 282-83
M. Pratello: 319
M. Pratolungo: 288
M. Pratone: 276-77
M. Purgatorio: 167
M. Querciabella: 234
M. Reale: 303-04
M. Reggiano: 291
M. Revole: 193-94
M. Ricci: 333-35

M. Rinaldo: 345
M. Romano: 195, 303-04, 307-09
M. Rotondo: 145, 154, 157, 164, 192
M. Ruazzo: 193
M. Sabbiuno: 509
M. Salvaro: 306-09
M. Sammucro: 149, 152-55, 157
M. Sarasiccia: 405-06
M. Scalari: 238
M. Scauri: 163, 193
M. Senario: 251, 261, 263, 265-66
M. Siserno: 198
M. Sole: 311-12, 497
M. Soprano: 132
M. Spadura: 302, 304, 306-10
M. Stanco: 296-97, 299-300, 302
M. Stelleto: 274
M. Taverna: 310-12, 339
M. Terminale: 423
M. Termine: 309-10
M. Testa: 319
M. Toncone: 288-89, 291
M. Tondo: 359
M. Trocchio: 161-62
M. Valbura: 433
M. Vase: 225-26
M. Vele: 195
M. Venere: 294, 296
M. Veruca: 271-72, 274, 277
M. Vigese: 294, 296
M. Villanova: 285
M. Vitalba: 224
M. L. Abele: 491
M. S. Bartalo: 323, 325
M. S. Biagio: 195
M. S. Michele: 234, 505
M. S. Barbara: 501, 503
M. S. Croce: 142-44, 146, 164, 196, 217
Maas River: 270-71, 276, 283-84, 291, 293, 297, 308, 316-19, 321, 325, 328, 331, 333, 340, 343, 351. See also Meuse River.
Maas-Waal Canal: 276, 278
Maashees: 283
Maastricht: 265-66, 270-71, 273, 275, 284, 353, 391
Mabalacat: 384
Mabalacat East Airfield: 384
Mabatang: 13
Mabatobato: 529
Mabini: 436, 440-41
Mabitac: 473
Mabompré: 376
Mabuni: 547-48
Macajalar Bay: 36, 520, 529, 535
Macalpe: 314
Macarite Island: 407
MacArthur, Gen. Douglas: 42, 135, 212-13, 314, 370, 377 379 381, 391, 394, 421, 505. See also Southwest Pacific Area; United States Army Forces, Far East.
appointed SCAP: 551
cancels Gasmata offensive: 145
cancels Hansa Bay assault: 178, 180
commands AFPAC: 472, 478
commands New Guinea offensive: 43, 54, 63
commands SWPA: 30, 33-34, 101
control of naval forces in P.I.: 20

MacArthur, Gen. Douglas—Continued
  decision to evacuate Manila: 8
  departure from Philippines: 25, 27, 29
  directives for Solomons: 122-23, 132, 135, 138
  inspects Bataan defenses: 13
  objection to stress on Marshalls: 113
  occupation plans for Japan: 546
  opens GHQ at Port Moresby: 6, 400
  plans for Admiralties and New Ireland: 172, 175-78
  plans for Arawe: 149
  plans for Formosa-Mindanao: 180, 209, 224, 230, 235, 237
  plans for recovery of Philippines: 266, 283, 294 301 ,341 ,367
  plans for Saidor assault: 155
  plans for TULSA: 43-45
  proposal on Bismarcks offensive: 40
  recommends offensive against Japan: 37, 44-45
  restores Philippine Government: 310
  retains control of P.I. operations after departure: 28
  role in Japanese surrender: 550-51
  transfers from Corregidor: 28-29
  warns of bombing of Manila: 248
Macatunao: 473
McAuliffe, Brig. Gen. Anthony C.: 208, 359
McBride, Brig. Gen. A. C.: 13, 17
McCabe, Col. Frederick: 52
McCain, Vice Adm. John S.: 49, 541
  commands COMAIRSOPAC: 38
  commands SOPAC land-based aircraft: 45
  and TF 63: 46-47
McCammon, Col. John E.: 199
McCawley: 59, 115
McClure, Brig. Gen. Robert B.: 126-27, 135, 339, 343, 354, 384, 544
McCreary, Lt. Col. Melvin: 72
McCreery, Lt. Gen. Sir Richard L. (Br.): 132-33, 292
Macedonia sector: 348
Macerata: 346
MacFarland: 59
Machang airfield: 4-5
Machinato: 504
Machinato airfield: 532
Machinato Inlet: 504
Machishi: 541
Machtum: 71
McKean: 147
MacKechnie, Col. Archibald R.: 101- 02, 114-15, 117
Macken: 438
Mackenbruch: 470
Mackwiller: 341-42
McLain, Maj. Gen. Raymond S.: 305, 337
MacLeod, Lt. Gen. D. K. (Br.): 5, 9
McMorris, Rear Adm. Charles H.: 82, 93, 100
McNair, Lt. Gen. Lesley J.: 28, 236
McNarney, Lt. Gen. Joseph T.: 309
MacNider, Brig. Gen. Hanford: 59, 69, 264, 383, 467, 538
Macon: 262
McSevney Point: 395, 398-400

Mactan Island: 460
Madagascar, operations in: 36-37, 40, 44, 53-57, 59-60, 63-64, 83
Madang: 74, 164, 178, 188
Madauk: 28
Madaya: 426
Madeleine River: 207
Maderbach Creek: 334, 336-38, 344
Madionen: 21
Madoera Strait: 22
Madon River: 264-65
Madonna di Brasa: 425
Madonna di Cerbiano: 310
Madrid: 128, 131
Maeda: 519-20
Maeda Escarpment: 519-20, 522, 524-25 527, 529-30, 532-34
Maegdesprung: 500, 502
Maeseyck: 317, 323
Maffin Airstrip No. 1: 196-97, 205
Maffin Bay: 222, 227, 230, 236, 261, 263- 64, 269
Magalang: 382, 386
Magat River: 544
Magdeburg: 486, 489, 491, 493, 495, 497, 499, 502, 506, 534
Mageret: 365, 367, 373-74
Mageri Point: 114
Magicienne Bay: 213-14, 217
Maginot Line: 320, 336-37, 345-47, 350, 366, 369, 372, 439
Magione: 217
Magliano: 210
MAGNET: 14,19
MAGNETO Conference: 392, 398, 400
Magneville: 205-06
Magny: 327
Magny en Vexin: 258
Magoster: 366
Magruder, Brig. Gen. John: 6
Magwe: 29-30, 33, 505
Mahan: 347
Maharès (Gumtree) Road: 99, 101-02
Mahlaing: 4 13
Mahlberg: 505
Mahogany Hill: 329-30, 333
Mahonag: 337 349
Maiana Island: 151
Maîche: 264
Maikop: 48, 49, 89
Mailar: 483
MAILFIST: 542. See also Singapore.
Main River: 451-55, 457, 459, 461, 463, 465, 469, 471, 475, 477, 479, 481, 485, 490
Mainaga: 436-37
Mainarde Ridge: 157
Mainbernheim: 477
Maingkwan: 168, 177-78, 187
Mainhardt: 503
Mainit River: 3 14
Mainneville: 258
Mainz: 44,24,44-45, 447-49, 452, 455, 457, 459, 461
Mainzlar: 458
Maiori: 133, 137
Mairy: 265
Maison Blanche: 64
Maison des Eaux: 92
Maison Rouge: 382-83
Maisoncelles-la-Jourdan: 246

Maixe: 273
Maizières-lès-Metz: 293-94, 296-99, 301- 02, 307, 312-15, 320-21, 326
Maizila Pass: 90
Majola Hill: 168
Majunga: 54-55, 57
Majuro Atoll: 164, I 66-67, 169, 172
Majuro Attack Group (TG 51.2): 164, 166
Makambo Island: 49
Makassar: 23
Makassar Strait: 17-18
Makin Atoll: 21, 50, 137-40, 147-49
Maknassy: 75, 89-90, 99-100, 102-04
Mako Ko: 375
Maktar: 86, 90, 93, 105
Makunsha: 225
Makuy Bum: 180
Malabang: 35, 446, 453, 488, 497, 501
Malabo: 525
Malabog: 488, 503
Malacca: 13-14
Malagang: 11
Malahang: 135
Malakawng: 187
Malamaui Island: 444-45
Malang: 21
Malarya Hill: 478, 480
Malaucourt: 320
Malay Barrier: 11
Malaya
  fall of
    AIF Malaya organized: 14
    air defense of: 4-5, 20
    airfields, British withdrawal from: 4
    Allied reinforcement of: 15
    armor reinforcement: 20
    capitulation: 24
    East Force organized: 14
    enemy air attacks: 3-4, 8, 17
    enemy control of waters and air: 4
    enemy landings: 3, 5, 7, 15-16, 19
    Indian forces regrouped: 7
    Singapore, withdrawal of force to: 18, 20-21
    Wavell visits front: 13-14
    West Force organized: 14
  recovery of: 3 116, 536, 541-43
    air support for: 531
    directive on: 391, 531
Malaya Command (Br.): 3-4
Malaybalay: 539-40
Malberg: 426
Malbergweich: 417, 419
Maldegem: 296, 298
Maldingen: 381
Malempré: 366
Maletto: 127
Malgobek: 58, 81
Malines: 269
Malinta Tunnel: 37
Malisiqui: 373
Mailing: 321-23, 325
MALLORY MAJOR: 228-29, 231
Malmédy: 354-58, 366, 373 375-78
Maloelap Atoll: 165-66
Malolos: 385, 387 390
Malsbenden: 422

[INDEX]

[621]

Malsfeld: 465, 467-68
Malta
   air reinforcement of: 37
   air support from: 116
   Axis invasion postponed: 38
   command controls designated: 28
   convoys, attacks on: 23, 29, 49, 67
   CRICKET Conference: 387, 390
   awarded George Cross: 33
   Italian surrender: 133, 138
   RAF forces absorbed by MAAF: 155
   supply situation: 28
Malta Air Command (RAF): 93
Maltot: 228, 234
Malvar: 455
Mamala River: 3 2
Mambare River: 74, 98
Mamburao: 358, 366
Mamien Pass: 192-93, 199-200
Mamming: 524, 526
Mananga River: 455, 488
Manauangan: 507
Manchuria, Soviet occupation of: 398, 550
Mandalay
   fall of: 25-26, 29-29, 33-35
   recovery of: 91, 93, 99, 150, 155, 257, 271, 293, 316, 327, 349, 374, 401, 412, 414, 421, 426, 430, 433, 435-36, 438, 442, 445-47, 467, 486
Mande St. Etienne: 365, 371
Manderfeld: 388-89, 412
Manderscheid: 410, 416, 432
Mandeville: 204
Mandog: 541-44
Mandom: 199
Mandray: 335
Mandurriao: 445
Mangaldan: 381
Mangatarem: 374
Mangima Canyon: 537, 539
Man-shih: 197, 206, 255, 322, 332
Manhay: 357-62, 368-70, 372
Manheim: 414
Manhton: 185
Maniagassa Island: 230
Manio Bridge: 205, 210
Manila
   conference on Japanese surrender: 551
   enemy advance on: 7, 11
   evacuation of: 8, 10
   declared open city: 9
   Pacific forces hq: 478, 490
   preservation of reservoirs: 505. See also Ipo Dam; Wawa Dam.
   recovery: 377, 379, 384-85, 387-97, 399-407 409-10, 412-14, 416-17, 419, 421, 423 426 439 484 542
   warning on U.S. bombing: 248
Manila Bay: 5, 10, 12, 391, 394, 401, 403, 406, 417, 423, 450, 499
Manipur: 47-48
Manipur River: 274
Manna: 504
MANNA: 285. See also Greece.
Manna Farm: 167-69, 171
Mannebach: 431
Mannerheim Line: 206-07, 213
Mannheim: 263, 267, 277, 318, 444, 446-47, 455, 459, 461, 463
Manning, Group Capt. E. R. (RAF): 11

Manoag: 371-72, 375
Manokwari Island: 201, 249
Manoncourt: 298
Manpin: 183, 188, 191
Mansfield, Rear Adm. J. M. (RN): 262
Manshausen: 385
Mansi: 304
Mantes-Gassicourt: 250-54, 256-58
Man-tha: 320, 326
Mantitang: 385
Manus Island: 129, 152, 164, 170, 172, 176-77, 179-81, 183-84, 186-87, 190, 303, 329
Manych River: 47, 86-87
Manzanares: 484, 493
Mapait Hills: 476, 478
Mapandan: 371
Mapia Islands: 327, 332
Maquis: 254. See also French Forces of the Interior.
Mar airfield: 227, 233, 236-39, 255, 262
Marxist, Col. Robert V.: 90
Marakei Island: 151
Maramag airfields: 53 4
Maran: 192
Marano: 513
Marano River: 264, 272, 274, 276-77
Maranola: 194
Marbache: 263-66
Marblehead: 22
Marburg: 385, 458, 460
Marches: 356, 358-59, 363, 365, 367
Marcoiano: 277, 279
Marcouray: 361, 369
Marcourt: 369
Marcus Island: 27, 130, 195, 299
Mardigny: 270, 273
Mardt Bibart: 488
Marecchia River: 282-83, 285-86
Mareth Line: 91-101
Marettimo Island: 123
Marghana: 111
Margut: 265
Mariadorf: 29 8, 3 27, 3 29
Mariana Islands
   air and naval actions: 175, 209-12, 214, 219, 222-23, 227, 234-37, 240, 242, 245
   armor support: 215, 217, 238, 244-45
   base for Japan air offensive: 336, 376, 458
   casualty summaries: 220, 227, 246
   enemy strength estimated: 209
   recovery of: 152, 162, 179, 208-27, 230, 234-46, 249
   staging area for Iwo Jima: 299, 373 385, 401-04
   underwater demolition teams: 210
Mariaweiler: 350, 352-53
Marienau: 424, 426, 428
Marienberg (eastern Germany): 384
Marienberg (western Germany): 292-93
Marienburg: 469, 471
Marienhausen: 454
Marienthal: 349
Marienwerder: 387
Marieulles: 275, 277
Marigny: 236-37
Marikina River. See Mariquina River.
Marilao: 390

Marimont: 330
Marimont Hill. See Hill 334 (France).
Marina di Pisa: 235
Marina di Ragusa: 118
Marinduque Island: 367, 372, 387, 389
Marine Corps Airdrome Battalion, 2d: 129-30
Marine Amphibious Corps
   I: 118, 135, 137, 140, 142-43, 145, 150, 154, 183
   III: 222, 225, 234, 241, 244-45, 249 263, 274, 278, 283, 301, 303, 307, 467-69, 471, 476, 478, 480, 482, 484, 486, 488, 493, 495, 497, 499, 501, 504, 508, 519,,531, 534-48
   V: 131, 135-36, 148, 150, 166-67, 173, 211, 217-18, 222-25, 303, 360, 366, 369, 406-09, 411-13, 415-17, 420-23, 425, 427-28, 430, 432-34 436-38, 440-41, 444-46, 449, 452-53, 455, 519
Marine Corps Aviation
   MAG 22: 26
   MAG 23: 50, 52
   MAG 25: 50
   1st MAW: 50, 59, 78
   2d MAW: 78
   VMF 211: 4, 7, 9, 26
   VMF 223: 50
   VMSB 17: 6
   VMSB 232: 50
Marine Corps Aviation personnel
   in defense of Bataan: 13, 17-18
   reinforce Midway: 4, 7, 9, 26
   in Philippines: 347, 544
   in defense of Wake: 4
Marine Corps Brigade, 1st Provisional 234-39, 243, 245
Marine Corps Defense Battalions
   1st: 4-5
   3d: 46-47
   4th: 8-9
   5th: 53-54, 57, 63
   6th: 3
   7th: 130
   9th: 71-72
   11th: 94
Marine Corps Divisions
   1st (1st, 5th, 7th): 35-73 93, 155-57, 159, 172, 178, 183, 188, 274, 283, 285-86, 301, 306, 338, 467-69, 471, 476, 525, 527, 529-30, 532-48
   2d (2d, 6th, 8th): 44, 74, 81-85, 89, 135, 148, 210-14, 216-24, 227, 230, 236-37, 239, 411, 427, 468, 546-47
   3d (4th, 22d, 29th): 137, 141, 143-50, 153-57, 161-63, 183, 234-46. 360, 408-09, 411-13, 415-17, 420-23, 427-28, 430, 432-34, 436-38, 440-42, 444, 456
   4th (3d, 9th, 21st): 167-68, 171, 173, 210-14, 216-27, 236-37, 239, 360, 407, 409, 411, 413, 415-16, 418, 420-21, 423, 428, 430, 432-34, 436-38, 440-42, 444-45
   5th (23d, 24th, 25th): 360, 407-09, 411-13, 415-16, 418, 420-21, 423, 428, 430, 432-34, 436-38, 440-42, 444-46, 449, 452-53, 456

Marine Corps Divisions—Continued
  6th (26th, 27th, 28th): 467-69, 471, 476, 478, 480, 482, 484, 486, 488, 493, 495, 497, 499, 501, 508, 531, 534-48, 551
Composite Army-Marine: 85-89
Marine Corps Engineer Battalions
  1st: 62
  2d: 74
Marine Corps Field Artillery Battalions
  10th: 89, 149, 226
  11th: 58
Marine Corps Parachute Infantry Battalions
  1st: 48-49, 54-56, 149
  2d: 142, 144
Marine Corps Parachute Infantry Regiment, 1st: 142, 152
Marine Corps Raider Battalions
  1st: 44, 48-49 53-59, 116-17
  2d: 50, 63, 66, 72
  3d :94, 144
  4th: 113, 115-16
Marine Corps Raider Regiments
  1st: 116
  2d Provisional: 143
Marine Corps Regiments
  1st: 35-73, 157, 172, 174, 274, 276-79, 281-83, 286, 468-69, 525, 527, 529 533-37, 539, 542-43, 545-46
  2d: 44, 49, 51, 55, 58, 62-63, 65, 84, 89, 148-49, 212, 216, 218, 223-24, 227
  3d: 143-45,427
  4th: 8, 10, 182, 234, 237-38, 468, 478, 495, 499, 539-44, 547, 551
  5th: 41, 49, 157, 159, 175-76, 178-79, 274, 276, 278, 281-82, 288-91, 296-97, 299-300, 468, 529, 53,3 535-39, 541-43, 546-47
  6th: 82, 84-89, 148-50, 212, 216, 218-21, 224, 227, 230
  7th: 45, 53-56, 156, 159, 162, 274, 276, 278-79, 281-82, 286, 288-89, 291-95, 297, 468, 533-39, 543-47
  8th: 63, 65, 71, 84-85, 89, 148-49, 212-13, 216-21, 224, 227, 236-37, 546-47
  9th: 143-44, 413, 415-17, 420-21, 423, 430, 432, 434, 436, 441, 444, 456, 474
  21st: 145-47, 154, 159, 408-09, 411, 413, 417, 420, 423, 428, 430, 432, 434, 436 441, 444, 451
  22d: 174-75, 234, 237-38, 468, 476, 478, 49,3 499, 534-3,8 541-42, 544, 547
  23d: 168, 211-13, 216-18, 224-25, 227, 407, 409, 413, 415-16, 418, 420, 423, 428, 430, 432-34, 441
  24th: 168, 212-13, 216-18, 220, 225-27, 407, 411, 413, 415, 420-21, 423, 428, 430, 433-34, 441-42, 444
  25th: 167-68, 211-14, 216, 220, 225, 227, 407, 409, .411, 415-16, 418, 420-21, 423, 428, 430, 434, 441, 442
  26th: 211, 407, 409, 411, 413, 415-16, 420-21, 423, 428, 436, 438, 441-42, 444-46, 449, 453,
  27th: 407, 409 416, 418, 420, 423, 428, 436, 438, 441, 449
  28th: 407-09, 411-13, 418, 420-21, 423, 428, 434, 436, 438, 440-42, 444-46, 449, 452-53
  29th: 212, 218, 478, 482, 484, 486, 495, 499, 537-39, 542-43, 547
Marine Corps Tank Battalions
  1st: 162 2d: 148, 149, 151
  4th: 173
Marisfeld: 481
Mariquina (Marikina) River: 407, 409-10, 457, 499, 501, 503, 510, 534, 540
Maritime Alps: 486
Mariupol: 133
Mariveles: 19, 403-05
Mark River: 314-17
Markbreit: 477
MARKET-GARDEN: 267, 276, 288. See also Rhine River.
Markham River and Valley: 120, 131, 136, 188
Markhausen: 462
Markolsheim: 386
Marksuhl: 473
Markt Nordheim: 490
Markt Oberdorf: 520
Markt Wald: 5, 119
Marktheidenfeld: 469
Marktl: 526
Marktredwitz: 506
Marktzeuln: 487, 490
Marl: 460, 462
Marly: 326-27
Marnach: 3 84
Marne River: 256-58, 266
Marne-Rhine Canal: 272-73, 275, 320
Maroth: 454
Marovovo: 91
Marpi Point: 224, 227
Marradi: 283, 285-87, 291-92
Marrakech: 66
MARS: 304, 441, 537
Marsal: 287
Marsala: 122
Marsanne: 254
Marsberg: 460
Marseilles 250-58, 307
Marshall, Gen. George C.: 40, 181, 205, 274, 517, 536, 545, 547. See also Combined Chiefs of Staff; Joint Chiefs of Staff; War Department.
  asks for air support for Rangoon: 462, 472
  authorizes mobile air force for SWPA and POA: 44
  at BOLERO conferences: 32-33
  on Calcutta-Assam LOC: 166-67, 171
  on division of CBI: 222-27, 230, 235, 266, 310
  establishes USAFIME: 41
  fosters Stilwell-Mountbatten meeting: 177

Marshall, Gen. George C.—Continued
  and King: 43
  and negotiations for use of Chinese Communists: 385
  orders Stratemeyer to command China air forces: 544
  proposes Stilwell as Chiang's chief of staff: 14
  proposes unified command for Far East: 9
  role in Japanese surrender: 550
  urges SLEDGEHAMMER: 46
Marshall, Brig. Gen. Richard J.: 12, 34, 46
Marshall Islands campaign: 112-13, 128-29, 139, 152, 159-60, 162, 164-75
  air and naval support: 21, 147, 164-69, 173-75
  armor support: 168-70
  casualty summaries: 170-71
  objection to stress on: 113
  staging area for Marianas: 204, 208
Martaban: 21, 23
Martelange: 359
Marthille: 325
Martigues: 255
Martin, Brig. Gen. Clarence A.: 72, 155, 157, 161, 195, 221, 229
Martin, Maj. Gen. Frederick L.: 6
Martinstein: 444
Martinville Ridge: 2 11, 228, 231-32
Martuba: 67
Marubian: 191-93
Maruyama Trail: 76
Marvie: 357, 363, 365, 370
Marzeno: 337
Marzeno River: 336-37
Masbate: 462, 471
Masbate Island: 462, 471, 480, 531
Maschio d'Ariano: 199-201
Mashiki: 476
Masholder: 416
Masilay: 436, 438, 442
Maspelt: 386
Massa: 296, 471, 475, 477, 483, 486, 490
Massa Lombardo: 490
Massaciuccioli: 275
Massacre Bay: 109-11
Massacre Valley: 109, 112
Massarosa: 275
Masseler: 377
Massenheim: 459
Massicault: 109
Mast, Brig. Gen. Charles E. (Fr.): 60
Masthorn: 400, 406
Masurian Lakes: 385
Mataba: 412
Matagob: 3 59-60
Mataling Rive: 3 5
Matanikau: 50, 57
Matanikau River: 49, 56-58, 60-63, 66, 68, 71, 74, 83, 85
Materborn: 398-400
Matese Mountains: 142
Mateur: 67, 70, 81, 95-96, 99, 106-09
Mati: 309
Matruh (Mersa Matruh): 42-43, 64
Matting: 517
Matzen: 416

[INDEX]

Matzerath: 414-15, 419
Mauban: 8, 13, 16-18, 480, 486, 488
Maubeuge: 261
Mauel: 414
Maungdaw: 75, 108, 110, 161, 178, 184
Mauo: 417, 421, 425
Maupertus: 217-19
Mauritius Island: 53
Mausbach: 273
Mawchi: 31, 33-34
Mawlaik: 344
Mawlu: 181, 316, 322
Mawpin: 311, 314
Maximiliansau: 453
Maxonchamp: 286
Maxwell, Maj. Gen. Russell L.: 42, 52, 63
Maybancal: 437, 467
Mayen: 431-32
Mayenne: 243-44, 247
Mayenne River: 242-44
Maymyo: 28, 32
Mayondon Point: 460
Mayotte Island: 44
Mayu Peninsula and River: 75, 78, 89, 98, 103, 152, 160, 351, 362
Mayu Range: 148
Mazagan: 66
Mazzarino: 118-19
Mbangai Island: 49
Meauffe: 213
Mechelen: 456
Mechelgruen: 498
Mecher: 382
Mecher-Dunkrodt: 362, 366
Mechili: 18-19, 22
Meckel: 416
Meckinghoven: 468
Mecklenburg: 523, 530
Mécleuges: 326
Medard: 444
Medebach: 464, 466, 468
Medeera: 547-48
Medel: 383
Medendorf: 386
Medendorp, Capt. Alfred: 58, 60, 70
Médenine: 93, 96-97, 100-101
Medicina: 492, 499, 501
Mediterranean Air Command (Allied): 93, 110
Mediterranean Allied Air Forces: 153, 155, 177, 246
Mediterranean Allied Tactical Air Force: 182, 228-29, 231
Mediterranean, Supreme Allied Commander. See Mediterranean Theater; Wilson, Gen. Sir Henry Maitland.
Mediterranean Theater. See also Wilson, Gen. Sir Henry Maitland.
 air reorganization: 156, 159
 CCS directive on unified command: 152-53, 155:
 landing craft allocation: 145, 155, 160, 172
 redesignated from NATOUSA: 316
 relinquishes North Africa to AMET: 419
 strategic planning: 150
 Wilson as SACMED: 156, 161

Medjerda River: 105, 108
Medjez el Bab: 68-72, 74, 78-79, 95, 101-08
Medyn: 15
Meerssen: 275, 277
Meeuwen: 355
Megara: 301-02
Meggen: 485
Mehdia: 65
Mehr: 398, 450
Mehr River: 452
Mehrum: 451
Meijel: 291, 313-14, 319-20, 327
Meiktila: 34-35, 348, 372, 408-09, 412, 414, 416-17, 425, 430, 439, 450, 459, 461, 463, 490
Meinbrexen: 481
Meindorf: 446
Meine: 484
Meiningen: 467-68, 475, 479 481
Meisburg: 426
Meisdorf: 502
Meisenheim: 444
Meisenthal: 346, 366
Meisert: 275
Meitesheim: 342-43
Meldola: 311, 313-15
Melfa River: 196-98
Melfi: 136
Mélisey: 285
Melitopol: 140, 142
Mellingen: 490
Mellu Island: 167
Melsbach: 449
Melun: 252, 254-56
Memel: 300, 302, 386
Memmingen: 518, 520
Mempakul: 12
Menado: 14
Menarmont: 315
Menate: 486, 488
Menaurupt: 319
Mendaropo: 63
Menden: 446, 451, 496
Menfi: 121
Mengeringhausen: 460
Mengerschied: 443
Mengmao: 212
Mengta Ferry: 191
Ménil: 361
Menne: 464
Mennekrath: 414
Menton: 266
Menzel Djemil: 109
Méounes: 252
Meppel: 493
Meppen: 480
Merauke: 42
Merbeck: 416
Mercato Saraceno: 299
Merchingen: 475
Merderet River: 203-08
Merduma: 75
Merefa: 131
Merenberg: 458
Mereveldhoven: 279
Mergui: 16, 18
Merheim: 427
Merken: 350, 395
Merkenich: 427
Merkers: 473

Merkols: 382
Merkstein: 295, 297
Merlscheid: 07
Mermuth: 439
Merode: 330-32, 340, 346, 349-50
Merrill, Rear Adm. A. Stanton: 143
Merrill, Brig. Gen. Frank D.: 160, 175, 178-79, 184, 189
Merrill's Marauders: 160, 163, 168, 175, 188-89, 191, 194-98
Mersa Bou Zedjar: 65
Mersa Matruh: 42-43, 64
Mersch: 357, 410, 412
Merscheid: 383
Merseburg: 492, 494, 496
Merseburg-Leuna: 192
Mersing: 15, 17
Merten: 340, 425, 427
Mertesdorf: 434-36
Mertloch: 437
Mertzdorf: 428
Mertzwiller: 340, 345-46. 349, 441
Merville: 203
Merviller: 315
Merxem: 294
Merxheim: 444, 518
Merxplas: 291
Merzbach: 427
Merzenhausen: 333-34, 338
Merzenich: 412, 422, 424
Merzien: 498
Merzig: 330-32, 341, 357, 359, 396, 410, 440, 442
Meschede: 480, 483
Meschenich: 427
Messdorf: 430
Messe, Marshal Giovanni (It.): 88, 94, 110
Messerich: 414
Messervy, Lt. Gen. Frank W.: 347
Messina: 114, 119-20, 124, 126, 128
Messina Strait: 128, 131-32
Messnerschlag: 526
Metapona River: 62-64
Metauro River: 253-54, 256–57
Metlaoui: 93, 97
Métrich: 321-23
Metropolitan Road (Luzon): 539
Mettendorf: 407-09, 413
Metterich: 422
Metternich: 425
Mettlach: 440
Mettmann: 497, 500
Metz: 260, 265-68, 270, 272-73, 275, 277, 288-89, 293, 315-18, 320-21, 324-32, 334, 340, 342, 345-47, 349, 351, 353, 357, 359, 399-400, 423
Metzeresche: 328
Metzervisse: 327
Metzingen: 510, 513-14
Meurich: 407
Meurthe River: 270, 272-73, 275, 280-81, 283-84, 300, 315, 319, 321-22, 324, 328, 330-33
Meuse River: 258-64, 266-67, 271, 277, 305, 320-21, 353, 356, 360-62, 366, 374, 396-407, 415. See also Maas River.
Meuse-Escaut Canal: 264, 267-68, 270, 276, 278

[623]

Mexican-U.S. Joint Defense Commission: 26
Meximieux: 259-62
Meycauayan: 391
Meyenheim: 395
Meyerode: 384
Meyrargues: 252
Mézidon: 246, 429
Mézières: 263
Mga: 164
Michael, King of Rumania: 255
MICHAELMAS: 155, 157-59, 172. *See also* Saidor.
Michaelstein: 508
Michamps: 365-66, 376
Michelan: 463
Michelbach: 427, 495, 505
Michelfeld: 500, 503
Michldorf: 512
Middelburg: 319
Middle East: 5, 9
  aircraft reinforcements for: 42
  U.S. mission to: 42
Middle East Air Command (RAF): 93
Middle East Air Force: 43
Middle East Command (Br.): 16, 25
  assumes control of Eritrea: 21
  control of Iran and Iraq: 12, 15
  diversion of aircraft from: 9, 155
  diversion of ground units from: 5, 24
Middle East Force (Br.): 55
  alerted for defense of Iran: 38
  Alexander succeeds Auchinleck: 49-50
  control of Malta: 28
  operations in Libya: 3
  preparation for defense of Anatolia: 35
Middle East Theater (U.S.), established: 41
Middleburg Island: 239, 241, 248, 251
Midway
  Battle of: 39-40
  enemy air losses: 28
  enemy bombardment: 3, 18, 22-23, 36
  garrison reinforced: 6, 8-9, 38
  MAG 22 formed: 26
  Nimitz inspects defenses: 36
  Seventh Air Force in defense of: 38
Miehelau: 490
Miel, 427
Mielec: 236
Miesbach: 527-28
Mieux: 257
Mignano: 141, 144
Mignano Gap: 144, 147, 155
Mignéville: 316
Migyaungye: 33
Mike Hill (Leyte): 311
Milan: 61, 523, 525, 527
Milburn, Maj. Gen. Frank W.: 361, 373
Milchenbach: 480
Military highway to Alaska: 23, 62
Military Liaison Headquarters, Greece (Allied): 262, 305, 325, 331
Military missions. *See countries by name.*
Mille Atoll: 166
Millerovo: 45, 85
Millich: 415

Milligen: 398
Milliken, Maj. Gen. John: 300, 441
Millingen: 430, 453
Millomont: 369
Mills, Maj. Herbert N.: 273, 281-82, 284, 327-29
Milne Bay: 40-45, 47, 50-54, 57-58 95, 97, 104, 114, 129, 141
Mils: 531
Milspe: 491
Miltonberger, Brig. Gen. Butler B.: 381, 386
Minami: 416, 418, 420-21, 423, 428
Minami-Uebaru: 480
Minatoga: 543-44.
Minatoga River: 543
Mindanao City: 434
Mindanao Island aircraft evacuated to Australia: 6
  capitulation: 37
  enemy assault on: 7-8, 33, 35-37
  FEAF transferred from Luzon to: 6
  MacArthur arrives: 28-29
  recovery of: 179, 211, 224, 235, 244, 275, 417, 419, 431, 433-34, 436-38, 440-42, 444-46, 452-53, 457, 462, 486, 488, 493, 497, 501, 503, 505-07, 510-13, 515, 517, 519-20, 522-23, 525, 527, 529-41, 543-44, 547-50
  Sharp commands garrison: 27
Mindanao River: 503, 506
Mindanao Sea: 351
Mindelheim: 518, 520
Minden: 403, 470, 472, 474, 476, 478, 480
Mindoro Attack Group: 339
Mindoro Island fall of: 22, 26
  recovery of: 302, 315, 331, 338-41, 350-58, 360, 362-69, 373, 375-76, 378-79, 381, 383, 385-87, 389, 405, 411, 415, 417, 419, 434, 488
Mineralnye Vody: 84
Minesweeping and Hydrographic Group (TG 77.6): 366-68
Mingaladon: 5, 528
Mingolsheim: 467
Minhla: 32-33
Minna Island: 491, 497
Minsk: 216, 218-20, 222-23
Mint Building (Manila): 410
Mintal: 529, 534, 536-37, 539-40
Minturno: 163-64, 186, 191
Mios Woendi: 200, 205
Miquelon Island: 8
Mirabeau: 252
Mirbach: 429
Mirecourt: 268, 272
Mirfeld: 383
Mirgorod: 216
Miri: 6
Miri Detachment: 5
Misano: 262
Misima Island: 37
Misinsman: 527
Miskolc: 341-44, 349, 355, 382
Mission Trail (Bougainville): 144, 146
Missouri: 551
Missy: 242, 256
Misterbianco: 120, 125

Mistretta: 123-24
Misurata: 85
Mitchell, Maj. Gen. Ralph J. (USMC) 148
Miteiriya Ridge: 61
Mitlesheim: 439
Mitrovica: 344
Mitry Mory: 258
Mitscher, Vice Adm. Marc A.: 122, 166, 175, 541
Mitsensk: 121
Mittel Gruendau: 463
Mittel Sorpe: 478
Mittelwihr: 346, 348
Mittenwald: 527, 530
Mitterfels: 515
Mittersheim: 331, 334-35
Mitterteich: 508
Mittl Isar Kanal: 524, 526
Mittweida: 496
Miyako Island: 519
Mnichov: 533
Moa: 103
Model, Field Marshal Walter: 228, 250, 502
Modena: 250, 511
Modenheim: 395
Moder River: 340, 379, 381, 383, 385, 389-91, 393, 402, 419, 439
Moderscheid: 382-83
Modica: 118
Modigliana: 321, 327
Moeckern: 494
Moeckmuehl: 475, 477
Moedrath: 416, 418, 420, 422, 425
Moehne Dam: 111
Moehra: 473
Moellen: 451
Moerdijk: 319-2 0
Moers: 422-23
Moetsch: 416
Mogaung Valley: 180, 185, 187, 195, 197, 200, 207, 210-11, 216, 219, 257
Mogilev: 150, 182, 219-20
Mogok: 446, 463
Mohacs: 340
Mo-hlaing: 346, 348-49, 353
Mohn: 419
Mohne River: 472, 478, 480, 482, 487
Mohnyin: 307
Mohon: 263
Moinet: 376, 379
Moircy: 364-65
Moivron: 288, 298
Mokerang Plantation: 181, 184, 187
Mokerang Point: 184
Mokmer: 198, 202, 204-09, 211, 213, 216, 219-20, 241
Mokpalin: 25
Moletta River: 164, 170-71, 173
Molo: 445-46
Molucca Passage: 17-18
Momauk: 326, 362
Mombaru: 469
Momerstroff: 336
Mommenheim: 445
Momote: 164, 170, 176-79, 181, 187
Monastery Hill: 151-52, 171-72, 174, 180-81, 192

[INDEX]

Moncada: 378, 381
Monceau: 358
Moncel: 283-84
Moncourt: 272, 281, 287, 308, 320
Mondelange: 265
Monfalcone: 527
Mong Pawn: 34
Mong Wi: 364, 368-69
Monghidoro: 292-93
Mongiorgio: 505
Monglo: 484, 490, 493, 495
Mongmit: 293, 359, 388 391, 434
Mono Island: 142, 146
Monoebaboe: 208
Monrovia: 118
Montrone: 280
Mons: 261-65
Monsabert, Lt. Gen. Aimè de Goislard de (Fr.): 261
Monschau: 271, 273, 278, 295, 353, 355 358, 388
Monschau Forest: 351, 353 358-59, 387-90
Monselice: 522
Monssen: 66
Monsummano: 264
Mont: 369, 374
Mont Castre Forest: 226, 225
Mont de Cadenbronn: 344
Mont de Fosse: 367
Mont le Ban: 372-73
Mont Pincon: 240-41, 243-44, 246
Montabaur: 454
Montaione: 232
Montalban: 409, 412, 440, 442, 450
Montalbano, Italy: 291
Montalbano, Sicily: 127
Montaquila: 145
Montarello: 287-88
Montargis: 254, 266
Montbéliard: 328-29
Montbronn: 346, 366
Montcornet: 260
Montdidier: 259, 333
Montebello: 285-86
Montebourg: 204-09, 213
Montebourg Station: 206
Montecarelli: 274
Montecchio: 292, 344
Montecodruzzo: 298
Montecorvino: 133
Montefiascone: 207
Montefredente: 290
Montélimar: 254, 256-59
Montelupo: 234, 250
Montemarano: 138
Montenau: 378, 394
Montenegro area: 347
Montenero: 233
Montenovo: 301
Montepiano: 284-85
Montepulciano: 221
Montereau: 252, 254-56
Monterenzio hills: 299-305
Monterosso: 119
Monterotondo: 204
Montescudo: 274, 276-77
Montese: 495
Montevarchi: 233
Montfort: 380-82

Montgomery, Rear Adm. Alfred L.: 145-46
Montgomery, Field Marshal Sir Bernard L.: 50, 54, 58, 60-63, 70, 74, 82-84, 86-87, 94-95, 100, 102, 104-05, 107, 118, 121, 126, 133-34, 137, 140, 142, 147
  CG of Eighth Army: 49-50
  CG of 21
  Army Group: 156
  commands Allied land forces in Normandy: 203
  directives on drive to Germany: 262, 271, 289, 292, 304, 317, 356, 363
  directives on Normandy breakout: 212-14, 221, 227, 240-41, 243, 245-46, 248, 252, 256
  directives on Rhine River crossing: 432
  relinquishes control of 12th Army Group: 260
  role in German surrender: 529
Montiano: 301
Monticello: 194
Montigny: 204, 315, 325
Montilgallo: 297
Montmartin-en-Graignes: 208-10
Montone River: 321, 323-26, 328, 333, 335-37, 342-43, 430
Montpellier: 259
Montrevel: 262
Monywa: 35-36, 381, 449
Monzelfeld: 444
Monzuno: 296
Mook: 396
Moore, Maj. Gen. George F.: 27
Moore, Maj. Gen. James (USMC): 186
Moore, Lt. Col. Malcolm A.: 125
Moosbrugger, Comdr. Frederick (USN) 125
Moosburg: 521-22, 524, 526
Moosham: 519
Mor: 451
Moranao: 547
Morava River: 477, 481
Moravian Gap: 465, 473, 481, 525
Moravska Ostrava: 505, 511, 523, 525
Morciano: 262
Morello Hill: 155, 157
Morenhoven: 427
Morgan, Lt. Gen. Sir Frederick E., named COSSAC: 106. *See also* Chief of Staff to Supreme Allied Commander (designate).
Morgorod: 201
Morhange: 325-26, 405
Morhange Plateau: 320
Moriviller: 278
Morlaix: 243-44, 251
Moro River: 151-53
Morobe Harbor: 101-02, 114, 116
Morocco, Allied landings in: 64-65. *See also* Algiers; Northwest Africa Campaign. Moron: 14-15, 17
Morondava: 54
Morong: 437
Morong River and Valley: 438, 441-42
Morotai Covering Force: 271
Morotai Island
  air and naval actions: 274, 276

Morotai Island—Continued
  assault on: 211, 233, 235, 249, 253-54, 261-64, 269-71, 274, 276-77, 279, 281-83, 286-87, 291, 295, 297, 302 390, 449, 491
  enemy air raids: 390, 449
  staging area for Philippines: 297, 400
Morris, Gen. Basil M. (Aus.): 43, 46, 50
Morris Force: 210, 230, 234
Morris, Brig. G. R. (Indian Army): 210
Morrona: 231
Morsbach: 392, 394
Morscheid: 437
Morschenich: 412, 414
Morshausen: 438-39
Morshead, Lt. Gen. Sir Leslie (Br.): 139
Morsott: 88, 104
Mortagne: 252-53, 310
Mortagne River: 275, 278, 280, 307-10
Mortain: 241-47
Mortars, first use in Pacific: 133
Morteaux: 250
Mortlock Atoll: 162
Morvillars: 330
Morville-lès-Vic: 321
Moscou Farm: 327
Moscow: 97, 166, 269
  Churchill arrival: 49
  Foreign Ministers Conference: 141, 143
  German assault on: 3-4, 10
  USSR-France treaty: 349
Moselkern: 438
Moselle River crossings: 260-61, 263-70, 273, 275, 277-78, 280-85, 287, 292, 295-97, 300 318, 320-23, 325-30, 360, 371, 374, 382, 406-09, 414, 419, 421-24, 432, 434-45
Moselotte River: 299-300, 304
Moselweiss: 441
Mosles: 204
Mossoux: 285
Mostroff: 360, 362
Moten, Brig. M. J. (Aus.): 85
Motobu Peninsula: 480, 482, 484, 486, 488 493 495 497 501, 508
Motor Torpedo Boat Squadron, 3d: 59
Motor torpedo boats: 17, 59
Motoyama: 409, 417, 420, 423, 430
Mott, Col. John W.: 70, 72
Mouen: 219
Moulins-lès-Metz: 329
Moulmein: 12, 17-18, 20-22, 155, 511, 515
Mountbatten, Adm. Lord Louis: 152, 155, 160, 170, 172, 178, 180-81, 187, 195, 206, 435, 463. *See also* Burma; China; India-Burma Theater; South East Asia Command.
  Cairo conference with Churchill: 299, 304, 316
  Calcutta commanders' conference: 358
  commands SEAC: 129, 141-42, 147
  directives on Burma and Malaya: 271, 274, 391, 531
  directives on recovery of Rangoon and Singapore: 395, 455, 469, 501
  establishes Air-Ground Supply Committee: 459

Mountbatten, Adm. Lord Louis—Continued
  offers British troops for training of Chinese: 163
  organizes Eastern Air Command: 153
  plan for Arakan offensive: 161, 321
  Plans for recovery of Malaya and Singapore: 542-43, 546
  plans for reinforcement of China by air: 449
  plans for SEAC strategy: 235, 241, 254, 293, 299, 304, 307, 316, 329
  and Stilwell conferences: 177, 185
  on transfer of Chinese from Burma: 341, 344
Mourmelon: 337
Mousson Hill: 272-73, 275
Mouterhouse: 346, 365, 439, 442
Moyland: 402-03, 408
Moyen: 238
Moyenmoutier: 333
Moyenvic: 284, 287, 320
Mozambique Channel: 54, 57
Mozdok: 53, 81
Mozhaisk: 16
Mozyr: 161-62
Mozzagrogna: 150
Msus: 19-20
Mt. Alava: 379
Mt. Alifan: 235
Mt. Alutom: 238
Mt. Austen: 48-49, 56, 61, 66, 75-78, 82, 88
Mt. Badian: 339
Mt. Balidbiran: 449
Mt. Banahao: 517
Mt. Barrigada: 241-44
Mt. Batulao: 390
Mt. Baytangan: 443, 445, 460
Mt. Bermodo: 421
Mt. Bijang: 435-36, 443, 445
Mt. Binicayan: 532-35
Mt. Cabungaan: 349-50, 352
Mt. Calugong: 482
Mt. Capisan: 438, 452
Mt. Cariliao: 390
Mt. Caumes: 253
Mt. Caymayuman: 445-46, 448
Mt. Cenis: 471, 473
Mt. Chachao: 235, 238
Mt. Coudon: 253
Mt. Daho: 501, 512
Mt. Dalaga: 499
Mt. Etna: 120-21, 126, 128
Mt. Faron: 254
Mt. Haruna: 530-31
Mt. Isarog: 529-30
Mt. Lasso: 237
Mt. Macolod: 445-46, 448, 450-53, 455, 460-61, 464-65, 471, 490, 493, 503, 505, 507, 510
Mt. Magabaag: 430-31, 433
Mt. Malepunyo: 469, 473, 476, 478, 480, 482, 484, 488, 490, 493, 497, 499, 511, 517, 523, 525
Mt. Mataasna Bundoc: 482, 488, 493, 499, 501, 505, 507, 511, 513, 517, 520, 522
Mt. Mataba: 413-14, 416, 431, 438, 450, 457, 460-61, 463-64, 475, 477, 482, 484, 486, 501, 503, 510

Mt. Minoro: 335
Mt. Mirador: 511, 513, 515, 517, 519
Mt. Montalban: 471
Mt. Myoko: 439, 442, 448-49, 453, 460, 463, 465, 467, 484, 486, 490, 493, 503, 505, 509-10, 515, 520, 522
Mt. Nafutan: 217-18
Mt. Natib: 15, 408
Mt. Oro: 419, 477 505
Mt. Pacawagan: 413-14, 416-17, 431, 477 503, 505, 507, 510-11, 513, 517, 520, 525, 527, 529, 533-34, 538
Mt. Petosukara: 225
Mt. Pinatubo: 440, 484, 497
Mt. Popa: 34, 507
Mt. Pulungbatu: 462
Mt. Saksin: 214, 225
Mt. St. Jean: 288, 298
Mt. Samat: 19, 31-32
Mt. Santa Rosa: 242-43, 245
Mt. Sapia: 59
Mt. Sembrano: 471
Mt. Silanganan: 16
Mt. Suribachi: 407-09, 411-13, 418
Mt. Tambu: 121, 129
Mt. Tanauan: 443, 445-46, 448-50
Mt. Tapotchau: 216-20, 222
Mt. Tenjo: 238
Mt. Thabor: 419
Mt. Tipo Pale: 216, 218-20, 222
Mt. Toulon: 272-73, 298
Mt. Vesuvius: 138
Mt. Yabang: 448
Muar: 14-17
Muar River: 15
Muara Island: 545-46
Mubo: 46, 53, 83, 90-91, 98, 106, 114-15, 117-18
Muchhausen: 422
Muda River: 6
Mudburch River: 313
Mueddersheim: 418
Mueggenhausen: 425
Muehl River: 528
Muehlacker: 477
Muehlberg: 472
Muehldorf: 528
Muehlen: 517
Muehlhausen: 481, 485, 521
Muehlheim: 455
Mueldorf: 465
Muelhausen: 421
Muelheim: 420, 431, 443-44
Muelldorf: 446
Muellendorf: 332-33, 344 355
Mueller, Maj. Gen. Paul J.: 279, 282, 307
Muenchberg: 494
Muendersbach: 454
Muensingen: 513-14
Muenster: 466, 468, 470, 472, 476, 497
Muenster Plain: 466
Muensterbusch: 278, 280-82, 284
Muentz: 412
Muenzenberg: 459
Muenzingen: 335
Muerlenbach: 428
Muerringen: 386-87
Muesse: 474
Muetzenich: 389

Mugford: 48
Muhlhausen: 383, 465, 470, 472, 474-75, 477, 479
Muhlheim: 511
Muids: 257
Mukacevo: 312
Mulazzano: 276
Mulcahy, Brig. Gen. Francis P. (USMC): 127
Mulde River: 492, 494, 496, 498, 500, 502, 508, 510, 514-15, 522, 524, 526
Muldenau: 418
Mulheim: 487
Mulhouse: 332-34, 336, 395
Munassib: 61
Munchen-Gladbach: 416, 418, 420, 422
Munda Point: 82, 97, 110, 113-29, 139, 156
Munda Trail: 116-18, 121
Munda-Bairoko Occupation Force: 116
Mundenheim: 448
Munich: 509, 512, 519, 521, 523-24, 526
Munoz: 388, 390-91, 393-96
Munster: 331, 334
Munstereiffel: 429
Muntzenheim: 386-87
Munzingen: 406
Murakumo: 58-59
Murg River: 488
Murnau: 525
Murphy, Robert: 60
Murr River: 503, 505
Murrhardt: 505
Musa River: 59-60
Musashino aircraft plant: 370, 425
Mu-se: 379, 386
Musita Island: 75, 77-79
MUSKET: 115. *See also* Taranto.
Musket block (New Guinea): 81-85
Mussau Island: 182
Mussolini, Benito: 88
  appeal to Italians: 120
  execution of: 521
  fall of: 122
Mussolini Canal: 164-65, 167, 177, 196
Mussomeli: 121
Mustert: 443
Musweiler: 432
Mutcho Point: 224
Mutterstadt: 447-48
Muxerath: 411
Myawadi: 16
Myebon: 372
Myebon Peninsula: 372-73, 378, 380
Myers, Brig. Gen. Donald J.: 262
Myhl: 415
Myingan: 450
Myingun: 505
Myinmu: 381, 401
Myitkyina conference on air organization: 375
  fall of: 36-38
  recovery of: 61-62, 64, 71, 91, 93, 145, 170, 175, 185-90, 193-201, 204, 207, 209-11, 213-14, 219-21, 223, 226, 229-31, 234, 236-39, 242 255, 266, 270, 274, 291, 293, 297, 304, 354, 375, 379, 382

[INDEX]   [627]

Myitson: 388-89, 397, 399
Myitta: 15
Myohaung: 384, 387
Myola: 58
Myotha: 436
Myothit: 314, 326
Mytilene (Lesbos) Island: 292

Naa Island: 150
Naab River: 510, 512, 514
Naaf River: 178, 290, 367
Nabburg: 510
Nachtmanderscheid: 381-82
Nackenheim: 449
Nadrin: 373
Nadzab: 131-33, 135-36, 154
Nafutan Point: 213-20
Naga: 6-7
Naga Trail: 168
Nagasaki: 550
Nago: 480
Nagold: 500
Nagold River: 496, 498
Nagoya :34
Naguilian: 443, 447, 455, 457, 482, 484, 546-47
Nagumo, Vice Adm. Chuichi: 39
Naha: 536, 540-44
Naha Inlet: 543
Nahe River: 439-46, 481
Naiden, Brig. Gen. Earl L.: 43
Nakagusuku Bay: 469
Nakama: 519
Nalbach: 444
Nalchik: 61, 77, 82
Nalimbiu River: 63-64
Nalut: 94
Nam Kawng Chaung: 183
Nambalan: 378
Namber: 225, 229-30
Nambyu Stream: 178-79
Namely: 444
Namhkam: 293, 342, 345, 353, 368, 371, 375-78
Namhpakka: 371, 376-79, 384-85
Namkwi: 193, 195
Namkwi River: 193, 195
Namkwin: 197
Namma: 286, 304, 311
Namur: 263-64, 363
Namur (Camouflage) Island. *See* Roi-Namur Islands.
Namyung: 391
Nan Hill (Leyte): 311
Nan Hill (Okinawa): 533-35
Nancy: 263, 267-70, 272-73, 275, 277-78, 280, 289
Nangis: 259
Nanning: 336, 541, 545
Nanod: 512-13
Nanomea Island: 128, 130, 132
Nanpo Shoto. *See* Volcano Islands.
Nantes: 245-47
Nanyaseik: 200
Napapo: 73, 75-76, 78
Napier: 11
Napilas: 484
Naples: 72, 115, 119, 121-23, 127, 129-40, 147, 163, 171, 187, 210, 224, 226, 248, 528
Naples-Foggia Campaign: 128-63

Narbefontaine: 336
Naranjo Island: 415
Narew River: 246, 272, 374
Narni: 209
Naro: 118
Narva: 168, 171, 237
Narva River: 170-71
Nashville: 351
Nasingen: 411
Naso: 126
Nassandres: 255
Nassau: 456
Nassau Bay: 114-17, 120
Nassereith: 530
Nassig: 463
Nastatten: 459
Nasugbu: 372, 379, 381, 385, 389
Natamo: 175
Nate Road (Kwajalein): 169
Nathan Road (Kwajalein): 169
National Military Advisory Council, China: 146, 246
National Redoubt (Germany): 520
Natmauk: 33
Natsugumo: 58-59
Nattenheim: 416-17
Natunga: 61-62, 65-67
Naubum: 188
Nauheim: 451
Naumberg: 487, 489 491
Naumburg: 466, 470
Nauplia: 298
Naurath: 431
Nauro: 54
Nauro Peninsula: 130-31
Nauru Island: 3, 121, 136-39, 147
Nautilus: 40, 148
Naval Coastal Frontiers, U.S.: 10, 22
Naval Construction Battalions: 63, 71
  in Admiralties: 187
  authorized: 9
  on Ellice Islands: 130
  in Solomons: 156
  6th: 53, 57
  18th: 74
  19th: 72
Naval District, 17th: 186
Naval forces, Allied. 22. *See also* Royal Navy; Navy, United States.
Naviglio Canal: 351-53, 356-58, 364, 366
Navy, United States. *See also* Fleets; Task Forces, Navy; United States Fleet.
  air units withdrawn from P.I.: 3, 6
  controls ANZAC area: 20
  coastal frontiers redesignated: 22
  Construction Battalions authorized: 9
  death of Knox: 189
  Europe forces headed by Stark: 28
  Forrestal appointed Secretary: 191
  in ground defense of Bataan: 13, 17-19
  King appointed CinC of Fleet and CNO: 7, 28
  Pacific forces headed by Nimitz: 472
  Pacific forces redesignated: 541
  Pearl Harbor warship losses: 3
  WAVES established: 47
Nawngmi Stream: 190

Ndeni: 57-58, 60
Ndrilo Island: 184
Nebra: 48
Neckar River: 459, 461, 463 ,66, 471, 473, 475, 477, 481, 500, 503, 505, 509, 513-14
Neckargemund: 465
Neckargartach: 473, 475
Neder Rijn (Lower Rhine) River: 276, 281, 284, 286-88, 342, 474
Nederweert: 313-16
Nederweert-Wessem Canal: 287, 315-16, 325
Needle Rock: 519
Neesen: 476
Nefaar: 189
Neffe: 365, 369
Neffel River: 4 115, 417-18
Negritos: 464, 497, 506, 510
Negros Island: 34, 05, 419, 430 452-53, 460-61, 464-65, 467, 469, 471, 473, 476, 480, 482, 484, 486, 488, 493, 497, 499, 501, 503, 506-08, 510, 517, 519-20, 522-23, 525, 527, 529-34, 536, 538, 540, 542-43, 547-48
Negros Occidental Province: 452, 460-61, 519, 522, 527, 529, 533-34, 536, 538, 540, 543
Negros Oriental Province: 430, 517, 519, 522, 527, 529-34, 542, 548
Neheim: 485, 487
Néhou: 211, 225
Neidenbach: 426
Neidhausen: 385
Neidingen: 386
Neilson Field: 4, 401
Neisse River: 498, 505
Nelben: 491
Nelson: 138
Nelson, Donald M.: 246-47, 263-65
Nelson, Maj. Gen. Frederick L.: 160
Nemi: 199, 201
Nemmenich: 422
Nennig: 334, 338, 375, 380-82
Neosho: 37
NEPTUNE: 168, 187. *See also* Normandy Campaign, landing phase.
Nero Point: 169
Neschen: 449
Nesselbach: 496
Netherlands operations in: 265-517. *See also* Western Europe.
  surrender of German forces in: 530
  U.S. air operations begin: 44
Netherlands Air Force, in Borneo: 6
Netherlands Army
  in Borneo: 549
  Royal Netherlands Brigade: 259, 266
Netherlands District (Br.): 468, 493
Netherlands East Indies
  ABDA directive for defense of: 11
  Allied air reinforcement: 6, 18
  casualty summaries: 295
  enemy landings: 14, 17-18
  fall of: 11-46
  government moves to Bandoeng: 27
  Malaya air force moved to: 20
  recovery of: 193, 233, 235-36, 249, 253-54, 261-64, 269-71, 274,

Netherlands East Indies—Continued
  recover of—Continued
    276-77, 279, 281-83, 286-87, 291, 295, 297, 302, 327, 331-32, 527, 545-47, 549-50
  SWPA control of: 30
Netphen: 468, 470, 472, 474
Netterden: 460
Nettuno: 164, 170-71. *See also* Anzio Campaign.
Neu Astenberg: 468, 470
Neu Ulm: 516, 518
Neuberg: 496
Neubourg: 383
Neudorf: 461
Neuenburg: 486, 511-12
Neuendorf: 398
Neuenkirchen: 464, 468
Neuenrade: 489, 494
Neuenstadt: 492
Neuenstein: 417, 490, 492
Neuerburg, 411, 413
Neuf-Brisach: 343, 389-93, 395
Neufchâteau, Belgium: 357-60, 365, 380
Neufchâteau, France: 268-70, 272
Neufchef: 266
Neufelden: 528-29
Neuffen: 513
Neuhaus: 468, 470, 506, 528-29, 531
Neuheilenbach: 424
Neuhof: 388, 390, 463, 487
Neuhoffen: 365
Neukirchen: 425, 446, 515, 522
Neumarkt, eastern Germany: 401
Neumarkt, western Germany: 507-08, 511-12, 531
Neumuhl: 458
Neundorf: 381-82
Neunhoffen: 442
Neunkirchen: 447
Neuoetting: 528-29
Neupfotz: 451
Neurath: 408, 420, 422
Neuss: 411, 416, 418, 420, 462, 466
Neustadt: 447 ,469, 477, 479, 485, 487, 490, 492, 496, 498, 518-19
Neustettin: 417
Neustrassburg: 424
Neuviller-sur-Moselle: 268
Neuwied: 448, 452
Neville: 375
Nevinnomyssk: 48
New Bosoboso: 448, 450-51, 453, 461. *See also* Bosoboso River and Valley
New Bosoboso River: 448
New Britain Island
  air offensive against: 140, 143-47, 155-56, 174
  Allied assault on: 139, 141, 143-47, 149, 151-56, 159-63, 166, 172-73, 175-76, 179-79, 181, 183, 198, 190
  armor actions on: 159-60, 163
  enemy air attacks on: 12, 16-17
  enemy landings on: 17
  JCS directive on: 44
  MacArthur proposed offensive: 43
  naval actions: 144, 146

New Britain Island—Continued
  plans for: 43-45, 92, 96-98, 101, 106, 108, 118, 136, 139, 10, 143, 151, 154
New Caledonia, as staging area: 26-28, 155, 322
New Delhi
  conference on Burma recovery: 90
  SEAC removed from: 187
NEW GALAHAD: 209, 221, 237. *See also* Long Range Penetration Groups.
New Georgia campaign: 113-36, 179
  air and naval actions: 72, 78, 97, 110, 115-18, 122, 125, 127-29, 138-39
  armor support: 119, 123, 135
  enemy move from Guadalcanal to: 82, 84
  Kolombangara naval battle: 118
  Kula Gulf naval battles: 116, 118
  supply situation: 117-18
  Vella Gulf naval battles: 125, 139, 363,
New Georgia Air Command: 127
New Georgia Attack Force: 119
New Georgia Occupation Force: 113, 116, 119, 126
New Guinea Campaign: 88-364, 536
  advance base established: 49
  air and naval actions: 51-52, 67-68, 70-74 77-78, 82-83, 90-91, 96, 104, 110, 117, 125-31, 135, 37, 147, 159, 161, 164, 173, 176-77, 180-81, 184-85, 187-91, 193, 197-98, 202, 205-06, 209, 211-12, 215-16, 220, 222-23, 225, 227, 230, 232, 235-36, 241, 247, 251, 256, 262, 267
  air supply: 74
  airborne operations: 131, 223-24
  Allied air attacks on shipping: 46-47
  Allied armor support: 74-79, 82, 84, 147, 196, 198, 200, 205, 215, 221
  Allied reinforcements: 39, 56, 58-59 63-66, 69-70, 72-76, 78-79, 85, 89, 91, 95-96 129, 131-32, 161, 163, 188, 198, 200, 202, 206, 208-10, 212-13, 220, 223, 229, 234, 247
  Australians take control: 342
  Blarney commands Allied forces: 56
  casualty summaries: 81, 87, 190, 195, 202, 216, 223, 238, 240, 253, 256, 260
  Eichelberger takes command: 71-72
  enemy air attacks: 17, 21, 27-28 .
  enemy armor support: 2 11
  enemy ground offensives: 17, 25, 31, 47
  enemy landings: 17, 25, 31
  enemy reinforcements: 49-53, 68, 71, 74, 77, 82, 96, 141, 178, 151
  first Army troops arrive: 55
  flame throwers: 73
  JCS directive on: 44
  MacArthur proposed to head offensive: 43
  naval attacks on enemy shipping: 46
  New Guinea Force controls all units: 48
  Papua Campaign: 46-87

New Guinea Campaign—Continued
  plans for offensive: 54, 57, 63, 92, 96-98, 101, 106, 108, 152-53, 155, 176, 178-80, 189-91, 201, 211, 214-15, 227, 230
  staging area for Morotai: 261-64, 269
  staging area for P.I.: 302
  supply situations: 72-74, 188-89, 201, 204-05, 217
  SWPA control of: 30
New Guinea Volunteer Reserve (Aus.): 12, 38
New Hebrides, as staging area: 29, 50, 53-55, 57, 61, 141, 145-46
New Ireland campaign air and naval actions: 149, 159-60, 162, 174-75
  Allied assault: 129, 155-56, 159-60, 162, 172, 174-75, 178, 180, 182
  Cape St. George naval battle: 149
  enemy air attacks on: 16-17
  enemy landings: 17
  JCS directive on: 44
  offensive plan for: 43-45 92, 96-98 101, 106, 108, 155
New Strip (New Guinea): 69-72, 76
NEW YORK: 453-54
New Zealand, U.S. troops arrive: 39, 41
New Zealand Army units
  Corps, New Zealand: 99-101, 169, 171-75, 180-83
  Divisions
    2d: 50, 53, 61, 63-66, 74-76, 84, 96, 99, 102-03, 105, 140, 150-51, 153, 156, 169, 174, 180, 183, 197-98, 207, 227-28, 230-31, 234-38, 240, 247, 250, 252, 268, 285, 288, 301-04, 306, 309, 338, 352-54, 357, 430, 484, 486, 492, 495, 497, 501, 503, 507, 513, 515, 518, 522-23, 525, 527-28
    3d: 134-35, 140, 142-43, 146, 172-75
  Brigades
    6th: 46
    8th: 134, 140, 142, 146
    14th: 135
Newel: 139, 154, 229, 419
Ney: 439
Nezhin: 135
Ngahgahtawng: 183
Ngajatzup: 144
Ngakyedauk Pass: 172, 175, 177
Ngam Ga: 177-78
Ngao Ga: 191
Ngarekeukl: 286
Ngazun: 412
Ngesebus Island: 226, 290-91
Ngulu Island: 184, 305
Nhpum Ga: 183-85, 196
Nicastro: 132-33
Nice: 249, 259
Nichols Field: 4-5, 395-96, 398-402
Nicholson, Brig. C. G. G. (Br.): 94-95
Nicosia: 121-25
Nida River: 374
Nidda: 461
Nideggen: 394, 398, 215
Nied Allemande Rive: 331
Nied Française River: 23-24, 327-29

[INDEX]   [629]

Nied River: 324, 329-30, 332, 336, 341
Niedaltdorf: 341
Nieder Bettingen: 427
Nieder Breisig: 433 435
Nieder Breitbach: 449
Nieder Dollendorf: 442
Nieder Emmel: 443
Nieder Emmels: 380
Nieder Erlenbach: 459
Nieder Eschbach: 459
Nieder Fell: 438, 440
Nieder Gailbach: 355
Nieder Gandern: 481
Nieder Gebraching: 517
Nieder Geckler: 409-10
Nieder Gladbach: 459, 461
Nieder Gondershausen: 439
Nieder Heimbach: 443
Nieder Hersdorf: 424
Nieder Jossa: 465
Nieder Kastenholz: 427
Nieder Lauch: 421
Nieder Losheim: 440
Nieder Mehlen: 398
Nieder Mendig: 441-42
Nieder Pierscheid: 411
Nieder Pruem: 399-400, 421-22
Nieder Schlettenbach: 445-46
Nieder Seemen: 463, 465
Nieder Stedem: 414
Nieder Uttfeld: 406-07
Nieder Viebach: 526
Nieder Vorschutz: 465
Nieder Winkel: 434
Nieder Zissen: 433
Niederau: 411-12
Niederaual: 463
Niederaussem: 420
Niederbach: 427
Niederberg: 420, 422
Niederbronn: 347-48, 442
Niederbruch: 422
Niedergegen: 406
Niederhone: 475, 477
Niederkail: 429
Niederkyll: 427
Niedermerz: 331
Niedermodern: 380
Niedernhausen: 456
Niederpleis: 446
Niederrad: 454-55
Niederroeblingen: 489
Niederroedern: 351
Niederschaeffolsheim :340
Niederschlettenbach: 443
Niederselters: 461
Niedersfeld: 472
Niederspay: 442
Niedersteinbach: 442
Niederstetten: 485
Niederwalgern: 458
Niederwampach: 374-75
Niederweiler: 417
Niederweis: 416
Niederzeuzheim: 456.
Niederzier: 410-11
Nieffern: 383
Niehl: 408, 427
Niel: 398
Niemen River: 300

Nienburg: 480, 489
Nierfeld: 426
Niers Canal: 418, 420
Niers River: 399 421
Niersbach: 431
Nierstein: 447
Nieukerk: 420
Nieuport: 266
Nievenhein: 425
Nigia River: 188-89, 207, 250
Nijmegen: 276, 278-79, 281-82, 289-90, 292, 321, 353, 356, 396, 398, 468, 474
Nikolaev: 153, 184
Nikopol: 142, 171
Nile River Delta: 43, 50
Nimes: 259
Nimitz, Adm. Chester W.: 60, 81, 102, 314
  CINCPOA: 30
  commands all Navy forces in Pacific: 472
  directives on recovery of Gilberts and Nauru: 121, 137
  inspects Midway defenses: 36
  JCS directives on Formosa and Mindanao: 180, 209, 224, 230, 235, 237
  orders offensive in Solomons: 45
  plans for New Guinea: 181
  plans for occupying Japan: 546
  plans for Pacific offensive: 139, 162, 211, 224, 230, 235, 237
  plans for recovery of Palaus: 226, 230
  plans for recovery of P.I.: 266, 294, 340
  plans for seizure of Volcanos: 297, 299 337, 385
  role in Japanese surrender: 550
  succeeds Kimmel: 6
Nims River: 413-14, 416-17, 419, 421-122, 424
Ningbyen: 175
Ningru Ga: 163
Ninni Island: 167-68
Ninth War Area, China: 208-09, 341
Niroemoar Island: 194
Nis: 300, 304, 324
Niscemi: 118- 19
Nisei troops. See Infantry Battalions (Separate), 100th; Infantry Regiments, 442d.
Nishi: 08, 421, 423
Nishibaru: 510, 512-13
Nishibaru Ridge: 506, 508, 510, 512, 515
Nissan Island: 173
Nister River: 454
Nittel: 408, 414
Nitra: 465
Nitra River: 463
Niumen Creek: 207, 240-43
Nob Pier: 169
Noble, Brig. Gen. Alfred H. (USMC): 182
Noble, Rear Adm. Albert G.: 501
Nocera: 133, 137-38
Nocher: 377
Nochern: 454
Nodake: 474

Noemfoor Island: 201-02, 206, 211, 214-17, 220-25, 228-30, 232, 235-36 246, 249 251, 255 257,260, 262, 264, 267
Noerde: 464
Noerdershausen: 438
Noertrange: 380
Noethen: 427
Nofilia: 76
Nogent-sur-Seine: 256
Nomeny: 277, 292, 320-21
Nompatelize: 315, 317
Nonancourt: 252-53
Nonhigny: 328
Nonnenweier: 498
Nonnweiler: 440
Nora Road (Kwajalein): 168-69
Nordborchen: 462, 464
Norddorf: 472
Nordenau: 474
Nordhausen: 483, 485, 487, 489, 491
Nordheim: 481
NORDWIND: 365. See also Armies, Seventh. Norfolk House (London): 116, 164
Normandy Campaign: 203-35
  air attack phase: 33, 39, 42, 49, 114, 161, 179, 183, 186-87, 199, 191, 195, 197, 203, 225-26, 232
  airborne operations: 164, 203-04
  amphibious plan issued: 168
  artificial moonlight employed: 231
  Battle of the Hedgerows: 223-32
  CCS approves BOLERO: 33
  CCS establishes staff structure: 106
  code names defined: 168
  conferences on air support: 39, 42, 46, 49
  contact with Seventh Army: 267
  D-Day determination: 129, 164, 167, 172, 183, 191, 202
  Eisenhower commands Allied forces 152, 156, 163, 203
  Italy offensive in support of: 187
  landing craft allocation: 164, 172
  landing phase: 199-201, 203-04, 216-27
  Marshall-Hopkins-King conferences: 32, 46
  naval attack phase: 189, 203, 218
  planning phase: 30, 32-33, 39, 42, 49, 106, 112, 129, 150, 164, 167-68, 172, 179, 183, 187, 189, 191, 202
  stabilization phase: 227-35
  U.K. accepts BOLERO plan: 33
North Africa, military mission to: 8, 21, 42
North African Air Force: 109, 113-15, 119, 124, 130, 140-41
North African Theater of Operations. See also Northwest Africa campaign.
  activated under Eisenhower: 91
  air organization: 155-56
  AMET, merger with: 419
  Devers heads: 161
  Germany-to-England, first shuttle raid: 114
  McNarney succeeds Devers: 309

North Africa Theater of Operations—Continued
  designated MTOUSA: 316
  SOS established: 92
  Southern France, plans for: 159
North Apennines Campaign: 267-473
North Carolina: 55
North Force, New Guinea: 229-32, 235-36, 239-40
North Gugegwe Island: 170
North Luzon Force: 8-10, 12
North Pacific, control by POA: 30
North Pacific Force: 48, 81, 102, 111, 135
North Sea: 449
Northampton: 71
Northeim: 483
Northern Assault Force, Salerno: 132
Northern Attack Force, Gilberts: 143-44, 147
Northern Attack Force, Marshalls: 167
Northern Attack Force (TF 53): 467
Northern Attack Group, French Morocco: 65
Northern Combat Area Command: 168, 170, 173-98, 200-201, 204, 207, 210-11, 213-14, 216, 219-21, 223, 226, 229-31, 234, 236-37, 239, 242, 244, 257, 274, 286, 293, 297, 304, 307, 311, 313-14, 318-19, 322-23, 326-28, 333, 337-39, 341-42, 345-48, 351-54, 358-59, 362-64, 366-69, 371-72, 375-78, 380-92, 397, 399, 402, 405-06, 430, 434, 438, 441, 446, 463, 467
Northern France Campaign: 235-71
  air support of: 236, 240, 244-45, 260
  breakout phase: 247-55
  pursuit phase: 259-65
  supply situation: 256-58, 260-62, 265
Northern Ireland, U.S. troops arrive in: 14, 19
Northern Landing Force, Attu: 109-12
Northern Landing Force, Marshalls: 167-68, 170-71
Northern Landing Force, New Georgia: 115, 126-29, 131, 140, 143, 146
Northern Landing Group, New Georgia 116
Northern Solomons Campaign: 95-332
Northern Troops and Landing Force, Marianas: 212, 227
Northwest Africa campaign. *See also* Algiers; Tunisia.
  air support of. *See* Air Forces, Twelfth; North African Air Force; Northwest African Allied Air Force. Algeria-French Morocco Campaign: 64-66
  AFHQ activated: 55
  attacks on shipping: 64-66, 73, 75
  civil government restored: 98
  CCS agrees upon command structure: 46
  convoy departures for: 59-61, 64
  Darlan orders cease fire: 66
  D-Day determination: 56
  decision on landing sites: 53

Northwest Africa Campaign—Continued
  decision to seize: 14, 42
  directive to Eisenhower: 50
  Egypt-Libya Campaign: 41-92
  Eighth Air Force diverted from: 33
  Eisenhower as commander: 48, 55
  outline plan issued: 56
  Stilwell proposed as commander: 14
  Tunisia Campaign: 66-110
  U.S.-French conference on: 60
  warship departures for: 61, 64
Northwest African Air Forces, activated: 93, 96
Northwest Sea Frontier: 186
Northwestern France. *See* Normandy Campaign; Northern France Campaign.
Nortons Knob: 437, 439, 446, 455, 457
Norway
  first U.S. assault on: 122
  German island bases raided: g
  operations in: g, 122, 308, 311, 326, 334
  Quisling establishes government: 21
Norzagaray: 390
Nossoncourt: 315
Nostorf: 526
Noswendel: 440
Nosy Bé Island: 54
Nothberg: 333
Nothweiler: 354
Notre Dame de Cenilly: 237
Notre Dame de la Garde: 257
Notre Dame d'Elle: 237, 242
Notscheid: 437-39
Nouméa: 50
Novaliches: 407, 503
Noveant: 264-65, 267
Novgorod: 163, 170
Novgorod Severski: 133, 135
Noville: 370-71, 374
Novo Belitsa: 140
Novocherkassk: 47, 92
Novograd Volyinsk: 159
Novorossisk: 48, 52-54, 57, 83, 86-87, 89, 91-92, 135
Novosokolniki: 176
Nowy Sacz: 379
Nowy Targ: 387, 473
Noyers: 231-32, 242
Noyes, Rear Adm. Leigh: 45, 47
Noyon: 261
Nueha River: 88-89
Nuembrecht: 482, 485
Nuetterden: 398
Nugent, Brig. Gen Richard E.: 271
Nugu Point: 89
Nukufetau: 129-30, 139
Numa Numa Trail: 144, 146, 157
Number 3 airstrip, New Guinea: 52
Numundo Plantation: 181
Nunkirchen: 442
Nure River: 518
Nuremberg: 184, 483, 487, 492, 494, 496, 498, 500, 502, 504, 507, 508-09, 513, 521, 530
Nusbaum: 405-07
Nutheim: 270
Nuttlar: 478
Nyaparake: 189-90, 192-93, 195
Nyaparake Force: 190

Nyaunglebin: 26
Nyaungu: 402, 408-09
Nyebon: 94
Nyrsko: 521-22

Oahu, Japanese attack on: 27
Oak Hill (Okinawa): 542
OB WEST. *See* Commander in Chief, West.
Ober Beisheim: 463
Ober Bettingen: 427
Ober Bieber: 451
Ober Breisig: 435
Ober Buchfeld: 511
Ober Dollendorf: 442
Ober Drees: 427
Ober Ehe: 429
Ober Eisenbach: 409-10
Ober Elspe: 485
Ober Elvenich: 422
Ober Emmels: 380
Ober Felden: 500
Ober Fleckenberg: 476
Ober Forstbach: 270
Ober Gartzem: 426
Ober Geckler: 410-11
Ober Gladbach: 459, 461
Ober Gondershausen: 439
Ober Henneborn: 483
Ober Hersdorf: 424
Ober Kappel: 524
Ober Kessach: 475
Ober Lahnstein: 452, 454
Ober Landenbeck: 483
Ober Lauch: 421
Ober Liblar: 424
Ober Mehlen: 396-97
Ober Meiser: 472
Ober Morscholz: 440
Ober Olmer Wald: 445
Ober Otterbach: 445
Ober Pierscheid: 411
Ober Ramstadt: 451
Ober Rot: 503
Ober Sorpe: 478
Ober Spiesheim: 485
Ober Stadtfeld: 428
Ober Stedem: 414
Ober Steinbach: 452
Ober Uttfeld: 406-07
Ober Wichterich: 422
Ober Windhagen: 442
Ober Winkel: 434 492
Ober Wolfert: 427
Ober Wurzbach: 446
Oberaasheim: 395
Oberau: 523
Oberbronn: 441
Oberbruegge: 489
Obercassel: 444
Oberembt: 414
Oberentzen: 393, 395
Oberesch: 336
Oberfeulen: 357
Obergailbach: 352
Obergartzem: 426
Obergeich: 349
Oberhausen: 386, 427, 440
Oberhof: 470, 477, 479, 483
Oberhoffen: 388-93, 395-402, 419, 439

[INDEX]

Oberhundem: 478
Oberkail: 426, 428
Oberkassel: 420, 422
Oberkirch: 500
Oberkirchen: 470, 472, 474, 476, 478
Oberkossa: 494
Oberleuken: 335-36, 338, 406
Oberlind: 490
Obermaubach: 358, 360-61, 363
Obermuhlthal: 370, 372, 376
Obernai: 338
Obernau: 459
Obernbreit: 473, 477
Oberndorf: 517
Obernkirchen: 482
Oberode: 479
Oberpleis: 445
Oberroeblingen: 489
Obersachswerfen: 487
Obersdorf: 489, 528
Obersehr: 417, 419
Obersgegen: 409
Oberspay: 44
Obersteinbach: 365
Obertal: 503
Obertiefenbach: 454
Obervellmar: 472
Oberwampach: 376-77, 379
Oberweiler: 419
Oberweis: 413
Oberwesel: 441, 443, 454
Oberwiehl: 482
Oberzenn: 509
Oberzier: 411-12
Object Hill (Luzon): 400, 406
Oboe Hill (Okinawa): 540-42
Obojan sector: 117
Obringhausen: 480
Observation Hill (New Guinea): 117
Observatory Hill (Germany): 302-03, 305
Obspringen: 380
Ocean Islands: 3
Ochakov: 184
Ochsenfurt: 465, 469, 471, 473, 477
Ochtendung: 429
Ockfen: 409-11, 413-14, 416-17
Ocoy River: 519, 529
OCTAGON Conference: 269, 271, 274, 280, 285, 290
Octeville: 217-19
Oda, Maj. Gen. Kensaku: 74, 76, 86
O'Daniel, Maj. Gen. John W.: 173
Odeigne: 367-68
Odekoven: 430
Odenbach: 444
Odendorf: 426
Odenhausen: 458
Odenwald: 459
Oder River: 382-84, 389, 394-95, 400, 425, 435, 438, 446, 467, 498, 505, 518
Odessa: 184, 186
Odheim: 481, 488
Odingen: 485
Odlumon: 529, 533-34
Odon River: 219-21, 224, 228, 231-32
Odrimont: 367
Oedt: 418, 420
Oehringen: 492, 494
Oels: 384

Oelsnitz: 498, 502
Oepping: 526, 528
Oerlinghausen: 466, 468, 470
Oermingen: 343
Oesel (Saarema) Island: 296, 330, 335
Oesthaven: 24
Oestringen: 469
Oeting: 404-05
Ofanto River: 137
Offenau: 475, 477, 479, 481, 483, 485
Offenbach: 455, 457
Offenburg: 496
Offendorf: 368, 376, 390, 393, 395-96
Offenthal: 455
Office of Strategic Services units: 139, 545-46
Offingen: 516
Offwiller: 381
Ognon River: 266
Ohe River: 515
Ohlau: 395
Ohr: 474 476
Ohrdorf: 486
Ohrdruf: 473, 477
Oidtweiler: 298, 327
Oirschot: 281
Oise River: 259
Oituz Pass: 258
Oivi: 47, 62-65
Oker River: 482, 484, 486
Okinawa campaign: 462-549
  Ryukyus Campaign.
  airborne operations: 540-41
  armor actions: 488, 506, 510, 519-20, 522, 538-40, 543-46
  East China Sea naval battle: 480
  effect of seizure: 548
  enemy air and naval attacks: 456, 458, 468, 478, 480, 488, 491, 499, 512, 520, 525, 532, 540-42, 548
  psychological warfare employed: 547
  spigot mortar, first use of: 482
  underwater demolition teams: 453, 462, 493
  U.S. air and naval actions: 300, 380-81, 449, 453, 456, 462, 464, 467, 471, 480, 482, 486, 493, 495, 497, 499, 506, 517, 525, 538, 540-41, 544-46, 548,
Okino Daito: 420
Oktwin: 511
Old Rossum: 181
Old Spanish Trail: 428, 434, 436, 441, 453, 548
Old Strip (New Guinea): 77-78, 81
Oldenburg: 480, 484, 495, 501
Oldendorf, Rear Adm. Jesse B.: 210
Oleana: 115
Olef River: 393-94, 424
Oleron Island: 525, 527
Olevsk: 159
Oliva: 453
OLIVE: 242. *See also* Gothic Line.
Oliver, Commodore G. N. (RN): 132
Oliveto: 136-37
Olk: 419
Olkenbach: 436
Ollheim: 427
Ollmuth: 426
Olmuetz: 523, 534
Olmscheid: 408, 410

Olongapo: 13, 22, 388, 403
Olpe: 482
Olsberg: 483
Olsdorf: 413
OLYMPIC: 541. *See also* Japan, preparations for invasion of.
Olzheim: 397, 400
Omaha: 254
OMAHA Beach: 203. *See also* Normandy Campaign, landing phase.
Ombrone River: 210, 214, 217
Ommersheim: 443
On Chong's Wharf (Butaritari): 148
Onaga: 517, 524 527
One-hundred-meter Hill (Okinawa): 542-43
Onaiavisi Entrance: 115
Onaiavisi Occupation Unit, New Georgia: 115
Ona-Yama Island: 542-43
Ondava River: 342-43
Ondenval: 376, 379
Ondonga: 139
Onipa River: 478
Oos: 426-27
Oosterbeek: 281-82
Oosterhout: 315
Opherten: 415
Ophoven: 416
Opladen: 495, 497
Oploo: 291
Opochka: 231
Opon airfield: 460
Oppau: 459
Oppeln: 383, 395, 449
Oppenau: 503
Oppenhausen: 438
Oppenheim: 318, 445, 447-48, 450, 452, 457, 465
Opperode: 502
Oran: 53, 64-65
Oradea: 301
Oraison: 252
Orange: 257
Orani: 403
Orani River: 14
Oranienbaum: 163
Oranienburg: 513
Orbec: 254
Orbetello: 208
Orbey: 353
Orcia River: 214-16, 218-19
Ordorf: 424
Ordzhonikidze: 64
Oregon: 42, 54
Orel: 90-91, 95-96, 99, 116-18, 120-21, 125, 128
Orenhofen: 424, 429, 431
Orete Cove: 130
Orglandes: 210
Orgon: 256
Orion: 15, 18
Orioung: 545-46
Orioung Pass: 545-46
Ork: 451
Orléans: 191, 247-51, 257, 261
Orlo River: 234
Ormoc: 316, 318-22, 326-29, 337, 341-42, 344-53, 358, 360, 363
Ormoc Bay: 334, 346-47, 349-50, 352
Ormoc Valley: 317-18, 355, 358

[632]   [INDEX]

Ormont: 414, 416, 419, 421-22
Orne River: 203, 216, 228, 231-33, 242-46
Oro Bay: 67, 74, 76-79, 88, 97, 104, 159, 176, 188, 225
Oroku Peninsula: 543-46
Oron: 324
Orote Peninsula: 235-39, 241
Orreux: 372
Orsara: 310, 312
Orsbeck: 415, 418
Orsberg: 429
Orscheid: 442
Orscholz: 379-80, 407-08, 410
Orscholz Switch Line: 330, 332, 334-36
Orsfeld: 426
Orsha: 219
Orsogna: 153, 156
Orsova: 291
Orsoy: 422, 425, 427-28, 456
Ortelsburg: 382
Ortona: 147, 152-53, 155-57
Orvieto: 204-06, 209-10
Osboy Ridge: 538-39
Osburger Hoch Wald: 438
Oscariz: 546
Oschersleben: 161
Osima: 225
Oskol: 45
Osmena, Sergio: 310
Osnabrueck: 460, 466, 468, 470, 472, 474, 501
Ospel: 317
Oss River: 290
Ossenberg: 428, 430, 432
Ossendorf: 464
Ost Buederich: 480
Ost Oennen: 476
Ostend: 266, 315-16
Osterath: 418
Osterburken: 475
Osterhagen: 487
Osterheide: 470
Osterhofen: 526
Osteria Finocchio: 201
Osterode: 487
Ostheim: 346, 381-82, 459, 469
Ostiglia: 505
Osterpai: 441
Ostroleka: 264
Ostrov: 229, 233-34
Ostrow: 384
Osweiler: 354-55, 358
Ostwig: 478
Ottbergen: 474
Otterskirchen: 522
Ottmarsheim: 397
Ottre: 369
Ottweiler: 444, 446-47
Otzenrath: 415-16
Oubourcy: 365, 375
Oudelande: 312
Oudna: 71
Oudref: 101
Oudrenne: 323-25
Oued ben Hassine: 109
Oued Zarga: 67-68, 103
Ouffet: 358
Ouistreham: 203
Oujda: 82
Ouki: 474, 482 486, 488

Ouki Hill: 508
Our River: 268-69, 353, 377-79, 381-83, 385-90, 392, 394, 396-402, 404-10
Ourthe: 380-81
Ourthe River: 359, 367, 371, 373-78
Ousseltia: 86, 88, 104
Ousseltia River and Valley: 8.6-89
Outscheid: 411
Overbruch: 451
Overhagen: 472
Overloon: 291, 293-95, 301-02
OVERLORD: 112, 114, 129, 150, 152, 156,161, 164, 168, 172, 183, 187, 199, 203, 258, 267. *See also* Normandy Campaign.
Overpelt: 267
Overton: 168
Ovruch: 147
Owen, Lt. Col. William T. (Aus.): 46
Owen Stanley Range: 43-44, 52-54, 58, 71, 131
Owl Island: 200-201, 206, 212, 215
Ozato: 545
Ozeville: 206, 208

Paan: 181 23
Pachino town and Peninsula: 118-19
Pachten: 334-46
Pacific Air Command, AAF: 22
Pacific Fleet (RN): 531
Pacific Fleet (U.S.), Nimitz Kimmel: 6
Pacific Military Conference, Washington: 97-98
Pacific Ocean Areas. *See also* Nimitz, Adm. Chester W.; Pacific theater; South Pacific theater; Southwest Pacific Area.
  absorbs part of SOPAC: 183
  control of Army units: 314
  directive on seizure of Gilberts-Nauru: 121, 137
  directive on missions: 30
  JCS directive on advance to Luzon-Formosa: 180
  Nimitz commands Navy forces: 6, 30, 472
  orders for recovery of Solomons: 45
  plans for occupation of Japan: 546
  plans for operations in New Guinea: 181
  plans for Pacific offensive: 139, 162, 221, 224, 230, 235, 237
  plans for recovery of Philippines: 266, 294 340
  plans for seizure of Formosa: 180, 209, 224, 230, 235, 237
  plans for seizure of Palaus: 226, 230
  plans for seizure of Volcanos: 297, 299 337 385
  reorganized: 183
  support for Guadalcanal: 60
Pacific theater
  air build-up: 126, 128-30, 132, 211, 224, 227, 235 282, 294
  Central Pacific Campaign: 3-152
  China as supply base for: 190, 200, 204-05, 242, 517, 536 540
  CCS establishes: 30
  controls SE Pacific area: 30-31

Pacific theater—Continued
  Eastern Mandates Campaign: 152-210
  hostilities cease: 551
  mobile air force authorized: 44
  plans for drive through to Japan: 112, 126, 129-30, 132, 135, 139, 147, 152, 162, 204, 209, 224, 230, 235, 237, 274, 294, 299
  redeployment of forces to: 528, 530, 550
  SWPA command problems: 43-44
  VJ-Day proclaimed: 551
  Western Pacific Campaign: 187-551
Pacific War Council, Allied: 23, 31
Pacijan Island: 379, 391
Pack Howitzer Battalion, 2d Separate: 174
Paderborn: 458, 460, 462, 464, 466, 468, 470
Padignon: 30
Padua: 224, 522-23
Paclasan: 368
Paco station: 400
Paernu: 285
Paestum: 132, 134, 136
Paffendorf: 415-16, 418
Pagan: 403
Pagani Valley: 133, 137
Pagbilao: 8-9
Paget, Gen. Sir Bernard (Br.): 156
Paglieta: 145
Pagny-lès-Goin: 322
Pagny-sur-Moselle: 263, 268
Pago Bay: 241
Pagsangahan River: 359
Pagsanjan: 464
Pagsanjan River: 475
Pahang: 9
Paidado Islands: 200
Paidu Pulangi: 506
Paima Shan: 509, 536
Pain de Sucre: 278, 280
Painten: 514
Pak Island: 186
Pakokku: 348, 372, 403
Pakriki: 249
Palacpalac: 378
Palaia: 232-34
Palanas River: 335, 345-46
Palatinate sector: 439,53
Palau Islands
  Allied seizure of: 264, 270, 274, 276-79, 281-83, 285-86, 288-97, 299-303, 305-08, 310-12, 317, 338-39, 342, 350
  air and naval actions: 264, 268, 270, 274, 278, 283, 286
  casualty summaries: 306, 308, 312, 338
  plans for seizure of: 179, 184, 211, 226, 230, 240, 249, 259, 263
  underwater demolition teams: 270
Palauan: 358, 366, 368
Palauig: 405
Palauru: 205-06, 233-34, 236, 238-39, 242
Palawan Island: 37, 395, 405, 415, 417, 419-21, 423, 425, 427-28, 430, 432, 442, 457, 484, 503, 512, 547, 549

[INDEX]

Palazzo: 314-15
Palazzolo: 118
Palazzuolo: 285, 286-87, 291-92
Palel: 189, 191, 416
Palembang: 8, 18, 24
Palena: 183
Palenberg: 292, 295
Palermo: 120-24
Palestrina: 201
Paliano: 201
Palimpinon: 520, 522-23, 525
Palma: 110
Palma di Montechiaro: 118
Palmersheim: 427
Palo: 307-11
Palombara Pass: 199
Palompon: 348, 356-64
Palzem: 407
Pamati: 194-95
Pampanga River: 110-11, 384, 388-89, 403, 409
Pampelonne Bay: 249
Panacan: 539
Panaon strait: 307, 315-16
Panaro River: 505, 509, 511, 513
Panay Island: 22, 33-34, 415, 419, 440-41, 443, 445-46, 448-50, 460, 547
Pandan: 4
Pandanan Island: 432, 512
Panheel: 325
Paniqui: 378
Pansfeld: 500
Panningen: 330
Pansipit River: 428
Pantabangan: 413
Pantalan River: 370
Pantangan: 401
Pantalbangan: 406, 409-10
Pantay: 442
Pantelleria Island: 109-14
Pantenburg: 432
Panther: 163. *See also* Garigliano River.
Pantingan River: 19
Paoching: 211, 481, 492, 509, 536, 544
Papa: 455
Papitalai Mission: 178, 181-82
Papua: 60
Papua Campaign: 46-87
Parachute Infantry battalions
   509th: 255
   551st: 255
Parachute Infantry Regiments
   503d: 65, 93, 131, 133, 135, 223-24, 229-30, 232, 235-36, 246, 251, 255 257, 302, 353, 357-58, 366, 368, 375, 404-06, 411-12, 415, 421, 480, 484, 493 501, 527, 533-34, 536
   504th: 164-65, 167, 184
   505th: 446
   508th: 380, 386-87, 397-99
   509th: 65-70, 72, 75, 134, 146, 164, 177, 185, 195-96
   511th: 337, 349, 352-54, 357, 389-90, 392-96, 398 434-35, 437, 445, 450-52 471, 478, 490, 497, 501, 522-23, 548
   517th: 212, 219, 254-55, 373, 389, 392, 394-95, 397-99

Paradise Valley (Saipan): 225, 227
Parai: 198-99, 201, 205
Parai Defile: 198-99, 201-02, 205, 207-08
Parakovio: 195, 199
Paramushiro Island: 117, 132
Parang: 35, 44, 453, 488, 497, 501, 503, 506, 531
Paranaque: 393-94
Pardo: 455
Parfouru-l'Eclin: 210
Parian Gate (Manila): 00
Paris: 251-58, 261, 328
Paris: 456, 458
Parker, Maj. Gen. George M., Jr.: 5, 8
Parkstein: 508
Parma: 515-16, 518
Parocchia di M. Maggiore: 351
Parmignola Canal: 492, 501
Parroy: 278
Parry Island: 174-75
Parsberg: 518
Partenkirchen: 523, 525
Partisan forces. *See* French Forces of the Interior; Guerrilla forces.
Pasananca: 436-38, 440, 442
Pasananca Reservoir: 440
Pasay: 401
Paschel: 417, 419
Pas-de-Calais: 256, 262, 268
Pasig River: 392, 394-97, 399-400, 410
Passau: 521-22, 526, 528-29
Passo Corese: 205
Pastena: 196-97
Pastina: 228-29
Pastrana: 311-13
Pasugi-Pianag: 357-58
Patani: 3
Patch, Lt. Gen. Alexander M.
   activates Americal Division: 39, 81
   CG of XI V Corps: 81
   CG of Seventh Army: 177
   commands on Guadalcanal: 73-74, 78, 82
   commands New Caledonia TF: 27-28
Paterno: 120-21, 125
Patersberg: 454
Pathfinders, use in bomber aircraft: 137, 144
Patik: 461
Patog: 464, 476, 497, 533-34
Patok: 318, 320-22
Patras: 285-86
Patrick, Brig. Gen. Edwin D.: 197-200, 215, 223
Pattensen: 486
Pattern: 334, 338, 410, 412
Patti: 126-27
Patton, Lt. Gen. George S., Jr.
   commands II Corps: 97, 100, 102, 104-05
   commands Third Army: 240, 247, 263, 286-87, 290-91, 316, 319-20, 343, 357, 442
   commands Seventh Army: 117, 119, 124, 501, 522-23, 548
   commands Western Assault Force: 65
Paustenbach: 355, 392, 394-95, 397-99
Pauli River: 523

Pauk: 385
Paulus, Field Marshal: 83
Paungde: 30-31
Paup villages: 228
Pausa: 496
Pavia: 527
Pavlograd: 94, 136
Pavuvu: 94
Pawing: 308-09
Payagyi: 26
Peabody, Capt. Maurice E., Jr.: 272,
Peabody Peak: 272
Pearl Harbor. *See also* Hawaiian Islands.
   attack on: 3
   conference on Pacific offensive: 230, 237
   Fletcher TF arrives: 39
   Spruance TF arrives: 38
Peary: 25
Peccia River: 160
Pecs: 340, 342
Pedaso: 214
Peel Marshes: 284, 287, 289-90, 292, 294, 296-97 301, 315
Peenemuende: 128
Peffingen: 405, 413
Pegau: 489, 491-92
Pegu: 24-27, 511, 523, 525, 529
Pegu Yomas: 26
Peilstein: 526, 528
Peine: 482
Peiping-Hankow railway: 187
Peirse, Air Chief Marshal Sir Richard 153
Peising: 519
Peleliu Island: 226, 268, 274, 276-79, 281-83, 285-86, 288-97, 299-303, 305-06, 311-12, 317, 338
Peleliu Island Garrison Force: 301
Peljesac Peninsula: 272
Pellingen: 416-17, 428
Peloponnesus sector: 275, 285, 298
Penablanca: 548
Penfoie: 24-25
Penadjim Point: 549
Penang Island: 4, 6
Penfeld River: 277
Penig: 494
Pensacola: 5, 8
Perak Flotilla (RN): 6
Perak River: 6-8
Percival, Lt. Gen. Sir Arthur E. (Br.) 6-7, 13-14, 23-24
   in Johore operations: 13, 18
   orders withdrawal to Singapore: 19
   surrenders Malaya forces: 24
Percy: 238-41
Perekop Isthmus: 143
Pergola: 352-54
Périers: 208-09, 224-27, 229, 231-32, 236-38
Perl: 406
Perlesreut: 515
Persano: 133-34, 136
Persecution: 182. *See also* Aitape operation.
Persecution Covering Force (New Guinea): 227-33, 236, 238, 241, 246-47, 249. *See also* Task Forces, Army, Persecution, Aitape.

Persia. *See* Iran.
Persian Corridor. *See* Persian Gulf Infantry Divisions Command; Persian Gulf Service 41st: 5, 13-16, 18-19, 21, 31
Persian Gulf Command: 141, 153, 156
Persian Gulf Service Command
 approval of plan for use: 56-57
 Connolly commands: 57, 60
 mission directive: 52
 redesignated PGC: 153
 personnel structure: 60
 operates under USAFIME: 49, 57
 Shingler commands: 50
 as supply route to USSR: 20
Persons, Maj. Gen. John C.: 233, 262, 274
Perth: 26
Pertuis: 252
Perugia: 210-14, 346
Pervomaisk: 182
Pesaro: 259-60, 262
Pescadores Islands: 367, 370, 375, 380
Pescara: 142, 207
Pescia: 277, 282, 288
Pescia River: 217-18, 221
Pesch: 415, 427
Pest: 349
Pétain, Marshal Henri-Philippe: 33
Petersau: 447
Petersroda: 504
Petit Landau: 397
Petit-Magny: 336
Petit Réderching: 349-50
Petit St. Bernard Pass: 457, 461
Petit Thier: 355, 376-77
Petite-Hettange: 321-23
Petite Langlir: 370-72
Petite Mormont: 373
Petite Tailles: 372
Petralia: 120-22
Petrignano: 221
Petsamo: 280, 303, 308
Pettoncourt: 289-90, 292
Pettstaedt: 489
Peuschen: 494
Peyrolles: 252
Pfaffenheck: 438, 440
Pfalz: 504, 512, 516
Pfatter: 519
Pfedelbach: 496
Pfeffer River: 442, 452
Pferdsfeld: 443
Pfettrach: 522
Pforzheim: 471, 475, 477, 481, 498, 503
Pfullendorf: 521
Pfullingen: 513
Pfungstadt: 451
Phalsbourg: 332-33, 335
Phantom Ridge (Italy): 192, 194
Philippine Army units
 Corps
  I: 12-25, 28, 30, 32
  II: 12-22, 24-25, 30-32
 Infantry Divisions
  1st: 12-13, 16-23, 35
  2d Philippine Constabulary: 13
  11th: 4, 7, 10-13, 19-22
  21st: 7, 9-13, 16, 18-19, 31-32
  31st: 12-13, 15-16, 18-20

Philippine Army units—Continued
 Infantry Divisions—Continued
  51st: 5, 10-11, 13-1 5, 18-20, 22, 28
  71st: 7, 9-12
  91st: 9-12, 17, 19, 22
  92d: 400
  101st: 35
  102d: 35-36
  106th: 549-50
  108th: 549-50
 Field Artillery Regiments
  51st: 10
  61st: 36
  81st: 36
  101st: 35
  102d: 35
 Infantry Regiments
  1st: 9, 13, 15, 403, 411, 417, 433
  1st Philippine Constabulary: 19
  2d: 35
  2d Philippine Constabulary: 10
  3d: 13
  11th: 20
  12th: 20
  21st: 14
  23d: 15
  32d: 15
  33d: 19, 31-32
  41st: 19, 32
  42d: 32
  43d: 32, 36
  52d: 9
  53d: 9
  61st: 35-36
  62d: 36-37
  71st: 7, 12
  72d: 12
  73d: 36
  82d: 32
  83d: 33
  92d: 16, 22
  93d: 36
  94th: 391
  102d: 35
  103d: 36
  104th: 35
  116th: 549-50
  118th: 549
  121st: 380, 446-47
 Engineer Battalion, 31st: 21
 Field Artillery Battalion, 31st: 13
 Philippine Constabulary Battalion, 1st: 20
 Philippine Constabulary, and defense of Bataan: 17, 20, 22, 32
Philippine Constabulary units. *See* Philippine Army units.
Philippine Guerrilla Forces, North Luzon: 419, 426, 447, 546
Philippine Islands
 fall of: 3-37, 41
  ABDA directive for defense of islands: 11
  aircraft moved to Australia: 6
  all elements assigned to USAFFE: 95

Philippine Islands—Continued
 fall of—Continued
  attacks on enemy shipping: 4
  Bataan Defense Force: 8, 12-13
  Corregidor as hq for USFIP: 29
  Death March: 32
  enemy air attack: 3-4
  enemy landings: 3-4
  final capitulation: 37
  first action by Australia-based planes: 7
  government moved to Corregidor: 8
  Luzon Force: 28-29, 31-32
  MacArthur controls islands after departure: 28, 30
  MacArthur controls naval forces 20
  MacArthur departs: 25, 27, 29
  MacArthur transfers to Mindanao: 28-29
  Mindanao seized by enemy: 7
  naval forces moved to Corregidor: 9
  naval forces withdrawn: 3, 6
  naval operations under Rockwell: 9
  Philippine Islands Campaign: 1-37
  PT boat operations: 17
  rations reduced: 12
  reorganization of forces: 27-28
  Service Area Command: 13, 17-18
  SWPA controls: 30
  TF South Pacific dispatched to P.I.: 5
  Visayan-Mindanao Force: 33
  Wainwright commands all forces: 29-30
  Yamashita succeeds Homma: 28
 naval battles
  Leyte Gulf: 310-12
  Philippine Sea: 212, 214-15
 recovery of: 302-549
  air actions: 244, 270, 297, 301, 304, 307-11, 315, 318-19, 322, 340, 344, 347, 350, 352-54, 356, 358, 360-61, 364, 366-70, 373, 375 379, 381, 395, 406, 408-09, 415, 417, 419, 428, 430, 434, 436-38, 441, 445-46, 448, 450, 455, 467, 469, 471, 479, 482, 484, 495, 497, 499, 501, 503, 505, 510, 513, 520, 527, 533-38, 540, 542, 544, 548
  airborne operations: 372, 379, 381, 385, 389, 390-92, 404, 410, 548
  armor actions: 310-11, 319, 376, 381, 471, 517, 540, 545-47
  artificial moonlight employed 503
  casualty summaries: 364, 389, 408, 411, 421, 423, 433, 448, 476, 503, 523, 531
  civil administration restored: 310
  enemy reinforcements: 316, 318, 321-22, 347-48, 350, 358, 368

[INDEX]

Philippine Islands—Continued
  fall of—Continued
    guerrilla activities: 356-58, 366-68, 372-73, 375, 399-400, 419, 426, 433-34, 436, 441, 443, 445-48, 453, 455, 457, 462, 469, 471, 476, 480, 482, 486, 497, 501, 503, 510, 513, 519, 522-23, 531, 535-36, 538, 540-43, 546-50
    kamikaze attacks: 347, 351, 366-68
    Leyte Campaign: 305-549
    Luzon Campaign: 353-549
    naval actions: 212, 214-15, 305-07, 310-12, 339, 351, 355, 362, 366-70, 372-73, 375, 380, 385, 403, 415, 417, 433-34, 436, 441, 443, 455, 462, 467, 469, 484, 499, 501, 535
    plans for: 95, 179, 209, 211, 224, 235, 237, 266, 274, 276, 283, 287, 291, 294, 301, 304, 315, 350
    Southern Philippines Campaign 415-549
    supply situation: 310-11, 323, 326, 332-33, 339, 342
    underwater demolition teams: 306-07 369
Philippine Islands Campaign: 1-37
Philippine Scouts: 21-22. *See also* Cavalry Regiments, 26th Philippine Scouts; Engineer Battalion, 14th Philippine Scouts; Field Artillery Regiments, 88th Philippine Scouts; Infantry Regiments, 45th and 57th Philippine Scouts.
Philippine Sea naval battle: 212, 214-15
Philippines, U.S. Forces in: 542
Philippsbourg: 365-68, 442
Philippsheim: 421, 426
Phillips, Adm. Sir Tom (RN): 4
Phillipsweiler: 414
Phyket Island: 531
Piacenza: 231, 518, 521
Pian dei Cerri: 239
Pian di Castello: 264
Piana di Caiazzo: 140
Pianoro: 499 501, 503
Piave River and Valley: 523, 525, 527
Piazza Armerina: 119-209
Pick, Brig. Gen. Lewis A.: 157, 392, 426
PICCADILLY: 178. *See also* Indian Army units, Divisions, 3d, and Brigades, 77th LRP (Chindits).
Picauville: 206
Pichon: 92, 97, 102-04
Pico: 194-96
Piedimonte: 164, 170, 195, 197
Piedimonte d'Alife: 140-41
Piedura: 344-45 347
Pier: 349-50 360
Pierrefontaine: 264
Piesbach: 444
Piesport: 435-36
Piet Hein: 25
Pietra Colora: 423, 425
Pietraperzia: 120
Pietrasanta: 279-80

PIGSTICK: 152, 160. *See also* Mayu Peninsula and River
Pikard: 342
Pikas: 310
Piket: 35
Pilar: 403, 405
Pilar River: 17-21
Pilelo Island: 154
Pili: 529
Pillsbury: 26
Pilsen (Plzen): 530, 532-33, 536
Pim: 188
Pimple Hill (Luzon): 490
Pin Chaung: 33-34
Pinamalayan: 365, 367-68, 373, 389
Pinamola: 548
Pinamopoan: 318-19, 322, 344, 358
Pinbaw: 257.
Pindale: 445
Pingka: 193, 196-97, 202, 286
Pingkian: 548
Pingsheim: 418
Pinlebu: 354
Pinnacle, The (Ie Shima): 501, 504, 506, 508, 510
Pinnacles, The, East and West (Okinawa): 508, 510
Pinsamont: 364, 367
Pinsk: 147, 230
Pintsch: 383
Pinwe: 322-23, 328, 337-38, 341
Pio: 11
Piombino: 218, 220
Piraeus: 301-02, 304
Pirmasens: 447
Pironpré: 367, 371
Piru Plantation: 129
Piryatin: 136, 201
Pisa: 162, 190, 202, 204, 210, 231, 234-35, 253, 261
Pisciatello: 304, 306
Pisek: 533
Pisignano: 309
Pistoia: 162, 204, 230, 234, 269, 279, 284, 288, 370
Pithiviers: 253
Piti Navy Yard: 235
Pitoe airfield: 274, 276, 279, 281, 286, 291
Pityilu Island: 184
Piva River: 148-49
Piva Uncle, and Piva Yoke, airstrips (Bougainville): 150, 157, 161, 179-80
Pivitsheide: 470, 472
Pizzo: 132
Plaine River: 329-31
Plana: 532
Plancher-lès-Mines: 332
Planice: 533
Planois: 300
Plaridel: 10-11, 385, 387, 389-90
Platt, Lt. Gen. Sir William (Br.): 44, 55, 57, 59, 83
Platting: 521-22, 524, 526
Plauen: 496, 498
Pleinting: 526
Pleiserhohn: 447
Plettenberg: 491
Pliesse River: 498, 502

Ploessberg: 510
Ploesti: 259
  air raids on: 41, 112, 124, 185, 234, 237 244
Plouvien: 245
Pluetscheid: 419, 421
PLUNDER: 449 *See also* Rhine River, Allied river crossing; Ruhr sector.
Po di Volano: 511
Po River and Valley air offensive against bridges: 228-29, 231
  drive to: 167, 224-520
Po Valley Campaign: 475-534
Pock, Lt. Hugh A.: 379
Podolski: 182
Pofi: 199
Poggibonsi: 226, 230-31
Poggio all'Olmo: 225
Poggio Berni: 285-86
Poggio Cavalmagra: 285
Poggio Prefetto: 271-72, 274
Poggio Renatico: 509
Poha River: 58, 62, 84-85, 87-88
Poikam: 514
Point Cruz: 57-58, 62-63, 68-69, 82, 84-86
POINTBLANK: 113, 129, 161. *See also* Combined Bomber Offensive against Europe.
Pointe d'Arceau: 525
Pointe de Corsen: 258
Pointe de Grave: 328, 496, 498, 503, 505, 507
Pointe du Hoe: 203-05
Poix: 259
Poland Combined Bomber Offensive against: 219, 236, 244
  operations in: 159, 176, 228-29, 237-39, 246, 248, 251, 264, 271-72, 279, 293, 306, 372, 374-87, 389, 403, 406, 410, 428, 435, 443, 473
  revolt against Germans: 240, 248, 271-72, 279, 293
Polch: 429
Polesella: 517
Polich: 434
Polish Army units
  Army, Second: 505
  Corps, 2: 183, 187, 189, 191-95, 197-99, 204, 212, 214-16, 221, 225, 227, 232, 233, 247, 251-63, 289, 303, 305-06, 308, 312-13, 315, 317, 319, 321, 324, 327, 329-30, 333-38, 344-45, 352-54, 358, 369, 402, 430, 435, 483, 486, 488, 490, 492, 495, 497, 499, 501, 505, 507, 509
  Divisions
    1st Armored: 245, 248, 250-53, 260-65, 268-69, 274, 279, 284, 287, 290-92, 307, 309, 314-15, 317-19, 480, 486
    3d Carpathian: 194, 210, 225, 251-52, 261, 319, 321, 330, 333, 354, 358, 402, 483, 486, 490, 509
    5th Kresowa: 251, 305-06, 308, 312-13, 319, 321, 330, 354, 358, 369, 430

[635]

Polish Army Units—Continued
    Brigade, 1st Parachute: 276, 279, 281–82, 284–86
Poll: 420
Polle: 478
Polloc Harbor: 501
Polong: 371
Polotsk: 156–57, 224
Polsfeld: 489
Polsum: 460, 462
Poltava: 93, 126, 137, 201, 215
Pomerania: 387–88, 410, 417, 425–26, 428, 435–36, 439, 443, 446, 520
Pongani: 59, 63, 65–66
Ponggor River: 19
Ponsacco: 232
Ponson Island: 375, 378
Pont: 374
Pont à Mousson: 263, 268, 292
Pont d'Aspach: 346
Pont de l'Arche: 257
Pont de la Roche: 23 8
Pont-du-Fahs: 106–07, 109
Pont Evêque: 253
Pont Hébert: 228–31
Pont l'Abbé: 206–10, 212–13
Pont Remy: 262
Pont St. Vincent: 268
Pont Sainte Maxence: 260
Pont-sur-Meuse: 260
Pont-sur-Saône: 268
Pontassieve: 250, 256, 258
Pontaubault: 239–40
Ponte Cavour: 202
Ponte a Moriano: 279
Ponte del Duca d'Aosta: 202
Ponte dells Pietra: 306
Ponte Grande: 117–18
Ponte Margherita: 202
Ponte Milvio: 202
Ponte Olivo: 117–18
Ponte Rotto: 165, 177
Ponte Samoggia: 507
Ponte Sele: 133, 136
Ponte Vecchio: 243, 248
Ponte Vedra Beach, German agents landed at: 42–43
Pontecorvo: 194–96
Pontedera: 232–33, 244
Pontelagoscuro: 513, 515
Pontianak: 20
Pontine Marshes: 196
Pontorson: 240.
Pope: 26
Popondetta: 68–69, 74–75, 79
Poppenweiler: 492
Poprad: 386
Porac: 11–12
Poritz: 486
Porkhov: 176
Porkkala Peninsula: 280
Porlaka: 178
Porlock Harbor: 74, 97
Poro Island: 378, 382, 389, 391
Poros Bay: 292
Porquerolles Island: 254
Port Cros Island: 249–50
Port Dickson: 13
Port-en-Bessin: 204–05
Port-Joie: 257
Port-Lyautey: 65–66

Port Moresby: 40, 42–43, 46–47, 50–56, 59, 72, 89, 97, 104, 131
    advance GHQ opens: 64
    advanced base established: 49
    Allied reinforcement: 38
    enemy air attack: 21, 28
    enemy invasion suspended: 37
    enemy landing attempt: 35, 37
    strategic conferences: 155
Port Sual: 370, 372
Port Swettenham: 13
Portal, Air Chief Marshal Sir Charles: 39,42
Porter: 61
Porter, Maj. Gen. Ray E.: 90, 368
Portico: 298
Porto di Pantelleria: 111
Porto Empedocle: 120
Porto Gruaro: 525
Posen: 381, 384–85, 387, 389, 394–95, 401, 410
Postroff: 335
Poteau: 355, 358, 377–78
Potenza: 135–36
Potsdam: 516, 520
    TERMINAL Conference: 550
Pouppeville: 203
Pournoy-la-Chévite: 278, 281, 283–85, 287, 324
Poussay: 269–70, 272
Pownall, Rear Adm. Charles A.: 136
Pownall, Lt. Gen. Sir Henry (Br.): 9
Pozorrubio: 374, 376–78, 382–83, 390, 402
Pozzallo: 119
Pozzilli: 145
Pozzo Alto: 261
Pra del Bianco Basin: 495
Prada: 297
Pradura: 505
Praga: 272
Prague: 531–35
Prairies Marcagéuses: 224
Prasily: 532
Prata: 143
Pratella: 142
Prates Reef: 375
Prato: 271, 273
Prayelle Farm: 325
Pré-Alps: 255
Prechlau: 417
Predappio Nuovo: 312–13
Prefetto Hill: 271–72, 274
Preischeid: 409
Preist: 424
Prenzlau: 520
Presenzano: 144
President Coolidge: 61
Presov: 379
Pressath: 506
Prether River: 393, 415, 417, 419, 422
Pretzetze: 508
Pretzsch: 517
Preussisch Eylau: 399
Prex: 502
Priluki: 136
Primasole: 119
Prims River: 352, 440, 442
Prince of Wales: 4
Princeton: 136, 312
Pringle: 499

Prinz Eugen: 23
Priola Gargallo: 118
Prisoners of war: 34. *See also* Death March.
Priverno: 197
Pro Mission: 188
Prochorovka: 118
Profen: 492
Prokhladny: 52
Proletarskaya: 47, 86
Prombach: 515
Prome: 29–31, 384, 404, 467, 522, 528, 537
Pronsfeld: 388, 392, 405–06, 417
Propoisk: 150
Proskurov: 183
Protville: 109
Provedroux: 369
PROVIDENCE: 46. *See also* Buna.
Providero Defile: 197
Provisional Groupment, New Guinea: 193–94
Provisional Mountain Force, Leyte: 363–64
Provisional Service Command, Bougainville: 160
Pruem: 275, 393–95, 397 399–401
Pruem River: 275, 277, 391, 398–400, 402–03, 405–11, 413–14, 416–17, 419, 421–22, 424
Prummern: 329–31, 333
Prut River: 183, 185, 257
Przemysl: 238
Pskov: 176, 233, 235
Psychological warfare, effect of: 547
PT boats: 17, 59
Pucot Hill: 17–19
Puderbach: 454
Puerto Princesa: 415, 417, 420
Puetzborn: 428–29, 432, 434
Puetzlohn: 333–35
Puffendorf: 327–28, 330
Puget: 250
PUGILIST: 95, too. *See also* Mareth Line; Tunisia Campaign.
Pugo Valley: 382, 482, 490, 505, 513
Pulangi River: 537, 541
Pulheim: 422
Pulie River: 155
Pulkovo: 163
Pullenried: 514
Pulo Anna Island: 307
Pulsnitz: 513
Pulupandan: 461, 464, 450
Pulversheim: 391
Puncan: 401, 409, 413, 417, 419, 421, 423, 426
Puntian: 36–37
Purple Heart Ridge (Saipan): 217–22
Pursuit Squadrons
    17th: 19–20
    1st: 22
Puruata Island: 143
Pussade: 510
Putanges: 251
Putbroek: 383
Putlan: 428, 430–31, 433–34, 437, 443
Putlan River and Valley: 449, 460, 463
Putscheid: 386
Puttelange: 336, 343–44, 359
Pyatigorsk: 49, 84

[INDEX]

Pyawbwe: 29, 35, 463, 486, 488
Pyinbon: 27
Pyinmana: 30-34, 503, 509
Pyingaing: 360
Pyinzi: 445
Pyle, Ernest T. (Ernie): 503
Pyritz: 425
Pyu: 517

Qattara Depression: 44
Quadrath: 4 118
QUADRANT Conference: 127-29
Quartermaster Port Battalion, 393d: 38
Quebec Conferences. See OCTAGON Conference; QUADRANT Conference.
Queckenberg: 427
QUEEN: 327, 336
Quedlinburg: 502, 512
Queichambach: 447
Quellendorf: 496
Querceta: 303
Question Mark Hill (Luzon): 406, 409
Quezon, Manuel: 8, 10
Quezon Bridge: 392
Quezon Gate: 410
Quezon Hill: 517
Quinan, Lt. Gen. E. P. (Br.): 12
Quinauan Point: 27-22
Quincy: 49
Quinéville: 204, 206-09
Quingentole: 513, 515
Quint: 430
Quinzano: 294-95
Quioeng: 497
Quisling, Vidkun: 21

Raamsdonk: 315
Raba River and Valley: 465
Rabaul
  Allied air attacks: 25, 45
  coastal battery destroyed: 17
  enemy air-naval reinforcement: 141, 144, 146
  enemy air attacks on: 12, 16-17
  enemy landings: 17
  enemy staging area for Bougainville: 144-46
  garrison and defenses of: 12
  Guadalcanal, enemy escape from 91
  JCS directive on offensive: 44
  neutralization of: 92, 96-98, 101, 106, 108, 115, 129, 140, 143-46, 153-55, 172, 174-75, 180
  operations plan drawn: 51
  17th Army in control: 50
  U.S. naval attack: 25
Rabbi River and Valley: 308, 312, 315-16,321
Rabi: 51
Rabon: 372-73
Rachamps: 374, 376
Rackwitz: 506
Radar, use of in air bombardment: 154, 166
Radda in Chianti: 233
Radewell: 504
Ramdhapur: 195, 198
Radicofani: 213
Radicosa Pass: 284-85, 290

Radio countermeasures, use of in air bombardment: 139
Radom: 237, 376
Radomyshl: 154
Radscheid: 270, 390
Raenkam: 517
Raesfeld: 456
Raffadali: 120
Ragay: 6
Ragusa: 118
Rahm: 449
Rahman: 61, 63
Rahrbach: 482
Raids (French town): 229
Raihu River: 188
RAINCOAT: 151-53
Ralshoven: 412
Rambervillers: 282, 291-92, 315
Rambouillet: 253
Rambrouch: 359-60
Rambutyo Island: 185, 188
Ramcke, Maj. Gen. Hermann Bernhard (Ger.): 279
Ramecourt: 272
Ramey, Brig. Gen. Rufus S.: 208, 215, 227, 232, 234, 236 ,240, 248
Ramgarh training center: 52, 60, 151
Rampan: 292
Ramrath: 422
Ramree Island: 380, 384, 399
Ramree River: 95
Ramsay, Adm. Sir Bertram H. (RN) 117, 203
Ramsbeck: 480
Ramscheid: 290-92
Ramu Valley: 164, 178, 188
Randau: 489
Randazzo: 125-28
Randerath: 383-84
Ranes: 248-49
Ranger Battalions
  1st: 64, 91-92, 98-99, 117, 119, 121, 133-34, 137-38, 145-46, 167
  2d: 203-05, 250, 256, 258, 325, 343, 345-47, 353, 355, 408, 418
  3d: 117, 119-20, 127, 133-34, 137-38, 151-53, 167
  4th: 117, 119, 121, 133-34, 137-38, 144, 167
  5th: 203-05, 250, 342, 362, 398, 406, 408-11, 413-14, 419, 494
  6th: 301, 305-06, 547-48
Ranger Force, 6615th Provisional: 164
Ranger units: 50, 119. *See also* Commandos; Ranger Battalions; Ranger Force, 6615th Provisional.
Rangoon
  British request for air support: 462, 472
  enemy air attacks: 8, 18
  enemy reinforcements: 32
  enemy seizure: 7-9, 18, 26-28, 32
  recovery of: 149, 155, 235, 260, 271, 293, 316, 395, 410, 426, 455, 467, 469, 486, 501, 511, 517-18, 525, 528, 530, 532-33, 536-37, 541, 546
  Tulsa Incident: 7, 9
Rangoon River: 5, 28, 530
Rankin: 83-84
Rankin, Capt. Pinkney R.: 83

Ransbach: 454
Raoe Island: 283
Raon-l'Etape: 309, 312, 314-15, 319, 321, 324, 326, 328-29, 331-32
Rapido Plain: 162
Rapido River: 162-67, 173, 191-93
Rappelsdorf: 481
RASHNESS: 508. *See also* Canton; Hong Kong.
Rastatt: 375
Rastatt: 488, 490
Rastenburg: 2,3
Rath: 414-15, 418, 420, 422, 489
Rathedaung: 78, 82, 86, 90, 98, 363
Ratheim: 415
Rathenow: 520
Ratibor: 457, 465
Ratingen: 500, 502
Ratzebuhr: 389
Ratzwiller: 343, 345
Rau de Vaux: 375
Raub: 12
Raubach: 454
Raunheim: 453, 455
Rauray: 218-19
Rauth: 527
Ravels Hill: 304
Ravenna: 162, 276, 344
RAVENOUS: 64, 73. *See also* British Army units, Corps, 4.
Ravensburg: 521
Ravolzhausen: 461
Rawang: 12
Rawlings, Vice Adm. Sir Bernard (RN): 450
Rawicz: 383
Razabil: 180
Rebaa Oulad Yahia: 86, 89
Rebaa Valley: 86, 89
Rebaou Pass: 104
Recanati: 340
Rechitsa: 146-47
Rechrival: 364-65, 367, 369
Recht: 355 375-78
RECKLESS: 182. *See also* Hollandia; Task Forces, Army, RECKLESS, Hollandia.
Recklinghausen: 466, 489
Recodo: 436
Recogne: 370, 374
Reconnaissance Squadrons, Army
  25th: 335
  41st: 396, 401, 442-44, 447-489, 463, 465, 526, 530, 532, 534
  42d: 336
  86th: 256, 401, 455
  91st: 123, 125, 197, 200, 202, 205,208, 261, 266-67, 284, 296
  94th 346-47, 349
  117th: 202, 208, 217, 220, 257, 262, 316, 331, 349, 389, 393
  Provisional, 1st Cavalry Division: 388-89
Reconnaissance Squadron, 110th Army Air: 206
Recouvrance: 257-58, 270, 274
Red Army. *See* Soviet Army; Soviet Army units.
Redeployment of units to Pacific: 528, 530, 550
Redeyef: 97

Redoute des Fourches: 217-18
Rees: 449-50, 452-53
Regalbuto: 124
Regen: 514-15, 519, 522, 529
Regen Pass: 532-33
Regen River: 514
Regensburg: 128, 175-76, 506, 512, 516-19, 521, 526
Regenstauf: 511
Reggio: 515
Reggio di Calabria: 131
Regimental combat teams. *See* Regiments
Regimental Objective Hill (Luzon): 539
Regiments. *See* Cavalry Regiments; Engineer Boat and Shore Regiments; Engineer Combat Regiments; Engineer General Service Regiments; Field Artillery Regiments; Glider Infantry Regiments; Infantry Regiments; Marine Corps Infantry Regiments; Marine Corps Parachute Infantry Regiment, 1st; Marine Corps Raider Regiments; Parachute Infantry Regiments.
Regne, Belgium: 267
Regne, France: 358, 369, 372
Reguisheim: 395
Rehau: 504, 506
Rehlingen: 345 408
Rehsiepen: 478
Reichenbach: 500, 514
Reichenhausen: 467
Reichensachen: 468, 470
Reichlos: 465
Reichshoffen: 349, 441-42
Reichswald: 278, 396, 398, 400-402
Reidenhausen: 440
Reiff: 408
Reifferscheid: 427, 432
Reifsnider, Rear Adm. Lawrence F.: 181, 467
Reigneville: 210
Reims: 257-58, 260, 405, 407, 534
Reinhausen: 481
Reinsfeld: 439
Reinsport: 443
Reipeldingen: 408
Reipertsweiler: 366-67, 371, 377
Reisach: 529
Reisbach: 526
Reisdorf: 377-78, 445 447
Reitano: 124
Reith: 528
Remagen: 364, 429, 431-33, 435-36, 440, 449
Remering: 336
Remich: 287, 292
Remilly: 323
Remiremont: 277, 282-86, 300
Remonval: 375
Rems River: 505, 507, 509, 511, 513
Remscheid: 495
Remsfeld: 463
Rendova Island: 115-18, 122, 126-27
Rengershausen: 475
Renglez: 378
Rengsdorf: 449
Renkum: 286
Rennell Island: 58

Rennes: 240-42, 247
Reno: 475
RENO: 95, 211.
Reno River: 304, 368, 469, 475, 477, 479, 486, 495, 503, 505, 507, 511, 513
Renuamont: 372
Repelen: 423, 435
Repulse: 4
Requancourt: 245
Rescheid: 417
Resia Pass: 531
Rethel: 260
Rethem: 486, 489, 491
Rethicourt-la-Petite: 280, 287
Retonfey: 330
Rettel: 323
Rettenbach: 516
Rettigny: 375, 378
Reuden: 496, 502
Reuland: 421-22
Reuler: 383
Reuth: 422, 424, 426
Reutlingen: 513, 516
Reutte: 523, 525
Reyersviller: 439
Rezonville: 264
Rheder: 426, 474
Rheinbach: 425-27
Rheinbay: 440
Rheinbeck: 433, 435
Rheinberg: 423, 425, 427, 433, 450, 452
Rheinbreitbach: 432
Rheinbrohl: 444, 447
Rheindahlen: 415
Rhein-Durkheim: 447 455
Rheine: 453, 460, 464, 466, 468, 470, 472, 476
Rheingonheim: 448
Rheinhausen: 423, 425
Rheinkamp: 425
Rheinprovinz: 512
Rheinzabern: 451
Rhens: 441-42
Rheurdt: 423
Rheydt: 415
Rhidma: 101
Rhine-Clove Canal: 399-400
Rhine-Herne Canal: 460, 466, 468, 472, 476, 478, 480, 482
Rhine-Main airport: 455
Rhine-Marne Canal: 272-73, 275, 320
Rhine Plain: 381, 389
Rhine-Rhône Canal. *See* Rhône-Rhine Canal. Rhine River: 258, 262-63, 277, 282, 330-31,362 366-68, 390, 392-93, 395-96, 468, 470-71, 476, 480, 485, 492, 496, 502, 504, 509, 512, 514-16, 530
Allied airborne crossing: 402, 450-52
Allied river crossing: 267, 271, 305, 307-09 313, 318-19, 333 335-38, 342-43, 345, 347, 349, 351, 353, 356, 386, 388-89, 393-94, 396-99, 402, 409, 415-16, 418-70
Rhineland Campaign: 271-447
Rhône-Rhine Canal: 330, 332, 386-90, 392-93, 395-97
Rhône River and Valley: 246, 253-55, 257-61

Rians: 252
Ribano Hill: 309
Ribeauville: 337, 386
Ribera: 121
Rice Anchorage: 116
Richardson, Lt. Gen. Robert C., Jr.: 126, 127, 130, 241
Richardson, Lt. Col. Walter B.: 335-38, 415, 420, 447, 454, 462
Richelsbusch: 382, 385
Richelskaul: 297, 299-300, 317
Rickelrath: 115
Ridge 300 (Saipan): 218
Ried: 529
Riedheim: 516
Riedseltz: 352
Riedwihr: 383-84
Riegling: 514
Riesa: 515
Riesi: 118
Riesweiler: 441
Rieti: 202-04
Rievenich: 432
Riez: 251-52
Riga: 229, 236, 253, 256, 275, 280, 295, 302
Riggs, Rear Adm. R. S.: 415
Rigo Track: 57
Rigossa River: 301-02
Rijsbergen: 313
Rilland: 311
Rimbach: 468
Rimbeck: 464, 466
Rimburg: 293-94, 296
Rimini: 190, 202, 210, 262, 266, 274, 276, 283
Rimini Line: 274, 276, 279-80, 282
Rimling: 352, 365, 369-70, 403, 439
Rimlingen: 440
Ringel: 362-63
Ringenberg: 453-54
Ringhuscheid: 411
Ringleben: 487
Rinnen: 427
Rinnthal: 447
Rinsecke: 480
Rinteln: 472
Rio de Janeiro, conference of American republics at: 15, 19
Riol: 434
Ripsdorf: 429, 431
Risle River: 255
Ritchie, Gen. Sir Neil M. (Br.): 18, 21, 28, 39, 41-42
Ritpong: 189-91
Rittersdorf: 413-14
Rittershoffen: 369-78
Riva: 525
Rizal, Leyte: 315
Rizal, Luzon: 391, 394 401-02, 409
RO: 141. *See also* Rabaul, enemy air-naval reinforcement.
Road Junction 471 (Huertgen Forest): 302-03
Roads Nos. 1, 2 and 3 (Manus Island): 180-81, 183
ROAST: 467. *See also* Comacchio Spit.
Roberts, Lt. Gen. O. L. (Br.): 536
Rocca d'Evandro: 153
Rocca di Roffeno: 495
Rocca Massima: 199

[INDEX]

Rocca Pipirozzi: 144
Rocca San Casciano: 313
Roccadaspide: 133, 135
Roccagorga: 198
Roccamonfina: 143
Roccaravindola: 144
Roccaromana: 141
Roccasecca: 196-97
Rochefort: 359, 363, 367
Rochelinval: 369
Rocherath: 353, 387-89
Roches-lès-Blâmont: 328
Rochesson: 319
Rocheville: 213
Rochlitz: 494, 496
Rockenhausen: 444, 453, 463
Rockwell, Rear Adm. R. W.: 9, 102, 111, 127
Rocky Crags (Okinawa): 506, 508, 510, 512-13
Rocky Point (Angaur): 278-79
Rodalbe: 323-24, 331
Rodder: 432
Rodenkirchen: 429
Rodershausen: 411
Rodgen: 387, 462
Rodgers, Rear Adm. B J.: 403
Rodheim: 458
Roding: 514
Rodingen: 412
Rodriguez Island: 53
Roedenweiler: 505
Roehl: 417
Roelsdorf: 354
Roenkhausen: 489
Roer Dam: 351
Roer Plain: 327, 336
Roer River and Valley: 295-96, 323, 327, 330, 332-33, 337-41, 343-44, 346-52, 354-56, 374, 384, 387, 389, 391-93, 395, 398-400, 402, 409-12, 414-20, 422-27
Roerdorf: 342, 409
Roermond: 290, 293, 325, 328, 332-33, 374-84, 415, 418
Roesberg: 425, 427
Roeschwoog: 377
Roetgen: 269-70, 272
Roetgen Forest: 271
Roettingen: 488
Roetz: 515
Roevenich: 420
Rogachev: 176
Rogden: 416
ROGER: 531
Rogery: 380
Roggendorf: 422, 424
Roggersing: 521
Rognac: 253, 255
Rognes: 254
Rohe: 331-32
Rohn Point: 188
Rohr River: 489
Rohrbach: 444, 528
Rohrbach-lès-Bitches: 345, 349
Rohrbusch: 376-77
Rohrdorf: 486
Rohren: 387, 389
Rohrenspring: 489
Rohrsen: 474
Rohrweiler: 368-70, 376-78, 390

Roi-Namur (Burlesque-Camouflage) Islands: 21, 166-68
Roisdorf: 429-30
Roitzheim: 426
Roitzsch: 500, 504
Rokossovski, Gen. Konstantin (USSR): 83
Rollesbroich: 278, 280, 353, 393
Roma: 133
Romblon: 436
Romblon Island: 427, 434, 436, 440, 448, 471, 476
Rome: 115, 121, 131-32, 136-37, 142, 159, 161-62, 213
  air attacks on: 120-21, 127
  declared open city: 127
  drive on: 176, 190-205
Rome-Arno Campaign: 164-267
Romelfing: 335
ROMEO: 249-50
Romlinghoven: 444
Rommel, Field Marshal Erwin: 39, 43, 91-92, 94-95. *See also* Egypt, operations in; Libya.
  commands Army Group, Africa: 95
  commands Axis forces in Libya: 3
  departure from Africa: 97
  relieved at Army Group B: 232
  relieved at German-Italian Panzer Army: 88
Rommelfangen: 407
Rommelsheim: 412, 414
Rommersheim: 422, 444
Rommerskirchen: 422
Romni: 135
Romrod: 463
ROMULUS: 316, 321, 351. *See also* Arakan coast.
Roncalla: 226
Ronce River: 370, 372
Ronco River: 310-13, 315-16, 318
Roncobilaccio: 286
Roncofreddo: 297-99
Roncourt: 268
Roney: 238
Ronsdorf: 495
Ronsperk: 526
Rooke Island: 172, 174
Rosendaal: 313
Roosevelt, Franklin D.: 42, 181
  agrees to cancellation of BUCCANEER: 152-53
  appeal to Italians: 120, 124
  asks commitment of Yunnan Force: 162
  attends ARCADIA Conference: 8
  Chiang's demands on: 59, 153, 155, 163, 165, 169, 171, 280, 285
  at conference on Pacific strategy: 230, 237
  on control of Calcutta-Assam LOC: 166-67, 171
  criticized for failure in China: 299
  death of: 491
  on division of CBI: 224-27, 230, 235, 90
  on Eisenhower as commander for OVERLORD: 152, 156
  on Eisenhower as commander for TORCH: 48
  at EUREKA Conference: 150-51

Roosevelt, Franklin D.—Continued
  and Giraud conference: 116
  JCS proposal to, for recovery of Burma: 73
  on observer mission to Chinese Communists: 171, 214, 217, 343
  and political representatives in China: 220, 226-27, 230, 235, 246-47
  protests Salween withdrawal: 276
  at QUADRANT Conference: 127-29
  and recovery of Burma: 176
  at SEXTANT Conference: 148, 150-52
  transmits OCTAGON decisions to Chiang: 280, 285
  signs SPARS bill: 69
  on Stilwell as commander of Chinese: 222-27, 230, 235, 255, 276, 296, 302
  on Stilwell recall: 220, 296, 301-02, 306
  on Stratemeyer as commander of India-Burma air affairs: 116
  at TRIDENT Conference: 110-12
Roosevelt Ridge (New Guinea): 121, 127
ROOSTER: 509. *See also* Chihchiang.
Rosario: 7, 373, 374-77, 380, 385, 390, 402, 407, 482
Rosario Heights: 400
Roscheid: 270, 272-73, 408
Rose: 466. *See also* Ruhr sector
Rose, Maj. Gen. Maurice: 462
Roselle River: 344-45
Rosenau: 331
Rosenberg: 510
Rosenkranz: 384
Rosenthal: 416
ROSIE: 466. *See also* Cannes; French Naval Assault Group.
Rosignano: 223-27, 237
Roslavl: 137
Rossbach: 449, 508, 510
Rossburg: 505
Rossendorf: 489, 492, 494
Rosslershof Castle: 334
Rossosh: 45, 85
Rossum: 181, 183
Rosteig: 366
Rostov: 45-46, 48, 81, 83, 85, 87-92
Rot am See: 505
Rota Island: 212
Roth: 391, 394, 408 ,427, 456, 458, 460, 475, 477, 507
Roth River: 418, 420
Rotha: 510
Rothau: 336
Rothbach: 340, 380, 382
Rothbach Rau: 379
Rothbach River: 419, 439
Rothenberga: 487
Rothenbergen: 461
Rothenburg: 488, 490, 494, 496, 498, 500, 505
Rothenstein: 490, 492
Rott: 270, 397, 447 ,521
Rottbitz: 438
Rotte Creek: 324
Rottenbach: 487
Rottenburg: 503
Rottenegg: 529-30
Rotterdam: 270

Rottersdorf: 492
Rottgen: 429
Rottweil: 509
Roubion River: 255-57
Rouen: 50, 253, 256, 258-59, 262
Rouffach: 351, 391-93
Rougemont: 268
Rougemont Ridge: 325
Rougemont-le-Château: 336
ROUNDUP: 30, 33. *See also* Normandy Campaign, planning phase.
Route Napoléon. *See* Highways, 85
Routes. *See Highways by number.*
Rouxeville: 237
Roversano: 306
Rovigo: 518
Rovno: 170, 181
Row, Brig. R. A. (NZ): 142
Rowell, Maj. Gen. Sydney F. (Aus.): 49-50
Roya River: 490, 500
Royal Air Force
 around-the-clock assault on Germany: 95
 attacks on Continent: 3, 54, 58, 61. *See also* Combined Bomber Offensive against Europe.
 attacks on V-weapons sites: 128
 Bomber Command: 191, 225, 239, 245, 248, 293
 in defense of Malaya: 4
 diversion of aircraft from ME to FE: 9
 Eagle Squadrons transferred to AAF: 57
 first shuttle raid on Germany: 114
 Malta Command absorbed by MAAF: 155
 Middle East Command absorbed by MAAF: 155
 Second Tactical Air Force: 150, 186
 sinks *Admiral Scheer*: 482
 sinks *Luetzow*: 497
 withdrawal from Singapore: 15-16
 224 Group: 536
Royal Australian Air Force
 at New Britain: 146
 responsibility assigned: 53
 in support of P.I. operations: 315
 Wing 71: 206
Royal Indian Navy: 89, 94-95
Royal Marines. *See* Commando forces, British.
Royal Navy. *See also* ships by name.
 Aircraft Carrier Squadron 11: 531
 East Indies Fleet: 384
 Eastern Fleet: 4, 12, 193, 236
 Pacific Fleet: 531, 550
 Special Boat Service: 473
 TF 57: 450, 456
Royan: 328, 494, 496, 498, 500, 503
Royce, Maj. Gen. Ralph: 133
Rubenach: 431
Rubercy: 206
Rubicone River: 301
Rudersdorf: 462
Rudingshain: 463
Rudisleben: 485
Rudolec: 533
Rudolstadt: 490
Ruebhausen: 447

Rueblingen: 492
Rueckingen: 461
Ruesselsheim: 453
Ruethen: 464
Rufina: 258
RUGBY: 249-51
Ruhla: 479
Ruhland: 215
Ruhmansfelden: 517
Ruhr River: 468, 470, 476, 478, 480, 482, 484, 486-87, 489, 491, 493, 495-96, 510, 515
Ruhr sector: 111, 114, 262, 270-71, 283-84, 287-88 , 292, 305, 432, 449, 456-66, 470, 472, 474, 476, 478-84, 487, 489, 493, 495-96, 498, 500, 502, 506, 510, 512, 517
Ruhrberg: 392-93
Rumania
 agreement with USSR on division of territory: 269
 air assault on: 111-121, 124, 185, 203, 207, 234, 237, 242, 244-45
 declares war on Germany: 256
 joins Allies: 269, 471
 King surrenders to USSR: 255
 operations in: 252, 254-55, 257-60, 264, 269, 291, 295, 300-301
 U.S. declares war on: 40
Rumbeck: 487
Rumersheim: 397
Rumlange: 380
Rumpenheim: 455
Rundstedt, Field Marshal Gerd von: 223, 262, 353, 527
Runzhausen: 458
Rupertus, Maj. Gen. William H. (USMC): 63, 155-57, 276
Ruppertshofen: 503
Rupt: 282, 285-86
Rurich: 410-11
Russell Islands: 93-94, 97, 102, 155
Russi: 344
Russian Army. *See* Soviet Army; Soviet Army units.
Ruthenia: 313
Ruttershausen: 458
Ruviano: 141
Ruweisat Ridge: 45
Ruwer: 428
Ruwer River: 423-24, 426, 428, 430-32, 434 437
Ruyter, de: 26
Ru-ywa: 404-06, 437
Rybnik: 457
Ryder, Maj. Gen. Charles W.: 64
Ryuju: 51
Ryukyus Campaign: 264, 456-549
 air and naval actions: 294, 300, 367, 370, 380-81, 420, 449-50, 452-53, 456, 462, 464, 467 486, 493, 495, 497, 499, 506, 517, 525, 538, 540-41, 544-46, 548-49
 casualty summaries: 465, 478, 480, 488, 510, 515, 525, 530, 548
 plan for invasion: 204, 294
 supported by raids on Japan: 444, 462
Rzhev: 14, 18, 47-49, 70, 95-96

S. Agata: 125-26

S. Andrea: 192
S. Andriano: 291
S. Angelo: 163-64, 302-03
S. Angelo d'Alife: 14-42
S. Angelo Hill: 170
S. Apollinare: 192
S. Arcangelo: 285-88
S. Barnaba: 337
S. Benedetto: 286-87, 291
S. Benedetto del Tronto: 138
S. Benedetto in Alpe: 286
S. Benedetto Po: 511
S. Biagio: 198
S. Carlo: 307-08
S. Casciano: 236-37
S. Cataldo: 120
S. Caterina: 120-21
S. Cesareo: 201
S. Chierlo: 503
S. Clemente: 263, 304
S. Constanzo: 252
S. Domenico Ridge: 191
S. Donato: 233
S. Elia: 150, 155, 157, 162
S. Fortunato: 274, 277, 279-80, 282-83
S. Fratello Ridge: 125
S. Giacomo Hill: 154
S. Gimignano: 226, 229
S. Giorgio: 193
S. Giovanni: 235, 509
S. Giovanni Incarico: 197
S. Giuseppe: 121
S. Giusta: 160
S. Ippolito: 254, 286
S. Lorenzo: 297-98
S. Lucia, Italy: 276-77, 282-84, 324
S. Margherita: 121
S. Maria Infante: 191-93
S. Maria Oliveto: 144
S. Maria Ridge: 191-92
S. Martello: 290
S. Martino: 274, 276-77, 292-93, 295-96
S. Martino Hill: 191-92
S. Martino in Strada: 320-21
S. Mauro: 123
S. Mauro di Romagna: 289
S. Michele Pass: 154
S. Oliva: 194, 196
S. Paola: 298-99
S. Patrignano: 274
S. Pellegrino: 282
S. Piero: 305
S. Pietro: 151-55
S. Pieve di Luce: 230
S. Prospero: 501
S Ridge, Italy: 191-93
S. Salvo: 144
S. Savino: 263-64, 266-67, 270-72
S. Severino: 137
S. Severo: 366, 368, 423, 430, 484
S. Stefano, Italy: 131, 234
S. Stefano, Sicily: 119, 121-24
S. Tome: 324
S. Varano: 321, 325
S. Vito: 151
S. Vittore: 155, 157, 160-61
Saale River: 479 485 487, 489-92, 494-99
Saale Stau Lake: 494
Saales: 332, 334-35

[INDEX]

Saales Pass: 282
Saalfeld: 492, 494
Saalhausen: 480, 483
Saar River. *See* Sarre River.
Saar sector: 262, 338, 340, 439-53
Saarbruecken: 278, 280, 346, 404, 408-10, 423, 426, 439, 445-46
Saarburg. *See* Sarrebourg.
Saarholzbach: 439-40
Saarland Province: 512, 514, 516
Saarlautern: 334, 340-44, 346-56, 374, 379, 384, 386, 389-400, 402-05, 410-11, 414, 417, 433, 435, 437-38, 442-44, 446
Saarlautern-Roden: 343, 345-46, 350, 396, 445
Saarlouis. *See* Saarlautern.
Saarlouis-Roden. *See* Saarlautern-Roden.
Saarwellingen: 444
Saase: 508
Sabalayan: 358
Sabang, Luzon: 390
Sabang, Sumatra: 236
Sabatai River: 282
Sablan: 486
Sabria: 101
Sabron: 188
Sachsa: 489
Sachsenburg: 487
Sachsenhausen: 454, 466
Sacignano: 290
Sacobia Ridge: 02
Sacobia River: 484
Sadler, Brig. Gen. Percy L.: 262
Sadzot: 362-63, 366
Saeffelen: 378
Saeffler Creek: 293-94
Saegmuhl: 367, 371, 383
Saffig: 431
Safi: 65-66
Sagekarasa Island: 134-36
Sagkanan: 316
Saguing: 515
Sahmaw: 244
Sahy: 353
Saidor: 131, 153, 155, 157-61, 163-64, 166, 172, 174-75
Saigon: 372
Saillancourt: 258
Sainscheid: 456
St. Amé: 286-87
St. André-de-l'Epine: 228
St. André-sur-Orne: 233
St. Anton: 531
St. Antonis: 287
St. Avold: 337-38, 342, 357, 362
St. Barbara: 340-42
St. Benoit: 315
St. Blaise: 334-35
St. Brieux: 243
St. Calais: 247
St. Christophe-du-Foc: 213
St. Clair-sur-Elle: 209
St. Clement: 283
St. Cloud: 65
St. Côme-du-Mont: 203-05
St. Cyprien: 109
St. Denis-le-Gast: 238
St. Dié: 282, 286, 300, 303, 306-10, 312-19, 324-26, 328, 332-34

St. Dizier: 191, 259
St. Eny: 227-28
St. Florentin: 255
St. Floxel: 207
St. Fraimbault-de-Prières: 244
St. Georges: 331
St. Georges-d'Elle: 228
St. Georges-du-Vièrve: 255
St. Germain-de-Varreville: 203
St. Germain-sur-Sèves: 234
St. Gilles: 226, 228, 236-37
St. Goar: 440-41
St. Goarer Stradtwald: 441
St. Goarshausen: 454
St. Hilaire-du-Harcourt: 241
St. Hippolyte: 264
St. Hubert: 265, 357 366 371, 373
St. Hubert Farm: 288-89, 327
St. Ilgen: 465
St. Ingbert: 446
St. Jacques: 367
St. Jean-de-Baisants: 238
St. Jean-de-Day: 226
St. Jean d'Ormont: 333
St. Jean-du-Bois: 243, 248
St. Jean-Rohrbach: 334-35
St. Joeris: 330
St. Johann: 443-44
St. Joost: 378
St. Lambert-sur-Dives: 251
St. Laurent-sur-Mer: 203-04
St. Leonard, Belgium: 286, 292
St. Leonard, France: 333
St. Lô: 207-09, 211, 213, 221, 227-33, 236-37
St. Louis: 332
St. Malo: 241-43, 245-50, 260
St. Martin-de-Varreville: 203
St. Martin-le-Gréard: 213-14
St. Matthias Islands: 180-82, 186
St. Médard: 324-25
St. Michel: 332
St. Mihiel: 261
St. Nazaire: 30, 365, 458, 464
St. Nicolas: 269, 273, 345
St. Oedenrode: 279, 282, 286, 288
St. Omer: 262-64
St. Oskol: 91
St. Paul: 252
St. Peter: 534
St. Pierre: 341
St. Pierre d' Oleron: 525
St. Pierre-du-Mont: 204
St. Pierre-Eglise: 215
St. Pierre Island: 8
St. Pierre-la-Vieille: 246
St. Pierre-sur-Dives: 249
St. Pois: 240-44
St. Pol: 260-61
St. Privat: 265
St. Quentin: 260-61
St. Raphaël: 249-50
St. Saens: 259
St. Sauveur-de-Chaulieu: 246-48
St. Sauveur-le-Vicomte: 210-11, 219, 221
St. Sever-Calvados: 242
St. Sulpice: 203
St. Sylvain: 245
St. Thomas: 426
St. Tonis: 420

St. Trond: 265, 356
St. Tropez: 249-51
St. Tropez Peninsula: 249
St. Valery-en-Caux: 197, 260-62
St. Vallier: 255
St. Vith: 269, 353-59, 370, 375-86
St. Wendel: 443-44
Ste. Anne: 205
Ste. Colombe: 209, 211
Ste. Croix en Plaine: 391
Ste. Geneviève: 269-70, 272-73, 275
Ste. Honorine: 216
Ste. Marguerite: 327
Ste. Marguerite-d'Elle: 208
Ste. Marie: 328, 335 337-39
Ste. Marie-aux-Chênes: 264-65
Ste. Maxime: 249
Ste. Mère-Eglise: 203-04
Ste. Pôle: 325
Ste. Suzanne-sur-Vire: 238
Saipan Island: 208-27, 230
  base for raids on Japan: 227
  staging area for Iwo: 403-04
Sakishima Islands: 380, 450, 456, 519
Sakket: 102
Sala: 138
Salacsac passes: 419, 426, 428, 435-36, 453, 457, 465, 477, 479, 482, 484, 486, 488, 501, 505, 527
Salamaua: 17, 18, 27-28, 43, 53, 117, 120, 129, 131-34
Salami Plantation: 178-79, 186
Salango River: 12
Salat: 473, 477, 479, 482, 486
Salazar: 428, 435-36, 441
Salchendorf: 464
Salerno: 122, 127-40, 163
Salival: 321
Salkau: 508
Salle: 373
Salm: 426, 428-29
Salm River: 358-59, 367 369-71 ,373-75,382 431-34
Salm Wald: 429
Salmbach: 352
Salmchâteau: 368-70, 372, 374 393397
Salonika: 316, 321
Salsk: 48
Salso River: 120, 125
Salt Lake City: 58
Salvaro: 439 457
Salvatito Hill: 163
Salvator Hill: 302, 306
Salween River: 18, 21-23, 37, 170, 181, 186, 189, 191-93, 195-200, 202, 205-08, 210-14, 216, 218-20, 223, 226-29, 235 237 241-43, 246-47, 253-55, 264-66, 270, 274, 276, 286, 314, 332, 342, 349, 357, 367, 379, 383
Salzburg: 528-29, 531
Salzwedel: 493 499 508
Samal: 13
Samal Island: 531, 534-39
Samar Island: 34, 310, 326, 361, 374, 388-400, 403, 406-07, 411-12, 415, 417, 421, 425, 433
Samarinda: 22
Sambro Valley: 292
Sambuco: 288-89

[641]

Sambodja: 550
Samland Peninsula: 406, 483, 498, 516
Samoa, as staging area: 53
Samoggia River: 326, 495, 503, 507
Samos Island: 135, 139
Sampoloc: 9
Samrée: 369-70
San Agustin, Luzon: 460, 465, 529
San Agustin, Mindoro: 353, 357
San Andres: 461
San Antonio: 519
San Bernardino Strait: 5, 306, 310-11, 403 406-07, 412, 415, 469, 499
San Carlos: 371
San Clemente: 375
San Fabian: 8, 370
San Fernando: 7, 10-11, 32, 386, 426, 443 446-47, 460
San Francisco, California, U.N. organization: 517, 548
Francisco, Luzon: 484, 486, 490,492, 495, 497, 499
San Isidro, Leyte: 362-63
San Isidro, Luzon: 393, 401, 412, 442, 531
San Jacinto: 370-71
San Joaquin: 311
San Jose, Leyte: 307, 354, 358
San Jose, Luzon: 9, 11-12, 387, 389 392, 393, 401-02, 427
San Jose, Mindoro: 301, 353, 364-65, 369, 386-87
San Jose, Panay: 34
San Juan, Luzon: 390
San Juan, Negros: 493
San Juanico Strait: 310-11
San Luis: 546
San Mandrier Peninsula: 257-58
San Manuel: 378–79, 381, 383, 385-86,403
San Marino, Republic of: 279, 282
San Mateo: 410, 413, 442
San Miguel, Leyte: 314, 364
San Miguel, Luzon: 380-81
San Nicolas: 390, 403
San Pablo, Leyte: 310-11
San Pablo, Luzon: 469, 473
San River: 235, 238
San Roque, Leyte: 309
San Roque, Mindanao: 434, 436-38, 440, 442
San Vicente: 313, 315
San Vicente Hill: 312-13
San Vicente River: 32
Sanananda Point and Village: 67-77, 81-87, 96
Sandakan: 15-16
Sandbach: 526, 529
Sandersdorf: 496, 500
Sandhausen: 465
Sandhofen: 455, 457
Sandomierz: 251, 372
Sandoway: 535
Sanfatucchio: 215
Sanga Sanga Island: 469, 478, 549
Sangerberg: 533
Sangerhausen: 489, 517
Sanggau: 10
Sangro River: 145, 147, 149-51
Sanip River: 162-63
Sanipon: 537-38, 541

Sannerville: 240
Sanok: 375
Sanry-sur-Nied: 323-24, 326
Sansapor Plantation and village: 227, 233, 236, 238, 240, 255, 260
Sansepolcro: 226
Sansonnet: 3 28
Santa Ana: 530
Santa Anastasia: 434
Santa Barbara, California, shelled by Japanese: 25
Santa Barbara, Luzon: 371-72
Santa Barbara, Panay: 443
Santa Cruz, Leyte: 310-11, 314
Santa Cruz, Luzon: 12, 477
Santa Cruz Island: 44-45, 52, 61
Santa Fe, Leyte: 312, 314
Santa Fe, Luzon: 390, 428, 453, 529, 536, 539-43
Santa Ignacia: 9
Santa Lucia, Luzon: 545
Santa Maria: 390, 394-95, 430
Santa Maria River, Mindanao: 440
Santa Maria River and Valley, Luzon 465 473
Santa Rita: 391
Santa Rosa: 388-89
Santerno River and Valley: 279-80, 282-85, 299, 344, 486, 488, 490, 492, 495
Santiago: 10, 546
Santo Tomas: 451, 453
Sanzenbach: 503
Saône River: 262
Sapangbato: 388
Sapois: 298
Sapri: 135
Sarana Pass and Valley: 111-12
Sarande: 301
Sarangani Bay: 549-50
Saratoga: 9, 44, 51-52
Sarawak: 5-6, 13, 547
Sardinia: 115, 121, 133, 136
Sargenroth: 443
Sariaya: 9, 480
Sark Island: 57
Sarmi: 177, 180, 189-90, 195-99, 208, 210, 213-20, 221, 224-25, 227, 230, 238, 249, 253, 262
Sarno River: 138
Sarny: 157, 162
Sarraltroff: 381
Sarre River: 318, 320, 325, 328-32, 334-42, 344-57, 374, 396, 406-110, 413-14, 416, 419, 423, 428, 435, 437-39, 442, 445
Sarre-Union: 339 341-44
Sarrebourg: 318-19, 325-26, 331-33, 335-36, 338, 408, 414, 419, 421 430-31, 434, 437
Sarreguemines: 278, 281, 345-50, 447, 455
Sarreinsberg: 366
Sarreinsming: 347
Sarstedt: 478
Sart: 369
Sarthe River: 243, 245
Sart-lez-St. Vith: 380
Sarzana: 501
Sasa airfield: 539
Sasavele Island: 115, 124

Sasebo: 226
Sassel: 380
Sassetta: 221
Sassoleone: 294-95
SATIN: 81, 85-86. *See also* Sfax.
Sattelberg: 138, 141-42, 147, 149
Sattler, Brig. Gen. Robert (Ger.): 219
Satzvey: 426
SAUCY: 118. See also India-Burma Theater, land supply route to China from.
Saudi Arabia: 52
Sauer River: 272, 287, 297, 360-63, 376-80, 382, 392, 396, 398, 400-401, 404, 409, 421
Saulcy: 334
Saulgrub: 523, 525
Saulxures: 299, 335
Saunnu: 18
Sava River: 344 346
Saverne: 282, 319, 331-32, 334-35, 366, 437
Savignano di Romagna: 288-89, 291, 297 300
Savio River: 301, 303-04, 306-10
Savo Island: 49, 53, 66-67
Savo Sound: 71
Savojaards Plaat: 284, 302, 306
Savoureuse River: 334
Sayre, Francis B.: 8
Sayre Highway: 35-36, 511, 513, 515, 519-20, 522-23, 525, 527 529-30, 532-37, 539-40
Sbeïtla: 86, 89-90, 92-93, 96, 98, 100-101, 104
Sbiba: 88, 93-94, 98
Sbiba Pass: 94
Scafati: 138
Scaldino: 337
Scattered Trees Ridge: 400
Scauri: 191, 193
Schaefstall: 518
Schaephuysen: 421
Schaerding: 528-29
Schaffhausen: 509, 511
Schaffhouse: 365
Schaidt: 450
Schainbach: 505
Schalbach: 336
Schalkau: 487
Schankweiler: 402-03, 405
Scharfbillig: 417
Scharnhorst: 23
Scharnhorst Line: 272-73
Schaueburg Lippe: 526
Schaufenberg: 298
Schauffenberg: 415
Schautzhofen: 523
Schaven: 426
Scheggia: 232
Scheibenhard: 445
Scheid: 424
Scheidel: 361
Scheiden: 439
Scheiditz: 490
Scheifendahl: 381
Schelde Estuary and River: 274, 276, 283-84, 289, 297, 304, 317
Scheller: 496
Scherfede: 462, 464, 470
Schermbeck: 456

Scherpenseel: 327-29
Scheuren: 392-94, 413, 432, 457
Schevenhuette: 275, 278, 280, 284, 311, 327
Schiebenhardt: 352
Schiefbahn: 420
Schierwaldenrath: 293-94, 297, 379
Schijndel: 282
Schilberg: 377
Schill Line: 273
Schilla: 131
Schillersdorf: 383-84
Schillingen: 439
Schimsheim: 444
Schippach: 463
Schirmeck: 333, 336
Schirnding: 508
Schkauditz: 492
Schladen: 484
Schladitz: 506
Schlausen Bacher Wald: 393
Schlebach: 427
Schleid: 419
Schleiden: 330, 382, 388, 390-91, 410, 422, 424, 427
Schleidweiler: 429
Schleithal: 445
Schlem: 432
Schlerthal: 352
Schleswig-Holstein: 527
Schleusingen: 477, 479
Schlicht: 349-50
Schlieben, Maj. Gen. Karl-Wilhelm von (Ger.): 215, 219
Schlier Lake: 531
Schlierbach: 356, 463
Schliersee: 531
Schlindermanderscheid: 384
Schlitz: 467
Schlossberg (Pillkalen): 374, 378
Schlotheim: 474, 485
Schlucht Pass: 252
Schluchtern: 471
Schmachtendorf: 456
Schmalkalden: 473, 475
Schmallenberg: 478
Schmidt: 295-98, 303, 311, 315, 317-19, 330, 342, 394-95, 397-98, 418
Schmidt, Maj. Gen. Harry (USMC) 168, 303, 406
Schmidtheim: 429
Schmidthof: 269
Schmiedefeld: 481
Schmitten: 463, 465
Schmittviller: 345
Schmorda: 494
Schnee Eifel: 270, 272-73, 275, 277, 280, 350, 354, 356, 389, 392-95
Schneidemuehl: 389, 401
Schneidhausen: 356, 358
Schneppenheim: 425
Schney: 490
Schnorrenberg: 419
Schoden: 411
Schoenbach: 428, 533
Schoenbronn: 505
Schoenebeck: 489, 495, 506
Schoenecken: 422
Schoenfeld: 424
Schoengras: 512
Schoenhofen: 514

Schoenlanke: 387
Schoensee: 516
Schoenthal: 335, 515
Schomerich: 419
Schonberg: 355 387-88
Schondorf: 437
Schoneberg: 452
Schoneseiffen: 390
Schongau: 520-21, 523
Schonnebeck: 480
Schonstedt: 477
Schophoven: 349-50, 360, 410
Schoppen: 378, 380
Schoppenstedt: 486
Schorbach: 439
Schorndorf: 509
Schostorf: 506
Schoven: 460
Schroeck: 458
Schrozberg: 492
Schueller: 427
Schulenberg: 476
Schuppach: 500
Schwabach: 505
Schwabenheim: 461
Schwabstadl: 520-21, 523
Schwadorf: 427
Schwaebisch Gmuend: 505, 507, 509, 511
Schwaebisch Hall: 498, 500, 503, 505, 507
Schwaiganger: 524
Schwall: 439
Schwammenauel Dam: 295, 391-93, 397-99
Schwandorf: 512
Schwanenstadt: 531
Schwanheim: 455
Schwarbsdorf: 487
Schwarza: 492
Schwarzach: 515
Schwarzach River: 515
Schwarzbach: 470
Schwarzenau: 470
Schwarzenbach: 508
Schwarzenfeld: 510
Schwarzmaar: 425
Schwartzenborn: 428-29, 431
Schwarzwald. See Black Forest.
Schwebenried: 481
Schweifeld: 439
Schweighausen: 342, 383, 385
Schweiler: 389
Schweinberg: 460
Schweinfurt: 128, 140, 176, 465, 475, 477, 479, 481, 483, 485, 487-88, 490
Schweinheim: 427, 453, 459, 461, 463
Schwelm: 491, 493, 496
Schwerdorff: 329
Schwerfen: 425
Schwerin: 527-28
Schwiebus: 388
Schwirzheim: 424
Sciacca: 121
Scobie, Lt. Gen. R. M. (Br.): 262, 288, 304, 331
Scoglitti: 117
Scoones, Lt. Gen. Sir Geoffrey (Br.): 347

Scott, Rear Adm. Norman: 58
Scout Company, 7th: 104, 110
Scout Ridge (New Guinea): 121, 132
Scudder, Col. Irwin C.: 32
Sea Frontiers, redesignated: 22
Sea Horse (Guadalcanal): 83-84
SEA LION: 3
Sea of Azov: 3
Sea Witch: 26
Seabees. *See* Naval Construction Battalions.
Sealark Channel: 53, 59
Sebkra d'Oran: 65
Sebkret en Noual: 103
Sebkret et Kourzia: 106
Sebou River: 65
Sebree, Brig. Gen. Edmund B.: 63, 68, 81, 90, 273, 277-78, 280
Secchia River: 513
Sechtem: 429
Second Front, Churchill-Stalin discussions: 49
Secret weapons, German. *See* V weapons.
Sedan: 261-65, 364
Sedjenane: 96, 101
Sedjenane River: 107
See: 512
Sée River: 239-40
Seeadler Harbor: 177-79
Seebach: 481
Seebergen: 479
Seefeld: 527, 530
Seehausen: 499
Seelbach: 476, 478
Sées: 245-48, 253
Seesbach: 443
Seesen: 484
Séez: 266
Seffers River: 440
Sefferweich: 417, 419
Segamat: 14-17
Segamat River: 16
Segendorf Rodenbach: 448
Segi Point: 114-15, 118, 139
Sehlem: 431, 434
's Hertogenbosch: 290, 308, 312
Seidfeld: 489
Seikpyu: 399
Seille River: 277-78, 280-82, 284-86, 288, 291-92, 298-99, 307, 316, 320-21, 324
Seine River: 243, 245, 248-49, 251-60
Seingbouse: 338
Seinsfeld: 426
Seinsheim: 475
Seiwerath: 424
Selange: 267
Selangor: 12
Selb: 504, 506
Selbagnone: 311, 316
Selbecke: 480
Selbitz: 494
Selbitz River: 492, 494
Sele River: 132-34
Selective Service System: 72
Seleo Island: 188
Sélestat: 337-39, 341-44, 381
Selgersdorf: 410
Selhausen: 410
Selkentrop: 480

Sellerich: 275, 393-94
Selsent: 379
Seltz: 351
Selune River: 239-40
Selzen: 445
Semécourt: 321
Sendenhorst: 476
Sened Station and Village: 88-90, 98-99
Sengerich: 407
Sengkofen: 5 19
Senio River: 353-55, 357-58, 364, 366, 368, 423, 483-84, 486, 488
Sennern: 462
Senonchamps: 365
Senones: 333-34
Sens: 252-54
Sensburg: 386
Sentani airdrome: 189
Sepolno: 386
Seppois: 331, 335
Serafimovich: 68
Serbia sector: 347-48
Serchio River and Valley: 261, 266, 267, 271, 273, 277 288-91, 296, 299, 313, 318, 361-64, 371, 392, 394, 397, 401, 481
Seremban: 13
Seria: 6
Serkenrode: 487
Sermide: 505, 515
Serravalle: 279-80
Serrest: 412
Serre: 136
Serrières: 261, 285, 293
Serrig: 409-11, 413-14, 416-17
Servance: 294
Service Command Area, Bataan: 13, 17-18
Services of Supply. *See theater, area, or command.*
Services of Supply, U.S. Army, constituted: 28
Sessa Aurunca: 138
Sessenheim: 368, 377-78, 452
Sesto: 261
Sesto Campano: 143
Sesupe River: 250
Seton: 195, 197, 200
Setta Creek: 290, 304, 311, 503
Setterich: 328-30
Setz: 386
Sevastopol: 3, 6, 10-12, 21, 40-44, 191
Sevelen: 420-21, 433
Seven Dwarfs forts (France): 325
Sevenig: 269, 411
Sevenum: 333
Sèves River: 229-30, 237
Sevizzano Ridge: 499, 501
Sevsk: 130
SEXTANT Conference: 148, 150-52
Seychelles Island: 53
Sezze: 198
Sfax: 75, 81, 85, 104
Sferro: 121
Shaberg: 424
Shaduzup: 183-85
Shaggy Ridge (New Guinea): 164
Shakhty: 92
Shan Hills: 545-46
Shan States: 28

Shanghai International Settlement: 4
Shanmen: 536
Sharaw Ga: 144
Sharp, Brig. Gen. William F.: 22, 27, 37
Shede: 458
Shemya Island: 112, 114
Shepetovka: 172
Shepherd, Brig. Gen. Lemuel C. (USMC): 159. *See also* ADC Group (USMC).
Sherman, Rear Adm. Frederick C.: 143, 156, 159-60
Shichina: 543
Shihtien: 198
Shimabuku: 469
Shimbu Line: 410, 419, 425, 430-31, 434, 436, 438-39, 441-42, 467, 471
Shimpach: 376
Shinchiku: 149
Shingbwiyang: 157, 168, 177
SHINGLE: 149, 159, 163. *See also* Anzio Campaign.
Shingler, Col. Don G.: 31, 42, 50, 52, 60
Shipping, Allied, attacks on: 55, 79
Shipping routes: 51
SHO: 306
Shoestring Ridge (Leyte): 335-36, 338-39 341
Shoho: 37
Shoaku: 37
Short, Lt. Gen. Walter C.: 6
Shortland Islands: 115-17, 123, 132, 143
Shuganu: 274
Shuri: 540-43
Shuri Castle: 540, 542
Shuri defense line: 484, 488, 506, 515, 519, 524 532 534-38 540-42
Shuttle bombing: 114, 138-39, 143. *See also* Combined Bomber Offensive against Europe; FRANTIC.
  Italy as base for: 139, 175, 201, 207, 219, 237, 244-45, 271
  U.K. as base for: 215, 219, 245
  USSR as base for: 201, 203, 207, 215, 219, 234, 236-37, 242 244-45, 268, 271
Shwebo: 369, 371
Shwedaung: 30-31
Shwegu: 304, 318, 320, 349
Shwegugale: 319
Shwegyin: 28, 36-37
Shwekyina: 333
Shweli River and Valley: 193, 200, 213-14, 216, 346, 349, 366-68, 371, 375, 388-90, 397, 402, 405
Shwemyo: 499
Shwemyo Bluff: 499, 503
Siain: 8
Sialum: 159
Sian: 453 520
Siauliai: 250-51, 295
Sibenik: 118
Sibert, Maj. Gen. Franklin C.: 208, 213, 217, 233, 239, 255, 308, 326, 497, 503
Siboney: 8, 21, 24

Sicily Campaign: 84, 87, 97, 105, 109-28
  air and naval actions: 110, 113-17, 119-20, 125-26, 128
  airborne operations: 117-19
  armor actions: 118, 126, 128
  enemy withdrawal: 126-28
Sicily Strait: 114
Sid: 346
Siddessen: 474
Sidi Amor el Kenani: 88
Sidi Barrani: 43, 65
Sidi Bou Zid: 89-93, 96, 104
Sidi Ferruch: 64
Sidi Muftah: 39-40
Sidi Nsir: 95, 104
Sidi Rezegh: 41-42
Sidi Said: 89
Siebenaler: 384
Siedlce: 239
Siedlinghausen: 476
Siefersheim: 444
Sieg River: 441, 445-47, 452, 454, 456, 458, 460, 462, 464, 466, 468, 470, 472, 474, 476, 478, 480, 482, 485, 487
Siegburg: 446, 482, 485
Siegen: 462, 464, 466, 468, 470, 472, 474, 476
Siegfried Line: 260-61, 265, 267-73, 275, 278, 280-82, 284, 288, 290, 292-94, 296-99, 334, 338, 344-46, 348, 351, 354, 374, 384-92, 394-400, 402, 405-09, 412, 428, 431, 436-39, 441-43, 445-48, 450
Siegmar: 496
Siena: 219, 222-23
Sienne River: 238-39
Sierck-les-Bains: 300
Sierra Bullones: 490
Sierra Madre Mountains: 549-50
Siersdorf: 327-29
Siersthal: 350
Sieve River: 267-69
Sievernich: 418
Sievsk: 96
Sigmaringen: 507, 509, 514, 516
Sigolsheim: 379, 382
Sikaw: 293
Sikorski, Gen. Wladislaw (Pol.): 116
Silaiim: 20
Silaiim Bay: 22
Silaiim Point: 23-24
Silaiim River: 20-23
Silay: 469, 471
Silbach: 474
Silchar: 186, 189
Silesia, operations in: 377, 379-84, 386, 394-95, 400-404, 406, 410, 417, 450, 457, 46,3 465, 467, 481, 518, 534
Silkerode: 485
Sillaro River: 292-94, 302, 305, 312, 490 495 497
Sillegny: 275, 278, 280-81
Silly-en-Saulnois: 322
Silvester, Maj. Gen. Lindsay McD.: 315
Silz: 448
Simara Island: 434, 436, 448
Simbach: 526
Simemi Creek: 76-77, 79, 81

[INDEX]   [645]

Simemi Village: 68, 73
Simeto River: 119-21, 126
Simignano: 222
Simmer River: 429, 439
Simmern: 439-40
Simmern unter Dhaun: 443
Simmons, Maj. Gen. F. Keith (Br.): 21
Simonskall: 318
Simpelveld: 277
Sims: 37
Sinaloan: 473
Sinalunga: 213, 222
Sindelsdorf: 525
Sindorf: 415-16
Singapore: 3-6, 11-24, 395, 542
Singkaling Hkamti: 177
Singkawang: 8, 19
Singling: 346, 348
Singora: 3-5
Sinn: 456
Sinnersdorf: 422
Sinonog River: 452
Sinsheim: 471
Sinspelt: 409-10
Sinsteden: 422
Sinthern: 424
Sintria River: 353
Sinz: 335, 384-85, 396-98
Sinzenich: 422
Sinzig: 429, 432
Sinzweya: 171-72, 175
Sio: 153, 160, 162
Sipoco: 7
Sirte: 76-77
Sison: 378, 383, 406
Sisserno Hill: 199
Sisteron: 252
Sitapur: 220, 223
SITKA: 249. See also Port Cros Island; Special Service Force, 1st.
Sittang River: 25-26, 28-29, 31, 33-34
Sittard: 277-78, 377
Sittaung: 244, 263, 331
Si-u: 326-27
Sivry: 293-94, 298
Siwori Creek: 71
Siwori Village: 75-76, 82
Skoda Works: 533
Skoplje: 261, 324, 326
Skyline Drive (Luxembourg-St. Vith road): 383
Skyline Ridge (Okinawa): 506, 508, 510, 512-13
SLAPSTICK: 131-32. See also Taranto.
Slavyansk: 49, 93, 96
SLEDGEHAMMER: 30, 46. See also Normandy Campaign, planning phase.
Slim, Lt. Gen. William J. Mr.): 29, 238, 244 263
Slim River: 8, 11-13
Slocum, Brig. Gen. L. H.: 400
Slooe Channel: 317-18
Slot, The (Guadalcanal): 91
Slovenia sector: 347
Smallwood, Maj. Gen. G. R. (Br.): 53, 59
Smela: 152, 166, 178
Smith, Maj. Gen. Holland M. (USMC): 131, 212, 215, 218, 225, 299
Smith, Maj. Gen. Julian C. (USMC): 148-49, 152

Smith, Maj. Gen. Ralph C.: 147-48, 215, 218
Smith, Lt. Gen. Walter Bedell: 159
Smith, Rear Adm. W. W.: 48, 82
Smoke, first wide-scale use of: 267
Smolensk: 25, 44, 97, 127, 130, 135-37, 218
Snake Hill North (Luzon): 396, 398-99, 401
Snake Hill West (Luzon): 400
Snake Ridge (Guadalcanal): 85, 87
Snaky River: 198, 214-15
Sobe: 468
Soegel: 484
Soena Plantation: 74
Soerabaja: 21, 193
Soest: 470, 474 476 478 480
Soetenich: 427
Sofia: 275, 304
Sogliano al Rubicone: 295-96
Soissons: 257-58, 260, 337
Solacciano: 191-92
Solano: 544
Solarolo: 486
Solingen: 495 497-500
Soller: 414, 417
Sollum: 14, 43
Solomon Islands air and naval actions: 48, 119, 122, 142, 156, 161
  Cape Esperance air-naval battle: 58-59
  casualty summaries: 129, 136, 139
  Eastern Solomons air-naval battle: 51
  Ghormley proposed as commander: 43
  Guadalcanal Campaign: 45-94, 115
  Guadalcanal naval battle: 66-67
  Harmon's offensive plans: 57
  JCS directive on: 44
  last enemy offensive in: 182-83
  native forces in: 124
  New Hebrides as staging area for: 53-55, 57, 61
  Northern Solomons Campaign: 95-332
  planning phase: 113-14, 126, 132, 138, 140
  recovery ordered: 45
  Samoa as staging area for: 53
  Santa Cruz air-naval battle: 61
  SOPAC control of: 44
  staging area for Palaus: 263
  SWPA control of: 30-31
  tactical orders issued: 46-47
  Tassafaronga naval battle: 71
  U.S. air strength in: 122
Solomons Air Support Force: 45, 47, 49
Solomons Amphibious Force: 45
Solomons Expeditionary Force: 45
"Solomons-New Guinea Ladder." See New Britain Island; New Guinea Campaign; New Ireland campaign; Solomon Islands.
Solscheid: 441, 444
Soltau: 484, 491, 493, 495, 497, 499, 501
Somaliland forces join Allies: 70, 78
Sombernon: 267
Sombor: 309

Someren: 281
Somme River and Valley: 258-62
Sommerain: 373, 375
Sommerau: 437
Sommervell, Lt. Gen. Brehon B.: 28, 90
Sommerviller: 273
Son: 276, 278-79, 281
Sonderhofen: 471
Song River: 136
Sonlez: 371-72
Sonneberg: 490
Sonnino: 196
Sonsbeck: 418, 425, 427
Sonthofen: 527
Soong, T. V.
  on, Allied strategy: 299
  approves selection of Wheeler: 64
  at Kunming conference:. 357 362
  named premier and foreign minister: 344
  plans for Yunnan Force: 66, 89
  proposal for U.S. commander of Chinese: 276
  on 30-division program: 89
  urges recall of Stilwell: 134-35
Sopron: 465, 467
Soputa: 46, 68-75, 77, 82, 84-87
Sora: 198, 200
Sorbey: 325-26
Sorido: 214, 244, 247, 249
Sorinne: 360-61
Sorong: 31
Sorong Island: 191, 212, 249
Sorpe Staubecken Lake: 489, 491
Sorrento: 133
Sorrivoli: 301-02
Sorsogon Province: 477, 484, 490, 492, 503
Sortini: 118
Soryu: 40
Sosoral Islands: 307
Soufflenheim: 335, 351
Souk Ahras 93
Souk el Arba: 67-68
Soulac: 503
Soulevre River: 238, 24
Soultz: 441
Soultz-sous-Forêts: 351, 369
Sourdeval: 244, 246-48
Sousse: 104-05, 112
South African units Divisions
  1st: 39, 41, 61
  2d: 10-11, 14, 39, 41
  6th: 202
  6th Armored: 191, 197-98, 202, 204-10, 215, 217, 219-22, 224, 226, 233-36, 252, 257, 261, 264, 266, 267, 269, 271, 273, 275, 277, 279, 282-84, 286-97, 299-300, 302-04, 306-12, 314-15, 318-19, 361, 375, 377, 410, 497 499, 501, 503, 505, 507, 509, 511, 513, 515-16, 518, 521, 523
  Regiment, Pretoria: 57
South America: 31 See also American republics.
South China Sea naval actions: 370, 372, 375-76, 380

South East Asia Command activated: 129, 147
  amphibious operations plans: 152
  Calcutta commanders conference: 358
  control of India Command: 147
  control of LOC troops: 168
  control of NCAC: 214
  delegation to SEXTANT Conference: 150
  directive on airlift supply of China: 200, 271, 293, 517
  directives on operations: 176, 293, 299, 304, 316
  Eastern Air Command activated: 153
  final air reorganization: 542
  hq transferred to Kandy: 187
  landing craft allocation: 152, 160
  Leigh-Mallory succeeded by Garrod: 326
  mission of Supreme Commander outlined: 142
  mission to U.S. and U.K.: 170
  plans for Burma: 145
  plans for Malaya-Singapore: 542
  plans for Rangoon: 410
  plans for Sumatra: 160-61, 176, 188
  strategy denounced by Chiang: 299
  Troop Carrier Command activated: 154
  Wheeler succeeds Stilwell: 146, 324
South Force, New Guinea: 42, 229-36, 238-44
South Gugegwe Island: 170
South Luzon Force: 5, 8-11
South Pacific Amphibious Force: 115, 119
South Pacific Scouts, U.S.: 124
South Pacific theater
  absorbed by SWPA and POA: 183
  air reinforcement: 60
  boundary defined: 44
  commanded by Ghormley: 33, 42
  Ghormley-MacArthur conference: 44-45
  Halsey succeeds Ghormley: 59
  Harmon commands USAF: 45
  McCain commands AIRSOPAC: 38
  plans for New Britain-New Guinea-New Ireland: 92, 96-98, 101, 106, 108, 155, 172, 175-76, 178, 180, 189
  plans for P.I. operations: 95
  POA control of: 30-31
South Seas Detachment: 52-74
Southeast Algerian Command (Br.): 97, 99-104
Southeast Area: 175
Southeast Asia Command. *See* South East Asia Command.
Southern Assault Force, Salerno: 132
Southern Attack Force, Gilberts: 145-46, 148
Southern Attack Force, Marianas: 213, 227
Southern Attack Force, Marshalls: 167
Southern Attack Force, Okinawa: 467
Southern Attack Group, Northwest Africa: 65
Southern Defense Command: 365

Southern France Campaign: 248-73
  air preparation: 246
  airborne operations: 249-51
  contact with OVERLORD forces: 267
  D-Day date: 183
  effect on operations in Italy: 171, 176, 182, 222
  exploitation phase: 263-73
  landing phase: 247-62
  Lattre commands French forces: 187
  planning phase: 150, 152, 155, 157, 162, 164, 171, 176-77, 182-83, 187, 189, 207, 212, 217, 220, 222, 240 246-47
  tactical air support: 256-58
Southern Landing Force, Attu: 109, 111-12
Southern Landing Force, Guam: 234
Southern Landing Force, Marshalls: 167-70
Southern Landing Group, New Georgia: 116, 142
Southern Philippines Campaign: 415-549
Southern Troops and Landing Force, Marianas: 222
Southwest Pacific Area: 135
  absorbs part of SOPAC: 183
  activated under MacArthur: 30-31
  air directive: 44, 53
  Army or Navy to control offensive in: 43-44
  Bismarck Archipelago Campaign: 154-338
  Blarney heads land forces: 34
  boundary defined: 44
  Brett heads air forces: 34, 45
  control of USF IL: 34
  first tank battle in: 198-99
  GHQ at Manila: 490
  GHQ moves to P.I.: 307
  GHQ at Port Moresby: 64
  Kennedy succeeds Brett: 45, 48
  Leary heads naval forces: 34
  Marshall heads SOS: 46
  naval elements become Seventh Fleet: 94
  order of battle reorganized: 183
  Philippine Army units assigned to USAFFE: 95
  plans for Cape Gloucester: 136
  plans for Hollandia: 176
  plans for Morotai: 233
  plans for New Britain-New Guinea-New Ireland: 92, 96-98, 101, 106, 108, 118, 136, 139, 141, 143, 151-55: 172, 175-76, 178, 180, 191 201-02: 230
  plans for P.I.: 95, 211, 230, 235, 137, 315, 395, 400
  replaces USAFFE: 34
  staff designated: 34
  supply role under USAFIA: 34
Soven: 447
Soviet Army
  meetings with Allied forces
    Austria: 535-36
    Czechoslovakia: 536
    Germany: 496, 498, 512-19, 521-23, 526-30, 532-34 536
  occupies Korea: 551

Soviet Army—Continued
  occupies Manchuria: 550
Soviet Army units
  Fronts
    First Baltic: 224, 239, 290, 295, 300, 386
    First Ukrainian: 166, 170, 172, 181-84, 187, 230, 232, 235-38, 242, 251, 372, 374-80, 382-86, 395, 400, 403, 448-50, 457, 465, 467, 509 511, 513, 516, 518, 534-35
    First White Russian: 176, 221-23, 225-26, 230, 232, 234-35, 237-39, 272, 374, 376- 82, 387, 425-26, 428, 436, 443, 446, 509, 511, 513, 515-16, 518, 520, 530, 534
    Second Baltic: 175, 229, 231, 236-37, 295, 302
    Second Ukrainian: 153-54, 166, 174, 182-83, 252, 254, 257-60, 295, 300-301, 308, 312-13, 316, 318, 340-44, 348-49, 351, 354, 362, 364, 377, 382, 453, 455, 457, 459, 463, 465, 467, 471, 473, 477, 481, 492, 498, 516, 518, 523, 535
    Second White Russian: 220, 231, 237, 239, 246, 271, 374, 377, 379-84, 399, 40,3 424-25, 428, 436, 448-50, 453, 455, 457, 459, 463, 518, 520, 523, 527, 530, 535
    Third Baltic: 232, 234-35, 247, 256, 280, 295, 302
    Third Ukrainian: 171, 180, 184, 186, 252, 254, 257 259 275 291, 300-301, 307, 340, 342, 343, 345-49 351, 354 35862, 364, 451, 453, 455, 457, 461, 463, 465, 467, 473, 477, 479, 481, 492, 535
    Third White Russian: 222-23, 227-29, 231, 239-41, 250, 305, 378-84, 399, 439, 446, 448-50, 453, 455 461, 471, 481, 483, 498, 516, 518, 535
    Fourth Ukrainian: 171, 306, 312-13, 343-44, 375, 378-79, 382, 385-87, 457, 47,3 511, 525, 534-35
    Bryansk: 125
    Central: 125, 1 41, 146
    Don: 68-69, 83
    Kalinin: 81
    Karelian: 215, 303, 308, 311, 326
    Leningrad: 84, 86, 162-63, 175, 206, 214, 237, 275 294 296, 534
    Northwest: 96
    Southern: 86-87, 91, 120
    Stalingrad: 68-70, 86
    Steppes: 125
    Volkhov: 84, 86
    Voronezh: 87, 125
    West: 125
  Armies
    5th Guard: 524
    62d: 62

[INDEX]

Soviet Army—Continued
  Armies—Continued
    64th: 62
      Independent Maritime: 187
  Corps
    III: 68
    III Cavalry: 530
    III Tank: 527-28
    VI: 65
  Divisions
    58th Guards: 517
    121st: 524
Soy: 359-61
Spaatz, Lt. Gen. Carl: 82
  commands Eighth Air Force: 36, 42, 72
  commands Twelfth Air Force: 96
  commands Western Desert Air Force: 94
  CG of NAAF: 72, 93, 155-56
  CG of USSAF: 156, 550
  CG of USSAFE and USSTAF: 160
  named deputy CinC, MAAF: 155-56,
Spaccato: 300
Spadafora: 128
Spandau: 520
Spang: 429
Spangenberg: 467
Spangdalem: 429
SPARS activated: 69
Spartan: 166
Spas Demensk: 127
Special Boat Squadron, RN: 285-86
Special Security Force, 37th Division: 396
Special Service Force,
  1st: 127, 149, 151-53, 156, 157-62, 170), 196-98, 200-202, 249-50, 254-55, 339
Spedaletto: 292
Speicher: 424, 426
Spell: 414
Spellen: 451
Sperlonga: 195
Spessart Mountains: 473
Speyer: 447-48 450-51, 459, 465
Speyer Landkreis: 516
Spezia: 114
Spicheren: 408
Spielberg: 465
Spielmannsholz Hill: 275
Spiesheim: 446
Spigno: 192-93
Spigot mortar, first use: 482
Spinazzola: 136
Spineux: 368-69
Spitzendorf: 522
Split: 314
Spora: 494
Sprague, Capt. Albert T. (USN): 453
Sprendlingen: 441, 443-44
Sprichra: 468
Sprimont: 372
Springlingen: 448, 455
Spruance, Adm. Raymond A.: 38-40, 137, 139, 142, 160, 162, 167, 212, 224, 230, 235 237,299
Staadt: 409

Stadtilm: 487
Stalltkyll: 427
Stadtlohn: 460
Stadt-Meckenheim: 425, 427, 432
Stadt-Schwarzach: 485
Staffeln: 427
Stahl: 414
Stainwald Woods: 389, 391
Stalbach: 408
STALEMATE: 230. *See also* Palau Islands.
Stalin, Joseph. See also Union of Soviet Socialist Republics.
  agreement on air bases: 169, 279
  and Churchill conferences: 49
  at EUREKA Conference: 150-51
Stalingrad, Battle of: 45, 47-55, 57, 61-62, 64-65, 68-71, 74-75, 77, 81, 83, 85-88, 90
Stalino: 92, 95, 129-30, 132
Stalzenburg: 268
Stammeln: 410
Standdaarbuiten: 315, 317
Standish, Lt. Col. Miles L.: 327, 332, 334
Stanislawow: 237
Stapp: 451
Staraya Russa: 25, 27, 30-32, 97, 174
Stargard: 425-26
Stark, Brig. Gen. Alexander N., Jr.: 88, 221, 383
Stark, Adm. Harold R.: 28
Starnberg: 526
Starr, Col. Edward M.: 240
Station Hospital, 159th: 38
Stattmatten: 368, 377
Staufen: 525
Staufenberg: 458, 460
Stavelot: 355-58, 361, 372
Stazzema: 290
Stegenthumbach: 506
Steckenborn: 393-94, 397
Steele: 474, 482
Steenbergen: 317-18
Steffeshausen: 387
Steige: 337
Steige Pass: 335-36
Steimke: 502
Stein: 477
Stein Bockenheim: 447
Steinach: 490, 492, 515, 521
Steinbach: 375, 380, 461, 492, 521
Steinberg: 492
Steinborn: 426
Steinfeld: 446-48
Steinfurth: 500
Steingaden: 523
Steinhau: 384, 401
Steinheid: 487
Steinheim: 409,421
Steinkirchen: 416, 496
Stein-Kopf: 387
Steinmehlen: 396, 398-99
Steinstrass: 411-12, 414
Sterkrade Buschhausen: 462
Sterkrade Holten: 456, 460
Sterpigny: 374-76
Stetternich: 411
Stettfeld: 466
Stettin: 424, 426, 436, 446, 518
Stettin Bay: 443

[647]

Stevenson, Air Vice Marshal D. F. (RAF): 11, 29
Stevensweerd: 378
Steyr: 176, 532-33
Stieldorferhohn: 445
Stienta: 515
Stiepelse: 524
Stilwell, Lt. Gen. Joseph W.: 30-31, 33-36 42, 98, 142, 145, 150, 159-60, 163, 170, 174, 179, 181, 184, 187-88, 190, 195, 197, 202, 204-05, 214, 219, 270, 272, 274, 279 280, 282, 303, 548. *See also* Burma; China; China-Burma-India Theater; China Theater; India; India-Burma Theater; South East Asia Command.
  agrees on SOS base at Calcutta: 53
  arrival in India: 25
  blamed for loss of east China: 299
  as China Theater chief of staff: 21
  at command conferences: 26-27, 177, 185
  commands Chinese in Burma: 28-29, 297
  commands Chinese in India: 33, 44, 155
  commands Yoke Force: 114
  control of NCAC: 168
  control of XX Bomber Command: 166
  defines command structure of CBI: 44
  deputy to Mountbatten: 129
  directive on China task force: 20-21
  on division of CBI: 222-27, 230, 235, 266
  establishes Hq, CBI: 27
  heads AGF: 384
  and lend-lease: 297
  ordered to halt offensive: 178
  plans for recovery of Burma: 46-48, 60-61, 63, 70, 155
  plans for CATF operations: 55, 60, 71
  plans for Yunnan Force: 66, 89, 146
  proposed as commander of Chinese in China: 222-27, 230, 235, 255 265-66, 271, 276, 287, 296, 302
  proposed as commander of GYMNAST: 14
  recall of: 134-35, 220, 296, 301-02, 306, 324
  relation to Chiang: 14, 17, 129
  reports on threat to air bases: 276
  retreat from Burma: 36, 38
  role in Chiang's demands: 43, 48, 59
  role in support of Communist forces: 132, 271
  selects Wheeler to head SOS: 64, 70
  division plan: 138
  on support of Chinese: 235
  temporarily commander of SEAC: 241, 254
  division plan: 59, 89
  warns on bombing of Manila: 248
  on Yunnan offensive: 144, 297
Stilwell Road: 386. *See also* Ledo Road.
Stima Peninsula: 131, 135
Stimson, Henry L.: 36
Stiring Wendel: 405, 408, 423-24, 426

Stirling Island: 142, 155-56
Stirpe: 472
Stivers, Col. Charles P.: 34
Stockach: 509, 511
Stockem: 275, 380, 406
Stocken: 509
Stockhausen: 442
Stockheim: 410-12, 414, 496
Stockigt: 273, 405
Stockstadt: 451
Stockum: 451, 482, 484
Stokes, Lt. Col. William M.: 275, 279
Stolberg: 269-71, 273, 275, 278, 281-82, 284, 327, 415
Stolzenau: 478
Stolzenburg: 387
Stommeln: 422
Stone, Maj. Gen. Charles B.: 550
Stone Pier (Makin): 148
Stopford, Lt. Gen. Sir Montagu (Br.) 185, 541
Storm King Mountain: 395-96
Stotzheim: 425-26
Stoubach: 386
Stoumont: 355-59
Stracking: 521
Strada San Zeno: 308
Straelen: 420
Straeten: 381
Strait Settlements Volunteer Force (Br.): 21
Strakonice: 533
Stralsund: 523, 527
Strangle: 182, 201
Strasbourg: 313, 319, 331-33, 335-36, 338-39, 347, 366-67, 369
Strass: 349
Strassebersbach: 462
Strassfeld: 425
Strasskirchen: 524
Strategic Air Forces, Allied: 186, 550
Stratemeyer, Lt. Gen. George E.: 116, 125, 147, 166, 173, 333
  and air organization conference: 375
  CG Eastern Air Command: 154, 342
  commands air forces in China: 527, 532, 537, 540, 544, 547
Straubing: 518-19
Strauch: 393 397
Strauscheid: 449
Straussfurt: 485
Streett, Maj. Gen. St. Clair: 186
Strehla: 518
Strehlen: 457
Streitau: 494
Strengberg: 534
Strettoia: 479
Stribro: 532
Strickscheid: 408
Strigara: 296
Strip Point (New Guinea): 76
Strodt: 440-42
Stroh, Maj. Gen. Donald A.: 339
Strohn: 434
Stromberg: 456
Stromberg Forest: 477
Strong: 116
Strotzbusch: 434
Struble, Rear Adm. Arthur D.: 339, 351, 353, 388, 403, 443
Strueth: 457

Struth: 479
Stundweiler: 369
Stupbach: 386
Stuppelburg: 398
Sturges, Maj. Gen. (Br.): 36
Stuttgart: 132, 176, 503, 505, 507, 509, 511, 513-14, 516
Stutzenbach: 481
Stutzhaus: 483, 485
Stuzelbronn: 442
Styr River: 176
Suarce: 330, 333
Subbawng: 333
Subiaco: 204
Subic: 388, 403
Subic Bay: 388, 403, 452
Submarines, German, land agents in U.S.: 41-43
Submarines, Japanese: 25
Subotica: 301, 309
Sudak: 12
Sudlingen: 417
Sudlohn: 460
Suechteln: 418, 420
Sueggerath: 329-30, 333
Suelm: 417
Suelz: 498, 500
Sugar Loaf Hill (Luzon): 438, 440-42, 445, 448, 532-35
Sugar Loaf Hill (Okinawa): 536-40
Suhl: 470, 473, 479
Suichwan: 324, 375, 387, 409
Suicide air attacks. *See* Kamikaze attacks.
Suicide Creek (New Britain): 159
Suikerbrood Hill: 188
Suippes: 366
Suisse: 325
Sukhinichi: 20
Sulac: 478, 482
Sully: 205
Sulmonte: 503
Sultan, Lt. Gen. Daniel I.: 159-60, 381
  air organization conference: 375
  commands in Burma: 222-27, 230, 235, 276
  commands China airlift: 297
  heads IBT: 310, 548
Sulu Archipelago: 8-9, 395, 419, 469, 478, 484, 499, 501, 512, 549
Suluan Island: 305
Sulzbach: 461, 503, 505, 507-08, 510, 518, 530
Sulzheim: 444
Sumatra: 15-16, 18, 24, 160-61, 176, 188, 236
Sumprabum: 96, 98, 181
Sumy: 95, 130
Sundhoffen: 391
Sung Shan: 198, 202, 211, 218, 220, 225-26, 228-29, 235, 237 242, 246-47, 253-54, 264-65
Sungei Patani: 4
SUPERCHARGE: 63, 100. *See also* El' Alamein; Mareth Line.
Supino: 200
Support Carrier Group, TF 52: 403
Supreme Allied Commander, Chief of Staff to. *See* Chief of Staff to Supreme Allied Commander.

Supreme Allied Commander, Mediterranean: 189, 262, 288, 354. *See also* Alexander, Gen. Sir Harold R. L. G.; Wilson, Gen. Sir Henry Maitland; Mediterranean Theater.
Supreme Allied Commander, South East Asia Command. *See* Mountbatten, Adm. Lord Louis; South East Asia Command.
Supreme Commander, Allied Powers, Far East. *See* MacArthur, Gen. Douglas.
Supreme Headquarters, Allied Expeditionary Force. *See also* Allied Force Headquarters; Eisenhower, Gen. Dwight D.
  army regroupment by: 236
  CCS directive to: 172
  control of 6th Army Group: 273
  control of 12th Army Group: 260
  COSSAC redesignated as: 163
  Eisenhower takes command: 152, 156, 163
  hq established: 172
  hq at Reims: 407
  planning for Normandy: 106, 112, 129, 150, 164, 167-68, 202
Surbourg: 443
Sure River: 368
Surigao Strait: 5, 306, 310, 351
Surovikino: 49
Surre: 362
Surth: 429
Susteren: 374, 376-77
Susuga Pass: 548
Sutherland, Lt. Gen. Richard K.: 34, 98
Suzuki, Gen. (Japanese): 486
Suzuki, Adm. Kantaro (Japanese): 476
Suzzano: 495 497
Svatovo: 90
Sverdrup, Col. Leif J.: 56, 60, 63
Swabian Jura Mountains: 511, 514, 516
Swatow: 376
Sweich: 421, 423-24, 429-32, 435-36
Swift, Maj. Gen. Innis P.: 176-78, 481
Swinemuende: 497
Switzerland, operations near: 332-33, 349, 419, 500, 509, 511, 514, 516, 518, 521
SWORD Beach: 203. *See also* Normandy Campaign, landing phase.
Sychevka: 97
Sydney: 39
Syffret, Rear Adm. (RN): 36
Syracuse: 110, 117-18
Syria, British forces in: 12
Syrian: 24, 530
Szeged: 295, 300, 308
Szekesfehervar: 346-47, 359-60, 379 382, 441, 451
Szentgotthard: 465
Szigetvar: 3 45
Szolnok: 318
Szombathely: 461

Taal: 428, 430
Tabali River: 115
Tabango Bay: 363
Tabarka: 67, 96
Tabawng Ga: 162

[INDEX]

Taben: 409-11, 413
Tabgas: 345
Tabgas River: 347
Tabontabon: 311-14
Tabuclan: 512-13
Tachiiwi Point: 409, 434
Tacloban: 307-10, 361
Tactical Air Commands
  IX: 240, 280-82, 292
  XII: 332, 398
  XIX: 240, 267-68, 270-71, 288, 307, 530
  XXIX: 271, 292
Tadji Plantation: 188-89, 196, 206, 250
Tadji Defense Perimeter and Covering Force: 249
Tafaraoui: 65, 70
Taganrog: 129-30
Tagaytay Ridge: 381, 389-92, 488
Tagbilaran: 486, 488
Taglawigan: 362
Tagoloan River: 36
Tagum River: 540
Taihpa Ga: 159, 161, 163, 168, 170
Taiping: 4, 7
Taira: 480
Taivu Point: 50, 54
Taiwan. *See* Formosa.
Ta-kawn: 376
Takrouna: 105
Talaga: 431
Talais: 498
Talaud Islands: 235, 274
Talamban: 469
Talange: 265
Talasea: 178-79, 183
Talavera: 388
Talheim: 494
Talisay, Cebu: 455
Talisay, Luzon: 476, 478
Talisay, Negros: 465, 467, 469
Talisayan River: 344, 347, 354
Tallinn: 256, 275, 280, 284
Talomo: 549
Talomo River and Valley: 534-38, 540-41, 549
Talomo Trail: 515, 520, 525, 530, 535, 537-38, 541, 548
TALON: 316, 367. *See also* Akyab operation.
Tamakau River: 116
Taman Peninsula: 137, 140
Tamandu: 426
Tamanthi: 206
Tamatave: 56
Tambalego River: 91
Tambongan: 540
Tambu Bay: 120
Tambuco: 355
Tamera: 96-98
Tamo: 191
Tamontaca: 503
Tampin: 13
Tamu: 179-80, 191, 243, 263, 347
Tanabaru: 513, 533-34
Tanabaru Ridge escarpment: 515, 533
Tanaga: 51
Tanahmerah Bay: 188
Tanai River and Valley: 96, 156, 159, 161, 163, 165-66, 177, 181
Tanambogo: 48-49

Tananarive: 54-57
Tanapag Harbor: 209, 211, 213, 219-20, 223, 230
Tanapag Plain: 224
Tanauan, Leyte: 311-12, 354, 361
Tanauan, Luzon: 455, 457
Tanbach: 479
Tanchuk: 550
Tandel: 379
Tangermuende: 489, 491, 493
Tanimbar (Tenimbar) Island: 47
Tanjong Malim: 13
Tank, Mark VI "Tiger," first appearance of: 86
Tank Battalions
  70th: 204
  191st: 133, 135, 172
  192d: 21
  193d: 147-48
  194th: 9
  702d: 422
  707th: 319
  743d: 332
  746th: 203-04
  751st: 109
  756th: 165, 488
  761st: 447
  767th: 310
  771st: 415
  777th: 492
  781st: 383, 513
  813th: 102
Tank battle, first in SWPA: 198-99
Tank Destroyer Battalions
  607th: 454
  704th: 308
  705th: 357
  804th: 219, 233
  827th: 369
  894th: 109
Tank Destroyer Group, 8th: 449, 464, 470, 502
Tank Group, 1st Provisional (Chinese-American): 177-82
Tankulan: 37, 536, 41, 549
Tanne: 500
Tannenberg: 379-80
Tannroda: 490
Tano Hill: 201
Taormina: 128
Tapananja: 84
Taping River: 314, 322, 326
Tarahoha: 220
Tarakan Island: 14, 527, 548
Tarakena: 75-76, 82-83
Taranto: 115, 131-32, 134-37, 140
Tarawa Atoll: 136, 139, 141, 146-50, 152
Tarchamps: 371
Target Hill (New Britain) 159-60
Tarhuna: 86-87
Tarlac: 5, 9-10, 379-80, 403, 405
Tarnopol: 179, 182-83, 187
Tarnow: 378
Taro Plain: 157, 165-66, 177
Taro River: 515
Taroa airstrip: 166
Tarquinia: 205-06
Tarragona: 345
Tarrenz: 527-28, 530

Tartu: 256
Tarung River: 143, 157, 160, 162-63
TARZAN: 145, 152. *See also* Burma, recovery of.
Tasimboko: 54
Task Forces, AAF
  Second: 125-26
  Third: 164
  Thirteenth: 186, 251
  China: 44 Desert: 60
  East China: 324
Task Forces, Army
  I, 92d Div: 397
  1st Airborne: 249-50, 252-55, 258-59, 261, 266, 333, 337
  45, 45th Div: 237, 252, 261, 266-67, 269, 273, 275, 277, 279-80, 283, 296, 319, 336, 370, 374, 386, 412
  77, 77th Div: 253, 274
  92, 92d Div: 287-91, 295-301, 305, 309
  A, VI Corps: 368
  A, 2d Armd Div: 328
  A, 6th Armd Div: 241-45, 251
  A, 82d A/B Div: 395 400
  Aola, 147th Inf: 63-64, 72
  Artman, 8th Armd Div: 470
  B, VI Corps: 368
  B, 29th Div: 256, 259
  Bacon, 95th Div: 326-30
  Baldy, XI Corps: 471, 479, 490, 530
  Barber, 4th Div: 206-07
  Beatty, 7th Armd Div: 460, 462
  Bell, 5th Div: 341-42
  Benson, 1st Armd Div: 98, 101-03
  Bibo, 45th Div: 257-58, 260-61
  Biddle, 834 Div: 472, 486
  Birks, 9th Div: 472, 474, 476, 478, 480, 483
  Boerem, 324 Div: 65, 69
  Boles, 3d Armd Div: 464, 474
  Boyer, 5th Armd Div: 343-45
  Bradford, 27th Div: 512, 515
  Breckenridge, 5th Div: 440-41, 443-44
  Brett, Fifth Army: 197
  BREWER, 1st Cav Div: 176-78
  Brown, 7th Armd Div: 454, 458, 460, 462
  Buna, 32d Div: 73
  Butler, VI Corps: 251-54, 256-59
  Byrne, 35th Div: 416, 418, 420-21, 423, 425, 430, 432-33
  C, 29th Div: 232-33
  Carrier, 28th Div: 65, 68-69
  Chamberlain, 10th Armd Div: 327, 332, 334
  Chappuis, 7th Armd Div: 458, 462
  Cheadle, 94th Div: 448, 450
  Church, 84th Div: 415, 418
  Coane, 41st Div: 113, 116, 120
  Connolly, 334 Div: 542, 547-48
  Cox, 30th Div: 294-96
  Crater, 89th Div: 487, 490, 492
  CYCLONE, New Guinea: 215, 217, 222-23, 225, 228-30, 260, 264
  26th Div: 437, 440
  Darby, Fifth Army: 516, 518
  Davisson, 1st Div: 417

Task Forces, Army—Continued
- DIRECTOR, New Britain: 114, 151, 154
- Disney, 2d Armd Div: 294
- Doan, 3d Armd Div: 414-15, 420, 427, 452, 454, 460, 462, 464
- Dull, 10th Mtn Div: 509, 511
- East, 6th Div: 403, 405-06, 408
- Ellis, Fifth Army: 205
- END RUN. *See* Myitkyina.
- Engel, 89th Div: 454, 459
- Erlenbusch, 7th Armd Div: 458
- Faith, 95th Div: 478, 480, 482, 485, 487, 489, 491
- Fickett, Third Army: 342, 353, 356, 360, 366, 368-69, 371, 373, 382, 386-87, 454, 457, 459, 461, 463, 465
- Field, 12th Armd Div: 444, 446-47
- Freeman, 7th Div: 352
- Gassman, 90th Div: 406-08
- Graham, 5th Div: 431, 434
- Griffin, 7th Armd Div: 454, 458, 460
- Guillaume, Fifth Army: 210, 217
- Gypsy, Sixth Army: 548
- H, Burma: 191, 193-94
- Hamberg, 5th Armd Div: 340, 342-43
- Hankins, 10th Armd Div: 490
- Harmon, Fifth Army: 174
- Harris, 63d Div: 349, 362, 364-65, 389, 446-47
- Herren, 10th Div: 357, 362, 365-67, 369-70, 373-74, 376, 383, 391
- Higgins, 101st A/B Div: 366
- Hinds, 2d Armd Div, 294
- Hogan, 3d Armd Div: 275, 277, 280-81, 284, 305-06, 372, 415, 420, 427, 454, 462
- Howze, 1st Armd Div: 197-98, 200-201, 205, 216
- Hudelson, Seventh Army: 362, 365-66
- HURRICANE, Biak: 196-202, 204-08, 210-13, 217, 220, 222, 234
- Johnson, 89th Div: 454, 459, 461
- K, Burma: 189-92, 194-95
- Kane, 3d Armd Div: 415-16, 420, 427, 452, 454, 460, 466, 474
- Kedrovsky, 90th Div: 427
- Keller, 104th Div: 491, 494 500, 502, 504
- King, 3d Armd Div: 273
- King, 7th Armd Div: 454
- Lagrew, 6th Armd Div: 376
- Laundon, 104th Div: 464, 476
- Linden, 42d Div: 349, 362, 366-68, 370, 377, 385, 404
- Lohse, 7th Armd Div: 462
- Lovelady, 3d Armd Div: 271, 273, 282, 284, 327, 414, 422, 424, 452, 458, 462, 464 474
- M, Burma: 194-95
- MacKechnie, 41st Div: 101-02, 114-15, 117
- MacNider, Sixth Army: 383
- MARS, Burma: 304, 441, 537
- McClure, 25th Div: 126-27, 135
- Medendorp, 32d Div: 58, 60, 70
- MICHAELMAS, 32d Div: 155, 157-59, 172

Task Forces, Army—Continued
- Mills, 3d Armd Div: 273, 281-82, 284, 327-29
- Miltonberger, 35th Div: 381, 386
- Muir, 87th Div: 426-27, 429
- Murray, 8th Armd Div: 425, 428, 430, 432-33
- Norton, 12th Armd Div: 444, 446
- Nyaparake, New Guinea: 189-91, 195-96, 199
- Oboe, 4th Armd Div: 390
- Onaway, XII Corps: 422, 426, 428-29, 431-32
- Palawan, 41st Div: 405, 417, 432
- Paratroop, Algeria: 66
- PERSECUTION, Aitape: 182, 187-88, 190, 195, 290-202, 206-07, 220-21, 227-28
- Polk, 3d Cav Gp: 280, 287, 289, 296, 300, 332, 396, 406, 408-11, 416, 419
- Pope, 86th Div: 489, 526, 528
- Porter, Fifth Army: 313, 337 350
- Provisional, Americal Div: 403, 406-07, 415
- Provisional, X Corps: 403
- Ramey, Fifth Army: 208, 215, 227, 232, 234, 236, 240, 248
- RECKLESS, Hollandia: 182-83, 186-88, 210
- Reed, 2d Cav Gp: 360
- Rhea, 7th Armd Div: 454
- Rhine, 4th Div: 431-32
- Richardson, 3d Armd Div: 335-38, 415, 420, 447, 454, 462
- Ripple, First Army: 319
- Rock, VI Corps: 404-06, 411-12, 415, 421
- Rodwell, 4th Div: 509, 511, 513-14
- Samar, Americal Div: 399-400
- Sarangani, 24th Div: 549-50
- SATIN, II Corps: 85-86
- Schwartz, 32d Div: 75-76
- Scott, 26th Div: 371
- Sebree, 35th Div: 273, 277-78, 280
- Smith, 80th Div: 531
- South, 38th Div: 403, 405-06, 408
- Spiess, 90th Div: 408, 410, 440-41, 443-45, 447-48, 453, 455, 465
- Standish, 10th Armd Div: 327, 332, 334
- Stark, 43d Div: 383
- Stokes, 2d Armd Div: 275, 279
- S, 2d Div: 09, 422, 424-26
- Sugar, 29th Div: 256-58
- Sundt, 87th Div: 454, 459, 461, 463, 485, 490, 494, 496, 498, 500
- Taylor, 1st Div: 478-79, 481
- TED, New Guinea: 240-45
- TORNADO, New Guinea: 193, 195-97, 199, 202, 205-06, 208-09, 217, 221, 233, 262
- TRADEWIND, Morotai: 249, 254, 263-64, 269-71, 274, 277, 287
- Twaddle, 95th Div: 478, 480, 482, 484-85, 487, 489, 491
- TYPHOON, Sansapor: 233, 236, 239 249, 255-56
- Urbana, 32d Div: 69-79, 81, 84
- VICTOR IV, 41st Div: 417
- VICTOR V, X Corps: 446

Task Forces, Army—Continued
- Wahl, 79th Div: 369, 383-84
- Walker, 8th Armd Div: 470
- Warnock, 5th Div: 295-97
- Warren, 32d Div: 56, 59, 63-64, 67-79, 81
- Welborn, 3d Armd Div: 414, 422, 452, 458, 462, 464, 474
- Wemple, 7th Armd Div: 454
- Western Visayan, Sixth Army: 302, 353, 356, 365, 387
- Wheeler, Fifth Army: 280
- Williamson, Fifth Army: 233
- Wingard, 11th Armd Div: 532
- Wolfe, 7th Armd Div: 462
- X, Darby's Rangers: 121-22
- X, 9th Div: 502, 504
- Yoke: 114
- Yon, 6th Div: 383

Task Force, British, Lind, Fifth Army: 280

Task Forces, Marine Corps
- BACKHANDER, New Britain: 155-56
- Liversedge, New Georgia: 116-18, 121, 124-26

Task Forces, Navy
- 8: 3, 48, 81, 102
- 14: 6-8, 139
- 15: 136
- 16: 102, 111
- 31: 115-16, 119, 126-29, 131, 140, 142-43, 146, 291
- 32: 119, 270, 291
- 38
  - China coast: 375-76
  - Formosa: 149, 165, 276, 302-03, 367, 370, 375, 380
  - Indochina: 372
  - New Britain: 143-44, 146, 156, 159-60
  - Pescadores: 367, 370, 375, 380
  - Philippines: 270, 301, 304-05, 367-68, 370, 372, 380
  - Ryukyus: 294, 300, 367, 370, 380-81
  - Sakishima Gunto: 380
  - scouts South China Sea: 370, 372 375, 380
  - and TF 58: 541
- 39: 143
- 50: 167, 299
- 51: 159, 167, 299, 373, 404, 467, 538
- 52: 143-44, 147, 167, 403-04
- 53: 145-46, 148, 167, 467
- 54: 403-04, 430
- 55: 467
- 56: 299
- 57: 303
- 58: 224
  - Hollandia: 187
  - Japan air offensive: 404-06, 413, 444-45, 462, 497, 499
  - Marianas: 208-10, 212, 214-15
  - Marshalls and Carolines: 166, 172-75, 184, 189, 204
  - Ryukyus: 420, 444, 449, 462, 488, 491, 499, 541
- 61: 45-50
- 62: 45-50
- 63: 45-47, 49-50
- 65: 55-55

[INDEX]   [651]

Task Forces, Navy—Continued
  76: 131, 154
  77: 222, 339 366-67, 370, 373
  88: 124
  Center: 64-65
  Eastern: 64, 117
  South Pacific: 5, 8
  Western: 60-61, 65, 117, 127, 132
Task Groups, Navy
  31.24: 548
  38.4: 268, 270
  50.15: 166
  51.2: 164, 166
  51.11: 172-73
  51.19: 486
  56.1: 303, 406
  58.4: 173
  74.2: 415
  77.2: 367-68
  77.3: 351, 355
  77.6: 366-68
  77.12: 351, 355
  78.2: 385, 415, 417, 501
  78.3: 339, 351, 353, 355, 403, 443
  78.4: 467
  94.9: 383
Tassafaronga naval battle: 71
Tassafaronga Point: 59, 67, 71, 89-90
Tassigny, Gen. Jean de Lattre de. *See* Lattre de Tassigny, Gen. Jean de.
Tata: 453
Tatangtzu Pass: 192, 197, 200
Tate, Capt. Jackson R. (USN): 152
Tategahtawng: 188
Tauali: 157
Tauber River: 479, 490
Taucha: 508
Taukkyan: 27-28
Taung Bazaar: 170, 172
Taungdwingyi: 29, 32-34, 492
Taunggyi: 33-37
Taungtha: 412, 430, 461
Taungup: 384, 437, 522, 535
Taup: 488
Taupota Bay: 186
Taute River: 210, 224, 227, 230, 237
Tavernaux: 374
Tavernelle: 231, 235
Tavigny: 379-80
Tavoy airdrome: 5, 15-16
Tawi Tawi Islands: 469
Tayabas Bay: 8, 372, 379
Taytay: 409-10, 437
Tayug: 8
Teano: 143
Teardrop (New Guinea): 215-19
Tebano: 355
Tébessa: 89, 94-95 98
Tebourba: 70-72, 108
Teboursouk: 78, 104
TED: 240-45. *See also* Aitape operation.
Tedder, Air Chief Marshal Sir Arthur W. (RAF): 93, 155-56
Tegern See: 528, 530-31
Tegernsee: 531
Tehran
  EUREKA Conference: 150-51
  hq for mission to USSR: 21
  movement of supplies to: 56-57
Tel el Aqqaqir: 63

Tel el Eisa: 45
Telfs: 530
Telgte: 466
Telok Anson: 11
Tementoe Creek: 193, 199, 210
Temmels: 408
Templeton's Crossing (New Guinea): 58-59
Temryuk: 137
Tenaro: 91
Tenaru River: 48-49
Tenasserim: 5, 13, 16
Tenavatu River: 48
Tendon: 287, 296
Tengah: 11, 22-23
Teng-chung: 71, 194, 205, 213, 216, 218-19, 223, 227, 237, 241-43, 272, 291, 379
Tenholt: 414
Tenney, Col. Clesen H. (USMC): 149
Tenth Military Region, French: 515
Teora: 137-38
Tepla River: 532
Tera: 545
Teramo: 212
Terek: 56
Terek River: 52-53, 71, 75
Terelle: 164
Terere: 122
Teresa: 440-41
Terheeg: 414
TERMINAL Conference: 550
Termini Imerese: 122
Termoli: 138-39
Ternate: 391, 406, 417, 423
Terneuzen: 284, 312
Terni: 136, 138, 162, 202, 204, 206-07, 209-10
Terra del Sole: 321
Terracina: 195-96
Terrette River: 231
Terricciola: 230-31
Terukini Ridge: 536
Tessel: 218
Tessy-sur-Vire: 238-41
Tetelrath: 416
Tetere: 63-64
Teterev River: 146
Teton: 476
Tettenborn: 487
Tettingen: 334-36, 338, 374-75, 377, 380, 389, 396-97
Teugn: 519
Teunz: 514
Teutoburger Wald: 466, 468, 470
Teveren: 291, 323
Thabaikkyin: 293, 374
Thabutkon: 414, 416
Thailand Allied air attacks: 202
  fall of: 3-4, 10, 33
  declares war on U.S.: 18
Thakutpin: 530
Thal: 481
Thala: 88, 94-95
Thale: 504
Thalexweiler: 443
Thalheim: 496, 502
Thalichtenberg: 443
Thalmassing: 521
Thanet: 19

Thankirchen: 526
Thann: 346-49
Thaon: 283
Tharrawaddy: 28
Thaton: 23-24
Thazi: 34, 348
Theater designations Alaska Defense Command redesignated Alaskan Dept: 143
  ABDA activated and inactivated: 15, 26
  CBI divided into IBT and China Theater: 222-27, 230, 235, 266, 310
  CBI activated: 27, 44 China Theater activated: 310
  CINCPOA activated: 30-31
  ETO supersedes USAFBI: 41
  India-Burma Theater activated: 310
  Islands Area (Br) activated: 59
  MTO activated: 152-53, 155
  NATO activated: 91, 316
  Pacific Theater activated: 30
  PGSC redesignated PGC: 153
  SEAC activated: 129, 147
  SOPAC absorbed by SWPA and POA: 183
  SWPA replaces USAFFE: 30-31, 34
  USAFFE inactivated and reactivated: 29, 95
  USAFIME activated: 41
  USAFIPOA supersedes USAFCPA: 241
  USAFISPA activated: 43
  USFIP inactivated: 41
Thélepte: 93
Themar: 477, 479
Theobald, Rear Adm. Robert A.: 38, 48, 81
Theoule-sur-Mer: 249-50
Theuerbronn: 505
Theuma: 500
Thicourt: 325
Thiéfosse: 299
Thielt: 265
Thier: 489
Thierbach: 496
Thionville: 191, 265-70, 272, 280, 287, 321-23, 325
Thirimont: 373-74
Thomas Stone: 64
Thommen: 380, 382
Thompson, Maj. Gen. Charles F.: 42
Thompsons Post: 62
Thonnbrunn: 510
Thorn, Germany: 407
Thorn, Poland: 384-85
Thrace Province: 321
Thrall Hill: 388
Three Peaks (Luzon): 484, 486, 488
Thuelen: 460
Thuir: 418
Thum: 415, 417
THUNDERBOLT: 277. *See also* Metz.
Thur River: 389, 391-92
Thuringer Wald: 467, 470, 475, 481, 485
Thurland: 496
Thurmansbang: 521
Thurnau: 492
Thury-Harcourt: 228, 243-48

Tiaong: 425, 471, 473
Tiawir River: 19
Tiber River and Valley: 202-07, 212, 214, 217, 220, 226, 229-30
Tibungko: 539
Tibur: 363
Ticala: 529
Ticala Valley: 529
Ticao Island: 421, 423, 436
Tichwin: 4
Ticino River: 523, 527
Ticonderoga: 380
TIDALWAVE: 124. *See also* Ploesti, air raids on
Tiddim: 179, 186, 189, 230, 240, 274, 295, 306, 317, 321
Tiefen Creek: 341, 343
Tiefenbach: 340, 342, 441
Tigbao: 308-09
Tigbauan: 443
TIGER: 189
Tigliano: 258
Tikhoretsk: 48, 89
Tilburg: 295, 307-08, 313-14
Tilic: 419
Tilin: 381
Tillet: 369-70
Tilly: 256
Tilly-la-Campagne: 232, 240
Tilly-sur-Seulles: 206-09, 218, 222
Tilsit: 379-80
Timor Island: 24-25, 360
Timoshenko, Marshal Semyon K. (USSR): 96
Tinchebray: 243, 246-49
Tine River and Valley: 106-08
Tinghawk Sakan: 168
Tingib: 314
Tingkrukawng: 192
Tingring: 187
Tingyaing: 359
Tinian Island base for air offensive against Japan: 458
 recovery of: 209, 234-41
 staging area for Iwo: 401-02
Tinian Town: 239
Tinker, Maj. Gen. Clarence L.: 6, 40
Tinsukia: 153
Tintage: 361
Tipolo: 364
Tippelskirch, Lt. Gen. von (Ger.): 528
Tirana: 329
Tirfoam River: 196-97, 199, 205-06, 210, 213-14
Tirlemont: 264
Tirschenreuth: 508, 512, 514
Tisza River: 300, 316
Titerno Creek: 141
Titi: 89-91
Tito, Marshal: 166, 307, 337, 527
Tittling: 5 115
Titz: 414
Tiyan airfield: 241
Tjilatjap: 26
Tmimi Line: 22
Toba: 483
Tobacco Factory (Salerno): 133-34
Tobruk: 3-4, 21, 40-42, 55, 67, 82
Todi: 210, 212

Toem: 195, 198-99, 202, 208, 210, 221, 236
Toenisberg: 421
Togbong River: 357-59
TOGO: 198. *See also* China, air bases, threats to.
Togo, Shigenori: 53
Toguchi: 486
Tojo, Hideki: 53, 233
Tokashiki Island: 457-58, 460, 462
Tokashiki Town: 460
Tokyo, air assaults on: 34, 336, 370, 405, 413, 425
Tokyo Bay, site of Japanese surrender: 551
Tokyo Express: 64
Tokyo Plain, plans for seizure of: 274
Tole: 499
Toledo: 32-33, 512
Tollevast: 216
Tollhausen: 415
Tom Hill (Okinawa): 542
Tomb Hill (Okinawa): 482, 484
Tomba di Pesaro: 261
Tombstone Ridge (Okinawa): 506, 508
Tomigusuki: 544
Tomlinson, Col. Clarence M.: 73, 76
Tongatabu Island: 37, 52
Tongres: 266
Tonk-wa: 346-49, 351-53, 364
Tonndorf: 487
Tonny: 372
Tooc: 513
Top of the World (Luzon): 388, 398
Tor River: 193-96, 199, 205, 222
Tor Sapienza: 201
TORCH: 46, 48, 53, 55-56, 59-61, 64. *See also* Northwest Africa campaign.
Torcheville: 331
TOREADOR: 150. *See also* Mandalay, recovery of.
Torgau: 513, 515-18
Torigny-sur-Vire: 238-39
TORNADO: 193, 195-97, 199, 202, 205, 206. *See also* Sarmi; Task Forces, Army, TORNADO; Wakde Island.
Tornitz: 495
Torraccia: 280, 282
Torre di Primaro: 425
Torre Iussi: 495
Torre Poggiolli: 287-89
Torrenuovo: 126
Torres: 373
Torricella Hill: 271, 274, 276-77, 279, 283
Torricelli Mountains: 242
Torten: 496, 498, 500, 502, 504
Torun: 389
Tosno: 165
Tossignano: 350-52
Tôtes: 259
Toul: 263, 273
Toulon: 70, 249-58
Toungoo: 22, 26, 28-31, 509, 511, 515
Touques River: 253
Tourane: 372
Tour-en-Bessin: 205
Tourlaville: 216-17, 257
Tournai: 261-62
Towers, Rear Adm. John H.: 39, 42
Tozeur: 93, 97

Trachenberg: 383
TRADEWIND: 249. *See also* Morotai Island.
TRADEWIND Assault Force, Morotai: 274
Traintrux: 315
Traps-en-Provence: 250
TRANSFIGURE: 257. *See also* Seine River.
Transylvanian Alps: 291
Trapani: 122-23
Traubling: 519
Traun Gmundner See: 533
Traun River: 531-32
Trautmannshofen: 507
Treasury Islands: 132, 134, 136, 140, 142, 145-46, 155-56
Trebisov: 342
Trebur: 449
Tredozio: 298, 312
Treis: 432, 438
Tremensuoli: 191
Trémery: 327
Trengganu: 9
Trentelhof: 371
Treuen: 500
Trévières: 206
Treviso: 523, 525
Treysa: 463
Triangle, The (New Guinea): 69-71, 75-78
Triangulation Hill (Okinawa): 482
Tribola: 291
TRIDENT Conference: 110-12, 114, 118, 129
Trier: 414, 416-17, 419, 421, 435, 437, 442, 446
Trieste: 523, 525, 527-28
Trieux: 265
Triflisco Gap: 140
Trigno River: 139, 142-43
Trimport: 417, 422
Trinal: 366
Trincomalee: 32
Tripoli: 16, 69, 83-88, 96
Tripolitania: 391
Trippelsdorf: 427
Tripsrath: 329
Triri: 117
Trivio: 194
Troarn: 232-33, 240
Trobriand Islands: 101, 114-15, 119-20, 122
Troina: 124-26
Troine: 380
Trois Ponts: 358-59, 361, 369
Trois Vierges: 354, 381-82
Troisdorf: 414, 487
Troisgots: 239
Trondheim: 122
Troop Carrier Command, CBI: 190, 194, 441
Troop Carrier Command, SEAC: 154
Troop Carrier Group, 90th: 66
Troop Carrier Squadrons
 21st: 38
 27th: 197, 199
Troop Carrier Wing, 51st: 302
Troppau: 511
Trossenfurt: 500
Trostau: 504
Trougemont: 299

[INDEX]

Troyes: 255-57, 259, 272
Trpanj: 272
Trustenice: 532
Trubenhausen: 477
Truk Atoll: 144, 162, 172-74, 189-90
Truman, Harry S.: 534, 551
Trun: 250-51
Truscott, Lt. Gen. Lucian K.: 65, 117-19, 173, 175, 249, 253, 282, 285, 311, 354
Truttemer-le-Grand: 247
Truttemer-le-Petit: 248
Trzebinia: 244
Tsamat Ga: 178
Tsimlyansk: 46, 82
Tsugen Shima: 486, 488
Tsutsuuran: 214
Tuapse: 56-57, 62
Tuba: 316
Tuebingen: 511
Tufillo: 145
Tufo: 164
Tugbok: 538-39, 547
Tuguegarao: 3, 5, 547-48
Tuitum: 274, 277
Tuktuk: 359
Tukums: 253
Tulagi Island: 36, 44-45 47-49 51-52, 55, 57, 59, 62
Tulear: 57
TULSA I, II, II-A: 43-45, 51. *See also* Admiralty Islands; New Britain Island; New Ireland campaign.
Tulsa Incident: 7, 9
Tumauini: 548
Tumleo Island: 188
Tumon Bay: 242
Tunga: 316
Tungkow: 509, 536
Tung-ting Lake: 152
Tunis
  conference on Anzio: 156
  drive on: 65-77, 86, 99-110
Tunisia Campaign: 66-110. *See also* Northwest Africa campaign.
  air actions: 71, 75, 87, 90, 92, 95, 982 100, 103, 105,108
  airborne operations: 65-71
  Allied reinforcements: 74, 89, 92-95, 98
  armor actions: 70-71, 74, 81, 86, 89, 92, 94, 97, 100, 103, 105-07
  attack plan approved: 73
  Axis air transport to: 105
  Axis aircraft losses: 70
  Axis strength: 71
  British forces enter: 67
  division of Allied control: 69
  18 Army Group disbanded: 112
  final offensive: 104-10
  U.S. forces enter: 70
Tuori: 225
Turin: 525
Turkey, internment of U.S. aircraft in: 41, 124
Turkheim: 518
Turkismuhle: 442
Turnage, Maj. Gen. Allen H. (USMC): 143

Turner, Adm. Richmond K.: 94, 113, 115, 119, 143, 148, 159, 167, 169, 227, 299, 433 467 538
  commands Fifth Amphibious Force: 129
  commands Solomons Amphibious Force: 45, 47
  on strengthening Lunga defenses: 54
Turnhout: 279, 286, 291
Turnhout-Antwerp Canal: 286, 292
Turnu-Severin: 264, 291
Turqueville: 203
Tusa: 123
Tu-shan: 343
Tutlingen: 518
Tuttlingen: 507, 509
Twenthe Canal: 468, 474
TWILIGHT: 147, 150. *See also* China Theater, air reinforcement
Twin Peaks, Luzon: 538
Twingon: 34
Twining, Maj. Gen. Nathan F.: 84, 122, 148
Twinnge: 382, 391
TYPHOON: 233. *See also* Mar airfield; Sansapor Plantation and Village; Vogelkop Peninsula.
Tyrrhenian Sea sector: 191

Ubstadt: 466, 469
Uchitomari: 474, 476
Uckange: 320-22, 324
Uckerath: 450-52
Udaic: 385
Udem: 407, 413-15
Uden: 284-85
Udenrath: 390
Udenhausen: 438
Udesheim: 427
Udine: 525
Udingen: 414
Udler: 434
Udo: 547
Uebach: 283-96
Uedorsdarf: 428, 431
Uekerath: 424
Uelpenich: 424
Uelzen: 491, 493, 495, 497, 499, 501, 508, 506, 509
Uerdingen: 418, 420, 422-25
Uetterath: 382
Uetze: 482
Uffenheim: 488, 490
Uffing: 526, 528
Ugong: 407
Ujelang Atoll: 164
Ukhrul: 154, 199, 191, 223, 228, 230
Ukiangong Point: 148
Ukraine sector: 166, 169, 171, 175, 178, 313. *See also* Dnieper Basin and River.
Ulandang: 506-07
Ulau Mission: 192-93
Ulithi Island: 184, 226, 268, 283, 285, 287, 305, 315, 350
  base for Ryukyus offensive: 350, 450, 488
Ullekoven: 427
Ulm: 501, 503-14, 506, 508
Ulmen: 428-29

Ulrichshalben: 487
Ulrichstein: 461
Ulster River: 475
Uman: 160, 179
Umanday: 371
Umasani River: 90-91
Umbertide: 213, 225-26
Umboi Island. *See* Rooke Island.
Umingan: 388, 390-91
Umm Qasr: 24, 31
Umnak Island: 38
Umtingalu: 154
Umurbrogol Mountains Pocket: 286, 288-97, 299-303, 305-06, 312, 317
Unconditional surrender policy: 143
Underground forces, air supply of: 160. *See also* French forces of the Interior; Guerrilla forces.
UNDERTONE: 439 *See also* Palatinate sector; Saar sector; Siegfried Line.
Underwater demolition teams
  first used in Pacific: 167, 173
  at Iwo Jima: 405
  in Marianas: 210
  in Palaus: 270
  in Philippines: 306-07, 369
  in Ryukyus: 453, 462, 493
Ungvar: 313
Union of Soviet Socialist Republics. *See also* Stalin, Joseph; Soviet Army; Soviet Army units.
  agreement with Finland on territory: 280
  agreement with Rumania on territory: 269
  aircraft supply through Iran: 102
  announces dissolution of Comintern: 112
  armistice with Finland: 181, 263
  armistice with Hungary: 378
  Axis armor losses in: 118
  Axis progress in, 1941: 3
  convoys attacked on way to: 55, 79
  and Foreign Ministers conference: 141, 143
  hostilities with Bulgaria: 264, 266
  hostilities with Japan: 151, 475, 550
  issues Yalta declaration: 400
  Manchuria as sphere of influence: 398
  mutual aid agreement with U.S. and U.K.: 39, 41
  and Potsdam Conference: 550
  as shuttle base in Combined Bomber Offensive: 201, 203, 207, 215, 219, 234, 236-37, 242, 244-45, 268, 271
  supply through Persian Corridor: 56, 57. *See also* Persia; Gulf Command; Persian Gulf Service Command.
  treaty with France: 349
  treaty with Iran: 20
  U.S. aid to: 25, 41, 56, 57, 141, 499
  U.S. Air bases in: 143, 169, 176, 216, 279
  U.S. military mission to: 8, 21, 36, 143
United Kingdom. *See also* Churchill, Winston S.; British Chiefs of Staff.

United Kingdom—Continued
  AAF in. *See* U.S. Army Air Forces in United Kingdom.
  accepts BOLERO plan: 33
  air conference in London: 39, 42
  amphibious training for Normandy operation: 189
  armistice with Hungary: 378
  bombings of Luftwaffe: 3, 34
  China lend-lease diverted to: 6, 9
  Churchill-Roosevelt conferences: 42
  declares war on Japan: 3
  Eaker commands USAAF in: 134
  and Foreign Ministers conference: 141, 143
  Hitler abandons plans to invade: 3
  issues Yalta declaration: 400
  lend-lease agreements with U.S.: 6, 25
  mutual aid agreements with U.S.: 39, 41
  at Potsdam Conference: 550
  recognizes Ethiopia: 21
  refuses U.S. proposal on SLEDGEHAMMER: 46
  as shuttle base for Combined Bomber Offensive: 114, 215, 219, 245
  treaty with Iran: 20
  U.S.-U.K. agreement on food and production: 41
United Nations: 11, 507, 548
United States Army Air Forces in United Kingdom: 134, 141, 160, 163
United States Army Air Forces, NATO: 159
United States Army Forces, British Isles
  commanded by Chaney: 25
  Eighth Air Force controls air units: 38
  superseded by ETO: 41
United States Army Forces, Far East: 13, 15, 18-19, 22
  absorbs AFPAC: 478, 545
  control of Panay and Mindoro: 22
  Corregidor as hq: 89
  in defense of Bataan: 12-13
  last elements leave Manila: 10
  Philippine Army assigned to: 95
  Philippine Division as reserve: 18-19
  staff nominations: 160
  superseded by USFIP: 29
  SWPA replaces: 34
United States Army Forces, Pacific. *See also* MacArthur, Gen. Douglas.
  activated: 472, 478
  AFPAC and USAFPOA absorbed: 478
  consolidated with USAFFE: 545
United States Army Forces in Australia
  air services established for: 506
  Brett commands: 10, 12
  Claggett temporarily commands: 9
  redesignated from TF South Pacific: 8
  replaced by USASOS SWPA: 46
  supply element of SWPA: 34
United States Army Forces in Central Pacific Area
  activated: 127
  superseded by USAFPOA: 241

United States Army Forces in the Middle East
  activated: 41-42
  Andrews succeeds Maxwell: 63
  Brereton succeeds Andrews: 90
  control of Iran-Iraq Service Command: 42
  Iran and Iraq included: 41
  Maxwell commands: 42
  personnel arrive: 74
  PGC detached from: 153
  PGSC administers: 49, 57
  redesignated AMET: 09
  replaces North African mission: 42
  Royce succeeds Brereton: 133
United States Army Forces in Pacific Ocean Areas
  absorbed by AFPAC: 478
  Richardson commands: 241
  supersedes USAFICPA: 241
United States Army Forces in the Philippines (Northern Luzon): 542-43
United States Army Forces in the South Pacific Area
  activated: 43
  Harmon commands tactical units: 45, 47
  hq moves to New Caledonia: 47
United States Fleet. *See also* Navy, United States; Fleets; Task Forces, Navy.
  control of Naval Coastal Frontiers: 10
  King appointed CinC.: 7, 28
United States Forces in the Philippines
  ceases to exist: 41
  controlled by SWPA: 34
  supersedes USAFFE: 29
United States Strategic Air Forces
  in Combined Bomber Offensive: 175
  commanded by Spaatz: 153, 160
  controls all air units in U.K.: 163
  USSAFE redesignated: 160
United States Strategic Air Forces in Europe
  commanded by Spaatz: 153, 160
  redesignated USSTAF: 160
United States Task Force in China: 20, 21
Units, independent
  5303d: 166, 168
  5307th Provisional: 146, 175-88. *See* Infantry Regiments, 475th.
Unjo: 472
Unna: 480, 482, 485, 487, 489
Unstrut River: 489
Unter Boebingen: 501
Unter Grainet: 507
Unter Gruppenbach: 496
Unter Heinriet: 494
Unter Kochen: 503
Unter Schaeftlarn: 526, 528
Unter Spiesheim: 485
Unter Tuerken: 526
Unterammergau: 523
Unterferrieden: 507
Untermaubach: 356, 358
Upperhausen: 410
Urach: 503-14
Urasoe-Mura Escarpment: 474, 506, 508, 510, 512-13, 509

Urb: 389
Urbach: 487
Urbiztondo: 372, 378
Urdaneta: 375-78
Urfahr: 530, 532
Urft Lake: 392, 397-98
Urft River and Dams: 350, 389, 424
Urschenheim: 387
Urspelt: 382-83
Urville: 212-13
Usch: 426
Ushi Point airfield: 236-38
Ushijima, Lt. Gen. Mitsuru: 548
Usigliano: 230-31
Ursingen: 459, 463 465 467
Uslar: 483
Uso River: 285-88, 295
Usterling: 524
UTAH Beach: 203, 210. *See also* Normandy Campaign, landing phase.
Utan Melentang: 11
Utap: 308
Uthweiler: 447
Uttenhofen: 503
Uttfeld: 269, 272, 275
Uyong: 370, 372

V weapons
  against Antwerp: 302
  attacks on launching sites of: 128, 130, 152, 156
Vaake: 476
Vac: 348
Vacha: 463, 470
Vachdorf: 468
Vachon, Brig. Gen. Joseph P.: 36
Vaerst, Gen. Gustav von (Ger.): 97
Vagney: 294-98
Vaiano: 215, 217-18
Valbert: 485
Valbonne: 255
Valdai Hills: 18
Valencia: 354-56, 359
Valender: 385
Valentano: 207
Valette: 336
Valga: 275, 280
Valguarnera: 121
Valiano: 221
Valkenburg: 271, 275, 277
Valkenswaard: 268, 276
Valle di Commachio: 295
Vallecchia: 277
Vallecorsa: 196-97
Valledolmo: 121
Vallelunga: 121
Vallendar: 452, 454
Vallerange: 329
Vallières: 330
Vallo: 135
Vallois: 280
Valmestroff: 323
Valmontone: 197-98, 200-201
Valognes: 210, 213, 216
Valuiki: 44, 86
Van Fleet, Maj. Gen. James A.: 441
Van River: 465
Vandegrift, Lt. Gen. Alexander A.: 46, 54, 56, 58-60, 73, 118, 135, 140, 143, 145

[INDEX]

Vandières: 263
Vanemont: 322
Vangunu Island: 115-16
Vannes: 242-43, 247-48
Var River: 258
Varenne River: 248
VARSITY: 402. *See also* Rhine River, Allied airborne crossing.
Vasey, Maj. Gen. George A. (Aus.): 68, 84
Vassy: 241, 248
Vasteville: 214
Vasto: 145
Vasvar: 465
Vathiménil: 280, 284
Vatimont: 359
Vaux: 374, 376
Vaux-les-Rosières: 359 361
Vaux-sur-Aure: 203
Vaux-sur-Seulles: 203
Vaxoncourt: 283
Vecchiano: 266-67
Vecciano: 274
Veckerhagen: 476-77, 479
Veckring: 435
VE-Day proclaimed: 534
Vedriano: 309-10
Veen: 427-28, 430, 432
Vegesack: 139
Veghel: 276, 279, 282, 284-86, 288
Vel Bor: 533
Vela Cela Island: 127
Velbert: 498
Velden: 507, 526
Veldhoven: 279
Velika Plana: 300
Velikie Luki: 18, 70, 77, 81
Velizh: 136
Vella Gulf naval battle: 125, 139
Vella Lavella Island: 121, 123, 125-30, 134-37, 139
Vellereux: 375-76
Velletri: 196-201
Velmede: 480
Venafro: 138, 140, 144-45
Vendersheim: 444
Venice: 224, 522-23, 525
Venlo: 313, 325, 331-33, 340, 343, 416, 418, 420
Vennebeck: 470
Venray: 283, 301-02, 304-05
Vensac: 496
Ventosa: 192
Ventotene Island: 132
Verahue: 90
Verberie: 260
Verde Island: 411-12, 416, 419, 423
Verdenne: 360-62
Verdun: 250-61, 356, 366
Vergato: 426, 431, 495, 497, 499
VERITABLE: 396, 403, 433. *See also* Canadian Army units, Army, First; Meuse River; Rhine River, Allied river crossing.
Verlautenheide: 273, 298
Verleumont: 369
Verneuil: 252-54
Verneville: 265
Vernio: 284
Vernon: 256-57
Verona: 224, 515-16, 518

Versailles: 254, 256, 283
Verse River dam: 487
Vervezelle: 307
Verviers: 266-68
Vervins: 260
Vesoul: 267-69, 271-72
Vesqueville: 371
Veszprem: 451
Vettelschoss: 440-42, 454
Vettweiss: 415
Vezouse River: 326, 328, 331
Via Flaminia: 202-03, 232
Via Prenestina: 202
Via Reggio: 246
Via Salaria: 203
Vianden: 382, 396, 401, 406, 409
Viareggio: 269, 273
Vicchio: 268
Vicenza: 518, 521
Vicht: 271, 275
Vicht River: 271, 273, 278
Vichy France
  Axis seizes unoccupied areas: 66
  Laval restored as Premier: 33
  Leahy recalled: 33-34
  U.S. breaks with: 65
Vic-sur-Seille: 287, 320
Victor Emmanuel, King of Italy: 122
VICTOR I: 443 547 *See also* Negros Occidental Province; Panay Island.
VICTOR I Attack Group: 443
VICTOR II: 547. *See also* Bohol Island; Cebu; Negros Oriental Province.
VICTOR III: 395 417, 547 *See also* Palawan Island.
VICTOR III Attack Group: 415, 417
VICTOR IV: 395 07, 547 *See also* Sulu Archipelago; Zamboanga Peninsula.
VICTOR V: 446, 501. *See also* Mindanao Island.
VICTOR V Attack: Group: 501
Victoria: 479-80
Victoria Point: 6
Vidouville: 237
Vielsalm: 355 357-58 361, 376
Vienna: 295, 441, 467 471, 473, 477, 479, 481, 483, 492, 498, 505
Vier Linden: 451
Viersen: 418
Viertelsheide: 422, 424
Vierville-sur-Mer: 203
Vietinghoff, Gen. Heinrich von
  succeeds Kesselring in Italy: 450
  surrenders forces in Italy: 523, 528
Vietri sul Mare: 133
Vieux Brisach: 509
Vigan: 4, 7, 372, 426
Vignola: 513
Vigny: 322
Viipuri: 2 114
Vila: 97, 110, 115-16, 121, 126
Vilbel: 459
Villa Basilica: 267
Villa Crocetta: 201
Villa Grandi: 156
Villa San Giovanni: 131
Villa Verde Trail: 390, 394-96, 398-401, 403, 409, 411-12, 419, 421, 426, 428, 430, 433, 435-36, 439, 449-50, 453, 457, 465, 467, 479,

[655]

Villa Verde Trail—Continued
  482, 484, 501, 505, 511, 529, 536, 541
Villaba: 363-64, 406, 412
Villafranca: 333, 515-16
Villamagna: 227, 230
Villapriola: 121
Ville: 337
Villebaudon: 238
Villedieu-lès-Poëles: 239, 241
Villefranche: 262
Villeneuve: 259
Villers-Bocage: 209, 221, 240-42
Villers-Cotterêts: 260
Villers-la-Bonne-Eau: 363-66, 368-71, 374
Villersexel: 266-69, 271-72
Ville-sur-Illon: 270
Villers-sur-Nied: 325
Villiers-Fossard: 212, 214, 221, 228
Villingen: 516
Vilno: 228-29
Vils: 523
Vils River: 526
Vilsbiburg: 526
Vilshofen: 526
Vilvenich: 350
Vimont: 246
Vincennes: 49
Vinchiaturo: 138-39, 141-42
Vinkovci: 349
Vinnitsa: 162, 182
Vipiteno: 531
Vire: 240-50
Vire River and Estuary: 203, 206, 208-10, 226, 228, 230-32, 238-39, 241
Vire-Taute Canal: 208, 211, 226
Virgne Ridge: 527, 529, 533
Virming: 330-31
Viru Harbor: 115-16
Viru Occupation Force: 115
Vis: 166
Visayan Islands: 27, 3334
Visayan-Mindanao Force: 33, 37
Visayan-Mindoro Force: 22, 27
Visayan Passage: 401, 435-36, 476
Vise: 268-69
Visso: 138
Vistula River: 237, 242, 244, 251, 272, 372, 374, 389, 428
Vital Corner (Burma): 317
Vitebsk: 139, 154, 156-58, 164, 176, 216, 218-19
Viterbo: 162, 202, 204-06
Vitiaz Strait: 71, 120
Vitry-le-François: 258
Vittel: 268-70, 313
Vittersbourg: 335-36
Vittonville: 273, 275
Vittoria: 117
Viviers: 322
Vizzini: 119
Vladivostok, U.S. air crews interned at: 34
Vlatava River: 533
Vlatten: 420, 424
Vlodrop: 384, 416, 418
Voecklabruck: 531-32
Voehringen: 516, 518
Voellerdingen: 343-44
Voellinghausen: 472

Vogelkop Peninsula: 211, 222, 227, 230, 233, 236, 238-41, 248-49, 251, 255-56, 260, 262
Vohenstrauss: 514
Vohrum: 482
Voiron: 258, 260
Voitsumra: 502
Volary: 532
Volcano Islands: 211, 224, 294, 297, 299, 303, 323, 337, 348, 360, 363, 456
Volchansk: 92
Volckmann, Lt. Col. Russell W.: 419
Volga River: 51
Volkach: 479, 481
Volkerode: 479, 481
Volkhov: 44, 84, 86, 92
Volkhov River: 12
Volkrange: 268
Volkrode: 481
Volmershoven: 429
Volonne: 253
Volterra: 226
Volturno River and Valley: 131, 135, 138-44
Volupai: 178
Volxheim: 443-44
Vorarlberg: 521
Vorde: 491
Voremberg: 474
Voronezh: 43-44, 85-89, 92, 125
Voroshilovgrad: 46, 48, 92, 120
Voroshilovsk: 87
Vorst: 416
Vortum: 291, 293
Vosges sector: 282, 304, 319, 335, 337-38, 340, 365-66, 375, 391, 395
Vossenack: 300-301, 315, 317, 319-20, 330, 343
Voyenne: 260
Voza: 142
Vseruby: 528-29
Vukovar: 345, 347
VULCAN: 104-05, 108. *See also* Tunisia, final offensive.
Vurai: 83-84
Vyazma: 97-98
Vynen: 423

Waal River: 276, 281, 284, 342
Wachendorf: 427
Wachtendonk: 420-21
Wackernheim: 445
Wadern: 463
Wadern Forest: 437
Wadi Akarit: 101-103
Wadi el Chebir: 78
Wadi Tamet: 78
Wadi Zem Zem: 85
Wadi Zigzaou: 99-100
Waga Waga: 53
Wahl: 359
Wahlbach: 460
Wahlen.: 440
Wahlenau: 442
Wahlhausen: 385
Wahlrod: 454
Wahnerheide: 487
Wahrenberg: 508
Waidhaus: 514, 530

Waimes: 355, 378, 400
Wainwright, Lt. Gen. Jonathan M.: 8, 14, 19, 28-30
  commands I Corps: 28
  commands Luzon Force: 28-29
  commands all forces in P.I.: 29-30
  moves hq to Corregidor: 29
  surrenders all of P.I.: 37
Wairopi: 46, 54, 57, 61, 67-68, 70
Wairopi Patrol, 32d Division: 60, 68
Waitanan Creek: 188, 190
Waizenkirchen: 529
Wakde Island: 177, 180, 189-91, 193-95, 197-99, 208, 210, 212-20, 221, 224-25, 227, 230, 238, 249, 253, 262
Wake
  fall of: 3-8
  U.S. air attacks on: 25, 139, 196
Wala: 157, 189
Walawbum: 163, 177-79
Walberberg: 425, 427
Walcheren Island: 293-94, 315
Walbeck: 421
Waldbillig: 357-58, 360-62
Waldboeckelheim: 441
Waldbreitbach: 449
Waldbrol: 480
Waldenburg: 496
Waldenrath: 38
Waldensberg: 469
Walderbach: 514
Waldesch: 440-41
Waldfeucht: 378
Waldhambach: 343
Waldholzbach: 439
Waldkenigen: 429
Waldkirchen: 517
Waldmuenchen: 515, 517, 524, 526
Waldniel: 415-16, 418
Waldorf: 427, 431, 433, 514, 516
Waldrach: 438-39
Waldron, Brig. Gen. Albert W.: 72-73
Waldsassen: 508
Waldthurn: 512
Walhalla: 516
Walheim: 405
Walker, Maj. Gen. Walton H.: 243 265, 277, 288, 338
Wallace, Henry A.: 114, 217, 220
Wallace Road (Kwajalein): 167
Wallach: 432, 450
Walldorf: 452, 457
Wallenborn: 426, 428
Wallendorf: 270, 272, 275, 277, 280, 282, 396-401
Wallenrode: 463
Wallerfangen: 345
Wallerode: 383
Wallersheim: 424
Wallerstaedten: 449
Wallertheim: 444
Wallgau: 530
Wallhausen: 489
Wallmerath: 388
Walney: 65
Walroth: 465
Walsdorf: 381
Walsrode: 496-97
Walsum: 451
Waltershausen: 477, 487

Waltrop: 472
Wama Drome: 281, 286, 291, 295
Wana Ridge and Draw: 536-40, 542
Wana Wana Lagoon: 131
Wandesbourcy: 379
Wanfried: 470
Wangen: 523
Wanigela: 58-59, 63-64
Wankum: 420
Wanne: 368-70
Wanneranval: 369-70
Wanting: 349 357 367 376-77, 379
Wantrange: 371
Wapil: 188
War Department: 24, 29, 42, 59, 70, 73, 143, 144, 153, 160, 161, 162, 171, 188, 255. *See also* Marshall, Gen. George C.; Roosevelt, Franklin D.
War Department General Staff: 28, 30, 144, 161, 188
War Manpower Commission: 72
Warang: 163
Warazup: 187
Warbeyen: 401
Warburg: 464, 466, 470
Ward: 347
Ward, Maj. Gen. Orlando: 100, 103
Warden: 329
Wardin: 364-67, 369-72, 374-75
Wardo Bay: 251
Warendorf: 466
Wareo: 138, 150, 153
Waria River: 101-02
Warndt: 342
Warnock: 360
Warnock, Brig. Gen. A. D.: 295-97
Warong: 190, 195
Warsaw: 239-40, 248, 271-72, 279, 293, 374, 377
Wart, The (Luzon): 493, 497, 503, 510-11
Warta River: 377
Warza: 475
Washang: 193
Wascheid: 395
Washington conferences
  ARCADIA: 8-10, 14
  Giraud-Roosevelt: 116
  Pacific Military: 97-98
  TRIDENT: 110-12
Wasp: 37, 44, 55
Wassenberg: 415
Wasserbillig: 374, 376, 382, 414
Wasserburg: 526, 528
Wasungen: 468, 473
Watien: 213-14
Watten: 130
Wattermal: 384
Watut River Valley: 125
Watzerath: 400
Wau: 38, 85, 89-91, 97
Waurichen: 296, 327
Wavell, Field Marshal Sir Archibald P.: 19
  arrival in Java: 13
  arrival at Singapore: 13, 23
  CG of ABDA Command: 10, 15
  commands India forces: 15, 26, 114
  in defense of Burma: 5, 22, 26, 31, 60-61, 63, 70, 90
  named Viceroy of India: 114

[INDEX]

Wavell, Field Marshal Sir Archibald P.
—Continued
 orders Moulmein held: 18
 visits Malayan front: 13-14
WAVES, activated: 47
Waw: 26-27
Wawa, Luzon: 373, 389, 413, 448, 503, 530-31, 534-35, 539, 541
Wawa, Mindoro: 373
Wawa Dam: 413, 539-42
Wawern: 408, 424
Wa-wu-tang: 525
Waxweiler: 410, 414, 417, 419
Weaver, Brig. Gen. William G.: 339, 345
Webenheim: 445
WEBFOOT: 163
Weckinghausen: 470
Wedemeyer, Gen. Albert C.: 322, 341-42, 348-49, 384, 405, 517
 accepted as Chiang's chief of staff: 306
 air organization plans: 375, 454, 527, 532, 536-37, 547
 announces loss of Indochina: 390
 heads China Theater: 310, 316, 352, 357
 negotiations for use of Chinese Communists: 338, 343, 385, 387
 plans for Canton-Hong Kong: 545
 plans for Chinese offensive force: 387
 plans for Kunming and Chungking: 333, 348, 350, 357, 362, 365
 plans for Kweilin-Liuchow-Canton: 403
 role in Japanese surrender: 550
 on Stratemeyer as air commander: 527, 532, 544, 547
 warned of Chennault relief: 538
Weerd: 382
Weert: 283-84, 291, 314
Weetzen: 480
Weeze: 411-12, 415, 420
Wega: 462
Wegberg: 415-16, 418, 420
Wegeringhausen: 485
Wegscheid: 524
Wehe Creek: 331-33
Wehlau: 382
Wehlen: 443
Wehofen: 456
Wehr: 407, 515
Wehrden: 481
Wehre River: 468, 470, 475, 477, 479
Wehrstapel: 480
Wei, Gen. Li-huang: 189, 198, 314, 383
Weicherdange: 380, 382
Weida: 494
Weida River: 496
Weiden:. 424, 508, 510, 530
Weidenau: 476
Weidenbach: 426
Weidesheim: 426
Weigenheim: 485
Weihenzell: 500
Weilburg: 456, 458, 460, 463, 466
Weiler: 380, 385, 420, 440, 494
Weilerswist: 422, 424
Weilheim: 521, 523, 525
Weimar: 465, 487, 490, 494

Weingarten: 450
Weinsfeld: 400
Weinsheim: 421-22, 447
Weisenau: 448
Weisenfels: 449
Weisel: 454
Weiskirchen: 438-39
Weirs: 429
Weirs River: 382, 384
Weissbach: 483, 488, 490
Weisse River: 494, 502
Weisse-Elster River: 489, 491-92, 494, 496, 498
Weissenbach: 525
Weissenberg Hill: 275, 277-78, 280-81
Weissenfels: 489, 491-92, 494
Weissenstadt: 502
Weisser Weh Creek: 281, 335
Weisten: 381
Weiswampach: 383-84, 396
Weisweiler: 330, 334-38
Weiszenburg: 507
Weiszenhorn: 518
Weiten: 407
Weiterbach: 396-99
Weitersborn: 433
Weitzetze: 510
Welborn, Lt. Col. John: 329
Welchenhausen: 386-87
Weldingsfeld: 483
Welferding: 412
Welgesheim: 444
Welldorf: 412
Wellesburg: 449
Wellmich: 454
Wels: 531
Welschbillig: 416
Welscheid: 380
Welsh, Air Marshal Sir William L. (RAF): 64
Welz: 340
Wenau: 330-31
Wendelsheim: 444
Weninghausen: 487
Wenne River: 485, 487
Wennigloh: 489
Wenns: 531
Weppeler: 388
Werben: 489
Werbomont: 356, 358
Werdau: 498, 500
Werdauer Wald: 498
Werden: 480, 500
Wereth: 385-86
Weringhausen: 487
Werk Kanal: 518, 520
Werkel: 465
Werkleitz: 495
Werl: 478, 480
Werlau: 440
Wermelskirchen: 493
Wernberg: 510
Werneck: 381
Wernham Cove: 95
Werntrop: 480
Werpin: 361
Werra River: 467-68, 470, 473-75, 477, 479, 481
Wertach: 521, 523, 525
Wertach River: 518-19, 521
Werth: 327

Wertheim: 465, 469
Wertingen: 514, 516
Wesel: 423, 425, 427-28, 430, 432-33, 435, 449-52, 454, 464, 470
Wesel Forest: 456
Weser Gebirge: 476
Weser River: 466; 468, 470, 472, 474, 476-84, 504
Weslarn: 474
Wessels, Brig. Gen. Theodore F.: 219, 223
Wessem: 287, 290, 293, 328
Wessem-Nederweert Canal: 287, 31516, 325
West Caves (Biak): 208, 210-18, 220
West Tank Barrier (Makin): 148
West Onnen: 478
West Pinnacle. *See* Pinnacles, The, East and West (Okinawa). West River (China): 116
West Wala: 192
Westen: 486
Westerburg: 456
Westerfeld: 487
Westerhausen: 447
Westerheusen: 495
Western Assault Force, Morocco: 65
Western Attack Force, Pilaus: 270, 291
Western Defense Area and Sector, New Guinea: 221, 227
Western Defense Command: 28, 102, 143
Western Desert: 58. *See also* Egypt, operations in; Libya.
Western Desert Air Force: 74, 94, 103, 105
Western Dorsal: 93-94
Western Europe, operations in: 261-534
 airborne operations: 276, 278-79, 281-82, 284-88, 353 450-52
 Allied air offensive begins: 44. *See also* Combined Bomber Offensive against Europe.
 Ardennes-Alsace Campaign: 353-83
 critical supply situations: 270, 281-82, 284-86, 302, 305, 331, 337, 348, 358-59
 Normandy Campaign: 203-36
 Northern France Campaign: 236-71
 Rhineland Campaign: 271-447
 smoke, first wide-scale use of: 267
 Southern France Campaign: 247-73
 tactical air support: 267-68, 270, 273, 277, 279-82, 286, 288-90, 295, 300-301, 307, 316, 321, 327, 332, 336, 339, 341-43, 347-48, 351, 359, 361, 365, 397-98, 406, 408, 419, 422, 433, 444, 447-50, 454-55, 463, 472, 478-80, 483, 485, 494, 496, 499, 502, 504, 516, 525, 530
Western Fire Support Group, Pilaus: 270, 274
Western Force, New Georgia: 115
Western Landing Group, Marianas: 210
Western Pacific Campaign: 187-551
Western Sea Frontier: 186
Westernach: 496
Westernboedefeld: 480
Westernheim: 509
Westervoort: 488

Westfeld: 470, 480, 484
Westhausen: 513
Westheim: 496
Westhemmerde: 482
Westhofen: 489, 491
Westkapelle: 316-17
Westkapelle Dike: 293-94, 316
Weston: 12
Westphalia: 510, 526
Westwall. *See* Siegfried Line.
Wesu Ga: 178-79
Wethen: 464
Wetter: 493
Wetteldorf: 422
Wettewitz: 498
Wettlingen: 275, 277, 413
Wetzlar: 454, 456, 458, 460 462, 466
Wevelinghoven: 422
Weversdorp: 189
Wewak: 125, 128-29, 135, 176, 181, 183, 189, 536
Wewe River: 239
Weweler: 386
Wewer: 462, 464
Weyer: 454
Weyersheim: 368, 370, 376, 378, 390
Whaling, Col. William J. (USMC): 58
Whaling Group: 58, 62-63
Wheeler Field: 3
Wheeler, Lt. Gen. Raymond A. and Assam airfield: 109, 112
    in charge of Ledo Road: 93
    heads Iran mission: 31
    heads SOS, CBI: 26, 146
    heads SOS, China: 64, 70
    recommended as deputy to Mountbatten: 224-27, 230, 235
    SEAC administrative officer: 146
    succeeds Stilwell at SEAC: 324
    succeeds Sultan in IBT: 548
Whitlock, Col. Lester J.: 34
Wibrin: 373
Wicterich: 420
Wickau: 496
Wickede: 480
Wicker: 459
Wickerswihr: 385-86
Wickham Anchorage: 115-16
Wicourt: 376
Widdau: 388-89
Widdern: 475, 479
Widdersdorf: 424
Wieblingen: 463
Wied: 452
Wied River: 440-42, 448-49, 451-52
Widenfeld: 420, 422
Wiemeringhausen: 474
Wiener Neustadt: 138, 144, 465 467, 471, 481
Wiershausen: 479
Wies: 375, 382
Wiesbaden: 457, 459, 461
Wiesbaum: 429
Wieseck: 458
Wiesenacker: 511
Wiesenfeld: 485
Wiesloch: 429
Wihr-en-Plaine: 387
Wijk: 270
Wildenburg: 427
Wildenguth: 367, 371

Wildenholz: 505
Wilderdange: 382
Wildenranna: 526
Wildenrath: 416, 418
Wildenreuth: 508
Wilferding: 403
Wilhelmina Canal: 278
Wilhelmshaven: 89, 113, 144, 520
Wilhelmshaven-Emden Peninsula: 520
Wilhelmshoehe: 334-36
Wilkau: 494 502
Wilkinson, Rear Adm. Theodore S.: 126-27, 131, 136, 140, 142-43, 146, 172, 180, 291
Will Road (Kwajalein): 167
Willaumez Peninsula: 175, 151
Willegassen: 474
Willems Vaart Canal: 275
Williamson, Brig. Gen. Raymond: 233
Willich: 418
Willingen: 464, 474
Willkie, Wendell L.: 58
Willoughby, Maj. Gen. Charles A.: 34
Willroth: 452
Willwerath: 398
Wilma Road (Kwajalein): 167
Wilogne: 373
Wilsecker: 428
Wilsenroth: 456
Wilson, Gen. Sir Henry Maitland: 12, 262, 273, 288. *See also* Mediterranean Theater.
    commands Ninth Army: 12
    directive on support of OVERLORD 187
    heads British Joint Staff Mission: 354
    plans for Southern France: 171, 182, 246
    succeeded by Alexander as SACMED 156, 161, 224, 354
Wiltingen: 419
Wiltrop: 474
Wiltz: 267, 354, 356, 363-64, 366, 371, 380-81
Wiltz River: 363, 374-75, 379-80, 382
Wilwerwiltz: 382-83
Wimmenau: 345, 366-67
Wincheringen: 406-08
Wincrange: 380
Windecken: 461
Winden: 356, 359-61
Windhagen: 441-42
Windischeschenbach: 508
Windsheim: 492, 502, 507
Wing, Maj. Gen. Leonard F.: 116, 249
Wingate, Brig. Orde Charles (Br.): 91, 111, 170, 183
Wingen: 345 366-69
Wingeshausen: 474, 476
Winhoering: 528
Winkhausen: 474
Winnekendonk: 420
Winnenden: 507, 509
Winningen: 440-41
Winnweiler: 444
Winringen: 421
Winseler: 370-71, 380
Winter Line: 144-47, 149-62, 368
Winterbach: 443
Winterberg: 464, 466, 468, 470, 472
Winterscheid: 389

Winterspelt: 388
Winterswijk: 460, 462
Wintrich: 443
Wipperfuerth: 489, 491, 493
Wirtheim: 470
Wirtzfeld: 357, 387
Wiskirchen: 426
Wismar: 527-28, 530
Wissembourg: 354, 369, 372, 445
Wissembourg Gap: 445-46
Wissersheim: 418
Wissmannsdorf: 416
Wissmar: 458, 460
Witlingen: 408
Wittelsheim: 391
Witten: 484, 486-87, 489, 491
Wittenberg: 466, 530
Wittenberge: 489, 510, 530
Witterschlick: 429
Wittingen: 486, 499, 506
Wittlich: 424, 429, 434-35, 443
Wittlingen: 514
Wittring: 345-46
Wittscheidt: 299-300, 303
Witzenhausen: 479
Witzerath: 393
Witzleben: 487
Wockerath: 414
Wodzislaw: 457
Woelfis: 479
Woensdrecht: 297-98, 304
Woerrstadt: 446
Woerth: 442, 461, 463
Woffelsbach: 393
Woffleben: 487
Woippy: 326-27
Woldenberg: 387
Woleai Island: 184, 187
Wolfe airfield: 434
Wolfen: 496, 502, 504, 506
Wolfenacker: 449
Wolfenbuettel: 486, 491
Wolfershausen: 465
Wolferstedt: 489
Wolfgantzen: 393
Wolfhound Ridge: 531-32
Wolfratshausen: 525, 527
Wolfsberg Pass: 332-33
Wolfsbusch: 376-77
Wolfsheim: 443-44
Wolfskirchen: 337-38
Wolfsoelden: 485
Wolken: 431
Wolkenberg: 492, 494
Wollaberg: 517, 524
Wollersheim: 418, 420
Wollseifen: 392
Wollstein: 443-44
Wolsfeld: 414, 06
Women's Auxiliary Army Corps activated: 38
Women's Reserve, USCG, activated: 69
Wonsheim: 444
Wood, Brig. Gen. John S.: 287
Woodlark Island: 114-15, 119, 122
Woodpecker Ridge (Luzon): 499 501, 517, 525 529-32 534-35, 537-39
Wootten, Brig. George F. (Aus.): 7375
Worde: 451
Worgl: 531

[INDEX]

World War II, total Army strength and casualties: 551
Wormbach: 480
Wormeldange: 297
Wormersdorf: 427
Worms: 441-44, 446-47 450 455
Worringen: 424-25
Woske River: 222
Wotje Atoll: 21, 166
Wrexen: 462
Wuelfrath: 496, 498, 500
Wuellenrath: 414-15
Wuerselen: 297-98, 300 327-28
Wuerzburg: 465-66, 469, 471, 473, 475, 494, 502
Wuescheim: 424
Wuestems: 461
Wukang: 509, 517
Wulfen: 458
Wullmeringhausen: 474
Wullscheid: 441-42
Wundwin: 447 450
Wunsiedel: 504
Wunthe: 356
Wupper River: 495, 497
Wuppertal: 496, 498, 500
Wurdinghausen: 480
Wurm: 330, 332, 334, 344, 354
Wurm River and Valley: 278, 292-93, 297-98, 302, 304, 323, 327, 330, 374, 383
Wurzen: 514
Wustenbrand: 494
Wutha: 479
Wuyang Valley: 529
Wy-dit-Joli-Village: 258
Wye Point: 85
Wyler: 281, 396

Xanrey: 289, 291
Xanten: 403, 423, 425, 427-28, 430, 432-33, 450
Xermaménil: 280
X-ray River: 207, 229

Y Force. *See* Yunnan Force.
Y-FOS: 189-90
Yabuchi Shima: 476
Yaeju-Dake Escarpment: 543-46
Yae-Take hills: 486, 488, 493, 495, 497, 499, 501
Yafusu: 520, 522, 533
Yagyagan: 499
Yahagi: 480
Yakabi Island: 456
Yakamul: 196, 199-262, 14, 228
Yalta: 187
Yalta Conference and Declaration: 392, 398, 400
Yalau Plantation: 178, 182
Yamagata, Maj. Gen. Tsuyuo: 78; 86
Yamamoto, Col. Hiroshi: 81
Yamamoto, Adm. Isoroko: 39, 105
Yamashita, Gen. Tomoyuki: 24, 28
Yamato: 480
Yamethin: 488
Yampol: 181
Yangtze River: 97, 105, 113
Yap Island: 184, 226, 268, 274, 305
Yartsevo: 136

Yasuda, Capt. Yoshitatsu: 67
Yawata: 211
Yawngbang: 170, 173-75
Yazagyo: 295
Yazawa, Col. Kiyomi: 71, 86
Yedashe: 30
Yeisk: 91
Yellow Line (Sicily).: 118-19
Yellow River: 187, 189
Yelnya: 130
Yenan Province, U.S. observer group in: 171, 214, 217, 343. *See also* Chinese Communist forces.
Yenangyaung: 33-34, 402 510, 511
Yeremenko, Gen. Andrei I. (USSR) 186
Ye-u: 36, 367
Yigo: 241, 245
YOKE: 114. *See also* China; Burma; India.
Yokohama: 34
Yokosuka naval base: 551
Yokoyama, Col. Yosuke: 67, 76
Yon, Brig. Gen. Everett M.: 383
Yona: 240
Yonabaru: 534 538 540-42
Yonawa: 542
Yong Peng: 15-17
Yonne River: 252, 256
Yontan airfield: 468-69, 471, 541
Yontan-Zan: 469, 471
Yorktown: 28, 36-37, 39-40
Youk-les-Bains: 67
Yoyang: 97
Ypad: 314
Yugoslavia
  agreement with Bulgaria on territory: 313-14
  air attacks on: 261
  Allied reinforcements: 272
  Allied bases in: 166, 337
  commando raids on. *See* British Army units, Battalions, 9th Commando.
  guerrilla forces: 307, 314, 317-18, 340
  meeting of Allied forces: 527
  operations in: 165, 261, 264, 272, 275, 291, 300-301, 303-04, 307, 309, 314, 316-18, 324, 326, 337, 340, 344, 346-47, 349, 374, 463, 471 473
Yugoslavian Partisan Army: 307, 314, 317-18, 340
Yukhnov: 27
Yunagusuku: 544
Yung-ning: 495, 541
Yunnan Force: 59-61, 63, 70, 90, 102, 111, 118, 125, 144-46, 150, 155, 162, 169, 170, 186, 189, 191, 194, 197, 274, 296, 322, 349, 353, 357, 379, 384-85
Yunnan Province
  Allied drive from: 60-61, 63, 66, 70, 73, 87-91, 110, 125, 144, 152, 170, 194
  as base for Burma operations: 47-48
  Stilwell commands Chinese in: 297
Yun-nan-i: 197, 219
Yupbang Ga: 144, 156, 158, 162, 168
Yuwa: 206
Yuza: 544-45

Yuza-Dake Escarpment: 544-47

Z Day, use of term: 151, 191
Zachopau River: 496
Zagarolo: 201.
Zaghouan: 69, 109-10
Zahrensdorf: 526
Zaluchie: 96
Zamami Island: 456-57, 460, 462, 465
Zambales Mountains: 376, 408, 411-12, 414-15, 425
Zamboanga City: 346
Zamboanga Peninsula: 405, 417, 431, 433-34, 441-42, 444-46, 462, 520, 531, 547, 549
Zanana: 116, 119-20
Zandpol: 397
Zannouch: 98-99
Zaporodzhe: 140
Zappulla River: 126
Zara: 317
Zautendorf: 500
Zavia: 88
ZEBRA: 144-45, 159
ZEBRA Force, U.S.-Sponsored: 144-45, 154, 159
Zebra Hill (Okinawa): 534-37
Zeebrugge: 268
Zeholfing: 522-524
Zeilin: 59
Zeitldorn: 515
Zeitz: 192, 489-92, 494 496
Zelezna Ruda: 532
Zell: 485
Zella Mehlis: 477, 481
Zellerfeld: 489
Zemmer: 429
Zena Creek: 304
Zenn River: 496
Zenner: 463
Zenobia da Costa, Brig. Gen. Euclydes: (Braz.): 273
Zerbst: 521-22
Zerf: 411, 413-14, 416, 428, 437
Zeulenroda: 496, 498
Zevenbergen: 315, 317
Zhitomir: 146-47, 156, 158
Zhlobin: 155, 161, 176, 219
Zhmerinka: 181
Zieta: 125, 128
Zieverich: 415-16
Zig Canal: 327
Zigyun: 194
Zigzag Pass (Luzon): 388, 390-91, 393-95, 398-99, 401-03, 405
Zimovniki: 83
Zingsheid: 427
Zingsheim: 427
Zinkovy: 533
Zinnia (Bogon) Island: 173
Zinswiller: 342-43, 439, 441
Zintzel River: 349 ,441
Zinzing: 407
ZIPPER: 531, 536, 541-43, 546. *See also* Malaya, recovery of.
Zirc: 451
Zirl: 530
Zliten: 86
Zmiev: 129
Znamenka: 151-53
Zon. *See* Son.

Zorge: 500
Zorn Canal: 393
Zorn River: 372
Zory: 457
Zotzenheim: 441
Zschernitz: 504
Zuara: 89
Zuellichau: 388
Zueschen: 468, 470
Zuid Beveland: 294, 297-98, 304

Zuider Zee: 276, 495, 499, 501
Zulling: 524
Zulpich: 422, 429
Zundert: 311-13
Zutphen: 468, 480
Zwackau: 494
Zweedorf: 526
Zweibrucken: 346, 439, 442, 445-46
Zweibruggen: 294-95
Zweifall: 271, 281, 288, 319, 401-02

Zweig Canal: 466, 468
Zwenkau: 498, 502
Zwettl: 529-30, 532
Zwick Mulde River: 492, 494, 496-98, 500, 502
Zwickau: 192, 500, 502
Zwiesel: 515, 522, 532
Zwinge: 485
Zwolle: 493
Zyfflich: 397